## *Writing about Drama*



## *Writing from a Critical Perspective*

# Literature

x 2

Wild Nights – Wild Nights!
Were I with thee
Wild Nights should be
Our luxury!

Futile – the winds –
To a Heart in port –
Done with the Compass –
Done with the Chart!

Rowing in Eden –
Ah! the Sea!
Might I but moor –
Tonight –
In thee!

Page from Dickinson's notebooks, showing "Wild Nights." See page 1127.

# Literature

## *Thinking, Reading, and Writing Critically*

SECOND EDITION

*Edited by*
Sylvan Barnet
*Tufts University*

Morton Berman
*Boston University*

William Burto
*University of Lowell*

William E. Cain
*Wellesley College*

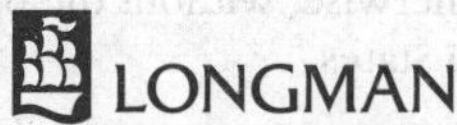


An imprint of Addison Wesley Longman, Inc.

New York • Reading, Massachusetts • MenloPark, California • Harlow, England
Don Mills, Ontario • Sydney • Mexico City • Madrid • Amsterdam

Acquisitions Editor: Lisa Moore
Developmental Editor: Katharine Glynn
Project Editor: Brigitte Pelner
Text Design: Mary Archondes/Nancy Sabato
Cover Designer: Mary Archondes
Cover Photo: © John Shaw/Tom Stack & Associates
Photo Researcher: Mira Schachne
Art Studio: Paul Lacy
Electronic Production Manager: Valerie A. Sawyer
Desktop Administrator: Jim Sullivan
Manufacturing Manager: Helene G. Landers
Electronic Page Makeup: American-Stratford Graphic Services, Inc.
Printer and Binder: RR Donnelley & Sons Company
Cover Printer: The Lehigh Press Inc.
Insert Printer: The Lehigh Press Inc.

For permission to use copyrighted material, grateful acknowledgment is made to the copyright holders on pp. 1981–1993, which are hereby made part of this copyright page.



Library of Congress Cataloging-in-Publication Data
Literature : thinking, reading, and writing critically / edited by
Sylvan Barnet . . . [et al.]. – 2nd ed.
p. cn.
Includes index.
ISBN 0-673-52523-6 (alk. paper)
1. College readers. 2. English language–Rhetoric–Problems,
exercises, etc. 3. Criticism–Authorship–Problems, exercises, etc.
thinking. I. Barnet, Sylvan.
PE1417.L643 1996
808–dc20 96-18848
CIP



ISBN 0-673-52523-6

123456789 —DOC—99989796

# CONTENTS

# PREFACE

*Literature: Thinking, Reading, and Writing Critically,* Second Edition, begins with three introductory chapters concerning reading, thinking, and writing (drawing on stories and poems ranging from the Parable of the Prodigal Son to works by William Blake, W. B. Yeats, Elizabeth Bishop, Toni Cade Bambara, and Pat Mora), and then offers an anthology of literature arranged by genre (fiction, poetry, drama). This genre anthology, like the introductory chapters, includes ample material that helps students to become active readers and careful, engaged writers.

## NEW FEATURES: AN OVERVIEW

The new edition of *Literature: Thinking, Reading, and Writing Critically* includes several key features for reading and writing about literature.

- Three opening chapters provide guidance in writing analyses, interpretations, and evaluations of literature, with a special emphasis on argument and critical thinking.
- Every chapter covering the elements includes a checklist on writing.
- 21 student papers, including essays in each casebook, provide guidance for writing.
- Every genre ends with a casebook. In Fiction, there are two—"Critical Perspectives on Joyce Carol Oates" and a *new* casebook "Critical Perspectives on Joseph Conrad." In Poetry, there are three casebooks—"Critical Perspectives on Emily Dickinson," "Critical Perspectives on Robert Frost," and a *new* casebook "Critical Perspectives on Langston Hughes." Finally, a *new* casebook appears in Drama—"Critical Perspectives on Shakespeare's *The Tempest.*"
- Two new chapters, "Writing about Issues: Perspectives on Gender" in Fiction and "Writing about Issues: Perspectives on a Multicultural America" in Poetry, provide a vibrant selection of stories and poems with a focus for writing.

- The unit on Poetry includes a new chapter, "Variations on Themes," which has a full-color 16-page insert pairing poems and paintings. This chapter also includes a unit on translating poems, which allows students competent in a language other than English to draw on their experience.
- The representation of contemporary authors has been increased.

## ABOUT THE LITERATURE

- **Canonical works** The book contains 68 stories, one novel (Kate Chopin's *The Awakening*), 281 poems, and 16 plays. Perhaps a third of the selections are canonical works that for many decades—in some cases even for centuries—have given readers great pleasure. Writers such as Sophocles, Shakespeare, Walt Whitman, Emily Dickinson, and Kate Chopin have stood the test of time, including the test of today's students and teachers in introductory courses in literature and composition. No editor and no instructor need apologize for asking students to read, think, and write about these authors. In "Tradition and the Individual Talent" T. S. Eliot makes the point well: "Someone said, 'The dead writers are remote from us because we *know* so much more than they did.' Precisely, and they are that which we know."
- **A new canon** The remaining two-thirds is contemporary material, some of it by writers who established their reputations several decades ago (for instance John Updike and Alice Walker), but much of it by writers who are still young (for instance, Amy Tan and Sandra Cisneros). We have tried to read widely in today's writing, and we think we have found important new stories, poems, and plays—pieces worth the time of busy students and busy instructors. Again, no editor and no instructor need apologize for asking students to study and take pleasure in these authors, *and* often to see how they return us to the authors of the past, the authors whose place in the canon is established and secure.

## THINKING AND READING CRITICALLY ABOUT LITERATURE

- **New introductory chapters on the nature of literature and on analysis, interpretation, and evaluation** These early chapters, which include several poems and stories, immediately engage students in reacting critically and arguing effectively.
- **In-depth representations, casebooks, and critical perspectives** Two fiction writers, Flannery O'Connor and Raymond Carver, are represented in depth, and we include casebooks on works by two others, Joseph Conrad (*Heart of Darkness*) and Joyce Carol Oates ("Where Are You Going, Where Have You Been?"). Among the poets, we represent in depth Emily Dickinson (poems, letters, modern criticism, and an essay by a student), Robert Frost (poems, comments on poetry, and three critical essays by students), and Langston Hughes (poems, comments on poetry, modern criticism, and an essay by a student). These authors are rep-

resented not only in depth but also by casebooks which offer multiple critical perspectives on single works. Of the dramatists, we give two plays by Sophocles, three by Shakespeare, and a casebook of criticism (including a student essay) on *The Tempest.* We think these features of the book are especially valuable, and that the kinds of writing assignments we have developed—assignments that have emerged from our own efforts and experiments in the classroom—will interest students and be productive for them.

- **Fiction unit on gender** We mentioned at the outset that the book is arranged by genre, but the fiction unit, after introducing such elements as plot, character, and point of view, includes a thematic chapter, "Writing about Issues: Perspectives on Gender." This chapter, which begins with suggestions for writing, enables students to see how a variety of authors have explored a challenging, multifaceted issue through stories, fictional narratives that focus on personal, familial, and social life.
- **Poetry units on multiculturalism, poems and paintings, and translating poetry** In addition to containing chapters on such topics as "The Lyric" and "The Speaking Tone of Voice," the poetry unit includes two unusual chapters, both associated with writing assignments. The first of these, "Writing about Issues: Perspectives on Multicultural America," contains 31 poems, including such familiar items as Phillis Wheatley's "On Being Brought from Africa to America" and Emma Lazarus's "The New Colossus" and poems by Gwendolyn Brooks and Robert Frost, but it also includes poems that perhaps have never before been anthologized in a book of this sort—for example, two anonymous Native American songs and several contemporary poems by Native Americans and by Chicano authors. These poems are accompanied by handsome pictures (chiefly photographs) that help to suggest aspects of the history of our multicultural society. For instance, the poems by Emma Lazarus, Thomas Bailey Aldrich, and Joseph Bruchac concerning immigration from Europe in the late nineteenth and early twentieth centuries are accompanied by three impressive photographs of the Statue of Liberty, of the Registry Room at Ellis Island, and of Slavic women immigrants. Similarly, with Mitsuye Yamada's "The Question of Loyalty" we reproduce Dorothea Lange's photograph of a Japanese family on its way to an internment camp in 1942; with the poems by Robert Frost, Paula Gunn Allen, Sherman Alexie, and Nila northSun—all on Native American life—we reproduce a nineteenth-century painting of Pocahontas and John Smith, and two contrasting photographs.
- **Variations on themes** This unusual unit consists of nine poems specifically derived from paintings; each poem is accompanied by a full-color reproduction of the painting.
- **Translating poetry** Students are introduced to the problems of translating poetry (Latin, French, Japanese, and Spanish poems are given), with the idea that the students will themselves translate a poem and write an essay setting forth the problems that they encountered in moving from one language to another.
- **Perspectives on plays** Most of the plays are accompanied by comments made by their authors—comments that themselves invite commentary.
- **Critical approaches** A chapter on "Critical Approaches," sketching such approaches as Reader-Response criticism and the New Historicism, will help students to develop a repertoire of points of view.

## WRITING ABOUT LITERATURE

Instructors know that one of the best ways to become an active reader is to read with a pencil in hand—that is, to annotate a text, to make jottings in a journal, and ultimately to draft and revise essays. We think that students, too, will find themselves saying of their experiences with literature what the philosopher Arthur C. Danto said about his experience with works of art:

> I get a lot more out of art, now that I am writing about it, than I ever did before. I think what is true of me must be true of everyone, that until one tries to write about it, the work of art remains a sort of aesthetic blur. . . . I think in a way everyone might benefit from becoming a critic in his or her own right. After seeing the work, write about it. You cannot be satisfied for very long in simply putting down what you felt. You have to go further.
>
> *Embodied Meanings* (1994), page 14.

- **Ten chapters on writing,** including samples of annotated pages, entries in journals, 17 checklists, and 21 essays by students are included.
- **Samples of annotated pages, journal entries, and student essays** To assist students to respond to the works of literature in this book, and then to think and write critically about their responses, we include not only a chapter devoted to the concepts of analyzing, interpreting, and evaluating (Chapter 3), but also examples of annotated pages, entries in journals, and 21 essays by students (some with the students' preliminary journal entries, and some with questions asking the reader to evaluate certain aspects of the essays). A research paper is included.
- **Explorative questions** About a third of the selections in the book are equipped with *questions* intended to help draw attention to matters that deserve careful thinking.
- **Casebooks** The representation of authors in depth, and the six critical perspectives already mentioned (on Oates's "Where Are You Going, Where Have You Been?", Conrad's *Heart of Darkness,* poems by Dickinson, Frost and Hughes, and on *The Tempest*), as well as the perspectives afforded by dramatists on their plays, provide abundant opportunities for writing. (Samples of student writing are included in some of the casebooks.)
- **Topics for critical thinking and writing** Hundreds of suggested topics provide a stimulus to writing.
- **Glossary** Literary terms, defined and discussed throughout the text, are concisely defined in a convenient glossary at the rear of the book, with page references to the fuller discussions.
- **Manuscript form** An appendix includes pages on the form of an essay, e.g. margins, capitalization in a title, and so on.
- **Writing a research paper** Another appendix gives information on doing research and on presenting one's findings in a documented essay (MLA form). This appendix includes material about writing with a word processor, and about the uses and misuses of a photocopier.

# INSTRUCTOR'S MANUAL AND MULTIMEDIA TEACHING RESOURCES

*Literature: Thinking, Reading, and Writing Critically* is accompanied by an extensive multimedia teaching resource package. We have prepared an instructor's manual, *Teaching Literature,* with suggestions for teaching every selection in the book. Longman can also provide numerous videotapes and audiotapes of literary works that will enhance the student's experience of literature. To receive more information, and to request a copy of *Teaching Literature,* contact your Longman representative, or write to

Humanities Marketing Manager
Addison Wesley Longman Publishers
10 East 53rd Street
New York, New York 10022

As we have worked together on this volume, we have often quoted to one another—it's a good source of motivation—observations that writers have made about the pleasure, pain, and wonder of literature. We think, for example, of Samuel Johnson's remark that "literature is a kind of intellectual light which, like the light of the sun, may sometimes enable us to see what we do not like." But we recall, too, Richard Wright's tribute to literature, presented in the final pages of *Black Boy,* as he tells of the inspiration and encouragement he received from reading:

> I hungered for books, new ways of looking and seeing. It was not a matter of believing or disbelieving what I read, but of feeling something new, of being affected by something that made the look of the world different.

We hope that the teachers and students who use *Literature: Thinking, Reading, and Writing Critically,* Second Edition, will feel some of the excitement and enthusiasm that Wright memorably describes.

# ACKNOWLEDGMENTS

We wish to thank the people who helped us to write this book. We are particularly indebted to Tim Armstrong, Katharine Glynn, Lynn Huddon, Lisa Moore, Brigitte Pelner, and Jim Sullivan of Longman. The book in many ways reflects their guidance.

For expert assistance in obtaining permission to reprint copyrighted material, we are greatly indebted to Virginia Creeden.

The following instructors read the manuscript and offered invaluable advice: Lucien L. Agosta, California State University, Sacramento; Ken Anderson, Floyd College; Alfred Arteaga, University of California, Berkeley; Rance Baker, San Antonio College; Jan Ballantine, St. Petersburgh Junior College; Lois Birky, Illinois Central College; Carol Boyd, Black Hawk College; Lois Bragg, Gallaudet University; Jane Gibson Brown, North Carolina Agricultural and Technical State University; Conrad Carroll, Northern Kentucky University; Jean W. Cash, James

Madison University; Robert Coltrane, Lock Haven University; Charles Darling, Greater Hartford Community College; Richard Dietrich, University of South Florida; Gail Duffy, Dean Junior College; Marilyn Edelstein, Santa Clara University; Toni Empringham, El Camino College; Craig Etchison, Glenville State College; Robert Farrell, Housatonic Community College; Elaine Fitzpatrick, Massasoit College; James E. Ford, University of Nebraska–Lincoln; Toni M. Forsyth, De Anza College; Donna Galati, University of South Dakota; Lois Gardner, Farleigh Dickinson University; Marvin P. Garrett, University of Cincinnati; Russell Greer, University of Georgia; Francis B. Hanify, Luzerne County Community College; Blair Hemstock, Keyano College (Canada); Paula Hester, Indian Hills Community College; Gloria Hochstein, University of Wisconsin–Eau Claire; Maura Ives, Texas A & M University; James L. Johnson, California State University, Fresno; Tammy Jones, University of Memphis; Edwina Jordan, Illinois Central College; Kate Keifer, Colorado State University; Sandra Lakey, Pennsylvania College of Technology; Wayne P. Lindquist, University of Wisconsin–Eau Claire; Paul McVeigh, Northern Virginia Community College; Cecilia G. Martyn, Montclair State College; Elizabeth Metzger, University of South Florida; Lawrence Milbourn, El Paso Community College; William S. Nicholson, Eastern Shore Community College; Stephen O'Neill, Bucks County Community College; Richard Pepp, Massasoit Community College; Frank Perkins, Quincy College; Betty Jo Hicks Peters, Morehead State University; Barbara Pokdowka, Commonwealth College; John C. Presley, Central Virginia Community College; Nancy Rayl, Cypress College; Betty Rhodes, Faulkner State College; Michelle Rogge, University of South Dakota; Patricia Rochester, University of Southwestern Louisiana; Leonard Sapienza, Red Rock Community College; Martha Saunders, West Georgia College; Allsion Shumsky, Northwestern Michigan College; Isabel B. Stanley, East Tennessee State University; Phillip Sterling, Ferris State University; Lisa M. Stroud, Liberty University; LaVonne Swanson, National College; Beverly Taylor, University of North Carolina, Chapel Hill; Merle Thompson, North Virginia Community College; Cyrilla Vessey, North Virginia Community College; Louise Vest, El Paso Community College; Mildred White, Oholone College; Margaret Whitt, University of Denver; Betty J. Williams, East Tennessee State University; Donald R. Williams, North Shore Community College; and Donnie Yeilding, Central Texas College.

Our thanks also to the many users of the earlier editions who gave us advice on how and where to make improvements: Linda Bamber, David Cavitch, Robert Cyr, Arthur Friedman, Nancy Grayson, Martha Hicks-Courant, Billie Ingram, Martha Lappen, Judy Maas, Deirdra McDonald, Patricia Meier, Ronald E. Pepin, William Roberts, Clair Seng-Niemoeller, Virginia Shine, and Charles L. Walker.

We are especially grateful for the comments and suggestions offered by the following scholars: Priscilla B. Bellair, Carroll Birtch, Don Brunn, Malcolm B. Clark, Terence A. Dalrymple, Franz Douskey, Gerald Duchovnay, Peter Dumanis, Estelle Easterly, Adam Fischer, Martha Flint, Robert H. Fossum, Gerald Hasham, Richard Henze, Catherine M. Hoff, Grace S. Kehrer, Nancy E. Kensicki, Linda Kraus, Juanita Laing, Vincent J. Liesenfeld, Martha McGowan, John H. fg-Meagher III, Stuart Millner, Edward Anthony Nagel, Peter L. Neff, Robert F. Panara, Ronald E. Pepin, Jane Pierce, Robert M. Post, Kris Rapp, Mark Reynolds, John Richardson, Donald H. Sanborn, Marlene Sebeck, Frank E. Sexton, Peggy

Skaggs, David Stuehler, James E. Tamer, Carol Teaff, C. Uejio, Hugh Witemeyer, Manfred Wolf, Joseph Zaitchik.

Finally, we are also grateful for valuable suggestions made by Charles Christensen, Joan Feinberg, Barbara Harman, X. J. Kennedy, Carolyn Potts, Marcia Stubbs, Helen Vendler, and Ann Chalmers Watts.

Sylvan Barnet
Morton Berman
William Burto
William E. Cain

# PART ONE

# *Reading, Thinking, and Writing Critically about Literature*

# CHAPTER 1

# *Reading and Responding to Literature*

## WHAT IS LITERATURE?

Large books have been written on this subject, and large books will continue to be written on it. But we can offer a few brief generalizations that may be useful.

First, the word "literature" can be used to refer to anything written. The Department of Agriculture will, upon request, send an applicant "literature on canning tomatoes." People who ask for such material expect it to be clear and informative, but they do not expect it to be interesting in itself. They do not read it for the experience of reading it; they read it only if they are thinking about canning tomatoes.

There is, however, a sort of literature that people *do* read without expecting a practical payoff. They read the sort of writing that is in *An Introduction to Literature* because they expect it to hold their interest and to provide pleasure. They may vaguely feel that it will be good for them, but they don't read it *because* it will be good for them, any more than they dance because dancing provides healthful exercise. Dancing may indeed be healthful, but that's not why people dance. They dance because dancing affords a special kind of pleasure. For similar reasons people watch athletic contests and go to concerts or to the theater. We participate in activities such as these not because we expect some sort of later reward but because we know that the experience of participating is in itself rewarding. Perhaps the best explanation is that the experiences are absorbing—which is to say they take us out of ourselves for a while—and that (especially in the case of concerts, dance performances, and athletic contests) they allow us to appreciate excellence, to admire achievement. Most of us can swim or toss a ball and maybe even hit a ball, but when we go to a swimming meet or to a ball game we see a level of performance that evokes our admiration.

## Looking at an Example: Robert Frost's "Immigrants"

Let's begin, then, by thinking of literature as (to quote Robert Frost) "a performance in words." And let's begin with a very short poem by Frost (1874-1963), probably America's best-known poet. Frost wrote these lines for a pageant at Plymouth, Massachusetts, celebrating the three-hundredth anniversary of the arrival of the *Mayflower* from England.

### *Immigrants*

No ship of all that under sail or steam
Have gathered people to us more and more
But Pilgrim-manned the Mayflower in a dream
Has been her anxious convoy in to shore.

[*1920*]

To find this poem—this performance in words—of any interest, a reader probably has to know that the *Mayflower* brought the Pilgrims to America. Second, a reader has to grasp a slightly unfamiliar construction: "No ship . . . but . . . has . . . ," which means, in effect, "every ship has." (Compare: "No human being but is born of woman," which means "Every human being is born of woman.")

If, then, we *paraphrase* the poem—translate it into other words in the same language—we get something roughly along these lines:

> Every ship of all the ships (whether sailing vessels or steamships) that have collected people in increasing numbers and brought them to this country has had the Mayflower, with its Pilgrims, as its eager (or worried?) escort to the coast.

We have tried to make this paraphrase as accurate and as concise as possible, but for reasons that we'll explain in a moment, we have omitted giving an equivalent for Frost's "in a dream." Why, one might ask, is our paraphrase so much less interesting than the original?

*Performance* First, the poem is metrical. With only a few exceptions, every second syllable is accented more than the preceding syllable. Take the first line. Although "No" probably receives at least as much stress as the word that follows it, "ship," in the rest of the line the pattern is clear:

Nó shíp ŏf áll thăt ún dĕr sáil ŏr stéam

(Of course not all of the stresses are equally heavy. When you read the line aloud you will probably put less emphasis on the first syllable of "under," for instance, than you put on "sail" or "steam.")

The language, then, is highly patterned, and you doubtless have experienced the force of patterned language—of rhythmic thought—whether from other poems or songs ("We shall overcome, / We shall overcome") or football chants ("Block that kick! Block that kick!"). Take a moment to reread the first line, without heavily emphasizing the stressed syllables but with some awareness of them. (Don't read the line mechanically; read it for sense, not for fixed pattern—but you'll *feel* a pattern.)

No ship of all that under sail or steam . . .

Further, repetition is not limited to the pattern of stresses in the lines. We get the same number of syllables (ten) in each line. (There may be a few variations. For instance, in the third line if we pronounce "Mayflower" with three syllables, the line has eleven syllables. Probably we should pronounce it with two syllables: "Mayflow'r," maybe something like "Mayflar.") And of course we also get repetitions of sounds at the ends of the lines: "steam" rhymes with "dream," and "more" with "shore."

Probably, too, the repetition of *s* in "*s*ail or *s*team" catches the ear. The two words are somewhat alike in that they are both monosyllables, they both begin with the same sound, and they both evoke images of ships. Compare "sail or steam" with "sail or gas" or "sail or engine" and you will probably agree that the original is more pleasing and more interesting.

One can see what Frost meant when he said that a poem is a performance in words: four lines, each with the same basic pattern of stresses, each ending with a word that rhymes, and all this in a single grammatical sentence. The thing looks easy enough, but we know that it took great skill to make the words behave properly, that is, to get the right words in the right order. Frost went into the lions' cage, did his act, and came out unharmed.

*Significance* We've been talking about Frost's skill in handling words, but we haven't said anything (except in our clumsy paraphrase) about *what* Frost is saying in "Immigrants." One of the things that literature does is to make us see—hear, feel, love—what the author thinks is a valuable part of the experience of living. A thousand years ago a Japanese writer, Lady Murasaki, made this point when she had one of the characters in her book talk about what motivates an author:

> Again and again something in one's own life or in that around one will seem so important that one cannot bear to let it pass into oblivion. There must never come a time, the writer feels, when people do not know about this.

We can probably agree with Lady Murasaki that writers of literature try to get at something important in their experiences, emotions, or visions, and try to make the reader feel the importance. And so writers show us what it is like (for instance) to be in love (plenty of room for comedy as well as tragedy here), or what forgiveness is like, or what is at the heart of immigration to America.

We can't be certain about what Frost really thought of the Pilgrims and of the *Mayflower*, but we do have the poem, and that's what we are concerned with. It celebrates the anniversary, of course, but it also celebrates at least two other things: the continuing arrival of new immigrants and the close connection between the early and the later immigrants.

Persons whose ancestors came over on the *Mayflower* have a reputation for being rather sniffy about later arrivals, but Frost reminds his Yankee audience that their ancestors, the *Mayflower* passengers, were themselves immigrants. However greatly the histories and the experiences of the early immigrants differed from those of later immigrants, the experience of emigration and the hopes for a better life link the Mayflower passengers with more recent arrivals.

The poem says, if our paraphrase is roughly accurate, that the *Mayflower* and its passengers accompany all later immigrants. Now, what does this mean?

Literally, of course, it is nonsense. The Mayflower and its passengers disappeared centuries ago.

##  TOPICS FOR CRITICAL THINKING AND WRITING

1. In our paraphrase, in an effort to avoid complexities, we did not give any equivalent for "in a dream." The time has now come to face this puzzle in line 3: "But Pilgrim-manned the *Mayflower* in a dream." Some readers take Frost to be saying that the long-deceased passengers of the *Mayflower* still dream of others following them. Other readers, however, interpret the line as saying that later immigrants dream of the *Mayflower*. Now, this paraphrase, even if accurate, makes an assertion that is not strictly true, since many later immigrants probably had never even heard of the *Mayflower*. But in a larger sense the statement is true. The later immigrants—with the terrible exception of involuntary immigrants from Africa who were brought here in chains—dreamed of a better life, just as the Mayflower passengers did. Some hoped for religious freedom, some hoped to escape political oppression or starvation, but again, all were seeking a better life. What do you make of line 3?
2. In our paraphrase we mentioned that "anxious" might be paraphrased either as "eager" or as "worried." (Contrast, for instance, "She was anxious to serve the community" and "She was anxious about the exam.") Is Frost's "anxious convoy" *eagerly* accompanying the ships with immigrants, or is it *nervously* accompanying them, perhaps worried that these new arrivals may not be the right sort of people, or worried that the new arrivals may not be able to get on in the new country? Or does the word "anxious," which seems to modify "convoy" (here, the *Mayflower*), really refer to the new immigrants, who are worried that they may not succeed? Or perhaps they are worried that America may not in fact correspond to their hopes.

   Read the poem aloud two or three times, and then think about which of these meanings—or some other meanings that you come up with—you find most rewarding. You might consider, too, whether more than one meaning can be present. Frost himself in a letter wrote that he liked to puzzle his readers a bit—to baffle them and yet (or thereby) propel them forward:

   > My poems—I should suppose everybody's poems—are all set to trip the reader head foremost into the boundless. Ever since infancy I have had the habit of leaving my blocks carts chairs and such like ordinaries where people would be pretty sure to fall forward over them in the dark. Forward, you understand, *and* in the dark.

   What we have been saying is this: a reader of a work of literature finds meanings in the work, but also (even when the meaning is uncertain) takes delight in the details, takes delight in the way that the work has been constructed, takes delight in (again) the performance. When we have got at what we think may be the "meaning" of a work, we do not value or hold on to the meaning only and turn away from the work itself; rather, we value even more the craftsmanship that the work displays. And we come to see that the meaning is inseparable from all of the details that go to make up the work.

3. "Pilgrim-manned" may disturb some readers. Conscious of sexist language, today we try to avoid saying things like "This shows the greatness of man" or "Man is a rational animal" when we are speaking not about males but about all people. Does Frost's "Pilgrim-manned" strikes you as slighting women? If not, why not?
4. We have already mentioned that Frost's poem cannot possibly be thought to describe involuntary immigrants. Is this a weakness in the poem? If so, how serious a weakness?
5. Frost's poem celebrates immigration and does not consider its effect on the Native American population. The poem does not, so to speak, tell the whole truth; but no statement, however long, could tell the "whole truth" about such a complex topic. Do you agree that if the poem doesn't give us the whole truth, perhaps we get enough if the poem reminds us of *a* truth?

## Looking at a Second Example: Pat Mora's "Immigrants"

*Pat Mora, after graduating from Texas Western College, earned a master's degree at the University of Texas at El Paso. She is best known for her poems, but she has also published essays on Chicano culture.*

### *Immigrants*

wrap their babies in the American flag,
feed them mashed hot dogs and apple pie,
name them Bill and Daisy,
buy them blonde dolls that blink blue
eyes or a football and tiny cleats
before the baby can even walk,
speak to them in thick English,
    hallo, babee, hallo.
whisper in Spanish or Polish
when the babies sleep, whisper
in a dark parent bed, that dark
parent fear, "Will they like
our boy, our girl, our fine american
boy, our fine american girl?"

[*1986*]

Pat Mora's experience—that of a Mexican-American woman in the United States—obviously must be very different from that of Frost, an Anglo-Saxon male and almost the official poet of the country. Further, Mora is writing in our own time, not three-quarters of a century ago. A reader expects, and finds, a very different sort of poem. We won't discuss this poem at length, but we will say that in our view she too gets at something important. Among the many things in this verbal performance that give us pleasure are these:

1. The wit of making the title part of the first sentence. A reader expects the title to be relevant to the poem but does not expect it to be grammatically the first word of the poem. We like the fresh way in which the title is used.
2. We also like the aptness with which Mora has caught the immigrants' eager yet worried attempt to make their children "100% American."
3. We like the mimicry of the immigrants talking to their children: "hallo, babee, hallo." Of course if this mimicry came from an outsider it would be condescending and offensive, but since it is written by someone known for her concern with Mexican-American culture, it probably is not offensive. It is almost affectionate.

## TOPICS FOR CRITICAL THINKING AND WRITING

1. The last comment may be right, so far as it goes, but isn't it too simple? Reread the poem—preferably aloud—and then try to decide exactly what Mora's attitude is toward the immigrants. Do you think that she fully approves of their hopes? On what do you base your answer?
2. What does it mean to say that someone—a politician, for instance—"wraps himself in the American flag"? What does Mora mean when she says that immigrants "wrap their babies in the American flag"? How would you paraphrase the line?
3. After reading the poem aloud two or three times, what elements of "verbal performance"—we might say of skillful play—do you notice? Mora does not use rhyme, but she does engage in some verbal play. What examples can you point to?
4. What is your own attitude toward the efforts of some immigrants to assimilate themselves to an Anglo-American model? How does your attitude affect your reading of the poem?

## THINKING ABOUT A STORY: THE PARABLE OF THE PRODIGAL SON

Good prose narratives, too, like good poems, are carefully constructed. Let's look at a story, one told by Jesus, and reported in the fifteenth chapter of the Gospel according to St. Luke. Jesus here tells a **parable,** a short story from which a lesson is to be drawn. Luke reports that just before Jesus told the story, the Pharisees and scribes—persons whom the Gospels depict as opposed to Jesus because he sometimes found their traditions and teachings inadequate—complained that Jesus was a man of loose morals, one who "receives sinners and eats with them." According to Luke, Jesus responded thus:

> And he said, "A certain man had two sons: and the younger of them said to his father, 'Father, give me the portion of goods that falleth to

> me.' And he divided unto them his living. And not many days after, the younger son gathered all together, and took his journey into a far country, and there wasted his substance with riotous living.
>
> And when he had spent all, there arose a mighty famine in that land, and he began to be in want. And he went and joined himself to a citizen of that country, and he sent him into his fields to feed swine. And he would fain have filled his belly with the husks that the swine did eat: and no man gave unto him.
>
> And when he came to himself he said, 'How many hired servants of my father's have bread enough and to spare, and I perish with hunger? I will arise and go to my father, and will say unto him, "Father, I have sinned against heaven, and before thee. And am no more worthy to be called thy son: make me as one of thy hired servants."'
>
> And he arose, and came to his father. But when he was yet a great way off, his father saw him, and had compassion, and ran, and fell on his neck, and kissed him. And the son said unto him, 'Father, I have sinned against heaven, and in thy sight, and am no more worthy to be called thy son.' But the father said to his servants, 'Bring forth the best robe, and put it on him, and put a ring on his hand, and shoes on his feet. And bring hither the fatted calf and kill it, and let us eat, and be merry. For this my son was dead, and is alive again; he was lost, and is found.' And they began to be merry.
>
> Now his elder son was in the field, and as he came and drew nigh to the house, he heard music and dancing. And he called one of the servants, and asked what these things meant. And he said unto him, 'Thy brother is come, and thy father hath killed the fatted calf, because he hath received him safe and sound.' And he was angry, and would not go in: therefore came his father out, and entreated him. And he answering said to his father, 'Lo, these many years do I serve thee, neither transgressed I at any time thy commandment, and yet thou never gavest me a kid, that I might make merry with my friends: but as soon as this thy son was come, which hath devoured thy living with harlots, thou has killed for him the fatted calf.' And he said unto him, 'Son, thou art ever with me, and all that I have is thine. It was meet that we should make merry, and be glad: for this thy brother was dead, and is alive again: and was lost, and is found."' (Luke 15:11–32, King James Version)

Now, to begin with a small point, it is not likely that any but strictly observant Jews, or perhaps Muslims (who, like these Jews, do not eat pork), can feel the disgust that Jesus' audience must have felt at the thought that the son was reduced to feeding swine and that he even envied the food that swine ate. Further, some of us may be vegetarians; if so, we are not at all delighted at the thought that the father kills the fatted calf (probably the wretched beast has been force-fed) in order to celebrate the son's return.

And, of course, some of us do not believe in God, and hence are not prepared to take the story, as many people take it, as a story whose message is that we, like God (the father in this parable is usually taken to stand for God), ought to rejoice in the restoration of the sinner. Probably, then, for all sorts of obvious reasons none of us can put ourselves back into the first century A.D. and hear the story exactly as Jesus' hearers heard it.

Still, most of us can probably agree on what we take to be the gist of the story, and, second, we can enjoy the skillful way in which it is told. This skill will become apparent, however, only after several readings. What are some examples of superb storytelling here, and what can a reader gain from a thoughtful reading? We can begin by noting a few points:

1. Although the story is customarily called "The Parable of the Prodigal Son" or "The Parable of the Lost Son," it tells of two sons, not of one. When we reread the story, we increasingly see that these brothers are compared and contrasted: the prodigal leaves his father's house for a different way of life—he thus seems lost to the father—but then he repents and returns to the father, whereas the older son, who physically remains with the father, is spiritually remote from the father, or is lost in a different way. By virtue of his self-centeredness the older son is remote from the father in feeling or spirit.
2. Again, reading and rereading reveal small but telling details. For instance, when the prodigal plans to return home, he thinks of what he will say to his father. He has come to his senses and repudiated his folly, but he still does not understand his father, for we will see in a moment that the prodigal has no need of this speech. Jesus tells us that as soon as the father saw the prodigal returning, he "had compassion, and ran, and fell on his neck, and kissed him." And (another very human touch) the prodigal—although already forgiven—nevertheless cannot refrain from uttering his heartfelt but, under the circumstances, unnecessary speech of repentance.
3. The elder son, learning that the merrymaking is for the returning prodigal, "was angry, and would not go in." This character is sketched only briefly, but a reader immediately recognizes the type: self-centered, unforgiving, and petulant. The older son does not realize it, but he is as distant from his father as the younger son had been. What is the father's response to this son, who is so different from the forgiving father?

    Therefore came his father out, and entreated him.

    The father goes out to the dutiful son, just as he had gone out to the prodigal son. (What the father *does* is as important as what he *says*.) Notice, too, speaking of sons, that the older son, talking to his father, somewhat distances himself from his brother, disdainfully referring to the prodigal as "this thy son." And what is the father's response? To the elder son's "this thy son," the father replies, "this thy brother."

No matter how closely we look, however, we will not be able to find certain pieces of information; certain **blanks** or **gaps** will remain. For instance, we are not given information about the relationship of the brothers before the story begins. Nor are we told if the older son learns a lesson, and repents of his nasty behavior. We can offer guesses based on our understanding of others and based on our own nature, but the story is not explicit about these matters, and other readers may offer different guesses. We may even, perhaps, deny that the stay-at-home's behavior *is* nasty, and we may say that the father was sentimental and foolish to forgive the prodigal so easily.

There may also be **indeterminacies** in a story, passages that remain unclear even to careful readers of the story. Thus, the father says to the older son, "All that I have is thine," but is this true? After all, he has just killed the fatted calf, and has never offered even "a kid" (young goat) to the older son. And—a very large issue—readers may even question the historical accuracy of the picture of the Pharisees and scribes, for sources other than the Gospels depict them more sympathetically.

Such thoughts may come to mind, because, again, we inevitably bring ourselves to all that we experience (and reading is an experience). It may turn out that, finally, we will (so to speak) go against the grain of the story and give it a **counter-reading,** a reading that challenges or replaces the more obvious meaning we might at first give it. Just as a reader of Frost's "Immigrants" might argue that it gives a white New Englander's view of immigration and overlooks the disastrous effects of colonization on Native Americans and on black slaves, so a reader may feel that the Parable of the Prodigal Son obscures another story and that the son should show his repentance in more than words. Or a reader may interpret the story from a psychoanalytic perspective as a story of sibling rivalry. We may come to feel that this whole story of a father and his two sons is an example of the sort of male-dominated or patriarchal thinking that (one might argue) gives little or no value to women; these sons seem to have no mother, and the only women mentioned are harlots.

Thoughtful, plausible responses of this sort, based on a close reading, can be valuable, and it is useful to set them forth in writing so that we share them with our colleagues. If, however, we let the work of literature merely trigger our stock responses rather than try to let it induce new, deeper responses, we may be the losers. We may, to put it bluntly, simply retain our prejudices and miss the experience of encountering something more important, more substantial.

## TOPIC FOR CRITICAL THINKING AND WRITING

This story is traditionally called the Parable of the Prodigal Son. Can a case be made for the view that it ought to be called the Parable of the Prodigal Father? Forget, if you can, the traditional title, and ask yourself if the story tells of a father who is prodigal with his property and who at the end is prodigal with his love. Explain why you accept or reject this interpretation.

# STORIES TRUE AND FALSE

The word "story" comes from "history"; the stories that historians, biographers, and journalists narrate are supposed to be true accounts of what happened. The stories of novelists and short-story writers, however, are admittedly untrue; they are "fiction," things made up, imagined, manufactured. As readers, we come to a supposedly true story with expectations different from those we bring to fiction.

Consider the difference between reading a narrative in a newspaper and one in a book of short stories. If, while reading a newspaper, we come across a story of, say, a subway accident, we assume that the account is true, and we read it for the information about a relatively unusual event. Anyone hurt? What sort of people? In our neighborhood? Whose fault? When we read a book of fiction, however, we do not expect to encounter literal truths; we read novels and short stories not for facts but for pleasure and for some insight or for a sense of what an aspect of life means to the writer. Consider the following short story by Grace Paley.

## GRACE PALEY

*Born in 1922 in New York City, Grace Paley attended Hunter College and New York University, but left without a degree. (She now teaches at Sarah Lawrence College.) While raising two children she wrote poetry and then, in the 1950s, turned to writing fiction.*

*Paley's chief subject is the life of little people struggling in the Big City. Of life she has said, "How daily life is lived is a mystery to me. You write about what's mysterious to you. What is it like? Why do people do this?" Of the short story she has said, "It can be just telling a little tale, or writing a complicated philosophical story. It can be a song, almost."*

*On page 490 we give another story by Paley.*

### *Samuel*

Some boys are very tough. They're afraid of nothing. They are the ones who climb a wall and take a bow at the top. Not only are they brave on the roof, but they make a lot of noise in the darkest part of the cellar where even the super hates to go. They also jiggle and hop on the platform between the locked doors of the subway cars.

Four boys are jiggling on the swaying platform. Their names are Alfred, Calvin, Samuel, and Tom. The men and the women in the cars on either side watch them. They don't like them to jiggle or jump but don't want to interfere. Of course some of the men in the cars were once brave boys like these. One of them had ridden the tail of a speeding truck from New York to Rockaway Beach without getting off, without his sore fingers losing hold. Nothing happened to him then or later. He had made a compact with other boys who preferred to watch: Starting at Eighth Avenue and Fifteenth Street, he would get to some specified place, maybe Twenty-third and the river, by hopping the tops of the moving trucks. This was hard to do when one truck turned a corner in the wrong direction and the nearest truck was a couple of feet too high. He made three or four starts before succeeding. He had gotten his idea from a film at school called *The Romance of Logging.* He had finished high school, married a good friend, was in a responsible job and going to night school.

These two men and others looked at the four boys jumping and jiggling on the platform and thought, It must be fun to ride that way, especially now the weather is nice and we're out of the tunnel and way high over the Bronx. Then they thought, These kids do seem to be acting sort of stupid. They *are* little. Then they thought of some of the brave things they had done when they were boys and jiggling didn't seem so risky.

The ladies in the car became very angry when they looked at the four boys. Most of them brought their brows together and hoped the boys could see their extreme disapproval. One of the ladies wanted to get up and say, Be careful you dumb kids, get off that platform or I'll call a cop. But three of the boys were Negroes and the fourth was something else she couldn't tell for sure. She was afraid they'd be fresh and laugh at her and embarrass her. She wasn't afraid they'd hit her, but she was afraid of embarrassment. Another lady thought, Their mothers never know where they are. It wasn't true in this particular case. Their mothers all knew that they had gone to see the missile exhibit on Fourteenth Street.

5 Out on the platform, whenever the train accelerated, the boys would raise their hands and point them up to the sky to act like rockets going off, then they rat-tat-tatted the shatterproof glass pane like machine guns, although no machine guns had been exhibited.

For some reason known only to the motorman, the train began a sudden slowdown. The lady who was afraid of embarrassment saw the boys jerk forward and backward and grab the swinging guard chains. She had her own boy at home. She stood up with determination and went to the door. She slid it open and said, "You boys will be hurt. You'll be killed. I'm going to call the conductor if you don't just go into the next car and sit down and be quiet."

Two of the boys said, "Yes'm," and acted as though they were about to go. Two of them blinked their eyes a couple of times and pressed their lips together. The train resumed its speed. The door slid shut, parting the lady and the boys. She leaned against the side door because she had to get off at the next stop.

The boys opened their eyes wide at each other and laughed. The lady blushed. The boys looked at her and laughed harder. They began to pound each other's back. Samuel laughed the hardest and pounded Alfred's back until Alfred coughed and the tears came. Alfred held tight to the chain hook. Samuel pounded him even harder when he saw the tears. He said, "Why you bawling? You a baby, huh?" and laughed. One of the men whose boyhood had been more watchful than brave became angry. He stood up straight and looked at the boys for a couple of seconds. Then he walked in a citizenly way to the end of the car, where he pulled the emergency cord. Almost at once, with a terrible hiss, the pressure of air abandoned the brakes and the wheels were caught and held.

People standing in the most secure places fell forward, then backward. Samuel had let go of his hold on the chain so he could pound Tom as well as Alfred. All the passengers in the cars whipped back and forth, but he pitched only forward and fell head first to be crushed and killed between the cars.

10 The train had stopped hard, halfway into the station, and the conductor called at once for the trainmen who knew about this kind of death and how to take the body from the wheels and brakes. There was silence except for passengers from other cars who asked, What happened! What happened! The ladies waited around wondering if he might be an only child. The men recalled other afternoons with very bad endings. The little boys stayed close to each other, leaning and touching shoulders and arms and legs.

When the policeman knocked at the door and told her about it, Samuel's mother began to scream. She screamed all day and moaned all night, though the doctors tried to quiet her with pills.

Oh, oh, she hopelessly cried. She did not know how she could ever find another boy like that one. However, she was a young woman and she became pregnant. Then for a few months she was hopeful. The child born to her was a boy. They brought him to be seen and nursed. She smiled. But immediately she saw that this baby wasn't Samuel. She and her husband together have had other children, but never again will a boy exactly like Samuel be known.

[*1968*]

You might think about the ways in which "Samuel" differs from a newspaper story of an accident in a subway. (You might even want to write a newspaper version of the happening.) In some ways, of course, Paley's story faintly resembles an account that might appear in a newspaper. Journalists are taught to give information about Who, What, When, Where and Why, and Paley does provide this. Thus, the *characters* (Samuel and others) are the journalist's Who; the *plot* (the boys were jiggling on the platform, and when a man pulled the emergency cord one of them was killed) is the What; the *setting* (the subway, presumably in modern times) is the When and the Where; the *motivation* (the irritation of the man who pulls the emergency cord) is the Why.

Ask yourself questions about each of these elements, and think about how they work in Paley's story. You might also think about responses to the following questions. Your responses will teach you a good deal about what literature is and about some of the ways in which it works.

## TOPICS FOR CRITICAL THINKING AND WRITING

1. Paley wrote the story, but an unspecified person *tells* it. Describe the voice of this narrator in the first paragraph. Is the voice neutral and objective, or do you hear some sort of attitude, a point of view? If you do hear an attitude, what words or phrases in the story indicate it?
2. What do you know about the setting of "Samuel"? What can you infer about the neighborhood?
3. In the fourth paragraph we are told that "three of the boys were Negroes and the fourth was something else." Is race important in this story? Is Samuel "Negro" or "something else"? Does it matter?
4. Exactly *why* did a man walk "in a citizenly way to the end of the car, where he pulled the emergency cord"? Do you think the author blames him? What evidence can you offer to support your view? Do *you* blame him? Or do you blame the boys? Or anyone? Explain.
5. The story is called "Samuel," and it is, surely, about him. But what happens after Samuel dies? (You might want to list the events.) What else is the story about? (You might want to comment on why you believe the items in your list are important.)
6. Can you generalize about what the men think of the jigglers and about what the women think? Is Paley saying something about the sexes? About the attitudes of onlookers in a big city?

# WHAT'S PAST IS PROLOGUE

The two poems and two stories that you have just read cannot, of course, stand for all works of literature. For one thing, although Mora's "Immigrants" and the two prose fictions include some dialogue, none of these works is in dramatic form, designed for presentation on a stage. Still, these four examples, as well as works of literature that you are already familiar with, will provide something of a background against which you can read the other works in this book. For instance, if you read a story that, like the Parable of the Prodigal Son, seems strongly to imply a moral, think about how the moral is controlled by what the characters *do* as well as by what they *say,* and how one character is defined by being set against another. If you read a poem that, like Mora's "Immigrants," seems to play one tone of voice against another (for instance, the voice of the speaker of the poem against a voice quoted within the poem), think about how the voices relate to each other and how they perhaps harmonize to create a complex vision.

In short, a work of literature is not a nut to be cracked open so that a kernel of meaning can be extracted and devoured, and the rest thrown away; the whole—a performance in words—is something to be experienced and enjoyed.

We end this chapter with one additional short work.

## COUNTEE CULLEN

*Countee Cullen (1903-46) was born Countee Porter in New York City, raised by his grandmother, and then adopted by the Reverend Frederick A. Cullen, a Methodist minister in Harlem. Cullen received a bachelor's degree from New York University (Phi Beta Kappa) and a master's degree from Harvard. He earned his living as a high school teacher of French, but his literary gifts were recognized in his own day.*

### *Incident*

*(For Eric Walrond)*

Once riding in old Baltimore,
  Heart-filled, head-filled with glee,
I saw a Baltimorean
  Keep looking straight at me.

Now I was eight and very small,
  And he was no whit bigger,
And so I smiled, but he poked out
  His tongue, and called me, "Nigger."

I saw the whole of Baltimore
  From May until December;
Of all the things that happened there
  That's all that I remember.

[*1925*]

## TOPICS FOR CRITICAL THINKING AND WRITING

1. How would you define an "incident"? A serious occurrence? A minor occurrence, or what? Think about the word, and then think about

Cullen's use of it as a title for the event recorded in this poem. Test out one or two other possible titles as a way of helping yourself to see the strengths or weaknesses of Cullen's title.

2. The dedicatee, Eric Walrond (1898–1966), was an African-American essayist and writer of fiction, who in an essay, "On Being Black," had described his experiences of racial prejudice. How does the presence of the dedication bear on our response to Cullen's account of the "incident"?
3. What is the tone of the poem? Indifferent? Angry? Or what? What do you think is the speaker's attitude toward the "incident"? What is your attitude?
4. Ezra Pound, poet and critic, once defined literature as "news that *stays* news." What do you think he meant by this? Do you think that the definition fits Cullen's poem?

# CHAPTER 2

# *Writing about Literature: From Idea to Essay*

## WHY WRITE?

If you have ever put exclamation points or question marks or brief annotations ("this is ridiculous," or "great!") in the margins of your books, you are aware of the *pleasure* one gets from putting responses into writing. But people also write about literature—not only in margins of books but, let's say, in notebooks or journals and ultimately in essays—in order to clarify and account for their responses to works that interest or excite or frustrate them.

In putting words on paper you will have to take a second and a third look at what is in front of you and what is within you. Writing, then, is not only a way of expressing pleasure but also a way of *learning*. The last word about complex thoughts and feelings is never said, but when we write we hope to make at least a little progress in the difficult but rewarding job of talking about our responses. We learn, and then we hope to interest our readers because we are communicating to them our responses to something that for one reason or another is worth talking about.

This communication is, in effect, teaching. You may think that you are writing for the teacher, but that is a misconception; when you write, *you* are the teacher. An essay on literature is an attempt to help someone see the work as you see it. If this chapter had to be boiled down to a single sentence, that sentence would be: Because you are teaching, your essay should embody those qualities that you value in teachers—intelligence, open-mindedness, effort; and a desire to offer what help one can.

# GETTING IDEAS: PRE-WRITING

"All there is to writing," Robert Frost said, "is having ideas. To learn to write is to learn to have ideas." But how does one "learn to have ideas"? Among the methods are these: reading with a pen or pencil in hand, so that you can annotate the text; keeping a journal, in which you jot down reflections about your reading; talking with others (including your instructor) about the reading. Let's look at the first of these, annotating.

## Annotating a Text

In reading, if you own the book don't hesitate to mark it up, indicating (by highlighting or underlining or by making marginal notes) what puzzles you, what pleases or interests you, and what displeases or bores you. Later, of course, you'll want to think further about these responses, asking yourself, on rereading, if you still feel that way, and if not, why not, but these first responses will get you started.

One kind of annotation is a question mark in the margin, jotted down in order to indicate your uncertainty about the meaning of a word. It's a good idea to keep a **dictionary** nearby while you are reading. Of course you won't look up every word that you are unsure about—this might spoil the fun of reading—but sometimes you will sense that you need to know the precise meanings and implications of the writer's words in order to feel and appreciate the effects he or she is trying to create. And the more you become aware of how richly meaningful the words can be in a literary text, the more sensitive and self-aware you will be about the words you use in your own prose.

We have already looked at Pat Mora's short poem, "Immigrants" (page 4), but here it is again, with a student's first annotations.

### *Immigrants*

wrap their babies in the American flag,
feed them mashed hot dogs and apple pie,
name them Bill and Daisy,
buy them blonde dolls that blink blue
eyes or a football and tiny cleats
before the baby can even walk,
speak to them in thick English,
hallo, babee, hallo.
whisper in Spanish or Polish
when the babies sleep, whisper
in a dark parent bed, that dark
parent fear. Will they like
our boy, our girl, our fine american
boy, our fine american girl?

unusual to use title as first word?

so what's wrong with hot dogs and mashed potatoes?

Anglo types—not Asian-American or Latino types

Is Mora making fun of immigrants?

do only immigrants show a "parent fear"? Don't all parents fear for their children?

why not a capital letter?

Notice that most of these annotations are questions that the student is asking herself. Asking questions is an excellent way to get yourself thinking. We will return to this method shortly.

## Brainstorming for Ideas for Writing

Unlike annotating, which consists of making brief notes and small marks on the printed page, "brainstorming"—the free jotting down of ideas—asks that you jot down at length whatever comes to mind, without inhibition. But before we talk further about brainstorming, read the following short story.

## KATE CHOPIN

*Kate Chopin (1851-1904)—the name is pronounced in the French way, somewhat like "show pan"—was born in St. Louis, with the name Katherine O'Flaherty. Her father was an immigrant from Ireland, and her mother was descended from an old Creole family. (In the United States, a Creole is a person descended from the original French settlers in Louisiana or the original Spanish settlers in the Gulf States.) At the age of nineteen she married Oscar Chopin, a cotton broker in New Orleans. They had six children, and though Kate Chopin had contemplated a literary career, she did not turn seriously to writing until after her husband's death in 1883. Most of her fiction concerns the lives of the descendants of the French who had settled in Louisiana. On page 607 we print Chopin's novel,* The Awakening.

## *The Story of an Hour*

Knowing that Mrs. Mallard was afflicted with a heart trouble, great care was taken to break to her as gently as possible the news of her husband's death.

It was her sister Josephine who told her, in broken sentences, veiled hints that revealed in half concealing. Her husband's friend Richards was there, too, near her. It was he who had been in the newspaper office when intelligence of the railroad disaster was received, with Brently Mallard's name leading the list of "killed." He had only taken the time to assure himself of its truth by a second telegram, and had hastened to forestall any less careful, less tender friend in bearing the sad message.

She did not hear the story as many women have heard the same, with a paralyzed inability to accept its significance. She wept at once, with sudden, wild abandonment, in her sister's arms. When the storm of grief had spent itself she went away to her room alone. She would have no one follow her.

There stood, facing the open window, a comfortable, roomy armchair. Into this she sank, pressed down by a physical exhaustion that haunted her body and seemed to reach into her soul.

5 She could see in the open square before her house the tops of trees that were all aquiver with the new spring life. The delicious breath of rain was in the air. In the street below a peddler was crying his wares. The notes of a distant song which some one was singing reached her faintly, and countless sparrows were twittering in the eaves.

There were patches of blue sky showing here and there through the clouds that had met and piled above the other in the west facing her window.

She sat with her head thrown back upon the cushion of the chair quite motionless, except when a sob came up into her throat and shook her, as a child who has cried itself to sleep continues to sob in its dreams.

She was young, with a fair, calm face, whose lines bespoke repression and even a certain strength. But now there was a dull stare in her eyes, whose gaze was fixed away off yonder on one of those patches of blue sky. It was not a glance of reflection, but rather indicated a suspension of intelligent thought.

There was something coming to her and she was waiting for it, fearfully. What was it? She did not know; it was too subtle and elusive to name. But she felt it, creeping out of the sky, reaching toward her through the sounds, the scents, the color that filled the air.

10 Now her bosom rose and fell tumultuously. She was beginning to recognize this thing that was approaching to possess her, and she was striving to beat it back with her will—as powerless as her two white slender hands would have been.

When she abandoned herself a little whispered word escaped her slightly parted lips. She said it over and over under her breath: "Free, free, free!" The vacant stare and the look of terror that had followed it went from her eyes. They stayed keen and bright. Her pulses beat fast, and the coursing blood warmed and relaxed every inch of her body.

She did not stop to ask if it were not a monstrous joy that held her. A clear and exalted perception enabled her to dismiss the suggestion as trivial.

She knew that she would weep again when she saw the kind, tender hands folded in death; the face that had never looked save with love upon her, fixed and gray and dead. But she saw beyond that bitter moment a long procession of years to come that would belong to her absolutely. And she opened and spread her arms out to them in welcome.

There would be no one to live for her during those coming years; she would live for herself. There would be no powerful will bending her in that blind persistence with which men and women believe they have a right to impose a private will upon a fellow creature. A kind intention or a cruel intention made the act seem no less a crime as she looked upon it in that brief moment of illumination.

15 And yet she had loved him—sometimes. Often she had not. What did it matter! What could love, the unsolved mystery, count for in face of this possession of self-assertion which she suddenly recognized as the strongest impulse of her being.

"Free! Body and soul free!" she kept whispering.

Josephine was kneeling before the closed door with her lips to the keyhole, imploring for admission. "Louise, open the door! I beg; open the door—you will make yourself ill. What are you doing, Louise? For heaven's sake open the door."

"Go away. I am not making myself ill." No; she was drinking in a very elixir of life through that open window.

Her fancy was running riot along those days ahead of her. Spring days, and summer days, and all sorts of days that would be her own. She breathed a quick prayer that life might be long. It was only yesterday she had thought with a shudder that life might be long.

20 She arose at length and opened the door to her sister's importunities. There was a feverish triumph in her eyes, and she carried herself unwittingly like a goddess of Victory. She clasped her sister's waist, and together they descended the stairs. Richards stood waiting for them at the bottom.

Some one was opening the front door with a latchkey. It was Brently Mallard who entered, a little travel-stained, composedly carrying his gripsack and umbrella. He had been far from the scene of accident, and did not even know there had been one. He stood amazed at Josephine's piercing cry; at Richards' quick motion to screen him from the view of his wife.

But Richards was too late.

When the doctors came they said she had died of heart disease—of joy that kills.

[*1894*]

In brainstorming, don't worry about spelling, about writing complete sentences, or about unifying your thoughts; just let one thought lead to another. Later you can review your jottings, deleting some, connecting with arrows others that are related, expanding still others, but for now you want to get going, and so there is no reason to look back. Thus you might jot down something about the title.

Title speaks of an hour, and story covers an hour, but maybe takes five minutes to read

And then, perhaps prompted by "an hour," you might happen to add something to this effect:

Doubt that a woman who got news of the death of her husband could move from grief to joy within an hour

Your next jotting might have little or nothing to do with this issue; it might simply say:

Enjoyed "Hour" especially because "Hour" is so shocking

And then you might ask yourself:

By shocking, do I mean "improbable," or what? Come to think of it, maybe it's not so improbable. A lot depends on what the marriage was like.

## Focused Free Writing

Focused, or directed, free writing is a method related to brainstorming that some writers use to uncover ideas they may want to write about. Concentrating on one issue—for instance, a question that strikes them as worth puzzling over

(What kind of person is Mrs. Mallard?)—they write at length, nonstop, for perhaps five or ten minutes.

Writers who find free writing helpful put down everything they can think of that has bearing on the one issue or question they are examining. They do not stop at this stage to evaluate the results, and they do not worry about niceties of sentence structure or of spelling. They just pour out their ideas in a steady stream of writing, drawing on whatever associations come to mind. If they pause in their writing, it is only to refer to the text, to search for more detail—perhaps a quotation—that will help them answer their question.

After the free-writing session, these writers usually go back and reread what they have written, highlighting or underlining what seems to be of value. Of course they find much that is of little or no use, but they also usually find that some strong ideas have surfaced and have received some development. At this point the writers are often able to make a scratch outline and then begin a draft.

Here is an example of one student's focused free writing, again on Chopin's "The Story of an Hour."

> What do I know about Mrs. Mallard? Let me put everything down here I know about her or can figure out from what Kate Chopin tells me. When she finds herself alone after the death of her husband, she says, "Free. Body and soul free" and before that she said, "Free, free, free." Three times. So she has suddenly perceived that she has not been free: she has been under the influence of a "powerful will." In this case it has been her husband, but she says no one, man nor woman, should impose their will on anyone else. So it's not a feminist issue--it's a power issue. No one should push anyone else around is what I guess Chopin means, force someone to do what the other person wants. I used to have a friend that did that to me all the time; he had to run everything. They say that fathers--before the women's movement--used to run things, with the father in charge of all the decisions, so maybe this is an honest reaction to having been pushed around by a husband. I think Mrs. Mallard is a believable

character, even if the plot is not all that believable--all those things happening in such quick succession.

## Listing and Clustering

In your preliminary thinking you may find it useful to make lists or to jot down clusters of your ideas, insights, comments, questions. For "The Story of an Hour" you might list Mrs. Mallard's traits, or you might list the stages of her development. (Such a list is not the same as a summary of a plot. The list helps the writer to see the sequence of psychological changes.)

```
weeps (when she gets the news)
goes to room, alone
"pressed down by a physical exhaustion"
"dull stare"
"something coming to her"
strives to beat back "this thing"
"Free, free, free!" The "vacant stare went from her
    eyes"
"A clear and exalted perception"
rejects Josephine
"she was drinking in a very elixir of life"
gets up, opens door, "a feverish triumph in her eyes"
sees B, and dies
```

Of course, unlike brainstorming and annotating, which let you go in all directions, listing requires that you first make a decision about what you will be listing—traits of character, images, puns, or whatever. Once you make the decision, you can then construct the list, and, with a list in front of you, you will probably see patterns that you were not fully conscious of earlier.

On the other hand, don't be unduly concerned if something does not seem to fit into a list or cluster. You can return to it, and give it more thought—maybe it will come to fit later. But you might also realize that this point needs to be placed to the side. As far as you can tell, it doesn't appear to belong in one of your lists or to link well to other points you have begun to make, and in this way you may come to realize that it is not relevant to your development of possible topics for your essay.

## Developing an Awareness of the Writer's Use of Language

In the first line of the story, Chopin notes that "Mrs. Mallard was afflicted with a heart trouble." You might want to look up "afflicted" in your dictionary. Why do you think that Chopin chose this word, as opposed to other words she might have chosen? How would the effect of the opening line be different if, for example, Chopin had written "Mrs. Mallard had a heart problem" or "Mrs. Mallard's heart was weak"?

Earlier we recommended that you keep a dictionary at hand when you read. It will help you, especially if you get into the habit of asking questions about the writer's choice of language. And this brings us to our next point.

## Asking Questions

If you feel stuck, ask yourself questions. We suggest questions for fiction on pages 149–52, for poetry on pages 957–59, and for drama on pages 1044–47. If, for instance, you are thinking about a work of fiction, you might ask yourself questions about the plot and the characters—are they believable, are they interesting, and what does it all add up to? What does the story mean *to you?* One student found it helpful to jot down the following questions:

```
Plot
  Ending false? unconvincing? or prepared for?
Character?
  Mrs. M. unfeeling? Immoral?
  Mrs. M. unbelievable character?
    What might her marriage have been like? Many
      gaps. (Can we tell what her husband was like?)
      "And yet she loved him--sometimes." Fickle?
      Realistic?
    What is "this thing that was approaching to
      possess her"?
Symbolism
    Set on spring day = symbolic of new life?
```

But, again, you don't have to be as tidy as this student was. You can begin by jotting down notes and queries about what you like or dislike and about what puzzles or amuses you. Here are the jottings of another student. They are, obviously, in no particular order—the student is "brainstorming," putting down whatever occurs to her—though it is equally obvious that one note sometimes led to the next:

```
Title nothing special. What might be better title?

Could a woman who loved her husband be so heartless?

Is she heartless? Did she love him?

What are (were) Louise's feelings about her husband?

Did she want too much? What did she want?

Could this story happen today? Feminist
   interpretation?

Sister (Josephine)--a busybody?

Tricky ending--but maybe it could be true

"And yet she loved him--sometimes. Often she had
   not."

Why does one love someone "sometimes"?

Irony: plot has reversal. Are characters ironic too?
```

These jottings will help the reader-writer to think about the story, to find a special point of interest and to develop a thoughtful argument about it.

## Keeping a Journal

A journal is not a diary, a record of what the writer did each day ("today I read Chopin's 'Hour'"); rather, a journal is a place to store some of the thoughts that you may have inscribed on a scrap of paper or in the margin of the text—for instance, your initial response to the title of a work or to the ending. It's also a place to jot down some further reflections. These reflections may include thoughts about what the work means to you or what was said in the classroom about writing in general or about specific works. You may, for instance, want to reflect on why your opinion is so different from that of another student, or you may want to apply a concept such as "character" or "irony" or "plausibility" to a story that later you may write an essay about.

You might even make an entry in the form of a letter to the author or in the form of a letter from one character to another. Similarly, you might write a dialogue between characters in two works or between two authors, or you might record an experience of your own that is comparable to something in the work.

A student who wrote about "The Story of an Hour" began with the following entry in his journal. In reading this entry, notice that one idea stimulates another. The student was, quite rightly, concerned with getting and exploring ideas, not with writing a unified paragraph.

Apparently a "well-made" story, but seems clever rather than moving or real. Doesn't seem plausible. Mrs. M's change comes out of the blue--maybe some women might respond like this, but probably not most.

Does literature deal with unusual people, or with usual (typical?) people? Shouldn't it deal with typical? Maybe not. (Anyway, how can I know?) Is "typical" same as "plausible"? Come to think of it, prob. not.

Anyway, whether Mrs. M. is typical or not, is her change plausible, believable?

Why did she change? Her husband dominated her life and controlled her action; he did "impose a private will upon a fellow creature." She calls this a crime. Why? Why not?

## Arriving at a Thesis

Having raised some questions, a reader goes back to the story, hoping to read it now with increased awareness. Some of the jottings will be dead ends, but some will lead to further ideas that can be arranged in lists. What the **thesis** of the essay will be—the idea that will be asserted and supported—is still in doubt, but there is no doubt about one thing: A good essay will have a thesis, a point, an argument. (We will discuss the argumentative element in Chapter 3.) You ought to be able to state your point in a **thesis sentence.**

Consider these candidates as possible thesis sentences:

1. Mrs. Mallard dies soon after hearing that her husband has died.

   True, but scarcely a point that can be argued, or even developed. About the most the essayist can do with this sentence is to amplify it by summarizing the plot of the story, a task not worth doing. An analysis may include a sentence or two of summary, to give readers their bearings, but a summary is not an essay.

2. The story is a libel on women.

   In contrast to the first statement, this one can be developed into an argument. Probably the writer will try to demonstrate that Mrs. Mallard's behavior is despicable. Whether this point can be convincingly argued is another matter; the thesis may be untenable, but it is a thesis. A second problem, however, is this: Even if the writer demonstrates that Mrs. Mallard's behavior is despicable, he or she will have to go on to demonstrate that the presentation of one despicable woman constitutes a libel on women in general. That's a pretty big order.

3. The story is clever but superficial because it is based on an unreal character.

   Here, too, is a thesis, a point of view that can be argued. Whether or not this thesis is true is another matter. The writer's job will be to support it by presenting evidence. Probably the writer will have no difficulty in finding evidence that the story is "clever"; the difficulty probably will be in establishing a case that the characterization of Mrs. Mallard is "unreal." The writer will have to set forth some ideas about what makes a character real and then will have to show that Mrs. Mallard is an "unreal" (unbelievable) figure.

4. The irony of the ending is believable partly because it is consistent with earlier ironies in the story.

   It happens that the student who wrote the essay printed on page 32 began by drafting an essay based on the third of these thesis topics, but as she worked on a draft she found that she couldn't support her assertion that the character was unconvincing. In fact, she came to believe that although Mrs. Mallard's joy was the reverse of what a reader might expect, several early reversals in the story helped to make Mrs. Mallard's shift from grief to joy acceptable.

## WRITING A DRAFT

After jotting down notes and then adding more notes stimulated by rereading and further thinking, you'll probably be able to formulate a tentative thesis. At this point most writers find it useful to clear the air by glancing over their preliminary notes and by jotting down the thesis and a few especially promising notes—brief statements of what they think their key points may be. These notes may include some brief key quotations that the writer thinks will help to support the thesis.

Here are the notes (not the original brainstorming notes, but a later selection from them, with additions) and a draft (following) that makes use of them. The final version of the essay—the product produced by the process—is given on page 32.

```
title? Ironies in an Hour (?) An Hour of Irony (?)
   Kate Chopin's Irony (?)
thesis: irony at the end is prepared for by earlier
   ironies
chief irony: Mrs. M. dies just as she is beginning to
   enjoy life
```

smaller ironies: 1. "sad message" brings her joy
2. Richards is "too late" at end;
3. Richards is too early at start

## Sample Draft of an Essay on Kate Chopin's "The Story of an Hour"

Now for the student's draft—not the first version, but a revised draft with some of the irrelevancies of the first draft omitted and some evidence added.

The digits within the parentheses refer to the page numbers from which the quotations are drawn, though with so short a work as "The Story of an Hour," page references are hardly necessary. Unless instructed otherwise, always provide page numbers for your quotations. This will enable your readers quickly to locate the passages to which you refer. (Detailed information about how to document a paper is given on pages 1955-67.)

IRONIES IN AN HOUR

After we know how the story turns out, if we reread it we find irony at the very start, as is true of many other stories. Mrs. Mallard's friends assume, mistakenly, that Mrs. Mallard was deeply in love with her husband, Brently Mallard. They take great care to tell her gently of his death. The friends mean well, and in fact they <u>do</u> well. They bring her an hour of life, an hour of freedom. They think their news is sad. Mrs. Mallard at first expresses grief when she hears the news, but soon she finds joy in it. So Richards's "sad message" (35), though sad in Richards's eyes, is in fact a happy message.

Among the ironic details is the statement that when Mallard entered the house, Richards tried to conceal him from Mrs. Mallard, but "Richards was too late" (36). This is ironic because earlier Richards "hastened" (35) to bring his sad message; if he had at the start been "too late" (36), Brently Mallard would have arrived at home first, and Mrs. Mallard's life would not have ended an hour later but would simply have gone on as it had before. Yet another irony at the end of the story is the diagnosis of the doctors. The doctors say she died of "heart disease--of joy that kills" (36). In one sense the doctors are right: Mrs. Mallard has experienced a great joy. But of course the doctors totally misunderstood the joy that kills her.

The central irony resides not in the well-intentioned but ironic actions of Richards, or in the unconsciously ironic words of the doctors, but in her own life. In a way she has been dead. She "sometimes" (36) loved her husband, but in a way she has been dead. Now, his apparent death brings her new life. This new life comes to her at the season of the year when "the tops of trees . . . were all aquiver with the new spring life" (35). But, ironically, her new life will last only an hour. She looks forward to "summer days" (36) but she will not see even the end of this spring day. Her years of marriage were ironic. They brought her a sort of living death instead of joy. Her new life is ironic too. It grows out of her moment of grief for her supposedly dead husband, and her vision of a new life is cut short.

WORK CITED

Chopin, Kate. "The Story of an Hour." <u>Literature: Thinking, Reading, and Writing Critically</u>. Ed. Sylvan Barnet et al. 2nd ed. New York: Longman, 1997. 19-21

## Revising a Draft

The draft, although thoughtful and clear, is not yet a finished essay. The student went on to improve it in many small but important ways.

First, the draft needs a good introductory paragraph, a paragraph that will let readers know where the writer will be taking them. Doubtless you know from your own experience as a reader that readers can follow an argument more easily—and with more pleasure—if early in the discussion the writer alerts them to the gist of the argument. (The title, too, can strongly suggest the thesis.) Second, some of the paragraphs could be clearer.

In revising paragraphs—or, for that matter, in revising an entire draft—writers unify, organize, clarify, and polish. Let's look at the nouns implicit in these verbs.

1. **Unity** is achieved partly by eliminating irrelevancies. Notice that in the final version, printed on page 32, the writer has deleted "as is true of many other stories" from the first sentence of the draft.
2. **Organization** is largely a matter of arranging material into a sequence that will assist the reader to grasp the point.
3. **Clarity** is achieved largely by providing concrete details and quotations to support generalizations and by providing helpful transitions ("for instance," "furthermore," "on the other hand," "however").
4. **Polish** is small-scale revision. For instance, one deletes unnecessary repetitions. In the second paragraph of the draft, the phrase "the doctors" appears three times, but it appears only once in the final version of the paragraph. Similarly, in polishing, a writer combines choppy sentences into longer sentences, and breaks overly long sentences into shorter sentences.

Later, after producing a draft that seems close to a finished essay, writers engage in yet another activity.

5. **Editing** concerns such things as checking the accuracy of quotations by comparing them with the original, checking a dictionary for the spelling of doubtful words, checking a handbook for doubtful punctuation—for instance, whether a comma or a semicolon is needed in a particular sentence.

## Peer Review

Your instructor may encourage (or even require) you to discuss your draft with another student or with a small group of students. That is, you may be asked to get a review from your peers. Such a procedure is helpful in several ways. First, it gives the writer a real audience, readers who can point to what pleases or puzzles them, who make suggestions, who may often disagree (with the writer or with each other), and who frequently, though not intentionally, *misread.* Though writers don't necessarily like everything they hear (they seldom hear "This is perfect. Don't change a word!"), reading and discussing their work with others almost always gives them a fresh perspective on their work, and a fresh perspective may stimulate thoughtful revision. (Having your intentions *misread* because your writing isn't clear enough can be particularly stimulating.)

The writer whose work is being reviewed is not the sole beneficiary. When students regularly serve as readers for each other, they become better readers of their own work and consequently better revisers.

When you produce a draft of your paper for peer review, it will not, of course, be in final form; the draft is an important step toward shaping the paper and bringing it to final form. But aim to do the best job possible on your draft; let your classmates respond to the best work you can do at this stage of the process.

```
Questions for Peer Review                    English 125a

Read each draft once, quickly. Then read it again,
    with the following questions in mind.
  1. What is the essay's topic? Is it one of the
     assigned topics, or a variation from it? Does
     the draft show promise of fulfilling the
     assignment?
  2. Looking at the essay as a whole, what thesis
     (main idea) is stated or implied? If implied,
     try to state it in your own words.
  3. Is the thesis plausible? How might the argument
     be strengthened?
  4. Looking at each paragraph separately:
     a.  What is the basic point? (If it isn't clear
         to you, ask for clarification.
     b.  How does the paragraph relate to the
         essay's main idea or to the previous para-
         graph?
     c.  Should some paragraphs be deleted? Be di-
         vided into two or more paragraphs? Be com-
         bined? Be put elsewhere? (If you outline the
         essay by jotting down the gist of each
         paragraph, you will get help in answering
         these questions.)
     d.  Is each sentence clearly related to the
         sentence that precedes and to the sentence
         that follows?
     e.  Is each paragraph adequately developed?
     f.  Are there sufficient details, perhaps brief
         supporting quotations from the text?
  5. What are the paper's chief strengths?
  6. Make at least two specific suggestions that you
     think will assist the author to improve the
     paper.
```

You will have more work to do on this paper—you know that. But you don't want your classmates to be pointing out mistakes that you know are in the draft and that you could have fixed yourself.

If peer review is a part of the writing process in your course, the instructor may distribute a sheet with some suggestions and questions. Above is an example of such a sheet.

## THE FINAL VERSION

Here is the final version of the student's essay. The essay that was submitted to the instructor had been retyped, but here, so that you can easily see how the

**draft has been revised, we print the draft with the final changes written in by hand.**

Ironies of Life in Kate Chopin's "The Story of an Hour"

~~Ironies in an Hour~~

Despite its title, Kate Chopin's "The Story of an Hour" ironically takes only a few minutes to read. In addition, the story turns out to have an ironic ending, but on rereading it one sees that the irony is not concentrated only in the outcome of the plot—Mrs. Mallard dies just when she is beginning to live—but is also present in many details.

After we know how the story turns out, if we reread it we find irony at the very start. ~~as is true of many other stories.~~ Because Mrs. Mallard's friends and her sister assume, mistakenly, that ~~Mrs. Mallard~~ she was deeply in love with her husband, Brently Mallard, ~~They~~ they take great care to tell her gently of his death. ~~The friends~~ They mean well, and in fact they do well, ~~They~~ bringing her an hour of life, an hour of joyous freedom, but it is ironic that they think their news is sad. True, Mrs. Mallard at first expresses grief when she hears the news, but soon (unknown to her friends) she finds joy in it. So Richards's "sad message" (19), though sad in Richards's eyes, is in fact a happy message.

Among the small but significant ironic details is the statement near the end of the story that when Mallard entered the house, Richards tried to conceal him from Mrs. Mallard, but "Richards was too late" (21). This is ironic because almost at the start of the story, in the second paragraph, ~~earlier~~ Richards "hastened" (19) to bring his sad message; if he had at the start been "too late" (21), Brently Mallard would have arrived at home first, and Mrs. Mallard's life would not have ended an hour later but would simply have gone on as it had before. Yet another irony at the end of the story is the diagnosis of the doctors. ~~The doctors~~ They say she died of "heart disease--of joy that kills" (21). In one sense ~~the doctors~~ they are right: Mrs. Mallard for the last hour experienced a great joy. But of course the doctors totally misunderstand the joy that kills her. It is not joy at seeing her husband alive, but her realization that the great joy she experienced during the last hour is over.

All of these ironic details add richness to the story, but the central irony resides not in the well-intentioned but ironic actions of Richards, nor in the unconsciously ironic words of the doctors, but in Mrs. Mallard's ~~her~~ own life. ~~In a way she has been dead.~~ She "sometimes" (20) loved her husband, but in a way she has been a body subjected to her husband's will dead. Now, his apparent death brings her new life. This new life comes to her at the season of the year when "the tops of trees . . . were all aquiver with the new spring life" (19). But, ironically, her new life will last only an hour. She is "free, free, free"—but only until her husband walks through the doorway. She looks forward to "summer days" (20) but she will not see even the end of this spring day. If her years of marriage were ironic, bringing ~~They brought~~ her a sort of living death instead of joy, her new life is ironic too, not only because it grows out of her moment of grief for her supposedly dead husband, but also because her vision of "a long progression of years" and her vision of a new life is cut short within an hour on a spring day.

Work Cited

Chopin, Kate. "The Story of an Hour." Literature: Thinking, Reading, and Writing Critically. Eds. Sylvan Barnet et al. New York: Longman, 1997. 19-21.

## A Brief Overview of the Final Version

Finally, as a quick review, let's look at several principles illustrated by this essay.

1. The **title of the essay** is not merely the title of the work discussed; rather, it gives the reader a clue, a small idea of the essayist's topic.
2. The **opening** or **introductory paragraph** does not begin by saying "In this story . . .". Rather, by naming the author and the title, it lets the reader know exactly what story is being discussed. It also develops the writer's thesis so readers know where they will be going.
3. The **organization** is effective. The smaller ironies are discussed in the second and third paragraphs, the central (chief) irony in the last paragraph. That is, the essay does not dwindle or become anticlimactic;

rather, it builds up from the least important to the most important point.

4. Some **brief quotations** are used, both to provide evidence and to let the reader hear—even if only fleetingly—Kate Chopin's writing.
5. The essay is chiefly devoted to **analysis** (how the parts relate to each other), not to summary (a brief restatement of the happenings). The writer, properly assuming that the reader has read the work, does not tell the plot in great detail. But, aware that the reader has not memorized the story, the writer gives helpful reminders.
6. The **present tense** is used in narrating the action: "Mrs. Mallard dies"; "Mrs. Mallard's friends and relatives all assume."
7. Although a **concluding paragraph** is often useful—if it does more than merely summarize what has already been clearly said—it is not essential in a short analysis. In this essay, the last sentence explains the chief irony and therefore makes an acceptable ending.

## EXPLICATION

A line-by-line commentary on what is going on in a text is an explication (literally, unfolding, or spreading out). Although your explication will for the most part move steadily from the beginning to the end of the selection, try to avoid writing along these lines (or, one might say, along this one line): "In line one. . . . In the second line. . . . In the third line . . . ." That is, don't hesitate to write such things as

```
The poem begins. . . . In the next line. . . . The speaker
immediately adds. . . . He then introduces. . . . The next
stanza begins by saying . . . .
```

And of course you can discuss the second line before the first if that seems the best way of handling the passage.

An explication is not concerned with the writer's life or times, and it is not a paraphrase (a rewording)—though it may include paraphrase if a passage in the original seems unclear, perhaps because of an unusual word or an unfamiliar expression. On the whole, however, an explication goes beyond paraphrase, seeking to make explicit what the reader perceives as implicit in the work. To this end it calls attention, as it proceeds, to the implications of words (for instance, to their tone), the function of rhymes (for instance, how they may connect ideas, as in *throne* and *alone*), the development of contrasts, and any other contributions to the meaning.

Obviously you will have ideas about the merit and the meaning of the poem, and your paper will implicitly have a *thesis*—an argument, for instance this poem is very difficult, or this poem begins effectively but quickly goes downhill, or this poem is excessively sentimental. Your essay, however, is largely devoted not to making assertions of this sort but to explaining how the details make the meaning.

A good way to stimulate responses to the poem is to ask some of the questions given on pages 957–59.

Many students find that by copying the poem (by hand, or on a typewriter, or, preferably, on a computer) they gain an understanding of the uses of language in a literary work. *Don't* photocopy the poem; the act of writing or typing it will help you to get into the piece, word by word, comma by comma. Double-space, so that you have ample room for annotations.

If you use a word processing program, you can highlight key words, lines, stanzas. You can also rearrange lines and stanzas, and perhaps substitute different words for the words that the poet has selected. Some students like to make multiple printouts for contrast and comparison—the poem as the poet wrote it, the poem as the student has marked it up by using the highlighting feature of the computer program, the poem as it stands after the student has somewhat rearranged it.

A computer cannot interpret a poem or story for you. But you can employ it as a tool to deepen your own sense of how a poem is structured—why this or that word or image is crucial at this juncture, why this or that stanza or passage belongs here and could not be placed elsewhere, and so on. Your goal is to gain insight into how writers of literary texts use their artistic medium, and often a computer can be a good complement to the dictionary that you always keep nearby.

## A Sample Explication

Read this short poem (published in 1917) by the Irish poet William Butler Yeats (1865-1939). The "balloon" in the poem is a dirigible, a blimp.

### WILLIAM BUTLER YEATS

### *The Balloon of the Mind*

Hands, do what you're bid:
Bring the balloon of the mind
That bellies and drags in the wind
Into its narrow shed.

[*1917*]

A student began thinking about the poem by copying it, double-spaced. Then she jotted down her first thoughts.

sounds abrupt

Hands, do what you're bid:

Bring the balloon of the mind

That bellies and drags in the wind

Into its narrow shed.

—balloon imagined by the mind? Or a mind like a balloon?

no real rhymes?

line seems to drag—it's so long!

Later she wrote some notes in a journal.

I'm still puzzled about the meaning of the words, "The balloon of the mind." Does "balloon of the mind" mean a balloon that belongs to the mind, sort of like "a disease of the heart"? If so, it means a balloon that the mind has, a balloon that the mind possesses, I guess by imagining it. Or does it mean that the mind is like a balloon, as when you say "he's a pig of a man," meaning he is like a pig, he is a pig? Can it mean both? What's a balloon that the mind imagines? Something like dreams of fame, wealth? Castles in Spain.

Is Yeats saying that the "hands" have to work hard to make dreams a reality? Maybe. But maybe the idea really is that the mind is like a balloon--hard to keep under control, floating around. Very hard to keep the mind on the job. If the mind is like a balloon, it's hard to get it into the hangar (shed).

"Bellies." Is there such a verb? In this poem it seems to mean something like "puffs out" or "flops around in the wind." Just checked The American Heritage Dictionary, and it says "belly" can be a verb, "to swell out," "to bulge." Well, you learn something every day.

A later entry:

OK; I think the poem is about a writer trying to keep his balloon-like mind from floating around, trying to keep the mind under control, trying to keep it working at the job of writing something, maybe writing something with the "clarity, unity, and coherence" I keep hearing about in this course.

Here is the student's final version of the explication.

Yeats's "Balloon of the Mind" is about writing poetry, specifically about the difficulty of getting one's floating thoughts down in lines on the page. The first line, a short, stern, heavily stressed command to the speaker's hands, perhaps implies by its severe or impatient tone that these hands will be disobedient or inept or careless if not watched closely: the poor bumbling body so often fails to achieve the goals of the mind. The bluntness of the command in the first line is emphasized by the fact that all the subsequent lines have more syllables. Furthermore, the first line is a grammatically complete sentence, whereas the thought of line 2 spills over into the next lines, implying the difficulty of fitting ideas into confining spaces, that is, of getting one's thoughts into order, especially into a coherent poem.

Lines 2 and 3 amplify the metaphor already stated in the title (the product of the mind is an airy but unwieldy balloon), and they also contain a second command, "Bring." Alliteration ties this command, "Bring," to the earlier "bid"; it also ties both of these verbs to their object, "balloon," and to the verb that most effectively describes the balloon, "bellies." In comparison with the abrupt first line of the poem, lines 2 and 3 themselves seem almost swollen, bellying and dragging, an effect aided by using adjacent unstressed syllables ("of the," "[bell]ies and," "in the") and by using an eye rhyme ("mind" and "wind") rather than an exact rhyme. And then comes the short last line: almost before we could expect it, the cumbersome balloon--here, the idea that is to be packed into the stanza--is successfully lodged in its "narrow shed."

Aside from the relatively colorless "into," the only words of more than one syllable in the poem are "balloon," "bellies," and "narrow," and all three emphasize the difficulty of the task. But after "narrow"--the word itself almost looks long and narrow, in this context like a hangar--we get the simplicity of the monosyllable "shed." The difficult job is done, the thought is safely packed away, the poem is completed--but again with an off rhyme ("bid" and "shed"), for neatness can go only so far when hands and mind and a balloon are involved.

*Note:* The reader of an explication needs to see the text, and because the explicated text is usually short, it is advisable to quote it all. (Remember, your imagined audience probably consists of your classmates; even if they have already read the work you are explicating, they have not memorized it, and so you helpfully remind them of the work by quoting it.) You can quote the entire text at the outset, or you can quote the first unit (for example, a stanza), then explicate that unit, and then quote the next unit, and so on. And if the poem or passage of prose is longer than, say, six lines, it is advisable to number every fifth line at the right for easy reference, or every fourth line if the poem is written in four-line stanzas.

## COMPARISON AND CONTRAST

Something should be said about an essay organized around a **comparison** or a **contrast,** say, of the settings in two short stories, of two characters in a novel, or of the symbolism in two poems. (A comparison emphasizes resemblances whereas a contrast emphasizes differences, but we can use the word "comparison" to cover both kinds of writing.) Probably the student's first thought, after making some jottings, is to discuss one-half of the comparison and then go on to the second half. Instructors and textbooks (though not this one) usually condemn such an organization, arguing that the essay breaks into two parts and that the second part involves a good deal of repetition of categories set up in the first part. Usually they recommend that students organize their thoughts differently, making point-by-point comparisons. For example, if one wishes to compare *Huckleberry Finn* with *The Catcher in the Rye,* one may organize the material thus:

1. First similarity: the narrator and his quest
   a. Huck
   b. Holden
2. Second similarity: the corrupt world surrounding the narrator
   a. society in *Huckleberry Finn*
   b. society in *Catcher*

3. First difference: degree to which the narrator fulfills his quest and escapes from society
    a. Huck's plan to "light out" to the frontier
    b. Holden's breakdown

Here is another way of organizing a comparison and contrast:

1. First point: the narrator and his quest
    a. similarities between Huck and Holden
    b. differences between Huck and Holden
2. Second point: the corrupt world
    a. similarities between the worlds in *Huck* and *Catcher*
    b. differences between the worlds in *Huck* and *Catcher*
3. Third point: degree of success
    a. similarities between Huck and Holden
    b. differences between Huck and Holden

But a comparison need not employ either of these structures. There is even the danger that an essay employing either of them may not come into focus until the essayist stands back from the seven-layer cake and announces, in the concluding paragraph, that the odd layers taste better. In one's preparatory thinking, one may want to make comparisons in pairs, but one must come to some conclusions about what these add up to before writing the final version. This final version should not duplicate the thought processes; rather, it should be organized to make the point clearly and effectively.

The point of the essay presumably is not to list pairs of similarities or differences, but to illuminate a work or works by making thoughtful comparisons. Although in a long essay one cannot postpone until page 30 a discussion of the second half of the comparison, in an essay of, say, fewer than ten pages nothing is wrong with setting forth one-half of the comparison and then, in light of it, the second half. The essay will break into two unrelated parts if the second half makes no use of the first or if it fails to modify the first half, but not if the second half looks back to the first half and calls attention to differences that the new material reveals. One ought to learn how to write an essay with interwoven comparisons, but one ought also to know that there is another, simpler and clearer way to write a comparison.

## REVIEW: HOW TO WRITE AN EFFECTIVE ESSAY

Everyone must work out his or her own procedures and rituals (Hemingway liked to sharpen pencils; John C. Calhoun liked to plough his farm before writing), but the following suggestions may provide some help.

1. **Read the work carefully.**
2. **Choose a worthwhile and compassable subject,** something that interests you and is not so big that your handling of it must be superficial. As you work, shape and narrow your topic—for example, from "The Character of Hester Prynne" to "The Effects of Alienation on Hester Prynne."
3. **Reread the work, jotting down notes** of all relevant matters. As you read, reflect on your reading and record your reflections. If you have a

feeling or an idea, jot it down; don't assume that you will remember it when you get around to writing your essay. The margins of the book are a good place for initial jottings, but many people find that in the long run it is easiest to transfer these notes to $3 \times 5$ cards, writing on one side only, or to a disk in a word processor.

4. **Sort out your cards into some kind of reasonable divisions,** and reject cards irrelevant to your topic. If you are writing an explication, the order probably is essentially the order of the lines or of the episodes, but if you are writing an analysis you almost surely will want to rearrange your notes. If you took notes on a word processor, print them and—well, here the authors of this text differ. One author recommends that you make jottings on the printout ("put this with X," "put this at end of file; probably not useful") so that you can, by block movements, rearrange the sequence in your file and thus have something fairly well organized to scan and think about on-screen. Another author, aiming for the same end result, recommends that you scissor the jottings apart, reorganize them just as you would reorganize index cards, and then, after much fiddling, rearrange the sequence in your file.

   Whichever method you use, get the notes into order. For instance, you may wish to organize your essay from the lesser material to the greater (to avoid anticlimax) or from the simple to the complex (to ensure intelligibility). If, for instance, you are discussing the roles of three characters in a story, it may be best to build up to the one of the three that you think the most important. If you are comparing two characters it may be best to move from the most obvious contrasts to the least obvious. When you have arranged your notes into a meaningful sequence of packets, you have approximately divided your material into paragraphs, though of course two or three notes may be combined into one paragraph, or one packed note may turn into two or more paragraphs.

5. **Get it down on paper.** Most essayists find it useful to jot down some sort of outline, indicating the main idea of each paragraph and, under each main idea, supporting details that give it substance. An outline—not necessarily anything highly formal with capital and lowercase letters and roman and arabic numerals but merely key phrases in some sort of order—will help you to overcome the paralysis called "writer's block" that commonly afflicts professionals as well as students. A page of paper with ideas in some sort of sequence, however rough, ought to encourage you to realize that you do have something to say. And so, despite the temptation to sharpen another pencil or put a new ribbon into the printer or check your e-mail, the best thing to do at this point is to sit down and start writing.

   If you don't feel that you can work from note cards and a rough outline, try another method: get something down on paper (or on a disk), writing freely, sloppily, automatically, or whatever, but allowing your ideas about what the work means to you and how it conveys its meaning—rough as your ideas may be—to begin to take visible form. If you are like most people, you can't do much precise thinking until you have committed to paper at least a rough sketch of your initial ideas. Later you can push and polish your ideas into shape, perhaps even deleting all of them and starting over, but it's a lot easier to improve your ideas once you see them in front of you than it is to do the job in your head. On paper or on the screen of a word processor one word leads to another; in your head one word often blocks another.

Just keep going; you may realize, as you near the end of a sentence, that you no longer believe it. OK, be glad that your first idea led you to a better one, and pick up your better one and keep going with it. What you are doing is, in a sense, by trial and error pushing your way not only toward clear expression but also toward sharper ideas and richer responses.

6. If there is time, **reread the work,** looking for additional material that strengthens or weakens your main point; take account of it in your outline or draft.
7. **By now your thesis should be clear to you,** and you ought to be able to give your essay an informative title—*not* simply the title of the story, poem, or play, but something that lets your reader know where you will be going.

   **With a thesis and title clearly in mind, improve your draft,** checking your notes for fuller details, such as supporting quotations. If, as you work, you find that some of the points in your earlier jottings are no longer relevant, eliminate them, but make sure that the argument flows from one point to the next. As you write, your ideas will doubtless become clearer; some may prove to be poor ideas. (We rarely know exactly what our ideas are until we have them set down on paper. As the little girl said, replying to the suggestion that she should think before she spoke, "How do I know what I think until I say it?") Not until you have written a draft do you really have a strong sense of what your ideas are and how good your essay may be.
8. After a suitable interval, preferably a few days, **read the draft with a view toward revising it,** not with a view toward congratulating yourself. A revision, after all, is a re-vision, a second (and presumably sharper) view. When you revise, you will be in the company of Picasso, who said that in painting he advanced by a series of destructions. A revision—say, the substitution of a precise word for an imprecise one—is not a matter of prettifying but of thinking. As you read, correct things that disturb you (for example, awkward repetitions that bore, inflated utterances that grate), add supporting detail where the argument is undeveloped (a paragraph of only one or two sentences is usually an undeveloped paragraph), and ruthlessly delete irrelevancies however well written they may be. But remember that a deletion probably requires some adjustment in the preceding and subsequent material.

   Make sure that the argument, aided by **transitions,** runs smoothly. The **details** should be relevant, the organization reasonable, the argument clear. **Check all quotations** for accuracy. Quotations are evidence, usually intended to support your assertions, and it is not nice to alter the evidence, even unintentionally. If there is time (there almost never is), put the revision aside, reread it in a day or two, and revise it again, especially with a view toward deleting wordiness and, on the other hand, supporting generalizations with evidence.
9. **Type or write or print a clean copy,** following the principles concerning margins, pagination, footnotes, and so on set forth on pages 1943–48. If you have borrowed any ideas, be sure to give credit, usually

in footnotes, to your sources. Remember that plagiarism is not limited to the unacknowledged borrowing of words; a borrowed idea, even when put into your own words, requires acknowledgment.

10. **Proofread and make corrections** as explained on pages 1943–48. Remember that writing is a form of self-representation. Fairly or unfairly, readers will make judgments about you based on how you present yourself to them in your writing. With this in mind, proofread your work carefully, making sure that there are no misspellings, misquotations, and the like. The trick, of course, is not to feel so good about the paper that you find yourself skimming and congratulating yourself on your ideas, rather than reading word by word, with an eye for small errors.

# ADDITIONAL READINGS

## KATE CHOPIN

*For a biographical sketch, see page 19.*

### *Ripe Figs*

Maman-Nainaine said that when the figs were ripe Babette might go to visit her cousins down on the Bayou-Lafourche where the sugar cane grows. Not that the ripening of figs had the least thing to do with it, but that is the way Maman-Nainaine was.

It seemed to Babette a very long time to wait; for the leaves upon the trees were tender yet, and the figs were like little hard, green marbles.

But warm rains came along and plenty of strong sunshine, and though Maman-Nainaine was as patient as the statue of la Madone, and Babette as restless as a humming-bird, the first thing they both knew it was hot summer-time. Every day Babette danced out to where the fig-trees were in a long line against the fence. She walked slowly beneath them, carefully peering between the gnarled, spreading branches. But each time she came disconsolate away again. What she saw there finally was something that made her sing and dance the whole long day.

When Maman-Nainaine sat down in her stately way to breakfast, the following morning, her muslin cap standing like an aureole about her white, placid face, Babette approached. She bore a dainty porcelain platter, which she set down before her godmother. It contained a dozen purple figs, fringed around with their rich, green leaves.

5 "Ah," said Maman-Nainaine arching her eyebrows, "how early the figs have ripened this year!"

"Oh," said Babette, "I think they have ripened very late."

"Babette," continued Maman-Nainaine, as she peeled the very plumpest figs with her pointed silver fruit-knife, "you will carry my love to them all down on Bayou-Lafourche. And tell your Tante[1] Frosine I shall look for her at Toussaint—when the chrysanthemums are in bloom."

[*1893*]

[1]**Tante** aunt (French)

## TOPICS FOR CRITICAL THINKING AND WRITING

1. Compare and contrast Maman-Nainaine and Babette.
2. Two questions here: What, if anything, "happens" in "Ripe Figs"? And what, in your opinion, is the story about?
3. What, if anything, would be lost if the last line were omitted? (If you can think of a better final line, write it, and explain why your version is preferable.)

## WILLIAM BLAKE

*William Blake (1757-1827) was born in London and at fourteen was apprenticed for seven years to an engraver. A Christian visionary poet, he made his living by giving drawing lessons and by illustrating books, including his own* Songs of Innocence *(1789) and* Songs of Experience *(1794). These two books represent, he said, "two contrary states of the human soul." ("Infant Joy" comes from* Innocence, *"Infant Sorrow" from* Experience.*) In 1809 Blake exhibited his art, but the show was a failure. Not until he was in his sixties, when he stopped writing poetry, did he achieve any public recognition—and then it was as a painter.*

# *Infant Joy*

"I have no name,
I am but two days old."
What shall I call thee?
"I happy am,
Joy is my name."
Sweet joy befall thee!

Pretty joy!
Sweet joy but two days old,
Sweet joy I call thee;
Thou dost smile,
I sing the while—
Sweet joy befall thee.

[*1789*]

## *Infant Sorrow*

My mother groaned! my father wept.
Into the dangerous world I leapt,
Helpless, naked, piping loud;
Like a fiend hid in a cloud.

Struggling in my father's hands,
Striving against my swadling bands;
Bound and weary I thought best
To sulk upon my mother's breast.

[*1794*]

## TOPICS FOR CRITICAL THINKING AND WRITING

1. A two-day-old infant cannot know her or his name, much less utter it. How, then, can you explain—make sense of—the first five lines of "Infant Joy"? What aspect of real life is the poet presenting?
2. In line 9 the mother says, "Sweet joy I call thee." Why does the mother give this name to the child? Do you think that the final line of the poem adds a somewhat dark note, implying that joy may *not* befall the child? Explain your position.
3. In "Infant Sorrow," why is the infant sorrowful? What does he or she struggle against? (Can you grant that, from a baby's point of view, it may be horrible to be powerless and utterly at the mercy of adults?) Does "like a fiend" suggest that the infant is inherently wicked and therefore should be repressed? Or does the adult world repress energy, and thus make the baby seem fiendlike?
4. Why does the mother groan? Why does the father weep? Is the world "dangerous" to the infant in other than an obviously physical sense? To what degree are his or her parents enemies? To what degree does the infant yield to them? In the last line, one might expect a newborn baby to nurse. What does this infant do?
5. Compare and contrast "Infant Joy" with "Infant Sorrow." For example, each poem consists of two stanzas, but are the patterns of the two poems similar? (A two-stanza pattern might, for instance, be a question and an answer, or a generalization and a specific example, or a mental action and then a physical action.) Examine each poem closely, and then, so to speak, stand back and see if you find a pattern in each. (By the way, notice how much more active "Infant Sorrow" is—with "pip*ing*," "struggl*ing*," and so forth—than is "Infant Joy.")

# CHAPTER 3

# *Thinking Critically, Arguing Effectively*

## *Analysis, Interpretation, and Evaluation*

When you write about literature, you will almost always be advancing an argument. This does not mean that you will be raising your voice and confidently insisting that you are right, in the manner of a participant in a televised debate, but it does mean that you will usually be setting forth a **thesis** (a position, a point of view), and will be trying to persuade your reader to see things the way you see them. We say "usually" rather than "always" because sometimes you may simply be quoting, and sometimes you may simply be stating matters of fact, such as biographical material. The essence of an argument is that certain statements are offered as *reasons* for other statements. We will see, as we discuss this matter of argument, that in writing about literature you will find yourself *offering evidence* in support of your thesis: "Juliet is more intelligent than Romeo" (that's the thesis) "as we can see when we compare their responses in two scenes" (that's the beginning of the evidence). You probably will even help the reader to see that you are arguing, by occasionally using such key terms as "because," "therefore," "so," and "it follows, then."

If you were trying to instruct someone in how to walk, you might begin by demonstrating certain motions of the legs, and only later might you demonstrate that motions of the arms are also involved in the act of walking. Similarly, for pedagogic reasons we will treat analysis, interpretation, and evaluation separately, though in practice the three are often combined.

## ANALYSIS

When you analyze a work, you show how the parts fit together, or how one part relates to the whole. Analysis is of course not a practice limited to the study of literature. Suppose a friend has invited you to visit during the summer vacation

("Stay as long as you want"), and on the third evening there you are served an unfamiliar soup. You engage in polite chatter, but you are thinking, "What *is* this? It's a chicken base, yes, but certainly this is not mother's chicken soup. It's sort of thick, a bit starchy; there's probably some potato in it. And curry. But are there also turnips? No, I think I taste carrot. Yes, it must be carrot soup, with curry." And then maybe you come up with an evaluation: "It's delicious." (Here, then, we have analysis and evaluation. We can't claim that you will interpret the soup—unless perhaps you conclude that they are serving you some perfectly awful stuff in order for you to get the idea that you overstayed your welcome.)

Remember, too, that your analysis of parts depends on what you take the whole to be. In this case, we have taken a bowl of soup to be the whole, but a dietician might take the whole to be the meal, of which the soup is one part. How nourishing is it? Is it too fattening—or will that depend on what the rest of the meal consists of? Or, even putting aside nutritional matters, one might say that the soup in itself is excellent, but it really goes better with fish than with beef.

## An Example: Analyzing "The Judgment of Solomon"

Let's look at a short work, and then at an analysis of it. This story, customarily called "The Judgment of Solomon," tells how King Solomon decided which of two women was the mother of a child. It appears in the Hebrew Bible and in the Old Testament, in the latter part of the third chapter of the book called 1 Kings or First Kings, probably written in the mid-sixth century B.C.E.

The translation is from the King James Version of the Bible (1611). Two expressions in the story need clarification: (1) The woman who "overlaid" her child in her sleep rolled over on the child and suffocated it; (2) it is said of one of the women that her "bowels yearned upon her son," that is, her heart longed for her son. (In the psychology of the time, the bowels were thought to be the seat of emotion. In the Jerusalem Bible, a modern translation, the passage is translated less literally, as "She burned with pity for her son.")

### *The Judgment of Solomon*

Then came there two women, that were harlots, unto the king, and stood before him. And the one woman said, "O my lord, I and this woman dwell in one house, and I was delivered of a child with her in the house. And it came to pass the third day after that I was delivered, that this woman was delivered also, and we were together; there was no stranger in the house, save we two in the house. And this woman's child died in the night, because she overlaid it. And she rose at midnight, and took my son from beside me, while thine handmaid slept, and laid it in her bosom, and laid her dead child in my bosom. And when I rose in the morning to give my child suck, behold, it was dead; but when I considered it in the morning, behold, it was not my son, which I did bear."

And the other woman said, "Nay, but the living son is my son, and the dead is thy son." And this said, "No, but the dead is thy son, and the living is my son." Thus they spoke before the king.

Then said the king, "The one said, 'This is my son that liveth, and thy son is dead.' And the other said, 'Nay, but thy son is the dead, and my son is the living."' And the king said, "Bring me a sword." And they brought a sword before the king. And the king said, "Divide the living child in two and give half to the one, and half to the other."

Then spake the woman whose the living child was unto the king, for her bowels yearned upon her son, and she said, "O my lord, give her the living child, and in no wise slay it." But the other said, "Let it be neither mine nor thine, but divide it."

5 Then the king answered and said, "Give her the living child, and in no wise slay it. She is the mother thereof."

And all Israel heard of the judgment which the king had judged, and they feared the king, for they saw that the wisdom of God was in him, to do judgment.

We have said that analysis examines the parts, and their relation to the whole. Now, much depends on what one thinks the whole is. For instance, one might take as the whole the Hebrew Bible or the Old Testament, and try to analyze the function, within that whole, of this short story. Or one might take as the whole biblical book (First Kings) in which this story appears. Or (and this is what we will do now) one might take the story itself as the whole, and examine its components in order to see the form or shape of the story. (The implicit thesis of the essay will be that the story does—or does not—have a coherent shape, and probably the essayist will argue that if it does not have a coherent shape it is flawed and ineffective.)

One form or shape that we notice is this: The story moves from a problem to a solution. We can also say, still speaking of the overall form, that the story moves from quarreling (or divisiveness) and talk of death to harmony (or unity) and talk of life. In short, it moves from a troubled situation to a happy ending, a form that (because it provides an optimistic view of life and also provides a sense of completeness) gives most people pleasure.

Second, we can say—or, rather, we can argue—that "The Judgment of Solomon" is a sort of detective story: There is a death, followed by a conflict in the testimony of the witnesses, and a solution by a shrewd outsider. Consider Solomon's predicament. In literature, characters usually are sharply defined and individualized, yet the essence of a detective story is that the culprit should not be easily recognized as wicked. Here nothing seems to distinguish the two petitioners. Solomon is confronted by "two women, that were harlots." Until late in the story—that is, up to the time Solomon suggests dividing the child—they are described only as "the one woman," "the other woman," "the one," "the other."

Do we want to argue, then, that the story suffers from weak characterization? (Here—as soon as we speak of *weak* characterization—we are slipping into evaluation.) No, one might argue, the characterization is not weak; on the contrary, *because* the point is to show Solomon's wisdom, the women must be as alike as possible, so that readers cannot tell which of the two is speaking the truth. Like Solomon, readers have nothing to go on; neither witness is known to be more honest than the other, and there are no other witnesses to support or refute either woman. (If you agree with this analysis, we hope you will agree that intelligent evaluation depends on *understanding,* and analysis seeks to help the reader to understand.)

Solomon wisely contrives a situation in which these two claimants, who seem so similar, will reveal their different natures: The mother will reveal her maternal love, and the other woman will reveal her hard heart. The early symmetry (the identity of the two women) pleases a reader, and so does the ingenious device by which we can at last distinguish between the two women who seem so alike.

But even near the end there is a further symmetry. In order to save the child's life, the true mother gives up her claim, crying out, "Give her the living child, and in no wise slay it." The author (or, rather, the seventeenth-century translator who produced this part of the King James Version) takes these very words, with no change whatsoever, and puts them into Solomon's mouth as the king's final judgment. Solomon too says, "Give her the living child, and in no wise slay it," but now the sentence takes on a new meaning. In the first sentence, "her" refers to the false claimant (the true mother will give the child to "her"); in Solomon's sentence, "her" refers to the true mother: "Give her the living child . . . ." If we were writing an analysis of the story, we would say—argue—that readers take special pleasure in the fact that the very words by which the mother renounces her child are the words that (1) reveal she is the true mother, and that (2) Solomon appropriately uses these words to restore the child to his mother.

In short, if you wrote an analysis along these lines, it would be rooted in several premises that need to be stated persuasively:

- The story pleases *because* it has an almost tangible symmetry.
- It pleases *because* it offers a surprising solution to a seemingly insoluble problem.
- It pleases *because* the anguished cry of the mother becomes the very language of Solomon's verdict.
- It pleases *because* it has a happy ending.

Your readers may of course disagree, but you have argued your case—given reasons—and have not merely asserted it.

## Other Possible Topics for Analysis

We have already mentioned that another possible kind of analytic essay might go beyond the structure of the individual work, to the relation of the work to some larger whole. For instance, one might approach "The Judgment of Solomon" from the point of view of gender criticism (discussed in Chapter 9), which often concentrates on the ways in which women are represented. In this story, one might argue, wisdom is an attribute only of a male; women are either deceitful or emotional. Here is an essay that is an example of gender criticism. It was written by Alice McCauley, a first-year college student who tried to look at the story without preconceptions, with fresh eyes, forgetting all that she had heard about the wisdom of Solomon, or, rather, remembering it but questioning it.

## A Sample Student Essay

Alice McCauley

English 101b

September 20, 1996

HOW WISE WAS SOLOMON?

The point of the story of Solomon, in 1 Kings 3.16-28, apparently is to show that "the wisdom of God" was in Solomon. But if it shows something about Solomon's nature, it also shows the nature of two women. What does it show them to be? First, that neither woman is wise; wisdom is reserved for Solomon. One woman, in the obvious interpretation of the story, is a loving mother, willing to sacrifice her own happiness for the good of her child. The other woman, again in the traditional interpretation of the story, is cruel, spiteful, willing to kill the baby rather than to allow her rival to have it. Given the depiction of these two women, what is a reader to conclude about women? Women are emotional; women act on impulses--in one case, the maternal instinct and in the other case a selfish instinct ("If-I-can't-have-it-nobody-will-have-it").

That is, in this world run by men, men have all of the wisdom and women have all of the emotion. Some of this emotion is good (maternal love) and some of it is nasty (selfishness or spitefulness), but in any case women cannot (the story seems to show us) be trusted to be fair or to be wise.

And what of Solomon's justice? Solomon, by threatening to do violence with a sword, evokes the two responses from the women. It is interesting to see that his proposal evokes no exclamations of horror from members of his court. Presumably the king can do whatever he wishes. It happens that Solomon does not proceed to divide the child because the responses of the women convince him that he knows who is the true mother. But what would he have done if the women had not responded as they did? We don't know, but the fact that both women assume he really will divide the child gives us a clear sense that the women live in a world in which men rule by violence, a world in which indeed the judge might have solved the problem with the sword, just as he threatened to do.

In such a world, the woman who told Solomon to divide the child might have been daring him to act in accordance with his speech. That is, although the usual interpretation is that she is acting spitefully--this is the way her act is perceived in a world with patriarchal views--she might have been acting from a very different motive. If we look at the story through eyes opened by the Women's Movement, maybe we can see an unconventional woman who was in effect saying, "Violence is at the heart of your way of life, and you make all of the rules here. Go ahead, divide the child, if you dare; see if you can live with your decision." That is, if we free ourselves from the traditional view that Solomon is wise, we see that she bravely (and intelligently) challenges Solomon, and in effect reveals the violence on which his "justice" and his "wisdom"

```
rest. The fact that she is a harlot--a woman whose
whole life is spent in subordination to men--makes
her bold defiance of the powerful king especially
impressive.
```

## TOPICS FOR CRITICAL THINKING AND WRITING

1. Do you find the essay convincing? Why? If you do not find it convincing, do you nevertheless find it interesting? Why?
2. If you watch a soap opera, take one day's episode and analyze the relation of the parts to the whole. For instance, are segments of young lovers balanced with segments of older lovers? Are romantic segments balanced with segments of adventure or intrigue?

## The Whole or the Part: The Chicken or the Egg?

The question of the relation of the parts to the whole, or the whole to the parts, may resemble the question, "Which came first, the chicken or the egg?" After all, to have any understanding of the whole of a literary work (or a piece of music, or of any complex thing) one must understand the parts that make up the whole; but to understand the parts—to see how each part functions—one must have a working sense of the whole. Tentatively one can say here that in reading a work we sometimes begin with some preconceptions of the whole; for instance, even if we have never before read *Hamlet* or seen it, we may know at the outset that we are reading a tragedy, and so we have a sense of the whole (it will end unhappily). But as we read and reread the work, line by line, our response to the parts may cause us to alter our preconceptions about the whole. We may, for instance, find some scenes that are comic. There is nothing strange about this continual adjustment that we make as we read a work. Think of the way we respond to daily experiences, such as meeting someone new. We form an overall impression, perhaps based on a few details (manner of speech, kind of clothing, line of work, and so forth), and as we get to know the person better we may find that our first impression is confirmed by countless additional details—or, on the other hand, we may modify our first impression (our view of the whole) as we encounter more and more details.

---

## ✔ Questions to Stimulate Analytic Thinking

- What does each part contribute to the whole?
- How is the work organized? (For instance, by repetition, or by contrast?)
- Does the work belong to a traditional type, such as the detective story, the ghost story, the love poem, or tragedy? If so, does the work depart from type in significant ways?

---

## Literature for Analysis

### PATRICIA GRACE

*Patricia Grace was born in Wellington, New Zealand, in 1937, of Ngati Raukawa, Ngati Toa, and Te Ati Awa descent. In 1974 she received the first grant awarded to a Maori writer, and in 1975 she became the first Maori woman to publish a book of stories. She is the author of five novels, a play, a book of poems, and several volumes of short stories.*

## *Butterflies*

The grandmother plaited her granddaughter's hair and then she said, "Get your lunch. Put it in your bag. Get your apple. You come straight back after school, straight home here. Listen to the teacher," she said. "Do what she say."

Her grandfather was out on the step. He walked down the path with her and out onto the footpath. He said to a neighbor, "Our granddaughter goes to school. She lives with us now."

"She's fine," the neighbor said. "She's terrific with her two plaits in her hair."

"And clever," the grandfather said. "Writes every day in her book."

"She's fine," the neighbor said.

The grandfather waited with his granddaughter by the crossing and then he said, "Go to school. Listen to the teacher. Do what she say."

When the granddaughter came home from school her grandfather was hoeing around the cabbages. Her grandmother was picking beans. They stopped their work.

"You bring your book home?" the grandmother asked.

"Yes."

"You write your story?"

"Yes."

"What's your story?"

"About the butterflies."

"Get your book then. Read your story."

The granddaughter took her book from her schoolbag and opened it.

"I killed all the butterflies," she read. "This is me and this is all the butterflies."

"And your teacher like your story, did she?"

"I don't know."

"What your teacher say?"

"She said butterflies are beautiful creatures. They hatch out and fly in the sun. The butterflies visit all the pretty flowers, she said. They lay their eggs and then they die. You don't kill butterflies, that's what she said."

The grandmother and the grandfather were quiet for a long time, and their granddaughter, holding the book, stood quite still in the warm garden.

"Because you see," the grandfather said, "your teacher, she buy all her cabbages from the supermarket and that's why."

[*1987*]

## TOPICS FOR CRITICAL THINKING AND WRITING

1. On the basis of the first six paragraphs, how would you characterize the grandparents? How would you characterize the grandfather at the end of the story?
2. Why do you suppose Grace makes the relationship between a girl and her grandparents rather than between the girl and her parents? Or, for that matter, why not a boy and his parents? Would the story have a different feel? Explain.
3. Analysis calls for close attention to shifts—sometimes slight and understated, sometimes sudden and startling—in tone. Consider the possibility that the granddaughter's words, "I killed all the butterflies," reveals a shift in the story's tone. What is your response?
4. The story is told not from the position of one of the characters but from an objective point of view, as though it was captured by a camcorder. Suppose Grace had told it from the grandfather's point of view. Rewrite the final paragraph, giving us the grandfather's point of view, and compare your version with Grace's. Which do you prefer? Why?

## LINDA PASTAN

*Linda Pastan was born in New York City in 1932 and educated at Radcliffe College, Simmons College, and Brandeis University. The author of ten books of poems, she has won numerous prizes and has received a grant from the National Endowment for the Arts.*

## *Marks*

My husband gives me an A
for last night's supper,
an incomplete for my ironing,
a B plus in bed.
My son says I am average,
an average mother, but if
I put my mind to it
I could improve.
My daughter believes
in Pass/Fail and tells me
I pass. Wait 'til they learn
I'm dropping out.

[*1978*]

## TOPICS FOR CRITICAL THINKING AND WRITING

1. Think about some of the "marks" you have received for your academic work. A mark or grade is of course an evaluation, but is it (at least sometimes) also an analysis? For instance, have some marks been based on "form" and others on "content"? Think of the marking of a paper that you have recently written, and consider the degree to which the mark was based on analytic thinking.
2. In addition to the A and B that are mentioned, where else in the poem does Pastan use the language of the world of the school? The speaker of the poem receives grades, but does she also give a grade, or imply one?
3. What would be gained or lost if Pastan's first sentence came last?

# INTERPRETATION

When we **interpret** a work we are trying to set forth its *meaning*. For instance, we may say what we think it adds up to: "King Solomon shows his wisdom"—or, to take a different interpretation, "King Solomon tends to solve problems by the threat of violence." Admittedly, interpretation is not clearly distinct from analysis—hidden beneath an analysis is an idea of what the work means, of what it is about—but in analysis the writer's emphasis is on explaining, not on arguing.

## Making Sense of Experience

When we interpret a work we give our sense of what it means. Human beings are always trying to make sense of their experience, and we can hardly fail to interpret any given event in terms of our overall beliefs. Our beliefs, of course, are shaped by such things as our sex, age, ethnic background, and religious heritage. Different people see the same thing differently. As an old saying has it, for the pessimist the glass is half-empty, but for the optimist the same glass is half full. Similarly, if we believe that people are basically untrustworthy, we will in our daily experience have ample occasion to say, "I told you so," but if on the other hand we believe that people are basically decent we will also find that experience supports our view. Freudians, Marxists, and so on will all find experience confirming their beliefs—though many of them will also concede that sometimes experience forces them to reconsider their beliefs and modify or change them somewhat. Earlier in this chapter we looked at the analysis of a student who, in "The Judgment of Solomon," found not the traditional meaning (implied in the title) but a rather different meaning, rooted in what she saw as a patriarchal culture that regarded women only as irrational and untrustworthy persons, at best governed by a useful maternal instinct.

## Looking at an Interpretation of the Parable of the Prodigal Son

In Chapter 1 we suggested that, according to the commonest interpretation of the Parable of the Prodigal Son, the parable argues that, like God, we should rejoice in the restoration of a sinner, or, to put the matter in more secular terms, that we should welcome back into our midst someone who repents his or her misdeeds. In the Middle Ages the story was usually interpreted in a very specific anti-Semitic manner: The older brother represents the Jews, who resent the conversion of the Gentiles; the fact that he is in the fields when the prodigal returns stands for the remoteness of the Jews from the grace of God; the younger brother represents the Gentiles, who served the devil (the owner of the swine) by tending the devil's demons (the swine); the pods that the prodigal ate represent the vices (which cannot satisfy); the father represents God the Father; his going forth to meet the prodigal stands for Christ's incarnation.

Few biblical scholars today accept such a detailed, one-to-one interpretation of the story, and they usually support their view by arguing that historical evidence shows that in Jesus' day rabbis used clear-cut stories as a way of commenting on a moral problem, not as a way of teaching in detail. Most of the details in the stories, it is said, are present in order to add vividness, and they are not to be explained as precise equivalents to something else (for instance, the pods as equal to the vices). Still, everyone probably agrees that the parables are open to some variation in interpretation, and we cannot be too confident that a given explanation is wrong and another is right. One of our students wrote an essay offering an unusual but highly interesting interpretation, arguing that although the parable is traditionally called The Parable of the Prodigal Son, it ought to be called The Parable of the Shrewd Son. Here is part of his essay:

The son's speech is carefully rehearsed. We are told that when the son came to his senses, he planned to say, "'father, I have sinned against heaven, and before thee. And am no more worthy to be called thy son: make me as one of thy hired servants,'" but in fact when he sees his father coming to meet him, he <u>omits from his speech</u> the passage suggesting that he deserves to be treated not as a member of the family but only as a hired servant. This boy is quick; why bring up the possibility of service, now that he's apparently been forgiven. (He never much liked the idea of being out in the fields with the older brother, much less doing the work the older brother was supervising.) Looking back even further, we see that when the prodigal son comes to himself, he realizes not that he has done wrong, but that he is hungry, and that his father's servants are eating better than he. No other man will give unto him,

```
so what choice does he have but to play up to the
old man?
```

## TOPICS FOR CRITICAL THINKING AND WRITING

1. Do you agree with this interpretation? If not, why not?
2. If you do not agree with this interpretation, do you think it can be proven to be wrong? Why?

## In Brief

When we consider a range of interpretations of a literary work (as you will be asked to do for some works printed at the end of this chapter), we sometimes may feel that one interpretation is as good as another, and that all that counts is that there be evidence for it. But really the point is different from this. All of the evidence—each word on the page—has to be considered carefully. The text provides a check or limit on the interpretations that we consider, making us clarify and sharpen them, and it often leads us to conclude that one interpretation is indeed more persuasive than another. It is important to understand interpretation as a process—a process of weighing one interpretation against another, of constantly returning to the literary work to consider the evidence that the language itself offers, of seeking to reach the interpretation that is the most accurate and compelling.

---

## ✔ Questions to Stimulate Interpretations

- Is the meaning of the work obvious? If not, why not?
- Do you think that the race, gender, or ethnicity of the reader plays a strong role in the reader's interpretation of the work?
- Do there seem to be multiple meanings—perhaps even contradictory meanings—in the work?
- Do you think the meaning(s) for the original audience differed from the meaning(s) that you now find?

---

## Literature for Interpretation

### TONI CADE BAMBARA

*Toni Cade Bambara (1939–95), an African-American writer, was born in New York City and grew up in black districts of the city. After studying at the University of Florence and at City College in New York, where she received a master's degree, she worked for a while as a case investigator for the New York State Welfare Department.*

*Later she directed a recreation program for hospital patients. Now that her literary reputation is established, she spends most of her time writing, though she has also served as writer in residence at Spelman College in Atlanta.*

## *The Lesson*

Back in the days when everyone was old and stupid or young and foolish and me and Sugar were the only ones just right, this lady moved on our block with nappy hair and proper speech and no makeup. And quite naturally we laughed at her, laughed the way we did at the junk man who went about his business like he was some big-time president and his sorry-ass horse his secretary. And we kinda hated her too, hated the way we did the winos who cluttered up our parks and pissed on our handball walls and stank up our hallways and stairs so you couldn't halfway play hide-and-seek without a goddamn gas mask. Miss Moore was her name. The only woman on the block with no first name. And she was black as hell, cept for her feet, which were fish-white and spooky. And she was always planning these boring-ass things for us to do, us being my cousin, mostly, who lived on the block cause we all moved North the same time and to the same apartment then spread out gradual to breathe. And our parents would yank our heads into some kinda shape and crisp up our clothes so we'd be presentable for travel with Miss Moore, who always looked like she was going to church, though she never did. Which is just one of the things the grownups talked about when they talked behind her back like a dog. But when she came calling with some sachet she'd sewed up or some gingerbread she'd made or some book, why then they'd all be too embarrassed to turn her down and we'd get handed over all spruced up. She'd been to college and said it was only right that she should take responsibility for the young ones' education, and she not even related by marriage or blood. So they'd go for it. Specially Aunt Gretchen. She was the main gofer in the family. You got some old dumb shit foolishness you want somebody to go for, you send for Aunt Gretchen. She been screwed into the go-along for so long, it's a blood-deep natural thing with her. Which is how she got saddled with me and Sugar and Junior in the first place while our mothers were in a la-de-da apartment up the block having a good ole time.

So this one day Miss Moore rounds us all up at the mailbox and it's puredee hot and she's knockin herself out about arithmetic. And school suppose to let up in summer I heard, but she don't never let up. And the starch in my pinafore scratching the shit outta me and I'm really hating this nappy-head bitch and her goddamn college degree. I'd much rather go to the pool or to the show where it's cool. So me and Sugar leaning on the mailbox being surly, which is a Miss Moore word. And Flyboy checking out what everybody brought for lunch. And Fat Butt already wasting his peanut-butter-and-jelly sandwich like the pig he is. And Junebug punchin on Q.T.'s arm for potato chips. And Rosie Giraffe shifting from one hip to the other waiting for somebody to step on her foot or ask her if she from Georgia so she can kick ass, preferably Mercedes'. And Miss Moore asking us do we know what money is, like we a bunch of retards. I mean real money, she say, like it's only poker chips or monopoly papers we lay on the grocer. So right away I'm tired of this and say so. And would much rather snatch Sugar and go to the Sunset and terrorize the West Indian kids and take their hair ribbons and their money too. And Miss Moore files that remark away for next week's lesson on brotherhood, I can tell. And finally I say we oughta get to the subway cause it's cooler and besides we might meet some cute boys. Sugar done swiped her mama's lipstick, so we ready.

So we heading down the street and she's boring us silly about what things cost and what our parents make and how much goes for rent and how money ain't divided up right in this country. And then she gets to the part about we all poor and live in the slums, which I don't feature. And I'm ready to speak on that, but she steps out in the street and hails two cabs just like that. Then she hustles half the crew in with her and hands me a five-dollar bill and tells me to calculate 10 percent tip for the driver. And we're off. Me and Sugar and Junebug and Flyboy hangin out the window and hollering to everybody, putting lipstick on each other cause Flyboy a faggot anyway, and making farts with our sweaty armpits. But I'm mostly trying to figure how to spend this money. But they all fascinated with the meter ticking and Junebug starts laying bets as to how much it'll read when Flyboy can't hold his breath no more. Then Sugar lays bets as to how much it'll be when we get there. So I'm stuck. Don't nobody want to go for my plan, which is to jump out at the next light and run off to the first bar-b-que we can find. Then the driver tells us to get the hell out cause we there already. And the meter reads eighty-five cents. And I'm stalling to figure out the tip and Sugar say give him a dime. And I decide he don't need it bad as I do, so later for him. But then he tries to take off with Junebug foot still in the door so we talk about his mama something ferocious. Then we check out that we on Fifth Avenue and everybody dressed up in stockings. One lady in a fur coat, hot as it is. White folks crazy.

"This is the place," Miss Moore say, presenting it to us in the voice she uses at the museum. "Let's look in the windows before we go in."

5 "Can we steal?" Sugar asks very serious like she's getting the ground rules squared away before she plays. "I beg your pardon," say Miss Moore, and we fall out. So she leads us around the windows of the toy store and me and Sugar screamin, "This is mine, that's mine. I gotta have that, that was made for me. I was born for that," till Big Butt drowns us out.

"Hey, I'm goin to buy that there."

"That there? You don't even know what it is, stupid."

"I do so," he say punchin on Rosie Giraffe. "It's a microscope."

"Whatcha gonna do with a microscope, fool?"

10 "Look at things."

"Like what, Ronald?" ask Miss Moore. And Big Butt ain't got the first notion. So here go Miss Moore gabbing about the thousands of bacteria in a drop of water and the somethinorother in a speck of blood and the million and one living things in the air around us is invisible to the naked eye. And what she say that for? Junebug go to town on that "naked" and we rolling. Then Miss Moore ask what it cost. So we all jam into the window smudgin it up and the price tag say $300. So then she ask how long'd take for Big Butt and Junebug to save up their allowances. "Too long," I say. "Yeh," adds Sugar, "outgrown it by that time." And Miss Moore say no, you never outgrow learning instruments. "Why, even medical students and interns and," blah, blah, blah. And we ready to choke Big Butt for bringing it up in the first damn place.

"This here costs four hundred eighty dollars," say Rosie Giraffe. So we pile up all over her to see what she pointin out. My eyes tell me it's a chunk of glass cracked with something heavy, and different-color inks dripped into the splits, then the whole thing put into a oven or something. But for $480 it don't make sense.

"That's a paperweight made of semi-precious stones fused together under tremendous pressure," she explains slowly, with her hands doing the mining and all the factory work.

"So what's a paperweight?" asks Rosie Giraffe.

15 "To weigh paper with, dumbbell," say Flyboy, the wise man from the East.

"Not exactly," say Miss Moore, which is what she say when you warm or way off too. "It's to weigh paper down so it won't scatter and make your desk untidy." So right away me and Sugar curtsy to each other and then to Mercedes who is more the tidy type.

"We don't keep paper on top of the desk in my class," say Junebug, figuring Miss Moore crazy or lyin one.

"At home, then," she say. "Don't you have a calendar and a pencil case and a blotter and a letter-opener on your desk at home where you do your homework?" And she know damn well what our homes look like cause she nosys around in them every chance she gets.

"I don't even have a desk," say Junebug. "Do we?"

20 "No. And I don't get no homework neither," says Big Butt.

"And I don't even have a home," say Flyboy like he do at school to keep the white folks off his back and sorry for him. Send this poor kid to camp posters, is his specialty.

"I do," says Mercedes. "I have a box of stationery on my desk and a picture of my cat. My godmother bought the stationery and the desk. There's a big rose on each sheet and the envelopes smell like roses."

"Who wants to know about your smelly-ass stationery," say Rosie Giraffe fore I can get my two cents in.

"It's important to have a work area all your own so that . . ."

25 "Will you look at this sailboat, please," say Flyboy, cuttin her off and pointin to the thing like it was his. So once again we tumble all over each other to gaze at this magnificent thing in the toy store which is just big enough to maybe sail two kittens across the pond if you strap them to the posts tight. We all start reciting the price tag like we in assembly. "Handcrafted sailboat of fiberglass at one thousand one hundred ninety-five dollars."

"Unbelievable," I hear myself say and am really stunned. I read it again for myself just in case the group recitation put me in a trance. Same thing. For some reason this pisses me off. We look at Miss Moore and she lookin at us, waiting for I dunno what.

"Who'd pay all that when you can buy a sailboat set for a quarter at Pop's, a tube of glue for a dime, and a ball of string for eight cents? It must have a motor and a whole lot else besides," I say. "My sailboat cost me about fifty cents."

"But will it take water?" say Mercedes with her smart ass.

"Took mine to Alley Pond Park once," say Flyboy. "String broke. Lost it. Pity."

"Sailed mine in Central Park and it keeled over and sank. Had to ask my father for another dollar."

"And you got the strap," laugh Big Butt. "The jerk didn't even have a string on it. My old man wailed on his behind."

Little Q.T. was staring hard at the sailboat and you could see he wanted it bad. But he too little and somebody'd just take it from him. So what the hell. "This boat for kids, Miss Moore?"

"Parents silly to buy something like that just to get all broke up," say Rosie Giraffe.

"That much money it should last forever," I figure.

"My father'd buy it for me if I wanted it."

"Your father, my ass," say Rosie Giraffe getting a chance to finally push Mercedes.

"Must be rich people shop here," say Q.T.

"You are a very bright boy," say Flyboy. "What was your first clue?" And he rap him on the head with the back of his knuckles, since Q.T. the only one he could get away with. Thought Q.T. liable to come up behind you years later and get his licks in when you half expect it.

"What I want to know is," I says to Miss Moore though I never talk to her, I wouldn't give the bitch that satisfaction, "is how much a real boat costs? I figure a thousand'd get you a yacht any day."

"Why don't you check that out," she says, "and report back to the group?" Which really pains my ass. If you gonna mess up a perfectly good swim day least you could do is have some answers. "Let's go in," she say like she got something up her sleeve. Only she don't lead the way. So me and Sugar turn the corner to where the entrance is, but when we get there I kinda hang back. Not that I'm scared, what's there to be afraid of, just a toy store. But I feel funny, shame. But what I got to be shamed about? Got as much right to go in as anybody. But somehow I can't seem to get hold of the door, so I step away for Sugar to lead. But she hangs back too. And I look at her and she looks at me and this is ridiculous. I mean, damn, I have never ever been shy about doing nothing or going nowhere. But then Mercedes steps up and then Rosie Giraffe and Big Butt crowd in behind and shove, and next thing we all stuffed into the doorway with only Mercedes squeezing past us, smoothing out her jumper and walking right down the aisle. Then the rest of us tumble in like a glued-together jigsaw done all wrong. And people lookin at us. And it's like the time me and Sugar crashed into the Catholic church on a dare. But once we got in there and everything so hushed and holy and the candles and the bowin and the handkerchiefs on all the drooping heads, I just couldn't go through with the plan. Which was for me to run up to the altar and do a tap dance while Sugar played the nose flute and messed around in the holy water. And Sugar kept givin me the elbow. Then later teased me so bad I tied her up in the shower and turned it on and locked her in. And she'd be there till this day if Aunt Gretchen hadn't finally figured I was lying about the boarder takin a shower.

Same thing in the store. We all walkin on tiptoe and hardly touchin the games and puzzles and things. And I watched Miss Moore who is steady watchin us like she waiting for a sign. Like Mama Drewery watches the sky and sniffs the air and takes note of just how much slant is in the bird formation. Then me and Sugar bump smack into each other, so busy gazing at the toys, 'specially the sailboat. But we don't laugh and go into our fat-lady bump-stomach routine. We just stare at that price tag. Then Sugar run a finger over the whole boat. And I'm jealous and want to hit her. Maybe not her, but I sure want to punch somebody in the mouth.

"Watcha bring us here for, Miss Moore?"

"You sound angry, Sylvia. Are you mad about something?" Givin me one of them grins like she tellin a grown-up joke that never turns out to be funny. And she's looking very closely at me like maybe she plannin to do my portrait from memory. I'm mad, but I won't give her that satisfaction. So I slouch around the store being very bored and say, "Let's go."

Me and Sugar at the back of the train watchin the tracks whizzin by large then small then gettin gobbled up in the dark. I'm thinkin about this tricky toy I saw in the store. A clown that somersaults on a bar then does chin-ups just cause you yank lightly at his leg. Cost $35. I could see me askin my mother for a $35 birthday clown. "You wanna who that costs what?" she'd say, cocking her head to the side to get a better view of the hole in my head. Thirty-five dollars could buy new bunk beds for Junior and Gretchen's boy. Thirty-five dollars and the whole household could go visit Granddaddy Nelson in the country. Thirty-five dollars would pay for the rent and the piano bill too. Who are these people that spend that much for performing clowns and $1000 for toy sailboats? What kinda work they do and how they live and how come we ain't in on it? Where we are is who we are, Miss Moore always pointin out. But it don't necessarily have to be that way, she always adds then waits for somebody to say that poor people have to wake up and demand their share of the pie and don't none of us know what kind of pie she talkin about in the first damn place. But she ain't so smart cause I still got her four dollars from the taxi and she sure ain't gettin it. Messin up my day with this shit. Sugar nudges me in my pocket and winks.

45 Miss Moore lines us up in front of the mailbox where we started from, seem like years ago, and I got a headache for thinkin so hard. And we lean all over each other so we can hold up under the draggy-ass lecture she always finishes off with at the end before we thank her for borin us to tears. But she just looks at us like she readin tea leaves. Finally she say, "Well, what did you think of F. A. O. Schwarz?"

Rosie Giraffe mumbles, "White folks crazy."

"I'd like to go there again when I get my birthday money," says Mercedes, and we shove her out the pack so she has to lean on the mailbox by herself.

"I'd like a shower. Tiring day," say Flyboy.

Then Sugar surprises me by saying, "You know, Miss Moore, I don't think all of us here put together eat in a year what that sailboat costs." And Miss Moore lights up like somebody goosed her. "And?" she say, urging Sugar on. Only I'm standin on her foot so she don't continue.

50 "Imagine for a minute what kind of society it is in which some people can spend on a toy what it would cost to feed a family of six or seven. What do you think?"

"I think," say Sugar pushing me off her feet like she never done before, cause I whip her ass in a minute, "that this is not much of a democracy if you ask me. Equal chance to pursue happiness means an equal crack at the dough, don't it?" Miss Moore is beside herself and I am disgusted with Sugar's treachery. So I stand on her foot one more time to see if she'll shove me. She shuts up, and Miss Moore looks at me, sorrowfully I'm thinkin. And somethin weird is goin on, I can feel it in my chest.

"Anybody else learn anything today?" lookin dead at me. I walk away and Sugar has to run to catch up and don't even seem to notice when I shrug her arm off my shoulder.

"Well, we got four dollars anyway," she says.

"Uh hunh."

55 "We could go to Hascombs and get half a chocolate layer and then go to the Sunset and still have plenty money for potato chips and ice cream sodas."

"Uh hunh."

"Race you to Hascombs," she say.

We start down the block and she gets ahead which is O.K. by me cause I'm going to the West End and then over to the Drive to think this day through. She can run if she want to and even run faster. But ain't nobody gonna beat me at nuthin.

[*1972*]

## TOPICS FOR CRITICAL THINKING AND WRITING

1. What is "the lesson" that Miss Moore is trying to teach the children? How much, if any, of this lesson does Sylvia learn? Point to specific passages to support your answers.
2. Since Miss Moore intends the lesson for the children's own good, why is Sylvia so resistant to it, so impatient and exasperated?
3. Toward the end of the story, Sylvia says that she is "disgusted with Sugar's treachery." Describe their relationship. What would be missing from the story if Bambara had not included Sugar among its characters?

## WILLIAM WORDSWORTH

***William Wordsworth (1770-1850) grew up in the Lake District in England. After graduating from Cambridge University in 1791, he spent a year in France, where he fell in love with a French girl and fathered her child. His enthusiasm for the French Revolution waned, and he returned alone to England, where he devoted his life to poetry. We print a poem, written in 1799, that is one of five poems customarily called "Lucy poems," even though this particular poem, unlike the other four, does not mention the woman's name. It is not known if the poems refer to a real person.***

## *A Slumber Did My Spirit Seal*

A slumber did my spirit seal;
    I had no human fears;

She seemed a thing that could not feel
  The touch of earthly years.

No motion has she now, no force;
  She neither hears nor sees;
Rolled round in earth's diurnal course,
With rocks, and stones, and trees.

[*1799*]

##  TOPICS FOR CRITICAL THINKING AND WRITING

Each of the following assertions represents a brief interpretation. Evaluate each, citing evidence to support or rebut it.

1. The first stanza expresses the speaker's comforting but naive view (his *spirit,* i.e., his intelligence, was in a *slumber*) that his beloved was exempt from the pressures of this world; the second stanza expresses his horrified realization that, now dead, she is mere inanimate matter mechanistically hurled into violent motion.
2. The poem, by a pantheist—someone who identifies the Deity with everything in the universe—is about the poet's realization that the woman whom he loved, and who seemed to be apart from everything else, is now (through her death) assimilated into the grandeur of all that is on the earth; her death is a return to the life of nature.
3. The poem is ambiguous—just as, say, the following sentence is ambiguous: "Martha's mother died when she was twenty." (Who was twenty, Martha or her mother?) There is no way to decide between the first and second views expressed.
4. The word *diurnal* ("daily") adds a solemnity that makes it impossible to see the poem as a statement about the brutality of Lucy's death. Further, *diurnal* contains the word *urn,* thereby affirming that the entire earth is her funeral urn.
5. Even if the second view correctly summarizes Wordsworth's pantheism, *for today's readers* the poem is about the brute fact of death.
6. The language is ambiguous, so the only intelligent way to decide between conflicting interpretations is to choose the interpretation that best fits in with what we know about the author.
7. Here, as in most poetry by males, the female is allowed no significant identity. She is a "thing" (line 3), she is the object of the poet's love, she seems to be above nature (thus she is the traditional woman on a pedestal), she is a nature spirit, she is the poet's inspiration—she is lots of things, but she is not a person.

If none of the preceding statements seems to you to be just what you would say if you were asked to summarize your interpretation, set forth your own view, in 50–75 words, and then support it by pointing to details in the poem.

# EVALUATION

An evaluation or judgment claims that something is good or bad, better or worse than something else. Here are some evaluative statements.

- The lyrics of country music deserve to be taken seriously.
- *Death of a Salesman* is Arthur Miller's best play.
- Alice Walker's short stories are better than her novels.
- The film version of *The Color Purple* is inferior to the book.

These are *claims of value,* and we make such claims every day, for instance when we recommend one movie rather than another, or one course rather than another. We are almost always making choices based on the feeling that one thing is better than another.

We have just used the word *feeling,* but is this the best word? Let's make some distinctions. First, we can put to one side matters of taste, such as "Vanilla is better than chocolate." The word *better* makes this statement seem to be a claim of value, but the sentence probably really means only, "I like vanilla more than I like chocolate." If indeed the speaker is talking about a personal preference, it is hard to imagine how someone else could refute it. Of course if by *better* the speaker is asserting that vanilla is more healthful than chocolate, or that one should eat vanilla in order to give employment to persons who grow vanilla beans, we might be able to argue the issue. But, again, if *better* merely means "I prefer it," one probably can do no better than reply with the Latin proverb, *De gustibus non est disputandum* ("There is no disputing about tastes").

But are all assertions of aesthetic value—"The film version of *The Color Purple* is inferior to the book," and so on—really nothing more than disguised statements of preference, deceptive or inflated ways of saying "I prefer vanilla to chocolate"? Probably not. When we say we prefer vanilla to chocolate, we are not suggesting that our preference can be checked against any *standard,* anything anyone can examine. We are in effect saying only, "Well, that's my feeling (or opinion)," rather than "That's my *judgment.*" On the other hand, when we make an aesthetic judgment—that is, when we say that a book or a film or a performer is good or bad or is better or worse than something comparable—we are suggesting that we have thought about the matter and that there are *external standards*—things out there, so to speak—against which we can measure the works or the performers.

Judgments are statements that imply a standard and that can be supported—or rebutted—by reasons. For instance, if we say that a film is a good film, we probably can go on to give our reasons:

- The characters are psychologically interesting.
- They are also physically attractive.
- The setting is convincing (or exotic, or whatever).
- The story is plausible.
- The special effects are unusual and are exciting.

Further, different standards or criteria are offered for different kinds of works of art. If we are talking about a comedy, we will ask how funny it is, whether the humor is offensively racist, and so forth; if we are talking about a mystery, we will ask how ingenious the solution is.

What are some of the standards commonly used in judging works of literature? Among them are:

- truth, that is, resemblance to reality (the work is good because it makes us say, "Yes, that's the way things are")

- morality (the work is good because it shows us what is right or wrong, and it helps us to live a decent life)
- craftsmanship or technique (the work is good because it is well-made)

## Truth, Morality, Craftsmanship

Let's spend a moment or two looking at each of these criteria.

*Truth* For certain kinds of works, including most short stories and novels, we usually expect plausible characters, characters of whom we might say, "Yes, that's just the way people are." If the characters change suddenly, or if their speeches do not sound natural, we find fault with them. Similarly, we usually expect the plot of a novel to be plausible. Now, in the real world a child may fall out of a third-floor window and land unharmed in an empty baby carriage below, but such stuff is scarcely typical of the way life proceeds. If a plot includes material of this sort, we may say that the writer does not have a firm grasp of reality: Life, we feel, just isn't like *that.*

*Morality* Many readers feel that, when it comes right down to it, a work of literature is not just a matter of interesting combinations of words; it sets forth a vision of how people live and (at least by implication) how they ought to live, and we must judge the writer's morals—not so much as they are evident in his or her daily behavior but as they are evident in the literary work. Thus, if a work seems to be racist, or if it implies that women ought to be subject to the will of their fathers or husbands, it is (some people hold) deficient, no matter how realistic the dialogue, or how effective the rhymes. Similarly, for some readers a poem praising lesbian love, or a story that does not condemn an adulterous relation, is unacceptable. (The opposing view, usually summarized as "Art for art's sake," holds that a work of art is to be judged only in terms of beauty, shapeliness, as one might judge a porcelain vase.)

*Craftsmanship* It's easy enough to see craftsmanship or technical skill when, say, we hear a singer, or when we see a quilt or sit in a chair. Flat notes, irregular stitches, and wobbly legs are obvious faults, even though the singer and the makers of the quilt and the chair had the best of intentions. The creators may be nice people, but we judge their work to be inferior stuff. Similarly, in reading a work of literature a reader may become aware that the writer simply doesn't have the necessary skill. Perhaps the rhymes seem forced, or the dialogue seems stilted, or the plot contains some inconsistencies that are due to the writer's failure to remember what he or she wrote in earlier pages. Let's look at this poem by Elizabeth Bishop (1911–79), a major writer of our century.

### *To a Tree*

Oh, tree outside my window, we are kin,
　　For you ask nothing of a friend but this:
To lean against the window and peer in
　　And watch me move about! Sufficient bliss

For me, who stand behind its framework stout,
    Full of my tiny tragedies and grotesque grieves,
To lean against the window and peer out,
    Admiring infinites'mal leaves. 8

There is much of interest here, but perhaps you will agree with a reader who is disturbed by what may be considered lapses in craftsmanship. For instance, the inversion in "framework stout" (instead of "stout framework") looks like a sign of the poet's desperate attempt to get a rhyme. Second, "grieves" (instead of "griefs") seems another example of the poet reaching for a rhyme. Third, "infinites'mal" suggests a willingness to squeeze a word unbecomingly in order to get it to fit into the metrical pattern.

If you agree that these are weaknesses in craftsmanship, in technical mastery, you may agree that the poem therefore cannot be rated very highly. On the other hand, when we realize that Bishop wrote this poem when she was only sixteen years old—she published it in the school's literary magazine—we probably are inclined to alter our judgment, and to say that *for a sixteen-year-old,* it is highly accomplished, However, her later work, as you can see by reading some of it elsewhere in this book, is far more technically accomplished.

We have looked briefly at three criteria (truth, morality, craftsmanship), but of course there are others. For instance, some readers have valued works because they seemed sincere, or because they dealt with subjects that other writers neglected, or because they represented a new kind of writing for the particular author.

When you make a judgment about a literary work, and seek to explain and demonstrate it in an essay, you are trying to persuade your reader to see the work as you do. You are, in a sense, something of a judge and something of a teacher.

Perhaps this point helps to remind us that judgments are not really as personal and private as they might seem. We find we want to share our judgments, argue for them, support them with evidence, bring others around to agreeing with us. Maybe you will succeed, or maybe, instead, you will find that readers and other students in the classroom will test and challenge your judgment. In this sense, judgment is an activity that occurs within a community. It is a process, it is (one could even say) an example of good conversation. Making judgments, sharing them, getting responses, returning to our judgments to reconsider them, finding our minds changing a lot or a little as we listen to others' judgments—all of this is part of the intellectual excitement and reward of reading, responding to, discussing, and writing about literature.

In arguing about evaluation, you will probably want to

- specify your standards
- perhaps explain *why* you hold these standards
- point to particular passages in the work and show how they do or do not meet the standards

---

## ✔ Questions to Stimulate Evaluations

- Why does the work interest you or not interest you?
- Do you think that the race, gender, or ethnicity of the reader plays a strong role in the reader's evaluation of the work?

- Can you share the author's values? To what extent does your understanding of the author's values affect your evaluation of the work?
- Do you think the work is good or bad? Why?
- Do you believe it is possible to say of a given work that it is good and yet not to like or admire it?

---

## Literature for Evaluation

Here are three poems, in chronological order, all of which concern the felling of a tree or trees. Read and reread them, and then evaluate them. Remember to connect your observations to details in the language of the poems. Cite evidence from the texts to support your evaluations.

1. Do you think that one poem clearly is the best and that another clearly is the poorest? If so, why?
2. Do you think that one poem is good in one way, another good in a different way? If so, explain.
3. Is it possible for you to say that you believe X is the best poem but that you like Y better? Explain.

### GEORGE POPE MORRIS

*George Pope Morris (1802–64) was born in Philadelphia, and as a boy worked in a printing office. When he was only twenty-one he founded and edited a magazine, and when he was twenty-four he wrote a play that was successfully produced. In 1830 he gained additional fame with the publication of "The Oak," popularly known as "Woodman, Spare That Tree." He continued to write poetry, but primarily he was an editor of magazines and newspapers.*

### *The Oak*

Woodman, spare that tree!
 Touch not a single bough!
In youth it sheltered me,
 And I'll protect it now.
'Twas my forefather's hand
 That placed it near his cot;
There, woodman, let it stand,
 Thy axe shall harm it not!

That old familiar tree,
 Whose glory and renown
Are spread o'er land and sea,
 And wouldst thou hack it down?
Woodman, forbear thy stroke!
 Cut not its earth-bound ties;

Oh, spare that aged oak,
  Now towering to the skies!

When but an idle boy
  I sought its grateful shade;
In all their gushing joy
  Here too my sisters played.
My mother kiss'd me here;
  My father press'd my hand—
Forgive this foolish tear,
  But let that old oak stand!

My heart-strings round thee cling,
  Close as thy bark, old friend!
Here shall the wild-bird sing,
  And still thy branches bend.
Old tree! the storm still brave!
  And, woodman, leave the spot;
While I've a hand to save,
  Thy axe shall harm it not.

[*1830*]

## GERARD MANLEY HOPKINS

*Gerard Manley Hopkins (1844-89) was born near London and was educated at Oxford, where he studied the classics. A convert from Anglicanism to Roman Catholicism, he was ordained a Jesuit priest in 1877. After serving as a parish priest and teacher, he was appointed Professor of Greek at the Catholic University in Dublin.*

*Hopkins published only a few poems during his lifetime, partly because he believed that the pursuit of literary fame was incompatible with his vocation as a priest, and partly because he was aware that his highly individual style—for instance his habit of coining words, and of using words with multiple meanings—might puzzle readers. In the following poem* unselve *is Hopkins's invention. It apparently means (1) to rob it of itself, and (2) to deforest (the Latin word for* forest *is* silva *or* sylva*).*

### *Binsey Poplars*

felled 1879

My aspens dear, whose airy cages quelled,
Quelled or quenched in leaves the leaping sun,
All felled, felled, are all felled;
  Of a fresh and following folded rank
          Not spared, not one
          That dandled a sandalled
      Shadow that swam or sank

On meadow and river and wind-wandering
weed-winding bank.

O if we but knew what we do
When we delve° or hew—
Hack and rack° the growing green!
Since country is so tender
To touch, her being só slender,
That, like this sleek and seeing ball°
But a prick will make no eye at all,

Where we, even where we mean
To mend her we end her,
When we hew or delve:
After-comers cannot guess the beauty been.
Ten or twelve, only ten or twelve
Strokes of havoc únselve
The sweet especial scene,
Rural scene, a rural scene,
Sweet especial rural scene.

[*1879*]

**11 delve** dig **12 hack and rack** torture **15 ball** eyeball

## ADRIENNE RICH

*Adrienne Rich, born in Baltimore in 1929, published "For the Felling of an Elm in the Harvard Yard" in her first book of poems,* A Change of World, *in 1951, when she was still an undergraduate at Radcliffe College. (Radcliffe is the women's college at Harvard University.) In the intervening years she has established herself as one of the chief American poets of the second half of the century.*

*In line 9,* James *and* Whitehead *are William James (1842–1910) and Alfred North Whitehead (1861–1947), both of whom taught philosophy at Harvard.*

# *For the Felling of an Elm in the Harvard Yard*

They say the ground precisely swept
No longer feeds with rich decay
The roots enormous in their age
That long and deep beneath have slept.

So the great spire is overthrown,
And sharp saws have gone hurtling through
The rings that three slow centuries wore;
The second oldest elm is down.

The shade where James and Whitehead strolled
Becomes a litter on the green.
The young men pause along the paths
To see the axes glinting bold.

Watching the hewn trunk dragged away,
Some turn the symbol to their own,
And some admire the clean dispatch
With which the aged elm came down.

[*1951*]

# PART TWO

## *Fiction*

# CHAPTER 4

# *Approaching Fiction: Responding in Writing*

The next four chapters will look at specific elements, one by one, in fiction—plot, character, symbolism, and so on—but first let's read a brief story by Ernest Hemingway and then talk about it (and see how one student talked about it) with little or no technical language.

## ERNEST HEMINGWAY

*Ernest Hemingway (1899–1961) was born in Oak Park, Illinois. After graduating from high school in 1917 he worked on the Kansas City* Star, *but left to serve as a volunteer ambulance driver in Italy, where he was wounded in action. He returned home, married, and then served as European correspondent for the* Toronto Star, *but he soon gave up journalism for fiction. In 1922 he settled in Paris, where he moved in a circle of American expatriates that included Ezra Pound, Gertrude Stein, and F. Scott Fitzgerald. It was in Paris that he wrote stories and novels about what Gertrude Stein called a "lost generation" of rootless Americans in Europe. (For Hemingway's reminiscences of the Paris years, see his posthumously published* A Moveable Feast.*) He served as a journalist during the Spanish Civil War and during the Second World War, but he was also something of a private soldier.*

*After the Second World War his reputation sank, though he was still active as a writer (for instance, he wrote* The Old Man and the Sea *in 1952). In 1954 Hemingway was awarded the Nobel Prize in Literature, but in 1961, depressed by a sense of failing power, he took his own life.*

## Cat in the Rain

There were only two Americans stopping at the hotel. They did not know any of the people they passed on the stairs on their way to and from their room. Their room was on the second floor facing the sea. It also faced the public garden and the war monument. There were big palms and green benches in the public garden. In the good weather there was always an artist with his easel. Artists liked the way the palms grew and the bright colors of the hotels facing the gardens and the sea. Italians came from a long way off to look up at the war monument. It was made of bronze and glistened in the rain. It was raining. The rain dripped from the palm trees. Water stood in pools on the gravel paths. The sea broke in a long line in the rain and slipped back down the beach to come up and break again in a long line in the rain. The motor cars were gone from the square by the war monument. Across the square in the doorway of the café a waiter stood looking out at the empty square.

The American wife stood at the window looking out. Outside right under their window a cat was crouched under one of the dripping green tables. The cat was trying to make herself so compact that she would not be dripped on.

"I'm going down and get that kitty," the American wife said.

"I'll do it," her husband offered from the bed.

"No, I'll get it. The poor kitty out trying to keep dry under a table."

The husband went on reading, lying propped up with the two pillows at the foot of the bed.

"Don't get wet," he said.

The wife went downstairs and the hotel owner stood up and bowed to her as she passed the office. His desk was at the far end of the office. He was an old man and very tall.

"Il piove,"[1] the wife said. She liked the hotel-keeper.

"Si, si, Signora, brutto tempo. It is very bad weather."

He stood behind his desk in the far end of the dim room. The wife liked him. She liked the deadly serious way he received any complaints. She liked his dignity. She liked the way he wanted to serve her. She liked the way he felt about being a hotel-keeper. She liked his old, heavy face and big hands.

Liking him she opened the door and looked out. It was raining harder. A man in a rubber cape was crossing the empty square to the café. The cat would be around to the right. Perhaps she could go along under the eaves. As she stood in the doorway an umbrella opened behind her. It was the maid who looked after their room.

"You must not get wet," she smiled, speaking Italian. Of course, the hotel-keeper had sent her.

With the maid holding the umbrella over her, she walked along the gravel path until she was under their window. The table was there, washed

[1]**Il piove** It's raining (Italian)

bright green in the rain, but the cat was gone. She was suddenly disappointed. The maid looked up at her.

"Ha perduto qualque cosa, Signora?"[2]

"There was a cat," said the American girl.

"A cat?"

"Si, il gatto."

"A cat?" the maid laughed. "A cat in the rain?"

"Yes," she said, "under the table." Then, "Oh, I wanted it so much. I wanted a kitty."

When she talked English the maid's face tightened.

"Come, Signora," she said. "We must get back inside. You will be wet."

"I suppose so," said the American girl.

They went back along the gravel path and passed in the door. The maid stayed outside to close the umbrella. As the American girl passed the office, the padrone bowed from his desk. Something felt very small and tight inside the girl. The padrone made her feel very small and at the same time really important. She had a momentary feeling of being of supreme importance. She went on up the stairs. She opened the door of the room. George was on the bed, reading.

"Did you get the cat?" he asked, putting the book down.

"It was gone."

"Wonder where it went to," he said, resting his eyes from reading.

She sat down on the bed.

"I wanted it so much," she said. "I don't know why I wanted it so much. I wanted that poor kitty. It isn't any fun to be a poor kitty out in the rain."

George was reading again.

She went over and sat in front of the mirror of the dressing table looking at herself with the hand glass. She studied her profile, first one side and then the other. Then she studied the back of her head and her neck.

"Don't you think it would be a good idea if I let my hair grow out?" she asked, looking at her profile again.

George looked up and saw the back of her neck, clipped close like a boy's.

"I like it the way it is."

"I get so tired of it," she said. "I get so tired of looking like a boy."

George shifted his position in the bed. He hadn't looked away from her since she started to speak.

"You look pretty darn nice," he said.

She laid the mirror down on the dresser and went over to the window and looked out. It was getting dark.

"I want to pull my hair back tight and smooth and make a big knot at the back that I can feel," she said. "I want to have a kitty to sit on my lap and purr when I stroke her."

"Yeah?" George said from the bed.

"And I want to eat at a table with my own silver and I want candles. And I want it to be spring and I want to brush my hair out in front of a mirror and I want a kitty and I want some new clothes."

"Oh, shut up and get something to read," George said. He was reading again.

[2]**Ha . . . Signora** Have you lost something, Madam?

His wife was looking out of the window. It was quite dark now and still raining in the palm trees.

"Anyway, I want a cat," she said, "I want a cat. I want a cat now. If I can't have long hair or any fun, I can have a cat."

George was not listening. He was reading his book. His wife looked out of the window where the light had come on in the square.

Someone knocked at the door.

"Avanti,"[3] George said. He looked up from his book.

In the doorway stood the maid. She held a big tortoise-shell cat pressed tight against her and swung down against her body.

"Excuse me," she said, "the padrone asked me to bring this for the Signora."

[*1925*]

[3] **Avanti** Come in

# RESPONSES: ANNOTATIONS AND JOURNAL ENTRIES

When you read a story—or, perhaps more accurately, when you reread a story before discussing it or writing about it—you'll find it helpful to jot an occasional note (for instance, a brief response or a question) in the margins and to underline or highlight passages that strike you as especially interesting. Here is part of the story, with a student's annotations.

The cat was trying to make herself so compact that she would not be dripped on.

"I'm going down and get that kitty," the American wife said.

"I'll do it," her husband offered from the bed.

He doesn't make a move

"No, I'll get it. The poor kitty out trying to keep dry under a table."

The husband went on reading, lying propped up with the two pillows at the foot of the bed.

still doesn't move!

"Don't get wet," he said.

Is he making a joke? Or maybe he just isn't even thinking about what he is saying?

The wife went downstairs and the hotel owner stood up and bowed to her as she passed the office. His desk was at the far end of the office. He was an old man and very tall.

contrast with the husband

"Il piove," the wife said. She liked the hotel-keeper.

"Si, si, Signora, brutto tempo. It is very bad weather."

He stood behind his desk in the far end of the dim room. The wife liked him. She liked the deadly serious way he received any complaints. She liked his dignity. She liked the way he wanted to serve her. She liked the way he felt about being a hotel-keeper. She liked his old, heavy face and big hands.

*She respects him and she is pleased by the attention he shows*

Liking him she opened the door and looked out. It was raining harder. A man in a rubber cape was crossing the empty square to the café. The cat would be around to the right.

*to emphasize the bad weather??*

Of course *everything* in a story presumably is important, but having read the story once, probably something has especially interested (or puzzled) you, such as the relationship between two people, or the way the end of the story is connected to the beginning. On rereading, then, pen in hand, you'll find yourself noticing things that you missed or didn't find especially significant on your first reading. Now that you know the end of the story, you will read the beginning in a different way.

And of course if your instructor asks you to think about certain questions, you'll keep these in mind while you reread, and you will find ideas coming to you. In "Cat in the Rain," suppose you are asked (or you ask yourself) if the story might just as well be about a dog in the rain. Would anything be lost?

Here are a few questions that you can ask of almost any story. After scanning the questions, you will want to reread the story, pen in hand, and then jot down your responses on a sheet of paper. As you write, doubtless you will go back and reread the story or at least parts of it.

1. *What happens?* In two or three sentences—say 25–50 words—summarize the gist of what happens in the story.
2. *What sorts of people are the chief characters?* In "Cat in the Rain" the chief characters are George, George's wife, and the innkeeper (the padrone). Jot down the traits that each seems to possess, and next to each trait briefly give some supporting evidence.
3. *What especially pleased or displeased you in the story?* Devote at least a sentence or two to the end of the story. Do you find the end satisfying? Why or why not?
4. *Have you any thoughts about the title?* If so, what are they? If the story did not have a title, what would you call it?

*After* you have made your own jottings, compare them with these responses by a student. No two readers will respond in exactly the same way, but all readers can examine their responses and try to account for them, at least in part. If your responses are substantially different, how do you account for the differences?

1. A summary. A young wife, stopping with her husband at an Italian hotel, from her room sees a cat in the rain. She goes to get it, but it is gone, and

so she returns empty-handed. A moment later the maid knocks at the door, holding a tortoise-shell cat.

2. The characters: The woman.

   kind-hearted (pities cat in rain)

   appreciates innkeeper's courtesy ("liked the way he wanted to serve her") and admires him ("She liked his dignity")

   unhappy (wants a cat, wants to change her hair, wants to eat at a table with her own silver)

   The husband, George.

   not willing to put himself out (says he'll go to garden to get cat but doesn't move)

   doesn't seem very interested in wife (hardly talks to her--he's reading; tells her to "shut up")

   but he does say he finds her attractive ("You look pretty darn nice")

   The innkeeper.

   serious, dignified ("She liked the deadly serious way he received any complaints. She liked his dignity")

   courteous, helpful (sends maid with umbrella; at end sends maid with cat)

3. Dislikes and likes. "Dislikes" is too strong, but I was disappointed that more didn't happen at the end. What is the husband's reaction to the cat? Or his final reaction to his wife? I mean, what did he think about his wife when the maid brings the cat? And, for that matter, what is the wife's reaction? Is she satisfied? Or does she realize

that the cat can't really make her happy? Now for the <u>likes</u>. (1) I guess I did like the way it turned out; it's sort of a happy ending, I think, since she wants the cat and gets it. (2) I also especially like the innkeeper. Maybe I like him partly because the wife likes him, and if she likes him he must be nice. And he <u>is</u> nice--very helpful. And I also like the way Hemingway shows the husband. I don't mean that I like the man himself, but I like the way Hemingway shows he is such a bastard--not getting off the bed to get the cat, telling his wife to shut up and read.

Another thing about him is that the one time he says something nice about her, it's about her hair, and she isn't keen on the way her hair is. She says it makes her look "like a boy," and she is "tired" of looking like a boy. There's something wrong with this marriage. George hardly pays attention to his wife, but he wants her to look like a boy. Maybe the idea is that this macho guy wants to keep her looking like an inferior (immature) version of himself. Anyway, he certainly doesn't seem interested in letting her fulfill herself as a woman.

<u>I think my feelings add up to this</u>: I like the way Hemingway shows us the relation between the husband and wife (even though the relation is pretty bad), and I like the innkeeper. Even if the relation with the couple ends unhappily, the story has a sort of happy ending, so far as it goes, since the innkeeper does what he can to please his

guest: he sends the maid, with the cat. There's really nothing more that he can do.

More about the ending. The more I think about it, the more I feel that the ending is as happy as it can be. George is awful. When his wife says "I want a cat and I want a cat now," Hemingway tells us "George was not listening." And then, a moment later, almost like a good fairy the maid appears and grants the wife's wish.

4. The title. I don't suppose that I would have called it "Cat in the Rain," but I don't know what I would have called it. Maybe "An American Couple in Italy." Or maybe "The Innkeeper." I really do think that the innkeeper is very important, even though he only has a few lines. He's very impressive--not only to the girl, but to me (and maybe to all readers), since at the end of the story we see how careful the innkeeper is.

But the more I think about Hemingway's title, the more I think that maybe it also refers to the girl. Like the "poor kitty" in the rain, the wife is in a pretty bad situation. "It isn't any fun to be a poor kitty out in the rain." Of course the woman is indoors, but her husband generates lots of unpleasant weather. She may as well be out in the rain. She says "I want to have a kitty to sit on my lap and purr when I stroke it." This shows that she wants to be affectionate and that she also wants to have someone respond to her affection. She _is_ like a cat in the rain.

Oh, I just noticed that the wife at first

calls the cat "her" rather than "it." ("The cat was trying to make herself compact . . . .") Later she says "it," but at first she thinks of the cat as female--because (I think) she identifies with the cat.

The responses of this student probably include statements that you want to take issue with. Or perhaps you feel that the student did not even mention some things that you think are important. You may want to jot down some notes and raise some questions in class.

## A SAMPLE STUDENT ESSAY

The responses that we have quoted were written by Bill Yanagi, who later wrote an essay developing one of them. Here is the essay.

Bill Yanagi

English 10B

20 October 1996

HEMINGWAY'S AMERICAN WIFE

My title alludes not to any of the three women to whom Hemingway was married, but to "the American wife" who is twice called by this term in his short story, "Cat in the Rain." We first meet her in the first sentence of the story ("There were only two Americans stopping at the hotel"), and the next time she is mentioned (apart from a reference to the wife and her husband as "they") it is as "the American wife," at the beginning of the second paragraph of the story. The term is used again at the end of the third paragraph.

She is, then, at least in the early part of this story, just an American or an American wife--someone identified only by her nationality and her marital status, but not at all by her personality, her individuality, her inner self. She first becomes something of an individual when she separates herself from her husband by leaving the hotel room and going to look for a cat that she has seen in the garden, in the rain. This act of separation, however, has not the slightest effect on her husband, who "went on reading" (74).

When she returns, without the cat, he puts down his book and speaks to her, but it is obvious that he has no interest in her, beyond as a physical object ("You look pretty darn nice"). This comment is produced when she says she is thinking of letting her hair grow out, because she is "so tired of looking like a boy" (75). Why, a reader wonders, does her husband, who has paid almost no attention to her up to now, assure her that she looks "pretty darn nice"? I think it is reasonable to conclude that he _wants_ her to look like someone who is not truly a woman, in particular someone who is immature. That she does not feel she has much identity is evident when she continues to talk about letting her hair grow, and she says "I want to pull my hair back tight and smooth and make a big knot at the back that I can feel" (75). Long hair is, or at least was, the traditional sign of a woman; she wants long hair, and at the same time she wants to keep it under her control by tying it in a "big knot," a knot that she can feel, a knot whose presence reminds her, because she can feel it, of her feminine nature.

She goes on to say that she wants to brush her hair "in front of a mirror." That is, she wants to see and to feel her femininity, since her husband apparently--so far as we can see in the story, at least--scarcely recognizes it or her. Perhaps her desire for the cat ("I want a cat") is a veiled way of saying that she wants to express her animal nature, and not be simply a neglected woman who is made by her husband to look like a boy. Hemingway tells us, however, that when she looked for the cat in the garden she could not find it, a sign, I think, of her failure to break from the man. At the end of the story the maid brings her the cat, but a woman cannot just be handed a new nature and accept it, just like that. She has to find it herself, and in herself, so I think the story ends with "the American wife" still nothing more than an American wife.

WORK CITED

Literature: Thinking, Reading, and Writing Critically. Ed. Sylvan Barnet et al. 2nd ed. New York: Longman, 1997.

A few comments and questions may be useful.

- Do you find the essay interesting? Explain your response.
- Do you find the essay well-written? Explain.
- Do you find the essay convincing? Can you suggest ways of strengthening it, or do you think its argument is mistaken? Carefully reread "Cat in the Rain," taking note of passages that give further support to this student's argument, or that seem to challenge or qualify it.
- We often say that a good critical essay sends us back to the literary work with a fresh point of view. Our rereading differs from our earlier reading. Does this essay change your reading of Hemingway's story?

## TOPICS FOR CRITICAL THINKING AND WRITING

1. Can we be certain that the cat at the end of the story is the cat that the woman saw in the rain? (When we first hear about the cat in the rain we are not told anything about its color, and at the end of the story we are not told that the tortoise-shell cat is wet.) Does it matter if there are two cats?

2. One student argued that the cat represents the child that the girl wants to have. Do you think there is something to this idea? How might you support or refute it?
3. Consider the following passage:

   > As the American girl passed the office, the padrone bowed from his desk. Something felt very small and tight inside the girl. The padrone made her feel very small and at the same time really important. She had a momentary feeling of being of supreme importance.

   Do you think there is anything sexual here? And if so, that the passage tells us something about her relations with her husband? Support your view.
4. What do you suppose Hemingway's attitude was toward each of the three chief characters? How might you support your hunch?
5. Hemingway wrote the story in Italy, when his wife Hadley was pregnant. In a letter to F. Scott Fitzgerald he said,

   > Cat in the Rain wasn't about Hadley. . . . When I wrote that we were at Rapallo but Hadley was 4 months pregnant with Bumby. The Inn Keeper was the one at Cortina D'Ampezzo. . . . Hadley never made a speech in her life about wanting a baby because she had been told various things by her doctor and I'd—no use going into all that. (*Letters,* p. 180)

   According to some biographers, the story shows that Hemingway knew his marriage was going on the rocks (Hemingway and Hadley divorced). Does knowing that Hemingway's marriage turned out unhappily help you to understand the story? Does it make the story more interesting? And do you think that the story tells a biographer something about Hemingway's life?
6. It is sometimes said that a good short story does two things at once: It provides a believable picture of the surface of life, and it also illuminates some moral or psychological complexity that we feel is part of the essence of human life. This dual claim may not be true, but for the moment accept it. Do you think that Hemingway's story fulfills either or both of these specifications? Support your view.

Later chapters will offer some technical vocabulary and will examine specific elements of fiction, but familiarity with technical vocabulary will not in itself ensure that you will understand and enjoy fiction. There is no substitute for reading carefully, thinking about your responses, and (pen in hand) rereading the text, looking for evidence that accounts for your responses or that will lead you to different and perhaps richer responses. The essays that you will submit to your instructor are, finally, rooted in the annotations that you make in your text and the notes in which you record and explore your responses.

# CHAPTER 5

# *Stories and Meanings: Plot, Character, Theme*

People tell stories for many reasons, including the sheer delight of talking, but probably most of the best storytelling proceeds from one of two more commendable desires: a desire to entertain or a desire to instruct. Among the most famous of the stories designed to instruct are the parables that Jesus told, including The Parable of the Prodigal Son, which we discussed in Chapter 1. (*Parable* comes from the Greek word meaning "to throw beside," that is, "to compare." We are to compare these little stories with our own behavior.) We can say that the parable is told for the sake of the point; we also can say that it is told for our sake, because we are implicitly invited to see ourselves in the story, and to live our lives in accordance with it. This simple but powerful story, with its memorable characters—though nameless and briefly sketched—makes us feel the point in our hearts.

Even older than Jesus' parables are the fables attributed to Aesop, some of which go back to the seventh century before Jesus. These stories also teach lessons by recounting brief incidents from which homely morals may easily be drawn, even though the stories are utterly fanciful. Among famous examples are the stories of the hare and the tortoise, the boy who cried "Wolf," the ant and the grasshopper, and a good many others that stick in the mind because of the sharply contrasted characters in sharply imagined situations. The fables just mentioned take only four or five sentences apiece, but, brief as they are, Aesop told some briefer ones. Here is the briefest of all:

> A vixen sneered at a lioness because she never bore more than one cub. "Only one," the lioness replied, "but a lion."

Just that: a situation with a conflict (the mere confrontation of a fox and a lion brings together the ignoble and the noble) and a resolution (*something* must come out of such a confrontation). There is no setting (we are not told that "one day in June a vixen, walking down a road, met a lioness"), but none is needed here. What there is—however briefly set forth—is characterization. The fox's baseness is effectively communicated through the verb "sneered" and through her taunt, and the lioness's nobility is even more effectively communicated through the brevity and decisiveness of her reply. This reply at first seems to agree with the fox ("Only one") and then, after a suspenseful delay provided by the words "the lioness replied," the reply is tersely and powerfully completed ("but a lion"), placing the matter firmly in a new light. Granted that the story is not much of a story, still, it is finely told, and more potent—more memorable, more lively, we might even say more real, despite its talking animals—than the mere moral: "Small-minded people confuse quantity with quality."

Here is a much later short tale, from nineteenth-century Japan. It is said to be literally true, but whether it really occurred or not is scarcely of any importance. It is the story, not the history, that counts.

> Two monks, Tanzan and Ekido, were once traveling together down a muddy road. A heavy rain was still falling.
>
> Coming around a bend, they met a lovely girl in a silk kimono and sash, unable to cross the intersection.
>
> "Come on, girl," said Tanzan at once. Lifting her in his arms, he carried her over the mud.
>
> Ekido did not speak again until that night when they reached a lodging temple. Then he no longer could restrain himself. "We monks don't go near females," he told Tanzan, "especially not young and lovely ones. It is dangerous. Why did you do that?"
>
> "I left the girl there," said Tanzan. "Are you still carrying her?"

A superb story. The opening paragraph, though simple and matter-of-fact, holds our attention: we sense that something interesting is going to happen during this journey along a muddy road on a rainy day. Perhaps we even sense, somehow, by virtue of the references to the mud and the rain, that the journey itself rather than the travelers' destination will be the heart of the story: getting there will be more than half the fun. And then, after the introduction of the two **characters** and the **setting,** we quickly get the **complication,** the encounter with the girl. Still there is apparently no **conflict,** though in "Ekido did not speak again until that night" we sense an unspoken conflict, an action (or, in this case, an inaction) that must be explained, an imbalance that must be righted before we are finished. At last Ekido, no longer able to contain his thoughts, lets his indignation burst out: "We monks don't go near females, especially not young and lovely ones. It is dangerous. Why did you do that?" His statement and his question reveal not only his moral principles, but also his insecurity and the anger that grows from it. And now, when the conflict is out in the open, comes the brief reply that reveals Tanzan's very different character as clearly as the outburst revealed Ekido's. This reply—though we could not have predicted it—strikes us as exactly right, bringing the story to a perfect end, that is to a point (like the ends of Jesus' parable and Aesop's fable) at which there is no more to be said. It provides the **dénouement** (literally, "unknotting"), or **resolution.**

Let's look now at another short piece, though this one is somewhat longer than the stories we have just read, and it is less concerned than they are with teaching a lesson.

## ANTON CHEKHOV

*Anton Chekhov (1860–1904) was born in Russia, the son of a shopkeeper. While a medical student at Moscow University, Chekhov wrote stories, sketches, and reviews to help support his family and to finance his education. In 1884 he received his medical degree, began to practice medicine, published his first book of stories, and suffered the first of a series of hemorrhages from tuberculosis. In his remaining twenty years, in addition to writing several hundred stories, he wrote plays, half a dozen of which have established themselves as classics. He died from tuberculosis at the age of forty-four.*

# Misery

*Translated by Constance Garnett*

*"To Whom Shall I Tell My Grief?"*

The twilight of evening. Big flakes of wet snow are whirling lazily about the street lamps, which have just been lighted, and lying in a thin soft layer on roofs, horses' backs, shoulders, caps. Iona Potapov, the sledgedriver, is all white like a ghost. He sits on the box without stirring, bent as double as the living body can be bent. If a regular snowdrift fell on him it seems as though even then he would not think it necessary to shake it off. . . . His little mare is white and motionless too. Her stillness, the angularity of her lines, and the stick-like straightness of her legs make her look like a halfpenny gingerbread horse. She is probably lost in thought. Anyone who has been torn away from the plough, from the familiar gray landscapes, and cast into this slough, full of monstrous lights, of unceasing uproar and hurrying people, is bound to think.

It is a long time since Iona and his nag have budged. They came out of the yard before dinner-time and not a single fare yet. But now the shades of evening are falling on the town. The pale light of the street lamps changes to a vivid color, and the bustle of the street grows noisier.

"Sledge to Vyborgskaya!" Iona hears. "Sledge!"

Iona starts, and through his snow-plastered eyelashes sees an officer in a military overcoat with a hood over his head.

5 "To Vyborgskaya," repeats the officer. "Are you asleep? To Vyborgskaya!"

In token of assent Iona gives a tug at the reins which sends cakes of snow flying from the horse's back and shoulders. The officer gets into the sledge. The sledge-driver clicks to the horse, cranes his neck like a swan, rises in his seat, and more from habit than necessity brandishes his whip. The mare cranes her neck, too, crooks her stick-like legs, and hesitatingly sets off. . . .

"Where are you shoving, you devil?" Iona immediately hears shouts from the dark mass shifting to and fro before him. "Where the devil are you going? Keep to the r-right!"

"You don't know how to drive! Keep to the right," says the officer angrily.

A coachman driving a carriage swears at him; a pedestrian crossing the road and brushing the horse's nose with his shoulder looks at him angrily and shakes the snow off his sleeve. Iona fidgets on the box as though he were sitting on thorns, jerks his elbows, and turns his eyes about like one possessed, as though he did not know where he was or why he was there.

10 "What rascals they all are!" says the officer jocosely. "They are simply doing their best to run up against you or fall under the horse's feet. They must be doing it on purpose."

Iona looks at his fare and moves his lips. . . . Apparently he means to say something, but nothing comes out but a sniff.

"What?" inquires the officer.

Iona gives a wry smile, and straining his throat, brings out huskily: "My son . . . , er . . . my son died this week, sir."

"H'm! What did he die of?"

15 Iona turns his whole body round to his fare, and says:

"Who can tell! It must have been from fever. . . . He lay three days in the hospital and then he died. . . . God's will."

"Turn round, you devil!" comes out of the darkness. "Have you gone cracked, you old dog? Look where you are going!"

"Drive on! drive on! . . ." says the officer. "We shan't get there till tomorrow going on like this. Hurry up!"

The sledge-driver cranes his neck again, rises in his seat, and with heavy grace swings his whip. Several times he looks round at the officer, but the latter keeps his eyes shut and is apparently disinclined to listen. Putting his fare down at Vyborgskaya, Iona stops by a restaurant, and again sits huddled up on the box. . . . Again the wet snow paints him and his horse white. One hour passes, and then another. . . .

20 Three young men, two tall and thin, one short and hunchbacked, come up, railing at each other and loudly stamping on the pavement with their galoshes.

"Cabby, to the Police Bridge!" the hunchback cries in a cracked voice. "The three of us, . . . twenty kopecks!"

Iona tugs at the reins and clicks to his horse. Twenty kopecks is not a fair price, but he has no thoughts for that. Whether it is a rouble or whether it is five kopecks does not matter to him now so long as he has a fare. . . . The three young men, shoving each other and using bad language, go up to the sledge, and all three try to sit down at once. The question remains to be settled: Which are to sit down and which one is to stand? After a long altercation, ill-temper, and abuse, they come to the conclusion that the hunchback must stand because he is the shortest.

"Well, drive on," says the hunchback in his cracked voice, settling himself and breathing down Iona's neck. "Cut along! What a cap you've got, my friend! You wouldn't find a worse one in all Petersburg . . . ."

"He-he! . . . he-he! . . ." laughs Iona. "It's nothing to boast of!"

25 "Well, then, nothing to boast of, drive on! Are you going to drive like this all the way? Eh? Shall I give you one in the neck?"

"My head aches," says one of the tall ones. "At the Dukmasovs' yesterday Vaska and I drank four bottles of brandy between us."

"I can't make out why you talk such stuff," says the other tall one angrily. "You lie like a brute."

"Strike me dead, it's the truth! . . ."

"It's about as true as that a louse coughs."

"He-he!" grins Iona. "Me-er-ry gentlemen!"

"Tfoo! the devil take you!" cries the hunchback indignantly. "Will you get on, you old plague, or won't you? Is that the way to drive? Give her one with the whip. Hang it all, give it her well."

Iona feels behind his back the jolting person and quivering voice of the hunchback. He hears abuse addressed to him, he sees people, and the feeling of loneliness begins little by little to be less heavy on his heart. The hunchback swears at him, till he chokes over some elaborately whimsical string of epithets and is overpowered by his cough. His tall companions begin talking of a certain Nadyezhda Petrovna. Iona looks round at them. Waiting till there is a brief pause, he looks round once more and says:

"This week . . . er . . . my . . . er . . . son died!"

"We shall all die, . . ." says the hunchback with a sigh, wiping his lips after coughing. "Come, drive on! drive on! My friends, I simply cannot stand crawling like this! When will he get us there?"

"Well, you give him a little encouragement . . . one in the neck!"

"Do you hear, you old plague? I'll make you smart. If one stands on ceremony with fellows like you one may as well walk. Do you hear, you old dragon? Or don't you care a hang what we say?"

And Iona hears rather than feels a slap on the back of his neck.

"He-he! . . ." he laughs. "Merry gentlemen . . . God give you health!"

"Cabman, are you married?" asks one of the tall ones.

"I? He-he! Me-er-ry gentlemen. The only wife for me now is the damp earth. . . . He-ho-ho! . . . The grave that is! . . . Here my son's dead and I am alive. . . . It's a strange thing, death has come in at the wrong door. . . . Instead of coming for me it went for my son . . ."

And Iona turns round to tell them how his son died, but at that point the hunchback gives a faint sigh and announces that, thank God! they have arrived at last. After taking his twenty kopecks, Iona gazes for a long while after the revelers, who disappear into a dark entry. Again he is alone and again there is silence for him. . . . The misery which has been for a brief space eased comes back again and tears his heart more cruelly than ever. With a look of anxiety and suffering Iona's eyes stray restlessly among the crowds moving to and fro on both sides of the street: can he not find among those thousands someone who will listen to him? But the crowds flit by heedless of him and his misery. . . . His misery is immense, beyond all bounds. If Iona's heart were to burst and his misery to flow out, it would flood the whole world, it seems, but yet it is not seen. It has found a hiding-place in such an insignificant shell that one would not have found it with a candle by daylight. . . .

Iona sees a house-porter with a parcel and makes up his mind to address him.

"What time will it be, friend?" he asks.

"Going on for ten. . . . Why have you stopped here? Drive on!"

Iona drives a few paces away, bends himself double, and gives himself up to his misery. He feels it is no good to appeal to people. But before five minutes have passed he draws himself up, shakes his head as though he feels a sharp pain, and tugs at the reins. . . . He can bear it no longer.

"Back to the yard!" he thinks. "To the yard!"

And his little mare, as though she knew his thoughts, falls to trotting. An hour and a half later Iona is sitting by a big dirty stove. On the stove, on the floor, and on the benches are people snoring. The air is full of smells and stuffiness. Iona looks at the sleeping figures, scratches himself, and regrets that he has come home so early. . . .

"I have not earned enough to pay for the oats, even," he thinks. "That's why I am so miserable. A man who knows how to do his work, . . . who has had enough to eat, and whose horse has had enough to eat, is always at ease. . . ."

In one of the corners a young cabman gets up, clears his throat sleepily, and makes for the waterbucket.

"Want a drink?" Iona asks him.

"Seems so."

"May it do you good. . . . But my son is dead, mate. . . . Do you hear? This week in the hospital. . . . It's queer business. . . ."

Iona looks to see the effect produced by his words, but he sees nothing. The young man has covered his head over and is already asleep. The old man sighs and scratches himself. . . . Just as the young man had been thirsty for water, he thirsts for speech. His son will soon have been dead a week, and he has not really talked to anybody yet. . . . He wants to talk of it properly, with deliberation. . . . He wants to tell how his son was taken ill, how he suffered, what he said before he died, how he died. . . . He wants to describe the funeral, and how he went to the hospital to get his son's clothes. He still has his daughter Anisya in the country. . . . And he wants to talk about her too. . . . Yes, he has plenty to talk about now. His listener ought to sigh and exclaim and lament. . . . It would be even better to talk to women. Though they are silly creatures, they blubber at the first word.

"Let's go out and have a look at the mare," Iona thinks. "There is always time for sleep. . . . You'll have sleep enough, no fear. . . ."

He puts on his coat and goes into the stables where his mare is standing. He thinks about oats, about hay, about the weather. . . . He cannot think about his son when he is alone. . . . To talk about him with someone is possible, but to think of him and picture him is insufferable anguish. . . .

"Are you munching?" Iona asks his mare, seeing her shining eyes. "There, munch away, munch away. . . . Since we have not earned enough for oats, we will eat hay. . . . Yes, . . . I have grown too old to drive. . . . My son ought to be driving, not I. . . . He was a real coachman. . . . He ought to have lived. . . ."

Iona is silent for a while, and then he goes on:

"That's how it is, old girl. . . . Kuzma Ionitch is gone. . . . He said good-by to me. . . . He went and died for no reason. . . . Now, suppose you had a little colt, and you were mother to that little colt. . . . And all at once that same little colt went and died. . . . You'd be sorry, wouldn't you? . . ."

The little mare munches, listens, and breathes on her master's hands. Iona is carried away and tells her all about it.

[*1886*]

Let's look at Chekhov's "Misery" as a piece of craftsmanship. The happenings (here, a cabman seeks to tell his grief to several people, but is rebuffed and finally tells it to his horse) are the **plot;** the participants (cabman, officer, drunks, etc.) are the **characters;** the locale, time, and social circumstances (a snowy city in Russia, in the late nineteenth century) are the **setting;** and (though, as we will urge later, this word should be used with special caution) the meaning or point is the **theme.**

The traditional plot has this structure:

1. **Exposition** (setting forth of the initial situation)
2. **Conflict** (a complication that moves to a climax)
3. **Dénouement** (the outcome of the conflict; the resolution)

Chekhov's first paragraph, devoted to **exposition,** begins by introducing a situation that seems to be static: It briefly describes a motionless cabdriver, who "is all white like a ghost," and the cabdriver's mare, whose immobility and angularity "make her look like a halfpenny gingerbread horse." A reader probably anticipates that something will intrude into this apparently static situation; some sort of conflict will be established, and then in all probability will be (in one way or another) resolved. In fact, the inertia described at the very beginning is disturbed even before the paragraph ends, when Chekhov rather surprisingly takes us into the mind not of the cabdriver but of the horse, telling us that if we were in such a situation as the horse finds itself, we "too would find it difficult not to think."

By the middle of the first paragraph, we have been given a brief but entirely adequate view of the **setting:** a Russian city in the days of horse-drawn sleighs, that is, in Chekhov's lifetime. Strictly speaking, the paragraph does not specify Russia or the period, but the author is a Russian writing in the late nineteenth century, the character has a Russian name, and there is lots of snow so one concludes that the story is set in Russia. (A reader somewhat familiar with Chekhov does not even have to read the first paragraph of this story to know the setting, since all of Chekhov's work is set in the Russia of his day.)

One might almost say that by the end of the first paragraph we have met all the chief **characters**—though we can't know this until we finish the story. In later paragraphs we will meet additional figures, but the chief characters—the characters whose fates we are concerned with—are simply the cabdriver and the horse. It's odd, of course, to call the horse a character, but, as we noticed, even in the first paragraph Chekhov takes us into the mind of the horse. Notice, too, how Chekhov establishes connections between the man and the horse; for instance, when the first fare gets into the sleigh, the driver "cranes his neck" and then "the mare cranes her neck, too." By the end of the story, the horse seems almost a part of Iona. Perhaps the horse will be the best possible listener, since perhaps grief of Iona's sort can be told only to the self.

Before talking further about the characters, we should point out that the word "character" has two chief meanings:

1. A figure in a literary work (thus Iona is a character, the officer who hires the cab is another character, and the drunks are additional characters).

2. Personality, as when we say that Iona's character is described only briefly, or that Hamlet's character is complex, or that So-and-So's character is unpleasant.

Usually the context makes clear the sense in which the word is used, but in your own writing, make sure that there is no confusion.

It is sometimes said that figures in literature are either **flat characters** (one-dimensional figures, figures with simple personalities) or **round characters** (complex figures). The usual implication is that good writers give us round characters, believable figures who are more than cardboard cutouts holding up signs saying "jealous lover," "cruel landlord," "kind mother," and so forth. But a short story scarcely has space to show the complexity or roundness of several characters, and in fact, many good stories do not give even their central characters much complexity. In "Misery," for instance, Iona is shown chiefly as a grieving father aching to speak of the death of his son. We don't know what sort of food he likes, whether he ever gets drunk, what he thinks of the Czar, or whether he belongs to the church. But it is hard to imagine that knowing any of these things would be relevant and would increase our interest in him. Similarly, the other characters in the story are drawn with a few simple lines. The officer who first hires the cab is arrogant ("Sledge to Vyborgskaya! . . . Are you asleep? To Vyborgskaya!"), and though he at first makes a little joke that leads Iona to think the officer will listen to his story, the officer quickly changes the subject. We know of him only that he wants to get to Vyborg. The three noisy drunks whom Iona next picks up can be fairly characterized as just that—three noisy drunks. Again, we can hardly imagine that the story would be better if we knew much more about these drunks.

On the other hand, Iona is not quite so flat as we have perhaps implied. A careful reader notices, for instance, that Iona reveals other things about himself in addition to his need to express his grief. For instance, he treats his horse as kindly as possible. When the officer gets into the cab, Iona "more from habit than necessity brandishes his whip"—but he gets the horse moving by making a clicking sound, and he actually whips the horse only when the officer tells him to hurry. Later the hunchback will say of the mare, "Give her one with the whip. Hang it all, give it her well," but we feel that Iona uses his horse as gently as is possible.

It should be noted, however, that the drunks, though they are not much more than drunks, are not less than drunks either. They are quarrelsome and they even display touches of cruelty, but we cannot call them villains. In some degree, the fact that they are drunk excuses their "bad language," their "ill-tempers," and even their displays of cruelty. If these characters are fairly flat, they nevertheless are thoroughly believable, and we know as much about them as we need to know for the purposes of the story. Furthermore, the characters in a story help to characterize other characters, by their resemblances or their differences. How Iona might behave if he were an officer, or if he were drunk, we do not know, but he is in some degree contrasted with the other characters and thus gains some complexity, to the extent that we can at least say that he is *not* drunk, arrogant, or quarrelsome.

We need hardly ask if there is **motivation** (compelling grounds, external and also within one's personality) for Iona's final action. He has tried to express his grief to the officer, and then to the drunks. Next, his eyes search the crowds to "find someone who will listen to him." After speaking to the house-porter,

Iona sees, Chekhov tells us, that "it is no good to appeal to people." When we read this line, we probably do not think, or at least do not think consciously, that he will turn from people to the mare, but when at the end of the story he does turn to the mare, the action seems entirely natural, inevitable.

In some stories, we are chiefly interested in plot (the arrangement of happenings or doings), in others we are chiefly interested in character (the personalities of the doers), but on the whole the two are so intertwined that interest in one involves interest in the other. Happenings occur (people cross paths), and personalities respond, engendering further happenings. As Henry James rhetorically asked, "What is character but the determination of incident? What is incident but the illustration of character?" Commonly, as a good story proceeds and we become increasingly familiar with the characters, we get intimations of what they may do in the future. We may not know precisely how they will act, but we have a fairly good idea, and when we see their subsequent actions, we usually recognize the appropriateness. Sometimes there are hints of what is to come, and because of this **foreshadowing,** we are not shocked by what happens later, but rather we experience suspense as we wait for the expected to come about. Coleridge had Shakespeare's use of foreshadowing in mind when he praised him for giving us not surprise, but expectation—the active reader participates in the work by reading it responsively—and then the fulfillment of expectation. E. M. Forster, in *Aspects of the Novel,* has a shrewd comment on the importance of both fulfilling expectation and offering a slight surprise: "Shock, followed by the feeling, 'Oh, that's all right,' is a sign that all is well with plot: characters, to be real, ought to run smoothly, but a plot ought to cause surprise."

Finally, a few words about **theme.** Usually we feel that a story is about something, it has a point—a theme. (What happens is the plot; what the happenings add up to is the theme.) But a word of caution is needed here. What is the theme of "Misery"? One student formulated the theme thus:

> Human beings must utter their grief, even if only to an animal.

Another student formulated it thus:

> Human beings are indifferent to the sufferings of others.

Still another student offered this:

> Deep suffering is incommunicable, but the sufferer must try to find an outlet.

Many other formulations are possible. Probably there is no "right" statement of the theme of "Misery" or of any other good story: a story is not simply an illustration of an abstract statement of theme. A story has a complex variety of details that modify any summary statement we may offer when we try to say what it is about. And what lives in our memory is not an abstract statement—certainly not a thesis, that is, a proposition offered and argued, such as "We should pay attention to the suffering of others." What lives is an image that by every word in the story has convinced us that it is a representation, if not of "reality," of at least an aspect of reality.

Still, the writer is guided by a theme in the choice of details; of many possible details, Chekhov decided to present only a few. The musical sense of the word "theme" can help us to understand what a theme in literature is: "a melody constituting the basis of variation, development, or the like." The variations and the development cannot be random, but must have a basis. (We have already suggested that the episodes in "Misery"—the movement from the officer to the drunks and then to the house-porter and the other cabman—are not random, but somehow seem exactly "right," just as the remarks about the man and the horse both stretching their necks seem "right.") What is it, Robert Frost asks, that prevents the writer from jumping "from one chance suggestion to another in all directions as of a hot afternoon in the life of a grasshopper?" Frost's answer: "Theme alone can steady us down."

We can, then, talk about the theme—again, what the story adds up to—as long as we do not think a statement of the theme is equivalent to or is a substitute for the whole story. As Flannery O'Connor said, "Some people have the notion that you can read the story and then climb out of it into the meaning, but for the fiction writer himself the whole story is the meaning." A theme, she said, is not like a string tying a sack of chicken feed, to be pulled out so that the feed can be got at. "A story is a way to say something that can't be said any other way." That "something"—which can't be said in any other way—is the theme. (On theme, see also pages 151–52.)

## TOPICS FOR CRITICAL THINKING AND WRITING

1. What do you admire or not admire about Chekhov's story? Why?
2. Try to examine in detail your response to the ending. Do you think the ending is, in a way, a happy ending? Would you prefer a different ending? For instance, should the story end when the young cabman falls asleep? Or when Iona sets out for the stable? Or can you imagine a better ending? If so, what?

## KATE CHOPIN: TWO STORIES

*For a biographical note, see page 19.*

# *The Storm*

### *I*

The leaves were so still that even Bibi thought it was going to rain. Bobinôt, who was accustomed to converse on terms of perfect equality with his little son, called the child's attention to certain sombre clouds that were rolling with sinister intention from the west, accompanied by a sullen, threatening roar. They were at Friedheimer's store and decided to remain there till the storm had passed. They sat within the door on two empty kegs. Bibi was four years old and looked very wise.

"Mama'll be 'fraid, yes," he suggested with blinking eyes.

"She'll shut the house. Maybe she got Sylvie helpin' her this evenin'," Bobinôt responded reassuringly.

"No; she ent got Sylvie. Sylvie was helpin' her yistiday," piped Bibi.

5 Bobinôt arose and going across to the counter purchased a can of shrimps, of which Calixta was very fond. Then he returned to his perch on

the keg and sat stolidly holding the can of shrimps while the storm burst. It shook the wooden store and seemed to be ripping great furrows in the distant field. Bibi laid his little hand on his father's knee and was not afraid.

## II

Calixta, at home, felt no uneasiness for their safety. She sat at a side window sewing furiously on a sewing machine. She was greatly occupied and did not notice the approaching storm. But she felt very warm and often stopped to mop her face on which the perspiration gathered in beads. She unfastened her white sacque at the throat. It began to grow dark, and suddenly realizing the situation she got up hurriedly and went about closing windows and doors.

Out on the small front gallery she had hung Bobinôt's Sunday clothes to air and she hastened out to gather them before the rain fell. As she stepped outside, Alcée Laballière rode in at the gate. She had not seen him very often since her marriage, and never alone. She stood there with Bobinôt's coat in her hands, and the big rain drops began to fall. Alcée rode his horse under the shelter of a side projection where the chickens had huddled and there were plows and a harrow piled up in the corner.

"May I come and wait on your gallery till the storm is over, Calixta?" he asked.

"Come 'long in, M'sieur Alcée."

His voice and her own startled her as if from a trance, and she seized Bobinôt's vest. Alcée, mounting to the porch, grabbed the trousers and snatched Bibi's braided jacket that was about to be carried away by a sudden gust of wind. He expressed an intention to remain outside, but it was soon apparent that he might as well have been out in the open: the water beat in upon the boards in driving sheets, and he went inside, closing the door after him. It was even necessary to put something beneath the door to keep the water out.

"My! what a rain! It's good two years sense it rain' like that," exclaimed Calixta as she rolled up a piece of bagging and Alcée helped her to thrust it beneath the crack.

She was a little fuller of figure than five years before when she married; but she had lost nothing of her vivacity. Her blue eyes still retained their melting quality; and her yellow hair, dishevelled by the wind and rain, kinked more stubbornly than ever about her ears and temples.

The rain beat upon the low, shingled roof with a force and clatter that threatened to break an entrance and deluge them there. They were in the dining room—the sitting room—the general utility room. Adjoining was her bed room, with Bibi's couch along side her own. The door stood open, and the room with its white, monumental bed, its closed shutters, looked dim and mysterious.

Alcée flung himself into a rocker and Calixta nervously began to gather up from the floor the lengths of a cotton sheet which she had been sewing.

"If this keeps up, *Dieu sait*[1] if the levees goin' to stan' it!" she exclaimed.

[1]***Dieu sait*** God only knows (French)

"What have you got to do with the levees?"

"I got enough to do! An' there's Bobinôt with Bibi out in that storm—if he only didn' left Friedheimer's!"

"Let us hope, Calixta, that Bobinôt's got sense enough to come in out of a cyclone."

She went and stood at the window with a greatly disturbed look on her face. She wiped the frame that was clouded with moisture. It was stiflingly hot. Alcée got up and joined her at the window, looking over her shoulder. The rain was coming down in sheets obscuring the view of far-off cabins and enveloping the distant wood in a gray mist. The playing of the lightning was incessant. A bolt struck a tall chinaberry tree at the edge of the field. It filled all visible space with a blinding glare and the crash seemed to invade the very boards they stood upon.

20 Calixta put her hands to her eyes, and with a cry, staggered backward. Alcée's arm encircled her, and for an instant he drew her close and spasmodically to him.

*"Bonte!"*[2] she cried, releasing herself from his encircling arm and retreating from the window, "the house'll go next! If I only knew w'ere Bibi was!" She would not compose herself; she would not be seated. Alcée clasped her shoulders and looked into her face. The contact of her warm, palpitating body when he had unthinkingly drawn her into his arms, had aroused all the old-time infatuation and desire for her flesh.

"Calixta," he said, "don't be frightened. Nothing can happen. The house is too low to be struck, with so many tall trees standing about. There! aren't you going to be quiet? say, aren't you?" He pushed her hair back from her face that was warm and steaming. Her lips were as red and moist as pomegranate seed. Her white neck and a glimpse of her full, firm bosom disturbed him powerfully. As she glanced up at him the fear in her liquid blue eyes had given place to a drowsy gleam that unconsciously betrayed a sensuous desire. He looked down into her eyes and there was nothing for him to do but to gather her lips in a kiss. It reminded him of Assumption.[3]

"Do you remember—in Assumption, Calixta?" he asked in a low voice broken by passion. Oh! she remembered; for in Assumption he had kissed her and kissed and kissed her; until his senses would well nigh fail, and to save her he would resort to a desperate flight. If she was not an immaculate dove in those days, she was still inviolate; a passionate creature whose very defenselessness had made her defense, against which his honor forbade him to prevail. Now—well, now—her lips seemed in a manner free to be tasted, as well as her round, white throat and her whiter breasts.

They did not heed the crashing torrents, and the roar of the elements made her laugh as she lay in his arms. She was a revelation in that dim, mysterious chamber; as white as the couch she lay upon. Her firm, elastic flesh that was knowing for the first time its birthright, was like a creamy lily that the sun invites to contribute its breath and perfume to the undying life of the world.

[2]***Bonte!*** Heavens!

[3]**Assumption** a town named for a church feast on 15 August celebrating Mary's bodily ascent to heaven

25 The generous abundance of her passion, without guile or trickery, was like a white flame which penetrated and found response in depths of his own sensuous nature that had never yet been reached.

When he touched her breasts they gave themselves up in quivering ecstasy, inviting his lips. Her mouth was a fountain of delight. And when he possessed her, they seemed to swoon together at the very borderland of life's mystery.

He stayed cushioned upon her, breathless, dazed, enervated, with his heart beating like a hammer upon her. With one hand she clasped his head, her lips lightly touching his forehead. The other hand stroked with a soothing rhythm his muscular shoulders.

The growl of the thunder was distant and passing away. The rain beat softly upon the shingles, inviting them to drowsiness and sleep. But they dared not yield.

The rain was over; and the sun was turning the glistening green world into a palace of gems. Calixta, on the gallery, watched Alcée ride away. He turned and smiled at her with a beaming face; and she lifted her pretty chin in the air and laughed aloud.

## *III*

30 Bobinôt and Bibi, trudging home, stopped without at the cistern to make themselves presentable.

"My! Bibi, w'at will yo' mama say! You ought to be ashame'. You oughtn' put on those good pants. Look at 'em! An' that mud on yo' collar! How you got that mud on yo' collar, Bibi? I never saw such a boy!" Bibi was the picture of pathetic resignation. Bobinôt was the embodiment of serious solicitude as he strove to remove from his own person and his son's the signs of their tramp over heavy roads and through wet fields. He scraped the mud off Bibi's bare legs and feet with a stick and carefully removed all traces from his heavy brogans. Then, prepared for the worst—the meeting with an over-scrupulous housewife, they entered cautiously at the back door.

Calixta was preparing supper. She had set the table and was dripping coffee at the hearth. She sprang up as they came in.

"Oh, Bobinôt! You back! My! but I was uneasy. W'ere you been during the rain? An' Bibi? he ain't wet? he ain't hurt?" She had clasped Bibi and was kissing him effusively. Bobinôt's explanations and apologies which he had been composing all along the way, died on his lips as Calixta felt him to see if he were dry, and seemed to express nothing but satisfaction at their safe return.

"I brought you some shrimps, Calixta," offered Bobinôt, hauling the can from his ample side pocket and laying it on the table.

35 "Shrimps! Oh, Bobinôt! you too good fo' anything!" and she gave him a smacking kiss on the cheek that resounded. "*J'vous reponds,*[4] we'll have a feas' to night! umph-umph!"

[4]***J'vous reponds*** Take my word; let me tell you

Bobinôt and Bibi began to relax and enjoy themselves, and when the three seated themselves at table they laughed much and so loud that anyone might have heard them as far away as Laballière's.

## *IV*

Alcée Laballière wrote to his wife, Clarisse, that night. It was a loving letter, full of tender solicitude. He told her not to hurry back, but if she and the babies liked it at Biloxi, to stay a month longer. He was getting on nicely; and though he missed them, he was willing to bear the separation a while longer—realizing that their health and pleasure were the first things to be considered.

## *V*

As for Clarisse, she was charmed upon receiving her husband's letter. She and the babies were doing well. The society was agreeable; many of her old friends and acquaintances were at the bay. And the first free breath since her marriage seemed to restore the pleasant liberty of her maiden days. Devoted as she was to her husband, their intimate conjugal life was something which she was more than willing to forgo for a while.

So the storm passed and everyone was happy.

[*1898*]

## TOPICS FOR CRITICAL THINKING AND WRITING

1. How would you characterize Calixta?
2. In Part III do you think Calixta is insincere in her expressions of solicitude for Bobinôt? Why, or why not?
3. Do you take Part IV to imply that Alcée and Calixta will continue their affair for another month? Support your answer.
4. Why does Chopin bother, in Part V, to tell us about Clarisse? And exactly what do you make of the last line of the story?
5. It is fair to say that the story is cynical? Explain.
6. Do you think the story is immoral and, if so, ought not to be assigned in a course in literature? Explain.

# *Désirée's Baby*

As the day was pleasant, Madame Valmondé drove over to L'Abri to see Désirée and the baby.

It made her laugh to think of Désirée with a baby. Why, it seemed but yesterday that Désirée was little more than a baby herself; when Monsieur in riding through the gateway of Valmondé had found her lying asleep in the shadow of the big stone pillar.

The little one awoke in his arms and began to cry for "Dada." That was as much as she could do or say. Some people thought she might have strayed there of her own accord, for she was of the toddling age. The prevailing belief was that she had been purposely left by a party of Texans, whose canvas-covered wagon, late in the day, had crossed the ferry that Coton Maïs kept, just below the plantation. In time Madame Valmondé abandoned every speculation but the one that Désirée had been sent to her by a beneficent Providence to be the child of her affection, seeing that she was without child of the flesh. For the girl grew to be beautiful and gentle, affectionate and sincere,—the idol of Valmondé.

It was no wonder, when she stood one day against the stone pillar in whose shadow she had lain asleep, eighteen years before, that Armand Aubigny riding by and seeing her there, had fallen in love with her. That was the way all the Aubignys fell in love, as if struck by a pistol shot. The wonder was that he had not loved her before; for he had known her since his father brought him home from Paris, a boy of eight, after his mother died there. The passion that awoke in him that day, when he saw her at the gate, swept along like an avalanche, or like a prairie fire, or like anything that drives headlong over all obstacles.

5 Monsieur Valmondé grew practical and wanted things well considered: that is, the girl's obscure origin. Armand looked into her eyes and did not care. He was reminded that she was nameless. What did it matter about a name when he could give her one of the oldest and proudest in Louisiana? He ordered the *corbeille*[1] from Paris, and contained himself with what patience he could until it arrived; then they were married.

Madame Valmondé had not seen Désirée and the baby for four weeks. When she reached L'Abri she shuddered at the first sight of it, as she always did. It was a sad looking place, which for many years had not known the gentle presence of a mistress, old Monsieur Aubigny having married and buried his wife in France, and she having loved her own land too well ever to leave it. The roof came down steep and black like a cowl, reaching out beyond the wide galleries that encircled the yellow stuccoed house. Big, solemn oaks grew close to it, and their thick-leaved, far-reaching branches shadowed it like a pall. Young Aubigny's rule was a strict one, too, and under it his negroes had forgotten how to be gay, as they had been during the old master's easy-going and indulgent lifetime.

The young mother was recovering slowly, and lay full length, in her soft white muslins and laces, upon a couch. The baby was beside her, upon her arm, where he had fallen asleep, at her breast. The yellow nurse woman sat beside a window fanning herself.

Madame Valmondé bent her portly figure over Désirée and kissed her, holding her an instant tenderly in her arms. Then she turned to the child.

"This is not the baby!" she exclaimed, in startled tones. French was the language spoken at Valmondé in those days.

10 "I knew you would be astonished," laughed Désirée, "at the way he has

[1]***corbeille*** wedding gifts from the groom to the bride

grown. The little *cochon de lait!*[2] Look at his legs, mamma, and his hands and fingernails,—real fingernails. Zandrine had to cut them this morning. Isn't it true, Zandrine?"

The woman bowed her turbaned head majestically, "Mais si,[3] Madame."

"And the way he cries," went on Désirée, "is deafening. Armand heard him the other day as far away as La Blanche's cabin."

Madame Valmondé had never removed her eyes from the child. She lifted it and walked with it over to the window that was lightest. She scanned the baby narrowly, then looked as searchingly at Zandrine, whose face was turned to gaze across the fields.

"Yes, the child has grown, has changed," said Madame Valmondé, slowly, as she replaced it beside its mother. "What does Armand say?"

Désirée's face became suffused with a glow that was happiness itself.

"Oh, Armand is the proudest father in the parish, I believe, chiefly because it is a boy, to bear his name; though he says not,—that he would have loved a girl as well. But I know it isn't true. I know he says that to please me. And mamma," she added, drawing Madame Valmondé's head down to her, and speaking in a whisper, "he hasn't punished one of them—not one of them—since baby is born. Even Négrillon, who pretended to have burnt his leg that he might rest from work—he only laughed, and said Négrillon was a great scamp. Oh, mamma, I'm so happy; it frightens me."

What Désirée said was true. Marriage, and later the birth of his son had softened Armand Aubigny's imperious and exacting nature greatly. This was what made the gentle Désirée so happy, for she loved him desperately. When he frowned she trembled, but loved him. When he smiled, she asked no greater blessing of God. But Armand's dark, handsome face had not often been disfigured by frowns since the day he fell in love with her.

When the baby was about three months old, Désirée awoke one day to the conviction that there was something in the air menacing her peace. It was at first too subtle to grasp. It had only been a disquieting suggestion; an air of mystery among the blacks; unexpected visits from far-off neighbors who could hardly account for their coming. Then a strange, an awful change in her husband's manner, which she dared not ask him to explain. When he spoke to her, it was with averted eyes, from which the old love-light seemed to have gone out. He absented himself from home; and when there, avoided her presence and that of her child, without excuse. And the very spirit of Satan seemed suddenly to take hold of him in his dealings with the slaves. Désirée was miserable enough to die.

She sat in her room, one hot afternoon, in her *peignoir,* listlessly drawing through her fingers the strands of her long, silky brown hair that hung about her shoulders. The baby, half naked, lay asleep upon her own great mahogany bed, that was like a sumptuous throne, with its satin-lined half-canopy. One of La Blanche's little quadroon boys—half naked too—stood fanning the child slowly with a fan of peacock feathers. Désirée's eyes had been fixed absently and sadly upon the baby, while she was striving to penetrate the threatening mist that she felt closing about her. She looked from her child to the boy who stood beside him, and back again; over and over. "Ah!" It was a cry that she could not help; which she was not conscious of

[2]***cochon de lait*** suckling pig (French)

[3]**Mais si** certainly (French)

having uttered. The blood turned like ice in her veins, and a clammy moisture gathered upon her face.

She tried to speak to the little quadroon boy; but no sound would come, at first. When he heard his name uttered, he looked up, and his mistress was pointing to the door. He laid aside the great, soft fan, and obediently stole away, over the polished floor, on his bare tiptoes.

She stayed motionless, with gaze riveted upon her child, and her face the picture of fright.

Presently her husband entered the room, and without noticing her, went to a table and began to search among some papers which covered it.

"Armand," she called to him, in a voice which must have stabbed him, if he was human. But he did not notice. "Armand," she said again. Then she rose and tottered towards him. "Armand," she panted once more, clutching his arm, "look at our child. What does it mean? tell me."

He coldly but gently loosened her fingers from about his arm and thrust the hand away from him. "Tell me what it means!" she cried despairingly.

"It means," he answered lightly, "that the child is not white; it means that you are not white."

A quick conception of all that this accusation meant for her nerved her with unwonted courage to deny it. "It is a lie; it is not true, I am white! Look at my hair, it is brown; and my eyes are gray, Armand, you know they are gray. And my skin is fair," seizing his wrist. "Look at my hand; whiter than yours, Armand," she laughed hysterically.

"As white as La Blanche's," he returned cruelly; and went away leaving her alone with their child.

When she could hold a pen in her hand, she sent a despairing letter to Madame Valmondé.

"My mother, they tell me I am not white. Armand has told me I am not white. For God's sake tell them it is not true. You must know it is not true. I shall die. I must die. I cannot be so unhappy, and live."

The answer that came was as brief:

"My own Désirée: Come home to Valmondé; back to your mother who loves you. Come with your child."

When the letter reached Désirée she went with it to her husband's study, and laid it open upon the desk before which he sat. She was like a stone image: silent, white, motionless after she placed it there.

In silence he ran his cold eyes over the written words. He said nothing. "Shall I go, Armand?" she asked in tones sharp with agonized suspense.

"Yes, go."

"Do you want me to go?"

"Yes, I want you to go."

He thought Almighty God had dealt cruelly and unjustly with him; and felt, somehow, that he was paying Him back in kind when he stabbed thus into his wife's soul. Moreover he no longer loved her, because of the unconscious injury she had brought upon his home and his name.

She turned away like one stunned by a blow, and walked slowly towards the door, hoping he would call her back.

"Good-by, Armand," she moaned.

He did not answer her. That was his last blow at fate.

Désirée went in search of her child. Zandrine was pacing the sombre gallery with it. She took the little one from the nurse's arms with no word of explanation, and descending the steps, walked away, under the live-oak branches.

It was an October afternoon; the sun was just sinking. Out in the still fields the negroes were picking cotton.

Désirée had not changed the thin white garment nor the slippers which she wore. Her hair was uncovered and the sun's rays brought a golden gleam from its brown meshes. She did not take the broad, beaten road which led to the far-off plantation of Valmondé. She walked across a deserted field, where the stubble bruised her tender feet, so delicately shod, and tore her thin gown to shreds.

She disappeared among the reeds and willows that grew thick along the banks of the deep, sluggish bayou; and she did not come back again.

45 Some weeks later there was a curious scene enacted at L'Abri. In the centre of the smoothly swept back yard was a great bonfire. Armand Aubigny sat in the wide hallway that commanded a view of the spectacle; and it was he who dealt out to a half dozen negroes the material which kept this fire ablaze.

A graceful cradle of willow, with all its dainty furbishings, was laid upon the pyre, which had already been fed with the richness of a priceless *layette.* Then there were silk gowns, and velvet and satin ones added to these; laces, too, and embroideries; bonnets and gloves; for the *corbeille* had been of rare quality.

The last thing to go was a tiny bundle of letters; innocent little scribblings that Désirée had sent to him during the days of their espousal. There was the remnant of one back in the drawer from which he took them. But it was not Désirée's; it was part of an old letter from his mother to his father. He read it. She was thanking God for the blessing of her husband's love:—

> "But, above all," she wrote, "night and day, I thank the good God for having so arranged our lives that our dear Armand will never know that his mother, who adores him, belongs to the race that is cursed with the brand of slavery."

[*1892*]

## TOPICS FOR CRITICAL THINKING AND WRITING

1. Let's start with the ending. Readers find the ending powerful, but they differ in their interpretations of it. Do you think that when Armand reads the letter he learns something he had never suspected, or, instead, something that he had sensed about himself all along? Find evidence in the text to support your view.
2. Describe Desirée's feelings toward Armand. Do you agree with the student who told us, "She makes him into a God"?
3. Chopin writes economically: each word counts, each phrase and sentence is significant. What is she revealing about Armand (and perhaps about the discovery he has made) when she writes, "And the very spirit of Satan seemed suddenly to take hold of him in his dealings with the slaves"?

4. Is this story primarily a character study, or is Chopin seeking to make larger points in it about race, slavery, and gender?

---

# ✔ Checklist: Writing about Plot, Character, and Theme

## Plot

1. Does the plot grow out of the characters, or does it depend on chance or coincidence? Did something at first strike you as irrelevant that later you perceived as relevant? Do some parts continue to strike you as irrelevant?
2. Does surprise play an important role, or does foreshadowing? If surprise is very important, can the story be read a second time with any interest? If so, what gives it this further interest?
3. What conflicts does the story include? Conflicts of one character against another? Of one character against the setting, or against society? Conflicts within a single character?
4. Are certain episodes narrated out of chronological order? If so, were you puzzled? Annoyed? On reflection, does the arrangement of episodes seem effective? Why or why not? Are certain situations repeated? If so, what do you make out of the repetitions?

## Character

1. Which character chiefly engages your interest? Why?
2. What purposes do minor characters serve? Do you find some who by their similarities and differences help to define each other or help to define the major character? How else is a particular character defined—by his or her words, actions (including thoughts and emotions), dress, setting, narrative point of view? Do certain characters act differently in the same, or in a similar, situation?
3. How does the author reveal character? By explicit authorial comment, for instance, or, on the other hand, by revelation through dialogue? Through depicted action? Through the actions of other characters? How are the author's methods especially suited to the whole of the story?
4. Is the behavior plausible—that is, are the characters well motivated?
5. If a character changes, why and how does he or she change? (You may want to jot down each event that influences a change.) Or did you change your attitude toward a character not because the character changes but because you came to know the character better?
6. Are the characters round or flat? Are they complex, or, on the other hand, highly typical (for instance, one-dimensional representatives of a social class or age group)? Are you chiefly interested in a character's psychology, or does the character strike you as standing for something, such as honesty or the arrogance of power?

7. How has the author caused you to sympathize with certain characters? How does your response—your sympathy or lack of sympathy—contribute to your judgment of the conflict?

## Theme

1. Is the title informative? What does it mean or suggest? Did the meaning seem to change after you read the story? Does the title help you to formulate a theme? If you had written the story, what title would you use?
2. Do certain passages—dialogue or description—seem to you to point especially toward the theme? Do you find certain repetitions of words or pairs of incidents highly suggestive and helpful in directing your thoughts toward stating a theme? Flannery O'Connor, in *Mystery and Manners,* says, "In good fiction, certain of the details will tend to accumulate meaning from the action of the story itself, and when that happens, they become symbolic in the way they work." Does this story work that way?
3. Is the meaning of the story embodied in the whole story, or does it seem stuck in, for example in certain passages of authorial comment?
4. Suppose someone asked you to state the point—the theme—of the story. Could you? And if you could, would you say that the theme of a particular story reinforces values you hold, or does it to some degree challenge them? (It is sometimes said that the best writers are subversive, forcing readers to see something that they do not want to see.)

---

# CHAPTER 6

# *Narrative Point of View*

Every story is told by someone. Mark Twain wrote *Adventures of Huckleberry Finn,* but he does not tell the story; Huck tells the story, and he begins thus:

> You don't know about me without you have read a book by the name of *The Adventures of Tom Sawyer,* but that ain't no matter. That book was made by Mr. Mark Twain, and he told the truth, mainly. There was things which he stretched, but mainly he told the truth.

Similarly, Edgar Allan Poe wrote "The Cask of Amontillado," but the story is told by a man whose name, we learn later, is Montresor. Here is the opening:

> The thousand injuries of Fortunato I had borne as I best could, but when he ventured upon insult, I vowed revenge.

Each of these passages gives a reader a very strong sense of the narrator, that is, of the invented person who tells the story, and it turns out that the works are chiefly about the speakers. Compare those opening passages, however, with two others, which sound far more objective. The first comes from Chekhov's "Misery" (page 87):

> The twilight of evening. Big flakes of wet snow are whirling lazily about the street lamps, which have just been lighted, and lying in a thin soft layer on roofs, horses' backs, shoulders, caps. Iona Potapov, the sledge-driver, is all white like a ghost. He sits on the box without stirring, bent as double as the living body can be bent.

And another example, this one from Hawthorne's "Young Goodman Brown" (page 127):

> Young Goodman Brown came forth at sunset into the street at Salem village; but put his head back, after crossing the threshold, to exchange a parting kiss with his young wife. And Faith, as the wife was aptly

> named, thrust her own pretty head into the street, letting the wind play with the pink ribbons of her cap while she called to Goodman Brown.

In each of these two passages, a reader is scarcely aware of the personality of the narrator; our interest is almost entirely in the scene that each speaker reveals, not in the speaker's response to the scene.

The narrators of *Huckleberry Finn* and of "The Cask of Amontillado" immediately impress us with their distinctive personalities. We realize that whatever happenings they report will be colored by the special ways in which such personalities see things. But what can we say about the narrators of "Misery" and of "Young Goodman Brown"? A reader hardly notices them, at least in comparison with Huck and Montresor. We look, so to speak, not *at* these narrators, but at others (the cabman and Goodman Brown and Faith).

Of course, it is true that as we read "Misery" and "Young Goodman Brown" we are looking through the eyes of the narrators, but these narrators seem (unlike Huck and Montresor) to have 20/20 vision. This is not to say, however, that these apparently colorless narrators really are colorless or invisible. The narrator of "Misery" seems, at least if we judge from the opening sentences, to want to evoke an atmosphere. He describes the setting in some detail, whereas the narrator of "Young Goodman Brown" seems chiefly concerned with reporting the actions of people whom he sees. Moreover, if we listen carefully to Hawthorne's narrator, perhaps we can say that when he mentions that Faith was "aptly" named, he makes a judgment. Still, it is clear that the narrative voices we hear in "Misery" and "Young Goodman Brown" are relatively impartial and inconspicuous; when we hear them, we feel, for the most part, that they are talking about something objective, about something "out there." These narrative voices will produce stories very different from the narrative voices used by Twain and Poe. The voice that the writer chooses, then, will in large measure shape the story; different voices, different stories.

The narrative point of view of *Huckleberry Finn* and of "The Cask of Amontillado" (and of any other story in which a character in the story tells the story) is a **participant** (or **first-person**) point of view. The point of view of "Young Goodman Brown" (and of any other story in which a nearly invisible outsider tells the story) is a **nonparticipant** (or **third-person**) point of view.

## PARTICIPANT (OR FIRST-PERSON) POINTS OF VIEW

In John Updike's "A & P" on page 109 the narrator is, like Mark Twain's Huck and Poe's Montresor, a major character. Updike has invented an adolescent boy who undergoes certain experiences and who comes to certain perceptions. Since the story is narrated by one of its characters, we can say that the author uses a first-person (or participant) point of view.

It happens that in Updike's "A & P" the narrator is the central character, the character whose actions—whose life, we might say—most interests the reader. But sometimes a first-person narrator tells a story that focuses on another character; the narrator still says "I" (thus the point of view is first person), but the reader feels that the story is not chiefly about this "I" but is about some other figure. For instance, the narrator may be a witness to a story about Jones, and our interest is in what happens to Jones, though we get the story of Jones filtered through, say, the eyes of Jones's friend, or brother, or cat.

When any of us tells a story (for instance, why we quit a job), our hearers may do well to take what we say with a grain of salt. After all, we are giving *our* side, our version of what happened. And so it is with first-person narrators of fiction. They may be reliable, in which case the reader can pretty much accept what they say, or they may be **unreliable narrators,** perhaps because they have an ax to grind, perhaps because they are not perceptive enough to grasp the full implications of what they report, or perhaps because they are mentally impaired, even insane. Poe's Montresor, in "The Cask of Amontillado," is so obsessed that we cannot be certain that Fortunato really did inflict a "thousand injuries" on him.

One special kind of unreliable first-person narrator (whether major or minor) is the **innocent eye:** the narrator is naive (usually a child, or a not-too-bright adult), telling what he or she sees and feels; the contrast between what the narrator perceives and what the reader understands produces an ironic effect. Such a story, in which the reader understands more than the teller himself does, is Ring Lardner's "Haircut," a story told by a garrulous barber who does not perceive that the "accident" he is describing is in fact a murder.

## NONPARTICIPANT (OR THIRD-PERSON) POINTS OF VIEW

In a nonparticipant (third-person) point of view, the teller of the tale is not a character in the tale. The narrator has receded from the story. If the point of view is **omniscient,** the narrator relates what he or she wishes about the thoughts as well as the deeds of the characters. The omniscient teller can at any time enter the mind of any or all of the characters; whereas the first-person narrator can only say, "I was angry," or "Jones seemed angry to me," the omniscient narrator can say, "Jones was inwardly angry but gave no sign; Smith continued chatting, but he sensed Jones's anger."

Furthermore, a distinction can be made between **neutral omniscience** (the narrator recounts deeds and thoughts, but does not judge) and **editorial omniscience** (the narrator not only recounts, but also judges). The narrator in Hawthorne's "Young Goodman Brown" knows what goes on in the mind of Brown, and he comments approvingly or disapprovingly: "With this excellent resolve for the future, Goodman Brown felt himself justified in making more haste on his present evil purpose."

Because a short story can scarcely hope to develop effectively a picture of several minds, an author may prefer to limit his or her omniscience to the minds of only a few of the characters, or even to that of one of the characters; that is, the author may use **selective omniscience** as the point of view. Selective omniscience provides a focus, especially if it is limited to a single character. When thus limited, the author hovers over the shoulder of one character, seeing him or her from outside and from inside and seeing other characters only from the outside and from the impact they make on the mind of this selected receptor. In "Young Goodman Brown" the reader sees things mostly as they make their impact on the protagonist's mind.

> He could have well-nigh sworn that the shape of his own dead father beckoned him to advance, looking downward from a smoke wreath,

> while a woman, with dim features of despair, threw out her hand to warn him back. Was it his mother? But he had no power to retreat one step, nor to resist, even in thought, when the minister and good old Deacon Gookin seized his arms and led him to the blazing rock.

When selective omniscience attempts to record mental activity ranging from consciousness to the unconscious, from clear perceptions to confused longings, it is sometimes labeled the **stream-of-consciousness** point of view. In an effort to reproduce the unending activity of the mind, some authors who use the stream-of-consciousness point of view dispense with conventional word order, punctuation, and logical transitions. The last forty-six pages in James Joyce's *Ulysses* are an unpunctuated flow of one character's thoughts.

Finally, sometimes a third-person narrator does not enter even a single mind, but records only what crosses a dispassionate eye and ear. Such a point of view is **objective** (sometimes called **the camera** or **fly-on-the-wall**). The absence of editorializing and of dissection of the mind often produces the effect of a play; we see and hear the characters in action. Much of Hemingway's "Cat in the Rain" (page 74) is objective, consisting of bits of dialogue that make the story look like a play:

> "I'm going down and get the kitty," the American wife said.
>
> "I'll do it," her husband offered from the bed.
>
> "No, I'll get it. The poor kitty out trying to keep dry under a table."
>
> The husband went on reading, lying propped up with the two pillows at the foot of the bed.
>
> "Don't get wet," he said.

The absence of comment on the happenings forces readers to make their own evaluations of the happenings. In the passage just quoted, when Hemingway writes "'Don't get wet,' he said," readers probably are forced to think (and to sense that Hemingway is guiding them to think) that the husband is indifferent to his wife. After all, how can she go out into the rain and not get wet? A writer can use an objective point of view, then, and still control the feelings of the reader.

## THE POINT OF A POINT OF VIEW

Generalizations about the effect of a point of view are risky, but two have already been made: that the innocent eye can achieve an ironic effect otherwise unattainable, and that an objective point of view (because we hear dialogue but get little or no comment about it) is dramatic. Three other generalizations are often made: (1) that a first-person point of view lends a sense of immediacy or reality, (2) that an omniscient point of view suggests human littleness, and (3) that the point of view must be consistent.

To take the first of these: it is true that when Poe begins a story "The thousand injuries of Fortunato I had borne as I best could, but when he ventured upon insult, I vowed revenge," we feel that the author has gripped us by the lapels; but, on the other hand, we know that we are only reading a piece of fiction, and we do not really believe in the existence of the "I" or of Fortunato; and furthermore, when we pick up a story that begins with *any* point of view, we agree (by picking up the book) to pretend to believe the fictions we are being told. That is, all fiction—whether in the first person or not—is known to be literally false but is read with the pretense that it is true (probably because we hope to get some sort of insight, or truth). The writer must hold our attention, and make us feel that the fiction is meaningful, but the use of the first-person pronoun does not of itself confer reality.

The second generalization, that an omniscient point of view can make puppets of its characters, is equally misleading; this point of view also can reveal in them a depth and complexity quite foreign to the idea of human littleness.

The third generalization, that the narrator's point of view must be consistent lest the illusion of reality be shattered, has been much preached by the followers of Henry James. But E. M. Forster has suggested, in *Aspects of the Novel,* that what is important is not consistency but "the power of the writer to bounce the reader into accepting what he says." Forster notes that in *Bleak House* Dickens uses in Chapter I an omniscient point of view, in Chapter II a selective omniscient point of view, and in Chapter III a first-person point of view. "Logically," Forster says, "*Bleak House* is all to pieces, but Dickens bounces us, so that we do not mind the shiftings of the viewpoint."

Perhaps the only sound generalizations possible are these:

1. Because point of view is one of the things that give form to a story, a good author chooses the point (or points) of view that he or she feels best for the particular story.
2. The use of any other point or points of view would turn the story into a different story.

## JOHN UPDIKE: TWO STORIES

*John Updike (b. 1932) grew up in Shillington, Pennsylvania, where his father was a teacher and his mother a writer. After receiving a B.A. degree in 1954 from Harvard, where he edited the* Harvard Lampoon *(for which he both wrote and drew), he studied drawing at Oxford for a year, but an offer from* The New Yorker *brought him back to the United States. He was hired as a reporter for the magazine but soon began contributing poetry, essays, and fiction. In 1957 he left* The New Yorker *in order to write independently fulltime, though his stories and book reviews appear regularly in it.*

*In 1959 Updike published his first book of stories (*The Same Door*) and also his first novel (*The Poorhouse Fair*); the next year he published* Rabbit, Run, *a highly successful novel whose protagonist, "Rabbit" Angstrom, has reappeared in three later novels,* Rabbit Redux *(1971),* Rabbit Is Rich *(1981), and* Rabbit at Rest *(1990). The first and the last Rabbit books each won a Pulitzer Prize.*

## *A & P*

In walks these three girls in nothing but bathing suits. I'm in the third checkout slot, with my back to the door, so I don't see them until they're over by the bread. The one that caught my eye first was the one in the plaid green two-piece. She was a chunky kid, with a good tan and a sweet broad soft-looking can with those two crescents of white just under it, where the sun never seems to hit, at the top of the backs of her legs. I stood there with my hand on a box of HiHo crackers trying to remember if I rang it up or not. I ring it up again and the customer starts giving me hell. She's one of these cash-register-watchers, a witch about fifty with rouge on her cheekbones and no eyebrows, and I know it made her day to trip me up. She'd been watching cash registers for fifty years and probably never seen a mistake before.

By the time I got her feathers smoothed and her goodies into a bag—she gives me a little snort in passing, if she'd been born at the right time they would have burned her over in Salem—by the time I get her on her way the girls had circled around the bread and were coming back, without a pushcart, back my way along the counters, in the aisle between the check-outs and the Special bins. They didn't even have shoes on. There was this chunky one, with the two-piece—it was bright green and the seams on the bra were still sharp and her belly was still pretty pale so I guessed she just got it (the suit)—there was this one, with one of those chubby berry-faces, the lips all bunched together under her nose, this one, and a tall one, with black hair that hadn't quite frizzed right, and one of these sunburns right across under the eyes, and a chin that was too long—you know, the kind of girl other girls think is very "striking" and "attractive" but never quite makes it, as they very well know, which is why they like her so much—and then the third one, that wasn't quite so tall. She was the queen. She kind of led them, the other two peeking around and making their shoulders round. She didn't look around, not this queen, she just walked straight on slowly, on these long white prima-donna legs. She came down a little hard on her heels, as if she didn't walk in her bare feet that much, putting down her heels and then letting the weight move along to her toes as if she was testing the floor with every step, putting a little deliberate extra action into it. You never know for sure how girls' minds work (do they really think it's a mind in there or just a little buzz like a bee in a glass jar?) but you got the idea she had talked the other two into coming in here with her, and now she was showing them how to do it, walk slow and hold yourself straight.

She had on a kind of dirty pink—beige maybe, I don't know—bathing suit with a little nubble all over it and, what got me, the straps were down. They were off her shoulders looped loose around the cool tops of her arms, and I guess as a result the suit had slipped on her, so all around the top of the cloth there was this shining rim. If it hadn't been there you wouldn't have known there could have been anything whiter than those shoulders. With the straps pushed off, there was nothing between the top of the suit and the top of her head except just *her,* this clean bare plane of the top of her chest down from the shoulder bones like a dented sheet of metal tilted in the light. I mean, it was more than pretty.

She had sort of oaky hair that the sun and salt had bleached, done up in a bun that was unravelling, and a kind of prim face. Walking into the A & P with your straps down, I suppose it's the only kind of face you *can* have. She held her head so high her neck, coming up out of those white shoulders, looked kind of stretched, but I didn't mind. The longer her neck was, the more of her there was.

5 She must have felt in the corner of her eye me and over my shoulder

Stokesie in the second slot watching, but she didn't tip. Not this queen. She kept her eyes moving across the racks, and stopped, and turned so slow it made my stomach rub the inside of my apron, and buzzed to the other two, who kind of huddled against her for relief, and then they all three of them went up the cat and dog food-breakfast cereal-macaroni-rice-raisins-seasonings-spreads-spaghetti-soft drinks-crackers-and-cookies aisle. From the third slot I look straight up this aisle to the meat counter, and I watched them all the way. The fat one with the tan sort of fumbled with the cookies, but on second thought she put the package back. The sheep pushing their carts down the aisle—the girls were walking against the usual traffic (not that we have one-way signs or anything)—were pretty hilarious. You could see them, when Queenie's white shoulders dawned on them, kind of jerk, or hop, or hiccup, but their eyes snapped back to their own baskets and on they pushed. I bet you could set off dynamite in the A & P and the people would by and large keep reaching and checking oatmeal off their lists and muttering "Let me see, there was a third thing, began with A, asparagus, no, ah, yes, applesauce!" or whatever it is they do mutter. But there was no doubt, this jiggled them. A few house slaves in pin curlers even look around after pushing their carts past to make sure what they had seen was correct.

You know, it's one thing to have a girl in a bathing suit down on the beach, where what with the glare nobody can look at each other much anyway, and another thing in the cool of the A & P, under the fluorescent lights, against all those stacked packages, with her feet paddling along naked over our checker-board green-and-cream rubber-tile floor.

"Oh, Daddy," Stokesie said beside me. "I feel so faint."

"Darling," I said. "Hold me tight." Stokesie's married, with two babies chalked up on his fuselage already, but as far as I can tell that's the only difference. He's twenty-two, and I was nineteen this April.

"Is it done?" he asks, the responsible married man finding his voice. I forgot to say he thinks he's going to be a manager some sunny day, maybe in 1990 when it's called the Great Alexandrov and Petrooshki Tea Company or something.

10 What he meant was, our town is five miles from a beach, with a big summer colony out on the Point, but we're right in the middle of town, and the women generally put on a shirt or shorts or something before they get out of the car into the street. And anyway these are usually women with six children and varicose veins mapping their legs and nobody, including them, could care less. As I say, we're right in the middle of town, and if you stand at our front doors you can see two banks and the Congregational church and the newspaper store and three real estate offices and about twenty-seven old freeloaders tearing up Central Street because the sewer broke again. It's not as if we're on the Cape; we're north of Boston and there's people in this town haven't seen the ocean for twenty years.

The girls had reached the meat counter and were asking McMahon something. He pointed, they pointed, and they shuffled out of sight behind a pyramid of Diet Delight peaches. All that was left for us to see was old McMahon patting his mouth and looking after them sizing up their joints. Poor kids, I began to feel sorry for them, they couldn't help it.

Now here comes the sad part of the story, at least my family says it's sad, but I don't think it's so sad myself. The store's pretty empty, it being Thursday afternoon, so there was nothing much to do except lean on the register and wait for the girls to show up again. The whole store was like a pinball machine and I didn't know which tunnel they'd come out of. After a while they come around out of the far aisle, around the light bulbs, records at discount of the Caribbean Six or Tony Martin Sings or some such gunk you wonder they waste the wax on, sixpacks of candy bars, and plastic toys done up in cellophane that fall apart when a kid·looks at them anyway. Around they come, Queenie still leading the way, and holding a little gray jar in her hand. Slots Three through Seven are unmanned and I could see her wondering between Stokes and me, but Stokesie with his usual luck draws an old party in baggy gray pants who stumbles up with four giant cans of pineapple juice (what do these bums *do* with all that pineapple juice? I've often asked myself) so the girls come to me. Queenie puts down the jar and I take it into my fingers icy cold. Kingfish Fancy Herring Snacks in Pure Sour Cream: 49¢. Now her hands are empty, not a ring or a bracelet, bare as God made them, and I wonder where the money's coming from. Still with the prim look she lifts a folded dollar bill out of the hollow at the center of her nubbled pink top. The jar went heavy in my hand. Really, I thought that was so cute.

Then everybody's luck begins to run out. Lengel comes in from haggling with a truck full of cabbages on the lot and is about to scuttle into the door marked MANAGER behind which he hides all day when the girls touch his eye. Lengel's pretty dreary, teaches Sunday school and the rest, but he doesn't miss that much. He comes over and says, "Girls, this isn't the beach."

Queenie blushes, though maybe it's just a brush of sunburn I was noticing for the first time, now that she was so close. "My mother asked me to pick up a jar of herring snacks." Her voice kind of startled me, the way voices do when you see the people first, coming out so flat and dumb yet kind of tony, too, the way it ticked over "pick up" and "snacks." All of a sudden I slid right down her voice into her living room. Her father and the other men were standing around in ice-cream coats and bow ties and the women were in sandals picking up herring snacks on toothpicks off a big glass plate and they were all holding drinks the color of water with olives and sprigs of mint in them. When my parents have somebody over they get lemonade and if it's a real racy affair Schlitz in tall glasses with "They'll Do It Every Time" cartoons stencilled on.

15 "That's all right," Lengel said. "But this isn't the beach." His repeating this struck me as funny, as if it had just occurred to him, and he had been thinking all these years the A & P was a great big dune and he was the head lifeguard. He didn't like my smiling—as I say he doesn't miss much—but he concentrates on giving the girls that sad Sunday-school-superintendent stare.

Queenie's blush is no sunburn now, and the plump one in plaid, that I liked better from the back—a really sweet can—pipes up, "We weren't doing any shopping. We just came in for the one thing."

"That makes no difference," Lengel tells her, and I could see from the way his eyes went that he hadn't noticed she was wearing a two-piece before. "We want you decently dressed when you come in here."

"We *are* decent," Queenie says suddenly, her lower lip pushing, getting sore now that she remembers her place, a place from which the crowd that runs the A & P must look pretty crummy. Fancy Herring Snacks flashed in her very blue eyes.

"Girls, I don't want to argue with you. After this come in here with your shoulders covered. It's our policy." He turns his back. That's policy for you. Policy is what the kingpins want. What the others want is juvenile delinquency.

20 All this while, the customers had been showing up with their carts but, you know, sheep, seeing a scene, they had all bunched up on Stokesie, who shook open a paper bag as gently as peeling a peach, not wanting to miss a word. I could feel in the silence everybody getting nervous, most of all Lengel, who asks me, "Sammy, have you rung up this purchase?"

I thought and said "No" but it wasn't about that I was thinking. I go through the punches, 4, 9, GROC, TOT—it's more complicated than you think and after you do it often enough, it begins to make a little song, that you hear words to, in my case "Hello *(bing)* there, you *(gung)* hap-py *pee*pul *(splat)!*"—the *splat* being the drawer flying out. I uncrease the bill, tenderly as you may imagine, it just having come from between the two smoothest scoops of vanilla I had ever known were there, and pass a half and a penny into her narrow pink palm and nestle the herrings in a bag and twist its neck and hand it over, all the time thinking.

The girls, and who'd blame them, are in a hurry to get out, so I say "I quit" to Lengel quick enough for them to hear, hoping they'll stop and watch me, their unsuspected hero. They keep right on going, into the electric eye; the door flies open and they flicker across the lot to their car, Queenie and Plaid and Big Tall Goony-Goony (not that as raw material she was so bad), leaving me with Lengel and a kink in his eyebrow.

"Did you say something, Sammy?"

"I said I quit."

25 "I thought you did."

"You didn't have to embarrass them."

"It was they who were embarrassing us."

I started to say something that came out "Fiddle-de-doo." It's a saying of my grandmother's, and I know she would have been pleased.

"I don't think you know what you're saying," Lengel said.

30 "I know you don't," I said. "But I do." I pull the bow at the back of my apron and start shrugging it off my shoulders. A couple customers that had been heading for my slot begin to knock against each other, like scared pigs in a chute.

Lengel sighs and begins to look very patient and old and gray. He's been a friend of my parents for years. "Sammy, you don't want to do this to your Mom and Dad," he tells me. It's true, I don't. But it seems to me that once you begin a gesture it's fatal not to go through with it. I fold the apron, "Sammy" stitched in red on the pocket, and put it on the counter, and drop the bow tie on top of it. The bow tie is theirs, if you've ever wondered. "You'll feel this for the rest of your life," Lengel says, and I know that's true, too, but remembering how he made that pretty girl blush makes me so scrunchy inside I punch the No Sale tab and the machine whirs "pee-pul" and the drawer slats out. One advantage to this scene taking place in summer, I can follow this up with a clean exit, there's no fumbling around getting your coat and galoshes, I just saunter into the electric eye in my white shirt that my mother ironed the night before, and the door heaves itself open, and outside the sunshine is skating around on the asphalt.

I look around for my girls, but they're gone, of course. There wasn't anybody but some young married screaming with her children about some candy they didn't get by the door of a powder-blue Falcon station wagon. Looking back in the big windows, over the bags of peat moss and aluminum lawn furniture stacked on the pavement, I could see Lengel in my place in the slot, checking the sheep through. His face was dark gray and his back stiff, as if he'd just had an injection of iron, and my stomach kind of fell as I felt how hard the world was going to be to me hereafter.

[*1962*]

## TOPICS FOR CRITICAL THINKING AND WRITING

1. What is Sammy's image of himself? What is your image of Sammy?
2. What is Sammy's social background? (Point to some passages in which Sammy's language provides clues.)
3. In your opinion, why does Sammy defy Lengel? As a matter of principle? To impress the girls? Both, or neither?
4. Write a paragraph from Lengel's point of view, describing some part of the episode.

Here is a second story by Updike, written from a different point of view.

# *The Rumor*

Frank and Sharon Whittier had come from the Cincinnati area and, with an inheritance of hers and a sum borrowed from his father, had opened a small art gallery on the fourth floor of a narrow building on West Fifty-seventh Street. They had known each other as children; their families had been in the same country-club set. They had married in 1971, when Frank was freshly graduated from Oberlin and Vietnam-vulnerable and Sharon was only nineteen, a sophomore at Antioch majoring in dance. By the time, six years later, they arrived in New York, they had two small children; the birth of a third led them to give up their apartment and the city struggle and move to a house in Hastings, a low stucco house with a wide-eaved Wright-style roof and a view, through massive beeches at the bottom of the yard, of the leaden, ongliding Hudson. They were happy, surely. They had dry midwestern taste, and by sticking to representational painters and abstract sculptors they managed to survive the uglier Eighties styles—faux graffiti, neo-German expressionism, cathode-ray prole play, ecological-protest trash art—and bring their quiet, chaste string of fourth-floor rooms into the calm lagoon of Nineties eclectic revivalism and subdued recession chic. They prospered; their youngest child turned twelve, their oldest was filling out college applications.

When Sharon first heard the rumor that Frank had left her for a young homosexual with whom he was having an affair, she had to laugh, for, far from having left her, there he was, right in the lamplit study with her, ripping pages out of *ARTnews.*

"I don't think so, Avis," she said to the graphic artist on the other end of the line. "He's right here with me. Would you like to say hello?" The easy refutation was made additionally sweet by the fact that, some years before, there had been a brief (Sharon thought) romantic flare-up between her husband and this caller, an overanimated redhead with protuberant cheeks and chin. Avis was a second-wave appropriationist who made color Xeroxes of masterpieces out of art books and then signed them in an ink mixed of her own blood and urine. How could she, who had actually slept with Frank, be imagining this grotesque thing?

The voice on the phone gushed as if relieved and pleased. "I know, it's wildly absurd, but I heard it from two sources, with absolutely solemn assurance."

"Who were these sources?"

"I'm not sure they'd like you to know. But it was Ed Jaffrey and then that boy who's been living with Walton Forney, what does he call himself, one of those single names like Madonna—Jojo!"

"Well, then," Sharon began.

"But I've heard it from still others," Avis insisted. "All over town—it's in the air. Couldn't you and Frank *do* something about it, if it's not true?"

"If," Sharon protested, and her thrust of impatience carried, when she put down the receiver, into her conversation with Frank. "Avis says you're supposed to have run off with your homosexual lover."

"I don't have a homosexual lover," Frank said, too calmly, ripping an auction ad out of the magazine.

"She says all New York says you do."

"Well, what are you going to believe, all New York or your own experience? Here I sit, faithful to a fault, straight as a die, whatever that means. We made love just two nights ago."

It seemed possibly revealing to her that he so distinctly remembered, as if heterosexual performance were a duty he checked off. He was—had always been, for over twenty years—a slim blond man several inches under six feet tall, with a narrow head he liked to keep trim, even during those years when long hair was in fashion, milky-blue eyes set at a slight tilt, such as you see on certain taut Slavic or Norwegian faces, and a small, precise mouth he kept pursed over teeth a shade too prominent and yellow. He was reluctant to smile, as if giving something away, and was vain of his flat belly and lithe collegiate condition. He weighed himself every morning on the bathroom scale, and if he weighed a pound more than yesterday, he skipped lunch. In this, and in his general attention to his own person, he was as quietly fanatic as—it for the first time occurred to her—a woman.

"You know I've never liked the queer side of this business," he went on. "I've just gotten used to it. I don't even think anymore, who's gay and who isn't."

"Avis was *ju*bilant," Sharon said. "How could she think it?"

It took him a moment to focus on the question and realize that his answer was important to her. He became nettled. "Ask *her* how," he said. "Our brief and regrettable relationship, if that's what interests you, seemed satisfactory to me at least. What troubles and amazes me, if I may say so, is how *you* can be taking this ridiculous rumor so seriously."

"I'm *not,* Frank," she insisted, then backtracked. "But why would such a rumor come out of thin air? Doesn't there have to be *something?* Since we moved up here, we're not together so much, naturally, some days when I can't come into town you're gone sixteen hours. . . ."

"But *Shar*on," he said, like a teacher restoring discipline, removing his reading glasses from his almond-shaped eyes, with their stubby fair lashes. "Don't you *know* me? Ever since after that dance when you were sixteen, that time by the lake? . . ."

She didn't want to reminisce. Their early sex had been difficult for her; she had submitted to his advances out of a larger, more social, rather idealistic attraction. She knew that together they would have the strength to get out of Cincinnati and, singly or married to others, they would stay. "Well," she said, enjoying this sensation, despite the chill the rumor had awakened in her, of descending to a deeper level of intimacy than usual, "how well do you know even your own spouse? People are fooled all the time. Peggy Jacobson, for instance, when Henry ran off with that physical therapist, couldn't believe, even when the evidence was right there in front of her—"

20 "I'm *deeply* insulted," Frank interrupted, his mouth tense in that way he had when making a joke but not wanting to show his teeth. "My masculinity is insulted." But he couldn't deny himself a downward glance into his magazine; his tidy white hand jerked, as if wanting to tear out yet another item that might be useful to their business. Intimacy had always made him nervous. She kept at it, rather hopelessly. "Avis said two separate people had solemnly assured her."

"Who, exactly?"

When she told him, he said, exactly as she had done, "Well, then." He added, "You know how gays are. Malicious. Mischievous. They have all that time and money on their hands."

"You sound jealous." Something about the way he was arguing with her strengthened Sharon's suspicion that, outrageous as the rumor was—indeed, *because* it was outrageous—it was true.

In the days that followed, now that she was alert to the rumor's vaporous presence, she imagined it everywhere—on the poised young faces of their staff, in the delicate negotiatory accents of their artists' agents, in the heartier tones of their repeat customers, even in the gruff, self-occupied ramblings of the artists themselves. People seemed startled when she and Frank entered a room together: The desk receptionist and the security guard in their gallery halted their daily morning banter, and the waiters in their pet restaurant, over on Fifty-ninth, appeared especially effusive and attentive. Handshakes lasted a second too long, women embraced her with an extra squeeze, she felt herself ensnared in a soft net of unspoken pity.

25 Frank sensed her discomfort and took a certain malicious pleasure in it, enacting all the while his perfect innocence. He composed himself to appear, from her angle, aloof above the rumor. Dealing professionally in so much absurdity—the art world's frantic attention-getting, studied grotesqueries—he merely intensified the fastidious dryness that had sustained their gallery through wave after wave of changing fashion, and that had, like a rocket's heat-resistant skin, insulated their launch, their escape from the comfortable riverine smugness of this metropolis of dreadful freedom. The rumor amused him, and it amused him, too, to notice how she helplessly watched to see if in the metropolitan throngs his eyes now followed young men as once they had noticed and followed young women. She observed

his gestures—always a bit excessively graceful and precise—distrustfully, and listened for the buttery, reedy tone of voice that might signal an invisible sex change.

That even in some small fraction of her she was willing to believe the rumor justified a certain maliciousness on his part. He couldn't help teasing her—glancing over at her, say, when an especially magnetic young waiter served them, or at home, in their bedroom, pushing more brusquely than was his style at her increasing sexual unwillingness. More than once, at last away from the countless knowing eyes of their New York milieu, in the privacy of their Hastings upstairs, beneath the wide midwestern eaves, she burst into tears and struck out at him, his infuriating, impervious apparent blamelessness. He was like one of those photo-realist nudes, merciless in every detail and yet subtly, defiantly not there, not human. "You're distant," she accused him. "You've always been."

"I don't mean to be. You didn't used to mind my manner. You thought it was quietly masterful."

"I was a teenage girl. I deferred to you."

"It worked out," he pointed out, lifting his hands in an effete, disclaiming way from his sides, to take in their room, their expensive house, their joint career. "What is it that bothers you, Sharon? The idea of losing me? Or the insult to your female pride? The people who started this ridiculous rumor don't even *see* women. Women to them are just background noise."

"It's *not* ridiculous—if it were, why does it keep on and on, even though we're seen together all the time?"

For, ostensibly to quiet her and to quench the rumor, he had all but ceased to go to the city alone, and took her with him even though it meant some neglect of the house and their sons.

Frank asked, "Who *says* it keeps on all the time? I've *never* heard it, never once, except from you. Who's mentioned it lately?"

"Nobody."

"Well, then." He smiled, his lips not quite parting on his curved teeth, tawny like a beaver's.

"You bastard!" Sharon burst out. "You have some stinking little secret!"

"I don't," he serenely half-lied.

The rumor had no factual basis. But was there, Frank asked himself, some truth to it after all? Not circumstantial truth, but some higher, inner truth? As a young man, slight of build, with artistic interests, had he not been fearful of being mistaken for a homosexual? Had he not responded to homosexual overtures as they arose, in bars and locker rooms, with a disproportionate terror and repugnance? Had not his early marriage, and then, ten years later, his flurry of adulterous womanizing, been an escape of sorts, into safe, socially approved terrain? When he fantasized, or saw a pornographic movie, was not the male organ the hero of the occasion for him, at the center of every scene? Were not those slavish, lapping starlets his robotlike delegates, with glazed eyes and undisturbed coiffures venturing where he did not dare? Did he not, perhaps, envy women their privilege of worshipping the phallus? But, Frank asked himself, in fairness, arguing both sides of the case, can homosexual strands be entirely disentangled from heterosexual in that pink muck of carnal excitement, of dream made flesh, of return to the presexual womb?

More broadly, had he not felt more comfortable with his father than with his mother? Was not this in itself a sinister reversal of the usual biology? His father had been a genteel Fourth Street lawyer, of no particular effectuality save that most of his clients were from the same social class, with the same accents and comfortably narrowed aspirations, here on this plateau by the swelling Ohio. Darker and taller than Frank, with the same long teeth and primly set mouth, his father had had the lawyer's gift of silence, of judicious withholding, and in his son's scattered memories of times together—a trip downtown on the trolley to buy Frank his first suit, each summer's one or two excursions to see the Reds play at old Crosley Field—the man said little. This prim reserve, letting so much go unstated and unacknowledged, was a relief after the daily shower of words and affection and advice Frank received from his mother. As an adult he was attracted, he had noticed, to stoical men, taller than he and nursing an unexpressed sadness; his favorite college roommate had been of this saturnine type, and his pet tennis partner in Hastings, and artists he especially favored and encouraged—dour, weathered landscapists and virtually illiterate sculptors, welded solid into their crafts and stubborn obsessions. With these men he became a catering, wifely, subtly agitated presence that Sharon would scarcely recognize.

Frank's mother, once a fluffy belle from Louisville, had been gaudy, strident, sardonic, volatile, needy, demanding, loving; from her he had inherited his "artistic" side, as well as his pretty blondness, but he was not especially grateful. Less—as was proposed by a famous formula he didn't know as a boy—would have been more. His mother had given him an impression of women as complex, brightly-colored traps, attractive but treacherous, their petals apt to harden in an instant into knives. A certain wistful pallor, indeed, a limp helplessness, had drawn him to Sharon and, after the initial dazzlement of the Avises of the world faded and fizzled, always drew him back. Other women asked more than he could provide; he was aware of other, bigger, warmer men they had had. But with Sharon he had been a rescuing knight, slaying the dragon of the winding Ohio. Yet what more devastatingly, and less forgivably, confirmed the rumor's essential truth than her willingness, she who knew him best and owed him most, to entertain it? Her instinct had been to believe Avis even though, far from run off, he was sitting there right in front of her eyes.

He was unreal to her, he could not help but conclude: all those years of uxorious cohabitation, those nights of lovemaking and days of homemaking ungratefully absorbed and now suddenly dismissed because of an apparition, a shadow of gossip. On the other hand, now that the rumor existed, Frank had become more real in the eyes of José, the younger, daintier of the two security guards, whose daily greetings had edged beyond the perfunctory; a certain mischievous dance in the boy's sable eyes animated their employer-employee courtesies. And Jennifer, too, the severely beautiful receptionist, with her rather Sixties-reminiscent bangs and shawls and serapes, now treated him more relaxedly, even offhandedly, as if he had somehow dropped out of her calculations. She assumed with him a comradely slanginess—"The boss was in earlier but she went out to exchange something at Bergdorf's"—as if both he and she were in roughly parallel ironic bondage to "the boss." Frank's heart felt a reflex loyalty to Sharon, a single sharp beat, but then he too relaxed, as if his phantom male lover and the weightless, scandal-veiled life that lived with him in some glowing apartment had bestowed at last what the city had withheld from the overworked, child-burdened married couple who had arrived fourteen years ago—a halo of glamour, of debonair uncaring.

In Hastings, when he and his wife attended a suburban party, the effect was less flattering. The other couples, he imagined, were slightly unsettled by the Whittiers' stubbornly appearing together and became disjointed in their presence, the men drifting off in distaste, the women turning supernormal and laying up a chinkless wall of conversation about children's college applications, local zoning, and Wall Street layoffs. The women, it seemed to Frank, edged, with an instinctive animal movement, a few inches closer to Sharon and touched her with a deft, protective flicking on the shoulder or forearm, to express solidarity and sympathy.

Wes Robertson, Frank's favorite tennis partner, came over to him and grunted, "How's it going?"

"*Fine,*" Frank said, staring up at Wes with what he hoped weren't unduly starry eyes. Wes, who had recently turned fifty, had an old motorcycle-accident scar on one side of his chin, a small pale rose of discoloration that seemed to concentrate the man's self-careless manliness. Frank gave him more of an answer than he might have wanted: "In the art game we're feeling the slowdown like everybody else, but the Japanese are keeping the roof from caving in. The trouble with the Japanese, though, is, from the standpoint of a marginal gallery like ours, they aren't adventurous—they want blue chips, they want guaranteed value, they can't grasp that in art, value has to be subjective to an extent. Look at their own stuff—it's all standardized. Who the hell can tell a Hiroshige from a Hokusai?[1] When you think about it, their whole society, their whole success, really, is based on everybody being alike, everybody agreeing. The notion of art as a struggle, a gamble, as the dynamic embodiment of an existential problem, they just don't get it." He was talking too much, he knew, but he couldn't help it; Wes's scowling presence, his melancholy scarred face, and his stringy alcoholic body, which nevertheless could still whip a backhand right across the forecourt, perversely excited Frank, made him want to flirt.

Wes grimaced and contemplated Frank glumly. "Be around for a game Sunday?" Meaning, had he really run off?

"Of course. Why wouldn't I be?" This was teasing the issue, and Frank tried to sober up, to rein in. He felt a flush on his face and a stammer coming on. He asked, "The usual time? Ten forty-five, more or less?"

Wes nodded. "Sure."

Frank chattered on: "Let's try to get court 5 this time. Those brats having their lessons on court 2 drove me crazy last time. We spent all our time retrieving their damn balls. And listening to their moronic chatter."

Wes didn't grant this attempt at evocation of past liaisons even a word, just continued his melancholy, stoical nodding. This was one of the things, it occurred to Frank, that he liked about men: their relational minimalism, their gender-based realization that the cupboard of life, emotionally speaking, was pretty near bare. There wasn't that tireless, irksome, bright-eyed *hope* women kept fluttering at you.

[1]**Hiroshige . . . Hokusai** Ando Hiroshige (1797–1858) and Katsushika Hokusai (1760–1849) are chiefly known as designers of landscape prints.

Once, years ago, on a stag golfing trip to Bermuda, he and Wes had shared a room with two single beds, and Wes had fallen asleep within a minute and started snoring, keeping Frank awake for much of the night. Contemplating the unconscious male body on its moonlit bed, Frank had been struck by the tragic dignity of this supine form, like a stone knight eroding on a tomb—the snoring profile in motionless gray silhouette, the massive, sacred warrior weight helpless as Wes's breathing struggled from phase to phase of the sleep cycle, from deep to REM to a near-wakefulness that brought a few merciful minutes of silence. The next morning, Wes said Frank should have reached over and poked him in the side; that's what his wife did. But he wasn't his wife, Frank thought, though in the course of that night's ordeal, he had felt his heart make many curious motions, among them the heaving, all-but-impossible effort women's hearts make in overcoming men's heavy grayness and achieving—a rainbow born of drizzle—love.

50 At the opening of Ned Forschheimer's show—Forschheimer, a shy, rude, stubborn, and now elderly painter of tea-colored, wintry Connecticut landscapes, was one of Frank's pets, unfashionable yet sneakily salable—none other than Walton Forney came up to Frank, his round face lit by white wine and odd, unquenchable self-delight, and said, "Say, Frank, old boy. Methinks I owe you an apology. It was Charlie Wit*field*, who used to run that framing shop down on Eighth Street, who left his wife suddenly, with some little Guatemalan boy he was putting through CCNY on the side. They took off for Mexico and left the missus sitting with the shop mortgaged up to its attic and about a hundred prints of wild ducks left unframed. The thing that must have confused me, Charlie came from Ohio, too—Columbus or Cleveland, one of those. It was—what do they call it—a Freudian slip, an understandable confusion. Avis Wasserman told me Sharon wasn't all that thrilled to get the word a while ago, and you must have wondered yourself what the hell was up."

"We ignored it," Frank said, in a voice firmer and less catering than his usual one. "We rose above it." Walton was a number of inches shorter than Frank, with yet a bigger head; his gleaming, thin-skinned face, bearing smooth jowls that had climbed into his sideburns, was shadowed blue here and there, like the moon. His bruised and powdered look somehow went with his small, spaced teeth and the horizontal red tracks his glasses had left in the fat in front of his ears.

The man gazed at Frank with a gleaming, sagging lower lip, his near-sighted little eyes trying to assess the damage, the depth of the grudge. "Well, mea culpa, mea culpa, I guess, though I *didn't* tell Jojo and that *poisonous* Ed Jaffrey to go blabbing it all over town."

"Well, thanks for telling me, Wally, I guess." Depending on which man he was standing with, Frank felt large and straight and sonorous or, as with Wes, gracile and flighty. Sharon, scenting blood amid the vacuous burble of the party, pushed herself through the crowd and joined the two men. To deny Walton the pleasure, Frank quickly told her, "Wally just confessed to me he started the rumor because Charlie Whitfield downtown, who did run off with somebody, came from Ohio, too. Toledo, as I remember."

"Oh, that rumor," Sharon said, blinking once, as if her party mascara were sticking. "I'd forgotten it. Who could believe it, of Frank?"

55 "Everybody, evidently," Frank said. It was possible, given the strange,

willful ways of women, that she had forgotten it, even while Frank had been brooding over its possible justice. If the rumor were truly dispersed—and Walton would undoubtedly tell the story of his Freudian slip around town as a self-promoting joke on himself—Frank would feel diminished. He would lose that small sadistic power to make her watch him watching waiters in restaurants, and to bring her into town as his chaperon. He would feel emasculated if she no longer thought he had a secret. Yet that night, at the party, Walton Forney's Jojo had come up to him. He had seemed, despite an earring the size of a faucet washer and a stripe of bleach in the center of his hair, unexpectedly intelligent and low-key, offering, not in so many words, a kind of apology, and praising the tea-colored landscapes being offered for sale. "I've been thinking, in my own work, of going, you know, more traditional. You get this feeling of, like, a dead end with abstraction." The boy had a bony, rueful face, with a silvery line of a scar under one eye, and seemed uncertain in manner, hesitantly murmurous, as if at a point in life where he needed direction. The fat fool Forney could certainly not provide that, and it pleased Frank to imagine that Jojo was beginning to realize it.

The car as he and Sharon drove home together along the Hudson felt close; the heater fan blew oppressively, parchingly. "*You* were willing to believe it at first," he reminded her.

"Well, Avis seemed so definite. But you convinced me."

"How?"

She placed her hand high on his thigh and dug her fingers in, annoyingly, infuriatingly. "You know," she said, in a lower register, meant to be sexy, but almost inaudible with the noise of the heater fan.

"That could be mere performance," he warned her. "Women are fooled that way all the time."

"Who says?"

"Everybody. Books. Proust.[2] People aren't that simple."

"They're simple enough," Sharon said, in a neutral, defensive tone, removing her presumptuous hand.

"If you say so," he said, somewhat stoically, his mind drifting. That silvery line of a scar under Jojo's left eye . . . lean long muscles snugly wrapped in white skin . . . lofts . . . Hellenic fellowship,[3] exercise machines . . . direct negotiations, a simple transaction among equals. The rumor might be dead in the world, but in him it had come alive.

[*1990*]

[2]**Proust** Marcel Proust (1871–1922), French homosexual novelist

[3]**Hellenic fellowship** Greek friendship, with the implication of erotic love between a mature man and a youth

## TOPICS FOR CRITICAL THINKING AND WRITING

1. What point of view is used in the first paragraph of the story?
2. Consider the following line from the story:

   > "I don't have a homosexual lover," Frank said, too calmly, ripping an auction ad out of the catalog.

   What is the point of view?

3. How would you characterize the point of view in the following passage, from near the end of the story?

> She placed her hand high on his thigh and dug her fingers in, annoyingly, infuriatingly. "You know," she said in a lower register, meant to be sexy, but almost inaudible with the noise of the heater fan.

4. Suppose the story had been told entirely from Sharon's point of view. What might have been gained? What might have been lost?
5. In an essay on fiction, Updike wrote:

> I want stories to startle and engage me within the first few sentences, and in their middle to widen or deepen or sharpen my knowledge of human activity, and to end by giving me a sensation of completed statement.

Is this what you want from stories? If not, in what ways do your desires differ from Updike's? A second question: Do you think "The Rumor" meets Updike's criteria? Explain.

---

## ✔ Checklist: Writing about Point of View

1. Who tells the story? How much does the narrator know? Does the narrator strike you as reliable? What effect is gained by using this narrator?
2. How does the point of view help shape the theme? After all, the basic story of "Little Red Riding Hood"—what happens—remains unchanged whether told from the wolf's point of view or the girl's, but if we hear the story from the wolf's point of view, we may feel that the story is about terrifying yet pathetic compulsive behavior; if from the girl's point of view, about terrified innocence and male violence.
3. Does the narrator's language help you to construct a picture of the narrator's character, class, attitude, strengths, and limitations? (Jot down some evidence, such as colloquial or—on the other hand—formal expressions, ironic comments, figures of speech.) How far can you trust the narrator? Why?

---

# CHAPTER 7

# Allegory and Symbolism

In Chapter 5 we looked at some fables, short fictions that were meant to teach us: the characters clearly stood for principles of behavior, and the fictions as a whole evidently taught lessons. If you think of a fable such as "The Ant and the Grasshopper" (the ant wisely collects food during the summer in order to provide for the winter, whereas the grasshopper foolishly sings all summer and goes hungry in the winter), you can easily see that the characters may stand for something other than themselves. The ant, let's say, is the careful, foresighted person, and the grasshopper is the person who lives for the moment. Similarly, in the fable of the tortoise and the hare, the tortoise represents the person who is slow but steady, the rabbit the person who is talented but overly confident and, in the end, foolish.

A story in which each character is understood to have an equivalent is an **allegory.** Further, in an allegory, not only characters but also things (roads, forests, houses) have fairly clear equivalents. Thus, in John Bunyan's *The Pilgrim's Progress,* we meet characters with names such as Christian, Mr. Worldly Wiseman, and the Giant Despair; and we also encounter places such as Vanity Fair, City of Destruction, and, finally (Christian's goal), the Celestial City. Bunyan tells us of a man named Christian, who, on the road to the Celestial City, comes to a place called Vanity Fair and encounters, among others, Giant Despair, Mr. Worldly Wiseman, and Faithful. What all of these are equivalent to is clear from their names. It is also clear that Christian's journey stands for the trials of the soul in this world. There is, so to speak, a one-to-one relationship: A =, B =, and so on. If, for example, we are asked what the road represents in *The Pilgrim's Progress,* we can confidently say that it stands for the journey of life. Thus, *The Pilgrim's Progress* tells two stories, the surface story of a man making a trip, during which he meets various figures and visits various places, and a second story, understood through the first, of the trials that afflict the soul during its quest for salvation.

Modern short stories rarely have the allegory's clear system of equivalents, but we may nevertheless feel that certain characters and certain things in the story stand for more than themselves, or hint at larger meanings. We feel, that is, that they are **symbolic.** But here we must be careful. How does one know that this or that figure or place is symbolic? In Hemingway's "Cat in the Rain" (page 74), is the cat symbolic? Is the innkeeper? Is the rain? Reasonable people may differ in their answers. Again, in Chopin's "The Story of an Hour" (page 19), is the railroad accident a symbol? Is Josephine a symbol? Is the season (springtime) a symbol? And again, reasonable people may differ in their responses.

Let's assume for the moment, however, that if writers use symbols, they want readers to perceive—at least faintly—that certain characters or places or seasons or happenings have rich implications, stand for something more than what they are on the surface. How do writers help us to perceive these things? By emphasizing them—for instance, by describing them at some length, or by introducing them at times when they might not seem strictly necessary, or by calling attention to them repeatedly.

Consider, for example, Chopin's treatment of the season in which "The Story of an Hour" takes place. The story has to take place at *some* time, but Chopin does not simply say, "On a spring day," or an autumn day, and let things go at that. Rather, she tells us about the sky, the trees, the rain, the twittering sparrows—and all of this in an extremely short story where we might think there is no time for talk about the setting. After all, none of this material is strictly necessary to a story about a woman who has heard that her husband was killed in an accident, who grieves, then recovers, and then dies when he suddenly reappears.

Why, then, does Chopin give such emphasis to the season? Because, we think, she is using the season symbolically. In this story, the spring is not just a bit of detail added for realism. It is rich with suggestions of renewal, of the new life that Louise achieves for a moment. But here, a caution. We think that the spring in this story is symbolic, but this is not to say that whenever spring appears in a story, it always stands for renewal, any more than whenever winter appears it always symbolizes death. Nor does it mean that since spring recurs, Louise will be reborn. In short, in *this* story Chopin uses the season to convey specific implications.

Is the railroad accident also a symbol? Our answer is no—though we don't expect all readers to agree with us. We think that the railroad accident in "The Story of an Hour" is just a railroad accident. It's our sense that Chopin is *not* using this event to say something about (for instance) modern travel, or about industrialism. The steam-propelled railroad train could of course be used, symbolically, to say something about industrialism displacing an agrarian economy, but does Chopin give her train any such suggestion? We don't think so. Had she wished to do so, she would probably have talked about the enormous power of the train, the shriek of its whistle, the smoke pouring out of the smokestack, the intense fire burning in the engine, its indifference as it charged through the countryside, and so forth. Had she done so, the story would be a different story. Or she might have made the train a symbol of fate overriding human desires. But, again in our opinion, Chopin does not endow her train with such suggestions. She gives virtually no emphasis to the train, and so we believe it has virtually no significance for the reader.

What of Chopin's "Ripe Figs" (page 42)? Maman-Nainaine tells Babette that when the figs are ripe Babette can visit her cousins. Of course Maman may merely be setting an arbitrary date, but as we read the story we probably feel—because of the emphasis on the *ripening* of the figs, which occurs in the spring or early summer—that the ripening of the figs in some way suggests the maturing of Babette. If we do get such ideas, we will in effect be saying that the story is not simply an anecdote about an old woman whose behavior is odd. True, the narrator of the story, after telling us of Maman-Nainaine's promise, adds, "Not that the ripening of figs had the least thing to do with it, but that is the way Maman-Nainaine was." The narrator sees nothing special—merely Maman-Nainaine's eccentricity—in the connection between the ripening of the figs and Babette's visit to her cousins. Readers, however, may see more than the narrator sees or says. They may see in Babette a young girl maturing; they may see in Maman-Nainaine an older woman who, almost collaborating with nature, helps Babette to mature.

And here, of course, as we talk about symbolism we are getting into the theme of the story. An apparently inconsequential and even puzzling action, such as is set forth in "Ripe Figs," may cast a long shadow. As Robert Frost once said,

> There is no story written that has any value at all, however straightforward it looks and free from doubleness, double entendre, that you'd value at all if it didn't have intimations of something more than itself.

The stranger, the more mysterious the story, the more likely we are to suspect some sort of significance, but even realistic stories such as Chopin's "The Storm" and "The Story of an Hour" may be rich in suggestions. This is not to say, however, that the suggestions (rather than the details of the surface) are what count. A reader does not discard the richly detailed, highly specific narrative (Mrs. Mallard learned that her husband was dead and reacted in such-and-such a way) in favor of some supposedly universal message or theme that it implies. We do not throw away the specific narrative—the memorable characters or the interesting things that happen in the story—and move on to some "higher truth." Robert Frost went on to say, "The anecdote, the parable, the surface meaning has got to be good and got to be sufficient in itself."

Between these two extremes—on the one hand, writing that is almost all a richly detailed surface and, on the other hand, writing that has a surface so thin that we are immediately taken up with the implications or meanings—are stories in which we strongly feel both the surface happenings and their implications. In *Place in Fiction,* Eudora Welty uses an image of a china lamp to explain literature that presents an interesting surface texture filled with rich significance. When unlit, the lamp showed London; when lit, it showed the Great Fire of London. Like a painted porcelain lamp that, when illuminated, reveals an inner picture shining through the outer, the physical details in a work are illuminated from within by the author's imaginative vision. The outer painting (the literal details) presents "a continuous, shapely, pleasing, and finished surface to the eye," but this surface is not the whole. Welty happens to be talking about the novel, but her words apply equally to the short story:

> The lamp alight is the combination of internal and external, glowing at the imagination as one; and so is the good novel. . . . The good novel should be steadily alight, revealing.

Details that glow, that are themselves and are also something more than themselves, are symbols. Readers may disagree about whether in any particular story something is or is not symbolic—let's say the figs and chrysanthemums in

Chopin's "Ripe Figs," or the season in "The Story of an Hour." And an ingenious reader may overcomplicate or overemphasize the symbolism of a work or may distort it by omitting some of the details and by unduly focusing on others. In many works the details glow, but the glow is so gentle and subtle that even to talk about the details is to overstate them and to understate other equally important aspects of the work.

Yet if it is false to overstate the significance of a detail, it is also false to understate a significant detail. The let's-have-no-nonsense literal reader who holds that "the figure of a man" whom Brown meets in the forest in Hawthorne's "Young Goodman Brown" is simply a man—rather than the Devil—impoverishes the story by neglecting the rich implications just as much as the symbol-hunter impoverishes "The Story of an Hour" by losing sight of Mrs. Mallard in an interpretation of the story as a symbolic comment on industrialism. To take only a single piece of evidence: the man whom Brown encounters holds a staff, "which bore the likeness of a great black snake, so curiously wrought that it might almost be seen to twist and wriggle itself like a living serpent." If we are familiar with the story of Adam and Eve, in which Satan took the form of a serpent, it is hard not to think that Hawthorne is here implying that Brown's new acquaintance is Satan. And, to speak more broadly, as one reads the story one can hardly not set up opposing meanings (or at least suggestions) for the village (from which Brown sets out) and the forest (into which he enters). The village is associated with daylight, faith, and goodness; the forest with darkness, loss of faith, and evil. This is not to say that the story sets up neat categories. If you read the story, you will find that Hawthorne is careful to be ambiguous. Even in the passage quoted, about the serpent-staff, you'll notice that he does not say it twisted and wriggled, but that it "might almost be seen to twist and wriggle."

## A NOTE ON SETTING

The **setting** of a story—not only the physical locale but also the time of day or the year or the century—may or may not be symbolic. Sometimes the setting is lightly sketched, presented only because the story has to take place somewhere and at some time. Often, however, the setting is more important, giving us the feel of the people who move through it. But if scenery is drawn in detail, yet adds up to nothing, we share the impatience Robert Louis Stevenson expressed in a letter: "'Roland approached the house; it had green doors and window blinds; and there was a scraper on the upper step.' To hell with Roland and the scraper."

Yes, of course, but if the green doors and the scraper were to tell us something about the tenant, they could be important. As the novelist Elizabeth Bowen said, "Nothing can happen nowhere. The locale of the happening always colors the happening, and often, to a degree, shapes it." And as Henry James neatly said, in fiction "landscape is character." But don't believe it simply because Bowen and James say it. Read the stories, and test the view for yourself.

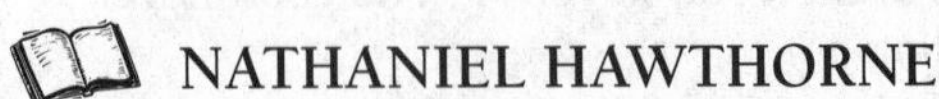

## NATHANIEL HAWTHORNE

*Nathaniel Hawthorne (1804-64) was born in Salem, Massachusetts, the son of a sea captain and a descendant of a judge who had persecuted Quakers and of another judge who had served at the Salem witch trials. After graduating from Bowdoin College in Maine, he returned to Salem, Massachusetts, in order to write in relative seclusion. In 1835 he published "Young Goodman Brown" in a magazine.*

*In his stories and novels Hawthorne keeps returning to the Puritan past, studying guilt, sin, and isolation.*

# Young Goodman Brown

Young Goodman[1] Brown came forth, at sunset, into the street at Salem village; but put his head back, after crossing the threshold, to exchange a parting kiss with his young wife. And Faith, as the wife was aptly named, thrust her pretty head into the street, letting the wind play with the pink ribbons of her cap while she called to Goodman Brown.

"Dearest heart," whispered she, softly and rather sadly, when her lips were close to his ear, "prithee put off your journey until sunrise and sleep in your own bed to-night. A lone woman is troubled with such dreams and such thoughts that she's afeared of herself sometimes. Pray tarry with me this night, dear husband, of all nights in the year."

"My love and my Faith," replied young Goodman Brown, "of all nights in the year, this one night must I tarry away from thee. My journey, as thou callest it, forth and back again, must needs be done 'twixt now and sunrise. What, my sweet, pretty wife, dost thou doubt me already, and we but three months married?"

"Then God bless you!" said Faith, with the pink ribbons; "and may you find all well when you come back."

5 "Amen!" cried Goodman Brown. "Say thy prayers, dear Faith, and go to bed at dusk, and no harm will come to thee."

So they parted; and the young man pursued his way until, being about to turn the corner by the meeting-house, he looked back and saw the head of Faith still peeping after him with a melancholy air, in spite of her pink ribbons.

"Poor little Faith!" thought he, for his heart smote him. "What a wretch am I to leave her on such an errand! She talks of dreams, too. Methought as she spoke there was trouble in her face, as if a dream had warned her what work is to be done to-night. But no, no; 'twould kill her to think it. Well, she's a blessed angel on earth; and after this one night, I'll cling to her skirts and follow her to heaven."

With this excellent resolve for the future, Goodman Brown felt himself justified in making more haste on his present evil purpose. He had taken a dreary road, darkened by all the gloomiest trees of the forest, which barely stood aside to let the narrow path creep through, and closed immediately behind. It was all as lonely as could be; and there is this peculiarity in such a solitude, that the traveller knows not who may be concealed by the innumerable trunks and the thick boughs overhead; so that with lonely footsteps he may yet be passing through an unseen multitude.

[1]**Goodman** polite term of address for a man of humble standing

"There may be a devilish Indian behind every tree," said Goodman Brown, to himself and he glanced fearfully behind him as he added, "What if the devil himself should be at my very elbow!"

10 His head being turned back, he passed a crook of the road, and, looking forward again, beheld the figure of a man, in grave and decent attire, seated at the foot of an old tree. He arose at Goodman Brown's approach and walked onward side by side with him.

"You are late, Goodman Brown," said he. "The clock of the Old South was striking as I came through Boston, and that is full fifteen minutes agone."

"Faith kept me back a while," replied the young man, with a tremor in his voice, caused by the sudden appearance of his companion, though not wholly unexpected.

It was now deep dusk in the forest, and deepest in that part of it where these two were journeying. As nearly as could be discerned, the second traveller was about fifty years old, apparently in the same rank of life as Goodman Brown, and bearing a considerable resemblance to him, though perhaps more in expression than features. Still they might have been taken for father and son. And yet, though the elder person was as simply clad as the younger, and as simple in manner too, he had an indescribable air of one who knew the world, and who would not have felt abashed at the governor's dinner table, or in King William's court, were it possible that his affairs should call him thither. But the only thing about him that could be fixed upon as remarkable was his staff, which bore the likeness of a great black snake, so curiously wrought that it might almost be seen to twist and wriggle itself like a living serpent. This, of course, must have been an ocular deception, assisted by the uncertain light.

"Come, Goodman Brown," cried his fellow-traveller, "this is a dull pace for the beginning of a journey. Take my staff, if you are so soon weary."

15 "Friend," said the other, exchanging his slow pace for a full stop, "having kept covenant by meeting thee here, it is my purpose now to return whence I came. I have scruples touching the matter thou wot'st[2] of."

"Sayest thou so?" replied he of the serpent, smiling apart. "Let us walk on, nevertheless, reasoning as we go; and if I convince thee not thou shalt turn back. We are but a little way in the forest yet."

"Too far! too far!" exclaimed the goodman, unconsciously resuming his walk. "My father never went into the woods on such an errand, nor his father before him. We have been a race of honest men and good Christians since the days of the martyrs; and shall I be the first of the name of Brown that ever took this path and kept—"

"Such company, thou wouldst say," observed the elder person, interpreting his pause. "Well said, Goodman Brown! I have been as well acquainted with your family as with ever a one among the Puritans; and that's no trifle to say. I helped your grandfather, the constable, when he lashed the Quaker woman so smartly through the streets of Salem; and it was I that brought your father a pitch-pine knot, kindled at my own hearth, to set fire to an Indian village, in King Philip's war.[3] They were my good friends, both;

[2]**wot'st** knowest

[3]**King Philip's war** war waged by the Colonists (1675–76) against the Wampanoag Indian leader Metacom, known as "King Philip"

and many a pleasant walk have we had along this path, and returned merrily after midnight. I would fain be friends with you for their sake."

"If it be as thou sayest," replied Goodman Brown, "I marvel they never spoke of these matters, or, verily, I marvel not, seeing that the least rumor of the sort would have driven them from New England. We are a people of prayer, and good works to boot, and abide no such wickedness."

20 "Wickedness or not," said the traveller with the twisted staff, "I have a very general acquaintance here in New England. The deacons of many a church have drunk the communion wine with me; the selectmen of divers towns make me their chairman; and a majority of the Great and General Court are firm supporters of my interest. The governor and I, too—But these are state secrets."

"Can this be so!" cried Goodman Brown, with a stare of amazement at his undisturbed companion. "Howbeit, I have nothing to do with the governor and council; they have their own ways, and are no rule for a simple husbandman[4] like me. But, were I to go on with thee, how should I meet the eye of that good old man, our minister, at Salem village? Oh, his voice would make me tremble both Sabbath day and lecture day!"

Thus far the elder traveller had listened with due gravity; but now burst into a fit of irrepressible mirth, shaking himself so violently that his snake-like staff actually seemed to wriggle in sympathy.

"Ha! ha! ha!" shouted he again and again; then composing himself, "Well, go on, Goodman Brown, go on; but, prithee, don't kill me with laughing."

"Well, then, to end the matter at once," said Goodman Brown, considerably nettled, "there is my wife, Faith. It would break her dear little heart; and I'd rather break my own."

25 "Nay, if that be the case," answered the other, "e'en go thy ways, Goodman Brown. I would not for twenty old women like the one hobbling before us that Faith should come to any harm."

As he spoke he pointed his staff at a female figure on the path, in whom Goodman Brown recognized a very pious and exemplary dame, who had taught him his catechism in youth, and was still his moral and spiritual adviser, jointly with the minister and Deacon Gookin.

"A marvel, truly, that Goody[5] Cloyse should be so far in the wilderness at night fall," said he. "But with your leave, friend, I shall take a cut through the woods until we have left this Christian woman behind. Being a stranger to you, she might ask whom I was consorting with and whither I was going."

"Be it so," said his fellow-traveller. "Betake you the woods, and let me keep the path."

Accordingly the young man turned aside, but took care to watch his companion, who advanced softly along the road until he had come within a staff's length of the old dame. She, meanwhile, was making the best of her way, with singular speed for so aged a woman, and mumbling some indistinct words—a prayer, doubtless—as she went. The traveller put forth his staff and touched her withered neck with what seemed the serpent's tail.

[4]**husbandman** farmer, or, more generally, any man of humble standing
[5]**Goody** contraction of Goodwife, a polite term of address for a married woman of humble standing

30 "The devil!" screamed the pious old lady.

"Then Goody Cloyse knows her old friend?" observed the traveller, confronting her and leaning on his writhing stick.

"Ah, forsooth, and is it your worship indeed?" cried the good dame. "Yea, truly is it, and in the very image of my old gossip, Goodman Brown, the grandfather of the silly fellow that now is. But—would your worship believe it?—my broomstick hath strangely disappeared, stolen, as I suspect, by that unhanged witch, Goody Cory, and that, too, when I was all anointed with the juice of smallage and cinquefoil and wolf's bane—"

"Mingled with fine wheat and the fat of a new-born babe," said the shape of old Goodman Brown.

"Ah, your worship knows the recipe," cried the old lady, cackling aloud. "So, as I was saying, being all ready for the meeting, and no horse to ride on, I made up my mind to foot it; for they tell me there is a nice young man to be taken into communion to-night. But now your good worship will lend me your arm, and we shall be there in a twinkling."

35 "That can hardly be," answered her friend. "I may not spare you my arm, Goody Cloyse; but here is my staff, if you will."

So saying, he threw it down at her feet, where, perhaps, it assumed life, being one of the rods which its owner had formerly lent to the Egyptian magi. Of this fact, however, Goodman Brown could not take cognizance. He had cast up his eyes in astonishment, and, looking down again, beheld neither Goody Cloyse nor the serpentine staff but his fellow-traveller alone, who waited for him as calmly as if nothing had happened.

"That old woman taught me my catechism," said the young man; and there was a world of meaning in this simple comment.

They continued to walk onward, while the elder traveller exhorted his companion to make good speed and persevere in the path, discoursing so aptly that his arguments seemed rather to spring up in the bosom of his auditor than to be suggested by himself. As they went, he plucked a branch of maple to serve for a walking-stick, and began to strip it of the twigs and little boughs, which were wet with evening dew. The moment his fingers touched them they became strangely withered and dried up as with a week's sunshine. Thus the pair proceeded, at a good free pace, until suddenly, in a gloomy hollow of the road, Goodman Brown sat himself down on the stump of a tree and refused to go any farther.

"Friend," said he, stubbornly, "my mind is made up. Not another step will I budge on this errand. What if a wretched old woman do choose to go to the devil when I thought she was going to heaven: is that any reason why I should quit my dear Faith and go after her?"

40 "You will think better of this by and by," said his acquaintance, composedly. "Sit here and rest yourself a while; and when you feel like moving again, there is my staff to help you along."

Without more words, he threw his companion the maple stick, and was as speedily out of sight as if he had vanished into the deepening gloom. The young man sat a few moments by the roadside, applauding himself greatly, and thinking with how clear a conscience he should meet the minister in his morning walk, nor shrink from the eye of good old Deacon Gookin. And what calm sleep would be his that very night, which was to have been spent so wickedly, but so purely and sweetly now, in the arms of

Faith! Amidst these pleasant and praiseworthy meditations, Goodman Brown heard the tramp of horses along the road, and deemed it advisable to conceal himself within the verge of the forest, conscious of the guilty purpose that had brought him thither, though now so happily turned from it.

On came the hoof-tramps and the voices of the riders, two grave old voices, conversing soberly as they drew near. These mingled sounds appeared to pass along the road, within a few yards of the young man's hiding-place; but, owing doubtless to the depth of the gloom at that particular spot, neither the travellers nor their steeds were visible. Though their figures brushed the small boughs by the wayside, it could not be seen that they intercepted, even for a moment, the faint gleam from the strip of bright sky athwart which they must have passed. Goodman Brown alternately crouched and stood on tiptoe, pulling aside the branches and thrusting forth his head as far as he durst without discerning so much as a shadow. It vexed him the more, because he could have sworn, were such a thing possible, that he recognized the voices of the minister and Deacon Gookin, jogging along quietly, as they were wont to do, when bound to some ordination or ecclesiastical council. While yet within hearing, one of the riders stopped to pluck a switch.

"Of the two, reverend sir," said the voice like the deacon's, "I had rather miss an ordination dinner than to-night's meeting. They tell me that some of our community are to be here from Falmouth and beyond, and others from Connecticut and Rhode Island, besides several of the Indian powwows, who, after their fashion, know almost as much deviltry as the best of us. Moreover, there is a goodly young woman to be taken into communion."

"Mighty well, Deacon Gookin!" replied the solemn old tones of the minister. "Spur up, or we shall be late. Nothing can be done, you know, until I get on the ground."

45 The hoofs clattered again; and the voices, talking so strangely in the empty air, passed on through the forest, where no church had ever been gathered or solitary Christian prayed. Whither, then, could these holy men be journeying so deep into the heathen wilderness? Young Goodman Brown caught hold of a tree for support, being ready to sink down on the ground, faint and overburdened with the heavy sickness of his heart. He looked up to the sky, doubting whether there really was a heaven above him. Yet, there was the blue arch, and the stars brightening in it.

"With heaven above, and Faith below, I will yet stand firm against the devil!" cried Goodman Brown.

While he still gazed upward into the deep arch of the firmament and had lifted his hands to pray, a cloud, though no wind was stirring, hurried across the zenith and hid the brightening stars. The blue sky was still visible, except directly overhead, where this black mass of cloud was sweeping swiftly northward. Aloft in the air, as if from the depths of the cloud, came a confused and doubtful sound of voices. Once the listener fancied that he could distinguish the accents of towns-people of his own, men and women, both pious and ungodly, many of whom he had met at the communion table, and had seen others rioting at the tavern. The next moment, so indistinct were the sounds, he doubted whether he had heard aught but the murmur of the old forest, whispering without a wind. Then came a stronger swell of those familiar tones, heard daily in the sunshine at Salem village, but never until now from a cloud of night. There was one voice, of a young woman, uttering lamentations, yet with an uncertain sorrow, and entreating for some favor, which, perhaps, it would grieve her to obtain; and all the unseen multitude, both saints and sinners, seemed to encourage her onward.

"Faith!" shouted Goodman Brown, in a voice of agony and desperation; and the echoes of the forest mocked him, crying, "Faith! Faith!" as if bewildered wretches were seeking her all through the wilderness.

The cry of grief, rage, and terror was yet piercing the night, when the unhappy husband held his breath for a response. There was a scream, drowned immediately in a louder murmur of voices, fading into far-off laughter, as the dark cloud swept away, leaving the clear and silent sky above Goodman Brown. But something fluttered lightly down through the air and caught on the branch of a tree. The young man seized it, and beheld a pink ribbon.

50 "My Faith is gone!" cried he, after one stupefied moment. "There is no good on earth; and sin is but a name. Come, devil; for to thee is this world given."

And, maddened with despair, so that he laughed loud and long, did Goodman Brown grasp his staff and set forth again, at such a rate that he seemed to fly along the forest path, rather than to walk or run. The road grew wilder and drearier and more faintly traced, and vanished at length, leaving him in the heart of the dark wilderness, still rushing onward with the instinct that guides mortal man to evil. The whole forest was peopled with frightful sounds—the creaking of the trees, the howling of wild beasts, and the yell of Indians; while sometimes the wind tolled like a distant church bell, and sometimes gave a broad roar around the traveller, as if all Nature were laughing him to scorn. But he was himself the chief horror of the scene, and shrank not from its other horrors.

"Ha! ha! ha!" roared Goodman Brown when the wind laughed at him. "Let us hear which will laugh loudest! Think not to frighten me with your deviltry! Come witch, come wizard, come Indian powwow, come devil himself, and here comes Goodman Brown. You may as well fear him as he fear you!"

In truth, all through the haunted forest there could be nothing more frightful than the figure of Goodman Brown. On he flew among the black pines, brandishing his staff with frenzied gestures, now giving vent to an inspiration of horrid blasphemy, and now shouting forth such laughter as set all the echoes of the forest laughing like demons around him. The fiend in his own shape is less hideous than when he rages in the breast of man. Thus sped the demoniac on his course, until, quivering among the trees, he saw a red light before him, as when the felled trunks and branches of a clearing have been set on fire, and throw up their lurid blaze against the sky, at the hour of midnight. He paused, in a lull of the tempest that had driven him onward, and heard the swell of what seemed a hymn, rolling solemnly from a distance with the weight of many voices. He knew the tune; it was a familiar one in the choir of the village meeting-house. The verse died heavily away, and was lengthened by a chorus, not of human voices, but of all the sounds of the benighted wilderness pealing in awful harmony together. Goodman Brown cried out; and his cry was lost to his own ear by its unison with the cry of the desert.

In the interval of silence he stole forward until the light glared full upon his eyes. At one extremity of an open space, hemmed in by the dark wall of the forest, arose a rock, bearing some rude, natural resemblance either to an altar or a pulpit, and surrounded by four blazing pines, their tops aflame, their stems untouched, like candles at an evening meeting. The mass of foliage that had overgrown the summit of the rock was all on fire, blazing high into the night and fitfully illuminating the whole field. Each pendent twig and leafy festoon was in a blaze. As the red light arose and fell, a numerous congregation alternately shone forth, then disappeared in shadow, and again grew, as it were, out of the darkness, peopling the heart of the solitary woods at once.

55 "A grave and dark-clad company," quoth Goodman Brown.

In truth, they were such. Among them, quivering to-and-fro between gloom and splendor, appeared faces that would be seen next day at the council board of the province, and others which, Sabbath after Sabbath, looked devoutly heavenward, and benignantly over the crowded pews, from the holiest pulpits in the land. Some affirm that the lady of the governor was there. At least there were high dames well known to her, and wives of honored husbands, and widows, a great multitude, and ancient maidens, all of excellent repute, and fair young girls, who trembled lest their mothers should espy them. Either the sudden gleams of light flashing over the obscure field bedazzled Goodman Brown, or he recognized a score of the church-members of Salem village famous for their especial sanctity. Good old Deacon Gookin had arrived, and waited at the skirts of that venerable saint, his revered pastor. But, irreverently consorting with these grave, reputable, and pious people, these elders of the church, these chaste dames and dewy virgins, there were men of dissolute lives and women of spotted fame, wretches given over to all mean and filthy vice, and suspected even of horrid crimes. It was strange to see, that the good shrank not from the wicked, nor were the sinners abashed by the saints. Scattered also among their pale-faced enemies were the Indian priests, or powwows, who had often scared their native forest with more hideous incantations than any known to English witchcraft.

"But, where is Faith?" thought Goodman Brown; and, as hope came into his heart, he trembled.

Another verse of the hymn arose, a slow and mournful strain, such as the pious love, but joined to words which expressed all that our nature can conceive of sin, and darkly hinted at far more. Unfathomable to mere mortals is the lore of fields. Verse after verse was sung; and still the chorus of the desert swelled between, like the deepest tone of a mighty organ; and with the final peal of that dreadful anthem there came a sound, as if the roaring wind, the rushing streams, the howling beasts, and every other voice of the unconcerted wilderness were mingling and according with the voice of guilty man in homage to the prince of all. The four blazing pines threw up a loftier flame, and obscurely discovered shapes and visages of horror on the smoke wreaths above the impious assembly. At the same moment the fire on the rock shot redly forth and formed a glowing arch above its base, where now appeared a figure. With reverence be it spoken, the figure bore no slight similitude, both in garb and manner, to some grave divine of the New England churches.

"Bring forth the converts!" cried a voice that echoed through the field and rolled into the forest.

60 At the word, Goodman Brown stepped forth from the shadow of the trees and approached the congregation, with whom he felt a loathful brotherhood by the sympathy of all that was wicked in his heart. He could have well nigh sworn that the shape of his own dead father beckoned him to advance, looking downward from a smoke wreath, while a woman, with dim features of despair, threw out her hand to warn him back. Was it his mother? But he had no power to retreat one step, nor to resist, even in thought, when the minister and good old Deacon Gookin seized his arms and led him to the blazing rock. Thither came also the slender form of a veiled female, led between Goody Cloyse, that pious teacher of the catechism, and Martha Carrier, who had received the devil's promise to be queen of hell. A rampant hag was she. And there stood the proselytes beneath the canopy of fire.

"Welcome, my children," said the dark figure, "to the communion of your race. Ye have found thus young your nature and your destiny. My children, look behind you!"

They turned; and flashing forth, as it were, in a sheet of flame, the fiend worshippers were seen; the smile of welcome gleamed darkly on every visage.

"There," resumed the sable form, "are all whom ye have reverenced from youth. Ye deemed them holier than yourselves, and shrank from your own sin, contrasting it with their lives of righteousness and prayerful aspirations heavenward. Yet here are they all in my worshipping assembly. This night it shall be granted you to know their secret deeds: how hoary-bearded elders of the church have whispered wanton words to the young maids of their households; how many a woman, eager for widow's weeds, has given her husband a drink at bedtime, and let him sleep his last sleep in her bosom; how beardless youths have made haste to inherit their fathers' wealth; and how fair damsels—blush not, sweet ones—have dug little graves in the garden, and bidden me, the sole guest, to an infant's funeral. By the sympathy of your human hearts for sin ye shall scent out all the places—whether in church, bedchamber, street, field, or forest—where crime has been committed, and shall exult to behold the whole earth one stain of guilt, one mighty blood spot. Far more than this. It shall be yours to penetrate, in every bosom, the deep mystery of sin, the fountain of all wicked arts, and which inexhaustibly supplies more evil impulses than human power—than my power at its utmost—can make manifest in deeds. And now, my children, look upon each other."

They did so; and, by the blaze of the hell-kindled torches, the wretched man beheld his Faith, and the wife her husband, trembling before that unhallowed altar.

65 "Lo, there ye stand, my children," said the figure, in a deep and solemn tone, almost sad with its despairing awfulness, as if his once angelic nature could yet mourn for our miserable race. "Depending upon one another's hearts, ye had still hoped that virtue were not all a dream. Now are ye undeceived. Evil is the nature of mankind. Evil must be your only happiness. Welcome, again, my children, to the communion of your race."

"Welcome," repeated the fiend worshippers, in one cry of despair and triumph.

And there they stood, the only pair, as it seemed, who were yet hesitating on the verge of wickedness in this dark world. A basin was hollowed, naturally, in the rock. Did it contain water, reddened by the lurid light? or was it blood? or, perchance, a liquid flame? Herein did the shape of evil dip his hand and prepare to lay the mark of baptism upon their foreheads, that they might be partakers of the mystery of sin, more conscious of the secret guilt of others, both in deed and thought, than they could now be of their own. The husband cast one look at his pale wife, and Faith at him. What polluted wretches would the next glance show them to each other, shuddering alike at what they disclosed and what they saw!

"Faith! Faith!" cried the husband, "look up to heaven, and resist the wicked one."

Whether Faith obeyed he knew not. Hardly had he spoken when he found himself amid calm night and solitude, listening to a roar of the wind which died heavily away through the forest. He staggered against the rock, and felt it chill and damp; while a hanging twig, that had been all on fire, besprinkled his cheek with the coldest dew.

The next morning young Goodman Brown came slowly into the street of Salem village, staring around him like a bewildered man. The good old minister was taking a walk along the graveyard to get an appetite for breakfast and meditate his sermon, and bestowed a blessing, as he passed, on Goodman Brown. He shrank from the venerable saint as if to avoid an anathema. Old Deacon Gookin was at domestic worship, and the holy words of his prayer were heard through the open window. "What God doth the wizard pray to?" quoth Goodman Brown. Goody Cloyse, that excellent old Christian, stood in the early sunshine at her own lattice, catechizing a little girl who had brought her a pint of morning's milk. Goodman Brown snatched away the child as from the grasp of the fiend himself. Turning the corner by the meeting-house, he spied the head of Faith, with the pink ribbons, gazing anxiously forth, and bursting into such joy at sight of him that she skipped along the street and almost kissed her husband before the whole village. But Goodman Brown looked sternly and sadly into her face, and passed on without a greeting.

Had Goodman Brown fallen asleep in the forest and only dreamed a wild dream of a witch-meeting?

Be it so, if you will; but, alas! it was a dream of evil omen for young Goodman Brown. A stern, a sad, a darkly meditative, a distrustful, if not a desperate man did he become from the night of that fearful dream. On the Sabbath day, when the congregation were singing a holy psalm, he could not listen because an anthem of sin rushed loudly upon his ear and drowned all the blessed strain. When the minister spoke from the pulpit with power and fervid eloquence, and, with his hand on the open Bible, of the sacred truths of our religion, and of saint-like lives and triumphant deaths, and of future bliss or misery unutterable, then did Goodman Brown turn pale, dreading lest the roof should thunder down upon the gray blasphemer and his hearers. Often, awakening suddenly at midnight, he shrank from the bosom of Faith; and at morning or eventide, when the family knelt down at prayer, he scowled and muttered to himself, and gazed sternly at his wife, and turned away. And when he had lived long, and was borne to his grave a hoary corpse, followed by Faith, an aged woman, and children and grandchildren, a goodly procession, besides neighbors, not a few, they carved no hopeful verse upon his tombstone, for his dying hour was gloom.

[*1835*]

## TOPICS FOR CRITICAL THINKING AND WRITING

1. Do you take Faith to stand only for religious faith, or can she here also stand for one's faith in one's fellow human beings? Explain.
2. Hawthorne describes the second traveler as "about fifty years old, apparently in the same rank as Goodman Brown, and bearing a considerable resemblance to him." Further, "they might have been taken for father and son." What do you think Hawthorne is getting at here?
3. In the forest Brown sees (or thinks he sees) Goody Cloyse, the minister, Deacon Gookin, and others. Does he in fact meet them, or does he dream of them? Or does he encounter "figures" and "forms" (rather than real people) whom the devil conjures up in order to deceive Brown?
4. Evaluate the view that when Brown enters the dark forest he is really entering his own evil mind.

## EUDORA WELTY

*Eudora Welty (b. 1909) was born in Jackson, Mississippi. Although she earned a bachelor's degree at the University of Wisconsin and spent a year studying advertising in New York City at the Columbia University Graduate School of Business, she has lived almost all of her life in Jackson. In the preface to her* Collected Stories *she says,*

> *I have been told, both in approval and in accusation, that I seem to love all my characters. What I do in writing of any character is to try to enter into the mind, heart and skin of a human being who is not myself. Whether this happens to be a man or a woman, old or young, with skin black or white, the primary challenge lies in making the jump itself. It is the act of a writer's imagination that I set most high.*

*In addition to writing stories and novels, Welty has written a book about fiction,* The Eye of the Story *(1977), and a memoir,* One Writer's Beginnings *(1984).*

# *A Worn Path*

It was December—a bright frozen day in the early morning. Far out in the country there was an old Negro woman with her head tied in a red rag, coming along a path through the pinewoods. Her name was Phoenix Jackson. She was very old and small and she walked slowly in the dark pine shadows, moving a little from side to side in her steps, with the balanced heaviness and lightness of a pendulum in a grandfather clock. She carried a thin, small cane made from an umbrella, and with this she kept tapping the frozen earth in front of her. This made a grave and persistent noise in the still air, that seemed meditative like the chirping of a solitary little bird.

She wore a dark striped dress reaching down to her shoe tops, and an equally long apron of bleached sugar sacks, with a full pocket: all neat and tidy, but every time she took a step she might have fallen over her shoelaces, which dragged from her unlaced shoes. She looked straight ahead. Her eyes were blue with age. Her skin had a pattern all its own of numberless branching wrinkles and as though a whole little tree stood in the middle of her forehead, but a golden color ran underneath, and the two knobs of her cheeks were illuminated by a yellow burning under the dark. Under the red rag her hair came down on her neck in the frailest of ringlets, still black, and with an odor like copper.

Now and then there was a quivering in the thicket. Old Phoenix said, "Out of my way, all you foxes, owls, beetles, jack rabbits, coons, and wild animals! . . . Keep out from under these feet, little bob-whites. . . . Keep the big wild hogs out of my path. Don't let none of those come running my direction. I got a long way." Under her small black-freckled hand her cane, limber as a buggy whip, would switch at the brush as if to rouse up any hiding things.

On she went. The woods were deep and still. The sun made the pine needles almost too bright to look at, up where the wind rocked. The cones dropped as light as feathers. Down in the hollow was the mourning dove—it was not too late for him.

5 The path ran up a hill. "Seem like there is chains about my feet, time I get this far," she said, in the voice of argument old people keep to use with themselves. "Something always take a hold of me on this hill—pleads I should stay."

After she got to the top she turned and gave a full, severe look behind her were she had come. "Up through pines," she said at length. "Now down through oaks."

Her eyes opened their widest, and she started down gently. But before she got to the bottom of the hill a bush caught her dress.

Her fingers were busy and intent, but her skirts were full and long, so that before she could pull them free in one place they were caught in another. It was not possible to allow the dress to tear. "I in the thorny bush," she said. "Thorns, you doing your appointed work. Never want to let folks pass—no sir. Old eyes thought you was a pretty little *green* bush."

Finally, trembling all over, she stood free, and after a moment dared to stoop for her cane.

10 "Sun so high!" she cried, leaning back and looking, while the thick tears went over her eyes. "The time getting all gone here."

At the foot of this hill was a place where a log was laid across the creek. "Now comes the trial," said Phoenix.

Putting her right foot out, she mounted the log and shut her eyes. Lifting her skirt, levelling her cane fiercely before her, like a festival figure in some parade, she began to march across. Then she opened her eyes and she was safe on the other side.

"I wasn't as old as I thought," she said.

15 But she sat down to rest. She spread her skirts on the bank around her and folded her hands over her knees. Up above her was a tree in a pearly cloud of mistletoe. She did not dare to close her eyes, and when a little boy brought her a little plate with a slice of marble-cake on it she spoke to him. "That would be acceptable," she said. But when she went to take it there was just her own hand in the air.

So she left that tree, and had to go through a barbed-wire fence. There she had to creep and crawl, spreading her knees and stretching her fingers like a baby trying to climb the steps. But she talked loudly to herself: she could not let her dress be torn now, so late in the day, and she could not pay for having her arm or leg sawed off if she got caught fast where she was.

At last she was safe through the fence and risen up out in the clearing. Big dead trees, like black men with one arm, were standing in the purple stalks of the withered cotton field. There sat a buzzard.

"Who you watching?"

In the furrow she made her way along.

20 "Glad this not the season for bulls," she said, looking sideways, "and the good Lord made his snakes to curl up and sleep in the winter. A pleasure I don't see no two-headed snake coming around that tree, where it come once. It took a while to get by him, back in the summer."

She passed through the old cotton and went into a field of dead corn. It whispered and shook and was taller than her head. "Through the maze now," she said, for there was no path.

Then there was something tall, black, and skinny there, moving before her.

At first she took it for a man. It could have been a man dancing in the field. But she stood still and listened, and it did not make a sound. It was as silent as a ghost.

"Ghost," she said sharply, "who be you the ghost of? For I have heard of nary death close by."

25 But there was no answer—only the ragged dancing in the wind.

She shut her eyes, reached out her hand, and touched a sleeve. She found a coat and inside that an emptiness, cold as ice.

"You scarecrow," she said. Her face lighted. "I ought to be shut up for good," she said with laughter. "My senses is gone, I too old. I the oldest people I ever know. Dance, old scarecrow," she said, "while I dancing with you."

She kicked her foot over the furrow, and with mouth drawn down, shook her head once or twice in a little strutting way. Some husks blew down and whirled in streamers about her skirts.

Then she went on, parting her way from side to side with the cane, through the whispering field. At last she came to the end, to a wagon track where the silver grass blew between the red ruts. The quail were walking around like pullets, seeming all dainty and unseen.

30 "Walk pretty," she said. "This the easy place. This the easy going."

She followed the track, swaying through the quiet bare fields, through the little strings of trees silver in their dead leaves, past cabins silver from weather, with the doors and windows boarded shut, all like old women under a spell sitting there. "I walking in their sleep," she said, nodding her head vigorously.

In a ravine she went where a spring was silently flowing through a hollow log. Old Phoenix bent and drank. "Sweet-gum makes the water sweet," she said, and drank more. "Nobody know who made this well, for it was here when I was born."

The track crossed a swampy part where the moss hung as white as lace from every limb. "Sleep on, alligators, and blow your bubbles." Then the track went into the road.

Deep, deep the road went down between the high green-colored banks. Overhead the live-oaks met, and it was as dark as a cave.

35 A black dog with a lolling tongue came up out of the weeds by the ditch. She was meditating, and not ready, and when he came at her she only hit him a little with her cane. Over she went in the ditch, like a little puff of milk-weed.

Down there, her senses drifted away. A dream visited her, and she reached her hand up, but nothing reached down and gave her a pull. So she lay there and presently went to talking. "Old woman," she said to herself, "that black dog come up out of the weeds to stall you off, and now there he sitting on his fine tail, smiling at you."

A white man finally came along and found her—a hunter, a young man, with his dog on a chain.

"Well, Granny!" he laughed. "what are you doing there?"

"Lying on my back like a June-bug waiting to be turned over, mister," she said, reaching up her hand.

40 He lifted her up, gave her a swing in the air, and set her down. "Anything broken, Granny?"

"No sir, them old dead weeds is springy enough," said Phoenix, when she had got her breath. "I thank you for your trouble."

"Where do you live, Granny?" he asked, while the two dogs were growling at each other.

"Away back yonder, sir, behind the ridge. You can't even see it from here."

"On your way home?"

45 "No, sir, I going to town."

"Why, that's too far! That's as far as I walk when I come out myself, and I get something for my trouble." He patted the stuffed bag he carried, and there hung down a little closed claw. It was one of the bob-whites, with its beak hooked bitterly to show it was dead. "Now you go on home, Granny!"

"I bound to go to town, mister," said Phoenix. "The time come around."

He gave another laugh, filling the whole landscape. "I know you old colored people! Wouldn't miss going to town to see Santa Claus!"

But something held Old Phoenix very still. The deep lines in her face went into a fierce and different radiation. Without warning, she had seen with her own eyes a flashing nickel fall out of the man's pocket onto the ground.

50 "How old are you, Granny?" he was saying.

"There is no telling, mister," she said, "no telling."

Then she gave a little cry and clapped her hands and said, "Git on away from here, dog! Look! Look at that dog!" She laughed as if in admiration. "He ain't scared of nobody. He a big black dog." She whispered, "Sic him!"

"Watch me get rid of that cur," said the man. "Sic him, Pete! Sic him!"

Phoenix heard the dogs fighting, and heard the man running and throwing sticks. She even heard a gunshot. But she was slowly bending forward by that time, further and further forward, the lids stretched down over her eyes, as if she were doing this in her sleep. Her chin was lowered almost to her knees. The yellow palm of her hand came out from the fold of her apron. Her fingers slid down and along the ground under the piece of money with the grace and care they would have in lifting an egg from under a sitting hen. Then she slowly straightened up, she stood erect, and the nickel was in her apron pocket. A bird flew by. Her lips moved. "God watching me the whole time. I come to stealing."

The man came back, and his own dog panted about them. "Well, I scared him off that time," he said, and then he laughed and lifted his gun and pointed it at Phoenix.

She stood straight and faced him.

"Doesn't the gun scare you?" he said, still pointing it.

"No, sir, I seen plenty go off closer by, in my day, and for less than what I done," she said, holding utterly still.

He smiled, and shouldered the gun. "Well, Granny," he said, "you must be a hundred years old, and scared of nothing. I'd give you a dime if I had any money with me. But you take my advice and stay home, and nothing will happen to you."

"I bound to go on my way, mister," said Phoenix. She inclined her head in the red rag. Then they went in different directions, but she could hear the gun shooting again and again over the hill.

She walked on. The shadows hung from the oak trees to the road like curtains. Then she smelled wood-smoke, and smelled the river, and she saw a steeple and the cabins on their steep steps. Dozens of little black children whirled around her. There ahead was Natchez shining. Bells were ringing. She walked on.

In the paved city it was Christmas time. There were red and green electric lights strung and crisscrossed everywhere, and all turned on in the daytime. Old Phoenix would have been lost if she had not distrusted her eyesight and depended on her feet to know where to take her.

She paused quietly on the sidewalk where people were passing by. A lady came along in the crowd, carrying an armful of red-, green-, and silver-wrapped presents; she gave off perfume like the red roses in hot summer, and Phoenix stopped her.

"Please, missy, will you lace up my shoe?" She held up her foot.

"What do you want, Grandma?"

"See my shoe," said Phoenix. "Do all right for out in the country, but wouldn't look right to go in a big building."

"Stand still then, Grandma," said the lady. She put her packages down on the sidewalk beside her and laced and tied both shoes tightly.

"Can't lace 'em with a cane," said Phoenix. "Thank you, missy. I doesn't mind asking a nice lady to tie up my shoe, when I gets out on the street."

Moving slowly and from side to side, she went into the big building and into a tower of steps, where she walked up and around and around until her feet knew to stop.

She entered a door, and there she saw nailed up on the wall the document that had been stamped with the gold seal and framed in the gold frame, which matched the dream that was hung up in her head.

"Here I be," she said. There was a fixed and ceremonial stiffness over her body.

"A charity case, I suppose," said an attendant who sat at the desk before her.

But Phoenix only looked above her head. There was sweat on her face, the wrinkles in her skin shone like a bright net.

"Speak up, Grandma," the woman said. "What's your name? We must have your history, you know. Have you been here before? What seems to be the trouble with you?"

Old Phoenix only gave a twitch to her face as if a fly were bothering her.

"Are you deaf?" cried the attendant.

But then the nurse came in.

"Oh, that's just old Aunt Phoenix," she said. "She doesn't come for herself—she has a little grandson. She makes these trips just as regular as clockwork. She lives away back off the old Natchez Trace." She bent down. "Well, Aunt Phoenix, why don't you just take a seat? We won't keep you standing after your long trip." She pointed.

The old woman sat down, bolt upright in the chair.

"Now, how is the boy?" asked the nurse.

Old Phoenix did not speak.

"I said, how is the boy?"

But Phoenix only waited and stared straight ahead, her face very solemn and withdrawn into rigidity.

"Is his throat any better?" asked the nurse. "Aunt Phoenix, don't you hear me? Is your grandson's throat any better since the last time you came for the medicine?"

With her hands on her knees, the old woman waited, silent, erect and motionless, just as if she were in armor.

"You mustn't take up our time this way, Aunt Phoenix," the nurse said. "Tell us quickly about your grandson, and get it over. He isn't dead, is he?"

At last there came a flicker and then a flame of comprehension across her face, and she spoke.

"My grandson. It was my memory had left me. There I sat and forgot why I made my long trip."

"Forgot?" The nurse frowned. "After you came so far?"

Then Phoenix was like an old woman begging a dignified forgiveness for waking up frightened in the night. "I never did go to school, I was too old at the Surrender," she said in a soft voice. "I'm an old woman without an education. It was my memory fail me. My little grandson, he is just the same, and I forgot it in the coming."

"Throat never heals, does it?" said the nurse, speaking in a loud, sure voice to Old Phoenix. By now she had a card with something written on it, a little list. "Yes. Swallowed lye. When was it—January—two-three years ago—"

Phoenix spoke unasked now. "No, missy, he not dead, he just the same. Every little while his throat begin to close up again, and he not able to swallow. He not get his breath. He not able to help himself. So the time come around, and I go on another trip for the soothing medicine."

"All right. The doctor said as long as you came to get it, you could have it," said the nurse. "But it's an obstinate case."

"My little grandson, he sit up there in the house all wrapped up, waiting by himself," Phoenix went on. "We is the only two left in the world. He suffer and it don't seem to put him back at all. He got a sweet look. He going to last. He wear a little patch quilt and peep out holding his mouth open like a little bird. I remembers so plain now. I not going to forget him again, no, the whole enduring time. I could tell him from all the others in creation."

95 "All right." The nurse was trying to hush her now. She brought her a bottle of medicine. "Charity," she said, making a check mark in a book.

Old Phoenix held the bottle close to her eyes and then carefully put it into her pocket.

"I thank you," she said.

"It's Christmas time, Grandma," said the attendant. "Could I give you a few pennies out of my purse?"

"Five pennies is a nickel," said Phoenix stiffly.

100 "Here's a nickel," said the attendant.

Phoenix rose carefully and held out her hand. She received the nickel and then fished the other nickel out of her pocket and laid it beside the new one. She stared at her palm closely, with her head on one side.

Then she gave a tap with her cane on the floor.

"This is what come to me to do," she said. "I going to the store and buy my child a little windmill they sells, made out of paper. He going to find it hard to believe there such a thing in the world. I'll march myself back where he waiting, holding it straight up in his hand."

She lifted her free hand, gave a little nod, turned round, and walked out of the doctor's office. Then her slow step began on the stairs, going down.

[*1941*]

## TOPICS FOR CRITICAL THINKING AND WRITING

1. If you do not know the legend of the Phoenix, look it up in a dictionary or, better, in an encyclopedia. Then carefully reread the story, to learn whether the story in any way connects with the legend.
2. What do you think of the hunter?
3. Is Christmas a particularly appropriate time in which to set the story? Why or why not?
4. What do you make of the title?

# A SAMPLE STUDENT ESSAY WITH DOCUMENTATION

The literary work that you are writing about is your primary material, but sometimes you may make use of secondary material—published discussions—perhaps in order to get some background or to see how your interpretation compares with what other readers have said. If you do make use of sources, you will want to quote or summarize only as much as is necessary to your own argument, and you will of course give credit to whatever sources you use. We print a moderately long research paper, on *Death of a Salesman,* on page 1476, and we discuss writing (and documenting) a research paper in Appendix B. But even a short paper may use a few sources. Here is an example of such a paper.

Jean Lee

Professor McCabe

English 102, sec. B

October 18, 1995

DO THE PINK RIBBONS
IN "YOUNG GOODMAN BROWN" HAVE A MEANING?

In the first six paragraphs of "Young Goodman Brown," Hawthorne mentions three times that Faith, Brown's wife, wears a cap with pink ribbons (127). The pink ribbons are mentioned twice more in the story. The first of these later references occurs when Brown is in the forest. Having recognized Faith's voice, Brown gazes heavenward, calls to her, sees something fluttering down, seizes it, and finds that it is "a pink ribbon" (132). "My Faith is gone!" he immediately calls out. "There is no good on earth; and sin is but a name. Come devil! for to thee the world is given" (132). The next (and final) reference to the pink ribbons occurs near the end of the story. When he entered Salem village on "the next morning," Brown "spied the head of Faith, with the pink ribbons" (135), not surprising since he now sees the townspeople in their usual dress and activities.

No one can doubt that Brown's wife, named Faith, symbolizes Brown's religious faith, but many scholars have expressed some doubt about the meaning of her pink ribbons. More precisely, scholars have usually expressed doubt about someone else's interpretation of the ribbons, and then confidently offered their own. According to E. Arthur Robinson, "Faith's pink ribbons symbolize passion" (223). Robinson compares the pink ribbon to "crimson or purple" symbols of "woman's physical nature" in other stories by Hawthorne, particularly Georgiana's flaw in "The Birthmark" and Beatrice's poisonous plant in "Rappaccini's Daughter" (224). But the connection with Goodman Brown's faith is unclear. A pink ribbon worn by Faith, if clarified by other details in the story, might serve to tell a reader what to make out of this woman--for instance, that she <u>really</u> is highly sexual, or that this faith <u>really</u> is "faith in the flesh," or some such thing--but Robinson does not offer these arguments, and the text does nothing to support them with additional details. Robinson's conclusion is that Brown comes to realize that "his father was a man like himself and his mother a woman like Faith" (222), and that Brown glumly accepts sensuality in his wife's nature as well as in his own.

But given that pink suggests, if anything, innocent little baby girls, why conclude that here it suggests "passion"? If one wants to argue that Faith pretends to be sweet and innocent but is not, one would argue that she is hypocritical, and might even argue that the ribbons symbolize hypocrisy disguised as innocence, but there is no evidence that the ribbons symbolize sexual passion. Further, if they do symbolize Brown's wife's sexual passion, what is their connection with Brown? What do they tell us about Brown's religious faith? In the forest, he takes the pink ribbon as evidence that his wife is of the devil's party, and he therefore announces that he has lost his faith, but if the pink color is to suggest passion, Brown's loss of faith would be a loss of belief in passion--an interpretation that makes no sense in the story.

Another school of thought argues that the pink symbolizes not passion but youthful femininity, and by extension, the weakness, superficiality, or frivolity of Brown's religious beliefs. Thomas E. Connolly argues that "the ribbons seem to be symbolic of [Brown's] initial illusion . . . that his faith will lead him to heaven. The pink ribbons on a Puritan lady's cap, signs of youth, joy, and happiness, are actually entirely out of keeping with the severity of the rest of her dress. . ." (374). James W. Mathews offers a roughtly similar view, arguing that "the insubstantiality of Brown's religious faith manifests itself in the pink ribbons of his wife's cap; their texture is aery and their color the pastel of infancy" (74).

Not all recent critics, of course, accept the view that the ribbons are a sign of the superficiality of Brown's faith. Edward Wagenknecht suggests (62) that Mathews's argument would be more convincing if Brown, rather than his wife, wore a ribbon. Against Wagenknecht's view, however, one might argue that allegory works in a different way. If in this allegory Faith stands for Brown's religious faith, then what is said about Faith--for instance what is said about her clothing--is understood to be said about Brown himself.

I think it is wrong to insist that the color of the ribbons is symbolic of passion (or insubstantial faith). Neither of these interpretations is traditional and therefore immediately plausible even without additional supporting detail. And no such additional detail is offered in the story to make them plausible. For instance, none of Faith's pious (or apparently pious) neighbors objects to the ribbons, nor does Brown find the ribbons out of keeping with Puritan dress. Similarly, the alleged association of pink with superficiality is not traditional, and Hawthorne does not establish it by giving related details.

Looking at the unconvincing allegorical interpretations, I think the first thing to say is that we should not make too much of these ribbons. Perhaps the second thing to say is that the early references to the ribbons do not serve to characterize Faith as lustful, superficial, or whatever (and certainly not to characterize Brown's religious faith as marked by any of these traits). Rather, the ribbons serve to identify Faith as a specific person--the woman who wears pink ribbons in her cap. In the forest, then, when the ribbon drifts down, Brown cannot doubt that his wife is present, is a participant in the wicked assembly. (Of course Brown may be deceived; maybe he has dreamed the episode, or maybe he has been duped by a show conjured up by the devil, but that's another issue.)

Convinced that even Faith is a worshipper of evil, Brown loses his faith not so much in God as in his fellow creatures. "Young Goodman Brown" of course has allegorical elements, but there is no reason to insist that every detail, down to the color of the ribbons, is allegorical. Nothing is gained by insisting that the pink ribbons "mean" something. Their function is to convince Brown that his wife is in the forest, and that is enough for some ribbons to do.

WORKS CITED

Connolly, Thomas E. "Hawthorne's 'Young Goodman Brown': An Attack on Puritanic Calvinism." American Literature 28 (1956): 370-75.

Hawthorne, Nathaniel. "Young Goodman Brown." Literature: Thinking, Reading, and Writing Critically. Ed. Sylvan Barnet et al. 2nd ed. New York: Longman, 1997: 127-35.

Mathews, James W. "Antinomianism in 'Young Goodman Brown.'" Studies in Short Fiction 3 (1965): 73-75.

Robinson, E. Arthur. "The Vision of Goodman Brown: A Source and Interpretation." American Literature 35 (1963): 218-25.

Wagenknecht, Edward. Nathaniel Hawthorne: The Man, His Tales and Romances. New York: Continuum, 1989.

Some comments about the essay may be useful. Secondary sources can help you to present and develop your argument—but remember that it is above all *your* argument that counts. By citing scholarly studies, you can sharpen and explain more effectively what *you* want to say about the literary work that you examine. Reread this essay on "Young Goodman Brown," and notice the following points in particular:

- The quotations constitute only a small proportion of the paper. Quote when you need to. Do not quote more than is required.
- The author does not simply quote passages; rather, she makes certain to introduce, comment on, and evaluate them.

In short, remember that whether you are quoting from a primary or a secondary source, you must interpret the quotation. Do *not* assume that its meaning is obvious and that it interprets itself.

## ✔ Checklist: Writing about Allegory and Symbolism

When we refer to a "symbol" in a literary work, we have in mind a character or detail of the setting or moment in the action that carries a range of meaning beyond itself. The letter "A" in Hawthorne's *The Scarlet Letter,* the white whale in Melville's *Moby-Dick,* Walden Pond in Thoreau's masterpiece—each of these means something in itself but much more as well. This range of meanings can be complex, even—so it often seems—ambiguous, and readers may be drawn to debate one another about what a symbol means, what range of associations it calls up and explores. It is important not to be rigid when examining a symbol in a literary work. Don't assume that it means one thing only. For Hawthorne, Melville, and Thoreau, for example, symbols are rich and complicated, elements of the literary work that readers are invited to linger over and think carefully about.

1. Do certain characters seem to you to stand for something in addition to themselves? Does the setting—whether a house, a farm, a landscape, a town, a period—have an extra dimension?
2. If you do believe that the story has symbolic elements, do you think they are adequately integrated within the story, or do they strike you as being too obviously stuck in?

# CHAPTER 8

# *Review: Writing about Fiction*

The following questions will help to stimulate ideas about stories. Not every question is, of course, relevant to every story, but if after reading a story and thinking about it, you then run your eye over these pages, you will find some questions that will help you to think further about the story—in short, that will help you to get ideas.

It's best to do your thinking with a pen or pencil in hand. If some of the following questions seem to you to be especially relevant to the story you will be writing about, jot down—freely, without worrying about spelling—your initial responses, interrupting your writing only to glance again at the story when you feel the need to check the evidence.

## PLOT

1. Does the plot grow out of the characters, or does it depend on chance or coincidence? Did something at first strike you as irrelevant that later you perceived as relevant? Do some parts continue to strike you as irrelevant?
2. Does surprise play an important role, or does foreshadowing? If surprise is very important, can the story be read a second time with any interest? If so, what gives it this further interest?
3. What conflicts does the story include? Conflicts of one character against another? Of one character against the setting, or against society? Conflicts within a single character?
4. Are certain episodes narrated out of chronological order? If so, were you puzzled? Annoyed? On reflection, does the arrangement of episodes seem effective? Why or why not? Are certain situations repeated? If so, what do you make out of the repetitions?

## CHARACTER

1. Which character chiefly engages your interest? Why?
2. What purposes do minor characters serve? Do you find some who by their similarities and differences help to define each other or help to define the major character? How else is a particular character defined—by his or her words, actions (including thoughts and emotions), dress, setting, narrative point of view? Do certain characters act differently in the same, or in a similar, situation?
3. How does the author reveal character? By explicit authorial (editorial) comment, for instance, or, on the other hand, by revelation through dialogue? Through depicted action? Through the actions of other characters? How are the author's methods especially suited to the whole of the story?
4. Is the behavior plausible—that is, are the characters well motivated?
5. If a character changes, why and how does he or she change? (You may want to jot down each event that influences a change.) Or did you change your attitude toward a character not because the character changes but because you came to know the character better?
6. Are the characters round or flat? Are they complex, or, on the other hand, highly typical (for instance, one-dimensional representatives of a social class or age)? Are you chiefly interested in a character's psychology, or does the character strike you as standing for something, such as honesty or the arrogance of power?
7. How has the author caused you to sympathize with certain characters? How does your response—your sympathy or lack of sympathy—contribute to your judgment of the conflict?

## POINT OF VIEW

1. Who tells the story? How much does the narrator know? Does the narrator strike you as reliable? What effect is gained by using this narrator?
2. How does the point of view help shape the theme? After all, the basic story of "Little Red Riding Hood"—what happens—remains unchanged whether told from the wolf's point of view or the girl's, but if we hear the story from the wolf's point of view we may feel that the story is about terrifying yet pathetic compulsive behavior; if from the girl's point of view, about terrified innocence and male violence.
3. Does the narrator's language help you to construct a picture of the narrator's character, class, attitude, strengths, and limitations? (Jot down some evidence, such as colloquial or—on the other hand—formal expressions, ironic comments, figures of speech.) How far can you trust the narrator? Why?

## SETTING

1. Do you have a strong sense of the time and place? Is the story very much about, say, New England Puritanism, or race relations in the

South in the late nineteenth century, or midwestern urban versus small-town life? If time and place are important, how and at what points in the story has the author conveyed this sense? If you do not strongly feel the setting, do you think the author should have made it more evident?

2. What is the relation of the setting to the plot and the characters? (For instance, do houses or rooms or their furnishings say something about their residents?) Would anything be lost if the descriptions of the setting were deleted from the story or if the setting were changed?

## SYMBOLISM

1. Do certain characters seem to you to stand for something in addition to themselves? Does the setting—whether a house, a farm, a landscape, a town, a period—have an extra dimension?
2. If you do believe that the story has symbolic elements, do you think they are adequately integrated within the story, or do they strike you as being too obviously stuck in?

## STYLE

(Style may be defined as *how* the writer says what he or she says. It is the writer's manner of expression. The writer's choice of words, of sentence structure, and of sentence length are all aspects of style. Example: "Shut the door," and "Would you mind closing the door, please," differ substantially in style. Another example: Lincoln begins the Gettysburg Address by speaking of "Four score and seven years ago," that is, by using language that has a Biblical overtone. If he had said "Eighty-seven years ago," his style would have been different.)

1. How would you characterize the style? Simple? Understated? Figurative?
2. How has the point of view shaped or determined the style?
3. Do you think that the style is consistent? If it isn't—for instance, if there are shifts from simple sentences to highly complex ones—what do you make of the shifts?

## THEME

1. Is the title informative? What does it mean or suggest? Did the meaning change after you read the story? Does the title help you to formulate a theme? If you had written the story, what title would you use?
2. Do certain passages—dialogue or description—seem to you to point especially toward the theme? Do you find certain repetitions of words or pairs of incidents highly suggestive and helpful in directing your thoughts toward stating a theme? Flannery O'Connor, in *Mystery and Manners,* says, "In good fiction, certain of the details will tend to accumulate meaning from the action of the story itself, and when that happens, they become symbolic in the way they work." Does this story work that way?

3. Is the meaning of the story embodied in the whole story, or does it seem stuck in, for example in certain passages of editorializing?
4. Suppose someone asked you to state the point—the theme—of the story. Could you? And if you could, would you say that the theme of a particular story reinforces values you hold, or does it to some degree challenge them? (It is sometimes said that the best writers are subversive, forcing readers to see something that they do not want to see.)

## A STORY, NOTES, AND AN ESSAY

In Chapter 2, we demonstrate the importance of annotating a text and of keeping a journal. The chapter also contains a sample draft, and the revision of the draft, for an essay on a short story, Kate Chopin's "The Story of an Hour." Chapter 4 includes annotations, journal entries, and a sample essay on Hemingway's "Cat in the Rain."

The purpose of the present chapter is both broader and narrower, broader in the sense that we have in the preceding pages covered a range of aspects of fiction that will provide topics for writing, but narrower in the sense that we are not here concerned with annotating a text or keeping a journal. We will give only the last stage of a student's preliminary notes and the final version of the essay that grew out of these notes. The student's topic is the personality of the narrator in Poe's story, "The Cask of Amontillado." Other topics are possible choices, such as symbolism in the story, or irony. But before looking at what the student wrote, read the story.

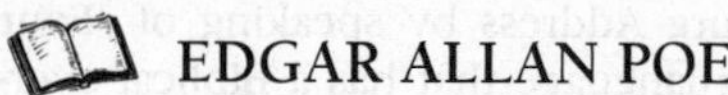

### EDGAR ALLAN POE

*Edgar Allan Poe (1809-49) was the son of traveling actors. His father abandoned the family almost immediately, and his mother died when he was two. The child was adopted—though never legally—by a prosperous merchant and his wife in Richmond. The tensions were great, aggravated by Poe's drinking and heavy gambling, and in 1827 Poe left Richmond for Boston. He wrote, served briefly in the army, attended West Point but left within a year, and became an editor for the remaining eighteen years of his life. It was during these years, too, that he wrote the poems, essays, and fiction—especially detective stories and horror stories—that have made him famous.*

## *The Cask of Amontillado*

The thousand injuries of Fortunato I had borne as I best could, but when he ventured upon insult, I vowed revenge. You, who so well know the nature of my soul, will not suppose, however, that I gave utterance to a threat. At *length* I would be avenged; this was a point definitely settled—but the very definitiveness with which it was resolved precluded the idea of risk. I must not only punish, but punish with impunity. A wrong is unredressed when retribution overtakes its redresser. It is equally unredressed when the avenger fails to make himself felt as such to him who has done the wrong.

It must be understood that neither by word nor deed had I given Fortunato cause to doubt my good will. I continued, as was my wont, to smile in his face, and he did not perceive that my smile *now* was at the thought of his immolation.

He had a weak point—this Fortunato—although in other regards he was a man to be respected and even feared. He prided himself on his connoisseurship in wine. Few Italians have the true virtuoso spirit. For the most part their enthusiasm is adopted to suit the time and opportunity to practice imposture upon the British and Austrian *millionaires.* In painting and gemmary Fortunato, like his countrymen, was a quack, but in the matter of old wines he was sincere. In this respect I did not differ from him materially;—I was skillful in the Italian vintages myself, and bought largely whenever I could.

It was about dusk, one evening during the supreme madness of the carnival season, that I encountered my friend. He accosted me with excessive warmth, for he had been drinking much. The man wore motley. He had on a tight-fitting parti-striped dress, and his head was surmounted by the conical cap and bells. I was so pleased to see him, that I thought I should never have done wringing his hand.

I said to him—"My dear Fortunato, you are luckily met. How remarkably well you are looking to-day! But I have received a pipe[1] of what passes for Amontillado, and I have my doubts."

"How?" said he, "Amontillado? A pipe? Impossible! And in the middle of the carnival?"

"I have my doubts," I replied; "and I was silly enough to pay the full Amontillado price without consulting you in the matter. You were not to be found, and I was fearful of losing a bargain."

"Amontillado!"

"I have my doubts."

"Amontillado!"

"And I must satisfy them."

"Amontillado!"

"As you are engaged, I am on my way to Luchesi. If any one has a critical turn, it is he. He will tell me—"

"Luchesi cannot tell Amontillado from Sherry."

"And yet some fools will have it that his taste is a match for your own."

"Come, let us go."

"Whither?"

"To your vaults."

"My friend, no; I will not impose upon your good nature. I perceive you have an engagement. Luchesi—"

"I have no engagement; come."

"My friend, no. It is not the engagement, but the severe cold with which I perceive you are afflicted. The vaults are insufferably damp. They are encrusted with nitre."

[1]**pipe** wine cask

"Let us go, nevertheless. The cold is merely nothing. Amontillado! You have been imposed upon; and as for Luchesi, he cannot distinguish Sherry from Amontillado."

Thus speaking, Fortunato possessed himself of my arm. Putting on a mask of black silk, and drawing a *roquelaure*[2] closely about my person, I suffered him to hurry me to my palazzo.

There were no attendants at home; they had absconded to make merry in honor of the time. I had told them that I should not return until the morning, and had given them explicit orders not to stir from the house. These orders were sufficient, I well knew, to insure their immediate disappearance, one and all, as soon as my back was turned.

25 I took from their sconces two flambeaux, and giving one to Fortunato, bowed him through several suites of rooms to the archway that led into the vaults. I passed down a long and winding staircase, requesting him to be cautious as he followed. We came at length to the foot of the descent, and stood together on the damp group of the catacombs of the Montresors.

The gait of my friend was unsteady, and the bells upon his cap jingled as he strode.

"The pipe," said he.

"It is farther on," said I; "but observe the white web-work which gleams from these cavern walls."

He turned towards me, and looked into my eyes with two filmy orbs that distilled the rheum of intoxication.

30 "Nitre?" he asked, at length.

"Nitre," I replied, "How long have you had that cough?"

"Ugh! ugh! ugh!—ugh! ugh! ugh!—ugh! ugh! ugh!—ugh! ugh! ugh!—ugh! ugh! ugh!"

My poor friend found it impossible to reply for many minutes.

"It is nothing," he said, at last.

35 "Come," I said, with decision, "we will go back; your health is precious. You are rich, respected, admired, beloved; you are happy, as once I was. You are a man to be missed. For me it is no matter. We will go back; you will be ill, and I cannot be responsible. Besides, there is Luchesi—"

"Enough," he said; "the cough is a mere nothing: it will not kill me. I shall not die of a cough."

"True—true," I replied; "and, indeed, I had no intention of alarming you unnecessarily—but you should use all proper caution. A draught of this Medoc will defend us from the damps."

Here I knocked off the neck of a bottle which I drew from a long row of its fellows that lay upon the mould.

"Drink," I said, presenting him the wine.

40 He raised it to his lips with a leer. He paused and nodded to me familiarly, while his bells jingled.

"I drink," he said, "to the buried that repose around us."

"And I to your long life."

He again took my arm, and we proceeded.

[2] ***roquelaure*** short cloak

"These vaults," he said, "are extensive."

45 "The Montresors," I replied, "were a great and numerous family."

"I forget your arms."

"A huge human foot d'or, in a field azure; the foot crushes a serpent rampant whose fangs are imbedded in the heel."

"And the motto?"

*"Nemo me impune lacessit."*[3]

50 "Good!" he said.

The wine sparkled in his eyes and the bells jingled. My own fancy grew warm with the Medoc. We had passed through walls of piled bones, with casks and puncheons intermingling, into the inmost recesses of the catacombs. I paused again, and this time I made bold to seize Fortunato by an arm above the elbow.

"The nitre!" I said; "see, it increases. It hangs like moss upon the vaults. We are below the river's bed. The drops of moisture trickle among the bones. Come, we will go back ere it is too late. Your cough—"

"It is nothing," he said; "let us go on. But first, another draught of the Medoc."

I broke and reached him a flagon of De Grâve. He emptied it at a breath. His eyes flashed with a fierce light. He laughed and threw the bottle upwards with a gesticulation I did not understand.

55 I looked at him in surprise. He repeated the movement—a grotesque one.

"You do not comprehend?" he said.

"Not I," I replied.

"Then you are not of the brotherhood."

"How?"

60 "You are not of the masons."

"Yes, yes," I said, "yes, yes."

"You? Impossible! A mason?"

"A mason," I replied.

"A sign," he said.

65 "It is this," I answered, producing a trowel from beneath the folds of my *roquelaure.*

"You jest," he exclaimed, recoiling a few paces. "But let us proceed to the Amontillado."

"Be it so," I said, replacing the tool beneath the cloak, and again offering him my arm. He leaned upon it heavily. We continued our route in search of the Amontillado. We passed through a range of low arches, descended, passed on, and descending again, arrived at a deep crypt, in which the foulness of the air caused our flambeaux rather to glow than flame.

At the most remote end of the crypt there appeared another less spacious. Its walls had been lined with human remains piled to the vault overhead, in the fashion of the great catacombs of Paris. Three sides of this interior crypt were still ornamented in this manner. From the fourth the bones

[3]***Nemo me impune lacessit*** No one dare attack me with impunity (the motto of Scotland)

had been thrown down, and lay promiscuously upon the earth, forming at one point a mound of some size. Within the wall thus exposed by the displacing of the bones, we perceived a still interior recess, in depth about four feet, in width three, in height six or seven. It seemed to have been constructed for no especial use within itself, but formed merely the interval between two of the colossal supports of the roof of the catacombs, and was backed by one of their circumscribing walls of solid granite.

It was in vain that Fortunato, uplifting his dull torch, endeavored to pry into the depths of the recess. Its termination the feeble light did not enable us to see.

70 "Proceed," I said; "herein is the Amontillado. As for Luchesi—"

"He is an ignoramus," interrupted my friend, as he stepped unsteadily forward, while I followed immediately at his heels. In an instant he had reached the extremity of the niche, and finding his progress arrested by the rock, stood stupidly bewildered. A moment more and I had fettered him to the granite. In its surface were two iron staples, distant from each other about two feet, horizontally. From one of these depended a short chain, from the other a padlock. Throwing the links about his waist, it was but the work of a few seconds to secure it. He was too much astounded to resist. Withdrawing the key I stepped back from the recess.

"Pass your hand," I said, "over the wall; you cannot help feeling the nitre. Indeed it is *very* damp. Once more let me *implore* you to return. No? Then I must positively leave you. But I must first render you all the little attentions in my power."

"The Amontillado!" ejaculated my friend, not yet recovered from his astonishment.

"True," I replied; "the Amontillado."

75 As I said these words I busied myself among the pile of bones of which I have before spoken. Throwing them aside, I soon uncovered a quantity of building-stone and mortar. With these materials and with the aid of my trowel, I began vigorously to wall up the entrance of the niche.

I had scarcely laid the first tier of masonry when I discovered that the intoxication of Fortunato had in a great measure worn off. The earliest indication I had of this was a low moaning cry from the depth of the recess. It was *not* the cry of a drunken man. There was then a long and obstinate silence. I laid the second tier, and the third, and the fourth; and then I heard the furious vibrations of the chain. The noise lasted for several minutes, during which, that I might hearken to it with the more satisfaction, I ceased my labors and sat down upon the bones. When at last the clanking subsided, I resumed the trowel, and finished without interruption the fifth, the sixth, and the seventh tier. The wall was now nearly upon a level with my breast. I again paused, and holding the flambeaux over the masonwork, threw a few feeble rays upon the figure within.

A succession of loud and shrill screams, bursting suddenly from the throat of the chained form, seemed to thrust me violently back. For a brief moment I hesitated—I trembled. Unsheathing my rapier, I began to grope with it about the recess; but the thought of an instant reassured me. I placed my hand upon the solid fabric of the catacombs, and felt satisfied. I reapproached the wall. I replied to the yells of him who clamored. I re-echoed—I aided—I surpassed them in volume and in strength. I did this, and the clamorer grew still.

It was now midnight, and my task was drawing to a close. I had completed the eighth, the ninth, and the tenth tier. I had finished a portion of the last and the eleventh; there remained but a single stone to be fitted and plastered in. I struggled with its weight; I placed it partially in its destined position. But now there came from out the niche a low laugh that erected the hairs upon my head. It was succeeded by a sad voice, which I had difficulty in recognizing as that of the noble Fortunato. The voice said—

"Ha! ha! ha!—he! he! he!—a very good joke indeed—an excellent jest. We will have many a rich laugh about it at the palazzo—he! he! he!—over our wine—he! he! he!"

80 "The Amontillado!" I said.

"He! he! he!—he! he! he!—yes, the Amontillado. But is it not getting late? Will not they be awaiting us at the palazzo, the Lady Fortunato and the rest? Let us be gone."

"Yes," I said, "let us be gone."

*"For the love of God, Montresor!"*

"Yes," I said, "for the love of God!"

85 But to these words I hearkened in vain for a reply. I grew impatient. I called aloud;

"Fortunato!"

No answer. I called again;

"Fortunato!"

No answer still, I thrust a torch through the remaining aperture and let it fall within. There came forth in return only a jingling of the bells. My heart grew sick—on account of the dampness of the catacombs. I hastened to make an end of my labor. I forced the last stone into its position; I plastered it up. Against the new masonry I reerected the old rampart of bones. For the half of a century no mortal has disturbed them. *In pace requiescat!*[4]

[*1846*]

[4]***In pace requiescat!*** May he rest in peace!

# A STUDENT'S WRITTEN RESPONSE TO A STORY

## Notes

If your instructor assigns a topic in advance, such as "Irony in 'The Cask of Amontillado'" or "Is Montresor Insane?," even on your first reading of the story you will be thinking in a specific direction, looking for relevant evidence. But if a topic is not assigned, it will be up to you to find something that you think is worth talking about to your classmates. (All writers must imagine a fairly specific audience, such as the readers of *Ms.*, or the readers of *Playboy*—these audiences are quite different—or the readers of the high school newspaper, or the readers of a highly technical professional journal, and so on. It's a good idea to imagine your classmates as your audience.)

You may want to begin by asking yourself (and responding in your journal) what you like or dislike in the story, or you may want to think about some of the questions mentioned at the beginning of this chapter, on plot, character, point of view, setting, symbolism, style, and theme. Or you may have annotated some passage that puzzled you, and, on rereading, you may feel that *this* passage is what you want to talk about. In any case, after several readings of the story you will settle not only on a *topic* (for instance, symbolism) but also on a *thesis,* an argument, a point (for instance, the symbolism is for the most part effective but in two places is annoyingly obscure).

It happens that the student whose essay we reprint decided to write about the narrator. The following notes are not her earliest jottings but are the jottings she recorded after she had tentatively chosen her topic.

Two characters: narrator (Montresor) and his enemy, Fortunato

1st person narrator, so we know Fort. only through what M. tells us

Fortunato

has wronged Montresor ("thousand injuries"; but is M. telling the truth?)

drinks a lot ("he had been drinking much")

vain (Fort. insists he knows much more than Luchesi)

courteous (in the vaults, drinks to M's buried relatives)

foolish (?? hard to be sure about this)

Montresor

first parag. tells us he seeks vengeance ("I vowed revenge") for "the thousand injuries" he suffered from Fort. ("I would be avenged")

of high birth

1) he comes from a family with a motto: Nemo me impune lacessit (No one dare attack me with impunity)

2) has coat of arms (human foot crushing serpent whose fangs are in heel). But what's the connection? Is the idea that he and his

noble family are like the <u>foot</u> crushing a serpent that has bitten them, or on the other hand is the idea that he and family are like the <u>serpent</u>—if stepped on (attacked, insulted), they will fight back? Maybe we are supposed to think that <u>he</u> thinks he is like the human foot, but <u>we</u> see that he is like the serpent.

highly educated? At least he uses hard words ("unredressed," "the thought of his immolation"). (Check "<u>immolation</u>")

Dictionary says it is a sacrifice, a ritual killing

cunning: knows how to work on Fortunato (implies that Luchesi is more highly regarded than F)

rich: lives in a "palazzo," and has servants

crazy:

1) murders for vengeance
2) enjoys hearing the sound of Fort. shaking chains ("that I might hearken to it with the more satisfaction, I ceased my labors")
3) when he hears the screams of F., <u>he</u> screams ("I surpassed them in volume and in strength")

Can we possibly sympathize with him? Can he possibly be acting fairly? Do we judge him? Do we judge (condemn) ourselves for liking the story? Why do I find the story interesting instead of repulsive? Because (<u>thesis</u> here) his motive is good, he thinks he is upholding family honor (in his eyes the killing is a family duty, a sacrifice; "immolation")

## Essay

**Here is the final version of the essay that grew out of the notes.**

Ann Geraghty

REVENGE, NOBLE AND IGNOBLE

Because Poe's "The Cask of Amontillado"[1] is told by a first-person narrator, a man named Montresor, we cannot be sure that what the narrator tells us is true. There are some things in the story, however, that we can certainly believe. For instance, we can accept the fact that there is a character (even though we never see him) named Luchesi, because the narrator mentions him and the other character in the story--Fortunato--also talks about him. But how sure can we be that Fortunato is the sort of man that the narrator says Fortunato is?

In the first paragraph, Montresor says that Fortunato has done him a "thousand injuries" (152). He is never specific about these, and Fortunato never says anything that we can interpret as evidence that he has injured Montresor. Further, Fortunato is courteous when he meets Montresor, which seems to suggest that he is not aware that he has injured Montresor. It seems fair to conclude, then, that Fortunato has not really injured Montresor, and that

[1]Reprinted in Sylvan Barnet et al., eds., Literature: Thinking, Reading, and Writing Critically, 2nd ed. (New York: Longman, 1997), 152-57. Page references to the story will be given parenthetically within the body of the essay.

Montresor has insanely imagined that Fortunato has injured him.

What evidence is there that Montresor is insane? First, we should notice the intensity with which Montresor speaks, especially in the first paragraph. He tells us that he "vowed revenge" (152) and that he "would be avenged" (152) and that he would "punish with impunity" (153). He also tells us, all in the first paragraph, that he himself must not get punished for his act of vengeance ("A wrong is unredressed when retribution overtakes its redresser"), and, second, that "It is equally unredressed when the avenger fails to make himself felt as such to him who has done the wrong." There is a common saying, "Don't get mad, get even," but Montresor is going way beyond getting even, and anyway it's not certain that he was injured in the first place. He _is_ getting "mad," not in the sense of "angry" but in the sense of "crazy."

If we agree that Montresor is insane, we can ask ourselves two questions about this story. First, is "The Cask of Amontillado" just a story about a mysterious madman, a story that begins and ends with a madman and does not even try to explain his madness? Second, why have people read this story for almost a hundred and fifty years? If we can answer the first question negatively, we may be able to answer the second.

I think that Montresor is insane, but his insanity is understandable, and it is even based on a concept of honor. He comes from a noble family, a family with a coat of arms (a foot is crushing a serpent that is biting the heel) and a motto (<u>Nemo me impune lacessit</u>, which means "No one dare attack me with impunity"). Fortunato may not have really injured him, but for some reason Montresor thinks he has been injured. As a nobleman who must uphold the honor of his family, Montresor acts with a degree of energy that is understandable for someone in his high position. That is, he must live up to his coat of arms, which shows a gold foot (symbolizing a nobleman) crushing a serpent. The motto in effect means that Montresor <u>must</u> take vengeance if he is to uphold his family honor. In fact, the unusual word "immolation" (153) in the second paragraph tells us a good deal about Montresor's action. To "immolate" is to "sacrifice," to perform a ritual killing. Since Montresor says his vengeance will be the "immolation" of Fortunato, we can assume that Montresor thinks that he has a duty, imposed by his noble family, to kill Fortunato. He sees himself as a priest performing a solemn sacrifice.

Interestingly, however, the <u>reader</u> can interpret the motto in a different way. The reader may see Montresor as the serpent, viciously stinging an enemy, and Fortunato is an almost innocent victim who has somehow accidentally offended (stepped on) Montresor. In reading the story we take pleasure in hearing, and seeing, a passionate nobleman performing what he thinks is a duty imposed on him by his rank. We also take pleasure in judging him accurately, that is, in seeing that his action is not really noble but is serpent-like, or base. We thus can eat our cake and have it too; we see a wicked action, a clever murder (and we enjoy seeing it), and, on the other hand, we can sit back and judge it as wicked (we see Montresor as a serpent) and therefore we can feel that we are highly moral.

In reading this essay, you may want to ask yourself the following questions (with an eye toward applying them also to your own writing):

1. Is the title appropriate and at least moderately interesting?
2. Does the essay have a thesis? If so, what is it?
3. Is the thesis (if there is one) adequately supported by evidence?
4. Is the organization satisfactory? Does one paragraph lead easily into the next, and is the argument presented in a reasonable sequence?

# CHAPTER 9

# *Writing about Issues: Perspectives on Gender*

In *The Nature of Woman: An Encyclopedia and Guide to the Literature* (1980), Mary Anne Warren notes that the term *gender* is often used as a synonym for *sex,* that is, for "biological maleness or femaleness." But, as Warren explains, most feminist critics—and now, following their lead, many others—make a distinction between sex and gender. *Sex* is physiological, the biologically fixed sex divisions between male and female (a matter of chromosomes, hormones, and anatomical differences). *Gender* is cultural, "the socially imposed dichotomy of masculine and feminine roles and character traits." These roles, it is now argued, are not "natural" or innate, but rather are "constructed" by the society in which we live. According to this view, society exaggerates the biological sexual difference (male, female), producing patterns of gender (masculinity, femininity) and of sexuality (for instance, the idea that heterosexuality is the only natural behavior). Thus, it is a biological fact (we think) that the female hormone estrogen inhibits aggression and the male hormone androgen influences aggression, but it is society that inculcates the idea that (for instance) young girls should be docile and young boys should be aggressive. Sayings such as "A woman's place is in the home," "*Kinder, Küche, Kirche*" (German for "children, cooking, and the church"), and "*Fatti maschii, parole femine*" (Italian for "Manly deeds, womanly words," the motto of the State of Maryland), reflect what was once thought to be the obvious fact that biology determines one's identity, and that males should be strong, self-assured, rational, competitive, and that women should be weak, dependent, emotional. We can now see how sayings such as these are *social ideals that create identity.* Against such statements that assume a fixed identity we can cite the now-famous words of Simone de Beauvoir in *The Second Sex* (1953), "One is not born, but rather becomes a woman."

As you read the following stories, you will want of course to reflect upon the technical points that you have been learning about—plot, character, point of view, setting, symbolism, style, theme. But for this group of stories, especially keep in mind the distinction we have just set forth between physiological and social or cultural differences.

## TOPICS FOR CONSIDERATION

You will find other stories in this volume that explore gender issues and themes, but we think the stories in this chapter form an interesting group that can be studied with profit as a whole. After reading a story, you may find it stimulating to ponder the following questions.

- How does the author describe men and women? Is their behavior in the story meant to illustrate something typical about men's and women's beliefs, attitudes, values?
- Does it make a difference to the story whether its author is a man or a woman? If you did not know the identity of the author, could you tell whether a man or a woman wrote it? If so, how?
- Does the author suggest that men and women are simply "the way they are," or, instead, that their understanding of themselves is the result of social pressures and circumstances—that they act out the roles that their societies assign to them?
- Do you see moments in the story when men and women resist the gender roles to which they have been accustomed?
- Think about stories, such as Margaret Atwood's "Rape Fantasies" and Doris Lessing's "Woman on a Roof" that touch on similar themes, and examine the similarities and differences between the authors' perspectives on gender.
- The study of gender also involves attention to gay and lesbian identities and to the special social and personal situations that same-sex lovers face, illustrated here by David Leavitt's "Territory" and Gloria Naylor's "The Two." Compare the presentation of men in love in Leavitt's story to that of women in love in Naylor's. Can these two stories be connected not only to one another, but, in the feelings about love and sexual desire they depict, to the stories gathered here about heterosexual love?
- After you have read several of the stories in this chapter, review and reread them according to their dates of publication, beginning with Guy de Maupassant's "Mademoiselle" and Gilman's "The Yellow Wallpaper." Do you see signs of a development or evolution in the treatment of gender?
- Does fiction strike you as a good means for exploring gender? What can a short story accomplish that a prose essay cannot? Can you imagine instances in which an essay or an autobiography might be more effective?
- In *On Deconstruction* (1982), a study of contemporary literary theory, Jonathan Culler remarks that feminist criticism has often stressed "reading as a woman." This concept, Culler states, affirms the "continuity between women's experience of social and familial structures and their experiences as readers." Do you agree with Culler's suggestion that men and women often interpret characters and incidents in stories differently? Locate moments in these stories when you think that men and women readers might differ in their responses.

- Culler's point (see the preceding item) is intriguing, but some people have criticized it for not taking into account the differences *within* groups of women and groups of men, differences that involve social class, race, ethnicity, religion. These critics have maintained that gender is only one dimension of who we are, and that good writers and careful readers perceive that gender is thus always connected to other things. Where in these stories do you observe gender being portrayed in relation to other important facets of personal identity and social life?

## GUY DE MAUPASSANT

*Guy de Maupassant (1850–93) was born in Dieppe, France. (In speaking of him by his last name only, the name is Maupassant,* not *de Maupassant.) He studied law briefly, served in the Franco-Prussian War (1870–71), and then lived in Paris, where he met such distinguished writers as Émile Zola and Gustave Flaubert. Maupassant for a time worked as a civil servant, but he resigned his job in 1880 when he published (in an anthology edited by Zola) the first of his two hundred or so stories. He had meanwhile contracted syphilis, which in later years affected his mind. He attempted suicide in 1891 and was confined to an asylum, where he died two years later.*

# *Mademoiselle*

***English version by Jane Saretta***

He had been registered under the names of Jean Marie[1] Mathieu Valot, but he was never called anything but "Mademoiselle." He was the village simpleton, but not one of those wretched, ragged simpletons who live on public charity. He lived comfortably on a small income which his mother had left him, and which his guardian paid him regularly, and so he was rather envied than pitied. And then, he was not one of those idiots with wild looks and the manners of an animal, for he was by no means unattractive, with his half-open lips and smiling eyes, and especially in his constant make-up in female dress. For he dressed like a girl, and thus showed how little he objected to being called Mademoiselle.

And why should he not like the nickname which his mother had given him affectionately, when he was a mere child, so delicate and weak, and with a fair complexion—poor little diminutive lad not as tall as many girls of the same age? It was in pure love that, in his earlier years, his mother whispered that tender Mademoiselle to him, while his old grandmother used to say jokingly:

[1]**Jean Marie** Although this name may strike American readers as a female name, in French it is unambiguously a male name.

"The fact is, as for his male equipment, it's really not worth mentioning—no offense to God in saying so." And his grandfather, who was equally fond of a joke, used to add: "I only hope it won't disappear as he grows up."

And they treated him as if he had really been a girl and coddled him, the more so as they were very prosperous and did not have to worry about making ends meet.

5 When his mother and grandparents were dead, Mademoiselle was almost as happy with his paternal uncle, an unmarried man, who had carefully attended the simpleton and who had grown more and more attached to him by dint of looking after him; and the worthy man continued to call Jean Marie Mathieu Valot, Mademoiselle.

He was called so in all the country round as well, not with the slightest intention of hurting his feelings, but, on the contrary, because all thought they would please the poor gentle creature who harmed nobody by his behavior.

The very street boys meant no harm by it, accustomed as they were to call the tall idiot in a frock and cap by the nickname; but it would have struck them as very extraordinary, and would have led them to crude jokes, if they had seen him dressed like a boy.

Mademoiselle, however, took care of that, for his dress was as dear to him as his nickname. He delighted in wearing it, and, in fact, cared for nothing else, and what gave it a particular zest was that he knew that he was not a girl, and that he was living in disguise. And this was evident by the exaggerated feminine bearing and walk he put on; as if to show that it was not natural to him. His enormous, carefully arranged cap was adorned with large variegated ribbons. His petticoat, with numerous flounces, was distended behind by many hoops. He walked with short steps, and with exaggerated swaying of the hips, while his folded arms and crossed hands were distorted into pretensions of comical coquetry.

On such occasions, if anybody wished to make friends with him, it was necessary to say:

10 "Ah! Mademoiselle, what a nice girl you make."

That put him into a good humor, and he used to reply, much pleased: "Don't I? But people can see I only do it for a joke."

But, nevertheless, when they were dancing at village festivals in the neighborhood, he would always be invited to dance as Mademoiselle, and would never ask any of the girls to dance with him; and one evening when somebody asked him the reason for this, he opened his eyes wide, laughed as if the man had said something stupid, and replied:

"I cannot ask the girls, because I am not dressed like a boy. Just look at my dress, you fool!"

15 As his interrogator was a judicious man, he said to him:

"Then dress like one, Mademoiselle."

He thought for a moment, and then said with a cunning look:

"But if I dress like a boy, I won't be a girl anymore; and then I am a girl," and he shrugged his shoulders as he said it.

But the remark seemed to make him think.

20 For some time afterward, when he met the same person, he would ask him abruptly:

"If I dress like a boy, will you still call me Mademoiselle?"

"Of course, I will," the other replied. "You will always be called so."

The simpleton appeared delighted, for there was no doubt that he thought more of his nickname than he did of his dress, and the next day he made his appearance in the village square, without his petticoats and dressed as a man. He had taken a pair of trousers, a coat, and a hat from his guardian's closet. This created quite a disturbance in the neighborhood, for the people who had been in the habit of smiling at him kindly when he was dressed as a woman, looked at him in astonishment and almost in fear, while the indulgent could not help laughing, and visibly making fun of him.

The involuntary hostility of some, and the too evident ridicule of others, the disagreeable surprise of all, were too palpable for him not to see it, and to be hurt by it, and it was still worse when a street urchin said to him in a jeering voice, as he danced round him:

25 "Oh! oh! Mademoiselle, you wear trousers! Oh! oh! Mademoiselle!"

And it grew worse and worse, when a whole band of these vagabonds were on his heels, hooting and yelling after him, as if he had been somebody in a masquerading dress during the Carnival.

It was quite certain that the unfortunate creature looked more in disguise now than he had formerly. By dint of living like a girl, and by even exaggerating the feminine walk and manners, he had totally lost all masculine looks and ways. His smooth face, his long flax-like hair, required a cap with ribbons, and became a caricature under the high stove-pipe hat of the old doctor, his grandfather.

Mademoiselle's shoulders, and especially his swelling stern, danced about wildly in this old-fashioned coat and wide trousers. And nothing was as funny as the contrast between his odd dress and delicate walk, the winning way he used his head, and the elegant movements of his hands, with which he fanned himself like a girl.

Soon the older lads and girls, the old women, men of ripe age and even the Judicial Councilor, joined the little brats, and hooted Mademoiselle, while the astonished fellow ran away, and rushed into the house with terror. There he put both hands to his poor head, and tried to comprehend the matter. Why were they angry with him? For it was quite evident that they were angry with him. What wrong had he done, and whom had he injured, by dressing as a boy? Was he not a boy, after all? For the first time in his life, he felt a horror for his nickname, for had he not been insulted through it? But immediately he was seized with a horrible doubt.

30 "Suppose that, after all, I am a girl?"

He wanted to ask his guardian about it but he was reluctant to do so, for he somehow felt, although only obscurely, that he, worthy man, might not tell him the truth, out of kindness. And, besides, he preferred to find out for himself, without asking anyone.

All his idiot's cunning, which had been lying latent up till then, because he never had any occasion to make use of it, now came out and urged him to a solitary and dark action.

The next day he dressed himself as a girl again, and made his appearance as if he had perfectly forgotten his escapade of the day before, but the people, especially the street boys, had not forgotten it. They looked at him sideways, and, even the best of them, could not help smiling, while the little blackguards ran after him and said:

"Oh! oh! Mademoiselle, you were wearing pants!"

35 But he pretended not to hear, or even to guess what they were alluding

to. He seemed as happy and glad to look about him as he usually did, with half-open lips and smiling eyes. As usual, he wore an enormous cap with variegated ribbons, and the same large petticoats; he walked with short, mincing steps, swaying and wriggling his hips and gesticulating like a coquette, and licked his lips when they called him Mademoiselle, while really he would have liked to have jumped at the throats of those who called him so.

Days and months passed, and by degrees people forgot all about his strange escapade. But he had never left off thinking about it, or trying to find out—for which he was always on the alert—how he could ascertain his qualities as a boy, and how to assert them victoriously. Really innocent, he had reached the age of twenty without knowing anything or without ever having any natural impulse, but being tenacious of purpose, curious and dissembling, he asked no questions, but observed all that was said and done.

Often at their village dances, he had heard young fellows boasting about girls whom they had seduced, and girls praising such and such a young fellow, and often, also, after a dance, he saw the couples go away together, with their arms round each other's waists. They paid no attention to him, and he listened and watched, until, at last, he discovered what was going on.

And then, one night, when dancing was over, and the couples were going away with their arms round each other's waists, a terrible screaming was heard at the corner of the woods through which those going to the next village had to pass. It was Josephine, pretty Josephine, and when her screams were heard, they ran to her assistance, and arrived only just in time to rescue her, half strangled, from Mademoiselle's clutches.

The idiot had watched her and had thrown himself upon her in order to treat her as the other young fellows did the girls, but she resisted him so stoutly that he took her by the throat and squeezed it with all his might until she could not breathe, and was nearly dead.

In rescuing Josephine from him, they had thrown him on the ground, but he jumped up again immediately, foaming at the mouth and slobbering, and exclaimed:

"I am not a girl any longer, I'm a man, I'm a man, I tell you."

[*1885*]

##  CHARLOTTE PERKINS GILMAN

***Charlotte Perkins Gilman (1860–1935), née Charlotte Perkins, was born in Hartford, Connecticut. Her father deserted the family soon after Charlotte's birth; she was brought up by her mother, who found it difficult to make ends meet. For a while Charlotte worked as an artist and teacher of art, and in 1884, when she was twenty-four, she married an artist. In 1885 she had a daughter, but soon after the birth of the girl Charlotte had a nervous breakdown. At her husband's urging she spent a month in the sanitarium of Dr. S. Weir Mitchell, a physician who specialized in treating women with nervous disorders.***

*(Mitchell is specifically named in "The Yellow Wallpaper.") Because the treatment—isolation and total rest—nearly drove her to insanity, she fled Mitchell and her husband. In California she began a career as a lecturer and writer on feminist topics. (She also supported herself by teaching school and by keeping a boardinghouse.) Among her books are* Women and Economics *(1899) and* The Man-Made World *(1911), which have been revived by the feminist movement. In 1900 she married a cousin, George Gilman. From all available evidence, the marriage was successful. Certainly it did not restrict her activities as a feminist. In 1935, suffering from inoperable cancer, she took her own life.*

*"The Yellow Wallpaper," written in 1892—that is, written after she had been treated by S. Weir Mitchell for her nervous breakdown—was at first interpreted either as a ghost story or as a Poe-like study of insanity. Only in recent years has it been seen as a feminist story. (One might ask oneself if these interpretations are mutually exclusive.)*

# The Yellow Wallpaper

It is very seldom that mere ordinary people like John and myself secure ancestral halls for the summer.

A colonial mansion, a hereditary estate, I would say a haunted house, and reach the height of romantic felicity—but that would be asking too much of fate!

Still I will proudly declare that there is something queer about it.

Else, why should it be let so cheaply? And why have stood so long untenanted?

5 John laughs at me, of course, but one expects that in marriage.

John is practical in the extreme. He has no patience with faith, an intense horror of superstition, and he scoffs openly at any talk of things not to be felt and seen and put down in figures.

John is a physician, and *perhaps*—(I would not say it to a living soul, of course, but this is dead paper and a great relief to my mind)—*perhaps* that is one reason I do not get well faster.

You see he does not believe I am sick!

And what can one do?

10 If a physician of high standing, and one's own husband, assures friends and relatives that there is really nothing the matter with one but temporary nervous depression—a slight hysterical tendency—what is one to do?

My brother is also a physician, and also of high standing, and he says the same thing.

So I take phosphates or phosphites—whichever it is, and tonics, and journeys, and air, and exercise, and am absolutely forbidden to "work" until I am well again.

Personally, I disagree with their ideas.

Personally, I believe that congenial work, with excitement and change, would do me good.

15 But what is one to do?

I did write for a while in spite of them; but it *does* exhaust me a good deal—having to be so sly about it, or else meet with heavy opposition.

I sometimes fancy that in my condition if I had less opposition and more society and stimulus—but John says the very worst thing I can do is to think about my condition, and I confess it always makes me feel bad.

So I will let it alone and talk about the house.

The most beautiful place! It is quite alone, standing well back from the road, quite three miles from the village. It makes me think of English places that you read about, for there are hedges and walls and gates that lock, and lots of separate little houses for the gardeners and people.

20 There is a *delicious* garden! I never saw such a garden—large and shady, full of box-bordered paths, and lined with long grapecovered arbors with seats under them.

There were greenhouses, too, but they are all broken now. There was some legal trouble, I believe, something about the heirs and coheirs; anyhow, the place has been empty for years.

That spoils my ghostliness, I am afraid, but I don't care—there is something strange about the house—I can feel it.

I even said so to John one moonlight evening, but he said what I felt was a *draught,* and shut the window.

I get unreasonably angry with John sometimes. I'm sure I never used to be so sensitive. I think it is due to this nervous condition.

25 But John says if I feel so, I shall neglect proper self-control; so I take pains to control myself—before him, at least, and that makes me very tired.

I don't like our room a bit. I wanted one downstairs that opened on the piazza and had roses all over the window, and such pretty old-fashioned chintz hangings! but John would not hear of it.

He said there was only one window and not room for two beds, and no near room for him if he took another.

He is very careful and loving, and hardly lets me stir without special direction.

I have a schedule prescription for each hour in the day; he takes all care from me, and so I feel basely ungrateful not to value it more.

30 He said we came here solely on my account, that I was to have perfect rest and all the air I could get. "Your exercise depends on your strength, my dear," said he, "and your food somewhat on your appetite; but air you can absorb all the time." So we took the nursery at the top of the house.

It is a big, airy room, the whole floor nearly, with windows that look all ways, and air and sunshine galore. It was nursery first and then playroom and gymnasium, I should judge; for the windows are barred for little children, and there are rings and things in the walls.

The paint and paper look as if a boys' school had used it. It is stripped off—the paper—in great patches all around the head of my bed, about as far as I can reach, and in a great place on the other side of the room low down. I never saw a worse paper in my life.

One of those sprawling flamboyant patterns committing every artistic sin.

It is dull enough to confuse the eye in following, pronounced enough to constantly irritate and provoke study, and when you follow the lame uncertain curves for a little distance they suddenly commit suicide—plunge off at outrageous angles, destroy themselves in unheard of contradictions.

35 The color is repellent, almost revolting; a smouldering unclean yellow, strangely faded by the slow-turning sunlight.

It is a dull yet lurid orange in some places, a sickly sulphur tint in others.

No wonder the children hated it! I should hate it myself if I had to live in this room long.

There comes John, and I must put this away,—he hates to have me write a word.

We have been here two weeks, and I haven't felt like writing before, since that first day.

40 I am sitting by the window now, up in this atrocious nursery, and there is nothing to hinder my writing as much as I please, save lack of strength.

John is away all day, and even some nights when his cases are serious.

I am glad my case is not serious!

But these nervous troubles are dreadfully depressing.

John does not know how much I really suffer. He knows there is no *reason* to suffer, and that satisfies him.

45 Of course it is only nervousness. It does weigh on me so not to do my duty in any way!

I meant to be such a help to John, such a real rest and comfort, and here I am a comparative burden already!

Nobody would believe what an effort it is to do what little I am able,—to dress and entertain, and order things.

It is fortunate Mary is so good with the baby. Such a dear baby!

And yet I *cannot* be with him, it makes me so nervous.

50 I suppose John never was nervous in his life. He laughs at me so about this wallpaper!

At first he meant to repaper the room, but afterwards he said that I was letting it get the better of me, and that nothing was worse for a nervous patient than to give way to such fancies.

He said that after the wallpaper was changed it would be the heavy bedstead, and then the barred windows, and then that gate at the head of the stairs, and so on.

"You know the place is doing you good," he said, "and really, dear, I don't care to renovate the house just for a three months' rental."

"Then do let us go downstairs," I said, "there are such pretty rooms there."

55 Then he took me in his arms and called me a blessed little goose, and said he would go down to the cellar, if I wished, and have it whitewashed into the bargain.

But he is right enough about the beds and windows and things.

It is an airy and comfortable room as any one need wish, and, of course, I would not be so silly as to make him uncomfortable just for a whim.

I'm really getting quite fond of the big room, all but that horrid paper.

Out of one window I can see the garden, those mysterious deep-shaded arbors, the riotous old-fashioned flowers, and bushes and gnarly trees.

60 Out of another I get a lovely view of the bay and a little private wharf belonging to the estate. There is a beautiful shaded lane that runs down there from the house. I always fancy I see people walking in these numerous paths and arbors, but John has cautioned me not to give way to fancy in

the least. He says that with my imaginative power and habit of story-making, a nervous weakness like mine is sure to lead to all manner of excited fancies, and that I ought to use my will and good sense to check the tendency. So I try.

I think sometimes that if I were only well enough to write a little it would relieve the press of ideas and rest me.

But I find I get pretty tired when I try.

It is so discouraging not to have any advice and companionship about my work. When I get really well, John says we will ask Cousin Henry and Julia down for a long visit; but he says he would as soon put fireworks in my pillow-case as to let me have those stimulating people about now.

I wish I could get well faster.

65 But I must not think about that. This paper looks to me as if it *knew* what a vicious influence it had!

There is a recurrent spot where the pattern lolls like a broken neck and two bulbous eyes stare at you upside down.

I get positively angry with the impertinence of it and the everlastingness. Up and down and sideways they crawl, and those absurd, unblinking eyes are everywhere. There is one place where two breadths didn't match, and the eyes go all up and down the line, one a little higher than the other.

I never saw so much expression in an inanimate thing before, and we all know how much expression they have! I used to lie awake as a child and get more entertainment and terror out of blank walls and plain furniture than most children could find in a toystore.

I remember what a kindly wink the knobs of our big, old bureau used to have, and there was one chair that always seemed like a strong friend.

70 I used to feel that if any of the other things looked too fierce I could always hop into that chair and be safe.

The furniture in this room is no worse than inharmonious, however, for we had to bring it all from downstairs. I suppose when this was used as a playroom they had to take the nursery things out, and no wonder! I never saw such ravages as the children have made here.

The wallpaper, as I said before, is torn off in spots, and it sticketh closer than a brother—they must have had perseverance as well as hatred.

Then the floor is scratched and gouged and splintered, the plaster itself is dug out here and there, and this great heavy bed which is all we found in the room, looks as if it had been through the wars.

But I don't mind it a bit—only the paper.

75 There comes John's sister. Such a dear girl as she is, and so careful of me! I must not let her find me writing.

She is a perfect and enthusiastic housekeeper, and hopes for no better profession. I verily believe she thinks it is the writing which made me sick!

But I can write when she is out, and see her a long way off from these windows.

There is one that commands the road, a lovely shaded winding road, and one that just looks off over the country. A lovely country, too, full of great elms and velvet meadows.

This wallpaper has a kind of sub-pattern in a different shade, a particularly irritating one, for you can only see it in certain lights, and not clearly then.

80 But in the places where it isn't faded and where the sun is just so—I

can see a strange, provoking, formless sort of figure, that seems to skulk about behind that silly and conspicuous front design.

There's sister on the stairs!

Well, the Fourth of July is over! The people are all gone and I am tired out. John thought it might do me good to see a little company, so we just had mother and Nellie and the children down for a week.

Of course I didn't do a thing. Jennie sees to everything now. But it tired me all the same.

John says if I don't pick up faster he shall send me to Weir Mitchell in the fall.

But I don't want to go there at all. I had a friend who was in his hands once, and she says he is just like John and my brother, only more so!

Besides, it is such an undertaking to go so far.

I don't feel as if it was worth while to turn my hand over for anything, and I'm getting dreadfully fretful and querulous.

I cry at nothing, and cry most of the time.

Of course I don't when John is here, or anybody else, but when I am alone.

And I am alone a good deal just now. John is kept in town very often by serious cases, and Jennie is good and lets me alone when I want her to.

So I walk a little in the garden or down that lovely lane, sit on the porch under the roses, and lie down up here a good deal.

I'm getting really fond of the room in spite of the wallpaper. Perhaps *because* of the wallpaper.

It dwells in my mind so!

I lie here on this great immovable bed—it is nailed down, I believe—and follow that pattern about by the hour. It is as good as gymnastics, I assure you. I start, we'll say, at the bottom, down in the corner over there where it has not been touched, and I determine for the thousandth time that I *will* follow that pointless pattern to some sort of a conclusion.

I know a little of the principle of design, and I know this thing was not arranged on any laws of radiation, or alternation, or repetition, or symmetry, or anything else that I ever heard of.

It is repeated, of course, by the breadths, but not otherwise.

Looked at in one way each breadth stands alone, the bloated curves and flourishes—a kind of "debased Romanesque" with *delirium tremens*—go waddling up and down in isolated columns of fatuity.

But, on the other hand, they connect diagonally, and the sprawling outlines run off in great slanting waves of optic horror, like a lot of wallowing seaweeds in full chase.

The whole thing goes horizontally, too, at least it seems so, and I exhaust myself in trying to distinguish the order of its going in that direction.

They have used a horizontal breadth for a frieze, and that adds wonderfully to the confusion.

There is one end of the room where it is almost intact, and there, when the crosslights fade and the low sun shines directly upon it, I can almost fancy radiation after all,—the interminable grotesques seem to form around a common center and rush off in headlong plunges of equal distraction.

It makes me tired to follow it. I will take a nap I guess.

I don't know why I should write this.

I don't want to.

I don't feel able.

And I know John would think it absurd. But I *must* say what I feel and think in some way—it is such a relief.

But the effort is getting to be greater than the relief!

Half the time now I am awfully lazy, and lie down ever so much.

John says I mustn't lose my strength, and has me take cod liver oil and lots of tonics and things, to say nothing of ale and wine and rare meat.

Dear John! He loves me very dearly, and hates to have me sick. I tried to have a real earnest reasonable talk with him the other day, and tell him how I wish he would let me go and make a visit to Cousin Henry and Julia.

But he said I wasn't able to go, nor able to stand it after I got there; and I did not make out a very good case for myself, for I was crying before I had finished.

It is getting to be a great effort for me to think straight. Just this nervous weakness I suppose.

And dear John gathered me up in his arms, and just carried me upstairs and laid me on the bed, and sat by me and read to me till it tired my head.

He said I was his darling and his comfort and all he had, and that I must take care of myself for his sake, and keep well.

He says no one but myself can help me out of it, that I must use my will and self-control and not let any silly fancies run away with me.

There's one comfort, the baby is well and happy, and does not have to occupy this nursery with the horrid wallpaper.

If we had not used it, that blessed child would have! What a fortunate escape! Why, I wouldn't have a child of mine, an impressionable little thing, live in such a room for worlds.

I never thought of it before, but it is lucky that John kept me here after all, I can stand it so much easier than a baby, you see.

Of course I never mention it to them any more—I am too wise,—but I keep watch of it all the same.

There are things in that paper that nobody knows but me, or ever will.

Behind that outside pattern the dim shapes get clearer every day.

It is always the same shape, only very numerous.

And it is like a woman stooping down and creeping about behind that pattern. I don't like it a bit. I wonder—I begin to think—I wish John would take me away from here!

It is so hard to talk with John about my case, because he is so wise, and because he loves me so.

But I tried last night.

It was moonlight. The moon shines in all around just as the sun does.

I hate to see it sometimes, it creeps so slowly, and always comes in by one window or another.

John was asleep and I hated to waken him, so I kept still and watched the moonlight on that undulating wallpaper till I felt creepy.

The faint figure behind seemed to shake the pattern, just as if she wanted to get out.

I got up softly and went to feel and see if the paper *did* move, and when I came back John was awake.

"What is it, little girl?" he said. "Don't go walking about like that—you'll get cold."

I thought it was a good time to talk, so I told him that I really was not gaining here, and that I wished he would take me away.

"Why darling!" said he, "our lease will be up in three weeks, and I can't see how to leave before."

"The repairs are not done at home, and I cannot possibly leave town just now. Of course if you were in any danger, I could and would, but you really are better, dear, whether you can see it or not. I am a doctor, dear, and I know. You are gaining flesh and color, your appetite is better, I feel really much easier about you."

135 "I don't weigh a bit more," said I, "nor as much; and my appetite may be better in the evening when you are here, but it is worse in the morning when you are away!"

"Bless her little heart!" said he with a big hug, "she shall be as sick as she pleases! But now let's improve the shining hours by going to sleep, and talk about it in the morning!"

"And you won't go away?" I asked gloomily.

"Why, how can I, dear? It is only three weeks more and then we will take a nice little trip of a few days while Jennie is getting the house ready. Really dear you are better!"

"Better in body perhaps—" I began, and stopped short, for he sat up straight and looked at me with such a stern, reproachful look that I could not say another word.

140 "My darling," said he, "I beg of you, for my sake and for our child's sake, as well as for your own, that you will never for one instant let that idea enter your mind! There is nothing so dangerous, so fascinating, to a temperament like yours. It is a false and foolish fancy. Can you not trust me as a physician when I tell you so?"

So of course I said no more on that score, and we went to sleep before long. He thought I was asleep first, but I wasn't and lay there for hours trying to decide whether that front pattern and the back pattern really did move together or separately.

On a pattern like this, by daylight, there is a lack of sequence, a defiance of law, that is a constant irritant to a normal mind.

The color is hideous enough, and unreliable enough, and infuriating enough, but the pattern is torturing.

You think you have mastered it, but just as you get well underway in following, it turns a back-somersault and there you are. It slaps you in the face, knocks you down, and tramples upon you. It is like a bad dream.

145 The outside pattern is a florid arabesque, reminding one of a fungus. If you can imagine a toadstool in joints, an interminable string of toadstools, budding and sprouting in endless convolutions—why, that is something like it.

That is, sometimes!

There is one marked peculiarity about this paper, a thing nobody seems to notice but myself, and that is that it changes as the light changes.

When the sun shoots in through the east window—I always watch for that first long, straight ray—it changes so quickly that I never can quite believe it.

That is why I watch it always.

150 By moonlight—the moon shines in all night when there is a moon—I wouldn't know it was the same paper.

At night in any kind of light, in twilight, candle light, lamplight, and worst of all by moonlight, it becomes bars! The outside pattern I mean, and the woman behind it is as plain as can be.

I didn't realize for a long time what the thing was that showed behind, that dim sub-pattern, but now I am quite sure it is a woman.

By daylight she is subdued, quiet. I fancy it is the pattern that keeps her so still. It is so puzzling. It keeps me quiet by the hour.

I lie down ever so much now. John says it is good for me, and to sleep all I can.

155 Indeed he started the habit by making me lie down for an hour after each meal.

It is a very bad habit I am convinced, for you see I don't sleep.

And that cultivates deceit, for I don't tell them I'm awake—O no!

The fact is I am getting a little afraid of John.

He seems very queer sometimes, and even Jennie has an inexplicable look.

160 It strikes me occasionally, just as a scientific hypothesis,—that perhaps it is the paper!

I have watched John when he did not know I was looking, and come into the room suddenly on the most innocent excuses, and I've caught him several times *looking at the paper!* And Jennie too. I caught Jennie with her hand on it once.

She didn't know I was in the room, and when I asked her in a quiet, a very quiet voice, with the most restrained manner possible, what she was doing with the paper—she turned around as if she had been caught stealing, and looked quite angry—asked me why I should frighten her so!

Then she said that the paper stained everything it touched, that she had found yellow smooches on all my clothes and John's, and she wished we would be more careful!

Did not that sound innocent? But I know she was studying that pattern, and I am determined that nobody shall find it out but myself!

165 Life is very much more exciting now than it used to be. You see I have something more to expect, to look forward to, to watch. I really do eat better, and am more quiet than I was.

John is so pleased to see me improve! He laughed a little the other day, and said I seemed to be flourishing in spite of my wallpaper.

I turned it off with a laugh. I had no intention of telling him it was *because* of the wallpaper—he would make fun of me. He might even want to take me away.

I don't want to leave now until I have found it out. There is a week more, and I think that will be enough.

I'm feeling ever so much better! I don't sleep much at night, for it is so interesting to watch developments; but I sleep a good deal in the daytime.

170 In the daytime it is tiresome and perplexing.

There are always new shoots on the fungus, and new shades of yellow all over it. I cannot keep count of them, though I have tried conscientiously.

It is the strangest yellow, that wallpaper! It makes me think of all the yellow things I ever saw—not beautiful ones like buttercups, but old foul, bad yellow things.

But there is something else about that paper—the smell! I noticed it the moment we came into the room, but with so much air and sun it was not bad. Now we have had a week of fog and rain, and whether the windows are open or not, the smell is here.

It creeps all over the house.

I find it hovering in the dining-room, skulking in the parlor, hiding in the hall, lying in wait for me on the stairs.

It gets into my hair.

Even when I go to ride, if I turn my head suddenly and surprise it—there is that smell!

Such a peculiar odor, too! I have spent hours in trying to analyze it, to find what it smelled like.

It is not bad—at first, and very gentle, but quite the subtlest, most enduring odor I ever met.

In this damp weather it is awful, I wake up in the night and find it hanging over me.

It used to disturb me at first. I thought seriously of burning the house—to reach the smell.

But now I am used to it. The only thing I can think of that it is like is the *color* of the paper! A yellow smell.

There is a very funny mark on this wall, low down, near the mopboard. A streak that runs round the room. It goes behind every piece of furniture, except the bed, a long, straight, even *smooch,* as if it had been rubbed over and over.

I wonder how it was done and who did it, and what they did it for. Round and round and round—round and round and round—it makes me dizzy!

I really have discovered something at last.

Through watching so much at night, when it changes so, I have finally found out.

The front pattern *does* move—and no wonder! The woman behind shakes it!

Sometimes I think there are a great many women behind, and sometimes only one, and she crawls around fast, and her crawling shakes it all over.

Then in the very bright spots she keeps still, and in the very shady spots she just takes hold of the bars and shakes them hard.

And she is all the time trying to climb through. But nobody could climb through that pattern—it strangles so; I think that is why it has so many heads.

They get through, and then the pattern strangles them off and turns them upside down, and makes their eyes white!

If those heads were covered or taken off it would not be half so bad.

I think that woman gets out in the daytime!

And I'll tell you why—privately—I've seen her!

I can see her out of every one of my windows!

It is the same woman, I know, for she is always creeping, and most women do not creep by daylight.

I see her on that long road under the trees, creeping along, and when a carriage comes she hides under the blackberry vines.

I don't blame her a bit. It must be very humiliating to be caught creeping by daylight!

I always lock the door when I creep by daylight. I can't do it at night, for I know John would suspect something at once.

And John is so queer now, that I don't want to irritate him. I wish he would take another room! Besides, I don't want anybody to get that woman out at night but myself.

I often wonder if I could see her out of all the windows at once.

But, turn as fast as I can, I can only see out of one at one time. And though I always see her, she *may* be able to creep faster than I can turn!

I have watched her sometimes away off in the open country, creeping as fast as a cloud shadow in a high wind.

If only that top pattern could be gotten off from the under one! I mean to try it, little by little.

I have found out another funny thing, but I shan't tell at this time! It does not do to trust people too much.

There are only two more days to get this paper off, and I believe John is beginning to notice. I don't like the look in his eyes.

And I heard him ask Jennie a lot of professional questions about me. She had a very good report to give.

She said I slept a good deal in the daytime.

John knows I don't sleep very well at night, for all I'm so quiet!

He asked me all sorts of questions, too, and pretended to be very loving and kind.

As if I couldn't see through him!

Still, I don't wonder he acts so, sleeping under this paper for three months.

It only interests me, but I feel sure John and Jennie are secretly affected by it.

Hurrah! This is the last day, but it is enough. John is to stay in town over night, and won't be out until this evening.

Jennie wanted to sleep with me—the sly thing! But I told her I should undoubtedly rest better for a night all alone.

That was clever, for really I wasn't alone a bit! As soon as it was moonlight and that poor thing began to crawl and shake the pattern, I got up and ran to help her.

I pulled and she shook, I shook and she pulled, and before morning we had peeled off yards of that paper.

A strip about as high as my head and half round the room. And then when the sun came and that awful pattern began to laugh at me, I declared I would finish it to-day!

We go away to-morrow, and they are moving all the furniture down again to leave things as they were before.

Jennie looked at the wall in amazement, but I told her merrily that I did it out of pure spite at the vicious thing.

She laughed and said she wouldn't mind doing it herself, but I must not get tired.

How she betrayed herself that time!

But I am here, and no person touches this paper but me—not *alive!*

She tried to get me out of the room—it was too patent! But I said it was so quiet and empty and clean now that I believed I would lie down again and sleep all I could; and not to wake me even for dinner—I would call when I woke.

So now she is gone, and the servants are gone, and the things are gone, and there is nothing left but that great bedstead nailed down, with the canvas mattress we found on it.

We shall sleep downstairs to-night, and take the boat home to-morrow.

I quite enjoy the room, now it is bare again.

How those children did tear about here!

This bedstead is fairly gnawed!

But I must get to work.

I have locked the door and thrown the key down into the front path.

I don't want to go out, and I don't want to have anybody come in, till John comes.

I want to astonish him.

I've got a rope up here that even Jennie did not find. If that woman does get out, and tries to get away, I can tie her!

But I forgot I could not reach far without anything to stand on! This bed will *not* move!

I tried to lift and push it until I was lame, and then I got so angry I bit off a little piece at one corner—but it hurt my teeth.

Then I peeled off all the paper I could reach standing on the floor. It sticks horribly and the pattern just enjoys it! All those strangled heads and bulbous eyes and waddling fungus growths just shriek with derision!

I am getting angry enough to do something desperate. To jump out of the window would be admirable exercise, but the bars are too strong even to try.

Besides I wouldn't do it. Of course not. I know well enough that a step like that is improper and might be misconstrued.

I don't like to *look* out of the windows even—there are so many of those creeping women, and they creep so fast.

I wonder if they all come out of that wallpaper as I did?

But I am securely fastened now by my well-hidden rope—you don't get *me* out in the road there!

I suppose I shall have to get back behind the pattern when it comes night, and that is hard!

It is so pleasant to be out in this great room and creep around as I please!

I don't want to go outside. I won't, even if Jennie asks me to.

For outside you have to creep on the ground, and everything is green instead of yellow.

But here I can creep smoothly on the floor, and my shoulder just fits in that long smooch around the wall, so I cannot lose my way.

Why there's John at the door!

It is no use, young man, you can't open it!

How he does call and pound!

Now he's crying for an axe.

It would be a shame to break down that beautiful door!

"John dear!" said I in the gentlest voice, "the key is down by the front steps, under a plantain leaf!"

That silenced him for a few moments.

"Then he said—very quietly indeed, "Open the door, my darling!"

I can't," said I. "The key is down by the front door under a plantain leaf!"

And then I said it again, several times, very gently and slowly, and said it so often that he had to go and see, and he got it of course, and came in. He stopped short by the door.

"What is the matter?" he cried. "For God's sake, what are you doing!"

I kept on creeping just the same, but I looked at him over my shoulder.

"I've got out at last," said I, "in spite of you and Jane. And I've pulled off most of the paper, so you can't put me back!"

Now why should that man have fainted? But he did, and right across my path by the wall, so that I had to creep over him every time!

[*1892*]

## D. H. LAWRENCE

*D[avid] H[erbert] Lawrence (1885–1930) was born in a Nottinghamshire (England) coal-mining district. His father was a miner, his mother a schoolteacher with cultural aspirations. When his father died, David had to leave high school, though he later earned a degree and completed a two-year program (1908) at Nottingham University College. Encouraged by his mother, he wrote and painted; in 1911, a year after his mother's death, he published his first novel,* The White Peacock, *and in the following year he published another novel,* The Trespasser. *His first major novel,* Sons and Lovers *(1913), draws heavily on his experiences with his parents: it concerns the conflicts between a coarse but vital father and a refined mother who seeks to possess her son with her love.*

*In addition to writing stories and such novels as* Women in Love *(1920) and* Lady Chatterley's Lover *(1928) Lawrence produced travel books, criticism (*Studies in Classic American Literature*), and poetry.*

*"My great religion," he wrote, "is a belief in the blood, the flesh, as being wiser than the intellect."*

# *The Horse Dealer's Daughter*

"Well, Mabel, and what are you going to do with yourself?" asked Joe, with foolish flippancy. He felt quite safe himself. Without listening for an answer, he turned aside, worked a grain of tobacco to the tip of his tongue and spat it out. He did not care about anything, since he felt safe himself.

The three brothers and the sister sat round the desolate breakfast table, attempting some sort of desultory consultation. The morning's post had given the final tap to the family fortune, and all was over. The dreary dining room itself, with its heavy mahogany furniture, looked as if it were waiting to be done away with.

But the consultation amounted to nothing. There was a strange air of ineffectuality about the three men, as they sprawled at table, smoking and reflecting vaguely on their own condition. The girl was alone, a rather short, sullen-looking young woman of twenty-seven. She did not share the same life as her brothers. She would have been good-looking, save for the impassive fixity of her face, "bull-dog," as her brothers called it.

There was a confused tramping of horses' feet outside. The three men all sprawled round in their chairs to watch. Beyond the dark holly bushes that separated the strip of lawn from the highroad, they could see a cavalcade of shire horses swinging out of their own yard, being taken for exercise. This was the last time. These were the last horses that would go through their hands. The young men watched with critical, callous looks. They were all frightened at the collapse of their lives, and the sense of disaster in which they were involved left them no inner freedom.

5 Yet they were three fine, well-set fellows enough. Joe, the eldest, was a man of thirty-three, broad and handsome in a hot, flushed way. His face was red, he twisted his black moustache over a thick finger, his eyes were shallow and restless. He had a sensual way of uncovering his teeth when he laughed, and his bearing was stupid. Now he watched the horses with a glazed look of helplessness in his eyes, a certain stupor of downfall.

The great draught-horses swung past. They were tied head to tail, four of them, and they heaved along to where a lane branched off from the highroad, planting their great hoofs floutingly in the fine black mud, swinging their great rounded haunches sumptuously, and trotting a few sudden steps as they were led into the lane, round the corner. Every movement showed a massive, slumbrous strength, and a stupidity which held them in subjection. The groom at the head looked back, jerking the leading rope. And the cavalcade moved out of sight up the lane, the tail of the last horse, bobbed up tight and stiff, held out taut from the swinging great haunches as they rocked behind the hedges in a motion-like sleep.

Joe watched with glazed hopeless eyes. The horses were almost like his own body to him. He felt he was done for now. Luckily he was engaged to a woman as old as himself, and therefore her father, who was steward of a neighboring estate, would provide him with a job. He would marry and go into harness. His life was over, he would be a subject animal now.

He turned uneasily aside, the retreating steps of the horses echoing in his ears. Then, with foolish restlessness, he reached for the scraps of bacon rind from the plates, and making a faint whistling sound, flung them to the terrier that lay against the fender. He watched the dog swallow them, and waited till the creature looked into his eyes. Then a faint grin came on his face, and in a high, foolish voice he said:

"You won't get much more bacon, shall you, you little bitch?"

10 The dog faintly and dismally wagged its tail, then lowered its haunches, circled round, and lay down again.

There was another helpless silence at the table. Joe sprawled uneasily in his seat, not willing to go till the family conclave was dissolved. Fred Henry, the second brother, was erect, cleanlimbed, alert. He had watched the passing of the horses with more sangfroid. If he was an animal, like Joe, he was an animal which controls, not one which is controlled. He was master of any horse, and he carried himself with a well-tempered air of mastery. But he was not master of the situations of life. He pushed his coarse brown moustache upwards, off his lip, and glanced irritably at his sister, who sat impassive and inscrutable.

"You'll go and stop with Lucy for a bit, shan't you?" he asked. The girl did not answer.

"I don't see what else you can do," persisted Fred Henry.

"Go as a skivvy," Joe interpolated laconically.

The girl did not move a muscle.

"If I was her, I should go in for training for a nurse," said Malcolm, the youngest of them all. He was the baby of the family, a young man of twenty-two, with a fresh, jaunty *museau*.[1]

But Mabel did not take any notice of him. They had talked at her and round her for so many years, that she hardly heard them at all.

The marble clock on the mantelpiece softly chimed the half-hour, the dog rose uneasily from the hearthrug and looked at the party at the breakfast table. But still they sat on in effectual conclave.

"Oh, all right," said Joe suddenly, apropos of nothing. "I'll get a move on."

He pushed back his chair, straddled his knees with a downward jerk, to get them free, in horsey fashion, and went to the fire. Still he did not go out of the room; he was curious to know what the others would do or say. He began to charge his pipe, looking down at the dog and saying, in a high, affected voice:

"Going wi' me? Going wi' me are ter? Tha'rt goin' further tha that counts on just now, dost hear?"

The dog faintly wagged its tail, the man stuck out his jaw and covered his pipe with his hands, and puffed intently, losing himself in the tobacco, looking down all the while at the dog with an absent brown eye. The dog looked at him in mournful distrust. Joe stood with his knees stuck out, in real horsey fashion.

"Have you had a letter from Lucy?" Fred Henry asked of his sister.

"Last week," came the neutral reply.

"And what does she say?"

There was no answer.

"Does she *ask* you to go and stop there?" persisted Fred Henry.

"She says I can if I like."

"Well, then, you'd better. Tell her you'll come on Monday." This was received in silence.

"That's what you'll do then, is it?" said Fred Henry, in some exasperation.

But she made no answer. There was a silence of futility and irritation in the room. Malcolm grinned fatuously.

"You'll have to make up your mind between now and next Wednesday," said Joe loudly, "or else find yourself lodgings on the curbstone."

The face of the young woman darkened, but she sat on immutable.

"Here's Jack Fergusson!" exclaimed Malcolm, who was looking aimlessly out of the window.

"Where?" exclaimed Joe, loudly.

"Just gone past."

"Coming in?"

[1] ***museau*** jaw (literally muzzle or snout of a beast)

Malcolm craned his neck to see the gate.

"Yes," he said.

There was a silence. Mabel sat on like one condemned, at the head of the table. Then a whistle was heard from the kitchen. The dog got up and barked sharply. Joe opened the door and shouted:

"Come on."

After a moment a young man entered. He was muffled up in overcoat and a purple woolen scarf, and his tweed cap, which he did not remove, was pulled down on his head. He was of medium height, his face was rather long and pale, his eyes looked tired.

"Hello, Jack! Well, Jack!" exclaimed Malcolm and Joe. Fred Henry merely said, "Jack."

"What's doing?" asked the newcomer, evidently addressing Fred Henry.

"Same. We've got to be out by Wednesday. Got a cold?"

"I have—got it bad, too."

"Why don't you stop in?"

"*Me* stop in? When I can't stand on my legs, perhaps I shall have a chance." The young man spoke huskily. He had a slight Scotch accent.

"It's a knock-out, isn't it," said Joe, boisterously, "if a doctor goes round croaking with a cold. Looks bad for the patients, doesn't it?"

The young doctor looked at him slowly.

"Anything the matter with *you,* then?" he asked sarcastically.

"Not as I know of. Damn your eyes, I hope not. Why?"

"I thought you were very concerned about the patients, wondered if you might be one yourself."

"Damn it, no, I've never been patient to no flaming doctor, and hope I never shall be," returned Joe.

At this point Mabel rose from the table, and they all seemed to become aware of her existence. She began putting the dishes together. The young doctor looked at her, but did not address her. He had not greeted her. She went out of the room with the tray, her face impassive and unchanged.

"When are you off then, all of you?" asked the doctor.

"I'm catching the eleven-forty," replied Malcolm. "Are you goin' down wi' th' trap, Joe?"

"Yes, I've told you I'm going down wi' th' trap, haven't I?"

"We'd better be getting her in then. So long, Jack, if I don't see you before I go," said Malcolm, shaking hands.

He went out, followed by Joe, who seemed to have his tail between his legs.

"Well, this is the devil's own," exclaimed the doctor, when he was left alone with Fred Henry. "Going before Wednesday, are you?"

"That's the orders," replied the other.

"Where, to Northampton?"

"That's it."

"The devil!" exclaimed Fergusson, with quiet chagrin.

And there was silence between the two.

"All settled up, are you?" asked Fergusson.

"About."

There was another pause.

"Well, I shall miss yer, Freddy, boy," said the young doctor.

"And I shall miss thee, Jack," returned the other.

"Miss you like hell," mused the doctor.

Fred Henry turned aside. There was nothing to say. Mabel came in again, to finish clearing the table.

"What are *you* going to do, then, Miss Pervin?" asked Fergusson. "Going to your sister's, are you?"

Mabel looked at him with her steady, dangerous eyes, that always made him uncomfortable, unsettling his superficial ease.

"No," she said.

"Well, what in the name of fortune *are* you going to do? Say what you mean to do," cried Fred Henry, with futile intensity.

But she only averted her head, and continued her work. She folded the white table-cloth, and put on the chenille cloth.

"The sulkiest bitch that ever trod!" muttered her brother.

But she finished her task with perfectly impassive face, the young doctor watching her interestedly all the while. Then she went out.

Fred Henry stared after her, clenching his lips, his blue eyes fixing in sharp antagonism, as he made a grimace of sour exasperation.

"You could bray her into bits, and that's all you'd get out of her," he said in a small, narrowed tone.

The doctor smiled faintly.

"What's she *going* to do, then?" he asked.

"Strike me if *I* know!" returned the other.

There was a pause. Then the doctor stirred.

"I'll be seeing you to-night, shall I?" he said to his friend.

"Ay—where's it to be? Are we going over to Jessdale?"

"I don't know. I've got such a cold on me. I'll come round to the Moon and Stars, anyway."

"Let Lizzie and May miss their night for once, eh?"

"That's it—if I feel as I do now."

"All's one—"

The two young men went through the passage and down to the back door together. The house was large, but it was servantless now, and desolate. At the back was a small bricked house-yard, and beyond that a big square, graveled fine and red, and having stables on two sides. Sloping, dank, winter-dark fields stretched away on the open sides.

But the stables were empty. Joseph Pervin, the father of the family, had been a man of no education, who had become a fairly large horse dealer. The stables had been full of horses, there was a great turmoil and come-and-go of horses and of dealers and grooms. Then the kitchen was full of servants. But of late things had declined. The old man had married a second time, to retrieve his fortunes. Now he was dead and everything was gone to the dogs, there was nothing but debt and threatening.

For months, Mabel had been servantless in the big house, keeping the home together in penury for her ineffectual brothers. She had kept house for ten years. But previously it was with unstinted means. Then, however brutal and coarse everything was, the sense of money had kept her proud, confident. The men might be foul-mouthed, the women in the kitchen might have bad reputations, her brothers might have illegitimate children. But so long as there was money, the girl felt herself established, and brutally proud, reserved.

No company came to the house, save dealers and coarse men. Mabel had no associates of her own sex, after her sister went away. But she did not mind. She went regularly to church, she attended to her father. And she lived in the memory of her mother, who had died when she was fourteen, and whom she had loved. She had loved her father, too, in a different way, depending upon him, and feeling secure in him, until at the age of fifty-four he married again. And then she had set hard against him. Now he had died and left them all hopelessly in debt.

She had suffered badly during the period of poverty. Nothing, however, could shake the curious sullen, animal pride that dominated each member of the family. Now, for Mabel, the end had come. Still she would not cast about her. She would follow her own way just the same. She would always hold the keys of her own situation. Mindless and persistent, she endured from day to day. Why should she think? Why should she answer anybody? It was enough that this was the end, and there was no way out. She need not pass any more darkly along the main street of the small town, avoiding every eye. She need not demean herself any more, going into the shops and buying the cheapest food. This was at an end. She thought of nobody, not even of herself. Mindless and persistent, she seemed in a sort of ecstasy to be coming nearer to her fulfillment, her own glorification, approaching her dead mother, who was glorified.

In the afternoon she took a little bag, with shears and sponge and a small scrubbing brush, and went out. It was a gray, wintry day, with saddened, dark green fields and an atmosphere blackened by the smoke of foundries not far off. She went quickly, darkly along the causeway, heeding nobody, through the town to the church-yard.

There she always felt secure, as if no one could see her, although as a matter of fact she was exposed to the stare of every one who passed along under the churchyard wall. Nevertheless, once under the shadow of the great looming church, among the graves, she felt immune from the world, reserved within the thick churchyard wall as in another country.

Carefully she clipped the grass from the grave, and arranged the pinky white, small chrysanthemums in the tin cross. When this was done, she took an empty jar from a neighboring grave, brought water, and carefully, most scrupulously sponged the marble headstone and the coping-stone. It gave her sincere satisfaction to do this. She felt in immediate contact with the world of her mother. She took minute pains, went through the park in a state bordering on pure happiness, as if in performing this task she came into a subtle, intimate connection with her mother. For the life she followed here in the world was far less real than the world of death she inherited from her mother.

The doctor's house was just by the church. Fergusson, being a mere hired assistant, was slave to the countryside. As he hurried now to attend to the outpatients in the surgery, glancing across the graveyard with his quick eyes, he saw the girl at her task at the grave. She seemed so intent and remote, it was like looking into another world. Some mystical element was touched in him. He slowed down as he walked, watching her as if spellbound.

She lifted her eyes, feeling him looking. Their eyes met. And each looked away again at once, each feeling, in some way, found out by the other. He lifted his cap and passed on down the road. There remained distinct in his consciousness, like a vision, the memory of her face, lifted from the tombstone in the churchyard, and looking at him with slow, large, portentous eyes. It *was* portentous, her face. It seemed to mesmerize him. There was a heavy power in her eyes which laid hold of his whole being, as if he had drunk some powerful drug. He had been feeling weak and done before. Now the life came back into him, he felt delivered from his own fretted, daily self.

He finished his duties at the surgery as quickly as might be, hastily filling up the bottles of the waiting people with cheap drugs. Then, in perpetual haste, he set off again to visit several cases in another part of his round, before teatime. At all times he preferred to walk if he could, but particularly when he was not well. He fancied the motion restored him.

The afternoon was falling. It was gray, deadened, and wintry, with a slow, moist, heavy coldness sinking in and deadening all the faculties. But why should he think or notice? He hastily climbed the hill and turned across the dark green fields, following the black cindertrack. In the distance, across a shallow dip in the country, the small town was clustered like smouldering ash, a tower, a spire, a heap of low, raw, extinct houses. And on the nearest fringe of the town, sloping into the dip, was Oldmeadow, the Pervins's house. He could see the stables and the outbuildings distinctly, as they lay towards him on the slope. Well, he would not go there many more times! Another resource would be lost to him, another place gone: the only company he cared for in the alien, ugly little town he was losing. Nothing but work, drudgery, constant hastening from dwelling to dwelling among the colliers and the iron-workers. It wore him out, but at the same time he had a craving for it. It was a stimulant to him to be in the homes of the working people, moving as it were through the innermost body of their life. His nerves were excited and gratified. He could come so near, into the very lives of the rough, inarticulate, powerfully emotional men and women. He grumbled, he said he hated the hellish hole. But as a matter of fact it excited him, the contact with the rough, strongly-feeling people was a stimulant applied direct to his nerves.

Below Oldmeadow, in the green, shallow, soddened hollow of fields, lay a square, deep pond. Roving across the landscape, the doctor's quick eye detected a figure in black passing through the gate of the field, down towards the pond. He looked again. It would be Mabel Pervin. His mind suddenly became alive and attentive.

Why was she going down there? He pulled up on the path on the slope above, and stood staring. He could just make sure of the small black figure moving in the hollow of the failing day. He seemed to see her in the midst of such obscurity, that he was like a clairvoyant, seeing rather with the mind's eye than with ordinary sight. Yet he could see her positively enough, while he kept his eye attentive. He felt, if he looked away from her, in the thick, ugly falling dusk, he would lose her altogether.

He followed her minutely as she moved, direct and intent, like something transmitted rather than stirring in voluntary activity, straight down the field towards the pond. There she stood on the bank for a moment. She never raised her head. Then she waded slowly into the water.

He stood motionless as the small black figure walked slowly and deliberately towards the center of the pond, very slowly, gradually moving deeper into the motionless water, and still moving forward as the water got up to her breast. Then he could see her no more in the dusk of the dead afternoon.

"There!" he exclaimed. "Would you believe it?"

110 And he hastened straight down, running over the wet, soddened fields, pushing through the hedges, down into the depression of callous wintry obscurity. It took him several minutes to come to the pond. He stood on the bank, breathing heavily. He could see nothing. His eyes seemed to penetrate the dead water. Yes, perhaps that was the dark shadow of her black clothing beneath the surface of the water.

He slowly ventured into the pond. The bottom was deep, soft clay, he sank in, and the water clasped dead cold round his legs. As he stirred he could smell the cold, rotten clay that fouled up into the water. It was objectionable in his lungs. Still, repelled and yet not heeding, he moved deeper into the pond. The cold water rose over his thighs, over his loins, upon his abdomen. The lower part of his body was all sunk in the hideous cold element. And the bottom was so deeply soft and uncertain he was afraid of pitching with his mouth underneath. He could not swim, and was afraid.

He crouched a little, spreading his hands under the water and moving them round, trying to feel for her. The dead cold pond swayed upon his chest. He moved again, a little deeper, and again, with his hands underneath, he felt all around under the water. And he touched her clothing. But it evaded his fingers. He made a desperate effort to grasp it.

And so doing he lost his balance and went under, horribly, suffocating in the foul earthy water, struggling madly for a few moments. At last, after what seemed an eternity, he got his footing, rose again into the air and looked around. He gasped, and knew he was in the world. Then he looked at the water. She had risen near him. He grasped her clothing, and drawing her nearer, turned to take his way to land again.

He went very slowly, carefully, absorbed in the slow progress. He rose higher, climbing out of the pond. The water was now only about his legs; he was thankful, full of relief to be out of the clutches of the pond. He lifted her and staggered on to the bank, out of the horror of wet, gray clay.

115 He laid her down on the bank. She was quite unconscious and running with water. He made the water come from her mouth, he worked to restore her. He did not have to work very long before he could feel the breathing begin again in her; she was breathing naturally. He worked a little longer. He could feel her live beneath his hands; she was coming back. He wiped her face, wrapped her in his overcoat, looked round into the dim, dark gray world, then lifted her and staggered down the bank and across the fields.

It seemed an unthinkably long way, and his burden so heavy he felt he would never get to the house. But at last he was in the stableyard, and then in the house-yard. He opened the door and went into the house. In the kitchen he laid her down on the hearthrug, and called. The house was empty. But the fire was burning in the grate.

Then again he kneeled to attend to her. She was breathing regularly, her eyes were wide open and as if conscious, but there seemed something missing in her look. She was conscious in herself, but unconscious of her surroundings.

He ran upstairs, took blankets from a bed, and put them before the fire to warm. Then he removed her saturated, earthy-smelling clothing, rubbed her dry with a towel, and wrapped her naked in the blankets. Then he went into the dining-room, to look for spirits. There was a little whisky. He drank a gulp himself, and put some into her mouth.

The effect was instantaneous. She looked full into his face, as if she had been seeing him for some time, and yet had only just become conscious of him.

120 "Dr. Fergusson?" she said.

"What?" he answered.

He was divesting himself of his coat, intending to find some dry clothing upstairs. He could not bear the smell of the dead, clayey water, and he was mortally afraid of his own health.

"What did I do?" she asked.

"Walked into the pond," he replied. He had begun to shudder like one sick, and could hardly attend to her. Her eyes remained full on him, he seemed to be going dark in his mind, looking back at her helplessly. The shuddering became quieter in him, his life came back in him, dark and unknowing, but strong again.

125 "Was I out of my mind?" she asked, while her eyes were fixed on him all the time.

"Maybe, for the moment," he replied. He felt quiet, because his strength came back. The strange fretful strain had left him.

"Am I out of my mind now?" she asked.

"Are you?" he reflected a moment. "No," he answered truthfully. "I don't see that you are." He turned his face aside. He was afraid now, because he felt dazed, and felt dimly that her power was stronger than his, in this issue. And she continued to look at him fixedly all the time. "Can you tell me where I shall find some dry things to put on?" he asked.

"Did you dive into the pond for me?" she asked.

130 "No," he answered. "I walked in. But I went in overhead as well."

There was silence for a moment. He hesitated. He very much wanted to go upstairs to get into dry clothing. But there was another desire in him. And she seemed to hold him. His will seemed to have gone to sleep, and left him, standing there slack before her. But he felt warm inside himself. He did not shudder at all, though his clothes were sodden on him.

"Why did you?" she asked.

"Because I didn't want you to do such a foolish thing," he said.

"It wasn't foolish," she said, still gazing at him as she lay on the floor, with a sofa cushion under her head. "It was the right thing to do. *I* knew best, then."

135 "I'll go and shift these wet things," he said. But still he had not the power to move out of her presence, until she sent him. It was as if she had the life of his body in her hands, and he could not extricate himself. Or perhaps he did not want to.

Suddenly she sat up. Then she became aware of her own immediate condition. She felt the blankets about her, she knew her own limbs. For a moment it seemed as if her reason were going. She looked round, with wild eye, as if seeking something. He stood still with fear. She saw her clothing lying scattered.

"Who undressed me?" she asked, her eyes resting full and inevitable on his face.

"I did," he replied, "to bring you round."

For some moments she sat and gazed at him awfully, her lips parted.

140 "Do you love me, then?" she asked.

He only stood and stared at her, fascinated. His soul seemed to melt.

She shuffled forward on her knees, and put her arms round him, round his legs, as he stood there, pressing her breasts against his knees and thighs, clutching him with strange, convulsive certainty, pressing his thighs against her, drawing him to her face, her throat, as she looked up at him with flaring, humble eyes of transfiguration, triumphant in first possession.

"You love me," she murmured, in strange transport, yearning and triumphant and confident. "You love me. I know you love me, I know."

And she was passionately kissing his knees, through the wet clothing, passionately and indiscriminately kissing his knees, his legs, as if unaware of everything.

145 He looked down at the tangled wet hair, the wild, bare, animal shoulders. He was amazed, bewildered, and afraid. He had never thought of loving her. He had never wanted to love her. When he rescued her and restored her, he was a doctor, and she was a patient. He had had no single personal thought of her. Nay, this introduction of the personal element was very distasteful to him, a violation of his professional honor. It was horrible to have her there embracing his knees. It was horrible. He revolted from it, violently. And yet—and yet—he had not the power to break away.

She looked at him again, with the same supplication of powerful love, and that same transcendent, frightening light of triumph. In view of the delicate flame which seemed to come from her face like a light, he was powerless. And yet he had never intended to love her. He had never intended. And something stubborn in him could not give way.

"You love me," she repeated, in a murmur of deep, rhapsodic assurance. "You love me."

Her hands were drawing him, drawing him down to her. He was afraid, even a little horrified. For he had, really, no intention of loving her. Yet her hands were drawing him towards her. He put out his hand quickly to steady himself, and grasped her bare shoulder. A flame seemed to burn the hand that grasped her soft shoulder. He had no intention of loving her: his whole will was against his yielding. It was horrible. And yet wonderful was the touch of her shoulders, beautiful the shining of her face. Was she perhaps mad? He had a horror of yielding to her. Yet something in him ached also.

He had been staring away at the door, away from her. But his hand remained on her shoulder. She had gone suddenly very still. He looked down at her. Her eyes were now wide with fear, with doubt, the light was dying from her face, a shadow of terrible grayness was returning. He could not bear the touch of her eyes' question upon him, and the look of death behind the question.

150 With an inward groan he gave way, and let his heart yield towards her. A sudden gentle smile came on his face. And her eyes, which never left his face, slowly, slowly filled with tears. He watched the strange water rise in

her eyes, like some slow fountain coming up. And his heart seemed to burn and melt away in his breast.

He could not bear to look at her any more. He dropped on his knees and caught her head with his arms and pressed her face against his throat. She was very still. His heart, which seemed to have broken, was burning with a kind of agony in his breast. And he felt her slow, hot tears wetting his throat. But he could not move.

He felt the hot tears wet his neck and the hollows of his neck, and he remained motionless, suspended through one of man's eternities. Only now it had become indispensable to him to have her face pressed close to him; he could never let her go again. He could never let her head go away from the close clutch of his arm. He wanted to remain like that for ever, with his heart hurting him in a pain that was also life to him. Without knowing, he was looking down on her damp, soft brown hair.

Then, as it were suddenly, he smelt the horrid stagnant smell of that water. And at the same moment she drew away from him and looked at him. Her eyes were wistful and unfathomable. He was afraid of them, and he fell to kissing her, not knowing what he was doing. He wanted her eyes not to have that terrible, wistful, unfathomable look.

When she turned her face to him again, a faint delicate flush was glowing, and there was again dawning that terrible shining of joy in her eyes, which really terrified him, and yet which he now wanted to see, because he feared the look of doubt still more.

155 "You love me?" she said, rather faltering.

"Yes." The word cost him a painful effort. Not because it wasn't true. But because it was too newly true, the *saying* seemed to tear open again his newly torn heart. And he hardly wanted it to be true, even now.

She lifted her face to him, and he bent forward and kissed her on the mouth, gently, with the one kiss that is an eternal pledge. And as he kissed her his heart strained again in his breast. He never intended to love her. But now it was over. He had crossed over the gulf to her, and all that he had left behind had shriveled and become void.

After the kiss, her eyes again slowly filled with tears. She sat still, away from him, with her face drooped aside, and her hands folded in her lap. The tears fell very slowly. There was complete silence. He too sat there motionless and silent on the hearthrug. The strange pain of his heart that was broken seemed to consume him. That he should love her? That this was love! That he should be ripped open in this way! Him, a doctor! How they would all jeer if they knew! It was agony to him to think they might know.

In the curious naked pain of the thought he looked again to her. She was sitting there drooped into a muse. He saw a tear fall, and his heart flared hot. He saw for the first time that one of her shoulders was quite uncovered, one arm bare, he could see one of her small breasts; dimly, because it had become almost dark in the room.

160 "Why are you crying?" he asked, in an altered voice.

She looked up at him, and behind her tears the consciousness of her situation for the first time brought a dark look of shame to her eyes.

"I'm not crying, really," she said, watching him half frightened.

He reached his hand, and softly closed it on her bare arm.

"I love you! I love you!" he said in a soft, low vibrating voice, unlike himself.

165 She shrank, and dropped her head. The soft, penetrating grip of his hand on her arm distressed her. She looked up at him.

"I want to go," she said. "I want to go and get you some dry things."

"Why?" he said. "I'm all right."

"But I want to go," she said. "And I want you to change your things."

He released her arm, and she wrapped herself in the blanket, looking at him rather frightened. And still she did not rise.

170 "Kiss me," she said wistfully.

He kissed her, but briefly, half in anger.

Then, after a second, she rose nervously, all mixed up in the blanket. He watched her in her confusion, as she tried to extricate herself and wrap herself up so that she could walk. He watched her relentlessly, as she knew. And as she went, the blanket trailing, and as he saw a glimpse of her feet and her white leg, he tried to remember her as she was when he had wrapped her in the blanket. But then he didn't want to remember, because she had been nothing to him then, and his nature revolted from remembering her as she was when she was nothing to him.

A tumbling, muffled noise from within the dark house startled him. Then he heard her voice:—"There are clothes." He rose and went to the foot of the stairs, and gathered up the garments she had thrown down. Then he came back to the fire, to rub himself down and dress. He grinned at his own appearance when he had finished.

The fire was sinking, so he put on coal. The house was now quite dark, save for the light of a street-lamp that shone in faintly from beyond the holly trees. He lit the gas with matches he found on the mantelpiece. Then he emptied the pockets of his own clothes, and threw all his wet things in a heap into the scullery. After which he gathered up her sodden clothes, gently, and put them in a separate heap on the copper-top in the scullery.

175 It was six o'clock on the clock. His own watch had stopped. He ought to go back to the surgery. He waited, and still she did not come down. So he went to the foot of the stairs and called:

"I shall have to go."

Almost immediately he heard her coming down. She had on her best dress of black voile, and her hair was tidy, but still damp. She looked at him—and in spite of herself, smiled.

"I don't like you in those clothes," she said.

"Do I look a sight?" he answered.

180 They were shy of one another.

"I'll make you some tea," she said.

"No, I must go."

"Must you?" And she looked at him again with the wide, strained, doubtful eyes. And again, from the pain of his breast, he knew how he loved her. He went and bent to kiss her, gently, passionately, with his heart's painful kiss.

"And my hair smells so horrible," she murmured in distraction. "And I'm so awful, I'm so awful! Oh, no, I'm too awful." And she broke into bitter, heart-broken sobbing. "You can't want to love me, I'm horrible."

185 "Don't be silly, don't be silly," he said, trying to comfort her, kissing her, holding her in his arms. "I want you, I want to marry you, we're going to be married, quickly, quickly—tomorrow if I can."

But she only sobbed terribly, and cried:

"I feel awful. I feel awful. I feel I'm horrible to you."

"No, I want you, I want you," was all he answered, blindly, with that terrible intonation which frightened her almost more than her horror lest he should *not* want her.

## DORIS LESSING

*Doris Lessing (b. 1919, née Tayler), was born of British parents in Kermanshah, Persia (now Iran), where her father ran a bank. In 1924 her family moved to a farm in Rhodesia (now Zimbabwe), where she educated herself by reading the classics of European and American literature. During her twenty-five years in Rhodesia she married, was active in the Communist Party, held various jobs, divorced, married and divorced a second time (though she retains the last name of her second husband), and wrote. (She says she had always wanted to be a writer, but didn't seriously get down to the business of writing until she was twenty-six or twenty-seven.) In 1949 she moved with her son to London (where she separated from the Communist Party) and has continued to live in London. In 1950 she published her first novel,* The Grass Is Singing. *Her best-known novels are* Martha Quest *(1952),* The Golden Notebook *(1962) and* The Four-Gated City *(1969).*

*In a collection of her nonfiction,* A Small Personal Voice *(1975), she says that when she reads a contemporary work of fiction she looks for "the warmth, the compassion, the humanity, the love of people which illuminates the literature of the nineteenth century. . . . Literature should be committed. It is these qualities which I demand."*

# *A Woman on a Roof*

It was during the week of hot sun, that June.

Three men were at work on the roof, where the leads got so hot they had the idea of throwing water on to cool them. But the water steamed, then sizzled; and they made jokes about getting an egg from some woman in the flats under them, to poach it for their dinner. By two it was not possible to touch the guttering they were replacing, and they speculated about what workmen did in regularly hot countries. Perhaps they should borrow kitchen gloves with the egg? They were all a bit dizzy, not used to the heat; and they shed their coats and stood side by side squeezing themselves into a foot-wide patch of shade against a chimney, careful to keep their feet in the thick socks and boots out of the sun. There was a fine view across several acres of roofs. Not far off a man sat in a deck chair reading the newspapers. Then they saw her, between chimneys, about fifty yards away. She lay face down on a brown blanket. They could see the top part of her: black hair, a flushed solid back, arms spread out.

"She's stark naked," said Stanley, sounding annoyed.

Harry, the oldest, a man of about forty-five, said: "Looks like it."

5 Young Tom, seventeen, said nothing, but he was excited and grinning.

Stanley said: "Someone'll report her if she doesn't watch out."

"She thinks no one can see," said Tom, craning his head all ways to see more.

At this point the woman, still lying prone, brought her two hands up behind her shoulders with the ends of a scarf in them, tied it behind her back, and sat up. She wore a red scarf tied around her breasts and brief red bikini pants. This being the first day of the sun she was white, flushing red. She sat smoking, and did not look up when Stanley let out a wolf whistle. Harry said: "Small things amuse small minds," leading the way back to their part of the roof, but it was scorching. Harry said: "Wait, I'm going to rig up some shade," and disappeared down the skylight into the building. Now that he'd gone, Stanley and Tom went to the farthest point they could to peer at the woman. She had moved, and all they could see were two pink legs stretched on the blanket. They whistled and shouted but the legs did not move. Harry came back with a blanket and shouted: "Come on, then." He sounded irritated with them. They clambered back to him and he said to Stanley: "What about your missus?" Stanley was newly married, about three months. Stanley said, jeering: "What about my missus?"—preserving his independence. Tom said nothing, but his mind was full of the nearly naked woman. Harry slung the blanket, which he had borrowed from a friendly woman downstairs, from the stem of a television aerial to a row of chimney-pots. This shade fell across the piece of gutter they had to replace. But the shade kept moving, they had to adjust the blanket, and not much progress was made. At last some of the heat left the roof, and they worked fast, making up for lost time. First Stanley, then Tom, made a trip to the end of the roof to see the woman. "She's on her back," Stanley said, adding a jest which made Tom snicker, and the older man smile tolerantly. Tom's report was that she hadn't moved, but it was a lie. He wanted to keep what he had seen to himself: he had caught her in the act of rolling down the little red pants over her hips, till they were no more than a small triangle. She was on her back, fully visible, glistening with oil.

Next morning, as soon as they came up, they went to look. She was already there, face down, arms spread out, naked except for the little red pants. She had turned brown in the night. Yesterday she was a scarlet-and-white woman, today she was a brown woman. Stanley let out a whistle. She lifted her head, startled, as if she'd been asleep, and looked straight over at him. The sun was in her eyes, she blinked and stared, then she dropped her head again. At this gesture of indifference, they all three, Stanley, Tom and old Harry, let out whistles and yells. Harry was doing it in parody of the younger men, making fun of them, but he was also angry. They were all angry because of her utter indifference to the three men watching her.

10 "Bitch," said Stanley.

"She should ask us over," said Tom, snickering.

Harry recovered himself and reminded Stanley: "If she's married, her old man wouldn't like that."

"Christ," said Stanley virtuously, "if my wife lay about like that, for everyone to see, I'd soon stop her."

Harry said, smiling: "How do you know, perhaps she's sunning herself at this very moment?"

"Not a chance, not on our roof." The safety of his wife put Stanley into a good humor, and they went to work. But today it was hotter than yesterday; and several times one or the other suggested they should tell Matthew, the foreman, and ask to leave the roof until the heat wave was over. But they didn't. There was work to be done in the basement of the big block of flats, but up here they felt free, on a different level from ordinary humanity shut in the streets or the buildings. A lot more people came out on to the roofs that day, for an hour at midday. Some married couples sat side by side in deck chairs, the women's legs stockingless and scarlet, the men in vests with reddening shoulders.

The woman stayed on her blanket, turning herself over and over. She ignored them, no matter what they did. When Harry went off to fetch more screws, Stanley said: "Come on." Her roof belonged to a different system of roofs, separated from theirs at one point by about twenty feet. It meant a scrambling climb from one level to another, edging along parapets, clinging to chimneys, while their big boots slipped and slithered, but at last they stood on a small square projecting roof looking straight down at her, close. She sat smoking, reading a book. Tom thought she looked like a poster, or a magazine cover, with the blue sky behind her and her legs stretched out. Behind her a great crane at work on a new building in Oxford Street swung its black arm across roofs in a great arc. Tom imagined himself at work on the crane, adjusting the arm to swing over and pick her up and swing her back across the sky to drop her near him.

They whistled. She looked up at them, cool and remote, then went on reading. Again, they were furious. Or, rather, Stanley was. His sun-heated face was screwed into a rage as he whistled again and again, trying to make her look up. Young Tom stopped whistling. He stood beside Stanley, excited, grinning; but he felt as if he were saying to the woman: Don't associate me with *him,* for his grin was apologetic. Last night he had thought of the unknown woman before he slept, and she had been tender with him. This tenderness he was remembering as he shifted his feet by the jeering, whistling Stanley, and watched the indifferent, healthy brown woman a few feet off, with the gap that plunged to the street between them. Tom thought it was romantic, it was like being high on two hilltops. But there was a shout from Harry, and they clambered back. Stanley's face was hard, really angry. The boy kept looking at him and wondered why he hated the woman so much, for by now he loved her.

They played their little games with the blanket, trying to trap shade to work under; but again it was not until nearly four that they could work seriously, and they were exhausted, all three of them. They were grumbling about the weather by now. Stanley was in a thoroughly bad humor. When they made their routine trip to see the woman before they packed up for the day, she was apparently asleep, face down, her back all naked save for the scarlet triangle on her buttocks. "I've got a good mind to report her to the police," said Stanley, and Harry said: "What's eating you? What harm's she doing?"

"I tell you, if she was my wife!"

"But she isn't, is she?" Tom knew that Harry, like himself, was uneasy at Stanley's reaction. He was normally a sharp young man, quick at his work, making a lot of jokes, good company.

"Perhaps it will be cooler tomorrow," said Harry.

But it wasn't; it was hotter, if anything, and the weather forecast said the good weather would last. As soon as they were on the roof, Harry went over to see if the woman was there, and Tom knew it was to prevent Stanley going, to put off his bad humor. Harry had grownup children, a boy the same age as Tom, and the youth trusted and looked up to him.

Harry came back and said: "She's not there."

"I bet her old man has put his foot down," said Stanley, and Harry and Tom caught each other's eyes and smiled behind the young married man's back.

Harry suggested they should get permission to work in the basement, and they did, that day. But before packing up Stanley said: "Let's have a breath of fresh air." Again Harry and Tom smiled at each other as they followed Stanley up to the roof, Tom in the devout conviction that he was there to protect the woman from Stanley. It was about five-thirty, and a calm, full sunlight lay over the roofs. The great crane still swung its black arm from Oxford Street to above their heads. She was not there. Then there was a flutter of white from behind a parapet, and she stood up, in a belted, white dressing-gown. She had been there all day, probably, but on a different patch of roof, to hide from them. Stanley did not whistle; he said nothing, but watched the woman bend to collect papers, books, cigarettes, then fold the blanket over her arm. Tom was thinking: If they weren't here, I'd go over and say . . . what? But he knew from his nightly dreams of her that she was kind and friendly. Perhaps she would ask him down to her flat? Perhaps . . . He stood watching her disappear down the skylight. As she went, Stanley let out a shrill derisive yell; she started, and it seemed as if she nearly fell. She clutched to save herself, they could hear things falling. She looked straight at them, angry. Harry said, facetiously: "Better be careful on those slippery ladders, love." Tom knew he said it to save her from Stanley, but she could not know it. She vanished, frowning. Tom was full of a secret delight, because he knew her anger was for the others, not for him.

"Roll on some rain," said Stanley, bitter, looking at the blue evening sky.

Next day was cloudless, and they decided to finish the work in the basement. They felt excluded, shut in the grey cement basement fitting pipes, from the holiday atmosphere in London in a heat wave. At lunchtime they came up for some air, but while the married couples, and the men in shirt-sleeves or vests, were there, she was not there, either on her usual patch of roof or where she had been yesterday. They all, even Harry, clambered about, between chimney-pots, over parapets, the hot leads stinging their fingers. There was not a sign of her. They took off their shirts and vests and exposed their chests, feeling their feet sweaty and hot. They did not mention the woman. But Tom felt alone again. Last night she had him into her flat: it was big and had fitted white carpets and a bed with a padded white leather headboard. She wore a black filmy negligée and her kindness to Tom thickened his throat as he remembered it. He felt she had betrayed him by not being there.

And again after work they climbed up, but still there was nothing to be seen of her. Stanley kept repeating that if it was as hot as this tomorrow he wasn't going to work and that's all there was to it. But they were all there next day. By ten the temperature was in the middle seventies, and it was eighty long before noon. Harry went to the foreman to say it was impossible to work on the leads in that heat; but the foreman said there was nothing else he could put them on, and they'd have to. At midday they stood, silent, watching the skylight on her roof open, and then she slowly emerged in her white gown, holding a bundle of blanket. She looked at them, gravely, then went to the part of the roof where she was hidden from them. Tom was pleased. He felt she was more his when the other men couldn't see her. They had taken off their shirts and vests, but now they put them back again, for they felt the sun bruising their flesh. "She must have the hide of a rhino," said Stanley, tugging at guttering and swearing. They stopped work, and sat in the shade, moving around behind chimney stacks. A woman came to water a yellow window box opposite them. She was middleaged, wearing a flowered summer dress. Stanley said to her: "We need a drink more than them." She smiled and said: "Better drop down to the pub quick, it'll be closing in a minute." They exchanged pleasantries, and she left them with a smile and a wave.

"Not likely Lady Godiva," said Stanley. "She can give us a bit of a chat and a smile."

"You didn't whistle at *her,*" said Tom, reproving.

"Listen to him," said Stanley, "you didn't whistle, then?"

But the boy felt as if he hadn't whistled, as if only Harry and Stanley had. He was making plans, when it was time to knock off work, to get left behind and somehow make his way over to the woman. The weather report said the hot spell was due to break, so he had to move quickly. But there was no chance of being left. The other two decided to knock off work at four, because they were exhausted. As they went down, Tom quickly climbed a parapet and hoisted himself higher by pulling his weight up a chimney. He caught a glimpse of her lying on her back, her knees up, eyes closed, a brown woman lolling in the sun. He slipped and clattered down, as Stanley looked for information: "She's gone down," he said. He felt as if he had protected her from Stanley, and that she must be grateful to him. He could feel the bond between the woman and himself.

Next day, they stood around on the landing below the roof, reluctant to climb up into the heat. The woman who had lent Harry the blanket came out and offered them a cup of tea. They accepted gratefully, and sat around Mrs. Pritchett's kitchen an hour or so, chatting. She was married to an airline pilot. A smart blonde, of about thirty, she had an eye for the handsome sharp-eyed Stanley; and the two teased each other while Harry sat in a corner, watching, indulgent, though his expression reminded Stanley that he was married. And young Tom felt envious of Stanley's ease in badinage;[1]

[1] **badinage** teasing conversation (French)

felt, too, that Stanley's getting off with Mrs. Pritchett left his romance with the woman on the roof safe and intact.

"I thought they said the heat wave'd break," said Stanley, sullen, as the time approached when they really would have to climb up into the sunlight.

"You don't like it, then?" asked Mrs. Pritchett.

"All right for some," said Stanley. "Nothing to do but lie about as if it was a beach up there. Do you ever go up?"

"Went up once," said Mrs. Pritchett. "But it's a dirty place up there, and it's too hot."

"Quite right too," said Stanley.

Then they went up, leaving the cool neat little flat and the friendly Mrs. Pritchett.

As soon as they were up they saw her. The three men looked at her, resentful at her ease in this punishing sun. Then Harry said, because of the expression on Stanley's face: "Come on, we've got to pretend to work, at least."

They had to wrench another length of guttering that ran beside a parapet out of its bed, so that they could replace it. Stanley took it in his two hands, tugged, swore, stood up. "Fuck it," he said, and sat down under a chimney. He lit a cigarette. "Fuck them," he said. "What do they think we are, lizards? I've got blisters all over my hands." Then he jumped up and climbed over the roofs and stood with his back to them. He put his fingers either side of his mouth and let out a shrill whistle. Tom and Harry squatted, not looking at each other, watching him. They could just see the woman's head, the beginnings of her brown shoulders. Stanley whistled again. Then he began stamping with his feet, and whistled and yelled and screamed at the woman, his face getting scarlet. He seemed quite mad, as he stamped and whistled, while the woman did not move, she did not move a muscle.

"Barmy," said Tom.

"Yes," said Harry, disapproving.

Suddenly the older man came to a decision. It was, Tom knew, to save some sort of scandal or real trouble over the woman. Harry stood up and began packing tools into a length of oily cloth. "Stanley," he said, commanding. At first Stanley took no notice, but Harry said: "Stanley, we're packing it in, I'll tell Matthew."

Stanley came back, cheeks mottled, eyes glaring.

"Can't go on like this," said Harry. "It'll break in a day or so. I'm going to tell Matthew we've got sunstroke, and if he doesn't like it, it's too bad." Even Harry sounded aggrieved, Tom noted. The small, competent man, the family man with his grey hair, who was never at a loss, sounded really off balance. "Come on," he said, angry. He fitted himself into the open square in the roof, and went down, watching his feet on the ladder. Then Stanley went, with not a glance at the woman. Then Tom, who, his throat beating with excitement, silently promised her on a backward glance: Wait for me, wait, I'm coming.

On the pavement Stanley said: "I'm going home." He looked white now, so perhaps he really did have sunstroke. Harry went off to find the foreman, who was at work on the plumbing of some flats down the street. Tom slipped back, not into the building they had been working on, but the building on whose roof the woman lay. He went straight up, no one stopping him. The skylight stood open, with an iron ladder leading up. He emerged on to the roof a couple of yards from her. She sat up, pushing back her black hair with both hands. The scarf across her breasts bound them tight, and brown flesh bulged around it. Her legs were brown and smooth. She stared at him in silence. The boy stood grinning, foolish, claiming the tenderness he expected from her.

"What do you want?" she asked.

"I . . . I came to . . . make your acquaintance," he stammered, grinning, pleading with her.

They looked at each other, the slight, scarlet-faced excited boy, and the serious, nearly naked woman. Then, without a word, she lay down on her brown blanket, ignoring him.

"You like the sun, do you?" he enquired of her glistening back.

Not a word. He felt panic, thinking of how she had held him in her arms, stroked his hair, brought him where he sat, lordly, in her bed, a glass of some exhilarating liquor he had never tasted in life. He felt that if he knelt down, stroked her shoulders, her hair, she would turn and clasp him in her arms.

He said: "The sun's all right for you, isn't it?"

She raised her head, set her chin on two small fists: "Go away," she said. He did not move. "Listen," she said, in a slow reasonable voice, where anger was kept in check, though with difficulty; looking at him, her face weary with anger, "if you get a kick out of seeing women in bikinis, why don't you take a sixpenny bus ride to the Lido? You'd see dozens of them, without all this mountaineering."

She hadn't understood him. He felt her unfairness pale him. He stammered: "But I like you, I've been watching you and . . ."

"Thanks," she said, and dropped her face again, turned away from him.

She lay there. He stood there. She said nothing. She had simply shut him out. He stood, saying nothing at all, for some minutes. He thought: She'll have to say something if I stay. But the minutes went past, with no sign of them in her, except in the tension of her back, her thighs, her arms—the tension of waiting for him to go.

He looked up at the sky, where the sun seemed to spin in heat; and over the roofs where he and his mates had been earlier. He could see the heat quivering where they had worked. And they expect us to work in these conditions! he thought, filled with righteous indignation. The woman hadn't moved. A bit of hot wind blew her black hair softly; it shone, and was iridescent. He remembered how he had stroked it last night.

Resentment of her at last moved him off and away down the ladder, through the building, into the street. He got drunk then, in hatred of her.

Next day when he woke the sky was grey. He looked at the wet grey and thought, vicious: Well, that's fixed you, hasn't it now? That's fixed you good and proper.

The three men were at work early on the cool leads, surrounded by damp drizzling roofs where no one came to sun themselves, black roofs, slimy with rain. Because it was cool now, they would finish the job that day, if they hurried.

[*1963*]

## ALICE MUNRO

*Alice Munro was born in 1931 in Wingham, Ontario, Canada, a relatively rural community and the sort of place in which she sets much of her fiction. She began publishing stories when she was an undergraduate at the University of Western Ontario. She left Western after two years, worked in a library and in a bookstore, then married, moved to Victoria, British Columbia, and founded a bookstore there. She continued to write while raising three children. Divorced and remarried, she often focuses on marriage or divorce, which is to say her writing concerns shifting relationships in a baffling world.*

*Her first collection of stories,* Dance of the Happy Shades *(1968), was highly successful, and she has continued to produce work (including a novel,* Lives of Girls and Women *[1971]) that has been both popular and highly esteemed.*

# *Boys and Girls*

My father was a fox farmer. That is, he raised silver foxes, in pens; and in the fall and early winter, when their fur was prime, he killed them and skinned them and sold their pelts to the Hudson's Bay Company or the Montreal Fur Traders. These companies supplied us with heroic calendars to hang, one on each side of the kitchen door. Against a background of cold blue sky and black pine forests and treacherous northern rivers, plumed adventurers planted the flags of England or of France; magnificent savages bent their backs to the portage.

For several weeks before Christmas, my father worked after supper in the cellar of our house. The cellar was whitewashed, and lit by a hundred-watt bulb over the worktable. My brother Laird and I sat on the top step and watched. My father removed the pelt inside-out from the body of the fox, which looked surprisingly small, mean and rat-like, deprived of its arrogant weight of fur. The naked, slippery bodies were collected in a sack and buried at the dump. One time the hired man, Henry Bailey, had taken a swipe at me with this sack, saying, "Christmas present!" My mother thought that was not funny. In fact she disliked the whole pelting operation—that was what the killing, skinning, and preparation of the furs was called—and wished it did not have to take place in the house. There was the smell. After the pelt had been stretched inside-out on a long board my father scraped away delicately, removing the little clotted webs of blood vessels, the bubbles of fat; the smell of blood and animal fat, with the strong primitive odor of the fox itself, penetrated all parts of the house. I found it reassuringly seasonal, like the smell of oranges and pine needles.

Henry Bailey suffered from bronchial troubles. He would cough and cough until his narrow face turned scarlet, and his light blue, derisive eyes filled up with tears; then he took the lid off the stove, and, standing well back, shot out a great clot of phlegm—hsss—straight into the heart of the flames. We admired him for this performance and for his ability to make his stomach growl at will, and for his laughter, which was full of high whistlings and gurglings and involved the whole faulty machinery of his chest. It was sometimes hard to tell what he was laughing at, and always possible that it might be us.

After we had been sent to bed we could still smell fox and still hear Henry's laugh, but these things, reminders of the warm, safe, brightly lit downstairs world, seemed lost and diminished, floating on the stale cold air upstairs. We were afraid at night in the winter. We were not afraid of *outside* though this was the time of year when snowdrifts curled around our house like sleeping whales and the wind harassed us all night, coming up from the buried fields, the frozen swamp, with its old bugbear chorus of threats and misery. We were afraid of *inside,* the room where we slept. At this time the upstairs of our house was not finished. A brick chimney went up one wall. In the middle of the floor was a square hole, with a wooden railing around it; that was where the stairs came up. On the other side of the stairwell were the things that nobody had any use for any more—a soldiery roll of linoleum, standing on end, a wicker baby carriage, a fern basket, china jugs and basins with cracks in them, a picture of the Battle of Balaclava, very sad to look at. I had told Laird, as soon as he was old enough to understand such things, that bats and skeletons lived over there; whenever a man escaped from the county jail, twenty miles away, I imagined that he had somehow let himself in the window and was hiding behind the linoleum. But we had rules to keep us safe. When the light was on, we were safe as long as we did not step off the square of worn carpet which defined our bedroom-space; when the light was off no place was safe but the beds themselves. I had to turn out the light kneeling on the end of my bed, and stretching as far as I could to reach the cord.

5 In the dark we lay on our beds, our narrow life rafts, and fixed our eyes on the faint light coming up the stairwell, and sang songs. Laird sang "Jingle Bells," which he would sing any time, whether it was Christmas or not, and I sang "Danny Boy." I loved the sound of my own voice, frail and supplicating, rising in the dark. We could make out the tall frosted shapes of the windows now, gloomy and white. When I came to the part, ***When I am dead, as dead I well may be***—a fit of shivering caused not by the cold sheets but by pleasurable emotion almost silenced me. ***You'll kneel and say, an Ave there about me***—What was an Ave? Every day I forgot to find out.

Laird went straight from singing to sleep. I could hear his long, satisfied, bubbly breaths. Now for the time that remained to me, the most perfectly private and perhaps the best time of the whole day, I arranged myself tightly under the covers and went on with one of the stories I was telling myself from night to night. These stories were about myself, when I had grown a little older; they took place in a world that was recognizably mine, yet one that presented opportunities for courage, boldness and self-sacrifice, as mine never did. I rescued people from a bombed building (it discouraged me that the real war had gone on so far away from Jubilee). I shot two rabid wolves who were menacing the schoolyard (the teachers cowered terrified at my back). I rode a fine horse spiritedly down the main street of Jubilee, acknowledging the townspeople's gratitude for some yet-to-be-worked-out piece of heroism (nobody ever rode a horse there, except

King Billy in the Orangemen's Day[1] parade). There was always riding and shooting in these stories, though I had only been on a horse twice—bareback because we did not own a saddle—and the second time I had slid right around and dropped under the horse's feet; it had stepped placidly over me. I really was learning to shoot, but could not hit anything yet, not even tin cans on fence posts.

Alive, the foxes inhabited a world my father made for them. It was surrounded by a high guard fence, like a medieval town, with a gate that was padlocked at night. Along the streets of this town were ranged large, sturdy pens. Each of them had a real door that a man could go through, a wooden ramp along the wire, for the foxes to run up and down on, and a kennel—something like a clothes chest with airholes—where they slept and stayed in winter and had their young. There were feeding and watering dishes attached to the wire in such a way that they could be emptied and cleaned from the outside. The dishes were made of old tin cans, and the ramps and kennels of odds and ends of old lumber. Everything was tidy and ingenious; my father was tirelessly inventive and his favorite book in the world was Robinson Crusoe. He had fitted a tin drum on a wheelbarrow, for bringing water down to the pens. This was my job in summer, when the foxes had to have water twice a day. Between nine and ten o'clock in the morning, and again after supper. I filled the drum at the pump and trundled it down through the barnyard to the pens, where I parked it, and filled my watering can and went along the streets. Laird came too, with his little cream and green gardening can, filled too full and knocking against his legs and slopping water on his canvas shoes. I had the real watering can, my father's, though I could only carry it three-quarters full.

The foxes all had names, which were printed on a tin plate and hung beside their doors. They were not named when they were born, but when they survived the first year's pelting and were added to the breeding stock. Those my father had named were called names like Prince, Bob, Wally and Betty. Those I had named were called Star or Turk, or Maureen or Diana. Laird named one Maud after a hired girl we had when he was little, one Harold after a boy at school, and one Mexico, he did not say why.

Naming them did not make pets out of them, or anything like it. Nobody but my father ever went into the pens, and he had twice had blood-poisoning from bites. When I was bringing them their water they prowled up and down on the paths they had made inside their pens, barking seldom—they saved that for nighttime, when they might get up a chorus of community frenzy—but always watching me, their eyes burning, clear gold, in their pointed, malevolent faces. They were beautiful for their delicate legs and heavy, aristocratic tails and the bright fur sprinkled on dark down their backs—which gave them their name—but especially for their faces, drawn exquisitely sharp in pure hostility, and their golden eyes.

10 Besides carrying water I helped my father when he cut the long grass, and the lamb's quarter and flowering money-musk, that grew between the pens. He cut with the scythe and I raked into piles. Then he took a pitch-

[1]**Orangemen's Day** The Orange Society is named for William of Orange, who, as King William III of England, defeated James II of England at the Battle of the Boyne on 12 July 1689. It sponsors an annual procession on 12 July.

fork and threw fresh-cut grass all over the top of the pens to keep the foxes cooler and shade their coats, which were browned by too much sun. My father did not talk to me unless it was about the job we were doing. In this he was quite different from my mother, who, if she was feeling cheerful, would tell me all sorts of things—the name of a dog she had had when she was a little girl, the names of boys she had gone out with later on when she was grown up, and what certain dresses of hers had looked like—she could not imagine now what had become of them. Whatever thoughts and stories my father had were private, and I was shy of him and would never ask him questions. Nevertheless I worked willingly under his eyes, and with a feeling of pride. One time a feed salesman came down into the pens to talk to him and my father said, "Like to have you meet my new hired hand." I turned away and raked furiously, red in the face with pleasure.

"Could of fooled me," said the salesman. "I thought it was only a girl."

After the grass was cut, it seemed suddenly much later in the year. I walked on stubble in the earlier evening, aware of the reddening skies, the entering silences, of fall. When I wheeled the tank out of the gate and put the padlock on, it was almost dark. One night at this time I saw my mother and father standing talking on the little rise of ground we called the gangway, in front of the barn. My father had just come from the meathouse; he had his stiff bloody apron on, and a pail of cut-up meat in his hand.

It was an odd thing to see my mother down at the barn. She did not often come out of the house unless it was to do something—hang out the wash or dig potatoes in the garden. She looked out of place, with her bare lumpy legs, not touched by the sun, her apron still on and damp across the stomach from the supper dishes. Her hair was tied up in a kerchief, wisps of it falling out. She would tie her hair up like this in the morning, saying she did not have time to do it properly, and it would stay tied up all day. It was true, too; she really did not have time. These days our back porch was piled with baskets of peaches and grapes and pears, bought in town, and onions and tomatoes and cucumbers grown at home, all waiting to be made into jelly and jam and preserves, pickles and chili sauce. In the kitchen there was a fire in the stove all day, jars clinked in boiling water, sometimes a cheesecloth bag was strung on a pole between two chairs straining blue-back grape pulp for jelly. I was given jobs to do and I would sit at the table peeling peaches that had been soaked in hot water, or cutting up onions, my eyes smarting and streaming. As soon as I was done I ran out of the house, trying to get out of earshot before my mother thought of what she wanted me to do next. I hated the hot dark kitchen in summer, the green blinds and the flypapers, the same old oilcloth table and wavy mirror and bumpy linoleum. My mother was too tired and preoccupied to talk to me, she had no heart to tell about the Normal School Graduation Dance; sweat trickled over her face and she was always counting under her breath, pointing at jars, dumping cups of sugar. It seemed to me that work in the house was endless, dreary and peculiarly depressing; work done out of doors, and in my father's service, was ritualistically important.

I wheeled the tank up to the barn, where it was kept, and I heard my mother saying, "Wait till Laird gets a little bigger, then you'll have a real help."

15 What my father said I did not hear. I was pleased by the way he stood listening, politely as he would to a salesman or a stranger, but with an air of

wanting to get on with his real work. I felt my mother had no business down here and I wanted him to feel the same way. What did she mean about Laird? He was no help to anybody. Where was he now? Swinging himself sick on the swing, going around in circles, or trying to catch caterpillars. He never once stayed with me till I was finished.

"And then I can use her more in the house," I heard my mother say. She had a dead-quiet, regretful way of talking about me that always made me uneasy. "I just get my back turned and she runs off. It's not like I had a girl in the family at all."

I went and sat on a feed bag in the corner of the barn, not wanting to appear when this conversation was going on. My mother, I felt, was not to be trusted. She was kinder than my father and more easily fooled, but you could not depend on her, and the real reasons for the things she said and did were not to be known. She loved me, and she sat up late at night making a dress of the difficult style I wanted, for me to wear when school started, but she was also my enemy. She was always plotting. She was plotting now to get me to stay in the house more, although she knew I hated it (*because* she knew I hated it) and keep me from working for my father. It seemed to me she would do this simply out of perversity, and to try her power. It did not occur to me that she could be lonely, or jealous. No grown-up could be; they were too fortunate. I sat and kicked my heels monotonously against a feed bag, raising dust, and did not come out till she was gone.

At any rate, I did not expect my father to pay any attention to what she said. Who could imagine Laird doing my work—Laird remembering the padlock and cleaning out the watering dishes with a leaf on the end of a stick, or even wheeling the tank without it tumbling over? It showed how little my mother knew about the way things really were.

I have forgotten to say what the foxes were fed. My father's bloody apron reminded me. They were fed horsemeat. At this time most farmers still kept horses, and when a horse got too old to work, or broke a leg or got down and would not get up, as they sometimes did, the owner would call my father, and he and Henry went out to the farm in the truck. Usually they shot and butchered the horse there, paying the farmer from five to twelve dollars. If they had already too much meat on hand, they would bring the horse back alive, and keep it for a few days or weeks in our stable, until the meat was needed. After the war the farmers were buying tractors and gradually getting rid of horses altogether, so it sometimes happened that we got a good healthy horse, that there was just no use for any more. If this happened in the winter we might keep the horse in our stable till spring, for we had plenty of hay and if there was a lot of snow—and the plow did not always get our road cleared—it was convenient to be able to go to town with a horse and cutter.[2]

20 The winter I was eleven years old we had two horses in the stable. We did not know what names they had had before, so we called them Mack and Flora. Mack was an old black workhorse, sooty and indifferent. Flora was a sorrel mare, a driver. We took them both out in the cutter. Mack was slow and easy to handle. Flora was given to fits of violent alarm, veering at cars

[2] **cutter** a small sleigh

and even at other horses, but we loved her speed and high-stepping, her general air of gallantry and abandon. On Saturdays we went down to the stable and as soon as we opened the door on its cozy, animal-smelling darkness Flora threw up her head, rolled her eyes, whinnied despairingly and pulled herself through a crisis of nerves on the spot. It was not safe to go into her stall; she would kick.

This winter also I began to hear a great deal more on the theme my mother had sounded when she had been talking in front of the barn. I no longer felt safe. It seemed that in the minds of the people around me there was a steady undercurrent of thought, not to be deflected, on this one subject. The word *girl* had formerly seemed to me innocent and unburdened, like the word *child;* now it appeared that it was no such thing. A girl was not, as I had supposed, simply what I was; it was what I had to become. It was a definition, always touched with emphasis, with reproach and disappointment. Also it was a joke on me. Once Laird and I were fighting, and for the first time ever I had to use all my strength against him; even so, he caught and pinned my arm for a moment, really hurting me. Henry saw this, and laughed, saying, "Oh, that there Laird's gonna show you, one of these days!" Laird was getting a lot bigger. But I was getting bigger too.

My grandmother came to stay with us for a few weeks and I heard other things. "Girls don't slam doors like that." "Girls keep their knees together when they sit down." And worse still, when I asked some questions, "That's none of girls' business." I continued to slam the doors and sit as awkwardly as possible, thinking that by such measures I kept myself free.

When spring came, the horses were let out in the barnyard. Mack stood against the barn wall trying to scratch his neck and haunches, but Flora trotted up and down and reared at the fences, clattering her hooves against the rails. Snow drifts dwindled quickly, revealing the hard gray and brown earth, the familiar rise and fall of the ground, plain and bare after the fantastic landscape of winter. There was a great feeling of opening-out, of release. We just wore rubbers now, over our shoes; our feet felt ridiculously light. One Saturday we went to the stable and found all the doors open, letting in the unaccustomed sunlight and fresh air. Henry was there, just idling around looking at his collection of calendars which were tacked up behind the stalls in a part of the stable my mother had probably never seen.

"Come to say goodbye to your old friend Mack?" Henry said. "Here, you give him a taste of oats." He poured some oats into Laird's cupped hands and Laird went to feed Mack. Mack's teeth were in bad shape. He ate very slowly, patiently shifting the oats around in his mouth, trying to find a stump of a molar to grind it on. "Poor old Mack," said Henry mournfully. "When a horse's teeth's gone, he's gone. That's about the way."

"Are you going to shoot him today?" I said. Mack and Flora had been in the stable so long I had almost forgotten they were going to be shot.

Henry didn't answer me. Instead he started to sing in a high, trembly, mocking-sorrowful voice. *Oh, there's no more work, for poor Uncle Ned, he's gone where the good darkies go.* Mack's thick, blackish tongue worked diligently at Laird's hand. I went out before the song was ended and sat down on the gangway.

I had never seen them shoot a horse, but I knew where it was done. Last summer Laird and I had come upon a horse's entrails before they were buried. We had thought it was a big black snake, coiled up in the sun. That was around in the field that ran up beside the barn. I thought that if we went inside the barn, and found a wide crack or a knothole to look through, we would be able to see them do it. It was not something I wanted to see; just the same, if a thing really happened, it was better to see, and know.

My father came down from the house, carrying a gun.

"What are you doing here?" he said.

30 "Nothing."

"Go on up and play around the house."

He sent Laird out of the stable. I said to Laird, "Do you want to see them shoot Mack?" and without waiting for an answer led him around to the front door of the barn, opened it carefully, and went in. "Be quiet or they'll hear us." I said. We could hear Henry and my father talking in the stable; then the heavy, shuffling steps of Mack being backed out of his stall.

In the loft it was cold and dark. Thin crisscrossed beams of sunlight fell through the cracks. The hay was low. It was rolling country, hills and hollows, slipping under our feet. About four feet up was a beam going around the walls. We piled hay up in one corner and I boosted Laird up and hoisted myself. The beam was not very wide; we crept along it with our hands flat on the barn walls. There were plenty of knotholes, and I found one that gave me the view I wanted—a corner of the barnyard, the gate, part of the field. Laird did not have a knothole and began to complain.

I showed him a widened crack between two boards. "Be quiet and wait. If they hear you you'll get us in trouble."

35 My father came in sight carrying the gun. Henry was leading Mack by the halter. He dropped it and took out his cigarette papers and tobacco; he rolled cigarettes for my father and himself. While this was going on Mack nosed around in the old, dead grass along the fence. Then my father opened the gate and they took Mack through. Henry led Mack way from the path to a patch of ground and they talked together, not loud enough for us to hear. Mack again began searching for a mouthful of fresh grass, which was not to be found. My father walked away in a straight line, and stopped short at a distance which seemed to suit him. Henry was walking away from Mack too, but sideways, still negligently holding on to the halter. My father raised the gun and Mack looked up as if he had noticed something and my father shot him.

Mack did not collapse at once but swayed, lurched sideways and fell, first on his side; then he rolled over on his back and, amazingly, kicked his legs for a few seconds in the air. At this Henry laughed, as if Mack had done a trick for him. Laird, who had drawn a long, groaning breath of surprise when the shot was fired, said out loud, "He's not dead." And it seemed to me it might be true. But his legs stopped, he rolled on his side again, his muscles quivered and sank. The two men walked over and looked at him in a businesslike way; they bent down and examined his forehead where the bullet had gone in, and now I saw his blood on the brown grass.

"Now they just skin him and cut him up," I said. "Let's go." My legs were a little shaky and I jumped gratefully down into the hay. "Now you've seen how they shoot a horse," I said in a congratulatory way, as if I had seen it many times before. "Let's see if any barn cat's had kittens in the hay." Laird jumped. He seemed young and obedient again. Suddenly I remembered how, when he was little, I had brought him into the barn and told him to climb the ladder to the top beam. That was in the spring, too, when the hay was low. I had done it out of a need for excitement, a desire for something to happen so that I could tell about it. He was wearing a little bulky brown and white checked coat, made down from one of mine. He went all the way up just as I told him, and sat down on the top beam with the hay far below him on one side, and the barn floor and some old machinery on the other. Then I ran screaming to my father. "Laird's up on the top beam!" My father came, my mother came, my father went up the ladder talking very quietly and brought Laird down under his arm, at which my mother leaned against the ladder and began to cry. They said to me, "Why weren't you watching him?" but nobody ever knew the truth. Laird did not know enough to tell. But whenever I saw the brown and white checked coat hanging in the closet, or at the bottom of the rag bag, which was where it ended up, I felt a weight in my stomach, the sadness of unexorcised guilt.

I looked at Laird, who did not even remember this, and I did not like the look on this thin, winter-paled face. His expression was not frightened or upset, but remote, concentrating. "Listen," I said, in an unusually bright and friendly voice, "you aren't going to tell, are you?"

"No," he said absently.

"Promise."

"Promise," he said. I grabbed the hand behind his back to make sure he was not crossing his fingers. Even so, he might have a nightmare; it might come out that way. I decided I had better work hard to get all thoughts of what he had seen out of his mind—which, it seemed to me, could not hold very many things at a time. I got some money I had saved and that afternoon we went into Jubilee and saw a show with Judy Canova,[3] at which we both laughed a great deal. After that I thought it would be all right.

Two weeks later I knew they were going to shoot Flora. I knew from the night before, when I heard my mother ask if the hay was holding out all right, and my father said, "Well, after tomorrow there'll just be the cow, and we should be able to put her out to grass in another week." So I knew it was Flora's turn in the morning.

This time I didn't think of watching it. That was something to see just one time. I had not thought about it very often since, but sometimes when I was busy, working at school, or standing in front of the mirror combing my hair and wondering if I would be pretty when I grew up, the whole scene would flash into my mind: I would see the easy, practiced way my father raised the gun, and hear Henry laughing when Mack kicked his legs in the air. I did not have any great feeling of horror and opposition, such as a city child might have had; I was too used to seeing the death of animals as a necessity by which we lived. Yet I felt a little ashamed, and there was a new wariness, a sense of holding-off, in my attitude to my father and his work.

It was a fine day, and we were going around the yard picking up tree branches that had been torn off in winter storms. This was something we had been told to do, and also we wanted to use them to make a teepee. We heard Flora whinny, and then my father's voice and Henry's shouting, and we ran down to the barnyard to see what was going on.

The stable door was open. Henry had just brought Flora out, and she

[3]**Judy Canova** American comedian, popular in films of the 1940s

had broken away from him. She was running free in the barnyard, from one end to the other. We climbed on the fence. It was exciting to see her running, whinnying, going up on her hind legs, prancing and threatening like a horse in a Western movie, an unbroken ranch horse, though she was just an old driver, an old sorrel mare. My father and Henry ran after her and tried to grab the dangling halter. They tried to work her into a corner, and they had almost succeeded when she made a run between them, wild-eyed, and disappeared round the corner of the barn. We heard the rails clatter down as she got over the fence, and Henry yelled. "She's into the field now!"

That meant she was in the long L-shaped field that ran up by the house. If she got around the center, heading towards the lane, the gate was open; the truck had been driven into the field this morning. My father shouted to me, because I was on the other side of the fence, nearest the lane, "Go shut the gate!"

I could run very fast. I ran across the garden, past the tree where our swing was hung, and jumped across a ditch into the lane. There was the open gate. She had not got out, I could not see her up on the road; she must have run to the other end of the field. The gate was heavy. I lifted it out of the gravel and carried it across the roadway. I had it halfway across when she came in sight, galloping straight toward me. There was just time to get the chain on. Laird came scrambling through the ditch to help me.

Instead of shutting the gate, I opened it as wide as I could. I did not make any decision to do this, it was just what I did. Flora never slowed down; she galloped straight past me, and Laird jumped up and down, yelling, "Shut it, shut it!" even after it was too late. My father and Henry appeared in the field a moment too late to see what I had done. They only saw Flora heading for the township road. They would think I had not got there in time.

They did not waste any time asking about it. They went back to the barn and got the gun and the knives they used, and put these in the truck; then they turned the truck around and came bouncing up the field toward us. Laird called to them, "Let me go too, let me go too!" and Henry stopped the truck and they took him in. I shut the gate after they were all gone.

I supposed Laird would tell. I wondered what would happen to me. I had never disobeyed my father before, and I could not understand why I had done it. Flora would not really get away. They would catch up with her in the truck. Or if they did not catch her this morning somebody would see her and telephone us this afternoon or tomorrow. There was no wild country here for her to run to, only farms. What was more, my father had paid for her, we needed the meat to feed the foxes, we needed the foxes to make our living. All I had done was make more work for my father who worked hard enough already. And when my father found out about it he was not going to trust me any more; he would know that I was not entirely on his side. I was on Flora's side, and that made me no use to anybody, not even to her. Just the same, I did not regret it; when she came running at me and I held the gate open, that was the only thing I could do.

I went back to the house, and my mother said, "What's all the commotion?" I told her that Flora had kicked down the fence and got away. "Your poor father," she said, "now he'll have to go chasing over the countryside.

Well, there isn't any use planning dinner before one." She put up the ironing board. I wanted to tell her, but thought better of it and went upstairs and sat on my bed.

Lately I had been trying to make my part of the room fancy, spreading the bed with old lace curtains, and fixing myself a dressing table with some leftovers of cretonne for a skirt. I planned to put up some kind of barricade between my bed and Laird's, to keep my section separate from his. In the sunlight, the lace curtains were just dusty rags. We did not sing at night any more. One night when I was singing Laird said, "You sound silly," and I went right on but the next night I did not start. There was not so much need to anyway, we were no longer afraid. We knew it was just old furniture over there, old jumble and confusion. We did not keep to the rules. I still stayed awake after Laird was asleep and told myself stories, but even in these stories something different was happening, mysterious alterations took place. A story might start off in the old way, with a spectacular danger, a fire or wild animals, and for a while I might rescue people; then things would change around, and instead, somebody would be rescuing me. It might be a boy from our class at school, or even Mr. Campbell, our teacher, who tickled girls under the arms. And at this point the story concerned itself at great length with what I looked like—how long my hair was, and what kind of dress I had on; by the time I had these details worked out the real excitement of the story was lost.

It was later than one o'clock when the truck came back. The tarpaulin was over the back, which meant there was meat in it. My mother had to heat dinner up all over again. Henry and my father had changed from their bloody overalls into ordinary working overalls in the barn, and they washed arms and necks and faces at the sink, and splashed water on their hair and combed it. Laird lifted his arm to show off a streak of blood. "We shot old Flora," he said, "and cut her up in fifty pieces."

"Well I don't want to hear about it," my mother said. "And don't come to my table like that."

My father made him go and wash the blood off.

We sat down and my father said grace and Henry pasted his chewing gum on the end of his fork, the way he always did; when he took it off he would have us admire the pattern. We began to pass the bowls of steaming, overcooked vegetables. Laird looked across the table at me and said proudly, distinctly, "Anyway it was her fault Flora got away."

"What?" my father said.

"She could of shut the gate and she didn't. She just open' it up and Flora run out."

"Is that right?" my father said.

Everybody at the table was looking at me. I nodded, swallowing food with great difficulty. To my shame, tears flooded my eyes.

My father made a curt sound of disgust. "What did you do that for?"

I did not answer. I put down my fork and waited to be sent from the table, still not looking up.

But this did not happen. For some time nobody said anything, then Laird said matter-of-factly, "She's crying."

"Never mind," my father said. He spoke with resignation, even good humor, the words which absolved and dismissed me for good. "She's only a girl," he said.

I didn't protest that, even in my heart. Maybe it was true.

[*1968*]

## MARGARET ATWOOD

***Margaret Atwood was born in 1939 in Ottawa, Ontario, Canada. She did her undergraduate work at Victoria College and graduate work at Radcliffe College. She has worked as a cashier, waitress, film writer, and teacher, but she began writing as a child and established herself as a writer in the middle 1960s. In addition to films, stories, writing novels, poetry, and criticism, she has edited anthologies of Canadian literature. Atwood's range is wide, but she is especially esteemed for her comic work.***

# *Rape Fantasies*

The way they're going on about it in the magazines you'd think it was just invented, and not only that but it's something terrific, like a vaccine for cancer. They put it in capital letters on the front cover, and inside they have these questionnaires like the ones they used to have about whether you were a good enough wife or an endomorph or an ectomorph,[1] remember that? with the scoring upside down on page 73, and then these numbered do-it-yourself dealies, you know? RAPE, TEN THINGS TO DO ABOUT IT, like it was ten new hairdos or something. I mean, what's so new about it?

So at work they all have to talk about it because no matter what magazine you open, there it is, staring you right between the eyes, and they're beginning to have it on the television, too. Personally I'd prefer a June Allyson[2] movie anytime but they don't make them anymore and they don't even have them that much on the Late Show. For instance, day before yesterday, that would be Wednesday, thank god it's Friday as they say, we were sitting around in the women's lunch room—the *lunch* room, I mean you'd think you could get some peace and quiet in there—and Chrissy closes up the magazine she's been reading and says, "How about it, girls, do you have rape fantasies?"

The four of us were having our game of bridge the way we always do, and I had a bare twelve points counting the singleton with not that much of a bid in anything. So I said one club, hoping Sondra would remember about the one club convention, because the time before when I used that she thought I really meant clubs and she bid us up to three, and all I had was four little ones with nothing higher than a six, and we went down two and

[1]**endomorph, ectomorph** body-types. An endomorph possesses a short, wide body; an ectomorph, a tall, narrow body.

[2]**June Allyson** actress who portrayed the friendly, healthy girl in musical-comedy films of the 1940s and 1950s

on top of that we were vulnerable. She is not the world's best bridge player. I mean, neither am I but there's a limit.

Darlene passed but the damage was done, Sondra's head went round like it was on ball bearings and she said, "*What* fantasies?"

5 "Rape fantasies," Chrissy said. She's a receptionist and she looks like one; she's pretty but cool as a cucumber, like she's been painted all over with nail polish, if you know what I mean. Varnished. "It says here all women have rape fantasies."

"For Chrissake, I'm eating an egg sandwich," I said, "and I bid one club and Darlene passed."

"You mean, like some guy jumping you in an alley or something," Sondra said. She was eating her lunch, we all eat our lunches during the game, and she bit into a piece of that celery she always brings and started to chew away on it with this thoughtful expression in her eyes and I knew we might as well pack it in as far as the game was concerned.

"Yeah, sort of like that," Chrissy said. She was blushing a little, you could see it even under her makeup.

"I don't think you should go out alone at night," Darlene said, "you put yourself in a position," and I may have been mistaken but she was looking at me. She's the oldest, she's forty-one though you wouldn't know it and neither does she, but I looked it up in the employees' file. I like to guess a person's age and then look it up to see if I'm right. I let myself have an extra pack of cigarettes if I am, though I'm trying to cut down. I figure it's harmless as long as you don't tell. I mean, not everyone has access to that file, it's more or less confidential. But it's all right if I tell you, I don't expect you'll ever meet her, though you never know, it's a small world. Anyway.

10 "For *heaven's* sake, it's only *Toronto,*" Greta said. She worked in Detroit for three years and she never lets you forget it, it's like she thinks she's a war hero or something, we should all admire her just for the fact that she's still walking this earth, though she was really living in Windsor the whole time, she just worked in Detroit. Which for me doesn't really count. It's where you sleep, right?

"Well, do you?" Chrissy said. She was obviously trying to tell us about hers but she wasn't about to go first, she's cautious, that one.

"I certainly don't," Darlene said, and she wrinkled up her nose, like this, and I had to laugh. "I think it's disgusting." She's divorced, I read that in the file too, she never talks about it. It must've been years ago anyway. She got up and went over to the coffee machine and turned her back on us as though she wasn't going to have anything more to do with it.

"Well," Greta said. I could see it was going to be between her and Chrissy. They're both blondes, I don't mean that in a bitchy way but they do try to outdress each other. Greta would like to get out of Filing, she'd like to be a receptionist too so she could meet more people. You don't meet much of anyone in Filing except other people in Filing. Me, I don't mind it so much, I have outside interests.

"Well," Greta said, "I sometimes think about, you know my apartment? It's got this little balcony, I like to sit out there in the summer and I have a few plants out there. I never bother that much about locking the door to the balcony, it's one of those sliding glass ones, I'm on the eighteenth floor for heaven's sake, I've got a good view of the lake and the CN Tower and all. But I'm sitting around one night in my housecoat, watching TV with my shoes off, you know how you do, and I see this guy's feet, coming down past the window, and the next thing you know he's standing on the balcony, he's let himself down by a rope with a hook on the end of it from the floor above, that's the nineteenth, and before I can even get up off the chesterfield he's inside the apartment. He's all dressed in black with black gloves on"—I knew right away what show she got the black gloves off because I saw the same one—"and then he, well, you know."

15 "You know what?" Chrissy said, but Greta said, "And afterwards he tells me that he goes all over the outside of the apartment building like that, from one floor to another, with his rope and his hook . . . and then he goes out to the balcony and tosses his rope, and he climbs up it and disappears."

"Just like Tarzan," I said, but nobody laughed.

"Is that all?" Chrissy said. "Don't you ever think about, well, I think about being in the bathtub, with no clothes on . . ."

"So who takes a bath in their clothes?" I said, you have to admit it's stupid when you come to think of it, but she just went on, ". . . with lots of bubbles, what I use is Vitabath, it's more expensive but it's so relaxing, and my hair pinned up, and the door opens and this fellow's standing there . . ."

"How'd he get in?" Greta said.

20 "Oh, I don't know, through a window or something. Well, I can't very well get out of the bathtub, the bathroom's too small and besides he's blocking the doorway, so I just lie there, and he starts to very slowly take his own clothes off, and then he gets into the bathtub with me."

"Don't you scream or anything?" said Darlene. She'd come back with her cup of coffee, she was getting really interested. "I'd scream like bloody murder."

"Who'd hear me?" Chrissy said. "Besides, all the articles say it's better not to resist, that way you don't get hurt."

"Anyway you might get bubbles up your nose," I said, "from the deep breathing," and I swear all four of them looked at me like I was in bad taste, like I'd insulted the Virgin Mary or something. I mean, I don't see what's wrong with a little joke now and then. Life's too short, right?

"Listen," I said, "those aren't *rape* fantasies. I mean, you aren't getting *raped,* it's just some guy you haven't met formally who happens to be more attractive than Derek Cummins"—he's the Assistant Manager, he wears elevator shoes or at any rate they have these thick soles and he has this funny way of talking, we call him Derek Duck—"and you have a good time. Rape is when they've got a knife or something and you don't want to."

25 "So what about you, Estelle," Chrissy said, she was miffed because I laughed at her fantasy, she thought I was putting her down. Sondra was miffed too, by this time she'd finished her celery and she wanted to tell about hers, but she hadn't got in fast enough.

"All right, let me tell you one," I said. "I'm walking down this dark street at night and this fellow comes up and grabs my arm. Now it so happens that I have a plastic lemon in my purse, you know how it always says you should carry a plastic lemon in your purse? I don't really do it, I tried it once but the darn thing leaked all over my checkbook, but in this fantasy I have one, and I say to him, 'You're intending to rape me, right?' and he nods, so I open my purse to get the plastic lemon, and I can't find it! My purse is full of all this junk, Kleenex and cigarettes and my change purse and my lipstick and my driver's license, you know the kind of stuff; so I ask him to hold out his hands, like this, and I pile all this junk into them and down at the bottom there's the plastic lemon, and I can't get the top off. So I hand it to him and he's very obliging, he twists the top off and hands it back to me, and I squirt him in the eye."

I hope you don't think that's too vicious. Come to think of it, it is a bit mean, especially when he was so polite and all.

"*That's* your rape fantasy?" Chrissy says. "I don't believe it."

"She's a card," Darlene says, she and I are the ones that've been here the longest and she never will forget the time I got drunk at the office party and insisted I was going to dance under the table instead of on top of it, I did a sort of Cossack number but then I hit my head on the bottom of the table—actually it was a desk—when I went to get up, and I knocked myself out cold. She's decided that's the mark of an original mind and she tells everyone new about it and I'm not sure that's fair. Though I did do it.

"I'm being totally honest," I say. I always am and they know it. There's no point in being anything else, is the way I look at it, and sooner or later the truth will come out so you might as well not waste the time, right? "You should hear the one about the Easy-Off Oven Cleaner."

But that was the end of the lunch hour, with one bridge game short to hell, and the next day we spent most of the time arguing over whether to start a new game or play out the hands we had left over from the day before, so Sondra never did get a chance to tell about her rape fantasy.

It started me thinking though, about my own rape fantasies. Maybe I'm abnormal or something, I mean I have fantasies about handsome strangers coming in through the window too, like Mr. Clean, I wish one would, please god somebody without flat feet and big sweat marks on his shirt, and over five feet five, believe me being tall is a handicap though it's getting better, tall guys are starting to like someone whose nose reaches higher than their belly button. But if you're being totally honest you can't count those as rape fantasies. In a real rape fantasy, what you should feel is this anxiety, like when you think about your apartment building catching on fire and whether you should use the elevator or the stairs or maybe just stick your head under a wet towel, and you try to remember everything you've read about what to do but you can't decide.

For instance, I'm walking along this dark street at night and this short, ugly fellow comes up and grabs my arm, and not only is he ugly, you know, with a sort of puffy nothing face, like those fellows you have to talk to in the bank when your account's overdrawn—of course I don't mean they're all like that—but he's absolutely covered in pimples. So he gets me pinned against the wall, he's short but he's heavy, and he starts to undo himself and the zipper gets stuck. I mean, one of the most significant moments in a girl's life, it's almost like getting married or having a baby or something, and he sticks the zipper.

So I say, kind of disgusted, "Oh for Chrissake," and he starts to cry. He tells me he's never been able to get anything right in his entire life, and this is the last straw, he's going to jump off a bridge.

35 "Look," I say, I feel so sorry for him, in my rape fantasies I always end up feeling sorry for the guy, I mean there has to be something *wrong* with them, if it was Clint Eastwood it'd be different but worse luck it never is. I was the kind of little girl who buried dead robins, know what I mean? It used to drive my mother nuts, she didn't like me touching them, because of the germs I guess. So I say, "Listen, I know how you feel. You really should do something about those pimples, if you got rid of them you'd be quite good looking, honest; then you wouldn't have to go around doing stuff like this. I had them myself once," I say, to comfort him, but in fact I did, and it ends up I give him the name of my old dermatologist, the one I had in high school, that was back in Leamington, except I used to go to St. Catharine's for the dermatologist. I'm telling you, I was really lonely when I first came here; I thought it was going to be such a big adventure and all, but it's a lot harder to meet people in a city. But I guess it's different for a guy.

Or I'm lying in bed with this terrible cold, my face is all swollen up, my eyes are red and my nose is dripping like a leaky tap, and this fellow comes in through the window and *he* has a terrible cold too, it's a new kind of flu that's been going around. So he says, "I'b goig do rabe you"—I hope you don't mind me holding my nose like this but that's the way I imagine it—and he lets out this terrific sneeze, which slows him down a bit, also I'm no object of beauty myself, you'd have to be some kind of pervert to want to rape someone with a cold like mine, it'd be like raping a bottle of LePage's mucilage the way my nose is running. He's looking wildly around the room, and I realize it's because he doesn't have a piece of Kleenex! "Id's ride here," I say, and I pass him the Kleenex, god knows why he even bothered to get out of bed, you'd think if you were going to go around climbing in windows you'd wait till you were healthier, right? I mean, that takes a certain amount of energy. So I ask him why doesn't he let me fix him a Neo-Citran and scotch, that's what I always take, you still have the cold but you don't feel it, so I do and we end up watching the Late Show together. I mean, they aren't all sex maniacs, the rest of the time they must lead a normal life. I figure they enjoy watching the Late Show just like anybody else.

I do have a scarier one though . . . where the fellow says he's hearing angel voices that're telling him he's got to kill me, you know, you read about things like that all the time in the papers. In this one I'm not in the apartment where I live now, I'm back in my mother's house in Leamington and the fellow's been hiding in the cellar, he grabs my arm when I go downstairs to get a jar of jam and he's got hold of the axe too, out of the garage, that one is really scary. I mean, what do you say to a nut like that?

So I start to shake but after a minute I get control of myself and I say, is he sure the angel voices have got the right person, because I hear the same angel voices and they've been telling me for some time that I'm going to give birth to the reincarnation of St. Anne who in turn has the Virgin Mary and right after that comes Jesus Christ and the end of the world, and he wouldn't want to interfere with that, would he? So he gets confused and listens some more, and then he asks for a sign and I show him my vaccination mark, you can see it's sort of an odd-shaped one, it got infected because I scratched the top off and that does it, he apologizes and climbs out the coal chute again, which is how he got in in the first place, and I say to myself there's some advantage in having been brought up a Catholic even though I haven't been to church since they changed the service into English, it just isn't the same, you might as well be a Protestant. I must write to Mother and tell her to nail up that coal chute, it always has bothered me. Funny, I couldn't tell you at all what this man looks like but I know exactly what kind of shoes he's wearing, because that's the last I see of him, his shoes going up the coal chute, and they're the old-fashioned kind that lace up the ankles, even though he's a young fellow. That's strange, isn't it?

Let me tell you though I really sweat until I see him safely out of there and I go upstairs right away and make myself a cup of tea. I don't think about that one much. My mother always said you shouldn't dwell on unpleasant things and I generally agree with that, I mean, dwelling on them doesn't make them go away. Though not dwelling on them doesn't make them go away either, when you come to think of it.

40 Sometimes I have these short ones where the fellow grabs my arm but I'm really a Kung-Fu expert, can you believe it, in real life I'm sure it would just be a conk on the head and that's that, like getting your tonsils out, you'd wake up and it would be all over except for the sore places, and you'd be lucky if your neck wasn't broken or something, I could never even hit the volleyball in gym and a volleyball is fairly large, you know?—and I just go *zap* with my fingers into his eyes and that's it, he falls over, or I flip him against a wall or something. But I could never really stick my fingers in anyone's eyes, could you? It would feel like hot jello and I don't even like cold jello, just thinking about it gives me the creeps. I feel a bit guilty about that one, I mean how would you like walking around knowing someone's been blinded for life because of you?

But maybe it's different for a guy.

The most touching one I have is when the fellow grabs my arm and I say, sad and kind of dignified, "You'd be raping a corpse." That pulls him up short and I explain that I've just found out I have leukemia and the doctors have only given me a few months to live. That's why I'm out pacing the streets alone at night, I need to think, you know, come to terms with myself. I don't really have leukemia but in the fantasy I do, I guess I chose that particular disease because a girl in my grade four class died of it, the whole class sent her flowers when she was in the hospital. I didn't understand then that she was going to die and I wanted to have leukemia too so I could get flowers. Kids are funny, aren't they? Well, it turns out that he has leukemia himself, and *he* only has a few months to live, that's why he's going around raping people, he's very bitter because he's so young and his life is being taken from him before he's really lived it. So we walk along gently under the street lights, it's spring and sort of misty, and we end up going for coffee, we're happy we've found the only other person in the world who can understand what we're going through, it's almost like fate, and after a while we just sort of look at each other and our hands touch, and he comes back with me and moves into my apartment and we spend our last months together before we die, we just sort of don't wake up in the morning, though I've never decided which one of us gets to die first. If it's him I have to go on and fantasize about the funeral, if it's me I don't have to worry about that, so it just about depends on how tired I am at the time. You may not believe this but sometimes I even start crying. I cry at the ends of movies, even the ones that aren't all that sad, so I guess it's the same thing. My mother's like that too.

The funny thing about these fantasies is that the man is always someone I don't know, and the statistics in the magazines, well, most of them anyway, they say it's often someone you do know, at least a little bit, like your boss or something—I mean, it wouldn't be *my* boss, he's over sixty and I'm sure he couldn't rape his way out of a paper bag, poor old thing, but it might be someone like Derek Duck, in his elevator shoes, perish the thought—or someone you just met, who invites you up for a drink, it's getting so you can hardly be sociable anymore, and how are you supposed to meet people if you can't trust them even that basic amount? You can't spend your whole life in the Filing Department or cooped up in your own apartment with all the doors and windows locked and the shades down. I'm not what you would call a drinker but I like to go out now and then for a drink or two in a nice place, even if I am by myself, I'm with Women's Lib on that even though I can't agree with a lot of other things they say. Like here for instance, the waiters all know me and if anyone, you know, bothers me. . . . I don't know why I'm telling you all this, except I think it helps you get to know a person, especially at first, hearing some of the things they think about. At work they call me the office worry wart, but it isn't so much like worrying, it's more like figuring out what you should do in an emergency, like I said before.

Anyway, another thing about it is that there's a lot of conversation, in fact I spend most of my time, in the fantasy that is, wondering what I'm going to say and what he's going to say, I think it would be better if you could get a conversation going. Like, how could a fellow do that to a person he's just had a long conversation with, once you let them know you're human, you have a life too, I don't see how they could go ahead with it, right? I mean, I know it happens but I just don't understand it, that's the part I really don't understand.

[*1975*]

##  BOBBIE ANN MASON

*Bobbie Ann Mason, born in 1940 in rural western Kentucky and a graduate of the University of Kentucky, now lives in Pennsylvania. She took a master's degree at the State University of New York at Binghamton, and a Ph.D. at the University of Connecticut, writing a dissertation on a novel by Vladimir Nabokov. Between graduate degrees she worked for various magazines, including* T.V. Star Parade. *In 1974 she published her first book—the dissertation on Nabokov—and in 1975 she published her second,* The Girl Sleuth: A Guide to the Bobbsey Twins, Nancy Drew and Their Sisters. *She is, however, most widely known for her fiction, which usually deals with blue-collar people in rural Kentucky. "I write," she says, about people trapped in circumstances. . . . I identify with people who are ambivalent about their situation. And I guess in my stories, I'm in a way imagining myself as I would have felt if I had not gotten away and gotten a different perspective on things—if, for example, I had gotten pregnant in high school and had to marry a truck driver as the woman did in my story "Shiloh."*

# Shiloh

Leroy Moffitt's wife, Norma Jean, is working on her pectorals. She lifts three-pound dumbbells to warm up, then progresses to a twenty-pound barbell. Standing with her legs apart, she reminds Leroy of Wonder Woman.

"I'd give anything if I could just get these muscles to where they're real hard," says Norma Jean. "Feel this arm. It's not as hard as the other one."

"That's 'cause you're right-handed," says Leroy, dodging as she swings the barbell in an arc.

"Do you think so?"

5 "Sure."

Leroy is a truckdriver. He injured his leg in a highway accident four months ago, and his physical therapy, which involves weights and a pulley, prompted Norma Jean to try building herself up. Now she is attending a body-building class. Leroy has been collecting temporary disability since his tractor-trailer jackknifed in Missouri, badly twisting his left leg in its socket. He has a steel pin in his hip. He will probably not be able to drive his rig again. It sits in the backyard, like a gigantic bird that has flown home to roost. Leroy has been home in Kentucky for three months, and his leg is almost healed, but the accident frightened him and he does not want to drive any more long hauls. He is not sure what to do next. In the meantime, he makes things from craft kits. He started by building a miniature log cabin from notched Popsicle sticks. He varnished it and place it on the TV set, where it remains. It reminds him of a rustic Nativity scene. Then he tried string art (sailing ships on black velvet), a macramé owl kit, a snap-together B-17 Flying Fortress, and a lamp made out of a model truck, with a light fixture screwed in the top of the cab. At first the kits were diversions, something to kill time, but now he is thinking about building a full-scale log house from a kit. It would be considerably cheaper than building a regular house, and besides, Leroy has grown to appreciate how things are put together. He has begun to realize that in all the years he was on the road he never took time to examine anything. He was always flying past scenery.

"They won't let you build a long cabin in any of the new subdivisions," Norma Jean tells him.

"They will if I tell them it's for you," he says, teasing her. Ever since they were married, he has promised Norma Jean he would build her a new home one day. They have always rented, and the house they live in is small and nondescript. It does not even feel like a home, Leroy realizes now.

Norma Jean works at the Rexall drugstore, and she has acquired an amazing amount of information about cosmetics. When she explains to Leroy the three stages of complexion care, involving creams, toners, and moisturizers, he thinks happily of other petroleum products—axle grease, diesel fuel. This is a connection between him and Norma Jean. Since he has been home, he has felt unusually tender about his wife and guilty over his long absences. But he can't tell what she feels about him. Norma Jean has never complained about his traveling; she has never made hurt remarks, like calling his truck a "widow-maker." He is reasonably certain she has been faithful to him, but he wishes she would celebrate his permanent home-coming more happily. Norma Jean is often startled to find Leroy at home, and he thinks she seems a little disappointed about it. Perhaps he reminds her too much of the early days of their marriage, before he went on the road. They had a child who died as an infant, years ago. They never speak about their memories of Randy, which have almost faded, but now that Leroy is home all the time, they sometimes feel awkward around each other, and Leroy wonders if one of them should mention the child. He has the feeling that they are waking up out of a dream together—that they must create a new marriage, start afresh. They are lucky they are still married. Leroy has read that for most people losing a child destroys the marriage—or else he heard this on *Donahue.* He can't always remember where he learns things anymore.

10 At Christmas, Leroy bought an electric organ for Norma Jean. She used to play the piano when she was in high school. "It don't leave you," she told him once. "It's like riding a bicycle."

The new instrument had so many keys and buttons that she was bewildered by it at first. She touched the keys tentatively, pushed some buttons, then pecked out "Chopsticks." It came out in an amplified fox-trot rhythm, with marimba sounds.

"It's an orchestra!" she cried.

The organ had a pecan-look finish and eighteen preset chords, with optional flute, violin, trumpet, clarinet, and banjo accompaniements. Norma Jean mastered the organ almost immediately. At first she played Christmas songs. Then she bought *The Sixties Songbook* and learned every tune in it, adding variations to each with the rows of brightly colored buttons.

"I didn't like these old songs back then," she said. "But I have this crazy feeling I missed something."

15 "You didn't miss a thing," said Leroy.

Leroy likes to lie on the couch and smoke a joint and listen to Norma Jean play "Can't Take My Eyes Off You" and "I'll Be Back." He is back again. After fifteen years on the road, he is finally settling down with the woman he loves. She is still pretty. Her skin is flawless. Her frosted curls resemble pencil trimmings.

Now that Leroy has come home to stay, he notices how much the town has changed. Subdivisions are spreading across western Kentucky like an oil slick. The sign at the edge of town says "Pop: 11,500"—only seven hundred more than it said twenty years before. Leroy can't figure out who is living in all the new houses. The farmers who used to gather around the courthouse square on Saturday afternoons to play checkers and spit tobacco juice have gone. It has been years since Leroy has thought about the farmers, and they have disappeared without his noticing.

Leroy meets a kid named Stevie Hamilton in the parking lot at the new shopping center. While they pretend to be strangers meeting over a stalled car, Stevie tosses an ounce of marijuana under the front seat of Leroy's car. Stevie is wearing orange jogging shoes and a T-shirt that says CHATTAHOOCHEE SUPER-RAT. His father is a prominent doctor who lives in one of the expensive subdivisions in a new white-columned brick house that looks like a funeral parlor. In the phone book under his name there is a separate number, with the listing "Teenagers."

"Where do you get this stuff?" asks Leroy. "From your pappy?"

"That's for me to know and you to find out," Stevie says. He is slit-eyed and skinny.

"What else you got?"

"What you interested in?"

"Nothing special. Just wondered."

Leroy used to take speed on the road. Now he has to go slowly. He needs to be mellow. He leans back against the car and says, "I'm aiming to build me a log house, soon as I get time. My wife, though, I don't think she likes the idea."

"Well, let me know when you want me again," Stevie says. He has a cigarette in his cupped palm, as though sheltering it from the wind. He takes a long drag, then stomps it on the asphalt and slouches away.

Stevie's father was two years ahead of Leroy in high school. Leroy is thirty-four. He married Norma Jean when they were both eighteen, and their child Randy was born a few months later, but he died at the age of four months and three days. He would be about Stevie's age now. Norma Jean and Leroy were at the drive-in, watching a double feature (*Dr. Strangelove* and *Lover Come Back*), and the baby was sleeping in the back seat. When the first movie ended, the baby was dead. It was the sudden infant death syndrome. Leroy remembers handing Randy to a nurse at the emergency room, as though he were offering her a large doll as a present. A dead baby feels like a sack of flour. "It just happens sometimes," said the doctor, in what Leroy always recalls as a nonchalant tone. Leroy can hardly remember the child anymore, but he still sees vividly a scene from *Dr. Strangelove* in which the President of the United States was talking in a folksy voice on the hot line to the Soviet premier about the bomber accidentally headed toward Russia. He was in the War Room, and the world map was lit up. Leroy remembers Norma Jean standing catatonically beside him in the hospital and himself thinking: Who is this strange girl? He had forgotten who she was. Now scientists are saying that crib death is caused by a virus. Nobody knows anything, Leroy thinks. The answers are always changing.

When Leroy gets home from the shopping center, Norma Jean's mother, Mabel Beasley, is there. Until this year, Leroy has not realized how much time she spends with Norma Jean. When she visits, she inspects the closets and then the plants, informing Norma Jean when a plant is droopy or yellow. Mabel calls the plants "flowers," although there are never any blooms. She also notices if Norma Jean's laundry is piling up. Mabel is a short, overweight woman whose tight, brown-dyed curls look more like a wig than the actual wig she sometimes wears. Today she has brought

Norma Jean an off-white dust ruffle she made for the bed; Mabel works in a custom-upholstery shop.

"This is the tenth one I made this year," Mabel says. "I got started and couldn't stop."

"It's real pretty," says Norma Jean.

30 "Now we can hide things under the bed," says Leroy, who gets along with his mother-in-law primarily by joking with her. Mabel has never really forgiven him for disgracing her by getting Norma Jean pregnant. When the baby died, she said that fate was mocking her.

"What's that thing?" Mabel says to Leroy in a loud voice, pointing to a tangle of yarn on a piece of canvas.

Leroy holds it up for Mabel to see. "It's my needlepoint," he explains. "This is a *Star Trek* pillow cover."

"That's what a woman would do," says Mabel. "Great day in the morning!"

"All the big football players on TV do it," he says.

35 "Why, Leroy, you're always trying to fool me. I don't believe you for one minute. You don't know what to do with yourself—that's the whole trouble. Sewing!"

"I'm aiming to build us a log house," says Leroy. "Soon as my plans come."

"Like *heck* you are," says Norma Jean. She takes Leroy's needlepoint and shoves it into a drawer. "You have to find a job first. Nobody can afford to build now anyway."

Mabel straightens her girdle and says, "I still think before you get tied down y'all ought to take a little run to Shiloh."

"One of these days, Mama," Norma Jean says impatiently.

40 Mabel is talking about Shiloh, Tennessee. For the past few years, she has been urging Leroy and Norma Jean to visit the Civil War battleground there. Mabel went there on her honeymoon—the only real trip she ever took. Her husband died of a perforated ulcer when Norma Jean was ten, but Mabel, who was accepted into the United Daughters of the Confederacy in 1975, is still preoccupied with going back to Shiloh.

"I've been to kingdom come and back in that truck out yonder," Leroy says to Mabel, "but we never yet set foot in that battleground. Ain't that something? How did I miss it?"

"It's not even that far," Mabel says.

After Mabel leaves, Norma Jean reads to Leroy from a list she has made. "Things you could do," she announces. "You could get a job as a guard at Union Carbide, where they'd let you set on a stool. You could get on at the lumberyard. You could do a little carpenter work, if you want to build so bad. You could—"

"I can't do something where I'd have to stand up all day."

45 "You ought to try standing up all day behind a cosmetics counter. It's amazing that I have strong feet, coming from two parents that never had strong feet at all." At the moment Norma Jean is holding on to the kitchen counter, raising her knees one at a time as she talks. She is wearing two-pound ankle weights.

"Don't worry," says Leroy. "I'll do something."

"You could truck calves to slaughter for somebody. You wouldn't have to drive any big old truck for that."

"I'm going to build you this house," says Leroy. "I want to make you a real home."

"I don't want to live in any log cabin."

50 "It's not a cabin. It's a house."

"I don't care. It looks like a cabin."

"You and me together could lift those logs. It's just like lifting weights."

Norma Jean doesn't answer. Under her breath, she is counting. Now she is marching through the kitchen. She is doing goose steps.

Before his accident, when Leroy came home he used to stay in the house with Norma Jean, watching TV in bed and playing cards. She would cook fried chicken, picnic ham, chocolate pie—all his favorites. Now he is home alone much of the time. In the mornings, Norma Jean disappears, leaving a cooling place in the bed. She eats a cereal called Body Buddies, and she leaves the bowl on the table, with the soggy tan balls floating in a milk puddle. He sees things about Norma Jean that he never realized before. When she chops onions, she stares off into a corner, as if she can't bear to look. She puts on her house slippers almost precisely at nine o'clock every evening and nudges her jogging shoes under the couch. She saves bread heels for the birds. Leroy watches the birds at the feeder. He notices the peculiar way goldfinches fly past the window. They close their wings, then fall, then spread their wings to catch and lift themselves. He wonders if they close their eyes when they fall. Norma Jean closes her eyes when they are in bed. She wants the lights turned out. Even then, he is sure she closes her eyes.

55 He goes for long drives around town. He tends to drive a car rather carelessly. Power steering and an automatic shift make a car feel so small and inconsequential that his body is hardly involved in the driving process. His injured leg stretches out comfortably. Once or twice he has almost hit something, but even the prospect of an accident seems minor in a car. He cruises the new subdivisions, feeling like a criminal rehearsing for a robbery. Norma Jean is probably right about a log house being inappropriate here in the new subdivision. All the houses look grand and complicated. They depress him.

One day when Leroy comes home from a drive he finds Norma Jean in tears. She is in the kitchen making a potato and mushroom-soup casserole, with grated cheese topping. She is crying because her mother caught her smoking.

"I didn't hear her coming. I was standing here puffing away pretty as you please," Norma Jean says, wiping her eyes.

"I knew it would happen sooner or later," says Leroy, putting his arm around her.

"She don't know the meaning of the word 'knock,'" says Norma Jean. "It's a wonder she hadn't caught me years ago."

60 "Think of it this way," Leroy says. "What if she caught me with a joint?"

"You better not let her!" Norma Jean shrieks. "I'm warning you, Leroy Moffitt!"

"I'm just kidding. Here, play me a tune. That'll help you relax."

Norma Jean puts the casserole in the oven and sets the timer. Then she plays a ragtime tune, with horns and banjo, as Leroy lights up a joint and lies on the couch, laughing to himself about Mabel's catching him at it. He thinks of Stevie Hamilton—a doctor's son pushing grass. Everything is funny. The whole town seems crazy and small. He is reminded of Virgil Mathis, a boastful policeman Leroy used to shoot pool with. Virgil recently led a drug bust in a back room at a bowling alley, where he seized ten thousand dollars' worth of marijuana. The newspaper had a picture of him holding up the bags of grass and grinning widely. Right now, Leroy can imagine Virgil breaking down the door and arresting him with a lungful of smoke. Virgil would probably have been alerted to the scene because of all the racket Norma Jean is making. Now she sounds like a hard-rock band. Norma Jean is terrific. When she switches to a Latin-rhythm version of "Sunshine Superman," Leroy hums along. Norma Jean's foot goes up and down, up and down.

"Well, what do you think?" Leroy says, when Norma Jean pauses to search through her music.

65 "What do I think about what?"

His mind has gone blank. Then he says, "I'll sell my rig and build us a house." That wasn't what he wanted to say. He wanted to know what she thought—what she *really* thought—about them.

"Don't start in on that again," says Norma Jean. She begins playing "Who'll Be the Next in Line?"

Leroy used to tell hitchhikers his whole life story—about his travels, his hometown, the baby. He would end with a question: "Well, what do you think?" It was just a rhetorical question. In time, he had the feeling that he'd been telling the same story over and over to the same hitchhikers. He quit talking to hitchhikers when he realized how his voice sounded—whining and self-pitying, like some teenage-tragedy song. Now Leroy has the sudden impulse to tell Norma Jean about himself, as if he had just met her. They have known each other so long they have forgotten a lot about each other. They could become reacquainted. But when the oven timer goes off and she runs to the kitchen, he forgets why he wants to do this.

The next day, Mabel drops by. It is Saturday and Norma Jean is cleaning. Leroy is studying the plans of his log house, which have finally come in the mail. He has them spread out on the table—big sheets of stiff blue paper, with diagrams and numbers printed in white. While Norma Jean runs the vacuum, Mabel drinks coffee. She sets her coffee cup on a blueprint.

70 "I'm just waiting for time to pass," she says to Leroy, drumming her fingers on the table.

As soon as Norma Jean switches off the vacuum, Mabel says in a loud voice, "Did you hear about the datsun dog that killed the baby?"

Norma Jean says, "The word is 'dachshund.'"

"They put the dog on trial. It chewed the baby's legs off. The mother was in the next room all the time." She raises her voice. "They thought it was neglect."

Norma Jean is holding her ears. Leroy manages to open the refrigerator and get some Diet Pepsi to offer Mabel. Mabel still has some coffee and she waves away the Pepsi.

75 "Datsuns are like that," Mabel says. "They're jealous dogs. They'll tear a place to pieces if you don't keep an eye on them."

"You better watch out what you're saying, Mabel," says Leroy.

"Well, facts is facts."

Leroy looks out the window at his rig. It is like a huge piece of furniture gathering dust in the backyard. Pretty soon it will be an antique. He hears the vacuum cleaner. Norma Jean seems to be cleaning the living room rug again.

Later, she says to Leroy, "She just said that about the baby because she caught me smoking. She's trying to pay me back."

80 "What are you talking about?" Leroy says, nervously shuffling blueprints.

"You know good and well," Norma Jean says. She is sitting in a kitchen chair with her feet up and her arms wrapped around her knees. She looks small and helpless. She says, "The very idea, her bringing up a subject like that! Saying it was neglect."

"She didn't mean that," Leroy says.

"She might not have *thought* she meant it. She always says things like that. You don't know how she goes on."

"But she didn't really mean it. She was just talking."

85 Leroy opens a king-sized bottle of beer and pours it into two glasses, dividing it carefully. He hands a glass to Norma Jean and she takes it from him mechanically. For a long time, they sit by the kitchen window watching the birds at the feeder.

Something is happening. Norma Jean is going to night school. She has graduated from her six-week body-building course and now she is taking an adult-education course in composition at Paducah Community College. She spends her evenings outlining paragraphs.

"First, you have a topic sentence," she explains to Leroy. "Then you divide it up. Your secondary topic has to be connected to your primary topic."

To Leroy, this sounds intimidating. "I never was any good in English," he says.

"It makes a lot of sense."

90 "What are you doing this for, anyhow?"

She shrugs. "It's something to do." She stands up and lifts her dumbbells a few times.

"Driving a rig, nobody cared about my English."

"I'm not criticizing your English."

Norma Jean used to say, "If I lose ten minutes' sleep, I just drag all day." Now she stays up late, writing compositions. She got a B on her first paper—a how-to theme on soup-based casseroles. Recently Norma Jean has been cooking unusual foods—tacos, lasagna, Bombay chicken. She doesn't play the organ anymore, though her second paper was called "Why Music Is Important to Me." She sits at the kitchen table, concentrating on her outlines, while Leroy plays with his log house plans, practicing with a set of Lincoln Logs. The thought of getting a truckload of notched, numbered logs scares him, and he wants to be prepared. As he and Norma Jean work together at the kitchen table, Leroy has the hopeful thought that they are sharing something, but he knows he is a fool to think this. Norma Jean is miles away. He knows he is going to lose her. Like Mabel, he is just waiting for time to pass.

95 One day, Mabel is there before Norma Jean gets home from work, and Leroy finds himself confiding in her. Mabel, he realizes, must know Norma Jean better than he does.

"I don't know what's got into that girl," Mabel says. "She used to go to bed with the chickens. Now you say she's up all hours. Plus her a-smoking. I like to died."

"I want to make her this beautiful home," Leroy says, indicating the Lincoln Logs. "I don't think she even wants it. Maybe she was happier with me gone."

"She don't know what to make of you, coming home like this."

"Is that it?"

100 Mabel takes the roof off his Lincoln Log cabin. "You couldn't get *me* in a log cabin," she says. "I was raised in one. It's no picnic, let me tell you."

"They're different now," says Leroy.

"I tell you what," Mabel says, smiling oddly at Leroy.

"What?"

"Take her on down to Shiloh. Y'all need to get out together, stir a little. Her brain's all balled up over them books."

105 Leroy can see traces of Norma Jean's features in her mother's face. Mabel's worn face has the texture of crinkled cotton, but suddenly she looks pretty. It occurs to Leroy that Mabel has been hinting all along that she wants them to take her with them to Shiloh.

"Let's all go to Shiloh," he says. "You and me and her. Come Sunday."

Mabel throws up her hand in protest. "Oh, no, not me. Young folks want to be by theirselves."

When Norma Jean comes in with groceries, Leroy says excitedly, "Your mama here's been dying to go to Shiloh for thirty-five years. It's about time we went, don't you think?"

"I'm not going to butt in on anybody's second honeymoon," Mabel says.

110 "Who's going on a honeymoon, for Christ's sake?" Norma Jean says loudly.

"I never raised no daughter of mine to talk that-a-way," Mabel says.

"You ain't seen nothing yet," says Norma Jean. She starts putting away boxes and cans, slamming cabinet doors.

"There's a log cabin at Shiloh," Mabel says. "It was there during the battle. There's bullet holes in it."

"When are you going to *shut up* about Shiloh, Mama?" asks Norma Jean.

115 "I always thought Shiloh was the prettiest place, so full of history," Mabel goes on. "I just hoped y'all could see it once before I die, so you could tell me about it." Later, she whispers to Leroy, "You do what I said. A little change is what she needs."

"Your name means 'the king,'" Norma Jean says to Leroy that evening. He is trying to get her to go to Shiloh, and she is reading a book about another century.

"Well, I reckon I ought to be right proud."

"I guess so."

"Am I still king around here?"

120 Norma Jean flexes her biceps and feels them for hardness. "I'm not fooling around with anybody, if that's what you mean," she says.

"Would you tell me if you were?"

"I don't know."

"What does *your* name mean?"

"It was Marilyn Monroe's real name."

125 "No kidding!"

"Norma comes from the Normans. They were invaders," she says. She closes her book and looks hard at Leroy. "I'll go to Shiloh with you if you'll stop staring at me."

On Sunday, Norma Jean packs a picnic and they go to Shiloh. To Leroy's relief Mabel says she does not want to come with them. Norma Jean drives, and Leroy, sitting beside her, feels like some boring hitchhiker she has picked up. He tries some conversation, but she answers him in monosyllables. At Shiloh, she drives aimlessly through the park, past bluffs and trails and steep ravines. Shiloh is an immense place, and Leroy cannot see it as a battleground. It is not what he expected. He thought it would look like a golf course. Monuments are everywhere, showing through the thick clusters of trees. Norma Jean passes the log cabin Mabel mentioned. It is surrounded by tourists looking for bullet holes.

"That's not the kind of log house I've got in mind," says Leroy apologetically.

"I know *that.*"

130 "This is a pretty place. Your mama was right."

"It's O.K.," says Norma Jean. "Well, we've seen it. I hope she's satisfied."

They burst out laughing together.

At the park museum, a movie on Shiloh is shown every half hour, but they decide that they don't want to see it. They buy a souvenir Confederate flag for Mabel, and then they find a picnic spot near the cemetery. Norma Jean has brought a picnic cooler, with pimento sandwiches, soft drinks, and Yodels. Leroy eats a sandwich and then smokes a joint, hiding it behind the picnic cooler. Norma Jean has quit smoking altogether. She is picking cake crumbs from the cellophane wrapper, like a fussy bird.

Leroy says, "So the boys in gray ended up in Corinth. The Union soldiers zapped 'em finally. April 7, 1862."

135 They both know that he doesn't know any history. He is just talking about some of the historical plaques they have read. He feels awkward, like a boy on a date with an older girl. They are still just making conversation.

"Corinth is where Mama eloped to," says Norma Jean.

They sit in silence and stare at the cemetery for the Union dead and, beyond, at a tall cluster of trees. Campers are parked nearby, bumper to bumper, and small children in bright clothing are cavorting and squealing. Norma Jean wads up the cake wrapper and squeezes it tightly in her hand. Without looking at Leroy, she says, "I want to leave you."

Leroy takes a bottle of Coke out of the cooler and flips off the cap. He holds the bottle poised near his mouth but cannot remember to take a drink. Finally he says, "No, you don't."

"Yes, I do."

140 "I won't let you."

"You can't stop me."

"Don't do me that way."

Leroy knows Norma Jean will have her own way. "Didn't I promise to be home from now on?" he says.

"In some ways, a woman prefers a man who wanders," says Norma Jean. "That sounds crazy, I know."

145 "You're not crazy."

Leroy remembers to drink from his Coke. Then he says, "Yes, you *are* crazy. You and me could start all over again. Right back at the beginning."

"We *have* started all over again," says Norma Jean. "And this is how it turned out."

"What did I do wrong?"

"Nothing."

150 "Is this one of those women's lib things?" Leroy asks.

"Don't be funny."

The cemetery, a green slope dotted with white markers, looks like a subdivision site. Leroy is trying to comprehend that his marriage is breaking up, but for some reason he is wondering about white slabs in a graveyard.

"Everything was fine till Mama caught me smoking," says Norma Jean, standing up. "That set something off."

"What are you talking about?"

155 "She won't leave me alone—*you* won't leave me alone." Norma Jean seems to be crying, but she is looking away from him. "I feel eighteen again. I can't face that all over again." She starts walking away. "No, it *wasn't* fine. I don't know what I'm saying. Forget it."

Leroy takes a lungful of smoke and closes his eyes as Norma Jean's words sink in. He tries to focus on the fact that thirty-five hundred soldiers died on the grounds around him. He can only think of that war as a board game with plastic soldiers. Leroy almost smiles, as he compares the Confederates' daring attack on the Union camps and Virgil Mathis's raid on the bowling alley. General Grant, drunk and furious, shoved the Southerners back to Corinth, where Mabel and Jet Beasley were married years later, when Mabel was still thin and good-looking. The next day, Mabel and Jet visited the battleground, and then Norma Jean was born, and then she married Leroy and they had a baby, which they lost, and now Leroy and Norma Jean are here at the same battleground. Leroy knows he is leaving out a lot. He is leaving out the insides of history. History was always just names and dates to him. It occurs to him that building a house of logs is similarly empty—too simple. And the real inner workings of a marriage, like most of history, have escaped him. Now he sees that building a log house is the dumbest idea he could have had. It was clumsy of him to think Norma Jean would want a log house. It was a crazy idea. He'll have to think of something else, quickly. He will wad the blueprints into tight balls and fling them into the lake. Then he'll get moving again. He opens his eyes. Norma Jean has moved away and is walking through the cemetery, following a serpentine brick path.

Leroy gets up to follow his wife, but his good leg is asleep and his bad leg still hurts him. Norma Jean is far away, walking rapidly toward the bluff by the river, and he tries to hobble toward her. Some children run past him, screaming noisily. Norma Jean has reached the bluff, and she is looking out over the Tennessee River. Now she turns toward Leroy and waves her arms. Is she beckoning to him? She seems to be doing an exercise for her chest muscles. The sky is unusually pale—the color of the dust ruffle Mabel made for their bed.

[*1982*]

## TOBIAS WOLFF

***Tobias Wolff was born in Alabama in 1945, but he grew up in the state of Washington. He left high school before graduating, served as an apprentice seaman and as a weight-guesser in a carnival, and then joined the army, where he served four years as a paratrooper. After his discharge from the army, he hired private tutors to enable him to pass the entrance examination to Oxford University. At Oxford he did spectacularly well, graduating with First Class Honors in English. Wolff has written stories, novels, and an autobiography (*****This Boy's Life*****); he now teaches writing at Syracuse University.***

# *Say Yes*

They were doing the dishes, his wife washing while he dried. He'd washed the night before. Unlike most men he knew, he really pitched in on the housework. A few months earlier he'd overheard a friend of his wife's congratulate her on having such a considerate husband, and he thought, *I try.* Helping out with the dishes was a way he had of showing how considerate he was.

They talked about different things and somehow got on the subject of whether white people should marry black people. He said that all things considered, he thought it was a bad idea.

"Why?" she asked.

Sometimes his wife got this look where she pinched her brows together and bit her lower lip and stared down at something. When he saw her like this he knew he should keep his mouth shut, but he never did. Actually it made him talk more. She had that look now.

5 "Why?" she asked again, and stood there with her hand inside a bowl, not washing it but just holding it above the water.

"Listen," he said, "I went to school with blacks, and I've worked with blacks and lived on the same street with blacks, and we've always gotten along just fine. I don't need you coming along now and implying that I'm a racist."

"I didn't imply anything," she said, and began washing the bowl again, turning it around in her hand as though she were shaping it. "I just don't see what's wrong with a white person marrying a black person, that's all."

"They don't come from the same culture as we do. Listen to them sometime—they even have their own language. That's okay with me, I *like* hearing them talk"—he did; for some reason it always made him feel happy—"but it's different. A person from their culture and a person from our culture could never really *know* each other."

"Like you know me?" his wife asked.

10 "Yes. Like I know you."

"But if they love each other," she said. She was washing faster now, not looking at him.

Oh boy, he thought. He said, "Don't take my word for it. Look at the statistics. Most of those marriages break up."

"Statistics." She was piling dishes on the drainboard at a terrific rate, just swiping at them with the cloth. Many of them were greasy, and there were flecks of food between the tines of the forks. "All right," she said, "what about foreigners? I suppose you think the same thing about two foreigners getting married."

"Yes," he said, "as a matter of fact I do. How can you understand someone who comes from a completely different background?"

15 "Different," said his wife. "Not the same, like us."

"Yes, different," he snapped, angry with her for resorting to this trick of repeating his words so that they sounded crass, or hypocritical. "These are dirty," he said, and dumped all the silverware back into the sink.

The water had gone flat and gray. She stared down at it, her lips pressed tight together, then plunged her hands under the surface. "Oh!" she cried, and jumped back. She took her right hand by the wrist and held it up. Her thumb was bleeding.

"Ann, don't move," he said. "Stay right there." He ran upstairs to the bathroom and rummaged in the medicine chest for alcohol, cotton, and a Band-Aid. When he came back down she was leaning against the refrigerator with her eyes closed, still holding her hand. He took the hand and dabbed at her thumb with the cotton. The bleeding had stopped. He squeezed it to see how deep the wound was and a single drop of blood welled up, trembling and bright, and fell to the floor. Over the thumb she stared at him accusingly. "It's shallow," he said. "Tomorrow you won't even know it's there." He hoped that she appreciated how quickly he had come to her aid. He'd acted out of concern for her, with no thought of getting anything in return, but now the thought occurred to him that it would be a nice gesture on her part not to start up that conversation again, as he was tired of it. "I'll finish up here," he said. "You go and relax."

"That's okay," she said. "I'll dry."

20 He began to wash the silverware again, giving a lot of attention to the forks.

"So," she said, "you wouldn't have married me if I'd been black."

"For Christ's sake, Ann!"

"Well, that's what you said, didn't you?"

"No, I did not. The whole question is ridiculous. If you had been black we probably wouldn't even have met. You would have had your friends and I would have had mine. The only black girl I ever really knew was my partner in the debating club, and I was already going out with you by then."

25 "But if we had met, and I'd been black?"

"Then you probably would have been going out with a black guy." He picked up the rinsing nozzle and sprayed the silverware. The water was so hot that the metal darkened to pale blue, then turned silver again.

"Let's say I wasn't," she said. "Let's say I am black and unattached and we meet and fall in love."

He glanced over at her. She was watching him and her eyes were bright. "Look," he said, taking a reasonable tone, "this is stupid. If you were black you wouldn't be you." As he said this he realized it was absolutely true. There was no possible way of arguing with the fact that she would not be herself if she were black. So he said it again: "If you were black you wouldn't be you."

"I know," she said, "but let's just say."

He took a deep breath. He had won the argument but he still felt cornered. "Say what?" he asked.

"That I'm black, but still me, and we fall in love. Will you marry me?"

He thought about it.

"Well?" she said, and stepped close to him. Her eyes were even brighter. "Will you marry me?"

"I'm thinking," he said.

"You won't, I can tell. You're going to say no."

"Let's not move too fast on this," he said. "There are lots of things to consider. We don't want to do something we would regret for the rest of our lives."

"No more considering. Yes or no."

"Since you put it that way—"

"Yes or no."

"Jesus, Ann. All right. No."

She said, "Thank you," and walked from the kitchen into the living room. A moment later he heard her turning the pages of a magazine. He knew that she was too angry to be actually reading it, but she didn't snap through the pages the way he would have done. She turned them slowly, as if she were studying every word. She was demonstrating her indifference to him, and it had the effect he knew she wanted it to have. It hurt him.

He had no choice but to demonstrate his indifference to her. Quietly, thoroughly, he washed the rest of the dishes. Then he dried them and put them away. He wiped the counters and the stove and scoured the linoleum where the drop of blood had fallen. While he was at it, he decided, he might as well mop the whole floor. When he was done the kitchen looked new, the way it looked when they were first shown the house, before they had ever lived here.

He picked up the garbage pail and went outside. The night was clear and he could see a few stars to the west, where the lights of the town didn't blur them out. On El Camino the traffic was steady and light, peaceful as a river. He felt ashamed that he had let his wife get him into a fight. In another thirty years or so they would both be dead. What would all that stuff matter then? He thought of the years they had spent together, and how close they were, and how well they knew each other, and his throat tightened so that he could hardly breathe. His face and neck began to tingle. Warmth flooded his chest. He stood there for a while, enjoying these sensations, then picked up the pail and went out the back gate.

The two mutts from down the street had pulled over the garbage can again. One of them was rolling around on his back and the other had something in her mouth. Growling, she tossed it into the air, leaped up and caught it, growled again and whipped her head from side to side. When they saw him coming they trotted away with short, mincing steps. Normally he would heave rocks at them, but this time he let them go.

The house was dark when he came back inside. She was in the bathroom. He stood outside the door and called her name. He heard bottles clinking, but she didn't answer him. "Ann, I'm really sorry," he said. "I'll make it up to you, I promise."

"How?" she said.

He wasn't expecting this. But from a sound in her voice, a level and definite note that was strange to him, he knew that he had to come up with the right answer. He leaned against the door. "I'll marry you," he whispered.

"We'll see," she said. "Go on to bed. I'll be out in a minute."

He undressed and got under the covers. Finally he heard the bathroom door open and close.

"Turn off the light," she said from the hallway.

"What?"

"Turn off the light."

He reached over and pulled the chain on the bedside lamp. The room went dark. "All right," he said. He lay there, but nothing happened. "All right," he said again. Then he heard a movement across the room. He sat up, but he couldn't see a thing. The room was silent. His heart pounded the way it had on their first night together, the way it still did when he woke at a noise in the darkness and waited to hear it again—the sound of someone moving through the house, a stranger.

[*1985*]

## GLORIA NAYLOR

***Gloria Naylor (b. 1950), a native of New York City, holds a bachelor's degree from Brooklyn College and a master's degree in Afro-American Studies from Yale University. "The Two" comes from*** The Women of Brewster Place ***(1982), a book that won the American Book Award for First Fiction. Naylor has subsequently published two novels and*** Centennial ***(1986), a work of nonfiction.***

# *The Two*

At first they seemed like such nice girls. No one could remember exactly when they had moved into Brewster. It was earlier in the year before Ben[1] was killed—of course, it had to be before Ben's death. But no one remembered if it was in the winter or spring of that year that the two had come. People often came and went on Brewster Place like a restless night's dream, moving in and out in the dark to avoid eviction notices or neighborhood bulletins about the dilapidated condition of their furnishings. So it wasn't until the two were clocked leaving in the mornings and returning in the evenings at regular intervals that it was quietly absorbed that they now

[1]The custodian of Brewster Place

claimed Brewster as home. And Brewster waited, cautiously prepared to claim them, because you never knew about young women, and obviously single at that. But when no wild music or drunken friends careened out of the corner building on weekends, and especially, when no slightly eager husbands were encouraged to linger around that first-floor apartment and run errands for them, a suspended sigh of relief floated around the two when they dumped their garbage, did their shopping, and headed for the morning bus.

The women of Brewster had readily accepted the lighter, skinny one. There wasn't much threat in her timid mincing walk and the slightly protruding teeth she seemed so eager to show everyone in her bell-like good mornings and evenings. Breaths were held a little longer in the direction of the short dark one—too pretty, and too much behind. And she insisted on wearing those thin Qiana dresses that the summer breeze molded against the maddening rhythm of the twenty pounds of rounded flesh that she swung steadily down the street. Through slitted eyes, the women watched their men watching her pass, knowing the bastards were praying for a wind. But since she seemed oblivious to whether these supplications went answered, their sighs settled around her shoulders too. Nice girls.

And so no one even cared to remember exactly when they had moved into Brewster Place, until the rumor started. It had first spread through the block like a sour odor that's only faintly perceptible and easily ignored until it starts growing in strength from the dozen mouths it had been lying in, among clammy gums and scum-coated teeth. And then it was everywhere—lining the mouths and whitening the lips of everyone as they wrinkled up their noses at its pervading smell, unable to pinpoint the source or time of its initial arrival. Sophie could—she had been there.

It wasn't that the rumor had actually begun with Sophie. A rumor needs no true parent. It only needs a willing carrier, and it found one in Sophie. She had been there—on one of those August evenings when the sun's absence is a mockery because the heat leaves the air so heavy it presses the naked skin down on your body, to the point that a sheet becomes unbearable and sleep impossible. So most of Brewster was outside that night when the two had come in together, probably from one of those air-conditioned movies downtown, and had greeted the ones who were loitering around their building. And they had started up the steps when the skinny one tripped over a child's ball and the darker one had grabbed her by the arm and around the waist to break her fall. "Careful, don't wanna lose you now." And the two of them had laughed into each other's eyes and went into the building.

5 The smell had begun there. It outlined the image of the stumbling woman and the one who had broken her fall. Sophie and a few other women sniffed at the spot and then, perplexed, silently looked at each other. Where had they seen that before? They had often laughed and touched each other—held each other in joy or its dark twin—but where had they seen *that* before? It came to them as the scent drifted down the steps and entered their nostrils on the way to their inner mouths. They had seen that—done that—with their men. That shared moment of invisible communion reserved for two and hidden from the rest of the world behind laughter or tears or a touch. In the days before babies, miscarriages, and other broken dreams, after stolen caresses in barn stalls and cotton houses, after intimate walks from church and secret kisses with boys who were

now long forgotten or permanently fixed in their lives—that was where. They could almost feel the odor moving about in their mouths, and they slowly knitted themselves together and let it out into the air like a yellow mist that began to cling to the bricks on Brewster.

So it got around that the two in 312 were *that* way. And they had seemed like such nice girls. Their regular exits and entrances to the block were viewed with a jaundiced eye. The quiet that rested around their door on the weekends hinted of all sorts of secret rituals, and their friendly indifference to the men on the street was an insult to the women as a brazen flaunting of unnatural ways.

Since Sophie's apartment windows faced theirs from across the air shaft, she became the official watchman for the block, and her opinions were deferred to whenever the two came up in conversation. Sophie took her position seriously and was constantly alert for any telltale signs that might creep out around their drawn shades, across from which she kept a religious vigil. An entire week of drawn shades was evidence enough to send her flying around with reports that as soon as it got dark they pulled their shades down and put on the lights. Heads nodded in knowing unison—a definite sign. If doubt was voiced with a "But I pull my shades down at night too," a whispered "Yeah, but you're not *that* way" was argument enough to win them over.

Sophie watched the lighter one dumping their garbage, and she went outside and opened the lid. Her eyes darted over the crushed tin cans, vegetable peelings, and empty chocolate chip cookie boxes. What do they do with all them chocolate chip cookies? It was surely a sign, but it would take some time to figure that one out. She saw Ben go into their apartment, and she waited and blocked his path as he came out, carrying his toolbox.

"What ya see?" She grabbed his arm and whispered wetly in his face.

Ben stared at her squinted eyes and drooping lips and shook his head slowly. "Uh, uh, uh, it was terrible."

"Yeah?" She moved in a little closer.

"Worst busted faucet I seen in my whole life." He shook her hand off his arm and left her standing in the middle of the block.

"You old sop bucket," she muttered, as she went back up on her stoop. A broken faucet, huh? Why did they need to use so much water?

Sophie had plenty to report that day. Ben had said it was terrible in there. No, she didn't know exactly what he had seen, but you can imagine—and they did. Confronted with the difference that had been thrust into their predictable world, they reached into their imaginations and, using an ancient pattern, weaved themselves a reason for its existence. Out of necessity they stitched all of their secret fears and lingering childhood nightmares into this existence, because even though it was deceptive enough to try and look as they looked, talk as they talked, and do as they did, it had to have some hidden stain to invalidate it—it was impossible for them both to be right. So they leaned back, supported by the sheer weight of their numbers and comforted by the woven barrier that kept them protected from the yellow mist that enshrouded the two as they came and went on Brewster Place.

Lorraine was the first to notice the change in the people on Brewster Place. She was a shy but naturally friendly woman who got up early, and had read the morning paper and done fifty sit-ups before it was time to leave for work. She came out of her apartment eager to start her day by greeting any of her neighbors who were outside. But she noticed that some of the people who had spoken to her before made a point of having something else to do with their eyes when she passed, although she could almost feel them staring at her back as she moved on. The ones who still spoke only did so after an uncomfortable pause, in which they seemed to be peering through her before they begrudged her a good morning or evening. She wondered if it was all in her mind and she thought about mentioning it to Theresa, but she didn't want to be accused of being too sensitive again. And how would Tee even notice anything like that anyway? She had a lousy attitude and hardly ever spoke to people. She stayed in that bed until the last moment and rushed out of the house fogged-up and grumpy, and she was used to being stared at—by men at least—because of her body.

Lorraine thought about these things as she came up the block from work, carrying a large paper bag. The group of women on her stoop parted silently and let her pass.

"Good evening," she said, as she climbed the steps.

Sophie was standing on the top step and tried to peek into the bag. "You been shopping, huh? What ya buy?" It was almost an accusation.

"Groceries." Lorraine shielded the top of the bag from view and squeezed past her with a confused frown. She saw Sophie throw a knowing glance to the others at the bottom of the stoop. What was wrong with this old woman? Was she crazy or something?

20 Lorraine went into her apartment. Theresa was sitting by the window, reading a copy of *Mademoiselle.* She glanced up from her magazine. "Did you get my chocolate chip cookies?"

"Why good evening to you, too, Tee. And how was my day? Just wonderful." She sat the bag down on the couch. "The little Baxter boy brought in a puppy for show-and-tell, and the damn thing pissed all over the floor and then proceeded to chew the heel off my shoe, but, yes, I managed to hobble to the store and bring you your chocolate chip cookies."

Oh, Jesus, Theresa thought, she's got a bug up her ass tonight.

"Well, you should speak to Mrs. Baxter. She ought to train her kid better than that." She didn't wait for Lorraine to stop laughing before she tried to stretch her good mood. "Here, I'll put those things away. Want me to make dinner so you can rest? I only worked half a day, and the most tragic thing that went down was a broken fingernail and that got caught in my typewriter."

Lorraine followed Theresa into the kitchen. "No, I'm not really tired, and fair's fair, you cooked last night. I didn't mean to tick off like that; it's just that . . . well, Tee, have you noticed that people aren't as nice as they used to be?"

25 Theresa stiffened. Oh, God, here she goes again. "What people, Lorraine? Nice in what way?"

"Well, the people in this building and on the street. No one hardly speaks anymore. I mean, I'll come in and say good evening—and just silence. It wasn't like that when we first moved in. I don't know, it just makes you wonder; that's all. What are they thinking?"

"I personally don't give a shit what they're thinking. And their good evenings don't put any bread on my table."

"Yeah, but you didn't see the way that woman looked at me out there. They must feel something or know something. They probably—"

"They, they, they!" Theresa exploded. "You know, I'm not starting up with this again, Lorraine. Who in the hell are they? And where in the hell are we? Living in some dump of a building in this God-forsaken part of town around a bunch of ignorant niggers with the cotton still under their fingernails because of you and your theys. They knew something in Linden Hills, so I gave up an apartment for you that I'd been in for the last four years. And then they knew in Park Heights, and you made me so miserable there we had to leave. Now these mysterious theys are on Brewster Place. Well, look out that window, kid. There's a big wall down that block, and this is the end of the line for me. I'm not moving anymore, so if that's what you're working yourself up to—save it!"

30 When Theresa became angry she was like a lump of smoldering coal, and her fierce bursts of temper always unsettled Lorraine.

"You see, that's why I didn't want to mention it." Lorraine began to pull at her fingers nervously. "You're always flying up and jumping to conclusions—no one said anything about moving. And I didn't know your life has been so miserable since you met me. I'm sorry about that," she finished tearfully.

Theresa looked at Lorraine, standing in the kitchen door like a wilted leaf, and she wanted to throw something at her. Why didn't she ever fight back? The very softness that had first attracted her to Lorraine was now a frequent cause for irritation. Smoked honey. That's what Lorraine had reminded her of, sitting in her office clutching that application. Dry autumn days in Georgia woods, thick bloated smoke under a beehive, and the first glimpse of amber honey just faintly darkened about the edges by the burning twigs. She had flowed just that heavily into Theresa's mind and had stuck there with a persistent sweetness.

But Theresa hadn't known then that this softness filled Lorraine up to the very middle and that she would bend at the slightest pressure, would be constantly seeking to surround herself with the comfort of everyone's goodwill, and would shrivel up at the least touch of disapproval. It was becoming a drain to be continually called upon for this nurturing and support that she just didn't understand. She had supplied it at first out of love for Lorraine, hoping that she would harden eventually, even as honey does when exposed to the cold. Theresa was growing tired of being clung to—of being the one who was leaned on. She didn't want a child—she wanted someone who could stand toe to toe with her and be willing to slug it out at times. If they practiced that way with each other, then they could turn back to back and beat the hell out of the world for trying to invade their territory. But she had found no such sparring partner in Lorraine, and the strain of fighting alone was beginning to show on her.

"Well, if it was that miserable, I would have been gone a long time ago," she said, watching her words refresh Lorraine like a gentle shower.

35 "I guess you think I'm some sort of sick paranoid, but I can't afford to have people calling my job or writing letters to my principal. You know I've already lost a position like that in Detroit. And teaching is my whole life, Tee."

"I know," she sighed, not really knowing at all. There was no danger of that ever happening on Brewster Place. Lorraine taught too far from this neighborhood for anyone here to recognize her in that school. No, it wasn't her job she feared losing this time, but their approval. She wanted to stand out there and chat and trade makeup secrets and cake recipes. She wanted to be secretary of their block association and be asked to mind their kids while they ran to the store. And none of that was going to happen if they couldn't even bring themselves to accept her good evenings.

Theresa silently finished unpacking the groceries. "Why did you buy cottage cheese? Who eats that stuff?"

"Well, I thought we should go on a diet."

"If *we* go on a diet, then you'll disappear. You've got nothing to lose but your hair."

"Oh, I don't know. I thought that we might want to try and reduce our hips or something." Lorraine shrugged playfully.

"No, thank you. We are very happy with our hips the way they are," Theresa said, as she shoved the cottage cheese to the back of the refrigerator. "And even when I lose weight, it never comes off there. My chest and arms just get smaller, and I start looking like a bottle of salad dressing."

The two women laughed, and Theresa sat down to watch Lorraine fix dinner. "You know, this behind has always been my downfall. When I was coming up in Georgia with my grandmother, the boys used to promise me penny candy if I would let them pat my behind. And I used to love those jawbreakers—you know, the kind that lasted all day and kept changing colors in your mouth. So I was glad to oblige them, because in one afternoon I could collect a whole week's worth of jawbreakers."

"Really. That's funny to you? Having some boy feeling all over you."

Theresa sucked her teeth. "We were only kids, Lorraine. You know, you remind me of my grandmother. That was one straight-laced old lady. She had a fit when my brother told her what I was doing. She called me into the smokehouse and told me in this real scary whisper that I could get pregnant from letting little boys pat my butt and that I'd end up like my cousin Willa. But Willa and I had been thick as fleas, and she had already given me a step-by-step summary of how she'd gotten into her predicament. But I sneaked around to her house that night just to double-check her story, since that old lady had seemed so earnest. 'Willa, are you sure?' I whispered through her bedroom window. 'I'm tellin' ya, Tee,' she said. 'Just keep both feet on the ground and you home free.' Much later I learned that advice wasn't too biologically sound, but it worked in Georgia because those country boys didn't have much imagination."

Theresa's laughter bounced off of Lorraine's silent, rigid back and died in her throat. She angrily tore open a pack of the chocolate chip cookies. "Yeah," she said, staring at Lorraine's back and biting down hard into the cookie, "it wasn't until I came up north to college that I found out there's a whole lot of things that a dude with a little imagination can do to you even with both feet on the ground. You see, Willa forgot to tell me not to bend over or squat or—"

"Must you!" Lorraine turned around from the stove with her teeth clenched tightly together.

"Must I what, Lorraine? Must I talk about things that are as much a part of life as eating or breathing or growing old? Why are you always so uptight about sex or men?"

"I'm not uptight about anything. I just think its disgusting when you go on and on about—"

"There's nothing disgusting about it, Lorraine. You've never been with a man, but I've been with quite a few—some better than others. There were a couple who I still hope to this day will die a slow, painful death, but then there were some who were good to me—in and out of bed."

"If they were so great, then why are you with me?" Lorraine's lips were trembling.

"Because—" Theresa looked steadily into her eyes and then down at the cookie she was twirling on the table. "Because," she continued slowly, "you can take a chocolate chip cookie and put holes in it and attach it to your ears and call it an earring, or hang it around your neck on a silver chain and pretend it's a necklace—but it's still a cookie. See—you can toss it in the air and call it a Frisbee or even a flying saucer, if the mood hits you, and it's still just a cookie. Send it spinning on a table—like this—until it's a wonderful blur of amber and brown light that you can imagine to be a topaz or rusted gold or old crystal, but the law of gravity has got to come into play, sometime, and it's got to come to rest—sometime. Then all the spinning and pretending and hoopla is over with. And you know what you got?"

"A chocolate chip cookie," Lorraine said.

"Uh-huh." Theresa put the cookie in her mouth and winked. "A lesbian." She got up from the table. "Call me when dinner's ready, I'm going back to read." She stopped at the kitchen door. "Now, why are you putting gravy on that chicken, Lorraine? You know it's fattening."

[*1982*]

## ANJANA APPACHANA

*Anjana Appachana, a graduate of Delhi University, published "To Rise Above" in 1989, when she was an M.F.A. candidate at Pennsylvania State University. She is the author of a book of short stories,* Incantations and Other Stories *(1991).*

## *To Rise Above*

Last evening my husband told me that he was tired of seeing me looking so washed out and sick. He said, when I come back from the office, the least I can expect is a smiling face. You don't even give me that. It's bad enough that the house is in a mess, but you don't even seem to have time to entertain my friends properly when they come home. They must be wondering what sort of a wife I have. I tell you, I'm tired of all this. And he walked out of the room, slamming the door behind him.

My baby looked up and went back to her toy. My darling, I told her, my *rani beti,* do you like the toy, do you like it baby? Next time I'll get you a big doll that will open and close its eyes just like you. I nuzzled her and she gurgled with pleasure.

What I say doesn't even affect you, groaned my husband, returning to the room. Look at you, your face unwashed, your hair uncombed, lying on the bed like that. That's not what I married you for. For heaven's sake, get up and prepare something, my friends are coming home for tea. I said, today? He mimicked, yes, today, today. Is the *Maharani*[1] too busy to look after them? I got up and went to the kitchen. O God, where to begin? The dishes had to be washed, the dinner to be made, also snacks for his friends. I put the potatoes to boil, best to make some *aloo sabji* and use the rest of them for *tikkies.* Then I took out the *sooji* to make *halwa.* That should be enough for them. Why did they have to come today? Even I was tired after a day at the office. The dishes were so dirty. I didn't expect my mother-in-law to wash them, but she could have soaked them in water at least. I suppose I should be thankful she remembered to fill the buckets before the water finished. Please God, I prayed, don't let the electricity go off too, these power cuts will be the death of me. I put the *dal* in the pressure cooker and began the dishes. How could I smile? What was there to smile about?

The bus back home had been so crowded. More so than usual, because the previous bus was held up by some college boys who were protesting about the irregular service. I could hardly get in and once I got in I couldn't move. It was horrible. I don't understand these men. Even if you are sitting they edge closer and closer to you and you can't do a thing. When the bus reached my stop I couldn't get out because I was stuck in the crowd and by the time I reached the door, the bus had started moving again. I told the driver to stop and he said something rude, but did. The air, how fresh it was, and the slight breeze against my face, so cleansing. I walked home slowly. This is the only time I ever get to myself. Sometimes I wished that I didn't know typing so that I didn't have to work, but if I didn't work we couldn't make ends meet. In my husband's matrimonial advertisement his family had insisted that they wanted a working girl, so I suppose it wouldn't be fair at this point to say that I just couldn't cope. When I was working before marriage, Ma would pack me a lunch of soft *parathas* with *sabji.* And when I came back she would make me a cup of hot tea and ask me how her *rani beti* was. Then she would talk to me and give me all the day's gossip—how lazy the *jamardani* was—how Mrs. Sharma next door had a fight with her husband. I always had a good laugh about Mrs. Sharma's fights, she had such a loud voice that very often we could hear her in the house. I wondered what she fought about. Sometimes I wish that I could fight, but I don't know how to, so whenever I'm upset I just go to the bathroom and cry instead. They all think that nothing bothers me. Let them. I long for Ma to come here and stay with me, but when I last wrote to her and asked her to do so she was very angry. Beti, she wrote, now you are a married woman and you must understand that a mother does not stay with her daughters, it is not the right thing to do. I miss her so much. No one talks to me here. Oh, they do in one sense, but not like Ma.

[1]***Maharani*** princess. The other Hindi words in the paragraph designate various foods. For the rest of the story, we annotate only words that are not the names of foods.

5 My mother-in-law called me, and I went to her room where she was lying down. She is always lying down. What are you doing, she asked me. She always wants to know what I am doing, whether I am in the kitchen or in the bathroom. Cooking, I said. Do you want any help, she asked as she did every day. No, *Mataji,*[2] you rest, I replied as I did every day and returned to the kitchen. I remember once when I had said that I did need some help (some people were coming over for dinner that day) she never let me live it down. She kept telling the guests, the child is still young, she just cannot cope with the housework. She smiled gently as she said this and the guests all looked pityingly at me. Later my husband reproached me for letting her take on so much of my work. I felt so guilty.

The potatoes were ready. I kept half of them for the *sabji* and began to mash the other half for the *tikkies.* Vegetables were so expensive these days, not to mention essentials like sugar. One needs another emergency to get our country out of this mess, my husband had said as he cast his vote. But with the new government, prices have gone up still further. Once economy meant buying a *saree*[3] or two less, now we have to cut down on things like fruits and sugar. Household stuff is almost impossible to buy. At the time of my marriage my parents gave me a refrigerator and a T.V. We would never have been able to buy them on our own. In the beginning my family was against giving the T.V., but my husband's side insisted, and as they were not taking any cash, my parents said that they might as well. Still, it was all so expensive, they spent about 50,000 *rupees* on the wedding and even then people said that they could have married me off in better style, considering that there were just my sister and I. Now my husband has taken out a policy for our daughter so that when it matures in another twenty years, we will have one *lakh rupees*[4] for the marriage expenses. The price of gold has gone up so much. My parents gave me three sets of jewelry. I doubt if I can give my daughter even two. God knows how we'll ever have money to build a house after that. And house rents are soaring too, our tiny two-bedroom house costs us 1,500 *rupees* and that is supposed to be cheap! No wonder people are corrupt. How else can they build such huge houses in a city like this? That way my husband isn't bad—he doesn't take bribes, but when he sees other people doing it, he gets mad and takes it out on me.

I put the oil on the gas and began frying the *tikkies.* They should be here any minute. Oh, God, time for baby's milk. I put the milk to heat and got the bottle ready. Is everything ready? asked my husband from the next room. Almost, I replied. He never entered the kitchen. On principle. He can't even heat a glass of milk. That's a woman's job, he said when I once asked him to heat the milk for Baby while I was engaged in some other work. Once, when I was ill and my mother-in-law away, there was no one to look after the house. What chaos. My husband lived for three whole days on bread, butter and cheese, while I, in bed, was given the same. I had no alternative but to get well and stagger about the house, cleaning up the place and washing the dishes which had mounted alarmingly. During those two

[2]***Mataji*** Mother (the suffix *ji* is a term of respect)

[3]***saree*** an outer garment of lightweight cloth, worn draped over one shoulder or covering the head

[4]***lakh rupees*** 100,000 rupees

days he used twelve mugs, six plates, seven glasses, four knives, eight spoons and two forks—all of which awaited me. Also two trousers, two shirts, four banyans, one pair of *pyjama kurta* and three handkerchiefs. Thank God you're all right, he sighed when he heard me in the kitchen that evening. It is the nearest he has come to paying me a compliment—if you can call it one.

Well, the *tikkies* were ready. Just a few minutes for the *halwa.* I quickly gave Baby her bottle, went back to the kitchen and heard my husband yell that they had come. For heaven's sake, get dressed, he said, coming into the kitchen. You should have finished everything by now. Once you get stuck in the kitchen, you get stuck. Learn to be systematic. I rushed to the bedroom and feverishly washed my face and combed my hair. Should I change my *saree* or not . . . might as well, or he'd say something again. I changed and went to the drawing room with a smile.

*Namaste, Bhabiji, Namaste,*[5] his friends said, what wonderful smells coming from the kitchen. Oh, it's nothing, I murmured, what will you have, tea or coffee? Please don't bother, they said. No bother at all, I replied, you must have something. Oh, well, said one, I'll have tea, the other said he would have coffee, but not to bother about anything else, no formality please. No, no, not at all, I said and went to the kitchen. I put one vessel for the tea and another for the coffee. Why couldn't they have asked for the same thing? Sometimes I felt glad that I was working, it provided some variety to this life of cooking and washing and cleaning. In the morning I get up at 5 a.m., make tea for everyone, milk for Baby, then get breakfast ready for the family. Sometimes my husband wants *parathas,* sometimes toast and eggs, sometimes he gets this craving for *dosas.* Then I pack our lunches for the office, make the beds and rush to catch the bus to work. No time to talk to Baby or cuddle her.

10 I took the tea and coffee to the drawing room. Thank you, thank you, they said, perfect weather for hot drinks. I looked out of the window. It was raining . . . I hadn't even known. Yes, perfect weather for tea and *pakodas,* they exclaimed. Good idea, excellent idea, beamed my husband, let us have some *pakodas.* Ah, this is what you would call doing poetic justice to the weather. So I went to the kitchen to do poetic justice to the weather. When they were ready I put the *pakodas, tikkies* and *halwa* on the tray and took it to them. Wonderful, wonderful, they said. What a feast you have laid out for us, you really shouldn't have bothered. No bother, no bother at all, I said. So, they enquired, how is your office? Fine, I smiled. It wasn't. Not now. In the beginning, when I started working, it was all so interesting. I met new people, got a salary, felt independent. But people are so strange. One day I happened to talk to one of my colleagues longer than I usually do. He was telling me about a book he was reading and I got so caught up in what he was saying that I hardly realized how time passed. That evening the girl who sits next to me said, so you had a nice chat did you? Yes, I replied, and then the way she was looking at me made me go red. The next day when he lent me the book I noticed another of my colleagues (male) looking meaningfully at me. Now whenever by chance I happen to talk to him everyone in the office watches and I feel so wretched. The men, especially,

[5]***Namaste, Bhabiji, Namaste*** greetings, sister-in-law, greetings (said with folded hands)

gossip so much. At lunchtime they sit among themselves and giggle. They seem to know everything—who is talking to whom, who is wearing what and who the boss favours . . . everything. They never seem to discuss books or music . . . and I miss both. We get bored *yar,*[6] they say, we don't know what to do on weekends. Oh, how I long to be bored. Or just lie in bed with a book and listen to music. That's my idea of heaven.

It's nice to be independent, said my husband's friend, women like you will change the face of this country. Very nice *pakodas,* very nice indeed. Thank you, you're very kind, I murmured. We don't feel like leaving, he added as he settled more comfortably into his chair. Stay for dinner, said my husband at once, then we can all relax and *gup-shup.*[7] That will be too much of a bother for your wife, said his friend. No problem, no problem, said my husband heartily. What is there? The food is ready, there is no such formality in this house. They all looked at me. Of course, I said, it's no bother. I excused myself and went to the kitchen. Would there be enough food for them? I felt like flinging the *dal* and *sabji* into their faces and was shocked at the force of the feeling. My husband followed me into the kitchen. Will the food be enough for them? I replied, it had better be. He hissed, what is the matter with you, stop acting difficult. I said, stop breathing down my neck. You invited them, not I. My husband said, this is the limit, I don't understand you. Is this the time to make a scene? Why don't you make another *sabji* and some *khir?* Because there is no other *sabji* and no milk for *khir,* I replied. We stared into each other's faces. I should have expected this, said my husband. Even my friends are not welcome in this house. If you are not prepared to look after them, you should have warned me earlier. This last-minute hysteria I will not stand for. I sank back against the sink. I said, then go and get the milk and *sabji.* Furious, he replied, how do you expect me to go; then who will look after them? I said, that's your problem. We don't have a servant. My husband said, you're always creating problems, this is what comes of being unsystematic. I reminded him, but you told me not to buy more vegetables and milk than was absolutely necessary because of the prices going up. This made him even angrier. What is the matter, can I help you, said my husband's friend, walking into the kitchen. I said, no, no, please. I can manage. I wondered what he would do if I had said yes, please help. The thought made me smile and my husband, seeing my face, gave a sigh of relief and ushered his friend out of the kitchen.

For dinner there were *puris, aloo, dal, karelas,* and mangoes with the cream that I had been collecting for the week's butter. I was so tired by the end of it that I could hardly eat. Then I put Baby to sleep and gave them all coffee. They finished the coffee, and said, *chalo, chalo,*[8] let us go for a movie. Now? I asked. Of course, they replied. If we rush we can get tickets for the night show, *chalo,* let us go. Let us, agreed my husband, these impromptu decisions are always so enjoyable, one shouldn't always plan. I said, I have to wash the dishes. They replied, oh, do that tomorrow, you mustn't always work so hard. I said, but I have to go to the office tomorrow,

[6]***yar*** a somewhat meaningless term, like *you know,* or *eh*
[7]***gup-shup*** gossip
[8]***chalo, chalo*** let's go, let's go

and I'm tired. My husband replied, don't make a fuss, you are not the only one who has to go to office, even I have to go. That is the trouble with you. You don't know how to enjoy yourself. And *Mataji* will look after the baby. Don't make *her* an excuse now. *Chalo, chalo,* let us hurry.

I put the dishes in the sink, and then we rushed. The tickets were not available so we bought them in black—ten *rupees* each. In spite of that, we were just four rows away from the screen. As the hero and heroine sang their first song to each other I fell asleep. A deep sleep. My husband woke me up when it was over. They were all amused. Even here she sleeps, said my husband indulgently.

We reached out colony at 1 a.m., just managed to get the night service bus back home. I slept in the bus, too. As we walked back home from the bus stop, my husband's mood expanded. What a night, what a night, he exclaimed. He stopped and looked up at the heavens,

> Palace-roof of cloudless nights!
> Paradise of golden lights!
> Deep, immeasurable, vast . . .

he quoted dreamily. I leaned sleepily against his arm and he looked at me with something akin to pain. Sleep, always sleep, he said. Why can't you rise above such purely physical reactions? You lack soul.

15 When we reached home, I made the beds and sank into mine with a groan of satisfaction. Heaven. The trouble with you, said my husband, is that your whole attitude to work is wrong. You'll never get tired if you change your attitude to work. Learn from Khalil Gibran, and he quoted:

> Always you have been told that work is a curse, and labour a misfortune.
> But I say to you that when you work you fulfill a part of earth's further dream, assigned to you when that dream was born,
> And in keeping yourself with labour you are in truth loving life,
> And to love life through labour is to be intimate with life's innermost secret.

That is poetry, philosophy, truth, mused my husband. So were the *pakodas,* I sighed and slept.

[*1989*]

## DAVID LEAVITT

*David Leavitt was twenty and still an undergraduate at Yale when in 1982 he published "Territory" in* The New Yorker. The New Yorker *had been publishing serious fiction for decades, but "Territory" was the first openly gay story to appear in the magazine. Two years later the story was reprinted in a collection of Leavitt's stories,* Family Dancing. *In addition to publishing stories, Leavitt has also published two novels (*The Lost Language of Cranes *[1986] and* Equal Affections *[1989]), both about gay life.*

## Territory

Neil's mother, Mrs. Campbell, sits on her lawn chair behind a card table outside the food co-op. Every few minutes, as the sun shifts, she moves the chair and table several inches back so as to remain in the shade. It is a hundred degrees outside, and bright white. Each time someone goes in or out of the co-op a gust of air-conditioning flies out of the automatic doors, raising dust from the cement.

Neil stands just inside, poised over a water fountain, and watches her. She has on a sun hat, and a sweatshirt over her tennis dress; her legs are bare, and shiny with cocoa butter. In front of her, propped against the table, a sign proclaims: MOTHERS, FIGHT FOR YOUR CHILDREN'S RIGHTS—SUPPORT A NON-NUCLEAR FUTURE. Women dressed exactly like her pass by, notice the sign, listen to her brief spiel, finger pamphlets, sign petitions or don't sign petitions, never give money. Her weary eyes are masked by dark glasses. In the age of Reagan, she has declared, keeping up the causes of peace and justice is a futile, tiresome, and unrewarding effort; it is therefore an effort fit only for mothers to keep up. The sun bounces off the window glass through which Neil watches her. His own reflection lines up with her profile.

Later that afternoon, Neil spreads himself out alongside the pool and imagines he is being watched by the shirtless Chicago gardener. But the gardener, concentrating on his pruning, is neither seductive or seducible. On the lawn, his mother's large Airedales—Abigail, Lucille, Fern—amble, sniff, urinate. Occasionally, they accost the gardener, who yells at them in Spanish.

After two years' absence, Neil reasons, he should feel nostalgia, regret, gladness upon returning home. He closes his eyes and tries to muster the proper background music for the cinematic scene of return. His rhapsody, however, is interrupted by the noises of his mother's trio—the scratchy cello, whining violin, stumbling piano—as she and Lillian Havalard and Charlotte Feder plunge through Mozart. The tune is cheery, in a Germanic sort of way, and utterly inappropriate to what Neil is trying to feel. Yet it *is* the music of his adolescence; they have played it for years, bent over the notes, their heads bobbing in silent time to the metronome.

5 It is getting darker. Every few minutes, he must move his towel so as to remain within the narrowing patch of sunlight. In four hours, Wayne, his lover of ten months and the only person he has ever imagined he could spend his life with, will be in this house, where no lover of his has ever set foot. The thought fills him with a sense of grand terror and curiosity. He stretches, tries to feel seductive, desirable. The gardener's shears whack at the ferns; the music above him rushes to a loud, premature conclusion. The women laugh and applaud themselves as they give up for the day. He hears Charlotte Feder's full nasal twang, the voice of a fat woman in a pink pants suit—odd, since she is a scrawny, arthritic old bird, rarely clad in anything other than tennis shorts and a blouse. Lillian is the fat woman in the pink pants suit; her voice is thin and warped by too much crying. Drink in hand, she calls out from the porch, "Hot enough!" and waves. He lifts himself up and nods to her.

The women sit on the porch and chatter; their voices blend with the clink of ice in glasses. They belong to a small circle of ladies all of whom, with the exception of Neil's mother, are widows and divorcées. Lillian's husband left her twenty-two years ago, and sends her a check every month to live on; Charlotte has been divorced twice as long as she was married, and has a daughter serving a long sentence for terrorist acts committed when she was nineteen. Only Neil's mother has a husband, a distant sort of husband, away often on business. He is away on business now. All of them feel betrayed—by husbands, by children, by history.

Neil closes his eyes, tries to hear the words only as sounds. Soon, a new noise accosts him: his mother arguing with the gardener in Spanish. He leans on his elbows and watches them; the syllables are loud, heated, and compressed, and seem on the verge of explosion. But the argument ends happily; they shake hands. The gardener collects his check and walks out the gate without so much as looking at Neil.

He does not know the gardener's name; as his mother has reminded him, he does not know most of what has gone on since he moved away. Her life has gone on, unaffected by his absence. He flinches at his own egotism, the egoism of sons.

"Neil! Did you call the airport to make sure the plane's coming in on time?"

10 "Yes," he shouts to her. "It is."

"Good. Well, I'll have dinner ready when you get back."

"Mom—"

"What?" The word comes out in a weary wail that is more of an answer than a question.

"What's wrong?" he says, forgetting his original question.

15 "Nothing's wrong," she declares in a tone that indicates that everything is wrong. "The dogs have to be fed, dinner has to be made, and I've got people here. Nothing's wrong."

"I hope things will be as comfortable as possible when Wayne gets here."

"Is that a request or a threat?"

"Mom—"

Behind her sunglasses, her eyes are inscrutable. "I'm tired," she says. "It's been a long day. I . . . I'm anxious to meet Wayne. I'm sure he'll be wonderful, and we'll all have a wonderful, wonderful time. I'm sorry. I'm just tired."

20 She heads up the stairs. He suddenly feels an urge to cover himself; his body embarrasses him, as it has in her presence since the day she saw him shirtless and said with delight, "Neil! You're growing hair under your arms!"

Before he can get up, the dogs gather round him and begin to sniff and lick at him. He wriggles to get away from them, but Abigail, the largest and stupidest, straddles his stomach and nuzzles his mouth. He splutters and, laughing, throws her off. "Get away from me, you goddamn dogs," he shouts, and swats at them. They are new dogs, not the dog of his childhood, not dogs he trusts.

He stands, and the dogs circle him, looking up at his face expectantly. He feels renewed terror at the thought that Wayne will be here so soon: Will they sleep in the same room? Will they make love? He has never had sex in his parents' house. How can he be expected to be a lover here, in this place of his childhood, of his earliest shame, in this household of mothers and dogs?

"Dinnertime! Abbylucyferny, Abbylucyferny, dinnertime!"

"Do you realize," he shouts to her, "that no matter how much those dogs love you they'd probably kill you for the leg of lamb in the freezer?"

25 Neil was twelve the first time he recognized in himself something like sexuality. He was lying outside, on the grass, when Rasputin—the dog, long dead, of his childhood—began licking his face. He felt a tingle he did not recognize, pulled off his shirt to give the dog access to more of him. Rasputin's tongue tickled coolly. A wet nose started to sniff down his body, toward his bathing suit. What he felt frightened him, but he couldn't bring himself to push the dog away. Then his mother called out, "Dinner," and Rasputin was gone, more interested in food than in him.

It was the day after Rasputin was put to sleep, years later, that Neil finally stood in the kitchen, his back turned to his parents, and said, with unexpected ease, "I'm a homosexual." The words seemed insufficient, reductive. For years, he had believed his sexuality to be detachable from the essential him, but now he realized that it was part of him. He had the sudden, despairing sensation that though the words had been easy to say, the fact of their having been aired was incurably damning. Only then, for the first time, did he admit that they were true, and he shook and wept in regret for what he would not be for his mother, for having failed her. His father hung back, silent; he was absent for that moment as he was mostly absent—a strong absence. Neil always thought of him sitting on the edge of the bed in his underwear, captivated by something on television. He said, "It's O.K., Neil." But his mother was resolute; her lower lip didn't quaver. She had enormous reserves of strength to which she only gained access at moments like this one. She hugged him from behind, wrapped him in the childhood smells of perfume and brownies, and whispered, "It's O.K., honey." For once, her words seemed as inadequate as his. Neil felt himself shrunk to an embarrassed adolescent, hating her sympathy, not wanting her to touch him. It was the way he would feel from then on whenever he was in her presence—even now, at twenty-three, bringing home his lover to meet her.

All through his childhood, she had packed only the most nutritious lunches, had served on the PTA, had volunteered at the children's library and at his school, had organized a successful campaign to ban a racist history textbook. The day after he told her, she located and got in touch with an organization called the Coalition of Parents of Lesbians and Gays. Within a year, she was president of it. On weekends, she and the other mothers drove their station wagons to San Francisco, set up their card tables in front of the Bulldog Baths, the Liberty Baths, passed out literature to men in leather and denim who were loath to admit they even had mothers. These men, who would habitually do violence to each other, were strangely cowed by the suburban ladies with their informational booklets, and bent their heads. Neil was a sophomore in college then, and lived in San Francisco. She brought him pamphlets detailing the dangers of bathhouses and back rooms, enemas and poppers, wordless sex in alleyways. His excursion into that world had been brief and lamentable, and was over. He winced at the thought that she knew all his sexual secrets, and vowed to move to the East Coast to escape her. It was not very different from the days when she had campaigned for a better playground, or tutored the Hispanic children in the audiovisual room. Those days, as well, he had run away from her concern. Even today, perched in front of the co-op, collecting signatures for nuclear disarmament, she was quintessentially a mother. And if the lot of mothers was to expect nothing in return, was the lot of sons to return nothing?

Driving across the Dumbarton Bridge on his way to the airport, Neil thinks, I have returned nothing; I have simply returned. He wonders if she would have given birth to him had she known what he would grow up to be.

Then he berates himself: Why should he assume himself to be the cause of her sorrow? She has told him that her life is full of secrets. She has changed since he left home—grown thinner, more rigid, harder to hug. She has given up baking, taken up tennis; her skin has browned and tightened. She is no longer the woman who hugged him and kissed him, who said, "As long as you're happy, that's all that's important to us."

30 The flats spread out around him; the bridge floats on purple and green silt, and spongy bay fill, not water at all. Only ten miles north, a whole city has been built on gunk dredged up from the bay.

He arrives at the airport ten minutes early, to discover that the plane has landed twenty minutes early. His first view of Wayne is from behind, by the baggage belt. Wayne looks as he always looks—slightly windblown—and is wearing the ratty leather jacket he was wearing the night they met. Neil sneaks up on him and puts his hands on his shoulders; when Wayne turns around, he looks relieved to see him.

They hug like brothers; only in the safety of Neil's mother's car do they dare to kiss. They recognize each other's smells, and grow comfortable again. "I never imagined I'd actually see you out here," Neil says, "but you're exactly the same here as there."

"It's only been a week."

They kiss again. Neil wants to go to a motel, but Wayne insists on being pragmatic. "We'll be there soon. Don't worry."

35 "We could go to one of the bathhouses in the city and take a room for a couple of aeons," Neil says. "Christ, I'm hard up. I don't even know if we're going to be in the same bedroom."

"Well, if we're not," Wayne says, "we'll sneak around. It'll be romantic."

They cling to each other for a few more minutes, until they realize that people are looking in the car window. Reluctantly, they pull apart. Neil reminds himself that he loves this man, that there is a reason for him to bring this man home.

He takes the scenic route on the way back. The car careers over foothills, through forests, along white four-lane highways high in the mountains. Wayne tells Neil that he sat next to a woman on the plane who was once Marilyn Monroe's psychiatrist's nurse. He slips his foot out of his shoe and nudges Neil's ankle, pulling Neil's sock down with his toe.

"I have to drive," Neil says. "I'm very glad you're here."

40 There is a comfort in the privacy of the car. They have a common fear of walking hand in hand, of publicly showing physical affection, even in the permissive West Seventies of New York—a fear that they have admitted only to one another. They slip through a pass between two hills, and are suddenly in residential Northern California, the land of expensive ranch-style houses.

As they pull into Neil's mother's driveway, the dogs run barking toward the car. When Wayne opens the door, they jump and lap at him, and he tries to close it again. "Don't worry. Abbylucyferny! Get in the house, damn it!"

His mother descends from the porch. She has changed into a blue flower-print dress, which Neil doesn't recognize. He gets out of the car and halfheartedly chastises the dogs. Crickets chirp in the trees. His mother looks radiant, even beautiful, illuminated by the headlights, surrounded by the now quiet dogs, like a Circe with her slaves. When she walks over to Wayne, offering her hand, and says, "Wayne, I'm Barbara," Neil forgets that she is his mother.

"Good to meet you, Barbara," Wayne says, and reaches out his hand. Craftier than she, he whirls around to kiss her cheek.

*Barbara!* He is calling his mother Barbara! Then he remembers that Wayne is five years older than he is. They chat by the open car door, and Neil shrinks back—the embarrassed adolescent, uncomfortable, unwanted.

45 So the dreaded moment passes and he might as well not have been there. At dinner, Wayne keeps the conversation smooth, like a captivated courtier seeking Neil's mother's hand. A faggot son's sodomist—such words spit into Neil's head. She has prepared tiny meatballs with fresh coriander, fettucine with pesto. Wayne talks about the street people in New York; El Salvador is a tragedy; if only Sadat had lived; Phyllis Schlafly[1]—what can you do?

"It's a losing battle," she tells him. "Every day I'm out there with my card table, me and the other mothers, but I tell you, Wayne, it's a losing battle. Sometimes I think us old ladies are the only ones with enough patience to fight."

Occasionally, Neil says something, but his comments seem stupid and clumsy. Wayne continues to call her Barbara. No one under forty has ever called her Barbara as long as Neil can remember. They drink wine; he does not.

Now is the time for drastic action. He contemplates taking Wayne's hand, then checks himself. He has never done anything in her presence to indicate that the sexuality he confessed to five years ago was a reality and not an invention. Even now, he and Wayne might as well be friends, college roommates. Then Wayne, his savior, with a single, sweeping gesture, reaches for his hand, and clasps it, in the midst of a joke he is telling about Saudi Arabians. By the time he is laughing, their hands are joined. Neil's throat contracts; his heart begins to beat violently. He notices his mother's eyes flicker, glance downward; she never breaks the stride of her sentence. The dinner goes on, and every taboo nurtured since childhood falls quietly away.

She removes the dishes. Their hands grow sticky; he cannot tell which fingers are his and which Wayne's. She clears the rest of the table and rounds up the dogs.

50 "Well, boys, I'm very tired, and I've got a long day ahead of me tomorrow, so I think I'll hit the sack. There are extra towels for you in Neil's bathroom. Wayne. Sleep well."

"Good night, Barbara," Wayne calls out. "It's been wonderful meeting you."

They are alone. Now they can disentangle their hands.

"No problem about where we sleep, is there?"

[1]**Phyllis Schlafly** a vigorous opponent of feminist movements

"No," Neil says. "I just can't imagine sleeping with someone in this house."

55 His leg shakes violently. Wayne takes Neil's hand in a firm grasp and hauls him up.

Later that night, they lie outside, under redwood trees, listening to the hysteria of the crickets, the hum of the pool cleaning itself. Redwood leaves prick their skin. They fell in love in bars and apartments, and this is the first time that they have made love outdoors. Neil is not sure he has enjoyed the experience. He kept sensing eyes, imagined that the neighborhood cats were staring at them from behind a fence of brambles. He remembers he once hid in this spot when he and some of the children from the neighborhood were playing sardines, remembers the intoxication of small bodies packed together, the warm breath of suppressed laughter on his neck. "The loser had to go through the spanking machine," he tells Wayne.

"Did you lose often?"

"Most of the time. The spanking machine never really hurt—just a whirl of hands. If you moved fast enough, no one could actually get you. Sometimes, though, late in the afternoon, we'd get naughty. We'd chase each other and pull each other's pants down. That was all. Boys and girls together!"

"Listen to the insects," Wayne says, and closes his eyes.

60 Neil turns to examine Wayne's face, notices a single, small pimple. Their lovemaking usually begins in a wrestle, a struggle for dominance, and ends with a somewhat confusing loss of identity—as now, when Neil sees a foot on the grass, resting against his leg, and tries to determine if it is his own or Wayne's.

From inside the house, the dogs begin to bark. Their yelps grow into alarmed falsettos. Neil lifts himself up. "I wonder if they smell something," he says.

"Probably just us," says Wayne.

"My mother will wake up. She hates getting waked up."

Lights go on in the house; the door to the porch opens.

65 "What's wrong, Abby? What's wrong?" his mother's voice calls softly.

Wayne clamps his hand over Neil's mouth. "Don't say anything," he whispers.

"I can't just—" Neil begins to say, but Wayne's hand closes over his mouth again. He bites it, and Wayne starts laughing.

"What was that?" Her voice projects into the garden. "Hello?" she says.

The dogs yelp louder. "Abbylucyferny, it's O.K., it's O.K." Her voice is soft and panicked. "Is anyone there?" she asks loudly.

70 The brambles shake. She takes a flashlight, shines it around the garden. Wayne and Neil duck down; the light lands on them and hovers for a few seconds. Then it clicks off and they are in the dark—a new dark, a darker dark, which their eyes must readjust to.

"Let's go to bed, Abbylucyferny," she says gently. Neil and Wayne hear her pad into the house. The dogs whimper as they follow her, and the lights go off.

Once before, Neil and his mother had stared at each other in the glare of bright lights. Four years ago, they stood in the arena created by the headlights of her car, waiting for the train. He was on his way back to San Francisco, where he was marching in a Gay Pride Parade the next day. The train station was next door to the food co-op and shared its parking lot. The co-op, familiar and boring by day, took on a certain mystery in the night. Neil recognized the spot where he had skidded on his bicycle and broken his leg. Through the glass doors, the brightly lit interior of the store glowed, its rows and rows of cans and boxes forming their own horizon, each can illuminated so that even from outside Neil could read the labels. All that was missing was the ladies in tennis dresses and sweatshirts, pushing their carts past bins of nuts and dried fruits.

"Your train is late," his mother said. Her hair fell loosely on her shoulders, and her legs were tanned. Neil looked at her and tried to imagine her in labor with him—bucking and struggling with his birth. He felt then the strange, sexless love for women which through his whole adolescence he had mistaken for heterosexual desire.

A single bright light approached them; it preceded the low, haunting sound of the whistle. Neil kissed his mother, and waved goodbye as he ran to meet the train. It was an old train, with windows tinted a sort of horrible lemon-lime. It stopped only long enough for him to hoist himself on board, and then it was moving again. He hurried to a window, hoping to see her drive off, but the tint of the window made it possible for him to make out only vague patches of light—street lamps, cars, the co-op.

He sank into the hard, green seat. The train was almost entirely empty; the only other passenger was a dark-skinned man wearing bluejeans and a leather jacket. He sat directly across the aisle from Neil, next to the window. He had rough skin and a thick mustache. Neil discovered that by pretending to look out the window he could study the man's reflection in the lemon-lime glass. It was only slightly hazy—the quality of a bad photograph. Neil felt his mouth open, felt sleep closing in on him. Hazy red and gold flashes through the glass pulsed in the face of the man in the window, giving the curious impression of muscle spasms. It took Neil a few minutes to realize that the man was staring at him, or, rather, staring at the back of his head—staring at his staring. The man smiled as though to say, I know exactly what you're staring at, and Neil felt the sickening sensation of desire rise in his throat.

Right before they reached the city, the man stood up and sat down in the seat next to Neil's. The man's thigh brushed deliberately against his own. Neil's eyes were watering; he felt sick to his stomach. Taking Neil's hand, the man said, "Why so nervous, honey? Relax."

Neil woke up the next morning with the taste of ashes in his mouth. He was lying on the floor, without blankets or sheets or pillows. Instinctively, he reached for his pants, and as he pulled them on came face to face with the man from the train. His name was Luis; he turned out to be a dog groomer. His apartment smelled of dog.

"Why such a hurry?" Luis said.

"The parade. The Gay Pride Parade. I'm meeting some friends to march."

"I'll come with you," Luis said. "I think I'm too old for these things, but why not?"

Neil did not want Luis to come with him, but he found it impossible to say so. Luis looked older by day, more likely to carry diseases. He dressed again in a torn T-shirt, leather jacket, bluejeans. "It's my everyday apparel," he said, and laughed. Neil buttoned his pants, aware that they had been washed by his mother the day before. Luis possessed the peculiar combination of hypermasculinity and effeminacy which exemplifies faggotry. Neil wanted to be rid of him, but Luis's mark was on him, he could see that much. They would become lovers whether Neil liked it or not.

They joined the parade midway. Neil hoped he wouldn't meet anyone he knew; he did not want to have to explain Luis, who clung to him. The parade was full of shirtless men with oiled, muscular shoulders. Neil's back ached. There were floats carrying garishly dressed prom queens and cheerleaders, some with beards, some actually looking like women. Luis said, "It makes me proud, makes me glad to be what I am." Neil supposed that by darting into the crowd ahead of him he might be able to lose Luis forever, but he found it difficult to let him go; the prospect of being alone seemed unbearable.

Neil was startled to see his mother watching the parade, holding up a sign. She was with the Coalition of Parents of Lesbians and Gays; they had posted a huge banner on the wall behind them proclaiming: OUR SONS AND DAUGHTERS, WE ARE PROUD OF YOU. She spotted him; she waved, and jumped up and down.

"Who's that woman?" Luis asked.

"My mother. I should go say hello to her."

"O.K.," Luis said. He followed Neil to the side of the parade. Neil kissed his mother. Luis took off his shirt, wiped his face with it, smiled.

"I'm glad you came," Neil said.

"I wouldn't have missed it, Neil. I wanted to show you I cared."

He smiled, and kissed her again. He showed no intention of introducing Luis, so Luis introduced himself.

"Hello, Luis," Mrs. Campbell said. Neil looked away. Luis shook her hand, and Neil wanted to warn his mother to wash it, warned himself to check with a V.D. clinic first thing Monday.

"Neil, this is Carmen Bologna, another one of the mothers," Mrs. Campbell said. She introduced him to a fat Italian woman with flushed cheeks, and hair arranged in the shape of a clamshell.

"Good to meet you, Neil, good to meet you," said Carmen Bologna. "You know my son, Michael? I'm so proud of Michael! He's doing so well now. I'm proud of him, proud to be his mother I am, and your mother's proud, too!"

The woman smiled at him, and Neil could think of nothing to say but "Thank you." He looked uncomfortably toward his mother, who stood listening to Luis. It occurred to him that the worst period of his life was probably about to begin and he had no way to stop it.

A group of drag queens ambled over to where the mothers were standing. "Michael! Michael!" shouted Carmen Bologna, and embraced a sticklike man wrapped in green satin. Michael's eyes were heavily dosed with green eyeshadow, and his lips were painted pink.

Neil turned and saw his mother staring, her mouth open. He marched over to where Luis was standing, and they moved back into the parade. He turned and waved to her. She waved back; he saw pain in her face, and then, briefly, regret. That day, he felt she would have traded him for any other son. Later, she said to him, "Carmen Bologna really was proud, and, speaking as a mother, let me tell you, you have to be brave to feel such pride."

Neil was never proud. It took him a year to dump Luis, another year to leave California. The sick taste of ashes was still in his mouth. On the plane, he envisioned his mother sitting alone in the dark, smoking. She did not leave his mind until he was circling New York, staring down at the dawn rising over Queens. The song playing in his earphones would remain hovering on the edges of his memory, always associated with her absence. After collecting his baggage, he took a bus into the city. Boys were selling newspapers in the middle of highways, through the windows of stopped cars. It was seven in the morning when he reached Manhattan. He stood for ten minutes on East Thirty-fourth Street, breathed the cold air, and felt bubbles rising in his blood.

Neil got a job as a paralegal—a temporary job, he told himself. When he met Wayne a year later, the sensations of that first morning returned to him. They'd been up all night, and at six they walked across the park to Wayne's apartment with the nervous, deliberate gait of people aching to make love for the first time. Joggers ran by with their dogs. None of them knew what Wayne and he were about to do, and the secrecy excited him. His mother came to mind, and the song, and the whirling vision of Queens coming alive below him. His breath solidified into clouds, and he felt happier than he had ever felt before in his life.

The second day of Wayne's visit, he and Neil go with Mrs. Campbell to pick up the dogs at the dog parlor. The grooming establishment is decorated with pink ribbons and photographs of the owner's champion pit bulls. A fat, middle-aged woman appears from the back, leading the newly trimmed and fluffed Abigail, Lucille, and Fern by three leashes. The dogs struggle frantically when they see Neil's mother, tangling the woman up in their leashes. "Ladies, behave!" Mrs. Campbell commands, and collects the dogs. She gives Fern to Neil and Abigail to Wayne. In the car on the way back, Abigail begins pawing to get on Wayne's lap.

"Just push her off," Mrs. Campbell says. "She knows she's not supposed to do that."

"You never groomed Rasputin," Neil complains.

"Rasputin was a mutt."

"Rasputin was a beautiful dog, even if he did smell."

"Do you remember when you were a little kid, Neil, you used to make Rasputin dance with you? Once you tried to dress him up in one of my blouses."

"I don't remember that," Neil says.

"Yes. I remember," says Mrs. Campbell. "Then you tried to organize a dog beauty contest in the neighborhood. You wanted to have runners-up—everything."

"A dog beauty contest?" Wayne says.

"Mother, do we have to—"

"I think it's a mother's privilege to embarrass her son," Mrs. Campbell says, and smiles.

When they are about to pull into the driveway, Wayne starts screaming, and pushes Abigail off his lap. "Oh, my God!" he says. "The dog just pissed all over me."

Neil turns around and sees a puddle seeping into Wayne's slacks. He suppresses his laughter, and Mrs. Campbell hands him a rag.

"I'm sorry, Wayne," she says. "It goes with the territory."

"This is really disgusting," Wayne says, swatting at himself with the rag.

Neil keeps his eyes on his own reflection in the rearview mirror and smiles.

At home, while Wayne cleans himself in the bathroom, Neil watches his mother cook lunch—Japanese noodles in soup. "When you went off to college," she says, "I went to the grocery store. I was going to buy you ramen noodles, and I suddenly realized you weren't going to be around to eat them. I started crying right then, blubbering like an idiot."

Neil clenches his fists inside his pockets. She has a way of telling him little sad stories when he doesn't want to hear them—stories of dolls broken by her brothers, lunches stolen by neighborhood boys on the way to school. Now he has joined the ranks of male children who have made her cry.

"Mama, I'm sorry," he says.

She is bent over the noodles, which steam in her face. "I didn't want to say anything in front of Wayne, but I wish you had answered me last night. I was very frightened—and worried."

"I'm sorry," he says, but it's not convincing. His fingers prickle. He senses a great sorrow about to be born.

"I lead a quiet life," she says. "I don't want to be a disciplinarian. I just don't have the energy for these—shenanigans. Please don't frighten me that way again."

"If you were so upset, why didn't you say something?"

"I'd rather not discuss it. I lead a quiet life. I'm not used to getting woken up late at night. I'm not used—"

"To my having a lover?"

"No, I'm not used to having other people around, that's all. Wayne is charming. A wonderful young man."

"He likes you, too."

"I'm sure we'll get along fine."

She scoops the steaming noodles into ceramic bowls. Wayne returns, wearing shorts. His white, hairy legs are a shocking contrast to hers, which are brown and sleek.

"I'll wash those pants, Wayne," Mrs. Campbell says. "I have a special detergent that'll take out the stain."

She gives Neil a look to indicate that the subject should be dropped. He looks at Wayne, looks at his mother; his initial embarrassment gives way to a fierce pride—the arrogance of mastery. He is glad his mother knows that he is desired, glad it makes her flinch.

Later, he steps into the back yard; the gardener is back, whacking at the bushes with his shears. Neil walks by him in his bathing suit, imagining he is on parade.

That afternoon, he finds his mother's daily list on the kitchen table:

TUESDAY
7:00—breakfast
Take dogs to groomer
Groceries (?)

Campaign against Draft—4-7

Buy underwear
Trios—2:00
Spaghetti
Fruit

Asparagus if sale
Peanuts
Milk

Doctor's Appointment (make)
Write Cranston/Hayakawa
re disarmament

Handi-Wraps
Mozart
Abigail
Top Ramen
Pedro

Her desk and trash can are full of such lists; he remembers them from the earliest days of his childhood. He had learned to read from them. In his own life, too, there have been endless lists—covered with check marks and arrows, at least one item always spilling over onto the next day's agenda. From September to November, "Buy plane ticket for Christmas" floated from list to list to list.

The last item puzzles him: Pedro. Pedro must be the gardener. He observes the accretion of names, the arbitrary specifics that give a sense of his mother's life. He could make a list of his own selves: the child, the adolescent, the promiscuous faggot son, and finally the good son, settled, relatively successful. But the divisions wouldn't work; he is today and will always be the child being licked by the dog, the boy on the floor with Luis; he will still be everything he is ashamed of. The other lists—the lists of things done and undone—tell their own truth: that his life is measured more properly in objects than in stages. He knows himself as "jump rope," "book," "sunglasses," "underwear."

"Tell me about your family, Wayne," Mrs. Campbell says that night, as they drive toward town. They are going to see an Esther Williams movie at the local revival house: an underwater musical, populated by mermaids, underwater Rockettes.

"My father was a lawyer," Wayne says. "He had an office in Queens, with a neon sign. I think he's probably the only lawyer in the world who had a neon sign. Anyway, he died when I was ten. My mother never remarried. She lives in Queens. Her great claim to fame is that when she was twenty-two she went on 'The $64,000 Question.' Her category was mystery novels. She made it to sixteen thousand before she got tripped up."

"When I was about ten, I wanted you to go on 'Jeopardy,'" Neil says to his mother. "You really should have, you know. You would have won."

You certainly loved 'Jeopardy,'" Mrs. Campbell says. "You used to watch it during dinner. Wayne, does your mother work?"

"No," he says. "She lives off investments."

"You're both only children," Mrs. Campbell says. Neil wonders if she is ruminating on the possible connection between that coincidence and their "alternative life style."

The movie theater is nearly empty. Neil sits between Wayne and his mother. There are pillows on the floor at the front of the theater, and a cat is prowling over them. It casts a monstrous shadow every now and then on the screen, disturbing the sedative effect of water ballet. Like a teen-ager, Neil cautiously reaches his arm around Wayne's shoulder. Wayne takes his hand immediately. Next to them, Neil's mother breathes in, out, in, out. Neil timorously moves his other arm and lifts it behind his mother's neck. He does not look at her, but he can tell from her breathing that she senses what he is doing. Slowly, carefully, he lets his hand drop on her shoulder; it twitches spasmodically, and he jumps, as if he had received an electric shock. His mother's quiet breathing is broken by a gasp; even Wayne notices. A sudden brightness on the screen illuminates the panic in her eyes, Neil's arm frozen above her, about to fall again. Slowly, he lowers his arm until his fingertips touch her skin, the fabric of her dress. He has gone too far to go back now; they are all too far.

140 "Wayne and Mrs. Campbell sink into their seats, but Neil remains stiff, holding up his arms, which rest on nothing. The movie ends, and they go on sitting just like that.

"I'm old," Mrs. Campbell says later, as they drive back home. "I remember when those films were new. Your father and I went to one on our first date. I loved them, because I could pretend that those women underwater were flying—they were so graceful. They really took advantage of Technicolor in those days. Color was something to appreciate. You can't know what it was like to see a color movie for the first time, after years of black-and-white. It's like trying to explain the surprise of snow to an East Coaster. Very little is new anymore, I fear."

Neil would like to tell her about his own nostalgia, but how can he explain that all of it revolves around her? The idea of her life before he was born pleases him. "Tell Wayne how you used to look like Esther Williams," he asks her.

She blushes. "I was told I looked like Esther Williams, but really more like Gene Tierney," she says. "Not beautiful, but interesting. I like to think I had a certain magnetism."

"You still do," Wayne says, and instantly recognizes the wrongness of his comment. Silence and a nervous laugh indicate that he has not yet mastered the family vocabulary.

145 When they got home, the night is once again full of the sound of crickets. Mrs. Campbell picks up a flashlight and calls the dogs. "Abbylucyferny, Abbylucyferny," she shouts, and the dogs amble from their various corners. She pushes them out the door to the back yard and follows them. Neil follows her. Wayne follows Neil, but hovers on the porch. Neil walks behind her as she tramps through the garden. She holds out her flashlight, and snails slide from behind bushes, from under rocks, to where she stands. When the snails become visible, she crushes them underfoot. They make a wet, cracking noise, like eggs being broken.

"Nights like this," she says, "I think of children without pants on, in hot South American countries. I have nightmares about tanks rolling down our street."

"The weather's never like this in New York," Neil says. "When it's hot, it's humid and sticky. You don't want to go outdoors."

"I could never live anywhere else but here. I think I'd die. I'm too used to the climate."

"Don't be silly."

"No, I mean it," she says. "I have adjusted too well to the weather."

The dogs bark and howl by the fence. "A cat, I suspect," she says. She aims her flashlight at a rock, and more snails emerge—uncountable numbers, too stupid to have learned not to trust light.

"I know what you were doing at the movie," she says.

"What?"

"I know what you were doing."

"What? I put my arm around you."

"I'm sorry, Neil," she says. "I can only take so much. Just so much."

"What do you mean?" he says. "I was only trying to show affection."

"Oh, affection—I know about affection."

He looks up at the porch, sees Wayne moving toward the door, trying not to listen.

"What do you mean?" Neil says to her.

She puts down the flashlight and wraps her arms around herself. "I remember when you were a little boy," she says. "I remember, and I have to stop remembering. I wanted you to grow up happy. And I'm very tolerant, very understanding. But I can only take so much."

His heart seems to have risen into his throat. "Mother," he says, "I think you know my life isn't your fault. But for God's sake, don't say that your life is my fault."

"It's not a question of fault," she says. She extracts a Kleenex from her pocket and blows her nose. "I'm sorry, Neil. I guess I'm just an old woman with too much on her mind and not enough to do." She laughs halfheartedly. "Don't worry. Don't say anything," she says. "Abbylucyferny, Abbylucyferny, time for bed!"

He watches her as she walks toward the porch, silent and regal. There is the pad of feet, the clinking of dog tags as the dogs run for the house.

He was twelve the first time she saw him march in a parade. He played the tuba, and as his elementary-school band lumbered down the streets of their then small town she stood on the sidelines and waved. Afterward, she had taken him out for ice cream. He spilled some on his red uniform, and she swiped at it with a napkin. She had been there for him that day, as well as years later, at that more memorable parade; she had been there for him every day.

Somewhere over Iowa, a week later, Neil remembers this scene, remembers other days, when he would find her sitting in the dark, crying. She had to take time out of her own private sorrow to appease his anxiety. "It was part of it," she told him later. "Part of being a mother."

"The scariest thing in the world is the thought that you could unknowingly ruin someone's life," Neil tells Wayne. "Or even change someone's life. I hate the thought of having such control. I'd make a rotten mother."

"You're crazy," Wayne says. "You have this great mother, and all you do is complain. I know people whose mothers have disowned them."

"Guilt goes with the territory," Neil says.

"Why?" Wayne asks, perfectly seriously.

Neil doesn't answer. He lies back in his seat, closes his eyes, imagines he grew up in a house in the mountains of Colorado, surrounded by snow—endless white snow on hills. No flat places, and no trees; just white hills.

Every time he has flown away, she has come into his mind, usually sitting alone in the dark, smoking. Today she is outside at dusk, skimming leaves from the pool.

"I want to get a dog," Neil says.

Wayne laughs. "In the city? It'd suffocate."

The hum of the airplane is druglike, dazing. "I want to stay with you a long time," Neil says.

"I know." Imperceptibly, Wayne takes his hand.

"It's very hot there in the summer, too. You know, I'm not thinking about my mother now."

"It's O.K."

For a moment, Neil wonders what the stewardess or the old woman on the way to the bathroom will think, but then he laughs and relaxes.

Later, the plane makes a slow circle over New York City, and on it two men hold hands, eyes closed, and breathe in unison.

[*1982*]

## ALICE ELLIOTT DARK

***Alice Elliott Dark received a B.A. in Oriental studies from the University of Pennsylvania, and an M.F.A. in creative writing from Antioch University. She has published a book of stories,* Naked to the Waist *(1991), and she teaches at The Writer's Voice, in New York City.***

# *In the Gloaming*

Her son wanted to talk again, suddenly. During the days, he still brooded, scowling at the swimming pool from the vantage point of his wheelchair, where he sat covered with blankets despite the summer heat. In the evenings, though, Laird became more like his old self—his *old* old self, really. He became sweeter, the way he'd been as a child, before he began to cloak himself with layers of irony and clever remarks. He spoke with an openness that astonished her. No one she knew talked that way—no man, at least. After he was asleep, Janet would run through the conversations in her mind, and realize what it was she wished she had said. She knew she was generally considered sincere, but that had more to do with her being a good listener than with how she expressed herself. She found it hard work to keep up with him, but it was the work she had pined for all her life.

A month earlier, after a particularly long and grueling visit with a friend who'd come up on the train from New York, Laird had declared a new policy: no visitors, no telephone calls. She didn't blame him. People who hadn't seen him for a while were often shocked to tears by his appearance, and, rather than having them cheer him up, he felt obliged to comfort them. She'd overheard bits of some of those conversations. The final one was no worse than the others, but he was fed up. He had said more than once that he wasn't cut out to be the brave one, the one who would inspire everybody to walk away from a visit with him feeling uplifted, shaking their heads in wonder. He had liked being the most handsome and missed it very much; he was not a good victim. When he had had enough he went into a self-imposed retreat, complete with a wall of silence and other ascetic practices that kept him busy for several weeks.

Then he softened. Not only did he want to talk again; he wanted to talk to *her*.

It began the night they ate outside on the terrace for the first time all summer. Afterward, Martin—Laird's father—got up to make a telephone call, but Janet stayed in her wicker chair, resting before clearing the table. It was one of those moments when she felt nostalgic for cigarettes. On nights like this, when the air was completely still, she used to blow her famous smoke rings for the children, dutifully obeying their commands to blow one through another or three in a row, or to make big, ropy circles that expanded as they floated up to the heavens. She did exactly what they wanted, for as long as they wanted, sometimes going through a quarter of a pack before they allowed her to stop. Incredibly, neither Anne nor Laird became smokers. Just the opposite; they nagged at her to quit, and were pleased when she finally did. She wished they had been just a little bit sorry; it was a part of their childhood coming to an end, after all.

Out of habit, she took note of the first lightning bug, the first star. The lawn darkened, and the flowers that had sulked in the heat all day suddenly released their perfumes. She laid her head back on the rim of the chair and closed her eyes. Soon she was following Laird's breathing, and found herself picking up the vital rhythms, breathing along. It was so peaceful, being near him like this. How many mothers spend so much time with their thirty-three-year-old sons? she thought. She had as much of him now as she had had when he was an infant; more, in a way, because she had the memory of the intervening years as well, to round out her thoughts about him. When they sat quietly together she felt as close to him as she ever had. It was still him in there, inside the failing shell. *She still enjoyed him.*

"The gloaming," he said, suddenly.

She nodded dreamily, automatically, then sat up. She turned to him. "What?" Although she had heard.

"I remember when I was little you took me over to the picture window and told me that in Scotland this time of day was called the 'gloaming.'"

Her skin tingled. She cleared her throat, quietly, taking care not to make too much of an event of his talking again. "You thought I said 'gloomy.'"

He gave a smile, then looked at her searchingly. "I always thought it hurt you somehow that the day was over, but you said it was a beautiful time because for a few moments the purple light made the whole world look like the Scottish Highlands on a summer night."

"Yes. As if all the earth were covered with heather."

"I'm sorry I never saw Scotland," he said.

"You're a Scottish lad nonetheless," she said. "At least on my side." She remembered offering to take him to Scotland once, but Laird hadn't been interested. By then, he was in college and already sure of his own destinations, which had diverged so thoroughly from hers. "I'm amazed you remember that conversation. You couldn't have been more than seven."

"I've been remembering a lot lately."

"Have you?"

"Mostly about when I was very small. I suppose it comes from having you take care of me again. Sometimes, when I wake up and see your face, I feel I can remember you looking in on me when I was in my crib. I remember your dresses."

"Oh, no!" She laughed lightly.

"You always had the loveliest expressions," he said.

She was astonished, caught off guard. Then, she had a memory, too—of her leaning over Laird's crib and suddenly having a picture of looking up at her own mother. "I know what you mean," she said.

"You do, don't you?"

He looked at her in a close, intimate way that made her self-conscious. She caught herself swinging her leg nervously, like a pendulum, and stopped.

"Mom," he said. "There are still a few things I need to do. I have to write a will, for one thing."

Her heart went flat. In his presence she had always maintained that he would get well. She wasn't sure she could discuss the other possibility.

"Thank you," he said.

"For what?"

"For not saying that there's plenty of time for that, or some similar sentiment."

"The only reason I didn't say it was to avoid the cliché, not because I don't believe it."

"You believe there is plenty of time?"

She hesitated; he noticed, and leaned forward slightly. "I believe there is time," she said.

"Even if I were healthy, it would be a good idea."

"I suppose."

"I don't want to leave it until it's too late. You wouldn't want me to suddenly leave everything to the nurses, would you?"

She laughed, pleased to hear him joking again. "All right, all right, I'll call the lawyer."

"That would be great." There was a pause. "Is this still your favorite time of day, Mom?"

"Yes, I suppose it is," she said, "although I don't think in terms of favorites anymore."

"Never mind favorites, then. What else do you like?"

"What do you mean?" she asked.

"I mean exactly that."

"I don't know. I care about all the ordinary things. You know what I like."

"Name one thing."

"I feel silly."

"Please?"

"All right. I like my patch of lilies of the valley under the trees over there. Now can we change the subject?"

"Name one more thing."

"Why?"

"I want to get to know you."

"Oh, Laird, there's nothing to know."

"I don't believe that for a minute."

"But it's true. I'm average. The only extraordinary thing about me is my children."

"All right," he said. "Then let's talk about how you feel about me."

"Do you flirt with your nurses like this when I'm not around?"

"I don't dare. They've got me where they want me." He looked at her. "You're changing the subject."

She smoothed her skirt. "I know how you feel about church, but if you need to talk I'm sure the minister would be glad to come over. Or if you would rather have a doctor . . ."

He laughed.

"What?"

"That you still call psychiatrists 'doctors.'"

She shrugged.

"I don't need a professional, Ma." He laced his hands and pulled at them as he struggled for words.

"What can I do?" she asked.

He met her gaze. "You're where I come from. I need to know about you."

That night she lay awake, trying to think of how she could help, of what, aside from her time, she had to offer. She couldn't imagine.

She was anxious the next day when he was sullen again, but the next night, and on each succeeding night, the dusk worked its spell. She set dinner on the table outside, and afterward, when Martin had vanished into the maw of his study, she and Laird began to speak. The air around them seemed to crackle with the energy they were creating in their effort to know and be known. Were other people so close, she wondered. She never had been, not to anybody. Certainly she and Martin had never really connected, not soul to soul, and with her friends, no matter how loyal and reliable, she always had a sense of what she could do that would alienate them. Of course, her friends had the option of cutting her off, and Martin could always ask for a divorce, whereas Laird was a captive audience. Parents and children were all captive audiences to each other; in view of this, it was amazing how little comprehension there was of one another's stories. Everyone stopped paying attention so early on, thinking they had figured it all out. She recognized that she was as guilty of this as anyone. She was still surprised whenever she went over to her daughter's house and saw how neat she was; in her mind, Anne was still a sloppy teenager who threw sweaters into the corner of her closet and candy wrappers under her bed. It still surprised her that Laird wasn't interested in girls. He had been, hadn't he? She remembered lying awake listening for him to come home, hoping that he was smart enough to apply what he knew about the facts of life, to take precautions.

Now she had the chance to let go of these old notions. It wasn't that she liked everything about Laird—there was much that remained foreign to her—but she wanted to know about all of it. As she came to her senses every morning in the moment or two after she awoke, she found herself aching with love and gratitude, as if he were a small, perfect creature again and she could look forward to a day of watching him grow. Quickly, she became greedy for their evenings. She replaced her half-facetious, half-hopeful reading of the horoscope in the daily newspaper with a new habit of tracking the time the sun would set, and drew satisfaction from seeing it come earlier as the summer waned; it meant she didn't have to wait as long. She took to sleeping late, shortening the day even more. It was ridiculous, she knew. She was behaving like a girl with a crush, behaving absurdly. It was a feeling she had thought she'd never have again, and now here it was. She immersed herself in it, living her life for the twilight moment when his eyes would begin to glow, the signal that he was stirring into consciousness. Then her real day would begin.

"Dad ran off quickly," he said one night. She had been wondering when he would mention it.

"He had a phone call to make," she said automatically.

Laird looked directly into her eyes, his expression one of gentle reproach. He was letting her know he had caught her in the central lie of her life, which was that she understood Martin's obsession with his work. She averted her gaze. The truth was that she had never understood. Why couldn't he sit with her for half an hour after dinner, or, if not with her, why not with his dying son?

She turned sharply to look at Laird. The word "dying" had sounded so loudly in her mind that she wondered if she had spoken it, but he showed no reaction. She wished she hadn't even thought it. She tried to stick to good thoughts in his presence. When she couldn't, and he had a bad night afterward, she blamed herself, as her efficient memory dredged up all the books and magazine articles she had read emphasizing the effect of psychological factors on the course of the disease. She didn't entirely believe it, but she felt compelled to give the benefit of the doubt to every theory that might help. It couldn't do any harm to think positively. And if it gave him a few more months . . .

"I don't think Dad can stand to be around me."

"That's not true." It was true.

"Poor Dad. He's always been a hypochondriac—we have that in common. He must hate this."

"He just wants you to get well."

"If that's what he wants, I'm afraid I'm going to disappoint him again. At least this will be the last time I let him down."

He said this merrily, with the old, familiar light darting from his eyes. She allowed herself to be amused. He had always been fond of teasing, and held no subject sacred. As the de facto authority figure in the house—Martin hadn't been home enough to be the real disciplinarian—she had often been forced to reprimand Laird, but, in truth, she shared his sense of humor. She responded to it now by leaning over to cuff him on the arm. It was an automatic response, prompted by a burst of high spirits that took no notice of the circumstances. It was a mistake. Even through the thickness of his terrycloth robe, her knuckles knocked on bone. There was nothing left of him.

"It's his loss," she said, the shock of Laird's thinness making her serious again. It was the furthest she would go in criticizing Martin. She had always felt it her duty to maintain a benign image of him for the children. He had become a character of her invention, with a whole range of postulated emotions whereby he missed them when he was away on a business trip and thought of them every few minutes when he had to work late. Some years earlier, when she was secretly seeing a doctor—a psychiatrist—she had finally admitted to herself that Martin was never going to be the lover she had dreamed of. He was an ambitious, competitive, self-absorbed man who probably should never have got married. It was such a relief to be able to face it that she wanted to share the news with her children, only to discover that they were dependent on the myth. They could hate his work, but they could not bring themselves to believe he had any choice in the matter. She had dropped the subject.

75 "Thank you, Ma. It's his loss in your case, too."

A throbbing began behind her eyes, angering her. The last thing she wanted to do was cry. There would be plenty of time for that. "It's not all his fault," she said when she had regained some measure of control. "I'm not very good at talking about myself. I was brought up not to."

"So was I," he said.

"Yes, I suppose you were."

"Luckily, I didn't pay any attention." He grinned.

80 "I hope not," she said, and meant it. "Can I get you anything?"

"A new immune system?"

She rolled her eyes, trying to disguise the way his joke had touched on her prayers. "Very funny. I was thinking more along the lines of an iced tea or an extra blanket."

"I'm fine. I'm getting tired, actually."

Her entire body went on the alert, and she searched his face anxiously for signs of deterioration. Her nerves darted and pricked whenever he wanted anything; her adrenaline rushed. The fight-or-flight response, she supposed. She had often wanted to flee, but had forced herself to stay, to fight with what few weapons she had. She responded to his needs, making sure there was a fresh, clean set of sheets ready when he was tired, food when he was hungry. It was what she could do.

85 "Shall I get a nurse?" She pushed her chair back from the table.

"O.K.," Laird said weakly. He stretched out his hand to her, and the incipient moonlight illuminated his skin so it shone like alabaster. His face had turned ashy. It was a sight that made her stomach drop. She ran for Maggie, and by the time they returned Laird's eyes were closed, his head lolling to one side. Automatically, Janet looked for a stirring in his chest. There it was: his shoulders expanded; he still breathed. Always, in the second before she saw movement, she became cold and clinical as she braced herself for the possibility of discovering that he was dead.

Maggie had her fingers on his wrist and was counting his pulse against the second hand on her watch, her lips moving. She laid his limp hand back on his lap. "Fast," she pronounced.

"I'm not surprised," Janet said, masking her fear with authority. "We had a long talk."

Maggie frowned. "Now I'll have to wake him up again for his meds."

90 "Yes, I suppose that's true. I forgot about that."

Janet wheeled him into his makeshift room downstairs and helped Maggie lift him into the rented hospital bed. Although he weighed almost nothing, it was really a job for two; his weight was dead weight. In front of Maggie, she was all brusque efficiency, except for the moment when her fingers strayed to touch Laird's pale cheek and she prayed she hadn't done any harm.

"Who's your favorite author?" he asked one night.

"Oh, there are so many," she said.

"Your real favorite."

She thought. "The truth is there are certain subjects I find attractive more than certain authors. I seem to read in cycles, to fulfill an emotional yearning."

"Such as?"

"Books about people who go off to live in Africa or Australia or the South Seas."

He laughed. "That's fairly self-explanatory. What else?"

"When I really hate life I enjoy books about real murders. 'True crime,' I think they're called now. They're very punishing."

"Is that what's so compelling about them? I could never figure it out. I just know that at certain times I loved the gore, even though I felt absolutely disgusted with myself for being interested in it."

"You need to think about when those times were. That will tell you a lot." She paused. "I don't like reading about sex."

"Big surprise!"

"No, no," she said. "It's not for the reason you think, or not only for that reason. You see me as a prude, I know, but remember, it's part of a mother's job to come across that way. Although perhaps I went a bit far . . ."

He shrugged amiably. "Water under the bridge. But go on about sex."

"I think it should be private. I always feel as though these writers are showing off when they describe a sex scene. They're not really trying to describe sex, but to demonstrate that they're not afraid to write about it. As if they're thumbing their noses at their mothers."

He made a moue.

Janet went on. "You don't think there's an element of that? I *do* question their motives, because I don't think sex can ever actually be portrayed—the sensations and the emotions are . . . beyond language. If you only describe the mechanics, the effect is either clinical or pornographic, and if you try to describe intimacy instead, you wind up with abstractions. The only sex you could describe fairly well is bad sex—and who wants to read about that, for God's sake, when everyone is having bad sex of their own?"

"Mother!" He was laughing helplessly, his arms hanging limply over the sides of his chair.

"I mean it. To me it's like reading about someone using the bathroom."

"Good grief!"

"Now who's the prude?"

"I never said I wasn't," he said. "Maybe we should change the subject."

She looked out across the land. The lights were on in other people's houses, giving the evening the look of early fall. The leaves were different, too, becoming droopy. The grass was dry, even with all the watering and tending from the gardener. The summer was nearly over.

"Maybe we shouldn't," she said. "I've been wondering. Was that side of life satisfying for you?"

115 "Ma, tell me you're not asking me about my sex life."

She took her napkin and folded it carefully, lining up the edges and running her fingers along the hems. She felt very calm, very pulled together and all of a piece, as if she'd finally got the knack of being a dignified woman. She threaded her fingers and laid her hands in her lap. "I'm asking about your love life," she said. "Did you love, and were you loved in return?"

"Yes."

"I'm glad."

"That was easy," he said.

120 "Oh, I've gotten very easy, in my old age."

"Does Dad know about this?" His eyes were twinkling wickedly.

"Don't be fresh," she said.

"You started it."

"Then I'm stopping it. Now."

125 He made a funny face, and then another, until she could no longer keep from smiling. His routine carried her back to memories of his childhood efforts to charm her: watercolors of her favorite vistas (unrecognizable without the captions), bouquets of violets self-consciously flung into her lap, chores performed without prompting. He had always gone too far, then backtracked to regain even footing. She had always allowed herself to be wooed.

Suddenly she realized: Laird had been the love of her life.

One night it rained hard. Janet decided to serve the meal in the kitchen, since Martin was out. They ate in silence; she was freed from the compulsion to keep up the steady stream of chatter that she used to affect when Laird hadn't talked at all; now she knew she could save her words for afterward. He ate nothing but comfort foods lately: mashed potatoes, vanilla ice cream, rice pudding. The days of his strict macrobiotic regime, and all the cooking classes she had taken in order to help him along with it, were past. His body was essentially a thing of the past, too; when he ate, he was feeding what was left of his mind. He seemed to want to recapture the cosseted feeling he'd had when he'd been sick as a child and she would serve him flat ginger ale, and toast soaked in cream, and play endless card games with him, using his blanket-covered legs as a table. In those days, too, there'd been a general sense of giving way to illness: then, he let himself go completely because he knew he would soon be better and active and have a million things expected of him again. Now he let himself go because he had fought long enough.

Finally, he pushed his bowl toward the middle of the table, signaling that he was finished. (His table manners had gone to pieces. Who cared?) She felt a light, jittery excitement, the same jazzy feeling she got when she was in a plane that was picking up speed on the runway. She arranged her fork and knife on the rim of her plate and pulled her chair in closer. "I had an odd dream last night," she said.

His eyes remained dull.

130 She waited uncertainly, thinking that perhaps she had started to talk too soon. "Would you like something else to eat?"

He shook his head. There was no will in his expression; his refusal was purely physical, a gesture coming from the satiation in his stomach. An animal walking away from its bowl, she thought.

To pass the time, she carried the dishes to the sink, gave them a good hot rinse, and put them in the dishwasher. She carried the ice cream to the counter, pulled a spoon from the drawer and scraped off a mouthful of the thick, creamy residue that stuck to the inside of the lid. She ate it without thinking, so the sudden sweetness caught her by surprise. All the while she kept track of Laird, but every time she thought she noticed signs of his readiness to talk and hurried back to the table, she found his face still blank.

She went to the window. The lawn had become a floodplain and was filled with broad pools; the branches of the evergreens sagged, and the sky was the same uniform grayish yellow it had been since morning. She saw him focus his gaze on the line where the treetops touched the heavens, and she understood. There was no lovely interlude on this rainy night, no heathered dusk. The gray landscape had taken the light out of him.

"I'm sorry," she said aloud, as if it were her fault.

135 He gave a tiny, helpless shrug.

She hovered for a few moments, hoping, but his face was slack, and she gave up. She felt utterly forsaken, too disappointed and agitated to sit with him and watch the rain. "It's all right," she said. "It's a good night to watch television."

She wheeled him to the den and left him with Maggie, then did not know what to do with herself. She had no contingency plan for this time. It was usually the one period of the day when she did not need the anesthesia of tennis games, bridge lessons, volunteer work, errands. She had not considered the present possibility. For some time, she hadn't given any thought to what Martin would call "the big picture." Her conversations with Laird had lulled her into inventing a parallel big picture of her own. She realized that a part of her had worked out a whole scenario: the summer evenings would blend into fall; then, gradually, the winter would arrive, heralding chats by the fire, Laird resting his feet on the pigskin ottoman in the den while she dutifully knitted her yearly Christmas sweaters for Anne's children.

She had allowed herself to imagine a future. That had been her mistake. This silent, endless evening was her punishment, a reminder of how things really were.

She did not know where to go in her own house, and ended up wandering through the rooms, propelled by a vague, hunted feeling. Several times, she turned around, expecting someone to be there, but, of course, no one ever was. She was quite alone. Eventually, she realized that she was imagining a person in order to give material properties to the source of her wounds. She was inventing a villain. There should be a villain, shouldn't there? There should be an enemy, a devil, an evil force that could be driven out. Her imagination had provided it with aspects of a corporeal presence so she could pretend, for a moment, that there was a real enemy hovering around her, someone she could have the police come and take away. But the enemy was part of Laird, and neither he nor she nor any of the doctors or experts or ministers could separate the two.

140 She went upstairs and took a shower. She barely paid attention to her own body anymore, and only noticed abstractly that the water was too hot,

her skin turning pink. Afterward, she sat on the chaise longue in her bedroom and tried to read. She heard something; she leaned forward and cocked her head toward the sound. Was that Laird's voice? Suddenly she believed that he had begun to talk after all—she believed he was talking to Maggie. She dressed and went downstairs. He was alone in the den, alone with the television. He didn't hear or see her. She watched him take a drink from a cup, his hand shaking badly. It was a plastic cup with a straw poking through the lid, the kind used by small children while they are learning to drink. It was supposed to prevent accidents, but it couldn't stop his hands from trembling. He managed to spill the juice anyway.

Laird had always coveted the decadent pile of cashmere lap blankets she had collected over the years in the duty-free shops of the various British airports. Now he wore one around his shoulders, one over his knees. She remembered similar balmy nights when he would arrive home from soccer practice after dark, a towel slung around his neck.

"I suppose it has to be in the church," he said.

"I think it should," she said, "but it's up to you."

"I guess it's not the most timely moment to make a statement about my personal disbeliefs. But I'd like you to keep it from being too lugubrious. No lilies, for instance."

145 "God forbid."

"And have some decent music."

"Such as?"

"I had an idea, but now I can't remember."

He pressed his hands to his eyes. His fingers were so transparent that they looked as if he were holding them over a flashlight.

150 "Please buy a smashing dress, something mournful yet elegant."

"All right."

"And don't wait until the last minute."

She didn't reply.

Janet gave up on the idea of a rapprochement between Martin and Laird; she felt freer when she stopped hoping for it. Martin rarely came home for dinner anymore. Perhaps he was having an affair? It was a thought she'd never allowed herself to have before, but it didn't threaten her now. Good for him, she even decided, in her strongest, most magnanimous moments. Good for him if he's actually feeling bad and trying to do something to make himself feel better.

155 Anne was brave and chipper during her visits, yet when she walked back out to her car, she would wrap her arms around her ribs and shudder. "I don't know how you do it, Mom. Are you really all right?" she always asked, with genuine concern.

"Anne's become such a hopeless matron," Laird always said, with fond exasperation, when he and his mother were alone again later. Once, Janet began to tease him for finally coming to friendly terms with his sister, but she cut it short when she saw that he was blinking furiously.

They were exactly the children she had hoped to have: a companionable girl, a mischievous boy. It gave her great pleasure to see them together. She did not try to listen to their conversations but watched from a distance, usually from the kitchen as she prepared them a snack reminiscent of their childhood, like watermelon boats or lemonade. Then she would walk Anne to the car, their similar good shoes clacking across the gravel. They hugged, pressing each other's arms, and their brief embraces buoyed them up—forbearance and grace passing back and forth between them like a piece of shared clothing, designated for use by whoever needed it most. It was the kind of parting toward which she had aimed her whole life, a graceful, secure parting at the close of a peaceful afternoon. After Anne left, Janet always had a tranquil moment or two as she walked back to the house through the humid September air. Everything was so still. Occasionally there were the hums and clicks of a lawnmower or the shrieks of a band of children heading home from school. There were the insects and the birds. It was a straightforward, simple life she had chosen. She had tried never to ask for too much, and to be of use. Simplicity had been her hedge against bad luck. It had worked for so long. For a brief moment, as she stepped lightly up the single slate stair and through the door, her legs still harboring all their former vitality, she could pretend her luck was still holding.

Then she would glance out the window and there would be the heart-catching sight of Laird, who would never again drop by for a casual visit. Her chest would ache and flutter, a cave full of bats.

Perhaps she had asked for too much, after all.

160 "What did you want to be when you grew up?" Laird asked.

"I was expected to be a wife and mother. I accepted that. I wasn't a rebel."

"There must have been something else."

"No," she said. "Oh, I guess I had all the usual fantasies of the day, of being the next Amelia Earhart or Margaret Mead, but that was all they were—fantasies. I wasn't even close to being brave enough. Can you imagine me flying across the ocean on my own?" She laughed and looked over for his laughter, but he had fallen asleep.

A friend of Laird's had somehow got the mistaken information that Laird had died, so she and Martin received a condolence letter. There was a story about a time a few years back when the friend was with Laird on a bus in New York. They had been sitting behind two older women, waitresses who began to discuss their income taxes, trying to decide how much of their tip income to declare to sound realistic so they wouldn't attract an audit. Each woman offered up bits of folk wisdom on the subject, describing in detail her particular situation. During a lull in the conversation, Laird stood up.

165 "Excuse me, I couldn't help overhearing," he said, leaning over them. "May I have your names and addresses, please? I work for the IRS."

The entire bus fell silent as everyone watched to see what would happen next. Laird took a small notebook and pen from the inside pocket of his jacket. He faced his captive audience. "I'm part of a new IRS outreach program," he told the group. "For the next ten minutes I'll be taking confessions. Does anyone have anything he or she wants to tell me?"

Smiles. Soon the whole bus was talking, comparing notes—when they'd first realized he was kidding, and how scared they had been before they caught on. It was difficult to believe these were the same New Yorkers who were supposed to be so gruff and isolated.

"Laird was the most vital, funniest person I ever met," his friend wrote.

Now, in his wheelchair, he faced off against slow-moving flies, waving them away.

170 "The gloaming," Laird said.

Janet looked up from her knitting, startled. It was midafternoon, and the living room was filled with bright October sun. "Soon," she said.

He furrowed his brow. A little flash of confusion passed through his eyes, and she realized that for him it was already dark.

He tried to straighten his shawl, his hands shaking. She jumped up to help; then, when he pointed to the fireplace, she quickly laid the logs as she wondered what was wrong. Was he dehydrated. She thought she recalled that a dimming of vision was a sign of dehydration. She tried to remember what else she had read or heard, but even as she grasped for information, facts, her instincts kept interrupting with a deeper, more dreadful thought that vibrated through her, rattling her and making her gasp as she often did when remembering her mistakes, things she wished she hadn't said or done, wished she had the chance to do over. She knew what was wrong, and yet she kept turning away from the truth, her mind spinning in every other possible direction as she worked on the fire, only vaguely noticing how wildly she made the sparks fly as she pumped the old bellows.

Her work was mechanical—she had made hundreds of fires—and soon there was nothing left to do. She put the screen up and pushed him close, then leaned over to pull his flannel pajamas down to meet his socks, protecting his bare shins. The sun streamed in around him, making him appear trapped between bars of light. She resumed her knitting, with mechanical hands.

175 "The gloaming," he said again. It did sound somewhat like "gloomy," because his speech was slurred.

"When all the world is purple," she said, hearing herself sound falsely bright. She wasn't sure whether he wanted her to talk. It was some time since he had talked—not long, really, in other people's lives, perhaps two weeks—but she had gone on with their conversations, gradually expanding into the silence until she was telling him stories and he was listening. Sometimes, when his eyes closed, she trailed off and began to drift. There would be a pause that she didn't always realize she was making, but if it went on too long he would call out "Mom?" with an edge of panic in his voice, as if he were waking from a nightmare. Then she would resume, trying to create a seamless bridge between what she had been thinking and where she had left off.

"It was really your grandfather who gave me my love for the gloaming," she said. "Do you remember him talking about it?" She looked up politely, expectantly, as if Laird might offer her a conversational reply. He seemed to like hearing the sound of her voice, so she went on, her needles clicking. Afterward, she could never remember for sure at what point she had stopped talking and had floated off into a jumble of her own thoughts, afraid to move, afraid to look up, afraid to know at which exact moment she became alone. All she knew was that at a certain point the fire was in danger of dying out entirely, and when she got up to stir the embers she glanced at him in spite of herself and saw that his fingers were making knitting motions over his chest, the way people did as they were dying. She knew that if she went to get the nurse, Laird would be gone by the time she returned, so she went and stood behind him, leaning over to press her face against his, sliding her hands down his busy arms, helping him along with his fretful stitches until he finished this last piece of work.

Later, after the most pressing calls had been made and Laird's body had been taken away, Janet went up to his old room and lay down on one of the twin beds. She had changed the room into a guest room when he went off to college, replacing his things with guest room decor, thoughtful touches such as luggage racks at the foot of each bed, a writing desk stocked with paper and pens, heavy wooden hangers and shoe trees. She made an effort to remember the room as it had been when he was a little boy; she had chosen a train motif, then had to redecorate when Laird decided trains were silly. He had wanted it to look like a jungle, so she had hired an art student to paint a jungle mural on the walls. When he decided *that* was silly, he hadn't bothered her to do anything about it, but had simply marked time until he could move on.

Anne came over, offered to stay, but was relieved to be sent home to her children.

Presently, Martin came in. Janet was watching the trees turn to mere silhouettes against the darkening sky, fighting the urge to pick up a true-crime book, a debased urge. He lay down on the other bed.

"I'm sorry," he said.

"It's so wrong," she said angrily. She hadn't felt angry until that moment; she had saved it up for him. "A child shouldn't die before his parents. A young man shouldn't spend his early thirties wasting away talking to his mother. He should be out in the world. He shouldn't be thinking about me, or what I care about, or my opinions. He shouldn't have had to return my love to me—it was his to squander. Now I have it all back and I don't know what I'm supposed to do with it," she said.

She could hear Martin weeping in the darkness. He sobbed, and her anger veered away.

They were quiet for some time.

"Is there going to be a funeral?" Martin asked finally.

"Yes. We should start making the arrangements."

"I suppose he told you what he wanted."

"In general. He couldn't decide about the music."

She heard Martin roll onto his side, so that he was facing her across the narrow chasm between the beds. He was still in his office clothes. "I remember being very moved by the bagpipes at your father's funeral."

It was an awkward offering, to be sure, awkward and late, and seemed to come from someone on the periphery of her life who knew her only slightly. It didn't matter; it was perfectly right. Her heart rushed toward it.

"I think Laird would have liked that idea very much," she said.

It was the last moment of the gloaming, the last moment of the day her son died. In a breath, it would be night; the moon hovered behind the trees, already rising to claim the sky, and she told herself she might as well get on with it. She sat up and was running her toes across the bare floor, searching for her shoes, when Martin spoke again, in a tone she used to hear on those long-ago nights when he rarely got home until after the children were in bed and he relied on her to fill him in on what they'd done that day. It was the same curious, shy, deferential tone that had always made her feel as though all the frustrations and boredom and mistakes and rushes of feeling in her days as a mother did indeed add up to something of importance, and she decided that the next round of telephone calls could wait while she answered the question he asked her: "Please tell me—what else did my boy like?"

[*1993*]

## A SAMPLE STUDENT ESSAY

A student, Bob Williams, was assigned in a literature course to write a short essay about "gender conflict" in Tobias Wolff's story "Say Yes." After reading the story carefully, he noted some impressions in his journal:

I'm not sure how I am supposed to feel about the husband. Sometimes he seems to be basically a good guy who loves his wife even though they are having problems. But then sometimes he seems to _be_ the problem himself, in this scene just itching for a fight. But she's no prize either.

I can't figure out why Wolff has included the conversation about interracial marriages. Why did he pick this subject for the couple to fight about?

Here is the final version of the essay that Bob wrote about "Say Yes." Notice how he keyed it to the opening paragraph of the story.

Bob Williams

Literature 100

October 1, 1996

He's the Problem: The Husband in "Say Yes"

Tobias Wolff's insights into "gender conflict" are evident in the first paragraph of his story. He starts by showing the couple doing something together--"they were washing the dishes"--but then in the next phrase he indicates that they performed separate tasks--"his wife washing while he dried." It seems like a small point, but in its own way I think this sentence is already revealing the emotional divide between the husband and the wife, and is foreshadowing the angry argument to come.

The next sentences seem to portray the husband in a positive light. He helped with the dishes the night before, and that time _he_ washed, so it seems that this couple shares the domestic chores each night. Wolff appears, then, to be bringing them back together a bit after separating them, through their different activities, in the first sentence of the story. This husband is a good, sensitive person who doesn't expect his wife to handle all of the messy chores in the kitchen.

But maybe Wolff wants us to realize that the husband is taken with himself--that not only does he help his wife with the chores, but also likes to compliment himself, as though he were doing her a favor. He likes to think of himself as better than other husbands; when Wolff writes how the husband "pitches in," I can hear the husband saying these words to himself as evidence of what a decent, down-to-earth guy he is. I notice that the husband also enjoys hearing other people compliment him: "he'd overheard a friend of his wife's congratulate her on having such a considerate husband." Is Wolff's main point that the husband _is_ considerate, or that he is a little too proud of himself?

When Wolff writes in the final sentence of this paragraph that "helping out with the dishes was a way he had of showing how considerate he was," he makes clear how we are to respond to the husband. What matters to the husband is not what he feels toward his wife, but, instead, _showing_ what he feels. He wants to prove to the world that unlike other men, he treats his wife as an equal; he won't take advantage of her or insist that because she is the wife, she ought to do the household duties. From one point of view, this sounds appealing. But Wolff's aim is to make the reader understand the difference between doing something for its own sake and doing something for the purpose of self-approval. For this husband, washing the dishes is just another opportunity for feeling pleased with himself.

Here are a few comments and questions about this student's essay:

- He pays close attention to Wolff's language in the opening paragraph. Do you agree with his interpretations—for example, his explanation of the meaning of "showing how considerate he was"?
- Do you think it is effective to focus the entire paper on this single opening paragraph? Should the student have included references to later passages, or does his point not require them?
- The student several times uses underlining to give extra emphasis to a word. Is this a good idea?
- In his journal, the student said that he didn't know how to make sense of the subject of interracial marriages that takes up so much of the story, and this no doubt explains why his essay makes no mention of it. Is this a wise or a risky strategy? Explain.
- Notice, too, that the student wrote in his journal that the wife's "no prize either." Should he have addressed this issue in his essay? Can you find evidence in the text that might support such a claim?

# CHAPTER 10

# Two Fiction Writers in Depth: Flannery O'Connor and Raymond Carver

We read stories by authors we are unfamiliar with, just as we try new foods or play new games or listen to the music of new groups, because we want to extend our experience. But we also sometimes stay with the familiar, for pretty much the same reason, oddly. We want, so to speak, to taste more fully, to experience not something utterly unfamiliar but a variation on a favorite theme. Having read, say, one story by Poe or by Alice Walker, we want to read another, and another, because we like the sort of thing that this author does, and we find that with each succeeding story we get deeper into an interesting mind talking about experiences that interest us.

This chapter includes three stories by Flannery O'Connor, along with some of her comments on her own work. It also includes three stories by Raymond Carver, along with an interview of Carver. You'll find that each of O'Connor's stories takes on a richer significance when thought of along with the others and with her comments, just as Carver's stories gain something by being seen as parts of a larger body of work.

## Flannery O'Connor: Three Stories, and Observations on Literature

***Flannery O'Connor (1925-1964)—her first name was Mary but she did not use it—was born in Savannah, Georgia, but spent most of her life in Milledgeville, Georgia, where her family moved when she was twelve. She***

*was educated in parochial schools and at the local college and then went to the School for Writers at the University of Iowa where she earned an M.F.A. in 1946. For a few months she lived at a writers' colony in Saratoga Springs, New York, and then for a few weeks she lived in New York City, but most of her life was spent back in Milledgeville, where she tended her peacocks and wrote stories, novels, essays (posthumously published as* Mystery and Manners *[1970]), and letters (posthumously published under the title of* The Habit of Being *[1979]).*

*In 1951, when she was twenty-five, Flannery O'Connor discovered that she was a victim of lupus erythematosus, an incurable degenerative blood disease that had crippled and then killed her father ten years before. She died at the age of thirty-nine. O'Connor faced her illness with stoic courage, Christian fortitude—and tough humor. Here is a glimpse, from one of her letters, of how she dealt with those who pitied her:*

> *An old lady got on the elevator behind me and as soon as I turned around she fixed me with a moist gleaming eye and said in a loud voice, "Bless you, darling!" I felt exactly like the Misfit [in "A Good Man Is Hard To Find"] and I gave her a weakly lethal look, whereupon greatly encouraged she grabbed my arm and whispered (very loud) in my ear, "Remember what they said to John at the gate, darling!" It was not my floor but I got off and I suppose the old lady was astounded at how quick I could get away on crutches. I have a one-legged friend and I asked her what they said to John at the gate. She said she reckoned they said, "The lame shall enter first." This may be because the lame will be able to knock everybody else aside with their crutches.*

*A devout Catholic, O'Connor forthrightly summarized the relation between her belief and her writing:*

> *I see from the standpoint of Christian orthodoxy. This means that for me the meaning of life is centered in our Redemption by Christ and what I see in the world I see in its relation to that.*

## *A Good Man Is Hard to Find*

The grandmother didn't want to go to Florida. She wanted to visit some of her connections in east Tennessee and she was seizing at every chance to change Bailey's mind. Bailey was the son she lived with, her only boy. He was sitting on the edge of his chair at the table, bent over the orange sports section of the *Journal.* "Now look here, Bailey," she said, "see here, read

2

[the grandmother] ~~Of course she~~ was the first one ready to load up the next morning at six o'clock. She had Baby Brother's bucking bronco ~~that~~ and ~~[illegible]~~ what she called her "~~valise~~ [grip]" and Pitty Sing, the cat, ~~[illegible]~~ packed in the car before Boatwrite had a chance to ~~[illegible]~~ [get the] ~~come out of the door with the~~ rest of the luggage out of the hall. They got off at seven-thirty, Boatwrite and ~~[illegible]~~ the children's mother in the front and Granny, John Wesley, Baby Brother, Little Sister Mary Ann, Pitty Sing, and the bucking bronco in the back.

"Why the hell did you bring that goddam rocking horse?" Boatwrite asked because as soon as ~~the car began to move,~~ [they were out of the city + on the smooth highway] Baby Brother began to squall to get on the bucking bronco. "He can't get on that thing in this car and that's final," his father who was a stern man said.

"Can we open the lunch now?" Little Sister ~~[illegible]~~ asked. "It'll shut Baby Brother up. Mamma, can we open up the lunch?"

"No," their grandmother said. [It's only eight-thirty]

Their mother was ~~[illegible]~~ reading SCREEN MOTHERS AND THEIR CHILDREN. "Yeah, sure," she said without looking up. She was all dressed up today. She had on a purple silk dress and a hat and ~~[illegible]~~ a choker of pink beads and a new [her red] pocket book, and high heel pumps.

"Let's go through Georgia quick so we won't have to look at it much," John Wesley said. ~~"I seen enough of it myself."~~

"You should see Tennessee," his grandmother said. "Now there is a [beautiful] state."

"Like hell," John Wesley said. "That's just a hillbilly dumping ground."

"Ha~~h~~[w]," his mother said, and nudged Boatwrite. "Didjer hear that?" [She was from Arkansas]

They ate their lunch and got along fine ~~after that~~ for a while until Pitty Sing who had been asleep jumped into the front of the car and caused Boatwrite to swerve to the right into a ditch. Pitty Sing was a large grey-striped cat with a yellow hind leg and a ~~large~~ [big] soiled white face. Granny thought that she was the only person in the world that he really loved but [the truth was] he had never ~~really~~ looked ~~[illegible]~~ [up] farther than her middle and he didn't even like other cats. He jumped snarling into the front seat and Boatwrite's shoulders

this," and she stood with one hand on her thin hip and the other rattling the newspaper at his bald head. "Here this fellow that calls himself The Misfit is aloose from the Federal Pen and headed toward Florida and you read here what it says he did to these people. Just you read it. I wouldn't take my children in any direction with a criminal like that aloose in it. I couldn't answer to my conscience if I did."

Bailey didn't look up from his reading so she wheeled around then and faced the children's mother, a young woman in slacks, whose face was as broad and innocent as a cabbage and was tied round with a green headkerchief that had two points on the top like rabbit's ears. She was sitting on the sofa, feeding the baby his apricots out of a jar. "The children have been to Florida before," the old lady said. "You all ought to take them somewhere else for a change so they would see different parts of the world and be broad. They never have been to east Tennessee."

The children's mother didn't seem to hear her but the eight-year-old boy, John Wesley, a stocky child with glasses, said, "If you don't want to go to Florida, why dontcha stay at home?" He and the little girl, June Star, were reading the funny papers on the floor.

"She wouldn't stay at home to be queen for a day," June Star said without raising her yellow head.

5 "Yes and what would you do if this fellow, The Misfit, caught you?" the grandmother said.

"I'd smack his face," John Wesley said.

"She wouldn't stay at home for a million bucks," June Star said. "Afraid she'd miss something. She has to go everywhere we go."

"All right, Miss," the grandmother said. "Just remember that the next time you want me to curl your hair."

June Star said her hair was naturally curly.

10 The next morning the grandmother was the first one in the car, ready to go. She had her big black valise that looked like the head of a hippopotamus in one corner, and underneath it she was hiding a basket with Pitty Sing, the cat, in it. She didn't intend for the cat to be left alone in the house for three days because he would miss her too much and she was afraid he might brush against one of the gas burners and accidentally asphyxiate himself. Her son, Bailey, didn't like to arrive at a motel with a cat.

She sat in the middle of the back seat with John Wesley and June Star on either side of her. Bailey and the children's mother and the baby sat in front and they left Atlanta at eight forty-five with the mileage on the car at 55890. The grandmother wrote this down because she thought it would be interesting to say how many miles they had been when they got back. It took them twenty minutes to reach the outskirts of the city.

The old lady settled herself comfortably, removing her white cotton gloves and putting them up with her purse on the shelf in front of the back window. The children's mother still had on slacks and still had her hair tied up in a green kerchief, but the grandmother had on a navy blue straw sailor hat with a bunch of white violets on the brim and a navy blue dress with a small white dot in the print. Her collars and cuffs were white organdy trimmed with lace and at her neckline she had pinned a purple spray of cloth violets containing a sachet. In case of an accident, anyone seeing her dead on the highway would know at once that she was a lady.

She said she thought it was going to be a good day for driving, neither too hot nor too cold, and she cautioned Bailey that the speed limit was fifty-five miles an hour and that the patrolmen hid themselves behind billboards and small clumps of trees and sped out after you before you had a chance to slow down. She pointed out interesting details of the scenery: Stone Mountain; the blue granite that in some places came up to both sides of the highway; the brilliant red clay banks slightly streaked with purple; and the various crops that made rows of green lace-work on the ground. The trees were full of silver-white sunlight and the meanest of them sparkled. The children were reading comic magazines and their mother had gone back to sleep.

"Let's go through Georgia fast so we won't have to look at it much," John Wesley said.

"If I were a little boy," said the grandmother, "I wouldn't talk about my native state that way. Tennessee has the mountains and Georgia has the hills."

"Tennessee is just a hillbilly dumping ground," John Wesley said, "and Georgia is a lousy state too."

"You said it," June Star said.

"In my time," said the grandmother, folding her thin veined fingers, "children were more respectful of their native states and their parents and everything else. People did right then. Oh look at the cute little pickaninny!" she said and pointed to a Negro child standing in the door of a shack. "Wouldn't that make a picture, now?" she asked and they all turned and looked at the little Negro out of the back window. He waved.

"He didn't have any britches on," June Star said.

"He probably didn't have any," the grandmother explained. "Little niggers in the country don't have things like we do. If I could paint, I'd paint that picture," she said.

The children exchanged comic books.

The grandmother offered to hold the baby and the children's mother passed him over the front seat to her. She set him on her knee and bounced him and told him about the things they were passing. She rolled her eyes and screwed up her mouth and stuck her leathery thin face into his smooth bland one. Occasionally he gave her a faraway smile. They passed a large cotton field with five or six graves fenced in the middle of it, like a small island. "Look at the graveyard!" the grandmother said, pointing it out. "That was the old family burying ground. That belonged to the plantation."

"Where's the plantation?" John Wesley asked.

"Gone With the Wind," said the grandmother. "Ha. Ha."

When the children finished all the comic books they had brought, they opened the lunch and ate it. The grandmother ate a peanut butter sandwich and an olive and would not let the children throw the box and the paper napkins out the window. When there was nothing else to do they played a game by choosing a cloud and making the other two guess what shape it suggested. John Wesley took one the shape of a cow and June Star guessed a cow and John Wesley said, no, an automobile, and June Star said he didn't play fair, and they began to slap each other over the grandmother.

The grandmother said she would tell them a story if they would keep quiet. When she told a story, she rolled her eyes and waved her head and was very dramatic. She said once when she was a maiden lady she had been courted by a Mr. Edgar Atkins Teagarden from Jasper, Georgia. She said he was a very good-looking man and a gentleman and that he brought her a watermelon every Saturday afternoon with his initials cut in it, E. A. T. Well, one Saturday, she said, Mr. Teagarden brought the watermelon and there was nobody at home and he left it on the front porch and returned in his buggy to Jasper, but she never got the watermelon, she said, because a nigger boy ate it when he saw the initials, E. A. T.! This story tickled John Wesley's funny bone and he giggled and giggled but June Star didn't think it was any good. She said she wouldn't marry a man that just brought her a watermelon on Saturday. The grandmother said she would have done well to marry Mr. Teagarden because he was a gentleman and had bought Coca-Cola stock when it first came out and that he had died only a few years ago, a very wealthy man.

They stopped at The Tower for barbecued sandwiches. The Tower was a part stucco and part wood filling station and dance hall set in a clearing outside of Timothy. A fat man named Red Sammy Butts ran it and there were signs stuck here and there on the building and for miles up and down the highway saying, TRY RED SAMMY'S FAMOUS BARBECUE. NONE LIKE FAMOUS RED SAMMY'S! RED SAM! THE FAT BOY WITH THE HAPPY LAUGH. A VETERAN! RED SAMMY'S YOUR MAN!

Red Sammy was lying on the bare ground outside The Tower with his head under a truck while a gray monkey about a foot high, chained to a small chinaberry tree, chattered nearby. The monkey sprang back into the tree and got on the highest limb as soon as he saw the children jump out of the car and run toward him.

Inside, The Tower was a long dark room with a counter at one end and tables at the other and dancing space in the middle. They all sat down at a broad table next to the nickelodeon and Red Sam's wife, a tall burnt-brown woman with hair and eyes lighter than her skin, came and took their order. The children's mother put a dime in the machine and played "The Tennessee Waltz," and the grandmother said that tune always made her want to dance. She asked Bailey if he would like to dance but he only glared at her. He didn't have a naturally sunny disposition like she did and trips made him nervous. The grandmother's brown eyes were very bright. She swayed her head from side to side and pretended she was dancing in her chair. June Star said play something she could tap to so the children's mother put in another dime and played a fast number and June Star stepped out onto the dance floor and did her tap routine.

30 "Ain't she cute?" Red Sam's wife said, leaning over the counter. "Would you like to come be my little girl?"

"No I certainly wouldn't," June Star said. "I wouldn't live in a broken-down place like this for a million bucks!" and she ran back to the table.

"Ain't she cute?" the woman repeated, stretching her mouth politely.

"Aren't you ashamed?" hissed the grandmother.

Red Sam came in and told his wife to quit lounging on the counter and hurry with these people's order. His khaki trousers reached just to his hip bones and his stomach hung over them like a sack of meal swaying under his shirt. He came over and sat down at a table nearby and let out a combination sigh and yodel. "You can't win," he said. "You can't win," and he wiped his sweating red face off with a gray handkerchief. "These days you don't know who to trust," he said. "Ain't that the truth?"

35 "People are certainly not nice like they used to be," said the grandmother.

"Two fellers come in here last week," Red Sammy said, "driving a Chrysler. It was a old beat-up car but it was a good one and these boys looked all right to me. Said they worked at the mill and you know I let them fellers charge the gas they bought? Now why did I do that?"

"Because you're a good man!" the grandmother said at once.

"Yes'm, I suppose so," Red Sam said as if he were struck with this answer.

His wife brought the orders, carrying the five plates all at once without a tray, two in each hand and one balanced on her arm. "It isn't a soul in this green world of God's that you can trust," she said. "And I don't count nobody out of that, not nobody," she repeated, looking at Red Sammy.

40 "Did you read about that criminal, The Misfit, that's escaped?" asked the grandmother.

"I wouldn't be a bit surprised if he didn't attack this place right here," said the woman. "If he hears about it being here, I wouldn't be none surprised to see him. If he hears it's two cent in the cash register, I wouldn't be a tall surprised if he . . ."

"That'll do," Red Sam said. "Go bring these people their Co'Colas," and the woman went off to get the rest of the order.

"A good man is hard to find," Red Sammy said. "Everything is getting terrible. I remember the day you could go off and leave your screen door unlatched. Not no more."

He and the grandmother discussed better times. The old lady said that in her opinion Europe was entirely to blame for the way things were now. She said the way Europe acted you would think we were made of money and Red Sam said it was no use talking about it, she was exactly right. The children ran outside into the white sunlight and looked at the monkey in the lacy chinaberry tree. He was busy catching fleas on himself and biting each one carefully between his teeth as if it were a delicacy.

45 They drove off again into the hot afternoon. The grandmother took cat naps and woke up every five minutes with her own snoring. Outside of Toombsboro she woke up and recalled an old plantation that she had visited in this neighborhood once when she was a young lady. She said the house had six white columns across the front and that there was an avenue of oaks leading up to it and two little wooden trellis arbors on either side in front where you sat down with your suitor after a stroll in the garden. She recalled exactly which road to turn off to get to it. She knew that Bailey would not be willing to lose any time looking at an old house, but the more she talked about it, the more she wanted to see it once again and find out if the little twin arbors were still standing. "There was a secret panel in this house," she said craftily, not telling the truth but wishing that she were, "and the story went that all the family silver was hidden in it when Sherman came through but it was never found . . ."

"Hey!" John Wesley said. "Let's go see it! We'll find it! We'll poke all the woodwork and find it! Who lives there? Where do you turn off at? Hey, Pop, can't we turn off there?"

"We never have seen a house with a secret panel!" June Star shrieked. "Let's go to the house with the secret panel! Hey Pop, can't we go see the house with the secret panel!"

"It's not far from here, I know," the grandmother said. "It wouldn't take over twenty minutes."

Bailey was looking straight ahead. His jaw was as rigid as a horseshoe. "No," he said.

50 The children began to yell and scream that they wanted to see the house with the secret panel. John Wesley kicked the back of the front seat and June Star hung over her mother's shoulder and whined desperately into her ear that they never had any fun even on their vacation, that they could never do what THEY wanted to do. The baby began to scream and John Wesley kicked the back of the seat so hard that his father could feel the blows in his kidney.

"All right!" he shouted and drew the car to a stop at the side of the road. "Will you all shut up? Will you all just shut up for one second? If you don't shut up, we won't go anywhere."

"It would be very educational for them," the grandmother murmured.

"All right," Bailey said, "but get this: this is the only time we're going to stop for anything like this. This is the one and only time."

"The dirt road that you have to turn down is about a mile back," the grandmother directed. "I marked it when we passed."

55 "A dirt road," Bailey groaned.

After they had turned around and were headed toward the dirt road, the grandmother recalled other points about the house, the beautiful glass over the front doorway and the candle-lamp in the hall. John Wesley said that the secret panel was probably in the fireplace.

"You can't go inside this house," Bailey said. "You don't know who lives there."

"While you all talk to the people in front, I'll run around behind and get in a window," John Wesley suggested.

"We'll all stay in the car," his mother said.

60 They turned onto the dirt road and the car raced roughly along in a swirl of pink dust. The grandmother recalled the times when there were no paved roads and thirty miles was a day's journey. The dirt road was hilly and there were sudden washes in it and sharp curves on dangerous embankments. All at once they would be on a hill, looking down over the blue tops of trees for miles around, then the next minute, they would be in a red depression with the dust-coated trees looking down on them.

"This place had better turn up in a minute," Bailey said, "or I'm going to turn around."

The road looked as if no one had traveled on it in months.

"It's not much farther," the grandmother said and just as she said it, a horrible thought came to her. The thought was so embarrassing that she turned red in the face and her eyes dilated and her feet jumped up, upsetting her valise in the corner. The instant the valise moved, the newspaper top she had over the basket under it rose with a snarl and Pitty Sing, the cat, sprang onto Bailey's shoulder.

The children were thrown to the floor and their mother, clutching the baby, was thrown out the door onto the ground, the old lady was thrown into the front seat. The car turned over once and landed rightsideup in a gulch on the side of the road. Bailey remained in the driver's seat with the cat—gray-striped with a broad white face and an orange nose—clinging to his neck like a caterpillar.

65 As soon as the children saw they could move their arms and legs, they scrambled out of the car, shouting, "We've had an ACCIDENT!" The grandmother was curled up under the dashboard, hoping she was injured so that Bailey's wrath would not come down on her all at once. The horrible thought she had had before the accident was that the house she had remembered so vividly was not in Georgia but in Tennessee.

Bailey removed the cat from his neck with both hands and flung it out the window against the side of a pine tree. Then he got out of the car and started looking for the children's mother. She was sitting against the side of the red gutted ditch, holding the screaming baby, but she only had a cut down her face and a broken shoulder. "We've had an ACCIDENT!" the children screamed in a frenzy of delight.

"But nobody's killed," June Star said with disappointment as the grandmother limped out of the car, her hat still pinned to her head but the broken front brim standing up at a jaunty angle and the violet spray hanging off the side. They all sat down in the ditch, except the children, to recover from the shock. They were all shaking.

"Maybe a car will come along," said the children's mother hoarsely.

"I believe I have injured an organ," said the grandmother, pressing her side, but no one answered her. Bailey's teeth were clattering. He had on a yellow sport shirt with bright blue parrots designed in it and his face was as yellow as the shirt. The grandmother decided that she would not mention that the house was in Tennessee.

70 The road was about ten feet above and they could see only the tops of the trees on the other side of it. Behind the ditch they were sitting in there were more woods, tall and dark and deep. In a few minutes they saw a car some distance away on top of a hill, coming slowly as if the occupants were watching them. The grandmother stood up and waved both her arms dramatically to attract their attention. The car continued to come on slowly, disappeared around a bend and appeared again, moving even slower, on top of the hill they had gone over. It was a big black battered hearse-like automobile. There were three men in it.

It came to a stop just over them and for some minutes, the driver looked down with a steady expressionless gaze to where they were sitting, and didn't speak. Then he turned his head and muttered something to the other two and they got out. One was a fat boy in black trousers and a red sweat shirt with a silver stallion embossed on the front of it. He moved around on the right side of them and stood staring, his mouth partly open in a kind of loose grin. The other had on khaki pants and a blue striped coat and a gray hat pulled down very low, hiding most of his face. He came around slowly on the left side. Neither spoke.

The driver got out of the car and stood by the side of it, looking down at them. He was an older man than the other two. His hair was just beginning to gray and he wore silver-rimmed spectacles that gave him a scholarly look. He had a long creased face and didn't have on any shirt or undershirt. He had on blue jeans that were too tight for him and was holding a black hat and a gun. The two boys also had guns.

"We've had an ACCIDENT!" the children screamed.

The grandmother had the peculiar feeling that the bespectacled man was someone she knew. His face was as familiar to her as if she had known him all her life but she could not recall who he was. He moved away from the car and began to come down the embankment, placing his feet carefully so that he wouldn't slip. He had on tan and white shoes and no socks, and his ankles were red and thin. "Good afternoon," he said. "I see you all had you a little spill."

75 "We turned over twice!" said the grandmother.

"Oncet," he corrected. "We seen it happen. Try their car and see will it run, Hiram," he said quietly to the boy with the gray hat.

"What you got that gun for?" John Wesley asked. "Whatcha gonna do with that gun?"

"Lady," the man said to the children's mother, "would you mind calling them children to sit down by you? Children make me nervous. I want all you all to sit down right together there where you're at."

"What are you telling us what to do for?" June Star asked.

80 Behind them the line of woods gaped like a dark open mouth. "Come here," said their mother.

"Look here now," Bailey began suddenly, "we're in a predicament! We're in . . ."

The grandmother shrieked. She scrambled to her feet and stood staring. "You're The Misfit!" she said. "I recognized you at once!"

"Yes'm," the man said, smiling slightly as if he were pleased in spite of himself to be known, "but it would have been better for all of you, lady, if you hadn't of recognized me."

Bailey turned his head sharply and said something to his mother that shocked even the children. The old lady began to cry and The Misfit reddened.

85 "Lady," he said, "don't you get upset. Sometimes a man says things he don't mean. I don't reckon he meant to talk to you thataway."

"You wouldn't shoot a lady, would you?" the grandmother said and removed a clean handkerchief from her cuff and began to slap at her eyes with it.

The Misfit pointed the toe of his shoe into the ground and made a little hole and then covered it up again. "I would hate to have to," he said.

"Listen," the grandmother almost screamed, "I know you're a good man. You don't look a bit like you have common blood. I know you must come from nice people!"

"Yes ma'm," he said, "finest people in the world." When he smiled he showed a row of strong white teeth. "God never made a finer woman than my mother and my daddy's heart was pure gold," he said. The boy with the red sweat shirt had come around behind them and was standing with his gun at his hip. The Misfit squatted down on the ground. "Watch them children, Bobby Lee," he said. "You know they make me nervous." He looked at the six of them huddled together in front of him and he seemed to be embarrassed as if he couldn't think of anything to say. "Ain't a cloud in the sky," he remarked, looking up at it. "Don't see no sun but don't see no cloud neither."

90 "Yes, it's a beautiful day," said the grandmother. "Listen," she said, "you shouldn't call yourself The Misfit because I know you're a good man at heart. I can just look at you and tell."

"Hush!" Bailey yelled. "Hush! Everybody shut up and let me handle this!" He was squatting in the position of a runner about to sprint forward but he didn't move.

"I pre-chate that, lady," The Misfit said and drew a little circle in the ground with the butt of his gun.

"It'll take a half a hour to fix this here car," Hiram called, looking over the raised hood of it.

"Well, first you and Bobby Lee get him and that little boy to step over yonder with you," The Misfit said, pointing to Bailey and John Wesley. "The boys want to ask you something," he said to Bailey. "Would you mind stepping back in them woods there with them?"

95 "Listen," Bailey began, "we're in a terrible predicament. Nobody realizes what this is," and his voice cracked. His eyes were as blue and intense as the parrots in his shirt and he remained perfectly still.

The grandmother reached up to adjust her hat brim as if she were going to the woods with him but it came off in her hand. She stood staring at it and after a second she let it fall on the ground. Hiram pulled Bailey up by the arm as if he were assisting an old man. John Wesley caught hold of his father's hand and Bobby Lee followed. They went off toward the woods and just as they reached the dark edge, Bailey turned and supporting himself against a gray naked pine trunk, he shouted, "I'll be back in a minute, Mamma, wait on me!"

"Come back this instant!" his mother shrilled but they all disappeared into the woods.

"Bailey Boy!" the grandmother called in a tragic voice but she found she was looking at The Misfit squatting on the ground in front of her. "I just know you're a good man," she said desperately. "You're not a bit common!"

"Nome, I ain't a good man," The Misfit said after a second as if he had considered her statement carefully, "but I ain't the worst in the world neither. My daddy said I was a different breed of dog from my brothers and sisters. 'You know,' Daddy said, 'it's some that can live their whole life out without asking about it and it's others has to know why it is, and this boy is one of the latters. He's going to be into everything!'" He put on his black hat and looked up suddenly and then away deep into the woods as if he were embarrassed again. "I'm sorry I don't have on a shirt before you ladies," he said, hunching his shoulders slightly. "We buried our clothes that we had on when we escaped and we're just making do until we can get better. We borrowed these from some folks we met," he explained.

100 "That's perfectly all right," the grandmother said. "Maybe Bailey has an extra shirt in his suitcase."

"I'll look and see terrectly," The Misfit said.

"Where are they taking him?" the children's mother screamed.

"Daddy was a card himself," The Misfit said. "You couldn't put anything over on him. He never got in trouble with the Authorities though. Just had the knack of handling them."

"You could be honest too if you'd only try," said the grandmother. "Think how wonderful it would be to settle down and live a comfortable life and not have to think about somebody chasing you all the time."

105 The Misfit kept scratching in the ground with the butt of his gun as if he were thinking about it. "Yes'm, somebody is always after you," he murmured.

The grandmother noticed how thin his shoulder blades were just behind his hat because she was standing up looking down on him. "Do you ever pray?" she asked.

He shook his head. All she saw was the black hat wiggle between shoulder blades. "Nome," he said.

There was a pistol shot from the woods, followed closely by another. Then silence. The old lady's head jerked around. She could hear the wind move through the tree tops like a long satisfied insuck of breath. "Bailey Boy!" she called.

"I was a gospel singer for a while," The Misfit said. "I been most everything. Been in the arm service, both land and sea, at home and abroad, been twict married, been an undertaker, been with the railroads, plowed Mother Earth, been in a tornado, seen a man burnt alive oncet," and he looked up at the children's mother and the little girl who were sitting close together, their faces white and their eyes glassy; "I even seen a woman flogged," he said.

110 "Pray, pray," the grandmother began, "pray, pray. . . ."

"I never was a bad boy that I remember of," The Misfit said in an almost dreamy voice, "but somewheres along the line I done something wrong and got sent to the penitentiary. I was buried alive," and he looked up and held her attention to him by a steady stare.

"That's when you should have started to pray," she said. "What did you do to get sent up to the penitentiary that first time?"

"Turn to the right, it was a wall," The Misfit said, looking up again at the cloudless sky. "Turn to the left, it was a wall. Look up it was a ceiling, look down it was a floor. I forget what I done, lady. I set there and set there, trying to remember what it was I done and I ain't recalled it to this day. Oncet in a while, I would think it was coming to me, but it never come."

"Maybe they put you in by mistake," the old lady said vaguely.

115 "Nome," he said. "It wasn't no mistake. They had the papers on me."

"You must have stolen something," she said.

The Misfit sneered slightly. "Nobody had nothing I wanted," he said. "It was a head-doctor at the penitentiary said what I had done was kill my daddy but I know that for a lie. My daddy died in nineteen ought nineteen of the epidemic flu and I never had a thing to do with it. He was buried in the Mount Hopewell Baptist churchyard and you can go there and see for yourself."

"If you would pray," the old lady said, "Jesus would help you."

"That's right," The Misfit said.

120 "Well then, why don't you pray?" she asked trembling with delight suddenly.

"I don't want no hep," he said. "I'm doing all right by myself."

Bobby Lee and Hiram came ambling back from the woods. Bobby Lee was dragging a yellow shirt with bright blue parrots in it.

"Throw me that shirt, Bobby Lee," The Misfit said. The shirt came flying at him and landed on his shoulder and he put it on. The grandmother couldn't name what the shirt reminded her of. "No, lady," The Misfit said while he was buttoning it up, "I found out the crime don't matter. You can do one thing or you can do another, kill a man or take a tire off his car, because sooner or later you're going to forget what it was you done and just be punished for it."

The children's mother had begun to make heaving noises as if she couldn't get her breath. "Lady," he asked, "would you and that little girl like to step off yonder with Bobby Lee and Hiram and join your husband."

125 "Yes, thank you," the mother said faintly. Her left arm dangled helplessly and she was holding the baby, who had gone to sleep, in the other. "Hep that lady up, Hiram," The Misfit said as she struggled to climb out of the ditch, "and Bobby Lee, you hold onto that little girl's hand."

"I don't want to hold hands with him," June Star said. "He reminds me of a pig."

The fat boy blushed and laughed and caught her by the arm and pulled her off into the woods after Hiram and her mother.

Alone with The Misfit, the grandmother found that she had lost her voice. There was not a cloud in the sky nor any sun. There was nothing around her but woods. She wanted to tell him that he must pray. She opened and closed her mouth several times before anything came out. Finally she found herself saying, "Jesus, Jesus," meaning, Jesus will help you, but the way she was saying it, it sounded as if she might be cursing.

"Yes'm," The Misfit said as if he agreed. "Jesus thown everything off balance. It was the same case with Him as with me except He hadn't committed any crime and they could prove I had committed one because they had the papers on me. Of course," he said, "they never shown me my papers. That's why I sign myself now. I said long ago, you get you a signature and sign everything you do and keep a copy of it. Then you'll know what you done and you can hold up the crime to the punishment and see do they match and in the end you'll have something to prove you ain't been treated right. I call myself The Misfit," he said, "because I can't make what all I done wrong fit what all I gone through in punishment."

130 There was a piercing scream from the woods, followed closely by a pistol report. "Does it seem right to you, lady, that one is punished a heap and another ain't punished at all?"

"Jesus!" the old lady cried. "You've got good blood! I know you wouldn't shoot a lady! I know you come from nice people! Pray! Jesus, you ought not to shoot a lady. I'll give you all the money I've got!"

"Lady," The Misfit said, looking beyond her far into the woods, "there never was a body that give the undertaker a tip."

There were two more pistol reports and the grandmother raised her head like a parched old turkey hen crying for water and called, "Bailey Boy, Bailey Boy!" as if her heart would break.

"Jesus was the only One that ever raised the dead," The Misfit continued, "and He shouldn't have done it. He thrown everything off balance. If He did what He said, then it's nothing for you to do but thow away everything and follow Him, and if He didn't, then it's nothing for you to do but enjoy the few minutes you got left the best way you can—by killing somebody or burning down his house or doing some other meanness to him. No pleasure but meanness," he said and his voice had become almost a snarl.

135 "Maybe He didn't raise the dead," the old lady mumbled, not knowing what she was saying and feeling so dizzy that she sank down in the ditch with her legs twisted under her.

"I wasn't there so I can't say He didn't," The Misfit said. "I wisht I had of been there," he said, hitting the ground with his fist. "It ain't right I wasn't there because if I had of been there I would of known. Listen lady," he said in a high voice, "if I had of been there I would of known and I wouldn't be like I am now." His voice seemed about to crack and the grandmother's head cleared for an instant. She saw the man's face twisted close to her own as if he were going to cry and she murmured, "Why you're one of my babies. You're one of my own children!" She reached out and touched him on the shoulder. The Misfit sprang back as if a snake had bitten him and shot her three times through the chest. Then he put his gun down on the ground and took off his glasses and began to clean them.

Hiram and Bobby Lee returned from the woods and stood over the ditch, looking down at the grandmother who half sat and half lay in a puddle of blood with her legs crossed under her like a child's and her face smiling up at the cloudless sky.

Without his glasses, The Misfit's eyes were red-rimmed and pale and defenseless-looking. "Take her off and thow her where you thown the others," he said, picking up the cat that was rubbing itself against his leg.

"She was a talker, wasn't she?" Bobby Lee said, sliding down the ditch with a yodel.

140 "She would of been a good woman," The Misfit said, "if it had been somebody there to shoot her every minute of her life."

"Some fun!" Bobby Lee said.

"Shut up, Bobby Lee," The Misfit said. "It's no real pleasure in life."

[*1953*]

## *Revelation*

The doctor's waiting room, which was very small, was almost full when the Turpins entered and Mrs. Turpin, who was very large, made it look even smaller by her presence. She stood looming at the head of the magazine table set in the center of it, a living demonstration that the room was inadequate and ridiculous. Her little bright black eyes took in all the patients as she sized up the seating situation. There was one vacant chair and a place on a sofa occupied by a blond child in a dirty blue romper who should have been told to move over and make room for the lady. He was five or six, but Mrs. Turpin saw at once that no one was going to tell him to move over. He was slumped down in the seat, his arms idle at his sides and his eyes idle in his head; his nose ran unchecked.

Mrs. Turpin put a firm hand on Claud's shoulder and said in a voice that included anyone who wanted to listen, "Claud, you sit in that chair there," and gave him a push down into the vacant one. Claud was florid and bald and sturdy, somewhat shorter than Mrs. Turpin, but he sat down as if he were accustomed to doing what she told him to.

Mrs. Turpin remained standing. The only man in the room besides Claud was a lean stringy old fellow with a rusty hand spread out on each knee, whose eyes were closed as if he were asleep or dead or pretending to be so as not to get up and offer her his seat. Her gaze settled agreeably on a well-dressed grey-haired lady whose eyes met hers and whose expression said: If that child belonged to me, he would have some manners and move over—there's plenty of room there for you and him too.

Claud looked up with a sigh and made as if to rise.

5 "Sit down," Mrs. Turpin said. "You know you're not supposed to stand on that leg. He has an ulcer on his leg," she explained.

Claud lifted his foot onto the magazine table and rolled his trouser leg up to reveal a purple swelling on a plump marble-white calf.

"My!" the pleasant lady said. "How did you do that?"

"A cow kicked him," Mrs. Turpin said.

"Goodness!" said the lady.

10 Claud rolled his trouser leg down.

"Maybe the little boy would move over," the lady suggested, but the child did not stir.

"Somebody will be leaving in a minute," Mrs. Turpin said. She could not understand why a doctor—with as much money as they made charging five dollars a day to just stick their head in the hospital door and look at you—couldn't afford a decent-sized waiting room. This one was hardly bigger than a garage. The table was cluttered with limp-looking magazines and at one end of it there was a big green glass ash tray full of cigaret butts and cotton wads with little blood spots on them. If she had had anything to do with the running of the place, that would have been emptied every so often. There were no chairs against the wall at the head of the room. It had a rectangular-shaped panel in it that permitted a view of the office where the nurse came and went and the secretary listened to the radio. A plastic fern in a gold pot sat in the opening and trailed its fronds down almost to the floor. The radio was softly playing gospel music.

Just then the inner door opened and a nurse with the highest stack of yellow hair Mrs. Turpin had ever seen put her face in the crack and called for the next patient. The woman sitting beside Claud grasped the two arms of her chair and hoisted herself up; she pulled her dress free from her legs and lumbered through the door where the nurse had disappeared.

Mrs. Turpin eased into the vacant chair, which held her tight as a corset. "I wish I could reduce," she said, and rolled her eyes and gave a comic sigh.

15 "Oh, *you* aren't fat," the stylish lady said.

"Ooooo I am too," Mrs. Turpin said. "Claud he eats all he wants to and never weighs over one hundred and seventy-five pounds, but me I just look at something good to eat and I gain some weight," and her stomach and shoulders shook with laughter. "You can eat all you want to, can't you, Claud?" she asked, turning to him.

Claud only grinned.

"Well, as long as you have such a good disposition," the stylish lady said, "I don't think it makes a bit of difference what size you are. You just can't beat a good disposition."

Next to her was a fat girl of eighteen or nineteen, scowling into a thick blue book which Mrs. Turpin saw was entitled *Human Development.* The girl raised her head and directed her scowl at Mrs. Turpin as if she did not like her looks. She appeared annoyed that anyone should speak while she tried to read. The poor girl's face was blue with acne and Mrs. Turpin thought how pitiful it was to have a face like that at that age. She gave the girl a friendly smile but the girl only scowled the harder. Mrs. Turpin herself was fat but she had always had good skin, and, though she was forty-seven years old, there was not a wrinkle in her face except around her eyes from laughing too much.

20 Next to the ugly girl was the child, still in exactly the same position, and next to him was a thin leathery old woman in a cotton print dress. She and Claud had three sacks of chicken feed in their pump house that was in the same print. She had seen from the first that the child belonged with the

old woman. She could tell by the way they sat—kind of vacant and white-trashy, as if they would sit there until Doomsday if nobody called and told them to get up. And at right angles but next to the well-dressed pleasant lady was a lank-faced woman who was certainly the child's mother. She had on a yellow sweat shirt and wine-colored slacks, both gritty-looking, and the rims of her lips were stained with snuff. Her dirty yellow hair was tied behind with a little piece of red paper ribbon. Worse than niggers any day, Mrs. Turpin thought.

The gospel hymn playing was, "When I looked up and He looked down," and Mrs. Turpin, who knew it, supplied the last line mentally, "And wona these days I know I'll we-era crown."

Without appearing to, Mrs. Turpin always noticed people's feet. The well-dressed lady had on red and grey suede shoes to match her dress. Mrs. Turpin had on her good black patent leather pumps. The ugly girl had on Girl Scout shoes and heavy socks. The old woman had on tennis shoes and the white-trashy mother had on what appeared to be bedroom slippers, black straw with gold braid threaded through them—exactly what you would have expected her to have on.

Sometimes at night when she couldn't go to sleep, Mrs. Turpin would occupy herself with the question of who she would have chosen to be if she couldn't have been herself. If Jesus had said to her before he made her, "There's only two places available for you. You can either be a nigger or white-trash," what would she have said? "Please, Jesus, please," she would have said, "just let me wait until there's another place available," and he would have said, "No, you have to go right now and I have only those two places so make up your mind." She would have wiggled and squirmed and begged and pleaded but it would have been no use and finally she would have said, "All right, make me a nigger then—but that don't mean a trashy one." And he would have made her a neat clean respectable Negro-woman, herself but black.

Next to the child's mother was a red-headed youngish woman, reading one of the magazines and working a piece of chewing gum, hell for leather, as Claud would say. Mrs. Turpin could not see the woman's feet. She was not white-trash, just common. Sometimes Mrs. Turpin occupied herself at night naming the classes of people. On the bottom of the heap were most colored people, not the kind she would have been if she had been one, but most of them; then next to them—not above, just away from—were the white-trash; then above them were the homeowners, and above them the home-and-land owners, to which she and Claud belonged. Above she and Claud were people with a lot of money and much bigger houses and much more land. But here the complexity of it would begin to bear in on her, for some of the people with a lot of money were common and ought to be below she and Claud and some of the people who had good blood had lost their money and had to rent and then there were colored people who owned their homes and land as well. There was a colored dentist in town who had two red Lincolns and a swimming pool and a farm with registered white-face cattle on it. Usually by the time she had fallen asleep all the classes of people were moiling and roiling around in her head, and she would dream they were all crammed in together in a box car, being ridden off to be put in a gas oven.

25 "That's a beautiful clock," she said and nodded to her right. It was a big wall clock, the face encased in a brass sunburst.

"Yes, it's very pretty," the stylish lady said agreeably. "And right on the dot too," she added, glancing at her watch.

The ugly girl beside her cast an eye upward at the clock, smirked, then looked directly at Mrs. Turpin and smirked again. Then she returned her eyes to her book. She was obviously the lady's daughter because, although they didn't look anything alike as to disposition, they both had the same shape of face and the same blue eyes. On the lady they sparkled pleasantly but in the girl's seared face they appeared alternately to smolder and to blaze.

What if Jesus had said, "All right, you can be white-trash or a nigger or ugly"!

Mrs. Turpin felt an awful pity for the girl, though she thought it was one thing to be ugly and another to act ugly.

30 The woman with the snuff-stained lips turned around in her chair and looked up at the clock. Then she turned back and appeared to look a little to the side of Mrs. Turpin. There was a cast in one of her eyes. "You want to know wher you can get one of themther clocks?" she asked in a loud voice.

"No, I already have a nice clock," Mrs. Turpin said. Once somebody like her got a leg in the conversation, she would be all over it.

"You can get you one with green stamps," the woman said. "That's most likely wher he got hisn. Save you up enough, you can get you most anything. I got me some joo'ry."

Ought to have got you a wash rag and some soap, Mrs. Turpin thought.

"I get contour sheets with mine," the pleasant lady said.

35 The daughter slammed her book shut. She looked straight in front of her, directly through Mrs. Turpin and on through the yellow curtain and the plate glass window which made the wall behind her. The girl's eyes seemed lit all of a sudden with a peculiar light, an unnatural light like night road signs give. Mrs. Turpin turned her head to see if there was anything going on outside that she should see, but she could not see anything. Figures passing cast only a pale shadow through the curtain. There was no reason the girl should single her out for her ugly looks.

"Miss Finley," the nurse said, cracking the door. The gum chewing woman got up and passed in front of her and Claud and went into the office. She had on red high-heeled shoes.

Directly across the table, the ugly girl's eyes were fixed on Mrs. Turpin as if she had some very special reason for disliking her.

"This is wonderful weather, isn't it?" the girl's mother said.

"It's good weather for cotton if you can get the niggers to pick it," Mrs. Turpin said, "but niggers don't want to pick cotton any more. You can't get the white folks to pick it and now you can't get the niggers—because they got to be right up there with the white folks."

40 "They gonna *try* anyways," the white-trash woman said, leaning forward.

"Do you have one of those cotton-picking machines?" the pleasant lady asked.

"No," Mrs. Turpin said, "they leave half the cotton in the field. We don't have much cotton anyway. If you want to make it farming now, you have to have a little of everything. We got a couple of acres of cotton and a few hogs and chickens and just enough white-face that Claud can look after them himself."

"One thang I don't want," the white-trash woman said, wiping her mouth with the back of her hand. "Hogs. Nasty stinking things, a-gruntin and a-rootin all over the place."

Mrs. Turpin gave her the merest edge of her attention. "Our hogs are not dirty and they don't stink," she said. "They're cleaner than some children I've seen. Their feet never touch the ground. We have a pig-parlor—that's where you raise them on concrete," she explained to the pleasant lady, "and Claud scoots them down with the hose every afternoon and washes off the floor." Cleaner by far than that child right there, she thought. Poor nasty little thing. He had not moved except to put the thumb of his dirty hand into his mouth.

45 The woman turned her face away from Mrs. Turpin. "I know I wouldn't scoot down no hog with no hose," she said to the wall.

You wouldn't have no hog to scoot down, Mrs. Turpin said to herself.

"A-gruntin and a-rootin and a-groanin," the woman muttered.

"We got a little of everything," Mrs. Turpin said to the pleasant lady. "It's no use in having more than you can handle yourself with help like it is. We found enough niggers to pick our cotton this year but Claud he has to go after them and take them home again in the evening. They can't walk that half a mile. No they can't. I tell you," she said and laughed merrily, "I sure am tired of buttering up niggers, but you got to love em if you want em to work for you. When they come in the morning, I run out and I say, 'Hi yawl this morning?' and when Claud drives them off to the field I just wave to beat the band and they just wave back." And she waved her hand rapidly to illustrate.

"Like you read out of the same book," the lady said, showing she understood perfectly.

50 "Child, yes," Mrs. Turpin said. "And when they come in from the field, I run out with a bucket of icewater. That's the way it's going to be from now on," she said. "You may as well face it."

"One thang I know," the white-trash woman said. "Two thangs I ain't going to do: love no niggers or scoot down no hog with no hose." And she let out a bark of contempt.

The look that Mrs. Turpin and the pleasant lady exchanged indicated they both understood that you had to *have* certain things before you could *know* certain things. But every time Mrs. Turpin exchanged a look with the lady, she was aware that the ugly girl's peculiar eyes were still on her, and she had trouble bringing her attention back to the conversation.

"When you got something," she said, "you got to look after it." And when you ain't got a thing but breath and britches, she added to herself, you can afford to come to town every morning and just sit on the Court House coping and spit.

A grotesque revolving shadow passed across the curtain behind her and was thrown palely on the opposite wall. Then a bicycle clattered down against the outside of the building. The door opened and a colored boy glided in with a tray from the drug store. It had two large red and white paper cups on it with tops on them. He was a tall, very black boy in discolored white pants and a green nylon shirt. He was chewing gum slowly, as if to music. He set the tray down in the office opening next to the fern and stuck his head through to look for the secretary. She was not in there. He rested his arms on the ledge and waited, his narrow bottom stuck out, swaying slowly to the left and right. He raised a hand over his head and scratched the base of his skull.

55 "You see that button there, boy?" Mrs. Turpin said. "You can punch that and she'll come. She's probably in the back somewhere."

"Is that right?" the boy said agreeably, as if he had never seen the button before. He leaned to the right and put his finger on it. "She sometime out," he said and twisted around to face his audience, his elbows behind him on the counter. The nurse appeared and he twisted back again. She handed him a dollar and he rooted in his pocket and made the change and counted it out to her. She gave him fifteen cents for a tip and he went out with the empty tray. The heavy door swung to slowly and closed at length with the sound of suction. For a moment no one spoke.

"They ought to send all them niggers back to Africa," the white-trash woman said. "That's wher they come from in the first place."

"Oh, I couldn't do without my good colored friends," the pleasant lady said.

"There's a heap of things worse than a nigger," Mrs. Turpin agreed. "It's all kinds of them just like it's all kinds of us."

60 "Yes, and it takes all kinds to make the world go round," the lady said in her musical voice.

As she said it, the raw-complexioned girl snapped her teeth together. Her lower lip turned downwards and inside out, revealing the pale pink inside of her mouth. After a second it rolled back up. It was the ugliest face Mrs. Turpin had ever seen anyone make and for a moment she was certain that the girl had made it at her. She was looking at her as if she had known and disliked her all her life—all of Mrs. Turpin's life, it seemed too, not just all the girl's life. Why, girl, I don't even know you, Mrs. Turpin said silently.

She forced her attention back to the discussion. "It wouldn't be practical to send them back to Africa," she said. "They wouldn't want to go. They got it too good here."

"Wouldn't be what they wanted—if I had anythang to do with it," the woman said.

"It wouldn't be a way in the world you could get all the niggers back over there," Mrs. Turpin said. "They'd be hiding out and lying down and turning sick on you and wailing and hollering and raring and pitching. It wouldn't be a way in the world to get them over there."

65 "They got over here," the trashy woman said. "Get back like they got over."

"It wasn't so many of them then," Mrs. Turpin explained.

The woman looked at Mrs. Turpin as if here was an idiot indeed but Mrs. Turpin was not bothered by the look, considering where it came from.

"Nooo," she said, "they're going to stay here where they can go to New York and marry white folks and improve their color. That's what they all want to do, every one of them, improve their color."

"You know what comes of that, don't you?" Claud asked.

70 "No, Claud, what?" Mrs. Turpin said.

Claud's eyes twinkled. "White-faced niggers," he said with never a smile.

Everybody in the office laughed except the white-trash and the ugly girl. The girl gripped the book in her lap with white fingers. The trashy woman looked around her from face to face as if she thought they were all idiots. The old woman in the feed sack dress continued to gaze expressionless across the floor at the high-top shoes of the man opposite her, the one who had been pretending to be asleep when the Turpins came in. He was laughing heartily, his hands still spread out on his knees. The child had fallen to the side and was lying now almost face down in the old woman's lap.

While they recovered from their laughter, the nasal chorus on the radio kept the room from silence.

You go to blank blank  
And I'll go to mine  
But we'll all blank along  
To-geth-ther,  
And all along the blank  
We'll hep each other out  
Smile-ling in any kind of  
Weath-ther!

Mrs. Turpin didn't catch every word but she caught enough to agree with the spirit of the song and it turned her thoughts sober. To help anybody out that needed it was her philosophy of life. She never spared herself when she found somebody in need, whether they were white or black, trash or decent. And of all she had to be thankful for, she was most thankful that this was so. If Jesus had said, "You can be high society and have all the money you want and be thin and svelte-like, but you can't be a good woman with it," she would have had to say, "Well don't make me that then. Make me a good woman and it don't matter what else, how fat or how ugly or how poor!" Her heart rose. He had not made her a nigger or white-trash or ugly! He had made her herself and given her a little of everything. Jesus, thank you! she said. Thank you thank you thank you! Whenever she counted her blessings she felt as buoyant as if she weighed one hundred and twenty-five pounds instead of one hundred and eighty.

75 "What's wrong with your little boy?" the pleasant lady asked the white-trashy woman.

"He has a ulcer," the woman said proudly. "He ain't give me a minute's peace since he was born. Him and her are just alike," she said, nodding at the old woman, who was running her leathery fingers through the child's pale hair. "Look like I can't get nothing down them two but Co'Cola and candy."

That's all you try to get down em, Mrs. Turpin said to herself. Too lazy to light the fire. There was nothing you could tell her about people like them that she didn't know already. And it was not just that they didn't have anything. Because if you gave them everything, in two weeks it would all be broken or filthy or they would have chopped it up for lightwood. She knew all this from her own experience. Help them you must, but help them you couldn't.

All at once the ugly girl turned her lips inside out again. Her eyes were fixed like two drills on Mrs. Turpin. This time there was no mistaking that there was something urgent behind them.

Girl, Mrs. Turpin exclaimed silently, I haven't done a thing to you! The girl might be confusing her with somebody else. There was no need to sit by and let herself be intimidated. "You must be in college," she said boldly, looking directly at the girl. "I see you reading a book there."

80 The girl continued to stare and pointedly did not answer.

Her mother blushed at this rudeness. "The lady asked you a question, Mary Grace," she said under her breath.

"I have ears," Mary Grace said.

The poor mother blushed again. "Mary Grace goes to Wellesley College," she explained. She twisted one of the buttons on her dress. "In Massachusetts," she added with a grimace. "And in the summer she just keeps right on studying. Just reads all the time, a real book worm. She's done real well at Wellesley; she's taking English and Math and History and Psychology and Social Studies," she rattled on, "and I think it's too much. I think she ought to get out and have fun."

The girl looked as if she would like to hurl them all through the plate glass window.

85 "Way up north," Mrs. Turpin murmured and thought, well, it hasn't done much for her manners.

"I'd almost rather to have him sick," the white-trash woman said, wrenching the attention back to herself. "He's so mean when he ain't. Look like some children just take natural to meanness. It's some gets bad when they get sick but he was the opposite. Took sick and turned good. He don't give me no trouble now. It's me waitin to see the doctor," she said.

If I was going to send anybody back to Africa, Mrs. Turpin thought, it would be your kind, woman. "Yes, indeed," she said aloud, but looking up at the ceiling, "it's a heap of things worse than a nigger." And dirtier than a hog, she added to herself.

"I think people with bad dispositions are more to be pitied than anyone on earth," the pleasant lady said in a voice that was decidedly thin.

"I thank the Lord he has blessed me with a good one," Mrs. Turpin said. "The day has never dawned that I couldn't find something to laugh at."

90 "Not since she married me anyways," Claud said with a comical straight face.

Everybody laughed except the girl and the white-trash.

Mrs. Turpin's stomach shook. "He's such a caution," she said, "that I can't help but laugh at him."

The girl made a loud ugly noise through her teeth.

Her mother's mouth grew thin and tight. "I think the worst thing in the world," she said, "is an ungrateful person. To have everything and not appreciate it. I know a girl," she said, "who has parents who would give her anything, a little brother who loves her dearly, who is getting a good education, who wears the best clothes, but who can never say a kind word to anyone, who never smiles, who just criticizes and complains all day long."

95 "Is she too old to paddle?" Claud asked.

The girl's face was almost purple.

"Yes," the lady said, "I'm afraid there's nothing to do but leave her to her folly. Some day she'll wake up and it'll be too late."

"It never hurt anyone to smile," Mrs. Turpin said. "It just makes you feel better all over."

Of course," the lady said sadly, "but there are just some people you can't tell anything to. They can't take criticism."

100 ""If it's one thing I am," Mrs. Turpin said with feeling, "it's grateful. When I think who all I could have been besides myself and what all I got, a little of everything, and a good disposition besides, I just feel like shouting, 'Thank you, Jesus, for making everything the way it is!' It could have been different!" For one thing, somebody else could have got Claud. At the thought of this, she was flooded with gratitude and a terrible pang of joy ran through her. "Oh thank you, Jesus, Jesus, thank you!" she cried aloud.

The book struck her directly over her left eye. It struck almost at the same instant that she realized the girl was about to hurl it. Before she could utter a sound, the raw face came crashing across the table toward her, howling. The girl's fingers sank like clamps into the soft flesh of her neck. She heard the mother cry out and Claud shout, "Whoa!" There was an instant when she was certain that she was about to be in an earthquake.

All at once her vision narrowed and she saw everything as if it were happening in a small room far away, or as if she were looking at it through the wrong end of a telescope. Claud's face crumpled and fell out of sight. The nurse ran in, then out, then in again. Then the gangling figure of the doctor rushed out of the inner door. Magazines flew this way and that as the table turned over. The girl fell with a thud and Mrs. Turpin's vision suddenly reversed itself and she saw everything large instead of small. The eyes of the white-trashy woman were staring hugely at the floor. There the girl, held down on one side by the nurse and on the other by her mother, was wrenching and turning in their grasp. The doctor was kneeling astride her, trying to hold her arm down. He managed after a second to sink a long needle into it.

Mrs. Turpin felt entirely hollow except for her heart which swung from side to side as if it were agitated in a great empty drum of flesh.

Somebody that's not busy call for the ambulance," the doctor said in the off-hand voice young doctors adopt for terrible occasions.

105 Mrs. Turpin could not have moved a finger. The old man who had been sitting next to her skipped nimbly into the office and made the call, for the secretary still seemed to be gone.

"Claud!" Mrs. Turpin called.

He was not in his chair. She knew she must jump up and find him but she felt like some one trying to catch a train in a dream, when everything moves in slow motion and the faster you try to run the slower you go.

"Here I am," a suffocated voice, very unlike Claud's, said.

He was doubled up in the corner on the floor, pale as paper, holding his leg. She wanted to get up and go to him but she could not move. Instead, her gaze was drawn slowly downward to the churning face on the floor, which she could see over the doctor's shoulder.

110 The girl's eyes stopped rolling and focused on her. They seemed a much lighter blue than before, as if a door that had been tightly closed behind them was now open to admit light and air.

Mrs. Turpin's head cleared and her power of motion returned. She leaned forward until she was looking directly into the fierce brilliant eyes.

There was no doubt in her mind that the girl did know her, knew her in some intense and personal way, beyond time and place and condition. "What you got to say to me?" she asked hoarsely and held her breath, waiting, as for a revelation.

The girl raised her head. Her gaze locked with Mrs. Turpin's. "Go back to hell where you came from, you old wart hog," she whispered. Her voice was low but clear. Her eyes burned for a moment as if she saw with pleasure that her message had struck its target.

Mrs. Turpin sank back in her chair.

After a moment the girl's eyes closed and she turned her head wearily to the side.

115 The doctor rose and handed the nurse the empty syringe. He leaned over and put both hands for a moment on the mother's shoulders, which were shaking. She was sitting on the floor, her lips pressed together, holding Mary Grace's hand in her lap. The girl's fingers were gripped like a baby's around her thumb. "Go on to the hospital," he said. "I'll call and make the arrangements."

"Now let's see that neck," he said in a jovial voice to Mrs. Turpin. He began to inspect her neck with his first two fingers. Two little moonshaped lines like pink fish bones were indented over her windpipe. There was the beginning of an angry red swelling above her eye. His fingers passed over this also.

"Lea' me be," she said thickly and shook him off. "See about Claud. She kicked him."

"I'll see about him in a minute," he said and felt her pulse. He was a thin gray-haired man, given to pleasantries. "Go home and have yourself a vacation the rest of the day," he said and patted her on the shoulder.

Quit your pattin me, Mrs. Turpin growled to herself.

120 "And put an ice pack over that eye," he said. Then he went and squatted down beside Claud and looked at his leg. After a moment he pulled him up and Claud limped after him into the office.

Until the ambulance came, the only sounds in the room were the tremulous moans of the girl's mother, who continued to sit on the floor. The white-trash woman did not take her eyes off the girl. Mrs. Turpin looked straight ahead at nothing. Presently the ambulance drew up, a long dark shadow, behind the curtain. The attendants came in and set the stretcher down beside the girl and lifted her expertly onto it and carried her out. The nurse helped the mother gather up her things. The shadow of the ambulance moved silently away and the nurse came back in the office.

"That ther girl is going to be a lunatic, ain't she?" the white-trash woman asked the nurse, but the nurse kept on to the back and never answered her.

"Yes, she's going to be a lunatic," the white-trash woman said to the rest of them.

"Po' critter," the old woman murmured. The child's face was still in her lap. His eyes looked idly out over her knees. He had not moved during the disturbance except to draw one leg up under him.

125 "I thank Gawd," the white-trash woman said fervently, "I ain't a lunatic."

Claud came limping out and the Turpins went home.

As their pick-up truck turned into their own dirt road and made the crest of the hill, Mrs. Turpin gripped the window ledge and looked out suspiciously. The land sloped gracefully down through a field dotted with lavender weeds and at the start of the rise their small yellow frame house, with its little flower beds spread out around it like a fancy apron, sat primly in its accustomed place between two giant hickory trees. She would not have been startled to see a burnt wound between two blackened chimneys.

Neither of them felt like eating so they put on their house clothes and lowered the shade in the bedroom and lay down, Claud with his leg on a pillow and herself with a damp washcloth over her eye. The instant she was flat on her back, the image of a razor-backed hog with warts on its face and horns coming out behind its ears snorted into her head. She moaned, a low quiet moan.

"I am not," she said tearfully, "a wart hog. From hell." But the denial had no force. The girl's eyes and her words, even the tone of her voice, low but clear, directed only to her, brooked no repudiation. She had been singled out for the message, though there was trash in the room to whom it might justly have been applied. The full force of this fact struck her only now. There was a woman there who was neglecting her own child but she had been overlooked. The message had been given to Ruby Turpin, a respectable, hard-working, church-going woman. The tears dried. Her eyes began to burn instead with wrath.

130 She rose on her elbow and the washcloth fell into her hand. Claud was lying on his back, snoring. She wanted to tell him what the girl had said. At the same time she did not wish to put the image of herself as a wart hog from hell into his mind.

"Hey, Claud," she muttered and pushed his shoulder.

Claud opened one pale baby blue eye.

She looked into it warily. He did not think about anything. He just went his way.

"Wha, whasit?" he said and closed the eye again.

135 "Nothing," she said. "Does your leg pain you?"

"Hurts like hell," Claud said.

"It'll quit terreckly," she said and lay back down. In a moment Claud was snoring again. For the rest of the afternoon they lay there. Claud slept. She scowled at the ceiling. Occasionally she raised her fist and made a small stabbing motion over her chest as if she was defending her innocence to invisible guests who were like the comforters of Job, reasonable-seeming but wrong.

About five-thirty Claud stirred. "Got to go after those niggers," he sighed, not moving.

She was looking straight up as if there were unintelligible handwriting on the ceiling. The protuberance over her eye had turned a greenish-blue. "Listen here," she said.

140 "What?"

"Kiss me."

Claud leaned over and kissed her loudly on the mouth. He pinched her side and their hands interlocked. Her expression of ferocious concentration did not change. Claud got up, groaning and growling, and limped off. She continued to study the ceiling.

She did not get up until she heard the pick-up truck coming back with the Negroes. Then she rose and thrust her feet in her brown oxfords, which she did not bother to lace, and stumped out onto the back porch and got her red plastic bucket. She emptied a tray of ice cubes into it and filled it half full of water and went out into the back yard. Every afternoon after Claud brought the hands in, one of the boys helped him put out hay and the rest waited in the back of the truck until he was ready to take them home. The truck was parked in the shade under one of the hickory trees.

"Hi yawl this evening?" Mrs. Turpin asked grimly, appearing with the bucket and the dipper. There were three women and a boy in the truck.

145 "Us doin nicely," the oldest woman said. "Hi you doin?" and her gaze stuck immediately on the dark lump on Mrs. Turpin's forehead. "You done fell down, ain't you?" she asked in a solicitous voice. The old woman was dark and almost toothless. She had on an old felt hat of Claud's set back on her head. The other two women were younger and lighter and they both had new bright green sun hats. One of them had hers on her head; the other had taken hers off and the boy was grinning beneath it.

Mrs. Turpin set the bucket down on the floor of the truck. "Yawl hep yourselves," she said. She looked around to make sure Claud had gone. "No. I didn't fall down," she said, folding her arms. "It was something worse than that."

"Ain't nothing bad happen to you!" the old woman said. She said it as if they all knew Mrs. Turpin was protected in some special way by Divine Providence. "You just had you a little fall."

"We were in town at the doctor's office for where the cow kicked Mr. Turpin," Mrs. Turpin said in a flat tone that indicated they could leave off their foolishness. "And there was this girl there. A big fat girl with her face all broke out. I could look at that girl and tell she was peculiar but I couldn't tell how. And me and her mama were just talking and going along and all of a sudden WHAM! She throws this big book she was reading at me and . . ."

"Naw!" the old woman cried out.

150 "And then she jumps over the table and commences to choke me."

"Naw!" they all exclaimed, "naw!"

"Hi come she do that?" the old woman asked. "What ail her?"

Mrs. Turpin only glared in front of her.

"Somethin ail her," the old woman said.

155 "They carried her off in an ambulance," Mrs. Turpin continued, "but before she went she was rolling on the floor and they were trying to hold her down to give her a shot and she said something to me." She paused. "You know what she said to me?"

"What she say?" they asked.

"She said," Mrs. Turpin began, and stopped, her face very dark and heavy. The sun was getting whiter and whiter, blanching the sky overhead so that the leaves of the hickory tree were black in the face of it. She could not bring forth the words. "Something real ugly," she muttered.

"She sho shouldn't said nothin ugly to you," the old woman said. "You so sweet. You the sweetest lady I know."

"She pretty too," the one with the hat on said.

160 "And stout," the other one said. "I never knowed no sweeter white lady."

"That's the truth befo' Jesus," the old woman said. "Amen! You des as sweet and pretty as you can be."

Mrs. Turpin knew just exactly how much Negro flattery was worth and it added to her rage. "She said," she began again and finished this time with a fierce rush of breath, "that I was an old wart hog from hell."

There was an astounded silence.

"Where she at?" the youngest woman cried in a piercing voice.

165 "Lemme see her. I'll kill her!"

"I'll kill her with you!" the other one cried.

"She b'long in the sylum," the old woman said emphatically. "You the sweetest white lady I know."

"She pretty too," the other two said. "Stout as she can be and sweet. Jesus satisfied with her!"

"Deed he is," the old woman declared.

170 Idiots! Mrs. Turpin growled to herself. You could never say anything intelligent to a nigger. You could talk at them but not with them. "Yawl ain't drunk your water," she said shortly. "Leave the bucket in the truck when you're finished with it. I got more to do than just stand around and pass the time of day," and she moved off and into the house.

She stood for a moment in the middle of the kitchen. The dark protuberance over her eye looked like a miniature tornado cloud which might any moment sweep across the horizon of her brow. Her lower lip protruded dangerously. She squared her massive shoulders. Then she marched into the front of the house and out the side door and started down the road to the pig parlor. She had the look of a woman going single-handed, weaponless, into battle.

The sun was a deep yellow now like a harvest moon and was riding westward very fast over the far tree line as if it meant to reach the hogs before she did. The road was rutted and she kicked several good-sized stones out of her path as she strode along. The pig parlor was on a little knoll at the end of a lane that ran off from the side of the barn. It was a square of concrete as large as a small room, with a board fence about four feet high around it. The concrete floor sloped slightly so that the hog wash could drain off into a trench where it was carried to the field for fertilizer. Claud was standing on the outside, on the edge of the concrete, hanging onto the top board, hosing down the floor inside. The hose was connected to the faucet of a water trough nearby.

Mrs. Turpin climbed up beside him and glowered down at the hogs inside. There were seven long-snouted bristly shoats in it—tan with liver-colored spots—and an old sow a few weeks off from farrowing. She was lying on her side grunting. The shoats were running about shaking themselves like idiot children, their little slit pig eyes searching the floor for anything left. She had read that pigs were the most intelligent animal. She doubted it. They were supposed to be smarter than dogs. There had even been a pig astronaut. He had performed his assignment perfectly but died of a heart attack afterwards because they left him in his electric suit, sitting upright throughout his examination when naturally a hog should be on all fours.

A-gruntin and a-rootin and a-groanin.

175 "Gimme that hose," she said, yanking it away from Claud. "Go on and carry them niggers home and then get off that leg."

"You look like you might have swallowed a mad dog," Claud observed, but he got down and limped off. He paid no attention to her humors.

Until he was out of earshot, Mrs. Turpin stood on the side of the pen, holding the hose and pointing the stream of water at the hind quarter of any shoat that looked as if it might try to lie down. When he had had time to get over the hill, she turned her head slightly and her wrathful eyes scanned the path. He was nowhere in sight. She turned back again and seemed to gather herself up. Her shoulders rose and she drew in her breath.

"What do you send me a message like that for?" she said in a low fierce voice, barely above a whisper but with the force of a shout in its concentrated fury. "How am I a hog and me both? How am I saved and from hell too?" Her free fist was knotted and with the other she gripped the hose, blindly pointing the stream of water in and out of the eye of the old sow whose outraged squeal she did not hear.

The pig parlor commanded a view of the back pasture where their twenty beef cows were gathered around the hay-bales Claud and the boy had put out. The freshly cut pasture sloped down to the highway. Across it was their cotton field and beyond that a dark green dusty wood which they owned as well. The sun was behind the wood, very red, looking over the paling of trees like a farmer inspecting his own hogs.

180 "Why me?" she rumbled. "It's no trash around here, black or white, that I haven't given to. And break my back to the bone every day working. And do for the church."

She appeared to be the right size woman to command the arena before her. "How am I a hog?" she demanded. "Exactly how am I like them?" and she jabbed the stream of water at the shoats. "There was plenty of trash there. It didn't have to be me."

"If you like trash better, go get yourself some trash then," she railed. "You could have made me trash. Or a nigger. If trash is what you wanted why didn't you make me trash?" She shook her fist with the hose in it and a watery snake appeared momentarily in the air. "I could quit working and take it easy and be filthy," she growled. "Lounge about the sidewalks all day drinking root beer. Dip snuff and spit in every puddle and have it all over my face. I could be nasty."

"Or you could have made me a nigger. It's too late for me to be a nigger," she said with deep sarcasm, "but I could act like one. Lay down in the middle of the road and stop traffic. Roll on the ground."

In the deepening light everything was taking on a mysterious hue. The pasture was growing a peculiar glassy green and the streak of highway had turned lavender. She braced herself for a final assault and this time her voice rolled out over the pasture. "Go on," she yelled, "call me a hog! Call me a hog again. From hell. Call me a wart hog from hell. Put that bottom rail on top. There'll still be a top and bottom!"

185 A garbled echo returned to her.

A final surge of fury shook her and she roared, "Who do you think you are?"

The color of everything, field and crimson sky, burned for a moment with a transparent intensity. The question carried over the pasture and across the highway and the cotton field and returned to her clearly like an answer from beyond the wood.

She opened her mouth but no sound came out of it.

A tiny truck, Claud's, appeared on the highway, heading rapidly out of sight. Its gears scraped thinly. It looked like a child's toy. At any moment a bigger truck might smash into it and scatter Claud's and the niggers' brains all over the road.

190 Mrs. Turpin stood there, her gaze fixed on the highway, all her muscles rigid, until in five or six minutes the truck reappeared, returning. She waited until it had had time to turn into their own road. Then like a monumental statue coming to life, she bent her head slowly and gazed, as if through the very heart of the mystery, down into the pig parlor at the hogs. They had settled all in one corner around the old sow who was grunting softly. A red glow suffused them. They appeared to pant with a secret life.

Until the sun slipped finally behind the tree line, Mrs. Turpin remained there with her gaze bent to them as if she were absorbing some abysmal life-giving knowledge. At last she lifted her head. There was only a purple streak in the sky, cutting through a field of crimson and leading, like an extension of the highway, into the descending dusk. She raised her hands from the side of the pen in a gesture hieratic and profound. A visionary light settled in her eyes. She saw the streak as a vast swinging bridge extending upward from the earth through a field of living fire. Upon it a vast horde of souls were rumbling toward heaven. There were whole companies of white-trash, clean for the first time in their lives, and bands of black niggers in white robes, and battalions of freaks and lunatics shouting and clapping and leaping like frogs. And bringing up the end of the procession was a tribe of people whom she recognized at once as those who, like herself and Claud, had always had a little of everything and the God-given wit to use it right. She leaned forward to observe them closer. They were marching behind the others with great dignity, accountable as they had always been for good order and common sense and respectable behavior. They alone were on key. Yet she could see by their shocked and altered faces that even their virtues were being burned away. She lowered her hands and gripped the rail of the hog pen, her eyes small but fixed unblinkingly on what lay ahead. In a moment the vision faded but she remained where she was, immobile.

At length she got down and turned off the faucet and made her slow way on the darkening path to the house. In the woods around her the invisible cricket choruses had struck up, but what she heard were the voices of the souls climbing upward into the starry field and shouting hallelujah.

[*1964*]

## *Parker's Back*

Parker's wife was sitting on the front porch floor, snapping beans. Parker was sitting on the step, some distance away, watching her sullenly. She was plain, plain. The skin on her face was thin and drawn as tight as the skin on an onion and her eyes were grey and sharp like the points of two icepicks. Parker understood why he had married her—he couldn't have got her any other way—but he couldn't understand why he stayed with her now. She was pregnant and pregnant women were not his favorite kind. Nevertheless, he stayed as if she had him conjured. He was puzzled and ashamed of himself.

The house they rented sat alone save for a single tall pecan tree on a high embankment overlooking a highway. At intervals a car would shoot past below and his wife's eyes would swerve suspiciously after the sound of it and then come back to rest on the newspaper full of beans in her lap. One of the things she did not approve of was automobiles. In addition to her other bad qualities, she was forever sniffing up sin. She did not smoke or dip,[1] drink whiskey, use bad language or paint her face, and God knew some paint would have improved it, Parker thought. Her being against color, it was the more remarkable she had married him. Sometimes he supposed that she had married him because she meant to save him. At other times he had a suspicion that she actually liked everything she said she didn't. He could account for her one way or another; it was himself he could not understand.

She turned her head in his direction and said, "It's no reason you can't work for a man. It don't have to be a woman."

"Aw shut your mouth for a change," Parker muttered.

5 If he had been certain she was jealous of the woman he worked for he would have been pleased but more likely she was concerned with the sin that would result if he and the woman took a liking to each other. He had told her that the woman was a hefty young blonde; in fact she was nearly seventy years old and too dried up to have an interest in anything except getting as much work out of him as she could. Not that an old woman didn't sometimes get an interest in a young man, particularly if he was as attractive as Parker felt he was, but this old woman looked at him the way she looked at her old tractor—as if she had to put up with it because it was all she had. The tractor had broken down the second day Parker was on it and she had set him at once to cutting bushes, saying out of the side of her mouth to the nigger, "Everything he touches, he breaks." She also asked him to wear his shirt when he worked; Parker had removed it even though the day was not sultry; he put it back on reluctantly.

This ugly woman Parker married was his first wife. He had had other women but he had planned never to get himself tied up legally. He had first seen her one morning when his truck broke down on the highway. He had managed to pull it off the road into a neatly swept yard on which sat a peeling two-room house. He got out and opened the hood of the truck and began to study the motor. Parker had an extra sense that told him when there was a woman nearby watching him. After he had leaned over the motor a few minutes, his neck began to prickle. He cast his eye over the empty yard and porch of the house. A woman he could not see was either nearby beyond a clump of honeysuckle or in the house, watching him out the window.

Suddenly Parker began to jump up and down and fling his hand about as if he had mashed it in the machinery. He doubled over and held his hand close to his chest. "God dammit!" he hollered, "Jesus Christ in hell! Jesus

[1]**dip** use snuff.

God Almighty damm! God dammit to hell!" he went on, flinging out the same few oaths over and over as loud as he could.

Without warning a terrible bristly claw slammed the side of his face and he fell backwards on the hood of the truck. "You don't talk no filth here!" a voice close to him shrilled.

Parker's vision was so blurred that for an instant he thought he had been attacked by some creature from above, a giant hawk-eyed angel wielding a hoary weapon. As his sight cleared, he saw before him a tall raw-boned girl with a broom.

10 "I hurt my hand," he said. "I HURT my hand." He was so incensed that he forgot that he hadn't hurt his hand. "My hand may be broke," he growled although his voice was still unsteady.

"Lemme see it," the girl demanded.

Parker stuck out his hand and she came closer and looked at it. There was no mark on the palm and she took the hand and turned it over. Her own hand was dry and hot and rough and Parker felt himself jolted back to life by her touch. He looked more closely at her. I don't want nothing to do with this one, he thought.

The girl's sharp eyes peered at the back of the stubby reddish hand she held. There emblazoned in red and blue was a tattooed eagle perched on a cannon. Parker's sleeve was rolled to the elbow. Above the eagle a serpent was coiled about a shield and in the spaces between the eagle and the serpent there were hearts, some with arrows through them. Above the serpent there was a spread hand of cards. Every space on the skin of Parker's arm, from wrist to elbow, was covered in some loud design. The girl gazed at this with an almost stupefied smile of shock, as if she had accidentally grasped a poisonous snake; she dropped the hand.

"I got most of my other ones in foreign parts," Parker said. "These here I mostly got in the United States. I got my first one when I was only fifteen year old."

15 "Don't tell me," the girl said, "I don't like it. I ain't got any use for it."

"You ought to see the ones you can't see," Parker said and winked.

Two circles of red appeared like apples on the girl's cheeks and softened her appearance. Parker was intrigued. He did not for a minute think that she didn't like the tattoos. He had never yet met a woman who was not attracted to them.

Parker was fourteen when he saw a man in a fair, tattooed from head to foot. Except for his loins which were girded with a panther hide, the man's skin was patterned by what seemed from Parker's distance—he was near the back of the tent, standing on a bench—a single intricate design of brilliant color. The man, who was small and sturdy, moved about on the platform, flexing his muscles so that the arabesque of men and beasts and flowers on his skin appeared to have a subtle motion of its own. Parker was filled with emotion, lifted up as some people are when the flag passes. He was a boy whose mouth habitually hung open. He was heavy and earnest, as ordinary as a loaf of bread. When the show was over, he had remained standing on the bench, staring where the tattooed man had been, until the tent was almost empty.

Parker had never before felt the least motion of wonder in himself. Until he saw the man at the fair, it did not enter his head that there was anything out of the ordinary about the fact that he existed. Even then it did not enter his head, but a peculiar unease settled in him. It was as if a blind boy had been turned so gently in a different direction that he did not know his destination had been changed.

20 He had his first tattoo some time after—the eagle perched on the cannon. It was done by a local artist. It hurt very little, just enough to make it appear to Parker to be worth doing. This was peculiar too for before he had thought that only what did not hurt was worth doing. The next year he quit school because he was sixteen and could. He went to the trade school for a while, then he quit the trade school and worked for six months in a garage. The only reason he worked at all was to pay for more tattoos. His mother worked in a laundry and could support him, but she would not pay for any tattoo except her name on a heart, which he had put on, grumbling. However, her name was Betty Jean and nobody had to know it was his mother. He found out that the tattoos were attractive to the kind of girls he liked but who had never liked him before. He began to drink beer and get in fights. His mother wept over what was becoming of him. One night she dragged him off to a revival with her, not telling him where they were going. When he saw the big lighted church, he jerked out of her grasp and ran. The next day he lied about his age and joined the navy.

Parker was large for the tight sailor's pants but the silly white cap, sitting low on his forehead, made his face by contrast look thoughtful and almost intense. After a month or two in the navy, his mouth ceased to hang open. His features hardened into the features of a man. He stayed in the navy five years and seemed a natural part of the grey mechanical ship, except for his eyes, which were the same pale slate-color as the ocean and reflected the immense spaces around him as if they were a microcosm of the mysterious sea. In port Parker wandered about comparing the rundown places he was in to Birmingham, Alabama. Everywhere he went he picked up more tattoos.

He had stopped having lifeless ones like anchors and crossed rifles. He had a tiger and a panther on each shoulder, a cobra coiled about a torch on his chest, hawks on his thighs, Elizabeth II and Philip over where his stomach and liver were respectively. He did not care much what the subject was so long as it was colorful; on his abdomen he had a few obscenities but only because that seemed the proper place for them. Parker would be satisfied with each tattoo about a month, then something about it that had attracted him would wear off. Whenever a decent-sized mirror was available, he would get in front of it and study his overall look. The effect was not of one intricate arabesque of colors but of something haphazard and botched. A huge dissatisfaction would come over him and he would go off and find another tattooist and have another space filled up. The front of Parker was almost completely covered but there were no tattoos on his back. He had no desire for one anywhere he could not readily see it himself. As the space on the front of him for tattoos decreased, his dissatisfaction grew and became general.

After one of his furloughs, he didn't go back to the navy but remained away without official leave, drunk, in a rooming house in a city he did not know. His dissatisfaction, from being chronic and latent, had suddenly become acute and raged in him. It was as if the panther and the lion and the serpents and the eagles and the hawks had penetrated his skin and lived inside him in a raging warfare. The navy caught up with him, put him in the brig for nine months and then gave him a dishonorable discharge.

After that Parker decided that country air was the only kind fit to breathe. He rented the shack on the embankment and bought the old truck and took various jobs which he kept as long as it suited him. At the time he met his future wife, he was buying apples by the bushel and selling them for the same price by the pound to isolated homesteaders on back country roads.

25 "All that there," the woman said, pointing to his arm, "is no better than what a fool Indian would do. It's a heap of vanity." She seemed to have found the word she wanted. "Vanity of vanities,"[2] she said.

Well what the hell do I care what she thinks of it? Parker asked himself, but he was plainly bewildered. "I reckon you like one of these better than another anyway," he said, dallying until he thought of something that would impress her. He thrust the arm back at her. "Which you like best?"

"None of them," she said, "but the chicken is not as bad as the rest."

"What chicken?" Parker almost yelled.

She pointed to the eagle.

30 "That's an eagle," Parker said. "What fool would waste their time having a chicken put on themself?"

"What fool would have any of it?" the girl said and turned away. She went slowly back to the house and left him there to get going. Parker remained for almost five minutes, looking agape at the dark door she had entered.

The next day he returned with a bushel of apples. He was not one to be outdone by anything that looked like her. He liked women with meat on them, so you didn't feel their muscles, much less their bones. When he arrived, she was sitting on the top step and the yard was full of children, all as thin and poor as herself; Parker remembered it was Saturday. He hated to be making up to a woman when there were children around, but it was fortunate he had brought the bushel of apples off the truck. As the children approached him to see what he carried, he gave each child an apple and told it to get lost; in that way he cleared out the whole crowd.

The girl did nothing to acknowledge his presence. He might have been a stray pig or goat that had wandered into the yard and she too tired to take up the broom and send it off. He set the bushel of apples down next to her on the step. He sat down on a lower step.

"Hep yourself," he said, nodding at the basket; then he lapsed into silence.

35 She took an apple quickly as if the basket might disappear if she didn't make haste. Hungry people made Parker nervous. He had always had plenty to eat himself. He grew very uncomfortable. He reasoned he had nothing to say so why should he say it? He could not think now why he had come or why he didn't go before he wasted another bushel of apples on the crowd of children. He supposed they were her brothers and sisters.

She chewed the apple slowly but with a kind of relish of concentration, bent slightly but looking out ahead. The view from the porch stretched off

[2]**Vanity of vanities** a quotation from Ecclesiastes 1:2

across a long incline studded with iron weed and across the highway to a vast vista of hills and one small mountain. Long views depressed Parker. You look out into space like that and you begin to feel as if someone were after you, the navy or the government or religion.

"Who them children belong to, you?" he said at length.

"I ain't married yet," she said. "They belong to momma." She said it as if it were only a matter of time before she would be married.

Who in God's name would marry her? Parker thought.

A large barefooted woman with a wide gap-toothed face appeared in the door behind Parker. She had apparently been there for several minutes.

"Good evening," Parker said.

The woman crossed the porch and picked up what was left of the bushel of apples. "We thank you," she said and returned with it into the house.

"That your old woman?" Parker muttered.

The girl nodded. Parker knew a lot of sharp things he could have said like "You got my sympathy," but he was gloomily silent. He just sat there, looking at the view. He thought he must be coming down with something.

"If I pick up some peaches tomorrow I'll bring you some," he said.

"I'll be much obliged to you," the girl said.

Parker had no intention of taking any basket of peaches back there but the next day he found himself doing it. He and the girl had almost nothing to say to each other. One thing he did say was, "I ain't got any tattoo on my back."

"What you got on it?" the girl said.

"My shirt," Parker said. "Haw."

"Haw, haw," the girl said politely.

Parker thought he was losing his mind. He could not believe for a minute that he was attracted to a woman like this. She showed not the least interest in anything but what he brought until he appeared the third time with two cantaloups. "What's your name?" she asked.

"O. E. Parker," he said.

"What does the O. E. stand for?"

"You can just call me O. E.," Parker said. "Or Parker. Don't nobody call me by my name."

"What's it stand for?" she persisted.

"Never mind," Parker said. "What's yours?"

"I'll tell you when you tell me what them letters are the short of," she said. There was just a hint of flirtatiousness in her tone and it went rapidly to Parker's head. He had never revealed the name to any man or woman, only to the files of the navy and the government, and it was on his baptismal record which he got at the age of a month; his mother was a Methodist. When the name leaked out of the navy files, Parker narrowly missed killing the man who used it.

"You'll go blab it around," he said.

"I'll swear I'll never tell nobody," she said. "On God's holy word I swear it."

Parker sat for a few minutes in silence. Then he reached for the girl's neck, drew her ear close to his mouth and revealed the name in a low voice.

"Obadiah," she whispered. Her face slowly brightened as if the name came as a sign to her. "Obadiah," she said.

The name still stank in Parker's estimation.

"Obadiah Elihue,"[3] she said in a reverent voice.

"If you call me that aloud, I'll bust your head open," Parker said. "What's yours?"

65 "Sarah Ruth Cates," she said.

"Glad to meet you, Sarah Ruth," Parker said.

Sarah Ruth's father was a Straight Gospel preacher but he was away, spreading it in Florida. Her mother did not seem to mind his attention to the girl so long as he brought a basket of something with him when he came. As for Sarah Ruth herself, it was plain to Parker after he had visited three times that she was crazy about him. She liked him even though she insisted that pictures on the skin were vanity of vanities and even after hearing him curse, and even after she had asked him if he was saved and he had replied that he didn't see it was anything in particular to save him from. After that, inspired, Parker had said, "I'd be saved enough if you was to kiss me."

She scowled. "That ain't being saved," she said.

Not long after that she agreed to take a ride in his truck. Parker parked it on a deserted road and suggested to her that they lie down together in the back of it.

70 "Not until after we're married," she said—just like that.

"Oh that ain't necessary," Parker said and as he reached for her, she thrust him away with such force that the door of the truck came off and he found himself flat on his back on the ground. He made up his mind then and there to have nothing further to do with her.

They were married in the County Ordinary's office because Sarah Ruth thought churches were idolatrous. Parker had no opinion about that one way or the other. The Ordinary's office was lined with cardboard file boxes and record books with dusty yellow slips of paper hanging on out of them. The Ordinary was an old woman with red hair who had held office for forty years and looked as dusty as her books. She married them from behind the iron-grill of a stand-up desk and when she finished, she said with a flourish, "Three dollars and fifty cents and till death do you part!" and yanked some forms out of a machine.

Marriage did not change Sarah Ruth a jot and it made Parker gloomier than ever. Every morning he decided he had had enough and would not return that night; every night he returned. Whenever Parker couldn't stand the way he felt, he would have another tattoo, but the only surface left on him now was his back. To see a tattoo on his own back he would have to get two mirrors and stand between them in just the correct position and this seemed to Parker a good way to make an idiot of himself. Sarah Ruth who, if she had had better sense, could have enjoyed a tattoo on his back, would not even look at the ones he had elsewhere. When he attempted to point out especial details of them, she would shut her eyes tight and turn her back as well. Except in total darkness, she preferred Parker dressed and with his sleeves rolled down.

[3]**Obadiah Elihue** Both names occur in the Hebrew Bible. Obadiah ("worshipper," or "servant of Yahweh") is used of at least eleven different people, including a prophet. Elihue, a young man who claims divine inspiration but who chiefly repeats what others have said, appears in Job 32–37.

"At the judgement seat of God, Jesus is going to say to you, 'What you been doing all your life besides have pictures drawn all over you?"' she said.

75 "You don't fool me none," Parker said, "you're just afraid that hefty girl I work for'll like me so much she'll say, 'Come on, Mr. Parker, let's you and me . . .'"

"You're tempting sin," she said, "and at the judgement seat of God you'll have to answer for that too. You ought to go back to selling the fruits of the earth."

Parker did nothing much when he was at home but listen to what the judgement seat of God would be like for him if he didn't change his ways. When he could, he broke in with tales of the hefty girl he worked for. "'Mr. Parker,'" he said she said, "'I hired you for your brains.'" (She had added, "So why don't you use them?")

"And you should have seen her face the first time she saw me without my shirt," he said. "'Mr. Parker,' she said, 'you're a walking panner-rammer!'" This had, in fact, been her remark but it had been delivered out of one side of her mouth.

Dissatisfaction began to grow so great in Parker that there was no containing it outside of a tattoo. It had to be his back. There was no help for it. A dim half-formed inspiration began to work in his mind. He visualized having a tattoo put there that Sarah Ruth would not be able to resist—a religious subject. He thought of an open book with HOLY BIBLE tattooed under it and an actual verse printed on the page. This seemed just the thing for a while; then he began to hear her say, "Ain't I already got a real Bible? What you think I want to read the same verse over and over for when I can read it all?" He needed something better even than the Bible! He thought about it so much that he began to lose sleep. He was already losing flesh—Sarah Ruth just threw food in the pot and let it boil. Not knowing for certain why he continued to stay with a woman who was both ugly and pregnant and no cook made him generally nervous and irritable, and he developed a little tic in the side of his face.

80 Once or twice he found himself turning around abruptly as if someone were trailing him. He had had a granddaddy who had ended in the state mental hospital, although not until he was seventy-five, but as urgent as it might be for him to get a tattoo, it was just as urgent that he get exactly the right one to bring Sarah Ruth to heel. As he continued to worry over it, his eyes took on a hollow preoccupied expression. The old woman he worked for told him that if he couldn't keep his mind on what he was doing, she knew where she could find a fourteen-year-old colored boy who could. Parker was too preoccupied to be offended. At any time previous, he would have left her then and there, saying drily, "Well, you go ahead on and get him then."

Two or three mornings later he was baling hay with the old woman's sorry baler and her broken down tractor in a large field, cleared save for one enormous old tree standing in the middle of it. The old woman was the kind who would not cut down a large old tree because it was a large old tree. She had pointed it out to Parker as if he didn't have eyes and told him to be careful not to hit it as the machine picked up hay near it. Parker began at the outside of the field and made circles inward toward it. He had to get off the tractor every now and then and untangle the baling cord or kick a rock out of the way. The old woman had told him to carry the rocks to the edge of the field, which he did when she was there watching. When he thought he could make it, he ran over them. As he circled the field his mind was on a suitable design for his back. The sun, the size of a golf ball, began to switch regularly from in front to behind him, but he appeared to see it both places as if he had eyes in the back of his head. All at once he saw the tree reaching out to grasp him. A ferocious thud propelled him into the air, and he heard himself yelling in an unbelievably loud voice, "GOD ABOVE!"

He landed on his back while the tractor crashed upside-down into the tree and burst into flame. The first thing Parker saw were his shoes, quickly being eaten by the fire; one was caught under the tractor, the other was some distance away, burning by itself. He was not in them. He could feel the hot breath of the burning tree on his face. He scrambled backwards, still sitting, his eyes cavernous, and if he had known how to cross himself he would have done it.

His truck was on a dirt road at the edge of the field. He moved toward it, still sitting, still backwards, but faster and faster; halfway to it he got up and began a kind of forward-bent run from which he collapsed on his knees twice. His legs felt like two old rusted rain gutters. He reached the truck finally and took off in it, zigzagging up the road. He drove past his house on the embankment and straight for the city, fifty miles distant.

Parker did not allow himself to think on the way to the city. He only knew that there had been a great change in his life, a leap forward into a worse unknown, and that there was nothing he could do about it. It was for all intents accomplished.

85 The artist had two large cluttered rooms over a chiropodist's office on a back street. Parker, still barefooted, burst silently in on him at a little after three in the afternoon. The artist, who was about Parker's own age—twenty-eight—but thin and bald, was behind a small drawing table, tracing a design in green ink. He looked up with an annoyed glance and did not seem to recognize Parker in the hollow-eyed creature before him.

"Let me see the book you got with all the pictures of God in it," Parker said breathlessly. "The religious one."

The artist continued to look at him with his intellectual, superior stare. "I don't put tattoos on drunks," he said.

"You know me!" Parker cried indignantly. "I'm O. E. Parker! You done work for me before and I always paid!"

The artist looked at him another moment as if he were not altogether sure. "You've fallen off some," he said. "You must have been in jail."

90 "Married," Parker said.

"Oh," said the artist. With the aid of mirrors the artist had tattooed on the top of his head a miniature owl, perfect in every detail. It was about the size of a half-dollar and served him as a show piece. There were cheaper artists in town but Parker had never wanted anything but the best. The artist went over to a cabinet at the back of the room and began to look over some art books. "Who are you interested in?" he said, "saints, angels, Christs or what?"

"God," Parker said.

"Father, Son or Spirit?"

"Just God," Parker said impatiently. "Christ. I don't care. Just so it's God."

95 The artist returned with a book. He moved some papers off another table and put the book down on it and told Parker to sit down and see what he liked. "The up-t-date ones are in the back," he said.

Parker sat down with the book and wet his thumb. He began to go through it, beginning at the back where the up-to-date pictures were. Some of them he recognized—The Good Shepherd, Forbid Them Not, The Smiling Jesus, Jesus the Physician's Friend, but he kept turning rapidly backwards and the pictures became less and less reassuring. One showed a gaunt green dead face streaked with blood. One was yellow with sagging purple eyes. Parker's heart began to beat faster and faster until it appeared to be roaring inside him like a great generator. He flipped the pages quickly, feeling that when he reached the one ordained, a sign would come. He continued to flip through until he had almost reached the front of the book. On one of the pages a pair of eyes glanced at him swiftly. Parker sped on, then stopped. His heart too appeared to cut off; there was absolute silence. It said as plainly as if silence were a language itself, GO BACK.

Parker returned to the picture—the haloed head of a flat stern Byzantine Christ[4] with all-demanding eyes. He sat there trembling; his heart began slowly to beat again as if it were being brought to life by a subtle power.

"You found what you want?" the artist asked.

Parker's throat was too dry to speak. He got up and thrust the book at the artist, opened at the picture.

100 "That'll cost you plenty," the artist said. "You don't want all those little blocks though, just the outline and some better features."

"Just like it is," Parker said, "just like it is or nothing."

"It's your funeral," the artist said, "but I don't do that kind of work for nothing."

"How much?" Parker asked.

"It'll take maybe two days work."

105 "How much?" Parker said.

"On time or cash?" the artist asked. Parker's other jobs had been on time, but he had paid.

"Ten down and ten for every day it takes," the artist said.

Parker drew ten dollar bills out of his wallet; he had three left in.

"You come back in the morning," the artist said, putting the money in his own pocket. "First I'll have to trace that out of the book."

110 "No no!" Parker said. "Trace it now or gimme my money back," and his eyes blared as if he were ready for a fight.

The artist agreed. Any one stupid enough to want a Christ on his back, he reasoned, would be just as likely as not to change his mind the next minute, but once the work was begun he could hardly do so.

While he worked on the tracing, he told Parker to go wash his back at the sink with the special soap he used there. Parker did it and returned to

[4]**Byzantine Christ** In Byzantine art (fifth to thirteenth century) the usual image of Christ is not the incarnate Messiah (the humble and humane teacher) but the all-powerful ruler enthroned in heaven. The most famous of such images, in San Vitale, Ravenna, is a sixth-century mosaic, hence the reference a little later in the story to "all those little blocks," that is, inlaid bits of colored stone or tile set in mortar to form a picture.

pace back and forth across the room, nervously flexing his shoulders. He wanted to go look at the picture again but at the same time he did not want to. The artist got up finally and had Parker lie down on the table. He swabbed his back with ethyl chloride and then began to outline the head on it with his iodine pencil. Another hour passed before he took up his electric instrument. Parker felt no particular pain. In Japan he had had a tattoo of the Buddha done on his upper arm with ivory needles; in Burma, a little brown root of a man had made a peacock on each of his knees using thin pointed sticks, two feet long; amateurs had worked on him with pins and soot. Parker was usually so relaxed and easy under the hand of the artist that he often went to sleep, but this time he remained awake, every muscle taut.

At midnight the artist said he was ready to quit. He propped one mirror, four feet square, on a table by the wall and took a smaller mirror off the lavatory wall and put it in Parker's hands. Parker stood with his back to the one on the table and moved the other until he saw a flashing burst of color reflected from his back. It was almost completely covered with little red and blue and ivory and saffron squares; from them he made out the lineaments of the face—a mouth, the beginning of heavy brows, a straight nose, but the face was empty; the eyes had not yet been put in. The impression for the moment was almost as if the artist had tricked him and done the Physician's Friend.

"It don't have eyes," Parker cried out.

115 "That'll come," the artist said, "in due time. We have another day to go on it yet."

Parker spent the night on a cot at the Haven of Light Christian Mission. He found these the best places to stay in the city because they were free and included a meal of sorts. He got the last available cot and because he was still barefooted, he accepted a pair of second-hand shoes which, in his confusion, he put on to go to bed; he was still shocked from all that had happened to him. All night he lay awake in the long dormitory of cots with lumpy figures on them. The only light was from a phosphorescent cross glowing at the end of the room. The tree reached out to grasp him again, then burst into flame; the shoe burned quietly by itself; the eyes in the book said to him distinctly GO BACK and at the same time did not utter a sound. He wished that he were not in this city, not in this Haven of Light Mission, not in a bed by himself. He longed miserably for Sarah Ruth. Her sharp tongue and icepick eyes were the only comfort he could bring to mind. He decided he was losing it. Her eyes appeared soft and dilatory compared with the eyes in the book, for even though he could not summon up the exact look of those eyes, he could still feel their penetration. He felt as though, under their gaze, he was as transparent as the wing of a fly.

The tattooist had told him not to come until ten in the morning, but when he arrived at that hour, Parker was sitting in the dark hallway on the floor, waiting for him. He had decided upon getting up that, once the tattoo was on him, he would not look at it, that all his sensations of the day and night before were those of a crazy man and that he would return to doing things according to his own sound judgement.

The artist began where he left off. "One thing I want to know," he said presently as he worked over Parker's back, "why do you want this on you? Have you gone and got religion? Are you saved?" he asked in a mocking voice.

Parker's throat felt salty and dry. "Naw," he said, "I ain't got no use for none of that. A man can't save his self from whatever it is he don't deserve none of my sympathy." These words seemed to leave his mouth like wraiths and to evaporate at once as if he had never uttered them.

120 "Then why. . ."

"I married this woman that's saved," Parker said. "I never should have done it. I ought to leave her. She's done gone and got pregnant."

"That's too bad," the artist said. "Then it's her making you have this tattoo."

"Naw," Parker said, "she don't know nothing about it. It's a surprise for her."

"You think she'll like it an lay off you a while?"

125 "She can't hep herself," Parker said. "She can't say she don't like the looks of God." He decided he had told the artist enough of his business. Artists were all right in their place but he didn't like them poking their noses into the affairs of regular people. "I didn't get no sleep last night," he said. "I think I'll get some now."

That closed the mouth of the artist but it did not bring him any sleep. He lay there, imagining how Sarah Ruth would be struck speechless by the face on his back and every now and then this would be interrupted by a vision of the tree of fire and his empty shoe burning beneath it.

The artist worked steadily until nearly four o'clock, not stopping to have lunch, hardly pausing with the electric instrument except to wipe the dripping dye off Parker's back as he went along. Finally he finished. "You can get up and look at it now," he said.

Parker sat up but he remained on the edge of the table.

The artist was pleased with his work and wanted Parker to look at it at once. Instead Parker continued to sit on the edge of the table, bent forward slightly but with a vacant look. "What ails you?" the artist said. "Go look at it."

130 "Ain't nothing ail me," Parker said in a sudden belligerent voice. "That tattoo ain't going nowhere. It'll be there when I get there." He reached for his shirt and began gingerly to put it on.

The artist took him roughly by the arm and propelled him between the two mirrors. "Now *look,*" he said, angry at having his work ignored.

Parker looked, turned white and moved away. The eyes in the reflected face continued to look at him—still, straight, all-demanding, enclosed in silence.

"It was your idea, remember," the artist said. "I would have advised something else."

Parker said nothing. He put on his shirt and went out the door while the artist shouted, "I'll expect all of my money!"

135 Parker headed toward a package shop on the corner. He bought a pint of whiskey and took it into a nearby alley and drank it all in five minutes. Then he moved on to a pool hall nearby which he frequented when he came to the city. It was a well-lighted barn-like place with a bar up one side and gambling machines on the other and pool tables in the back. As soon as Parker entered, a large man in a red and black checkered shirt hailed him by slapping him on the back and yelling, "Yeyyyyyy bo! O. E. Parker!"

Parker was not yet ready to be struck on the back. "Lay off," he said, "I got a fresh tattoo there."

"What you got this time?" the man asked and then yelled to a few at the machines. "O. E.'s got him another tattoo."

"Nothing special this time," Parker said and slunk over to a machine that was not being used.

"Come on," the big man said, "let's have a look at O. E.'s tattoo," and while Parker squirmed at their hands, they pulled up his shirt. Parker felt all the hands drop away instantly and his shirt fell again like a veil over the face. There was a silence in the pool room which seemed to Parker to grow from the circle around him until it extended to the foundations under the building and upward through the beams in the roof.

140 Finally some one said, "Christ!" Then they all broke into noise at once. Parker turned around, an uncertain grin on his face.

"Leave it to O. E.!" the man in the checkered shirt said. "That boy's a real card!"

"Maybe he's gone and got religion," some one yelled.

"Not on your life," Parker said.

"O. E.'s got religion and is witnessing for Jesus, ain't you, O. E.?" a little man with a piece of cigar in his mouth said wryly. "An original way to do it if I ever saw one."

145 "Leave it to Parker to think of a new one!" the fat man said.

"Yyeeeeeeyyyyyy bo!" someone yelled and they all began to whistle and curse in compliment until Parker said, "Aaa shut up."

"What'd you do it for?" somebody asked.

"For laughs," Parker said. "What's it to you?"

"Why ain't you laughing then?" somebody yelled. Parker lunged into the midst of them and like a whirlwind on a summer's day there began a fight that raged and overturned tables and swinging fists until two of them grabbed him and ran to the door with him and threw him out. Then a calm descended on the pool hall as nerve shattering as if the long barn-like room were the ship from which Jonah had been cast into the sea.

150 Parker sat for a long time on the ground in the alley behind the pool hall, examining his soul. He saw it as a spider web of facts and lies that was not at all important to him but which appeared to be necessary in spite of his opinion. The eyes that were now forever on his back were eyes to be obeyed. He was as certain of it as he had ever been of anything. Throughout his life, grumbling and sometimes cursing, often afraid, once in rapture, Parker had obeyed whatever instinct of this kind had come to him—in rapture when his spirit had lifted at the sight of the tattooed man at the fair, afraid when he had joined the navy, grumbling when he had married Sarah Ruth.

The thought of her brought him slowly to his feet. She would know what he had to do. She would clear up the rest of it, and she would at least be pleased. It seemed to him that, all along, that was what he wanted, to please her. His truck was still parked in front of the building where the artist had his place, but it was not far away. He got in it and drove out of the city and into the country night. His head was almost clear of liquor and he observed that his dissatisfaction was gone, but he felt not quite like himself. It was as if he were himself but a stranger to himself, driving into a new country though everything he saw was familiar to him, even at night.

He arrived finally at the house on the embankment, pulled the truck under the pecan tree and got out. He made as much noise as possible to assert that he was still in charge here, that his leaving her for a night without word meant nothing except it was the way he did things. He slammed the car door, stamped up the two steps and across the porch and rattled the door knob. It did not respond to his touch. "Sarah Ruth!" he yelled, "let me in."

There was no lock on the door and she had evidently placed the back of a chair against the knob. He began to beat on the door and rattle the knob at the same time.

He heard the bed springs creak and bent down and put his head to the keyhole, but it was stopped up with paper. "Let me in!" he hollered, bamming on the door again. "What you got me locked out for?"

155 A sharp voice close to the door said, "Who's there?"

"Me," Parker said, "O. E."

He waited a moment.

"Me," he said impatiently, "O.E."

Still no sound from inside.

160 He tried once more. "O. E.," he said, bamming the door two or three more times. "O. E. Parker. You know me."

There was a silence. Then the voice said slowly, "I don't know no O. E."

"Quit fooling," Parker pleaded. "You ain't got any business doing me this way. It's me, old O. E., I'm back. You ain't afraid of me."

"Who's there?" the same unfeeling voice said.

Parker turned his head as if he expected someone behind him to give him the answer. The sky had lightened slightly and there were two or three streaks of yellow floating above the horizon. Then as he stood there, a tree of light burst over the skyline.

165 Parker fell back against the door as if he had been pinned there by a lance.

"Who's there?" the voice from inside said and there was a quality about it now that seemed final. The knob rattled and the voice said peremptorily, "Who's there, I ast you?"

Parker bent down and put his mouth near the stuffed keyhold. "Obadiah," he whispered and all at once he felt the light pouring through him, turning his spider web soul into a perfect arabesque of colors, a garden of trees and birds and beasts.

"Obadiah Elihue!" he whispered.

The door opened and he stumbled in. Sarah Ruth loomed there, hands on her hips. She began at once, "That was no hefty blonde woman you was working for and you'll have to pay her every penny on her tractor you busted up. She don't keep insurance on it. She came here and her and me had a long talk and I . . ."

170 Trembling, Parker set about lighting the kerosene lamp.

"What's the matter with you, wasting that kerosene this near daylight?" she demanded. "I ain't got to look at you."

A yellow glow enveloped them. Parker put the match down and began to unbutton his shirt.

"And you ain't going to have none of me this near morning," she said.

"Shut your mouth," he said quietly. "Look at this and then I don't want to hear no more out of you." He removed the shirt and turned his back to her.

"Another picture," Sarah Ruth growled. "I might have known you was off after putting some more trash on yourself."

Parker's knees went hollow under him. He wheeled around and cried, "Look at it! Don't just say that! *Look* at it!"

"I done looked," she said.

"Don't you know who it is?" he cried in anguish.

"No, who is it?" Sarah Ruth said. "It ain't anybody I know."

"It's him," Parker said.

"Him who?"

"God!" Parker cried.

"God? God don't look like that!"

"What do you know how he looks?" Parker moaned. "You ain't seen him."

"He don't *look,*" Sarah Ruth said. "He's a spirit. No man shall see his face."

"Aw listen," Parker groaned, "this is just a picture of him."

"Idolatry!" Sarah Ruth screamed. "Idolatry! Enflaming yourself with idols under every green tree! I can put up with lies and vanity but I don't want no idolator in this house!" and she grabbed up the broom and began to thrash him across the shoulders with it.

Parker was too stunned to resist. He sat there and let her beat him until she had nearly knocked him senseless and large welts had formed on the face of the tattooed Christ. Then he staggered up and made for the door.

She stamped the broom two or three times on the floor and went to the window and shook it out to get the taint of him off it. Still gripping it, she looked toward the pecan tree and her eyes hardened still more. There he was—who called himself Obadiah Elihue—leaning against the tree, crying like a baby.

[*1964*]

# ON FICTION: REMARKS FROM ESSAYS AND LETTERS

## from "The Fiction Writer and His Country"

In the greatest fiction, the writer's moral sense coincides with his dramatic sense, and I see no way for it to do this unless his moral judgment is part of the very act of seeing, and he is free to use it. I have heard it said that belief in Christian dogma is a hindrance to the writer, but I myself have found nothing further from the truth. Actually, it frees the storyteller to observe. It is not a set of rules which fixes what he sees in the world. It affects his writing primarily by guaranteeing his respect for mystery. . . .

When I look at stories I have written I find that they are, for the most part, about people who are poor, who are afflicted in both mind and body, who have little—or at best a distorted—sense of spiritual purpose, and whose actions do not apparently give the reader a great assurance of the joy of life.

Yet how is this? For I am no disbeliever in spiritual purpose and no vague believer. I see from the standpoint of Christian orthodoxy. This means that for me the meaning of life is centered in our Redemption by Christ and what I see in the world I see in its relation to that. . . .

The novelist with Christian concerns will find in modern life distortions which are repugnant to him, and his problem will be to make these appear as distortions to an audience which is used to seeing them as natural; and he may well be forced to take ever more violent means to get his vision across to this hostile audience. When you can assume that your audience holds the same beliefs you do, you can relax a little and use more normal means of talking to it; when you have to assume that it does not, then you have to make your vision apparent by shock—to the hard of hearing you shout, and for the almost-blind you draw large and startling figures.

## from "Some Aspects of the Grotesque in Southern Fiction"

If the writer believes that our life is and will remain essentially mysterious, if he looks upon us as beings existing in a created order to whose laws we freely respond, then what he sees on the surface will be of interest to him only as he can go through it into an experience of mystery itself. His kind of fiction will always be pushing its own limits outward toward the limits of mystery, because for this kind of writer, the meaning of a story does not begin except at a depth where adequate motivation and adequate psychology and the various determinations have been exhausted. Such a writer will be interested in what we don't understand rather than in what we do. He will be interested in possibility rather than in probability. He will be interested in characters who are forced out to meet evil and grace and who act on a trust beyond themselves—whether they know very clearly what it is they act upon or not. To the modern mind, this kind of character, and his creator, are typical Don Quixotes, tilting at what is not there.

## from "The Nature and Aim of Fiction"

The novel works by a slower accumulation of detail than the short story does. The short story requires more drastic procedures than the novel because more has to be accomplished in less space. The details have to carry more immediate weight. In good fiction, certain of the details will tend to accumulate meaning from the story itself, and when this happens, they become symbolic in their action.

Now the word *symbol* scares a good many people off, just as the word *art* does. They seem to feel that a symbol is some mysterious thing put in arbitrarily by the writer to frighten the common reader—sort of a literary Masonic grip that is only for the initiated. They seem to think that it is a way of saying something that you aren't actually saying, and so if they can be got to read a reputedly symbolic work at all, they approach it as if it were a problem in algebra. Find *x*. And when they do find or think they find this abstraction, *x*, then they go off with an elaborate sense of satisfaction and the notion that they have "understood" the story. Many students confuse the *process* of understanding a thing with understanding it.

I think that for the fiction writer himself, symbols are something he uses simply as a matter of course. You might say that these are details that, while having their essential place in the literal level of the story, operate in depth as well as on the surface, increasing the story in every direction . . . .

People have a habit of saying, "What is the theme of your story?" and they expect you to give them a statement: "The theme of my story is the economic pressure of the machine on the middle class"—or some such absurdity. And when they've got a statement like that, they go off happy and feel it is no longer necessary to read the story.

Some people have the notion that you read the story and then climb out of it into the meaning, but for the fiction writer himself the whole story is the meaning, because it is an experience, not an abstraction.

## from "Writing Short Stories"

Being short does not mean being slight. A short story should be long in depth and should give us an experience of meaning. . . .

Meaning is what keeps the short story from being short. I prefer to talk about the meaning in a story rather than the theme of a story. People talk about the theme of a story as if the theme were like the string that a sack of chicken feed is tied with. They think that if you can pick out the theme, the way you pick the right thread in the chicken-feed sack, you can rip the story open and feed the chickens. But this is not the way meaning works in fiction.

When you can state the theme of a story, when you can separate it from the story itself, then you can be sure the story is not a very good one. The meaning of a story has to be embodied in it, has to be made concrete in it. A story is a way to say something that can't be said any other way, and it takes every word in the story to say what the meaning is. You tell a story because a statement would be inadequate. When anybody asks what a story is about, the only proper thing is to tell him to read the story. The meaning of fiction is not abstract meaning but experienced meaning, and the purpose of making statements about the meaning of a story is only to help you to experience that meaning more fully.

## "A Reasonable Use of the Unreasonable"

Last fall I received a letter from a student who said she would be "graciously appreciative" if I would tell her "just what enlightenment" I expected her to get from each of my stories. I suspect she had a paper to write. I wrote her back to forget about the enlightenment and just try to enjoy them. I knew that was the most unsatisfactory answer I could have given because, of course, she didn't want to enjoy them, she just wanted to figure them out.

In most English classes the short story has become a kind of literary specimen to be dissected. Every time a story of mine appears in a Freshman anthology, I have a vision of it, with its little organs laid open, like a frog in a bottle.

I realize that a certain amount of this what-is-the-significance has to go on, but I think something has gone wrong in the process when, for so many students, the story becomes simply a problem to be solved, something which you evaporate to get Instant Enlightenment.

A story really isn't any good unless it successfully resists paraphrase, unless it hangs on and expands in the mind. Properly, you analyze to enjoy, but it's equally true that to analyze with any discrimination, you have to have enjoyed already, and I think that the best reason to hear a story read is that it should stimulate that primary enjoyment.

I don't have any pretensions to being an Aeschylus or Sophocles and providing you in this story with a cathartic experience out of your mythic background, though this story I'm going to read certainly calls up a good deal of the South's mythic background, and it should elicit from you a degree of pity and terror, even though its way of being serious is a comic one. I do think, though, that like the Greeks you should know what is going to happen in this story so that any element of suspense in it will be transferred from its surface to its interior.

I would be most happy if you have already read it, happier still if you knew it well, but since experience has taught me to keep my expectations along these lines modest, I'll tell you that this is the story of a family of six which, on its way driving to Florida, gets wiped out by an escaped convict who calls himself the Misfit. The family is made up of the Grandmother and her son, Bailey, and his children, John Wesley and June Star and the baby, and there is also the cat and the children's mother. The cat is named Pitty Sing, and the Grandmother is taking him with them, hidden in a basket.

Now I think it behooves me to try to establish with you the basis on which reason operates in this story. Much of my fiction takes its character from a reasonable use of the unreasonable, though the reasonableness of my use of it may not always be apparent. The assumptions that underlie this use of it, however, are those of the central Christian mysteries. These are assumptions to which a large part of the modern audience takes exception. About this I can only say that there are perhaps other ways than my own in which this story could be read, but none other by which it could have been written. Belief, in my own case anyway, is the engine that makes perception operate.

The heroine of this story, the Grandmother, is in the most significant position life offers the Christian. She is facing death. And to all appearances she, like the rest of us, is not too well prepared for it. She would like to see the event postponed. Indefinitely.

I've talked to a number of teachers who use this story in class and who tell their students that the Grandmother is evil, that in fact, she's a witch, even down to the cat. One of these teachers told me that his students, and particularly his Southern students, resisted this interpretation with a certain bemused vigor, and he didn't understand why. I had to tell him that they resisted it because they all had grandmothers or great-aunts just like her at home, and they knew, from personal experience, that the old lady lacked comprehension, but that she had a good heart. The Southerner is usually tolerant of those weaknesses that proceed from innocence, and he knows that a taste for self-preservation can be readily combined with the missionary spirit.

This same teacher was telling his students that morally the Misfit was several cuts above the Grandmother. He had a really sentimental attachment to the Misfit. But then a prophet gone wrong is almost always more interesting than your grandmother, and you have to let people take their pleasures where they find them.

It is true that the old lady is a hypocritical old soul; her wits are no match for the Misfit's, nor is her capacity for grace equal to his; yet I think the unprejudiced reader will feel that the Grandmother has a special kind of triumph in this story which instinctively we do not allow to someone altogether bad.

I often ask myself what makes a story work, and what makes it hold up as a story, and I have decided that it is probably some action, some gesture of a character that is unlike any other in the story, one which indicates where the real heart of the story lies. This would have to be an action or a gesture which was both totally right and totally unexpected; it would have to be one that was both in character and beyond character; it would have to suggest both the world and eternity. The action or gesture I'm talking about would have to be on the anagogical level, that is, the level which has to do with the Divine life and our participation in it. It would be a gesture that transcended any neat allegory that might have been intended or any pat moral categories a reader could make. It would be a gesture which somehow made contact with mystery.

There is a point in this story where such a gesture occurs. The Grandmother is at last alone, facing the Misfit. Her head clears for an instant and she realizes, even in her limited way, that she is responsible for the man before her and joined to him by ties of kinship which have their roots deep in the mystery she has been merely prattling about so far. And at this point, she does the right thing, she makes the right gesture.

I find that students are often puzzled by what she says and does here, but I think myself that if I took out this gesture and what she says with it, I would have no story. What was left would not be worth your attention. Our age not only does not have a very sharp eye for the almost imperceptible intrusions of grace, it no longer has much feeling for the nature of the violences which precede and follow them. The devil's greatest wile, Baudelaire has said, is to convince us that he does not exist.

I suppose the reasons for the use of so much violence in modern fiction will differ with each writer who uses it, but in my own stories I have found that violence is strangely capable of returning my characters to reality and preparing them to accept their moment of grace. Their heads are so hard that almost nothing else will do the work. This idea, that reality is something to which we must be returned at considerable cost, is one which is seldom understood by the casual reader, but it is one which is implicit in the Christian view of the world.

I don't want to equate the Misfit with the devil. I prefer to think that, however unlikely this may seem, the old lady's gesture, like the mustard-seed, will grow to be a great crow-filled tree in the Misfit's heart, and will be enough of a pain to him there to turn him into the prophet he was meant to become. But that's another story.

This story has been called grotesque, but I prefer to call it literal. A good story is literal in the same sense that a child's drawing is literal. When a child draws, he doesn't intend to distort but to set down exactly what he sees, and as his gaze is direct, he sees the lines that create motion. Now the lines of motion that interest the writer are usually invisible. They are lines of spiritual motion. And in this story you should be on the lookout for such things as the action of grace in the Grandmother's soul, and not for the dead bodies.

We hear many complaints about the prevalence of violence in modern fiction, and it is always assumed that this violence is a bad thing and meant to be an end in itself. With the serious writer, violence is never an end in itself. It is the extreme situation that best reveals what we are essentially, and I believe these are times when writers are more interested in what we are essentially than in the tenor of our daily lives. Violence is a force which can be used for good or evil, and among other things taken by it is the kingdom of heaven. But regardless of what can be taken by it, the man in the violent situation reveals those qualities least dispensable in his personality, those qualities which are all he will have to take into eternity with him; and since the characters in this story are all on the verge of eternity, it is appropriate to think of what they take with them. In any case, I hope that if you consider these points in connection with the story, you will come to see it as something more than an account of a family murdered on the way to Florida.

[*1957*]

## ON INTERPRETING "A GOOD MAN IS HARD TO FIND"

*A professor of English had sent Flannery the following letter: "I am writing as spokesman for three members of our department and some ninety university students in three classes who for a week now have been discussing your story 'A Good Man Is Hard to Find.' We have debated at length several possible interpretations, none of which fully satisfies us. In general we believe that the appearance of the Misfit is not 'real' in the same sense that the incidents of the first half of the story are real. Bailey, we believe, imagines the appearance of the Misfit, whose activities have been called to his attention on the night before the trip and again during the stopover at the roadside restaurant. Bailey, we further believe, identifies himself with the Misfit and so plays two roles in the imaginary last half of the story. But we cannot, after great effort, determine the point at which reality fades into illusion or reverie. Does the accident literally occur, or is it a part of Bailey's dream? Please believe me when I say we are not seeking an easy way out of our difficulty. We admire your story and have examined it with great care, but we are convinced that we are missing something important which you intended for us to grasp. We will all be very grateful if you comment on the interpretation which I have outlined above and if you will give us further comments about your intention in writing 'A Good Man Is Hard to Find.'"*

*She replied:*

To a Professor of English

28 March 61

The interpretation of your ninety students and three teachers is fantastic and about as far from my intentions as it could get to be. If it were a legitimate interpretation, the story would be little more than a trick and its interest would be simply for abnormal psychology. I am not interested in abnormal psychology.

There is a change of tension from the first part of the story to the second where the Misfit enters, but this is no lessening of reality. This story is, of course, not meant to be realistic in the sense that it portrays the everyday doings of people in Georgia. It is stylized and its conventions are comic even though its meaning is serious.

Bailey's only importance is as the Grandmother's boy and the driver of the car. It is the Grandmother who first recognizes the Misfit and who is most concerned with him throughout. The story is a duel of sorts between the Grandmother and her superficial beliefs and the Misfit's more profoundly felt involvement with Christ's action which set the world off balance for him.

The meaning of a story should go on expanding for the reader the more he thinks about it, but meaning cannot be captured in an interpretation. If teachers are in the habit of approaching a story as if it were a research problem for which any answer is believable so long as it is not obvious, then I think students will never learn to enjoy fiction. Too much interpretation is certainly worse than too little and where feeling for a story is absent, theory will not supply it.

My tone is not meant to be obnoxious. I am in a state of shock.

# *Raymond Carver: Three Stories, and Talking about Stories*

*Raymond Carver (1938–88) was born in Clatskanie, a logging town in Oregon. In 1963 he graduated from Humboldt State College in northern California and then did further study at the University of Iowa.*

*His early years were not easy—he married while still in college, divorced a little later, and sometimes suffered from alcoholism. In his last years he found domestic happiness, but he died of cancer at the age of fifty.*

*As a young man he wrote poetry while working at odd jobs (janitor, deliveryman, etc.); later he turned to fiction, though he continued to write poetry. Most of his fiction is of a sort called "minimalist," narrating in a spare, understated style stories about bewildered and sometimes exhausted men and women. His later work,*

***beginning with "Cathedral" in 1983, by his own admission was "larger."***

## *Popular Mechanics*

Early that day the weather turned and the snow was melting into dirty water. Streaks of it ran down from the little shoulder-high window that faced the backyard. Cars slushed by on the street outside, where it was getting dark. But it was getting dark on the inside too.

He was in the bedroom pushing clothes into a suitcase when she came to the door.

I'm glad you're leaving! I'm glad you're leaving! she said. Do you hear?

He kept on putting his things into the suitcase.

Son of a bitch! I'm so glad you're leaving! She began to cry. You can't even look me in the face, can you?

Then she noticed the baby's picture on the bed and picked it up.

He looked at her and she wiped her eyes and stared at him before turning and going back to the living room.

Bring that back, he said.

Just get your things and get out, she said.

He did not answer. He fastened the suitcase, put on his coat, looked around the bedroom before turning off the light. Then he went out to the living room.

She stood in the doorway of the little kitchen, holding the baby.

I want the baby, he said.

Are you crazy?

No, but I want the baby. I'll get someone to come by for his things.

You're not touching this baby, she said.

The baby had begun to cry and she uncovered the blanket from around his head.

Oh, oh, she said, looking at the baby.

He moved toward her.

For God's sake! she said. She took a step back into the kitchen.

I want the baby.

Get out of here!

She turned and tried to hold the baby over in a corner behind the stove.

But he came up. He reached across the stove and tightened his hands on the baby.

Let go of him, he said.

Get away, get away! she cried.

The baby was red-faced and screaming. In the scuffle they knocked down a flowerpot that hung behind the stove.

He crowded her into the wall then, trying to break her grip. He held on to the baby and pushed with all his weight.

Let go of him, he said.

Don't, she said. You're hurting the baby, she said.

I'm not hurting the baby, he said.

The kitchen window gave no light. In the near-dark he worked on her fisted fingers with one hand and with the other hand he gripped the screaming baby up under an arm near the shoulder.

She felt her fingers being forced open. She felt the baby going from her.

No! she screamed just as her hands came loose.

She would have it, this baby. She grabbed for the baby's other arm. She caught the baby around the wrist and leaned back.

35 But he would not let go. He felt the baby slipping out of his hands and he pulled back very hard.

In this manner, the issue was decided.

[*1981*]

# *What We Talk about When We Talk about Love*

My friend Mel McGinnis was talking. Mel McGinnis is a cardiologist, and sometimes that gives him the right.

The four of us were sitting around his kitchen table drinking gin. Sunlight filled the kitchen from the big windows behind the sink. There were Mel and me and his second wife, Teresa—Terri, we called her—and my wife, Laura. We lived in Albuquerque then. But we were all from somewhere else.

There was an ice bucket on the table. The gin and the tonic water kept going around, and we somehow got on the subject of love. Mel thought real love was nothing less than spiritual love. He said he'd spent five years in a seminary before quitting to go to medical school. He said he still looked back on those years in the seminary as the most important years in his life.

Terri said the man she lived with before she lived with Mel loved her so much he tried to kill her. Then Terri said, "He beat me up one night. He dragged me around the living room by my ankles. He kept saying, 'I love you, I love you, you bitch.' He went on dragging me around the living room. My head kept knocking on things." Terri looked around the table. "What do you do with love like that?"

5 She was a bone-thin woman with a pretty face, dark eyes, and brown hair that hung down her back. She liked necklaces made of turquoise, and long pendant earrings.

"My God, don't be silly. That's not love, and you know it," Mel said. "I don't know what you'd call it, but I sure know you wouldn't call it love."

"Say what you want to, but I know it was," Terri said. "It may sound crazy to you, but it's true just the same. People are different, Mel. Sure, sometimes he may have acted crazy. Okay. But he loved me. In his own way maybe, but he loved me. There was love there, Mel. Don't say there wasn't."

Mel let out his breath. He held his glass and turned to Laura and me. "The man threatened to kill me," Mel said. He finished his drink and reached for the gin bottle. "Terri's a romantic. Terri's of the kick-me-so-I'll-know-you-love-me school. Terri, hon, don't look that way." Mel reached across the table and touched Terri's cheek with his fingers. He grinned at her.

"Now he wants to make up," Terri said.

10 "Make up what?" Mel said. "What is there to make up? I know what I know. That's all."

"How'd we get started on this subject, anyway?" Terri said. She raised her glass and drank from it. "Mel always has love on his mind," she said. "Don't you, honey?" She smiled, and I thought that was the last of it.

"I just wouldn't call Ed's behavior love. That's all I'm saying, honey," Mel said. "What about you guys?" Mel said to Laura and me. "Does that sound like love to you?"

"I'm the wrong person to ask," I said. "I didn't even know the man. I've only heard his name mentioned in passing. I wouldn't know. You'd have to know the particulars. But I think what you're saying is that love is an absolute."

Mel said, "The kind of love I'm talking about is. The kind of love I'm talking about, you don't try to kill people."

15 Laura said, "I don't know anything about Ed, or anything about the situation. But who can judge anyone else's situation?"

I touched the back of Laura's hand. She gave me a quick smile. I picked up Laura's hand. It was warm, the nails polished, perfectly manicured. I encircled the broad wrist with my fingers, and I held her.

"When I left, he drank rat poison," Terri said. She clasped her arms with her hands. "They took him to the hospital in Santa Fe. That's where we lived then, about ten miles out. They saved his life. But his gums went crazy from it. I mean they pulled away from his teeth. After that, his teeth stood out like fangs. My God," Terri said. She waited a minute, then let go of her arms and picked up her glass.

"What people won't do!" Laura said.

"He's out of the action now," Mel said. "He's dead."

20 Mel handed me the saucer of limes. I took a section, squeezed it over my drink, and stirred the ice cubes with my finger.

"It gets worse," Terri said. "He shot himself in the mouth. But he bungled that too. Poor Ed," she said. Terri shook her head.

"Poor Ed nothing," Mel said. "He was dangerous."

Mel was forty-five years old. He was tall and rangy with curly soft hair. His face and arms were brown from the tennis he played. When he was sober, his gestures, all his movements, were precise, very careful.

"He did love me though, Mel. Grant me that," Terri said. "That's all I'm asking. He didn't love me the way you love me. I'm not saying that. But he loved me. You can grant me that, can't you?"

25 "What do you mean, he bungled it?" I said.

Laura leaned forward with her glass. She put her elbows on the table and held her glass in both hands. She glanced from Mel to Terri and waited with a look of bewilderment on her open face, as if amazed that such things happened to people you were friendly with.

"How'd he bungle it when he killed himself?" I said.

"I'll tell you what happened," Mel said. "He took this twenty-two pistol he'd bought to threaten Terri and me with. Oh, I'm serious, the man was always threatening. You should have seen the way we lived in those days. Like fugitives. I even bought a gun myself. Can you believe it? A guy like me? But I did. I bought one for self-defense and carried it in the glove compartment. Sometimes I'd have to leave the apartment in the middle of the night. To go to the hospital, you know? Terri and I weren't married then, and my first wife had the house and kids, the dog, everything, and Terri and I were living in this apartment here. Sometimes, as I say, I'd get a call in the middle of the night and have to go into the hospital at two or three in the morning. It'd be dark out there in the parking lot, and I'd break into a sweat before I could even get to my car. I never knew if he was going to come up out of the shrubbery or from behind a car and start shooting. I mean, the man was crazy. He was capable of wiring a bomb, anything. He used to call my service at all hours and say he needed to talk to the doctor, and when I'd return the call, he'd say, 'Son of a bitch, your days are numbered.' Little things like that. It was scary, I'm telling you."

"I still feel sorry for him," Terri said.

30 "It sounds like a nightmare," Laura said. "But what exactly happened after he shot himself?"

Laura is a legal secretary. We'd met in a professional capacity. Before we knew it, it was a courtship. She's thirty-five, three years younger than I am. In addition to being in love, we like each other and enjoy one another's company. She's easy to be with.

"What happened?" Laura said.

Mel said, "He shot himself in the mouth in his room. Someone heard the shot and told the manager. They came in with a passkey, saw what had happened, and called an ambulance. I happened to be there when they brought him in, alive but past recall. The man lived for three days. His head swelled up to twice the size of a normal head. I'd never seen anything like it, and I hope I never do again. Terri wanted to go in and sit with him when she found out about it. We had a fight over it. I didn't think she should see him like that. I didn't think she should see him, and I still don't."

"Who won the fight?" Laura said.

35 "I was in the room with him when he died," Terri said. "He never came up out of it. But I sat with him. He didn't have anyone else."

"He was dangerous," Mel said. "If you call that love, you can have it."

"It was love," Terri said. "Sure, it's abnormal in most people's eyes. But he was willing to die for it. He did die for it."

"I sure as hell wouldn't call it love," Mel said. "I mean, no one knows what he did it for. I've seen a lot of suicides, and I couldn't say anyone ever knew what they did it for."

Mel put his hands behind his neck and tilted his chair back. "I'm not interested in that kind of love," he said. "If that's love, you can have it."

40 Terri said, "We were afraid. Mel even made a will out and wrote to his brother in California who used to be a Green Beret. Mel told him who to look for if something happened to him."

Terri drank from her glass. She said, "But Mel's right—we lived like fugitives. We were afraid. Mel was, weren't you, honey? I even called the police at one point, but they were no help. They said they couldn't do anything until Ed actually did something. Isn't that a laugh?" Terri said.

She poured the last of the gin into her glass and waggled the bottle. Mel got up from the table and went to the cupboard. He took down another bottle.

"Well, Nick and I know what love is," Laura said. "For us, I mean," Laura said. She bumped my knee with her knee. "You're supposed to say something now," Laura said, and turned her smile on me.

For an answer, I took Laura's hand and raised it to my lips. I made a big production out of kissing her hand. Everyone was amused.

"We're lucky," I said.

"You guys," Terri said. "Stop that now. You're making me sick. You're still on the honeymoon, for God's sake. You're still gaga, for crying out loud. Just wait. How long have you been together now? How long has it been? A year? Longer than a year?"

"Going on a year and a half," Laura said, flushed and smiling.

"Oh, now," Terri said. "Wait awhile."

She held her drink and gazed at Laura.

"I'm only kidding," Terri said.

Mel opened the gin and went around the table with the bottle.

"Here, you guys," he said. "Let's have a toast. I want to propose a toast. A toast to love. To true love," Mel said.

We touched glasses.

"To love," we said.

Outside in the backyard, one of the dogs began to bark. The leaves of the aspen that leaned past the window ticked against the glass. The afternoon sun was like a presence in this room, the spacious light of ease and generosity. We could have been anywhere, somewhere enchanted. We raised our glasses again and grinned at each other like children who had agreed on something forbidden.

"I'll tell you what real love is," Mel said. "I mean, I'll give you a good example. And then you can draw your own conclusions." He poured more gin into his glass. He added an ice cube and a sliver of lime. We waited and sipped our drinks. Laura and I touched knees again. I put a hand on her warm thigh and left it there.

"What do any of us really know about love?" Mel said. "It seems to me we're just beginners at love. We say we love each other and we do, I don't doubt it. I love Terri and Terri loves me, and you guys love each other too. You know the kind of love I'm talking about now. Physical love, that impulse that drives you to someone special, as well as love of the other person's being, his or her essence, as it were. Carnal love and, well, call it sentimental love, the day-to-day caring about the other person. But sometimes I have a hard time accounting for the fact that I must have loved my first wife too. But I did, I know I did. So I suppose I am like Terri in that regard. Terri and Ed." He thought about it and then he went on. "There was a time when I thought I loved my first wife more than life itself. But now I hate her guts. I do. How do you explain that? What happened to that love? What happened to it, is what I'd like to know. I wish someone could tell me. Then there's Ed. Okay, we're back to Ed. He loves Terri so much he tries to kill her and he winds up killing himself." Mel stopped talking and swallowed from his glass. "You guys have been together eighteen months and you love each other. It shows all over you. You glow with it. But you both loved other people before you met each other. You've both been married before, just like us. And you probably loved other people before that too, even. Terri and I have been together five years, been married for four. And the terrible thing, the terrible thing is, but the good thing too, the saving grace, you might say, is that if something happened to one of us—excuse me for saying this—but if something happened to one of us tomorrow, I think the other one, the other person, would grieve for a while, you know, but then the surviving party would go out and love again, have someone else soon enough. All this, all of this love we're talking about, it would just be a memory. Maybe not even a memory. Am I wrong? Am I way off base? Because I want you to set me straight if you think I'm wrong. I want to know. I mean, I don't know anything, and I'm the first one to admit it."

"Mel, for God's sake," Terri said. She reached out and took hold of his wrist. "Are you getting drunk? Honey? Are you drunk?"

"Honey, I'm just talking," Mel said. "All right? I don't have to be drunk to say what I think. I mean, we're all just talking, right?" Mel said. He fixed his eyes on her.

60 "Sweetie, I'm not criticizing," Terri said.

She picked up her glass.

"I'm not on call today," Mel said. "Let me remind you of that. I am not on call," he said.

"Mel, we love you," Laura said.

Mel looked at Laura. He looked at her as if he could not place her, as if she was not the woman she was.

65 "Love you too, Laura," Mel said. "And you, Nick, love you too. You know something?" Mel said. "You guys are our pals," Mel said.

He picked up his glass.

Mel said, "I was going to tell you about something. I mean, I was going to prove a point. You see, this happened a few months ago, but it's still going on right now, and it ought to make us feel ashamed when we talk like we know what we're talking about when we talk about love."

"Come on now," Terri said. "Don't talk like you're drunk if you're not drunk."

"Just shut up for once in your life," Mel said very quietly. "Will you do me a favor and do that for a minute? So as I was saying, there's this old couple who had this car wreck out on the interstate. A kid hit them and they were all torn to shit and nobody was giving them much chance to pull through."

70 Terri looked at us and then back at Mel. She seemed anxious, or maybe that's too strong a word.

Mel was handing the bottle around the table.

"I was on call that night," Mel said. "It was May or maybe it was June. Terri and I had just sat down to dinner when the hospital called. There'd been this thing out on the interstate. Drunk kid, teenager, plowed his dad's pickup into this camper with this old couple in it. They were up in their mid-seventies, that couple. The kid—eighteen, nineteen, something—he was DOA. Taken the steering wheel through his sternum. The old couple, they were alive, you understand. I mean, just barely. But they had everything. Multiple fractures, internal injuries, hemorrhaging, contusions, lacerations, the works, and they each of them had themselves concussions. They were in a bad way, believe me. And, of course, their age was two strikes against them. I'd say she was worse off than he was. Ruptured spleen along with everything else. Both kneecaps broken. But they'd been wearing their seatbelts and, God knows, that's what saved them for the time being."

"Folks, this is an advertisement for the National Safety Council," Terri said. "This is your spokesman, Dr. Melvin R. McGinnis, talking." Terri laughed. "Mel," she said, "sometimes you're just too much. But I love you, hon," she said.

"Honey, I love you," Mel said.

75 He leaned across the table. Terri met him halfway. They kissed.

"Terri's right," Mel said as he settled himself again. "Get those seatbelts on. But seriously, they were in some shape, those oldsters. By the time I got down there, the kid was dead, as I said. He was off in a corner, laid out on a gurney. I took one look at the old couple and told the ER nurse to get me a neurologist and an orthopedic man and a couple of surgeons down there right away."

He drank from his glass. "I'll try to keep this short," he said. "So we took the two of them up to the OR and worked like fuck on them most of the night. They had these incredible reserves, those two. You see that once in a while. So we did everything that could be done, and toward morning we're giving them a fifty-fifty chance, maybe less than that for her. So here they are, still alive the next morning. So, okay, we move them into the ICU, which is where they both kept plugging away at it for two weeks, hitting it better and better on all the scopes. So we transfer them out to their own room."

Mel stopped talking. "Here," he said, "let's drink this cheapo gin the hell up. Then we're going to dinner, right? Terri and I know a new place. That's where we'll go, to this new place we know about. But we're not going until we finish up this cut-rate, lousy gin."

Terri said, "We haven't actually eaten there yet. But it looks good. From the outside, you know."

80 "I like food," Mel said. "If I had it to do all over again, I'd be a chef, you know? Right? Terri?" Mel said.

He laughed. He fingered the ice in his glass.

"Terri knows," he said. "Terri can tell you. But let me say this. If I could come back again in a different life, a different time and all, you know what? I'd like to come back as a knight. You were pretty safe wearing all that armor. It was all right being a knight until gunpowder and muskets and pistols came along."

"Mel would like to ride a horse and carry a lance," Terri said.

"Carry a woman's scarf with you everywhere," Laura said.

85 "Or just a woman," Mel said.

"Shame on you," Laura said.

Terri said, "Suppose you came back as a serf. The serfs didn't have it so good in those days," Terri said.

"The serfs never had it good," Mel said. "But I guess even the knights were vessels to someone. Isn't that the way it worked? But then everyone is always a vessel to someone. Isn't that right? Terri? But what I liked about knights, besides their ladies, was that they had that suit of armor, you know, and they couldn't get hurt very easy. No cars in those days, you know? No drunk teenagers to tear into your ass."

"Vassals," Terri said.

90 "What?" Mel said.

"Vassals," Terri said. "They were called vassals, not vessels."

"Vassals, vessels," Mel said, "what the fuck's the difference? You knew what I meant anyway. All right," Mel said. "So I'm not educated. I learned my stuff. I'm a heart surgeon, sure, but I'm just a mechanic. I go in and fuck around and fix things. Shit," Mel said.

"Modesty doesn't become you," Terri said.

"He's just a humble sawbones," I said. "But sometimes they suffocated in all that armor, Mel. They'd even have heart attacks if it got too hot and they were too tired and worn out. I read somewhere that they'd fall off their horses and not be able to get up because they were too tired to stand with all that armor on them. They got trampled by their own horses sometimes."

95 "That's terrible," Mel said. "That's a terrible thing, Nicky. I guess they'd just lay there and wait until somebody came along and made a shish kebab out of them."

"Some other vessel," Terri said.

"That's right," Mel said. "Some vassal would come along and spear the bastard in the name of love. Or whatever the fuck it was they fought over in those days."

"Same things we fight over these days," Terri said.

Laura said, "Nothing's changed."

100 The color was still high in Laura's cheeks. Her eyes were bright. She brought her glass to her lips.

Mel poured himself another drink. He looked at the label closely as if studying a long row of numbers. Then he slowly put the bottle down on the table and slowly reached for the tonic water.

"What about the old couple?" Laura said. "You didn't finish that story you started."

Laura was having a hard time lighting her cigarette. Her matches kept going out.

The sunshine inside the room was different now, changing, getting thinner. But the leaves outside the window were still shimmering, and I stared at the pattern they made on the panes and on the Formica counter. They weren't the same patterns, of course.

105 "What about the old couple?" I said.

"Older but wiser," Terri said.

Mel stared at her.

Terri said, "Go on with your story, hon. I was only kidding. Then what happened?"

"Terri, sometimes," Mel said.

110 "Please, Mel." Terri said. "Don't always be so serious, sweetie. Can't you take a joke?"

"Where's the joke?" Mel said.

He held his glass and gazed steadily at his wife.

"What happened?" Laura said.

Mel fastened his eyes on Laura. He said, "Laura, if I didn't have Terri and if I didn't love her so much, and if Nick wasn't my best friend, I'd fall in love with you. I'd carry you off, honey," he said.

115 "Tell your story," Terri said. "Then we'll go to that new place, okay?"

"Okay?" Mel said. "Where was I?" he said. He stared at the table and then he began again.

"I dropped in to see each of them every day, sometimes twice a day if I was up doing other calls anyway. Casts and bandages, head to foot, the both of them. You know, you've seen it in the movies. That's just the way they looked, just like in the movies. Little eye-holes and nose-holes and mouth-holes. And she had to have her legs slung up on top of it. Well, the husband was very depressed for the longest while. Even after he found out that his wife was going to pull through, he was still very depressed. Not about the accident, though. I mean, the accident was one thing, but it wasn't everything. I'd get up to his mouth-hole, you know, and he'd say no, it wasn't the accident exactly but it was because he couldn't see her through his eye-holes. He said that was what was making him feel so bad. Can you imagine? I'm telling you, the man's heart was breaking because he couldn't turn his goddman head and *see* his goddamn wife."

Mel looked around the table and shook his head at what he was going to say.

"I mean, it was killing the old fart just because he couldn't *look* at the fucking woman."

We all look at Mel.

"Do you see what I'm saying?" he said.

Maybe we were a little drunk by then. I know it was hard keeping things in focus. The light was draining out of the room, going back through the window where it had come from. Yet nobody made a move to get up from the table to turn on the overhead light.

"Listen," Mel said. "Let's finish this fucking gin. There's about enough left here for one shooter all around. Then let's go eat. Let's go to the new place."

"He's depressed," Terri said. "Mel, why don't you take a pill?"

Mel shook his head. "I've taken everything there is."

"We all need a pill now and then," I said.

"Some people are born needing them," Terri said.

She was using her finger to rub at something on the table. Then she stopped rubbing.

"I think I want to call my kids," Mel said. "Is that all right with everybody? I'll call my kids," he said.

Terri said, "What if Marjorie answers the phone? You guys, you've heard us on the subject of Marjorie? Honey, you know you don't want to talk to Marjorie. It'll make you feel even worse."

"I don't want to talk to Marjorie," Mel said. "But I want to talk to my kids."

"There isn't a day goes by that Mel doesn't say he wishes she'd get married again. Or else die," Terri said. "For one thing," Terri said, "she's bankrupting us. Mel says it's just to spite him that she won't get married again. She has a boyfriend who lives with her and the kids, so Mel is supporting the boyfriend too."

"She's allergic to bees," Mel said. "If I'm not praying she'll get married again, I'm praying she'll get herself stung to death by a swarm of fucking bees."

"Shame on you," Laura said.

"Bzzzzzzz," Mel said, turning his fingers into bees and buzzing them at Terri's throat. Then he let his hands drop all the way to his sides.

"She's vicious," Mel said. "Sometimes I think I'll go up there dressed like a beekeeper. You know, that hat that's like a helmet with the plate that comes down over your face, the big gloves, and the padded coat? I'll knock on the door and let a loose hive of bees in the house. But first I'd make sure the kids were out, of course."

He crossed one leg over the other. It seemed to take him a lot of time to do it. Then he put both feet on the floor and leaned forward, elbows on the table, his chin cupped in his hands.

"Maybe I won't call the kids, after all. Maybe it isn't such a hot idea. Maybe we'll just go eat. How does that sound?"

"Sounds fine to me," I said. "Eat or not eat. Or keep drinking. I could head right on out into the sunset."

"What does that mean, honey?" Laura said.

"It just means what I said," I said. "It means I could just keep going. That's all it means."

"I could eat something myself," Laura said. "I don't think I've ever been so hungry in my life. Is there something to nibble on?"

"I'll put out some cheese and crackers," Terri said.

But Terri just sat there. She did not get up to get anything.

Mel turned his glass over. He spilled it out on the table.

"Gin's gone," Mel said.

Terri said, "Now what?"

I could hear my heart beating. I could hear everyone's heart. I could hear the human noise we sat there making, not one of us moving, not even when the room went dark.

[*1981*]

# *Cathedral*

This blind man, an old friend of my wife's, he was on his way to spend the night. His wife had died. So he was visiting the dead wife's relatives in Connecticut. He called my wife from his in-laws'. Arrangements were made. He would come by train, a five-hour trip, and my wife would meet him at the station. She hadn't seen him since she worked for him one summer in Seattle ten years ago. But she and the blind man had kept in touch. They made tapes and mailed them back and forth. I wasn't enthusiastic about his visit. He was no one I knew. And his being blind bothered me. My idea of blindness came from the movies. In the movies, the blind moved slowly and never laughed. Sometimes they were led by seeing-eye dogs. A blind man in my house was not something I looked forward to.

That summer in Seattle she had needed a job. She didn't have any money. The man she was going to marry at the end of the summer was in officers' training school. He didn't have any money, either. But she was in love with the guy, and he was in love with her, etc. She'd seen something in the paper: HELP WANTED—*Reading to Blind Man,* and a telephone number. She phoned and went over, was hired on the spot. She'd worked with this blind man all summer. She read stuff to him, case studies, reports, that sort of thing. She helped him organize his little office in the county social-service department. They'd become good friends, my wife and the blind man. How do I know these things? She told me. And she told me something else. On her last day in the office, the blind man asked if he could touch her face. She agreed to this. She told me he touched his fingers to every part of her face, her nose—even her neck! She never forgot it. She even tried to write a poem about it. She was always trying to write a poem. She wrote a poem or two every year, usually after something really important had happened to her.

When we first started going out together, she showed me the poem. In the poem, she recalled his fingers and the way they had moved around over her face. In the poem, she talked about what she had felt at the time, about what went through her mind when the blind man touched her nose and lips. I can remember I didn't think much of the poem. Of course, I didn't tell her that. Maybe I just don't understand poetry. I admit it's not the first thing I reach for when I pick up something to read.

Anyway, this man who'd first enjoyed her favors, the officer-to-be, he'd been her childhood sweetheart. So okay. I'm saying that at the end of the summer she let the blind man run his hands over her face, said goodbye to him, married her childhood etc., who was now a commissioned officer, and she moved away from Seattle. But they'd kept in touch, she and the blind man. She made the first contact after a year or so. She called him up one night from an Air Force base in Alabama. She wanted to talk. They talked. He asked her to send a tape and tell him about her life. She did this. She sent the tape. On the tape, she told the blind man about her husband and about their life together in the military. She told the blind man she loved her husband but she didn't like it where they lived and she didn't like it that he was part of the military-industrial thing. She told the blind man she'd written a poem and he was in it. She told him that she was writing a poem about what it was like to be an Air Force officer's wife. The poem wasn't finished yet. She was still writing it. The blind man made a tape. He sent her the tape. She made a tape. This went on for years. My wife's officer was posted to one base and then another. She sent tapes from Moody AFB, McGuire, McConnell, and finally Travis, near Sacramento, where one night she got to feeling lonely and cut off from people she kept losing in that moving-around life. She got to feeling she couldn't go it another step. She went in and swallowed all the pills and capsules in the medicine chest and washed them down with a bottle of gin. Then she got into a hot bath and passed out.

5 But instead of dying, she got sick. She threw up. Her officer—why should he have a name? he was the childhood sweetheart, and what more does he want?—came home from somewhere, found her, and called the ambulance. In time, she put it all on a tape and sent the tape to the blind man. Over the years, she put all kinds of stuff on tapes and sent the tapes off lickety-split. Next to writing a poem every year, I think it was her chief means of recreation. On one tape, she told the blind man she'd decided to live away from her officer for a time. On another tape, she told him about her divorce. She and I began going out, and of course she told her blind man about it. She told him everything, or so it seemed to me. Once she asked me if I'd like to hear the latest tape from the blind man. This was a year ago. I was on the tape, she said. So I said okay, I'd listen to it. I got us drinks and we settled down in the living room. We made ready to listen. First she inserted the tape into the player and adjusted a couple of dials. Then she pushed a lever. The tape squeaked and someone began to talk in this loud voice. She lowered the volume. After a few minutes of harmless

chitchat, I heard my own name in the mouth of this stranger, this blind man I didn't even know! And then this: "From all you've said about him, I can only conclude—" But we were interrupted, a knock at the door, something, and we didn't ever get back to the tape. Maybe it was just as well. I'd heard all I wanted to.

Now this same blind man was coming to sleep in my house.

"Maybe I could take him bowling," I said to my wife. She was at the draining board doing scalloped potatoes. She put down the knife she was using and turned around.

"If you love me," she said, "you can do this for me. If you don't love me, okay. But if you had a friend, any friend, and the friend came to visit, I'd make him feel comfortable." She wiped her hands with the dish towel.

"I don't have any blind friends," I said.

10 "You don't have *any* friends," she said. "Period. Besides," she said, "goddamn it, his wife's just died! Don't you understand that? The man's lost his wife!"

I didn't answer. She'd told me a little about the blind man's wife. Her name was Beulah. Beulah! That's a name for a colored woman.

"Was his wife a Negro?" I asked.

"Are you crazy?" my wife said. "Have you just flipped or something?" She picked up a potato. I saw it hit the floor, then roll under the stove. "What's wrong with you?" she said. "Are you drunk?"

"I'm just asking," I said.

15 Right then my wife filled me in with more detail than I cared to know. I made a drink and sat at the kitchen table to listen. Pieces of the story began to fall into place.

Beulah had gone to work for the blind man the summer after my wife had stopped working for him. Pretty soon Beulah and the blind man had themselves a church wedding. It was a little wedding—who'd want to go to such a wedding in the first place?—just the two of them, plus the minister and the minister's wife. But it was a church wedding just the same. It was what Beulah had wanted, he'd said. But even then Beulah must have been carrying the cancer in her glands. After they had been inseparable for eight years—my wife's word, *inseparable*—Beulah's health went into a rapid decline. She died in a Seattle hospital room, the blind man sitting beside the bed and holding on to her hand. They'd married, lived and worked together, slept together—had sex, sure—and then the blind man had to bury her. All this without his having ever seen what the goddamned woman looked like. It was beyond my understanding. Hearing this, I felt sorry for the blind man for a little bit. And then I found myself thinking what a pitiful life this woman must have led. Imagine a woman who could never see herself as she was seen in the eyes of her loved one. A woman who could go on day after day and never receive the smallest compliment from her beloved. A woman whose husband could never read the expression on her face, be it misery or something better. Someone who could wear makeup or not—what difference to him? She could, if she wanted, wear green eye-shadow around one eye, a straight pin in her nostril, yellow slacks, and purple shoes, no matter. And then to slip off into death, the blind man's hand on her hand, his blind eyes streaming tears—I'm imagining now—her last thought maybe this: that he never even knew what she looked like, and she on an express to the grave. Robert was left with a small insurance policy and a half of a twenty-peso Mexican coin. The other half of the coin went into the box with her. Pathetic.

So when the time rolled around, my wife went to the depot to pick him up. With nothing to do but wait—sure, I blamed him for that—I was having a drink and watching the TV when I heard the car pull into the drive. I got up from the sofa with my drink and went to the window to have a look.

I saw my wife laughing as she parked the car. I saw her get out of the car and shut the door. She was still wearing a smile. Just amazing. She went around to the other side of the car to where the blind man was already starting to get out. This blind man, feature this, he was wearing a full beard! A beard on a blind man! Too much, I say. The blind man reached into the back seat and dragged out a suitcase. My wife took his arm, shut the car door, and, talking all the way, moved him down the drive and then up the steps to the front porch. I turned off the TV. I finished my drink, rinsed the glass, dried my hands. Then I went to the door.

My wife said, "I want you to meet Robert. Robert, this is my husband. I've told you all about him." She was beaming. She had this blind man by his coat sleeve.

20 The blind man let go of his suitcase and up came his hand. I took it. He squeezed hard, held my hand, and then he let it go.

"I feel like we've already met," he boomed.

"Likewise," I said. I didn't know what else to say. Then I said, "Welcome. I've heard a lot about you." We began to move then, a little group, from the porch into the living room, my wife guiding him by the arm. The blind man was carrying his suitcase in his other hand. My wife said things like, "To your left here, Robert. That's right. Now watch it, there's a chair. That's it. Sit down right here. This is the sofa. We just bought this sofa two weeks ago."

I started to say something about the old sofa. I'd liked that old sofa. But I didn't say anything. Then I wanted to say something else, small-talk, about the scenic ride along the Hudson. How going *to* New York, you should sit on the right-hand side of the train, and coming *from* New York, the left-hand side.

"Did you have a good train ride?" I said. "Which side of the train did you sit on, by the way?"

25 "What a question, which side!" my wife said. "What's it matter which side?" she said.

"I just asked," I said.

"Right side," the blind man said. "I hadn't been on a train in nearly forty years. Not since I was a kid. With my folks. That's been a long time. I'd nearly forgotten the sensation. I have winter in my beard now," he said. "So I've been told, anyway. Do I look distinguished, my dear?" the blind man said to my wife.

"You look distinguished, Robert," she said. "Robert," she said. "Robert, it's just so good to see you."

My wife finally took her eyes off the blind man and looked at me. I had the feeling she didn't like what she saw. I shrugged.

30 I've never met, or personally known, anyone who was blind. This blind man was late forties, a heavy-set, balding man with stooped shoulders, as if he carried a great weight there. He wore brown slacks, brown shoes, a light-brown shirt, a tie, a sports coat. Spiffy. He also had this full beard. But

he didn't use a cane and he didn't wear dark glasses. I'd always thought dark glasses were a must for the blind. Fact was, I wished he had a pair. At first glance, his eyes looked like anyone else's eyes. But if you looked close, there was something different about them. Too much white in the iris, for one thing, and the pupils seemed to move around in the sockets without his knowing it or being able to stop it. Creepy. As I stared at his face, I saw the left pupil turn in toward his nose while the other made an effort to keep in one place. But it was only an effort, for that eye was on the roam without his knowing it or wanting it to be.

I said, "Let me get you a drink. What's your pleasure? We have a little of everything. It's one of our pastimes."

"Bub, I'm a Scotch man myself," he said fast enough in this big voice.

"Right," I said. Bub! "Sure you are. I knew it."

He let his fingers touch his suitcase, which was sitting alongside the sofa. He was taking his bearings. I didn't blame him for that.

35 "I'll move that up to your room," my wife said.

"No, that's fine," the blind man said loudly. "It can go up when I go up."

"A little water with the Scotch?" I said.

"Very little," he said.

"I knew it," I said.

40 He said, "Just a tad. The Irish actor, Barry Fitzgerald? I'm like that fellow. When I drink water, Fitzgerald said, I drink water. When I drink whiskey, I drink whiskey." My wife laughed. The blind man brought his hand up under his beard. He lifted his beard slowly and let it drop.

I did the drinks, three big glasses of Scotch with a splash of water in each. Then we made ourselves comfortable and talked about Robert's travels. First the long flight from the West Coast to Connecticut, we covered that. Then from Connecticut up here by train. We had another drink concerning that leg of the trip.

I remembered having read somewhere that the blind didn't smoke because, as speculation had it, they couldn't see the smoke they exhaled. I thought I knew that much and that much only about blind people. But this blind man smoked his cigarette down to the nubbin and then lit another one. This blind man filled his ashtray and my wife emptied it.

When we sat down at the table for dinner, we had another drink. My wife heaped Robert's plate with cube steak, scalloped potatoes, green beans. I buttered him up two slices of bread. I said, "Here's bread and butter for you." I swallowed some of my drink. "Now let us pray," I said, and the blind man lowered his head. My wife looked at me, her mouth agape. "Pray the phone won't ring and the food doesn't get cold," I said.

We dug in. We ate everything there was to eat on the table. We ate like there was no tomorrow. We didn't talk. We ate. We scarfed. We grazed that table. We were into serious eating. The blind man had right away located his foods, he knew just where everything was on his plate. I watched with admiration as he used his knife and fork on the meat. He'd cut two pieces of meat, fork the meat into his mouth, and then go all out for the scalloped potatoes, the beans next, and then he'd tear off a hunk of buttered bread and eat that. He'd follow this up with a big drink of milk. It didn't seem to bother him to use his fingers once in a while, either.

45 We finished everything, including half a strawberry pie. For a few mo-

ments, we sat as if stunned. Sweat beaded on our faces. Finally, we got up from the table and left the dirty places. We didn't look back. We took ourselves into the living room and sank into our places again. Robert and my wife sat on the sofa. I took the big chair. We had us two or three more drinks while they talked about the major things that had come to pass for them in the past ten years. For the most part, I just listened. Now and then I joined in. I didn't want him to think I'd left the room, and I didn't want her to think I was feeling left out. They talked of things that had happened to them—to them!—these past ten years. I waited in vain to hear my name on my wife's sweet lips: "And then my dear husband came into my life"—something like that. But I heard nothing of the sort. More talk of Robert. Robert had done a little of everything, it seemed, a regular blind jack-of-all-trades. But most recently he and his wife had had an Amway distributorship, from which, I gathered, they'd earned their living, such as it was. The blind man was also a ham radio operator. He talked in his loud voice about conversations he'd had with fellow operators in Guam, in the Philippines, in Alaska, and even in Tahiti. He said he'd have a lot of friends there if he ever wanted to go visit those places. From time to time, he'd turn his blind face toward me, put his hand under his beard, ask me something. How long had I been in my present position? (Three years.) Did I like my work? (I didn't.) Was I going to stay with it? (What were the options?) Finally, when I thought he was beginning to run down, I got up and turned on the TV.

My wife looked at me with irritation. She was heading toward a boil. Then she looked at the blind man and said, "Robert, do you have a TV?"

The blind man said, "My dear, I have two TVs. I have a color set and a black-and-white thing, an old relic. It's funny, but if I turn the TV on, and I'm always turning it on, I turn on the color set. It's funny, don't you think?"

I didn't know what to say to that. I had absolutely nothing to say to that. No opinion. So I watched the news program and tried to listen to what the announcer was saying.

"This is a color TV," the blind man said. "Don't ask me how, but I can tell."

50 "We traded up a while ago," I said.

The blind man had another taste of his drink. He lifted his beard, sniffed it, and let it fall. He leaned forward on the sofa. He positioned his ashtray on the coffee table, then put the lighter to his cigarette. He leaned back on the sofa and crossed his legs at the ankles.

My wife covered her mouth, and then she yawned. She stretched. She said, "I think I'll go upstairs and put on my robe. I think I'll change into something else. Robert, you make yourself comfortable," she said.

"I'm comfortable," the blind man said.

"I want you to feel comfortable in this house," she said.

55 "I am comfortable," the blind man said.

After she'd left the room, he and I listened to the weather report and then to the sports roundup. By that time, she'd been gone so long I didn't know if she was going to come back. I thought she might have gone to bed. I wished she'd come back downstairs. I didn't want to be left alone with a blind man. I asked him if he wanted another drink, and he said sure. Then I asked if he wanted to smoke some dope with me. I said I'd just rolled a number. I hadn't, but I planned to do so in about two shakes.

"I'll try some with you," he said.

"Damn right," I said. "That's the stuff."

I got our drinks and sat down on the sofa with him. Then I rolled us two fat numbers. I lit one and passed it. I brought it to his fingers. He took it and inhaled.

60 "Hold it as long as you can," I said. I could tell he didn't know the first thing.

My wife came back downstairs wearing her pink robe and her pink slippers.

"What do I smell?" she said.

"We thought we'd have us some cannabis," I said.

My wife gave me a savage look. Then she looked at the blind man and said, "Robert, I didn't know you smoked."

65 He said, "I do now, my dear. There's a first time for everything. But I don't feel anything yet."

"This stuff is pretty mellow," I said. "This stuff is mild. It's dope you can reason with," I said. "It doesn't mess you up."

"Not much it doesn't, bub," he said, and laughed.

My wife sat on the sofa between the blind man and me. I passed her the number. She took it and toked and then passed it back to me. "Which way is this going?" she said. Then she said, "I shouldn't be smoking this. I can hardly keep my eyes open as it is. That dinner did me in. I shouldn't have eaten so much."

"It was the strawberry pie," the blind man said. "That's what did it," he said, and he laughed his big laugh. Then he shook his head.

70 "There's more strawberry pie," I said.

"Do you want some more, Robert?" my wife said.

"Maybe in a little while," he said.

We gave our attention to the TV. My wife yawned again. She said, "Your bed is made up when you feel like going to bed, Robert. I know you must have had a long day. When you're ready to go to bed, say so." She pulled his arm. "Robert?"

He came to and said, "I've had a real nice time. This beats tapes, doesn't it?"

75 I said, "Coming at you," and I put the number between his fingers. He inhaled, held the smoke, and then let it go. It was like he'd been doing it since he was nine years old.

"Thanks, bub," he said. "But I think this is all for me. I think I'm beginning to feel it," he said. He held the burning roach out for my wife.

"Same here," she said. "Ditto. Me, too." She took the roach and passed it to me. "I may just sit here for a while between you two guys with my eyes closed. But don't let me bother you, okay? Either one of you. If it bothers you, say so. Otherwise, I may just sit here with my eyes closed until you're ready to go to bed," she said. "Your bed's made up, Robert, when you're ready. It's right next to our room at the top of the stairs. We'll show you up when you're ready. You wake me up now, you guys, if I fall asleep." She said that and then she closed her eyes and went to sleep.

The news program ended. I got up and changed the channel. I sat back down on the sofa. I wished my wife hadn't pooped out. Her head lay across the back of the sofa, her mouth open. She'd turned so that her robe slipped away from her legs, exposing a juicy thigh. I reached to draw her robe back over her, and it was then that I glanced at the blind man. What the hell! I flipped the robe open again.

"You say when you want some strawberry pie," I said.

80 "I will," he said.

I said, "Are you tired? Do you want me to take you up to your bed? Are you ready to hit the hay?"

"Not yet," he said. "No, I'll stay up with you, bub. If that's all right. I'll stay up until you're ready to turn in. We haven't had a chance to talk. Know what I mean? I feel like me and her monopolized the evening." He lifted his beard and he let it fall. He picked up his cigarettes and his lighter.

"That's all right," I said. Then I said, "I'm glad for the company."

And I guess I was. Every night I smoked dope and stayed up as long as I could before I fell asleep. My wife and I hardly ever went to bed at the same time. When I did go to sleep, I had these dreams. Sometimes I'd wake up from one of them, my heart going crazy.

85 Something about the church and the Middle Ages was on the TV. Not your run-of-the-mill TV fare. I wanted to watch something else. I turned to the other channels. But there was nothing on them, either. So I turned back to the first channel and apologized.

"Bub, it's all right," the blind man said. "It's fine with me. Whatever you want to watch is okay. I'm always learning something. Learning never ends. It won't hurt me to learn something tonight. I got ears," he said.

We didn't say anything for a time. He was leaning forward with his head turned at me, his right ear aimed in the direction of the set. Very disconcerting. Now and then his eyelids drooped and then they snapped open again. Now and then he put his fingers into his beard and tugged, like he was thinking about something he was hearing on the television.

On the screen, a group of men wearing cowls was being set upon and tormented by men dressed in skeleton costumes and men dressed as devils. The men dressed as devils wore devil masks, horns, and long tails. This pageant was part of a procession. The Englishman who was narrating the thing said it took place in Spain once a year. I tried to explain to the blind man what was happening.

"Skeletons," he said. "I know about skeletons," he said, and he nodded.

90 The TV showed this one cathedral. Then there was a long, slow look at another one. Finally, the picture switched to the famous one in Paris, with its flying buttresses and its spires reaching up to the clouds. The camera pulled away to show the whole of the cathedral rising above the skyline.

There were times when the Englishman who was telling the thing would shut up, would simply let the camera move around the cathedrals. Or else the camera would tour the countryside, men in fields walking behind oxen. I waited as long as I could. Then I felt I had to say something. I said, "They're showing the outside of this cathedral now. Gargoyles. Little statues carved to look like monsters. Now I guess they're in Italy. Yeah, they're in Italy. There's paintings on the walls of this one church."

"Are those fresco paintings, bub?" he asked, and he sipped from his drink.

I reached for my glass. But it was empty. I tried to remember what I could remember. "You're asking me are those frescoes?" I said. "That's a good question. I don't know."

The camera moved to a cathedral outside Lisbon. The differences in the Portuguese cathedral compared with the French and Italian were not that great. But they were there. Mostly the interior stuff. Then something occurred to me, and I said, "Something has occurred to me. Do you have any idea what a cathedral is? What they look like, that is? Do you follow me? If somebody says cathedral to you, do you have any notion what they're talking about? Do you know the difference between that and a Baptist church, say?"

95 He let the smoke dribble from his mouth. "I know they took hundreds of workers fifty or a hundred years to build," he said. "I just heard the man say that, of course. I know generations of the same families worked on a cathedral. I heard him say that, too. The men who began their life's work on them, they never lived to see the completion of their work. In that wise, bub, they're no different from the rest of us, right?" He laughed. Then his eyelids drooped again. His head nodded. He seemed to be snoozing. Maybe he was imagining himself in Portugal. The TV was showing another cathedral now. This one was in Germany. The Englishman's voice droned on. "Cathedrals," the blind man said. He sat up and rolled his head back and forth. "If you want the truth, bub, that's about all I know. What I just said. What I heard him say. But maybe you could describe one to me? I wish you'd do it. I'd like that. If you want to know, I really don't have a good idea."

I stared hard at the shot of the cathedral on the TV. How could I even begin to describe it? But say my life depended on it. Say my life was being threatened by an insane guy who said I had to do it or else.

I stared some more at the cathedral before the picture flipped off into the countryside. There was no use. I turned to the blind man and said, "To begin with, they're very tall." I was looking around the room for clues. "They reach way up. Up and up. Toward the sky. They're so big, some of them, they have to have these supports. To help hold them up, so to speak. These supports are called buttresses. They remind me of viaducts, for some reason. But maybe you don't know viaducts, either? Sometimes the cathedrals have devils and such carved into the front. Sometimes lords and ladies. Don't ask me why this is," I said.

He was nodding. The whole upper part of his body seemed to be moving back and forth.

"I'm not doing so good, am I?" I said.

100 He stopped nodding and leaned forward on the edge of the sofa. As he listened to me, he was running his fingers through his beard. I wasn't getting through to him, I could see that. But he waited for me to go on just the same. He nodded, like he was trying to encourage me. I tried to think what else to say. "They're really big," I said. "They're massive. They're built of stone. Marble, too, sometimes. In those olden days, when they built cathedrals, men wanted to be close to God. In those olden days, God was an important part of everyone's life. You could tell this from their cathedral-building. I'm sorry," I said, "but it looks like that's the best I can do for you. I'm just no good at it."

"That's all right, bub," the blind man said. "Hey, listen. I hope you don't mind my asking you. Can I ask you something? Let me ask you a simple question, yes or no. I'm just curious and there's no offense. You're my host. But let me ask if you are in any way religious? You don't mind my asking?"

I shook my head. He couldn't see that, though. A wink is the same as a nod to a blind man. "I guess I don't believe in it. In anything. Sometimes it's hard. You know what I'm saying?"

"Sure, I do," he said.

"Right," I said.

105 The Englishman was still holding forth. My wife sighed in her sleep. She drew a long breath and went on with her sleeping.

"You'll have to forgive me," I said. "But I can't tell you what a cathedral looks like. It just isn't in me to do it. I can't do any more than I've done."

The blind man sat very still, his head down, as he listened to me.

I said, "The truth is, cathedrals don't mean anything special to me. Nothing. Cathedrals. They're something to look at on late-night TV. That's all they are."

It was then that the blind man cleared his throat. He brought something up. He took a handkerchief from his back pocket. Then he said, "I get it, bub. It's okay. It happens. Don't worry about it," he said. "Hey, listen to me. Will you do me a favor? I got an idea. Why don't you find us some heavy paper? And a pen. We'll do something. We'll draw one together. Get us a pen and some heavy paper. Go on, bub, get the stuff," he said.

110 So I went upstairs. My legs felt like they didn't have any strength in them. They felt like they did after I'd done some running. In my wife's room, I looked around. I found some ballpoints in a little basket on her table. And then I tried to think where to look for the kind of paper he was talking about.

Downstairs, in the kitchen, I found a shopping bag with onion skins in the bottom of the bag. I emptied the bag and shook it. I brought it into the living room and sat down with it near his legs. I moved some things, smoothed the wrinkles from the bag, spread it out on the coffee table.

The blind man got down from the sofa and sat next to me on the carpet.

He ran his fingers over the paper. He went up and down the sides of the paper. The edges, even the edges. He fingered the corners.

"All right," he said. "All right, let's do her."

115 He found my hand, the hand with the pen. He closed his hand over my hand. "Go ahead, bub, draw," he said. "Draw. You'll see. I'll follow along with you. It'll be okay. Just begin now like I'm telling you. You'll see. Draw," the blind man said.

So I began. First I drew a box that looked like a house. It could have been the house I lived in. Then I put a roof on it. At either end of the roof, I drew spires. Crazy.

"Swell," he said. "Terrific. You're doing fine," he said. "Never thought anything like this could happen in your lifetime, did you, bub? Well, it's a strange life, we all know that. Go on now. Keep it up."

I put in windows with arches. I drew flying buttresses. I hung great doors. I couldn't stop. The TV station went off the air. I put down the pen and closed and opened my fingers. The blind man felt around over the paper. He moved the tips of his fingers over the paper, all over what I had drawn, and he nodded.

"Doing fine," the blind man said.

120 I took up the pen again, and he found my hand. I kept at it. I'm no artist. But I kept drawing just the same.

My wife opened up her eyes and gazed at us. She sat up on the sofa, her robe hanging open. She said, "What are you doing? Tell me, I want to know."

I didn't answer her.

The blind man said, "We're drawing a cathedral. Me and him are working on it. Press hard," he said to me. "That's right. That's good," he said. "Sure. You got it, bub, I can tell. You didn't think you could. But you can, can't you? You're cooking with gas now. You know what I'm saying? We're going to really have us something here in a minute. How's the old arm?" he said. "Put some people in there now. What's a cathedral without people?"

My wife said, "What's going on? Robert, what are you doing? What's going on?"

"It's all right," he said to her. "Close your eyes now," the blind man said to me.

I did it. I closed them just like he said.

"Are they closed?" he said. "Don't fudge."

"They're closed," I said.

"Keep them that way," he said. He said, "Don't stop now. Draw."

So we kept on with it. His fingers rode my fingers as my hand went over the paper. It was like nothing else in my life up to now.

Then he said, "I think that's it. I think you got it," he said. "Take a look. What do you think?"

But I had my eyes closed. I thought I'd keep them that way for a little longer. I thought it was something I ought to do.

"Well?" he said. "Are you looking?"

My eyes were still closed. I was in my house. I knew that. But I didn't feel like I was inside anything.

"It's really something," I said.

[*1983*]

## TALKING ABOUT STORIES

*Larry McCaffery and Sinda Gregory have interviewed many contemporary authors and have published some of the interviews in a collection entitled* Alive and Writing *(1987). In the following selections from a long interview, Carver talks about his life and work.*

SINDA GREGORY. Your newfound "belief in love for the things of this world" is very evident in some of the stories in *Cathedral,* especially in the title story.

RAYMOND CARVER. That story was very much an "opening up" process for me—I mean that in every sense. "Cathedral" *was* a larger, grander story than anything I had previously written. When I began writing that story I felt that I was breaking out of something I had put myself into, both personally and aesthetically. I simply couldn't go on any farther in the direction I had been going in *What We Talk About When We Talk About Love.* Oh, I *could* have, I suppose, but I didn't want to. Some of the stories were becoming too attenuated. I didn't write anything for five or six months after that book came out. I literally wrote nothing except letters. So it was especially pleasing to me that, when I finally sat down to write again, I wrote *that* story, "Cathedral." It felt like I had never written anything that way before. I could let myself *go* in some way, I didn't have to impose the restrictions on myself that I had in the earlier stories. The last story I wrote for the collection was "Fever," which was also just about the longest story I've ever written. And it's affirmative, I think, positive in its outlook. Really, the whole collection is different, and the next book is going to be different as well!

LARRY MCCAFFERY. What does it mean to a writer like you to find yourself, relatively suddenly, in such a different frame of mind? Do you find it difficult today to write about the despair, emotional turmoil, and hopelessness that is so much a part of the vision of your earlier fiction?

RC. No, because when I need to open this door to my imagination—stare out over the window casement, what Keats called his "magic casements"—I can remember exactly the texture of that despair and hopelessness, I can still taste it, feel it. The things that are emotionally meaningful to me are still very much alive and available to me, even though the circumstances of my personal life have changed. Merely because my physical surroundings and my mental state are different today doesn't mean, of course, that I still don't know exactly what I was talking about in the earlier stories. I can bring all that back if I choose to, but I'm finding that I am not driven to write about it exclusively. That's not to say I'm interested in writing about life here, where I live in Four Seasons Ranch, this chichi development. If you look carefully at *Cathedral,* you'll find that many of those stories have to do with that other life, which is still very much with me. But not all of them do, which is why the book feels different to me. . . .

SG. Many of your stories either open with the ordinary being slightly disturbed by this sense of menace you've just mentioned, or they develop in that direction. Is this tendency the result of your conviction that the world *is* menacing for most people? Or does it have more to do with an aesthetic choice—that menace contains more interesting possibilities for storytelling?

RC. The world is a menacing place for many of the people in my stories, yes. The people I've chosen to write about *do* feel menace, and I think many, if not most, people feel the world is a menacing place. Probably not so many people who will see this interview feel menace in the sense I'm talking about. Most of our friends and acquaintances, yours and mine, don't feel this way. But try living on the other side of the tracks for a while. Menace is there, and it's palpable. As to the second part of your question, that's true, too. Menace does contain, for me at least, more interesting possibilities to explore. . . .

SG. A reader is immediately struck with the "pared down" quality of your work, especially your work before *Cathedral.* Was this style something that evolved, or had it been with you from the beginning?

RC. From the very beginning I loved the rewriting process as much as the initial execution. I've always loved taking sentences and playing with them, rewriting them, paring them down to where they seem solid somehow. This may have resulted from being John Gardner's student, because he told me something I immediately responded to: If you can say it in fifteen words rather than twenty or thirty words, then say it in fifteen words. That struck me with the force of revelation. There I was, groping to find my own way, and here someone was telling me something that somehow conjoined with what I already wanted to do. It was the most natural thing in the world for me to go back and refine what was happening on the page and eliminate the padding. The last few days I've been reading Flaubert's letters, and he says some things that seem relevant to my own aesthetic. At one point when Flaubert was writing *Madame Bovary,* he would knock off at midnight or one in the morning and write letters to his mistress, Louise Colet, about the construction of the book and his general notion of aesthetics. One passage he wrote her that really struck me was when he said, "The artist in his work must be like God in his creation—invisible and all powerful; he must be everywhere felt but nowhere seen." I like the last part of that especially. There's another interesting remark when Flaubert is writing to his editors at the magazine that published the book in installments. They were just getting ready to serialize *Madame Bovary* and were going to make a lot of cuts in the text because they were afraid they were going to be closed down by the government if they published it just as Flaubert wrote it, so Flaubert tells them that if they make the cuts they can't publish the book, but they'll still be friends. The last line of this letter is: "I know how to distinguish between literature and literary business"—another insight I respond to. Even in these letters his prose is astonishing: "Prose must stand upright from one end to the other, like a wall whose ornamentation continues down to its very base." "Prose is architecture." "Everything must be done coldly, with poise." "Last week I spent five days writing one page." One of the interesting things about the Flaubert book is the way it demonstrates how self-consciously he was setting out to do something very special and different with prose. He consciously tried to make prose an art form. If you look at what else was being published in Europe in 1855, when *Madame Bovary* was published, you realize what an achievement the book really is. . . .

LM. Another distinctive feature of your work is that you usually present characters that most writers don't deal with—that is, people who are basically inarticulate, who can't verbalize their plights, who often don't seem to really grasp what is happening to them.

RC. I don't think of this as being especially "distinctive" or nontraditional because I feel perfectly comfortable with these people while I'm working. I've known people like this all my life. Essentially, I *am* one of those confused, befuddled people, I come from people like that, those are the people I've worked with and earned my living beside for years. That's why I've never had any interest whatsoever in writing a story or a poem that has anything to do with the academic life, with teachers or students and so forth. I'm just not that interested. The things that have made an indelible impression on me are the things I saw in lives I witnessed being lived around me, and in the life I myself lived. These were lives where people really *were* scared when someone knocked on their door, day or night, or when the telephone rang; they didn't know how they were going to pay the rent or what they could do if their refrigerator went out. Anatole Broyard tries to criticize my story "Preservation" by saying, "So the refrigerator breaks—why don't they just call a repairman and get it fixed?" That kind of remark is dumb. You bring a repairman out to fix your refrigerator and it's sixty bucks to *fix* it; and who knows how much if the thing is completely broken? Well, Broyard may not be aware of it, but some people can't afford to bring in a repairman if it's going to cost them sixty bucks, just like they don't get to a doctor if they don't have insurance, and their teeth go bad because they can't afford to go to a dentist when they need one. That kind of situation doesn't seem unrealistic or artificial to me. It also doesn't seem that, in focusing on this group of people, I have really been doing anything all that different from other writers. Chekhov was writing about a submerged population a hundred years ago. Short story writers have always been doing that. Not all of Chekhov's stories are about people who are down and out, but a significant number of them deal with that submerged population I'm talking about. He wrote about doctors and businessmen and teachers sometimes, but he also gave voice to people who were not so articulate. He found a means of letting those people have their say as well. So in writing about people who aren't so articulate and who are confused and scared, I'm not doing anything radically different.

LM. Aren't there formal problems in writing about this group of people? I mean, you can't have them sit around in drawing rooms endlessly analyzing their situations, the way James does, or, in a different sense, the way Bellow does. I suppose setting the scene, composing it, must be especially important from a technical standpoint.

RC. If you mean literally just setting the scene, that's the least of my worries. The scene is easy to set: I just open the door and see what's inside. I pay a lot of attention to trying to make the people talk the right way. By this I don't mean just *what* they say, but *how* they say it, and *why*. I guess *tone* is what I'm talking about, partly. There's never any chit-chat in my stories. Everything said is for a reason and adds, I want to think, to the overall impression of the story.

SG. People usually emphasize the realistic aspects of your work, but I feel there's a quality about your fiction that is *not* basically realistic. It's as if something is happening almost off the page, a dreamy sense of irrationality, almost like Kafka's fiction.

RC. Presumably my fiction is in the realistic tradition (as opposed to the really far-out side), but just telling it like it is bores me. It really does. People couldn't possibly read pages of description about the way people *really* talk, about what *really* happens in their lives. They'd just snore away, of course. If you look carefully at my stories, I don't think you'll find people talking the way people do in real life. People always say that Hemingway had a great ear for dialogue, and he did. But no one ever talked in real life like they do in Hemingway's fiction. At least not until after they've *read* Hemingway.

# CHAPTER 11

# A Collection of Short Fiction

The stories of Cain and Abel, Ruth, Samson, and Joseph in the Hebrew Bible and the parables of Jesus in the New Testament are sufficient evidence that brief narratives existed in ancient times. The short tales in Boccaccio's *Decameron* and Chaucer's *Canterbury Tales* (the latter an amazing variety of narrative poems ranging from bawdy stories to legends of saints) are medieval examples of the ancient form. But, speaking generally, short narratives before the nineteenth century were either didactic pieces, with the narrative existing for the sake of a moral point, or they were "curious and striking" tales (to use Somerset Maugham's words for his favorite kind of story) recounted in order to entertain.

The contemporary short story is rather different from both of these genres, which can be called the parable and the anecdote. Like the parable, the contemporary short story has a point, a meaning; but unlike the parable, it has a richness of surface as well as depth, so that it is interesting whether or not the reader goes on to ponder "the meaning." Like the anecdote, the short story relates a happening, but whereas the happening in the anecdote is curious and is the center of interest, the happening in the contemporary story often is less interesting in itself than as a manifestation of a character's state of mind. A good short story usually has a psychological interest that an anecdote lacks.

The anecdotal story is what "story" means for most readers. It is an interesting happening or series of happenings, usually with a somewhat surprising ending. The anecdotal story, however, is quite different from most of the contemporary short stories in this book. The anecdote is good entertainment, and good entertainment should not be lightly dismissed. But it has two elements within it that prevent it (unless it is something in addition to an anecdote) from taking a high place among the world's literature. First, it cannot be reread with increasing or even continued pleasure. Even when it is well told, once we know the happening we may lose patience with the telling. Second, effective anecdotes are often highly implausible. Now, implausible anecdotes alleged to be true have a special impact by virtue of their alleged truth: they make us say to ourselves, "Truth is stranger than fiction." But the invented anecdote lacks this power; its unlikely coincidence, its unconvincing ironic situation, its surprise ending, are both untrue and unbelievable. It is entertaining but it is usually not especially meaningful.

The short story of the last hundred and fifty years is not an anecdote and is not an abbreviated novel. If it were the latter, *Reader's Digest* condensations of novels would be short stories. But they aren't; they are only eviscerated novels. Novelists usually cover a long period of time, presenting not only a few individuals but also something of a society. They often tell of the development of several many-sided figures. In contrast, short-story writers, having only a few pages, usually focus on a single figure in a single episode, revealing a character rather than recording its development.

Whereas the novel is narrative, the contemporary short story often seems less narrative than lyric or dramatic: in the short story we have a sense of a present mood or personality revealed, rather than the sense of a history reported. The revelation in a story is presented through incidents, of course, but the interest commonly resides in the character revealed through the incidents, rather than in the incidents themselves. Little "happens," in the sense that there is little rushing from place to place. What does "happen" is usually a mental reaction to an experience, and the mental reaction, rather than the external experience, is the heart of the story. In older narratives the plot usually involves a conflict that is resolved, bringing about a change in the protagonist's condition; in contemporary stories the plot usually is designed to reveal a protagonist's state of mind. This de-emphasis of overt actions results in a kinship with the lyric and the drama.

One way of looking at the matter is to distinguish between literature of *resolution* and literature of *revelation,* that is, between (1) literature that resolves a plot (literature that stimulates us to ask, "And what happened next?" and that finally leaves us with a settled state of affairs), and (2) literature that reveals a condition (literature that causes us to say, "Ah, now I understand how these people feel"). Two great writers of the later nineteenth century can be taken as representatives of the two kinds: Guy de Maupassant (1850–93) usually puts the emphasis on resolution, Anton Chekhov (1860–1904) usually on revelation. Maupassant's tightly plotted stories move to a decisive end, ordinarily marked by a great change in fortune (usually to the characters' disadvantage). Chekhov's stories, on the other hand, seem loosely plotted and may end with the characters pretty much in the condition they were in at the start, but *we* see them more clearly, even if *they* have not achieved any self-knowledge.

A slightly different way of putting the matter is this: much of the best short fiction from Chekhov onward is less concerned with *what happens* than it is with how a character (often the narrator) *feels* about the happenings. Thus the emphasis is not on external action but on inner action, feeling. Perhaps one can say that the reader is left with a mood rather than with an awareness of a decisive happening.

The distinction between a story of resolution and a story of revelation will probably be clear enough if you are familiar with stories by Maupassant and Chekhov, but of course the distinction should not be overemphasized. These are poles; most stories exist somewhere in between, closer to one pole or the other, but not utterly apart from the more remote pole. Consider again The Parable of the Prodigal Son, in Chapter 1. Insofar as the story stimulates responses such as

"The son left, *and then what happened? Did he prosper?*" it is a story of resolution. Insofar as it makes increasingly evident the unchanging love of the father, it is a story of revelation.

The de-emphasis on narrative in the contemporary short story is not an invention of the twentieth-century mind. It goes back at least to three important American writers of the early nineteenth century—Washington Irving, Nathaniel Hawthorne, and Edgar Allan Poe. In 1824 Irving wrote:

> I fancy much of what I value myself upon in writing, escapes the observation of the great mass of my readers: who are intent more upon the story than the way in which it is told. For my part I consider a story merely as a frame on which to stretch my materials. It is the play of thought, and sentiments and language; the weaving in of characters, lightly yet expressively delineated; the familiar and faithful exhibition of scenes in common life; and the half-concealed vein of humor that is often playing through the whole—these are among what I aim at, and upon which I felicitate myself in proportion as I think I succeed.

Hawthorne and Poe may seem stranger than Irving as forebears of the contemporary short story: both are known for their fantastic narratives (and, in addition, Poe is known as the inventor of the detective story, a genre in which there is strong interest in curious happenings). But because Hawthorne's fantastic narratives are, as he said, highly allegorical, the reader's interest is pushed beyond the narrative to the moral significance. Poe's "arabesques," as he called his fanciful tales (in distinction from his detective tales of "ratiocination"), are aimed at revealing and arousing unusual mental states. The weird happenings and personages are symbolic representations of the mind or soul. In "The Cask of Amontillado," for instance, perhaps the chief interest is not in what happens but rather in the representation of an almost universal fear of being buried alive. But, it must be noted, in both Hawthorne and Poe we usually get what is commonly called the tale rather than the short story: We get short prose fiction dealing with the strange rather than the usual. (The distinction between the wondrous and the ordinary is discussed at some length in Chapter 12 "The Novel," page 602.)

A paragraph from Poe's review (1842) of Hawthorne's *Twice Told Tales,* though more useful in revealing Poe's theory of fiction than Hawthorne's, illuminates something of the kinship between the contemporary short story and the best short fictions of the earlier nineteenth century. In the review Poe has been explaining that because "unity of effect or impression" is essential, a tale (Poe doubtless uses "tale" to mean short fiction in general, rather than the special type just discussed) that can be read at a single sitting has an advantage over the novel.

> A skillful artist has constructed a tale. He has not fashioned his thoughts to accommodate his incidents, but having deliberately conceived a certain single effect to be wrought, he then invents such incidents, he then combines such events, and discusses them in such tone as may best serve him in establishing this preconceived effect. If his very first sentence tends not to be outbringing of this effect, then in his very first step has he committed a blunder. In the whole composition there should be no word written of which the tendency, direct or indirect, is not to the one pre-established design. And by such means, with such

> care and skill a picture is at length painted which leaves in the mind of him who contemplates it with a kindred art, a sense of the fullest satisfaction. The idea of the tale, its thesis, has been presented unblemished, because undisturbed—an end absolutely demanded, yet, in the novel, altogether unattainable.

Nothing that we have said should be construed as suggesting that short fiction from the mid-nineteenth century to the present is necessarily better than older short narratives. The object of these comments has been less to evaluate than to call attention to the characteristics dominating short fiction of the last century and a half. Not that all of this fiction is of a piece; the stories in this book demonstrate something of its variety. Readers who do not like one need not despair; they need only (in the words of an early writer of great short fiction) "turne over the leef and chese another tale."

## LEO TOLSTOY

*Leo Tolstoy (1828–1910) was born into a noble family on his parents' estate near Tula, Russia. Orphaned early, he was brought up by aunts and privately tutored. For a while he studied law at the University of Kazan, but he left without a degree and returned to his estate, where he made some unsuccessful efforts at educating the serfs. He then went to St. Petersburg and later to Moscow, where for a while he lived the life of a rake. While serving in the army (1851–55) he wrote his first book, an autobiographical work called* Childhood *(1852). After leaving the military Tolstoy shuttled between St. Petersburg and the family estate. His diary records his unhappiness with the loose life he was living. He then set up a school for peasants, which was unsuccessful. In 1862 he married, but his abundant infidelities made the marriage unhappy. During this period he wrote* War and Peace *(1869)—a prose epic on Napoleon's 1812 invasion of Russia—and* Anna Karenina *(1877), a novel about a woman tragically destroyed by her faith in romantic love.*

*About 1876 Tolstoy began a reexamination of his life, which led to a conversion to the Christian doctrine of love and to a doctrine of nonresistance to evil. Obsessed with trying to live a simple and saintly life, he decided to leave his family, intending to enter a monastery. His journey ended in the waiting room of a nearby railway station where he was fatally stricken. According to one report, as Tolstoy lay dying on the station master's couch, he whispered these last words to his son: "I love Truth . . . very much. . . . I love Truth." Another version of his last words: "I wonder how a peasant would die."*

*Yet another quotation, this one setting forth his view of the qualities of a writer, is of special interest. Tolstoy said that his brother Nicholas*

> *was a wonderful boy, and later a wonderful man. Turgenev used to say of him, very truly, that he lacked only certain faults to be a great writer. He lacked the chief fault necessary for authorship—vanity—and was not at all interested in what people thought of him. The qualities of a writer that he possessed were, first of all, a fine artistic sense, an extremely developed sense of proportion, a good-natured, gay sense of humor, an extraordinary, inexhaustible imagination, and a truthful and highly moral view of life.*

## *The Death of Ivan Ilych*

*Translated by Louise and Aylmer Maude*

### I

During an interval in the Melvinski trial in the large building of the Law Courts, the members and public prosecutor met in Ivan Egorovich Shebek's private room, where the conversation turned on the celebrated Krasovski case. Fëdor Vasilievich warmly maintained that it was not subject to their jurisdiction, Ivan Egorovich maintained the contrary, while Peter Ivanovich, not having entered into the discussion at the start, took no part in it but looked through the *Gazette* which had just been handed in.

"Gentlemen," he said, "Ivan Ilych has died!"

"You don't say so!"

"Here, read it yourself," replied Peter Ivanovich, handing Fëdor Vasilievich the paper still damp from the press. Surrounded by a black border were the words: "Praskovya Fëdorovna Golovina, with profound sorrow, informs relatives and friends of the demise of her beloved husband Ivan Ilych Golovin, Member of the Court of Justice, which occurred on February the 4th of this year 1882. The funeral will take place on Friday at one o'clock in the afternoon."

5 Ivan Ilych had been a colleague of the gentlemen present and was liked by them all. He had been ill for some weeks with an illness said to be incurable. His post had been kept open for him, but there had been conjectures that in case of his death Alexeev might receive his appointment, and that either Vinnikov or Shtabel would succeed Alexeev. So on receiving the news of Ivan Ilych's death the first thought of each of the gentlemen in that private room was of the changes and promotions it might occasion among themselves or their acquaintances.

"I shall be sure to get Shtabel's place or Vinnikov's," thought Fëdor Vasilievich. "I was promised that long ago, and the promotion means an extra eight hundred rubles a year for me besides the allowance."

"Now I must apply for my brother-in-law's transfer from Kaluga," thought Peter Ivanovich. "My wife will be very glad, and then she won't be able to say that I never do anything for her relations."

"I thought he would never leave his bed again," said Peter Ivanovich aloud. "It's very sad."

"But what really was the matter with him?"

10 "The doctors couldn't say—at least they could, but each of them said something different. When last I saw him I thought he was getting better."

"And I haven't been to see him since the holidays. I always meant to go."

"Had he any property?"

"I think his wife had a little—but something quite trifling."

"We shall have to go to see her, but they live so terribly far away."

15 "Far away from you, you mean. Everything's far away from your place."

"You see, he never can forgive my living on the other side of the river," said Peter Ivanovich, smiling at Shebek. Then, still talking of the distances between different parts of the city, they returned to the Court.

Besides considerations as to the possible transfers and promotions likely to result from Ivan Ilych's death, the mere fact of the death of a near acquaintance aroused, as usual, in all who heard of it the complacent feeling that "it is he who is dead and not I."

Each one thought or felt, "Well, he's dead but I'm alive!" But the more intimate of Ivan Ilych's acquaintances, his so-called friends, could not help thinking also that they would now have to fulfill the very tiresome demands of propriety by attending the funeral service and paying a visit of condolence to the widow.

Fëdor Vasilievich and Peter Ivanovich had been his nearest acquaintances. Peter Ivanovich had studied law with Ivan Ilych and had considered himself to be under obligations to him.

20 Having told his wife at dinner-time of Ivan Ilych's death and of his conjecture that it might be possible to get her brother transferred to their circuit, Peter Ivanovich sacrificed his usual nap, put on his evening clothes, and drove to Ivan Ilych's house.

At the entrance stood a carriage and two cabs. Leaning against the wall in the hall downstairs near the cloak-stand was a coffin-lid covered with cloth of gold, ornamented with gold cord and tassels, that had been polished up with metal powder. Two ladies in black were taking off their fur cloaks. Peter Ivanovich recognized one of them as Ivan Ilych's sister, but the other was a stranger to him. His colleague Schwartz was just coming downstairs, but on seeing Peter Ivanovich enter he stopped and winked at him, as if to say: "Ivan Ilych has made a mess of things—not like you and me."

Schwartz's face with his Piccadilly whiskers[1] and his slim figure in evening dress, had as usual an air of elegant solemnity which contrasted with the playfulness of his character and had a special piquancy here, or so it seemed to Peter Ivanovich.

Peter Ivanovich allowed the ladies to precede him and slowly followed them upstairs. Schwartz did not come down but remained where he was, and Peter Ivanovich understood that he wanted to arrange where they

[1]**Piccadilly whiskers** English-style sideburns

should play bridge that evening. The ladies went upstairs to the widow's room, and Schwartz with seriously compressed lips but a playful look in his eyes, indicated by a twist of his eyebrows the room to the right where the body lay.

Peter Ivanovich, like everyone else on such occasions, entered feeling uncertain what he would have to do. All he knew was that at such times it is always safe to cross oneself. But he was not quite sure whether one should make obeisances while doing so. He therefore adopted a middle course. On entering the room he began crossing himself and made a slight movement resembling a bow. At the same time, as far as the motion of his head and arm allowed, he surveyed the room. Two young men—apparently nephews, one of whom was a high-school pupil—were leaving the room, crossing themselves as they did so. An old woman was standing motionless, and a lady with strangely arched eyebrows was saying something to her in a whisper. A vigorous, resolute Church Reader, in a frock-coat, was reading something in a loud voice with an expression that precluded any contradiction. The butler's assistant, Gerasim, stepping lightly in front of Peter Ivanovich, was strewing something on the floor. Noticing this, Peter Ivanovich was immediately aware of a faint odor of a decomposing body. The last time he had called on Ivan Ilych, Peter Ivanovich had seen Gerasim in the study. Ivan Ilych had been particularly fond of him and he was performing the duty of a sick nurse.

Peter Ivanovich continued to make the sign of the cross, slightly inclining his head in an intermediate direction between the coffin, the Reader, and the icons[2] on the table in a corner of the room. Afterwards, when it seemed to him that this movement of his arm in crossing himself had gone on too long, he stopped and began to look at the corpse.

The dead man lay, as dead men always lie, in a specially heavy way, his rigid limbs sunk in the soft cushions of the coffin, with the head forever bowed on the pillow. His yellow waxen brow with bald patches over his sunken temples was thrust up in the way peculiar to the dead, the protruding nose seeming to press on the upper lip. He was much changed and had grown even thinner since Peter Ivanovich had last seen him, but, as is always the case with the dead, his face was handsomer and above all more dignified than when he was alive. The expression on his face said that what was necessary had been accomplished, and accomplished rightly. Besides this there was in that expression a reproach and a warning to the living. This warning seemed to Peter Ivanovich out of place, or at least not applicable to him. He felt a certain discomfort and so he hurriedly crossed himself once more and turned and went out the door—too hurriedly and too regardless of propriety, as he himself was aware.

Schwartz was waiting for him in the adjoining room with legs spread wide apart and both hands toying with his top-hat behind his back. The mere sight of that playful, well-groomed, and elegant figure refreshed Peter Ivanovich. He felt that Schwartz was above all these happenings and would not surrender to any depressing influences. His very look said that this incident of a church service for Ivan Ilych could not be a sufficient reason for infringing the order of the session—in other words, that it would certainly

[2] **icons** religious images, usually painted on small wooden panels

not prevent his unwrapping a new pack of cards and shuffling them that evening while a footman placed four fresh candles on the table: in fact, that there was no reason for supposing that this incident would hinder their spending the evening agreeably. Indeed he said this in a whisper as Peter Ivanovich passed him, proposing that they should meet for a game at Fëdor Vasilievich's. But apparently Peter Ivanovich was not destined to play bridge that evening. Praskovya Fëdorovna (a short, fat woman who despite all efforts to the contrary had continued to broaden steadily from her shoulders downwards and who had the same extraordinarily arched eyebrows as the lady who had been standing by the coffin), dressed all in black, her head covered with lace, came out of her own room with some other ladies, conducted them to the room where the dead body lay, and said: "The service will begin immediately. Please go in."

Schwartz, making an indefinite bow, stood still, evidently neither accepting nor declining this invitation. Praskovya Fëdorovna, recognizing Peter Ivanovich, sighed, went close up to him, took his hand, and said: "I know you were a true friend of Ivan Ilych . . ." and looked at him awaiting some suitable response. And Peter Ivanovich knew that, just as it had been the right thing to cross himself in that room, so what he had to do here was to press her hand, sigh, and say, "Believe me . . . ." So he did all this and as he did it felt that the desired result had been achieved: that both he and she were touched.

"Come with me. I want to speak to you before it begins," said the widow. "Give me your arm."

Peter Ivanovich gave her his arm and they went to the inner rooms, passing Schwartz, who winked at Peter Ivanovich compassionately.

"That does for our bridge! Don't object if we find another player. Perhaps you can cut in when you do escape," said his playful look.

Peter Ivanovich sighed still more deeply and despondently, and Praskovya Fëdorovna pressed his arm gratefully. When they reached the drawing-room, upholstered in pink cretonne and lighted by a dim lamp, they sat down at the table—she on a sofa and Peter Ivanovich on a low pouffe, the springs of which yielded spasmodically under his weight. Praskovya Fëdorovna had been on the point of warning him to take another seat, but felt that such a warning was out of keeping with her present condition and so changed her mind. As he sat down on the pouffe Peter Ivanovich recalled how Ivan Ilych had arranged this room and had consulted him regarding this pink cretonne with green leaves. The whole room was full of furniture and knick-knacks, and on her way to the sofa the lace of the widow's black shawl caught on the carved edge of the table. Peter Ivanovich rose to detach it, and the springs of the pouffe, relieved of his weight, rose also and gave him a push. The widow began detaching her shawl herself, and Peter Ivanovich again sat down, suppressing the rebellious springs of the pouffe under him. But the widow had not quite freed herself and Peter Ivanovich got up again, and again the pouffe rebelled and even creaked. When this was all over she took out a clean cambric handkerchief and began to weep. The episode with the shawl and the struggle with the pouffe had cooled Peter Ivanovich's emotions and he sat there with a sullen look on his face. This awkward situation was interrupted by Sokolov, Ivan Ilych's butler, who came to report that the plot in the cemetery that Praskovya Fëdorovna had chosen would cost two hundred rubles. She stopped weeping and, looking at Peter Ivanovich with the air of a victim, remarked in French that it was very hard for her. Peter Ivanovich made a silent gesture signifying his full conviction that it must indeed be so.

"Please smoke," she said in a magnanimous yet crushed voice, and turned to discuss with Sokolov the price of the plot for the grave.

35 Peter Ivanovich while lighting his cigarette heard her inquiring very circumstantially into the price of different plots in the cemetery and finally decided which she would take. When that was done she gave instructions about engaging the choir. Sokolov then left the room.

"I look after everything myself," she told Peter Ivanovich, shifting the albums that lay on the table; and noticing that the table was endangered by his cigarette-ash, she immediately passed him an ashtray, saying as she did so: "I consider it an affectation to say that my grief prevents my attending to practical affairs. On the contrary, if anything can—I won't say console me, but—distract me, it is seeing to everything concerning him." She again took out her handkerchief as if preparing to cry, but suddenly, as if mastering her feeling, she shook herself and began to speak calmly. "But there is something I want to talk to you about."

Peter Ivanovich bowed, keeping control of the springs of the pouffe, which immediately began quivering under him.

"He suffered terribly the last few days."

"Did he?" said Peter Ivanovich.

40 "Oh, terribly! He screamed unceasingly, not for minutes but for hours. For the last three days he screamed incessantly. It was unendurable. I cannot understand how I bore it; you could hear him three rooms off. Oh, what I have suffered!"

"Is it possible that he was conscious all that time?" asked Peter Ivanovich.

"Yes," she whispered. "To the last moment. He took leave of us a quarter of an hour before he died, and asked us to take Vasya away."

The thought of the sufferings of this man he had known so intimately, first as a merry little boy, then as a school-mate, and later as a grown-up colleague, suddenly struck Peter Ivanovich with horror, despite an unpleasant consciousness of his own and this woman's dissimulation. He again saw that brow, and that nose pressing down on the lip, and felt afraid for himself.

"Three days of frightful suffering and then death! Why, that might suddenly, at any time, happen to me," he thought, and for a moment felt terrified. But—he did not himself know how—the customary reflection at once occurred to him that this had happened to Ivan Ilych and not to him, and that it should not and could not happen to him, and that to think that it could would be yielding to depression which he ought not to do, as Schwartz's expression plainly showed. After which reflection Peter Ivanovich felt reassured, and began to ask with interest about the details of Ivan Ilych's death, as though death was an accident natural to Ivan Ilych but certainly not to himself.

45 After many details of the really dreadful physical sufferings Ivan Ilych had endured (which details he learnt only from the effect those sufferings had produced on Praskovya Fëdorovna's nerves) the widow apparently found it necessary to get to business.

"Oh, Peter Ivanovich, how hard it is! How terribly, terribly hard!" and she again began to weep.

Peter Ivanovich sighed and waited for her to finish blowing her nose. When she had done so he said, "Believe me . . ." and she again began talking and brought out what was evidently her chief concern with him—namely, to question him as to how she could obtain a grant of money from the government on the occasion of her husband's death. She made it appear that she was asking Peter Ivanovich's advice about her pension, but he soon saw that she already knew about that to the minutest detail, more even than he did himself. She knew how much could be got out of the government in consequence of her husband's death, but wanted to find out whether she could not possibly extract something more. Peter Ivanovich tried to think of some means of doing so, but after reflecting for a while and, out of propriety, condemning the government for its niggardliness, he said he thought that nothing more could be got. Then she sighed and evidently began to devise means of getting rid of her visitor. Noticing this, he put out his cigarette, rose, pressed her hand, and went out into the anteroom.

In the dining-room where the clock stood that Ivan Ilych had liked so much and had bought at an antique shop, Peter Ivanovich met a priest and a few acquaintances who had come to attend the service, and he recognized Ivan Ilych's daughter, a handsome young woman. She was in black and her slim figure appeared slimmer than ever. She had a gloomy, determined, almost angry expression, and bowed to Peter Ivanovich as though he were in some way to blame. Behind her, with the same offended look, stood a wealthy young man, an examining magistrate, whom Peter Ivanovich also knew and who was her fiancé, as he had heard. He bowed mournfully to them and was about to pass into the death-chamber, when from under the stairs appeared the figure of Ivan Ilych's schoolboy son, who was extremely like his father. He seemed a little Ivan Ilych, such as Peter Ivanovich remembered when they studied law together. His tear-stained eyes had in them the look that is seen in the eyes of boys of thirteen or fourteen who are not pure-minded. When he saw Peter Ivanovich he scowled morosely and shamefacedly. Peter Ivanovich nodded to him and entered the death-chamber. The service began: candles, groans, incense, tears, and sobs. Peter Ivanovich stood looking gloomily down at his feet. He did not look once at the dead man, did not yield to any depressing influence, and was one of the first to leave the room. There was no one in the anteroom, but Gerasim darted out of the dead man's room, rummaged with his strong hands among the fur coats to find Peter Ivanovich's, and helped him on with it.

"Well, friend Gerasim," said Peter Ivanovich, so as to say something. "It's a sad affair, isn't it?"

50 "It's God's will. We shall all come to it some day," said Gerasim, displaying his teeth—the even, white teeth of a healthy peasant—and, like a man in the thick of urgent work, he briskly opened the front door, called the coachman, helped Peter Ivanovich into the sledge, and sprang back to the porch as if in readiness for what he had to do next.

Peter Ivanovich found the fresh air particularly pleasant after the smell of incense, the dead body, and carbolic acid.

"Where to, sir?" asked the coachman.

"It's not too late even now . . . I'll call round on Fëdor Vasilievich."

He accordingly drove there and found them just finishing the first rubber, so that it was quite convenient for him to cut in.

## II

55 Ivan Ilych's life had been most simple and most ordinary and therefore most terrible.

He had been a member of the Court of Justice, and died at the age of forty-five. His father had been an official who after serving in various ministries and departments in Petersburg[3] had made the sort of career which brings men to positions from which by reason of their long service they cannot be dismissed, though they are obviously unfit to hold any responsible position, and for whom therefore posts are specially created, which though fictitious carry salaries of from six to ten thousand rubles that are not fictitious, and in receipt of which they live on to a great age.

Such was the Privy Councillor and superfluous member of various superfluous institutions, Ilya Epimovich Golovin.

He had three sons, of whom Ivan Ilych was the second. The eldest son was following in his father's footsteps only in another department, and was already approaching that stage in the service at which a similar sinecure would be reached. The third son was a failure. He had ruined his prospects in a number of positions and was now serving in the railway department. His father and brothers, and still more their wives, not merely disliked meeting him, but avoided remembering his existence unless compelled to do so. His sister had married Baron Greff, a Petersburg official of her father's type. Ivan Ilych was *le phénix de la famille*[4] as people said. He was neither as cold and formal as his elder brother nor as wild as the younger, but was a happy mean between them—an intelligent, polished, lively, and agreeable man. He had studied with his younger brother at the School of Law, but the latter had failed to complete the course and was expelled when he was in the fifth class. Ivan Ilych finished the course well. Even when he was at the School of Law he was just what he remained for the rest of his life: a capable, cheerful, good-natured, and sociable man, though strict in the fulfillment of what he considered to be his duty, and he considered his duty, to be what was so considered by those in authority. Neither as a boy nor as a man was he a toady, but from early youth was by nature attracted to people of high station as a fly is drawn to the light, assimilating their ways and views of life and establishing friendly relations with them. All the enthusiasms of childhood and youth passed without leaving much trace on him; he succumbed to sensuality, to vanity, and latterly among the highest classes to liberalism, but always within limits which his instinct unfailingly indicated to him as correct.

[3]**Petersburg** the capital of Russia and its social and intellectual center from the eighteenth century until 1918. It was named for Peter the Great, who built it.

[4]***le phénix de la famille*** French (members of the upper class often spoke French, a sign of their sophistication), literally meaning "the phoenix of the family," i.e., the prodigy of the family

At school he had done things which had formerly seemed to him very horrid and made him feel disgusted with himself when he did them; but when later on he saw that such actions were done by people of good position and that they did not regard them as wrong, he was able not exactly to regard them as right, but to forget about them entirely or not be at all troubled at remembering them.

60 Having graduated from the School of Law and qualified for the tenth rank of the civil service, and having received money from his father for his equipment, Ivan Ilych ordered himself clothes at Scharmer's, the fashionable tailor, hung a medallion inscribed *respice finem*[5] on his watch-chain, took leave of his professor and the prince who was patron of the school, had a farewell dinner with his comrades at Donon's first-class restaurant, and with his new and fashionable portmanteau, linen, clothes, shaving and other toilet appliances, and a traveling rug, all purchased at the best shops, he set off for one of the provinces where, through his father's influence, he had been attached to the Governor as an official for special service.

In the province Ivan Ilych soon arranged as easy and agreeable a position for himself as he had had at the School of Law. He performed his official tasks, made his career, and at the same time amused himself pleasantly and decorously. Occasionally he paid official visits to country districts, where he behaved with dignity both to his superiors and inferiors, and performed the duties entrusted to him, which related chiefly to the sectarians,[6] with an exactness and incorruptible honesty of which he could not but feel proud.

In official matters, despite his youth and taste for frivolous gaiety, he was exceedingly reserved, punctilious, and even severe; but in society he was often amusing and witty, and always good-natured, correct in his manner, and *bon enfant*,[7] as the governor and his wife—with whom he was like one of the family—used to say of him.

In the province he had an affair with a lady who made advances to the elegant young lawyer, and there was also a milliner; and there were carousals with aides-de-camp who visited the district, and after-supper visits to a certain outlying street of doubtful reputation; and there was too some obsequiousness to his chief and even to his chief's wife, but all this was done with such a tone of good breeding that no hard names could be applied to it. It all came under the heading of the French saying: *"Il faut que jeunesse se passe."*[8] It was all done with clean hands, in clean linen, with French phrases, and above all among people of the best society and consequently with the approval of people of rank.

So Ivan Ilych served for five years and then came a change in his official life. The new and reformed judicial institutions were introduced, and new men were needed. Ivan Ilych became such a new man. He was offered the

[5]***respice finem*** Latin, "Consider the end" (i.e., keep death in mind)

[6]**sectarians** Old Believers, a sect that in the seventeenth century had broken with the Orthodox Church

[7]***bon enfant*** French, literally "good child," here "well-behaved"

[8]***Il faut que jeunesse se passe*** French, "Youth will have its fling."

post of examining magistrate, and he accepted it though the post was in another province and obliged him to give up the connections he had formed and to make new ones. His friends met to give him a send-off; they had a group-photograph taken and presented him with a silver cigarette-case, and he set off to his new post.

65 As examining magistrate Ivan Ilych was just as *comme il faut*[9] and decorous a man, inspiring general respect and capable of separating his official duties from his private life, as he had been when acting as an official on special service. His duties now as examining magistrate were far more interesting and attractive than before. In his former position it had been pleasant to wear an undress uniform made by Scharmer, and to pass through the crowd of petitioners and officials who were timorously awaiting an audience with the governor, and who envied him as with free and easy gait he went straight into his chief's private room to have a cup of tea and a cigarette with him. But not many people had been directly dependent on him—only police officials and the sectarians when he went on special missions—and he liked to treat them politely, almost as comrades, as if he were letting them feel that he who had the power to crush them was treating them in this simple, friendly way. There were then but few such people. But now, as an examining magistrate, Ivan Ilych felt that everyone without exception, even the most important and self-satisfied, was in his power, and that he need only write a few words on a sheet of paper with a certain heading, and this or that important, self-satisfied person would be brought before him in the role of an accused person or a witness, and if he did not choose to allow him to sit down, would have to stand before him and answer his questions. Ivan Ilych never abused his power; he tried on the contrary to soften its expression, but the consciousness of it and of the possibility of softening its effect, supplied the chief interest and attraction of his office. In his work itself, especially in his examinations, he very soon acquired a method of eliminating all considerations irrelevant to the legal aspect of the case, and reducing even the most complicated case to a form in which it would be presented on paper only in its externals, completely excluding his personal opinion of the matter, while above all observing every prescribed formality. The work was new and Ivan Ilych was one of the first men to apply the new Code of 1864.[10]

On taking up the post of examining magistrate in a new town, he made new acquaintances and connections, placed himself on a new footing, and assumed a somewhat different tone. He took up an attitude of rather dignified aloofness towards the provincial authorities, but picked out the best circle of legal gentlemen and wealthy gentry living in the town and assumed a tone of slight dissatisfaction with the government, of moderate liberalism, and of enlightened citizenship. At the same time, without at all altering the elegance of his toilet, he ceased shaving his chin and allowed his beard to grow as it pleased.

Ivan Ilych settled down very pleasantly in this new town. The society there, which inclined towards opposition to the governor, was friendly, his salary was larger, and he began to play *vint*,[11] which he found added not a

[9]***comme il faut*** French, "proper"
[10]**Code of 1864** body of statutes governing judicial processes
[11]***vint*** a card game similar to bridge

little to the pleasure of life, for he had a capacity for cards, played good-humoredly, and calculated rapidly and astutely, so that he usually won.

After living there for two years he met his future wife, Praskovya Fëdorovna Mikhel, who was the most attractive, clever, and brilliant girl of the set in which he moved, and among other amusements and relaxations from his labors as examining magistrate, Ivan Ilych established light and playful relations with her.

While he had been an official on special service he had been accustomed to dance, but now as an examining magistrate it was exceptional for him to do so. If he danced now, he did it as if to show that though he served under the reformed order of things, and had reached the fifth official rank, yet when it came to dancing he could do it better than most people. So at the end of an evening he sometimes danced with Praskovya Fëdorovna, and it was chiefly during these dances that he captivated her. She fell in love with him. Ivan Ilych had at first no definite intention of marrying, but when the girl fell in love with him he said to himself: "Really, why shouldn't I marry?"

Praskovya Fëdorovna came of a good family, was not bad-looking, and had some little property. Ivan Ilych might have aspired to a more brilliant match, but even this was good. He had his salary, and she, he hoped, would have an equal income. She was well connected, and was a sweet, pretty, and thoroughly correct young woman. To say that Ivan Ilych married because he fell in love with Praskovya Fëdorovna and found that she sympathized with his views of life would be as incorrect as to say that he married because his social circle approved of the match. He was swayed by both these considerations: the marriage gave him personal satisfaction, and at the same time it was considered the right thing by the most highly placed of his associates.

So Ivan Ilych got married.

The preparations for marriage and the beginning of married life, with its conjugal caresses, the new furniture, new crockery, and new linen, were very pleasant until his wife became pregnant—so that Ivan Ilych had begun to think that marriage would not impair the easy, agreeable, gay, and always decorous character of his life, approved of by society and regarded by himself as natural, but would even improve it. But from the first months of his wife's pregnancy, something new, unpleasant, depressing, and unseemly, and from which there was no way of escape, unexpectedly showed itself.

His wife, without any reason—*de gaieté de coeur*[12] as Ivan Ilych expressed it to himself—began to disturb the pleasure and propriety of their life. She began to be jealous without any cause, expected him to devote his whole attention to her, found fault with everything, and made coarse and ill-mannered scenes.

At first Ivan Ilych hoped to escape from the unpleasantness of this state of affairs by the same easy and decorous relation to life that had served him heretofore: he tried to ignore his wife's disagreeable moods, continued to live in his usual easy and pleasant way, invited friends to his house for a game of cards, and also tried going out to his club or spending his evenings with friends. But one day his wife began upbraiding him so vigorously, using such coarse words, and continued to abuse him every time he did not

[12]***de gaieté de coeur*** French, "from sheer whim"

fulfill her demands, so resolutely and with such evident determination not to give way till he submitted—that is, till he stayed at home and was bored just as she was—that he became alarmed. He now realized that matrimony—at any rate with Praskovya Fëdorovna—was not always conducive to the pleasures and amenities of life, but on the contrary often infringed both comfort and propriety, and that he must therefore entrench himself against such infringement. And Ivan Ilych began to seek for means of doing so. His official duties were the one thing that imposed upon Praskovya Fëdorovna, and by means of his official work and the duties attached to it he began struggling with his wife to secure his own independence.

75 With the birth of their child, the attempts to feed it and the various failures in doing so, and with the real and imaginary illnesses of mother and child, in which Ivan Ilych's sympathy was demanded but about which he understood nothing, the need of securing for himself an existence outside his family life became still more imperative.

As his wife grew more irritable and exacting and Ivan Ilych transferred the center of gravity of his life more and more to his official work so did he grow to like his work better and became more ambitious than before.

Very soon, within a year of his wedding, Ivan Ilych had realized that marriage, though it may add some comforts to life, is in fact a very intricate and difficult affair towards which in order to perform one's duty, that is, to lead a decorous life approved of by society, one must adopt a definite attitude just as towards one's official duties.

And Ivan Ilych evolved such an attitude towards married life. He only required of it those conveniences—dinner at home, housewife, and bed—which it could give him, and above all that propriety of external forms required by public opinion. For the rest he looked for light-hearted pleasure and propriety, and was very thankful when he found them, but if he met with antagonism and querulousness he at once retired into his separate fenced-off world of official duties, where he found satisfaction.

Ivan Ilych was esteemed a good official, and after three years was made Assistant Public Prosecutor. His new duties, their importance, the possibility of indicting and imprisoning anyone he chose, the publicity his speeches received, and the success he had in all these things made his work still more attractive.

80 More children came. His wife became more and more querulous and ill-tempered, but the attitude Ivan Ilych had adopted towards his home life rendered him almost impervious to her grumbling.

After seven years' service in that town he was transferred to another province as Public Prosecutor. They moved, but were short of money and his wife did not like the place they moved to. Though the salary was higher the cost of living was greater, besides which two of their children died and family life became still more unpleasant for him.

Praskovya Fëdorovna blamed her husband for every inconvenience they encountered in their new home. Most of the conversations between husband and wife, especially as to the children's education, led to topics which recalled former disputes, and those disputes were apt to flare up again at any moment. There remained only those rare periods of amorousness which still came to them at times but did not last long. These were islets at which they anchored for a while and then again set out upon that ocean of veiled hostility which showed itself in their aloofness from one another. This aloofness might have grieved Ivan Ilych had he considered that it ought not to exist, but he now regarded the position as normal, and even made it the goal at which he aimed in family life. His aim was to free himself more and more from those unpleasantnesses and to give them a semblance of harmlessness and propriety. He attained this by spending less and less time with his family, and when obliged to be at home he tried to safeguard his position by the presence of outsiders. The chief thing however was that he had his official duties. The whole interest of his life now centered in the official world and that interest absorbed him. The consciousness of his power, being able to ruin anybody he wished to ruin, the importance, even the external dignity of his entry into court, or meetings with his subordinates, his success with superiors and inferiors, and above all his masterly handling of cases, of which he was conscious—all this gave him pleasure and filled his life, together with chats with his colleagues, dinners, and bridge. So that on the whole Ivan Ilych's life continued to flow as he considered it should do—pleasantly and properly.

So things continued for another seven years. His eldest daughter was already sixteen, another child had died, and only one son was left, a schoolboy and a subject of dissension. Ivan Ilych wanted to put him in the School of Law, but to spite him Praskovya Fëdorovna entered him at the High School. The daughter had been educated at home and had turned out well: the boy did not learn badly either.

## III

So Ivan Ilych lived for seventeen years after his marriage. He was already a Public Prosecutor of long standing, and had declined several proposed transfers while awaiting a more desirable post, when an unanticipated and unpleasant occurrence quite upset the peaceful course of his life. He was expecting to be offered the post of presiding judge in a University town, but Happe somehow came to the front and obtained the appointment instead. Ivan Ilych became irritable, reproached Happe, and quarreled both with him and with his immediate superiors—who became colder to him and again passed him over when other appointments were made.

85 This was in 1880, the hardest year of Ivan Ilych's life. It was then that it became evident on the one hand that his salary was insufficient for them to live on, and on the other that he had been forgotten, and not only this, but that what was for him the greatest and most cruel injustice appeared to others a quite ordinary occurrence. Even his father did not consider it his duty to help him. Ivan Ilych felt himself abandoned by everyone, and that they regarded his position with a salary of 3,500 rubles as quite normal and even fortunate. He alone knew that with the consciousness of the injustices done him, with his wife's incessant nagging, and with the debts he had contracted by living beyond his means, his position was far from normal.

In order to save money that summer he obtained leave of absence and went with his wife to live in the country at her brother's place.

In the country, without his work, he experienced *ennui* for the first time in his life, and not only *ennui* but intolerable depression, and he decided that it was impossible to go on living like that, and that it was necessary to take energetic measures.

Having passed a sleepless night pacing up and down the veranda, he decided to go to Petersburg and bestir himself, in order to punish those who had failed to appreciate him and to get transferred to another ministry.

Next day, despite many protests from his wife and her brother, he started for Petersburg with the sole object of obtaining a post with a salary of five thousand rubles a year. He was no longer bent on any particular department, or tendency, or kind of activity. All he now wanted was an appointment to another post with a salary of five thousand rubles, either in the administration, in the banks, with the railways, in one of the Empress Marya's Institutions, or even in the customs—but it had to carry with it a salary of five thousand rubles and be in a ministry other than that in which they had failed to appreciate him.

90 And this quest of Ivan Ilych's was crowned with remarkable and unexpected success. At Kursk an acquaintance of his, F. I. Ilyin, got into the first-class carriage, sat down beside Ivan Ilych, and told him of a telegram just received by the Governor of Kursk announcing that a change was about to take place in the ministry: Peter Ivanovich was to be superseded by Ivan Semënovich.

The proposed change, apart from its significance for Russia, had a special significance for Ivan Ilych, because by bringing forward a new man, Peter Petrovich, and consequently his friend Zachar Ivanovich, it was highly favorable for Ivan Ilych, since Zachar Ivanovich was a friend and colleague of his.

In Moscow this news was confirmed, and on reaching Petersburg Ivan Ilych found Zachar Ivanovich and received a definite promise of an appointment in his former department of Justice.

A week later he telegraphed to his wife: "Zachar in Miller's place. I shall receive appointment on presentation of report."

Thanks to this change of personnel, Ivan Ilych had unexpectedly obtained an appointment in his former ministry which placed him two stages above his former colleagues besides giving him five thousand rubles salary and three thousand five hundred rubles for expenses connected with his removal. All his ill humor towards his former enemies and the whole department vanished, and Ivan Ilych was completely happy.

95 He returned to the country more cheerful and contented than he had been for a long time. Praskovya Fëdorovna also cheered up and a truce was arranged between them. Ivan Ilych told of how he had been fêted by everybody in Petersburg, how all those who had been his enemies were put to shame and now fawned on him, how envious they were of his appointment, and how much everybody in Petersburg had liked him.

Praskovya Fëdorovna listened to all this and appeared to believe it. She did not contradict anything, but only made plans for their life in the town to which they were going. Ivan Ilych saw with delight that these plans were his plans, that he and his wife agreed, and that, after a stumble, his life was regaining its due and natural character of pleasant lightheartedness and decorum.

Ivan Ilych had come back for a short time only, for he had to take up his new duties on the 10th of September. Moreover, he needed time to settle into the new place, to move all his belongings from the province, and to buy and order many additional things: in a word, to make such arrangements as he had resolved on, which were almost exactly what Praskovya Fëdorovna too had decided on.

Now that everything had happened so fortunately, and that he and his wife were at one in their aims and moreover saw so little of one another, they got on together better than they had done since the first years of marriage. Ivan Ilych had thought of taking his family away with him at once, but the insistence of his wife's brother and her sister-in-law, who had suddenly become particularly amiable and friendly to him and his family, induced him to depart alone.

So he departed, and the cheerful state of mind induced by his success and by the harmony between his wife and himself, the one intensifying the other, did not leave him. He found a delightful house, just the thing both he and his wife had dreamt of. Spacious, lofty reception rooms in the old style, a convenient and dignified study, rooms for his wife and daughter, a study for his son—it might have been specially built for them. Ivan Ilych himself superintended the arrangements, chose the wallpapers, supplemented the furniture (preferably with antiques which he considered particularly *comme il faut*), and supervised the upholstering. Everything progressed and progressed and approached the ideal he had set himself: even when things were only half completed they exceeded his expectations. He saw what a refined and elegant character, free from vulgarity, it would all have when it was ready. On falling asleep he pictured to himself how the reception-room would look. Looking at the yet unfinished drawing-room he could see the fireplace, the screen, the what-not, the little chairs dotted here and there, the dishes and plates on the walls, and the bronzes, as they would be when everything was in place. He was pleased by the thought of how his wife and daughter, who shared his taste in this matter, would be impressed by it. They were certainly not expecting as much. He had been particularly successful in finding, and buying cheaply, antiques which gave a particularly aristocratic character to the whole place. But in his letters he intentionally understated everything in order to be able to surprise them. All this so absorbed him that his new duties—though he liked his official work—interested him less than he had expected. Sometimes he even had moments of absent-mindedness during the Court Sessions, and would consider whether he should have straight or curved cornices for his curtains. He was so interested in it all that he often did things himself, rearranging the furniture, or rehanging the curtains. Once when mounting a step-ladder to show the upholsterer, who did not understand, how he wanted the hangings draped, he made a false step and slipped, but being a strong and agile man he clung on and only knocked his side against the knob of the window frame. The bruised place was painful but the pain soon passed, and he felt particularly bright and well just then. He wrote: "I feel fifteen years younger." He thought he would have everything ready by September, but it dragged on till mid-October. But the result was charming not only in his eyes but to everyone who saw it.

In reality it was just what is usually seen in the houses of people of moderate means who want to appear rich, and therefore succeed only in resembling others like themselves: there were damasks, dark wood, plants, rugs, and dull and polished bronzes—all the things people of a certain class have in order to resemble other people of that class. His house was so like the others that it would never have been noticed, but to him it all seemed to be quite exceptional. He was very happy when he met his family at the station and brought them to the newly furnished house all lit up, where a footman in a white tie opened the door into the hall decorated with plants, and when they went on into the drawing-room and the study uttering exclamations of delight. He conducted them everywhere, drank in their praises eagerly, and beamed with pleasure. At tea that evening, when Praskovya Fëdorovna among other things asked him about his fall, he laughed and showed them how he had gone flying and had frightened the upholsterer.

"It's a good thing I'm a bit of an athlete. Another man might have been killed, but I merely knocked myself, just here; it hurts when it's touched, but it's passing off already—it's only a bruise."

So they began living in their new home—in which, as always happens, when they got thoroughly settled in they found they were just one room short—and with the increased income, which as always was just a little (some five hundred rubles) too little, but it was all very nice.

Things went particularly well at first, before everything was finally arranged and while something had still to be done: this thing bought, that thing ordered, another thing moved, and something else adjusted. Though there were some disputes between husband and wife, they were both so well satisfied and had so much to do that it all passed off without any serious quarrels. When nothing was left to arrange it became rather dull and something seemed to be lacking, but they were then making acquaintances, forming habits, and life was growing fuller.

Ivan Ilych spent his mornings at the law court and came home to dinner, and at first he was generally in a good humor, though he occasionally became irritable just on account of his house. (Every spot on the tablecloth or the upholstery, and every broken windowblind string, irritated him. He had devoted so much trouble to arranging it all that every disturbance of it distressed him.) But on the whole his life ran its course as he believed life should do: easily, pleasantly, and decorously.

105 He got up at nine, drank his coffee, read the paper, and then put on his undress uniform and went to the law courts. There the harness in which he worked had already been stretched to fit him and he donned it without a hitch: petitioners, inquiries at the chancery, the chancery itself, and the sittings public and administrative. In all this the thing was to exclude everything fresh and vital, which always disturbs the regular course of official business, and to admit only official relations with people, and then only on official grounds. A man would come, for instance, wanting some information. Ivan Ilych, as one in whose sphere the matter did not lie, would have nothing to do with him: but if the man had some business with him in his official capacity, something that could be expressed on officially stamped paper, he would do everything, positively everything he could within the limits of such relations, and in doing so would maintain the semblance of friendly human relations, that is, would observe the courtesies of life. As soon as the official relations ended, so did everything else. Ivan Ilych possessed this capacity to separate his real life from the official side of affairs and not mix the two, in the highest degree, and by long practice and natural aptitude had brought it to such a pitch that sometimes, in the manner of a virtuoso, he would even allow himself to let the human and official relations mingle. He let himself do this just because he felt that he could at any time he chose resume the strictly official attitude again and drop the human relation. And he did it all easily, pleasantly, correctly, and even artistically. In the intervals between the sessions he smoked, drank tea, chatted a little about politics, a little about general topics, a little about cards, but most of all about official appointments. Tired, but with the feelings of a virtuoso—

one of the first violins who has played his part in an orchestra with precision—he would return home to find that his wife and daughter had been out paying calls, or had a visitor, and that his son had been to school, had done his homework with his tutor, and was duly learning what is taught at High Schools. Everything was as it should be. After dinner, if they had no visitors, Ivan Ilych sometimes read a book that was being much discussed at the time, and in the evening settled down to work, that is, read official papers, compared the depositions of witnesses, and noted paragraphs of the Code applying to them. This was neither dull nor amusing. It was dull when he might have been playing bridge, but if no bridge was available it was at any rate better than doing nothing or sitting with his wife. Ivan Ilych's chief pleasure was giving little dinners to which he invited men and women of good social position, and just as his drawing-room resembled all other drawing-rooms so did his enjoyable little parties resemble all other such parties.

Once they even gave a dance. Ivan Ilych enjoyed it and everything went off well, except that it led to a violent quarrel with his wife about the cakes and sweets. Praskovya Fëdorovna had made her own plans, but Ivan Ilych insisted on getting everything from an expensive confectioner and ordered too many cakes, and the quarrel occurred because some of those cakes were left over and the confectioner's bill came to forty-five rubles. It was a great and disagreeable quarrel. Praskovya Fëdorovna called him "a fool and an imbecile," and he clutched at his head and made angry allusions to divorce.

But the dance itself had been enjoyable. The best people were there, and Ivan Ilych had danced with Princess Trufonova, a sister of the distinguished founder of the Society "Bear My Burden."

The pleasures connected with his work were pleasures of ambition; his social pleasures were those of vanity; but Ivan Ilych's greatest pleasure was playing bridge. He acknowledged that whatever disagreeable incident happened in his life, the pleasure that beamed like a ray of light above everything else was to sit down to bridge with good players, not noisy partners, and of course to four-handed bridge (with five players it was annoying to have to stand out, though one pretended not to mind), to play a clever and serious game (when the cards allowed it), and then to have supper and drink a glass of wine. After a game of bridge, especially if he had won a little (to win a large sum was unpleasant), Ivan Ilych went to bed in specially good humor.

So they lived. They formed a circle of acquaintances among the best people and were visited by people of importance and by young folk. In their views as to their acquaintances, husband, wife, and daughter were entirely agreed, and tacitly and unanimously kept at arm's length and shook off the various shabby friends and relations who, with much show of affection, gushed into the drawing-room with its Japanese plates on the walls. Soon these shabby friends ceased to obtrude themselves and only the best people remained in the Golovins' set.

110 Young men made up to Lisa, and Petrischev, an examining magistrate and Dmitri Ivanovich Petrischev's son and sole heir, began to be so attentive to her that Ivan Ilych had already spoken to Praskovya Fëdorovna about it, and considered whether they should not arrange a party for them, or get up some private theatricals.

So they lived, and all went well, without change, and life flowed pleasantly.

## IV

They were all in good health. It could not be called ill health if Ivan Ilych sometimes said that he had a queer taste in his mouth and felt some discomfort in his left side.

But this discomfort increased and, though not exactly painful, grew into a sense of pressure in his side accompanied by ill humor. And his irritability became worse and worse and began to mar the agreeable, easy, and correct life that had established itself in the Golovin family. Quarrels between husband and wife became more and more frequent, and soon the ease and amenity disappeared and even the decorum was barely maintained. Scenes again became frequent, and very few of those islets remained on which husband and wife could meet without an explosion. Praskovya Fëdorovna now had good reason to say that her husband's temper was trying. With characteristic exaggeration she said he had always had a dreadful temper, and that it had needed all her good nature to put up with it for twenty years. It was true that now the quarrels were started by him. His bursts of temper always came just before dinner, often just as he began to eat his soup. Sometimes he noticed that a plate or dish was chipped, or the food was not right, or his son put his elbow on the table, or his daughter's hair was not done as he liked it, and for all this he blamed Praskovya Fëdorovna. At first she retorted and said disagreeable things to him, but once or twice he fell into such a rage at the beginning of dinner that she realized it was due to some physical derangement brought on by taking food, and so she restrained herself and did not answer, but only hurried to get the dinner over. She regarded this self-restraint as highly praiseworthy. Having come to the conclusion that her husband had a dreadful temper and made her life miserable, she began to feel sorry for herself, and the more she pitied herself the more she hated her husband. She began to wish he would die; yet she did not want him to die because then his salary would cease. And this irritated her against him still more. She considered herself dreadfully unhappy just because not even his death could save her, and though she concealed her exasperation, that hidden exasperation of hers increased his irritation also.

After one scene in which Ivan Ilych had been particularly unfair and after which he had said in explanation that he certainly was irritable but that it was due to his not being well, she said that if he was ill it should be attended to, and insisted on his going to see a celebrated doctor.

115 He went. Everything took place as he had expected and as it always does. There was the usual waiting and the important air assumed by the doctor, with which he was so familiar (resembling that which he himself assumed in court), and the sounding and listening, and the questions which called for answers that were foregone conclusions and were evidently unnecessary, and the look of importance which implied that "if only you put yourself in our hands we will arrange everything—we know indubitably how it has to be done, always in the same way for everybody alike." It was all just as it was in the law courts. The doctor put on just the same air towards him as he himself put on towards an accused person.

The doctor said that so-and-so indicated that there was so-and-so inside the patient, but if the investigation of so-and-so did not confirm this, then he must assume that and that. If he assumed that and that, then . . . and so on. To Ivan Ilych only one question was important: was his case serious or not? But the doctor ignored that inappropriate question. From his point of view it was not the one under consideration, the real question was to decide between a floating kidney, chronic catarrh, or appendicitis. It was not a question of Ivan Ilych's life or death, but one between a floating kidney and appendicitis. And that question the doctor solved brilliantly, as it seemed to Ivan Ilych, in favor of the appendix, with the reservation that should an examination of the urine give fresh indications the matter would be reconsidered. All this was just what Ivan Ilych had himself brilliantly accomplished a thousand times in dealing with men on trial. The doctor summed up just as brilliantly, looking over his spectacles triumphantly and even gaily at the accused. From the doctor's summing up Ivan Ilych concluded that things were bad, but that for the doctor, and perhaps for everybody else, it was a matter of indifference, though for him it was bad. And this conclusion struck him painfully, arousing in him a great feeling of pity for himself and of bitterness towards the doctor's indifference to a matter of such importance.

He said nothing of this, but rose, placed the doctor's fee on the table, and remarked with a sigh: "We sick people probably often put inappropriate questions. But tell me, in general, is this complaint dangerous, or not? . . ."

The doctor looked at him sternly over his spectacles with one eye, as if to say: "Prisoner, if you will not keep to the questions put to you, I shall be obliged to have you removed from the court."

"I have already told you what I consider necessary and proper. The analysis may show something more." And the doctor bowed.

Ivan Ilych went out slowly, seated himself disconsolately in his sledge, and drove home. All the way home he was going over what the doctor had said, trying to translate those complicated, obscure, scientific phrases into plain language and find in them an answer to the question: "Is my condition bad? Is it very bad? Or is there as yet nothing much wrong?" And it seemed to him that the meaning of what the doctor had said was that it was very bad. Everything in the streets seemed depressing. The cabmen, the houses, the passers-by, and the shops, were dismal. His ache, this dull gnawing ache that never ceased for a moment, seemed to have acquired a new and more serious significance from the doctor's dubious remarks. Ivan Ilych now watched it with a new and oppressive feeling.

He reached home and began to tell his wife about it. She listened, but in the middle of his account his daughter came in with her hat on, ready to go out with her mother. She sat down reluctantly to listen to this tedious story, but could not stand it long, and her mother too did not hear him to the end.

"Well, I am very glad," she said. "Mind now to take your medicine regularly. Give me the prescription and I'll send Gerasim to the chemist's."[13] And she went to get ready to go out.

[13]**chemist's** pharmacist's

While she was in the room Ivan Ilych had hardly taken time to breathe, but he sighed deeply when she left it.

"Well," he thought, "perhaps it isn't so bad after all."

125 He began taking his medicine and following the doctor's directions, which had been altered after the examination of the urine. But then it happened that there was a contradiction between the indications drawn from the examination of the urine and the symptoms that showed themselves. It turned out that what was happening differed from what the doctor had told him, and that he had either forgotten, or blundered, or hidden something from him. He could not, however, be blamed for that, and Ivan Ilych still obeyed his orders implicitly and at first derived some comfort from doing so.

From the time of his visit to the doctor, Ivan Ilych's chief occupation was the exact fulfillment of the doctor's instructions regarding hygiene and the taking of medicine, and the observation of his pain and his excretions. His chief interests came to be people's ailments and people's health. When sickness, deaths, or recoveries were mentioned in his presence, especially when the illness resembled his own, he listened with agitation which he tried to hide, asked questions, and applied what he heard to his own case.

The pain did not grow less, but Ivan Ilych made efforts to force himself to think that he was better. And he could do this so long as nothing agitated him. But as soon as he had any unpleasantness with his wife, any lack of success in his official work, or held bad cards at bridge, he was at once acutely sensible of his disease. He had formerly borne such mischances, hoping soon to adjust what was wrong, to master it and attain success, or make a grand slam. But now every mischance upset him and plunged him into despair. He would say to himself: "There now, just as I was beginning to get better and the medicine had begun to take effect, comes this accursed misfortune, or unpleasantness. . . ." And he was furious with the mishap, or with the people who were causing the unpleasantness and killing him, for he felt that this fury was killing him but could not restrain it. One would have thought that it should have been clear to him that this exasperation with circumstances and people aggravated his illness, and that he ought therefore to ignore unpleasant occurrences. But he drew the very opposite conclusion: he said that he needed peace, and he watched for everything that might disturb it and became irritable at the slightest infringement of it. His condition was rendered worse by the fact that he read medical books and consulted doctors. The progress of his disease was so gradual that he could deceive himself when comparing one day with another—the difference was so slight. But when he consulted the doctors it seemed to him that he was getting worse, and even very rapidly. Yet despite this he was continually consulting them.

That month he went to see another celebrity, who told him almost the same as the first had done but put his questions rather differently, and the interview with this celebrity only increased Ivan Ilych's doubts and fears. A friend of a friend of his, a very good doctor, diagnosed his illness again quite differently from the others, and though he predicted recovery, his questions and suppositions bewildered Ivan Ilych still more and increased his doubts. A homeopathist diagnosed the disease in yet another way, and prescribed medicine which Ivan Ilych took secretly for a week. But after a week, not feeling any improvement and having lost confidence both in the former doctor's treatment and in this one's, he became still more despondent. One day a lady acquaintance mentioned a cure effected by a wonder-working icon. Ivan Ilych caught himself listening attentively and beginning to believe that it had occurred. This incident alarmed him. "Has my mind really weakened to such an extent?" he asked himself. "Nonsense! It's all rubbish. I mustn't give way to nervous fears but having chosen a doctor must keep strictly to his treatment. That is what I will do. Now it's all settled. I won't think about it, but will follow the treatment seriously till summer, and then we shall see. From now there must be no more of this wavering!" This was easy to say but impossible to carry out. The pain in his side oppressed him and seemed to grow worse and more incessant, while the taste in his mouth grew stranger and stranger. It seemed to him that his breath had a disgusting smell, and he was conscious of a loss of appetite and strength. There was no deceiving himself: something terrible, new, and more important than anything before in his life, was taking place within him of which he alone was aware. Those about him did not understand or would not understand it, but thought everything in the world was going on as usual. That tormented Ivan Ilych more than anything. He saw that his household, especially his wife and daughter who were in a perfect whirl of visiting, did not understand anything of it and were annoyed that he was so depressed and so exacting, as if he were to blame for it. Though they tried to disguise it he saw that he was an obstacle in their path, and that his wife had adopted a definite line in regard to his illness and kept to it regardless of anything he said or did. Her attitude was this: "You know," she would say to her friends, "Ivan Ilych can't do as other people do, and keep to the treatment prescribed for him. One day he'll take his drops and keep strictly to his diet and go to bed in good time, but the next day unless I watch him he'll suddenly forget his medicine, eat sturgeon—which is forbidden—and sit up playing cards till one o'clock in the morning."

"Oh, come, when was that?" Ivan Ilych would ask in vexation. "Only once at Peter Ivanovich's."

"And yesterday with Shebek."

"Well, even if I hadn't stayed up, this pain would have kept me awake."

"Be that as it may you'll never get well like that, but will always make us wretched."

Praskovya Fëdorovna's attitude to Ivan Ilych's illness, as she expressed it both to others and to him, was that it was his own fault and was another of the annoyances he caused her. Ivan Ilych felt that this opinion escaped her involuntarily—but that did not make it easier for him.

At the law courts too, Ivan Ilych noticed, or thought he noticed, a strange attitude towards himself. It sometimes seemed to him that people were watching him inquisitively as a man whose place might soon be vacant. Then again, his friends would suddenly begin to chaff him in a friendly way about his low spirits, as if the awful, horrible, and unheard-of thing that was going on within him, incessantly gnawing at him and irresistibly drawing him away, was a very agreeable subject for jests. Schwartz in particular irritated him by his jocularity, vivacity, and *savoir-faire,* which reminded him of what he himself had been ten years ago.

Friends came to make up a set and they sat down to cards. They dealt, bending the new cards to soften them, and he sorted the diamonds in his hand and found he had seven. His partner said "No trumps" and supported him with two diamonds. What more could be wished for? It ought to be jolly and lively. They would make a grand slam. But suddenly Ivan Ilych was conscious of that gnawing pain, that taste in his mouth, and it seemed ridiculous that in such circumstances he should be pleased to make a grand slam.

He looked at his partner Mikhail Mikhaylovich, who rapped the table with his strong hand and instead of snatching up the tricks pushed the cards courteously and indulgently towards Ivan Ilych that he might have the pleasure of gathering them up without the trouble of stretching out his hand for them. "Does he think I am too weak to stretch out my arm?" thought Ivan Ilych, and forgetting what he was doing he over-trumped his partner, missing the grand slam by three tricks. And what was most awful of all was that he saw how upset Mikhail Mikhaylovich was about it but did not himself care. And it was dreadful to realize why he did not care.

They all saw that he was suffering, and said: "We can stop if you are tired. Take a rest." Lie down? No, he was not at all tired, and he finished the rubber. All were gloomy and silent. Ivan Ilych felt that he had diffused this gloom over them and could not dispel it. They had supper and went away, and Ivan Ilych was left alone with the consciousness that his life was poisoned and was poisoning the lives of others, and that this poison did not weaken but penetrated more and more deeply into his whole being.

With this consciousness, and with physical pain besides the terror, he must go to bed, often to lie awake the greater part of the night. Next morning he had to get up again, dress, go to the law courts, speak, and write; or if he did not go out, spend at home those twenty-four hours a day each of which was a torture. And he had to live thus all alone on the brink of an abyss, with no one who understood or pitied him.

## V

So one month passed and then another. Just before the New Year his brother-in-law came to town and stayed at their house. Ivan Ilych was at the law courts and Praskovya Fëdorovna had gone shopping. When Ivan Ilych came home and entered his study he found his brother-in-law there—a healthy, florid man—unpacking his portmanteau himself. He raised his head on hearing Ivan Ilych's footsteps and looked up at him for a moment without a word. That stare told Ivan Ilych everything. His brother-in-law opened his mouth to utter an exclamation of surprise but checked himself, and that action confirmed it all.

"I have changed, eh?"

"Yes, there is a change."

And after that, try as he would to get his brother-in-law to return to the subject of his looks, the latter would say nothing about it. Praskovya Fëdorovna came home and her brother went out to her. Ivan Ilych locked the door and began to examine himself in the glass, first full face, then in profile. He took up a portrait of himself taken with his wife, and compared it with what he saw in the glass. The change in him was immense. Then he bared his arms to the elbow, looked at them, drew the sleeves down again, sat down on an ottoman, and grew blacker than night.

"No, no, this won't do!" he said to himself, and jumped up, went to the table, took up some law papers, and began to read them, but could not continue. He unlocked the door and went into the reception-room. The door leading to the drawing-room was shut. He approached it on tiptoe and listened.

"No, you are exaggerating!" Praskovya Fëdorovna was saying.

"Exaggerating! Don't you see it? Why, he's a dead man! Look at his eyes—there's no light in them. But what is it that is wrong with him?"

"No one knows. Nikolaevich said something, but I don't know what. And Leshchetitsky said quite the contrary. . . ."

Ivan Ilych walked away, went to his own room, lay down, and began musing: "The kidney, a floating kidney." He recalled all the doctors had told him of how it detached itself and swayed about. And by an effort of imagination he tried to catch that kidney and arrest it and support it. So little was needed for this, it seemed to him. "No, I'll go to see Peter Ivanovich again." He rang, ordered the carriage, and got ready to go.

"Where are you going, Jean?"[14] asked his wife, with a specially sad and exceptionally kind look.

This exceptionally kind look irritated him. He looked morosely at her.

"I must go to see Peter Ivanovich."

He went to see Peter Ivanovich, and together they went to see his friend, the doctor. He was in, and Ivan Ilych had a long talk with him.

Reviewing the anatomical and physiological details of what in the doctor's opinion was going on inside him, he understood it all.

There was something, a small thing, in the vermiform appendix. It might all come right. Only stimulate the energy of one organ and check the activity of another, then absorption would take place and everything would come right. He got home rather late for dinner, ate his dinner, and conversed cheerfully, but could not for a long time bring himself to go back to work in his room. At last, however, he went to his study and did what was necessary, but the consciousness that he had put something aside—an important, intimate matter which he would revert to when his work was done—never left him. When he had finished his work he remembered that this intimate matter was the thought of his vermiform appendix. But he did not give himself up to it, and went to the drawing-room for tea. There were callers there, including the examining magistrate who was a desirable match for his daughter, and they were conversing, playing the piano, and singing. Ivan Ilych, as Praskovya Fëdorovna remarked, spent that evening more cheerfully than usual, but he never for a moment forgot that he had postponed the important matter of the appendix. At eleven o'clock he said good-night and went to his bedroom. Since his illness he had slept alone in a small room next to his study. He undressed and took up a novel by Zola,[15] but instead of reading it he fell into thought, and in his imagination that desired improvement in the vermiform appendix occurred. There were the absorption and evacuation and the re-establishment of normal activity. "Yes, that's it!" he said to himself. "One need only assist nature, that's all." He remembered his medicine, rose, took it, and lay down on his back watching for the beneficent action of the medicine and for it to lessen the pain. "I need only take it regularly and avoid all injurious influences. I am already

[14]**Jean** French form of Ivan

[15]**Émile Zola** French novelist and social critic

feeling better, much better." He began touching his side: it was not painful to the touch. "There, I really don't feel it. It's much better already." He put out the light and turned on his side. . . . "The appendix is getting better, absorption is occurring." Suddenly he felt the old, familiar, dull, gnawing pain, stubborn and serious. There was the same familiar loathsome taste in his mouth. His heart sank and he felt dazed. "My God! My God!" he muttered. "Again, again! and it will never cease." And suddenly the matter presented itself in a quite different aspect. "Vermiform appendix! Kidney!" he said to himself. "It's not a question of appendix or kidney, but of life and . . . death. Yes, life was there and now it is going, going and I cannot stop it. Yes. Why deceive myself? Isn't it obvious to everyone but me that I'm dying, and that it's only a question of weeks, days . . . it may happen this moment. There was light and now there is darkness. I was here and now I'm going there! Where?" A chill came over him, his breathing ceased, and he felt only the throbbing of his heart.

"When I am not, what will there be? There will be nothing. Then where shall I be when I am no more? Can this be dying? No, I don't want to!" He jumped up and tried to light the candle, felt for it with trembling hands, dropped candle and candlestick on the floor, and fell back on his pillow.

155 "What's the use? It makes no difference," he said to himself, staring with wide-open eyes into the darkness. "Death. Yes, death. And none of them know or wish to know it, and they have no pity for me. Now they are playing." (He heard through the door the distant sound of a song and its accompaniment.) "It's all the same to them, but they will die too! Fools! I first, and they later, but it will be the same for them. And now they are merry . . . the beasts!"

Anger choked him and he was agonizingly, unbearably miserable. "It is impossible that all men have been doomed to suffer this awful horror!" He raised himself.

"Something must be wrong. I must calm myself—must think it all over from the beginning." And he again began thinking. "Yes, the beginning of my illness: I knocked my side, but I was still quite well that day and the next. It hurt a little, then rather more. I saw the doctors, then followed despondency and anguish, more doctors, and I drew nearer to the abyss. My strength grew less and I kept coming nearer and nearer, and now I have wasted away and there is no light in my eyes. I think of the appendix—but this is death! I think of mending the appendix, and all the while here is death! Can it really be death?" Again terror seized him and he gasped for breath. He leant down and began feeling for the matches, pressing with his elbow on the stand beside the bed. It was in his way and hurt him, he grew furious with it, pressed on it still harder, and upset it. Breathless and in despair he fell on his back, expecting death to come immediately.

Meanwhile the visitors were leaving. Praskovya Fëdorovna was seeing them off. She heard something fall and came in.

"What has happened?"

160 "Nothing. I knocked it over accidentally."

She went out and returned with a candle. He lay there panting heavily, like a man who has run a thousand yards, and stared upwards at her with a fixed look.

"What is it, Jean?"

"No . . . no . . . thing. I upset it." ("Why speak of it? She won't understand," he thought.)

And in truth she did not understand. She picked up the stand, lit his candle, and hurried away to see another visitor off. When she came back he still lay on his back, looking upwards.

"What is it? Do you feel worse?"

"Yes."

She shook her head and sat down.

"Do you know, Jean, I think we must ask Leshchetitsky to come and see you here."

This meant calling in the famous specialist, regardless of expense. He smiled malignantly and said "No." She remained a little longer and then went up to him and kissed his forehead.

While she was kissing him he hated her from the bottom of his soul and with difficulty refrained from pushing her away.

"Good-night. Please God you'll sleep."

"Yes."

## VI

Ivan Ilych saw that he was dying, and he was in continual despair.

In the depth of his heart he knew he was dying, but not only was he not accustomed to the thought, he simply did not and could not grasp it.

The syllogism he had learnt from Kiezewetter's Logic:[16] "Caius is a man, men are mortal, therefore Caius is mortal," had always seemed to him correct as applied to Caius, but certainly not as applied to himself. That Caius—man in the abstract—was mortal, was perfectly correct, but he was not Caius, not an abstract man, but a creature quite, quite separate from all others. He had been little Vanya,[17] with a mama and a papa, with Mitya and Volodya, with the toys, a coachman and a nurse, afterwards with Katenka and with all the joys, griefs, and delights of childhood, boyhood, and youth. What did Caius know of the smell of that striped leather ball Vanya had been so fond of? Had Caius kissed his mother's hand like that, and did the silk of her dress rustle so for Caius? Had he rioted like that at school when the pastry was bad? Had Caius been in love like that? Could Caius preside at a session as he did? "Caius really was mortal, and it was right for him to die; but for me, little Vanya, Ivan Ilych, with all my thoughts and emotions, it's altogether a different matter. It cannot be that I ought to die. That would be too terrible."

Such was his feeling.

"If I had to die like Caius I should have known it was so. An inner voice would have told me so, but there was nothing of the sort in me and I and all my friends felt that our case was quite different from that of Caius. And now here it is!" he said to himself. "It can't be. It's impossible! But here it is. How is this? How is one to understand it?"

[16]**Kiezewetter's Logic** *The Outline of Logic According to Kantian Principles,* a widely used text in Russia, written by Klaus Kiezewetter and based on the philosophy of Immanuel Kant (1722–1804)

[17]**Vanya** diminutive of Ivan

He could not understand it, and tried to drive this false, incorrect, morbid thought away and to replace it by other proper and healthy thoughts. But that thought, and not the thought only but the reality itself, seemed to come and confront him.

And to replace that thought he called up a succession of others, hoping to find in them some support. He tried to get back into the former current of thoughts that had once screened the thought of death from him. But strange to say, all that had formerly shut off, hidden, and destroyed his consciousness of death, no longer had that effect. Ivan Ilych now spent most of his time in attempting to re-establish that old current. He would say to himself: "I will take up my duties again—after all I used to live by them." And banishing all doubts he would go to the law courts, enter into conversation with his colleagues, and sit carelessly as was his wont, scanning the crowd with a thoughtful look and leaning both his emaciated arms on the arms of his oak chair; bending over as usual to a colleague and drawing his papers nearer he would interchange whispers with him, and then suddenly raising his eyes and sitting erect would pronounce certain words and open the proceedings. But suddenly in the midst of those proceedings the pain in his side, regardless of the stage the proceedings had reached, would begin its own gnawing work. Ivan Ilych would turn his attention to it and try to drive the thought of it away, but without success. *It* would come and stand before him and look at him, and he would be petrified and the light would die out of his eyes, and he would again begin asking himself whether *It* alone was true. And his colleagues and subordinates would see with surprise and distress that he, the brilliant and subtle judge, was becoming confused and making mistakes. He would shake himself, try to pull himself together, manage somehow to bring the sitting to a close, and return home with the sorrowful consciousness that his judicial labors could not as formerly hide from him what he wanted them to hide, and could not deliver him from *It.* And what was worst of all was that *It* drew his attention to itself not in order to make him take some action but only that he should look at *It,* look it straight in the face: look at it and, without doing anything, suffer inexpressibly.

180 And to save himself from this condition Ivan Ilych looked for consolation—new screens—and new screens were found and for a while seemed to save him, but then they immediately fell to pieces or rather became transparent, as if *It* penetrated them and nothing could veil *It.*

In these latter days he would go into the drawing-room he had arranged—that drawing-room where he had fallen and for the sake of which (how bitterly ridiculous it seemed) he had sacrificed his life—for he knew that his illness originated with that knock. He would enter and see that something had scratched the polished table. He would look for the cause of this and find that it was the bronze ornamentation of an album, that had got bent. He would take up the expensive album which he had lovingly arranged, and feel vexed with his daughter and her friends for their untidiness—for the album was torn here and there and some of the photographs turned upside down. He would put it carefully in order and bend the ornamentation back into position. Then it would occur to him to place all those things in another corner of the room, near the plants. He could call the footman, but his daughter or wife would come to help him. They would not agree, and his wife would contradict him, and he would dispute and grow angry. But that was all right, for then he did not think about *It*. *It* was invisible.

But then, when he was moving something himself, his wife would say: "Let the servants do it. You will hurt yourself again." And suddenly *It* would flash through the screen and he would see it. It was just a flash, and he hoped it would disappear, but he would involuntarily pay attention to his side. "It sits there as before, gnawing just the same!" And he could no longer forget *It*, but could distinctly see it looking at him from behind the flowers. "What is it all for?"

"It really is so! I lost my life over that curtain as I might have done when storming a fort. Is that possible? How terrible and how stupid. It can't be true! It can't, but it is."

He would go to his study, lie down, and again be alone with *It:* face to face with *It*. And nothing could be done with *It* except to look at it and shudder.

## VII

185 How it happened it is impossible to say because it came about step by step, unnoticed, but in the third month of Ivan Ilych's illness, his wife, his daughter, his son, his acquaintances, the doctors, the servants, and above all he himself, were aware that the whole interest he had for other people was whether he would soon vacate his place, and at last release the living from the discomfort caused by his presence and be himself released from his sufferings.

He slept less and less. He was given opium and hypodermic injections of morphine, but this did not relieve him. The dull depression he experienced in a somnolent condition at first gave him a little relief, but only as something new, afterwards it became as distressing as the pain itself or even more so.

Special foods were prepared for him by the doctors' orders, but all those foods became increasingly distasteful and disgusting to him.

For his excretions also special arrangements had to be made, and this was a torment to him every time—a torment from the uncleanliness, the unseemliness, and the smell, and from knowing that another person had to take part in it.

But just through this most unpleasant matter, Ivan Ilych obtained comfort. Gerasim, the butler's young assistant, always came in to carry the things out. Gerasim was a clean, fresh peasant lad, grown stout on town food and always cheerful and bright. At first the sight of him, in his clean Russian peasant costume, engaged on that disgusting task embarrassed Ivan Ilych.

190 Once when he got up from the commode too weak to draw up his trousers, he dropped into a soft armchair and looked with horror at his bare, enfeebled thighs with the muscles so sharply marked on them.

Gerasim with a firm light tread, his heavy boots emitting a pleasant smell of tar and fresh winter air, came in wearing a clean Hessian apron, the sleeves of his print shirt tucked up over his strong bare young arms; and refraining from looking at his sick master out of consideration for his feelings, and restraining the joy of life that beamed from his face, he went up to the commode.

"Gerasim!" said Ivan Ilych in a weak voice.

Gerasim started, evidently afraid he might have committed some blunder, and with a rapid movement turned his fresh, kind, simple young face which just showed the first downy signs of a beard.

"Yes, sir?"

195 "That must be very unpleasant for you. You must forgive me. I am helpless."

"Oh, why, sir," and Gerasim's eyes beamed and he showed his glistening white teeth, "what's a little trouble? It's a case of illness with you, sir."

And his deft strong hands did their accustomed task, and he went out of the room stepping lightly. Five minutes later he as lightly returned.

Ivan Ilych was still sitting in the same position in the armchair.

"Gerasim," he said when the latter had replaced the freshly-washed utensil. "Please come here and help me." Gerasim went up to him. "Lift me up. It is hard for me to get up, and I have sent Dmitri away."

200 Gerasim went up to him, grasped his master with his strong arms deftly but gently, in the same way that he stepped—lifted him, supported him with one hand, and with the other drew up his trousers and would have set him down again, but Ivan Ilych asked to be led to the sofa. Gerasim, without an effort and without apparent pressure, led him, almost lifting him, to the sofa, and placed him on it.

"Thank you. How easily and well you do it all!"

Gerasim smiled again and turned to leave the room. But Ivan Ilych felt his presence such a comfort that he did not want to let him go.

"One thing more, please move up that chair. No, the other one—under my feet. It is easier for me when my feet are raised."

Gerasim brought the chair, set it down gently in place, and raised Ivan Ilych's legs on to it. It seemed to Ivan Ilych that he felt better while Gerasim was holding up his legs.

205 "It's better when my legs are higher," he said. "Place that cushion under them."

Gerasim did so. He again lifted the legs and placed them, and again Ivan Ilych felt better while Gerasim held his legs. When he set them down Ivan Ilych fancied he felt worse.

"Gerasim," he said. "Are you busy now?"

"Not at all, sir," said Gerasim, who had learnt from the townsfolk how to speak to gentlefolk.

"What have you still to do?"

210 "What have I to do? I've done everything except chopping the logs for tomorrow."

"Then hold my legs up a bit higher, can you?"

"Of course I can. Why not?" And Gerasim raised his master's legs higher and Ivan Ilych thought that in that position he did not feel any pain at all.

"And how about the logs?"

"Don't trouble about that, sir. There's plenty of time."

215 Ivan Ilych told Gerasim to sit down and hold his legs, and began to talk to him. And strange to say it seemed to him that he felt better while Gerasim held his legs up.

After that Ivan Ilych would sometimes call Gerasim and get him to hold his legs on his shoulders, and he liked talking to him. Gerasim did it all easily, willingly, simply, and with a good nature that touched Ivan Ilych. Health, strength, and vitality in other people were offensive to him, but Gerasim's strength and vitality did not mortify but soothed him.

What tormented Ivan Ilych most was the deception, the lie, which for some reason they all accepted, that he was not dying but was simply ill, and that he only need keep quiet and undergo a treatment and then something very good would result. He however knew that do what they would nothing would come of it, only still more agonizing suffering and death. This deception tortured him—their not wishing to admit what they all knew and what he knew, but wanting to lie to him concerning his terrible condition, and wishing and forcing him to participate in that lie. Those lies—lies enacted over him on the eve of his death and destined to degrade this awful, solemn act to the level of their visitings, their curtains, their sturgeon for dinner—were a terrible agony for Ivan Ilych. And strangely enough, many times when they were going through their antics over him he had been within a hairbreadth of calling out to them: "Stop lying! You know and I know that I am dying. Then at least stop lying about it!" But he had never had the spirit to do it. The awful, terrible act of his dying was, he could see, reduced by those about him to the level of a casual, unpleasant, and almost indecorous incident (as if someone entered a drawing-room diffusing an unpleasant odor) and this was done by that very decorum which he had served all his life long. He saw that no one felt for him, because no one even wished to grasp his position. Only Gerasim recognized it and pitied him. And so Ivan Ilych felt at ease only with him. He felt comforted when Gerasim supported his legs (sometimes all night long) and refused to go to bed, saying: "Don't you worry, Ivan Ilych. I'll get sleep enough later on," or when he suddenly became familiar and exclaimed: "If you weren't sick it would be another matter, but as it is, why should I grudge a little trouble?" Gerasim alone did not lie; everything showed that he alone understood the facts of the case and did not consider it necessary to disguise them, but simply felt sorry for his emaciated and enfeebled master. Once when Ivan Ilych was sending him away he even said straight out: "We shall all of us die, so why should I grudge a little trouble?"—expressing the fact that he did not think his work burdensome, because he was doing it for a dying man and hoped someone would do the same for him when his time came.

Apart from this lying, or because of it, what most tormented Ivan Ilych was that no one pitied him as he wished to be pitied. At certain moments after prolonged suffering he wished most of all (though he would have been ashamed to confess it) for someone to pity him as a sick child is pitied. He longed to be petted and comforted. He knew he was an important functionary, that he had a beard turning grey, and that therefore what he longed for was impossible, but still he longed for it. And in Gerasim's attitude towards him there was something akin to what he wished for, and so that attitude comforted him. Ivan Ilych wanted to weep, wanted to be petted and cried over, and then his colleague Shebek would come, and instead of weeping and being petted, Ivan Ilych would assume a serious, severe, and profound air, and by force of habit would express his opinion on a decision of the Court of Cassation and would stubbornly insist on that view. This falsity around him and within him did more than anything else to poison his last days.

## VIII

It was morning. He knew it was morning because Gerasim had gone, and Peter the footman had come and put out the candles, drawn back one of the curtains, and begun quietly to tidy up. Whether it was morning or evening, Friday or Sunday, made no difference, it was all just the same: the gnawing, unmitigated, agonizing pain, never ceasing for an instant, the consciousness of life inexorably waning but not yet extinguished, the approach of that ever dreaded and hateful Death which was the only reality, and always the same falsity. What were days, weeks, hours, in such a case?

"Will you have some tea, sir?"

"He wants things to be regular, and wishes the gentlefolk to drink tea in the morning," thought Ivan Ilych, and only said "No."

"Wouldn't you like to move onto the sofa, sir?"

"He wants to tidy up the room, and I'm in the way. I am uncleanliness and disorder," he thought, and said only:

"No, leave me alone."

The man went on bustling about. Ivan Ilych stretched out his hand. Peter came up, ready to help.

"What is it, sir?"

"My watch."

Peter took the watch which was close at hand and gave it to his master.

"Half-past eight. Are they up?"

"No, sir, except Vasily Ivanich" (the son) "who has gone to school. Praskovya Fëdorovna ordered me to wake her if you asked for her. Shall I do so?"

"No, there's no need to." "Perhaps I'd better have some tea," he thought, and added aloud: "Yes, bring me some tea."

Peter went to the door, but Ivan Ilych dreaded being left alone. "How can I keep him here? Oh yes, my medicine." "Peter, give me my medicine." "Why not? Perhaps it may still do me some good." He took a spoonful and swallowed it. "No, it won't help. It's all tomfoolery, all deception," he decided as soon as he became aware of the familiar, sickly, hopeless taste. "No, I can't believe in it any longer. But the pain, why this pain? If it would only cease just for a moment!" And he moaned. Peter turned towards him. "It's all right. Go and fetch me some tea."

Peter went out. Left alone Ivan Ilych groaned not so much with pain, terrible though that was, as from mental anguish. Always and for ever the same, always these endless days and nights. If only it would come quicker! If only *what* would come quicker? Death, darkness? . . . No, no! Anything rather than death!

When Peter returned with the tea on a tray, Ivan Ilych stared at him for a time in perplexity, not realizing who and what he was. Peter was disconcerted by that look and his embarrassment brought Ivan Ilych to himself.

"Oh, tea! All right, put it down. Only help me to wash and put on a clean shirt."

And Ivan Ilych began to wash. With pauses for rest, he washed his hands and then his face, cleaned his teeth, brushed his hair, and looked in the glass. He was terrified by what he saw, especially by the limp way in which his hair clung to his pallid forehead.

While his shirt was being changed he knew that he would be still more frightened at the sight of his body, so he avoided looking at it. Finally he was ready. He drew on a dressing-gown, wrapped himself in a plaid, and sat down in the armchair to take his tea. For a moment he felt refreshed, but soon as he began to drink the tea he was again aware of the same taste, and the pain also returned. He finished it with an effort, and then lay down stretching out his legs, and dismissed Peter.

Always the same. Now a spark of hope flashes up, then a sea of despair rages, and always pain; always pain, always despair, and always the same. When alone he had a dreadful and distressing desire to call someone, but he knew beforehand that with others present it would be still worse. "Another dose of morphine—to lose consciousness. I will tell him, the doctor, that he must think of something else. It's impossible, impossible, to go on like this."

An hour and another pass like that. But now there is a ring at the door bell. Perhaps it's the doctor? It is. He comes in fresh, hearty, plump, and cheerful, with that look on his face that seems to say: "There now, you're in a panic about something, but we'll arrange it all for you directly!" The doctor knows this expression is out of place here, but he has put it on once for all and can't take it off—like a man who has put on a frock-coat in the morning to pay a round of calls.

The doctor rubs his hands vigorously and reassuringly.

"Brr! How cold it is! There's such a sharp frost; just let me warm myself!" he says, as if it were only a matter of waiting till he was warm, and then he would put everything right.

"Well now, how are you?"

Ivan Ilych feels that the doctor would like to say: "Well, how are our affairs?" but that even he feels that this would not do, and says instead: "What sort of a night have you had?"

Ivan Ilych looks at him as much as to say: "Are you really never ashamed of lying?" But the doctor does not wish to understand this question, and Ivan Ilych says: "Just as terrible as ever. The pain never leaves me and never subsides. If only something . . ."

"Yes, you sick people are always like that. . . There, now I think I am warm enough. Even Praskovya Fëdorovna, who is so particular, could find no fault with my temperature. Well, now I can say good-morning," and the doctor presses his patient's hand.

Then, dropping his former playfulness, he begins with a most serious face to examine the patient, feeling his pulse and taking his temperature, and then begins the sounding and auscultation.[18]

Ivan Ilych knows quite well and definitely that all this is nonsense and pure deception, but when the doctor, getting down on his knee, leans over him, putting his ear first higher then lower, and performs various gymnastic movements over him with a significant expression on his face, Ivan Ilych submits to it all as he used to submit to the speeches of the lawyers, though he knew very well that they were all lying and why they were lying.

The doctor, kneeling on the sofa, is still sounding him when Praskovya Fëdorovna's silk dress rustles at the door and she is heard scolding Peter for not having let her know of the doctor's arrival.

She comes in, kisses her husband, and at once proceeds to prove that she has been up a long time already, and only owing to a misunderstanding failed to be there when the doctor arrived.

[18]**auscultation** diagnosing the sounds made by internal organs

250 Ivan Ilych looks at her, scans her all over, sets against her the whiteness and plumpness and cleanness of her hands and neck, the gloss of her hair, and the sparkle of her vivacious eyes. He hates her with his whole soul. And the thrill of hatred he feels for her makes him suffer from her touch.

Her attitude towards him and his disease is still the same. Just as the doctor had adopted a certain relation to his patient which he could not abandon, so had she formed one towards him—that he was not doing something he ought to do and was himself to blame, and that she reproached him lovingly for this—and she could not now change that attitude.

"You see he doesn't listen to me and doesn't take his medicine at the proper time. And above all he lies in a position that is no doubt bad for him—with his legs up."

She described how he made Gerasim hold his legs up.

The doctor smiled with a contemptuous affability that said: "What's to be done? These sick people do have foolish fancies of that kind, but we must forgive them."

255 When the examination was over the doctor looked at his watch, and then Praskovya Fëdorovna announced to Ivan Ilych that it was of course as he pleased, but she had sent today for a celebrated specialist who would examine him and have a consultation with Michael Danilovich (their regular doctor).

"Please don't raise any objections. I am doing this for my own sake," she said ironically, letting it be felt that she was doing it all for his sake and only said this to leave him no right to refuse. He remained silent, knitting his brows. He felt that he was so surrounded and involved in a mesh of falsity that it was hard to unravel anything.

Everything she did for him was entirely for her own sake, and she told him she was doing for herself what she actually was doing for herself, as if that was so incredible that he must understand the opposite.

At half-past eleven the celebrated specialist arrived. Again the sounding began and the significant conversations in his presence and in another room, about the kidneys and the appendix, and the questions and answers, with such an air of importance that again, instead of the real question of life and death which now alone confronted him, the question arose of the kidney and appendix which were not behaving as they ought to and would now be attacked by Michael Danilovich and the specialist and forced to amend their ways.

The celebrated specialist took leave of him with a serious though not hopeless look, and in reply to the timid question Ivan Ilych, with eyes glistening with fear and hope, put to him as to whether there was a chance of recovery, said that he could not vouch for it but there was a possibility. The look of hope with which Ivan Ilych watched the doctor out was so pathetic that Praskovya Fëdorovna, seeing it, even wept as she left the room to hand the doctor his fee.

260 The gleam of hope kindled by the doctor's encouragement did not last long. The same room, the same pictures, curtains, wallpaper, medicine bottles, were all there, and the same aching suffering body, and Ivan Ilych began to moan. They gave him a subcutaneous injection and he sank into oblivion.

It was twilight when he came to. They brought him his dinner and he swallowed some beef tea with difficulty, and then everything was the same again and night was coming on.

After dinner, at seven o'clock, Praskovya Fëdorovna came into the room in evening dress, her full bosom pushed up by her corset, and with traces of powder on her face. She had reminded him in the morning that they were going to the theater. Sarah Bernhardt was visiting the town and they had a box, which he had insisted on their taking. Now he had forgotten about it and her toilet offended him, but he concealed his vexation when he remembered that he had himself insisted on their securing a box and going because it would be an instructive and aesthetic pleasure for the children.

Praskovya Fëdorovna came in, self-satisfied but yet with a rather guilty air. She sat down and asked how he was, but, as he saw, only for the sake of asking and not in order to learn about it, knowing that there was nothing to learn—and then went on to what she really wanted to say: that she would not on any account have gone but that the box had been taken and Helen and their daughter were going, as well as Petrishchev (the examining magistrate, their daughter's fiancé), and that it was out of the question to let them go alone; but that she would have much preferred to sit with him for a while; and he must be sure to follow the doctor's orders while she was away.

"Oh, and Fëdor Petrovich" (the fiancé) "would like to come in. May he? And Lisa?"

265 "All right."

Their daughter came in in full evening dress, her fresh young flesh exposed (making a show of that very flesh which in his own case caused so much suffering), strong, healthy, evidently in love, and impatient with illness, suffering, and death, because they interfered with her happiness.

Fëdor Petrovich came in too, in evening dress, his hair curled *à la Capoul,*[19] a tight stiff collar round his long sinewy neck, an enormous white shirt-front, and narrow black trousers tightly stretched over his strong thighs. He had one white glove tightly drawn on, and was holding his opera hat in his hand.

Following him the schoolboy crept in unnoticed, in a new uniform, poor little fellow, and wearing gloves. Terribly dark shadows showed under his eyes, the meaning of which Ivan Ilych knew well.

His son had always seemed pathetic to him, and now it was dreadful to see the boy's frightened look of pity. It seemed to Ivan Ilych that Vasya was the only one besides Gerasim who understood and pitied him.

270 They all sat down and again asked how he was. A silence followed. Lisa asked her mother about the opera-glasses, and there was an altercation between mother and daughter as to who had taken them and where they had been put. This occasioned some unpleasantness.

Fëdor Petrovich inquired of Ivan Ilych whether he had ever seen Sarah Bernhardt. Ivan Ilych did not at first catch the question, but then replied: "No, have you seen her before?"

"Yes, in *Adrienne Lecouvreur.*"[20]

Praskovya Fëdorovna mentioned some rôles in which Sarah Bernhardt was particularly good. Her daughter disagreed. Conversation sprang up as

[19]**hair curled *à la Capoul*** an elaborate hairstyle for men, named after a French singer

[20]***Adrienne Lecouvreur*** tragedy (1849) by the French dramatist Eugène Scribe

to the elegance and realism of her acting—the sort of conversation that is always repeated and is always the same.

In the midst of the conversation Fëdor Petrovich glanced at Ivan Ilych and became silent. The others also looked at him and grew silent. Ivan Ilych was staring with glittering eyes straight before him, evidently indignant with them. This had to be rectified, but it was impossible to do so. The silence had to be broken, but for a time no one dared to break it and they all became afraid that the conventional deception would suddenly become obvious and the truth become plain to all. Lisa was the first to pluck up courage and break that silence, but by trying to hide what everybody was feeling, she betrayed it.

"Well, if we are going it's time to start," she said, looking at her watch, a present from her father, and with a faint and significant smile at Fëdor Petrovich relating to something known only to them. She got up with a rustle of her dress.

They all rose, said good-night, and went away.

When they had gone it seemed to Ivan Ilych that he felt better; the falsity had gone with them. But the pain remained—that same pain and that same fear that made everything monotonously alike, nothing harder and nothing easier. Everything was worse.

Again minute followed minute and hour followed hour. Everything remained the same and there was no cessation. And the inevitable end of it all became more and more terrible.

"Yes, send Gerasim here," he replied to a question Peter asked.

## IX

His wife returned late at night. She came in on tiptoe, but he heard her, opened his eyes, and made haste to close them again. She wished to send Gerasim away and to sit with him herself, but he opened his eyes and said: "No, go away."

"Are you in great pain?"

"Always the same."

"Take some opium."

He agreed and took some. She went away.

Till about three in the morning he was in a state of stupefied misery. It seemed to him that he and his pain were being thrust into a narrow, deep black sack, but though they were pushed further and further in they could not be pushed to the bottom. And this, terrible enough in itself, was accompanied by suffering. He was frightened yet wanted to fall through the sack, he struggled but yet cooperated. And suddenly he broke through, fell, and regained consciousness. Gerasim was sitting at the foot of the bed dozing quietly and patiently, while he himself lay with his emaciated stockinged legs resting on Gerasim's shoulders; the same shaded candle was there and the same unceasing pain.

"Go away, Gerasim," he whispered.

"It's all right, sir. I'll stay a while."

"No. Go away."

He removed his legs from Gerasim's shoulders, turned sideways onto his arm, and felt sorry for himself. He only waited till Gerasim had gone into the next room and then restrained himself no longer but wept like a child.

He wept on account of his helplessness, his terrible loneliness, the cruelty of man, the cruelty of God, and the absence of God.

"Why hast Thou done all this? Why hast Thou brought me here? Why, why dost Thou torment me so terribly?"

He did not expect an answer and yet wept because there was no answer and could be none. The pain grew more acute, but he did not stir and did not call. He said to himself: "Go on! Strike me! But what is it for? What have I done to Thee? What is it for?"

Then he grew quiet and not only ceased weeping but even held his breath and became all attention. It was as though he was listening not to an audible voice but to the voice of his soul, to the current of thoughts arising within him.

"What is it you want?" was the first clear conception capable of expression in words, that he heard.

"What do you want? What do you want?" he repeated to himself.

"What do I want? To live and not to suffer," he answered.

And again he listened with such concentrated attention that even his pain did not distract him.

"To live? How?" asked his inner voice.

"Why, to live as I used to—well and pleasantly."

"As you lived before, well and pleasantly?" the voice repeated.

And in imagination he began to recall the best moments of his pleasant life. But strange to say none of those best moments of his pleasant life now seemed at all what they had then seemed—none of them except the first recollections of childhood. There, in childhood, there had been something really pleasant with which it would be possible to live if it could return. But the child who had experienced that happiness existed no longer, it was like a reminiscence of somebody else.

As soon as the period began which had produced the present Ivan Ilych, all that had then seemed joys now melted before his sight and turned into something trivial and often nasty.

And the further he departed from childhood and the nearer he came to the present the more worthless and doubtful were the joys. This began with the School of Law. A little that was really good was still found there—there was lightheartedness, friendship, and hope. But in the upper classes there had already been fewer of such good moments. Then during the first years of his official career, when he was in the service of the Governor, some pleasant moments again occurred: they were the memories of love for a woman. Then all became confused and there was still less of what was good; later on again there was still less that was good, and the further he went the less there was. His marriage, a mere accident, then the disenchantment that followed it, his wife's bad breath and the sensuality and hypocrisy; then the deadly official life and those preoccupations about money, a year of it, and two, and ten, and twenty, and always the same thing. And the longer it lasted the more deadly it became. "It is as if I had been going downhill while I imagined I was going up. And that is really what it was. I was going up in public opinion, but to the same extent life was ebbing away from me. And now it is all done and there is only death."

"Then what does it mean? Why? It can't be that life is so senseless and horrible. But if it really has been so horrible and senseless, why must I die and die in agony? There is something wrong!

"Maybe I did not live as I ought to have done," it suddenly occurred to him. "But how could that be, when I did everything properly?" he replied, and immediately dismissed from his mind this, the sole solution of all the riddles of life and death, as something quite impossible.

305 "Then what do you want now? To live? Live how? Live as you lived in the law courts when the usher proclaimed 'The judge is coming!' The judge is coming, the judge!" he repeated to himself. "Here he is, the judge. But I am not guilty!" he exclaimed angrily. "What is it for?" And he ceased crying, but turning his face to the wall continued to ponder on the same question: Why, and for what purpose, is there all this horror? But however much he pondered he found no answer. And whenever the thought occurred to him, as it often did, that it all resulted from his not having lived as he ought to have done, he at once recalled the correctness of his whole life and dismissed so strange an idea.

## X

Another fortnight passed. Ivan Ilych now no longer left his sofa. He would not lie in bed but lay on the sofa, facing the wall nearly all the time. He suffered ever the same unceasing agonies and in his loneliness pondered always on the same insoluble question: "What is this? Can it be that it is Death?" And the inner voice answered: "Yes, it is Death."

"Why these sufferings?" And the voice answered, "For no reason—they just are so." Beyond and besides this there was nothing.

From the very beginning of his illness, ever since he had first been to see the doctor, Ivan Ilych's life had been divided between two contrary and alternating moods: now it was despair and the expectation of this uncomprehended and terrible death, and now hope and an intently interested observation of the functioning of his organs. Now before his eyes there was only a kidney or an intestine that temporarily evaded its duty, and now only that incomprehensible and dreadful death from which it was impossible to escape.

These two states of mind had alternated from the very beginning of his illness, but the further it progressed the more doubtful and fantastic became the conception of the kidney, and the more real the sense of impending death.

310 He had but to call to mind what he had been three months before and what he was now, to call to mind with what regularity he had been going downhill, for every possibility of hope to be shattered.

Latterly during that loneliness in which he found himself as he lay facing the back of the sofa, a loneliness in the midst of a populous town and surrounded by numerous acquaintances and relations but that yet could not have been more complete anywhere—either at the bottom of the sea or under the earth—during that terrible loneliness Ivan Ilych had lived only in memories of the past. Pictures of his past rose before him one after another. They always began with what was nearest in time and then went back to what was most remote—to his childhood—and rested there. If he thought of the stewed prunes that had been offered him that day, his mind went back to the raw shrivelled French plums of his childhood, their peculiar flavor and the flow of saliva when he sucked their stones, and along with the memory of that taste came a whole series of memories of those days: his nurse, his brother, and their toys. "No, I mustn't think of that. . . . It is too painful," Ivan Ilych said to himself, and brought himself back to the present—to the button on the back of the sofa and the creases in its morocco.[21] "Morocco is expensive, but it does not wear well: there had been a quarrel about it. It was a different kind of quarrel and a different kind of morocco that time when we tore father's portfolio and were punished, and mama brought us some tarts. . . ." And again his thoughts dwelt on his childhood, and again it was painful and he tried to banish them and fix his mind on something else.

Then again together with that chain of memories another series passed through his mind—of how his illness had progressed and grown worse. There also the further back he looked the more life there had been. There had been more of what was good in life and more of life itself. The two merged together. "Just as the pain went on getting worse and worse, so my life grew worse and worse," he thought. "There is one bright spot there at the back, at the beginning of life, and afterwards all becomes blacker and blacker and proceeds more and more rapidly—in inverse ratio to the square of the distance from death," thought Ivan Ilych. And the example of a stone falling downwards with increasing velocity entered his mind. Life, a series of increasing sufferings, flies further and further towards its end—the most terrible suffering. "I am flying. . . ." He shuddered, shifted himself, and tried to resist, but was already aware that resistance was impossible, and again, with eyes weary of gazing but unable to cease seeing what was before them, he stared at the back of the sofa and waited—awaiting that dreadful fall and shock and destruction.

"Resistance is impossible!" he said to himself. "If I could only understand what it is all for! But that too is impossible. An explanation would be possible if it could be said that I have not lived as I ought to. But it is impossible to say that," and he remembered all the legality, correctitude, and propriety of his life. "That at any rate can certainly not be admitted," he thought, and his lips smiled ironically as if someone could see that smile and be taken in by it. "There is no explanation! Agony, death. . . . What for?"

## *XI*

Another two weeks went by in this way and during that fortnight an event occurred that Ivan Ilych and his wife had desired. Petrishchev formally proposed. It happened in the evening. The next day Praskovya Fëdorovna came into her husband's room considering how best to inform him of it, but that very night there had been a fresh change for the worse in his condition. She found him still lying on the sofa but in a different position. He lay on his back, groaning and staring fixedly straight in front of him.

She began to remind him of his medicines, but he turned his eyes towards her with such a look that she did not finish what she was saying; so great an animosity, to her in particular, did that look express.

"For Christ's sake let me die in peace!" he said.

She would have gone away, but just then their daughter came in and went up to say good morning. He looked at her as he had done at his wife,

[21]**morocco** soft, fine leather made of goatskin

and in reply to her inquiry about his health said dryly that he would soon free them all of himself. They were both silent and after sitting with him for a while went away.

"Is it our fault?" Lisa said to her mother. "It's as if we were to blame! I am sorry for papa, but why should we be tortured?"

The doctor came at his usual time. Ivan Ilych answered "Yes" and "No," never taking his angry eyes from him, and at last said: "You know you can do nothing for me, so leave me alone."

320 "We can ease your sufferings."

"You can't even do that. Let me be."

The doctor went into the drawing-room and told Praskovya Fëdorovna that the case was very serious and that the only resource left was opium to allay her husband's sufferings, which must be terrible.

It was true, as the doctor said, that Ivan Ilych's physical sufferings were terrible, but worse than the physical sufferings were his mental sufferings, which were his chief torture.

His mental sufferings were due to the fact that one night, as he looked at Gerasim's sleepy, good-natured face with its prominent cheekbones, the question suddenly occurred to him: "What if my whole life has really been wrong?"

325 It occurred to him that what had appeared perfectly impossible before, namely that he had not spent his life as he should have done, might after all be true. It occurred to him that his scarcely perceptible attempts to struggle against what was considered good by the most highly placed people, those scarcely noticeable impulses which he had immediately suppressed, might have been the real thing, and all the rest false. And his professional duties and the whole arrangement of his life and of his family, and all his social and official interests, might all have been false. He tried to defend all those things to himself and suddenly felt the weakness of what he was defending. There was nothing to defend.

"But if that is so," he said to himself, "and I am leaving this life with the consciousness that I have lost all that was given me and it is impossible to rectify it—what then?"

He lay on his back and began to pass his life in review in quite a new way. In the morning when he saw first his footman, then his wife, then his daughter, and then the doctor, their every word and movement confirmed to him the awful truth that had been revealed to him during the night. In them he saw himself—all that for which he had lived—and saw clearly that it was not real at all, but a terrible and huge deception which had hidden both life and death. This consciousness intensified his physical suffering tenfold. He groaned and tossed about, and pulled at his clothing which choked and stifled him. And he hated them on that account.

He was given a large dose of opium and became unconscious, but at noon his sufferings began again. He drove everybody away and tossed from side to side.

His wife came to him and said:

330 "Jean, my dear, do this for me. It can't do any harm and often helps. Healthy people often do it."

He opened his eyes wide.

"What? Take communion? Why? It's unnecessary! However. . . ."

She began to cry.

"Yes, do, my dear. I'll send for our priest. He is such a nice man."

335 "All right. Very well," he muttered.

When the priest came and heard his confession, Ivan Ilych was softened and seemed to feel a relief from his doubts and consequently from his sufferings, and for a moment there came a ray of hope. He again began to think of the vermiform appendix and the possibility of correcting it. He received the sacrament with tears in his eyes.

When they laid him down again afterwards he felt a moment's ease, and the hope that he might live awoke in him again. He began to think of the operation that had been suggested to him. "To live! I want to live!" he said to himself.

His wife came in to congratulate him after his communion, and when uttering the usual conventional words she added:

"You feel better, don't you?"

340 Without looking at her he said "Yes."

Her dress, her figure, the expression of her face, the tone of her voice, all revealed the same thing. "This is wrong, it is not as it should be. All you have lived for and still live for is falsehood and deception, hiding life and death from you." And as soon as he admitted that thought, his hatred and his agonizing physical suffering again sprang up, and with that suffering a consciousness of the unavoidable, approaching end. And to this was added a new sensation of grinding shooting pain and a feeling of suffocation.

The expression of his face when he uttered that "yes" was dreadful. Having uttered it, he looked her straight in the eyes, turned on his face with a rapidity extraordinary in his weak state and shouted:

"Go away! Go away and leave me alone!"

## *XII*

From that moment the screaming began that continued for three days, and was so terrible that one could not hear it through two closed doors without horror. At the moment he answered his wife he realized that he was lost, that there was no return, that the end had come, the very end, and his doubts were still unsolved and remained doubts.

345 "Oh! Oh! Oh!" he cried in various intonations. He had begun by screaming "I won't!" and continued screaming on the letter *O.*

For three whole days, during which time did not exist for him, he struggled in that black sack into which he was being thrust by an invisible, resistless force. He struggled as a man condemned to death struggles in the hands of the executioner, knowing that he cannot save himself. And every moment he felt that despite all his efforts he was drawing nearer and nearer to what terrified him. He felt that his agony was due to his being thrust into that black hole and still more to his not being able to get right into it. He was hindered from getting into it by his conviction that his life had been a good one. That very justification of his life held him fast and prevented his moving forward, and it caused him most torment of all.

Suddenly some force struck him in the chest and side, making it still harder to breathe, and he fell through the hole and there at the bottom was a light. What had happened to him was like the sensation one sometimes experiences in a railway carriage when one thinks one is going backwards while one is really going forwards and suddenly becomes aware of the real direction.

"Yes, it was all not the right thing," he said to himself, "but that's no matter. It can be done. But what *is* the right thing?" he asked himself, and suddenly grew quiet.

This occurred at the end of the third day, two hours before his death. Just then his schoolboy son had crept softly in and gone up to the bedside. The dying man was still screaming desperately and waving his arms. His hand fell on the boy's head, and the boy caught it, pressed it to his lips, and began to cry.

At that very moment Ivan Ilych fell through and caught sight of the light, and it was revealed to him that though his life had not been what it should have been, this could still be rectified. He asked himself, "What *is* the right thing?" and grew still, listening. Then he felt that someone was kissing his hand. He opened his eyes, looked at his son, and felt sorry for him. His wife came up to him and he glanced at her. She was gazing at him open-mouthed, with undried tears on her nose and cheek and a despairing look on her face. He felt sorry for her too.

"Yes, I am making them wretched," he thought. "They are sorry, but it will be better for them when I die." He wished to say this but had not the strength to utter it. "Besides, why speak? I must act," he thought. With a look at his wife he indicated his son and said: "Take him away . . . sorry for him . . . sorry for you too. . . ." He tried to add, "forgive me," but said "forgo" and waved his hand, knowing that He whose understanding mattered would understand.

And suddenly it grew clear to him that what had been oppressing him and would not leave him was all dropping away at once from two sides, from ten sides, and from all sides. He was sorry for them, he must act so as not to hurt them: release them and free himself from these sufferings. "How good and how simple!" he thought. "And the pain?" he asked himself. "What has become of it? Where are you, pain?"

He turned his attention to it.

"Yes, here it is. Well, what of it? Let the pain be."

"And death . . . where is it?"

He sought his former accustomed fear of death and did not find it. "Where is it? What death?" There was no fear because there was no death. In place of death there was light.

"So that's what it is!" he suddenly exclaimed aloud. "What joy!"

To him all this happened in a single instant, and the meaning of that instant did not change. For those present his agony continued for another two hours. Something rattled in his throat, his emaciated body twitched, then the gasping and rattle became less and less frequent.

"It is finished!" said someone near him.

He heard these words and repeated them in his soul.

"Death is finished," he said to himself. "It is no more!"

He drew in a breath, stopped in the midst of a sigh, stretched out, and died.

[*1886*]

## SARAH ORNE JEWETT

*Sarah Orne Jewett (1849–1909) was born and raised in South Berwick, Maine. A sickly girl, Jewett received little formal education, but her father, a doctor, introduced her to British and American fiction. Inspired by the writings of Harriet Beecher Stowe, in her teens Jewett determined to become a writer and began writing sketches and stories about the rural people of her native region. (Although South Berwick in Jewett's day was beginning to become industrialized, it had once been a busy port in a rural setting; Jewett's grandfather had been a sea captain and a leading owner of ships.) When she was twenty, she published her first story in the* Atlantic Monthly, *and she continued to publish in national magazines stories about the vanishing life of her childhood.*

# *A White Heron*

### *I*

The woods were already filled with shadows one June evening, just before eight o'clock, though a bright sunset still glimmered faintly among the trunks of the trees. A little girl was driving home her cow, a plodding, dilatory, provoking creature in her behavior, but a valued companion for all that. They were going away from whatever light there was, and striking deep into the woods, but their feet were familiar with the path, and it was no matter whether their eyes could see it or not.

There was hardly a night the summer through when the old cow could be found waiting at the pasture bars; on the contrary, it was her greatest pleasure to hide herself away among the huckleberry bushes, and though she wore a loud bell she had made the discovery that if one stood perfectly still it would not ring. So Sylvia had to hunt for her until she found her, and call Co'! Co'! with never an answering Moo, until her childish patience was quite spent. If the creature had not given good milk and plenty of it, the case would have seemed very different to her owners. Besides, Sylvia had all the time there was, and very little use to make of it. Sometimes in pleasant weather it was a consolation to look upon the cow's pranks as an intelligent attempt to play hide and seek, and as the child had no playmates she lent herself to this amusement with a good deal of zest. Though this chase had been so long that the wary animal herself had given an unusual signal of her whereabouts, Sylvia had only laughed when she came upon Mistress Molly at the swampside, and urged her affectionately homeward with a twig of birch leaves. The old cow was not inclined to wander farther, she even turned in the right direction for once as they left the pasture, and stepped along the road at a good pace. She was quite ready to be milked now, and seldom stopped to browse. Sylvia wondered what her grandmother would say because they were so late. It was a great while since she had left home at half-past five o'clock, but everybody knew the difficulty of making this errand a short one. Mrs. Tilley had chased the horned torment too many summer evenings herself to blame any one else for lingering, and was only thankful as she waited that she had Sylvia, nowadays, to give such valuable assistance. The good woman suspected that Sylvia loitered occasionally on her own account; there never was such a child for straying about out-of-doors since the world was made! Everybody said that it was a good change for a little maid who had tried to grow for eight years in a crowded manufacturing town, but as for Sylvia herself, it seemed as if she never had been alive at all before she came to live at the farm. She thought often with wistful compassion of a wretched geranium that belonged to a town neighbor.

"'Afraid of folks,'" old Mrs. Tilley said to herself, with a smile, after she had made the unlikely choice of Sylvia from her daughter's houseful of children, and was returning to the farm. "'Afraid of folks,' they said! I guess she won't be troubled no great with 'em up to the old place!" When they reached the door of the lonely house and stopped to unlock it, and the cat came to purr loudly, and rub against them, a deserted pussy, indeed, but fat with young robins, Sylvia whispered that this was a beautiful place to live in, and she never should wish to go home.

The companions followed the shady woodroad, the cow taking slow steps and the child very fast ones. The cow stopped long at the brook to drink, as if the pasture were not half a swamp, and Sylvia stood still and waited, letting her bare feet cool themselves in the shoal water, while the great twilight moths struck softly against her. She waded on through the brook as the cow moved away, and listened to the thrushes with a heart that beat fast with pleasure. There was a stirring in the great boughs overhead. They were full of little birds and beasts that seemed to be wide awake, and going about their world, or else saying goodnight to each other in sleepy twitters. Sylvia herself felt sleepy as she walked along. However, it was not much farther to the house, and the air was soft and sweet. She was not often in the woods so late as this, and it made her feel as if she were a part of the gray shadows and the moving leaves. She was just thinking how long it seemed since she first came to the farm a year ago, and wondering if everything went on in the noisy town just the same as when she was there; the thought of the great red-faced boy who used to chase and frighten her made her hurry along the path to escape from the shadow of the trees.

5 Suddenly this little woods-girl is horror-stricken to hear a clear whistle not very far away. Not a bird's-whistle, which would have a sort of friendliness, but a boy's whistle, determined, and somewhat aggressive. Sylvia left the cow to whatever sad fate might await her, and stepped discreetly aside into the brushes, but she was just too late. The enemy had discovered her, and called out in a very cheerful and persuasive tone, "Halloa, little girl, how far is it to the road?" and trembling Sylvia answered almost inaudibly, "A good ways."

She did not dare to look boldly at the tall young man, who carried a gun over his shoulder, but she came out of her bush and again followed the cow, while he walked alongside.

"I have been hunting for some birds," the stranger said kindly, "and I have lost my way, and need a friend very much. Don't be afraid," he added gallantly. "Speak up and tell me what your name is, and whether you think I can spend the night at your house, and go out gunning early in the morning."

Sylvia was more alarmed than before. Would not her grandmother consider her much to blame? But who could have foreseen such an accident as this? It did not seem to be her fault, and she hung her head as if the stem of it were broken, but managed to answer "Sylvy," with much effort when her companion again asked her name.

Mrs. Tilley was standing in the doorway when the trio came into view. The cow gave a loud moo by way of explanation.

10 "Yes, you'd better speak up for yourself, you old trial! Where'd she tucked herself away this time, Sylvy?" But Sylvia kept an awed silence; she knew by instinct that her grandmother did not comprehend the gravity of the situation. She must be mistaking the stranger for one of the farmer-lads of the region.

The young man stood his gun beside the door, and dropped a lumpy game-bag beside it; then he bade Mrs. Tilley good-evening, and repeated his wayfarer's story, and asked if he could have a night's lodging.

"Put me anywhere you like," he said. "I must be off early in the morning, before day; but I am very hungry, indeed. You can give me some milk at any rate, that's plain."

"Dear sakes, yes," responded the hostess, whose long slumbering hospitality seemed to be easily awakened. "You might fare better if you went out to the main road a mile or so, but you're welcome to what we've got. I'll milk right off, and you make yourself at home. You can sleep on husks or feathers," she proffered graciously. "I raised them all myself. There's good pasturing for geese just below here towards the ma'sh. Now step round and set a plate for the gentleman, Sylvy!" And Sylvia promptly stepped. She was glad to have something to do, and she was hungry herself.

It was a surprise to find so clean and comfortable a little dwelling in this New England wilderness. The young man had known the horrors of its most primitive housekeeping, and the dreary squalor of that level of society which does not rebel at the companionship of hens. This was the best thrift of an old-fashioned farmstead, though on such a small scale that it seemed like a hermitage. He listened eagerly to the old woman's quaint talk, he watched Sylvia's pale face and shining gray eyes with ever growing enthusiasm, and insisted that this was the best supper he had eaten for a month, and afterward the new-made friends sat down in the doorway together while the moon came up.

15 Soon it would be berry-time, and Sylvia was a great help at picking. The cow was a good milker, though a plaguy thing to keep track of, the hostess gossiped frankly, adding presently that she had buried four children, so Sylvia's mother, and a son (who might be dead) in California were all the children she had left. "Dan, my boy, was a great hand to go gunning," she explained sadly. "I never wanted for pa'tridges or gray squer'ls while he was to home. He's been a great wand'rer, I expect, and he's no hand to write letters. There, I don't blame him, I'd ha' seen the world myself if it had been so I could."

"Sylvy takes after him," the grandmother continued affectionately, after a minute's pause. "There ain't a foot o' ground she don't know her way over, and the wild creaturs counts her one o' themselves. Squer'ls she'll tame to come an' feed right out o' her hands, and all sorts o' birds. Last winter she got the jaybirds to bangeing here, and I believe she'd 'a' scanted herself of her own meals to have plenty to throw out amongst 'em, if I hadn't kep' watch. Anything but crows, I tell her, I'm willin' to help support—though Dan he had a tamed one o' them that did seem to have reason same as folks. It was round here a good spell after he went away. Dan an' his father they didn't hitch,—but he never held up his head ag'in after Dan had dared him an' gone off."

The guest did not notice this hint of family sorrows in his eager interest in something else.

"So Sylvy knows all about birds, does she?" he exclaimed, as he looked round at the little girl who sat, very demure but increasingly sleepy, in the moonlight. "I am making a collection of birds myself. I have been at it ever since I was a boy." (Mrs. Tilley smiled.) "There are two or three very rare ones I have been hunting for these five years. I mean to get them on my own ground if they can be found."

"Do you cage 'em up?" asked Mrs. Tilley doubtfully, in response to this enthusiastic announcement.

20 "Oh no, they're stuffed and preserved, dozens and dozens of them," said the ornithologist, "and I have shot or snared every one myself. I caught a glimpse of a white heron a few miles from here on Saturday, and I have followed it in this direction. They have never been found in this district at all. The little white heron, it is," and he turned again to look at Sylvia with the hope of discovering that the rare bird was one of her acquaintances.

But Sylvia was watching a hop-toad in the narrow footpath.

"You would know the heron if you saw it," the stranger continued eagerly. "A queer tall white bird with soft feathers and long thin legs. And it would have a nest perhaps in the top of a high tree, made of sticks, something like a hawk's nest."

Sylvia's heart gave a wild beat; she knew that strange white bird, and had once stolen softly near where it stood in some bright green swamp grass, away over at the other side of the woods. There was an open place where the sunshine always seemed strangely yellow and hot, where tall, nodding rushes grew, and her grandmother had warned her that she might sink in the soft black mud underneath and never be heard of more. Not far beyond were the salt marshes just this side the sea itself, which Sylvia wondered and dreamed much about, but never had seen, whose great voice could sometimes be heard above the noise of the woods on stormy nights.

"I can't think of anything I should like so much as to find that heron's nest," the handsome stranger was saying. "I would give ten dollars to anybody who could show it to me," he added desperately, "and I mean to spend my whole vacation hunting for it if need be. Perhaps it was only migrating, or had been chased out of its own region by some bird of prey."

25 Mrs. Tilley gave amazed attention to all this, but Sylvia still watched the toad, not divining, as she might have done at some calmer time, that the creature wished to get to its hole under the door-step, and was much hindered by the unusual spectators at that hour of the evening. No amount of thought, that night, could decide how many wished-for treasures the ten dollars, so lightly spoken of, could buy.

The next day the young sportsman hovered about the woods, and Sylvia kept him company, having lost her first fear of the friendly lad, who proved to be most kind and sympathetic. He told her many things about the birds and what they knew and where they lived and what they did with themselves. And he gave her a jack-knife, which she thought as great a treasure as if she were a desert-islander. All day long he did not once make her troubled or afraid except when he brought down some unsuspecting singing creature from its bough. Sylvia would have liked him vastly better without his gun: she could not understand why he killed the very birds he seemed to like so much. But as the day waned, Sylvia still watched the young man with loving admiration. She had never seen anybody so charming and delightful; the woman's heart, asleep in the child, was vaguely thrilled by a dream of love. Some premonition of that great power stirred and swayed these young creatures who traversed the solemn woodlands with soft-footed silent care. They stopped to listen to a bird's song; they pressed forward again eagerly, parting the branches—speaking to each other rarely and in whispers; the young man going first and Sylvia following, fascinated, a few steps behind, with her gray eyes dark with excitement.

She grieved because the longed-for white heron was elusive, but she did not lead the guest, she only followed, and there was no such thing as speaking first. The sound of her own unquestioned voice would have terrified her—it was hard enough to answer yes or no when there was need of that. At last evening began to fall, and they drove the cow home together, and Sylvia smiled with pleasure when they came to the place where she heard the whistle and was afraid only the night before.

## *II*

Half a mile from home, at the farther edge of the woods, where the land was highest, a great pine-tree stood, the last of its generation. Whether it was left for a boundary mark, or for what reason, no one could say; the woodchoppers who had felled its mates were dead and gone long ago, and a whole forest of sturdy trees, pines and oaks and maples, had grown again. But the stately head of this old pine towered above them all and made a landmark for sea and shore miles and miles away. Sylvia knew it well. She had always believed that whoever climbed to the top of it could see the ocean; and the little girl had often laid her hand on the great rough trunk and looked up wistfully at those dark boughs that the wind always stirred, no matter how hot and still the air might be below. Now she thought of the tree with a new excitement, for why, if one climbed it at break of day could not one see all the world, and easily discover from whence the white heron flew, and mark the place, and find the hidden nest?

What a spirit of adventure, what wild ambition! What fancied triumph and delight and glory for the later morning when she could make known the secret! It was almost too real and too great for the childish heart to bear.

All night the door of the little house stood open and the whippoorwills came and sang upon the very step. The young sportsman and his old hostess were sound asleep, but Sylvia's great design kept her broad awake and watching. She forgot to think of sleep. The short summer night seemed as long as the winter darkness, and at last when the whippoorwills ceased, and she was afraid the morning would after all come too soon, she stole out of the house and followed the pasture path through the woods, hastening toward the open ground beyond, listening with a sense of comfort and companionship to the drowsy twitter of a half-awakened bird, whose perch she had jarred in passing. Alas, if the great wave of human interest which flooded for the first time this dull little life should sweep away the satisfactions of an existence heart to heart with nature and the dumb life of the forest!

There was the huge tree asleep yet in the paling moonlight, and small and silly Sylvia began with utmost bravery to mount to the top of it, with tingling, eager blood coursing the channels of her whole frame, with her bare feet and fingers, that pinched and held like bird's claws to the monstrous ladder reaching up, up, almost to the sky itself. First she must mount the white oak tree that grew alongside, where she was almost lost among the dark branches and the green leaves heavy and wet with dew; a bird fluttered off its nest, and a red squirrel ran to and fro and scolded pettishly at the harmless housebreaker. Sylvia felt her way easily. She had often climbed there, and knew that higher still one of the oak's upper branches chafed against the pine trunk, just where its lower boughs were set close together. There, when she made the dangerous pass from one tree to the other, the great enterprise would really begin.

She crept out along the swaying oak limb at last, and took the daring step across into the old pine-tree. The way was harder than she thought; she must reach far and hold fast, the sharp dry twigs caught and held her and scratched her like angry talons, the pitch made her thin little fingers clumsy and stiff as she went round and round the tree's great stem, higher and higher upward. The sparrows and robins in the woods below were beginning to wake and twitter to the dawn, yet it seemed much lighter there aloft in the pine-tree, and the child knew she must hurry if her project were to be of any use.

The tree seemed to lengthen itself out as she went up, and to reach farther and farther upward. It was like a great main-mast to the voyaging earth; it must truly have been amazed that morning through all its ponderous frame as it felt this determined spark of human spirit wending its way from higher branch to branch. Who knows how steadily the least twigs held themselves to advantage this light, weak creature on her way! The old pine must have loved his new dependent. More than all the hawks, and bats, and moths, and even the sweet voiced thrushes, was the brave, beating heart of the solitary gray-eyed child. And the tree stood still and frowned away the winds that June morning while the dawn grew bright in the east.

Sylvia's face was like a pale star, if one had seen it from the ground, when the last thorny bough was past, and she stood trembling and tired but wholly triumphant, high in the treetop. Yes, there was the sea with the dawning sun making a golden dazzle over it, and toward that glorious east flew two hawks with slow-moving pinions. How low they looked in the air from that height when one had only seen them before far up, and dark against the blue sky. Their gray feathers were as soft as moths; they seemed only a little way from the tree, and Sylvia felt as if she too could go flying away among the clouds. Westward, the woodlands and farms reached miles and miles into the distance; here and there were church steeples, and white villages, truly it was a vast and awesome world!

The birds sang louder and louder. At last the sun came up bewilderingly bright. Sylvia could see the white sails of ships out at sea, and the clouds that were purple and rose-colored and yellow at first began to fade away. Where was the white heron's nest in the sea of green branches, and was this wonderful sight and pageant of the world the only reward for having climbed to such a giddy height? Now look down again, Sylvia, where the green marsh is set among the shining birches and dark hemlocks; there where you saw the white heron once you will see him again; look, look! a white spot of him like a single floating feather comes up from the dead hemlock and grows larger, and rises, and comes close at last, and goes by the landmark pine with steady sweep of wing and outstretched slender neck and crested head. And wait! wait! do not move a foot or a finger, little girl, do not send an arrow of light and consciousness from your two eager eyes, for the heron has perched on a pine bough not far beyond yours, and cries back to his mate on the nest and plumes his feathers for the new day!

The child gives a long sigh a minute later when a company of shouting catbirds comes also to the tree, and vexed by their fluttering and lawlessness the solemn heron goes away. She knows his secret now, the wild, light, slender bird that floats and wavers, and goes back like an arrow presently to his home in the green world beneath. Then Sylvia, well satisfied, makes her perilous way down again, not daring to look far below the branch she stands on, ready to cry sometimes because her fingers ache and her lamed feet slip. Wondering over and over again what the stranger would say to her, and what he would think when she told him how to find his way straight to the heron's nest.

"Sylvy, Sylvy!" called the busy old grandmother again and again, but nobody answered, and the small husk bed was empty and Sylvia had disappeared.

The guest waked from a dream, and remembering his day's pleasure hurried to dress himself that might it sooner begin. He was sure from the way the shy little girl looked once or twice yesterday that she had at least seen the white heron, and now she must really be made to tell. Here she comes now, paler than ever, and her worn old frock is torn and tattered, and smeared with pine pitch. The grandmother and the sportsman stand in the door together and question her, and the splendid moment has come to speak of the dead hemlock-tree by the green marsh.

But Sylvia does speak after all, though the old grandmother fretfully rebukes her, and the young man's kind, appealing eyes are looking straight in her own. He can make them rich with money; he has promised it, and they are poor now. He is so well worth making happy, and he waits to hear the story she can tell.

No, she must keep silence! What is it that suddenly forbids her and makes her dumb? Has she been nine years growing and now, when the great world for the first time puts out a hand to her, must she thrust it aside for a bird's sake? The murmur of the pine's green branches is in her ears, she remembers how the white heron came flying through the golden air and how they watched the sea and the morning together, and Sylvia cannot speak; she cannot tell the heron's secret and give its life away.

Dear loyalty, that suffered a sharp pang as the guest went away disappointed later in the day, that could have served and followed him and loved him as a dog loves! Many a night Sylvia heard the echo of his whistle haunting the pasture path as she came home with the loitering cow. She forgot even her sorrow at the sharp report of his gun and the sight of thrushes and sparrows dropping silent to the ground, their songs hushed and their pretty feathers stained and wet with blood. Were the birds better friends than their hunter might have been,—who can tell? Whatever treasures were lost to her, woodlands and summer-time, remember! Bring your gifts and graces and tell your secrets to this lonely country child!

[*1886*]

## WILLA CATHER

*Willa Cather (1873-1947) was born in Gore, Virginia, but when she was nine her family moved to rural Nebraska. While an undergraduate at the University of Nebraska she published short stories and served as a drama critic for the* Nebraska State Journal. *From 1895 to 1906 she lived in Pittsburgh, working first as a journalist and later as a teacher. In 1906 she went to New York to work for* McClure's Magazine; *in 1911 she left the magazine in order to devote all of her time to writing. "Paul's Case," written in 1904, is an early work. Her most widely known works, novels, were written later:* O Pioneers! *(1913),* The Song of the Lark *(1915),* My Antonia *(1918),* A Lost Lady *(1923), and* Death Comes for the Archbishop *(1927).*

# *Paul's Case*

It was Paul's afternoon to appear before the faculty of the Pittsburgh High School to account for his various misdemeanors. He had been suspended a week ago, and his father had called at the Principal's office and confessed his perplexity about his son. Paul entered the faculty room suave and smiling. His clothes were a trifle outgrown and the tan velvet on the collar of his open overcoat was frayed and worn; but for all that there was something of the dandy about him, and he wore an opal pin in his neatly knotted black four-in-hand, and a red carnation in his buttonhole. This latter adornment the faculty somehow felt was not properly significant of the contrite spirit befitting a boy under the ban of suspension.

Paul was tall for his age and very thin, with high, cramped shoulders and a narrow chest. His eyes were remarkable for a certain hysterical brilliancy and he continually used them in a conscious, theatrical sort of way, peculiarly offensive in a boy. The pupils were abnormally large, as though he were addicted to belladonna, but there was a glassy glitter about them which that drug does not produce.

When questioned by the Principal as to why he was there, Paul stated, politely enough, that he wanted to come back to school. This was a lie, but Paul was quite accustomed to lying; found it, indeed, indispensable for overcoming friction. His teachers were asked to state their respective charges against him, which they did with such a rancor and aggrievedness as evinced that this was not a usual case. Disorder and impertinence were among the offenses named, yet each of his instructors felt that it was scarcely possible to put into words the real cause of the trouble, which lay in a sort of hysterically defiant manner of the boy's; in the contempt which they all knew he felt for them, and which he seemingly made not the least effort to conceal. Once, when he had been making a synopsis of a paragraph at the blackboard, his English teacher had stepped to his side and attempted to guide his hand. Paul had started back with a shudder and thrust his hands violently behind him. The astonished woman could scarcely have been more hurt and embarrassed had he struck at her. The insult was so involuntary and definitely personal as to be unforgettable. In one way and another, he had made all his teachers, men and women alike, conscious of the same feeling of physical aversion. In one class he habitually sat with his hand shading his eyes; in another he always looked out of the window during the recitation; in another he made a running commentary on the lecture, with humorous intention.

His teachers felt this afternoon that his whole attitude was symbolized by his shrug and his flippantly red carnation flower, and they fell upon him without mercy, his English teacher leading the pack. He stood through it smiling, his pale lips parted over his white teeth. (His lips were continually twitching, and he had a habit of raising his eyebrows that was contemptuous and irritating to the last degree.) Older boys than Paul had broken down and shed tears under that baptism of fire, but his set smile did not once desert him, and his only sign of discomfort was the nervous trembling of the fingers that toyed with the buttons of his overcoat, and an occasional jerking of the other hand that held his hat. Paul was always smiling, always glancing about him, seeming to feel that people might be watching him and trying to detect something. This conscious expression, since it was as far as possible from boyish mirthfulness, was usually attributed to insolence or "smartness."

5 As the inquisition proceeded, one of his instructors repeated an impertinent remark of the boy's, and the Principal asked him whether he thought that a courteous speech to have made a woman. Paul shrugged his shoulders slightly and his eyebrows twitched.

"I don't know," he replied. "I didn't mean to be polite or impolite, either. I guess it's a sort of way I have of saying things regardless."

The Principal, who was a sympathetic man, asked him whether he didn't think that a way it would be well to get rid of. Paul grinned and said he guessed so. When he was told that he could go, he bowed gracefully and went out. His bow was but a repetition of the scandalous red carnation.

His teachers were in despair, and his drawing master voiced the feeling of them all when he declared there was something about the boy which none of them understood. He added: "I don't really believe that smile of his comes altogether from insolence; there's something sort of haunted about it. The boy is not strong, for one thing. I happen to know that he was born in Colorado, only a few months before his mother died out there of a long illness. There is something wrong about the fellow."

The drawing master had come to realize that, in looking at Paul, one saw only his white teeth and the forced animation of his eyes. One warm afternoon the boy had gone to sleep at his drawing-board, and his master had noted with amazement what a white, blue-veined face it was; drawn and wrinkled like an old man's about the eyes, the lips twitching even in his sleep, and stiff with a nervous tension that drew them back from his teeth.

10 His teachers left the building dissatisfied and unhappy; humiliated to have felt so vindictive toward a mere boy, to have uttered this feeling in cutting terms, and to have set each other on, as it were, in the gruesome game of intemperate reproach. Some of them remembered having seen a miserable street cat set at bay by a ring of tormentors.

As for Paul, he ran down the hill whistling the Soldiers' Chorus from *Faust* looking wildly behind him now and then to see whether some of his teachers were not there to writhe under his light-heartedness. As it was now late in the afternoon and Paul was on duty that evening as usher at Carnegie Hall, he decided that he would not go home to supper. When he reached the concert hall the doors were not yet open and, as it was chilly outside, he decided to go up into the picture gallery—always deserted at this hour—where there were some of Raffaelli's gay studies of Paris streets and an airy blue Venetian scene or two that always exhilarated him. He was delighted to find no one in the gallery but the old guard, who sat in one corner, a newspaper on his knee, a black patch over one eye and the other closed. Paul possessed himself of the place and walked confidently up and down, whistling under his breath. After a while he sat down before a blue Rico and lost himself. When he bethought him to look at his watch, it was after seven o'clock, and he rose with a start and ran downstairs, making a face at Augustus, peering out from the cast-room, and an evil gesture at the Venus of Milo as he passed her on the stairway.

When Paul reached the ushers' dressing-room half-a-dozen boys were there already, and he began excitedly to tumble into his uniform. It was one of the few that at all approached fitting, and Paul thought it very becoming—though he knew that the tight, straight coat accentuated his narrow chest, about which he was exceedingly sensitive. He was always considerably excited while he dressed, twanging all over to the tuning of the strings and the preliminary flourishes of the horns in the music-room; but to-night he seemed quite beside himself, and he teased and plagued the boys until, telling him that he was crazy, they put him down on the floor and sat on him.

Somewhat calmed by his suppression, Paul dashed out to the front of the house to seat the early comers. He was a model usher; gracious and smiling he ran up and down the aisles; nothing was too much trouble for him; he carried messages and brought programmes as though it were his greatest pleasure in life, and all the people in his section thought him a charming boy, feeling that he remembered and admired them. As the house filled, he grew more and more vivacious and animated, and the color came to his cheeks and lips. It was very much as though this were a great reception and Paul were the host. Just as the musicians came out to take their places, his English teacher arrived with checks for the seats which a prominent manufacturer had taken for the season. She betrayed some embarrassment when she handed Paul the tickets, and a *hauteur* which subsequently made her feel very foolish. Paul was startled for a moment, and had the feeling of wanting to put her out; what business had she here among all these fine people and gay colors? He looked her over and decided that she was not appropriately dressed and must be a fool to sit downstairs in such togs. The tickets had probably been sent her out of kindness, he reflected as he put down a seat for her, and she had about as much right to sit there as he had.

When the symphony began Paul sank into one of the rear seats with a long sigh of relief, and lost himself as he had done before the Rico. It was not that symphonies, as such, meant anything in particular to Paul, but the first sigh of the instruments seemed to free some hilarious and potent spirit within him; something that struggled there like the Genius in the bottle found by the Arab fisherman. He felt a sudden zest of life; the lights danced before his eyes and the concert hall blazed into unimaginable splendor. When the soprano soloist came on, Paul forgot even the nastiness of his teacher's being there and gave himself up to the peculiar stimulus such personages always had for him. The soloist chanced to be a German woman, by no means in her first youth, and the mother of many children; but she wore an elaborate gown and a tiara, and above all she had that indefinable air of achievement, that world-shine upon her, which, in Paul's eyes, made her a veritable queen of Romance.

15 After a concert was over Paul was always irritable and wretched until he got to sleep, and tonight he was even more than usually restless. He had the feeling of not being able to let down, of its being impossible to give up this delicious excitement which was the only thing that could be called living at all. During the last number he withdrew and, after hastily changing his clothes in the dressing-room, slipped out to the side door where the soprano's carriage stood. Here he began pacing rapidly up and down the walk, waiting to see her come out.

Over yonder the Schenley, in its vacant stretch, loomed big and square through the fine rain, the windows of its twelve stories glowing like those of a lighted cardboard house under a Christmas tree. All the actors and singers of the better class stayed there when they were in the city, and a number of the big manufacturers of the place lived there in the winter. Paul had often hung about the hotel, watching the people go in and out, longing to enter and leave school-masters and dull care behind him forever.

At last the singer came out, accompanied by the conductor, who helped her into her carriage and closed the door with a cordial *auf wiedersehen* which set Paul to wondering whether she were not an old sweetheart of his. Paul followed the carriage over to the hotel, walking so rapidly as not to be far from the entrance when the singer alighted and disappeared behind the swinging glass doors that were opened by a negro in a tall hat and a long coat. In the moment that the door was ajar it seemed to Paul that he, too, entered. He seemed to feel himself go after her up the steps, into the warm, lighted building, into an exotic, a tropical world of shiny, glistening surfaces and basking ease. He reflected upon the mysterious dishes that were brought into the dining-room, the green bottles in buckets of ice, as he had seen them in the supper party pictures of the *Sunday World* supplement. A quick gust of wind brought the rain down with sudden vehemence, and Paul was startled to find that he was still outside in the slush of the gravel driveway; that his boots were letting in the water and his scanty overcoat was clinging wet about him; that the lights in front of the concert hall were out, and that the rain was driving in sheets between him and the orange glow of the windows above him. There it was, what he wanted—tangibly before him, like the fairy world of a Christmas pantomime, but mocking spirits stood guard at the doors, and, as the rain beat in his face, Paul wondered whether he were destined always to shiver in the black night outside, looking up at it.

He turned and walked reluctantly toward the car tracks. The end had to come sometime; his father in his night-clothes at the top of the stairs, explanations that did not explain, hastily improvised fictions that were forever tripping him up, his upstairs room and its horrible yellow wall-paper, the creaking bureau with the greasy plush collar-box, and over his painted wooden bed the pictures of George Washington and John Calvin, and the framed motto, "Feed my Lambs," which had been worked in red worsted by his mother.

Half an hour later, Paul alighted from his car and went slowly down one of the side streets off the main thoroughfare. It was a highly respectable street, where all the houses were exactly alike, and where businessmen of moderate means begot and reared large families of children, all of whom went to Sabbath-school and learned the shorter catechism, and were interested in arithmetic; all of whom were as exactly alike as their homes, and of a piece with the monotony in which they lived. Paul never went up Cordelia Street without a shudder of loathing. His home was next to the house of the Cumberland minister. He approached it tonight with the nerveless sense of defeat, the hopeless feeling of sinking back forever into ugliness and commonness that he had always had when he came home. The moment he turned into Cordelia Street he felt the waters close above his head. After each of these orgies of living, he experienced all the physical depression which follows a debauch; the loathing of respectable beds, of common food, of a house penetrated by kitchen odors; a shuddering repulsion for the flavorless, colorless mass of everyday existence; a morbid desire for cool things and soft lights and fresh flowers.

The nearer he approached the house, the more absolutely unequal Paul felt to the sight of it all; his ugly sleeping chamber; the cold bathroom with the grimy zinc tub, the cracked mirror, the dripping spigots; his father, at the top of the stairs, his hairy legs sticking out from his night-shirt, his feet thrust into carpet slippers. He was so much later than usual that there would certainly be inquiries and reproaches. Paul stopped short before the door. He felt that he could not be accosted by his father tonight; that he could not toss again on that miserable bed. He would not go in. He would tell his father that he had no car fare, and it was raining so hard he had gone home with one of the boys and stayed all night.

Meanwhile, he was wet and cold. He went around to the back of the house and tried one of the basement windows, found it open, raised it cautiously, and scrambled down the cellar wall to the floor. There he stood, holding his breath, terrified by the noise he had made, but the floor above him was silent, and there was no creak on the stairs. He found a soap-box, and carried it over to the soft ring of light that streamed from the furnace door, and sat down. He was horribly afraid of rats, so he did not try to sleep, but sat looking distrustfully at the dark, still terrified lest he might have awakened his father. In such reactions, after one of the experiences which made days and nights out of the dreary blanks of the calendar, when his senses were deadened, Paul's head was always singularly clear. Suppose his father had heard him getting in at the window and had come down and shot him for a burglar? Then, again, suppose his father had come down, pistol in hand, and he had cried out in time to save himself, and his father had been horrified to think how nearly he had killed him? Then, again, suppose a day should come when his father would remember that night, and wish there had been no warning cry to stay his hand? With this last supposition Paul entertained himself until daybreak.

The following Sunday was fine; the sodden November chill was broken by the last flash of autumnal summer. In the morning Paul had to go to church and Sabbath-school, as always. On seasonable Sunday afternoons the burghers of Cordelia Street always sat out on their front "stoops," and talked to their neighbors on the next stoop, or called to those across the street in neighborly fashion. The men usually sat on gay cushions placed upon the steps that led down to the sidewalk, while the women, in their Sunday "waists," sat in rockers on the cramped porches, pretending to be greatly at their ease. The children played in the streets; there were so many of them that the place resembled the recreation grounds of a kindergarten. The men on the steps—all in their shirt sleeves, their vests unbuttoned—sat with their legs well apart, their stomachs comfortably protruding, and talked of the prices of things, or told anecdotes of the sagacity of their various chiefs and overlords. They occasionally looked over the multitude of squabbling children, listened affectionately to their high-pitched, nasal voices, smiling to see their own proclivities reproduced in their offspring, and interspersed their legends of the iron kings with remarks about their sons' progress at school, their grades in arithmetic, and the amounts they had saved in their toy banks.

On this last Sunday of November, Paul sat all the afternoon on the lowest step of his "stoop," staring into the street, while his sisters, in their rockers, were talking to the minister's daughters next door about how many shirt-waists they had made in the last week, and how many waffles some one had eaten at the last church supper. When the weather was warm, and his father was in a particularly jovial frame of mind, the girls made lemonade, which was always brought out in a red-glass pitcher, ornamented with forget-me-nots in blue enamel. This the girls thought very fine, and the neighbors always joked about the suspicious color of the pitcher.

Today Paul's father sat on the top step, talking to a young man who shifted a restless baby from knee to knee. He happened to be the young man who was daily held up to Paul as a model, and after whom it was his father's dearest hope that he would pattern. This young man was of a ruddy complexion, with a compressed, red mouth, and faded, near-sighted eyes, over which he wore thick spectacles, with gold bows that curved about his ears. He was clerk to one of the magnates of a great steel corporation, and was looked upon in Cordelia Street as a young man with a future. There was a story that, some five years ago—he was now barely twenty-six—he had been a trifle dissipated but in order to curb his appetites and save the loss of time and strength that a sowing of wild oats might have entailed, he had taken his chief's advice, oft reiterated to his employees, and at twenty-one had married the first woman whom he could persuade to share his fortunes. She happened to be an angular school-mistress, much older than he, who also wore thick glasses, and who had now borne him four children, all near-sighted, like herself.

The young man was relating how his chief, now cruising in the Mediterranean, kept in touch with all the details of the business, arranging his office hours on his yacht just as though he were at home, and "knocking off work enough to keep two stenographers busy." His father told, in turn, the plan his corporation was considering, of putting in an electric railway plant at Cairo. Paul snapped his teeth; he had an awful apprehension that they might spoil it all before he got there. Yet he rather liked to hear these legends of the iron kings, that were told and retold on Sundays and holidays; these stories of palaces in Venice, yachts on the Mediterranean, and high play at Monte Carlo appealed to his fancy, and he was interested in the triumphs of these cash boys who had become famous, though he had no mind for the cash-boy stage.

After supper was over, and he had helped to dry the dishes, Paul nervously asked his father whether he could go to George's to get some help in his geometry, and still more nervously asked for car fare. This latter request he had to repeat, as his father, on principle, did not like to hear requests for money, whether much or little. He asked Paul whether he could not go to some boy who lived nearer, and told him that he ought not to leave his school work until Sunday; but he gave him the dime. He was not a poor man, but he had a worthy ambition to come up in the world. His only reason for allowing Paul to usher was, that he thought a boy ought to be earning a little.

Paul bounded upstairs, scrubbed the greasy odor of the dish-water from his hands with the ill-smelling soap he hated, and then shook over his fingers a few drops of violet water from the bottle he kept hidden in his drawer. He left the house with his geometry conspicuously under his arm, and the moment he got out of Cordelia Street and boarded a downtown car, he shook off the lethargy of two deadening days, and began to live again.

The leading juvenile of the permanent stock company which played at one of the downtown theatres was an acquaintance of Paul's, and the boy had been invited to drop in at the Sunday-night rehearsals whenever he could. For more than a year Paul had spent every available moment loitering about Charley Edwards's dressing-room. He had won a place among Edwards's following not only because the young actor, who could not afford to employ a dresser, often found him useful, but because he recognized in Paul something akin to what churchmen term "vocation."

It was at the theatre and at Carnegie Hall that Paul really lived; the rest was but a sleep and a forgetting. This was Paul's fairy tale, and it had for him all the allurement of a secret love. The moment he inhaled the gassy, painty, dusty odor behind the scenes, he breathed like a prisoner set free, and felt within him the possibility of doing or saying splendid, brilliant, poetic things. The moment the cracked orchestra beat out the overture from *Martha,* or jerked at the serenade from *Rigoletto,* all stupid and ugly things slid from him, and his senses were deliciously, yet delicately fired.

Perhaps it was because, in Paul's world, the natural nearly always wore the guise of ugliness, that a certain element of artificiality seemed to him necessary in beauty. Perhaps it was because his experience of life elsewhere was so full of Sabbath-school picnics, petty economies, wholesome advice as to how to succeed in life, and the unescapable odors of cooking, that he found this existence so alluring, these smartly-clad men and women so attractive, that he was so moved by these starry apple orchards that bloomed perennially under the lime-light.

It would be difficult to put it strongly enough how convincingly the stage entrance of that theatre was for Paul the actual portal of Romance. Certainly none of the company ever suspected it, least of all Charley Edwards. It was very like the old stories that used to float about London of fabulously rich Jews, who had subterranean halls there, with palms, and fountains, and soft lamps and richly apparelled women who never saw the disenchanting light of London day. So, in the midst of that smoke-palled city, enamored of figures and grimy toil, Paul had his secret temple, his wishing carpet, his bit of blue-and-white Mediterranean shore bathed in perpetual sunshine.

Several of Paul's teachers had a theory that his imagination had been perverted by garish fiction, but the truth was that he scarcely ever read at all. The books at home were not such as would either tempt or corrupt a youthful mind, and as for reading the novels that some of his friends urged upon him—well, he got what he wanted much more quickly from music; any sort of music, from an orchestra to a barrel organ. He needed only the spark, the indescribable thrill that made his imagination master of his senses, and he could make plots and pictures enough of his own. It was equally true that he was not stage struck—not, at any rate, in the usual acceptation of that expression. He had no desire to become an actor, any more than he had to become a musician. He felt no necessity to do any of these things; what he wanted was to see, to be in the atmosphere, float on the wave of it, to be carried out, blue league after blue league, away from everything.

After a night behind the scenes, Paul found the school-room more than ever repulsive; the bare floors and naked walls; the prosy men who never wore frock coats, or violets in their buttonholes; the women with their dull gowns, shrill voices, and pitiful seriousness about prepositions that govern the dative. He could not bear to have the other pupils think, for a moment, that he took these people seriously; he must convey to them that he considered it all trivial, and was there only by way of a jest, anyway. He had autographed pictures of all the members of the stock company which he showed his classmates, telling them the most incredible stories of his familiarity with these people, of his acquaintance with the soloists who came to Carnegie Hall, his suppers with them and the flowers he sent them. When these stories lost their effect, and his audience grew listless, he became desperate and would bid all the boys good-bye, announcing that he was going to travel for a while; going to Naples, to Venice, to Egypt. Then, next Monday, he would slip back, conscious and nervously smiling; his sister was ill, and he should have to defer his voyage until spring.

Matters went steadily worse with Paul at school. In the itch to let his instructors know how heartily he despised them and their homilies, and how thoroughly he was appreciated elsewhere, he mentioned once or twice that he had no time to fool with theorems; adding—with a twitch of the eyebrows and a touch of that nervous bravado which so perplexed them—that he was helping the people down at the stock company; they were old friends of his.

35 The upshot of the matter was that the Principal went to Paul's father, and Paul was taken out of school and put to work. The manager at Carnegie Hall was told to get another usher in his stead; the door-keeper at the theatre was warned not to admit him to the house; and Charley Edwards remorsefully promised the boy's father not to see him again.

The members of the stock company were vastly amused when some of Paul's stories reached them—especially the women. They were hardworking women, most of them supporting indigent husbands or brothers, and they laughed rather bitterly at having stirred the boy to such fervid and florid inventions. They agreed with the faculty and with his father that Paul's was a bad case.

The east-bound train was ploughing through a January snow-storm; the dull dawn was beginning to show grey when the engine whistled a mile out of Newark. Paul started up from the seat where he had lain curled in uneasy slumber, rubbed the breath-misted window glass with his hand, and peered out. The snow was whirling in curling eddies above the white bottom lands, and the drifts lay already deep in the fields and along the fences, while here and there the long dead grass and dried weed stalks protruded black above it. Lights shone from the scattered houses, and a gang of laborers who stood beside the track waved their lanterns.

Paul had slept very little, and he felt grimy and uncomfortable. He had made the all-night journey in a day coach, partly because he was ashamed, dressed as he was, to go into a Pullman, and partly because he was afraid of being seen there by some Pittsburgh businessman, who might have noticed him in Denny & Carson's office. When the whistle awoke him, he clutched quickly at his breast pocket, glancing about him with an uncertain smile. But the little, clay-bespattered Italians were still sleeping, the slatternly women across the aisle were in open-mouthed oblivion, and even the crumby, crying babies were for the nonce stilled. Paul settled back to struggle with his impatience as best as he could.

When he arrived at the Jersey City station, he hurried through his breakfast, manifestly ill at ease and keeping a sharp eye about him. After he reached the Twenty-third Street station, he consulted a cabman, and had himself driven to a men's furnishing establishment that was just opening for the day. He spent upward of two hours there, buying with endless reconsidering and great care. His new street suit he put on in the fitting-room; the frock coat and dress clothes he had bundled into the cab with his linen. Then he drove to a hatter's and a shoe house. His next errand was at Tiffany's, where he selected his silver and a new scarf-pin. He would not wait to have his silver marked, he said. Lastly, he stopped at a trunk shop on Broadway, and had his purchases packed into various travelling bags.

It was a little after one-o'clock when he drove up to the Waldorf, and after settling with the cabman, went into the office. He registered from Washington; said his mother and father had been abroad, and that he had come down to await the arrival of their steamer. He told his story plausibly and had no trouble, since he volunteered to pay for them in advance, in engaging his rooms; a sleeping-room, sitting-room and bath.

Not once, but a hundred times Paul had planned this entry into New York. He had gone over every detail of it with Charley Edwards, and in his scrap book at home there were pages of description about New York hotels, cut from the Sunday papers. When he was shown to his sitting-room on the eighth floor, he saw at a glance that everything was as it should be; there was but one detail in his mental picture that the place did not realize, so he rang for the bell boy and sent him down for flowers. He moved about nervously until the boy returned, putting away his new linen and fingering it delightedly as he did so. When the flowers came, he put them hastily into water, and then tumbled into a hot bath. Presently he came out of his white bath-room, resplendent in his new silk underwear, and playing with the tassels of his red robe. The snow was whirling so fiercely outside his windows that he could scarcely see across the street, but within the air was deliciously soft and fragrant. He put the violets and jonquils on the taboret beside the couch, and threw himself down, with a long sigh, covering himself with a Roman blanket. He was thoroughly tired; he had been in such haste, he had stood up to such a strain, covered so much ground in the last twenty-four hours, that he wanted to think how it had all come about. Lulled by the sound of the wind, the warm air, and the cool fragrance of the flowers, he sank into deep, drowsy retrospection.

It had been wonderfully simple; when they had shut him out of the theatre and concert hall, when they had taken away his bone, the whole thing was virtually determined. The rest was a mere matter of opportunity. The only thing that at all surprised him was his own courage—for he realized well enough that he had always been tormented by fear, a sort of apprehensive dread that, of late years, as the meshes of the lies he had told closed about him, had been pulling the muscles of his body tighter and tighter. Until now, he could not remember the time when he had not been dreading something. Even when he was a little boy, it was always there—behind him, or before, or on either side. There had always been the shadowed corner, the dark place into which he dared not look, but from which something seemed always to be watching him—and Paul had done things that were not pretty to watch, he knew.

But now he had a curious sense of relief, as though he had at last thrown down the gauntlet to the thing in the corner.

Yet it was but a day since he had been sulking in the traces; but yesterday afternoon that he had been sent to the bank with Denny & Carson's deposit, as usual—but this time he was instructed to leave the book to be balanced. There was above two thousand dollars in checks, and nearly a thousand in the bank notes which he had taken from the book and quietly transferred to his pocket. At the bank he had made out a new deposit slip. His nerves had been steady enough to permit of his returning to the office, where he had finished his work and asked for a full day's holiday tomorrow, Saturday, giving a perfectly reasonable pretext. The bank book, he knew, would not be returned before Monday or Tuesday, and his father would be out of town for the next week. From the time he slipped the bank notes into his pocket until he boarded the night train for New York, he had not known a moment's hesitation. It was not the first time Paul had steered through treacherous waters.

How astonishingly easy it had all been; here he was, the thing done; and this time there would be no awakening, no figure at the top of the stairs. He watched the snow flakes whirling by his window until he fell asleep.

When he awoke, it was three o'clock in the afternoon. He bounded up with a start; half of one of his precious days gone already! He spent more than an hour in dressing, watching every stage of his toilet carefully in the mirror. Everything was quite perfect; he was exactly the kind of boy he had always wanted to be.

When he went downstairs, Paul took a carriage and drove up Fifth Avenue toward the Park. The snow had somewhat abated; carriages and tradesmen's wagons were hurrying soundlessly to and fro in the winter twilight; boys in woollen mufflers were shovelling off the doorsteps; the avenue stages made fine spots of color against the white street. Here and there on the corners were stands, with whole flower gardens blooming under glass cases, against the sides of which the snow flakes stuck and melted; violets, roses, carnations, lilies of the valley—somewhat vastly more lovely and alluring that they blossomed thus unnaturally in the snow. The Park itself was a wonderful stage winterpiece.

When he returned, the pause of the twilight had ceased, and the tune of the streets had changed. The snow was falling faster, lights streamed from the hotels that reared their dozen stories fearlessly up into the storm, defying the raging Atlantic winds. A long, black stream of carriages poured down the avenue, intersected here and there by other streams, tending horizontally. There were a score of cabs about the entrance of his hotel, and his driver had to wait. Boys in livery were running in and out of the awning stretched across the sidewalk, up and down the red velvet carpet laid from the door to the street. Above, about, within it all was the rumble and roar, the hurry and toss of thousands of human beings as hot for pleasure as himself, and on every side of him towered the glaring affirmation of the omnipotence of wealth.

The boy set his teeth and drew his shoulders together in a spasm of realization: the plot of all dramas, the text of all romances, the nerve-stuff of all sensations was whirling about him like the snow flakes. He burnt like a faggot in a tempest.

50 When Paul went down to dinner, the music of the orchestra came floating up the elevator shaft to greet him. His head whirled as he stepped into the thronged corridor, and he sank back into one of the chairs against the wall to get his breath. The lights, the chatter, the perfumes, the bewildering medley of color—he had, for a moment, the feeling of not being able to stand it. But only for a moment; these were his own people, he told himself. He went slowly about the corridors, through the writing-rooms, smoking-rooms, reception-rooms, as though he were exploring the chambers of an enchanted palace, built and peopled for him alone.

When he reached the dining-room he sat down at a table near a window. The flowers, the white linen, the many-colored wine glasses, the gay toilettes of the women, the low popping of corks, the undulating repetitions of the *Blue Danube* from the orchestra, all flooded Paul's dream with bewildering radiance. When the roseate tinge of his champagne was added—that cold, precious, bubbling stuff that creamed and foamed in his glass—Paul wondered that there were honest men in the world at all. This was what all the world was fighting for, he reflected; this was what all the struggle was about. He doubted the reality of his past. Had he ever known a place called Cordelia Street, a place where fagged-looking businessmen got on the early car; mere rivets in a machine they seemed to Paul—sickening men, with combings of children's hair always hanging to their coats, and the smell of cooking in their clothes. Cordelia Street—Ah! that belonged to another time and country; had he not always been thus, had he not sat here night after night, from as far back as he could remember, looking pensively over just such shimmering textures, and slowly twirling the stem of a glass like this one between his thumb and middle finger? He rather thought he had.

He was not in the least abashed or lonely. He had no especial desire to meet or to know any of these people; all he demanded was the right to look on and conjecture, to watch the pageant. The mere stage properties were all he contended for. Nor was he lonely later in the evening, in his loge at the Metropolitan. He was now entirely rid of his nervous misgivings, of his forced aggressiveness, of the imperative desire to show himself different from his surroundings. He felt now that his surroundings explained him. Nobody questioned the purple; he had only to wear it passively. He had only to glance down at his attire to reassure himself that here it would be impossible for anyone to humiliate him.

He found it hard to leave his beautiful sitting-room to go to bed that night, and sat long watching the raging storm from his turret window. When he went to sleep it was with the lights turned on in his bedroom; partly because of his old timidity, and partly so that, if he should wake in the night, there would be no wretched moment of doubt, no horrible suspicion of yellow wall-paper, or of Washington and Calvin above his bed.

Sunday morning the city was practically snow-bound. Paul breakfasted late, and in the afternoon he fell in with a wild San Francisco boy, a freshman at Yale, who said he had run down for a "little flyer" over Sunday. The young man offered to show Paul the night side of the town, and the two boys went out together after dinner, not returning to the hotel until seven o'clock the next morning. They had started out in the confiding warmth of a champagne friendship, but their parting in the elevator was singularly cool. The freshman pulled himself together to make his train, and Paul went to bed. He awoke at two o'clock in the afternoon, very thirsty and dizzy, and rang for ice-water, coffee, and the Pittsburgh papers.

55 On the part of the hotel management, Paul excited no suspicion. There was this to be said for him, that he wore his spoils with dignity and in no way made himself conspicuous. Even under the glow of his wine he was never boisterous, though he found the stuff like a magician's wand for wonder-building. His chief greediness lay in his ears and eyes, and his excesses were not offensive ones. His dearest pleasures were the grey winter twilights in his sitting-room; his quiet enjoyment of his flowers, his clothes, his wide divan, his cigarette, and his sense of power. He could not remember a time when he had felt so at peace with himself. The mere release from the necessity of petty lying, lying every day and every day, restored his self-respect. He had never lied for pleasure, even at school; but to be noticed and admired, to assert his difference from other Cordelia Street boys; and he felt a good deal more manly, more honest, even, now that he had no need for boastful pretensions, now that he could, as his actor friends used to say, "dress the part." It was characteristic that remorse did not occur to him. His golden days went by without a shadow, and he made each as perfect as he could.

On the eighth day after his arrival in New York, he found the whole affair exploited in the Pittsburgh papers, exploited with a wealth of detail which indicated that local news of a sensational nature was at a low ebb. The firm of Denny & Carson announced that the boy's father had refunded the full amount of the theft, and that they had no intention of prosecuting. The Cumberland minister had been interviewed, and expressed his hope of yet reclaiming the motherless lad, and his Sabbath-school teacher declared that she would spare no effort to that end. The rumor had reached Pittsburgh that the boy had been seen in a New York hotel, and his father had gone East to find him and bring him home.

Paul had just come in to dress for dinner; he sank into a chair, weak to the knees, and clasped his head in his hands. It was to be worse than jail, even; the tepid waters of Cordelia Street were to close over him finally and forever. The grey monotony stretched before him in hopeless, unrelieved years; Sabbath-school, Young People's Meeting, the yellow-papered room, the damp dish-towels; it all rushed back upon him with a sickening vividness. He had the old feeling that the orchestra had suddenly stopped, the sinking sensation that the play was over. The sweat broke out on his face, and he sprang to his feet, looked about him with his white, conscious smile, and winked at himself in the mirror. With something of the old childish belief in miracles with which he had so often gone to class, all his lessons unlearned, Paul dressed and dashed whistling down the corridor to the elevator.

He had no sooner entered the dining-room and caught the measure of the music than his remembrance was lightened by his old elastic power of claiming the moment, mounting with it, and finding it all sufficient. The glare and glitter about him, the mere scenic accessories had again, and for the last time, their old potency. He would show himself that he was game, he would finish the thing splendidly. He doubted, more than ever, the existence of Cordelia Street, and for the first time he drank his wine recklessly. Was he not, after all, one of those fortunate beings born to the purple, was he not still himself and in his own place? He drummed a nervous accompaniment to the Pagliacci music and looked about him, telling himself over and over that it had paid.

He reflected drowsily, to the swell of the music and the chill sweetness of his wine, that he might have done it more wisely. He might have caught an outboard steamer and been well out of their clutches before now. But the other side of the world had seemed too far away and too uncertain then; he could not have waited for it; his need had been too sharp. If he had to choose over again, he would do the same thing tomorrow. He looked affectionately about the dining-room, now gilded with a soft mist. Ah, it had paid indeed!

60 Paul was awakened next morning by a painful throbbing in his head and feet. He had thrown himself across the bed without undressing, and had slept with his shoes on. His limbs and hands were lead heavy, and his tongue and throat were parched and burnt. There came upon him one of those fateful attacks of clear-headedness that never occurred except when he was physically exhausted and his nerves hung loose. He lay still and closed his eyes and let the tide of things wash over him.

His father was in New York; "stopping at some joint or other," he told himself. The memory of successive summers on the front stoop fell upon him like a weight of black water. He had not a hundred dollars left; and he knew now, more than ever, that money was everything, the wall that stood between all he loathed and all he wanted. The thing was winding itself up; he had thought of that on his first glorious day in New York, and had even provided a way to snap the thread. It lay on his dressing-table now; he had got it out last night when he came blindly up from dinner, but the shiny metal hurt his eyes, and he disliked the looks of it.

He rose and moved about with a painful effort, succumbing now and again to attacks of nausea. It was the old depression exaggerated; all the world had become Cordelia Street. Yet somehow he was not afraid of anything, was absolutely calm; perhaps because he had looked into the dark corner at last and knew. It was bad enough, what he saw there, but somehow not so bad as his long fear of it had been. He saw everything clearly now. He had a feeling that he had made the best of it, that he had lived the sort of life he was meant to live, and for half an hour he sat staring at the revolver. But he told himself that was not the way, so he went downstairs and took a cab to the ferry.

When Paul arrived at Newark, he got off the train and took another cab, directing the driver to follow the Pennsylvania tracks out of the town. The snow lay heavy on the roadways and had drifted deep in the open fields. Only here and there the dead grass or dried weed stalks projected, singularly black, above it. Once well into the country, Paul dismissed the carriage and walked, floundering along the tracks, his mind a medley of irrelevant things. He seemed to hold in his brain an actual picture of everything he had seen that morning. He remembered every feature of both his drivers, of the toothless old woman from whom he had bought the red flowers in his coat, the agent from whom he had got his ticket, and all of his fellow-passengers on the ferry. His mind, unable to cope with vital matters near at hand, worked feverishly and deftly at sorting and grouping these images. They made for him a part of the ugliness of the world, of the ache in his head, and the bitter burning on his tongue. He stooped and put a handful of snow into his mouth as he walked, but that, too, seemed hot. When he reached a little hillside, where the tracks ran through a cut some twenty feet below him, he stopped and sat down.

The carnations in his coat were drooping with the cold, he noticed; their red glory all over. It occurred to him that all the flowers he had seen in the glass cases that first night must have gone the same way, long before this. It was only one splendid breath they had, in spite of their brave mockery at the winter outside the glass; and it was a losing game in the end, it seemed, this revolt against the homilies by which the world is run. Paul took one of the blossoms carefully from his coat and scooped a little hole in the snow, where he covered it up. Then he dozed a while, from his weak condition, seemingly insensible to the cold.

65 The sound of an approaching train awoke him, and he started to his feet, remembering only his resolution, and afraid lest he should be too late. He stood watching the approaching locomotive, his teeth chattering, his lips drawn away from them in a frightened smile; once or twice he glanced nervously sidewise, as though he were being watched. When the right moment came, he jumped. As he fell, the folly of his haste occurred to him with merciless clearness, the vastness of what he had left undone. There flashed through his brain, clearer than ever before, the blue of Adriatic water, the yellow of Algerian sands.

He felt something strike his chest, and that his body was being thrown swiftly through the air, on and on, immeasurably far and fast, while his limbs were gently relaxed. Then, because the picture-making mechanism was crushed, the disturbing visions flashed into black, and Paul dropped back into the immense design of things.

[*1904*]

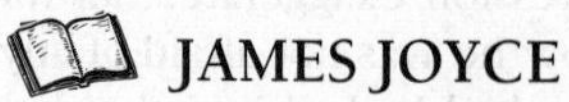

## JAMES JOYCE

*James Joyce (1882–1941) was born into a middle-class family in Dublin, Ireland. His father drank, became increasingly irresponsible and unemployable, and the family sank in the social order. Still, Joyce received a strong classical education at excellent Jesuit schools and at University College, Dublin, where he studied modern languages. In 1902, at the age of twenty, he left Ireland so that he might spend the rest of his life writing about life in Ireland. ("The shortest way to Tara," he said, "is via Holyhead," i.e., the shortest way to the heart of Ireland is to take ship away.) In Trieste, Zurich, and Paris he supported his family in a variety of ways, sometimes teaching English in a Berlitz language school. His fifteen stories, collected under the title of* Dubliners, *were written between 1904 and 1907, but he could not get them published until 1914. Next came a highly autobiographical novel,* A Portrait of the Artist As a Young Man *(1916).* Ulysses *(1922), a large novel covering eighteen hours in Dublin, was for some years banned by the United States Post Office, though few if any readers today find it offensive. Joyce spent most of the rest of his life working on* Finnegans Wake *(1939).*

*Nine years before he succeeded in getting* Dubliners *published he described the manuscript in these terms:*

> *My intention was to write a chapter of the moral history of my country and I chose Dublin for the scene because that city seemed to me the centre of paralysis. . . . I have written it for the most part in a style of scrupulous meanness and with the conviction that he is a very bold man who dares to alter in the presentment, still more to deform, whatever he has seen and heard.*

# *Araby*

North Richmond Street, being blind,[1] was a quiet street except at the hour when the Christian Brothers' School set the boys free. An uninhabited house of two stories stood at the blind end, detached from its neighbors in a square ground. The other houses of the street, conscious of decent lives within them, gazed at one another with brown imperturbable faces.

[1]**blind** a dead-end street

The former tenant of our house, a priest, had died in the back drawing-room. Air, musty from having long been enclosed, hung in all the rooms, and the waste room behind the kitchen was littered with old useless papers. Among these I found a few papercovered books, the pages of which were curled and damp: *The Abbot,* by Walter Scott, *The Devout Communicant* and *The Memoirs of Vidocq.*[2] I liked the last best because its leaves were yellow. The wild garden behind the house contained a central apple-tree and a few straggling bushes under one of which I found the late tenant's rusty bicycle-pump. He had been a very charitable priest; in his will he had left all his money to institutions and the furniture of his house to his sister.

When the short days of winter came dusk fell before we had well eaten our dinners. When we met in the street the houses had grown sombre. The space of sky above us was the colour of everchanging violet and towards it the lamps of the street lifted their feeble lanterns. The cold air stung us and we played till our bodies glowed. Our shouts echoed in the silent street. The career of our play brought us through the dark muddy lanes behind the houses where we ran the gauntlet of the rough tribes from the cottages, to the back doors of the dark dripping gardens where odours arose from the ashpits, to the dark odorous stables where a coachman smoothed and combed the horse or shook music from the buckled harness. When we returned to the street light from the kitchen windows had filled the areas. If my uncle was seen turning the corner we hid in the shadow until we had seen him safely housed. Or if Mangan's sister came out on the doorstep to call her brother in to his tea we watched her from our shadow peer up and down the street. We waited to see whether she would remain or go in and, if she remained, we left our shadow and walked up to Mangan's steps resignedly. She was waiting for us, her figure defined by the light from the half-opened door. Her brother always teased her before he obeyed and I stood by the railings looking at her. Her dress swung as she moved her body and the soft rope of her hair tossed from side to side.

Every morning I lay on the floor in the front parlour watching her door. The blind was pulled down to within an inch of the sash so that I could not be seen. When she came out on the doorstep my heart leaped. I ran to the hall, seized my books and followed her. I kept her brown figure always in my eye and, when we came near the point at which our ways diverged, I quickened my pace and passed her. This happened morning after morning. I had never spoken to her, except for a few casual words, and yet her name was like a summons to all my foolish blood.

5 Her image accompanied me even in places the most hostile to romance. On Saturday evenings when my aunt went marketing I had to go to carry some of the parcels. We walked through the flaring streets, jostled by drunken men and bargaining women, amid the curses of labourers, the shrill litanies of shop-boys who stood on guard by the barrels of pigs' cheeks, the nasal chanting of street-singers, who sang a *come-all-you* about O'Donovan Rossa,[3] or a ballad about the troubles in our native land. These

[2]*The Abbot* was one of Scott's popular historical romances. *The Devout Communicant* was a Catholic religious manual; *The Memoirs of Vidocq* were the memoirs of the chief of the French detective force.

[3]Jeremiah O'Donovan (1831–1915), a popular Irish leader who was jailed by the British for advocating violent rebellion. A "come-all-you" was a topical song that began "Come all you gallant Irishmen."

noises converged in a single sensation of life for me: I imagined that I bore my chalice safely through a throng of foes. Her name sprang to my lips at moments in strange prayers and praises which I myself did not understand. My eyes were often full of tears (I could not tell why) and at times a flood from my heart seemed to pour itself out into my bosom. I thought little of the future. I did not know whether I would ever speak to her or not or, if I spoke to her, how I could tell her of my confused adoration. But my body was like a harp and her words and gestures were like fingers running upon the wires.

One evening I went into the back drawing-room in which the priest had died. It was a dark rainy evening and there was no sound in the house. Through one of the broken panes I heard the rain impinge upon the earth, the fine incessant needles of water playing in the sodden beds. Some distant lamp or lighted window gleamed below me. I was thankful that I could see so little. All my senses seemed to desire to veil themselves and, feeling that I was about to slip from them, I pressed the palms of my hands together until they trembled, murmuring: *O love! O love!* many times.

At last she spoke to me. When she addressed the first words to me I was so confused that I did not know what to answer. She asked me was I going to Araby.

I forget whether I answered yes or no. It would be a splendid bazaar, she said; she would love to go.

—And why can't you? I asked.

10 While she spoke she turned a silver bracelet round and round her wrist. She could not go, she said, because there would be a retreat that week in her convent. Her brother and two other boys were fighting for their caps and I was alone at the railings. She held one of the spikes, bowing her head towards me. The light from the lamp opposite our door caught the white curve of her neck, lit up her hair that rested there and, falling, lit up the hand upon the railing. It fell over one side of her dress and caught the white border of a petticoat, just visible as she stood at ease.

—It's well for you, she said.

—If I go, I said, I will bring you something.

What innumerable follies laid waste my waking and sleeping thoughts after that evening! I wished to annihilate the tedious intervening days. I chafed against the work of school. At night in my bedroom and by day in the classroom her image came between me and the page I strove to read. The syllables of the word *Araby* were called to me through the silence in which my soul luxuriated and cast an Eastern enchantment over me. I asked for leave to go to the bazaar on Saturday night. My aunt was surprised and hoped it was not some Freemason[4] affair. I answered few questions in class, I watched my master's face pass from amiability to sternness; he hoped I was not beginning to idle. I could not call my wandering thoughts together. I had hardly any patience with the serious work of life which, now that it stood between me and my desire, seemed to me child's play, ugly monotonous child's play.

On Saturday morning I reminded my uncle that I wished to go to the bazaar in the evening. He was fussing at the hallstand, looking for the hat-brush, and answered me curtly:

[4]Irish Catholics viewed the Masons as their Protestant enemies.

15 —Yes, boy, I know.

As he was in the hall I could not go into the front parlour and lie at the window. I left the house in bad humour and walked slowly towards the school. The air was pitilessly raw and already my heart misgave me.

When I came home to dinner my uncle had not yet been home. Still it was early. I sat staring at the clock for some time and, when its ticking began to irritate me, I left the room. I mounted the staircase and gained the upper part of the house. The high cold empty gloomy rooms liberated me and I went from room to room singing. From the front window I saw my companions playing below in the street. Their cries reached me weakened and indistinct and, leaning my forehead against the cool glass, I looked over at the dark house where she lived. I may have stood there for an hour, seeing nothing but the brown-clad figure cast by my imagination, touched discreetly by the lamplight at the curved neck, at the hand upon the railings and at the border below the dress.

When I came downstairs again I found Mrs Mercer sitting at the fire. She was an old garrulous woman, a pawnbroker's widow, who collected used stamps for some pious purpose. I had to endure the gossip of the tea-table. The meal was prolonged beyond an hour and still my uncle did not come. Mrs Mercer stood up to go: she was sorry she couldn't wait any longer, but it was after eight o'clock and she did not like to be out late, as the night air was bad for her. When she had gone I began to walk up and down the room, clenching my fists. My aunt said:

—I'm afraid you may put off your bazaar for this night of Our Lord.

20 At nine o'clock I heard my uncle's latchkey in the halldoor. I heard him talking to himself and heard the hallstand rocking when it had received the weight of his overcoat. I could interpret these signs. When he was midway through his dinner I asked him to give me the money to go to the bazaar. He had forgotten.

—The people are in bed and after their first sleep now, he said.

I did not smile. My aunt said to him energetically:

—Can't you give him the money and let him go? You've kept him late enough as it is.

My uncle said he was very sorry he had forgotten. He said he believed in the old saying: *All work and no play makes Jack a dull boy*. He asked me where I was going and, when I had told him a second time he asked me did I know *The Arab's Farewell to His Steed*.[5] When I left the kitchen he was about to recite the opening lines of the piece to my aunt.

25 I held a florin tightly in my hand as I strode down Buckingham Street towards the station. The sight of the streets thronged with buyers and glaring with gas recalled to me the purpose of my journey. I took my seat in a third-class carriage of a deserted train. After an intolerable delay the train moved out of the station slowly. It crept onward among ruinous houses and over the twinkling river. At Westland Row Station a crowd of people pressed to the carriage doors; but the porters moved them back, saying that it was a special train for the bazaar. I remained alone in the bare carriage. In a few minutes the train drew up beside an improvised wooden platform. I passed out on to the road and saw by the lighted dial of a clock that it was

[5]"The Arab to His Favorite Steed" was a popular sentimental poem by Caroline Norton (1808–77).

ten minutes to ten. In front of me was a large building which displayed the magical name.

I could not find any sixpenny entrance and, fearing that the bazaar would be closed, I passed in quickly through a turnstile, handing a shilling to a weary-looking man. I found myself in a big hall girdled at half its height by a gallery. Nearly all the stalls were closed and the greater part of the hall was in darkness. I recognised a silence like that which pervades a church after a service. I walked into the center of the bazaar timidly. A few people were gathered about the stalls which were still open. Before a curtain, over which the words *Café Chantant* were written in coloured lamps, two men were counting money on a salver. I listened to the fall of the coins.

Remembering with difficulty why I had come I went over to one of the stalls and examined porcelain vases and flowered teasets. At the door of the stall a young lady was talking and laughing with two young gentlemen. I remarked their English accents and listened vaguely to their conversation.

—O, I never said such a thing!

—O, but you did!

—O, but I didn't!

—Didn't she say that?

—Yes! I heard her.

—O, there's a . . . fib!

Observing me the young lady came over and asked me did I wish to buy anything. The tone of her voice was not encouraging; she seemed to have spoken to me out of a sense of duty. I looked humbly at the great jars that stood like eastern guards at either side of the dark entrance to the stall and murmured:

—No, thank you.

The young lady changed the position of one of the vases and went back to the two young men. They began to talk of the same subject. Once or twice the young lady glanced at me over her shoulder.

I lingered before her stall, though I knew my stay was useless, to make my interest in her wares seem the more real. Then I turned away slowly and walked down the middle of the bazaar. I allowed the two pennies to fall against the sixpence in my pocket. I heard a voice call from one end of the gallery that the light was out. The upper part of the hall was now completely dark.

Gazing up into the darkness I saw myself as a creature driven and derided by vanity; and my eyes burned with anguish and anger.

[*1905*]

## FRANZ KAFKA

*Franz Kafka (1883–1924) was born in Prague, Austro-Hungarian Empire (now the Czech Republic), the son of a German Jew who had risen from peddler to prosperous businessman. A Jew in a Gentile world, a speaker of German in a predominantly Slavic community, an artist in a bourgeois society, he was very much an outsider—a feeling strengthened by his difficult relations with a dominating father. Yielding to his father, he studied law and*

***after receiving his degree he worked as a civil servant investigating insurance claims, a job that he hated. He was several times engaged to be married, but the engagements were broken. Because he was regularly dissatisfied with what he wrote, he published very little before his death from tuberculosis, and the little that he published was suppressed by the Nazis in the 1930s. Readers owe much to Kafka's editor, Max Brod, who rejected Kafka's wish that Brod destroy the manuscripts of the unpublished stories and novels. Not until after the Second World War did Kafka become known internationally.***

# *The Metamorphosis*

*Translated by Willa and Edwin Muir*

## *I*

As Gregor Samsa awoke one morning from uneasy dreams he found himself transformed in his bed into a gigantic insect. He was lying on his hard, as it were armor-plated, back and when he lifted his head a little he could see his dome-like brown belly divided into stiff arched segments on top of which the bed quilt could hardly keep in position and was about to slide off completely. His numerous legs, which were pitifully thin compared to the rest of his bulk, waved helplessly before his eyes.

What has happened to me? he thought. It was no dream. His room, a regular human bedroom, only rather too small, lay quiet between the four familiar walls. Above the table on which a collection of cloth samples was unpacked and spread out—Samsa was a commercial traveler—hung the picture which he had recently cut out of an illustrated magazine and put into a pretty gilt frame. It showed a lady, with a fur cap on and a fur stole, sitting upright and holding out to the spectator a huge fur muff into which the whole of her forearm had vanished!

Gregor's eyes turned next to the window, and the overcast sky—one could hear rain drops beating on the window gutter—made him quite melancholy. What about sleeping a little longer and forgetting all this nonsense, he thought, but it could not be done, for he was accustomed to sleep on his right side and in his present condition he could not turn himself over. However violently he forced himself towards his right side he always rolled on to his back again. He tried it at least a hundred times, shutting his eyes to keep from seeing his struggling legs, and only desisted when he began to feel in his side a faint dull ache he had never experienced before.

Oh God, he thought, what an exhausting job I've picked on! Traveling about day in, day out. It's much more irritating work than doing the actual business in the office, and on top of that there's the trouble of constant traveling, of worrying about train connections, the bed and irregular meals, casual acquaintances that are always new and never become intimate friends. The devil take it all! He felt a slight itching up on his belly; slowly pushed himself on his back nearer to the top of the bed so that he could lift his head more easily; identified the itching place which was surrounded by many small white spots the nature of which he could not understand and made to touch it with a leg, but drew the leg back immediately, for the contact made a cold shiver run through him.

He slid down again into his former position. This getting up early, he thought, makes one quite stupid. A man needs his sleep. Other commercials live like harem women. For instance, when I come back to the hotel of a morning to write up the orders I've got, these others are only sitting down to breakfast. Let me just try that with my chief; I'd be sacked on the spot. Anyhow, that might be quite a good thing for me, who can tell? If I didn't have to hold my hand because of my parents I'd have given notice long ago, I'd have gone to the chief and told him exactly what I think of him. That would knock him endways from his desk! It's a queer way of doing, too, this sitting on high at a desk and talking down to employees, especially when they have to come quite near because the chief is hard of hearing. Well, there's still hope; once I've saved enough money to pay back my parents' debts to him—that should take another five or six years—I'll do it without fail. I'll cut myself completely loose then. For the moment, though, I'd better get up, since my train goes at five.

He looked at the alarm clock ticking on the chest. Heavenly Father! he thought. It was half-past six o'clock and the hands were quietly moving on, it was even past the half-hour, it was getting on toward a quarter to seven. Had the alarm clock not gone off? From the bed one could see that it had been properly set for four o'clock; of course it must have gone off. Yes, but was it possible to sleep quietly through that ear-splitting noise? Well, he had not slept quietly, yet apparently all the more soundly for that. But what was he to do now? The next train went at seven o'clock; to catch that he would need to hurry like mad and his samples weren't even packed up, and he himself wasn't feeling particularly fresh and active. And even if he did catch the train he wouldn't avoid a row with the chief, since the firm's porter would have been waiting for the five o'clock train and would have long since reported his failure to turn up. The porter was a creature of the chief's, spineless and stupid. Well, supposing he were to say he was sick? But that would be most unpleasant and would look suspicious, since during his five years' employment he had not been ill once. The chief himself would be sure to come with the sick-insurance doctor, would reproach his parents with their son's laziness and would cut all excuses short by referring to the insurance doctor, who of course regarded all mankind as perfectly healthy malingerers. And would he be so far wrong on this occasion? Gregor really felt quite well, apart from a drowsiness that was utterly superfluous after such a long sleep, and he was even unusually hungry.

As all this was running through his mind at top speed without his being able to decide to leave his bed—the alarm clock had just struck a quarter to seven—there came a cautious tap at the door behind the head of his bed. "Gregor," said a voice—it was his mother's—"it's a quarter to seven. Hadn't you a train to catch?" That gentle voice! Gregor had a shock as he heard his own voice answering hers, unmistakably his own voice, it was true, but with a persistent horrible twittering squeak behind it like an undertone, that left the words in their clear shape only for the first moment and then rose up reverberating round them to destroy their sense, so that one could not be sure one had heard them rightly. Gregor wanted to answer at length and explain everything, but in the circumstances he confined himself to saying: "Yes, yes, thank you, Mother, I'm getting up now." The wooden door between them must have kept the change in his voice from being noticeable outside, for his mother contented herself with this statement and shuffled away. Yet this brief exchange of words had made the other members of the family aware that Gregor was still in the house, as they had not expected, and at one of the side doors his father was already knocking, gently, yet with his fist. "Gregor, Gregor," he called, "what's the matter with you?" And after a little while he called again in a deeper voice: "Gregor! Gregor!" At the other side door his sister was saying in a low, plaintive tone: "Gregor? Aren't you well? Are you needing anything?" He answered them both at once: "I'm just ready," and did his best to make his voice sound as normal as possible by enunciating the words very clearly and leaving long pauses between them. So his father went back to his breakfast, but his sister whispered: "Gregor, open the door, do." However, he was not thinking of opening the door, and felt thankful for the prudent habit he had acquired in traveling of locking all doors during the night, even at home.

His immediate intention was to get up quietly without being disturbed, to put on his clothes and above all eat his breakfast, and only then to consider what else was to be done, since in bed, he was well aware, his meditations would come to no sensible conclusion. He remembered that often enough in bed he had felt small aches and pains, probably caused by awkward postures, which had proved purely imaginary once he got up, and he looked forward eagerly to seeing this morning's delusions gradually fall away. That the change in his voice was nothing but the precursor of a severe chill, a standing ailment of commercial travelers, he had not the least possible doubt.

To get rid of the quilt was quite easy; he had only to inflate himself a little and it fell off by itself. But the next move was difficult, especially because he was so uncommonly broad. He would have needed arms and hands to hoist himself up; instead he had only the numerous little legs which never stopped waving in all directions and which he could not control in the least. When he tried to bend one of them it was the first to stretch itself straight; and did he succeed at last in making it do what he wanted, all the other legs meanwhile waved the more wildly in a high degree of unpleasant agitation. "But what's the use of lying idle in bed," said Gregor to himself.

10 He thought that he might get out of bed with the lower part of his body first, but this lower part, which he had not yet seen and of which he could form no clear conception, proved too difficult to move; it shifted so slowly; and when finally, almost wild with annoyance, he gathered his forces together and thrust out recklessly, he had miscalculated the direction and bumped heavily against the lower end of the bed, and the stinging pain he felt informed him that precisely this lower part of his body was at the moment probably the most sensitive.

So he tried to get the top part of himself out first, and cautiously moved his head towards the edge of the bed. That proved easy enough, and despite its breadth and mass the bulk of his body at last slowly followed the movement of his head. Still, when he finally got his head free over the edge of the bed he felt too scared to go on advancing, for after all if he let himself fall in this way it would take a miracle to keep his head from being injured. And at all costs he must not lose consciousness now, precisely now; he would rather stay in bed.

But when after a repetition of the same efforts he lay in his former position again, sighing, and watched his little legs struggling against each other more wildly than ever, if that were possible, and saw no way of bringing any order into this arbitrary confusion, he told himself again that it was impossible to stay in bed and that the most sensible course was to risk everything for the smallest hope of getting away from it. At the same time he did not forget meanwhile to remind himself that cool reflection, the coolest possible, was much better than desperate resolves. In such moments he focused his eyes as sharply as possible on the window, but, unfortunately, the prospect of the morning fog, which muffled even the other side of the narrow street, brought him little encouragement and comfort. "Seven o'clock already," he said to himself when the alarm clock chimed again, "seven o'clock already and still such a thick fog." And for a little while he lay quiet, breathing lightly, as if perhaps expecting such complete repose to restore all things to their real and normal condition.

But then he said to himself: "Before it strikes a quarter past seven I must be quite out of this bed, without fail. Anyhow, by that time someone will have come from the office to ask for me, since it opens before seven." And he set himself to rocking his whole body at once in a regular rhythm, with the idea of swinging it out of the bed. If he tipped himself out in that way he could keep his head from injury by lifting it at an acute angle when he fell. His back seemed to be hard and was not likely to suffer from a fall on the carpet. His biggest worry was the loud crash he would not be able to help making, which would probably cause anxiety, if not terror, behind all the doors. Still, he must take the risk.

When he was already half out of the bed—the new method was more a game than an effort, for he needed only to hitch himself across by rocking to and fro—it struck him how simple it would be if he could get help. Two strong people—he thought of his father and the servant girl—would be amply sufficient; they would only have to thrust their arms under his convex back, lever him out of the bed, bend down with their burden and then be patient enough to let him turn himself right over on to the floor, where it was to be hoped his legs would then find their proper function. Well, ignoring the fact that the doors were all locked, ought he really to call for help? In spite of his misery he could not suppress a smile at the very idea of it.

He had got so far that he could barely keep his equilibrium when he rocked himself strongly, and he would have to nerve himself very soon for the final decision since in five minutes' time it would be a quarter past seven—when the front doorbell rang. "That's someone from the office," he said to himself, and grew almost rigid, while his little legs only jigged about all the faster. For a moment everything stayed quiet. "They're not going to open the door," said Gregor to himself, catching at some kind of irrational hope. But then of course the servant girl went as usual to the door with her heavy tread and opened it. Gregor needed only to hear the first good morning of the visitor to know immediately who it was—the chief clerk himself. What a fate, to be condemned to work for a firm where the smallest omission at once gave rise to the gravest suspicion! Were all employees in a body nothing but scoundrels, was there not among them one single loyal devoted man who, had he wasted only an hour or so of the firm's time in a morning, was so tormented by conscience as to be driven out of his mind and actually incapable of leaving his bed? Wouldn't it really have been sufficient to send an apprentice to inquire—if any inquiry were necessary at all—did the chief clerk himself have to come and thus indicate to the entire family, an innocent family, that this suspicious circumstance could be investigated by no one less versed in affairs than himself? And more through the agitation caused by these reflections than through any act of will Gregor swung himself out of bed with all his strength. There was a loud thump, but it was not really a crash. His fall was broken to some extent by the carpet, his back, too, was less stiff than he thought, and so there was merely a dull thud, not so very startling. Only he had not lifted his head carefully enough and had hit it; he turned it and rubbed it on the carpet in pain and irritation.

"That was something falling down in there," said the chief clerk in the next room to the left. Gregor tried to suppose to himself that something like what had happened to him today might some day happen to the chief clerk; one really could not deny that it was possible. But as if in brusque reply to this supposition the chief clerk took a couple of firm steps in the next-door room and his patent leather boots creaked. From the right-hand room his sister was whispering to inform him of the situation: "Gregor, the chief clerk's here." "I know," muttered Gregor to himself; but he didn't dare to make his voice loud enough for his sister to hear it.

"Gregor," said his father now from the left-hand room, "the chief clerk has come and wants to know why you didn't catch the early train. We don't know what to say to him. Besides, he wants to talk to you in person. So open the door, please. He will be good enough to excuse the untidiness of your room." "Good morning, Mr. Samsa," the chief clerk was calling amiably meanwhile. "He's not well," said his mother to the visitor, while his father was still speaking through the door, "he's not well, sir, believe me. What else would make him miss a train! The boy thinks about nothing but his work. It makes me almost cross the way he never goes out in the evenings; he's been here the last eight days and has stayed at home every single evening. He just sits there quietly at the table reading a newspaper or looking through railway timetables. The only amusement he gets is doing fretwork. For instance, he spent two or three evenings cutting out a little picture frame; you would be surprised to see how pretty it is; it's hanging in his room; you'll see it in a minute when Gregor opens the door. I must say I'm glad you've come, sir; we should never have got him to unlock the door by ourselves; he's so obstinate; and I'm sure he's unwell, though he wouldn't have it to be so this morning." "I'm just coming," said Gregor slowly and carefully, not moving an inch for fear of losing one word of the conversation. "I can't think of any other explanation, madam," said the chief clerk, "I hope it's nothing serious. Although on the other hand I must say that we men of business—fortunately or unfortunately—very often simply have to ignore any slight indisposition, since business must be attended to." "Well, can the chief clerk come in now?" asked Gregor's father impatiently, again knocking on the door. "No," said Gregor. In the left-hand room a painful silence followed this refusal, in the right-hand room his sister began to sob.

Why didn't his sister join the others? She was probably newly out of bed and hadn't even begun to put on her clothes yet. Well, why was she crying? Because he wouldn't get up and let the chief clerk in, because he was in danger of losing his job, and because the chief would begin dunning his parents again for the old debts? Surely these were things one didn't need to worry about for the present. Gregor was still at home and not in the least thinking of deserting the family. At the moment, true, he was lying on the carpet and no one who knew the condition he was in could seriously expect him to admit the chief clerk. But for such a small discourtesy, which could plausibly be explained away somehow later on, Gregor could hardly be dismissed on the spot. And it seemed to Gregor that it would be much more sensible to leave him in peace for the present than to trouble him with tears and entreaties. Still, of course, their uncertainty bewildered them all and excused their behavior.

"Mr. Samsa," the chief clerk called now in a louder voice, "what's the matter with you? Here you are, barricading yourself in your room, giving only 'yes' and 'no' for answers, causing your parents a lot of unnecessary trouble and neglecting—I mention this only in passing—neglecting your business duties in an incredible fashion. I am speaking here in the name of your parents and of your chief, and I beg you quite seriously to give me an immediate and precise explanation. You amaze me, you amaze me. I thought you were a quiet, dependable person, and now all at once you seem bent on making a disgraceful exhibition of yourself. The chief did hint to me early this morning a possible explanation for your disappearance—with reference to the cash payments that were entrusted to you recently—but I almost pledged my solemn word of honor that this could not be so. But now that I see how incredibly obstinate you are, I no longer have the slightest desire to take your part at all. And your position in the firm is not so unassailable. I came with the intention of telling you all this in private, but since you are wasting my time so needlessly I don't see why your parents shouldn't hear it too. For some time past your work has been most unsatisfactory; this is not the season of the year for a business boom, of course, we admit that, but a season of the year for doing no business at all, that does not exist, Mr. Samsa, must not exist."

20 "But, sir," cried Gregor, beside himself and in his agitation forgetting everything else. "I'm just going to open the door this very minute. A slight illness, an attack of giddiness, has kept me from getting up. I'm still lying in bed. But I feel all right again. I'm getting out of bed now. Just give me a moment or two longer! I'm not quite so well as I thought. But I'm all right, really. How a thing like that can suddenly strike one down! Only last night I was quite well, my parents can tell you, or rather I did have a slight presentiment. I must have showed some sign of it. Why didn't I report it at the office! But one always thinks that an indisposition can be got over without staying in the house. Oh sir, do spare my parents! All that you're reproaching me with now has no foundation; no one has ever said a word to me about it. Perhaps you haven't looked at the last orders I sent in. Anyhow, I can still catch the eight o'clock train, I'm much the better for my few hours' rest. Don't let me detain you here, sir; I'll be attending to business very soon, and do be good enough to tell the chief so and to make my excuses to him!"

And while all this was tumbling out pell-mell and Gregor hardly knew what he was saying, he had reached the chest quite easily, perhaps because of the practice he had had in bed, and was now trying to lever himself upright by means of it. He meant actually to open the door, actually to show himself and speak to the chief clerk; he was eager to find out what the others, after all their insistence, would say at the sight of him. If they were horrified then the responsibility was no longer his and he could stay quiet. But if they took it calmly, then he had no reason either to be upset, and could really get to the station for the eight o'clock train if he hurried. At first he slipped down a few times from the polished surface of the chest, but at length with a last heave he stood upright; he paid no more attention to the pains in the lower part of his body, however they smarted. Then he let himself fall against the back of a nearby chair, and clung with his little legs to the edges of it. That brought him into control of himself again and he stopped speaking, for now he could listen to what the chief clerk was saying.

"Did you understand a word of it?" the chief clerk was asking; "surely he can't be trying to make fools of us?" "Oh dear," cried his mother, in tears, "perhaps he's terribly ill and we're tormenting him. Grete! Grete!" she called out then. "Yes Mother?" called his sister from the other side. They were calling to each other across Gregor's room. "You must go this minute for the doctor. Gregor is ill. Go for the doctor, quick. Did you hear how he was speaking?" "That was no human voice," said the chief clerk in a voice noticeably low beside the shrillness of the mother's. "Anna! Anna!" his father was calling through the hall to the kitchen, clapping his hands, "get a locksmith at once!" And the two girls were already running through the hall with a swish of skirts—how could his sister have got dressed so quickly?—and were tearing the front door open. There was no sound of its closing again; they had evidently left it open as one does in houses where some great misfortune has happened.

But Gregor was now much calmer. The words he uttered were no longer understandable, apparently, although they seemed clear enough to him, even clearer than before, perhaps because his ear had grown accustomed to the sound of them. Yet at any rate people now believed that something was wrong with him, and were ready to help him. The positive certainty with which these first measures had been taken comforted him. He felt himself drawn once more into the human circle and hoped for great and remarkable results from both the doctor and the locksmith, without really distinguishing precisely between them. To make his voice as clear as possible for the decisive conversation that was now imminent he coughed a little, as quietly as he could, of course, since this noise too might not sound like a human cough for all he was able to judge. In the next room meanwhile there was complete silence. Perhaps his parents were sitting at the table with the chief clerk, whispering, perhaps they were all leaning against the door and listening.

Slowly Gregor pushed the chair towards the door, then let go of it, caught hold of the door for support—the soles at the end of his little legs were somewhat sticky—and rested against it for a moment after his efforts. Then he set himself to turning the key in the lock with his mouth. It seemed, unhappily, that he hadn't really any teeth—what could he grip the key with?—but on the other hand his jaws were certainly very strong; with their help he did manage to set the key in motion, heedless of the fact that he was undoubtedly damaging them somewhere, since a brown fluid issued from his mouth, flowed over the key and dripped on the floor. "Just listen to that," said the chief clerk next door; "he's turning the key." That was a great encouragement to Gregor; but they should all have shouted encouragement to him, his father and mother too: "Go on, Gregor," they should have called out, "keep going, hold on to that key!" And in the belief that they were all following his efforts intently, he clenched his jaws recklessly on the key with all the force at his command. As the turning of the key progressed he circled round the lock, holding on now only with his mouth, pushing on the key, as required, or pulling it down again with all the weight of his body. The louder click of the finally yielding lock literally quickened Gregor. With a deep breath of relief he said to himself. "So I didn't need the locksmith," and laid his head on the handle to open the door wide.

Since he had to pull the door towards him, he was still invisible when it was really wide open. He had to edge himself very slowly round the near half of the double door, and to do it very carefully if he was not to fall plump upon his back just on the threshold. He was still carrying out this difficult manoeuvre, with no time to observe anything else, when he heard the chief clerk utter a loud "Oh!"—it sounded like a gust of wind—and now he could see the man, standing as he was nearest to the door, clapping one hand before his open mouth and slowly backing away as if driven by some invisible steady pressure. His mother—in spite of the chief clerk's being there her hair was still undone and sticking up in all directions—first clasped her hands and looked at his father, then took two steps towards Gregor and fell on the floor among her outspread skirts, her face quite hidden on her breast. His father knotted his fist with a fierce expression on his face as if he meant to knock Gregor back into his room, then looked uncertainly round the living room, covered his eyes with his hands and wept till his great chest heaved.

Gregor did not go now into the living room, but leaned against the inside of the firmly shut wing of the door, so that only half his body was visible and his head above it bending sideways to look at the others. The light had meanwhile strengthened; on the other side of the street one could see clearly a section of the endlessly long, dark gray building opposite—it was a hospital—abruptly punctuated by its row of regular windows; the rain was still falling, but only in large singly discernible and literally singly splashing drops. The breakfast dishes were set out on the table lavishly, for breakfast was the most important meal of the day to Gregor's father, who lingered it out for hours over various newspapers. Right opposite Gregor on the wall hung a photograph of himself on military service, as a lieutenant, hand on sword, a carefree smile on his face, inviting one to respect his uniform and military bearing. The door leading to the hall was open, and one could see that the front door stood open too, showing the landing beyond and the beginning of the stairs going down.

"Well," said Gregor, knowing perfectly that he was the only one who had retained any composure, "I'll put my clothes on at once, pack up my samples and start off. Will you only let me go? You see, sir, I'm not obstinate, and I'm willing to work; traveling is a hard life, but I couldn't live without it. Where are you going, sir? To the office? Yes? Will you give a true account of all this? One can be temporarily incapacitated, but that's just the moment for remembering former services and bearing in mind that later on, when the incapacity has been got over, one will certainly work with all the more industry and concentration. I'm loyally bound to serve the chief, you know that very well. Besides, I have to provide for my parents and my sister. I'm in great difficulties, but I'll get out of them again. Don't make things any worse for me than they are. Stand up for me in the firm. Travelers are not popular there, I know. People think they earn sacks of money and just have a good time. A prejudice there's no particular reason for revising. But you, sir, have a more comprehensive view of affairs than the rest of the staff, yes, let me tell you in confidence, a more comprehensive view than the chief himself, who, being the owner, lets his judgment easily be swayed against one of his employees. And you know very well that the traveler, who is never seen in the office almost the whole year round, can so easily fall a victim to gossip and ill luck and unfounded complaints, which he mostly knows nothing about, except when he comes back exhausted from his rounds, and only then suffers in person from their evil consequences, which he can no longer trace back to the original causes. Sir, sir, don't go away without a word to me to show that you think me in the right at least to some extent!"

But at Gregor's very first words the chief clerk had already backed away and only stared at him with parted lips over one twitching shoulder. And while Gregor was speaking he did not stand still one moment but stole away towards the door, without taking his eyes off Gregor, yet only an inch at a time, as if obeying some secret injunction to leave the room. He was already at the hall, and the suddenness with which he took his last step out of the living room would have made one believe he had burned the sole of his foot. Once in the hall he stretched his right arm before him towards the staircase, as if some supernatural power were waiting there to deliver him.

Gregor perceived that the chief clerk must on no account be allowed to go away in this frame of mind if his position in the firm were not to be endangered to the utmost. His parents did not understand this so well; they had convinced themselves in the course of years that Gregor was settled for life in this firm, and besides they were so occupied with their immediate troubles that all foresight had forsaken them. Yet Gregor had this foresight. The chief clerk must be detained, soothed, persuaded and finally won over; the whole future of Gregor and his family depended on it! If only his sister had been there! She was intelligent; she had begun to cry while Gregor was still lying quietly on his back. And no doubt the chief clerk, so partial to ladies, would have been guided by her; she would have shut the door of the flat and in the hall talked him out of his horror. But she was not there, and Gregor would have to handle the situation himself. And without remembering that he was still unaware what powers of movement he possessed, without even remembering that his words in all possibility, indeed in all likelihood, would again be unintelligible, he let go the wing of the door, pushed himself through the opening, started to walk towards the chief clerk, who was already ridiculously clinging with both hands to the railing on the landing; but immediately, as he was feeling for a support, he fell down with a little cry upon all his numerous legs. Hardly was he down when he experienced for the first time this morning a sense of physical comfort; his legs had firm ground under them; they were completely obedient, as he noted with joy; they even strove to carry him forward in whatever direction he chose; and he was inclined to believe that a final relief from all his sufferings was at hand. But in the same moment as he found himself on the floor, rocking with suppressed eagerness to move, not far from his mother, indeed just in front of her, she, who had seemed so completely crushed, sprang all at once to her feet, her arms and fingers outspread, cried: "Help, for God's sake, help!" bent her head down as if to see Gregor better, yet on the contrary kept backing senselessly away; had quite forgotten that the laden table stood behind her; sat upon it hastily, as if in absence of mind, when she bumped into it; and seemed altogether unaware that the big coffee pot beside her was upset and pouring coffee in a flood over the carpet.

30 "Mother, Mother," said Gregor in a low voice, and looked up at her. The chief clerk, for the moment, had quite slipped from his mind; instead he could not resist snapping his jaws together at the sight of the streaming coffee. That made his mother scream again, she fled from the table and fell into the arms of his father, who hastened to catch her. But Gregor had now no time to spare for his parents; the chief clerk was already on the stairs; with his chin on the banisters he was taking one last backward look. Gregor made a spring, to be as sure as possible of overtaking him; the chief clerk must have divined his intention, for he leaped down several steps and vanished; he was still yelling "Ugh!" and it echoed through the whole staircase.

Unfortunately, the flight of the chief clerk seemed completely to upset Gregor's father, who had remained relatively calm until now, for instead of running after the man himself, or at least not hindering Gregor in his pursuit, he seized in his right hand the walking stick which the chief clerk had left behind on a chair, together with a hat and greatcoat, snatched in his left hand a large newspaper from the table and began stamping his feet and flourishing the stick and the newspaper to drive Gregor back into his room. No entreaty of Gregor's availed, indeed no entreaty was even understood; however humbly he bent his head his father only stamped on the floor the more loudly. Behind his father his mother had torn open a window, despite the cold weather, and was leaning far out of it with her face in her hands. A strong draught set in from the street to the staircase, the window curtain blew in, the newspapers on the table fluttered, stray pages whisked over the floor. Pitilessly Gregor's father drove him back, hissing and crying "Shoo!" like a savage. But Gregor was quite unpracticed in walking backwards, it really was a slow business. If he only had a chance to turn round he could get back to his room at once, but he was afraid of exasperating his father by the slowness of such a rotation and at any moment the stick in his father's hand might hit him a fatal blow on the back or on the head. In the end, however, nothing else was left for him to do since to his horror he observed that in moving backwards he could not even control the direction he took; and so, keeping an anxious eye on his father all the time over his shoulder, he began to turn round as quickly as he could, which was in reality very slowly. Perhaps his father noted his good intentions, for he did not interfere except every now and then to help in the manoeuvre from a distance with the point of the stick. If only he would have stopped making that unbearable hissing noise! It made Gregor quite lose his head. He had turned almost completely round when the hissing noise so distracted him that he even turned a little the wrong way again. But when at last his head was fortunately right in front of the doorway, it appeared that his body was too broad simply to get through the opening. His father, of course, in his present mood was far from thinking of such a thing as opening the other half of the door, to let Gregor have enough space. He had merely the fixed idea of driving Gregor back into his room as quickly as possible. He would have never suffered Gregor to make the circumstantial preparations for standing up on end and perhaps slipping his way through the door. Maybe he was now making more noise than ever to urge Gregor forward as if no obstacle impeded him; to Gregor, anyhow, the noise in his rear sounded no longer like the voice of one single father; this was really no joke, and Gregor thrust himself—come what might—into the doorway. One side of his body rose up, he was tilted at an angle in the doorway, his flank was quite bruised, horrid blotches stained the white door, soon he was stuck fast and, left to himself, could not have moved at all, his legs on one side fluttered trembling in the air, those on the other were crushed painfully to the floor—when from behind his father gave him a strong push which was literally a deliverance and he flew far into the room, bleeding freely. The door was slammed behind him with the stick, and then at last there was silence.

## *II*

Not until it was twilight did Gregor awake out of a deep sleep, more like a swoon than a sleep. He would certainly have waked up of his own accord not much later, for he felt himself sufficiently rested and well-slept, but it seemed to him as if a fleeting step and a cautious shutting of the door leading into the hall had aroused him. The electric lights in the street cast a pale sheen here and there on the ceiling and the upper surfaces of the furniture, but down below, where he lay, it was dark. Slowly, awkwardly trying out his feelers, which he now first learned to appreciate, he pushed his way to the door to see what had been happening there. His left side felt like one single long, unpleasantly tense scar, and he had actually to limp on his two rows of legs. One little leg, moreover, had been severely damaged in the course of that morning's events—it was almost a miracle that only one had been damaged—and trailed uselessly behind him.

He had reached the door before he discovered what had really drawn him to it: the smell of food. For there stood a basin filled with fresh milk in which floated little sops of white bread. He could almost have laughed with joy, since he was now still hungrier than in the morning, and dipped his head almost over the eyes straight into the milk. But soon in disappointment he withdrew it again; not only did he find it difficult to feed because of his tender left side—and he could only feed with the palpitating collaboration of his whole body—he did not like the milk either, although milk had been his favorite drink and that was certainly why his sister had set it there for him, indeed it was almost with repulsion that he turned away from the basin and crawled back to the middle of the room.

He could see through the crack of the door that the gas was turned on in the living room, but while usually at this time his father made a habit of reading the afternoon newspaper in a loud voice to his mother and occasionally to his sister as well, not a sound was now to be heard. Well, perhaps his father had recently given up his habit of reading aloud, which his sister had mentioned so often in conversation and in her letters. But there was the same silence all around, although the flat was certainly not empty of occupants. "What a quiet life our family has been leading," said Gregor to himself, and as he sat there motionless staring into the darkness he felt great pride in the fact that he had been able to provide such a life for his parents and sister in such a fine flat. But what if all the quiet, the comfort, the contentment were now to end in horror? To keep himself from being lost in such thoughts Gregor took refuge in movement and crawled up and down the room.

Once during the long evening one of the side doors was opened a little and quickly shut again, later the other side door too; someone had apparently wanted to come in and then thought better of it. Gregor now stationed himself immediately before the living room door, determined to persuade any hesitating visitor to come in or at least to discover who it might be; but the door was not opened again and he waited in vain. In the early morning, when the doors were locked, they had all wanted to come in, now that he had opened one door and the other had apparently been opened during the day, no one came in and even the keys were on the other side of the doors.

It was late at night before the gas went out in the living room, and Gregor could easily tell that his parents and his sister had all stayed awake until then, for he could clearly hear the three of them stealing away on tiptoe. No one was likely to visit him, not until the morning, that was certain; so he had plenty of time to meditate at his leisure on how he was to arrange his life afresh. But the lofty, empty room in which he had to lie flat on the floor filled him with an apprehension he could not account for, since it had been his very own room for the past five years—and with a half-unconscious action, not without a slight feeling of shame, he scuttled under the sofa, where he felt comfortable at once, although his back was a little cramped and he could not lift his head up, and his only regret was that his body was too broad to get the whole of it under the sofa.

He stayed there all night, spending the time partly in a light slumber, from which his hunger kept waking him up with a start, and partly in worrying and sketching vague hopes, which all led to the same conclusion, that he must lie low for the present and, by exercising patience and the utmost consideration, help the family to bear the inconvenience he was bound to cause them in his present condition.

Very early in the morning, it was still almost night, Gregor had the chance to test the strength of his new resolutions, for his sister, nearly fully dressed, opened the door from the hall and peered in. She did not see him at once, yet when she caught sight of him under the sofa—well, he had to be somewhere, he couldn't have flown away, could he?—she was so startled that without being able to help it she slammed the door shut again. But as if regretting her behavior she opened the door again immediately and came in on tiptoe, as if she were visiting an invalid or even a stranger. Gregor had pushed his head forward to the very edge of the sofa and watched her. Would she notice that he had left the milk standing, and not for lack of hunger, and would she bring in some other kind of food more to his taste? If she did not do it of her own accord, he would rather starve than draw her attention to the fact, although he felt a wild impulse to dart out from under the sofa, throw himself at her feet and beg her for something to eat. But his sister at once noticed, with surprise, that the basin was still full, except for a little milk that had been spilt all around it, she lifted it immediately, not with her bare hands, true, but with a cloth and carried it away. Gregor was wildly curious to know what she would bring instead, and made various speculations about it. Yet what she actually did next, in the goodness of her heart, he could never have guessed at. To find out what he liked she brought him a whole selection of food, all set out on an old newspaper. There were old, half-decayed vegetables, bones from last night's supper covered with a white sauce that had thickened; some raisins and almonds; a piece of cheese that Gregor would have called uneatable two days ago; a dry roll of bread, a buttered roll, and a roll both buttered and salted. Besides all that, she set down again the same basin, into which she had poured some water, and which was apparently to be reserved for his exclusive use. And with fine tact, knowing that Gregor would not eat in her presence, she withdrew quickly and even turned the key, to let him understand that he could take his ease as much as he liked. Gregor's legs all whizzed towards the food. His wounds must have healed completely, moreover, for he felt no disability, which amazed him and made him reflect how more than a month ago he had cut one finger a little with a knife and had still suffered pain from the wound only the day before yesterday. Am I less sensitive now? he thought, and sucked greedily at the cheese, which above all the other edibles attracted him at once and strongly. One after another and with tears of satisfaction in his eyes he quickly devoured the cheese, the vegetables and the sauce; the fresh food, on the other hand, had no charms for him, he could not even stand the smell of it and actually dragged away to some little distance the things he could eat. He had long finished his meal and was only lying lazily on the same spot when his sister turned the key slowly as a sign for him to retreat. That roused him at once, although he was nearly asleep, and he hurried under the sofa again. But it took considerable self-control for him to stay under the sofa, even for the short time his sister was in the room, since the large meal had swollen his body somewhat and he was so cramped he could hardly breathe. Slight attacks of breathlessness afflicted him and his eyes were starting a little out of his head as he watched his unsuspecting sister sweeping together with a broom not only the remains of what he had eaten but even the things he had not touched, as if these were now of no use to anyone, and hastily shoveling it all into a bucket, which she covered with a wooden lid and carried away. Hardly had she turned her back when Gregor came from under the sofa and stretched and puffed himself out.

In this manner Gregor was fed, once in the early morning while his parents and the servant girl were still asleep, and a second time after they had all had their midday dinner, for then his parents took a short nap and the servant girl could be sent out on some errand or other by his sister. Not that they would have wanted him to starve, of course, but perhaps they could not have borne to know more about his feeding than from hearsay, perhaps too his sister wanted to spare them such little anxieties wherever possible, since they had quite enough to bear as it was.

Under what pretext the doctor and the locksmith had been got rid of on that first morning Gregor could not discover, for since what he said was not understood by the others it never struck any of them, not even his sister, that he could understand what they said, and so whenever his sister came into his room he had to content himself with hearing her utter only a sigh now and then and an occasional appeal to the saints. Later on, when she had got a little used to the situation—of course she could never get completely used to it—she sometimes threw out a remark which was kindly meant or could be so interpreted. "Well, he liked his dinner today," she would say when Gregor had made a good clearance of his food; and when he had not eaten, which gradually happened more and more often, she would say almost sadly: "Everything's been left standing again."

But although Gregor could get no news directly, he overheard a lot from the neighboring rooms, and as soon as voices were audible, he would run to the door of the room concerned and press his whole body against it. In the first few days especially there was no conversation that did not refer to him somehow, even if only indirectly. For two whole days there were family consultations at every mealtime about what should be done; but also between meals the same subject was discussed, for there were always at least two members of the family at home, since no one wanted to be alone in the flat and to leave it quite empty was unthinkable. And on the very first of these days the household cook—it was not quite clear what and how much she knew of the situation—went down on her knees to his mother and begged leave to go, and when she departed, a quarter of an hour later, gave thanks for her dismissal with tears in her eyes as if for the greatest benefit that could have been conferred on her, and without any prompting swore a solemn oath that she would never say a single word to anyone about what had happened.

Now Gregor's sister had to cook too, helping her mother; true, the cooking did not amount to much, for they ate scarcely anything. Gregor was always hearing one of the family vainly urging another to eat and getting no answer but: "Thanks, I've had all I want," or something similar. Perhaps they drank nothing either. Time and again his sister kept asking if he wouldn't like some beer and offered kindly to go and fetch it herself, and when he made no answer suggested that she could ask the concierge to fetch it, so that he need feel no sense of obligation, but then a round "No" came from his father and no more was said about it.

In the course of that very first day Gregor's father explained the family's financial position and prospects to both his mother and his sister. Now and then he rose from the table to get some voucher or memorandum out of the small safe he had rescued from the collapse of his business five years earlier. One could hear him opening the complicated lock and rustling papers out and shutting it again. This statement made by his father was the first cheerful information Gregor had heard since his imprisonment. He had been of the opinion that nothing at all was left over from his father's business, at least his father had never said anything to the contrary, and of course he had not asked him directly. At that time Gregor's sole desire was to do his utmost to help the family to forget as soon as possible the catastrophe which had overwhelmed the business and thrown them all into a state of complete despair. And so he had set to work with unusual ardor and almost overnight had become a commercial traveler instead of a little clerk, with of course much greater chances of earning money, and his success was immediately translated into good round coin which he could lay on the table for his amazed and happy family. These had been fine times, and they had never recurred, at least not with the same sense of glory, although later on Gregor had earned so much money that he was able to meet the expenses of the whole household and did so. They had simply got used to it, both the family and Gregor; the money was gratefully accepted and gladly given, but there was no special uprush of warm feeling. With his sister alone had he remained intimate, and it was a secret plan of his that she, who loved music, unlike himself, and could play movingly on the violin, should be sent next year to study at the Conservatorium, despite the great expense that would entail, which must be made up in some other way. During his brief visits home the Conservatorium was often mentioned in the talks he had with his sister, but always merely as a beautiful dream which could never come true, and his parents discouraged even these innocent references to it; yet Gregor had made up his mind firmly about it and meant to announce the fact with due solemnity on Christmas Day.

Such were the thoughts, completely futile in his present condition, that went through his head as he stood clinging upright to the door and listening. Sometimes out of sheer weariness he had to give up listening and let his head fall negligently against the door, but he always had to pull himself together again at once, for even the slight sound his head made was audible next door and brought all conversation to a stop. "What can he be doing now?" his father would say after a while, obviously turning towards the door, and only then would the interrupted conversation gradually be set going again.

45 Gregor was now informed as amply as he could wish—for his father tended to repeat himself in his explanations, partly because it was a long time since he had handled such matters and partly because his mother could not always grasp things at once—that a certain amount of investments, a very small amount it was true, had survived the wreck of their fortunes and had even increased a little because the dividends had not been touched meanwhile. And besides that, the money Gregor brought home every month—he had kept only a few dollars for himself—had never been quite used up and now amounted to a small capital sum. Behind the door Gregor nodded his head eagerly, rejoiced at this evidence of unexpected thrift and foresight. True, he could really have paid off some more of his father's debts to the chief with this extra money, and so brought much nearer the day on which he could quit his job, but doubtless it was better the way his father had arranged it.

Yet this capital was by no means sufficient to let the family live on the interest of it; for one year, perhaps, or at the most two, they could live on the principal, that was all. It was simply a sum that ought not to be touched and should be kept for a rainy day; money for living expenses would have to be earned. Now his father was still hale enough but an old man, and he had done no work for the past five years and could not be expected to do much; during these five years, the first years of leisure in his laborious though unsuccessful life, he had grown rather fat and become sluggish. And Gregor's old mother, how was she to earn a living with her asthma, which troubled her even when she walked through the flat and kept her lying on a sofa every other day panting for breath beside an open window? And was his sister to earn her bread, she who was still a child of seventeen and whose life hitherto had been so pleasant, consisting as it did in dressing herself nicely, sleeping long, helping in the housekeeping, going out to a few modest entertainments and above all playing the violin? At first whenever the need for earning money was mentioned Gregor let go his hold on the door and threw himself down on the cool leather sofa beside it, he felt so hot with shame and grief.

Often he just lay there the long nights through without sleeping at all, scrabbling for hours on the leather. Or he nerved himself to the great effort of pushing an armchair to the window, then crawled up over the window sill and, braced against the chair, leaned against the window panes, obviously in some recollection of the sense of freedom that looking out of a window always used to give him. For in reality day by day things that were even a little way off were growing dimmer to his sight; the hospital across the street, which he used to execrate for being all too often before his eyes, was now quite beyond his range of vision, and if he had not known that he lived in Charlotte Street, a quiet street but still a city street, he might have believed that his window gave on a desert waste where gray sky and gray land blended indistinguishably into each other. His quick-witted sister only needed to observe twice that the armchair stood by the window; after that whenever she had tidied the room she always pushed the chair back to the same place at the window and even left the inner casements open.

If he could have spoken to her and thanked her for all she had to do for him, he could have borne her ministrations better; as it was, they oppressed him. She certainly tried to make as light as possible of whatever was disagreeable in her task, and as time went on she succeeded, of course, more and more, but time brought more enlightenment to Gregor too. The very way she came in distressed him. Hardly was she in the room when she rushed to the window, without even taking time to shut the door, careful as she was usually to shield the sight of Gregor's room from the others, and as if she were almost suffocating tore the casements open with hasty fingers, standing them in the open draught for a while even in the bitterest cold and drawing deep breaths. This noisy scurry of hers upset Gregor twice a day; he would crouch trembling under the sofa all the time, knowing quite well that she would certainly have spared him such a disturbance had she found it at all possible to stay in his presence without opening the window.

On one occasion, about a month after Gregor's metamorphosis, when there was surely no reason for her to be still startled at his appearance, she came a little earlier than usual and found him gazing out of the window, quite motionless, and thus well placed to look like a bogey. Gregor would not have been surprised had she not come in at all, for she could not immediately open the window while he was there, but not only did she retreat, she jumped back as if in alarm and banged the door shut; a stranger might well have thought that he had been lying in wait for her there meaning to bite her. Of course he hid himself under the sofa at once, but he had to wait until midday before she came again, and she seemed more ill at ease than usual. This made him realize how repulsive the sight of him still was to her, and that it was bound to go on being repulsive, and what an effort it must cost her not to run away even from the sight of the small portion of his body that stuck out from under the sofa. In order to spare her that, therefore, one day he carried a sheet on his back to the sofa—it cost him four hours' labor—and arranged it there in such a way as to hide him completely, so that even if she were to bend down she could not see him. Had she considered the sheet unnecessary, she would certainly have stripped it off the sofa again, for it was clear enough that this curtaining and confining of himself was not likely to conduce Gregor's comfort, but she left it where it was, and Gregor even fancied that he caught a thankful glance from her eye when he lifted the sheet carefully a very little with his head to see how she was taking the new arrangement.

50 For the first fortnight his parents could not bring themselves to the

point of entering his room, and he often heard them expressing their appreciation of his sister's activities, whereas formerly they had frequently scolded her for being as they thought a somewhat useless daughter. But now, both of them often waited outside the door, his father and his mother, while his sister tidied his room, and as soon as she came out she had to tell them exactly how things were in the room, what Gregor had eaten, how he had conducted himself this time and whether there was not perhaps some slight improvement in his condition. His mother, moreover, began relatively soon to want to visit him, but his father and sister dissuaded her at first with arguments which Gregor listened to very attentively and altogether approved. Later, however, she had to be held back by main force, and when she cried out: "Do let me in to Gregor, he is my unfortunate son! Can't you understand that I must go to him?" Gregor thought that it might be well to have her come in, not every day, of course, but perhaps once a week; she understood things, after all, much better than his sister, who was only a child despite the efforts she was making and had perhaps taken on so difficult a task merely out of childish thoughtlessness.

Gregor's desire to see his mother was soon fulfilled. During the daytime he did not want to show himself at the window, out of consideration for his parents, but he could not crawl very far around the few square yards of floor space he had, nor could he bear lying quietly at rest all during the night, while he was fast losing any interest he had ever taken in food, so that for mere recreation he had formed the habit of crawling criss-cross over the walls and ceiling. He especially enjoyed hanging suspended from the ceiling; it was much better than lying on the floor. One could breathe more freely; one's body swung and rocked lightly; and in the almost blissful absorption induced by this suspension it could happen to his own surprise that he let go and fell plump on the floor. Yet he now had his body much better under control than formerly, and even such a big fall did him no harm. His sister at once remarked the new distraction Gregor had found for himself—he left traces behind him of the sticky stuff on his soles wherever he crawled—and she got the idea in her head of giving him as wide a field as possible to crawl in and of removing the pieces of furniture that hindered him, above all the chest of drawers and the writing desk. But that was more than she could manage all by herself, she did not dare ask her father to help her; and as for the servant girl, a young creature of sixteen who had had the courage to stay on after the cook's departure, she could not be asked to help, for she had begged as an especial favor that she might keep the kitchen door locked and open it only on a definite summons; so there was nothing left but to apply to her mother at an hour when her father was out. And the old lady did come, with exclamations of joyful eagerness, which, however, died away at the door of Gregor's room. Gregor's sister, of course, went in first, to see that everything was in order before letting his mother enter. In great haste Gregor pulled the sheet lower and tucked it more in folds so that it really looked as if it had been thrown accidentally over the sofa. And this time he did not peer out from under it; he renounced the pleasure of seeing his mother on this occasion and was only glad that she had come at all. "Come in, he's out of sight," said his sister, obviously leading her mother by the hand. Gregor could now hear the two women struggling to shift the heavy old chest from its place, and his sister claiming the greater part of the labor for herself, without listening to the admonitions of her mother who feared she might overstrain herself. It took a long time. After at least a quarter of an hour's tugging his mother objected that the chest had better be left where it was, for in the first place it was too heavy and could never be got out before his father came home, and standing in the middle of the room like that it would only hamper Gregor's movements, while in the second place it was not at all certain that removing the furniture would be doing a service to Gregor. She was inclined to think to the contrary; the sight of the naked walls made her own heart heavy, and why shouldn't Gregor have the same feeling, considering that he had been used to his furniture for so long and might feel forlorn without it. "And doesn't it look," she concluded in a low voice—in fact she had been almost whispering all the time as if to avoid letting Gregor, whose exact whereabouts she did not know, hear even the tones of her voice, for she was convinced that he could not understand her words—"doesn't it look as if we were showing him, by taking away his furniture, that we have given up hope of his ever getting better and are just leaving him coldly to himself? I think it would be best to keep his room exactly as it has always been, so that when he comes back to us he will find everything unchanged and be able all the more easily to forget what has happened in between."

On hearing these words from his mother Gregor realized that the lack of all direct human speech for the past two months together with the monotony of family life must have confused his mind, otherwise he could not account for the fact that he had quite earnestly looked forward to having his room emptied of furnishing. Did he really want his warm room, so comfortably fitted with old family furniture, to be turned into a naked den in which he would certainly be able to crawl unhampered in all directions but at the price of shedding simultaneously all recollection of his human background? He had indeed been so near the brink of forgetfulness that only the voice of his mother, which he had not heard for so long, had drawn him back from it. Nothing should be taken out of his room; everything must stay as it was; he could not dispense with the good influence of the furniture on his state of mind; and even if the furniture did hamper him in his senseless crawling round and round, that was no drawback but a great advantage.

Unfortunately his sister was of the contrary opinion; she had grown accustomed, and not without reason, to consider herself an expert in Gregor's affairs as against her parents, and so her mother's advice was now enough to make her determined on the removal not only of the chest and the writing desk, which had been her first intention, but of all the furniture except the indispensable sofa. This determination was not, of course, merely the outcome of childish recalcitrance and of the self-confidence she had recently developed so unexpectedly and at such cost; she had in fact perceived that Gregor needed a lot of space to crawl about in, while on the other hand he never used the furniture at all, so far as could be seen. Another factor might have been also the enthusiastic temperament of an adolescent girl, which seeks to indulge itself on every opportunity and which now tempted Grete to exaggerate the horror of her brother's circumstances in order that she might do all the more for him. In a room where Gregor lorded it all alone over empty walls no one save herself was likely ever to set foot.

And so she was not to be moved from her resolve by her mother who seemed moreover to be ill at ease in Gregor's room and therefore unsure of herself, was soon reduced to silence and helped her daughter as best she could to push the chest outside. Now, Gregor could do without the chest, if need be, but the writing desk he must retain. As soon as the two women had got the chest out of his room, groaning as they pushed it, Gregor stuck his head out from under the sofa to see how he might intervene as kindly and cautiously as possible. But as bad luck would have it, his mother was the first to return, leaving Grete clasping the chest in the room next door where she was trying to shift it all by herself, without of course moving it from the spot. His mother however was not accustomed to the sight of him, it might sicken her and so in alarm Gregor backed quickly to the other end of the sofa, yet could not prevent the sheet from swaying a little in front. That was enough to put her on the alert. She paused, stood still for a moment and then went back to Grete.

55 Although Gregor kept reassuring himself that nothing out of the way was happening, but only a few bits of furniture were being changed round, he soon had to admit that all this trotting to and fro of the two women, their little ejaculations and the scraping of furniture along the floor affected him like a vast disturbance coming from all sides at once, and however much he tucked in his head and legs and cowered to the very floor he was bound to confess that he would not be able to stand it for long. They were clearing his room out; taking away everything he loved; the chest in which he kept his fret saw and other tools was already dragged off, they were now loosening the writing desk which had almost sunk into the floor, the desk at which he had done all his homework when he was at the commercial academy, at the grammar school before that, and, yes, even at the primary school—he had no more time to waste in weighing the good intentions of the two women, whose existence he had by now almost forgotten, for they were so exhausted that they were laboring in silence and nothing could be heard but the heavy scuffling of their feet.

And so he rushed out—the women were just leaning against the writing desk in the next room to give themselves a breather—and four times changed his direction, since he really did not know what to rescue first, then on the wall opposite, which was already otherwise cleared, he was struck by the picture of the lady muffled in so much fur and quickly crawled up to it and pressed himself to the glass, which was a good surface to hold on to and comforted his hot belly. This picture at least, which was entirely hidden beneath him, was going to be removed by nobody. He turned his head towards the door of the living room so as to observe the women when they came back.

They had not allowed themselves much of a rest and were already coming; Grete had twined her arm round her mother and was almost supporting her. "Well, what shall we take now?" said Grete, looking round. Her eyes met Gregor's from the wall. She kept her composure, presumably because of her mother, bent her head down to her mother, to keep her from looking up, and said, although in a fluttering, unpremeditated voice: "Come, hadn't we better go back to the living room for a moment?" Her intentions were clear enough to Gregor, she wanted to bestow her mother in safety and then chase him down from the wall. Well, just let her try it! He clung to his picture and would not give it up. He would rather fly in Grete's face.

But Grete's words had succeeded in disquieting her mother, who took a step to one side, caught sight of the huge brown mass on the flowered wallpaper, and before she was really conscious that what she saw was Gregor screamed in a loud, hoarse voice: "Oh God, oh God!" fell with outspread arms over the sofa as if giving up and did not move. "Gregor!" cried his sister, shaking her fist and glaring at him. This was the first time she had directly addressed him since his metamorphosis. She ran into the next room for some aromatic essence with which to rouse her mother from her fainting fit. Gregor wanted to help too—there was still time to rescue the picture—but he was stuck fast to the glass and had to tear himself loose; he then ran after his sister into the next room as if he could advise her, as he used to do; but then had to stand helplessly behind her; she meanwhile searched among various small bottles and when she turned round started in alarm at the sight of him; one bottle fell on the floor and broke; a splinter of glass cut Gregor's face and some kind of corrosive medicine splashed him; without pausing a moment longer Grete gathered up all the bottles she could carry and ran to her mother with them; she banged the door shut with her foot. Gregor was now cut off from his mother, who was perhaps nearly dying because of him; he dared not open the door for fear of frightening away his sister, who had to stay with her mother; there was nothing he could do but wait; and harassed by self-reproach and worry he began now to crawl to and fro, over everything, walls, furniture and ceiling, and finally in his despair, when the whole room seemed to be reeling round him, fell down on to the middle of the big table.

A little while elapsed, Gregor was still lying there feebly and all around was quiet, perhaps that was a good omen. Then the doorbell rang. The servant girl was of course locked in her kitchen, and Grete would have to open the door. It was his father. "What's been happening?" were his first words; Grete's face must have told him everything. Grete answered in a muffled voice, apparently hiding her head on his breast: "Mother has been fainting, but she's better now. Gregor's broken loose." "Just what I expected," said his father, "just what I've been telling you, but you women would never listen." It was clear to Gregor that his father had taken the worst interpretation of Grete's all too brief statement and was assuming that Gregor had been guilty of some violent act. Therefore Gregor must now try to propitiate his father, since he had neither time nor means for an explanation. And so he fled to the door of his own room and crouched against it, to let his father see as soon as he came in from the hall that his son had the good intention of getting back into his room immediately and that it was not necessary to drive him there, but that if only the door were opened he would disappear at once.

60 Yet his father was not in the mood to perceive such fine distinctions. "Ah!" he cried as soon as he appeared, in a tone which sounded at once angry and exultant. Gregor drew his head back from the door and lifted it to look at his father. Truly, this was not the father he had imagined to himself, admittedly he had been too absorbed of late in his new recreation of crawling over the ceiling to take the same interest as before in what was happening elsewhere in the flat, and he ought really to be prepared for some changes. And yet, and yet, could that be his father? The man who used to lie wearily sunk in bed whenever Gregor set out on a business journey; who welcomed him back of an evening lying in a long chair in a dressing gown; who could not really rise to his feet but only lifted his arms in greeting, and on the rare occasions when he did go out with his family, on one or two

Sundays a year and on high holidays, walked between Gregor and his mother, who were slow walkers anyhow, even more slowly than they did, muffled in his old greatcoat, shuffling laboriously forward with the help of his crook-handled stick which he set down most cautiously at every step and, whenever he wanted to say anything, nearly always came to a full stop and gathered his escort around him? Now he was standing there in fine shape; dressed in a smart blue uniform with gold buttons, such as bank messengers wear; his strong double chin bulged over the stiff high collar of his jacket; from under his bushy eyebrows his black eyes darted fresh and penetrating glances; his one-time tangled white hair had been combed flat on either side of a shining and carefully exact parting. He pitched his cap, which bore a gold monogram, probably the badge of some bank, in a wide sweep across the whole room on to a sofa and with the tail-ends of his jacket thrown back, his hands in his trouser pockets, advanced with a grim visage towards Gregor. Likely enough he did not himself know what he meant to do; at any rate he lifted his feet uncommonly high, and Gregor was dumbfounded at the enormous size of his shoe soles. But Gregor could not risk standing up to him, aware as he had been from the very first day of his new life that his father believed only the severest measures suitable for dealing with him. And so he ran before his father, stopping when he stopped and scuttling forward again when his father made any kind of move. In this way they circled the room several times without anything decisive happening, indeed the whole operation did not even look like a pursuit because it was carried out so slowly. And so Gregor did not leave the floor, for he feared that his father might take as a piece of peculiar wickedness any excursion of his over the walls or the ceiling. All the same, he could not stay this course much longer, for while his father took one step he had to carry out a whole series of movements. He was already beginning to feel breathless, just as in his former life his lungs had not been very dependable. As he was staggering along, trying to concentrate his energy on running, hardly keeping his eyes open; in his dazed state never even thinking of any other escape than simply going forward; and having almost forgotten that the walls were free to him, which in his room were well provided with finely carved pieces of furniture full of knobs and crevices—suddenly something lightly flung landed close behind him and rolled before him. It was an apple; a second apple followed immediately; Gregor came to a stop in alarm; there was no point in running on, for his father was determined to bombard him. He had filled his pockets with fruit from the dish on the sideboard and was now shying apple after apple, without taking particularly good aim for the moment. The small red apples rolled about the floor as if magnetized and cannoned into each other. An apple thrown without much force grazed Gregor's back and glanced off harmlessly. But another following immediately landed right on his back and sank in; Gregor wanted to drag himself forward, as if this startling, incredible pain could be left behind him; but he felt as if nailed to the spot and flattened himself out in a complete derangement of all his senses. With his last conscious look he saw the door of his room being torn open and his mother rushing out ahead of his screaming sister, in her underbodice, for her daughter had loosened her clothing to let her breathe more freely and recover from her swoon, he saw his mother rushing towards his father, leaving one after another behind her on the floor her loosened petticoats, stumbling over her petticoats straight to his father and embracing him, in complete union with him—but here Gregor's sight began to fail—with her hands clasped round his father's neck as she begged for her son's life.

## *III*

The serious injury done to Gregor, which disabled him for more than a month—the apple went on sticking in his body as a visible reminder, since no one ventured to remove it—seemed to have made even his father recollect that Gregor was a member of the family, despite his present unfortunate and repulsive shape, and ought not to be treated as an enemy, that, on the contrary, family duty required the suppression of disgust and the exercise of patience, nothing but patience.

And although his injury had impaired, probably for ever, his power of movement, and for the time being it took him long, long minutes to creep across his room like an old invalid—there was no question now of crawling up the wall—yet in his own opinion he was sufficiently compensated for this worsening of his condition by the fact that towards evening the living-room door, which he used to watch intently for an hour or two beforehand, was always thrown open, so that lying in the darkness of his room, invisible to the family, he could see them all at the lamplit table and listen to their talk, by general consent as it were, very different from his earlier eavesdropping.

True, their intercourse lacked the lively character of former times, which he had always called to mind with a certain wistfulness in the small hotel bedrooms where he had been wont to throw himself down, tired out, on damp bedding. They were now mostly very silent. Soon after supper his father would fall asleep in his armchair; his mother and sister would admonish each other to be silent; his mother, bending low over the lamp, stitched at fine sewing for an underwear firm; his sister, who had taken a job as a salesgirl, was learning shorthand and French in the evenings on the chance of bettering herself. Sometimes his father woke up, and as if quite unaware that he had been sleeping said to his mother: "What a lot of sewing you're doing today!" and at once fell asleep again, while the two women exchanged a tired smile.

With a kind of mulishness his father persisted in keeping his uniform on even in the house; his dressing gown hung uselessly on its peg and he slept fully dressed where he sat, as if he were ready for service at any moment and even here only at the beck and call of his superior. As a result, his uniform, which was not brand-new to start with, began to look dirty, despite all the loving care of the mother and sister to keep it clean, and Gregor often spent whole evenings gazing at the many greasy spots on the garment, gleaming with gold buttons always in a high state of polish, in which the old man sat sleeping in extreme discomfort and yet quite peacefully.

65 As soon as the clock struck ten his mother tried to rouse his father with gentle words and to persuade him after that to get into bed, for sitting there he could not have a proper sleep and that was what he needed most, since he had to go to duty at six. But with the mulishness that had obsessed him since he became a bank messenger he always insisted on staying longer at the table, although he regularly fell asleep again and in the end only with the greatest trouble could be got out of his armchair and into his bed. How-

ever insistently Gregor's mother and sister kept urging him with gentle reminders, he would go on slowly shaking his head for a quarter of an hour, keeping his eyes shut, and refuse to get to his feet. The mother plucked at his sleeve, whispering endearments in his ear, the sister left her lessons to come to her mother's help, but Gregor's father was not to be caught. He would only sink down deeper in his chair. Not until the two women hoisted him up by the armpits did he open his eyes and look at them both, one after the other, usually with the remark: "This is a life. This is the peace and quiet of my old age." And leaning on the two of them he would heave himself up, with difficulty, as if he were a great burden to himself, suffer them to lead him as far as the door and then wave them off and go on alone, while the mother abandoned her needlework and the sister her pen in order to run after him and help him farther.

Who could find time, in this overworked and tired-out family, to bother about Gregor more than was absolutely needful? The household was reduced more and more; the servant girl was turned off; a gigantic bony charwoman with white hair flying round her head came in morning and evening to do the rough work; everything else was done by Gregor's mother, as well as great piles of sewing. Even various family ornaments, which his mother and sister used to wear with pride at parties and celebrations, had to be sold, as Gregor discovered of an evening from hearing them all discuss the prices obtained. But what they lamented most was the fact that they could not leave the flat which was too big for their present circumstances, because they could not think of any way to shift Gregor. Yet Gregor saw well enough that consideration for him was not the main difficulty preventing the removal, for they could have easily shifted him in some suitable box with a few air holes in it; what really kept them from moving into another flat was rather their own complete hopelessness and the belief that they had been singled out for a misfortune such as had never happened to any of their relations or acquaintances. They fulfilled to the uttermost all that the world demands of poor people, the father fetched breakfast for the small clerks in the bank, the mother devoted her energy to making underwear for strangers, the sister trotted to and fro behind the counter at the behest of customers, but more than this they had not the strength to do. And the wound in Gregor's back began to nag at him afresh when his mother and sister, after getting his father into bed, came back again, left their work lying, drew close to each other and sat cheek by cheek; when his mother, pointing towards his room, said: "Shut that door now, Grete," and he was left again in darkness, while next door the women mingled their tears or perhaps sat dry-eyed staring at the table.

Gregor hardly slept at all by night or by day. He was often haunted by the idea that next time the door opened he would take the family's affairs in hand again just as he used to do; once more, after this long interval, there appeared in his thoughts the figures of the chief and the chief clerk, the commercial travelers and the apprentices, the porter who was so dull-witted, two or three friends in other firms, a chambermaid in one of the rural hotels, a sweet and fleeting memory, a cashier in a milliner's shop, whom he had wooed earnestly but too slowly—they all appeared, together with strangers or people he had quite forgotten, but instead of helping him and his family they were one and all unapproachable and he was glad when they vanished. At other times he would not be in the mood to bother about his family, he was only filled with rage at the way they were neglecting him, and although he had no clear idea of what he might care to eat he would make plans for getting into the larder to take the food that was after all his due, even if he were not hungry. His sister no longer took thought to bring him what might especially please him, but in the morning and at noon before she went to business hurriedly pushed into his room with her foot any food that was available, and in the evening cleared it out again with one sweep of the broom, heedless of whether it had been merely tasted, or—as most frequently happened—left untouched. The cleaning of his room, which she now did always in the evenings, could not have been more hastily done. Streaks of dirt stretched along the walls, here and there lay balls of dust and filth. At first Gregor used to station himself in some particularly filthy corner when his sister arrived, in order to reproach her with it, so to speak. But he could have sat there for weeks without getting her to make any improvements; she could see the dirt as well as he did, but she had simply made up her mind to leave it alone. And yet, with a touchiness that was new to her, which seemed anyhow to have infected the whole family, she jealously guarded her claim to be the sole caretaker of Gregor's room. His mother once subjected his room to a thorough cleaning, which was achieved only by means of several buckets of water—all this dampness of course upset Gregor too and he lay widespread, sulky and motionless on the sofa—but she was well punished for it. Hardly had his sister noticed the changed aspect of his room that evening than she rushed in high dudgeon into the living room and, despite the imploringly raised hands of her mother, burst into a storm of weeping, while her parents—her father had of course been startled out of his chair—looked on at first in helpless amazement; then they too began to go into action; the father reproached the mother on his right for not having left the cleaning of Gregor's room to his sister; shrieked at the sister on his left that never again was she to be allowed to clean Gregor's room; while the mother tried to pull the father into his bedroom, since he was beyond himself with agitation; the sister, shaken with sobs, then beat upon the table with her small fists; and Gregor hissed loudly with rage because not one of them thought of shutting the door to spare him such a spectacle and so much noise.

Still, even if the sister, exhausted by her daily work, had grown tired of looking after Gregor as she did formerly, there was no need for his mother's intervention or for Gregor's being neglected at all. The charwoman was there. This old widow, whose strong bony frame had enabled her to survive the worst a long life could offer, by no means recoiled from Gregor. Without being in the least curious she had once by chance opened the door of his room and at the sight of Gregor, who, taken by surprise, began to rush to and fro although no one was chasing him, merely stood there with her arms folded. From that time she never failed to open his door a little for a moment, morning and evening, to have a look at him. At first she even used to call him to her, with words which apparently she took to be friendly; such as: "Come along, then, you old dung beetle!" or "Look at the old dung beetle, then!" To such allocutions Gregor made no answer, but stayed motionless where he was, as if the door had never been opened. Instead of being allowed to disturb him so senselessly whenever the whim took her, she should rather have been ordered to clean out his room daily, that charwoman! Once, early in the morning—heavy rain was lashing on the windowpanes, perhaps a sign that spring was on the way—Gregor was so exasperated when she began addressing him again that he ran for her, as if to attack her, although slowly and feebly enough. But the charwoman instead of showing fright merely lifted high a chair that happened to be beside the door, and as she stood there with her mouth wide open it was clear that she meant to shut it only when she brought the chair down on Gregor's back. "So you're not coming any nearer?" she asked, as Gregor turned away again, and quietly put the chair back into the corner.

Gregor was now eating hardly anything. Only when he happened to pass the food laid out for him did he take a bit of something in his mouth as a pastime, kept it there for an hour at a time and usually spat it out again. At first he thought it was chagrin over the state of his room that prevented him from eating, yet he soon got used to the various changes in his room. It had become a habit in the family to push into his room things there was no room for elsewhere, and there were plenty of these now, since one of the rooms had been let to three lodgers. These serious gentlemen—all three of them with full beards, as Gregor once observed through a crack in the door—had a passion for order, not only in their own room but, since they were now members of the household, in all its arrangements, especially in the kitchen. Superfluous, not to say dirty, objects they could not bear. Besides, they had brought with them most of the furnishings they needed. For this reason many things could be dispensed with that it was no use trying to sell but that should not be thrown away either. All of them found their way into Gregor's room. The ash can likewise and the kitchen garbage can. Anything that was not needed for the moment was simply flung into Gregor's room by the charwoman, who did everything in a hurry; fortunately Gregor usually saw only the object, whatever it was, and the hand that held it. Perhaps she intended to take the things away again as time and opportunity offered, or to collect them until she could throw them all out in a heap, but in fact they just lay wherever she happened to throw them, except when Gregor pushed his way through the junk heap and shifted it somewhat, at first out of necessity, because he had not room enough to crawl, but later with increasing enjoyment, although after such excursions, being sad and weary to death, he would lie motionless for hours. And since the lodgers often ate their supper at home in the common living room, the living-room door stayed shut many an evening, yet Gregor reconciled himself quite easily to the shutting of the door, for often enough on evenings when it was opened he had disregarded it entirely and lain in the darkest corner of his room, quite unnoticed by the family. But on one occasion the charwoman left the door open a little and it stayed ajar even when the lodgers came in for supper and the lamp was lit. They set themselves at the top end of the table where formerly Gregor and his father and mother had eaten their meals, unfolded their napkins and took knife and fork in hand. At once his mother appeared in the doorway with a dish of meat and close behind her his sister with a dish of potatoes piled high. The food steamed with a thick vapor. The lodgers bent over the food set before them as if to scrutinize it before eating, in fact the man in the middle, who seemed to pass for an authority with the other two, cut a piece of meat as it lay on the dish, obviously to discover if it were tender or should be sent back to the kitchen. He showed satisfaction, and Gregor's mother and sister, who had been watching anxiously, breathed freely and began to smile.

70 The family itself took its meals in the kitchen. None the less, Gregor's father came into the living room before going into the kitchen and with one prolonged bow, cap in hand, made a round of the table. The lodgers all stood up and murmured something in their beards. When they were alone again they ate their food in almost complete silence. It seemed remarkable to Gregor that among the various noises coming from the table he could always distinguish the sound of their masticating teeth, as if this were a sign to Gregor that one needed teeth in order to eat, and that with toothless jaws even of the finest make one could do nothing. "I'm hungry enough," said Gregor sadly to himself, "but not for that kind of food. How these lodgers are stuffing themselves, and here am I dying of starvation!"

On that very evening—during the whole of his time there Gregor could not remember ever having heard the violin—the sound of violin-playing came from the kitchen. The lodgers had already finished their supper, the one in the middle had brought out a newspaper and given the other two a page apiece, and now they were leaning back at ease reading and smoking. When the violin began to play they pricked up their ears, got to their feet, and went on tiptoe to the hall door where they stood huddled together. Their movements must have been heard in the kitchen, for Gregor's father called out: "Is the violin-playing disturbing you gentlemen? It can be stopped at once." "On the contrary," said the middle lodger, "could not Fräulein Samsa come and play in this room, beside us, where it is much more convenient and comfortable?" "Oh certainly," cried Gregor's father, as if he were the violin player. The lodgers came back into the living room and waited. Presently Gregor's father arrived with the music stand, his mother carrying the music and his sister with the violin. His sister quietly made everything ready to start playing; his parents, who had never let rooms before and so had an exaggerated idea of the courtesy due to lodgers, did not venture to sit down on their own chairs; his father leaned against the door, the right hand thrust between two buttons of his livery coat, which was formally buttoned up; but his mother was offered a chair by one of the lodgers and, since she left the chair just where he had happened to put it, sat down in a corner to one side.

Gregor's sister began to play; the father and mother, from either side, intently watched the movements of her hands. Gregor, attracted by the playing, ventured to move forward a little until his head was actually inside the living room. He felt hardly any surprise at his growing lack of consideration for the others; there had been a time when he prided himself on being considerate. And yet just on this occasion he had more reason than ever to hide himself, since owing to the amount of dust which lay thick in his room and rose into the air at the slightest movement, he too was covered with dust; fluff and hair and remnants of food trailed with him, caught on his back and along his sides; his indifference to everything was much too great for him to turn on his back and scrape himself clean on the carpet, as once he had done several times a day. And in spite of his condition, no shame deterred him from advancing a little over the spotless floor of the living room.

To be sure, no one was aware of him. The family was entirely absorbed in the violin-playing; the lodgers, however, who first of all had stationed themselves, hands in pockets, much too close behind the music stand so that they could all have read the music, which must have bothered his sister, had soon retreated to the window, half-whispering with downbent heads, and stayed there while his father turned an anxious eye on them. Indeed, they were making it more than obvious that they had been disappointed in their expectation of hearing good or enjoyable violin-playing, that they had had more than enough of the performance and only out of courtesy suffered a continued disturbance of their peace. From the way they all kept blowing the smoke of their cigars high in the air through nose and mouth one could divine their irritation. And yet Gregor's sister was playing so beautifully. Her face leaned sideways, intently and sadly her eyes followed the notes of music. Gregor crawled a little farther forward and lowered his head to the ground so that it might be possible for his eyes to meet hers. Was he an animal, that music had such an effect upon him? He felt as if the way were opening before him to the unknown nourishment he craved. He was determined to push forward till he reached his sister, to pull at her skirt and so let her know that she was to come into his room with her violin, for no one here appreciated her playing as he would appreciate it. He would never let her out of his room, at least, not so long as he lived; his frightful appearance would become, for the first time, useful to him; he would watch all the doors of his room at once and spit at intruders; but his sister should need no constraint, she should stay with him of her own free will; she should sit beside him on the sofa, bend down her ear to him and hear him confide that he had had the firm intention of sending her to the Conservatorium, and that, but for his mishap, last Christmas—surely Christmas was long past?—he would have announced it to everybody without allowing a single objection. After this confession his sister would be so touched that she would burst into tears, and Gregor would then raise himself to her shoulder and kiss her on the neck, which, now that she went to business, she kept free of any ribbon or collar.

"Mr. Samsa!" cried the middle lodger, to Gregor's father, and pointed, without wasting any more words, at Gregor, now working himself slowly forwards. The violin fell silent, the middle lodger first smiled to his friends with a shake of the head and then looked at Gregor again. Instead of driving Gregor out, his father seemed to think it more needful to begin by soothing down the lodgers, although they were not at all agitated and apparently found Gregor more entertaining than the violin-playing. He hurried towards them and, spreading out his arms, tried to urge them back into their own room and at the same time to block their view of Gregor. They now began to be really a little angry, one could not tell whether because of the old man's behavior or because it just dawned on them that all unwittingly they had such a neighbor as Gregor next door. They demanded explanations of his father, they waved their arms like him, tugged uneasily at their beards, and only with reluctance backed towards their room. Meanwhile Gregor's sister, who stood there as if lost when her playing was so abruptly broken off, came to life again, pulled herself together all at once after standing for a while holding violin and bow in nervelessly hanging hands and staring at her music, pushed her violin into the lap of her mother, who was still sitting in her chair fighting asthmatically for breath, and ran into the lodgers' room to which they were now being shepherded by her father rather more quickly than before. One could see the pillows and blankets on the beds flying under her accustomed fingers and being laid in order. Before the lodgers had actually reached their room she had finished making the beds and slipped out.

75 The old man seemed once more to be so possessed by his mulish self-assertiveness that he was forgetting all the respect he should show to his lodgers. He kept driving them on and driving them on until in the very door of the bedroom the middle lodger stamped his foot loudly on the floor and so brought him to a halt. "I beg to announce," said the lodger, lifting one hand and looking also at Gregor's mother and sister, "that because of the disgusting conditions prevailing in this household and family"—here he spat on the floor with emphatic brevity—"I give you notice on the spot. Naturally I won't pay you a penny for the days I have lived here, on the contrary I shall consider bringing an action for damages against you, based on claims—believe me—that will be easily susceptible of proof." He ceased and stared straight in front of him, as if he expected something. In fact his two friends at once rushed into the breach with these words: "And we too give notice on the spot." On that he seized the door-handle and shut the door with a slam.

Gregor's father, groping with his hands, staggered forward and fell into his chair; it looked as if he were stretching himself there for his ordinary evening nap, but the marked jerkings of his head, which was as if uncontrollable, showed that he was far from asleep. Gregor had simply stayed quietly all the time on the spot where the lodgers had espied him. Disappointment at the failure of his plan, perhaps also the weakness arising from extreme hunger, made it impossible for him to move. He feared, with a fair degree of certainty, that at any moment the general tension would discharge itself in a combined attack upon him, and he lay waiting. He did not react even to the noise made by the violin as it fell off his mother's lap from under her trembling fingers and gave out a resonant note.

"My dear parents," said his sister, slapping her hand on the table by way of introduction, "things can't go on like this. Perhaps you don't realize that, but I do. I won't utter my brother's name in the presence of this creature, and so all I say is: we must try to get rid of it. We've tried to look after it and to put up with it as far as is humanly possible, and I don't think anyone could reproach us in the slightest."

"She is more than right," said Gregor's father to himself. His mother, who was still choking for lack of breath, began to cough hollowly into her hand with a wild look in her eyes.

His sister rushed over to her and held her forehead. His father's thoughts seemed to have lost their vagueness at Grete's words, he sat more upright, fingering his service cap that lay among the plates still lying on the table from the lodgers' supper, and from time to time looked at the still form of Gregor.

80 "We must try to get rid of it," his sister now said explicitly to her father, since her mother was coughing too much to hear a word, "it will be the death of both of you. I can see that coming. When one has to work as hard as we do, all of us, one can't stand this continual torment at home on top of it. At least I can't stand it any longer." And she burst into such a passion of sobbing that her tears dropped on her mother's face, where she wiped them off mechanically.

"My dear," said the old man sympathetically, and with evident understanding, "but what can we do?"

Gregor's sister merely shrugged her shoulders to indicate the feeling of helplessness that had now overmastered her during her weeping fit, in contrast to her former confidence.

"If he could understand us," said her father, half questioningly; Grete, still sobbing, vehemently waved a hand to show how unthinkable that was.

"If he could understand us," repeated the old man, shutting his eyes to consider his daughter's conviction that understanding was impossible, "then perhaps we might come to some agreement with him. But as it is—"

85 "He must go," cried Gregor's sister, "that's the only solution, Father. You must just try to get rid of the idea that this is Gregor. The fact that we've believed it for so long is the root of all our trouble. But how can it be Gregor? If this were Gregor, he would have realized long ago that human beings can't live with such a creature, and he'd have gone away on his own accord. Then we wouldn't have any brother, but we'd be able to go on living and keep his memory in honor. As it is, this creature persecutes us, drives away our lodgers, obviously wants the whole apartment to himself and would have us all sleep in the gutter. Just look, Father," she shrieked all at once, "he's at it again!" And in an access of panic that was quite incomprehensible to Gregor she even quitted her mother, literally thrusting the chair from her as if she would rather sacrifice her mother than stay so near to Gregor, and rushed behind her father, who also rose up, being simply upset by her agitation, and half-spread his arms out as if to protect her.

Yet Gregor had not the slightest intention of frightening anyone, far less his sister. He had only begun to turn round in order to crawl back to his room, but it was certainly a startling operation to watch, since because of his disabled condition he could not execute the difficult turning movements except by lifting his head and then bracing it against the floor over and over again. He paused and looked around. His good intentions seemed to have been recognized; the alarm had only been momentary. Now they were all watching him in melancholy silence. His mother lay in her chair, her legs stiffly outstretched and pressed together, her eyes almost closing for sheer weariness; his father and his sister were sitting beside each other, his sister's arm around the old man's neck.

Perhaps I can go on turning round now, thought Gregor, and began his labors again. He could not stop himself from panting with the effort, and had to pause now and then to take breath. Nor did anyone harass him, he was left entirely to himself. When he had completed the turn-round he began at once to crawl straight back. He was amazed at the distance separating him from his room and could not understand how in his weak state he had managed to accomplish the same journey so recently, almost without remarking it. Intent on crawling as fast as possible, he barely noticed that not a single word, not an ejaculation from his family, interfered with his progress. Only when he was already in the doorway did he turn his head round, not completely, for his neck muscles were getting stiff, but enough to see that nothing had changed behind him except that his sister had risen to her feet. His last glance fell on his mother, who was not quite overcome by sleep.

Hardly was he well inside his room when the door was hastily pushed shut, bolted and locked. The sudden noise in his rear startled him so much that his little legs gave beneath him. It was his sister who had shown such haste. She had been standing ready waiting and had made a light spring forward. Gregor had not even heard her coming, and she cried "At last!" to her parents as she turned the key in the lock.

"And what now?" said Gregor to himself, looking round in the darkness. Soon he made the discovery that he was now unable to stir a limb.

This did not surprise him, rather it seemed unnatural that he should ever actually have been able to move on these feeble little legs. Otherwise he felt relatively comfortable. True, his whole body was aching, but it seemed that the pain was gradually growing less and would finally pass away. The rotting apple in his back and the inflamed area around it, all covered with soft dust, already hardly troubled him. He thought of his family with tenderness and love. The decision that he must disappear was one that he held to even more strongly than his sister, if that were possible. In this state of vacant and peaceful meditation he remained until the tower clock struck three in the morning. The first broadening of light in the world outside the window entered his consciousness once more. Then his head sank to the floor of its own accord and from his nostrils came the last faint flicker of his breath.

90 When the charwoman arrived early in the morning—what between her strength and her impatience she slammed all the doors so loudly, never mind how often she had been begged not to do so, that no one in the whole apartment could enjoy any quiet sleep after her arrival—she noticed nothing unusual as she took her customary peep into Gregor's room. She thought he was lying motionless on purpose, pretending to be in the sulks; she credited him with every kind of intelligence. Since she happened to have the longhandled broom in her hand she tried to tickle him up with it from the doorway. When that too produced no reaction she felt provoked and poked at him a little harder, and only when she had pushed him along the floor without meeting any resistance was her attention aroused. It did not take her long to establish the truth of the matter, and her eyes widened, she let out a whistle, yet did not waste much time over it but tore open the door of the Samsas' bedroom and yelled into the darkness at the top of her voice: "Just look at this, it's dead; it's lying here dead and done for!"

Mr. and Mrs. Samsa started up in their double bed and before they realized the nature of the charwoman's announcement had some difficulty in overcoming the shock of it. But then they got out of bed quickly, one on either side, Mr. Samsa throwing a blanket over his shoulders, Mrs. Samsa in nothing but her nightgown; in this array they entered Gregor's room. Meanwhile the door of the living room opened, too, where Grete had been sleeping since the advent of the lodgers; she was completely dressed as if she had not been to bed, which seemed to be confirmed also by the paleness of her face. "Dead?" said Mrs. Samsa, looking questioningly at the charwoman, although she could have investigated for herself, and the fact was obvious enough without investigation. "I should say so," said the charwoman, proving her words by pushing Gregor's corpse a long way to one side with her broomstick. Mrs. Samsa made a movement as if to stop her, but checked it. "Well," said Mr. Samsa, "now thanks be to God." He crossed himself, and the three women followed his example. Grete, whose eyes never left the corpse, said: "Just see how thin he was. It's such a long time since he's eaten anything. The food came out again just as it went in." Indeed, Gregor's body was completely flat and dry, as could only now be seen when it was no longer supported by the legs and nothing prevented one from looking closely at it.

"Come in beside us, Grete, for a little while," said Mrs. Samsa with a tremulous smile, and Grete, not without looking back at the corpse, followed her parents into their bedroom. The charwoman shut the door and opened the window wide. Although it was so early in the morning a certain softness was perceptible in the fresh air. After all, it was already the end of March.

The three lodgers emerged from their room and were surprised to see no breakfast; they had been forgotten. "Where's our breakfast?" said the middle lodger peevishly to the charwoman. But she put her finger to her lips and hastily, without a word, indicated by gestures that they should go into Gregor's room. They did so and stood, their hands in the pockets of their somewhat shabby coats, around Gregor's corpse in the room where it was now fully light.

At that the door of the Samsas' bedroom opened and Mr. Samsa appeared in his uniform, his wife on one arm, his daughter on the other. They all looked a little as if they had been crying; from time to time Grete hid her face on her father's arm.

95 "Leave my house at once!" said Mr. Samsa, and pointed to the door without disengaging himself from the women. "What do you mean by that?" said the middle lodger, taken somewhat aback, with a feeble smile. The two others put their hands behind them and kept rubbing them together, as if in gleeful expectation of a fine set-to in which they were bound to come off the winners. "I mean just what I say," answered Mr. Samsa, and advanced in a straight line with his two companions towards the lodger. He stood his ground at first quietly, looking at the floor as if his thoughts were taking a new pattern in his head. "Then let us go, by all means," he said and looked up at Mr. Samsa as if in a sudden access of humility he were expecting some renewed sanction for this decision. Mr. Samsa merely nodded briefly once or twice with meaning eyes. Upon that the lodger really did go with long strides into the hall, his two friends had been listening and had quite stopped rubbing their hands for some moments and now went scuttling after him as if afraid that Mr. Samsa might get into the hall before them and cut them off from their leader. In the hall they all three took their hats from the rack, their sticks from the umbrella stand, bowed in silence and quitted the apartment. With a suspiciousness which proved quite unfounded Mr. Samsa and the two women followed them out to the landing; leaning over the banister they watched the three figures slowly but surely going down the long stairs, vanishing from sight at a certain turn of the staircase on every floor and coming into view again after a moment or so; the more they dwindled, the more the Samsa family's interest in them dwindled, and when a butcher's boy met them and passed them on the stairs coming up proudly with a tray on his head, Mr. Samsa and the two women soon left the landing and as if a burden had been lifted from them went back into their apartment.

They decided to spend this day in resting and going for a stroll; they had not only deserved such a respite from work, but absolutely needed it. And so they sat down at the table and wrote three notes of excuse, Mr. Samsa to his board of management, Mrs. Samsa to her employer and Grete to the head of her firm. While they were writing, the charwoman came in to say that she was going now, since her morning's work was finished. At first they only nodded without looking up, but as she kept hovering there they eyed her irritably. "Well?" said Mr. Samsa. The charwoman stood grinning in the doorway as if she had good news to impart to the family but meant not to say a word unless properly questioned. The small ostrich feather standing upright on her hat, which had annoyed Mr. Samsa ever since she was engaged, was waving gaily in all directions. "Well, what is it then?" asked Mrs. Samsa, who obtained more respect from the charwoman than the others. "Oh," said the charwoman, giggling so amiably that she could not at once continue, "just this, you don't need to bother about how to get rid of the thing next door. It's been seen to already." Mrs. Samsa and Grete bent over their letters again, as if preoccupied; Mr. Samsa, who perceived that she was eager to begin describing it all in detail, stopped her with a decisive hand. But since she was not allowed to tell her story, she remembered the great hurry she was in, being obviously deeply huffed: "Bye, everybody," she said, whirling off violently, and departed with a frightful slamming of doors.

"She'll be given notice tonight," said Mr. Samsa, but neither from his wife nor his daughter did he get any answer, for the charwoman seemed to have shattered again the composure they had barely achieved. They rose, went to the window and stayed there, clasping each other tight. Mr. Samsa turned in his chair to look at them and quietly observed them for a little. Then he called out: "Come along, now, do. Let bygones be bygones. And you might have some consideration for me." The two of them complied at once, hastened to him, caressed him and quickly finished their letters.

Then they all three left the apartment together, which was more than they had done for months, and went by tram into the open country outside the town. The tram, in which they were the only passengers, was filled with warm sunshine. Leaning comfortably back in their seats they canvassed their prospects for the future, and it appeared on closer inspection that these were not at all bad, for the jobs they had got, which so far they had never really discussed with each other, were all three admirable and likely to lead to better things later on. The greatest immediate improvement in their condition would of course arise from moving to another house; they wanted to take a smaller and cheaper but also better situated and more easily run apartment than the one they had, which Gregor had selected. While they were thus conversing, it struck both Mr. and Mrs. Samsa, almost at the same moment, as they became aware of their daughter's increasing vivacity, that in spite of all the sorrow of recent times, which had made her cheeks pale, she had bloomed into a pretty girl with a good figure. They grew quieter and half unconsciously exchanged glances of complete agreement, having come to the conclusion that it would soon be time to find a good husband for her. And it was like a confirmation of their new dreams and excellent intentions that at the end of their journey their daughter sprang to her feet first and stretched her young body.

[*1915*]

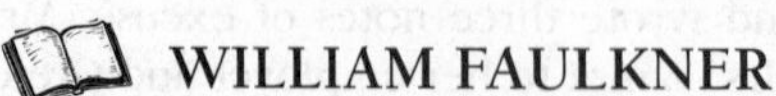

## WILLIAM FAULKNER

*William Faulkner (1897–1962) was brought up in Oxford, Mississippi. His great-grandfather had been a Civil War hero, and his father was treasurer of the University of Mississippi, in Oxford; the family was no longer rich, but it was still respected. During the First World War he enrolled in the Royal Canadian Air Force, though he never saw overseas service. After the war he returned to Mississippi, went to the university for two years, and then went to New Orleans, where he became friendly with Sherwood Anderson, already an established writer. In New Orleans Faulkner worked for* The Times-Picayune; *still later, even after he had established himself as a major novelist with* The Sound and the Fury *(1929), he had to do some work in Hollywood in order to make ends meet. In 1950 he was awarded the Nobel Prize in Literature.*

*Almost all of Faulkner's writing is concerned with the people of Yoknapatawpha, an imaginary county in Mississippi. "I discovered," he said, "that my own little postage stamp of native soil was worth writing about and that I would never live long enough to exhaust it." Though he lived for brief periods in Canada, New Orleans, New York, Hollywood, and Virginia (where he died), he spent most of his life in his native Mississippi.*

# A Rose for Emily

## I

When Miss Emily Grierson died, our whole town went to her funeral: the men through a sort of respectful affection for a fallen monument, the women mostly out of curiosity to see the inside of her house, which no one save an old manservant—a combined gardener and cook—had seen in at least ten years.

It was a big, squarish frame house that had once been white, decorated with cupolas and spires and scrolled balconies in the heavily lightsome style of the seventies, set on what had once been our most select street. But garages and cotton gins had encroached and obliterated even the august names of that neighborhood; only Miss Emily's house was left, lifting its stubborn and coquettish decay above the cotton wagons and the gasoline pumps—an eyesore among eyesores. And now Miss Emily had gone to join the representatives of those august names where they lay in the cedar-bemused cemetery among the ranked and anonymous graves of Union and Confederate soldiers who fell at the battle of Jefferson.

Alive, Miss Emily had been a tradition, a duty, and a care; a sort of hereditary obligation upon the town, dating from that day in 1894 when Colonel Sartoris, the mayor—he who fathered the edict that no Negro woman should appear on the streets without an apron—remitted her taxes, the dispensation dating from the death of her father on into perpetuity. Not that Miss Emily would have accepted charity. Colonel Sartoris invented an involved tale to the effect that Miss Emily's father had loaned money to the town, which the town, as a matter of business, preferred this way of repaying. Only a man of Colonel Sartoris' generation and thought could have invented it, and only a woman could have believed it.

When the next generation, with its more modern ideas, became mayors and aldermen, this arrangement created some little dissatisfaction. On the first of the year they mailed her a tax notice. February came, and there was no reply. They wrote her a formal letter, asking her to call at the sheriff's office at her convenience. A week later the mayor wrote her himself, offering to call or to send his car for her, and received in reply a note on paper of an archaic shape, in a thin, flowing calligraphy in faded ink, to the effect that she no longer went out at all. The tax notice was also enclosed, without comment.

They called a special meeting of the Board of Aldermen. A deputation waited upon her, knocked at the door through which no visitor had passed since she ceased giving china-painting lessons eight or ten years earlier. They were admitted by the old Negro into a dim hall from which a staircase mounted into still more shadow. It smelled of dust and disuse—a close, dank smell. The Negro led them into the parlor. It was furnished in heavy, leather-covered furniture. When the Negro opened the blinds of one window, they could see that the leather was cracked; and when they sat down, a faint dust rose sluggishly about their thighs, spinning with slow motes in the single sunray. On a tarnished gilt easel before the fireplace stood a crayon portrait of Miss Emily's father.

They rose when she entered—a small, fat woman in black, with a thin gold chain descending to her waist and vanishing into her belt, leaning on an ebony cane with a tarnished gold head. Her skeleton was small and spare; perhaps that was why what would have been merely plumpness in another was obesity in her. She looked bloated, like a body long submerged in motionless water, and of that pallid hue. Her eyes, lost in the fatty ridges of her face, looked like two small pieces of coal pressed into a lump of dough as they moved from one face to another while the visitors stated their errand.

She did not ask them to sit. She just stood in the door and listened quietly until the spokesman came to a stumbling halt. Then they could hear the invisible watch ticking at the end of the gold chain.

Her voice was dry and cold. "I have no taxes in Jefferson. Colonel Sartoris explained it to me. Perhaps one of you can gain access to the city records and satisfy yourselves."

"But we have. We are the city authorities. Miss Emily. Didn't you get a notice from the sheriff, signed by him?"

"I received a paper, yes," Miss Emily said. "Perhaps he considers himself the sheriff. . . . I have no taxes in Jefferson."

"But there is nothing on the books to show that, you see. We must go by the—"

"See Colonel Sartoris. I have no taxes in Jefferson."

"But, Miss Emily—"

"See Colonel Sartoris." (Colonel Sartoris had been dead almost ten years.) "I have no taxes in Jefferson. Tobe!" The Negro appeared. "Show these gentlemen out."

## II

So she vanquished them, horse and foot, just as she had vanquished their fathers thirty years before about the smell. That was two years after her father's death and a short time after her sweetheart—the one we believed would marry her—had deserted her. After her father's death she went out very little; after her sweetheart went away, people hardly saw her at all. A few of the ladies had the temerity to call, but were not received, and the only sign of life about the place was the Negro man—a young man then—going in and out with a market basket.

"Just as if a man—any man—could keep a kitchen properly," the ladies said; so they were not surprised when the smell developed. It was another link between the gross, teeming world and the high and mighty Griersons.

A neighbor, a woman, complained to the mayor, Judge Stevens, eighty years old.

"But what will you have me do about it, madam?" he said.

"Why, send her word to stop it," the woman said. "Isn't there a law?"

20 "I'm sure that won't be necessary," Judge Stevens said. "It's probably just a snake or a rat that nigger of hers killed in the yard. I'll speak to him about it."

The next day he received two more complaints, one from a man who came in diffident deprecation. "We really must do something about it, Judge. I'd be the last one in the world to bother Miss Emily, but we've got to do something." That night the Board of Aldermen met—three gray-beards and one younger man, a member of the rising generation.

"It's simple enough," he said. "Send her word to have her place cleaned up. Give her a certain time to do it in, and if she don't . . ."

"Dammit, sir," Judge Stevens said, "will you accuse a lady to her face of smelling bad?"

So the next night, after midnight, four men crossed Miss Emily's lawn and slunk about the house like burglars, sniffing along the base of the brick-work and at the cellar openings while one of them performed a regular sowing motion with his hand out of a sack slung from his shoulder. They broke open the cellar door and sprinkled lime there, and in all the outbuildings. As they recrossed the lawn, a window that had been dark was lighted and Miss Emily sat in it, the light behind her, and her upright torso motionless as that of an idol. They crept quietly across the lawn and into the shadow of the locusts that lined the street. After a week or two the smell went away.

25 That was when people had begun to feel really sorry for her. People in our town, remembering how old lady Wyatt, her great-aunt, had gone completely crazy at last, believed that the Griersons held themselves a little too high for what they really were. None of the young men were quite good enough for Miss Emily and such. We had long thought of them as a tableau; Miss Emily a slender figure in white in the background, her father a spraddled silhouette in the foreground, his back to her and clutching a horsewhip, the two of them framed by the back-flung front door. So when she got to be thirty and was still single, we were not pleased exactly, but vindicated; even with insanity in the family she wouldn't have turned down all of her chances if they had really materialized.

When her father died, it got about that the house was all that was left to her; and in a way, people were glad. At last they could pity Miss Emily. Being left alone, and a pauper, she had become humanized. Now she too would know the old thrill and the old despair of a penny more or less.

The day after his death all the ladies prepared to call at the house and offer condolence and aid, as is our custom. Miss Emily met them at the door, dressed as usual and with no trace of grief on her face. She told them that her father was not dead. She did that for three days, with the ministers calling on her, and the doctors, trying to persuade her to let them dispose of the body. Just as they were about to resort to law and force, she broke down, and they buried her father quickly.

We did not say she was crazy then. We believed she had to do that. We remembered all the young men her father had driven away, and we knew that with nothing left, she would have to cling to that which had robbed her, as people will.

## *III*

She was sick for a long time. When we saw her again, her hair was cut short, making her look like a girl, with a vague resemblance to those angels in colored church windows—sort of tragic and serene.

30 The town had just let the contracts for paving the sidewalks, and in the summer after her father's death they began the work. The construction company came with niggers and mules and machinery, and a foreman named Homer Barron, a Yankee—a big, dark, ready man, with a big voice and eyes lighter than his face. The little boys would follow in groups to hear him cuss the niggers, and the niggers singing in time to the rise and fall of picks. Pretty soon he knew everybody in town. Whenever you heard a lot of laughing anywhere about the square, Homer Barron would be in the center of the group. Presently we began to see him and Miss Emily on Sunday afternoons driving in the yellow-wheeled buggy and the matched team of bays from the livery stable.

At first we were glad that Miss Emily would have an interest, because the ladies all said, "Of course a Grierson would not think seriously of a Northerner, a day laborer." But there were still others, older people, who said that even grief could not cause a real lady to forget *noblesse oblige*—without calling it *noblesse oblige.* They just said, "Poor Emily. Her kinsfolk should come to her." She had some kin in Alabama; but years ago her father had fallen out with them over the estate of old lady Wyatt, the crazy woman, and there was no communication between the two families. They had not even been represented at the funeral.

And as soon as the old people said, "Poor Emily," the whispering began. "Do you suppose it's really so?" they said to one another. "Of course it is. What else could . . ." This behind their hands; rustling of craned silk and satin behind jalousies closed upon the sun of Sunday afternoon as the thin, swift clop-clop-clop of the matched team passed: "Poor Emily."

She carried her head high enough—even when we believed that she was fallen. It was as if she demanded more than ever the recognition of her dignity as the last Grierson; as if it had wanted that touch of earthiness to reaffirm her imperviousness. Like when she bought the rat poison, the arsenic. That was over a year after they had begun to say "Poor Emily," and while the two female cousins were visiting her.

"I want some poison," she said to the druggist. She was over thirty then, still a slight woman, though thinner than usual, with cold, haughty black eyes in a face the flesh of which was strained across the temples and about the eyesockets as you imagine a lighthousekeeper's face ought to look. "I want some poison," she said.

35 "Yes, Miss Emily. What kind? For rats and such? I'd recom—"

"I want the best you have. I don't care what kind."

The druggist named several. "They'll kill anything up to an elephant. But what you want is—"

"Arsenic," Miss Emily said. "Is that a good one?"

"Is . . . arsenic? Yes, ma'am. But what you want—"

40 "I want arsenic."

The druggist looked down at her. She looked back at him, erect, her face like a strained flag. "Why, of course," the druggist said. "If that's what you want. But the law requires you to tell what you are going to use it for."

Miss Emily just stared at him, her head tilted back in order to look him eye for eye, until he looked away and went and got the arsenic and wrapped it up. The Negro delivery boy brought her the package; the druggist didn't come back. When she opened the package at home there was written on the box, under the skull and bones: "For rats."

## IV

So the next day we all said, "She will kill herself"; and we said it would be the best thing. When she had first begun to be seen with Homer Barron, we had said, "She will marry him." Then we said, "She will persuade him yet," because Homer himself had remarked—he liked men, and it was known that he drank with the younger men in the Elks' Club—that he was not a marrying man. Later we said, "Poor Emily" behind the jalousies as they passed on Sunday afternoon in the glittering buggy, Miss Emily with her head high and Homer Barron with his hat cocked and a cigar in his teeth, reins and whip in a yellow glove.

Then some of the ladies began to say that it was a disgrace to the town and a bad example to the young people. The men did not want to interfere, but at last the ladies forced the Baptist minister—Miss Emily's people were Episcopal—to call upon her. He would never divulge what happened during that interview, but he refused to go back again. The next Sunday they again drove about the streets, and the following day the minister's wife wrote to Miss Emily's relations in Alabama.

45 So she had blood-kin under her roof again and we sat back to watch developments. At first nothing happened. Then we were sure that they were to be married. We learned that Miss Emily had been to the jeweler's and ordered a man's toilet set in silver, with the letters H. B. on each piece. Two days later we learned that she had bought a complete outfit of men's clothing, including a nightshirt, and we said, "They are married." We were really glad. We were glad because the two female cousins were even more Grierson than Miss Emily had ever been.

So we were surprised when Homer Barron—the streets had been finished some time since—was gone. We were a little disappointed that there was not a public blowing-off, but we believed that he had gone on to prepare for Miss Emily's coming, or to give her a chance to get rid of the cousins. (By that time it was a cabal, and we were all Miss Emily's allies to help circumvent the cousins.) Sure enough, after another week they departed. And, as we had expected all along, within three days Homer Barron was back in town. A neighbor saw the Negro man admit him at the kitchen door at dusk one evening.

And that was the last we saw of Homer Barron. And of Miss Emily for some time. The Negro man went in and out with the market basket, but the front door remained closed. Now and then we would see her at a window for a moment, as the men did that night when they sprinkled the lime, but for almost six months she did not appear on the streets. Then we knew that this was to be expected too; as if that quality of her father which had thwarted her woman's life so many times had been too virulent and too furious to die.

When we next saw Miss Emily, she had grown fat and her hair was turning gray. During the next few years it grew grayer and grayer until it attained an even pepper-and-salt iron-gray, when it ceased turning. Up to the day of her death at seventy-four it was still that vigorous iron-gray, like the hair of an active man.

From that time on her front door remained closed, save for a period of six or seven years, when she was about forty, during which she gave lessons in china-painting. She fitted up a studio in one of the downstairs rooms, where the daughters and grand-daughters of Colonel Sartoris' contemporaries were sent to her with the same regularity and in the same spirit that they were sent to church on Sundays with a twenty-five-cent piece for the collection plate. Meanwhile her taxes had been remitted.

50 Then the newer generation became the backbone and the spirit of the town, and the painting pupils grew up and fell away and did not send their children to her with boxes of color and tedious brushes and pictures cut from the ladies' magazines. The front door closed upon the last one and remained closed for good. When the town got free postal delivery, Miss Emily alone refused to let them fasten the metal numbers above her door and attach a mailbox to it. She would not listen to them.

Daily, monthly, yearly we watched the Negro grow grayer and more stooped, going in and out with the market basket. Each December we sent her a tax notice, which would be returned by the post office a week later, unclaimed. Now and then we would see her in one of the downstairs windows—she had evidently shut up the top floor of the house—like the carven torso of an idol in a niche, looking or not looking at us, we could never tell which. Thus she passed from generation to generation—dear, inescapable, impervious, tranquil, and perverse.

And so she died. Fell ill in the house filled with dust and shadows, with only a doddering Negro man to wait on her. We did not even know she was sick; we had long since given up trying to get any information from the Negro. He talked to no one, probably not even to her, for his voice had grown harsh and rusty, as if from disuse.

She died in one of the downstairs rooms, in a heavy walnut bed with a curtain, her gray head propped on a pillow yellow and moldy with age and lack of sunlight.

## V

The Negro met the first of the ladies at the front door and let them in, with their hushed, sibilant voices and their quick, curious glances, and then he disappeared. He walked right through the house and out the back and was not seen again.

55 The two female cousins came at once. They held the funeral on the second day, with the town coming to look at Miss Emily beneath a mass of bought flowers, with the crayon face of her father musing profoundly above the bier and the ladies sibilant and macabre; and the very old men—some in their brushed Confederate uniforms—on the porch and the lawn, talking of Miss Emily as if she had been a contemporary of theirs, believing that they

had danced with her and courted her perhaps, confusing time with its mathematical progression, as the old do, to whom all the past is not a diminishing road but, instead, a huge meadow which no winter ever quite touches, divided from them now by the narrow bottleneck of the most recent decade of years.

Already we knew that there was one room in that region above stairs which no one had seen in forty years, and which would have to be forced. They waited until Miss Emily was decently in the ground before they opened it.

The violence of breaking down the door seemed to fill this room with pervading dust. A thin, acrid pall as of the tomb seemed to lie everywhere upon this room decked and furnished as for a bridal: upon the valance curtains of faded rose color, upon the rose-shaded lights, upon the dressing table, upon the delicate array of crystal and the man's toilet things backed with tarnished silver, silver so tarnished that the monogram was obscured. Among them lay collar and tie, as if they had just been removed, which, lifted, left upon the surface a pale crescent in the dust. Upon a chair hung the suit, carefully folded; beneath it the two mute shoes and the discarded socks.

The man himself lay in the bed.

For a long while we just stood there, looking down at the profound and fleshless grin. The body had apparently once lain in the attitude of an embrace, but now the long sleep that outlasts love, that conquers even the grimace of love, had cuckolded him. What was left of him, rotted beneath what was left of the nightshirt, had become inextricable from the bed in which he lay; and upon him and upon the pillow beside him lay that even coating of the patient and biding dust.

60 Then we noticed that in the second pillow was the indentation of a head. One of us lifted something from it, and leaning forward, that faint and invisible dust dry and acrid in the nostrils, we saw a long strand of iron-gray hair.

[*1930*]

## FRANK O'CONNOR

*"Frank O'Connor" was the pen name of Michael O'Donovan (1903-66), who was born in Cork, Ireland. Poverty compelled his family to take him out of school after the fourth grade. He worked at odd jobs and then, during "the troubles"—the armed conflict of 1918-21 that led to the establishment (1922) of the Irish Free State—he served in the Irish Republican Army, fighting the British, until he was captured. After his release from prison he worked as a librarian and as a director (1935-39) of the Abbey Theatre in Dublin. Still later, in the 1950s, he lived in the United States, teaching at Northwestern University and Harvard University.*

*Among his books—stories, novels, autobiographies, plays, translations of Gaelic poetry, and criticism—is* The Lonely Voice, *a study of the short story.*

# *Guests of the Nation*

## *I*

At dusk the big Englishman, Belcher, would shift his long legs out of the ashes and say, "Well, chums, what about it?" and Noble or me would say "All right, chum" (for we had picked up some of their curious expressions), and the little Englishman, Hawkins, would light the lamp and bring out the cards. Sometimes Jeremiah Donovan would come up and supervise the game and get excited over Hawkins's cards, which he always played badly, and shout at him as if he was one of our own "Ah, you divil, you, why didn't you play the tray?"

But ordinarily Jeremiah was a sober and contented poor devil like the big Englishman, Belcher, and was looked up to only because he was a fair hand at documents, though he was slow enough even with them. He wore a small cloth hat and big gaiters over his long pants, and you seldom saw him with his hands out of his pockets. He reddened when you talked to him, tilting from toe to heel and back, and looking down all the time at his big farmer's feet. Noble and me used to make fun of his broad accent, because we were from the town.

I couldn't at the time see the point of me and Noble guarding Belcher and Hawkins at all, for it was my belief that you could have planted that pair down anywhere from this to Claregalway and they'd have taken root there like a native weed. I never in my short experience seen two men to take to the country as they did.

They were handed on to us by the Second Battalion when the search for them became too hot, and Noble and myself, being young, took over with a natural feeling of responsibility, but Hawkins made us look like fools when he showed that he knew the country better than we did.

5 "You're the bloke they calls Bonaparte," he says to me. "Mary Brigid O'Connell told me to ask you what you done with the pair of her brother's socks you borrowed."

For it seemed, as they explained it, that the Second used to have little evenings, and some of the girls of the neighborhood turned in, and, seeing they were such decent chaps, our fellows couldn't leave the two Englishmen out of them. Hawkins learned to dance "The Walls of Limerick," "The Siege of Ennis," and "The Waves of Tory" as well as any of them, though, naturally, we couldn't return the compliment, because our lads at that time did not dance foreign dances on principle.

So whatever privileges Belcher and Hawkins had with the Second they just naturally took with us, and after the first day or two we gave up all pretense of keeping a close eye on them. Not that they could have got far, for they had accents you could cut with a knife and wore khaki tunics and overcoats with civilian pants and boots. But it's my belief that they never had any idea of escaping and were quite content to be where they were.

It was a treat to see how Belcher got off with the old woman of the house where we were staying. She was a great warrant to scold, and cranky even with us, but before ever she had a chance of giving our guests, as I may call them, a lick of her tongue, Belcher had made her his friend for life. She was breaking sticks, and Belcher, who hadn't been more than ten minutes in the house, jumped up from his seat and went over to her.

"Allow me, madam," he says, smiling his queer little smile, "please allow me"; and he takes the bloody hatchet. She was struck too paralytic to speak, and after that, Belcher would be at her heels, carrying a bucket, a basket, or a load of turf, as the case might be. As Noble said, he got into looking before she leapt, and hot water, or any little thing she wanted, Belcher would have it ready for her. For such a huge man (and though I am five foot ten myself I had to look up at him) he had an uncommon shortness—or should I say lack?—of speech. It took us some time to get used to him, walking in and out, like a ghost, without a word. Especially because Hawkins talked enough for a platoon, it was strange to hear big Belcher with his toes in the ashes come out with a solitary "Excuse me, chum," or "That's right, chum." His one and only passion was cards, and I will say for him that he was a good cardplayer. He could have fleeced myself and Noble, but whatever we lost to him Hawkins lost to us, and Hawkins played with the money Belcher gave him.

10 Hawkins lost to us because he had too much old gab, and we probably lost to Belcher for the same reason. Hawkins and Noble would spit at one another about religion into the early hours of the morning, and Hawkins worried the soul out of Noble, whose brother was a priest, with a string of questions that would puzzle a cardinal. To make it worse, even in treating of holy subjects, Hawkins had a deplorable tongue. I never in all my career met a man who could mix such a variety of cursing and bad language into an argument. He was a terrible man, and a fright to argue. He never did a stroke of work, and when he had no one else to talk to, he got stuck in the old woman.

He met his match in her, for one day when he tried to get her to complain profanely of the drought, she gave him a great comedown by blaming it entirely on Jupiter Pluvius (a deity neither Hawkins nor I had ever heard of, though Noble said that among the pagans it was believed that he had something to do with the rain). Another day he was swearing at the capitalists for starting the German war when the old lady laid down her iron, puckered up her little crab's mouth, and said: "Mr. Hawkins, you can say what you like about the war, and think you'll deceive me because I'm only a simple poor countrywoman, but I know what started the war. It was the Italian Count that stole the heathen divinity out of the temple in Japan. Believe me, Mr. Hawkins, nothing but sorrow and want can follow the people that disturb the hidden powers."

A queer old girl, all right.

## II

We had our tea one evening, and Hawkins lit the lamp and we all sat into cards. Jeremiah Donovan came in too, and sat down and watched us for a while, and it suddenly struck me that he had no great love for the two Englishmen. It came as a great surprise to me, because I hadn't noticed anything about him before.

Late in the evening a really terrible argument blew up between Hawkins and Noble, about capitalists and priests and love of your country.

15 "The capitalists," says Hawkins with an angry gulp, "pays the priests to tell you about the next world so as you won't notice what the bastards are up to in this."

"Nonsense, man!" says Noble, losing his temper. "Before ever a capitalist was thought of, people believed in the next world."

Hawkins stood up as though he was preaching a sermon.

"Oh, they did, did they?" he says with a sneer. "They believed all the things you believe, isn't that what you mean? And you believe that God created Adam, and Adam created Shem, and Shem created Jehoshaphat. You believe all that silly old fairytale about Eve and Eden and the apple. Well, listen to me, chum. If you're entitled to hold a silly belief like that, I'm entitled to hold my silly belief—which is that the first thing your God created was a bleeding capitalist, with morality and Rolls-Royce complete. Am I right, chum?" he says to Belcher.

"You're right, chum," says Belcher with his amused smile, and got up from the table to stretch his long legs into the fire and stroke his moustache. So, seeing that Jeremiah Donovan was going, and that there was no knowing when the argument about religion would be over, I went out with him. We strolled down to the village together, and then he stopped and started blushing and mumbling and saying I ought to be behind, keeping guard on the prisoners. I didn't like the tone he took with me, and anyway I was bored with life in the cottage, so I replied by asking him what the hell we wanted guarding them at all for. I told him I'd talked it over with Noble, and that we'd both rather be out with a fighting column.

"What use are those fellows to us?" says I.

He looked at me in surprise and said: "I thought you knew we were keeping them as hostages."

"Hostages?" I said.

"The enemy have prisoners belonging to us," he says, "and now they're talking of shooting them. If they shoot our prisoners, we'll shoot theirs."

"Shoot them?" I said.

"What else did you think we were keeping them for?" he says.

"Wasn't it very unforeseen of you not to warn Noble and myself of that in the beginning?" I said.

"How was it?" says he. "You might have known it."

"We couldn't know it, Jeremiah Donovan," says I. "How could we when they were on our hands so long?"

"The enemy have our prisoners as long and longer," says he.

"That's not the same thing at all," says I.

"What difference is there?" says he.

I couldn't tell him, because I knew he wouldn't understand. If it was only an old dog that was going to the vet's, you'd try and not get too fond of him, but Jeremiah Donovan wasn't a man that would ever be in danger of that.

"And when is this thing going to be decided?" says I.

"We might hear tonight," he says. "Or tomorrow or the next day at latest. So if it's only hanging round here that's a trouble to you, you'll be free soon enough."

It wasn't the hanging round that was a trouble to me at all by this time. I had worse things to worry about. When I got back to the cottage the argument was still on. Hawkins was holding forth in his best style, maintaining that there was no next world, and Noble was maintaining that there was; but I could see that Hawkins had had the best of it.

"Do you know what, chum?" he was saying with a saucy smile. "I think you're just as big a bleeding unbeliever as I am. You say you believe in the next world, and you know just as much about the next world as I do, which is sweet damn-all. What's heaven? You don't know. Where's heaven? You don't know. You know sweet damn-all! I ask you again, do they wear wings?"

"Very well, then," says Noble, "they do. Is that enough for you? They do wear wings."

"Where do they get them, then? Who makes them? Have they a factory for wings? Have they a sort of store where you hands in your chit and takes your chit and takes your bleeding wings?"

"You're an impossible man to argue with," says Noble. "Now, listen to me—" And they were off again.

40 It was long after midnight when we locked up and went to bed. As I blew out the candle I told Noble what Jeremiah Donovan was after telling me. Noble took it very quietly. When we'd been in bed about an hour he asked me did I think we ought to tell the Englishmen. I didn't think we should, because it was more than likely that the English wouldn't shoot our men, and even if they did, the brigade officers, who were always up and down with the Second Battalion and knew the Englishmen well, wouldn't be likely to want them plugged. "I think so too," says Noble. "It would be great cruelty to put the wind up them now."

"It was very unforeseen of Jeremiah Donovan anyhow," says I.

It was next morning that we found it so hard to face Belcher and Hawkins. We went about the house all day scarcely saying a word. Belcher didn't seem to notice; he was stretched into the ashes as usual, with his usual look of waiting in quietness for something unforeseen to happen, but Hawkins noticed and put it down to Noble's being beaten in the argument of the night before.

"Why can't you take a discussion in the proper spirit?" he says severely. "You and your Adam and Eve! I'm a Communist, that's what I am. Communist or anarchist, it all comes to much the same thing." And for hours he went round the house, muttering when the fit took him. "Adam and Eve! Adam and Eve! Nothing better to do with their time than picking bleeding apples!"

## *III*

I don't know how we got through that day, but I was very glad when it was over, the tea things were cleared away, and Belcher said in his peaceable way: "Well, chums, what about it?" We sat round the table and Hawkins took out the cards, and just then I heard Jeremiah Donovan's footsteps on the path and a dark presentiment crossed my mind. I rose from the table and caught him before he reached the door.

45 "What do you want?" I asked.

"I want those two soldier friends of yours," he says, getting red.

"Is that the way, Jeremiah Donovan?" I asked.

"That's the way. There were four of our lads shot this morning, one of them a boy of sixteen."

"That's bad," I said.

50 At that moment Noble followed me out, and the three of us walked down the path together, talking in whispers. Feeney, the local intelligence officer, was standing by the gate.

"What are you going to do about it?" I asked Jeremiah Donovan.

"I want you and Noble to get them out; tell them they're being shifted again; that'll be the quietest way."

"Leave me out of that," says Noble under his breath.

Jeremiah Donovan looks at him hard.

55 "All right," he says. "You and Feeney get a few tools from the shed and dig a hole by the far end of the bog. Bonaparte and myself will be after you. Don't let anyone see you with the tools. I wouldn't like it to go beyond ourselves."

We saw Feeney and Noble go round to the shed and went in ourselves. I left Jeremiah Donovan to do the explanations. He told them that he had orders to send them back to the Second Battalion. Hawkins let out a mouthful of curses, and you could see that though Belcher didn't say anything, he was a bit upset too. The old woman was for having them stay in spite of us, and she didn't stop advising them until Jeremiah Donovan lost his temper and turned on her. He had a nasty temper, I noticed. It was pitch-dark in the cottage by this time, but no one thought of lighting the lamp, and in the darkness the two Englishmen fetched their topcoats and said good-bye to the old woman.

"Just as a man makes a home of a bleeding place, some bastard at headquarters thinks you're too cushy and shunts you off," says Hawkins, shaking her hand.

"A thousand thanks, madam," says Belcher. "A thousand thanks for everything"—as though he'd made it up.

We went round to the back of the house and down towards the bog, it was only then that Jeremiah Donovan told them. He was shaking with excitement.

60 "There were four of our fellows shot in Cork this morning and now you're to be shot as a reprisal."

"What are you talking about?" snaps Hawkins. "It's bad enough being mucked about as we are without having to put up with your funny jokes."

"It isn't a joke," says Donovan. "I'm sorry, Hawkins, but it's true," and begins on the usual rigmarole about duty and how unpleasant it is.

I never noticed that people who talk a lot about duty find it much of a trouble to them.

"Oh, cut it out!" says Hawkins.

65 "Ask Bonaparte," says Donovan, seeing that Hawkins isn't taking him seriously. "Isn't it true, Bonaparte?"

"It is," I say, and Hawkins stops.

"Ah, for Christ's sake, chum."

"I mean it, chum," I say.

"You don't sound as if you meant it."

70 "If he doesn't mean it, I do," says Donovan, working himself up.

"What have you against me, Jeremiah Donovan?"

"I never said I had anything against you. But why did your people take out four of our prisoners and shoot them in cold blood?"

He took Hawkins by the arm and dragged him on, but it was impossible to make him understand that we were in earnest. I had the Smith and Wesson in my pocket and I kept fingering it and wondering what I'd do if they put up a fight for it or ran, and wishing to God they'd do one or the other. I knew if they did run for it, that I'd never fire on them. Hawkins wanted to know was Noble in it, and when we said yes, he asked us why Noble wanted to plug him. Why did any of us want to plug him? What had he done to us? Weren't we all chums? Didn't we understand him and didn't he understand us? Did we imagine for an instant that he'd shoot us for all the so-and-so officers in the so-and-so British Army?

By this time we'd reached the bog, and I was so sick I couldn't even answer him. We walked along the edge of it in the darkness, and every now and then Hawkins would call a halt and begin all over again, as if he was wound up, about our being chums, and I knew that nothing but the sight of the grave would convince him that we had to do it. And all the time I was hoping that something would happen; that they'd run for it or that Noble would take over the responsibility from me. I had the feeling that it was worse on Noble than on me.

## IV

At last we saw the lantern in the distance and made towards it. Noble was carrying it, and Feeney was standing somewhere in the darkness behind him, and the picture of them so still and silent in the bogland brought it home to me that we were in earnest, and banished the last bit of hope I had.

Belcher, on recognizing Noble, said: "Hallo, chum," in his quiet way, but Hawkins flew at him at once, and the argument began all over again, only this time Noble had nothing to say for himself and stood with his head down, holding the lantern between his legs.

It was Jeremiah Donovan who did the answering. For the twentieth time, as though it was haunting his mind, Hawkins asked if anybody thought he'd shoot Noble.

"Yes, you would," says Jeremiah Donovan.

"No, I wouldn't, damn you!"

"You would, because you'd know you'd be shot for not doing it."

"I wouldn't, not if I was to be shot twenty times over. I wouldn't shoot a pal. And Belcher wouldn't—isn't that right, Belcher?"

"That's right, chum," Belcher said, but more by way of answering the question than of joining in the argument. Belcher sounded as though whatever unforeseen thing he'd always been waiting for had come at last.

"Anyway, who says Noble would be shot if I wasn't? What do you think I'd do if I was in his place, out in the middle of a blasted bog?"

"What would you do?" asks Donovan.

"I'd go with him wherever he was going, of course. Share my last bob with him and stick by him through thick and thin. No one can ever say of me that I let down a pal."

"We had enough of this," says Jeremiah Donovan, cocking his revolver. "Is there any message you want to send?"

"No, there isn't."

"Do you want to say your prayers?"

Hawkins came out with a cold-blooded remark that even shocked me and turned on Noble again.

"Listen to me, Noble," he says. "You and me are chums. You can't come over to my side, so I'll come over to your side. That show you I mean what I say? Give me a rifle and I'll go along with you and the other lads."

Nobody answered him. We knew that was no way out.

"Hear what I'm saying?" he says. "I'm through with it. I'm a deserter or anything else you like. I don't believe in your stuff, but it's no worse than mine. That satisfy you?"

Noble raised his head, but Donovan began to speak and he lowered it again without replying.

"For the last time, have you any messages to send?" says Donovan in a cold, excited sort of voice.

"Shut up, Donovan! You don't understand me, but these lads do. They're not the sort to make a pal and kill a pal. They're not the tools of any capitalist."

I alone of the crowd saw Donovan raise his Webley to the back of Hawkins's neck, and as he did so I shut my eyes and tried to pray. Hawkins had begun to say something else when Donovan fired, and as I opened my eyes at the bang, I saw Hawkins stagger at the knees and lie out flat at Noble's feet, slowly and as quiet as a kid falling asleep, with the lantern-light on his lean legs and bright farmer's boots. We all stood very still, watching him settle out in the last agony.

Then Belcher took out a handkerchief and began to tie it about his own eyes (in our excitement we'd forgotten to do the same for Hawkins), and, seeing it wasn't big enough, turned and asked for the loan of mine. I gave it to him and he knotted the two together and pointed with his foot at Hawkins.

"He's not quite dead," he says. "Better give him another." Sure enough, Hawkins's left knee is beginning to rise. I bend down and put my gun to his head; then, recollecting myself, I get up again. Belcher understands what's in my mind.

"Give him his first," he says. "I don't mind. Poor bastard, we don't know what's happening to him now."

I knelt and fired. By this time I didn't seem to know what I was doing. Belcher, who was fumbling a bit awkwardly with the handkerchiefs, came out with a laugh as he heard the shot. It was the first time I heard him laugh and it sent a shudder down my back; it sounded so unnatural.

"Poor bugger!" he said quietly. "And last night he was so curious about it all. It's very queer, chums, I always think. Now he knows as much about it as they'll ever let him know, and last night he was all in the dark."

Donovan helped him to tie the handkerchiefs about his eyes. "Thanks, chum," he said. Donovan asked if there were any messages he wanted sent.

"No, chum," he says. "Not for me. If any of you would like to write to Hawkins's mother, you'll find a letter from her in his pocket. He and his mother were great chums. But my missus left me eight years ago. Went away with another fellow and took the kid with her. I like the feeling of a home, as you may have noticed, but I couldn't start again after that."

It was an extraordinary thing, but in those few minutes Belcher said more than in all the weeks before. It was just as if the sound of the shot had started a flood of talk in him and he could go on the whole night like that, quite happily, talking about himself. We stood round like fools now that he couldn't see us any longer. Donovan looked at Noble, and Noble shook his head. Then Donovan raised his Webley, and at that moment Belcher gives his queer laugh again. He may have thought we were talking about him, or perhaps he noticed the same thing I'd noticed and couldn't understand it.

"Excuse me, chums," he says. "I feel I'm talking the hell of a lot, and so silly, about my being so handy about a house and things like that. But this thing came on me suddenly. You'll forgive me, I'm sure."

"You don't want to say a prayer?" asked Donovan.

"No, chum," he says. "I don't think it would help. I'm ready, and you boys want to get it over."

"You understand that we're only doing our duty?" says Donovan.

Belcher's head was raised like a blind man's, so that you could only see his chin and the tip of his nose in the lantern-light.

"I never could make out what duty was myself," he said. "I think you're all good lads, if that's what you mean. I'm not complaining."

Noble, just as if he couldn't bear any more of it, raised his fist at Donovan, and in a flash Donovan raised his gun and fired. The big man went over like a sack of meal, and this time there was no need of a second shot.

I don't remember much about the burying, but that it was worse than all the rest because we had to carry them to the grave. It was all mad lonely with nothing but a patch of lantern-light between ourselves and the dark, and birds hooting and screeching all round, disturbed by the guns. Noble went through Hawkins's belongings to find the letter from his mother, and then joined his hands together. He did the same with Belcher. Then, when we'd filled in the grave, we separated from Jeremiah Donovan and Feeney and took our tools back to the shed. All the way we didn't speak a word. The kitchen was dark and cold as we'd left it, and the old woman was sitting over the hearth, saying her beads. We walked past her into the room, and Noble struck a match to light the lamp. She rose quietly and came to the doorway with all her cantankerousness gone.

"What did ye do with them?" she asked in a whisper, and Noble started so that the match went out in his hand.

"What's that?" he asked without turning round.

"I heard ye," she said.

"What did you hear?" asked Noble.

"I heard ye. Do ye think I didn't hear ye, putting the spade back in the houseen?"

Noble struck another match and this time the lamp lit for him.

"Was that what ye did to them?" she asked.

Then, by God, in the very doorway, she fell on her knees and began praying, and after looking at her for a minute or two Noble did the same by the fireplace. I pushed my way out past her and left them at it. I stood at the door, watching the stars and listening to the shrieking of the birds dying out over the bogs. It is so strange what you feel at times like that you can't describe it. Noble says he saw everything ten times the size, as though there were nothing in the whole world but that little patch of bog with the two Englishmen stiffening into it, but with me it was as if the patch of bog where the Englishmen were was a million miles away, and even Noble and the old woman, mumbling behind me, and the birds and the bloody stars were all far away, and I was somehow very small and very lost and lonely like a child astray in the snow. And anything that happened to me afterwards, I never felt the same about again.

[*1931*]

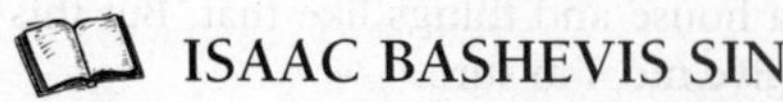

## ISAAC BASHEVIS SINGER

*Isaac Bashevis Singer (1904-91) was born in a Jewish village in Poland. His father and both of his grandfathers were Hasidic rabbis, and Singer received a traditional Jewish education in a rabbinical seminary in Warsaw, although he left the seminary after one year and turned to writing fiction and journalism. In 1935 he immigrated to New York, where he wrote articles and essays for the Yiddish* Daily Forward *as well as radio scripts for Yiddish soap operas.*

*Singer wrote many stories and novels, as well as books for juveniles and four autobiographies (including* Lost in America, *1981). In 1978 his work received world attention when he was awarded the Nobel Prize in Literature.*

# *The Son from America*

The village of Lentshin was tiny—a sandy marketplace where the peasants of the area met once a week. It was surrounded by little huts with thatched roofs or shingles green with moss. The chimneys looked like pots. Between the huts there were fields, where the owners planted vegetables or pastured their goats.

In the smallest of these huts lived old Berl, a man in his eighties, and his wife, who was called Berlcha (wife of Berl). Old Berl was one of the Jews who had been driven from their villages in Russia and had settled in Poland. In Lentshin, they mocked the mistakes he made while praying aloud. He spoke with a sharp "r." He was short, broad-shouldered, and had a small white beard, and summer and winter he wore a sheepskin hat, a padded cotton jacket, and stout boots. He walked slowly, shuffling his feet. He had a half acre of field, a cow, a goat, and chickens.

The couple had a son, Samuel, who had gone to America forty years ago. It was said in Lentshin that he became a millionaire there. Every month, the Lentshin letter carrier brought old Berl a money order and a letter that no one could read because many of the words were English. How much money Samuel sent his parents remained a secret. Three times a year, Berl and his wife went on foot to Zakroczym and cashed the money orders there. But they never seemed to use the money. What for? The garden, the cow, and the goat provided most of their needs. Besides, Berlcha sold chickens and eggs, and from these there was enough to buy flour for bread.

No one cared to know where Berl kept the money that his son sent him. There were no thieves in Lentshin. The hut consisted of one room, which contained all their belongings: the table, the shelf for meat, the shelf for milk foods, the two beds, and the clay oven. Sometimes the chickens roosted in the woodshed and sometimes, when it was cold, in a coop near the oven. The goat, too, found shelter inside when the weather was bad. The more prosperous villages had kerosene lamps, but Berl and his wife did not believe in newfangled gadgets. What was wrong with a wick in a dish of oil? Only for the Sabbath would Berlcha buy three tallow candles at the store. In summer, the couple got up at sunrise and retired with the chickens. In the long winter evenings, Berlcha spun flax at her spinning wheel and Berl sat beside her in the silence of those who enjoy their rest.

5 Once in a while when Berl came home from the synagogue after evening prayers, he brought news to his wife. In Warsaw there were strikers who demanded that the czar abdicate. A heretic by the name of Dr. Herzl[1] had come up with the idea that Jews should settle again in Palestine. Berlcha listened and shook her bonneted head. Her face was yellowish and wrinkled like a cabbage leaf. There were bluish sacks under her eyes. She was half deaf. Berl had to repeat each word he said to her. She would say, "The things that happen in the big cities!"

Here in Lentshin nothing happened except usual events: a cow gave birth to a calf, a young couple had a circumcision party, or a girl was born and there was no party. Occasionally, someone died. Lentshin had no cemetery, and the corpse had to be taken to Zakroczym. Actually, Lentshin had become a village with few young people. The young men left for Zakroczym, for Nowy Dwor, for Warsaw, and sometimes for the United States. Like Samuel's, their letters were illegible, the Yiddish mixed with the languages of the countries where they were now living. They sent photographs in which the men wore top hats and the women fancy dresses like squiresses.

Berl and Berlcha also received such photographs. But their eyes were failing and neither he nor she had glasses. They could barely make out the pictures. Samuel had sons and daughters with gentile names—and grandchildren who had married and had their own offspring. Their names were so strange that Berl and Berlcha could never remember them. But what difference do names make? America was far, far away on the other side of the ocean, at the edge of the world. A Talmud[2] teacher who came to Lentshin had said that Americans walked with their heads down and their feet up. Berl and Berlcha could not grasp this. How was it possible? But since the teacher said so it must be true. Berlcha pondered for some time and then she said, "One can get accustomed to everything."

And so it remained. From too much thinking—God forbid—one may lose one's wits.

One Friday morning, when Berlcha was kneading the dough for the Sabbath loaves, the door opened and a nobleman entered. He was so tall that he had to bend down to get through the door. He wore a beaver hat and a cloak bordered with fur. He was followed by Chazkel, the coachman from Zakroczym, who carried two leather valises with brass locks. In astonishment Berlcha raised her eyes.

10 The nobleman looked around and said to the coachman in Yiddish,

[1]**Dr. Herzl** Theodore Herzl (1860–1904), the founder of Zionism

[2]**Talmud** the collection of ancient rabbinic writings that constitute the basis of traditional Judaism

"Here it is." He took out a silver ruble and paid him. The coachman tried to hand him change but he said, "You can go now."

When the coachman closed the door, the nobleman said, "Mother, it's me, your son Samuel—Sam."

Berlcha heard the words and her legs grew numb. Her hands, to which pieces of dough were sticking, lost their power. The nobleman hugged her, kissed her forehead, both her cheeks. Berlcha began to cackle like a hen, "My son!" At that moment Berl came in from the woodshed, his arms piled with logs. The goat followed him. When he saw a nobleman kissing his wife, Berl dropped the wood and exclaimed, "What is this?"

The nobleman let go of Berlcha and embraced Berl. "Father!"

For a long time Berl was unable to utter a sound. He wanted to recite holy words that he had read in the Yiddish Bible, but he could remember nothing. Then he asked, "Are you Samuel?"

15 "Yes, Father, I am Samuel."

"Well, peace be with you." Berl grasped his son's hand. He was still not sure that he was not being fooled. Samuel wasn't as tall and heavy as this man, but then Berl reminded himself that Samuel was only fifteen years old when he had left home. He must have grown in that faraway country. Berl asked, "Why didn't you let us know that you were coming?"

"Didn't you receive my cable?" Samuel asked.

Berl did not know what a cable was.

Berlcha had scraped the dough from her hands and enfolded her son. He kissed her again and asked, "Mother, didn't you receive a cable?"

20 "What? If I lived to see this, I am happy to die," Berlcha said, amazed by her own words. Berl, too, was amazed. These were just the words he would have said earlier if he had been able to remember. After a while Berl came to himself and said, "Pescha, you will have to make a double Sabbath pudding in addition to the stew."

It was years since Berl had called Berlcha by her given name. When he wanted to address her, he would say, "Listen," or "Say." It is the young or those from the big cities who call a wife by her name. Only now did Berlcha begin to cry. Yellow tears ran from her eyes, and everything became dim. Then she called out, "It's Friday—I have to prepare for the Sabbath." Yes, she had to knead the dough and braid the loaves. With such a guest, she had to make a larger Sabbath stew. The winter day is short and she must hurry.

Her son understood what was worrying her, because he said, "Mother, I will help you."

Berlcha wanted to laugh, but a choked sob came out. "What are you saying? God forbid."

The nobleman took off his cloak and jacket and remained in his vest, on which hung a solid-gold watch chain. He rolled up his sleeves and came to the trough. "Mother, I was a baker for many years in New York," he said, and he began to knead the dough.

25 "What! You are my darling son who will say Kaddish[3] for me." She wept raspingly. Her strength left her, and she slumped onto the bed.

Berl said, "Women will always be women." And he went to the shed to get more wood. The goat sat down near the oven; she gazed with surprise at this strange man—his height and his bizarre clothes.

[3]**Kaddish** the prayer for the dead

The neighbors had heard the good news that Berl's son had arrived from America and they came to greet him. The women began to help Berlcha prepare for the Sabbath. Some laughed, some cried. The room was full of people, as at a wedding. They asked Berl's son, "What is new in America?" And Berl's son answered, "America is all right."

"Do Jews make a living?"

"One eats white bread there on weekdays."[4]

"Do they remain Jews?"

"I am not a gentile."

After Berlcha blessed the candles, father and son went to the little synagogue across the street. A new snow had fallen. The son took large steps, but Berl warned him, "Slow down."

In the synagogue the Jews recited "Let Us Exult" and "Come, My Groom." All the time, the snow outside kept falling. After prayers, when Berl and Samuel left the Holy Place, the village was unrecognizable. Everything was covered in snow. One could see only the contours of the roofs and the candles in the windows. Samuel said, "Nothing has changed here."

Berlcha had prepared gefilte fish, chicken soup with rice, meat, carrot stew. Berl recited the benediction over a glass of ritual wine. The family ate and drank, and when it grew quiet for a while one could hear the chirping of the house cricket. The son talked a lot, but Berl and Berlcha understood little. His Yiddish was different and contained foreign words.

After the final blessing Samuel asked, "Father, what did you do with all the money I sent you?"

Berl raised his white brows. "It's here."

"Didn't you put it in a bank?"

"There is no bank in Lentshin."

"Where do you keep it?"

Berl hesitated. "One is not allowed to touch money on the Sabbath but I will show you." He crouched beside the bed and began to shove something heavy. A boot appeared. Its top was stuffed with straw. Berl removed the straw and the son saw that the boot was full of gold coins. He lifted it.

"Father, this is a treasure!" he called out.

"Well."

"Why didn't you spend it?"

"On what? Thank God, we have everything."

"Why didn't you travel somewhere?"

"Where to? This is our home."

The son asked one question after the other, but Berl's answer was always the same: they wanted for nothing. The garden, the cow, the goat, the chickens provided them with all they needed. The son said, "If thieves knew about this, your lives wouldn't be safe."

"There are no thieves here."

"What will happen to the money?"

"You take it."

Slowly, Berl and Berlcha grew accustomed to their son and his American Yiddish. Berlcha could hear him better now. She even recognized his voice. He was saying, "Perhaps we should build a larger synagogue."

[4]**One eats white bread there on weekdays** in the poor communities of Europe white bread was a luxury reserved for holidays such as the Sabbath

"The synagogue is big enough," Berl replied.

"Perhaps a home for old people."

"No one sleeps in the street."

The next day after the Sabbath meal was eaten, a gentile from Zakroczym brought a paper—it was the cable. Berl and Berlcha lay down for a nap. They soon began to snore. The goat, too, dozed off. The son put on his cloak and his hat and went for a walk. He strode with his long legs across the marketplace. He stretched out a hand and touched a roof. He wanted to smoke a cigar, but he remembered it was forbidden on the Sabbath. He had a desire to talk to someone, but it seemed that the whole of Lentshin was asleep. He entered the synagogue. An old man was sitting there, reciting psalms. Samuel asked, "Are you praying?"

"What else is there to do when one gets old?"

"Do you make a living?"

The old man did not understand the meaning of those words. He smiled, showing his empty gums, and then he said, "If God gives health, one keeps on living."

Samuel returned home. Dusk had fallen. Berl went to the synagogue for the evening prayers and the son remained with his mother. The room was filled with shadows.

Berlcha began to recite in a solemn singsong, "God of Abraham, Isaac, and Jacob, defend the poor people of Israel and Thy name. The Holy Sabbath is departing; the welcome week is coming to us. Let it be one of health, wealth, and good deeds."

"Mother, you don't need to pray for wealth," Samuel said. "You are wealthy already."

Berlcha did not hear—or pretended not to. Her face had turned into a cluster of shadows.

In the twilight Samuel put his hand into his jacket pocket and touched his passport, his checkbook, his letters of credit. He had come here with big plans. He had a valise filled with presents for his parents. He wanted to bestow gifts on the village. He brought not only his own money but funds from the Lentshin Society in New York, which had organized a ball for the benefit of the village. But this village in the hinterland needed nothing. From the synagogue one could hear hoarse chanting. The cricket, silent all day, started again its chirping. Berlcha began to sway and utter holy rhymes inherited from mothers and grandmothers:

Thy holy sheep
In mercy keep,
In Torah[5] good deeds;
Provide for all their needs,
Shoes, clothes, and bread
And the Messiah's tread.

[*1973*]

[5]**Torah** Jewish teachings, especially the first five books of the Hebrew Bible

## NAGUIB MAHFOUZ

***Naguib Mahfouz, born in Cairo, Egypt, in 1911, studied philosophy at Cairo University and then worked as a civil servant, chiefly in the division controlling the nationalized film industry. He published his first story in 1934 (the year he graduated from the university) and went on to write more than thirty novels and fourteen volumes of short stories. In the Arab world he was long recognized as a leading novelist, but he did not achieve international fame until he received the Nobel Prize in Literature in 1988. We reprint a story that he first published soon after receiving the prize.***

# *The Answer Is No*

*Translated by Denys Johnson-Davies*

The important piece of news that the new headmaster had arrived spread through the school. She heard of it in the women teachers' common room as she was casting a final glance at the day's lessons. There was no getting away from joining the other teachers in congratulating him, and from shaking him by the hand too. A shudder passed through her body, but it was unavoidable.

"They speak highly of his ability," said a colleague of hers. "And they talk too of his strictness."

It had always been a possibility that might occur, and now it had. Her pretty face paled, and a staring look came to her wide black eyes.

When the time came, the teachers went in single file, decorously attired, to his open room. He stood behind his desk as he received the men and women. He was of medium height, with a tendency to portliness, and had a spherical face, hooked nose, and bulging eyes; the first thing that could be seen of him was a thick, puffed-up mustache, arched like a foam-laden wave. She advanced with her eyes fixed on his chest. Avoiding his gaze, she stretched out her hand. What was she to say? Just what the others had said? However, she kept silent, uttered not a word. What, she wondered, did his eyes express? His rough hand shook hers, and he said in a gruff voice, "Thanks." She turned elegantly and moved off.

5 She forgot her worries through her daily tasks, though she did not look in good shape. Several of the girls remarked, "Miss is in a bad mood." When she returned to her home at the beginning of the Pyramids Road, she changed her clothes and sat down to eat with her mother. "Everything all right?" inquired her mother, looking her in the face.

"Badran, Badran Badawi," she said briefly. "Do you remember him? He's been appointed our headmaster."

"Really!"

Then, after a moment of silence, she said, "It's of no importance at all—it's an old and long-forgotten story."

After eating, she took herself off to her study to rest for a while before correcting some exercise books. She had forgotten him completely. No, not completely. How could he be forgotten completely? When he had first come to give her a private lesson in mathematics, she was fourteen years of age. In fact not quite fourteen. He had been twenty-five years older, the same age as her father. She had said to her mother, "His appearance is a mess, but he explains things well." And her mother had said, "We're not concerned with what he looks like; what's important is how he explains things."

He was an amusing person, and she got on well with him and benefited from his knowledge. How, then, had it happened? In her innocence she had not noticed any change in his behavior to put her on her guard. Then one day he had been left on his own with her, her father having gone to her aunt's clinic. She had not the slightest doubts about a man she regarded as a second father. How, then, had it happened? Without love or desire on her part the thing had happened. She had asked in terror about what had occurred, and he had told her, "Don't be frightened or sad. Keep it to yourself and I'll come and propose to you the day you come of age."

And he had kept his promise and had come to ask for her hand. By then she had attained a degree of maturity that gave her an understanding of the dimensions of her tragic position. She had found that she had no love or respect for him and that he was as far as he could be from her dreams and from the ideas she had formed of what constituted an ideal and moral person. But what was to be done? Her father had passed away two years ago, and her mother had been taken aback by the forwardness of the man. However, she had said to her, "I know your attachment to your personal independence, so I leave the decision to you."

She had been conscious of the critical position she was in. She had either to accept or to close the door forever. It was the sort of situation that could force her into something she detested. She was the rich, beautiful girl, a byword in Abbasiyya for her nobility of character, and now here she was struggling helplessly in a well-sprung trap, while he looked down at her with rapacious eyes. Just as she had hated his strength, so too did she hate her own weakness. To have abused her innocence was one thing, but for him to have the upper hand now that she was fully in possession of her faculties was something else. He had said, "So here I am, making good my promise because I love you." He had also said, "I know of your love of teaching, and you will complete your studies at the College of Science."

She had felt such anger as she had never felt before. She had rejected coercion in the same way as she rejected ugliness. It had meant little to her to sacrifice marriage. She had welcomed being on her own, for solitude accompanied by self-respect was not loneliness. She had also guessed he was after her money. She had told her mother quite straightforwardly, "No," to which her mother had replied, "I am astonished you did not make this decision from the first moment."

The man had blocked her way outside and said, "How can you refuse? Don't you realize the outcome?" And she had replied with an asperity he had not expected, "For me any outcome is preferable to being married to you."

After finishing her studies, she had wanted something to do to fill her spare time, so she had worked as a teacher. Chances to marry had come time after time, but she had turned her back on them all.

"Does no one please you?" her mother asked her.

"I know what I'm doing," she had said gently.

"But time is going by."

"Let it go as it pleases, I am content."

Day by day she becomes older. She avoids love, fears it. With all her strength she hopes that life will pass calmly, peacefully, rather than happily. She goes on persuading herself that happiness is not confined to love and motherhood. Never has she regretted her firm decision. Who knows what the morrow holds? But she was certainly unhappy that he should again make his appearance in her life, that she would be dealing with him day after day, and that he would be making of the past a living and painful present.

Then, the first time he was alone with her in his room, he asked her, "How are you?"

She answered coldly, "I'm fine."

He hesitated slightly before inquiring, "Have you not . . . I mean, did you get married?"

In the tone of someone intent on cutting short a conversation, she said, "I told you, I'm fine."

[*1988*]

## JOHN STEINBECK

*John Steinbeck (1902–1968) was born in Salinas, California, and much of his fiction concerns this landscape and its people. As a young man he worked on ranches, farms, and road gangs, and sometimes attended Stanford University—he never graduated—but he wrote whenever he could find the time. His early efforts at writing, however, were uniformly rejected by publishers. Even when he did break into print, he did not achieve much notice for several years: a novel in 1929, a book of stories in 1932, and another novel in 1933 attracted little attention. But the publication of* Tortilla Flat *(1935), a novel about Mexican Americans, changed all that. It was followed by other successful novels—*In Dubious Battle *(1936) and* Of Mice and Men *(1937)—and by* The Long Valley *(1938), a collection of stories that included "The Chrysanthemums." His next book,* The Grapes of Wrath *(1939), about dispossessed sharecropper migrants from the Oklahoma dustbowl, was also immensely popular and won a Pulitzer Prize. During the Second World War*

*Steinbeck sent reports from battlefields in Italy and Africa. In 1962 he was awarded the Nobel Prize in Literature.*

# The Chrysanthemums

The high grey-flannel fog of winter closed off the Salinas Valley[1] from the sky and from all the rest of the world. On every side it sat like a lid on the mountains and made of the great valley a closed pot. On the broad, level land floor the gang plows bit deep and left the black earth shining like metal where the shares had cut. On the foothill ranches across the Salinas River, the yellow stubble fields seemed to be bathed in pale cold sunshine, but there was no sunshine in the valley now in December. The thick willow scrub along the river flamed with sharp and positive yellow leaves.

It was a time of quiet and of waiting. The air was cold and tender. A light wind blew up from the southwest so that the farmers were mildly hopeful of a good rain before long; but fog and rain do not go together.

Across the river, on Henry Allen's foothill ranch there was little work to be done, for the hay was cut and stored and the orchards were plowed up to receive the rain deeply when it should come. The cattle on the higher slopes were becoming shaggy and rough-coated.

Elisa Allen, working in her flower garden, looked down across the yard and saw Henry, her husband, talking to two men in business suits. The three of them stood by the tractor shed, each man with one foot on the side of the little Fordson.[2] They smoked cigarettes and studied the machine as they talked.

5 Elisa watched them for a moment and then went back to her work. She was thirty-five. Her face was lean and strong and her eyes were as clear as water. Her figure looked blocked and heavy in her gardening costume, a man's black hat pulled low down over her eyes, clod-hopper shoes, a figured print dress almost completely covered by a big corduroy apron with four big pockets to hold the snips, the trowel and scratcher, the seeds and the knife she worked with. She wore heavy leather gloves to protect her hands while she worked.

She was cutting down the old year's chrysanthemum stalks with a pair of short and powerful scissors. She looked down toward the men by the tractor shed now and then. Her face was eager and mature and handsome; even her work with the scissors was over-eager, over-powerful. The chrysanthemum stems seemed too small and easy for her energy.

She brushed a cloud of hair out of her eyes with the back of her glove, and left a smudge of earth on her cheek in doing it. Behind her stood the neat white farm house with red geraniums close-banked around it as high as the windows. It was a hard-swept looking little house with hard-polished windows, and a clean mud-mat on the front steps.

Elisa cast another glance toward the tractor shed. The strangers were getting into their Ford coupe. She took off a glove and put her strong fin-

[1]**the Salinas Valley** a fertile area in central California
[2]**Fordson** a two-door Ford car

gers down into the forest of new green chrysanthemum sprouts that were growing around the old roots. She spread the leaves and looked down among the close-growing stems. No aphids were there, no sowbugs or snails or cutworms. Her terrier fingers destroyed such pests before they could get started.

Elisa started at the sound of her husband's voice. He had come near quietly, and he leaned over the wire fence that protected her flower garden from cattle and dogs and chickens.

10 "At it again," he said. "You've got a strong new crop coming."

Elisa straightened her back and pulled on the gardening glove again. "Yes. They'll be strong this coming year." In her tone and on her face there was a little smugness.

"You've got a gift with things," Henry observed. "Some of those yellow chrysanthemums you had this year were ten inches across. I wish you'd work out in the orchard and raise some apples that big."

Her eyes sharpened. "Maybe I could do it, too. I've a gift with things, all right. My mother had it. She could stick anything in the ground and make it grow. She said it was having planters' hands that knew how to do it."

"Well, it sure works with flowers," he said.

15 "Henry, who were those men you were talking to?"

"Why, sure, that's what I came to tell you. They were from the Western Meat Company. I sold those thirty head of three-year-old steers. Got nearly my own price, too."

"Good," she said. "Good for you."

"And I thought," he continued, "I thought how it's Saturday afternoon, and we might go into Salinas for dinner at a restaurant, and then to a picture show—to celebrate, you see."

"Good," she repeated. "Oh, yes. That will be good."

20 "Henry put on his joking tone. "There's fights tonight. How'd you like to go to the fights?"

Oh, no," she said breathlessly. "No, I wouldn't like fights."

"Just fooling, Elisa. We'll go to a movie. Let's see. It's two now. I'm going to take Scotty and bring down those steers from the hill. It'll take us maybe two hours. We'll go in town about five and have dinner at the Cominos Hotel. Like that?"

"Of course I'll like it. It's good to eat away from home."

"All right, then. I'll go get up a couple of horses."

25 She said, "I'll have plenty of time to transplant some of these sets, I guess."

She heard her husband calling Scotty down by the barn. And a little later she saw the two men ride up the pale yellow hillside in search of the steers.

There was a little square sandy bed kept for rooting the chrysanthemums. With her trowel she turned the soil over and over, and smoothed it and patted it firm. Then she dug ten parallel trenches to receive the sets. Back at the chrysanthemum bed she pulled out the little crisp shoots, trimmed off the leaves of each one with her scissors and laid it on a small orderly pile.

A squeak of wheels and plod of hoofs came from the road. Elisa looked up. The country road ran along the dense bank of willows and cottonwoods that bordered the river, and up this road came a curious vehicle, curiously drawn. It was an old springwagon, with a round canvas top on it like the cover of a prairie schooner. It was drawn by an old bay horse and a little grey-and-white burro. A big stubble-bearded man sat between the cover flaps and drove the crawling team. Underneath the wagon, between the hind wheels, a lean and rangy mongrel dog walked sedately. Words were painted on the canvas, in clumsy, crooked letters. "Pots, pans, knives, sisors, lawn mores, Fixed." Two rows of articles, and the triumphantly definitive "Fixed" below. The black paint had run down in little sharp points beneath each letter.

Elisa, squatting on the ground, watched to see the crazy, loose-jointed wagon pass by. But it didn't pass. It turned into the farm road in front of her house, crooked old wheels skirling and squeaking. The rangy dog darted from between the wheels and ran ahead. Instantly the two ranch shepherds flew out at him. Then all three stopped, and with stiff and quivering tails, with taut straight legs, with ambassadorial dignity, they slowly circled, sniffing daintily. The caravan pulled up to Elisa's wire fence and stopped. Now the newcomer dog, feeling out-numbered, lowered his tail and retired under the wagon with raised hackles and bared teeth.

30 The man on the wagon seat called out, "That's a bad dog in a fight when he gets started."

Elisa laughed. "I see he is. How soon does he generally get started?"

The man caught up her laughter and echoed it heartily. "Sometimes not for weeks and weeks," he said. He climbed stiffly down, over the wheel. The horse and the donkey drooped like unwatered flowers.

Elisa saw that he was a very big man. Although his hair and beard were greying, he did not look old. His worn black suit was wrinkled and spotted with grease. The laughter had disappeared from his face and eyes the moment his laughing voice ceased. His eyes were dark, and they were full of the brooding that gets in the eyes of teamsters and of sailors. The calloused hands he rested on the wire fence were cracked, and every crack was a black line. He took off his battered hat.

"I'm off my general road, ma'am," he said. "Does this dirt road cut over across the river to the Los Angeles highway?"

35 Elisa stood up and shoved the thick scissors in her apron pocket. "Well, yes, it does, but it winds around and then fords the river. I don't think your team could pull through the sand."

He replied with some asperity. "It might surprise you what them beasts can pull through."

"When they get started?" she asked.

He smiled for a second. "Yes. When they get started."

"Well," said Elisa, "I think you'll save time if you go back to the Salinas road and pick up the highway there."

40 He drew a big finger down the chicken wire and made it sing. "I ain't in any hurry, ma'am. I go from Seattle to San Diego and back every year. Takes all my time. About six months each way. I aim to follow nice weather."

Elisa took off her gloves and stuffed them in the apron pocket with the scissors. She touched the under edge of her man's hat, searching for fugitive hairs. "That sounds like a nice kind of way to live," she said.

He leaned confidentially over the fence. "Maybe you noticed the writing on my wagon. I mend pots and sharpen knives and scissors. You got any of them things to do?"

"Oh, no," she said quickly. "Nothing like that." Her eyes hardened with resistance.

"Scissors is the worst thing," he explained. "Most people just ruin scissors trying to sharpen 'em, but I know how. I got a special tool. It's a little bobbit kind of thing, and patented. But it sure does the trick."

"No. My scissors are all sharp."

"All right, then. Take a pot," he continued earnestly, "a bent pot, or a pot with a hole. I can make it like new so you don't have to buy no new ones. That's a saving for you."

"No," she said shortly. "I tell you I have nothing like that for you to do."

His face fell to an exaggerated sadness. His voice took on a whining undertone. "I ain't had a thing to do today. Maybe I won't have no supper tonight. You see I'm off my regular road. I know folks on the highway clear from Seattle to San Diego. They save their things for me to sharpen up because they know I do it so good and save them money."

"I'm sorry," Elisa said irritably. "I haven't anything for you to do."

His eyes left her face and fell to searching the ground. They roamed about until they came to the chrysanthemum bed where she had been working. "What's them plants, ma'am?"

The irritation and resistance melted from Elisa's face. "Oh, those are chrysanthemums, giant whites and yellows. I raise them every year, bigger than anybody around here."

"Kind of a long-stemmed flower? Looks like a quick puff of colored smoke?" he asked.

"That's it. What a nice way to describe them."

"They smell kind of nasty till you get used to them," he said.

"It's a good bitter smell," she retorted, "not nasty at all."

He changed his tone quickly. "I like the smell myself."

"I had ten-inch blooms this year," she said.

The man leaned farther over the fence. "Look. I know a lady down the road a piece, has got the nicest garden you ever seen. Got nearly every kind of flower but no chrysantheums. Last time I was mending a copper-bottom wash-tub for her (that's a hard job but I do it good), she said to me, 'If you ever run acrost some nice chrysanthemums I wish you'd try to get me a few seeds.' That's what she told me."

Elisa's eyes grew alert and eager. "She couldn't have known much about chrysanthemums. You *can* raise them from seed, but it's much easier to root the little sprouts you see there."

"Oh," he said. "I s'pose I can't take none to her, then."

"Why yes you can," Elisa cried. "I can put some in damp sand, and you can carry them right along with you. They'll take root in the pot if you keep them damp. And then she can transplant them."

"She'd sure like to have some, ma'am. You say they're nice ones?"

"Beautiful," she said. "Oh, beautiful." Her eyes shone. She tore off the battered hat and shook out her dark pretty hair. "I'll put them in a flower pot, and you can take them right with you. Come into the yard."

While the man came through the picket gate Elisa ran excitedly along the geranium-bordered path to the back of the house. And she returned carrying a big red flower pot. The gloves were forgotten now. She kneeled on the ground by the starting bed and dug up the sandy soil with her fingers and scooped it into the bright new flower pot. Then she picked up the little pile of shoots she had prepared. With her strong fingers she pressed them into the sand and tamped around them with her knuckles. The man stood over her. "I'll tell you what to do," she said. "You remember so you can tell the lady."

65 "Yes, I'll try to remember."

"Well, look. These will take root in about a month. Then she must set them out, about a foot apart in good rich earth like this, see?" She lifted a handful of dark soil for him to look at. "They'll grow fast and tall. Now remember this: In July tell her to cut them down, about eight inches from the ground."

"Before they bloom?" he asked.

"Yes, before they bloom." Her face was tight with eagerness. "They'll grow right up again. About the last of September the buds will start."

She stopped and seemed perplexed. "It's the budding that takes the most care," she said hesitantly. "I don't know how to tell you." She looked deep into his eyes, searchingly. Her mouth opened a little, and she seemed to be listening. "I'll try to tell you," she said. "Did you ever hear of planting hands?"

70 "Can't say I have, ma'am."

"Well, I can only tell you what it feels like. It's when you're picking off the buds you don't want. Everything goes right down into your fingertips. You watch your fingers work. They do it themselves. You can feel how it is. They pick and pick the buds. They never make a mistake. They're with the plant. Do you see? Your fingers and the plant. You can feel that, right up your arm. They know. They never make a mistake. You can feel it. When you're like that you can't do anything wrong. Do you see that? Can you understand that?"

She was kneeling on the ground looking up at him. Her breast swelled passionately.

The man's eyes narrowed. He looked away self-consciously. "Maybe I know," he said. "Sometimes in the night in the wagon there—"

Elisa's voice grew husky. She broke in on him, "I've never lived as you do, but I know what you mean. When the night is dark—why, the stars are sharp-pointed, and there's quiet. Why, you rise up and up! Every pointed star gets driven into your body. It's like that. Hot and sharp and—lovely."

75 Kneeling there, her hand went out toward his legs in the greasy black trousers. Her hesitant fingers almost touched the cloth. Then her hand dropped to the ground. She crouched low like a fawning dog.

He said, "It's nice, just like you say. Only when you don't have no dinner, it ain't."

She stood up then, very straight, and her face was ashamed. She held the flower pot out to him and placed it gently in his arms. "Here. Put it in your wagon, on the seat, where you can watch it. Maybe I can find something for you to do."

At the back of the house she dug in the can pile and found two old and battered aluminum saucepans. She carried them back and gave them to him. "Here, maybe you can fix these."

His manner changed. He became professional. "Good as new I can fix them." At the back of his wagon he set a little anvil, and out of an oily tool box dug a small machine hammer. Elisa came through the gate to watch him while he pounded out the dents in the kettles. His mouth grew sure and knowing. At a difficult part of the work he sucked his under-lip.

80 "You sleep right in the wagon?" Elisa asked.

"Right in the wagon, ma'am. Rain or shine I'm dry as a cow in there."

"It must be nice," she said. "It must be very nice. I wish women could do such things."

"It ain't the right kind of a life for a woman."

Her upper lip raised a little, showing her teeth. "How do you know? How can you tell?" she said.

85 "I don't know, ma'am," he protested. "Of course I don't know. Now here's your kettles, done. You don't have to buy no new ones."

"How much?"

"Oh, fifty cents'll do. I keep my prices down and my work good. That's why I have all them satisfied customers up and down the highway."

Elisa brought him a fifty-cent piece from the house and dropped it in his hand. "You might be surprised to have a rival some time. I can sharpen scissors, too. And I can beat the dents out of little pots. I could show you what a woman might do."

He put his hammer back in the oily box and shoved the little anvil out of sight. "It would be a lonely life for a woman, ma'am, and a scarey life, too, with animals creeping under the wagon all night." He climbed over the singletree, steadying himself with a hand on the burro's white rump. He settled himself in the seat, picked up the lines. "Thank you kindly, ma'am," he said. "I'll do like you told me; I'll go back and catch the Salinas road."

90 "Mind," she called, "if you're long in getting there, keep the sand damp."

"Sand, ma'am? . . . Sand? Oh, sure. You mean around the chrysantheums. Sure I will." He clucked his tongue. The beasts leaned luxuriously into their collars. The mongrel dog took his place between the back wheels. The wagon turned and crawled out the entrance road and back the way it had come, along the river.

Elisa stood in front of her wire fence watching the slow progress of the caravan. Her shoulders were straight, her head thrown back, her eyes half-closed, so that the scene came vaguely into them. Her lips moved silently, forming the words "Good-bye—good-bye." Then she whispered, "That's a bright direction. There's a glowing there." The sound of her whisper startled her. She shook herself free and looked about to see whether anyone had been listening. Only the dogs had heard. They lifted their heads toward her from their sleeping in the dust, and then stretched out their chins and settled asleep again. Elisa turned and ran hurriedly into the house.

In the kitchen she reached behind the stove and felt the water tank. It was full of hot water from the noonday cooking. In the bathroom she tore off her soiled clothes and flung them into the corner. And then she scrubbed herself with a little block of pumice, legs and thighs, loins and chest and arms, until her skin was scratched and red. When she had dried herself she stood in front of a mirror in her bedroom and looked at her body. She tightened her stomach and threw out her chest. She turned and looked over her shoulder at her back.

After a while she began to dress, slowly. She put on her newest underclothing and her nicest stockings and the dress which was the symbol of her prettiness. She worked carefully on her hair, penciled her eyebrows and rouged her lips.

95 Before she was finished she heard the little thunder of hoofs and the shouts of Henry and his helper as they drove the red steers into the corral. She heard the gate bang shut and set herself for Henry's arrival.

His step sounded on the porch. He entered the house calling, "Elisa, where are you?"

"In my room, dressing. I'm not ready. There's hot water for your bath. Hurry up. It's getting late."

When she heard him splashing in the tub, Elisa laid his dark suit on the bed, and shirt and socks and tie beside it. She stood his polished shoes on the floor beside the bed. Then she went to the porch and sat primly and stiffly down. She looked toward the river road where the willow-line was still yellow with frosted leaves so that under the high grey fog they seemed a thin band of sunshine. This was the only color in the grey afternoon. She sat unmoving for a long time. Her eyes blinked rarely.

Henry came banging out of the door shoving his tie inside his vest as he came. Elisa stiffened and her face grew tight. Henry stopped short and looked at her. "Why—why, Elisa. You look so nice!"

100 "Nice? You think I look nice? What do you mean by 'nice'?"

Henry blundered on. "I don't know. I mean you look different, strong and happy."

"I am strong? Yes, strong. What do you mean 'strong'?"

He looked bewildered. "You're playing some kind of a game," he said helplessly. "It's a kind of a play. You look strong enough to break a calf over your knee, happy enough to eat it like a watermelon."

For a second she lost her rigidity. "Henry! Don't talk like that. You didn't know what you said." She grew complete again. "I'm strong," she boasted. "I never knew before how strong."

105 Henry looked down toward the tractor shed, and when he brought his eyes back to her, they were his own again. "I'll get out the car. You can put on your coat while I'm starting."

Elisa went into the house. She heard him drive to the gate and idle down his motor, and then she took a long time to put on her hat. She pulled it here and pressed it there. When Henry turned the motor off she slipped into her coat and went out.

The little roadster bounced along on the dirt road by the river, raising the birds and driving the rabbits into the brush. Two cranes flapped heavily over the willow-line and dropped into the river-bed.

Far ahead on the road Elisa saw a dark speck. She knew.

She tried not to look as they passed it, but her eyes would not obey. She whispered to herself sadly, "He might have thrown them off the road. That wouldn't have been much trouble, not very much. But he kept the pot," she explained. "He had to keep the pot. That's why he couldn't get them off the road."

110 The roadster turned a bend and she saw the caravan ahead. She swung full around toward her husband so she could not see the little covered wagon and the mismatched team as the car passed them.

In a moment it was over. The thing was done. She did not look back.

She said loudly, to be heard above the motor, "It will be good, tonight, a good dinner."

"Now you're changed again," Henry complained. He took one hand from the wheel and patted her knee. "I ought to take you in to dinner oftener. It would be good for both of us. We get so heavy out on the ranch."

"Henry," she asked, "could we have wine at dinner?"

115 "Sure we could. Say! That will be fine."

She was silent for a while; then she said, "Henry, at those prize fights, do the men hurt each other very much?"

"Sometimes a little, not often. Why?"

"Well, I've read how they break noses, and blood runs down their chests. I've read how the fighting gloves get heavy and soggy with blood."

He looked around at her. "What's the matter, Elisa? I didn't know you read things like that." He brought the car to a stop, then turned to the right over the Salinas River bridge.

120 "Do any women ever go to the fights?" she asked.

"Oh, sure, some. What's the matter, Elisa? Do you want to go? I don't think you'd like it, but I'll take you if you really want to go."

She relaxed limply in the seat. "Oh, no. No. I don't want to go. I'm sure I don't." Her face was turned away from him. "It will be enough if we can have wine. It will be plenty." She turned up her coat collar so he could not see that she was crying weakly—like an old woman.

[*1937*]

## RALPH ELLISON

*Ralph Ellison (1914-94) was born in Oklahoma City. His father died when Ellison was three, and his mother supported herself and her child by working as a domestic. A trumpeter since boyhood, after graduating from high school Ellison went to study music at Tuskegee Institute, a black college in Alabama founded by Booker T. Washington. In 1936 he dropped out of Tuskegee and went to Harlem to study music composition and the visual arts; there he met Langston Hughes and Richard Wright, who encouraged him to turn to fiction. Ellison published stories and essays, and in 1942 became the managing editor of* Negro Quarterly. *During the Second World War he served in the Merchant Marine. After the war he returned to writing and later taught in universities.*

*"Battle Royal" was first published in 1947 and slightly revised (a transitional paragraph was added at the end of the story) for the opening chapter of Ellison's novel,* The Invisible Man *(1952), a book cited by* Book-Week *as "the most significant work of fiction written by an American" in the years between 1945 and 1965. In addition to publishing stories and one novel, Ellison*

*published critical essays, which are brought together in* The Collected Essays of Ralph Ellison *(1995).*

## Battle Royal

It goes a long way back, some twenty years. All my life I had been looking for something, and everywhere I turned someone tried to tell me what it was. I accepted their answers too, though they were often in contradiction and even self-contradictory. I was naïve. I was looking for myself and asking everyone except myself questions which I, and only I, could answer. It took me a long time and much painful boomeranging of my expectations to achieve a realization everyone else appears to have been born with: That I am nobody but myself. But first I had to discover that I am an invisible man!

And yet I am no freak of nature, nor of history. I was in the cards, other things having been equal (or unequal) eighty-five years ago. I am not ashamed of my grandparents for having been slaves. I am only ashamed of myself for having at one time been ashamed. About eighty-five years ago they were told that they were free, united with others of our country in everything pertaining to the common good, and, in everything social, separate like the fingers of the hand. And they believed it. They exulted in it. They stayed in their place, worked hard, and brought up my father to do the same. But my grandfather is the one. He was an odd old guy, my grandfather, and I am told I take after him. It was he who caused the trouble. On his deathbed he called my father to him and said, "Son, after I'm gone I want you to keep up the good fight. I never told you, but our life is a war and I have been a traitor all my born days, a spy in the enemy's country ever since I give up my gun back in the Reconstruction. Live with your head in the lion's mouth. I want you to overcome 'em with yeses, undermine 'em with grins, agree 'em to death and destruction, let 'em swoller you till they vomit or bust wide open." They thought the old man had gone out of his mind. He had been the meekest of men. The younger children were rushed from the room, the shades drawn and the flame of the lamp turned so low that it sputtered on the wick like the old man's breathing. "Learn it to the younguns," he whispered fiercely; then he died.

But my folks were more alarmed over his last words than over his dying. It was as though he had not died at all, his words caused so much anxiety. I was warned emphatically to forget what he had said and, indeed, this is the first time it has been mentioned outside the family circle. It had a tremendous effect upon me, however. I could never be sure of what he meant. Grandfather had been a quiet old man who never made any trouble, yet on his deathbed he had called himself a traitor and a spy, and he had spoken of his meekness as a dangerous activity. It became a constant puzzle which lay unanswered in the back of my mind. And whenever things went well for me I remembered my grandfather and felt guilty and uncomfortable. It was as though I was carrying out his advice in spite of myself. And to make it worse, everyone loved me for it. I was praised by the most lily-white men of the town. I was considered an example of desirable conduct—just as my grandfather had been. And what puzzled me was that the old man had defined it as *treachery.* When I was praised for my conduct I felt a guilt that in some way I was doing something that was really against the wishes of the white folks, that if they had understood they would have desired me to act just the opposite, that I should have been sulky and mean, and that that really would have been what they wanted, even though they were fooled and thought they wanted me to act as I did. It made me afraid that some day they would look upon me as a traitor and I would be lost. Still I was more afraid to act any other way because they didn't like that at all. The old man's words were like a curse. On my graduation day I delivered an oration in which I showed that humility was the secret, indeed, the very essence of progress. (Not that I believed this—how could I, remembering my grandfather?—I only believed that it worked.) It was a great success. Everyone praised me and I was invited to give the speech at a gathering of the town's leading white citizens. It was a triumph for our whole community.

It was in the main ballroom of the leading hotel. When I got there I discovered that it was on the occasion of a smoker, and I was told that since I was to be there anyway I might as well take part in the battle royal to be fought by some of my schoolmates as part of the entertainment. The battle royal came first.

5 All of the town's big shots were there in their tuxedoes, wolfing down the buffet foods, drinking beer and whiskey and smoking black cigars. It was a large room with a high ceiling. Chairs were arranged in neat rows around three sides of a portable boxing ring. The fourth side was clear, revealing a gleaming space of polished floor. I had some misgivings over the battle royal, by the way. Not from a distaste for fighting, but because I didn't care too much for the other fellows who were to take part. They were tough guys who seemed to have no grandfather's curse worrying their minds. No one could mistake their toughness. And besides, I suspected that fighting a battle royal might detract from the dignity of my speech. In those pre-invisible days I visualized myself as a potential Booker T. Washington. But the other fellows didn't care too much for me either, and there were nine of them. I felt superior to them in my way, and I didn't like the manner in which we were all crowded together into the servants' elevator. Nor did they like my being there. In fact, as the warmly lighted floors flashed past the elevator we had words over the fact that I, by taking part in the fight, had knocked one of their friends out of a night's work.

We were led out of the elevator through a rococo hall into an anteroom and told to get into our fighting togs. Each of us was issued a pair of boxing gloves and ushered out into the big mirrored hall, which we entered looking cautiously about us and whispering, lest we might accidentally be heard above the noise of the room. It was foggy with cigar smoke. And already the whiskey was taking effect. I was shocked to see some of the most important men of the town quite tipsy. They were all there—bankers, lawyers, judges, doctors, fire chiefs, teachers, merchants. Even one of the more fashionable pastors. Something we could not see was going on up front. A clarinet was vibrating sensuously and the men were standing up and moving eagerly forward. We were a small tight group, clustered together, our bare upper bodies touching and shining with anticipatory sweat; while up front the big shots were becoming increasingly excited over something we still could not see. Suddenly I heard the school superintendent, who had told me to come, yell, "Bring up the shines, gentlemen! Bring up the little shines!"

We were rushed up to the front of the ballroom, where it smelled even more strongly of tobacco and whiskey. Then we were pushed into place. I almost wet my pants. A sea of faces, some hostile, some amused, ringed around us, and in the center, facing us, stood a magnificent blonde—stark naked. There was dead silence. I felt a blast of cold air chill me. I tried to back away, but they were behind me and around me. Some of the boys stood with lowered heads, trembling. I felt a wave of irrational guilt and fear. My teeth chattered, my skin turned to goose flesh, my knees knocked. Yet I was strongly attracted and looked in spite of myself. Had the price of looking been blindness, I would have looked. The hair was yellow like that of a circus kewpie doll, the face heavily powdered and rouged, as though to form an abstract mask, the eyes hollow and smeared a cool blue, the color of a baboon's butt. I felt a desire to spit upon her as my eyes brushed slowly over her body. Her breasts were firm and round as the domes of East Indian temples, and I stood so close as to see the fine skin texture and beads of pearly perspiration glistening like dew around the pink and erected buds of her nipples. I wanted at one and the same time to run from the room, to sink through the floor, or go to her and cover her from my eyes and the eyes of the others with my body; to feel the soft thighs, to caress her and destroy her, to love her and murder her, to hide from her, and yet to stroke where below the small American flag tattooed upon her belly her thighs formed a capital V. I had a notion that of all in the room she saw only me with her impersonal eyes.

And then she began to dance, a slow sensuous movement; the smoke of a hundred cigars clinging to her like the thinnest of veils. She seemed like a fair bird-girl girdled in veils calling to me from the angry surface of some gray and threatening sea. I was transported. Then I became aware of the clarinet playing and the big shots yelling at us. Some threatened us if we looked and others if we did not. On my right I saw one boy faint. And now a man grabbed a silver pitcher from a table and stepped close as he dashed ice water upon him and stood him up and forced two of us to support him as his head hung and moans issued from his thick bluish lips. Another boy began to plead to go home. He was the largest of the group, wearing dark red fighting trunks much too small to conceal the erection which projected from him as though in answer to the insinuating low-registered moans of the clarinet. He tried to hide himself with his boxing gloves.

And all the while the blonde continued dancing, smiling faintly at the big shots who watched her with fascination, and faintly smiling at our fear. I noticed a certain merchant who followed her hungrily, his lips loose and drooling. He was a large man who wore diamond studs in a shirtfront which swelled with the ample paunch underneath, and each time the blonde swayed her undulating hips he ran his hand through the thin hair of his bald head and, with his arms upheld, his posture clumsy like that of an intoxicated panda, wound his belly in a slow and obscene grind. This creature was completely hypnotized. The music had quickened. As the dancer flung herself about with a detached expression on her face, the men began reaching out to touch her. I could see their beefy fingers sink into her soft flesh. Some of the others tried to stop them and she began to move around the floor in graceful circles, as they gave chase, slipping and sliding over the polished floor. It was mad. Chairs went crashing, drinks were spilt, as they ran laughing and howling after her. They caught her just as she reached a door, raised her from the floor, and tossed her as college boys are tossed at a hazing, and above her red, fixed-smiling lips I saw the terror and disgust in her eyes, almost like my own terror and that which I saw in some of the other boys. As I watched, they tossed her twice and her soft breasts seemed to flatten against the air and her legs flung wildly as she spun. Some of the more sober ones helped her to escape. And I started off the floor, heading for the anteroom with the rest of the boys.

10 Some were still crying and in hysteria. But as we tried to leave we were stopped and ordered to get into the ring. There was nothing to do but what we were told. All ten of us climbed under the ropes and allowed ourselves to be blindfolded with broad bands of white cloth. One of the men seemed to feel a bit sympathetic and tried to cheer us up as we stood with our backs against the ropes. Some of us tried to grin. "See that boy over there?" one of the men said. "I want you to run across at the bell and give it to him right in the belly. If you don't get him, I'm going to get you. I don't like his looks." Each of us was told the same. The blindfolds were put on. Yet even then I had been going over my speech. In my mind each word was as bright as flame. I felt the cloth pressed into place, and frowned so that it would be loosened when I relaxed.

But now I felt a sudden fit of blind terror. I was unused to darkness. It was as though I had suddenly found myself in a dark room filled with poisonous cotton-mouths. I could hear the bleary voices yelling insistently for the battle royal to begin.

"Get going in there!"

"Let me at that big nigger!"

I strained to pick up the school superintendent's voice, as though to squeeze some security out of that slightly more familiar sound.

15 "Let me at those black sonsabitches!" someone yelled.

"No, Jackson, no!" another voice yelled. "Here, somebody, help me hold Jack."

"I want to get at that ginger-colored nigger. Tear him limb from limb," the first voice yelled.

I stood against the ropes trembling. For in those days I was what they called ginger-colored, and he sounded as though he might crunch me between his teeth like a crisp ginger cookie.

Quite a struggle was going on. Chairs were being kicked about and I could hear voices grunting as with a terrific effort. I wanted to see, to see more desperately than ever before. But the blindfold was as tight as a thick skin-puckering scab and when I raised my gloved hands to push the layers of white aside a voice yelled, "Oh, no you don't, black bastard! Leave that alone!"

20 "Ring the bell before Jackson kills him a coon!" someone boomed in the sudden silence. And I heard the bell clang and the sound of the feet scuffling forward.

A glove smacked against my head. I pivoted, striking out stiffly as someone went past, and felt the jar ripple along the length of my arm to my shoulder. Then it seemed as though all nine of the boys had turned upon me at once. Blows pounded me from all sides while I struck out as best I could. So many blows landed upon me that I wondered if I were not the only blindfolded fighter in the ring, or if the man called Jackson hadn't succeeded in getting me after all.

Blindfolded, I could no longer control my motions. I had no dignity. I stumbled about like a baby or a drunken man. The smoke had become thicker and with each new blow it seemed to sear and further restrict my lungs. My saliva became like hot bitter glue. A glove connected with my head, filling my mouth with warm blood. It was everywhere. I could not tell if the moisture I felt upon my body was sweat or blood. A blow landed hard against the nape of my neck. I felt myself going over, my head hitting the floor. Streaks of blue light filled the black world behind the blindfold. I lay prone, pretending that I was knocked out, but felt myself seized by hands and yanked to my feet. "Get going, black boy! Mix it up!" My arms were like lead, my head smarting from blows. I managed to feel my way to the ropes and held on, trying to catch my breath. A glove landed in my mid-section and I went over again, feeling as though the smoke had become a knife jabbed into my guts. Pushed this way and that by the legs milling around me, I finally pulled erect and discovered that I could see the black, sweat-washed forms weaving in the smoky-blue atmosphere like drunken dancers weaving to the rapid drum-like thuds of blows.

Everyone fought hysterically. It was complete anarchy. Everybody fought everybody else. No group fought together for long. Two, three, four, fought one, then turned to fight each other, were themselves attacked. Blows landed below the belt and in the kidney, with the gloves open as well as closed, and with my eye partly opened now there was not so much terror. I moved carefully, avoiding blows, although not too many to attract attention, fighting from group to group. The boys groped about like blind, cautious crabs crouching to protect their mid-sections, their heads pulled in short against their shoulders, their arms stretched nervously before them, with their fists testing the smoke-filled air like the knobbed feelers of hypersensitive snails. In one corner I glimpsed a boy violently punching the air and heard him scream in pain as he smashed his hand against a ring post. For a second I saw him bent over holding his hand, then going down as a blow caught his unprotected head. I played one group against the other, slipping and throwing a punch then stepping out of range while pushing the others into the melee to take the blows blindly aimed at me. The smoke was agonizing and there were no rounds, no bells at three minute intervals to relieve our exhaustion. The room spun round me, a swirl of lights, smoke, sweating bodies surrounded by tense white faces. I bled from both nose and mouth, the blood spattering upon my chest.

The men kept yelling, "Slug him, black boy! Knock his guts out!"

"Uppercut him! Kill him! Kill that big boy!"

Taking a fake fall, I saw a boy going down heavily beside me as though we were felled by a single blow, saw a sneaker-clad foot shoot into his groin as the two who had knocked him down stumbled upon him. I rolled out of range, feeling a twinge of nausea.

The harder we fought the more threatening the men became. And yet, I had begun to worry about my speech again. How would it go? Would they recognize my ability? What would they give me?

I was fighting automatically and suddenly I noticed that one after another of the boys was leaving the ring. I was surprised, filled with panic, as though I had been left alone with an unknown danger. Then I understood. The boys had arranged it among themselves. It was the custom for the two men left in the ring to slug it out for the winner's prize. I discovered this too late. When the bell sounded two men in tuxedoes leaped into the ring and removed the blindfold. I found myself facing Tatlock, the biggest of the gang. I felt sick at my stomach. Hardly had the bell stopped ringing in my ears than it clanged again and I saw him moving swiftly toward me. Thinking of nothing else to do I hit him smash on the nose. He kept coming, bringing the rank sharp violence of stale sweat. His face was a black bank of a face, only his eyes alive—with hate of me and aglow with a feverish terror from what had happened to us all. I became anxious. I wanted to deliver my speech and he came at me as though he meant to beat it out of me. I smashed him again and again, taking his blows as they came. Then on a sudden impulse I struck him lightly as we clinched, I whispered, "Fake like I knocked you out, you can have the prize."

"I'll break your behind," he whispered hoarsely.

"For *them?*"

"For *me,* sonofabitch!"

They were yelling for us to break it up and Tatlock spun me half around with a blow, and as a joggled camera sweeps in a reeling scene, I saw the howling red faces crouching tense beneath the cloud of blue-gray smoke. For a moment the world wavered, unraveled, flowed, then my head cleared and Tatlock bounced before me. That fluttering shadow before my eyes was his jabbing left hand. Then falling forward, my head against his damp shoulder, I whispered,

"I'll make it five dollars more."

"Go to hell!"

But his muscles relaxed a trifle beneath my pressure and I breathed, "Seven!"

"Give it to your ma," he said, ripping me beneath the heart.

And while I still held him I butted him and moved away. I felt myself bombarded with punches. I fought back with hopeless desperation. I wanted to deliver my speech more than anything else in the world, because I felt that only these men could judge truly my ability, and now this stupid clown was ruining my chances. I began fighting carefully now, moving in to punch him and out again with my greater speed. A lucky blow to his chin and I had him going too—until I heard a loud voice yell, "I got my money on the big boy."

Hearing this, I almost dropped my guard. I was confused: Should I try to win against the voice out there? Would not this go against my speech, and was not this a moment for humility, for nonresistance? A blow to my head as I danced about sent my right eye popping like a jack-in-the-box and settled my dilemma. The room went red as I fell. It was a dream fall, my body languid and fastidious as to where to land, until the floor became impatient and smashed up to meet me. A moment later I came to. An hypnotic voice said FIVE emphatically. And I lay there, hazily watching a dark red spot of my own blood shaping itself into a butterfly, glistening and soaking into the soiled gray world of the canvas.

When the voice drawled TEN I was lifted up and dragged to a chair. I sat dazed. My eye pained and swelled with each throb of my pounding heart and I wondered if now I would be allowed to speak. I was wringing wet, my mouth still bleeding. We were grouped along the wall now. The other boys ignored me as they congratulated Tatlock and speculated as to how much they would be paid. One boy whimpered over his smashed hand.

Looking up front, I saw attendants in white jackets rolling the portable ring away and placing a small square rug in the vacant space surrounded by chairs. Perhaps, I thought, I will stand on the rug to deliver my speech.

40 Then the M.C. called to us, "Come on up here boys and get your money."

We ran forward to where the men laughed and talked in their chairs, waiting. Everyone seemed friendly now.

"There it is on the rug," the man said. I saw the rug covered with coins of all dimensions and a few crumpled bills. But what excited me, scattered here and there, were the gold pieces.

"Boys, it's all yours," the man said. "You get all you grab."

"That's right, Sambo," a blond man said, winking at me confidentially.

45 I trembled with excitement, forgetting my pain. I would get the gold and the bills, I thought. I would use both hands. I would throw my body against the boys nearest me to block them from the gold.

"Get down around the rug now," the man commanded, "and don't anyone touch it until I give the signal."

"This ought to be good," I heard.

As told, we got around the square rug on our knees. Slowly the man raised his freckled hand as we followed it upward with our eyes.

I heard, "These niggers look like they're about to pray!"

50 Then, "Ready," the man said. "Go!"

I lunged for a yellow coin lying on the blue design of the carpet, touching it and sending a surprised shriek to join those rising around me. I tried frantically to remove my hand but could not let go. A hot, violent force tore through my body, shaking me like a wet rat. The rug was electrified. The hair bristled up on my head as I shook myself free. My muscles jumped, my nerves jangled, writhed. But I saw that this was not stopping the other boys. Laughing in fear and embarrassment, some were holding back and scooping up the coins knocked off by the painful contortions of the others. The men roared above us as we struggled.

"Pick it up, goddamnit, pick it up!" someone called like a bass-voiced parrot. "Go on, get it!"

I crawled rapidly around the floor, picking up the coins, trying to avoid the coppers and to get greenbacks and the gold. Ignoring the shock by laughing, as I brushed the coins off quickly, I discovered that I could contain the electricity—a contradiction, but it works. Then the men began to push us onto the rug. Laughing embarrassedly, we struggled out of their hands and kept after the coins. We were all wet and slippery and hard to hold. Suddenly I saw a boy lifted into the air, glistening with sweat like a circus seal, and dropped, his wet back landing flush upon the charged rug, heard him yell and saw him literally dance upon his back, his elbows beating a frenzied tatoo upon the floor, his muscles twitching like the flesh of a horse stung by many flies. When he finally rolled off, his face was gray and no one stopped him when he ran from the floor amid booming laughter.

"Get the money," the M.C. called. "That's good hard American cash!"

55 And we snatched and grabbed, snatched and grabbed. I was careful not to come too close to the rug now, and when I felt the hot whiskey breath descend upon me like a cloud of foul air I reached out and grabbed the leg of a chair. It was occupied and I held on desperately.

"Leggo, nigger! Leggo!"

The huge face wavered down to mine as he tried to push me free. But my body was slippery and he was too drunk. It was Mr. Colcord, who owned a chain of movie houses and "entertainment palaces." Each time he grabbed me I slipped out of his hands. It became a real struggle. I feared the rug more than I did the drunk, so I held on, surprising myself for a moment by trying to topple *him* upon the rug. It was such an enormous idea that I found myself actually carrying it out. I tried not to be obvious, yet when I grabbed his leg, trying to tumble him out of the chair, he raised up roaring with laughter, and, looking at me with soberness dead in the eye, kicked me viciously in the chest. The chair leg flew out of my hand. I felt myself going and rolled. It was as though I had rolled through a bed of hot coals. It seemed a whole century would pass before I would roll free, a century in which I was seared through the deepest levels of my body to the fearful breath within me and the breath seared and heated to the point of explosion. It'll all be over in a flash, I thought as I rolled clear. It'll all be over in a flash.

But not yet, the men on the other side were waiting, red faces swollen as though from apoplexy as they bent forward in their chairs. Seeing their fingers coming toward me I rolled away as a fumbled football rolls off the receiver's fingertips, back into the coals. That time I luckily sent the rug sliding out of place and heard the coins ringing against the floor and the boys scuffling to pick them up and the M.C. calling, "All right, boys, that's all. Go get dressed and get your money."

I was limp as a dish rag. My back felt as though it had been beaten with wires.

When we had dressed the M.C. came in and gave us each five dollars, except Tatlock, who got ten for being the last in the ring. Then he told us to leave. I was not to get a chance to deliver my speech, I thought. I was going out into the dim alley in despair when I was stopped and told to go back. I returned to the ballroom, where the men were pushing back their chairs and gathering in groups to talk.

The M.C. knocked on a table for quiet. "Gentlemen," he said, "we almost forgot an important part of the program. A most serious part, gentlemen. This boy was brought here to deliver a speech which he made at his graduation yesterday. . . ."

"Bravo!"

"I'm told that he is the smartest boy we've got out there in Greenwood. I'm told that he knows more big words than a pocket-sized dictionary."

Much applause and laughter.

"So now, gentlemen, I want you to give him your attention."

There was still laughter as I faced them, my mouth dry, my eye throbbing. I began slowly, but evidently my throat was tense, because they began shouting, "Louder! Louder!"

"We of the younger generation extol the wisdom of that great leader and educator," I shouted, "who first spoke these flaming words of wisdom: 'A ship lost at sea for many days suddenly sighted a friendly vessel. From the mast of the unfortunate vessel was seen a signal: "Water, water; we die of thirst!" The answer from the friendly vessel came back: "Cast down your bucket where you are." The captain of the distressed vessel, at last heeding the injunction, cast down his bucket, and it came up full of fresh sparkling water from the mouth of the Amazon River.' And like him I say, and in his words, 'To those of my race who depend upon bettering their condition in a foreign land, or who underestimate the importance of cultivating friendly relations with the Southern white man, who is his next-door neighbor, I would say: "Cast down your bucket where you are"—cast it down in making friends in every manly way of the people of all races by whom we are surrounded. . . ."

I spoke automatically and with such fervor that I did not realize that the men were still talking and laughing until my dry mouth, filling up with blood from the cut, almost strangled me. I coughed, wanting to stop and go to one of the tall brass, sand-filled spittoons to relieve myself, but a few of the men, especially the superintendent, were listening and I was afraid. So I gulped it down, blood, saliva and all, and continued. (What powers of endurance I had during those days! What enthusiasm! What a belief in the rightness of things!) I spoke even louder in spite of the pain. But still they talked and still they laughed, as though deaf with cotton in dirty ears. So I spoke with greater emotional emphasis. I closed my ears and swallowed blood until I was nauseated. The speech seemed a hundred times as long as before, but I could not leave out a single word. All had to be said, each memorized nuance considered, rendered. Nor was that all. Whenever I uttered a word of three or more syllables a group of voices would yell for me to repeat it. I used the phrase "social responsibility" and they yelled:

"What's the word you say, boy?"

"Social responsibility," I said.

"What?"

"Social . . ."

"Louder."

". . . responsibility."

"More!"

"Respon—"

"Repeat!"

"—sibility."

The room filled with the uproar of laughter until, no doubt, distracted by having to gulp down my blood, I made a mistake and yelled a phrase I had often seen denounced in newspaper editorials, heard debated in private.

"Social . . ."

"What?" they yelled.

". . . equality—"

The laughter hung smokelike in the sudden stillness. I opened my eyes, puzzled. Sounds of displeasure filled the room. The M.C. rushed forward. They shouted hostile phrases at me. But I did not understand.

A small dry mustached man in the front row blared out, "Say that slowly, son!"

"What sir?"

"What you just said!"

"Social responsibility, sir," I said.

"You weren't being smart, were you, boy?" he said, not unkindly.

"No, sir!"

"You sure that about 'equality' was a mistake?"

"Oh, yes, sir," I said. "I was swallowing blood."

"Well, you had better speak more slowly so we can understand. We mean to do right by you, but you've got to know your place at all times. All right, now, go on with your speech."

I was afraid. I wanted to leave but I wanted also to speak and I was afraid they'd snatch me down.

"Thank you, sir," I said, beginning where I had left off, and having them ignore me as before.

95 Yet when I finished there was a thunderous applause. I was surprised to see the superintendent come forth with a package wrapped in white tissue paper, and gesturing for quiet, address the men.

"Gentlemen, you see that I did not overpraise this boy. He makes a good speech and some day he'll lead his people in the proper paths. And I don't have to tell you that that is important in these days and times. This is a good, smart boy, and so to encourage him in the right direction, in the name of the Board of Education I wish to present him a prize in the form of this . . ."

He paused, removing the tissue paper and revealing a gleaming calfskin brief case.

". . . in the form of this first-class article from Shad Whitmore's shop."

"Boy," he said, addressing me, "take this prize and keep it well. Consider it a badge of office. Prize it. Keep developing as you are and some day it will be filled with important papers that will help shape the destiny of your people."

100 I was so moved that I could hardly express my thanks. A rope of bloody saliva forming a shape like an undiscovered continent drooled upon the leather and I wiped it quickly away. I felt an importance that I had never dreamed.

"Open it and see what's inside," I was told.

My fingers a-tremble, I complied, smelling the fresh leather and finding an official-looking document inside. It was a scholarship to the state college for Negroes. My eyes filled with tears and I ran awkwardly off the floor.

## SHIRLEY JACKSON

*Shirley Jackson (1919–65) was born in San Francisco and went to college in New York, first at the University of Rochester and then at Syracuse University. Although one of her stories was published in The* Best American Short Stories 1944, *she did not receive national attention until 1948 when* The New Yorker *published "The Lottery." The magazine later reported that none of its earlier publications had produced so strong a response.*

*In 1962 she experienced a breakdown and was unable to write, but she recovered and worked on a new novel. Before completing the book, however, she died of cardiac arrest at the age of forty-six. The book was published posthumously under the title* Come Along With Me.

*Two of her books,* Life Among the Savages *(1953) and* Raising Demons *(1957), are engaging self-portraits of a harried mother in a house full of children. But what seems amusing also has its dark underside. After her breakdown Jackson said, "I think all my books laid end to end would be one long documentary of anxiety."*

*Her husband, Stanley Edgar Hyman (her college classmate and later a professor of English), said of Jackson, "If she uses the resources of supernatural terror, it was to provide metaphors for the all-too-real terrors of the natural."*

## *The Lottery*

The morning of June 27th was clear and sunny, with the fresh warmth of a full-summer day; the flowers were blossoming profusely and the grass was richly green. The people of the village began to gather in the square, between the post office and the bank, around ten o'clock; in some towns there were so many people that the lottery took two days and had to be started on June 26th, but in this village, where there were only about three hundred people, the whole lottery took less than two hours, so it could begin at ten o'clock in the morning and still be through in time to allow the villagers to get home for noon dinner.

The children assembled first, of course. School was recently over for the summer, and the feeling of liberty sat uneasily on most of them; they tended to gather together quietly for a while before they broke into boisterous play, and their talk was still of the classroom and the teacher, of books and reprimands. Bobby Martin had already stuffed his pockets full of stones, and the other boys soon followed his example, selecting the smoothest and roundest stones; Bobby and Harry Jones and Dickie Delacroix—the villagers pronounced this name "Dellacroy"—eventually made a great pile of stones in one corner of the square and guarded it against the raids of the other boys. The girls stood aside, talking among themselves, looking over their shoulders at the boys, and the very small children rolled in the dust or clung to the hands of their older brothers or sisters.

Soon the men began to gather, surveying their own children, speaking of planting and rain, tractors and taxes. They stood together, away from the pile of stones in the corner, and their jokes were quiet and they smiled rather than laughed. The women, wearing faded house dresses and sweaters, came shortly after their menfolk. They greeted one another and exchanged bits of gossip as they went to join their husbands. Soon the women, standing by their husbands, began to call to their children, and the children came reluctantly, having to be called four or five times. Bobby Martin ducked under his mother's grasping hand and ran, laughing, back to the pile of stones. His father spoke up sharply, and Bobby came quickly and took his place between his father and his oldest brother.

The lottery was conducted—as were the square dances, the teenage club, the Halloween program—by Mr. Summers, who had time and energy to devote to civic activities. He was a round-faced, jovial man and he ran the coal business, and people were sorry for him, because he had no children and his wife was a scold. When he arrived in the square, carrying the black wooden box, there was a murmur of conversation among the villagers and he waved and called, "Little late today, folks." The postmaster, Mr. Graves, followed him, carrying a three-legged stool, and the stool was put in the center of the square and Mr. Summers set the black box down on it. The villagers kept their distance, leaving a space between themselves and the stool, and when Mr. Summers said, "Some of you fellows want to give me a hand?" there was a hesitation before two men, Mr. Martin and his oldest son, Baxter, came forward to hold the box steady on the stool while Mr. Summers stirred up the papers inside it.

5 The original paraphernalia for the lottery had been lost long ago, and the black box now resting on the stool had been put into use even before Old Man Warner, the oldest man in town, was born. Mr. Summers spoke frequently to the villagers about making a new box, but no one liked to upset even as much tradition as was represented by the black box. There was a story that the present box had been made with some pieces of the box that had preceded it, the one that had been constructed when the first people settled down to make a village here. Every year, after the lottery, Mr. Summers began talking again about a new box, but every year the subject was allowed to fade off without anything's being done. The black box grew shabbier each year; by now it was no longer completely black but splintered badly along one side to show the original wood color, and in some places faded or stained.

Mr. Martin and his oldest son, Baxter, held the black box securely on the stool until Mr. Summers had stirred the papers thoroughly with his hand. Because so much of the ritual had been forgotten or discarded, Mr. Summers had been successful in having slips of paper substituted for the chips of wood that had been used for generations. Chips of wood, Mr. Summers had argued, had been all very well when the village was tiny, but now that the population was more than three hundred and likely to keep on growing, it was necessary to use something that would fit more easily into the black box. The night before the lottery, Mr. Summers and Mr. Graves made up the slips of paper and put them in the box, and it was then taken to the safe of Mr. Summers's coal company and locked up until Mr. Summers was ready to take it to the square next morning. The rest of the year, the box was put away, sometimes one place, sometimes another; it had spent one year in Mr. Graves's barn and another year underfoot in the post office, and sometimes it was set on a shelf in the Martin grocery and left there.

There was a great deal of fussing to be done before Mr. Summers declared the lottery open. There were lists to make up—of heads of families, heads of households in each family, members of each household in each family. There was the proper swearing-in of Mr. Summers by the postmaster, as the official of the lottery; at one time, some people remembered, there had been a recital of some sort, performed by the official of the lottery, a perfunctory, tuneless chant that had been rattled off duly each year; some people believed that the official of the lottery used to stand just so when he said or sang it, others believed that he was supposed to walk among the people, but years and years ago this part of the ritual had been allowed to lapse. There had been, also, a ritual salute, which the official of the lottery had had to use in addressing each person who came up to draw from the box, but this also had changed with time, until now it was felt necessary only for the official to speak to each person approaching. Mr. Summers was very good at all this; in his clean white shirt and blue jeans, with one hand resting carelessly on the black box, he seemed very proper and important as he talked interminably to Mr. Graves and the Martins.

Just as Mr. Summers finally left off talking and turned to the assembled villagers, Mrs. Hutchinson came hurriedly along the path to the square, her sweater thrown over her shoulders, and slid into place in the back of the crowd. "Clean forgot what day it was," she said to Mrs. Delacroix, who stood next to her, and they both laughed softly. "Thought my old man was out back stacking wood," Mrs. Hutchinson went on, "and then I looked out the window and the kids were gone, and then I remembered it was the twenty-seventh and came a-running." She dried her hands on her apron, and Mrs. Delacroix said, "You're in time, though. They're still talking away up there."

Mrs. Hutchinson craned her neck to see through the crowd and found her husband and children standing near the front. She tapped Mrs. Delacroix on the arm as a farewell and began to make her way through the crowd. The people separated good humoredly to let her through; two or three people said, in voices just loud enough to be heard across the crowd, "Here comes your Missus, Hutchinson," and "Bill, she made it after all." Mrs. Hutchinson reached her husband, and Mr. Summers, who had been waiting, said cheerfully, "Thought we were going to have to get on without you, Tessie." Mrs. Hutchinson said, grinning, "Wouldn't have me leave m'dishes in the sink, now would you, Joe?," and soft laughter ran through the crowd as the people stirred back into position after Mrs. Hutchinson's arrival.

10 "Well, now," Mr. Summers said soberly, "guess we better get started, get this over with, so's we can go back to work. Anybody ain't here?"

"Dunbar," several people said. "Dunbar, Dunbar."

Mr. Summers consulted his list. "Clyde Dunbar," he said. "That's right. He's broke his leg, hasn't he? Who's drawing for him?"

"Me, I guess," a woman said, and Mr. Summers turned to look at her. "Wife draws for her husband," Mr. Summers said. "Don't you have a grown boy to do it for you, Janey?" Although Mr. Summers and everyone else in the village knew the answer perfectly well, it was the business of the official of the lottery to ask such questions formally. Mr. Summers waited with an expression of polite interest while Mrs. Dunbar answered.

"Horace's not but sixteen yet," Mrs. Dunbar said regretfully. "Guess I gotta fill in for the old man this year."

15 "Right," Mr. Summers said. He made a note on the list he was holding. Then he asked, "Watson boy drawing this year?"

A tall boy in the crowd raised his hand. "Here," he said. "I'm drawing for m'mother and me." He blinked his eyes nervously and ducked his head as several voices in the crowd said things like "Good fellow, Jack," and "Glad to see your mother's got a man to do it."

"Well," Mr. Summers said, "guess that's everyone. Old Man Warner make it?"

"Here," a voice said, and Mr. Summers nodded.

A sudden hush fell on the crowd as Mr. Summers cleared his throat and looked at the list. "All ready?" he called. "Now, I'll read the names—heads of families first—and the men come up and take a paper out of the box.

Keep the paper folded in your hand without looking at it until everyone has had a turn. Everything clear?"

20 The people had done it so many times that they only half listened to the directions; most of them were quiet, wetting their lips, not looking around. Then Mr. Summers raised one hand high and said, "Adams." A man disengaged himself from the crowd and came forward. "Hi, Steve," Mr. Summers said, and Mr. Adams said, "Hi, Joe." They grinned at one another humorlessly and nervously. Then Mr. Adams reached into the black box and took out a folded paper. He held it firmly by one corner as he turned and went hastily back to his place in the crowd, where he stood a little apart from his family, not looking down at his hand.

"Allen," Mr. Summers said. "Anderson. . . . Bentham."

"Seems like there's no time at all between lotteries any more," Mrs. Delacroix said to Mrs. Graves in the back row. "Seems like we got through with the last one only last week."

"Time sure goes fast," Mrs. Graves said.

"Clark. . . . Delacroix."

25 "There goes my old man," Mrs. Delacroix said. She held her breath while her husband went forward.

"Dunbar," Mr. Summers said, and Mrs. Dunbar went steadily to the box while one of the women said, "Go on, Janey," and another said, "There she goes."

"We're next," Mrs. Graves said. She watched while Mr. Graves came around from the side of the box, greeted Mr. Summers gravely, and selected a slip of paper from the box. By now, all through the crowd there were men holding the small folded papers in their large hands, turning them over and over nervously. Mrs. Dunbar and her two sons stood together. Mrs. Dunbar holding the slip of paper.

"Harburt. . . . Hutchinson."

"Get up there, Bill," Mrs. Hutchinson said, and the people near her laughed.

30 "Jones."

"They do say," Mr. Adams said to Old Man Warner, who stood next to him, "that over in the north village they're talking of giving up the lottery."

Old Man Warner snorted. "Pack of crazy fools," he said. "Listening to the young folks, nothing's good enough for *them.* Next thing you know, they'll be wanting to go back to living in caves, nobody work any more, live *that* way for a while. Used to be a saying about 'Lottery in June, corn be heavy soon.' First thing you know, we'd all be eating stewed chickweed and acorns. There's *always* been a lottery," he added petulantly. "Bad enough to see young Joe Summers up there joking with everybody."

"Some places have already quit lotteries," Mrs. Adams said.

"Nothing but trouble in *that,*" Old Man Warner said stoutly. "Pack of young fools."

35 "Martin." And Bobby Martin watched his father go forward. "Overdyke. . . . Percy."

"I wish they'd hurry," Mrs. Dunbar said to her older son. "I wish they'd hurry."

"They're almost through," her son said.

"You get ready to run tell Dad," Mrs. Dunbar said.

Mr. Summers called his own name and then stepped forward precisely and selected a slip from the box. Then he called, "Warner."

40 "Seventy-seventh year I been in the lottery," Old Man Warner said as he went through the crowd. "Seventy-seventh time."

"Watson." The tall boy came awkwardly through the crowd. Someone said, "Don't be nervous, Jack," and Mr. Summers said, "Take your time, son."

"Zanini."

After that, there was a long pause, a breathless pause, until Mr. Summers, holding his slip of paper in the air, said, "All right, fellows." For a minute, no one moved, and then all the slips of paper were opened. Suddenly, all women began to speak at once, saying, "Who is it?" "Who's got it?" "Is it the Dunbars?" "Is it the Watsons?" Then the voices began to say, "It's Hutchinson. It's Bill." "Bill Hutchinson's got it."

"Go tell your father," Mrs. Dunbar said to her older son.

45 People began to look around to see the Hutchinsons. Bill Hutchinson was standing quiet, staring down at the paper in his hand. Suddenly, Tessie Hutchinson shouted to Mr. Summers, "You didn't give him time enough to take any paper he wanted. I saw you. It wasn't fair!"

"Be a good sport, Tessie," Mrs. Delacroix called, and Mrs. Graves said, "All of us took the same chance."

"Shut up, Tessie," Bill Hutchinson said.

"Well, everyone," Mr. Summers said, "that was done pretty fast, and now we've got to be hurrying a little more to get done in time." He consulted his next list. "Bill," he said, "you draw for the Hutchinson family. You got any other households in the Hutchinsons?"

"There's Don and Eva," Mrs. Hutchinson yelled. "Make *them* take their chance!"

50 "Daughters draw with their husbands' families, Tessie," Mr. Summers said gently. "You know that as well as anyone else."

"It wasn't fair," Tessie said.

"I guess not, Joe," Bill Hutchinson said regretfully. "My daughter draws with her husbands's family, that's only fair. And I've got no other family except the kids."

"Then, as far as drawing for families is concerned, it's you," Mr. Summers said in explanation, "and as far as drawing for households is concerned, that's you, too. Right?"

"Right," Bill Hutchinson said.

55 "How many kids, Bill?" Mr. Summers asked formally.

"Three," Bill Hutchinson said. "There's Bill, Jr., and Nancy, and little Dave. And Tessie and me."

"All right, then," Mr. Summers said. "Harry, you got their tickets back?"

Mr. Graves nodded and held up the slips of paper. "Put them in the box, then," Mr. Summers directed. "Take Bill's and put it in."

"I think we ought to start over," Mrs. Hutchinson said, as quietly as she could. "I tell you it wasn't *fair*. You didn't give him time enough to choose. *Every*body saw that."

60 Mr. Graves had selected the five slips and put them in the box, and he

dropped all the papers but those onto the ground, where the breeze caught them and lifted them off.

"Listen, everybody," Mrs. Hutchinson was saying to the people around her.

"Ready, Bill?" Mr. Summers asked, and Bill Hutchinson, with one quick glance around at his wife and children, nodded.

"Remember," Mr. Summers said, "take the slips and keep them folded until each person has taken one. Harry, you help little Dave." Mr. Graves took the hand of the little boy, who came willingly with him up to the box. "Take a paper out of the box, Davy," Mr. Summers said. Davy put his hand into the box and laughed. "Take just *one* paper," Mr. Summers said. "Harry, you hold it for him." Mr. Graves took the child's hand and removed the folded paper from the tight fist and held it while little Dave stood next to him and looked up at him wonderingly.

"Nancy next," Mr. Summers said. Nancy was twelve, and her school friends breathed heavily as she went forward, switching her skirt, and took a slip daintily from the box. "Bill, Jr.," Mr. Summers said, and Billy, his face red and his feet over-large, nearly knocked the box over as he got a paper out. "Tessie," Mr. Summers said. She hesitated for a minute, looking around defiantly, and then set her lips and went up to the box. She snatched a paper out and held it behind her.

65 "Bill," Mr. Summers said, and Bill Hutchinson reached into the box and felt around, bringing his hand out at last with the slip of paper in it.

The crowd was quiet. A girl whispered, "I hope it's not Nancy," and the sound of the whisper reached the edges of the crowd.

"It's not the way it used to be," Old Man Warner said clearly. "People ain't the way they used to be."

"All right," Mr. Summers said. "Open the papers. Harry, you open little Dave's."

Mr. Graves opened the slip of paper and there was a general sigh through the crowd as he held it up and everyone could see that it was blank. Nancy and Bill, Jr., opened theirs at the same time, and both beamed and laughed, turning around to the crowd and holding their slips of paper above their heads.

70 "Tessie," Mr. Summers said. There was a pause, and then Mr. Summers looked at Bill Hutchinson, and Bill unfolded his paper and showed it. It was blank.

"It's Tessie," Mr. Summers said, and his voice was hushed. "Show us her paper, Bill."

Bill Hutchinson went over to his wife and forced the slip of paper out of her hand. It had a black spot on it, the black spot Mr. Summers had made the night before with the heavy pencil in the coal-company office. Bill Hutchinson held it up, and there was a stir in the crowd.

"All right, folks," Mr. Summers said, "let's finish quickly."

Although the villagers had forgotten the ritual and lost the original black box, they still remembered to use stones. The pile of stones the boys had made earlier was ready; there were stones on the ground with the blowing scraps of paper that had come out of the box. Mrs. Delacroix selected a stone so large she had to pick it up with both hands and turned to Mrs. Dunbar. "Come on," she said. "Hurry up."

75 Mrs. Dunbar had small stones in both hands, and she said, gasping for breath, "I can't run at all. You'll have to go ahead and I'll catch up with you."

The children had stones already, and someone gave little Davy Hutchinson a few pebbles.

Tessie Hutchinson was in the center of a cleared space by now, and she held her hands out desperately as the villagers moved in on her. "It isn't fair," she said. A stone hit her on the side of the head.

Old Man Warner was saying, "Come on, come on, everyone." Steve Adams was in the front of the crowd of villagers, with Mrs. Graves beside him.

"It isn't fair, it isn't right," Mrs. Hutchinson screamed, and then they were upon her.

[*1948*]

## GRACE PALEY

*Born in 1922 in New York City, Grace Paley attended Hunter College and New York University, but left without a degree. (She now teaches at Sarah Lawrence College.) While raising two children she wrote poetry and then, in the 1950s, turned to writing fiction.*

*Paley's chief subject is the life of little people struggling in the Big City. She has said, "How daily life is lived is a mystery to me. You write about what's mysterious to you. What is it like? Why do people do this?" Of the short story she has said, "It can be just telling a little tale, or writing a complicated philosophical story. It can be a song, almost."*

*We reprint another story by Paley on page12.*

# A Conversation with My Father

My father is eighty-six years old and in bed. His heart, that bloody motor, is equally old and will not do certain jobs any more. It still floods his head with brainy light. But it won't let his legs carry the weight of his body around the house. Despite my metaphors, this muscle failure is not due to his old heart, he says, but to a potassium shortage. Sitting on one pillow, leaning on three, he offers last-minute advice and makes a request.

"I would like you to write a simple story just once more," he says, "the kind de Maupassant wrote, or Chekhov, the kind you used to write. Just recognizable people and then write down what happened to them next."

I say, "Yes, why not? That's possible." I want to please him, though I don't remember writing that way. I *would* like to try to tell such a story, if he means the kind that begins: "There was a woman . . ." followed by plot, the absolute line between two points which I've always despised. Not for literary reasons, but because it takes all hope away. Everyone, real or invented, deserves the open destiny of life.

Finally I thought of a story that had been happening for a couple of years right across the street. I wrote it down, then read it aloud. “Pa,” I said, “how about this? Do you mean something like this?”

5 Once in my time there was a woman and she had a son. They lived nicely, in a small apartment in Manhattan. This boy at about fifteen became a junkie, which is not unusual in our neighborhood. In order to maintain her close friendship with him, she became a junkie too. She said it was part of the youth culture, with which she felt very much at home. After a while, for a number of reasons, the boy gave it all up and left the city and his mother in disgust. Hopeless and alone, she grieved. We all visit her.

O.K., Pa, that’s it,” I said, “an unadorned and miserable tale.”

“But that’s not what I mean,” my father said. “You misunderstood me on purpose. You know there’s a lot more to it. You know that. You left everything out. Turgenev[1] wouldn’t do that. Chekhov wouldn’t do that. There are in fact Russian writers you never heard of, you don’t have an inkling of, as good as anyone, who can write a plain ordinary story, who would not leave out what you have left out. I object not to facts but to people sitting in trees talking senselessly, voices from who knows where . . .”

“Forget that one, Pa, what have I left out now? In this one?”

“Her looks, for instance.”

10 ““Oh. Quite handsome, I think. Yes.”

Her hair?”

“Dark, with heavy braids, as though she were a girl or a foreigner.”

“What were her parents like, her stock? That she became such a person. It’s interesting, you know.”

“From out of town. Professional people. The first to be divorced in their county. How’s that? Enough?” I asked.

15 “With you, it’s all a joke,” he said. “What about the boy’s father. Why didn’t you mention him? Who was he? Or was the boy born out of wedlock?”

“Yes,” I said. “He was born out of wedlock.”

“For Godsakes, doesn’t anyone in your stories get married? Doesn’t anyone have the time to run down to City Hall before they jump into bed?”

“No,” I said. “In real life, yes. But in my stories, no.”

“Why do you answer me like that?”

20 “Oh, Pa, this is a simple story about a smart woman who came to N.Y.C. full of interest love trust excitement very up to date, and about her son, what a hard time she had in this world. Married or not, it’s of small consequence.”

“It is of great consequence,” he said.

“O.K.,” I said.

“O.K. O.K. yourself,” he said, “but listen. I believe you that she’s good-looking, but I don’t think she was so smart.”

“That’s true,” I said. “Actually that’s the trouble with stories. People start out fantastic. You think they’re extraordinary, but it turns out as the

[1]**Turgenev** Ivan Sergevich Turgenev (1818–83), Russian novelist whose best-known work, *Fathers and Sons,* deals with the conflict between the generations

work goes along, they're just average with a good education. Sometimes the other way around, the person's a kind of dumb innocent, but he outwits you and you can't even think of an ending good enough."

25 "What do you do then?" he asked. He had been a doctor for a couple of decades and then an artist for a couple of decades and he's still interested in details, craft, technique.

"Well, you just have to let the story lie around till some agreement can be reached between you and the stubborn hero."

"Aren't you talking silly, now?" he asked. "Start again," he said. "It so happens I'm not going out this evening. Tell the story again. See what you can do this time."

"O.K.," I said. "But it's not a five-minute job." Second attempt:

> Once, across the street from us, there was a fine handsome woman, our neighbor. She had a son whom she loved because she'd known him since birth (in helpless chubby infancy, and in the wrestling, hugging ages, seven to ten, as well as earlier and later). This boy, when he fell into the fist of adolescence, became a junkie. He was not a hopeless one. He was in fact hopeful, an ideologue and successful converter. With his busy brilliance, he wrote persuasive articles for his high-school newspaper. Seeking a wider audience, using important connections, he drummed into Lower Manhattan newsstand distribution a periodical called *Oh! Golden Horse!*
>
> 30 In order to keep him from feeling guilty (because guilt is the stony heart of nine tenths of all clinically diagnosed cancers in America today, she said), and because she had always believed in giving bad habits room at home where one could keep an eye on them, she too became a junkie. Her kitchen was famous for a while—a center for intellectual addicts who knew what they were doing. A few felt artistic like Coleridge and others were scientific and revolutionary like Leary.[2] Although she was often high herself, certain good mothering reflexes remained, and she saw to it that there was lots of orange juice around and honey and milk and vitamin pills. However, she never cooked anything but chili, and that no more than once a week. She explained, when we talked to her, seriously, with neighborly concern, that it was her part in the youth culture and she would rather be with the young, it was an honor, than with her own generation.
>
> One week, while nodding through an Antonioni film, this boy was severely jabbed by the elbow of a stern and proselytizing girl, sitting beside him. She offered immediate apricots and nuts for his sugar level, spoke to him sharply, and took him home.
>
> She had heard of him and his work and she herself published, edited, and wrote a competitive journal called *Man Does Live By Bread Alone.* In the organic heat of her continuous presence he could not help but become interested once more in his muscles,

[2]**Coleridge . . . Leary** Samuel Taylor Coleridge (1772–1834), English poet, wrote "Kubla Khan" (see page 914) after taking opium; Timothy Leary (1920–96) was an American psychologist known for his use of psychedelic drugs

his arteries, and nerve connections. In fact he began to love them, treasure them, praise them with funny little songs in *Man Does Live* . . .

the fingers of my flesh transcend
my transcendental soul
the tightness in my shoulders end
my teeth have made me whole

To the mouth of his head (that glory of will and determination) he brought hard apples, nuts, wheat germ, and soybean oil. He said to his old friends, From now on, I guess I'll keep my wits about me. I'm going on the natch. He said he was about to begin a spiritual deep-breathing journey. How about you too, Mom? he asked kindly.

His conversion was so radiant, splendid, that neighborhood kids his age began to say that he had never been a real addict at all, only a journalist along for the smell of the story. The mother tried several times to give up what had become without her son and his friends a lonely habit. This effort only brought it to supportable levels. The boy and his girl took their electronic mimeograph and moved to the bushy edge of another borough. They were very strict. They said they would not see her again until she had been off drugs for sixty days.

At home alone in the evening, weeping, the mother read and reread the seven issues of *Oh! Golden Horse!* They seemed to her as truthful as ever. We often crossed the street to visit and console. But if we mentioned any of our children who were at college or in the hospital or dropouts at home, she would cry out, My baby! My baby! and burst into terrible, face-scarring, time-consuming tears. The End.

First my father was silent, then he said, "Number One: You have a nice sense of humor. Number Two: I see you can't tell a plain story. So don't waste time." Then he said sadly, "Number Three: I suppose that means she was alone, she was left like that, his mother. Alone. Probably sick?"

I said, "Yes."

"Poor woman. Poor girl, to be born in a time of fools, to live among fools. The end. The end. You were right to put that down. The end."

I didn't want to argue, but I had to say, "Well, it is not necessarily the end, Pa."

"Yes," he said, "what a tragedy. The end of a person."

"No, Pa," I begged him. "It doesn't have to be. She's only about forty. She could be a hundred different things in this world as time goes on. A teacher or a social worker. An ex-junkie! Sometimes it's better than having a master's in education."

"Jokes," he said. "As a writer that's your main trouble. You don't want to recognize it. Tragedy! Plain tragedy! Historical tragedy! No hope. The end."

"Oh, Pa," I said. "She could change."

"In your own life, too, you have to look it in the face." He took a couple of nitroglycerin. "Turn to five," he said, pointing to the dial on the oxygen tank. He inserted the tubes into his nostrils and breathed deep. He closed his eyes and said, "No."

45 I had promised the family to always let him have the last word when arguing, but in this case I had a different responsibility. That woman lives across the street. She's my knowledge and my invention. I'm sorry for her. I'm not going to leave her there in that house crying. (Actually neither would Life, which unlike me has no pity.)

Therefore: She did change. Of course her son never came home again. But right now, she's the receptionist in a storefront community clinic in the East Village. Most of the customers are young people, some old friends. The head doctor said to her, "If we only had three people in this clinic with your experiences . . ."

"The doctor said that?" My father took the oxygen tubes out of his nostrils and said, "Jokes. Jokes again."

"No, Pa, it could really happen that way, it's a funny world nowadays."

"No," he said. "Truth first. She will slide back. A person must have character. She does not."

50 "No, Pa," I said. "That's it. She's got a job. Forget it. She's in that storefront working."

"How long will it be?" he asked. "Tragedy! You too. When will you look it in the face?"

[*1974*]

## GABRIEL GARCÍA MÁRQUEZ

*Gabriel García Márquez (b. 1928) was born in Aracataca, a small village in Colombia. After being educated in Bogota, where he studied journalism and law, he worked as a journalist in Latin America, Europe, and the United States. He began writing fiction when he was in Paris, and at twenty-seven he published his first novel,* La hojarasca (Leaf Storm, *1955). During most of the 1960s he lived in Mexico, where he wrote film scripts and the novel that made him famous:* Cien años de soledad *(1967, translated in 1970 as* A Hundred Years of Solitude*). In 1982 Márquez was awarded the Nobel Prize in Literature.*

*In addition to writing stories and novels—often set in Macondo, a town modeled on Aracataca—Márquez has written screenplays. A socialist, he now lives in Mexico because his presence is not welcome in Colombia.*

# *A Very Old Man with Enormous Wings: A Tale for Children*

*Translated by Gregory Rabassa*

On the third day of rain they had killed so many crabs inside the house that Pelayo had to cross his drenched courtyard and throw them into the sea, because the newborn child had a temperature all night and they thought it was due to the stench. The world had been sad since Tuesday. Sea and sky were a single ash-gray thing and the sands of the beach, which on March nights glimmered like powdered light, had become a stew of mud and rotten shellfish. The light was so weak at noon that when Pelayo was coming back to the house after throwing away the crabs, it was hard for him to see what it was that was moving and groaning in the rear of the courtyard. He had to go very close to see that it was an old man, a very old man, lying face down in the mud, who, in spite of his tremendous efforts, couldn't get up, impeded by his enormous wings.

Frightened by that nightmare, Pelayo ran to get Elisenda, his wife, who was putting compresses on the sick child, and he took her to the rear of the courtyard. They both looked at the fallen body with mute stupor. He was dressed like a ragpicker. There were only a few faded hairs left on his bald skull and very few teeth in his mouth, and his pitiful condition of a drenched great-grandfather had taken away any sense of grandeur he might have had. His huge buzzard wings, dirty and half-plucked, were forever entangled in the mud. They looked at him so long and so closely that Pelayo and Elisenda very soon overcame their surprise and in the end found him familiar. Then they dared speak to him, and he answered in an incomprehensible dialect with a strong sailor's voice. That was how they skipped over the inconvenience of the wings and quite intelligently concluded that he was a lonely castaway from some foreign ship wrecked by the storm. And yet, they called in a neighbor woman who knew everything about life and death to see him, and all she needed was one look to show them their mistake.

"He's an angel," she told them. "He must have been coming for the child, but the poor fellow is so old that the rain knocked him down."

On the following day everyone knew that a flesh-and-blood angel was held captive in Pelayo's house. Against the judgment of the wise neighbor woman, for whom angels in those times were the fugitive survivors of a celestial conspiracy, they did not have the heart to club him to death. Pelayo watched over him all afternoon from the kitchen, armed with his bailiff's club, and before going to bed he dragged him out of the mud and locked him up with the hens in the wire chicken coop. In the middle of the night, when the rain stopped, Pelayo and Elisenda were still killing crabs. A short time afterward the child woke up without a fever and with a desire to eat. Then they felt magnanimous and decided to put the angel on a raft with fresh water and provisions for three days and leave him to his fate on the high seas. But when they went out into the courtyard with the first light of dawn, they found the whole neighborhood in front of the chicken coop having fun with the angel, without the slightest reverence, tossing him things to eat through the openings in the wire as if he weren't a supernatural creature but a circus animal.

5 Father Gonzaga arrived before seven o'clock, alarmed at the strange news. By that time onlookers less frivolous than those at dawn had already arrived and they were making all kinds of conjectures concerning the captive's future. The simplest among them thought that he should be named mayor of the world. Others of sterner mind felt that he should be promoted to the rank of five-star general in order to win all wars. Some visionaries hoped that he could be put to stud in order to implant on earth a race of

winged wise men who could take charge of the universe. But Father Gonzaga, before becoming a priest, had been a robust woodcutter. Standing by the wire, he reviewed his catechism in an instant and asked them to open the door so that he could take a close look at that pitiful man who looked more like a huge decrepit hen among the fascinated chickens. He was lying in a corner drying his open wings in the sunlight among the fruit peels and breakfast leftovers that the early risers had thrown him. Alien to the impertinences of the world, he only lifted his antiquarian eyes and murmured something in his dialect when Father Gonzaga went into the chicken coop and said good morning to him in Latin. The parish priest had his first suspicion of an imposter when he saw that he did not understand the language of God or know how to greet His ministers. Then he noticed that seen close up he was much too human: he had an unbearable smell of the outdoors, the back side of his wings was strewn with parasites and his main feathers had been mistreated by terrestrial winds, and nothing about him measured up to the proud dignity of angels. Then he came out of the chicken coop and in a brief sermon warned the curious against the risks of being ingenuous. He reminded them that the devil had the bad habit of making use of carnival tricks in order to confuse the unwary. He argued that if wings were not the essential element in determining the difference between a hawk and an airplane, they were even less so in the recognition of angels. Nevertheless, he promised to write a letter to his bishop so that the latter would write to his primate so that the latter would write to the Supreme Pontiff in order to get the final verdict from the highest courts.

His prudence fell on sterile hearts. The news of the captive angel spread with such rapidity that after a few hours the courtyard had the bustle of a marketplace and they had to call in troops with fixed bayonets to disperse the mob that was about to knock the house down. Elisenda, her spine all twisted from sweeping up so much marketplace trash, then got the idea of fencing in the yard and charging five cents admission to see the angel.

The curious came from far away. A traveling carnival arrived with a flying acrobat who buzzed over the crowd several times, but no one paid any attention to him because his wings were not those of an angel but, rather, those of a sidereal bat. The most unfortunate invalids on earth came in search of health: a poor woman who since childhood had been counting her heartbeats and had run out of numbers; a Portuguese man who couldn't sleep because the noise of the stars disturbed him; a sleepwalker who got up at night to undo the things he had done while awake; and many others with less serious ailments. In the midst of that shipwreck disorder that made the earth tremble, Pelayo and Elisenda were happy with fatigue, for in less than a week they had crammed their rooms with money and the line of pilgrims waiting their turn to enter still reached beyond the horizon.

The angel was the only one who took no part in his own act. He spent his time trying to get comfortable in his borrowed nest, befuddled by the hellish heat of the oil lamps and sacramental candles that had been placed along the wire. At first they tried to make him eat some mothballs, which, according to the wisdom of the wise neighbor woman, were the food prescribed for angels. But he turned them down, just as he turned down the papal lunches that the penitents brought him, and they never found out whether it was because he was an angel or because he was an old man that in the end he ate nothing but eggplant mush. His only supernatural virtue seemed to be patience. Especially during the first days, when the hens pecked at him, searching for the stellar parasites that proliferated in his wings, and the cripples pulled out feathers to touch their defective parts with, and even the most merciful threw stones at him, trying to get him to rise so they could see him standing. The only time they succeeded in arousing him was when they burned his side with an iron for branding steers, for he had been motionless for so many hours that they thought he was dead. He awoke with a start, ranting in his hermetic language and with tears in his eyes, and he flapped his wings a couple of times, which brought on a whirlwind of chicken dung and lunar dust and a gale of panic that did not seem to be of this world. Although many thought that his reaction had been one not of rage but of pain, from then on they were careful not to annoy him, because the majority understood that his passivity was not that of a hero taking his ease but that of a cataclysm in repose.

Father Gonzaga held back the crowd's frivolity with formulas of maidservant inspiration while awaiting the arrival of a final judgment on the nature of the captive. But the mail from Rome showed no sense of urgency. They spent their time finding out if the prisoner had a navel, if his dialect had any connection with Aramaic, how many times he could fit on the head of a pin, or whether he wasn't just a Norwegian with wings. Those meager letters might have come and gone until the end of time if a providential event had not put an end to the priest's tribulations.

10 It so happened that during those days, among so many other carnival attractions, there arrived in town the traveling show of the woman who had been changed into a spider for having disobeyed her parents. The admission to see her was not only less than the admission to see the angel, but people were permitted to ask her all manner of questions about her absurd state and to examine her up and down so that no one would ever doubt the truth of her horror. She was a frightful tarantula the size of a ram and with the head of a sad maiden. What was most heart-rending, however, was not her outlandish shape but the sincere affliction with which she recounted the details of her misfortune. While still practically a child she had sneaked out of her parents' house to go to a dance, and while she was coming back through the woods after having danced all night without permission, a fearful thunderclap rent the sky in two and through the crack came the lightning bolt of brimstone that changed her into a spider. Her only nourishment came from the meatballs that charitable souls chose to toss into her mouth. A spectacle like that, full of so much human truth and with such a fearful lesson, was bound to defeat without even trying that of a haughty angel who scarcely deigned to look at mortals. Besides, the few miracles attributed to the angel showed a certain mental disorder, like the blind man who didn't recover his sight but grew three new teeth, or the paralytic who didn't get to walk but almost won the lottery, and the leper whose sores sprouted sunflowers. Those consolation miracles, which were more like mocking fun, had already ruined the angel's reputation when the woman who had been changed into a spider finally crushed him completely. That was how Father Gonzaga was cured forever of his insomnia and Pelayo's courtyard went back to being as empty as during the time it had rained for three days and crabs walked through the bedrooms.

The owners of the house had no reason to lament. With the money they saved they built a two-story mansion with balconies and gardens and high netting so that crabs wouldn't get in during the winter, and with iron bars on the windows so that angels couldn't get in. Pelayo also set up a rabbit warren close to town and gave up his job as bailiff for good, and Elisenda bought some satin pumps with high heels and many dresses of iridescent silk, the kind worn on Sunday by the most desirable women in those times. The chicken coop was the only thing that didn't receive any attention. If they washed it down with creolin and burned tears of myrrh inside it every so often, it was not in homage to the angel but to drive away the dungheap stench that still hung everywhere like a ghost and was turning the new house into an old one. At first, when the child learned to walk, they were careful that he not get too close to the chicken coop. But then they began to lose their fears and got used to the smell, and before the child got his second teeth he'd gone inside the chicken coop to play, where the wires were falling apart. The angel was no less standoffish with him than with other mortals, but he tolerated the most ingenious infamies with the patience of a dog who had no illusions. They both came down with chicken pox at the same time. The doctor who took care of the child couldn't resist the temptation to listen to the angel's heart, and he found so much whistling in the heart and so many sounds in his kidneys that it seemed impossible for him to be alive. What surprised him most, however, was the logic of his wings. They seemed so natural on that completely human organism that he couldn't understand why other men didn't have them too.

When the child began school it had been some time since the sun and rain had caused the collapse of the chicken coop. The angel went dragging himself about here and there like a stray dying man. They would drive him out of the bedroom with a broom and a moment later find him in the kitchen. He seemed to be in so many places at the same time that they grew to think that he'd been duplicated, that he was reproducing himself all through the house, and the exasperated and unhinged Elisenda shouted that it was awful living in that hell full of angels. He could scarcely eat and his antiquarian eyes had also become so foggy that he went about bumping into posts. All he had left were the bare cannulae of his last feathers. Pelayo threw a blanket over him and extended him the charity of letting him sleep in the shed, and only then did they notice that he had a temperature at night, and was delirious with the tongue twisters of an old Norwegian. That was one of the few times they became alarmed, for they thought he was going to die and not even the wise neighbor woman had been able to tell them what to do with dead angels.

And yet he not only survived his worst winter, but seemed improved with the first sunny days. He remained motionless for several days in the farthest corner of the courtyard, where no one would see him, and at the beginning of December some large, stiff feathers began to grow on his wings, the feathers of a scarcecrow, which looked more like another misfortune of decrepitude. But he must have known the reason for those changes, for he was quite careful that no one should notice them, that no one should hear the sea chanteys that he sometimes sang under the stars. One morning Elisenda was cutting some bunches of onions for lunch when a wind that seemed to come from the high seas blew into the kitchen. Then she went to the window and caught the angel in his first attempts at flight. They were so clumsy that his fingernails opened a furrow in the vegetable patch and he was on the point of knocking the shed down with the ungainly flapping that slipped on the light and couldn't get a grip on the air. But he did manage to gain altitude. Elisenda let out a sigh of relief, for herself and for him, when she saw him pass over the last houses, holding himself up in some way with the risky flapping of a senile vulture. She kept watching him even when she was through cutting the onions and she kept on watching until it was no longer possible for her to see him, because then he was no longer an annoyance in her life but an imaginary dot on the horizon of the sea.

[*1968*]

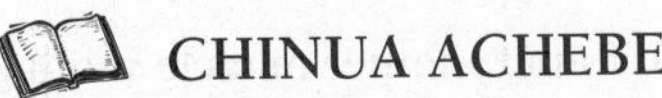

## CHINUA ACHEBE

*Chinua Achebe (b. 1930), whose name is pronounced CHIN-oo-ah Ah-CHEE-bee, was born in Eastern Nigeria, which at that time was a British colony. In 1963 Nigeria became a republic, but in 1967 the Eastern Region seceded, taking the name of Biafra. Civil war ensued until 1970, when the secessionists capitulated. Achebe's story, "Civil Peace," takes place after the capitulation.*

*Achebe's first novel,* Things Fall Apart *(1958), a realistic picture of the conflicts of African and European culture in Nigeria, was an immediate success. Since then he has written other novels and short stories as well as two collections of essays on literary and cultural topics,* Morning Yet on Creation Day *(1975) and* Hopes and Impediments: Selected Essays 1965-87 *(1988).*

# *Civil Peace*

Jonathan Iwegbu counted himself extraordinarily lucky. "Happy survival!" meant so much more to him than just a current fashion of greeting old friends in the first hazy days of peace. It went deep to his heart. He had come out of the war with five inestimable blessings—his head, his wife Maria's head, and the heads of three out of their four children. As a bonus he also had his old bicycle—a miracle too but naturally not to be compared to the safety of five human heads.

The bicycle had a little history of its own. One day at the height of the war it was commandeered "for urgent military action." Hard as its loss would have been to him he would still have let it go without a thought had he not had some doubts about the genuineness of the officer. It wasn't his disreputable rags, nor the toes peeping out of one blue and one brown canvas shoe, nor yet the two stars of his rank done obviously in a hurry in biro[1] that troubled Jonathan; many good and heroic soldiers looked the same or worse. It was rather a certain lack of grip and firmness in his manner. So Jonathan, suspecting he might be amenable to influence, rummaged in his raffia bag and produced the two pounds with which he had been going to buy firewood which his wife, Maria, retailed to camp officials for extra stockfish and cornmeal, and got his bicycle back. That night he buried it in

[1]**biro** ballpoint

the little clearing in the bush where the dead of the camp, including his own youngest son, were buried. When he dug it up again a year later after the surrender all it needed was a little palm-oil greasing. "Nothing puzzles God," he said in wonder.

He put it to immediate use as a taxi and accumulated a small pile of Biafran money ferrying camp officials and their families across the four-mile stretch to the nearest tarred road. His standard charge per trip was six pounds and those who had the money were only glad to be rid of some of it in this way. At the end of a fortnight he had made a small fortune of one hundred and fifteen pounds.

Then he made the journey to Enugu and found another miracle waiting for him. It was unbelievable. He rubbed his eyes and looked again and it was still standing there before him. But, needless to say, even that monumental blessing must be accounted also totally inferior to the five heads in the family. This newest miracle was his little house in Ogui Overside. Indeed nothing puzzles God! Only two houses away a huge concrete edifice some wealthy contractor had put up just before the war was a mountain of rubble. And here was Jonathan's little zinc house of no regrets built with mud blocks quite intact! Of course the doors and windows were missing and five sheets off the roof. But what was that? And anyhow he had returned to Enugu early enough to pick up bits of old zinc and wood and soggy sheets of cardboard lying around the neighborhood before thousands more came out of their forest holes looking for the same things. He got a destitute carpenter with one old hammer, a blunt plane, and a few bent and rusty nails in his tool bag to turn this assortment of wood, paper, and metal into door and window shutters for five Nigerian shillings or fifty Biafran pounds. He paid the pounds, and moved in with his overjoyed family carrying five heads on their shoulders.

5 His children picked mangoes near the military cemetery and sold them to soldiers' wives for a few pennies—real pennies this time—and his wife started making breakfast akara balls[2] for neighbors in a hurry to start life again. With his family earnings he took his bicycle to the villages around and bought fresh palm wine which he mixed generously in his rooms with the water which had recently started running again in the public tap down the road, and opened up a bar for soldiers and other lucky people with good money.

At first he went daily, then every other day, and finally once a week, to the offices of the Coal Corporation where he used to be a miner, to find out what was what. The only thing he did find out in the end was that that little house of his was even a greater blessing than he had thought. Some of his fellow ex-miners who had nowhere to return at the end of the day's waiting just slept outside the doors of the offices and cooked what meal they could scrounge together in Bournvita tins. As the weeks lengthened and still nobody could say what was what, Jonathan discontinued his weekly visits altogether and faced his palm-wine bar.

But nothing puzzles God. Came the day of the windfall when after five days of endless scuffles in queues and counterqueues in the sun outside the Treasury he had twenty pounds counted into his palms as ex gratia award

[2]**akara balls** peppered dough fried in palm oil

for the rebel money he had turned in. It was like Christmas for him and for many others like him when the payments began. They called it (since few could manage its proper official name) *egg-rasher*.[3]

As soon as the pound notes were placed in his palm Jonathan simply closed it tight over them and buried fist and money inside his trouser pocket. He had to be extra careful because he had seen a man a couple of days earlier collapse into near-madness in an instant before that oceanic crowd because no sooner had he got his twenty pounds than some heartless ruffian picked it off him. Though it was not right that a man in such an extremity of agony should be blamed yet many in the queues that day were able to remark quietly at the victim's carelessness, especially after he pulled out the innards of his pocket and revealed a hole in it big enough to pass a thief's head. But of course he had insisted that the money had been in the other pocket, pulling it out too to show its comparative wholeness. So one had to be careful.

Jonathan soon transferred the money to his left hand and pocket so as to leave his right free for shaking hands should the need arise, though by fixing his gaze at such an elevation as to miss all approaching human faces he made sure that the need did not arise, until he got home.

10 He was normally a heavy sleeper but that night he heard all the neighborhood noises die down one after another. Even the night watchman who knocked the hour on some metal somewhere in the distance had fallen silent after knocking one o'clock. That must have been the last thought in Jonathan's mind before he was finally carried away himself. He couldn't have been gone for long, though, when he was violently awakened again.

"Who is knocking?" whispered his wife lying beside him on the floor.

"I don't know," he whispered back breathlessly.

The second time the knocking came it was so loud and imperious that the rickety old door could have fallen down.

"Who is knocking?" he asked them, his voice parched and trembling.

15 "Na tief-man and him people," came the cool reply. "Make you hopen de door." This was followed by the heaviest knocking of all.

Maria was the first to raise the alarm, then he followed and all their children.

*"Police-o! Thieves-o! Neighbors-o! Police-o! We are lost! We are dead! Neighbors, are you asleep? Wake up! Police-o!"*

"You done finish?" asked the voice outside. "Make we help you small. Oya, everybody!"

*"Police-o! Tief-man-so! Neighbors-o! we done loss-o! Police-o! . . ."*

20 There were at least five other voices besides the leader's.

Jonathan and his family were now completely paralyzed by terror. Maria and the children sobbed inaudibly like lost souls. Jonathan groaned continuously.

The silence that followed the thieves' alarm vibrated horribly. Jonathan all but begged their leader to speak again and be done with it.

"My frien," said he at long last, "we don try our best for call dem but I tink say dem all done sleep-o . . . So wetin we go do now? Sometaim you

[3]***egg-rasher:*** the official name is *ex gratia,* Nigerian money given in exchange for rebel (and now worthless) Biafran money

wan call soja? Or you wan make we call dem for you? Soja better pass police. No be so?"

"Na so!" replied his men. Jonathan thought he heard even more voices now than before and groaned heavily. His legs were sagging under him and his throat felt like sandpaper.

25 "My frien, why you no de talk again. I de ask you say you wan make we call soja?"

"No."

"Awrighto. Now make we talk business. We no be bad tief. We no like for make trouble. Trouble done finish. War done finish and all the katakata[4] wey de for inside. No Civil War again. This time na Civil Peace. No be so?"

"Na so!" answered the horrible chorus.

"What do you want from me? I am a poor man. Everything I had went with this war. Why do you come to me? You know people who have money. We . . ."

30 "Awright! We know say you no get plenty money. But we sef no get even anini.[5] So derefore make you open dis window and give us one hundred pound and we go commot. Otherwise we de come for inside now to show you guitar-boy like dis . . ."

A volley of automatic fire rang through the sky. Maria and the children began to weep aloud again.

"Ah, missisi de cry again. No need for dat. We done talk say we na good tief. We just take our small money and go nwayorly. No molest. Abi we de molest?"

"At all!" said the chorus.

"My friends," began Jonathan hoarsely. "I hear what you say and I thank you. If I had one hundred pounds . . ."

35 "Lookia my frien, no be play we come play for your house. If we make mistake and step for inside you no go like am-o. So derefore . . ."

"To God who made me; if you come inside and find one hundred pounds, take and shoot me and shoot my wife and children. I swear to God. The only money I have in this life is this twenty-pounds *egg-rasher* they gave me today . . ."

"OK. Time de go. Make you open dis window and bring the twenty pound. We go manage am like dat."

There were now loud murmurs of dissent among the chorus: "Na lie de man de lie; e get plenty money . . . Make we go inside and search properly well . . . Wetin be twenty pound? . . ."

"Shurrup!" rang the leader's voice like a lone shot in the sky and silenced the murmuring at once. "Are you dere? Bring the money quick!"

40 "I am coming," said Jonathan fumbling in the darkness with the key of the small wooden box he kept by his side on the mat.

At the first sign of light as neighbors and others assembled to commiserate with him he was already strapping his five-gallon demijohn to his bicycle carrier and his wife, sweating in the open fire, was turning over akara balls in a wide clay bowl of boiling oil. In the corner his eldest son was rinsing out dregs of yesterday's palm wine from old beer bottles.

[4]**katakata** shit
[5]**anini** penny

"I count it as nothing," he told his sympathizers, his eyes on the rope he was tying. "What is egg-rasher? Did I depend on it last week? Or is it greater than other things that went with the war? I say, let egg-rasher perish in the flames! Let it go where everything else has gone. Nothing puzzles God."

[*1971*]

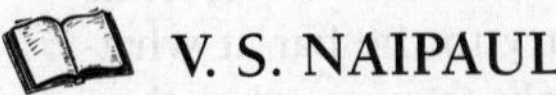

## V. S. NAIPAUL

*V[idiadhar] S[urajprasad] Naipaul was born in 1932 in Trinidad. After completing his early education in Trinidad he emigrated to England and graduated from Oxford in 1954. A prolific novelist and a far-traveler, he writes about the United States, Africa, India—where his grandfather was born—and, especially, about the Caribbean.*

# *The Night Watchman's Occurrence Book*

*November 21.* 10.30 p.m. C. A. Cavander take over duty at C——Hotel all corrected. *Cesar Alwyn Cavander*

7 a.m. C. A. Cavander hand over duty to Mr Vignales at C——Hotel no report. *Cesar Alwyn Cavander*

*November 22.* 10.30 p.m. C. A. Cavander take over duty at C——Hotel no report. *Cesar Alwyn Cavander*

7 a.m. C. A. Cavander hand over duty to Mr Vignales at C——Hotel all corrected. *Cesar Alwyn Cavander*

This is the third occasion on which I have found C. A. Cavander, Night Watchman, asleep on duty. Last night, at 12.45 a.m., I found him sound asleep in a rocking chair in the hotel lounge. Night Watchman Cavander has therefore been dismissed. Night Watchman Hillyard: This book is to be known in future as "The Night Watchman's Occurrence Book." In it I shall expect to find a detailed account of everything that happens in the hotel tonight. Be warned by the example of ex-Night Watchman Cavander, *W. A. G. Inskip, Manager*

Mr Manager, remarks noted. You have no worry where I am concern sir. *Charles Ethelbert Hillyard, Night Watchman*

5 *November 23.* 11 p.m. Night Watchman Hillyard take over duty at C—— Hotel with one torch light 2 fridge keys and room keys 1, 3, 6, 10 and 13. Also 25 cartoons Carib Beer and 7 cartoons Heineken[1] and 2 cartoons American cigarettes. Beer cartoons intact Bar intact all corrected no report. *Charles Ethelbert Hillyard*

[1]**Heineken** a Dutch beer

7 a.m. Night Watchman Hillyard hand over duty to Mr Vignales at C——Hotel with one torch light 2 fridge keys and room keys, 1, 3, 6, 10 and 13, 32 cartoons beer. Bar intact all corrected no report. *Charles Ethelbert Hillyard*

> Night Watchman Hillyard: Mr Wills complained bitterly to me this morning that last night he was denied entry to the bar by you. I wonder if you know exactly what the purpose of this hotel is. In future all hotel guests are to be allowed entry to the bar at whatever time they choose. It is your duty simply to note what they take. This is one reason why the hotel provides a certain number of beer cartons (please note the spelling of this word). *W. A. G. Inskip*

Mr Manager, remarks noted. I sorry I didn't get the chance to take some education sir. *Chas. Ethelbert Hillyard*

*November 24.* 11 p.m. N. W. Hillyard take over duty with one Torch, 1 Bar Key, 2 Fridge Keys, 32 cartoons Beer, all intact. 12 Midnight Bar close and Barman left leaving Mr Wills and others in Bar, and they left at 1 a.m. Mr Wills took 16 Carib Beer, Mr Wilson 8, Mr Percy 8. At 2 a.m. Mr Wills come back in the bar and take 4 Carib and some bread, he cut his hand trying to cut the bread, so please dont worry about the stains on the carpet sir. At 6 a.m. Mr Wills come back for some soda water. It didn't have any so he take a ginger beer instead. Sir you see it is my intention to do this job good sir, I cant see how Night Watchman Cavander could fall asleep on this job sir. *Chas. Ethelbert Hillyard*

> You always seems sure of the time, and guests appear to be in the habit of entering the bar on the hour. You will kindly note the exact time. The clock from the kitchen is left on the window near the switches. You can use this clock but you MUST replace it every morning before you go off duty. *W. A. G. Inskip*

Noted. *Chas. Ethelbert Hillyard*

*November 25.* Midnight Bar close and 12.23 a.m. Barman left leaving Mr Wills and others in Bar. Mr Owen take 5 bottles Carib, Mr Wilson 6 bottles Heineken, Mr Wills 18 Carib and they left at 2.52 a.m. Nothing unusual. Mr. Wills was helpless, I don't see how anybody could drink so much, eighteen one man alone, this work enough to turn anybody Seventh Day Adventist, and another man come in the bar, I dont know his name, I hear they call him Paul, he assist me because the others couldn't do much, and we take Mr Wills up to his room and take off his boots and slack his other clothes and then we left. Don't know sir if they did take more while I was away, nothing was mark on the Pepsi Cola board, but they was drinking still, it looks as if they come back and take some more, but with Mr Wills I want some extra assistance sir.

Mr Manager, the clock break I find it break when I come back from Mr Wills room sir. It stop 3.19 sir. *Chas. E. Hillyard*

> More than 2 lbs of veal were removed from the Fridge last night, and a cake that was left in the press was cut. It is your duty, Night Watchman Hillyard, to keep an eye on these things. I ought to

warn you that I have also asked the Police to check on all employees leaving the hotel, to prevent such occurrences in the future. *W. A. G. Inskip*

Mr Manager, I don't know why people so anxious to blame servants sir. About the cake, the press lock at night and I dont have the key sir, everything safe where I am concern sir. *Chas. Hillyard*

*November 26.* Midnight Bar close and Barman left. Mr Wills didn't come, I hear he at the American base tonight, all quiet, nothing unusual.

Mr Manager, I request one thing. Please inform the Barman to let me know sir when there is a female guest in the hotel sir. *C. E. Hillyard*

This morning I received a report from a guest that there were screams in the hotel during the night. You wrote All Quiet. Kindly explain in writing. *W. A. G. Inskip* Write Explanation here:

EXPLANATION. Not long after midnight the telephone ring and a woman ask for Mr Jimminez. I try to tell her where he was but she say she cant hear properly. Fifteen minutes later she came in a car, she was looking vex and sleepy, and I went up to call him. The door was not lock, I went in and touch his foot and call him very soft, and he jump up and begin to shout. When he come to himself he said he had Night Mere, and then he come down and went away with the woman, was not necessary to mention.

Mr Manager, I request you again, please inform the Barman to let me know sir when there is a female guest in the Hotel. *C. Hillyard*

*November 27.* 1 a.m. Bar close, Mr Wills and a American 19 Carib and 2.30 a.m. a Police come and ask for Mr Wills, he say the American report that he was robbed of $200.00¢, he was last drinking at the C——with Mr Wills and others. Mr Wills and the Police ask to open the Bar to search it, I told them I cannot open the Bar for you like that, the Police must come with the Manager. Then the American say it was only joke he was joking, and they try to get the Police to laugh, but the Police looking the way I feeling. Then laughing Mr Wills left in a garage car as he couldn't drive himself and the American was waiting outside and they both fall down as they was getting in the car, and Mr Wills saying any time you want a overdraft you just come to my bank kiddo. The Police left walking by himself. *C. Hillyard*

Night Watchman Hillyard: "Was not necessary to mention"!! You are not to decide what is necessary to mention in this night watchman's occurrence book. Since when have you become sole owner of the hotel as to determine what is necessary to mention? If the guest did not mention it I would never have known that there were screams in the hotel during the night. Also will you kindly tell me who Mr Jimminez is? And what rooms he occupied or occupies? And by what right? You have been told by me personally that the names of all hotel guests are on the slate next to the light switches. If you find Mr Jimminez's name on this slate, or could give me some information about him, I will be most warmly obliged to you. The lady you ask about is Mrs Roscoe, Room 12, as you very well know. It is your duty to see that guests are not pestered by unauthorized callers. You should give no information

> about guests to such people, and I would be glad if in future you could direct such callers straight to me. *W. A. G. Inskip*

Sir was what I ask you two times, I dont know what sort of work I take up, I always believe that nightwatchman work is a quiet work and I dont like meddling in white people business, but the gentleman occupy Room 12 also, was there that I went up to call him, I didn't think it necessary to mention because was none of my business sir. *C.E.H.*

*November 28.* 12 Midnight Bar close and Barman left at 12.20 a.m. leaving Mr Wills and others, and they all left at 1.25 a.m. Mr Wills 8 Carib, Mr Wilson 12, Mr Percy 8, and the man they call Paul 12. Mrs Roscoe join the gentlemen at 12.33 a.m., four gins, everybody calling her Minnie from Trinidad, and then they start singing that song, and some others. Nothing unusual. Afterwards there were mild singing and guitar music in Room 12. A man come in and ask to use the phone at 2.17 a.m. and while he was using it about 7 men come in and wanted to beat him up, so he put down the phone and they all ran away. At 3 a.m. I notice the padlock not on the press, I look inside, no cake, but the padlock was not put on in the first place sir. Mr Wills come down again at 6 a.m. to look for his sweet, he look in the Fridge and did not see any. He took a piece of pineapple. A plate was covered in the Fridge, but it didn't have anything in it. Mr Wills put it out, the cat jump on it and it fall down and break. The garage bulb not burning. *C.E.H.*

> You will please sign your name at the bottom of your report. You are in the habit of writing Nothing Unusual. Please take note and think before making such a statement. I want to know what is meant by nothing unusual. I gather, not from you, needless to say, that the police have fallen into the habit of visiting the hotel at night. I would be most grateful to you if you could find the time to note the times of these visits. *W. A. G. Inskip*

Sir, nothing unusual means everything usual. I dont know, nothing I writing you liking. I dont know what sort of work this night watchman work getting to be, since when people have to start getting Cambridge certificate to get night watchman job, I ain't educated and because of this everybody think they could insult me. *Charles Ethelbert Hillyard*

*November 29.* Midnight Bar close and 12.15 Barman left leaving Mr Wills and Mrs Roscoe and others in the Bar. Mr Wills and Mrs Roscoe left at 12.30 a.m. leaving Mr Wilson and the man they call Paul, and they all left at 1.00 a.m. Twenty minutes to 2 Mr Wills and party return and left again at 5 to 3. At 3.45 Mr Wills return and take break and milk and olives and cherries, he ask for nutmeg too, I said we had none, he drink 2 Carib, and left ten minutes later. He also collect Mrs Roscoe bag. All the drinks, except the 2 Carib, was taken by the man they call Paul. I don't know sir I don't like this sort of work, you better hire a night barman. At 5.30 Mrs Roscoe and the man they call Paul come back to the bar, they was having a quarrel, Mr Paul saying you make me sick, Mrs Roscoe saying I feel sick, and then she vomit all over the floor, shouting I didn't want that damned milk. I was cleaning up when Mr Wills come down to ask for soda water, we got to lay in more soda for Mr Wills, but I need extra assistance with Mr Wills Paul and party sir.

The police come at 2, 3.48 and 4.52. They sit down in the bar a long time. Firearms discharge 2 times in the back yard. Detective making inquiries. I dont know sir, I thinking it would be better for me to go back to some other sort of job. At 3 I hear somebody shout Thief, and I see a man running out of the back, and Mr London, Room 9, say he miss 80 cents and a pack of cigarettes which was on his dressing case. I don't know when the people in this place does sleep. *Chas. Ethelbert Hillyard*

Night Watchman Hillyard: A lot more than 80 cents was stolen. Several rooms were in fact entered during the night, including my own. You are employed to prevent such things occurring. Your interest in the morals of our guests seems to be distracting your attention from your duties. Save your preaching for your roadside prayer meetings. Mr Pick, Room 7, reports that in spite of the most pressing and repeated requests, you did not awaken him at 5. He has missed his plane to British Guiana as a result. No newspapers were delivered to the rooms this morning. I am again notifying you that papers must be handed personally to Doorman Vignales. And the messenger's bicycle, which I must remind you is the property of the hotel, has been damaged. What do you *do* at nights? *W. A. G. Inskip*

Please don't ask me sir.

Relating to the damaged bicycle: I left the bicycle the same place where I meet it, nothing took place so as to damage it. I always take care of all property sir. I don't know how you could think I have time to go out for bicycle rides. About the papers, sir, the police and them read it and leave them in such a state that I didn't think it would be nice to give them to guests. I wake up Mr Pick, room 7, at 4.50 a.m. 5 a.m. 5.15 a.m. and 5.30. He told me to keep off, he would not get up, and one time he pelt a box of matches at me, matches scatter all over the place. I always do everything to the best of my ability sir but God is my Witness I never find a night watchman work like this, so much writing I dont have time to do anything else, I dont have four hands and six eyes and I want this extra assistance with Mr Wills and party sir. I am a poor man and you could abuse me, but you must not abuse my religion sir because the good Lord sees All and will have His revenge sir, I don't know what sort of work and trouble I land myself in, all I want is a little quiet night work and all I getting is abuse. *Chas. E. Hillyard*

*November 30.* 12.25 a.m. Bar close and Barman left 1.00 a.m. leaving Mr Wills and party in Bar. Mr Wills take 12 Carib, Mr Wilson 6, Mr Percy 14. Mrs Roscoe five gins. At 1.30 a.m. Mrs Roscoe left and there were a little singing and mild guitar playing in Room 12. Nothing unusual. The police came at 1.35 and sit down in the bar for a time, not drinking, not talking, not doing anything except watching. At 1.45 the man they call Paul come in with Mr McPherson of the SS Naparoni, they was both falling down and laughing whenever anything break and the man they call Paul say Fireworks about to begin tell Minnie Malcolm coming the ship just dock. Mr Wills and party scatter leaving one or two bottles half empty and then the man they call Paul tell me to go up to Room 12 and tell Minnie Roscoe that Malcolm coming. I don't know how people could behave so the thing enough to make anybody turn priest. I notice the padlock on the bar door break off it hanging on only by a little piece of wood. And when I went up to Room 12 and tell Mrs Roscoe that Malcolm coming the ship just dock the woman get sober straight away like she dont want to hear no more guitar music and she asking me where to hide where to go. I dont know, I feel the day of reckoning is at hand, but she not listening to what I saying, she busy straightening up the room one minute packing the next, and then she run out into the corridor and before I could stop she she run straight down the back stairs to the annexe. And then 5 past 2, still in the corridor, I see a big red man running up to me and he sober as a judge and he mad as a drunkard and he asking me where she is where she is. I ask whether he is a authorized caller, he say you don't give me any of that crap now, where she is, where she is. So remembering about the last time Mr Jimminez I direct him to the manager office in the annexe. He hear a little scuffling inside Mr Inskip room and I make out Mr Inskip sleepy voice and Mrs Roscoe voice and the red man run inside and all I hearing for the next five minutes is bam bam bodow bodow bow and this woman screaming. I dont know what sort of work this night watchman getting I want something quiet like the police. In time things quiet down and the red man drag Mrs Roscoe out of the annexe and they take a taxi, and the Police sitting down quiet in the bar. Then Mr Percy and the others come back one by one to the bar and they talking quiet and they not drinking and they left 3 a.m. 3.15 Mr Wills return and take one whisky and 2 Carib. He asked for pineapple or some sweet fruit but it had nothing.

6 a.m. Mr Wills come in the bar looking for soda but it aint have none. We have to get some soda for Mr Wills sir.

6.30 a.m. the papers come and I deliver them to Doorman Vignales at 7 a.m. *Chas. Hillyard*

> Mr Hillyard: In view of the unfortunate illness of Mr. Inskip, I am temporarily in charge of the hotel. I trust you will continue to make your nightly reports, but I would be glad if you could keep your entries as brief as possible. *Robt. Magnus, Acting Manager*

*December 1.* 10.30 p.m. C. E. Hillyard take over duty at C———Hotel all corrected 12 Midnight Bar close 2 a.m. Mr Wills 2 Carib, 1 bread 6 a.m. Mr Wills 1 soda 7 a.m. Night Watchman Hillyard hand over duty to Mr Vignales with one torch light 2 Fridge keys and Room Keys 1, 3, 6 and 12. Bar intact all corrected no report. *C.E.H.*

[*1967*]

## JACK FORBES

*Jack Forbes was born in California in 1934 of Powhattan and Delaware background. He teaches anthropology and Native American studies at the University of California, Davis, and is the author of fiction and nonfiction, including* Columbus and Other Cannibals *(1992) and* African and Native Americans *(1993), a study of Red-Black peoples.*

# *Only Approved Indians Can Play: Made in USA*

The All-Indian Basketball Tournament was in its second day. Excitement was pretty high, because a lot of the teams were very good or at least eager and hungry to win. Quite a few people had come to watch, mostly Indians. Many were relatives or friends of the players. A lot of people were betting money and tension was pretty great.

A team from the Tucson Inter-Tribal House was set to play against a group from the Great Lakes region. The Tucson players were mostly very dark young men with long black hair. A few had little goatee beards or mustaches though, and one of the Great Lakes fans had started a rumor that they were really Chicanos. This was a big issue since the Indian Sports League had a rule that all players had to be of one-quarter or more Indian blood and that they had to have their BIA[1] roll numbers available if challenged.

And so a big argument started. One of the biggest, darkest Indians on the Tucson team had been singled out as a Chicano, and the crowd wanted him thrown out. The Great Lakes players, most of whom were pretty light, refused to start. They all had their BIA identification cards, encased in plastic. This proved that they were all real Indians, even a blonde-haired guy. He was really only about one-sixteenth but the BIA rolls had been changed for his tribe so legally he was one-fourth. There was no question about the Great Lakes team. They were all land-based, federally-recognized Indians, although living in a big midwestern city, and they had their cards to prove it.

Anyway, the big, dark Tucson Indian turned out to be a Papago. He didn't have a BIA card but he could talk Papago so they let him alone for the time being. Then they turned towards a lean, very Indian-looking guy who had a pretty big goatee. He seemed to have a Spanish accent, so they demanded to see his card.

5 Well, he didn't have one either. He said he was a full-blood Tarahumara Indian and he could also speak his language. None of the Great Lakes Indians could talk their languages so they said that was no proof of anything, that you had to have a BIA roll number.

The Tarahumara man was getting pretty angry by then. He said his father and uncle had been killed by the whites in Mexico and that he did not expect to be treated with prejudice by other Indians.

But all that did no good. Someone demanded to know if he had a reservation and if his tribe was recognized. He replied that his people lived high up in the mountains and that they were still resisting the Mexicanos, that the government was trying to steal their land.

"What state do your people live in," they wanted to know. When he said that his people lived free, outside of the control of any state, they only shook their fists at him. "You're not an official Indian. All official Indians are under the whiteman's rule now. We all have a number given to us, to show that we are recognized."

Well, it all came to an end when someone shouted that "Tarahumaras don't exist. They're not listed in the BIA dictionary." Another fan yelled, "He's a Mexican. He can't play. This tournament is only for Indians."

10 The officials of the tournament had been huddling together. One blew his whistle and an announcement was made. "The Tucson team is disqualified. One of its members is a Yaqui. One is a Tarahumara. The rest are Papagos. None of them have BIA enrollment cards. They are not Indians within the meaning of the laws of the government of the United States. The Great Lakes team is declared the winner by default."

[1]**BIA** Bureau of Indian Affairs

A tremendous roar of applause swept through the stands. A white BIA official wiped the tears from his eyes and said to a companion, "God Bless America. I think we've won."

[*1983*]

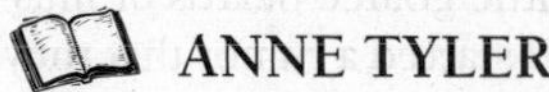

## ANNE TYLER

*Anne Tyler was born in 1941 in Minneapolis, brought up in various Quaker communes, and educated at Duke University and then at Columbia University, where she did graduate work in Russian. On several occasions she has said that her favorite writer is Eudora Welty: "Reading [Welty] taught me there were stories to be written about the mundane life around me," and "Reading Eudora Welty when I was growing up showed me that very small things are often really larger than the large things."*

# The Artificial Family

The first full sentence that Mary ever said to him was, "Did you know I have a daughter?" Toby was asking her to dinner. He had just met her at a party—a long-haired girl in a floor-length gingham dress—and the invitation was instant, offered out of desperation because she was already preparing to leave and he wasn't sure he could ever find her again. Now, how did her daughter enter into this? Was she telling him that she was married? Or that she couldn't go out in the evenings? "No," said Toby. "I didn't know."

"Well, now you do," she said. Then she wrote her address down for him and left, and Toby spent the rest of the evening clutching the scrap of paper in his pocket for fear of losing it.

The daughter was five years old. Her name was Samantha, and it suited her: she was an old-fashioned child with two thick braids and a solemn face. When she and her mother stood side by side, barefoot, wearing their long dresses, they might have been about to climb onto a covered wagon. They presented a solid front. Their eyes were a flat, matching blue. "Well!" Toby would say, after he and Samantha knew each other better. "Shall we all *three* go somewhere? Shall we take a picnic lunch? Visit the zoo?" Then the blue would break up into darker colors, and they would smile—but it was the mother who smiled first. The child was the older of the two. She took longer to think things over.

They would go to the Baltimore Zoo and ride the tiny passenger train. Sitting three abreast on the narrow seat—Toby's arm around Mary, Samantha scrunched between them—they rattled past dusty-looking deer fenced in among the woods, through a tunnel where the younger children screamed, alongside a parade of wooden cartoon animals which everyone tried to identify. "That's Bullmoose! There's Bugs Bunny!" Only Samantha said nothing. She had no television set. Bugs Bunny was a stranger to her. She sat very straight, with her hands clasped between her knees in her long skirt, and Toby looked down at her and tried to piece out her father from the curve of her cheek and the tilt of her nose. Her eyes were her mother's, but surely that rounded chin came from her father's side. Had her father had red hair? Was that what gave Samantha's brown braids that coppery sheen? He didn't feel that he could ask straight out because Mary had slammed a door on the subject. All she said was that she had run away with Samantha after two years of marriage. Then once, discussing some earlier stage in Samantha's life, she pulled out a wallet photo to show him: Samantha as a baby, in her mother's lap. "Look at you!" Toby said. "You had your hair up! You had lipstick on! You were wearing a sweater and skirt! Look at Samantha in her party dress!" The photo stunned him, but Mary hardly noticed. "Oh, yes," she said, closing her wallet, "I was very straight back then." And that was the last time she mentioned her marriage. Toby never saw the husband, or heard anything about him. There seemed to be no visiting arrangements for the child.

5 Mornings Mary worked in an art gallery. She had to leave Samantha with a teenage babysitter after kindergarten closed for the summer. "Summers! I hate them" she said. "All the time I'm at work I'm wondering how Samantha is." Toby said, "Why not let *me* stay with her. You know how Samantha and I get along." He was a graduate student with a flexible schedule; and besides, he seized on every excuse to entrench himself deeper in Mary's life. But Mary said, "No, I couldn't ask you to do that." And she went on paying Carol, and paying her again in the evenings when they went out somewhere. They went to dinner, or to movies, or to Toby's rambling apartment. They always came back early. "Carol's mother will kill me!" Mary would say, and she would gather up her belongings and run ahead of Toby to his car. When he returned from taking her home his apartment always smelled of her: a clean, straw smell, like burlap. Her bobby pins littered the bed and the crevices of the sofa. Strands of her long hairs tended to get wound around the rollers of his carpet sweeper. When he went to sleep the cracked bell of her voice threaded through all his dreams.

At the end of August, they were married in a civil ceremony. They had known each other five months. *Only* five months, Toby's parents said. They wrote him a letter pointing out all their objections. How would he support three on a university grant? How would he study? What did he want with someone else's child? The child: that was what they really minded. The ready-made grandchild. How could he love some other man's daughter? But Toby had never been sure he would know how to love his *own* children; so the question didn't bother him. He liked Samantha. And he liked the idea of her: the single, solitary treasure carried away from the disaster of the sweater-and-skirt marriage. If he himself ever ran away, what would he choose to take? His grandfather's watch, his favorite chamois shirt, eight cartons of books, some still unread, his cassette tape recorder—each object losing a little more worth as the list grew longer. Mary had taken Samantha, and nothing else. He envied both of them.

They lived in his apartment, which was more than big enough. Mary quit her job. Samantha started first grade. They were happy but guarded, still, working too hard at getting along. Mary turned the spare bedroom into a study for Toby, with a "Private" sign on the door. "Never go in there," she told Samantha. "That's Toby's place to be alone." "But I don't *want* to be alone," Toby said. "I'm alone all day at the lab." Nobody seemed to believe him. Samantha passed the doorway of his study on tiptoe, never even peeking inside. Mary scrupulously avoided littering the apartment with her own possessions. Toby was so conscientious a father that he might have written himself a timetable: At seven, play Old Maid. At seven-thirty, read a story. At eight o'clock, offer a piggyback ride to bed. Mary he treated like glass. He kept thinking of her first marriage; his greatest fear was that she would leave him.

Every evening, Samantha walked around to Toby's lab to call him for supper. In the midst of reaching for a beaker or making a notation he would look up to find her standing there, absolutely silent. Fellow students gave her curious looks. She ignored them. She concentrated on Toby, watching him with a steady blue gaze that gave all his actions a new importance. Would he feel this flattered if she were his own? He didn't think so. In their peculiar situation—nearly strangers, living in the same house, sharing Mary—they had not yet started to take each other for granted. Her coming for him each day was purely a matter of choice, which he imagined her spending some time over before deciding; and so were the sudden, rare smiles which lit her face when he glanced down at her during the walk home.

At Christmastime Toby's parents flew down for a visit. They stayed four days, each one longer than the day before. Toby's mother had a whole new manner which kept everyone at arm's length. She would look at Samantha and say, "My, she's thin! Is her father thin, Mary? Does her father have those long feet?" She would go out to the kitchen and say, "I see you've done something with Toby's little two-cup coffeepot. Is this *your* pot, Mary? May I use it?" Everything she said was meant to remind them of their artificiality: the wife was someone else's first, the child was not Toby's. But her effect was to draw them closer together. The three of them formed an alliance against Mrs. Scott and her silent husband, who lent her his support merely by not shutting her up. On the second evening Toby escaped to his study and Samantha and Mary joined him, one by one, sliding through the crack in his door to sit giggling silently with him over a game of dominoes. One afternoon they said they had to take Samantha to her art lesson and they snuck off to a Walt Disney movie instead, and stayed there in the dark for two hours eating popcorn and Baby Ruths and endless strings of licorice.

10 Toby's parents went home, but the alliance continued. The sense of effort had disappeared. Toby's study became the center of the apartment, and every evening while he read Mary sat with him and sewed and Samantha played with cut-outs at their feet. Mary's pottery began lining the mantel and the bookshelves. She pounded in nails all over the kitchen and hung up her saucepans. Samantha's formal bedtime ritual changed to roughhousing, and she and Toby pounded through the rooms and pelted each other with sofa cushions and ended up in a tangle on the hallway carpet.

Now Samantha was growing unruly with her mother. Talking back. Disobeying. Toby was relieved to see it. Before she had been so good that she seemed pathetic. But Mary said, "I don't know what I'm going to do with that child. She's getting out of hand."

"She seems all right to *me,*" said Toby.

"I knew you'd say that. It's your fault she's changed like this, too. You've spoiled her."

"*Spoiled* her?"

15 "You dote on her, and she knows it," Mary said. She was folding the laundry, moving crisply around the bedroom with armloads of sheets and

towels. Nowadays she wore sweaters and skirts—more practical for house work—and her loafers tapped across the floor with an efficient sound that made him feel she knew what she was talking about. “You give her everything she asks for,” she said. “Now she doesn't listen to *me* any more.

“But there's nothing wrong with giving her things. Is there?”

“If you had to live with her all day long,” Mary said, “eighteen hours a day, the way I do, you'd think twice before you said that.”

But how could he refuse anything to Samantha? With him, she was never disobedient. She shrieked with him over pointless riddles, she asked him unanswerable questions on their walks home from the lab, she punched at him ineffectually, her thumbs tucked inside her fists, when he called her Sam. The only time he was ever angry with her was once when she stepped into the path of a car without looking. “Samantha!” he yelled, and he yanked her back and shook her until she cried. Inside he had felt his stomach lurch, his heart sent out a wave of heat and his knees shook. The purple marks of his fingers stayed on Samantha's arm for days afterward. Would he have been any more terrified if the child were his own? New opportunities for fear were everywhere, now that he was a family man. Samantha's walk from school seemed long and under-policed, and every time he called home without an answer he imagined that Mary had run away from him and he would have to get through life without her. “I think we should have another baby,” he told Mary, although of course he knew that increasing the number of people he loved would not make any one of them more expendable. All Mary said was, “Do you?”

“I love that little girl. I really love her. I'd like to have a whole *armload* of little girls. Did you ever think I would be so good at loving people?”

“Yes,” said Mary.

“I didn't. Not until I met you. I'd like to *give* you things. I'd like to sit you and Samantha down and pile things in your laps. Don't you ever feel that way?”

“Women don't,” said Mary. She slid out of his hands and went to the sink, where she ran cold water over some potatoes. Lately she had started wearing her hair pinned up, out of the way. She looked carved, without a stray wisp or an extra line, smooth to the fingertips, but when Toby came up behind her again she ducked away and went to the stove. “Men are the only ones who have that much feeling left to spare,” she said. “Women's love gets frittered away: every day a thousand little demands for milk and Band-Aids and swept floors and clean towels.”

“I don't believe that,” said Toby.

But Mary was busy regulating the flame under the potatoes now, and she didn't argue with him.

For Easter, Toby bought Samantha a giant prepacked Easter basket swaddled in pink cellophane. It was a spur-of-the-moment purchase—he had gone to the all-night drugstore for pipe tobacco, seen this basket and remembered suddenly that tomorrow was Easter Sunday. Wouldn't Samantha be expecting some sort of celebration? He hated to think of her returning to school empty-handed, when everyone else had chocolate eggs or stuffed rabbits. But when he brought the basket home—rang the doorbell and waited, obscured behind the masses of cellophane like some comical florist's-messenger—he saw that he had made a mistake. Mary didn't like the basket. “How come you bought a thing like that?” she asked him.

"Tomorrow's Easter."

"Easter? Why Easter? We don't even go to church."

"We celebrated Christmas, didn't we?"

"Yes, but—and Easter's not the question," Mary said. "It's this basket." She reached out and touched the cellophane, which shrank beneath her fingers. "We never *used* to buy baskets. Before I've always hidden eggs and let her hunt for them in the morning, and then she dyes them herself."

"Oh, I thought people had jellybeans and things," Toby said.

"*Other* people, maybe. Samantha and I do it differently."

"Wouldn't she like to have what her classmates have?"

"She isn't trying to keep up with the *Joneses,* Toby," Mary said. "And how about her teeth? How about her stomach? Do I always have to be the heavy, bringing these things up? Why is it you get to shower her with love and gifts, and then it's me that takes her to the dentist?"

"Oh, let's not go into *that* again," Toby said.

Then Mary, who could never be predicted, said, "All right," and stopped the argument. "It was nice of you to think of it, anyway," she said formally, taking the basket. "I know Samantha will like it."

Samantha did like it. She treasured every jellybean and marshmallow egg and plastic chick; she telephoned a friend at seven in the morning to tell her about it. But even when she threw her arms around Toby's neck, smelling of sugar and cellophane, all he felt was a sense of defeat. Mary's face was serene and beautiful, like a mask. She continued to move farther and farther away from him, with her lips perpetually curved in a smile and no explanations at all.

In June, when school closed, Mary left him for good. He came home one day to find a square of paper laid flat on a club sandwich. The sight of it thudded instantly against his chest, as if he had been expecting it all along. "I've gone," the note said. His name was nowhere on it. It might have been the same note she sent her first husband—retrieved, somehow, and saved in case she found another use for it. Toby sat down and read it again, analyzed each loop of handwriting for any sign of indecision or momentary, reversible anger. Then he ate the club sandwich, every last crumb, without realizing he was doing so, and after that he pushed his plate away and lowered his head into his hands. He sat that way for several minutes before he thought of Samantha.

It was Monday evening—the time when she would just be finishing with her art lesson. He ran all the way, jaywalking and dodging cars and waving blindly at the drivers who honked. When he arrived in the dingy building where the lessons were given he found he was too early. The teacher still murmured behind a closed door. Toby sat down, panting, on a bench beneath a row of coat hooks. Flashes of old TV programs passed through his head. He saw himself blurred and bluish on a round-cornered screen—one of those mysteriously partnerless television parents who rear their children with more grace and tact and unselfishness than any married couple could ever hope for. Then the classroom door opened. The teacher came out in her smock, ringed by six-year-olds. Toby stood up and said, "Mrs.—um. Is Samantha Glover here?"

The teacher turned. He knew what she was going to say as soon as she took a breath; he hated her so much he wanted to grab her by the neck and slam her head against the wall. "Samantha?" she said. "Why, no, Mr. Scott, Samantha didn't come today."

40 On the walk back, he kept his face stiff and his eyes unfocused. People stared at him. Women turned to look after him, frowning, curious to see the extent of the damage. He barely noticed them. He floundered up the stairs to his apartment, felt his way to the sofa and sat down heavily. There was no need to turn the lights on. He knew already what he would find: toys and saucepans, Mary's skirts and sweaters, Samantha's new short dresses. All they would have taken with them, he knew, was their long gingham gowns and each other.

[*1980*]

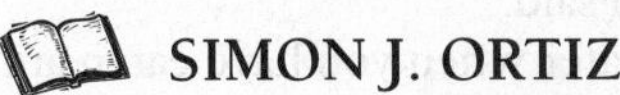

## SIMON J. ORTIZ

*Simon J. Ortiz, of the Acona Pueblo in New Mexico, was born in Albuquerque in 1941, and educated at Fort Lewis College, the University of New Mexico, and the University of Iowa. Although Ortiz is known primarily for his poetry, he has also written short fiction, and he has edited an anthology of Native American short fiction,* Earth Power Coming *(1983). He sums up his chief concern thus: "What I want is a full life / for my son, / for myself / for my Mother, / the Earth.*

# *The San Francisco Indians*

The Chief and a couple of members of his tribe went to the American Indian Center at Mission and 16th. They had walked all the way from their street. A lock hung on the door of the Center, and they stood by the door wondering whether they should go back, call somebody up, or wait around.

"I wonder where they're all at," one of them said.

"Maybe it's a day off or something," another offered.

The Chief pushed against the door again and searched for a notice or something. He read the Fuck FBIs scribble again and felt said. "I guess there isn't going to be anybody here," he said and pulled his blanket tighter to ward off the cold. He motioned to the others and they began to leave. "We'll come back later," the Chief said.

5 At that moment a man walked around the corner and looked up at the plastic sign reading American Indian Center.

One of the Chief's companions called, "Hey, Chief Black Bear." The Chief and the others stopped and watched the man.

The man was around seventy years old. His gray suit was wrinkled and his shoes were scuffed. He looked at the door with the lock and then stepped back into the street. He held a grip bag in his hand.

"Hey, there's an Indian," one of the tribal members said. He smiled happily.

"Yes, there's an Indian," Chief Black Bear said. He straightened up and walked toward the Indian. The Indian man watched them approach.

10 "Hello," the Chief said. He offered a handshake.

"Hello," the Indian said, shaking hands lightly. He was nervous, and he looked at the pavement and then at the young man with the blanket and beads before him. The others, both young men also, stood to one side. They were not as dressed in Indian attire as their chief was.

The Chief and his companions noticed that the Indian was very tired. They felt his tiredness and his age. The Chief said, "We want to invite you to our home. It is not far from here."

"Yes," the Indian said. "But first, I have to find out where all the Indians go. Is this where all the Indians go?" He indicated the locked-up Center.

"Yes," Chief Black Bear said. "They come here, but not all of them. They're all over the city. Some are up on the street."

15 "Yes, Indians are everywhere," the Indian said.

"Come with us, and you can come back later when you have eaten and rested."

The Indian thought about this for a while. He didn't know where to go. He had come this far, and he didn't know where to go.

"I came to look for my grandchild. She came to go to school in Oakland, to learn about business work, months ago. She wrote to tell us she was O.K. But we got letters from the school that she was not going any more, and then she stopped writing. I asked the government, but they don't know about her any more. I came to see her, to find her, but I haven't found her. Someone said she came to San Francisco. That's why I came to where the Indians come. Maybe somebody knows her and where she lives."

The Chief and his tribe were saddened by the old man's search. They wanted to comfort him somehow. "There are Indians on our street," the youthful chief said. "Maybe they will know."

20 The Indian and Chief Black Bear and his tribe walked through gray streets busy with traffic. Some people stared at them, and some didn't. They walked up and down hills. The walking reminded the Indian of the hills and mesas at home. He couldn't see much except buildings and traffic and Chinamen hurrying to some place. Once in a while he could see the ocean to the west. He wanted to ask questions of the young men, but they were intent in their walking and were quiet.

Haight Street was crowded as usual. The Indian saw that some people were just sitting, some were walking around or driving past. He wondered if it was Sunday or a day off. There were a few dressed like the young men he walked with. Chief Black Bear and his companions called greetings to people they met. They walked into a building and up some stairs and entered a room.

"You are welcome here," Chief Black Bear said. He pointed to a small cot. "You can sit down there and sleep there, too." The other two left the room.

The Indian sat down, and he wondered if he would find his grandchild here. There was fast music coming from somewhere behind the walls, and muffled sounds came from the street. The Chief offered him a boloney sandwich and a bottle of wine.

"I'll see if I can find some Indian kids," Chief Black Bear said, and left.

25 After he had finished eating, the Indian lay down and closed his eyes. He was very tired. He had almost fallen asleep when a girl's voice called,

"Chief." He came fully awake to face a girl with blond hair, wearing a colored band around her head.

"Hi," she said. "I'm looking for Chief Black Bear. I heard he brought an Indian back." She was smiling.

"Hello," the Indian said and sat up.

They watched each other. "We have some peyote from Mexico," the girl said. She brought a large coffee can filled with some of the dried buttons. "We have some songs," she said and showed him some records of Indian chants. "This will be the first time, and we wanted someone who knows how to show us." The girl fingered her beads.

The Indian had never seen peyote before, but he had heard songs and prayers for the ceremonials. Maybe it will do O.K., he thought, but he was doubtful. He didn't know the labels on the records, but he thought the chants were not what they would need.

"We want it to be good," the girl said. She felt some of the old man's tiredness too, and his searching and sadness, even without his telling her. She reached out and touched him.

The Chief came back. "There are no Indians around," he said.

The Indian thought, Maybe they have all left for their homes. He looked about the room and wondered if he should leave too. Yes, maybe he should, he thought. But he had come this far, to some place, he was tired, he had seen glimpses of the ocean he had heard about, he had not found his grandchild, and he did not really know where else to look. He had come to look for her because the girl's parents had not. They said, She'll be all right, she's grown up, our people are going some place every day, there are Indians all over the place, she'll be O.K. And that's why he had come.

The People were going all over the world. Indians were everywhere. He had met some at bus stations in Arizona and California. They stood around looking into jukeboxes, magazines in their hands, and getting on and off the buses. And he had met these San Francisco Indians. He looked over at the Chief and the girl who sat on the floor opposite him. They smiled at him.

"I think I'll go now," he said. And he got up to get his bag. "Thank you for your food and wine."

"Wait," Chief Black Bear said. The girl looked worried. And they both looked as if they would grab and hold the Indian. "Won't you stay tonight? We want you to be with us. We have all the things ready," the Chief said.

The Indian looked at the coffee can. "I don't know anything about the peyote stuff. I have heard the songs and prayers, but I think you need more than that. I think I will go," he said.

"But your granddaughter, aren't you going to wait and see if you can find somebody who knows where she is?" Chief Black Bear asked.

"I came to look for my grandchild, but I haven't been able to find her. I am getting to be an old man, and I am tired, and I should be home. My grandchild will be all right, I think. Indians are everywhere."

The Chief and the girl watched helplessly as the Indian left. When he got down to the street, he called a cab from a bar. The cab drove him to the bus station.

As the bus went south toward Palo Alto, the day was getting dark. He thought of a scene a long time back. My prayers were for rain. Pray for rain, my mother said. The *koshare*[1] were going to the east. They were going home. Let us go home, brothers, they sang. I watched them with my prayers.

[*1974*]

[1] ***koshare*** sacred clowns (performers in a religious ritual)

## LILIANA HEKER

***Liliana Heker, born in Argentina in 1943, achieved fame in 1966 with the publication of her first book. She has continued to write fiction, and she has also been influential in her role as the editor of a literary magazine. "The Stolen Party," first published in Spanish in 1982, was translated and printed in*** **Other Fires: Short Fiction by Latin American Women** ***(1985), edited and translated by Alberto Manguel.***

# *The Stolen Party*

As soon as she arrived she went straight to the kitchen to see if the monkey was there. It was: what a relief! She wouldn't have liked to admit that her mother had been right. *Monkeys at a birthday?* her mother had sneered. *Get away with you, believing any nonsense you're told!* She was cross, but not because of the monkey, the girl thought; it's just because of the party.

"I don't like you going," she told her. "It's a rich people's party."

"Rich people go to Heaven too," said the girl, who studied religion at school.

"Get away with Heaven," said the mother. "The problem with you, young lady, is that you like to fart higher than your ass."

5 The girl didn't approve of the way her mother spoke. She was barely nine, and one of the best in her class.

"I'm going because I've been invited," she said. "And I've been invited because Luciana is my friend. So there."

"Ah yes, your friend," her mother grumbled. She paused. "Listen, Rosaura," she said at last. "That one's not your friend. You know what you are to them? The maid's daughter, that's what."

Rosaura blinked hard: she wasn't going to cry. Then she yelled: "Shut up! You know nothing about being friends!"

Every afternoon she used to go to Luciana's house and they would both finish their homework while Rosaura's mother did the cleaning. They had their tea in the kitchen and they told each other secrets. Rosaura loved everything in the big house, and she also loved the people who lived there.

10 "I'm going because it will be the most lovely party in the whole world, Luciana told me it would. There will be a magician, and he will bring a monkey and everything."

The mother swung around to take a good look at her child, and pompously put her hands on her hips.

"Monkeys at a birthday?" she said. "Get away with you, believing any nonsense you're told!"

Rosaura was deeply offended. She thought it unfair of her mother to accuse other people of being liars simply because they were rich. Rosaura too wanted to be rich, of course. If one day she managed to live in a beautiful palace, would her mother stop loving her? She felt very sad. She wanted to go to that party more than anything else in the world.

"I'll die if I don't go," she whispered, almost without moving her lips.

And she wasn't sure whether she had been heard, but on the morning of the party she discovered that her mother had starched her Christmas dress. And in the afternoon, after washing her hair, her mother rinsed it in apple vinegar so that it would be all nice and shiny. Before going out, Rosaura admired herself in the mirror, with her white dress and glossy hair, and thought she looked terribly pretty.

Señora Ines also seemed to notice. As soon as she saw her, she said: "How lovely you look today, Rosaura."

Rosaura gave her starched skirt a slight toss with her hands and walked into the party with a firm step. She said hello to Luciana and asked about the monkey. Luciana put on a secretive look and whispered into Rosaura's ear: "He's in the kitchen. But don't tell anyone, because it's a surprise."

Rosaura wanted to make sure. Carefully she entered the kitchen and there she saw it: deep in thought, inside its cage. It looked so funny that the girl stood there for a while, watching it, and later, every so often, she would slip out of the party unseen and go and admire it. Rosaura was the only one allowed into the kitchen. Señora Ines had said: "You yes, but not the others, they're much too boisterous, they might break something." Rosaura had never broken anything. She even managed the jug of orange juice, carrying it from the kitchen into the dining room. She held it carefully and didn't spill a single drop. And Señora Ines had said: "Are you sure you can manage a jug as big as that?" Of course she could manage. She wasn't a butterfingers, like the others. Like that blonde girl with the bow in her hair. As soon as she saw Rosaura, the girl with the bow had said:

"And you? Who are you?"

"I'm a friend of Luciana," said Rosaura.

"No," said the girl with the bow, "you are not a friend of Luciana because I'm her cousin and I know all her friends. And I don't know you."

"So what," said Rosaura. "I come here every afternoon with my mother and we do our homework together."

"You and your mother do your homework together?" asked the girl, laughing.

"I and Luciana do our homework together," said Rosaura, very seriously.

The girl with the bow shrugged her shoulders.

"That's not being friends," she said. "Do you go to school together?"

"No."

"So where do you know her from?" said the girl, getting impatient.

Rosaura remembered her mother's words perfectly. She took a deep breath.

"I'm the daughter of the employee," she said.

Her mother had said very clearly: "If someone asks, you say you're the daughter of the employee; that's all." She also told her to add: "And proud of it." But Rosaura thought that never in her life would she dare say something of the sort.

"What employee?" said the girl with the bow. "Employee in a shop?"

"No," said Rosaura angrily. "My mother doesn't sell anything in any shop, so there."

35 "So how come she's an employee?" said the girl with the bow.

Just then Señora Ines arrived saying *shh shh,* and asked Rosaura if she wouldn't mind helping serve out the hotdogs, as she knew the house so much better than the others.

"See?" said Rosaura to the girl with the bow, and when no one was looking she kicked her in the shin.

Apart from the girl with the bow, all the others were delightful. The one she liked best was Luciana, with her golden birthday crown; and then the boys. Rosaura won the sack race, and nobody managed to catch her when they played tag. When they split into two teams to play charades, all the boys wanted her for their side. Rosaura felt she had never been so happy in all her life.

But the best was still to come. The best came after Luciana blew out the candles. First the cake. Señora Ines had asked her to help pass the cake around, and Rosaura had enjoyed the task immensely, because everyone called out to her, shouting "Me, me!" Rosaura remembered a story in which there was a queen who had the power of life or death over her subjects. She had always loved that, having the power of life or death. To Luciana and the boys she gave the largest pieces, and to the girl with the bow she gave a slice so thin one could see through it.

40 After the cake came the magician, tall and bony, with a fine red cape. A true magician: he could untie handkerchiefs by blowing on them and make a chain with links that had no openings. He could guess what cards were pulled out from a pack, and the monkey was his assistant. He called the monkey "partner." "Let's see here, partner," he would say, "turn over a card." And, "Don't run away, partner: time to work now."

The final trick was wonderful. One of the children had to hold the monkey in his arms and the magician said he would make him disappear.

"What, the boy?" they all shouted.

"No, the monkey!" shouted back the magician.

Rosaura thought that this was truly the most amusing party in the whole world.

45 The magician asked a small fat boy to come and help, but the small fat boy got frightened almost at once and dropped the monkey on the floor. The magician picked him up carefully, whispered something in his ear, and the monkey nodded almost as if he understood.

"You mustn't be so unmanly, my friend," the magician said to the fat boy.

"What's unmanly?" said the fat boy.

The magician turned around as if to look for spies.

"A sissy," said the magician. "Go sit down."

50 Then he stared at all the faces, one by one. Rosaura felt her heart tremble.

"You with the Spanish eyes," said the magician. And everyone saw that he was pointing at her.

She wasn't afraid. Neither holding the monkey, nor when the magician made him vanish; not even when, at the end, the magician flung his red cape over Rosaura's head and uttered a few magic words . . . and the monkey reappeared, chattering happily, in her arms. The children clapped furiously. And before Rosaura returned to her seat, the magician said:

"Thank you very much, my little countess."

She was so pleased with the compliment that a while later, when her mother came to fetch her, that was the first thing she told her.

"I helped the magician and he said to me, 'Thank you very much, my little countess."

It was strange because up to then Rosaura had thought that she was angry with her mother. All along Rosaura had imagined that she would say to her: "See that the monkey wasn't a lie?" But instead she was so thrilled that she told her mother all about the wonderful magician.

Her mother tapped her on the head and said: "So now we're a countess!"

But one could see that she was beaming.

And now they both stood in the entrance, because a moment ago Señora Ines, smiling, had said: "Please wait here a second."

Her mother suddenly seemed worried.

"What is it?" she asked Rosaura.

"What is what?" said Rosaura. "It's nothing; she just wants to get the presents for those who are leaving, see?"

She pointed at the fat boy and at a girl with pigtails who were also waiting there, next to their mothers. And she explained about the presents. She knew, because she had been watching those who left before her. When one of the girls was about to leave, Señora Ines would give her a bracelet. When a boy left, Señora Ines gave him a yo-yo. Rosaura preferred the yo-yo because it sparkled, but she didn't mention that to her mother. Her mother might have said: "So why don't you ask for one, you blockhead?" That's what her mother was like. Rosaura didn't feel like explaining that she'd be horribly ashamed to be the odd one out. Instead she said:

"I was the best-behaved at the party."

And she said no more because Señora Ines came out into the hall with two bags, one pink and one blue.

First she went up to the fat boy, gave him a yo-yo out of the blue bag, and the fat boy left with his mother. Then she went up to the girl and gave her a bracelet out of the pink bag, and the girl with the pigtails left as well.

Finally she came up to Rosaura and her mother. She had a big smile on her face and Rosaura liked that. Señora Ines looked down at her, then looked up at her mother, and then said something that made Rosaura proud:

"What a marvelous daughter you have, Herminia."

For an instant, Rosaura thought that she'd give her two presents: the bracelet and the yo-yo. Señora Ines bent down as if about to look for something. Rosaura also leaned forward, stretching out her arm. But she never completed the movement.

Señora Ines didn't look in the pink bag. Nor did she look in the blue bag. Instead she rummaged in her purse. In her hand appeared two bills.

"You really and truly earned this," she said handing them over. "Thank you for all your help, my pet."

Rosaura felt her arms stiffen, stick close to her body, and then she noticed her mother's hand on her shoulder. Instinctively she pressed herself against her mother's body. That was all. Except her eyes. Rosaura's eyes had a cold, clear look that fixed itself on Señora Ines's face.

Señora Ines, motionless, stood there with her hand outstretched. As if she didn't dare draw it back. As if the slightest change might shatter an infinitely delicate balance.

[*1982*]

## ALICE WALKER

*Alice Walker was born in 1944 in Eatonton, Georgia, where her parents eked out a living as sharecroppers and dairy farmers; her mother also worked as a domestic. (In a collection of essays,* In Search of Our Mothers' Gardens *[1984], Walker celebrates women who, like her mother, passed on a "respect for the possibilities [of life]—and the will to grasp them.") Walker attended Spelman College in Atlanta, and in 1965 finished her undergraduate work at Sarah Lawrence College near New York City. She then became active in the welfare rights movement in New York and in the voter registration movement in Georgia. Later she taught writing and literature in Mississippi, at Jackson State College and Tougaloo College, and at Wellesley College, the University of Massachusetts, and Yale University.*

*Walker has written essays, poetry, and fiction. Her best-known novel,* The Color Purple *(1982), won a Pulitzer Prize and the National Book Award. She has said that her chief concern is "exploring the oppressions, the insanities, the loyalties, and the triumphs of black women."*

# *Everyday Use*

*For your grandmama*

I will wait for her in the yard that Maggie and I made so clean and wavy yesterday afternoon. A yard like this is more comfortable than most people know. It is not just a yard. It is like an extended living room. When the hard clay is swept clean as a floor and the fine sand around the edges lined with tiny, irregular grooves anyone can come and sit and look up into the elm tree and wait for the breezes that never come inside the house.

Maggie will be nervous until after her sister goes: she will stand hopelessly in corners homely and ashamed of the burn scars down her arms and legs, eyeing her sister with a mixture of envy and awe. She thinks her sister has held life always in the palm of one hand, that "no" is a word the world never learned to say to her.

You've no doubt seen those TV shows where the child who has "made it" is confronted, as a surprise, by her own mother and father, tottering in weakly from backstage. (A pleasant surprise, of course: What would they do if parent and child came on the show only to curse out and insult each other?) On TV mother and child embrace and smile into each other's faces. Sometimes the mother and father weep, the child wraps them in her arms and leans across the table to tell how she would not have made it without their help. I have seen these programs.

Sometimes I dream a dream in which Dee and I are suddenly brought together on a TV program of this sort. Out of a dark and soft-seated limousine I am ushered into a bright room filled with many people. There I meet a smiling, gray, sporty man like Johnny Carson who shakes my hand and tells me what a fine girl I have. Then we are on the stage and Dee is embracing me with tears in her eyes. She pins on my dress a large orchid, even though she has told me once that she thinks orchids are tacky flowers.

5 In real life I am large, big-boned woman with rough, man-working hands. In the winter I wear flannel nightgowns to bed and overalls during the day. I can kill and clean a hog as mercilessly as a man. My fat keeps me hot in zero weather. I can work outside all day, breaking ice to get water for washing. I can eat pork liver cooked over the open fire minutes after it comes steaming from the hog. One winter I knocked a bull calf straight in the brain between the eyes with a sledge hammer and had the meat hung up to chill before nightfall. But of course all this does not show on television. I am the way my daughter would want me to be: a hundred pounds lighter, my skin like an uncooked barley pancake. My hair glistens in the hot bright lights. Johnny Carson has much to do to keep up with my quick and witty tongue.

But that is a mistake. I know even before I wake up. Who ever knew a Johnson with a quick tongue? Who can even imagine me looking a strange white man in the eye? It seems to me I have talked to them always with one foot raised in flight, with my head turned in whichever way is farthest from them. Dee, though. She would always look anyone in the eye. Hesitation was no part of her nature.

"How do I look, Mama?" Maggie says, showing just enough of her thin body enveloped in pink skirt and red blouse for me to know she's there, almost hidden by the door.

"Come out into the yard," I say.

Have you ever seen a lame animal, perhaps a dog run over by some careless person rich enough to own a car, sidle up to someone who is ignorant enough to be kind to him? That is the way my Maggie walks. She has been like this, chin on chest, eyes on ground, feet in shuffle, ever since the fire that burned the other house to the ground.

10 Dee is lighter than Maggie, with nicer hair and a fuller figure. She's a woman now, though sometimes I forget. How long ago was it that the other house burned? Ten, twelve years? Sometimes I can still hear the flames and feel Maggie's arms sticking to me, her hair smoking and her dress falling off her in little black papery flakes. Her eyes seemed stretched open, blazed

open by the flames reflected in them. And Dee. I see her standing off under the sweet gum tree she used to dig gum out of; a look of concentration on her face as she watched the last dingy gray board of the house fall in toward the red-hot brick chimney. Why don't you do a dance around the ashes? I'd wanted to ask her. She had hated the house that much.

I used to think she hated Maggie, too. But that was before we raised the money, the church and me, to send her to Augusta to school. She used to read to us without pity; forcing words, lies, other folks' habits, whole lives upon us two, sitting trapped and ignorant underneath her voice. She washed us in a river of make-believe, burned us with a lot of knowledge we didn't necessarily need to know. Pressed us to her with the serious way she read, to shove us away at just the moment, like dimwits, we seemed about to understand.

Dee wanted nice things. A yellow organdy dress to wear to her graduation from high school; black pumps to match a green suit she'd made from an old suit somebody gave me. She was determined to stare down any disaster in her efforts. Her eyelids would not flicker for minutes at a time. Often I fought off the temptation to shake her. At sixteen she had a style of her own: and knew what style was.

I never had an education myself. After second grade the school was closed down. Don't ask me why: in 1927 colored asked fewer questions than they do now. Sometimes Maggie reads to me. She stumbles along good-naturedly but can't see well. She knows she is not bright. Like good looks and money, quickness passed her by. She will marry John Thomas (who has mossy teeth in an earnest face) and then I'll be free to sit here and I guess just sing church songs to myself. Although I never was a good singer. Never could carry a tune. I was always better at a man's job. I used to love to milk till I was hoofed in the side in '49. Cows are soothing and slow and don't bother you, unless you try to milk them the wrong way.

I have deliberately turned my back on the house. It is three rooms, just like the one that burned, except the roof is tin; they don't make shingle roofs any more. There are no real windows, just some holes cut in the sides, like the portholes in a ship, but not round and not square, with rawhide holding the shutters up on the outside. This house is in a pasture, too, like the other one. No doubt when Dee sees it she will want to tear it down. She wrote me once that no matter where we "choose" to live, she will manage to come see us. But she will never bring her friends. Maggie and I thought about this and Maggie asked me, "Mama, when did Dee ever *have* any friends?"

15 She had a few. Furtive boys in pink shirts hanging about on washday after school. Nervous girls who never laughed. Impressed with her they worshiped the well-turned phrase, the cute shape, the scalding humor that erupted like bubble in lye. She read to them.

When she was courting Jimmy T she didn't have much time to pay to us, but turned all her faultfinding power on him. He *flew* to marry a cheap gal from a family of ignorant flashy people. She hardly had time to recompose herself.

When she comes I will meet—but there they are!

Maggie attempts to make a dash for the house, in her shuffling way, but I stay her with my hand. "Come back here," I say. And she stops and tries to dig a well in the sand with her toe.

It is hard to see them clearly through the strong sun. But even the first glimpse of leg out of the car tells me it is Dee. Her feet were always neat-looking, as if God himself had shaped them with a certain style. From the other side of the car comes a short, stocky man. Hair is all over his head a foot long and hanging from his chin like a kinky mule tail. I hear Maggie suck in her breath. "Uhnnnh," is what it sounds like. Like when you see the wriggling end of a snake just in front of your foot on the road. "Uhnnh."

20 Dee next. A dress down to the ground, in this hot weather. A dress so loud it hurts my eyes. There are yellows and oranges enough to throw back the light of the sun. I feel my whole face warming from the heat waves it throws out. Earrings, too, gold and hanging down to her shoulders. Bracelets dangling and making noises when she moves her arm up to shake the folds of the dress out of her armpits. The dress is loose and flows, and as she walks closer, I like it. I hear Maggie go "Uhnnnh" again. It is her sister's hair. It stands straight up like the wool on a sheep. It is black as night and around the edges are two long pigtails that rope about like small lizards disappearing behind her ears.

"Wa-su-zo-Tean-o!" she says, coming on in that gliding way the dress makes her move. The short stocky fellow with the hair to his navel is all grinning and he follows up with "Asalamalakim, my mother and sister!" He moves to hug Maggie but she falls back, right up against the back of my chair. I feel her trembling there and when I look up I see the perspiration falling off her chin.

"Don't get up," says Dee. Since I am stout it takes something of a push. You can see me trying to move a second or two before I make it. She turns, showing white heels through her sandals, and goes back to the car. Out she peeks next with a Polaroid. She stoops down quickly and lines up picture after picture of me sitting there in front of the house with Maggie cowering behind me. She never takes a shot without making sure the house is included. When a cow comes nibbling around the edge of the yard she snaps it and me and Maggie *and* the house. Then she puts the Polaroid in the back seat of the car, and comes up and kisses me on the forehead.

Meanwhile Asalamalakim is going through the motions with Maggie's hand. Maggie's hand is as limp as a fish, and probably as cold, despite the sweat, and she keeps trying to pull it back. It looks like Asalamalakim wants to shake hands but wants to do it fancy. Or maybe he don't know how people shake hands. Anyhow, he soon gives up on Maggie.

"Well," I say. "Dee."

25 "No, Mama," she says. "Not 'Dee,' Wangero Leewanika Kemanjo!"

"What happened to 'Dee'?" I wanted to know.

"She's dead," Wangero said. "I couldn't bear it any longer being named after the people who oppress me."

"You know as well as me you was named after your aunt Dicie," I said. Dicie is my sister. She named Dee. We called her "Big Dee" after Dee was born.

"But who was *she* named after?" asked Wangero.

30 "I guess after Grandma Dee," I said.

"And who was she named after?" asked Wangero.

"Her mother," I said, and saw Wangero was getting tired. "That's about as far back as I can trace it," I said. Though, in fact, I probably could have carried it back beyond the Civil War through the branches.

"Well," said Asalamalakim, "there you are."

"Uhnnnh," I heard Maggie say.

35 "There I was not," I said, "before 'Dicie' cropped up in our family, so why should I try to trace it that far back?"

He just stood there grinning, looking down on me like somebody inspecting a Model A car. Every once in a while he and Wangero sent eye signals over my head.

"How do you pronounce this name?" I asked.

"You don't have to call me by it if you don't want to," said Wangero.

"Why shouldn't I?" I asked. "If that's what you want us to call you, we'll call you."

40 "I know it might sound awkward at first," said Wangero.

"I'll get used to it," I said. "Ream it out again."

Well, soon we got the name out of the way. Asalamalakim had a name twice as long and three times as hard. After I tripped over it two or three times he told me just to call him Hakim-a-barber. I wanted to ask him was he a barber, but I didn't really think he was, so I didn't ask.

"You must belong to those beef-cattle peoples down the road," I said. They said "Asalamalakim" when they met you, too, but they didn't shake hands. Always too busy: feeding the cattle, fixing the fences, putting up salt-lick shelters, throwing down hay. When the white folks poisoned some of the herd the men stayed up all night with rifles in their hands. I walked a mile and a half just to see the sight.

Hakim-a-barber said, "I accept some of their doctrines, but farming and raising cattle is not my style." (They didn't tell me, and I didn't ask, whether Wangero [Dee] had really gone and married him.)

45 We sat down to eat and right away he said he didn't eat collards and pork was unclean. Wangero, though, went on through the chitlins and corn bread, the greens and everything else. She talked a blue streak over the sweet potatoes. Everything delighted her. Even the fact that we still used the benches her daddy made for the table when we couldn't afford to buy chairs.

"Oh, Mama!" she cried. Then turned to Hakim-a-barber. "I never knew how lovely these benches are. You can feel the rump prints," she said, running her hands underneath her and along the bench. Then she gave a sigh and her hand closed over Grandma Dee's butter dish. "That's it!" she said. "I knew there was something I wanted to ask you if I could have." She jumped up from the table and went over in the corner where the churn stood, the milk in it clabber by now. She looked at the churn and looked at it.

"This churn top is what I need," she said. "Didn't Uncle Buddy whittle it out of a tree you all used to have?"

"Yes," I said.

"Uh huh," she said happily. "And I want the dasher, too."

50 "Uncle Buddy whittle that, too?" asked the barber.

Dee (Wangero) looked up at me.

"Aunt Dee's first husband whittled the dash," said Maggie so low you almost couldn't hear her. "His name was Henry, but they called him Stash."

"Maggie's brain is like an elephant's," Wangero said, laughing. "I can use the churn top as a centerpiece for the alcove table," she said, sliding a plate over the churn, "and I'll think of something artistic to do with the dasher."

When she finished wrapping the dasher the handle stuck out. I took it for a moment in my hands. You didn't even have to look close to see where hands pushing the dasher up and down to make butter had left a kind of sink in the wood. In fact, there were a lot of small sinks; you could see where thumbs and fingers had sunk into the wood. It was beautiful light yellow wood, from a tree that grew in the yard where Big Dee and Stash had lived.

55 After dinner Dee (Wangero) went to the trunk at the foot of my bed and started rifling through it. Maggie hung back in the kitchen over the dishpan. Out came Wangero with two quilts. They had been pieced by Grandma Dee and then Big Dee and me had hung them on the quilt frames on the front porch and quilted them. One was in the Lone Star pattern. The other was Walk Around the Mountain. In both of them were scraps of dresses Grandma Dee had worn fifty and more years ago. Bits and pieces of Grandpa Jarrell's paisley shirts. And one teeny faded blue piece, about the piece of a penny matchbox, that was from Great Grandpa Ezra's uniform that he wore in the Civil War.

"Mama," Wangero said sweet as a bird. "Can I have these old quilts?"

I heard something fall in the kitchen, and a minute later the kitchen door slammed.

"Why don't you take one or two of the others?" I asked. "These old things was just done by me and Big Dee from some tops your grandma pieced before she died."

"No," said Wangero. "I don't want those. They are stitched around the borders by machine."

60 "That's make them last better," I said.

"That's not the point," said Wangero. "These are all pieces of dresses Grandma used to wear. She did all this stitching by hand. Imagine!" She held the quilts securely in her arms, stroking them.

"Some of the pieces, like those lavender ones, come from old clothes her mother handed down to her," I said, moving up to touch the quilts. Dee (Wangero) moved back just enough so that I couldn't reach the quilts. They already belonged to her.

"Imagine!" she breathed again, clutching them closely to her bosom.

"The truth is," I said, "I promised to give them quilts to Maggie, for when she marries John Thomas."

65 She gasped like a bee had stung her.

"Maggie can't appreciate these quilts!" she said. "She'd probably be backward enough to put them to everyday use."

"I reckon she would," I said. "God knows I been saving 'em for long enough with nobody using 'em. I hope she will!" I didn't want to bring up how I had offered Dee (Wangero) a quilt when she went away to college. Then she had told me they were old-fashioned, out of style.

"But they're *priceless!*" she was saying now, furiously; for she has a temper. "Maggie would put them on the bed and in five years they'd be in rags. Less than that!"

"She can always make some more," I said. "Maggie knows how to quilt."

70 Dee (Wangero) looked at me with hatred. "You just will not understand. The point is these quilts, *these* quilts!"

"Well," I said, stumped. "What would *you* do with them?"

"Hang them," she said. As if that was the only thing you *could* do with quilts.

Maggie by now was standing in the door. I could almost hear the sound her feet made as they scraped over each other.

"She can have them, Mama," she said, like somebody used to never winning anything, or having anything reserved for her. "I can 'member Grandma Dee without the quilts."

75 I looked at her hard. She had filled her bottom lip with checkerberry snuff and it gave her face a kind of dopey, hangdog look. It was Grandma Dee and Big Dee who taught her how to quilt herself. She stood there with her scarred hands hidden in the folds of her skirt. She looked at her sister with something like fear but she wasn't mad at her. This was Maggie's portion. This was the way she knew God to work.

When I looked at her like that something hit me in the top of my head and ran down to the soles of my feet. Just like when I'm in church and the spirit of God touches me and I get happy and shout. I did something I never had done before: hugged Maggie to me, then dragged her on into the room, snatched the quilts out of Miss Wangero's hands and dumped them into Maggie's lap. Maggie just sat there on my bed with her mouth open.

"Take one or two of the others," I said to Dee.

But she turned without a word and went out to Hakim-a-barber.

"You just don't understand," she said, as Maggie and I came out to the car.

80 "What don't I understand?" I wanted to know.

"Your heritage," she said. And then she turned to Maggie, kissed her, and said, "You ought to try to make something of yourself, too, Maggie. It's really a new day for us. But from the way you and Mama still live you'd never know it."

She put on some sunglasses that hid everything above the tip of her nose and her chin.

Maggie smiled; maybe at the sunglasses. But a real smile, not scared. After we watched the car dust settle I asked Maggie to bring me a dip of snuff. And then the two of us sat there just enjoying, until it was time to go in the house and go to bed.

[*1973*]

## TOBIAS WOLFF

*Tobias Wolff was born in Alabama in 1945, but he grew up in the state of Washington. He left high school before graduating, served as an apprentice seaman and as a weight-guesser in a carnival, and then joined the army, where he served four years as a paratrooper. After his discharge from the army, he hired private tutors to enable him to pass the entrance degree to Oxford University. At Oxford he did spectacularly well, graduating with First Class Honors in English. Wolff has written stories, novels, and an autobiography (*This Boy's Life*); he now teaches writing at Syracuse University.*

# Powder

Just before Christmas my father took me skiing at Mount Baker. He'd had to fight for the privilege of my company, because my mother was still angry with him for sneaking me into a nightclub during his last visit, to see Thelonius Monk.

He wouldn't give up. He promised, hand on heart, to take good care of me and have me home for dinner on Christmas Eve, and she relented. But as we were checking out of the lodge that morning it began to snow, and in this snow he observed some quality that made it necessary for us to get in one last run. We got in several last runs. He was indifferent to my fretting. Snow whirled around us in bitter, blinding squalls, hissing like sand, and still we skied. As the lift bore us to the peak yet again, my father looked at his watch and said: "Criminey. This'll have to be a fast one."

By now I couldn't see the trail. There was no point in trying. I stuck to him like white on rice and did what he did and somehow made it to the bottom without sailing off a cliff. We returned our skis and my father put chains on the Austin-Healy while I swayed from foot to foot, clapping my mittens and wishing I were home. I could see everything. The green tablecloth, the plates with the holly pattern, the red candles waiting to be lit.

We passed a diner on our way out. "You want some soup?" my father asked. I shook my head. "Buck up," he said. "I'll get you there. Right, doctor?"

5 I was supposed to say, "Right, doctor," but I didn't say anything.

A state trooper waved us down outside the resort. A pair of sawhorses were blocking the road. The trooper came up to our car and bent down to my father's window. His face was bleached by the cold. Snowflakes clung to his eyebrows and to the fur trim of his jacket and cap.

"Don't tell me," my father said.

The trooper told him. The road was closed. It might get cleared, it might not. Storm took everyone by surprise. So much, so fast. Hard to get people moving. Christmas Eve. What can you do?

My father said: "Look. We're talking about four, five inches. I've taken this car through worse than that."

10 The trooper straightened up, boots creaking. His face was out of sight but I could hear him. "The road is closed."

My father sat with both hands on the wheel, rubbing the wood with his thumbs. He looked at the barricade for a long time. He seemed to be trying to master the idea of it. Then he thanked the trooper, and with a weird, old-maidy show of caution turned the car around. "Your mother will never forgive me for this," he said.

"We should have left before," I said. "Doctor."

He didn't speak to me again until we were in a booth at the diner, waiting for our burgers. "She won't forgive me," he said. "Do you understand? Never."

"I guess," I said, but no guesswork was required; she wouldn't forgive him.

15 "I can't let that happen." He bent toward me. "I'll tell you what I want. I want us to be all together again. Is that what you want?"

"Yes, sir."

He bumped my chin with his knuckles. "That's all I needed to hear."

When we finished eating he went to the pay phone in the back of the diner, then joined me in the booth again. I figured he'd called my mother, but he didn't give a report. He sipped at his coffee and stared out the window at the empty road. "Come on, come on," he said. A little while later he said, "Come on!" When the trooper's car went past, lights flashing, he got up and dropped some money on the check. "O.K. Vámonos."

The wind had died. The snow was falling straight down, less of it now; lighter. We drove away from the resort, right up to the barricade. "Move it," my father told me. When I looked at him he said, "What are you waiting for?" I got out and dragged one of the sawhorses aside, then put it back after he drove through. He pushed the door open for me. "Now you're an accomplice," he said. "We go down together." He put the car into gear and gave me a look. "Joke, doctor."

"Funny, doctor."

Down the first long stretch I watched the road behind us, to see if the trooper was on our tail. The barricade vanished. Then there was nothing but snow: snow on the road, snow kicking up from the chains, snow on the trees, snow in the sky; and our trail in the snow. I faced around and had a shock. The lie of the road behind us had been marked by our own tracks, but there were no tracks ahead of us. My father was breaking virgin snow between a line of tall trees. He was humming "Stars Fell on Alabama." I felt snow brush along the floorboards under my feet. To keep my hands from shaking, I clamped them between my knees.

My father grunted in a thoughtful way and said, "Don't ever try this yourself."

"I won't."

"That's what you say now, but someday you'll get your license and then you'll think you can do anything. Only you won't be able to do this. You need, I don't know—a certain instinct."

"Maybe I have it."

"You don't. You have your strong points, but not . . . this. I only mention it, because I don't want you to get the idea this is something just anybody can do. I'm a great driver. That's not a virtue, O.K.? It's just a fact, and one you should be aware of. Of course you have to give the old heap some credit, too—there aren't many cars I'd try this with. Listen!"

I listened. I heard the slap of the chains, the stiff, jerky rasps of the wipers, the purr of the engine. It really did purr. The car was almost new. My father couldn't afford it, and kept promising to sell it, but here it was.

I said, "Where do you think that policeman went to?"

"Are you warm enough?" He reached over and cranked up the blower. Then he turned off the wipers. We didn't need them. The clouds had brightened. A few sparse, feathery flakes drifted into our slipstream and were swept away. We left the trees and entered a broad field of snow that ran level for a while and then tilted sharply downward. Orange stakes had been planted at intervals in two parallel lines and my father steered a course between them, though they were far enough apart to leave considerable doubt in my mind as to where exactly the road lay. He was humming again, doing little scat riffs around the melody.

"O.K. then. What are my strong points?"

"Don't get me started," he said. "It'd take all day."

"Oh, right. Name one."

"Easy. You always think ahead."

True. I always thought ahead. I was a boy who kept his clothes on numbered hangers to insure proper rotation. I bothered my teachers for homework assignments far ahead of their due dates so I could make up schedules. I thought ahead, and that was why I knew that there would be other troopers waiting for us at the end of our ride, if we got there. What I did not know was that my father would wheedle and plead his way past them—he didn't sing "O Tannenbaum" but just about—and get me home for dinner, buying a little more time before my mother decided to make the split final. I knew we'd get caught; I was resigned to it. And maybe for this reason I stopped moping and began to enjoy myself.

Why not? This was one for the books. Like being in a speedboat, but better. You can't go downhill in a boat. And it was all ours. And it kept coming, the laden trees, the unbroken surface of snow, the sudden white vistas. Here and there I saw hints of the road, ditches, fences, stakes, but not so many that I could have found my way. But then I didn't have to. My father was driving. My father in his 48th year, rumpled, kind, bankrupt of honor, flushed with certainty. He was a great driver. All persuasion, no coercion. Such subtlety at the wheel, such tactful pedalwork. I actually trusted him. And the best was yet to come—the switchbacks and hairpins. Impossible to describe. Except maybe to say this: If you haven't driven fresh powder, you haven't driven.

[*1992*]

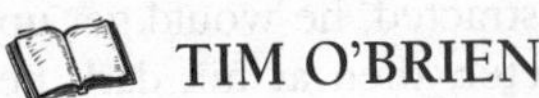

## TIM O'BRIEN

*Tim O'Brien, born in 1947 in Austin, Minnesota, was drafted into the army in 1968 and served as an infantryman in Vietnam. Drawing on this experience he wrote a memoir,* If I Die in a Combat Zone *(1973), in which he explains that he did not believe in the Vietnam War, considered dodging the draft, but, lacking the courage to do so, he served, largely out of fear and embarrassment. A later book, a novel called* Going after Cacciato, *won the National Book Award in 1979.*

*"The Things They Carried," first published in 1986, in 1990 was republished as one of a series of interlocking stories in a book entitled* The Things They Carried. *In one of the stories, entitled "How To Tell a True War Story," he writes,*

> *A true war story is never moral. It does not instruct, nor encourage virtue, nor suggest models of proper human behavior. . . . If a story seems moral, do not believe it. If at the end of a war story you feel uplifted, or if you feel that some small bit of rectitude has been salvaged from the larger waste, then you have been made the victim of a very old and terrible lie. There is no rectitude whatsoever. There is no virtue. As a first rule of thumb, therefore, you can tell a true war*

***story by its absolute and uncompromising allegiance to obscenity and evil.***

## *The Things They Carried*

First Lieutenant Jimmy Cross carried letters from a girl named Martha, a junior at Mount Sebastian College in New Jersey. They were not love letters, but Lieutenant Cross was hoping, so he kept them folded in plastic at the bottom of his rucksack. In the late afternoon, after a day's march, he would dig his foxhole, wash his hands under a canteen, unwrap the letters, hold them with the tips of his fingers, and spend the last hour of light pretending. He would imagine romantic camping trips into the White Mountains in New Hampshire. He would sometimes taste the envelope flaps, knowing her tongue had been there. More than anything, he wanted Martha to love him as he loved her, but the letters were mostly chatty, elusive on the matter of love. She was a virgin, he was almost sure. She was an English major at Mount Sebastian, and she wrote beautifully about her professors and roommates and midterm exams, about her respect for Chaucer and her great affection for Virginia Woolf. She often quoted lines of poetry; she never mentioned the war, except to say, Jimmy, take care of yourself. The letters weighed ten ounces. They were signed "Love, Martha," but Lieutenant Cross understood that Love was only a way of signing and did not mean what he sometimes pretended it meant. At dusk, he would carefully return the letters to his rucksack. Slowly, a bit distracted, he would get up and move among his men, checking the perimeter, then at full dark he would return to his hole and watch the night and wonder if Martha was a virgin.

The things they carried were largely determined by necessity. Among the necessities or near-necessities were P-38 can openers, pocket knives, heat tabs, wrist watches, dog tags, mosquito repellent, chewing gum, candy, cigarettes, salt tablets, packets of Kool-Aid, lighters, matches, sewing kits, Military Payment Certificates, C rations, and two or three canteens of water. Together, these items weighed between fifteen and twenty pounds, depending upon a man's habits or rate of metabolism. Henry Dobbins, who was a big man, carried extra rations; he was especially fond of canned peaches in heavy syrup over pound cake. Dave Jensen, who practiced field hygiene, carried a toothbrush, dental floss, and several hotel-size bars of soap he'd stolen on R&R[1] in Sydney, Australia. Ted Lavender, who was scared, carried tranquilizers until he was shot in the head outside the village of Than Khe in mid-April. By necessity, and because it was SOP,[2] they all carried steel helmets that weighed five pounds including the liner and camouflage cover. They carried the standard fatigue jackets and trousers. Very few carried underwear. On their feet they carried jungle boots—2.1 pounds—and Dave Jensen carried three pairs of socks and a can of Dr. Scholl's foot powder as a precaution against trench foot. Until he was shot,

[1]**R&R** rest and rehabilitation leave
[2]**SOP** standard operating procedure

Ted Lavender carried six or seven ounces of premium dope, which for him was a necessity. Mitchell Sanders, the RTO,[3] carried condoms. Norman Bowker carried a diary. Rat Kiley carried comic books. Kiowa, a devout Baptist, carried an illustrated New Testament that had been presented to him by his father, who taught Sunday school in Oklahoma City, Oklahoma. As a hedge against bad times, however, Kiowa also carried his grandmother's distrust of the white man, his grandfather's old hunting hatchet. Necessity dictated. Because the land was mined and booby-trapped, it was SOP for each man to carry a steel-centered, nylon-covered flak jacket, which weighed 6.7 pounds, but which on hot days seemed much heavier. Because you could die so quickly, each man carried at least one large compress bandage, usually in the helmet band for easy access. Because the nights were cold, and because the monsoons were wet, each carried a green plastic poncho that could be used as a raincoat or groundsheet or makeshift tent. With its quilted liner, the poncho weighed almost two pounds, but it was worth every ounce. In April, for instance, when Ted Lavender was shot, they used his poncho to wrap him up, then to carry him across the paddy, then to lift him into the chopper that took him away.

They were called legs or grunts.

To carry something was to "hump" it, as when Lieutenant Jimmy Cross humped his love for Martha up the hills and through the swamps. In its intransitive form, "to hump" meant "to walk," or "to march," but it implied burdens far beyond the intransitive.

5 Almost everyone humped photographs. In his wallet, Lieutenant Cross carried two photographs of Martha. The first was a Kodachrome snapshot signed "Love," though he knew better. She stood against a brick wall. Her eyes were gray and neutral, her lips slightly open as she stared straight-on at the camera. At night, sometimes, Lieutenant Cross wondered who had taken the picture, because he knew she had boyfriends, because he loved her so much, and because he could see the shadow of the picture taker spreading out against the brick wall. The second photograph had been clipped from the 1968 Mount Sebastian yearbook. It was an action shot—women's volleyball—and Martha was bent horizontal to the floor, reaching, the palms of her hands in sharp focus, the tongue taut, the expression frank and competitive. There was no visible sweat. She wore white gym shorts. Her legs, he thought, were almost certainly the legs of a virgin, dry and without hair, the left knee cocked and carrying her entire weight, which was just over one hundred pounds. Lieutenant Cross remembered touching that left knee. A dark theater, he remembered, and the movie was *Bonnie and Clyde,* and Martha wore a tweed skirt, and during the final scene, when he touched her knee, she turned and looked at him in a sad, sober way that made him pull his hand back, but he would always remember the feel of the tweed skirt and the knee beneath it and the sound of the gunfire that killed Bonnie and Clyde, how embarrassing it was, how slow and oppressive. He remembered kissing her goodnight at the dorm door. Right then, he thought, he should've done something brave. He should've carried her up the stairs to her room and tied her to the bed and touched that left knee all

[3]**RTO** radio and telephone operator

night long. He should've risked it. Whenever he looked at the photographs, he thought of new things he should've done.

What they carried was partly a function of rank, partly of field specialty.

As a first lieutenant and platoon leader, Jimmy Cross carried a compass, maps, code books, binoculars, and a .45-caliber pistol that weighed 2.9 pounds fully loaded. He carried a strobe light and the responsibility for the lives of his men.

As an RTO, Mitchell Sanders carried the PRC-25 radio, a killer, twenty-six pounds with its battery.

As a medic, Rat Kiley carried a canvas satchel filled with morphine and plasma and malaria tablets and surgical tape and comic books and all the things a medic must carry, including M&M's[4] for especially bad wounds, for a total weight of nearly twenty pounds.

10 As a big man, therefore a machine gunner, Henry Dobbins carried the M-60, which weighed twenty-three pounds unloaded, but which was almost always loaded. In addition, Dobbins carried between ten and fifteen pounds of ammunition draped in belts across his chest and shoulders.

As PFCs or Spec 4s, most of them were common grunts and carried the standard M-16 gas-operated assault rifle. The weapon weighed 7.5 pounds unloaded, 8.2 pounds with its full twenty-round magazine. Depending on numerous factors, such as topography and psychology, the riflemen carried anywhere from twelve to twenty magazines, usually in cloth bandoliers, adding on another 8.4 pounds at minimum, fourteen pounds at maximum. When it was available, they also carried M-16 maintenance gear—rods and steel brushes and swabs and tubes of LSA oil—all of which weighed about a pound. Among the grunts, some carried the M-79 grenade launcher, 5.9 pounds unloaded, a reasonably light weapon except for the ammunition, which was heavy. A single round weighed ten ounces. The typical load was twenty-five rounds. But Ted Lavender, who was scared, carried thirty-four rounds when he was shot and killed outside. Than Khe, and he went down under an exceptional burden, more than twenty pounds of ammunition, plus the flak jacket and helmet and rations and water and toilet paper and tranquilizers and all the rest, plus the unweighed fear. He was dead weight. There was no twitching or flopping. Kiowa, who saw it happen, said it was like watching a rock fall, or a big sandbag or something—just boom, then down—not like the movies where the dead guy rolls around and does fancy spins and goes ass over teakettle—not like that, Kiowa said, the poor bastard just flat-fuck fell. Boom. Down. Nothing else. It was a bright morning in mid-April. Lieutenant Cross felt the pain. He blamed himself. They stripped off Lavender's canteens and ammo, all the heavy things, and Rat Kiley said the obvious, the guy's dead, and Mitchell Sanders used his radio to report one U.S. KIA[5] and to request a chopper. Then they wrapped Lavender in his poncho. They carried him out to a dry paddy, established security, and sat smoking the dead man's dope until the chopper came. Lieutenant Cross

[4]**M&M** joking term for medical supplies

[5]**KIA** killed in action

kept to himself. He pictured Martha's smooth young face, thinking he loved her more than anything, more than his men, and now Ted Lavender was dead because he loved her so much and could not stop thinking about her. When the dust-off arrived, they carried Lavender aboard. Afterward they burned Than Khe. They marched until dusk, then dug their holes, and that night Kiowa kept explaining how you had to be there, how fast it was, how the poor guy just dropped like so much concrete. Boom-down, he said. Like cement.

In addition to the three standard weapons—the M-60, M-16, and M-79—they carried whatever presented itself, or whatever seemed appropriate as a means of killing or staying alive. They carried catch-as-catch-can. At various times, in various situations, they carried M-14s and CAR-15s and Swedish Ks and grease guns and captured AK-47s and Chi-Coms and RPGs and Simonov carbines and black-market Uzis and .38-caliber Smith & Wesson handguns and 66 mm LAWs and shotguns and silencers and blackjacks and bayonets and C-4 plastic explosives. Lee Strunk carried a slingshot; a weapon of last resort, he called it. Mitchell Sanders carried brass knuckles. Kiowa carried his grandfather's feathered hatchet. Every third or fourth man carried a Claymore antipersonnel mine—3.5 pounds with its firing device. They all carried fragmentation grenades—fourteen ounces each. They all carried at least one M-18 colored smoke grenade—twenty-four ounces. Some carried CS or tear-gas grenades. Some carried white-phosphorus grenades. They carried all they could bear, and then some, including a silent awe for the terrible power of the things they carried.

In the first week of April, before Lavender died, Lieutenant Jimmy Cross received a good-luck charm from Martha. It was a simple pebble, an ounce at most. Smooth to the touch, it was a milky-white color with flecks of orange and violet, oval-shaped, like a miniature egg. In the accompanying letter, Martha wrote that she had found the pebble on the Jersey shoreline, precisely where the land touched water at high tide, where things came together but also separated. It was this separate-but-together quality, she wrote, that had inspired her to pick up the pebble and to carry it in her breast pocket for several days, where it seemed weightless, and then to send it through the mail, by air, as a token of her truest feelings for him. Lieutenant Cross found this romantic. But he wondered what her truest feelings were, exactly, and what she meant by separate-but-together. He wondered how the tides and waves had come into play on that afternoon along the Jersey shoreline when Martha saw the pebble and bent down to rescue it from geology. He imagined bare feet. Martha was a poet, with the poet's sensibilities, and her feet would be brown and bare, the toenails unpainted, the eyes chilly and somber like the ocean in March, and though it was painful, he wondered who had been with her that afternoon. He imagined a pair of shadows moving along the strip of sand where things came together but also separated. It was phantom jealousy, he knew, but he couldn't help himself. He loved her so much. On the march, through the hot days of early April, he carried the pebble in his mouth, turning it with his tongue, tasting sea salts and moisture. His mind wandered. He had difficulty keeping his attention on the war. On occasion he would yell at his men to spread out the column, to keep their eyes open, but then he would slip away into daydreams, just pretending, walking barefoot along the Jersey shore, with Martha, carrying nothing. He would feel himself rising. Sun and waves and gentle winds, all love and lightness.

What they carried varied by mission.

15 When a mission took them to the mountains, they carried mosquito netting, machetes, canvas tarps, and extra bugjuice.

If a mission seemed especially hazardous, or if it involved a place they knew to be bad, they carried everything they could. In certain heavily mined AOs,[6] where the land was dense with Toe Poppers and Bouncing Betties, they took turns humping a twenty-eight-pound mine detector. With its headphones and big sensing plate, the equipment was a stress on the lower back and shoulders, awkward to handle, often useless because of the shrapnel in the earth, but they carried it anyway, partly for safety, partly for the illusion of safety.

On ambush, or other night missions, they carried peculiar little odds and ends. Kiowa always took along his New Testament and a pair of moccasins for silence. Dave Jensen carried night-sight vitamins high in carotin. Lee Strunk carried his slingshot; ammo, he claimed, would never be a problem. Rat Kiley carried brandy and M&M's. Until he was shot, Ted Lavender carried the starlight scope, which weighed 6.3 pounds with its aluminum carrying case. Henry Dobbins carried his girlfriend's panty hose wrapped around his neck as a comforter. They all carried ghosts. When dark came, they would move out single file across the meadows and paddies to their ambush coordinates, where they would quietly set up the Claymores and lie down and spend the night waiting.

Other missions were more complicated and required special equipment. In mid-April, it was their mission to search out and destroy the elaborate tunnel complexes in the Than Khe area south of Chu Lai. To blow the tunnels, they carried one-pound blocks of pentrite high explosives, four blocks to a man, sixty-eight pounds in all. They carried wiring, detonators, and battery-powdered clackers. Dave Jensen carried earplugs. Most often, before blowing the tunnels, they were ordered by higher command to search them, which was considered bad news, but by and large they just shrugged and carried out orders. Because he was a big man, Henry Dobbins was excused from tunnel duty. The others would draw numbers. Before Lavender died there were seventeen men in the platoon, and whoever drew the number seventeen would strip off his gear and crawl in headfirst with a flashlight and Lieutenant Cross's .45-caliber pistol. The rest of them would fan out as security. They would sit down or kneel, not facing the hole, listening to the ground beneath them, imagining cobwebs and ghosts, whatever was down there—the tunnel walls squeezing in—how the flashlight seemed impossibly heavy in the hand and how it was tunnel vision in the very strictest sense, compression in all ways, even time, and how you had to wiggle in—ass and elbows—a swallowed-up feeling—and how you found yourself worrying about odd things—will your flashlight go dead? Do rats

[6]**AOs** areas of operation

carry rabies? If you screamed, how far would the sound carry? Would your buddies hear it? Would they have the courage to drag you out? In some respects, though not many, the waiting was worse than the tunnel itself. Imagination was a killer.

On April 16, when Lee Strunk drew the number seventeen, he laughed and muttered something and went down quickly. The morning was hot and very still. Not good, Kiowa said. He looked at the tunnel opening, then out across a dry paddy toward the village of Than Khe. Nothing moved. No clouds or birds or people. As they waited, the men smoked and drank Kool-Aid, not talking much, feeling sympathy for Lee Strunk but also feeling the luck of the draw. You win some, you lose some, said Mitchell Sanders, and sometimes you settle for a rain check. It was a tired line and no one laughed.

20 Henry Dobbins ate a tropical chocolate bar. Ted Lavender popped a tranquilizer and went off to pee.

After five minutes, Lieutenant Jimmy Cross moved to the tunnel, leaned down, and examined the darkness. Trouble, he thought—a cave-in maybe. And then suddenly, without willing it, he was thinking about Martha. The stresses and fractures, the quick collapse, the two of them buried alive under all that weight. Dense, crushing love. Kneeling, watching the hole, he tried to concentrate on Lee Strunk and the war, all the dangers, but his love was too much for him, he felt paralyzed, he wanted to sleep inside her lungs and breathe her blood and be smothered. He wanted her to be a virgin and not a virgin, all at once. He wanted to know her. Intimate secrets—why poetry? Why so sad? Why that grayness in her eyes? Why so alone? Not lonely, just alone—riding her bike across campus or sitting off by herself in the cafeteria. Even dancing, she danced alone—and it was the aloneness that filled him with love. He remembered telling her that one evening. How she nodded and looked away. And how, later, when he kissed her, she received the kiss without returning it, her eyes wide open, not afraid, not a virgin's eyes, just flat and uninvolved.

Lieutenant Cross gazed at the tunnel. But he was not there. He was buried with Martha under the white sand at the Jersey shore. They were pressed together, and the pebble in his mouth was her tongue. He was smiling. Vaguely, he was aware of how quiet the day was, the sullen paddies, yet he could not bring himself to worry about matters of security. He was beyond that. He was just a kid at war, in love. He was twenty-two years old. He couldn't help it.

A few moments later Lee Strunk crawled out of the tunnel. He came up grinning, filthy but alive. Lieutenant Cross nodded and closed his eyes while the others clapped Strunk on the back and made jokes about rising from the dead.

Worms, Rat Kiley said. Right out of the grave. Fuckin' zombie.

25 The men laughed. They all felt great relief.

Spook City, said Mitchell Sanders.

Lee Strunk made a funny ghost sound, a kind of moaning, yet very happy, and right then, when Strunk made that high happy moaning sound, when he went *Ahhooooo,* right then Ted Lavender was shot in the head on his way back from peeing. He lay with his mouth open. The teeth were broken. There was a swollen black bruise under his left eye. The cheekbone was gone. Oh shit, Rat Kiley said, the guy's dead. The guy's dead, he kept saying, which seemed profound—the guy's dead. I mean really.

The things they carried were determined to some extent by superstition. Lieutenant Cross carried his good-luck pebble. Dave Jensen carried a rabbit's foot. Norman Bowker, otherwise a very gentle person, carried a thumb that had been presented to him as a gift by Mitchell Sanders. The thumb was dark brown, rubbery to the touch, and weighed four ounces at most. It had been cut from a VC corpse, a boy of fifteen or sixteen. They'd found him at the bottom of an irrigation ditch, badly burned, flies in his mouth and eyes. The boy wore black shorts and sandals. At the time of his death he had been carrying a pouch of rice, a rifle, and three magazines of ammunition.

You want my opinion, Mitchell Sanders said, there's a definite moral here.

30 He put his hand on the dead boy's wrist. He was quiet for a time, as if counting a pulse, then he patted the stomach, almost affectionately, and used Kiowa's hunting hatchet to remove the thumb.

Henry Dobbins asked what the moral was.

Moral?

You know. *Moral.*

Sanders wrapped the thumb in toilet paper and handed it across to Norman Bowker. There was no blood. Smiling, he kicked the boy's head, watched the flies scatter, and said, It's like with that old TV show—Paladin. Have gun, will travel.

35 Henry Dobbins thought about it.

Yeah, well, he finally said. I don't see no moral.

There it *is,* man.

Fuck off.

They carried USO stationery and pencils and pens. They carried Sterno, safety pins, trip flares, signal flares, spools of wire, razor blades, chewing tobacco, liberated joss sticks and statuettes of the smiling Buddha, candles, grease pencils, *The Stars and Stripes,* fingernail clippers, Psy Ops leaflets, bush hats, bolos, and much more. Twice a week, when the resupply choppers came in, they carried hot chow in green Mermite cans and large canvas bags filled with iced beer and soda pop. They carried plastic water containers, each with a two gallon capacity. Mitchell Sanders carried a set of starched tiger fatigues for special occasions. Henry Dobbins carried Black Flag insecticide. Dave Jensen carried empty sandbags that could be filled at night for added protection. Lee Strunk carried tanning lotion. Some things they carried in common. Taking turns, they carried the big PRC-77 scrambler radio, which weighed thirty pounds with its battery. They shared the weight of memory. They took up what others could no longer bear. Often, they carried each other, the wounded or weak. They carried infections. They carried chess sets, basketballs, Vietnamese-English dictionaries, insignia of rank, Bronze Stars and Purple Hearts, plastic cards imprinted with the Code of Conduct. They carried diseases, among them malaria and dysentery. They carried lice and ringworm and leeches and paddy algae and various rots and molds. They carried the land itself—Vietnam, the place, the soil—a powdery orange-red dust that covered their boots and fatigues and faces. They carried the sky. The whole atmosphere, they carried it, the humidity, the monsoons, the stink of fungus and decay, all of it, they carried gravity. They moved like mules. By daylight they took sniper fire, at night they were mortared, but it was not battle, it was just the endless march, village to village, without purpose, nothing won or lost. They marched for the sake of the march. They plodded along slowly, dumbly, leaning forward against the heat, unthinking, all blood and bone, simple grunts, soldiering with their legs, toiling up the hills and down into the paddies and across the rivers and up again and down, just humping, one step and then the next and then another, but no volition, no will, because it was automatic, it was anatomy, and the war was entirely a matter of posture and carriage, the hump was everything, a kind of inertia, a kind of emptiness, a dullness of desire and intellect and conscience and hope and human sensibility. Their principles were in their feet. Their calculations were biological. They had no sense of strategy or mission. They searched the villages without knowing what to look for, nor caring, kicking over jars of rice, frisking children and old men, blowing tunnels, sometimes setting fires and sometimes not, then forming up and moving on to the next village, then other villages, where it would always be the same. They carried their own lives. The pressures were enormous. In the heat of early afternoon, they would remove their helmets and flak jackets, walking bare, which was dangerous but which helped ease the strain. They would often discard things along the route of march. Purely for comfort, they would throw away rations, blow their Claymores and grenades, no matter, because by nightfall the resupply choppers would arrive with more of the same, then a day or two later still more, fresh watermelons and crates of ammunition and sunglasses and woolen sweaters—the resources were stunning—sparklers for the Fourth of July, colored eggs for Easter. It was the great American war chest—the fruits of sciences, the smoke stacks, the canneries, the arsenals at Hartford, the Minnesota forests, the machine shops, the vast fields of corn and wheat—they carried like freight trains; they carried it on their backs and shoulders—and for all the ambiguities of Vietnam, all the mysteries and unknowns, there was at least the single abiding certainty that they would never be at a loss for things to carry.

40 After the chopper took Lavender away, Lieutenant Jimmy Cross led his men into the village of Than Khe. They burned everything. They shot chickens and dogs, they trashed the village well, they called in artillery and watched the wreckage, then they marched for several hours through the hot afternoon, and then at dusk, while Kiowa explained how Lavender died, Lieutenant Cross found himself trembling.

He tried not to cry. With his entrenching tool, which weighed five pounds, he began digging a hole in the earth.

He felt shame. He hated himself. He had loved Martha more than his men, and as a consequence Lavender was now dead, and this was something he would have to carry like a stone in his stomach for the rest of the war.

All he could do was dig. He used his entrenching tool like an ax, slashing, feeling both love and hate, and then later, when it was full dark, he sat at the bottom of his foxhole and wept. It went on for a long while. In part, he was grieving for Ted Lavender, but mostly it was for Martha, and for himself, because she belonged to another world, which was not quite real, and because she was a junior at Mount Sebastian College in New Jersey, a poet and a virgin and uninvolved, and because he realized she did not love him and never would.

Like cement, Kiowa whispered in the dark. I swear to God—boom-down. Not a word.

45 I've heard this, said Norman Bowker.

A pisser, you know? Still zipping himself up. Zapped while zipping.

All right, fine. That's enough.

Yeah, but you had to see it, the guy just—

I *heard,* man. Cement. So why not shut the fuck *up?*

50 Kiowa shook his head sadly and glanced over at the hole where Lieutenant Jimmy Cross sat watching the night. The air was thick and wet. A warm, dense fog had settled over the paddies and there was the stillness that precedes rain.

After a time Kiowa sighed.

One thing for sure, he said. The lieutenant's in some deep hurt. I mean that crying jag—the way he was carrying on—it wasn't fake or anything, it was real heavy-duty hurt. The man cares.

Sure, Norman Bowker said.

Say what you want, the man does care.

55 We all got problems.

Not Lavender.

No, I guess not, Bowker said. Do me a favor, though.

Shut up?

That's a smart Indian. Shut up.

60 Shrugging, Kiowa pulled off his boots. He wanted to say more, just to lighten up his sleep, but instead he opened his New Testament and arranged it beneath his head as a pillow. The fog made things seem hollow and unattached. He tried not to think about Ted Lavender, but then he was thinking how fast it was, no drama, down and dead, and how it was hard to feel anything except surprise. It seemed unchristian. He wished he could find some great sadness, or even anger, but the emotion wasn't there and he couldn't make it happen. Mostly he felt pleased to be alive. He liked the smell of the New Testament under his cheek, the leather and ink and paper and glue, whatever the chemicals were. He liked hearing the sounds of night. Even his fatigue, it felt fine, the stiff muscles and the prickly awareness of his own body, a floating feeling. He enjoyed not being dead. Lying there, Kiowa admired Lieutenant Jimmy Cross's capacity for grief. He wanted to share the man's pain, he wanted to care as Jimmy Cross cared. And yet when he closed his eyes, all he could think was Boom-down, and all he could feel was the pleasure of having his boots off and the fog curling in around him and the damp soil and the Bible smells and the plush comfort of night.

After a moment Norman Bowker sat up in the dark.

What the hell, he said. You want to talk, *talk.* Tell it to me.

Forget it.

No, man, go on. One thing I hate, it's a silent Indian.

65 For the most part they carried themselves with poise, a kind of dignity. Now and then, however, there were times of panic, when they squealed or wanted to squeal but couldn't, when they twitched and made moaning sounds and covered their heads and said Dear Jesus and flopped around on

the earth and fired their weapons blindly and cringed and sobbed and begged for the noise to stop and went wild and made stupid promises to themselves and to God and to their mothers and fathers, hoping not to die. In different ways, it happened to all of them. Afterward, when the firing ended, they would blink and peek up. They would touch their bodies, feeling shame, then quickly hiding it. They would force themselves to stand. As if in slow motion, frame by frame, the world would take on the old logic—absolute silence, then the wind, then sunlight, then voices. It was the burden of being alive. Awkwardly, the men would reassemble themselves, first in private, then in groups, becoming soldiers again. They would repair the leaks in their eyes. They would check for casualties, call in dustoffs, light cigarettes, try to smile, clear their throats and spit and begin cleaning their weapons. After a time someone would shake his head and say. No lie, I almost shit my pants, and someone else would laugh, which meant it was bad, yes, but the guy had obviously not shit his pants, it wasn't that bad, and in any case nobody would ever do such a thing and then go ahead and talk about it. They would squint into the dense, oppressive sunlight. For a few moments, perhaps, they would fall silent, lighting a joint and tracking its passage from man to man, inhaling, holding in the humiliation. Scary stuff, one of them might say. But then someone else would grin or flick his eyebrows and say, Roger-dodger, almost cut me a new asshole, *almost.*

There were numerous such poses. Some carried themselves with a sort of wistful resignation, others with pride or stiff soldierly discipline or good humor or macho zeal. They were afraid of dying but they were even more afraid to show it.

They found jokes to tell.

They used a hard vocabulary to contain the terrible softness. *Greased,* they'd say. *Offed, lit up, zapped while zipping.* It wasn't cruelty, just stage presence. They were actors and the war came at them in 3-D. When someone died, it wasn't quite dying, because in a curious way it seemed scripted, and because they had their lines mostly memorized, irony mixed with tragedy, and because they called it by other names, as if to encyst and destroy the reality of death itself. They kicked corpses. They cut off thumbs. They talked grunt lingo. They told stories about Ted Lavender's supply of tranquilizers, how the poor guy didn't feel a thing, how incredibly tranquil he was.

There's a moral here, said Mitchell Sanders.

70 They were waiting for Lavender's chopper, smoking the dead man's dope.

The moral's pretty obvious, Sanders said, and winked. Stay away from drugs. No joke, they'll ruin your day every time.

Cute, said Henry Dobbins.

Mind-blower, get it? Talk about wiggy—nothing left, just blood and brains.

They made themselves laugh.

75 There it is, they'd say, over and over, as if the repetition itself were an act of poise, a balance between crazy and almost crazy, knowing without going. There it is, which meant be cool, let it ride, because oh yeah, man, you can't change what can't be changed, there it is, there it absolutely and positively and fucking well *is.*

They were tough.

They carried all the emotional baggage of men who might die. Grief, terror, love, longing—these were intangibles, but the intangibles had their own mass and specific gravity, they had tangible weight. They carried shameful memories. They carried the common secret of cowardice barely restrained, the instinct to run or freeze or hide, and in many respects this was the heaviest burden of all, for it could never be put down, it required perfect balance and perfect posture. They carried their reputations. They carried the soldier's greatest fear, which was the fear of blushing. Men killed, and died, because they were embarrassed not to. It was what had brought them to the war in the first place, nothing positive, no dreams of glory or honor, just to avoid the blush of dishonor. They died so as not to die of embarrassment. They crawled into tunnels and walked point and advanced under fire. Each morning, despite the unknowns, they made their legs move. They endured. They kept humping. They did not submit to the obvious alternative, which was simply to close the eyes and fall. So easy, really. Go limp and tumble to the ground and let the muscles unwind and not speak and not budge until your buddies picked you up and lifted you into the chopper that would roar and dip its nose and carry you off to the world. A mere matter of falling, yet no one ever fell. It was not courage, exactly; the object was not valor. Rather, they were too frightened to be cowards.

By and large they carried these things inside, maintaining the masks of composure. They sneered at sick call. They spoke bitterly about guys who had found release by shooting off their own toes or fingers. Pussies, they'd say. Candyasses. It was fierce, mocking talk, with only a trace of envy or awe, but even so, the image played itself out behind their eyes.

They imagined the muzzle against flesh. They imagined the quick, sweet pain, then the evacuation to Japan, then a hospital with warm beds and cute geisha nurses.

80 They dreamed of freedom birds.

At night, on guard, staring into the dark, they were carried away by jumbo jets. They felt the rush of takeoff. *Gone!* they yelled. And then velocity, wings and engines, a smiling stewardess—but it was more than a plane, it was a real bird, a big sleek silver bird with feathers and talons and high screeching. They were flying. The weights fell off, there was nothing to bear. They laughed and held on tight, feeling the cold slap of wind and altitude, soaring, thinking *It's over, I'm gone!*—they were naked, they were light and free—it was all lightness, bright and fast and buoyant, light as light, a helium buzz in the brain, a giddy bubbling in the lungs as they were taken up over the clouds and the war, beyond duty, beyond gravity and mortification and global entanglements—*Sin loi!*[7] they yelled, *I'm sorry, motherfuckers, but I'm out of it, I'm goofed, I'm on a space cruise, I'm gone!*—and it was a restful, disencumbered sensation, just riding the light waves, sailing that big silver freedom bird over the mountains and oceans, over America, over the farms and great sleeping cities and cemeteries and highways and the Golden Arches of McDonald's. It was flight, a kind of fleeing, a kind of falling, falling higher and higher, spinning off the edge of the earth and beyond the sun and through the vast, silent vacuum where there were no burdens and where everything weighed exactly nothing. *Gone!*

[7] ***Sin loi*** Sorry

they screamed, *I'm sorry but I'm gone!* And so at night, not quite dreaming, they gave themselves over to lightness, they were carried, they were purely borne.

On the morning after Ted Lavender died, First Lieutenant Jimmy Cross crouched at the bottom of his foxhole and burned Martha's letters. Then he burned the two photographs. There was a steady rain falling, which made it difficult, but he used heat tabs and Sterno to build a small fire, screening it with his body, holding the photographs over the tight blue flame with the tips of his fingers.

He realized it was only a gesture. Stupid, he thought. Sentimental, too, but mostly just stupid.

Lavender was dead. You couldn't burn the blame.

85 Besides, the letters were in his head. And even now, without photographs, Lieutenant Cross could see Martha playing volleyball in her white gym shorts and yellow T-shirt. He could see her moving in the rain.

When the fire died out, Lieutenant Cross pulled his poncho over his shoulders and ate breakfast from a can.

There was no great mystery, he decided.

In those burned letters Martha had never mentioned the war, except to say, Jimmy, take care of yourself. She wasn't involved. She signed the letters "Love," but it wasn't love, and all the fine lines and technicalities did not matter.

The morning came up wet and blurry. Everything seemed part of everything else, the fog and Martha and the deepening rain.

90 It was a war, after all.

Half smiling, Lieutenant Jimmy Cross took out his maps. He shook his head hard, as if to clear it, then bent forward and began planning the day's march. In ten minutes, or maybe twenty, he would rouse the men and they would pack up and head west, where the maps showed the country to be green and inviting. They would do what they had always done. The rain might add some weight, but otherwise it would be one more day layered upon all the other days.

He was realistic about it. There was that new hardness in his stomach. No more fantasies, he told himself.

Henceforth, when he thought about Martha, it would be only to think that she belonged elsewhere. He would shut down the daydreams. This was not Mount Sebastian, it was another world, where there were no pretty poems or midterm exams, a place where men died because of carelessness and gross stupidity. Kiowa was right. Boom-down, and you were dead, never partly dead.

95 Briefly, in the rain, Lieutenant Cross saw Martha's gray eyes gazing back at him.

He understood.

It was very sad, he thought. The things men carried inside. The things men did or felt they had to do.

He almost nodded at her, but didn't.

Instead he went back to his maps. He was now determined to perform his duties firmly and without negligence. It wouldn't help Lavender, he knew that, but from this point on he would comport himself as a soldier. He would dispose of his good-luck pebble. Swallow it, maybe, or use Lee

Strunk's slingshot, or just drop it along the trail. On the march he would impose strict field discipline. He would be careful to send out flank security, to prevent straggling or bunching up, to keep his troops moving at the proper pace and at the proper interval. He would insist on clean weapons. He would confiscate the remainder of Lavender's dope. Later in the day, perhaps, he would call the men together and speak to them plainly. He would accept the blame for what had happened to Ted Lavender. He would be a man about it. He would look them in the eyes, keeping his chin level, and he would issue the new SOPs in a calm, impersonal tone of voice, an officer's voice, leaving no room for argument or discussion. Commencing immediately, he'd tell them, they would no longer abandon equipment along the route of march. They would police up their acts. They would get their shit together, and keep it together, and maintain it neatly and in good working order.

He would not tolerate laxity. He would show strength, distancing himself.

Among the men there would be grumbling, of course, and maybe worse, because their days would seem longer and their loads heavier, but Lieutenant Cross reminded himself that his obligation was not to be loved but to lead. He would dispense with love; it was not now a factor. And if anyone quarreled or complained, he would simply tighten his lips and arrange his shoulders in the correct command posture. He might give a curt little nod. Or he might not. He might just shrug and say Carry on, then they would saddle up and form into a column and move out toward the villages west of Than Khe.

[*1986*]

## LESLIE MARMON SILKO

*Leslie Marmon Silko was born in 1948 in Albuquerque, New Mexico, and grew up on the Laguna Pueblo Reservation some fifty miles to the west. Of her family she says,*

> *We are mixed blood—Laguna, Mexican, white. . . . All those languages, all those ways of living are combined, and we live somewhere on the fringes of all three. But I don't apologize for this any more—not to whites, not to full bloods—our origin is unlike any other. My poetry, my storytelling rise out of this source.*

*After graduating from the University of New Mexico in 1969, Silko entered law school but soon left to become a writer. She taught for two years at Navajo Community College at Many Farms, Arizona, and then went to Alaska for two years where she studied Eskimo-Aleut culture and worked on a novel,* Ceremony. *After returning to the Southwest, she taught at the University of Arizona and then at the University of New Mexico.*

*In addition to writing stories, a novel, and poems, Silko has written the screenplay for Marlon Brando's film,* Black Elk. *In 1981 she was awarded one of the so-called "genius grants" from the MacArthur Foundation, which supports "exceptionally talented individuals."*

# *The Man to Send Rain Clouds*

## *One*

They found him under a big cottonwood tree. His Levi jacket and pants were faded light-blue so that he had been easy to find. The big cottonwood tree stood apart from a small grove of winterbare cottonwoods which grew in the wide, sandy arroyo. He had been dead for a day or more, and the sheep had wandered and scattered up and down the arroyo. Leon and his brother-in-law, Ken, gathered the sheep and left them in the pen at the sheep camp before they returned to the cottonwood tree. Leon waited under the tree while Ken drove the truck through the deep sand to the edge of the arroyo. He squinted up at the sun and unzipped his jacket—it sure was hot for this time of year. But high and northwest the blue mountains were still deep in snow. Ken came sliding down the low, crumbling bank about fifty yards down, and he was bringing the red blanket.

Before they wrapped the old man, Leon took a piece of string out of his pocket and tied a small gray feather in the old man's long white hair. Ken gave him the paint. Across the brown wrinkled forehead he drew a streak of white and along the high cheekbones he drew a strip of blue paint. He paused and watched Ken throw pinches of corn meal and pollen into the wind that fluttered the small gray feather. Then Leon painted with yellow under the old man's broad nose, and finally, when he had painted green across the chin, he smiled.

"Send us rain clouds, Grandfather." They laid the bundle in the back of the pickup and covered it with a heavy tarp before they started back to the pueblo.

They turned off the highway onto the sandy pueblo road. Not long after they passed the store and post office they saw Father Paul's car coming toward them. When he recognized their faces he slowed his car and waved for them to stop. The young priest rolled down the car window.

"Did you find old Teofilo?" he asked loudly.

Leon stopped the truck. "Good morning, Father. We were just out to the sheep camp. Everything is O.K. now."

"Thank God for that. Teofilo is a very old man. You really shouldn't allow him to stay at the sheep camp alone."

"No, he won't do that any more now."

"Well, I'm glad you understand. I hope I'll be seeing you at Mass this week—we missed you last Sunday. See if you can get old Teofilo to come with you." The priest smiled and waved at them as they drove away.

## *Two*

Louise and Teresa were waiting. The table was set for lunch, and the coffee was boiling on the black iron stove. Leon looked at Louise and then at Teresa.

"We found him under a cottonwood tree in the big arroyo near sheep camp. I guess he sat down to rest in the shade and never got up again." Leon walked toward the old man's head. The red plaid shawl had been shaken and spread carefully over the bed, and a new brown flannel shirt and pair of stiff new Levis were arranged neatly beside the pillow. Louise held the screen door open while Leon and Ken carried in the red blanket. He looked small and shriveled, and after they dressed him in the new shirt and pants he seemed more shrunken.

It was noontime now because the church bells rang the Angelus.[1] They ate the beans with hot bread, and nobody said anything until after Teresa poured the coffee.

Ken stood up and put on his jacket. "I'll see about the gravediggers. Only the top layer of soil is frozen. I think it can be ready before dark."

Leon nodded his head and finished his coffee. After Ken had been gone for a while, the neighbors and clanspeople came quietly to embrace Teofilo's family and to leave food on the table because the grave-diggers would come to eat when they were finished.

## *Three*

15 The sky in the west was full of pale-yellow light. Louise stood outside with her hands in the pockets of Leon's green army jacket that was too big for her. The funeral was over, and the old men had taken their candles and medicine bags and were gone. She waited until the body was laid into the pickup before she said anything to Leon. She touched his arm, and he noticed that her hands were still dusty from the corn meal that she had sprinkled around the old man. When she spoke, Leon could not hear her.

"What did you say? I didn't hear you."

"I said that I had been thinking about something."

"About what?"

"About the priest sprinkling holy water for Grandpa. So he won't be thirsty."

20 Leon stared at the new moccasins that Teofilo had made for the ceremonial dances in the summer. They were nearly hidden by the red blanket. It was getting colder, and the wind pushed gray dust down the narrow pueblo road. The sun was approaching the long mesa where it disappeared during the winter. Louise stood there shivering and watching his face. Then he zipped up his jacket and opened the truck door. "I'll see if he's there."

Ken stopped the pickup at the church, and Leon got out; and then Ken drove down the hill to the graveyard where people were waiting. Leon knocked at the old carved door with its symbols of the Lamb. While he waited he looked up at the twin bells from the king of Spain with the last sunlight pouring around them in their tower.

The priest opened the door and smiled when he saw who it was. "Come in! What brings you here this evening?"

The priest walked toward the kitchen, and Leon stood with his cap in his hand, playing with the earflaps and examining the living room—the

[1]**Angelus** a devotional prayer commemorating the Annunciation (the angel Gabriel's announcement of the Incarnation of God in the human form of Jesus)

brown sofa, the green armchair, and the brass lamp that hung down from the ceiling by links of chain. The priest dragged a chair out of the kitchen and offered it to Leon.

"No thank you, Father. I only came to ask you if you would bring your holy water to the graveyard."

25 The priest turned away from Leon and looked out the window at the patio full of shadows and the dining-room windows of the nuns' cloister across the patio. The curtains were heavy, and the light from within faintly penetrated; it was impossible to see the nuns inside eating supper. "Why didn't you tell me he was dead? I could have brought the Last Rites anyway."

Leon smiled. "It wasn't necessary, Father."

The priest stared down at his scuffed brown loafers and the worn hem of his cassock. "For a Christian burial it was necessary."

His voice was distant, and Leon thought that his blue eyes looked tired.

"It's O.K., Father, we just want him to have plenty of water."

30 The priest sank down in the green chair and picked up a glossy missionary magazine. He turned the colored pages full of lepers and pagans without looking at them.

"You know I can't do that, Leon. There should have been the Last Rites and a funeral Mass at the very least."

Leon put on his green cap and pulled the flaps down over his ears. "It's getting late, Father. I've got to go."

When Leon opened the door Father Paul stood up and said, "Wait." He left the room and came back wearing a long brown overcoat. He followed Leon out the door and across the dim churchyard to the adobe steps in front of the church. They both stooped to fit through the low adobe entrance. And when they started down the hill to the graveyard only half of the sun was visible above the mesa.

The priest approached the grave slowly, wondering how they had managed to dig into the frozen ground and then he remembered that this was New Mexico, and saw the pile of cold loose sand beside the hole. The people stood close to each other with little clouds of steam puffing from their faces. The priest looked at them and saw a pile of jackets, gloves, and scarves in the yellow, dry tumbleweeds that grew in the graveyard. He looked at the red blanket, not sure that Teofilo was so small, wondering if it wasn't some perverse Indian trick—something they did in March to ensure a good harvest—wondering if maybe old Teofilo was actually at sheep camp corraling the sheep for the night. But there he was, facing into a cold dry wind and squinting at the last sunlight, ready to bury a red wool blanket while the faces of the parishioners were in shadow with the last warmth of the sun on their backs.

35 His fingers were stiff, and it took them a long time to twist the lid off the holy water. Drops of water fell on the red blanket and soaked into dark icy spots. He sprinkled the grave and the water disappeared almost before it touched the dim, cold sand; it reminded him of something—he tried to remember what it was, because he thought if he could remember he might understand this. He sprinkled more water; he shook the container until it was empty, and the water fell through the light from sundown like August rain that fell while the sun was still shining, almost evaporating before it touched the wilted squash flowers.

The wind pulled at the priest's brown Franciscan robe and swirled away the corn meal and pollen that had been sprinkled on the blanket. They lowered the bundle into the ground, and they didn't bother to untie the stiff pieces of new rope that were tied around the ends of the blanket. The sun was gone, and over on the highway the eastbound lane was full of headlights. The priest walked away slowly. Leon watched him climb the hill, and when he had disappeared within the tall, thick walls, Leon turned to look up at the high blue mountains in the deep snow that reflected a faint red light from the west. He felt good because it was finished, and he was happy about the sprinkling of the holy water, now the old man could send them big thunderclouds for sure.

[*1969*]

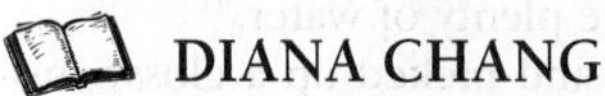

## DIANA CHANG

*Diana Chang, author of several novels and books of poems, teaches creative writing at Barnard College. She identifies herself as as American writer whose background is mostly Chinese.*

# *The Oriental Contingent*

Connie couldn't remember whose party it was, whose house. She had an impression of kerosene lamps on brown wicker tables, of shapes talking in doorways. It was summer, almost the only time Connie has run into her since, too, and someone was saying, "You must know Lisa Mallory."

"I don't think so."

"She's here. You must know her."

Later in the evening, it was someone else who introduced her to a figure perched on the balustrade of the steps leading to the lawn where more shapes milled. In stretching out a hand to shake Connie's, the figure almost fell off sideways. Connie pushed her back upright onto her perch and, peering, took in the fact that Lisa Mallory had a Chinese face. For a long instant, she felt nonplussed, and was rendered speechless.

5 But Lisa Mallory was filling in the silence. "Well, now, Connie Sung," she said, not enthusiastically but with a kind of sophisticated interest. "I'm not in music myself, but Paul Wu's my cousin. Guilt by association!" She laughed. "No-tone music, I call his. He studied with John Cage, Varese, and so forth."

Surprised that Lisa knew she was a violinist, Connie murmured something friendly, wondering if she should simply ask outright, "I'm sure I should know, but what do you do?" but she hesitated, taking in her appearance instead, while Lisa went on with, "It's world class composing. Nothing's wrong with the level. But it's hard going for the layman, believe me."

Lisa Mallory wore a one-of-a-kind kimono dress, but it didn't make her look Japanese at all, and her hair was drawn back tightly in a braid which stood out from close to the top of her head horizontally. You could probably lift her off her feet by grasping it, like the handle of a pot.

"You should give a concert here, Connie," she said, using her first name right away, Connie noticed, like any American. "Lots of culturati around." Even when she wasn't actually speaking, she pursued her own line of thought actively and seemed to find herself mildly amusing.

"I'm new to the area," Connie said, deprecatingly. "I've just been a weekend guest, actually, till a month ago."

10 "It's easy to be part of it. Nothing to it. I should know. You'll see."

"I wish it weren't so dark," Connie found herself saying, waving her hand in front of her eyes as if the night were a veil to brush aside. She recognized in herself that intense need to see, to see into fellow Orientals, to fathom them. So far, Lisa Mallory had not given her enough clues, and the darkness itself seemed to be interfering.

Lisa dropped off her perch. "It's important to be true to oneself," she said. "Keep the modern stuff out of your repertory. Be romantic. Don't look like that! You're best at the romantics. Anyhow, take it from me. I know. And *I* like what I like."

Released by her outspokenness, Connie laughed and asked, "I'm sure I should know, but what is it that you do?" She was certain Lisa would say something like, "I'm with a public relations firm." "I'm in city services."

But she replied, "What do all Chinese excel at?" Not as if she'd asked a rhetorical question, she waited, then answered herself. "Well, aren't we all physicists, musicians, architects, or in software?"

15 At that point a voice broke in, followed by a large body which put his arms around both women, "The Oriental contingent! I've got to break this up."

Turning, Lisa kissed him roundly, and said over her shoulder to Connie, "I'll take him away before he tells us we look alike!"

They melted into the steps below, and Connie, feeling put off balance and somehow slow-witted, was left to think over her new acquaintance.

"Hello, Lisa Mallory," Connie Sung always said on the infrequent occasions when they ran into one another. She always said "Hello, Lisa Mallory," with a shyness she did not understand in herself. It was strange, but they had no mutual friends except for Paul Wu, and Connie had not seen him in ages. Connie had no one of whom to ask her questions. But sometime soon, she'd be told Lisa's maiden name. Sometime she'd simply call her Lisa. Sometime what Lisa did with her life would be answered.

Three, four years passed, with their running into one another at receptions and openings, and still Lisa Mallory remained an enigma. Mildly amused herself, Connie wondered if other people, as well, found her inscrutable. But none of her American friends (though, of course, Lisa and she were Americans, too, she had to remind herself), none of their Caucasian friends seemed curious about backgrounds. In their accepting way, they did not wonder about Lisa's background, or about Connie's or Paul Wu's. Perhaps they assumed they were all cut from the same cloth. But to Connie, the Orientals she met were unread books, books she never had the right occasion or time to fully pursue.

20 She didn't even see the humor in her situation—it was such an issue with her. The fact was she felt less, much less, sure of herself when she was with real Chinese.

As she was realizing this, the truth suddenly dawned on her. Lisa Mallory never referred to her own background because it was more Chinese than Connie's, and therefore of a higher order. She was tact incarnate. All along, she had been going out of her way not to embarrass Connie. Yes, yes. Her assurance was definitely uppercrust (perhaps her father had been in the diplomatic service), and her offhand didacticness, her lack of self-doubt, was indeed characteristically Chinese-Chinese. Connie was not only impressed by these traits, but also put on the defensive because of them.

Connie let out a sigh—a sigh that follows the solution to a nagging problem . . . Lisa's mysteriousness. But now Connie knew only too clearly that her own background made her decidedly inferior. Her father was a second-generation gynecologist who spoke hardly any Chinese. Yes, inferior and totally without recourse.

Of course, at one of the gatherings, Connie met Bill Mallory, too. He was simply American, maybe Catholic, possibly lapsed. She was not put off balance by him at all. But most of the time he was away on business, and Lisa cropped up at functions as single as Connie.

Then one day, Lisa had a man in tow—wiry and tall, he looked Chinese from the Shantung area, or perhaps from Beijing, and his styled hair made him appear vaguely artistic.

25 "Connie, I'd like you to meet Eric Li. He got out at the beginning of the *detente,* went to Berkeley, and is assimilating a mile-a-minute," Lisa said, with her usual irony. "Bill found him and is grooming him, though he came with his own charisma."

Eric waved her remark aside. "Lisa has missed her calling. She was born to be in PR," he said, with an accent.

"Is that what she does?" Connie put in at once, looking only at him. "Is that her profession?"

"You don't know?" he asked, with surprise.

Though she was greeting someone else, Lisa turned and answered, "I'm a fabrics tycoon, I think I can say without immodesty." She moved away and continued her conversation with the other friend.

30 Behind his hand, he said, playfully, as though letting Connie in on a secret, "Factories in Hongkong and Taipei, and now he's—Bill, that is—is exploring them on the mainland."

"With her fabulous contacts over there!" Connie exclaimed, now seeing it all. "Of course, what a wonderful business combination they must make."

Eric was about to utter something, but stopped, and said flatly, "I have all the mainland contacts, even though I was only twenty when I left, but my parents . . ."

"How interesting," Connie murmured lamely. "I see," preoccupied as she was with trying to put two and two together.

Lisa was back and said without an introduction, continuing her line of thought, "You two look good together, if I have to say so myself. Why don't you ask him to one of your concerts? And you, Eric, you're in America now, so don't stand on ceremony, or you'll be out in left field." She walked away with someone for another drink.

35 Looking uncomfortable, but recovering himself with a smile, Eric said, "Lisa makes me feel more Chinese than I am becoming—it is her directness, I suspect. In China, we'd say she is too much like a man."

At which Connie found herself saying, "She makes me feel *less* Chinese."

"Less!"

"Less Chinese than she is."

"That is not possible," Eric said, with a shade of contempt—for whom? Lisa or Connie? He barely suppressed a laugh, cold as Chinese laughter could be.

Connie blurted out, "I'm a failed Chinese. Yes, and it's to you that I need to say it." She paused and repeated emphatically, "I am a failed Chinese." Her heart was beating quicker, but she was glad to have got that out, a confession and a definition that might begin to free her. "Do you know you make me feel that, too? You've been here only about ten years, right?"

"Right, and I'm thirty-one."

"You know what I think? I think it's harder for a Chinese to do two things."

At that moment, an American moved in closer, looking pleased somehow to be with them.

She continued, "It's harder for us to become American than, say, for a German, and it's also harder not to remain residually Chinese, even if you are third generation."

Eric said blandly, "Don't take yourself so seriously. You can't help being an American product."

Trying to be comforting, the American interjected with, "The young lady is not a product, an object. She is a human being, and there is no difference among peoples that I can see."

"I judge myself both as a Chinese and as an American," Connie said.

"You worry too much," Eric said, impatiently. Then he looked around and though she wasn't in sight, he lowered his voice. "She is what she is. I know what she is. But she avoids going to Hongkong. She avoids it."

Connie felt turned around. "Avoids it?"

"Bill's in Beijing right now. She's here. How come?"

"I don't know," Connie replied, as though an answer had been required of her.

"She makes up many excuses, reasons. Ask her. Ask her yourself," he said, pointedly.

"Oh, I couldn't do that. By the way, I'm going on a concert tour next year in three cities—Shanghai, Beijing and Nanking," Connie said. "It'll be my first time in China."

"Really! You must be very talented to be touring at your age," he said, genuinely interested for the first time. Because she was going to China, or because she now came across as an over-achiever, even though Chinese American?

"I'm just about your age," she said, realizing then that maybe Lisa Mallory had left them alone purposely.

"You could both pass as teenagers!" the American exclaimed.

Two months later, she ran into Lisa again. As usual, Lisa began in the middle of her own thoughts. "Did he call?"

"Who? Oh. No, no."

"Well, it's true he's been in China the last three weeks with Bill. They'll be back this weekend."

Connie saw her opportunity. "Are you planning to go to China yourself?"

For the first time, Lisa seemed at a loss for words. She raised her shoulders, than let them drop. Too airily, she said, "You know, there's always Paris. I can't bear not to go to Paris, if I'm to take a trip."

"But you're Chinese. You *have* been to China, you came from China originally, didn't you?"

"I could go to Paris twice a year, I love it so," Lisa said. "And then there's London, Florence, Venice."

"But—but your business contacts?"

65 "*My* contacts? Bill, he's the businessman who makes the contacts. Always has. I take care of the New York office, which is a considerable job. We have a staff of eighty-five."

Connie said, "I told Eric I'll be giving a tour in China. I'm taking Chinese lessons right now."

Lisa Mallory laughed. "Save your time. They'll still be disdainful over there. See, *they* don't care," and she waved her hand at the crowd. "Some of them have been born in Buffalo, too! It's the Chinese you can't fool. They know you're not the genuine article—you and I."

Her face was suddenly heightened in color, and she was breathing as if ready to flee from something. "Yes, you heard right. I was born in Buffalo."

"You were!" Connie exclaimed before she could control her amazement.

70 "Well, what about you?" Lisa retorted. She was actually shaking and trying to hide it by making sudden gestures.

"Westchester."

"But your parents at least were Chinese."

"Well, so were, so are, yours!"

"I was adopted by Americans. My full name is Lisa Warren Mallory."

75 Incredulous, Connie said, "I'm more Chinese than you!"

"Who isn't?" She laughed, unhappily. "Having Chinese parents makes all the difference. We're worlds apart."

"And all the time I thought . . . never mind what I thought."

"You have it over me. It's written all over you. I could tell even in the dark that night."

"Oh, Lisa," Connie said to comfort her, "none of this matters to anybody except us. Really and truly. They're too busy with their own problems."

80 "The only time I feel Chinese is when I'm embarrassed I'm not more Chinese—which is a totally Chinese reflex I'd give anything to be rid of!"

"I know what you mean."

"And as for Eric looking down his nose at me, he's knocking himself out to be so American, *but as a secure Chinese!* What's so genuine about that article?"

Both of them struck their heads laughing, but their eyes were not merry.

"Say it again," Connie asked of her, "say it again that my being more Chinese is written all over me."

85 "Consider it said," Lisa said. "My natural mother happened to be there at the time—I can't help being born in Buffalo."

"I know, I know," Connie said with feeling. "If only you had had some say in the matter."

"It's only Orientals who haunt me!" Lisa stamped her foot. "Only them!"

"I'm so sorry," Connie Sung said, for all of them. "It's all so turned around."

"So I'm made in America, so there!" Lisa Mallory declared, making a sniffing sound, and seemed to be recovering her sangfroid.

Connie felt tired—as if she'd traveled—but a lot had been settled on the way.

[*1989*]

## JAMAICA KINCAID

*Jamaica Kincaid (b. 1949) was born in St. John's, Antigua, in the West Indies. She was educated at the Princess Margaret School in Antigua, and, briefly, at Westchester Community College and Franconia College. Since 1974 she has been a contributor to* The New Yorker.

*Kincaid is the author of four books,* At the Bottom of the River *(1983, a collection of short pieces, including "Girl"),* Annie John *(1985, a second book recording a girl's growth, including "Columbus in Chains"),* A Small Place *(1988, a passionate essay about the destructive effects of colonialism), and* Lucy *(1990, a short novel about a young black woman who comes to the United States from the West Indies).*

# *Girl*

Wash the white clothes on Monday and put them on the stone heap; wash the color clothes on Tuesday and put them on the clothesline to dry; don't walk barehead in the hot sun; cook pumpkin fritters in very hot sweet oil; soak your little clothes right after you take them off; when buying cotton to make yourself a nice blouse, be sure that it doesn't have gum on it, because that way it won't hold up well after a wash; soak salt fish overnight before you cook it; is it true that you sing benna[1] in Sunday School?; always eat your food in such a way that it won't turn someone else's stomach; on Sundays try to walk like a lady and not like the slut you are so bent on becoming; don't sing benna in Sunday School; you mustn't speak to wharf-rat boys, not even to give directions; don't eat fruits on the street—flies will follow you; *but I don't sing benna on Sundays at all and never in Sunday school;* this is how to sew on a button; this is how to make a buttonhole for the button you have just sewed on; this is how to hem a dress when you see the hem coming down and so to prevent yourself from looking like the slut I know you are so bent on becoming; this is how you iron your father's khaki shirt so that it doesn't have a crease; this is how you

[1]**benna** Calypso music

iron your father's khaki pants so that they don't have a crease; this is how you grow okra—far from the house, because okra tree harbors red ants; when you are growing dasheen, make sure it gets plenty of water or else it makes your throat itch when you are eating it; this is how you sweep a corner; this is how you sweep a whole house; this is how you sweep a yard; this is how you smile to someone you don't like too much; this is how you set a table for dinner with an important guest; this is how you smile to someone you don't like at all; this is how you smile to someone you like completely; this is how you set a table for tea; this is how you set a table for dinner; this is how you set a table for lunch; this is how you set a table for breakfast; this is how to behave in the presence of men who don't know you very well, and this way they won't recognize immediately the slut I have warned you against becoming; be sure to wash every day, even if it is with your own spit; don't squat down to play marbles—you are not a boy, you know; don't pick people's flowers—you might catch something; don't throw stones at blackbirds, because it might not be a blackbird at all; this is how to make a bread pudding; this is how to make doukona[2]; this is how to make pepper pot; this is how to make a good medicine for a cold; this is how to make a good medicine to throw away a child before it even becomes a child; this is how to catch a fish; this is how to throw back a fish you don't like, and that way something bad won't fall on you; this is how to bully a man; this is how a man bullies you; this is how to love a man, and if this doesn't work there are other ways, and if they don't work don't feel too bad about giving up; this is how to spit up in the air if you feel like it, and this is how to move quick so that it doesn't fall on you; this is how to make ends meet; always squeeze bread to make sure it's fresh; *but what if the baker won't let me feel the bread?;* you mean to say that after all you are really going to be the kind of woman who the baker won't let near the bread?

[*1978*]

[2]**doukona** a spicy pudding made of plantains

## AMY TAN

*Amy Tan was born in Oakland, California, in 1952, and grew up in the San Francisco Bay area. She graduated from high school in Montreux, Switzerland, and received her master's degree in linguistics from San Jose State University. Tan is the author of* The Joy Luck Club, The Kitchen God's Wife, *and two books for children,* The Moon Lady *and* The Chinese Siamese Cat. *Her work has been translated into 20 languages. She has been married for the past 21 years to Lou DeMattei. They live in San Francisco and New York with their cat, Sagwa, and their dog, Mr. Zo.*

# *Two Kinds*

My mother believed you could be anything you wanted to be in America. You could open a restaurant. You could work for the government and get good retirement. You could buy a house with almost no money down. You could become rich. You could become instantly famous.

"Of course you can be prodigy, too," my mother told me when I was nine. "You can be best anything. What does Auntie Lindo know? Her daughter, she is only best tricky."

America was where all my mother's hopes lay. She had come here in 1949 after losing everything in China: her mother and father, her family home, her first husband, and two daughters, twin baby girls. But she never looked back with regret. There were so many ways for things to get better.

We didn't immediately pick the right kind of prodigy. At first my mother thought I could be a Chinese Shirley Temple. We'd watch Shirley's old movies on TV as though they were training films. My mother would poke my arm and say. "*Ni kan*"—You watch. And I would see Shirley tapping her feet, or singing a sailor song, or pursing her lips into a very round O while saying, "Oh my goodness."

5 "*Ni kan,*" said my mother as Shirley's eyes flooded with tears. "You already know how. Don't need talent for crying!"

Soon after my mother got this idea about Shirley Temple, she took me to a beauty training school in the Mission district and put me in the hands of a student who could barely hold the scissors without shaking. Instead of getting big fat curls, I emerged with an uneven mass of crinkly black fuzz. My mother dragged me off to the bathroom and tried to wet down my hair. "You look like Negro Chinese," she lamented, as if I had done this on purpose.

The instructor of the beauty training school had to lop off these soggy clumps to make my hair even again. "Peter Pan is very popular these days," the instructor assured my mother. I now had hair the length of a boy's, with straight-across bangs that hung at a slant two inches above my eyebrows. I liked the haircut and it made me actually look forward to my future fame.

In fact, in the beginning, I was just as excited as my mother, maybe even more so. I pictured this prodigy part of me as many different images, trying each one on for size. I was a dainty ballerina girl standing by the curtains, waiting to hear the right music that would send me floating on my tiptoes. I was like the Christ child lifted out of the straw manger, crying with holy indignity. I was Cinderella stepping from her pumpkin carriage with sparkly cartoon music filling the air.

10 In all of my imaginings, I was filled with a sense that I would soon become *perfect.* My mother and father would adore me. I would be beyond reproach. I would never feel the need to sulk for anything.

But sometimes the prodigy in me became impatient. "If you don't hurry up and get me out of here, I'm disappearing for good," it warned. "And then you'll always be nothing."

Every night after dinner, my mother and I would sit at the Formica kitchen table. She would present new tests, taking her examples from stories of amazing children she had read in *Ripley's Believe It or Not,* or *Good Housekeeping, Reader's Digest,* and a dozen other magazines she kept in a pile in our bathroom. My mother got these magazines from people whose houses she cleaned. And since she cleaned many houses each week, we had a great assortment. She would look through them all, searching for stories about remarkable children.

The first night she brought out a story about a three-year-old boy who knew the capitals of all the states and even most of the European countries. A teacher was quoted as saying the little boy could also pronounce the names of the foreign cities correctly.

"What's the capital of Finland?" my mother asked me, looking at the magazine story.

All I knew was the capital of California, because Sacramento was the name of the street we lived on in Chinatown. "Naimbil" I guessed, saying the most foreign word I could think of. She checked to see if that was possibly one way to pronounce "Helsinki" before showing me the answer.

15 The tests got harder—multiplying numbers in my head, finding the queen of hearts in a deck of cards, trying to stand on my head without using my hands, predicting the daily temperatures in Los Angeles, New York, and London.

One night I had to look at a page from the Bible for three minutes and then report everything I could remember. "Now Jehoshaphat had riches and honor in abundance and . . . that's all I remember, Ma," I said.

And after seeing my mother's disappointed face once again, something inside of me began to die. I hated the tests, the raised hopes and failed expectations. Before going to bed that night, I looked in the mirror above the bathroom sink and when I saw only my face staring back—and that it would always be this ordinary face—I began to cry. Such a sad, ugly girl! I made high-pitched noises like a crazed animal, trying to scratch out the face in the mirror.

And then I saw what seemed to be the prodigy side of me—because I had never seen that face before. I looked at my reflection, blinking so I could see more clearly. The girl staring back at me was angry, powerful. This girl and I were the same. I had new thoughts, willful thoughts, or rather thoughts filled with lots of won'ts. I won't let her change me, I promised myself. I won't be what I'm not.

So now on nights when my mother presented her tests, I performed listlessly, my head propped on one arm. I pretended to be bored. And I was. I got so bored I started counting the bellows of the foghorns out on the bay while my mother drilled me in other areas. The sound was comforting and reminded me of the cow jumping over the moon. And the next day, I played a game with myself, seeing if my mother would give up on me before eight bellows. After a while I usually counted only one, maybe two bellows at most. At last she was beginning to give up hope.

Two or three months had gone by without any mention of my being a prodigy again. And then one day my mother was watching *The Ed Sullivan Show* on TV. The TV was old and the sound kept shorting out. Every time my mother got halfway up from the sofa to adjust the set, the sound would go back on and Ed would be talking. As soon as she sat down, Ed would go silent again. She got up, the TV broke into loud piano music. She sat down. Silence. Up and down, back and forth, quiet and loud. It was like a stiff embraceless dance between her and the TV set. Finally she stood by the set with her hand on the sound dial.

20 She seemed entranced by the music, a little frenzied piano piece with this mesmerizing quality, sort of quick passages and then teasing lilting ones before it returned to the quick playful parts.

"*Ni kan,*" my mother said, calling me over with hurried hand gestures, "Look here."

I could see why my mother was fascinated by the music. It was being pounded out by a little Chinese girl, about nine years old, with a Peter Pan haircut. The girl had the sauciness of a Shirley Temple. She was proudly modest like a proper Chinese child. And she also did this fancy sweep of a curtsy, so that the fluffy skirt of her white dress cascaded slowly to the floor like the petals of a large carnation.

In spite of these warning signs, I wasn't worried. Our family had no piano and we couldn't afford to buy one, let alone reams of sheet music and piano lessons. So I could be generous in my comments when my mother bad-mouthed the little girl on TV.

"Play note right, but doesn't sound good! No singing sound," complained my mother.

25 "What are you picking on her for?" I said carelessly. "She's pretty good. Maybe she's not the best, but she's trying hard." I knew almost immediately I would be sorry I said that.

"Just like you," she said. "Not the best. Because you not trying." She gave a little huff as she let go of the sound dial and sat down on the sofa.

The little Chinese girl sat down also to play an encore of "Anitra's Dance" by Grieg. I remember the song, because later on I had to learn how to play it.

Three days after watching *The Ed Sullivan Show,* my mother told me what my schedule would be for piano lessons and piano practice. She had talked to Mr. Chong, who lived on the first floor of our apartment building. Mr. Chong was a retired piano teacher and my mother had traded housecleaning services for weekly lessons and a piano for me to practice on every day, two hours a day, from four until six.

When my mother told me this, I felt as though I had been sent to hell. I whined and then kicked my foot a little when I couldn't stand it anymore.

30 "Why don't you like me the way I am? I'm *not* a genius! I can't play the piano. And even if I could, I wouldn't go on TV if you paid me a million dollars!" I cried.

My mother slapped me. "Who ask you be genius?" she shouted. "Only ask you be your best. For you sake. You think I want you be genius? Hanh! What for! Who ask you!"

"So ungrateful," I heard her mutter in Chinese. "If she had as much talent as she has temper, she would be famous now."

Mr. Chong, whom I secretly nicknamed Old Chong, was very strange, always tapping his fingers to the silent music of an invisible orchestra. He looked ancient in my eyes. He had lost most of the hair on top of his head and he wore thick glasses and had eyes that always looked tired and sleepy.

But he must have been younger than I thought, since he lived with his mother and was not yet married.

I met Old Lady Chong once and that was enough. She had this peculiar smell like a baby that had done something in its pants. And her fingers felt like a dead person's, like an old peach I once found in the back of the refrigerator; the skin just slid off the meat when I picked it up.

35 I soon found out why Old Chong had retired from teaching piano. He was deaf. "Like Beethoven!" he shouted to me. "We're both listening only in our head!" And he would start to conduct his frantic silent sonatas.

Our lessons went like this. He would open the book and point to different things, explaining their purpose: "Key! Treble! Bass! No sharps or flats! So this is C major! Listen now and play after me!"

And then he would play the C scale a few times, a simple chord, and then, as if inspired by an old, unreachable itch, he gradually added more notes and running trills and a pounding bass until the music was really something quite grand.

I would play after him, the simple scale, the simple chord, and then I just played some nonsense that sounded like a cat running up and down on top of garbage cans. Old Chong smiled and applauded and then said, "Very good! But now you must learn to keep time!"

So that's how I discovered that Old Chong's eyes were too slow to keep up with the wrong notes I was playing. He went through the motions in half-time. To help me keep rhythm, he stood behind me, pushing down on my right shoulder for every beat. He balanced pennies on top of my wrists so I would keep them still as I slowly played scales and arpeggios. He had me curve my hand around an apple and keep that shape when playing chords. He marched stiffly to show me how to make each finger dance up and down, staccato like an obedient little soldier.

40 He taught me all these things, and that was how I also learned I could be lazy and get away with mistakes, lots of mistakes. If I hit the wrong notes because I hadn't practiced enough, I never corrected myself. I just kept playing in rhythm. And Old Chong kept conducting his own private reverie.

So maybe I never really gave myself a fair chance. I did pick up the basics pretty quickly, and I might have become a good pianist at that young age. But I was so determined not to try, not to be anybody different that I learned to play only the most ear-splitting preludes, the most discordant hymns.

Over the next year, I practiced like this, dutifully in my own way. And then one day I heard my mother and her friend Lindo Jong both talking in a loud bragging tone of voice so others could hear. It was after church, and I was leaning against the brick wall wearing a dress with stiff white petticoats. Auntie Lindo's daughter, Waverly, who was about my age, was standing farther down the wall about five feet away. We had grown up together and shared all the closeness of two sisters squabbling over crayons and dolls. In other words, for the most part, we hated each other. I thought she was snotty. Waverly Jong had gained a certain amount of fame as "Chinatown's Littlest Chinese Chess Champion."

"She bring home too many trophy," lamented Auntie Lindo that Sunday. "All day she play chess. All day I have no time do nothing but dust off her winnings." She threw a scolding look at Waverly, who pretended not to see her.

"You lucky you don't have this problem," said Auntie Lindo with a sigh to my mother.

45 And my mother squared her shoulders and bragged: "Our problem worser than yours. If we ask Jing-mei wash dish, she hear nothing but music. It's like you can't stop this natural talent."

And right then, I was determined to put a stop to her foolish pride.

A few weeks later, Old Chong and my mother conspired to have me play in a talent show which would be held in the church hall. By then, my parents had saved up enough to buy me a secondhand piano, a black Wurlitzer spinet with a scarred bench. It was the showpiece of our living room.

For the talent show, I was to play a piece called "Pleading Child" from Schumann's *Scenes from Childhood.* It was a simple, moody piece that sounded more difficult than it was. I was supposed to memorize the whole thing, playing the repeat parts twice to make the piece sound longer. But I dawdled over it, playing a few bars and then cheating, looking up to see what notes followed. I never really listened to what I was playing. I daydreamed about being somewhere else, about being someone else.

The part I liked to practice best was the fancy curtsy: right foot out, touch the rose on the carpet with a pointed foot, sweep to the side, left leg bends, look up and smile.

My parents invited all the couples from the Joy Luck Club to witness my debut. Auntie Lindo and Uncle Tin were there. Waverly and her two older brothers had also come. The first two rows were filled with children both younger and older than I was. The littlest ones got to go first. They recited simple nursery rhymes, squawked out tunes on miniature violins, twisted Hula Hoops, pranced in pink ballet tutus, and when they bowed or curtsied, the audience would sigh in unison, "Awww," and then clap enthusiastically.

50 When my turn came, I was very confident. I remember my childish excitement. It was as if I knew, without a doubt, that the prodigy side of me really did exist. I had no fear whatsoever, no nervousness. I remember thinking to myself, This is it! This is it! I looked out over the audience, at my mother's blank face, my father's yawn, Auntie Lindo's stiff-lipped smile, Waverly's sulky expression. I had on a white dress layered with sheets of lace, and a pink bow in my Peter Pan haircut. As I sat down I envisioned people jumping to their feet and Ed Sullivan rushing up to introduce me to everyone on TV.

And I started to play. It was so beautiful. I was so caught up in how lovely I looked that at first I didn't worry how I would sound. So it was a surprise to me when I hit the first wrong note and I realized something didn't sound quite right. And then I hit another and another followed that. A chill started at the top of my head and began to trickle down. Yet I couldn't stop playing, as though my hands were bewitched. I kept thinking my fingers would adjust themselves back, like a train switching to the right track. I played this strange jumble through two repeats, the sour notes staying with me all the way to the end.

When I stood up, I discovered my legs were shaking. Maybe I had just been nervous and the audience, like Old Chong, had seen me go through the right motions and had not heard anything wrong at all. I swept my right foot out, went down on my knee, looked up and smiled. The room was quiet, except for Old Chong, who was beaming and shouting, "Bravo! Bravo! Well done!" But then I saw my mother's face, her stricken face. The audience clapped weakly, and as I walked back to my chair, with my whole face quivering as I tried not to cry, I heard a little boy whisper loudly to his mother, "That was awful," and the mother whispered back, "Well, she certainly tried."

And now I realized how many people were in the audience, the whole world it seemed. I was aware of eyes burning into my back. I felt the shame of my mother and father as they sat stiffly throughout the rest of the show.

We could have escaped during intermission. Pride and some strange sense of honor must have anchored my parents to their chairs. And so we watched it all: the eighteen-year-old boy with a fake mustache who did a magic show and juggled flaming hoops while riding a unicycle. The breasted girl with white makeup who sang from *Madama Butterfly* and got honorable mention. And the eleven-year-old boy who won first prize playing a tricky violin song that sounded like a busy bee.

55 After the show, the Hsus, the Jongs, and the St. Clairs from the Joy Luck Club came up to my mother and father.

"Lots of talented kids," Auntie Lindo said vaguely, smiling broadly.

"That was somethin' else," said my father, and I wondered if he was referring to me in a humorous way, or whether he even remembered what I had done.

Waverly looked at me and shrugged her shoulders. "You aren't a genius like me," she said matter-of-factly. And if I hadn't felt so bad, I would have pulled her braids and punched her stomach.

But my mother's expression was what devastated me: a quiet, blank look that said she had lost everything. I felt the same way, and it seemed as if everybody were now coming up, like gawkers at the scene of an accident, to see what parts were actually missing. When we got on the bus to go home, my father was humming the busy-bee tune and my mother was silent. I kept thinking she wanted to wait until we got home before shouting at me. But when my father unlocked the door to our apartment, my mother walked in and then went to the back, into the bedroom. No accusations. No blame. And in a way, I felt disappointed. I had been waiting for her to start shouting, so I could shout back and cry and blame her for all my misery.

60 I assumed my talent-show fiasco meant I never had to play the piano again. But two days later, after school, my mother came out of the kitchen and saw me watching TV.

"Four clock," she reminded me as if it were any other day. I was stunned, as though she were asking me to go through the talent-show torture again. I wedged myself more tightly in front of the TV.

"Turn off TV," she called from the kitchen five minutes later.

I didn't budge. And then I decided. I didn't have to do what my mother said anymore. I wasn't her slave. This wasn't China. I had listened to her before and look what happened. She was the stupid one.

She came out from the kitchen and stood in the arched entryway of the living room. "Four clock," she said once again, louder.

65 "I'm not going to play anymore," I said nonchalantly. "Why should I? I'm not a genius."

She walked over and stood in front of the TV. I saw her chest was heaving up and down in an angry way.

"No!" I said, and I now felt stronger, as if my true self had finally emerged. So this was what had been inside me all along.

"No! I won't!" I screamed.

She yanked me by the arm, pulled me off the floor, snapped off the TV. She was frighteningly strong, half pulling, half carrying me toward the piano as I kicked the throw rugs under my feet. She lifted me up and onto the hard bench. I was sobbing by now, looking at her bitterly. Her chest was heaving even more and her mouth was open, smiling crazily as if she were pleased I was crying.

70 "You want me to be someone that I'm not!" I sobbed. "I'll never be the kind of daughter you want me to be!"

"Only two kinds of daughters," she shouted in Chinese. "Those who are obedient and those who follow their own mind! Only one kind of daughter can live in this house. Obedient daughter!"

"Then I wish I wasn't your daughter. I wish you weren't my mother," I shouted. As I said these things I got scared. It felt like worms and toads and slimy things crawling out of my chest, but it also felt good, as if this awful side of me had surfaced, at last.

"Too late change this," said my mother shrilly.

And I could sense her anger rising to its breaking point. I wanted to see it spill over. And that's when I remembered the babies she had lost in China, the ones we never talked about. "Then I wish I'd never been born!" I shouted. "I wish I were dead! Like them."

75 It was as if I had said the magic words. Alakazam!—and her face went blank, her mouth closed, her arms went slack, and she backed out of the room, stunned, as if she were blowing away like a small brown leaf, thin, brittle, lifeless.

It was not the only disappointment my mother felt in me. In the years that followed, I failed her so many times, each time asserting my own will, my right to fall short of expectations. I didn't get straight As. I didn't become class president. I didn't get into Stanford. I dropped out of college.

For unlike my mother, I did not believe I could be anything I wanted to be. I could only be me.

And for all those years, we never talked about the disaster at the recital or my terrible accusations afterward at the piano bench. All that remained unchecked, like a betrayal that was now unspeakable. So I never found a way to ask her why she had hoped for something so large that failure was inevitable.

And even worse, I never asked her what frightened me the most: Why had she given up hope?

80 For after our struggle at the piano, she never mentioned my playing again. The lessons stopped. The lid to the piano was closed, shutting out the dust, my misery, and her dreams.

So she surprised me. A few years ago, she offered to give me the piano, for my thirtieth birthday. I had not played in all those years. I saw the offer as a sign of forgiveness, a tremendous burden removed.

"Are you sure?" I asked shyly. "I mean, won't you and Dad miss it?"

"No, this your piano," she said firmly. "Always your piano. You only one can play."

"Well, I probably can't play anymore," I said. "It's been years."

85 "You pick up fast," said my mother, as if she knew this was certain. "You have natural talent. You could been genius if you want to."

"No I couldn't."

"You just not trying," said my mother. And she was neither angry nor sad. She said it as if to announce a fact that could never be disproved. "Take it," she said.

But I didn't at first. It was enough that she had offered it to me. And after that, every time I saw it in my parents' living room, standing in front of the bay windows, it made me feel proud, as if it were a shiny trophy I had won back.

Last week I sent a tuner over to my parents' apartment and had the piano reconditioned, for purely sentimental reasons. My mother had died a few months before and I had been getting things in order for my father, a little bit at a time. I put the jewelry in special silk pouches. The sweaters she had knitted in yellow, pink, bright orange—all the colors I hated—I put those in moth-proof boxes. I found some old Chinese silk dresses, the kind with little slits up the sides. I rubbed the old silk against my skin, then wrapped them in tissue and decided to take them home with me.

90 After I had the piano tuned, I opened the lid and touched the keys. It sounded even richer than I remembered. Really, it was a very good piano. Inside the bench were the same exercise notes with handwritten scales, the same secondhand music books with their covers held together with yellow tape.

I opened up the Schumann book to the dark little piece I had played at the recital. It was on the left-hand side of the page, "Pleading Child." It looked more difficult than I remembered. I played a few bars, surprised at how easily the notes came back to me.

And for the first time, or so it seemed, I noticed the piece on the right-hand side. It was called "Perfectly Contented." I tried to play this one as well. It had a lighter melody but the same flowing rhythm and turned out to be quite easy. "Pleading Child" was shorter but slower; "Perfectly Contented" was longer, but faster. And after I played them both a few times, I realized they were two halves of the same song.

[*1989*]

## RITA DOVE

*Rita Dove (b. 1952) is chiefly known as a poet—we give one of her poems on page 1115—but she has also published short stories and, most recently, a novel. In 1993 she was appointed the nation's poet laureate for 1993-94.*

# *Second-Hand Man*

Virginia couldn't stand it when someone tried to shorten her name—like *Ginny,* for example. But James Evans didn't. He set his twelve-string guitar down real slow.

"Miss Virginia," he said, "you're a fine piece of woman."

Seemed he'd been asking around. Knew everything about her. Knew she was bold and proud and didn't cotton to no silly niggers. Vir-gin-ee-a he said, nice and slow. Almost Russian, the way he said it. Right then and there she knew this man was for her.

He courted her just inside a year, came by nearly every day. First she wouldn't see him for more than half an hour at a time. She'd send him away; he knew better than to try to force her. Another fellow did that once—kept coming by when she said she had other things to do. She told him he do it once more, she'd be waiting at the door with a pot of scalding water to teach him some manners. Did, too. Fool didn't believe her—she had the pot waiting on the stove and when he came up those stairs, she was standing in the door. He took one look at her face and turned and ran. He was lucky those steps were so steep. She only got a little piece of his pant leg.

5 No, James knew his stuff. He'd come on time and stay till she told him he needed to go.

She'd met him out at Summit Beach one day. In the Twenties, that was the place to go on hot summer days! Clean yellow sand all around the lake, and an amusement park that ran from morning to midnight. She went there with a couple of girl friends. They were younger than her and a little silly. But they were sweet. Virginia was nineteen then. "High time," everyone used to say to her, but she'd just lift her head and go on about her business. She weren't going to marry just any old Negro. He had to be perfect.

There was a man who was chasing her around about that time, too. Tall dark Negro—Sterling Williams was his name. Pretty as a panther. Married, he was. Least that's what everyone said. Left a wife in Washington, D.C. A little crazy, the wife—poor Sterling was trying to get a divorce.

Well, Sterling was at Summit Beach that day, too. He followed Virginia around, trying to buy her root beer. Everybody loved root beer that summer. Root beer and vanilla ice cream—the Boston Cooler. But she wouldn't pay him no mind. People said she was crazy—Sterling was the best catch in Akron, they said.

"Not for me," Virginia said. "I don't want no second-hand man."

10 But Sterling wouldn't give up. He kept buying root beers and having to drink them himself.

Then she saw James. He'd just come up from Tennessee, working his way up on the riverboats. Folks said his best friend had been lynched down there and he turned his back on the town and said he was never coming back. Well, when she saw this cute little man in a straw hat and a twelve-string guitar under his arm, she got a little flustered. Her girlfriends whispered around to find out who he was, but she acted like she didn't even see him.

He was the hit of Summit Beach. Played that twelve-string guitar like a devil. They'd take off their shoes and sit on the beach toward evening. All the girls loved James. "Oh, Jimmy," they'd squeal, "play us a *loooove* song!" He'd laugh and pick out a tune:

I'll give you a dollar if you'll come out tonight
If you'll come out tonight,
If you'll come out tonight.
I'll give you a dollar if you'll come out tonight
And dance by the light of the moon.

Then the girls would giggle. "Jimmy," they screamed, "you outta be 'shamed of yourself!" He'd sing the second verse then:

I danced with a girl with a hole in her stockin',
And her heel kep' a-rockin',
And her heel kep' a-rockin';
I danced with a girl with a hole in her stockin',
And we danced by the light of the moon.

Then they'd all priss and preen their feathers and wonder which would be best—to be in fancy clothes and go on being courted by these dull factory fellows, or to have a hole in their stockings and dance with James.

Virginia never danced. She sat a bit off to one side and watched them make fools of themselves.

Then one night near season's end, they were all sitting down by the water, and everyone had on sweaters and was in a foul mood because the cold weather was coming and there wouldn't be no more parties. Someone said something about hating having the good times end, and James struck up a nice and easy tune, looking across the fire straight at Virginia:

As I was lumb'ring down de street,
Down de street, down de street,
A han'some gal I chanced to meet,
Oh, she was fair to view!

I'd like to make dat gal my wife,
Gal my wife, gal my wife.
I'd be happy all my life
If I had her by me.

She knew he was the man. She'd known it a long while, but she was just biding her time. He called on her the next day. She said she was busy canning peaches. He came back the day after. They sat on the porch and watched the people go by. He didn't talk much, except to say her name like that:

"Vir-gin-ee-a," he said, "you're a mighty fine woman."

She sent him home a little after that. He showed up again a week later. She was angry at him and told him she didn't have time for playing around. But he'd brought his twelve-string guitar, and he said he'd been practicing all week just to play a couple of songs for her. She let him in then and made him sit on the stool while she sat on the porch swing. He sang the first song. It was a floor thumper.

There is a gal in our town,
She wears a yellow striped gown,

And when she walks the streets aroun',
The hollow of her foot makes a hole in the ground.

Ol' folks, young folks, cl'ar the kitchen,
Ol' folks, young folks, cl'ar the kitchen,
Ol' Virginny never tire.

20 She got a little mad then, but she knew he was baiting her. Seeing how much she would take. She knew he wasn't singing about her, and she'd already heard how he said her name. It was time to let the dog in out of the rain, even if he shook his wet all over the floor. So she leaned back and put her hands on her hips, real slow.

"I just *know* you ain't singing about me."

"Virginia," he replied, with a grin would've put Rudolph Valentino to shame, "I'd *never* sing about you that way."

He pulled a yellow scarf out of his trouser pocket. Like melted butter it was, with fringes.

"I saw it yesterday and thought how nice it would look against your skin," he said.

25 That was the first present she ever accepted from a man. Then he sang his other song:

I'm coming, I'm coming!
Virginia, I'm coming to stay.
Don't hold it agin' me
For running away.

And if I can win ya,
I'll never more roam,
I'm coming Virginia,
My dixie land home.

She was gone for him. Not like those girls on the beach: she had enough sense left to crack a joke or two. "You saying I look like the state of Virginia?" she asked, and he laughed. But she was gone.

She didn't let him know it, though, not for a long while. Even when he asked her to marry him, eight months later, he was trembling and thought she just might refuse out of some woman's whim. No, he courted her proper. Every day for a little while. They'd sit on the porch until it got too cold and then they'd sit in the parlor with two or three bright lamps on. Her mother and father were glad Virginia'd found a beau, but they weren't taking any chances. Everything had to be proper.

He got down, all trembly, on one knee and asked her to be his wife. She said yes. There's a point when all this dignity and stuff get in the way of Destiny. He kept on trembling; he didn't believe her.

"What?" he said.

30 "I said yes," Virginia answered. She was starting to get angry. Then he saw that she meant it, and he went into the other room to ask her father for her hand in marriage.

But people are too curious for their own good, and there's some things they never need to know, but they're going to find them out one way or the other. James had come all the way up from Tennessee and that should have been far enough, but he couldn't hide that snake any more. It just crawled out from under the rock when it was good and ready.

The snake was Jeremiah Morgan. Some fellows from Akron had gone off for work on the riverboats, and some of these fellows had heard about James. That twelve-string guitar and straw hat of his had made him pretty popular. So, story got to town that James had a baby somewhere. And joined up to this baby—but long dead and buried—was a wife.

Virginia had been married six months when she found out from sweet-talking, side-stepping Jeremiah Morgan who never liked her no-how after she'd laid his soul to rest one night when he'd taken her home from a dance. (She always carried a brick in her purse—no man could get the best of her!)

Jeremiah must have been the happiest man in Akron the day he found out. He found it out later than most people—things like that have a way of circulating first among those who know how to keep it from spreading to the wrong folks—then when the gossip's gotten to everyone else, it's handed over to the one who knows what to do with it.

"Ask that husband of your'n what else he left in Tennessee besides his best friend," was all Jeremiah said at first.

No no-good Negro like Jeremiah Morgan could make Virginia beg for information. She wouldn't bite.

"I ain't got no need for asking my husband nothing," she said, and walked away. She was going to choir practice.

He stood where he was, yelled after her like any old common person. "Mrs. Evans always talking about being Number 1! It looks like she's Number 2 after all."

Her ears burned from the shame of it. She went on to choir practice and sang her prettiest; and straight when she was back home she asked:

"What's all this number two business?"

James broke down and told her the whole story—how he'd been married before, when he was seventeen, and his wife dying in childbirth and the child not quite right because of being blue when it was born. And how when his friend was strung up he saw no reason for staying. And how when he met Virginia, he found out pretty quick what she'd done to Sterling Williams and that she'd never have no second-hand man, and he had to have her, so he never said a word about his past.

She took off her coat and hung it in the front closet. She unpinned her hat and set it in its box on the shelf. She reached in the back of the closet and brought out his hunting rifle and the box of bullets. She didn't see no way out but to shoot him.

"Put that down!" he shouted. "I love you!"

"You were right not to tell me," she said, "because I sure as sin wouldn't have married you. I don't want you now."

"Virginia!" he said. He was real scared. "How can you shoot me down like this?"

No, she couldn't shoot him when he stood there looking at her with those sweet brown eyes, telling her how much he loved her.

"You have to sleep sometime," she said, and sat down to wait.

He didn't sleep for three nights. He knew she meant business. She sat up in their best chair with the rifle across her lap, but he wouldn't sleep. He sat at the table and told her over and over that he loved her and he hadn't known what else to do at the time.

"When I get through killing you," she told him, "I'm going to write to Tennessee and have them send that baby up here. It won't do, farming a child out to any relative with an extra plate."

She held onto that rifle. Not that he would have taken it from her—not that that would've saved him. No, the only thing would've saved him was running away. But he wouldn't run either.

Sitting there, Virginia had lots of time to think. He was afraid of what she might do, but he wouldn't leave her, either. Some of what he was saying began to sink in. He had lied, but that was the only way to get her—she could see the reasoning behind that. And except for that, he was perfect. It was hardly like having a wife before at all. And the baby—anyone could see the marriage wasn't meant to be anyway.

On the third day about midnight, she laid down the rifle.

"You will join the choir and settle down instead of plucking on that guitar anytime anyone drop a hat," she said. "And we will write to your aunt in Tennessee and have that child sent up here." Then she put the rifle back in the closet.

The child never made it up to Ohio—it had died a month before Jeremiah ever opened his mouth. That hit James hard. He thought it was his fault and all, but Virginia made him see the child was sick and was probably better off with its Maker than it would be living out half a life.

James made a good tenor in the choir. The next spring, Virginia had her first baby and they decided to name her Belle. That's French for beautiful. And she was, too.

[*1985*]

## LOUISE ERDRICH

***Louise Erdrich was born in North Dakota in 1954; her father (born in Germany) and her mother (a Chippewa) both worked for the Bureau of Indian Affairs. After graduating from Dartmouth College in 1976, she returned to North Dakota to teach in the Poetry in the Schools Program. In 1979 she received a master's degree in creative writing from Johns Hopkins University. She now lives in New Hampshire with her husband and collaborator, Michael Dorris, a professor of Native American Studies at Dartmouth, and their five children.***

***Erdrich has written three novels—*Love Medicine *(1984),* The Beet Queen *(1986), and* Tracks *(1988)—about several generations of characters who live on or close to a Chippewa reservation in North Dakota, near a mythical town called Argus. Most of these people are Native Americans who have been displaced by the white civilization. "Fleur"—named for a character who is a mystic with strange powers—appeared first as a short story and***

*later appeared as part of* Tracks. *The novel covers the period from 1912 to 1924.*

## Fleur

The first time she drowned in the cold and glassy waters of Lake Turcot, Fleur Pillager was only a girl. Two men saw the boat tip, saw her struggle in the waves. They rowed over to the place she went down, and jumped in. When they dragged her over the gunwales, she was cold to the touch and stiff, so they slapped her face, shook her by the heels, worked her arms back and forth, and pounded her back until she coughed up lake water. She shivered all over like a dog, then took a breath. But it wasn't long afterward that those two men disappeared. The first wandered off, and the other, Jean Hat, got himself run over by a cart.

It went to show, my grandma said. It figured to her, all right. By saving Fleur Pillager, those two men had lost themselves.

The next time she fell in the lake, Fleur Pillager was twenty years old and no one touched her. She washed onshore, her skin a dull dead gray, but when George Many Women bent to look closer, he saw her chest move. Then her eyes spun open, sharp black riprock, and she looked at him. "You'll take my place," she hissed. Everybody scattered and left her there, so no one knows how she dragged herself home. Soon after that we noticed Many Women changed, grew afraid, wouldn't leave his house, and would not be forced to go near water. For his caution, he lived until the day that his sons brought him a new tin bathtub. Then the first time he used the tub he slipped, got knocked out, and breathed water while his wife stood in the other room frying breakfast.

Men stayed clear of Fleur Pillager after the second drowning. Even though she was good-looking, nobody dared to court her because it was clear that Misshepeshu, the waterman, the monster, wanted her for himself. He's a devil, that one, love-hungry with desire and maddened for the touch of young girls, the strong and daring especially, the ones like Fleur.

5 Our mothers warn us that we'll think he's handsome, for he appears with green eyes, copper skin, a mouth tender as a child's. But if you fall into his arms, he sprouts horns, fangs, claws, fins. His feet are joined as one and his skin, brass scales, rings to the touch. You're fascinated, cannot move. He casts a shell necklace at your feet, weeps gleaming chips that harden into mica on your breasts. He holds you under. Then he takes the body of a lion or a fat brown worm. He's made of gold. He's made of beach moss. He's a thing of dry foam, a thing of death by drowning, the death a Chippewa cannot survive.

Unless you are Fleur Pillager. We all knew she couldn't swim. After the first time, we thought she'd never go back to Lake Turcot. We thought she'd keep to herself, live quiet, stop killing men off by drowning in the lake. After the first time, we thought she'd keep the good ways. But then, after the second drowning, we knew that we were dealing with something much more serious. She was haywire, out of control. She messed with evil, laughed at the old women's advice, and dressed like a man. She got herself into some half-forgotten medicine, studied ways we shouldn't talk about. Some say she kept the finger of a child in her pocket and a powder of unborn rabbits in a leather thong around her neck. She laid the heart of an owl on her tongue so she could see at night, and went out, hunting, not even in her own body. We know for sure because the next morning, in the snow or dust, we followed the tracks of her bare feet and saw where they changed, where the claws sprang out, the pad broadened and pressed into the dirt. By night we heard her chuffing cough, the bear cough. By day her silence and the wide grin she threw to bring down our guard made us frightened. Some thought that Fleur Pillager should be driven off the reservation, but not a single person who spoke like this had the nerve. And finally, when people were just about to get together and throw her out, she left on her own and didn't come back all summer. That's what this story is about.

During that summer, when she lived a few miles south in Argus, things happened. She almost destroyed that town.

When she got down to Argus in the year of 1920, it was just a small grid of six streets on either side of the railroad depot. There were two elevators, one central, the other a few miles west. Two stores competed for the trade of the three hundred citizens, and three churches quarreled with one another for their souls. There was a frame building for Lutherans, a heavy brick one for Episcopalians, and a long narrow shingled Catholic church. This last had a tall slender steeple, twice as high as any building or tree.

No doubt, across the low, flat wheat, watching from the road as she came near Argus on foot, Fleur saw that steeple rise, a shadow thin as a needle. Maybe in that raw space it drew her the way a lone tree draws lightning. Maybe, in the end, the Catholics are to blame. For if she hadn't seen that sign of pride, that slim prayer, that marker, maybe she would have kept walking.

10 But Fleur Pillager turned, and the first place she went once she came into town was to the back door of the priest's residence attached to the landmark church. She didn't go there for a handout, although she got that, but to ask for work. She got that too, or the town got her. It's hard to tell which came out worse, her or the men or the town, although the upshot of it all was that Fleur lived.

The four men who worked at the butcher's had carved up about a thousand carcasses between them, maybe half of that steers and the other half pigs, sheep, and game animals like deer, elk, and bear. That's not even mentioning the chickens, which were beyond counting. Pete Kozka owned the place, and employed Lily Veddar, Tor Grunewald, and my stepfather, Dutch James, who had brought my mother down from the reservation the year before she disappointed him by dying. Dutch took me out of school to take her place. I kept house half the time and worked the other in the butcher shop, sweeping floors, putting sawdust down, running a hambone across the street to a customer's bean pot or a package of sausage to the corner. I was a good one to have around because until they needed me, I was invisible. I blended into the stained brown walls, a skinny, big-nosed girl with staring eyes. Because I could fade into a corner or squeeze beneath a shelf, I knew everything, what the men said when no one was around, and what they did to Fleur.

Kozka's Meats served farmers for a fifty-mile area, both to slaughter, for it had a stock pen and chute, and to cure the meat by smoking it or spicing it in sausage. The storage locker was a marvel, made of many thicknesses of brick, earth insulation, and Minnesota timber, lined inside with sawdust and vast blocks of ice cut from Lake Turcot, hauled down from home each winter by horse and sledge.

A ramshackle board building, part slaughterhouse, part store, was fixed to the low, thick square of the lockers. That's where Fleur worked. Kozka hired her for her strength. She could lift a haunch or carry a pole of sausages without stumbling, and she soon learned cutting from Pete's wife, a string-thin blonde who chain-smoked and handled the razor-sharp knives with nerveless precision, slicing close to her stained fingers. Fleur and Fritzie Kozka worked afternoons, wrapping their cuts in paper, and Fleur hauled the packages to the lockers. The meat was left outside the heavy oak doors that were only opened at 5:00 each afternoon, before the men ate supper.

Sometimes Dutch, Tor, and Lily ate at the lockers, and when they did I stayed too, cleaned floors, restoked the fires in the front smokehouses, while the men sat around the squat cast-iron stove spearing slats of herring onto hardtack bread. They played long games of poker or cribbage on a board made from the planed end of a salt crate. They talked and I listened, although there wasn't much to hear since almost nothing ever happened in Argus. Tor was married, Dutch had lost my mother, and Lily read circulars. They mainly discussed about the auctions to come, equipment, or women.

Every so often, Pete Kozka came out front to make a whist, leaving Fritzie to smoke cigarettes and fry raised doughnuts in the back room. He sat and played a few rounds but kept his thoughts to himself. Fritzie did not tolerate him talking behind her back, and the one book he read was the New Testament. If he said something, it concerned weather or a surplus of sheep stomachs, a ham that smoked green or the markets for corn and wheat. He had a good-luck talisman, the opal-white lens of a cow's eye. Playing cards, he rubbed it between his fingers. That soft sound and the slap of cards was about the only conversation.

Fleur finally gave them a subject.

Her cheeks were wide and flat, her hands large, chapped, muscular. Fleur's shoulders were broad as beams, her hips fishlike, slippery, narrow. An old green dress clung to her waist, worn thin where she sat. Her braids were thick like the tails of animals, and swung against her when she moved, deliberately, slowly in her work, held in and half-tamed, but only half. I could tell, but the others never saw. They never looked into her sly brown eyes or noticed her teeth, strong and curved and very white. Her legs were bare, and since she padded around in beadwork moccasins they never saw that her fifth toes were missing. They never knew she'd drowned. They were blinded, they were stupid, they only saw her in the flesh.

And yet it wasn't just that she was a Chippewa, or even that she was a woman, it wasn't that she was good-looking or even that she was alone that made their brains hum. It was how she played cards.

Women didn't usually play with men, so the evening that Fleur drew a chair up to the men's table without being so much as asked, there was a shock of surprise.

"What's this," said Lily. He was fat, with a snake's cold pale eyes and precious skin, smooth and lily-white, which is how he got his name. Lily had a dog, a stumpy mean little bull of a thing with a belly drum-tight from eating pork rinds. The dog liked to play cards just like Lily, and straddled his barrel thighs through games of stud, rum poker, vingt-un. The dog snapped at Fleur's arm that first night, but cringed back, its snarl frozen, when she took her place.

"I thought," she said, her voice soft and stroking, "you might deal me in."

There was a space between the heavy bin of spiced flour and the wall where I just fit. I hunkered down there, kept my eyes open, saw her black hair swing over the chair, her feet solid on the wood floor. I couldn't see up on the table where the cards slapped down, so after they were deep in their game I raised myself up in the shadows, and crouched on a sill of wood.

I watched Fleur's hands stack and ruffle, divide the cards, spill them to each player in a blur, rake them up and shuffle again. Tor, short and scrappy, shut one eye and squinted the other at Fleur. Dutch screwed his lips around a wet cigar.

"Gotta see a man," he mumbled, getting up to go out back to the privy. The others broke, put their cards down, and Fleur sat alone in the lamplight that glowed in a sheen across the push of her breasts. I watched her closely, then she paid me a beam of notice for the first time. She turned, looked straight at me, and grinned the white wolf grin a Pillager turns on its victims, except that she wasn't after me.

"Pauline there," she said, "how much money you got?"

We'd all been paid for the week that day. Eight cents was in my pocket.

"Stake me," she said, holding out her long fingers. I put the coins in her palm and then I melted back to nothing, part of the walls and tables. It was a long time before I understood that the men would not have seen me no matter what I did, how I moved. I wasn't anything like Fleur. My dress hung loose and my back was already curved, an old woman's. Work had roughened me, reading made my eyes sore, caring for my mother before she died had hardened my face. I was not much to look at, so they never saw me.

When the men came back and sat around the table, they had drawn together. They shot each other small glances, stuck their tongues in their cheeks, burst out laughing at odd moments, to rattle Fleur. But she never minded. They played their vingt-un, staying even as Fleur slowly gained. Those pennies I had given her drew nickels and attracted dimes until there was a small pile in front of her.

Then she hooked them with five-card draw, nothing wild. She dealt, discarded, drew, and then she sighed and her cards gave a little shiver. Tor's eyes gleamed, and Dutch straightened in his seat.

"I'll pay to see that hand," said Lily Veddar.

Fleur showed, and she had nothing there, nothing at all.

Tor's thin smile cracked open, and he threw his hand in too.

"Well, we know one thing," he said, leaning back in his chair, "the squaw can't bluff."

With that I lowered myself into a mound of swept sawdust and slept. I woke up during the night, but none of them had moved yet, so I couldn't either. Still later, the men must have gone out again, or Fritzie come out to break the game, because I was lifted, soothed, cradled in a woman's arms and rocked so quiet that I kept my eyes shut while Fleur rolled me into a closet of grimy ledgers, oiled paper, balls of string, and thick files that fit beneath me like a mattress.

The game went on after work the next evening. I got my eight cents back five times over, and Fleur kept the rest of the dollar she'd won for a stake. This time they didn't play so late, but they played regular, and then kept going at it night after night. They played poker now, or variations, for one week straight, and each time Fleur won exactly one dollar, no more and no less, too consistent for luck.

By this time, Lily and the other men were so lit with suspense that they got Pete to join the game with them. They concentrated, the fat dog sitting tense in Lily Veddar's lap, Tor suspicious, Dutch stroking his huge square brow, Pete steady. It wasn't that Fleur won that hooked them in so, because she lost hands too. It was rather that she never had a freak hand or even anything above a straight. She only took on her low cards, which didn't sit right. By chance, Fleur should have gotten a full or flush by now. The irritating thing was she beat with pairs and never bluffed, because she couldn't, and still she ended up each night with exactly one dollar. Lily couldn't believe, first of all, that a woman could be smart enough to play cards, but even if she was, that she would then be stupid enough to cheat for a dollar a night. By day I watched him turn the problem over, his hard white face dull, small fingers probing at his knuckles, until he finally thought he had Fleur figured out as a bit-time player, caution her game. Raising the stakes would throw her.

More than anything now, he wanted Fleur to come away with something but a dollar. Two bits less or ten more, the sum didn't matter, just so he broke he streak.

Night after night she played, won her dollar, and left to stay in a place that just Fritzie and I knew about. Fleur bathed in the slaughtering tub, then slept in the unused brick smokehouse behind the lockers, a windowless place tarred on the inside with scorched fats. When I brushed against her skin I noticed that she smelled of the walls, rich and woody, slightly burnt. Since that night she put me in the closet I was no longer afraid of her, but followed her close, stayed with her, became her moving shadow that the men never noticed, the shadow that could have saved her.

August, the month that bears fruit, closed around the shop, and Pete and Fritzie left for Minnesota to escape the heat. Night by night, running, Fleur had won thirty dollars, and only Pete's presence had kept Lily at bay. But Pete was gone now, and one payday, with the heat so bad no one could move but Fleur, the men sat and played and waited while she finished work. The cards sweat, limp in their fingers, the table was slick with grease, and even the walls were warm to the touch. The air was motionless. Fleur was in the next room boiling heads.

Her green dress, drenched, wrapped her like a transparent sheet. A skin of lakeweed. Black snarls of veining clung to her arms. Her braids were loose, half-unraveled, tied behind her neck in a thick loop. She stood in steam, turning skulls through a vat with a wooden paddle. When scraps boiled to the surface, she bent with a round tin sieve and scooped them out. She'd filled two dishpans.

"Ain't that enough now?" called Lily. "We're waiting." The stump of a dog trembled in his lap, alive with rage. It never smelled me or noticed me above Fleur's smoky skin. The air was heavy in my corner, and pressed me down. Fleur sat with them.

"Now what do you say?" Lily asked the dog. It barked. That was the signal for the real game to start.

"Let's up the ante," said Lily, who had been stalking this night all month. He had a roll of money in his pocket. Fleur had five bills in her dress. The men had each saved their full pay.

"Ante a dollar then," said Fleur, and pitched hers in. She lost, but they let her scrape along, cent by cent. And then she won some. She played unevenly, as if chance was all she had. She reeled them in. The game went on. The dog was stiff now, poised on Lily's knees, a ball of vicious muscle with its yellow eyes slit in concentration. It gave advice, seemed to sniff the lay of Fleur's cards, twitched and nudged. Fleur was up, then down, saved by a scratch. Tor dealt seven cards, three down. The pot grew, round by round, until it held all the money. Nobody folded. Then it all rode on one last card and they went silent. Fleur picked hers up and blew a long breath. The heat lowered like a bell. Her card shook, but she stayed in.

Lily smiled and took the dog's head tenderly between his palms.

"Say, Fatso," he said, crooning the words, "you reckon that girl's bluffing?"

The dog whined and Lily laughed. "Me too," he said, "let's show." He swept his bills and coins into the pot and then they turned their cards over.

Lily looked once, looked again, then he squeezed the dog up like a fist of dough and slammed it on the table.

Fleur threw her arms out and drew the money over, grinning that same wolf grin that she'd used on me, the grin that had them. She jammed the bills in her dress, scooped the coins up in waxed white paper that she tied with string.

"Let's go another round," said Lily, his voice choked with burrs. But Fleur opened her mouth and yawned, then walked out back to gather slops for the one big hog that was waiting in the stock pen to be killed.

The men sat still as rocks, their hands spread on the oiled wood table. Dutch had chewed his cigar to damp shreds. Tor's eye was dull. Lily's gaze was the only one to follow Fleur. I didn't move. I felt them gathering, saw my stepfather's veins, the ones in his forehead that stood out in anger. The dog had rolled off the table and curled in a knot below the counter, where none of the men could touch it.

Lily rose and stepped out back to the closet of ledgers where Pete kept his private stock. He brought back a bottle, uncorked and tipped it between his fingers. The lump in his throat moved, then he passed it on. They drank, quickly felt the whiskey's fire, and planned with their eyes things they couldn't say out loud.

When they left, I followed. I hid out back in the clutter of broken boards and chicken crates beside the stock pen, where they waited. Fleur could not be seen at first, and then the moon broke and showed her, slipping cautiously along the rough board chute with a bucket in her hand. Her hair fell, wild and coarse, to her waist, and her dress was a floating patch in the dark. She made a pig-calling sound, rang the tin pail lightly against the wood, froze suspiciously. But too late. In the sound of the ring Lily moved, fat and nimble, stepped right behind Fleur and put out his creamy hands. At his first touch, she whirled and doused him with the bucket of sour slops. He pushed her against the big fence and the package of coins split, went clinking and jumping, winked against the wood. Fleur rolled over once and vanished in the yard.

The moon fell behind a curtain of ragged clouds, and Lily followed into the dark muck. But he tripped, pitched over the huge flank of the pig, who lay mired to the snout, heavily snoring. I sprang out of the weeds and climbed the side of the pen, stuck like glue. I saw the sow rise to her neat, knobby knees, gain her balance, and sway, curious, as Lily stumbled forward. Fleur had backed into the angle of rough wood just beyond, and when Lily tried to jostle past, the sow tipped up on her hind legs and struck, quick and hard as a snake. She plunged her head into Lily's thick side and snatched a mouthful of his shirt. She lunged again, caught him lower, so that he grunted in pained surprise. He seemed to ponder, breathing deep. Then he launched his huge body in a swimmer's dive.

The sow screamed as his body smacked over hers. She rolled, striking out with her knife-sharp hooves, and Lily gathered himself upon her, took her foot-long face by the ears and scraped her snout and cheeks against the trestles of the pen. He hurled the sow's tight skull against an iron post, but instead of knocking her dead, he merely woke her from her dream.

She reared, shrieked, drew him with her so that they posed standing upright. They bowed jerkily to each other, as if to begin. Then his arms swung and flailed. She sank her black fangs into his shoulder, clasping him, dancing him forward and backward through the pen. Their steps picked up pace, went wild. The two dipped as one, box-stepped, tripped each other. She ran her split foot through his hair. He grabbed her kinked tail. They went down and came up, the same shape and then the same color, until the men couldn't tell one from the other in that light and Fleur was able to launch herself over the gates, swing down, hit gravel.

The men saw, yelled, and chased her at a dead run to the smokehouse. And Lily too, once the sow gave up in disgust and freed him. That is where I should have gone to Fleur, saved her, thrown myself on Dutch. But I went stiff with fear and couldn't unlatch myself from the trestles or move at all. I closed my eyes and put my head in my arms, tried to hide, so there is nothing to describe but what I couldn't block out, Fleur's hoarse breath, so loud it filled me, her cry in the old language, and my name repeated over and over among the words.

The heat was still dense the next morning when I came back to work. Fleur was gone but the men were there, slack-faced, hung over. Lily was paler and softer than ever, as if his flesh had steamed on his bones. They smoked, took pulls off a bottle. It wasn't noon yet. I worked awhile, waiting shop and sharpening steel. But I was sick, I was smothered, I was sweating so hard that my hands slipped on the knives, and I wiped my fingers clean of the greasy touch of the customers' coins. Lily opened his mouth and roared once, not in anger. There was no meaning to the sound. His boxer dog, sprawled limp beside his foot, never lifted its head. Nor did the other men.

They didn't notice when I stepped outside, hoping for a clear breath. And then I forget them because I knew that we were all balanced, ready to tip, to fly, to be crushed as soon as the weather broke. The sky was so low that I felt the weight of it like a yoke. Clouds hung down, witch teats, a tornado's green-brown cones, and as I watched one flicked out and became a delicate probing thumb. Even as I picked up my heels and ran back inside, the wind blew suddenly, cold, and then came rain.

60 Inside, the men had disappeared already and the whole place was trembling as if a huge hand was pinched at the rafters, shaking it. I ran straight through, screaming for Dutch or for any of them, and then I stopped at the heavy doors of the lockers, where they had surely taken shelter. I stood there a moment. Everything went still. Then I heard a cry building in the wind, faint at first, a whistle and then a shrill scream that tore through the walls and gathered around me, spoke plain so I understood that I should move, put my arms out, and slam down the great iron bar that fit across the hasp and lock.

Outside, the wind was stronger, like a hand held against me. I struggled forward. The bushes tossed, the awnings flapped off storefronts, the rails of porches rattled. The odd cloud became a fat snout that nosed along the earth and sniffled, jabbed, picked at things, sucked them up, blew them apart, rooted around as if it was following a certain scent, then stopped behind me at the butcher shop and bored down like a drill.

I went flying, landed somewhere in a ball. When I opened my eyes and looked, stranger things were happening.

A herd of cattle flew through the air like giant birds, dropping dung, their mouths opened in stunned bellows. A candle, still lighted, blew past, and tables, napkins, garden tools, a whole school of drifting eyeglasses, jackets on hangers, hams, a checkerboard, a lampshade, and at last the sow from behind the lockers, on the run, her hooves a blur, set free, swooping, diving, screaming as everything in Argus fell apart and got turned upside down, smashed, and thoroughly wrecked.

Days passed before the town went looking for the men. They were bachelors, after all, except for Tor, whose wife had suffered a blow to the head that made her forgetful. Everyone was occupied with digging out, in high relief because even though the Catholic steeple had been torn off like a peaked cap and sent across five fields, those huddled in the cellar were unhurt. Walls had fallen, windows were demolished, but the stores were intact and so were the bankers and shop owners who had taken refuge in their safes or beneath their cash registers. It was a fair-minded disaster, no one could be said to have suffered much more than the next, at least not until Fritzie and Pete came home.

65 Of all the businesses in Argus, Kozka's Meats had suffered worst. The boards of the front building had been split to kindling, piled in a huge pyramid, and the shop equipment was blasted far and wide. Pete paced off the distance the iron bathtub had been flung—a hundred feet. The glass candy case went fifty, and landed without so much as a cracked pane. There were other surprises as well, for the back rooms where Fritzie and Pete lived were undisturbed. Fritzie said the dust still coated her china figures, and upon her kitchen table, in the ashtray, perched the last cigarette she'd put out in haste. She lit it up and finished it, looking through the window. From there, she could see that the old smokehouse Fleur had slept in was crushed to a reddish sand and the stockpens were completely torn apart, the rails stacked helter-skelter. Fritzie asked for Fleur. People shrugged. Then she asked about the others and, suddenly, the town understood that three men were missing.

There was a rally of help, a gathering of shovels and volunteers. We passed boards from hand to hand, stacked them, uncovered what lay beneath the pile of jagged splinters. The lockers, full of the meat that was Pete and Fritzie's investment, slowly came into sight, still intact. When enough room was made for a man to stand on the roof, there were calls, a general urge to hack through and see what lay below. But Fritzie shouted that she wouldn't allow it because the meat would spoil. And so the work continued, board by board, until at last the heavy oak doors of the freezer were revealed and people pressed to the entry. Everyone wanted to be the first, but since it was my stepfather lost, I was let go in when Pete and Fritzie wedged through into the sudden icy air.

Pete scraped a match on his boot, lit the lamp Fritzie held, and then the three of us stood still in its circle. Light glared off the skinned and hanging carcasses, the crates of wrapped sausages, the bright and cloudy blocks of lake ice, pure as winter. The cold bit into us, pleasant at first, then numbing. We must have stood there a couple of minutes before we saw the men, or more rightly, the humps of fur, the iced and shaggy hides they wore, the bearskins they had taken down and wrapped around themselves. We stepped closer and tilted the lantern beneath the flaps of fur into their faces. The dog was there, perched among them, heavy as a doorstop. The three had hunched around a barrel where the game was still laid out, and a dead lantern and an empty bottle, too. But they had thrown down their last hands and hunkered tight, clutching one another, knuckles raw from beating at the door they had also attacked with hooks. Frost stars gleamed off their eyelashes and the stubble of their beards. Their faces were set in concentration, mouths open as if to speak some careful thought, some agreement they'd come to in each other's arms.

Power travels in the bloodlines, handed out before birth. It comes down through the hands, which in the Pillagers were strong and knotted, big, spidery, and rough, with sensitive fingertips good at dealing cards. It comes through the eyes, too, belligerent, darkest brown, the eyes of those in the bear clan, impolite as they gaze directly at a person.

In my dreams, I look straight back at Fleur, at the men. I am no longer the watcher on the dark sill, the skinny girl.

70 The blood draws us back, as if it runs through a vein of earth. I've come home and, except for talking to my cousins, live a quiet life. Fleur lives quiet too, down on Lake Turcot with her boat. Some say she's married to the waterman, Misshepeshu, or that she's living in shame with white men or windigos, or that she's killed them all. I'm about the only one here who ever goes to visit her. Last winter, I went to help out in her cabin when she bore the child, whose green eyes and skin the color of an old penny made more talk, as no one could decide if the child was mixed blood or what, fathered in a smokehouse, or by a man with brass scales, or by the lake. The girl is bold, smiling in her sleep, as if she knows what people wonder, as if she hears the old men talk, turning the story over. It comes up different every time and has no ending, no beginning. They get the middle wrong too. They only know that they don't know anything.

[*1986*]

## KAZUO ISHIGURO

*Kazuo Ishiguro was born in Japan in 1954, and at the age of six was brought by his parents to England, where he continues to live. Of his stories and novels he has said, "I try to put in as little plot as possible." In 1989 his novel* The Remains of the Day *won the prestigious Booker Prize in England.*

# *A Family Supper*

Fugu is a fish caught off the Pacific shores of Japan. The fish has held a special significance for me ever since my mother died after eating one. The poison resides in the sex glands of the fish, inside two fragile bags. These bags must be removed with caution when preparing the fish, for any clumsiness will result in the poison leaking into the veins. Regrettably, it is not easy to tell whether or not this operation has been carried out successfully. The proof is, as it were, in the eating.

Fugu poisoning is hideously painful and almost always fatal. If the fish has been eaten during the evening, the victim is usually overtaken by pain during his sleep. He rolls about in agony for a few hours and is dead by morning. The fish became extremely popular in Japan after the war. Until stricter regulations were imposed, it was all the rage to perform the hazardous gutting operation in one's own kitchen, then to invite neighbors and friends round for the feast.

At the time of my mother's death, I was living in California. My relationship with my parents had become somewhat strained around that period and consequently I did not learn of the circumstances of her death until I returned to Tokyo two years later. Apparently, my mother had always refused to eat fugu, but on this particular occasion she had made an exception, having been invited by an old school friend whom she was anxious not to offend. It was my father who supplied me with the details as we drove from the airport to his house in the Kamakura district. When we finally arrived, it was nearing the end of a sunny autumn day.

"Did you eat on the plane?" my father asked. We were sitting on the tatami floor of his tearoom.

5 "They gave me a light snack."

"You must be hungry. We'll eat as soon as Kikuko arrives."

My father was a formidable-looking man with a large stony jaw and furious black eyebrows. I think now, in retrospect, that he much resembled Chou En-lai, although he would not have cherished such a comparison, being particularly proud of the pure samurai blood that ran in the family. His general presence was not one that encouraged relaxed conversation; neither were things helped much by his odd way of stating each remark as if it were the concluding one. In fact, as I sat opposite him that afternoon, a boyhood memory came back to me of the time he had struck me several times around the head for "chattering like an old woman." Inevitably, our conversation since my arrival at the airport had been punctuated by long pauses.

"I'm sorry to hear about the firm," I said when neither of us had spoken for some time. He nodded gravely.

"In fact, the story didn't end there," he said. "After the firm's collapse, Watanabe killed himself. He didn't wish to live with the disgrace."

10 "I see."

"We were partners for seventeen years. A man of principle and honor. I respected him very much."

"Will you go into business again?" I asked.

"I am . . . in retirement. I'm too old to involve myself in new ventures now. Business these days has become so different. Dealing with foreigners. Doing things their way. I don't understand how we've come to this. Neither did Watanabe." He sighed. "A fine man. A man of principle."

The tearoom looked out over the garden. From where I sat I could make out the ancient well that as a child I had believed to be haunted. It was just visible now through the thick foliage. The sun had sunk low and much of the garden had fallen into shadow.

"I'm glad in any case that you've decided to come back," my father said. "More than a short visit, I hope."

"I'm not sure what my plans will be."

"I, for one, am prepared to forget the past. Your mother, too, was always ready to welcome you back—upset as she was by your behavior."

"I appreciate your sympathy. As I say, I'm not sure what my plans are."

"I've come to believe now that there were no evil intentions in your mind," my father continued. "You were swayed by certain . . . influences. Like so many others."

"Perhaps we should forget it, as you suggest."

"As you will. More tea?"

Just then a girl's voice came echoing through the house.

"At last." My father rose to his feet. "Kikuko has arrived."

Despite our difference in years, my sister and I had always been close. Seeing me again seemed to make her excessively excited, and for a while she did nothing but giggle nervously. But she calmed down somewhat when my father started to question her about Osaka and her university. She answered him with short, formal replies. She in turn asked me a few questions, but she seemed inhibited by the fear that her questions might lead to awkward topics. After a while, the conversation had become even sparser than prior to Kikuko's arrival. Then my father stood up, saying: "I must attend to the supper. Please excuse me for being burdened by such matters. Kikuko will look after you."

My sister relaxed quite visibly once he had left the room. Within a few minutes, she was chatting freely about her friends in Osaka and about her classes at university. Then quite suddenly she decided we should walk in the garden and went striding out onto the veranda. We put on some straw sandals that had been left along the veranda rail and stepped out into the garden. The light in the garden had grown very dim.

"I've been dying for a smoke for the last half hour," she said, lighting a cigarette.

"Then why didn't you smoke?"

She made a furtive gesture back toward the house, then grinned mischievously.

"Oh, I see," I said.

"Guess what? I've got a boyfriend now."

"Oh, yes?"

"Except I'm wondering what to do. I haven't made up my mind yet."

"Quite understandable."

"You see, he's making plans to go to America. He wants me to go with him as soon as I finish studying."

"I see. And you want to go to America?"

"If we go, we're going to hitchhike." Kikuko waved a thumb in front of my face. "People say it's dangerous, but I've done it in Osaka and it's fine."

"I see. So what is it you're unsure about?"

We were following a narrow path that wound through the shrubs and finished by the old well. As we walked, Kikuko persisted in taking unnecessarily theatrical puffs on her cigarette.

"Well, I've got lots of friends now in Osaka. I like it there. I'm not sure I want to leave them all behind just yet. And Suichi . . . I like him, but I'm not sure I want to spend so much time with him. Do you understand?"

"Oh, perfectly."

She grinned again, then skipped on ahead of me until she had reached the well. "Do you remember," she said as I came walking up to her, "how you used to say this well was haunted?"

"Yes, I remember."

We both peered over the side.

"Mother always told me it was the old woman from the vegetable store you'd seen that night," she said. "But I never believed her and never came out here alone."

"Mother used to tell me that too. She even told me once the old woman had confessed to being the ghost. Apparently, she'd been taking a shortcut through our garden. I imagine she had some trouble clambering over these walls."

Kikuko gave a giggle. She then turned her back to the well, casting her gaze about the garden.

"Mother never really blamed you, you know," she said, in a new voice. I remained silent. "She always used to say to me how it was their fault, hers and Father's, for not bringing you up correctly. She used to tell me how much more careful they'd been with me, and that's why I was so good." She looked up and the mischievous grin had returned to her face. "Poor Mother," she said.

"Yes. Poor Mother."

"Are you going back to California?"

"I don't know. I'll have to see."

"What happened to . . . to her? To Vicki?"

"That's all finished with," I said. "There's nothing much left for me now in California."

"Do you think I ought to go there?"

"Why not? I don't know. You'll probably like it." I glanced toward the house. "Perhaps we'd better go in soon. Father might need a hand with the supper."

But my sister was once more peering down into the well. "I can't see any ghosts," she said. Her voice echoed a little.

"Is Father very upset about his firm collapsing?"

"Don't know. You never can tell with Father." Then suddenly she straightened up and turned to me. "Did he tell you about old Watanabe? What he did?"

"I heard he committed suicide."

"Well, that wasn't all. He took his whole family with him. His wife and his two little girls."

"Oh, yes?"

"Those two beautiful little girls. He turned on the gas while they were all asleep. Then he cut his stomach with a meat knife."

"Yes, Father was just telling me how Watanabe was a man of principle."

"Sick." My sister turned back to the well.

"Careful. You'll fall right in."

"I can't see any ghost," she said. "You were lying to me all that time."

"But I never said it lived down the well."

"Where is it then?"

We both looked around at the trees and shrubs. The daylight had almost gone. Eventually I pointed to a small clearing some ten yards away.

"Just there I saw it. Just there."

We stared at the spot.

"What did it look like?"

"I couldn't see very well. It was dark."

"But you must have seen something."

"It was an old woman. She was just standing there, watching me."

We kept staring at the spot as if mesmerized.

"She was wearing a white kimono," I said. "Some of her hair came undone. It was blowing around a little."

Kikuko pushed her elbow against my arm. "Oh, be quiet. You're trying to frighten me all over again." She trod on the remains of her cigarette, then for a brief moment stood regarding it with a perplexed expression. She kicked some pine needles over it, then once more displayed her grin. "Let's see if supper's ready," she said.

We found my father in the kitchen. He gave us a quick glance, then carried on with what he was doing.

"Father's become quite a chef since he's had to manage on his own," Kikuko said with a laugh.

He turned and looked at my sister coldly. "Hardly a skill I'm proud of," he said. "Kikuko, come here and help."

For some moments my sister did not move. Then she stepped forward and took an apron hanging from a drawer.

"Just these vegetables need cooking now," he said to her. "The rest just needs watching." Then he looked up and regarded me strangely for some seconds. "I expect you want to look around the house," he said eventually. He put down the chopsticks he had been holding. "It's a long time since you've seen it."

As we left the kitchen I glanced toward Kikuko, but her back was turned.

"She's a good girl," my father said.

I followed my father from room to room. I had forgotten how large the house was. A panel would slide open and another room would appear. But the rooms were all startlingly empty. In one of the rooms the lights did not come on, and we stared at the stark walls and tatami in the pale light that came from the windows.

"This house is too large for a man to live in alone," my father said. "I don't have much use for most of these rooms now."

But eventually my father opened the door to a room packed full of books and papers. There were flowers in vases and pictures on the walls. Then I noticed something on a low table in the corner of the room. I came nearer and saw it was a plastic model of a battleship, the kind constructed by children. It had been placed on some newspaper; scattered around it were assorted pieces of gray plastic.

My father gave a laugh. He came up to the table and picked up the model.

"Since the firm folded," he said, "I have a little more time on my hands." He laughed again, rather strangely. For a moment his face looked almost gentle. "A little more time."

90 "That seems odd," I said. "You were always so busy."

"Too busy, perhaps." He looked at me with a small smile. "Perhaps I should have been a more attentive father."

I laughed. He went on contemplating his battleship. Then he looked up. "I hadn't meant to tell you this, but perhaps it's best that I do. It's my belief that your mother's death was no accident. She had many worries. And some disappointments."

We both gazed at the plastic battleship.

"Surely," I said eventually, "my mother didn't expect me to live here forever."

95 "Obviously you don't see. You don't see how it is for some parents. Not only must they lose their children, they must lose them to things they don't understand." He spun the battleship in his fingers. "These little gunboats here could have been better glued, don't you think?"

"Perhaps. I think it looks fine."

"During the war I spent some time on a ship rather like this. But my ambition was always the air force. I figured it like this: If your ship was struck by the enemy, all you could do was struggle in the water hoping for a lifeline. But in an airplane—well, there was always the final weapon." He put the model back onto the table. "I don't suppose you believe in war."

"Not particularly."

He cast an eye around the room. "Supper should be ready by now," he said. "You must be hungry."

100 Supper was waiting in a dimly lit room next to the kitchen. The only source of light was a big lantern that hung over the table, casting the rest of the room in shadow. We bowed to each other before starting the meal.

There was little conversation. When I made some polite comment about the food, Kikuko giggled a little. Her earlier nervousness seemed to have returned to her. My father did not speak for several minutes. Finally he said:

"It must feel strange for you, being back in Japan."

"Yes, it is a little strange."

"Already, perhaps, you regret leaving America."

105 "A little. Not so much. I didn't leave behind much. Just some empty rooms."

"I see."

I glanced across the table. My father's face looked stony and forbidding in the half-light. We ate on in silence.

Then my eye caught something at the back of the room. At first I continued eating, then my hands became still. The others noticed and looked at me. I went on gazing into the darkness past my father's shoulder.

"Who is that? In that photograph there?"

"Which photograph?" My father turned slightly, trying to follow my gaze.

"The lowest one. The old woman in the white kimono."

My father put down his chopsticks. He looked first at the photograph, then at me.

"Your mother." His voice had become very hard. "Can't you recognize your own mother?"

"My mother. You see, it's dark. I can't see it very well."

No one spoke for a few seconds, then Kikuko rose to her feet. She took the photograph down from the wall, came back to the table, and gave it to me.

"She looks a lot older," I said.

"It was taken shortly before her death," said my father.

"It was the dark. I couldn't see very well."

I looked up and noticed my father holding out a hand. I gave him the photograph. He looked at it intently, then held it toward Kikuko. Obediently, my sister rose to her feet once more and returned the picture to the wall.

There was a large pot left unopened at the center of the table. When Kikuko had seated herself again, my father reached forward and lifted the lid. A cloud of steam rose up and curled toward the lantern. He pushed the pot a little toward me.

"You must be hungry," he said. One side of his face had fallen into shadow.

"Thank you." I reached forward with my chopsticks. The steam was almost scalding. "What is it?"

"Fish."

"It smells very good."

In the soup were strips of fish that had curled almost into balls. I picked one out and brought it to my bowl.

"Help yourself. There's plenty."

"Thank you." I took a little more, then pushed the pot toward my father. I watched him take several pieces to his bowl. Then we both watched as Kikuko served herself.

My father bowed slightly. "You must be hungry," he said again. He took some fish to his mouth and started to eat. Then I, too, chose a piece and put it in my mouth. It felt soft, quite fleshy against my tongue.

The three of us ate in silence. Several minutes went by. My father lifted the lid and once more steam rose up. We all reached forward and helped ourselves.

"Here," I said to my father, "you have this last piece."

"Thank you."

When we had finished the meal, my father stretched out his arms and yawned with an air of satisfaction. "Kikuko," he said, "prepare a pot of tea, please."

My sister looked at him, then left the room without comment. My father stood up.

"Let's retire to the other room. It's rather warm in here."

135 I got to my feet and followed him into the tearoom. The large sliding windows had been left open, bringing in a breeze from the garden. For a while we sat in silence.

"Father," I said, finally.

"Yes?"

"Kikuko tells me Watanabe-son took his whole family with him."

My father lowered his eyes and nodded. For some moments he seemed deep in thought. "Watanabe was very devoted to his work," he said at last. "The collapse of the firm was a great blow to him. I fear it must have weakened his judgment."

140 "You think what he did . . . it was a mistake?"

"Why, of course. Do you see it otherwise?"

"No, no. Of course not."

"There are other things besides work," my father said.

"Yes."

145 We fell silent again. The sound of locusts came in from the garden. I looked out into the darkness. The well was no longer visible.

"What do you think you will do now?" my father asked. "Will you stay in Japan for a while?"

"To be honest, I hadn't thought that far ahead."

"If you wish to stay here, I mean here in this house, you would be very welcome. That is, if you don't mind living with an old man."

"Thank you. I'll have to think about it."

150 I gazed out once more into the darkness.

"But of course," said my father, "this house is so dreary now. You'll no doubt return to America before long."

"Perhaps. I don't know yet."

"No doubt you will."

For some time my father seemed to be studying the back of his hands. Then he looked up and sighed.

155 "Kikuko is due to complete her studies next spring," he said. "Perhaps she will want to come home then. She's a good girl."

"Perhaps she will."

"Things will improve then."

"Yes, I'm sure they will."

We fell silent once more, waiting for Kikuko to bring the tea.

[*1990*]

## SANDRA CISNEROS

*Sandra Cisneros, daughter of a Mexican father and a Mexican-American mother, was born in Chicago in 1954. A graduate of the Iowa Writers Workshop and a National Endowment for the Arts Fellow, she has taught creative writing at several universities and also in Chicago at an alternative high school for dropouts. Cisneros has published two collections of stories and a volume of poetry.*

# *One Holy Night*

> About the truth, if you give it to a person, then he has power over you. And if someone gives it to you, then they have made themselves your slave. It is a strong magic. You can never take it back.
>
> Chaq Uxmal Paloquín

He said his name was Chaq. Chaq Uxmal Paloquín. That's what he told me. He was of an ancient line of Mayan kings. Here, he said, making a map with the heel of his boot, this is where I come from, the Yucatán, the ancient cities. This is what Boy Baby said.

It's been eighteen weeks since Abuelita[1] chased him away with the broom, and what I'm telling you I never told nobody, except Rachel and Lourdes, who know everything. He said he would love me like a revolution, like a religion. Abuelita burned the pushcart and sent me here, miles from home, in this town of dust, with one wrinkled witch woman who rubs my belly with jade, and sixteen nosy cousins.

I don't know how many girls have gone bad from selling cucumbers. I know I'm not the first. My mother took the crooked walk too, I'm told, and I'm sure my Abuelita has her own story, but it's not my place to ask.

Abuelita says it's Uncle Lalo's fault because he's the man of the family and if he had come home on time like he was supposed to and worked the pushcart on the days he was told to and watched over his goddaughter, who is too foolish to look after herself, nothing would've happened, and I wouldn't have to be sent to Mexico. But Uncle Lalo says if they had never left Mexico in the first place, shame enough would have kept a girl from doing devil things.

5 I'm not saying I'm not bad. I'm not saying I'm special. But I'm not like the Allport Street girls, who stand in doorways and go with men into alleys.

All I know is I didn't want it like that. Not against the bricks or hunkering in somebody's car. I wanted it come undone like gold thread, like a tent full of birds. The way it's supposed to be, the way I knew it would be when I met Boy Baby.

But you must know, I was no girl back then. And Boy Baby was no boy. Chaq Uxmal Paloquín. Boy Baby was a man. When I asked him how old he was he said he didn't know. The past and the future are the same thing. So he seemed boy and baby and man all at once, and the way he looked at me, how do I explain?

I'd park the pushcart in front of the Jewel food store Saturdays. He bought a mango on a stick the first time. Paid for it with a new twenty. Next Saturday he was back. Two mangoes, lime juice, and chili powder, keep the change. The third Saturday he asked for a cucumber spear and ate it slow. I didn't see him after that till the day he brought me Kool-Aid in a plastic cup. Then I knew what I felt for him.

Maybe you wouldn't like him. To you he might be a bum. Maybe he looked it. Maybe. He had broken thumbs and burnt fingers. He had thick greasy fingernails he never cut and dusty hair. And all his bones were strong

[1]**Abuelita** Grandma (Spanish)

ones like a man's. I waited every Saturday in my same blue dress. I sold all the mango and cucumber, and then Boy Baby would come finally.

10 What I knew of Chaq was only what he told me, because nobody seemed to know where he came from. Only that he could speak a strange language that no one could understand, said his name translated into boy, or boy-child, and so it was the street people nicknamed him Boy Baby.

I never asked about his past. He said it was all the same and didn't matter, past and the future all the same to his people. But the truth has a strange way of following you, of coming up to you and making you listen to what it has to say.

Night time. Boy Baby brushes my hair and talks to me in his strange language because I like to hear it. What I like to hear him tell is how he is Chaq, Chaq of the people of the sun, Chaq of the temples, and what he says sounds sometimes like broken clay, and at other times like hollow sticks, or like the swish of old feathers crumbling into dust.

He lived behind Esparza & Sons Auto Repair in a little room that used to be a closet—pink plastic curtains on a narrow window, a dirty cot covered with newspapers, and a cardboard box filled with socks and rusty tools. It was there, under one bald bulb, in the back room of the Esparza garage, in the single room with pink curtains, that he showed me the guns—twenty-four in all. Rifles and pistols, one rusty musket, a machine gun, and several tiny weapons with mother-of-pearl handles that looked like toys. So you'll see who I am, he said, laying them all out on the bed of newspapers. So you'll understand. But I didn't want to know.

The stars foretell everything, he said. My birth. My son's. The boy-child who will bring back the grandeur of my people from those who have broken the arrows, from those who have pushed the ancient stones off their pedestals.

15 Then he told how he had prayed in the Temple of the Magician years ago as a child when his father had made him promise to bring back the ancient ways. Boy Baby had cried in the temple dark that only the bats made holy. Boy Baby who was man and child among the great and dusty guns lay down on the newspaper bed and wept for a thousand years. When I touched him, he looked at me with the sadness of stone.

You must not tell anyone what I am going to do, he said. And what I remember next is how the moon, the pale moon with its one yellow eye, the moon of Tikal, and Tulum, and Chichén, stared through the pink plastic curtains. Then something inside bit me, and I gave out a cry as if the other, the one I wouldn't be anymore, leapt out.

So I was initiated beneath an ancient sky by a great and mighty heir—Chaq Uxmal Paloquín. I, Ixchel, his queen.

The truth is, it wasn't a big deal. It wasn't any deal at all. I put my bloody panties inside my T-shirt and ran home hugging myself. I thought about a lot of things on the way home. I thought about all the world and how suddenly I became a part of history and wondered if everyone on the street, the sewing machine lady and the *panadería*[2] saleswomen and the woman with two kids sitting on the bus bench didn't all know. *Did I look*

[2]***panadería*** bakery

*any different? Could they tell?* We were all the same somehow, laughing behind our hands, waiting the way all women wait, and when we find out, we wonder why the world and a million years made such a big deal over nothing.

I know I was supposed to feel ashamed, but I wasn't ashamed. I wanted to stand on top of the highest building, the top-top floor, and yell, *I know.*

20 Then I understood why Abuelita didn't let me sleep over at Lourdes's house full of too many brothers, and why the Roman girl in the movies always runs away from the soldier, and what happens when the scenes in love stories begin to fade, and why brides blush, and how it is that sex isn't simply a box you check *M* or *F* on in the test we get at school.

I was wise. The corner girls were still jumping into their stupid little hopscotch squares. I laughed inside and climbed the wooden stairs two by two to the second floor rear where me and Abuelita and Uncle Lalo live. I was still laughing when I opened the door and Abuelita asked, "Where's the pushcart?"

And then I didn't know what to do.

It's a good thing we live in a bad neighborhood. There are always plenty of bums to blame for your sins. If it didn't happen the way I told it, it really could've. We looked and looked all over for the kids who stole my pushcart. The story wasn't the best, but since I had to make it up right then and there with Abuelita staring a hole through my heart, it wasn't too bad.

For two weeks I had to stay home. Abuelita was afraid the street kids who had stolen the cart would be after me again. Then I thought I might go over to the Esparza garage and take the pushcart out and leave it in some alley for the police to find, but I was never allowed to leave the house alone. Bit by bit the truth started to seep out like a dangerous gasoline.

25 First the nosy woman who lives upstairs from the laundromat told my Abuelita she thought something was fishy, the pushcart wheeled into Esparza & Sons every Saturday after dark, how a man, the same dark Indian one, the one who never talks to anybody, walked with me when the sun went down and pushed the cart into the garage, that one there, and yes we went inside, there where the fat lady named Concha, whose hair is dyed a hard black, pointed a fat finger.

I prayed that we would not meet Boy Baby, and since the gods listen and are mostly good, Esparza said yes, a man like that had lived there but was gone, had packed a few things and left the pushcart in a corner to pay for his last week's rent.

We had to pay $20 before he would give us our pushcart back. Then Abuelita made me tell the real story of how the cart had disappeared, all of which I told this time, except for that one night, which I would have to tell anyway, weeks later, when I prayed for the moon of my cycle to come back, but it would not.

When Abuelita found out I was going to *dar a luz,*[3] she cried until her eyes were little, and blamed Uncle Lalo, and Uncle Lalo blamed this country, and Abuelita blamed the infamy of men. That is when she burned the cucumber pushcart and called me a *sinvergüenza* because I *am* without shame.

[3]***dar a luz*** have a baby

Then I cried too—Boy Baby was lost from me—until my head was hot with headaches and I fell asleep. When I woke up, the cucumber pushcart was dust and Abuelita was sprinkling holy water on my head.

30 Abuelita woke up early every day and went to the Esparza garage to see if news about that *demonio* had been found, had Chaq Uxmal Paloquín sent any letters, any, and when the other mechanics heard that name they laughed, and asked if we had made it up, that we could have some letters that had come for Boy Baby, no forwarding address, since he had gone in such a hurry.

There were three. The first, addressed "Occupant," demanded immediate payment for a four-month-old electric bill. The second was one I recognized right away—a brown envelope fat with cake-mix coupons and fabric-softener samples—because we'd gotten one just like it. The third was addressed in a spidery Spanish to a Señor C. Cruz, on paper so thin you could read it unopened by the light of the sky. The return address a convent in Tampico.

This was to whom my Abuelita wrote in hopes of finding the man who could correct my ruined life, to ask if the good nuns might know the whereabouts of a certain Boy Baby—and if they were hiding him it would be of no use because God's eyes see through all souls.

We heard nothing for a long time. Abuelita took me out of school when my uniform got tight around the belly and said it was a shame I wouldn't be able to graduate with the other eighth graders.

Except for Lourdes and Rachel, my grandma and Uncle Lalo, nobody knew about my past. I would sleep in the big bed I share with Abuelita same as always. I could hear Abuelita and Uncle Lalo talking in low voices in the kitchen as if they were praying the rosary, how they were going to send me to Mexico, to San Dionisio de Tlaltepango, where I have cousins and where I was conceived and would've been born had my grandma not thought it wise to send my mother here to the United States so that neighbors in San Dionisio de Tlaltepango wouldn't ask why her belly was suddenly big.

35 I was happy. I liked staying home. Abuelita was teaching me to crochet the way she had learned in Mexico. And just when I had mastered the tricky rosette stitch, the letter came from the convent which gave the truth about Boy Baby—however much we didn't want to hear.

He was born on a street with no name in a town called Miseria. His father, Eusebio, is a knife sharpener. His mother, Refugia, stacks apricots into pyramids and sells them on a cloth in the market. There are brothers. Sisters too of which I know little. The youngest, a Carmelite, writes me all this and prays for my soul, which is why I know it's all true.

Boy Baby is thirty-seven years old. His name is Chato which means fat-face. There is no Mayan blood.

I don't think they understand how it is to be a girl. I don't think they know how it is to have to wait your whole life. I count the months for the baby to be born, and it's like a ring of water inside me reaching out and out until one day it will tear from me with its own teeth.

Already I can feel the animal inside me stirring in his own uneven sleep. The witch woman says it's the dreams of weasels that make my child sleep the way he sleeps. She makes me eat white bread blessed by the priest, but

I know it's the ghost of him inside me that circles and circles, and will not let me rest.

40 Abuelita said they sent me here just in time, because a little later Boy Baby came back to our house looking for me, and she had to chase him away with the broom. The next thing we hear, he's in the newspaper clippings his sister sends. A picture of him looking very much like stone, police hooked on either arm . . . *on the road to* Las Grutas de Xtacumbilxuna, *the Caves of the Hidden Girl . . . eleven female bodies . . . the last seven years . . .*

Then I couldn't read but only stare at the little black-and-white dots that make up the face I am in love with.

All my girl cousins here either don't talk to me, or those who do, ask questions they're too young to know *not* to ask. What they want to know really is how it is to have a man, because they're too ashamed to ask their married sisters.

They don't know what it is to lay so still until his sleep breathing is heavy, for the eyes in the dim dark to look and look without worry at the man-bones and the neck, the man-wrist and man-jaw thick and strong, all the salty dips and hollows, the stiff hair of the brow and sour swirl of sideburns, to lick the fat earlobes that taste of smoke, and stare at how perfect is a man.

I tell them, "It's a bad joke. When you find out you'll be sorry."

45 I'm going to have five children. Five. Two girls. Two boys. And one baby.

The girls will be called Lisette and Maritza. The boys I'll name Pablo and Sandro.

And my baby. My baby will be named Alegre, because life will always be hard.

Rachel says that love is like a big black piano being pushed off the top of a three-story building and you're waiting on the bottom to catch it. But Lourdes says it's not that way at all. It's like a top, like all the colors in the world are spinning so fast they're not colors anymore and all that's left is a white hum.

There was a man, a crazy who lived upstairs from us when we lived on South Loomis. He couldn't talk, just walked around all day with this harmonica in his mouth. Didn't play it. Just sort of breathed through it, all day long, wheezing, in and out, in and out.

50 This is how it is with me. Love I mean.

[*1988*]

## HELENA MARIA VIRAMONTES

*Helena Maria Viramontes was born in East Los Angeles in 1954. After completing her undergraduate studies at Immaculate Heart College, she did graduate work at California State University, Los Angeles, and further work (1979–81) in the MFA Creative Writing Program at the University of California, Irvine. Viramontes has won first prize in several fiction contests, including the Irvine Chicano Literary Contest. In 1989, the year in which she was awarded a Creative Writing Fellowship from the National Endowment for the Arts, she participated in a "Storytelling for Film" workshop at the Sundance Film Institute. She now teaches writing at Cornell.*

*Viramontes writes chiefly about women whose lives are circumscribed by a patriarchal Latino society. Eight of her stories have been collected in* "The Moths" and Other Stories *(1985); she is also the author of a widely praised novel,* Under the Feet of Jesus *(1995).*

# *The Moths*

I was fourteen years old when Abuelita[1] requested my help. And it seemed only fair. Abuelita had pulled me through the rages of scarlet fever by placing, removing and replacing potato slices on the temples of my forehead; she had seen me through several whippings, an arm broken by a dare jump off Tío Enrique's toolshed, puberty, and my first lie. Really, I told Amá, it was only fair.

Not that I was her favorite granddaughter or anything special. I wasn't even pretty or nice like my older sisters and I just couldn't do the girl things they could do. My hands were too big to handle the fineries of crocheting or embroidery and I always pricked my fingers or knotted my colored threads time and time again while my sisters laughed and called me bull hands with their cute waterlike voices. So I began keeping a piece of jagged brick in my sock to bash my sisters or anyone who called me bull hands. Once, while we all sat in the bedroom, I hit Teresa on the forehead, right above her eyebrow and she ran to Amá with her mouth open, her hand over her eye while blood seeped between her fingers. I was used to the whippings by then.

I wasn't respectful either. I even went so far as to doubt the power of Abuelita's slices, the slices she said absorbed my fever. "You're still alive, aren't you?" Abuelita snapped back, her pasty gray eye beaming at me and burning holes in my suspicions. Regretful that I had let secret questions drop out of my mouth, I couldn't look into her eyes. My hands began to fan out, grow like a liar's nose until they hung by my side like low weights. Abuelita made a balm out of dried moth wings and Vicks and rubbed my hands, shaped them back to size and it was the strangest feeling. Like bones melting. Like sun shining through the darkness of your eyelids. I didn't mind helping Abuelita after that, so Amá would always send me over to her.

In the early afternoon Amá would push her hair back, hand me my sweater and shoes, and tell me to go to Mama Luna's. This was to avoid another fight and another whipping, I knew. I would deliver one last direct shot on Marisela's arm and jump out of our house, the slam of the screen door burying her cries of anger, and I'd gladly go help Abuelita plant her

[1]**Abuelita** Grandma (Spanish); other Spanish words for relatives mentioned in the story are *Tío,* Uncle, *Amá,* Mother, and *Apá,* Dad.

wild lilies or jasmine or heliotrope or cilantro or hierbabuena in red Hills Brothers coffee cans. Abuelita would wait for me at the top step of her porch holding a hammer and nail and empty coffee cans. And although we hardly spoke, hardly looked at each other as we worked over root transplants, I always felt her gray eye on me. It made me feel, in a strange sort of way, safe and guarded and not alone. Like God was supposed to make you feel.

5 On Abuelita's porch, I would puncture holes in the bottom of the coffee cans with a nail and a precise hit of a hammer. This completed, my job was to fill them with red clay mud from beneath her rose bushes, packing it softly, then making a perfect hole, four fingers round, to nest a sprouting avocado pit, or the spidery sweet potatoes that Abuelita rooted in mayonnaise jars with toothpicks and daily water, or prickly chayotes[2] that produced vines that twisted and wound all over her porch pillars, crawling to the roof, up and over the roof, and down the other side, making her small brick house look like it was cradled within the vines that grew pear-shaped squashes ready for the pick, ready to be steamed with onions and cheese and butter. The roots would burst out of the rusted coffee cans and search for a place to connect. I would then feed the seedlings with water.

But this was a different kind of help, Amá said, because Abuelita was dying. Looking into her gray eye, then into her brown one, the doctor said it was just a matter of days. And so it seemed only fair that these hands she had melted and formed found use in rubbing her caving body with alcohol and marihuana, rubbing her arms and legs, turning her face to the window so that she could watch the Bird of Paradise blooming or smell the scent of clove in the air. I toweled her face frequently and held her hand for hours. Her gray wiry hair hung over the mattress. Since I could remember, she'd kept her long hair in braids. Her mouth was vacant and when she slept, her eyelids never closed all the way. Up close, you could see her gray eye beaming out the window, staring hard as if to remember everything. I never kissed her. I left the window open when I went to the market.

Across the street from Jay's Market there was a chapel. I never knew its denomination, but I went in just the same to search for candles. I sat down on one of the pews because there were none. After I cleaned my fingernails, I looked up at the high ceiling. I had forgotten the vastness of these places, the coolness of the marble pillars and the frozen statues with blank eyes. I was alone. I knew why I had never returned.

That was one of Apá's biggest complaints. He would pound his hands on the table, rocking the sugar dish or spilling a cup of coffee and scream that if I didn't go to mass every Sunday to save my goddamn sinning soul, then I had no reason to go out of the house, period. Punto final.[3] He would grab my arm and dig his nails into me to make sure I understood the importance of catechism. Did he make himself clear? Then he strategically directed his anger at Amá for her lousy ways of bringing up daughters, being disrespectful and unbelieving, and my older sisters would pull me aside and tell me if I didn't get to mass right this minute, they were all going to kick the holy shit out of me. Why am I so selfish? Can't you see what it's doing to

[2]**chayotes** squash-like fruit
[3]**Punto final** period

Amá, you idiot? So I would wash my feet and stuff them in my black Easter shoes that shone with Vaseline, grab a missal and veil, and wave good-bye to Amá.

I would walk slowly down Lorena to First to Evergreen, counting the cracks on the cement. On Evergreen I would turn left and walk to Abuelita's. I liked her porch because it was shielded by the vines of the chayotes and I could get a good look at the people and car traffic on Evergreen without them knowing. I would jump up the porch steps, knock on the screen door as I wiped my feet and call Abuelita? mi Abuelita? As I opened the door and stuck my head in, I would catch the gagging scent of toasting chile on the placa.[4] When I entered the sala,[5] she would greet me from the kitchen, wringing her hands in her apron. I'd sit at the corner of the table to keep from being in her way. The chiles made my eyes water. Am I crying? No, Mama Luna, I'm sure not crying. I don't like going to mass, but my eyes watered anyway, the tears dropping on the tablecloth like candle wax. Abuelita lifted the burnt chiles from the fire and sprinkled water on them until the skins began to separate. Placing them in front of me, she turned to check the menudo.[6] I peeled the skins off and put the flimsy, limp looking green and yellow chiles in the molcajete[7] and began to crush and crush and twist and crush the heart out of the tomato, the clove of garlic, the stupid chiles that made me cry, crushed them until they turned into liquid under my bull hand. With a wooden spoon, I scraped hard to destroy the guilt, and my tears were gone. I put the bowl of chile next to a vase filled with freshly cut roses. Abuelita touched my hand and pointed to the bowl of menudo that steamed in front of me. I spooned some chile into the menudo and rolled a corn tortilla thin with the palms of my hands. As I ate, a fine Sunday breeze entered the kitchen and a rose petal calmly feathered down to the table.

10 I left the chapel without blessing myself and walked to Jay's. Most of the time Jay didn't have much of anything. The tomatoes were always soft and the cans of Campbell soups had rusted spots on them. There was dust on the tops of cereal boxes. I picked up what I needed: rubbing alcohol, five cans of chicken broth, a big bottle of Pine Sol. At first Jay got mad because I thought I had forgotten the money. But it was there all the time, in my back pocket.

When I returned from the market, I heard Amá crying in Abuelita's kitchen. She looked up at me with puffy eyes. I placed the bags of groceries on the table and began putting the cans of soup away. Amá sobbed quietly. I never kissed her. After a while, I patted her on the back for comfort. Finally: "¿Y mi Amá?"[8] she asked in a whisper, then choked again and cried into her apron.

Abuelita fell off the bed twice yesterday, I said, knowing that I shouldn't have said it and wondering why I wanted to say it because it only made Amá cry harder. I guess I became angry and just so tired of the quar-

[4]**placa** round cast-iron griddle
[5]**sala** living room
[6]**menudo** tripe soup
[7]**molcajete** mixing vessel, mortar
[8]**¿Y mi Amá?** And my Mother?

rels and beatings and unanswered prayers and my hands just there hanging helplessly by my side. Amá looked at me again, confused, angry, and her eyes were filled with sorrow. I went outside and sat on the porch swing and watched the people pass. I sat there until she left. I dozed off repeating the words to myself like rosary prayers: when do you stop giving when do you start giving when do you . . . and when my hands fell from my lap, I awoke to catch them. The sun was setting, an orange glow, and I knew Abuelita was hungry.

There comes a time when the sun is defiant. Just about the time when moods change, inevitable seasons of a day, transitions from one color to another, that hour or minute or second when the sun is finally defeated, finally sinks into the realization that it cannot with all its power to heal or burn, exist forever, there comes an illumination where the sun and earth meet, a final burst of burning red orange fury reminding us that although endings are inevitable, they are necessary for rebirths, and when that time came, just when I switched on the light in the kitchen to open Abuelita's can of soup, it was probably then that she died.

The room smelled of Pine Sol and vomit and Abuelita had defecated the remains of her cancerous stomach. She had turned to the window and tried to speak, but her mouth remained open and speechless. I heard you, Abuelita, I said, stroking her cheek, I heard you. I opened the windows of the house and let the soup simmer and overboil on the stove. I turned the stove off and poured the soup down the sink. From the cabinet I got a tin basin, filled it with lukewarm water and carried it carefully to the room. I went to the linen closet and took out some modest bleached white towels. With the sacredness of a priest preparing his vestments, I unfolded the towels one by one on my shoulders. I removed the sheets and blankets from her bed and peeled off her thick flannel nightgown. I toweled her puzzled face, stretching out the wrinkles, removing the coils of her neck, toweled her shoulders and breasts. Then I changed the water. I returned to towel the creases of her stretch-marked stomach, her sporadic vaginal hairs, and her sagging thighs. I removed the lint from between her toes and noticed a mapped birthmark on the fold of her buttock. The scars on her back which were as thin as the life lines on the palms of her hands made me realize how little I really knew of Abuelita. I covered her with a thin blanket and went into the bathroom. I washed my hands, and turned on the tub faucets and watched the water pour into the tub with vitality and steam. When it was full, I turned off the water and undressed. Then, I went to get Abuelita.

15 She was not as heavy as I thought and when I carried her in my arms, her body fell into a V, and yet my legs were tired, shaky, and I felt as if the distance between the bedroom and bathroom was miles and years away. Amá, where are you?

I stepped into the bathtub one leg first, then the other. I bent my knees slowly to descend into the water slowly so I wouldn't scald her skin. There, there, Abuelita, I said, cradling her, smoothing her as we descended, I heard you. Her hair fell back and spread across the water like eagle's wings. The water in the tub overflowed and poured onto the tile of the floor. Then the moths came. Small, gray ones that came from her soul and out through her mouth fluttering to light, circling the single dull light bulb of the bathroom. Dying is lonely and I wanted to go to where the moths were, stay with her and plant chayotes whose vines would crawl up her fingers and into the clouds; I wanted to rest my head on her chest with her stroking my hair, telling me about the moths that lay within the soul and slowly eat the spirit up; I wanted to return to the waters of the womb with her so that we would never be alone again. I wanted. I wanted my Amá. I removed a few strands of hair from Abuelita's face and held her small light head within the hollow of my neck. The bathroom was filled with moths, and for the first time in a long time I cried, rocking us, crying for her, for me, for Amá, the sobs emerging from the depths of anguish, the misery of feeling half born, sobbing until finally the sobs rippled into circles and circles of sadness and relief. There, there, I said to Abuelita, rocking us gently, there, there.

[*1982*]

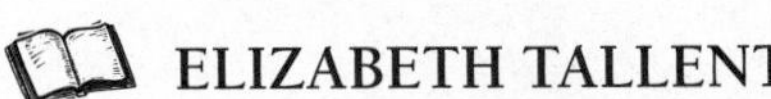

## ELIZABETH TALLENT

***Elizabeth Tallent was born in Washington, D.C., in 1954, and educated at Illinois State University at Normal. The author of novels and short stories, she has won many awards, including a fellowship from the National Endowment for the Arts, and the O. Henry Award.***

# *No One's a Mystery*

For my eighteenth birthday Jack gave me a five-year diary with a latch and a little key, light as a dime. I was sitting beside him scratching at the lock, which didn't seem to want to work, when he thought he saw his wife's Cadillac in the distance, coming toward us. He pushed me down onto the dirty floor of the pickup and kept one hand on my head while I inhaled the musk of his cigarettes in the dashboard ashtray and sang along with Rosanne Cash on the tape deck. We'd been drinking tequila and the bottle was between his legs, resting up against his crotch, where the seam of his Levi's was bleached linen-white, though the Levi's were nearly new. I don't know why his Levi's always bleached like that, along the seams and at the knees. In a curve of cloth his zipper glinted, gold.

"It's her," he said. "She keeps the lights on in the daytime. I can't think of a single habit in a woman that irritates me more than that." When he saw that I was going to stay still he took his hand from my head and ran it through his own dark hair.

"Why does she?" I said.

"She thinks it's safer. Why does she need to be safer? She's driving exactly fifty-five miles an hour. She believes in those signs: 'Speed Monitored by Aircraft.' It doesn't matter that you can look up and see that the sky is empty."

5 "She'll see your lips move, Jack. She'll know you're talking to someone."

"She'll think I'm singing along with the radio."

He didn't lift his head, just raised the fingers in salute while the pressure of his palm steadied the wheel, and I heard the Cadillac honk twice, musically; he was driving easily eighty miles an hour. I studied his boots. The elk heads stitched into the leather were bearded with frayed thread, the toes were scuffed, and there was a compact wedge of muddy manure between the heel and the sole—the same boots he'd been wearing for the two years I'd known him. On the tape deck Rosanne Cash sang, "Nobody's into me, no one's a mystery."

"Do you think she's getting famous because of who her daddy is or for herself?" Jack said.

"There are about a hundred pop tops on the floor, did you know that? Some little kid could cut a bare foot on one of these, Jack."

10 "No little kids get into this truck except for you."

"How come you let it get so dirty?"

"'How come,'" he mocked. "You even sound like a kid. You can get back into the seat now, if you want. She's not going to look over her shoulder and see you."

"How do you know?"

"I just know," he said. "Like I know I'm going to get meat loaf for supper. It's in the air. Like I know what you'll be writing in that diary."

15 "What will I be writing?" I knelt on my side of the seat and craned around to look at the butterfly of dust printed on my jeans. Outside the window Wyoming was dazzling in the heat. The wheat was fawn and yellow and parted smoothly by the thin dirt road. I could smell the water in the irrigation ditches hidden in the wheat.

"Tonight you'll write, 'I love Jack. This is my birthday present from him. I can't imagine anybody loving anybody more than I love Jack.'"

"I can't."

"In a year you'll write, 'I wonder what I ever really saw in Jack. I wonder why I spent so many days just riding around in his pickup. It's true he taught me something about sex. It's true there wasn't ever much else to do in Cheyenne.'"

"I won't write that."

20 "In two years you'll write, 'I wonder what that old guy's name was, the one with the curly hair and the filthy dirty pickup truck and time on his hands.'"

"I won't write that."

"No?"

"Tonight I'll write, 'I love Jack. This is my birthday present from him. I can't imagine anybody loving anybody more than I love Jack.'"

"No, you can't," he said. "You can't imagine it."

25 "In a year I'll write, 'Jack should be home any minute now. The table's set—my grandmother's linen and her old silver and the yellow candles left over from the wedding—but I don't know if I can wait until after the trout à la Navarra to make love to him.'"

"It must have been a fast divorce."

"In two years I'll write, 'Jack should be home by now. Little Jack is hungry for his supper. He said his first word today besides "Mama" and "Papa." He said "kaka."'"

Jack laughed. "He was probably trying to finger-paint with kaka on the bathroom wall when you heard him say it."

"In three years I'll write, 'My nipples are a little sore from nursing Eliza Rosamund.'"

30 "Rosamund. Every little girl should have a middle name she hates."

"'Her breath smells like vanilla and her eyes are just Jack's color of blue.'"

"That's nice," Jack said.

"So, which one do you like?"

"I like yours," he said. "But I believe mine."

35 "It doesn't matter. I believe mine."

"Not in your heart of hearts, you don't."

"You're wrong."

"I'm not wrong," he said. "And her breath would smell like your milk, and it's kind of a bittersweet smell, if you want to know the truth."

[*1985*]

## SUSAN MINOT

*Susan Minot was born in Manchester, Massachusetts, in 1956, and was educated at Boston University, Brown University, and Columbia University. Minot has written a novel,* Monkeys *(1986) and numerous stories, some of which have been collected in* Lust and Other Stories *(1989).*

# *Lust*

Leo was from a long time ago, the first one I ever saw nude. In the spring before the Hellmans filled their pool, we'd go down there in the deep end, with baby oil, and like that. I met him the first month away at boarding school. He had a halo from the campus light behind him. I flipped.

Roger was fast. In his illegal car, we drove to the reservoir, the radio blaring, talking fast, fast, fast. He was always going for my zipper. He got kicked out sophomore year.

By the time the band got around to playing "Wild Horses," I had tasted Bruce's tongue. We were clicking in the shadows on the other side of the amplifier, out of Mrs. Donovan's line of vision. It tasted like salt, with my neck bent back, because we had been dancing so hard before.

Tim's line: "I'd like to see you in a bathing suit." I knew it was his line when he said the exact same thing to Annie Hines.

5 You'd go on walks to get off campus. It was raining like hell, my sweater as sopped as a wet sheep. Tim pinned me to a tree, the woods light brown and dark brown, a white house half-hidden with the lights already on. The water was as loud as a crowd hissing. He made certain comments about my forehead, about my cheeks.

We started off sitting at one end of the couch and then our feet were squished against the armrest and then he went over to turn off the TV and came back after he had taken off his shirt and then we slid onto the floor and he got up again to close the door, then came back to me, a body waiting on the rug.

You'd try to wipe off the table or to do the dishes and Willie would untuck your shirt and get his hands up under in front, standing behind you, making puffy noises in your ear.

He likes it when I wash my hair. He covers his face with it and if I start to say something, he goes, "Shush."

For a long time, I had Philip on the brain. The less they noticed you, the more you got them on the brain.

My parents had no idea. Parents never really know what's going on, especially when you're away at school most of the time. If she met them, my mother might say, "Oliver seems nice" or "I like that one" without much of an opinion. If she didn't like them, "He's a funny fellow, isn't he?" or "Johnny's perfectly nice but a drink of water." My father was too shy to talk to them at all, unless they played sports and he'd ask them about that.

The sand was almost cold underneath because the sun was long gone. Eben piled a mound over my feet, patting around my ankles, the ghostly surf rumbling behind him in the dark. He was the first person I ever knew who died, later that summer, in a car crash. I thought about it for a long time.

"Come here," he says on the porch.

I go over to the hammock and he takes my wrist with two fingers.

"What?"

He kisses my palm then directs my hand to his fly.

Songs went with whichever boy it was. "Sugar Magnolia" was Tim, with the line "Rolling in the rushes/down by the riverside." With "Darkness Darkness," I'd picture Philip with his long hair. Hearing "Under My Thumb" there'd be the smell of Jamie's suede jacket.

We hid in the listening rooms during study hall. With a record cover over the door's window, the teacher on duty couldn't look in. I came out flushed and heady and back at the dorm was surprised how red my lips were in the mirror.

One weekend at Simon's brother's, we stayed inside all day with the shades down, in bed, then went out to Store 24 to get some ice cream. He stood at the magazine rack and read through *MAD* while I got butterscotch sauce, craving something sweet.

I could do some things well. Some things I was good at, like math or painting or even sports, but the second a boy put his arm around me, I forgot about wanting to do anything else, which felt like a relief at first until it became like sinking into a muck.

It was different for a girl.

When we were little, the brothers next door tied up our ankles. They held the door of the goat house and wouldn't let us out till we showed them our underpants. Then they'd forget about being after us and when we played whiffle ball, I'd be just as good as them.

Then it got to be different. Just because you have on a short skirt, they yell from the cars, slowing down for a while and if you don't look, they screech off and call you a bitch.

"What's the matter with me?" they say, point-blank.

Or else, "Why won't you go out with me? I'm not asking you to get married," about to get mad.

25 Or it'd be, trying to be reasonable, in a regular voice, "Listen, I just want to have a good time."

So I'd go because I couldn't think of something to say back that wouldn't be obvious, and if you go out with them, you sort of have to do something.

I sat between Mack and Eddie in the front seat of the pickup. They were having a fight about something. I've a feeling about me.

Certain nights you'd feel a certain surrender, maybe if you'd had wine. The surrender would be forgetting yourself and you'd put your nose to his neck and feel like a squirrel, safe, at rest, in a restful dream. But then you'd start to slip from that and the dark would come in and there'd be a cave. You make out the dim shape of the windows and feel yourself become a cave, filled absolutely with air, or with a sadness that wouldn't stop.

Teenage years. You know just what you're doing and don't see the things that start to get in the way.

30 Lots of boys, but never two at the same time. One was plenty to keep you in a state. You'd start to see a boy and something would rush over you like a fast storm cloud and you couldn't possibly think of anyone else. Boys took it differently. Their eyes perked up at any little number that walked by. You'd act like you weren't noticing.

The joke was that the school doctor gave out the pill like aspirin. He didn't ask you anything. I was fifteen. We had a picture of him in assembly, holding up an IUD shaped like a T. Most girls were on the pill, if anything, because they couldn't handle a diaphragm. I kept the dial in my top drawer like my mother and thought of her each time I tipped out the yellow tablets in the morning before chapel.

If they were too shy, I'd be more so. Andrew was nervous. We stayed up with his family album, sharing a pack of Old Golds. Before it got light, we turned on the TV. A man was explaining how to plant seedlings. His mouth jerked to the side in a tic. Andrew thought it was a riot and kept imitating him. I laughed to be polite. When we finally dozed off, he dared to put his arm around me but that was it.

You wait till they come to you. With half fright, half swagger, they stand one step down. They dare to touch the button on your coat then lose their nerve and quickly drop their hand so you—you'd do anything for them. You touch their cheek.

The girls sit around in the common room and talk about boys, smoking their heads off.

35 "What are you complaining about?" says Jill to me when we talk about problems.

"Yeah," says Giddy. "You always have a boyfriend."

I look at them and think, As if.

I thought the worst thing anyone could call you was a cockteaser. So, if you flirted, you had to be prepared to go through with it. Sleeping with someone was perfectly normal once you had done it. You didn't really worry about it. But there were other problems. The problems had to do with something else entirely.

Mack was during the hottest summer ever recorded. We were renting a house on an island with all sorts of other people. No one slept during the heat wave, walking around the house with nothing on which we were used to because of the nude beach. In the living room, Eddie lay on top of a coffee table to cool off. Mack and I, with the bedroom door open for air, sweated and sweated all night.

40 "I can't take this," he said at 3 A.M. "I'm going for a swim." He and some guys down the hall went to the beach. The heat put me on edge. I sat on a cracked chest by the open window and smoked and smoked till I felt even worse, waiting for something—I guess for him to get back.

One was on a camping trip in Colorado. We zipped our sleeping bags together, the coyotes' hysterical chatter far away. Other couples murmured in other tents. Paul was up before sunrise, starting a fire for breakfast. He wasn't much of a talker in the daytime. At night, his hand leafed about in the hair at my neck.

There'd be times when you overdid it. You'd get carried away. All the next day, you'd be in a total fog, delirious, absent-minded, crossing the street and nearly getting run over.

The more girls a boy has, the better. He has a bright look, having reaped fruits, blooming. He stalks around, sure-shouldered, and you have the feeling he's got more in him, a fatter heart, more stories to tell. For a girl, with each boy it's like a petal gets plucked each time.

Then you start to get tired. You begin to feel diluted, like watered-down stew.

45 Oliver came skiing with us. We lolled by the fire after everyone had gone to bed. Each creak you'd think was someone coming downstairs. The silver-loop bracelet he gave me had been a present from his girlfriend before.

On vacations, we went skiing, or you'd go south if someone invited you. Some people had apartments in New York that their families hardly ever used. Or summer houses, or older sisters. We always managed to find some place to go.

We made the plan at coffee hour. Simon snuck out and met me at Main Gate after lights-out. We crept to the chapel and spent the night in the balcony. He tasted like onions from a submarine sandwich.

The boys are one of two ways: either they can't sit still or they don't move. In front of the TV, they won't budge. On weekends they play touch football while we sit on the sidelines, picking blades of grass to chew on, and watch. We're always watching them run around. We shiver in the stands, knocking our boots together to keep our toes warm and they whizz across the ice, chopping their sticks around the puck. When they're in the rink, they refuse to look at you, only eyeing each other beneath low helmets. You cheer for them but they don't look up, even if it's a face-off when nothing's happening, even if they're doing drills before any game has started at all.

Dancing under the pink tent, he bent down and whispered in my ear. We slipped away to the lawn on the other side of the hedge. Much later, as he was leaving the buffet with two plates of eggs and sausage, I saw the grass stains on the knees of his white pants.

Tim's was shaped like a banana, with a graceful curve to it. They're all different. Willie's like a bunch of walnuts when nothing was happening, another's as thin as a thin hot dog. But it's like faces; you're never really surprised.

Still, you're not sure what to expect.

I look into his face and he looks back. I look into his eyes and they look back at mine. Then they look down at my mouth so I look at his mouth, then back to his eyes then, backing up, at his whole face. I think, Who? Who are you? His head tilts to one side.

I say, "Who are you?"

"What do you mean?"

"Nothing."

I look at his eyes again, deeper. Can't tell who he is, what he thinks.

"What?" he says. I look at his mouth.

"I'm just wondering," I say and go wandering across his face. Study the chin line. It's shaped like a persimmon.

"Who are you? What are you thinking?"

He says, "What the hell are you talking about?"

Then they get mad after when you say enough is enough. After, when it's easier to explain that you don't want to. You wouldn't dream of saying that maybe you weren't really ready to in the first place.

Gentle Eddie. We waded into the sea, the waves round and plowing in, buffalo-headed, slapping our thighs. I put my arms around his freckled shoulders and he held me up, buoyed by the water, and rocked me like a sea shell.

I had no idea whose party it was, the apartment jampacked, stepping over people in the hallway. The room with the music was practically empty, the bare floor, me in red shoes. This fellow slides onto one knee and takes me around the waist and we rock to jazzy tunes, with my toes pointing heavenward, and waltz and spin and dip to "Smoke Gets in Your Eyes" or "I'll Love You Just for Now." He puts his head to my chest, runs a sweeping hand down my inside thigh and we go loose-limbed and sultry and as smooth as silk and I stamp my red heels and he takes me into a swoon. I never saw him again after that but I thought, I could have loved that one.

You wonder how long you can keep it up. You begin to feel like you're showing through, like a bathroom window that only lets in grey light, the kind you can't see out of.

They keep coming around. Johnny drives up at Easter vacation from Baltimore and I let him in the kitchen with everyone sound asleep. He has friends waiting in the car.

"What are you crazy? It's pouring out there," I say.

"It's okay," he says. "They understand."

So he gets some long kisses from me, against the refrigerator, before he goes because I hate those girls who push away a boy's face as if she were made out of Ivory soap, as if she's that much greater than he is.

The note on my cubby told me to see the headmaster. I had no idea for what. He had received complaints about my amorous displays on the town green. It was Willie that spring. The headmaster told me he didn't care what I did but that Casey Academy had a reputation to uphold in the town. He lowered his glasses on his nose. "We've got twenty acres of woods on this campus," he said. "If you want to smooch with your boyfriend, there are twenty acres for you to do it out of the public eye. You read me?"

Everybody'd get weekend permissions for different places then we'd all go to someone's house whose parents were away. Usually there'd be more boys than girls. We raided the liquor closet and smoked pot at the kitchen table and you'd never know who would end up where, or with whom. There were always disasters. Ceci got bombed and cracked her head open on the bannister and needed stitches. Then there was the time Wendel Blair walked through the picture window at the Lowe's and got slashed to ribbons.

He scared me. In bed, I didn't dare look at him. I lay back with my eyes closed, luxuriating because he knew all sorts of expert angles, his hands never fumbling, going over my whole body, pressing the hair up and off the back of my head, giving an extra hip shove, as if to say *There.* I parted my eyes slightly, keeping the screen of my lashes low because it was too much to look at him, his mouth loose and pink and parted, his eyes looking through my forehead, or kneeling up, looking through my throat. I was ashamed but couldn't look him in the eye.

You wonder about things feeling a little off-kilter. You begin to feel like a piece of pounded veal.

At boarding school, everyone gets depressed. We go in and see the housemother, Mrs. Gunther. She got married when she was eighteen. Mr. Gunther was her high-school sweetheart, the only boyfriend she ever had.

"And you knew you wanted to marry him right off?" we ask her.

She smiles and says, "Yes."

"They always want something from you," says Jill, complaining about her boyfriend.

"Yeah," says Giddy. "You always feel like you have to deliver something."

"You do," says Mrs. Gunther. "Babies."

After sex, you curl up like a shrimp, something deep inside you ruined, slammed in a place that sickens at slamming, and slowly you fill up with an overwhelming sadness, an elusive gaping worry. You don't try to explain it, filled with the knowledge that it's nothing after all, everything filling up finally and absolutely with death. After the briskness of loving, loving stops. And you roll over with death stretched out alongside you like a feather boa, or a snake, light as air, and you . . . you don't even ask for anything or try to say something to him because it's obviously your own damn fault. You haven't been able to—to what? To open your heart. You open your legs but can't, or don't dare anymore, to open your heart.

It starts this way:

You stare into their eyes. They flash like all the stars are out. They look at you seriously, their eyes at a low burn and their hands no matter what starting off shy and with such a gentle touch that the only thing you can do is take that tenderness and let yourself be swept away. When, with one attentive finger they tuck the hair behind your ear, you—

You do everything they want.

Then comes after. After when they don't look at you. They scratch their balls, stare at the ceiling. Or if they do turn, their gaze is altogether changed. They are surprised. They turn casually to look at you, distracted, and get a mild distracted surprise. You're gone. Their blank look tells you that the girl they were fucking is not there anymore. You seem to have disappeared.

[*1990*]

# CHAPTER 12

# The Novel

## OBSERVATIONS ON THE NOVEL

Most of what has been said about short stories (on probability, narrative point of view, style) is relevant to the novel. And just as the short story of the last hundred years or so is rather different from earlier short fiction (see pages 342–45), the novel—though here we must say of the last few hundred years—is different from earlier long fiction.

The ancient epic is at best a distant cousin to the novel, for though a narrative, the epic is in verse, and deals with godlike men and women, and even with gods themselves. One has only to think of the *Iliad* or the *Odyssey,* or the *Aeneid* or *Beowulf* or *Paradise Lost* to recall that the epic does not deal with the sort of people one meets in *Tom Jones, David Copperfield, Crime and Punishment, The Return of the Native, The Portrait of a Lady, The Sun Also Rises, The Catcher in the Rye,* or *The Color Purple.*

The romance is perhaps a closer relative to the novel. Ancient romances were even in prose. But the hallmark of the romance, whether the romance is by a Greek sophist (Longus's *Daphnis and Chloe*) or by a medieval English poet (Chaucer's "The Knight's Tale") or by an American (Hawthorne's *The House of the Seven Gables*), is a presentation of the remote or the marvelous, rather than the local and the ordinary. The distinction is the same as that between the tale and the short story. "Tale" has the suggestion of a yarn, of unreality or of wondrous reality. (A case can be made for excluding Hawthorne's "Young Goodman Brown" from a collection of short stories on the ground that its remoteness and its allegorical implications mark it as a tale rather than a short story. This is not to say that it is inferior to a story, but only different.) In his preface to *The House of the Seven Gables* Hawthorne himself distinguishes between the romance and the novel:

> The latter form of composition is presumed to aim at a very minute fidelity, not merely to the possible, but to the probable and ordinary course of man's experience. The former—while, as a work of art, it must rigidly subject itself to laws, and while it sins unpardonably so far as it may swerve aside from the truth of the human heart—has fairly a right to present that truth under circumstances, to a great extent, of the writer's own choosing or creation.

In his preface to *The Marble Faun* Hawthorne explains that he chose "Italy as the site of his Romance" because it afforded him "a sort of poetic or fairy precinct, where actualities would not be so terribly insisted upon as they are . . . in America."

"Actualities . . . insisted upon." That, in addition to prose and length, is the hallmark of the novel. The novel is a sort of long newspaper story; the very word "novel" comes from an Italian word meaning a little new thing, and is related to the French word that gives us "news." (It is noteworthy that the French cognate of Hawthorne's "actualities," *actualités,* means "news" or "current events.") It is no accident that many novelists have been newspapermen: Defoe, Dickens, Crane, Dreiser, Joyce, Hemingway, Camus. And this connection with reportage perhaps helps to account for the relatively low esteem in which the novel is occasionally held: to some college students, a course in the novel does not seem quite up to a course in poetry, and people who read novels but not poetry are not likely to claim an interest in "literature."

Though Defoe's *Robinson Crusoe* is set in a far-off place, and thus might easily have been a romance, in Defoe's day it was close to current events, for it is a fictionalized version of events that had recently made news—Alexander Selkirk's life on the island of Juan Fernandez. And the story is not about marvelous happenings, but about a man's struggle for survival in dismal surroundings. Crusoe is not armed with a magic sword, nor does he struggle with monsters; he has a carpenter's chest of tools and he struggles against commonplace nature. This chest was "much more valuable than a shiploading of gold would have been at that time." The world of romance contains splendid castles and enchanted forests, but Crusoe's world contains not much more than a plot of ground, some animals and vegetables, and Friday. "I fancied I could make all but the wheel [of a wheelbarrow Crusoe needed], but that I had no notion of, neither did I know how to go about it; besides, I had no possible way to make the iron gudgeons for the spindle or axis of the wheel to run in, so I gave it over." The book, in short, emphasizes not the strange, but (given the initial situation) the usual, the commonsensical, the probable. The world of *Robinson Crusoe* is hardly different from the world we meet in the beginning of almost any novel:

> My father's family name being Pirrip, and my Christian name Philip, my infant tongue could make of both names nothing longer or more explicit than Pip. So I called myself Pip, and came to be called Pip.
>
> I give Pirrip as my father's family name, on the authority of his tombstone and my sister—Mrs. Joe Gargery, who married the blacksmith.
>
> Charles Dickens, *Great Expectations*

> If you really want to hear about it, the first thing you'll probably want to know is where I was born, and what my lousy childhood was like, and how my parents were occupied and all before they had me, and all

> that David Copperfield kind of crap, but I don't feel like going into it, if you want to know the truth.
>
> J. D. Salinger, *The Catcher in the Rye*

> It was June, 1933, one week after Commencement, when Kay Leiland Strong, Vassar '33, the first of her class to run around the table at the Class Day dinner, was married to Harald Petersen, Reed '27, in the chapel of St. George's Church, P.E., Karl F. Reiland, Rector. Outside, on Stuyvesant Square, the trees were in full leaf, and the wedding guests arriving by twos and threes in taxis heard the voices of children playing round the statue of Peter Stuyvesant in the park.
>
> Mary McCarthy, *The Group*

A man who explains his nickname; another boy who in boy's language seems reluctant to talk of his "lousy childhood"; a young woman who ran around the table at the Class Day dinner. In all these passages, and in the openings of most other novels, we are confronted with current biography. In contrast to these beginnings, look at the beginning of one of Chaucer's great romances:

> Whilom,[1] as olde stories tellen us,
> There was a duc that highte[2] Theseus;
> Of Atthenes he was lord and governour,
> And in his tyme swich[3] a conquerour,
> That gretter was ther noon under the sonne.

"Whilom." "Olde stories." "Gretter was ther noon under the sonne." We are in a timeless past, in which unusual people dwell. In contrast, the novel is almost always set in the present or very recent past, and it deals with ordinary people. It so often deals with ordinary people, and presents them, apparently, in so ordinary a fashion that we sometimes wonder what is the point of it. Although the romance is often "escape" literature, it usually is didactic, holding up to us images of noble and ignoble behavior, revealing the rewards of courage and the power of love. In the preface to *The Marble Faun,* for instance, Hawthorne says he "proposed to himself to merely write a fanciful story, evolving a thoughtful moral, and did not propose attempting a portraiture of Italian manners and character." But portraiture is what novelists give us. Intent on revealing the world of real men and women going about their daily work and play, they do not simplify their characters into representatives of vices and virtues as do the romancers who wish to evolve a thoughtful moral, but give abundant detail—some of it apparently irrelevant. The innumerable details add up to a long book, although there need not be many physical happenings. The novel tells a story, of course, but the story is not only about what people overtly do but also about what they think (i.e., their mental doings) and about the society in which they are immersed and by which they are in part shaped. In the much-quoted preface to *Pierre and Jean,* Maupassant says:

> Skill of the novelist's plan will not reside in emotional effects, in attractive writing, in a striking beginning or a moving dénouement, but in the artful building up of solid details from which the essential meaning of the work will emerge.

[1]**whilom** once
[2]**highte** was named
[3]**swich** such

As we read a novel we feel we are seeing not the "higher reality" or the "inner reality" so often mentioned by students of the arts, but the real reality.

The short story, too, is detailed, but commonly it reveals only a single character at a moment of crisis, whereas the novel commonly traces the development of an individual, a group of people, a world. Novelists have an attitude toward their world; they are not compiling an almanac but telling an invented story, making a work of art, offering not merely a representation of reality but a response to it, and they therefore select and shape their material. One way of selecting and shaping the material is through the chosen point of view: We do not get everything in nineteenth-century England, but only everything that Pip remembers or chooses to set down about his experiences, and what he sets down is colored by his personality. "I remember Mr. Hubble as a tough high-shouldered stooping old man, of a saw-dusty fragrance, with his legs extraordinarily wide apart: so that in my short days I always saw some miles of open country between them when I met him coming up the lane." In any case, the coherence in a novel seems inclusive rather than exclusive. Novelists usually convey the sense that they, as distinct from their characters, are—in the words of Christopher Isherwood's *The Berlin Stories*—"a camera with its shutter open, quite passive, recording not thinking. Recording the man shaving at the windows opposite and the woman in the kimono washing her hair. Some day, all of this will have to be developed, carefully fixed, printed."

It is not merely that the novel gives us details. *Gulliver's Travels* has plenty of details about people six inches tall and people sixty feet tall, and about a flying island and rational horses. But these things are recognized as fanciful inventions, though they do turn our mind toward the real world. *Gulliver* is a satire that presents us with a picture of a fantastic world by which, paradoxically, we come to see the real world a little more clearly. The diminutive stature of the Lilliputians is an amusing and potent metaphor for the littleness of man, the flying island for abstract thinkers who have lost touch with reality, and so on. But the novelist who wants to show us the littleness of human beings invents not Lilliputians but a world of normal-sized people who do little things and have little thoughts.

Having spent so much time saying that the novel is not the epic or romance or fable, we must mention that a work may hover on the borderlines of these forms. Insofar as *Moby-Dick* narrates with abundant realistic detail the experiences of a whaler ("This book," Dorothy Parker has said, "taught me more about whales than I ever wanted to know"), it is a novel; but in its evocation of mystery—Queequeg, the prophecies, Ishmael's miraculous rescue from the sea filled with sharks who "glided by as if with padlocks on their mouths"—it is a romance with strong symbolic implications.

The point is that although readers of a long piece of prose fiction can complain that they did not get what they paid for, they should find out what they did get. A remark by Bishop Butler, an eighteenth-century English moral philosopher, is relevant to literary criticism: "Everything is what it is and not another thing."

## READING KATE CHOPIN'S *THE AWAKENING*

Readers of novels often report on the way in which a favorite novel has absorbed their attention, taken them inside another world—not the rather private world of the lyric poem, but a social world, the life and times of a society other than our own. The novel that you will now turn to—Kate Chopin's *The Awakening*—is shorter than most novels, yet its detailed settings beautifully evoke the *feel* of late nineteenth-century New Orleans life and French Creole society. Chopin draws her characters acutely, closely studying how they speak and act, what they look like, how they dress and express themselves. And through her settings and characterizations, Chopin explores issues that are as vital and complicated today as they were when she wrote her book—relationships between men and women, marriage, motherhood, the family, the ways in which the structure of social life rewards and limits a woman's aspirations.

As you read *The Awakening,* enjoy the novel and find yourself challenged by it. But aim, too, as you read and reread it, to become an analytic reader. Keep in mind the key terms outlined in Chapter 8, "Review: Writing about Fiction": plot, character, point of view, setting, symbolism, and style. Novels are longer than short stories, but in a sense you can imagine them as *long* stories, or as works that tell multiple, intertwined stories. Remember that you can make use of the same terms that are important for responding to, thinking about, and writing on short stories. It's just that with a novel there is more to attend to.

This is why it is often essential (and pleasurable) to reread a novel, especially a good one like *The Awakening.* One of our teachers once made the helpful suggestion that novels need to be read at different speeds. On a first reading, we might find ourselves caught up in the plot, wondering what will happen next. But when we are done, we might then return to the opening chapter, in order to examine how the author begins his or her work, starting there to detail the settings and lay out the organizing themes. Or maybe we will wish to reread the novel with an eye toward how the author portrays the major characters or structures a crucial scene. What Degas said about painting a picture is true also of a novel: "A good picture requires as much planning as a crime."

As you read and reread *The Awakening,* make notes in the margins and underline words, phrases, images that strike you as interesting and important or puzzling and that you sense you will want to come back to for further thought and study. We suggest, too, that you keep a journal in which you record your responses and ideas. But most of all, we suggest that you read the novel not merely to fulfill an assignment but to enlarge your sense (by seeing through Chopin's eyes) of the range of human experience.

## KATE CHOPIN

***Kate Chopin (1851–1904) was born Katherine O'Flaherty in St. Louis; her father was an immigrant from Ireland, her mother a member of a French Creole family descended from the early colonizers of Louisiana. Chopin's father died when she was four, and she was raised by her mother's family and educated in Catholic schools. She read widely in French literature, especially admiring the stories of Guy de Maupassant. At nineteen she married Oscar Chopin (the name is pronounced in the French way, something like "show pan"), a New Orleans cotton broker, and for a while she lived an elegant life. When her husband's business failed, he moved the family to central Louisiana where he owned some land. Two years***

*later Oscar Chopin died, and with her six children his widow returned to St. Louis where, at the age of thirty-seven, she began to write stories of Creole life. These were published in national magazines and then collected into two books,* Bayou Folk *(1894) and* A Night in Acadie *(1899). Chopin's readers were pleased with her attention to the habits and language of a picturesque region, but her next publication, a novel entitled* The Awakening *(1899), was unfavorably received, largely because of its alleged immorality, and Chopin now found that she and her earlier works were looked on with disfavor.*

*"The Storm" (see page 94) was written after* The Awakening *but before the reviews of the novel were published; once the reviews of the novel appeared, the new story must have seemed unpublishable. In any case, "The Storm" was not published during Chopin's lifetime, although she did publish three other stories after the novel.*

# *The Awakening*

## *I*

A green and yellow parrot, which hung in a cage outside the door, kept repeating over and over:

"*Allez vous-en! Allez vous-en! Sapristi!*[1] That's all right!"

He could speak a little Spanish, and also a language which nobody understood, unless it was the mocking-bird that hung on the other side of the door, whistling his fluty notes out upon the breeze with maddening persistence.

Mr. Pontellier, unable to read his newspaper with any degree of comfort, arose with an expression and an exclamation of disgust. He walked down the gallery and across the narrow "bridges" which connected the Lebrun cottages one with the other. He had been seated before the door of the main house. The parrot and the mockingbird were the property of Madame Lebrun, and they had the right to make all the noise they wished. Mr. Pontellier had the privilege of quitting their society when they ceased to be entertaining.

5 He stopped before the door of his own cottage, which was the fourth one from the main building and next to the last. Seating himself in a wicker rocker which was there, he once more applied himself to the task of reading the newspaper. The day was Sunday; the paper was a day old. The Sunday papers had not yet reached Grand Isle.[2] He was already acquainted with the market reports, and he glanced restlessly over the editorials and bits of news which he had not had time to read before quitting New Orleans the day before.

[1]***Allez . . . Sapristi!*** Go away! go away! For God's sake! (French)
[2]**Grand Isle** a resort island fifty miles south of New Orleans

Mr. Pontellier wore eye-glasses. He was a man of forty, of medium height and rather slender build; he stooped a little. His hair was brown and straight, parted on one side. His beard was neatly and closely trimmed.

Once in a while he withdrew his glance from the newspaper and looked about him. There was more noise than ever over at the house. The main building was called "the house," to distinguish it from the cottages. The chattering and whistling birds were still at it. Two young girls, the Farival twins, were playing a duet from "Zampa"[3] upon the piano. Madame Lebrun was bustling in and out, giving orders in a high key to a yard-boy whenever she got inside the house, and directions in an equally high voice to a dining-room servant whenever she got outside. She was a fresh, pretty woman, clad always in white with elbow sleeves. Her starched skirts crinkled as she came and went. Farther down, before one of the cottages, a lady in black was walking demurely up and down, telling her beads. A good many persons of the *pension*[4] had gone over to the *Chênière Caminada* in Beaudelet's lugger[5] to hear mass. Some young people were out under the water-oaks playing croquet. Mr. Pontellier's two children were there—sturdy little fellows of four and five. A quadroon nurse followed them about with a far-away, meditative air.

Mr. Pontellier finally lit a cigar and began to smoke, letting the paper drag idly from his hand. He fixed his gaze upon a white sunshade that was advancing at snail's pace from the beach. He could see it plainly between the gaunt trunks of the water-oaks and across the stretch of yellow camomile. The gulf looked far away, melting hazily into the blue of the horizon. The sunshade continued to approach slowly. Beneath its pink-lined shelter were his wife, Mrs. Pontellier, and young Robert Lebrun. When they reached the cottage, the two seated themselves with some appearance of fatigue upon the upper step of the porch, facing each other, each leaning against a supporting post.

"What folly! to bathe at such an hour in such heat!" exclaimed Mr. Pontellier. He himself had taken a plunge at daylight. That was why the morning seemed long to him.

10 "You are burnt beyond recognition," he added, looking at his wife as one looks at a valuable piece of personal property which has suffered some damage. She held up her hands, strong, shapely hands, and surveyed them critically, drawing up her lawn[6] sleeves above the wrists. Looking at them reminded her of her rings, which she had given to her husband before leaving for the beach. She silently reached out to him, and he, understanding, took the rings from his vest pocket and dropped them into her open palm. She slipped them upon her fingers; then clasping her knees, she looked across at Robert and began to laugh. The rings sparkled upon her fingers. He sent back an answering smile.

"What is it?" asked Pontellier, looking lazily and amused from one to the other. It was some utter nonsense; some adventure out there in the water, and they both tried to relate it at once. It did not seem half so amusing

[3]**"Zampa"** opera by Louis Hérold (1791–1833). In the opera, a lover dies at sea.
[4]***pension*** small hotel
[5]**lugger** small boat
[6]**lawn** fine cotton or linen

when told. They realized this, and so did Mr. Pontellier. He yawned and stretched himself. Then he got up, saying he had half a mind to go over to Klein's hotel and play a game of billiards.

"Come go along, Lebrun," he proposed to Robert. But Robert admitted quite frankly that he preferred to stay where he was and talk to Mrs. Pontellier.

"Well, send him about his business when he bores you, Edna," instructed her husband as he prepared to leave.

"Here, take the umbrella," she exclaimed, holding it out to him. He accepted the sunshade, and lifting it over his head descended the steps and walked away.

"Coming back to dinner?" his wife called after him. He halted a moment and shrugged his shoulders. He felt in his vest pocket; there was a ten-dollar bill there. He did not know; perhaps he would return for the early dinner and perhaps he would not. It all depended upon the company which he found over at Klein's and the size of "the game." He did not say this, but she understood it, and laughed, nodding good-by to him.

Both children wanted to follow their father when they saw him starting out. He kissed them and promised to bring back bonbons and peanuts.

## II

Mrs. Pontellier's eyes were quick and bright; they were a yellowish brown, about the color of her hair. She had a way of turning them swiftly upon an object and holding them there as if lost in some inward maze of contemplation or thought.

Her eyebrows were a shade darker than her hair. They were thick and almost horizontal, emphasizing the depth of her eyes. She was rather handsome than beautiful. Her face was captivating by reason of a certain frankness of expression and a contradictory subtle play of features. Her manner was engaging.

Robert rolled a cigarette. He smoked cigarettes because he could not afford cigars, he said. He had a cigar in his pocket which Mr. Pontellier had presented him with, and he was saving it for his after-dinner smoke.

This seemed quite proper and natural on his part. In coloring he was not unlike his companion. A clean-shaved face made the resemblance more pronounced than it would otherwise have been. There rested no shadow of care upon his open countenance. His eyes gathered in and reflected the light and languor of the summer day.

Mrs. Pontellier reached over for a palm-leaf fan that lay on the porch and began to fan herself, while Robert sent between his lips light puffs from his cigarette. They chatted incessantly: about the things around them; their amusing adventure out in the water—it had again assumed its entertaining aspect; about the wind, the trees, the people who had gone to the *Chênière;* about the children playing croquet under the oaks, and the Farival twins, who were now performing the overture to "The Poet and the Peasant."[7]

[7]**"The Poet and the Peasant"** operetta by Franz von Suppé (1819–95)

Robert talked a good deal about himself. He was very young, and did not know any better. Mrs. Pontellier talked a little about herself for the same reason. Each was interested in what the other said. Robert spoke of his intention to go to Mexico in the autumn, where fortune awaited him. He was always intending to go to Mexico, but some way never got there. Meanwhile he held on to his modest position in a mercantile house in New Orleans, where an equal familiarity with English, French and Spanish gave him no small value as a clerk and correspondent.

He was spending his summer vacation, as he always did, with his mother at Grand Isle. In former times, before Robert could remember, "the house" had been a summer luxury of the Lebruns. Now, flanked by its dozen or more cottages, which were always filled with exclusive visitors from the *"Quartier Français,"*[8] it enabled Madame Lebrun to maintain the easy and comfortable existence which appeared to be her birthright.

Mrs. Pontellier talked about her father's Mississippi plantation and her girlhood home in the old Kentucky blue-grass country. She was an American woman, with a small infusion of French which seemed to have been lost in dilution. She read a letter from her sister, who was away in the East, and who had engaged herself to be married. Robert was interested, and wanted to know what manner of girls the sisters were, what the father was like, and how long the mother had been dead.

25 When Mrs. Pontellier folded the letter it was time for her to dress for the early dinner.

"I see Léonce isn't coming back," she said, with a glance in the direction whence her husband had disappeared. Robert supposed he was not, as there were a good many New Orleans club men over at Klein's.

When Mrs. Pontellier left him to enter her room, the young man descended the steps and strolled over toward the croquet players, where, during the half-hour before dinner, he amused himself with the little Pontellier children, who were very fond of him.

## *III*

It was eleven o'clock that night when Mr. Pontellier returned from Klein's hotel. He was in an excellent humor, in high spirits, and very talkative. His entrance awoke his wife, who was in bed and fast asleep when he came in. He talked to her while he undressed, telling her anecdotes and bits of news and gossip that he had gathered during the day. From his trousers pockets he took a fistful of crumpled banknotes and a good deal of silver coin, which he piled on the bureau indiscriminately with keys, knife, handkerchief, and whatever else happened to be in his pockets. She was overcome with sleep, and answered him with little half utterances.

He thought it very discouraging that his wife, who was the sole object of his existence, evinced so little interest in things which concerned him, and valued so little his conversation.

30 Mr. Pontellier had forgotten the bonbons and peanuts for the boys. Notwithstanding he loved them very much, and went into the adjoining room where they slept to take a look at them and make sure that they were

[8]***Quartier Français*** French Quarter, in New Orleans

resting comfortably. The result of his investigation was far from satisfactory. He turned and shifted the youngsters about in bed. One of them began to kick and talk about a basket full of crabs.

Mr. Pontellier returned to his wife with the information that Raoul had a high fever and needed looking after. Then he lit a cigar and went and sat near the open door to smoke it.

Mrs. Pontellier was quite sure Raoul had no fever. He had gone to bed perfectly well, she said, and nothing had ailed him all day. Mr. Pontellier was too well acquainted with fever symptoms to be mistaken. He assured her the child was consuming[9] at that moment in the next room.

He reproached his wife with her inattention, her habitual neglect of the children. If it was not a mother's place to look after children, whose on earth was it? He himself had his hands full with his brokerage business. He could not be in two places at once; making a living for his family on the street, and staying at home to see that no harm befell them. He talked in a monotonous, insistent way.

Mrs. Pontellier sprang out of bed and went into the next room. She soon came back and sat on the edge of the bed, leaning her head down on the pillow. She said nothing, and refused to answer her husband when he questioned her. When his cigar was smoked out he went to bed, and in half a minute he was fast asleep.

35 Mrs. Pontellier was by that time thoroughly awake. She began to cry a little, and wiped her eyes on the sleeve of her *peignoir.*[10] Blowing out the candle, which her husband had left burning, she slipped her bare feet into a pair of satin *mules* at the foot of the bed and went out on the porch, where she sat down in the wicker chair and began to rock gently to and fro.

It was then past midnight. The cottages were all dark. A single faint light gleamed out from the hallway of the house. There was no sound abroad except the hooting of an old owl in the top of a water-oak, and the everlasting voice of the sea, that was not uplifted at that soft hour. It broke like a mournful lullaby upon the night.

The tears came so fast to Mrs. Pontellier's eyes that the damp sleeve of her *peignoir* no longer served to dry them. She was holding the back of her chair with one hand; her loose sleeve had slipped almost to the shoulder of her uplifted arm. Turning, she thrust her face, steaming and wet, into the bend of her arm, and she went on crying there, not caring any longer to dry her face, her eyes, her arms. She could not have told why she was crying. Such experiences as the foregoing were not uncommon in her married life. They seemed never before to have weighed much against the abundance of her husband's kindness and a uniform devotion which had come to be tacit and self-understood.

An indescribable oppression, which seemed to generate in some unfamiliar part of her consciousness, filled her whole being with a vague anguish. It was like a shadow, like a mist passing across her soul's summer day. It was strange and unfamiliar; it was a mood. She did not sit there inwardly upbraiding her husband, lamenting at Fate, which had directed her footsteps to the path which they had taken. She was just having a good cry

[9]**consuming** being consumed, that is feverish
[10]***peignoir*** dressing gown

all to herself. The mosquitoes made merry over her, biting her firm, round arms and nipping at her bare insteps.

The little stinging, buzzing imps succeeded in dispelling a mood which might have held her there in the darkness half a night longer.

40 The following morning Mr. Pontellier was up in good time to take the rockaway[11] which was to convey him to the steamer at the wharf. He was returning to the city to his business, and they would not see him again at the Island till the coming Sunday. He had regained his composure, which seemed to have been somewhat impaired the night before. He was eager to be gone, as he looked forward to a lively week in Carondelet Street.[12]

Mr. Pontellier gave his wife half of the money which he had brought away from Klein's hotel the evening before. She liked money as well as most women, and accepted it with no little satisfaction.

"It will buy a handsome wedding present for Sister Janet!" she exclaimed, smoothing out the bills as she counted them one by one.

"Oh! we'll treat Sister Janet better than that, my dear," he laughed, as he prepared to kiss her good-by.

The boys were tumbling about, clinging to his legs, imploring that numerous things be brought back to them. Mr. Pontellier was a great favorite, and ladies, men, children, even nurses, were always on hand to say good-by to him. His wife stood smiling and waving, the boys shouting, as he disappeared in the old rockaway down the sandy road.

45 A few days later a box arrived for Mrs. Pontellier from New Orleans. It was from her husband. It was filled with *friandises,* with luscious and toothsome bits—the finest of fruits, *patés,* a rare bottle or two, delicious syrups, and bonbons in abundance.

Mrs. Pontellier was always very generous with the contents of such a box; she was quite used to receiving them when away from home. The *patés* and fruit were brought to the dining-room; the bonbons were passed around. And the ladies, selecting with dainty and discriminating fingers and a little greedily, all declared that Mr. Pontellier was the best husband in the world. Mrs. Pontellier was forced to admit that she knew of none better.

## IV

It would have been a difficult matter for Mr. Pontellier to define to his own satisfaction or any one else's wherein his wife failed in her duty toward their children. It was something which he felt rather than perceived, and he never voiced the feeling without subsequent regret and ample atonement.

If one of the little Pontellier boys took a tumble whilst at play, he was not apt to rush crying to his mother's arms for comfort; he would more likely pick himself up, wipe the water out of his eyes and the sand out of his mouth, and go on playing. Tots as they were, they pulled together and stood their ground in childish battles with doubled fists and uplifted voices, which usually prevailed against the other brother-tots. The quadroon nurse was looked upon as a huge encumbrance, only good to button up waists and panties and to brush and part hair; since it seemed to be a law of society that their hair must be parted and brushed.

[11]**rockaway** horse-drawn carriage
[12]**Carondelet Street** street in the financial district of New Orleans

In short, Mrs. Pontellier was not a mother-woman. The mother-women seemed to prevail that summer at Grand Isle. It was easy to know them, fluttering about with extended, protecting wings when any harm, real or imaginary, threatened their precious brood. They were women who idolized their children, worshiped their husbands, and esteemed it a holy privilege to efface themselves as individuals and grow wings as ministering angels.

50 Many of them were delicious in the rôle; one of them was the embodiment of every womanly grace and charm. If her husband did not adore her, he was a brute, deserving of death by slow torture. Her name was Adèle Ratignolle. There are no words to describe her save the old ones that have served so often to picture the bygone heroine of romance and the fair lady of our dreams. There was nothing subtle or hidden about her charms; her beauty was all there, flaming and apparent; the spun-gold hair that comb nor confining pin could restrain; the blue eyes that were like nothing but sapphires; two lips that pouted, that were so red one could only think of cherries or some other delicious crimson fruit in looking at them. She was growing a little stout, but it did not seem to detract an iota from the grace of every step, pose, gesture. One would not have wanted her white neck a mite less full or her beautiful arms more slender. Never were hands more exquisite than hers, and it was joy to look at them when she threaded her needle or adjusted her gold thimble to her taper middle finger as she sewed away on the little night-drawers or fashioned a bodice or a bib.

Madame Ratignolle was very fond of Mrs. Pontellier, and often she took her sewing and went over to sit with her in the afternoons. She was sitting there the afternoon of the day the box arrived from New Orleans. She had possession of the rocker, and she was busily engaged in sewing upon a diminutive pair of night-drawers.

She had brought the pattern of the drawers for Mrs. Pontellier to cut out—a marvel of construction, fashioned to enclose a baby's body so effectually that only two small eyes might look out from the garment, like an Eskimo's. They were designed for winter wear, when treacherous drafts came down chimneys and insidious currents of deadly cold found their way through key-holes.

Mrs. Pontellier's mind was quite at rest concerning the present material needs of her children, and she could not see the use of anticipating and making winter night garments the subject of her summer meditations. But she did not want to appear unamiable and uninterested, so she had brought forth newspapers, which she spread upon the floor of the gallery, and under Madame Ratignolle's directions she had cut a pattern of the impervious garment.

Robert was there, seated as he had been the Sunday before, and Mrs. Pontellier also occupied her former position on the upper step, leaning listlessly against the post. Beside her was a box of bonbons, which she held out at intervals to Madame Ratignolle.

55 That lady seemed at a loss to make a selection, but finally settled upon a stick of nougat, wondering if it were not too rich; whether it could possibly hurt her. Madame Ratignolle had been married seven years. About every two years she had a baby. At that time she had three babies, and was beginning to think of a fourth one. She was always talking about her "condition." Her "condition" was in no way apparent, and no one would have known a

thing about it but for her persistence in making it the subject of conversation.

Robert started to reassure her, asserting that he had known a lady who had subsisted upon nougat during the entire—but seeing the color mount into Mrs. Pontellier's face he checked himself and changed the subject.

Mrs. Pontellier, though she had married a Creole,[13] was not thoroughly at home in the society of Creoles; never before had she been thrown so intimately among them. There were only Creoles that summer at Lebrun's. They all knew each other, and felt like one large family, among whom existed the most amicable relations. A characteristic which distinguished them and which impressed Mrs. Pontellier most forcibly was their entire absence of prudery. Their freedom of expression was at first incomprehensible to her, though she had no difficulty in reconciling it with a lofty chastity which in the Creole woman seems to be inborn and unmistakable.

Never would Edna Pontellier forget the shock with which she heard Madame Ratignolle relating to old Monsieur Farival the harrowing story of one of her *accouchements,*[14] withholding no intimate detail. She was growing accustomed to like shocks, but she could not keep the mounting color back from her cheeks. Oftener than once her coming had interrupted the droll story with which Robert was entertaining some amused group of married women.

A book had gone the rounds of the *pension.* When it came her turn to read it, she did so with profound astonishment. She felt moved to read the book in secret and solitude, though none of the others had done so—to hide it from view at the sound of approaching footsteps. It was openly criticized and freely discussed at table. Mrs. Pontellier gave over being astonished, and concluded that wonders would never cease.

## V

60 They formed a congenial group sitting there that summer afternoon—Madame Ratignolle sewing away, often stopping to relate a story or incident with much expressive gesture of her perfect hands; Robert and Mrs. Pontellier sitting idle, exchanging occasional words, glances or smiles which indicated a certain advanced stage of intimacy and *camaraderie.*

He had lived in her shadow during the past month. No one thought anything of it. Many had predicted that Robert would devote himself to Mrs. Pontellier when he arrived. Since the age of fifteen, which was eleven years before, Robert each summer at Grand Isle had constituted himself the devoted attendant of some fair dame or damsel. Sometimes it was a young girl, again a widow; but as often as not it was some interesting married woman.

For two consecutive seasons he lived in the sunlight of Mademoiselle Duvigné's presence. But she died between summers; then Robert posed as an inconsolable, prostrating himself at the feet of Madame Ratignolle for whatever crumbs of sympathy and comfort she might be pleased to vouchsafe.

Mrs. Pontellier liked to sit and gaze at her fair companion as she might look upon a faultless Madonna.

[13]**Creole** aristocratic descendant of the French and Spanish settlers of New Orleans
[14]***accouchements*** birthings

"Could any one fathom the cruelty beneath that fair exterior?" murmured Robert. "She knew that I adored her once, and she let me adore her. It was 'Robert, come; go; stand up; sit down; do this; do that; see if the baby sleeps; my thimble, please, that I left God knows where. Come and read Daudet[15] to me while I sew."'

65 "*Par exemple!*[16] I never had to ask. You were always there under my feet, like a troublesome cat."

"You mean like an adoring dog. And just as soon as Ratignolle appeared on the scene, then it *was* like a dog. *'Passez! Adieu! Allez vous-en!'*"[17]

"Perhaps I feared to make Alphonse jealous," she interjoined, with excessive naïveté. That made them all laugh. The right hand jealous of the left! The heart jealous of the soul! But for that matter, the Creole husband is never jealous; with him the gangrene passion is one which has become dwarfed by disuse.

Meanwhile Robert, addressing Mrs. Pontellier, continued to tell of his one time hopeless passion for Madame Ratignolle; of sleepless nights, of consuming flames till the very sea sizzled when he took his daily plunge. While the lady at the needle kept up a little running, contemptuous comment:

*"Blagueur—farceur—gros bête, va!"*[18]

70 He never assumed this serio-comic tone when alone with Mrs. Pontellier. She never knew precisely what to make of it; at that moment it was impossible for her to guess how much of it was jest and what proportion was earnest. It was understood that he had often spoken words of love to Madame Ratignolle, without any thought of being taken seriously. Mrs. Pontellier was glad he had not assumed a similar rôle toward herself. It would have been unacceptable and annoying.

Mrs. Pontellier had brought her sketching materials, which she sometimes dabbled with in an unprofessional way. She liked the dabbling. She felt in it satisfaction of a kind which no other employment afforded her.

She had long wished to try herself on Madame Ratignolle. Never had that lady seemed a more tempting subject than at that moment, seated there like some sensuous Madonna, with the gleam of the fading day enriching her splendid color.

Robert crossed over and seated himself upon the step below Mrs. Pontellier, that he might watch her work. She handled her brushes with a certain ease and freedom which came, not from long and close acquaintance with them, but from a natural aptitude. Robert followed her work with close attention, giving forth little ejaculatory expressions of appreciation in French, which he addressed to Madame Ratignolle.

*"Mais ce n'est pas mal! Elle s'y connait, elle a de la force, oui."*[19]

75 During his oblivious attention he once quietly rested his head against Mrs. Pontellier's arm. As gently she repulsed him. Once again he repeated the offense. She could not but believe it to be thoughtlessness on his part; yet that was no reason she should submit to it. She did not remonstrate, except again to repulse him quietly but firmly. He offered no apology.

[15]**Daudet** Alphonse Daudet (1840–87), French novelist

[16]***Par exemple!*** Indeed!

[17]***Passez . . . vous-en!*** Go! Goodby! Go away!

[18]***Blagueur . . . va!*** Joker—clown—silly, cut it out!

[19]***Mais . . . oui*** Not bad! She knows what's she doing, she's really good.

The picture completed bore no resemblance to Madame Ratignolle. She was greatly disappointed to find that it did not look like her. But it was a fair enough piece of work, and in many respects satisfying.

Mrs. Pontellier evidently did not think so. After surveying the sketch critically she drew a broad smudge of paint across its surface, and crumpled the paper between her hands.

The youngsters came tumbling up the steps, the quadroon following at the respectful distance which they required her to observe. Mrs. Pontellier made them carry her paints and things into the house. She sought to detain them for a little talk and some pleasantry. But they were greatly in earnest. They had only come to investigate the contents of the bonbon box. They accepted without murmuring what she chose to give them, each holding out two chubby hands scoop-like, in the vain hope that they might be filled; and then away they went.

The sun was low in the west, and the breeze soft and languorous that came up from the south, charged with the seductive odor of the sea. Children, freshly befurbelowed,[20] were gathering for their games under the oaks. Their voices were high and penetrating.

Madame Ratignolle folded her sewing, placing thimble, scissors and thread all neatly together in the roll, which she pinned securely. She complained of faintness. Mrs. Pontellier flew for the cologne water and a fan. She bathed Madame Ratignolle's face with cologne, while Robert plied the fan with unnecessary vigor.

The spell was soon over, and Mrs. Pontellier could not help wondering if there were not a little imagination responsible for its origin, for the rose tint had never faded from her friend's face.

She stood watching the fair woman walk down the long line of galleries with the grace and majesty which queens are sometimes supposed to possess. Her little ones ran to meet her. Two of them clung about her white skirts, the third she took from its nurse and with a thousand endearments bore it along in her own fond, encircling arms. Though, as everybody well knew, the doctor had forbidden her to lift so much as a pin!

"Are you going bathing?" asked Robert of Mrs. Pontellier. It was not so much a question as a reminder.

"Oh, no," she answered with a tone of indecision. "I'm tired; I think not." Her glance wandered from his face away toward the Gulf, whose sonorous murmur reached her like a loving but imperative entreaty.

"Oh, come!" he insisted. "You mustn't miss your bath. Come on. The water must be delicious; it will not hurt you. Come."

He reached up for her big, rough straw hat that hung on a peg outside the door, and put it on her head. They descended the steps, and walked away together toward the beach. The sun was low in the west and the breeze was soft and warm.

## *VI*

Edna Pontellier could not have told why, wishing to go to the beach with Robert, she should in the first place have declined, and in the second place

[20]**befurbelowed** dressed in frills

have followed in obedience to one of the two contradictory impulses which impelled her.

A certain light was beginning to dawn dimly within her,—the light which, showing the way, forbids it.

At that early period it served but to bewilder her. It moved her to dreams, to thoughtfulness, to the shadowy anguish which had overcome her the midnight when she had abandoned herself to tears.

90 In short, Mrs. Pontellier was beginning to realize her position in the universe as a human being, and to recognize her relations as an individual to the world within and about her. This may seem like a ponderous weight of wisdom to descend upon the soul of a young woman of twenty-eight—perhaps more wisdom than the Holy Ghost is usually pleased to vouchsafe to any woman.

But the beginning of things, of a world especially, is necessarily vague, tangled, chaotic, and exceedingly disturbing. How few of us ever emerge from such beginning! How many souls perish in its tumult!

The voice of the sea is seductive; never ceasing, whispering, clamoring, murmuring, inviting the soul to wander for a spell in abysses of solitude; to lose itself in mazes of inward contemplation.

The voice of the sea speaks to the soul. The touch of the sea is sensuous, enfolding the body in its soft, close embrace.

## *VII*

Mrs. Pontellier was not a woman given to confidences, a characteristic hitherto contrary to her nature. Even as a child she had lived her own small life all within herself. At a very early period she had apprehended instinctively the dual life—that outward existence which conforms, the inward life which questions.

95 That summer at Grand Isle she began to loosen a little the mantle of reserve that had always enveloped her. There may have been—there must have been—influences, both subtle and apparent, working in their several ways to induce her to do this; but the most obvious was the influence of Adèle Ratignolle. The excessive physical charm of the Creole had first attracted her, for Edna had a sensuous susceptibility to beauty. Then the candor of the woman's whole existence, which every one might read, and which formed so striking a contrast to her own habitual reserve—this might have furnished a link. Who can tell what metals the gods use in forging the subtle bond which we call sympathy, which we might as well call love.

The two women went away one morning to the beach together, arm in arm, under the huge white sunshade. Edna had prevailed upon Madame Ratignolle to leave the children behind, though she could not induce her to relinquish a diminutive roll of needlework, which Adèle begged to be allowed to slip into the depths of her pocket. In some unaccountable way they had escaped from Robert.

The walk to the beach was no inconsiderable one, consisting as it did of a long, sandy path, upon which a sporadic and tangled growth that bordered it on either side made frequent and unexpected inroads. There were acres of yellow camomile reaching out on either hand. Further away still, vegetable gardens abounded, with frequent small plantations of orange or lemon trees intervening. The dark green clusters glistened from afar in the sun.

The women were both of goodly height, Madame Ratignolle possessing the more feminine and matronly figure. The charm of Edna Pontellier's physique stole insensibly upon you. The lines of her body were long, clean and symmetrical; it was a body which occasionally fell into splendid poses; there was no suggestion of the trim stereotyped fashion-plate about it. A casual and indiscriminating observer, in passing, might not cast a second glance upon the figure. But with more feeling and discernment he would have recognized the noble beauty of its modeling, and the graceful severity of poise and movement, which made Edna Pontellier different from the crowd.

She wore a cool muslin that morning—white, with a waving vertical line of brown running through it; also a white linen collar and the big straw hat which she had taken from the peg outside the door. The hat rested any way on her yellow-brown hair, that waved a little, was heavy, and clung close to her head.

100 Madame Ratignolle, more careful of her complexion, had twined a gauze veil about her head. She wore doeskin gloves, with gauntlets that protected her wrists. She was dressed in pure white, with a fluffiness of ruffles that became her. The draperies and fluttering things which she wore suited her rich, luxuriant beauty as a greater severity of line could not have done.

There were a number of bath-houses along the beach, of rough but solid construction, built with small, protecting galleries facing the water. Each house consisted of two compartments, and each family at Lebrun's possessed a compartment for itself, fitted out with all the essential paraphernalia of the bath and whatever other conveniences the owners might desire. The two women had no intention of bathing; they had just strolled down to the beach for a walk and to be alone and near the water. The Pontellier and Ratignolle compartments adjoined one another under the same roof.

Mrs. Pontellier had brought down her key through force of habit. Unlocking the door of her bath-room she went inside, and soon emerged, bringing a rug, which she spread upon the floor of the gallery, and two huge hair pillows covered with crash,[21] which she placed against the front of the building.

The two seated themselves there in the shade of the porch, side by side, with their backs against the pillows and their feet extended. Madame Ratignolle removed her veil, wiped her face with a rather delicate handkerchief, and fanned herself with the fan which she always carried suspended somewhere about her person by a long, narrow ribbon. Edna removed her collar and opened her dress at the throat. She took the fan from Madame Ratignolle and began to fan both herself and her companion. It was very warm, and for a while they did nothing but exchange remarks about the heat, the sun, the glare. But there was a breeze blowing, a choppy, stiff wind that whipped the water into froth. It fluttered the skirts of the two women and kept them for a while engaged in adjusting, readjusting, tucking in, securing hair-pins and hat-pins. A few persons were sporting some dis-

[21]**crash** heavy linen

tance away in the water. The beach was very still of human sound at that hour. The lady in black was reading her morning devotions on the porch of a neighboring bath-house. Two young lovers were exchanging their hearts' yearnings beneath the children's tent, which they had found unoccupied.

Edna Pontellier, casting her eyes about, had finally kept them at rest upon the sea. The day was clear and carried the gaze out as far as the blue sky went; there were a few white clouds suspended idly over the horizon. A lateen[22] sail was visible in the direction of Cat Island, and others to the south seemed almost motionless in the far distance.

105 "Of whom—of what are you thinking?" asked Adèle of her companion, whose countenance she had been watching with a little amused attention, arrested by the absorbed expression which seemed to have seized and fixed every feature into a statuesque repose.

"Nothing," returned Mrs. Pontellier, with a start, adding at once: "How stupid! But it seems to me it is the reply we make instinctively to such a question. Let me see," she went on, throwing back her head and narrowing her fine eyes till they shone like two vivid points of light. "Let me see. I was really not conscious of thinking of anything; but perhaps I can retrace my thoughts."

"Oh! never mind!" laughed Madame Ratignolle. "I am not quite so exacting. I will let you off this time. It is really too hot to think, especially to think about thinking."

"But for the fun of it," persisted Edna. "First of all, the sight of the water stretching so far away, those motionless sails against the blue sky, made a delicious picture that I just wanted to sit and look at it. The hot wind beating in my face made me think—without any connection that I can trace—of a summer day in Kentucky, of a meadow that seemed as big as the ocean to the very little girl walking through the grass, which was higher than her waist. She threw out her arms as if swimming when she walked, beating the tall grass as one strikes out in the water. Oh, I see the connection now!"

"Where were you going that day in Kentucky, walking through the grass?"

110 "I don't remember now. I was just walking diagonally across a big field. My sun-bonnet obstructed the view. I could see only the stretch of green before me, and I felt as if I must walk on forever, without coming to the end of it. I don't remember whether I was frightened or pleased. I must have been entertained.

"Likely as not it was Sunday," she laughed; "and I was running away from prayers, from the Presbyterian service, read in a spirit of gloom by my father that chills me yet to think of."

"And have you been running away from prayer ever since, *ma chère?*" asked Madame Ratignolle, amused.

"No! oh, no!" Edna hastened to say. "I was a little unthinking child in those days, just following a misleading impulse without question. On the contrary, during one period of my life religion took a firm hold upon me; after I was twelve and until—until—why, I suppose until now, though I never thought much about it—just driven along by habit. But do you know," she

[22]**lateen** triangular

broke off, turning her quick eyes upon Madame Ratignolle and leaning forward a little so as to bring her face quite close to that of her companion, "sometimes I feel this summer as if I were walking through the green meadow again; idly, aimlessly, unthinking and unguided."

Madame Ratignolle laid her hand over that of Mrs. Pontellier, which was near her. Seeing that the hand was not withdrawn, she clasped it firmly and warmly. She even stroked it a little fondly, with the other hand, murmuring in an undertone, *"Pauvre chérie."*[23]

115 The action was at first a little confusing to Edna, but she soon lent herself readily to the Creole's gentle caress. She was not accustomed to an outward and spoken expression of affection, either in herself or in others. She and her younger sister, Janet, had quarreled a good deal through force of unfortunate habit. Her older sister, Margaret, was matronly and dignified, probably from having assumed matronly and housewifely responsibilities too early in life, their mother having died when they were quite young. Margaret was not effusive: she was practical. Edna had had an occasional girl friend, but whether accidentally or not, they seemed to have been all of one type—the self-contained. She never realized that the reserve of her own character had much, perhaps everything, to do with this. Her most intimate friend at school had been one of rather exceptional intellectual gifts, who wrote fine-sounding essays, which Edna admired and strove to imitate; and with her she talked and glowed over the English classics, and sometimes held religious and political controversies.

Edna often wondered at one propensity which sometimes had inwardly disturbed her without causing any outward show or manifestation on her part. At a very early age—perhaps it was when she traversed the ocean of waving grass—she remembered that she had been passionately enamored of a dignified and sad-eyed cavalry officer who visited her father in Kentucky. She could not leave his presence when he was there, nor remove her eyes from his face, which was something like Napoleon's, with a lock of black hair falling across the forehead. But the cavalry officer melted imperceptibly out of her existence.

At another time her affections were deeply engaged by a young gentleman who visited a lady on a neighboring plantation. It was after they went to Mississippi to live. The young man was engaged to be married to the young lady, and they sometimes called upon Margaret, driving over of afternoons in a buggy. Edna was a little miss, just merging into her teens; and the realization that she herself was nothing, nothing, nothing to the engaged young man was a bitter affliction to her. But he, too, went the way of dreams.

She was a grown young woman when she was overtaken by what she supposed to be the climax of her fate. It was when the face and figure of a great tragedian began to haunt her imagination and stir her senses. The persistence of the infatuation lent it an aspect of genuineness. The hopelessness of it colored it with the lofty tones of a great passion.

The picture of the tragedian stood enframed upon her desk. Any one may possess the portrait of a tragedian without exciting suspicion or comment. (This was a sinister reflection which she cherished.) In the pres-

[23]***Pauvre chérie*** Poor dear

ence of others she expressed admiration for his exalted gifts, as she handed the photograph around and dwelt upon the fidelity of the likeness. When alone she sometimes picked it up and kissed the cold glass passionately.

120 Her marriage to Léonce Pontellier was purely an accident, in this respect resembling many other marriages which masquerade as the decrees of Fate. It was in the midst of her secret great passion that she met him. He fell in love, as men are in the habit of doing, and pressed his suit with an earnestness and an ardor which left nothing to be desired. He pleased her; his absolute devotion flattered her. She fancied there was a sympathy of thought and taste between them, in which fancy she was mistaken. Add to this the violent opposition of her father and her sister Margaret to her marriage with a Catholic, and we need seek no further for the motives which led her to accept Monsieur Pontellier for her husband.

The acme of bliss, which would have been a marriage with the tragedian, was not for her in this world. As the devoted wife of a man who worshiped her, she felt she would take her place with a certain dignity in the world of reality, closing the portals forever behind her upon the realm of romance and dreams.

But it was not long before the tragedian had gone to join the cavalry officer and the engaged young man and a few others; and Edna found herself face to face with the realities. She grew fond of her husband, realizing with some unaccountable satisfaction that no trace of passion or excessive and fictitious warmth colored her affection, thereby threatening its dissolution.

She was fond of her children in an uneven, impulsive way. She would sometimes gather them passionately to her heart; she would sometimes forget them. The year before they had spent part of the summer with their grandmother Pontellier in Iberville. Feeling secure regarding their happiness and welfare, she did not miss them except with an occasional intense longing. Their absence was a sort of relief, though she did not admit this, even to herself. It seemed to free her of a responsibility which she had blindly assumed and for which Fate had not fitted her.

Edna did not reveal so much as all this to Madame Ratignolle that summer day when they sat with faces turned to the sea. But a good part of it escaped her. She had put her head down on Madame Ratignolle's shoulder. She was flushed and felt intoxicated with the sound of her own voice and the unaccustomed taste of candor. It muddled her like wine, or like a first breath of freedom.

125 There was the sound of approaching voices. It was Robert, surrounded by a troop of children, searching for them. The two little Pontelliers were with him, and he carried Madame Ratignolle's little girl in his arms. There were other children beside, and two nurse-maids followed, looking disagreeable and resigned.

The women at once rose and began to shake out their draperies and relax their muscles. Mrs. Pontellier threw the cushions and rug into the bathhouse. The children all scampered off to the awning, and they stood there in a line, gazing upon the intruding lovers, still exchanging their vows and sighs. The lovers got up, with only a silent protest, and walked slowly away somewhere else.

The children possessed themselves of the tent, and Mrs. Pontellier went over to join them.

Madame Ratignolle begged Robert to accompany her to the house; she complained of cramp in her limbs and stiffness of the joints. She leaned draggingly upon his arm as they walked.

## *VIII*

"Do me a favor, Robert," spoke the pretty woman at his side, almost as soon as she and Robert had started on their slow, homeward way. She looked up in his face, leaning on his arm beneath the encircling shadow of the umbrella which he had lifted.

"Granted; as many as you like," he returned, glancing down into her eyes that were full of thoughtfulness and some speculation.

"I only ask for one; let Mrs. Pontellier alone."

*"Tiens!"* he exclaimed, with a sudden, boyish laugh. *"Voilá que Madame Ratignolle est jalouse!"*[24]

"Nonsense! I'm in earnest; I mean what I say. Let Mrs. Pontellier alone."

"Why?" he asked; himself growing serious at his companion's solicitation.

"She is not one of us; she is not like us. She might make the unfortunate blunder of taking you seriously."

His face flushed with annoyance, and taking off his soft hat he began to beat it impatiently against his leg as he walked. "Why shouldn't she take me seriously?" he demanded sharply. "Am I a comedian, a clown, a jack-in-the-box? Why shouldn't she? You Creoles! I have no patience with you! Am I always to be regarded as a feature of an amusing programme? I hope Mrs. Pontellier does take me seriously. I hope she has discernment enough to find in me something besides the *blagueur*.[25] If I thought there was any doubt—"

"Oh, enough, Robert!" she broke into his heated outburst. "You are not thinking of what you are saying. You speak with about as little reflection as we might expect from one of those children down there playing in the sand. If your intentions to any married women here were ever offered with any attention of being convincing, you would not be the gentleman we all know you to be, and you would be unfit to associate with the wives and daughters of the people who trust you."

Madame Ratignolle had spoken what she believed to be the law and the gospel. The young man shrugged his shoulders impatiently.

"Oh! well! That isn't it," slamming his hat down vehemently upon his head. "You ought to feel that such things are not flattering to say to a fellow."

"Should our whole intercourse consist of an exchange of compliments? *Ma foi!*"[26]

"It isn't pleasant to have a woman tell you—" he went on, unheedingly, but breaking off suddenly: "Now if I were like Arobin—you remember Alcée Arobin and that story of the consul's wife at Biloxi?" And he related the story of Alcée Arobin and the consul's wife; and another about the tenor of the French Opera, who received letters which should never have been writ-

[24]***Tiens . . . jalouse!*** Ah, so Madame Ratignolle is jealous!
[25]***blagueur*** joker
[26]***Ma foi!*** Good Lord!

ten; and still other stories, grave and gay, till Mrs. Pontellier and her possible propensity for taking young men seriously was apparently forgotten.

Madame Ratignolle, when they had regained her cottage, went in to take the hour's rest which she considered helpful. Before leaving her, Robert begged her pardon for the impatience—he called it rudeness—with which he had received her well-meant caution.

"You made one mistake, Adéle," he said, with a light smile; "there is no earthly possibility of Mrs. Pontellier ever taking me seriously. You should have warned me against taking myself seriously. Your advice might then have carried some weight and given me subject for some reflection. *Au revoir.* But you look tired," he added, solicitously. "Would you like a cup of bouillon? Shall I stir you a toddy? Let me mix you a toddy with a drop of Angostura."

She acceded to the suggestion of bouillon, which was grateful and acceptable. He went himself to the kitchen, which was a building apart from the cottages and lying to the rear of the house. And he himself brought her the golden-brown bouillon, in a dainty Sévres cup, with a flaky cracker or two on the saucer.

145 She thrust a bare, white arm from the curtain which shielded her open door, and received the cup from his hands. She told him he was a *bon garçon*[27] and she meant it. Robert thanked her and turned away toward "the house."

The lovers were just entering the grounds of the *pension.* They were leaning toward each other as the water-oaks bent from the sea. There was not a particle of earth beneath their feet. Their heads might have been turned upside-down, so absolutely did they tread upon blue ether. The lady in black, creeping behind them, looked a trifle paler and more jaded than usual. There was no sign of Mrs. Pontellier and the children. Robert scanned the distance for any such apparition. They would doubtless remain away till the dinner hour. The young man ascended to his mother's room. It was situated at the top of the house, made up of odd angles and a queer, sloping ceiling. Two broad dormer windows looked out toward the Gulf, and as far across it as man's eye might reach. The furnishings of the room were light, cool, and practical.

Madame Lebrun was busily engaged at the sewing-machine. A little black girl sat on the floor, and with her hands worked the treadle of the machine. The Creole woman does not take any chances which may be avoided of imperiling her health.

Robert went over and seated himself on the broad sill of one of the dormer windows. He took a book from his pocket and began energetically to read it, judging by the precision and frequency with which he turned the leaves. The sewing-machine made a resounding clatter in the room; it was of a ponderous, by-gone make. In the lulls, Robert and his mother exchanged bits of desultory conversation.

"Where is Mrs. Pontellier?"

150 "Down at the beach with the children."

"I promised to lend her the Goncourt.[28] Don't forget to take it down when you go; it's there on the bookshelf over the small table." Clatter, clatter, clatter, bang! for the next five or eight minutes.

[27]***bon garçon*** (1) nice fellow; (2) good waiter
[28]**the Goncourt** novel by Edmond Goncourt (1822–96)

"Where is Victor going with the rockaway?"

"The rockaway? Victor?"

"Yes; down there in front. He seems to be getting ready to drive away somewhere."

155 "Call him." Clatter, clatter!

Robert uttered a shrill, piercing whistle which might have been heard back at the wharf.

"He won't look up."

Madame Lebrun flew to the window. She called "Victor!" She waved a handkerchief and called again. The young fellow below got into the vehicle and started the horse off at a gallop.

Madame Lebrun went back to the machine, crimson with annoyance. Victor was the younger son and brother—a *tête montée,*[29] with a temper which invited violence and a will which no ax could break.

160 "Whenever you say the word I'm ready to thrash any amount of reason into him that he's able to hold."

"If your father had only lived!" Clatter, clatter, clatter, clatter, bang! It was a fixed belief with Madame Lebrun that the conduct of the universe and all things pertaining thereto would have been manifestly of a more intelligent and higher order had not Monsieur Lebrun been removed to other spheres during the early years of their married life.

"What do you hear from Montel?" Montel was a middle-aged gentleman whose vain ambition and desire for the past twenty years had been to fill the void which Monsieur Lebrun's taking off had left in the Lebrun household. Clatter, clatter, bang, clatter!

"I have a letter somewhere," looking in the machine drawer and finding the letter in the bottom of the work-basket. "He says to tell you he will be in Vera Cruz the beginning of next month"—clatter, clatter!—"and if you still have the intention of joining him"—bang! clatter, clatter, bang!

"Why didn't you tell me so before, mother? You know I wanted—" Clatter, clatter, clatter!

165 "Do you see Mrs. Pontellier starting back with the children? She will be in late to luncheon again. She never starts to get ready for luncheon till the last minute." Clatter, clatter! "Where are you going?"

"Where did you say the Goncourt was?"

## *IX*

Every light in the hall was ablaze; every lamp turned as high as it could be without smoking the chimney or threatening explosion. The lamps were fixed at intervals against the wall, encircling the whole room. Some one had gathered orange and lemon branches, and with these fashioned graceful festoons between. The dark green of the branches stood out and glistened against the white muslin curtains which draped the windows, and which puffed, floated, and flapped at the capricious will of a stiff breeze that swept up from the Gulf.

It was Saturday night a few weeks after the intimate conversation held between Robert and Mrs. Ratignolle on their way from the beach. An un-

[29]***tête montée*** impulsive fellow

usual number of husbands, fathers, and friends had come down to stay over Sunday; and they were being suitably entertained by their families, with the material help of Madame Lebrun. The dining tables had all been removed to one end of the hall, and the chairs ranged about in rows and in clusters. Each little family group had had its say and exchanged its domestic gossip earlier in the evening. There was now an apparent disposition to relax; to widen the circle of confidences and give a more general tone to the conversation.

Many of the children had been permitted to sit up beyond their usual bedtime. A small band of them were lying on their stomachs on the floor looking at the colored sheets of the comic papers which Mr. Pontellier had brought down. The little Pontellier boys were permitting them to do so, and making their authority felt.

170 Music, dancing, and a recitation or two were the entertainments furnished, or rather, offered. But there was nothing systematic about the programme, no appearance of prearrangement nor even premeditation.

At an early hour in the evening the Farival twins were prevailed upon to play the piano. They were girls of fourteen, always clad in the Virgin's colors, blue and white, having been dedicated to the Blessed Virgin at their baptism. They played a duet from "Zampa," and at the earnest solicitation of every one present followed it with the overture to "The Poet and the Peasant."

*"Allez vous-en! Sapristi!"* shrieked the parrot outside the door. He was the only being present who possessed sufficient candor to admit that he was not listening to these gracious performances for the first time that summer. Old Monsieur Farival, grandfather of the twins, grew indignant over the interruption, and insisted upon having the bird removed and consigned to regions of darkness. Victor Lebrun objected; and his decrees were as immutable as those of Fate. The parrot fortunately offered no further interruption to the entertainment, the whole venom of his nature apparently having been cherished up and hurled against the twins in that one impetuous outburst.

Later a young brother and sister gave recitations, which every one present had heard many times at winter evening entertainments in the city.

A little girl performed a skirt dance in the center of the floor. The mother played her accompaniments and at the same time watched her daughter with greedy admiration and nervous apprehension. She need have had no apprehension. The child was mistress of the situation. She had been properly dressed for the occasion in black tulle and black silk tights. Her little neck and arms were bare, and her hair, artificially crimped, stood out like fluffy black plumes over her head. Her poses were full of grace, and her little black-shod toes twinkled as they shot out and upward with a rapidity and suddenness which were bewildering.

175 But there was no reason why every one should not dance. Madame Ratignolle could not, so it was she who gaily consented to play for the others. She played very well, keeping excellent waltz time and infusing an expression into the strains which was indeed inspiring. She was keeping up her music on account of the children, she said; because she and her husband both considered it a means of brightening the home and making it attractive.

Almost every one danced but the twins, who could not be induced to separate during the brief period when one or the other should be whirling around the room in the arms of a man. They might have danced together, but they did not think of it.

The children were sent to bed. Some went submissively; others with shrieks and protests as they were dragged away. They had been permitted to sit up till after the ice-cream, which naturally marked the limit of human indulgence.

The ice-cream was passed around with cake—gold and silver cake arranged on platters in alternate slices; it had been made and frozen during the afternoon back of the kitchen by two black women, under the supervision of Victor. It was pronounced a great success—excellent if it had only contained a little less vanilla or a little more sugar, if it had been frozen a degree harder, and if the salt might have been kept out of portions of it. Victor was proud of his achievement, and went about recommending it and urging every one to partake of it to excess.

After Mrs. Pontellier had danced twice with her husband, once with Robert, and once with Monsieur Ratignolle, who was thin and tall and swayed like a reed in the wind when he danced, she went out on the gallery and seated herself on the low window-sill, where she commanded a view of all that went on in the hall and could look out toward the Gulf. There was a soft effulgence in the east. The moon was coming up, and its mystic shimmer was casting a million lights across the distant, restless water.

180 "Would you like to hear Mademoiselle Reisz play?" asked Robert, coming out on the porch where she was. Of course Edna would like to hear Mademoiselle Reisz play, but she feared it would be useless to entreat her.

"I'll ask her," he said. "I'll tell her that you want to hear her. She likes you. She will come." He turned and hurried away to one of the far cottages, where Mademoiselle Reisz was shuffling away. She was dragging a chair in and out of her room, and at intervals objecting to the crying of a baby, which a nurse in the adjoining cottage was endeavoring to put to sleep. She was a disagreeable little woman, no longer young, who had quarreled with almost every one, owing to a temper which was self-assertive and a disposition to trample upon the rights of others. Robert prevailed upon her without any too great difficulty.

She entered the hall with him during a lull in the dance. She made an awkward, imperious little bow as she went in. She was a homely woman, with a small weazened face and body and eyes that glowed. She had absolutely no taste in dress, and wore a batch of rusty black lace with a bunch of artificial violets pinned to the side of her hair.

"Ask Mrs. Pontellier what she would like to hear me play," she requested of Robert. She sat perfectly still before the piano, not touching the keys, while Robert carried her message to Edna at the window. A general air of surprise and genuine satisfaction fell upon every one as they saw the pianist enter. There was a settling down, and a prevailing air of expectancy everywhere. Edna was a trifle embarrassed at being thus signaled out for the imperious little woman's favor. She would not dare to choose, and begged that Mademoiselle Riesz would please herself in her selections.

Edna was what she herself called very fond of music. Musical strains, well rendered, had a way of evoking pictures in her mind. She sometimes liked to sit in the room of mornings when Madame Ratignolle played or practiced. One piece which that lady played Edna had entitled "Solitude." It was a short, plaintive, minor strain. The name of the piece was something else, but she called it "Solitude." When she heard it there came before her imagination the figure of a man standing beside a desolate rock on the seashore. He was naked. His attitude was one of hopeless resignation as he looked toward a distant bird winging its flight away from him.

185 Another piece called to her mind a dainty young woman clad in an Empire gown, taking mincing dancing steps as she came down a long avenue between tall hedges. Again, another reminded her of children at play, and still another of nothing on earth but a demure lady stroking a cat.

The very first chords which Mademoiselle Reisz struck upon the piano sent a keen tremor down Mrs. Pontellier's spinal column. It was not the first time she had heard an artist at the piano. Perhaps it was the first time she was ready, perhaps the first time her being was tempered to take an impress of the abiding truth.

She waited for the material pictures which she thought would gather and blaze before her imagination. She waited in vain. She saw no pictures of solitude, of hope, of longing, or of despair. But the very passions themselves were aroused within her soul, swaying it, lashing it, as the waves daily beat upon her splendid body. She trembled, she was choking, and the tears blinded her.

Mademoiselle had finished. She arose, and bowing her stiff, lofty bow, she went away, stopping for neither thanks nor applause. As she passed along the gallery she patted Edna upon the shoulder.

"Well, how did you like my music?" she asked. The young woman was unable to answer; she pressed the hand of the pianist convulsively. Mademoiselle Reisz perceived her agitation and even her tears. She patted her again upon the shoulder as she said:

190 "You are the only one worth playing for. Those others? Bah!" and she went shuffling and sidling on down the gallery toward her room.

But she was mistaken about "those others." Her playing had aroused a fever of enthusiasm. "What passion!" "What an artist!" "I have always said no one could play Chopin[30] like Mademoiselle Reisz!" "That last prelude! Bon Dieu![31] It shakes a man!"

It was growing late, and there was a general disposition to disband. But some one, perhaps it was Robert, thought of a bath at that mystic hour and under that mystic moon.

## X

At all events Robert proposed it, and there was not a dissenting voice. There was not one but was ready to follow when he led the way. He did not lead the way, however, he directed the way; and he himself loitered behind with the lovers, who had betrayed a disposition to linger and hold themselves apart. He walked between them, whether with malicious or mischievous intent was not wholly clear, even to himself.

The Pontelliers and Ratignolles walked ahead; the women leaning upon the arms of their husbands. Edna could hear Robert's voice behind them, and could sometimes hear what he said. She wondered why he did not join

[30]**Chopin** Fréderic François Chopin (1810–49), Polish pianist and composer
[31]**Bon Dieu!** Good Lord!

them. It was unlike him not to. Of late he had sometimes held away from her for an entire day, redoubling his devotion upon the next and the next, as though to make up for hours that had been lost. She missed him the days when some pretext served to take him away from her, just as one misses the sun on a cloudy day without having thought much about the sun when it was shining.

195 The people walked in little groups toward the beach. They talked and laughed; some of them sang. There was a band playing down at Klein's hotel, and the strains reached them faintly, tempered by the distance. There were strange, rare odors abroad—a tangle of the sea smell and of weeds and damp, new-plowed earth, mingled with the heavy perfume of a field of white blossoms somewhere near. But the night sat lightly upon the sea and the land. There was no weight of darkness, there were no shadows. The white light of the moon had fallen upon the world like the mystery and the softness of sleep.

Most of them walked into the water as though into a native element. The sea was quiet now, and swelled lazily in broad billows that melted into one another and did not break except upon the beach in little foamy crests that coiled back like slow, white serpents.

Edna had attempted all summer to learn to swim. She had received instructions from both the men and women; in some instances from the children. Robert had pursued a system of lessons almost daily; and he was nearly at the point of discouragement in realizing the futility of his efforts. A certain ungovernable dread hung about her when in the water, unless there was a hand near by that might reach out and reassure her.

But that night she was like the little tottering, stumbling, clutching child, who of a sudden realizes its powers, and walks for the first time alone, boldly and with over-confidence. She could have shouted for joy. She did shout for joy, as with a sweeping stroke or two she lifted her body to the surface of the water.

A feeling of exultation overtook her, as if some power of significant import had been given to her to control the working of her body and her soul. She grew daring and reckless, overestimating her strength. She wanted to swim far out, where no woman had swum before.

200 Her unlooked-for achievement was the subject of wonder, applause, and admiration. Each one congratulated himself that his special teachings had accomplished this desired end.

"How easy it is!" she thought. "It is nothing," she said aloud; "why did I not discover before that it was nothing? Think of the time I have lost splashing about like a baby!" She would not join the groups in their sports and bouts, but intoxicated with her newly conquered power, she swam out alone.

She turned her face seaward to gather in an impression of space and solitude, which the vast expanse of water, meeting and melting with the moonlit sky, conveyed to her excited fancy. As she swam she seemed to be reaching out for the unlimited in which to lose herself.

Once she turned and looked toward the shore, toward the people she had left there. She had not gone any great distance—that is, what would have been a great distance for an experienced swimmer. But to her unaccustomed vision the stretch of water behind her assumed the aspect of a barrier which her unaided strength would never be able to overcome.

A quick vision of death smote her soul, and for a second time appalled and enfeebled her senses. But by an effort she rallied her staggering faculties and managed to regain the land.

She made no mention of her encounter with death and her flash of terror, except to say to her husband, "I thought I should have perished out there alone."

"You were not so very far, my dear; I was watching you," he told her.

Edna went at once to the bath-house, and she had put on her dry clothes and was ready to return home before the others had left the water. She started to walk away alone. They all called to her and shouted to her. She waved a dissenting hand, and went on, paying no further heed to their renewed cries which sought to detain her.

"Sometimes I am tempted to think that Mrs. Pontellier is capricious," said Madame Lebrun, who was amusing herself immensely and feared that Edna's abrupt departure might put an end to the pleasure.

"I know she is," assented Mr. Pontellier; "sometimes, not often."

Edna had not traversed a quarter of the distance on her way home before she was overtaken by Robert.

"Did you think I was afraid?" she asked him, without a shade of annoyance.

"No; I knew you weren't afraid."

"Then why did you come? Why didn't you stay out there with the others?"

"I never thought of it."

"Thought of what?"

"Of anything. What difference does it make?"

"I'm very tired," she uttered, complainingly.

"I know you are."

"You don't know anything about it. Why should you know? I never was so exhausted in my life. But it isn't unpleasant. A thousand emotions have swept through me to-night. I don't comprehend half of them. Don't mind what I'm saying; I am just thinking aloud. I wonder if I shall ever be stirred again as Mademoiselle Reisz's playing moved me to-night. I wonder if any night on earth will ever again be like this one. It is like a night in a dream. The people about me are like some uncanny, half-human beings. There must be spirits abroad to-night."

"There are," whispered Robert. "Didn't you know this was the twenty-eighth of August?"

"The twenty-eight of August?"

"Yes. On the twenty-eighth of August, at the hour of midnight, and if the moon is shining—the moon must be shining—a spirit that has haunted these shores for ages rises up from the Gulf. With its own penetrating vision the spirit seeks some one mortal worthy to hold him company, worthy of being exalted for a few hours into realms of the semi-celestials. His search has always hitherto been fruitless, and he has sunk back, disheartened, into the sea. But to-night he found Mrs. Pontellier. Perhaps he will never wholly release her from the spell. Perhaps she will never again suffer a poor, unworthy earthling to walk in the shadow of her divine presence."

"Don't banter me," she said, wounded at what appeared to be his flippancy. He did not mind the entreaty, but the tone with its delicate note of pathos was like a reproach. He could not explain; he could not tell her that he had penetrated her mood and understood. He said nothing except to offer her his arm, for, by her own admission, she was exhausted. She had been walking alone with her arms hanging limp, letting her white skirts trail along the dewy path. She took his arm, but she did not lean upon it. She let her hand lie listlessly, as though her thoughts were elsewhere—somewhere in advance of her body, and she was striving to overtake them.

Robert assisted her into the hammock which swung from the post before her door out to the trunk of a tree.

"Will you stay out here and wait for Mr. Pontellier?" he asked.

"I'll stay out here. Good-night."

"Shall I get you a pillow?"

"There's one here," she said, feeling about, for they were in the shadow.

"It must be soiled; the children have been tumbling it about."

"No matter." And having discovered the pillow, she adjusted it beneath her head. She extended herself in the hammock with a deep breath of relief. She was not a supercilious or an over-dainty woman. She was not much given to reclining in the hammock, and when she did so it was with no cat-like suggestion of voluptuous ease, but with a beneficent repose which seemed to invade her whole body.

"Shall I stay with you till Mr. Pontellier comes?" asked Robert, seating himself on the outer edge of one of the steps and taking hold of the hammock rope which was fastened to the post.

"If you wish. Don't swing the hammock. Will you get my white shawl which I left on the window-sill over at the house?"

"Are you chilly?"

"No; but I shall be presently."

"Presently?" he laughed. "Do you know what time it is? How long are you going to stay out here?"

"I don't know. Will you get the shawl?"

"Of course I will," he said, rising. He went over to the house, walking along the grass. She watched his figure pass in and out of the strips of moonlight. It was past midnight. It was very quiet.

When he returned with the shawl she took it and kept it in her hand. She did not put it around her.

"Did you say I should stay till Mr. Pontellier came back?"

"I said you might if you wished to."

He seated himself again and rolled a cigarette, which he smoked in silence. Neither did Mrs. Pontellier speak. No multitude of words could have been more significant than those moments of silence, or more pregnant with the first-felt throbbings of desire.

When the voices of the bathers were heard approaching, Robert said goodnight. She did not answer him. He thought she was asleep. Again she watched his figure pass in and out of the strips of moonlight as he walked away.

## XI

"What are you doing out here, Edna? I thought I should find you in bed," said her husband, when he discovered her lying there. He had walked up with Madame Lebrun and left her at the house. His wife did not reply.

"Are you asleep?" he asked, bending down close to look at her.

245 "No." Her eyes gleamed bright and intense, with no sleepy shadows, as they looked into his.

"Do you know it is past one o'clock? Come on," and he mounted the steps and went into their room.

"Edna!" called Mr. Pontellier from within, after a few moments had gone by.

"Don't wait for me," she answered. He thrust his head through the door.

"You will take cold out there," he said irritably. "What folly is this? Why don't you come in?"

250 "It isn't cold; I have my shawl."

"The mosquitoes will devour you."

"There are no mosquitoes."

She heard him moving about the room; every sound indicating impatience and irritation. Another time she would have gone in at his request. She would, through habit, have yielded to his desire; not with any sense of submission or obedience to his compelling wishes, but unthinkingly, as we walk, move, sit, stand, go through the daily treadmill of the life which has been portioned out to us.

"Edna, dear, are you not coming in soon?" he asked again, this time fondly, with a note of entreaty.

255 "No; I am going to stay out here."

"This is more than folly," he blurted out. "I can't permit you to stay out there all night. You must come in the house instantly."

With a writhing motion she settled herself more securely in the hammock. She perceived that her will had blazed up, stubborn and resistant. She could not at that moment have done other than denied and resisted. She wondered if her husband had ever spoken to her like that before, and if she had submitted to his command. Of course she had; she remembered that she had. But she could not realize why or how she should have yielded, feeling as she then did.

"Léonce, go to bed," she said. "I mean to stay out here. I don't wish to go in, and I don't intend to. Don't speak to me like that again; I shall not answer you."

Mr. Pontellier had prepared for bed, but he slipped on an extra garment. He opened a bottle of wine, of which he kept a small and select supply in a buffet of his own. He drank a glass of wine and went out on the gallery and offered a glass to his wife. She did not wish any. He drew up a rocker, hoisted his slippered feet on the rail, and proceeded to smoke a cigar. He smoked two cigars; then he went inside and drank another glass of wine. Mrs. Pontellier again declined to accept a glass when it was offered to her. Mr. Pontellier once more seated himself with elevated feet, and after a reasonable interval of time smoked some more cigars.

260 Edna began to feel like one who awakens gradually out of a dream, a delicious, grotesque, impossible dream, to feel again the realities pressing into her soul. The physical need for sleep began to overtake her; the exuberance which had sustained and exalted her spirit left her helpless and yielding to the conditions which crowded her in.

The stillest hour of the night had come, the hour before dawn, when the world seems to hold its breath. The moon hung low, and had turned from silver to copper in the sleeping sky. The old owl no longer hooted, and the water-oaks had ceased to moan as they bent their heads.

Edna arose, cramped from lying so long and still in the hammock. She tottered up the steps, clutching feebly at the post before passing into the house.

"Are you coming in, Léonce?" she asked, turning her face toward her husband.

"Yes, dear," he answered, with a glance following a misty puff of smoke. "Just as soon as I have finished my cigar."

## *XII*

265 She slept but a few hours. They were troubled and feverish hours, disturbed with dreams that were intangible, that eluded her, leaving only an impression upon her half-awakened senses of something unattainable. She was up and dressed in the cool of the early morning. The air was invigorating and steadied somewhat her faculties. However, she was not seeking refreshment or help from any source, either external or from within. She was blindly following whatever impulse moved her, as if she had placed herself in alien hands for direction, and freed her soul of responsibility.

Most of the people at that early hour were still in bed and asleep. A few, who intended to go over to the *Chênière* for mass, were moving about. The lovers, who had laid their plans the night before, were already strolling toward the wharf. The lady in black, with her Sunday prayer-book, velvet and gold-clasped, and her Sunday silver beads, was following them at no great distance. Old Monsieur Farival was up, and was more than half inclined to do anything that suggested itself. He put on his big straw hat, and taking his umbrella from the stand in the hall, followed the lady in black, never overtaking her.

The little negro girl who worked Madame Lebrun's sewing-machine was sweeping the galleries with long, absent-minded strokes of the broom. Edna sent her up into the house to awaken Robert.

"Tell him I am going to the *Chênière*. The boat is ready; tell him to hurry."

He had soon joined her. She had never sent for him before. She had never asked for him. She had never seemed to want him before. She did not appear conscious that she had done anything unusual in commanding his presence. He was apparently equally unconscious of anything extraordinary in the situation. But his face was suffused with a quiet glow when he met her.

270 They went together back to the kitchen to drink coffee. There was no time to wait for any nicety of service. They stood outside the window and the cook passed them their coffee and a roll, which they drank and ate from the window-sill. Edna said it tasted good. She had not thought of coffee nor of anything. He told her he had often noticed that she lacked forethought.

"Wasn't it enough to think of going to the *Chênière* and waking you up?" she laughed. "Do I have to think of everything?—as Léonce says when he's in a bad humor. I don't blame him; he'd never be in a bad humor if it weren't for me."

They took a short cut across the sands. At a distance they could see the curious procession moving toward the wharf—the lovers, shoulder to shoulder, creeping; the lady in black, gaining steadily upon them; old Monsieur Farival, losing ground inch by inch, and a young barefooted Spanish girl, with a red kerchief on her head and a basket on her arm, bringing up the rear.

Robert knew the girl, and he talked to her a little in the boat. No one present understood what they said. Her name was Mariequita. She had a round, sly, piquant face and pretty black eyes. Her hands were small, and she kept them folded over the handle of her basket. Her feet were broad and coarse. She did not strive to hide them. Edna looked at her feet, and noticed the sand and slime between her brown toes.

Beaudelet grumbled because Mariequita was there, taking up so much room. In reality he was annoyed at having old Monsieur Farival, who considered himself the better sailor of the two. But he would not quarrel with so old a man as Monsieur Farival, so he quarreled with Mariequita. The girl was deprecatory at one moment, appealing to Robert. She was saucy the next, moving her head up and down, making "eyes" at Robert and making "mouths" at Beaudelet.

The lovers were all alone. They saw nothing, they heard nothing. The lady in black was counting her beads for the third time. Old Monsieur Farival talked incessantly of what he knew about handling a boat, and of what Beaudelet did not know on the same subject.

Edna liked it all. She looked Mariequita up and down, from her ugly brown toes to her pretty black eyes, and back again.

"Why does she look at me like that?" inquired the girl of Robert.

"Maybe she thinks you are pretty. Shall I ask her?"

"No. Is she your sweetheart?"

"She's a married lady, and has two children."

"Oh! well! Francisco ran away with Sylvano's wife, who had four children. They took all his money and one of the children and stole his boat."

"Shut up!"

"Does she understand?"

"Oh, hush!"

"Are those two married over there—leaning on each other?"

"Of course not," laughed Robert.

"Of course not," echoed Mariequita, with a serious, confirmatory bob of the head.

The sun was high up and beginning to bite. The swift breeze seemed to Edna to bury the sting of it into the pores of her face and hands. Robert held his umbrella over her.

As they went cutting sidewise through the water, the sails bellied taut, with the wind filling and overflowing them. Old Monsieur Farival laughed sardonically at something as he looked at the sails, and Beaudelet swore at the old man under his breath.

Sailing across the bay to the *Chênière Caminada,* Edna felt as if she were being borne away from some anchorage which had held her fast, whose chains had been loosening—had snapped the night before when the mystic spirit was abroad, leaving her free to drift whithersoever she chose to set her sails. Robert spoke to her incessantly; he no longer noticed Mariequita. The girl had shrimps in her bamboo basket. They were covered with Spanish moss. She beat the moss down impatiently, and muttered to herself sullenly.

"Let us go to Grand Terre to-morrow," said Robert in a low voice.

"What shall we do there?"

"Climb up the hill to the old fort and look at the little wriggling gold snakes, and watch the lizards sun themselves."

She gazed away toward Grande Terre and thought she would like to be alone there with Robert, in the sun, listening to the ocean's roar and watching the slimy lizards writhe in and out among the ruins of the old fort.

"And the next day or the next we can sail to the Bayou Brulow," he went on.

"What shall we do there?"

"Anything—cast bait for fish."

"No; we'll go back to Grande Terre. Let the fish alone."

"We'll go wherever you like," he said. "I'll have Tonie come over and help me patch and trim my boat. We shall not need Beaudelet nor any one. Are you afraid of the pirogue?"[32]

"Oh, no."

"Then I'll take you some night on the pirogue when the moon shines. Maybe your Gulf spirit will whisper to you in which of these islands the treasures are hidden—direct you to the very spot, perhaps."

"And in a day we should be rich!" she laughed. "I'd give it all to you, the pirate gold and every bit of treasure we could dig up. I think you would know how to spend it. Pirate gold isn't a thing to be hoarded or utilized. It is something to squander and throw to the four winds, for the fun of seeing the golden specks fly."

"We'd share it, and scatter it together," he said. His face flushed.

They all went together up to the quaint little Gothic church of Our Lady of Lourdes, gleaming all brown and yellow with paint in the sun's glare.

Only Beaudelet remained behind, tinkering at his boat, and Mariequita walked away with her basket of shrimps, casting a look of childish ill-humor and reproach at Robert from the corner of her eye.

## XIII

A feeling of oppression and drowsiness overcame Edna during the service. Her head began to ache, and the lights on the altar swayed before her eyes. Another time she might have made an effort to regain her composure; but her one thought was to quit the stifling atmosphere of the church and reach the open air. She arose, climbing over Robert's feet with a muttered apology. Old Monsieur Farival, flurried, curious, stood up, but upon seeing that Robert had followed Mrs. Pontellier, he sank back into his seat. He whispered an anxious inquiry of the lady in black, who did not notice him or reply, but kept her eyes fastened upon the pages of her velvet prayer-book.

"I felt giddy and almost overcome," Edna said, lifting her hands instinctively to her head and pushing her straw hat up from her forehead. "I couldn't have stayed through the service." They were outside in the shadow of the church. Robert was full of solicitude.

[32]**pirogue** canoe

"It was folly to have thought of going in the first place, let alone staying. Come over to Madame Antoine's; you can rest there." He took her arm and led her away, looking anxiously and continuously down into her face.

How still it was, with only the voice of the sea whispering through the reeds that grew in the salt-water pools! The long line of little gray, weather-beaten houses nestled peacefully among the orange trees. It must always have been God's day on that low, drowsy island, Edna thought. They stopped, leaning over a jagged fence made of sea-drift, to ask for water. A youth, a mild-faced Acadian,[33] was drawing water from the cistern, which was nothing more than a rusty buoy, with an opening on one side, sunk in the ground. The water which the youth handed to them in a tin pail was not cold to taste, but it was cool to her heated face, and it greatly revived and refreshed her.

Madame Antoine's cot[34] was at the far end of the village. She welcomed them with all the native hospitality, as she would have opened her door to let the sunlight in. She was fat, and walked heavily and clumsily across the floor. She could speak no English, but when Robert made her understand that the lady who accompanied him was ill and desired to rest, she was all eagerness to make Edna feel at home and to dispose of her comfortably.

The whole place was immaculately clean, and the big, four-posted bed, snow-white, invited one to repose. It stood in a small side room which looked out across a narrow grass plot toward the shed, where there was a disabled boat lying keel upward.

Madame Antoine had not gone to mass. Her son Tonie had, but she supposed he would soon be back, and she invited Robert to be seated and wait for him. But he went and sat outside the door and smoked. Madame Antoine busied herself in the large front room preparing dinner. She was boiling mullets over a few red coals in the huge fireplace.

Edna, left alone in the little side room, loosened her clothes, removing the greater part of them. She bathed her face, her neck and arms in the basin that stood between the windows. She took off her shoes and stockings and stretched herself in the very center of the high, white bed. How luxurious it felt to rest thus in a strange, quaint bed, with its sweet country odor of laurel lingering about the sheets and mattress! She stretched her strong limbs that ached a little. She ran her fingers through her loosened hair for a while. She looked at her round arms as she held them straight up and rubbed them one after the other, observing closely, as if it were something she saw for the first time, the fine, firm quality and texture of her flesh. She clasped her hands easily above her head, and it was thus she fell asleep.

She slept lightly at first, half awake and drowsily attentive to the things about her. She could hear Madame Antoine's heavy, scraping tread as she walked back and forth on the sanded floor. Some chickens were clucking outside the windows, scratching for bits of gravel in the grass. Later she half heard the voices of Robert and Tonie talking under the shed. She did not

[33]**Acadian** descendant of French Canadians whom the British expelled from eastern Canada (Acadia) in 1775

[34]**cot** cottage

stir. Even her eyelids rested numb and heavily over her sleepy eyes. The voices went on—Tonie's slow, Acadian drawl, Robert's quick, soft, smooth French. She understood French imperfectly unless directly addressed, and the voices were only part of the other drowsy, muffled sounds lulling her senses.

315 When Edna awoke it was with the conviction that she had slept long and soundly. The voices were hushed under the shed. Madame Antoine's step was no longer to be heard in the adjoining room. Even the chickens had gone elsewhere to scratch and cluck. The mosquito bar was drawn over her; the old woman had come in while she slept and let down the bar. Edna rose quietly from the bed, and looking between the curtains of the window, she saw by the slanting rays of the sun that the afternoon was far advanced. Robert was out there under the shed, reclining in the shade against the sloping keel of the overturned boat. He was reading from a book. Tonie was no longer with him. She wondered what had become of the rest of the party. She peeped out at him two or three times as she stood washing herself in the little basin between the windows.

Madame Antoine had lain some coarse, clean towels upon a chair, and had placed a box of *poudre de riz*[35] within easy reach. Edna dabbed the powder upon her nose and cheeks as she looked at herself closely in the little distorted mirror which hung on the wall above the basin. Her eyes were bright and wide awake and her face glowed.

When she had completed her toilet she walked into the adjoining room. She was very hungry. No one was there. But there was a cloth spread upon the table that stood against the wall, and a cover was laid for one, with a crusty brown loaf and a bottle of wine beside the plate. Edna bit a piece from the brown loaf, tearing it with her strong, white teeth. She poured some of the wine into the glass and drank it down. Then she went softly out of doors, and plucking an orange from the low-hanging bough of a tree, threw it at Robert, who did not know she was awake and up.

An illumination broke over his whole face when he saw her and joined her under the orange tree.

"How many years have I slept?" she inquired. "The whole island seems changed. A new race of beings must have sprung up, leaving only you and me as past relics. How many ages ago did Madame Antoine and Tonie die? and when did our people from Grand Isle disappear from the earth?"

320 He familiarly adjusted a ruffle upon her shoulder.

"You have slept precisely one hundred years. I was left here to guard your slumbers; and for one hundred years I have been out under the shed reading a book. The only evil I couldn't prevent was to keep a broiled fowl from drying up."

"If it has turned to stone, still will I eat it," said Edna, moving with him into the house. "But really, what has become of Monsieur Farival and the others?"

"Gone hours ago. When they found that you were sleeping they thought it best not to awake you. Any way, I wouldn't have let them. What was I here for?"

"I wonder if Léonce will be uneasy!" she speculated, as she seated herself at table.

[35]***poudre de riz*** talcum powder

325 "Of course not; he knows you are with me," Robert replied, as he busied himself among sundry pans and covered dishes which had been left standing on the hearth.

"Where are Madame Antoine and her son?" asked Edna.

"Gone to Vespers,[36] and to visit some friends, I believe. I am to take you back in Tonie's boat whenever you are ready to go."

He stirred the smoldering ashes till the broiled fowl began to sizzle afresh. He served her with no mean repast, dripping the coffee anew and sharing it with her. Madame Antoine had cooked little else than the mullets, but while Edna slept Robert had foraged the island. He was childishly gratified to discover her appetite, and to see the relish with which she ate the food which he had procured for her.

"Shall we go right away?" she asked, after draining her glass and brushing together the crumbs of the crusty loaf.

330 "The sun isn't as low as it will be in two hours," he answered.

"The sun will be gone in two hours."

"Well, let it go; who cares!"

They waited a good while under the orange trees, till Madame Antoine came back, panting, waddling, with a thousand apologies to explain her absence. Tonie did not dare to return. He was shy, and would not willingly face any woman except his mother.

It was very pleasant to stay there under the orange trees, while the sun dipped lower and lower, turning the western sky to flaming copper and gold. The shadows lengthened and crept out like stealthy, grotesque monsters across the grass.

335 Edna and Robert both sat upon the ground—that is, he lay upon the ground beside her, occasionally picking at the hem of her muslin gown.

Madame Antoine seated her fat body, broad and squat, upon a bench beside the door. She had been talking all the afternoon, and had wound herself up to the story-telling pitch.

And what stories she told them! But twice in her life she had left the *Chênière Caminada,* and then for the briefest span. All her years she had squatted and waddled there upon the island, gathering legends of the Baratarians[37] and the sea. The night came on, with the moon to lighten it. Edna could hear the whispering voices of dead men and the click of muffled gold.

When she and Robert stepped into Tonie's boat, with the red lateen sail, misty spirit forms were prowling in the shadows and among the reeds, and upon the water were phantom ships, speeding to cover.

## XIV

The youngest boy, Etienne, had been very naughty, Madame Ratignolle said, as she delivered him into the hands of his mother. He had been unwilling to go to bed and had made a scene; whereupon she had taken charge of him and pacified him as well as she could. Raoul had been in bed and asleep for two hours.

[36]**Vespers** evening church service

[37]**Baratarians** pirates (e.g., Jean Laffite) in the Baratarian Bay (in the Mississippi delta)

340 The youngster was in his long white nightgown, that kept tripping him up as Madame Ratignolle led him along by the hand. With the other chubby fist he rubbed his eyes, which were heavy with sleep and ill humor. Edna took him in her arms, and seating herself in the rocker, began to coddle and caress him, calling him all manner of tender names, soothing him to sleep.

It was not more than nine o'clock. No one had yet gone to bed but the children.

Léonce had been very uneasy at first, Madame Ratignolle said, and had wanted to start at once for the *Chênière.* But Monsieur Farival had assured him that his wife was only overcome with sleep and fatigue, that Tonie would bring her safely back later in the day; and he had thus been dissuaded from crossing the bay. He had gone over to Klein's, looking up some cotton broker whom he wished to see in regard to securities, exchanges, stocks, bonds, or something of the sort, Madame Ratignolle did not remember what. He said he would not remain away late. She herself was suffering from heat and oppression, she said. She carried a bottle of salts and a large fan. She would not consent to remain with Edna, for Monsieur Ratignolle was alone, and he detested above all things to be left alone.

When Etienne had fallen asleep Edna bore him into the back room, and Robert went and lifted the mosquito bar that she might lay the child comfortably in his bed. The quadroon had vanished. When they emerged from the cottage Robert bade Edna good-night.

"Do you know we have been together the whole livelong day, Robert—since early this morning?" she said at parting.

345 "All but the hundred years when you were sleeping. Good-night."

He pressed her hand and went away in the direction of the beach. He did not join any of the others, but walked alone toward the Gulf.

Edna stayed outside, awaiting her husband's return. She had no desire to sleep or to retire; nor did she feel like going over to sit with the Ratignolles, or to join Madame Lebrun and a group whose animated voices reached her as they sat in conversation before the house. She let her mind wander back over her stay at Grand Isle; and she tried to discover wherein this summer had been different from any and every other summer of her life. She could only realize that she herself—her present self—was in some way different from the other self. That she was seeing with different eyes and making the acquaintance of new conditions in herself that colored and changed her environment, she did not yet suspect.

She wondered why Robert had gone away and left her. It did not occur to her to think he might have grown tired of being with her the livelong day. She was not tired, and she felt that he was not. She regretted that he had gone. It was so much more natural to have him stay when he was not absolutely required to leave her.

As Edna waited for her husband she sang low a little song that Robert had sung as they crossed the bay. It began with "Ah! *Si tu savais,*"[38] and every verse ended with *"si tu savais."*

350 Robert's voice was not pretentious. It was musical and true. The voice, the notes, the whole refrain haunted her memory.

[38]***Si tu savais*** "Could'st thou but know" (title and refrain of a song by Michael William Balfe [1808–70])

## XV

When Edna entered the dining-room one evening a little late, as was her habit, an unusually animated conversation seemed to be going on. Several persons were talking at once, and Victor's voice was predominating, even over that of his mother. Edna had returned late from her bath, had dressed in some haste, and her face was flushed. Her head, set off by her dainty white gown, suggested a rich, rare blossom. She took her seat at table between old Monsieur Farival and Madame Ratignolle.

As she seated herself and was about to begin to eat her soup, which had been served when she entered the room, several persons informed her simultaneously that Robert was going to Mexico. She laid her spoon down and looked about her bewildered. He had been with her, reading to her all the morning, and had never even mentioned such a place as Mexico. She had not seen him during the afternoon; she had heard some one say he was at the house, upstairs with his mother. This she had thought nothing of, though she was surprised when he did not join her later in the afternoon, when she went down to the beach.

She looked across at him, where he sat beside Madame Lebrun, who presided. Edna's face was a blank picture of bewilderment, which she never thought of disguising. He lifted his eyebrows with the pretext of a smile as he returned her glance. He looked embarrassed and uneasy.

"When is he going?" she asked of everybody in general, as if Robert were not there to answer for himself.

355 "To-night!" "This very evening!" "Did you ever!" "What possesses him!" were some of the replies she gathered, uttered simultaneously in French and English.

"Impossible!" she exclaimed. "How can a person start off from Grand Isle to Mexico at a moment's notice, as if he were going over to Klein's or to the wharf or down to the beach?"

"I said all along I was going to Mexico; I've been saying so for years!" cried Robert, in an excited and irritable tone, with the air of a man defending himself against a swarm of stinging insects.

Madame Lebrun knocked on the table with her knife handle.

"Please let Robert explain why he is going, and why he is going to-night," she called out. "Really, this table is getting to be more and more like Bedlam every day, with everybody talking at once. Sometimes—I hope God will forgive me—but positively, sometimes I wish Victor would lose the power of speech."

360 Victor laughed sardonically as he thanked his mother for her holy wish, of which he failed to see the benefit to anybody, except that it might afford her a more ample opportunity and license to talk herself.

Monsieur Farival thought that Victor should have been taken out in midocean in his earliest youth and drowned. Victor thought there would be more logic in thus disposing of old people with an established claim for making themselves universally obnoxious. Madame Lebrun grew a trifle hysterical; Robert called his brother some sharp, hard names.

"There's nothing much to explain, mother," he said; though he explained, nevertheless—looking chiefly at Edna—that he could only meet the gentleman whom he intended to join at Vera Cruz by taking such and such a steamer, which left New Orleans on such a day; that Beaudelet was going out with his lugger-load of vegetables that night, which gave him an opportunity of reaching the city and making his vessel in time.

"But when did you make up your mind to all this?" demanded Monsieur Farival.

"This afternoon," returned Robert, with a shade of annoyance.

365 "At what time this afternoon?" persisted the old gentleman, with nagging determination, as if he were cross-questioning a criminal in a court of justice.

"At four o'clock this afternoon, Monsieur Farival," Robert replied, in a high voice and with a lofty air, which reminded Edna of some gentleman on the stage.

She had forced herself to eat most of her soup, and now she was picking the flaky bits of a *court bouillon*[39] with her fork.

The lovers were profiting by the general conversation on Mexico to speak in whispers of matters which they rightly considered were interesting to no one but themselves. The lady in black had once received a pair of prayer-beads of curious workmanship from Mexico, with very special indulgence[40] attached to them, but she had never been able to ascertain whether the indulgence extended outside the Mexican border. Father Fochel of the Cathedral had attempted to explain it; but he had not done so to her satisfaction. And she begged that Robert would interest himself, and discover, if possible, whether she was entitled to the indulgence accompanying the remarkably curious Mexican prayer-beads.

Madame Ratignolle hoped that Robert would exercise extreme caution in dealing with the Mexicans, who, she considered, were a treacherous people, unscrupulous and revengeful. She trusted she did them no injustice in thus condemning them as a race. She had known personally but one Mexican, who made and sold excellent tamales, and whom she would have trusted implicitly, so soft-spoken was he. One day he was arrested for stabbing his wife. She never knew whether he had been hanged or not.

370 Victor had grown hilarious, and was attempting to tell an anecdote about a Mexican girl who served chocolate one winter in a restaurant in Dauphine Street. No one would listen to him but old Monsieur Farival, who went into convulsions over the droll story.

Edna wondered if they had all gone mad, to be talking and clamoring at that rate. She herself could think of nothing to say about Mexico or the Mexicans.

"At what time do you leave?" she asked Robert.

"At ten," he told her. "Beaudelet wants to wait for the moon."

"Are you all ready to go?"

375 "Quite ready. I shall only take a hand-bag, and shall pack my trunk in the city."

He turned to answer some question put to him by his mother, and Edna, having finished her black coffee, left the table.

She went directly to her room. The little cottage was close and stuffy after leaving the outer air. But she did not mind; there appeared to be a hundred different things demanding her attention indoors. She began to set the

[39] ***court bouillon*** fish broth
[40] **indulgence** power to reduce the punishment for sins

toilet-stand to rights, grumbling at the negligence of the quadroon, who was in the adjoining room putting the children to bed. She gathered together stray garments that were hanging on the backs of chairs, and put each where it belonged in closet or bureau drawer. She changed her gown for a more comfortable and commodious wrapper. She rearranged her hair, combing and brushing it with unusual energy. Then she went in and assisted the quadroon in getting the boys to bed.

They were very playful and inclined to talk—to do anything but lie quiet and go to sleep. Edna sent the quadroon away to her supper and told her she need not return. Then she sat and told the children a story. Instead of soothing it excited them, and added to their wakefulness. She left them in heated argument, speculating about the conclusion of the tale which their mother promised to finish the following night.

The little black girl came in to say that Madame Lebrun would like to have Mrs. Pontellier go and sit with them over at the house till Mr. Robert went away. Edna returned answer that she had already undressed, that she did not feel quite well, but perhaps she would go over to the house later. She started to dress again, and got as far advanced as to remove her *peignoir.* But changing her mind once more she resumed the *peignoir,* and went outside and sat down before her door. She was over-heated and irritable, and fanned herself energetically for a while. Madame Ratignolle came down to discover what was the matter.

380 "All that noise and confusion at the table must have upset me," replied Edna, "and moreover, I hate shocks and surprises. The idea of Robert starting off in such a ridiculously sudden and dramatic way! As if it were a matter of life and death! Never saying a word about it all morning when he was with me."

"Yes," agreed Madame Ratignolle. "I think it was showing us all—you especially—very little consideration. It wouldn't have surprised me in any of the others; those Lebruns are all given to heroics. But I must say I should never have expected such a thing from Robert. Are you not coming down? Come on, dear; it doesn't look friendly."

"No," said Edna, a little sullenly. "I can't go to the trouble of dressing again; I don't feel like it."

"You needn't dress; you look all right; fasten a belt around your waist. Just look at me!"

"No," persisted Edna; "but you go on. Madame Lebrun might be offended if we both stayed away."

385 Madame Ratignolle kissed Edna good-night, and went away, being in truth rather desirous of joining in the general and animated conversation which was still in progress concerning Mexico and the Mexicans.

Somewhat later Robert came up, carrying his hand-bag.

"Aren't you feeling well?" he asked.

"Oh, well enough. Are you going right away?"

He lit a match and looked at his watch. "In twenty minutes," he said. The sudden and brief flare of the match emphasized the darkness for a while. He sat down upon a stool which the children had left out on the porch.

390 "Get a chair," said Edna.

"This will do," he replied. He put on his soft hat and nervously took it off again, and wiping his face with his handkerchief, complained of the heat.

"Take the fan," said Edna, offering it to him.

"Oh, no! Thank you. It does no good; you have to stop fanning some time, and feel all the more uncomfortable afterward."

"That's one of the ridiculous things which men always say. I have never known one to speak otherwise of fanning. How long will you be gone?"

"Forever, perhaps. I don't know. It depends upon a good many things."

"Well, in case it shouldn't be forever, how long will it be?"

"I don't know."

"This seems to me perfectly preposterous and uncalled for. I don't like it. I don't understand your motive for silence and mystery, never saying a word to me about it this morning." He remained silent, not offering to defend himself. He only said, after a moment:

"Don't part with me in an ill-humor. I never knew you to be out of patience with me before."

"I don't want to part in any ill-humor," she said. "But can't you understand? I've grown used to seeing you, to having you with me all the time, and your action seems unfriendly, even unkind. You don't even offer an excuse for it. Why, I was planning to be together, thinking of how pleasant it would be to see you in the city next winter."

"So was I," he blurted. "Perhaps that's the—" He stood up suddenly and held out his hand. "Good-by, my dear Mrs. Pontellier; good-by. You won't—I hope you won't completely forget me." She clung to his hand, striving to detain him.

"Write to me when you get there, won't you, Robert?" she entreated.

"I will, thank you. Good-by."

How unlike Robert! The merest acquaintance would have said something more emphatic than "I will, thank you; good-by," to such a request.

He had evidently already taken leave of the people over at the house, for he descended the steps and went to join Beaudelet, who was out there with an oar across his shoulder waiting for Robert. They walked away in the darkness. She could only hear Beaudelet's voice; Robert had apparently not even spoken a word of greeting to his companion.

Edna bit her handkerchief convulsively, striving to hold back and to hide, even from herself as she would have hidden from another, the emotion which was troubling—tearing—her. Her eyes were brimming with tears.

For the first time she recognized anew the symptoms of infatuation which she had felt incipiently as a child, as a girl in her earliest teens, and later as a young woman. The recognition did not lessen the reality, the poignancy of the revelation by any suggestion or promise of instability. The past was nothing to her; offered no lesson which she was willing to heed. The future was a mystery which she never attempted to penetrate. The present alone was significant; was hers, to torture her as it was doing then with the biting conviction that she had lost that which she had held, that she had been denied that which her impassioned, newly awakened being demanded.

## *XVI*

"Do you miss your friend greatly?" asked Mademoiselle Reisz one morning as she came creeping up behind Edna, who had just left her cottage on her way to the beach. She spent much of her time in the water since she had acquired finally the art of swimming. As their stay at Grand Isle drew near its close, she felt that she could not give too much time to a diversion which afforded her the only real pleasurable moments that she knew. When Mademoiselle Reisz came and touched her upon the shoulder and spoke to her, the woman seemed to echo the thought which was ever in Edna's mind; or better, the feeling which constantly possessed her.

Robert's going had some way taken the brightness, the color, the meaning out of everything. The conditions of her life were in no way changed, but her whole existence was dulled, like a faded garment which seems to be no longer worth wearing. She sought him everywhere—in others whom she induced to talk about him. She went up in the mornings to Madame Lebrun's room, braving the clatter of the old sewing-machine. She sat there and chatted at intervals as Robert had done. She gazed around the room at the pictures and photographs hanging upon the wall, and discovered in some corner an old family album, which she examined with the keenest interest, appealing to Madame Lebrun for enlightenment concerning the many figures and faces which she discovered between its pages.

410 There was a picture of Madame Lebrun with Robert as a baby, seated in her lap, a round-faced infant with a fist in his mouth. The eyes alone in the baby suggested the man. And that was he also in kilts, at the age of five, wearing long curls and holding a whip in his hand. It made Edna laugh, and she laughed, too, at the portrait in his first long trousers; while another interested her, taken when he left for college, looking thin, long-faced, with eyes full of fire, ambition and great intentions. But there was no recent picture, none which suggested the Robert who had gone away five days ago, leaving a void and wilderness behind him.

"Oh, Robert stopped having his pictures taken when he had to pay for them himself! He found wiser use for his money, he says," explained Madame Lebrun. She had a letter from him, written before he left New Orleans. Edna wished to see the letter, and Madame Lebrun told her to look for it either on the table or the dresser, or perhaps it was on the mantelpiece.

The letter was on the bookshelf. It possessed the greatest interest and attraction for Edna; the envelope, its size and shape, the post-mark, the handwriting. She examined every detail of the outside before opening it. There were only a few lines, setting forth that he would leave the city that afternoon, that he had packed his trunk in good shape, that he was well, and sent her his love and begged to be affectionately remembered to all. There was no special message to Edna except a postscript saying that if Mrs. Pontellier desired to finish the book which he had been reading to her, his mother would find it in his room, among other books there on the table. Edna experienced a pang of jealousy because he had written to his mother rather than to her.

Every one seemed to take for granted that she missed him. Even her husband, when he came down the Saturday following Robert's departure, expressed regret that he had gone.

"How do you get on without him, Edna?" he asked.

415 "It's very dull without him," she admitted. Mr. Pontellier had seen Robert in the city, and Edna asked him a dozen questions or more. Where had they met? On Carondelet Street, in the morning. They had gone "in"

and had a drink and a cigar together. What had they talked about? Chiefly about his prospects in Mexico, which Mr. Pontellier thought were promising. How did he look? How did he seem—grave, or gay, or how? Quite cheerful, and wholly taken up with the idea of his trip, which Mr. Pontellier found altogether natural in a young fellow about to seek fortune and adventure in a strange, queer country.

Edna tapped her foot impatiently, and wondered why the children persisted in playing in the sun when they might be under the trees. She went down and led them out of the sun, scolding the quadroon for not being more attentive.

It did not strike her as in the least grotesque that she should be making of Robert the object of conversation and leading her husband to speak of him. The sentiment which she entertained for Robert in no way resembled that which she felt for her husband, or had ever felt, or ever expected to feel. She had all her life long been accustomed to harbor thoughts and emotions which never voiced themselves. They had never taken the form of struggles. They belonged to her and were her own, and she entertained the conviction that she had a right to them and that they concerned no one but herself. Edna had once told Madame Ratignolle that she would never sacrifice herself for her children, or for any one. Then had followed a rather heated argument; the two women did not appear to understand each other or to be talking the same language. Edna tried to appease her friend, to explain.

"I would give up the unessential; I would give my money, I would give my life for my children; but I wouldn't give myself. I can't make it more clear; it's only something which I am beginning to comprehend, which is revealing itself to me."

"I don't know what you would call the essential, or what you mean by the unessential," said Madame Ratignolle, cheerfully; "but a woman who would give her life for her children could do no more than that—your Bible tells you so. I'm sure I couldn't do more than that."

"Oh, yes you could!" laughed Edna.

She was not surprised at Mademoiselle Reisz's question the morning that lady, following her to the beach, tapped her on the shoulder and asked if she did not greatly miss her young friend.

"Oh, good morning, Mademoiselle; is it you? Why, of course I miss Robert. Are you going down to bathe?"

"Why should I go down to bathe at the very end of the season when I haven't been in the surf all summer?" replied the woman, disagreeably.

"I beg your pardon," offered Edna, in some embarrassment, for she should have remembered that Mademoiselle Reisz's avoidance of the water had furnished a theme for much pleasantry. Some among them thought it was on account of her false hair, or the dread of getting the violets wet, while others attributed it to the natural aversion for water sometimes believed to accompany the artistic temperament. Mademoiselle offered Edna some chocolates in a paper bag, which she took from her pocket, by way of showing that she bore no ill feeling. She habitually ate chocolates for their sustaining quality; they contained much nutrient in small compass, she said. They saved her from starvation, as Madame Lebrun's table was utterly impossible; and no one save so impertinent a woman as Madame Lebrun could think of offering such food to people and requiring them to pay for it.

425 "She must feel very lonely without her son," said Edna, desiring to change the subject. "Her favorite son, too. It must have been quite hard to let him go."

Mademoiselle laughed maliciously.

"Her favorite son! Oh, dear! Who could have been imposing such a tale upon you? Aline Lebrun lives for Victor, and for Victor alone. She has spoiled him into the worthless creature he is. She worships him and the ground he walks on. Robert is very well in a way, to give up all the money he can earn to the family, and keep the barest pittance for himself. Favorite son, indeed! I miss the poor fellow myself, my dear. I liked to see him and to hear him about the place—the only Lebrun who is worth a pinch of salt. He comes to see me often in the city. I like to play to him. That Victor! hanging would be too good for him. It's a wonder Robert hasn't beaten him to death long ago."

"I thought he had great patience with his brother," offered Edna, glad to be talking about Robert, no matter what was said.

"Oh! he thrashed him well enough a year or two ago," said Mademoiselle. "It was about a Spanish girl, whom Victor considered that he had some sort of claim upon. He met Robert one day talking to the girl, or walking with her, or bathing with her, or carrying her basket—I don't remember what;—and he became so insulting and abusive that Robert gave him a thrashing on the spot that has kept him comparatively in order for a good while. It's about time he was getting another."

430 "Was her name Mariequita?" asked Edna.

"Mariequita—yes, that was it; Mariequita. I had forgotten. Oh, she's a sly one, and a bad one, that Mariequita!"

Edna looked down at Mademoiselle Reisz and wondered how she could have listened to her venom so long. For some reason she felt depressed, almost unhappy. She had not intended to go into the water; but she donned her bathing suit, and left Mademoiselle alone, seated under the shade of the children's tent. The water was growing cooler as the season advanced. Edna plunged and swam about with an abandon that thrilled and invigorated her. She remained a long time in the water, half hoping that Mademoiselle Reisz would not wait for her.

But Mademoiselle waited. She was very amiable during the walk back, and raved much over Edna's appearance in her bathing suit. She talked about music. She hoped that Edna would go to see her in the city, and wrote her address with the stub of a pencil on a piece of card which she found in her pocket.

"When do you leave?" asked Edna.

435 "Next Monday; and you?"

"The following week," answered Edna, adding, "It has been a pleasant summer, hasn't it, Mademoiselle?"

"Well," agreed Mademoiselle Reisz, with a shrug, "rather pleasant, if it hadn't been for the mosquitoes and the Farival twins."

## XVII

The Pontelliers possessed a very charming home on Esplanade Street[41] in New Orleans. It was a large, double cottage, with a broad front veranda,

[41]**Esplanade Street** fashionable street in New Orleans

whose round, fluted columns supported the sloping roof. The house was painted a dazzling white; the outside shutters, or jalousies, were green. In the yard, which was kept scrupulously neat, were flowers and plants of every description which flourish in South Louisiana. Within doors the appointments were perfect after the conventional type. The softest carpets and rugs covered the floors; rich and tasteful draperies hung at doors and windows. There were paintings, selected with judgment and discrimination, upon the walls. The cut glass, the silver, the heavy damask which daily appeared upon the table were the envy of many women whose husbands were less generous than Mr. Pontellier.

Mr. Pontellier was very fond of walking about his house examining its various appointments and details, to see that nothing was amiss. He greatly valued his possessions, chiefly because they were his, and derived genuine pleasure from contemplating a painting, a statuette, a rare lace curtain—no matter what—after he had bought it and placed it among his household goods.

440 On Tuesday afternoons—Tuesday being Mrs. Pontellier's reception day—there was a constant stream of callers—women who came in carriages or in the street cars, or walked when the air was soft and distance permitted. A light-colored mulatto boy, in dress coat and bearing a diminutive silver tray for the reception of cards, admitted them. A maid, in white fluted cap, offered the callers liqueur, coffee, or chocolate, as they might desire. Mrs. Pontellier, attired in a handsome reception gown, remained in the drawing-room the entire afternoon receiving her visitors. Men sometimes called in the evening with their wives.

This had been the programme which Mrs. Pontellier had religiously followed since her marriage, six years before. Certain evenings during the week she and her husband attended the opera or sometimes the play.

Mr. Pontellier left his home in the mornings between nine and ten o'clock, and rarely returned before half-past six or seven in the evening—dinner being served at half-past seven.

He and his wife seated themselves at table one Tuesday evening, a few weeks after their return from Grand Isle. They were alone together. The boys were being put to bed; the patter of their bare, escaping feet could be heard occasionally, as well as the pursuing voice of the quadroon, lifted in mild protest and entreaty. Mrs. Pontellier did not wear her usual Tuesday reception gown; she was in ordinary house dress. Mr. Pontellier, who was observant about such things, noticed it, as he served the soup and handed it to the boy in waiting.

"Tired out, Edna? Whom did you have? Many callers?" he asked. He tasted his soup and began to season it with pepper, salt, vinegar, mustard—everything within reach.

445 "There were a good many," replied Edna, who was eating her soup with evident satisfaction. "I found their cards when I got home; I was out."

"Out!" exclaimed her husband, with something like genuine consternation in his voice as he laid down the vinegar cruet and looked at her through his glasses. "Why, what could have taken you out on Tuesday? What did you have to do?"

"Nothing. I simply felt like going out, and I went out."

"Well, I hope you left some suitable excuse," said her husband, somewhat appeased, as he added a dash of cayenne pepper to the soup.

"No, I left no excuse. I told Joe to say I was out, that was all."

450 "Why, my dear, I should think you'd understand by this time that people don't do such things; we've got to observe *les convenances*[42] if we ever expect to get on and keep up with the procession. If you felt that you had to leave home this afternoon, you should have left some suitable explanation for your absence.

"This soup is really impossible; it's strange that woman hasn't learned yet to make a decent soup. Any free-lunch stand in town serves a better one. Was Mrs. Belthrop here?"

"Bring the tray with the cards, Joe. I don't remember who was here."

The boy retired and returned after a moment, bringing the tiny silver tray, which was covered with ladies' visiting cards. He handed it to Mrs. Pontellier.

"Give it to Mr. Pontellier," she said.

455 Joe offered the tray to Mr. Pontellier, and removed the soup.

Mr. Pontellier scanned the names of his wife's callers, reading some of them aloud, with comments as he read.

"'The Misses Delasidas.' I worked a big deal in futures[43] for their father this morning; nice girls; it's time they were getting married. 'Mrs. Belthrop.' I tell you what it is Edna; you can't afford to snub Mrs. Belthrop. Why, Belthrop could buy and sell us ten times over. His business is worth a good, round sum to me. You'd better write her a note. 'Mrs. James Highcamp.' Hugh! the less you have to do with Mrs. Highcamp, the better. 'Madame Laforcé.' Came all the way from Carrolton, too, poor old soul. 'Miss Wiggs,' 'Mrs. Eleanor Boltons.'" He pushed the cards aside.

"Mercy!" exclaimed Edna, who had been fuming. "Why are you taking the thing so seriously and making such a fuss over it?"

"I'm not making any fuss over it. But it's just such seeming trifles that we've got to take seriously; such things count."

460 The fish was scorched. Mr. Pontellier would not touch it. Edna said she did not mind a little scorched taste. The roast was in some way not to his fancy, and he did not like the manner in which the vegetables were served.

"It seems to me," he said, "we spend money enough in this house to procure at least one meal a day which a man could eat and retain his self-respect."

"You used to think the cook was a treasure," returned Edna, indifferently.

"Perhaps she was when she first came; but cooks are only human. They need looking after, like any other class of persons that you employ. Suppose I didn't look after the clerks in my office, just let them run things their own way; they'd soon make a nice mess of me and my business."

"Where are you going?" asked Edna, seeing that her husband arose from table without having eaten a morsel except a taste of the highly-seasoned soup.

465 "I'm going to get my dinner at the club. Good night." He went into the hall, took his hat and stick from the stand, and left the house.

[42]***les convenances*** the proprieties; social conventions

[43]**futures** stocks or commodities bought or sold for future delivery (a form of speculation)

She was somewhat familiar with such scenes. They had often made her very unhappy. On a few previous occasions she had been completely deprived of any desire to finish her dinner. Sometimes she had gone into the kitchen to administer a tardy rebuke to the cook. Once she went to her room and studied the cookbook during an entire evening, finally writing out a menu for the week, which left her harassed with a feeling that, after all, she had accomplished no good that was worth the name.

But that evening Edna finished her dinner alone, with forced deliberation. Her face was flushed and her eyes flamed with some inward fire that lighted them. After finishing her dinner she went to her room, having instructed the boy to tell any other callers that she was indisposed.

It was a large, beautiful room, rich and picturesque in the soft, dim light which the maid had turned low. She went and stood at an open window and looked out upon the deep tangle of the garden below. All the mystery and witchery of the night seemed to have gathered there amid the perfumes and the dusky and tortuous outlines of flowers and foliage. She was seeking herself and finding herself in just such sweet, half-darkness which met her moods. But the voices were not soothing that came to her from the darkness and the sky above and the stars. They jeered and sounded mournful notes without promise, devoid even of hope. She turned back into the room and began to walk to and fro down its whole length, without stopping, without resting. She carried in her hands a thin handkerchief, which she tore into ribbons, rolled into a ball, and flung from her. Once she stopped, and taking off her wedding ring, flung it upon the carpet. When she saw it lying there, she stamped her heel upon it, striving to crush it. But her small boot heel did not make an indenture, not a mark upon the little glittering circlet.

In a sweeping passion she seized a glass vase from the table and flung it upon the tiles of the hearth. She wanted to destroy something. The crash and clatter were what she wanted to hear.

A maid, alarmed at the din of breaking glass, entered the room to discover what was the matter.

"A vase fell upon the hearth," said Edna. "Never mind; leave it till morning."

"Oh! you might get some of the glass in your feet, ma'am," insisted the young woman, picking up bits of the broken vase that were scattered upon the carpet. "And here's your ring, ma'am, under the chair."

Edna held out her hand, and taking the ring, slipped it upon her finger.

## *XVIII*

The following morning Mr. Pontellier, upon leaving for his office, asked Edna if she would not meet him in town in order to look at some new fixtures for the library.

"I hardly think we need new fixtures, Léonce. Don't let us get anything new; you are too extravagant. I don't believe you ever think of saving or putting by."

"The way to become rich is to make money, my dear Edna, not to save it," he said. He regretted that she did not feel inclined to go with him and select new fixtures. He kissed her good-by, and told her she was not looking well and must take care of herself. She was unusually pale and very quiet.

She stood on the front veranda as he quitted the house, and absently picked a few sprays of jessamine that grew upon a trellis near by. She inhaled the odor of the blossoms and thrust them into the bosom of her white morning gown. The boys were dragging along the banquette[44] a small "express wagon," which they had filled with blocks and sticks. The quadroon was following them with little quick steps, having assumed a fictitious animation and alacrity for the occasion. A fruit vendor was crying his wares in the street.

Edna looked straight before her with a self-absorbed expression upon her face. She felt no interest in anything about her. The street, the children, the fruit vendor, the flowers growing there under her eyes, were all part and parcel of an alien world which had suddenly become antagonistic.

She went back into the house. She had thought of speaking to the cook concerning her blunders of the previous night; but Mr. Pontellier had saved her that disagreeable mission, for which she was so poorly fitted. Mr. Pontellier's arguments were usually convincing with those whom he employed. He left home feeling quite sure that he and Edna would sit down that evening, and possibly a few subsequent evenings, to a dinner deserving of the name.

Edna spent an hour or two in looking over some of her old sketches. She could see their shortcomings and defects, which were glaring in her eyes. She tried to work a little, but found she was not in the humor. Finally she gathered together a few of the sketches—those which she considered the least discreditable; and she carried them with her when, a little later, she dressed and left the house. She looked handsome and distinguished in her street gown. The tan of the seashore had left her face, and her forehead was smooth, white, and polished beneath her heavy, yellow-brown hair. There were a few freckles on her face, and a small, dark mole near the under lip and one on the temple, half-hidden in her hair.

As Edna walked along the street she was thinking of Robert. She was still under the spell of her infatuation. She had tried to forget him, realizing the inutility of remembering. But the thought of him was like an obsession, ever pressing itself upon her. It was not that she dwelt upon details of their acquaintance, or recalled in any special or peculiar way his personality; it was his being, his existence, which dominated her thought, fading sometimes as if it would melt into the mist of the forgotten, reviving again with an intensity which filled her with an incomprehensible longing.

Edna was on her way to Madame Ratignolle's. Their intimacy, begun at Grand Isle, had not declined, and they had seen each other with some frequency since their return to the city. The Ratignolles lived at no great distance from Edna's home, on the corner of a side street, where Monsieur Ratignolle owned and conducted a drug store which enjoyed a steady and prosperous trade. His father had been in the business before him, and Monsieur Ratignolle stood well in the community and bore an enviable reputation for integrity and clear-headedness. His family lived in commodious apartments over the store, having an entrance on the side within the *porte cochère.*[45] There was something which Edna thought very French, very foreign, about their whole manner of living. In the large and pleasant salon

[44]**banquette** sidewalk

[45]***porte cochère*** a roof supported by columns, serving to protect passengers who alight from a carriage

which extended across the width of the house, the Ratignolles entertained their friends once a fortnight with a *soirée musicale,*[46] sometimes diversified by card-playing. There was a friend who played upon the 'cello. One brought his flute and another his violin, while there were some who sang and a number who performed upon the piano with various degrees of taste and agility. The Ratignolles' *soirées musicales* were widely known, and it was considered a privilege to be invited to them.

Edna found her friend engaged in assorting the clothes which had returned that morning from the laundry. She at once abandoned her occupation upon seeing Edna, who had been ushered without ceremony into her presence.

"Cité can do it as well as I; it is really her business," she explained to Edna, who apologized for interrupting her. And she summoned a young black woman, whom she instructed, in French, to be very careful in checking off the list which she handed her. She told her to notice particularly if a fine linen handkerchief of Monsieur Ratignolle's, which was missing last week, had been returned; and to be sure to set to one side such pieces as required mending and darning.

485 Then placing an arm around Edna's waist, she led her to the front of the house, to the salon, where it was cool and sweet with the odor of great roses that stood upon the hearth in jars.

Madame Ratignolle looked more beautiful than ever there at home, in a négligée which left her arms almost wholly bare and exposed the rich, melting curves of her white throat.

"Perhaps I shall be able to paint your picture some day," said Edna with a smile when they were seated. She produced the roll of sketches and started to unfold them. "I believe I ought to work again. I feel as if I wanted to be doing something. What do you think of them? Do you think it worth while to take it up again and study some more? I might study for a while with Laidpore."

She knew that Madame Ratignolle's opinion in such a matter would be next to valueless, that she herself had not alone decided, but determined; but she sought the words of praise and encouragement that would help her to put heart into her venture.

"Your talent is immense, dear!"

490 "Nonsense!" protested Edna, well pleased.

"Immense, I tell you," persisted Madame Ratignolle, surveying the sketches one by one, at close range, then holding them at arm's length, narrowing her eyes, and dropping her head on one side. "Surely, this Bavarian peasant is worthy of framing; and this basket of apples! Never have I seen anything more lifelike. One might almost be tempted to reach out a hand and take one."

Edna could not control a feeling which bordered upon complacency at her friend's praise, even realizing, as she did, its true worth. She retained a few of the sketches, and gave all the rest to Madame Ratignolle, who appreciated the gift far beyond its value and proudly exhibited the pictures to her husband when he came up from the store a little later for his midday dinner.

Mr. Ratignolle was one of those men who are called the salt of the earth. His cheerfulness was unbounded, and it was matched by his good-

[46]***soirée musicale*** evening of music

ness of heart, his broad charity, and common sense. He and his wife spoke English with an accent which was only discernible through its un-English emphasis and a certain carefulness and deliberation. Edna's husband spoke English with no accent whatever. The Ratignolles understood each other perfectly. If ever the fusion of two human beings into one has been accomplished on this sphere it was surely in their union.

As Edna seated herself at table with them she thought, "Better a dinner of herbs," though it did not take her long to discover that it was no dinner of herbs, but a delicious repast, simple, choice, and in every way satisfying.
495 Monsieur Ratignolle was delighted to see her, though he found her looking not so well as at Grand Isle, and he advised a tonic. He talked a good deal on various topics, a little politics, some city news and neighborhood gossip. He spoke with an animation and earnestness that gave an exaggerated importance to every syllable he uttered. His wife was keenly interested in everything he said, laying down her fork the better to listen, chiming in, taking the words out of his mouth.

Edna felt depressed rather than soothed after leaving them. The little glimpse of domestic harmony which had been offered her, gave her no regret, no longing. It was not a condition of life which fitted her, and she could see in it but an appalling and hopeless ennui. She was moved by a kind of commiseration for Madame Ratignolle,—a pity for that colorless existence which never uplifted its possessor beyond the region of blind contentment, in which no moment of anguish ever visited her soul, in which she would never have the taste of life's delirium. Edna vaguely wondered what she meant by "life's delirium." It had crossed her thought like some unsought extraneous impression.

## *XIX*

Edna could not help but think that it was very foolish, very childish, to have stamped upon her wedding ring and smashed the crystal vase upon the tiles. She was visited by no more outbursts, moving her to such futile expedients. She began to do as she liked and to feel as she liked. She completely abandoned her Tuesdays at home, and did not return the visits of those who had called upon her. She made no ineffectual efforts to conduct her household *en bonne ménagère*,[47] going and coming as it suited her fancy, and, so far as she was able, lending herself to any passing caprice.

Mr. Pontellier had been a rather courteous husband so long as he met a certain tacit submissiveness in his wife. But her new and unexpected line of conduct completely bewildered him. It shocked him. Then her absolute disregard for her duties as a wife angered him. When Mr. Pontellier became rude, Edna grew insolent. She had resolved never to take another step backward.

"It seems to me the utmost folly for a woman at the head of a household, and the mother of children, to spend in an atelier[48] days which would be better employed contriving for the comfort of her family."

500 "I feel like painting," answered Edna. "Perhaps I shan't always feel like it."

[47]***en bonne ménagère*** as a good housewife
[48]**atelier** studio

"Then in God's name paint! but don't let the family go to the devil. There's Madame Ratignolle; because she keeps up her music, she doesn't let everything else go to chaos. And she's more of a musician than you are a painter."

"She isn't a musician, and I'm not a painter. It isn't on account of painting that I let things go."

"On account of what, then?"

"Oh! I don't know. Let me alone; you bother me."

505 It sometimes entered Mr. Pontellier's mind to wonder if his wife were not growing a little unbalanced mentally. He could see plainly that she was not herself. That is, he could not see that she was becoming herself and daily casting aside that fictitious self which we assume like a garment with which to appear before the world.

Her husband let her alone as she requested, and went away to his office. Edna went up to her atelier—a bright room in the top of the house. She was working with great energy and interest, without accomplishing anything, however, which satisfied her even in the smallest degree. For a time she had the whole household enrolled in the service of art. The boys posed for her. They thought it amusing at first, but the occupation soon lost its attractiveness when they discovered that it was not a game arranged especially for their entertainment. The quadroon sat for hours before Edna's palette, patient as a savage, while the house-maid took charge of the children, and the drawing-room went undusted. But the house-maid, too, served her term as model when Edna perceived that the young woman's back and shoulders were molded on classic lines, and that her hair, loosened from its confining cap, became an inspiration. While Edna worked she sometimes sang low the little air, *"Ah! si tu savais!"*

It moved her with recollections. She could hear again the ripple of the water, the flapping sail. She could see the glint of the moon upon the bay, and could feel the soft, gusty beating of the hot south wind. A subtle current of desire passed through her body, weakening her hold upon the brushes and making her eyes burn.

There were days when she was very happy without knowing why. She was happy to be alive and breathing, when her whole being seemed to be one with the sunlight, the color, the odors, the luxuriant warmth of some perfect Southern day. She liked then to wander alone into strange and unfamiliar places. She discovered many a sunny, sleepy corner, fashioned to dream in. And she found it good to dream and to be alone and unmolested.

There were days when she was unhappy, she did not know why,—when it did not seem worth while to be glad or sorry, to be alive or dead; when life appeared to her like a grotesque pandemonium and humanity like worms struggling blindly toward inevitable annihilation. She could not work on such a day, nor weave fancies to stir her pulses and warm her blood.

## XX

510 It was during such a mood that Edna hunted up Mademoiselle Reisz. She had not forgotten the rather disagreeable impression left upon her by their last interview; but she nevertheless felt a desire to see her—above all, to listen while she played upon the piano. Quite early in the afternoon she

started upon her quest for the pianist. Unfortunately she had mislaid or lost Mademoiselle Reisz's card, and looking up her address in the city directory, she found that the woman lived on Bienville Street, some distance away. The directory which fell into her hands was a year or more old, however, and upon reaching the number indicated, Edna discovered that the house was occupied by a respectable family of mulattoes who had *chambres garnies*[49] to let. They had been living there for six months, and knew absolutely nothing of a Mademoiselle Reisz. In fact, they knew nothing of any of their neighbors; their lodgers were all people of the highest distinction, they assured Edna. She did not linger to discuss class distinctions with Madame Pouponne, but hastened to a neighboring grocery store, feeling sure that Mademoiselle would have left her address with the proprietor.

He knew Mademoiselle Reisz a good deal better than he wanted to know her, he informed his questioner. In truth, he did not want to know her at all, or anything concerning her—the most disagreeable and unpopular woman who ever lived in Bienville Street. He thanked heaven she had left the neighborhood, and was equally thankful that he did not know where she had gone.

Edna's desire to see Mademoiselle Reisz had increased tenfold since these unlooked-for obstacles had arisen to thwart it. She was wondering who could give her the information she sought, when it suddenly occurred to her that Madame Lebrun would be the one most likely to do so. She knew it was useless to ask Madame Ratignolle, who was on the most distant terms with the musician, and preferred to know nothing concerning her. She had once been almost as emphatic in expressing herself upon the subject as the corner grocer.

Edna knew that Madame Lebrun had returned to the city, for it was the middle of November. And she also knew where the Lebruns lived, on Chartres Street.

Their home from the outside looked like a prison, with iron bars before the door and lower windows. The iron bars were a relic of the old *régime,*[50] and no one had ever thought of dislodging them. At the side was a high fence enclosing the garden. A gate or door opening upon the street was locked. Edna rang the bell at this side garden gate, and stood upon the banquette, waiting to be admitted.

515 It was Victor who opened the gate for her. A black woman, wiping her hands upon her apron, was close at his heels. Before she saw them Edna could hear them in altercation, the woman—plainly an anomaly—claiming the right to be allowed to perform her duties, one of which was to answer the bell.

Victor was surprised and delighted to see Mrs. Pontellier, and he made no attempt to conceal either his astonishment or his delight. He was a dark-browed, good-looking youngster of nineteen, greatly resembling his mother, but with ten times her impetuosity. He instructed the black woman to go at once and inform Madame Lebrun that Mrs. Pontellier desired to see her. The woman grumbled a refusal to do part of her duty when she had not been permitted to do it all, and started back to her interrupted task of weeding the garden. Whereupon Victor administered a rebuke in the form of a

[49]***chambres garnies*** furnished rooms
[50]**the old *régime*** that is, the days of the Spanish

volley of abuse, which, owing to its rapidity and incoherence, was all but incomprehensible to Edna. Whatever it was, the rebuke was convincing, for the woman dropped her hoe and went mumbling into the house.

Edna did not wish to enter. It was very pleasant there on the side porch, where there were chairs, a wicker lounge, and a small table. She seated herself, for she was tired from her long tramp; and she began to rock gently and smooth out the folds of her silk parasol. Victor drew up his chair beside her. He at once explained that the black woman's offensive conduct was all due to imperfect training, as he was not there to take her in hand. He had only come up from the island the morning before, and expected to return next day. He stayed all winter at the island; he lived there, and kept the place in order and got things ready for the summer visitors.

But a man needed occasional relaxation, he informed Mrs. Pontellier, and every now and again he drummed up a pretext to bring him to the city. My! but he had had a time of it the evening before! He wouldn't want his mother to know, and he began to talk in a whisper. He was scintillant with recollections. Of course, he couldn't think of telling Mrs. Pontellier all about it, she being a woman and not comprehending such things. But it all began with a girl peeping and smiling at him through the shutters as he passed by. Oh! but she was a beauty! Certainly he smiled back, and went up and talked to her. Mrs. Pontellier did not know him if she supposed he was once to let an opportunity like that escape him. Despite herself, the youngster amused her. She must have betrayed in her look some degree of interest or entertainment. The boy grew more daring, and Mrs. Pontellier might have found herself, in a little while, listening to a highly colored story but for the timely appearance of Madame Lebrun.

That lady was still clad in white, according to her custom of the summer. Her eyes beamed an effusive welcome. Would not Mrs. Pontellier go inside? Would she partake of some refreshment? Why had she not been there before? How was that dear Mr. Pontellier and how were those sweet children? Had Mrs. Pontellier ever known such a warm November?

Victor went and reclined on the wicker lounge behind his mother's chair, where he commanded a view of Edna's face. He had taken her parasol from her hands while he spoke to her, and he now lifted it and twirled it above him as he lay on his back. When Madame Lebrun complained that it was *so* dull coming back to the city; that she saw *so* few people now; that even Victor, when he came up from the island for a day or two, had *so* much to occupy him and engage his time; then it was that the youth went into contortions on the lounge and winked mischievously at Edna. She somehow felt like a confederate in crime, and tried to look severe and disapproving.

There had been but two letters from Robert, with little in them, they told her. Victor said it was really not worth while to go inside for the letters, when his mother entreated him to go in search of them. He remembered the contents, which in truth he rattled off very glibly when put to the test.

One letter was written from Vera Cruz and the other from the City of Mexico. He had met Montel, who was doing everything toward his advancement. So far, the financial situation was no improvement over the one he had left in New Orleans, but of course the prospects were vastly better. He wrote of the City of Mexico, the buildings, the people and their habits, the conditions of life which he found there. He sent his love to the family.

He inclosed a check to his mother, and hoped she would affectionately remember him to all his friends. That was about the substance of the two letters. Edna felt that if there had been a message for her, she would have received it. The despondent frame of mind in which she had left home began again to overtake her, and she remembered that she wished to find Mademoiselle Reisz.

Madame Lebrun knew where Mademoiselle Reisz lived. She gave Edna the address, regretting that she would not consent to stay and spend the remainder of the afternoon, and pay a visit to Mademoiselle Reisz some other day. The afternoon was already well advanced.

Victor escorted her out upon the banquette, lifted her parasol, and held it over her while he walked to the car[51] with her. He entreated her to bear in mind that the disclosures of the afternoon were strictly confidential. She laughed and bantered him a little, remembering too late that she should have been dignified and reserved.

525 "How handsome Mrs. Pontellier looked!" said Madame Lebrun to her son.

"Ravishing!" he admitted. "The city atmosphere has improved her. Some way she doesn't seem like the same woman."

## XXI

Some people contended that the reason Mademoiselle Reisz always chose apartments up under the roof was to discourage the approach of beggars, peddlers and callers. There were plenty of windows in her little front room. They were for the most party dingy, but as they were nearly always open it did not make so much difference. They often admitted into the room a good deal of smoke and soot; but at the same time all the light and air that there was came through them. From her windows could be seen the crescent of the river, the masts of ships and the big chimneys of the Mississippi steamers. A magnificent piano crowded the apartment. In the next room she slept, and in the third and last she harbored a gasoline stove on which she cooked her meals when disinclined to descend to the neighboring restaurant. It was there also that she ate, keeping her belongings in a rare old buffet, dingy and battered from a hundred years of use.

When Edna knocked at Mademoiselle Reisz's front room door and entered, she discovered that person standing beside the window, engaged in mending or patching an old prunella gaiter.[52] The little musician laughed all over when she saw Edna. Her laugh consisted of a contortion of the face and all the muscles of the body. She seemed strikingly homely, standing there in the afternoon light. She still wore the shabby lace and the artificial bunch of violets on the side of her head.

"So you remembered me at last," said Mademoiselle. "I had said to myself, 'Ah, bah! she will never come.'"

530 "Did you want me to come?" asked Edna with a smile.

"I had not thought much about it," answered Mademoiselle. The two had seated themselves on a little bumpy sofa which stood against the wall.

[51]**car** streetcar

[52]**prunella gaiter** ankle-high shoe, with the upper section made of cloth

"I am glad, however, that you came. I have the water boiling back there, and was just about to make some coffee. You will drink a cup with me. And how is *la belle dame?* Always handsome! always healthy! always contented!" She took Edna's hand between her strong wiry fingers, holding it loosely without warmth, and executing a sort of double theme upon the back and palm.

"Yes," she went on; "I sometimes thought: 'She will never come. She promised as those women in society always do, without meaning it. She will not come.' For I really don't believe you like me, Mrs. Pontellier."

"I don't know whether I like you or not," replied Edna, gazing down at the little woman with a quizzical look.

The candor of Mrs. Pontellier's admission greatly pleased Mademoiselle Reisz. She expressed her gratification by repairing forthwith to the region of the gasoline stove and rewarding her guest with the promised cup of coffee. The coffee and the biscuit accompanying it proved very acceptable to Edna, who had declined refreshment at Madame Lebrun's and was now beginning to feel hungry. Mademoiselle set the tray which she brought in upon a small table near at hand, and seated herself once again on the lumpy sofa.

535 "I have had a letter from your friend," she remarked, as she poured a little cream into Edna's cup and handed it to her.

"My friend?"

"Yes, your friend Robert. He wrote to me from the City of Mexico."

"Wrote to *you?*" repeated Edna in amazement, stirring her coffee absently.

"Yes, to me. Why not? Don't stir all the warmth out of your coffee; drink it. Though the letter might as well have been sent to you; it was nothing but Mrs. Pontellier from beginning to end."

540 "Let me see it," requested the young woman, entreatingly.

"No; a letter concerns no one but the person who writes it and the one to whom it is written."

"Haven't you just said it concerned me from beginning to end?"

"It was written about you, not to you. 'Have you seen Mrs. Pontellier? How is she looking?' he asks. 'As Mrs. Pontellier says,' or 'as Mrs. Pontellier once said.' 'If Mrs. Pontellier should call upon you, play for her that Impromptu of Chopin's, my favorite. I heard it here a day or two ago, but not as you play it. I should like to know how it affects her,' and so on, as if he supposed we were constantly in each other's society."

"Let me see the letter."

545 "Oh, no."

"Have you answered it?"

"No."

"Let me see the letter."

"No, and again, no."

550 "Then play the Impromptu for me."

"It is growing late; what time do you have to be home?"

"Time doesn't concern me. Your question seems a little rude. Play the Impromptu."

"But you have told me nothing of yourself. What are you doing?"

"Painting!" laughed Edna. "I am becoming an artist. Think of it!"

555 "Ah! an artist! You have pretensions, Madame."

"Why pretensions? Do you think I could not become an artist?"

"I do not know you well enough to say. I do not know your talent or your temperament. To be an artist includes much; one must possess many gifts—absolute gifts—which have not been acquired by one's own effort. And, moreover, to succeed, the artist must possess the courageous soul."

"What do you mean by the courageous soul?"

"Courageous, *ma foi!* The brave soul. The soul that dares and defies."

"Show me the letter and play for me the Impromptu. You see that I have persistence. Does that quality count for anything in art?"

"It counts with a foolish old woman whom you have captivated," replied Mademoiselle, with her wriggling laugh.

The letter was right there at hand in the drawer of the little table upon which Edna had just placed her coffee cup. Mademoiselle opened the drawer and drew forth the letter, the topmost one. She placed it in Edna's hands, and without further comment arose and went to the piano.

Mademoiselle played a soft interlude. It was an improvisation. She sat low at the instrument, and the lines of her body settled into ungraceful curves and angles that gave it an appearance of deformity. Gradually and imperceptibly the interlude melted into the soft opening minor chords of the Chopin Impromptu.

Edna did not know when the Impromptu began or ended. She sat in the sofa corner reading Robert's letter by the fading light. Mademoiselle had glided from the Chopin into the quivering love-notes of Isolde's song,[53] and back again to the Impromptu with its soulful and poignant longing.

The shadows deepened in the little room. The music grew strange and fantastic—turbulent, insistent, plaintive and soft with entreaty. The shadows grew deeper. The music filled the room. It floated out upon the night, over the housetops, the crescent of the river, losing itself in the silence of the upper air.

Edna was sobbing, just as she had wept one midnight at Grand Isle when strange, new voices awoke in her. She arose in some agitation to take her departure. "May I come again, Mademoiselle?" she asked at the threshold.

"Come whenever you feel like it. Be careful; the stairs and landings are dark; don't stumble."

Mademoiselle reentered and lit a candle. Robert's letter was on the floor. She stooped and picked it up. It was crumpled and damp with tears. Mademoiselle smoothed the letter out, restored it to the envelope, and replaced it in the table drawer.

## XXII

One morning on his way into town, Mr. Pontellier stopped at the house of his old friend and family physician, Doctor Mandelet. The Doctor was a semi-retired physician, resting, as the saying is, upon his laurels. He bore a reputation for wisdom rather than skill—leaving the active practice of medicine to his assistants and younger contemporaries—and was much sought

[53]**Isolde's song** that is, the Liebestod ("Love-Death") sung by Isolde in *Tristan und Isolde* (1857–59) by the German composer Richard Wagner. Isolde, holding her dead lover in her arms, bids him farewell and then dies.

for in matters of consultation. A few families, united to him by bonds of friendship, he still attended when they required the services of a physician. The Pontelliers were among these.

570 Mr. Pontellier found the Doctor reading at the open window of his study. His house stood rather far back from the street, in the center of a delightful garden, so that it was quiet and peaceful at the old gentleman's study window. He was a great reader. He stared up disapprovingly over his eye-glasses as Mr. Pontellier entered, wondering who had the temerity to disturb him at that hour of the morning.

"Ah, Pontellier! Not sick, I hope. Come and have a seat. What news do you bring this morning?" He was quite portly, with a profusion of gray hair, and small blue eyes which age had robbed of much of their brightness but none of their penetration.

"Oh! I'm never sick, Doctor. You know that I come of tough fiber—of that old Creole race of Pontelliers that dry up and finally blow away. I came to consult—no, not precisely to consult—to talk to you about Edna. I don't know what ails her."

"Madame Pontellier not well?" marveled the Doctor. "Why, I saw her—I think it was a week ago—walking along Canal Street, the picture of health, it seemed to me."

"Yes, yes; she seems quite well," said Mr. Pontellier, leaning forward and whirling his stick between his two hands; "but she doesn't act well. She's odd, she's not like herself. I can't make her out, and I thought perhaps you'd help me."

575 "How does she act?" inquired the doctor.

"Well, it isn't easy to explain," said Mr. Pontellier, throwing himself back in his chair. "She lets the housekeeping go to the dickens."

"Well, well; women are not all alike, my dear Pontellier. We've got to consider—"

"I know that; I told you I couldn't explain. Her whole attitude—toward me and everybody and everything—has changed. You know I have a quick temper, but I don't want to quarrel or be rude to a woman, especially my wife; yet I'm driven to it, and feel like ten thousand devils after I've made a fool of myself. She's making it devilishly uncomfortable for me," he went on nervously. "She's got some sort of notion in her head concerning the eternal rights of women; and—you understand—we meet in the morning at the breakfast table."

The old gentleman lifted his shaggy eyebrows, protruded his thick nether lip, and tapped the arms of his chair with his cushioned fingertips.

580 "What have you been doing to her, Pontellier?"

"Doing! *Parbleu!*"[54]

"Has she," asked the Doctor, with a smile, "has she been associating of late with a circle of pseudo-intellectual women—super-spiritual superior beings? My wife has been telling me about them."

"That's the trouble," broke in Mr. Pontellier, "she hasn't been associating with any one. She has abandoned her Tuesdays at home, has thrown over all her acquaintances, and goes tramping about by herself, moping in the street-cars, getting in after dark. I tell you she's peculiar. I don't like it; I feel a little worried over it."

[54]***Parbleu!*** For heaven's sake!

This was a new aspect for the Doctor. "Nothing hereditary?" he asked, seriously. "Nothing peculiar about her family antecedents, is there?"

585 "Oh, no indeed! She comes of sound old Presbyterian Kentucky stock. The old gentleman, her father, I have heard, used to atone for his weekday sins with his Sunday devotions. I know for a fact, that his race horses literally ran away with the prettiest bit of Kentucky farming land I ever laid eyes upon. Margaret—you know Margaret—she has all the Presbyterianism undiluted. And the youngest is something of a vixen. By the way, she gets married in a couple of weeks from now."

"Send your wife up to the wedding," exclaimed the Doctor, foreseeing a happy solution. "Let her stay among her own people for a while; it will do her good."

"That's what I want her to do. She won't go to the marriage. She says a wedding is one of the most lamentable spectacles on earth. Nice thing for a woman to say to her husband!" exclaimed Mr. Pontellier, fuming anew at the recollection.

"Pontellier," said the Doctor, after a moment's reflection, "let your wife alone for a while. Don't bother her, and don't let her bother you. Woman, my dear friend, is a very peculiar and delicate organism—a sensitive and highly organized woman, such as I know Mrs. Pontellier to be, is especially peculiar. It would require an inspired psychologist to deal successfully with them. And when ordinary fellows like you and me attempt to cope with their idiosyncrasies the result is bungling. Most women are moody and whimsical. This is some passing whim of your wife, due to some cause or causes which you and I needn't try to fathom. But it will pass happily over, especially if you let her alone. Send her around to see me."

"Oh! I couldn't do that; there'd be no reason for it," objected Mr. Pontellier.

590 "Then I'll go around and see her," said the Doctor. "I'll drop in to dinner some evening *en bon ami*."[55]

"Do! by all means," urged Mr. Pontellier. "What evening will you come? Say Thursday. Will you come Thursday?" he asked, rising to take his leave.

"Very well; Thursday. My wife may possibly have some engagement for me Thursday. In case she has, I shall let you know. Otherwise, you may expect me."

Mr. Pontellier turned before leaving to say:

"I am going to New York on business very soon. I have a big scheme on hand, and want to be on the field proper to pull the ropes and handle the ribbons.[56] We'll let you in on the inside if you say so, Doctor," he laughed.

595 "No, I thank you, my dear sir," returned the Doctor. "I leave such ventures to you younger men with the fever of life still in your blood."

"What I wanted to say," continued Mr. Pontellier, with his hand on the knob; "I may have to be absent a good while. Would you advise me to take Edna along?"

"By all means, if she wishes to go. If not, leave her here. Don't contradict her. The mood will pass, I assure you. It may take a month, two, three months—possibly longer, but it will pass; have patience."

[55]***en bon ami*** as a friend

[56]**handle the ribbons** control the reins, that is, run things

"Well, good-by, *à jeudi,*"[57] said Mr. Pontellier, as he let himself out.

The doctor would have liked during the course of conversation to ask, "Is there any man in the case?" but he knew his Creole too well to make such a blunder as that.

He did not resume his book immediately, but sat for a while meditatively looking out into the garden.

## *XXIII*

Edna's father was in the city, and had been with them several days. She was not very warmly or deeply attached to him, but they had certain tastes in common, and when together they were companionable. His coming was in the nature of a welcome disturbance; it seemed to furnish a new direction for her emotions.

He had come to purchase a wedding ring for his daughter, Janet, and an outfit for himself in which he might make a creditable appearance at her marriage. Mr. Pontellier had selected the bridal gift, as every one immediately connected with him always deferred to his taste in such matters. And his suggestions on the question of dress—which too often assumes the nature of a problem—were of inestimable value to his father-in-law. But for the past few days the old gentleman had been upon Edna's hands, and in his society she was becoming acquainted with a new set of sensations. He had been a colonel in the Confederate army, and still maintained, with the title, the military bearing which had always accompanied it. His hair and mustache were white and silky, emphasizing the rugged bronze of his face. He was tall and thin, and wore his coats padded, which gave a fictitious breadth and depth to his shoulders and chest. Edna and her father looked very distinguished together, and excited a good deal of notice during their perambulations. Upon his arrival she began by introducing him to her atelier and making a sketch of him. He took the whole matter very seriously. If her talent had been ten-fold greater than it was, it would not have surprised him, convinced as he was that he had bequeathed to all of his daughters the germs of a masterful capability, which only depended upon their own efforts to be directed toward successful achievement.

Before her pencil he sat rigid and unflinching, as he had faced the cannon's mouth in days gone by. He resented the intrusion of the children, who gaped with wondering eyes at him, sitting so stiff up there in their mother's bright atelier. When they drew near he motioned them away with an expressive action of the foot, loath to disturb the fixed lines of his countenance, his arms, or his rigid shoulders.

Edna, anxious to entertain him, invited Mademoiselle Reisz to meet him, having promised him a treat in her piano playing; but Mademoiselle declined the invitation. So together they attended a *soirée musicale* at the Ratignolles'. Monsieur and Madame Ratignolle made much of the Colonel, installing him as the guest of honor and engaging him at once to dine with them the following Sunday, or any day which he might select. Madame coquetted with him in the most captivating and naïve manner, with eyes, gestures, and a profusion of compliments, till the Colonel's old head felt thirty

[57] ***à jeudi*** until Thursday

years younger on his padded shoulders. Edna marveled, not comprehending. She herself was almost devoid of coquetry.

605 There were one or two men whom she observed at the *soirée musicale;* but she would never have felt moved to any kittenish display to attract their notice—to any feline or feminine wiles to express herself toward them. Their personality attracted her in an agreeable way. Her fancy selected them, and she was glad when a lull in the music gave them an opportunity to meet her and talk with her. Often on the street the glance of strange eyes had lingered in her memory, and sometimes had disturbed her.

Mr. Pontellier did not attend these *soirée musicales.* He considered them *bourgeois,* and found more diversion at the club. To Madame Ratignolle he said the music dispensed at her *soirées* was too "heavy," too far beyond his untrained comprehension. His excuse flattered her. But she disapproved of Mr. Pontellier's club, and she was frank enough to tell Edna so.

"It's a pity Mr. Pontellier doesn't stay home more in the evenings. I think you would be more—well, if you don't mind my saying it—more united, if he did."

"Oh! dear no!" said Edna, with a blank look in her eyes. "What should I do if he stayed home? We wouldn't have anything to say to each other."

She had not much of anything to say to her father, for that matter; but he did not antagonize her. She discovered that he interested her, though she realized that he might not interest her long; and for the first time in her life she felt as if she were thoroughly acquainted with him. He kept her busy serving him and ministering to his wants. It amused her to do so. She would not permit a servant or one of the children to do anything for him which she might do herself. Her husband noticed, and thought it was the expression of a deep filial attachment which he had never suspected.

610 The Colonel drank numerous "toddies" during the course of the day, which left him, however, imperturbed. He was an expert at concocting strong drinks. He had even invented some, to which he had given fantastic names, and for whose manufacture he required diverse ingredients that it devolved upon Edna to procure for him.

When Doctor Mandelet dined with the Pontelliers on Thursday he could discern in Mrs. Pontellier no trace of that morbid condition which her husband had reported to him. She was excited and in a manner radiant. She and her father had been to the race course, and their thoughts when they seated themselves at table were still occupied with the events of the afternoon, and their talk was still of the track. The Doctor had not kept pace with turf affairs. He had certain recollections of racing in what he called "the good old times" when the Lecompte stables flourished, and he drew upon this fund of memories so that he might not be left out and seem wholly devoid of the modern spirit. But he failed to impose upon the Colonel, and was even far from impressing him with this trumped-up knowledge of bygone days. Edna had staked her father on his last venture, with the most gratifying results to both of them. Besides, they had met some very charming people, according to the Colonel's impressions. Mrs. Mortimer Merriman and Mrs. James Highcamp, who were there with Alcée Arobin, had joined them and had enlivened the hours in a fashion that warmed him to think of.

Mr. Pontellier himself had no particular leaning toward horse-racing, and was even rather inclined to discourage it as a pastime, especially when he considered the fate of that blue-grass farm in Kentucky. He endeavored in a general way, to express a particular disapproval, and only succeeded in arousing the ire and opposition of his father-in-law. A petty dispute followed, in which Edna warmly espoused her father's cause and the Doctor remained neutral.

He observed his hostess attentively from under his shaggy brows, and noted a subtle change which had transformed her from the listless woman he had known into a being who, for the moment, seemed palpitant with the forces of life. Her speech was warm and energetic. There was no repression in her glance or gesture. She reminded him of some beautiful, sleek animal waking up in the sun.

The dinner was excellent. The claret was warm and the champagne was cold, and under their beneficent influence the threatened unpleasantness melted and vanished with the fumes of the wine.

Mr. Pontellier warmed up and grew reminiscent. He told some amusing plantation experiences, recollections of old Iberville and his youth, when he hunted 'possum in company with some friendly darky; thrashed the pecan trees, shot the grosbec, and roamed the woods and fields in mischievous idleness.

The Colonel, with little sense of humor and of the fitness of things, related a somber episode of those dark and bitter days, in which he had acted a conspicuous part and always formed a central figure. Nor was the Doctor happier in his selection, when he told the old, ever new and curious story of the waning of a woman's love, seeking strange, new channels, only to return to its legitimate source after days of fierce unrest. It was one of the many little human documents which had been unfolded to him during his long career as a physician. The story did not seem especially to impress Edna. She had one of her own to tell, of a woman who paddled away with her lover one night in a pirogue and never came back. They were lost amid the Baratarian Islands, and no one ever heard of them or found trace of them from that day to this. It was a pure invention. She said that Madame Antoine had related it to her. That, also, was an invention. Perhaps it was a dream she had had. But every glowing word seemed real to those who listened. They could feel the hot breath of the Southern night; they could hear the long sweep of the pirogue through the glistening moonlit water, the beating of birds' wings, rising startled from among the reeds in the salt-water pools; they could see the faces of the lovers, pale, close together, rapt in oblivious forgetfulness, drifting into the unknown.

The champagne was cold, and its subtle fumes played fantastic tricks with Edna's memory that night.

Outside, away from the glow of the fire and the soft lamplight, the night was chill and murky. The Doctor doubled his old-fashioned cloak across his breast as he strode home through the darkness. He knew his fellow-creatures better than most men; knew that inner life which so seldom unfolds itself to unanointed eyes. He was sorry he had accepted Pontellier's invitation. He was growing old, and beginning to need rest and an imperturbed spirit. He did not want the secrets of other lives thrust upon him.

"I hope it isn't Arobin," he muttered to himself as he walked. "I hope to heaven it isn't Alcée Arobin."

## XXIV

620 Edna and her father had a warm, and almost violent dispute upon the subject of her refusal to attend her sister's wedding. Mr. Pontellier declined to interfere, to interpose either his influence or his authority. He was following Doctor Mandelet's advice, and letting her do as she liked. The Colonel reproached his daughter for her lack of filial kindness and respect, her want of sisterly affection and womanly consideration. His arguments were labored and unconvincing. He doubted if Janet would accept any excuse—forgetting that Edna had offered none. He doubted if Janet would ever speak to her again, and he was sure Margaret would not.

Edna was glad to be rid of her father when he finally took himself off with his wedding garments and his bridal gifts, with his padded shoulders, his Bible reading, his "toddies" and ponderous oaths.

Mr. Pontellier followed him closely. He meant to stop at the wedding on his way to New York and endeavor by every means which money and love could devise to atone somewhat for Edna's incomprehensible action.

"You are too lenient, too lenient by far, Léonce," asserted the Colonel. "Authority, coercion are what is needed. Put you foot down good and hard; the only way to manage a wife. Take my word for it."

The Colonel was perhaps unaware that he had coerced his own wife into her grave. Mr. Pontellier had a vague suspicion of it which he thought it needless to mention at that late day.

625 Edna was not so consciously gratified at her husband's leaving home as she had been over the departure of her father. As the day approached when he was to leave her for a comparatively long stay, she grew melting and affectionate, remembering his many acts of consideration and his repeated expressions of an ardent attachment. She was solicitous about his health and his welfare. She bustled around, looking after his clothing, thinking about heavy underwear, quite as Madame Ratignolle would have done under similar circumstances. She cried when he went away, calling him her dear, good friend, and she was quite certain she would grow lonely before very long and go to join him in New York.

But after all, a radiant peace settled upon her when she at last found herself alone. Even the children were gone. Old Madame Pontellier had come herself and carried them off to Iberville with their quadroon. The old Madame did not venture to say she was afraid they would be neglected during Léonce's absence; she hardly ventured to think so. She was hungry for them—even a little fierce in her attachment. She did not want them to be wholly "children of the pavement," she always said when begging to have them for a space. She wished them to know the country, with its streams, its fields, its woods, its freedom, so delicious to the young. She wished them to taste something of the life their father had lived and known and loved when he, too, was a little child.

When Edna was at last alone, she breathed a big, genuine sigh of relief. A feeling that was unfamiliar but very delicious came over her. She walked all through the house, from one room to another, as if inspecting it for the first time. She tried the various chairs and lounges, as if she had never sat and reclined upon them before. And she perambulated around the outside of the house, investigating, looking to see if windows and shutters were secure and in order. The flowers were like new acquaintances; she approached them in a familiar spirit, and made herself at home among them. The garden walks were damp, and Edna called to the maid to bring out her rubber sandals. And there she stayed, and stooped, digging around the plants, trimming, picking dead, dry leaves. The children's little dog came out, interfering, getting in her way. She scolded him, laughed at him, played with him. The garden smelled so good and looked so pretty in the afternoon sunlight. Edna plucked all the bright flowers she could find, and went into the house with them, she and the little dog.

Even the kitchen assumed a sudden interesting character which she had never before perceived. She went in to give directions to the cook, to say that the butcher would have to bring much less meat, that they would require only half their usual quantity of bread, of milk and groceries. She told the cook that she herself would be greatly occupied during Mr. Pontellier's absence, and she begged her to take all thought and responsibility of the larder upon her own shoulders.

That night Edna dined alone. The candelabra, with a few candles in the center of the table, gave all the light she needed. Outside the circle of light in which she sat, the large dining-room looked solemn and shadowy. The cook, placed upon her mettle, served a delicious repast—a luscious tenderloin broiled *à point.*[58] The wine tasted good; the *marron glacé*[59] seemed to be just what she wanted. It was so pleasant, too, to dine in a comfortable *peignoir.*

She thought a little sentimentally about Léonce and the children, and wondered what they were doing. As she gave a dainty scrap or two to the doggie, she talked intimately to him about Etienne and Raoul. He was beside himself with astonishment and delight over these companionable advances, and showed his appreciation by his little quick, snappy barks and a lively agitation.

Then Edna sat in the library after dinner and read Emerson until she grew sleepy. She realized that she had neglected her reading, and determined to start anew upon a course of improving studies, now that her time was completely her own to do with as she liked.

After a refreshing bath, Edna went to bed. And as she snuggled comfortably beneath the eiderdown a sense of restfulness invaded her, such as she had not known before.

## XXV

When the weather was dark and cloudy Edna could not work. She needed the sun to mellow and temper her mood to the sticking point. She had reached a stage when she seemed to be no longer feeling her way, working,

[58]***à point*** to a turn
[59]***marron glacé*** glazed chestnuts

when in the humor, with sureness and ease. And being devoid of ambition, and striving not toward accomplishment, she drew satisfaction from the work in itself.

On rainy or melancholy days Edna went out and sought the society of the friends she had made at Grand Isle. Or else she stayed indoors and nursed a mood with which she was becoming too familiar for her own comfort and peace of mind. It was not despair; but it seemed to her as if life were passing by, leaving its promise broken and unfulfilled. Yet there were other days when she listened, was led on and deceived by fresh promises which her youth held out to her.

She went again to the races, and again. Alcée Arobin and Mrs. Highcamp called for her one bright afternoon in Arobin's drag.[60] Mrs. Highcamp was a worldly but unaffected, intelligent, slim, tall blonde woman in the forties, with an indifferent manner and blue eyes that stared. She had a daughter who served her as a pretext for cultivating the society of young men of fashion. Alcée Arobin was one of them. He was a familiar figure at the race course, the opera, the fashionable clubs. There was a perpetual smile in his eyes, which seldom failed to awaken a corresponding cheerfulness in any one who looked into them and listened to his good-humored voice. His manner was quiet, and at times a little insolent. He possessed a good figure, a pleasing face, not overburdened with depth of thought or feeling; and his dress was that of the conventional man of fashion.

He admired Edna extravagantly, after meeting her at the races with her father. He had met her before on other occasions, but she had seemed to him unapproachable until that day. It was at his instigation that Mrs. Highcamp called to ask her to go with them to the Jockey Club to witness the turf event of the season.

There were possibly a few track men out there who knew the race horse as well as Edna, but there was certainly none who knew it better. She sat between her two companions as one having authority to speak. She laughed at Arobin's pretensions, and deplored Mrs. Highcamp's ignorance. The race horse was a friend and intimate associate of her childhood. The atmosphere of the stable and the breath of the blue grass paddock revived in her memory and lingered in her nostrils. She did not perceive that she was talking like her father as the sleek geldings ambled in review before them. She played for very high stakes, and fortune favored her. The fever of the game flamed in her cheeks and eyes, and it got into her blood and into her brain like an intoxicant. People turned their heads to look at her, and more than one lent an attentive ear to her utterances, hoping thereby to secure the elusive but ever-desired "tip." Arobin caught the contagion of excitement which drew him to Edna like a magnet. Mrs. Highcamp remained, as usual, unmoved, with her indifferent stare and uplifted eyebrows.

Edna stayed and dined with Mrs. Highcamp upon being urged to do so. Arobin also remained and sent away his drag.

The dinner was quiet and uninteresting, save for the cheerful efforts of Arobin to enliven things. Mrs. Highcamp deplored the absence of her daughter from the races, and tried to convey to her what she had missed by

[60]**drag** heavy carriage

going to the "Dante[61] reading" instead of joining them. The girl held a geranium leaf up to her nose and said nothing, but looked knowing and noncommittal. Mr. Highcamp was a plain, bald-headed man, who only talked under compulsion. He was unresponsive. Mrs. Highcamp was full of delicate courtesy and consideration toward her husband. She addressed most of her conversation to him at table. They sat in the library after dinner and read the evening papers together under the droplight; while the younger people went into the drawing-room near by and talked. Miss Highcamp played some selections from Grieg[62] upon the piano. She seemed to have apprehended all of the composer's coldness and none of his poetry. While Edna listened she could not help wondering if she had lost her taste for music.

640 When the time came for her to go home, Mr. Highcamp grunted a lame offer to escort her, looking down at his slippered feet with tactless concern. It was Arobin who took her home. The car ride was long, and it was late when they reached Esplanade Street. Arobin asked permission to enter for a second to light his cigarette—his match safe[63] was empty. He filled his match safe, but did not light his cigarette until he left her, after she had expressed her willingness to go to the races with him again.

Edna was neither tired nor sleepy. She was hungry again, for the Highcamp dinner, though of excellent quality, had lacked abundance. She rummaged in the larder and brought forth a slice of Gruyère and some crackers. She opened a bottle of beer which she found in the icebox. Edna felt extremely restless and excited. She vacantly hummed a fantastic tune as she poked at the wood embers on the hearth and munched a cracker.

She wanted something to happen—something, anything; she did not know what. She regretted that she had not made Arobin stay a half hour to talk over the horses with her. She counted the money she had won. But there was nothing else to do, so she went to bed, and tossed there for hours in a sort of monotonous agitation.

In the middle of the night she remembered that she had forgotten to write her regular letter to her husband; and she decided to do so next day and tell him about her afternoon at the Jockey Club. She lay wide awake composing a letter which was nothing like the one which she wrote next day. When the maid awoke her in the morning Edna was dreaming of Mr. Highcamp playing the piano at the entrance of a music store on Canal Street, while his wife was saying to Alcée Arobin, as they boarded an Esplanade Street car:

"What a pity that so much talent has been neglected! but I must go."

645 When, a few days later, Alcée Arobin again called for Edna in his drag, Mrs. Highcamp was not with him. He said they would pick her up. But as that lady had not been apprised of his intention of picking her up, she was not at home. The daughter was just leaving the house to attend the meeting of a branch Folk Lore Society, and regretted that she could not accompany

[61]**Dante** Dante Alighieri (1265–1321), Italian poet
[62]**Grieg** Edvard Grieg (1843–1907), Norwegian composer
[63]**match safe** noncombustible box to hold friction matches

them. Arobin appeared nonplused, and asked Edna if there were any one else she cared to ask.

She did not deem it worth while to go in search of any of the fashionable acquaintances from whom she had withdrawn herself. She thought of Madame Ratignolle, but knew that her fair friend did not leave the house, except to take a languid walk around the block with her husband after nightfall. Mademoiselle Reisz would have laughed at such a request from Edna. Madame Lebrun might have enjoyed the outing, but for some reason Edna did not want her. So they went alone, she and Arobin.

The afternoon was intensely interesting to her. The excitement came back upon her like a remittent fever. Her talk grew familiar and confidential. It was no labor to become intimate with Arobin. His manner invited easy confidence. The preliminary stage of becoming acquainted was one which he always endeavored to ignore when a pretty and engaging woman was concerned.

He stayed and dined with Edna. He stayed and sat beside the wood fire. They laughed and talked; and before it was time to go he was telling her how different life might have been if he had known her years before. With ingenuous frankness he spoke of what a wicked, ill-disciplined boy he had been, and impulsively drew up his cuff to exhibit upon his wrist the scar from a saber cut which he had received in a duel outside of Paris when he was nineteen. She touched his hand as she scanned the red cicatrice[64] on the inside of his white wrist. A quick impulse that was somewhat spasmodic impelled her fingers to close in a sort of clutch upon his hand. He felt the pressure of her pointed nails in the flesh of his palm.

She arose hastily and walked toward the mantel.

"The sight of a wound or scar always agitates and sickens me," she said. "I shouldn't have looked at it."

"I beg your pardon," he entreated, following her; "it never occurred to me that it might be repulsive."

He stood close to her, and the effrontery in his eyes repelled the old, vanishing self in her, yet drew all her awakening sensuousness. He saw enough in her face to impel him to take her hand and hold it while he said his lingering good night.

"Will you go to the races again?" he asked.

"No," she said. "I've had enough of the races. I don't want to lose all the money I've won, and I've got to work when the weather is bright, instead of—"

"Yes; work; to be sure. You promised to show me your work. What morning may I come up to your atelier? To-morrow?"

"No!"

"Day after?"

"No, no."

"Oh, please don't refuse me! I know something of such things. I might help you with a stray suggestion or two."

"No. Good night. Why don't you go after you have said good night? I

[64]**cicatrice** scar

don't like you," she went on in a high, excited pitch, attempting to draw away her hand. She felt that her words lacked dignity and sincerity, and she knew that he felt it.

"I'm sorry you don't like me. I'm sorry I offended you. How have I offended you? What have I done? Can't you forgive me?" And he bent and pressed his lips upon her hand as if he wished never more to withdraw them.

"Mr. Arobin," she complained. "I'm greatly upset by the excitement of the afternoon; I'm not myself. My manner must have misled you in some way. I wish you to go, please." She spoke in a monotonous, dull tone. He took his hat from the table, and stood with eyes turned from her, looking into the dying fire. For a moment or two he kept an impressive silence.

"Your manner has not misled me, Mrs. Pontellier," he said finally. "My own emotions have done that. I couldn't help it. When I'm near you, how could I help it? Don't think anything of it, don't bother, please. You see, I go when you command me. If you wish me to stay away, I shall do so. If you let me come back, I—oh! you will let me come back?"

He cast one appealing glance at her, to which she made no response. Alcée Arobin's manner was so genuine that it often deceived even himself. Edna did not care or think whether it were genuine or not. When she was alone she looked mechanically at the back of her hand which he had kissed so warmly. Then she leaned her head down on the mantelpiece. She felt somewhat like a woman who in a moment of passion is betrayed into an act of infidelity, and realizes the significance of the act without being wholly awakened from its glamour. The thought was passing vaguely through her mind, "What would he think?"

She did not mean her husband; she was thinking of Robert Lebrun. Her husband seemed to her now like a person whom she had married without love as an excuse.

She lit a candle and went up to her room. Alcée Arobin was absolutely nothing to her. Yet his presence, his manners, the warmth of his glances, and above all the touch of his lips upon her hand had acted like a narcotic upon her.

She slept a languorous sleep, interwoven with vanishing dreams.

## XXVI

Alcée Arobin wrote Edna an elaborate note of apology, palpitant with sincerity. It embarrassed her; for in a cooler, quieter moment it appeared to her absurd that she should have taken his action so seriously, so dramatically. She felt sure that the significance of the whole occurrence had lain in her own self-consciousness. If she ignored his note it would give undue importance to a trivial affair. If she replied to it in a serious spirit it would still leave in his mind the impression that she had in a susceptible moment yielded to his influence. After all, it was no great matter to have one's hand kissed. She was provoked at his having written the apology. She answered in as light and bantering a spirit as she fancied it deserved, and said she would be glad to have him look in upon her at work whenever he felt the inclination and his business gave him the opportunity.

He responded at once by presenting himself at her home with all his disarming naïveté. And then there was scarcely a day which followed that she did not see him or was not reminded of him. He was prolific in pretexts. His attitude became one of good-humored subservience and tacit adoration. He was ready at all times to submit to her moods, which were as often kind as they were cold. She grew accustomed to him. They became intimate and friendly by imperceptible degrees, and then by leaps. He sometimes talked in a way that astonished her at first and brought the crimson into her face; in a way that pleased her at last, appealing to the animalism that stirred impatiently within her.

There was nothing which so quieted the turmoil in Edna's senses as a visit to Mademoiselle Reisz. It was then, in the presence of that personality which was offensive to her, that the woman, by her divine art, seemed to reach Edna's spirit and set it free.

It was misty, with heavy, lowering atmosphere, one afternoon, when Edna climbed the stairs to the pianist's apartments under the roof. Her clothes were dripping with moisture. She felt chilled and pinched as she entered the room. Mademoiselle was poking at a rusty stove that smoked a little and warmed the room indifferently. She was endeavoring to heat a pot of chocolate on the stove. The room looked cheerless and dingy to Edna as she entered. A bust of Beethoven, covered with a hood of dust, scowled at her from the mantelpiece.

"Ah! here comes the sunlight!" exclaimed Mademoiselle, rising from her knees before the stove. "Now it will be warm and bright enough; I can let the fire alone."

She closed the stove door with a bang, and approaching, assisted in removing Edna's dripping mackintosh.

675 "You are cold; you look miserable. The chocolate will soon be hot. But would you rather have a taste of brandy? I have scarcely touched the bottle which you brought me for my cold." A piece of red flannel was wrapped around Mademoiselle's throat; a stiff neck compelled her to hold her head on one side.

"I will take some brandy," said Edna, shivering as she removed her gloves and overshoes. She drank the liquor from the glass as a man would have done. Then flinging herself upon the uncomfortable sofa she said, "Mademoiselle, I am going to move away from my house on Esplanade Street."

"Ah!" ejaculated the musician, neither surprised nor especially interested. Nothing ever seemed to astonish her very much. She was endeavoring to adjust the bunch of violets which had become loose from its fastening in her hair. Edna drew her down upon the sofa, and taking a pin from her own hair, secured the shabby artificial flowers in their accustomed place.

"Aren't you astonished?"

"Passably. Where are you going? to New York? to Iberville? to your father in Mississippi? where?"

680 "Just two steps away," laughed Edna, "in a little four-room house around the corner. It looks so cozy, so inviting and restful, whenever I pass by; and it's for rent. I'm tired looking after that big house. It never seemed like mine, anyway—like home. It's too much trouble. I have to keep too many servants. I am tired bothering with them."

"That is not your true reason, *ma belle*. There is no use in telling me lies. I don't know your reason, but you have not told me the truth." Edna did not protest or endeavor to justify herself.

"The house, the money that provides for it, are not mine. Isn't that enough reason?"

"They are your husband's," returned Mademoiselle, with a shrug and a malicious elevation of the eyebrows.

"Oh! I see there is no deceiving you. Then let me tell you: It is a caprice. I have a little money of my own from my mother's estate, which my father sends me by driblets. I won a large sum this winter on the races, and I am beginning to sell my sketches. Laidpore is more and more pleased with my work; he says it grows in force and individuality. I cannot judge of that myself, but I feel that I have gained in ease and confidence. However, as I said, I have sold a good many through Laidpore. I can live in the tiny house for little or nothing, with one servant. Old Celestine, who works occasionally for me, says she will come stay with me and do my work. I know I shall like it, like the feeling of freedom and independence."

685 "What does your husband say?"

"I have not told him yet. I only thought of it this morning. He will think I am demented, no doubt. Perhaps you think so."

Mademoiselle shook her head slowly. "Your reason is not yet clear to me," she said.

Neither was it quite clear to Edna herself; but it unfolded itself as she sat for a while in silence. Instinct had prompted her to put away her husband's bounty in casting off her allegiance. She did not know how it would be when he returned. There would have to be an understanding, an explanation. Conditions would some way adjust themselves, she felt; but whatever came, she had resolved never again to belong to another than herself.

"I shall give a grand dinner before I leave the old house!" Edna exclaimed. "You will have to come to it, Mademoiselle. I will give you everything that you like to eat and drink. We shall sing and laugh and be merry for once." And she uttered a sigh that came from the very depths of her being.

690 If Mademoiselle happened to have received a letter from Robert during the interval of Edna's visits, she would give her the letter unsolicited. And she would seat herself at the piano and play as her humor prompted her while the young woman read the letter.

The little stove was roaring; it was red-hot, and the chocolate in the tin sizzled and sputtered. Edna went forward and opened the stove door, and Mademoiselle rising, took a letter from under the bust of Beethoven and handed it to Edna.

"Another! so soon!" she exclaimed, her eyes filled with delight. "Tell me, Mademoiselle, does he know that I see his letters?"

"Never in the world! He would be angry and would never write to me again if he thought so. Does he write to you? Never a line. Does he send you a message? Never a word. It is because he loves you, poor fool, and is trying to forget you, since you are not free to listen to him or to belong to him."

"Why do you show me his letters, then?"

695 "Haven't you begged for them? Can I refuse you anything? Oh! you cannot deceive me," and Mademoiselle approached her beloved instrument and began to play. Edna did not at once read the letter. She sat holding it in her hand, while the music penetrated her whole being like an effulgence,

warming and brightening the dark places of her soul. It prepared her for joy and exultation.

"Oh!" she exclaimed, letting the letter fall to the floor. "Why did you not tell me?" She went and grasped Mademoiselle's hands up from the keys. "Oh! unkind! malicious! Why did you not tell me?"

"That he was coming back? No great news, *ma foi.* I wonder he did not come long ago."

"But when, when?" cried Edna, impatiently. "He does not say when."

"He says 'very soon.' You know as much about it as I do; it is all in the letter."

"But why? Why is he coming? Oh, if I thought—" and she snatched the letter from the floor and turned the pages this way and that way, looking for the reason, which was left untold.

"If I were young and in love with a man," said Mademoiselle, turning on the stool and pressing her wiry hands between her knees as she looked down at Edna, who sat on the floor holding the letter, "it seems to me he would have to be some *grand esprit,*[65] a man with lofty aims and ability to reach them; one who stood high enough to attract the notice of his fellow-men. It seems to me if I were young and in love I should never deem a man of ordinary caliber worthy of my devotion."

"Now it is you who are telling lies and seeking to deceive me, Mademoiselle; or else you have never been in love, and know nothing about it. Why," went on Edna, clasping her knees and looking up into Mademoiselle's twisted face, "do you suppose a woman knows why she loves? Does she select? Does she say to herself: 'Go to! Here is a distinguished statesman with presidential possibilities; I shall proceed to fall in love with him.' Or, 'I shall set my heart upon this musician, whose fame is on every tongue?' Or, 'This financier, who controls the world's money markets?'"

"You are purposely misunderstanding me, *ma reine.*[66] Are you in love with Robert?"

"Yes," said Edna. It was the first time she had admitted it, and a glow overspread her face, blotching it with red spots.

"Why?" asked her companion. "Why do you love him when you ought not to?"

Edna, with a motion or two, dragged herself on her knees before Mademoiselle Reisz, who took the glowing face between her two hands.

"Why? Because his hair is brown and grows away from his temples; because he opens and shuts his eyes, and his nose is a little out of drawing; because he has two lips and a square chin, and a little finger which he can't straighten from having played baseball too energetically in his youth. Because—"

"Because you do, in short," laughed Mademoiselle. "What will you do when he comes back?" she asked.

"Do? Nothing, except feel glad and happy to be alive."

She was already glad and happy to be alive at the mere thought of his

[65]***grand esprit*** noble soul

[66]***ma reine*** my dear (literally, "my queen")

return. The murky, lowering sky, which had depressed her a few hours before, seemed bracing and invigorating as she splashed through the streets on her way home.

She stopped at a confectioner's and ordered a huge box of bonbons for the children in Iberville. She slipped a card in the box, on which she scribbled a tender message and sent an abundance of kisses.

Before dinner in the evening Edna wrote a charming letter to her husband, telling him of her intention to move for a while into the little house around the block, and to give a farewell dinner before leaving, regretting that he was not there to share it, to help her out with the menu and assist her in entertaining the guests. Her letter was brilliant and brimming with cheerfulness.

## *XXVII*

"What is the matter with you?" asked Arobin that evening. "I never found you in such a happy mood." Edna was tired by that time, and was reclining on the lounge before the fire.

"Don't you know the weather prophet has told us we shall see the sun pretty soon?"

715 "Well, that ought to be reason enough," he acquiesced. "You wouldn't give me another if I sat here all night imploring you." He sat close to her on a low tabouret, and as he spoke his fingers lightly touched the hair that fell a little over her forehead. She liked the touch of his fingers through her hair, and closed her eyes sensitively.

"One of these days," she said, "I'm going to pull myself together for a while and think—try to determine what character of a woman I am; for, candidly, I don't know. By all the codes which I am acquainted with, I am a devilishly wicked specimen of the sex. But some way I can't convince myself that I am. I must think about it."

"Don't. What's the use? Why should you bother thinking about it when I can tell you what manner of woman you are." His fingers strayed occasionally down to her warm, smooth cheeks and firm chin, which was growing a little full and double.

"Oh, yes! You will tell me that I am adorable; everything that is captivating. Spare yourself the effort."

"No; I shan't tell you anything of the sort, though I shouldn't be lying if I did."

720 "Do you know Mademoiselle Reisz?" she asked irrelevantly.

"The pianist? I know her by sight. I've heard her play."

"She says queer things sometimes in a bantering way that you don't notice at the time and you find yourself thinking about afterward."

"For instance?"

"Well, for instance, when I left her to-day, she put her arms around me and felt my shoulder blades, to see if my wings were strong, she said. 'The bird that would soar above the level plain of tradition and prejudice must have strong wings. It is a sad spectacle to see the weaklings bruised, exhausted, fluttering back to earth.'"

725 "Whither would you soar?"

"I'm not thinking of any extraordinary flights. I only half comprehend her."

"I've heard she's partially demented," said Arobin.

"She seems to me wonderfully sane," Edna replied.

"I'm told she's extremely disagreeable and unpleasant. Why have you introduced her at a moment when I desired to talk of you?"

"Oh! talk of me if you like," cried Edna, clasping her hands beneath her head; "but let me think of something else while you do."

"I'm jealous of your thoughts to-night. They're making you a little kinder than usual; but some way I feel as if they were wandering, as if they were not here with me." She only looked at him and smiled. His eyes were very near. He leaned upon the lounge with an arm extended across her, while the other hand still rested upon her hair. They continued silently to look into each other's eyes. When he leaned forward and kissed her, she clasped his head, holding his lips to hers.

It was the first kiss of her life to which her nature had really responded. It was a flaming torch that kindled desire.

## *XXVIII*

Edna cried a little that night after Arobin left her. It was only one phase of the multitudinous emotions which had assailed her. There was with her an overwhelming feeling of irresponsibility. There was the shock of the unexpected and the unaccustomed. There was her husband's reproach looking at her from the external things around her which he had provided for her external existence. There was Robert's reproach making itself felt by a quicker, fiercer, more overpowering love, which had awakened within her toward him. Above all, there was understanding. She felt as if a mist had been lifted from her eyes, enabling her to look upon and comprehend the significance of life, that monster made up of beauty and brutality. But among the conflicting sensations which assailed her, there was neither shame nor remorse. There was a dull pang of regret because it was not the kiss of love which had inflamed her, because it was not love which had held this cup of life to her lips.

## *XXIX*

Without even waiting for an answer from her husband regarding his opinion or wishes in the matter, Edna hastened her preparations for quitting her home on Esplanade Street and moving into the little house around the block. A feverish anxiety attended her every action in that direction. There was no moment of deliberation, no interval of repose between the thought and its fulfillment. Early upon the morning following those hours passed in Arobin's society, Edna set about securing her new abode and hurrying her arrangements for occupying it. Within the precincts of her home she felt like one who has entered and lingered within the portals of some forbidden temple in which a thousand muffled voices bade her begone.

Whatever was her own in the house, everything she had acquired aside from her husband's bounty, she caused to be transported to the other house, supplying simple and meager deficiencies from her own resources.

Arobin found her with rolled sleeves, working in company with the house-maid when he looked in during the afternoon. She was splendid and robust, and had never appeared handsomer than in the old blue gown, with a red silk handkerchief knotted at random around her head to protect her hair from the dust. She was mounted upon a high step-ladder, unhooking a picture from the wall when he entered. He had found the front door open, and had followed his ring by walking in unceremoniously.

"Come down!" he said. "Do you want to kill yourself?" She greeted him with affected carelessness, and appeared absorbed in her occupation.

If he had expected to find her languishing, reproachful, or indulging in sentimental tears, he must have been greatly surprised.

He was no doubt prepared for any emergency, ready for any one of the foregoing attitudes, just as he bent himself easily and naturally to the situation which confronted him.

"Please come down," he insisted, holding the ladder and looking up at her.

"No," she answered; "Ellen is afraid to mount the ladder. Joe is working over at the 'pigeon house'—that's the name Ellen gives it, because it's so small and looks like a pigeon house—and some one has to do this."

Arobin pulled off his coat, and expressed himself ready and willing to tempt fate in her place. Ellen brought him one of her dust-caps, and went into contortions of mirth, which she found it impossible to control, when she saw him put it on before the mirror as grotesquely as he could. Edna herself could not refrain from smiling when she fastened it at his request. So it was he who in turn mounted the ladder, unhooking pictures and curtains, and dislodging ornaments as Edna directed. When he had finished he took off his dust-cap and went out to wash his hands.

Edna was sitting on the tabouret, idly brushing the tips of a feather duster along the carpet when he came in again.

"Is there anything more you will let me do?" he asked.

"That is all," she answered. "Ellen can manage the rest." She kept the young woman occupied in the drawing-room, unwilling to be left alone with Arobin.

"What about the dinner?" he asked; "the grand event, the *coup d'état?*"

"It will be day after to-morrow. Why do you call it the *'coup d'état?'* Oh! it will be very fine; all my best of everything—crystal, silver and gold, Sèvres, flowers, music, and champagne to swim in. I'll let Léonce pay the bills. I wonder what he'll say when he sees the bills."

"And you ask me why I call it a *coup d'état?*" Arobin put on his coat, and he stood before her and asked if his cravat was plumb. She told him it was, looking no higher than the tip of his collar.

"When do you go to the 'pigeon house?'—with all due acknowledgement to Ellen."

"Day after to-morrow, after the dinner. I shall sleep there."

"Ellen, will you very kindly get me a glass of water?" asked Arobin. "The dust in the curtains, if you will pardon me for hinting such a thing, has parched my throat to a crisp."

"While Ellen gets the water," said Edna, rising, "I will say good-by and let you go. I must get rid of this grime, and I have a million things to do and think of."

"When shall I see you?" asked Arobin, seeking to detain her, the maid having left the room.

"At the dinner, of course. You are invited."

"Not before?—not to-night or to-morrow morning or to-morrow noon or night? or the day after morning or noon? Can't you see yourself, without my telling you, what an eternity it is?"

He had followed her into the hall and to the foot of the stairway, looking up at her as she mounted with her face half turned to him.

"Not an instant sooner," she said. But she laughed and looked at him with eyes that at once gave him courage to wait and made it torture to wait.

## XXX

Though Edna had spoken of the dinner as a grand affair, it was in truth a very small affair and very select, in so much as the guests invited were few and were selected with discrimination. She had counted upon an even dozen seating themselves at her round mahogany board, forgetting for the moment that Madame Ratignolle was to the last degree *souffrante*[67] and unpresentable, and not foreseeing that Madame Lebrun would send a thousand regrets at the last moment. So there were only ten, after all, which made a cozy, comfortable number.

There were Mr. and Mrs. Merriman, a pretty, vivacious little woman in the thirties; her husband, a jovial fellow, something of a shallow-pate, who laughed a good deal at other people's witticisms, and had thereby made himself extremely popular. Mrs. Highcamp had accompanied them. Of course, there was Alcée Arobin; and Mademoiselle Reisz had consented to come. Edna had sent her a fresh bunch of violets with black lace trimmings for her hair. Monsieur Ratignolle brought himself and his wife's excuses. Victor Lebrun, who happened to be in the city, bent upon relaxation, had accepted with alacrity. There was a Miss Mayblunt, no longer in her teens, who looked at the world through lorgnettes and with the keenest interest. It was thought and said that she was intellectual; it was suspected of her that she wrote under a *nom de guerre.*[68] She had come with a gentleman by the name of Gouvernail, connected with one of the daily papers, of whom nothing special could be said, except that he was observant and seemed quiet and inoffensive. Edna herself made the tenth, and at half-past eight they seated themselves at table, Arobin and Monsieur Ratignolle on either side of their hostess.

Mrs. Highcamp sat between Arobin and Victor Lebrun. Then came Mrs. Merriman, Mr. Gouvernail, Miss Mayblunt, Mr. Merriman, and Mademoiselle Reisz next to Monsieur Ratignolle.

There was something extremely gorgeous about the appearance of the table, an effect of splendor conveyed by a cover of pale yellow satin under strips of lacework. There were wax candles in massive brass candelabra, burning softly under yellow silk shades; full, fragrant roses, yellow and red, abounded. There were silver and gold, as she had said there would be, and crystal which glittered like the gems which the women wore.

The ordinary stiff dining chairs had been discarded for the occasion and replaced by the most commodious and luxurious which could be collected throughout the house. Mademoiselle Reisz, being exceedingly diminutive, was elevated upon cushions, as small children are sometimes hoisted at table upon bulky volumes.

[67] ***souffrante*** ill

[68] ***nom de guerre*** pseudonym (literally, "war name")

"Something new, Edna?" exclaimed Miss Mayblunt, with lorgnette directed toward a magnificent cluster of diamonds that sparkled, that almost sputtered, in Edna's hair, just over the center of her forehead.

"Quite new; 'brand' new, in fact; a present from my husband. It arrived this morning from New York. I may as well admit that this is my birthday, and that I am twenty-nine. In good time I expect you to drink my health. Meanwhile, I shall ask you to begin with this cocktail, composed—would you say 'composed?'" with an appeal to Miss Mayblunt—"composed by my father in honor of Sister Janet's wedding."

765 Before each guest stood a tiny glass that looked and sparkled like a garnet gem.

"Then, all things considered," spoke Arobin, "it might not be amiss to start out by drinking the Colonel's health in the cocktail which he composed, on the birthday of the most charming of women—the daughter whom he invented."

Mr. Merriman's laugh at this sally was such a genuine outburst and so contagious that it started the dinner with an agreeable swing that never slackened.

Miss Mayblunt begged to be allowed to keep her cocktail untouched before her, just to look at. The color was marvelous! She could compare it to nothing she had ever seen, and the garnet lights which it emitted were unspeakably rare. She pronounced the Colonel an artist, and stuck to it.

Monsieur Ratignolle was prepared to take things seriously: the *mets*, the *entremets*,[69] the service, the decorations, even the people. He looked up from his pompano[70] and inquired of Arobin if he were related to the gentleman of that name who formed one of the firm of Laitner and Arobin, lawyers. The young man admitted that Laitner was a warm personal friend, who permitted Arobin's name to decorate the firm's letterheads and to appear upon a shingle that graced Perdido Street.

770 "There are so many inquisitive people and institutions abounding," said Arobin, "that one is really forced as a matter of convenience these days to assume the virtue of an occupation if he has it not."

Monsieur Ratignolle stared a little, and turned to ask Mademoiselle Reisz if she considered the symphony concerts up to the standard which had been set the previous winter. Mademoiselle Reisz answered Monsieur Ratignolle in French, which Edna thought a little rude, under the circumstances, but characteristic. Mademoiselle had only disagreeable things to say of the symphony concerts, and insulting remarks to make of all the musicians of New Orleans, singly and collectively. All her interest seemed to be centered upon the delicacies placed before her.

Mr. Merriman said that Mr. Arobin's remark about inquisitive people reminded him of a man from Waco the other day at the St. Charles Hotel—but as Mr. Merriman's stories were always lame and lacking point, his wife seldom permitted him to complete them. She interrupted him to ask if he remembered the name of the author whose book she had bought the week before to send to a friend in Geneva. She was talking "books" with Mr. Gouvernail and trying to draw from him his opinion upon current literary top-

[69]***mets . . . entre-mets*** main courses . . . side dishes
[70]**pompano** kind of fish

ics. Her husband told the story of the Waco man privately to Miss Mayblunt, who pretended to be greatly amused and to think it extremely clever.

Mrs. Highcamp hung with languid but unaffected interest upon the warm and impetuous volubility of her left-hand neighbor, Victor Lebrun. Her attention was never for a moment withdrawn from him after seating herself at table; and when he turned to Mrs. Merriman, who was prettier and more vivacious than Mrs. Highcamp, she waited with easy indifference for an opportunity to reclaim his attention. There was the occasional sound of music, of mandolins, sufficiently removed to be an agreeable accompaniment rather than an interruption to the conversation. Outside the soft, monotonous splash of a fountain could be heard; the sound penetrated into the room with the heavy odor of jessamine that came through the open windows.

The golden shimmer of Edna's satin gown spread in rich folds on either side of her. There was a soft fall of lace encircling her shoulders. It was the color of her skin, without the glow, the myriad living tints that one may sometimes discover in vibrant flesh. There was something in her attitude, in her whole appearance when she leaned her head against the high-backed chair and spread her arms, which suggested the regal woman, the one who rules, who looks on, who stands alone.

But as she sat there amid her guests, she felt the old ennui overtaking her; the hopelessness which so often assailed her, which came upon her like an obsession, like something extraneous, independent of volition. It was something which announced itself; a chill breath that seemed to issue from some vast cavern wherein discords wailed. There came over her the acute longing which always summoned into her spiritual vision the presence of the beloved one, overpowering her at once with a sense of the unattainable.

The moments glided on, while a feeling of good fellowship passed around the circle like a mystic cord, holding and binding these people together with jest and laughter. Monsieur Ratignolle was the first to break the pleasant charm. At ten o'clock he excused himself. Madame Ratignolle was waiting for him at home. She was *bien souffrante,*[71] and she was filled with vague dread, which only her husband's presence could allay.

Mademoiselle Reisz arose with Monsieur Ratignolle, who offered to escort her to the car. She had eaten well; she had tasted the good, rich wines, and they must have turned her head, for she bowed pleasantly to all as she withdrew from table. She kissed Edna upon the shoulder, and whispered: *"Bonne nuit, ma reine; soyez sage."*[72] She had been a little bewildered upon rising, or rather, descending from her cushions, and Monsieur Ratignolle gallantly took her arm and led her away.

Mrs. Highcamp was weaving a garland of roses, yellow and red. When she had finished the garland, she laid it lightly upon Victor's black curls. He was reclining far back in the luxurious chair, holding a glass of champagne to the light.

As if a magician's wand had touched him, the garland of roses transformed him into a vision of Oriental beauty. His cheeks were the color of crushed grapes, and his dusky eyes glowed with a languishing fire.

[71]***bien souffrante*** very ill

[72]***Bonne . . . sage*** Good night, my love; be good.

*"Sapristi!"* exclaimed Arobin.

But Mrs. Highcamp had one more touch to add to the picture. She took from the back of her chair a white silken scarf, with which she had covered her shoulders in the early part of the evening. She draped it across the boy in graceful folds, and in a way to conceal his black, conventional evening dress. He did not seem to mind what she did to him, only smiled showing a faint gleam of white teeth, while he continued to gaze with narrowing eyes at the light through his glass of champagne.

"Oh! to be able to paint in color rather than in words!" exclaimed Miss Mayblunt, losing herself in a rhapsodic dream as she looked at him.

"'There was a graven image of Desire
Painted with red blood on a ground of gold.'"[73]

murmured Gouvernail, under his breath.

The effect of the wine upon Victor was to change his accustomed volubility into silence. He seemed to have abandoned himself to a reverie, and to be seeing pleasing visions in the amber bead.

"Sing," entreated Mrs. Highcamp. "Won't you sing to us?"

"Let him alone," said Arobin.

"He's posing," offered Mr. Merriman; "let him have it out."

"I believe he's paralyzed," laughed Mrs. Merriman. And leaning over the youth's chair, she took the glass from his hand and held it to his lips. He sipped the wine slowly, and when he had drained the glass she laid it upon the table and wiped his lips with her little filmy handkerchief.

"Yes, I'll sing for you," he said, turning in his chair toward Mrs. Highcamp. He clasped his hands behind his head, and looking up at the ceiling began to hum a little, trying his voice like a musician tuning an instrument. Then, looking at Edna, he began to sing:

"Ah! si tu savais!"

"Stop!" she cried, "don't sing that. I don't want you to sing it," and she laid her glass so impetuously and blindly upon the table as to shatter it against a carafe. The wine spilled over Arobin's legs and some of it trickled down upon Mrs. Highcamp's black gauze gown. Victor had lost all idea of courtesy, or else he thought his hostess was not in earnest, for he laughed and went on:

"Ah! si tu savais
Ce que tes yeux me disent"—[74]

"Oh! you mustn't! you mustn't," exclaimed Edna, and pushing back her chair she got up, and going behind him placed her hand over his mouth. He kissed the soft palm that pressed upon his lips.

"No, no, I won't, Mrs. Pontellier. I didn't know you meant it," looking up at her with caressing eyes. The touch of his lips was like a pleasing sting to her hand. She lifted the garland of roses from his head and flung it across the room.

[73]***"There was . . . gold"*** *first two lines of a sonnet entitled "A Cameo," by the English poet Algernon Charles Swinburne (1837–1909)*
[74]***Ab! . . . disent*** *"Oh, if you only knew what your eyes tell me"*

"Come, Victor; you've posed long enough. Give Mrs. Highcamp her scarf."

Mrs. Highcamp undraped her scarf from about him with her own hands. Miss Mayblunt and Mr. Gouvernail suddenly conceived the notion that it was time to say good night. And Mr. and Mrs. Merriman wondered how it could be so late.

Before parting from Victor, Mrs. Highcamp invited him to call upon her daughter, who she knew would be charmed to meet him and talk French and sing French songs with him. Victor expressed his desire and intention to call upon Miss Highcamp at the first opportunity which presented itself. He asked if Arobin were going his way. Arobin was not.

The mandolin players had long since stolen away. A profound stillness had fallen upon the broad, beautiful street. The voices of Edna's disbanding guests jarred like a discordant note upon the quiet harmony of the night.

## XXXI

"Well?" questioned Arobin, who had remained with Edna after the others had departed.

"Well," she reiterated, and stood up, stretching her arms, and feeling the need to relax her muscles after having been so long seated.

"What next?" he asked.

"The servants are all gone. They left when the musicians did. I have dismissed them. The house has to be closed and locked, and I shall trot around to the pigeon house, and shall send Celestine over in the morning to straighten things up."

He looked around, and began to turn out some of the lights.

"What about upstairs?" he inquired.

"I think it is all right; but there may be a window or two unlatched. We had better look; you might take a candle and see. And bring me my wrap and hat on the foot of the bed in the middle room."

He went up with the light, and Edna began closing doors and windows. She hated to shut in the smoke and the fumes of the wine. Arobin found her cape and hat, which he brought down and helped her to put on.

When everything was secured and the lights put out, they left through the front door, Arobin locking it and taking the key, which he carried for Edna. He helped her down the steps.

"Will you have a spray of jessamine?" he asked, breaking off a few blossoms as he passed.

"No; I don't want anything."

She seemed disheartened, and had nothing to say. She took his arm, which he offered her, holding up the weight of her satin gown with the other hand. She looked down, noticing the black line of his leg moving in and out so close to her against the yellow shimmer of her gown. There was the whistle of a railway train somewhere in the distance, and the midnight bells were ringing. They met no one in their short walk.

The "pigeon-house" stood behind a locked gate, and a shallow *parterre*[75] that had been somewhat neglected. There was a small front

[75]***parterre*** garden with geometric flower-beds and paths

porch, upon which a long window and the front door opened. The door opened directly into the parlor; there was no side entry. Back in the yard was a room for servants, in which old Celestine had been ensconced.

Edna had left a lamp burning low upon the table. She had succeeded in making the room look habitable and homelike. There were some books on the table and a lounge near at hand. On the floor was a fresh matting, covered with a rug or two; and on the walls hung a few tasteful pictures. But the room was filled with flowers. These were a surprise to her. Arobin had sent them, and had had Celestine distribute them during Edna's absence. Her bedroom was adjoining, and across a small passage were the dining-room and kitchen.

Edna seated herself with every appearance of discomfort.

"Are you tired?" he asked.

"Yes, and chilled, and miserable. I feel as if I had been wound up to a certain pitch—too tight—and something inside of me had snapped."

She had rested her head against the table upon her bare arm.

"You want to rest," he said, "and to be quiet. I'll go; I'll leave you and let you rest."

"Yes," she replied.

He stood up beside her and smoothed her hair with his soft, magnetic hand. His touch conveyed to her a certain physical comfort. She could have fallen quietly asleep there if he had continued to pass his hand over her hair. He brushed the hair upward from the nape of her neck.

"I hope you will feel better and happier in the morning," he said. "You have tried to do too much in the past few days. The dinner was the last straw; you might have dispensed with it."

"Yes," she admitted; "it was stupid."

"No, it was delightful; but it has worn you out." His hand strayed to her beautiful shoulders, and he could feel the response of her flesh to his touch. He seated himself beside her and kissed her lightly on the shoulder.

"I thought you were going away," she said, in an uneven voice.

"I am, after I have said good night."

"Good night," she murmured.

He did not answer, except to continue to caress her. He did not say good night until she had become supple to his gentle, seductive entreaties.

## *XXXII*

When Mr. Pontellier learned of his wife's intention to abandon her home and take up her residence elsewhere he immediately wrote her a letter of unqualified disapproval and remonstrance. She had given reasons which he was unwilling to acknowledge as adequate. He hoped she had not acted upon her rash impulse; and he begged her to consider first, foremost, and above all else, what people would say. He was not dreaming of scandal when he uttered this warning; that was a thing which would never have entered into his mind to consider in connection with his wife's name or his own. He was simply thinking of his financial integrity. It might get noised about that the Pontelliers had met with reverses, and were forced to conduct their *ménage*[76] on a humbler scale than heretofore. It might do incalculable mischief to his business prospects.

[76]***ménage*** household

825 But remembering Edna's whimsical turn of mind of late, and foreseeing that she had immediately acted upon her impetuous determination, he grasped the situation with his usual promptness and handled it with his well-known business tact and cleverness.

The same mail which brought to Edna his letter of disapproval carried instructions—the most minute instructions—to a well-known architect concerning the remodeling of his home, changes which he had long contemplated, and which he desired carried forward during his temporary absence.

Expert and reliable packers and movers were engaged to convey the furniture, carpets, pictures—everything movable, in short—to places of security. And in an incredibly short time the Pontellier house was turned over to the artisans. There was to be an addition—a small snuggery; there was to be frescoing, and hardwood flooring was to be put into such rooms as had not yet been subjected to this improvement.

Furthermore, in one of the daily papers appeared a brief notice to the effect that Mr. and Mrs. Pontellier were contemplating a summer sojourn abroad, and that their handsome residence on Esplanade Street was undergoing sumptuous alterations, and would not be ready for occupancy until their return. Mr. Pontellier had saved appearances!

Edna admired the skill of his maneuver, and avoided any occasion to balk his intentions. When the situation as set forth by Mr. Pontellier was accepted and taken for granted, she was apparently satisfied that it should be so.

830 The pigeon-house pleased her. It at once assumed the intimate character of a home, while she herself invested it with a charm which it reflected like a warm glow. There was with her a feeling of having descended in the social scale, with a corresponding sense of having risen in the spiritual. Every step which she took toward relieving herself from obligations added to her strength and expansion as an individual. She began to look with her own eyes; to see and to apprehend the deeper undercurrents of life. No longer was she content to "feed upon opinion" when her own soul had invited her.

After a little while, a few days, in fact, Edna went up and spent a week with her children in Iberville. They were delicious February days, with all the summer's promise hovering in the air.

How glad she was to see the children! She wept for very pleasure when she felt their little arms clasping her; their hard, ruddy cheeks pressed against her own glowing cheeks. She looked into their faces with hungry eyes that could not be satisfied with looking. And what stories they had to tell their mother! About the pigs, the cows, the mules! About riding to the mill behind Gluglu; fishing back in the lake with their Uncle Jasper; picking pecans with Lidie's little black brood, and hauling chips in their little express wagon. It was a thousand times more fun to haul real chips for old lame Susie's real fire than to drag painted blocks along the banquette on Esplanade Street!

She went with them herself to see the pigs and the cows, to look at the darkies laying the cane, to thrash the pecan trees, and catch fish in the back lake. She lived with them a whole week long, giving them all of herself, and gathering and filling herself with their young existence. They listened, breathless, when she told them the house in Esplanade Street was crowded with workmen, hammering, nailing, sawing, and filling the place with clatter. They wanted to know where their bed was; what had been done with their rocking-horse; and where did Joe sleep, and where had Ellen gone, and the cook? But, above all, they were fired with a desire to see the little house around the block. Was there any place to play? Were there any boys next door? Raoul, with pessimistic foreboding, was convinced that there were only girls next door. Where would they sleep, and where would papa sleep? She told them the fairies would fix it all right.

The old Madame was charmed with Edna's visit, and showered all manner of delicate attentions upon her. She was delighted to know that the Esplanade Street house was in a dismantled condition. It gave her the promise and pretext to keep the children indefinitely.

835 It was with a wrench and a pang that Edna left her children. She carried away with her the sound of their voices and the touch of their cheeks. All along the journey homeward their presence lingered with her like the memory of a delicious song. But by the time she had regained the city the song no longer echoed in her soul. She was again alone.

## *XXXIII*

It happened sometimes when Edna went to see Mademoiselle Reisz that the little musician was absent, giving a lesson or making some small necessary household purchase. The key was always left in a secret hiding-place in the entry, which Edna knew. If Mademoiselle happened to be away, Edna would usually enter and wait for her return.

When she knocked at Mademoiselle Reisz's door one afternoon there was no response; so unlocking the door, as usual, she entered and found the apartment deserted, as she had expected. Her day had been quite filled up, and it was for a rest, for a refuge, and to talk about Robert, that she sought out her friend.

She had worked at her canvas—a young Italian character study—all the morning, completing the work without the model; but there had been many interruptions, some incident to her modest housekeeping, and others of a social nature.

Madame Ratignolle had dragged herself over, avoiding the too public thoroughfares, she said. She complained that Edna had neglected her much of late. Besides, she was consumed with curiosity to see the little house and the manner in which it was conducted. She wanted to hear all about the dinner party; Monsieur Ratignolle had left *so* early. What had happened after he left? The champagne and grapes which Edna sent over were *too* delicious. She had so little appetite; they had refreshed and toned her stomach. Where on earth was she going to put Mr. Pontellier in that little house, and the boys? And then she made Edna promise to go to her when her hour of trial overtook her.

840 "At any time—any time of the day or night, dear," Edna assured her.

Before leaving Madame Ratignolle said:

"In some way you seem to me like a child, Edna. You seem to act without a certain amount of reflection which is necessary in this life. That is the reason I want to say you mustn't mind if I advise you to be a little careful while you are living here alone. Why don't you have some one come and stay with you? Wouldn't Mademoiselle Reisz come?"

"No; she wouldn't wish to come, and I shouldn't want her always with me."

"Well, the reason—you know how evil-minded the world is—some one was talking of Alcée Arobin visiting you. Of course, it wouldn't matter if Mr. Arobin had not such a dreadful reputation. Monsieur Ratignolle was telling me that his attentions alone are considered enough to ruin a woman's name."

845 "Does he boast of his successes?" asked Edna, indifferently, squinting at her picture.

"No, I think not. I believe he is a decent fellow as far as that goes. But his character is so well known among the men. I shan't be able to come back and see you; it was very, very imprudent to-day."

"Mind the step!" cried Edna.

"Don't neglect me," entreated Madame Ratignolle; "and don't mind what I said about Arobin, or having some one to stay with you."

"Of course not," Edna laughed. "You may say anything you like to me." They kissed each other good-by. Madame Ratignolle had not far to go, and Edna stood on the porch a while watching her walk down the street.

850 Then in the afternoon Mrs. Merriman and Mrs. Highcamp had made their "party call." Edna felt that they might have dispensed with the formality. They had also come to invite her to play *vingt-et-un*[77] one evening at Mrs. Merriman's. She was asked to go early, to dinner, and Mr. Merriman or Mr. Arobin would take her home. Edna accepted in a half-hearted way. She sometimes felt very tired of Mrs. Highcamp and Mrs. Merriman.

Late in the afternoon she sought refuge with Mademoiselle Reisz, and stayed there alone, waiting for her, feeling a kind of repose invade her with the very atmosphere of the shabby, unpretentious little room.

Edna sat at the window, which looked out over the house-tops and across the river. The window frame was filled with pots of flowers, and she sat and picked the dry leaves from a rose geranium. The day was warm, and the breeze which blew from the river was very pleasant. She removed her hat and laid it on the piano. She went on picking the leaves and digging around the plants with her hat pin. Once she thought she heard Mademoiselle Reisz approaching. But it was a young black girl, who came in, bringing a small bundle of laundry, which she deposited in the adjoining room, and went away.

Edna seated herself at the piano, and softly picked out with one hand the bars of a piece of music which lay open before her. A half-hour went by. There was the occasional sound of people going and coming in the lower hall. She was growing interested in her occupation of picking out the aria, when there was a second rap at the door. She vaguely wondered what these people did when they found Mademoiselle's door locked.

"Come in," she called, turning her face toward the door. And this time it was Robert Lebrun who presented himself. She attempted to rise; she could not have done so without betraying the agitation which mastered her at sight of him, so she fell back upon the stool, only exclaiming, "Why, Robert!"

855 He came and clasped her hand, seemingly without knowing what he was saying or doing.

"Mrs. Pontellier! How do you happen—oh! how well you look! Is Mademoiselle Reisz not here? I never expected to see you."

[77]***vingt-et-un*** twenty-one (card game)

"When did you come back?" asked Edna in an unsteady voice, wiping her face with her handkerchief. She seemed ill at ease on the piano stool, and he begged her to take the chair by the window. She did so, mechanically, while he seated himself on the stool.

"I returned day before yesterday," he answered, while he leaned his arm on the keys, bringing forth a crash of discordant sound.

"Day before yesterday!" she repeated, aloud; and went on thinking to herself, "day before yesterday," in a sort of an uncomprehending way. She had pictured him seeking her at the very first hour, and he had lived under the same sky since day before yesterday; while only by accident had he stumbled upon her. Mademoiselle must have lied when she said, "Poor fool, he loves you."

860 "Day before yesterday," she repeated, breaking off a spray of Mademoiselle's geranium; "then if you had not met me here to-day you wouldn't—when—that is, didn't you mean to come and see me?"

"Of course, I should have gone to see you. There have been so many things—" he turned the leaves of Mademoiselle's music nervously. "I started in at once yesterday with the old firm. After all there is as much chance for me here as there was there—that is, I might find it profitable some day. The Mexicans were not very congenial."

So he had come back because the Mexicans were not congenial; because business was as profitable here as there; because of reason, and not because he cared to be near her. She remembered the day she sat on the floor, turning the pages of his letter, seeking the reason which was left untold.

She had not noticed how he looked—only feeling his presence; but she turned deliberately and observed him. After all, he had been absent but a few months, and was not changed. His hair—the color of hers—waved back from his temples in the same way as before. His skin was not more burned than it had been at Grand Isle. She found in his eyes, when he looked at her for one silent moment, the same tender caress, with an added warmth and entreaty which had not been there before—the same glance which had penetrated to the sleeping places of her soul and awakened them.

A hundred times Edna had pictured Robert's return, and imagined their first meeting. It was usually at her home, whither he had sought her out at once. She always fancied him expressing or betraying in some way his love for her. And here, the reality was that they sat ten feet apart, she at the window, crushing geranium leaves in her hand and smelling them, he twirling around on the piano stool, saying:

865 "I was very much surprised to hear of Mr. Pontellier's absence; it's a wonder Mademoiselle Reisz did not tell me; and your moving—mother told me yesterday. I should think you would have gone to New York with him, or to Iberville with the children, rather than be bothered here with housekeeping. And you are going abroad, too, I hear. We shan't have you at Grand Isle next summer; it won't seem—do you see much of Mademoiselle Reisz? She often spoke of you in the few letters she wrote."

"Do you remember that you promised to write to me when you went away?" A flush overspread his whole face.

"I couldn't believe that my letters would be of any interest to you."

"That is an excuse; it isn't the truth." Edna reached for her hat on the piano. She adjusted it, sticking the hat pin through the heavy coil of hair with some deliberation.

"Are you not going to wait for Mademoiselle Reisz?" asked Robert.

"No; I have found when she is absent this long, she is liable not to come back till late." She drew on her gloves, and Robert picked up his hat.

"Won't you wait for her?" asked Edna.

"Not if you think she will not be back till late," adding, as if suddenly aware of some discourtesy in his speech, "and I should miss the pleasure of walking home with you." Edna locked the door and put the key back in its hiding-place.

They went together, picking their way across muddy streets and sidewalks encumbered with the cheap display of small tradesmen. Part of the distance they rode in the car, and after disembarking, passed the Pontellier mansion, which looked broken and half torn asunder. Robert had never known the house, and looked at it with interest.

"I never knew you in your home," he remarked.

"I am glad you did not."

"Why?" She did not answer. They went on around the corner, and it seemed as if her dreams were coming true after all, when he followed her into the little house.

"You must stay and dine with me, Robert. You see I am all alone, and it is so long since I have seen you. There is so much I want to ask you."

She took off her hat and gloves. He stood irresolute, making some excuse about his mother who expected him; he even muttered something about an engagement. She struck a match and lit the lamp in the table; it was growing dusk. When he saw her face in the lamp-light, looking pained, with all the soft lines gone out of it, he threw his hat aside and seated himself.

"Oh! you know I want to stay if you will let me!" he exclaimed. All the softness came back. She laughed, and went and put her hand on his shoulder.

"This is the first moment you have seemed like the old Robert. I'll go tell Celestine." She hurried away to tell Celestine to set an extra place. She even sent her off in search of some added delicacy which she had not thought of for herself. And she recommended great care in dripping the coffee and having the omelet done to a proper turn.

When she reentered, Robert was turning over magazines, sketches and things that lay upon the table in great disorder. He picked up a photograph, and exclaimed:

"Alcée Arobin! What on earth is his picture doing here?"

"I tried to make a sketch of his head one day," answered Edna, "and he thought the photograph might help me. It was at the other house. I thought it had been left there. I must have picked it up with my drawing materials."

"I should think you would give it back to him if you have finished with it."

"Oh! I have a great many such photographs. I never think of returning them. They don't amount to anything." Robert kept on looking at the picture.

"It seems to me—do you think his head worth drawing? Is he a friend of Mr. Pontellier's? You never said you knew him."

"He isn't a friend of Mr. Pontellier's; he's a friend of mine. I always knew him—that is, it is only of late that I know him pretty well. But I'd rather talk about you, and know what you have been seeing and doing and feeling out there in Mexico." Robert threw aside the picture.

"I've been seeing the waves and the white beach of Grand Isle; the quiet, grassy street of the *Chênière Caminada;* the old fort at Grande Terre. I've been working like a machine, and feeling like a lost soul. There was nothing interesting."

She leaned her head upon her hand to shade her eyes from the light.

890 "And what have you been seeing and doing and feeling all these days?" he asked.

"I've been seeing the waves and the white beach of Grand Isle; the quiet, grassy street of the *Chênière;* the old sunny fort at Grande Terre. I've been working with a little more comprehension than a machine, and still feeling like a lost soul. There was nothing interesting."

"Mrs. Pontellier, you are cruel," he said, with feeling, closing his eyes and resting his head back in his chair. They remained in silence till old Celestine announced dinner.

## *XXXIV*

The dining-room was very small. Edna's round mahogany would have almost filled it. As it was there was but a step or two from the little table to the kitchen, to the mantel, the small buffet, and the side door that opened out on the narrow brick-paved yard.

A certain degree of ceremony settled upon them with the announcement of dinner. There was no return to personalities. Robert related incidents of his sojourn in Mexico, and Edna talked of events likely to interest him, which had occurred during his absence. The dinner was of ordinary quality, except for the few delicacies which she had sent out to purchase. Old Celestine, with a bandana *tignon*[78] twisted about her head, hobbled in and out, taking a personal interest in everything; and she lingered occasionally to talk patois[79] with Robert, whom she had known as a boy.

895 He went out to a neighboring cigar stand to purchase cigarette papers, and when he came back he found that Celestine had served the black coffee in the parlor.

"Perhaps I shouldn't have come back," he said. "When you are tired of me, tell me to go."

"You never tire me. You must have forgotten the hours and hours at Grand Isle in which we grew accustomed to each other and used to being together."

"I have forgotten nothing at Grand Isle," he said, not looking at her, but rolling a cigarette. His tobacco pouch, which he laid upon the table, was a fantastic embroidered silk affair, evidently the handiwork of a woman.

"You used to carry your tobacco in a rubber pouch," said Edna, picking up the pouch and examining the needlework.

900 "Yes; it was lost."

"Where did you buy this one? In Mexico?"

[78]**bandana *tignon*** hair tied in a scarf
[79]**patois** regional dialect of French, English, Spanish, and American Indian

"It was given to me by a Vera Cruz girl; they are very generous," he replied, striking a match and lighting his cigarette.

"They are very handsome, I suppose, those Mexican women; very picturesque, with their black eyes and their lace scarfs."

"Some are; others are hideous. Just as you find women everywhere."

"What was she like—the one who gave you the pouch? You must have known her very well."

"She was very ordinary. She wasn't of the slightest importance. I knew her well enough."

"Did you visit at her house? Was it interesting? I should like to know and hear about the people you met, and the impressions they made on you."

"There are some people who leave impressions not so lasting as the imprint of an oar upon the water."

"Was she such a one?"

"It would be ungenerous for me to admit that she was of that order and kind." He thrust the pouch back in his pocket, as if to put away the subject with the trifle which had brought it up.

Arobin dropped in with a message from Mrs. Merriman, to say that the card party was postponed on account of the illness of one of her children.

"How do you do, Arobin?" said Robert, rising from the obscurity.

"Oh! Lebrun. To be sure! I heard yesterday you were back. How did they treat you down in Mexique?"

"Fairly well."

"But not well enough to keep you there. Stunning girls, though, in Mexico. I thought I should never get away from Vera Cruz when I was down there a couple of years ago."

"Did they embroider slippers and tobacco pouches and hat-bands and things for you?" asked Edna.

"Oh! my! no! I didn't get so deep in their regard. I fear they made more impression on me than I made on them."

"You were less fortunate than Robert, then."

"I am always less fortunate than Robert. Has he been imparting tender confidences?"

"I've been imposing myself long enough," said Robert, rising, and shaking hands with Edna. "Please convey my regards to Mr. Pontellier when you write."

He shook hands with Arobin and went away.

"Fine fellow, that Lebrun," said Arobin when Robert had gone. "I never heard you speak of him."

"I knew him last summer at Grand Isle," she replied. "Here is that photograph of yours. Don't you want it?"

"What do I want with it? Throw it away." She threw it back on the table.

"I'm not going to Mrs. Merriman's," she said. "If you see her, tell her so. But perhaps I had better write. I think I shall write now, and say that I am sorry her child is sick, and tell her not to count on me."

"It would be a good scheme," acquiesced Arobin. "I don't blame you; stupid lot!"

Edna opened the blotter, and having procured paper and pen, began to write the note. Arobin lit a cigar and read the evening paper, which he had in his pocket.

"What is the date?" she asked. He told her.

"Will you mail this for me when you go out?"

930 "Certainly." He read to her little bits out of the newspaper, while she straightened things on the table.

"What do you want to do?" he asked, throwing aside the paper. "Do you want to go out for a walk or a drive or anything? It would be a fine night to drive."

"No; I don't want to do anything but just be quiet. You go away and amuse yourself. Don't stay."

"I'll go away if I must; but I shan't amuse myself. You know that I only live when I am near you."

He stood up to bid her good night.

935 "Is that one of the things you always say to women?"

"I have said it before, but I don't think I ever came so near meaning it," he answered with a smile. There were no warm lights in her eyes; only a dreamy, absent look.

"Good night. I adore you. Sleep well," he said, and he kissed her hand and went away.

She stayed alone in a kind of reverie—a sort of stupor. Step by step she lived over every instant of the time she had been with Robert after he had entered Mademoiselle Reisz's door. She recalled his words, his looks. How few and meager they had been for her hungry heart! A vision—a transcendently seductive vision of a Mexican girl arose before her. She writhed with a jealous pang. She wondered when he would come back. He had not said he would come back. She had been with him, had heard his voice and touched his hand. But some way he had seemed nearer to her off there in Mexico.

## *XXXV*

The morning was full of sunlight and hope. Edna could see before her no denial—only the promise of excessive joy. She lay in bed awake, with bright eyes full of speculation. "He loves you, poor fool." If she could but get that conviction firmly fixed in her mind, what mattered about the rest? She felt she had been childish and unwise the night before in giving herself over to despondency. She recapitulated the motives which no doubt explained Robert's reserve. They were not insurmountable; they would not hold if he really loved her; they could not hold against her own passion, which he must come to realize in time. She pictured him going to his business that morning. She even saw how he was dressed; how he walked down one street, and turned the corner of another; saw him bending over his desk, talking to people who entered the office, going to his lunch, and perhaps watching for her on the street. He would come to her in the afternoon or evening, sit and roll his cigarette, talk a little, and go away as he had done the night before. But how delicious it would be to have him there with her! She would have no regrets, nor seek to penetrate his reserve if he still chose to wear it.

940 Edna ate her breakfast only half dressed. The maid brought her a delicious printed scrawl from Raoul, expressing his love, asking her to send him some bonbons, and telling her they had found that morning ten tiny white pigs all lying in a row beside Lidie's big white pig.

A letter also came from her husband, saying he hoped to be back early in March, and then they would get ready for that journey abroad which he had promised her so long, which he felt now fully able to afford; he felt able to travel as people should, without any thought of small economies—thanks to his recent speculations in Wall Street.

Much to her surprise she received a note from Arobin, written at midnight from the club. It was to say good morning to her, to hope she had slept well, to assure her of his devotion, which he trusted she in some faintest manner returned.

All these letters were pleasing to her. She answered the children in a cheerful frame of mind, promising them bonbons, and congratulating them upon their happy find of the little pigs.

She answered her husband with friendly evasiveness,—not with any fixed design to mislead him, only because all sense of reality had gone out of her life; she had abandoned herself to Fate, and awaited the consequences with indifference.

To Arobin's note she made no reply. She put it under Celestine's stove-lid.

Edna worked several hours with much spirit. She saw no one but a picture dealer, who asked her if it were true that she was going abroad to study in Paris.

She said possibly she might, and he negotiated with her for some Parisian studies to reach him in time for the holiday trade in December.

Robert did not come that day. She was keenly disappointed. He did not come the following day, nor the next. Each morning she awoke with hope, and each night she was a prey to despondency. She was tempted to seek him out. But far from yielding to the impulse, she avoided any occasion which might throw her in his way. She did not go to Mademoiselle Reisz's nor pass by Madame Lebrun's, as she might have done if he had still been in Mexico.

When Arobin, one night, urged her to drive with him, she went—out to the lake, on the Shell Road. His horses were full of mettle, and even a little unmanageable. She liked the rapid gait at which they spun along, and the quick, sharp sound of the horses' hoofs on the hard road. They did not stop anywhere to eat or to drink. Arobin was not needlessly imprudent. But they ate and they drank when they regained Edna's little dining-room—which was comparatively early in the evening.

It was late when he left her. It was getting to be more than a passing whim with Arobin to see her and be with her. He had detected the latent sensuality, which unfolded under his delicate sense of her nature's requirements like a torpid, torrid, sensitive blossom.

There was no despondency when she fell asleep that night; nor was there hope when she awoke in the morning.

## XXXVI

There was a garden out in the suburbs; a small, leafy corner, with a few green tables under the orange trees. An old cat slept all day on the stone step in the sun, and an old *mulatresse*[80] slept her idle hours away in her

[80]***mulatresse*** woman of black and white ancestry

chair at the open window, till some one happened to knock on one of the green tables. She had milk and cream cheese to sell, and bread and butter. There was no one who could make such excellent coffee or fry a chicken so golden brown as she.

The place was too modest to attract the attention of people of fashion, and so quiet as to have escaped the notice of those in search of pleasure and dissipation. Edna had discovered it accidentally one day when the high-board gate stood ajar. She caught sight of a little green table, blotched with the checkered sunlight that filtered through the quivering leaves overhead. Within she had found the slumbering *mulatresse,* the drowsy cat, and a glass of milk which reminded her of the milk she had tasted in Iberville.

She often stopped there during her perambulations; sometimes taking a book with her, and sitting an hour or two under the trees when she found the place deserted. Once or twice she took a quiet dinner there alone, having instructed Celestine beforehand to prepare no dinner at home. It was the last place in the city where she would have expected to meet any one she knew.

Still she was not astonished when, as she was partaking of a modest dinner late in the afternoon, looking into an open book, stroking the cat, which had made friends with her—she was not greatly astonished to see Robert come in at the tall garden gate.

"I am destined to see you only by accident," she said, shoving the cat off the chair beside her. He was surprised, ill at ease, almost embarrassed at meeting her thus so unexpectedly.

"Do you come here often?" he asked.

"I almost live here," she said.

"I used to drop in very often for a cup of Catiche's good coffee. This is the first time since I came back."

"She'll bring you a plate, and you will share my dinner. There's always enough for two—even three." Edna had intended to be indifferent and as reserved as he when she met him; she had reached the determination by a laborious train of reasoning, incident to one of her despondent moods. But her resolve melted when she saw him before her, seated there beside her in the little garden, as if a designing Providence had led him into her path.

"Why have you kept away from me, Robert?" she asked, closing the book that lay open upon the table.

"Why are you so personal, Mrs. Pontellier? Why do you force me to idiotic subterfuges?" he exclaimed with sudden warmth. "I suppose there's no use telling you I've been very busy, or that I've been sick, or that I've been to see you and not found you at home. Please let me off with any of these excuses."

"You are the embodiment of selfishness," she said. "You save yourself something—I don't know what—but there is some selfish motive, and in sparing yourself you never consider for a moment what I think, or how I feel your neglect and indifference. I suppose this is what you would call unwomanly; but I have got into a habit of expressing myself. It doesn't matter to me, and you may think me unwomanly if you like."

"No; I only think you cruel, as I said the other day. Maybe not intentionally cruel; but you seem to be forcing me into disclosures which can result in nothing; as if you would have me bare a wound for the pleasure of looking at it, without the intention or power of healing it."

965 "I'm spoiling your dinner, Robert; never mind what I say. You haven't eaten a morsel."

"I only came in for a cup of coffee." His sensitive face was all disfigured with excitement.

"Isn't this a delightful place?" she remarked. "I am so glad it has never actually been discovered. It is so quiet, so sweet, here. Do you notice there is scarcely a sound to be heard? It's so out of the way; and a good walk from the car. However, I don't mind walking. I always feel so sorry for women who don't like to walk; they miss so much—so many rare little glimpses of life; and we women learn so little of life on the whole.

"Catiche's coffee is always hot. I don't know how she manages it, here in open air. Celestine's coffee gets cold bringing it from the kitchen to the dining-room. Three lumps! How can you drink it so sweet? Take some of the cress with your chop; it's so biting and crisp. Then there's the advantage of being able to smoke with your coffee out here. Now, in the city—aren't you going to smoke?"

"After a while," he said, laying a cigar on the table.

970 "Who gave it to you?" she laughed.

"I bought it. I suppose I'm getting reckless; I bought a whole box." She was determined not to be personal again and make him uncomfortable.

The cat made friends with him, and climbed into his lap when he smoked his cigar. He stroked her silky fur, and talked a little about her. He looked at Edna's book, which he had read; and he told her the end, to save her the trouble of wading through it, he said.

Again he accompanied her back to her home; and it was after dusk when they reached the little "pigeon-house." She did not ask him to remain, which he was grateful for, as it permitted him to stay without the discomfort of blundering through an excuse which he had no intention of considering. He helped her to light the lamp; then she went into her room to take off her hat and to bathe her face and hands.

When she came back Robert was not examining the pictures and magazines as before; he sat off in the shadow, leaning his head back on the chair as if in a reverie. Edna lingered a moment beside the table, arranging the books there. Then she went across the room to where he sat. She bent over the arm of his chair and called his name.

975 "Robert," she said, "are you asleep?"

"No," he answered, looking up at her.

She leaned over and kissed him—a soft, cool, delicate kiss, whose voluptuous sting penetrated his whole being—then she moved away from him. He followed, and took her in his arms, just holding her close to him. She put her hand up to his face and pressed his cheek against her own. The action was full of love and tenderness. He sought her lips again. Then he drew her down upon the sofa beside him and held her hand in both of his.

"Now you know," he said, "now you know what I have been fighting against since last summer at Grand Isle; what drove me away and drove me back again."

"Why have you been fighting against it?" she asked. Her face glowed with soft lights.

980 "Why? Because you were not free; you were Léonce Pontellier's wife. I couldn't help loving you if you were ten times his wife; but so long as I went away from you and kept away I could help telling you so." She put her

free hand up to his shoulder, and then against his cheek, rubbing it softly. He kissed her again. His face was warm and flushed.

"There in Mexico I was thinking of you all the time, and longing for you."

"But not writing to me," she interrupted.

"Something put into my head that you cared for me; and I lost my senses. I forgot everything but a wild dream of your some way becoming my wife."

"Your wife!"

985 "Religion, loyalty, everything would give way if only you cared."

"Then you must have forgotten that I was Léonce Pontellier's wife."

"Oh! I was demented, dreaming of wild, impossible things, recalling men who had set their wives free, we have heard of such things."

"Yes, we have heard of such things."

"I came back full of vague, mad intentions. And when I got here—"

990 "When you got here you never came near me!" She was still caressing his cheek.

"I realized what a cur I was to dream of such a thing, even if you had been willing."

She took his face between her hands and looked into it as if she would never withdraw her eyes more. She kissed him on the forehead, the eyes, the cheeks, and the lips.

"You have been a very, very foolish boy, wasting your time dreaming of impossible things when you speak of Mr. Pontellier setting me free! I am no longer one of Mr. Pontellier's possessions to dispose of or not. I give myself where I choose. If he were to say, 'Here, Robert, take her and be happy; she is yours,' I should laugh at you both."

His face grew a little white. "What do you mean?" he asked.

995 There was a knock at the door. Old Celestine came in to say that Madame Ratignolle's servant had come around the back way with a message that Madame had been taken sick and begged Mrs. Pontellier to go to her immediately.

"Yes, yes," said Edna, rising; "I promised. Tell her yes—to wait for me. I'll go back with her."

"Let me walk over with you," offered Robert.

"No," she said; "I will go with the servant." She went into her room to put on her hat, and when she came in again she sat once more upon the sofa beside him. He had not stirred. She put her arms about his neck.

"Good-by, my sweet Robert. Tell me good-by." He kissed her with a degree of passion which had not before entered into his caress, and strained her to him.

1000 "I love you," she whispered, "only you; no one but you. It was you who woke me last summer out of a life-long, stupid dream. Oh! you have made me so unhappy with your indifference. Oh! I have suffered, suffered! Now you are here we shall love each other, my Robert. We shall be everything to each other. Nothing else in the world is of any consequence. I must go to my friend; but you will wait for me? No matter how late; you will wait for me, Robert?"

"Don't go; don't go! Oh! Edna, stay with me," he pleaded. "Why should you go? Stay with me, stay with me."

"I shall come back as soon as I can; I shall find you here." She buried her face in his neck, and said good-by again. Her seductive voice, together with his great love for her, had enthralled his senses, had deprived him of every impulse but the longing to hold her and keep her.

## XXXVII

Edna looked in at the drug store. Monsieur Ratignolle was putting up a mixture himself, very carefully, dropping a red liquid into a tiny glass. He was grateful to Edna for having come; her presence would be a comfort to his wife. Madame Ratignolle's sister, who had always been with her at such trying times, had not been able to come up from the plantation, and Adèle had been inconsolable until Mrs. Pontellier so kindly promised to come to her. The nurse had been with them at night for the past week, as she lived a great distance away. And Dr. Mandelet had been coming and going all the afternoon. They were then looking for him any moment.

Edna hastened upstairs by a private stairway that led from the rear of the store to the apartment above. The children were all sleeping in a back room. Madame Ratignolle was in the salon, whither she had strayed in her suffering impatience. She sat on the sofa, clad in an ample white *peignoir,* holding a handkerchief tight in her hand with a nervous clutch. Her face was drawn and pinched, her sweet blue eyes haggard and unnatural. All her beautiful hair had been drawn back and plaited. It lay in a long braid on the sofa pillow, coiled like a golden serpent. The nurse, a comfortable looking *Griffe*[81] woman in white apron and cap, was urging her to return to her bedroom.

"There is no use, there is no use," she said at once to Edna. "We must get rid of Mandelet; he is getting too old and careless. He said he would be here at half-past seven; now it must be eight. See what time it is, Joséphine."

The woman was possessed of a cheerful nature, and refused to take any situation too seriously, especially a situation with which she was so familiar. She urged Madame to have courage and patience. But Madame only set her teeth hard into her under lip, and Edna saw the sweat gather in beads on her white forehead. After a moment or two she uttered a profound sigh and wiped her face with the handkerchief rolled in a ball. She appeared exhausted. The nurse gave her a fresh handkerchief, sprinkled with cologne water.

"This is too much!" she cried. "Mandelet ought to be killed! Where is Alphonse? Is it possible I am to be abandoned like this—neglected by every one?"

"Neglected, indeed!" exclaimed the nurse. Wasn't she there? And here was Mrs. Pontellier leaving, no doubt, a pleasant evening at home to devote to her? And wasn't Monsieur Ratignolle coming that very instant through the hall? And Joséphine was quite sure she had heard Doctor Mandelet's coupé.[82] Yes, there it was, down at the door.

Adèle consented to go back to her room. She sat on the edge of a little low couch next to her bed.

[81]*Griffe* mixed-race
[82]**coupé** closed four-wheel carriage

1010 Doctor Mandelet paid no attention to Madame Ratignolle's upbraidings. He was accustomed to them at such times, and was too well convinced of her loyalty to doubt it.

He was glad to see Edna, and wanted her to go with him into the salon and entertain him. But Madame Ratignolle would not consent that Edna should leave her for an instant. Between agonizing moments, she chatted a little, and said it took her mind off her sufferings.

Edna began to feel uneasy. She was seized with a vague dread. Her own like experiences seemed far away, unreal, and only half remembered. She recalled faintly an ecstasy of pain, the heavy odor of chloroform, a stupor which had deadened sensation, and an awakening to find a little new life to which she had given being, added to the great unnumbered multitude of souls that come and go.

She began to wish she had not come; her presence was not necessary. She might have invented a pretext for staying away; she might even invent a pretext now for going. But Edna did not go. With an inward agony, with a flaming, outspoken revolt against the ways of Nature, she witnessed the scene of torture.

She was still stunned and speechless with emotion when later she leaned over her friend to kiss her and softly say good-by. Adèle, pressing her cheek, whispered in an exhausted voice: "Think of the children, Edna. Oh, think of the children! Remember them!"

## *XXXVIII*

1015 Edna still felt dazed when she got outside in the open air. The Doctor's coupé had returned for him and stood before the *porte cochère.* She did not wish to enter the coupé, and told Doctor Mandelet she would walk; she was not afraid, and would go alone. He directed his carriage to meet him at Mrs. Pontellier's, and he started to walk home with her.

Up—away up, over the narrow street between the tall houses, the stars were blazing. The air was mild and caressing, but cool with the breath of spring and the night. They walked slowly, the Doctor with a heavy, measured tread and his hands behind him; Edna, in an absent-minded way, as she had walked one night at Grand Isle, as if her thoughts had gone ahead of her and she was striving to overtake them.

"You shouldn't have been there, Mrs. Pontellier," he said. "That was no place for you. Adèle is full of whims at such times. There were a dozen women she might have had with her, unimpressionable women. I felt that it was cruel, cruel. You shouldn't have gone."

"Oh, well!" she answered, indifferently. "I don't know that it matters after all. One has to think of the children some time or other; the sooner the better."

"When is Léonce coming back?"

1020 "Quite soon. Some time in March."

"And you are going abroad?"

"Perhaps—no, I am not going. I'm not going to be forced into doing things. I don't want to go abroad. I want to be let alone. Nobody has any right—except children, perhaps—and even then, it seems to me—or it did seem—" She felt that her speech was voicing the incoherency of her thoughts, and stopped abruptly.

"The trouble is," sighed the Doctor, grasping her meaning intuitively, "that youth is given up to illusions. It seems to be a provision of Nature; a decoy to secure mothers for the race. And Nature takes no account of moral consequences, or arbitrary conditions which we create, and which we feel obliged to maintain at any cost."

"Yes," she said. "The years that are gone seem like dreams—if one might go on sleeping and dreaming—but to wake up and find—oh! well! perhaps it is better to wake up after all, even to suffer, rather than to remain a dupe to illusions all one's life."

1025 "It seems to me, my dear child," said the Doctor at parting, holding her hand, "you seem to me to be in trouble. I am not going to ask for your confidence. I will only say that if ever you feel moved to give it to me, perhaps I might help you. I know I would understand, and I tell you there are not many who would—not many, my dear."

"Some way I don't feel moved to speak of things that trouble me. Don't think I am ungrateful or that I don't appreciate your sympathy. There are periods of despondency and suffering which take possession of me. But I don't want anything but my own way. That is wanting a good deal, of course, when you have to trample upon the lives, the hearts, the prejudices of others—but no matter—still, I shouldn't want to trample upon the little lives. Oh! I don't know what I'm saying, Doctor. Good night. Don't blame me for anything."

"Yes, I will blame you if you don't come and see me soon. We will talk of things you never have dreamt of talking about before. It will do us both good. I don't want you to blame yourself, whatever comes. Good night, my child."

She let herself in at the gate, but instead of entering she sat upon the step of the porch. The night was quiet and soothing. All the tearing emotion of the last few hours seemed to fall away from her like a somber, uncomfortable garment, which she had but to loosen to be rid of. She went back to that hour before Adèle had sent for her; and her senses kindled afresh in thinking of Robert's words, the pressure of his arms, and the feeling of his lips upon her own. She could picture at that moment no greater bliss on earth than possession of the beloved one. His expression of love had already given him to her in part. When she thought that he was there at hand, waiting for her, she grew numb with the intoxication of expectancy. It was so late; he would be asleep perhaps. She would awaken him with a kiss. She hoped he would be asleep that she might arouse him with her caresses.

Still, she remembered Adèle's voice whispering, "Think of the children; think of them." She meant to think of them; that determination had driven into her soul like a death wound—but not to-night. To-morrow would be time to think of everything.

1030 Robert was not waiting for her in the little parlor. He was nowhere at hand. The house was empty. But he had scrawled on a piece of paper that lay in the lamplight:

"I love you. Good-by—because I love you."

Edna grew faint when she read the words. She went and sat on the sofa. Then she stretched herself out there, never uttering a sound. She did not sleep. She did not go to bed. The lamp sputtered and went out. She was still awake in the morning, when Celestine unlocked the kitchen door and came in to light the fire.

## XXXIX

Victor, with hammer and nails and scraps of scantling, was patching a corner of one of the galleries. Mariequita sat near by, dangling her legs, watching him work, and handing him nails from the tool-box. The sun was beating down upon them. The girl covered her head with her apron folded into a square pad. They had been talking for an hour or more. She was never tired of hearing Victor describe the dinner at Mrs. Pontellier's. He exaggerated every detail, making it appear a veritable Lucullean feast.[83] The flowers were in tubs, he said. The champagne was quaffed from huge golden goblets. Venus rising from the foam[84] could have presented no more entrancing a spectacle than Mrs. Pontellier, blazing with beauty and diamonds at the head of the board, while the other women were all of them youthful houris,[85] possessed of incomparable charms.

She got it into her head that Victor was in love with Mrs. Pontellier, and he gave her evasive answers, framed so as to confirm her belief. She grew sullen and cried a little, threatening to go off and leave him to his fine ladies. There were a dozen men crazy about her at the *Chênière;* and since it was the fashion to be in love with married people, why, she could run away any time she liked to New Orleans with Célina's husband.

1035 Célina's husband was a fool, a coward, and a pig, and to prove it to her, Victor intended to hammer his head into a jelly the next time he encountered him. This assurance was very consoling to Mariequita. She dried her eyes, and grew cheerful at the prospect.

They were still talking of the dinner and the allurements of city life when Mrs. Pontellier herself slipped around the corner of the house. The two youngsters stayed dumb with amazement before what they considered to be an apparition. But it was really she in flesh and blood, looking tired and a little travel-strained.

"I walked up from the wharf," she said, "and heard the hammering. I supposed it was you, mending the porch. It's a good thing. I was always tripping over those loose planks last summer. How dreary and deserted everything looks!"

It took Victor some time to comprehend that she had come in Beaudelet's lugger, that she had come alone, and for no purpose but to rest.

"There's nothing fixed up yet, you see. I'll give you my room; it's the only place."

1040 "Any corner will do," she assured him.

"And if you can stand Philomel's cooking," he went on, "though I might try to get her mother while you are here. Do you think she would come?" turning to Mariequita.

Mariequita thought that perhaps Philomel's mother might come for a few days, and money enough.

Beholding Mrs. Pontellier make her appearance, the girl had at once suspected a lovers' rendezvous. But Victor's astonishment was so genuine,

[83]**Lucullean feast** that is, splendid, in the manner of the feasts given by the Roman general Lucius Licinius Lucullus

[84]**Venus rising from the foam** goddess of love, said to have sprung from the foam of the sea

[85]**houris** beautiful virgins of the Koranic paradise

and Mrs. Pontellier's indifference so apparent, that the disturbing notion did not lodge long in her brain. She contemplated with the greatest interest this woman who gave the most sumptuous dinners in America, and who had all the men in New Orleans at her feet.

"What time will you have dinner?" asked Edna. "I'm very hungry; but don't get anything extra."

1045 "I'll have it ready in little or no time," he said, bustling and packing away his tools. "You may go to my room to brush up and rest yourself. Mariequita will show you."

"Thank you," said Edna. "But, do you know, I have a notion to go down to the beach and take a good wash and even a little swim, before dinner?"

"The water is too cold!" they both exclaimed. "Don't think of it."

"Well, I might go down and try—dip my toes in. Why, it seems to me the sun is hot enough to have warmed the very depths of the ocean. Could you get me a couple of towels? I'd better go right away, so as to be back in time. It would be a little too chilly if I waited till this afternoon."

Mariequita ran over to Victor's room, and returned with some towels, which she gave to Edna.

1050 "I hope you have fish for dinner," said Edna, as she started to walk away; "but don't do anything extra if you haven't."

"Run and find Philomel's mother," Victor instructed the girl. "I'll go to the kitchen and see what I can do. By Gimminy! Women have no consideration! She might have sent me word."

Edna walked on down to the beach rather mechanically, not noticing anything special except that the sun was hot. She was not dwelling upon any particular train of thought. She had done all the thinking which was necessary after Robert went away, when she lay awake upon the sofa till morning.

She had said over and over to herself: "To-day it is Arobin; to-morrow it will be some one else. It makes no difference to me, it doesn't matter about Léonce Pontellier—but Raoul and Etienne!" She understood now clearly what she had meant long ago when she said to Adèle Ratignolle that she would give up the unessential, but she would never sacrifice herself for her children.

Despondency had come upon her there in the wakeful night, and had never lifted. There was no one thing in the world that she desired. There was no human being whom she wanted near her except Robert; and she even realized that the day would come when he, too, and the thought of him would melt out of her existence, leaving her alone. The children appeared before her like antagonists who had overcome her; who had overpowered and sought to drag her into the soul's slavery for the rest of her days. But she knew a way to elude them. She was not thinking of these things when she walked down to the beach.

1055 The water of the Gulf stretched out before her, gleaming with the million lights of the sun. The voice of the sea is seductive, never ceasing, whispering, clamoring, murmuring, inviting the soul to wander in abysses of solitude. All along the white beach, up and down, there was no living thing in sight. A bird with a broken wing was beating the air above, reeling, fluttering, circling disabled down, down to the water.

Edna had found her old bathing suit still hanging, faded, upon its accustomed peg.

She put it on, leaving her clothing in the bath-house. But when she was there beside the sea, absolutely alone, she cast the unpleasant, pricking garments from her, and for the first time in her life she stood naked in the open air, at the mercy of the sun, the breeze that beat upon her, and the waves that invited her.

How strange and awful it seemed to stand naked under the sky! how delicious! She felt like some new-born creature, opening its eyes in a familiar world that it had never known.

The foamy wavelets curled up to her white feet, and coiled like serpents above her ankles. She walked out. The water was chill, but she walked on. The water was deep, but she lifted her white body and reached out for a long, sweeping stroke. The touch of the sea is sensuous, enfolding the body in its soft, close embrace.

1060 She went on and on. She remembered the night she swam far out, and recalled the terror that seized her at the fear of being unable to regain the shore. She did not look back now, but went on and on, thinking of the blue-grass meadow that she had traversed when a little child, believing that it had no beginning and no end.

Her arms and legs were growing tired.

She thought of Léonce and the children. They were a part of her life. But they need not have thought that they could possess her, body and soul. How Mademoiselle Reisz would have laughed, perhaps sneered, if she knew! "And you call yourself an artist! What pretensions, Madame! The artist must possess the courageous soul that dares and defies."

Exhaustion was pressing upon and overpowering her.

"Good-by—because I love you." He did not know; he did not understand. He would never understand. Perhaps Doctor Mandelet would have understood if she had seen him—but it was too late; the shore was far behind her, and her strength was gone.

1065 She looked into the distance, and the old terror flamed up for an instant, then sank again. Edna heard her father's voice and her sister Margaret's. She heard the barking of an old dog that was chained to the sycamore tree. The spurs of the cavalry officer clanged as he walked across the porch. There was the hum of bees, and the musky odor of pinks filled the air.

[*1899*]

## TOPICS FOR CRITICAL THINKING AND WRITING

1. Although the story was published with the title *The Awakening*, Chopin originally called it "A Solitary Soul." Which title do you prefer? Why?
2. Compare Edna, Mademoiselle Reisz, and Adèle. In what significant ways, if any, does Edna resemble each and in what significant ways does she differ? To what does each of her friends awaken Edna?
3. Edna says to Dr. Mandelet (p. 695), "I don't want anything but my own way. That is wanting a good deal, of course, when you have to trample upon the lives, the hearts, the prejudices of others—but no matter. . . ." Does this statement reveal the essential Edna? If not, why not?

4. Characterize Léonce. Do you see him as Edna presumably does, or do you see him somewhat more sympathetically? Why?
5. Readers have often debated the ending of the novel: Is it triumphant, tragic, or both? Examine the final chapter carefully, and set forth your understanding of what leads Edna to her fateful decision.
6. Like many novels, *The Awakening* explores and comments on the society that it describes. Focus in particular on Chopin's treatment of marriage, motherhood, and the family. What is her attitude toward these institutions?
7. Discuss the settings that Chopin presents. How does she convey to the reader a strong sense of a specific time and place?
8. When we read and talk about novels, one key source of interest is asking, What makes *this* writer special, different from this or that other one? Consider this question in relation to the style of *The Awakening*, to Chopin's choice of words, tone of voice, narrative point of view.

# CHAPTER 13

# Critical Perspectives on Joyce Carol Oates

# "Where Are You Going, Where Have You Been?": A Casebook

## A NOTE ON INTERPRETATION

We talked about interpretation in Chapter 3, but more can be said about the topic. We want to take the opportunity to add a few words here, before you read Oates's story and several related works.

Almost inevitably (and perhaps especially if we enjoy a literary work) we seek to interpret what we read. We find ourselves saying that the work expresses such-and-such a feeling, or it says such-and-such about life. When we say that it is "about" something or other, on what do we base our interpretation? On evidence, of course, just as we base our interpretations of the happenings of real life on evidence.

If, for instance, we visit a classroom and see that the attendance is sparse, that the instructor speaks in a monotone and does not look at the students, and that the students are yawning, we draw conclusions about the instructor. We are always interpreting signs—which is just what the narrator in James Joyce's "Araby" tells us he did as a youth. He informs us that when he was a child he impatiently awaited the arrival of his uncle so that he could get permission to go to a bazaar.

> At nine o'clock I heard my uncle's latchkey in the halldoor. I heard him talking to himself and heard the hallstand rocking when it had received the weight of his overcoat. I could interpret these signs. (406)

The narrator never explicitly sets forth his interpretation, but it's pretty clear that he understood from the signs that his uncle was drunk. What is the evidence? The uncle is unduly late, he is talking to himself, and when he hangs his coat on the coat tree he does it so forcefully or clumsily that the coat tree audibly rocks.

Now, readers who interpret the passage this way probably cannot absolutely *prove* that the uncle is drunk, but they can point to evidence and a discussion can ensue. The chief evidence is the text itself, the words on the page, but there may also be other kinds of evidence, such as a writer's letters or diary in which the writer comments on the work; or evidence may even be the testimony of other readers as well as one's own response. Probably one cannot *absolutely* prove any interpretation of a story. Nor can one absolutely *dis*prove any interpretation that a reader is determined to hold. Suppose, for instance, someone argues that Jack, in the story of Jack and the Beanstalk, really is a girl and not a boy, or that the giant is not a giant but only a figment of Jack's imagination. It's impossible to find anything in the story that specifically refutes such contentions, but surely most people will feel that *that* is not what the story is about. Or someone might say of Kate Chopin's "The Story of an Hour" (p. 19) that Mrs. Mallard did not really die; the doctors were faulty not only in their diagnosis of the cause of death but also in their diagnosis that she died. Or—a last example—someone might say that Brently Mallard *was* killed in the wreck and that the man who appears at the door is an impostor, or perhaps a demon in the shape of Brently. There probably is no way of disproving such interpretations. The best that one can do is to try to demonstrate, by pointing to the text, that there really is no evidence to support them.

On the other hand, to return to Jack and the Beanstalk, suppose someone says that the beanstalk is phallic, the giant represents male authority (e.g., Jack's father), and the story is "about" a boy who grows up and becomes a man by killing a father-figure. Is this psychoanalytic interpretation in the same class as the interpretations of Jack and the Beanstalk that we mentioned a moment ago? Or what of a Marxist interpretation that sees the story as showing the lowly proletariat overthrowing the apparently all-powerful bourgeoisie? How might we prove or disprove such an interpretation? Similarly, if a reader says that the story of Sleeping Beauty makes a patriarchal statement about the dependence of women on men (since in effect Sleeping Beauty is lifeless until the prince awakens her with a kiss), is this sociological interpretation far-fetched? Is the story "just a story," or can reasonable people agree that it includes this meaning, as well, perhaps, as other meanings?

In this chapter we give a story, Joyce Carol Oates's "Where Are You Going, Where Have You Been?," and we follow it with

1. a centuries-old anonymous poem that, at least very broadly, tells a somewhat similar story;
2. a story on this motif, by Elizabeth Bowen;
3. an interview in which Oates comments on the story;
4. an essay by Oates on her story and on the film that was based on it;
5. an essay by Mike Tierce and John Michael Crafton, chiefly taking issue with an interpretation offered by other readers;
6. an essay by Larry Rubin, suggesting that the story reports a sort of dream or "daymare" by the chief character;
7. an essay by A. R. Coulthard arguing that the story is realistic. For instance, Arnold Friend "is simply the sick killer who is going to murder"

Connie. "He doesn't 'represent' anything, except the kind of creep a girl like Connie . . . might have the bad luck to attract."

After reading this material, think about the degree to which each interpretation strikes you as valid. *Why* do you accept certain interpretations and reject others?

## JOYCE CAROL OATES

*Joyce Carol Oates was born in 1938 in Millerport, New York. She won a scholarship to Syracuse University, from which she graduated (Phi Beta Kappa and valedictorian) in 1960. She then did graduate work in English, first at the University of Wisconsin and then at Rice University, but she withdrew from Rice in order to be able to devote more time to writing. Her first collection of stories,* By the North Gate, *was published in 1963; since then she has published at least forty books—stories, poems, essays, and (in twenty-five years) twenty-two novels. She has received many awards, has been elected to the American Academy and Institute of Arts and Letters, and now teaches creative writing at Princeton University.*

# *Where Are You Going, Where Have You Been?*

*To Bob Dylan*

Her name was Connie. She was fifteen and she had a quick nervous giggling habit of craning her neck to glance into mirrors or checking other people's faces to make sure her own was all right. Her mother, who noticed everything and knew everything and who hadn't much reason any longer to look at her own face, always scolded Connie about it. "Stop gawking at yourself, who are you? You think you're so pretty?" she would say. Connie would raise her eyebrows at these familiar complaints and look right through her mother, into a shadowy vision of herself as she was right at that moment: she knew she was pretty and that was everything. Her mother had been pretty once too, if you could believe those old snapshots in the album, but now her looks were gone and that was why she was always after Connie.

"Why don't you keep your room clean like your sister? How've you got your hair fixed—what the hell stinks? Hair spray? You don't see your sister using that junk."

Her sister June was twenty-four and still lived at home. She was a secretary in the high school Connie attended, and if that wasn't bad enough—with her in the same building—she was so plain and chunky and steady that Connie had to hear her praised all the time by her mother and her mother's sisters. June did this, June did that, she saved money and helped clean the house and cooked and Connie couldn't do a thing, her mind was all filled with trashy daydreams. Their father was away at work most of the time and when he came home he wanted supper and he read the newspaper at supper and after supper he went to bed. He didn't bother talking much to them, but around his bent head Connie's mother kept picking at her until Connie wished her mother was dead and she herself was dead and it was all over. "She makes me want to throw up sometimes," she complained to her friends. She had a high, breathless, amused voice which made everything she said sound a little forced, whether it was sincere or not.

There was one good thing: June went places with girlfriends of hers, girls who were just as plain and steady as she, and so when Connie wanted to do that her mother had no objections. The father of Connie's best girlfriend drove the girls the three miles to town and left them off at a shopping plaza, so that they could walk through the stores or go to a movie, and when he came to pick them up again at eleven he never bothered to ask what they had done.

5 They must have been familiar sights, walking around that shopping plaza in their shorts and flat ballerina slippers that always scuffed the sidewalk, with charm bracelets jingling on their thin wrists; they would lean together to whisper and laugh secretly if someone passed by who amused or interested them. Connie had long dark blond hair that drew anyone's eye to it, and she wore part of it pulled up on her head and puffed out and the rest of it she let fall down her back. She wore a pull-over jersey blouse that looked one way when she was at home and another way when she was away from home. Everything about her had two sides to it, one for home and one for anywhere that was not home: her walk that could be childlike and bobbing, or languid enough to make anyone think she was hearing music in her head, her mouth which was pale and smirking most of the time, but bright and pink on these evenings out, her laugh which was cynical and drawling at home—"Ha, ha, very funny"—but high-pitched and nervous anywhere else, like the jingling of the charms on her bracelet.

Sometimes they did go shopping or to a movie, but sometimes they went across the highway, ducking fast across the busy road, to a drive-in restaurant where older kids hung out. The restaurant was shaped like a big bottle, though squatter than a real bottle, and on its cap was a revolving figure of a grinning boy who held a hamburger aloft. One night in midsummer they ran across, breathless with daring, and right away someone leaned out a car window and invited them over, but it was just a boy from high school they didn't like. It made them feel good to be able to ignore him. They went up through the maze of parked and cruising cars to the bright-lit, fly-infested restaurant, their faces pleased and expectant as if they were entering a sacred building that loomed out of the night to give them what haven and what blessing they yearned for. They sat at the counter and crossed their legs at the ankles, their thin shoulders rigid with excitement, and listened to the music that made everything so good: the music was always in the background like music at a church service, it was something to depend upon.

A boy named Eddie came in to talk with them. He sat backward on his stool, turning himself jerkily around in semicircles and then stopping and turning again, and after a while he asked Connie if she would like something to eat. She said she did and so she tapped her friend's arm on her way out—her friend pulled her face up into a brave droll look—and Connie said she would meet her at eleven, across the way. "I just hate to leave her like that," Connie said earnestly, but the boy said that she wouldn't be alone for long. So they went out to his car and on the way Connie couldn't help but let her eyes wander over the windshields and faces all around her, her face gleaming with a joy that had nothing to do with Eddie or even this place; it might have been the music. She drew her shoulders up and sucked in her breath with the pure pleasure of being alive, and just at that moment she happened to glance at a face just a few feet from hers. It was a boy with shaggy black hair, in a convertible jalopy painted gold. He stared at her and then his lips widened into a grin. Connie slit her eyes at him and turned away, but she couldn't help glancing back and there he was still watching her. He wagged a finger and laughed and said, "Gonna get you, baby," and Connie turned away again without Eddie noticing anything.

She spent three hours with him, at the restaurant where they ate hamburgers and drank Cokes in wax cups that were always sweating, and then down an alley a mile or so away, and when he left her off at five to eleven only the movie house was still open at the plaza. Her girlfriend was there, talking with a boy. When Connie came up the two girls smiled at each other and Connie said, "How was the movie?" and the girl said, "*You* should know." They rode off with the girl's father, sleepy and pleased, and Connie couldn't help but look at the darkened shopping plaza with its big empty parking lot and its signs that were faded and ghostly now, and over at the drive-in restaurant where cars were still circling tirelessly. She couldn't hear the music at this distance.

Next morning June asked her how the movie was and Connie said, "So-so."

10 She and that girl and occasionally another girl went out several times a week that way, and the rest of the time Connie spent around the house—it was summer vacation—getting in her mother's way and thinking, dreaming, about the boys she met. But all the boys fell back and dissolved into a single face that was not even a face, but an idea, a feeling, mixed up with the urgent insistent pounding of the music and the humid night air of July. Connie's mother kept dragging her back to the daylight by finding things for her to do or saying, suddenly, "What's this about the Pettinger girl?"

And Connie would say nervously, "Oh, her. That dope." She always drew thick clear lines between herself and such girls, and her mother was simple and kindly enough to believe her. Her mother was so simple, Connie thought, that it was maybe cruel to fool her so much. Her mother went scuffling around the house in old bedroom slippers and complained over the telephone to one sister about the other, then the other called up and the two of them complained about the third one. If June's name was mentioned her mother's tone was approving, and if Connie's name was mentioned it was disapproving. This did not really mean she disliked Connie and actually Connie thought that her mother preferred her to June because she was prettier, but the two of them kept up a pretense of exasperation, a sense that they were tugging and struggling over something of little value to either of them. Sometimes, over coffee, they were almost friends, but something would come up—some vexation that was like a fly buzzing suddenly around their heads—and their faces went hard with contempt.

One Sunday Connie got up at eleven—none of them bothered with church—and washed her hair so that it could dry all day long, in the sun. Her parents and sister were going to a barbecue at an aunt's house and Connie said no, she wasn't interested, rolling her eyes to let her mother know just what she thought of it. "Stay home alone then," her mother said sharply. Connie sat out back in a lawn chair and watched them drive away, her father quiet and bald, hunched around so that he could back the car out, her mother with a look that was still angry and not at all softened through the windshield, and in the back seat poor old June all dressed up as if she didn't know what a barbecue was, with all the running yelling kids and the flies. Connie sat with her eyes closed in the sun, dreaming and dazed with the warmth about her as if this were a kind of love, the caresses of love, and her mind slipped over onto thoughts of the boy she had been with the night before and how nice he had been, how sweet it always was, not the way someone like June would suppose but sweet, gentle, the way it was in movies and promised in songs; and when she opened her eyes she hardly knew where she was, the back yard ran off into weeds and a fence line of trees and behind it the sky was perfectly blue and still. The asbestos "ranch house" that was now three years old startled her—it looked small. She shook her head as if to get awake.

It was too hot. She went inside the house and turned on the radio to drown out the quiet. She sat on the edge of her bed, barefoot, and listened for an hour and a half to a program called XYZ Sunday Jamboree, record after record of hard, fast, shrieking songs she sang along with, interspersed by exclamations from "Bobby King": "An' look here you girls at Napoleon's—Son and Charley want you to pay real close attention to this song coming up!"

And Connie paid close attention herself, bathed in a glow of slow-pulsed joy that seemed to rise mysteriously out of the music itself and lay languidly about the airless little room, breathed in and breathed out with each gentle rise and fall of her chest.

15 After a while she heard a car coming up the drive. She sat up at once, startled, because it couldn't be her father so soon. The gravel kept crunching all the way in from the road—the driveway was long—and Connie ran to the window. It was a car she didn't know. It was an open jalopy, painted a bright gold that caught the sunlight opaquely. Her heart began to pound and her fingers snatched at her hair, checking it, and she whispered "Christ, Christ," wondering how bad she looked. The car came to a stop at the side door and the horn sounded four short taps as if this were a signal Connie knew.

She went into the kitchen and approached the door slowly, then hung out the screen door, her bare toes curling down off the step. There were two boys in the car and now she recognized the driver: he had shaggy, shabby black hair that looked crazy as a wig and he was grinning at her.

"I ain't late, am I?" he said.

"Who the hell do you think you are?" Connie said.

"Toldja I'd be out, didn't I?"

20 "I don't even know who you are."

She spoke sullenly, careful to show no interest or pleasure, and he spoke in a fast bright monotone. Connie looked past him to the other boy, taking her time. He had fair brown hair, with a lock that fell onto his forehead. His sideburns gave him a fierce, embarrassed look, but so far he hadn't even bothered to glance at her. Both boys wore sunglasses. The driver's glasses were metallic and mirrored everything in miniature.

"You wanta come for a ride?" he said.

Connie smirked and let her hair fall loose over one shoulder.

"Don'tcha like my car? New paint job," he said. "Hey."

25 "What?"

"You're cute."

She pretended to fidget, chasing flies away from the door.

"Don'tcha believe me, or what?" he said.

"Look, I don't even know who you are," Connie said in disgust.

30 "Hey, Ellie's got a radio, see. Mine's broke down." He lifted his friend's arm and showed her the little transistor the boy was holding, and now Connie began to hear the music. It was the same program that was playing inside the house.

"Bobby King?" she said.

"I listen to him all the time. I think he's great."

"He's kind of great." Connie said reluctantly.

"Listen, that guy's *great.* He knows where the action is."

35 Connie blushed a little, because the glasses made it impossible for her to see just what this boy was looking at. She couldn't decide if she liked him or if he was just a jerk, and so she dawdled in the doorway and wouldn't come down or go back inside. She said, "What's all that stuff painted on your car?"

"Can'tcha read it?" He opened the door very carefully, as if he was afraid it might fall off. He slid out just as carefully, planting his feet firmly on the ground, the tiny metallic world in his glasses slowing down like gelatine hardening and in the midst of it Connie's bright green blouse. "This here is my name, to begin with," he said. ARNOLD FRIEND was written in tarlike black letters on the side, with a drawing of a round grinning face that reminded Connie of a pumpkin, except it wore sunglasses. "I wanta introduce myself, I'm Arnold Friend and that's my real name and I'm gonna be your friend, honey, and inside the car's Ellie Oscar, he's kinda shy." Ellie brought his transistor radio up to his shoulder and balanced it there. "Now these numbers are a secret code, honey," Arnold Friend explained. He read off the numbers 33, 19, 17 and raised his eyebrows at her to see what she thought of that, but she didn't think much of it. The left rear fender had been smashed and around it was written, on the gleaming gold background: DONE BY CRAZY WOMAN DRIVER. Connie had to laugh at that. Arnold Friend was pleased at her laughter and looked up at her. "Around the other side's a lot more—you wanta come and see them?"

"No."

"Why not?"

"Why should I?"

40 "Don'tcha wanta see what's on the car? Don'tcha wanta go for a ride?"

"I don't know."

"Why not?"

"I got things to do."

"Like what?"

45 "Things."

He laughed as if she had said something funny. He slapped his thighs. He was standing in a strange way, leaning back against the car as if he were balancing himself. He wasn't tall, only an inch or so taller than she would be if she came down to him. Connie liked the way he was dressed, which was the way all of them dressed: tight faded jeans stuffed into black, scuffed boots, a belt that pulled his waist in and showed how lean he was, and a white pullover shirt that was a little soiled and showed the hard small muscles of his arms and shoulders. He looked as if he probably did hard work, lifting and carrying things. Even his neck looked muscular. And his face was a familiar face, somehow: the jaw and chin and cheeks slightly darkened, because he hadn't shaved for a day or two, and the nose long and hawklike, sniffing as if she were a treat he was going to gobble up and it was all a joke.

"Connie, you ain't telling the truth. This is your day set aside for a ride with me and you know it," he said, still laughing. The way he straightened and recovered from his fit of laughing showed that it had been all fake.

"How do you know what my name is?" she said suspiciously.

"It's Connie."

50 "Maybe and maybe not."

"I know my Connie," he said, wagging his finger. Now she remembered him even better, back at the restaurant, and her cheeks warmed at the thought of how she sucked in her breath just at the moment she passed him—how she must have looked to him. And he had remembered her. "Ellie and I come out here especially for you," he said. "Ellie can sit in back. How about it?"

"Where?"

"Where what?"

"Where're we going?"

55 He looked at her. He took off the sunglasses and she saw how pale the skin around his eyes was, like holes that were not in shadow but instead in light. His eyes were like chips of broken glass that catch the light in an amiable way. He smiled. It was as if the idea of going for a ride somewhere, to some place, was a new idea to him.

"Just for a ride, Connie sweetheart."

"I never said my name was Connie," she said.

"But I know what it is. I know your name and all about you, lots of things," Arnold Friend said. He had not moved yet but stood still leaning back against the side of his jalopy. "I took a special interest in you, such a pretty girl, and found out all about you like I know your parents and sister are gone somewheres and I know where and how long they're going to be gone, and I know who you were with last night, and your best girlfriend's name is Betty. Right?"

He spoke in a simple lilting voice, exactly as if he were reciting the words to a song. His smile assured her that everything was fine. In the car Ellie turned up the volume on his radio and did not bother to look around at them.

60 "Ellie can sit in the back seat," Arnold Friend said. He indicated his friend with a casual jerk of his chin, as if Ellie did not count and she should not bother with him.

"How'd you find out all that stuff?" Connie said.

"Listen: Betty Schultz and Tony Fitch and Jimmy Pettinger and Nancy Pettinger," he said, in a chant. "Raymond Stanley and Bob Hutter—"

"Do you know all those kids?"

"I know everybody."

65 "Look, you're kidding. You're not from around here."

"Sure."

"But—how come we never saw you before?"

"Sure you saw me before," he said. He looked down at his boots, as if he were a little offended. "You just don't remember."

"I guess I'd remember you," Connie said.

70 "Yeah?" He looked up at this, beaming. He was pleased. He began to mark time with the music from Ellie's radio, tapping his fists lightly together. Connie looked away from his smile to the car, which was painted so bright it almost hurt her eyes to look at it. She looked at that name, ARNOLD FRIEND. And up at the front fender was an expression that was familiar—MAN THE FLYING SAUCERS. It was an expression kids had used the year before, but didn't use this year. She looked at it for a while as if the words meant something to her that she did not yet know.

"What're you thinking about? Huh?" Arnold Friend demanded. "Not worried about your hair blowing around in the car, are you?"

"No."

"Think I maybe can't drive good?"

"How do I know?"

75 "You're a hard girl to handle. How come?" he said. "Don't you know I'm your friend? Didn't you see me put my sign in the air when you walked by?"

"What sign?"

"My sign." And he drew an X in the air, leaning out toward her. They were maybe ten feet apart. After his hand fell back to his side the X was still in the air, almost visible. Connie let the screen door close and stood perfectly still inside it, listening to the music from her radio and the boy's blend together. She stared at Arnold Friend. He stood there so stiffly relaxed, pretending to be relaxed, with one hand idly on the door handle as if he were keeping himself up that way and had no intention of ever moving again. She recognized most things about him, the tight jeans that showed his thighs and buttocks and the greasy leather boots and the tight shirt, and even that slippery friendly smile of his, that sleepy dreamy smile that all the boys used to get across ideas they didn't want to put into words. She recognized all this and also the singsong way he talked, slightly mocking, kidding, but serious and a little melancholy, and she recognized the way he tapped one fist against the other in homage to the perpetual music behind him. But all these things did not come together.

She said suddenly, "Hey, how old are you?"

His smile faded. She could see then that he wasn't a kid, he was much older—thirty, maybe more. At this knowledge her heart began to pound faster.

80 "That's a crazy thing to ask. Can'tcha see I'm your own age?"

"Like hell you are."

"Or maybe a coupla years older, I'm eighteen."

"Eighteen?" she said doubtfully.

He grinned to reassure her and lines appeared at the corners of his mouth. His teeth were big and white. He grinned so broadly his eyes became slits and she saw how thick the lashes were, thick and black as if painted with a black tarlike material. Then he seemed to become embarrassed, abruptly, and looked over his shoulder at Ellie. "*Him,* he's crazy," he said. "Ain't he a riot, he's a nut, a real character." Ellie was still listening to the music. His sunglasses told nothing about what he was thinking. He wore a bright orange shirt unbuttoned halfway to show his chest, which was a pale, bluish chest and not muscular like Arnold Friend's. His shirt collar was turned up all around and the very tips of the collar pointed out past his chin as if they were protecting him. He was pressing the transistor radio up against his ear and sat there in a kind of daze, right in the sun.

85 "He's kinda strange," Connie said.

"Hey, she says you're kinda strange! Kinda strange!" Arnold Friend cried. He pounded on the car to get Ellie's attention. Ellie turned for the first time and Connie saw with shock that he wasn't a kid either—he had a fair, hairless face, cheeks reddened slightly as if the veins grew too close to the surface of his skin, the face of a forty-year-old baby. Connie felt a wave of dizziness rise in her at this sight and she stared at him as if waiting for something to change the shock of the moment, make it all right again. Ellie's lips kept shaping words, mumbling along, with the words blasting in his ear.

"Maybe you two better go away," Connie said faintly.

"What? How come?" Arnold Friend cried. "We come out here to take you for a ride. It's Sunday." He had the voice of the man on the radio now. It was the same voice, Connie thought. "Don'tcha know it's Sunday all day and honey, no matter who you were with last night today you're with Arnold Friend and don't you forget it!—Maybe you better step out here," he said, and this last was in a different voice. It was a little flatter, as if the heat was finally getting to him.

"No. I got things to do."

90 "Hey."

"You two better leave."

"We ain't leaving until you come with us."

"Like hell I am—"

"Connie, don't fool around with me. I mean, I mean, don't fool *around,*" he said, shaking his head. He laughed incredulously. He placed his sunglasses on top of his head, carefully, as if he were indeed wearing a wig, and brought the stems down behind his ears. Connie stared at him, another wave of dizziness and fear rising in her so that for a moment he wasn't even in focus but was just a blur, standing there against his gold car, and she had the idea that he had driven up the driveway all right but had come from nowhere before that and belonged nowhere and that everything about him and even about the music that was so familiar to her was only half real.

95 "If my father comes and sees you—"

"He ain't coming. He's at barbecue."

"How do you know that?"

"Aunt Tillie's. Right now they're—uh—they're drinking. Sitting around," he said vaguely, squinting as if he were staring all the way to town and over to Aunt Tillie's back yard. Then the vision seemed to get clear and he nodded energetically. "Yeah. Sitting around. There's your sister in a blue dress, huh? And high heels, the poor sad bitch—nothing like you, sweetheart! And your mother's helping some fat woman with the corn, they're cleaning the corn—husking the corn—"

"What fat woman?" Connie cried.

100 "How do I know what fat woman. I don't know every goddam fat woman in the world!" Arnold Friend laughed.

"Oh, that's Mrs. Hornby. . . . Who invited her?" Connie said. She felt a little light-headed. Her breath was coming quickly.

"She's too fat. I don't like them fat. I like them the way you are, honey," he said, smiling sleepily at her. They stared at each other for a while, through the screen door. He said softly, "Now what you're going to do is this: you're going to come out that door. You're going to sit up front with me and Ellie's going to sit in the back, the hell with Ellie, right? This isn't Ellie's date. You're my date. I'm your lover, honey."

"What? You're crazy—"

"Yes, I'm your lover. You don't know what that is but you will," he said. "I know that too. I know all about you. But look: it's real nice and you couldn't ask for nobody better than me, or more polite. I always keep my word. I'll tell you how it is, I'm always nice at first, the first time. I'll hold you so tight you won't think you have to try to get away or pretend anything because you'll know you can't. And I'll come inside you where it's all secret and you'll give in to me and you'll love me—"

105 "Shut up! You're crazy!" Connie said. She backed away from the door. She put her hands against her ears as if she'd heard something terrible, something not meant for her. "People don't talk like that, you're crazy," she muttered. Her heart was almost too big now for her chest and its pumping made sweat break out all over her. She looked out to see Arnold Friend pause and then take a step toward the porch lurching. He almost fell. But, like a clever drunken man, he managed to catch his balance. He wobbled in his high boots and grabbed hold of one of the porch posts.

"Honey?" he said. "You still listening?"

"Get the hell out of here!"

"Be nice, honey. Listen."

"I'm going to call the police—"

110 He wobbled again and out of the side of his mouth came a fast spat curse, an aside not meant for her to hear. But even this "Christ!" sounded forced. Then he began to smile again. She watched this smile come, awkward as if he were smiling from inside a mask. His whole face was a mask, she thought wildly, tanned down onto his throat but then running out as if he had plastered makeup on his face but had forgotten about his throat.

"Honey—? Listen, here's how it is. I always tell the truth and I promise you this: I ain't coming in that house after you."

"You better not! I'm going to call the police if you—if you don't—"

"Honey," he said, talking right through her voice, "honey, I'm not coming in there but you are coming out here. You know why?"

She was panting. The kitchen looked like a place she had never seen before, some room she had run inside but which wasn't good enough, wasn't going to help her. The kitchen window had never had a curtain, after three years, and there were dishes in the sink for her to do—probably—and if you ran your hand across the table you'd probably feel something sticky there.

115 "You listening, honey? Hey?"

"—going to call the police—"

"Soon as you touch the phone I don't need to keep my promise and can come inside. You won't want that."

She rushed forward and tried to lock the door. Her fingers were shaking. "But why lock it," Arnold Friend said gently, talking right into her face.

"It's just a screen door. It's just nothing." One of his boots was at a strange angle, as if his foot wasn't in it. It pointed out to the left, bent at the ankle. "I mean, anybody can break through a screen door and glass and wood and iron or anything else if he needs to, anybody at all and specially Arnold Friend. If the place got lit up with a fire honey you'd come runnin' out into my arms, right into my arms an' safe at home—like you knew I was your lover and'd stopped fooling around. I don't mind a nice shy girl but I don't like no fooling around." Part of those words were spoken with a slight rhythmic lilt, and Connie somehow recognized them—the echo of a song from last year, about a girl rushing into her boyfriend's arms and coming home again—

Connie stood barefoot on the linoleum floor, staring at him. "What do you want?" she whispered.

120 "I want you," he said.

"What?"

"Seen you that night and thought, that's the one, yes sir. I never needed to look any more."

"But my father's coming back. He's coming to get me. I had to wash my hair first—" She spoke in a dry, rapid voice, hardly raising it for him to hear.

"No, your Daddy is not coming and yes, you had to wash your hair and you washed it for me. It's nice and shining and all for me, I thank you, sweetheart," he said, with a mock bow, but again he almost lost his balance. He had to bend and adjust his boots. Evidently his feet did not go all the way down; the boots must have been stuffed with something so that he would seem taller. Connie stared out at him and behind him Ellie in the car, who seemed to be looking off toward Connie's right into nothing. This Ellie said, pulling the words out of the air one after another as if he were just discovering them, "You want me to pull out the phone?"

125 "Shut your mouth and keep it shut," Arnold Friend said, his face red from bending over or maybe from embarrassment because Connie had seen his boots. "This ain't none of your business."

"What—what are you doing? What do you want?" Connie said. "If I call the police they'll get you, they'll arrest you—"

"Promise was not to come in unless you touch that phone, and I'll keep that promise," he said. He resumed his erect position and tried to force his shoulders back. He sounded like a hero in a movie, declaring something important. He spoke too loudly and it was as if he were speaking to someone behind Connie. "I ain't made plans for coming in that house where I don't belong but just for you to come out to me, the way you should. Don't you know who I am?"

"You're crazy," she whispered. She backed away from the door but did not want to go into another part of the house, as if this would give him permission to come through the door. "What do you . . . You're crazy, you . . ."

"Huh? What're you saying, honey?"

130 Her eyes darted everywhere in the kitchen. She could not remember what it was, this room.

"This is how it is, honey: you come out and we'll drive away, have a nice ride. But if you don't come out we're gonna wait till your people come home and then they're all going to get it."

"You want that telephone pulled out?" Ellie said. He held the radio away from his ear and grimaced, as if without the radio the air was too much for him.

"I toldja shut up, Ellie," Arnold Friend said, "you're deaf, get a hearing aid, right? Fix yourself up. This little girl's no trouble and's gonna be nice to me, so Ellie keep to yourself, this ain't your date—right? Don't hem in on me. Don't hog. Don't crush. Don't bird dog. Don't trail me," he said in a rapid meaningless voice, as if he were running through all the expressions he'd learned but was no longer sure which one of them was in style, then rushing on to new ones, making them up with his eyes closed, "Don't crawl under my fence, don't squeeze in my chipmunk hole, don't sniff my glue, suck my popsicle, keep your own greasy fingers on yourself!" He shaded his eyes and peered in at Connie, who was backed against the kitchen table. "Don't mind him honey he's just a creep. He's a dope. Right? I'm the boy for you and like I said you come out here nice like a lady and give me your hand, and nobody else gets hurt, I mean, your nice old bald-headed daddy and your mummy and your sister in her high heels. Because listen: why bring them in this?"

"Leave me alone," Connie whispered.

135 "Hey, you know that old woman down the road, the one with the chickens and stuff—you know her?"

"She's dead!"

"Dead? What? You know her?" Arnold Friend said.

"She's dead—"

"Don't you like her?"

140 "She's dead—she's—she isn't here any more—"

"But don't you like her, I mean, you got something against her? Some grudge or something?" Then his voice dipped as if he were conscious of a rudeness. He touched the sunglasses perched on top of his head as if to make sure they were still there. "Now you be a good girl."

"What are you going to do?"

"Just two things, or maybe three," Arnold Friend said. "But I promise it won't last long and you'll like me the way you get to like people you're close to. You will. It's all over for you here, so come on out. You don't want your people in any trouble, do you?"

She turned and bumped against a chair or something, hurting her leg, but she ran into the back room and picked up the telephone. Something roared in her ear, a tiny roaring, and she was so sick with fear that she could do nothing but listen to it—the telephone was clammy and very heavy and her fingers groped down to the dial but were too weak to touch it. She began to scream into the phone, into the roaring. She cried out, she cried for her mother, she felt her breath start jerking back and forth in her lungs as if it were something Arnold Friend were stabbing her with again and again with no tenderness. A noisy sorrowful wailing rose all about her and she was locked inside it the way she was locked inside the house.

145 After a while she could hear again. She was sitting on the floor with her wet back against the wall.

Arnold Friend was saying from the door, "That's a good girl. Put the phone back."

She kicked the phone away from her.

"No, honey. Pick it up. Put it back right."

She picked it up and put it back. The dial tone stopped.

150 "That's a good girl. Now come outside."

She was hollow with what had been fear, but what was now just an emptiness. All that screaming had blasted it out of her. She sat, one leg cramped under her, and deep inside her brain was something like a pinpoint of light that kept going and would not let her relax. She thought, I'm not going to see my mother again. She thought, I'm not going to sleep in my bed again. Her bright green blouse was all wet.

Arnold Friend said, in a gentle-loud voice that was like a stage voice, "The place where you came from ain't there any more, and where you had in mind to go is canceled out. This place you are now—inside your daddy's house—is nothing but a cardboard box I can knock down any time. You know that and always did know it. You hear me?"

She thought, I have got to think. I have to know what to do.

"We'll go out to a nice field, out in the country here where it smells so nice and it's sunny," Arnold Friend said. "I'll have my arms tight around you so you won't need to try to get away and I'll show you what love is like, what it does. The hell with this house! It looks solid all right," he said. He ran a fingernail down the screen and the noise did not make Connie shiver, as it would have the day before. "Now put your hand on your heart, honey. Feel that? That feels solid too but we know better, be nice to me, be sweet like you can because what else is there for a girl like you but to be sweet and pretty and give in?—and get away before her people come back?"

155 She felt her pounding heart. Her hand seemed to enclose it. She thought for the first time in her life that it was nothing that was hers, that belonged to her, but just a pounding, living thing inside this body that wasn't really hers either.

"You don't want them to get hurt," Arnold Friend went on. "Now get up, honey. Get up all by yourself."

She stood up.

"Now turn this way. That's right. Come over here to me—Ellie, put that away, didn't I tell you? You dope. You miserable creepy dope," Arnold Friend said. His words were not angry but only part of an incantation. The incantation was kindly. "Now come out through the kitchen to me honey, and let's see a smile, try it, you're a brave sweet little girl and now they're eating corn and hot dogs cooked to bursting over an outdoor fire, and they don't know one thing about you and never did and honey you're better than them because not a one of them would have done this for you."

Connie felt the linoleum under her feet; it was cool. She brushed her hair back out of her eyes. Arnold Friend let go of the post tentatively and opened his arms for her, his elbows pointing in toward each other and his wrists limp, to show that this was an embarrassed embrace and a little mocking, he didn't want to make her self-conscious.

160 She put out her hand against the screen. She watched herself push the door slowly open as if she were safe back somewhere in the other doorway, watching this body and this head of long hair moving out into the sunlight where Arnold Friend waited.

"My sweet little blue-eyed girl," he said, in a half-sung sigh that had nothing to do with her brown eyes but was taken up just the same by the vast sunlit reaches of the land behind him and on all sides of him, so much land that Connie had never seen before and did not recognize except to know that she was going to it.

[*1966*]

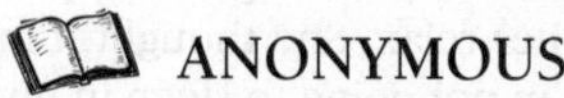

# ANONYMOUS

## *The Demon Lover*

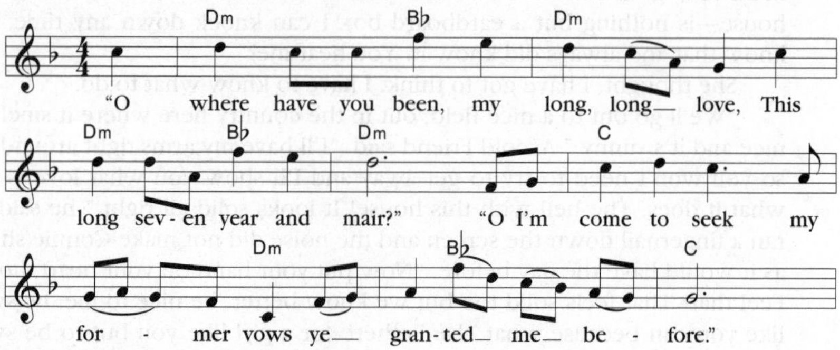


"O where have you been, my long, long love,
This long seven years and mair?"°
"O I'm come to seek my former vows
Ye granted me before."

"O hold your tongue of your former vows,
For they will breed sad strife;
O hold your tongue of your former vows,
For I am become a wife."

He turned him right and round about,
And the tear blinded his ee:
"I wad never hae trodden on Irish ground,
If it had not been for thee.

"I might hae had a king's daughter,
Far, far beyond the sea;
I might have had a king's daughter,
Had it not been for love o thee."

"If ye might have had a king's daughter,
Yer sel ye had to blame;
Ye might have taken the king's daughter,
For ye kend° that I was nane.

**2 mair** more **20 kend** knew

"If I was to leave my husband dear,
And my two babes also,
O what have you to take me to,
If with you I should go?"

"I hae seven ships upon the sea—
The eighth brought me to land—
With four-and-twenty bold mariners,
And music on every hand."

She has taken up her two little babes,
Kissed them baith cheek and chin:
"O fair ye weel, my ain two babes,
For I'll never see you again."

She set her foot upon the ship,
No mariners could she behold;
But the sails were o the taffetie,°
And the masts o the beaten gold.

They had not sailed a league, a league,
A league but barely three,
With dismal grew his countenance,
And drumlie° grew his ee.

They had not sailed a league, a league,
A league but barely three,
Until she espied his cloven foot,
And she wept right bitterlie.

"O hold your tongue of your weeping," says he,
"Of your weeping now let me be;
I will show you how the lilies grow
On the banks of Italy."

"O what hills are yon, yon pleasant hills,
That the sun shines sweetly on?"
"O yon are the hills of heaven," he said.
"Where you will never win."°

"O whaten mountain is yon," she said,
"All so dreary wi frost and snow?"
"O yon is the mountain of hell," he cried,
"Where you and I will go."

He strack the tap-mast wi his hand,
The fore-mast wi his knee,
And he brake that gallant ship in twain,
And sank her in the sea.

**35 taffetie** fabric used chiefly for women's clothing **40 drumlie** gloomy **52 win** gain, get to

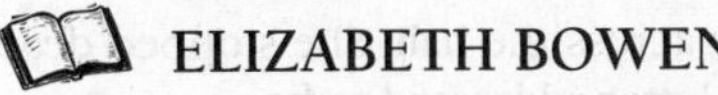

## ELIZABETH BOWEN

***Elizabeth Bowen (1899–1973) was born in Dublin, Ireland, of Anglo-Irish stock and received her schooling in***

*England. During the First World War she served as a nurse in a military hospital. In 1923 she married an Englishman and the same year published her first book,* Encounters, *a collection of stories. For twelve years she and her husband lived near Oxford. Later they moved to London where Bowen worked for the Ministry of Information during the Second World War. After the war she returned to her family home in Ireland, though she spent her last years in England.*

*Bowen wrote stories and novels—often with a hallucinatory quality that struck readers as a counterpart to the absurdity of life—as well as some critical essays.*

## The Demon Lover

Towards the end of her day in London Mrs. Drover went round to her shut-up house to look for several things she wanted to take away. Some belonged to herself, some to her family, who were by now used to their country life. It was late August; it had been a steamy, showery day: at the moment the trees down the pavement glittered in an escape of humid yellow afternoon sun. Against the next batch of clouds, already piling up ink-dark, broken chimneys and parapets stood out. In her once familiar street, as in any unused channel, an unfamiliar queerness had silted up: a cat wove itself in and out of railings, but no human eye watched Mrs. Drover's return. Shifting some parcels under her arm, she slowly forced round her latchkey in an unwilling lock, then gave the door, which had warped, a push with her knee. Dead air came out to meet her as she went in.

The staircase window having been boarded up, no light came down into the hall. But one door, she could just see, stood ajar, so she went quickly through into the room and unshuttered the big window in there. Now the prosaic woman, looking about her, was more perplexed than she knew by everything that she saw, by traces of her long former habit of life—the yellow smoke-stain up the white marble mantelpiece, the ring left by a vase on the top of the escritoire; the bruise in the wallpaper where, on the door being thrown open widely, the china handle had always hit the wall. The piano, having gone away to be stored, had left what looked like claw-marks on its part of the parquet. Though not much dust had seeped in, each object wore a film of another kind; and, the only ventilation being the chimney, the whole drawing-room smelled of the cold hearth. Mrs. Drover put down her parcels on the escritoire and left the room to proceed upstairs; the things she wanted were in a bedroom closet.

She had been anxious to see how the house was—the part-time caretaker she shared with some neighbours was away this week on his holiday, known to be not yet back. At the best of times he did not look in often, and she was never sure that she trusted him. There were some cracks in the structure, left by the last bombing, on which she was anxious to keep an eye. Not that one could do anything—

A shaft of refracted daylight now lay across the hall. She stopped dead and stared at the hall table—on this lay a letter addressed to her.

5 She thought first—then the caretaker *must* be back. All the same, who,

seeing the house shuttered, would have dropped a letter in at the box? It was not a circular, it was not a bill. And the post office redirected, in the address to the country, everything for her that came through the post. The caretaker (even if he *were* back) did not know she was due in London today—her call here had been planned to be a surprise—so his negligence in the manner of this letter, leaving it to wait in the dusk and the dust, annoyed her. Annoyed, she picked up the letter, which bore no stamp. But it cannot be important, or they would know . . . She took the letter rapidly upstairs with her, without a stop to look at the writing till she reached what had been her bedroom, where she let in light. The room looked over the garden and other gardens: the sun had gone in; as the clouds sharpened and lowered, the trees and rank lawns seemed already to smoke with dark. Her reluctance to look again at the letter came from the fact that she felt intruded upon—and by someone contemptuous of her ways. However, in the tenseness preceding the fall of rain she read it: it was a few lines.

> Dear Kathleen: You will not have forgotten that today is our anniversary, and the day we said. The years have gone by at once slowly and fast. In view of the fact that nothing has changed, I shall rely upon you to keep your promise. I was sorry to see you leave London, but was satisfied that you would be back in time. You may expect me, therefore, at the hour arranged. Until then . . .
>
> K.

Mrs. Drover looked for the date: it was today's. She dropped the letter on to the bed-springs, then picked it up to see the writing again—her lips, beneath the remains of lipstick, beginning to go white. She felt so much the change in her own face that she went to the mirror, polished a clear patch in it, and looked at once urgently and stealthily in. She was confronted by a woman of forty-four, with eyes starting out under a hat-brim that had been rather carelessly pulled down. She had not put on any more powder since she left the shop where she ate her solitary tea. The pearls her husband had given her on their marriage hung loose around her now rather thinner throat, slipping in the V of the pink wool jumper her sister knitted last autumn as they sat round the fire. Mrs. Drover's most normal expression was one of controlled worry, but of assent. Since the birth of the third of her little boys, attended by a quite serious illness, she had had an intermittent muscular flicker to the left of her mouth, but in spite of this she could always sustain a manner that was at once energetic and calm.

Turning from her own face as precipitately as she had gone to meet it, she went to the chest where the things were, unlocked it, threw up the lid, and knelt to search. But as rain began to come crashing down she could not keep from looking over her shoulder at the stripped bed on which the letter lay. Behind the blanket of rain the clock of the church that still stood struck six—with rapidly heightening apprehension she counted each of the slow strokes. "The hour arranged . . . My God," she said, "*what* hour? How should I . . . ? After twenty-five years . . ."

The young girl talking to the soldier in the garden had not ever completely seen his face. It was dark; they were saying goodbye under a tree. Now and then—for it felt, from not seeing him at this intense moment, as though she had never seen him at all—she verified his presence for these few moments longer by putting out a hand, which he each time pressed, without very much kindness, and painfully, on to one of the breast buttons of his uniform. That cut of the button on the palm of her hand was, principally, what she was to carry away. This was so near the end of a leave from France that she could only wish him already gone. It was August 1916. Being not kissed, being drawn away from and looked at intimidated Kathleen till she imagined spectral glitters in the place of his eyes. Turning away and looking back up the lawn she saw, through branches of trees, the drawing-room window light: she caught a breath for the moment when she could go running back there into the safe arms of her mother and sister, and cry: "What shall I do, what shall I do? He has gone."

Hearing her catch her breath, her finacé said, without feeling: "Cold?"

"You're going away such a long way."

"Not so far as you think."

"I don't understand?"

"You don't have to," he said. "You will. You know what we said."

"But that was—suppose you—I mean, suppose."

"I shall be with you," he said, "sooner or later. You won't forget that. You need do nothing but wait."

Only a little more than a minute later she was free to run up the silent lawn. Looking in through the window at her mother and sister, who did not for the moment perceive her, she already felt that unnatural promise drive down between her and the rest of all human kind. No other way of having given herself could have made her feel so apart, lost and foresworn. She could not have plighted a more sinister troth.

Kathleen behaved well when, some months later, her fiancé was reported missing, presumed killed. Her family not only supported her but were able to praise her courage without stint because they could not regret, as a husband for her, the man they knew almost nothing about. They hoped she would, in a year or two, console herself—and had it been only a question of consolation things might have gone much straighter ahead. But her trouble, behind just a little grief, was a complete dislocation from everything. She did not reject other lovers, for these failed to appear: for years she failed to attract men—and with the approach of her thirties she became natural enough to share her family's anxiousness on this score. She began to put herself out, to wonder; and at thirty-two she was very greatly relieved to find herself being courted by William Drover. She married him, and the two of them settled down in this quiet, arboreal part of Kensington: in this house the years piled up, her children were born, and they all lived till they were driven out by the bombs of the next war. Her movements as Mrs. Drover were circumscribed, and she dismissed any idea that they were still watched.

As things were—dead or living the letter-writer sent her only a threat. Unable, for some minutes, to go on kneeling with her back exposed to the empty room, Mrs. Drover rose from the chest to sit on an upright chair whose back was firmly against the wall. The desuetude of her former bedroom, her married London home's whole air of being a cracked cup from which memory, with its reassuring power, had either evaporated or leaked away, made a crisis—and at just this crisis the letter-writer had, knowledgeably, struck. The hollowness of the house this evening cancelled years on years of voices, habits, and steps. Through the shut windows she only heard rain fall on the roofs around. To rally herself, she said she was in a mood—and for two or three seconds shutting her eyes, told herself that she had imagined the letter. But she opened them—there it lay on the bed.

On the supernatural side of the letter's entrance she was not permitting her mind to dwell. Who, in London, knew she meant to call at the house today? Evidently, however, this had been known. The caretaker, *had* he come back, had had no cause to expect her: he would have taken the letter in his pocket, to forward it, at his own time, through the post. There was no other sign that the caretaker had been in—but, if not? Letters dropped in at doors of deserted houses do not fly or walk to tables in halls. They do not sit on the dust of empty tables with the air of certainty that they will be found. There is needed some human hand—but nobody but the caretaker had a key. Under circumstances she did not care to consider, a house can be entered without a key. It was possible that she was not alone now. She might be being waited for, downstairs. Waited for—until when? Until "the hour arranged." At least that was not six o'clock: six has struck.

She rose from the chair and went over and locked the door.

20 The thing was, to get out. To fly? No, not that: she had to catch her train. As a woman whose utter dependability was the keystone of her family life she was not willing to return to the country, to her husband, her little boys, and her sister, without the objects she had come up to fetch. Resuming work at the chest she set about making up a number of parcels in a rapid, fumbling-decisive way. These, with her shopping parcels, would be too much to carry; these meant a taxi—at the thought of the taxi her heart went up and her normal breathing resumed. I will ring up the taxi now; the taxi cannot come too soon: I shall hear the taxi out there running its engine, till I walk calmly down to it through the hall. I'll ring up—But no: the telephone is cut off . . . She tugged at a knot she had tied wrong.

The idea of flight . . . He was never kind to me, not really. I don't remember him kind at all. Mother said he never considered me. He was set on me, that was what it was—not love. Not love, not meaning a person well. What did he do, to make me promise like that? I can't remember—But she found that she could.

She remembered with such dreadful acuteness that the twenty-five years since then dissolved like smoke and she instinctively looked for the weal left by the button on the palm of her hand. She remembered not only all that he said and did but the complete suspension of *her* existence during that August week. I was not myself—they all told me so at the time. She remembered—but with one white burning blank as where acid has dropped on a photograph: *under no conditions* could she remember his face.

So, wherever he may be waiting, I shall not know him. You have no time to run from a face you do not expect.

The thing was to get to the taxi before any clock struck what could be the hour. She would slip down the street and round the side of the square to where the square gave on the main road. She would return in the taxi, safe, to her own door, and bring the solid driver into the house with her to pick up the parcels from room to room. The idea of the taxi driver made her decisive, bold: she unlocked her door, went to the top of the staircase, and listened down.

25 She heard nothing—but while she was hearing nothing the *passé*[1] air of the staircase was disturbed by a draught that travelled up to her face. It emanated from the basement: down there a door or window was being opened by someone who chose this moment to leave the house.

The rain had stopped; the pavements steamily shone as Mrs. Drover let herself out by inches from her own front door into the empty street. The unoccupied houses opposite continued to meet her look with their damaged stare. Making towards the thoroughfare and the taxi, she tried not to keep looking behind. Indeed, the silence was so intense—one of those creeks of London silence exaggerated this summer by the damage of war—that no tread could have gained on hers unheard. Where her street debouched on the square where people went on living, she grew conscious of, and checked, her unnatural pace. Across the open end of the square two buses impassively passed each other: women, a perambulator, cyclists, a man wheeling a barrow signalized, once again, the ordinary flow of life. At the square's most populous corner should be—and was—the short taxi rank. This evening, only one taxi—but this, although it presented its blank rump, appeared already to be alertly waiting for her. Indeed, without looking round the driver started his engine as she panted up from behind and put her hand on the door. As she did so, the clock struck seven. The taxi faced the main road: to make the trip back to her house it would have to turn—she had settled back on the seat and the taxi *had* turned before she, surprised by its knowing movement, recollected that she had not "said where." She leaned forward to scratch at the glass panel that divided the driver's head from her own.

The driver braked to what was almost a stop, turned round, and slid the glass panel back: the jolt of this flung Mrs. Drover forward till her face was almost into the glass. Through the aperture driver and passenger, not six inches between them, remained for an eternity eye to eye. Mrs. Drover's mouth hung open for some seconds before she could issue her first scream. After that she continued to scream freely and to beat with her gloved hands on the glass all round as the taxi, accelerating without mercy, made off with her into the hinterland of deserted streets.

[*1941*]

[1]***passé*** stuffy

## CHRISTOPHER R. REASKE AND JOHN R. KNOTT, JR.

# *Interview with Joyce Carol Oates*

EDITORS. How did you get the idea for the story?

MISS OATES. The story as it was originally published in *Epoch* was not dedicated to anyone, but after that I dedicated it "to Bob Dylan." I will explain this: after hearing for some weeks Dylan's song "It's All Over Now, Baby Blue," and after having read about a killer in some Southwestern state, and after having thought about the old legends and folk songs of Death and the Maiden, the story came to me more or less in a piece. Dylan's song is very beautiful, very disturbing.

EDITORS. How does Arnold Friend know so much about what Connie's parents are doing? About the woman down the street?

MISS OATES. Arnold Friend is a fantastic figure: he is Death, he is the "elf-Knight" of the ballads, he is the Imagination, he is a Dream, he is a Lover, a Demon, *and all that.* The story was originally called "Death and the Maiden," but I thought the title too pompous, too literary.

It is always frustrating to attempt to explain these things . . . the mind goes dead, the voice keeps on supplying words, familiar terms, a system of explanations. But the explanations are false, or inadequate. What is so terrifying about the world of dreams is its indeterminate quality; raised to a verbal level (what is verbalized is less of a threat . . . ?) so much is lost, at least to the rational mind. Still, it will not do to suggest that one writes in a trance, the way Jackson Pollock evidently did some of his violent paintings, because writing and painting (his kind of painting) are two quite different things. But the "writing" I do is a kind of reporting, a recalling, an approximation of things that have already happened. I never write until these things have already happened, and then I try to do justice to them.

[*1975*]

## JOYCE CAROL OATES

# *"Where Are You Going, Where Have You Been?" and* Smooth Talk*: Short Story into Film*

Some years ago in the American Southwest there surfaced a tabloid psychopath known as "The Pied Piper of Tucson." I have forgotten his name, but his speciality was the seduction and occasional murder of teen-aged girls. He may or may not have had actual accomplices, but his bizarre activities were known among a circle of teenagers in the Tucson area; for some reason they kept his secret, deliberately did not inform parents or police. It was this fact, not the fact of the mass murderer himself, that struck me at the time. And this was a pre-Manson time, early or mid-1960s.

The Pied Piper mimicked teenagers in their talk, dress, and behavior, but he was not a teenager—he was a man in his early thirties. Rather short, he stuffed rags in his leather boots to give himself height. (And sometimes walked unsteadily as a consequence: did none among his admiring constituency notice?) He charmed his victims as charismatic psychopaths have always charmed their victims, to the bewilderment of others who fancy themselves free of all lunatic attractions. The Pied Piper of Tucson: a trashy dream, a tabloid archetype, sheer artifice, comedy, cartoon—surrounded, however improbably, and finally tragically, by real people. You think that, if you look twice, he won't be there. But there he is.

I don't remember any longer where I first read about this Pied Piper—very likely in *Life* Magazine. I do recall deliberately not reading the full article because I didn't want to be distracted by too much detail. It was not after all the mass murderer himself who intrigued me, but the disturbing fact that a number of teenagers—from "good" families—aided and abetted his crimes. This is the sort of thing authorities and responsible citizens invariably call "inexplicable" because they can't find explanations for it. *They* would not have fallen under this maniac's spell, after all.

An early draft of my short story, "Where Are You Going, Where Have You Been?"—from which the film *Smooth Talk* was adapted by Joyce Chopra and Tom Cole—had the rather too explicit title "Death and the Maiden." It was cast in a mode of fiction to which I am still partial—indeed, every third or fourth story of mine is probably in this mode—"realistic allegory," it might be called. It is Hawthornean, romantic, shading into parable. Like the medieval German engraving from which my title was taken, the story was minutely detailed yet clearly an allegory of the fatal attractions of death (or the devil). An innocent young girl is seduced by way of her own vanity; she mistakes death for erotic romance of a particularly American/trashy sort.

5 In subsequent drafts the story changed its tone, its focus, its language, its title. It became "Where Are You Going, Where Have You Been?" Written at a time when the author was intrigued by the music of Bob Dylan, particularly the hauntingly elegiac song "It's All Over Now, Baby Blue," it was dedicated to Bob Dylan. The charismatic mass murderer drops into the background and his innocent victim, a fifteen-year-old, moves into the foreground. She becomes the true protagonist of the tale, courting and being courted by her fate, a self-styled 1950s pop figure, alternately absurd and winning. There is no suggestion in the published story that "Arnold Friend" has seduced and murdered other young girls, or even that he necessarily intends to murder Connie. Is his interest "merely" sexual? (Nor is there anything about the complicity of other teenagers. I saved that yet more provocative note for a current story, "Testimony.") Connie is shallow, vain, silly, hopeful, doomed—but capable nonetheless of an unexpected gesture of heroism at the story's end. Her smooth-talking seducer, who cannot lie, promises her that her family will be unharmed if she gives herself to him; and so she does. The story ends abruptly at the point of her "crossing over." We don't know the nature of her sacrifice, only that she is generous enough to make it.

In adapting a narrative so spare and thematically foreshortened as "Where Are You Going, Where Have You Been?" film director Joyce Chopra and screenwriter Tom Cole were required to do a good deal of filling in, expanding, inventing. Connie's story becomes lavishly, and lovingly, textured; she is not an allegorical figure so much as a "typical" teenaged girl (if Laura Dern, spectacularly good-looking, can be so defined). Joyce Chopra, who has done documentary films on contemporary teenage culture and, yet more authoritatively, has an adolescent daughter of her own, creates in *Smooth Talk* a vivid and absolutely believable world for Connie to inhabit. Or worlds: as in the original story there is Connie-at-home, and there is

Connie-with-her-friends. Two fifteen-year-old girls, two finely honed styles, two voices, sometimes but not often overlapping. It is one of the marvelous visual features of the film that we *see* Connie and her friends transform themselves, once they are safely free of parental observation. The girls claim their true identities in the neighborhood shopping mall. What freedom, what joy!

*Smooth Talk* is, in a way, as much Connie's mother's story as it is Connie's; its center of gravity, its emotional nexus, is frequently with the mother—warmly and convincingly played by Mary Kay Place. (Though the mother's sexual jealousy of her daughter is slighted in the film.) Connie's ambiguous relationship with her affable, somewhat mysterious father (well played by Levon Helm) is an excellent touch: I had thought, subsequent to the story's publication, that I should have built up the father, suggesting, as subtly as I could, an attraction there paralleling the attraction Connie feels for her seducer, Arnold Friend. And Arnold Friend himself—"A. Friend" as he says—is played with appropriately overdone sexual swagger by Treat Williams, who is perfect for the part; and just the right age. We see that Arnold Friend isn't a teenager even as Connie, mesmerized by his presumed charm, does not seem to *see* him at all. What is so difficult to accomplish in prose—nudging the reader to look over the protagonist's shoulder, so to speak—is accomplished with enviable ease in film.

Treat Williams as Arnold Friend is supreme in his very awfulness, as, surely, the original Pied Piper of Tucson must have been. (Though no one involved in the film knew about the original source.) Mr. Williams flawlessly impersonates Arnold Friend as Arnold Friend impersonates—is it James Dean? James Dean regarding himself in mirrors, doing James Dean impersonations? That Connie's fate is so trashy is in fact her fate.

What is outstanding in Joyce Chopra's *Smooth Talk* is its visual freshness, its sense of motion and life; the attentive intelligence the director has brought to the semi-secret world of the American adolescent—shopping mall flirtations, drive-in restaurant romances, highway hitchhiking, the fascination of rock music played very, very loud. (James Taylor's music for the film is wonderfully appropriate. We hear it as Connie hears it; it is the music of her spiritual being.) Also outstanding, as I have indicated, and numerous critics have noted, are the acting performances. Laura Dern is so dazzlingly right as "my" Connie that I may come to think I modeled the fictitious girl on her, in the way that writers frequently delude themselves about motions of causality.

10 My difficulties with *Smooth Talk* have primarily to do with my chronic hesitation—about seeing/hearing work of mine abstracted from its contexture of language. All writers know that language is their subject; quirky word choices, patterns of rhythm, enigmatic pauses, punctuation marks. Where the quick scanner sees "quick" writing, the writer conceals nine tenths of the iceberg. Of course we all have "real" subjects, and we will fight to the death to defend those subjects, but beneath the tale-telling it is the tale-telling that grips us so very fiercely. The writer works in a single dimension, the director works in three. I assume they are professionals to their fingertips; authorities in their medium as I am an authority (if I am) in

mine. I would fiercely defend the placement of a semicolon in one of my novels but I would probably have deferred in the end to Joyce Chopra's decision to reverse the story's conclusion, turn it upside down, in a sense, so that the film ends not with death, not with a sleepwalker's crossing over to her fate, but upon a scene of reconciliation, rejuvenation.

A girl's loss of virginity, bittersweet but not necessarily tragic. Not today. A girl's coming-of-age that involves her succumbing to, but then rejecting, the "trashy dreams" of her pop teenage culture. "Where Are You Going, Where Have You Been?" defines itself as allegorical in its conclusion: Death and Death's chariot (a funky souped-up convertible) have come for the Maiden. Awakening is, in the story's final lines, moving out into the sunlight where Arnold Friend waits:

> "My sweet little blue-eyed girl," he said in a half-sung sigh that had nothing to do with [Connie's] brown eyes but was taken up just the same by the vast sunlit reaches of the land behind him and on all sides of him—so much land that Connie had never seen before and did not recognize except to know that she was going to it.

—a conclusion impossible to transfigure into film.

[*1986*]

## MIKE TIERCE AND JOHN MICHAEL CRAFTON

# *Connie's Tambourine Man: A New Reading of Arnold Friend*

The critical reception of Joyce Carol Oates' "Where Are You Going, Where Have You Been?" reveals a consistent pattern for reducing that text to a manageable, univocal reading. Generally, this pattern involves two assumptions: Arnold *must* symbolize Satan and Connie *must* be raped and murdered. No critic has yet questioned Joyce Wegs' assertion that "Arnold is clearly a symbolic Satan."[1] Marie Urbanski argues that Arnold's "feet resemble the devil's cloven hoofs," Joan Winslow calls the story "an encounter with the devil," Tom Quirk maintains the story describes a "demoniac character," and Christina Marsden Gillis refers to "the satanic visitor's incantation."[2] Wegs' assertion that Arnold is "a criminal with plans to rape and probably murder Connie"[3] is also accepted at face value. Gillis assumes that

[1]Joyce M. Wegs, "'Don't You Know Who I Am?' The Grotesque in Oates' 'Where Are You Going, Where Have You Been?'" in *Critical Essays on Joyce Carol Oates,* ed. Linda W. Wagner (Boston: G.K. Hall, 1979), p. 90. First printed in *Journal of Narrative Technique,* 5 (1975), 66–72.

[2]Marie Urbanski, "Existential Allegory: Joyce Carol Oates' 'Where Are You Going, Where Have You Been?'" *Studies in Short Fiction,* 15 (1978), 202; Joan Winslow, "The Stranger Within: Two Stories by Oates and Hawthorne," *Studies in Short Fiction,* 17 (1980), 264; Tom Quirk "A Source for 'Where Are You Going, Where Have You Been?'" *Studies in Short Fiction,* 18 (1981), 416; Christina Marsden Gillis, "'Where Are You Going, Where Have You Been?': Seduction, Space, and a Fictional Mode," *Studies in Short Fiction,* 18 (1981), 70.

[3]Wegs, p. 89.

Arnold "leads his victim . . . to a quick and violent sexual assault,"[4] and Quirk refers to "the rape and subsequent murder of Connie."[5] Even though Gretchen Schulz and R. J. R. Rockwood correctly claim that the portrait of Arnold "is created in the mind of Connie . . . and that it exists *there only,*" they still persist in having Arnold as a demon and Connie as doomed: "But we know that he is still the Wolf, and that he still intends to 'gobble up' this 'little girl' as soon as he gets the chance. Connie is not going to live happily ever after. Indeed, it would seem that she is not going to live at all."[6]

While all of these critics insist on seeing satanic traces in Arnold, they refuse, on the other hand, to see that these traces are only part of a much more complex, more dynamic symbol. There are indeed diabolic shades to Arnold, but just as Blake and Shelley could see in Milton's Satan a positive, attractive symbol of the poet, the rebellious embodiment of creative energy, so we should also be sensitive to Arnold's multifaceted and creative nature. Within the frame of the story, the fiction of Arnold burns in the day as the embodiment of poetic energy. The story is dedicated to Bob Dylan, the troubadour, the artist. Friend is the artist, the actor, the rhetorician, the teacher, all symbolized by Connie's overheated imagination. We should not assume that Arnold is completely evil because she is afraid of him. Her limited perceptions remind us of Blake's questioner in "The Tyger" who begins to perceive the frightening element of the experiential world but also is rather duped into his fear by his own limitations. Like the figure in Blake, Connie is the framer, the story creator—and the diabolic traces in her fiction frighten her not because they are the manifestations of an outside evil but because they are the symbolic extrapolations of her own psyche.

If the adamant insistence that Arnold Friend is Satan is rejected, then who is this intriguing mysterious visitor? In *Enter Mysterious Stranger: American Cloistral Fiction,* Roy Male asserts that many mysterious intruders throughout American literature "are almost always potential saviors, destroyers, or ambiguous combinations of both, and their initial entrance, however much it may be displaced toward realism, amounts to the entrance of God or the devil on a machine."[7] And if Arnold Friend is *not* satanic, then his arrival could be that of a savior. This possibility moreover is suggested by Connie's whispering "Christ. Christ"[8] when Arnold first arrives in his golden "machine." Not only is "33" part of Arnold's "secret code" of numbers (p. 706), but his sign, an "X" that seems to hover in the air, is also one of the symbols for Christ. Because music is closely associated with religion—"the music was always in the background, like music at a church service" (p. 703)—it also adds a religious element to Arnold's arrival. The key question then is who is this musical messiah, and the key to the answer is

[4]Gillis, p. 65.

[5]Quirk, p. 416.

[6]Gretchen Schulz and R. J. R. Rockwood, "In Fairyland, Without a Map: Connie's Exploration Inward in Joyce Carol Oates' 'Where Are You Going, Where Have You Been?'" *Literature and Psychology,* 30 (1980), 156 & 165 & 166, respectively.

[7]Roy Male, *Enter Mysterious Stranger: American Cloistral Fiction* (Norman: University of Oklahoma Press, 1979), p. 21.

[8]Joyce Carol Oates, "Where Are You Going, Where Have You Been?" in *The Wheel of Love* (New York: Vanguard Press, 1970), p. 40. Hereafter cited parenthetically within the text.

the dedication "For Bob Dylan"—the element of the story so unsatisfactorily accounted for by our predecessors. Not only does the description of Arnold Friend also fit Bob Dylan—a type of rock-and-roll messiah—but three of Dylan's songs (popular when the story was written) are very similar to the story itself.

In the mid-sixties Bob Dylan's followers perceived him to be a messiah. According to his biographer, Dylan was "a rock-and-roll king."[9] It is no wonder then that Arnold speaks with "the voice of the man on the radio" (p. 709), the disc jockey whose name, Bobby King, is a reference to "Bobby" Dylan, the "king" of rock-and-roll. Dylan was more than just a "friend" to his listeners; he was "Christ revisited," "the prophet leading [his followers] into [a new] Consciousness."[10] In fact, "people were making him an idol; . . . thousands of men and women, young and old, felt their lives entwined with his because they saw him as a mystic, a messiah who would lead them to salvation."[11]

5 That Oates consciously associates Arnold Friend with Bob Dylan is clearly suggested by the similarities of their physical descriptions. Arnold's "shaggy, shabby black hair that looked crazy as a wig" (p. 705), his "long and hawklike nose" (p. 707), his unshavened face, his "big and white" teeth (p. 708), his lashes, "thick and black as if painted with a black tarlike material" (p. 708) and his size ("only an inch or so taller than Connie" [p. 706]) are all characteristic of Bob Dylan. Even Arnold's "fast, bright monotone voice" (p. 705) is suggestive of Dylan, especially since he speaks "in a simple lilting voice, exactly as if he were reciting the words to a song" (p. 707).

Dylan then provides a physical model for Arnold's appearance and a historical referent for Arnold's existence. Yet more profoundly, the myth of Dylan's being organized or somehow controlled by his music is reflected by Connie, Arnold, and Ellie being organized or perhaps even unified by the almost mystical music heard throughout the story. Connie, for example, notices the way Arnold "tapped one fist against another in homage to the perpetual music behind him" (p. 708). Since this "perpetual music" is the one thing that Connie can "depend upon" (p. 705), it even becomes her breath of life; she is "bathed in a glow of slow-pulsed joy that seemed to rise mysteriously out of the music itself, . . . breathed in and breathed out with each gentle rise of her chest" (p. 705). Paying "close attention" to the words and singing along with the songs played on the "XYZ Sunday Jamboree," Connie spends her Sunday afternoon worshipping "the music that made everything so good" (p. 703). And when her two visitors arrive, "the same program . . . playing inside the house" (p. 706) is also playing on Ellie Oscar's radio. In fact, "the music from [Connie's] radio and [Ellie's] blend together" (p. 708). Ellie is so closely associated with the radio that without it pressed up against his ear, he grimaces "as if . . . the air was too much for him" (p. 712). Both Ellie's and Arnold's existences seem to depend completely on the "perpetual music"; consequently, Oates appears to be suggesting that they are not literally present. They are instead part of Connie's musically induced fantasy—another of her so-called "trashy daydreams" (p. 702).

[9]Anthony Scaduto, *Bob Dylan* (New York: Grosset and Dunlop, 1971), p. 222.
[10]Scaduto, p. 274.
[11]Scaduto, p. 229.

Oates points out that Connie spends her summer "thinking, dreaming of the boys she met" (p. 704). But because of Connie's gradually changing desires, "all the boys fell back and dissolved into a single face that was not even a face but an idea, a feeling, mixed up with the urgent insistent pounding of the music" (p. 704). This "urgent" feeling reflects Connie's desire for something more sexually stimulating than the kissing sessions she spends with "boys" like Eddie. As Freud points out, "the motive forces of phantasies are unsatisfied wishes, and every single phantasy is the fulfillment of a wish, a correlation of unsatisfying reality. . . . In young women the erotic wishes predominate almost exclusively."[12] Although we acknowledge the sexist nature of Freud's generalization, his point seems to apply to Connie. Furthermore, Roy Male suggests that even though "there is no logical reason for the entrance of a stranger, it is equally true that he comes as if in answer to some unuttered call."[13] Arnold is described as "talking right through Connie's voice" (p. 710) because that is the only voice he has. His arrival is the answer to Connie's "unuttered" call and to her "erotic" desires. Arnold's "face" is therefore "familiar" (p. 710) because it is the "face" that replaces the "boys" in her fantasies. Not only is the emphasis placed on Arnold's face reinforced by "a drawing of a round grinning face" (p. 706) on his car, but when Connie first encounters Arnold at Napoleon's drive-in restaurant, he is described as "a face just a few feet from hers" (p. 704)—perhaps her own distorted reflection in a car windshield.

Connie not only turns away from Arnold's face "without Eddie noticing anything" (p. 704), but many other elements in the story suggest that Arnold is just another "shadowy vision of [Connie] herself" (p. 702). For example, Arnold is described as being "just a blur . . . that . . . had come from nowhere . . . and belonged nowhere and that everything about him . . . was only half real" (p. 709). His "fake" laughter suggests that his threatening presence is "all a joke" (p. 707). He opens the door to his car carefully because it might fall off, he cannot walk without stumbling, his feet seem not to be in his boots, and he wears a mask and make-up. He even touches his sunglasses "as if to make sure they were still there" (p. 712). He also magically knows Connie's name, her best friend's name, her other friends' names, and where her parents are and when they will return. Part of the action that takes place also suggests a dream-like experience. Arnold's asking Connie if she has something against a dead woman, Connie's inability to dial the telephone, and Arnold's promise not to come into the house are all tinged with a sense of unreality. Even the fact that the phrase "as if" is used over thirty times suggests that there is something dubious about Connie's experience.

In order to reinforce the idea that Arnold's visit is another fantasy, Oates parallels the actual description of one of Connie's other daydreams to the description of her finally joining Arnold Friend at the story's end:

> Connie sat with her eyes closed in the sun, dreaming and dazed with the warmth about her as if this were a kind of love, the caresses of love, and her mind slipped over onto thoughts of the boy she had been with the night before and how nice he had been,

[12]Sigmund Freud, "Creative Writers and Day-Dreamers," in *Criticism: The Major Statements,* ed. Charles Kaplan (New York: St. Martin's Press, 1975), p. 468.
[13]Male, p. 10.

> how sweet it always was, not the way someone like June would suppose but sweet, gentle, the way it was in movies and promised in songs; and when she opened her eyes she hardly knew where she was, the back yard ran off into weeds and a fence-like line of trees and behind it the sky was perfectly blue and still. The asbestos "ranch house" that was now three years old startled her—it looked small. She shook her head as if to get awake. (p. 705).
>
> "My sweet little blue-eyed girl," he said in a half-sung sigh that had nothing to do with her brown eyes but was taken up just the same by the vast sunlit reaches of the land behind him and on all sides of him—so much land that Connie had never seen before and did not recognize except to know that she was going to it. (pp. 713-14)

The fence-like line of trees is replaced by "the vast sunlit reaches of the land" surrounding Arnold Friend. Through her encounter with his mysterious stranger, Connie frees herself from the sense of confinement she feels in her father's house. As Roy Male so aptly explains it, the "mysterious strangers who are potential saviors" force the "insider" to undergo a transformation, which "may involve the effort of the insider to break out of his fixed orientation."[14] The Dylanesque music initiates such a breakthrough for Connie. She no longer has to "dawdle in the doorway" (p. 706). As Dylan suggests in "Mister Tambourine Man," once she answers the call by forcing open the screen door, "there are no fences facin'" her any longer. She broadens her horizons to include the "vast sunlit reaches of the land" all around her.

10 The reference to "Mister Tambourine Man" implies another connection between the story and Dylan. A few of his song lyrics are very similar to the story itself. Oates herself suggests that part of the story's inspiration was "hearing for some weeks Dylan's song 'It's All Over Now, Baby Blue.'"[15] Such lines as "you must leave now," "something calls for you," "the vagabond who's rapping at your door," and "go start anew" are suggestive of the impending change awaiting Connie. Two other Dylan songs are equally as applicable though. The following lines from "Like a Rolling Stone"—the second most popular song of 1965 (the story was first published in 1966)—are also very similar to Connie's situation at the end of the story:

> You used to be so amused
> At Napoleon in rags and the language that he used
> Go to him now, he calls you, you can't refuse
> When you got nothing, you got nothing to lose
> You're invisible now, you got no secrets to conceal.

But Dylan's "Mr. Tambourine Man"—the number ten song in 1965—is even more similar. The following stanza establishes the notion of using music to rouse one's imagination into a blissful fantasy world:

[14] Male, p. 10.

[15] "Interview with Joyce Carol Oates about 'Where Are You Going, Where have You Been?'" in *Mirrors: An Introduction to Literature,* eds. John R. Knott, Jr. and Christopher R. Reaske, 2nd ed. (San Francisco: Canfield Press, 1975), pp. 18-19.

Take me on a trip upon your magic swirlin' ship,
My senses have been stripped,
My hands can't feel to grip,
My toes too numb to step,
Wait only for my boot heels to be wanderin'.

I'm ready to go anywhere,
I'm ready for to fade
Into my own parade.
Cast your dancin' spell my way,
I promised to go under it.

Hey, Mister Tambourine Man, play a song for me,
I'm not sleepy and there ain't no place I'm going to.
Hey, Mister Tambourine Man, play a song for me.
In the jingle, jangle morning I'll come followin' you.

Arnold Friend's car—complete with the phrase "MAN THE FLYING SAUCERS" (p. 708)—is just such "a magic swirlin' ship." Arnold is the personification of popular music, particularly Bob Dylan's music; and as such, Connie's interaction with him is a musically induced fantasy, a kind of "magic carpet ride" in "a convertible jalopy painted gold." Rising out of Connie's radio, Arnold Friend/Bob Dylan is a magical, musical messiah; he persuades Connie to abandon her father's house. As a manifestation of her own desires, he frees her from the limitations of a fifteen-year-old girl, assisting her maturation by stripping her of her childlike vision.

[*1985*]

 LARRY RUBIN

## *Oates's "Where Are You Going, Where Have You Been?"*

In a recent essay Joyce M. Wegs brilliantly establishes the satanic identity of the sinister Arnold Friend, young Connie's abductor and probable rapist-murderer in Joyce Carol Oates's widely anthologized short story "Where Are You Going, Where Have You Been?"[1] On another level, the psychological level, she points out that Arnold is "the incarnation of Connie's unconscious erotic desires and dreams, but in uncontrollable nightmare form."[2] I would go a step further and suggest that, on still another level, the whole terrifying episode involving Arnold Friend is itself a dream—a fantasy that Connie falls into on a sleepy Sunday afternoon when she is left alone in the

[1]Joyce M. Wegs, "'Don't You Know Who I Am?' The Grotesque in Oates's 'Where Are You Going, Where Have You Been?'" in *Critical Essays on Joyce Carol Oates,* ed. Linda W. Wagner (Boston: G. K. Hall & Co., 1979), pp. 87–92. See also Joan D. Winslow, "The Stranger Within: Two Stories by Oates and Hawthorne," *Studies in Short Fiction,* 17 (1980), 263–68.

[2]Wegs, *Critical Essays,* p. 90.

house and decides to spend the entire day drying her hair.[3] For those of her readers who don't believe in devils, Oates has made the willing suspension of disbelief somewhat easier by imparting to her story a dreamlike, unreal atmosphere that makes it possible for the reader to view Connie's scary encounter with Arnold as a dream-vision or "daymare"—one in which Connie's intense desire for total sexual experience runs headlong into her innate fear of such experience.[4] We must remember that Connie is only fifteen; and the collision is gorgeous.

First of all, for all the talk of sex and boys in the story, we have no clear evidence that Connie is not still a virgin. Sophisticated, yes—but only in the most superficial ways, involving the heightening of her physical charms. Even the brief time Connie spends with a boy named Eddie in an alley[5] seems, in context, more in keeping with smooching or even heavy petting than with triple-x sex. Indeed, her horror at Arnold Friend's direct solicitation ("I'll come inside you where it's all secret and you'll give in to me and you'll love me—" [p. 710]) would appear to be owing to her basic lack of full sexual experience. In the repeated references to rock music in the shopping center she frequents and on the radio, both in Arnold's car and her own house, we find a powerful source of erotic suggestion and of Connie's intensified teen-age hungers, true; but nowhere are we given to feel that she is a fully experienced woman. Rather, we experience her as a somewhat childish and silly narcissistic adolescent, one who feels put down by her more mature older sister (a librarian, and a perfect foil to Connie in her primness) and by her mother, who accuses her of "trashy daydreams" (p. 702). Actually, the trashy daydream involving Arnold may, in a sense, have a certain sobering effect on her frivolousness. Like Dante's dream-vision of Hell, it might improve the situation.

But such speculation begs the question, which is, *Is* it all a daydream? The first clue that we get that it *is* comes even before the Arnold Friend episode, when Oates tells us: "But all the boys fell back and dissolved into a single face that was not even a face but an idea, a feeling, mixed up with the urgent insistent pounding of the music and the humid night air of July" (p. 704). As we shall see, that music provides a key link between her daydreams and their materialization in Arnold Friend. But first we have another important clue, in Connie's languid dreaminess when she is left alone in the house on that fateful, hot summer afternoon: "Connie sat with her eyes closed in the sun, dreaming and dazed with the warmth about her as if this were a kind of love, the caresses of love. . . . She shook her head as if to get awake" (p. 705). Because it is so hot she goes inside and, sitting on the edge of her bed [N.B.], listens for an hour and a half to rock songs on the radio, "bathed in a glow of slow-pulsed joy that seemed to rise mysteriously out of

[3]Winslow (*Stranger Within,* pp. 267–68) considers briefly the possibility of the Arnold Friend episode's being interpreted as a dream but focuses primarily on other similarities between Oates's story and Hawthorne's "Young Goodman Brown."

[4]Winslow (pp. 265–66) also discusses the virginal Connie's fear of total sexual experience.

[5]Joyce Carol Oates, "Where Are You Going, Where Have You Been?" in *The Wheel of Love and Other Stories* (New York: The Vanguard Press, 1970), p. 37. All subsequent references to the story are to this edition.

the music itself and lay languidly about the airless little room, breathed in and out with each gentle rise and fall of her chest" (p. 705). At this point Oates starts a new paragraph to tell us that "After a while she heard a car coming up the drive" (p. 705). This is Arnold driving up, just when the author has described certain physiological sounds and motions that sound suspiciously like those of sleep.

If Arnold is indeed the devil—and he may well be, on the level so perspicaciously analyzed by Joyce Wegs—he is certainly a comical one, with his wig, incompletely made-up face, stuffed boots, and stumbling gait. In the *threat* he represents to Connie, of course, he is indeed a figure of evil, but with all this fakery, what Oates seems to be showing us is the absurd emptiness and falseness of sexual fulfillment. Connie fears she will be destroyed by Arnold, and the critics (like Wegs) have concentrated on the immediate level of *physical* death; what makes the story so rich, it seems to me, is the possibility of seeing her pending destruction as a *moral* phenomenon. Her compulsive sex drive will destroy her, Oates seems to tell us, but not simply physically (which, if that were all there were to it, would make the story merely a luscious gumdrop for gothic horror fans). It is the potential destruction of Connie as a *person,* on a humanistic level, that is the real source of power in this story, and it is through the protagonist's daydream of fearful sexual fulfillment that this horror is conveyed.

5 The fact that Connie recognizes the sensual music being broadcast on Arnold's car radio as being the same as that emanating from her own in the house (p. 706) provides another strong clue to his real nature—that of a dream-like projection of her erotic fantasies. His music and hers, Oates tells us, blend perfectly (p. 706), and indeed Arnold's voice is perceived by Connie as being the same as that of the disc jockey on the radio (p. 707). Thus the protagonist's inner state of consciousness is being given physical form by her imagination. We should recall that Connie's initial response to her first view of Arnold the night before, in the shopping center, was one of intense sexual excitement (p. 704); now she discovers how dangerous that excitement can be to her survival as a person. Instinctively she recoils; but the conflict between excitement and desire, on the one hand, and fear, on the other, leaves her will paralyzed, and she cannot even dial the phone for help (p. 712). Such physical paralysis in the face of oncoming danger is a phenomenon familiar to all dreamers, like being unable to run from the monster because your legs won't respond to your will.

Finally, the rather un-devil-like tribute that Arnold pays Connie as she finally succumbs to his threats against her family and goes out of the house to him—". . . you're better than them [her family] because not a one of them would have done this for you" (p. 713)—is exactly what poor, unappreciated Connie wants to hear. She is making a noble sacrifice, and in her dream she gives herself full credit for it.

The episode with Arnold Friend, then, may be viewed as the vehicle for fulfillment of Connie's deep-rooted desire for ultimate sexual gratification, a fearsome business which, for the uninitiated female, may involve destruction of the person. Unsophisticated as she is, Connie's subconscious is aware of this danger, and her dream conveys this conflict. Thus, Oates's achievement in this story lies in her ability to convey all these subtleties while still creating the illusion of a real-life experience.

[*1984*]

## A. R. COULTHARD

# *Joyce Carol Oates's "Where Are You Going, Where Have You Been?" as Pure Realism*

The tendency among "Where Are You Going, Where Have You Been?" commentators is to equate Arnold Friend with the Devil himself and to "mysticize" the story into a dream allegory. This interpretation may have been largely inspired by the author's remark that "Arnold Friend is a fantastic figure: he is Death, he is the 'elf-knight' of the ballads, he is the Imagination, he is a Dream, he is a Lover, a Demon, and all that."[1] This is a lot of weight for one short man to carry. Arnold Friend *is* a fantastic character, but only in the slang sense of the word. Such sweeping pronouncements as Oates's, especially when a nonchalant "and all that" is appended, should be viewed with skepticism, and I suspect that the author was seizing upon an after-the-fact opportunity to make her story seem more "literary" than it really is. If so, I don't understand why Joyce Carol Oates should have been content to let "Where Are You Going?" stand on its solid realism.

That Oates is operating in a realistic mode is indicated by Tom Quirk in an article so revealing that its main details are worth repeating here.[2] Quirk convincingly demonstrates that Oates closely modeled her story on Charles Schmid's murder of Alleen Rowe in the fall of 1965, just prior to the 1966 publication of "Where Are You Going?" in *Epoch*.[3] Though the murder was publicized in several popular news magazines, Quirk even identifies the one which Oates most likely used, noting that the *Life* account alone mentioned that Alleen, like Connie, had just washed her hair before her assailants arrived (p. 416).

[1]Oates made this statement to John R. Knott and Christopher R. Reaske in an interview published in the second edition of their textbook *Mirrors: An Introduction to Literature* (San Francisco: Canfield Press, 1975), p. 19. James H. Pickering and Jeffrey D. Hoeper quote it in the Instructor's Manual to the second edition of *Literature* (New York: Macmillan, 1986), p. 47. Gretchen Schulz and J. R. Rockwood also quote it on the opening page of their article "In Fairyland Without a Map: Connie's Exploration Inward in Joyce Carol Oates' 'Where Are You Going, Where Have You Been?'" (*Literature and Psychology* 30 [1978], 155–67); this article is a fanciful explication of "Where Are You Going?" as a modernized witches' brew of popular fairy tales: "Arnold Friend is the Woodcutter as well as the Wolf" (p. 163), and Connie is Snow White (p. 160), Cinderella and Rapunzel (p. 162), as well as Little Red Riding Hood (p. 163). Oates apparently blessed even this interpretation. Schulz says that she asked Oates at the 1976 MLA convention "if the many allusions to various fairy tales in 'Where Are You Going, Where Have You Been?' were intentional," and "She replied that they were" (p. 166, n. 9).

[2]"A Source for 'Where Are You Going, Where Have You Been?'" *Studies in Short Fiction*, 18, No. 4 (1981), 413–19. Further citations are in the text.

[3]Oates mentioned this influence in the Knott and Reaske interview when she said that the story came to her "after reading about a killer in some Southwestern state" (p. 18), but the casual nature of this remark does not acknowledge the extent of the author's debt, a fact which Quirk's article makes plain.

Assailants is also revealing, in that Schmid murdered two other young girls, but the killing of Rowe was the only one in which he had an accomplice. Schmid and his friend John Saunders raped and murdered Alleen Rowe, then beat her to death and buried her in the desert outside Tucson, Arizona (p. 416). Arnold Friend's creepy cohort Ellie Oscar was no doubt suggested to Oates by John Saunders.

The parallels between "Where Are You Going?" and the Rowe account are so numerous that Oates's borrowing is inquestionable. For instance, Alleen was fifteen at the time of her death, the same age as Connie. Either by accident or by design, the murderers caught her at home alone on a night when her mother was working, just as Connie is found in helpless circumstances in her own house (p. 416).

5 But the most telling evidence is how faithfully Oates duplicated the bizarre facts about Charles Schmid in her characterization of Arnold Friend. When Schmid was arrested, he was twenty-three but still haunting teen hangouts. Like Friend, he was short (5′3″) and muscular, and he tried to appear younger and to disguise his lack of height by dying his hair black, wearing pancake makeup, and stuffing rags and even crumpled cans into his black leather boots (p. 414). He was also a rock-and-roll fan and identified Elvis as his "idol" (p. 417). Schmid, like Arnold, even drove a garish gold-colored car (p. 414).

But while the fact that Oates copied many of her details from the account of an actual murder suggests a realistic story, it does not prove that she did not transform Charles Schmid into a mystical Arnold Friend and, in so doing, mythologize "Where Are You Going?" What proves that she didn't is the story's consistent naturalism. Absolutely nothing occurs that can't be explained in purely literal terms or that isn't best explained so. Like all good stories, "Where Are You Going?" resonates in the mind, but its style is realistic, not allegorical. Its principal characters are not personifications of abstract qualities but a demented killer and giddy teenaged girl. Arnold Friend does not appear in a dream but at Connie's kitchen door.

Joan D. Winslow would disagree with this view.[4] Winslow argues that Connie's "repressed fear, uncertainty, and guilt finally emerge in the shape of Arnold Friend" (p. 268) and says that "The knowing reader can easily identify him as the devil" (p. 267). But Connie's problem is that she has no sexual fear, uncertainty, or guilt, not even in repressed form. There is nothing psychologically complex about her. She is simply a pathetic teen-ager who isn't being reared very well. Her church is a "bright-lit, fly-infested"[5] drive-in restaurant, and her inspirational music is mindnumbing rock-and-roll, both middle-class clichés of the early sixties. Connie's father doesn't care where she has been, and her mother, who the story implies was much like Connie when she was younger, takes only a perfunctory interest in where she's going. When Connie blithely distances herself from the disrep-

[4]The Stranger Within: Two Stories by Oates and Hawthorne," *Studies in Short Fiction,* 17, No. 3 (1980), 263–68. Further citations are in the text.

[5]"Where Are You Going, Where Have You Been?" in *Classic Short Fiction,* ed. Charles H. Bohner (Englewood Cliffs, NJ: Prentice-Hall, 1986), p. 822. Further citations are in the text.

utable Pettinger girl, Connie's mother, "who noticed everything and knew everything" (p. 702), pretends to accept her daughter's nice girl/bad girl distinction. Connie thinks that "it was maybe cruel to fool her so much" (p. 704), but she isn't fooled. She just doesn't care. This is the stuff of sociological naturalism, not psychosexual allegory.

Winslow sees "Where Are You Going?" as a dream allegory[6] comparable to Hawthorne's "Young Goodman Brown," but the stories differ markedly in style. The dream possibility is pronounced in Hawthorne's story ("Had Goodman Brown fallen asleep in the forest, and only dreamed a wild dream of a witch-meeting?"), and several of its events, such as the vanishing of the Satanic initiation rite, cannot be explained except in terms of dream or fantasy. No such narrative signals or unreal occurrences appear in Oates's story.

Connie exists in a dream-like state but never in a dream. Her mother is right when she says that Connie's "mind was all filled with trashy daydreams" (p. 702). Connie is never more than half awake to reality, but this is her natural mental state and not a temporary psychic phenomenon that conjures up Arnold Friend. Connie rides home from the mall "sleepy and pleased" (p. 704) because she has sated her appetite for cheap diversion for another night. Her "dreams" are mundane teen-age boy-girl reveries, enhanced by the hypnotic music she listens to constantly. She spends most of her waking hours "dreaming about the boys she met. But all the boys fell back and dissolved into a single face that was not even a face, but an idea, a feeling, mixed up with the urgent insistent pounding of the music" (p. 704)—which is merely to say that Connie, like many teen-agers, is in love with love.

10 Or maybe just sex. Not only is there nothing remotely fabulous about such daydreaming, but it may be inspired by a reality-based erotic impulse: "her mind slipped over onto thoughts of the boy she had been with the night before and how nice he had been, how sweet it always was . . ." (p. 705). There is a good possibility that "it" refers to sexual intercourse. (That Arnold Friend likes to think his victim is a virgin doesn't mean this is so.) Connie is in her characteristic semi-conscious state on the fateful Sunday of Arnold Friend's visit. She has "sat with her eyes closed in the sun, dreaming and dazed with the warmth about her" (p. 705), but she is merely indulging in her routine "trashy daydreams" about boys when Arnold arrives. He is not a dream but a brutal awakening.

Connie's dream-like state at the end of the story is of another type. It is the nightmare sense of unreality of a person who knows she is about to be murdered: "She thought, I'm not going to see my mother again. She thought, I'm not going to sleep in my bed again" (p. 713). Her final trance-like compliance signals the acceptance of the inevitable. The atrocious thing that is happening to her renders her empty. She is in effect "out of body" from despair and shock: "She watched herself push the door slowly open . . . , watching this body and this head of long hair moving out into the

[6]Marie Mitchell Olesen Urbanski also treats the story as an allegory in "Existential Allegory: Joyce Carol Oates's 'Where Are You Going, Where Have You Been?'" (*Studies in Short Fiction,* 15, No. 2 [1978], 200–03), and Christina Marsden Gillis refers to "elements of fairy tale and dream" (p. 65) in "'Where Are You Going, Where Have You Been?': Seduction, Space, and a Fictional Mode" (*Studies in Short Fiction,* 18, No. 1 [1981], 65–70).

sunlight where Arnold Friend waited" (p. 713). Connie's psychological reaction to her impending death is realistically detailed and completely believable. Allegorizing it into a mere bad dream not only strains the text but takes the edge off the genuine horror of Connie's fate.

Just as Connie is no more and no less than the pathetic girl who is about to be murdered, Arnold Friend is simply the sick killer who is going to murder her. He doesn't "represent" anything, except the kind of creep a girl like Connie (or even a girl unlike Connie) might have the bad luck to attract. The story even implies that Arnold has killed, or at least raped, before. "[T]he numbers 33, 19, 17" painted on the car may be "a secret code" (p. 706), as the miscreant himself boasts, but they are not demonic numerology. The numbers are most likely the ages of Arnold Friend's previous victims, suggested to Oates by the ages—seventeen, fifteen, and thirteen—of the girls killed by Charles Schmid. Assuming that Friend has listed his victims in chronological order, the number sequence is revealing. He started with a woman near his own age, dropped down to the last teen year, then picked a girl two years younger than the previous one, which parallels Schmid's youth fetish. Connie fits perfectly into the descending two-year age difference of nineteen, seventeen, and now fifteen. (Schmid's thirteen-year-old would be next for Arnold.) For Friend's "secret code," Oates used two of the three ages of Charles Schmid's victims, all of whom were two years apart in age.

That Arnold Friend seems to possess Satanic powers in the form of supernatural knowledge of Connie and her family is also explicable on a purely realistic level. Even Tom Quirk credits him with "intimate, even satanic knowledge of her family's doings" (p. 417), but Arnold really has no supernatural powers. He knows nothing about Connie that he could not have observed, learned by asking around, or guessed. That he knows about "that old woman down the road, the one with the chickens" (p. 712) suggests that he has cased the neighborhood; that he doesn't know she has recently died—"Dead? What?" (p. 712)—suggests the opposite of Satanic perception. It is true that when Connie tries to scare him off by saying that her father is due home, Arnold knows that the family is at a barbecue at Aunt Tillie's. But when Connie asks him how he knows this, his halting reply again suggests no mystical knowledge: "Right now they're—uh—they're drinking." As Arnold continues, Oates's "stage directions" make it clear that he is improvising: "'Sitting around,' he said vaguely, squinting as if he were staring all the way to town and over to Aunt Tillie's backyard" (p. 709). (Since Aunt Tillie's house is in town, it is quite possible that the cruising Arnold Friend has previously observed Connie's family—and maybe even Connie—there. Oates's locale seems a much smaller place than Charles Schmid's Tucson, a fact which would explain how Arnold has even learned the name of Connie's aunt.) Then he says something which reveals he has in fact watched the family depart: "Yeah. Sitting around. There's your sister in a blue dress, huh? And high heels" (p. 709). (If he has been this close, he could have overheard the family's destination and the aunt's name.)

The rest of Arnold Friend's "special knowledge" is simply guesswork, not all of it correct. He speculates that a family cookout is likely to have corn-on-the-cob (it may or may not) and that there is a "fat woman" present, an idea which startles Connie: "'What fat woman?' Connie cried." Friend, the omniscient Devil, replies, "How do I know what fat woman?" To complete this hint that Arnold's "powers" are totally fake, there isn't even a fat woman at the gathering. "Oh, that's Mrs. Hornby," the shaken girl replies, then adds, "Who invited her?" (p. 709) Arnold's scam has worked so well that Connie imagines an outsider at the barbecue, and then wonders why she is there!

15 Neither does Arnold Friend possess any supernatural knowledge about Connie. He boasts to her that "I know your name and all about you" (p. 707), and then proves it by reciting a list of her friends. But his information would be easily available to anyone who frequents teen gathering places, as Arnold does. That Arnold has gone to the trouble of "researching" Connie merely emphasizes that he has had his eye on her for some time: "I took a special interest in you, such a pretty girl, and found out all about you" (p. 707). When Arnold calls June "the poor sad bitch" (p. 709), he correctly guesses Connie's attitude toward her plain older sister, but his conjecture is likely enough, considering what he knows of Connie's narcissism. It is hard to believe that Oates intended special powers for a character who can't even get current teen slang right: Arnold runs through "all the expressions he'd learned but was no longer sure which one of them was in style . . ." (p. 712).

Other so-called symbols of Arnold Friend as supernatural Demon are also better explained as the trappings of a pathological pervert. His "sign" (p. 708), the X he draws in the air, is no arcane Satanic marking of Connie. It is, rather, the kind of banal, sexually aggressive gesture one would expect of an Arnold Friend, the body-language counterpart to his hackneyed "Gonna get you, baby" (p. 704). Friend's clumsy boots do not hide "the cloven feet of the devil," as Joan Winslow contends (p. 267) but the comically vain height-enhancing rags and cans of Charles Schmid. The phoney name of Arnold Friend does not bespeak Satan in disguise but is rather an ironically inappropriate alias, probably copied, as Quirk surmises, after Charles Schmid's pseudonym of Angel Rodriguez (p. 415).

The only "demonic" power Arnold Friend possesses is the ability to use fear to ravage his victim's humanity, but such power is within the province of any heartless killer. During their final moments, Charles Schmid's young victims may well have experienced the same hopeless disorientation as Connie does. To reduce "Where Are You Going, Where Have You Been?" to a teen-age dream and to raise Arnold Friend to a superhuman Symbol is to rob the story of its elemental power. Arnold Friends do exist (Charles Schmid is proof of that), and the evil they do is not safely confined to the literary dreamworld.

[*1989*]

# A SAMPLE STUDENT ESSAY

Elizabeth Debutts

English 150G

March 19, 1996

Why Connie "Can't Help But" Do Anything

In Joyce Carol Oates's "Where Are You Going, Where Have You Been?" the central character, Connie, tries to resist the advances of a strange character named Arnold Friend, but at the end of the story she opens the door and joins him, almost against her own will. This is the way Oates puts it in the next-to-last paragraph:

> She put out her hand against the screen. She watched herself push the door slowly open as if she were safe back somewhere in the other doorway, watching this body and this head of long hair moving out into the sunlight where Arnold Friend waited. (p. 713)

But <u>why</u> does Connie join Arnold? And does she have any choice? After all, when Oates says that Connie "watched herself push the door slowly open," she is telling us that Connie cannot control her own actions.

Connie's lack of self-control is seen at the start. In the first sentence Oates tells us that Connie "had a quick nervous giggling habit of craning her neck to glance into mirrors or checking other people's faces to make sure her own was all right" (p. 702). Nobody freely decides to giggle; when Joyce Carol Oates tells us that Connie has a "nervous giggling habit," she is telling us that Connie can't control herself. And in several other places in the story Oates makes the same point. For instance, early in the story, when she is crossing the parking lot with Eddie to go to his car, "Connie couldn't help but let her eyes wander over the windshields" (p. 704), and then, when she sees Arnold Friend, "she couldn't help glancing back and there he was still watching her" (p. 704). She "can't help" almost anything that she does.

Many other passages in the story suggest Connie has no control. For instance, in paragraph 12 she sits in the sun, "dreaming and dazed with the warmth" (p. 705). Later in this paragraph Oates says that Connie "shook her head as if to get awake," and it is almost as though Connie is sleepwalking or dreaming for the rest of the story.

We can't be sure exactly why Connie behaves like this, but probably part of the blame can be put on her parents. In the third paragraph Oates tells us that Connie's "father was away at work most of the time and when he came home he wanted supper and he read the newspaper at supper and after supper he went to bed. He didn't bother talking much to them . . ." (pp. 702-03). Connie's mother is jealous of Connie's good looks, and Connie and the mother often quarrel. Oates does not labor the point, but it seems clear that the parents are at least partly to blame for Connie's uncontrolled or irrational behavior.

There is, however, another reason for the reader's sense that Connie's actions lack free will. Oates's story is a rewriting of a traditional story, a story that appears in an old anonymous poem, "The Demon Lover," and is also the subject of a short story (also called "The Demon Lover") by Elizabeth Bowen. Of course Oates was free to make many changes, modernizing the setting, for instance, but no matter how many details she changed, if she was going to tell the old story in modern terms she had to follow the main line, telling about a girl who is carried off by a mysterious demon lover. This means that the girl in Oates's story <u>has</u> to behave in a way that suggests she has no free will, maybe partly because she is the neurotic or maybe even psychotic child of parents who have failed her, but primarily because she is <u>destined</u> to her fate, by the earlier versions of her story. It is as though someone today were to retell the story of, say, Pocahontas and John Smith. If the author truly respects the story, Pocahontas <u>has</u> to fall in love with Smith, and she <u>has</u> to risk her life to save him, because that's what the story is about.

It is interesting to notice that Oates, in an interview, sees herself as a writer who is almost lacking in free will when she writes a story of this sort. In the interview with Reaske and Knott she says that after having thought about "the old legends and folk songs of Death and the Maiden, the story came to me more or less in a piece" (p. 721). She goes on to say that "the 'writing' I do is a kind of reporting, a recalling, an approximation of things that have already happened. I never write until these things have already happened, and then I try to do justice to them" (p. 721).

Of course we must believe that Oates is free to write what she wants, and she freely chooses her subjects and she can change plots and characters if she wishes. But, if we take Oates at her word, <u>she</u> believes that once she has chosen her story--once she has settled on "things that have happened"--she feels she must tell the story as it is. It is almost as if the writer does not have free will. And so it is not at all surprising that Oates tells us a story about a girl who seems to move almost in a dream world, and who "cannot help but" behave the way she does. Connie "cannot help" it, because she is acting out a role that was destined hundreds of years ago, by the tale of the Demon Lover, and Oates "cannot help" it either, once she has decided to retell the story.

Works Cited

Barnet, Sylvan, et al., eds. Literature: Thinking, Reading, and Writing Critically, 2nd ed. New York: Longman, 1997.

Oates, Joyce Carol. "Where Are You Going, Where Have You Been?" Barnet et al. 702-14.

Reaske, Christopher R., and John R. Knott, Jr. "Interview with Joyce Carol Oates." Barnet et al. 720-21

## TOPICS FOR CRITICAL THINKING AND WRITING

1. What is the author's thesis?
2. Do you think the thesis is adequately supported? Explain.

# CHAPTER 14

# Critical Perspectives on Joseph Conrad

## Heart of Darkness: A Casebook

In this chapter we give the text of Conrad's short novel, along with the following material:

1. two comments by Conrad on fiction (one from the preface to a novel called *The Nigger of the "Narcissus"* and one from the preface to *Youth . . . and Two Other Stories,* the book that included *Heart of Darkness*)
2. extracts from an essay by the Nigerian novelist and critic Chinua Achebe, arguing that *Heart of Darkness* is a racist book
3. an extract from Elaine Showalter's *Sexual Anarchy*
4. an analysis of Conrad's use of symbolism, from Ian Watt's *Conrad in the Nineteenth Century*
5. an extract from Edward Said's *Culture and Imperialism,* describing Marlow as a representative of imperial discourse
6. extracts from an essay by Gerald Graff, expressing some disagreement with Achebe but indicating how Achebe's view has enlarged his own and has changed his way of teaching the book

## JOSEPH CONRAD

*Joseph Conrad (1857–1924) was born Josef Teodor Konrad Nalecz Korzeniowski in the Ukraine, Russian Poland. From his father, who translated Shakespeare and Dickens, he learned to read English but not to speak it. When Conrad was four, his parents were charged with conspiracy, and the family was deported into Russia. Both of his parents died before he was twelve, and he was brought up by a maternal uncle. Conrad left this home*

*when he was seventeen and served in the French marine service, making several voyages to the West Indies; in between them he apparently was involved in gun-running. At twenty-two he joined the English merchant marine; eight years later, in 1886, he won his master's papers and became a naturalized British citizen. In 1888 he took his first command of a ship.*

*Unable to obtain a second command, in 1890 Conrad took a post as a riverboat captain on the Congo River, where he acquired the experience that he turned into* Heart of Darkness. *The Congo (now Zaire) was nominally the Congo Free State; in fact it was not independent but was the property of Leopold II of Belgium, who exploited it mercilessly. When Conrad arrived in the Congo, he found that his assigned vessel was undergoing repairs, and he was sent as a supernumerary on another steamer, to learn the river. This vessel was sent to Stanley Falls, to pick up Georges Antoine Klein—the Kurtz of Conrad's novel—who died aboard the ship. Conrad then fell ill, and he returned to England, broken in health. (He did not write* Heart of Darkness *until 1899; it was published in 1902.)*

*Conrad began to write while still at sea, perhaps as early as 1889. In 1892 he showed the manuscript of* Almayer's Folly *to a passenger—the novelist John Galsworthy—who encouraged him to publish it. (It was published in 1895.) In 1896 Conrad married an English woman, settled in England, and devoted himself exclusively to writing.*

## *Heart of Darkness*

### I

The *Nellie,* a cruising yawl, swung to her anchor without a flutter of the sails, and was at rest. The flood had made, the wind was nearly calm, and being bound down the river, the only thing for it was to come to and wait for the turn of the tide.

The sea-reach of the Thames stretched before us like the beginning of an interminable waterway. In the offing the sea and the sky were welded together without a joint, and in the luminous space the tanned sails of the barges drifting up with the tide seemed to stand still in red clusters of canvas sharply peaked, with gleams of varnished sprits. A haze rested on the low shores that ran out to sea in vanishing flatness. The air was dark above Gravesend,[1] and farther back still seemed condensed into a mournful gloom, brooding motionless over the biggest, and the greatest, town on earth.

[1]**Gravesend** a port on the Thames River, about twenty-five miles east of London

The Director of Companies was our captain and our host. We four affectionately watched his back as he stood in the bows looking to seaward. On the whole river there was nothing that looked half so nautical. He resembled a pilot, which to a seaman is trustworthiness personified. It was difficult to realize his work was not out there in the luminous estuary, but behind him, within the brooding gloom.

Between us there was, as I have already said somewhere, the bond of the sea. Besides holding our hearts together through long periods of separation, it had the effect of making us tolerant of each other's yarns—and even convictions. The Lawyer—the best of old fellows—had, because of his many years and many virtues, the only cushion on deck, and was lying on the only rug. The accountant had brought out already a box of dominoes, and was toying architecturally with the bones. Marlow sat cross-legged right aft, leaning against the mizzen-mast. He had sunken cheeks, a yellow complexion, a straight back, and ascetic aspect, and, with his arms dropped, the palms of hands outwards, resembled an idol. The director, satisfied the anchor had good hold, made his way aft and sat down amongst us. We exchanged a few words lazily. Afterwards there was silence on board the yacht. For some reason or other we did not begin that game of dominoes. We felt meditative, and fit for nothing but placid staring. The day was ending in a serenity of still and exquisite brilliance. The water shone pacifically; the sky, without a speck, was a benign immensity of unstained light; the very mist on the Essex marshes was like a gauzy and radiant fabric, hung from the wooded rises inland, and draping the low shores in diaphanous folds. Only the gloom in the west, brooding over the upper reaches, became more somber every minute, as if angered by the approach of the sun.

5 And at last, in its curved and imperceptible fall, the sun sank low, and from glowing white changed to a dull red without rays and without heat, as if about to go out suddenly, stricken to death by the touch of that gloom brooding over a crowd of men.

Forthwith a change came over the water, and the serenity became less brilliant but more profound. The old river in its broad reach rested unruffled at the decline of day, after ages of good service done to the race that peopled its banks, spread out in the tranquil dignity of a waterway leading to the uttermost ends of the earth. We looked at the venerable stream not in the vivid flush of a short day that comes and departs forever, but in the august light of abiding memories. And indeed nothing is easier for a man who has, as the phrase goes, "followed the sea" with reverence and affection, than to evoke the great spirit of the past upon the lower reaches of the Thames. The tidal current runs to and fro in its unceasing service, crowded with memories of men and ships it had borne to the rest of home or to the battles of the sea. It had known and served all men of whom the nation is proud, from Sir Francis Drake to Sir John Franklin,[2] knights all, titled and untitled—the knights-errant of the sea. It had borne all the ships whose names

[2]**Sir Francis Drake . . . Sir John Franklin** Drake (1540–96), an English explorer, sailed around the world (1577–80) in a ship named *The Golden Hind;* Sir John Franklin (1786–1847) commanded an expedition consisting of ships named *Erebus* (in Greek mythology, the entrance to Hades) and *Terror,* searching for the Northwest passage. The ships never returned.

are like jewels flashing in the night of time, from the *Golden Hind* returning with her round flanks full of treasure, to be visited by the Queen's Highness and thus pass out of the gigantic tale, to the *Erebus* and *Terror*, bound on other conquests—and that never returned. It had known the ships and the men. They had sailed from Deptford, from Greenwich, from Erith—the adventures and the settlers; kings' ships and the ships of men on 'Change;[3] captains, admirals, the dark "interlopers" of the Eastern trade, and the commissioned "Generals" of East India fleets. Hunters for gold or pursuers of fame, they all had gone out on that stream, bearing the sword, and often the torch, messengers of the might within the land, bearers of a spark from the sacred fire. What greatness had not floated on the ebb of that river into the mystery of an unknown earth! . . . The dreams of men, the seed of commonwealths, the germs of empires.

The sun set; the dusk fell on the stream, and lights began to appear along the shore. The Chapman lighthouse, a three-legged thing erect on a mud-flat, shone strongly. Lights of ships moved in the fairway[4]—a great stir of lights going up and going down. And farther west on the upper reaches the place of the monstrous town was still marked ominously on the sky, a brooding gloom in sunshine, a lurid glare under the stars.

"And this also," said Marlow suddenly, "has been one of the dark places on the earth."

He was the only man of us who still "followed the sea." The worst that could be said of him was that he did not represent his class. He was a seaman, but he was a wanderer, too, while most seamen lead, if one may so express it, a sedentary life. Their minds are of the stay-at-home order, and their home is always with them—the ship; and so is their country—the sea. One ship is very much like another, and the sea is always the same. In the immutability of their surroundings the foreign shores, the foreign faces, the changing immensity of life, glide past, veiled not by a sense of mystery but by a slightly disdainful ignorance; for there is nothing mysterious to a seaman unless it be the sea itself, which is the mistress of his existence and as inscrutable as Destiny. For the rest, after his hours of work, a casual stroll or a casual spree on shore suffices to unfold for him the secret of a whole continent, and generally he finds the secret not worth knowing. The yarns of seamen have a direct simplicity, the whole meaning of which lies within the shell of a cracked nut. But Marlow was not typical (if his propensity to spin yarns be excepted), and to him the meaning of an episode was not inside like a kernel but outside, enveloping the tale which brought it out only as a glow brings out a haze, in the likeness of one of these misty halos that sometimes are made visible by the special illumination of moonshine.

10 His remark did not seem at all surprising. It was just like Marlow. It was accepted in silence. No one took the trouble to grunt even; and presently, he said, very slow—

"I was thinking of very old times, when the Romans first came here, nineteen hundred years ago—the other day. . . . Light came out of this river since—you say Knights? Yes; but it is like a running blaze on a plain, like a flash of lightning in the clouds. We live in the flicker—may it last as long as

[3]**men on 'Change** members of the London stock exchange
[4]**fairway** the navigable part of a river

the old earth keeps rolling! But darkness was here yesterday. Imagine the feelings of a commander of a fine—what d'ye call 'em?—trireme[5] in the Mediterranean, ordered suddenly to the north; run overland across the Gauls in a hurry; put in charge of one of these craft the legionaries—a wonderful lot of handy men they must have been, too—used to build, apparently by the hundred, in a month or two, if we may believe what we read. Imagine him here—the very end of the world, a sea the color of lead, a sky the color of smoke, a kind of ship about as rigid as a concertina—and going up this river with stores, or orders, or what you like. Sandbanks, marshes, forests, savages—precious little to eat fit for a civilized man, nothing but Thames water to drink. No Falernian wine here, no going ashore. Here and there a military camp lost in a wilderness, like a needle in a bundle of hay—cold, fog, tempests, disease, exile, and death—death skulking in the air, in the water, in the bush. They must have been dying like flies here. Oh, yes—he did it. Did it very well, too, no doubt, and without thinking much about it either, except afterwards to brag of what he had gone through in his time, perhaps. They were men enough to face the darkness. And perhaps he was cheered by keeping his eye on a chance of promotion to the fleet at Ravenna[6] by and by, if he had good friends in Rome and survived the awful climate. Or think of a decent young citizen in a toga—perhaps too much dice, you know—coming out here in the train of some prefect, or taxgatherer, or trader even, to mend his fortunes. Land in a swamp, march through the woods, and in some inland post feel the savagery, the utter savagery, had closed round him—all that mysterious life of the wilderness that stirs in the forest, in the jungles, in the hearts of wild men. There's no initiation either into such mysteries. He has to live in the midst of the incomprehensible, which is also detestable. And it has a fascination, too, that goes to work upon him. The fascination of the abomination—you know, imagine the growing regrets, the longing to escape, the powerless disgust, the surrender, the hate."

He paused.

"Mind," he began again, lifting one arm from the elbow, the palm of the hand outwards, so that, with his legs folded before him, he had the pose of a Buddha preaching in European clothes and without a lotus-flower—"Mind, none of us would feel exactly like this. What saves us is efficiency—the devotion to efficiency. But these chaps were not much account, really. They were no colonists; their administration was merely a squeeze, and nothing more, I suspect. They were conquerors, and for that you want only brute force—nothing to boast of, when you have it, since your strength is just an accident arising from the weakness of others. They grabbed what they could get for the sake of what was to be got. It was just robbery with violence, aggravated murder on a great scale, and men going at it blind—as is very proper for those who tackle a darkness. The conquest of the earth, which mostly means the taking it away from those who have a different complexion or slightly flatter noses than ourselves, is not a pretty thing when you look into it too much. What redeems it is the idea only. An idea at the back of it; not a sentimental pretense but an idea; and an unselfish belief

[5]**trireme** ancient Greek or Roman galley with three ranks of oars

[6]**Ravenna** in ancient Roman times an important naval station on the Adriatic Sea

in the idea—something you can set up, and bow down before, and offer a sacrifice to. . . ."

He broke off. Flames glided in the river, small green flames, red flames, white flames, pursuing, overtaking, joining, crossing each other—then separating slowly or hastily. The traffic of the great city went on in the deepening night upon the sleepless river. We looked on, waiting patiently—there was nothing else to do till the end of the flood; but it was more after a long silence, when he said, in a hesitating voice, "I suppose you fellows remember I did once turn fresh-water sailor for a bit," that we knew we were fated, before the ebb began to run, to hear one of Marlow's inconclusive experiences.

15 "I don't want to bother you much with what happened to me personally," he began, showing in this remark the weakness of many tellers of tales who seem so often unaware of what their audience would best like to hear; "yet to understand the effect of it on me you ought to know how I got out there, what I saw, how I went up that river to the place where I first met the poor chap. It was the farthest point of navigation and the culminating point of my experience. It seemed somehow to throw a kind of light on everything about me—and into my thoughts. It was somber enough, too—and pitiful—not extraordinary in any way—not very clear either. No, not very clear. And yet it seemed to throw a kind of light.

"I had then, as you remember, just returned to London after a lot of Indian Ocean, Pacific, China Seas—a regular dose of the East—six years or so, and I was loafing about, hindering you fellows in your work and invading your homes, just as though I had got a heavenly mission to civilize you. It was very fine for a time, but after a bit I did get tired of resting. Then I began to look for a ship—I should think the hardest work on earth. But the ships wouldn't even look at me. And I got tired of that game, too.

"Now when I was a little chap I had a passion for maps. I would look for hours at South America, or Africa, or Australia, and lose myself in all the glories of exploration. At that time there were many blank spaces on the earth, and when I saw one that looked particularly inviting on a map (but they all look that) I would put my finger on it and say, When I grow up I will go there. The North Pole was one of these places, I remember. Well, I haven't been there yet, and shall not try now. The glamour's off. Other places were scattered about the Equator, and in every sort of latitude all over the two hemispheres. I have been in some of them, and . . . well, we won't talk about that. But there was one yet—the biggest, the most blank, so to speak—that I had a hankering after.

"True, by this time it was not a blank space any more. It had got filled since my childhood with rivers and lakes and names. It had ceased to be a blank space of delightful mystery—a white patch for a boy to dream gloriously over. It had become a place of darkness. But there was in it one river especially, a mighty big river, that you could see on the map, resembling an immense snake uncoiled, with its head in the sea, its body at rest curving afar over a vast country, and its tail lost in the depths of the land. And as I looked at the map of it in a shop-window, it fascinated me as a snake would a bird—a silly little bird. Then I remembered there was a big concern, a Company for trade on that river. Dash it all! I thought to myself, they can't trade without using some kind of craft on that lot of fresh water—steamboats! Why shouldn't I try to get charge of one? I went on along Fleet Street, but could not shake off the idea. The snake had charmed me.

"You understand it was a Continental concern, that Trading society; but I have a lot of relations living on the Continent, because it's cheap and not so nasty as it looks, they say.

"I am sorry to own I began to worry them. This was already a fresh departure for me. I was not used to getting things that way, you know. I always went my own road and on my own legs where I had a mind to go. I wouldn't have believed it of myself; but, then—you see—I felt somehow I must get there by hook or by crook. So I worried them. The men said 'My dear fellow,' and did nothing. Then—would you believe it?—I tried the women. I, Charlie Marlow, set the women to work—to get a job. Heavens! Well, you see, the notion drove me. I had an aunt, a dear enthusiastic soul. She wrote: 'It will be delightful. I am ready to do anything, anything for you. It is a glorious idea. I know the wife of a very high personage in the Administration, and also a man who has lots of influence with,' etc., etc. She was determined to make no end of fuss to get me appointed skipper of a river steamboat, if such was my fancy.

"I got my appointment—of course; and I got it very quick. It appears the Company had received news that one of their captains had been killed in a scuffle with the natives. This was my chance, and it made me the more anxious to go. It was only months and months afterwards, when I made the attempt to recover what was left of the body, that I heard the original quarrel arose from a misunderstanding about some hens. Yes, two black hens. Fresleven—that was the fellow's name, a Dane—thought himself wronged somehow in the bargain, so he went ashore and started to hammer the chief of the village with a stick. Oh, it didn't surprise me in the least to hear this, and at the same time to be told that Fresleven was the gentlest, quietest creature that ever walked on two legs. No doubt he was; but he had been a couple of years already out there engaged in the noble cause, you know, and he probably felt the need at last of asserting his self-respect in some way. Therefore he whacked the old nigger mercilessly, while a big crowd of his people watched him, thunderstruck, till some man—I was told the chief's son—in desperation at hearing the old chap yell, made a tentative jab with a spear at the white man—and of course it went quite easy between the shoulder blades. Then the whole population cleared into the forest, expecting all kinds of calamities to happen, while, on the other hand, the steamer Fresleven commanded left also in a bad panic, in charge of the engineer, I believe. Afterwards nobody seemed to trouble much about Fresleven's remains, till I got out and stepped into his shoes. I couldn't let it rest, though; but when an opportunity offered at last to meet my predecessor, the grass growing through his ribs was tall enough to hide his bones. They were all there. The supernatural being had not been touched after he fell. And the village was deserted, the huts gaped black, rotting, all askew within the fallen enclosures. A calamity had come to it, sure enough. The people had vanished. Mad terror had scattered them, men, women, and children, through the bush, and they had never returned. What became of the hens I don't know either. I should think the cause of progress got them, anyhow. However, through this glorious affair I got my appointment, before I had fairly begun to hope for it.

"I flew around like mad to get ready, and before forty-eight hours I was crossing the Channel to show myself to my employers, and sign the contract. In a very few hours I arrived in a city that always makes me think of a whited sepulcher. Prejudice no doubt. I had no difficulty in finding the Company's offices. It was the biggest thing in the town, and everybody I met was full of it. They were going to run an over-sea empire, and make no end of coin by trade.

"A narrow and deserted street in deep shadow, high houses, innumerable windows with venetian blinds, a dead silence, grass sprouting between the stones, imposing carriage archways right and left, immense double doors standing ponderously ajar. I slipped through one of these cracks, went up a swept and ungarnished staircase, as arid as a desert, and opened the first door I came to. Two women, one fat and the other slim, sat on straw-bottomed chairs, knitting black wool. The slim one got up and walked straight at me—still knitting with downcast eyes—and only just as I began to think of getting out of her way, as you would for a somnambulist, stood still, and looked up. Her dress was as plain as an umbrella-cover, and she turned round without a word and preceded me into a waiting-room. I gave my name, and looked about. Deal table in the middle, plain chairs all around the walls, on one end a large shining map, marked with all the colors of a rainbow. There was a vast amount of red—good to see at any time, because one knows that some real work is done in there, a deuce of a lot of blue, a little green, smears of orange, and, on the East Coast, a purple patch, to show where the jolly pioneers of progress drink the jolly lagerbeer. However, I wasn't going into any of these. I was going into the yellow.[7] Dead in the center. And the river was there—fascinating—deadly—like a snake. Ough! A door opened, a white-haired secretarial head, but wearing a compassionate expression, appeared, and a skinny forefinger beckoned me into the sanctuary. Its light was dim, and a heavy writing-desk squatted in the middle. From behind that structure came out an impression of pale plumpness in a frock-coat. The great man himself. He was five feet six, I should judge, and had his grip on the handle-end of ever so many millions. He shook hands, I fancy, murmured vaguely, was satisfied with my French. *Bon voyage.*

"In above forty-five seconds I found myself again in the waiting-room with the compassionate secretary, who, full of desolation and sympathy, made me sign some document. I believe I undertook amongst other things not to disclose any trade secrets. Well, I am not going to.

25 "I began to feel slightly uneasy. You know I am not used to such ceremonies, and there was something ominous in the atmosphere. It was just as though I had been let into some conspiracy—I don't know—something not quite right; and I was glad to get out. In the outer room the two women knitted black wool feverishly. People were arriving, and the younger one was walking back and forth introducing them. The old one sat on her chair. Her flat cloth slippers were propped up on a footwarmer, and a cat reposed on her lap. She wore a starched white affair on her head, had a wart on one

[7]**red . . . yellow** the colors indicate the colonial powers controlling Africa: red, Great Britain; blue, France; green, Italy; orange, Portugal; purple, Germany; yellow, Belgium

cheek, and silver-rimmed spectacles hung on the tip of her nose. She glanced at me above the glasses. The swift and indifferent placidity of that look troubled me. Two youths with foolish and cheery countenances were being piloted over, and she threw at them the same quick glance of unconcerned wisdom. She seemed to know all about them and about me, too. An eerie feeling came over me. She seemed uncanny and fateful. Often far away there I thought of these two, guarding the door of Darkness, knitting black wool as for a warm pall, one introducing, introducing continuously to the unknown, the other scrutinizing the cheery and foolish faces with unconcerned old eyes. *Ave!* Old knitter of black wool. *Morituri te salutant.*[8] Not many of those she looked at ever saw her again—not half, by a long way.

"There was yet a visit to the doctor. 'A simple formality,' assured me the secretary, with an air of taking an immense part in all my sorrows. Accordingly a young chap wearing his hat over the left elbow, some clerk I suppose—there must have been clerks in the business, though the house was as still as a house in a city of the dead—came from somewhere upstairs, and led me forth. He was shabby and careless, with inkstains on the sleeves of his jacket, and his cravat was large and billowy, under a chin shaped like the toe of an old boot. It was a little too early for the doctor, so I proposed a drink, and thereupon he developed a vein of joviality. As we sat over our vermouths he glorified the Company's business, and by and by I expressed casually my surprise at him not going out there. He became very cool and collected all at once. 'I am not such a fool as I look, quoth Plato to his disciples,' he said sententiously, emptied his glass with great resolution, and we rose.

"The old doctor felt my pulse, evidently thinking of something else the while. 'Good, good for there,' he mumbled, and then with a certain eagerness asked me whether I would let him measure my head. Rather surprised, I said Yes, when he produced a thing like calipers and got the dimensions back and front and every way, taking notes carefully. He was an unshaven little man in a threadbare coat like a gaberdine, with his feet in slippers, and I thought him a harmless fool. 'I always ask leave, in the interests of science, to measure the crania of those going out there,' he said. 'And when they come back, too?' I asked, 'Oh, I never see them,' he remarked; 'and, moreover, the changes take place inside, you know.' He smiled, as if at some quiet joke. 'So you are going out there. Famous. Interesting, too.' He gave me a searching glance, and made another note. 'Ever any madness in your family?' he asked, in a matter-of-fact tone. I felt very annoyed. 'Is that question in the interests of science, too?' 'It would be,' he said, without taking notice of my irritation, 'interesting for science to watch the mental changes of individuals, on the spot, but. . . .' 'Are you an alienist?'[9] I interrupted. 'Every doctor should be—a little,' answered that original, imperturbably. 'I have a little theory which you Messieurs who go out there must help me to prove. This is my share in the advantages my country shall reap from the possession of such a magnificent dependency. The mere wealth I leave to others. Pardon my questions, but you are the first Englishman coming under

[8]***Ave! Morituri te salutant*** Hail! Those who are about to die salute you (Latin; the words of Roman gladiators on entering the arena, addressed to the emperor)
[9]**alienist** psychiatrist

my observation. . . .' I hastened to assure him I was not in the least typical. 'If I were,' said I, 'I wouldn't be talking like this with you.' 'What you say is rather profound, and probably erroneous,' he said, with a laugh. 'Avoid irritation more than the exposure to the sun. Adieu. How do you English say, eh? Good-by. Ah! Good-by. Adieu. In the tropics one must before everything keep calm.' . . . He lifted a warning forefinger. . . . *'Du calme, du calme. Adieu.'*[10]

"One thing more remained to do—say good-by to my excellent aunt. I found her triumphant. I had a cup of tea—the last decent cup of tea for many days—and in a room that most soothingly looked just as you would expect a lady's drawing-room to look, we had a long quiet chat by the fireside. In the course of these confidences it became quite plain to me I had been represented to the wife of the high dignitary, and goodness knows to how many more people besides, as an exceptional and gifted creature—a piece of good fortune for the Company—a man you don't get hold of every day. Good heavens! and I was going to take charge of a two-penny-half-penny river-steamboat with a penny whistle attached! It appeared, however, I was also one of the Workers, with a capital—you know. Something like an emissary of light, something like a lower sort of apostle. There had been a lot of such rot let loose in print and talk just about that time, and the excellent woman, living right in the rush of all that humbug, got carried off her feet. She talked about 'weaning those ignorant millions from their horrid ways,' till, upon my word, she made me quite uncomfortable. I ventured to hint that the Company was run for profit.

"'You forget, dear Charlie, that the laborer is worthy of his hire,' she said, brightly. It's queer how out of touch with truth women are. They live in a world of their own, and there has never been anything like it, and never can be. It is too beautiful altogether, and if they were to set it up it would go to pieces before the first sunset. Some confounded fact we men have been living contentedly with ever since the day of creation would start up and knock the whole thing over.

"After this I got embraced, told to wear flannel, be sure to write often, and so on—and I left. In the street—I don't know why—a queer feeling came to me that I was an impostor. Odd thing that I, who used to clear out for any part of the world at twenty-four hours' notice, with less thought than most men give to the crossing of a street, had a moment—I won't say of hesitation, but of startled pause, before this commonplace affair. The best way I can explain it to you is by saying that, for a second or two, I felt as though, instead of going to the center of a continent, I were about to set off for the center of the earth.

"I left in a French steamer, and she called in every blamed port they have out there, for, as far as I could see, the sole purpose of landing soldiers and custom-house officers. I watched the coast. Watching a coast as it slips by the ship is like thinking about an enigma. There it is before you—smiling, frowning, inviting, grand, mean, insipid, or savage, and always mute with an air of whispering, Come and find out. This one was almost featureless, as if still in the making, with an aspect of monotonous grimness. The edge of a colossal jungle, so dark-green as to be almost black, fringed with

[10]***Du calme, du calme. Adieu*** Keep calm, keep calm. Good-bye (French)

white surf, ran straight, like a ruled line, far, far away along a blue sea whose glitter was blurred by a creeping mist. The sun was fierce, the land seemed to glisten and drip with steam. Here and there grayish-whitish specks showed up clustered inside the white surf, with a flag flying above them perhaps. Settlements some centuries old, and still no bigger than pinheads on the untouched expanse of their background. We pounded along, stopped, landed soldiers; went on, landed custom-house clerks to levy toll in what looked like a God-forsaken wilderness, with a tin shed and a flag-pole lost in it; landed more soldiers—to take care of the custom-house clerks, presumably. Some, I heard, got drowned in the surf; but whether they did or not, nobody seemed particularly to care. They were just flung out there, and on we went. Every day the coast looked the same, as though we had not moved; but we passed various places—trading places—with names like Gran' Bassam, Little Popo; names that seemed to belong to some sordid farce acted in front of a sinister backcloth. The idleness of a passenger, my isolation amongst all these men with whom I had no point of contact, the oily and languid sea, the uniform somberness of the coast, seemed to keep me away from the truth of things, within the toil of a mournful and senseless delusion. The voice of the surf heard now and then was a positive pleasure, like the speech of a brother. It was something natural, that had its reason, that had a meaning. Now and then a boat from the shore gave one a momentary contact with reality. It was paddled by black fellows. You could see from afar the white of their eyeballs glistening. They shouted, sang; their bodies streamed with perspiration; they had faces like grotesque masks—these chaps; but they had bone, muscle, a wild vitality, an intense energy of movement, that was as natural and true as the surf along their coast. They wanted no excuse for being there. They were a great comfort to look at. For a time I would feel I belonged still to a world of straightforward facts, but the feeling would not last long. Something would turn up to scare it away. Once, I remember, we came upon a man-of-war anchored off the coast. There wasn't even a shed there, and she was shelling the bush. It appears the French had one of their wars going on thereabouts. Her ensign dropped limp like a rag; the muzzles of the long six-inch guns stuck out all over the low hull; the greasy, slimy swell swung her up lazily and let her down, swaying her thin masts. In the empty immensity of earth, sky, and water, there she was, incomprehensible, firing into a continent. Pop, would go one of the six-inch guns; a small flame would dart and vanish, a little white smoke would disappear, a tiny projectile would give a feeble screech—and nothing happened. Nothing could happen. There was a touch of insanity in the proceeding, a sense of lugubrious drollery in the sight; and it was not dissipated by somebody on board assuring me earnestly there was a camp of natives—he called them enemies!—hidden out of sight somewhere.

"We gave her her letters (I heard the men in that lonely ship were dying of fever at the rate of three a day) and went on. We called at some more places with farcical names, where the merry dance of death and trade goes on in a still and earthy atmosphere as of an overheated catacomb; all along the formless coast bordered by dangerous surf, as if Nature herself had tried to ward off intruders; in and out of rivers, streams of death in life, whose banks were rotting into mud, whose waters, thickened into slime, invaded the contorted mangroves, that seemed to writhe at us in the extremity of an impotent despair. Nowhere did we stop long enough to get a particularized impression, but the general sense of vague and oppressive wonder grew upon me. It was like a weary pilgrimage amongst hints for nightmares.

"It was upward of thirty days before I saw the mouth of the big river. We anchored off the seat of the government. But my work would not begin till some two hundred miles farther on. So as soon as I could I made a start for a place thirty miles higher up.

"I had my passage on a little sea-going steamer. Her captain was a Swede, and knowing me for a seaman, invited me on the bridge. He was a young man, lean, fair, and morose, with lanky hair and a shuffling gait. As we left the miserable little wharf, he tossed his head contemptuously at the shore. 'Been living there?' he asked. I said, 'Yes.' 'Fine lot these government chaps—are they not?' he went on, speaking English with great precision and considerable bitterness. 'It is funny what some people will do for a few francs a month. I wonder what becomes of that kind when it goes upcountry?' I said to him I expected to see that soon. 'So-o-o!' he exclaimed. He shuffled athwart, keeping one eye ahead vigilantly. 'Don't be too sure,' he continued. 'The other day I took up a man who hanged himself on the road. He was a Swede, too.' 'Hanged himself! Why, in God's name?' I cried. I kept on looking out watchfully. 'Who knows? The sun was too much for him, or the country perhaps.'

"At last we opened a reach. A rocky cliff appeared, mounds of turned-up earth by the shore, houses on a hill, others with iron roofs, amongst a waste of excavations, or hanging to the declivity. A continuous noise of the rapids above hovered over this scene of inhabited devastation. A lot of people, mostly black and naked, moved about like ants. A jetty projected into the river. A blinding sunlight drowned all this at times in a sudden recrudescence of glare. 'There's your Company's station,' said the Swede, pointing to three wooden barrack-like structures on the rocky slope. 'I will send your things up. Four boxes did you say? So. Farewell.'

"I came upon a boiler wallowing in the grass, then found a path leading up the hill. It turned aside for the boulders, and also for an undersized railway-truck lying there on its back with its wheels in the air. One was off. The thing looked as dead as the carcass of some animal. I came upon more pieces of decaying machinery, a stack of rusty rails. To the left a clump of trees made a shady spot, where dark things seemed to stir feebly. I blinked, the path was steep. A horn tooted to the right, and I saw the black people run. A heavy and dull detonation shook the ground, a puff of smoke came out of the cliff, and that was all. No change appeared on the face of the rock. They were building a railway. The cliff was not in the way of anything; but the objectless blasting was all the work going on.

"A slight clinking behind me made me turn my head. Six black men advanced in a file, toiling up the path. They walked erect and slow, balancing small baskets full of earth on their heads, and the clink kept time with their footsteps. Black rags were wound round their loins, and the short ends behind waggled to and fro like tails. I could see every rib, the joints of their limbs were like knots in a rope; each had an iron collar on his neck, and all were connected together with a chain whose bights swung between them, rhythmically clinking. Another report from the cliff made me think suddenly of that ship of war I had seen firing into a continent. It was the same kind of ominous voice; but these men could by no stretch of imagination be called enemies. They were called criminals, and the outraged law, like the bursting shells, had come to them, an insoluble mystery from the sea. All their meager breasts panted together, the violently dilated nostrils quivered, the eyes stared stonily uphill. They passed me within six inches, without a glance, with the complete, deathlike indifference of unhappy savages. Behind this raw matter one of the reclaimed, the product of the new forces at work, strolled despondently, carrying a rifle by its middle. He had a uniform jacket with one button off, and seeing a white man on the path, hoisted his weapon to his shoulder with alacrity. This was simple prudence, white men being so much alike at a distance that he could not tell who I might be. He was speedily reassured, and with a large, white, rascally grin, and a glance at his charge, seemed to take me into partnership in his exalted trust. After that, I also was a part of the great cause of these high and just proceedings.

"Instead of going up, I turned and descended to the left. My idea was to let that chain-gang get out of sight before I climbed the hill. You know I am not particularly tender, I've had to strike and to fend off. I've had to resist and to attack sometimes—that's only one way of resisting—without counting the exact cost, according to the demands of such sort of life as I had blundered into. I've seen the devil of violence, and the devil of greed, and the devil of hot desire; but, by all the stars! these were strong, lusty, red-eyed devils, that swayed and drove men—men, I tell you. But as I stood on this hillside, I foresaw that in the blinding sunshine of that land I would become acquainted with a flabby, pretending, weak-eyed devil of a rapacious and pitiless folly. How insidious he could be, too, I was only to find out several months later and a thousand miles farther. For a moment I stood appalled, as though by a warning. Finally I descended the hill, obliquely, towards the trees I had seen.

"I avoided a vast artificial hole somebody had been digging on the slope, the purpose of which I found it impossible to divine. It wasn't a quarry or a sandpit, anyhow. It was just a hole. It might have been connected with the philanthropic desire of giving the criminals something to do. I don't know. Then I nearly fell into a very narrow ravine, almost no more than a scar in the hillside. I discovered that a lot of imported drainage-pipes for the settlement had been tumbled in there. There wasn't one that was not broken. It was a wanton smash-up. At last I got under the trees. My purpose was to stroll into the shade for a moment; but no sooner within than it seemed to me I had stepped into the gloomy circle of some Inferno. The rapids were near, and an uninterrupted, uniform, headlong, rushing noise filled the mournful stillness of the grove, where not a breath stirred, not a leaf moved, with a mysterious sound—as though the tearing pace of the launched earth had suddenly become audible.

40 "Black shapes crouched, lay, sat between the trees leaning against the trunks, clinging to the earth, half coming out, half effaced within the dim light, in all the attitudes of pain, abandonment, and despair. Another mine on the cliff went off, followed by a slight shudder of the soil under my feet. The work was going on. The work! and this was the place where some of the helpers had withdrawn to die.

"They were dying slowly—it was very clear. They were not enemies, they were not criminals, they were nothing earthly now—nothing but black shadows of disease and starvation, lying confusedly in the greenish gloom. Brought from all the recesses of the coast in all the legality of time contracts, lost in uncongenial surroundings, fed on unfamiliar food, they sickened, became inefficient, and were then allowed to crawl away and rest. These moribund shapes were free as air—and nearly as thin. I began to distinguish the gleam of the eyes under the trees. Then, glancing down, I saw a face near my hand. The black bones reclined at full length with one shoulder against the tree, and slowly the eyelids rose and the sunken eyes looked up at me, enormous and vacant, a kind of blind, white flicker in the depths of the orbs, which died out slowly. The man seemed young—almost a boy—but you know with them it's hard to tell. I found nothing else to do but to offer him one of my good Swede's ship's biscuits I had in my pocket. The fingers closed slowly on it and held—there was no other movement and no other glance. He had tied a bit of white worsted round his neck—Why? Where did he get it? Was it a badge—an ornament—a charm—a propitiatory act? Was there any idea at all connected with it? It looked startling round his black neck, this bit of white thread from beyond the seas.

"Near the same tree two more bundles of acute angles sat with their legs drawn up. One, with his chin propped on his knees, stared at nothing, in an intolerable and appalling manner: his brother phantom rested its forehead, as if overcome with a great weariness; and all about others were scattered in every pose of contorted collapse, as in some picture of a massacre or a pestilence. While I stood horror-struck, one of these creatures rose to his hands and knees, and went off on all-fours towards the river to drink. He lapped out of his hand, then sat up in the sunlight, crossing his shins in front of him, and after a time let his woolly head fall on his breastbone.

"I didn't want any more loitering in the shade, and I made haste towards the station. When near the buildings I met a white man, in such an unexpected elegance of get-up that in the first moment I took him for a sort of vision. I saw a high starched collar, white cuffs, a light alpaca jacket, snowy trousers, a clean necktie, and varnished boots. No hat. Hair parted, brushed, oiled, under a green-lined parasol held in a big white hand. He was amazing, and had a penholder behind his ear.

"I shook hands with this miracle, and I learned he was the Company's chief accountant, and that all the bookkeeping was done at this station. He had come out for a moment, he said, 'to get a breath of fresh air.' The expression sounded wonderfully odd, with its suggestion of sedentary desk-life. I wouldn't have mentioned the fellow to you at all, only it was from his lips that I first heard the name of the man who is so indissolubly connected with the memories of that time. Moreover, I respected the fellow. Yes; I respected his collars, his vast cuffs, his brushed hair. His appearance was certainly that of a hairdresser's dummy; but in the great demoralization of the land he kept up his appearance. That's backbone. His starched collars and got-up shirt-fronts were achievements of character. He had been out nearly three years; and, later, I could not help asking him how he managed to sport such linen. He had just the faintest blush, and said modestly, 'I've been teaching one of the native women about the station. It was difficult. She had a distaste for the work.' Thus this man had verily accomplished something. And he was devoted to his books, which were in apple-pie order.

45 "Everything else in the station was in a muddle—heads, things, build-

ings. Strings of dusty niggers with splay feet arrived and departed; a stream of manufactured goods, rubbishy cottons, beads, and brass-wire set into the depths of darkness, and in return came a precious trickle of ivory.

"I had to wait in the station for ten days—an eternity. I lived in a hut in the yard, but to be out of the chaos I would sometimes get into the accountant's office. It was built of horizontal planks, and so badly put together that, as he bent over his high desk, he was barred from neck to heels with narrow strips of sunlight. There was no need to open the big shutter to see. It was hot there, too; big flies buzzed fiendishly, and did not sting, but stabbed. I sat generally on the floor, while, of faultless appearance (and even slightly scented), perching on a high stool, he wrote, he wrote. Sometimes he stood up for exercise. When a trucklebed with a sick man (some invalid agent from up-country) was put in there, he exhibited a gentle annoyance. 'The groans of this sick person,' he said, 'distract my attention. And without that it is extremely difficult to guard against clerical errors in this climate.'

"One day he remarked, without lifting his head, 'In the interior you will no doubt meet Mr. Kurtz.' On my asking who Mr. Kurtz was, he said he was a first-class agent; and seeing my disappointment at this information, he added slowly, laying down his pen, 'He is a very remarkable person.' Further questions elicited from him that Mr. Kurtz was at present in charge of a trading-post, a very important one, in the true ivory-country, at 'the very bottom of there. Sends in as much ivory as all the others put together. . . .' He began to write again. The sick man was too ill to groan. The flies buzzed in a great peace.

"Suddenly there was a growing murmur of voices and a great tramping of feet. A caravan had come in. A violent babble of uncouth sounds burst out on the other side of the planks. All the carriers were speaking together, and in the midst of the uproar the lamentable voice of the chief agent was heard 'giving it up' tearfully for the twentieth time that day. . . . He rose slowly. 'What a frightful row,' he said. He crossed the room gently to look at the sick man, and returning, said to me, 'He does not hear.' 'What! Dead?' I asked, startled. 'No, not yet,' he answered, with great composure. Then, alluding with a toss of the head to the tumult in the station-yard, 'When one has got to make correct entries, one comes to hate those savages—hate them to the death.' He remained thoughtful for a moment. 'When you see Mr. Kurtz,' he went on, 'tell him for me that everything here'—he glanced at the desk—'is very satisfactory. I don't like to write to him—with those messengers of ours you never know who may get hold of your letter—at that Central Station.' He stared at me for a moment with his mild, bulging eyes. 'Oh, he will go far, very far,' he began again. 'He will be a somebody in the Administration before long. They, above—the Council in Europe, you know—mean him to be.'

"He turned to his work. The noise outside had ceased, and presently in going out I stopped at the door. In the steady buzz of flies the homeward-bound agent was lying flushed and insensible; the other, bent over his books, was making correct entries of perfectly correct transactions; and fifty feet below the doorstep I could see the still tree-tops of the grove of death.

50 "Next day I left the station at last, with a caravan of sixty men, for a two-hundred-mile tramp.

"No use telling you much about that. Paths, paths, everywhere; a stamped-in network of paths spreading over the empty land, through long grass, through burnt grass, through thickets, down and up chilly ravines, up and down stony hills ablaze with heat; and a solitude, a solitude, nobody, not a hut. The population had cleared out a long time ago. Well, if a lot of mysterious niggers armed with all kinds of fearful weapons suddenly took to traveling on the road between Deal and Gravesend, catching the yokels right and left to carry heavy loads for them, I fancy every farm and cottage thereabouts would get empty very soon. Only here the dwellings were gone, too. Still I passed through several abandoned villages. There's something pathetically childish in the ruins of grass walls. Day after day, with the stamp and shuffle of sixty pair of bare feet behind me, each pair under a sixty-pound load. Camp, cook, sleep, strike camp, march. Now and then a carrier dead in harness, at rest in the long grass near the path, with an empty water-gourd and his long staff lying by his side. A great silence around and above. Perhaps on some quiet night the tremor of far-off drums, sinking, swelling, a tremor vast, faint; a sound weird, appealing, suggestive, and wild—and perhaps with as profound a meaning as the sound of bells in a Christian country. Once a white man in an unbuttoned uniform, camping on the path with an armed escort of lank Zanzibaris, very hospitable and festive—not to say drunk. Was looking after the upkeep of the road, he declared. Can't say I saw any road or any upkeep, unless the body of a middle-aged Negro, with a bullet-hole in the forehead, upon which I absolutely stumbled three miles farther on, may be considered as a permanent improvement. I had a white companion, too, not a bad chap, but rather too fleshy and with the exasperating habit of fainting on the hot hillsides, miles away from the least bit of shade and water. Annoying, you know, to hold your own coat like a parasol over a man's head while he is coming to. I couldn't help asking him once what he meant by coming there at all. 'To make money, of course. What do you think?' he said, scornfully. Then he got fever, and had to be carried in a hammock slung under a pole. As he weighed sixteen stone[11] I had no end of rows with the carriers. They jibbed, ran away, sneaked off with their loads in the night—quite a mutiny. So, one evening, I made a speech in English with gestures, not one of which was lost to the sixty pairs of eyes before me, and the next morning I started the hammock off in front all right. An hour afterwards I came upon the whole concern wrecked in a bush—man, hammock, groans, blankets, horrors. The heavy pole had skinned his poor nose. He was very anxious for me to kill somebody, but there wasn't the shadow of a carrier near. I remembered the old doctor—'It would be interesting for science to watch the mental changes of individuals, on the spot.' I felt I was becoming scientifically interesting. However, all that is to no purpose. On the fifteenth day I came in sight of the big river again, and hobbled into the Central Station. It was a backwater surrounded by scrub and forest, with a pretty border of smelly mud on one side, and on the three others enclosed by a crazy fence of rushes. A neglected gap was all the gate it had, and the first glance at the place was enough to let you see the flabby devil was running that show. White men with long staves in their hands appeared languidly from

[11]**sixteen stone** 224 pounds (a *stone* equals 14 pounds)

amongst the buildings, strolling up to take a look at me, and then retired out of sight somewhere. One of them, a stout, excitable chap with black mustaches, informed me with great volubility and many digressions, as soon as I told him who I was, that my steamer was at the bottom of the river. I was thunderstruck. What, how, why? Oh, it was 'all right.' The 'manager himself' was there. All quite correct. 'Everybody had behaved splendidly! splendidly!'—'you must,' he said in agitation, 'go and see the general manager at once. He is waiting!'

"I did not see the real significance of that wreck at once. I fancy I see it now, but I am not sure—not at all. Certainly the affair was too stupid—when I think of it—to be altogether natural. Still. . . . But at the moment it presented itself simply as a confounded nuisance. The steamer was sunk. They had started two days before in a sudden hurry up the river with the manager on board, in charge of some volunteer skipper, and before they had been out three hours they tore the bottom out of her on stones, and she sank near the south bank. I asked myself what I was to do there, now my boat was lost. As a matter of fact, I had plenty to do in fishing my command out of the river. I had to set about it the very next day. That, and the repairs when I brought the pieces to the station, took some months.

"My first interview with the manager was curious. He did not ask me to sit down after my twenty-mile walk that morning. He was commonplace in complexion, in feature, in manners, and in voice. He was of middle size and of ordinary build. His eyes, of the usual blue, were perhaps remarkably cold, and he certainly could make his glance fall on one as trenchant and heavy as an ax. But even at these times the rest of his person seemed to disclaim the intention. Otherwise there was only an indefinable, faint expression of his lips, something stealthy—a smile—not a smile—I remember it, but I can't explain. It was unconscious, this smile was, though just after he had said something it got intensified for a instant. It came at the end of his speeches like a seal applied on the words to make the meaning of the commonest phrase appear absolutely inscrutable. He was a common trader, from his youth up employed in these parts—nothing more. He was obeyed, yet he inspired neither love nor fear, nor even respect. He inspired uneasiness. That was it! Uneasiness. Not a definite mistrust—just uneasiness—nothing more. You have no idea how effective such a . . . a . . . faculty can be. He had no genius for organizing, for initiative, or for order even. That was evident in such things as the deplorable state of the station. He had no learning, and no intelligence. His position had come to him—why? Perhaps because he was never ill. . . . He had served three terms of three years out there. . . . Because triumphant health in the general rout of constitutions is a kind of power itself. When he went home on leave he rioted on a large scale—pompously. Jack ashore—with a difference—in externals only. This one could gather from his casual talk. He originated nothing, he could keep the routine going—that's all. But he was great. He was great by this little thing that it was impossible to tell what could control such a man. He never gave the secret away. Perhaps there was nothing within him. Such a suspicion made one pause—for out there there were no external checks. Once when various tropical diseases had laid low almost every 'agent' in the station, he was heard to say, 'Men who come out here should have no entrails.' He sealed the utterance with that smile of his, as though it had been a door opening into a darkness he had in his keeping. You fancied you had seen things—but the seal was on. When annoyed at meal-times by the constant quarrels of the white men about precedence, he ordered an immense round table to be made, for which a special house had to be built. This was the station's messroom. Where he sat was the first place—the rest were nowhere. One felt this to be his unalterable conviction. He was neither civil nor uncivil. He was quiet. He allowed his 'boy'—an overfed young Negro from the coast—to treat the white men, under his very eyes, with provoking insolence.

"He began to speak as soon as he saw me. I had been very long on the road. He could not wait. Had to start without me. The upriver stations had to be relieved. There had been so many delays already that he did not know who was dead and who was alive, and how they got on—and so on, and so on. He paid no attention to my explanations, and, playing with a stick of sealing-wax, repeated several times that the situation was 'very grave, very grave.' There were rumors that a very important station was in jeopardy, and its chief, Mr. Kurtz, was ill. Hoped it was not true. Mr. Kurtz was. . . . I felt weary and irritable. Hang Kurtz, I thought. I interrupted him by saying I had heard of Mr. Kurtz on the coast. 'Ah! So they talk of him down there,' he murmured to himself. Then he began again, assuring me Mr. Kurtz was the best agent he had, an exceptional man, of the greatest importance to the Company; therefore I could understand his anxiety. He was, he said, 'very, very uneasy.' Certainly he fidgeted on his chair a good deal, exclaimed, 'Ah, Mr. Kurtz!' broke the stick of sealing-wax and seemed dumfounded by the accident. Next thing he wanted to know 'how long it would take to. . . .' I interrupted him again. Being hungry, you know, and kept on my feet too, I was getting savage. 'How can I tell?' I said. 'I haven't even seen the wreck yet—some months, no doubt.' All this talk seemed to me so futile. 'Some months,' he said. 'Well, let us say three months before we can make a start. Yes. That ought to do the affair.' I flung out of his hut (he lived all alone in a clay hut with a sort of veranda) muttering to myself my opinion of him. He was a chattering idiot. Afterwards I took it back when it was borne in upon me startlingly with what extreme nicety he had estimated the time requisite for the 'affair.'

55 "I went to work the next day, turning, so to speak, my back on that station. In that way only it seemed to me I could keep my hold on the redeeming facts of life. Still, one must look about sometimes; and then I saw this station, these men strolling aimlessly about in the sunshine of the yard. I asked myself sometimes what it all meant. They wandered here and there with their absurd long staves in their hands, like a lot of faithless pilgrims bewitched inside a rotten fence. The word 'ivory' rang in the air, was whispered, was sighed. You would think they were praying to it. A taint of imbecile rapacity blew through it all, like a whiff from some corpse. By Jove! I've never seen anything so unreal in my life. And outside, the silent wilderness surrounding this cleared speck on the earth struck me as something great and invincible, like evil or truth, waiting patiently for the passing away of this fantastic invasion.

"Oh, these months! Well, never mind. Various things happened. One evening a grass shed full of calico, cotton prints, beads, and I don't know what else, burst into a blaze so suddenly that you would have thought the earth had opened to let an avenging fire consume all the trash. I was smoking my pipe quietly by my dismantled steamer, and saw them all cutting capers in the light, with their arms lifted high, when the stout man with mustaches came tearing down to the river, a tin pail in his hand, assured me that everybody was 'behaving splendidly, splendidly,' dipped about a quart of water and tore back again. I noticed there was a hole in the bottom of his pail.

"I strolled up. There was no hurry. You see the thing had gone off like a box of matches. It had been hopeless from the very first. The flame had leaped high, driven everybody back, lighted up everything—and collapsed. The shed was already a heap of embers glowing fiercely. A nigger was being beaten near by. They said he had caused the fire in some way; be that as it may, he was screeching most horribly. I saw him, later, for several days, sitting in a bit of shade looking very sick and trying to recover himself: afterwards he arose and went out—and the wilderness without a sound took him into its bosom again. As I approached the glow from the dark I found myself at the back of two men, talking. I heard the name of Kurtz pronounced, then the words, 'take advantage of this unfortunate accident.' One of the men was the manager. I wished him a good evening. 'Did you ever see anything like it—eh? it is incredible,' he said, and walked off. The other man remained. He was a first-class agent, young, gentlemanly, a bit reserved, with a forked little beard and a hooked nose. He was standoffish with the other agents, and they on their side said he was the manager's spy among them. As to me, I had hardly ever spoken to him before. We got into talk, and by and by we strolled away from the hissing ruins. Then he asked me to his room, which was in the main building of the station. He struck a match, and I perceived that this young aristocrat had not only a silver-mounted dressing-case but also a whole candle all to himself. Just at that time the manager was the only man supposed to have any right to candles. Native mats covered the clay walls; a collection of spears, assegais,[12] shields, knives was hung up in trophies. The business intrusted to this fellow was the making of bricks—so I had been informed; but there wasn't a fragment of a brick anywhere in the station, and he had been there more than a year—waiting. It seems he could not make bricks without something, I don't know what—straw, maybe. Anyways, it could not be found there, and as it was not likely to be sent from Europe, it did not appear clear to me what he was waiting for. An act of special creation perhaps. However, they were all waiting—all the sixteen or twenty pilgrims of them—for something; and upon my word it did not seem an uncongenial occupation, from the way they took it, though the only thing that ever came to them was disease—as far as I could see. They beguiled the time by backbiting and intriguing against each other in a foolish kind of way. There was an air of plotting about that station, but nothing came of it, of course. It was as unreal as everything else—as the philanthropic pretense of the whole concern, as their talk, as their government, as their show of work. The only real feeling was a desire to get appointed to a trading-post where ivory was to be had, so that they could earn percentages. They intrigued and slandered and hated each other only on that account—but as to effectually lifting a little finger—oh, no. By heavens! there is something after all in the world allowing one man to steal a horse while another must not look at the halter. Steal

[12]**assegais** light throwing spears of hard wood, usually with an iron tip

a horse straight out. Very well. He has done it. Perhaps he can ride. But there is a way of looking at a halter that would provoke the most charitable of saints into a kick.

"I had no idea why he wanted to be sociable, but as we chatted in there it suddenly occurred to me the fellow was trying to get at something—in fact, pumping me. He alluded constantly to Europe, to the people I was supposed to know there—putting leading questions as to my acquaintances in the sepulchral city, and so on. His little eyes glittered like mica discs—with curiosity—though he tried to keep up a bit of superciliousness. At first I was astonished, but very soon I became awfully curious to see what he would find out from me. I couldn't possibly imagine what I had in me to make it worth his while. It was very pretty to see how he baffled himself, for in truth my body was full only of chills, and my head had nothing in it but that wretched steamboat business. It was evident that he took me for a perfectly shameless prevaricator. At last he got angry, and, to conceal a movement of furious annoyance, he yawned. I rose. Then I noticed a small sketch in oils, on a panel, representing a woman, draped and blindfolded, carrying a lighted torch. The background was somber—almost black. The movement of the woman was stately, and the effect of the torchlight on the face was sinister.

"It arrested me, and he stood by civilly, holding an empty half-pint champagne bottle (medical comforts) with the candle stuck in it. To my question he said Mr. Kurtz had painted this—in this very station more than a year ago—while waiting for means to go to his trading-post. 'Tell me, pray,' said I, 'who is this Mr. Kurtz?'

60 "'The chief of the Inner Station,' he answered in a short tone, looking away. 'Much obliged,' I said, laughing. 'And you are the brickmaker of the Central Station. Everyone knows that.' He was silent for a while. 'He is a prodigy,' he said at last. 'He is an emissary of pity, and science, and progress, and devil knows what else. We want,' he began to declaim suddenly, 'for the guidance of the cause intrusted to us by Europe, so to speak, higher intelligence, wide sympathies, a singleness of purpose.' 'Who says that?' I asked. 'Lots of them,' he replied. 'Some even write that; and so *he* comes here, a special being, as you ought to know.' 'Why ought I to know?' I interrupted, really surprised. He paid no attention. 'Yes. Today he is chief of the best station, next year he will be assistant-manager, two years more and . . . but I daresay you know what he will be in two years' time. You are of the new gang—the gang of virtue. The same people who sent him specially also recommended you. Oh, don't say no. I've my own eyes to trust.' Light dawned upon me. My dear aunt's influential acquaintances were producing an unexpected effect upon that young man. I nearly burst into a laugh. 'Do you read the Company's confidential correspondence?' I asked. He hadn't a word to say. It was great fun. 'When Mr. Kurtz,' I continued, severely, 'is General Manager, you won't have the opportunity.'

"He blew the candle out suddenly, and we went outside. The moon had risen. Black figures strolled about listlessly, pouring water on the glow, whence proceeded a sound of hissing; steam ascended in the moonlight, the beaten nigger groaned somewhere. 'What a row the brute makes!' said the indefatigable man with the mustaches, appearing near us. 'Serves him right. Transgression—punishment—bang! Pitiless, pitiless. That's the only way. This will prevent all conflagrations for the future. I was just telling the manager. . . .' He noticed my companion, and became crestfallen all at once. 'Not in bed yet,' he said, with a kind of servile heartiness; 'it's so natural. Ha! Danger—agitation.' He vanished. I went on to the riverside, and the other followed me. I heard a scathing murmur at my ear, 'Heap of muffs—go to.' The pilgrims could be seen in knots gesticulating, discussing. Several had still their staves in their hands. I verily believe they took these sticks to bed with them. Beyond the fence the forest stood up spectrally in the moonlight, and through the dim stir, through the faint sounds of that lamentable courtyard, the silence of the land went home to one's very heart—its mystery, its greatness, the amazing reality of its concealed life. The hurt nigger moaned feebly somewhere near by, and then fetched a deep sigh that made me mend my pace away from there. I felt a hand introducing itself under my arm. 'My dear sir,' said the fellow, 'I don't want to be misunderstood, and especially by you, who will see Mr. Kurtz long before I can have that pleasure. I wouldn't like him to get a false idea of my disposition . . . .'

"I let him run on, this papier-mâché Mephistopheles, and it seemed to me that if I tried I could poke my forefinger through him, and would find nothing inside but a little loose dirt, maybe. He, don't you see, had been planning to be assistant-manager by and by under the present man, and I could see that the coming of that Kurtz had upset them both not a little. He talked precipitately, and I did not try to stop him. I had my shoulders against the wreck of my steamer, hauled up on the slope like a carcass of some big river animal. The smell of mud, of primeval mud, by Jove! was in my nostrils, the high stillness of primeval forest was before my eyes; there were shiny patches on the black creek. The moon had spread over everything a thin layer of silver—over the rank grass, over the mud, upon the wall of matted vegetation standing higher than the wall of a temple, over the great river I could see through a somber gap glittering, glittering, as it flowed broadly by without a murmur. All this was great, expectant, mute, while the man jabbered about himself. I wondered whether the stillness on the face of the immensity looking at us two were meant as an appeal or as a menace. What were we who had strayed in here? Could we handle that dumb thing, or would it handle us? I felt how big, how confoundedly big, was that thing that couldn't talk, and perhaps was deaf as well. What was in there? I could see a little ivory coming out from there, and I had heard Mr. Kurtz was in there. I had heard enough about it, too—God knows! Yet somehow it didn't bring an image with it—no more than if I had been told an angel or a fiend was in there. I believed it in the same way one of you might believe there are inhabitants in the planet Mars. I knew once a Scotch sailmaker who was certain, dead sure, there were people in Mars. If you asked him for some idea how they looked and behaved, he would get shy and mutter something about 'walking on all-fours.' If you as much as smiled, he would—though a man of sixty—offer to fight you. I would not have gone so far as to fight for Kurtz, but I went for him near enough to a lie. You know I hate, detest, and can't bear a lie, not because I am straighter than the rest of us, but simply because it appalls me. There is a taint of death, a flavor of mortality in lies—which is exactly what I hate and detest in the world—what I want to forget. It makes me miserable and sick, like biting something rotten would do. Temperament, I suppose. Well, I went near enough to it by letting the young fool there believe anything he liked to imagine as to my influence in Europe. I became in an instant as much of a pretense as the rest of the bewitched pilgrims. This simply because I had a notion it somehow would be of help to that Kurtz whom at the time I did not see—you understand. He was just a word for me. I did not see the man in the name any more than you do. Do you see him? Do you see the story? Do you see anything? It seems to me I am trying to tell you a dream—making a vain attempt, because no relation of a dream can convey the dream-sensation, that commingling of absurdity, surprise, and bewilderment in a tremor of struggling revolt, that notion of being captured by the incredible which is of the very essence of dreams. . . ."

He was silent for a while.

". . . No, it is impossible; it is impossible to convey the life-sensation of any given epoch of one's existence—that which makes its truth, its meaning—its subtle and penetrating essence. It is impossible. We live, as we dream—alone. . . ."

65 He paused again as if reflecting, then added—

"Of course in this you fellows see more than I could then. You see me, whom you know. . . ."

It had become so pitch dark that we listeners could hardly see one another. For a long time already he, sitting apart, had been no more to us than a voice. There was not a word from anybody. The others might have been asleep, but I was awake. I listened, I listened on the watch for the sentence, for the word, that would give me the clew of the faint uneasiness inspired by this narrative that seemed to shape itself without human lips in the heavy night-air of the river.

". . . Yes—I let him run on," Marlow began again, "and think what he pleased about the powers that were behind me. I did! And there was nothing behind me! There was nothing but that wretched, old, mangled steamboat I was leaning against, while he talked fluently about 'the necessity for every man to get on.' 'And when one comes out here, you conceive, it is not to gaze at the moon.' Mr. Kurtz was a 'universal genius,' but even a genius would find it easier to work with 'adequate tools—intelligent men.' He did not make bricks—why, there was a physical impossibility in the way—as I was well aware; and if he did secretarial work for the manager, it was because 'no sensible man rejects wantonly the confidence of his superiors.' Did I see it? I saw it. What more did I want? What I really wanted was rivets, by heavens! Rivets. To get on with the work—to stop the hole. Rivets I wanted. There were cases of them down at the coast—cases—piled up—burst—split! You kicked a loose rivet at every second step in that station yard on the hillside. Rivets had rolled into the grove of death. You could fill your pockets with rivets for the trouble of stooping down—and there wasn't one rivet to be found where it was wanted. We had plates that would do, but nothing to fasten them with. And every week the messenger, a lone Negro, letter-bag on shoulder and staff in hand, left our station for the coast. And several times a week a coast caravan came in with trade goods—ghastly glazed calico that made you shudder only to look at it; glass beads, valued about a penny a quart, confounded spotted cotton handkerchiefs. And no rivets. Three carriers could have brought all that was wanted to set that steamboat afloat.

"He was becoming confidential now, but I fancy my unresponsive attitude must have exasperated him at last, for he judged it necessary to inform me he feared neither God nor devil, let alone any mere man. I said I could see that very well, but what I wanted was a certain quantity of rivets—and rivets were what really Mr. Kurtz wanted, if he had only known it. Now letters went to the coast every week. . . . 'My dear sir,' he cried, 'I write from dictation.' I demanded rivets. There was a way—for an intelligent man. He changed his manner; became very cold, and suddenly began to talk about a hippopotamus; wondered whether sleeping on board the steamer (I stuck to my salvage night and day) I wasn't disturbed. There was an old hippo that had the bad habit of getting out on the bank and roaming at night over the station grounds. The pilgrims used to turn out in a body and empty every rifle they could lay hands on at him. Some even had sat up o' nights for him. All this energy was wasted, though. 'That animal had a charmed life,' he said; 'but you can say this only of brutes in this country. No man—you apprehend me?—no man here bears a charmed life.' He stood there for a moment in the moonlight with his delicate hooked nose set a little askew, and his mica eyes glittering without a wink, then, with a curt good night, he strode off. I could see he was disturbed and considerably puzzled, which made me feel more hopeful than I had been for days. It was a great comfort to turn from that chap to my influential friend, the battered, twisted, ruined, tin-pot steamboat. I clambered on board. She rang under my feet like an empty Huntley & Palmer biscuit-tin kicked along a gutter; she was nothing so solid in make, and rather less pretty in shape, but I had expended enough hard work on her to make me love her. No influential friend would have served me better. She had given me a chance to come out a bit—to find out what I could do. No, I don't like work. I had rather laze about and think of all the fine things that can be done. I don't like work—no man does—but I like what is in the work—the chance to find yourself. Your own reality—for yourself, not for others—what no other man can ever know. They can only see the mere show, and never tell me what it really means.

70 "I was not surprised to see somebody sitting aft, on the deck, with his legs dangling over the mud. You see I rather chummed with the few mechanics there were in that station, whom the other pilgrims naturally despised—on account of their imperfect manners, I suppose. This was the foreman—a boiler-maker by trade—a good worker. He was a lank, bony, yellow-faced man, with big intense eyes. His aspect was worried, and his head was as bald as the palm of my hand; but his hair in falling seemed to have stuck to his chin, and had prospered in the new locality, for his beard hung down to his waist. He was a widower with six young children (he had left them in charge of a sister of his to come out there), and the passion of his life was pigeon-flying. He was an enthusiast and a connoisseur. He would rave about pigeons. After work hours he used sometimes to come over from his hut for a talk about his children and his pigeons; at work, when he had to crawl in the mud under the bottom of the steamboat, he would tie up that beard of his in a kind of white serviette[13] he brought for the purpose. It had loops to go over his ears. In the evening he could be seen squatted on the bank rinsing that wrapper in the creek with great care, then spreading it solemnly on a bush to dry.

"I slapped him on the back and shouted, 'We shall have rivets!' He scrambled to his feet exclaiming, 'No! Rivets!' as though he couldn't believe his ears. Then in a low voice, 'You . . . eh?' I don't know why we behaved

[13] **serviette** napkin

like lunatics. I put my finger to the side of my nose and nodded mysteriously. 'Good for you!' he cried, snapped his fingers above his head, lifting one foot. I tried a jig. We capered on the iron deck. A frightful clatter came out of that hulk, and the virgin forest on the other bank of the creek sent it back in a thundering roll upon the sleeping station. It must have made some of the pilgrims sit up in their hovels. A dark figure obscured the lighted doorway of the manager's hut, vanished, then, a second or so after, the doorway itself vanished, too. We stopped, and the silence driven away by the stamping of our feet flowed back again from the recesses of the land. The great wall of vegetation, an exuberant and entangled mass of trunks, branches, leaves, boughs, festoons, motionless in the moonlight, was like a rioting invasion of soundless life, a rolling wave of plants, piled up, crested, ready to topple over the creek, to sweep every little man of us out of his little existence. And it moved not. A deadened burst of mighty splashes and snorts reached us from afar as though an ichthyosaurus had been taking a bath of glitter in the great river. 'After all,' said the boilermaker in a reasonable tone, 'why shouldn't we get the rivets?' Why not, indeed! I did not know of any reason why we shouldn't. 'They'll come in three weeks,' I said confidently.

"But they didn't. Instead of rivets there came an invasion, an infliction, a visitation. It came in sections during the next three weeks, each section headed by a donkey carrying a white man in new clothes and tan shoes, bowing from that elevation right and left to the impressed pilgrims. A quarrelsome band of footsore sulky niggers trod on the heels of the donkeys; a lot of tents, campstools, tin boxes, white cases, brown bales would be shot down in the courtyard, and the air of mystery would deepen a little over the muddle of the station. Five such installments came, with their absurd air of disorderly flight with the loot of innumerable outfit shops and provision stores, that, one would think, they were lugging, after a raid, into the wilderness for equitable division. It was an extricable mess of things decent in themselves but that human folly made look like the spoils of thieving.

"This devoted band called itself the Eldorado Exploring Expedition, and I believe they were sworn to secrecy. Their talk, however, was the talk of sordid buccaneers: it was reckless without hardihood, greedy without audacity, and cruel without courage; there was not an atom of foresight or of serious intention in the whole batch of them, and they did not seem aware these things are wanted for the work of the world. To tear treasure out of the bowels of the land was their desire, with no more moral purpose at the back of it than there is in burglars breaking into a safe. Who paid the expenses of the noble enterprise I don't know; but the uncle of our manager was leader of that lot.

"In exterior he resembled a butcher in a poor neighborhood, and his eyes had a look of sleepy cunning. He carried his fat paunch with ostentation on his short legs, and during the time his gang infested the station spoke to no one but his nephew. You could see these two roaming about all day long with their heads close together in an everlasting confab.

75 "I had given up worrying myself about the rivets. One's capacity for that kind of folly is more limited than you would suppose. I said Hang!—and let things slide. I had plenty of time for meditation, and now and then I would give some thought to Kurtz. I wasn't very interested in him. No. Still, I was curious to see whether this man, who had come out equipped with

moral ideas of some sort, would climb to the top after all and how he would set about his work when there."

## II

"One evening as I was lying flat on the deck of my steamboat, I heard voices approaching—and there were the nephew and the uncle strolling along the bank. I laid my head on my arm again, and had nearly lost myself in a doze, when somebody said in my ear, as it were: 'I am as harmless as a little child, but I don't like to be dictated to. Am I the manager—or am I not? I was ordered to send him there. It's incredible.' . . . I became aware that the two were standing on the shore alongside the forepart of the steamboat, just below my head. I did not move; it did not occur to me to move: I was sleepy. 'It *is* unpleasant,' grunted the uncle. 'He has asked the Administration to be sent there,' said the other, 'with the idea of showing what he could do; and I was instructed accordingly. Look at the influence that man must have. Is it not frightful?' They both agreed it was frightful, then made several bizarre remarks: 'Make rain and fine weather—one man—the Council—by the nose'—bits of absurd sentences that got the better of my drowsiness, so that I had pretty near the whole of my wits about me when the uncle said, 'The climate may do away with this difficulty for you. Is he alone there?' 'Yes,' answered the manager; 'he sent his assistant down the river with a note to me in these terms: "Clear this poor devil out of the country, and don't bother sending more of that sort. I had rather be alone than have the kind of men you can dispose of with me." It was more than a year ago. Can you imagine such impudence!' 'Anything since then?' asked the other, hoarsely. 'Ivory,' jerked the nephew; 'lots of it—prime sort—lots—most annoying, from him.' 'And with that?' questioned the heavy rumble. 'Invoice,' was the reply fired out, so to speak. Then silence. They had been talking about Kurtz.

"I was broad awake by this time, but, lying perfectly at ease, remained still, having no inducement to change my position. 'How did that ivory come all this way?' growled the elder man, who seemed very vexed. The other explained that it had come with a fleet of canoes in charge of an English half-caste clerk Kurtz had with him; that Kurtz had apparently intended to return himself, the station being by that time bare of goods and stores, but after coming three hundred miles, had suddenly decided to go back, which he started to do alone in a small dugout with four paddlers, leaving the half-caste to continue down the river with the ivory. The two fellows there seemed astounded at anybody attempting such a thing. They were at a loss for an adequate motive. As to me, I seemed to see Kurtz for the first time. It was a distinct glimpse: the dugout, four paddling savages, and the lone white man turning his back suddenly on the headquarters, on relief, on thoughts of home—perhaps; setting his face towards the depths of the wilderness, towards his empty and desolate station. I did not know the motive. Perhaps he was just simply a fine fellow who stuck to his work for its own sake. His name, you understand, had not been pronounced once. He was 'that man.' The half-caste, who, as far as I could see, had conducted a difficult trip with great prudence and pluck, was invariably alluded to as 'that scoundrel.' The 'scoundrel' had reported that the 'man' had been very ill—had recovered imperfectly. . . . The two below me moved away then a few paces, and strolled back and forth at some little distance. I heard: 'Military post—doctor—two hundred miles—quite alone now—unavoidable delays—nine months—no news—strange rumors.' They approached again, just as the manager was saying, 'No one, as far as I know, unless a species of wandering trader—a pestilential fellow, snapping ivory from the natives.' Who was it they were talking about now? I gathered in snatches that this was some man supposed to be in Kurtz's district, and of whom the manager did not approve. 'We will not be free from unfair competition till one of these fellows is hanged for an example,' he said. 'Certainly,' grunted the other; 'get him hanged! Why not? Anything—anything can be done in this country. That's what I say; nobody here, you understand, *here,* can endanger your position. And why? You stand the climate—you outlast them all. The danger is in Europe; but there before I left I took care to—' They moved off and whispered, then their voices rose again. 'The extraordinary series of delays is not my fault. I did my best.' The fat man sighed. 'Very sad.' 'And the pestiferous absurdity of his talk,' continued the other; 'he bothered me enough when he was here. "Each station should be like a beacon on the road towards better things, a center for trade, of course, but also for humanizing, improving, instructing." Conceive you—that ass! And he wants to be manager! No it's—' Here he got choked by excessive indignation, and I lifted my head the least bit. I was surprised to see how near they were—right under me. I could have spat upon their hats. They were looking on the ground, absorbed in thought. The manager was switching his leg with a slender twig: his sagacious relative lifted his head. 'You have been well since you came out this time?' he asked. The other gave a start. 'Who? I? Oh! Like a charm—like a charm. But the rest—oh, my goodness! All sick. They die so quick, too, that I haven't the time to send them out of the country—it's incredible!' 'H'm. Just so,' grunted the uncle. 'Ah! my boy, trust to this—I say, trust to this.' I saw him extend his short flipper of an arm for a gesture that took in the forest, the creek, the mud, the river—seemed to beckon with a dishonoring flourish before the sunlit face of the land a treacherous appeal to the lurking death, to the hidden evil, to the profound darkness of its heart. It was so startling that I leaped to my feet and looked back at the edge of the forest, as though I had expected an answer of some sort to that black display of confidence. You know the foolish notions that come to one sometimes. The high stillness confronted these two figures with its ominous patience, waiting for the passing away of a fantastic invasion.

"They swore aloud together—out of sheer fright, I believe—then pretending not to know anything of my existence, turned back to the station. The sun was low; and leaning forward side by side, they seemed to be tugging painfully uphill their two ridiculous shadows of unequal length, that trailed behind them slowly over the tall grass without bending a single blade.

"In a few days the Eldorado Expedition went into the patient wilderness, that closed upon it as the sea closes over a diver. Long afterwards the news came that all the donkeys were dead. I know nothing as to the fate of the less valuable animals. They, no doubt, like the rest of us, found what they deserved. I did not inquire. I was then rather excited at the prospect of meeting Kurtz very soon. When I say very soon I mean it comparatively. It was just two months from the day we left the creek when we came to the bank below Kurtz's station.

80 "Going up that river was like traveling back to the earliest beginnings of the world, when vegetation rioted on the earth and the big trees were kings. An empty stream, a great silence, an impenetrable forest. The air was warm, thick, heavy, sluggish. There was no joy in the brilliance of sunshine. The long stretches of the waterway ran on, deserted, into the gloom of overshadowed distances. On silvery sandbanks hippos and alligators sunned themselves side by side. The broadening waters flowed through a mob of wooded islands; you lost your way on that river as you would in a desert, and butted all day long against shoals, trying to find the channel, till you thought yourself bewitched and cut off forever from everything you had known once—somewhere—far away—in another existence perhaps. There were moments when one's past came back to one, as it will sometimes when you have not a moment to spare to yourself; but it came in the shape of an unrestful and noisy dream, remembered with wonder amongst the overwhelming realities of this strange world of plants, and water, and silence. And this stillness of life did not in the least resemble a peace. It was the stillness of an implacable force brooding over an inscrutable intention. It looked at you with a vengeful aspect. I got used to it afterwards; I did not see it any more; I had no time. I had to keep guessing at the channel; I had to discern, mostly by inspiration, the signs of hidden banks; I watched for sunken stones; I was learning to clap my teeth smartly before my heart flew out, when I shaved by a fluke some infernal sly old snag that would have ripped the life out of the tin-pot steamboat and drowned all the pilgrims; I had to keep a lookout for the signs of dead wood we could cut up in the night for next day's steaming. When you have to attend to things of that sort, to the mere incidents of the surface, the reality—the reality, I tell you—fades. The inner truth is hidden—luckily, luckily. But I felt it all the same; I felt often its mysterious stillness watching me at my monkey tricks, just as it watches you fellows performing on your respective tightropes for—what is it? half-a-crown a tumble—"

"Try to be civil, Marlow," growled a voice, and I knew there was at least one listener awake besides myself.

"I beg your pardon. I forgot the heartache which makes up the rest of the price. And indeed what does the price matter, if the trick be well done? You do your tricks very well. And I didn't do badly either, since I managed not to sink that steamboat on my first trip. It's a wonder to me yet. Imagine a blindfolded man set to drive a van over a bad road. I sweated and shivered over the business considerably, I can tell you. After all, for a seaman, to scrape the bottom of the thing that's supposed to float all the time under his care is the unpardonable sin. No one may know of it, but you never forget the thump—eh? A blow on the very heart. You remember it, you dream of it, you wake up at night and think of it—years after—and go hot and cold all over. I don't pretend to say that steamboat floated all the time. More than once she had to wade for a bit, with twenty cannibals splashing around and pushing. We had enlisted some of these chaps on the way for a crew. Fine fellows—cannibals—in their place. They were men one could work with, and I am grateful to them. And, after all, they did not eat each other before my face: they had brought along a provision of hippo-meat which went rotten, and made the mystery of the wilderness stink in my nostrils. Phoo! I can sniff it now. I had the manager on board and three or four pilgrims with their staves—all complete. Sometimes we came upon a station close by the bank, clinging to the skirts of the unknown, and the white men rushing out of a tumble-down hovel, with great gestures of joy and surprise and welcome, seemed very strange—had the appearance of being held there captive by a spell. The word ivory would ring in the air for a while—and on we went again into the silence, along empty reaches, round the still bends, between the high walls of our winding way, reverberating in hollow claps the ponderous beat of the stern-wheel. Trees, trees, millions of trees, massive, immense, running up high; and at their foot, hugging the bank against the stream, crept the little begrimed steamboat, like a sluggish beetle crawling on the floor of a lofty portico. It made you feel very small, very lost, and yet it was not altogether depressing, that feeling. After all, if you were small, the grimy beetle crawled on—which was just what you wanted it to do. Where the pilgrims imagined it crawled to I don't know. To some place where they expected to get something, I bet! For me it crawled towards Kurtz—exclusively; but when the steam-pipes started leaking we crawled very slow. The reaches opened before us and closed behind, as if the forest had stepped leisurely across the water to bar the way for our return. We penetrated deeper and deeper into the heart of darkness. It was very quiet there. At night sometimes the roll of drums behind the curtain of trees would run up the river and remained sustained faintly, as if hovering in the air high over our heads, till the first break of day. Whether it means war, peace, or prayer we could not tell. The dawns were heralded by the descent of a chill stillness; the wood-cutters slept, their fires burned low; the snapping of a twig would make you start. We were wanderers on a prehistoric earth, on an earth that wore the aspect of an unknown planet. We could have fancied ourselves the first men taking possession of an accursed inheritance, to be subdued at the cost of profound anguish and of excessive toil. But suddenly, as we struggled round a bend, there would be a glimpse of rush walls, of peaked grass-roofs, a burst of yells, a whirl of black limbs, a mass of hands clapping, of feet stamping, of bodies swaying, of eyes rolling, under the droop of heavy and motionless foliage. The steamer toiled along slowly on the edge of a black and incomprehensible frenzy. The prehistoric man was cursing us, praying to us, welcoming us—who could tell? We were cut off from the comprehension of our surroundings; we glided past like phantoms, wondering and secretly appalled, as sane men would be before an enthusiastic outbreak in a madhouse. We could not understand because we were too far and could not remember, because we were traveling in the night of first ages, of those ages that are gone, leaving hardly a sign—and no memories.

"The earth seemed unearthly. We are accustomed to look upon the shackled form of a conquered monster, but there—there you could look at a thing monstrous and free. It was unearthly, and the men were—No, they were not inhuman. Well, you know, that was the worst of it—this suspicion of their not being inhuman. It would come slowly to one. They howled and leaped, and spun, and made horrid faces; but what thrilled you was just the thought of their humanity—like yours—the thought of your remote kinship with this wild and passionate uproar. Ugly. Yes, it was ugly enough; but if you were man enough you would admit to yourself that there was in you just the faintest trace of a response to the terrible frankness of that noise, a dim suspicion of there being a meaning in it which you—you so remote from the night of first ages—could comprehend. And why not? The mind of man is capable of anything—because everything is in it, all the past as well as the future. What was there after all? Joy, fear, sorrow, devotion, valor, rage—who can tell?—but truth—truth stripped of its cloak of time. Let the fool gape and shudder—the man knows, and can look on without a wink. But he must at least be as much of a man as these on the shore. He must meet the truth with his own true stuff—with his own inborn strength. Principles won't do. Acquisitions, clothes, pretty rags—rags that would fly off at the first good shake. No; you want a deliberate belief. An appeal to me in this fiendish row—is there? Very well; I hear; I admit, but I have a voice, too, and for good or evil mine is the speech that cannot be silenced. Of course, a fool, what with sheer fright and fine sentiments, is always safe. Who's that grunting? You wonder I didn't go ashore for a howl and a dance? Well, no—I didn't. Fine sentiments, you say? Fine sentiments, be hanged! I had no time. I had to mess about with white-lead and strips of woolen blanket helping to put bandages on those leaky steam-pipes—I tell you. I had to watch the steering, and circumvent those snags, and get the tin-pot along by hook or by crook. There was surface-truth enough in these things to save a wiser man. And between whiles I had to look after the savage who was fireman. He was an improved specimen; he could fire up a vertical boiler. He was there below me, and, upon my word, to look at him was as edifying as seeing a dog in a parody of breeches and a feather hat, walking on his hindlegs. A few months of training had done for that really fine chap. He squinted at the steam-gauge and at the water-gauge with an evident effort of intrepidity—and he had filed teeth, too, the poor devil, and the wool of his pate shaved into queer patterns, and three ornamental scars on each of his cheeks. He ought to have been clapping his hands and stamping his feet on the bank, instead of which he was hard at work, a thrall to strange witchcraft, full of improving knowledge. He was useful because he had been instructed; and what he knew was this—that should the water in that transparent thing disappear, the evil spirit inside the boiler would get angry through the greatness of his thirst, and take a terrible vengeance. So he sweated and fired up and watched the glass fearfully (with an impromptu charm, made of rags, tied to his arm, and a piece of polished bone, as big as a watch, stuck flatways through his lower lip), while the wooden banks slipped past us slowly, the short noise was left behind, the interminable miles of silence—and we crept on, towards Kurtz. But the snags were thick, the water was treacherous and shallow, the boiler seemed indeed to have a sulky devil in it, and thus neither that fireman nor I had any time to peer into our creepy thoughts.

"Some fifty miles below the Inner Station we came upon a hut of reeds, an inclined and melancholy pole, with the unrecognizable tatters of what had been a flag of some sort flying from it, and a neatly stacked woodpile. This was unexpected. We came to the bank, and on the stack of firewood found a flat piece of board with some faded pencil-writing on it. When deciphered it said: 'Wood for you. Hurry up. Approach cautiously.' There was a signature, but it was illegible—not Kurtz—a much longer word. 'Hurry up.' Where? Up the river? 'Approach cautiously.' We had not done so. But the warning could not have been meant for the place where it could be only found after approach. Something was wrong above. But what—and how much? That was the question. We commented adversely upon the imbecility of that telegraphic style. The bush around said nothing, and would not let us look very far, either. A torn curtain of red twill hung in the doorway of the hut, and flapped sadly in our faces. The dwelling was dismantled; but we could see a white man had lived there not very long ago. There remained a rude table—a plank on two posts; a heap of rubbish reposed in a dark corner, and by the door I picked up a book. It had lost its covers, and the pages had been thumbed into a state of extremely dirty softness; but the back had been lovingly stitched afresh with white cotton thread, which looked clean yet. It was an extraordinary find. Its title was, *An Inquiry into Some Points of Seamanship,* by a man Towser, Towson—some such name—Master in his Majesty's Navy. The matter looked dreary reading enough, with illustrative diagrams and repulsive tables of figures, and the copy was sixty years old. I handled this amazing antiquity with the greatest possible tenderness, lest it should dissolve in my hands. Within, Towson or Towser was inquiring earnestly into the breaking strain of ships' chains and tackle, and other such matters. Not a very enthralling book; but at the first glance you could see there a singleness of intention, an honest concern for the right way of going to work, which made these humble pages, thought out so many years ago, luminous with another than a professional light. The simple old sailor, with his talk of chains and purchases,[14] made me forget the jungle and the pilgrims in a delicious sensation of having come upon something unmistakably real. Such a book being there was wonderful enough; but still more astounding were the notes penciled in the margin, and plainly referring to the text. I couldn't believe my eyes! They were in cipher! Yes, it looked like cipher. Fancy a man lugging with him a book of that description into this nowhere and studying it—and making notes—in cipher at that! It was an extravagant mystery.

85 "I had been dimly aware for some time of a worrying noise, and when I lifted my eyes I saw the woodpile was gone, and the manager, aided by all the pilgrims, was shouting at me from the riverside. I slipped the book into my pocket. I assure you to leave off reading was like tearing myself away from the shelter of an old and solid friendship.

"I started the lame engine ahead. 'It must be this miserable trader—this intruder,' exclaimed the manager, looking back malevolently at the place we had left. 'He must be English,' I said. 'It will not save him from getting into trouble if he is not careful,' muttered the manager darkly. I observed with assumed innocence that no man was safe from trouble in this world.

"The current was more rapid now, the steamer seemed at her last gasp, the stern-wheel flopped languidly, and I caught myself listening on tiptoe for the next beat of the float,[15] for in sober truth I expected the wretched thing to give up every moment. It was like watching the last flickers of a life. But still we crawled. Sometimes I would pick out a tree a little way ahead to measure our progress towards Kurtz by, but I lost it invariably before we got abreast. To keep the eyes so long on one thing was too much for human patience. The manager displayed a beautiful resignation. I fretted and fumed and took to arguing with myself whether or not I would talk openly with Kurtz; but before I could come to any conclusion it occurred to me that my speech or my silence, indeed any action of mine, would be a

[14]**purchases** tackles, levers, and other devices used to obtain a mechanical advantage

[15]**float** an automatic device that opens and closes a water-supply valve

mere futility. What did it matter what anyone knew or ignored? What did it matter who was manager? One gets sometimes such a flash of insight. The essentials of this affair lay deep under the surface, beyond my reach, and beyond my power of meddling.

"Towards the evening of the second day we judged ourselves about eight miles from Kurtz's station. I wanted to push on; but the manager looked grave, and told me the navigation up there was so dangerous that it would be advisable, the sun being very low already, to wait where we were till next morning. Moreover, he pointed out that if the warning to approach cautiously were to be followed, we must approach in daylight—not at dusk, or in the dark. This was sensible enough. Eight miles meant nearly three hours' steaming for us, and I could also see suspicious ripples at the upper end of the reach. Nevertheless, I was annoyed beyond expression at the delay, and most unreasonably, too, since one night more could not matter much after so many months. As we had plenty of wood, and caution was the word, I brought up in the middle of the stream. The reach was narrow, straight, with high sides like a railway cutting. The dusk came gliding into it long before the sun had set. The current ran smooth and swift, but a dumb immobility sat on the banks. The living trees, lashed together by the creepers and every living bush of the undergrowth, might have been changed into stone, even to the slenderest twig, to the lightest leaf. It was not sleep—it seemed unnatural, like a state of trance. Not the faintest sound of any kind could be heard. You looked on amazed, and began to suspect yourself of being deaf—then the night came suddenly, and struck you blind as well. About three in the morning some large fish leaped, and the loud splash made me jump as though a gun had been fired. When the sun rose there was a white fog, very warm and clammy, and more blinding than the night. It did not shift or drive; it was just there, standing all around you like something solid. At eight or nine, perhaps, it lifted as a shutter lifts. We had a glimpse of the towering multitude of trees, of the immense matted jungle, with the blazing little ball of the sun hanging over it—all perfectly still—and then the white shutter came down again, smoothly, as if sliding in greased grooves. I ordered the chain, which we had begun to heave in, to be paid out again. Before it stopped running with a muffled rattle, a cry, a very loud cry, as of infinite desolation, soared slowly in the opaque air. It ceased. A complaining clamor, modulated in savage discords, filled our ears. The sheer unexpectedness of it made my hair stir under my cap. I don't know how it struck the others: to me it seemed as though the mist itself had screamed, so suddenly, and apparently from all sides at once, did this tumultuous and mournful uproar arise. It culminated in a hurried outbreak of almost intolerably excessive shrieking, which stopped short, leaving us stiffened in a variety of silly attitudes, and obstinately listening to the nearly as appalling and excessive silence. 'Good God! What is the meaning—' stammered at my elbow one of the pilgrims—a little fat man, with sandy hair and red whiskers, who wore side-spring boots, and pink pajamas tucked into his socks. Two others remained open-mouthed a whole minute, then dashed into the little cabin, to rush out incontinently and stand darting scared glances, with Winchesters at 'ready' in their hands. What we could see was just the steamer we were on, her outlines blurred as though she had been on the point of dissolving, and a misty strip of water, perhaps two feet broad, around her—and that was all. The rest of the world was nowhere, as far as our eyes and ears were concerned. Just nowhere. Gone, disappeared; swept off without leaving a whisper or a shadow behind.

"I went forward, and ordered the chain to be hauled in short, so as to be ready to trip the anchor and move the steamboat at once if necessary. 'Will they attack?' whispered an awed voice. 'We will be all butchered in this fog,' murmured another. The faces twitched with the strain, the hands trembling slightly, the eyes forgot to wink. It was very curious to see the contrast of expressions of the white men and of the black fellows of our crew, who were as much strangers to that part of the river as we, though their homes were only eight hundred miles away. The whites, of course, greatly discomposed, had besides a curious look of being painfully shocked by such an outrageous row. The others had an alert, naturally interested expression; but their faces were essentially quiet, even those of the one or two who grinned as they hauled at the chain. Several exchanged short, grunting phrases, which seemed to settle the matter to their satisfaction. Their headman, a young, broad-chested black, severely draped in dark-blue fringed cloths, with fierce nostrils and his hair all done up artfully in oily ringlets, stood near me. 'Aha!' I said, just for good fellowship's sake. 'Catch 'em,' he snapped, with a bloodshot widening of his eyes and a flash of sharp teeth—'catch 'im. Give 'im to us.' 'To you, eh?' I asked; 'what would you do with them?' 'Eat 'em!' he said, curtly, and, leaning his elbow on the rail, looked out into the fog in a dignified and profoundly pensive attitude. I would no doubt have been properly horrified, had it not occurred to me that he and his chaps must be very hungry; that they must have been growing increasingly hungry for at least this month past. They had been engaged for six months (I don't think a single one of them had any clear idea of time, as we at the end of countless ages have. They still belonged to the beginnings of time—had no inherited experience to teach them as it were), and of course, as long as there was a piece of paper written over in accordance with some farcical law or other made down the river, it didn't enter anybody's head to trouble how they would live. Certainly they had brought with them some rotten hippo-meat, which couldn't have lasted very long, anyway, even if the pilgrims hadn't, in the midst of a shocking hullabaloo, thrown a considerable quantity of it overboard. It looked like a high-handed proceeding; but it was really a case of legitimate self-defense. You can't breathe dead hippo waking, sleeping, and eating, and at the same time keep your precarious grip on existence. Besides that, they had given them every week three pieces of brass wire, each about nine inches long; and the theory was they were to buy their provisions with that currency in riverside villages. You can see how *that* worked. There were either no villages, or the people were hostile, or the director, who like the rest of us fed out of tins, with an occasional old he-goat thrown in, didn't want to stop the steamer for some more or less recondite reason. So, unless they swallowed the wire itself, or made loops of it to snare the fishes with, I don't see what good their extravagant salary could be to them. I must say it was paid with a regularity worthy of a large and honorable trading company. For the rest, the only thing to eat—though it didn't look eatable in the least—I saw in their possession was a few lumps of some stuff like half-cooked dough, of a dirty lavender color, they kept wrapped in leaves, and now and then swallowed a piece of, but so small that it seemed done more for the looks of the thing than for any serious purpose of sustenance. Why in the name of all the gnawing devils of hunger they didn't go for us—they were thirty to five—and have a good tuck-in for once, amazes me now when I think of it. They were big powerful men, with not much capacity to weigh the consequences, with courage, with strength, even yet, though their skins were no longer glossy and their muscles no longer hard. And I saw that something restraining, one of those human secrets that baffle probability, had come into play there. I looked at them with a swift quickening of interest—not because it occurred to me I might be eaten by them before very long, though I own to you that just then I perceived—in a new light, as it were—how unwholesome the pilgrims looked, and I hoped, yes, I positively hoped, that my aspect was not so—what shall I say?—so—unappetizing: a touch of fantastic vanity which fitted well with the dream-sensation that pervaded all my days at that time. Perhaps I had a little fever, too. One can't live with one's finger everlastingly on one's pulse. I had often 'a little fever,' or a little touch of other things—the playful paw-strokes of the wilderness, the preliminary trifling before the more serious onslaught which came in due course. Yes; I looked at them as you would on any human being, with a curiosity of their impulses, motives, capacities, weaknesses, when brought to the test of an inexorable physical necessity. Restraint! What possible restraint? Was it superstition, disgust, patience, fear—or some kind of primitive honor? No fear can stand up to hunger, no patience can wear it out, disgust simply does not exist where hunger is; and as to superstition, beliefs, and what you may call principles, they are less than chaff in a breeze. Don't you know the devilry of lingering starvation, its exasperating torment, its black thoughts, its somber and brooding ferocity? Well, I do. It takes a man all his inborn strength to fight hunger properly. It's really easier to face bereavement, dishonor, and the perdition of one's soul—than this kind of prolonged hunger. Sad, but true. And these chaps, too, had no earthly reason for any kind of scruple. Restraint! I would just as soon have expected restraint from a hyena prowling amongst the corpses of a battlefield. But there was the fact facing me—the fact dazzling, to be seen, like the foam on the depths of the sea, like a ripple on an unfathomable enigma, a mystery greater—when I thought of it—than the curious, inexplicable note of desperate grief in this savage clamor that had swept by us on the riverbank, behind the blind whiteness of the fog.

90 "Two pilgrims were quarreling in hurried whispers as to which bank. 'Left.' 'No, no; how can you? Right, right, of course.' 'It is very serious,' said the manager's voice behind me; 'I would be desolated if anything should happen to Mr. Kurtz before we came up.' I looked at him, and had not the slightest doubt he was sincere. He was just the kind of man who would wish to preserve appearances. That was his restraint. But when he muttered something about going on at once, I did not even take the trouble to answer him. I knew, and he knew, that it was impossible. Were we to let go our hold of the bottom, we would be absolutely in the air—in space. We wouldn't be able to tell where we were going to—whether up or down stream, or across—till we fetched against one bank or the other—and then we wouldn't know at first which it was. Of course I made no move. I had no mind for a smash-up. You couldn't imagine a more deadly place for a shipwreck. Whether drowned at once or not, we were sure to perish speedily in

one way or another. 'I authorize you to take all the risks,' he said, after a short silence. 'I refuse to take any,' I said, shortly; which was just the answer he expected, though its tone might have surprised him. 'Well, I must defer to your judgment. You are captain,' he said, with marked civility. I turned my shoulder to him in sign of my appreciation, and looked into the fog. How long would it last? It was the most hopeless lookout. The approach to this Kurtz grubbing for ivory in the wretched bush was beset by as many dangers as though he had been an enchanted princess sleeping in a fabulous castle. 'Will they attack, do you think?' asked the manager, in a confidential tone.

"I did not think they would attack, for several obvious reasons. The thick fog was one. If they left the bank in their canoes they would get lost in it, as we would be if we attempted to move. Still, I had also judged the jungle of both banks quite impenetrable—and yet eyes were in it, eyes that had seen us. The riverside bushes were certainly very thick; but the undergrowth behind was evidently penetrable. However, during the short lift I had seen no canoes anywhere in the reach—certainly not abreast of the steamer. But what made the idea of attack inconceivable to me was the nature of the noise—of the cries we had heard. They had not the fierce character boding immediate hostile intention. Unexpected, wild, and violent as they had been, they had given me an irresistible impression of sorrow. The glimpse of the steamboat had for some reason filled those savages with unrestrained grief. The danger, if any, I expounded, was from our proximity to a great human passion let loose. Even extreme grief may ultimately vent itself in violence—but more generally takes the form of apathy. . . .

"You should have seen the pilgrims stare! They had no heart to grin, or even to revile me: but I believe they thought me gone mad—with fright, maybe. I delivered a regular lecture. My dear boys, it was no good bothering. Keep a lookout? Well, you may guess I watched the fog for the signs of lifting as a cat watches a mouse; but for anything else our eyes were of no more use to us than if we had been buried miles deep in a heap of cotton-wool. It felt like it, too—choking, warm, stifling. Besides, all I said, though it sounded extravagant, was absolutely true to fact. What we afterwards alluded to as an attack was really an attempt at repulse. The action was very far from being aggressive—it was not even defensive, in the usual sense: it was undertaken under the stress of desperation, and in its essence was purely protective.

"It developed itself, I should say, two hours after the fog lifted, and its commencement was at a spot, roughly speaking, about a mile and a half below Kurtz's station. We had just floundered and flopped round a bend, when I saw an islet, a mere grassy hummock of bright green, in the middle of the stream. It was the only thing of the kind; but as we opened the reach more, I perceived it was the head of a long sandbank, or rather of a chain of shallow patches stretching down the middle of the river. They were discolored, just awash, and the whole lot was seen just under the water, exactly as a man's backbone is seen running down the middle of his back under the skin. Now, as far as I did see, I could go to the right or to the left of this. I didn't know either channel, of course. The banks looked pretty well alike, the depth appeared the same; but as I had been informed the station was on the west side, I naturally headed for the western passage.

"No sooner had we fairly entered it than I became aware it was much narrower than I had supposed. To the left of us there was the long uninterrupted shoal, and to the right a high, steep bank heavily overgrown with bushes. Above the bush the trees stood in serried ranks. The twigs overhung the current thickly, and from distance to distance a large limb of some tree projected rigidly over the stream. It was then well on in the afternoon, the face of the forest was gloomy, and a broad strip of shadow had already fallen on the water. In this shadow we steamed up—very slowly, as you may imagine. I sheered her well inshore—the water being deepest near the bank, as the sounding-pole informed me.

95 "One of my hungry and forbearing friends was sounding in the bows just below me. This steamboat was exactly like a decked scow. On the deck, there were two little teak-wood houses, with doors and windows. The boiler was in the fore-end, and the machinery right astern. Over the whole there was a light roof, supported on stanchions. The funnel projected through that roof, and in front of the funnel a small cabin built of light planks served for a pilot-house. It contained a couch, two campstools, a loaded Martini-Henry[16] leaning in one corner, a tiny table, and the steering-wheel. It had a wide door in front and a broad shutter at each side. All these were always thrown open, of course. I spent my days perched up there on the extreme fore-end of that roof, before the door. At night I slept, or tried to, on the couch. An athletic black belonging to some coast tribe, and educated by my poor predecessor, was the helmsman. He sported a pair of brass earrings, wore a blue cloth wrapper from the waist to the ankles, and thought all the world of himself. He was the most unstable kind of fool I had ever seen. He steered with no end to a swagger while you were by; but if he lost sight of you, he became instantly the prey of an abject funk, and would let that cripple of a steamboat get the upper hand of him in a minute.

"I was looking down at the sounding-pole, and feeling much annoyed to see at each try a little more of it stick out that river, when I saw my poleman give up the business suddenly, and stretch himself flat on the deck, without even taking the trouble to haul his pole in. He kept hold on it though, and it trailed in the water. At the same time the fireman, whom I could also see below me, sat down abruptly before his furnace and ducked his head. I was amazed. Then I had to look at the river mighty quick, because there was a snag in the fairway. Sticks, little sticks, were flying about—thick: they were whizzing before my nose, dropping below me, striking behind me against my pilot-house. All this time the river, the shore, the woods, were very quiet—perfectly quiet. I could only hear the heavy splashing thump of the stern-wheel and the patter of these things. We cleared the snag clumsily. Arrows, by Jove! We were being shot at! I stepped in quickly to close the shutter on the land-side. That fool-helmsman, his hands on the spokes, was lifting his knees high, stamping his feet, champing his mouth, like a reined-in horse. Confound him! And we were staggering within ten feet of the bank. I had to lean right out to swing the heavy shutter, and I saw a face amongst the leaves on the level with my

[16]**Martini-Henry** a kind of rifle

own, looking at me very fierce and steady; and then suddenly, as though a veil had been removed from my eyes, I made out, deep in the tangled gloom, naked breasts, arms, legs, glaring eyes—the bush was swarming with human limbs in movement, glistening, of bronze color. The twigs shook, swayed, and rustled, the arrows flew out of them, and then the shutter came to. 'Steer her straight,' I said to the helmsman. He held his head rigid, face forward; but his eyes rolled, he kept on lifting and setting down his feet gently, his mouth foamed a little. 'Keep quiet!' I said in a fury. I might just as well have ordered a tree not to sway in the wind. I darted out. Below me there was a great scuffle of feet on the iron deck; confused exclamations; a voice screamed, 'Can you turn back?' I caught sight of a V-shaped ripple on the water ahead. What? Another snag! A fusillade burst out under my feet. The pilgrims had opened with their Winchesters, and were simply squirting lead into that bush. A deuce of a lot of smoke came up and drove slowly forward. I swore at it. Now I couldn't see the ripple or the snag either. I stood in the doorway, peering, and the arrows came in swarms. They might have been poisoned, but they looked as though they wouldn't kill a cat. The bush began to howl. Our wood-cutters raised a war-like whoop; the report of a rifle just at my back deafened me. I glanced over my shoulder, and the pilot-house was yet full of noise and smoke when I made a dash at the wheel. The fool-nigger had dropped everything to throw the shutter open and let off that Martini-Henry. He stood before the wide opening, glaring, and I yelled at him to come back, while I straightened the sudden twist out of that steamboat. There was no room to turn even if I had wanted to, the snag was somewhere very near ahead in the confounded smoke, there was no time to lose, so I just crowded her into the bank—right into the bank, where I knew the water was deep.

"We tore slowly along the overhanging bushes in a whirl of broken twigs and flying leaves. The fusillade below stopped short, as I had foreseen it would when the squirts got empty. I threw my head back to a glinting whizz that traversed the pilot-house, in at one shutter-hole and out at the other. Looking past that mad helmsman, who was shaking the empty rifle and yelling at the shore, I saw vague forms of men running bent double, leaping, gliding, distinct, incomplete, evanescent. Something big appeared in the air before the shutter, the rifle went overboard, and the man stepped back swiftly, looked at me over his shoulder in an extraordinary, profound, familiar manner, and fell upon my feet. The side of his head hit the wheel twice, and the end of what appeared a long cane clattered round and knocked over a little campstool. It looked as though after wrenching the thing from somebody ashore he had lost his balance in the effort. The thin smoke had blown away, we were clear of the snag, and looking ahead I could see that in another hundred yards or so I would be free to sheer off, away from the bank; but my feet felt so very warm and wet that I had to look down. The man had rolled on his back and stared straight up at me; both his hands clutched that cane. It was the shaft of a spear that, either thrown or lunged through the opening, had caught him in the side just below the ribs; the blade had gone in out of sight, after making a frightful gash; my shoes were full; a pool of blood lay very still, gleaming dark-red under the wheel; his eyes shown with an amazing luster. The fusillade burst out again. He looked at me anxiously, gripping the spear like something precious, with an air of being afraid I would try to take it away from him. I had to make an effort to free my eyes from his gaze and attend to steering. With one hand I felt above my head for the line of the steam-whistle, and jerked out screech after screech hurriedly. The tumult of angry and warlike yells was checked instantly, and then from the depths of the woods went out such a tremulous and prolonged wail of mournful fear and utter despair as may be imagined to follow the flight of the last hope from the earth. There was a great commotion in the bush; the shower of arrows stopped, a few dropping shots rang out sharply—then silence, in which the languid beat of the stern-wheel came plainly to my ears. I put the helm hard a-starboard at the moment when the pilgrim in pink pajamas, very hot and agitated, appeared in the doorway. 'The manager sends me—' he began in an official tone, and stopped short. 'Good God!' he said, glaring at the wounded man.

"We two whites stood over him, and his lustrous and inquiring glance enveloped us both. I declare it looked as though he would presently put to us some question in an understandable language; but he died without uttering a sound, without moving a limb, without twitching a muscle. Only in the very last moment, as though in response to some sign we could not see, to some whisper we could not hear, he frowned heavily, and that frown gave to his black death-mask an inconceivably somber, brooding, and menacing expression. The luster of inquiring glance faded swiftly into vacant glassiness. 'Can you steer?' I asked the agent eagerly. He looked very dubious; but I made a grab at his arm, and he understood at once I meant him to steer whether or no. To tell you the truth, I was morbidly anxious to change my shoes and socks. 'He is dead,' murmured the fellow, immensely impressed. 'No doubt about it,' said I tugging like mad at the shoe-laces. 'And by the way, I suppose Mr. Kurtz is dead as well by this time.'

"For the moment that was the dominant thought. There was a sense of extreme disappointment, as though I had found out I had been striving after something altogether without a substance. I couldn't have been more disgusted if I had traveled all this way for the sole purpose of talking with Mr. Kurtz. Talking with . . . I flung one shoe overboard, and became aware that that was exactly what I had been looking forward to—a talk with Kurtz. I made the strange discovery that I had never imagined him as doing, you know, but as discoursing. I didn't say to myself, 'Now I will never see him,' or 'Now I will never shake him by the hand,' but, 'Now I will never hear him.' The man presented himself as a voice. Not of course that I did not connect him with some sort of action. Hadn't I been told in all the tones of jealousy and admiration that he had collected, bartered, swindled, or stolen more ivory than all the other agents together? That was not the point. The point was in his being a gifted creature, and that of all his gifts the one that stood out preeminently, that carried with it a sense of real presence, was his ability to talk, his words—the gift of expression, the bewildering, the illuminating, the most exalted and the most contemptible, the pulsating stream of light, or the deceitful flow from the heart of an impenetrable darkness.

100 "The other shoe went flying unto the devil-god of that river. I thought, by Jove! it's all over. We are too late; he has vanished—the gift has vanished, by means of some spear, arrow, or club. I will never hear that chap speak after all—and my sorrow had a startling extravagance of emotion, even such as I had noticed in the howling sorrow of these savages in the bush. I couldn't have felt more lonely desolation somehow, had I been

robbed of a belief or had missed my destiny in life. . . . Why do you sigh in this beastly way, somebody? Absurd? Well, absurd. Good Lord! mustn't a man ever—Here, give me some tobacco." . . .

There was a pause of profound stillness, then a match flared, and Marlow's lean face appeared, worn, hollow, with downward folds and drooped eyelids, with an aspect of concentrated attention; and as he took vigorous draws at his pipe, it seemed to retreat and advance out of the night in the regular flicker of the tiny flame. The match went out.

"Absurd!" he cried. "This is the worst of trying to tell. . . . Here you all are, each moored with two good addresses, like a hulk with two anchors, a butcher round one corner, a policeman round another, excellent appetites, and temperature normal—you hear—normal from year's end to year's end. And you say, Absurd! Absurd be—exploded! Absurd! My dear boys, what can you expect from a man who out of sheer nervousness had just flung overboard a pair of new shoes! Now I think of it, it is amazing I did not shed tears. I am, upon the whole, proud of my fortitude. I was cut to the quick at the idea of having lost the inestimable privilege of listening to the gifted Kurtz. Of course I was wrong. The privilege was waiting for me. Oh, yes, I heard more than enough. And I was right, too. A voice. He was very little more than a voice. And I heard—him—it—this voice—other voices—all of them were so little more than voices—and the memory of that time itself lingers around me, impalpable, like a dying vibration of one immense jabber, silly, atrocious, sordid, savage, or simply mean, without any kind of sense. Voices, voices—even the girl herself—now—"

He was silent for a long time.

"I laid the ghost of his gifts at last with a lie," he began, suddenly. "Girl! What? Did I mention a girl? Oh, she is out of it—completely. They—the women I mean—are out of it—should be out of it. We must help them to stay in that beautiful world of their own, lest ours gets worse. Oh, she had to be out of it. You should have heard the disinterred body of Mr. Kurtz saying, 'My Intended.' You would have perceived directly then how completely she was out of it. And the lofty frontal bone of Mr. Kurtz! They say the hair goes on growing sometimes, but this—ah—specimen, was impressively bald. The wilderness had patted him on the head, and, behold, it was like a ball—an ivory ball; it had caressed him, and—lo!—he had withered; it had taken him, loved him, embraced him, got into his veins, consumed his flesh, and sealed his soul to its own by the inconceivable ceremonies of some devilish initiation. He was its spoiled and pampered favorite. Ivory? I should think so. Heaps of it, stacks of it. The old mud shanty was bursting with it. You would think here was not a single tusk left either above or below the ground in the whole country. 'Mostly fossil,' the manager had remarked, disparagingly. It was no more fossil than I am; but they call it fossil when it is dug up. It appears these niggers do bury the tusks sometimes—but evidently they couldn't bury this parcel deep enough to save the gifted Mr. Kurtz from his fate. We filled the steamboat with it, and had to pile a lot on the deck. Thus he could see and enjoy as long as he could see, because the appreciation of this favor had remained with him to the last. You should have heard him say, 'My ivory.' Oh, yes, I heard him. 'My Intended, my ivory, my station, my river, my—' everything belonged to him. It made me hold my breath in expectation of hearing the wilderness burst into a prodigious peal of laughter that would shake the fixed stars in their places. Everything belonged to him—but that was a trifle. The thing was to know what he belonged to, how many powers of darkness claimed him for their own. That was the reflection that made you creepy all over. It was impossible—it was not good for one either—trying to imagine. He had taken a high seat amongst the devils of the land—I mean literally. You can't understand. How could you?—with solid pavement under your feet, surrounded by kind neighbors ready to cheer you or to fall on you, stepping delicately between the butcher and the policeman, in the holy terror of scandal and gallows and lunatic asylums—how can you imagine what particular region of the first ages a man's untrammeled feet may take him into by the way of solitude—utter solitude without a policeman—by the way of silence—utter silence, where no warning voice of a kind neighbor can be heard whispering of public opinion? These little things make all the great difference. When they are gone you must fall back upon your own innate strength, upon your own capacity for faithfulness. Of course you may be too much of a fool to go wrong—too dull even to know you are being assaulted by the powers of darkness. I take it, no fool ever made a bargain for his soul with the devil: the fool is too much of a fool, or the devil too much of a devil—I don't know which. Or you may be such a thunderingly exalted creature as to be altogether deaf and blind to anything but heavenly sights and sounds. Then the earth for you is only a standing place—and whether to be like this is your loss or your gain I won't pretend to say. But most of us are neither one nor the other. The earth for us is a place to live in, where we must put up with sights, with sounds, with smells, too, by Jove!—breathe dead hippo, so to speak and not be contaminated. And there, don't you see? your strength comes in, the faith in your ability for the digging of unostentatious holes to bury the stuff in—your power of devotion, not to yourself, but to an obscure, back-breaking business. And that's difficult enough. Mind, I am not trying to excuse or even explain—I am trying to account to myself for—for—Mr. Kurtz—for the shade of Mr. Kurtz. This initiated wraith from the back of Nowhere honored me with its amazing confidence before it vanished altogether. This was because it could speak English to me. The original Kurtz had been educated partly in England, and—as he was good enough to say himself—his sympathies were in the right place. His mother was half-English, his father was half-French. All Europe contributed to the making of Kurtz; and by and by I learned that, most appropriately, the International Society for the Suppression of Savage Customs had intrusted him with the making of a report, for its future guidance. And he had written it, too. I've seen it. I've read it. It was eloquent, vibrating with eloquence, but too high-strung, I think. Seventeen pages of close writing he had found time for! But this must have been before his—let us say—nerves, went wrong, and caused him to preside at certain midnight dances ending with unspeakable rites, which—as far as I reluctantly gathered from what I heard at various times—were offered up to him—do you understand?—to Mr. Kurtz himself. But it was a beautiful piece of writing. The opening paragraph, however, in the light of later information, strikes me now as ominous. He began with the argument that we whites, from the point of development we had arrived at, 'must necessarily appear to them [savages] in the nature of supernatural beings—we approach them with the might as of a 'deity,' and so on, and so on. 'By the simple exercise of our will we can exert a power for good practically unbounded,' etc., etc. From that point he soared and took me with him. The peroration was magnificent, though difficult to remember, you know. It gave me the notion of an exotic Immensity ruled by an august Benevolence. It made me tingle with enthusiasm. This was the unbounded power of eloquence—of words—of burning noble words. There were no practical hints to interrupt the magic current of phrases, unless a kind of note at the foot of the last page, scrawled evidently much later, in an unsteady hand, may be regarded as the exposition of a method. It was very simple, and at the end of that moving appeal to every altruistic sentiment it blazed at you, luminous and terrifying, like a flash of lightning in a serene sky: 'Exterminate all the brutes!' The curious part was that he had apparently forgotten all about that valuable postscriptum, because, later on, when he in a sense came to himself, he repeatedly entreated me to take good care of 'my pamphlet' (he called it), as it was sure to have in the future a good influence upon his career. I had full information about all these things, and, besides, as it turned out, I was to have the care of his memory. I've done enough for it to give me the indisputable right to lay it, if I choose, for an everlasting rest in the dust-bin of progress, amongst all the sweepings and, figuratively speaking, all the dead cats of civilization. But then, you see, I can't choose. He won't be forgotten. Whatever he was, he was not common. He had the power to charm or frighten rudimentary souls into an aggravated witch-dance in his honor; he could also fill the small souls of the pilgrims with bitter misgivings: he had one devoted friend at least, and he had conquered one soul in the world that was neither rudimentary nor tainted with self-seeking. No; I can't forget him, though I am not prepared to affirm the fellow was exactly worth the life we lost in getting to him. I missed my late helmsman awfully—I missed him even while his body was still lying in the pilot-house. Perhaps you will think it passing strange this regret for a savage who was no more account than a grain of sand in a black Sahara. Well, don't you see, he had done something, he had steered; for months I had him at my back—a help—an instrument. It was a kind of partnership. He steered for me—I had to look after him, I worried about his deficiencies, and thus a subtle bond had been created, of which I only became aware when it was suddenly broken. And the intimate profundity of that look he gave me when he received his hurt remains to this day in my memory—like a claim of distant kinship affirmed in a supreme moment.

105 "Poor fool! If he had only left that shutter alone. He had no restraint, no restraint—just like Kurtz—a tree swayed by the wind. As soon as I had put on a dry pair of slippers, I dragged him out, after first jerking the spear out of his side, which operation I confess I performed with my eyes shut tight. His heels leaped together over the little door-step; his shoulders were pressed to my breast; I hugged him from behind desperately. Oh! he was heavy, heavy; heavier than any man on earth, I should imagine. Then without more ado I tipped him overboard. The current snatched him as though he had been a wisp of grass, and I saw the body roll over twice before I lost sight of it forever. All the pilgrims and the manager were then congregated on the awning-deck about the pilot-house, chattering at each other like a flock of excited magpies, and there was a scandalized murmur at my heartless promptitude. What they wanted to keep that body hanging about for I can't guess. Embalm it, maybe. But I had also heard another, and a very ominous, murmur on the deck below. My friends the wood-cutters were like-

wise scandalized, and with a better show of reason—though I admit that the reason itself was quite inadmissible. Oh, quite! I had made up my mind that if my late helmsman was to be eaten, the fishes alone should have him. He had been a very second-rate helmsman while alive, but now he was dead he might have become a first-class temptation, and possibly cause some startling trouble. Besides, I was anxious to take the wheel, the man in pink pajamas showing himself a hopeless duffer at the business.

"This I did directly the simple funeral was over. We were going half-speed, keeping right in the middle of the stream, and I listened to the talk about me. They had given up Kurtz, they had given up the station; Kurtz was dead, and the station had been burnt—and so on—and so on. The red-haired pilgrim was beside himself with the thought that at least this poor Kurtz had been properly avenged. 'Say! We must have made a glorious slaughter of them in the bush. Eh? What do you think? Say?' He positively danced, the blood-thirsty little gingery beggar. And he had nearly fainted when he saw the wounded man! I could not help saying, 'You made a glorious lot of smoke, anyhow.' I had seen, from the way the tops of the bushes rustled and flew, that almost all the shots had gone too high. You can't hit anything unless you take aim and fire from the shoulder; but these chaps fired from the hip with their eyes shut. The retreat, I maintained—and I was right—was caused by the screeching of the steam-whistle. Upon this they forgot Kurtz, and began to howl at me with indignant protests.

"The manager stood by the wheel murmuring confidentially about the necessity of getting well away down the river before dark at all events, when I saw in the distance a clearing on the riverside and the outlines of some sort of building. 'What's this?' I asked. He clapped his hands in wonder. 'The station!' he cried. I edged in at once, still going half-speed.

Through my glasses I saw the slope of a hill interspersed with rare trees and perfectly free from undergrowth. A long decaying building on the summit was half buried in the high grass; the large holes in the peaked roof gaped black from afar; the jungle and the woods made a background. There was no enclosure or fence of any kind; but there had been one apparently, for near the house half-a-dozen slim posts remained in a row, roughly trimmed, and with their upper ends ornamented with round carved balls. The rails, or whatever there had been between, had disappeared. Of course the forest surrounded all that. The riverbank was clear, and on the waterside I saw a white man under a hat like a cart-wheel beckoning persistently with his whole arm. Examining the edge of the forest above and below, I was almost certain I could see movements—human forms gliding here and there. I steamed past prudently, then stopped the engines and let her drift down. The man on the shore began to shout, urging us to land. 'We have been attacked,' screamed the manager. 'I know—I know. It's all right,' yelled back the other, as cheerful as you please. 'Come along. It's all right, I am glad.'

"His aspect reminded me of something I had seen—something funny I had seen somewhere. As I maneuvered to get alongside, I was asking myself, 'What does this fellow look like?' Suddenly I got it. He looked like a harlequin. His clothes had been made of some stuff that was brown holland probably, but it was covered with patches all over, with bright patches, blue, red, and yellow—patches on the back, patches on the front, patches on elbows, on knees; colored binding around his jacket, scarlet edging at the bottom of his trousers; and the sunshine made him look extremely gay and wonderfully neat withal, because you could see how beautifully all this patching had been done. A beardless, boyish face, very fair, no features to speak of, nose peeling, little blue eyes, smiles and frowns chasing each other over that open countenance like sunshine and shadow on a windswept plain. 'Look out, captain!' he cried; 'there's a snag lodged in here last night.' What! Another snag? I confess I swore shamefully. I had nearly holed my cripple, to finish off that charming trip. The harlequin on the bank turned his little pug-nose up to me. 'You English?' he asked, all smiles. 'Are you?' I shouted from the wheel. The smiles vanished, and he shook his head as if sorry for my disappointment. Then he brightened up. 'Never mind!' he cried, encouragingly. 'Are we in time?' I asked. 'He is up there,' he replied with a toss of the head up the hill, and becoming gloomy all of a sudden. His face was like the autumn sky, overcast one moment and bright the next.

110 "When the manager, escorted by the pilgrims, all of them armed to the teeth, had gone to the house this chap came on board. 'I say, I don't like this. These natives are in the bush,' I said. He assured me earnestly it was all right. 'They are simple people,' he added; 'well, I am glad you came. It took me all my time to keep them off.' 'But you said it was all right,' I cried. 'Oh, they meant no harm,' he said; and as I stared he corrected himself, 'Not exactly.' Then vivaciously, 'My faith, your pilothouse wants a clean-up!' In the next breath he advised me to keep enough steam on the boiler to blow the whistle in case of any trouble. 'One good screech will do more for you than all your rifles. They are simple people,' he repeated. He rattled away at such a rate he quite overwhelmed me. He seemed to be trying to make up for lots of silence, and actually hinted, laughing, that such was the case. 'Don't you talk with Mr. Kurtz?' I said. 'You don't talk with that man—you listen to him,' he exclaimed with severe exaltation. 'But now—' He waved his arm, and in the twinkling of an eye was in the uttermost depths of despondency. In a moment he came up again with a jump, possessed himself of both my hands, and shook them continuously, while he gabbled: 'Brother sailor . . . honor . . . pleasure . . . delight . . . introduce myself . . . Russian . . . son of an arch-priest . . . Government of Tambov . . . What? Tobacco! English tobacco; the excellent English tobacco! Now, that's brotherly. Smoke? Where's a sailor that does not smoke?'

"The pipe soothed him, and gradually I made out he had run away from school, had gone to sea in a Russian ship; ran away again; served some time in English ships; was now reconciled with the arch-priest. He made a point of that. 'But when one is young one must see things, gather experience, ideas; enlarge the mind.' 'Here!' I interrupted. 'You can never tell! Here I met Mr. Kurtz,' he said, youthfully solemn and reproachful. I held my tongue after that. It appears he had persuaded a Dutch trading-house on the coast to fit him out with stores and goods, and had started for the interior with a light heart, and no more idea of what would happen to him than a baby. He had been wandering about that river for nearly two years alone, cut off from everybody and everything. 'I am not so young as I look. I am twenty-five,' he said. 'At first old Van Shuyten would tell me to go to the devil,' he narrated with keen enjoyment; 'but I stuck to him, and talked and talked, till at last he got afraid I would talk the hind-leg off his favorite dog, so he gave me some cheap things and a few guns, and told me he hoped he would never see my face again. Good old Dutchman, Van Shuyten. I've sent him one small lot of ivory a year ago, so that he can't call me a little thief when I get back. I hope he got it. And for the rest I don't care. I had some wood stacked for you. That was my old house. Did you see?'

"I gave him Towson's book. He made as though he would kiss me, but restrained himself. 'The only book I had left, and I thought I had lost it,' he said, looking at it ecstatically. 'So many accidents happen to a man going about alone, you know. Canoes get upset sometimes—and sometimes you've got to clear out so quick when the people get angry.' He thumbed the pages. 'You made notes in Russian?' I asked. He nodded. 'I thought they were written in cipher,' I said. He laughed, then became serious. 'I had lots of trouble to keep these people off,' he said. 'Did they want to kill you?' I asked. 'Oh, no!' he cried, and checked himself. 'Why did they attack us?' I pursued. He hesitated, then said shamefacedly, 'They don't want him to go.' 'Don't they?' I said, curiously. He nodded a nod full of mystery and wisdom. 'I tell you,' he cried, 'this man has enlarged my mind.' He opened his arms wide, staring at me with his little blue eyes that were perfectly round."

## *III*

"I looked at him, lost in astonishment. There he was before me, in motley, as though he had absconded from a troupe of mimes, enthusiastic, fabulous. His very existence was improbable, inexplicable, and altogether bewildering. He was an insoluble problem. It was inconceivable how he had existed, how he had succeeded in getting so far, how he had managed to remain—why he did not instantly disappear. 'I went a little farther,' he said, 'then still a little farther—till I had gone so far that I don't know how I'll ever get back. Never mind. Plenty time. I can manage. You take Kurtz away quick—quick—I tell you.' The glamour of youth enveloped his parti-colored rags, his destitution, his loneliness, the essential desolation of his futile wanderings. For months—for years—his life hadn't been worth a day's purchase; and there he was gallantly, thoughtlessly alive, to all appearance indestructible solely by the virtue of his few years and of his unreflecting audacity. I was seduced into something like admiration—like envy. Glamour urged him on, glamour kept him unscathed. He surely wanted nothing from the wilderness but space to breathe in and to push on through. His need was to exist, and to move onwards at the greatest possible risk, and with a maximum of privation. If the absolutely pure, uncalculating, unpractical spirit of adventure had ever ruled a human being, it ruled this be-patched youth. I almost envied him the possession of this modest and clear flame. It seemed to have consumed all thought of self so completely, that even while he was talking to you, you forgot that it was he—the man before your eyes—who had gone through these things. I did not envy him his devotion to Kurtz, though. He had not meditated over it. It came to him and he accepted it with a sort of eager fatalism. I must say that to me it appeared about the most dangerous thing in every way he had come upon so far.

"They had come together unavoidably, like two ships becalmed near each other, and lay rubbing sides at last. I suppose Kurtz wanted an audience, because on a certain occasion, when encamped in the forest, they had talked all night, or more probably Kurtz had talked. 'We talked of everything,' he said, quite transported at the recollection. 'I forgot there was such a thing as sleep. The night did not seem to last an hour. Everything! Everything! . . . Of love, too.' 'Ah, he talked to you of love!' I said, much amused. 'It isn't what you think,' he cried, almost passionately. 'It was in general. He made me see things—things.'

115 "He threw his arms up. We were on deck at the time, and the headman of my wood-cutters, lounging near by, turned upon him his heavy and glittering eyes. I looked around, and I don't know why, but I assure you that never, never before, did this land, this river, this jungle, the very arch of this blazing sky, appear to me so hopeless and so dark, so impenetrable to human thought, so pitiless to human weakness. 'And, ever since, you have been with him, of course?' I said.

"On the contrary. It appears their intercourse had been very much broken by various causes. He had, as he informed me proudly, managed to nurse Kurtz through two illnesses (he alluded to it as you would to some risky feat), but as a rule Kurtz wandered alone far in the depths of the forest. 'Very often coming to this station, I had to wait days and days before he would turn up,' he said. 'Ah, it was worth waiting for!—sometimes.' 'What was he doing? exploring or what?' I asked. 'Oh, yes, of course'; he had discovered lots of villages, a lake, too—he did not know exactly in what direction; it was dangerous to inquire too much—but mostly his expeditions had been for ivory. 'But he had no goods to trade with by that time,' I objected. 'There's a good lot of cartridges left even yet,' he answered, looking away. 'To speak plainly, he raided the country,' I said. He nodded. 'Not alone, surely!' He muttered something about the villages round that lake. 'Kurtz got the tribe to follow him, did he?' I suggested. He fidgeted a little. 'They adored him,' he said. The tone of these words was so extraordinary that I looked at him searchingly. It was curious to see his mingled eagerness and reluctance to speak of Kurtz. The man filled his life, occupied his thoughts, swayed his emotions. 'What can you expect?' he burst out; 'he came to them with thunder and lightning, you know—and they had never seen anything like it—and very terrible. He could be very terrible. You can't judge Mr. Kurtz as you would an ordinary man. No, no, no! Now—just to give you an idea—I don't mind telling you, he wanted to shoot me, too, one day—but I don't judge him.' 'Shoot you!' I cried. 'What for?' 'Well, I had a small lot of ivory the chief of that village near my house gave me. You see I used to shoot game for them. Well, he wanted it, and wouldn't hear reason. He declared he would shoot me unless I gave him the ivory and then cleared out of the country, because he could do so, and had a fancy for it, and there was nothing on earth to prevent him killing whom he jolly well pleased. And it was true, too. I gave him the ivory. What did I care! But I didn't clear out. No, no. I couldn't leave him. I had to be careful, of course, till we got friendly again for a time. He had his second illness then. Afterwards I had to keep out of the way; but I didn't mind. He was living for the most part in those villages on the lake. When he came down to the river, sometimes he would take to me, and sometimes it was better for me to be careful. This man suffered too much. He hated all this, and somehow he couldn't get away. When I had a chance I begged him to try and leave while there was time; I offered to go back with him And he would say yes, and then he would remain; go off on another ivory hunt; disappear for weeks; forget himself amongst these people—forget himself—you know.' 'Why! he's mad,' I said. He protested indignantly. Mr. Kurtz couldn't be mad. If I had heard him talk, only two days ago, I wouldn't dare hint at such a thing. . . . I had taken up my binoculars while we talked, and was looking at the shore, sweeping the limit of the forest at each side and at the back of the house. The consciousness of there being people in that bush, so silent, so quiet—as silent and quiet as the ruined house on the hill—made me uneasy. There was no sign on the face of nature of this amazing tale that was not so much told as suggested to me in desolate exclamations, completed by shrugs, in interrupted phrases, in hints ending in deep sighs. The woods were unmoved, like a mask—heavy, like the closed door of a prison—they looked with their air of hidden knowledge, of patient expectation, of unapproachable silence. The Russian was explaining to me that it was only lately that Mr. Kurtz had come down to the river, bringing along with him all the fighting men of that lake tribe. He had been absent for several months—getting himself adored, I suppose—and had come down unexpectedly, with the intention to all appearance of making a raid either across the river or down stream. Evidently the appetite for more ivory had got the better of the—what shall I say?—less material aspirations. However he had got much worse suddenly. 'I heard he was lying helpless, and so I came up—took my chance,' said the Russian. 'Oh, he is bad, very bad.' I directed my glass to the house. There were no signs of life, but there was the ruined roof, the long mud wall peeping above the grass, with three little square window-holes, no two of the same size; all this brought within reach of my hand, as it were. And then I made a brusque movement, and one of the remaining posts of that vanished fence leaped up in the field of my glass. You remember I told you I had been struck at the distance by certain attempts at ornamentation, rather remarkable in the ruinous aspect of the place. Now I had suddenly a nearer view, and its first result was to make me throw my head back as if before a blow. Then I went carefully from post to post with my glass, and I saw my mistake. These round knobs were not ornamental but symbolic; they were expressive and puzzling, striking and disturbing—food for thought and also for vultures if there had been any looking down from the sky; but at all events for such ants as were industrious enough to ascend the pole. They would have been even more impressive, those heads on the stakes, if their faces had not been turned to the house. Only one, the first I had made out, was facing my way. I was not so shocked as you may think. The start back I had given was really nothing but a movement of surprise. I had expected to see a knob of wood there, you know. I returned deliberately to the first I had seen—and there it was, black, dried, sunken, with closed eyelids—a head that seemed to sleep at the top of that pole, and with the shrunken dry lips showing a narrow white line of the teeth, was smiling, too, smiling continuously at some endless and jocose dream of that eternal slumber.

"I am not disclosing any trade secrets. In fact, the manager said afterwards that Mr. Kurtz's methods had ruined the district. I have no opinion on that point, but I want you clearly to understand that there was nothing exactly profitable in these heads being there. They only showed that Mr. Kurtz lacked restraint in the gratification of his various lusts, that there was something wanting in him—some small matter which, when the pressing need arose, could not be found under his magnificent eloquence. Whether he knew of this deficiency himself I can't say. I think the knowledge came to him at last—only at the very last. But the wilderness had found him out early, and had taken on him a terrible vengeance for the fantastic invasion. I think it had whispered to him things about himself which he did not know, things of which he had no conception till he took counsel with this great solitude—and the whisper had proved irresistibly fascinating. It echoed loudly within him because he was hollow at the core. . . . I put down the glass, and the head that had appeared near enough to be spoken to seemed at once to have leaped away from me into inaccessible distance.

"The admirer of Mr. Kurtz was a bit crestfallen. In a hurried indistinct voice he began to assure me he had not dared to take these—say, symbols—down. He was not afraid of the natives; they would not stir till Mr. Kurtz gave the word. His ascendancy was extraordinary. The camps of these people surrounded the place, and the chiefs came every day to see him. They would crawl. . . . 'I don't want to know anything of the ceremonies used when approaching Mr. Kurtz,' I shouted. Curious, this feeling that came over me that such details would be more intolerable than those heads drying on the stakes under Mr. Kurtz's windows. After all, that was only a savage sight, while I seemed at one bound to have been transported into some lightless region of subtle horrors, where pure, uncomplicated savagery was a positive relief, being something that had a right to exist—obviously—in the sunshine. The young man looked at me with surprise. I suppose it did not occur to him that Mr. Kurtz was no idol of mine. He forgot I hadn't heard any of these special monologues on, what was it? on love, justice, conduct of life—or what not. If it had come to crawling before Mr. Kurtz, he crawled as much as the veriest savage of them all. I had no idea of the conditions, he said: these heads were the heads of rebels. I shocked him excessively by laughing. Rebels! What would be the next definition I was to hear? There had been enemies, criminals, workers—and these were rebels. Those rebellious heads looked very subdued to me on their sticks. 'You don't know how such a life tries a man like Kurtz,' cried Kurtz's last disciple. 'Well, and you?' I said. 'I! I! I am a simple man. I have no great thoughts. I want nothing from anybody. How can you compare me to . . . ?' His feelings were too much for speech, and suddenly he broke down. 'I don't understand,' he groaned. 'I've been doing my best to keep him alive, and that's enough. I had no hand in all this. I have no abilities. There hasn't been a drop of medicine or a mouthful of invalid food for months here. He was shamefully abandoned. A man like this, with such ideas. Shamefully! Shamefully! I—I—haven't slept for the last ten nights. . . .'

"His voice lost itself in the calm of the evening. The long shadows of the forest had slipped downhill while we talked, had gone far beyond the ruined hovel, beyond the symbolic row of stakes. All this was in the gloom, while we down there were yet in the sunshine, and the stretch of the river abreast of the clearing glittered in a still and dazzling splendor, with a murky and overshadowed bend above and below. Not a living soul was seen on the shore. The bushes did not rustle.

120 "Suddenly round the corner of the house a group of men appeared, as though they had come up from the ground. They waded waist-deep in the grass, in a compact body, bearing an improvised stretcher in their midst. Instantly, in the emptiness of the landscape, a cry arose whose shrillness pierced the still air like a sharp arrow flying straight to the very heart of the land; and, as if by enchantment, streams of human beings—of naked human beings—with spears in their hands, with bows, with shields, with wild

glances and savage movements, were poured into the clearing by the dark-faced and pensive forest. The bushes shook, the grass swayed for a time, and then everything stood still in attentive immobility.

"'Now, if he does not say the right thing to them we are all done for,' said the Russian at my elbow. The knot of men with the stretcher had stopped, too, halfway to the steamer, as if petrified. I saw the man on the stretcher sit up, lank and with an uplifted arm, above the shoulders of the bearers. 'Let us hope that the man who can talk so well of love in general will find some particular reason to spare us this time,' I said. I resented bitterly the absurd danger of our situation, as if to be at the mercy of that atrocious phantom had been a dishonoring necessity. I could not hear a sound, but through my glasses I saw the thin arm extended commandingly, the lower jaw moving, the eyes of that apparition shining darkly far in its bony head that nodded with grotesque jerks. Kurtz—Kurtz—that means short in German—don't it? Well, the name was as true as everything else in his life—and death. He looked at least seven feet long. His covering had fallen off, and his body emerged from it pitiful and appalling as from a winding-sheet. I could see the cage of his ribs all astir, the bones of his arm waving. It was as though an animated image of death carved out of old ivory had been shaking its hand with menaces at a motionless crowd of men made of dark and glittering bronze. I saw him open his mouth wide—it gave him a weirdly voracious aspect, as though he had wanted to swallow all the air, all the earth, all the men before him. A deep voice reached me faintly. He must have been shouting. He fell back suddenly. The stretcher shook as the bearers staggered forward again, and almost at the same time I noticed that the crowd of savages was vanishing without any perceptible movement of retreat, as if the forest that had ejected these beings so suddenly had drawn them in again as the breath is drawn in a long aspiration.

"Some of the pilgrims behind the stretcher carried his arms—two shotguns, a heavy rifle, and a light revolver-carbine—the thunderbolts of that pitiful Jupiter. The manager bent over him murmuring as he walked beside his head. They laid him down in one of the little cabins—just a room for a bedplace and a campstool or two, you know. We had brought his belated correspondence, and a lot of torn envelopes and open letters littered his bed. His hand roamed feebly amongst these papers. I was struck by the fire in his eyes and the composed languor of his expression. It was not so much the exhaustion of disease. He did not seem in pain. This shadow looked satiated and calm, as though for the moment it had had its fill of all the emotions.

"He rustled one of the letters, and looking straight in my face said, 'I am glad.' Somebody had been writing to him about me. These special recommendations were turning up again. The volume of tone he emitted without effort, almost without the trouble of moving his lips, amazed me. A voice! a voice! It was grave, profound, vibrating, while the man did not seem capable of a whisper. However, he had enough strength in him—factitious no doubt—to very nearly make an end of us, as you shall hear directly.

"The manager appeared silently in the doorway; I stepped out at once and he drew the curtain after me. The Russian, eyed curiously by the pilgrims, was staring at the shore. I followed the direction of his glance.

125 "Dark human shapes could be made out in the distance, flitting indistinctly against the gloomy border of the forest, and near the river two

bronze figures, leaning on tall spears, stood in the sunlight under fantastic headdresses of spotted skins, war-like and still in statuesque repose. And from right to left along the lighted shore moved a wild and gorgeous apparition of a woman.

"She walked with measured steps, draped in striped and fringed cloths, treading the earth proudly, with a slight jingle and flash of barbarous ornaments. She carried her head high; her hair was done in the shape of a helmet; she had brass leggings to the knee, brass wire gauntlets to the elbow, a crimson spot on her tawny cheek, innumerable necklaces of glass beads on her neck; bizarre things, charms, gifts of witchmen, that hung about her, glittered and trembled at every step. She must have had the value of several elephant tusks upon her. She was savage and superb, wild-eyed and magnificent; there was something ominous and stately in her deliberate progress. And in the hush that had fallen suddenly upon the whole sorrowful land, the immense wilderness, the colossal body of the fecund and mysterious life seemed to look at her, pensive, as though it had been looking at the image of its own tenebrous and passionate soul.

"She came abreast of the steamer, stood still, and faced us. Her long shadow fell to the water's edge. Her face had a tragic and fierce aspect of wild sorrow and of dumb pain mingled with the fear of some struggling, half-shaped resolve. She stood looking at us without a stir, and like the wilderness itself, with an air of brooding over an inscrutable purpose. A whole minute passed, and then she made a step forward. There was a low jingle, a glint of yellow metal, a sway of fringed draperies, and she stopped as if her heart had failed her. The young fellow by my side growled. The pilgrims murmured at my back. She looked at us all as if her life had depended upon the unswerving steadiness of her glance. Suddenly she opened her bared arms and threw them up rigid above her head, as though in an uncontrollable desire to touch the sky, and at the same time the swift shadows darted out on the earth, swept around on the river, gathering the steamer into a shadowy embrace. A formidable silence hung over the scene.

"She turned away slowly, walked on, following the bank, and passed into the bushes to the left. Once only her eyes gleamed back at us in the dusk of the thickets before she disappeared.

"'If she had offered to come abroad I really think I would have tried to shoot her,' said the man of patches, nervously. 'I have been risking my life every day for the last fortnight to keep her out of the house. She got in one day and kicked up a row about those miserable rags I picked up in the storeroom to mend my clothes with. I wasn't decent. At least it must have been that, for she talked like a fury to Kurtz for an hour, pointing at me now and then. I don't understand the dialect of this tribe. Luckily for me, I fancy Kurtz felt too ill that day to care, or there would have been mischief. I don't understand. . . . No—it's too much for me. Ah, well, it's all over now.'

130 "At this moment I heard Kurtz's deep voice behind the curtain: 'Save me!—save the ivory, you mean. Don't tell me. Save *me!* Why, I've had to save you. You are interrupting my plans now. Sick! Sick! Not so sick as you would like to believe. Never mind. I'll carry my ideas out yet—I will return. I'll show you what can be done. You with your little peddling notions—you are interfering with me. I will return. I. . . .'

"The manager came out. He did me the honor to take me under the arm and lead me aside. 'He is very low, very low,' he said. He considered it necessary to sigh, but neglected to be consistently sorrowful. 'We have done all we could for him—haven't we? But there is no disguising the fact, Mr. Kurtz has done more harm than good to the Company. He did not see the time was not ripe for vigorous action. Cautiously, cautiously—that's my principle. We must be cautious yet. The district is closed to us for a time. Deplorable! Upon the whole, the trade will suffer. I don't deny there is a remarkable quantity of ivory—mostly fossil. We must save it, at all events—but look how precarious the position is—and why? Because the method is unsound.' 'Do you,' said I, looking at the shore, 'call it "unsound method"?' 'Without doubt,' he exclaimed, hotly. 'Don't you?' . . . 'No method at all,' I murmured after a while. 'Exactly,' he exulted. 'I anticipated this. Shows a complete want of judgment. It is my duty to point it out in the proper quarter.' 'Oh,' said I, 'that fellow—what's his name?—the brickmaker, will make a readable report for you.' He appeared confounded for a moment. It seemed to me I had never breathed an atmosphere so vile, and I turned mentally to Kurtz for relief—positively for relief. 'Nevertheless I think Mr. Kurtz is a remarkable man,' I said with emphasis. He started, dropped on me a cold heavy glance, said very quietly, 'he *was*,' and turned his back on me. My hour of favor was over; I found myself lumped along with Kurtz as a partisan of methods for which the time was not ripe. I was unsound! Ah! but it was something to have at least a choice of nightmares.

"I had turned to the wilderness really, not to Mr. Kurtz, who, I was ready to admit, was as good as buried. And for a moment it seemed to me as if I also was buried in a vast grave full of unspeakable secrets. I felt an intolerable weight oppressing my breast, the smell of the damp earth, the unseen presence of victorious corruption, the darkness of an impenetrable night. . . . The Russian tapped me on the shoulder. I heard him mumbling and stammering something about 'brother seaman—couldn't conceal—knowledge of matters that would affect Mr. Kurtz's reputation.' I waited. For him evidently Mr. Kurtz was not in his grave; I suspect that for him Mr. Kurtz was one of the immortals. 'Well!' said I at last, 'speak out. As it happens, I am Mr. Kurtz's friend—in a way.'

"He stated with a good deal of formality that had we not been 'of the same profession,' he would have kept the matter to himself without regard to consequences. 'He suspected there was an active ill will towards him on the part of these white men that—' 'You are right,' I said, remembering a certain conversation I had overheard. 'The manager thinks you ought to be hanged.' He showed a concern at this intelligence which amused me at first. 'I had better get out of the way quietly,' he said, earnestly. 'I can do no more for Kurtz now, and they would soon find some excuse. What's to stop them? There's a military post three hundred miles from here.' 'Well, upon my word,' said I, 'perhaps you had better go if you have any friends amongst the savages near by.' 'Plenty,' he said. 'They are simple people—and I want nothing, you know.' He stood biting his lip, then: 'I don't want any harm to happen to these whites here, but of course I was thinking of Mr. Kurtz's reputation—but you are a brother seaman and—' 'All right,' said I, after a time. 'Mr. Kurtz's reputation is safe with me.' I did not know how truly I spoke.

"He informed me, lowering his voice, that it was Kurtz who had ordered the attack to be made on the steamer. 'He hated sometimes the idea of being taken away—and then again. . . . But I don't understand these matters. I am a simple man. He thought it would scare you away—that you would give it up, thinking him dead. I could not stop him. Oh, I had an awful time of it this last month.' 'Very well,' I said. 'He is all right now.' 'Ye-e-es,' he muttered, not very convinced apparently. 'Thanks,' said I; 'I shall keep my eyes open.' 'But quiet—eh?' he urged, anxiously. 'It would be awful for his reputation if anybody here—' I promised a complete discretion with great gravity. 'I have a canoe and three black fellows waiting not very far. I am off. Could you give me a few Martini-Henry cartridges?' I could, and did, with proper secrecy. He helped himself, with a wink at me, to a handful of my tobacco. 'Between sailors—you know—good English tobacco.' At the door of the pilot-house he turned round—'I say, haven't you a pair of shoes you could spare?' He raised one leg. 'Look.' The soles were tied with knotted strings sandal-wise under his bare feet. I rooted out an old pair, at which he looked with admiration before tucking them under his left arm. One of his pockets (bright red) was bulging with cartridges, from the other (dark blue) peeped 'Towson's Inquiry,' etc., etc. He seemed to think himself excellently well equipped for a renewed encounter with the wilderness. 'Ah! I'll never, never meet such a man again. You ought to have heard him recite poetry—his own, too, it was, he told me. Poetry!' He rolled his eyes at the recollection of these delights. 'Oh, he enlarged my mind!' 'Good-by,' said I. He shook hands and vanished in the night. Sometimes I ask myself whether I had ever really seen him—whether it was possible to meet such a phenomenon! . . .

135 "When I woke up shortly after midnight his warning came to my mind with its hint of danger that seemed, in the starred darkness, real enough to make me get up for the purpose of having a look around. On the hill a big fire burned, illuminating fitfully a crooked corner of the station-house. One of the agents with a picket of a few of our blacks, armed for the purpose, was keeping guard over the ivory; but deep within the forest, red gleams that wavered, that seemed to sink and rise from the ground amongst confused columnar shapes of intense blackness, showed the exact position of the camp where Mr. Kurtz's adorers were keeping their uneasy vigil. The monotonous beating of a big drum filled the air with muffled shocks and a lingering vibration. A steady droning sound of many men chanting each to himself some weird incantation came out from the black, flat wall of the wood as the humming of bees comes out of a hive, and had a strange narcotic effect upon my half-awake senses. I believe I dozed off leaning over the rail, till an abrupt burst of yells, an overwhelming outbreak of a pent-up and mysterious frenzy, woke me up in a bewildered wonder. It was cut short all at once, and the low droning went on with an effect of audible and soothing silence. I glanced casually into the little cabin. A light was burning within, but Mr. Kurtz was not there.

"I think I would have raised an outcry if I had believed my eyes. But I didn't believe them at first—the thing seemed so impossible. The fact is I was completely unnerved by a sheer blank fright, pure abstract terror, unconnected with any distinct shape of physical danger. What made this emotion so overpowering was—how shall I define it?—the moral shock I received, as if something altogether monstrous, intolerable to thought and odious to the soul, had been thrust upon me unexpectedly. This lasted of course the merest fraction of a second, and then the usual sense of commonplace, deadly danger, the possibility of a sudden onslaught and massacre, or something of the kind, which I saw impending, was positively welcome and composing. It pacified me, in fact, so much, that I did not raise an alarm.

"There was an agent buttoned up inside an ulster and sleeping on a chair on deck within three feet of me. The yells had not awakened him; he snored very slightly; I left him to his slumbers and leaped ashore. I did not betray Mr. Kurtz—it was ordered I should never betray him—it was written I should be loyal to the nightmare of my choice. I was anxious to deal with this shadow by myself alone—and to this day I don't know why I was so jealous of sharing with anyone the peculiar blackness of that experience.

"As soon as I got on the bank I saw a trail—a broad trail through the grass. I remember the exultation with which I said to myself, 'He can't walk—he is crawling on all-fours—I've got him.' The grass was wet with dew. I strode rapidly with clenched fists. I fancy I had some vague notion of falling upon him and giving him a drubbing. I don't know. I had some imbecile thoughts. The knitting old woman with the cat obtruded herself upon my memory as a most improper person to be sitting at the other end of such an affair. I saw a row of pilgrims squirting lead in the air out of Winchesters held to the hip. I thought I would never get back to the steamer, and imagined myself living alone and unarmed in the woods to an advanced age. Such silly things—you know. And I remember I confounded the beat of the drum with the beating of my heart, and was pleased at its calm regularity.

"I kept to the track though—then stopped to listen. The night was very clear; a dark blue space, sparkling with dew and starlight, in which black things stood very still. I thought I could see a kind of motion ahead of me. I was strangely cocksure of everything that night. I actually left the track and ran in a wide semicircle (I verily believe chuckling to myself) so as to get in front of that stir, of that motion I had seen—if indeed I had seen anything. I was circumventing Kurtz as though it had been a boyish game.

140 "I came upon him, and, if he had not heard me coming, I would have fallen over him, too, but he got up in time. He rose, unsteady, long, pale, indistinct, like a vapor exhaled by the earth, and swayed slightly, misty and silent before me; while at my back the fires loomed between the trees, and the murmur of many voices issued from the forest. I had cut him off cleverly; but when actually confronting him I seemed to come to my senses, I saw the danger in its right proportion. It was by no means over yet. Suppose he began to shout? Though he could hardly stand, there was still plenty of vigor in his voice. 'Go away—hide yourself,' he said, in that profound tone. It was very awful. I glanced back. We were within thirty yards from the nearest fire. A black figure stood up, strode on long black legs, waving long black arms, across the glow. It had horns—antelope horns, I think—on its head. Some sorcerer, some witchman, no doubt; it looked fiend-like enough. 'Do you know what you are doing?' I whispered. 'Perfectly,' he answered, raising his voice for that single word: it sounded to me far off and yet loud, like a hail through a speaking-trumpet. If he makes a row we are lost, I thought to myself. This clearly was not a case for fisticuffs, even apart from the very natural aversion I had to beat that Shadow—this wandering and tormented thing. 'You will be lost,' I said—'utterly lost.' One gets sometimes such a flash of inspiration, you know. I did say the right thing, though indeed he could not have been more irretrievably lost than he was at this very moment, when the foundations of our

intimacy were being laid—to endure—to endure—even to the end—even beyond.

"'I had immense plans,' he muttered irresolutely. 'Yes,' said I; 'but if you try to shout I'll smash your head with—' There was not a stick or a stone near. 'I will throttle you for good,' I corrected myself. 'I was on the threshold of great things,' he pleaded, in a voice of longing, with a wistfulness of tone that made my blood run cold. 'And now for this stupid scoundrel—' 'Your success in Europe is assured in any case,' I affirmed, steadily. I did not want to have the throttling of him, you understand—and indeed it would have been very little use for any practical purpose. I tried to break the spell—the heavy, mute spell of the wilderness—that seemed to draw him to its pitiless breast by the awakening of forgotten and brutal instincts, by the memory of gratified and monstrous passions. This alone, I was convinced, had driven him out to the edge of the forest, to the bush, towards the gleam of fires, the throb of drums, the drone of weird incantations; this alone had beguiled his unlawful soul beyond the bounds of permitted aspirations. And, don't you see, the terror of the position was not in being knocked on the head—though I had a very lively sense of that danger, too—but in this, that I had to deal with a being to whom I could not appeal in the name of anything high or low. I had, even like the niggers, to invoke him—himself—his own exalted and incredible degradation. There was nothing either above or below him, and I knew it. He had kicked himself loose of the earth. Confound the man! he had kicked the very earth to pieces. He was alone, and I before him did not know whether I stood on the ground or floated in the air. I've been telling you what we said—repeating the phrases we pronounced—but what's the good? They were common everyday words—the familiar, vague sounds exchanged on every waking day of life. But what of that? They had behind them, to my mind, the terrific suggestiveness of words heard in dreams, of phrases spoken in nightmares. Soul! If anybody had ever struggled with a soul, I am the man. And I wasn't arguing with a lunatic either. Believe me or not, his intelligence was perfectly clear—concentrated, it is true, upon himself with horrible intensity, yet clear; and therein was my only chance—barring, of course, the killing him there and then, which wasn't so good, on account of unavoidable noise. But his soul was mad. Being alone in the wilderness, it had looked within itself, and, by heavens! I tell you, it had gone mad. I had—for my sins, I suppose—to go through the ordeal of looking into it myself. No eloquence could have been so withering to one's belief in mankind as his final burst of sincerity. He struggled with himself, too. I saw it—I heard it. I saw the inconceivable mystery of a soul that knew no restraint, no faith, and no fear, yet struggling blindly with itself. I kept my head pretty well; but when I had him at last stretched on the couch, I wiped my forehead, while my legs shook under me as though I had carried half a ton on my back down the hill. And yet I had only supported him, his bony arm clasped round my neck—and he was not much heavier than a child.

"When next day we left at noon, the crowd, of whose presence behind the curtain of trees I had been acutely conscious all the time, flowed out of the woods again, filled the clearing, covered the slope with a mass of naked, breathing, quivering, bronze bodies. I steamed up a bit, then swung downstream, and two thousand eyes followed the evolutions of the splashing, thumping, fierce river-demon beating the water with its terrible tail and breathing black smoke into the air. In front of the first rank, along the river, three men, plastered with bright red earth from head to foot, strutted to and fro restlessly. When we came abreast again, they faced the river, stamped their feet, nodded their horned heads, swayed their scarlet bodies; they shook towards the fierce river-demon a bunch of black feathers, a mangy skin with a pendent tail—something that looked like a dried gourd; they shouted periodically together strings of amazing words that resembled no sounds of human language; and the deep murmurs of the crowd, interrupted suddenly, were like the responses of some satanic litany.

"We had carried Kurtz into the pilot-house; there was more air there. Lying on the couch, he stared through the open shutter. There was an eddy in the mass of human bodies, and the woman with helmeted head and tawny cheeks rushed out to the very brink of the stream. She put out her hands, shouted something, and all that wild mob took up the shout in a roaring chorus of articulated, rapid, breathless utterance.

"'Do you understand this?' I asked.

145 "He kept on looking out past me with fiery, longing eyes, with a mingled expression of wistfulness and hate. He made no answer, but I saw a smile, a smile of indefinable meaning, appear on his colorless lips that a moment after twitched convulsively. 'Do I not?' he said slowly, gasping, as if the words had been torn out of him by a supernatural power.

"I pulled the string of the whistle, and I did this because I saw the pilgrims on deck getting out their rifles with an air of anticipating a jolly lark. At the sudden screech there was a movement of abject terror through that wedged mass of bodies. 'Don't! don't you frighten them away,' cried someone on deck disconsolately. I pulled the string time after time. They broke and ran, they leaped, they crouched, they swerved, they dodged the flying terror of the sound. The three red chaps had fallen flat, face down on the shore, as though they had been shot dead. Only the barbarous and superb woman did not so much as flinch, and stretched tragically her bare arms after us over the somber and glittering river.

"And then that imbecile crowd down on the deck started their little fun, and I could see nothing more for smoke.

"The brown current ran swiftly out of the heart of darkness, bearing us down towards the sea with twice the speed of our upward progress; and Kurtz's life was running swiftly, too, ebbing, ebbing out of his heart into the sea of inexorable time. The manager was very placid, he had no vital anxieties now, he took us both in with a comprehensive and satisfied glance: the 'affair' had come off as well as could be wished. I saw the time approaching when I would be left alone of the party of 'unsound method.' The pilgrims looked upon me with disfavor. I was, so to speak, numbered with the dead. It is strange how I accepted this unforeseen partnership, this choice of nightmares forced upon me in the tenebrous land invaded by these mean and greedy phantoms.

"Kurtz discoursed. A voice! a voice! It rang deep to the very last. It survived his strength to hide in the magnificent folds of eloquence the barren darkness of his heart. Oh, he struggled! he struggled! The wastes of his weary brain were haunted by shadowy images now—images of wealth and fame revolving obsequiously round his unextinguishable gift of noble and lofty expression. My Intended, my station, my career, my ideas—these were the objects for the occasional utterances of elevated sentiments. The shade of the original Kurtz frequented the bedside of the hollow sham, whose fate it was to be buried presently in the mold of primeval earth. But both the diabolic love and the unearthly hate of the mysteries it had penetrated fought for the possession of that soul satiated with primitive emotions, avid of lying fame, of sham distinction, of all the appearances of success and power.

150 "Sometimes he was contemptibly childish. He desired to have kings meet him at railway stations on his return from some ghastly Nowhere, where he intended to acomplish great things. 'You show them you have in you something that is really profitable, and then there will be no limits to the recognition of your ability,' he would say. 'Of course you must take care of the motives—right motives—always.' The long reaches that were like one and the same reach, monotonous bends that were exactly alike, slipped past the steamer with their multitude of secular[17] trees looking patiently after this grimy fragment of another world, the forerunner of change, of conquest, of trade, of massacres, of blessings. I looked ahead—piloting. 'Close the shutter,' said Kurtz suddenly one day; 'I can't bear to look at this.' I did so. There was a silence. 'Oh, but I will wring your heart yet!' he cried at the invisible wilderness.

"We broke down—as I had expected—and had to lie up for repairs at the head of an island. This delay was the first thing that shook Kurtz's confidence. One morning he gave me a packet of papers and a photograph—the lot tied together with a shoestring. 'Keep this for me,' he said. 'This noxious fool' (meaning the manager) 'is capable of prying into my boxes when I am not looking.' In the afternoon I saw him. He was lying on his back with closed eyes, and I withdrew quietly, but I heard him mutter, 'Live rightly, die, die. . . .' I listened. There was nothing more. Was he rehearsing some speech in his sleep, or was it a fragment of a phrase from some newspaper article? He had been writing for the papers and meant to do so again, 'for the furthering of my ideas. It's a duty.'

"His was an impenetrable darkness. I looked at him as you peer down at a man who is lying at the bottom of a precipice where the sun never shines. But I had not much time to give him, because I was helping the engine-driver to take to pieces the leaky cylinders, to straighten a bent connecting-rod, and in other such matters. I lived in an infernal mess of rust, filings, nuts, bolts, spanners, hammers, ratchet-drills—things I abominate, because I don't get on with them. I tended the little forge we fortunately had aboard; I toiled wearily in a wretched scrap-heap—unless I had the shakes too bad to stand.

"One evening coming in with a candle I was startled to hear him say a little tremulously, 'I am lying here in the dark waiting for death.' The light was within a foot of his eyes. I forced myself to murmur, 'Oh, nonsense!' and stood over him as if transfixed.

"Anything approaching the change that came over his features I have never seen before, and hope never to see again. Oh, I wasn't touched. I was fascinated. It was as though a veil had been rent. I saw on that ivory face the expression of somber pride, of ruthless power, of craven terror—of an intense and hopeless despair. Did he live his life again in every detail of de-

[17]**secular** centuries-old

sire, temptation, and surrender during that supreme moment of complete knowledge? He cried in a whisper at some image, at some vision—he cried out twice, a cry that was no more than a breath—

155 "'The horror! The horror!'

"I blew the candle out and left the cabin. The pilgrims were dining in the messroom, and I took my place opposite the manager, who lifted his eyes to give me a questioning glance, which I successfully ignored. He leaned back, serene, with that peculiar smile of his sealing the unexpressed depths of his meanness. A continuous shower of small flies streamed upon the lamp, upon the cloth, upon our hands and faces. Suddenly the manager's boy put his insolent black head in the doorway, and said in a tone of scathing contempt—

"'Mistah Kurtz—he dead.'

"All the pilgrims rushed out to see. I remained, and went on with my dinner. I believe I was considered brutally callous. However, I did not eat much. There was a lamp in there—light, don't you know—and outside it was so beastly, beastly dark. I went no more near the remarkable man who had pronounced a judgment upon the adventures of his soul on this earth. The voice was gone. What else had been there? But I am of course aware that next day the pilgrims buried something in a muddy hole.

"And then they very nearly buried me.

160 "However, as you see, I did not go to join Kurtz there and then. I did not. I remained to dream the nightmare out to the end, and to show my loyalty to Kurtz once more. Destiny. My destiny! Droll thing life is—that mysterious arrangement of merciless logic for a futile purpose. The most you can hope from it is some knowledge of yourself—that comes too late—a crop of unextinguishable regrets. I have wrestled with death. It is the most unexciting contest you can imagine. It takes place in an impalpable grayness, with nothing underfoot, with nothing around, without spectators, without clamor, without glory, without the great desire of victory, without the great fear of defeat, in a sickly atmosphere of tepid skepticism, without much belief in your own right, and still less in that of your adversary. If such is the form of ultimate wisdom, then life is a greater riddle than some of us think it to be. I was within a hair's breadth of the last opportunity for pronouncement, and I found with humiliation that probably I would have nothing to say. This is the reason why I affirm that Kurtz was a remarkable man. He had something to say. He said it. Since I had peeped over the edge myself, I understand better the meaning of his stare, that could not see the flame of the candle, but was wide enough to embrace the whole universe, piercing enough to penetrate all the hearts that beat in the darkness. He had summed up—he had judged. 'The horror!' He was a remarkable man. After all, this was the expression of some sort of belief; it had candor, it had conviction, it had a vibrating note of revolt in its whisper, it had the appalling face of a glimpsed truth—the strange commingling of desire and hate. And it is not my own extremity I remember best—a vision of grayness without form filled with physical pain, and a careless contempt for the evanescence of all things—even of this pain itself. No! It is his extremity that I seem to have lived through. True, he had made that last stride, he had stepped over the edge, while I had been permitted to draw back my hesitating foot. And perhaps in this is the whole difference; perhaps all the wisdom, and all truth, and all sincerity, are just compressed into that inappreciable moment

of time in which we step over the threshold of the invisible. Perhaps! I like to think my summing-up would not have been a word of careless contempt. Better his cry—much better. It was an affirmation, a moral victory paid for by innumerable defeats, by abominable terrors, by abominable satisfactions. But it was a victory! That is why I have remained loyal to Kurtz to the last, and even beyond, when a long time after I heard once more, not his own choice, but the echo of his magnificent eloquence thrown to me from a soul as translucently pure as a cliff of crystal.

"No, they did not bury me, though there is a period of time which I remember mistily, with a shuddering wonder, like a passage through some inconceivable world that had no hope in it and no desire. I found myself back in the sepulchral city resenting the sight of people hurrying through the streets to filch a little money from each other, to devour their infamous cookery, to gulp their unwholesome beer, to dream their insignificant and silly dreams. They trespassed upon my thoughts. They were intruders whose knowledge of life was to me an irritating pretense, because I felt so sure they could not possibly know the things I knew. Their bearing, which was simply the bearing of commonplace individuals going about their business in the assurance of perfect safety, was offensive to me like the outrageous flauntings of folly in the face of a danger it is unable to comprehend. I had no particular desire to enlighten them, but I had some difficulty in restraining myself from laughing in their faces, so full of stupid importance. I daresay I was not very well at that time. I tottered about the streets—there were various affairs to settle—grinning bitterly at perfectly respectable persons. I admit my behavior was inexcusable, but then my temperature was seldom normal in these days. My dear aunt's endeavors to 'nurse up my strength' seemed altogether beside the mark. It was not my strength that wanted nursing, it was my imagination that wanted soothing. I kept the bundle of papers given me by Kurtz, not knowing exactly what to do with it. His mother had died lately, watched over, as I was told, by his Intended. A clean-shaven man, with an official manner and wearing gold-rimmed spectacles, called on me one day and made inquiries, at first circuitous, afterwards suavely pressing, about what he was pleased to denominate certain 'documents.' I was not surprised, because I had had two rows with the manager on the subject out there. I had refused to give up the smallest scrap out of that package, and I took the same attitude with the spectacled man. He became darkly menacing at last, and with much heat argued that the Company had the right to every bit of information about its 'territories.' And said he, 'Mr. Kurtz's knowledge of unexplored regions must have been necessarily extensive and peculiar—owing to his great abilities and to the deplorable circumstances in which he had been placed: therefore—' I assured him Mr. Kurtz's knowledge, however extensive, did not bear upon the problems of commerce or administration. He invoked then the name of science. 'It would be an incalculable loss if,' etc., etc. I offered him the report on the 'Suppression of Savage Customs,' with the postscriptum torn off. He took it up eagerly, but ended by sniffing at it with an air of contempt. 'This is not what we had a right to expect,' he remarked. 'Expect nothing else,' I said. 'There are only private letters.' He withdrew upon some threat of legal proceedings, and I saw him no more; but another fellow, calling himself Kurtz's cousin, appeared two days later, and was anxious to hear all the details about his dear relative's last moments. Incidentally he gave me to understand that Kurtz had been essentially a great musician. 'There was the making of an immense success,' said the man, who was an organist, I believe, with lank gray hair flowing over a greasy coat-collar. I had no reason to doubt his statement; and to this day I am unable to say what was Kurtz's profession, whether he ever had any—which was the greatest of his talents. I had taken him for a painter who wrote for the papers, or else for a journalist who could paint—but even the cousin (who took snuff during the interview) could not tell me what he had been—exactly. He was a universal genius—on that point I agreed with the old chap, who thereupon blew his nose noisily into a large cotton handkerchief and withdrew in senile agitation, bearing off some family letters and memoranda without importance. Ultimately a journalist anxious to know something of the fate of his 'dear colleague' turned up. This visitor informed me Kurtz's proper sphere ought to have been politics 'on the popular side.' He had furry straight eyebrows, bristly hair cropped short, an eye-glass on a broad ribbon, and, becoming expansive, confessed his opinion that Kurtz really couldn't write a bit—'But heavens! how that man could talk. He electrified large meetings. He had faith—don't you see?—he had the faith. He could get himself to believe anything—anything. He would have been a splendid leader of an extreme party.' 'What party?' I asked. 'Any party,' answered the other. 'He was an—an—extremist.' Did I not think so? I assented. Did I know, he asked, with a sudden flash of curiosity, 'what it was that had induced him to go out there?' 'Yes,' said I, and forthwith handed him the famous Report for publication, if he thought fit. He glanced through it hurriedly, mumbling all the time, judged 'it would do,' and took himself off with this plunder.

"Thus I was left at last with a slim packet of letters and the girl's portrait. She struck me as beautiful—I mean she had a beautiful expression. I know that the sunlight can be made to lie, too, yet one felt that no manipulation of light and pose could have conveyed the delicate shade of truthfulness upon those features. She seemed ready to listen without mental reservation, without suspicion, without a thought for herself. I concluded I would go and give her back her portrait and those letters myself. Curiosity? Yes; and also some other feeling perhaps. All that had been Kurtz's had passed out of my hands: his soul, his body, his station, his plans, his ivory, his career. There remained only this memory and his Intended—and I wanted to give that up, too, to the past; in a way—to surrender personally all that remained of him with me to that oblivion which is the last word of our common fate. I don't defend myself. I had no clear perception of what it was I really wanted. Perhaps it was an impulse of unconscious loyalty, or the fulfillment of one of those ironic necessities, that lurk in the facts of human existence. I don't know. I can't tell. But I went.

"I thought his memory was like the other memories of the dead that accumulate in every man's life—a vague impress on the brain of shadows that had fallen on it in their swift and final passage; but before the high and ponderous door, between the tall houses of a street as still and decorous as a well-kept alley in a cemetery, I had a vision of him on the stretcher, opening his mouth voraciously, as if to devour all the earth with all its mankind. He lived then before me; he lived as much as he had ever lived—a shadow insatiable of splendid appearances, of frightful realities; a shadow darker than the shadow of the night, and draped nobly in the folds of a gorgeous eloquence. The vision seemed to enter the house with me—the stretcher, the phantom-bearers, the wild crowd of obedient worshipers, the gloom of the forests, the glitter of the reach between the murky bends, the beat of the drum, regular and muffled like the beating of a heart—the heart of a conquering darkness. It was a moment of triumph for the wilderness, an invading and vengeful rush which, it seemed to me, I would have to keep back alone for the salvation of another soul. And the memory of what I had heard him say afar there, with the honored shapes stirring at my back, in the glow of fires, within the patient woods, those broken phrases came back to me, were heard again in their ominous and terrifying simplicity. I remember his abject pleading, his abject threats, the colossal scale of his vile desires, the meanness, the torment, the tempestuous anguish of his soul. And later on I seem to see his collected languid manner, when he said one day, 'This lot of ivory now is really mine. The Company did not pay for it. I collected it myself at a very great personal risk. I am afraid they will try to claim it as theirs though. H'm. It is a difficult case. What do you think I ought to do—resist? Eh? I want no more than justice.' . . . He wanted no more than justice—no more than justice. I rang the bell before a mahogany door on the first floor, and while I waited he seemed to stare at me out of the glassy panel—stare with that wide and immense stare embracing, condemning, loathing all the universe. I seemed to hear the whispered cry, 'The horror! The horror!'

"The dusk was falling. I had to wait in a lofty drawing-room with three long windows from floor to ceiling that were like three luminous and bedraped columns. The bent gilt legs and backs of the furniture shone in indistinct curves. The tall marble fireplace had a cold and monumental whiteness. A grand piano stood massively in a corner; with dark gleams on the flat surfaces like a somber and polished sarcophagus. A high door opened—closed. I rose.

165 "She came forward, all in black, with a pale head, floating towards me in the dusk. She was in mourning. It was more than a year since his death, more than a year since the news came; she seemed as though she would remember and mourn forever. She took both my hands in hers and murmured, 'I had heard you were coming.' I noticed she was not very young—I mean not girlish. She had a mature capacity for fidelity, for belief, for suffering. The room seemed to have grown darker, as if all the sad light of the cloudy evening had taken refuge on her forehead. This fair hair, this pale visage, this pure brow, seemed surrounded by an ashy halo from which the dark eyes looked out at me. Their glance was guileless, profound, confident, and trustful. She carried her sorrowful head as though she were proud of that sorrow, as though she would say, I—I alone know how to mourn him as he deserves. But while we were still shaking hands, such a look of awful desolation came upon her face that I perceived she was one of those creatures that are not the playthings of Time. For her he had died only yesterday. And, by Jove! the impression was so powerful that for me, too, he seemed to have died only yesterday—nay, this very minute. I saw her and

him in the same instant of time—his death and her sorrow—I saw her sorrow in the very moment of his death. Do you understand? I saw them together—I heard them together. She had said, with a deep catch of the breath, 'I have survived' while my strained ears seemed to hear distinctly, mingled with her tone of despairing regret, the summing up whisper of his eternal condemnation. I asked myself what I was doing there, with a sensation of panic in my heart as though I had blundered into a place of cruel and absurd mysteries not fit for a human being to behold. She motioned me to a chair. We sat down. I laid the packet gently on the little table, and she put her hand over it. . . . 'You knew him well,' she murmured, after a moment of mourning silence.

"'Intimacy grows quickly out there,' I said. 'I knew him as well as it is possible for one man to know another.'

"'And you admired him,' she said. 'It was impossible to know him and not to admire him. Was it?'

"'He was a remarkable man,' I said, unsteadily. Then before the appealing fixity of her gaze, that seemed to watch for more words on my lips, I went on, 'It was impossible not to—'

"'Love him,' she finished eagerly, silencing me into an appalled dumbness. 'How true! how true! But when you think that no one knew him so well as I! I had all his noble confidence. I knew him best.'

170 "'You knew him best,' I repeated. And perhaps she did. But with every word spoken the room was growing darker, and only her forehead, smooth and white, remained illumined by the unextinguishable light of belief and love.

"'You were his friend,' she went on. 'His friend,' she repeated, a little louder. 'You must have been, if he had given you this, and sent you to me. I feel I can speak to you—and oh! I must speak. I want you—you have heard his last words—to know I have been worthy of him. . . . It is not pride. . . . Yes! I am proud to know I understood him better than anyone on earth—he told me so himself. And since his mother died I have had no one—no one—to—to—'

"I listened. The darkness deepened. I was not even sure he had given me the right bundle. I rather suspect he wanted me to take care of another batch of his papers which, after his death, I saw the manager examining under the lamp. And the girl talked, easing her pain in the certitude of my sympathy; she talked as thirsty men drink. I had heard that her engagement with Kurtz had been disapproved by her people. He wasn't rich enough or something. And indeed I don't know whether he had not been a pauper all his life. He had given me some reason to infer that it was his impatience of comparative poverty that drove him out there.

"'. . . Who was not his friend who had heard him speak once?' she was saying. 'He drew men towards him by what was best in them.' She looked at me with intensity. 'It is the gift of the great,' she went on, and the sound of her low voice seemed to have the accompaniment of all the other sounds, full of mystery, desolation, and sorrow, I had ever heard—the ripple of the river, the soughing of the trees swayed by the wind, the murmurs of the crowds, the faint ring of incomprehensible words cried from afar, the whisper of a voice speaking from beyond the threshold of an eternal darkness. 'But you have heard him! You know!' she cried.

"'Yes, I know,' I said with something like despair in my heart, but bowing my head before the faith that was in her, before that great and saving illusion that shone with an unearthly glow in the darkness, in the triumphant darkness from which I could not have defended her—from which I could not even defend myself.

175 "'What a loss to me—to us!'—she corrected herself with beautiful generosity; then added in a murmur, 'To the world.' By the last gleams of twilight I could see the glitter of her eyes, full of tears—of tears that would not fall.

"'I have been very happy—very fortunate—very proud,' she went on. 'Too fortunate. Too happy for a little while. And now I am unhappy for—for life.'

"She stood up; her fair hair seemed to catch all the remaining light in a glimmer of gold. I rose, too.

"'And of all this,' she went on, mournfully, 'of all his promise, and of all his greatness, of his generous mind, of his noble heart, nothing remains—nothing but a memory. You and I—'

"'We shall always remember him,' I said, hastily.

180 "'No!' she cried. "It is impossible that all this should be lost—that such a life should be sacrificed to leave nothing—but sorrow. You know what vast plans he had. I knew of them, too—I could not perhaps understand—but others knew of them. Something must remain. His words, at least, have not died.'

"'His words will remain,' I said.

"'And his example,' she whispered to herself. 'Men looked up to him—his goodness shone in every act. His example—'

"'True,' I said; 'his example, too. Yes, his example. I forgot that.'

"'But I do not. I cannot—I cannot believe—not yet. I cannot believe that I shall never see him again, that nobody will see him again, never, never, never.'

185 "She put out her arms as if after a retreating figure, stretching them black and with clasped pale hands across the fading and narrow sheen of the window. Never see him! I saw him clearly enough then. I shall see this eloquent phantom as long as I live, and I shall see her, too, a tragic and familiar Shade, resembling in this gesture another one, tragic also, and bedecked with powerless charms, stretching bare arms over the glitter of the infernal stream, the stream of darkness. She said suddenly very low, 'He died as he lived.'

"'His end,' said I, with dull anger stirring in me, 'was in every way worthy of his life.'

"'And I was not with him,' she murmured. My anger subsided before a feeling of infinite pity.

"'Everything that could be done—' I mumbled.

"'Ah, but I believed in him more than anyone on earth—more than his own mother, more than—himself. He needed me! Me! I would have treasured every sigh, every word, every sign, every glance.'

190 "I felt like a chill grip on my chest. 'Don't,' I said, in a muffled voice.

"'Forgive me. I—I have mourned so long in silence—in silence. . . . You were with him—to the last? I think of his loneliness. Nobody near to understand him as I would have understood. Perhaps no one to hear. . .'

"'To the very end,' I said shakily. 'I heard his very last words. . . .' I stopped in a fright.

"'Repeat them,' she murmured in a heart-broken tone. 'I want—I want—something—something—to—live with.'

"I was on the point of crying at her, 'Don't you hear them?' The dusk was repeating them in a persistent whisper all around us, in a whisper that seemed to swell menacingly like the first whisper of a rising wind. 'The horror! The horror!'

195 "'His last word—to live with,' she insisted. 'Don't you understand I loved him—I loved him—I loved him!'

"I pulled myself together and spoke slowly.

"'The last word he pronounced was—your name.'

"I heard a light sigh and then my heart stood still, stopped dead short by an exulting and terrible cry, by the cry of inconceivable triumph and of unspeakable pain. 'I knew it—I was sure!' . . . She knew. She was sure. I heard her weeping, she had hidden her face in her hands. It seemed to me that the house would collapse before I could escape, that the heavens would fall upon my head. But nothing happened. The heavens do not fall for such a trifle. Would they have fallen, I wonder, if I had rendered Kurtz that justice which was his due? Hadn't he said he wanted only justice? But I couldn't. I could not tell her. It would have been too dark—too dark altogether. . . ."

Marlow ceased, and sat apart, indistinct and silent, in the pose of a meditating Buddha. Nobody moved for a time. "We have lost the first of the ebb," said the Director, suddenly. I raised my head. The offing was barred by a black bank of clouds, and the tranquil waterway leading to the uttermost ends of the earth flowed somber under an overcast sky—seemed to lead into the heart of an immense darkness.

[*1902*]

## TOPICS FOR CRITICAL THINKING AND WRITING

1. Conrad gives us a narrator's account of Marlow's narration. That is, he does not simply let Marlow tell the story directly to the reader. What effect does this indirect method have on you?
2. What do you make of the narrator's assertion that for Marlow "the meaning of an episode was not inside like a kernel but outside, enveloping the tale . . ."?
3. What is "the horror" that Kurtz perceives? Why does Marlow call Kurtz's cry "a moral victory"?
4. At the end of the story why does Marlow lie to the Intended?

## JOSEPH CONRAD

# *Remarks on Fiction*

### *From the* Preface *to* The Nigger of the "Narcissus"

A work that aspires, however humbly, to the condition of art should carry its justification in every line. And art itself may be defined as a single-minded attempt to render the highest kind of justice to the visible universe, by bringing to light the truth, manifold and one, underlying its every aspect. It is an attempt to find in its forms, in its colours, in its light, in its shadows, in the aspects of matter, and in the facts of life what of each is fundamental, what is enduring and essential—their one illuminating and convincing quality—the very truth of their existence. The artist, then, like the thinker or the scientist, seeks the truth and makes his appeal. Impressed by the aspect of the world the thinker plunges into ideas, the scientist into facts—whence, presently, emerging they make their appeal to those qualities of our being that fit us best for the hazardous enterprise of living. They speak authoritatively to our common sense, to our intelligence, to our desire of peace, or to our desire of unrest; not seldom to our prejudices, sometimes to our fears, often to our egoism—but always to our credulity. And their words are heard with reverence, for their concern is with weighty matters: with the cultivation of our minds and the proper care of our bodies, with the attainment of our ambitions, with the perfection of the means and the glorification of our precious aims.

It is otherwise with the artist.

Confronted by the same enigmatical spectacle the artist descends within himself, and in that lonely region of stress and strife, if he be deserving and fortunate, he finds the terms of his appeal. His appeal is made to our less obvious capacities: to that part of our nature which, because of the warlike conditions of existence, is necessarily kept out of sight within the more resisting and hard qualities—like the vulnerable body within a steel armour. His appeal is less loud, more profound, less distinct, more stirring—and sooner forgotten. Yet its effect endures for ever. The changing wisdom of successive generations discards ideas, questions facts, demolishes theories. But the artist appeals to that part of our being which is not dependent on wisdom; to that in us which is a gift and not an acquisition—and, therefore, more permanently enduring. He speaks to our capacity for delight and wonder, to the sense of mystery surrounding our lives; to our sense of pity, and beauty, and pain; to the latent feeling of fellowship with all creation—and to the subtle but invincible conviction of solidarity that knits together the loneliness of innumerable hearts, to the solidarity in dreams, in joy, in sorrow, in aspirations, in illusions, in hope, in fear, which binds men to each other, which binds together all humanity—the dead to the living and the living to the unborn.

. . .

. . . My task which I am trying to achieve is, by the power of the written word to make you hear, to make you feel—it is, before all, to make you see. That—and no more, and it is everything. If I succeed, you shall find there according to your deserts: encouragement, consolation, fear, charm—all you demand—and, perhaps, also that glimpse of truth for which you have forgotten to ask.

5 To snatch in a moment of courage, from the remorseless rush of time, a passing phase of life, is only the beginning of the task. The task approached in tenderness and faith is to hold up unquestioningly, without choice and without fear, the rescued fragment before all eyes in the light of a sincere mood. It is to show its vibration, its colour, its form; and through its movement, its form, and its colour, reveal the substance of its truth—disclose its inspiring secret: the stress and passion within the core of each convincing moment. In a single-minded attempt of that kind, if one be deserving and fortunate, one may perchance attain to such clearness of sincerity that at

last the presented vision of regret or pity, of terror or mirth, shall awaken in the hearts of the beholders that feeling of unavoidable solidarity; of the solidarity in mysterious origin, in toil, in joy, in hope, in uncertain fate, which binds men to each other and all mankind to the visible world.

[*1897*]

## *From the* Preface *to* Youth . . . *and Two Other Stories*

. . . *Heart of Darkness* also received a certain amount of notice from the first; and of its origins this much may be said: it is well known that curious men go prying into all sorts of places (where they have no business) and come out of them with all kinds of spoil. This story, and one other, not in this volume, are all the spoil I brought out from the centre of Africa, where, really, I had no sort of business. More ambitious in its scope and longer in the telling, *Heart of Darkness* is quite as authentic in fundamentals as *Youth.* It is, obviously, written in another mood, I won't characterize the mood precisely, but anybody can see that it is anything but the mood of wistful regret, of reminiscent tenderness.

One more remark may be added. *Youth* is a feat of memory. It is a record of experience; but that experience, in its facts, in its inwardness and in its outward colouring, begins and ends in myself. *Heart of Darkness* is experience, too; but it is experience pushed a little (and only very little) beyond the actual facts of the case for the perfectly legitimate, I believe, purpose of bringing it home to the minds and bosoms of the readers. There it was no longer a matter of sincere colouring. It was like another art altogether. That sombre theme had to be given a sinister resonance, a tonality of its own, a continued vibration that, I hoped, would hang in the air and dwell on the ear after the last note had been struck.

[*1917*]

## TOPICS FOR CRITICAL THINKING AND WRITING

1. In his first paragraph Conrad says that a work of art must "attempt to render . . . the truth. . . ." Do you agree? Suppose someone said that we cannot know the truth—we can at best give our version of what we perceive. What would you reply?
2. In the third paragraph Conrad says that the artist

   > speaks to our capacity for delight and wonder, to the sense of mystery surrounding our lives; to our sense of pity, and beauty, and pain; to the latent feeling of fellowship with all creation. . . .

   Point to episodes or passages in *Heart of Darkness* that might be used to support Conrad's claim.
3. In the final paragraph Conrad speaks of the "sombre theme" of *Heart of Darkness.* What would you say the theme is?

## CHINUA ACHEBE

*Chinua Achebe, born in Nigeria in 1930, is the author of* Things Fall Apart *(1958) and other distinguished books.*

*In 1975 he delivered a lecture on Conrad at the University of Massachusetts, Amherst. We reprint some extracts from the published lecture (1977), in which Achebe argues that the book is racist and is badly written.*

## *An Image of Africa: Racism in Conrad's* Heart of Darkness

. . . *Heart of Darkness* projects the image of Africa as 'the other world,' the antithesis of Europe and therefore of civilization, a place where man's vaunted intelligence and refinement are finally mocked by triumphant bestiality. The book opens on the River Thames, tranquil, resting peacefully 'at the decline of day after ages of good service done to the race that peopled its banks.' But the actual story will take place on the River Congo, the very antithesis of the Thames. The River Congo is quite decidedly not a River Emeritus. It has rendered no service and enjoys no old-age pension. We are told that 'going up that river was like travelling back to the earliest beginning of the world.'

Is Conrad saying then that these two rivers are very different, one good, the other bad? Yes, but that is not the real point. It is not the differentness that worries Conrad but the lurking hint of kinship, of common ancestry. For the Thames too 'has been one of the dark places of the earth.' It conquered its darkness, of course, and is now in daylight and at peace. But if it were to visit its primordial relative, the Congo, it would run the terrible risk of hearing grotesque echoes of its own forgotten darkness, and falling victim to an avenging recrudescence of the mindless frenzy of the first beginnings.

These suggestive echoes comprise Conrad's famed evocation of the African atmosphere in *Heart of Darkness.* In the final consideration his method amounts to no more than a steady, ponderous, fake-ritualistic repetition of two antithetical sentences, one about silence and the other about frenzy. We can inspect samples of this on pages 103 and 105 of the New American Library edition: (a) 'It was the stillness of an implacable force brooding over an inscrutable intention' and (b) 'The steamer toiled along slowly on the edge of a black and incomprehensible frenzy'. Of course there is a judicious change of adjective from time to time, so that instead of 'inscrutable', for example, you might have 'unspeakable', even plain 'mysterious', etc., etc.

The eagle-eyed English critic F. R. Leavis drew attention long ago to Conrad's 'adjectival insistence upon inexpressible and incomprehensible mystery'. That insistence must not be dismissed lightly, as many Conrad critics have tended to do, as a mere stylistic flaw; for it raises serious questions of artistic good faith. When a writer while pretending to record scenes, incidents and their impact is in reality engaged in inducing hypnotic stupor in his readers through a bombardment of emotive words and other forms of trickery, much more has to be at stake than stylistic felicity. Generally normal readers are well armed to detect and resist such underhand activity. But Conrad chose his subject well—one which was guaranteed not to put him in conflict with the psychological predisposition of his readers or raise the need for him to contend with their resistance. He chose the role of purveyor of comforting myths.

5 The most interesting and revealing passages in *Heart of Darkness* are, however, about people. I must crave the indulgence of my reader to quote almost a whole page from about the middle of the story when representatives of Europe in a steamer going down the Congo encounter the denizens of Africa:

> We were wanderers on a prehistoric earth, on an earth that wore the aspect of an unknown planet. We could have fancied ourselves the first of men taking possession of an accursed inheritance, to be subdued at the cost of profound anguish and of excessive toil. But suddenly, as we struggled round a bend, there would be a glimpse of rush walls, of peaked grass-roofs, a burst of yells, a whirl of black limbs, a mass of hands clapping, of feet stamping, of bodies swaying, of eyes rolling, under the droop of heavy and motionless foliage. The steamer toiled along slowly on the edge of the black and incomprehensible frenzy. The prehistoric man was cursing us, praying to us, welcoming us—who could tell? We were cut off from the comprehension of our surroundings; we glided past like phantoms, wondering and secretly appalled, as sane men would be before an enthusiastic outbreak in a madhouse. We could not understand because we were too far and could not remember because we were travelling in the night of first ages, of those ages that are gone, leaving hardly a sign—and no memories.
>
> The earth seemed unearthly. We are accustomed to look upon the shackled form of a conquered monster, but there—there you could look at a thing monstrous and free. It was unearthly, and the men were—No, they were not inhuman. Well, you know, that was the worst of it—this suspicion of their not being inhuman. It would come slowly to one. They howled and leaped, and spun, and made horrid faces; but what thrilled you was just the thought of their humanity—like yours—the thought of your remote kinship with this wild and passionate uproar. Ugly. Yes, it was ugly enough; but if you were man enough you would admit to yourself that there was in you just the faintest trace of a response to the terrible frankness of that noise, a dim suspicion of there being a meaning in it which you—you so remote from the night of first ages—could comprehend.

Herein lies the meaning of *Heart of Darkness* and the fascination it holds over the Western mind: 'What thrilled you was just the thought of their humanity—like yours . . . Ugly.'

Having shown us Africa in the mass, Conrad then zeros in, half a page later, on a specific example, giving us one of his rare descriptions of an African who is not just limbs or rolling eyes:

> And between whiles I had to look after the savage who was fireman. He was an improved specimen; he could fire up a vertical boiler. He was there below me, and, upon my word, to look at him was as edifying as seeing a dog in a parody of breeches and a feather hat, walking on his hind legs. A few months of training had

> done for that really fine chap. He squinted at the steam-gauge and at the water-gauge with an evident effort of intrepidity—and he had filed teeth, too, the poor devil, and the wool of his pate shaved into queer patterns, and three ornamental scars on each of his cheeks. He ought to have been clapping his hands and stamping his feet on the bank, instead of which he was hard at work, a thrall to strange witchcraft, full of improving knowledge.

As everybody knows, Conrad is a romantic on the side. He might not exactly admire savages clapping their hands and stamping their feet but they have at least the merit of being in their place, unlike this dog in a parody of breeches. For Conrad things being in their place is of the utmost importance.

'Fine fellows—cannibals—in their place,' he tells us pointedly. Tragedy begins when things leave their accustomed place, like Europe leaving its safe stronghold between the policeman and the baker to take a peep into the heart of darkness.

Before the story takes us into the Congo basin proper we are given this nice little vignette as an example of things in their place:

> Now and then a boat from the shore gave one a momentary contact with reality. It was paddled by black fellows. You could see from afar the white of their eyeballs glistening. They shouted, sang; their bodies streamed with perspiration; they had faces like grotesque masks—these chaps; but they had bone, muscle, a wild vitality, an intense energy of movement, that was as natural and true as the surf along their coast. They wanted no excuse for being there. They were a great comfort to look at.

Towards the end of the story Conrad lavishes a whole page quite unexpectedly on an African woman who has obviously been some kind of mistress to Mr Kurtz and now presides (if I may be permitted a little liberty) like a formidable mystery over the inexorable imminence of his departure:

> She was savage and superb, wild-eyed and magnificent . . . She stood looking at us without a stir, and like the wilderness itself, with an air of brooding over an inscrutable purpose.

This Amazon is drawn in considerable detail, albeit of a predictable nature, for two reasons. First, she is in her place and so can win Conrad's special brand of approval; and second, she fulfils a structural requirement of the story: a savage counterpart to the refined, European woman who will step forth to end the story:

> She came forward, all in black, with a pale head, floating towards me in the dusk. She was in mourning . . . She took both my hands in hers and murmured, 'I had heard you were coming' . . . She had a mature capacity for fidelity, for belief, for suffering.

The difference in the attitude of the novelist to these two women is conveyed in too many direct and subtle ways to need elaboration. But perhaps the most significant difference is the one implied in the author's bestowal of human expression to the one and the withholding of it from the other. It is clearly not part of Conrad's purpose to confer language on the 'rudimentary souls' of Africa. In place of speech they made 'a violent babble of uncouth sounds'. They 'exchanged short grunting phrases' even among themselves. But most of the time they were too busy with their frenzy. There are two occasions in the book, however, when Conrad departs somewhat from his practice and confers speech, even English speech, on the savages. The first occurs when cannibalism gets the better of them:

> 'Catch 'im,' he snapped, with a bloodshot widening of his eyes and a flash of sharp white teeth—'catch 'im. Give 'im to us.' 'To you, eh?' I asked; 'what would you do with them?' 'Eat 'im!' he said curtly.

The other occasion was the famous announcement: 'Mistah Kurtz—he dead'.

At first sight these instances might be mistaken for unexpected acts of generosity from Conrad. In reality they constitute some of his best assaults. In the case of the cannibals the incomprehensible grunts that had thus far served them for speech suddenly proved inadequate for Conrad's purpose of letting the European glimpse the unspeakable craving in their hearts. Weighing the necessity for consistency in the portrayal of the dumb brutes against the sensational advantages of securing their conviction by clear, unambiguous evidence issuing out of their own mouth Conrad chose the latter. As for the announcement of Mr Kurtz's death by the 'insolent black head in the doorway', what better or more appropriate *finis* could be written to the horror story of that wayward child of civilization who wilfully had given his soul to the powers of darkness and 'taken a high seat amongst the devils of the land' than the proclamation of his physical death by the forces he had joined?

10 It might be contended, of course, that the attitude to the African in *Heart of Darkness* is not Conrad's but that of his fictional narrator, Marlow, and that far from endorsing it Conrad might indeed be holding it up to irony and criticism. Certainly Conrad appears to go to considerable pains to set up layers of insulation between himself and the moral universe of his story. He has, for example, a narrator behind a narrator. The primary narrator is Marlow but his account is given to us through the filter of a second, shadowy person. But if Conrad's intention is to draw a cordon sanitaire between himself and the moral and psychological *malaise* of his narrator his care seems to me totally wasted because he neglects to hint, clearly and adequately, at an alternative frame of reference by which we may judge the actions and opinions of his characters. It would not have been beyond Conrad's power to make that provision if he had thought it necessary. Conrad seems to me to approve of Marlow, with only minor reservations—a fact reinforced by the similarities between their two careers.

Marlow comes through to us not only as a witness of truth, but one holding those advanced and humane views appropriate to the English liberal tradition which required all Englishmen of decency to be deeply shocked by atrocities in Bulgaria or the Congo of King Leopold of the Belgians or wherever.

Thus Marlow is able to toss out such bleeding-heart sentiments as these:

> They were all dying slowly—it was very clear. They were not enemies, they were not criminals, they were nothing earthly

> now—nothing but black shadows of disease and starvation, lying confusedly in the greenish gloom. Brought from all the recesses of the coast in all the legality of time contracts, lost in uncongenial surroundings, fed on unfamiliar food, they sickened, became inefficient, and were then allowed to crawl away and rest.

The kind of liberalism espoused here by Marlow/Conrad touched all the best minds of the age in England, Europe and America. It took different forms in the minds of different people but almost always managed to sidestep the ultimate question of equality between white people and black people. That extraordinary missionary, Albert Schweitzer, who sacrificed brilliant careers in music and theology in Europe for a life of service to Africans in much the same area as Conrad writes about, epitomizes the ambivalence. In a comment which has often been quoted Schweitzer says: 'The African is indeed my brother but my junior brother.' And so he proceeded to build a hospital appropriate to the needs of junior brothers with standards of hygiene reminiscent of medical practice in the days before the germ theory of disease came into being. Naturally he became a sensation in Europe and America. Pilgrims flocked, and I believe still flock even after he has passed on, to witness the prodigious miracle in Lamberene, on the edge of the primeval forest.

Conrad's liberalism would not take him quite as far as Schweitzer's, though. He would not use the word 'brother' however qualified; the farthest he would go was 'kinship'. When Marlow's African helmsman falls down with a spear in his heart he gives his white master one final disquieting look:

> And the intimate profundity of that look he gave me when he received his hurt remains to this day in my memory—like a claim of distant kinship affirmed in a supreme moment.

It is important to note that Conrad, careful as ever with his words, is concerned not so much about 'distant kinship' as about someone *laying a claim* on it. The black man lays a claim on the white man which is well-nigh intolerable. It is the laying of this claim which frightens and at the same time fascinates Conrad, 'the thought of their humanity—like yours . . . Ugly.'

The point of my observations should be quite clear by now, namely that Joseph Conrad was a thoroughgoing racist. That this simple truth is glossed over in criticisms of his work is due to the fact that white racism against Africa is such a normal way of thinking that its manifestations go completely unremarked. Students of *Heart of Darkness* will often tell you that Conrad is concerned not so much with Africa as with the deterioration of one European mind caused by solitude and sickness. They will point out to you that Conrad is, if anything, less charitable to the Europeans in the story than he is to the natives, that the point of the story is to ridicule Europe's civilizing mission in Africa. A Conrad student informed me in Scotland that Africa is merely a setting for the disintegration of the mind of Mr Kurtz.

15 Which is partly the point. Africa as setting and backdrop which eliminates the African as human factor. Africa as a metaphysical battlefield devoid of all recognizable humanity, into which the wandering European en-

ters at his peril. Can nobody see the preposterous and perverse arrogance in thus reducing Africa to the role of props for the break-up of one petty European mind? But that is not even the point. The real question is the dehumanization of Africa and Africans which this age-long attitude has fostered and continues to foster in the world. And the question is whether a novel which celebrates this dehumanization, which depersonalizes a portion of the human race, can be called a great work of art. My answer is: No, it cannot. I do not doubt Conrad's great talents. Even *Heart of Darkness* has its memorably good passages and moments:

> The reaches opened before us and closed behind, as if the forest had stepped leisurely across the water to bar the way for our return.

Its exploration of the minds of the European characters is often penetrating and full of insight. But all that has been more than fully discussed in the last fifty years. His obvious racism has, however, not been addressed. And it is high time it was!

. . .

There are two probable grounds on which what I have said so far may be contested. The first is that it is no concern of fiction to please people about whom it is written. I will go along with that. But I am not talking about pleasing people. I am talking about a book which parades in the most vulgar fashion prejudices and insults from which a section of mankind has suffered untold agonies and atrocities in the past and continues to do so in many ways and many places today. I am talking about a story in which the very humanity of black people is called in question.

Secondly, I may be challenged on the grounds of actuality. Conrad, after all, did sail down the Congo in 1890 when my own father was still a babe in arms. How could I stand up more than fifty years after his death and purport to contradict him? My answer is that as a sensible man I will not accept just any traveller's tales solely on the grounds that I have not made the journey myself. I will not trust the evidence even of a man's very eyes when I suspect them to be as jaundiced as Conrad's. And we also happen to know that Conrad was, in the words of his biographer, Bernard C. Meyer, 'notoriously inaccurate in the rendering of his own history.'

But more important by far is the abundant testimony about Conrad's savages which we could gather if we were so inclined from other sources and which might lead us to think that these people must have had other occupations besides merging into the evil forest or materializing out of it simply to plague Marlow and his dispirited band. For as it happened, soon after Conrad had written his book an event of far greater consequence was taking place in the art world of Europe. This is how Frank Willett, a British art historian, describes it:

> Gauguin had gone to Tahiti, the most extravagant individual act of turning to a non-European culture in the decades immediately before and after 1900, when European artists were avid for new artistic experiences, but it was only about 1904–5 that African art began to make its distinctive impact. One piece is still identifiable; it is a mask that had been given to Maurice Vlaminck in 1905. He records that Derain was 'speechless' and 'stunned' when he saw it,

> bought it from Vlaminck and in turn showed it to Picasso and Matisse, who were also greatly affected by it. Ambroise Vollard then borrowed it and had it cast in bronze . . . The revolution of twentieth century art was under way!

The mask in question was made by other savages living just north of Conrad's River Congo. They have a name too: the Fang people, and are without a doubt among the world's greatest masters of the sculptured form. The event Frank Willett is referring to marked the beginning of cubism and the infusion of new life into European art that had run completely out of strength.

The point of all this is to suggest that Conrad's picture of the peoples of the Congo seems grossly inadequate even at the height of their subjection to the ravages of King Leopold's International Association for the Civilization of Central Africa.

. . .

[*1977*]

## TOPICS FOR CRITICAL THINKING AND WRITING

1. In his third paragraph Achebe speaks of Conrad's "steady, ponderous, fake-ritualistic repetition of two antithetical sentences, one about silence and the other about frenzy." And in the next paragraph Achebe quotes the critic F. R. Leavis, who took a dim view of *Heart of Darkness.* Do you agree that the story is badly written? If so, point to some passages that you consider badly written, and explain why you think they are bad.
2. In paragraph 12 Achebe comments briefly on Albert Schweitzer. Compare Achebe's view with the view expressed in a brief biography, such as can be found in the *Encyclopaedia Britannica.*
3. In paragraph 14 Achebe summarizes the usual defenses offered in behalf of Conrad, and he goes on to find them unimpressive. What case, if any, *can* be made on behalf of Conrad?

## ELAINE SHOWALTER

*Elaine Showalter, a professor of English at Princeton University, has written and edited many books on nineteenth- and twentieth-century literature. Among her literary concerns are the representations of women in books and the responses of women as readers. (The title is the editors'.)*

# *The Double Worlds of Men and Women*

Like [Rider Haggard's] *She* and [Rudyard Kipling's] "The Man Who Would Be King," *Heart of Darkness* is both an exposé of imperialism and an allegory of male bonding and the flight from women. Conrad's story of a journey up the Congo to find the mad Kurtz, who has abandoned his idealistic vision of suppressing savage customs and instead has set himself up as a savage god, is the most famous and influential version of the male quest romance. When *Blackwood's Magazine,* familiarly known as *Maga,* commissioned it, the editors congratulated themselves on bringing out "the most notable book we have published since George Eliot." *Heart of Darkness* both took the genre to its artistic heights and brought out the seductiveness of a regression to the primitive. Although, like Haggard and Kipling, Conrad based his story on his personal experience in Africa and his protest against Leopold's exploitation of the Congolese, his eloquent pessimism, psychological complexity, and symbolic style have made his story the most enduring monument of fin-de-siècle disillusionment.

More insistently than the other quest romances, *Heart of Darkness* highlights the importance of narrative transmission from one man to another, in an interminable process. At the center of the narrative is Kurtz's story, available to us only in fragments. It is told by the seaman Charlie Marlow, who has traveled up the river in quest of Kurtz and in the process has discovered and revealed his own heart of complicity with falsehood, savagery, and greed. Moreover, Marlow's story, too, is contained within a narrative frame and told by someone else: an unnamed ex-seaman who, along with Marlow and three other men, a Lawyer, an Accountant, and a Director of Companies, is on a yacht in the Thames where they have gathered for their weekly reunion. This narrator, too, has his moment of enlightened identification with the story; and finally, the readers of the story, in reconstructing the case study of Kurtz, form their own relation to darkness, horror, and truth. Conrad had imagined these readers as the masculine audience for *Blackwood's:* "One was in decent company there," he commented, "and had a good sort of public. There isn't a single club and messroom and man-of-war in the British Seas and Dominions which hasn't its copy of Maga."

But while *male* readers in the club, messroom, and cabin can share in the narrative transmission of Conrad's story, it is much more difficult for a woman reader to identify with the process or themes of the quest. As the feminist critic Nina Pelikan Straus observes, "Marlow speaks in *Heart of Darkness* to other men, and although he speaks *about* women, there is no indication that women might be included among his hearers. . . . The peculiar density and inaccessibility of *Heart of Darkness* may be the result of its extremely masculine historical referentiality, its insistence on a male circle of readers."[1]

This is so not only because no women are named or specified in Marlow's audience, but because the terms in which Marlow sees the world exclude women from knowledge of the dark truth. From the very beginning, Marlow's quest is one which women can aid but never understand. Frustrated in his efforts to find a job that will take him to the "place of darkness" in the middle of the map, Marlow becomes so desperate that he uses the influence of his aunt: "I, Charlie Marlow, set the women to work—to get a job. Heavens!" Yet although his aunt can help him, she cannot understand

[1]Nina Pelikan Straus, "The Exclusion of the Intended from Secret Sharing in Conrad's *Heart of Darkness,*" *Novel* 20 (Winter 1987): 124.

what he is doing, and embarrasses him by babbling religious humbug about "weaning those ignorant millions from their horrid ways." "It's queer how out of touch with truth women are," Marlow ruminates. "They live in a world of their own, and there has never been anything like it, and never can be. It is too beautiful altogether, and if they were to set it up it would go to pieces before the first sunset."

5 His attitude towards women is one of many details that have led critics to see Marlow as Kurtz's double, a theme brilliantly emphasized in the plan Orson Welles had in the late 1930s for a film of *Heart of Darkness* in which he would play both Marlow and Kurtz. Marlow has a first glimpse of Kurtz as a kindred spirit when he sees a sketch that Kurtz has painted, "representing a woman, draped and blindfolded, carrying a lighted torch." This image of a woman bearing a light she cannot see strikes Marlow as "sinister," but he responds to it instantly with curiosity and a kind of empathy for Kurtz. As the stationmaster tells Marlow, "The same people who sent him specially also recommended you." In fact, the text holds out hints that Marlow will replace Kurtz, take over his life—either by becoming mad and assuming Kurtz's role as God in the Congo, or by marrying his Intended back in the Old World.

Despite his skepticism and revulsion, Marlow comes to feel that Kurtz is a "remarkable man," a man who dared to "step over the threshold of the invisible." His cry "the horror!" is "an affirmation, a moral victory paid for by innumerable defeats, by abominable terrors, by abominable satisfactions." In order for Marlow to be loyal to Kurtz's victory and to protect his world of empowering but awful knowledge, it must be kept from non-initiates. He does not immediately tell his story when he returns. First he is ill, wrestling with death as Kurtz has done and coming to appreciate the greater defiance with which Kurtz has faced the abyss. The fever is a "passage through some inconceivable world that had no hope in it and no desire"; it is a transition from the heart of darkness back to European "civilization." Returning to Brussels, Marlow feels a sense of election and specialness that distinguishes him from the irritating Belgians "hurrying through the streets to filch a little money from each other, to devour their infamous cookery, to gulp their unwholesome beer, to dream their insignificant and silly dreams." When Company officials and distant cousins of Kurtz appear, he refuses to give up information. But he has some letters and a portrait of Kurtz's fiancée, who strikes him as different from her countrymen; she is beautiful, honest, mature. Yet when Marlow calls on her he feels that he must protect her naive faith in Kurtz by lying about what he has seen and heard. The exchange between Marlow and the Intended, according to Conrad, was the most important part of the story: "The interview of the man and the girl locks in—as it were—the whole 30,000 words of narrative description into one suggestive view of a whole phase of life, and makes of that story something quite on another plane than an anecdote of a man who went mad in the Center of Africa."[2] Their dialogue is intensely ironic; Marlow is drawn repeatedly into colluding with her idealistic view of Kurtz, al-

[2]Quoted in *Heart of Darkness,* ed. Robert Kimbrough (New York: Norton Critical Edition, 1963), p. 124.

though all his responses have a double meaning for the reader: "'His end,' said I, with dull anger stirring in me, 'was in every way worthy of his life.'"

We may take this as a chivalrous white lie, meant to spare her feelings and leave her with her memories intact. But the symbolic dimensions of the story suggest otherwise. In keeping the truth about Kurtz from the Intended, Marlow ensures the continuation of the double worlds of men and women. "They—the women, I mean—are out of it—should be out of it. We must help them stay in that beautiful world of their own, lest ours get worse." Nina Straus interprets Marlow's gesture as his unconscious unwillingness to share his knowledge and love for Kurtz with a woman. "Marlow's protectiveness is no longer seen in the service of woman's deluded desires, but serves the therapeutic end of keeping the woman/intended mute."[3]

In this interview, the Intended reminds Marlow of Kurtz's African mistress, whom he has seen in the jungle: "She walked with measured steps, draped in striped and fringed cloths, treading the earth proudly, with a slight jingle and flash of barbarous ornaments. She carried her head high; her hair was done in the shape of a helmet; she had brass leggings to the knees, brass wire gauntlets to the elbow, a crimson spot on her tawny cheek, innumerable necklaces of glass beads on her neck; bizarre things, charms, gifts of witch-men, that hung about her, glittered and trembled at every step. . . . She was savage and superb, wild-eyed and magnificent; there was something ominous and stately in her deliberate progress." Ian Watt calls this woman "the most affirmative image in the narrative, the embodiment of the confident natural energy of the African wilderness"; but in another Conradian sense, while privileged Europeans are kept in the dark about the brute realities of imperialism, human greed, and cruelty, black women *are* the dark. As in the other tales, *Heart of Darkness* pursues the penetration of a female wilderness, here a place of lassitude, paralysis, darkness, and suffocation. Conrad told an interviewer in 1914 that the sight that had most impressed him in his life was "a certain woman, a Negress. That was in Africa. Hung with bracelets and necklaces, she was walking in front of a railroad station."[4] At the heart of the heart of darkness is this image of the black jungle queen.

Conrad's queen reappears as the "dark exogamous bride" of Levi-Strauss's *Tristes Tropiques,* who epitomizes the seductive and threatening Other and who has been allegorically allied with the notion of wilderness itself.[5] Not only modernist novelists but also twentieth-century anthropologists learned their narrative techniques from Conrad. While late-nineteenth-century British anthropologists such as W. H. R. Rivers were influenced by reading male quest romances by Haggard and Kipling, Conrad's dark story of the divided self in the culture of the Other became the model for a younger generation of modern ethnographers. "[W. H. R.]

[3]Straus, "The Exclusion of the Intended," p. 134.

[4]Edmund A. Bojarski, "Joseph Conrad's Sentimental Journey: A Fiftieth Anniversary Review," *Texas Quarterly* 7 (1964): 164.

[5]See Cleo McNelly, "Natives, Women, and Claude Levi-Strauss," *Massachusetts Review* 16 (1975): 6–29; and Nina Pelikan Straus, "Exclusion of the Intended," pp. 128–29.

Rivers is the Rider Haggard of Anthropology," Bronislaw Malinowski remarked at the beginning of his career; "I shall be the Conrad!"[6] By this vow Malinowski primarily meant that he would attempt to bring to his analysis of Trobriand people the subtlety, profundity, and wisdom of Conrad the artist. But he also experienced the gap between the serene and enlightened self of his ethnographic persona, and the Kurtz-like hostile and threatened self of his personal diaries.

10 Orson Welles never made the film he had planned, but Francis Ford Coppola's film revision of *Heart of Darkness* in *Apocalypse Now* (1979) provides a fascinating modern gloss on questions of male bonding, transference, and politics. By using Conrad's story and structures in a film about the American experience in Vietnam, Coppola revised the narrative forms of the male quest romance in contemporary terms. Most Conrad scholars, however, were looking for a reverent imitation and were highly critical of Coppola's free adaptation, in which Captain Willard (played by Martin Sheen), a character based on Marlow, is sent to Cambodia to assassinate Colonel Kurtz (played by Marlon Brando), a renegade Green Beret officer who has set himself up in a Montagnard compound as a god. Conrad specialists were both reluctant to give over the authority of their sacred work to a mere filmmaker and obtuse about the meaning of both film process and a Vietnam experience that might not be representable through modernist techniques. It was a spectacular display of academic snobbery. In a symposium in the journal *Conradiana* in 1981, for example, four scholars denounced the film as "fraudulent and glib" and "altogether confusing." Defending their Conrad against Coppola, the Hollywood hack who had previously made *The Godfather,* the academics compared the film to Disneyland, a "Horrorland" of wretched excess in contrast to Conrad's elegant modernist "restraint." They found the voice-over narration written by Michael Herr, author of the Vietnam memoir *Dispatches,* pedestrian compared to Conrad's impressionistic rhetoric, and cited the first line spoken by Willard—"Saigon. Shit."—as an instance of the way he "grunts in the tense amoral clichés of pulp detective fiction."[7]

But with every year since, the brilliance of Coppola's version has become more apparent—not as an adaptation of *Heart of Darkness,* but rather as a contemporary meditation and interpretation, a new work that alludes to Conrad but that also can be read back into the earlier work. Coppola finds extraordinary visual images for Conrad's impressionistic prose, such as the helicopter, used from the first frames of the film for its whirring blades and strange clicking noise, through its nightmarish end, when crashed helicopters seem like dead prehistoric birds burning in the jungle trees. Surrealistic scenes such as the cold-blooded helicopter attack on the beach, with its mechanized cavalry charge and rousing soundtrack of "The Ride of the Valkyrie," both shock the audience and also marshal all the ex-

[6]Bronislaw Malinowski, quoted in James Clifford, *The Predicament of Culture: Twentieth-Century Ethnography, Literature, and Art* (Cambridge: Harvard University Press, 1988), p. 96.

[7]See *Conradiana,* 13 (1981), pp. 37, 41, 55. 1981. But see also Garrett Stewart, "Coppola's Conrad: the Repetitions of Complicity," *Critical Inquiry* 7 (Spring 1981): 455–74. I am indebted to Garrett Stewart's brilliant and sympathetic analysis of *Apocalypse Now.*

citement we have learned to associate with such moments in a lifetime of watching adventure movies. Like Conrad, Coppola engages in a critique of imperialism, but he also ironically affirms the pleasure of the film medium and the spectacle of the epic screen.

[*1990*]

## TOPICS FOR CRITICAL THINKING AND WRITING

1. Do you agree with Showalter (paragraph 7) that "the symbolic dimensions of the story" prevent us from taking Marlow's report to the Intended as "a chivalrous white lie"? Explain.
2. In paragraph 7 Showalter quotes Nina Straus's interpretation of Marlow's lie. How convincing do you find this interpretation? Explain.
3. In paragraph 8 Showalter quotes Ian Watt's comment that Kurtz's mistress "is the most affirmative image in the narrative." Do you agree? Can you reconcile Watt's opinion with Achebe's comments, printed earlier in this chapter?
4. If you have seen Coppola's *Apocalypse Now,* do you agree with Showalter's evaluation? Explain.

## IAN WATT

*Ian Watt, emeritus professor of English at Stanford University, begins this discussion of Conrad's use of symbolism by quoting the passages on pages 748–49 that describe Marlow's trip to the trading company to receive his appointment. In this excerpt from* Conrad in the Nineteenth Century *(1979), Watt indicates how Conrad's symbolism arises from vivid, particular details of character, scene, and setting. (The title is the editors'.)*

# *The Symbolism of the Two Knitters*

Several critics have made the two knitters a primary basis for a large-scale symbolic interpretation of *Heart of Darkness* in which Marlow's whole journey becomes a version of the traditional descent into hell, such as that in the sixth book of Virgil's *Aeneid,*[1] and in Dante's *Inferno.* This kind of critical interpretation assumes that the symbolic reference of the verbal sign must be closed rather than open, and that it arises, not from the natural and inherent associations of the object, but from a preestablished body of ideas, stories, or myths. The present passage certainly makes symbolic reference to associations of this kind; Marlow presents his own experience in the general perspective of the pagan and Christian traditions of a journey to the underworld: this is made sufficiently explicit when he talks of the knitters "guarding the door of Darkness," and of the two youths "being piloted

[1]Lillian Feder, "Marlow's Descent into Hell," *Nineteenth-Century Fiction* 9 (1955): 280–92.

over." But this is not the only symbolic reference of the passage, nor the most important; and there is no reason to assume that the movement from the literal to the symbolic must be centripetal. Only some such assumption could have impelled one critic to assert that there is a "close structural parallel between *Heart of Darkness* and the *Inferno,*" and proceed to equate the company station with Limbo and the central station with the abode of the fraudulent, while making Kurtz both a "traitor to kindred" and a Lucifer.[2]

One obvious practical objection to this kind of symbolic interpretation is that it alerts our attention too exclusively to a few aspects of the narrative—to those which seem to provide clues that fit the assumed unitary and quasi-allegorical frame of symbolic reference. This leads us to interrogate the text only in those terms, and to ask such questions as: Why does Conrad give us only *two* fates? Which one is Clotho the spinner? and which Lachesis the weaver? Did the Greeks know about knitting anyway? Where are the shears? What symbolic meaning can there be in the fact that the thin one lets people *in* to the room and then *out* again—a birth and death ritual, perhaps? Lost in such unfruitful preoccupations, our imaginations will hardly be able to respond to the many other symbolic clues in the passage, or even to the many other meanings in those details which have secured our attention.

In fact a multiplicity of historical and literary associations pervades the scene in the anteroom; and this multiplicity surely combines to place the two knitters in a much more universal perspective. There is, most obviously, the heartless unconcern manifested throughout the ages by the spectators at a variety of ordeals that are dangerous or fatal to the protagonists. This unconcern is what the fates have in common with the two other main historical parallels evoked in the passage—the French *tricoteuses* callously knitting at the guillotine, and the Roman crowds to whom the gladiators address their scornful farewell in Marlow's rather pretentious interjection: "*Ave!* Old knitter of black wool, *Morituri te salutant.*"

Within the context of *Heart of Darkness* as a whole the function of these three examples of symbolic reference is local and circumscribed; like Marlow's earlier historical allusions to Drake and Franklin they are dropped as soon as made; they are not intended to link up with other allusions into a single cryptographic system which gives the main symbolic meaning of the work as a whole. One reason for this is surely that any continuing symbolic parallel would undermine the literal interest and significance of the narrative at every compositional level, from the essential conflict of the plot, to the details of its narrative presentation.

5 The present passage, then, gives clear evidence of how Conrad aimed at a continuous immediacy of detail which had symbolic reference that was primarily of a natural, open, and multivocal kind. Marlow presents a highly selective but vivid series of details; they are for the most part given as raw and unexplained observations, and the autonomy and isolation of each particular image seems to impel the reader to larger surmise. There is, for instance, the approach of the thin knitter who "got up and walked straight at me—still knitting with downcast eyes—and only just as I began to think of getting out of her way, as you would for a somnambulist, stood still, and looked up. Her dress was as plain as an umbrella-cover."

[2]Robert O. Evans, "Conrad's Underworld," *Modern Fiction Studies* 2 (1956):59; 60.

If we submit ourselves to the evocative particularity of these intensely visualised details, their symbolic connotations take us far beyond our primary sense of the fateful, uncanny, and impassive atmosphere of the scene; we are driven to a larger awareness of a rigid, mechanical, blind, and automatised world. If we attempt to explain the sources of this awareness we can point to the way that the thin knitter does not speak to Marlow, nor even, apparently, see him; her movements are unrelated to other human beings. The knitter's appearance increases this sense of the nonhuman; her shape recalls an umbrella and its tight black cover; there has been no effort to soften the functional contours of its hard and narrow ugliness with rhythmic movements, rounded forms, or pleasing colours. It is not that the knitter reminds us of the classical Fates which really matters, but that she is herself a fate—a dehumanised death in life to herself and to others, and thus a prefiguring symbol of what the trading company does to its creatures.

Some of the images in the passage are representative in a limited and mainly pictorial way; the older knitter, for example, with her wart and her flat cloth slippers, becomes a stark visual image of physical and spiritual deformity combined with imperturbable self-complacence. But there is another, larger, and to some extent contrary, tendency, where the extreme selectivity of Marlow's memory draws our attention to his state of mind at the time. For instance, when Marlow comments about the tycoon: "He shook hands I fancy," his uncertainty suggests that his consciousness was occupied with other matters. Marlow omits much that would certainly be mentioned in an autobiography, or a naturalist novel; we are not, for instance, given the details of Marlow's contract, or the name of the people. This omission of proper names is a particularly typical symbolist procedure—in Maeterlinck, for instance, or in Kafka. The general reason for the strategy is clear: most of the details about the narrative object are omitted, so that what details remain, liberated from the bonds and irrelevancies of the purely circumstantial and contingent, can be recognised as representatives of larger ideas and attitudes.

*[1979]*

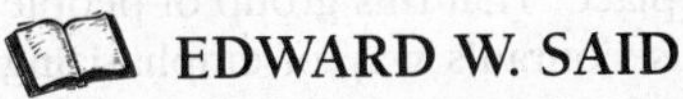

## EDWARD W. SAID

*Edward Said, University Professor at Columbia University, is best known for* Orientalism *(1978), and related studies of literature, literary theory, and cultural history. In this excerpt from his* Culture and Imperialism *(1993), Said notes how Conrad uses his character Marlow to present the worldview—dominant, all-pervasive, controlling—of imperialism. (The title is the editors'.)*

# *The Imperial Attitude*

This imperial attitude is, I believe, beautifully captured in the complicated and rich narrative form of Conrad's great novella *Heart of Darkness,* written between 1898 and 1899. On the one hand, the narrator Marlow acknowledges the tragic predicament of all speech—that "it is impossible to convey the life-sensation of any given epoch of one's existence—that which makes its truth, its meaning—its subtle and penetrating essence. . . . We live, as we dream—alone"—yet still manages to convey the enormous power of Kurtz's African experience through his own overmastering narrative of his voyage into the African interior toward Kurtz. This narrative in turn is connected directly with the redemptive force, as well as the waste and horror, of Europe's mission in the dark world. Whatever is lost or elided or even simply made up in Marlow's immensely compelling recitation is compensated for in the narrative's sheer historical momentum, the temporal forward movement—with digressions, descriptions, exciting encounters, and all. Within the narrative of how he journeyed to Kurtz's Inner Station, whose source and authority he now becomes, Marlow moves backward and forward materially in small and large spirals, very much the way episodes in the course of his journey up-river are then incorporated by the principal forward trajectory into what he renders as "the heart of Africa."

Thus Marlow's encounter with the improbably white-suited clerk in the middle of the jungle furnishes him with several digressive paragraphs, as does his meeting later with the semi-crazed, harlequin-like Russian who has been so affected by Kurtz's gifts. Yet underlying Marlow's inconclusiveness, his evasions, his arabesque meditations on his feelings and ideas, is the unrelenting course of the journey itself, which, despite all the many obstacles, is sustained through the jungle, through time, through hardship, to the heart of it all, Kurtz's ivory-trading empire. Conrad wants us to see how Kurtz's great looting adventure, Marlow's journey up the river, and the narrative itself all share a common theme: Europeans performing acts of imperial mastery and will in (or about) Africa.

What makes Conrad different from the other colonial writers who were his contemporaries is that, for reasons having partly to do with the colonialism that turned him, a Polish expatriate, into an employee of the imperial system, he was so self-conscious about what he did. Like most of his other tales, therefore, *Heart of Darkness* cannot just be a straightforward recital of Marlow's adventures: it is also a dramatization of Marlow himself, the former wanderer in colonial regions, telling his story to a group of British listeners at a particular time and in a specific place. That this group of people is drawn largely from the business world is Conrad's way of emphasizing the fact that during the 1890s the business of empire, once an adventurous and often individualistic enterprise, had become the empire of business. (Coincidentally we should note that at about the same time Halford Mackinder, an explorer, geographer, and Liberal Imperialist, gave a series of lectures on imperialism at the London Institute of Bankers: perhaps Conrad knew about this.) Although the almost oppressive force of Marlow's narrative leaves us with a quite accurate sense that there is no way out of the sovereign historical force of imperialism, and that it has the power of a system representing as well as speaking for everything within its dominion, Conrad shows us that what Marlow does is contingent, acted out for a set of like-minded British hearers, and limited to that situation.

Yet neither Conrad nor Marlow gives us a full view of what is *outside* the world-conquering attitudes embodied by Kurtz, Marlow, the circle of listeners on the deck of the *Nellie,* and Conrad. By that I mean that *Heart of Darkness* works so effectively because its politics and aesthetics are, so to speak, imperialist, which in the closing years of the nineteenth century seemed to be at the same time an aesthetic, politics, and even epistemology inevitable and unavoidable. For if we cannot truly understand someone else's experience and if we must therefore depend upon the assertive authority of the sort of power that Kurtz wields as a white man in the jungle or that Marlow, another white man, wields as narrator, there is no use looking for other, non-imperialist alternatives; the system has simply eliminated them and made them unthinkable. The circularity, the perfect closure of the whole thing is not only aesthetically but also mentally unassailable.

5 Conrad is so self-conscious about situating Marlow's tale in a narrative moment that he allows us simultaneously to realize after all that imperialism, far from swallowing up its own history, was taking place in and was circumscribed by a larger history, one just outside the tightly inclusive circle of Europeans on the deck of the *Nellie*. As yet, however, no one seemed to inhabit that region, and so Conrad left it empty.

[*1993*]

## GERALD GRAFF

*Gerald Graff, a professor of English at the University of Chicago, has been especially concerned with recent critical theory and with its effect on the ways in which literature is taught. In the following selection he talks about the effect Achebe's essay* *(see page 804)* *has had on his teaching.*

# *Teaching the Politics of* Heart of Darkness

Since I started teaching in the mid-1960s, a work I have assigned frequently is Joseph Conrad's classic *Heart of Darkness,* published in 1899. When I first assigned the novella in 1966 or 1967, I taught it in much the way it had been taught to me in college in the late 1950s, as a profound meditation on a universal moral theme. I presented Conrad's story of the destruction of the idealistic trader Mr. Kurtz as a universal parable of the precarious status of civilized reason in a world overly confident of its having outgrown the primitive and the irrational.

My reading of *Heart of Darkness* as a universal parable of reason and unreason pointed up something in the novel that I still think is important. But this reading also depended on my not seeing certain things or not treating them as worth thinking about. Of little interest to me were the facts that Conrad sets his novella in the Congo in the high period of European colonialism and that he chooses subjugated black Africans to represent the primitive, irrational forces that are Mr. Kurtz's undoing. Conrad, after all, could have chosen any number of ways to symbolize the forces of primitive unreason. That he happened to choose black Africa seemed incidental to his main intention, which was to make a statement about the human condition that would transcend mere questions of nationality and race.

. . . I had been trained to believe that literature is "an impartial phenomenon that addresses essential questions beyond and apart from politics," and I assumed that these transcendent concerns were what the teaching of literature is all about. The subjugation of black Africans was the sort of thing that might interest historians, sociologists, and political scientists, but if the job was to treat literature *as* literature, it was at best of ancillary interest. After all, if God had wanted us to raise political questions in teaching literature, why had he put the departments of English and sociology in separate buildings?

It never occurred to me to ask how a black person might read the story, and the fact that only a small number of black students appeared in my classes helped assure that the question did not come up. Had it come up, however, I would have found it beside the point. What difference did it make who you were and what your history was when you read a literary work? The point of studying literature was to rise above those traces of your upbringing and history. It was Conrad and his vision that mattered, and reflecting on the position from which you read Conrad could only distract attention from his vision to your own narcissistic special interests.

5 Today I teach *Heart of Darkness* very differently. One critical work that caused me to change my approach was an essay by the Nigerian novelist Chinua Achebe, entitled "An Image of Africa: Racism in Conrad's *Heart of Darkness.*" Achebe argues that Conrad's presentation of black Africa is thoroughly racist. And he is able to accumulate a painfully large number of quotations from both the novel and Conrad's letters and diaries that do reveal how cruelly stereotyped Conrad's thinking about the black African is. . . .

Even if Achebe's interpretation of Conrad is unfair, as I think it is, it forced me to rethink my assumptions about art and politics. For according to Achebe, Conrad's novel is not simply a disinterested work of art, but a text that played and may still be playing an active role in constructing the Western image of black Africa. "Conrad did not originate the image of Africa which we find in his book," Achebe writes. "It was and is the dominant image of Africa in the Western imagination and Conrad merely brought the peculiar gifts of his own mind to bear on it. For reasons which can certainly use close psychological inquiry the West seems to suffer deep anxieties about the precariousness of its civilization and to have a need for constant reassurance by comparison with Africa." Achebe's point is one that recent literary and cultural "theory" has been making, though I think with more complications and qualifications: that literary representations are not simply neutral aesthetic descriptions but interventions that act upon the world they describe. This, in fact, is the point underlying many recent critiques of the idea of *objectivity,* critiques that are poorly understood by their critics; the point is not that there is no truth but that descriptions influence the situations they describe, thereby complicating the problem of truth.

In short, I was forced to rethink not just my interpretation of *Heart of Darkness* but my theoretical assumptions about literature. First, I was forced to recognize that I *had* theoretical assumptions. I had previously thought I was simply teaching the truth about *Heart of Darkness,* "the text itself." I now had to recognize that I had been teaching an interpretation of the text, one that was shaped by a certain *theory* that told me what was and was not worth noticing and emphasizing in my classroom. I had been unable to see my theory *as* a theory because I was living so comfortably inside it.

. . .

Far from debasing the academic standards of my courses, teaching *Heart of Darkness* as I now teach it seems to me to have made my courses considerably *more* challenging than they were previously. For my students now have to be more reflective about their assumptions than they had to be before, and they are now asked to take part in a set of complex debates that I previously did not expect them to. Nor, I think, do the critical and theoretical debates I teach distract students from the close reading of literary works in themselves. When it seemed to me at one point that my students were agreeing too easily with Achebe, I corrected by restating the aesthetic reading of *Heart of Darkness* and the need to return constantly to the verbal particulars of the text.

In the end I think Achebe's critique pushes my students to a closer reading of the verbal and stylistic particularity of *Heart of Darkness* than they would achieve through an exclusively aesthetic approach. Then, too, I think it also enables them to understand more clearly just what an "aesthetic approach" is, since they now have something to compare it with. Before, students would look blank when I used words like "aesthetic" (or "traditional," "humanistic," etc.), as if to say, "'Aesthetic' as opposed to *what?*" Introducing a challenge to traditional values helps students understand what is at stake in embracing or rejecting them.

[*1992*]

## TOPICS FOR CRITICAL THINKING AND WRITING

1. In his first paragraph Graff summarizes his early view of the story. Does the rest of his discussion convince you that this view was inadequate?
2. In paragraph 4 Graff raises the question of whether black students reading *Heart of Darkness* respond differently from white students. To what extent do you think race, gender, and class influence *your* reading of this story? Of other literary works? For instance, if you are a woman, do you think you read, say, Updike's "A & P" or Poe's "The Cask of Amontillado" or a play by Shakespeare differently from a man? Explain.

# A SAMPLE STUDENT ESSAY

Edith Jones

English 101: Introduction to Literature

November 15, 1995

Is Joseph Conrad a Racist?

Some of Conrad's descriptions of African people bothered me when I was reading Heart of Darkness, and after I read Chinua Achebe's forceful essay they bothered me even more. But while I think that Achebe is right to criticize signs of Conrad's racism, I believe that the novella is more complicated than he suggests. In particular, Achebe seems to me much too quick to dismiss any evidence that might balance his negative judgment, and he strikes me as too determined to make the narrator Marlow into Conrad's spokesman.

Achebe does cite many passages that show Conrad's stereotyping of the natives, and there is even more evidence than he supplies. I remember feeling uncomfortable with Conrad's language about the helmsman, an "athletic black" who "sported a pair of brass earrings, wore a blue cloth wrapper from the waist to the ankles, and thought all the world of himself. He was the most unstable kind of fool I had ever seen" (p. 775). And then there is that passage about the shrieking natives as they come around the corner of the house: "streams of human beings--of naked human beings--with spears in their hands, with bows, with shields, with wild glances and savage movements" (pp. 786-87). In one instance, Conrad presents a picture of an individual African only to say what a contemptible fool the person was; in the other one, he makes the natives all the same--they are not individuals at all, just a savage stream.

It is misleading, however, to say "Conrad," since it is not Conrad, but Marlow, who is telling the tale. We should not forget that the author is not identical to his character, and that's the mistake that Achebe makes here. To give Achebe his due, he admits that we have to consider who presents the story to us--that it's not Conrad directly, but Marlow. Yet no sooner does Achebe make this point than he claims that Conrad himself approves of Marlow's descriptions and judgments. Maybe Achebe is correct, but he does not provide enough analysis and evidence to convince me.

Achebe needs to balance his interpretation with passages like this one from the first chapter, where Conrad gives Marlow's comparison of the Roman and European kinds of imperialism:

> They [i.e., the Romans] were conquerors, and for that you want only brute force. . . . It was just robbery with violence, aggravated murder on a great scale, and men going at it blind--as is very proper for those who tackle a darkness. The conquest of the earth, which mostly means the taking it away from those who have a different complexion or slightly flatter noses than ourselves, is not a pretty thing when you look into it too much. What redeems it is the idea only. (745)

Here Conrad's language calls attention to the way in which the imperialists, whether ancient Roman or modern European, use racism to justify their conquests. Marlow's words reveal that imperialism is nothing but raw theft--"taking it away."

Interestingly, Marlow tries to maintain that there is a _good_ imperialism--one that somehow, through an "idea," redeems the violent robbery of the native peoples' land. But I think that Conrad is being very subtle here; his point is that this is just the sort of thing that imperialists _want_ to believe. They want to believe that what they are doing is different from, and better than, what others have done. Marlow states that imperialism is based on racism--he admits that. But then he declares that it is acceptable as long as an idea saves it and makes it honorable. But what idea? Whose idea? Can any idea ever be important enough to make racist victimization of native people into something that is acceptable? These are the questions that Conrad expects the reader to ask about Marlow's words.

There are many similar passages in Heart of Darkness, and they tend to support the interpretations that Elaine Showalter and Edward W. Said give--that Conrad is exposing and criticizing imperialism, not endorsing it and the racist attitudes that reinforce it. Marlow is the racist, not Conrad.

Works Cited

Achebe, Chinua. Hopes and Impediments. London: Heinemann, 1988. 1-13.

Joseph Conrad, Heart of Darkness. In Literature: Thinking, Reading, and Writing Critically, 2nd ed. Eds. Sylvan Barnet et al. New York: HarperCollins, 1996. 742-801.

Said, Edward W. Culture and Imperialism. New York: Knopf, 1993.

Showalter, Elaine. Sexual Anarchy. New York: Viking, 1990.

## TOPICS FOR CRITICAL THINKING AND WRITING

1. The student refers to Achebe's essay and lists it in her Works Cited, but she does not quote from the essay. Nor does she quote Elaine Showalter and Edward W. Said, though she refers to their writings as well. Would quotation have strengthened this essay? Are there specific sentences in these critics' pieces (reprinted in this book) that you would have quoted if this were your essay?
2. Does the student make a convincing argument about the shortcomings of Achebe's interpretation? Can you locate passages in *Heart of Darkness* that give further support to her argument, or is it your view that

the weight of the evidence supports the position that Achebe has taken?

3. Focus on the third paragraph. This is the moment when the student states her main objection to Achebe's reading. Do you find her objection persuasive? Could this paragraph be improved in style and content? Note: In pondering these questions, you should refer back to Achebe's section on Marlow, which begins, "It might be contended, of course . . ." (p. 807).
4. What about the brief concluding paragraph? Is it effective? Should anything be added to it?

# PART THREE

## *Poetry*

# CHAPTER 15

# *Approaching Poetry: Responding in Writing*

The title of this chapter is a bit misleading, since we have already spent a few pages discussing two poems in Chapter 1, "Reading and Responding to Literature." But here we will begin again, taking a different approach.

First, some brief advice.

1. Read the poem aloud, or, if you can't bring yourself to read aloud, at least sound the poem in your mind's ear. Try to catch the speaker's tone of voice.
2. Pay attention not only to the black marks on the white paper but also to the white spaces between groups of lines. If a space follows some lines, pause briefly, and take the preceding lines as a unit of thought.
3. Read the poem a second and a third time. Now that you know how it ends, you'll be able to see the connections between the beginning and what follows.

## LANGSTON HUGHES

*The following short poem is by Langston Hughes (1902–67), an African-American writer, born in Joplin, Missouri, who lived part of his youth in Mexico, spent a year at Columbia University, served as a merchant seaman, and worked in a Paris nightclub, where he showed some of his poems to Dr. Alain Locke, a strong advocate of African-American literature. Encouraged by Locke, when Hughes returned to the United States he continued to write, publishing fiction, plays, essays, and biogra-*

*phies; he also founded theaters, gave public readings, and was, in short, a highly visible presence. The poem that we reprint, "Harlem" (1951), provided Lorraine Hansberry with the title of her well-known play,* A Raisin in the Sun *(1958). For a generous selection of poems by Langston Hughes, see Chapter 28.*

## *Harlem*

What happens to a dream deferred?

Does it dry up
like a raisin in the sun?
Or fester like a sore—
And then run?
Does it stink like rotten meat?
Or crust and sugar over—
like a syrupy sweet?

Maybe it just sags
like a heavy load.

*Or does it explode?*

[*1951*]

Read the poem at least twice, and then think about its effect on you.

1. Do you find the poem interesting? Why or why not?
2. Do some things in it interest you more than others? If so, why?
3. Does anything in it puzzle you? If so, what?

Before reading any further, you might jot down your responses to some of these questions. And, whatever your responses, can you point to features of the poem to account for them?

Of course, different readers will respond at least somewhat differently to any work. On the other hand, since writers want to communicate, they try to control their readers' responses, and they count on their readers to understand the meanings of words as they understand them. Thus, Hughes assumed that his readers knew that Harlem was the site of a large African-American community in New York City.

Let's assume that the reader understands Hughes is talking about Harlem, New York, and, further, that the reader understands the "dream deferred" to refer to the unfulfilled hopes of African-Americans who live in a dominant white society. But Hughes does not say "hopes," he says "dream," and he does not say "unfulfilled," he says "deferred." You might ask yourself exactly what differences there are between these words. Next, when you have read the poem several times, you might think about which expression is better in the context, "Unfulfilled Hopes" or "Dream Deferred," and why.

## Thinking about "Harlem"

Let's turn to an analysis of the poem, an examination of how the parts fit. As you look at the poem, think about the parts, and jot down whatever notes come to mind. After you have written your own notes, consider the annotations of one student.

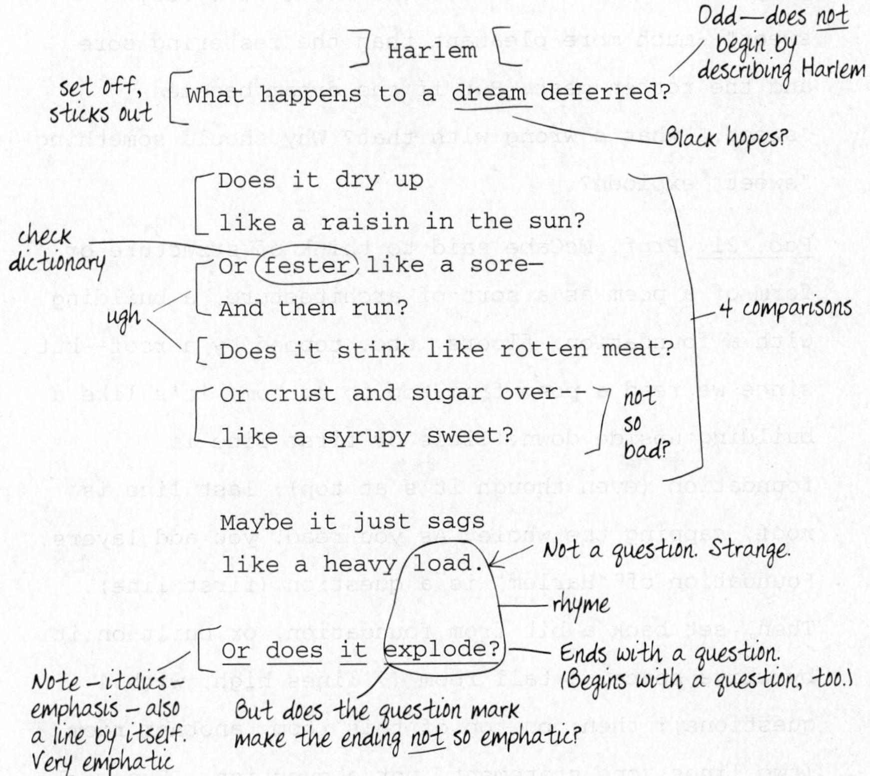

Harlem
What happens to a dream deferred?
Does it dry up
like a raisin in the sun?
Or fester like a sore—
And then run?
Does it stink like rotten meat?
Or crust and sugar over—
like a syrupy sweet?
Maybe it just sags
like a heavy load.
Or does it explode?
Odd—does not begin by describing Harlem
set off, sticks out
Black hopes?
check dictionary
ugh
4 comparisons
not so bad?
Not a question. Strange.
rhyme
Ends with a question. (Begins with a question, too.)
Note – italics – emphasis – also a line by itself. Very emphatic
But does the question mark make the ending not so emphatic?


These annotations chiefly get at the structure of the poem, the relationship of the parts. The student notices that the poem begins with a line set off by itself and ends with a line set off by itself, and he also notices that each of these lines is a question. Further, he indicates that each of these two lines is emphasized in other ways. The first begins further to the left than any of the other lines—as though the other lines are subheadings or are in some way subordinate—and the last is italicized. In short, he comments on the *structure* of the poem.

## Some Journal Entries

The student who made these annotations later wrote an entry in his journal:

> Feb. 18. Since the title is "Harlem," it's obvious that the "dream" is by African-American people. Also, obvious that Hughes thinks that if the "dream"

doesn't become real there may be riots ("explode"). I like "raisin in the sun" (maybe because I like the play), and I like the business about "a syrupy sweet"--much more pleasant than the festering sore and the rotten meat. But if the dream becomes "sweet," what's wrong with that? Why should something "sweet" explode?

Feb. 21. Prof. McCabe said to think of structure or form of a poem as a sort of architecture, a building with a foundation, floors, etc. topped by a roof--but since we read a poem from top to bottom, it's like a building upside down. Title or first line is foundation (even though it's at top); last line is roof, capping the whole. As you read, you add layers. Foundation of "Harlem" is a question (first line). Then, set back a bit from foundation, or built on it by white space, a tall room (7 lines high, with 4 questions); then, on top of this room, another room (two lines, one statement, not a question). Funny; I thought that in poems all stanzas are the same number of lines. Then--more white space, so another unit--the roof. Man, this roof is going to fall in--"explode." Not just the roof, maybe the whole house.

Feb. 21, pm. I get it; one line at start, one line at end; both are questions, but the last sort of says (because it is in italics) that it is the most likely answer to the question of the first line. The last line is also a question, but it's still an answer. The big stanza (7 lines) has 4 questions: 2 lines, 2 lines, 1 line, 2 lines. Maybe the switch to 1 line is to give some variety, so as not to be dull? It's exactly in the middle of the poem. I get the progress from raisin in the sun (dried, but not so terrible), to festering sore and to stinking meat, but I still don't see what's so bad about "a syrupy sweet." Is Hughes saying that after things are very bad they will get better? But why, then, the explosion at the end?

<u>Feb. 23.</u> "Heavy load" and "sags" in next-to-last stanza seems to me to suggest slaves with bales of cotton, or maybe poor cotton pickers dragging big sacks of cotton. Or maybe people doing heavy labor in Harlem. Anyway, very tired. Different from running sore and stinking meat earlier; not disgusting, but pressing down, deadening. Maybe <u>worse</u> than a sore or rotten meat--a hard, hopeless life. And then the last line. Just one line, no fancy (and disgusting) simile. Boom! Not just pressed down and tired, like maybe some racist whites think (hope?) blacks will be? Bang! Will there be survivors?

Drawing chiefly on these notes, the student jotted down some key ideas to guide him through a draft of an analysis of the poem. (The organization of the draft posed no problem; the student simply followed the organization of the poem.)

11 lines; short, but powerful; explosive
Question (first line)
Answers (set off by space & also indented)
"raisin in the sun": shrinking
"sore" } disgusting
"rotten meat"
"syrupy sweet": relief from disgusting comparisons
final question (last line): explosion?
  explosive (powerful) because:
    short, condensed, packed
    in italics
    stands by itself—like first line
    no fancy comparison; very direct

## Final Draft

**Here is the final analysis:**

Langston Hughes's "Harlem"

"Harlem" is a poem that is only eleven lines long, but it is charged with power. It explodes. Hughes sets the stage, so to speak, by telling us in the title that he is talking about Harlem, and then he begins by asking, "What happens to a dream deferred?" The rest of the poem is set off by being indented, as though it is the answer to his question. This answer is in three parts (three stanzas, of different lengths).

In a way, it's wrong to speak of the answer, since the rest of the poem consists of questions, but I think Hughes means that each question (for instance, does a "deferred" hope "dry up / like a raisin in the sun?") really is an answer, something that really has happened and that will happen again. The first question, "Does it dry up / like a raisin in the sun?," is a famous line. To compare hope to a raisin dried in the sun is to suggest a terrible shrinking. The next two comparisons are to a "sore" and to "rotten meat." These comparisons are less clever, but they are very effective because they are disgusting. Then, maybe because of the disgusting comparisons, he gives a comparison that is not at all disgusting. In this comparison he says that maybe the "dream deferred" will "crust and sugar over-- / like a syrupy sweet."

The seven lines with four comparisons are followed by a stanza of two lines with just one comparison:

Maybe it just sags
like a heavy load.

So if we thought that this postponed dream might finally turn into something "sweet," we were kidding ourselves. Hughes comes down to earth, in a short stanza, with an image of a heavy load, which probably also calls to mind images of people bent under heavy loads, maybe of cotton, or maybe just any sort of heavy load carried by African-Americans in Harlem and elsewhere.

The opening question ("What happens to a dream deferred?") was followed by four questions in seven lines, but now, with "Maybe it just sags/like a heavy load," we get a statement, as though the poet at last has found an answer. But at the end we get one more question, set off by itself and in italics: "Or does it explode?" This line itself is explosive for three reasons: it is short, it is italicized, and it is a stanza in itself. It's also interesting that this line, unlike the earlier lines, does not use a simile. It's almost as though Hughes is saying, "OK, we've had enough fancy ways of talking about this terrible situation; here it is, straight."

## TOPICS FOR CRITICAL THINKING AND WRITING

1. The student's analysis suggests that the comparison with "a syrupy sweet" is a deliberately misleading happy ending that serves to make the real ending even more powerful. In class another student suggested that Hughes may be referring to African-Americans who play the Uncle Tom, people who adopt a smiling manner in order to cope with an oppressive society. Which explanation do you prefer, and why? What do you think of combining the two? Or can you offer a different explanation?
2. Do you suppose that virtually all African-Americans respond to this poem in a way that is substantially different from the way virtually all Caucasians or Asian-Americans respond? Explain your position.

# CHAPTER 16

# *Lyric Poetry*

For the ancient Greeks, a **lyric** was a song accompanied by a lyre. It was short, and it usually expressed a single emotion, such as joy or sorrow. The word is now used more broadly, referring to a poem that, neither narrative (telling a story) nor strictly dramatic (performed by actors), is an emotional or reflective soliloquy. Still, it is rarely very far from a singing voice. James Joyce saw the lyric as the "verbal vesture of an instant of emotion, a rhythmical cry such as ages ago cheered on the man who pulled at the oar." Such lyrics, too, were sung more recently than "ages ago." Here is a song that American slaves sang when rowing heavy loads.

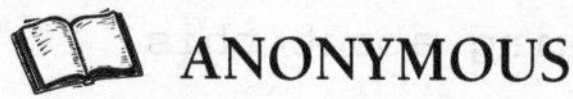

## *Michael Row the Boat Ashore*

Michael row the boat ashore, Hallelujah!
Michael's boat's a freedom boat, Hallelujah!
Sister, help to trim the sail, Hallelujah!
Jordan stream is wide and deep, Hallelujah!
Freedom stands on the other side, Hallelujah!

We might pause for a moment to comment on why people sing at work. There are at least three reasons: (1) work done rhythmically goes more efficiently; (2) the songs relieve the boredom of the work; and (3) the songs—whether narrative or lyrical—provide something of an outlet for the workers' frustrations.

Speaking roughly, we can say that whereas a narrative (whether in prose or poetry) is set in the past, telling what happened, a lyric is set in the present, catching a speaker in a moment of expression. But a lyric can, of course, glance backward or forward, as in this folk song, usually called "Careless Love."

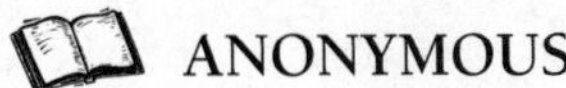

## ANONYMOUS

### *Careless Love*

Love, O love, O careless love,
You see what careless love can do.
When I wore my apron low,
Couldn't keep you from my do,°
  Fare you well, fare you well.
Now I wear my apron high,
Scarce see you passin' by,
  Fare you well, fare you well.

Notice, too, that a lyric, like a narrative, can have a plot: "Michael" moves toward the idea of freedom, and "Careless Love" implies a story of desertion—something has happened between the time that the singer could not keep the man from her door and now, when she "scarce" sees him passing by—but, again, the emphasis is on a present state of mind.

Lyrics are sometimes differentiated among themselves. For example, if a lyric is melancholy or mournfully contemplative, especially if it laments a death, it may be called an **elegy.** If a lyric is rather long, elaborate, and on a lofty theme such as immortality or a hero's victory, it may be called an **ode** or a **hymn.** Distinctions among lyrics are often vague, and one person's ode may be another's elegy. Still, when writers use one of these words in their titles, they are inviting the reader to recall the tradition in which they are working. Of the poet's link to tradition T. S. Eliot said:

> No poet, no artist of any art, has his complete meaning alone. His significance, his appreciation is the appreciation of his relation to the dead poets and artists. You cannot value him alone; you must set him, for contrast and comparison, among the dead.

Although the lyric is often ostensibly addressed to someone (the "you" in "Careless Love"), the reader usually feels that the speaker is really talking to himself or herself. In "Careless Love," the speaker need not be in the presence of her man; rather, her heart is overflowing (the reader senses) and she pretends to address him.

A comment by John Stuart Mill on poetry is especially true of the lyric:

> Eloquence is *heard,* poetry is *over*heard. Eloquence supposes an audience; the peculiarity of poetry appears to us to lie in the poet's utter unconsciousness of a listener. Poetry is feeling confessing itself to itself, in moments of solitude.

This is particularly true in work songs such as "Michael Row the Boat Ashore," where there is no audience: the singers sing for themselves, participating rather than performing. As one prisoner in Texas said: "They really be singing about

**4 do** door

the way they feel inside. Since they can't say it to nobody, they sing a song about it." The sense of "feeling confessing itself to itself, in moments of solitude" or of "singing about the way they feel inside" is strong and clear in this short cowboy song.

ANONYMOUS

## *The Colorado Trail*

Eyes like the morning star,
Cheeks like a rose,
Laura was a pretty girl
God Almighty knows.

Weep all ye little rains,
Wail winds wail,
All along, along, along
The Colorado trail.

When we read a lyric poem, no matter who the speaker is, for a moment—while we recite or hear the words—we become the speaker. That is, we get into the speaker's mind, or, perhaps more accurately, the speaker takes charge of our mind, and we undergo (comfortably seated in a chair or sprawled on a bed) the mental experience that is embodied in the words. Consider the following bit of folk literature, heard in Kentucky.

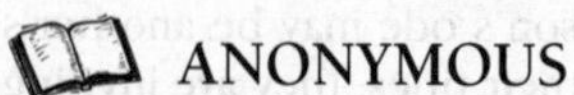

ANONYMOUS

## *Sally Goodin*

I had a piece of pie and a little piece of puddin',
I'd give it all away to hug Sally Goodin.
Night's so dark, road's so muddy,
I'm so drunk I can't walk steady.

The first two lines express a simple but charming sentiment: The boy is so in love (and so young) that he would give the girl the two things he apparently values most highly, a piece of pie and some pudding. The next two lines have no obvious connection with the first two, but they serve to let us see—to let us enter into the mind of—this drunken boy staggering along the road, filled with confused thoughts of food, Sally Goodin, and the uncertain path. We may disapprove of drinking, but we enjoy our moment of vicarious drunken love, and—perhaps especially if we ourselves have never been drunk—we get a sense of drunkenness in the marvelous drunken rhyme of *muddy* and *steady*.

Finally, one more anonymous love poem, this one written in England, probably in the early sixteenth century. In the title, "Western" is a modernized form of the first word of the poem.

## ANONYMOUS

### *Western Wind*

Westron wind, when will thou blow?
The small rain down can rain.
Christ, that my love were in my arms,
And I in my bed again.

## TOPICS FOR CRITICAL THINKING AND WRITING

1. In "Western Wind," what do you think is the tone of the speaker's voice in the first two lines? Angry? Impatient? Supplicating? Be as precise as possible. What is the tone in the next two lines?
2. In England, the west wind, warmed by the Gulf Stream, rises in the spring. What associations link the wind and rain of lines 1 and 2 with lines 3 and 4?
3. Ought we to have been told why the lovers are separated? Explain.

Love poems are by no means all the same—to take an obvious point, some are happy and some are sad—but those that are about the loss of a beloved or about the pains of love seem to be especially popular. Here is a seventeenth-century poem—actually a song—that makes use of the idea that the eyes of the mistress can dart fire, and that she can kill (or at least severely wound) the sighing, helpless male lover. The male speaker describes the appearance of Cupid, the tyrannic god of love, who (he claims) is equipped with darts and death-dealing fire taken from the eyes of the proud, cruel woman whom the speaker loves.

## APHRA BEHN

*Aphra Behn (1640-89) is regarded as the first English woman to have made a living by writing. Not much is known of her life, but she seems to have married a London merchant of Dutch descent, and after his death to have served as a spy in the Dutch Wars (1665-67). After her return to England she took up playwrighting, and she gained fame with* The Rover *(1677). Behn also wrote novels, the most important of which is* Oroonoko, or The Royal Slave *(1688), which is among the first works in English to express pity for enslaved Africans.*

## *Song: Love Armed*

Love in fantastic triumph sate,
  Whilst bleeding hearts around him flowed,
For whom fresh pains he did create,
  And strange tyrannic power he showed:
From thy bright eyes he took his fire,
  Which round about in sport he hurled;
But 'twas from mine he took desire,
  Enough to undo the amorous world.

From me he took his sighs and tears:
  From thee, his pride and cruelty;
From me, his languishments and fears;
  And every killing dart from thee.
Thus thou and I the god have armed
  And set him up a deity;
But my poor heart alone is harmed,
  Whilst thine the victor is, and free.

*[1676]*

## TOPICS FOR CRITICAL THINKING AND WRITING

1. The speaker talks of the suffering he is undergoing. Can we nevertheless feel that he enjoys his plight? *Why,* by the way, do we often enjoy songs of unhappy love?
2. The woman ("thee") is said to exhibit "pride and cruelty" (line 10). Is the poem sexist? Is it therefore offensive?
3. Do you suppose that men can enjoy the poem more than women? Explain.

We will temporarily end our concern with love poems ("temporarily" because other love poems will be included in later chapters) with a poem lamenting the death of the beloved.

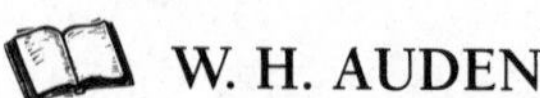

## W. H. AUDEN

*Wystan Hugh Auden (1907–73) was born in York, England, and educated at Oxford. In the 1930s his witty left-wing poetry earned him wide acclaim as the leading poet of his generation. In 1939 Auden came to America, and in 1946 he became a citizen of the United States, though he spent his last years in England.*

## *Stop All the Clocks, Cut Off the Telephone*

Stop all the clocks, cut off the telephone,
Prevent the dog from barking with a juicy bone,
Silence the pianos and with muffled drum
Bring out the coffin, let the mourners come.

Let aeroplanes circle moaning overhead
Scribbling on the sky the message He Is Dead,
Put the crepe bows round the white necks of the public doves,
Let the traffic policemen wear black cotton gloves.

He was my North, my South, my East and West,
My working week and my Sunday rest,
My noon, my midnight, my talk, my song;
I thought that love would last for ever: I was wrong.

The stars are not wanted now: put out every one;
Pack up the moon and dismantle the sun;
Pour away the ocean and sweep up the wood.
For nothing now can ever come to any good.

[*1936*]

## TOPICS FOR CRITICAL THINKING AND WRITING

1. Let's assume that poems are rooted in real-life situations, that is, they take their origin from responses to experience, whether the experience is falling in love or losing a loved one, or praising God or losing one's faith, or celebrating a war (as in "Battle Hymn of the Republic") or lamenting the tragic destruction of war. But of course the poet then shapes the experience into a memorable statement and somehow makes a distinctive work on a traditional theme. Cite some phrases in Auden's poem that you would *not* expect to find in a poem on the death of the beloved. (For example, would you expect to find a reference to a dog eating "a juicy bone" in a poem on this theme?) Do you think these passages are effective, or do you think they are just silly? Explain.
2. Perhaps another way of getting at the question we have just asked is this: Can you imagine reading this at the funeral of someone you love? Or would you want a lover to read it at your funeral? Why?
3. The words of the last line of the poem are simple, almost a cliché. Yet we find them very powerful, and we wonder if you agree. What is the relationship of this line to the preceding lines of the stanza, with its images of mighty actions and cosmic gestures, and to the poem as a whole?

Here is yet one more lyric dealing, as lyric usually does, with a deeply felt personal experience.

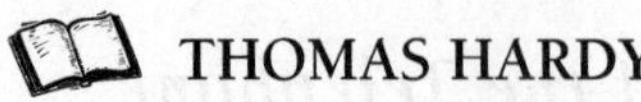

## THOMAS HARDY

*Thomas Hardy (1840–1928) was born in Dorset, England, the son of a stonemason. Best known for his novels, Hardy stopped writing fiction after the hostile reception of* Jude the Obscure *in 1896 and turned to writing lyric poetry.*

### *The Self-Unseeing*

Here is the ancient floor,  
Footworn and hollowed and thin,  
Here was the former door  
Where the dead feet walked in.

She sat here in her chair,  
Smiling into the fire;  
He who played stood there,  
Bowing it higher and higher.

Childlike, I danced in a dream;  
Blessings emblazoned that day;  
Everything glowed with a gleam;  
Yet we were looking away!

[*1901*]

## TOPICS FOR CRITICAL THINKING AND WRITING

1. In line 8, what does "Bowing it higher and higher" mean? Putting aside the issue of rhyme, what, if anything, would be lost if lines 7–8 were omitted?
2. What do you take the title of the poem to mean? And the last line?
3. Hardy chose to punctuate the final line with an exclamation point. Would the tone and meaning change if he had used a period?

Let's look now at much more public songs, beginning with a song about an issue of national importance.

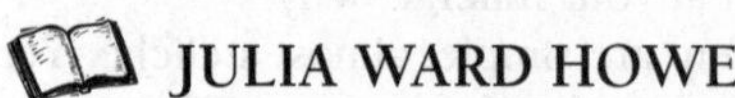

## JULIA WARD HOWE

*Julia Ward Howe (1819–1910) was born in New York City. A social reformer, her work for the emancipation of African-Americans and the right of women to vote is no-*

*table. She was the first woman to be elected to the American Academy of Arts and Letters.*

## Battle Hymn of the Republic

Mine eyes have seen the glory of the coming of the Lord:
He is trampling out the vintage where the grapes of wrath are stored;
He hath loosed the fateful lightning of his terrible swift sword;
  His truth is marching on.

*Chorus*
  Glory! glory! Hallelujah!
  Glory! glory! Hallelujah!
  Glory! glory! Hallelujah!
    His truth is marching on!

I have seen him in the watch-fires of a hundred circling camps;
They have builded him an altar in the evening dews and damps;
I can read his righteous sentence by the dim and flaring lamps:
  His day is marching on.

I have read a fiery gospel, writ in burnished rows of steel:
"As ye deal with my contemners, so with you my grace shall deal;
Let the Hero, born of woman, crush the serpent with his heel,
  Since God is marching on."

He has sounded forth the trumpet that shall never call retreat;
He is sifting out the hearts of men before his judgment-seat;
Oh, be swift, my soul, to answer him! be jubilant, my feet!
  Our God is marching on.

In the beauty of the lilies Christ was born across the sea,
With a glory in his bosom that transfigures you and me:
As he died to make men holy, let us die to make men free,
  While God is marching on.

[*1861*]

## TOPICS FOR CRITICAL THINKING AND WRITING

1. This poem of the Civil War, written to the tune of "John Brown's Body," draws some of its militant imagery from the Bible, especially from Isaiah 63.1–6 and Revelation 19.11–15. Do you think the lines about Christ are inappropriate here? Explain.
2. If you know the tune to which "Battle Hymn of the Republic" is sung, think about the interplay between the music and the words. Do we have a different response to Howe's words when her text is read as a poem, rather than experienced as a song?

We have already mentioned that the lyric can range from expressions of emotion focused on personal matters to expressions of emotion focused on public matters, and the latter are sometimes characterized as odes or hymns. Among the most memorable hymns produced in the United States are the spirituals, or Sorrow Songs, created by black slaves in the United States, chiefly in the first half of the nineteenth century. The origins of the spirituals are still a matter of some dispute, but most specialists agree that the songs represent a distinctive fusion of African rhythms with European hymns, and of course many of the texts derive ultimately from biblical sources. One of the chief themes is the desire for release, sometimes presented with imagery drawn from ancient Israel. Examples include references to crossing the River Jordan (a river that runs from north of the Sea of Galilee to the Dead Sea), the release of the Israelites from slavery in Egypt (Exodus), Jonah's release from the whale (Book of Jonah), and Daniel's deliverance from a fiery furnace and from the lions' den (Book of Daniel, chapters 3 and 6).

The texts were collected and published especially in the 1860s, for instance in *Slave Songs of the United States* (1867). These books usually sought to reproduce the singers' pronunciation, and we have followed the early texts in the two examples that we give here.

## ANONYMOUS

# *Deep River*

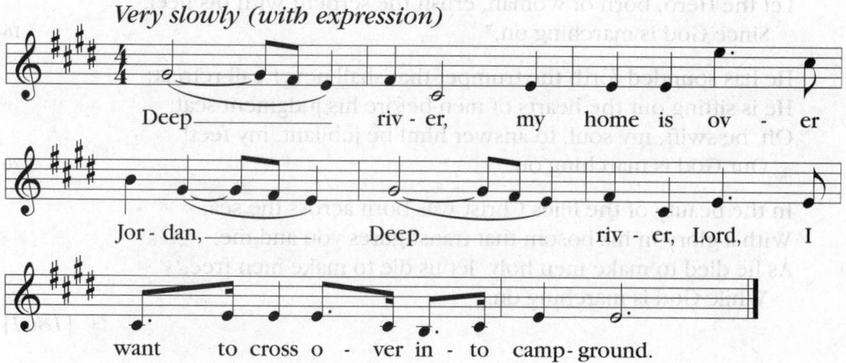


Deep river, my home is over Jordan, Deep river,
Lord, I want to cross over into campground,
Lord, I want to cross over into campground,
Lord, I want to cross over into campground.
Oh, chillun, Oh, don't you want to go to that gospel feast,
That promised land, that land, where all is peace?
Walk into heaven, and take my seat,
And cast my crown at Jesus feet,
Lord, I want to cross over into campground,
Lord, I want to cross over into campground,

Lord, I want to cross over into campground.
Deep river, my home is over Jordan, Deep river
Lord, I want to cross over into campground,
Lord, I want to cross over into campground,
Lord, I want to cross over into campground, Lord!

## ANONYMOUS

# *Didn't My Lord Deliver Daniel*

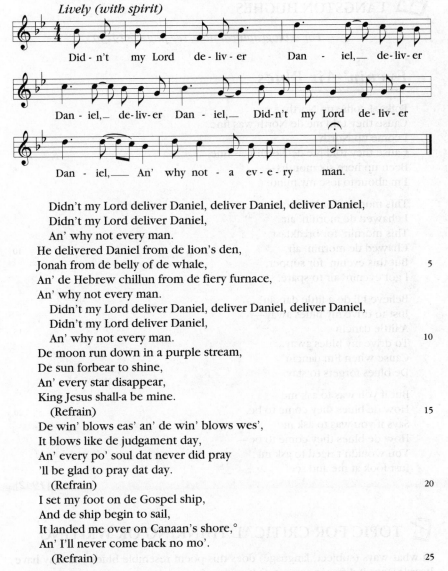

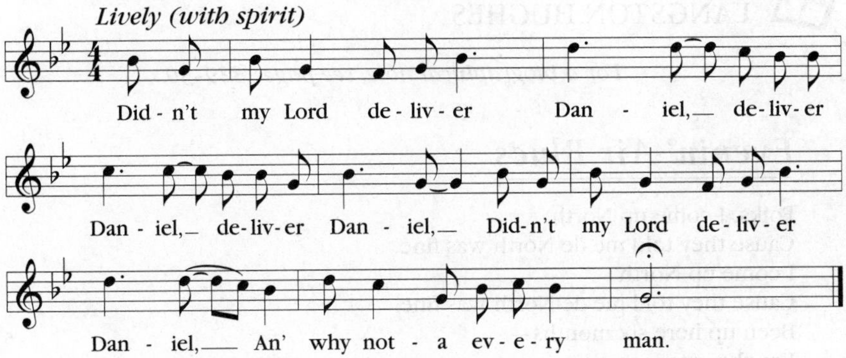

*Lively (with spirit)*

Did - n't my Lord de - liv - er Dan - iel,— de- liv- er
Dan - iel,— de- liv- er Dan - iel,— Did- n't my Lord de - liv - er
Dan - iel,— An' why not - a ev - e - ry man.

Didn't my Lord deliver Daniel, deliver Daniel, deliver Daniel,
Didn't my Lord deliver Daniel,
An' why not every man.
He delivered Daniel from de lion's den,
Jonah from de belly of de whale,
An' de Hebrew chillun from de fiery furnace,
An' why not every man.
Didn't my Lord deliver Daniel, deliver Daniel, deliver Daniel,
Didn't my Lord deliver Daniel,
An' why not every man.
De moon run down in a purple stream,
De sun forbear to shine,
An' every star disappear,
King Jesus shall-a be mine.
(Refrain)
De win' blows eas' an' de win' blows wes',
It blows like de judgament day,
An' every po' soul dat never did pray
'll be glad to pray dat day.
(Refrain)
I set my foot on de Gospel ship,
And de ship begin to sail,
It landed me over on Canaan's shore,°
An' I'll never come back no mo'.
(Refrain)

**23 Canaan's shore** Canaan is the ancient name of a territory that included part of what is now Israel

## TOPIC FOR CRITICAL THINKING OR WRITING

As we mentioned a moment ago, we give the texts of the songs as they were printed in the second half of the nineteenth century, when an effort to indicate pronunciation was made (e.g., *chillun* for *children*). If you were printing the songs, would you retain these attempts to indicate pronunciation? What, if anything, is gained by keeping them? What, if any, unintentional side effects do you think may be produced?

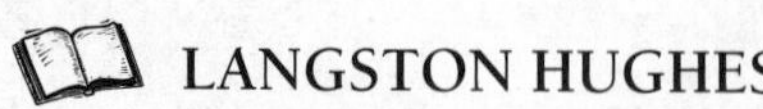

## LANGSTON HUGHES

*For a biographical note, see pages 829–30.*

### *Evenin' Air Blues*

Folks, I come up North  
Cause they told me de North was fine.  
I come up North  
Cause they told me de North was fine.  
Been up here six months—  
I'm about to lose my mind.

This mornin' for breakfast  
I chawed de mornin' air.  
This mornin' for breakfast  
Chawed de mornin' air.  
But this evenin' for supper,  
I got evenin' air to spare.

Believe I'll do a little dancin'  
Just to drive my blues away—  
A little dancin'  
To drive my blues away,  
Cause when I'm dancin'  
De blues forgets to stay.

But if you was to ask me  
How de blues they come to be,  
Says if you was to ask me  
How de blues they come to be—  
You wouldn't need to ask me:  
Just look at me and see!

[*1942*]

## TOPIC FOR CRITICAL THINKING OR WRITING

In what ways (subject, language) does this poem resemble blues you may have heard? Does it differ in any ways? If so, how?

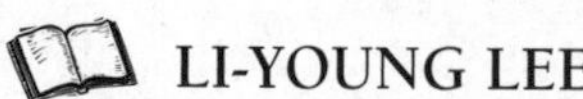

## LI-YOUNG LEE

*Li-Young Lee was born in 1957 in Jakarta, Indonesia, of Chinese parents. In 1964 his family brought him to the United States. He was educated at the University of Pitts-*

*burgh, the University of Arizona, and the State University of New York, Brockport. He now lives in Illinois, where he works as an artist.*

## *I Ask My Mother to Sing*

She begins, and my grandmother joins her.
Mother and daughter sing like young girls.
If my father were alive, he would play
his accordion and sway like a boat.

I've never been in Peking, or the Summer Palace,
nor stood on the great Stone Boat to watch
the rain begin on Kuen Ming Lake, the picnickers
running away in the grass.

But I love to hear it sung;
how the waterlilies fill with rain until
they overturn, spilling water into water,
then rock back, and fill with more.

Both women have begun to cry.
But neither stops her song.

[*1986*]

### TOPICS FOR CRITICAL THINKING AND WRITING

1. Why might the speaker ask the women to sing?
2. Why do the women cry? Why do they continue to sing?

## EDNA ST. VINCENT MILLAY

*Edna St. Vincent Millay (1892-1950) was born in Rockland, Maine. Even as a child she wrote poetry, and by the time she graduated from Vassar College (1917) she had achieved some notice as a poet. Millay settled for a while in Greenwich Village, a center of Bohemian activity in New York City, where she wrote, performed in plays, and engaged in feminist causes. In 1923, the year she married, she became the first woman to win the Pulitzer Prize for Poetry. Numerous other awards followed. Though she is best known as a lyric poet—especially as a writer of sonnets—she also wrote memorable political poetry and nature poetry as well as short stories, plays, and a libretto for an opera.*

## *The Spring and the Fall*

In the spring of the year, in the spring of the year,
I walked the road beside my dear.

The trees were black where the bark was wet.
I see them yet, in the spring of the year.
He broke me a bough of the blossoming peach
That was out of the way and hard to reach.

In the fall of the year, in the fall of the year,
I walked the road beside my dear.
The rooks went up with a raucous trill.
I hear them still, in the fall of the year.
He laughed at all I dared to praise,
And broke my heart, in little ways.

Year be springing or year be falling,
The bark will drip and the birds be calling.
There's much that's fine to see and hear
In the spring of a year, in the fall of a year.
'Tis not love's going hurts my days,
But that it went in little ways.

[*1923*]

## TOPICS FOR CRITICAL THINKING AND WRITING

1. The first stanza describes the generally happy beginning of a love story. Where do you find the first hint of an unhappy ending?
2. Describe the rhyme scheme of the first stanza, including internal rhymes. Do the second and third stanzas repeat the pattern, or are there some variations? What repetition of sounds other than rhyme do you note?
3. Put the last two lines into your own words. How do you react to them; that is, do you find the conclusion surprising, satisfying, recognizable from your own experience, anticlimactic, or what?
4. In two or three paragraphs explain how the imagery of the poem (drawn from the seasons of the year) contributes to its meaning.

## WILFRED OWEN

*Wilfred Owen (1893–1918) was born in Shropshire, in England, and studied at London University. He enlisted in the army at the outbreak of World War I and fought in the Battle of the Somme until he was hospitalized with shell shock. After his recuperation in England, he returned to the front, only to be killed in action one week before the end of the war. His collected poems were published posthumously.*

## *Anthem for Doomed Youth*

What passing-bells for these who die as cattle?
Only the monstrous anger of the guns.
Only the stuttering rifles' rapid rattle

Can patter out their hasty orisons.
No mockeries for them from prayers or bells,
Nor any voice of mourning save the choirs—
The shrill, demented choirs of wailing shells;
And bugles calling for them from sad shires.

What candles may be held to speed° them all?
Not in the hands of boys, but in their eyes
Shall shine the holy glimmers of good-byes.
The pallor of girls' brows shall be their pall;
Their flowers the tenderness of patient minds,
And each slow dusk a drawing-down of blinds.

[*1920*]

**9 speed** aid

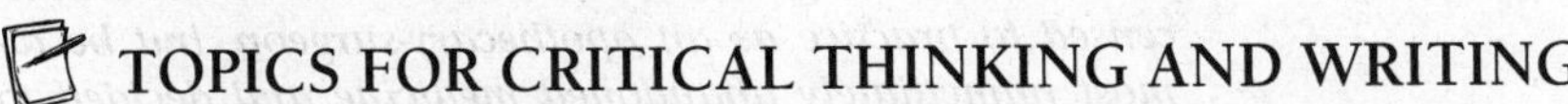

## TOPICS FOR CRITICAL THINKING AND WRITING

1. What is an anthem? What are some of the words or phrases in this poem that might be found in a traditional anthem? What are some of the words or phrases that you would not expect in an anthem?
2. How would you characterize the speaker's state of mind? (Your response probably will require more than one word.)

## WALT WHITMAN

*Walt Whitman (1819-92) was born on Long Island, the son of a farmer. The young Whitman taught school and worked as a carpenter, a printer, a newspaper editor, and, during the Civil War, as a volunteer nurse on the Union side. After the war he supported himself by doing secretarial jobs. In Whitman's own day his poetry was highly controversial because of its unusual form (formlessness, many people said) and (though not in the following poem) its abundant erotic implications.*

### *A Noiseless Patient Spider*

A noiseless patient spider,
I mark'd where on a little promontory it stood isolated,
Mark'd how to explore the vacant vast surrounding,
It launch'd forth filament, filament, filament, out of itself,
Ever unreeling them, ever tirelessly speeding them.

And you O my soul where you stand,
Surrounded, detached, in measureless oceans of space,
Ceaselessly musing, venturing, throwing, seeking the spheres to
  connect them,
Till the bridge you will need be form'd, till the ductile anchor hold,
Till the gossamer thread you fling catch somewhere, O my soul.

[*1862-63*]

## TOPICS FOR CRITICAL THINKING AND WRITING

1. How are the suggestions in "launch'd" (line 4) and "unreeling" (line 5) continued in the second stanza?
2. How are the varying lengths of lines 1, 4, and 8 relevant to their ideas?
3. The second stanza is not a complete sentence. Why? The poem is unrhymed. What effect does the near-rhyme (*bold: soul*) in the last two lines have on you?

## JOHN KEATS

*John Keats (1795-1821), son of a London stable keeper, was taken out of school when he was fifteen and was apprenticed to a surgeon and apothecary. In 1816 he was licensed to practice as an apothecary-surgeon, but he almost immediately abandoned medicine and decided to make a career as a poet. His progress was amazing; he published books of poems—to mixed reviews—in 1817, 1818, and 1820, before dying of tuberculosis at the age of twenty-five. Today he is esteemed as one of England's greatest poets.*

### *Ode on a Grecian Urn*

*I*

Thou still unravished bride of quietness,
  Thou foster-child of silence and slow time,
Sylvan historian, who canst thus express
  A flowery tale more sweetly than our rhyme:
What leaf-fringed legend haunts about thy shape
  Of deities or mortals, or of both,
    In Tempe or the dales of Arcady?
  What men or gods are these? What maidens loth?
What mad pursuit? What struggle to escape?
    What pipes and timbrels? What wild ecstasy?

*II*

Heard melodies are sweet, but those unheard
  Are sweeter; therefore, ye soft pipes, play on;
Not to the sensual° ear, but, more endeared,
  Pipe to the spirit ditties of no tone:
Fair youth, beneath the trees, thou canst not leave
  Thy song, nor ever can those trees be bare;
    Bold Lover, never, never canst thou kiss,

**13 sensual** sensuous

Though winning near the goal—yet, do not grieve;
She cannot fade, though thou hast not thy bliss,
For ever wilt thou love, and she be fair!

*III*

Ah, happy, happy boughs! that cannot shed
Your leaves, nor ever bid the Spring adieu;
And, happy melodist, unwearied,
For ever piping songs for ever new;
More happy love! more happy, happy love!
For ever warm and still to be enjoyed,
For ever panting, and for ever young;
All breathing human passion far above,
That leaves a heart high-sorrowful and cloyed,
A burning forehead, and a parching tongue.

*IV*

Who are these coming to the sacrifice?
To what green altar, O mysterious priest,
Lead'st thou that heifer lowing at the skies,
And all her silken flanks with garlands drest?
What little town by river or sea shore,
Or mountain-built with peaceful citadel,
Is emptied of this folk, this pious morn?
And, little town, thy streets for evermore
Will silent be; and not a soul to tell
Why thou art desolate can e'er return.

V

O Attic shape! Fair attitude! with brede°
Of marble men and maidens overwrought,
With forest branches and the trodden weed;
Thou, silent form, dost tease us out of thought
As doth eternity: Cold Pastoral!
When old age shall this generation waste,
Thou shalt remain, in midst of other woe
Than ours, a friend to man, to whom thou say'st,
"Beauty is truth, truth beauty,"—that is all
Ye know on earth, and all ye need to know.

[*1820*]

**41 brede** design

## TOPICS FOR CRITICAL THINKING AND WRITING

1. If you do not know the meaning of "sylvan," check a dictionary. Why does Keats call the urn a "sylvan" historian (line 3)? As the poem continues, what evidence is there that the urn cannot "express" (line 3) a tale so sweetly as the speaker said?

2. What do you make of lines 11–14?
3. What do you think the urn may stand for in the first three stanzas? In the third stanza, is the speaker caught up in the urn's world or is he sharply aware of his own?
4. Do you take "tease us out of thought" (line 44) to mean "draw us into a realm of imaginative experience superior to that of reason" or to mean "draw us into futile and frustrating questions"? Or both? Or neither? What suggestions do you find in "Cold Pastoral" (line 45)?
5. Do lines 49–50 perhaps mean that imagination, stimulated by the urn, achieves a realm richer than the daily world? Or perhaps that art, the highest earthly wisdom, suggests there is a realm wherein earthly troubles are resolved?

## E. E. CUMMINGS

*e. e. cummings was the pen name of Edwin Estlin Cummings (1894–1962), who grew up in Cambridge, Massachusetts, and was graduated from Harvard, where he became interested in modern literature and art, especially in the movements called cubism and futurism. His father, a conservative clergyman and a professor at Harvard, seems to have been baffled by the youth's interests, but Cummings's mother encouraged his artistic activities, including his use of unconventional punctuation and capitalization.*

*Politically liberal in his youth, Cummings became more conservative after a visit to Russia in 1931, but early and late his work emphasizes individuality and freedom of expression.*

### *anyone lived in a pretty how town*

anyone lived in a pretty how town
(with up so floating many bells down)
spring summer autumn winter
he sang his didn't he danced his did.

Women and men (both little and small)
cared for anyone not at all
they sowed their isn't they reaped their same
sun moon stars rain

children guessed (but only a few
and down they forgot as up they grew
autumn winter spring summer)
that noone loved him more by more

when by now and tree by leaf
she laughed his joy she cried his grief
bird by snow and stir by still
anyone's any was all to her

someones married their everyones
laughed their cryings and did their dance
(sleep wake hope and then) they
said their nevers they slept their dream

stars rain sun moon
(and only the snow can begin to explain
how children are apt to forget to remember
with up so floating many bells down)

one day anyone died i guess
(and noone stopped to kiss his face)
busy folk buried them side by side
little by little and was by was

all by all and deep by deep
and more by more they dream their sleep
noone and anyone earth by april
wish by spirit and if by yes.

Women and men (both dong and ding)
summer autumn winter spring
reaped their sowing and went their came
sun moon stars rain

[*1940*]

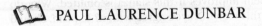

## TOPICS FOR CRITICAL THINKING AND WRITING

1. Put into normal order (as far as possible) the words of the first two stanzas and then compare your version with Cummings's. What does Cummings gain—or lose?
2. Characterize the "anyone" who "sang his didn't" and "danced his did." In your opinion, how does he differ from the people who "sowed their isn't they reaped their same"?
3. Some readers interpret "anyone died" (line 25) to mean that the child matured and became as dead as the other adults. How might you support or refute this interpretation?

## PAUL LAURENCE DUNBAR

*Paul Laurence Dunbar (1872-1906), born in Ohio to parents who had been slaves in Kentucky, achieved fame for his dialect poetry. He published early—even while in high school—and by 1896, with the publication of* Lyrics of Lowly Life, *he had three books to his credit. Because he often used black speech patterns and pronunciation, his work was sometimes thought to present demeaning racial stereotypes, but in recent years critics have seen the protest beneath the quaint surface. In the following poem, however, he works entirely within a traditional white idiom, although the subject is distinctively African-American.*

## *Sympathy*

I know what the caged bird feels, alas!
When the sun is bright on the upland slopes;
When the wind stirs soft through the spring grass,
And the river flows like a stream of glass.
When the first bird sings and the first bud opes,
And the faint perfume from its chalice steals—
I know what the caged bird feels!

I know why the caged bird beats his wing
Till its blood is red on the cruel bars;
For he must fly back to his perch and cling
When he fain would be on the bough a-swing;
And a pain still throbs in the old, old scars
And they pulse again with a keener sting—
I know why he beats his wing!

I know why the caged bird sings, ah me,
When his wing is bruised and his bosom sore,—
When he beats his bars and he would be free;
It is not a carol of joy or glee,
But a prayer that he sends from his heart's deep core,
But a plea, that upward to Heaven he flings—
I know why the caged bird sings

[*1899*]

## TOPICS FOR CRITICAL THINKING AND WRITING

1. Pay careful attention to Dunbar's use of language. Describe, for example, what the comparison "like a stream of glass" in the first stanza expresses about the river, and comment on the implications of the word "chalice."
2. Some readers have felt that the second stanza is the weakest in the poem, and that the poem improves if this stanza is omitted. Why do you suppose they hold this view? Do you agree with it? Explain. Should Dunbar have dropped this stanza?
3. After reading and rereading the poem, try to summarize its overall effect. Explain why the speaker sees such an intimate connection between himself and the "caged bird."

## LINDA PASTAN

*Linda Pastan was born in New York City in 1932. The author of ten books of poems, she has won numerous prizes and has received grants from the National Endow-*

*ment for the Arts. In the following poem she wittily plays with repetitions and with pauses.*

## *Jump Cabling*

When our cars          touched
When you lifted the hood          of mine
To see the intimate workings          underneath,
When we were bound          together
By a pulse of pure          energy,
When my car like the          princess
In the tale woke with a          start,
I thought why not ride the rest of the way together?

[*1984*]

### TOPICS FOR CRITICAL THINKING AND WRITING

1. Suppose someone argued that this is merely prose broken up into arbitrary units. Would you agree? Explain.
2. As you read the poem aloud, think about the spacing that Pastan designed for it. What is the effect of the space between the first and second parts of the first seven lines? Why does she do something different for the final line?

### DOROTHY PARKER

*Dorothy Parker (1893–1967), born in West End, New Jersey, but brought up in New York City, from 1917 to 1920 served as drama critic for the magazine* Vanity Fair, *where her witty, satiric reviews gained her the reputation of being hard to please. She distinguished between wit and wisecracking: "Wit has truth in it; wisecracking is simply calisthenics with words."*

*In addition to writing essays and stories, Parker also wrote light verse, especially about love.*

## *General Review of the Sex Situation*

Woman wants monogamy;
Man delights in novelty.
Love is woman's moon and sun;
Man has other forms of fun.

Woman lives but in her lord;
Count to ten, and man is bored.
With this the gist and sum of it,
What earthly good can come of it?

[*1926*]

## TOPICS FOR CRITICAL THINKING AND WRITING

1. How would you characterize Parker's message? (For instance, is it sad, happy, pitiful, or what?) How would you characterize her tone—her attitude, as you perceive it?
2. Take note of and describe Parker's use of language—for example, the contrast she makes between "monogamy" and "novelty," and the image she gives in line 3, "Love is woman's moon and sun." Where else in this short poem do you see evidence of careful handling of language?
3. How much truth do you think there is in Parker's lines? (Remember: No poem, or, for that matter, no novel—however long—can tell the whole truth about life.) As for truth, how would you compare it with the following passage, from Barbara Dafoe Whitehead's review (*The Times Literary Supplement*, 9 June 1995) of two sociological studies, *The Social Organization of Sexuality: Sexual Practice in the U.S.* and *Sex in America*?

> Men and women have different sexual interests, stakes and appetites, with men more oriented to the sex act and women more interested in sex as an expression of affiliative and romantic love.

## A SAMPLE ESSAY

The subject is Aphra Behn's "song" (p. 840). We begin with two entries in a journal, kept by a first-year student, Geoffrey Sullivan, and we follow these entries with Sullivan's completed essay.

October 10. The title "Love Armed" puzzled me at first; funny, I somehow was thinking of the expression "strong-armed" and at first I didn't understand that "Love" in this poem is a human--no, not a human, but the god Cupid, who has a human form--and that he is shown as armed, with darts and so forth.

October 13. This god of "Love" is Cupid, and so he is something like what is on a valentine card--Cupid with his bow and arrow. But valentine cards just show cute little Cupids, and in this poem Cupid is a real menace. He causes lots of pain ("bleeding hearts," "tears," "killing dart," etc.). So what is Aphra Behn telling us about the god of love, or love? That love hurts? And she is singing about it! But we do sing songs about how hard life is. But do we sing them when we are really hurting, or only when we are pretty well off and just thinking about being hurt?

When you love someone and they don't return your love, it hurts, but even when love isn't returned it still gives some intense pleasure. Strange, but I think true. I wouldn't say that love always has this two-sided nature, but I do see the idea that love can have two sides, pleasure and pain. And love takes two kinds of people, male and female. Well, for most people, anyway. Maybe there's also something to the idea that "opposites attract." Anyway, Aphra Behn seems to be talking about men vs. women, pain vs. pleasure, power vs. weakness, etc. Pairs, opposites. And in two stanzas (a pair of stanzas?).

The final essay makes use of some, but not of all, of the preliminary jottings, and it includes much that Sullivan did not think of until he reread his jottings, reread the poem, and began drafting the essay.

Geoffrey Sullivan

English 2G

15 October 1997

The Double Nature of Love

Aphra Behn's "Love Armed" is in two stanzas, and it is about two people, "me" and "thee," that is, you and I, the lover and the woman he loves. I think the speaker is a man, since according to the usual code men are supposed to be the active lovers and women are the (relatively) passive people who are loved. In this poem, the beloved--the woman, I think--has "bright eyes" (line 5) that provide the god of Love with fire, and she also provides the god with "pride and cruelty" (10). This of course is the way the man sees it if a woman doesn't respond to him; if she doesn't love him in return, she is (he thinks) arrogant and cruel. What does the man give to Love? He provides "desire" (7), "sighs and tears" (9), "languishments and fears" (11). None of this sounds very manly, but the joke is that the god of love--which means love--can turn a strong man into a crybaby when a woman does not respond to him.

Although both stanzas are clever <u>descriptions</u> of the god of love, the poem is not just a description. Of course there is not a plot in the way that a short story has a plot, but there is a sort of a switch at the end, giving the story something of a plot. The poem is, say, ninety percent expression of feeling and description of love, but during the course of expressing feelings and describing love something happens, so there is a tiny <u>story</u>. The first stanza sets the scene ("Love in fantastic triumph sate" [1]) and tells of some of the things that the speaker and the woman contributed to the god of Love. The woman's eyes provided Love with fire, and the man's feelings provided Love with "desire" (7). The second stanza goes on to mention other things that Love got from the speaker ("sighs and tears," etc. [9]), and other things that Love got from the beloved ("pride and cruelty," etc. [10]), and in line 13 the poet says, "Thus thou and I the god have armed," so the two humans share something. They have both given Love his weapons. But--and this is the story I spoke of--the poem ends by emphasizing their difference: Only the man is "harmed," and the woman is the "victor" because her heart is not captured, as the man's heart is. In the battle that Love presides over, the woman is the winner; the man's heart has fallen for the woman, but, according to the last line, the woman's heart remains "free."

We have all seen the god of Love on valentine cards, a cute little Cupid armed with a bow and arrow. But despite the bow and arrow that the Valentine Day Cupid carries, I think that until I read Aphra Behn's "Love Armed" I had never really thought about Cupid as <u>powerful</u> and as capable of causing real pain. On valentine cards, he is just cute, but when I think about it, I realize the truth of Aphra Behn's concept of love. Love <u>is</u> (or can be) two-sided, whereas the valentine cards show only the sweet side.

I think it is interesting to notice that although the poem is about the destructive power of love, it is fun to read. I am not bothered by the fact that the lover is miserable. Why? I think I enjoy the poem, rather than am bothered by it, because <u>he is enjoying his misery</u>. After all, he is singing about it, sort of singing in the rain, telling anyone who will listen about how miserable he is, and he is having a very good time doing it.

Work Cited

Behn, Aphra. "Love Armed." <u>Literature: Thinking, Reading, and Writing Critically</u>, 2nd ed. Ed. Sylvan Barnet et al. New York: Longman, 1997. 840.

## TOPICS FOR CRITICAL THINKING AND WRITING

1. What do you think of the title? Is it sufficiently interesting and focused?
2. What are the writer's chief points? Are they clear, and are they adequately developed?
3. Do you think the writer is too concerned with himself, and that he

loses sight of the poem? Or do you find it interesting that he connects the poem with life?

4. Focus on the writer's use of quotations. Does he effectively introduce and examine quoted lines and phrases?
5. What grade would you give the essay? Why?

---

## ✔ Checklist: Writing about Lyric Poetry

- How songlike is the poem? What makes it resemble or not resemble a song? (Suggestion: Read the poem aloud a few times. Could it conceivably be set to music?)
- How would you characterize the speaker?
- What is the situation? Is the speaker addressing a particular audience, or meditating to himself or herself? Has anything already happened?
- If the speaker expresses an emotion, is this emotion the result of something that has happened before the poem began?
- Does something *happen* within the poem—some change of mood, for instance?
- Pay close attention to the beginning, middle, and end of the poem. Can you trace some sort of development in it?

---

# CHAPTER 17

# *The Speaking Tone of Voice*

> Everything is as good as it is dramatic. . . . [A poem is] heard as sung or spoken by a person in a scene—in character, in a setting. By whom, where and when is the question. By the dreamer of a better world out in a storm in Autumn; by a lover under a window at night.
>
> —Robert Frost, Preface, *A Way Out*

If we fall into the habit of saying, "Julia Ward Howe says that her 'eyes have seen the glory of the coming of the Lord,'" or "Robert Frost says that he thinks he knows 'Whose woods these are,'" we neglect the important truth in Frost's comment about poetry as drama: A poem is written by an author (Howe, Frost), but it is spoken by an invented speaker. The author counterfeits the speech of a person in a particular situation.

The anonymous author of "Western Wind" (p. 839), for instance, invents the speech of an unhappy lover who longs for the spring ("Western wind, when will thou blow?"); Julia Ward Howe invents the speech of someone who has seen God working in this world; Robert Frost, in "Stopping by Woods on a Snowy Evening" (p. 1141), invents a speaker who, sitting in a horse-drawn sleigh, watches the woods fill up with snow.

The speaker's voice often has the ring of the author's own voice—certainly Robert Frost did a great deal to cultivate the idea that he was a farmer-poet—but even when the resemblance seems close, we should recall that in the poem we get a particular speaker in a particular situation. That is, we get, for instance, not the whole of Frost (the father, the competitive poet, the public lecturer, and so on), but only a man in a horse-drawn sleigh watching the woods fill up with snow. It is customary, then, in writing about the voice one hears in a poem, to write not about the author but about the **speaker,** or **voice,** or **mask,** or **persona** (Latin for "mask") that speaks the poem.

In reading a poem, the first and most important question to ask yourself is this: *Who is speaking?* If an audience and a setting are suggested, keep them in mind, too. Consider, for example, the following poem.

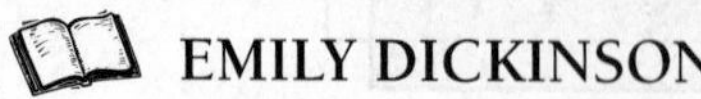

## EMILY DICKINSON

*Emily Dickinson (1830-86) was born into a proper New England family in Amherst, Massachusetts. Because she never married, and because in her last twenty years she may never have left her house, she has sometimes been pitied, but as the critic Allen Tate said, "All pity for Miss Dickinson's 'starved life' is misdirected. Her life was one of the richest and deepest ever lived on this continent." Her brother was probably right in saying that, having seen something of the rest of the world, "she could not resist the feeling that it was painfully hollow. It was to her so thin and unsatisfying in the face of the Great Realities of Life." For a fuller biographical account, and for a selection of Dickinson's poems and letters, see pages 1118-39. For additional poems by Dickinson, see Chapter 26.*

### *I'm Nobody! Who Are You?*

I'm Nobody! Who are you?
Are you—Nobody—too?
Then there's a pair of us!
Don't tell! they'd banish us—you know!

How dreary—to be—Somebody!
How public—like a Frog—
To tell your name—the livelong June—
To an admiring Bog!

[*1861?*]

Let's consider the sort of person we hear in "I'm Nobody! Who are you?" (Read it aloud, to see if you agree. In fact, you should test each of our assertions by reading the poem aloud.) The voice in line 1 is rather like that of a child playing a game with a friend. In lines 2 and 3 the speaker sees the reader as a fellow spirit ("Are you—Nobody—too?") and invites the reader to join her ("Then there's a pair of us!") in forming a sort of conspiracy of silence against outsiders ("Don't tell!"). In "they'd banish us," however, we hear a word that a child would not be likely to use, and we probably feel that the speaker is a shy but (with the right companion) playful adult, who here is speaking to an intimate friend. And since we hear this voice—we are reading the poem—we are or we become the friend. Because "banish" is a word that brings to mind images of a king's court, the speaker almost comically inflates and thereby makes fun of the "they" who are opposed to "us."

In the second stanza, or we might better say in the space between the two stanzas, the speaker puts aside the childlike manner. In "How dreary," the first words of the second stanza, we hear a sophisticated voice, one might even say a world-weary voice, or a voice with perhaps more than a touch of condescension. But since by now we are paired with the speaker in a conspiracy against outsiders, we enjoy the contrast that the speaker makes between the Nobodies and the Somebodies. Who are these Somebodies, these people who would imperiously "banish" the speaker and the friend? What are the Somebodies like?

> How dreary—to be—Somebody!
> How public—like a Frog—
> To tell your name—the livelong June—
> To an admiring Bog!

The last two lines do at least two things: They amusingly explain to the speaker's new friend (the reader) in what way a Somebody is public (it proclaims its presence all day), and they also indicate the absurdity of the Somebody-Frog's behavior (the audience is "an admiring Bog"). By the end of the poem we are quite convinced that it is better to be a Nobody (like Dickinson's speaker, and the reader?) than a Somebody (a loudmouth, like a croaking frog).

Often we tend to think of reading as something we do in private, and silently. But it is important to remember that writers, especially poets, care greatly about how their words *sound.* Poets pay attention not only to how the poem is arranged on the page—the length of the lines, for example—but also to how the poem sounds when actually read aloud, or, at least, when heard within the reader's mind.

One of the pleasures of reading literature, in fact, is the pleasure of listening to the sound of a voice, with its special rhythms, tones, accents, and emphases. Getting to know a poem, and becoming engaged by a poet's style, is very much a matter of getting to know a voice, acquiring a feeling for its familiar intonations, yet also being surprised, puzzled, even startled by it on occasion.

If you have done a little acting, you know from this experience how crucial it is to discover the way a character's lines in a play should sound. Directors and actors spend a great deal of time reading the lines, trying them in a variety of ways to catch their truest pace and verbal shape. And so do poets. We aren't making this up; in a letter, Robert Frost talks about "the sound of sense," a sort of abstraction in which an emotion or attitude comes through, even if the words are not clearly heard. He writes:

> The best place to get the abstract sound of sense is from voices behind a door that cuts off the words. Ask yourself how these sentences would sound without the words in which they are embodied:
>
> You mean to tell me you can't read?
> I said no such thing.
> Well read then.
> You're not my teacher.

In another letter, continuing the discussion of the topic, after giving some additional examples (for instance, "Unless I'm greatly mistaken," "No fool like an old fool"), Frost says, "It is so and not otherwise that we get the variety that makes it fun to write and read. *The ear does it.* The ear is the only true writer and the only true reader." (For a group of poems by Frost, see Chapter 27.)

In reading, then, your goal is to achieve a deeper sense of character—what this voice sounds like, what kind of person speaks like this. Read aloud; imagine how the writer might have meant his or her words to sound; read aloud again; and listen carefully all the while to the echoes and resonances of the words.

Consider the dramatic situation and the voice in the following short poem.

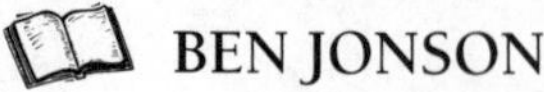

## BEN JONSON

*Ben Jonson (1572-1637), born in London, was Shakespeare's contemporary. Like Shakespeare, he wrote for the theater, and in fact Shakespeare acted in Jonson's first important play,* Every Man in His Humour *(1598). But unlike Shakespeare, Jonson produced a fairly large body of nondramatic poetry.*

## *The Hour-Glass*

Do but consider this small dust,
 Here running in the glass,
  By atoms moved;
 Could you believe that this,
  The body was
   Of one that loved?
And in his mistress' flame, played like a fly,
 Turned to cinders by her eye?
 Yes; and in death, as life unblessed,
   To have expressed,
 Even ashes of lovers find no rest.

[*1616*]

Who is speaking? A lover, of course. And this lover is to be imagined as male, since almost all poems written by men were conceived of as spoken by men, unless the invented speaker very clearly was characterized as a woman.

What is the dramatic situation? The lover is speaking to his beloved, telling her of a man who was destroyed ("Turned to cinders") by the eye—we might say by the killing looks—of the woman he loved. The victim has become the dust or sand that is constantly in motion ("Even ashes of lovers find no rest") in the hourglass. It is an easy step to conclude that the speaker, telling his beloved about the plight of the lover who was destroyed by the flame-darting eyes of his mistress, is implicitly comparing the faithful but unblessed lover to himself, and is thereby suggesting that his beloved should treat him more kindly.

But exactly how would you read each line? Is the first line, "Do but consider this small dust," spoken authoritatively, or pleadingly, or in some other way? And when the speaker asks his hearer if she can "believe that this, / The body was / Of one that loved," is the voice suffused with pity, or is there some playfulness in it? At the end of the poem, can we perhaps hear in the voice of this lover a note of satisfaction when he announces, "Even ashes of lovers find no rest"?

Although Jonson's poem deals with love and death—two thoroughly serious topics—it deals with them in a witty or perhaps playful fashion. The next poem deals with a different kind of love, and a different kind of death, and the tone is entirely different.

## GWENDOLYN BROOKS

***Gwendolyn Brooks was born in Topeka, Kansas, in 1917, but was raised in Chicago's South Side, where she has spent most of her life. In 1950, when she won the Pulitzer Prize for Poetry, she became the first African-American writer to win a Pulitzer Prize.***

## *The Mother*

Abortions will not let you forget.
You remember the children you got that you did not get,
The damp small pulps with a little or with no hair,
The singers and workers that never handled the air.
You will never neglect or beat
Them, or silence or buy with a sweet.
You will never wind up the sucking-thumb
Or scuttle off ghosts that come.
You will never leave them, controlling your luscious sigh,
Return for a snack of them, with gobbling mother-eye.

I have heard in the voices of the wind the voices of my dim killed
children.
I have contracted. I have eased
My dim dears at the breasts they could never suck.
I have said, Sweets, if I sinned, if I seized
Your luck
And your lives from your unfinished reach,
If I stole your births and your names,
Your straight baby tears and your games,
Your stilted or lovely loves, your tumults, your marriages, aches,
and your deaths,
If I poisoned the beginnings of your breaths,
Believe that even in my deliberateness I was not deliberate.
Though why should I whine,
Whine that the crime was other than mine?—
Since anyhow you are dead.
Or rather, or instead,
You were never made.
But that too, I am afraid,
Is faulty: oh, what shall I say, how is the truth to be said?
You were born, you had body, you died.
It is just that you never giggled or planned or cried.

Believe me, I loved you all.
Believe me, I knew you, though faintly, and I loved, I loved you
All.

[*1945*]

## TOPICS FOR CRITICAL THINKING AND WRITING

1. Who is being addressed?
2. The first ten lines sound like a chant. What gives them that quality? What makes them nonetheless serious?
3. In lines 20–23 the mother attempts to deny the "crime" but cannot. What is her reasoning here?
4. Do you find the last lines convincing? Explain.
5. The poem was first published in 1945. Do you think that the abundant debate about abortion in recent years has somehow made the poem seem dated, or more timely than ever? Explain.

Here is a second poem by Gwendolyn Brooks. Who is speaking?

### *We Real Cool*

The Pool Players.
Seven at the Golden Shovel.

We real cool. We
Left school. We

Lurk late. We
Strike straight. We

Sing sin. We
Thin gin. We

Jazz June. We
Die soon.

[*1960*]

## TOPICS FOR CRITICAL THINKING AND WRITING

1. Exactly why do you identify the speaker as you do?
2. The stanzas could have been written thus:

   We real cool.
   We left school.

   We lurk late.
   We strike straight.

   And so forth. Why do you think Brooks wrote them, or printed them, the way she did?

## THE READER AS THE SPEAKER

We have been arguing that the speaker of the poem usually is not the author but a dramatized form of the author, and that we overhear this speaker in some situation. But with poems of the sort that we have been looking at, we can also say that *the reader* is the speaker. That is, as we read the poem, at least to some degree *we* utter the thoughts, and *we* experience the sensations or emotions that the writer sets forth. We feel that Dickinson has allowed us to set forth our own feelings about what it is to be Nobody in a world where others are Somebody (and she has also helped us to say that the Somebody is a noisy frog); with Jonson we find (or at least we think we find) that we can express our own feelings about the complexities of love and loving; and with Brooks we hear or overhear thoughts and feelings that perhaps strike us as more relevant and more profound and more moving than most of what we hear on television or read in the newspapers about abortion.

In the following poem you will hear at least three voices—the voice of the person who begins the poem by telling us about a dead man ("Nobody heard him, the dead man"), the voice of the dead man ("I was much further out than you thought / And not waving but drowning"), and the collective voice of the dead man's friends ("Poor chap, he always loved larking"). But see if you don't find that all of the voices together say things that you have said (or almost said).

## STEVIE SMITH

*Stevie Smith (1902–71), christened Florence Margaret Smith, was born in England, in Hull. In addition to writing poems, she wrote stories, essays, and three novels. She is the subject of a film,* Stevie, *in which Glenda Jackson plays Smith.*

## *Not Waving but Drowning*

Nobody heard him, the dead man,
But still he lay moaning:
I was much further out than you thought
And not waving but drowning.

Poor chap, he always loved larking
And now he's dead
It must have been too cold for him his heart gave way,
They said.

Oh, no no no, it was too cold always
(Still the dead one lay moaning)
I was much too far out all my life
And not waving but drowning.

[*1957*]

## TOPICS FOR CRITICAL THINKING AND WRITING

1. Identify the speaker of each line.
2. What sort of man did the friends of the dead man think he was? What type of man do you think he was?
3. The first line, "Nobody heard him, the dead man," is literally true. Dead men do not speak. In what other ways is it true?

# THE DRAMATIC MONOLOGUE

We have said at some length that in most poems the speaker is not quite the author (say, Robert Frost) but is a dramatized version (a man sitting in a sleigh, watching the "woods fill up with snow"). We have also said that in most poems the reader can imagine himself or herself as the speaker; as we read Dickinson or even Jonson and Brooks, we say to ourselves that the poet is expressing thoughts and emotions that might be our own. But in some poems the poet creates so distinct a speaker that the character clearly is not us but is something Other. Such a poem is called a **dramatic monologue.** In it, a highly specific character speaks, in a clearly specified situation. The most famous example is Robert Browning's "My Last Duchess," where a Renaissance duke is addressing an emissary from a count.

## ROBERT BROWNING

*Born in a suburb of London into a middle-class family, Browning (1812–89) was educated primarily at home, where he read widely. For a while he wrote for the English stage, but after marrying Elizabeth Barrett in 1846—she too was a poet—he lived with her in Italy until her death in 1861. He then returned to England and settled in London with their son. Regarded as one of the most distinguished poets of the Victorian period, he is buried in Westminster Abbey.*

## *My Last Duchess*

Ferrara*

That's my last Duchess painted on the wall,
Looking as if she were alive. I call
That piece a wonder, now; Frà Pandolf's° hands
Worked busily a day, and there she stands.
Will't please you sit and look at her? I said
"Frà Pandolf" by design, for never read
Strangers like you that pictured countenance,
The depth and passion of its earnest glance,
But to myself they turned (since none puts by
The curtain I have drawn for you, but I)
And seemed as they would ask me, if they durst,
How such a glance came there; so, not the first
Are you to turn and ask thus. Sir, 'twas not
Her husband's presence only, called that spot
Of joy into the Duchess' cheek; perhaps
Frà Pandolf chanced to say "Her mantle laps

*__Ferrara__ town in Italy **3 Frà Pandolf** a fictitious painter

Over my Lady's wrist too much," or, "Paint
Must never hope to reproduce the faint
Half-flush that dies along her throat." Such stuff
Was courtesy, she thought, and cause enough
For calling up that spot of joy. She had
A heart—how shall I say?—too soon made glad,
Too easily impressed; she liked whate'er
She looked on, and her looks went everywhere.
Sir, 'twas all one! My favor at her breast,
The dropping of the daylight in the west,
The bough of cherries some officious fool
Broke in the orchard for her, the white mule
She rode with round the terrace—all and each
Would draw from her alike the approving speech,
Or blush, at least. She thanked men—good! but thanked
Somehow—I know not how—as if she ranked
My gift of a nine-hundred-years-old name
With anybody's gift. Who'd stoop to blame
This sort of trifling? Even had you skill
In speech—(which I have not)—to make your will
Quite clear to such an one, and say, "Just this
Or that in you disgusts me; here you miss,
Or there exceed the mark"—and if she let
Herself be lessoned so, nor plainly set
Her wits to yours, forsooth, and made excuse,
—E'en then would be some stooping; and I choose
Never to stoop. Oh, Sir, she smiled, no doubt,
Whene'er I passed her; but who passed without
Much the same smile? This grew; I gave commands;
Then all smiles stopped together. There she stands
As if alive. Will't please you rise? We'll meet
The company below, then. I repeat,
The Count your master's known munificence
Is ample warrant that no just pretense
Of mine for dowry will be disallowed;
Though his fair daughter's self, as I avowed
At starting, is my object. Nay, we'll go
Together down, Sir. Notice Neptune, though,
Taming a sea-horse, thought a rarity,
Which Claus of Innsbruck° cast in bronze for me!

[*1844*]

**55 Claus of Innsbruck** a fictitious sculptor

## TOPICS FOR CRITICAL THINKING AND WRITING

1. What is the occasion for the meeting?
2. What words or lines do you think especially convey the speaker's arrogance? What is your attitude toward the speaker? Loathing? Fascination? Respect? Explain.

3. The time and place are Renaissance Italy; how do they affect your attitude toward the duke? What would be the effect if the poem were set in the late twentieth century?
4. Years after writing this poem, Browning explained that the duke's "commands" (line 45) were "that she should be put to death, or he might have had her shut up in a convent." Do you think the poem should have been more explicit? Does Browning's later uncertainty indicate that the poem is badly thought out? Suppose we did not have Browning's comment on line 45. Do you think the line then could mean only that he commanded her to stop smiling and that she obeyed? Explain.

# DICTION AND TONE

From the whole of language, one consciously or unconsciously selects certain words and grammatical constructions; this selection constitutes one's **diction.** It is partly by the diction that we come to know the speaker of a poem. Stevie Smith's speaker used words such as "chap" and "larking," which are scarcely imaginable in the mouth of Browning's Renaissance duke. But of course some words are used in both poems: "I," "you," "thought," "the," and so on. The fact remains, however, that although a large part of language is shared by all speakers, certain parts of language are used only by certain speakers.

Like some words, some grammatical constructions are used only by certain kinds of speakers. Consider these two passages:

In Adam's fall
We sinned all.
—Anonymous, *The New England Primer*

Of Man's first disobedience, and the fruit
Of that forbidden tree whose mortal taste
Brought death into the World, and all our woe,
With loss of Eden, till one greater Man
Restore us, and regain the blissful seat,
Sing, Heavenly Muse, that, on the secret top
Of Oreb, or of Sinai, didst inspire
That shepherd who first taught the chosen seed
In the beginning how the heavens and earth
Rose out of Chaos. . . .
—Milton, *Paradise Lost*

There is an enormous difference in the diction of these two passages. Milton, speaking as an inspired poet, appropriately uses words and grammatical constructions somewhat removed from common life. Hence, while the anonymous author of the primer speaks directly of "Adam's fall," Milton speaks allusively of the fall, calling it "Man's first disobedience." Milton's sentence is nothing that any Englishman ever said in conversation; its genitive beginning, its length (the sentence continues for six lines beyond the quoted passage), and its postponement of the main verb ("Sing") until the sixth line mark it as the utterance of a poet working in the tradition of Latin poetry. The primer's statement, by its choice of words as well as by its brevity, suggests a far less sophisticated speaker.

Speakers have attitudes toward themselves, their subjects, and their audiences, and (consciously or unconsciously) they choose their words, pitch, and modulation accordingly; all these add up to the **tone.** In written literature, tone must be detected without the aid of the ear; the reader must understand by the selection and sequence of words the way in which they are meant to be heard (that is, playfully, angrily, confidentially, sarcastically, etc.). The reader must catch what Frost calls "the speaking tone of voice somehow entangled in the words and fastened to the page of the ear of the imagination."*

## ROBERT HERRICK

*Robert Herrick (1591-1674) was born in London, the son of a goldsmith. After taking an M.A. at Cambridge, he was ordained in the Church of England, and later he was sent to the country parish of Dean Prior in Devonshire, where he wrote most of his poetry. A loyal supporter of the king, in 1647 he was expelled from his parish by the Puritans, though in 1662 he was restored to Dean Prior.*

# *To the Virgins, to Make Much of Time*

Gather ye rosebuds while ye may,
    Old Time is still a-flying;
And this same flower that smiles today,
    Tomorrow will be dying.

The glorious lamp of heaven, the sun,
    The higher he's a-getting,
The sooner will his race be run,
    And nearer he's to setting.

That age is best which is the first,
    When youth and blood are warmer;
But being spent, the worse, and worst
    Times still succeed the former.

Then be not coy, but use your time;
    And while ye may, go marry:
For having lost but once your prime,
    You may for ever tarry.

[*1648*]

*Carpe diem* (Latin: "seize the day") is the theme. But if we want to get the full force of the poem, we must understand who is talking to whom. Look, for example, at "Old Time" in line 2. Time is "old" in the sense of having been around a long while, but doesn't "old" in this context suggest also that the speaker re-

*This discussion concentrates on the speaker's tone. But one can also talk of the author's tone, that is, of the author's attitude toward the invented speaker. The speaker's tone might, for example, be angry, but the author's tone (as detected by the reader) might be humorous.

gards Time with easy familiarity, almost affection? We visit the old school, and our friend is old George. Time is destructive, yes, and the speaker urges the young maidens to make the most of their spring, but the speaker is neither bitter nor importunate; rather, he seems to be the wise old man, the counselor, the man who has made his peace with Time and is giving advice to the young. Time moves rapidly in the poem (the rosebud of line 1 is already a flower in line 3), but the speaker is unhurried; in line 5 he has leisure to explain that the glorious lamp of heaven is the sun.

In "To the Virgins," the pauses, indicated by punctuation at the ends of the lines (except in line 11, where we tumble without stopping from "worst" to "Times"), slow the reader down. But even if there is no punctuation at the end of a line of poetry, the reader probably pauses slightly or gives the final word an additional bit of emphasis. Similarly, the space between stanzas slows a reader down, increasing the emphasis on the last word of one stanza and the first word of the next.

## THOMAS HARDY

*Thomas Hardy (1840–1928) was born in Dorset, England, the son of a stonemason. Despite great obstacles he studied the classics and architecture, and in 1862 he moved to London to study and practice as an architect. Ill health forced him to return to Dorset, where he continued to work as an architect and to write. Best known for his novels, Hardy ceased writing fiction after the hostile reception of* Jude the Obscure *in 1896 and turned to writing lyric poetry.*

### *The Man He Killed*

"Had he and I but met
By some old ancient inn,
We should have sat us down to wet
Right many a nipperkin°!

"But ranged as infantry,
And staring face to face,
I shot at him as he at me,
And killed him in his place.

"I shot him dead because—
Because he was my foe,
Just so: my foe of course he was;
That's clear enough; although

"He thought he'd 'list, perhaps,
Off-hand like—just as I—
Was out of work—had sold his traps°—
No other reason why.

**4 nipperkin** cup **15 traps** personal belongings

"Yes; quaint and curious war is!
You shoot a fellow down
You'd treat if met where any bar is,
Or help to half-a-crown."

[*1902*]

## TOPICS FOR CRITICAL THINKING AND WRITING

1. What do we learn about the speaker's life before he enlisted in the infantry? How does his diction characterize him?
2. What is the effect of the series of monosyllables in lines 7 and 8?
3. Consider the punctuation of the third and fourth stanzas. Why are the heavy, frequent pauses appropriate? What question is the speaker trying to answer?
4. In the last stanza, what attitudes toward war does the speaker express? What, from the evidence of this poem, would you infer Hardy's attitude toward war to be?

## WALTER DE LA MARE

*Walter de la Mare (1873–1956) was born in Kent, England. He worked for many years as an accountant for the Anglo-American Oil Company until a legacy enabled him to devote his life to writing lyric poetry and fiction.*

### *An Epitaph*

Here lies a most beautiful lady:
Light of step and heart was she;
I think she was the most beautiful lady
That ever was in the West Country.

But beauty vanishes; beauty passes;
However rare—rare it be;
And when I crumble, who will remember
This lady of the West Country?

[*1925*]

## TOPICS FOR CRITICAL THINKING AND WRITING

1. Who is the speaker of the poem?
2. Do you think that the simple language lacks dignity? In some older poetry, especially poetry that was passed down orally, a word of two syllables at the end of the line has the stress on the second syllable, as "sailór." In this poem, what is the effect of rhyming "country" and "she" and "be"?
3. Do you think that the last two lines introduce a new idea, or do they deepen the implications of the earlier lines? When you read aloud the

final stanza, pay special notice to the pause at the end of line 6. How does your voice register the movement from line 6 to line 7?

## ELIZABETH BISHOP

*Elizabeth Bishop (1911–79) was born in Worcester, Massachusetts. Because her father died when she was eight months old and her mother was confined to a sanitarium four years later, Bishop was raised by relatives in New England and Nova Scotia. After graduating from Vassar College in 1934, where she was co-editor of the student literary magazine, she lived (on a small private income) for a while in Key West, France, and Mexico, and then for much of her adult life in Brazil, before returning to the United States to teach at Harvard. Her financial independence enabled her to write without worrying about the sales of her books and without having to devote energy to distracting jobs.*

### *Filling Station*

Oh, but it is dirty!
—this little filling station,
oil-soaked, oil-permeated
to a disturbing, over-all
black translucency.
Be careful with that match!

Father wears a dirty,
oil-soaked monkey suit
that cuts him under the arms,
and several quick and saucy
and greasy sons assist him
(it's a family filling station),
all quite thoroughly dirty.

Do they live in the station?
It has a cement porch
behind the pumps, and on it
a set of crushed and grease-
impregnated wickerwork;
on the wicker sofa
a dirty dog, quite comfy.

Some comic books provide
the only note of color—
of certain color. They lie
upon a big dim doily
draping a taboret

(part of the set), beside
a big hirsute begonia.

Why the extraneous plant?
Why the taboret?
Why, oh why, the doily?
(Embroidered in daisy stitch
with marguerites, I think,
and heavy with gray crochet.)

Somebody embroidered the doily.
Somebody waters the plant,
or oils it, maybe. Somebody
arranges the rows of cans
so that they softly say:
ESSO°—SO—SO—SO
to high-strung automobiles.
Somebody loves us all.

[*1965*]

39 ESSO a brand of gasoline, now Exxon

## TOPICS FOR CRITICAL THINKING AND WRITING

1. Elizabeth Bishop might have chosen to invent a male speaker. But she didn't. What words or phrases in "Filling Station" convince you that the speaker is a woman?
2. Taking into account only the first 14 lines, how would you characterize the speaker?
3. Would you agree that in the third stanza a reader begins to feel more sympathetic toward the speaker? Why? Because the speaker seems to be somewhat more sympathetic toward the family and the gas station? What do you make of "comfy" in line 20? Is it the speaker's word? Or is the speaker using a word that might be used by the owners of the gas station?
4. In lines 21–30, what evidence suggests that the speaker feels that her taste is superior to the taste of the family? Do you think that she changes her tone later? A little, a lot, or not at all?

## GERARD MANLEY HOPKINS

*Gerard Manley Hopkins (1844–89) was born near London and was educated at Oxford, where he studied the classics. A convert from Anglicanism to Roman Catholicism, he was ordained a Jesuit priest in 1877. After serving as a parish priest and teacher, he was appointed Professor of Greek at the Catholic University in Dublin.*

*Hopkins published only a few poems during his lifetime, partly because he believed that the pursuit of literary fame was incompatible with his vocation as a priest, and partly because he was aware that his highly individual style might puzzle readers.*

## *Spring and Fall: To a Young Child*

Márgarét, are you gríeving
Over Goldengrove unleaving?
Léaves, líke the things of man, you
With your fresh thoughts care for, can you?
Áh! ás the heart grows older
It will come to such sights colder
By and by, nor spare a sigh
Though worlds of wanwood leafmeal lie;
And yet you will weep and know why.
Now no matter, child, the name:
Sórrow's spríngs áre the same.
Nor mouth had, no nor mind, expressed
What heart heard of, ghost° guessed:
It ís the blight man was born for,
It ís Margaret you mourn for.

[*1880*]

**13 ghost** spirit

## TOPICS FOR CRITICAL THINKING AND WRITING

1. About how old do you think the speaker is? What is his tone? What connection can you make between the title and the speaker and Margaret? What meanings do you think may be in "Fall"?
2. What is meant by Margaret's "fresh thoughts" (line 4)? Paraphrase (put into your own words) lines 3-4 and lines 12-13.
3. "Wanwood" and "leafmeal" are words coined by Hopkins. What do they suggest to you?
4. How can you explain the apparent contradiction that Margaret weeps for herself (line 15) after the speaker has said that she weeps for "Goldengrove unleaving" (line 2)?

## WILLIAM BLAKE

*William Blake (1757-1827) was born in London and at age 14 was apprenticed for seven years to an engraver. A Christian visionary poet, he made his living by giving drawing lessons and by illustrating books, including his own* Songs of Innocence *(1789) and* Songs of Experience *(1794). These two books represent, he said, "two contrary states of the human soul." ("The Clod and the Pebble" comes from* Experience.*) In 1809 Blake exhibited his art, but the show was a failure. Not until he was in his sixties, when he stopped writing poetry, did he achieve any public recognition—and then it was as a painter.*

## *The Clod and the Pebble*

"Love seeketh not Itself to please,
Nor for itself hath any care;
But for another gives its ease,
And builds a Heaven in Hell's despair."

So sang a little Clod of Clay,
Trodden with the cattle's feet;
But a Pebble of the brook,
Warbled out these meters meet:

"Love seeketh only Self to please,
To bind another to its delight;
Joys in another's loss of ease,
And builds a Hell in Heaven's despite."

[*1794*]

## TOPICS FOR CRITICAL THINKING AND WRITING

1. Can one reasonably say that the clod is feminine, the pebble masculine? Can one reasonably say that the clod needs the pebble, and the pebble needs the clod? Explain.
2. The clod and the pebble each express an uncompromising view. Does Blake express a preference for one or for the other? Or does he imply that both points of view have merit? Explain.

## COUNTEE CULLEN

*Countee Cullen (1903–46) was born Countee Porter in New York City, raised by his grandmother, and then adopted by the Reverend Frederick A. Cullen, a Methodist minister in Harlem. Cullen received a bachelor's degree from New York University (Phi Beta Kappa) and a master's degree from Harvard. He earned his living as a high school teacher of French, but his literary gifts were recognized in his own day. Cullen sometimes wrote about black life, but he also wrote on other topics, insisting that African-Americans need not work only in the literary tradition exemplified by such writers as Langston Hughes.*

## *For a Lady I Know*

She even thinks that up in heaven
  Her class lies late and snores,
While poor black cherubs rise at seven
  To do celestial chores.

[*1925*]

## TOPICS FOR CRITICAL THINKING AND WRITING

1. What is the gist of what Cullen is saying?
2. How would you characterize the tone? Furious? Indifferent?

## LYN LIFSHIN

***Born in Burlington, Vermont, in 1944, and educated at Syracuse University and the University of Vermont, Lyn Lifshin has written many books of poetry on a range of topics, from Shaker communities of early America to Eskimo culture in the Arctic. Much of her work shows a strong feminist concern.***

## *My Mother and the Bed*

No, not that way she'd
say when I was 7, pulling
the bottom sheet smooth,
you've got to    saying
hospital corners

I wet the bed much later
than I should, until
just writing this I
hadn't thought of
the connection

My mother would never
sleep on sheets someone
else had    I never
saw any stains on hers
tho her bedroom was
a maze of powder    hair
pins    black dresses
Sometimes she brings her
own sheets to my house,
carries toilet seat covers

Did anybody sleep
in my    she always asks
Her sheets    her hair
she says the rooms here
smell funny

We drive at 3 am
slowly into Boston and
strip what looks like
two clean beds as the
sky gets light    I

smooth on the form
fitted flower bottom,
she redoes it
She thinks of my life
as a bed only she
can make right

## TOPICS FOR CRITICAL THINKING AND WRITING

1. What do you make of the extra spaces—for instance, the space between "to" and "saying" in line 4? In reading the poem aloud, how do you "read" the spaces?
2. Would you agree that the poem is humorous and, on the whole, genial? Or do you think that bitterness overshadows the humor? Explain.
3. One student made the suggestion that the final stanza, perhaps because it seems to "explain" the poem to the reader, is the least effective part of the poem. Do you agree? If you do, write a new final stanza.

# THE VOICE OF THE SATIRIST

The writer of **satire,** in one way or another, ridicules an aspect or several aspects of human behavior, seeking to arouse in the reader some degree of amused contempt for the object. However urbane in tone, the satirist is always critical. By cleverly holding up foibles or vices for the world's derision, satire (Alexander Pope claimed) "heals with morals what it hurts with wit." The laughter of comedy is an end in itself; the laughter of satire is a weapon against the world: "The intellectual dagger," Frank O'Connor called satire, "opposing the real dagger." Jonathan Swift, of whom O'Connor is speaking, insisted that his satires were not malice but medicine:

His satire points at no defect
But what all mortals may correct. . . .
He spared a hump or crooked nose,
Whose owners set not up for beaux.

But Swift, although he claimed that satire is therapeutic, also saw its futility: "Satire is a sort of glass [i.e., mirror] wherein beholders do generally discover everybody's face but their own."

Sometimes the satirist speaks out directly as defender of public morals, abusively but wittily chopping off heads. Byron, for example, wrote:

> Prepare for rhyme—I'll publish, right or wrong:
> Fools are my theme, let Satire be my song.

But sometimes the satirist chooses to invent a speaker far removed from himself or herself, just as Browning chose to invent a Renaissance duke. The satirist may invent a callous brigadier general or a pompous judge who unconsciously annihilates himself. Consider this satirical poem by e. e. cummings (pen name of Edwin Estlin Cummings).

## E. E. CUMMINGS

*Edwin Estlin Cummings (1894–1962) grew up in Cambridge, Massachusetts, and was graduated from Harvard, where he became interested in modern literature and art, especially in the movements called cubism and futurism. His father, a conservative clergyman and a professor at Harvard, seems to have been baffled by the youth's interests, but Cummings's mother encouraged his artistic activities, including his use of unconventional punctuation as a means of expression.*

*Politically liberal in his youth, Cummings became more conservative after a visit to Russia in 1931, but early and late his work emphasizes individuality and freedom of expression.*

### *next to of course god america i*

"next to of course god america i
love you land of the pilgrims' and so forth oh
say can you see by the dawn's early my
country 'tis of centuries come and go
and are no more what of it we should worry
in every language even deafanddumb
thy sons acclaim your glorious name by gorry
by jingo by gee by gosh by gum
why talk of beauty what could be more beautiful than these heroic happy dead
who rushed like lions to the roaring slaughter
they did not stop to think they died instead
then shall the voice of liberty be mute?"

He spoke. And drank rapidly a glass of water

[*1926*]

Cummings might have written, in the voice of a solid citizen or a good poet, a direct attack on chauvinistic windbags; instead, he chose to invent a windbag whose rhetoric punctures itself. Yet the last line tells that we are really hearing someone who is recounting what the windbag said; that is, the speaker of all the lines but the last is a combination of the chauvinist *and* the satiric observer of the chauvinist. (When Cummings himself recited these lines, there was mockery in his voice.)

Only in the final line of the poem does the author seem to speak entirely on his own, and even here he adopts a matter-of-fact pose that is far more potent than **invective** (direct abuse) would be. Yet the last line is not totally free of explicit hostility. It might, for example, have run, "He spoke. And slowly poured a glass of water." Why does this version lack the punch of Cummings's? And what do you think is implied by the absence of a final period in line 14?

## JOHN UPDIKE

*John Updike (b. 1932) grew up in Shillington, Pennsylvania, where his father was a teacher and his mother a writer. After receiving a B.A. degree in 1954 from Harvard, he studied drawing at Oxford for a year, but returned to the United States to work for* The New Yorker. *Best noted for his novels, he has also published volumes of poetry and short stories.*

### *Youth's Progress*

Dick Schneider of Wisconsin . . . was elected "Greek God" for an interfraternity ball.

—*Life*

When I was born, my mother taped my ears
So they lay flat. When I had aged ten years,
My teeth were firmly braced and much improved.
Two years went by; my tonsils were removed.

At fourteen, I began to comb my hair
A fancy way. Though nothing much was there,
I shaved my upper lip—next year, my chin.
At seventeen, the freckles left my skin.

Just turned nineteen, a nicely molded lad,
I said goodbye to Sis and Mother; Dad
Drove me to Wisconsin and set me loose.
At twenty-one, I was elected Zeus.

[*1955*]

## TOPICS FOR CRITICAL THINKING AND WRITING

1. Suppose the first two lines ran thus:

   To keep them flat, my mother taped my ears;
   And then, at last, when I had aged ten years . . . .

How does this revision destroy the special tone of voice in the original two lines? (Notice that in the revision there is a heavy pause at the end of the first line.) Why, in the second line of the revision, is "at last" false to the "tone" or "voice" in the rest of the poem?

2. What do you think is the speaker's attitude toward himself? What is the author's attitude toward the speaker?

## MARGE PIERCY

*Marge Piercy, born in Detroit in 1936, was the first member of her family to attend college. After earning a bachelor's degree from the University of Michigan in 1957 and a master's degree from Northwestern University in 1958, she moved to Chicago. There she worked at odd jobs while writing novels (unpublished) and engaging in action on behalf of women and blacks and against the war in Vietnam. In 1970—the year she moved to Wellfleet, Massachusetts, where she still lives—she published her first book, a novel. Since then she has published other novels, as well as short stories, poems, and essays.*

### *Barbie Doll*

This girlchild was born as usual
and presented dolls that did pee-pee
and miniature GE stoves and irons
and wee lipsticks the color of cherry candy.
Then in the magic of puberty, a classmate said:
You have a great big nose and fat legs.

She was healthy, tested intelligent,
possessed strong arms and back,
abundant sexual drive and manual dexterity.
She went to and fro apologizing.
Everyone saw a fat nose on thick legs.

She was advised to play coy,
exhorted to come on hearty,
exercise, diet, smile and wheedle.
Her good nature wore out
like a fan belt.
So she cut off her nose and her legs
and offered them up.
In the casket displayed on satin she lay
with the undertaker's cosmetics painted on,
a turned-up putty nose,
dressed in a pink and white nightie.
Doesn't she look pretty? everyone said.
Consummation at last.
To every woman a happy ending.

[*1969*]

## TOPICS FOR CRITICAL THINKING AND WRITING

1. Why is the poem called "Barbie Doll"?
2. What voice do you hear in lines 1–4? Line 6 is, we are told, the voice of "a classmate." How do these voices differ? What voice do you hear in the first three lines of the second stanza?
3. Explain in your own words what Piercy is saying about women in this poem. Does her view seem to you fair, slightly exaggerated, or greatly exaggerated?

# *What's That Smell in the Kitchen?*

All over America women are burning dinners.
It's lambchops in Peoria; it's haddock
in Providence; it's steak in Chicago;
tofu delight in Big Sur; red
rice and beans in Dallas.
All over America women are burning
food they're supposed to bring with calico
smile on platters glittering like wax.
Anger sputters in her brainpan, confined
but spewing out missiles of hot fat.
Carbonized despair presses like a clinker
from a barbecue against the back of her eyes.
If she wants to grill anything, it's
her husband spitted over a slow fire.
If she wants to serve him anything
it's a dead rat with a bomb in its belly
ticking like the heart of an insomniac.
Her life is cooked and digested,
nothing but leftovers in Tupperware.
Look, she says, once I was roast duck
on your platter with parsley but now I am Spam.
Burning dinner is not incompetence but war.

[*1982*]

## TOPICS FOR CRITICAL THINKING AND WRITING

1. Suppose a friend told you that she didn't understand lines 21–22. How would you paraphrase the lines?
2. Who speaks the title?

3. If a poem begins, "All over America women are . . . ," what words might a reader reasonably expect next?
4. Do you take the poem to be chiefly comic? Superficially comic but a work with a serious purpose?

## MITSUYE YAMADA

***Mitsuye Yamada, the daughter of Japanese immigrants to the United States, was born in Japan in 1923, during her mother's return visit to her native land. Yamada was raised in Seattle, but in 1942 she and her family were incarcerated and then relocated in a camp in Idaho, when Executive Order 9066 gave military authorities the right to remove any and all persons from "military areas." In 1954 she became an American citizen. A professor of English at Cypress Junior College in San Luis Obispo, California, she is the author of poems and stories.***

### *To the Lady*

The one in San Francisco who asked:
Why did the Japanese Americans let
the government put them in
those camps without protest?

Come to think of it I
should've run off to Canada
should've hijacked a plane to Algeria
should've pulled myself up from my
bra straps
and kicked'm in the groin
should've bombed a bank
should've tried self-immolation
should've holed myself up in a
woodframe house
and let you watch me
burn up on the six o'clock news
should've run howling down the street
naked and assaulted you at breakfast
by AP wirephoto
should've screamed bloody murder
like Kitty Genovese°

Then
YOU would've
come to my aid in shining armor

**21 Kitty Genovese** In 1964 Kitty Genovese of Kew Gardens, New York, was stabbed to death when she left her car and walked toward her home. Thirty-eight persons heard her screams, but no one came to her assistance.

laid yourself across the railroad track
marched on Washington
tatooed a Star of David on your arm
written six million enraged
letters to Congress

But we didn't draw the line
anywhere
law and order Executive Order 9066°
social order moral order internal order

YOU let'm
I let'm
All are punished.

[*1976*]

**32 Executive Order 9066** an authorization, signed in 1941 by President Franklin D. Roosevelt, allowing military authorities to relocate Japanese and Japanese-Americans who resided on the Pacific Coast of the United States

## TOPICS FOR CRITICAL THINKING AND WRITING

1. Has the lady's question (lines 2–4) ever crossed your mind? If so, what answers did you think of?
2. What, in effect, is the speaker really saying in lines 5–21? And in lines 24–29?
3. Explain the last line.

## LOUISE ERDRICH

*Louise Erdrich was born in North Dakota in 1954; her father (born in Germany) and her mother (a Chippewa) both worked for the Bureau of Indian Affairs. After graduating from Dartmouth College in 1976, she returned to North Dakota to teach in the Poetry in the Schools Program. In 1979 she received a master's degree in creative writing from Johns Hopkins University. She now lives in New Hampshire with her husband and collaborator, Michael Dorris, a professor of Native American Studies at Dartmouth, and their five children. Although Erdrich is most widely known as a novelist, she has also won a reputation as a poet.*

### *Dear John Wayne*

August and the drive-in picture is packed.
We lounge on the hood of the Pontiac
surrounded by the slow-burning spirals they sell
at the window, to vanquish the hordes of mosquitoes.
Nothing works. They break through the smoke screen for blood.

Always the lookout spots the Indians first,
spread north to south, barring progress.
The Sioux or some other Plains bunch
in spectacular columns, ICBM missiles,
feathers bristling in the meaningful sunset.

The drum breaks. There will be no parlance.
Only the arrows whining, a death-cloud of nerves
swarming down on the settlers
who die beautifully, tumbling like dust weeds
into the history that brought us all here
together: this wide screen beneath the sign of the bear.

The sky fills, acres of blue squint and eye
that the crowd cheers. His face moves over us,
a thick cloud of vengeance, pitted
like the land that was once flesh. Each rut,
each scar makes a promise: *It is*
*not over, this fight, not as long as you resist.*

*Everything we see belongs to us.*

A few laughing Indians fall over the hood
slipping in the hot spilled butter.
*The eye sees a lot, John, but the heart is so blind.*
*Death makes us owners of nothing.*
He smiles, a horizon of teeth
the credits reel over, and then the white fields
again blowing in the true-to-life dark.
The dark films over everything.
We get into the car
scratching our mosquito bites, speechless and small
as people are when the movie is done.
We are back in our skins.
How can we help but keep hearing his voice,
the flip side of the sound track, still playing:
*Come on, boys, we got them*
*where we want them, drunk, running.*
*They'll give us what we want, what we need.*
Even his disease was the idea of taking everything.
Those cells, burning, doubling, splitting out of their skins.

[*1984*]

## TOPICS FOR CRITICAL THINKING AND WRITING

1. Who is the speaker of most of the poem? Who speaks the italicized lines?
2. There are curious shifts in the diction, for instance from "some other Plains bunch" (line 8) to "parlance" (line 11). Whose voice do we hear in "some . . . bunch"? Consider, too, the diction in "to vanquish the hordes of mosquitoes" (line 4). If you were talking about mosquitoes,

you probably would not use the word "vanquish." What do you think Erdrich is up to?

3. What do you make of lines 24–25, talking of Indians "slipping in the hot spilled butter"? What connection do these lines have with what presumably is going on in the film?

---

## ✔ Checklist: Writing about the Speaking Tone of Voice

### Speaker and Tone

1. Who is the speaker? (Consider age, sex, personality, frame of mind, and tone of voice.) Is the speaker defined fairly precisely (for instance, an older woman speaking to a child), or is the speaker simply a voice meditating? (Jot down your first impressions, then reread the poem and make further jottings, if necessary.)
2. How would you characterize the language—colloquial, or elevated, or what?
3. Do you think the speaker is fully aware of what he or she is saying, or does the speaker unconsciously reveal his or her personality and values? What is your attitude toward this speaker?
4. Is the speaker narrating or reflecting on an earlier experience or attitude? If so, does he or she convey a sense of new awareness, such as regret for innocence lost?

### Audience

1. To whom is the speaker speaking?
2. What is the situation (including time and place)? (In some poems, a listener is strongly implied, but in others, especially those in which the speaker is meditating, there may be no audience other than the reader, who "overhears" the speaker.)

---

# CHAPTER 18

# *Figurative Language: Simile, Metaphor, Personification, Apostrophe*

HIPPOLYTA. 'Tis strange, my Theseus, that these lovers speak of.
THESEUS. More strange than true. I never may believe
These antique fables, nor these fairy toys.
Lovers and madmen have such seething brains,
Such shaping fantasies, that apprehend
More than cool reason ever comprehends.
The lunatic, the lover, and the poet,
Are of imagination all compact.
One sees more devils than vast hell can hold,
That is the madman. The lover, all as frantic,
Sees Helen's beauty in a brow of Egypt.
The poet's eye, in a fine frenzy rolling,
Doth glance from heaven to earth, from earth to heaven;
And as imagination bodies forth
The forms of things unknown, the poet's pen
Turns them to shapes, and gives to airy nothing
A local habitation and a name.
—Shakespeare, *A Midsummer Night's Dream,* V.i.1–17

Theseus was neither the first nor the last to suggest that poets, like lunatics and lovers, freely employ their imagination. Terms such as *poetic license* and *poetic justice* imply that poets are free to depict a never-never land. One has only to leaf through any anthology of poetry to encounter numerous statements that are, from a logical point of view, lunacies. Here are two quotations:

Look like th' innocent flower,
But be the serpent under 't.
—Shakespeare

Each outcry from the hunted hare
A fiber from the brain does tear.
—William Blake

The first of these is spoken by Lady Macbeth, when she urges her husband to murder King Duncan. How can a human being "Look like th' innocent flower," and how can a human being "be the serpent"? But Macbeth knows, and we know exactly what she means. We see and we feel her point, in a way that we would not if she had said, "Put on an innocent-looking face, but in fact kill the king."

And in the quotation from Blake, when we read that the hunted hare's plaintive cry serves to "tear" a "fiber" from our brain, we almost wince, even though we know that the statement is literally untrue.

On a literal level, then, such assertions are nonsense (so, too, is Theseus's notion that reason is cool). But of course they are not to be taken literally; rather, they employ **figures of speech**—departures from logical usage that are aimed at gaining special effects. Consider the lunacies that Robert Burns heaps up here.

## ROBERT BURNS

***Robert Burns (1759-96) was born in Ayrshire in southwestern Scotland. Many of his best poems and songs were written in the Scots dialect, though he also wrote perfect English.***

# *A Red, Red Rose*

O, my luve is like a red, red rose,
  That's newly sprung in June.
O, my luve is like the melodie,
  That's sweetly played in tune.

As fair art thou, my bonnie lass,
  So deep in luve am I,
And I will luve thee still, my dear,
  Till a'° the seas gang° dry.

Till a' the seas gang dry, my dear,
  And the rocks melt wi' the sun!
And I will luve thee still, my dear,
  While the sands o' life shall run.

And fare thee weel, my only luve,
  And fare thee weel awhile!
And I will come again, my luve,
  Though it were ten thousand mile!

[*1796*]

**8 a'** all **gang** go

To the charge that these lines are lunacies or untruths, at least two replies can be made. First, it might be said that the speaker is not really making assertions about a woman; he is saying he feels a certain way. His words, it can be argued, are not assertions about external reality but expressions of his state of mind, just as a tune one whistles asserts nothing about external reality but expresses the whistler's state of mind. In this view, the nonlogical language of poetry (like a groan of pain or an exclamation of joy) is an expression of emotion; its further aim, if it has one, is to induce in the hearer an emotion.

Second, and more to the point here, it can be said that nonlogical language does indeed make assertions about external reality, and even gives the reader an insight into this reality that logical language cannot. The opening comparison in Burns's poem ("my luve is like a red, red rose") brings before our eyes the lady's beauty in a way that the reasonable assertion "She is beautiful" does not. By comparing the woman to a rose, the poet invites us to see the woman through a special sort of lens: she is fragrant; her lips (and perhaps her cheeks) are like a rose in texture and color; she will not keep her beauty long. Also, "my love is like a red, red rose" says something different from "like a red, red beet," or "a red, red cabbage."

The poet, then, has not only communicated a state of mind but also has discovered, through the lens of imagination, some things (both in the beloved and in the lover's own feelings) that interest us. The discovery is not world-shaking; it is less important than the discovery of America or the discovery that the meek are blessed, but it *is* a discovery and it leaves the reader with the feeling, "Yes, that's right. I hadn't quite thought of it that way, but that's right."

A poem, Robert Frost said, "assumes direction with the first line laid down, . . . runs a course of lucky events, and ends in a clarification of life—not necessarily a great clarification, such as sects and cults are founded on, but in a momentary stay against confusion." What is clarified? In another sentence Frost gives an answer: "For me the initial delight is in the surprise of remembering something I didn't know I knew." John Keats made a similar statement: "Poetry . . . should strike the Reader as a wording of his own highest thoughts, and appear almost a Remembrance."

Some figures of speech are, in effect, riddling ways of speech. To call fishermen "farmers of the sea"—a metaphor—is to give a sort of veiled description of fishermen, bringing out, when the term is properly understood, certain aspects of a fisherman's activities. And a riddle, after all, is a veiled description—though intentionally obscure or deceptive—calling attention to characteristics, especially similarities, not usually noticed. (*Riddle,* like *read,* is from Old English *redan,* "to guess," "to interpret," and thus its solution provides knowledge.) "Two sisters upstairs, often looking but never seeing each other" is (after the riddle is explained) a way of calling attention to the curious fact that the eye, the instrument of vision, never sees its mate.

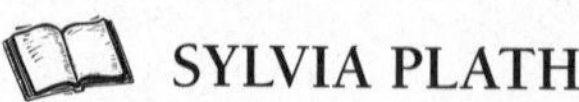

## SYLVIA PLATH

*Sylvia Plath (1932–63) was born in Boston, the daughter of German immigrants. While still an undergraduate at Smith College, she published in* Seventeen *and* Mademoiselle, *but her years at college, like her later years, were marked by manic-depressive periods. After graduating from college, she went to England to study at Cambridge University, where she met the English poet Ted Hughes, whom she married in 1956. The marriage was unsuccessful, and they separated. One day she committed suicide by turning on the kitchen gas.*

## *Metaphors*

I'm a riddle in nine syllables,
An elephant, a ponderous house,
A melon strolling on two tendrils.
O red fruit, ivory, fine timbers!
This loaf's big with its yeasty rising.
Money's new-minted in this fat purse.
I'm a means, a stage, a cow in calf.
I've eaten a bag of green apples,
Boarded the train there's no getting off.

[*1960*]

The riddling speaker says that she is, among other things, "a ponderous house" and "a cow in calf." What is she?

## SIMILE

In a **simile,** items from different classes are explicitly compared by a connective such as *like, as,* or *than* or by a verb such as *appears* or *seems.* (If the objects compared are from the same class, e.g., "New York is like Chicago," no simile is present.)

Sometimes I feel like a motherless child.
—Anonymous

It is a beauteous evening, calm and free.
The holy time is quiet as a Nun,
Breathless with adoration.
—Wordsworth

How sharper than a serpent's tooth it is
To have a thankless child.
—Shakespeare

Seems he a dove? His feathers are but borrowed.
—Shakespeare

## RICHARD WILBUR

*Richard Wilbur, born in New York City in 1921, was educated at Amherst and Harvard. He served in the army during World War II and in 1947 published* The Beautiful

Changes, *a book of poems that reflected some of his experience in Europe. This book and subsequent books of poetry established his literary reputation, but probably his most widely known works are the lyrics that he wrote for Leonard Bernstein's musical version of* Candide *(1956). In 1987 the Library of Congress named him U.S. Poet Laureate.*

## *A Simile for Her Smile*

Your smiling, or the hope, the thought of it,
Makes in my mind such pause and abrupt ease
As when the highway bridgegates fall,
Balking the hasty traffic, which must sit
On each side massed and staring, while
Deliberately the drawbridge starts to rise:

Then horns are hushed, the oilsmoke rarifies,
Above the idling motors one can tell
The packet's smooth approach, the slip,
Slip of the silken river past the sides,
The ringing of clear bells, the dip
And slow cascading of the paddle wheel.

[*1950*]

### TOPIC FOR CRITICAL THINKING OR WRITING

The title may lead you to think that the poet will compare the woman's smile to something. But, in fact, the comparison is not between her smile and the passing scene. What *is* being compared to the traffic?

## METAPHOR

A **metaphor** asserts the identity, without a connective such as *like* or a verb such as *appears,* of terms that are literally incompatible.

She is the rose, the glory of the day.
—Spenser

O western orb sailing the heaven.
—Whitman

Notice how in the second example only one of the terms ("orb") is stated; the other ("ship") is implied in "sailing."

### JOHN KEATS

*John Keats (1795–1821), son of a London stable keeper, was taken out of school when he was 15 and was ap-*

*prenticed to a surgeon and apothecary. In 1816 he was licensed to practice as an apothecary-surgeon, but he almost immediately abandoned medicine and decided to make a career as a poet. His progress was amazing; he quickly moved from routine verse to major accomplishments, publishing books of poems—to mixed reviews—in 1817, 1818, and 1820, before dying of tuberculosis at the age of 25.*

## *On First Looking into Chapman's Homer**

Much have I traveled in the realms of gold,
And many goodly states and kingdoms seen;
Round many western islands have I been
Which bards in fealty to Apollo° hold.
Oft of one wide expanse have I been told
That deep-browed Homer ruled as his demesne°;
Yet did I never breathe its pure serene°
Till I heard Chapman speak out loud and bold:
Then felt I like some watcher of the skies
When a new planet swims into his ken;
Or like stout Cortez when with eagle eyes
He stared at the Pacific—and all his men
Looked at each other with a wild surmise—
Silent, upon a peak in Darien.

[*1816*]

**4 Apollo** god of poetry **6 demesne** domain **7 serene** open space

## TOPICS FOR CRITICAL THINKING AND WRITING

1. In line 1, what do you think "realms of gold" stands for? Chapman was an Elizabethan; how does this fact add relevance to the metaphor in the first line?
2. Does line 9 introduce a totally new idea, or can you somehow connect it to the opening metaphor?

## MARGE PIERCY

*Two poems by Piercy (as well as a biographical note) appear on pages 882–83.*

*George Chapman (1559–1634?), Shakespeare's contemporary, is chiefly known for his translations (from the Greek) of Homer's *Odyssey* and *Iliad.* In lines 11–14 Keats mistakenly says that Cortez was the first European to see the Pacific, from the heights of Darien, in Panama. In fact, Balboa was the first.

## *A Work of Artifice*

The bonsai tree
in the attractive pot
could have grown eighty feet tall
on the side of a mountain
till split by lightning.
But a gardener
carefully pruned it.
It is nine inches high.
Every day as he
whittles back the branches
the gardener croons,
It is your nature
to be small and cozy,
domestic and weak;
how lucky, little tree,
to have a pot to grow in.
With living creatures
one must begin very early
to dwarf their growth:
the bound feet,
the crippled brain,
the hair in curlers,
the hands you
love to touch.

[*1973*]

## TOPICS FOR CRITICAL THINKING AND WRITING

1. Piercy uses a bonsai tree as a metaphor—but a metaphor for what? (If you have never seen a bonsai tree, try to visit a florist or a nursery to take a close look at one. You can find a picture of a bonsai in *The American Heritage Dictionary*.)
2. The gardener "croons" (line 11) a song to the bonsai tree. If the tree could respond, what might it say?
3. Explain lines 17–24 to someone who doesn't get the point. In your response, explain how these lines are connected with "hair in curlers." Explain, too, what "the hands you / love to touch" has to do with the rest of the poem. What tone of voice do you hear in "the hands you / love to touch"?
4. How does the form of the poem suggest its subject?

Two types of metaphor deserve special mention. In **metonymy,** something is named that replaces something closely related to it; "City Hall," for example, sometimes is used to stand for municipal authority. In the following passage James Shirley names certain objects (scepter and crown; scythe and spade), using them to replace social classes (royalty; agricultural labor) to which they are related:

Scepter and crown must tumble down
And in the dust be equal made
With the poor crooked scythe and spade.

In **synecdoche,** the whole is replaced by the part, or the part by the whole. For example, *bread* in "Give us this day our daily bread" replaces the whole class of edibles. Similarly, an automobile can be "wheels," and workers are "hands." Robert Frost was fond of calling himself "a Synecdochist" because he believed that it is the nature of poetry to "have intimations of something more than itself. It almost always comes under the head of synecdoche, a part, a hem of the garment for the whole garment."

## PERSONIFICATION

The attribution of human feelings or characteristics to abstractions or to inanimate objects is called **personification.**

But Time did beckon to the flowers, and they
By noon most cunningly did steal away.
—Herbert

Herbert attributes a human gesture to Time and shrewdness to flowers. Of all figures, personification most surely gives to airy nothings a local habitation and a name:

There's Wrath who has learnt every trick of guerrilla warfare,
The shamming dead, the night-raid, the feinted retreat.
—Auden

Hope, thou bold taster of delight.
—Crashaw

The alarm clock meddling in somebody's sleep.
—Brooks

. . . neon script leering from the shuddering asphalt.
—Dove

## APOSTROPHE

Crashaw's personification, "Hope, thou bold taster of delight," is also an example of the figure called **apostrophe,** an address to a person or thing not literally listening. Wordsworth begins a sonnet by apostrophizing John Milton:

Milton, thou shouldst be living at this hour,

And Shelley begins an ode by apostrophizing a skylark:

Hail to thee, blithe Spirit!

The following poem is largely built on apostrophe.

## EDMUND WALLER

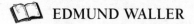

***Edmund Waller (1606–87), born into a country family of wealth in Buckinghamshire in England, attended Eton and Cambridge before spending most of his life as a member of parliament. When the Puritans came to power, he was imprisoned and eventually banished to France, although he was soon allowed to return to England. When the monarchy was restored to the throne, he returned to parliament.***

### *Song*

Go, lovely rose,
Tell her that wastes her time and me,
That now she knows,
When I resemble her to thee,
How sweet and fair she seems to be.

Tell her that's young,
And shuns to have her graces spied,
That hadst thou sprung
In deserts where no men abide,
Thou must have uncommended died.

Small is the worth
Of beauty from the light retired:
Bid her come forth,
Suffer her self to be desired,
And not blush so to be admired.

Then die, that she
The common fate of all things rare
May read in thee,
How small a part of time they share,
That are so wondrous sweet and fair.

[*1645*]

What conclusions, then, can we draw about **figurative language?** First, figurative language, with its literally incompatible terms, forces the reader to attend to the **connotations** (suggestions, associations) rather than to the **denotations** (dictionary definitions) of one of the terms.

Second, although figurative language is said to differ from ordinary discourse, it is found in ordinary discourse as well as in literature. "It rained cats and dogs," "War is hell," "Don't be a pig," and other tired figures are part of our daily utterances. But through repeated use, these (and most of the figures we use) have lost whatever impact they once had and are only a shade removed from expressions which, though once figurative, have become literal: the *eye* of a needle, a *branch* office, the *face* of a clock.

Third, good figurative language is usually (1) concrete, (2) condensed, and (3) interesting. The concreteness lends precision and vividness; when Keats writes that he felt "like some watcher of the skies / When a new planet swims into his ken," he more sharply characterizes his feelings than if he had said, "I felt excited." His simile isolates for us a precise kind of excitement, and the metaphoric "swims" vividly brings up the oceanic aspect of the sky. The second of these three qualities, condensation, can be seen by attempting to paraphrase some of the figures. A paraphrase or rewording will commonly use more words than the original and will have less impact—as the gradual coming of night usually has less impact on us than a sudden darkening of the sky or as a prolonged push has less impact than a sudden blow. The third quality, interest, largely depends on the previous two: the successful figure often makes us open our eyes wider and take notice. Keats's "deep-browed Homer" arouses our interest in Homer as "thoughtful Homer" or "meditative Homer" does not. Similarly, when W. B. Yeats says (p. 1071):

> An aged man is but a paltry thing,
> A tattered coat upon a stick, unless
> Soul clap its hands and sing, and louder sing
> For every tatter in its mortal dress,

the metaphoric identification of an old man with a scarecrow jolts us out of all our usual unthinking attitudes about old men as kind, happy folk content to have passed from youth to senior citizenship.

Finally, the point must be made that although figurative language is one of the poet's chief tools, a poem does not have to contain figures. The anonymous ballad "Edward" (p. 1047) contains no figures, yet surely it is a poem, and no one would say that the addition of figures would make it a better poem.

Here is a poem by William Carlos Williams. Does it contain any figures of speech?

## WILLIAM CARLOS WILLIAMS

*William Carlos Williams (1883–1963) was the son of an English traveling salesman and a Basque-Jewish woman. The couple met in Puerto Rico and settled in Rutherford, New Jersey, where Williams was born. He spent his life there, practicing as a pediatrician and writing poems in the moments between seeing patients who were visiting his office.*

### *The Red Wheelbarrow*

so much depends
upon

a red wheel
barrow

glazed with rain
water

beside the white
chickens.

[*1923*]

The following poems rely heavily on figures of speech.

## ALFRED, LORD TENNYSON

***Alfred, Lord Tennyson (1809–92), the son of an English clergyman, was born in Lincolnshire, where he began writing verse at age 5. Educated at Cambridge, he had to leave without a degree when his father died and Alfred had to accept responsibility for bringing up his brothers and sisters. In fact, the family had inherited ample funds, but for some years the money was tied up by litigation. In 1850 Tennyson was made poet laureate following Wordsworth's death. With his government pension he moved with his family to the Isle of Wight where he lived in vast comfort until his death.***

### *The Eagle*

Fragment

He clasps the crag with crooked hands;
Close to the sun in lonely lands,
Ringed with the azure world, he stands.
The wrinkled sea beneath him crawls:
He watches from his mountain walls,
And like a thunderbolt he falls.

[*1851*]

## TOPICS FOR CRITICAL THINKING AND WRITING

1. What figure is used in line 1? In line 4? In line 6? Can it be argued that the figures give us a sense of the eagle that is not to be found in a literal description?
2. In line 2 we get overstatement, or hyperbole, for the eagle is not really close to the sun. Suppose instead of "close to the sun" Tennyson had written "Waiting on high"? Do you think the poem would be improved or worsened?

## CHRISTINA ROSSETTI

***Christina Rossetti (1830–94) was the daughter of an exiled Italian patriot who lived in London and the sister of the poet and painter Dante Gabriel Rossetti. After her fa-***

*ther became an invalid, she led an extremely ascetic life, devoting most of her life to doing charitable work. Her first, and best known, volume of poetry,* Goblin Market and Other Poems, *was published in 1862.*

## *Uphill*

Does the road wind uphill all the way?
  Yes, to the very end.
Will the day's journey take the whole long day?
  From morn to night, my friend.

But is there for the night a resting-place?
  A roof for when the slow dark hours begin.
May not the darkness hide it from my face?
  You cannot miss that inn.

Shall I meet other wayfarers at night?
  Those who have gone before.
Then must I knock, or call when just in sight?
  They will not keep you standing at that door.

Shall I find comfort, travel-sore and weak?
  Of labor you shall find the sum.
Will there be beds for me and all who seek?
  Yea, beds for all who come.

[*1858*]

## TOPICS FOR CRITICAL THINKING AND WRITING

1. Suppose that someone told you this poem is about a person preparing to go on a hike. The person is supposedly making inquiries about the road and the possible hotel arrangements. What would you reply?
2. Who is the questioner? A woman? A man? All human beings collectively? Can one say that in "Uphill" the questioner and the answerer are the same person?
3. Are the answers unambiguously comforting? Or can it, for instance, be argued that the "roof" is (perhaps among other things) the lid of a coffin—hence the questioner will certainly not be kept "standing at the door"? If the poem can be read along these lines, is it chilling rather than comforting?

## RANDALL JARRELL

*Randall Jarrell (1914-65)—in the second name the accent is on the second syllable—was educated at Vanderbilt, where he majored in psychology. After serving with the air force in World War II, he taught in several colleges and universities, meanwhile establishing a reputation as a poet and as a literary critic.*

## *The Death of the Ball Turret Gunner*

From my mother's sleep I fell into the State,
And I hunched in its belly till my wet fur froze.
Six miles from earth, loosed from its dream of life,
I woke to black flak and the nightmare fighters.
When I died they washed me out of the turret with a hose.

[*1955*]

Jarrell has furnished an explanatory note: "A ball turret was a plexiglass sphere set into the belly of a B-17 or B-24, and inhabited by two .50 caliber machine-guns and one man, a short small man. When this gunner tracked with his machine-guns a fighter attacking his bomber from below, he revolved with the turret; hunched upside-down in his little sphere, he looked like the fetus in the womb. The fighters which attacked him were armed with cannon firing explosive shells. The hose was a steam hose."

## TOPICS FOR CRITICAL THINKING AND WRITING

1. What is implied in the first line? In "I woke to . . . nightmare"? Taking account of the title, do you think "wet fur" is literal or metaphoric or both? Do you find the simplicity of the last line anticlimactic? How does it continue the metaphor of birth?
2. Why do you think Jarrell ended each line with punctuation?

## SAMUEL JOHNSON

*Samuel Johnson (1709–84), essayist, poet, and dictionary maker, was regarded as the literary dictator of his day, but now he is best known as the subject of a wonderful biography by a friend, James Boswell. Readers who go beyond the biography will find that Johnson remains an impressive poet and literary critic.*

*The subject of the poem we print, Johnson's friend Robert Levet, was described by Boswell as "an obscure practiser in physick amongst the lower people." Levet, an unlicensed physician, paid house calls to the indigent, unlike most of his professional superiors.*

*Line 28 speaks of "the single talent." Johnson here is alluding to Jesus's parable of the talents, in Matthew 25.14–30. (In ancient times, in the classical and Middle Eastern world a* talent *was a unit of money.) Read the*

***parable and then think about the way in which Johnson adds a twist to the parable.***

## *On the Death of Mr. Robert Levet*

Condemned to Hope's delusive mine,
As on we toil from day to day,
By sudden blasts, or slow decline,
Our social comforts drop away.

Well tried through many a varying year,
See Levet to the grave descend,
Officious,° innocent, sincere,
Of every friendless name the friend.

Yet still he fills Affection's eye,
Obscurely wise and coarsely kind;
Nor, lettered Arrogance, deny
Thy praise to merit unrefined.

When fainting Nature called for aid,
And hovering Death prepared the blow,
His vigorous remedy displayed
The power of art without the show.

In Misery's darkest caverns known,
His useful care was ever nigh,
Where hopeless Anguish poured his groan,
And lonely Want retired to die.

No summons mocked by chill delay,
No petty gain disdained by pride;
The modest wants of every day
The toil of every day supplied.

His virtues walked their narrow round,
Nor made a pause, nor left a void;
And sure the Eternal Master found
The single talent well employed.

The busy day, the peaceful night,
Unfelt, uncounted, glided by;
His frame was firm, his powers were bright,
Though now his eightieth year was nigh.

Then with no throbbing, fiery pain,
No cold gradations of decay,
Death broke at once the vital chain,
And freed his soul the nearest way.

[*1783*]

7 **officious** obliging

## TOPICS FOR CRITICAL THINKING AND WRITING

1. How is the figure of the mine (line 1) continued in other stanzas?
2. Some readers find lines 9–12 out of place in a poem commemorating the death of a friend. What is your response?
3. Why is it appropriate that Levet's death was quick and easy?
4. Do you think that the lack of personal expression of grief suggests insincerity? Explain.

## SEAMUS HEANEY

*Seamus Heaney was born in Belfast, Northern Ireland, in 1939. He grew up on a farm, and then went to Queens University in Belfast. "Digging," the first poem in his first book, reveals his concern with getting to the bottom of things. Heaney has lectured widely in Ireland, England, and the United States, and he now lives half the year in Dublin and the other half in Cambridge, Massachusetts, where he teaches at Harvard. He is also Regius Professor of Poetry at Oxford, a post that has been held by Matthew Arnold and W. H. Auden. In addition to writing poetry he has written essays about poetry. In 1995 he was awarded the Nobel Prize for Literature.*

### *Digging*

Between my finger and my thumb
The squat pen rests; snug as a gun.

Under my window, a clean rasping sound
When the spade sinks into gravelly ground:
My father, digging, I look down

Till his straining rump among the flowerbeds
Bends low, comes up twenty years away
Stooping in rhythm through potato drills
Where he was digging.

The coarse boot nestled on the lug, the shaft
Against the inside knee was levered firmly.
He rooted out tall tops, buried the bright edge deep
To scatter new potatoes that we picked
Loving their cool hardness in our hands.
By God, the old man could handle a spade.
Just like his old man.

My grandfather cut more turf in a day
Than any other man on Toner's bog.
Once I carried him milk in a bottle
Corked sloppily with paper. He straightened up
To drink it, then fell to right away

Nicking and slicing neatly, heaving sods
Over his shoulder, going down and down
For the good turf. Digging.

The cold smell of potato mould, the
squelch and slap
Of soggy peat, the curt cuts of an edge
Through living roots awaken in my head.
But I've no spade to follow men like them.

Between my finger and my thumb
The squat pen rests.
I'll dig with it.

[*1966*]

## TOPICS FOR CRITICAL THINKING AND WRITING

1. The poem ends with the speaker saying that he will "dig" with his pen. Given all the preceding lines, what will he dig?
2. The first lines compare the pen with a gun. What implications are suggested by this comparison?

## LOUISE ERDRICH

*Louise Erdrich (b. 1954) is of German and Native American descent. For a fuller biography and another poem, see page 885.*

# *Indian Boarding School: The Runaways*

Home's the place we head for in our sleep.
Boxcars stumbling north in dreams
don't wait for us. We catch them on the run.
The rails, old lacerations that we love,
shoot parallel across the face and break
just under Turtle Mountains.° Riding scars
you can't get lost. Home is the place they cross.

The lame guard strikes a match and makes the dark
less tolerant. We watch through cracks in boards
as the land starts rolling, rolling till it hurts
to be here, cold in regulation clothes.
We know the sheriff's waiting at midrun
to take us back. His car is dumb and warm.
The highway doesn't rock, it only hums
like a wing of long insults. The worn-down welts
of ancient punishment lead back and forth.

**6 Turtle Mountains** mountains in North Dakota and Manitoba

All runaways wear dresses, long green ones,
the color you would think shame was. We scrub
the sidewalks down because it's shameful work.
Our brushes cut the stone in watered arcs
and in the soak frail outlines shiver clear
a moment, things us kids pressed on the dark
face before it hardened, pale, remembering
delicate old injuries, the spines of names and leaves.

[*1984*]

## TOPICS FOR CRITICAL THINKING AND WRITING

1. In line 4 the railroad tracks are called "old lacerations." What is the connection between the two?
2. What other imagery of injury do you find in the poem? In lines 20–24, what—literally—is "the dark / face" that "hardened, pale"?

---

## ✔ Checklist: Writing about Figurative Language

1. Are the figures of speech readily apparent, or were you unaware of them on first reading?
2. What kinds of figures of speech can you discover when you reread the poem carefully? (Note: Feel free to mark and circle examples in the text.) Are the figures predominantly of one kind? Or is one kind of figure (for example, personification) found in the early part of the poem and a different kind (for example, metaphor) found toward the end? If so, what do you make of the change?
3. How do the figures of speech contribute to the main theme or themes of the poem?

---

# CHAPTER 19

# *Imagery and Symbolism*

When we read the word "rose"—or, for that matter, "finger" or "thumb"—we may more or less call to mind a picture, an image. The term **imagery** is used to refer to whatever in a poem appeals to any of our sensations, including sensations of pressure and heat as well as of sight, smell, taste, touch, and sound.

Consider the opening lines of Seamus Heaney's "Digging" (p. 902):

> Between my finger and my thumb
> The squat pen rests; snug as a gun.

We may in our mind's eye see a finger, thumb, and pen; and perhaps, stimulated by "squat," we may almost feel the pen. Notice, too, that in Heaney's line the pen is compared to a gun, so there is yet another image in the line. In short, images are the sensory content of the work, whether literal (the finger, thumb, and pen) or figurative (the gun, to which the pen is compared). Edmund Waller's rose in "Go, Lovely Rose" (p. 896) is an image that happens to be compared in the first stanza to a woman ("I resemble her to thee"); later in the poem this image comes to stand for "all things rare." Yet we never forget that the rose is a rose, and that the poem is chiefly a revelation of the poet's attitude toward his beloved.

If a poet says "my rose" and is speaking about a rose, we have an image, even though we do not have a figure of speech. If a poet says "my rose" and, we gather, is speaking not really or chiefly about a rose but about something else—let's say the transience of beauty—we can say that the poet is using the rose as a symbol.

Some symbols are **natural symbols,** recognized as standing for something in particular even by people from different cultures. Rain, for instance, usually stands for fertility or the renewal of life. A forest often stands for mental darkness or chaos, a mountain for stability, a valley for a place of security, and so on. There are many exceptions, but by and large these meanings prevail.

Other symbols, however, are **conventional symbols,** which people have agreed to accept as standing for something other than themselves: A poem about the cross would probably be about Christianity. Similarly, the rose has long been a symbol for love. In Virginia Woolf's novel *Mrs. Dalloway,* the husband communicates his love by proffering this conventional symbol: "He was holding out flowers—roses, red and white roses. (But he could not bring himself to say he loved her; not in so many words.)" Objects that are not conventional symbols, however, also may give rise to rich, multiple, indefinable associations. The following poem uses the symbol of the rose but uses it in a nontraditional way.

## WILLIAM BLAKE

*A biography of Blake, along with one of his poems, appears on page 876. Additional poems by Blake appear on pages 1057–59.*

### *The Sick Rose*

O rose, thou are sick!
The invisible worm
That flies in the night
In the howling storm

Has found out thy bed
Of crimson joy,
And his dark secret love
Does thy life destroy.

[*1794*]

One might argue that the worm is "invisible" (line 2) merely because it is hidden within the rose, but an "invisible worm / That flies in the night" is more than a long, slender, soft-bodied creeping animal; and a rose that has, or is, a "bed / Of crimson joy" is more than a gardener's rose.

Blake's worm and rose suggest things beyond themselves—a stranger, more vibrant world than the world we are usually aware of. Many readers find themselves half-thinking, for example, that the worm is male, the rose female, and that the poem is about the violation of virginity. Or that the poem is about the destruction of beauty: woman's beauty, rooted in joy, is destroyed by a power that feeds on her. But these interpretations are not fully satisfying: the poem presents a worm and a rose, and yet it is not merely about a worm and a rose. These objects resonate, stimulating our thoughts toward something else, but the something else is elusive, whereas it is not elusive in Burns's "A Red, Red Rose" (p. 889).

A **symbol,** then, is an image so loaded with significance that it is not simply literal, and it does not simply stand for something else; it is both itself *and* something else that it richly suggests, a manifestation of something too complex or too elusive to be otherwise revealed. Blake's poem is about a blighted rose and at the same time about much more. In a symbol, as Thomas Carlyle wrote, "the Infinite is made to blend with the Finite, to stand visible, and as it were, attainable there." Probably it is not fanciful to say that the American slaves who sang

"Joshua fought the battle of Jericho, / And the walls came tumbling down" were singing both about an ancient occurrence *and* about a new embodiment of the ancient, the imminent collapse of slavery in the nineteenth century. Not one or the other, but both: the present partook of the past, and the past partook of the present.

## WALT WHITMAN

*Walt Whitman (1819–92) was born in a farmhouse in rural Long Island, New York, but was brought up in Brooklyn, then an independent city in New York. He attended public school for a few years (1825–30), apprenticed as a printer in the 1830s, and then worked as a typesetter, journalist, and newspaper editor. In 1855 he published the first edition of a collection of his poems,* Leaves of Grass, *a book that he revised and published throughout the remainder of his life. During the Civil War he served as a volunteer nurse for the Union army.*

*In the third edition of* Leaves of Grass *(1860) Whitman added two groups of poems, one called "Children of Adam" and the other (named for an aromatic grass that grows near ponds and swamps) called "Calamus." "Children of Adam" celebrates heterosexual relations, whereas "Calamus" celebrates what Whitman called "manly love." Although many of the "Calamus" poems seem clearly homosexual, perhaps the very fact that Whitman published them made them seem relatively innocent; in any case, those nineteenth-century critics who condemned Whitman for the sexuality of his writing concentrated on the poems in "Children of Adam."*

*"I Saw in Louisiana" is from the "Calamus" section. It was originally published in the third edition of* Leaves of Grass *and was revised into its final form in the 1867 edition. We give it in the 1867 version. We also give the manuscript, showing it in its earliest extant version.*

# *I Saw in Louisiana a Live-Oak Growing.*

I saw in Louisiana a live-oak growing,
All alone stood it and the moss hung down from the branches,
Without any companion it grew there uttering joyous leaves of
  dark green,
And its look, rude, unbending, lusty, made me think of myself,
But I wonder'd how it could utter joyous leaves standing alone
  there without its friend near, for I knew I could not,
And I broke off a twig with a certain number of leaves upon it,
  and twined around it a little moss,
And brought it away, and I have placed it in sight in my room,
It is not needed to remind me as of my own dear friends,

*(continued on page 910)*

Calamus 20
p 364

II

I saw in Louisiana a
live-oak growing,
All alone stood it, and the
moss hung down from the
branches,
Without any companion it grew
there, glistening out ~~with~~
joyous leaves of dark green,
And its look, rude, unbending,
lusty, made me think of
myself;
But I wondered how it could
utter joyous leaves, standing
alone there without its friend,
its lover — For I knew I could
not;
And I plucked a twig with
a certain number of leaves
upon it, and twined around
it a little moss, and brought
it away — And I have placed
it in sight in my room,

2

Walt Whitman, "I Saw in Louisiana a Live-Oak Growing," manuscript of 1860. On the first leaf, in line 3 Whitman deleted "with." On the second leaf, in the third line (line 8 of the printed text) he added, with a caret, "lately." In the sixth line on this leaf he deleted "I write

(*continued*)

It is not needed to remind
me as of my friends, (for I
believe lately think of little
else than of them,)
Yet it remains to me a
curious token – it makes ~~I write~~
me think of manly love;
~~these pieces and name~~
~~them after it~~;
For all that, and though the
live oak ~~tree~~ glistens there in Louisiana, solitary in a wide
flat space, uttering joyous
leaves all its life, without
a friend, a lover, near – I
know very well I could
not.

these pieces, and name them after it," replacing the deletion with "it makes me think of manly love." In the next line he deleted "tree" and inserted "live oak." When he reprinted the poem in the 1867 version of *Leaves of Grass,* he made further changes, as you will see if you compare the printed text with this manuscript version. (Walt Whitman Collection. Clifton Waller Library, Manuscript Division, University of Virginia Library)

(For I believe lately I think of little else than of them,)
Yet it remains to me a curious token, it makes me think of manly
 love;
For all that, and though the live-oak glistens there in Louisiana
 solitary in a wide flat space,
Uttering joyous leaves all its life without a friend a lover near,
I know very well I could not.

[*1867*]

## TOPIC FOR CRITICAL THINKING OR WRITING

Compare the final version (1867) of the poem with the manuscript version of 1860. Which version do you prefer? Why?

## JOHN HAINES

*John Haines was born in Norfok, Virginia, in 1925 and educated at National Art School in Washington, D.C.; American University; Hans Hoffman School of Fine Art; and the University of Washington. He has worked as a hunter, fisherman, gardener, writer, and (1954-69) homesteader in Alaska. Haines has also served as writer in residence at several institutions.*

# *The Whale in the Blue Washing Machine*

There are depths even in a household
where a whale can live . . . .

His warm bulk swims from room
to room, floating by on the stairway,
searching the drafts, the cold
currents of water and liberation.

He comes to the surface hungry,
sniffs at the table,
and sinks, his wake rocking the chairs.

His pulsebeat sounds at night
when the washer spins and the dryer
clanks on stray buttons . . . .

Alone in the kitchen darkness,
looking through steamy windows
at the streets draining away in fog;

watching and listening
for the wail of an unchained buoy,
the steep fall of his wave.

[*1977*]

## TOPICS FOR CRITICAL THINKING AND WRITING

1. Students have told us they find this poem intriguing but very strange, because it seems so incongruous to refer to a whale living "in a household." What does the whale symbolize? Does the poem persuade you that this is an effective choice of symbol or not?
2. Describe the poem's tone. One could imagine how a poem like this could be a humorous one, but it isn't. Or is it?

## EDGAR ALLAN POE

***Edgar Allan Poe (1809-49) was the son of traveling actors. His father abandoned the family almost immediately, and his mother died when Poe was two. The child was adopted—though never legally—by a prosperous merchant and his wife in Richmond. The tensions were great, aggravated by Poe's drinking and heavy gambling, and in 1827 Poe left Richmond for Boston. He wrote, served briefly in the army, attended West Point but left within a year, and became an editor for the remaining eighteen years of his life. It was during these years, too, that he wrote the poems, essays, and fiction—especially detective stories and horror stories—that have made him famous.***

### *To Helen**

Helen, thy beauty is to me
  Like those Nicean° barks of yore,
That gently, o'er a perfumed sea,
  The weary, way-worn wanderer bore
To his own native shore.

On desperate seas long wont to roam,
  Thy hyacinth° hair, thy classic face,
Thy Naiad° airs have brought me home
  To the glory that was Greece
And the grandeur that was Rome.

Lo! in yon brilliant window-niche
  How statue-like I see thee stand,
  The agate lamp within thy hand!

***Helen** Helen of Troy, considered the most beautiful woman of ancient times **2 Nicean** perhaps referring to Nicea, an ancient city associated with the god Dionysus, or perhaps meaning "victorious," from Nike, Greek goddess of Victory **7 hyacinth hair** naturally curling hair, like that of Hyacinthus, beautiful Greek youth beloved by Apollo **8 Naiad** a nymph associated with lakes and streams

Ah! Psyche,° from the regions which
  Are Holy Land!°

[*1831-43*]

**14 Psyche** Greek for "soul" **15 Holy Land** ancient Rome or Athens, i.e., a sacred realm of art

## TOPICS FOR CRITICAL THINKING AND WRITING

1. In the first stanza, to what is Helen's beauty compared? To whom does the speaker apparently compare himself? What does "way-worn" in line 4 suggest to you? To what in the speaker's experience might the "native shore" in line 5 correspond?
2. What do you take "desperate seas" to mean in line 6, and who has been traveling them? To what are they contrasted in line 8? How does "home" seem to be defined in this stanza (stanza 2)?
3. What further light is shed on the speaker's home or destination in stanza 3?
4. Do you think that "To Helen" can be a love poem and also a poem about spiritual beauty or about the love of art? Why or why not?

## D. H. LAWRENCE

*D. H. Lawrence (1885-1930) was born David Herbert Lawrence in Nottinghamshire, in England. He is chiefly known as a writer of fiction, but he also wrote plays, travel books, and poetry.*

# *Snake*

A snake came to my water-trough
On a hot, hot day, and I in pajamas for the heat,
To drink there.

In the deep, strange-scented shade of the great dark carob-tree
I came down the steps with my pitcher
And must wait, must stand and wait, for there he was at the trough
  before me.

He reached down from a fissure in the earth-wall in the gloom
And trailed his yellow-brown slackness soft-bellied down, over the
  edge of the stone trough
And rested his throat upon the stone bottom,
And where the water had dripped from the tap, in a small clearness,
He sipped with his straight mouth,
Softly drank through his straight gums, into his slack long body,
Silently.

Someone was before me at my water-trough,
And I, like a second comer, waiting.

He lifted his head from his drinking, as cattle do,
And looked at me vaguely, as drinking cattle do,

And flickered his two-forked tongue from his lips, and mused a moment,
And stooped and drank a little more,
Being earth-brown, earth-golden from the burning bowels of the earth
On the day of Sicilian July, with Etna smoking.

The voice of my education said to me
He must be killed,
For in Sicily the black, black snakes are innocent, the gold are venomous.

And voices in me said, If you were a man
You would take a stick and break him now, and finish him off.

But must I confess how I liked him,
How glad I was he had come like a guest in quiet, to drink at my
water-trough
And depart peaceful, pacified, and thankless,
Into the burning bowels of this earth?

Was it cowardice, that I dared not kill him?
Was it perversity, that I longed to talk to him?
Was it humility, to feel so honored?
I felt so honored.

And yet those voices:
*If you were not afraid, you would kill him!*

And truly I was afraid, I was most afraid,
But even so, honored still more
That he should seek my hospitality
From out the dark door of the secret earth.

He drank enough
And lifted his head, dreamily, as one who has drunken,
And flickered his tongue like a forked night on the air, so black,
Seeming to lick his lips,
And looked around like a god, unseeing, into the air,
And slowly turned his head,
And slowly, very slowly, as if thrice adream,
Proceeded to draw his slow length curving round
And climb again the broken bank of my wall-face.

And as he put his head into that dreadful hole,
And as he slowly drew up, snake-easing his shoulders, and entered
farther,
A sort of horror, a sort of protest against his withdrawing into that
horrid black hole,
Deliberately going into the blackness, and slowly drawing himself after,
Overcame me now his back was turned.

I looked round, I put down my pitcher,
I picked up a clumsy log
And threw it at the water-trough with a clatter.

I think it did not hit him,
But suddenly that part of him that was left behind convulsed in
undignified haste,
Writhed like lightning, and was gone

Into the black hole, the earth-lipped fissure in the wall-front,
At which, in the intense still noon, I stared with fascination.

And immediately I regretted it.
I thought how paltry, how vulgar, what a mean act!
I despised myself and the voices of my accursed human education.
And I thought of the albatross,
And I wished he would come back, my snake.
For he seemed to me again like a king,
Like a king in exile, uncrowned in the underworld,
Now due to be crowned again.

And so, I missed my chance with one of the lords
Of life.
And I have something to expiate:
A pettiness.

[*1923*]

## TOPICS FOR CRITICAL THINKING AND WRITING

1. In line 6 and later Lawrence calls the snake "he"; in line 14, "someone," thus elevating the snake. What other figures are used to give the snake dignity? How does Lawrence diminish himself?
2. What do you think Lawrence means by "The voice of my education" (line 22)? It explicitly speaks in lines 23–26. Where else in the poem do you hear this voice? What might you call the opposing voice?

## SAMUEL TAYLOR COLERIDGE

*Samuel Taylor Coleridge (1772–1834) was born in Devonshire in England, the son of a clergyman. He attended Christ's Hospital school in London and Cambridge University, which he left without receiving a degree. With his friend William Wordsworth in 1798 he published, anonymously, a volume of poetry,* Lyrical Ballads, *which became the manifesto of the Romantic movement.*

# *Kubla Khan*

Or, A Vision in a Dream. A Fragment.

In Xanadu did Kubla Khan
A stately pleasure-dome decree:
Where Alph, the sacred river, ran
Through caverns measureless to man
 Down to a sunless sea.
So twice five miles of fertile ground
With walls and towers were girdled round:
And here were gardens bright with sinuous rills,

Where blossomed many an incense-bearing tree;
And here were forests ancient as the hills,
Enfolding sunny spots of greenery.

But oh! that deep romantic chasm which slanted
Down the green hill athwart a cedarn cover!
A savage place! as holy and enchanted
As e'er beneath a waning moon was haunted
By woman wailing for her demon-lover!
And from this chasm, with ceaseless turmoil seething,
As if this earth in fast thick pants were breathing
A mighty fountain momently was forced;
Amid whose swift half-intermitted burst
Huge fragments vaulted like rebounding hail,
Or chaffy grain beneath the thresher's flail:
And 'mid these dancing rocks at once and ever
It flung up momently the sacred river.
Five miles meandering with a mazy motion
Through wood and dale the sacred river ran,
Then reached the caverns measureless to man,
And sank in tumult to a lifeless ocean:
And 'mid this tumult Kubla heard from far
Ancestral voices prophesying war!
The shadow of the dome of pleasure
Floated midway on the waves;
Where was heard the mingled measure
From the fountain and the caves.
It was a miracle of rare device,
A sunny pleasure-dome with caves of ice!
A damsel with a dulcimer
In a vision once I saw:
It was an Abyssinian maid,
And on her dulcimer she played,
Singing of Mount Abora.
Could I revive within me
Her symphony and song,
To such a deep delight 'twould win me,
That with music loud and long,
I would build that dome in air,
That sunny dome! those caves of ice!
And all who heard should see them there,
And all should cry, Beware! Beware!
His flashing eyes, his floating hair!
Weave a circle round him thrice,
And close your eyes with holy dread,
For he on honey-dew hath fed,
And drunk the milk of Paradise.

[*1798*]

When Coleridge published "Kubla Khan" in 1816, he prefaced it with this explanatory note:

The following fragment is here published at the request of a poet of great and deserved celebrity, and, as far as the author's own opinions are concerned, rather as a psychological curiosity, than on the ground of any supposed *poetic* merits.

In the summer of the year 1797, the author, then in ill health, had retired to a lonely farmhouse between Porlock and Linton, on the Exmoor confines of Somerset and Devonshire. In consequence of a slight indisposition, an anodyne had been prescribed, from the effects of which he fell asleep in his chair at the moment that he was reading the following sentence, or words of the same substance, in *Purcha's Pilgrimage:* "Here the Khan Kubla commanded a palace to be built, and a stately garden thereunto. And thus ten miles of fertile ground were inclosed with a wall." The author continued for about three hours in a profound sleep, at least of the external senses, during which time he has the most vivid confidence that he could not have composed less than from two to three hundred lines; if that indeed can be called composition in which all the images rose up before him as *things,* with a parallel production of the correspondent expressions, without any sensation or consciousness of effort. On awaking he appeared to himself to have a distinct recollection of the whole, and taking his pen, ink, and paper, instantly and eagerly wrote down the lines that are here preserved. At this moment he was unfortunately called out by a person on business from Porlock, and detained by him above an hour, and on his return to his room, found, to his no small surprise and mortification, that though he still retained some vague and dim recollection of the general purport of the vision, yet, with the exception of some eight or ten scattered lines and images, all the rest had passed away like the images on the surface of a stream into which a stone has been cast, but, alas! without the after restoration of the latter!

Then all the charm
Is broken—all that phantom world so fair
Vanishes, and a thousand circlets spread,
And each misshape[s] the other. Stay awhile,
Poor youth! who scarcely dar'st lift up thine eyes—
The stream will soon renew its smoothness, soon
The visions will return! And lo, he stays,
And soon the fragments dim of lovely forms
Come trembling back, unite, and now once more
The pool becomes a mirror.

—Coleridge, *The Picture; or, the Lover's Resolution,* lines 91–100

Yet from the still surviving recollections in his mind, the author has frequently purposed to finish for himself what had been originally, as it were, given to him. Σαμερου αδιου ασω [today I shall sing more sweetly]: "But the tomorrow is yet to come."

## TOPICS FOR CRITICAL THINKING AND WRITING

1. Coleridge changed the "palace" of his source into a "dome" (line 2). What do you think are the relevant associations of "dome"?
2. What pairs of contrasts (e.g., underground river, fountain) do you find? What do you think they contribute to the poem?

3. If Coleridge had not said that the poem is a fragment, might you take it as a complete poem, the first thirty-six lines describing the creative imagination, and the remainder lamenting the loss of poetic power?

## LORNA DEE CERVANTES

*Lorna Dee Cervantes, born in San Francisco in 1954, founded a press and a poetry magazine,* Mango, *chiefly devoted to Chicano literature. In 1978 she received a fellowship from the National Endowment for the Arts, and in 1981 she published her first book of poems. "Refugee Ship," originally written in 1974, was revised for the book. We print the revised version.*

# *Refugee Ship*

Like wet cornstarch, I slide
past my grandmother's eyes. Bible
at her side, she removes her glasses.
The pudding thickens.

Mama raised me without language.
I'm orphaned from my Spanish name.
The words are foreign, stumbling
on my tongue. I see in the mirror
my reflection: bronzed skin, black hair.

I feel I am a captive
aboard the refugee ship.
The ship that will never dock.
*El barco que nunca atraca.*°

[*1981*]

13 ***El barco que nunca atraca*** The ship that never docks

## TOPICS FOR CRITICAL THINKING AND WRITING

1. What do you think the speaker means by the comparison with "wet cornstarch" in line 1? And what do you take her to mean in line 7 when she says, "I'm orphaned from my Spanish name"?
2. Judging from the poem as a whole, why does the speaker feel she is "a captive / aboard the refugee ship"? How would you characterize such feelings?
3. In an earlier version of the poem, instead of "my grandmother's eyes" Cervantes wrote "*mi abuelita's* eyes"; that is, she used the Spanish words for "my grandmother." In line 5 instead of "Mama" she wrote "*mamá*" (again, the Spanish equivalent), and in line 9 she wrote "brown skin" instead of "bronzed skin." The final line of the original version was not in Spanish but in English, a repetition of the preceding line, which ran thus: "A ship that will never dock." How does each of these changes strike you?

## ADRIENNE RICH

*Adrienne Rich, born in 1929 in Baltimore, was educated at Radcliffe College. Her first book of poems,* A Change of World, *published in 1951 when she was still an undergraduate, was selected by W. H. Auden for the Yale Series of Younger Poets. In 1953 she married an economist and had three sons, but as she indicates in several books, she felt confined by the full-time domestic role that she was expected to play, and the marriage did not last. Much of her poetry is concerned with issues of gender and power. When her ninth book,* Diving into the Wreck *(1973), won the National Book Award, Rich accepted the award not as an individual but on behalf of women everywhere.*

### *Diving into the Wreck*

First having read the book of myths,
and loaded the camera,
and checked the edge of the knife-blade,
I put on
the body-armor of black rubber
the absurd flippers
the grave and awkward mask.
I am having to do this
not like Cousteau° with his
assiduous team
aboard the sun-flooded schooner
but here alone.

There is a ladder.
The ladder is always there
hanging innocently
close to the side of the schooner.
We know what it is for,
we who have used it.
Otherwise
it's a piece of maritime floss
some sundry equipment.

I go down.
Rung after rung and still
the oxygen immerses me
the blue light
the clear atoms
of our human air.

**9 Jacques Cousteau** (b. 1910) French underwater explorer

I go down.
My flippers cripple me,
I crawl like an insect down the ladder
and there is no one
to tell me when the ocean
will begin.

First the air is blue and then
it is bluer and then green and then
black I am blacking out and yet
my mask is powerful
it pumps my blood with power
the sea is another story
the sea is not a question of power
I have to learn alone
to turn my body without force
in the deep element.

And now: it is easy to forget
what I came for
among so many who have always
lived here
swaying their crenellated fans
between the reefs
and besides
you breathe differently down here.

I came to explore the wreck.
The words are purposes.
The words are maps.
I came to see the damage that was done
and the treasures that prevail.
I stroke the beam of my lamp
slowly along the flank
of something more permanent
than fish or weed

the thing I came for:
the wreck and not the story of the wreck
the thing itself and not the myth
the drowned face always staring
toward the sun
the evidence of damage
worn by salt and sway into this threadbare beauty
the ribs of the disaster
curving their assertion
among the tentative haunters.

This is the place.
And I am here, the mermaid whose dark hair
streams black, the merman in his armored body
We circle silently
about the wreck

we dive into the hold.
I am she: I am he

whose drowned face sleeps with open eyes
whose breasts still bear the stress
whose silver, copper, vermeil cargo lies
obscurely inside barrels
half-wedged and left to rot
we are the half-destroyed instruments
that once held to a course
the water-eaten log
the fouled compass

We are, I am, you are
by cowardice or courage
the one who find our way
back to this scene
carrying a knife, a camera
a book of myths
in which
our names do not appear.

[*1973*]

## WALLACE STEVENS

*Wallace Stevens (1879–1955), educated at Harvard and at New York Law School, earned his living as a lawyer and an insurance executive; at the time of his death he was a vice president of the Hartford Accident and Indemnity Company. While pursuing this career, however, he also achieved distinction as a poet, and today he is widely regarded as among the most important American poets of the twentieth century.*

# *The Emperor of Ice-Cream*

Call the roller of big cigars,
The muscular one, and bid him whip
In kitchen cups concupiscent curds.
Let the wenches dawdle in such dress
As they are used to wear, and let the boys
Bring flowers in last month's newspapers.
Let be be finale of seem.
The only emperor is the emperor of ice-cream.

Take from the dresser of deal,°
Lacking the three glass knobs, that sheet
On which she embroidered fantails once

And spread it so as to cover her face.
If her horny feet protrude, they come
To show how cold she is, and dumb.
Let the lamp affix its beam.
The only emperor is the emperor of ice-cream.

[*1923*]

**9 deal** fir or pine wood

## TOPIC FOR CRITICAL THINKING OR WRITING

What associations does the word "emperor" have for you? The word "ice-cream"? What, then, do you make of "the emperor of ice-cream"? The poem describes the preparations for a wake, and in line 15 ("Let the lamp affix its beam") it insists on facing the reality of death. In this context, then, what do you make of the last line of each stanza?

## A NOTE ON HAIKU

One form of poetry that puts a great emphasis on sharp images is the **haiku,** a Japanese poem of seventeen syllables, arranged in three lines of five, seven, and five syllables. Japanese poetry is unrhymed, but English versions sometimes rhyme the first and third lines. The subject matter can be high or low—the Milky Way or the screech of automobile brakes—but usually it is connected with the seasons, and it is described objectively and sharply. Most haiku set forth a sense of *where, what,* and *when*—but the when may be implicit, as in the first haiku.

On pages 1035–37 we discuss translating haiku, and we give some literal translations for you to improve.

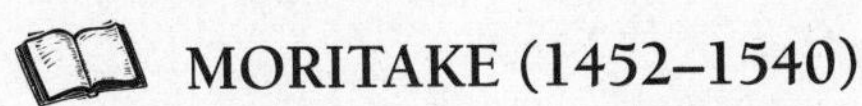

## MORITAKE (1452–1540)

### *Fallen petals rise*

*Translated by Harold G. Henderson*

Fallen petals rise
back to the branch—I watch
oh . . . butterflies!

Concentrating his attention on the phenomenon (butterflies moving upward), the poet nevertheless conveys an emotion through the images (wonder, and then the recognition of the familiar), stirring the reader's imagination to supply the emotion that completes the experience.

## SÔKAN (1465–1553)

### *If only we could*

*Translated by Kenneth Yasuda*

If only we could
Add a handle to the moon
It would make a good fan.

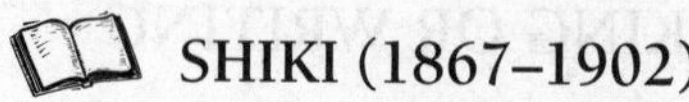

## SHIKI (1867–1902)

### *River in summer*

River in summer:
there is a bridge, but my horse
walks through the water.

## RICHARD WRIGHT (1908–60)

### *Four Haiku*

A balmy spring wind
Reminding me of something
I cannot recall.

The green cockleburrs
Caught in the thick wooly hair
Of the black boy's head.

Standing in the field,
I hear the whispering of
Snowflake to snowflake.

It is September
The month in which I was born,
And I have no thoughts.

## GARY SNYDER (b. 1930)

### *After weeks of watching the roof leak*

After weeks of watching the roof leak
I fixed it tonight
by moving a single board.

## Writing a Haiku

Although the haiku originated in Japan, it is now written throughout the world.

For a start, you may want to take some ordinary experience—tying your shoelaces, seeing a cat at the foot of the stairs, glancing out of a window and seeing unexpected snowflakes, hearing the alarm clock—and present it interestingly. One way to make it interesting is to construct the poem in two parts—the first line balanced against the next two lines, or the first two lines balanced against the last line. If you construct a poem on this principle, the two sections should be related to each other, but they should also in some degree make a contrast with each other. For instance, in the following poem by Taigi, there is a contrast between pleasant sociability (the first two lines) and loneliness (the last line).

 TAIGI (1723–76)

### *Look, O look, There Go*

*Translated by Kenneth Yasuda*

"Look, O look, there go
Fireflies," I would like to say—
But I am alone.

Basho said, "He who creates three to five haiku during a lifetime is a haiku poet. He who attains to ten is a master."

## ✔ Checklist: Writing about Imagery and Symbolism

Our comment (p. 148) about the importance of not being rigid in interpreting symbols in fiction—especially in interpreting them to mean one thing and one thing only—applies also to interpreting symbols in poetry.

1. What leads you to believe that something in a particular passage is symbolic rather than literal (or symbolic as well as literal)?
2. Do any of the symbols surprise you or prove unclear or confusing in their meanings?
3. Sometimes symbols are used in traditional ways, as when we say that a flower or the dew symbolizes transience, or that an oak or a stone symbolizes endurance. If the symbols in the poem are *traditional,* are they clichés, or has the poet somehow made them fresh? If the symbols are not traditional, do they effectively convey a special set of meanings that this particular poet has given to them?

# CHAPTER 20

# *Irony*

There is a kind of discourse which, though nonliteral, need not use similes, metaphors, apostrophes, personification, or symbols. Without using these figures, speakers may say things that are not to be taken literally. They may, in short, employ **irony.**

In Greek comedy, the *eiron* was the sly underdog who, by dissembling inferiority, outwitted his opponent. As Aristotle puts it, irony (employed by the *eiron*) is a "pretense tending toward the underside" of truth. Later, Cicero somewhat altered the meaning of the word: He defined it as saying one thing and meaning another, and he held that Socrates, who feigned ignorance and let his opponents entrap themselves in their own arguments, was the perfect example of an ironist.

In **verbal irony,** as the term is now used, what is *stated* is in some degree negated by what is *suggested.* A classic example is Lady Macbeth's order to get ready for King Duncan's visit: "He that's coming / Must be provided for." The words seem to say that she and Macbeth must busy themselves with household preparations so that the king may be received in appropriate style, but this suggestion of hospitality is undercut by an opposite meaning: preparations must be made for the murder of the king. Two other examples of verbal irony are Melville's comment

> What like a bullet can undeceive!

and the lover's assertion (in Marvell's "To His Coy Mistress") that

> The grave's a fine and private place,
> But none, I think, do there embrace.

Under Marvell's cautious words ("I think") we detect a wryness; the **understatement** masks yet reveals a deep-felt awareness of mortality and the barrenness of the grave. The self-mockery in this understatement proclaims modesty, but suggests assurance. The speaker here, like most ironists, is both playful and serious at once. Irony packs a great deal into a few words.* What we call irony here, it should be mentioned, is often called **sarcasm,** but a distinction can be made: sarcasm is notably contemptuous and crude or heavyhanded ("You're a great guy, a real friend," said to a friend who won't lend you ten dollars). Sarcasm is only one kind of irony, and a kind almost never found in literature.

**Overstatement (hyperbole),** like understatement, is ironic when it contains a contradictory suggestion:

For Brutus is an honorable man;
So are they all, all honorable men.

The sense of contradiction that is inherent in verbal irony is also inherent in a paradox. **Paradox** has several meanings for philosophers, but we need only be concerned with its meaning of an apparent contradiction. In Gerard Manley Hopkins's "Spring and Fall: To a Young Child" (p. 876), there is an apparent contradiction in the assertions that Margaret is weeping for the woods (line 2) and for herself (line 15), but the contradiction is not real: both the woods and Margaret are parts of the nature blighted by Adam's sin. Other paradoxes are

The child is father of the man;
—Wordsworth

and (on the soldiers who died to preserve the British Empire)

The saviors come not home tonight;
Themselves they could not save;
—Housman

and

One short sleep past, we wake eternally,
And Death shall be no more; Death, thou shalt die.
—Donne

Donne's lines are a reminder that paradox is not only an instrument of the poet. Christianity embodies several paradoxes: God became a human being; through the death on the cross, human beings can obtain eternal life; human beings do not live fully until they die.

Some critics have put a high premium on ironic and paradoxical poetry. Briefly, their argument runs that great poetry recognizes the complexity of experience, and that irony and paradox are ways of doing justice to this complexity. I. A. Richards uses "irony" to denote "The bringing in of the opposite, the complementary impulses," and suggests (in *The Principles of Literary Criticism*) that irony in this sense is a characteristic of poetry of "the highest order." It is dubious that all poets must always bring in the opposite, but it is certain that much poetry is ironic and paradoxical.

*A word of caution: We have been talking about verbal irony, not **irony of situation.** Like ironic words, ironic situations have in them an element of contrast. A clown whose heart is breaking must make his audience laugh; an author's worst book is her only financial success; a fool solves a problem that vexes the wise.

## SHARON OLDS

*Sharon Olds, born in San Francisco in 1942, and educated at Stanford University and Columbia University, has published several volumes of poetry and has received major awards.*

### *Rites of Passage*

As the guests arrive at my son's party
They gather in the living room—
short men, men in first grade
with smooth jaws and chins.
Hands in pockets, they stand around
jostling, jockeying for place, small fights
breaking out and calming. One says to another
*How old are you? Six. I'm seven. So?*
They eye each other, seeing themselves
tiny in the other's pupils. They clear their
throats a lot, a room of small bankers,
they fold their arms and frown. *I could beat you*
*up,* a seven says to a six,
the dark cake, round and heavy as a
turret, behind them on the table. My son,
freckles like specks of nutmeg on his cheeks,
chest narrow as the balsa keel of a
model boat, long hands
cool and thin as the day they guided him
out of me, speaks up as a host
for the sake of the group.
*We could easily kill a two-year-old,*
he says in his clear voice. The other
men agree, they clear their throats
like Generals, they relax and get down to
playing war, celebrating my son's life.

[*1983*]

## TOPICS FOR CRITICAL THINKING AND WRITING

1. Focus on the details that the speaker provides about the boys—how they look, how they speak. What do the details reveal about them?
2. Is the speaker's son the same as or different from the other boys?
3. Some readers find the ironies in this poem (e.g., "short men") to be somewhat comical, while others, noting such phrases as "kill a two-year-old" and "playing war," conclude that the poem as a whole is meant to be upsetting, even frightening. How would you describe the kinds of irony that Olds uses here?
4. An experiment in irony and point of view: Try writing a poem like this one, from the point of view of a father about the birthday party of his

son, and then try writing another one by either a father or mother about a daughter's party.

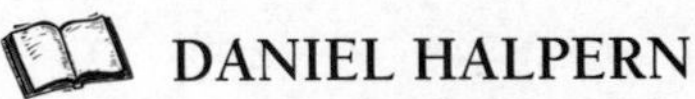

## DANIEL HALPERN

*Daniel Halpern, born in Syracuse, New York, in 1945, is editor in chief of Ecco Press, the author of several books of poems, and the editor of several anthologies of literature. Halpern has taught workshops in writing poetry and fiction at Columbia University and elsewhere.*

### *How to Eat Alone*

While it's still light out
set the table for one:
a red linen tablecloth,
one white plate, a bowl
for the salad
and the proper silverware.
Take out a three-pound leg of lamb,
rub it with salt, pepper and cumin,
then push in two cloves
of garlic splinters.
Place it in a 325-degree oven
and set the timer for an hour.
Put freshly cut vegetables
into a pot with some herbs
and the crudest olive oil
you can find.
Heat on a low flame.
Clean the salad.
Be sure the dressing is made
with fresh dill, mustard
and the juice of hard lemons.
Open a bottle of good late harvest zinfandel
and let it breathe on the table.
Pour yourself a glass
of cold California chardonnay
and go to your study and read.
As the story unfolds
you will smell the lamb
and the vegetables.
This is the best part of the evening:
the food cooking, the armchair,
the book and bright flavor
of the chilled wine.
When the timer goes off
toss the salad
and prepare the vegetables
and the lamb. Bring them out

to the table. Light the candles
and pour the red wine
into your glass.
Before you begin to eat,
raise your glass in honor
of yourself.
The company is the best you'll ever have.

[*1975*]

## TOPICS FOR CRITICAL THINKING AND WRITING

1. Note the reference to "you" in line 16. Who is this "you"? Is it the reader? How would the poem be different if all of the pronouns were in the first person "I"—that this is what I do, how I eat alone?
2. The directions given for "how to eat alone" are precise and fairly lengthy. Why is Halpern so specific?
3. Is the final line surprising? Is it meant to be ironic or simply true?

## JOHN HALL WHEELOCK

*John Hall Wheelock (1908–78) was born in Far Rockaway, Long Island, New York. In 1928, while an undergraduate at Harvard, he published a book of poems. After doing graduate work at the Universities of Berlin and Göttingen, he settled in New York, where he worked as an editor for Scribner's.*

### *Earth*

"A planet doesn't explode of itself," said drily
The Martian astronomer, gazing off into the air—
"That they were able to do it is proof that highly
Intelligent beings must have been living there."

[*1961*]

## TOPICS FOR CRITICAL THINKING AND WRITING

1. What is the "it" (line 3) that has been done?
2. How do you think the Martian astronomer would characterize himself or herself? How do you think the author would characterize the astronomer?

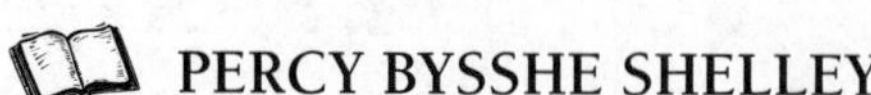

## PERCY BYSSHE SHELLEY

*Percy Bysshe Shelley (1792–1822) was born in Sussex in England, the son of a prosperous country squire. Edu-*

*cated at Eton, he went on to Oxford but was expelled for having written a pamphlet supporting a belief in atheism. Like John Keats he was a member of the second generation of English romantic poets. (The first generation included Wordsworth and Coleridge.) And like Keats, Shelley died young; he was drowned during a violent storm while sailing with a friend.*

## *Ozymandias*

I met a traveler from an antique land
Who said: Two vast and trunkless legs of stone
Stand in the desert . . . Near them, on the sand,
Half sunk, a shattered visage lies, whose frown,
And wrinkled lip, and sneer of cold command,
Tell that its sculptor well those passions read
Which yet survive, stamped on these lifeless things,
The hand that mocked them, and the heart that fed:
And on the pedestal these words appear:
"My name is Ozymandias, king of kings:
Look on my works, ye Mighty, and despair!"
Nothing beside remains. Round the decay
Of that colossal wreck, boundless and bare
The lone and level sands stretch far away.

[*1817*]

Lines 4–8 are somewhat obscure, but the gist is that the passions—still evident in the "shattered visage"—survive the sculptor's hand that "mocked"—that is, (1) imitated or copied, (2) derided—them, and the passions also survive the king's heart that had nourished them.

## TOPIC FOR CRITICAL THINKING OR WRITING

There is an irony of plot here: Ozymandias believed that he created enduring works, but his intentions came to nothing. However, another is also present: How are his words, in a way he did not intend, true?

## LINDA PASTAN

*Linda Pastan was born in New York City in 1932 and educated at Radcliffe College, Simmons College, and Brandeis University. The author of ten books of poems, she has won numerous prizes and has received a grant from the National Endowment for the Arts.*

## *Ethics*

In ethics class so many years ago
our teacher asked this question every fall:

if there were a fire in a museum
which would you save, a Rembrandt painting
or an old woman who hadn't many
years left anyhow? Restless on hard chairs
caring little for pictures or old age
we'd opt one year for life, the next for art
and always half-heartedly. Sometimes
the woman borrowed my grandmother's face
leaving her usual kitchen to wander
some drafty, half-imagined museum.
One year, feeling clever, I replied
why not let the woman decide herself?
Linda, the teacher would report, eschews
the burdens of responsibility.
This fall in a real museum I stand
before a real Rembrandt, old woman,
or nearly so, myself. The colors
within this frame are darker than autumn,
darker even than winter—the browns of earth,
though earth's most radiant elements burn
through the canvas. I know now that woman
and painting and season are almost one
and all beyond saving by children.

[*1980*]

## TOPICS FOR CRITICAL THINKING AND WRITING

1. What, if anything, do we know about the teacher in the poem? Do you think you would like to take a course with this teacher? Why?
2. Lines 3–6 report a question that a teacher asked. Does the rest of the poem answer the question? If so, what is the answer? If not, what does the rest of the poem do?
3. Do you assume that, for this poem, the responses of younger readers (say, ages 17–22) as a group would differ from those of older readers? If so, why?

## ANDREW MARVELL

*Born in 1621 near Hull in England, Marvell attended Trinity College, Cambridge, and graduated in 1638. During the English Civil War he was tutor to the daughter of Sir Thomas Fairfax in Yorkshire at Nun Appleton House, where most of his best-known poems were written. In 1657 he was appointed assistant to John Milton, the Latin Secretary for the Commonwealth. After the Restoration of the monarchy in 1659, Marvell represented Hull as a member of parliament until his death. Most of his poems were not published until after his death in 1678.*

## *To His Coy Mistress*

Had we but world enough, and time,
This coyness, lady, were no crime.
We would sit down, and think which way
To walk, and pass our long love's day.
Thou by the Indian Ganges' side
Should'st rubies find: I by the tide
Of Humber would complain.° I would
Love you ten years before the Flood,
And you should, if you please, refuse
Till the conversion of the Jews.
My vegetable° love should grow
Vaster than empires, and more slow.
An hundred years should go to praise
Thine eyes, and on thy forehead gaze:
Two hundred to adore each breast:
But thirty thousand to the rest.
An age at least to every part,
And the last age should show your heart.
For, lady, you deserve this state,
Nor would I love at lower rate.
    But at my back I always hear
Time's winged chariot hurrying near;
And yonder all before us lie
Deserts of vast eternity.
Thy beauty shall no more be found,
Nor in thy marble vault shall sound
My echoing song; then worms shall try
That long preserved virginity,
And your quaint honor turn to dust,
And into ashes all my lust.
The grave's a fine and private place,
But none, I think, do there embrace.
    Now therefore, while the youthful hue
Sits on thy skin like morning dew,
And while thy willing soul transpires
At every pore with instant fires,
Now let us sport us while we may;
And now, like am'rous birds of prey,
Rather at once our time devour,
Than languish in his slow-chapt° power,
Let us roll all our strength, and all
Our sweetness, up into one ball;
And tear our pleasures with rough strife
Thorough° the iron gates of life.

**7 complain** write love poems **11 vegetable** i.e., unconsciously growing **40 slow-chapt** slowly devouring **44 Thorough** through

Thus, though we cannot make our sun
Stand still, yet we will make him run.

[*1681*]

## TOPICS FOR CRITICAL THINKING AND WRITING

1. Do you find the assertions in lines 1–20 so inflated that you detect behind them a playfully ironic tone? Explain. Why does the speaker say, in line 8, that he would love "ten years before the Flood," rather than merely "since the Flood"?
2. Explain lines 21–24. Why is time behind the speaker, and eternity in front of him? Is this "eternity" the same as the period discussed in lines 1–20? What do you make of the change in the speaker's tone after line 20?
3. Do you agree with the comment on pages 924–25 about the understatement in lines 31–32? What more can you say about these lines, in context?
4. Why "am'rous birds of prey" (line 38) rather than the conventional doves? Is the idea of preying continued in the poem?
5. Try to explain the last two lines, and characterize the speaker's tone. Do you find these lines anticlimactic?
6. The poem is organized in the form of an argument. Trace the steps.

## JOHN DONNE

***John Donne (1572–1631) was born into a Roman Catholic family in England, but in the 1590s he abandoned that faith. In 1615 he became an Anglican priest and soon was known as a great preacher. A hundred and sixty of his sermons survive, including one with the famous line, "No man is an island, entire of itself; every man is a piece of the continent, a part of the main; if a clod be washed away by the sea, Europe is the less . . . ; and therefore never send to know for whom the bell tolls; it tolls for thee." From 1621 until his death he was dean of St. Paul's Cathedral in London. His love poems (often bawdy and cynical) are said to be his early work, and his "Holy Sonnets" (among the greatest religious poems written in English) his later work.***

# *Holy Sonnet XIV*

Batter my heart, three-personed God; for you
As yet but knock, breathe, shine, and seek to mend;
That I may rise and stand, o'erthrow me, and bend
Your force, to break, blow, burn, and make me new.

I, like an usurped town, to another due,
Labor to admit you, but oh, to no end,
Reason, your viceroy in me, me should defend,
But is captived, and proves weak or untrue.
Yet dearly I love you, and would be loved fain,
But am betrothed unto your enemy:
Divorce me, untie, or break that knot again,
Take me to you, imprison me, for I
Except you enthrall me, never shall be free,
Nor ever chaste, except you ravish me.

[*1633*]

## TOPICS FOR CRITICAL THINKING AND WRITING

1. Explain the paradoxes in lines 1, 3, 13, and 14. Explain the double meanings of "enthrall" (line 13) and "ravish" (line 14).
2. In lines 1–4, what is God implicitly compared to (considering especially lines 2 and 4)? How does this comparison lead into the comparison that dominates lines 5–8? What words in lines 9–12 are especially related to the earlier lines?
3. What do you think is gained by piling up verbs in lines 2–4?
4. Do you find sexual references irreverent in a religious poem? (As already mentioned, Donne was an Anglican priest.)

## LANGSTON HUGHES

*Other poems by Langston Hughes (1902–67) appear on pages 830, 846, and 1172, 1176–84. For a biography see page 829.*

## *Dream Boogie*

Good morning, daddy!
Ain't you heard
The boogie-woogie rumble
Of a dream deferred?
Listen closely:
You'll hear their feet
Beating out and beating out a—

*You think*
*It's a happy beat?*

Listen to it closely:
Ain't you heard
something underneath
like a—

*What did I say?*

Sure,
I'm happy!
Take it away!

*Hey, pop!*
*Re-bop!*
*Mop!*

*Y-e-a-h!*

*What don't bug*
*them white kids*
*sure bugs me:*
*We knows everybody*
*ain't free!*

Some of these young ones is cert'ly bad—
One batted a hard ball right through my window
and my gold fish et the glass.

*What's written down*
*for white folks*
*ain't for us a-tall:*
*"Liberty And Justice—*
*Huh—For All."*

*Oop-pop-a-da!*
*Skee! Daddle-de-do!*
*Be-bop!*

Salt'peanuts!
*De-dop!*

[*1951*]

## TOPICS FOR CRITICAL THINKING AND WRITING

1. What is boogie, or boogie-woogie?
2. Why did many whites assume that boogie was "a happy beat" (line 9)? In fact, what was boogie chiefly an expression of?
3. Why does Hughes in lines 33–34 quote part of the Pledge of Allegiance?

## MARTÍN ESPADA

*Martín Espada was born in Brooklyn in 1957. He received a bachelor's degree from the University of Wisconsin and a law degree from Northeastern University. He is now Outreach Coordinator and Supervisor of Lawyers of the Arts at the Artists' Foundation in Boston.*

## *Tony Went to the Bodega* but He Didn't Buy Anything*

*para Angel Guadalupe*

Tony's father left the family
and the Long Island city projects,
leaving a mongrel-skinny puertorriqueño boy
nine years old
who had to find work.

Makengo the Cuban
let him work at the bodega.
In grocery aisles
he learned the steps of the dry-mop mambo,
banging the cash register
like piano percussion
in the spotlight of Machito's orchestra,
polite with the abuelas° who bought on credit,
practicing the grin on customers
he'd seen Makengo grin
with his bad yellow teeth.

Tony left the projects too,
with a scholarship for law school.
But he cursed the cold primavera°
in Boston;
the cooking of his neighbors
left no smell in the hallway,
and no one spoke Spanish
(not even the radio).

So Tony walked without a map
through the city,
a landscape of hostile condominiums
and the darkness of white faces,
sidewalk-searcher lost
till he discovered the projects.

Tony went to the bodega
but he didn't buy anything:
he sat by the doorway satisfied
to watch la gente° (people
island-brown as him)
crowd in and out,
hablando español,°
thought: this is beautiful,

***Bodega** grocery and liquor store; in the dedication, after the title, *para* means "for"
**13 abuelas** grandmothers **19 primavera** spring season **34 la gente** the people
**37 hablando español** speaking Spanish

and grinned
his bodega grin.

This is a rice and beans
success story:
today Tony lives on Tremont Street,
above the bodega.

[*1987*]

## TOPICS FOR CRITICAL THINKING AND WRITING

1. Why do you suppose Espada included the information about Tony's father? The information about young Tony "practicing" a grin?
2. Why does Tony leave?
3. How would you characterize Tony?

## EDNA ST. VINCENT MILLAY

***For another poem by the American poet Edna St. Vincent Millay (1892–1950) as well as a brief biography, see pages 847–48.***

# *Love Is Not All: It Is Not Meat nor Drink*

Love is not all: it is not meat nor drink
Nor slumber nor a roof against the rain;
Nor yet a floating spar to men that sink
And rise and sink and rise and sink again;
Love can not fill the thickened lung with breath,
Nor clean the blood, nor set the fractured bone;
Yet many a man is making friends with death
Even as I speak, for lack of love alone.
It well may be that in a difficult hour,
Pinned down by pain and moaning for release,
Or nagged by want past resolution's power,
I might be driven to sell your love for peace,
Or trade the memory of this night for food.
It well may be. I do not think I would.

[*1931*]

## TOPICS FOR CRITICAL THINKING AND WRITING

1. "Love Is Not All" is a sonnet. Using your own words, briefly summarize the argument of the octet (the first 8 lines). Next, paraphrase the sestet (the six lines from line 9 through line 14), line by line. On the whole, does the sestet repeat the idea of the octet, or does it add a new idea? Whom did you imagine to be speaking the octet? What does the sestet

add to your knowledge of the speaker and the occasion? (And how did you paraphrase line 11?)

2. The first and last lines of the poem consist of words of one syllable, and both lines have a distinct pause in the middle. Do you imagine the lines to be spoken in the same tone of voice? If not, can you describe the difference and account for it?
3. Lines 7 and 8 appear to mean that the absence of love can be a cause of death. To what degree do you believe that to be true?
4. Would you call "Love Is Not All" a love poem? Why or why not? Describe the kind of person who might include the poem in a love letter or valentine, or who would be happy to receive it. (One of our friends recited it at her wedding. What do you think of that idea?)

---

## ✔ Checklist: Irony

1. Is the speaker fully aware of what he or she is saying?
2. Is the irony so heavy that it can be called sarcasm? If so, is this a weakness in the poem?
3. Is the irony *verbal* (a speaker says something but means something else), or is it *situational* (the irony results from the contrast between what is honestly thought or said and what the facts are)?

---

# CHAPTER 21

# *Rhythm and Versification*

Up and down the City Road,
In and out the Eagle;
That's the way the money goes,
Pop goes the weasel.

Probably very few of the countless children—and adults—who sometimes find themselves singing this ditty have the faintest idea of what it is about. It endures because it is catchy—a strong, easily remembered rhythm. Even if you just read it aloud without singing it, we think you will agree.

If you try to specify exactly what the rhythm is, for instance by putting an accent mark on each syllable that you stress heavily, you may run into difficulties. You may become unsure of whether you stress *up* and *down* equally; maybe you will decide that *up* is hardly stressed more than *and,* at least compared with the heavy stress that you put on *down.* Different readers (really, singers) will recite it differently. Does this mean that anything goes? Of course not. No one will emphasize *and* or *the*, just as no one will emphasize the second syllable in *city* or the second syllable in *money.* There may be some variations from reader to reader, but there will also be a good deal that all readers will agree on. And surely all readers agree that it is memorable.

Does this song have a meaning? Well, historians say that the Eagle was a tavern and music hall in the City Road, in Victorian London. People went there to eat, drink, and sing, with the result that they sometimes spent too much money and then had to pawn (or "pop") the "weasel"—though no one is sure what the weasel is. It doesn't really matter; the song lives by its rhythm.

Now consider this poem, by Ezra Pound (1885-1972), whose biography is given on page 1074. Pound's early work is highly rhythmical; later he became obsessed with fascistic ideas, with the result that for many readers his later work is much less interesting—just a lot of dated ideas, rather than memorable expressions. Pound ought to have remembered his own definition of literature: "Literature is news that *stays* news." One way of staying is to use unforgettable rhythms.

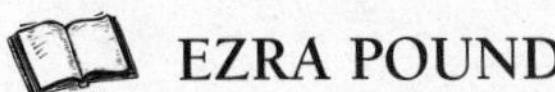

## EZRA POUND

## *An Immorality*

Sing we for love and idleness,
Naught else is worth the having.

Though I have been in many a land,
There is naught else in living.

And I would rather have my sweet,
Though rose-leaves die of grieving,

Than do high deeds in Hungary
To pass all men's believing.

[*1919*]

A good poem. To begin with, it sings; as Pound said, "Poetry withers and dries out when it leaves music, or at least imagined music, too far behind it. Poets who are not interested in music are, or become, bad poets." Hymns and ballads, it must be remembered, are songs, and other poetry, too, is sung, especially by children. Children reciting a counting-out rhyme, or singing on their way home from school, are enjoying poetry:

Pease-porridge hot,
  Pease-porridge cold,
Pease-porridge in the pot
  Nine days old.

Nothing very important is being said, but for generations children have enjoyed the music of these lines, and adults, too, have recalled them with pleasure—though few people know what pease-porridge is.

The "music"—the catchiness of certain sounds—should not be underestimated. Here are lines chanted by the witches in *Macbeth:*

Double, double, toil and trouble;
Fire burn and cauldron bubble.

This is rather far from words that mean approximately the same thing: "Twice, twice, work and care; / Fire ignite, and pot boil." The difference is more in the sounds than in the instructions. What is lost in the paraphrase is the magic, the incantation, which resides in elaborate repetitions of sounds and stresses.

**Rhythm** (most simply, in English poetry, stresses at regular intervals) has a power of its own. A good march, said John Philip Sousa (the composer of "Stars and Stripes Forever"), "should make even someone with a wooden leg step out." A highly pronounced rhythm is common in such forms of poetry as charms, college yells, and lullabies; all of them (like the witches' speech) are aimed at inducing a special effect magically. It is not surprising that *carmen,* the Latin word for "poem" or "song," is also the Latin word for *charm,* and the word from which *charm* is derived.

Rain, rain, go away;
Come again another day.

> Block that kick! Block that kick! Block that kick!

> Rock-a-bye baby, on the tree top,
> When the wind blows, the cradle will rock.

In much poetry rhythm is only half-heard, but its omnipresence is suggested by the fact that when poetry is printed it is customary to begin each line with a capital letter. Prose (from Latin *prorsus,* "forward," "straight on") keeps running across the paper until the right-hand margin is reached, and then, merely because the paper has given out, the writer or printer starts again at the left, with a small letter. But verse (Latin *versus,* "a turning") often ends well short of the right-hand margin, and the next line begins at the left—usually with a capital—not because paper has run out but because the rhythmic pattern begins again. Lines of poetry are continually reminding us that they have a pattern.

Before turning to some other highly rhythmic pieces, a word of caution: a mechanical, unvarying rhythm may be good to put the baby to sleep, but it can be deadly to readers who wish to keep awake. Poets vary their rhythm according to their purpose; a poet ought not to be so regular that he or she is (in W. H. Auden's words) an "accentual pest." In competent hands, rhythm contributes to meaning; it says something. The rhythm in the lines from *Macbeth,* for example, helps suggest the strong binding power of magic. Again Ezra Pound has a relevant comment: "Rhythm *must* have meaning. It can't be merely a careless dash off, with no grip and no real hold to the words and sense, a tumty tum tumty tum tum ta." Some examples will be useful.

Consider this description of Hell from John Milton's *Paradise Lost* (the heavier stresses are marked by ´):

> Rocks, caves, lakes, fens, bogs, dens, and shades of death.

Such a succession of stresses is highly unusual. Elsewhere in the poem Milton chiefly uses iambic feet—alternating unstressed and stressed syllables—but here he immediately follows one heavy stress with another, thereby helping to communicate the "meaning"—the impressive monotony of Hell. As a second example, consider the function of the rhythm in two lines by Alexander Pope:

> When Ajax strives some rock's vast weight to throw,
>
> The line too labors, and the words move slow.

The heavier stresses (again, marked by ´) do not merely alternate with the lighter ones (marked ˘); rather, the great weight of the rock is suggested by three consecutive stressed words, "rock's vast weight," and the great effort involved in moving it is suggested by another three consecutive stresses, "line too labors," and by yet another three, "words move slow." Note, also, the abundant pauses within the lines. In the first line, unless one's speech is slovenly, one must pause at least slightly after "Ajax," "strives," "rock's," "vast," "weight," and "throw." The grating sounds in "Ajax" and "rock's" do their work, too, and so do the explosive *t*'s. When Pope wishes to suggest lightness, he reverses his procedure and he groups *un*stressed syllables:

Not so, when swift Camilla scours the plain,
Flies o'er th'unbending corn, and skims along the main.

This last line has twelve syllables and is thus longer than the line about Ajax, but the addition of "along" helps to communicate lightness and swiftness because in this line (it can be argued) neither syllable of "along" is strongly stressed. If "along" is omitted, the line still makes grammatical sense and becomes more "regular," but it also becomes less imitative of lightness.

The very regularity of a line may be meaningful too. Shakespeare begins a sonnet thus:

When I do count the clock that tells the time.

This line about a mechanism runs with appropriate regularity. (It is worth noting, too, that "*c*ount the *c*lock" and "*t*ells the *t*ime" emphasize the regularity by the repetition of sounds and syntax.) But notice what Shakespeare does in the middle of the next line:

And see the brave day sunk in hideous night.

What has he done? And what is the effect?

Here is another poem that refers to a clock. In England, until capital punishment was abolished, executions regularly took place at 8:00 A.M.

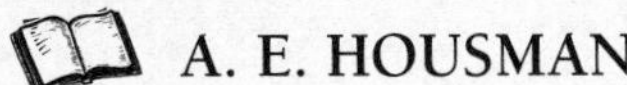

## A. E. HOUSMAN

*For another poem by the English poet A. E. Housman (1859–1936) and for a brief biography, see page 1069.*

## *Eight O'Clock*

He stood, and heard the steeple
  Sprinkle the quarters on the morning town.
One, two, three, four, to market-place and people
  It tossed them down.

Strapped, noosed, nighing his hour,
  He stood and counted them and cursed his luck;
And then the clock collected in the tower
  Its strength, and struck.

[*1922*]

The chief (but not unvarying) pattern is iambic; that is, the odd syllables are less emphatic than the even ones, as in

He stood, and heard the steeple

Try to mark the syllables, stressed and unstressed, in the rest of the poem. Be guided by your ear, not by a mechanical principle, and don't worry too much about difficult or uncertain parts; different readers may reasonably come up with different results.

## TOPICS FOR CRITICAL THINKING AND WRITING

1. Where do you find two or more consecutive stresses? What explanations (related to meaning) can be offered?
2. What do you think is the effect of the short line at the end of each stanza? And what significance can you attach to the fact that these lines (unlike the first and third lines in each stanza) end with a stress?

Following are some poems in which the strongly felt pulsations are highly important.

## THEODORE ROETHKE

*Theodore Roethke (1908–63) was born in Saginaw, Michigan, and educated at the University of Michigan and Harvard. From 1947 until his death he taught at the University of Washington in Seattle, where he exerted considerable influence on the next generation of poets. Many of Roethke's best poems are lyrical memories of his childhood.*

### *My Papa's Waltz*

The whiskey on your breath
Could make a small boy dizzy;
but I hung on like death:
Such waltzing was not easy.

We romped until the pans
Slid from the kitchen shelf;
My mother's countenance
Could not unfrown itself.

The hand that held my wrist
Was battered on one knuckle;
At every step you missed
My right ear scraped a buckle.

You beat time on my head
With a palm caked hard by dirt,
Then waltzed me off to bed
Still clinging to your shirt.

[*1948*]

## TOPICS FOR CRITICAL THINKING AND WRITING

1. Do the syntactical pauses vary much from stanza to stanza? Be specific. Would you say that the rhythm suggests lightness? Why?

2. Does the rhythm parallel or ironically contrast with the episode described? Was the dance a graceful waltz? Explain.
3. What would you say is the function of the stresses in lines 13–14?

## WILLIAM CARLOS WILLIAMS

*A poem by William Carlos Williams (1883-1963), along with a brief biography, appears on page 897.*

### *The Dance*

In Breughel's great picture, The Kermess,°
the dancers go round, they go round and
around, the squeal and the blare and the
tweedle of bagpipes, a bugle and fiddles
tipping their bellies (round as the thick-
sided glasses whose wash they impound)
their hips and their bellies off balance
to turn them. Kicking and rolling about
the Fair Grounds, swinging their butts, those
shanks must be sound to bear up under such
rollicking measures, prance as they dance
in Breughel's great picture, The Kermess.

[*1944*]

**1 Kermess** Carnival

Pieter Breughel, *The Carnival* (1520?–1569). (Kunsthistorisches Museum, Vienna)

## TOPICS FOR CRITICAL THINKING AND WRITING

1. Read Williams's poem aloud several times, and decide where the heavy stresses fall. Mark the heavily stressed syllables ´, the lightly stressed ones ^, and the unstressed ones ˇ. Are all the lines identical? What effect is thus gained, especially when read aloud? What does the parenthetical statement (lines 5–6) do to the rhythm? Does a final syllable often receive a heavy stress here? Are there noticeable pauses at the ends of the lines? What is the consequence? Are the dancers waltzing?
2. What syllables rhyme or are repeated (e.g., "round" in lines 2 and 5, and "-pound" in line 6; "-ing" in lines 5, 8, 9, and 11)? What effect do they have?
3. What do you think the absence at the beginning of each line of the customary capital contributes to the meaning? Why is the last line the same as the first?

## DYLAN THOMAS

*Dylan Thomas (1914–53) was born and grew up in Swansea, in Wales. His first volume of poetry, published in 1934, immediately made him famous. Endowed with a highly melodious voice, on three tours of the United States he was immensely successful as a reader both of his own and of other poets' work. He died in New York City.*

### *Do not go gentle into that good night*

Do not go gentle into that good night,
Old age should burn and rave at close of day;
Rage, rage against the dying of the light.

Though wise men at their end know dark is right,
Because their words had forked no lightning they
Do not go gentle into that good night.

Good men, the last wave by, crying how bright
Their frail deeds might have danced in a green bay,
Rage, rage against the dying of the light.

Wild men who caught and sang the sun in flight,
And learn, too late, they grieved it on its way,
Do not go gentle into that good night.

Grave men, near death, who see with blinding sight
Blind eyes could blaze like meteors and be gay,
Rage, rage against the dying of the light.

And you, my father, there on the sad height,
Curse, bless, me now with your fierce tears, I pray.
Do not go gentle into that good night.
Rage, rage against the dying of the light.

[*1952*]

This poem is written in an elaborate French form, the **villanelle,** that is, five tercets (stanzas of three lines each, the first and third lines rhyming) and a final quatrain (stanza of four lines, the first, third, and fourth lines all rhyming with the first and third lines of the tercets, and the second line rhyming with the middle lines of the tercets). Moreover, the first line of the poem is the last line of the second and fourth tercets; the third line of the poem is the last line of the third and fifth tercets, and these two lines reappear yet again as a pair of rhyming lines at the end of the poem.

## TOPIC FOR CRITICAL THINKING OR WRITING

The intricate form of the villanelle might seem too fussy for a serious poem about dying. Do you find it too fussy? Or does the form here somehow succeed?

## ROBERT FRANCIS

*Robert Francis (1901–87) was born in Upland, Pennsylvania, and educated at Harvard. He taught only briefly, a term here or there and an occasional summer, devoting himself for the most part to reading and writing.*

# *The Pitcher*

His art is eccentricity, his aim
How not to hit the mark he seems to aim at,

His passion how to avoid the obvious,
His technique how to vary the avoidance.

The others throw to be comprehended. He
Throws to be a moment misunderstood.

Yet not too much. Not errant, arrant, wild,
But every seeming aberration willed.

Not to, yet still, still to communicate
Making the batter understand too late.

[*1960*]

If you read this poem aloud, pausing appropriately where the punctuation tells you to, you will hear the poet trying to represent something of the pitcher's "eccentricity." ("Eccentric," you may know, literally means "off center.") A pitcher tries to deceive a batter, perhaps by throwing a ball that will unexpectedly curve over the plate; the poet playfully deceives the reader, for instance, with unexpected pauses. In line 5, for example, he puts a heavy pause (indicated by a period) not at the end of the line, but just before the end.

## TOPICS FOR CRITICAL THINKING AND WRITING

1. Notice that some lines contain no pauses, but the next-to-last line contains two within it (indicated by commas) and none at the end. What do you suppose Francis is getting at?
2. What significance can be attached to the fact that only the last two lines really rhyme (communicate / late) whereas other lines do not quite rhyme?

# VERSIFICATION: A GLOSSARY FOR REFERENCE

The technical vocabulary of **prosody** (the study of the principles of verse structure, including meter, rhyme, and other sound effects, and stanzaic patterns) is large. An understanding of these terms will not turn anyone into a poet, but it will enable one to discuss some aspects of poetry more efficiently. A knowledge of them, like a knowledge of most other technical terms (e.g., "misplaced modifier," "woofer," "automatic transmission"), allows for quick and accurate communication. The following are the chief terms of prosody.

## Meter

Most English poetry has a pattern of **stressed (accented)** sounds, and this pattern is the **meter** (from the Greek word for "measure"). Although in Old English poetry (poetry written in England before the Norman-French Conquest in 1066) a line may have any number of unstressed syllables in addition to four stressed syllables, most poetry written in England since the Conquest not only has a fixed number of stresses in a line, but also has a fixed number of unstressed syllables before or after each stressed one. (One really ought not to talk of "unstressed" or "unaccented" syllables, since to utter a syllable—however lightly—is to give it some stress. It is really a matter of *relative* stress, but the fact is that "unstressed" or "unaccented" are parts of the established terminology of versification.)

In a line of poetry, the **foot** is the basic unit of measurement. On rare occasions it is a single stressed syllable, but generally a foot consists of two or three syllables, one of which is stressed. (Stress is indicated by ´, lack of stress by ˘.) The repetition of feet, then, produces a pattern of stresses throughout the poem.

*Two cautions:*

1. A poem will seldom contain only one kind of foot throughout; significant variations usually occur, but one kind of foot is dominant.

2. In reading a poem one pays attention to the sense as well as to the metrical pattern. By paying attention to the sense, one often finds that the stress falls on a word that according to the metrical pattern would be unstressed. Or a word that according to the pattern would be stressed may be seen to be un-

stressed. Furthermore, by reading for sense, one finds that not all stresses are equally heavy; some are almost as light as unstressed syllables, and sometimes there is a **hovering stress;** that is, the stress is equally distributed over two adjacent syllables. To repeat: *read for sense*, allowing the meaning to help indicate the stresses.

***Metrical Feet.*** The most common feet in English poetry are the six listed below.

**Iamb** (adjective: **iambic**): one unstressed syllable followed by one stressed syllable. The iamb, said to be the most common pattern in English speech, is surely the most common in English poetry. The following example has four iambic feet:

> ˘ / ˘ / ˘ / ˘ /
> My heart is like a sing-ing bird.
> —Christina Rossetti

**Trochee (trochaic):** one stressed syllable followed by one unstressed.

> / ˘ / ˘ / ˘ / ˘ / ˘
> We were very tired, we were very merry
> —Edna St. Vincent Millay

**Anapest (anapestic):** two unstressed syllables followed by one stressed.

> ˘ ˘ / ˘ ˘ / ˘ ˘ / ˘ ˘ /
> There are man-y who say that a dog has his day.
> —Dylan Thomas

**Dactyl (dactylic):** one stressed syllable followed by two unstressed. This trisyllabic foot, like the anapest, is common in light verse or verse suggesting joy, but its use is not limited to such material, as Longfellow's *Evangeline* shows. Thomas Hood's sentimental "The Bridge of Sighs" begins:

> / ˘ ˘ / ˘ ˘
> Take her up tenderly.

**Spondee (spondaic):** two stressed syllables; most often used as a substitute for an iamb or trochee.

> / / ˘ / ˘ / ˘ /
> Smart lad, to slip betimes away.
> —A. E. Housman

**Pyrrhic:** two unstressed syllables; it is often not considered a legitimate foot in English.

***Metrical Lines.*** A metrical line consists of one or more feet and is named for the number of feet in it. The following names are used:

| | |
|---|---|
| **monometer:** one foot | **pentameter:** five feet |
| **dimeter:** two feet | **hexameter:** six feet |
| **trimeter:** three feet | **heptameter:** seven feet |
| **tetrameter:** four feet | **octameter:** eight feet |

A line is scanned for the kind and number of feet in it, and the **scansion** tells you if it is, say, anapestic trimeter (three anapests):

> ˘ ˘ / ˘ ˘ / ˘ ˘ /
> As I came to the edge of the woods.
> —Robert Frost

Or, in another example, iambic pentameter:

> ˘ / ˘ / ˘ / ˘ / ˘ /
> The sum-mer thun-der, like a wood-en bell
> —Louise Bogan

A line ending with a stress has a **masculine ending;** a line ending with an extra unstressed syllable has a **feminine ending.** The **caesura** (usually indicated by the symbol //) is a slight pause within the line. It need not be indicated by punctuation (notice the fourth and fifth lines in the following quotation), and it does not affect the metrical count:

Awake, my St. John! // leave all meaner things
To low ambition, // and the pride of kings.
Let us // (since life can little more supply
Than just to look about us // and to die)
Expatiate free // o'er all this scene of Man;
A mighty maze! // but not without a plan;
A wild, // where weeds and flowers promiscuous shoot;
Or garden, // tempting with forbidden fruit.
—Alexander Pope

The varying position of the caesura helps to give Pope's lines an informality that plays against the formality of the pairs of rhyming lines.

An **end-stopped line** concludes with a distinct syntactical pause, but a **run-on line** has its sense carried over into the next line without syntactical pause. (The running-on of a line is called **enjambment.**) In the following passage, only the first is a run-on line:

Yet if we look more closely we shall find
Most have the seeds of judgment in their mind:
Nature affords at least a glimmering light;
The lines, though touched but faintly, are drawn right.
—Alexander Pope

Meter produces **rhythm,** recurrences at equal intervals, but rhythm (from a Greek word meaning "flow") is usually applied to larger units than feet. Often it depends most obviously on pauses. Thus, a poem with run-on lines will have a different rhythm from a poem with end-stopped lines, even though both are in the same meter. And prose, though it is unmetrical, can have rhythm, too.

In addition to being affected by syntactical pause, rhythm is affected by pauses attributable to consonant clusters and to the length of words. Words of several syllables establish a different rhythm from words of one syllable, even in metrically identical lines. One can say, then, that rhythm is altered by shifts in meter, syntax, and the length and ease of pronunciation. But even with no such shift, even if a line is repeated word for word, a reader may sense a change in rhythm. The rhythm of the final line of a poem, for example, may well differ from that of the line before, even though in all other respects the lines are identical, as in Frost's "Stopping by Woods on a Snowy Evening" (p. 1141), which concludes by repeating "And miles to go before I sleep." One may simply sense that the final line ought to be spoken, say, more slowly and with more stress on "miles."

## Patterns of Sound

Though rhythm is basic to poetry, **rhyme**—the repetition of the identical or similar stressed sound or sounds—is not. Rhyme is, presumably, pleasant in itself; it suggests order; and it may also be related to meaning, for it brings two words sharply together, often implying a relationship, as in the now trite *dove* and *love,* or in the more imaginative *throne* and *alone.*

**Perfect,** or **exact, rhyme:** Differing consonant sounds are followed by identical stressed vowel sounds, and the following sounds, if any, are identical *(foe—toe; meet—fleet; buffer—rougher).* Notice that perfect rhyme involves identity of sound, not of spelling. *Fix* and *sticks,* like *buffer* and *rougher,* are perfect rhymes.

**Half-rhyme** (or **off-rhyme**): Only the final consonant sounds of the words are identical; the stressed vowel sounds as well as the initial consonant sounds, if any, differ *(soul—oil; mirth—forth; trolley—bully).*

**Eye-rhyme:** The sounds do not in fact rhyme, but the words look as though they would rhyme *(cough—bough).*

**Masculine rhyme:** The final syllables are stressed and, after their differing initial consonant sounds, are identical in sound *(stark—mark; support—retort).*

**Feminine rhyme** (or **double rhyme**): Stressed rhyming syllables are followed by identical unstressed syllables *(revival—arrival; flatter—batter).* **Triple rhyme** is a kind of feminine rhyme in which identical stressed vowel sounds are followed by two identical unstressed syllables *(machinery—scenery; tenderly—slenderly).*

**End rhyme** (or **terminal rhyme**): The rhyming words occur at the ends of the lines.

**Internal rhyme:** At least one of the rhyming words occurs within the line (Oscar Wilde's "Each narrow *cell* in which we *dwell*").

**Alliteration:** sometimes defined as the repetition of initial sounds ("*A*ll the *a*wful *a*uguries," or "*B*ring me my *b*ow of *b*urning gold"), and sometimes as the prominent repetition of a consonant ("a*f*ter li*f*e's *f*it*f*ul *f*ever").

**Assonance:** the repetition, in words of proximity, of identical vowel sounds preceded and followed by differing consonant sounds. Whereas *tide* and *hide* are rhymes, *tide* and *mine* are assonantal.

**Consonance:** the repetition of identical consonant sounds and differing vowel sounds in words in proximity *(fail—feel; rough—roof; pitter—patter).* Sometimes consonance is more loosely defined merely as the repetition of a consonant *(fail—peel).*

**Onomatopoeia:** the use of words that imitate sounds, such as *hiss* and *buzz.* There is a mistaken tendency to see onomatopoeia everywhere—for example in *thunder* and *horror.* Many words sometimes thought to be onomatopoeic are not clearly imitative of the thing they refer to; they merely contain some sounds that, when we know what the word means, seem to have some resemblance to the thing they denote. Tennyson's lines from "Come down, O maid" are usually cited as an example of onomatopoeia:

The moan of doves in immemorial elms
And murmuring of innumerable bees.

If you have read the preceding—and, admittedly, not entirely engaging—paragraphs, you may have found yourself mentally repeating some catchy sounds, let's say our example of internal rhyme ("Each narrow cell in which we dwell") or our example of alliteration ("Bring me my bow of burning gold"). As the creators of advertising slogans know, all of us—not just poets—can be hooked by the sounds of words, but probably poets are especially fond of savoring words. Consider the following poem.

## GALWAY KINNELL

*Born in 1927 in Providence, Rhode Island, Galway Kinnell was educated at Princeton and the University of Rochester. He is the author of several books of poems, and he has won many awards, including the Pulitzer Prize for Poetry and the American Book Award.*

### *Blackberry Eating*

I love to go out in late September
among the fat, overripe, icy, black blackberries
to eat blackberries for breakfast,
the stalks very prickly, a penalty
they earn for knowing the black art
of blackberry-making; and as I stand among them
lifting the stalks to my mouth, the ripest berries
fall almost unbidden to my tongue,
as words sometimes do, certain peculiar words
like *strengths* or *squinched,*
many-lettered, one-syllabled lumps,
which I squeeze, squinch open, and splurge well
in the silent, startled, icy, black language
of blackberry-eating in late September.

[*1980*]

Kinnell does not use rhyme, but he uses other kinds of aural repetition. For instance, in the first line we get "*l*ove" and "*l*ate," and the *l* sound (already present in the title of the poem) is picked up in the second line, in "black blackberries." The *k* sound is then continued in the next line, in "stalks" and the *l* and *k* in "prickly," and "prickly" contains not only the *k* and the *l* of "blackberry" but also the *r*.

In lines 7–9 Kinnell compares eating blackberries—an action involving the tongue and the lips, and the mind also, if one is savoring the berries—to speaking "certain peculiar words." There is no need for us to point out additional connections between words in the poem, but we do want to mention that the last line ends with the same two words as the first, providing closure, which is one of the things rhyme normally does.

## TOPICS FOR CRITICAL THINKING AND WRITING

1. Specify three words that you like to "squinch," and explain why.
2. Specify one poem, other than a poem in this chapter (the poem need not be in this book), in which you think the repetitions of sounds are especially important, and explain why you hold this view.

## Stanzaic Patterns

Lines of poetry are commonly arranged in a rhythmical unit called a stanza (from an Italian word meaning "room" or "stopping-place"). Usually all the stanzas in a poem have the same rhyme pattern. A stanza is sometimes called a **verse,** though *verse* may also mean a single line of poetry. (In discussing stanzas, rhymes are indicated by identical letters. Thus, *abab* indicates that the first and third lines rhyme with each other, while the second and fourth lines are linked by a different rhyme. An unrhymed line is denoted by *x*.) Common stanzaic forms in English poetry are the following:

**Couplet:** a stanza of two lines, usually but not necessarily with end-rhymes. *Couplet* is also used for a pair of rhyming lines. The **octosyllabic couplet** is iambic or trochaic tetrameter:

Had we but world enough and time,
This coyness, lady, were no crime.
—Andrew Marvell

**Heroic couplet:** a rhyming couplet of iambic pentameter, often "closed," that is, containing a complete thought, with a fairly heavy pause at the end of the first line and a still heavier one at the end of the second. Commonly, there is a parallel or an *antithesis* (contrast) within a line or between the two lines. It is called heroic because in England, especially in the eighteenth century, it was much used for heroic (epic) poems.

Some foreign writers, some our own despise;
The ancients only, or the moderns, prize.
—Alexander Pope

**Triplet** (or **tercet**): a three-line stanza, usually with one rhyme.

Whenas in silks my Julia goes
Then, then (methinks) how sweetly flows
That liquefaction of her clothes.
—Robert Herrick

**Quatrain:** a four-line stanza, rhymed or unrhymed. The **heroic** (or **elegiac**) **quatrain** is iambic pentameter, rhyming *abab.* That is, the first and third lines rhyme (so they are designated *a*), and the second and fourth lines rhyme (so they are designated *b*).

**Sonnet:** a fourteen-line poem, predominantly in iambic pentameter. The rhyme is usually according to one of two schemes. The **Italian** or **Petrarchan sonnet,** named for the Italian poet Francesco Petrarch (1304–74), has two divisions: The first eight lines (rhyming *abba abba*) are the octave, the last six (rhyming *cd cd cd,* or a variant) are the sestet. Gerard Manley Hopkins's "God's Grandeur" (p. 1068) is an Italian sonnet. The second kind of sonnet, the **English** or **Shakespearean sonnet,** is usually arranged into three quatrains and a couplet, rhyming *abab cdcd efef gg.* (For examples see pages 1051–52.) In many sonnets there is a marked correspondence between the rhyme scheme and the development of the thought. Thus an Italian sonnet may state a generalization in the octave and a specific example in the sestet. Or an English sonnet may give three examples—one in each quatrain—and draw a conclusion in the couplet.

Why poets choose to imprison themselves in fourteen tightly rhymed lines is something of a mystery. Tradition has a great deal to do with it: the form, having been handled successfully by major poets, stands as a challenge. In writing a sonnet a poet gains a little of the authority of Petrarch, Shakespeare, Milton, Wordsworth, and other masters who showed that the sonnet is not merely a trick. A second reason perhaps resides in the very tightness of the rhymes, which can help as well as hinder. Many poets have felt, along with Richard Wilbur (in *Mid-Century American Poets,* ed. John Ciardi), that the need for a rhyme has suggested

> . . . arbitrary connections of which the mind may take advantage if it likes. For example, if one has to rhyme with *tide,* a great number of rhyme-words at once come to mind (ride, bide, shied, confide, Akenside, etc.). Most of these, in combination with *tide,* will probably suggest nothing apropos, but one of them may reveal precisely what one wanted to say. If none of them does, *tide* must be dispensed with. Rhyme, austerely used, may be a stimulus to discovery and a stretcher of the attention.

Here is a sonnet by X. J. Kennedy, written in the Petrarchan form. Kennedy alludes (line 4) to Milton's *Paradise Lost,* VII, 205–07: "Heaven opened wide / Her ever-during gates, harmonious sound / On golden hinges moving . . . ." For an account of the slaughter of the innocents (line 5), see Matthew 2.16. The Venerable Bede (673–735), in line 6, was an English theologian and historian.

## X. J. KENNEDY

*X. J. Kennedy was born in New Jersey in 1929. He has taught at Tufts University and is the author of several books of poems, books for children, and college textbooks.*

# *Nothing in Heaven Functions as It Ought*

Nothing in Heaven functions as it ought:
Peter's bifocals, blindly sat on, crack;
His gates lurch wide with the cackle of a cock,
Not turn with a hush of gold as Milton had thought;
Gangs of the slaughtered innocents keep huffing
The nimbus off the Venerable Bede
Like that of an old dandelion gone to seed;
And the beatific choir keep breaking up, coughing.

But Hell, sleek Hell hath no freewheeling part:
None takes his own sweet time, none quickens pace.
Ask anyone, How come you here, poor heart?—
And he will slot a quarter through his face,

You'll hear an instant click, a tear will start
Imprinted with an abstract of his case.

[*1965*]

## TOPIC FOR CRITICAL THINKING AND WRITING

In the octave Kennedy uses off-rhymes *(crack, cock; huffing, coughing)* but in the sestet all the rhymes are exact. How do the rhymes help to convey the meaning? (Notice, too, that lines 3, 4, 5, 7, and 8 all have more than the usual ten syllables. Again, why?)

## Blank Verse and Free Verse

A good deal of English poetry is unrhymed, much of it in **blank verse,** that is, unrhymed iambic pentameter. Introduced into English poetry by Henry Howard, the Earl of Surrey, in the middle of the sixteenth century, late in the century it became the standard medium (especially in the hands of Marlowe and Shakespeare) of English drama. In the seventeenth century, Milton used it for *Paradise Lost,* and it has continued to be used in both dramatic and nondramatic literature. For an example see the first scene of *Hamlet* (pp. 1294-99). A passage of blank verse that has a rhetorical unity is sometimes called a **verse paragraph.**

The second kind of unrhymed poetry fairly common in English, especially in the twentieth century, is **free verse** (or **vers libre**): rhythmical lines varying in length, adhering to no fixed metrical pattern and usually unrhymed. Such poetry may seem formless; Robert Frost, who strongly preferred regular meter and rhyme, said that he would not consider writing free verse any more than he would consider playing tennis without a net. But free verse does have a form or pattern, often largely based on repetition and parallel grammatical structure. Whitman's "A Noiseless Patient Spider" (p. 849) is an example; Arnold's "Dover Beach" (p. 1065) is another example, though less typical because it uses rhyme. Thoroughly typical is Whitman's "When I Heard the Learn'd Astronomer."

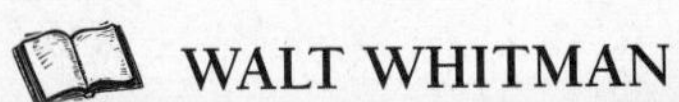

### WALT WHITMAN

*For a biography of the American poet Walt Whitman (1819-92), see the note prefacing "A Noiseless Patient Spider" (p. 849).*

## *When I Heard the Learn'd Astronomer*

When I heard the learn'd astronomer,
When the proofs, the figures, were ranged in columns before me,

When I was shown the charts and diagrams, to add, divide, and measure
them,
When I sitting heard the astronomer where he lectured with much
applause in the lecture-room,
How soon unaccountable I became tired and sick,
Till rising and gliding out I wander'd off by myself,
In the mystical moist night-air, and from time to time,
Look'd up in perfect silence at the stars.

[*1865*]

What can be said about the rhythmic structure of this poem? Rhymes are absent, and the lines vary greatly in the number of syllables, ranging from 9 (the first line) to 23 (the fourth line), but when we read the poem we sense a rhythmic structure. The first four lines obviously hang together, each beginning with "When"; indeed, three of these four lines begin "When I." We may notice, too, that each of these four lines has more syllables than its predecessor (the numbers are 9, 14, 18, and 23); this increase in length, like the initial repetition, is a kind of pattern. But then, with the fifth line, which speaks of fatigue and surfeit, there is a shrinkage to 14 syllables, offering an enormous relief from the previous swollen line with its 23 syllables. The second half of the poem—the pattern established by "When" in the first four lines is dropped, and in effect we get a new stanza, also of four lines—does not relentlessly diminish the number of syllables in each succeeding line, but it *almost* does so: 14, 14, 13, 10.

The second half of the poem thus has a pattern too, and this pattern is more or less the reverse of the first half of the poem. We may notice too that the last line (in which the poet, now released from the oppressive lecture hall, is in communion with nature) is very close to an iambic pentameter line; that is, the poem concludes with a metrical form said to be the most natural in English. The effect of naturalness or ease in this final line, moreover, is increased by the absence of repetitions (e.g., not only of "When I," but even of such syntactic repetitions as "charts and diagrams," "tired and sick," "rising and gliding") that characterize most of the previous lines. This final effect of naturalness is part of a carefully constructed pattern in which rhythmic structure is part of meaning. Though at first glance free verse may appear unrestrained, as T. S. Eliot (a practitioner) said, "No *vers* is *libre* for the man who wants to do a good job"—or for the woman who wants to do a good job.

## The Prose Poem

The term *prose poem* is sometimes applied to a short work that looks like prose but that is highly rhythmical or rich in images, or both. Here is a modern example.

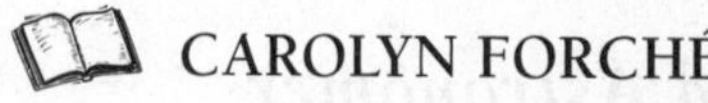

### CAROLYN FORCHÉ

*Carolyn Forché was born in Detroit in 1950. After earning a bachelor's degree from Michigan State University and a master's degree from Bowling Green State Univer-*

*sity, she traveled widely in the Southwest, living among Pueblo Indians. Between 1978 and 1986 she made several visits to El Salvador, documenting human rights violations for Amnesty International. Her first book of poems,* Gathering the Tribes, *won the Yale Younger Poets award in 1975. Her second book of poems,* The Country Between Us *(1981), includes "The Colonel," which has been called a prose poem.*

## *The Colonel*

What you have heard is true. I was in his house. His wife carried a tray of coffee and sugar. His daughter filed her nails, his son went out for the night. There were daily papers, pet dogs, a pistol on the cushion beside him. The moon swung bare on its black cord over the house. On the television was a cop show. It was in English. Broken bottles were embedded in the walls around the house to scoop the kneecaps from a man's legs or cut his hands to lace. On the windows there were gratings like those in liquor stores. We had dinner, rack of lamb, good wine, a gold bell was on the table for calling the maid. The maid brought green mangoes, salt, a type of bread. I was asked how I enjoyed the country. There was a brief commercial in Spanish. His wife took everything away. There was some talk then of how difficult it had become to govern. The parrot said hello on the terrace. The colonel told it to shutup, and pushed himself from the table. My friend said to me with his eyes: say nothing. The colonel returned with a sack used to bring groceries home. He spilled many human ears on the table. They were like dried peach halves. There is no other way to say this. He took one of them in his hands, shook it in our faces, dropped it into a water glass. It came alive there. I am tired of fooling around he said. As for the rights of anyone, tell your people they can go fuck themselves. He swept the ears to the floor with his arm and held the last of his wine in the air. Something for your poetry, no? he said. Some of the ears on the floor caught this scrap of his voice. Some of the ears on the floor were pressed to the ground.

*May 1978*

[*publ. 1981*]

## TOPICS FOR CRITICAL THINKING AND WRITING

1. How would you characterize the colonel in a few sentences?
2. We are told that the colonel spoke of "how difficult it had become to govern." What do you suppose the colonel assumes is the purpose of government? What do you assume its purpose is?
3. How much do we know about the narrator? Can we guess the narrator's purpose in visiting the colonel? How would you characterize the narrator's tone? Do you believe the narrator?
4. What is your response to the last sentence?

## ✔ Checklist: Writing about Rhythm and Versification

1. What is the role of sound effects, including repetitions of sound (for instance, alliteration) and of entire words, and shifts in versification?
2. If there are off-rhymes (*dizzy* and *easy,* or *home* and *come*), what effect do they have on you? Do they, for instance, add a note of tentativeness or uncertainty?
3. If there are unexpected stresses or pauses, what do they communicate about the speaker's experience? How do they affect you?
4. If the poem is in stanzas, do the stanzas represent stages in the development of the thought or emotion?

# CHAPTER 22

# *Review: Writing about Poetry*

If you are going to write about a fairly short poem (say, under 30 lines), it's not a bad idea to copy out the poem, writing or typing it double-spaced. By writing it out you will be forced to notice details, down to the punctuation. After you have copied the poem, proofread it carefully against the original. Catching an error—even the addition or omission of a comma—may help you to notice a detail in the original that you might otherwise have overlooked. And now that you have the poem with ample space between the lines, you have a worksheet with room for jottings.

A good essay is based on a genuine response to a poem; a response may be stimulated in part by first reading the poem aloud and then considering the following questions.

## FIRST RESPONSE

What was your response to the poem on first reading? Did some parts especially please or displease you, or puzzle you? After some study—perhaps checking the meanings of some of the words in a dictionary and reading the poem several times—did you modify your initial response to the parts and to the whole?

## SPEAKER AND TONE

1. Who is the speaker? (Consider age, sex, personality, frame of mind, and tone of voice.) Is the speaker defined fairly precisely (for instance, an older woman speaking to a child), or is the speaker simply a voice

meditating? (Jot down your first impressions, then reread the poem and make further jottings, if necessary.)

2. Do you think the speaker is fully aware of what he or she is saying, or does the speaker unconsciously reveal his or her personality and values? What is your attitude toward this speaker?
3. Is the speaker narrating or reflecting on an earlier experience or attitude? If so, does he or she convey a sense of new awareness, such as regret for innocence lost?

## AUDIENCE

To whom is the speaker speaking? What is the situation (including time and place)? (In some poems a listener is strongly implied, but in others, especially those in which the speaker is meditating, there may be no audience other than the reader, who "overhears" the speaker.)

## STRUCTURE AND FORM

1. Does the poem proceed in a straightforward way, or at some point or points does the speaker reverse course, altering his or her tone or perception? If there is a shift, what do you make of it?
2. Is the poem organized into sections? If so, what are these sections—stanzas, for instance—and how does each section (characterized, perhaps, by a certain tone of voice, or a group of rhymes) grow out of what precedes it?
3. What is the effect on you of the form—say, quatrains (stanzas of four lines) or blank verse (unrhymed lines of ten syllables of iambic pentameter)? If the sense overflows the form, running without pause from (for example) one quatrain into the next, what effect is created?

## CENTER OF INTEREST AND THEME

1. What is the poem about? Is the interest chiefly in a distinctive character, or in meditation? That is, is the poem chiefly psychological or chiefly philosophical?
2. Is the theme stated explicitly (directly) or implicitly? How might you state the theme in a sentence? What is lost by reducing the poem to a statement of a theme?

## DICTION

1. How would you characterize the language? Colloquial, or elevated, or what?
2. Do certain words have rich and relevant associations that relate to other words and help to define the speaker or the theme or both?

3. What is the role of figurative language, if any? Does it help to define the speaker or the theme?
4. What do you think is to be taken figuratively or symbolically, and what literally?

## SOUND EFFECTS

1. What is the role of sound effects, including repetitions of sound (for instance, alliteration) and of entire words, and shifts in versification?
2. If there are off-rhymes (for instance, *dizzy* and *easy*, or *home* and *come*), what effect do they have on you? Do they, for instance, add a note of tentativeness or uncertainty?
3. If there are unexpected stresses or pauses, what do they communicate about the speaker's experience? How do they affect you?

## A NOTE ON EXPLICATION

On page 34 we discuss the form known as *explication,* a line-by-line commentary seeking to make explicit or to explain the meaning that is implicit or hidden within the words. (*Explication* comes from the Latin *explicare,* meaning "to unfold," from *ex* = out + *plicare* = to fold.) The implication of such an activity is that writers "fold" a meaning into their words, and the reader perceives or unfolds the message. (*Implication,* also from the Latin word for "fold," means something entangled or involved in something else.)

An example will clarify these remarks. If we say to someone, "Shut the door," obviously we are conveying a message through these words. Also obviously, the message in "Shut the door" is *not* exactly the same as the message in "Would you mind shutting the door, please?" An explication would point out that the first sentence contains an authoritative tone that is not found in the second. In effect, the first sentence "says" (in addition to the point about the door) that the speaker may give orders to the hearer; or, to put it the other way around, folded into the second sentence (but not the first) is the speaker's awareness that the person receiving the words is the speaker's social equal. A slightly more complicated and much more interesting example is Julius Caesar's "I came, I saw, I conquered" (Latin: *veni, vidi, vici*). An explication would point out that in addition to the explicit meaning there are implicit meanings, for example that a man like Caesar does not waste words, that he is highly disciplined (the pattern of words suggests that he is a master of language), and that he is the sort of person who, on seeing something, immediately gets it under control by taking the appropriate action.

Because explication is chiefly concerned with making explicit what is implicit in a text, it is not concerned with such matters as the poet's place in history or the poet's biography, nor is it concerned with the reader's response to the poem—except to the degree that the reader's explication really may *not* be an objective decoding of the poem but may depend in large part on the reader's private associations. (Some literary critics would argue that the underlying premise of explication—that a writer puts a specific meaning into a work and that a reader can objectively recover that meaning—is based on the mistaken belief that readers can be objective.) If you look at the sample explication on page 35, you can decide for yourself whether the student unfolded implicit meanings that the author (William Butler Yeats) had tucked into the words of his poem or whether the explication really is a personal response to the poem.

# A STUDENT'S WRITTEN RESPONSE TO A POEM

What we give in this chapter is not an explication but a more personal response to a poem by Adrienne Rich. Like an explication, it is concerned with the author's meaning, but unlike an explication it does not hesitate to go beyond the poem and into "the real world." The essay is not so personal that the poem disappears (as it might in an essay that says something like "This poem reminds me of the time that I . . ."), but it does not claim merely to unfold meanings that Rich has embodied or entangled in her words.

First read the following biographical note and the poem.

## ADRIENNE RICH

*Adrienne Rich, born in Baltimore in 1929, published her first book of poems while she was an undergraduate at Radcliffe College. In 1953 she married, and she bore three children in rapid succession. In* Of Woman Born, *a prose work of 1976, she wrote of the conflict she felt between her roles as wife, mother, and writer. Rich was active in opposing the Vietnam War, and she became increasingly interested in feminist issues, including lesbian politics.*

## *Aunt Jennifer's Tigers*

Aunt Jennifer's tigers prance across a screen,
Bright topaz denizens of a world of green.
They do not fear the men beneath the tree;
They pace in sleek chivalric certainty.

Aunt Jennifer's fingers fluttering through her wool
Find even the ivory needle hard to pull.
The massive weight of Uncle's wedding band
Sits heavily upon Aunt Jennifer's hand.

When Aunt is dead, her terrified hands will lie
Still ringed with ordeals she was mastered by.
The tigers in the panel that she made
Will go on prancing, proud and unafraid.

[*1951*]

## Annotations

Here are the annotations that Maria Fuentes, a first-year student, produced in the course of thinking about the poem.

Aunt Jennifer's Tigers — *odd—arouses interest*

Aunt Jennifer's tigers prance across a screen,
? Bright topaz denizens of a world of green.
They do not fear the men beneath the tree;
They pace in sleek chivalric certainty. ??

Aunt Jennifer's fingers fluttering through her wool
Find even the ivory needle hard to pull.
The massive weight of Uncle's wedding band — *he tyrannized over her*
Sits heavily upon Aunt Jennifer's hand.

When Aunt is dead, her terrified hands will lie
Still ringed with ordeals she was mastered by.
The tigers in the panel that she made
Will go on prancing, proud and unafraid.

*her work embroidery?*

*We are told only that she was oppressed & that she created a lively work of art. That's about all we know of her.*

*contrast to the prancing tigers she created*

*Uncle?*

*in contrast to "terrified" Aunt J. BUT She created these "proud and unafraid" tigers. Her vision of a better life?*

## Essay

Ultimately Fuentes produced the following essay.

Maria Fuentes

Aunt Jennifer's Screen and Adrienne Rich's Poem

What especially pleases me in Adrienne Rich's "Aunt Jennifer's Tigers" is the combination of neat, tight, highly disciplined stanzas of four rhyming lines (like marching squadrons) with the explosive rebellious content of the poem. Somehow the message seems especially powerful because it is so tightly packed, because the form is so restrained.

The poem is, on the surface at least, about what the title says it is about, "Aunt Jennifer's Tigers." Aunt Jennifer has made a screen, in embroidery or needlepoint, showing tigers that "prance." Presumably Aunt Jennifer was a sweet old lady, but she has created a picture of enormous energy, expressing, through her work of art, her own repressed energy.

We learn in the second stanza that she was repressed by the man she was married to:

> The massive weight of Uncle's wedding
> band
> Sits heavily upon Aunt Jennifer's hand.

The wedding band for her, as for many women in the present as well as in the past, is like a heavy chain. Rich tells us that Aunt Jennifer was "terrified" and was "mastered," obviously by Uncle. Rich makes a pun on the word "ringed," but the joke is very bitter:

> When Aunt is dead, her terrified hands
> will lie
> Still ringed with ordeals she was
> mastered by.

And yet, Rich points out, this "terrified" woman created something beautiful, a picture of tigers who "go on prancing, proud and unafraid." Apparently Aunt Jennifer was able, despite being oppressed by Uncle, to make something that gives pleasure to a later generation--just as the poet, however unhappy she may be, produces a work of art that gives pleasure to those who later read it.

Aunt Jennifer's work of art shows, in the prancing tigers, an energy that she apparently felt and understood, but because of her husband and perhaps because of the period in which she lived, she could express herself only in a "ladylike" activity such as embroidering. Aunt Jennifer was "mastered" (line 10), but she has nevertheless "made" (line 11) something depicting creatures who are "proud and unafraid." She was "terrified" (line 9), as many women were terrified by the patriarchal society in which they lived (and still live), but in her art she created an image of energy. Adrienne Rich, too, makes a work of art--a highly patterned poem consisting of three rhymed quatrains--that is as elegantly crafted as a work of embroidery. Rich speaks matter-of-factly and in a disciplined way in her quatrains about Aunt Jennifer and her tigers, but in this elegant poem she conveys energy and outrage on behalf of her terrified aunt who could not openly protest against the role that society had assigned to her.

# CHAPTER 23

# *Writing about Issues: Perspectives on a Multicultural America*

The continents in this hemisphere were populated long before Columbus "discovered" them. And, as has often been pointed out, the inhabitants knew where they were; it was Columbus, who thought he was in India, who was lost. In the words of the literary scholar Sacvan Bercovitch, the so-called discovery of America needs to be understood in "symbolic" terms:

> The New World of America was neither new nor a world nor America. Symbolically, the continent did not exist until it was invented by Europeans. And that symbolic act was cognitive and ideological: it gave conceptual unity not only to the unknown terrain but to the people who lived there.*

As a number of the poems in this chapter illustrate, American history has often paid little heed to the presence, to the history, of the many different people who were already here when the Europeans arrived. We now commonly refer to them as Native Americans, which honors them in one sense but which, as Bercovitch has noted, does justice neither to their "multiplicity of customs, traditions, languages, and religions" nor to the fact that they too immigrated to this continent from northern Asia. There were many kinds of Americans then, and there are many more now.

In the twentieth century, as the novelist Gertrude Stein wryly observed, "in the United States there is more space where nobody is than where anybody is." The beauty and breadth and diversity of the landscape are common themes in commentary on, and literature about, America. Yet the new nation has never seemed big enough to contain all of its people peacefully, and many poets, as

*See "The Biblical Basis of American Myth," in *The Bible and American Arts and Letters,* ed. Giles Gunn (Philadelphia: Fortress Press, 1983).

some of these selections show, have written bitterly about how distant they feel from America's dream of prosperity and its promise of freedom and equality.

Indeed, much of American history can be understood as a debate, often played out in battles and wars, about who is *really* American, and to whom the land *really* belongs. It was Walt Whitman, in his preface to *Leaves of Grass* (1855), who affirmed that "the United States themselves are essentially the greatest poem." But if the nation is a poem, a work of art, it is open to many interpretations of its essential meaning, and disagreements about how the nation should be defined and who should enjoy its freedoms have led to much pain, suffering, and death.

Perhaps the most painful fact of all is the system of slavery that started in the Virginia colony in 1619 and lasted until the Civil War. When the Revolution began in 1775, in all of the colonies there were 500,000 slaves; by 1860, there were 4 million slaves living in the South. During the Civil War, more than 600,000 soldiers were killed—which exceeds the combined number of deaths in all of America's other wars.

With the horrors of the Civil War in mind, historians sometimes have proposed that we speak of the "Disunited" as well as the United States, for our nation's history has been marked by strife and division over settlement, slavery, immigration, war, civil rights. Even as poets, essayists, and political leaders have praised America as a land of opportunity for all and a "melting pot," others have invoked the same phrases ironically to dramatize their own sense of being marginalized, excluded, mistreated. They feel they are not welcome, that they do not belong.

The selections below include some soaring tributes to America and affirmations of its uniqueness as a land blessed by God, unlike any other on earth in its ideals. In view of the harsh facts of American history, from the enslavement of Africans to the internment of Japanese-Americans during World War II to forms of bias and bigotry that exist today, it is often difficult to respond to such language positively. Yet the promise of America is remarkably resilient, and one of the reasons its critics have assailed it is because their hopes for America remain high. In *Notes of a Native Son* (1955), the African-American novelist and essayist James Baldwin declared, "I love America more than any other country in the world, and, exactly for this reason, I insist on the right to criticize her perpetually."

## TOPICS FOR CONSIDERATION

- Remember the important formal features of poetry that you have been studying: tone of voice; figurative language (simile, metaphor, personification, apostrophe); imagery and symbolism; irony and paradox; rhythm and versification. Focus not only on what the writer says but on how he or she is saying it, recalling as you do that in the best poems, form and content are closely fitted together. You might try selecting a poem and giving a paraphrase of it. What has been lost when you translate the writer's ideas and observations from verse to nonfictional prose?
- Can you see recurring patterns in the language that writers use about America? Which of these poems seem, implicitly or explicitly, to be speaking to others in the group, offering yet another perspective, or possibly a similar one, on the same general issue?

- It has been said that the Civil War never really ended—that its issues of race and regional difference have lingered for over a century. How do the poets here who write about the Civil War describe it? How do they remember the dead?
- To whom does America belong? Do some groups merit inclusion more than others? Select poems from this group that challenge as well as support your answers.
- Is it possible to express the meaning or meanings of "America"? Locate poems and passages that seek to explain what America is, for better or worse. Consider, too, as you think about this issue, why we tend to use the word *America* most often, rather than *the United States.*
- Woodrow Wilson, elected president in 1912 and reelected in 1916, said that "America lives in the heart of every man everywhere who wishes to find a region where he will be free to work out his destiny as he chooses." How do the poems that follow celebrate or criticize this sense of American exceptionalism—the special quality and spirit not only of the nation but of the people who live (or want to live) here?
- In a number of these poems—for example, Lydia Sigourney's "The Indian's Welcome to the Pilgrim Fathers" and Robert Frost's "The Vanishing Red"—a member of one group speaks about or on behalf of another one. Do you think that this kind of poem works well, or do you believe that, as some have argued, only a member of a certain racial or ethnic group can be a spokesperson for it?
- Do you perceive among these poems any ideas, beliefs, attitudes that you have not encountered before? Do you find that these literary works are giving you new insights into American history?
- "Multicultural" can mean either many cultures within a single whole or, instead, many cultures, races, and ethnic and religious groups that have little or nothing in common. Which of these definitions do the poems in this group support?
- Other poems in this volume could also be part of this multicultural mosaic in verse, and you might enjoy finding examples and explaining why they belong and to what poems in this group they could be related.

## A Note on Sharing Your Responses

Many of the poems in this section deal with painful historical events and issues. Some of the poems will move you deeply, while others may upset and even anger you. When you discuss or write about your responses, you'll want to connect them to specific moments in the text, so that your classmates and readers will be able to understand how you came to feel that way. Your response matters because it is your own—it's important to you and says something about who you are. But when you share it with others, you need to help them to understand it clearly. Describe your feelings and, at the same time, refer back to the text to clarify and explain them well. Do full justice to the interest and worth of your response to the poem.

About half of the poems in this chapter were written in the second half of the twentieth century; about a quarter were written in the first half; of the remaining poems, most were written in the nineteenth century, but one is from the eighteenth (Phillis Wheatley's "On Being Brought from Africa to America") and one is from the seventeenth (Andrew Marvell's "Be rmudas"). Because most of the poems deal with the past, in preparing to write about a poem you may want to spend a few minutes on background reading. For instance, if you write about Joseph Bruchac's poem called "Ellis Island," you may want to check an encyclopedia in order to find out when this reception center for immigrants was in operation.

We print the earliest of the poems, followed by a student's essay.

## ANDREW MARVELL

*Born in 1621 near Hull in England, Marvell graduated from Trinity College, Cambridge, in 1638. After the Civil War in England he served in Oliver Cromwell's Commonwealth government, and after the Restoration of the monarchy he served as a member of parliament until his death. His best-known poem is "To His Coy Mistress" (p. 931), but he did not confine himself to love poetry, as the following work attests.*

*In 1609 some English colonists en route to Virginia were shipwrecked in the Bermudas (a fact known to Shakespeare when he wrote* The Tempest*), and later in the century others sailed from England to Bermuda, seeking refuge from "prelates' rage" (line 12). That is, like the Pilgrims who in 1620 founded Plymouth Colony on the coast of Massachusetts, these slightly later pilgrims to the New World are Puritans who are fleeing the persecution of the Church of England.*

### *Bermudas*

Where the remote Bermudas ride
In th' ocean's bosom unespied,
From a small boat that rowed along
The listening winds received this song.

"What should we do but sing his praise
That led us through the wat'ry maze,
Unto an isle so long unknown,
And yet far kinder than our own?
Where he the huge sea-monsters wracks,°
That lift the deep upon their backs,
He lands us on a grassy stage,
Safe from the storms' and prelates' rage.
He gave us this eternal spring,
Which here enamels everything,
And sends the fowls to us in care,
On daily visits through the air;
He hangs in shades the orange bright,
Like golden lamps in a green night;
And does in the pomegranates close
Jewels more rich than Ormus° shows.

**9 he the huge sea-monsters wracks** he strands whales

He makes the figs our mouths to meet,
And throws the melons at our feet;
But apples plants of such a price
No tree could ever bear them twice.
With cedars chosen by his hand
From Lebanon he stores the land,
And makes the hollow seas, that roar,
Proclaim the ambergris° on shore.
He cast (of which we rather boast)°
The Gospel's pearl upon our coast,
And in these rocks for us did frame
A temple, where to sound his name.
Oh, let our voice his praise exalt,
Till it arrive at heaven's vault,
Which, thence perhaps rebounding, may
Echo beyond the Mexique Bay."

Thus sung they, in the English boat,
An holy and a cheerful note;
And all the way, to guide their chime,
With falling oars they kept the time.

[*1653?*]

**20 Ormus** Hormuz, an island in the Persian gulf, important as a trade center with India **28 ambergris** a fragrant secretion of sperm whales, used in making perfume **29 boast** speak with pride (not a negative word)

# SAMPLE ESSAY ON A POEM

Barbara Medford

English 101B

November 1, 1997

Andrew Marvell and the Paradise of the New World

When I first read Andrew Marvell's "Bermudas" I was puzzled and disturbed. This poem about English people who, leaving England, flee "from the storms' and prelates' rage" to "the remote Bermudas" says not a word about the native people that the English settlers enslaved or killed. I checked the New Encyclopaedia Britannica to see exactly what the natives were called--and I found, to my surprise, that the islands were uninhabited until 1515, when a Spaniard, Juan de Bermudez, sighted them when he was blown off course on his trip from Spain to Cuba. The next to arrive were some Englishmen sailing for Virginia, who encountered a hurricane and in 1609 were shipwrecked in Bermuda. So at least the settlement of Bermuda was not an assault on indigenous people.

Marvell begins the poem a bit mysteriously, with four lines telling us about a song that was received by "the listening winds" (line 4). The song tells us that the people in the boat are refugees from "the prelates' rage" (12); that is, they are Puritans--Marvell too was a Puritan--who sought religious freedom. What is especially interesting is that, according to Marvell, the New World that these religious refugees found is like the Eden in which Adam and Eve lived. In Bermuda, Marvell says, there is "eternal spring" (13); God takes care that his followers have abundant food, and they do not seem to have to work for it. According to the Bible, after Adam and Eve sinned they and their descendants would have to earn their food by "the sweat of their brow," but Marvell's Bermudians apparently live in an unfallen world, a paradise just like the world of Adam and Eve before they sinned by eating the forbidden fruit. "He makes the figs our mouths to meet, / And throws the melons at our feet" (21-22).

So, the Bermudians live a life of ease, surrounded by delicious food, and, more important, they have "The Gospel's pearl" (30). Everything, again, is like the world before the Fall; it is a world in which human beings live in harmony with nature, and (more or less naturally) worship God directly, without "prelates," and in fact without a humanly constructed church. Nature, or, rather, the God who created nature, provides the church. Marvell says that, according to the singers in the boat, God "in these rocks for us did frame / A temple, where to sound his name" (31-32).

Other seventeenth-century Puritans, such as the passengers on the Mayflower, who settled in what later was to become the United States, also often thought of themselves as journeying to a second Eden, a new, unfallen world, and because they were fleeing from religious persecution, they thought of themselves as Israelites being led by God to a Promised Land. But one great difference between these other colonists and the Bermudians is, as I have said, that the Bermudians did not annihilate the natives in the land to which they journeyed.

On the other hand, although Marvell presents his Bermudians as God-fearing people who live in an earthly paradise, the serpent was there--not in the garden but in their own hearts and minds. According to the New Encyclopaedia Britannica, even before Marvell wrote his poem the English settlers in Bermuda had transported slaves from Africa to Bermuda, to do the agricultural labor that supported the white colonists. Marvell's lovely picture of an unfallen Eden, a world of natural abundance and of piety and of music, is therefore not the whole picture of Bermuda even in Marvell's day. What I find especially sad is that a society of men and women who devoutly worshiped God somehow saw nothing wrong with enslaving other men and women.

WORKS CITED

"Bermuda." New Encyclopaedia Britannica: Micropaedia. 15th ed. 1987.

Marvell, Andrew. "Bermudas." Literature: Thinking, Reading, and Writing Critically. Ed. Sylvan Barnet et al. 2nd ed. New York: Longman, 1997. 967-68.

A few comments on the paper may be useful.

- The student has made good use of some background reading, but she keeps her eye on the poem.
- Quotations are used, so that the reader hears the poet's voice, but the quotations are not so numerous or so extended that they strike a reader as padding.
- The writer makes her feelings felt, but she does not talk only about her feelings; she discusses the literary work.

## ROBERT FROST

*For a biographical note on Robert Frost (1875-1963), and for a selection of his poems and his comments on poetry, see page1140-70.*

# *The Gift Outright*

The land was ours before we were the land's.
She was our land more than a hundred years
Before we were her people. She was ours
In Massachusetts, in Virginia,
But we were England's, still colonials,
Possessing what we still were unpossessed by,
Possessed by what we now no more possessed.
Something we were withholding made us weak
Until we found it was ourselves
We were withholding from our land of living,
And forthwith found salvation in surrender.
Such as we were we gave ourselves outright
(The deed of gift was many deeds of war)
To the land vaguely realizing westward,
But still unstoried, artless, unenhanced,
Such as she was, such as she would become.

[*1942*]

## PHILLIS WHEATLEY

*Kidnapped in Africa when she was a child of about age 7, and brought to Boston on the schooner* Phillis, *Phillis Wheatley (1753?-84) owed her first name to the ship and her second to the family name of the merchant who bought her to attend on his wife. She was educated in*

*English, Latin, history, and geography, and especially in the Bible, and within a few years she was writing poetry in the approved manner, that is, the manner of eighteenth-century England. In 1773, the year she was granted freedom, she published a book of her poems in England.*

*Despite her education and the style of writing that she adopted, Wheatley of course did not move freely in the white world. But neither did she move freely in the black world, since her educators kept her away from other persons of African origin. Perhaps the best single sentence ever written about Phillis Wheatley is Richard Wright's: "Before the webs of slavery had so tightened as to snare nearly all Negroes in our land, one was freed by accident to give in clear, bell-like limpid cadence the hope of freedom in the New World." One other sentence about Wheatley, by another African-American writer, should also be quoted here. Alice Walker, commenting on Wheatley's much criticized assumption of white values, says, in an address to Wheatley, "It is not so much what you sang, as that you kept alive, in so many of our ancestors,* the notion of song."

*"On Being Brought from Africa to America" alludes to the story of Cain and Abel, in Genesis 4, which reports that Cain killed Abel, and that "the Lord set a mark upon Cain" (4.15). The biblical text explicitly says that the mark was to protect Cain from someone who might take vengeance on him, but it does not say what the mark was. Nevertheless, some Christians developed the idea that the color of Africans was the mark of Cain.*

*On the opposite page we reproduce a drawing of a slave ship.*

## *On Being Brought from Africa to America*

'Twas mercy brought me from my pagan land;
Taught my benighted soul to understand
That there's a God, that there's a Savior too:
Once I redemption neither sought nor knew.
Some view our sable race with scornful eye.
"Their color is a diabolic dye."
Remember, Christians, Negroes, black as Cain.
May be refined, and join the angelic train.

[*1772*]

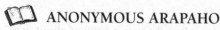

## ANONYMOUS ARAPAHO

*The Arapaho are North American Plains Indians of Algonquian (or Algonkian) linguistic stock. Their origins are uncertain, but according to tribal traditions they migrated from northern Minnesota. During their westward migra-*

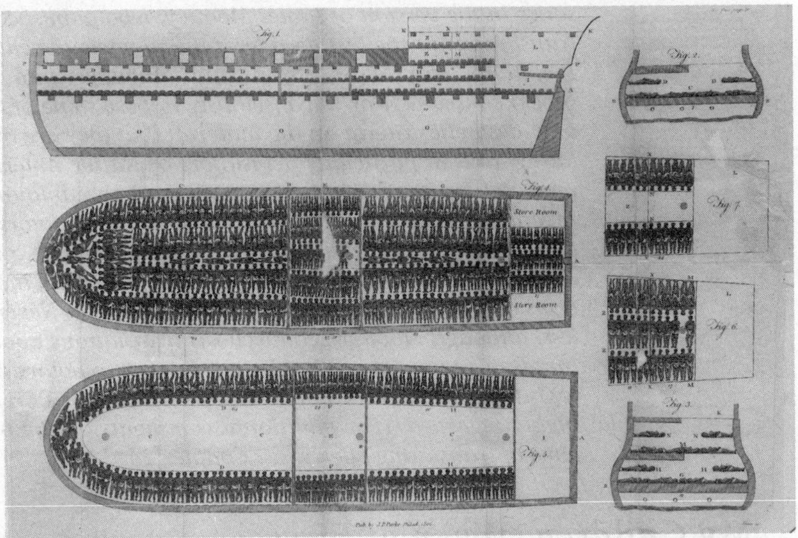

Phillis Wheatley probably was brought to America on a slave ship such as this one. Thomas Clarkson distributed this drawing with his *Essay on the Slavery and Commerce of the Human Species.* (1786. Boston Athenaeum)

*tion they divided into northern and southern groups, and they now live chiefly in Wyoming and Oklahoma.*

*The two songs that we reprint are both from the Ghost Dance ritual, part of a widespread messianic religion that originated in the late nineteenth century, and is especially associated with a Paiute, Wovoka (c. 1858-1932, known also as Jack Wilson), the son of a medicine man. Wovoka, influenced by his father as well as by a Christian family he worked for and by the revivalistic Shaker movement, in 1889 said he had a vision that the earth would soon die and be reborn: All whites would disappear, and all Indians (living and dead) would be reunited. (The "ghosts" of the dance are dead Indians.) The songs were sung throughout the night, by singers in trances. Although Wovoka was a pacifist, the movement became, or seemed to become, warlike, and its adherents wore magic shirts they deemed to be bullet-proof. On December 29, 1890, at Wounded Knee, South Dakota, a group of Sioux were ordered to disarm; a medicine man threw dust into the air; an Indian with a gun wounded an officer; U.S. troops opened fire, and almost two hundred Sioux men, women, and children were killed. The apocalyptic hopes of the Ghost Dance were over.*

*The songs constitute a dialogue between the Sun ("Father") and the Native Americans ("children"). It is essential to understand that these compositions, like all Native American poetry of the nineteenth century, are oral, not written, and like most oral literature they use repetition and parallelism, as well as contrast. We give two songs in the version of James Mooney, who published his translations in the last decade of the nineteenth century. Inevitably translators (from any language into any other) consciously or unconsciously impose some of their own aesthetic criteria on the material that they are translating, and in particular translators of Native American material have often somewhat reduced the amount of repetition. Further, many contemporary translators believe that oral material must be presented in such a way as to indicate how it was performed (i.e., with indications of pauses, changes of stress, and so forth). Nevertheless, although Mooney produced his translations about a hundred years ago, and although modern scholars have tools he never dreamed of, Mooney's translations are still highly regarded. (For additional comments on the problems of translating poetry, see Chapter 24.)*

# My Children, When at First I Liked the Whites

My children, when at first I liked the whites,
My children, when at first I liked the whites,
I gave them fruits,
I gave them fruits.

# Father, Have Pity on Me

Father, have pity on me,
Father, have pity on me;
I am crying for thirst,
I am crying for thirst;
All is gone—I have nothing to eat,
All is gone—I have nothing to eat.

"Ghost Dancers." (National Anthropological Archives/Smithsonian Institution)

## LYDIA HOWARD HUNTLEY SIGOURNEY

*Lydia Sigourney (1791-1865), born in Norwich, Connecticut, of humble family, was taken up by her father's employer as a child prodigy and was tutored in Latin and Hebrew. She wrote poetry chiefly on public issues, such as historical events and slavery, rather than personal lyric poetry. A fair number of her poems concern the displacement of Native Americans; she did not condemn the settling of the continent, but she did criticize the failure of whites to treat the Native Americans according to Christian ethics.*

# *The Indian's Welcome to the Pilgrim Fathers*

*"On Friday, March 16th, 1622, while the colonists were busied in their usual labors, they were much surprised to see a savage walk boldly towards them, and salute them with, 'much welcome, English, much welcome, Englishmen.'"*

Above them spread a stranger sky
Around, the sterile plain,
The rock-bound coast rose frowning nigh,
Beyond,—the wrathful main:
Chill remnants of the wintry snow
Still chok'd the encumber'd soil,
Yet forth these Pilgrim Fathers go,
To mark their future toil.

'Mid yonder vale their corn must rise
In Summer's ripening pride,
And there the church-spire woo the skies
Its sister-school beside.
Perchance 'mid England's velvet green
Some tender thought repos'd,—
Though nought upon their stoic mien
Such soft regret disclos'd.

When sudden from the forest wide
A red-brow'd chieftain came,
With towering form, and haughty stride,
And eye like kindling flame:
No wrath he breath'd, no conflict sought,
To no dark ambush drew,
But simply *to the Old World brought,*
*The welcome of the New.*

That *welcome* was a blast and ban
Upon thy race unborn.
Was there no seer, thou fated Man!
Thy lavish zeal to warn?

Thou in thy fearless faith didst hail
A weak, invading band,
But who shall heed thy children's wail,
Swept from their native land?

Thou gav'st the riches of thy streams,
The lordship o'er thy waves,
The region of thine infant dreams,
And of thy fathers' graves,
But who to yon proud mansions pil'd
With wealth of earth and sea,
Poor outcast from thy forest wild,
*Say, who shall welcome thee?*

[*1835*]

## PAULA GUNN ALLEN

*Part Sioux-Laguna and part Lebanese-Jewish, Paula Gunn Allen was born in 1939 in Cubero, New Mexico, into a family that used five languages. Allen, who holds a Ph.D. from the University of New Mexico, teaches Native American Studies at San Francisco State University. She has written several books of poems, a novel, a collection of traditional tales, and a collection of essays,* The Sacred Hoop: Recovering the Feminine in American Indian Traditions *(1986).*

# *Pocahontas to Her English Husband, John Rolfe*

Had I not cradled you in my arms,
oh beloved perfidious one,
you would have died.
And how many times did I pluck you
from certain death in the wilderness—
my world through which you stumbled
as though blind?
Had I not set you tasks
your masters far across the sea
would have abandoned you—
did abandon you, as many times they
left you to reap the harvest of their lies;
still you survived oh my fair husband
and brought them gold
wrung from a harvest I taught you
to plant: Tobacco. It
is not without irony that by this crop
your descendants die, for other powers
than those you know take part in this.
And indeed I did rescue you

Victor Nehlig, "Pocahontas and John Smith" (1870).
(© Courtesy of Museum of Art, Brigham Young University.)


not once but a thousand thousand times
and in my arms you slept, a foolish child,
and beside me you played,
chattering nonsense about a God
you had not wit to name;
and wondered you at my silence—
simple foolish wanton maid you saw,
dusky daughter of heathen sires
who knew not the ways of grace—
no doubt, no doubt.
I spoke little, you said.
And you listened less.
But played with your gaudy dreams
and sent ponderous missives to the throne
striving thereby to curry favor
with your king. I saw you well. I
understood the ploy and still protected you,
going so far as to die in your keeping—
a wasting, putrifying death, and you,
deceiver, my husband, father of my son,
survived, your spirit bearing crop
slowly from my teaching, taking
certain life from the wasting of my bones.

[*1988*]

## ROBERT FROST

*For a biographical note on Robert Frost (1875-1963), see page 1140.*

# *The Vanishing Red*

He is said to have been the last Red Man
In Acton.° And the Miller is said to have laughed—
If you like to call such a sound a laugh.
But he gave no one else a laugher's license.
For he turned suddenly grave as if to say,
'Whose business—if I take it on myself,
Whose business—but why talk round the barn?—
When it's just that I hold with getting a thing done
  with.'
You can't get back and see it as he saw it.
It's too long a story to go into now.
You'd have to have been there and lived it.
Then you wouldn't have looked on it as just a matter
Of who began it between the two races.

Some guttural exclamation of surprise
The Red Man gave in poking about the mill
Over the great big thumping shuffling mill-stone
Disgusted the Miller physically as coming
From one who had no right to be heard from.
'Come, John,' he said, 'you want to see the wheel pit?'°

He took him down below a cramping rafter,
And showed him, through a manhole in the floor,
The water in desperate straits like frantic fish,
Salmon and sturgeon, lashing with their tails.
Then he shut down the trap door with a ring in it
That jangled even above the general noise,
And came up stairs alone—and gave that laugh,
And said something to a man with a meal-sack
That the man with the meal-sack didn't catch—then.
Oh, yes, he showed John the wheel pit all right.

[*1916*]

**2 Acton** a town in Massachusetts, not far from where Frost spent part of his childhood **19 wheel pit** the pit containing the wheel that, agitated by the water, drives the mill

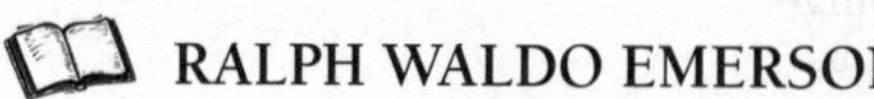

## RALPH WALDO EMERSON

*Ralph Waldo Emerson (1803-82), born in Boston and educated at Harvard, served briefly as a Unitarian preacher, but in 1832 he resigned his pastorate and de-*

*voted himself fully to lecturing and to writing essays and, to a much lesser extent, to writing poetry. In his period, he was probably the most influential man of letters in the United States, and he remains a towering figure.*

*The historical background of "Concord Hymn" is as follows: On April 19, 1775, near a wooden bridge (the "rude bridge" of line 1) that spanned the Concord River, the Minutemen (farmers who had pledged to resist the British on a minute's notice) resisted British soldiers. The British had killed eight men at nearby Lexington, but at Concord they were dispersed, and the American Revolution was evident to all ("the shot heard round the world"). The land where the skirmish occurred was owned by Emerson's step-grandfather, who later gave it to the town.*

*Emerson's poem was composed in 1836 for a ceremony dedicating a monument—an obelisk—on the site. At the dedicatory ceremony the poem was sung by a choir to the tune of "Old Hundredth," an immensely popular hymn tune written in the sixteenth century for Psalm 100 ("All people that on earth do dwell") in the English Psalter. The tune is also sometimes used for "Praise God, from whom all blessings flow." In 1875, at the one-hundredth anniversary of the battle, Daniel Chester French's statue* The Minute Man of Concord *was dedicated on the site, with the first stanza of Emerson's poem inscribed on the pedestal.*

# Concord Hymn

Sung at the Completion of the Battle Monument, July 4, 1837

By the rude bridge that arched the flood,
  Their flag to April's breeze unfurled,
Here once the embattled farmers stood
  And fired the shot heard round the world.

The foe long since in silence slept;
  Alike the conqueror silent sleeps;
And Time the ruined bridge has swept
  Down the dark stream which seaward creeps.

On this green bank, by this soft stream,
  We set today a votive stone;
That memory may their deed redeem,
  When, like our sires, our sons are gone.

Spirit, that made those heroes dare
  To die, and leave their children free,
Bid Time and Nature gently spare
  The shaft we raise to them and thee.

[*1836*]

## FRANCIS SCOTT KEY

*Francis Scott Key (1770–1843), born in Frederick County, Maryland, was a lawyer practicing in Washington at the time he wrote "The Defense of Fort McHenry," later renamed "The Star-Spangled Banner." More precisely, Key was on a British ship, seeking the release of an American who had been taken prisoner during the War of 1812. After Key boarded the ship, the British force began bombarding Fort McHenry, in Baltimore harbor, and Key was thus forced to remain on the ship throughout the night of September 13–14, 1814. Released the next morning, he drafted the poem while being taken ashore and revised it in his Baltimore hotel on the night of September 14. It was published anonymously in the* Baltimore Patriot *on September 20. The tune is that of what was then a popular drinking song, "The Anacreontic Song," known chiefly by its first words, "To Anacreon in Heaven."*

*Key's concern for whether the flag is flying ("does that star-spangled banner yet wave") is significant; if the British had conquered the fort during the night, the flag would have been lowered, and the British might have gone on to occupy Baltimore. But the British campaign failed, and three days after the attack on Fort McHenry the British fleet left Baltimore.*

*Although Key's song was widely popular, and in 1916 President Wilson issued an executive order designating it the national anthem, it did not officially achieve this status until 1931, when Congress confirmed Wilson's order.*

# *The Star-Spangled Banner*

O say, can you see, by the dawn's early light,
What so proudly we hailed at the twilight's last gleaming?
Whose broad stripes and bright stars, through the perilous fight,
O'er the ramparts we watched, were so gallantly streaming!
And the rockets' red glare, the bombs bursting in air,
Gave proof through the night that our flag was still there:
O say, does that star-spangled banner yet wave
O'er the land of the free and the home of the brave?

On the shore, dimly seen through the mists of the deep,
Where the foe's haughty host in dread silence reposes,
What is that which the breeze, o'er the towering steep,
As it fitfully blows, now conceals, now discloses?
Now it catches the gleam of the morning's first beam,

In full glory reflected now shines on the stream:
'Tis the star-spangled banner! O long may it wave
O'er the land of the free and the home of the brave!

And where is the band who so vauntingly swore
That the havoc of war and the battle's confusion
A home and a country should leave us no more?
Their blood has washed out their foul footsteps' pollution.
No refuge could save the hireling and slave
From the terror of flight, or the gloom of the grave:
And the star-spangled banner in triumph doth wave
O'er the land of the free and the home of the brave!

Oh! thus be it ever, when freemen shall stand
Between their loved homes and the war's desolation!
Blest with victory and peace, may the heaven-rescued land
Praise the Power that hath made and preserved us a nation.
Then conquer we must, for our cause it is just,
And this be our motto: "In God is our trust."
And the star-spangled banner in triumph shall wave
O'er the land of the free and the home of the brave!

[*1814*]

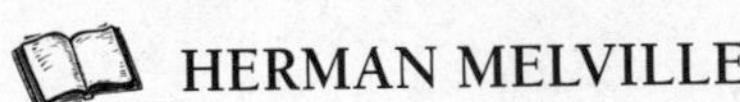

## HERMAN MELVILLE

*Herman Melville (1819–91) was born into a prosperous family in New York City. The bankruptcy and death of his father when Melville was 12 forced the boy to leave school. During his early years he worked first as a bank clerk, then as a farm laborer, then as a store clerk and a bookkeeper, and then as a schoolmaster. In 1837 he sailed to England as a cabin boy and signed on for other voyages, notably on whalers in the South Pacific, where he spent time in the Marquesas Islands and Tahiti. Out of his marine adventures he produced commercially successful books,* Typee *(1846),* Omoo *(1847),* Mardi *(1849), and* Redburn *(1849), but the book for which he is best known today,* Moby-Dick *(1851), was a commercial failure. In 1866 a book of poems about the Civil War—we print one of the poems here—was published, but it, too, was a failure. Abandoning his attempt to live by his pen, Melville survived on some inherited money, and on a political appointment as a customs inspector in New York City.*

*The poem that we reprint concerns the victory of the Confederate forces in the First Manassas or the First Battle of Bull Run (July 1861), fought near Manassas, Virginia. The final line of the poem alludes to the Second Battle of Manassas, fought in August 1862, when Union forces were again defeated.*

Timothy H. O'Sullivan, "John L. Burns with Gun and Crutches" (1863). (Library of Congress)

## *The March into Virginia,*

Ending in the First Manassas.
*(July, 1861.)*

Did all the lets° and bars appear
To every just or larger end,
Whence should come the trust and cheer?
Youth must its ignorant impulse lend—
Age finds place in the rear.
All wars are boyish, and are fought by boys,
The champions and enthusiasts of the state:
Turbid ardors and vain joys
Not barrenly abate—
Stimulants to the power mature,
Preparatives of fate.

Who here forecasteth the event?
What heart but spurns at precedent
And warnings of the wise,
Contemned foreclosures of surprise?
The banners play, the bugles call,
The air is blue and prodigal.
No berrying party, pleasure-wooed,

**1 lets** impediments

No picnic party in the May,
Ever went less loth than they
  Into that leafy neighborhood.
In Bacchic glee° they file toward Fate,
Moloch's° uninitiate;
Expectancy, and glad surmise
Of battle's unknown mysteries.
All they feel is this: 'tis glory,
A rapture sharp, though transitory,
Yet lasting in belaureled story.
So they gayly go to fight,
Chatting left and laughing right.

But some who this blithe mood present,
  As on in lightsome files they fare,
Shall die experienced ere three days are spent—
  Perish, enlightened by the vollied glare;
Or shame survive, and, like to adamant,
  The throe of Second Manassas share.

[*1866*]

**22 Bacchic glee** with the glee inspired by Bacchus, Roman god of wine
**23 Moloch** ancient Semite god to whom children were sacrificed

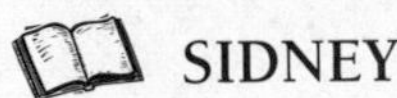

## SIDNEY LANIER

*Sidney Lanier (1842–81), born in Macon, Georgia, served with the Confederate Army and was taken as a prisoner of war. After the war, he wrote a novel based on his war experience (*Tiger-Lilies *[1867]), and he then turned to lecturing on English literature at Johns Hopkins. An accomplished musician, in* The Science of English Verse *(1880) Lanier set forth the theory that music and poetry are governed by the same principles, and that therefore time, not accent, is the chief element in poetry.*

*We reprint Lanier's poem on the death of General Thomas J. Jackson, known as Stonewall Jackson, the Confederate general who was accidentally killed by his own men at the Battle of Chancellorsville (1863). The Confederate Army won the battle, but it cost them one of their best officers, and it was their last important victory.*

# *The Dying Words of Jackson*

*"Order A. P. Hill to prepare for battle."*
*"Tell Major Hawks to advance the Commissary train."*
*"Let us cross the river and rest in the shade."*

The stars of Night contain the glittering Day,
And rain his glory down with sweeter grace

Women at the grave of Stonewall Jackson. (Photograph by Boude & Miley, 1912. Courtesy of Virginia Military Institute)

Upon the dark World's grand, enchanted face
All loth to turn away.

And so the Day, about to yield his breath,
Utters the Stars unto the listening Night
To stand for burning fare-thee-wells of light
Said on the verge of death.

O hero-life that lit us like the Sun!
O hero-words that glittered like the Stars
And stood and shone above the gloomy wars
When the hero-life was done!

The Phantoms of a battle came to dwell
I' the fitful vision of his dying eyes—
Yet even in battle-dreams, he sends supplies
To those he loved so well.

His army stands in battle-line arrayed:
His couriers fly: all's done—now God decide!
And not till then saw he the Other Side
Or would accept the Shade.

Thou Land whose Sun is gone, thy Stars remain!
Still shine the words that miniature his deeds—
O Thrice-Beloved, where'er thy great heart bleeds,
Solace hast thou for pain!

[*1865*]

## WALT WHITMAN

*Walt Whitman (1819–92) was born on Long Island, the son of a farmer. The young Whitman taught school, worked as a carpenter, a printer, a newspaper editor, and, during the Civil War, as a volunteer nurse on the Union side. After the war he supported himself by doing secretarial jobs. In Whitman's own day his poetry was highly controversial because of its unusual form (formlessness, many people said) and its abundant erotic implications.*

# *Reconciliation*

Word over all, beautiful as the sky,
Beautiful that war and all its deeds of carnage must in time be utterly lost.
That the hands of the sisters Death and Night incessantly softly wash again,
and ever again, this soil'd world;
For my enemy is dead, a man divine as myself is dead,
I look where he lies white-faced and still in the coffin—I draw near,
Bend down and touch lightly with my lips the white face in the coffin.

[*1865–1866*]

## AURORA LEVINS MORALES

*Aurora Levins Morales, born in Puerto Rico in 1954, came to the United States with her family in 1967. She has lived in Chicago and New Hampshire and now lives in the San Francisco Bay Area. Levins Morales has published stories, essays, prose poems, and poems.*

# *Child of the Americas*

I am a child of the Americas,
a light-skinned mestiza of the Caribbean,
a child of many diaspora,° born into this continent at a crossroads.

I am a U.S. Puerto Rican Jew,
a product of the ghettos of New York I have never known.
An immigrant and the daughter and granddaughter of immigrants.
I speak English with passion: it's the tongue of my consciousness,
a flashing knife blade of crystal, my tool, my craft.

3 **diaspora** literally, "scattering"; the term is used especially to refer to the dispersion of the Jews outside of Israel from the sixth century B.C., when they were exiled to Babylonia, to the present time.

I am Caribeña,° island grown. Spanish is in my flesh,
ripples from my tongue, lodges in my hips:
the language of garlic and mangoes,
the singing in my poetry, the flying gestures of my hands.
I am of Latinoamerica, rooted in the history of my continent:
I speak from that body.

I am not african. Africa is in me, but I cannot return.
I am not taína.° Taíno is in me, but there is no way back.
I am not european. Europe lives in me, but I have no home there.

I am new. History made me. My first language was spanglish.°
I was born at the crossroads
and I am whole.

[*1986*]

**9 Caribeña** Caribbean woman **16 taína** the Taínos were the Indian tribe native to Puerto Rico **18 spanglish** a mixture of Spanish and English

## EMMA LAZARUS

*Emma Lazarus (1849–87) was of German-Jewish descent on her mother's side, and of Sephardic descent on her father's side. (Sephardic Jews trace their ancestry back to Spain under Moslem rule, before the Jews were expelled by the Christians in 1492.)*

*In 1883 a committee was formed to raise funds for a pedestal for the largest statue in the world,* Liberty Enlightening the People, *to be installed on a small island in New York harbor. Authors were asked to donate manuscripts which then were auctioned to raise money. Emma Lazarus, keenly aware of ancient persecutions and of contemporary Jewish refugees fleeing Russian persecutions, contributed the following poem. It was read when the statue was unveiled in 1886, and the words of Liberty, spoken in the last five lines, were embossed on a plaque inside the pedestal.*

*For the ancients, a colossus was a statue larger than life. "The brazen giant of Greek fame," mentioned in Lazarus's first line, was a statue of the sun god, erected in the harbor of the Greek island of Rhodes, celebrating the island's success in resisting the Macedonians in 305–04* B.C. *More than 100 feet tall, it stood in the harbor until it toppled during an earthquake in 225* B.C. *In later years its size became mythical; it was said to have straddled the harbor (Lazarus speaks of "limbs astride from land to land"), so that ships supposedly entered the harbor by sailing between its legs.*

*In Lazarus's poem, the "imprisoned lightning" (line 5) in the torch is electricity. The harbor is said to be "air-bridged" because in 1883, the year of the poem, the*

Tseng Kwong Chi, "Statue of Liberty, New York City." (© 1995 Estate of Tseng Kwong Chi, MTDP/Artists Rights Society [ARS], New York)

*Brooklyn Bridge was completed, connecting Brooklyn with New York. (These are the "twin cities" of the poem.)*

## *The New Colossus*

Not like the brazen giant of Greek fame,
With conquering limbs astride from land to land;
Here at our sea-washed, sunset gates shall stand
A mighty woman with a torch, whose flame
Is the imprisoned lightning, and her name
Mother of Exiles. From her beacon-hand
Glows world-wide welcome; her mild eyes command
The air-bridged harbor that twin cities frame.
"Keep, ancient lands, your storied pomp!" cries she
With silent lips. "Give me your tired, your poor,
Your huddled masses yearning to breathe free,
The wretched refuse of your teeming shore.
Send these, the homeless, tempest-tost to me,
I lift my lamp beside the golden door!"

[*1883*]

## THOMAS BAILEY ALDRICH

*Thomas Bailey Aldrich (1836–1907) was born in Portsmouth, New Hampshire. He wrote poetry from his youth to his old age, and he also wrote short stories and essays, but his literary career was chiefly that of a journalist and an editor. (One magazine that he edited from 1881 to 1890,* Atlantic Monthly, *continues to be important.) As the following poem indicates, Aldrich was deeply conservative. The view that he here expresses is known as Nativism, or the Nativist view.*

# *The Unguarded Gates*

Wide open and unguarded stand our gates,
And through them press a wild, a motley throng—
Men from the Volga and the Tartar steppes,
Featureless figures of the Hoang-Ho,
Malayan, Scythian, Teuton, Kelt, and Slav,
Flying the Old World's poverty and scorn;
These bringing with them unknown gods and rites,
Those tiger passions, here to stretch their claws.
In street and alley what strange tongues are these,
Accents of menace alien to our air,
Voices that once the tower of Babel knew!
O, Liberty, white goddess, is it well
To leave the gate unguarded? On thy breast
Fold sorrow's children, soothe the hurts of fate,
Lift the downtrodden, but with the hand of steel
Stay those who to thy sacred portals come
To waste the fight of freedom. Have a care
Lest from thy brow the clustered stars be torn
And trampled in the dust. For so of old
The thronging Goth and Vandal trampled Rome,
And where the temples of the Caesars stood
The lean wolf unmolested made her lair.

[*1885*]

## JOSEPH BRUCHAC III

*Joseph Bruchac III (the name is pronounced "Brewshack") was born in Saratoga Springs, New York, in 1942, and educated at Cornell University, Syracuse University, and Union Graduate School. Like many other Americans, he has a multicultural ethnic heritage, and he includes Native Americans as well as Slovaks among his ancestors. Bruchac, who has taught in Ghana and also in the United States, has chiefly worked as an editor.*

The Registry Room, Ellis Island, ca. 1912. (William Williams Collection of Photographs, Miriam and Ira D. Wallach Division of Art, Prints and Photographs, New York Public Library)

*"Much of my writing and my life," Bruchac says, "relates to the problem of being an American. . . . While in college I was active in Civil Rights work and in the anti-war movement. . . . I went to Africa to teach—but more than that to be taught. It showed me many things. How much we have as Americans and take for granted. How much our eyes refuse to see because they are blinded to everything in a man's face except his color."*

## *Ellis Island*

Beyond the red brick of Ellis Island
where the two Slovak children
who became my grandparents
waited the long days of quarantine,
after leaving the sickness,
the old Empires of Europe,
a Circle Line ship slips easily
on its way to the island
of the tall woman, green
as dreams of forests and meadows
waiting for those who'd worked
a thousand years
yet never owned their own.

Slavic women arrive at Ellis Island in the winter of 1910. (Brown Brothers)

Like millions of others,
I too come to this island,
nine decades the answerer
of dreams.

Yet only one part of my blood loves that memory.
Another voice speaks
of native lands
within this nation.
Lands invaded
when the earth became owned.
Lands of those who followed
the changing Moon,
knowledge of the seasons
in their veins.

[*1978*]

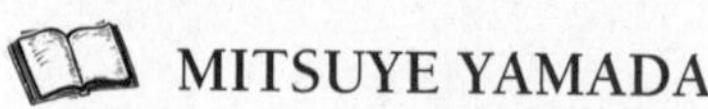

## MITSUYE YAMADA

*Mitsuye Yamada, the daughter of Japanese immigrants to the United States, was born in Japan in 1923, during her mother's return visit to her native land. Yamada was raised in Seattle, but in 1942 she and her family were incarcerated and then relocated in a camp in Idaho, when Executive Order 9066 gave military authorities the right to remove any and all persons from "military areas." In*

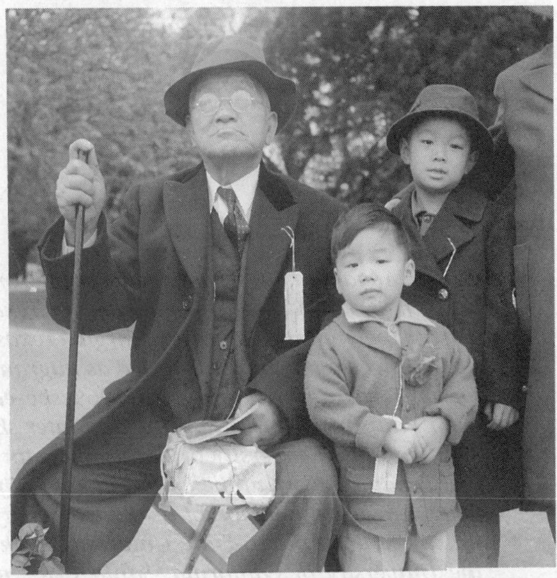

Dorothea Lange, "Grandfather and Grandchildren Awaiting Evacuation Bus." (War Relocation Authority/The National Archives)

*1954 she became an American citizen. A professor of English at Cypress Junior College in San Luis Obispo, California, she is the author of poems and stories.*

## *The Question of Loyalty*

I met the deadline
for alien registration
once before
was numbered fingerprinted
and ordered not to travel
without permit.

But alien still they said I must
forswear allegiance to the emperor.
for me that was easy
I didn't even know him
but my mother who did cried out
  If I sign this
  What will I be?
  I am doubly loyal
  to my American children
  also to my own people.
  How can double mean nothing?
  I wish no one to lose this war.
  Everyone does.

I was poor
at math.
I signed
my only ticket out.

[*1976*]

## GLORIA ANZALDÚA

*Gloria Anzaldúa, a seventh-generation American, was born in 1942 on a ranch settlement in Texas. When she was 11 her family moved to Hargill, Texas, and in the next few years the family traveled as migrant workers between Texas and Arkansas. In 1969 she earned a B.A. from Pan American University, and later she earned an M.A. from the University of Texas at Austin and did further graduate work at the University of California, Santa Cruz. Anzaldúa has taught at the University of Texas at Austin; San Francisco State University; Oakes College at the University of California, Santa Cruz; and Vermont College.*

*We give a poem from Anzaldúa's* Borderlands: La Frontera—The New Mestiza *(1987), a work that combines seven prose essays with poems. For Anzaldúa—a woman, a Latina, and a lesbian—the "borderlands" of course are spiritual as well as geographic.*

# *To live in the Borderlands means you*

To live in the Borderlands means you
are neither *hispana india negra española*
*ni gabacha, eres mestiza, mulata,*° half-breed
caught in the crossfire between camps
while carrying all five races on your back
not knowing which side to turn to, run from;

To live in the Borderlands means knowing
that the *india* in you, betrayed for 500 years,
is no longer speaking to you,
that *mexicanas* call you *rajetas,*°
that denying the Anglo inside you
is as bad as having denied the Indian or Black;

*Cuando vives en la frontera*°
people walk through you, the wind steals your voice,
you're a *burra, buey,*° scapegoat,
forerunner of a new race,

**2–3 neither . . . *mulata*** neither Spanish indian black Spanish woman, nor white, you are mixed, a mixed breed **10 *rajetas*** split, having betrayed your word [author's note] **13 *Cuando . . . frontera*** when you live in the borderlands **15 *burra, buey*** donkey, ox [author's note]

half and half—both woman and man, neither—
a new gender;

To live in the Borderlands means to
put *chile* in the borscht,
eat whole wheat *tortillas,*
speak Tex-Mex with a Brooklyn accent;
be stopped by *la migra*° at the border checkpoints;

Living in the Borderlands means you fight hard to
resist the gold elixer beckoning from the bottle,
the pull of the gun barrel,
the rope crushing the hollow of your throat;

In the Borderlands
you are the battleground
where enemies are kin to each other;
you are at home, a stranger,
the border disputes have been settled
the volley of shots have shattered the truce
you are wounded, lost in action
dead, fighting back;

To live in the Borderlands means
the mill with the razor white teeth wants to shred off
your olive-red skin, crush out the kernel, your heart
pound you pinch you roll you out
smelling like white bread but dead;

To survive the Borderlands
you must live *sin fronteras*°
be a crossroads.

[*1987*]

**23** ***la migra*** immigration officials **42** ***sin fronteras*** without borders

## BOB DYLAN

*Bob Dylan, born Robert Zimmerman in 1941 in Duluth, Minnesota, played the guitar as a child and learned the harmonica when he was 15. His chief models were Huddie Ledbetter (better known as Leadbelly), an African-American folk singer and guitarist, and Woody Guthrie, a white folksinger, guitarist, and harmonica player. Dylan's music ranges from folk to folk-rock to country blues, but perhaps his most influential songs were those of social protest, such as "Blowin' in the Wind" and "The Times They Are A-Changin'." He has written an autobiography,* Bob Dylan: Self-Portrait *(1970).*

# *The Times They Are A-Changin'*

Come gather 'round people
Wherever you roam

And admit that the waters
Around you have grown
And accept it that soon
You'll be drenched to the bone.
If your time to you
Is worth savin'
Then you better start swimmin'
Or you'll sink like a stone
For the times they are a-changin'.

Come writers and critics
Who prophesize with your pen
And keep your eyes wide
The chance won't come again
And don't speak too soon
For the wheel's still in spin
And there's no tellin' who
That it's namin'.
For the loser now
Will be later to win
For the times they are a-changin'.

Come senators, congressmen
Please heed the call
Don't stand in the doorway
Don't block up the hall
For he that gets hurt
Will be he who has stalled
There's a battle outside
And it is ragin'.
It'll soon shake your windows
And rattle your walls
For the times they are a-changin'.

Come mothers and fathers
Throughout the land
And don't criticize
What you can't understand
Your sons and your daughters
Are beyond your command
Your old road is
Rapidly agin'.
Please get out of the new one
If you can't lend your hand
For the times they are a-changin'.

The line it is drawn
The curse it is cast
The slow one now
Will later be fast
As the present now
Will later be past
The order is

Rapidly fadin'.
And the first one now
Will later be last
For the times they are a-changin'.

[*1963*]

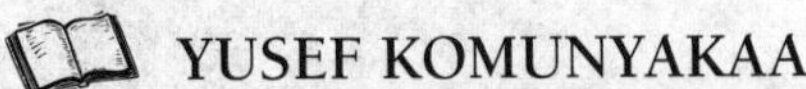

## YUSEF KOMUNYAKAA

*Yusef Komunyakaa was born in 1947 in Bogalusa, Louisiana. After graduating from high school he entered the army and served in Vietnam, where he was awarded the Bronze Star. On his return to the United States he earned a bachelor's degree at the University of Colorado, and then earned an M.A. at Colorado State University and an M.F.A. in creative writing at the University of California, Irvine. The author of several books of poetry, he has been teaching at Indiana University in Bloomington since 1985. "Facing It" is the last poem in a book of poems about Vietnam,* Dien Cai Dau *(1988). The title of the book is a slang word for* crazy.

### *Facing It*

My black face fades,
hiding inside the black granite.
I said I wouldn't,
dammit: No tears.
I'm stone. I'm flesh.
My clouded reflection eyes me
like a bird of prey, the profile of night
slanted against morning. I turn
this way—the stone lets me go.
I turn that way—I'm inside
the Vietnam Veterans Memorial
again, depending on the light
to make a difference.
I go down the 58,022 names,
half-expecting to find
my own in letters like smoke.
I touch the name Andrew Johnson;
I see the booby trap's white flash.
Names shimmer on a woman's blouse
but when she walks away
the names stay on the wall.
Brushstrokes flash, a red bird's
wings cutting across my stare.
The sky. A plane in the sky.
A white vet's image floats
closer to me, then his pale eyes

Vietnam Veterans Memorial. (AP/Wide World Photos)

look through mine. I'm a window.
He's lost his right arm
inside the stone. In the black mirror
a woman's trying to erase names:
No, she's brushing a boy's hair.

[*1988*]

## JAMES WELDON JOHNSON

*Born in Jacksonville, Florida, James Weldon Johnson (1871-1938) received a bachelor's and a master's degree from Atlanta University. Johnson taught school, served as a high school principal, and founded the* Daily American *(1895, the first black daily in America). Later he became active in the NAACP, served as consul to Venezuela and to Nicaragua, and taught creative writing at Fisk University. On the day of his death, in an automobile accident, he was appointed to teach black literature at New York University.*

*Johnson wrote dialect poems and also poems in standard English.*

## *To America*

How would you have us, as we are?
Or sinking 'neath the load we bear?
Our eyes fixed forward on a star?
Or gazing empty at despair?

Rising or falling? Men or things?
With dragging pace or footsteps fleet?
Strong, willing sinews in your wings?
Or tightening chains about your feet?

[*1917*]

## CLAUDE MCKAY

*Claude McKay (1890–1948), born in Jamaica, came to the United States when he was 23. McKay is known chiefly for his militant left-wing writings—novels and essays as well as poems—but he wrote a wide range of lyric poetry, and despite his radicalism he favored (like his friend Countee Cullen) traditional poetic forms such as the sonnet.*

## *America*

Although she feeds me bread of bitterness,
And sinks into my throat her tiger's tooth,
Stealing my breath of life, I will confess
I love this cultured hell that tests my youth!
Her vigor flows like tides into my blood,
Giving me strength against her hate.
Her bigness sweeps my being like a flood.
Yet as a rebel fronts a king in state,
I stand within her walls with not a shred
Of terror, malice, not a word of jeer.
Darkly I gaze into the days ahead,
And see her might and granite wonders there,
Beneath the touch of Time's unerring hand,
Like priceless treasures sinking in the sand.

[*1921*]

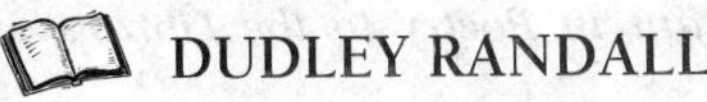

## DUDLEY RANDALL

*Born in Washington, D.C., in 1914, Randall graduated from Wayne State University and the University of Michigan, and worked as a reference librarian and as poet in residence at the University of Detroit. In 1965 he founded the Broadside Press, widely recognized as influential far beyond its size. Broadside Press issues excellent small books and single sheets with poems by African-Americans.*

## *The Melting Pot*

There is a magic melting pot
where any girl or man
can step in Czech or Greek or Scot,
step out American.

*Johann* and *Jan* and *Jean* and *Juan,*
*Giovanni* and *Ivan*
step in and then step out again
all freshly christened *John.*

Sam, watching, said, "Why, I was here
even before they came,"
and stepped in too, but was tossed out
before he passed the brim.

And every time Sam tried that pot
they threw him out again.

"Keep out. This is our private pot
We don't want your black stain."

At last, thrown out a thousand times,
Sam said, "I don't give a damn.
Shove your old pot. You can like it or not,
but I'll be just what I am."

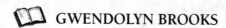

[*1968*]

# GWENDOLYN BROOKS

*Gwendolyn Brooks was born in Topeka, Kansas, in 1917 but was raised in Chicago's South Side, where she has spent most of her life. Brooks has taught in several colleges and universities and she has written a novel (*Maud Martha, *1953) and a memoir (*Report from Part One, *1972), but she is best known as a poet. In 1950, when she won the Pulitzer Prize for Poetry, she became the first African-American writer to win a Pulitzer Prize. In 1985 Brooks became Consultant in Poetry to the Library of Congress.*

*The subject of Brooks's poem, the civil rights leader Martin Luther King Jr. (1929–1968), was assassinated at the height of his career.*

## *Martin Luther King, Jr.*

A man went forth with gifts.
He was a prose poem.
He was a tragic grace.
He was a warm music.

He tried to heal the vivid volcanoes.
His ashes are
   reading the world.

His Dream still wishes to anoint
   the barricades of faith and of control.

His word still burns the center of the sun,
   above the thousands and the
   hundred thousands.

The word was Justice. It was spoken.

So it shall be spoken.
So it shall be done.

[*1970*]

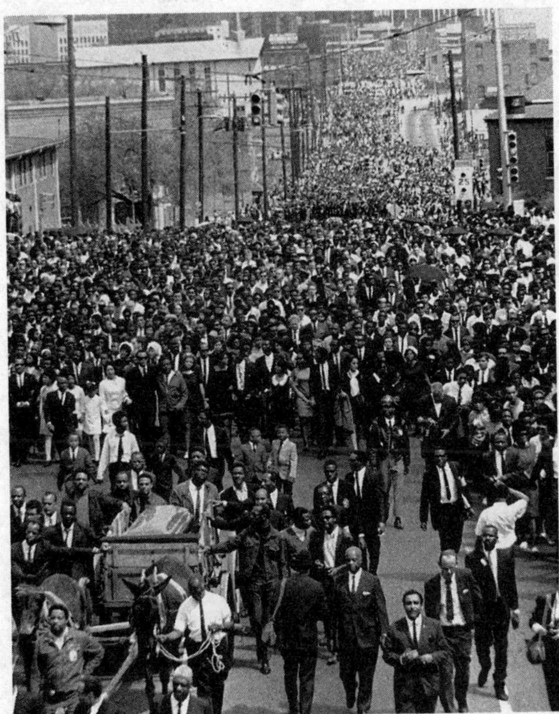

Funeral march for Martin Luther King Jr. (UPI/Bettmann Newsphotos)

## AMIRI BARAKA

*Amiri Baraka in his early years was Everett LeRoi (or LeRoy) Jones, but with an increasing awareness of his African heritage he altered his name, first to Imamu ("spiritual leader") Ameer ("blessed") Baraka ("prince") and then to Amiri Baraka. Baraka was educated at Howard University, Columbia University, and the New School for Social Research.*

*After serving in the United States Air Force, Baraka settled in Greenwich Village, in New York City, and became part of the (chiefly white) literary scene; he and his wife published a journal that included works by Jack Kerouac, Allen Ginsberg, and others. The assassination of Malcolm X in 1965 had a profound effect on Baraka, and in this year he left his white wife and the artistic life of Greenwich Village and moved to Harlem, where he established the Black Arts Repertory Theater/School. In 1966 he returned to Newark, where he founded a similar school and, perhaps because of his heightened socialism, dropped Imamu from his name. The author of many plays and books of poetry, he now teaches at the State University of New York, Stony Brook.*

*Malcolm X (1925–65), the subject of the following poem, was a militant black leader who rose to prominence in the Black Muslims. When in 1963 Elijah Muhammad suspended him, Malcolm formed his own organization, the Muslim Mosque. In 1964 he converted to orthodox Islam, and he proclaimed the brotherhood of blacks and whites, although he continued to support black nationalism. In February 1965 he was shot to death by an unidentified assassin.*

# *A Poem for Black Hearts*

For Malcolm's eyes, when they broke
the face of some dumb white man, For
Malcolm's hands raised to bless us
all black and strong in his image
of ourselves, For Malcolm's words
fire darts, the victor's tireless
thrusts, words hung above the world
change as it may, he said it, and
for this he was killed, for saying,
and feeling, and being / change, all
collected hot in his heart, For Malcolm's
heart, raising us above our filthy cities,
for his stride, and his beat, and his address
to the gray monsters of the world, For Malcolm's

pleas for your dignity, black men, for your life,
black man, for the filling of your minds
with righteousness, For all of him dead and
gone and vanished from us, and all of him which
clings to our speech black god of our time.
For all of him, and all of yourself, look up,
black man, quit stuttering and shuffling, look up,
black man, quit whining and stooping, for all of him,
For Great Malcolm a prince of the earth, let nothing in us rest
until we avenge ourselves for his death, stupid animals
that killed him, let us never breathe a pure breath if
we fail and white men call us faggots till the end of
the earth.

[*1965*]

## MARTÍN ESPADA

***Martín Espada was born in Brooklyn in 1957. He received a bachelor's degree from the University of Wisconsin and a law degree from Northeastern University. A poet who publishes regularly, Espada is also Outreach Coordinator and Supervisor of Lawyers of the Arts at the Artists' Foundation in Boston.***

### *Bully*

*Boston, Massachusetts, 1987*

In the school auditorium,
the Theodore Roosevelt statue
is nostalgic
for the Spanish-American War,
each fist lonely for a saber
or the reins of anguish-eyed horses,
or a podium to clatter with speeches
glorying in the malaria of conquest.

But now the Roosevelt school
is pronounced *Hernández.*
Puerto Rico has invaded Roosevelt
with its army of Spanish-singing children
in the hallways,
brown children devouring
the stockpiles of the cafeteria,
children painting *Taíno* ancestors
that leap naked across murals.

Roosevelt is surrounded
by all the faces
he ever shoved in eugenic spite

and cursed as mongrels, skin of one race,
hair and cheekbones of another.

Once Marines tramped
from the newsreel of his imagination;
now children plot to spray graffiti
in parrot-brilliant colors
across the Victorian mustache
and monocle.

[*1990*]

## JIMMY SANTIAGO BACA

*Jimmy Santiago Baca, of chicano and Apache descent, was born in 1952. When he was 2 his parents divorced, and a grandparent brought him up until he was 5, when he was placed in an orphanage in New Mexico. He ran away when he was 11, lived on the streets, took drugs, and at the age of 20 was convicted of drug possession. In prison he taught himself to read and write, and he began to compose poetry. A fellow inmate urged him to send some poems to* Mother Jones *magazine, and the work was accepted. In 1979 Louisiana State University Press published a book of his poems,* Immigrants in Our Own Land. *He has since published several other books.*

### *So Mexicans Are Taking Jobs from Americans*

O Yes? Do they come on horses
with rifles, and say,
Ese gringo,° gimmee your job?
And do you, gringo, take off your ring,
drop your wallet into a blanket
spread over the ground, and walk away?

I hear Mexicans are taking your jobs away.
Do they sneak into town at night,
and as you're walking home with a whore,
do they mug you, a knife at your throat,
saying, I want your job?

3 ***Ese gringo*** Hey, whitey

Even on TV, an asthmatic leader
crawls turtle heavy, leaning on an assistant,
and from a nest of wrinkles on his face,
a tongue paddles through flashing waves
of lightbulbs, of cameramen, rasping
"They're taking our jobs away."

Well, I've gone about trying to find them,
asking just where the hell are these fighters.

The rifles I hear sound in the night
are white farmers shooting blacks and browns
whose ribs I see jutting out
and starving children,
I see the poor marching for a little work,
I see small white farmers selling out
to clean-suited farmers living in New York,
who've never been on a farm,
don't know the look of a hoof or the smell
of a woman's body bending all day long in fields.

I see this, and I hear only a few people
got all the money in this world, the rest
count their pennies to buy bread and butter.

Below that cool green sea of money,
millions and millions of people fight to live,
search for pearls in the darkest depths
of their dreams, hold their breath for years
trying to cross poverty to just having something.

The children are dead already. We are killing them,
that is what America should be saying;
on TV, in the streets, in offices, should be saying,
"We aren't giving the children a chance to live."

Mexicans are taking our jobs, they say instead.
What they really say is, let them die,
and the children too.

[*1979*]

## NILA NORTHSUN

*Nila northSun was born in 1951 in Schurz, Nevada, of Shoshone-Chippewa stock. She studied at the California State University campuses at Hayward and Humboldt and the University of Montana at Missoula, beginning as a psychology major but switching to art history, specializing in Native American art. She is the author of three books of poetry and is director of an emergency youth shelter in Fallon, Nevada.*

Blackfoot travois. (Photograph by Edward S. Curtis. Vol. 18, No. 637, *The North American Indian.* Courtesy of Laboratory of Anthropology/Museum of Indian Arts & Culture)

## *Moving Camp Too Far*

i can't speak of
many moons
moving camp on travois°
i can't tell of
the last great battle
counting coup° or
taking scalp
i don't know what it
was to hunt buffalo
or do the ghost dance
but
i can see an eagle
almost extinct
on slurpee plastic cups
i can travel to powwows
in campers & winnebagos
i can eat buffalo meat
at the tourist burger stand
i can dance to indian music
rock-n-roll hey-a-hey-o

**1 travois** a frame slung between trailing poles that are pulled by a horse. Plains Indians used the device to transport their goods. **6 counting coup** recounting one's exploits in battle

i can
    & unfortunately
    i do

[*1977*]

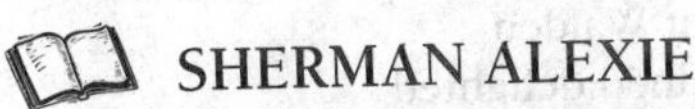

## SHERMAN ALEXIE

***Sherman Alexie, born in 1966 in Spokane, Washington, holds a B.A. from Washington State University. Author of novels, stories, and poems, Alexie has been awarded a grant from the National Endowment for the Arts. Of his life and his work he says, "I am a Spokane Coeur d'Alene Indian. . . . I live on the Spokane Indian Reservation. Everything I do now, writing and otherwise, has its origin in that."***

# *On the Amtrak from Boston to New York City*

The white woman across the aisle from me says, "Look,
look at all the history, that house
on the hill there is over two hundred years old,"
as she points out the window past me

into what she has been taught. I have learned
little more about American history during my few days
back East than what I expected and far less
of what we should all know of the tribal stories

whose architecture is 15,000 years older
than the corners of the house that sits
museumed on the hill. "Walden Pond,"°
the woman on the train asks, "Did you see Walden Pond?"

and I don't have a cruel enough heart to break
her own by telling her there are five Walden Ponds
on my little reservation out West
and at least a hundred more surrounding Spokane,

the city I pretend to call my home. "Listen,"
I could have told her. "I don't give a shit
about Walden. I know the Indians were living stories
around that pond before Walden's grandparents were born

**11 Walden Pond** site in Massachusetts where Henry David Thoreau (1817–62) lived from 4 July 1845 to 6 September 1847, and about which he wrote in his most famous book, *Walden* (1854)

and before his grandparents' grandparents were born.
I'm tired of hearing about Don-fucking-Henley° saving it, too,
because that's redundant. If Don Henley's brothers and sisters
and mothers and fathers hadn't come here in the first place
then nothing would need to be saved."
But I didn't say a word to the woman about Walden
Pond because she smiled so much and seemed delighted
that I thought to bring her an orange juice
back from the food car. I respect elders
of every color. All I really did was eat
my tasteless sandwich, drink my Diet Pepsi
and nod my head whenever the woman pointed out
another little piece of her country's history
while I, as all Indians have done
since this war began, made plans
for what I would do and say the next time
somebody from the enemy thought I was one of their own.

[*1993*]

**22 Don Henley** rock singer who was active in preserving Walden from building developers

## LAUREEN MAR

*Laureen Mar, a Chinese-American born in Seattle in 1953, studied creative writing at Columbia University. She has published poems in several national magazines.*

# *My Mother, Who Came from China, Where She Never Saw Snow*

In the huge, rectangular room, the ceiling
a machinery of pipes and fluorescent lights,
ten rows of women hunch over machines,
their knees pressing against pedals
and hands pushing the shiny fabric thick as tongues
through metal and thread.
My mother bends her head to one of these machines.
Her hair is coarse and wiry, black as burnt scrub.
She wears glasses to shield her intense eyes.
A cone of orange thread spins. Around her,
talk flutters harshly in Toisan wah.°
Chemical stings. She pushes cloth
through a pounding needle, under, around, and out,

**11 Toisan wah** a Chinese dialect

breaks thread with a snap against fingerbone, tooth.
Sleeve after sleeve, sleeve.
It is easy. The same piece.
For eight or nine hours, sixteen bundles maybe,
250 sleeves to ski coats, all the same.
It is easy, only once she's run the needle
through her hand. She earns money
by each piece, on a good day,
thirty dollars. Twenty-four years.
It is frightening how fast she works.
She and the women who were taught sewing
terms in English as Second Language.
Dull thunder passes through their fingers.

[*1977*]

# CHAPTER 24

# *Variations on Themes:*

## *Poems, Paintings, and Translations*

## WRITING ABOUT POEMS AND PAINTINGS

Are there, one may ask, significant correspondences between the arts? If we talk about *rhythm* in a painting, are we talking about a quality similar to *rhythm* in a poem? Are the painter's colors comparable to the poet's images? Does it make sense to say, as Goethe (1749-1832) said, that architecture is frozen music? Or to call architecture "music in space"? Many artists of one sort have felt that their abilities *ought* to enable them to move into a "sister art," and they have tried their hand at something outside their specialty, usually with no great success. (William Blake, represented in this book by several poems and pictures, is often said to be the only figure in English arts who is significant both as a poet and as a painter.) For instance, the painter Edgar Degas (1834-1917) tried to write sonnets, but could not satisfy even himself. When he complained to his friend, the poet Stéphane Mallarmé, that he couldn't write poems even though he had plenty of ideas, Mallarmé replied, "You don't write poems with ideas; you write them with words."

Painters have been moved, for many centuries, to illustrate texts. More than two thousand years ago the painters of Greek vases illustrated the Greek myths, and from the Middle Ages onward artists have illustrated the Bible. In this book we include a mid-twentieth-century painting by Charles Demuth, based on a poem by William Carlos Williams. Conversely, poets have been moved to write about paintings or sculptures. In this chapter we reprint several poems about paintings by Brueghel, van Gogh, and others.

Despite Mallarmé's witty remark that poems are made not with ideas but with words (and despite Archibald MacLeish's assertion, on page 1082, that "A poem should not mean/But be"), of course poems use ideas, and of course they have meanings. When you read the poems that we print along with paintings, you might think about some of the following questions:

- What is your own first response to the painting? In interpreting the painting, consider the subject matter, the composition (for instance, balanced masses, as opposed to an apparent lack of equilibrium), the technique (for instance, vigorous brushstrokes of thick paint, as opposed to thinly applied strokes that leave no trace of the artist's hand), the color, and the title.
- Now that you have read the poem, do you see the painting in a somewhat different way?
- To what extent does the poem illustrate the painting, and to what extent does it depart from the painting and make a very different statement?
- If the painting is based on a poem (see Demuth's painting on page 1014), to what extent does the painting capture the poem?
- Beyond the subject matter, what (if anything) do the two works have in common?

## A SAMPLE ESSAY

On page 1023 read (preferably aloud) Anne Sexton's "The Starry Night," which was inspired by van Gogh's painting of the same name. Then read the following essay.

Tina Washington

English 10G

November 12, 1996

TWO WAYS OF LOOKING AT A STARRY NIGHT

About a hundred years ago Vincent van Gogh looked up into the sky at night and painted what he saw, or what he felt. We know that he was a very religious man, but even if we had not heard this in an art course or read it in a book we would know it from his painting <u>The Starry Night,</u> which shows a glorious heaven, with stars so bright that they all have halos. Furthermore, almost in the lower center of the picture is a church, with its steeple rising above the hills and pointing to the heavens.

Anne Sexton's poem is about this painting, and also (we know from the line she quotes above the poem) about van Gogh's religious vision of the stars. But her poem is not about the heavenly comfort that the starry night offered van Gogh. It is a poem about her wish to die. As I understand the poem, she wants to die in a blaze of light, and to become extinct. She says, in the last line of the poem, that she wants to disappear with "no cry," but this seems to me to be very different from anything van Gogh is saying. His picture is about the glorious heavens, not about himself. Or if it is about himself, it is about how wonderful he feels when he sees God's marvelous creation. Van Gogh is concerned with praising God as God expresses himself in nature; Anne Sexton is concerned with expressing her anguish and with her hope that she can find extinction. Sexton's world is not ruled by a benevolent God but is ruled by an "old unseen serpent." The night is a "rushing beast," presided over by a "great dragon."

Sexton has responded to the painting in a highly unique way. She is not trying to put van Gogh's picture into words that he might approve of. Rather, she has boldly used the picture as a point of departure for her own word-picture.

## TOPICS FOR CRITICAL THINKING AND WRITING

1. Do you agree with this student's analysis, especially her point about Sexton's poem?
2. Has the student cited and examined passages from the poem in a convincing way?
3. A general question: Do you think poets are obliged to be faithful to the paintings that they write about, or do poets enjoy the freedom—a kind of poetic license—to interpret a painting just as they choose, doing with it whatever the purpose of the poem requires?

Niten (Miyamoto Musashi), *Shrike* (Ink on paper, 125.6 × 54.3 cm. Kuboso Memorial Museum of Arts, Osaka)

## Shrike on a Dead Tree

*After a painting by Miyamoto Musashi (1584-1645)*

Steadfastly
up the
single
brush stroke
of its
trunk

a worm
crawls
toward
a butcher
bird
perched
on

an upper
barren
branch.

[*1986*]

## JAMES MASAO MITSUI

*James Masao Mitsui, a nisei (second-generation) Japanese-American, was born in 1940 in Skykomish, Washington, and along with other Japanese and Japanese-Americans on the West Coast was incarcerated during World War II. He has published several volumes of poems.*

*We reprint a poem that describes a famous painting by a samurai (warrior) painter of seventeenth-century Japan. The picture shows a shrike on a branch. The shrike is also called the butcher bird because of its habit of impaling its victim on a thorn. The painter was famous as a swordsman, as a painter, and as a practitioner of Zen Buddhism.*

## TOPICS FOR CRITICAL THINKING AND WRITING

1. If you know little or nothing about Zen, do a bit of homework, perhaps beginning with a good encyclopedia, and find out what connection exists between Zen and the warrior class in Japan.
2. The painter Miyamoto Musashi was famous as a swordsman. Does this picture seem to you to be appropriate to his profession? Explain.
3. What, if anything, makes Mitsui's words a poem rather than a prose sentence?
4. Would you say that Mitsui's poem is a description or an interpretation of the painting, or a little of both? Point to evidence in the text for your response.

Vincent van Gogh, *Vincent's Bed in Arles.* (Oil on canvas, 72 × 90 cm. Vincent van Gogh Foundation/Van Gogh Museum, Amsterdam.

## JANE FLANDERS

*Jane Flanders, born in Waynesboro, Pennsylvania, in 1940, and educated at Bryn Mawr College and Columbia University, is the author of three books of poems. Among her awards are poetry fellowships from the National Endowment for the Arts and the New York Foundation for the Arts.*

# *Van Gogh's Bed*

is orange,
like Cinderella's coach, like
the sun when he looked it
straight in the eye.

is narrow,
he slept alone, tossing
between two pillows, while it carried him
bumpily to the ball.

is clumsy,
but friendly. A peasant
built the frame; an old wife beat
the mattress till it rose like meringue.

is empty,
morning light pours in
like wine, melody, fragrance,
the memory of happiness.

[*1985*]

## TOPICS FOR CRITICAL THINKING AND WRITING

Jane Flanders tells us that the poem is indebted not only to the painting but also to two comments in letters that van Gogh wrote to his brother, Theo:

> I can tell you that for my part I will try to keep a straight course, and will paint the most simple, the most common things.
>
> *(December 1884)*
>
> My eyes are still tired, but then I had a new idea in my head and here is the sketch of it. . . . It's just simply my bedroom, only here color is to do everything, and giving by its simplification a grander style to things, is to be suggestive here of *rest* or of sleep in general. In a word, to look at the picture ought to rest the brain or rather the imagination.
>
> *(September 1888)*

1. Does the painting convey "rest" to you? If not, has van Gogh failed to paint a picture of interest? What *does* the picture convey to you?
2. In an earlier version, the last stanza of the poem went thus:

    empty,
    morning light pours in
    like wine; the sheets are what they are,
    casting no shadows.

Which version do you prefer? Why?

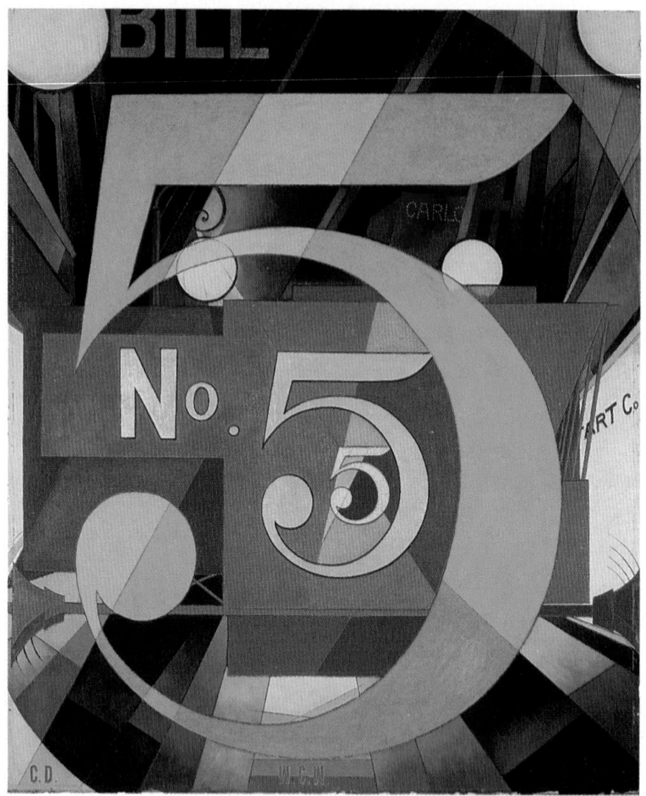


Charles Demuth. *I Saw the Figure 5 in Gold.* 1928. (Oil on composition board. 36 × 29 3/4 in. The Metropolitan Museum of Art, New York. The Alfred Stieglitz Collection, 1949)

## WILLIAM CARLOS WILLIAMS

*William Carlos Williams (1883-1963) was the son of an English traveling salesman and a Basque-Jewish woman. The couple met in Puerto Rico and settled in Rutherford, New Jersey, where Williams was born. He spent his life there, practicing as a pediatrician and writing poems in the moments between seeing patients who were visiting his office.*

*In his Autobiography Williams gives an account of the origin of this poem. He was walking in New York City, on his way to visit a friend:*

> *As I approached his number I heard a great clatter of bells and the roar of a fire engine passing the end of the street down Ninth Avenue. I turned just in time to see a golden 5 on a red background flash by. The impression was so sudden and forceful that I took a piece of paper out of my pocket and wrote a short poem about it.*

*Several years later his friend Charles Demuth (1883-1939), an American painter who has been called a cubist-realist, painted this picture, inspired by the poem. The picture is one of a series of paintings about Demuth's friends.*

## *The Great Figure*

Among the rain
and lights
I saw the figure 5
in gold
on a red
fire truck
moving
tense
unheeded
to gong clangs
siren howls
and wheels rumbling
through the dark city

[*1920*]

## TOPICS FOR CRITICAL THINKING AND WRITING

Williams's draft for the poem runs thus:

> Among the rain
> and lights
> I saw the figure 5
> gold on red
> moving
> to gong clangs
> siren howls
> and wheels rumbling
> tense
> unheeded
> through the dark city

Do you think the final version is better in all respects, some respects, or no respects? Explain.

Edwin Romanzo Elmer. *Mourning Picture.* 1890. (Oil on canvas, 28 × 36 in. [71.1 × 91.5 cm.] Smith College Museum of Art, Northampton, Massachusetts. Purchased 1953)

## ADRIENNE RICH

*Adrienne Rich, born in 1929 in Baltimore, was educated at Radcliffe College. Her first book of poems,* A Change of World, *published in 1951 when she was still an undergraduate, was selected by W. H. Auden for the Yale Series of Younger Poets.*

# Mourning Picture

*(The picture was painted by Edwin Romanzo Elmer (1850–1923) as a memorial to his daughter Effie. In the poem, it is the dead girl who speaks.)*

They have carried the mahogany chair and the cane rocker
out under the lilac bush,
and my father and mother darkly sit there, in black clothes.
Our clapboard house stands fast on its hill,
my doll lies in her wicker pram
gazing at western Massachusetts.
This was our world.
I could remake each shaft of grass
feeling its rasp on my fingers,
draw out the map of every lilac leaf
or the net of veins on my father's
grief-tranced hand.

Out of my head, half-bursting,
still filling, the dream condenses—
shadows, crystals, ceilings, meadows, globes of dew.
Under the dull green of the lilacs, out in the light
carving each spoke of the pram, the turned porch-pillars,
under high early-summer clouds,
I am Effie, visible and invisible,
remembering and remembered.

They will move from the house,
give the toys and pets away.
Mute and rigid with loss my mother
will ride the train to Baptist Corner,
the silk-spool will run bare.
I tell you, the thread that bound us lies
faint as a web in the dew.
Should I make you, world, again,
could I give back the leaf its skeleton, the air
its early-summer cloud, the house
its noonday presence, shadowless,
and leave *this* out? I am Effie, you were my dream.

[*1965*]

Kitagawa Utamaro, *Two Women Dressing Their Hair.* (Print collection, Miriam and Ira D. Wallach Division of Art, Prints and Photographs/ New York Public Library, Astor, Lenox and Tilden Foundations)*

## CATHY SONG

*Cathy Song was born in Honolulu in 1925 of a Chinese mother and a Korean father. She holds a bachelor's degree from Wellesley College and a master's degree in creative writing from Boston University. A manuscript that she submitted to the Yale Series of Younger Poets was chosen as the winner and in 1983 was published under the title of* Picture Bride.

*Kitagawa Utamaro (1754–1806) lived in Edo (now called Tokyo). He specialized in designing pictures of courtesans and actors that were then used to make woodblock prints. Brothels and the theater were important parts of what was called the Floating World, that is, the world of transient pleasure.

## *Beauty and Sadness*

*for Kitagawa Utamaro*

He drew hundreds of women
in studies unfolding
like flowers from a fan.
Teahouse waitresses, actresses,
geishas, courtesans and maids.
They arranged themselves
before this quick, nimble man
whose invisible presence
one feels in these prints
is as delicate
as the skinlike paper
he used to transfer
and retain their fleeting loveliness.

Crouching like cats,
they purred amid the layers of
kimono
swirling around them
as though they were bathing
in a mountain pool with irises
growing in the silken sunlit water.
Or poised like porcelain vases,
slender, erect and tall; their heavy
brocaded hair was piled high
with sandalwood combs and blossom
sprigs
poking out like antennae.
They resembled beautiful iridescent
insects,
creatures from a floating world.

Utamaro absorbed these women of
Edo
in their moments of melancholy
He captured the wisp of shadows,
the half-draped body
emerging from a bath; whatever
skin was exposed
was powdered white as snow.
A private space disclosed.
Portraying another girl
catching a glimpse of her own
vulnerable
face in the mirror, he transposed
the trembling plum lips
like a drop of blood
soaking up the white expanse of paper.

At times, indifferent to his inconsolable
eye, the women drifted
through the soft gray feathered light,
maintaining stillness, the moments in
between.
Like the dusty ash-winged moths
that cling to the screens in summer
and that the Japanese venerate
as ancestors reincarnated;
Utamaro graced these women with
immortality
in the thousand sheaves of prints
fluttering into the reverent hands of
keepers:
the dwarfed and bespectacled painter
holding up to a square of sunlight
what he had carried home beneath his
coat
one afternoon in winter.

[*1983*]

## TOPICS FOR CRITICAL THINKING AND WRITING

1. In the first stanza the women in Utamaro's prints possess a "fleeting loveliness." What does "fleeting" suggest here? What are Utamaro's characteristics in this stanza?
2. In the second stanza would you say that the women are beautiful, or not? And in the third stanza? What do they look like in each stanza?
3. In the last stanza, in the last few lines, we learn that Utamaro was a "dwarfed and bespectacled painter." We might have learned this earlier in the poem, or not at all. Why does Song wait until this late in the poem to tell us?

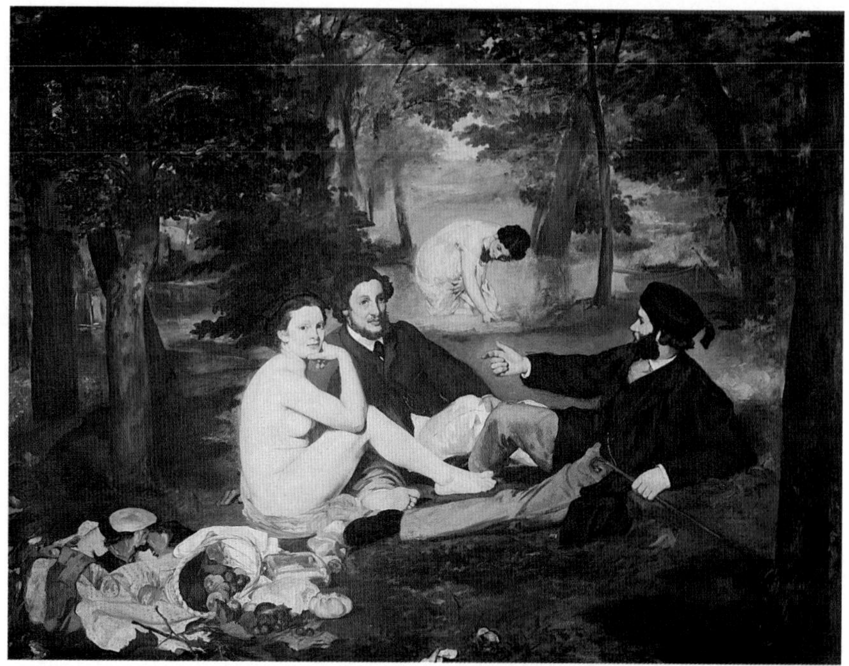

Édouard Manet, *Déjeuner sur l'herbe.* 1863. (Oil on canvas, 6′9″ × 8′10″. Louvre, Paris. Scala/Art Resource, NY)

## CARL PHILLIPS

*Carl Phillips was born in 1959 in Everett, Washington, and was educated at Harvard and at Boston University. African-American, gay, a scholar of classical Greek and Latin, and the author of two books of poetry, he has taught creative writing at Harvard, and he now teaches English and African-American Studies at Washington University in St. Louis.*

# Luncheon on the Grass

They're a curious lot, Manet's scandalous
lunch partners. The two men, lost
in cant and full dress, their legs sprawled
subway-style, as men's legs invariably are, seem
remarkably unruffled, all but oblivious to their nude
female companion. Her nudity is puzzling and
correct; clothes for her are surely only needed
to shrug a shoulder out of. She herself appears
baldly there-for-the-ride; her eyes, moving out
toward the viewer, are wide with the most banal,
detached surprise, as if to say, "where's
the *real* party?"

Now, in a comparable state of outdoor
undress, I'm beginning to have a fair idea
of what's going on in that scene. Watching
you, in clothes, remove one boot to work your
finger toward an itch in your athletic sock,
I look for any similarities between art
and our afternoon here on abandoned
property. The bather in the painting's
background, presumably there for a certain
balance of composition, is for us an ungainly,
rusted green dumpster, rising from overgrown
weeds that provide a contrast only remotely
pastoral. We are two to Manet's main group
of three, but the hum of the odd car or truck
on the highway below us offers a transient third.
Like the nude, I don't seem especially hungry,
partly because it's difficult eating naked when
everyone else is clothed, partly because
you didn't remember I hate chicken salad.
The beer you opened for me sits untouched,
going flat in the sun. I stroke the wet bottle
fitfully, to remind myself just how far
we've come or more probably have always been

from the shape of romance. My dear,
this is not art; we're not anywhere close
to Arcadia.

[*1993*]

**38 Arcadia** an ancient region in Greece, traditionally associated in art and literature with the simple, pastoral life, a Golden Age of unfailing romantic love.

## TOPICS FOR CRITICAL THINKING AND WRITING

1. The author is openly gay. Does knowledge of his sexual orientation affect the way in which you read the poem? Explain.
2. Do you agree that the speaker and the partner are "not anywhere close/to Arcadia"? Support your response with evidence.

Vincent van Gogh. *The Starry Night*. 1889. (Oil on canvas, 29 × 36 1/4 in. Collection, The Museum of Modern Art, New York. Acquired through the Lillie P. Bliss Bequest.Photograph © 1995 The Museum of Modern Art)

## ANNE SEXTON

*Anne Sexton (1928-75) was born in Newton, Massachusetts. She attended Garland Junior College, married at 20, and began a life as a housewife. After a mental breakdown at the age of 28 she took up writing poetry on the suggestion of a therapist. She published eight books of poetry, the third of which won a Pulitzer Prize. Despite her literary success, her life was deeply troubled, and she attempted suicide on several occasions. At last she succeeded, by carbon monoxide poisoning.*

# *The Starry Night*

*That does not keep me from having a terrible need of—shall I say the word—religion. Then I go out at night to paint the stars.*

Vincent van Gogh in a letter to his brother

The town does not exist
except where one black-haired tree slips
up like a drowned woman into the hot sky.
The town is silent. The night boils with eleven stars
Oh starry starry night! This is how
I want to die.

It moves. They are all alive.
Even the moon bulges in its orange irons
to push children, like a god, from its eye.
The old unseen serpent swallows up the stars.
Oh starry starry night! This is how
I want to die:

into that rushing beast of the night,
sucked up by that great dragon, to split
from my life with no flag,
no belly,
no cry.

[*1961*]

## TOPIC FOR CRITICAL THINKING AND WRITING

Sexton calls her poem "The Starry Night" and uses an epigraph from van Gogh. In what ways does her poem *not* describe or evoke van Gogh's painting? In what ways *does* it describe the painting?

Pieter Bruegel the Elder, *Landscape with the Fall of Icarus.* Copyright ACL, Brussels.

## W. H. AUDEN

*Wystan Hugh Auden (1907–73) was born in York, England, and educated at Oxford. In the 1930s his witty left-wing poetry earned him wide acclaim as the leading poet of his generation. He went to Spain during the Spanish Civil War, intending to serve as an ambulance driver for the Republicans in their struggle against Fascism, but he was so distressed by the violence of the Republicans that he almost immediately returned to England. In 1939 he came to America, and in 1946 he became a citizen of the United States, though he spent his last years in England. Much of his poetry is characterized by a combination of colloquial diction and technical dexterity.*

*In the following poem, Auden offers a meditation triggered by a painting in the Museum of Fine Arts in Brussels. The painting, by Pieter Bruegel (c. 1525–1569), is based on the legend of Icarus, told by the Roman poet Ovid (43* B.C.–A.D. *17) in his* Metamorphoses. *The story goes thus: Daedalus, father of Icarus, was confined with his son on the island of Crete. In order to escape, Daedalus made wings for himself and for Icarus by fastening feathers together with wax, but Icarus flew too near the sun, the wax melted, and Icarus fell into the sea. According to Ovid, the event—a boy falling through the sky—was witnessed with amazement by a ploughman, a shepherd, and an angler. In the painting, however, these figures seem to pay no attention to Icarus, who is represented not falling through the sky but already in the water (in the lower right corner, near the ship), with only his lower legs still visible.*

# *Musée des Beaux Arts*

About suffering they were never wrong,
The Old Masters: how well they understood
Its human position; how it takes place
While someone else is eating or opening a window or just walking dully along;
How, when the aged are reverently, passionately waiting
For the miraculous birth, there always must be
Children who did not specially want it to happen, skating
On a pond at the edge of the wood:
They never forgot
That even the dreadful martyrdom must run its course
Anyhow in a corner, some untidy spot
Where the dogs go on with their doggy life and the torturer's horse
Scratches its innocent behind on a tree.

In Brueghel's *Icarus,* for instance: how everything turns away
Quite leisurely from the disaster; the plowman may
Have heard the splash, the forsaken cry,
But for him it was not an important failure; the sun shone
As it had to on the white legs disappearing into the green
Water; and the expensive delicate ship that must have seen
Something amazing, a boy falling out of the sky,
Had somewhere to get to and sailed calmly on.

[*1938*]

## TOPICS FOR CRITICAL THINKING AND WRITING

1. In your own words sum up what, according to the speaker (in lines 1-13), the Old Masters understood about human suffering. (The Old Masters were the great European painters who worked from about 1500 to about 1750.)
2. Suppose the first lines read:

   The Old Masters were never wrong about suffering.
   They understood its human position well.

   What (beside the particular rhymes ) would change or be lost?
3. Reread the poem (preferably over the course of several days) a number of times, jotting down your chief responses after each reading. Then, in connection with a final reading, study your notes, and write an essay of 500 words setting forth the history of your final response to the poem. For example, you may want to report that certain difficulties soon were clarified and that your enjoyment increased. Or, conversely, you may want to report that the poem became less interesting (for reasons you will set forth) the more you studied it. Probably your history will be somewhat more complicated than these simple examples. Try to find a chief pattern in your experience, and shape it into a thesis.
4. Consider a picture, either in a local museum or reproduced in a book, and write a 500-word reflection on it. If the picture is not well known, include a reproduction (a postcard from the museum or a photocopy of a page of

Marcel Duchamp, *Nude Descending a Staircase, No. 2.* (1912. Oil on canvas. 58″ × 35″. Philadelphia Museum of Art: The Louise and Walter Arensberg Collection)

## X. J. KENNEDY

*X. J. Kennedy was born in New Jersey in 1929. He has taught at Tufts University and is the author of several books of poems, books for children, and college textbooks.*

*Marcel Duchamp's* Nude Descending a Staircase, No. 2 *(1912) was exhibited in 1913 in the Armory Show, an international exhibition held at an armory in New York, and later in Chicago and Boston. The Armory Show gave America its first good look at contemporary European art, for instance, cubism, which had influenced Duchamp's painting.*

# *Nude Descending a Staircase*

Toe upon toe, a snowing flesh,
A gold of lemon, root and rind,
She sifts in sunlight down the stairs
With nothing on. Nor on her mind.

We spy beneath the banister
A constant thresh of thigh on thigh—
Her lips imprint the swinging air
That parts to let her parts go by
One-woman waterfall, she wears
Her slow descent like a long cape
And pausing, on the final stair
Collects her motions into shape.

[*1961*]

## TOPICS FOR CRITICAL THINKING AND WRITING

1. To what extent does the poem describe the painting? To what extent does it do something else?
2. Some viewers have found Duchamp's painting strange and confusing. Does Kennedy's poem help you to understand Duchamp's style of art? Explain.

# POETRY AND TRANSLATION

During the course of reading this section you will be invited to translate several poems. If you are at ease in a language other than English, you will be asked to translate a poem of your choice from that language, and also to write about the particular difficulties you experienced while translating. Or you can choose to translate the French, Spanish, and Japanese poems that we print in this chapter; you don't have to know any of these languages, since we provide literal translations.

We will talk briefly about some theories concerning translation, but first let's look at a very brief Latin poem and some English versions of it.

## Five Versions of a Two-Line Poem by Catullus

We begin by looking at a poem by the Roman author Catullus (87?–55? B.C.). The subject is the paradoxical quality of the feelings of a lover. (There are countless poems about love as a pleasing pain, a heavenly hell, and about the lover as both active and passive, eagerly loving and yet tormented by love. See, for instance, Aphra Behn's poem on page 840.) Here is Catullus's poem:

Odi et amo, quare id faciam, fortasse requiris?
Nescio, sed fieri sentio et excrucior.

This can be translated more or less literally as:

I hate and love. Why do I do that, perhaps you ask.
I don't know, but I feel it to be happening, and I am tortured.

Notice that the language of this poem is not so remote from English as it may seem at first glance. The Latin *odi* ("I hate") is related to the English word *odious; amo* ("I love") is related to our word *amorous, requiris* ("you ask") to our *require* and *inquire;* in the second line, *sentio* ("I feel") is related to our *sentient,* and *excrucior* ("I am crucified" or "I am tortured") to our *excruciate.* (This last word includes *crux,* or "cross.")

Next—and here we get closer to our topic, poetry—notice the arrangement or pattern of the words, since one of the things literature does is to put experience into a pattern. In Catullus's little poem, there is a pattern of long and short syllables (but we need not discuss classical versification here), and also a pattern of verbs. Each line contains four verbs; those in the first line are active ("I hate," "I love," "I do," "you ask"), whereas those in the second line are passive or they describe a passive condition ("I don't know," "I feel it to be happening," "I am tortured"). And so we can say that Catullus catches an aspect—or, rather, two aspects—of love, the sense of activity and also the sense of helplessness. Each verb in the first line is echoed or balanced in the second; thus *Odi et amo* ("I hate and I love") at the beginning of the first line chimes with *sentio et excrucior* ("I feel . . . and I am tortured") at the end of the second. Moreover, the active *faciam* ("I do") in the first line connects with the passive form of the verb, *fieri* ("to be done," "to happen") in the second.

Having tried to convey something of the poetry of Catullus's two lines—something of their artful expressiveness—let's look at a few translations. The original does not rhyme, but many translators have believed that an English version needs to rhyme if it is to be seen and felt as a poem.

I hate and love—the why I cannot tell,
But by my tortures know the fact too well.
—Theodore Martin

In the next two versions the translators suggest particular tortures:

I hate and I love. Why do that? Good question.
No answer, save "I do." Nailed, through either hand.
—Frederic Raphael and Kenneth McLeish

I hate and I love. And if you ask me how,
I do not know: I only feel it, and I'm torn in two.
—Peter Whigham

The first of these versions, by Raphael and McLeish, clearly—perhaps too clearly?—evokes crucifixion. The second, with "I'm torn in two," catches the double nature of love that is the subject of Catullus's poem, and it evokes visions of the instrument of torture known as the rack, or perhaps of a victim whose limbs were tied to two or more horses which were then whipped into flight.

Here is one more version:

"At once I hate and love as well."
—"In heaven's name, Catullus, how?"
—"God knows! And yet I feel it now
Here in my heart: the whole of hell."
—M. H. Tattersall

Tattersall's version is free in that it converts the poem into a dialogue and names Catullus, but one can argue that it is true to the spirit of the poem. It is widely agreed that in the translation of poetry the spirit is more important than the letter. Some of the worst—least moving, indeed least readable—translations are word-by-word translations that can claim to be very close to the original but that are unlike anything we can imagine being spoken in English.

## Can Poetry Be Translated?

Having looked at a range of translations, we can perhaps now move from a particular work to a general problem or question. To translate is (literally) "to carry across"; a text is carried from one language into another. But can poetry be translated? Robert Frost once defined poetry as "what gets lost in translation." He was not the only person to think that poetry can't be translated. An Italian proverb generalizes, "Traduttori, traditori," that is, "Translators are traitors," or, more freely, "Translation betrays"—but, as you can see, much is lost in the translation.

The idea that poetry can't be translated is rooted in the fact that poets make use not only of the gist of the obvious meaning of a word but also of patterns of sound. We can see this most easily by first looking at a statement that is not a poem but that relies heavily on its sounds. Consider

Look before you leap.

The most obvious pattern is the alliteration (words that begin with the same sound), *l*ook and *l*eap, but there is also a pattern of stresses. The sentence begins and ends with a stress, and "before" and "you leap" each consist of an unstressed syllable followed by a stressed syllable. If you compare "Look before you leap" with "Watch out before you leap," or with "Before jumping, look around," you'll see that these translations of English words into other English words lose much of what counts in the original.

You might take a moment to try to put into other words such expressions as "There's no fool like an old fool," "Penny wise and pound foolish," or "A penny saved is a penny earned." Even better, if you are familiar with a memorable saying in a language other than English, try to capture the effectiveness in an English translation of your own.

Let's think now of some issues specific to translating poetry. Rhyme of course is a kind of pattern (a recurring sound), and it can cause a translator difficulty since effective rhyme often conveys some sort of meaning. It may bring together two words that not only sound alike but have some association in common, as in the greeting-card rhymes of *moon* and *June, dove* and *love.* Or a rhyme may achieve a poignant ironic effect by bringing together two words that sound alike but that differ sharply in meaning, such as *light* (with its associations of life) and *night* (with its associations of death). "Look before you leap" doesn't contain rhyme in the usual sense of the word, but the alliterating *l*'s can be called *initial rhyme,* and alliteration—because of the identity in sound—can imply some sort of identity between the alliterating words, or as here, it can make an effective contrast: *look* implies caution and probably motionlessness, whereas *leap* implies reckless activity.

Probably everyone will agree that translators should strive to capture the subtleties of the original, and probably everyone will agree—here we get back to Robert Frost's view—that inevitably much will be lost. But what is gained in translation, or what may be gained, is a new poem.

Something along these lines is suggested by Edwin Cranston, a leading translator of classical Japanese poetry, in *A Waka Anthology.* Translators have duties to their authors, but they also have duties to their own powers. Cranston makes this point by calling attention to a tenth-century Japanese poet's assertion that poems "have their seed in the human heart, and burgeon forth into the myriad leaves of words." In similar fashion, Cranston says, the translator "descends into the poem and lets something happen"; the translator serves "as a medium for the new growth." But of course the process of translating is not passive. As Cranston says, if translators enter into the work and listen to it, they also have their own ideas. The original is strongly there, but so is the translator's creative impulse, which has its own direction and has "its own life and integrity. Nothing is more persuasive than something that works, and if a line somehow works, it is hard to abandon it."

The result may be a translation that is free rather than faithful. Or if it is faithful, it is faithful to the spirit of literature rather than to the letter of the original work. If we push this view further than Cranston himself does, the translation—perhaps better called a *version* or an *adaptation*—is a success if it has life as a poem, however removed it may be from the original. More than one translator has defended his or her work as Edward FitzGerald (translator of *The Rubaiyat of Omar Khayyam*) did, by quoting from Ecclesiastes, "Better a live dog than a dead lion." One translator we know tells us he likes to think of the original as a "control." The original serves as a control on the act of translation, though it rests with the translator to decide whether he or she allows the original to control a lot or a little. Translators can give themselves a great deal of freedom, or only a little. But in either case, because their work is a translation of something else, they are always referring back to another text while they compose a new one.

# Looking at Translations of a Poem by Charles Baudelaire

In the following poem Charles Baudelaire (1821–67) compares the albatross—majestic when soaring above oceangoing ships, but pitiful when captured and flopping on the deck—with the poet, whose lofty imagination makes him unsuited for the workaday world. The poem was first published in the 1859 edition of Baudelaire's book, *The Flowers of Evil.*

## *L'Albatros*

Souvent, pour s'amuser, les hommes d'équipage
Prennent des albatros, vastes oiseaux des mers.
Qui suivent, indolents compagnons de voyage,
Le navire glissant sur les gouffres amers.

À peine les ont-ils déposés sur les planches,
Que ces rois de l'azur, maladroits et honteux,
Laissent piteusement leurs grandes ailes blanches
Comme des avirons traîner à côté d'eux.

Ce voyageur ailé, comme il est gauche et veule!
Luis, naguère si beau, qu'il est comique et laid!
L'un agace son bec avec un brûle-gueule,
L'autre mime, en boitant, l'infirme qui volait!

Le Poète est semblable au prince des nuées
Qui hante la tempêt se rit de l'archer;
Exilé sur le sol au milieu des huées,
Ses ailes de géant l'empêchent de marcher.

[*1859*]

A literal translation, almost word by word, would go something as follows. (We retain the lineation of the original, and we offer it not as a satisfactory version of the poem but only as a starting point, in order to help readers who do not know French to follow the poem.)

Often, to amuse themselves, sailors
capture albatrosses, great sea birds,
who follow, indolent companions of the journey,
the ship, gliding on the bitter deeps.

As soon as they stretch them out on the deck
these monarchs of the blue, awkward and ashamed,
pitifully let their large white wings
like oars drag by their sides.

The winged traveler, how awkward and feeble!
He who a short time ago was so beautiful,
one sailor teases his beak with a clay pipe,
and another, limping, mimics the cripple who flew.

The Poet is like the prince of the clouds
who is at home in the tempest and who scorns the archer:

exiled on the earth, an object of scorn,
his giant wings hinder him as he walks.

Let's look now at some verse translations of the first stanza. In the original, the first and third lines of each stanza rhyme, as do the second and fourth, the rhyme scheme thus being *abab.* The task of following Baudelaire's rhyme scheme is difficult, and it can lead to very strained lines; some translators therefore prefer to rhyme only two of the four lines, or to settle for an off-rhyme, as in the first example here, where *sea* and *indolently* rhyme, and where *selves* and *gulfs* chime less precisely:

Sometimes, sailors to amuse themselves
catch albatrosses, great birds of the sea,
which as companions follow indolently
the vessel gliding over bitter gulfs.
—C. F. MacIntyre

In the next version, all four lines rhyme closely, but, not surprisingly, the translation is somewhat freer:

Often, when bored, the sailors of the crew
Trap albatross, the great birds of the seas,
Mild travelers escorting in the blue
Ships gliding on the ocean's mysteries.
—James McGowan

We say this version is freer because, after all, Baudelaire spoke not of "the ocean's mysteries" but of *les gouffres amers,* the bitter deeps. In short, there often is a trade-off between closely following what might be called the formal properties of the poem (in this case, rhyme) and the precise meaning. On the other hand, here is a rhymed translation that is remarkably faithful to the original. We quote the entire version:

Often, for pastime, mariners will ensnare
The albatross, that vast sea-bird who sweeps
On high companionable pinion where
Their vessel glides upon the bitter deeps.

Torn from his native space, this captive king
Flounders upon the deck in stricken pride,
And pitiably lets his great white wing
Drag like a heavy paddle at his side.

This rider of winds, how awkward he is, and weak!
How droll he seems, who lately was all grace!
A sailor pokes a pipestem into his beak;
Another, hobbling, mocks his trammeled pace.

The Poet is like this monarch of the clouds,
Familiar of storms, of stars, and of all high things;
Exiled on earth amidst its hooting crowds,
He cannot walk, borne down by his giant wings.
—Richard Wilbur

***Exercise.*** Produce your own version—rhymed or unrhymed—of the final stanza of "The Albatross." For your convenience we offer some rhymes that other translators have used, but you are under no compulsion to use them. MacIntyre used *mocks, clouds, crowds, walk;* McGowan used *clouds, day, crowds, way.* George Dillon (who collaborated with Edna St. Vincent Millay on a translation of *The Flowers of Evil*) used *cloud, slings, crowd, wings.* Francis Duke, in his translation of *Flowers of Evil,* used *clouds, defiant, crowds, giant.*

## Translating a Poem of Your Choice, and Commenting on the Translation

If you are at ease in a language other than English, translate a short poem from that language into English. It may be a poem that you learned in school or on the street.

We suggest that you begin by jotting down a line-for-line prose translation, and then work on a poetic version. Your prose version of course will not be a word-for-word translation. After all, a word-for-word translation of the Spanish "Me llamo Juan" is "Me [or "Myself"] I call John," but no one speaking English says this. The English version of these words is "My name is John"—even though the Spanish word for *name* (*nombre*) does not appear in the original sentence. Similarly, a native speaker of French, when asked whether he or she is going to class this morning, may reply "Mais oui," which in a word-for-word translation would be "But yes." In English, however, we would simply say "Yes" or "Certainly," and therefore the "But" ought to be omitted in a translation. Or consider the phrase "les hommes d'équipage" in the first line of Baudelaire's "L'Albatros" (see page 1030). A word-for-word translation would be "men of the crew," but does one say this? Perhaps "members of the crew" is better? Or perhaps simply "the crew"? Or "crewmen"? Or, perhaps best of all, "sailors"? In any case, the French *équipage* certainly cannot be translated as "equipment." (Translators call words that look alike but that have different meanings "false friends." Examples: French *advertissement* means "warning"; German *also* means "therefore"; Spanish *constipado* means "having a head cold.")

The prose translation *ought to sound like English,* and this means going beyond a word-for-word translation, at least to a phrase-by-phrase translation. If English is not your native language, you may want to check your prose version with a native-born speaker of English. In any case, once you have a prose version that is in idiomatic English, try to put it into a poetic form.

This does not mean that (assuming your original uses rhyme) you must preserve the exact rhyme scheme. If the original rhymes *abab,* you may find it satisfactory to produce a version in which only the second and fourth lines rhyme. Similarly, even if the original line has 11 or 12 syllables, you may prefer to reduce the line to 10 syllables because the pentameter line (10 syllables) is so widely used in English that it seems natural. Admittedly, your task is easier if you choose an unrhymed poem, and much of the world's poetry—to cite only two instances, Native American poetry and Japanese poetry—does not use rhyme. (We discuss one Japanese form, the haiku, on page 921.)

When you have done your best, relax for a while, and then jot down (in preparation for drafting an essay that will accompany your translation) some notes about the particular problems involved in translating the work. Is there a pun in the original that is impossible to translate? Are there historical or mythological allusions that are clear to people who belong to the culture that produced the poem but that are obscure to outsiders? Are there qualities in the original language (specialists call it "the source language") that simply cannot be reproduced in the "host" (or "target") language? For instance, Japanese has several verbs meaning "to give"; the word used in "I gave you a book" differs from the word in "You gave me a book." It is rather as if one had to say, "You bestowed a book on me"—but of course no one *does* say this in English. What, then, is a translator to do?

In the end, you will produce a translation, and an essay of some 500 words, explaining the particular difficulties you encountered, and perhaps explaining the hardest decisions that you ultimately made.

## Last-Minute Help: Three Spanish Poems

If you don't know a poem in a language other than English, consider translating one or both of these Spanish folk songs, or, finally, the poem we print by the Chilean poet Gabriela Mistral.

| | |
|---|---|
| Ya se van los pastores, alla Estremadura | The shepherds are already leaving on their way to Estremadura |
| Ya se queda la Sierra triste y obscura. | And the mountain ridge is already sad and gloomy. |
| Ya se van los pastores ya se van marchando | The shepherds are already going, they are already departing |
| Ya las pobres niñas se quedan llorando. | And the poor girls remain there, crying. |

Here is the second song:

| | |
|---|---|
| Una gallina con pollos cinco duro me costó | I bought a hen and chicks for five duros |
| Corrocloclo corrocloclo | Corrocloclo corrocloclo |
| La compré por la mañana, y a la tarde se perdió | I bought her in the morning and in the afternoon it lost its way |
| Corrocloclo corrocloclo | Corrocloclo corrocloclo |
| Yo no siento la gallina ni el dinero que costó | I'm not sorry about the hen or the money it cost |
| Corrocloclo corrocloclo | Corrocloclo corrocloclo |
| Solo siento los pollitos que sin madre los quedó | I'm only sorry for the chicks who are left without a mother |
| Corrocloclo corrocloclo. | Corrocloclo corrocloclo. |

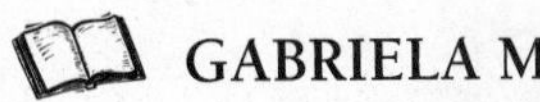

## GABRIELA MISTRAL

*Lucila Godoy Alacayaga (1889–1957) adopted the pseudonym Gabriela Mistral. A teacher and a director of schools in Chile, she achieved fame there in 1914, when she won first prize in a national poetry contest; she received international fame in 1945, when she was awarded the Nobel Prize for literature, the first Latin American writer to win the award. She was also distinguished in two other careers, as an educator—she is esteemed for her revision of the Mexican school system and she was a beloved professor at Barnard College in New York—and as a figure in the world of international politics, representing Chile in the League of Nations and the United Nations.*

*The poem originates in a response to a statue, Rodin's* The Thinker. *If you do work on a translation of Mistral's poem, you might keep in mind a comment by an earlier translator of her work, the poet Langston Hughes, who in his Introduction to* Selected Poems of Gabriela Mistral *(1957) wrote: "I have no theories of translation. I simply try to transfer into English as much as I can of the literal content, emotion, and style of each poem." Unfortunately Hughes did not include a translation of the following poem.*

## El Pensador de Rodin

Con el mentón caído sobre la mano ruda,
el Pensador se acuerda que es carne de la huesa,
carne fatal, delante del destino desnuda,
carne que odia la muerte, y tembló de belleza.

Y tembló de amor, toda su primavera ardiente,
y ahora, al otoño, anégase de verdad y tristeza.
El "de morir tenemos" pasa sobre su frente,
en todo agudo bronce, cuando la noche empieza.
Y en la angustia, sus músculos se hienden, sufridores.
Los surcos de su carne se llenan de terrores.
Se hiende, como la hoja de otoño, al Señor fuerte

que la llama en los bronces . . . Y no hay árbol torcido
de sol en la llanura, ni león de flanco herido,
crispados como este hombre que medita en la muerte.

## Rodin's Thinker

*Translated by Gustavo Alfaro**

With his chin fallen on his rough hand,
the Thinker, remembering that his flesh is of the grave,
mortal flesh, naked before its fate,
flesh that hates death, trembled for beauty.

And he trembled for love, his whole ardent spring,
and now in autumn, he is overcome with truth and sadness.
"We must die" passes across his brow,
in every piercing trumpet sound, when night begins to fall.

Auguste Rodin, *The Thinker.* (1910. Bronze, height 27½". The Metropolitan Museum of Art, Gift of Thomas F. Ryan)

And in his anguish, his long suffering muscles split.
The furrows of his flesh are filled with terrors.
It splits, like the autumn leaf before the mighty Lord

who calls it with trumpet calls . . . And there is no tree twisted 12
by the sun in the plain, nor lion wounded on its side,
as tense as this man who meditates on death.

******Translator's note:*** Mistral's ***bronce*** **in line 8 and** ***bronces*** **in line 12 I translate as** ***trumpet sound*** **and** ***trumpet calls.*** **Given the context, this reading seems to me to be more plausible than a reading that takes** ***bronce*** **and** ***bronces*** **to refer to the bronze sculpture itself.**

## Translating Haiku

The haiku, a Japanese poetic form, consists of 17 syllables, arranged into lines of 5, 7, and 5 syllables. (Strictly speaking, it is written in a continuous line, as we write prose, but it is conceived as three units, 5-7-5.) It is unrhymed, but some English translations and imitations use rhyme.

Here is the most famous of all haiku, in Japanese and with a word-by-word literal translation:

## BASHO (1644–94)

Furuike ya
kawazu tobikomu
mizu no oto

old pond
frog jumps in
water's sound

One of the things that made this poem remarkable was that it probably was the first Japanese poem about a frog that did *not* talk about the noise of the frog croaking, but instead talked about the noise of the water. (By the way, for an American poem that calls attention to the croaking of a frog, see Emily Dickinson's "I'm Nobody! Who are you?" on page 862.)

How to translate Basho's poem? We have already given a literal translation, but here are some efforts at more literary versions:

The old pond
A frog jumps in
The sound of water.

Old garden lake!
The frog jumps in,
And the waters wake.

The old pond;
A frog jumps;
The water slurps.

An old pond
a
frog
jumps
in—
Plop.

A bog
A frog
A sound
Drowned.

***Exercise.*** Offer your own translation or adaptation of the haiku, perhaps keeping the 5-7-5 arrangement of the original; or compose an original poem that responds to Basho's. Here are two examples of responses that our students have produced:

An old pond—
Basho jumps in;
No more noise.

An old pond—
If Basho were here
I'd push him in.

Here is another haiku by Basho, in Japanese and with a graceless word-by-word translations:

Kare-eda ni
karasu no tomari-keri
aki no kure

withered branch on
crow is perched
autumn evening

Japanese does not usually distinguish between the singular and the plural, so what we translate as "crow is perched" could equally be translated "crows are perched." Further, what we translated as "autumn evening" may equally be translated "late autumn."

The next poem, also by Basho, was composed at the site of a battle where one of Japan's most famous warriors committed suicide after being defeated by forces acting on behalf of his own brother. It is impossible to find an exact parallel in American history, but perhaps the death of Stonewall Jackson at the Battle of Chancellorsville (1863) comes close in feeling, especially because Jackson was mortally wounded by his own men.

| | |
|---|---|
| Natsu-gusa ya | Summer grasses |
| tsuwamono-domo ga | strong warriors' |
| yume no ato | dreams' relics |

In the second line, we use "warriors" rather than "soldiers" because the Japanese word has an archaic flavor. (By the way, in this instance, unlike the poem about the crow or crows, the word for "warriors" is plural.) The gist of the idea of the poem is that grasses (or weeds) now flourish where strong soldiers once fought; all that is left of the dreams (or ambitions) of the soldiers is the summer grass. Here are two versions that students produced, using off-rhymes:

| | |
|---|---|
| Summer grasses | Weeds flourish |
| All that is left | where soldiers nourished |
| where warriors passed. | dreams of glory. |

Here are two versions, again by students, that retain the 5-7-5 pattern of the original.

| | |
|---|---|
| On this grassy spot | Grasses grow today |
| Here once a noble army | Where heroic soldiers died |
| Dreamed its dream and died. | Leaving bones and dreams. |

### *Exercises*

1. Try your hand at translating Basho's poems about the crow(s) and about the dead warriors, or invent an adaptation of each poem. You might, for instance, write a poem about a bird in a season other than the fall, and a poem about the ironic implications of some local site.
2. Here are literal translations of two more haiku by Basho. Create versions that are more memorable.

   stillness
   rock into pierce
   locust-voice

   soon die
   no indication of
   locust's voice

## A Sample Essay with a Translation

George Guzman

English 101

November 10, 1996

García Lorca's "Despedida"

My father sometimes quotes, half-jokingly although it is a serious poem, Federico García Lorca's "Despedida," which he learned when he was a schoolboy in Cuba. Because it is short and because he quotes it so often, I know it by heart. In Spanish it goes like this:

Despedida

Si muero,
dejad el balcón abierto.

El niño come naranjas.
(Desde mi balcón lo veo.)

El segador siega el trigo.
(Desde mi balcón lo siento.)

¡Si muero,
dejad el balcón abierto!

When I translated the poem for this assignment, I didn't find any serious difficulties--probably because the poem does not rhyme. The only word in the poem that I think is especially hard to translate is the title, "Despedida." It comes from a verb, "despedir," which Spanish-English dictionaries define as "to take one's leave." In English, however, no one "takes one's leave"; we just say "Goodbye," and go. But "Goodbye" is too informal for "Despedida," so I settled on "Farewell." No one speaking English ever says "Farewell," but I think it catches the slight formality of the Spanish, and it has the right tone for this poem about a man who is talking about leaving the world.

Aside from the title, I at first found the poem easy to translate, but on further thinking about my translation, I found a few things that I wish I could do better. Here, for a start, is my literal translation.

Farewell

If I die,
leave the balcony open.

The boy eats oranges.
(From my balcony I see him.)

The reaper reaps the wheat.
(From my balcony I hear him.)

If I die,
leave the balcony open.

There are subtle things in this poem, but most of them can be translated easily. For instance, in the first and the last stanzas the poet speaks of "<u>el</u> balcón" (<u>the</u> balcony), but in the middle two stanzas he speaks of "<u>mi</u> balcón" (<u>my</u> balcony). That is, in the first and last stanzas, where he imagines himself dead, he realizes the balcony is not <u>his</u> any more, but is simply "the balcony." There is no difficulty in translating this idea from Spanish into English.

Because I knew the poem by heart, I translated it without first looking at the original on the page. But when I wrote it out in Spanish, too, I became aware of a small difficulty. In Spanish if a sentence ends with an exclamation point (or a question mark) it also begins with one, so the reader knows <u>at the beginning of the sentence</u> what sort of sentence it will be. We don't do this in English, and I think something is lost in English. The <u>two</u> exclamation marks in García Lorca's last sentence, one at the beginning and one at the end, seem to me to call more attention to the sentence, and make it more sad. And since the first and last sentences are identical <u>except</u> for the exclamation marks around the last sentence, the punctuation makes the last sentence different from the first. Superficially the poem begins and ends with the same sentence, but the last sentence is much more final.

A second difficulty is this: On rereading my translation, I wondered if it should try to catch the <u>o</u> sounds that in the original are at the end of every line except the third. It's hard to explain, but I think this repeated <u>o</u> sound has several effects. Certainly the repetition of the sound gives unity to the poem. But it also is part of the <u>meaning</u>, in two ways. First of all, the sound of <u>o</u> is like a lament or a cry. Second, because the sound is repeated again and again, in line after line, it is as if the poet wants the present to continue, doesn't want to stop, wants to keep living. Obviously he is not looking forward to dying. He doesn't says anything about hoping to go to heaven. All he thinks of is <u>what he sees now</u>, and he suggests that he would like to keep seeing it from his balcony.

<u>Balcón</u> in Spanish means, as I have translated it, "balcony," but to say "leave the balcony open"-- which is perfectly all right in Spanish--sounds a little funny in English, maybe especially because we don't have many balconies here, unlike (I am told)

Spain. The idea of course is to leave open the door, or if it is glass it is also a window, that leads to the balcony. Maybe, then, it makes better sense to be a little free in the translation, and to say, "Leave the window open," or even "Do not draw the curtain," or some such thing. In fact, if we can put "window" at the end of the line, we get the o sound of the original.

If I die,
Leave open the window.

But in the original the first line ("Si muero," literally "If I die") has this o sound also, and I can't think of any way of getting this into the translation. For a moment I thought of beginning,

If I go,
Leave open the window,

but "If I go" just isn't a moving way of saying "If I die," which is what "Si muero" means. Still, we might translate line 4 as "I see him from my window," and line 6 as "I hear him from my window." In the end, I decided not to begin by saying "If I go," but (even though I lose the o sound in the first line) to substitute "window" for "balcony" in lines 2, 4, and 6, in order to get the repetition and the sad o sound. My final version goes like this:

Farewell

If I die,
leave open the window.

The boy eats oranges.
(I see him from my window.)

The reaper reaps the wheat.
(I hear him from my window.)

If I die,
leave open the window.

Here are our responses. If yours differ, consider putting them into writing.

- This seems like an excellent translation to us. Do you agree?
- When the student shared his essay with others in the class, it was praised for being "thoughtful." What gives the essay this quality?

## A Note on Using the First-Person Pronoun

Some handbooks on writing tell students never to use *I* in an essay. But this rule is too rigid; in the case of the essay you have just read, the personal touches make it all the more interesting and engaging. Often the problem is not really with the use of *I,* but, rather, with the absence of explanation and evidence that make clear what prompted the "I" to respond as he or she does. This student does a good job of focusing on the poem, commenting on details of language, and keeping the nature of the assignment in mind. His use of *I* occurs as part of a careful analysis and argument.

# CHAPTER 25

# A Collection of Poems

## A NOTE ON FOLK BALLADS

**Folk ballads,** or **popular ballads,** are anonymous stories told in song. They acquired their distinctive flavor by being passed down orally from generation to generation, each singer consciously or unconsciously modifying his or her inheritance. Most ballad singers probably were composers only by accident; they intended to transmit what they had heard, but their memories were sometimes faulty and their imaginations active. The modifications effected by oral transmission generally give a ballad three noticeable qualities:

1. It is impersonal; even if there is an "I" who sings the tale, this "I" is usually characterless.
2. The ballad—like other oral literature such as the nursery rhyme or the counting-out rhyme ("one potato, two potato")—is filled with **repetition,** sometimes of lines, sometimes of words. Consider, for example, "Go saddle me the black, the black, / Go saddle me the brown," or "O wha is this has done this deid, / This ill deid don to me?" Sometimes, in fact, the story is told by repeating lines with only a few significant variations. This **incremental repetition** (repetition with slight variations advancing the narrative) is the heart of "Edward." Furthermore, **stock epithets** are repeated from ballad to ballad: "true love," "milk-white steed," "golden hair." Oddly, these clichés do not bore us, but by their impersonality often lend a simplicity that effectively contrasts with the violence of the tale.
3. Because the ballads were transmitted orally, residing in the memory rather than on the printed page, weak stanzas were often dropped, leaving a series of sharp scenes, frequently with dialogue:

The king sits in Dumferling toune,
Drinking the blude-reid wine:
"O whar will I get guid sailor,
To sail this schip of mine?"

Because ballads were sung rather than printed, and because singers made alterations, no one version of a ballad is the "correct" one. The versions printed here have become such favorites that they are almost regarded as definitive, but the reader should consult a collection of ballads to get some idea of the wide variety.

Popular ballads have been much imitated by professional poets, especially since the late eighteenth century. Two such **literary ballads** are Keats's "La Belle Dame sans Merci" (p. 1061) and Coleridge's "The Rime of the Ancient Mariner." In a literary ballad the story is often infused with multiple meanings, with insistent symbolic implications. Ambiguity can be present in the popular ballad also, but it is of a different sort. Whether it is due to the loss of stanzas or to the creator's unconcern with some elements of the narrative, the ambiguity of the popular ballad commonly lies in the narrative itself rather than in the significance of the narrative.

Here are five popular ballads.

 ANONYMOUS

## *Sir Patrick Spence*

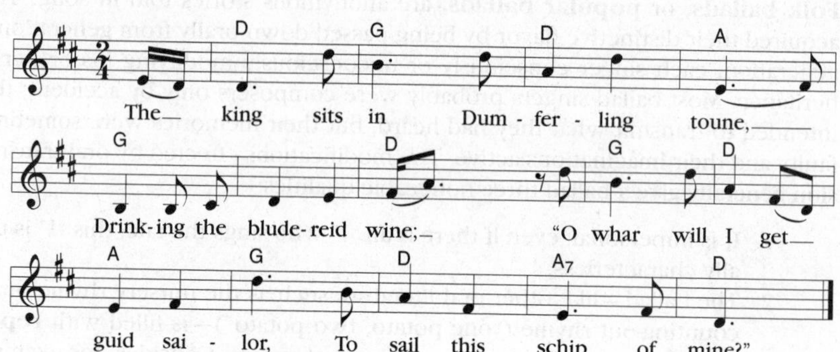


The king sits in Dumferling toune,
Drinking the blude-reid wine:
"O whar will I get guid sailor,
To sail this schip of mine?"

Up and spak an eldern knicht,
Sat at the kings richt kne:
"Sir Patrick Spence is the best sailor,
That sails upon the se."

The king has written a braid° letter,
And signed it wi' his hand,

9 **braid** broad, open

And sent it to Sir Patrick Spence,
  Was walking on the sand.

The first line that Sir Patrick red,
  A loud lauch° lauched he;
The next line that Sir Patrick red,
  The teir blinded his ee.

"O wha is this has done this deid,
  This ill deid don to me,
To send me out this time o' the yeir,
  To sail upon the se?

"Mak hast, mak hast, my mirry men all,
  Our guid schip sails the morne":
"O say na sae, my master deir,
  For I feir a deadlie storme.

"Late late yestreen I saw the new moone,
  Wi' the auld moone in hir arme,
And I feir, I feir, my deir master,
  That we will cum to harme."

O our Scots nobles wer richt laith°
  To weet their cork-heild schoone;°
Bot lang owre° a' the play wer playd,
  Thair hats they swam aboone.°

O lang, lang may their ladies sit,
  Wi' thair fans into their hand,
Or eir° they se Sir Patrick Spence
  Cum sailing to the land.

O lang, lang may the ladies stand,
  Wi' thair gold kems in their hair,
Waiting for their ain deir lords,
  For they'll se thame na mair.

Have owre° have owre to Aberdour,
  It's fiftie fadom deip,
And thair lies guid Sir Patrick Spence,
  Wi' the Scots lords at his feit.

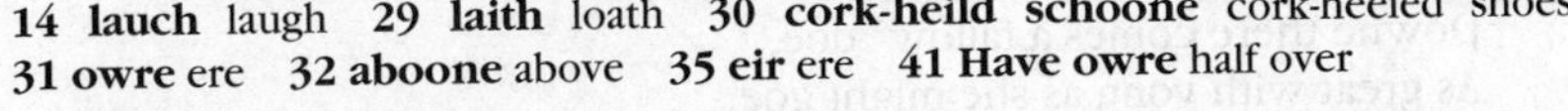
**14 lauch** laugh **29 laith** loath **30 cork-heild schoone** cork-heeled shoes **31 owre** ere **32 aboone** above **35 eir** ere **41 Have owre** half over

 ANONYMOUS

## *The Three Ravens*

There were three ravens sat on a tree,
  *Downe a downe, hay downe, hay downe*
There were three ravens sat on a tree,
  *With a downe*

There were three ravens sat on a tree,
They were as blacke as they might be,
*With a downe derrie, derrie, derrie, downe, downe.*

The one of them said to his mate,
"Where shall we our breakfast take?"
"Down in yonder greene field,
There lies a knight slain under his shield.

"His hounds they lie downe at his feete,
So well they can their master keepe.

"His haukes they flie so eagerly,
There's no fowle dare him come nie."

Downe there comes a fallow° doe,
As great with yong as she might goe.

She lift up his bloudy hed,
And kist his wounds that were so red.

She got him up upon her backe,
And carried him to earthen lake.°

**16 fallow** brown **16 doe** The "doe," often taken as a suggestive description of the knight's beloved, is probably a vestige of the folk belief that an animal may be an enchanted human being. **21 lake** pit

She buried him before the prime,°
She was dead herselfe ere even-song time.

God send every gentleman
Such haukes, such hounds, and such a leman.°

**22 prime** about nine A.M. **25 leman** sweetheart

## ANONYMOUS

# *The Twa Corbies*

As I was walking all alane,
I heard twa corbies° making a mane;°
The tane° unto the t' other say,
"Where sall we gang° and dine to-day?"

"In behint yon auld fail dyke,°
I wot° there lies a new-slain knight;
And naebody kens° that he lies there,
But his hawk, his hound, and lady fair.

"His hound is to the hunting gane,
His hawk, to fetch the wild-fowl hame,
His lady's ta'en another mate,
So we may mak our dinner sweet.

"Ye'll sit on his white hause-bane,°
And I'll pike out his bonny blue een.°
Wi' ae° lock o' his gowden° hair
We'll theek° our nest when it grows bare.

"Mony a one for him makes mane,
But nane sall ken whare he is gane;
O'er his white banes, when they are bare,
The wind sall blaw for evermair."

**2 twa corbies** two ravens. **mane** lament **3 tane** one **4 sall we gang** shall we go **5 auld fail dyke** old turf wall **6 wot** know **7 kens** knows **13 hause-bane** neck bone **14 een** eyes **15 Wi' ae** with one. **gowden** golden **16 theek** thatch

## ANONYMOUS

# *Edward*

"Why dois your brand° sae° drap wi' bluid,
    Edward, Edward?
Why dois your brand sae drap wi' bluid?
    And why sae sad gang° yee, O?"

**1 brand** sword. **sae** so **4 gang** go

"O, I hae killed my hauke sae guid,
Mither, mither,
O, I hae killed my hauke sae guid,
And I had nae mair bot hee, O."
"Your haukis bluid was nevir sae reid,
Edward, Edward,
Your haukis bluid was nevir sae reid,
My deir son I tell thee, O."
"O, I hae killed my reid-roan steid,
Mither, mither,
O, I hae killed my reid-roan steid,
That erst° was sae fair and frie,° O."

"Your steid was auld, and ye hae gat mair,
Edward, Edward,
Your steid was auld, and ye hae gat mair,
Sum other dule° ye drie,° O."
"O, I hae killed my fadir deir,
Mither, mither,
O, I hae killed my fadir deir,
Alas, and wae is mee, O!"

"And whatten penance wul ye drie for that,
Edward, Edward?
And whatten penance wul ye drie for that?
My deir son, now tell me, O."
"Ile set my feit in yonder boat,
Mither, mither,
Ile set my feit in yonder boat,
And Ile fare ovir the sea, O."

"And what wul ye doe wi' your towirs and your ha',°
Edward, Edward,
And what wul ye doe wi' your towirs and your ha',
That were sae fair to see, O?"
"Ile let thame stand tul they doun fa',°
Mither, mither,
Ile let thame stand tul they doun fa',
For here nevir mair maun° I bee, O."
"And what wul ye leive to your bairns° and your wife,
Edward, Edward?
And what wul ye leive to your bairns and your wife,
When ye gang ovir the sea, O?"
"The warldis° room, late° them beg thrae° life,
Mither, mither,
The warldis room, late them beg thrae life,
For thame nevir mair wul I see, O."

**16 erst** once. **frie** spirited **20 dule** grief **drie** suffer **33 ha'** hall **37 fa'** fall **40 maun** must **41 bairns** children **45 warldis** world's. **late** let. **thrae** through

"And what wul ye leive to your ain mither deir,
Edward, Edward?
And what wul ye leive to your ain mither deir?
My deir son, now tell me, O."
"The curse of hell frae me sall ye beir,
Mither, mither,
The curse of hell frae me sall ye beir.
Sic° counseils ye gave to me, O."

**56 Sic** such

## ANONYMOUS

# *John Henry**

John Henry was a very small boy,
Sitting on his mammy's knee;
He picked up a hammer and a little piece of steel,
Saying, "A hammer'll be the death of me, O Lord,
A hammer'll be the death of me."

John Henry went up on the mountain
And he came down on the side.
The mountain was so tall and John Henry was so small
That he laid down his hammer and he cried, "O Lord,"
He laid down his hammer and he cried.

John Henry was a man just six feet in height,
Nearly two feet and a half across the breast.
He'd take a nine-pound hammer and hammer all day long
And never get tired and want to rest, O Lord,
And never get tired and want to rest.

John Henry was a steel-driving man, O Lord,
He drove all over the world.
He come to Big Bend Tunnel on the C. & O. Road
Where he beat the steam drill down, O Lord,
Where he beat the steam drill down.

John Henry said to the captain,
"Captain, you go to town,
Bring me back a twelve-pound hammer
And I'll beat that steam drill down, O Lord,
And I'll beat that steam drill down."

They placed John Henry on the right-hand side,
The steam drill on the left;
He said, "Before I let that steam drill beat me down

*John Henry, a black steel driver from West Virginia, worked on the Chesapeake and Ohio's Big Bend Tunnel around 1870. The steel driver hammered a drill (held by his assistant, the "shaker") into rocks so that explosives could then be poured in. In the 1870s, mechanical steel drills were introduced, displacing the steel driver.

I'll die with my hammer in my hand, O Lord,
And send my soul to rest."

The white folks all got scared,
Thought Big Bend was a-fallin' in;
John Henry hollered out with a very loud shout,
"It's my hammer a-fallin' in the wind, O Lord,
It's my hammer a-fallin' in the wind."

John Henry said to his shaker,
"Shaker, you better pray,
For if I miss that little piece of steel
Tomorrow'll be your buryin' day, O Lord,
Tomorrow'll be your buryin' day."

The man that invented that steam drill
He thought he was mighty fine.
John Henry sunk the steel fourteen feet
While the steam drill only made nine, O Lord,
While the steam drill only made nine.

John Henry said to his loving little wife,
"I'm sick and want to go to bed.
Fix me a place to lay down, Child;
There's a roarin' in my head, O Lord,
There's a roarin' in my head."

## SIR THOMAS WYATT

***Sir Thomas Wyatt (1503–42) was born in England in Kent and educated at Cambridge University. As a member of the court of Henry VIII, he served as ambassador to Spain and to the court of Emperor Charles V. Interested in foreign literature, he introduced the sonnet form into English from Italian. Although his poems circulated in manuscripts, most of them were not published until after his death.***

### *They Flee from Me*

They flee from me that sometime did me seek
With naked foot stalking in my chamber.
I have seen them gentle, tame, and meek
That now are wild and do not remember
That sometime they put themselves in danger
To take bread at my hand; and now they range
Busily seeking with a continual change.

Thankèd be Fortune, it hath been otherwise
Twenty times better; but once in special,
In thin array after a pleasant guise,
When her loose gown from her shoulders did fall,

And she me caught in her arms long and small,°
And therewithall sweetly did me kiss,
And softly said, "Dear heart, how like you this?"

It was no dream; I lay broad waking.
But all is turned thorough my gentleness
Into a strange fashion of forsaking;
And I have leave to go of her goodness,
And she also to use newfangleness.
But since that I so kindely° am served,
I fain would know what she hath deserved.

[*1557*]

**12 small** narrow **20 kindely** naturally, kindly (ironic)

## WILLIAM SHAKESPEARE

***William Shakespeare (1564–1616), born in Stratford-upon-Avon in England, is chiefly known as a dramatic poet, but he also wrote nondramatic poetry. In 1609 a volume of 154 of his sonnets was published, apparently without his permission. Probably he chose to keep his sonnets unpublished not because he thought that they were of little value, but because it was more prestigious to be an amateur poet (unpublished) than a professional (published) poet. Although the sonnets were published in 1609, they were probably written in the mid-1590s, when there was a vogue for sonneteering. A contemporary writer in 1598 said that Shakespeare's "sugred Sonnets [circulate] among his private friends."***

## *Sonnet 29*

When, in disgrace with Fortune and men's eyes,
I all alone beweep my outcast state,
And trouble deaf heaven with my bootless° cries,
And look upon myself and curse my fate,
Wishing me like to one more rich in hope,
Featured like him, like him° with friends possessed,
Desiring this man's art, and that man's scope,
With what I most enjoy contented least;
Yet in these thoughts myself almost despising,
Haply° I think on thee, and then my state,
Like to the lark at break of day arising
From sullen earth, sings hymns at heaven's gate;
For thy sweet love rememb'red such wealth brings,
That then I scorn to change my state with kings.

**3 bootless** useless **6 like him, like him** like a second man, like a third man
**10 Haply** perchance

## Sonnet 73

That time of year thou mayst in me behold
When yellow leaves, or none, or few, do hang
Upon those boughs which shake against the cold,
Bare ruined choirs° where late the sweet birds sang.
In me thou see'st the twilight of such day
As after sunset fadeth in the west,
Which by-and-by black night doth take away,
Death's second self that seals up all in rest,
In me thou see'st the glowing of such fire
That on the ashes of his youth doth lie,
As the deathbed whereon it must expire,
Consumed with that which it was nourished by.
  This thou perceiv'st, which makes thy love more strong,
  To love that well which thou must leave ere long.

**4 choir** the part of the church where services were sung

## Sonnet 116

Let me not to the marriage of true minds
Admit impediments; love is not love
Which alters when it alteration finds,
Or bends with the remover to remove.
O, no, it is an ever-fixèd mark°
That looks on tempests and is never shaken;
It is the star° to every wand'ring bark,
Whose worth's unknown, although his height be taken.
Love's not Time's fool,° though rosy lips and cheeks
Within his bending sickle's compass° come;
Love alters not with his° brief hours and weeks
But bears° it out even to the edge of doom.°
  If this be error and upon me proved,
  I never writ, nor no man ever loved.

**5 mark** guide to mariners **7 star** the North Star **9 fool** plaything **10 compass** range **11 his** Time's **12 bears** endures. **doom** Judgment Day

## Sonnet 146

Poor soul, the center of my sinful earth,
My sinful earth° these rebel pow'rs that thee array,
Why dost thou pine within and suffer dearth,
Painting thy outward walls so costly gay?

**2 My sinful earth** doubtless an error made by the printer of the first edition (1609), who mistakenly repeated the end of the first line. Among suggested corrections are "Thrall to," "Fooled by," "Rebuke these," "Leagued with," and "Feeding."

Why so large cost,° having so short a lease,
Dost thou upon thy fading mansion spend?
Shall worms, inheritors of this excess,
Eat up thy charge? Is this thy body's end?
Then, soul, live thou upon thy servant's loss,
And let that pine to aggravate thy store;
Buy terms divine° in selling hours of dross;
Within be fed, without be rich no more.
  So shalt thou feed on Death, that feeds on men,
  And death once dead, there's no more dying then.

**5 cost** expense **11 Buy terms divine** buy ages of immortality

## JOHN DONNE

*John Donne (1572–1631) was born into a Roman Catholic family in England, but in the 1590s he abandoned that faith. In 1615 he became an Anglican priest and soon was known as a great preacher. A hundred and sixty of his sermons survive, including one with the famous line "No man is an island, entire of itself; every man is a piece of the continent, a part of the main; if a clod be washed away by the sea, Europe is the less . . . ; and therefore never send to know for whom the bell tolls; it tolls for thee." From 1621 until his death he was dean of St. Paul's Cathedral in London. Most of his love poems (often bawdy and cynical) are said to be his early work, and his "Holy Sonnets" (among the greatest religious poems written in English) his later work.*

### *A Valediction: Forbidding Mourning*

As virtuous men pass mildly away;
  And whisper to their souls, to go,
Whilst some of their sad friends do say,
  "The breath goes now," and some say, "No":

So let us melt, and make no noise.
  No tear-floods, nor sigh-tempests move.
'Twere profanation of our joys
  To tell the laity our love.

Moving of the earth° brings harms and fears,
  Men reckon what it did and meant;
But trepidation of the spheres,
  Though greater far, is innocent.°

**9 moving of the earth** an earthquake **12 But . . . innocent** But the movement of the heavenly spheres (in Ptolemaic astronomy), though far greater, is harmless.

Dull sublunary° lovers' love
(Whose soul is sense) cannot admit
Absence, because it doth remove
Those things which elemented it.

But we, by a love so much refined
That our selves know not what it is,
Inter-assuréd of the mind,
Care less, eyes, lips, and hands to miss.

Our two souls therefore, which are one,
Though I must go, endure not yet
A breach, but an expansion,
Like gold to airy thinness beat.

If they be two, they are two so
As stiff twin compasses° are two:
Thy soul, the fixed foot, makes no show
To move, but doth, if the other do.

And though it in the center sit,
Yet when the other far doth roam,
It leans, and hearkens after it,
And grows erect, as that comes home.

Such wilt thou be to me, who must
Like the other foot, obliquely run:
Thy firmness makes my circle just,
And makes me end where I begun.

[*1633*]

**13 sublunary** under the moon, i.e., earthly **26 twin compasses** a carpenter's compass, used for making circles

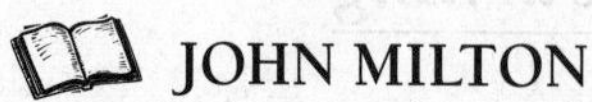

## JOHN MILTON

***John Milton (1608–74) was born into a well-to-do family in London, where from childhood he was a student of languages, mastering at an early age Latin, Greek, Hebrew and most modern languages. He graduated from Cambridge University with a B.A. and an M.A. Instead of becoming a minister in the Anglican Church, he resolved to become a poet and spent the next five years at his family's country home, reading. His attacks against the monarchy secured him a position in Oliver Cromwell's Puritan government as Secretary of Foreign Tongues to the Council of State. He became totally blind, but he continued his work through secretaries, one of whom was Andrew Marvell, author of "To His Coy Mistress" (page 931). With the restoration of the monarchy in 1660, Milton was for a time confined but was later pardoned in the general amnesty. Until his death he continued to work on many subjects, including his greatest poem, the***

*epic* Paradise Lost, *and a poetic drama,* Samson Agonistes, *about the blind Hebrew hero.*

## *When I consider how my light is spent*

When I consider how my light is spent
  Ere half my days, in this dark world and wide,
  And that one talent which is death to hide°
  Lodged with me useless,° though my soul more bent
To serve therewith my Maker, and present
  My true account, lest he returning chide;
  "Doth God exact day-labor, light denied?"
  I fondly° ask; but Patience to prevent°
That murmur, soon replies, "God doth not need
  Either man's work or his own gifts; who best
  Bear his mild yoke, they serve him best. His state
Is kingly. Thousands at his bidding speed
  And post o'er land and ocean without rest:
  They also serve who only stand and wait."

[*1673*]

**3 talent . . . hide** There is a pun here, relating Milton's literary talent to Christ's "Parable of the Talents" (Matthew 25.14 ff.), in which a servant is rebuked for not putting his talent (a unit of money) to use. **4 useless** a pun on *use,* i.e., usury, interest **8 fondly** foolishly. **prevent** forestall

## JOSEPH ADDISON

*Joseph Addison (1672–1719), an English essayist and poet, was perhaps the most influential literary critic of his day. His essays, written chiefly for two newspapers (*The Tatler *and* The Spectator*), were immensely popular and they remain highly esteemed today, at least by teachers of English.*

*In one issue of* The Spectator *(No. 465, August 23, 1712) Addison published the poem that we reprint here, a version of Psalm 19: He called it simply "Ode." (An ode is a song of praise, specifically of an exalted subject such as heroism, or one's nation, or God.) In the essay he introduced the poem thus:*

> *The Supream Being has made the best Arguments for his own Existence, in the Formation of the Heavens and the Earth, and these are Arguments which a Man of Sense cannot forbear attending to, who is out of the Noise and Hurry of Human Affairs. Aristotle says, that should a Man live under Ground, and there converse with Works of Art and Mechanism, and should afterwards be brought up into the open Day, and see the several Glories of the Heav'n and Earth, he*

*would immediately pronounce them the Works of such a Being as we define God to be.*

*What Addison is here offering is his version of the Argument from Design, the argument that the world obviously is a designed thing, like, say, a watch, and therefore there must be a designer, God.*

## *Ode*

The Spacious Firmament on high,
With all the blue Etherial Sky,
And spangled Heav'ns, a Shining Frame,
Their great Original proclaim:
Th'unwearied Sun, from Day to Day,
Does his Creator's Power display,
And publishes to every land
The Work of an Almighty Hand.

Soon as the Evening Shades prevail,
The Moon takes up the wondrous Tale,
And nightly to the listning Earth
Repeats the Story of her Birth:
Whilst all the Stars that round her burn,
And all the Planets, in their turn,
Confirm the Tidings as they rowl,
And spread the truth from Pole to Pole.

What Though, in solemn Silence, all
Move round the dark terrestrial Ball?
What tho' nor real Voice nor Sound
Amid their radiant Orbs be found?
In Reason's Ear they all rejoice,
And utter forth a glorious Voice,
For ever singing, as they shine,
"The Hand that made us is Divine."

[*1712*]

# WILLIAM BLAKE

*William Blake (1757–1827) was born in London and at age 14 was apprenticed for seven years to an engraver. A Christian visionary poet, he made his living by giving drawing lessons and by illustrating books, including his own* Songs of Innocence *(1789) and* Songs of Experience *(1794). These two books represent, he said, "two contrary states of the human soul." ("The Lamb" comes from* Innocence, *"The Tyger" from* Experience.*) In 1809 Blake exhibited his art, but the show was a failure. Not until he*

***was in his sixties, when he stopped writing poetry, did he achieve any public recognition—and then it was as a painter.***

## *The Lamb*

Little Lamb, who made thee?
Dost thou know who made thee?
Gave thee life, and bid thee feed
By the stream and o'er the mead;
Gave thee clothing of delight,
Softest clothing, wooly, bright;
Gave thee such a tender voice,
Making all the vales rejoice?
Little Lamb, who made thee?
Dost thou know who made thee?

Little Lamb, I'll tell thee,
Little Lamb, I'll tell thee:
He is calléd by thy name,
For he calls himself a Lamb.
He is meek, and he is mild;
He became a little child.
I a child, and thou a lamb,
We are calléd by his name.
Little Lamb, God bless thee!
Little Lamb, God bless thee!

[*1789*]

## *The Tyger*

Tyger! Tyger! burning bright
In the forests of the night,
What immortal hand or eye
Could frame thy fearful symmetry?

In what distant deeps or skies
Burnt the fire of thine eyes?
On what wings dare he aspire?
What the hand dare seize the fire?

And what shoulder, and what art,
Could twist the sinews of thy heart?
And, when thy heart began to beat,
What dread hand? and what dread feet?

What the hammer? what the chain?
In what furnace was thy brain?
What the anvil? what dread grasp
Dare its deadly terrors clasp?

When the stars threw down their spears,
And watered heaven with their tears,
Did he smile his work to see?
Did he who made the lamb make thee?

Tyger! Tyger! burning bright
In the forests of the night,
What immortal hand or eye,
Dare frame thy fearful symmetry?

[*1793*]

## *London*

I wander thro' each charter'd street,
Near where the charter'd Thames does flow,
And mark in every face I meet
Marks of weakness, marks of woe.

In every cry of every Man,
In every Infant's cry of fear,
In every voice, in every ban,
The mind-forg'd manacles I hear.

How the Chimney-sweeper's cry
Every black'ning Church appalls;
And the hapless Soldier's sigh
Runs in blood down Palace walls.

But most thro' midnight streets I hear
How the youthful Harlot's curse
Blasts the new-born Infant's tear,
And blights with plagues the Marriage hearse.

[*1794*]

## *The Echoing Green*

The Sun does arise,
And make happy the skies;
The merry bells ring
To welcome the Spring;
The skylark and thrush,
The birds of the bush,
Sing louder around
To the bells' cheerful sound,
While our sports shall be seen
On the Echoing Green.

Old John, with white hair,
Does laugh away care,
Sitting under the oak,
Among the old folk.
They laugh at our play,

And soon they all say:
"Such, such were the joys
When we all, girls and boys,
In our youth time were seen
On the Echoing Green."

Till the little ones, weary,
No more can be merry;
The sun does descend,
And our sports have an end.
Round the laps of their mothers
Many sisters and brothers,
Like birds in their nest,
Are ready for rest,
And sport no more seen
On the darkening Green.

[*1789*]

## WILLIAM WORDSWORTH

*William Wordsworth (1770–1850), the son of an attorney, grew up in the Lake District of England. After graduating from Cambridge University in 1791, he spent a year in France, falling in love with a French girl, by whom he had a daughter. His enthusiasm for the French Revolution waned, and he returned alone to England where, with the help of a legacy, he devoted his life to poetry. With his friend, Samuel Taylor Coleridge, in 1798 he published anonymously a volume of poetry,* Lyrical Ballads, *which changed the course of English poetry. In 1799 he and his sister Dorothy settled in Grasmere in the Lake District, where he married and was given the office of distributor of stamps. In 1843 he was appointed poet laureate.*

# *The World Is Too Much with Us*

The world is too much with us; late and soon,
Getting and spending, we lay waste our powers;
Little we see in Nature that is ours;
We have given our hearts away, a sordid boon!°
This Sea that bares her bosom to the moon,
The winds that will be howling at all hours,
And are up-gathered now like sleeping flowers,
For this, for everything, we are out of tune;
It moves us not.—Great God! I'd rather be
A Pagan suckled in a creed outworn;

**4 boon** gift

So might I, standing on this pleasant lea,
Have glimpses that would make me less forlorn;
Have sight of Proteus° rising from the sea;
Or hear old Triton° blow his wreathéd horn.

[*1807*]

**13, 14 Proteus, Triton** sea gods

# *I Wandered Lonely as a Cloud*

I wandered lonely as a cloud
That floats on high o'er vales and hills,
When all at once I saw a crowd,
A host, of golden daffodils,
Beside the lake, beneath the trees,
Fluttering and dancing in the breeze.

Continuous as the stars that shine
And twinkle on the milky way,
They stretched in never-ending line
Along the margin of a bay;
Ten thousand saw I at a glance,
Tossing their heads in sprightly dance.

The waves beside them danced, but they
Outdid the sparkling waves in glee;
A poet could not but be gay,
In such a jocund company;
I gazed—and gazed—but little thought
What wealth the show to me had brought:

For oft, when on my couch I lie
In vacant or in pensive mood,
They flash upon that inward eye
Which is the bliss of solitude;
And then my heart with pleasure fills,
And dances with the daffodils.

[*1807*]

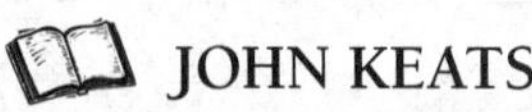

## JOHN KEATS

*John Keats (1795–1821), son of a London stable keeper, was taken out of school when he was 15 and was apprenticed to a surgeon and apothecary. In 1816 he was licensed to practice as an apothecary-surgeon, but he almost immediately abandoned medicine and decided to make a career as a poet. His progress was amazing; he quickly moved from routine verse to major accomplishments, publishing books of poems—to mixed reviews—in 1817, 1818, and 1820, before dying of tuberculosis at the age of 25. Today he is esteemed as one of England's greatest poets.*

# *La Belle Dame sans Merci**

O what can ail thee, knight-at-arms,
Alone and palely loitering?
The sedge has withered from the lake,
And no birds sing.

O what can ail thee, knight-at-arms,
So haggard and so woe-begone?
The squirrel's granary is full,
And the harvest's done.

I see a lily on thy brow,
With anguish moist and fever dew,
And on thy cheeks a fading rose
Fast withereth too.

"I met a lady in the meads,
Full beautiful—a faery's child,
Her hair was long, her foot was light,
And her eyes were wild.

"I made a garland for her head,
And bracelets too, and fragrant zone;°
She looked at me as she did love,
And made sweet moan.

"I set her on my pacing steed,
And nothing else saw all day long,
For sidelong would she bend and sing
A faery's song.

"She found me roots of relish sweet,
And honey wild, and manna dew,
And sure in language strange she said
'I love thee true.'

"She took me to her elfin grot,
And there she wept and sighed full sore,
And there I shut her wild wild eyes
With kisses four.

"And there she lulléd me asleep,
And there I dreamed—Ah! woe betide!
The latest dream I ever dreamt
On the cold hill side.

"I saw pale kings and princes too,
Pale warriors, death-pale were they all;
They cried, 'La Belle Dame sans Merci
Thee hath in thrall!'

***La Belle Dame sans Merci** the beautiful pitiless lady **18 fragrant zone** belt of flowers

"I saw their starved lips in the gloam
With horrid warning gapéd wide,
And I awoke, and found me here,
On the cold hill's side.

"And this is why I sojourn here,
Alone and palely loitering,
Though the sedge is withered from the lake,
And no birds sing."

[*1819*]

## *To Autumn*

### *I*

Season of mists and mellow fruitfulness,
Close bosom-friend of the maturing sun;
Conspiring with him how to load and bless
With fruit the vines that round the thatch-eaves run;
To bend with apples the mossed cottage-trees,
And fill all fruit with ripeness to the core;
To swell the gourd, and plump the hazel shells
With a sweet kernel; to set budding more,
And still more, later flowers for the bees,
Until they think warm days will never cease,
For summer has o'er-brimmed their clammy cells.

### *II*

Who hath not seen thee oft amid thy store?
Sometimes whoever seeks abroad may find
Thee sitting careless on a granary floor,
Thy hair soft-lifted by the winnowing wind;
Or on a half-reaped furrow sound asleep,
Drowsed with the fume of poppies, while thy hook
Spares the next swath and all its twinéd flowers:
And sometime like a gleaner thou dost keep
Steady thy laden head across a brook;
Or by a cider-press, with patient look,
Thou watchest the last oozings hours by hours.

### *III*

Where are the songs of Spring? Ay, where are they?
Think not of them, thou hast thy music too,—
While barred clouds bloom the soft-dying day,
And touch the stubble-plains with rosy hue;
Then in a wailful choir the small gnats mourn
Among the river sallows, borne aloft
Or sinking as the light wind lives or dies;

And full-grown lambs loud bleat from hilly bourn;
Hedge-crickets sing; and now with treble soft
The red-breast whistles from a garden-croft;
And gathering swallows twitter in the skies.

[*1819*]

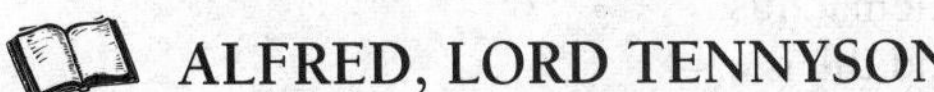

## ALFRED, LORD TENNYSON

*Alfred, Lord Tennyson (1809–92), the son of an English clergyman, was born in Lincolnshire, where he began writing verse at age 5. Educated at Cambridge, he had to leave without a degree when his father died and Alfred had to accept responsibility for bringing up his brothers and sisters. In fact, the family had inherited ample funds, but for some years the money was tied up by litigation. Following Wordsworth's death in 1850, Tennyson was made poet laureate. With his government pension he moved with his family to the Isle of Wight, where he lived in comfort until his death.*

### *Ulysses**

It little profits that an idle king,
By this still hearth, among these barren crags,
Matched with an aged wife, I mete and dole
Unequal laws unto a savage race,
That hoard, and sleep, and feed, and know not me.
I cannot rest from travel; I will drink
Life to the lees. All times I have enjoyed
Greatly, have suffered greatly, both with those
That loved me, and alone; on shore, and when
Thro' scudding drifts the rainy Hyades
Vext the dim sea. I am become a name;
For always roaming with a hungry heart
Much have I seen and known,—cities of men
And manners, climates, councils, governments,
Myself not least, but honored of them all,—
And drunk delight of battle with my peers,
Far on the ringing plains of windy Troy.
I am a part of all that I have met;
Yet all experience is an arch wherethro'
Gleams that untravelled world whose margin fades
For ever and for ever when I move.
How dull it is to pause, to make an end,
To rust unburnished, not to shine in use!
As tho' to breathe were life! Life piled on life
Were all too little, and of one to me
Little remains; but every hour is saved
From that eternal silence, something more,

***Ulysses** Odysseus, King of Ithaca, a leader of the Greeks in the Trojan War, famous for his ten years of journeying to remote places.

A bringer of new things; and vile it were
For some three suns to store and hoard myself,
And this gray spirit yearning in desire
To follow knowledge like a sinking star,
Beyond the utmost bound of human thought.

This is my son, mine own Telemachus,
To whom I leave the scepter and the isle,—
Well-loved of me, discerning to fulfill
This labor, by slow prudence to make mild
A rugged people, and thro' soft degrees
Subdue them to the useful and the good.
Most blameless is he, centered in the sphere
Of common duties, decent not to fail
In offices of tenderness, and pay
Meet adoration to my household gods,
When I am gone. He works his work, I mine.

There lies the port; the vessel puffs her sail;
There gloom the dark, broad seas. My mariners,
Souls that have toiled, and wrought, and thought with me,—
That ever with a frolic welcome took
The thunder and the sunshine, and opposed
Free hearts, free foreheads,—you and I are old;
Old age hath yet his honor and his toil.
Death closes all; but something ere the end,
Some work of noble note, may yet be done,
Not unbecoming men that strove with Gods.
The lights begin to twinkle from the rocks;
The long day wanes; the slow moon climbs; the deep
Moans round with many voices. Come, my friends.
'Tis not too late to seek a newer world.
Push off, and sitting well in order smite
The sounding furrows; for my purpose holds
To sail beyond the sunset, and the baths
Of all the western stars, until I die.
It may be that the gulfs will wash us down;
It may be we shall touch the Happy Isles,
And see the great Achilles, whom we knew.
Tho' much is taken, much abides; and tho'
We are not now that strength which in old days
Moved earth and heaven, that which we are, we are.
One equal temper of heroic hearts,
Made weak by time and fate, but strong in will
To strive, to seek, to find, and not to yield.

[*1833*]

## MATTHEW ARNOLD

*Matthew Arnold (1822-88) was the son of a famous educator, Dr. Thomas Arnold, the headmaster of Rugby*

*School. After graduating from Oxford, Matthew Arnold became an inspector of schools, a post he held until two years before his death. Besides writing poetry, Arnold wrote literary criticism and was appointed professor of poetry at Oxford from 1857 to 1867. He traveled widely on the Continent and lectured in the United States.*

## *Dover Beach*

The sea is calm to-night.
The tide is full, the moon lies fair
Upon the straits;—on the French coast the light
Gleams and is gone; the cliffs of England stand,
Glimmering and vast, out in the tranquil bay.
Come to the window, sweet is the night-air!
Only, from the long line of spray
Where the sea meets the moon-blanch'd land,
Listen! you hear the grating roar
Of pebbles which the waves draw back, and fling,
At their return, up the high strand,
Begin, and cease, and then again begin,
With tremulous cadence slow, and bring
The eternal note of sadness in.

Sophocles long ago
Heard it on the Ægean, and it brought
Into his mind the turbid ebb and flow
Of human misery; we
Find also in the sound a thought,
Hearing it by this distant northern sea.

The Sea of Faith
Was once, too, at the full, and round earth's shore
Lay like the folds of a bright girdle furl'd.
But now I only hear
Its melancholy, long, withdrawing roar,
Retreating, to the breath
Of the night-wind, down the vast edges drear
And naked shingles° of the world.

Ah, love, let us be true
To one another! for the world, which seems
To lie before us like a land of dreams,
So various, so beautiful, so new,
Hath really neither joy, nor love, nor light,
Nor certitude, nor peace, nor help for pain;
And we are here as on a darkling plain
Swept with confused alarms of struggle and flight,
Where ignorant armies clash by night.

[*c. 1851*]

**28 shingles** pebbled beaches

## THOMAS HARDY

*Thomas Hardy (1840–1928) was born in Dorset, England, the son of a stonemason. Despite great obstacles he studied the classics and architecture, and in 1862 he moved to London to study and practice as an architect. Ill health forced him to return to Dorset, where he continued to work as an architect and to write. Best known for his novels, Hardy ceased writing fiction after the hostile reception of* Jude the Obscure *in 1896 and turned to writing lyric poetry.*

## *Ah, Are You Digging on My Grave?*

"Ah, are you digging on my grave,
  My loved one?—planting rue?"
—"No: yesterday he went to wed
One of the brightest wealth has bred.
'It cannot hurt her now,' he said,
  'That I should not be true.'"

"Then who is digging on my grave?
  My nearest dearest kin?"
—"Ah, no: they sit and think, 'What use!
What good will planting flowers produce?
No tendance of her mound can loose
  Her spirit from Death's gin.'"

"But some one digs upon my grave?
  My enemy?—prodding sly?"
—"Nay: When she heard you had passed the Gate
That shuts on all flesh soon or late,
She thought you no more worth her hate,
  And cares not where you lie."

"Then, who is digging on my grave?
  Say—since I have not guessed!"
—"O it is I, my mistress dear,
Your little dog, who still lives near,
And much I hope my movements here
  Have not disturbed your rest?"

"Ah, yes! *You* dig upon my grave . . .
  Why flashed it not on me
That one true heart was left behind!
What feeling do we ever find
To equal among human kind
  A dog's fidelity!"

"Mistress, I dug upon your grave
  To bury a bone, in case
I should be hungry near this spot

When passing on my daily trot.
I am sorry, but I quite forgot
It was your resting-place."

[*1914*]

# *The Convergence of the Twain*

Lines on the Loss of the Titanic

### *I*

In a solitude of the sea
Deep from human vanity,
And the Pride of Life that planned her, stilly couches she.

### *II*

Steel chambers, late the pyres
Of her salamandrine fires,
Cold currents thrid,° and turn to rhythmic tidal lyres.

### *III*

Over the mirrors meant
To glass the opulent
The sea-worm crawls—grotesque, slimed, dumb, indifferent.

### *IV*

Jewels in joy designed
To ravish the sensuous mind
Lie lightless, all their sparkles bleared and black and blind.

### *V*

Dim moon-eyed fishes near
Gaze at the gilded gear
And query: "What does this vaingloriousness down here?"

### *VI*

Well: while was fashioning
This creature of cleaving wing,
The Immanent Will that stirs and urges everything

**6 thrid** thread

### *VII*

Prepared a sinister mate
For her—so gaily great—
A Shape of Ice, for the time far and dissociate.

### *VIII*

And as the smart ship grew
In stature, grace, and hue,
In shadowy silent distance grew the Iceberg too.

### *IX*

Alien they seemed to be:
No mortal eye could see
The intimate welding of their later history,

### *X*

Or sign that they were bent
By paths coincident
On being anon twin halves of one august event,

### *XI*

Till the Spinner of the Years
Said "Now!" And each one hears,
And consummation comes, and jars two hemispheres.

[*1912*]

## GERARD MANLEY HOPKINS

*Gerard Manley Hopkins (1844–89) was born near London and was educated at Oxford, where he studied the classics. A convert from Anglicanism to Roman Catholicism, he was ordained a Jesuit priest in 1877. After serving as a parish priest and teacher, he was appointed Professor of Greek at the Catholic University in Dublin.*

*Hopkins published only a few poems during his lifetime, partly because he believed that the pursuit of literary fame was incompatible with his vocation as a priest, and partly because he was aware that his highly individual style might puzzle readers.*

## *God's Grandeur*

The world is charged with the grandeur of God.
It will flame out, like shining from shook foil;
It gathers to a greatness, like the ooze of oil

Crushed. Why do men then now not reck his rod?
Generations have trod, have trod, have trod;
And all is seared with trade; bleared, smeared with toil;
And wears man's smudge and shares man's smell: the soil
Is bare now, nor can foot feel, being shod.

And for all this, nature is never spent;
There lives the dearest freshness deep down things;
And though the last lights off the black West went
Oh, morning, at the brown brink eastward, springs—
Because the Holy Ghost over the bent
World broods with warm breast and with ah! bright wings.

[*1877*]

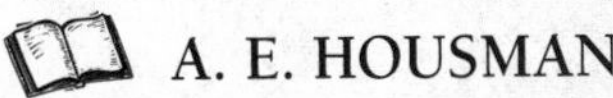

## A. E. HOUSMAN

*Alfred Edward Housman (1859-1936) was born in rural Shropshire, England, and educated in classics and philosophy at Oxford University. Although he was a brilliant student, his final examination was unexpectedly weak—in fact, he failed—and he did not receive the academic appointment that he had anticipated. He began working as a civil servant at the British Patent Office, but in his spare time he wrote scholarly articles on Latin literature, and these writings in 1892 won him an appointment as Professor of Latin at the University of London. In 1911 he was appointed to Cambridge. During his lifetime he published (in addition to his scholarly writings) only two thin books of poetry,* A Shropshire Lad *(1898) and* Last Poems *(1922), and a highly readable lecture called* The Name and Nature of Poetry *(1933). After his death a third book of poems,* More Poems *(1936), was published.*

## *Shropshire Lad #19 (To an Athlete Dying Young)*

The time you won your town the race
We chaired you through the market-place;
Man and boy stood cheering by,
And home we brought you shoulder-high.

Today, the road all runners come,
Shoulder-high we bring you home,
And set you at your threshold down,
Townsman of a stiller town.

Smart lad, to slip betimes away
From fields where glory does not stay
And early though the laurel grows
It withers quicker than the rose.

Eyes the shady night has shut
Cannot see the record cut,
And silence sounds no worse than cheers
After earth has stopped the ears:

Now you will not swell the rout
Of lads that wore their honors out,
Runners whom renown outran
And the name died before the man.

So set, before its echoes fade,
The fleet foot on the sill of shade,
And hold to the low lintel° up
The still-defended challenge-cup.

And round that early-laureled head
Will flock to gaze the strengthless dead,
And find unwithered on its curls
The garland briefer than a girl's.

[*1896*]

**23 lintel** beam over a doorway

## WILLIAM BUTLER YEATS

*William Butler Yeats (1865–1939) was born in Dublin, Ireland. The early Yeats was much interested in highly lyrical, romantic poetry, often drawing on Irish mythology. The later poems, from about 1910 (and especially after Yeats met Ezra Pound in 1911), are often more colloquial. Although these later poems often employ mythological references, too, one feels that the poems are more down-to-earth. He was awarded the Nobel Prize in Literature in 1923.*

### *Leda and the Swan**

A sudden blow: the great wings beating still
Above the staggering girl, her thighs caressed
By the dark webs, her nape caught in his bill,
He holds her helpless breast upon his breast.

How can those terrified vague fingers push
The feathered glory from her loosening thighs?
And how can body, laid in that white rush,
But feel the strange heart beating where it lies?

***Leda and the Swan** According to Greek mythology, Zeus fell in love with Leda, disguised himself as a swan, and raped her. Among the offspring of this union were Helen and Clytemnestra. Paris, a Trojan, abducted Helen, causing the Greeks to raze Troy; Clytemnestra, wife of the Greek general Agamemnon, murdered her husband on his triumphant return to Greece.

A shudder in the loins engenders there
The broken wall, the burning roof and tower
And Agamemnon dead.
                                        Being so caught up,
So mastered by the brute blood of the air,
Did she put on his knowledge with his power
Before the indifferent beak could let her drop?

[*1923*]

## *Sailing to Byzantium**

### I

That is no country for old men. The young
In one another's arms, birds in the trees
—Those dying generations—at their song,
The salmon-falls, the mackerel-crowded seas,
Fish, flesh, or fowl, commend all summer long
Whatever is begotten, born, and dies.
Caught in that sensual music all neglect
Monuments of unaging intellect.

### II

An aged man is but a paltry thing,
A tattered coat upon a stick, unless
Soul clap its hands and sing, and louder sing
For every tatter in its mortal dress.
Nor is there singing school but studying
Monuments of its own magnificence;
And therefore I have sailed the seas and come
To the holy city of Byzantium.

### III

O sages standing in God's holy fire
As in the gold mosaic of a wall,
Come from the holy fire, perne° in a gyre,
And be the singing-masters of my soul.
Consume my heart away; sick with desire
And fastened to a dying animal
It knows not what it is; and gather me
Into the artifice of eternity.

### IV

Once out of nature I shall never take
My bodily form from any natural thing,

***Byzantium** The modern Istanbul. Byzantium was the chief city of the Roman Empire in the east and the capital of Eastern Christianity. **19 perne** whirl down

But such a form as Grecian goldsmiths make
Of hammered gold and gold enameling
To keep a drowsy Emperor awake;
Or set upon a golden bough to sing
To lords and ladies of Byzantium
Of what is past, or passing, or to come.

[*1926*]

## *For Anne Gregory**

"Never shall a young man,
Thrown into despair
By those great honey-coloured
Ramparts at your ear
Love you for yourself alone
And not your yellow hair."

"But I can get a hair-dye
And set such colour there,
Brown, or black, or carrot,
That young men in despair
May love me for myself alone
And not my yellow hair."

"I heard an old religious man
But yesternight declare
That he had found a text to prove
That only God, my dear,
Could love you for yourself alone
And not your yellow hair."

[*1930*]

***Anne Gregory** Yeats was 65 when he wrote this poem for Anne Gregory, the 19-year-old granddaughter of Lady Augusta Gregory, a woman whom Yeats had admired.

# EDWIN ARLINGTON ROBINSON

*Edwin Arlington Robinson (1869–1935) grew up in Gardiner, Maine, spent two years at Harvard, and then returned to Maine, where he published his first book of poetry in 1896. Though he received encouragement from neighbors, his finances were precarious, even after President Theodore Roosevelt, having been made aware of the book, secured for him an appointment as customs inspector in New York from 1905 to 1909. Additional books won fame for Robinson, and in 1922 he was awarded the first of the three Pulitzer Prizes for poetry that he would win.*

## *Richard Cory*

Whenever Richard Cory went down town,
We people on the pavement looked at him:
He was a gentleman from sole to crown,
Clean favored, and imperially slim.

And he was always quietly arrayed,
And he was always human when he talked;
But still he fluttered pulses when he said,
"Good-morning," and he glittered when he walked.

And he was rich—yes, richer than a king—
And admirably schooled in every grace:
In fine, we thought that he was everything
To make us wish that we were in his place.

So on we worked, and waited for the light,
And went without the meat, and cursed the bread;
And Richard Cory, one calm summer night,
Went home and put a bullet through his head.

[*1896*]

# WILLIAM CARLOS WILLIAMS

***William Carlos Williams (1883-1963) was the son of an English traveling salesman and a Basque-Jewish woman. The couple met in Puerto Rico and settled in Rutherford, New Jersey, where William was born. He spent his life there, practicing as a pediatrician and writing poems in the moments between seeing patients who visited his office.***

## *Spring and All*

By the road to the contagious hospital
under the surge of the blue
mottled clouds driven from the
northeast—a cold wind. Beyond, the
waste of broad, muddy fields
brown with dried weeds, standing and fallen

patches of standing water
the scattering of tall trees

All along the road the reddish
purplish, forked, upstanding, twiggy
stuff of bushes and small trees
with dead, brown leaves under them
leafless vines—

Lifeless in appearance, sluggish
dazed spring approaches—

They enter the new world naked,
cold, uncertain of all
save that they enter. All about them
the cold, familiar wind—

Now the grass, tomorrow
the stiff curl of wildcarrot leaf
One by one objects are defined—
It quickens: clarity, outline of leaf

But now the stark dignity of
entrance—Still, the profound change
has come upon them: rooted, they
grip down and begin to awaken

[*1923*]

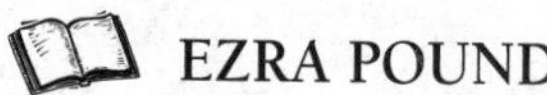

## EZRA POUND

*Ezra Pound (1885-1972), born in Hailey, Idaho, and raised in Philadelphia, was one of the most influential American poets of the twentieth century. He prepared to be a teacher of medieval and Renaissance Spanish, Italian, and French literature, but his career as an academician ended abruptly when he was fired from Wabash College for having a woman in his room overnight. Pound went to Venice, where he did odd jobs, and then to London, where he met T. S. Eliot and played a large role in editing Eliot's long poem,* The Waste Land. *Among the other poets whom he assisted was Robert Frost, who was then living in England. In 1924 Pound settled in Italy. He espoused Mussolini's cause, was arrested by the American forces in 1944, and (having been declared insane and therefore not fit to be tried for treason) was confined in a mental institution in Washington, D.C. Released in 1958, he spent the remainder of his life in Italy.*

*"The River-Merchant's Wife" is based on an English translation of a Chinese poem by Li Po (700?-762). "In a Station of the Metro" is an "Imagist poem," a poem based on (in Pound's words) a "luminous detail" presented concretely and directly.*

## *The River-Merchant's Wife: A Letter*

While my hair was still cut straight across my forehead
I played about the front gate, pulling flowers.
You came by on bamboo stilts, playing horse,

You walked about my seat, playing with blue plums.
And we went on living in the village of Chokan:°
Two small people, without dislike or suspicion.
At fourteen I married My Lord you.
I never laughed, being bashful.
Lowering my head, I looked at the wall.
Called to, a thousand times, I never looked back.

At fifteen I stopped scowling,
I desired my dust to be mingled with yours
Forever and forever and forever.
Why should I climb the lookout?

At sixteen you departed,
You went into far Ku-to-yen,° by the river of swirling eddies,
And you have been gone five months.
The monkeys make sorrowful noise overhead.

You dragged your feet when you went out.
By the gate now, the moss is grown, the different mosses,
Too deep to clear them away!
The leaves fall early this autumn, in wind.
The paired butterflies are already yellow with August
Over the grass in the West garden;
They hurt me. I grow older.
If you are coming down through the narrows of the river Kiang,
Please let me know before hand,
And I will come out to meet you
  As far as Cho-fu-sa.°

[*1915*]

**5 Chokan** Chang-kan, near Nanking **16 Ku-to-yen** an island several hundred miles up the river Kiang from Nanking **29 Cho-fu-sa** a beach near Ku-to-yen

## *In a Station of the Metro**

The apparition of these faces in the crowd;
Petals on a wet, black bough.

[*1916*]

***metro** subway in Paris

## H. D.

*H. D. was the* nom de plume *of Hilda Doolittle (1886–1961). Doolittle, born in Bethlehem, Pennsylvania, of a socially prominent family, met Ezra Pound (see the two preceding poems) when she was 15 and he was 16. Their relationship was complicated—Doolittle was sexually attracted to women as well as to men—and met with opposition from her family. She further distressed her family when she dropped out of Bryn Mawr College. In*

*1911 H. D. and a female friend who had once loved Doolittle and now loved Pound followed Pound to England, where Doolittle was active in various literary movements.*

*We print a poem about a Greek mythological figure, Helen, wife of Menelaus, king of the Greek city-state of Sparta. Paris, a Trojan prince, abducted her and thereby initiated the Trojan War. Poets—ever since the days of ancient Greece—have been interested in this story, but H. D. had an especially strong interest in classical Greece and in psychoanalytic and feminist interpretations of mythology.*

## *Helen*

All Greece hates
the still eyes in the white face,
the lustre as of olives
where she stands,
and the white hands.

All Greece reviles
the wan face when she smiles,
hating it deeper still
when it grows wan and white,
remembering past enchantments
and past ills.

Greece sees unmoved,
God's daughter, born of love,
the beauty of cool feet
and slenderest knees,
could love indeed the maid,
only if she were laid,
white ash amid funereal cypresses.

[*1924*]

## MARIANNE MOORE

*Marianne Moore (1887-1972) graduated from Bryn Mawr College, in Pennsylvania, and then for a while taught business courses at the U.S. Indian School in Carlisle, Pennsylvania. By 1915 her poems began to attract attention, and as the editor (1925-29) of* The Dial, *an important literary magazine, she became an influential figure in the world of letters.*

*Moore's method of composition was unusual; she would write a stanza and revise it until the cadences sounded right, and she would then write subsequent stanzas with the same number of syllables.*

# *Poetry**

I, too, dislike it: there are things that are important beyond all
this fiddle.
Reading it, however, with a perfect contempt for it, one
discovers in
it after all, a place for the genuine.
Hands that can grasp, eyes
that can dilate, hair that can rise
if it must, these things are important not because a
high-sounding interpretation can be put upon them but because
they are
useful. When they become so derivative as to become
unintelligible,
the same thing may be said for all of us, that we
do not admire what
we cannot understand: the bat
holding on upside down or in quest of something to
eat, elephants pushing, a wild horse taking a roll, a tireless
wolf under
a tree, the immovable critic twitching his skin like a horse
that feels a flea, the base-
ball fan, the statistician—
nor is it valid
to discriminate against "business documents and
school-books"; all these phenomena are important. One must
make a distinction
however: when dragged into prominence by half poets, the
result is not poetry,
nor till the poets among us can be
"literalists of
the imagination"—above
insolence and triviality and can present
for inspection, "imaginary gardens with real toads in them"
shall we have
it. In the meantime, if you demand on the one hand,
the raw material of poetry in
all its rawness and
that which is on the other hand
genuine, you are interested in poetry.

[*1921*]

*In a note to this poem, Moore says that the quotation in lines 17–18 is derived from *The Diaries of Leo Tolstoy;* the quotation in lines 21–22, from W. B. Yeats's *Ideas of Good and Evil.*

A comment in *Predilections,* her volume of literary essays, affords some insight into her style: "My own fondness for the unaccepted rhyme derives, I think, from an instinctive effort to ensure naturalness. Even elate and fearsome rightness like Shakespeare's is only preserved from the offense of being 'poetic' by his well-nested effects of helpless naturalness."

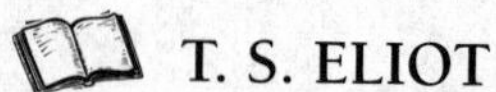

## T. S. ELIOT

*Thomas Stearns Eliot (1888–1965) was born into a New England family that had moved to St. Louis. He attended a preparatory school in Massachusetts, then graduated from Harvard and did further study in literature and philosophy in France, Germany, and England. In 1914 he began working for Lloyd's Bank in London, and three years later he published his first book of poems (it included "Prufrock"). In 1925 he joined a publishing firm, and in 1927 he became a British citizen and a member of the Church of England. Much of his later poetry, unlike "The Love Song of J. Alfred Prufrock," is highly religious. In 1948 Eliot received the Nobel Prize for Literature.*

# *The Love Song of J. Alfred Prufrock*

*S'io credesse che mia risposta fosse*
*A persona che mai tornasse al mondo,*
*Questa fiamma staria senza più scosse.*
*Ma perciocchè giammai di questo fondo*
*Non torno vivo alcun, s' i' odo il vero,*
*Senza tema d'infamia ti rispondo.**

Let us go then, you and I,
When the evening is spread out against the sky
Like a patient etherised upon a table;
Let us go, through certain half-deserted streets,
The muttering retreats
Of restless nights in one-night cheap hotels
And sawdust restaurants with oyster-shells;
Streets that follow like a tedious argument
Of insidious intent
To lead you to an overwhelming question . . .

*In Dante's *Inferno* XXVII:61–66, a damned soul who had sought absolution before committing a crime addresses Dante, thinking that his words will never reach the earth: "If I believed that my answer were to a person who could ever return to the world, this flame would no longer quiver. But because no one ever returned from this depth, if what I hear is true, without fear of infamy, I answer you."

Explanations of allusions in the poem may be helpful. "Works and days" (line 29) is the title of a poem on farm life by Hesiod (eighth century B.C.); "dying fall" (line 52) echoes *Twelfth Night* I.i.4; lines 81–83 allude to John the Baptist (see Matthew 14.1–11); line 92 echoes lines 41–42 of Marvell's "To His Coy Mistress" (see page 931); for "Lazarus" (line 94) see Luke 16 and John 11; lines 112–117 allude to Polonius and perhaps to other figures in *Hamlet*; "full of high sentence" (line 117) comes from Chaucer's description of the Clerk of Oxford in the *Canterbury Tales.*

Oh, do not ask, "What is it?"
Let us go and make our visit.

In the room the women come and go
Talking of Michelangelo.

The yellow fog that rubs its back upon the window panes,
The yellow smoke that rubs its muzzle on the window panes
Licked its tongue into the corners of the evening,
Lingered upon the pools that stand in drains,
Let fall upon its back the soot that falls from chimneys,
Slipped by the terrace, made a sudden leap,
And seeing that it was a soft October night,
Curled once about the house, and fell asleep.

And indeed there will be time
For the yellow smoke that slides along the street,
Rubbing its back upon the window-panes;
There will be time, there will be time
To prepare a face to meet the faces that you meet;
There will be time to murder and create,
And time for all the works and days of hands
That lift and drop a question on your plate;
Time for you and time for me,
And time yet for a hundred indecisions,
And for a hundred visions and revisions,
Before the taking of a toast and tea.

In the room the women come and go
Talking of Michelangelo.

And indeed there will be time
To wonder, "Do I dare?" and, "Do I dare?"—
Time to turn back and descend the stair,
With a bald spot in the middle of my hair—
(They will say: "How his hair is growing thin!")
My morning coat, my collar mounting firmly to the chin,
My necktie rich and modest, but asserted by a simple pin—
(They will say: "But how his arms and legs are thin!")
Do I dare
Disturb the universe?
In a minute there is time
For decisions and revisions which a minute will reverse.

For I have known them all already, known them all:—
Have known the evenings, mornings, afternoons,
I have measured out my life with coffee spoons;
I know the voices dying with a dying fall
Beneath the music from a farther room.
    So how should I presume?

And I have known the eyes already, known them all—
The eyes that fix you in a formulated phrase.

And when I am formulated, sprawling on a pin,
When I am pinned and wriggling on the wall,
Then how should I begin
To spit out all the butt-ends of my days and ways?
  And how should I presume?

And I have known the arms already, known them all—
Arms that are braceleted and white and bare
(But in the lamplight, downed with light brown hair!)
Is it perfume from a dress
That makes me so digress?
Arms that lie along a table, or wrap about a shawl.
  And should I then presume?
  And how should I begin?

Shall I say, I have gone at dusk through narrow streets
And watched the smoke that rises from the pipes
Of lonely men in shirt-sleeves, leaning out of windows? . . .

I should have been a pair of ragged claws
Scuttling across the floors of silent seas.

And the afternoon, the evening, sleeps so peacefully!
Smoothed by long fingers,
Asleep . . . tired . . . or it malingers,
Stretched on the floor, here beside you and me.
Should I, after tea and cakes and ices,
Have the strength to force the moment to its crisis?
But though I have wept and fasted, wept and prayed,
Though I have seen my head (grown slightly bald)
  brought in upon a platter,
I am no prophet—and here's no great matter;
I have seen the moment of my greatness flicker,
And I have seen the eternal Footman hold my coat, and
  snicker,
And in short, I was afraid.

And would it have been worth it, after all,
After the cups, the marmalade, the tea,
Among the porcelain, among some talk of you and me,
Would it have been worth while,
To have bitten off the matter with a smile,
To have squeezed the universe into a ball
To roll it toward some overwhelming question,
To say: "I am Lazarus, come from the dead,
Come back to tell you all, I shall tell you all"—
If one, settling a pillow by her head,
  Should say: "That is not what I meant at all;
  That is not it, at all."

And would it have been worth it, after all,
Would it have been worth while,

After the sunsets and the dooryards and the sprinkled streets,
After the novels, after the teacups, after the skirts
that trail along the floor—
And this, and so much more?—
It is impossible to say just what I mean!
But as if a magic lantern threw the nerves in patterns
on a screen:
Would it have been worth while
If one, settling a pillow or throwing off a shawl,
And turning toward the window, should say:
"That is not it at all,
That is not what I meant, at all."

No! I am not Prince Hamlet, nor was meant to be;
Am an attendant lord, one that will do
To swell a progress, start a scene or two,
Advise the prince; no doubt, an easy tool,
Deferential, glad to be of use,
Politic, cautious, and meticulous;
Full of high sentence, but a bit obtuse;
At times, indeed, almost ridiculous—
Almost, at times, the Fool.

I grow old . . . I grow old . . .
I shall wear the bottoms of my trousers rolled.

Shall I part my hair behind? Do I dare to eat a peach?
I shall wear white flannel trousers, and walk upon the beach.
I have heard the mermaids singing, each to each.

I do not think that they will sing to me.

I have seen them riding seaward on the waves
Combing the white hair of the waves blown back
When the wind blows the water white and black.

We have lingered in the chambers of the sea
By sea-girls wreathed with seaweed red and brown,
Till human voices wake us, and we drown.

[*1917*]

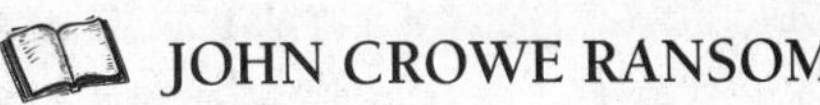

## JOHN CROWE RANSOM

*John Crowe Ransom (1888–1974) studied classics at Vanderbilt and (as a Rhodes scholar) at Oxford. After military service in World War I, he returned to Vanderbilt to teach and then moved on to Kenyon College, where he founded* The Kenyon Review. *A contemporary critic, Helen Vendler, aptly has said that in his poems Ransom "combined faultless irony with a faultless civility and tenderness."*

## *Piazza Piece*

—I am a gentleman in a dustcoat trying
To make you hear. Your ears are soft and small
And listen to an old man not at all,
They want the young men's whispering and sighing.
But see the roses on your trellis dying
And hear the spectral singing of the moon;
For I must have my lovely lady soon,
I am a gentleman in a dustcoat trying.

—I am a lady young in beauty waiting
Until my truelove comes, and then we kiss.
But what gray man among the vines is this
Whose words are dry and faint as in a dream?
Back from my trellis, Sir, before I scream!
I am a lady young in beauty waiting.

[*1925*]

# ARCHIBALD MACLEISH

*Archibald MacLeish (1892–1982) was educated at Harvard and at Yale Law School. His early poetry (say, to about 1930), including "Ars Poetica," often is condensed and allusive, though his later poems and his plays are readily accessible. Under Franklin Delano Roosevelt, MacLeish served as librarian of Congress (1939–44) and as assistant secretary of state (1944–45). He then taught at Harvard and at Amherst until he retired in 1967.*

## *Ars Poetica*

A poem should be palpable and mute
As a globed fruit,

Dumb
As old medallions to the thumb,

Silent as the sleeve-worn stone
Of casement ledges where the moss has grown—

A poem should be wordless
As the flight of birds.

A poem should be motionless in time
As the moon climbs,

Leaving, as the moon releases
Twig by twig the night-entangled trees,

Leaving, as the moon behind the winter leaves,
Memory by memory the mind—

A poem should be motionless in time
As the moon climbs.

A poem should be equal to:
Not true.

For all the history of grief
An empty doorway and a maple leaf.

For love
The leaning grasses and two lights above the sea—

A poem should not mean
But be.

[*1926*]

## WILFRED OWEN

*Wilfred Owen (1893–1918) was born in Shropshire, in England, and studied at London University. He enlisted in the army at the outbreak of World War I and fought in the Battle of the Somme until he was hospitalized with shell shock. After his recuperation in England, he returned to the front only to be killed in action one week before the end of the war. His collected poems were published posthumously.*

# *Dulce et Decorum Est**

Bent double, like old beggars under sacks,
Knock-kneed, coughing like hags, we cursed through sludge,
Till on the haunting flares we turned our backs
And towards our distant rest began to trudge.
Men marched asleep. Many had lost their boots
But limped on, blood-shod. All went lame; all blind;
Drunk with fatigue; deaf even to the hoots
Of tired, outstripped Five-Nines° that dropped behind.

Gas! Gas! Quick, boys!—An ecstasy of fumbling,
Fitting the clumsy helmets just in time;
But someone still was yelling out and stumbling
And flound'ring like a man in fire or lime . . .
Dim, through the misty panes and thick green light,
As under a green sea, I saw him drowning.

***Dulce et Decorum Est** From the Latin poet Horace's *Odes* (III:2.13): *Dulce et decorum est pro patria mori*—"It is sweet and honorable to die for your country."
**8 Five-Nines** shells containing poison gas

In all my dreams, before my helpless sight,
He plunges at me, guttering, choking, drowning.

If in some smothering dreams you too could pace
Behind the wagon that we flung him in,
And watch the white eyes writhing in his face,
His hanging face, like a devil's sick of sin;
If you could hear, at every jolt, the blood
Come gargling from the froth-corrupted lungs,
Obscene as cancer, bitter as the cud
Of vile, incurable sores on innocent tongues,—
My friend,° you would not tell with such high zest
To children ardent for some desperate glory,
The old Lie: Dulce et decorum est
Pro patria mori.

[*1917*]

**25 friend** Early drafts of "Dulce et Decorum Est" are dedicated to Jessie Pope, author of children's books and conventional patriotic verse.

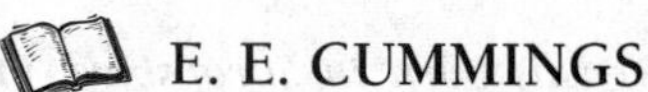

## E. E. CUMMINGS

*Edwin Estlin Cummings (1894–1962), who used the pen name e. e. cummings, grew up in Cambridge, Massachusetts, and was graduated from Harvard, where he became interested in modern literature and art, especially in the movements called cubism and futurism. His father, a conservative clergyman and a professor at Harvard, seems to have been baffled by the youth's interests, but Cummings's mother encouraged his artistic activities, including unconventional punctuation.*

*Politically liberal in his youth, Cummings became more conservative after a visit to Russia in 1931, but early and late his work emphasizes individuality and freedom of expression.*

### *in Just-*

in Just-
spring when the world is mud-
luscious the little
lame balloonman

whistles far and wee

and eddieandbill come
running from marbles and
piracies and it's
spring

when the world is puddle-wonderful
the queer
old balloonman whistles

far and wee
and bettyandisbel come dancing

from hop-scotch and jump-rope and

it's
spring
and
  the
    goat-footed

balloonMan whistles
far
and
wee

[*1920*]

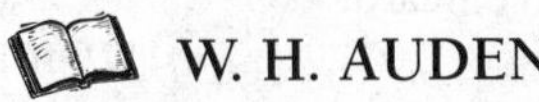

## W. H. AUDEN

*Wystan Hugh Auden (1907–1973) was born in York, England, and educated at Oxford. In the 1930s his witty left-wing poetry earned him wide acclaim as the leading poet of his generation. He went to Spain during the Spanish Civil War, intending to serve as an ambulance driver for the Republicans in their struggle against fascism, but he was so distressed by the violence of the Republicans that he almost immediately returned to England. In 1939 he came to America, and in 1946 he became a citizen of the United States, though he returned to England for his last years. Much of his poetry is characterized by a combination of colloquial diction and technical dexterity.*

# *The Unknown Citizen*

*(To JS/07/M/378*
*This Marble Monument*
*Is Erected by the State)*

He was found by the Bureau of Statistics to be
One against whom there was no official complaint,
And all the reports on his conduct agree
That, in the modern sense of an old-fashioned word, he was a saint,
For in everything he did he served the Greater Community.
Except for the War till the day he retired
He worked in a factory and never got fired,
But satisfied his employers, Fudge Motors Inc.
Yet he wasn't a scab or odd in his views,
For his Union reports that he paid his dues,
(Our report on his Union shows it was sound)
And our Social Psychology workers found
That he was popular with his mates and liked a drink.
The Press are convinced that he bought a paper every day

And that his reactions to advertisements were normal in every way.
Policies taken out in his name prove that he was fully insured,
And his Health-card shows he was once in hospital but left it cured.
Both Producers Research and High-Grade Living declare
He was fully sensible to the advantages of the Installment Plan
And had everything necessary to the Modern Man,
A phonograph, radio, a car and a frigidaire.
Our researchers into Public Opinion are content
That he held the proper opinions for the time of year;
When there was peace, he was for peace; when there was war, he went.
He was married and added five children to the population,
Which our Eugenist says was the right number for a parent of his
generation,
And our teachers report that he never interfered with their education.
Was he free? Was he happy? The question is absurd:
Had anything been wrong, we should certainly have heard.

[*1940*]

## ELIZABETH BISHOP

***Elizabeth Bishop (1911-79) was born in Worcester, Massachusetts. Because her father died when she was eight months old and her mother was confined to a sanitarium four years later, Bishop was raised by relatives in New England and Nova Scotia. After graduating from Vassar College in 1934, where she was co-editor of the student literary magazine, she lived (on a small private income) for a while in Key West, France, and Mexico, and then for much of her adult life in Brazil, before returning to the United States to teach at Harvard. Her financial independence enabled her to write without worrying about the sales of her books and without having to devote energy to distracting jobs.***

### *The Fish*

I caught a tremendous fish
and held him beside the boat
half out of water, with my hook
fast in a corner of his mouth.
He didn't fight.
He hadn't fought at all.
He hung a grunting weight,
battered and venerable
and homely. Here and there
his brown skin hung in strips
like ancient wall-paper,
and its pattern of darker brown
was like wall-paper:

shapes like full-blown roses
stained and lost through age.
He was speckled with barnacles,
fine rosettes of lime,
and infested
with tiny white sea-lice,
and underneath two or three
rags of green weed hung down.
While his gills were breathing in
the terrible oxygen
—the frightening gills,
fresh and crisp with blood,
that can cut so badly—
I thought of the coarse white flesh
packed in like feathers,
the big bones and the little bones,
the dramatic reds and blacks
of his shiny entrails,
and the pink swim-bladder
like a big peony.
I looked into his eyes
which were far larger than mine
but shallower, and yellowed,
the irises backed and packed
with tarnished tinfoil
seen through the lenses
of old scratched isinglass.
They shifted a little, but not
to return my stare.
—It was more like the tipping
of an object toward the light.
I admired his sullen face,
the mechanism of his jaw,
and then I saw
that from his lower lip
—if you could call it a lip—
grim, wet, and weapon-like,
hung five old pieces of fish-line,
or four and a wire leader
with the swivel still attached,
with all their five big hooks
grown firmly in his mouth.
A green line, frayed at the end
where he broke it, two heavier lines,
and a fine black thread
still crimped from the strain and snap
when it broke and he got away.
Like medals with their ribbons
frayed and wavering,
a five-haired beard of wisdom
trailing from his aching jaw.

I stared and stared
and victory filled up
the little rented boat,
from the pool of bilge
where oil had spread a rainbow
around the rusted engine
to the bailer rusted orange,
the sun-cracked thwarts,
the oarlocks on their strings,
the gunnels—until everything
was rainbow, rainbow, rainbow!
And I let the fish go.

[*1946*]

## *Poem*

About the size of an old-style dollar bill,
American or Canadian,
mostly the same whites, gray greens, and steel grays
—this little painting (a sketch for a larger one?)
has never earned any money in its life.
Useless and free, it has spent seventy years
as a minor family relic
handed along collaterally to owners
who looked at it sometimes, or didn't bother to.

It must be Nova Scotia; only there
does one see gabled wooden houses
painted that awful shade of brown.
The other houses, the bits that show, are white.
Elm trees, low hills, a thin church steeple
—that gray-blue wisp—or is it? In the foreground
a water meadow with some tiny cows,
two brushstrokes each, but confidently cows;
two minuscule white geese in the blue water,
back-to-back, feeding, and a slanting stick.
Up closer, a wild iris, white and yellow,
fresh-squiggled from the tube.
The air is fresh and cold; cold early spring
clear as gray glass; a half inch of blue sky
below the steel-gray storm clouds.
(They were the artist's specialty.)
A specklike bird is flying to the left.
Or is it a flyspeck looking like a bird?

Heavens, I recognize the place, I know it!
It's behind—I can almost remember the farmer's name.
His barn backed on that meadow. There it is,
titanium white, one dab. The hint of steeple,
filaments of brush-hairs, barely there,

must be the Presbyterian church.
Would that be Miss Gillespie's house?
Those particular geese and cows
are naturally before my time.
A sketch done in an hour, "in one breath,"
once taken from a trunk and handed over.
*Would you like this? I'll probably never*
*have room to hang these things again.*
*Your Uncle George, no, mine, my Uncle George,*
*he'd be your great-uncle, left them all with Mother*
*when he went back to England.*
*You know, he was quite famous, an R.A.°* . . .

I never knew him. We both knew this place,
apparently, this literal small backwater,
looked at it long enough to memorize it,
our years apart. How strange. And it's still loved,
or its memory is (it must have changed a lot).
Our visions coincided—"visions" is
too serious a word—our looks, two looks:
art "copying from life" and life itself,
life and the memory of it so compressed
they've turned into each other. Which is which?
Life and the memory of it cramped,
dim, on a piece of Bristol board,
dim, but how live, how touching in detail
—the little that we get for free,
the little of our earthly trust. Not much.
About the size of our abidance
along with theirs: the munching cows,
the iris, crisp and shivering, the water
still standing from spring freshets,
the yet-to-be-dismantled elms, the geese.

[*1976*]

**44 R. A.** a member of the Royal Academy

## ROBERT HAYDEN

*Robert Hayden (1913–80) was born in Detroit, Michigan. His parents divorced when he was a child, and he was brought up by a neighboring family, whose name he adopted. In 1942, at the age of 29, he graduated from Detroit City College (now Wayne State University), and he received a master's degree from the University of Michigan. He taught at Fisk University from 1946 to 1969 and after that, for the remainder of his life, at the University of Michigan. In 1979 he was appointed Consultant in Poetry to the Library of Congress, the first African-American to hold the post.*

## *Frederick Douglass**

When it is finally ours, this freedom, this liberty, this beautiful
and terrible thing, needful to man as air,
usable as earth; when it belongs at last to all,
when it is truly instinct, brain matter, diastole, systole,
reflex action; when it is finally won; when it is more
than the gaudy mumbo jumbo of politicians:
this man, this Douglass, this former slave, this Negro
beaten to his knees, exiled, visioning a world
where none is lonely, none hunted, alien,
this man, superb in love and logic, this man
shall be remembered. Oh, not with statues' rhetoric,
not with legends and poems and wreaths of bronze alone,
but with the lives grown out of his life, the lives
fleshing his dream of the beautiful, needful thing.

[*1947*]

***Frederick Douglass** (1818–95) Born a slave, Douglass escaped and became an important spokesman for the abolitionist movement and later for civil rights for African-Americans.

## *Those Winter Sundays*

Sundays too my father got up early
and put his clothes on in the blueblack cold,
then with cracked hands that ached
from labor in the weekday weather made
banked fires blaze. No one ever thanked him.

I'd wake and hear the cold splintering, breaking.
When the rooms were warm, he'd call,
and slowly I would rise and dress,
fearing the chronic angers of that house,

Speaking indifferently to him,
who had driven out the cold
and polished my good shoes as well.
What did I know, what did I know
of love's austere and lonely offices?

[*1962*]

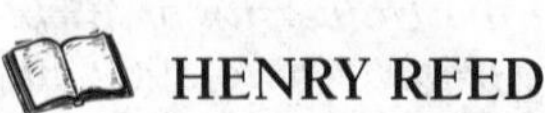

## HENRY REED

*Henry Reed (b. 1914) was born in Birmingham, England, and educated at Birmingham University. During World War II he served in the army before being trans-*

***ferred to the diplomatic service. Most of his poems are based on his war experiences.***

## *Naming of Parts*

To-day we have naming of parts. Yesterday,
We had daily cleaning. And to-morrow morning,
We shall have what to do after firing. But to-day,
To-day we have naming of parts. Japonica°
Glistens like coral in all of the neighboring gardens,
  And to-day we have naming of parts.

This is the lower sling swivel. And this
Is the upper sling swivel, whose use you will see,
When you are given your slings. And this is the piling swivel,
Which in your case you have not got. The branches
Hold in the gardens their silent, eloquent gestures,
  Which in our case we have not got.

This is the safety-catch, which is always released
With an easy flick of the thumb. And please do not let me
See anyone using his finger. You can do it quite easy
If you have any strength in your thumb. The blossoms
Are fragile and motionless, never letting anyone see
  Any of them using their finger.

And this you can see is the bolt. The purpose of this
Is to open the breech, as you see. We can slide it
Rapidly backwards and forwards: we call this
Easing the spring. And rapidly backwards and forwards
The early bees are assaulting and fumbling the flowers:
  They call it easing the Spring.

They call it easing the Spring: it is perfectly easy
If you have any strength in your thumb: like the bolt,
And the breech, and the cocking-piece, and the point of balance,
Which in our case we have not got; and the almond-blossom
Silent in all of the gardens and the bees going backwards and forwards,
  For to-day we have naming of parts.

[*1946*]

**4 Japonica** Japanese quince

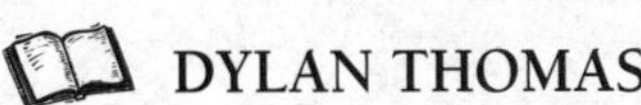

## DYLAN THOMAS

***Dylan Thomas (1914–53) was born and grew up in Swansea, in Wales. His first volume of poetry, published in 1934, immediately made him famous. Endowed with a highly melodious voice, on three tours of the United States***

*he was immensely successful as a reader both of his own and of other poets' work. He died in New York City.*

## *Fern Hill*

Now as I was young and easy under the apple boughs
About the lilting house and happy as the grass was green,
    The night above the dingle starry,
        Time let me hail and climb
    Golden in the heydays of his eyes,
And honored among wagons I was prince of the apple towns
And once below a time I lordly had the trees and leaves
        Trail with daisies and barley
    Down the rivers of the windfall light.

And as I was green and carefree, famous among the barns
About the happy yard and singing as the farm was home,
    In the sun that is young once only,
        Time let me play and be
    Golden in the mercy of his means,
And green and golden I was huntsman and herdsman,
    the calves
Sang to my horn, the foxes on the hills barked clear and cold,
        And the sabbath rang slowly
    In the pebbles of the holy streams.

All the sun long it was running, it was lovely, the hay
Fields high as the house, the tunes from the chimneys,
      it was air
    And playing, lovely and watery
      And fire green as grass.
    And nightly under the simple stars
As I rode to sleep the owls were bearing the farm away,
All the moon long I heard, blessed among stables, the night-
      jars
    Flying with the ricks, and the horses
      Flashing into the dark.
And then to awake, and the farm, like a wanderer white
With the dew, come back, the cock on his shoulder: it was all
    Shining, it was Adam and maiden,
      The sky gathered again
    And the sun grew round that very day.
So it must have been after the birth of the simple light
In the first, spinning place, the spellbound horses walking warm
    Out of the whinnying green stable
      On to the fields of praise.

And honored among foxes and pheasants by the gay house
Under the new made clouds and happy as the heart was long,
    In the sun born over and over,
      I ran my heedless ways,
    My wishes raced through the house high hay
And nothing I cared, at my sky blue trades, that time allows

In all his tuneful turning so few and such morning songs
Before the children green and golden
Follow him out of grace,

Nothing I cared, in the lamb white days, that time would take me
Up to the swallow thronged loft by the shadow of my hand,
In the moon that is always rising,
Nor that riding to sleep
I should hear him fly with the high fields
And wake to the farm forever fled from the childless land.
Oh as I was young and easy in the mercy of his means,
Time held me green and dying
Though I sang in my chains like the sea.

[*1946*]

## WILLIAM STAFFORD

*William Stafford (1914-93) was born in Hutchinson, Kansas, and was educated at the University of Kansas and the State University of Iowa. A conscientious objector during World War II, he worked for the Brethren Service and the Church World Service. After the war he taught at several universities and then settled at Lewis and Clark College in Portland, Oregon. In addition to writing several books of poems, Stafford wrote* Down in My Heart *(1947), an account of his experiences as a conscientious objector.*

# *Traveling Through the Dark*

Traveling through the dark I found a deer
dead on the edge of the Wilson River road.
It is usually best to roll them into the canyon:
the road is narrow; to swerve might make more dead.

By glow of the tail-light I stumbled back of the car
and stood by the heap, a doe, a recent killing;
she had stiffened already, almost cold.
I dragged her off; she was large in the belly.

My fingers touching her side brought me the reason—
her side was warm; her fawn lay there waiting,
alive, still, never to be born.
Beside that mountain road I hesitated.

The car aimed ahead its lowered parking lights;
under the hood purred the steady engine.
I stood in the glare of the warm exhaust turning red;
around our group I could hear the wilderness listen.

I thought hard for us all—my only swerving—
then pushed her over the edge into the river.

[*1960*]

## LAWRENCE FERLINGHETTI

*Lawrence Ferlinghetti (b. 1919) has been much concerned with bringing poetry to the people. To this end he has not only written poetry but has also been the editor and publisher of City Lights Books in San Francisco and (since 1953) has operated a bookstore, the City Lights Bookshop, the first all-paperback bookstore in the United States. In 1956 Ferlinghetti achieved national fame when, as the publisher of Allen Ginsberg's* Howl, *he was arrested (and later acquitted) on an obscenity charge.*

# *Constantly Risking Absurdity*

Constantly risking absurdity
and death
whenever he performs
above the heads
of his audience
the poet like an acrobat
climbs on rime
to a high wire of his own making
and balancing on eyebeams
above a sea of faces
paces his way
to the other side of day
performing *entrechats*°
and sleight-of-foot tricks
and other high theatrics
and all without mistaking
any thing
for what it may not be
For he's the super realist
who must perforce perceive
taut truth
before the taking of each stance or step
in his supposed advance
toward that still higher perch
where Beauty stands and waits
with gravity
to start her death-defying leap
And he
a little charleychaplin man
who may or may not catch

**13** ***entrechats*** a leap in ballet

her fair eternal form
spreadeagled in the empty air
of existence

[*1958*]

## RICHARD WILBUR

*Richard Wilbur, born in New York City in 1921, was educated at Amherst and Harvard. He served in the army during World War II, and in 1947 published* The Beautiful Changes, *a book of poems that reflected some of his experience in Europe. This book and subsequent books of poetry established his literary reputation, but probably his most widely known works are the lyrics that he wrote for Leonard Bernstein's musical version of* Candide *(1956).*

# *Love Calls Us to the Things of This World*

The eyes open to a cry of pulleys,
And spirited from sleep, the astounded soul
Hangs for a moment bodiless and simple
As false dawn.
Outside the open window
The morning air is all awash with angels.

Some are in bed-sheets, some are in blouses,
Some are in smocks: but truly there they are.
Now they are rising together in calm swells
Of halcyon feeling, filling whatever they wear
With the deep joy of their impersonal breathing;

Now they are flying in place, conveying
The terrible speed of their omnipresence, moving
And staying like white water; and now of a sudden
They swoon down into so rapt a quiet
That nobody seems to be there.
The soul shrinks

From all that it is about to remember,
From the punctual rape of every blessèd day,
And cries,
"Oh, let there be nothing on earth but laundry,
Nothing but rosy hands in the rising steam
And clear dances done in the sight of heaven."

Yet, as the sun acknowledges
With a warm look the world's hunks and colors,
The soul descends once more in bitter love

To accept the waking body, saying now
In a changed voice as the man yawns and rises,

"Bring them down from their ruddy gallows;
Let there be clean linen for the backs of thieves;
Let lovers go fresh and sweet to be undone,
And the heaviest nuns walk in a pure floating
Of dark habits,
keeping their difficult balance."

[*1956*]

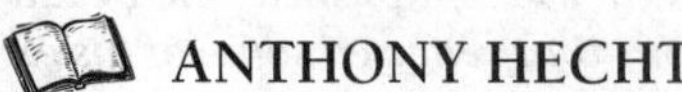

## ANTHONY HECHT

***Anthony Hecht was born in New York City in 1923, and educated at Bard College and Columbia University. He has taught at several institutions (since 1985 he has been at Georgetown University), and he has served as poetry consultant to the Library of Congress.***

***Like "The Dover Bitch," which assumes a reader's familiarity with Matthew Arnold's "Dover Beach" (p. 1065), much of Hecht's work glances at earlier literature.***

### *The Dover Bitch*

A Criticism of Life
For Andrews Wanning

So there stood Matthew Arnold and this girl
With the cliffs of England crumbling away behind them,
And he said to her, "Try to be true to me,
And I'll do the same for you, for things are bad
All over, etc., etc."
Well now, I knew this girl. It's true she had read
Sophocles in a fairly good translation
And caught that bitter allusion to the sea,
But all the time he was talking she had in mind
The notion of what his whiskers would feel like
On the back of her neck. She told me later on
That after a while she got to looking out
At the lights across the channel, and really felt sad,
Thinking of all the wine and enormous beds
And blandishments in French and the perfumes.
And then she got really angry. To have been brought
All the way down from London, and then be addressed
As sort of a mournful cosmic last resort
Is really tough on a girl, and she was pretty.
Anyway, she watched him pace the room
And finger his watch-chain and seem to sweat a bit,
And then she said one or two unprintable things.

But you mustn't judge her by that. What I mean to say is,
She's really all right. I still see her once in a while
And she always treats me right.
We have a drink
And I give her a good time, and perhaps it's a year
Before I see her again, but there she is,
Running to fat, but dependable as they come,
And sometimes I bring her a bottle of *Nuit d'Amour.*

[*1967*]

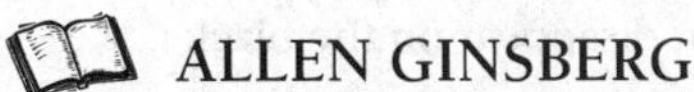

## ALLEN GINSBERG

*Allen Ginsberg, born in Newark, New Jersey, in 1926, graduated from Columbia University in 1948. After eight months in Columbia Psychiatric Institute—Ginsberg had pleaded insanity to avoid prosecution when the police discovered that a friend stored stolen goods in Ginsberg's apartment—he worked at odd jobs and finally left the nine-to-five world for a freer life in San Francisco. In the 1950s he established a reputation as an uninhibited declamatory poet whose chief theme was a celebration of those who were alienated from a repressive America. Ginsberg has received many awards and, though he now lives on a farm in New Jersey, often reads at college campuses throughout the country.*

# *A Supermarket in California*

What thoughts I have of you tonight, Walt Whitman, for I walked down the sidestreets under the trees with a headache self-conscious looking at the full moon.

In my hungry fatigue, and shopping for images, I went into the neon fruit supermarket, dreaming of your enumerations!

What peaches and what penumbras! Whole families shopping at night! Aisles full of husbands! Wives in the avocados, babies in the tomatoes!—and you, García Lorca,° what were you doing down by the watermelons?

I saw you, Walt Whitman, childless, lonely old grubber, poking among the meats in the refrigerator and eyeing the grocery boys.

I heard you asking questions of each: Who killed the pork chops? What price bananas? Are you my Angel?

I wandered in and out of the brilliant stacks of cans following you, and followed in my imagination by the store detective.

We strode down the open corridors together in our solitary fancy tasting artichokes, possessing every frozen delicacy, and never passing the cashier.

**3 García Lorca** Federico García Lorca (1899–1936), Spanish poet (and, like Whitman and Ginsberg, a homosexual)

Where are we going, Walt Whitman? The doors close in an hour. Which way does your beard point tonight?

(I touch your book and dream of our odyssey in the supermarket and feel absurd.)

Will we walk all night through solitary streets? The trees add shade to shade, lights out in the houses, we'll both be lonely.

Will we stroll dreaming of the lost America of love past blue automobiles in driveways, home to our silent cottage?

Ah, dear father, graybeard, lonely old courage-teacher, what America did you have when Charon quit poling his ferry and you got out on a smoking bank and stood watching the boat disappear on the black water of Lethe?°

[*1956*]

**12 Lethe** In classical mythology, Charon ferried the souls of the dead across the river Styx, to Hades, where, after drinking from the river Lethe, they forgot the life they had lived.

## JAMES WRIGHT

*James Wright (1927–80) was born in Martins Ferry, Ohio, which provided him with the locale for many of his poems. He is often thought of as a poet of the Midwest, but (as in the example that we give) his poems move beyond the scenery. Wright was educated at Kenyon College in Ohio and at the University of Washington. He wrote several books of poetry and published many translations of European and Latin American poetry.*

## *Lying in a Hammock at William Duffy's Farm in Pine Island, Minnesota*

Over my head, I see the bronze butterfly,
Asleep on the black trunk,
Blowing like a leaf in green shadow.
Down the ravine behind the empty house,
The cowbells follow one another
Into the distances of the afternoon.
To my right,
In a field of sunlight between two pines,
The droppings of last year's horses
Blaze up into golden stones.
I lean back, as the evening darkens and comes on.
A chicken hawk floats over, looking for home.
I have wasted my life.

[*1963*]

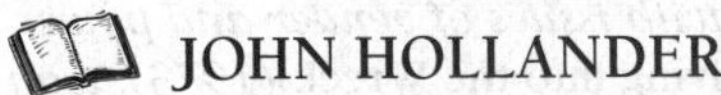

## JOHN HOLLANDER

*John Hollander, born in 1929, is a professor of English at Yale University and the author of several books of poetry and of several books about poetry, including* Rhyme's Reason, *an engaging treatment of versification.*

# *Disagreements*

We are all at sixes and sevens not just about
The state of the nation but our state of contention
Itself, you maintaining that repose is a snaffle
In exuberance's mouth, I that quarreling is
A cave where the spirit sits deafened and dumbfounded.
You rise to the bait of what I refuse to stand for.

Arguments of heat cool off in bed where arguments
Of light are dimmed in horizontal ways of being
At odds. Rough, pleasurable strife resolves nothing but
Minimizes differences for the while we lie
Silent together in apposition that is true
Friendship.—*No,* you say, as if to awaken sleeping
Amity to its daily work of debate once more.

*Nay,* calls strife's reveille. I disagree; and we're at
A new kind of odds, in which my braying out of *Yea*
Shivers the morning air into little blasts of wind.
But this smacks far less than ever of domestic farce—
No fear lest dinner burn, say, while unheated, genial
Discourse propound itself in the next room; no fear lest
Argument drop idly to the floor like a dishrag
The while Judy throws what was to have been lunch at Punch.

Your side of the story? Starting out with unhoarse nay-
Saying? Well, without me, you would never have it told:
Your tacit dissents are heard only in inference
From my affirmatives, yeas echoing unheard nays.
I'll give you eight to five that at bottom we agree.

[*1982*]

## ADRIENNE RICH

*Adrienne Rich, born in 1929 in Baltimore, was educated at Radcliffe College. Her first book of poems,* A Change of World, *published in 1951 when she was still an undergraduate, was selected by W. H. Auden for the Yale Series of Younger Poets. In 1953 she married an economist and had three sons, but as she indicates in several books, she felt confined by the full-time domestic role that she was expected to play, and the marriage did not last. Much of her poetry is concerned with issues of gender and power. When her ninth book,* Diving into the Wreck *(1973), won the National Book Award, Rich accepted the award not as an individual but on behalf of women everywhere.*

## *Living in Sin*

She had thought the studio would keep itself,
no dust upon the furniture of love.
Half heresy, to wish the taps less vocal,
the panes relieved of grime. A plate of pears,
a piano with a Persian shawl, a cat
stalking the picturesque amusing mouse
had risen at his urging.
Not that at five each separate stair would writhe
under the milkman's tramp; that morning light
so coldly would delineate the scraps
of last night's cheese and three sepulchral bottles;
that on the kitchen shelf among the saucers
a pair of beetle-eyes would fix her own—
envoy from some black village in the mouldings . . .
Meanwhile, he, with a yawn,
sounded a dozen notes upon the keyboard,
declared it out of tune, shrugged at the mirror,
rubbed at his beard, went out for cigarettes;
while she, jeered by the minor demons,
pulled back the sheets and made the bed and found
a towel to dust the table-top,
and let the coffee-pot boil over on the stove.
By evening she was back in love again,
though not so wholly but throughout the night
she woke sometimes to feel the daylight coming
like a relentless milkman up the stairs.

[*1955*]

## *Rape*

There is a cop who is both prowler and father:
he comes from your block, grew up with your brothers,
had certain ideals.
You hardly know him in his boots and silver badge,
on horseback, one hand touching his gun.

You hardly know him but you have to get to know him:
he has access to machinery that could kill you.
He and his stallion clop like warlords among the trash,
his ideals stand in the air, a frozen cloud
from between his unsmiling lips.

And so, when the time comes, you have to turn to him,
the maniac's sperm still greasing your thighs,

your mind whirling like crazy. You have to confess
to him, you are guilty of the crime
of having been forced.

And you see his blue eyes, the blue eyes of all the family
whom you used to know, grow narrow and glisten,
his hand types out the details
and he wants them all
but the hysteria in your voice pleases him best.

You hardly know him but now he thinks he knows you:
he has taken down your worst moment
on a machine and filed it in a file.
He knows, or thinks he knows, how much you imagined;
he knows, or thinks he knows, what you secretly wanted.

He has access to machinery that could get you put away;
and if, in the sickening light of the precinct,
your details sound like a portrait of your confessor,
will you swallow, will you deny them, will you lie your way home?

[*1972*]

## DEREK WALCOTT

*Derek Walcott, born in 1930 on the Caribbean island of St. Lucia, in 1992 was awarded the Nobel Prize for Literature. Although in the United States he is known chiefly as a poet, Walcott is also an important playwright and director of plays. Much of his work is concerned with his mixed heritage—a black writer from the Caribbean, whose language is English and who lives part of the year in New England, where he teaches at Boston University.*

# *A Far Cry from Africa*

A wind is ruffling the tawny pelt
Of Africa. Kikuyu,° quick as flies,
Batten upon the bloodstreams of the veldt.°
Corpses are scattered through a paradise.
Only the worm, colonel of carrion, cries:
'Waste no compassion on these separate dead!'
Statistics justify and scholars seize
The salients of colonial policy.
What is that to the white child hacked in bed?
To savages, expendable as Jews?

Threshed out by beaters, the long rushes break
In a white dust of ibises whose cries

**2 Kikuyu** an African tribe who fought against British colonialists **3 veldt** grassland in southern Africa

Have wheeled since civilization's dawn
From the parched river or beast-teeming plain.
The violence of beast on beast is read
As natural law, but upright man
Seeks his divinity by inflicting pain.
Delirious as these worried beasts, his wars
Dance to the tightened carcass of a drum,
While he calls courage still that native dread
Of the white peace contracted by the dead.

Again brutish necessity wipes its hands
Upon the napkins of a dirty cause, again
A waste of our compassion, as with Spain,°
The gorilla wrestles with the superman.

I who am poisoned with the blood of both,
Where shall I turn, divided to the vein?
I who have cursed
The drunken officer of British rule, how choose
Between this Africa and the English tongue I love?
Betray them both, or give back what they give?
How can I face such slaughter and be cool?
How can I turn from Africa and live?

**24 Spain** a reference to the triumph of fascism in Spain after the Civil War of 1936–39

## SYLVIA PLATH

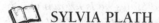

*Sylvia Plath (1932–63) was born in Boston, the daughter of German immigrants. While still an undergraduate at Smith College, she published in* Seventeen *and* Mademoiselle, *but her years at college, like her later years, were marked by manic-depressive periods. After graduating from college she went to England to study at Cambridge University, where she met the English poet Ted Hughes, whom she married in 1956. The marriage was unsuccessful, and they separated. One day she committed suicide by turning on the kitchen gas.*

### *Daddy*

You do not do, you do not do
Any more, black shoe
In which I have lived like a foot
For thirty years, poor and white,
Barely daring to breathe or Achoo.

Daddy, I have had to kill you.
You died before I had time—
Marble-heavy, a bag full of God,

Ghastly statue with one gray toe
Big as a Frisco seal

And a head in the freakish Atlantic
Where it pours bean green over blue
In the waters off beautiful Nauset.
I used to pray to recover you.
Ach, du.°

In the German tongue, in the Polish town
Scraped flat by the roller
Of wars, wars, wars.
But the name of the town is common.
My Polack friend

Says there are a dozen or two.
So I never could tell where you
Put your foot, your root,
I never could talk to you.
The tongue stuck in my jaw.

It stuck in a barb wire snare.
Ich, ich, ich, ich,°
I could hardly speak.
I thought every German was you.
And the language obscene

An engine, an engine
Chuffing me off like a Jew.
A Jew to Dachau, Auschwitz, Belsen.°
I began to talk like a Jew.
I think I may well be a Jew.

The snows of the Tyrol, the clear beer of Vienna
Are not very pure or true.
With my gypsy ancestress and my weird luck
And my Taroc pack and my Taroc pack
I may be a bit of a Jew.

I have always been scared of *you*,
With your Luftwaffe,° your gobbledygoo.
And your neat moustache
And your Aryan eye, bright blue,
Panzer-man,° panzer-man, O You—

Not God but a swastika
So black no sky could squeak through.
Every woman adores a Fascist,
The boot in the face, the brute
Brute heart of a brute like you.

**15 Ach, du** O, you (German) **27 Ich, ich, ich, ich** I, I, I, I **33 Dachau . . . Belsen** concentration camps **42 Luftwaffe** German air force **45 Panzer-man** member of a tank crew

You stand at the blackboard, daddy,
In the picture I have of you,
A cleft in your chin instead of your foot
But no less a devil for that, no not
Any less the black man who

Bit my pretty red heart in two.
I was ten when they buried you.
At twenty I tried to die
And get back, back, back to you.
I thought even the bones would do.

But they pulled me out of the sack,
And they stuck me together with glue,
And then I knew what to do.
I made a model of you,
A man in black with a Meinkampf° look

And a love of the rack and the screw.
And I said I do, I do.
So daddy, I'm finally through.
The black telephone's off at the root,
The voices just can't worm through.

If I've killed one man, I've killed two—
The vampire who said he was you
And drank my blood for a year,
Seven years, if you want to know.
Daddy, you can lie back now.

There's a stake in your fat black heart
And the villagers never liked you.
They are dancing and stamping on you.
They always *knew* it was you.
Daddy, daddy, you bastard, I'm through.

[*1965*]

**65 Meinkampf** My Struggle (title of Hitler's autobiography)

## MARY OLIVER

*Mary Oliver, born in Cleveland in 1935, attended Ohio State University and Vassar College. She is the author of six books of poetry—*American Primitive *received the Pulitzer Prize for Poetry in 1984, and* New and Selected Poems *received a National Book Award in 1992—and she has served as a visiting professor or a poet in residence at several colleges.*

*Two of her prose comments may be of special interest. Of today's readers she has said, "The question asked today is: What does it mean? Nobody says, how does it feel?" And of her work she has said, "I am trying in my poems to vanish and have the reader be the experiencer. I do not want to be there. It is not even a walk we take together."*

## *The Black Walnut Tree*

My mother and I debate:
we could sell
the black walnut tree
to the lumberman,
and pay off the mortgage.
Likely some storm anyway
will churn down its dark boughs,
smashing the house. We talk
slowly, two women trying
in a difficult time to be wise.
Roots in the cellar drains,
I say, and she replies
that the leaves are getting heavier
every year, and the fruit
harder to gather away.
But something brighter than money
moves in our blood—an edge
sharp and quick as a trowel
that wants us to dig and sow.
So we talk, but we don't do
anything. That night I dream
of my fathers out of Bohemia
filling the blue fields
of fresh and generous Ohio
with leaves and vines and orchards.
What my mother and I both know
is that we'd crawl with shame
in the emptiness we'd made
in our own and our fathers' backyard.
So the black walnut tree
swings through another year
of sun and leaping winds,
of leaves and bounding fruit,
and, month after month, the whip-
crack of the mortgage.

[*1992*]

## LUCILLE CLIFTON

*Lucille Clifton (née Sayles) was born in New York State in 1936 and was educated at Howard University and Fredonia State Teachers College. In addition to publishing seven books of poetry, she has written fifteen children's books. Clifton has received numerous awards, including a grant from the National Endowment for the*

*Arts. She teaches creative writing at the University of California, Santa Cruz.*

## *in the inner city*

in the inner city
or
like we call it
home
we think a lot about uptown
and the silent nights
and the houses straight as
dead men
and the pastel lights
and we hang on to our no place
happy to be alive
and in the inner city
or
like we call it
home

[*1969*]

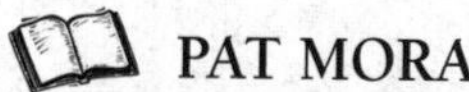

## PAT MORA

*Pat Mora, after graduating from Texas Western College, earned a master's degree at the University of Texas at El Paso. She is best known for her poems, but she has also published essays on Chicano culture.*

## *Sonrisas**

I live in a doorway
between two rooms. I hear
quiet clicks, cups of black
coffee, *click, click* like facts
   budgets, tenure, curriculum,
from careful women in crisp beige
suits, quick beige smiles
that seldom sneak into their eyes.

I peek
in the other room señoras
in faded dresses stir sweet
milk coffee, laughter whirls
with steam from fresh *tamales*
   *sh, sh, mucho ruido,*°

***Sonrisas** smiles (Spanish) **4 *mucho ruido*** lots of noise

they scold one another,
press their lips, trap smiles
in their dark, Mexican eyes.

[*1986*]

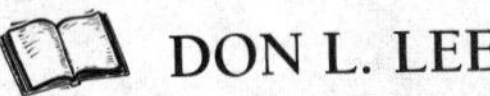

## DON L. LEE

*Don L. Lee (Haki R. Madhubuti) was born in Little Rock, Arkansas, in 1942, but he grew up in Chicago, where he studied at the University of Illinois, Chicago, Chicago City College, and Roosevelt University. In 1984 he earned an M.F.A. from the University of Iowa. Lee has taught at several colleges and universities and now teaches at Chicago State University. He has published widely and has made a recording,* Rappin' and Readin' *(1971).*

### *But He Was Cool or: He Even Stopped for Green Lights*

super-cool
ultrablack
a tan / purple
had a beautiful shade.
he had a double-natural
that wd put the sisters to shame.
his dashikis were tailor made
& his beads were imported sea shells
  (from some blk / country i never heard of)
he was triple-hip.

his tikis were hand carved
out of ivory
& came express from the motherland.
he would greet u in swahili
& say good-by in yoruba.

woooooooooooo-jim he bes so cool & ill tel li gent
  cool-cool is so cool he was un-cooled by other niggers' cool
  cool-cool ultracool was bop-cool / ice box cool so cool cold
    cool
  his wine didn't have to be cooled, him was air conditioned
    cool
  cool-cool / real cool made me cool—now ain't that cool
  cool-cool so cool him nick-named refrigerator.

cool-cool so cool
he didn't know,
after detroit, newark, chicago &c.,
we had to hip
  cool-cool / super-cool / real cool
  that

to be black
is
to be
very-hot.

[*1969*]

## LOUISE GLÜCK

*Louise Glück (b. 1943) was born in New York City and attended Sarah Lawrence College and Columbia University. She has taught at Goddard College in Vermont and at Warren Wilson College in North Carolina. Her volume of poems,* The Triumph of Achilles *(1985), won the National Book Critics Circle Award for poetry.*

### *The School Children*

The children go forward with their little satchels.
And all morning the mothers have labored
to gather the late apples, red and gold,
like words of another language.

And on the other shore
are those who wait behind great desks
to receive these offerings.

How orderly they are—the nails
on which the children hang
their overcoats of blue or yellow wool.

And the teachers shall instruct them in silence
and the mothers shall scour the orchards for a way out,
drawing to themselves the gray limbs of the fruit trees
bearing so little ammunition.

[*1975*]

## TESS GALLAGHER

*Tess Gallagher, born in 1943 in Port Angeles, Washington, was educated at the University of Washington and the University of Iowa. The author of books of poems and of short stories, she has taught creative writing at several major universities.*

### *The Hug*

A woman is reading a poem on the street
and another woman stops to listen. We stop too.
with our arms around each other. The poem
is being read and listened to out here

in the open. Behind us
no one is entering or leaving the houses.

Suddenly a hug comes over me and I'm
giving it to you, like a variable star shooting light
off to make itself comfortable, then
subsiding. I finish but keep on holding
you. A man walks up to us and we know he hasn't
come out of nowhere, but if he could, he
would have. He looks homeless because of how
he needs. "Can I have one of those?" he asks you,
and I feel you nod. I'm surprised,
surprised you don't tell him how
it is—that I'm yours, only
yours, etc., exclusive as a nose to
its face. Love—that's what we're talking about, love
that nabs you with "for me
only" and holds on.

So I walk over to him and put my
arms around him and try to
hug him like I mean it. He's got an overcoat on
so thick I can't feel
him past it. I'm starting the hug
and thinking, "How big a hug is this supposed to be?
How long shall I hold this hug?" Already
we could be eternal, his arms falling over my
shoulders, my hands not
meeting behind his back, he is so big!

I put my head into his chest and snuggle
in. I lean into him. I lean my blood and my wishes
into him. He stands for it. This is his
and he's starting to give it back so well I know he's
getting it. This hug. So truly, so tenderly
we stop having arms and I don't know if
my lover has walked away or what, or
if the woman is still reading the poem, or the houses—
what about them?—the houses.

Clearly, a little permission is a dangerous thing.
But when you hug someone you want it
to be a masterpiece of connection, the way the button
on his coat will leave the imprint of
a planet in my cheek
when I walk away. When I try to find some place
to go back to.

[*1987*]

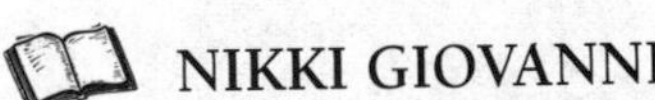

## NIKKI GIOVANNI

*Nikki Giovanni was born in Knoxville, Tennessee, in 1943 and educated at Fisk University, the University of*

*Pennsylvania School of Social Work, and Columbia University. She has taught at Queens College, Rutgers University, and Ohio State University, and she now teaches creative writing at Mt. St. Joseph on the Ohio. Giovanni has published many books of poems, an autobiography* (Gemini: An Extended Autobiographical Statement on My First Twenty-Five Years of Being a Black Poet), *a book of essays, and a book consisting of a conversation with James Baldwin.*

## Nikki-Rosa

childhood rememberances are always a drag
if you're Black
you always remember things like living in Woodlawn
with no inside toilet
and if you become famous or something
they never talk about how happy you were to have your mother
all to yourself and
how good the water felt when you got your bath from one of those
big tubs that folk in chicago barbecue in
and somehow when you talk about home
it never gets across how much you
understood their feelings
as the whole family attended meetings about Hollydale
and even though you remember
your biographers never understand
your father's pain as he sells his stock
and another dream goes
and though you're poor it isn't poverty that
concerns you
and though they fought a lot
it isn't your father's drinking that makes any difference
but only that everybody is together and you
and your sister have happy birthdays and very good christmasses
and I really hope no white person ever has cause to write about me
because they never understand Black love is Black wealth
  and they'll
probably talk about my hard childhood and never understand that
all the while I was quite happy

[*1968*]

## Master Charge Blues

its wednesday night baby
and i'm all alone
wednesday night baby
and i'm all alone
sitting with myself
waiting for the telephone

wanted you baby
but you said you had to go
wanted you yeah
but you said you had to go
called your best friend
but he can't come 'cross no more

did you ever go to bed
at the end of a busy day
look over and see the smooth
where your hump usta lay
feminine odor and no reason why
i said feminine odor and no reason why
asked the lord to help me
he shook his head "not i"

but i'm a modern woman baby
ain't gonna let this get me down
i'm a modern woman
ain't gonna let this get me down
gonna take my master charge
and get everything in town

[*1970*]

## CRAIG RAINE

*Born in England in 1945, Raine graduated from Oxford, where after his graduation he was appointed a lecturer. Since 1981 he has been poetry editor for the English publisher Faber and Faber. He gives frequent readings of his poetry both in England and in America.*

*Much of his poetry, including the poem we reprint here, is designed to help the reader to see the world from a fresh point of view.*

### A Martian Sends a Postcard Home

Caxtons° are mechanical birds with many wings
and some are treasured for their markings—

they cause the eyes to melt
or the body to shriek without pain.

I have never seen one fly, but
sometimes they perch on the hand.

Mist is when the sky is tired of flight
and rests its soft machine on ground:

then the world is dim and bookish
like engravings under tissue paper.

**1 Caxtons** William Caxton (c. 1422–1491) the first English printer of books

Rain is when the earth is television.
It has the property of making colours darker.

Model T° is a room with the lock inside—
a key is turned to free the world

for movement, so quick there is a film
to watch for anything missed.

But time is tied to the wrist
or kept in a box, ticking with impatience.

In homes, a haunted apparatus sleeps,
that snores when you pick it up.

If the ghost cries, they carry it
to their lips and soothe it to sleep

with sounds. And yet, they wake it up
deliberately, by tickling with a finger.

Only the young are allowed to suffer
openly. Adults go to a punishment room

with water but nothing to eat.
They lock the door and suffer the noises

alone. No one is exempt
and everyone's pain has a different smell.

At night, when all the colours die,
they hide in pairs

and read about themselves—
in colour, with their eyelids shut.

[*1979*]

**13 Model T** A Ford automobile made between 1908 and 1928.

## WENDY ROSE

*Wendy Rose, of Hopi and Miwok ancestry, was born in 1948 in Oakland, California. A graduate of the University of California, Berkeley, she has been editor of* American Indian Quarterly. *She teaches American Indian Studies at Fresno City College and is active as a poet, artist, and anthologist.*

### *Three Thousand Dollar Death Song*

*Nineteen American Indian Skeletons from Nevada . . . valued at $3000 . . .*
*—Museum invoice, 1975*

Is it in cold hard cash? the kind
that dusts the insides of men's pockets
lying silver-polished surface along the cloth.

Or in bills? papering the wallets of they
who thread the night with dark words. Or
checks? paper promises weighing the same
as words spoken once on the other side
of the grown grass and damned rivers
of history. However it goes, it goes
Through my body it goes assessing each nerve, running its edges
along my arteries, planning ahead
for whose hands will rip me
into pieces of dusty red paper,
whose hands will smooth or smatter me
into traces of rubble. Invoiced now,
it's official how our bones are valued
that stretch out pointing to sunrise
or are flexed into one last foetal bend,
that are removed and tossed about,
catalogued, numbered with black ink
on newly-white foreheads.
As we were formed to the white soldier's voice,
so we explode under white students' hands.
Death is a long trail of days
in our fleshless prison.

From this distant point we watch our bones
auctioned with our careful beadwork,
our quilled medicine bundles, even the bridles
of our shot-down horses. You: who have
priced us, you who have removed us: at what cost?
What price the pits where our bones share
a single bit of memory, how one century
turns our dead into specimens, our history
into dust, our survivors into clowns.
Our memory might be catching, you know;
picture the mortars, the arrowheads, the labrets°
shaking off their labels like bears
suddenly awake to find the seasons have ended
while they slept. Watch them touch each other,
measure reality, march out the museum door!
Watch as they lift their faces
and smell about for us; watch our bones rise
to meet them and mount the horses once again!
The cost, then, will be paid
for our sweetgrass-smelling having-been
in clam shell beads and steatite,°
dentalia° and woodpecker scalp, turquoise
and copper, blood and oil, coal
and uranium, children, a universe
of stolen things.

[*1980*]

**36 labrets** wood or bone ornaments inserted into a perforation in the lip
**46 steatite** soapstone **47 dentalia** plural of *dentalium,* a kind of shellfish

## JOY HARJO

*Joy Harjo, a Creek Indian, was born in Tulsa, Oklahoma, in 1951. She was educated at the Institute of American Indian Arts in Santa Fe, New Mexico, and at the University of Iowa Writers' Workshop. She now teaches at the University of Colorado in Boulder. Her chief books are* The Last Song, What Moon Drove Me to This, She Had Some Horses, *and* Secrets from the Center of the World.

### *Vision*

The rainbow touched down
"somewhere in the Rio Grande,"
we said. And saw the light of it
from your mother's house in Isleta.°
How it curved down between earth
and the deepest sky to give us horses
of color
horses that were within us all of this time
but we didn't see them because
we wait for the easiest vision
to save us.

In Isleta the rainbow was a crack
in the universe. We saw the barest
of all life that is possible.
Bright horses rolled over
and over the dusking sky.
I heard the thunder of their beating
hearts. Their lungs hit air
and sang. All the colors of horses
formed the rainbow,
and formed us
watching them.

[*1983*]

**4 Isleta** a pueblo in New Mexico

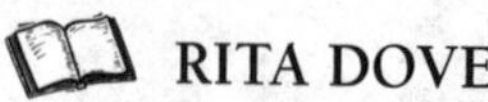

## RITA DOVE

*Rita Dove was born in 1952 in Akron, Ohio. After graduating* summa cum laude *from Miami University (Ohio), she earned an M.F.A. at the Iowa Writers' Workshop. She has been awarded fellowships from the Guggenheim Foundation and the National Endowment for the Arts, and she now teaches at the University of Virginia. In 1993 she was appointed poet laureate for 1993-94. Dove is currently writing a book about the experiences of an*

*African-American volunteer regiment in France during World War I.*

## Daystar

She wanted a little room for thinking:
but she saw diapers steaming on the line,
a doll slumped behind the door.
So she lugged a chair behind the garage
to sit out the children's naps.

Sometimes there were things to watch—
the pinched armor of a vanished cricket,
a floating maple leaf. Other days
she stared until she was assured
when she closed her eyes
she'd see only her own vivid blood.

She had an hour, at best, before Liza appeared
pouting from the top of the stairs.
And just *what* was mother doing
out back with the field mice? Why,
building a palace. Later
that night when Thomas rolled over and
lurched into her, she would open her eyes
and think of the place that was hers
for an hour—where
she was nothing,
pure nothing, in the middle of the day.

[*1986*]

# JUDITH ORTIZ COFER

*Born in Puerto Rico in 1952 of a Puerto Rican mother and a United States mainland father who served in the Navy, Judith Ortiz Cofer was educated both in Puerto Rico and on the mainland. After earning a bachelor's and a master's degree in English, she did further graduate work at Oxford and then taught English in Florida. She has published seven volumes of poetry.*

## My Father in the Navy: A Childhood Memory

Stiff and immaculate
in the white cloth of his uniform
and a round cap on his head like a halo,
he was an apparition on leave from a shadow-world

and only flesh and blood when he rose from below
the waterline where he kept watch over the engines
and dials making sure the ship parted the waters
on a straight course.
Mother, brother and I kept vigil
on the nights and dawns of his arrivals,
watching the corner beyond the neon sign of a quasar
for the flash of white our father like an angel
heralding a new day.
His homecomings were the verses
we composed over the years making up
the siren's song that kept him coming back
from the bellies of iron whales
and into our nights
like the evening prayer.

[*1987*]

## DAVID MURA

*David Mura (b. 1952) is a* sansei, *a third-generation Japanese-American. In addition to publishing a book of poems, he has published* A Male Grief *(an essay on pornography) and* Turning Japanese *(a memoir of his visit to Japan). Mura has received several awards, including a US/Japan Creative Artist Fellowship, and an NEA Literature Fellowship.*

## *An Argument: On 1942*

*For my mother*

*Near Rose's Chop Suey and Jinosuke's grocery,*
*the temple where incense hovered and inspired*
*dense evening chants (prayers for Buddha's mercy,*
*colorless and deep), that day he was fired . . .*

—No, no, no, she tells me. Why bring it back?
The camps are over. (Also overly dramatic.)
Forget *shoyu*-stained *furoshiki,*° *mochi*° on a stick:
You're like a terrier, David, gnawing a bone, an old, old trick . . .

Mostly we were bored. Women cooked and sewed,
men played blackjack, dug gardens, a *benjo.*°
Who noticed barbed wire, guards in the towers?
We were children, hunting stones, birds, wild flowers.

Yes, Mother hid tins of *tsukemono*° and eel
beneath the bed. And when the last was peeled,

**7 *shoyu*-stained *furoshiki*** a soy-sauce-stained scarf that is used to carry things ***mochi*** rice cakes **10 *benjo*** toilet **13 *tsukemono*** Japanese pickles [Author's notes]

clamped tight her lips, growing thinner and thinner.
But cancer not the camps made her throat blacker

. . . And she didn't die then . . . after the war, in St. Paul,
you weren't even born. Oh I know, I know, it's all
part of your job, your way, but why can't you glean
how far we've come, how much I can't recall—

David, it was so long ago—how useless it seems . . .

[*1989*]

# CHAPTER 26

# *Critical Perspectives on Emily Dickinson*

## *A Casebook*

## ON READING AUTHORS REPRESENTED IN DEPTH

If you have read several works by an author, whether tragedies by Shakespeare or detective stories about Sherlock Holmes by Arthur Conan Doyle, you know that authors return again and again to certain themes (tragedy for Shakespeare, crime for Conan Doyle), yet each treatment is different. *Hamlet, Macbeth,* and *Romeo and Juliet* are all tragedies, and they all share certain qualities that we think of as Shakespearean, yet each is highly distinctive.

When we read several works by an author, we find ourselves thinking about resemblances and differences. We enjoy seeing the author return to some theme (for instance, God, or nature, or love) or to some literary form (for instance, the sonnet, or blank verse, or pairs of rhyming lines); and we may find, to our delight, that the author has handled things differently and that we are getting a sense of the writer's variety and perhaps even of the writer's development. Indeed, we sometimes speak of the *shape* or *design* of the author's career, meaning that our careful study of the writings has led us to an understanding of the story—with its beginning, middle, and end—that the writings tell across a period of time. Often, once we read one poem by an author and find it intriguing or compelling, we want to read more: Are there other poems like this one? What kinds of poems were written before or after this one? Our enjoyment and understanding of one poem helps us to enjoy and understand others, and makes us curious about the place that each one occupies in a larger structure, the shape of the author's career.

We can go further and say that the reading of a second author can help us—perhaps by way of contrast—to understand the first. In the preface to one of his volumes of poetry Robert Frost put it this way:

> A poem is best read in the light of all the other poems ever written. We read A the better to read B (we have to start somewhere; we may get very little out of A). We read B the better to read C, C the better to read D, D the better to go back and get something more out of A. Progress is not the aim, but circulation. The thing is to get among the poems where they hold each other apart in their places as the stars do.

In an Introduction to Literature course, although you'll often be asked to write analytical papers about a single poem, story, or play, sometimes you'll be assigned a paper that requires a comparison and contrast of, for example, two poems by different authors. Less frequent perhaps, but equally important, is the paper that examines a central theme or idea as it is expressed and explored in three or more works.

At first this might seem a daunting task, but there are helpful ways of getting in control of the assignment. One of the best is to begin with a single work and then to move outward from it, making connections to works that show interesting similarities to, or differences from, it.

For a paper printed in Chapter 28, a student named Mark Bradley was assigned to write on a theme (which he had to define himself) in a selection of poems by Langston Hughes. Mark started by closely studying a poem by Hughes that had caught his attention when he made his way through the group of poems for the first time. In one of his journal entries, Mark wrote:

> The poem "The South" surprised me. It wasn't what I expected. I thought Hughes would attack the South for being so racist--he wrote the poem in the 1920s, when segregation was everywhere in the South. He says some tough stuff about the South, that's for sure: "Beast strong, / Idiot-brained." But he also says that the South is attractive in some ways, and I'm not convinced that when he brings in the North at the end, he really believes that the North is superior.

Intrigued by this poem, Mark made it his point of departure for the thematic paper he was assigned. He judged that if he worked intensively on this poem and came to know it well, he could review other Hughes poems and see how they were both like and unlike the poem with which he began.

In this chapter, and in the next two chapters (on Robert Frost and Langston Hughes), we present an author in depth, so that you can have the pleasure of deepening your understanding of each of these writers. In reading their works, and in preparing to write about any of them, you may find it useful to keep in mind the following questions:

- What subject matter recurs in the author's work?
- Do certain views—attitudes toward life—emerge?
- Does a particular personality emerge?

- Does the author show a fondness for certain literary devices, for instance, irony, or symbolism, or off-rhymes?
- Do any of the poems strike you as highly *un*representative of the author?
- The works are arranged chronologically. Do you detect changing views or changing techniques?
- Does any one poem especially help you to interpret another poem?
- It is often rewarding to compare the career of one poet with that of another. How does studying two authors in depth enable you to perceive the distinctive features of each one more clearly? Does one show greater range in style and subject?

When you write an essay on several works, keep two points especially in mind: the length of the assignment, and the choice of examples. You want to treat the right number of examples for the space you are given, and, furthermore, to provide sufficient detail in your analysis of each of them. You might call this the **principle of proportion.**

Preparing an outline can be valuable. It will lead you to think carefully about which examples you have selected for your argument and the main idea about each one that you will present. You might begin by examining one poem in depth, and then proceed to relate it to key passages in other poems. Or maybe you'll find one passage in a poem so significant that it—rather than the poem in its entirety—can serve as a good beginning. Whichever strategy you choose, when you review the rough draft, use a pen to mark off the amount of space that you have devoted to each example. Ask yourself:

- Is this example clearly connected to my argument in the paper as a whole?
- Have I not only referred to the example, but also provided adequate quotation from it?
- Have I made certain to comment on the passage? (Remember that passages do not interpret themselves. You have to explicate and explain them.)
- Has each example received its due?

There is no easy rule of thumb for knowing how much space each example should be given. Some passages are more complicated than others; some demand more intensive scrutiny. But you'll be well on the way toward handling this aspect of the paper effectively if you are self-aware about your choices, alert to the principle of proportion.

## EMILY DICKINSON

*Emily Dickinson (1830–86) was born into a proper New England family in Amherst, Massachusetts. Although she spent her seventeenth year a few miles away, at Mount Holyoke Seminary (now Mount Holyoke College), in the next twenty years she left Amherst only five or six times, and in her last twenty years she may never have left her house. Her brother was probably right when he said that having seen something of the rest of the world—she had visited Washington with her father, when he was a mem-*

*ber of Congress—"she could not resist the feeling that it was painfully hollow. It was to her so thin and unsatisfying in the face of the Great Realities of Life." Dickinson lived with her parents (a somewhat reclusive mother and an austere, remote father) and a younger sister; a married brother lived in the house next door. She formed some passionate attachments, to women as well as men, but there is no evidence that they found physical expression.*

*By the age of twelve Dickinson was writing witty letters, but she apparently did not write more than an occasional poem before her late twenties. At her death—she died in the house where she was born—she left 1,775 poems, only seven of which had been published (anonymously) during her lifetime.*

*We first give one of her poems, "The Soul selects her own Society," followed by four discussions by modern critics. We then give sixteen additional poems, and finally comments from three of her letters.*

## *The Soul selects her own Society*

The Soul selects her own Society—
Then—shuts the Door—
To her divine Majority—
Present no more—

Unmoved—she notes the Chariots—pausing—
At her low Gate—
Unmoved—an Emperor be kneeling
Upon her Mat—

I've known her—from an ample nation—
Choose One—
Then—close the Valves° of her attention—
Like Stone—

[*1862*]

**11 Valves** the two halves of a hinged door, such as is now found on old telephone booths. Possibly also an allusion to a bivalve, such as an oyster or a clam, having a shell consisting of two hinged parts

 ELIZABETH BOWMAN

## *An Interpretation of "The Soul selects her own Society"*

The problem in Emily Dickinson's poem "The Soul Selects Her Own Society" is to decide whether the poet's attitude toward the behavior described

The Soul selects - her own Society -
Then - Shuts the Door -
+To her divine Majority -
+Present - no more -

Unmoved - She notes the Chariots - pausing
At - her low Gate -
Unmoved - an Emperor be kneeling
+Opon her Mat -

I've known her - from an ample
nation -
Choose One -
Then - Close the Valves of
her attention -
Like Stone -
+ On + obtrude + On + Rush mat - + Lids

Page from Dickinson's notebooks, showing "The Soul selects her own Society."

is one of approval, disapproval, or neutrality. Since the poem employs no overt expression of praise, or blame, one could see on its surface, with Simon Tugwell (Exp., Jan., 1969, XXVII, 37) only "a rather trite, comfortable truth," and look to deeper levels for the significance of the poem.

A. A. Hill ("Poetry and Stylistics," as reprinted in Seymour Chatman and Samuel R. Levin: *Essays on the Language of Literature*, Boston, 1967), without arguing the point, regards the poet's attitude as one of approval and reaches the ingenious conclusion that, from a large multitude, the soul selects one, of whom she makes a friend, as an oyster (the thing with valves) selects a grain of sand, of which it makes a pearl.

No one seems to have tried the assumption that the poet condemns the behavior, but this assumption fits the poem equally well and also explains it. The shut door symbolizes the closed mind. The term "divine majority" is ironic. As Mr. Hill suggests, the soul is seen as a parliamentary body, casting votes over the candidates for membership in her society. But we should note this is a majority of one over nothing, and where is the victory when there is no opposition? "Divine" is the soul's arrogant estimate of herself: like God, she knows all in advance and can safely reject without examining. In the second stanza, the soul, in her modest circumstances (another version has "rush mat," one made of the cheapest material), could benefit from the acquaintance of her callers, people of wealth and power. Here the length of the lines is symbolic, the long lines mentioning the opulent visitors, the short lines the soul's lowly dwelling. It is now probable that the "society" is one of ideas rather than people, the rejected postulants, then, being rich and powerful ideas. The last stanza presents the extreme case where the soul, with "an ample nation" available, limits herself to only one. That such behavior could be subject to disapproval is readily apparent.

It is to be noticed that in the short lines of the first two stanzas the two strong-stressed syllables are cushioned, so to speak, by the presence of weak-stressed ones, but in the last stanza the two strong-stressed syllables stand as starkly alone as the soul with her single companion. This is deliberate: "I've known her choose" is rather deviant; one would expect "*to* choose."

Another version has "lids" instead of "valves," thus presenting the image of a stone statue with its eyes closed, and obviating all possibility of a pearl. "Valves" is more insulting, because it completely dehumanizes the subject. We may also note that in the present version the last image we are left with is that of an impermeable stone.

The conclusive feature is that in the very first line of the poem there are five *s*'s within the compass of ten syllables. Since four of them are in morphemes for which *s*-less synonyms could easily have been found, they are here for a purpose. They are hardly decorative, nor do they mark rhythm, since three of them are in weak-stressed positions. The poet is announcing her subject with the hiss that greeted the villain in old-time melodrama.

One can imagine that, after trying to present an idea to someone who rejected it out of hand, Miss Dickinson, muttering "You might as well talk to a stone, or a statue," sat down and in exasperation wrote this poem, a portrait of bigotry.

[*1970*]

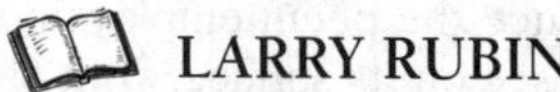

## LARRY RUBIN

# *Response to Elizabeth Bowman's Interpretation of "The Soul selects her own Society"*

Elizabeth Bowman's able explication of Emily Dickinson's "The Soul Selects Her Own Society" (EXP., Oct., 1970, XXIX, 13) as a poem which implicitly castigates people with closed minds invites rebuttal on the basis of the overall *tone* of the poem—a tone which would seem to substantiate the more traditional interpretation that the poet is here projecting a vision of the exclusiveness of the inner person (the soul). Whether such an exclusiveness is morally defensible or not does not seem to be much at issue in the poem; the *tone,* in its rather stern, matter-of-fact way, says, "Take it or leave it—that's the way it is, baby."

Aside from admittedly hazy intuitive responses to tone, one can point to some fairly objective evidence in support of this view. For one thing, the poet speaks, not of *some* souls only, but of "The Soul" in general. It is difficult to believe that she is attempting to slander the entire human race—including, presumably, herself—by accusing everyone of having closed minds. When she does criticize her fellow human beings (and that is rarely), she is much more specific about the target of her displeasure—the hypocritical minister or church-goers (Poem 324), for example, the "gentlewomen" with their "dimity convictions" (Poem 401), or the fame-hungry types who enjoy telling their names "the livelong June / To an admiring Bog" (Poem 288). In such poems there is no mistaking the particular type of person she is attempting to tell off.

Reference to the last poem brings up another point. There *is* a strong note of what some might consider haughty exclusiveness in both Emily Dickinson's life and her work. The derogatory tone of "an admiring Bog" as a reference to the celebrity-adoring general public is a clear example. What the poet seems to be doing in "The Soul Selects Her Own Society," then, is simply to be asserting the right and privilege of an individual sensitive enough to be said to *have* a soul, to retreat, retire, withdraw from the mass of mankind into the exclusive company of a single congenial soulmate (or the memory of such a person), and this despite whatever exalted rank, by the materialistic standards of the world, others who seek that individual's company or want to share her privacy might possess. Thus even emperors are kept outside the door.

As for the melodramatic hissing sound of the "*s*'s" in the first line—a sound Miss Bowman uses to cap her case—one can only remark that sound effects in poetry are particularly tricky things to interpret from a psychological point of view; when there is a clear case of onomatopoeia in question, and some audible sound in the real world is being described by the sound of the words the poet uses (as in the textbook examples of "dull thud" or "buzz" or "crackle," or in any line of Poe's "Bells"), the critic is entitled to crow triumphantly over his (or her) discovery. But when there is anything at issue as subtle as Emily Dickinson's attitude toward the aristocratic exclusiveness of the soul, as in the poem in question, one must proceed with extreme care and above all avoid trying to cinch one's case by referring in positive and final terms to a thing so delicate and elusive. Actually, the "*s*'s" sound villainous here only if one has *already* decided that the poem is a slam at narrow-minded people—it's an *ex post facto* judgment. Another listener might well find no more hateful hissing in those "*s*'s" than in the first line of "Success is counted sweetest" (Poem 67), in which such a judgment about those same sounds would be patently inappropriate.

Finally, there is the evidence of Poem 306, whose first stanza alone—

The Soul's Superior instants
Occur to Her—alone
When friend—and Earth's occasion
Have infinite withdrawn

should suffice to suggest how Emily Dickinson thought about these matters. However, should that not suffice, the doubter might explore Poem 664:

Of all the Souls that stand create—
I have elected—One—

etc.

[*1972*]

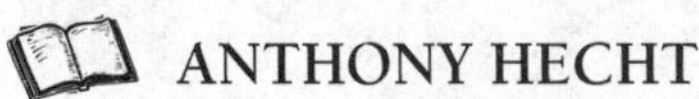

## ANTHONY HECHT

## *On Dickinson's "The Soul selects her own Society"*

"The Soul selects her own Society" has always been understood as a covert declaration of love. And it might be that. I suspect myself that it is not. It has to do, certainly, with the affinities one has with a very few people and how the soul, or anybody, makes exclusions and inclusions that are quite arbitrary; but I think this is meant to parallel the question of the Elect of God. So the soul in choosing its friends does very much what the deity does in discriminating between the saved and the damned. There is something very frightening about that; when we think of how ruthless we are about who our friends and enemies might be, at least inwardly, we are performing . . . the same act that God performs when he cuts us off from all hope of salvation. The poem, I think, hovers on the brink of those curious mysteries which are interior and psychological, but are also exterior and theological.

[*1987*]

## JUDITH FARR

## *The Passion of Emily Dickinson*

Emily Dickinson's willingness to write about "the Soul" may have been prepared by her knowledge of the sermons of Jonathan Edwards or the essays of Emerson. In both, the comprehensive rational, volitional, and emotional faculties of the human being are expressed by that term; most important, though, "the Soul" underscores the relation of the human spirit to God. Thus, when Dickinson writes

> The Soul selects her own Society—
> Then—shuts the Door—
> To her divine Majority—
> Present no more—

she is reporting on an election of suitable fellowship, made by that quintessential spark, the anima, composed in God's image and therefore divine. This best known of her poems about the soul seems to crystallize her personal attitude to society, the world outside the self. Readings of this poem have usually stressed the adamant fastidiousness and exclusivity of the speaker; she is made out to be the archetypical cool Puritan. It is important, however, to note the *kind* of society the Soul rejects here; she will not receive the potentates of time and this world, having chosen instead the One—a private lover/friend/Christ or Christ figure—who represents the sum of value, the mystical number I:

> Unmoved—she notes the Chariots—pausing
> At her low Gate—
> Unmoved—an Emperor be kneeling
> Upon her Mat—
>
> I've known her—from an ample nation—
> Choose One—
> Then—close the Valves of her attention—
> Like Stone—

The heart has valves, and they are turned to stone against all but the beloved. The Soul's basic humility, not her pride, is emphasized; for her gate, the entrance to her inmost nature, is "low" and the mat before it is not the crimson or purple rug that might be appointed to receive an emperor. Nevertheless, this gate, however modest, is related to the gate of heaven that Jacob recognizes as leading to the house of God in Genesis 18:17; and it is the same gate that Dickinson will write of to Master in the first of her three famous letters to him. (Thus she exults in her choice of such a lover by saying, "Indeed it is God's house—and these are gates of Heaven": her life has been made heavenly by having admitted him at her gate.)

[*1992*]

# ADDITIONAL POEMS

## *These are the days when Birds come back*

These are the days when Birds come back—
A very few—a Bird or two—
To take a backward look.

These are days when skies resume
The old—old sophistries° of June—
A blue and gold mistake.

O fraud that cannot cheat the Bee—
Almost thy plausibility
Induces my belief.

Till ranks of seeds their witness bear—
And softly thro' the altered air
Hurries a timid leaf.

Oh Sacrament of summer days,
Oh Last Communion in the Haze—
Permit a child to join.

Thy sacred emblems to partake—
Thy consecrated bread to take
And thine immortal wine!

[*1859*]

**5 sophistries** deceptively subtle arguments

## *Papa above!*

Papa above!
Regard a Mouse
O'erpowered by the Cat!
Reserve within thy kingdom
A "Mansion" for the Rat!

Snug in seraphic Cupboards
To nibble all the day,
While unsuspecting Cycles°
Wheel solemnly away!

[*c. 1859*]

**8 cycles** long periods, eons

## *Wild Nights—Wild Nights!*

Wild Nights—Wild Nights!
Were I with thee
Wild Nights should be
Our luxury!

Futile—the Winds—
To a Heart in port—
Done with the Compass—
Done with the Chart!

Rowing in Eden—
Ah, the Sea!
Might I but moor—Tonight—
In Thee!

[*1861*]

## *There's a certain Slant of light*

There's a certain Slant of light,
Winter Afternoons—
That oppresses, like the Heft°
Of Cathedral Tunes—

Heavenly Hurt, it gives us—
We can find no scar,
But internal difference,
Where the Meanings, are—

None may teach it—Any—
'Tis the Seal Despair—
An imperial affliction
Sent us of the Air—

When it comes, the Landscape listens—
Shadows—hold their breath—
When it goes, 'tis like the Distance
On the look of Death—

[*c. 1861*]

**3 Heft** weight

## *I got so I could hear his name—*

I got so I could hear his name—
Without—Tremendous gain—
That Stop-sensation—on my Soul—
And Thunder—in the Room—

I got so I could walk across
That Angle in the floor,
Where he turned so, and I turned—how—
And all our Sinew tore—

I got so I could stir the Box—
In which his letters grew
Without that forcing, in my breath—
As Staples—driven through—

Could dimly recollect a Grace—
I think, they call it "God"—
Renowned to ease Extremity—
When Formula, had failed—

And shape my Hands—
Petition's way,
Tho' ignorant of a word
That Ordination°—utters—

My Business, with the Cloud,
If any Power behind it, be,
Not subject to Despair—

It care, in some remoter way,
For so minute affair
As Misery—
Itself, too great, for interrupting—more—

[*1861*]

**20 Ordination** the ministry

## *This was a Poet—It is That*

This was a Poet—It is That
Distills amazing sense
From Ordinary Meanings—
And Attar so immense

From the familiar species
That perished by the Door—
We wonder it was not Ourselves
Arrested it—before—

Of Pictures, the Discloser—
The Poet—it is He—
Entitles Us—by Contrast—
To ceaseless Poverty—

Of Portion—so unconscious—
The Robbing—could not harm—
Himself—to Him—a Fortune—
Exterior—to Time—

[*1862*]

## *I heard a Fly buzz—when I died*

I heard a Fly buzz—when I died—
The Stillness in the Room
Was like the Stillness in the Air—
Between the Heaves of Storm—

The Eyes around—had wrung them dry—
And Breaths were gathering firm
For the last Onset—when the King
Be witnessed—in the Room—

I willed my Keepsakes—Signed away
What portion of me be
Assignable—and then it was
There interposed a Fly—

With Blue—uncertain stumbling Buzz—
Between the light—and me—
And then the Windows failed—and then
I could not see to see—

[*1862*]

## *This World is not Conclusion*

This World is not Conclusion.
A Species stands beyond—
Invisible, as Music—
But positive, as Sound—
It beckons, and it baffles—
Philosophy—dont know—
And through a Riddle, at the last—
Sagacity, must go—
To guess it, puzzles scholars—
To gain it, Men have borne
Contempt of Generations
And Crucifixion, shown—
Faith slips—and laughs, and rallies—
Blushes, if any see—
Plucks at a twig of Evidence—
And asks a Vane, the way—
Much Gesture, from the Pulpit—
Strong Hallelujahs roll—
Narcotics cannot still the Tooth
That nibbles at the soul—

[*c. 1862*]

## *I like to see it lap the Miles*

I like to see it lap the Miles—
And lick the Valleys up—
And stop to feed itself at Tanks—
And then—prodigious step

Around a Pile of Mountains—
And supercilious peer
In Shanties—by the sides of Roads—
And then a Quarry pare

To fit its Ribs
And crawl between
Complaining all the while
In horrid—hooting stanza—
Then chase itself down Hill—

And neigh like Boanerges°
Then—punctual as a Star
Stop—docile and omnipotent
At its own stable door—

[*1862*]

**14 Boanerges** a name said (in Mark 3.17) to mean "Sons of Thunder"

## *Because I could not stop for Death*

Because I could not stop for Death—
He kindly stopped for me—
The Carriage held but just Ourselves—
And Immortality.

We slowly drove—He knew no haste
And I had put away
My labor and my leisure too,
For His Civility—

We passed the School, where Children strove
At Recess—in the Ring—
We passed the Fields of Gazing Grain—
We passed the Setting Sun—

Or rather—He passed Us—
The Dews drew quivering and chill—
For only Gossamer, my Gown—
My Tippet°—only Tulle°—

We paused before a House that seemed
A Swelling of the Ground—
The Roof was scarcely visible—
The Cornice—in the Ground—

Since then—'tis Centuries—and yet
Feels shorter than the Day
I first surmised the Horses' Heads
Were toward Eternity—

[*c. 1863*]

**16 Tippet** shawl. **Tulle** net of silk

## *A narrow Fellow in the Grass*

A narrow Fellow in the Grass
Occasionally rides—
You may have met Him—did you not
His notice sudden is—

The Grass divides as with a Comb—
A spotted shaft is seen—
And then it closes at your feet
And opens further on—

He likes a Boggy Acre
A Floor too cool for Corn—
Yet when a Boy, and Barefoot—
I more than once at Noon
Have passed, I thought, a Whip lash
Unbraiding in the Sun

When stopping to secure it
It wrinkled, and was gone—

Several of Nature's People
I know, and they know me—
I feel for them a transport
Of cordiality—

But never met this Fellow
Attended, or alone
Without a tighter breathing
And Zero at the Bone—

[*c. 1865*]

## *Further in Summer than the Birds*

Further in Summer than the Birds
Pathetic from the Grass
A minor Nation celebrates
Its unobtrusive Mass.

No Ordinance° be seen
So gradual the Grace
A pensive Custom it becomes
Enlarging Loneliness.

Antiquest felt at Noon
When August burning low
Arise this spectral Canticle°
Repose to typify

Remit as yet no Grace
No Furrow on the Glow
Yet a Druidic° Difference
Enhances Nature now

[*1866*]

**5 Ordinance** religious rite of Holy Communion **11 Canticle** hymn **15 Druidic** pertaining to pre-Christian Celtic priests

## *Tell all the Truth but tell it slant*

Tell all the Truth but tell it slant—
Success in Circuit lies
Too bright for our infirm Delight
The Truth's superb surprise

As Lightning to the Children eased
With explanation kind
The Truth must dazzle gradually
Or every man be blind—

[*c. 1868*]

## *A Route of Evanescence**

A Route of Evanescence
With a revolving Wheel—
A Resonance of Emerald—
A Rush of Cochineal°—
And every Blossom on the Bush
Adjusts its tumbled Head—
The mail from Tunis,° probably,
An easy Morning's Ride—

[*c. 1879*]

***A Route of Evanescence** In letters to friends Dickinson said the poem referred to a hummingbird **4 Cochineal** bright red **7 Tunis** city in North Africa

## *Those—dying, then*

Those—dying, then
Knew where they went
They went to God's Right Hand—
The Hand is amputated now
And God cannot be found—
The abdication of Belief
Makes the Behavior small—
Better an ignis fatuus°
Than no illume at all—

[*1882*]

**8 ignis fatuus** a phosphorescent light that hovers over swampy ground, hence something deceptive

## *Apparently with no surprise*

Apparently with no surprise
To any happy Flower
The Frost beheads it at its play—
In accidental power—
The blonde Assassin passes on—
The Sun proceeds unmoved
To measure off another Day
For an Approving God.

[*c. 1884*]

## LETTERS ABOUT POETRY

We include three of Dickinson's letters, the first of which is addressed to Susan Gilbert, probably her dearest friend and the wife of Dickinson's brother, Austin. The two other letters are addressed to Thomas Wentworth Higginson, a writer and leading abolitionist. After reading in *Atlantic Monthly* (April 1862) Higginson's article offering advice to young authors, Dickinson (31 at the time) sent Higginson some of her poems along with a letter, and a correspondence ensued, lasting until Dickinson's death.

## *To Susan Gilbert (Dickinson)*

late April 1852

So sweet and still, and Thee, Oh Susie, what need I more, to make my heaven whole?

Sweet Hour, blessed Hour, to carry me to you, and to bring you back to me, long enough to snatch one kiss, and whisper Good bye, again.

I have thought of it all day, Susie, and I fear of but little else, and when I was gone to meeting it filled my mind so full, I could not find a *chink* to put the worthy pastor; when he said "Our Heavenly Father," I said "Oh Darling Sue"; when he read the 100th Psalm, I kept saying your precious letter all over to myself, and Susie, when they sang—it would have made you laugh to hear one little voice, piping to the departed. I made up words and kept singing how I loved you, and you had gone, while all the rest of the choir were singing Hallelujahs. I presume nobody heard me, because I sang *so small,* but it was a kind of a comfort to think I might put them out, singing of you. I a'nt there this afternoon, tho', because I am here, writing a little letter to my dear Sue, and I am very happy. I think of ten weeks—Dear One, and I think of love, and you, and my heart grows full and warm, and my breath stands still. The sun does'nt shine at all, but I can feel a sunshine stealing into my soul and making it all summer, and every thorn, a *rose.* And I pray that such summer's sun shine on my Absent One, and cause her bird to sing!

You have been happy, Susie, and now are sad—and the whole world seems lone; but it wont be so always, "some days *must* be dark and dreary"! You wont cry any more, will you, Susie, for my father will be your father, and my home will be your home, and where you go, I will go, and we will lie side by side in the kirkyard.

I have parents on earth, dear Susie, but your's are in the skies, and I have an earthly fireside, but you have one above, and you have a "Father in Heaven," where I have *none*—and *sister* in heaven, and I know they love you dearly, and think of you every day.

Oh I wish I had half so many dear friends as you in heaven—I could'nt spare them now—but to know they had got there safely, and should suffer nevermore—Dear Susie! . . .

Emilie—

## *To T. W. Higginson*

25 April 1862

Mr Higginson,

Your kindness claimed earlier gratitude—but I was ill—and write today, from my pillow.

Thank you for the surgery[1]—it was not so painful as I supposed. I bring you others—as you ask—though they might not differ—

While my thought is undressed—I can make the distinction, but when I put them in the Gown—they look alike, and numb.

You asked how old I was? I made no verse—but one or two—until this winter—Sir—

I had a terror—since September—I could tell to none—and so I sing, as the Boy does by the Burying Ground—because I am afraid—You inquire my Books—For Poets—I have Keats—and Mr and Mrs Browning. For Prose—Mr Ruskin—Sir Thomas Browne—and the Revelations.[2] I went to school—but in your manner of the phrase—had no education. When a little Girl, I had a friend, who taught me Immortality—but venturing too near, himself—he never returned—Soon after, my Tutor, died—and for several years, my Lexicon—was my only companion—Then I found one more—but he was not contented I be his scholar—so he left the Land.

You ask of my Companions Hills—Sir—and the Sundown—and a Dog—large as myself, that my Father bought me—They are better than Beings—because they know—but do not tell—and the noise in the Pool, at Noon—excels my Piano. I have a Brother and Sister—My Mother does not care for thought—and Father, too busy with his Briefs[3]—to notice what we do—He buys me many Books—but begs me not to read them—because he fears they joggle the Mind. They are religious—except me—and address an Eclipse, every morning—whom they call their "Father." But I fear my story fatigues you—I would like to learn—Could you tell me how to grow—or is it unconveyed—like Melody—or Witchcraft?

You speak of Mr Whitman—I never read his Book[4]—but was told that he was disgraceful—

I read Miss Prescott's "Circumstance,"[5] but it followed me, in the Dark—so I avoided her—

Two Editors of Journals came to my Father's House, this winter—and asked me for my Mind—and when I asked them "Why," they said I was penurious—and they, would use it for the World—

I could not weigh myself—Myself—

My size felt small—to me—I read your Chapters in the Atlantic—and experienced honor for you—I was sure you would not reject a confiding question—

Is this—Sir—what you asked me to tell you?

Your friend,
E—Dickinson.

[1]**surgery** probably cuts that Higginson suggested be made in her poems

[2]**Keats . . . Revelations** John Keats, Robert Browning, and Elizabeth Barrett Browning were nineteenth-century English poets; Thomas Browne was a seventeenth-century English writer of prose; John Ruskin was a nineteenth-century English art critic and social critic; Revelations is the last book of the New Testament.

[3]**Briefs** legal documents (Dickinson's father was a lawyer)

[4]**Mr Whitman . . . Book** Walt Whitman's *Leaves of Grass* was first published in 1855. Its unconventional punctuation and its celebration of Whitman's passions shocked many readers.

[5]**Miss Prescott's "Circumstance"** Harriet Prescott Spofford's story, published in *Atlantic Monthly* in May, 1860. It tells of a woman who, returning from a visit to a sick friend, is held hostage by a beast who is calmed only when she sings to him. Her husband eventually rescues her, but when they arrive home they find that their house has burned down.

## *To T. W. Higginson*

1876

**Nature is a Haunted House—but Art—a House that tries to be haunted.**

# SAMPLE ESSAY BY A STUDENT

Peter Gottsegen

English 150G

April 12, 1996

Religion and Religious Imagery in Emily Dickinson

Emily Dickinson was not a preacher but a poet, so if we read her poetry about God we should not be surprised if we do not find a simple, consistent view, or even a clear development from one view--for instance, belief--to another--for instance, loss of faith. Rather, judging from some examples of her poetry, she explored various views, and we should not try to convert this variety into unity.

We can begin by looking at extreme views, first two poems of faith, and then a poem of doubt. One of the poems of faith, "Papa above" (1127), begins with a childlike or almost playful version of the Lord's Prayer. (In Matthew 6.9 Jesus begins a prayer by saying, "Our father who art in heaven.") I think this poem says that God will see to it that even a mouse or rat will get into heaven, and will remain there for eternity. But Dickinson's God is not always concerned for all of the creatures of the world. In another poem that expresses belief in the existence of God, "Apparently with no surprise" (1133), Dickinson describes the frost as beheading a flower--that is, beauty perishes--and she goes on to make the point that this occurs under the eyes of "an Approving God." Here she seems to be saying that evil takes place, and God approves of it. It is important to realize that in this poem Dickinson still says that God exists, even if he is indifferent to suffering.

In another poem, "Those--dying, then" (1133), Dickinson expresses doubt that God exists. In olden days, she says, people mistakenly thought that God would protect them, but now, she says, "God cannot be found." She uses a particularly terrifying image to convey the loss of God. In the past, Dickinson says, the faithful went to "God's Right Hand," but, she goes on to say, "The Hand is amputated now . . . ." The faith in God that earlier people had was an illusion, but it was something, and it was "better" than the nothingness we now experience. This nothingness, or something not much more than nothingness, is the subject of "I heard a Fly buzz--when I died" (1129). In this poem, the speaker expects "the King" (God) to appear to her as she dies, but all she sees is a fly, and then she hears its buzz. God ("the King") never appears.

Even these few poems show that Dickinson held a variety of views about God and religion, and it is difficult or perhaps impossible for us to say exactly what her religious beliefs were. But what is certain is that religious ideas were so important to her, so much a part of her mind, that even when she was not explicitly writing about the existence of a benevolent God or the absence of God, she used religious imagery--for instance, to describe impressive things in the natural world around her. In "These are the days when Birds come back" (1126), she talks about what we call Indian summer, fall days that are like summer days. But the poem is filled with religious words: "belief," "Sacrament," "Communion," "consecrated bread," "immortal wine." The fifth stanza goes like this:

> Oh Sacrament of summer days,
> Oh Last Communion in the Haze--
> Permit a child to join.

I don't think Dickinson is really talking about traditional religion here. Instead, she is using religious imagery to talk about a particular precious moment in the seasons. As a second example of her use of religious imagery in a poem that is about nature and not about God, we might look at "There's a certain Slant of light" (1128). In this poem she says that on "Wintry Afternoons" this particular light has "the Heft / Of Cathedral Tunes." That is, the wintry light has the solidity, the feel, the "heft" of religious music. When we see this light, Dickinson says, we are moved, in a way that we are moved by music in church. She is not saying anything here about whether God is benevolent or not, or whether he exists or not. Rather, she is drawing on experiences in church--probably experiences shared by many people even today--to help us to see nature more effectively.

Speaking as someone who was brought up with traditional religious beliefs but who does not go to church now, I can say that Dickinson effectively represents the ideas of a believer and also of a non-believer. But what I think is especially impressive is that she sees that someone who no longer is a believer can't help but still think in religious terms when he or she sees something exceptionally beautiful, for instance on a winter day "a certain Slant of light."

WORK CITED

Barnet, Sylvan, et al. Literature: Thinking, Reading, and Writing Critically. 2nd ed. New York: Longman, 1997.

## TOPICS FOR CRITICAL THINKING AND WRITING

1. In this essay Gottsegen comments on the following poems: "Papa above," "Apparently with no surprise," "Those—dying, then," "These are the days when Birds come back," and "There's a certain Slant of light." Read or reread each of these poems to see if you agree with Gottsegen's interpretations.
2. Are there other poems in the casebook that you think Gottsegen could have used with better effect than some that he did use? Explain.
3. Reread the concluding pararaph. Do you think it is effective? Explain.

# CHAPTER 27

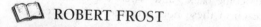

# Critical Perspectives on Robert Frost

## A Casebook

## ROBERT FROST

*Robert Frost (1874–1963) was born in California. After his father's death in 1885 Frost's mother brought the family to New England, where she taught in high schools in Massachusetts and New Hampshire. Frost studied for part of one term at Dartmouth College in New Hampshire, then did odd jobs (including teaching), and from 1897 to 1899 was enrolled as a special student at Harvard. He then farmed in New Hampshire, published a few poems in local newspapers, left the farm and taught again, and in 1912 left for England, where he hoped to achieve more popular success as a writer. By 1915 he had won a considerable reputation, and he returned to the United States, settling on a farm in New Hampshire and cultivating the image of the country-wise farmer-poet. In fact he was well read in the classics, the Bible, and English and American literature.*

*Among Frost's many comments about literature, here are three: "Writing is unboring to the extent that it is dramatic"; "Every poem is . . . a figure of the will braving alien entanglements"; and, finally, a poem "begins in delight and ends in wisdom . . . It runs a course of lucky events, and ends in a clarification of life—not necessarily a great clarification, such as sects and cults are founded on, but in a momentary stay against confusion."*

*And for good measure, here is Frost, in a letter, writing about his own work. "You get more credit for think-*

*ing if you restate formulae or cite cases that fall in easily under formulae, but all the fun is outside[,] saying things that suggest formulae that won't formulate—that almost but don't quite formulate. I should like to be so subtle at this game as to seem to the casual person altogether obvious. The casual person would assume I meant nothing or else I came near enough meaning something he was familiar with to mean it for all practical purposes. Well, well, well."*

*We begin by giving one of Frost's best-known poems, "Stopping by Woods on a Snowy Evening," along with the manuscript of the poem (p. 1142), some remarks by Frost about the poem, and three essays by students. We then give sixteen additional poems, and some of Frost's comments about poetry in general.*

## *Stopping by Woods on a Snowy Evening*

Whose woods these are I think I know.
His house is in the village, though;
He will not see me stopping here
To watch his woods fill up with snow.

My little horse must think it queer
To stop without a farmhouse near
Between the woods and frozen lake
The darkest evening of the year.

He gives his harness bells a shake
To ask if there is some mistake.
The only other sound's the sweep
Of easy wind and downy flake.

The woods are lovely, dark and deep,
But I have promises to keep,
And miles to go before I sleep,
And miles to go before I sleep.

[*1923*]

## *Remarks about "Stopping by Woods on a Snowy Evening"*

[Frost made these comments after reading the poem to an audience at Middlebury College on 30 June, 1955.]

Now, you see, the first thing about that is to take it right between the eyes just as it is, and that's the ability to do that: to take it right between the eyes like a little blow and not, you know, take it in neuter sort of. And then, you know, the next thing is your inclinations with it. I never read anything, in Latin, say, without a constant expectation of meaning that I'm

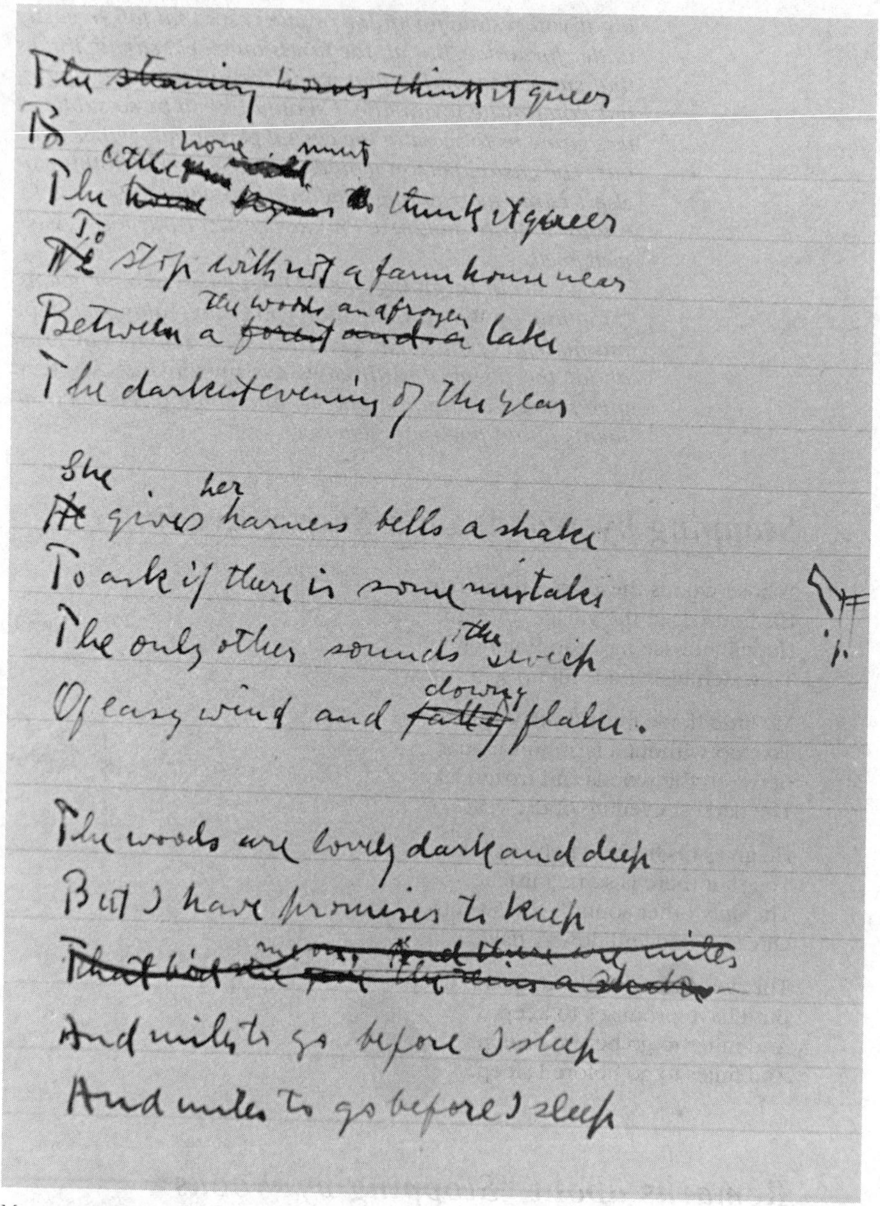

Manuscript version of Frost's "Stopping by Woods on a Snowy Evening." The first part is lost. (Courtesy of the Jones Library, Inc., Amherst, Mass.)

either getting justified in or corrected. See. Confirmed in or corrected. I've got that going on all the time or else I'd be a dead translator. I've got to have something that's a little aggressive to it, but that's so with a poem. Right away you begin to take it your way. And you can almost say in a poem that you see in it the place where it begins to be ulterior, you know, where it goes a little with you, carries you on somewhere. And if you're very strong about it—of course, it may not be the same day. I know that's the way with me. I hear a talk like this from somebody else, see, and I may not be able to hold my own with it—not then. I think to myself that when this is over I'll get going again. [*Laughter*] My own stream-of-consciousness will get going again. I'll be all right. I'll be all right on Monday after hearing it on Sunday. Many a time I thought that. This is putting it all over but I'm still there, you know. I'll resume my thread, and no matter what's said to me I want to be sure if I differ with it a little that I know what it is that I'm differing with.

Now this little thing ["Stopping by Woods"] you see very simply as I wrote it—night, evening, snowstorm, woods, dark, late, snow falling among the alders, and trees, and with a little poetic exaggeration, you know (to see the woods fill up with snow). Did they fill up? How high? See. You want to know. Don't ask me. [*Laughter*] And I've been asked such things, you know. [*Laughter*] I've had people say—somebody who ought to know better—quote me as saying [in] that poem, "the coldest evening of the year." See. Now that's getting a thermometer into it. [*Laughter*] And "The darkest evening of the year" 's better—more poetical some way. Never mind why. I don't know. More foolish. That's where the foolishness comes in. Got to be a little foolish or a good deal foolish. But then it goes on and says "The woods are lovely, dark and deep," and then if I were reading it for somebody else, I'd begin to wonder what he's up to. See. Not what he means but what he's up to.

The woods are lovely, dark and deep.
But I have promises to keep,
And miles to go before I sleep.

There are so many things that have happened, too, that way. People have come to me to ask me what were the promises [to keep], and I've joined in on that. Let them have their say, and I took it my way. I remember telling one committee that came to me about that from a college—committee of students—and I said, promises may be divided into two kinds: those that I myself make for myself and those that my ancestors made for me, known as the social contract. [*Laughter*] Now did I think of that when I wrote it? You know better. I've just got to say something. Just take it. [*Laughter*] They take it their way and I take it my way. But this is the thing I finally said about it—partly in self-defense; I said: What does it say there? "The woods are lovely, dark and deep." That's just as I might be getting along. That's all. That's the nicest way out of it—if you've got to get out of it.

## THREE INTERPRETATIONS BY STUDENTS

### Annotated Text and Essay

Here are the annotations that a student named Darrel MacDonald jotted down, followed by the final version of the essay that he developed from the annotations.

Whose woods these are I think I know.
His house is in the village, though;
He will not see me stopping here
To watch his woods fill up with snow.

afraid of being seen? Why? Because on private property? Or because not going about his business?

My little horse must think it queer
To stop without a farmhouse near
Between the woods and frozen lake
The darkest evening of the year.

odd? gay?

He gives his harness bells a shake
To ask if there is some mistake.
The only other sound's the sweep
Of easy wind and downy flake.

what is the mistake? Is it a mistake to enjoy nature?

The woods are lovely, dark and deep,
But I have promises to keep,
And miles to go before I sleep,
And miles to go before I sleep.

a woman's word? But isn't the speaker a man? Maybe a woman?

Why twice? Is he emphatically telling himself to get moving?

apparently he does not stay to see the "woods fill up with snow."

**Now for the essay that the student developed out of these annotations.**

Darrel MacDonald

Stopping by Woods--and Going On

Robert Frost's "Stopping by Woods on a Snowy Evening" is about what the title says it is. It is also about something more than the title says.

When I say it is about what the title says, I mean that the poem really does give us the thoughts of a person who pauses (that is, a person who is "stopping") by woods on a snowy evening. This person probably is a man, since Robert Frost wrote the poem and nothing in the poem clearly indicates that the speaker is not a man. But, and this point will be important, the speaker perhaps feels that he is not a very masculine man. As we will see, the word "queer" appears in the poem, and, also, the speaker uses the word "lovely," which sounds more like the word a woman would use than a man. In line 3 the speaker says he is "stopping here," and it is clear that "here" is by woods, since "woods" is mentioned not only in the title but also in the first line of the poem, and again in the second stanza, and still again in the last stanza.

But in what sense is the poem about more than the title? The title does not tell us anything about the man who is "stopping by woods," but the poem--the man's meditation--tells us a lot about him. In the first stanza he reveals that he is uneasy at the thought that the owner of the woods may see him stopping by the woods. Maybe he is uneasy because he is trespassing, but the poem does not actually say that he has illegally entered someone else's property. More likely, he feels uneasy, almost ashamed, of watching the "woods fill up with snow." That is, he would not want anyone to see that he actually is enjoying a beautiful aspect of nature and is not hurrying about whatever his real business is in thrifty Yankee style.

The second stanza gives more evidence that he feels guilty about enjoying beauty. He feels so guilty that he even thinks the horse thinks there is something odd about him. In fact, he says that the horse thinks he is "queer," which of course may just mean odd, but also (as is shown by The American Heritage Dictionary) it can mean "gay," "homosexual." A real man, he sort of suggests, wouldn't spend time looking at snow in the woods.

So far, then, the speaker in two ways has indicated that he feels insecure. First, he expresses uneasiness that someone might see him watching the woods fill up with snow. Second, he expresses uneasiness when he suggests that even the horse thinks he is strange, maybe even "queer." And so in the last stanza, even though he finds the woods beautiful, he decides not to stop and to see the woods fill up with snow. And his description of the woods as "lovely"--a woman's word--sounds as though he may be something less than a he-man. He seems to feel ashamed of himself for enjoying the sight of the snowy woods and for seeing them as "lovely," and so he tells himself that he has spent enough time looking at the woods and that he must go on about his business. In fact, he tells himself twice that he has business to attend to.

Frost gives us, then, a man who indeed is seen "stopping by woods on a snowy evening," but a man who, afraid of what society will think of him, is also afraid to "stop" long enough to fully enjoy the sight that attracts him, because he is driven by a sense that he may be seen to be trespassing and also may be thought to be unmanly. So after only a brief stop in the woods he forces himself to go on, a victim (though he probably doesn't know it) of the work ethic and of an over-simple idea of manliness.

## TOPICS FOR CRITICAL THINKING AND WRITING

1. In a sentence or two state the thesis of the essay.
2. Is the thesis adequately supported? Explain, pointing out strengths, if any, and weaknesses, if any.
3. Do you find the organization satisfactory? Why, or why not?
4. Do you find the title and the opening paragraph of interest? If not, how might you improve them?
5. Given the thesis and the development of it, is the final paragraph satisfactory? Why, or why not?
6. If you think that, on the whole, the essay is effectively written, take two or three sentences and explain what their strengths are. If you think that, on the whole, the writing could be more effective, take two or three sentences and revise them into more effective sentences. (It's not a matter of agreeing or disagreeing with the argument; we are talking chiefly about style.)

# Journal Entry and Essay

The second student, Sara Fong, kept a journal. We give an entry from her journal concerning Frost's poem and then the final version of her essay.

Journal entry: I think that when the class talked about "the death wish" in "Stopping by Woods," they were on to something, but they went too far. It's not really a "death wish." The poet wants to lose himself, so to speak, by merging himself with the woods ("the woods are lovely, dark and deep"), or maybe with the soft white snow ("downy flake"), but that's not really the same as saying he wishes for death. Still, the beauty of the woods--we might say the world of peaceful solitude--is set against the world of the living, the world of "promises" to other humans.

We have already studied short stories this term, and I think it is a good idea to see this poem as a very short short story. As I see it, the plot has three stages: (1) the character (the poet) has fairly ordinary thoughts as he looks at the wood (he thinks of the person who owns it and of the owner's house in the village), but soon he begins to feel that there is something special, something odd ("queer") in looking at the woods on what is, in fact, a special day ("The darkest evening of the year"). Then (2) he seems to get almost fully caught up with (or drawn in by) the beauty of the scene ("easy wind and downy flake," "The woods are lovely, dark and deep"), and then, finally, (3) he shakes off the pull of nature, the appeal of nature that has almost made him forget everything else.

I'm not so sure, come to think of it, that at the very end he does completely reject the impulse to give himself up to nature. He repeats the last line ("And miles to go before I sleep, / And miles to go before I sleep."), and it seems to me that maybe this repetition is sort of hypnotic, almost as though he is drowsing off. I <u>feel</u> this, and when I read the lines aloud I can make them sound almost as though the speaker is drowsing off, but I'm not really sure that I'm right. After all, I can also read them aloud so they sound sort of perky or chipper, with a sense of "Well, I've put that behind me." I wonder if there is any way of deciding exactly how the last two lines should be read.

Now for the student's essay. You'll notice that it draws heavily on the journal, but it differs in two important ways. First, whereas in the journal the student saw the story as having three stages, in the final essay she sees four stages. (What in the journal is said to be the first stage of the poem, in the essay becomes two stages.) Second, you'll notice that the point made in the last paragraph of the journal is not included in the essay. Why? Here are three possibilities: (1) the writer came to feel that the point was not sound; (2) she came to feel that the point was sound but not worth making; (3) she came to feel that the point, though interesting and sound and worth making, required more space than was available. It was, so to speak, the material for a different paper.

Sara Fong

## "Stopping by Woods on a Snowy Evening" as a Short Story

Robert Frost's "Stopping by Woods on a Snowy Evening" can be read as a poem about a man who pauses to observe the beauty of nature, and it can also be read as a poem about a man with a death wish, a man who seems to long to give himself up completely to nature and thus escape his responsibilities as a citizen. A lot depends on what a reader wants to emphasize. For instance, a reader can emphasize lines about the beauty of nature: "The only other sound's the sweep / Of easy wind and downy flake," and "The woods are lovely, dark and deep." On the other hand, a reader can emphasize lines that show the speaker is fully aware of the responsibilities that most of us agree we have. At the very start of the poem he recognizes that the woods are not his but are owned by someone else, and at the end of the poem he recognizes that he has "promises to keep" and that before he sleeps (dies?) he must accomplish many things (go for "miles").

Does a reader have to choose between these two interpretations? I don't think so; to the contrary, I think it makes sense to read the poem as a kind of very short story, with a character whose developing thoughts make up a plot with four stages. In the first stage, the central figure is an ordinary person with rather ordinary thoughts. His very first thought is of the owner of the woods. He knows who the owner is, and since the owner lives in the village, the poet feels safe in trespassing, or at least in watching the woods "fill up with snow." Then, very subtly, the poet begins to tell us that although this seems to be an ordinary person thinking ordinary thoughts, he is a somewhat special person in a special situation. This is the second stage. Frost tells us that the horse thinks something is strange. He shakes his bells, wondering why the driver doesn't keep moving, as presumably ordinary drivers would. Moreover, we are told that this is "the darkest evening of the year." Frost could simply have said that the evening is dark, but he goes out of his way to make the evening a special evening.

We have now seen two stages in the first ten lines, and only six lines remain, yet in these six lines the story goes through two additional phases. The first three of these lines ("The only other sound's the sweep / Of easy wind and downy flake" and "The woods are lovely, dark and deep") are probably the most beautiful lines, the ones that make us say, "I wish I were there," or "I'd love to experience this." We feel that the poet has moved from the ordinary thoughts of the first stanza, about such business-like things as who owns the woods and where the owner's house is, to less materialistic thoughts, thoughts about the beauty of the nonhuman world of nature. And now, with the three final lines, we get the fourth stage of the story, the return to the ordinary world of people, the world of "promises." But this world that we get at the end is not exactly the same as the world we got at the beginning. The world at the beginning of the poem is a world of property (who owns the woods, and where the house is), but the world at the end of the poem is a world of unspecified and rather mysterious responsibilities ("promises to keep," "miles to go before I sleep"). It is almost as though the poet's experience of the beauty of nature--a beauty that for a moment made him forget the world of property--has served to sharpen his sense that human beings have responsibilities.

He clearly sees that "The woods are lovely, dark and deep," and then he says (I add the italics) "*But* I have promises to keep." The "but" would be logical if after saying that the woods are lovely, dark and deep, he had said something like "But in the daylight they look different," or "But one can freeze to death in them." The logic of what Frost says, however, is not at all clear: "The woods are lovely, dark and deep, / But I have promises to keep." What is the logical connection? We have to supply one, something like "but, *because we are human beings we have responsibilities;* we can refresh ourselves by perceiving the beauties of nature, and we can even for a moment get so caught up that we seem to enter an enchanted forest, but we cannot forget our responsibilities."

My point is not that Frost ends with an important moral. Rather, my point is that the poem takes us through several stages. The speaker undergoes mental experiences--goes through a plot with a conflict (the appeal of the snowy woods versus the call to return to the human world). It's not a matter of good versus evil and of one side winning. Frost doesn't suggest that it is wrong to feel the beauty of nature. But the poem is certainly not simply a praise of the beauty of nature. Frost shows us, in this ministory or minidrama, one character who sees the woods as property, then sees them as a place of almost overwhelming beauty, and then (maybe refreshed by this experience) rejoins the world of chores and responsibilities.

## TOPICS FOR CRITICAL THINKING AND WRITING

We can ask of this essay the same questions we asked of the previous essay:

1. In a sentence or two state the thesis of the essay.
2. Is the thesis adequately supported? Explain, pointing out strengths, if any, and weaknesses, if any.
3. Do you find the organization satisfactory? Why, or why not?
4. Do you find the title and the opening paragraph of interest? If not, how might you improve them?
5. Given the thesis and the development of it, is the final paragraph satisfactory? Why, or why not?
6. If you think that, on the whole, the essay is effectively written, take two or three sentences in it and explain what their strengths are. If you think that, on the whole, the writing could be more effective, take two or three sentences and revise them into more effective sentences. (It's not a matter of agreeing or disagreeing with the argument; we are talking chiefly about style.)

## Journal Entry and Essay

We preface the third student essay with Peter Franken's entry from his journal. The final essay does not include every point that the journal makes; on the contrary, it includes many points that the journal does not make, but you'll easily see that the journal provided a starting point for the thinking that ended up in the essay.

Journal entry: When we studied this poem in school last year, most students agreed with the instructor that it was about Robert Frost's belief that we can love nature but we must also love our fellow persons and recognize that we have responsibilities to them.

It doesn't matter which man owns the woods. We have a duty to God to fulfill our responsibilities. We also discussed the view that the poem takes place around Christmas, because of the snow. One student brought up the point that the true owner of the woods (and of everything else) is God, and I now feel on reading the poem again that the author makes this point very clear, and that the owner's house that he mentions is the village church. We also discussed the possibility that the man is thinking about how hard life is, and that he wants to give up, and be close to nature, and be buried under the peaceful pure snow. One student brought up the point that God owns the woods and everything else.

The student's final essay follows.

Peter Franken

The Meaning of
"Stopping by Woods on a Snowy Evening"

Although on the surface there is nothing about religion in Robert Frost's "Stopping by Woods on a Snowy Evening," I think the poem is basically about a person's realization that he or she has a religious duty to help other people.

In stanza 1 the poet tells us that he knows who owns the woods. The owner is God. Of course some individual may, during his lifetime, think that he owns the woods, but he is only the steward of the woods, a sort of caretaker. The true owner is God, whose "house is in the village," that is, who has a church in the village. At this stage in the poem, the poet is mistaken when he says that God will not see him, because God sees everything. So the poet's statement here is an example of unconscious irony.

In stanzas 2 and 3 the poet tells us that God sent a sort of message to him, through the horse. The horse shakes his harness bells, telling the speaker that he (the speaker) is making a "mistake." It may also be that in the picture of a snowy night and a domestic animal Robert Frost is trying to subtly suggest that we remember the scene of the birth of Jesus, in a manger, with domestic animals. In any case, although the scene is very peaceful and quiet (except for the harness bells and the sound of the "easy wind"), God is watching over the speaker of this poem.

In stanza 4, in the first line ("The woods are lovely, dark and deep") Robert Frost tells us of man's love of God's creation, and in the other lines of the stanza he says that proper love of the creation leads to an awareness of our responsibilities to other human beings. Robert Frost is very effective because he uses the device of understatement. He does not tell us exactly what these responsibilities are, so he leaves it to our imagination, but we can easily think of our many duties to our family and our fellow citizens and our country.

## TOPICS FOR CRITICAL THINKING AND WRITING

We can ask of this essay the same questions that we asked of the two previous essays.

1. In a sentence or two state the thesis of the essay.
2. Is the thesis adequately supported? Explain, pointing out strengths, if any, and weaknesses, if any.
3. Do you find the organization satisfactory? Why, or why not?

4. Do you find the title and the opening paragraph of interest? If not, how might you improve them?
5. Given the thesis and the development of it, is the final paragraph satisfactory? Why, or why not?
6. If you think that, on the whole, the essay is effectively written, take two or three sentences and explain what their strength is. If you think that, on the whole, the writing could be more effective, take two or three sentences and revise them into more effective sentences. (It's not a matter of agreeing or disagreeing with the argument; we are talking chiefly about style.)

## ADDITIONAL POEMS

### *The Pasture*

I'm going out to clean the pasture spring;
I'll only stop to rake the leaves away
(And wait to watch the water clear, I may):
I sha'n't be gone long.—You come too.

I'm going out to fetch the little calf
That's standing by the mother. It's so young,
It totters when she licks it with her tongue.
I sha'n't be gone long.—You come too.

[*1913*]

### *Mending Wall*

Something there is that doesn't love a wall,
That sends the frozen-ground-swell under it,
And spills the upper boulder in the sun;
And makes gaps even two can pass abreast.
The work of hunters is another thing:
I have come after them and made repair
Where they have left not one stone on a stone,
But they would have the rabbit out of hiding,
To please the yelping dogs. The gaps I mean,
No one has seen them made or heard them made,
But at spring mending-time we find them there.
I let my neighbor know beyond the hill;
And on a day we meet to walk the line
And set the wall between us once again.
We keep the wall between us as we go.
To each the boulders that have fallen to each.
And some are loaves and some so nearly balls
We have to use a spell to make them balance:
'Stay where you are until our backs are turned!'
We wear our fingers rough with handling them.
Oh, just another kind of outdoor game,
One on a side. It comes to little more:

There where it is we do not need the wall:
He is all pine and I am apple orchard.
My apple trees will never get across
And eat the cones under his pines, I tell him.
He only says, 'Good fences make good neighbours.'
Spring is the mischief in me, and I wonder
If I could put a notion in his head:
'*Why* do they make good neighbours? Isn't it
Where there are cows? But here there are no cows.
Before I built a wall I'd ask to know
What I was walling in or walling out,
And to whom I was like to give offence.
Something there is that doesn't love a wall,
That wants it down.' I could say 'Elves' to him,
But it's not elves exactly, and I'd rather
He said it for himself. I see him there
Bringing a stone grasped firmly by the top
In each hand, like an old-stone savage armed.
He moves in darkness as it seems to me,
Not of woods only and the shade of trees.
He will not go behind his father's saying,
And he likes having thought of it so well
He says again, 'Good fences make good neighbours.'

[*1914*]

## *The Wood-Pile*

Out walking in the frozen swamp one grey day,
I paused and said, 'I will turn back from here.
No, I will go on farther—and we shall see.'
The hard snow held me, save where now and then
One foot went through. The view was all in lines
Straight up and down of tall slim trees
Too much alike to mark or name a place by
So as to say for certain I was here
Or somewhere else: I was just far from home.
A small bird flew before me. He was careful
To put a tree between us when he lighted,
And say no word to tell me who he was
Who was so foolish as to think what *he* thought.
He thought that I was after him for a feather—
The white one in his tail; like one who takes
Everything said as personal to himself.
One flight out sideways would have undeceived him.
And then there was a pile of wood for which
I forgot him and let his little fear
Carry him off the way I might have gone,
Without so much as wishing him good-night.
He went behind it to make his last stand.
It was a cord of maple, cut and split

And piled—and measured, four by four by eight.
And not another like it could I see.
No runner tracks in this year's snow looped near it.
And it was older sure than this year's cutting,
Or even last year's or the year's before.
The wood was grey and the bark warping off it
And the pile somewhat sunken. Clematis
Had wound strings round and round it like a bundle.
What held it though on one side was a tree
Still growing, and on one a stake and prop,
These latter about to fall. I thought that only
Someone who lived in turning to fresh tasks
Could so forget his handiwork on which
He spent himself, the labour of his axe,
And leave it there far from a useful fireplace
To warm the frozen swamps as best it could
With the slow smokeless burning of decay.

[*1914*]

## *The Road Not Taken*

Two roads diverged in a yellow wood,
And sorry I could not travel both
And be one traveler, long I stood
And looked down one as far as I could
To where it bent in the undergrowth;

Then took the other, as just as fair,
And having perhaps the better claim,
Because it was grassy and wanted wear;
Though as for that the passing there
Had worn them really about the same,

And both that morning equally lay
In leaves no step had trodden black.
Oh, I kept the first for another day!
Yet knowing how way leads on to way,
I doubted if I should ever come back.

I shall be telling this with a sigh
Somewhere ages and ages hence:
Two roads diverged in a wood, and I—
I took the one less traveled by,
And that has made all the difference.

[*1916*]

## *The Telephone*

'When I was just as far as I could walk
From here to-day
There was an hour

All still
When leaning with my head against a flower
I heard you talk.
Don't say I didn't, for I heard you say—
You spoke from that flower on the window sill—
Do you remember what it was you said?'

'First tell me what it was you thought you heard.'

'Having found the flower and driven a bee away,
I leaned my head,
And holding by the stalk,
I listened and I thought I caught the word—
What was it? Did you call me by my name?
Or did you say—
*Someone* said "Come"—I heard it as I bowed.'

'I may have thought as much, but not aloud.'

'Well, so I came.'

[*1916*]

## The Oven Bird

There is a singer everyone has heard,
Loud, a mid-summer and a mid-wood bird,
Who makes the solid tree trunks sound again.
He says that leaves are old and that for flowers
Mid-summer is to spring as one to ten.
He says the early petal-fall is past
When pear and cherry bloom went down in showers
On sunny days a moment overcast;
And comes that other fall we name the fall.
He says the highway dust is over all.
The bird would cease and be as other birds
But that he knows in singing not to sing.
The question that he frames in all but words
Is what to make of a diminished thing.

[*1916*]

## The Aim Was Song

Before man came to blow it right
  The wind once blew itself untaught,
And did its loudest day and night
  In any rough place where it caught.

Man came to tell it what was wrong:
  It hadn't found the place to blow;
It blew too hard—the aim was song.
  And listen—how it ought to go!

He took a little in his mouth,
  And held it long enough for north
To be converted into south,
  And then by measure blew it forth.

By measure. It was word and note,
  The wind the wind had meant to be—
A little through the lips and throat.
  The aim was song—the wind could see.

[*1923*]

## *Two Look at Two*

Love and forgetting might have carried them
A little further up the mountain side
With night so near, but not much further up.
They must have halted soon in any case
With thoughts of the path back, how rough it was
With rock and washout, and unsafe in darkness;
When they were halted by a tumbled wall
With barbed-wire binding. They stood facing this,
Spending what onward impulse they still had
In one last look the way they must not go,
On up the failing path, where, if a stone
Or earthslide moved at night, it moved itself;
No footstep moved it. 'This is all,' they sighed,
'Good-night to woods.' But not so; there was more.
A doe from round a spruce stood looking at them
Across the wall, as near the wall as they.
She saw them in their field, they her in hers.
The difficulty of seeing what stood still,
Like some up-ended boulder split in two,
Was in her clouded eyes: they saw no fear there.
She seemed to think that two thus they were safe.
Then, as if they were something that, though strange,
She could not trouble her mind with too long,
She sighed and passed unscared along the wall.
'*This*, then, is all. What more is there to ask?'
But no, not yet. A snort to bid them wait.
A buck from round the spruce stood looking at them
Across the wall as near the wall as they.
This was an antlered buck of lusty nostril,
Not the same doe come back into her place.
He viewed them quizzically with jerks of head,
As if to ask, 'Why don't you make some motion?
Or give some sign of life? Because you can't.
I doubt if you're as living as you look.'
Thus till he had them almost feeling dared
To stretch a proffering hand—and a spell-breaking.
Then he too passed unscared along the wall.

Two had seen two, whichever side you spoke from.
'This *must* be all.' It was all. Still they stood,
A great wave from it going over them,
As if the earth in one unlooked-for favor
Had made them certain earth returned their love.

[*1923*]

## *The Need of Being Versed in Country Things*

The house had gone to bring again
To the midnight sky a sunset glow.
Now the chimney was all of the house that stood,
Like a pistil after the petals go.

The barn opposed across the way,
That would have joined the house in flame
Had it been the will of the wind, was left
To bear forsaken the place's name.

No more it opened with all one end
For teams that came by the stony road
To drum on the floor with scurrying hoofs
And brush the mow with the summer load.

The birds that came to it through the air
At broken windows flew out and in,
Their murmur more like the sigh we sigh
From too much dwelling on what has been.

Yet for them the lilac renewed its leaf,
And the aged elm, though touched with fire;
And the dry pump flung up an awkward arm;
And the fence post carried a strand of wire.

For them there was really nothing sad.
But though they rejoiced in the nest they kept,
One had to be versed in country things
Not to believe the phoebes wept.

[*1923*]

## *Acquainted with the Night*

I have been one acquainted with the night.
I have walked out in rain—and back in rain.
I have outwalked the furthest city light.

I have looked down the saddest city lane.
I have passed by the watchman on his beat
And dropped my eyes, unwilling to explain.

I have stood still and stopped the sound of feet
When far away an interrupted cry
Came over houses from another street,

But not to call me back or say good-bye;
And further still at an unearthly height,
One luminary clock against the sky

Proclaimed the time was neither wrong nor right.
I have been one acquainted with the night.

[*1928*]

## *Desert Places*

Snow falling and night falling fast oh fast
In a field I looked into going past,
And the ground almost covered smooth in snow,
But a few weeds and stubble showing last.

The woods around it have it—it is theirs.
All animals are smothered in their lairs.
I am too absent-spirited to count;
The loneliness includes me unawares.

And lonely as it is that loneliness
Will be more lonely ere it will be less—
A blanker whiteness of benighted snow
With no expression, nothing to express.

They cannot scare me with their empty spaces
Between stars—on stars where no human race is.
I have it in me so much nearer home
To scare myself with my own desert places.

[*1936*]

## *Design*

I found a dimpled spider, fat and white,
On a white heal-all, holding up a moth
Like a white piece of rigid satin cloth—
Assorted characters of death and blight
Mixed ready to begin the morning right,
Like the ingredients of a witches' broth—
A snow-drop spider, a flower like froth,
And dead wings carried like a paper kite.

What had that flower to do with being white,
The wayside blue and innocent heal-all?
What brought the kindred spider to that height,

Then steered the white moth thither in the night?
What but design of darkness to appall?—
If design govern in a thing so small.

[*1936*]

## *The Silken Tent*

She is as in a field a silken tent
At midday when a sunny summer breeze
Has dried the dew and all its ropes relent,
So that in guys it gently sways at ease,
And its supporting central cedar pole,
That is its pinnacle to heavenward
And signifies the sureness of the soul,
Seems to owe naught to any single cord,
But strictly held by none, is loosely bound
By countless silken ties of love and thought
To everything on earth the compass round,
And only by one's going slightly taut
In the capriciousness of summer air
Is of the slightest bondage made aware.

[*1942*]

## *Come In*

As I came to the edge of the woods.
Thrush music—hark!
Now if it was dusk outside,
Inside it was dark.

Too dark in the woods for a bird
By sleight of wing
To better its perch for the night,
Though it still could sing.

The last of the light of the sun
That had died in the west
Still lived for one song more
In a thrush's breast.

Far in the pillared dark
Thrush music went—
Almost like a call to come in
To the dark and lament.

But no, I was out for stars:
I would not come in.
I meant not even if asked,
And I hadn't been.

[*1942*]

## *The Most of It*

He thought he kept the universe alone;
For all the voice in answer he could wake
Was but the mocking echo of his own
From some tree-hidden cliff across the lake.
Some morning from the boulder-broken beach
He would cry out on life, that what it wants
Is not its own love back in copy speech,
But counter-love, original response.
And nothing ever came of what he cried
Unless it was the embodiment that crashed
In the cliff's talus on the other side,
And then in the far distant water splashed,
But after a time allowed for it to swim,
Instead of proving human when it neared
And someone else additional to him,
As a great buck it powerfully appeared,
Pushing the crumpled water up ahead,
And landed pouring like a waterfall,
And stumbled through the rocks with horny tread,
And forced the underbrush—and that was all.

[*1942*]

## *The Draft Horse*

With a lantern that wouldn't burn
In too frail a buggy we drove
Behind too heavy a horse
Through a pitch-dark limitless grove.

And a man came out of the trees
And took our horse by the head
And reaching back to his ribs
Deliberately stabbed him dead.

The ponderous beast went down
With a crack of a broken shaft.
And the night drew through the trees
In one long invidious draft.

The most unquestioning pair
That ever accepted fate
And the least disposed to ascribe
Any more than we had to to hate,

We assumed that the man himself
Or someone he had to obey
Wanted us to get down
And walk the rest of the way.

[*1962*]

# ROBERT FROST ON POETRY

We give five passages in which Frost talks about poetry. The first two are letters addressed to John Bartlett, who had been a pupil when Frost taught at Pinkerton Academy from 1907–09. Frost wrote these two letters during his stay in England, before he returned and established a career in the United States.

In addition to the letters, we reprint an essay, a portion of another essay, and some brief comments on Emily Dickinson. Frost wrote the first of these, "The Figure a Poem Makes," for the 1939 edition of his *Collected Poems* (the 1930 edition did not have the essay), and he reprinted it in later volumes. Our next selection is an extract—two paragraphs—from "The Constant Symbol," first published in the *Atlantic Monthly* for October 1946. Our final selection, three comments on Dickinson, gives a reader a sense of Frost's platform manner.

## *To John Bartlett*

Dear John:— Fourth of July [1913] Beaconsfield

Those initials you quote from T.P.'s belong to a fellow named Buckley and the explanation of Buckley is this that he has recently issued a book with David Nutt, but at his own expense, whereas in my case David Nutt assumed the risks. *And* those other people Buckley reviewed are his personal friends or friends of his friends or if not that simply examples of the kind of wrong horse most fools put their money on. You will be sorry to hear me say so but they are not even craftsmen. Of course there are two ways of using the word the good and the bad one. To be on the safe side it is best to call such dubs mechanics. To be perfectly frank with you I am one of the most notable craftsmen of my time. That will transpire presently. I am possibly the only person going who works on any but a worn out theory (principle I had better say) of versification. You see the great successes in recent poetry have been made on the assumption that the music of words was a matter of harmonised vowels and consonants. Both Swinburne and Tennyson arrived largely at effects in assonation. But they were on the wrong track or at any rate on a short track. They went the length of it. Any one else who goes that way must go after them. And that's where most are going. I alone of English writers have consciously set myself to make music out of what I may call the sound of sense. Now it is possible to have sense without the sound of sense (as in much prose that is supposed to pass muster but makes very dull reading) and the sound of sense without sense (as in Alice in Wonderland which makes anything but dull reading). The best place to get the abstract sound of sense is from voices behind a door that cuts off the words. Ask yourself how these sentences would sound without the words in which they are embodied:

You mean to tell me you can't read?
I said no such thing.
Well read then.
You're not my teacher.

———

He says it's too late.
Oh, say!
Damn an Ingersoll watch anyway.

———

One-two-three—go!
No good! Come back—come back.
Haslam go down there and make those kids get out of the track.

---

Those sounds are summoned by the audile [audial] imagination and they must be positive, strong, and definitely and unmistakeably indicated by the context. The reader must be at no loss to give his voice the posture proper to the sentence. The simple declarative sentence used in making a plain statement is one sound. But Lord love ye it mustn't be worked to death. It is against the law of nature that whole poems should be written in it. If they are written they won't be read. The sound of sense, then. You get that. It is the abstract vitality of our speech. It is pure sound—pure form. One who concerns himself with it more than the subject is an artist. But remember we are still talking merely of the raw material of poetry. An ear and an appetite for these sounds of sense is the first qualification of a writer, be it of prose or verse. But if one is to be a poet he must learn to get cadences by skillfully breaking the sounds of sense with all their irregularity of accent across the regular beat of the metre. Verse in which there is nothing but the beat of the metre furnished by the accents of the polysyllabic words we call doggerel. Verse is not that. Neither is it the sound of sense alone. It is a resultant from those two. There are only two or three metres that are worth anything. We depend for variety on the infinite play of accents in the sound of sense. The high possibility of emotional expression all lets in this mingling of sense-sound and word-accent. A curious thing. And all this has its bearing on your prose me boy. Never if you can help it write down a sentence in which the voice will not know how to posture *specially.*

That letter head shows how far we have come since we left Pink. Editorial correspondent of the Montreal Star sounds to me. Gad, we get little mail from you.

Affectionately R.F.

Maybe you'll keep this discourse on the sound of sense till I can say more on it.

## *To John Bartlett*

Dear John: 22 February 1914 Beaconsfield

[ . . . ] I set a good deal of store by the magazine work you are doing or going to do. That is your way out of bondage. You can—must write better for a magazine than there is any inducement to do for a daily.

My notion is that your work is coming on. Your style tightens up. What you will have to guard against is the lingo of the newspaper, words that nobody but a journalist uses, and worse still, phrases. John Cournos who learned his trade on the Philadelphia Record, where he went by the nickname of Gorky, has come over here to write short stories. He is thirty. His worst enemy is going to be his habit of saying cuticle for skin.

I really liked what you wrote about me. Your sentences go their distance, straight and sure and they relay each other well. You always had ideas and apprehended ideas. You mustnt lose that merit. You must find some way to show people that you have initiative and judgement. You must "get up" new things as new even as a brand new department for some paper.

[ . . . ] I want to write down here two or three cardinal principles that I wish you would think over and turn over now and again till we *can* protract talk.

I give you a new definition of a sentence:

A sentence is a sound in itself on which other sounds called words may be strung.

You may string words together without a sentence-sound to string them on just as you may tie clothes together by the sleeves and stretch them without a clothes line between two trees, but—it is bad for the clothes.

The number of words you may string on one sentence-sound is not fixed but there is always danger of overloading.

The sentence-sounds are very definite entities. (This is no literary mysticism I am preaching.) They are as definite as words. It is not impossible that they could be collected in a book though I don't at present see on what system they would be catalogued.

They are apprehended by the ear. They are gathered by the ear from the vernacular and brought into books. Many of them are already familiar to us in books. I think no writer invents them. The most original writer only catches them fresh from talk, where they grow spontaneously.

A man is all a writer if *all* his words are strung on definite recognizable sentence sounds. The voice of the imagination, the speaking voice must know certainly how to behave how to posture in every sentence he offers.

A man is a marked writer if his words are largely strung on the more striking sentence sounds.

A word about recognition: In literature it is our business to give people the thing that will make them say, "Oh yes I know what you mean." It is never to tell them something they dont know, but something they know and hadnt thought of saying. It must be something they recognize.

A Patch of Old Snow

In the corner of the wall where the bushes haven't been trimmed, there is a patch of old snow like a blow-away newspaper that has come to rest there. And it is dirty as with the print and news of a day I have forgotten, if I ever read it.

Now that is no good except for what I may call certain points of recognition in it: patch of old snow in a corner of the wall,—you know what that is. You know what a blow-away newspaper is. You know the curious dirt on old snow and last of all you know how easily you forget what you read in papers.*

Now for the sentence sounds: We will look for the marked ones because they are easiest to discuss. The first sentence sound will do but it is

*Editors' note: Here is the final version of the poem, called "A Patch of Snow":

There's a patch of old snow in a corner,  
  That I should have guessed  
Was a blow-away paper the rain  
  Had brought to rest.

It is speckled with grime as if  
  Small print overspread it.  
The news of a day I've forgotten—  
  If I ever read it.

merely ordinary and bookish: it is entirely subordinate in interest to the meaning of the words strung on it. But half the effectiveness of the second sentence is in the very special tone with which you must say—news of a day I have forgotten—if I ever read it. You must be able to say Oh yes one knows how that goes. (There is some adjective to describe the intonation or cadence, but I won't hunt for it.)

One of the least successful of the poems in my book is almost saved by a final striking sentence-sound (Asking for Roses.)

Not caring so very much *what* she supposes.

Take My November Guest. Did you know at once how we say such sentences as these when we talk?

She thinks I have no eye for these.

Not yesterday I learned etc.

But it were vain to tell her so

Get away from the sing-song. You must hear and recognize in the last line the sentence sound that supports, No use in telling him so.

Let's have some examples pell-mell in prose and verse because I don't want you to think I am setting up as an authority on verse alone.

My father used to say—
You're a liar!
If a hen and a half lay an egg and a half etc.
A long long time ago—
Put it there, old man! (Offering your hand)
I aint a going [to] hurt you, so you needn't be scared.

Suppose Henry Horne says something offensive to a young lady named Rita when her brother Charles is by to protect her. Can you hear the two different tones in which she says their respective names. "Henry Horne! Charles!" I can hear it better than I can say it. And by oral practice I get further and further away from it.

Never you say a thing like that to a man!
And such they are and such they will be found.
Well I swan!
Unless I'm greatly mistaken—
Hence with denial vain and coy excuse
A soldier and afraid (afeared)
Come, child, come home.
The thing for me to do is to get right out of here while I am able.
No fool like an old fool.

It is so and not otherwise that we get the variety that makes it fun to write and read. *The ear does it.* The ear is the only true writer and the only true reader. I have known people who could read without hearing the sentence sounds and they were the fastest readers. Eye readers we call them. They can get the meaning by glances. But they are bad readers because they miss the best part of what a good writer puts into his work.

Remember that the sentence sound often says more than the words. It may even as in irony convey a meaning opposite to the words.

I wouldn't be writing all this if I didn't think it the most important thing I know. I write it partly for my own benefit, to clarify my ideas for an essay or two I am going to write some fine day (not far distant).

To judge a poem or piece of prose you go the same way to work—apply the one test—greatest test. You listen for the sentence sounds. If you find some of those not bookish, caught fresh from the mouths of people, some of them striking, all of them definite and recognizable, so recognizable that with a little trouble you can place them and even name them, you know you have found a writer. [ . . . ]

## *The Figure a Poem Makes*

Abstraction is an old story with the philosophers, but it has been like a new toy in the hands of the artists of our day. Why can't we have any one quality of poetry we choose by itself? We can have in thought. Then it will go hard if we can't in practice. Our lives for it.

Granted no one but a humanist much cares how sound a poem is if it is only *a* sound. The sound is the gold in the ore. Then we will have the sound out alone and dispense with the inessential. We do till we make the discovery that the object in writing poetry is to make all poems sound as different as possible from each other, and the resources for that of vowels, consonants, punctuation, syntax, words, sentences, meter are not enough. We need the help of context—meaning—subject matter. That is the greatest help towards variety. All that can be done with words is soon told. So also with meters—particularly in our language where there are virtually but two, strict iambic and loose iambic. The ancients with many were still poor if they depended on meters for all tune. It is painful to watch our sprung-rhythmists straining at the point of omitting one short from a foot for relief from monotony. The possibilities for tune from the dramatic tones of meaning struck across the rigidity of a limited meter are endless. And we are back in poetry as merely one more art of having something to say, sound or unsound. Probably better if sound, because deeper and from wider experience.

Then there is this wildness whereof it is spoken. Granted again that it has an equal claim with sound to being a poem's better half. If it is a wild tune, it is a poem. Our problem then is, as modern abstractionists, to have the wildness pure: to be wild with nothing to be wild about. We bring up as aberrationists, giving way to undirected associations and kicking ourselves from one chance suggestion to another in all directions as of a hot afternoon in the life of a grasshopper. Theme alone can steady us down. Just as the first mystery was how a poem could have a tune in such a straightness as meter, so the second mystery is how a poem can have wildness and at the same time a subject that shall be fulfilled.

It should be of the pleasure of a poem itself to tell how it can. The figure a poem makes. It begins in delight and ends in wisdom. The figure is the same as for love. No one can really hold that the ecstasy should be static and stand still in one place. It begins in delight, it inclines to the impulse, it assumes direction with the first line laid down, it runs a course of lucky events, and ends in a clarification of life—not necessarily a great clarification, such as sects and cults are founded on, but in a momentary stay against confusion. It has denouement. It has an outcome that though unforeseen was predestined from the first image of the original mood—and indeed from the very mood. It is but a trick poem and no poem at all if the best of it was thought of first and saved for the last. It finds its own name as it goes and discovers the best waiting for it in some final phrase at once wise and sad—the happy-sad blend of the drinking song.

No tears in the writer, no tears in the reader. No surprise for the writer, no surprise for the reader. For me the initial delight is in the surprise of remembering something I didn't know I knew. I am in a place, in a situation, as if I had materialized from cloud or risen out of the ground. There is a glad recognition of the long lost and the rest follows. Step by step the wonder of unexpected supply keeps growing. The impressions most useful to my purpose seem always those I was unaware of and so made no note of at the time when taken, and the conclusion is come to that like giants we are always hurling experience ahead of us to pave the future with against the day when we may want to strike a line of purpose across it for somewhere. The line will have the more charm for not being mechanically straight. We enjoy the straight crookedness of a good walking stick. Modern instruments of precision are being used to make things crooked as if by eye and hand in the old days.

I tell how there may be a better wildness of logic than of inconsequence. But the logic is backward, in retrospect, after the act. It must be more felt than seen ahead like prophecy. It must be a revelation, or a series of revelations, as much for the poet as for the reader. For it to be that there must have been the greatest freedom of the material to move about in it and to establish relations in it regardless of time and space, previous relation, and everything but affinity. We prate of freedom. We call our schools free because we are not free to say away from them till we are sixteen years of age. I have given up my democratic prejudices and now willingly set the lower classes free to be completely taken care of by the upper classes. Political freedom is nothing to me. I bestow it right and left. All I would keep for myself is the freedom of my material—the condition of body and mind now and then to summons aptly from the vast chaos of all I have lived through.

Scholars and artists thrown together are often annoyed at the puzzle of where they differ. Both work from knowledge; but I suspect they differ most importantly in the way their knowledge is come by. Scholars get theirs with conscientious thoroughness along projected lines of logic; poets theirs cavalierly and as it happens in and out of books. They stick to nothing deliberately, but let what will stick to them like burrs where they walk in the fields. No acquirement is on assignment, or even self-assignment. Knowledge of the second kind is much more available in the wild free ways of wit and art. A school boy may be defined as one who can tell you what he knows in the order in which he learned it. The artist must value himself as he snatches a thing from some previous order in time and space into a new order with not so much as a ligature clinging to it of the old place where it was organic.

More than once I should have lost my soul to radicalism if it had been the originality it was mistaken for by young converts. Originality and initiative are what I ask for my country. For myself the originality need be no more than the freshness of a poem run in the way I have described: from delight to wisdom. The figure is the same as for love. Like a piece of ice on a hot stove the poem must ride on its own melting. A poem may be worked over once it is in being, but may not be worried into being. Its most precious quality will remain its having run itself and carried away the poet with it. Read it a hundred times: it will forever keep its freshness as a metal keeps its fragrance. It can never lose its sense of a meaning that once unfolded by surprise as it went.

## *From "The Constant Symbol"*

There are many other things I have found myself saying about poetry, but the chiefest of these is that it is metaphor, saying one thing and meaning another, saying one thing in terms of another, the pleasure of ulteriority. Poetry is simply made of metaphor. So also is philosophy—and science, too, for that matter, if it will take the soft impeachment from a friend. Every poem is a new metaphor inside or it is nothing. And there is a sense in which all poems are the same old metaphor always.

Every single poem written regular is a symbol small or great of the way the will has to pitch into commitments deeper and deeper to a rounded conclusion and then be judged for whether any original intention it had has been strongly spent or weakly lost; be it in art, politics, school, church, business, love, or marriage—in a piece of work or in a career. Strongly spent is synonymous with kept.

## *Three Comments on the Poetry of Emily Dickinson*

[The first of these comments was made at Middlebury College on 9 November 1945, during a lecture-reading. The other two comments were made in conversation with Daniel Smythe on 28 June 1960.]

1. One of the great things in life is being true within the conventions. I deny in a good poem or a good life that there is compromise. When there is, it is an attempt to so flex the lines that no suspicion can be cast upon what the poet does. Emily Dickinson's poems are examples of this. When the rhyme begins to bother, she says, "Here I come with my truth. Let the rhyme take care of itself." This makes me feel her strength.

2. I try to make good sentences fit the meter. That is important. Good grammar. I don't like to twist the order around in order to fit a form. I try to keep to regular structure and good rhymes. Though I admit that Emily Dickinson, for one, didn't do this always. When she started a poem, it was "Here I come!" and she came plunging through. The meter and rhyme often had to take care of itself.

3. [In response to an interviewer's remark that Dickinson "didn't study technique"] But she should have been more careful. She was more interested in getting the poem down and writing a new one. I feel that she left some to be revised later, and she never revised them. . . . She has all kinds of off rhymes. Some that do not rhyme. Her meter does not always go together.

# CHAPTER 28

# *Critical Perspectives on Langston Hughes*

## *A Casebook*

### LANGSTON HUGHES

*Langston Hughes (1902–67) was an accomplished poet, short-story writer, dramatist, essayist, and editor. He was born in Joplin, Missouri; he grew up in Lawrence, Kansas, and Cleveland, Ohio; and he spent a year living in Mexico before entering Columbia University in 1921. He left Columbia the following year and traveled extensively in Europe, returning to the United States in the mid-1920s. During these years, Hughes pursued his academic studies at Lincoln University in Pennsylvania (graduating in 1929) and published his first two books of verse,* The Weary Blues *(1926) and* Fine Clothes to the Jew *(1927). His many achievements in literature, drawing upon spirituals, blues, jazz, and folk expression, and his rich, productive career have led his biographer, Arnold Rampersad, to describe him as "perhaps the most representative black American writer."*

*Here we provide a selection of Hughes's poetry that shows the range of his themes and the variety of his speaking voices. We begin with one of his best-known works, "The Negro Speaks of Rivers," a poem first published in the June 1921 issue of* The Crisis, *the official magazine of the NAACP. We follow this poem with Hughes's own account of its composition; the response to it by Jessie Fauset, literary editor of* The Crisis; *critical commentaries by Onwuchekwa Jemie, Arnold Rampersad, and R. Baxter Miller; and additional poems and prose by Hughes.*

## The Negro Speaks of Rivers

I've known rivers:
I've known rivers ancient as the world and older than the
  flow of human blood in human veins.

My soul has grown deep like the rivers.

I bathed in the Euphrates when dawns were young.
I built my hut near the Congo and it lulled me to sleep.
I looked upon the Nile and raised the pyramids above it.
I heard the singing of the Mississippi when Abe Lincoln
  went down to New Orleans, and I've seen its muddy
  bosom turn all golden in the sunset.

I've known rivers:
Ancient, dusky rivers.

My soul has grown deep like the rivers.

[*1921*]

## On Writing "The Negro Speaks of Rivers"

[Hughes gave this account in *The Big Sea* (1940), the first volume of his autobiography.]

The one of my poems that has perhaps been most often reprinted in anthologies, was written on the train during this trip to Mexico when I was feeling very bad. It's called "The Negro Speaks of Rivers" and was written just outside St. Louis, as the train rolled toward Texas.

It came about in this way. All day on the train I had been thinking about my father and his strange dislike of his own people. I didn't understand it, because I was a Negro, and I liked Negroes very much. One of the happiest jobs I had ever had was during my freshman year in high school, when I worked behind the soda fountain for a Mrs. Kitzmiller, who ran a refreshment parlor on Central Avenue in the heart of the colored neighborhood. People just up from the South used to come in for ice cream and sodas and watermelon. And I never tired of hearing them talk, listening to the thunderclaps of their laughter, to their troubles, to their discussions of the war and the men who had gone to Europe from the Jim Crow South, their complaints over the high rent and the long overtime hours that brought what seemed like big checks, until the weekly bills were paid. They seemed to me like the gayest and the bravest people possible—these Negroes from the Southern ghettos—facing tremendous odds, working and laughing and trying to get somewhere in the world.

I had been in to dinner early that afternoon on the train. Now it was just sunset, and we crossed the Mississippi, slowly, over a long bridge. I looked out the window of the Pullman at the great muddy river flowing down toward the heart of the South, and I began to think what that river, the old Mississippi, had meant to Negroes in the past—how to be sold down the river was the worst fate that could overtake a slave in times of bondage. Then I remembered reading how Abraham Lincoln had made a trip down the Mississippi on a raft to New Orleans, and how he had seen slavery at its worst, and had decided within himself that it should be removed from American life. Then I began to think about other rivers in our past—the Congo, and the Niger, and the Nile in Africa—and the thought came to me: "I've known rivers," and I put it down on the back of an envelope I had in my pocket, and within the space of ten or fifteen minutes, as the train gathered speed in the dusk, I had written this poem, which I called "The Negro Speaks of Rivers":

I've known rivers:
I've known rivers ancient as the world and older than the
  flow of human blood in human veins.

My soul has grown deep like the rivers.

I bathed in the Euphrates when dawns were young.
I built my hut near the Congo and it lulled me to sleep.
I looked upon the Nile and raised the pyramids above it.
I heard the singing of the Mississippi when Abe Lincoln
  went down to New Orleans, and I've seen its muddy
  bosom turn all golden in the sunset.

I've known rivers:
Ancient, dusky rivers.

My soul has grown deep like the rivers.

No doubt I changed a few words the next day, or maybe crossed out a line or two. But there are seldom many changes in my poems, once they're down. Generally, the first two or three lines come to me from something I'm thinking about, or looking at, or doing, and the rest of the poem (if there is to be a poem) flows from those first few lines, usually right away. If there is a chance to put the poem down then, I write it down. If not, I try to remember it until I get to a pencil and paper; for poems are like rainbows: they escape you quickly.

[*1940*]

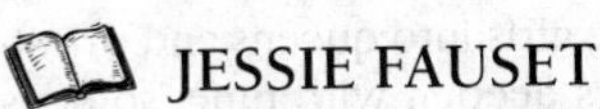

## JESSIE FAUSET

*Fauset (1882-1961) was the literary editor of* The Crisis *and W. E. B. Du Bois its general editor. In her comments, from a review of Hughes's* The Weary Blues *(1926), Fauset refers to* Brownies' Book, *a monthly for children that she and Du Bois had begun in October, 1919, in which Hughes had already published poems.*

## *On Reading "The Negro Speaks of Rivers"*

Very perfect is the memory of my first literary acquaintance with Langston Hughes. In the unforgettable days when we were publishing *The Brownies' Book* we had already appreciated a charming fragile conceit which read:

Out of the dust of dreams,
Fairies weave their garments;
Out of the purple and rose of old memories,
They make purple wings.
No wonder we find them such marvelous
things.

Then one day came "The Negro Speaks of Rivers." I took the beautiful dignified creation to Dr. Du Bois and said: "What colored person is there, do you suppose, in the United States who writes like that and yet is unknown to us?" And I wrote and found him to be a Cleveland high school graduate who had just gone to live in Mexico. Already he had begun to assume that remote, so elusive quality which permeates most of his work. Before long we had the pleasure of seeing the work of the boy, whom we had sponsored, copied and recopied in journals far and wide. "The Negro Speaks of Rivers" even appeared in translation in a paper printed in Germany.

[*1926*]

 ONWUCHEKWA JEMIE

## *On the Power of "The Negro Speaks of Rivers"*

"The Negro Speaks of Rivers" is perhaps the most profound of these poems of heritage and strength. Composed when Hughes was a mere 17 years old, and dedicated to W. E. B. DuBois, it is a sonorous evocation of transcendent essences so ancient as to appear timeless, predating human existence, longer than human memory. The rivers are part of God's body, and participate in his immortality. They are the earthly analogues of eternity: deep, continuous, mysterious. They are named in the order of their association with black history. The black man has drunk of their life-giving essences, and thereby borrowed their immortality. He and the rivers have become one. The magical transformation of the Mississippi from mud to gold by the sun's radiance is mirrored in the transformation of slaves into free men by Lincoln's Proclamation (and, in Hughes's poems, the transformation of shabby cabarets into gorgeous palaces, dancing girls into queens and priestesses by the spell of black music). As the rivers deepen with time, so does the black man's soul; as their waters ceaselessly flow, so will the black soul endure. The black man has seen the rise and fall of civilizations from the earliest times, seen the beauty and death-changes of the world over the thousands of years, and will survive even this America. The poem's meaning is related to Zora Neale Hurston's judgment of the mythic High John de Conquer, whom she held as a symbol of the triumphant spirit of black America: that John was of the "Be" class. "*Be* here when the ruthless man comes, and *be* here when he is gone." In a time and place where black life is held cheap and the days of black men appear to be numbered, the poem is a majestic reminder of the strength and fullness of history, of the source of that life which transcends even ceaseless labor and burning crosses.

[*1973*]

ARNOLD RAMPERSAD

## *Parricide and Peace in "The Negro Speaks of Rivers"*

Within a year, before he was nineteen, Hughes had written at least three of the poems on which his revered position among black readers would rest. The most important, and the one most illustrative of his poetic process, was composed on a train in July 1920, when, after graduating from high school, he traveled to Mexico to attempt a reconciliation with his father. According to the poet, the place was a train crossing the Mississippi River near St. Louis, the time was near sunset, and his mood something like despair after a long dwelling on his unhappiness with his father and his father's contempt for blacks. A phrase came to Hughes, then the whole poem, "The Negro Speaks of Rivers."

If the details of its inspiration are true (and they appear to be), then "The Negro Speaks of Rivers" reflects the classic motion of Hughes's creativity as a poet. The poem begins in a sense of hurt mingled with indignation, but the affliction and the rage are transcended. In this case, the image of his father, the primal source of anxiety, even of a death-wish, dissolves into the superior power with which it would contend, the beauty and historicity of the black race, which nourishes the poet as a mother nourishes her child. Quietly, without anger, much less invective, the father (the hurt) is liquidated in the inexorable flow of the river, whose despised "muddy bosom," irradiated by the poet's filial vision, turns now "all golden" in the sunset of the poem. Buried deep within the work, deep in the river, is an act of violence—parricide—which nevertheless brings peace both to the brown river-race and to the poet who honors it.

Published in Du Bois's *Crisis* magazine in June 1921, when Hughes was nineteen, "The Negro Speaks of Rivers" would remain in some ways the centerpiece of his verse to the end of his life.

[*1987*]

R. BAXTER MILLER

## *Africa as the Source of Civilization and History*

"Rivers" presents the narrator's skill in retracing known civilization back to the source in East Africa. Within thirteen lines and five stanzas, through the suggestion of wisdom by anagoge, we re-project ourselves into aboriginal consciousness. Then the speaker affirms the spirit distilled from human history, ranging from 3000 B.C. through the mid-nineteenth century to the author himself at the brink of the Harlem Renaissance. The powerful repetend "I've known rivers. / Ancient, dusky rivers" closes the human narrative in nearly a circle, for the verse has turned itself subtly from an external focus to a unified and internal one: "My soul has grown deep like the rivers." Except for the physical and spiritual dimensions, the subjective "I" and the "river" read the same.

When the Euphrates flows from eastern Turkey southeast and southwest into the Tigris, it recalls the rise as well as the fall of the Roman Empire. For over two thousand years the water helped delimit that domain. Less so did the Congo, which south of the Sahara demarcates the natural boundaries between white and Black Africa. The latter empties into the Atlantic Ocean; the Nile flows northward from Uganda into the Mediterranean; in the United States the Mississippi River flows southeast from north central Minnesota to the Gulf of Mexico. Whether north or south, east or west, "River" signifies the fertility as well as the dissemination of life in concentric half-circles. The liquid, as the externalized form of the contemplative imagination, has both depth and flow. "The Negro Speaks of Rivers" reclaims the origins in Africa of both physical and spiritual humanity.

[*1989*]

# ADDITIONAL POEMS

## *Mother to Son*

Well, son, I'll tell you:
Life for me ain't been no crystal stair.
It's had tacks in it,
And splinters,
And boards torn up,
And places with no carpet on the floor—
Bare.
But all the time
I'se been a-climbin' on,
And reachin' landin's,
And turnin' corners,
And sometimes goin' in the dark
Where there ain't been no light.
So boy, don't you turn back.
Don't you set down on the steps
'Cause you finds it's kinder hard.
Don't you fall now—
For I'se still goin', honey,
I'se still climbin',
And life for me ain't been no crystal stair.

[*1922*]

## *The Weary Blues*

Droning a drowsy syncopated tune,
Rocking back and forth to a mellow croon,
  I heard a Negro play.
Down on Lenox Avenue the other night
By the pale dull pallor of an old gas light
  He did a lazy sway. . . .
  He did a lazy sway. . . .
To the tune o' those Weary Blues.
With his ebony hands on each ivory key
He made that poor piano moan with melody.
  O Blues!
Swaying to and fro on his rickety stool
He played that sad raggy tune like a musical fool.
  Sweet Blues!
Coming from a black man's soul.
  O Blues!
In a deep song voice with a melancholy tone
I heard that Negro sing, that old piano moan—
  "Ain't got nobody in all this world,
    Ain't got nobody but ma self.
    I's gwine to quit ma frownin'
    And put ma troubles on the shelf."

Thump, thump, thump, went his foot on the floor.
He played a few chords then he sang some more—
  "I got the Weary Blues
    And I can't be satisfied.
    Got the Weary Blues
    And can't be satisfied—
    I ain't happy no mo'
    And I wish that I had died."
And far into the night he crooned that tune.
The stars went out and so did the moon.
The singer stopped playing and went to bed
While the Weary Blues echoed through his head.
He slept like a rock or a man that's dead.

[*1925*]

## *The South*

The lazy, laughing South
With blood on its mouth.
The sunny-faced South,
  Beast-strong,
  Idiot-brained.

The child-minded South
Scratching in the dead fire's ashes
For a Negro's bones.
  Cotton and the moon,
  Warmth, earth, warmth,
  The sky, the sun, the stars,
  The magnolia-scented South.
Beautiful, like a woman,
Seductive as a dark-eyed whore,
  Passionate, cruel,
  Honey-lipped, syphilitic—
  That is the South.
And I, who am black, would love her
But she spits in my face.
And I, who am black,
Would give her many rare gifts
But she turns her back upon me.
  So now I seek the North—
  The cold-faced North,
  For she, they say,
  Is a kinder mistress,
And in her house my children
May escape the spell of the South.

[*1922*]

## *Ruby Brown*

She was young and beautiful
And golden like the sunshine
That warmed her body.
And because she was colored
Mayville had no place to offer her,
Nor fuel for the clean flame of joy
That tried to burn within her soul.

One day,
Sitting on old Mrs. Latham's back porch
Polishing the silver,
She asked herself two questions
And they ran something like this:
What can a colored girl do
On the money from a white woman's kitchen?
And ain't there any joy in this town?

Now the streets down by the river
Know more about this pretty Ruby Brown,
And the sinister shuttered houses of the bottoms
Hold a yellow girl
Seeking an answer to her questions.
The good church folk do not mention
Her name any more.

But the white men,
Habitués of the high shuttered houses,
Pay more money to her now
Than they ever did before,
When she worked in their kitchens.

[*1926*]

# *Let America Be America Again*

Let America be America again.
Let it be the dream it used to be.
Let it be the pioneer on the plain
Seeking a home where he himself is free.

(America never was America to me.)

Let America be the dream the dreamers dreamed—
Let it be that great strong land of love
Where never kings connive nor tyrants scheme
That any man be crushed by one above.

(It never was America to me.)

O, let my land be a land where Liberty
Is crowned with no false patriotic wreath,
But opportunity is real, and life is free,
Equality is in the air we breathe.

(There's never been equality for me,
Nor freedom in this "homeland of the free.")

*Say, who are you that mumbles in the dark?*
*And who are you that draws your veil across the stars?*

I am the poor white, fooled and pushed apart,
I am the Negro bearing slavery's scars.
I am the red man driven from the land,
I am the immigrant clutching the hope I seek—
And finding only the same old stupid plan
Of dog eat dog, of mighty crush the weak.

I am the young man, full of strength and hope,
Tangled in that ancient endless chain
Of profit, power, gain, of grab the land!
Of grab the gold! Of grab the ways of satisfying need!
Of work the men! Of take the pay!
Of owning everything for one's own greed!

I am the farmer, bondsman to the soil.
I am the worker sold to the machine.
I am the Negro, servant to you all.
I am the people, humble, hungry, mean—
Hungry yet today despite the dream.
Beaten yet today—O, Pioneers!

I am the man who never got ahead,
The poorest worker bartered through the years.

Yet I'm the one who dreamt our basic dream
In that Old World while still a serf of kings,
Who dreamt a dream so strong, so brave, so true,
That even yet its mighty daring sings
In every brick and stone, in every furrow turned
That's made America the land it has become.
O, I'm the man who sailed those early seas
In search of what I meant to be my home—
For I'm the one who left dark Ireland's shore,
And Poland's plain, and England's grassy lea,
And torn from Black Africa's strand I came
To build a "homeland of the free."

The free?

Who said the free? Not me?
Surely not me? The millions on relief today?
The millions shot down when we strike?
The millions who have nothing for our pay?
For all the dreams we've dreamed
And all the songs we've sung
And all the hopes we've held
And all the flags we've hung,
The millions who have nothing for our pay—
Except the dream that's almost dead today.

O, let America be America again—
The land that never has been yet—
And yet must be—the land where *every* man is free.
The land that's mine—the poor man's, Indian's, Negro's, ME—
Who made America,
Whose sweat and blood, whose faith and pain,
Whose hand at the foundry, whose plow in the rain,
Must bring back our mighty dream again.

Sure, call me any ugly name you choose—
The steel of freedom does not stain.
From those who live like leeches on the people's lives,
We must take back our land again,
America!

O, yes,
I say it plain,
America never was America to me,
And yet I swear this oath—
America will be!

Out of the rack and ruin of our gangster death,
The rape and rot of graft, and stealth, and lies,
We, the people, must redeem
The land, the mines, the plants, the rivers.
The mountains and the endless plain—

All, all the stretch of these great green states—
And make America again!

[*1936*]

## *Poet to Patron*

What right has anyone to say
That I
Must throw out pieces of my heart
For pay?

For bread that helps to make
My heart beat true,
I must sell myself
To you?

A factory shift's better,
A week's meagre pay,
Than a perfumed note asking:
*What poems today?*

[*1939*]

## *Ballad of the Landlord*

Landlord, landlord,
My roof has sprung a leak.
Don't you 'member I told you about it
Way last week?

Landlord, landlord,
These steps is broken down.
When you come up yourself
It's a wonder you don't fall down.

Ten Bucks you say I owe you?
Ten Bucks you say is due?
Well, that's Ten Bucks more'n I'll pay you
Till you fix this house up new.

What? You gonna get eviction orders?
You gonna cut off my heat?
You gonna take my furniture and
Throw it in the street?

Um-huh! You talking high and mighty.
Talk on—till you get through.
You ain't gonna be able to say a word
If I land my fist on you.

*Police! Police!*
*Come and get this man!*
*He's trying to ruin the government*
*And overturn the land!*

Copper's whistle!
Patrol bell!
Arrest.

Precinct Station.
Iron cell.
Headlines in press:

MAN THREATENS LANDLORD

•
• •

TENANT HELD NO BAIL

•
• •

JUDGE GIVES NEGRO 90 DAYS IN COUNTY JAIL.

[*1940*]

## *Too Blue*

I got those sad old weary blues.
I don't know where to turn.
I don't know where to go.
Nobody cares about you
When you sink so low.

What shall I do?
What shall I say?
Shall I take a gun
And put myself away?

I wonder if
*One* bullet would do?
As hard as my head is,
It would probably take two.

But I ain't got
Neither bullet nor gun—
And I'm too blue
To look for one.

[*1943*]

## *Harlem [1]*

Here on the edge of hell
Stands Harlem—
Remembering the old lies,
The old kicks in the back,
The old "Be patient"
They told us before.

Sure, we remember.
Now when the man at the corner store

Says sugar's gone up another two cents,
And bread one,
And there's a new tax on cigarettes—
We remember the job we never had,
Never could get,
And can't have now
Because we're colored.

So we stand here
On the edge of hell
In Harlem
And look out on the world
And wonder
What we're gonna do
In the face of what
We remember.

[*1949*]

## *Theme for English B*

The instructor said,

*Go home and write*
*a page tonight.*
*And let that page come out of you—*
*Then, it will be true.*

I wonder if it's that simple?
I am twenty-two, colored, born in Winston-Salem.
I went to school there, then Durham, then here
to this college on the hill above Harlem.
I am the only colored student in my class.
The steps from the hill lead down into Harlem,
through a park, then I cross St. Nicholas,
Eighth Avenue, Seventh, and I come to the Y,
the Harlem Branch Y, where I take the elevator
up to my room, sit down, and write this page:

It's not easy to know what is true for you or me
at twenty-two, my age. But I guess I'm what
I feel and see and hear, Harlem, I hear you:
hear you, hear me—we two—you, me, talk on this page.
(I hear New York, too.) Me—who?
Well, I like to eat, sleep, drink, and be in love.
I like to work, read, learn, and understand life.
I like a pipe for a Christmas present,
or records—Bessie, bop, or Bach.
I guess being colored doesn't make me *not* like
the same things other folks like who are other races.
So will my page be colored that I write?
Being me, it will not be white.
But it will be

a part of you, instructor.
You are white—
yet a part of me, as I am a part of you.
That's American.
Sometimes perhaps you don't want to be a part of me.
Nor do I often want to be a part of you.
But we are, that's true!
As I learn from you,
I guess you learn from me—
although you're older—and white—
and somewhat more free.

This is my page for English B.

[*1949*]

## *Poet to Bigot*

I have done so little
For you,
And you have done so little
For me,
That we have good reason
Never to agree.

I, however,
Have such meagre
Power,
Clutching at a
Moment,
While you control
An hour.

But your hour is
A stone.

My moment is
A flower.

[*1953*]

# LANGSTON HUGHES ON POETRY

## *Making Poetry Pay: On Public Reading*

[This selection comes from *I Wonder as I Wander,* Hughes's second volume of autobiography.]

By midwinter I had worked out a public routine of reading my poetry that almost never failed to provoke, after each poem, some sort of audible audience response—laughter, applause, a grunt, a groan, a sigh, or an "Amen!" I began my programs quite simply by telling where I was born in Missouri, that I grew up in Kansas in the geographical heart of the country, and was, therefore very American, that I belonged to a family that was always moving; and I told something of my early travels about the Midwest and how, at fourteen, in Lincoln, Illinois, I was elected Class Poet for the eighth-grade graduating exercises, and from then on I kept writing poetry.

After this biographical introduction I would read to my audiences the first of my poems, written in high school, and show how my poetry had changed over the years. To start my reading, I usually selected some verses written when I was about fifteen:

I had my clothes cleaned
Just like new.
I put 'em on but
I still feels blue.

I bought a new hat,
Sho is fine,
But I wish I had back that
Old gal o' mine.

I got new shoes,
They don't hurt my feet,
But I ain't got nobody
To call me sweet.

Then I would say, "That's a sad poem, isn't it?" Everybody would laugh. Then I would read some of my jazz poems so my listeners could laugh more. I wanted them to laugh a lot early in the program, so that later in the evening they would not laugh when I read poems like "Porter":

I must say,
Yes, sir,
To you all the time.
Yes, sir!
Yes, sir!

All my days
Climbing up a great big mountain
Of yes, sirs!

Rich old white man
Owns the world.
Gimme yo' shoes to shine.

Yes, sir, boss!
Yes, sir!

By the time I reached this point in the program my nonliterary listeners would be ready to think in terms of their own problems. Then I read poems about women domestics, workers on the Florida roads, poor black students wanting to shatter the darkness of ignorance and prejudice, and one about the sharecroppers of Mississippi:

Just a herd of Negroes
Driven to the field,
Plowing, planting, hoeing,
To make the cotton yield.

When the cotton's picked
And the work is done,
Boss man takes the money
And you get none.

Just a herd of Negroes
Driven to the field.
Plowing, planting, hoeing,
To make the cotton yield.

Many of my verses were documentary, journalistic and topical. All across the South that winter I read my poems about the plight of the Scottsboro boys:

Justice is a blind goddess.
To this we blacks are wise:
Her bandage hides two festering sores
That once perhaps were eyes.

Usually people were deeply attentive. But if at some point in the program my audience became restless—as audiences sometimes will, no matter what a speaker is saying—or if I looked down from the platform and noticed someone about to go to sleep, I would pull out my ace in the hole, a poem called "Cross." This poem, delivered dramatically, I had learned, would make anybody, white or black, sit up and take notice. It is a poem about miscegenation—a very provocative subject in the South. The first line—intended to awaken all sleepers—I would read in a loud voice:

My old man's a white old man . . . .

And this would usually arouse any who dozed. Then I would pause before continuing in a more subdued tone:

My old mother's black.

Then in a low, sad, thoughtful tragic vein:

But if ever I cursed my white old man
I take my curses back.

If ever I cursed my black old mother
And wished she were in hell,
I'm sorry for that evil wish
And now I wish her well.

My old man died in a fine big house,
My ma died in a shack.
I wonder where I'm gonna die,
Being neither white nor black.

Here I would let my voice trail off into a lonely silence. Then I would stand quite still for a long time, because I knew I had the complete attention of my listeners again.

Usually after a résumé of the racial situation in our country, with an optimistic listing of past achievements on the part of Negroes, and future possibilities, I would end the evening with:

I, too, sing America.

I am the darker brother.
They send me
To eat in the kitchen
When company comes,
But I laugh,
And eat well,
And grow strong.

Tomorrow
I'll sit at the table
When company comes.
Nobody'll dare
Say to me,
"Eat in the kitchen,"
Then.

Besides,
They'll see
How beautiful I am
And be ashamed.

I, too, am America.

[*1956*]

## *"The Negro and the Racial Mountain"*

[Hughes often examined the challenges he faced in writing both as an American and an African-American, as in this provocative essay published in 1926.]

One of the most promising of the young Negro poets said to me once, "I want to be a poet—not a Negro poet," meaning, I believe, "I want to write like a white poet"; meaning subconsciously, "I would like to be a white poet"; meaning behind that, "I would like to be white." And I was sorry the young man said that, for no great poet has ever been afraid of being himself. And I doubted then that, with his desire to run away spiritually from his race, this boy would ever be a great poet. But this is the mountain standing in the way of any true Negro art in America—this urge within the race toward whiteness, the desire to pour racial individuality into the mold of American standardization, and to be as little Negro and as much American as possible.

But let us look at the immediate background of this young poet. His family is of what I suppose one would call the Negro middle class: people who are by no means rich yet never uncomfortable nor hungry—smug, contented, respectable folk, members of the Baptist church. The father goes to work every morning. He is a chief steward at a large white club. The mother sometimes does fancy sewing or supervises parties for the rich families of the town. The children go to a mixed school. In the home they read white papers and magazines. And the mother often says "Don't be like niggers" when the children are bad. A frequent phrase from the father is, "Look how well a white man does things." And so the word white comes to be unconsciously a symbol of all the virtues. It holds for the children beauty, morality, and money. The whisper of "I want to be white" runs silently through their minds. This young poet's home is, I believe, a fairly typical home of the colored middle class. One sees immediately how difficult it would be for an artist born in such a home to interest himself in interpreting the beauty of his own people. He is never taught to see that beauty. He is taught rather not to see it, or if he does, to be ashamed of it when it is not according to Caucasian patterns.

For racial culture the home of a self-styled "high-class" Negro has nothing better to offer. Instead there will perhaps be more aping of things white than in a less cultured or less wealthy home. The father is perhaps a doctor, lawyer, landowner, or politician. The mother may be a social worker, or a teacher, or she may do nothing and have a maid. Father is often dark but he has usually married the lightest woman he could find. The family attend a fashionable church where few really colored faces are to be found. And they themselves draw a color line. In the North they go to white theaters and white movies. And in the South they have at least two cars and a house "like white folks." Nordic manners, Nordic faces, Nordic hair, Nordic art (if any), and an Episcopal heaven. A very high mountain indeed for the would-be racial artist to climb in order to discover himself and his people.

But then there are the low-down folks, the so-called common element, and they are the majority—may the Lord be praised! The people who have their nip of gin on Saturday nights and are not too important to themselves or the community, or too well fed, or too learned to watch the lazy world go round. They live on Seventh Street in Washington or State Street in Chicago and they do not particularly care whether they are like white folks or anybody else. Their joy runs, bang! into ecstasy. Their religion soars to a shout. Work maybe a little today, rest a little tomorrow. Play awhile. Sing awhile. O, let's dance! These common people are not afraid of spirituals, as for a long time their more intellectual brethren were, and jazz is their child. They furnish a wealth of colorful, distinctive material for any artist because they still hold their own individuality in the face of American standardizations. And perhaps these common people will give to the world its truly great Negro artist, the one who is not afraid to be himself. Whereas the better-class Negro would tell the artist what to do, the people at least let him alone when he does appear. And they are not ashamed of him—if they know he exists at all. And they accept what beauty is their own without question.

5 Certainly there is, for the American Negro artist who can escape the restrictions the more advanced among his own group would put upon him, a great field of unused material ready for his art. Without going outside his race and even among the better classes with their "white" culture and conscious American manners, but still Negro enough to be different, there is sufficient matter to furnish a black artist with a lifetime of creative work. And when he chooses to touch on the relations between Negroes and whites in this country with their innumerable overtones and undertones, surely, and especially for literature and the drama, there is an inexhaustible supply of themes at hand. To these the Negro artist can give his racial individuality, his heritage of rhythm and warmth, and his incongruous humor

that so often, as in the Blues, becomes ironic laughter mixed with tears. But let us look again at the mountain.

A prominent Negro clubwoman in Philadelphia paid eleven dollars to hear Raquel Meller sing Andalusian popular songs. But she told me a few weeks before she would not think of going to hear "that woman," Clara Smith, a great black artist, sing Negro folksongs. And many an upper-class Negro church, even now, would not dream of employing a spiritual in its services. The drab melodies in white folks' hymnbooks are much to be preferred. "We want to worship the Lord correctly and quietly. We don't believe in 'shouting.' Let's be dull like the Nordics," they say, in effect.

The road for the serious black artist, then, who would produce a racial art is most certainly rocky and the mountain is high. Until recently he received almost no encouragement for his work from either white or colored people. The fine novels of Chestnutt[1] go out of print with neither race noticing their passing. The quaint charm and humor of Dunbar's[2] dialect verse brought to him, in his day, largely the same kind of encouragement one would give a sideshow freak (A colored man writing poetry! How odd!) or a clown (How amusing!).

The present vogue in things Negro, although it may do as much harm as good for the budding colored artist, has at least done this: it has brought him forcibly to the attention of his own people among whom for so long, unless the other race had noticed him beforehand, he was a prophet with little honor. I understand that Charles Gilpin acted for years in Negro theaters without any special acclaim from his own, but when Broadway gave him eight curtain calls, Negroes, too, began to beat a tin pan in his honor. I know a young colored writer, a manual worker by day, who had been writing well for the colored magazines for some years, but it was not until he recently broke into the white publications and his first book was accepted by a prominent New York publisher that the "best" Negroes in his city took the trouble to discover that he lived there. Then almost immediately they decided to give a grand dinner for him. But the society ladies were careful to whisper to his mother that perhaps she'd better not come. They were not sure she would have an evening gown.

The Negro artist works against an undertow of sharp criticism and misunderstanding from his own group and unintentional bribes from the whites. "O, be respectable, write about nice people, show how good we are," say the Negroes. "Be stereotyped, don't go too far, don't shatter our illusions about you, don't amuse us too seriously. We will pay you," say the whites. Both would have told Jean Toomer not to write "Cane." The colored people did not praise it. The white people did not buy it. Most of the colored people who did read "Cane" hate it. They are afraid of it. Although the critics gave it good reviews the public remained indifferent. Yet (excepting the work of DuBois[3]) "Cane" contains the finest prose written by a Negro in America. And like the singing of Robeson,[4] it is truly racial.

10 But in spite of the Nordicized Negro intelligentsia and the desires of

[1]**Chestnutt** Charles Chestnutt (1858–1932), African-American novelist [2]**Dunbar** Paul Laurence Dunbar (1872–1906), African-American poet (for an example of his work, see page 854) [3]**DuBois** William Edward DuBois (1868–1963), African-American historian, sociologist, writer [4]**Robeson** Paul Robeson (1898–1976), African-American singer and actor

some white editors we have an honest American Negro literature already with us. Now I await the rise of the Negro theater. Our folk music, having achieved world-wide fame, offers itself to the genius of the great individual American Negro composer who is to come. And within the next decade I expect to see the work of a growing school of colored artists who paint and model the beauty of dark faces and create with new technique the expressions of their own soul-world. And the Negro dancers who will dance like flame and the singers who will continue to carry our songs to all who listen—they will be with us in even greater numbers tomorrow.

Most of my own poems are racial in theme and treatment, derived from the life I know. In many of them I try to grasp and hold some of the meanings and rhythms of jazz. I am sincere as I know how to be in these poems and yet after every reading I answer questions like these from my own people: Do you think Negroes should always write about Negroes? I wish you wouldn't read some of your poems to white folks. How do you find anything interesting in a place like a cabaret? Why do you write about black people? You aren't black. What makes you do so many jazz poems?

But jazz to me is one of the inherent expressions of Negro life in America: the eternal tom-tom beating in the Negro soul—the tom-tom of revolt against weariness in a white world, a world of subway trains, and work, work, work; the tom-tom of joy and laughter, and pain swallowed in a smile. Yet the Philadelphia clubwoman is ashamed to say that her race created it and she does not like me to write about it. The old subconscious "white is best" runs through her mind. Years of study under white teachers, a lifetime of white books, pictures, and papers, and white manners, morals, and Puritan standards made her dislike the spirituals. And now she turns up her nose at jazz and all its manifestations—likewise almost everything else distinctly racial. She doesn't care for the Winold Reiss portraits of Negroes because they are "too Negro." She does not want a true picture of herself from anybody. She wants the artist to flatter her, to make the white world believe that all Negroes are as smug and as near white in soul as she wants to be. But, to my mind, it is the duty of the younger Negro artist, if he accepts any duties at all from outsiders, to change through the force of his art that old whispering "I want to be white," hidden in the aspirations of his people, to "Why should I want to be white? I am a Negro—and beautiful!"

So I am ashamed for the black poet who says, "I want to be a poet, not a Negro poet," as though his own racial world were not as interesting as any other world. I am ashamed, too, for the colored artist who runs from the painting of Negro faces to the painting of sunsets after the manner of the academicians because he fears the strange un-whiteness of his own features. An artist must be free to choose what he does, certainly, but he must also never be afraid to do what he might choose.

Let the blare of Negro jazz bands and the bellowing voice of Bessie Smith singing Blues penetrate the closed ears of the colored near-intellectuals until they listen and perhaps understand. Let Paul Robeson singing Water Boy, and Rudolph Fisher writing about the streets of Harlem, and Jean Toomer holding the heart of Georgia in his hands, and Aaron Douglas drawing strange black fantasies cause the smug Negro middle class to turn from their white, respectable, ordinary books and papers to catch a glimmer of their own beauty. We younger Negro artists who create now intend to express our individual dark-skinned selves without fear or shame. If white people are pleased we are glad. If they are not, it doesn't matter. We know we are beautiful. And ugly too. The tom-tom cries and the tom-tom laughs. If colored people are pleased we are glad. If they are not, their displeasure doesn't matter either. We build our temples for tomorrow, strong as we know how, and we stand on top of the mountain, free within ourselves.

[*1926*]

## *On Writing and Singing Poems*

[This passage comes from Hughes's *The Big Sea: An Autobiography.* The title of the extract is the editors'.]

My two years in Washington were unhappy years, except for poetry and the friends I made through poetry. I wrote many poems. I always put them away new for several weeks in a bottom drawer. Then I would take them out and re-read them. If they seemed bad, I would throw them away. They would all seem good when I wrote them and, usually, bad when I would look at them again. So most of them were thrown away.

The blues poems I would often make up in my head and sing on the way to work. (Except that I could never carry a tune. But when I sing to myself, I think I am singing.) One evening, I was crossing Rock Creek Bridge, singing a blues I was trying to get right before I put it down on paper. A man passing on the opposite side of the bridge stopped, looked at me, then turned around and cut across the roadway.

He said: "Son, what's the matter? Are you ill?"

"No," I said. "Just singing."

"I thought you were groaning," he commented. "Sorry!" And went his way.

So after that I never sang my verses aloud in the street any more.

[*1924–1925*]

## *Writers: Black and White*

[Hughes presented this paper at the First Conference of Negro Writers, in March 1959. It was published in *The American Negro Writer and His Roots* (American Society of African Culture, 1960) and reprinted in the collection *Black Voices: An Anthology of Afro-American Literature,* ed. Abraham Chapman (New York: New American Library, 1968).]

Even to sell *bad* writing you have to be good.

There was a time when, if you were colored, you might sell bad writing a little easier than if you were white. But no more. The days of the Negro's passing as a writer and getting by purely because of his "negritude" are past.

Even pure Africans find it hard to get published in the U.S.A. You have to be a Nadine Gordimer or an Alan Paton. For the general public, "the blacker the berry, the sweeter the juice" may be true in jazz, but not in prose. These days I would hate to be a Negro writer depending on race to get somewhere.

To create a market for your writing you have to be consistent, professional, a continuing writer—not just a one-article or a one-story or a one-book man. Those expert vendors, the literary agents, do not like to be bothered with a one-shot writer. No money in them. Agents like to help build a career, not light a flash in the pan. With one-shot writers, literary hucksters cannot pay their income taxes. Nor can publishers get their money back on what they lose on the first book. Even if you are a good writer, but *not* consistent, you probably will not get far. Color has nothing to do with writing as such. So I would say, in your mind don't be a *colored* writer even when dealing in racial material. Be a *writer* first. Like an egg: first, egg; then an Easter egg, the color applied.

5 To write about yourself, you should first be outside yourself—objective. To write well about Negroes, it might be wise, occasionally at least, to look at them with white eyes—then the better will you see how distinctive we are. Sometimes I think whites are more appreciative of our *uniqueness* than we are ourselves. The white "black" artists—dealing in Negro material—have certainly been financially more successful than any of us real Negroes have ever been. Who wrote the most famous "Negro" (in quotes) music? George Gershwin, who looked at Harlem from a downtown penthouse, while Duke Ellington still rode the "A" train. Who wrote the best selling plays and novels and thereby made money's mammy? White Eugene O'Neill, white Paul Green, white Lillian Smith, white Marc Connelly, and Du Bose Heyward: *Emperor Jones, In Abraham's Bosom, Strange Fruit, Green Pastures, Porgy.* Who originated the longest running Negro radio and TV show? The various white authors of the original *Amos and Andy* scripts, not Negroes. Who wrote all those Negro and interracial pictures that have swept across the Hollywood screen from *Hallelujah* to *Anna Lucasta,* from *Pinky* to *Porgy and Bess?* Not Negroes. Not you, not I, not any colored-body here.

Our eyes are not white enough to look at Negroes clearly in terms of popular commercial marketing. Not even white enough to see as Faulkner sees—through Mississippi-Nobel-Prize-winning-Broadway eyes in his play "Requiem for a Nun." There his "nigger dope-fiend whore" of a mammy, Nancy Manningoe, "cullud," raises the curtain with three traditional "Yas, Lawd's," and when asked later by a white actor, "What would a person like you be doing in heaven?" humbly replies, "Ah kin work." Since Faulkner repeatedly calls Nancy "a nigger dope-fiend whore," all I can add is she is also a liar—because the *last* thing a Negro thinks of doing in heaven is working. Nancy knows better, even if Faulkner doesn't.

Nigger dope-fiend Nancy, Porgy's immoral Bess, Mamba's immoral daughter, street-walking Anna Lucasta, whorish Carmen Jones! Lawd, let me be a member of the wedding! "White folks Ah kin work!" In fact, yas, Lawd, I have to work because—

You've done taken my blues and gone—
Sure have! You sing 'em on Broadway,
And you sing 'em in Hollywood Bowl.
You mixed 'em up with symphonies,
And you fixed 'em so they don't sound like me.
Yep, you done taken my blues and gone!
You also took my spirituals and gone.

Now you've rocked-and-rolled 'em to death!
You put me in *Macbeth,*
In *Carmen Jones,* and *Anna Lucasta,*
And all kinds of *Swing Mikados*
And in everything but what's about me—
But someday somebody'll
Stand up and talk about me,
And write about me—
Black and beautiful—
And sing about me,
And put on plays about me!
I reckon it'll be me myself!
Yes, it'll be me.

Of course, it may be a long time before we finance big Broadway shows or a seven-million-dollar movie like *Porgy and Bess* on which, so far as I know, not a single Negro writer was employed. The *Encyclopaedia Britannica* declares *Porgy and Bess* "the greatest American musical drama ever written." The *Encyclopaedia Britannica* is white. White is right. So shoot the seven million! 7 come 11! Dice, gin, razors, knives, dope, watermelon, whores—7-11! Come 7!

Yet, surely Negro writing, even when commercial, need not be in terms of stereotypes. The interminable crap game at the beginning of *Porgy and Bess* is just because its authors could not see beyond the *surface* of Negro color. But the author of the original novel did see, with his white eyes, wonderful, poetic human qualities in the inhabitants of Catfish Row that made them come alive in his book, half alive on the stage, and I am sure, bigger than life on the screen. Du Bose Heyward was a *writer* first, white second, and this you will have to be, too: *writer* first, *colored* second. That means losing nothing of your racial identity. It is just that in the great sense of the word, anytime, any place, good art transcends land, race, or nationality, and color drops away. If you are a good writer, in the end neither blackness nor whiteness makes a difference to readers.

10 Greek the writer of *Oedipus* might have been, but *Oedipus* shakes Booker T. Washington High School. Irish was Shaw, but he rocks Fisk University. Scottish was Bobby Burns, but kids like him at Tuskegee. The more regional or national an art is in its origins, the more universal it may become in the end. What could be more Spanish than *Don Quixote:* yet what is more universal? What more Italian than Dante? Or more English than Shakespeare? Advice to Negro writers: Step *outside yourself,* then look back—and you will see how human, yet how beautiful and black you are. How very black—even when you're integrated.

As to marketing, however, blackness seen through black eyes may be too black for wide white consumption—unless coupled with greatness or its approximation. What should a Negro writer do, then, in a land where we have no black literary magazines, no black publishers, no black producers, no black investors able to corral seven million dollars to finance a movie? Sell what writing you can, get a job teaching, and give the rest of your talent away. Or else try becoming a good *bad* writer or a black *white* writer, in which case you might, with luck, do as well as white *black* writers do. If you are good enough in a *bad* way, or colored enough in a *good* way, you stand a chance perhaps, maybe, of becoming *even,* commercially successful. At any rate, I would say, keep writing. Practice will do you no harm.

Second, be not dismayed! Keep sending your work out, magazine after magazine, publisher after publisher. Collect rejection slips as some people collect stamps. When you achieve a publication or two, try to get a literary agent—who will seek to collect checks for you instead of rejection slips. See along the way how few editors or agents will ask what color you are physically if you have something good to sell. I would say very few or NONE. Basically they do not care about race, if what you write is readable, new, different, exciting, alive on the printed page. Almost nobody knows Frank Yerby is colored. Few think about Willard Motley's complexion. Although how you treat the materials of race may narrow your market, I do not believe your actual race will. Certainly racial or regional subject matter has its marketing limitations. Publishers want only so many Chinese books a year. The same is true of Negro books.

However, if you want a job as a free-lance writer in Hollywood, on radio, or in TV, that now is sometimes possible—in contrast to the years before the War. But in the entertainment field, regular full-time staff jobs are still not too easy to come by if you are colored. Positions are valuable in the U.S.A., so commercial white culture would rather allow a colored writer a book than a job, even fame rather than an ordinary, decent, dependable living. But if you are so constituted as to wish a dependable living, with luck you might possibly nowadays achieve that too, purely as a writer. I hope so—because *starving* writers are stereotypes. And a stereotype is the last thing a Negro wants to be.

But you can't be a member of the Beat Generation, the fashionable word at the moment in marketing, *unless* you starve a little. Yet who wants to be "beat?" Not Negroes. That is what this conference is all about—how *not* to be "beat." So don't worry about beatness. That is easy enough to come by. Instead, let your talent bloom! You say you are mired in manure? Manure fertilizes. As the old saying goes, "Where the finest roses bloom, there is always a lot of manure around."

15 Of course, to be highly successful in a white world—commercially successful—in writing or anything else, you really should *be* white. But until you get white, *write.*

[*1959*]

## *On the Cultural Achievements of African-Americans*

[On June 26, 1960, Hughes was awarded the Spingarn Medal—the most prestigious award given to an African-American—at the fifty-first convention of the NAACP. He said that he accepted this honor "in the name of the Negro people" who had been both the main source of and audience for his art.]

Without them, on my part, there would have been no poems; without their hopes and fears and dreams, no stories; without their struggles, no dramas; without their music, no songs.

Had I not heard as a child in the little churches of Kansas and Missouri,

"Deep river, my home is over Jordan," or "My Lord, what a morning when the stars begin to fall," I might not have come to realize the lyric beauty of *living* poetry. . . .

There is so much richness in Negro humor, so much beauty in black dreams, so much dignity in our struggle, and so much universality in our problems, in *us*—in each living human being of color—that I do not understand the tendency today that some American Negro artists have of seeking to run away from themselves, of running away from *us,* of being afraid to sing our own songs, paint our pictures, write about ourselves—when it is our music that has given America its greatest music, our humor that has enriched its entertainment media for the past 100 years, our rhythm that has guided its dancing feet from plantation days to the Charleston. . . . Yet there are some of us who say, "Why write about Negroes? Why not be *just a writer?*" And why not—if one wants to be "just a writer?" Negroes in a free world should be whatever each wants to be—even if it means being "just a writer." . . .

There is nothing to be ashamed of in the strength and dignity and laughter of the Negro people. And there is nothing to be afraid of in the use of their material.

Could you be possibly afraid that the rest of the world will not accept it? Our spirituals are sung and loved in the great concert halls of the whole world. Our blues are played from Topeka to Tokyo. Harlem's jive talk delights Hong Kong and Paris. Those of our writers who have *most* concerned themselves with our very special problems are translated and read around the world. The local, the regional can—and does—become universal. Sean O'Casey's Irishmen are an example. So I would say to young Negro writers, do not be afraid of yourself. *You* are the world . . . .

[*1960*]

## A SAMPLE ESSAY

As we mentioned on page 1119, a student, Mark Bradley, decided to write about a theme in a group of poems by Langston Hughes. Because Bradley was taken by a poem called "The South," in his journal he wrote an entry (printed on page 1119) about this poem. From this poem and the entry, he went on to explore some of Hughes's other poems. Below we print part of his essay—we have omitted Bradley's final page.

Mark Bradley

English 1C: Critical Interpretation

December 5, 1994

A National Problem: Race and Racism in the Poetry of Langston Hughes

One of Langston Hughes's key concerns in his poetry is to show that racism is a national problem, and that it is mistaken to pretend that racism affects only the South.[1] In his poem "The South," Hughes criticizes the racist attitudes that pervade the Southern states, yet he ends with only a hesitant embrace of the North. In other poems, such as "Ruby Brown" and "Ballad of the Landlord," it is not racism in the South that is the crucial fact: it is instead the presence of racism everywhere in the United States. "Let America Be America Again" summarizes Hughes's position--that the nation must change its ways and at long last live up to and fulfill its highest ideals.

"The South" begins with a line that sounds appealing: "The lazy, laughing South." But then Hughes turns sharply to a different kind of image in the second line: "With blood on its mouth." Line 3 echoes line 1: "The sunny-faced South"; and then the next two lines challenge it: "Beast-strong, / idiot-brained." Hughes continues:

> The child-minded South
> Scratching in the dead fire's ashes
> For a Negro's bones.

Here Hughes is attacking the evil of lynching, by which black men were hung, shot, or burned to death on the mere suspicion of having committed a crime or somehow threatened white supremacy. According to one source that I consulted, from 1882 to 1901, the annual number of lynchings "usually

[1]All references to Hughes's poems are to poems in Literature: Thinking, Reading, and Writing Critically, 2nd ed. Ed. Sylvan Barnet et al. (1997), 1172-84.

exceeded 100"; and though the numbers declined somewhat in the twentieth century, there were still 83 lynchings in 1919, just several years before Hughes published his poem (Foner and Garraty 685).

Hughes is moved by the beauties of the Southern landscape, but he knows that the South is cruel and contemptuous, and that it will not return to him the love he feels for it:

> And I, who am black, would love her
> But she spits in my face.

Hughes then says that he will "seek the North," but I find his words are very qualified and cautious:

> So now I seek the North--
> The cold-faced North,
> For she, they say,
> Is a kinder mistress,
> And in her house my children
> May escape the spell of the South.

"Cold-faced" is not only a reference to the cold Northern weather, but also implies something "cold" about Northern interactions with other people. The South, Hughes says at one point, is dangerously "seductive" (line 14), but the North may be at the other extreme--distant, chilly in its response to newcomers. Hughes does not know for certain how he will be treated in the North. He has heard reports--"they say"; but possibly the reports will prove inaccurate. "May escape the spell of the South," he writes, which is more tentative than saying "will escape." Most important of all, he doesn't expect his own life will be better, though maybe his children's will.

It is possible that "Ruby Brown" is a Southern poem, a story about life in the South, but I think it is interesting that Hughes doesn't say explicitly that it is. This is the story of a "young and beautiful" woman who wants the good things of life. She wants happiness and pleasure, but will never be able to afford them on the wages she receives for working as a servant. So she becomes a prostitute.

Hughes intends for readers to understand Ruby Brown's story as one that has occurred countless times. It's a story about racism--how racism drives people to despair and corruption. "Mayville" sounded to me at first like the name of a Southern town, but according to an atlas that I consulted, all of the towns named Mayville in the United States are in the North (Michigan, New York, North Dakota, Wisconsin). For Hughes, racism is a problem for the United States as a whole, because its effects are evident throughout the nation.

"Ballad of the Landlord" is also about despair, but it is about anger and resistance, too, and, like "Ruby Brown," it recounts an incident that could happen anywhere. The speaker of the first twenty lines is indignant at the shabby condition of the building he lives in; he talks back to the landlord and even threatens him with violence--"If I land my fist on you." But Hughes's real point in this poem is that an African-American who stands up for his rights is immediately perceived as a danger to the community. Everybody calls for the police and declares that this black man is a revolutionary who aims to overthrow the government and hurl the country into chaos. The final lines, in capital letters, indicate how the media broadcast a version of events that confirms racist stereotypes. But while it is true that the man does threaten the landlord, that's only because he has been mistreated himself.

Someone could differ with my interpretation, I suppose, and claim that Hughes locates "Ballad of the Landlord" in the North, just as it could be argued that "Ruby Brown" is a poem about a woman in a Southern locale. But, again, if Hughes had wanted to make this clear to his readers, he could have done so. He chooses not to, because he is aiming to make readers aware of the national evil of racism, a view that he repeats in detail and vividly conveys in the long poem "Let America Be America Again." . . .

Works Cited

Foner, Eric, and John A. Garraty, eds. The Reader's Companion to American History. Boston: Houghton Mifflin, 1991.

Literature: Thinking, Reading, and Writing Critically. Eds. Sylvan Barnet et al. 2nd ed. New York: Longman, 1997.

The New Cosmopolitan World Atlas. Chicago: Rand McNally, 1992.

## TOPICS FOR CRITICAL THINKING AND WRITING

1. Focus on Mark Bradley's opening paragraph. Is it an effective one? What are the elements of a good opening paragraph?
2. Write an additional page or two for Mark Bradley's essay, which is missing its final section as we have reprinted it here. Comment on the relevance of "Let America Be America Again" for Bradley's thesis—make

certain that you quote and examine passages from the poem—and provide a conclusion for the essay as a whole.

3. Note on writing the concluding paragraph: Aim to summarize the overall argument of the paper, but without simply repeating what has already been said. Summarize *and* present one final insight about, or perspective on, the paper's argument.
4. Reread the poems by Hughes included in this chapter. Has Mark Bradley chosen the best examples for his argument? Are there additional poems that he could have included?
5. Bradley uses two reference works. Do you think that these make his analysis more convincing? Explain.

# PART FOUR

## *Drama*

# CHAPTER 29

# *Elements of Drama*

## THINKING ABOUT THE LANGUAGE OF DRAMA

The earlier parts of this book have dealt with fiction and poetry. A third chief literary type is drama, texts written to be performed.

A play is written to be seen and to be heard. We go to *see* a play in a theater (*theater* is derived from a Greek word meaning "to watch"), but in the theater we also *hear* it because we become an audience (*audience* is derived from a Latin word meaning "to hear"). Hamlet was speaking the ordinary language of his day when he said, "We'll hear a play tomorrow." When we read a play rather than see and hear it in a theater, we lose a good deal. We must see it in the mind's eye and hear it in the mind's ear.

In reading a play it's not enough mentally to hear the lines. We must try to see the characters, costumed and moving within a specified setting, and we must try to hear not only their words but their tone, their joy or hypocrisy or tentativeness or aggression. Our job is much easier when we are in the theater and we have only to pay attention to the performers; as readers on our own, however, we must do what we can to perform the play in the theater under our hats.

If as a reader you develop the following principles into habits, you will get far more out of a play than if you read it as though it were a novel consisting only of dialogue.

1. *Pay attention to the* ***list of characters*** *and carefully read whatever* ***descriptions*** *the playwright has provided.* Early dramatists, such as Shakespeare, did not provide much in the way of description ("Othello, the Moor" or "Ariel, an airy spirit" is about as much as we find in Elizabethan texts), but later playwrights often are very forthcoming. Here,

for instance, is Tennessee Williams introducing us to Amanda Wingfield in *The Glass Menagerie.* (We give only the beginning of his longish description.)

> *Amanda Wingfield,* the mother. A little woman of great but confused vitality clinging frantically to another time and place.

And here is Susan Glaspell introducing us to all the characters in her one-act play, *Trifles:*

> . . . the Sheriff comes in, followed by the County Attorney and Hale. The Sheriff and Hale are men in middle life, the County Attorney is a young man; all are much bundled up and go at once to the stove. They are followed by the two women—the Sheriff's Wife, [Mrs. Peters] first; she is a slight wiry woman, a thin nervous face. Mrs. Hale is larger and would ordinarily be called more comfortable looking, but she is disturbed now and looks fearfully about as she enters. The women have come in slowly and stand close together near the door.

Glaspell's description of her characters is not nearly so explicit as Tennessee Williams's, but Glaspell does reveal much to a reader. What do we know about the men? They differ in age, they are bundled up, and they "go at once to the stove." What do we know about the women? Mrs. Peters is slight, and she has a "nervous face"; Mrs. Hale is "larger" but she too is "disturbed." The women enter "slowly," and they "stand close together near the door." In short, the men, who take over the warmest part of the room, are more confident than the women, who nervously huddle together near the door. It's a man's world.

2. *Pay attention to* ***gestures and costumes*** *that are specified in stage directions or are implied by the dialogue.* We have just seen how Glaspell distinguishes between the men and the women by what they do—the men take over the warm part of the room, the women stand insecurely near the door. Most dramatists from the late nineteenth century to the present have been fairly generous with their stage directions, but when we read the works of earlier dramatists we often have to deduce the gestures from the speeches. For instance, although the texts of Shakespeare's day have an occasional direction, such as "Enter Hamlet reading on a book," "Leaps in the grave," and "in scuffling, again, they change rapiers," such directions are rare. In reading Shakespeare, we must, again, see the action *in the mind's eye* (a phrase from *Hamlet,* by the way). Here, for instance, are Horatio's words when he sees the Ghost:

> But soft, behold! Lo, where it comes again!
> I'll cross it, though it blast me. [*It spreads his arms.*] Stay, *illusion!*

As a footnote indicates, the "his" in the stage direction is the Ghost's; today we would say "its." There is no doubt about what the Ghost does, but what does Horatio do when he says "I'll cross it"? Conceivably "I'll cross it" means "I'll confront it, I'll stand in its path," and Horatio then walks up to the Ghost. Or perhaps the words mean "I'll make the sign of the cross, to protect myself from this creature from another world." If so, does Horatio make the sign of the cross with his hand, or does he perhaps hold up his sword, an object that by virtue of the sword guard at right angles to the blade is itself a cross? The words "Stay, *illusion*" similarly must be accompanied by a gesture; perhaps Horatio reaches out, to try to take hold of the Ghost.

*The Tempest* is relatively rich in stage directions (the play begins with "*A Tempestuous Noise of Thunder and Lightning Heard. Enter a Shipmaster and a Boatswain*"), but even in this play readers must often provide the stage directions for themselves. Thus, in the second scene of the first act, the magician Prospero is telling his innocent daughter Miranda how the two of them came to be on this remote island. He says:

> Lend thy hand
> And pluck my magic garment from me. So,
> Lie there, my art.

From these lines we understand that Miranda takes the robe from off his shoulders and—perhaps jointly with Prospero—places it on the ground. Later in the scene Ariel reports that he has left one of the victims of the shipwreck with "his arms in this sad knot," and presumably while speaking these words Ariel illustrates the "sad knot" by folding his arms across his chest and perhaps by bending his trunk forward, thus imitating the "knot" that the distressed victim has made of his own body.

Or consider the first reunion of Hamlet and Horatio, in the second scene of the play:

> HORATIO. Hail to your lordship!
> HAMLET. I am glad to see you well.
> Horatio!—or I do forget myself.

One cannot be positive, but it seems that the melancholy Hamlet, hearing a greeting ("Hail to your lordship"), at first replies with routine politeness ("I am glad to see you well") and, when an instant later he recognizes that this greeting comes from an old friend whom he has not seen for a while, he responds with an enthusiastic "Horatio!" and perhaps with an embrace.

In addition to thinking about gestures, don't forget the costumes that the characters wear. Costumes identify the characters as soldiers or kings or farmers or whatever, and changes of costume can be especially symbolic. Prospero has his magic cloak (never described in the play, but perhaps a rich color adorned with silver astrological symbols, or some such thing). In one engaging direction, we are told that Ariel enters, "invisible"; perhaps he wore a special garment (maybe black?) that was understood by the audience to render him invisible.

Costumes are always important, because they tell us something about the people who wear them. As even the fatuous Polonius knows, "the apparel oft proclaims the man." We have already noticed that in the first act of *The Tempest* Prospero takes off a robe that indicates he has magic powers; the final act, in which he brings his plans to completion, begins with a stage direction, "*Enter Prospero in His Magic*

*Robes* . . . ," a sign that he is master of the situation. In *Hamlet,* the use of symbolic costume is equally evident; Hamlet is dressed in black (we hear of his "nighted color" and his "inky cloak"), a color that sets him apart from the courtiers, who presumably are dressed in colorful robes. Later in the play, when, having escaped from a sea journey that was supposed to end in his death, Hamlet is seen in the graveyard, perhaps he wears the "sea gown" that he mentions, and we feel that he is now a more energetic character, freed from his constricting suit of mourning.

3. *Keep in mind the* ***kind of theater*** for which the play was written. The plays in this book were written for various kinds of theaters. Sophocles, author of *Antigone* and *Oedipus Rex,* wrote for the ancient Greek theater, essentially a space where performers acted in front of an audience seated on a hillside. (See the illustration on page 1227.) This theater was open to the heavens, with a structure representing a palace or temple behind the actors, in itself a kind of image of a society governed by the laws of the state and the laws of the gods. Moreover, the chorus entered the playing space by marching down the side aisles, close to the audience, thus helping to unite the world of the audience and of the players. On the other hand, the audience in most modern theaters sits in a darkened area and looks through a proscenium arch at performers who move in a boxlike setting. The box set of the late nineteenth century and the twentieth century is, it often seems, an appropriate image of the confined lives of the unheroic characters of the play.
4. *If the playwright describes a set, try to* ***envision the set*** *clearly.* Glaspell, for instance, tells us a good deal about the set. We quote only the first part.

> The kitchen in the now abandoned farmhouse of John Wright, a gloomy kitchen, and left without having been put in order. . . .

These details about a gloomy and disordered kitchen may seem to be mere realism—after all, the play has to take place *somewhere*—but it turns out that the disorder and, for that matter, the gloominess are extremely important. You'll have to read the play to find out why.

Another example of a setting that provides important information is Arthur Miller's in *Death of a Salesman.* Again we quote only the beginning of the description.

> Before us is the Salesman's house. We are aware of towering, angular shapes behind it, surrounding it on all sides. Only the blue light of the sky falls upon the house and forestage; the surrounding area shows an angry glow of orange.

If we read older drama, we find that playwrights do *not* give us much help, but by paying attention to the words we can to some degree visualize the locale. For instance, the first stage direction in *Hamlet* ("*Enter Bernardo and Francisco, two sentinels*"), along with the opening dialogue ("Who's there?", "Nay, answer me. Stand and unfold yourself"), indicates that we are in some sort of public place where anyone may suddenly appear. Elizabethan plays were staged in daylight, and there was no way of darkening the stage, so if the scene is a night scene the playwright has to convey this information. In this instance, the audience understands that the meeting takes place at night because the characters can hear but cannot see each other; to make certain, however, a few lines later Shakespeare has Bernardo say, " 'Tis now struck twelve. Get thee to bed, Francisco."

5. *Pay attention to whatever* ***sound effects*** *are specified in the play.* In *Hamlet,* when the king (called "Denmark" in the speech we quote) drinks, he does so to the rather vulgar accompaniment of a cannonade:

   No jocund health that Denmark drinks today
   But the great cannon to the clouds shall tell,
   And the King's rouse the heaven shall bruit again,
   Respeaking earthly thunder.

   The point is made again several times, but these salutes to King Claudius are finally displaced by a military salute to Hamlet; "*a peal of ordnance is shot off,*" we are told, when his body is carried off the stage at the end of the play. Thus, the last sound that we hear in *Hamlet* is a validation of Hamlet as a hero.

   In *Death of a Salesman,* before the curtain goes up, "A melody is heard, played upon a flute. It is small and fine, telling of grass and trees and the horizon." Then the curtain rises, revealing the Salesman's house, with "towering, angular shapes behind it, surrounding it on all sides." Obviously the sound of the flute is meant to tell us of the world that the Salesman is shut off from.

   A sound effect, however, need not be so evidently symbolic to be important in a play. In Glaspell's *Trifles,* almost at the very end of the play we hear the "sound of a knob turning in the other room." The sound has an electrifying effect on the audience, as it does on the two women on the stage, and it precedes a decisive action.

6. *Pay attention to what the characters say, and keep in mind that (like real people)* ***dramatic characters are not always to be trusted.*** An obvious case is Shakespeare's Iago, an utterly unscrupulous villain who knows that he is a liar, but a character may be self-deceived, or, to put it a bit differently, characters may say what they honestly think but may not know what they are talking about.

## PLOT AND CHARACTER

Although **plot** is sometimes equated with the gist of the narrative—the story—it is sometimes reserved to denote the writer's *arrangement* of the happenings in the story. Thus, all plays about the assassination of Julius Caesar have pretty much the same story, but by beginning with a scene of workmen enjoying a holiday (and thereby introducing the motif of the fickleness of the mob), Shakespeare's play has a plot different from a play that omits such a scene.

Handbooks on the drama often suggest that a plot (arrangement of happenings) should have a **rising action,** a **climax,** and a **falling action.** This sort of plot can be diagrammed as a pyramid, the tension rising through complications, or **crises,** to a climax, at which point the fate of the **protagonist** (chief character) is firmly established; the climax is the apex, and the tension allegedly slackens as we witness the **dénouement** (unknotting). Shakespeare sometimes used a pyramidal structure, placing his climax neatly in the middle of what seems to us to be the third of five acts.* Roughly the first half of *Julius Caesar* shows Brutus rising, reaching his height in 3.1 with the death of Caesar; but later in this scene he gives Marc Antony permission to speak at Caesar's funeral and thus he sets in motion his own fall, which occupies the second half of the play. In *Macbeth,* the protagonist attains his height in 3.1 ("Thou hast it now: King"), but he soon perceives that he is going downhill:

I am in blood
Stepped in so far, that, should I wade no more,
Returning were as tedious as go o'er.

Of course, no law demands such a structure, and a hunt for the pyramid usually causes the hunter to overlook all the crises but the middle one. William Butler Yeats once suggestively diagrammed a good plot not as a pyramid but as a line moving diagonally upward, punctuated by several crises. Perhaps it is sufficient to say that a good plot has its moments of tension, but the location of these will vary with the play. They are the product of **conflict,** but not all conflict produces tension; there is conflict but little tension in a ball game when the score is 10–0 in the ninth inning with two out and no one on base.

Regardless of how a plot is diagrammed, the **exposition** is that part that tells the audience what it has to know about the past, the **antecedent action.** When two gossiping servants tell each other that after a year away in Paris the young master is coming home tomorrow with a new wife, they are giving the audience the exposition by introducing characters and establishing relationships. The Elizabethans and the Greeks sometimes tossed out all pretense at dialogue and began with a **prologue,** like the one spoken by the Chorus at the outset of *Romeo and Juliet:*

Two households, both alike in dignity
In fair Verona, where we lay our scene,
From ancient grudge break to new mutiny,
Where civil blood makes civil hands unclean.
From forth the fatal loins of these two foes
A pair of star-crossed lovers take their life. . . .

And in Tennessee Williams's *The Glass Menagerie,* Tom's first speech is a sort of prologue. However, the exposition also may extend far into the play, so that the audience keeps getting bits of information that both clarify the present and build suspense about the future. Occasionally the **soliloquy** (speech of a character alone on the stage, revealing his or her thoughts) or the **aside** (speech in the

*An **act** is a main division in a drama or opera. Act divisions probably stem from Roman theory and derive ultimately from the Greek practice of separating episodes in a play by choral interludes, but Greek (and probably Roman) plays were performed without interruption, for the choral interludes were part of the plays themselves. Elizabethan plays, too, may have been performed without breaks; the division of Elizabethan plays into five acts is usually the work of editors rather than of authors. Frequently an act division today (commonly indicated by lowering the curtain and turning up the houselights) denotes change in locale and lapse of time. A **scene** is a smaller unit, either (1) a division with no change of locale or abrupt shift of time, or (2) a division consisting of an actor or group of actors on the stage; according to the second definition, the departure or entrance of an actor changes the composition of the group and thus introduces a new scene. (In an entirely different sense, the scene is the locale where a work is set.)

presence of others but unheard by them) is used to do the job of putting the audience in possession of the essential facts. The soliloquy and the aside are not limited to exposition, of course; they are used to reveal the private thoughts of characters who, like people in real life, do not always tell others what their inner thoughts are. The soliloquy is especially used for meditation, where we might say the character is interacting not with another character but with himself or herself.

Because a play is not simply words but words spoken with accompanying gestures by performers who are usually costumed and in a particular setting, it may be argued that to read a play (rather than to see and hear it) is to falsify it. Drama is not literature, some people hold, but theater. However, there are replies: a play can be literature as well as theater, and readers of a play can perhaps enact in the theater of their mind a more effective play than the one put on by imperfect actors. After all, as Shakespeare's Duke Theseus, in *A Midsummer Night's Dream,* says of actors, "The best in this kind are but shadows." In any case, we need not wait for actors to present a play; we can do much on our own.

## SUSAN GLASPELL

*Susan Glaspell (1882–1948) was born in Davenport, Iowa, and educated at Drake University in Des Moines. In 1903 she married George Cram Cook and, with Cook and other writers, actors, and artists, in 1915 founded the Provincetown Players, a group that remained vital until 1929. Glaspell wrote* Trifles *(1916) for the Provincetown Players, but she also wrote stories, novels, and a biography of her husband. In 1931 she won a Pulitzer Prize for* Alison's House, *a play about the family of a deceased poet who in some ways resembles Emily Dickinson.*

# *Trifles*

**SCENE:** *The kitchen in the now abandoned farmhouse of John Wright, a gloomy kitchen, and left without having been put in order—unwashed pans under the sink, a loaf of bread outside the breadbox, a dish towel on the table—other signs of incompleted work. At the rear the outer door opens, and the Sheriff comes in, followed by the County Attorney and Hale. The Sheriff and Hale are men in middle life, the County Attorney is a young man; all are much bundled up and go at once to the stove. They are followed by the two women—the Sheriff's Wife first; she is a slight wiry woman, a thin nervous face. Mrs. Hale is larger and would ordinarily be called more comfortable looking, but she is disturbed now and looks fearfully about as she enters. The women have come in slowly and stand close together near the door.*

Marjorie Vonnegut, Elinor M. Cox, John King, Arthur F. Hole, and T. W. Gibson in *Trifles*, as published in *Theatre Magazine*, January 1917. (Courtesy of The Billy Rose Theatre Collection/New York Public Library)

COUNTY ATTORNEY (*rubbing his hands*). This feels good. Come up to the fire, ladies.

MRS. PETERS (*after taking a step forward*). I'm not—cold.

SHERIFF (*unbuttoning his overcoat and stepping away from the stove as if to the beginning of official business*). Now, Mr. Hale, before we move things about, you explain to Mr. Henderson just what you saw when you came here yesterday morning.

COUNTY ATTORNEY. By the way, has anything been moved? Are things just as you left them yesterday?

SHERIFF (*looking about*). It's just the same. When it dropped below zero last night, I thought I'd better send Frank out this morning to make a fire for us—no use getting pneumonia with a big case on; but I told him not to touch anything except the stove—and you know Frank.

COUNTY ATTORNEY. Somebody should have been left here yesterday.

SHERIFF. Oh—yesterday. When I had to send Frank to Morris Center for that man who went crazy—I want you to know I had my hands full yesterday. I knew you could get back from Omaha by today, and as long as I went over everything here myself—

COUNTY ATTORNEY. Well, Mr. Hale, tell just what happened when you came here yesterday morning.

HALE. Harry and I had started to town with a load of potatoes. We came along the road from my place; and as I got here, I said, "I'm going to see if I can't get John Wright to go in with me on a party telephone." I spoke to Wright about it once before, and he put me off, saying folks talked too much anyway, and all he asked was peace and quiet—I guess you know about how much he talked himself; but I thought maybe if I went to the house and talked about it before his wife, though I said to Harry that I didn't know as what his wife wanted made much difference to John—

COUNTY ATTORNEY. Let's talk about that later, Mr. Hale. I do want to talk about that, but tell now just what happened when you got to the house.

HALE. I didn't hear or see anything; I knocked at the door, and still it was all quiet inside. I knew they must be up, it was past eight o'clock. So I knocked again, and I thought I heard somebody say, "Come in." I wasn't sure, I'm not sure yet, but I opened the door—this door (*indicating the door by which the two women are still standing*), and there in that rocker—(*pointing to it*) sat Mrs. Wright. (*They all look at the rocker.*)

COUNTY ATTORNEY. What—was she doing?

HALE. She was rockin' back and forth. She had her apron in her hand and was kind of—pleating it.

COUNTY ATTORNEY. And how did she—look?

HALE. Well, she looked queer.

COUNTY ATTORNEY. How do you mean—queer?

HALE. Well, as if she didn't know what she was going to do next. And kind of done up.

COUNTY ATTORNEY. How did she seem to feel about your coming?

HALE. Why, I don't think she minded—one way or other. She didn't pay much attention. I said, "How do, Mrs. Wright, it's cold, ain't it?" And she said, "Is it?"—and went on kind of pleating at her apron. Well, I was surprised; she didn't ask me to come up to the stove, or to set down, but just sat there, not even looking at me, so I said, "I want to see John." And then she—laughed. I guess you would call it a laugh. I thought of Harry and the team outside, so I said a little sharp: "Can't I see John?" "No," she says, kind o' dull like. "Ain't he home?" says I. "Yes," says she, "he's home." "Then why can't I see him?" I asked her, out of patience. " 'Cause he's dead," says she. "*Dead?*" says I. She just nodded her head, not getting a bit excited, but rockin' back and forth. "Why—where is he?" says I, not knowing what to say. She just pointed upstairs—like that (*himself pointing to the room above*). I got up, with the idea of going up there. I walked from there to here—then I says, "Why, what did he die of?" "He died of a rope around his neck," says she, and just went on pleatin' at her apron. Well, I went out and called Harry. I thought I might—need help. We went upstairs, and there he was lyin'—

COUNTY ATTORNEY. I think I'd rather have you go into that upstairs, where you can point it all out. Just go on now with the rest of the story.

HALE. Well, my first thought was to get that rope off. I looked . . . (*Stops, his face twitches.*) . . . but Harry, he went up to him, and he said, "No, he's dead all right, and we'd better not touch anything." So we went back downstairs. She was still sitting that same way. "Has anybody been notified?" I asked. "No," says she, unconcerned. "Who did this, Mrs.

Wright?" said Harry. He said it business-like—and she stopped pleatin' of her apron. "I don't know," she says. "You don't *know?*" says Harry. "No," says she. "Weren't you sleepin' in the bed with him?" says Harry. "Yes," says she, "but I was on the inside." "Somebody slipped a rope round his neck and strangled him, and you didn't wake up?" says Harry. "I didn't wake up," she said after him. We must 'a looked as if we didn't see how that could be, for after a minute she said, "I sleep sound." Harry was going to ask her more questions, but I said maybe we ought to let her tell her story first to the coroner, or the sheriff, so Harry went fast as he could to Rivers' place, where there's a telephone.

COUNTY ATTORNEY. And what did Mrs. Wright do when she knew that you had gone for the coroner?

HALE. She moved from that chair to this over here . . . (*Pointing to a small chair in the corner.*) . . . and just sat there with her hands held together and looking down. I got a feeling that I ought to make some conversation, so I said I had come in to see if John wanted to put in a telephone, and at that she started to laugh, and then she stopped and looked at me—scared. (*The County Attorney, who has had his notebook out, makes a note.*) I dunno, maybe it wasn't scared. I wouldn't like to say it was. Soon Harry got back, and then Dr. Lloyd came, and you, Mr. Peters, and so I guess that's all I know that you don't.

COUNTY ATTORNEY (*looking around*). I guess we'll go upstairs first—and then out to the barn and around there. (*To the Sheriff.*) You're convinced that there was nothing important here—nothing that would point to any motive?

SHERIFF. Nothing here but kitchen things.

(*The County Attorney, after again looking around the kitchen, opens the door of a cupboard closet. He gets up on a chair and looks on a shelf. Pulls his hand away, sticky.*)

COUNTY ATTORNEY. Here's a nice mess.

(*The women draw nearer.*)

MRS. PETERS (*to the other woman*). Oh, her fruit; it did freeze. (*To the Lawyer.*) She worried about that when it turned so cold. She said the fir'd go out and her jars would break.

SHERIFF. Well, can you beat the women! Held for murder and worryin' about her preserves.

COUNTY ATTORNEY. I guess before we're through she may have something more serious than preserves to worry about.

HALE. Well, women are used to worrying over trifles.

(*The two women move a little closer together.*)

COUNTY ATTORNEY (*with the gallantry of a young politician*). And yet, for all their worries, what would we do without the ladies? (*The women do not unbend. He goes to the sink, takes a dipperful of water from the pail and, pouring it into a basin, washes his hands. Starts to wipe them on the roller towel, turns it for a cleaner place.*) Dirty towels! (*Kicks his foot against the pans under the sink.*) Not much of a housekeeper, would you say, ladies?

MRS. HALE (*stiffly*). There's a great deal of work to be done on a farm.

COUNTY ATTORNEY. To be sure. And yet . . . (*With a little bow to her.*) . . . I know there are some Dickson county farmhouses which do not have such roller towels. (*He gives it a pull to expose its full length again.*)

MRS. HALE. Those towels get dirty awful quick. Men's hands aren't always as clean as they might be.

COUNTY ATTORNEY. Ah, loyal to your sex, I see. But you and Mrs. Wright were neighbors. I suppose you were friends, too.

MRS. HALE (*shaking her head*). I've not seen much of her of late years. I've not been in this house—it's more than a year.

COUNTY ATTORNEY. And why was that? You didn't like her?

MRS. HALE. I liked her all well enough. Farmers' wives have their hands full, Mr. Henderson. And then—

COUNTY ATTORNEY. Yes—?

MRS. HALE (*looking about*). It never seemed a very cheerful place.

COUNTY ATTORNEY. No—it's not cheerful. I shouldn't say she had the home-making instinct.

MRS. HALE. Well, I don't know as Wright had, either.

COUNTY ATTORNEY. You mean that they didn't get on very well?

MRS. HALE. No, I don't mean anything. But I don't think a place'd be any cheerfuler for John Wright's being in it.

COUNTY ATTORNEY. I'd like to talk more of that a little later. I want to get the lay of things upstairs now. (*He goes to the left, where three steps lead to a stair door.*)

SHERIFF. I suppose anything Mrs. Peters does'll be all right. She was to take in some clothes for her, you know, and a few little things. We left in such a hurry yesterday.

COUNTY ATTORNEY. Yes, but I would like to see what you take, Mrs. Peters, and keep an eye out for anything that might be of use to us.

MRS. PETERS. Yes, Mr. Henderson.

(*The women listen to the men's steps on the stairs, then look about the kitchen.*)

MRS. HALE. I'd hate to have men coming into my kitchen, snooping around and criticizing. (*She arranges the pans under sink which the Lawyer had shoved out of place.*)

MRS. PETERS. Of course it's no more than their duty.

MRS. HALE. Duty's all right, but I guess that deputy sheriff that came out to make the fire might have got a little of this on. (*Gives the roller towel a pull.*) Wish I'd thought of that sooner. Seems mean to talk about her for not having things slicked up when she had to come away in such a hurry.

MRS. PETERS (*who has gone to a small table in the left rear corner of the room, and lifted one end of a towel that covers a pan*). She had bread set. (*Stands still.*)

MRS. HALE (*eyes fixed on a loaf of bread beside the breadbox, which is on a low shelf at the other side of the room. Moves slowly toward it*). She was going to put this in there. (*Picks up loaf, then abruptly drops it. In a manner of returning to familiar things.*) It's a shame about her fruit. I wonder if it's all gone. (*Gets up on the chair and looks.*) I think there's some here that's all right, Mrs. Peters. Yes—here; (*Holding it toward the window.*) this is cherries, too. (*Looking again.*) I declare I believe that's the only one. (*Gets down, bottle in her hand. Goes to the sink and wipes it off on the outside.*) She'll feel awful bad after all her hard work in the hot weather. I remember the afternoon I put up my cherries last summer. (*She puts the bottle on the big kitchen table, center of the room, front table. With a sigh, is about to sit down in the rocking chair. Before she is seated realizes what chair it is; with a slow look at it, steps back. The chair, which she has touched, rocks back and forth.*)

MRS. PETERS. Well, I must get those things from the front room closet. (*She goes to the door at the right, but after looking into the other room steps back.*) You coming with me, Mrs. Hale? You could help me carry them. (*They go into the other room; reappear, Mrs. Peters carrying a dress and skirt, Mrs. Hale following with a pair of shoes.*)

MRS. PETERS. My, it's cold in there. (*She puts the cloth on the big table, and hurries to the stove.*)

MRS. HALE (*examining the skirt*). Wright was close. I think maybe that's why she kept so much to herself. She didn't even belong to the Ladies' Aid. I suppose she felt she couldn't do her part, and then you don't enjoy things when you feel shabby. She used to wear pretty clothes and be lively, when she was Minnie Foster, one of the town girls singing in the choir. But that—oh, that was thirty years ago. This all you was to take in?

MRS. PETERS. She said she wanted an apron. Funny thing to want, for there isn't much to get you dirty in jail, goodness knows. But I suppose just to make her feel more natural. She said they was in the top drawer in this cupboard. Yes, here. And then her little shawl that always hung behind the door. (*Opens stair door and looks.*) Yes, here it is. (*Quickly shuts door leading upstairs.*)

MRS. HALE (*abruptly moving toward her*). Mrs. Peters?

MRS. PETERS. Yes, Mrs. Hale?

MRS. HALE. Do you think she did it?

MRS. PETERS (*in a frightened voice*). Oh, I don't know.

MRS. HALE. Well, I don't think she did. Asking for an apron and her little shawl. Worrying about her fruit.

MRS. PETERS (*starts to speak, glances up, where footsteps are heard in the room above. In a low voice*). Mr. Peters says it looks bad for her. Mr. Henderson is awful sarcastic in speech, and he'll make fun of her sayin' she didn't wake up.

MRS. HALE. Well, I guess John Wright didn't wake when they was slipping that rope under his neck.

MRS. PETERS. No, it's strange. It must have been done awful crafty and still. They say it was such a—funny way to kill a man, rigging it all up like that.

MRS. HALE. That's just what Mr. Hale said. There was a gun in the house. He says that's what he can't understand.

MRS. PETERS. Mr. Henderson said coming out that what was needed for the case was a motive; something to show anger, or—sudden feeling.

MRS. HALE (*who is standing by the table*). Well, I don't see any signs of anger around here. (*She puts her hand on the dish towel which lies on the table, stands looking down at the table, one half of which is clean, the other half messy.*) It's wiped here. (*Makes a move as if to finish work, then turns and looks at loaf of bread outside the bread-box. Drops towel. In that voice of coming back to familiar things.*) Wonder how they are finding things upstairs? I hope she had it a little more red-up there. You know, it seems kind of *sneaking.* Locking her up in town and then coming out here and trying to get her own house to turn against her!

MRS. PETERS. But, Mrs. Hale, the law is the law.

MRS. HALE. I s'pose 'tis. (*Unbuttoning her coat.*) Better loosen up your things, Mrs. Peters. You won't feel them when you go out.

(*Mrs. Peters takes off her fur tippet, goes to hang it on hook at the back of room, stands looking at the under part of the small corner table.*)

MRS. PETERS. She was piecing a quilt. (*She brings the large sewing basket, and they look at the bright pieces.*)

MRS. HALE. It's log cabin pattern. Pretty, isn't it? I wonder if she was goin' to quilt or just knot it?

(*Footsteps have been heard coming down the stairs. The Sheriff enters, followed by Hale and the County Attorney.*)

SHERIFF. They wonder if she was going to quilt it or just knot it. (*The men laugh, the women look abashed.*)

COUNTY ATTORNEY (*rubbing his hands over the stove*). Frank's fire didn't do much up there, did it? Well, let's go out to the barn and get that cleared up.

(*The men go outside.*)

MRS. HALE (*resentfully*). I don't know as there's anything so strange, our takin' up our time with little things while we're waiting for them to get the evidence. (*She sits down at the big table, smoothing out a block with decision.*) I don't see as it's anything to laugh about.

MRS. PETERS (*apologetically*). Of course they've got awful important things on their minds. (*Pulls up a chair and joins Mrs. Hale at the table.*)

MRS. HALE (*examining another block*). Mrs. Peters, look at this one. Here, this is the one she was working on, and look at the sewing! All the rest of it has been so nice and even. And look at this! It's all over the place! Why, it looks as if she didn't know what she was about! (*After she has said this, they look at each other, then started to glance back at the door. After an instant Mrs. Hale has pulled at a knot and ripped the sewing.*)

MRS. PETERS. Oh, what are you doing, Mrs. Hale?

MRS. HALE (*mildly*). Just pulling out a stitch or two that's not sewed very good. (*Threading a needle.*) Bad sewing always made me fidgety.

MRS. PETERS (*nervously*). I don't think we ought to touch things.

MRS. HALE. I'll just finish up this end. (*Suddenly stopping and leaning forward.*) Mrs. Peters?

MRS. PETERS. Yes, Mrs. Hale?

MRS. HALE. What do you suppose she was so nervous about?

MRS. PETERS. Oh—I don't know. I don't know as she was nervous. I sometimes sew awful queer when I'm just tired. (*Mrs. Hale starts to say something, looks at Mrs. Peters, then goes on sewing.*) Well, I must get these things wrapped up. They may be through sooner than we think. (*Putting apron and other things together.*) I wonder where I can find a piece of paper, and string.

MRS. HALE. In that cupboard, maybe.

MRS. PETERS (*looking in cupboard*). Why, here's a birdcage. (*Holds it up.*) Did she have a bird, Mrs. Hale?

MRS. HALE. Why, I don't know whether she did or not—I've not been here for so long. There was a man around last year selling canaries cheap, but I don't know as she took one; maybe she did. She used to sing real pretty herself.

MRS. PETERS (*glancing around*). Seems funny to think of a bird here. But she must have had one, or why should she have a cage? I wonder what happened to it?

MRS. HALE. I s'pose maybe the cat got it.

MRS. PETERS. No, she didn't have a cat. She's got that feeling some people have about cats—being afraid of them. My cat got in her room, and she was real upset and asked me to take it out.

MRS. HALE. My sister Bessie was like that. Queer, ain't it?

MRS. PETERS (*examining the cage*). Why, look at this door. It's broke. One hinge is pulled apart.

MRS. HALE (*looking, too*). Looks as if someone must have been rough with it.

MRS. PETERS. Why, yes. (*She brings the cage forward and puts it on the table.*)

MRS. HALE. I wish if they're going to find any evidence they'd be about it. I don't like this place.

MRS. PETERS. But I'm awful glad you came with me, Mrs. Hale. It would be lonesome for me sitting here alone.

MRS. HALE. It would, wouldn't it? (*Dropping her sewing.*) But I tell you what I do wish, Mrs. Peters. I wish I had come over sometimes when *she* was here. I—(*Looking around the room.*)—wish I had.

MRS. PETERS. But of course you were awful busy, Mrs. Hale—your house and your children.

MRS. HALE. I could've come. I stayed away because it weren't cheerful—and that's why I ought to have come. I—I've never liked this place. Maybe because it's down in a hollow, and you don't see the road. I dunno what it is, but it's a lonesome place and always was. I wish I had come over to see Minnie Foster sometimes. I can see now—(*Shakes her head.*)

MRS. PETERS. Well, you mustn't reproach yourself, Mrs. Hale. Somehow we just don't see how it is with other folks until—something comes up.

MRS. HALE. Not having children makes less work—but it makes a quiet house, and Wright out to work all day, and no company when he did come in. Did you know John Wright, Mrs. Peters?

MRS. PETERS. Not to know him; I've seen him in town. They say he was a good man.

MRS. HALE. Yes—good; he didn't drink, and kept his word as well as most, I guess, and paid his debts. But he was a hard man, Mrs. Peters. Just to pass the time of day with him. (*Shivers.*) Like a raw wind that gets to the bone. (*Pauses, her eye falling on the cage.*) I should think she would 'a wanted a bird. But what do you suppose went with it?

MRS. PETERS. I don't know, unless it got sick and died. (*She reaches over and swings the broken door, swings it again; both women watch it.*)

MRS. HALE. You weren't raised round here, were you? (*Mrs. Peters shakes her head.*) You didn't know—her?

MRS. PETERS. Not till they brought her yesterday.

MRS. HALE. She—come to think of it, she was kind of like a bird herself—real sweet and pretty, but kind of timid and—fluttery. How—she—did—change. (*Silence; then as if struck by a happy thought and relieved to get back to everyday things.*) Tell you what, Mrs. Peters, why don't you take the quilt in with you? It might take up her mind.

MRS. PETERS. Why, I think that's a real nice idea, Mrs. Hale. There couldn't possibly be any objection to it, could there? Now, just what would I take? I wonder if her patches are in here—and her things. (*They look in the sewing basket.*)

MRS. HALE. Here's some red. I expect this has got sewing things in it (*Brings out a fancy box.*) What a pretty box. Looks like something somebody would give you. Maybe her scissors are in here. (*Opens box. Suddenly puts her hand to her nose.*) Why—(*Mrs. Peters bends nearer, then turns her face away.*) There's something wrapped up in this piece of silk.

MRS. PETERS. Why, this isn't her scissors.

MRS. HALE (*lifting the silk*). Oh, Mrs. Peters—it's—(*Mrs. Peters bends closer.*)

MRS. PETERS. It's the bird.

MRS. HALE (*jumping up*). But, Mrs. Peters—look at it. Its neck! Look at its neck! It's all—other side *to.*

MRS. PETERS. Somebody—wrung—its neck.

(*Their eyes meet. A look of growing comprehension of horror. Steps are heard outside. Mrs. Hale slips box under quilt pieces, and sinks into her chair. Enter Sheriff and County Attorney. Mrs. Peters rises.*)

COUNTY ATTORNEY (*as one turning from serious things to little pleasantries*). Well, ladies, have you decided whether she was going to quilt it or knot it?

MRS. PETERS. We think she was going to—knot it.

COUNTY ATTORNEY. Well, that's interesting, I'm sure. (*Seeing the birdcage.*) Has the bird flown?

MRS. HALE (*putting more quilt pieces over the box*). We think the—cat got it.

COUNTY ATTORNEY (*preoccupied*). Is there a cat?

(*Mrs. Hale glances in a quick covert way at Mrs. Peters.*)

MRS. PETERS. Well, not now. They're superstitious, you know. They leave.

COUNTY ATTORNEY (*to Sheriff Peters, continuing an interrupted conversation*). No sign at all of anyone having come from the outside. Their own rope. Now let's go up again and go over it piece by piece. (*They start upstairs.*) It would have to have been someone who knew just the—

(*Mrs. Peters sits down. The two women sit there not looking at one another, but as if peering into something and at the same time holding back. When they talk now, it is the manner of feeling their way over strange ground, as if afraid of what they are saying, but as if they cannot help saying it.*)

MRS. HALE. She liked the bird. She was going to bury it in that pretty box.

MRS. PETERS (*in a whisper*). When I was a girl—my kitten—there was a boy took a hatchet, and before my eyes—and before I could get there—(*Covers her face an instant.*) If they hadn't held me back, I would have—(*Catches herself, looks upstairs where steps are heard, falters weakly.*)—hurt him.

MRS. HALE (*with a slow look around her*). I wonder how it would seem never to have had any children around. (*Pause.*) No, Wright wouldn't like the bird—a thing that sang. She used to sing. He killed that, too.

MRS. PETERS (*moving uneasily*). We don't know who killed the bird.

MRS. HALE. I knew John Wright.

MRS. PETERS. It was an awful thing was done in this house that night, Mrs. Hale. Killing a man while he slept, slipping a rope around his neck that choked the life out of him.

MRS. HALE. His neck. Choked the life out of him.

(*Her hand goes out and rests on the birdcage.*)

MRS. PETERS (*with a rising voice*). We don't know who killed him. We don't *know.*

MRS. HALE (*her own feeling not interrupted*). If there'd been years and years of nothing, then a bird to sing to you, it would be awful—still, after the bird was still.

MRS. PETERS (*something within her speaking*). I know what stillness is. When we homesteaded in Dakota, and my first baby died—after he was two years old, and me with no other then—

MRS. HALE (*moving*). How soon do you suppose they'll be through, looking for evidence?

MRS. PETERS. I know what stillness is. (*Pulling herself back.*) The law has got to punish crime, Mrs. Hale.

MRS. HALE (*not as if answering that*). I wish you'd seen Minnie Foster when she wore a white dress with blue ribbons and stood up there in the choir and sang. (*A look around the room.*) Oh, I *wish* I'd come over here once in a while! That was a crime! That was a crime! Who's going to punish that?

MRS. PETERS (*looking upstairs*). We mustn't—take on.

MRS. HALE. I might have known she needed help! I know how things can be—for women. I tell you, it's queer, Mrs. Peters. We live close together and we live far apart. We all go through the same things—it's all just a different kind of the same thing. (*Brushes her eyes, noticing the bottle of fruit, reaches out for it.*) If I was you, I wouldn't tell her her fruit was gone. Tell her it *ain't.* Tell her it's all right. Take this in to prove it to her. She—she may never know whether it was broke or not.

MRS. PETERS (*takes the bottle, looks about for something to wrap it in; takes petticoat from the clothes brought from the other room, very ner-*

*vously begins winding this around the bottle. In a false voice*). My, it's a good thing the men couldn't hear us. Wouldn't they just laugh! Getting all stirred up over a little thing like a—dead canary. As if that could have anything to do with—with—wouldn't they *laugh!*

(*The men are heard coming downstairs.*)

MRS. HALE (*under her breath*). Maybe they would—maybe they wouldn't.

COUNTY ATTORNEY. No, Peters, it's all perfectly clear except a reason for doing it. But you know juries when it comes to women. If there was some definite thing. Something to show—something to make a story about—a thing that would connect up with this strange way of doing it.

(*The women's eyes meet for an instant. Enter Hale from outer door.*)

HALE. Well, I've got the team around. Pretty cold out there.

COUNTY ATTORNEY. I'm going to stay here awhile by myself. (*To the Sheriff.*) You can send Frank out for me, can't you? I want to go over everything. I'm not satisfied that we can't do better.

SHERIFF. Do you want to see what Mrs. Peters is going to take in?

(*The Lawyer goes to the table, picks up the apron, laughs.*)

COUNTY ATTORNEY. Oh I guess they're not very dangerous things the ladies have picked up. (*Moves a few things about, disturbing the quilt pieces which cover the box. Steps back.*) No, Mrs. Peters doesn't need supervising. For that matter, a sheriff's wife is married to the law. Ever think of it that way, Mrs. Peters?

MRS. PETERS. Not—just that way.

SHERIFF (*chuckling*). Married to the law. (*Moves toward the other room.*) I just want you to come in here a minute, George. We ought to take a look at these windows.

COUNTY ATTORNEY (*scoffingly*). Oh, windows!

SHERIFF. We'll be right out, Mr. Hale.

(*Hale goes outside. The Sheriff follows the County Attorney into the other room. Then Mrs. Hale rises, hands tight together, looking intensely at Mrs. Peters, whose eyes take a slow turn, finally meeting Mrs. Hale's. A moment Mrs. Hale holds her, then her own eyes point the way to where the box is concealed. Suddenly Mrs. Peters throws back quilt pieces and tries to put the box in the bag she is wearing. It is too big. She opens box, starts to take the bird out, cannot touch it, goes to pieces, stands there helpless. Sound of a knob turning in the other room. Mrs. Hale snatches the box and puts it in the pocket of her big coat. Enter County Attorney and Sheriff.*)

COUNTY ATTORNEY (*facetiously*). Well, Henry, at least we found out that she was not going to quilt it. She was going to—what is it you call it, ladies?

MRS. HALE (*her hand against her pocket*). We call it—knot it, Mr. Henderson.

CURTAIN

*[1916]*

## TOPICS FOR CRITICAL THINKING AND WRITING

1. Briefly describe the setting, indicating what it "says" and what atmosphere it evokes.
2. How would you characterize Mr. Henderson, the county attorney?
3. In what way or ways are Mrs. Peters and Mrs. Hale different from each other?
4. Several times the men "laugh" or "chuckle." In their contexts, what do these expressions of amusement convey?
5. On page 1219, "*the women's eyes meet for an instant.*" What do you think this bit of action "says"? What do you understand by the exchange of glances?
6. On page 1218, when Mrs. Peters tells of the boy who killed her cat, she says, "If they hadn't held me back, I would have—(*Catches herself, looks upstairs where steps are heard, falters weakly.*)—hurt him." What do you think she was about to say before she faltered? Why do you suppose Glaspell included this speech about Mrs. Peters's girlhood?
7. On page 1215, Mrs. Hale, looking at a quilt, wonders whether Mrs. Wright "was goin' to quilt or just knot it." The men are amused by the women's concern with this topic, and the last line of the play returns to the issue. What do you make of this emphasis on the matter?
8. We never see Mrs. Wright on stage. Nevertheless, by the end of *Trifles* we know a great deal about her. In an essay of 500–750 words explain both what we know about her—physical characteristics, habits, interests, personality, life before her marriage and after—and *how* we know these things.
9. The title of the play is ironic—the "trifles" are important. What other ironies do you find in the play? (On irony, see pages 1225–26.)
10. Do you think the play is immoral? Explain.
11. Assume that the canary has been found, thereby revealing a possible motive, and that Minnie is indicted for murder. You are the defense attorney. In 500 words set forth your defense. (Take any position you wish. For instance, you may want to argue that she committed justifiable homicide or that—on the basis of her behavior as reported by Mr. Hale—she is innocent by reason of insanity.)
12. Assume that the canary had been found and Minnie Wright convicted. Compose the speech you think she might have delivered before the sentence was given.

---

## ✔ Checklist: Writing about Plot, Character, and Nonverbal Language

### Plot

1. Does the exposition introduce elements that will be ironically fulfilled? During the exposition do you perceive things differently from the way the characters perceive them?
2. Are certain happenings or situations recurrent? If so, what significance do you attach to them?

3. If there is more than one plot, do the plots seem to you to be related? Is one plot clearly the main plot and another plot a sort of subplot, a minor variation on the theme?
4. Do any scenes strike you as irrelevant?
5. Are certain scenes so strongly foreshadowed that you anticipated them? If so, did the happenings in these scenes merely fulfill your expectations, or did they also in some way surprise you?
6. What kinds of conflict are there? One character against another, one group against another, one part of a personality against another part in the same person?
7. How is the conflict resolved? By an unambiguous triumph of one side or by a triumph that is also in some degree a loss for the triumphant side? Do you find the resolution satisfying, or unsettling, or what? Why?

## Character

1. A dramatic character is not likely to be thoroughly realistic, a copy of someone we might know. Still, we can ask if the character is consistent and coherent. We can also ask if the character is complex or is, on the other hand, a rather simple representative of some human type.
2. How is the character defined? Consider what the character says and does and what others say about him or her and do to him or her. Also consider other characters who more or less resemble the character in question, because the similarities—and the differences—may be significant.
3. How trustworthy are the characters when they characterize themselves? When they characterize others?
4. Do characters change as the play goes on, or do we simply know them better at the end?
5. What do you make of the minor characters? Are they merely necessary to the plot, or are they foils to other characters? Or do they serve some other functions?
6. If a character is tragic, does the tragedy seem to you to proceed from a moral flaw, from an intellectual error, from the malice of others, from sheer chance, or from some combination of these?
7. What are the character's goals? To what degree do you sympathize with them? If a character is comic, do you laugh *with* or *at* the character?
8. Do you think the characters are adequately motivated?
9. Is a given character so meditative that you feel he or she is engaged less in a dialogue with others than in a dialogue with the self? If so, do you feel that this character is in large degree a spokesperson for the author, commenting not only on the world of the play but also on the outside world?

## Nonverbal Language

1. If the playwright does not provide full stage directions, imagine for at least one scene what gestures and tones might accompany each speech. (The first scene is usually a good one to try your hand at.)

2. What do you make of the setting? Does it help to reveal character? Do changes of scene strike you as symbolic? If so, symbolic of what?
3. Do certain costumes (dark suits, flowery shawls, stiff collars, etc.) or certain properties (books, pictures, toys, candlesticks, etc.) strike you as symbolic? If so, symbolic of what?

---

# CHAPTER 30

# *Tragedy*

The Greek philosopher Aristotle defined "tragedy" as a dramatization of a serious happening—not necessarily one ending with the death of the protagonist—and his definition remains among the best. But many plays have been written since Aristotle defined tragedy. When we think of Shakespeare's tragedies, we cannot resist narrowing Aristotle's definition by adding something like "showing a struggle that rends the protagonist's whole being"; and when we think of the "problem plays" of the last hundred years—the serious treatments of such sociological problems as alcoholism and race prejudice—we might be inclined to exclude some of them by adding to the definition something about the need for universal appeal.

The question remains: Is there a single quality present in all works that we call tragedy and absent from works not called tragedy? If there is, no one has yet pointed it out to general satisfaction. But this failure does not mean that there is no such classification as "tragedy." We sense that tragedies resemble each other as members of the same family resemble each other: two children have the mother's coloring and eyes, a third child has the mother's coloring but the father's eyes, a fourth child has the mother's eyes but the father's coloring.

The next few pages will examine three comments on tragedy, none of which is entirely acceptable, but each of which seems to have some degree of truth, and each of which can help us detect resemblances and differences among tragedies. The first comment is by Cyril Tourneur, a tragic dramatist of the early seventeenth century:

When the bad bleed, then is the tragedy good.

We think of Macbeth ("usurper," "butcher"). Macbeth is much more than a usurper and butcher, but it is undeniable that he is an offender against the moral order. Whatever the merits of Tourneur's statement, however, if we think of

*Romeo and Juliet* (to consider only one play), we realize its inadequacy. Tourneur so stresses the guilt of the protagonist that his or her suffering becomes mere retributive justice. But we cannot plausibly say, for example, that Romeo and Juliet deserved to die because they married without their parents' consent; it is much too simple to call them "bad." Romeo and Juliet are young, in love, nobler in spirit than their parents.

Tourneur's view is probably derived ultimately from an influential passage in Aristotle's *Poetics* in which Aristotle speaks of **hamartia,** sometimes literally translated as "missing the target," sometimes as "vice" or "flaw" or "weakness," but perhaps best translated as "mistake." Aristotle seems to imply that the hero is undone because of some mistake he or she commits, but this mistake need not be the result of a moral fault; it may be simply a miscalculation—for example, failure to foresee the consequences of a deed. Brutus makes a strategic mistake when he lets Marc Antony speak at Caesar's funeral, but we can hardly call it a vice.

Because Aristotle's *hamartia* includes mistakes of this sort, the common translation "tragic flaw" is erroneous. In many Greek tragedies the hero's hamartia is **hubris** (or **hybris**), usually translated as "overweening pride." The hero forgets that he or she is fallible, acts as though he or she has the power and wisdom of the gods, and is later humbled for this arrogance. But one can argue that this self-assertiveness is not a vice but a virtue, not a weakness but a strength; if the hero is destroyed for self-assertion, he or she is nevertheless greater than the surrounding people, just as the person who tries to stem a lynch mob is greater than the mob, although that person also may be lynched for his or her virtue. Or a hero may be undone by a high-mindedness that makes him or her vulnerable. Hamlet is vulnerable because he is, as his enemy says, "most generous and free from all contriving"; because Hamlet is high-minded, he will not suspect that the proposed fencing match is a murderous plot. Othello can be tricked into murdering Desdemona not simply because he is jealous but because he is (in the words of the villainous Iago) "of a free and open nature / That thinks men honest that but seem so." Iago knows, too, that out of Desdemona's "goodness" he can "make the net / That shall enmesh them all."

Next, here is a statement more or less the reverse of Tourneur's, by a Russian critic, L. I. Timofeev:

> Tragedy in Soviet literature arouses a feeling of pride for the man who has accomplished a great deed for the people's happiness; it calls for continued struggle against the things which brought about the hero's death.

The distortions in Soviet criticism are often amusing: Hamlet is seen as an incipient Communist, undone by the decadent aristocracy; or Romeo and Juliet as young people of the future, undone by bourgeois parents. Soviet drama in the third quarter of the twentieth century so consistently showed the triumph of the worker that Western visitors to Russia commented on the absence of contemporary tragic plays. Still, there is much in the idea that the tragic hero accomplishes "a great deed," and perhaps we do resent "the things which brought about the hero's death." The stubbornness of the Montagues and Capulets, the fury of the mob that turns against Brutus, the crimes of Claudius in *Hamlet*—all these would seem to call for our indignation.

The third comment is by Arthur Miller:

> If it is true to say that in essence the tragic hero is intent upon claiming his whole due as a personality, and if this struggle must be total and

> without reservation, then it automatically demonstrates the indestructible will of man to achieve his humanity. . . . It is curious, although edifying, that the plays we revere, century after century, are the tragedies. In them, and in them alone, lies the belief—optimistic, if you will—in the perfectibility of man.

There is much in Miller's suggestions that the tragic hero makes a large and total claim and that the audience often senses triumph rather than despair in tragedies. We often feel that we have witnessed human greatness—that the hero, despite profound suffering, has lived according to his or her ideals. We may feel that we have achieved new insight into human greatness. But the perfectibility of man? Do we feel that *Julius Caesar* or *Macbeth* or *Hamlet* have to do with human perfectibility? Don't these plays suggest rather that people, whatever their nobility, have within them the seeds of their own destruction? Without overstressing the guilt of the protagonists, don't we feel that in part the plays dramatize the *im*perfectibility of human beings? In much tragedy, after all, the destruction comes from within, not from without:

> In tragic life, God wot,
> No villain need be! Passions spin the plot:
> We are betrayed by what is false within.
> —George Meredith

What we are talking about is **tragic irony,** the contrast between what is believed to be so and what is so, or between expectations and accomplishments.* Several examples from *Macbeth* illustrate something of the range of tragic irony within a single play. In the first act, King Duncan bestows on Macbeth the title of Thane of Cawdor. By his kindness Duncan seals his own doom, for Macbeth, having achieved this rank, will next want to achieve a higher one. In the third act, Macbeth, knowing that Banquo will soon be murdered, hypocritically urges Banquo to "fail not our feast." But Macbeth's hollow request is ironically fulfilled: the ghost of Banquo terrorizes Macbeth during the feast. The most pervasive irony of all, of course, is that Macbeth aims at happiness when he kills Duncan and takes the throne, but he wins only sorrow.

Aristotle's discussion of **peripeteia (reversal)** and **anagnorisis (recognition)** may be a way of getting at this sort of irony. He may simply have meant a reversal of fortune (for example, good luck ceases) and a recognition of who is who (for example, the pauper is really the prince), but more likely he meant profounder things. One can say that the reversal in *Macbeth* lies in the sorrow that Macbeth's increased power brings. The recognition comes when he realizes the consequences of his deeds:

> I have lived long enough: my way of life
> Is fall'n into the sere, the yellow leaf;
> And that which should accompany old age,
> As honor, love, obedience, troops of friends,
> I must not look to have; but, in their stead,
> Curses, not loud but deep, mouth-honor, breath
> Which the poor heart would fain deny, and dare not.

*Tragic irony is sometimes called **dramatic irony** or **Sophoclean irony.** The terms are often applied to speeches or actions that the audience understands in a sense fuller than or different from the sense in which the dramatic characters understand them.

That our deeds often undo us, that we can aim at our good and produce our ruin, was not, of course, a discovery of the tragic dramatists. The archetype is the story of Adam and Eve: these two aimed at becoming like God, and as a consequence, they brought upon themselves corruption, death, the loss of their earthly paradise. The Bible is filled with stories of tragic irony. A brief quotation from Ecclesiastes (10.8–9) can stand as an epitome of these stories:

> He that diggeth a pit shall fall into it; and whoso breaketh an hedge, a serpent shall bite him.
>
> Whoso removeth stones shall be hurt therewith; and he that cleaveth wood shall be endangered thereby.

"He that cleaveth wood shall be endangered thereby." Activity involves danger. To be inactive is, often, to be ignoble, but to be active is necessarily to imperil oneself. Perhaps we can attempt a summary of tragic figures: they act, and they suffer, usually as a consequence of their action. The question is not of the action's being particularly bad (Tourneur's view) or particularly good (Timofeev's view); the action is often both good and bad, a sign of courage and also of arrogance, a sign of greatness and also of limitations.

Finally, a brief consideration of the pleasure of tragedy: Why do we enjoy plays about suffering? Aristotle has some obscure comments on **catharsis (purgation)** that are often interpreted as saying that tragedy arouses in us both pity and fear and then purges us of these emotions. The idea, perhaps, is that just as we can (it is said) harmlessly discharge our aggressive impulses by witnessing a prizefight or by shouting at an umpire, so we can harmlessly discharge our impulses to pity and to fear by witnessing the dramatization of a person's destruction. The theater in this view is an outlet for emotions that elsewhere would be harmful. But, it must be repeated, Aristotle's comments on catharsis are obscure; perhaps, too, they are wrong.

Most later theories on the pleasure of tragedy are footnotes to Aristotle's words on catharsis. Some say that our pleasure is sadistic (we enjoy the sight of suffering); some, that our pleasure is masochistic (we enjoy lacerating ourselves); some, that it lies in sympathy (we enjoy extending pity and benevolence to the wretched); some, that it lies in self-congratulation (we are reminded, when we see suffering, of our own good fortune); some, that we take pleasure in tragedy because the tragic hero acts out our secret desires, and we rejoice in his or her aggression, expiating our guilt in his or her suffering; and so on.

But this is uncertain psychology, and it mostly neglects the distinction between real suffering and dramatized suffering. In the latter, surely, part of the pleasure is in the contemplation of an aesthetic object, an object that is unified and complete. The chaos of real life seems, for a few moments in drama, to be ordered: the protagonist's action, his or her subsequent suffering, and the total cosmos seem somehow related. Tragedy has no use for the passerby who is killed by a falling brick. The events (the person's walk, the brick's fall) have no meaningful relation. But suppose a person chooses to climb a mountain, and in making the ascent sets in motion an avalanche that destroys that person. Here we find (however simple the illustration) something closer to tragedy. We do not say that people should avoid mountains, or that mountain climbers deserve to die by avalanches. But we feel that the event is unified, as the accidental conjunction of brick and passerby is not.

Tragedy thus presents some sort of ordered action; tragic drama itself is orderly. As we see or read it, we feel it cannot be otherwise; word begets word, deed begets deed, and every moment is exquisitely appropriate. Whatever the

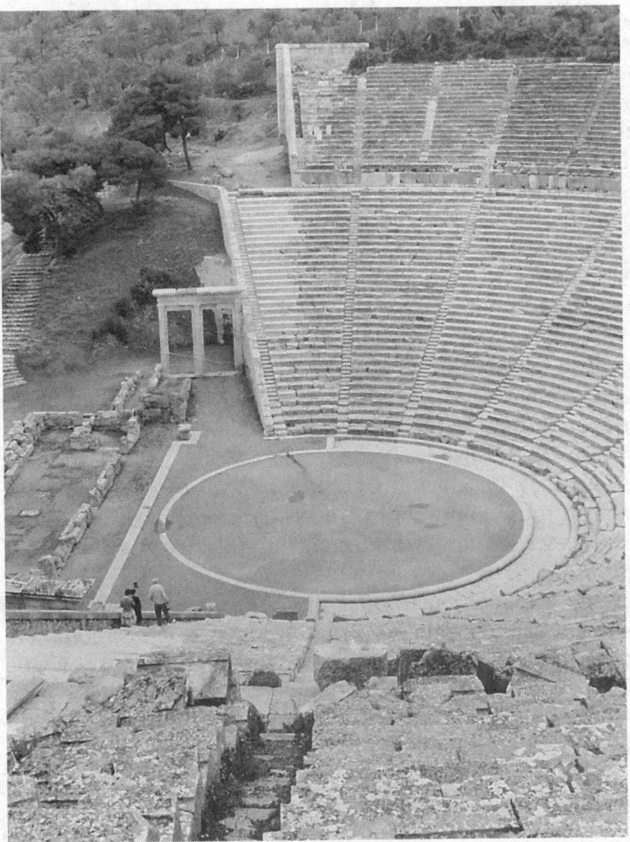

Greek theater of Epidauras on the Peloponnesus east of Nauplia. (Frederick Ayer/Photo Researchers)

relevance of sadism, masochism, sympathy, and the rest, the pleasure of tragedy surely comes in part from the artistic shaping of the material.

## A NOTE ON GREEK TRAGEDY

Little or nothing is known for certain of the origin of Greek tragedy. The most common hypothesis holds that it developed from improvised speeches during choral dances honoring Dionysus, a Greek nature god associated with spring, fertility, and wine. Thespis (who perhaps never existed) is said to have introduced an actor into these choral performances in the sixth century B.C. Aeschylus (525–456 B.C.), Greece's first great writer of tragedies, added the second actor, and Sophocles (495?–406 B.C.) added the third actor and fixed the size of the chorus at fifteen. (Because the chorus leader often functioned as an additional actor, and because the actors sometimes doubled in their parts, a Greek tragedy could have more characters than might at first be thought.)

All the extant great Greek tragedy is of the fifth century B.C. It was performed at religious festivals in the winter and early spring, in large outdoor amphitheaters built on hillsides. Some of these theaters were enormous; the one at

Epidaurus held about fifteen thousand people. The audience sat in tiers, looking down on the **orchestra** (a dancing place), with the acting area behind it and the **skene** (the scene building) yet farther back. The scene building served as dressing room, background (suggesting a palace or temple), and place for occasional entrances and exits. Furthermore, this building helped to provide good acoustics, for speech travels well if there is a solid barrier behind the speakers and a hard, smooth surface in front of them, and if the audience sits in tiers. The wall of the scene building provided the barrier; the orchestra provided the surface in front of the actors; and the seats on the hillside fulfilled the third requirement. Moreover, the acoustics were somewhat improved by slightly elevating the actors above the orchestra, but it is not known exactly when this platform was first constructed in front of the scene building.

A tragedy commonly begins with a **prologos** (prologue), during which the exposition is given. Next comes the **párodos,** the chorus's ode of entrance, sung while the chorus marches into the theater through the side aisles and onto the orchestra. The **epeisodion** (episode) is the ensuing scene; it is followed by a **stasimon** (choral song, ode). Usually there are four or five *epeisodia,* alternating with *stasima.* Each of these choral odes has a **strophe** (lines presumably sung while the chorus dances in one direction) and an **antistrophe** (lines presumably sung while the chorus retraces its steps). Sometimes a third part, an **epode,** concludes an ode. (In addition to odes that are *stasima,* there can be odes within episodes; the fourth episode of *Antigonê* contains an ode complete with *epode.*) After the last part of the last ode comes the **exodos,** the epilogue or final scene.

The actors (all male) wore masks, and they seem to have chanted much of the play. Perhaps the total result of combining speech with music and dancing was a sort of music-drama roughly akin to opera with some spoken dialogue, such as Mozart's *Magic Flute.*

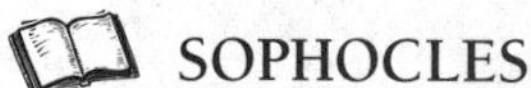

## SOPHOCLES

*One of the three great writers of tragedies in ancient Greece, Sophocles (496?–406 B.C.) was born in Colonus, near Athens, into a well-to-do family. Well educated, he first won public acclaim as a tragic poet at the age of 27, in 468 B.C., when he defeated Aeschylus in a competition for writing a tragic play. He is said to have written some 120 plays, but only 7 tragedies are extant; among them are* Oedipus Rex, Antigonê, *and* Oedipus at Colonus. *He died, much honored, in his ninetieth year, in Athens, where he had lived his entire life.*

# *Oedipus Rex*

*An English Version by Dudley Fitts and Robert Fitzgerald*

LIST OF CHARACTERS

OEDIPUS

A PRIEST

CREON

Laurence Olivier in *Oedipus Rex.* (Photograph by John Vickers)

TEIRESIAS
IOCASTÊ
MESSENGER
SHEPHERD OF LAÏOS
SECOND MESSENGER
CHORUS OF THEBAN ELDERS

**SCENE:** ***Before the palace of Oedipus, King of Thebes. A central door and two lateral doors open onto a platform which runs the length of the facade. On the platform, right and left, are altars; and three steps lead down into the "orchestra," or chorus-ground. At the beginning of the action these steps are crowded by Suppliants who have brought branches and chaplets of olive leaves and who lie in various attitudes of despair. Oedipus enters.***

## *Prologue*

OEDIPUS. My children, generations of the living
In the line of Kadmos,° nursed at his ancient hearth;
Why have you strewn yourselves before these altars
In supplication, with your boughs and garlands?
The breath of incense rises from the city
With a sound of prayer and lamentation.
Children,
I would not have you speak through messengers,
And therefore I have come myself to hear you—
I, Oedipus, who bear the famous name.
(*To a Priest.*) You, there, since you are eldest in the company,
Speak for them all, tell me what preys upon you,

**2 Kadmos** mythical founder of Thebes

Whether you come in dread, or crave some blessing:
Tell me, and never doubt that I will help you
In every way I can; I should be heartless
Were I not moved to find you suppliant here.

PRIEST. Great Oedipus, O powerful King of Thebes!
You see how all the ages of our people
Cling to your altar steps: here are boys
Who can barely stand alone, and here are priests
By weight of age, as I am a priest of God,
And young men chosen from those yet unmarried;
As for the others, all that multitude,
They wait with olive chaplets in the squares,
At the two shrines of Pallas,° and where Apollo°
Speaks in the glowing embers.
Your own eyes
Must tell you: Thebes is in her extremity
And cannot lift her head from the surge of death.
A rust consumes the buds and fruits of the earth;
The herds are sick; children die unborn,
And labor is vain. The god of plague and pyre
Raids like detestable lightning through the city,
And all the house of Kadmos is laid waste,
All emptied, and all darkened: Death alone
Battens upon the misery of Thebes.
You are not one of the immortal gods, we know;
Yet we have come to you to make our prayer
As to the man of all men best in adversity
And wisest in the ways of God. You saved us
From the Sphinx,° that flinty singer, and the tribute
We paid to her so long; yet you were never
Better informed than we, nor could we teach you:
It was some god breathed in you to set us free.

Therefore, O mighty King, we turn to you:
Find us our safety, find us a remedy,
Whether by counsel of the gods or the men.
A king of wisdom tested in the past
Can act in a time of troubles, and act well.
Noblest of men, restore
Life to your city! Think how all men call you
Liberator for your triumph long ago;
Ah, when your years of kingship are remembered,
Let them not say *We rose, but later fell—*
Keep the State from going down in the storm!
Once, years ago, with happy augury,

**24 Pallas** Athena, goddess of wisdom, protectress of Athens **Apollo** god of light and healing **39 Sphinx** a monster (body of a lion, wings of a bird, face of a woman) who asked the riddle "What goes on four legs in the morning, two at noon, and three in the evening?" and who killed those who could not answer. When Oedipus responded correctly that man crawls on all fours in infancy, walks upright in maturity, and uses a staff in old age, the Sphinx destroyed herself.

You brought us fortune; be the same again!
No man questions your power to rule the land:
But rule over men, not over a dead city!
Ships are only hulls, citadels are nothing,
When no life moves in the empty passageways.

OEDIPUS. Poor children! You may be sure I know
All that you longed for in your coming here.
I know that you are deathly sick; and yet,
Sick as you are, not one is as sick as I.
Each of you suffers in himself alone
His anguish, not another's; but my spirit
Groans for the city, for myself, for you.

I was not sleeping, you are not waking me.
No, I have been in tears for a long while
And in my restless thought walked many ways.
In all my search, I found one helpful course,
And that I have taken: I have sent Creon,
Son of Menoikeus, brother of the Queen,
To Delphi, Apollo's place of revelation,
To learn there, if he can,
What act or pledge of mine may save the city.
I have counted the days, and now, this very day,
I am troubled, for he has overstayed his time.
What is he doing? He has been gone too long.
Yet whenever he comes back, I should do ill
To scant whatever hint the god may give.

PRIEST. It is a timely promise. At this instant
They tell me Creon is here.

OEDIPUS. O Lord Apollo!
May his news be fair as his face is radiant!

PRIEST. It could not be otherwise: he is crowned with bay,
The chaplet is thick with berries.

OEDIPUS. We shall soon know;
He is near enough to hear us now.
*Enter Creon.*
O Prince:
Brother: son of Menoikeus:
What answer do you bring us from the god?

CREON. It is favorable. I can tell you, great afflictions
Will turn out well, if they are taken well.

OEDIPUS. What was the oracle? These vague words
Leave me still hanging between hope and fear.

CREON. Is it your pleasure to hear me with all these
Gathered around us? I am prepared to speak,
But should we not go in?

OEDIPUS. Let them all hear it.
It is for them I suffer, more than myself.

CREON. Then I will tell you what I heard at Delphi.

In plain words
The god commands us to expel from the land of Thebes

An old defilement that it seems we shelter.
It is a deathly thing, beyond expiation.
We must not let it feed upon us longer.
OEDIPUS. What defilement? How shall we rid ourselves of it?
CREON. By exile or death, blood for blood. It was
Murder that brought the plague-wind on the city.
OEDIPUS. Murder of whom? Surely the god has named him?
CREON. My lord: long ago Laïos was our king,
Before you came to govern us.
OEDIPUS. I know;
I learned of him from others; I never saw him.
CREON. He was murdered; and Apollo commands us now
To take revenge upon whoever killed him.
OEDIPUS. Upon whom? Where are they? Where shall we find a clue
To solve that crime, after so many years?
CREON. Here in this land, he said.
If we make enquiry,
We may touch things that otherwise escape us.
OEDIPUS. Tell me: Was Laïos murdered in his house,
Or in the fields, or in some foreign country?
CREON. He said he planned to make a pilgrimage.
He did not come home again.
OEDIPUS. And was there no one,
No witness, no companion, to tell what happened?
CREON. They were all killed but one, and he got away
So frightened that he could remember one thing only.
OEDIPUS. What was that one thing? One may be the key
To everything, if we resolve to use it.
CREON. He said that a band of highwaymen attacked them,
Outnumbered them, and overwhelmed the King.
OEDIPUS. Strange, that a highwayman should be so daring—
Unless some faction here bribed him to do it.
CREON. We thought of that. But after Laïos' death
New troubles arose and we had no avenger.
OEDIPUS. What troubles could prevent your hunting down the killers?
CREON. The riddling Sphinx's song
Made us deaf to all mysteries but her own.
OEDIPUS. Then once more I must bring what is dark to light.
It is most fitting that Apollo shows,
As you do, this compunction for the dead.
You shall see how I stand by you, as I should,
To avenge the city and the city's god,
And not as though it were for some distant friend,
But for my own sake, to be rid of evil.
Whoever killed King Laïos might—who knows?—
Decide at any moment to kill me as well.
By avenging the murdered king I protect myself.
Come, then, my children: leave the altar steps,
Lift up your olive boughs!
One of you go
And summon the people of Kadmos to gather here.

I will do all that I can; you may tell them that.
(*Exit a Page.*)

So, with the help of God,
We shall be saved—or else indeed we are lost.

PRIEST. Let us rise, children. It was for this we came,
And now the King has promised it himself.
Phoibos° has sent us an oracle; may he descend
Himself to save us and drive out the plague.

*Exeunt Oedipus and Creon into the palace by the central door. The Priest and the Suppliants disperse right and left. After a short pause the Chorus enters the orchestra.*

## *Párodos*

CHORUS. What is God singing in his profound *Strophe 1*
Delphi of gold and shadow?
What oracle for Thebes, the sunwhipped city?
Fear unjoints me, the roots of my heart tremble.
Now I remember, O Healer, your power, and wonder;
Will you send doom like a sudden cloud, or weave it
Like nightfall of the past?
Speak, speak to us, issue of holy sound:
Dearest to our expectancy: be tender!

Let me pray to Athenê, the immortal daughter *Antistrophe 1*
of Zeus,
And to Artemis her sister
Who keeps her famous throne in the market ring,
And to Apollo, bowman at the far butts of heaven—

O gods, descend! Like three streams leap against
The fires of our grief, the fires of darkness;
Be swift to bring us rest!

As in the old time from the brilliant house
Of air you stepped to save us, come again!

Now our afflictions have no end, *Strophe 2*
Now all our stricken host lies down
And no man fights off death with his mind;

The noble plowland bears no grain,
And groaning mothers cannot bear—
See, how our lives like birds take wing,
Like sparks that fly when a fire soars,
To the shore of the god of evening.

The plague burns on, it is pitiless *Antistrophe 2*
Though pallid children laden with death
Lie unwept in the stony ways,
And old gray women by every path
Flock to the strand about the altars

**152 Phoibos** Phoebus Apollo, the sun god

There to strike their breasts and cry
Worship of Phoibos in wailing prayers:
Be kind, God's golden child!

*Strophe 3*

There are no swords in this attack by fire,
No shields, but we are ringed with cries.
Send the besieger plunging from our homes
Into the vast sea-room of the Atlantic
Or into the waves that foam eastward of Thrace—
For the day ravages what the night spares—

Destroy our enemy, lord of the thunder!
Let him be riven by lightning from heaven!

*Antistrophe 3*

Phoibos Apollo, stretch the sun's bowstring,
That golden cord, until it sing for us,
Flashing arrows in heaven!
Artemis, Huntress,
Race with flaring lights upon our mountains!
O scarlet god, O golden-banded brow,
O Theban Bacchos° in a storm of Maenads,°

*Enter Oedipus, center.*

Whirl upon Death, that all the Undying hate!
Come with blinding cressets, come in joy!

## *Scene I*

OEDIPUS. Is this your prayer? It may be answered. Come,
Listen to me, act as the crisis demands,
And you shall have relief from all these evils.

Until now I was a stranger to this tale,
As I had been a stranger to the crime.
Could I track down the murderer without a clue?
But now, friends,
As one who became a citizen after the murder,
I make this proclamation to all Thebans:
If any man knows by whose hand Laïos, son of Labdakos,
Met his death, I direct that man to tell me everything,
No matter what he fears for having so long withheld it.
Let it stand as promised that no further trouble
Will come to him, but he may leave the land in safety.

Moreover: If anyone knows the murderer to be foreign,
Let him not keep silent: he shall have his reward from me.
However, if he does conceal it; if any man
Fearing for his friend or for himself disobeys this edict,
Hear what I propose to do:

I solemnly forbid the people of this country,
Where power and throne are mine, ever to receive that man

**48 Bacchos** Dionysos, god of wine, thus scarlet-faced **Maenads** Dionysos's female attendants

Or speak to him, no matter who he is, or let him
Join in sacrifice, lustration, or in prayer.
I decree that he be driven from every house,

Being, as he is, corruption itself to us: the Delphic
Voice of Zeus has pronounced this revelation.
Thus I associate myself with the oracle
And take the side of the murdered king.

As for the criminal, I pray to God—
Whether it be a lurking thief, or one of a number—
I pray that that man's life be consumed in evil and wretchedness.
And as for me, this curse applies no less
If it should turn out that the culprit is my guest here,
Sharing my hearth.
You have heard the penalty.
I lay it on you now to attend to this
For my sake, for Apollo's, for the sick
Sterile city that heaven has abandoned.
Suppose the oracle had given you no command:
Should this defilement go uncleansed for ever?
You should have found the murderer: your king,
A noble king, had been destroyed!
Now I,
Having the power that he held before me,
Having his bed, begetting children there
Upon his wife, as he would have, had he lived—
Their son would have been my children's brother,
If Laïos had had luck in fatherhood!
(But surely ill luck rushed upon his reign)—
I say I take the son's part, just as though
I were his son, to press the fight for him
And see it won! I'll find the hand that brought
Death to Labdakos' and Polydoros' child,
Heir of Kadmos' and Agenor's line.
And as for those who fail me,
May the gods deny them the fruit of the earth,
Fruit of the womb, and may they rot utterly!
Let them be wretched as we are wretched, and worse!

For you, for loyal Thebans, and for all
Who find my actions right, I pray the favor
Of justice, and of all the immortal gods.

CHORAGOS.° Since I am under oath, my lord, I swear
I did not do the murder, I cannot name
The murderer. Might not the oracle
That has ordained the search tell where to find him?

OEDIPUS. An honest question. But no man in the world
Can make the gods do more than the gods will.

CHORAGOS. There is one last expedient—

**60 Choragos** leader of the Chorus

OEDIPUS. Tell me what it is.
Though it seem slight, you must not hold it back.
CHORAGOS. A lord clairvoyant to the lord Apollo,
As we all know, is the skilled Teiresias.
One might learn much about this from him, Oedipus.
OEDIPUS. I am not wasting time:
Creon spoke of this, and I have sent for him—
Twice, in fact; it is strange that he is not here.
CHORAGOS. The other matter—that old report—seems useless.
OEDIPUS. Tell me. I am interested in all reports.
CHORAGOS. The King was said to have been killed by highwaymen.
OEDIPUS. I know. But we have no witnesses to that.
CHORAGOS. If the killer can feel a particle of dread,
Your curse will bring him out of hiding!
OEDIPUS. No.
The man who dared that act will fear no curse.

*Enter the blind seer Teiresias, led by a Page.*

CHORAGOS. But there is one man who may detect the criminal.
This is Teiresias, this is the holy prophet
In whom, alone of all men, truth was born.
OEDIPUS. Teiresias: seer: student of mysteries,
Of all that's taught and all that no man tells,
Secrets of Heaven and secrets of the earth:
Blind though you are, you know the city lies
Sick with plague; and from this plague, my lord,
We find that you alone can guard or save us.

Possibly you did not hear the messengers?
Apollo, when we sent to him,
Sent us back word that this great pestilence
Would lift, but only if we established clearly
The identity of those who murdered Laïos.
They must be killed or exiled.
Can you use
Birdflight or any art of divination
To purify yourself, and Thebes, and me
From this contagion? We are in your hands.
There is no fairer duty
Than that of helping others in distress.
TEIRESIAS. How dreadful knowledge of the truth can be
When there's no help in truth! I knew this well,
But did not act on it: else I should not have come.
OEDIPUS. What is troubling you? Why are your eyes so cold?
TEIRESIAS. Let me go home. Bear your own fate, and I'll
Bear mine. It is better so: trust what I say.
OEDIPUS. What you say is ungracious and unhelpful
To your native country. Do not refuse to speak.
TEIRESIAS. When it comes to speech, your own is neither temperate
Nor opportune. I wish to be more prudent.
OEDIPUS. In God's name, we all beg you—
TEIRESIAS. You are all ignorant.

No; I will never tell you what I know.
Now it is my misery; then, it would be yours.
OEDIPUS. What! You do know something, and will not tell us?
You would betray us all and wreck the State?
TEIRESIAS. I do not intend to torture myself, or you.
Why persist in asking? You will not persuade me.
OEDIPUS. What a wicked man you are! You'd try a stone's
Patience! Out with it! Have you no feeling at all?
TEIRESIAS. You call me unfeeling. If you could only see
The nature of your feelings . . .
OEDIPUS. Why,
Who would not feel as I do? Who could endure
Your arrogance toward the city?
TEIRESIAS. What does it matter!
Whether I speak or not, it is bound to come.
OEDIPUS. Then, if "it" is bound to come, you are bound to tell me.
TEIRESIAS. No, I will not go on. Rage as you please.
OEDIPUS. Rage? Why not!
And I'll tell you what I think:
You planned it, you had it done, you all but
Killed him with your own hands: if you had eyes,
I'd say the crime was yours, and yours alone.
TEIRESIAS. So? I charge you, then,
Abide by the proclamation you have made.
From this day forth
Never speak again to these men or to me;
You yourself are the pollution of this country.
OEDIPUS. You dare say that! Can you possibly think you have
Some way of going free, after such insolence?
TEIRESIAS. I have gone free. It is the truth sustains me.
OEDIPUS. Who taught you shamelessness? It was not your craft.
TEIRESIAS. You did. You made me speak. I did not want to.
OEDIPUS. Speak what? Let me hear it again more clearly.
TEIRESIAS. Was it not clear before? Are you tempting me?
OEDIPUS. I did not understand it. Say it again.
TEIRESIAS. I say that you are the murderer whom you seek.
OEDIPUS. Now twice you have spat out infamy. You'll pay for it!
TEIRESIAS. Would you care for more? Do you wish to be really angry?
OEDIPUS. Say what you will. Whatever you say is worthless.
TEIRESIAS. I say you live in hideous shame with those
Most dear to you. You cannot see the evil.
OEDIPUS. It seems you can go on mouthing like this for ever.
TEIRESIAS. I can, if there is power in truth.
OEDIPUS. There is:
But not for you, not for you,
You sightless, witless, senseless, mad old man!
TEIRESIAS. You are the madman. There is no one here
Who will not curse you soon, as you curse me.
OEDIPUS. You child of endless night! You cannot hurt me
Or any other man who sees the sun.
TEIRESIAS. True: it is not from me your fate will come.

That lies within Apollo's competence,
As it is his concern.
OEDIPUS. Tell me:
Are you speaking for Creon, or for yourself?
TEIRESIAS. Creon is no threat. You weave your own doom.
OEDIPUS. Wealth, power, craft of statesmanship!
Kingly position, everywhere admired!
What savage envy is stored up against these,
If Creon, whom I trusted, Creon my friend,
For this great office which the city once
Put in my hands unsought—if for this power
Creon desires in secret to destroy me!

He has brought this decrepit fortune-teller, this
Collector of dirty pennies, this prophet fraud—
Why, he is no more clairvoyant than I am!
Tell us:
Has your mystic mummery ever approached the truth?
When that hellcat the Sphinx was performing here,
What help were you to these people?
Her magic was not for the first man who came along:
It demanded a real exorcist. Your birds—
What good were they? or the gods, for the matter of that?
But I came by,
Oedipus, the simple man, who knows nothing—
I thought it out for myself, no birds helped me!
And this is the man you think you can destroy,
That you may be close to Creon, when he's king!
Well, you and your friend Creon, it seems to me,
Will suffer most. If you were not an old man,
You would have paid already for your plot.
CHORAGOS. We cannot see that his words or yours
Have spoken except in anger, Oedipus,
And of anger we have no need. How can God's will
Be accomplished best? That is what most concerns us.
TEIRESIAS. You are a king. But where argument's concerned
I am your man, as much a king as you.
I am not your servant, but Apollo's.
I have no need of Creon to speak for me.

Listen to me. You mock my blindness, do you?
But I say that you, with both your eyes, are blind:
You cannot see the wretchedness of your life,
Not in whose house you live, no, nor with whom.
Who are your father and mother? Can you tell me?
You do not even know the blind wrongs
That you have done them, on earth and in the world below.
But the double lash of your parents' curse will whip you
Out of this land some day, with only night
Upon your precious eyes.

Your cries then—where will they not be heard?
What fastness of Kithairon° will not echo them?
And that bridal-descant of yours—you'll know it then,
The song they sang when you came here to Thebes
And found your misguided berthing.
All this, and more, that you cannot guess at now,
Will bring you to yourself among your children.
Be angry, then. Curse Creon. Curse my words.
I tell you, no man that walks upon the earth
Shall be rooted out more horribly than you.

OEDIPUS. Am I to bear this from him?—Damnation
Take you! Out of this place! Out of my sight!

TEIRESIAS. I would not have come at all if you had not asked me.

OEDIPUS. Could I have told that you'd talk nonsense, that
You'd come here to make a fool of yourself, and of me?

TEIRESIAS. A fool? Your parents thought me sane enough.

OEDIPUS. My parents again!—Wait: who were my parents?

TEIRESIAS. This day will give you a father, and break your heart.

OEDIPUS. Your infantile riddles! Your damned abracadabra!

TEIRESIAS. You were a great man once at solving riddles.

OEDIPUS. Mock me with that if you like; you will find it true.

TEIRESIAS. It was true enough. It brought about your ruin.

OEDIPUS. But if it saved this town.

TEIRESIAS (*to the Page*). Boy, give me your hand.

OEDIPUS. Yes, boy; lead him away.
—While you are here
We can do nothing. Go; leave us in peace.

TEIRESIAS. I will go when I have said what I have to say.
How can you hurt me? And I tell you again:
The man you have been looking for all this time,
The damned man, the murderer of Laïos,
That man is in Thebes. To your mind he is foreignborn,
But it will soon be shown that he is a Theban,
A revelation that will fail to please.
A blind man,
Who has his eyes now; a penniless man, who is rich now;
And he will go tapping the strange earth with his staff;
To the children with whom he lives now he will be
Brother and father—the very same; to her
Who bore him, son and husband—the very same
Who came to his father's bed, wet with his father's blood.

Enough. Go think that over.
If later you find error in what I have said,
You may say that I have no skill in prophecy.

*Exit Teiresias, led by his Page. Oedipus goes into the palace.*

**206 fastness of Kithairon** stronghold in a mountain near Thebes

## *Ode I*

CHORUS. The Delphic stone of prophecies *Strophe 1*
Remembers ancient regicide
And a still bloody hand.
That killer's hour of flight has come.
He must be stronger than riderless
Coursers of untiring wind,
For the son of Zeus° armed with his father's thunder
Leaps in lightning after him;
And the Furies° follow him, the sad Furies.

Holy Parnassos' peak of snow *Antistrophe 1*
Flashes and blinds that secret man,
That all shall hunt him down:
Though he may roam the forest shade
Like a bull gone wild from pasture
To rage through glooms of stone.
Doom comes down on him; flight will not avail him;
For the world's heart calls him desolate,
And the immortal Furies follow, for ever follow.

But now a wilder thing is heard *Strophe 2*
From the old man skilled at hearing Fate in the wingbeat of a bird.
Bewildered as a blown bird, my soul hovers and cannot find
Foothold in this debate, or any reason or rest of mind.
But no man ever brought—none can bring
Proof of strife between Thebes' royal house,
Labdakos' line,° and the son of Polybos;°
And never until now has any man brought word
Of Laïos' dark death staining Oedipus the King.

Divine Zeus and Apollo hold *Antistrophe 2*
Perfect intelligence alone of all tales ever told;
And well though this diviner works, he works in his own night;
No man can judge that rough unknown or trust in second sight,
For wisdom changes hands among the wise.
Shall I believe my great lord criminal.
At a raging word that a blind old man let fall?
I saw him, when the carrion woman faced him of old,
Prove his heroic mind! These evil words are lies.

## *Scene II*

CREON. Men of Thebes:
I am told that heavy accusations
Have been brought against me by King Oedipus.
I am not the kind of man to bear this tamely.

**7 son of Zeus** Apollo **9 Furies** avenging deities **25 Labdakos' line** family of Laïos **25 son of Polybos** Oedipus (so the Chorus believes)

If in these present difficulties
He holds me accountable for any harm to him
Through anything I have said or done—why, then,
I do not value life in this dishonor.
It is not as though this rumor touched upon
Some private indiscretion. The matter is grave.
The fact is that I am being called disloyal
To the State, to my fellow citizens, to my friends.

CHORAGOS. He may have spoken in anger, not from his mind.

CREON. But did you hear him say I was the one
Who seduced the old prophet into lying?

CHORAGOS. The thing was said; I do not know how seriously.

CREON. But you were watching him! Were his eyes steady?
Did he look like a man in his right mind?

CHORAGOS. I do not know.
I cannot judge the behavior of great men.
But here is the King himself.

*Enter Oedipus.*

OEDIPUS. So you dared come back.
Why? How brazen of you to come to my house,
You murderer!
Do you think I do not know
That you plotted to kill me, plotted to steal my throne?
Tell me, in God's name: am I coward, a fool,
That you should dream you could accomplish this?
A fool who could not see your slippery game?
A coward, not to fight back when I saw it?
You are the fool, Creon, are you not? hoping
Without support or friends to get a throne?
Thrones may be won or bought: you could do neither.

CREON. Now listen to me. You have talked; let me talk, too.
You cannot judge unless you know the facts.

OEDIPUS. You speak well: there is one fact; but I find it hard
To learn from the deadliest enemy I have.

CREON. That above all I must dispute with you.

OEDIPUS. That above all I will not hear you deny.

CREON. If you think there is anything good in being stubborn
Against all reason, then I say you are wrong.

OEDIPUS. If you think a man can sin against his own kind
And not be punished for it, I say you are mad.

CREON. I agree. But tell me: what have I done to you?

OEDIPUS. You advised me to send for that wizard, did you not?

CREON. I did. I should do it again.

OEDIPUS. Very well. Now tell me:
How long has it been since Laïos—

CREON. What of Laïos?

OEDIPUS. Since he vanished in that onset by the road?

CREON. It was long ago, a long time.

OEDIPUS. And this prophet,
Was he practicing here then?

CREON. He was; and with honor, as now.
OEDIPUS. Did he speak of me at that time?
CREON. He never did;
At least, not when I was present.
OEDIPUS. But . . . the enquiry?
I suppose you held one?
CREON. We did, but we learned nothing.
OEDIPUS. Why did the prophet not speak against me then?
CREON. I do not know; and I am the kind of man
Who holds his tongue when he has no facts to go on.
OEDIPUS. There's one fact that you know, and you could tell it.
CREON. What fact is that? If I know it, you shall have it.
OEDIPUS. If he were not involved with you, he could not say
That it was I who murdered Laïos.
CREON. If he says that, you are the one that knows it!—
But now it is my turn to question you.
OEDIPUS. Put your questions. I am no murderer.
CREON. First, then: You married my sister?
OEDIPUS. I married your sister.
CREON. And you rule the kingdom equally with her?
OEDIPUS. Everything that she wants she has from me.
CREON. And I am the third, equal to both of you?
OEDIPUS. That is why I call you a bad friend.
CREON. No. Reason it out, as I have done.
Think of this first. Would any sane man prefer
Power, with all a king's anxieties,
To that same power and the grace of sleep?
Certainly not I.
I have never longed for the king's power—only his rights.
Would any wise man differ from me in this?
As matters stand, I have my way in everything
With your consent, and no responsibilities.
If I were king, I should be a slave to policy.
How could I desire a scepter more
Than what is now mine—untroubled influence?
No, I have not gone mad; I need no honors,
Except those with the perquisites I have now.
I am welcome everywhere; every man salutes me,
And those who want your favor seek my ear,
Since I know how to manage what they ask.
Should I exchange this ease for that anxiety?
Besides, no sober mind is treasonable.
I hate anarchy
And never would deal with any man who likes it.

Test what I have said. Go to the priestess
At Delphi, ask if I quoted her correctly.
And as for this other thing: if I am found
Guilty of treason with Teiresias,
Then sentence me to death! You have my word
It is a sentence I should cast my vote for—

But not without evidence!
You do wrong
When you take good men for bad, bad men for good.
A true friend thrown aside—why, life itself
Is not more precious!
In time you will know this well:
For time, and time alone, will show the just man,
Though scoundrels are discovered in a day.
CHORAGOS. This is well said, and a prudent man would ponder it.
Judgments too quickly formed are dangerous.
OEDIPUS. But is he not quick in his duplicity?
And shall I not be quick to parry him?
Would you have me stand still, hold my peace, and let
This man win everything, through my inaction?
CREON. And you want—what is it, then? To banish me?
OEDIPUS. No, not exile. It is your death I want,
So that all the world may see what treason means.
CREON. You will persist, then? You will not believe me?
OEDIPUS. How can I believe you?
CREON. Then you are a fool.
OEDIPUS. To save myself?
CREON. In justice, think of me.
OEDIPUS. You are evil incarnate.
CREON. But suppose that you are wrong?
OEDIPUS. Still I must rule.
CREON. But not if you rule badly.
OEDIPUS. O city, city!
CREON. It is my city, too!
CHORAGOS. Now, my lords, be still. I see the Queen,
Iocastê, coming from her palace chambers;
And it is time she came, for the sake of you both.
This dreadful quarrel can be resolved through her.

*Enter Iocastê.*

IOCASTÊ. Poor foolish men, what wicked din is this?
With Thebes sick to death, is it not shameful
That you should rake some private quarrel up?
(*To Oedipus.*) Come into the house.
—And you, Creon, go now:
Let us have no more of this tumult over nothing.
CREON. Nothing? No, sister: what your husband plans for me
Is one of two great evils: exile or death.
OEDIPUS. He is right.
Why, woman, I have caught him squarely
Plotting against my life.
CREON. No! Let me die
Accurst if ever I have wished you harm!
IOCASTÊ. Ah, believe it, Oedipus!
In the name of the gods, respect this oath of his
For my sake, for the sake of these people here!

CHORAGOS. Open your mind to her, my lord. Be ruled by her, I beg you! *Strophe 1*
OEDIPUS. What would you have me do?
CHORAGOS. Respect Creon's word. He has never spoken like a fool,
And now he has sworn an oath.
OEDIPUS. You know what you ask?
CHORAGOS. I do.
OEDIPUS. Speak on, then.
CHORAGOS. A friend so sworn should not be baited so,
In blind malice, and without final proof.
OEDIPUS. You are aware, I hope, that what you say
Means death for me, or exile at the least.

CHORAGOS. No, I swear by Helios,° first in Heaven! *Strophe 2*
May I die friendless and accurst,
The worst of deaths, if ever I meant that!
It is the withering fields
That hurt my sick heart:
Must we bear all these ills,
And now your bad blood as well?
OEDIPUS. Then let him go. And let me die, if I must,
Or be driven by him in shame from the land of Thebes.
It is your unhappiness, and not his talk,
That touches me.
As for him—
Wherever he is, I will hate him as long as I live.
CREON. Ugly in yielding, as you were ugly in rage!
Natures like yours chiefly torment themselves.
OEDIPUS. Can you not go? Can you not leave me?
CREON. I can.
You do not know me; but the city knows me,
And in its eyes I am just, if not in yours.
(*Exit Creon.*)

CHORAGOS. Lady Iocastê, did you not ask the King to go to his chambers? *Antistrophe 1*
IOCASTÊ. First tell me what has happened.
CHORAGOS. There was suspicion without evidence; yet it rankled
As even false charges will.
IOCASTÊ. On both sides?
CHORAGOS. On both.
IOCASTÊ. But what was said?
CHORAGOS. Oh let it rest, let it be done with!
Have we not suffered enough?
OEDIPUS. You see to what your decency has brought you:
You have made difficulties where my heart saw none.

CHORAGOS. Oedipus, it is not once only I have told you— *Antistrophe 2*
You must know I should count myself unwise

**139 Helios** sun god

To the point of madness, should I now forsake you—
You, under whose hand,
In the storm of another time,
Our dear land sailed out free,
But now stand fast at the helm!
IOCASTÊ. In God's name, Oedipus, inform your wife as well:
Why are you so set in this hard anger?
OEDIPUS. I will tell you, for none of these men deserves
My confidence as you do. It is Creon's work,
His treachery, his plotting against me.
IOCASTÊ. Go on, if you can make this clear to me.
OEDIPUS. He charges me with the murder of Laïos.
IOCASTÊ. Has he some knowledge? Or does he speak from hearsay?
OEDIPUS. He would not commit himself to such a charge,
But he has brought in that damnable soothsayer
To tell his story.
IOCASTÊ. Set your mind at rest.
If it is a question of soothsayers, I tell you
That you will find no man whose craft gives knowledge
Of the unknowable.
Here is my proof.

An oracle was reported to Laïos once
(I will not say from Phoibos himself, but from
His appointed ministers, at any rate)
That his doom would be death at the hands of his own son—
His son, born of his flesh and of mine!

Now, you remember the story: Laïos was killed
By marauding strangers where three highways meet;
But his child had not been three days in this world
Before the King had pierced the baby's ankles
And left him to die on a lonely mountainside.

Thus, Apollo never caused that child
To kill his father, and it was not Laïos fate
To die at the hands of his son, as he had feared.
This is what prophets and prophecies are worth!
Have no dread of them.
It is God himself
Who can show us what he wills, in his own way.
OEDIPUS. How strange a shadowy memory crossed my mind,
Just now while you were speaking; it chilled my heart.
IOCASTÊ. What do you mean? What memory do you speak of?
OEDIPUS. If I understand you, Laïos was killed
At a place where three roads meet.
IOCASTÊ. So it was said;
We have no later story.
OEDIPUS. Where did it happen?
IOCASTÊ. Phokis, it is called: at a place where the Theban Way
Divides into the roads towards Delphi and Daulia.
OEDIPUS. When?

IOCASTÊ. We had the news not long before you came
And proved the right to your succession here.
OEDIPUS. Ah, what net has God been weaving for me?
IOCASTÊ. Oedipus! Why does this trouble you?
OEDIPUS. Do not ask me yet.
First, tell me how Laïos looked, and tell me
How old he was.
IOCASTÊ. He was tall, his hair just touched
With white; his form was not unlike your own.
OEDIPUS. I think that I myself may be accurst
By my own ignorant edict.
IOCASTÊ. You speak strangely.
It makes me tremble to look at you, my King.
OEDIPUS. I am not sure that the blind man cannot see.
But I should know better if you were to tell me—
IOCASTÊ. Anything—though I dread to hear you ask it.
OEDIPUS. Was the King lightly escorted, or did he ride
With a large company, as a ruler should?
IOCASTÊ. There were five men with him in all: one was a herald;
And a single chariot, which he was driving.
OEDIPUS. Alas, that makes it plain enough!
But who—
Who told you how it happened?
IOCASTÊ. A household servant,
The only one to escape.
OEDIPUS. And is he still
A servant of ours?
IOCASTÊ. No; for when he came back at last
And found you enthroned in the place of the dead king,
He came to me, touched my hand with his, and begged
That I would send him away to the frontier district
Where only the shepherds go—
As far away from the city as I could send him.
I granted his prayer; for although the man was a slave,
He had earned more than this favor at my hands.
OEDIPUS. Can he be called back quickly?
IOCASTÊ. Easily.
But why?
OEDIPUS. I have taken too much upon myself
Without enquiry; therefore I wish to consult him.
IOCASTÊ. Then he shall come.
But am I not one also
To whom you might confide these fears of yours!
OEDIPUS. That is your right; it will not be denied you,
Now least of all; for I have reached a pitch
Of wild foreboding. Is there anyone
To whom I should sooner speak?
Polybos of Corinth is my father.
My mother is a Dorian: Meropê.
I grew up chief among the men of Corinth

Until a strange thing happened—
Not worth my passion, it may be, but strange.

At a feast, a drunken man maundering in his cups
Cries out that I am not my father's son!

I contained myself that night, though I felt anger
And a sinking heart. The next day I visited
My father and mother, and questioned them. They stormed,
Calling it all the slanderous rant of a fool;
And this relieved me. Yet the suspicion
Remained always aching in my mind;
I knew there was talk; I could not rest;
And finally, saying nothing to my parents,
I went to the shrine at Delphi.
The god dismissed my question without reply;
He spoke of other things.
Some were clear,
Full of wretchedness, dreadful, unbearable:
As, that I should lie with my own mother, breed
Children from whom all men would turn their eyes;
And that I should be my father's murderer.

I heard all this, and fled. And from that day
Corinth to me was only in the stars
Descending in that quarter of the sky,
As I wandered farther and farther on my way
To a land where I should never see the evil
Sung by the oracle. And I came to this country
Where, so you say, King Laïos was killed.
I will tell you all that happened there, my lady.

There were three highways
Coming together at a place I passed;
And there a herald came towards me, and a chariot
Drawn by horses, with a man such as you describe
Seated in it. The groom leading the horses
Forced me off the road at his lord's command;
But as this charioteer lurched over toward me
I struck him in my rage. The old man saw me
And brought his double goad down upon my head
As I came abreast.
He was paid back, and more!
Swinging my club in this right hand I knocked him
Out of his car, and he rolled on the ground.
I killed him.

I killed them all.
Now if that stranger and Laïos were—kin,
Where is a man more miserable than I?
More hated by the gods? Citizen and alien alike
Must never shelter me or speak to me—

I must be shunned by all.
And I myself
Pronounced this malediction upon myself!

Think of it: I have touched you with these hands,
These hands that killed your husband. What defilement!

Am I all evil, then? It must be so,
Since I must flee from Thebes, yet never again
See my own countrymen, my own country,
For fear of joining my mother in marriage
And killing Polybos, my father.
Ah,
If I was created so, born to this fate,
Who could deny the savagery of God?

O holy majesty of heavenly powers!
May I never see that day! Never!
Rather let me vanish from the race of men
Than know the abomination destined me!

CHORAGOS. We too, my lord, have felt dismay at this.
But there is hope: you have yet to hear the shepherd.

OEDIPUS. Indeed, I fear no other hope is left me.

IOCASTÊ. What do you hope from him when he comes?

OEDIPUS. This much:
If his account of the murder tallies with yours,
Then I am cleared.

IOCASTÊ. What was it that I said
Of such importance?

OEDIPUS. Why, "marauders," you said,
Killed the King, according to this man's story.
If he maintains that still, if there were several,
Clearly the guilt is not mine: I was alone.
But if he says one man, singlehanded, did it,
Then the evidence all points to me.

IOCASTÊ. You may be sure that he said there were several;
And can he call back that story now? He cannot.
The whole city heard it as plainly as I.
But suppose he alters some detail of it:
He cannot ever show that Laïos' death
Fulfilled the oracle: for Apollo said
My child was doomed to kill him; and my child—
Poor baby!—it was my child that died first.

No. From now on, where oracles are concerned,
I would not waste a second thought on any.

OEDIPUS. You may be right.
But come: let someone go
For the shepherd at once. This matter must be settled.

IOCASTÊ. I will send for him.
I would not wish to cross you in anything,

And surely not in this.—Let us go in.

*Exeunt into the palace.*

## *Ode II*

CHORUS. Let me be reverent in the ways of right, *Strophe 1*
Lowly the paths I journey on;
Let all my words and actions keep
The laws of the pure universe
From highest Heaven handed down.
For Heaven is their bright nurse,
Those generations of the realms of light;
Ah, never of mortal kind were they begot,
Nor are they slaves of memory, lost in sleep:
Their Father is greater than Time, and ages not.

The tyrant is a child of Pride *Antistrophe 1*
Who drinks from his great sickening cup
Recklessness and vanity,
Until from his high crest headlong
He plummets to the dust of hope.
That strong man is not strong.
But let no fair ambition be denied;
May God protect the wrestler for the State
In government, in comely policy,
Who will fear God, and on His ordinance wait.

Haughtiness and the high hand of disdain *Strophe 2*
Tempt and outrage God's holy law;
And any mortal who dares hold
No immortal Power in awe
Will be caught up in a net of pain:
The price for which his levity is sold.
Let each man take due earnings, then,
And keep his hands from holy things,
And from blasphemy stand apart—
Else the crackling blast of heaven
Blows on his head, and on his desperate heart;
Though fools will honor impious men,
In their cities no tragic poet sings.

Shall we lose faith in Delphi's obscurities, *Antistrophe 2*
We who have heard the world's core
Discredited, and the sacred wood
Of Zeus at Elis praised no more?
The deeds and the strange prophecies
Must make a pattern yet to be understood.
Zeus, if indeed you are lord of all,
Throned in light over night and day,
Mirror this in your endless mind:
Our masters call the oracle
Words on the wind, and the Delphic vision blind!

Their hearts no longer know Apollo,
And reverence for the gods has died away.

## *Scene III*

*Enter Iocastê.*

IOCASTÊ. Princes of Thebes, it has occurred to me
To visit the altars of the gods, bearing
These branches as a suppliant, and this incense.
Our King is not himself: his noble soul
Is overwrought with fantasies of dread,
Else he would consider
The new prophecies in the light of the old.
He will listen to any voice that speaks disaster,
And my advice goes for nothing.

*She approaches the altar, right.*

To you, then, Apollo,
Lycean lord, since you are nearest, I turn in prayer.
Receive these offerings, and grant us deliverance
From defilement. Our hearts are heavy with fear
When we see our leader distracted, as helpless sailors
Are terrified by the confusion of their helmsman.

*Enter Messenger.*

MESSENGER. Friends, no doubt you can direct me:
Where shall I find the house of Oedipus,
Or, better still, where is the King himself?
CHORAGOS. It is this very place, stranger; he is inside.
This is his wife and mother of his children.
MESSENGER. I wish her happiness in a happy house,
Blest in all the fulfillment of her marriage.
IOCASTÊ. I wish as much for you: your courtesy
Deserves a like good fortune. But now, tell me:
Why have you come? What have you to say to us?
MESSENGER. Good news, my lady, for your house and your husband.
IOCASTÊ. What news? Who sent you here?
MESSENGER. I am from Corinth.
The news I bring ought to mean joy for you,
Though it may be you will find some grief in it.
IOCASTÊ. What is it? How can it touch us in both ways?
MESSENGER. The people of Corinth, they say,
Intend to call Oedipus to be their king.
IOCASTÊ. But old Polybos—is he not reigning still?
MESSENGER. No. Death holds him in his sepulchre.
IOCASTÊ. What are you saying? Polybos is dead?
MESSENGER. If I am not telling the truth, may I die myself.
IOCASTÊ (*to a Maidservant*). Go in, go quickly; tell this to your master.
O riddlers of God's will, where are you now!
This was the man whom Oedipus, long ago,
Feared so, fled so, in dread of destroying him—
But it was another fate by which he died.

*Enter Oedipus, center.*

OEDIPUS. Dearest Iocastê, why have you sent for me?
IOCASTÊ. Listen to what this man says, and then tell me
What has become of the solemn prophecies.
OEDIPUS. Who is this man? What is his news for me?
IOCASTÊ. He has come from Corinth to announce your father's death!
OEDIPUS. Is it true, stranger? Tell me in your own words.
MESSENGER. I cannot say it more clearly: the King is dead.
OEDIPUS. Was it by treason? Or by an attack of illness?
MESSENGER. A little thing brings old men to their rest.
OEDIPUS. It was sickness, then?
MESSENGER. Yes, and his many years.
OEDIPUS. Ah!
Why should a man respect the Pythian hearth,° or
Give heed to the birds that jangle above his head?
They prophesied that I should kill Polybos,
Kill my own father; but he is dead and buried,
And I am here—I never touched him, never,
Unless he died in grief for my departure,
And thus, in a sense, through me. No, Polybos
Has packed the oracles off with him underground.
They are empty words.
IOCASTÊ. Had I not told you so?
OEDIPUS. You had; it was my faint heart that betrayed me.
IOCASTÊ. From now on never think of those things again.
OEDIPUS. And yet—must I not fear my mother's bed?
IOCASTÊ. Why should anyone in this world be afraid,
Since Fate rules us and nothing can be foreseen?
A man should live only for the present day.
Have no more fear of sleeping with your mother.
How many men, in dreams, have lain with their mothers!
No reasonable man is troubled by such things.
OEDIPUS. That is true; only—
If only my mother were not still alive!
But she is alive. I cannot help my dread.
IOCASTÊ. Yet this news of your father's death is wonderful.
OEDIPUS. Wonderful. But I fear the living woman.
MESSENGER. Tell me, who is this woman that you fear?
OEDIPUS. It is Meropê, man; the wife of King Polybos.
MESSENGER. Meropê? Why should you be afraid of her?
OEDIPUS. An oracle of the gods, a dreadful saying.
MESSENGER. Can you tell me about it or are you sworn to silence?
OEDIPUS. I can tell you, and I will.
Apollo said through his prophet that I was the man
Who should marry his own mother, shed his father's blood
With his own hands. And so, for all these years
I have kept clear of Corinth, and no harm has come—
Though it would have been sweet to see my parents again.

**52 Pythian hearth** Delphi (also called Pytho because a great snake had lived there), where Apollo spoke through a priestess

MESSENGER. And is this the fear that drove you out of Corinth?
OEDIPUS. Would you have me kill my father?
MESSENGER. As for that
You must be reassured by the news I gave you.
OEDIPUS. If you could reassure me, I would reward you.
MESSENGER. I had that in mind, I will confess: I thought
I could count on you when you returned to Corinth.
OEDIPUS. No: I will never go near my parents again.
MESSENGER. Ah, son, you still do not know what you are doing—
OEDIPUS. What do you mean? In the name of God tell me!
MESSENGER. —If these are your reasons for not going home—
OEDIPUS. I tell you, I fear the oracle may come true.
MESSENGER. And guilt may come upon you through your parents?
OEDIPUS. That is the dread that is always in my heart.
MESSENGER. Can you not see that all your fears are groundless?
OEDIPUS. How can you say that? They are my parents, surely?
MESSENGER. Polybos was not your father.
OEDIPUS. Not my father?
MESSENGER. No more your father than the man speaking to you.
OEDIPUS. But you are nothing to me!
MESSENGER. Neither was he.
OEDIPUS. Then why did he call me son?
MESSENGER. I will tell you:
Long ago he had you from my hands, as a gift.
OEDIPUS. Then how could he love me so, if I was not his?
MESSENGER. He had no children, and his heart turned to you.
OEDIPUS. What of you? Did you buy me? Did you find me by chance?
MESSENGER. I came upon you in the crooked pass of Kithairon.
OEDIPUS. And what were you doing there?
MESSENGER. Tending my flocks.
OEDIPUS. A wandering shepherd?
MESSENGER. But your savior, son, that day.
OEDIPUS. From what did you save me?
MESSENGER. Your ankles should tell you that.
OEDIPUS. Ah, stranger, why do you speak of that childhood pain?
MESSENGER. I cut the bonds that tied your ankles together.
OEDIPUS. I have had the mark as long as I can remember.
MESSENGER. That was why you were given the name you bear.°
OEDIPUS. God! Was it my father or my mother who did it?
Tell me!
MESSENGER. I do not know. The man who gave you to me
Can tell you better than I.
OEDIPUS. It was not you that found me, but another?
MESSENGER. It was another shepherd gave you to me.
OEDIPUS. Who was he? Can you tell me who he was?
MESSENGER. I think he was said to be one of Laïos' people.
OEDIPUS. You mean the Laïos who was king here years ago?
MESSENGER. Yes; King Laïos; and the man was one of his herdsmen.
OEDIPUS. Is he still alive? Can I see him?
MESSENGER. These men here

**116 name you bear** *Oedipus* means "swollen-foot"

Know best about such things.

OEDIPUS. Does anyone here
Know this shepherd that he is talking about?
Have you seen him in the fields, or in the town?
If you have, tell me. It is time things were made plain.

CHORAGOS. I think the man he means is that same shepherd
You have already asked to see. Iocastê perhaps
Could tell you something.

OEDIPUS. Do you know anything
About him, Lady? Is he the man we have summoned?
Is that the man this shepherd means?

IOCASTÊ. Why think of him?
Forget this herdsman. Forget it all.
This talk is a waste of time.

OEDIPUS. How can you say that,
When the clues to my true birth are in my hands?

IOCASTÊ. For God's love, let us have no more questioning!
Is your life nothing to you?
My own is pain enough for me to bear.

OEDIPUS. You need not worry. Suppose my mother a slave,
And born of slaves: no baseness can touch you.

IOCASTÊ. Listen to me, I beg you: do not do this thing!

OEDIPUS. I will not listen; the truth must be made known.

IOCASTÊ. Everything that I say is for your own good!

OEDIPUS. My own good
Snaps my patience, then: I want none of it.

IOCASTÊ. You are fatally wrong! May you never learn who you are!

OEDIPUS. Go, one of you, and bring the shepherd here.
Let us leave this woman to brag of her royal name.

IOCASTÊ. Ah, miserable!
That is the only word I have for you now.
That is the only word I can ever have.

*Exit into the palace.*

CHORAGOS. Why has she left us, Oedipus? Why has she gone
In such a passion of sorrow? I fear this silence:
Something dreadful may come of it.

OEDIPUS. Let it come!
However base my birth, I must know about it.
The Queen, like a woman, is perhaps ashamed
To think of my low origin. But I
Am a child of luck; I cannot be dishonored.
Luck is my mother; the passing months, my brothers,
Have seen me rich and poor. If this is so,
How could I wish that I were someone else?
How could I not be glad to know my birth?

## *Ode III*

CHORUS. If ever the coming time were known *Strophe*
To my heart's pondering,
Kithairon, now by Heaven I see the torches
At the festival of the next full moon,

And see the dance, and hear the choir sing
A grace to your gentle shade:
Mountain where Oedipus was found,
O mountain guard of a noble race!
May the god who heals us lend his aid,
And let that glory come to pass
For our king's cradling-ground.

*Antistrophe*

Of the nymphs that flower beyond the years.
Who bore you, royal child,
To Pan of the hills or the timberline Apollo,
Cold in delight where the upland clears.
Or Hermês for whom Kyllenê's° heights are piled?
Or flushed as evening cloud,
Great Dionysos, roamer of mountains,
He—was it he who found you there,
And caught you up in his own proud
Arms from the sweet god-ravisher°
Who laughed by the Muses' fountains?

## *Scene IV*

OEDIPUS. Sirs: though I do not know the man,
I think I see him coming, this shepherd we want:
He is old, like our friend here, and the men
Bringing him seem to be servants of my house.
But you can tell, if you have ever seen him.

*Enter Shepherd escorted by servants.*

CHORAGOS. I know him, he was Laïos' man. You can trust him.
OEDIPUS. Tell me first, you from Corinth: is this the shepherd
We were discussing?
MESSENGER. This is the very man.
OEDIPUS (*to Shepherd*). Come here. No, look at me. You must answer
Everything I ask.—You belonged to Laïos?
SHEPHERD. Yes: born his slave, brought up in his house.
OEDIPUS. Tell me: what kind of work did you do for him?
SHEPHERD. I was a shepherd of his, most of my life.
OEDIPUS. Where mainly did you go for pasturage?
SHEPHERD. Sometimes Kithairon, sometimes the hills near-by.
OEDIPUS. Do you remember ever seeing this man out there?
SHEPHERD. What would he be doing there? This man?
OEDIPUS. This man standing here. Have you ever seen him before?
SHEPHERD. No. At least, not to my recollection.
MESSENGER. And that is not strange, my lord. But I'll refresh
His memory: he must remember when we two
Spent three whole seasons together, March to September,
On Kithairon or thereabouts. He had two flocks;

**16 Hermês . . . Kyllenê's** Hermês, messenger of the gods, was said to have been born on Mt. Kyllenê. **21 the sweet god-ravisher** the presumed mother, the nymph whom the god found irresistible

I had one. Each autumn I'd drive mine home
And he would go back with his to Laïos' sheepfold.—
Is this not true, just as I have described it?
SHEPHERD. True, yes; but it was all so long ago.
MESSENGER. Well, then: do you remember, back in those days
That you gave me a baby boy to bring up as my own?
SHEPHERD. What if I did? What are you trying to say?
MESSENGER. King Oedipus was once that little child.
SHEPHERD. Damn you, hold your tongue!
OEDIPUS. No more of that!
It is your tongue needs watching, not this man's.
SHEPHERD. My King, my Master, what is it I have done wrong?
OEDIPUS. You have not answered his question about the boy.
SHEPHERD. He does not know . . . He is only making trouble . . .
OEDIPUS. Come, speak plainly, or it will go hard with you.
SHEPHERD. In God's name, do not torture an old man!
OEDIPUS. Come here, one of you; bind his arms behind him.
SHEPHERD. Unhappy king! What more do you wish to learn?
OEDIPUS. Did you give this man the child he speaks of?
SHEPHERD. I did.
And I would to God I had died that very day.
OEDIPUS. You will die now unless you speak the truth.
SHEPHERD. Yet if I speak the truth, I am worse than dead.
OEDIPUS. Very well; since you insist upon delaying—
SHEPHERD. No! I have told you already that I gave him the boy.
OEDIPUS. Where did you get him? From your house?
From somewhere else?
SHEPHERD. Not from mine, no. A man gave him to me.
OEDIPUS. Is that man here? Do you know whose slave he was?
SHEPHERD. For God's love, my King, do not ask me any more!
OEDIPUS. You are a dead man if I have to ask you again.
SHEPHERD. Then . . . Then the child was from the palace of Laïos.
OEDIPUS. A slave child? or a child of his own line?
SHEPHERD. Ah, I am on the brink of dreadful speech!
OEDIPUS. And I of dreadful hearing. Yet I must hear.
SHEPHERD. If you must be told, then . . .
They said it was Laïos' child,
But it is your wife who can tell you about that.
OEDIPUS. My wife!—Did she give it to you?
SHEPHERD. My lord, she did.
OEDIPUS. Do you know why?
SHEPHERD. I was told to get rid of it.
OEDIPUS. An unspeakable mother!
SHEPHERD. There had been prophecies . . .
OEDIPUS. Tell me.
SHEPHERD. It was said that the boy would kill his own father.
OEDIPUS. Then why did you give him over to this old man?
SHEPHERD. I pitied the baby, my King,
And I thought that this man would take him far away
To his own country.
He saved him—but for what a fate!

For if you are what this man says you are,
No man living is more wretched than Oedipus.

OEDIPUS. Ah God!
It was true!
All the prophecies!
—Now,
O Light, may I look on you for the last time!
I, Oedipus,
Oedipus, damned in his birth, in his marriage damned,
Damned in the blood he shed with his own hand!

*He rushes into the palace.*

## *Ode IV*

CHORUS. Alas for the seed of men. *Strophe 1*

What measure shall I give these generations
That breathe on the void and are void
And exist and do not exist?

Who bears more weight of joy
Than mass of sunlight shifting in images,
Or who shall make his thought stay on
That down time drifts away?

Your splendor is all fallen.

O naked brow of wrath and tears,
O change of Oedipus!
I who saw your days call no man blest—
Your great days like ghósts góne.

That mind was a strong bow. *Antistrophe 1*
Deep, how deep you drew it then, hard archer,
At a dim fearful range,
And brought dear glory down!

You overcame the stranger—
The virgin with her hooking lion claws—
And though death sang, stood like a tower
To make pale Thebes take heart.

Fortress against our sorrow!

Divine king, giver of laws,
Majestic Oedipus!
No prince in Thebes had ever such renown,
No prince won such grace of power.

And now of all men ever known *Strophe 2*
Most pitiful is this man's story:
His fortunes are most changed, his state
Fallen to a low slave's
Ground under bitter fate.

O Oedipus, most royal one!
The great door that expelled you to the light

Gave it night—ah, gave night to your glory:
As to the father, to the fathering son.

All understood too late.

How could that queen whom Laïos won,
The garden that he harrowed at his height,
Be silent when that act was done?

But all eyes fail before time's eye, *Antistrophe 2*
All actions come to justice there.
Though never willed, though far down the deep past,
Your bed, your dread sirings,
Are brought to book at last.
Child by Laïos doomed to die,
Then doomed to lose that fortunate little death,
Would God you never took breath in this air
That with my wailing lips I take to cry:

For I weep the world's outcast.

I was blind, and now I can tell why:
Asleep, for you had given ease of breath
To Thebes, while the false years went by.

## *Exodos*

*Enter, from the palace, Second Messenger.*

SECOND MESSENGER. Elders of Thebes, most honored in this land,
What horrors are yours to see and hear, what weight
Of sorrow to be endured, if, true to your birth,
You venerate the line of Labdakos!
I think neither Istros nor Phasis, those great rivers,
Could purify this place of the corruption
It shelters now, or soon must bring to light—
Evil not done unconsciously, but willed.

The greatest griefs are those we cause ourselves.

CHORAGOS. Surely, friend, we have grief enough already;
What new sorrow do you mean?

SECOND MESSENGER. The Queen is dead.

CHORAGOS. Iocastê? Dead? But at whose hand?

SECOND MESSENGER. Her own.
The full horror of what happened you cannot know,
For you did not see it; but I, who did, will tell you
As clearly as I can how she met her death.

When she had left us,
In passionate silence, passing through the court,
She ran to her apartment in the house,
Her hair clutched by the fingers of both hands.
She closed the doors behind her; then, by that bed
Where long ago the fatal son was conceived—
That son who should bring about his father's death—
We heard her call upon Laïos, dead so many years,

And heard her wail for the double fruit of her marriage,
A husband by her husband, children by her child.

Exactly how she died I do not know:
For Oedipus burst in moaning and would not let us
Keep vigil to the end: it was by him
As he stormed about the room that our eyes were caught.
From one to another of us he went, begging a sword,
Cursing the wife who was not his wife, the mother
Whose womb had carried his own children and himself.
I do not know: it was none of us aided him,
But surely one of the gods was in control!
For with a dreadful cry
He hurled his weight, as though wrenched out of himself,
At the twin doors: the bolts gave, and he rushed in.
And there we saw her hanging, her body swaying
From the cruel cord she had noosed about her neck.
A great sob broke from him heartbreaking to hear,
As he loosed the rope and lowered her to the ground.

I would blot out from my mind what happened next!
For the King ripped from her gown the golden brooches
That were her ornament, and raised them, and plunged them down
Straight into his own eyeballs, crying, "No more,
No more shall you look on the misery about me,
The horrors of my own doing! Too long you have known
The faces of those whom I should never have seen,
Too long been blind to those for whom I was searching!
From this hour, go in darkness!" And as he spoke,
He struck at his eyes—not once, but many times;
And the blood spattered his beard,
Bursting from his ruined sockets like red hail.

So from the unhappiness of two this evil has sprung,
A curse on the man and woman alike. The old
Happiness of the house of Labdakos
Was happiness enough: where is it today?
It is all wailing and ruin, disgrace, death—all
The misery of mankind that has a name—
And it is wholly and for ever theirs.

CHORAGOS. Is he in agony still? Is there no rest for him?

SECOND MESSENGER. He is calling for someone to lead him to the gates
So that all the children of Kadmos may look upon
His father's murderer, his mother's—no,
I cannot say it!
And then he will leave Thebes,
Self-exiled, in order that the curse
Which he himself pronounced may depart from the house.
He is weak, and there is none to lead him,
So terrible is his suffering.
But you will see:
Look, the doors are opening; in a moment
You will see a thing that would crush a heart of stone.

*The central door is opened; Oedipus, blinded, is led in.*

CHORAGOS. Dreadful indeed for men to see.
Never have my own eyes
Looked on a sight so full of fear.

Oedipus!
What madness came upon you, what daemon°
Leaped on your life with heavier
Punishment than a mortal man can bear?
No: I cannot even
Look at you, poor ruined one.
And I would speak, question, ponder,
If I were able. No.
You make me shudder.

OEDIPUS. God. God.
Is there a sorrow greater?
Where shall I find harbor in this world?
My voice is hurled far on a dark wind.
What has God done to me?

CHORAGOS. Too terrible to think of, or to see.

OEDIPUS. O cloud of night, *Strophe 1*
Never to be turned away: night coming on,
I cannot tell how: night like a shroud!
My fair winds brought me here.
Oh God. Again
The pain of the spikes where I had sight,
The flooding pain
Of memory, never to be gouged out.

CHORAGOS. This is not strange.
You suffer it all twice over, remorse in pain,
Pain in remorse.

OEDIPUS. Ah dear friend *Antistrophe 1*
Are you faithful even yet, you alone?
Are you still standing near me, will you stay here,
Patient, to care for the blind?
The blind man!
Yet even blind I know who it is attends me,
By the voice's tone—
Though my new darkness hide the comforter.

CHORAGOS. Oh fearful act!
What god was it drove you to rake black
Night across your eyes?

OEDIPUS. Apollo. Apollo. Dear *Strophe 2*
Children, the god was Apollo.
He brought my sick, sick fate upon me.
But the blinding hand was my own!
How could I bear to see
When all my sight was horror everywhere?

**76 daemon** a spirit, not necessarily evil

CHORAGOS. Everywhere; that is true.
OEDIPUS. And now what is left?
Images? Love? A greeting even,
Sweet to the senses? Is there anything?
Ah, no, friends: lead me away.
Lead me away from Thebes.
Lead the great wreck
And hell of Oedipus, whom the gods hate.
CHORAGOS. Your fate is clear, you are not blind to that.
Would God you had never found it out!

*Antistrophe 2*

OEDIPUS. Death take the man who unbound
My feet on that hillside
And delivered me from death to life! What life?
If only I had died,
This weight of monstrous doom
Could not have dragged me and my darlings down.
CHORAGOS. I would have wished the same.
OEDIPUS. Oh never to have come here
With my father's blood upon me! Never
To have been the man they call his mother's husband!
Oh accurst! O child of evil,
To have entered that wretched bed—
the selfsame one!
More primal than sin itself, this fell to me.
CHORAGOS. I do not know how I can answer you.
You were better dead than alive and blind.
OEDIPUS. Do not counsel me any more. This punishment
That I have laid upon myself is just.
If I had eyes,
I do not know how I could bear the sight
Of my father, when I came to the house of Death,
Or my mother: for I have sinned against them both
So vilely that I could not make my peace
By strangling my own life.
Or do you think my children,
Born as they were born, would be sweet to my eyes?
Ah never, never! Nor this town with its high walls,
Nor the holy images of the gods.
For I,
Thrice miserable—Oedipus, noblest of all the line
Of Kadmos, have condemned myself to enjoy
These things no more, by my own malediction
Expelling that man whom the gods declared
To be a defilement in the house of Laïos.
After exposing the rankness of my own guilt,
How could I look men frankly in the eyes?
No, I swear it,
If I could have stifled my hearing at its source,
I would have done it and made all this body
A tight cell of misery, blank to light and sound:

So I should have been safe in a dark agony
Beyond all recollection.
Ah Kithairon!
Why did you shelter me? When I was cast upon you,
Why did I not die? Then I should never
Have shown the world my execrable birth.

Ah Polybos! Corinth, city that I believed
The ancient seat of my ancestors: how fair
I seemed, your child! And all the while this evil
Was cancerous within me!
For I am sick
In my daily life, sick in my origin.

O three roads, dark ravine, woodland and way
Where three roads met: you, drinking my father's blood,
My own blood, spilled by my own hand: can you remember
The unspeakable things I did there, and the things
I went on from there to do?
O marriage, marriage!
The act that engendered me, and again the act
Performed by the son in the same bed—
Ah, the net
Of incest, mingling fathers, brothers, sons,
With brides, wives, mothers: the last evil
That can be known by men: no tongue can say
How evil!
No. For the love of God, conceal me
Somewhere far from Thebes; or kill me; or hurl me
Into the sea, away from men's eyes for ever.
Come, lead me. You need not fear to touch me.
Of all men, I alone can bear this guilt.

*Enter Creon.*

CHORAGOS. We are not the ones to decide; but Creon here
May fitly judge of what you ask. He only
Is left to protect the city in your place.

OEDIPUS. Alas, how can I speak to him? What right have I
To beg his courtesy whom I have deeply wronged?

CREON. I have not come to mock you, Oedipus,
Or to reproach you, either.
(*To Attendants.*) —You, standing there:
If you have lost all respect for man's dignity,
At least respect the flame of Lord Helios:
Do not allow this pollution to show itself
Openly here, an affront to the earth
And Heaven's rain and the light of day. No, take him
Into the house as quickly as you can.
For it is proper
That only the close kindred see his grief.

OEDIPUS. I pray you in God's name, since your courtesy
Ignores my dark expectation, visiting

With mercy this man of all men most execrable:
Give me what I ask—for your good, not for mine.

CREON. And what is it that you would have me do?

OEDIPUS. Drive me out of this country as quickly as may be
To a place where no human voice can ever greet me.

CREON. I should have done that before now—only,
God's will had not been wholly revealed to me.

OEDIPUS. But his command is plain: the parricide
Must be destroyed. I am that evil man.

CREON. That is the sense of it, yes; but as things are,
We had best discover clearly what is to be done.

OEDIPUS. You would learn more about a man like me?

CREON. You are ready now to listen to the god.

OEDIPUS. I will listen. But it is to you.
That I must turn for help. I beg you, hear me.

The woman in there—
Give her whatever funeral you think proper:
She is your sister.
—But let me go, Creon!
Let me purge my father's Thebes of the pollution
Of my living here, and go out to the wild hills,
To Kithairon, that has won such fame with me,
The tomb my mother and father appointed for me,
And let me die there, as they willed I should.
And yet I know
Death will not ever come to me through sickness
Or in any natural way: I have been preserved
For some unthinkable fate. But let that be.
As for my sons, you need not care for them.
They are men, they will find some way to live.
But my poor daughters, who have shared my table,
Who never before have been parted from their father—
Take care of them, Creon; do this for me.
And will you let me touch them with my hands
A last time, and let us weep together?
Be kind, my lord,
Great prince, be kind!
Could I but touch them,
They would be mine again, as when I had my eyes.

*Enter Antigonê and Ismenê, attended.*

Ah, God!
Is it my dearest children I hear weeping?
Has Creon pitied me and sent my daughters?

CREON. Yes, Oedipus: I knew that they were dear to you
In the old days, and know you must love them still.

OEDIPUS. May God bless you for this—and be a friendlier
Guardian to you than he has been to me!

Children, where are you?
Come quickly to my hands: they are your brother's—

Hands that have brought your father's once clear eyes
To this way of seeing—
Ah dearest ones,
I had neither sight nor knowledge then, your father
By the woman who was the source of his life!
And I weep for you—having no strength to see you—,
I weep for you when I think of the bitterness
That men will visit upon you all your lives.
What homes, what festivals can you attend
Without being forced to depart again in tears?
And when you come to marriageable age,
Where is the man, my daughters, who would dare
Risk the bane that lies on all my children?
Is there any evil wanting? Your father killed
His father; sowed the womb of her who bore him;
Engendered you at the fount of his own existence!
That is what they will say of you.
Then, whom
Can you ever marry? There are no bridegrooms for you,
And your lives must wither away in sterile dreaming.
O Creon, son of Menoikeus!
You are the only father my daughters have,
Since we, their parents, are both of us gone for ever.
They are your own blood: you will not let them
Fall into beggary and loneliness;
You will keep them from the miseries that are mine!
Take pity on them; see, they are only children,
Friendless except for you. Promise me this,
Great Prince, and give me your hand in token of it.

*Creon clasps his right hand.*

Children:
I could say much, if you could understand me,
But as it is, I have only this prayer for you:
Live where you can, be as happy as you can—
Happier, please God, than God has made your father!

CREON. Enough. You have wept enough. Now go within.
OEDIPUS. I must; but it is hard.
CREON. Time eases all things.
OEDIPUS. But you must promise—
CREON. Say what you desire.
OEDIPUS. Send me from Thebes!
CREON. God grant that I may!
OEDIPUS. But since God hates me . . .
CREON. No, he will grant your wish.
OEDIPUS. You promise?
CREON. I cannot speak beyond my knowledge.
OEDIPUS. Then lead me in.
CREON. Come now, and leave your children.
OEDIPUS. No! Do not take them from me!
CREON. Think no longer

That you are in command here, but rather think
How, when you were, you served your own destruction.

*Exeunt into the house all but the Chorus; the Choragos chants directly to the audience.*

CHORAGOS. Men of Thebes: look upon Oedipus.
This is the king who solved the famous riddle
And towered up, most powerful of men.
No mortal eyes but looked on him with envy,
Yet in the end ruin swept over him.
Let every man in mankind's frailty
Consider his last day; and let none
Presume on his good fortune until he find
Life, at his death, a memory without pain.

[*c. 430* B.C.]

## TOPICS FOR CRITICAL THINKING AND WRITING

1. On the basis of the Prologue, characterize Oedipus. What additional traits are revealed in Scene I and Ode I?
2. How fair is it to say that Oedipus is morally guilty? Does he argue that he is morally innocent because he did not intend to do immoral deeds? Can it be said that he is guilty of hubris but that hubris has nothing to do with his fall?
3. Oedipus says that he blinds himself in order not to look upon people he should not. What further reasons can be given? Why does he not (like his mother) commit suicide?
4. How fair is it to say that the play shows the contemptibleness of human efforts to act intelligently?
5. How fair is it to say that in *Oedipus* the gods are evil?
6. Are the choral odes lyrical interludes that serve to separate the scenes, or do they advance the dramatic action?
7. Matthew Arnold said that Sophocles saw life steadily and saw it whole. But in this play is Sophocles facing the facts of life, or, on the contrary, is he avoiding life as it usually is and presenting a series of unnatural and outrageous coincidences?
8. Can you describe your emotions at the end of the play? Do they include pity for Oedipus? Pity for all human beings, including yourself? Fear that you might be punished for some unintended transgression? Awe, engendered by a perception of the interrelatedness of things? Relief that the story is only a story? Exhilaration?

# *Antigonê*

*An English Version by Dudley Fitts and Robert Fitzgerald*

LIST OF CHARACTERS

ANTIGONÊ
ISMENÊ
EURYDICÊ
CREON

Jane Lapotaire in *Antigonê,* National Theater, London, 1984. (© Donald Cooper/Photostage)

HAIMON
TEIRESIAS
A SENTRY
A MESSENGER
CHORUS

**SCENE:** *Before the palace of Creon, King of Thebes. A central double door, and two lateral doors. A platform extends the length of the façade, and from this platform three steps lead down into the "orchestra," or chorus-ground.*

**TIME:** *Dawn of the day after the repulse of the Argive army from the assault on Thebes.*

## *Prologue*

*Antigonê and Ismenê enter from the central door of the palace.*

ANTIGONÊ. Ismenê, dear sister,
You would think that we had already suffered enough
For the curse on Oedipus.°
I cannot imagine any grief
That you and I have not gone through. And now—
Have they told you of the new decree of our King Creon?

**3 Oedipus,** once King of Thebes, was the father of Antigonê and Ismenê, and of their brothers Polyneicês and Eteoclês. Oedipus unwittingly killed his father, Laïos, and married his own mother, Iocastê. When he learned what he had done, he blinded himself and left Thebes. Eteoclês and Polyneicês quarreled; Polyneicês was driven out but returned to assault Thebes. In the battle each brother killed the other; Creon became king and ordered that Polyneicês be left to rot unburied on the battlefield as a traitor.

ISMENÊ. I have heard nothing: I know
That two sisters lost two brothers, a double death
In a single hour; and I know that the Argive army
Fled in the night; but beyond this, nothing.
ANTIGONÊ. I thought so. And this is why I wanted you
To come out here with me. There is something we must do.
ISMENÊ. Why do you speak so strangely?
ANTIGONÊ. Listen, Ismenê:
Creon buried our brother Eteoclês
With military honors, gave him a soldier's funeral,
And it was right that he should; but Polyneicês,
Who fought as bravely and died as miserably,—
They say that Creon has sworn
No one shall bury him, no one mourn for him,
But his body must lie in the fields, a sweet treasure
For carrion birds to find as they search for food.
That is what they say, and our good Creon is coming here
To announce it publicly; and the penalty—
Stoning to death in the public square!
There it is,
And now you can prove what you are:
A true sister, or a traitor to your family.
ISMENÊ. Antigonê, you are mad! What could I possibly do?
ANTIGONÊ. You must decide whether you will help me or not.
ISMENÊ. I do not understand you. Help you in what?
ANTIGONÊ. Ismenê. I am going to bury him. Will you come?
ISMENÊ. Bury him! You have just said the new law forbids it.
ANTIGONÊ. He is my brother. And he is your brother, too.
ISMENÊ. But think of the danger! Think what Creon will do!
ANTIGONÊ. Creon is not strong enough to stand in my way.
ISMENÊ. Ah sister!
Oedipus died, everyone hating him
For what his own search brought to light, his eyes
Ripped out by his own hand; and Iocastê died,
His mother and wife at once: she twisted the cords
That strangled her life; and our two brothers died,
Each killed by the other's sword. And we are left:
But oh, Antigonê,
Think how much more terrible than these
Our own death would be if we should go against Creon
And do what he has forbidden! We are only women,
We cannot fight with men, Antigonê!
The law is strong, we must give in to the law
In this thing, and in worse. I beg the Dead
To forgive me, but I am helpless: I must yield
To those in authority. And I think it is dangerous business
To be always meddling.
ANTIGONÊ. If that is what you think,
I should not want you, even if you asked to come.
You have made your choice, you can be what you want to be.
But I will bury him; and if I must die,

I say that this crime is holy: I shall lie down
With him in death, and I shall be as dear
To him as he to me.
It is the dead,
Not the living, who make the longest demands:
We die for ever. . . .
You may do as you like.
Since apparently the laws of the gods mean nothing to you.

ISMENÊ. They mean a great deal to me; but I have no strength
To break laws that were made for the public good.

ANTIGONÊ. That must be your excuse, I suppose. But as for me,
I will bury the brother I love.

ISMENÊ. Antigonê,
I am so afraid for you!

ANTIGONÊ. You need not be:
You have yourself to consider, after all.

ISMENÊ. But no one must hear of this, you must tell no one!
I will keep it a secret, I promise!

ANTIGONÊ. O tell it! Tell everyone!
Think how they'll hate you when it all comes out
If they learn that you knew about it all the time!

ISMENÊ. So fiery! You should be cold with fear.

ANTIGONÊ. Perhaps. But I am doing only what I must.

ISMENÊ. But can you do it? I say that you cannot.

ANTIGONÊ. Very well: when my strength gives out,
I shall do no more.

ISMENÊ. Impossible things should not be tried at all.

ANTIGONÊ. Go away, Ismenê:
I shall be hating you soon, and the dead will too,
For your words are hateful. Leave me my foolish plan:
I am not afraid of the danger; if it means death,
It will not be the worst of deaths—death without honor.

ISMENÊ. Go then, if you feel that you must.
You are unwise,
But a loyal friend indeed to those who love you.

*Exit into the palace. Antigonê goes off, left. Enter the Chorus.*

## *Párodos*

CHORUS. Now the long blade of the sun, lying *Strophe 1*
Level east to west, touches with glory
Thebes of the Seven Gates. Open, unlidded
Eye of golden day! O marching light
Across the eddy and rush of Dircê's stream,°
Striking the white shields of the enemy
Thrown headlong backward from the blaze of morning!

CHORAGOS.° Polyneicês their commander
Roused them with windy phrases,

**5 Dircê's stream** a stream west of Thebes **8 Choragos** leader of the Chorus

He the wild eagle screaming
Insults above our land,
His wings their shields of snow,
His crest their marshalled helms.

CHORUS. Against our seven gates in a yawning ring *Antistrophe 1*
The famished spears came onward in the night:
But before his jaws were sated with our blood,
Or pine fire took the garland of our towers,
He was thrown back; and as he turned, great Thebes—
No tender victim for his noisy power—
Rose like a dragon behind him, shouting war.

CHORAGOS. For God hates utterly
The bray of bragging tongues;
And when he beheld their smiling,
Their swagger of golden helms,
The frown of his thunder blasted
Their first man from our walls.

CHORUS. We heard his shout of triumph high in the air *Strophe 2*
Turn to a scream; far out in a flaming arc
He fell with his windy torch, and the earth struck him.
And others storming in fury no less than his
Found shock of death in the dusty joy of battle.

CHORAGOS. Seven captains at seven gates
Yielded their clanging arms to the god
That bends the battle-line and breaks it.
These two only, brothers in blood,
Face to face in matchless rage,
Mirroring each the other's death,
Clashed in long combat.

CHORUS. But now in the beautiful morning of victory *Antistrophe 2*
Let Thebes of the many chariots sing for joy!
With hearts for dancing we'll take leave of war:
Our temples shall be sweet with hymns of praise,
And the long nights shall echo with our chorus.

## *Scene I*

CHORAGOS. But now at last our new King is coming:
Creon of Thebes, Menoikeus' son.
In this auspicious dawn of his reign
What are the new complexities
That shifting Fate has woven for him?
What is his counsel? Why has he summoned
The old men to hear him?

*Enter Creon from the palace, center. He addresses the Chorus from the top step.*

CREON. Gentlemen: I have the honor to inform you that our Ship of State, which recent storms have threatened to destroy, has come safely to harbor at last, guided by the merciful wisdom of Heaven. I have summoned you here this morning because I know that I can depend upon you: your devotion to King Laïos was absolute; you never hesitated in your duty to our late ruler Oedipus; and when Oedipus died, your loyalty was transferred to his children. Unfortunately, as you know, his two sons, the princes Eteoclês and Polyneicês, have killed each other in battle; and I, as the next in blood, have succeeded to the full power of the throne.

I am aware, of course, that no Ruler can expect complete loyalty from his subjects until he has been tested in office. Nevertheless, I say to you at the very outset that I have nothing but contempt for the kind of Governor who is afraid, for whatever reason, to follow the course that he knows is best for the State; and as for the man who sets private friendship above the public welfare,—I have no use for him, either. I call God to witness that if I saw my country headed for ruin, I should not be afraid to speak out plainly; and I need hardly remind you that I would never have any dealings with an enemy of the people. No one values friendship more highly than I: but we must remember that friends made at the risk of wrecking our Ship are not real friends at all.

These are my principles, at any rate, and that is why I have made the following decision concerning the sons of Oedipus: Eteoclês, who died as a man should die, fighting for his country, is to be buried with full military honors, with all the ceremony that is usual when the greatest heroes die; but his brother Polyneicês, who broke his exile to come back with fire and sword against his native city and the shrines of his fathers' gods, whose one idea was to spill the blood of his blood and sell his own people into slavery—Polyneicês, I say, is to have no burial: no man is to touch him or say the least prayer for him; he shall lie on the plain, unburied; and the birds and the scavenging dogs can do with him whatever they like.

This is my command, and you can see the wisdom behind it. As long as I am King, no traitor is going to be honored with the loyal man. But whoever shows by word and deed that he is on the side of the State—he shall have my respect while he is living and my reverence when he is dead.

CHORAGOS. If that is your will, Creon son of Menoikeus,
You have the right to enforce it: we are yours.

CREON. That is my will. Take care that you do your part.

CHORAGOS. We are old men: let the younger ones carry it out.

CREON. I do not mean that: the sentries have been appointed.

CHORAGOS. Then what is it that you would have us do?

CREON. You will give no support to whoever breaks this law.

CHORAGOS. Only a crazy man is in love with death!

CREON. And death it is; yet money talks, and the wisest
Have sometimes been known to count a few coins too many.

*Enter Sentry from left.*

SENTRY. I'll not say that I'm out of breath from running, King, because every time I stopped to think about what I have to tell you, I felt like going back. And all the time a voice kept saying, "You fool, don't you know you're walking straight into trouble?"; and then another voice: "Yes, but if you let somebody else get the news to Creon first, it will be even worse than that for you!" But good sense won out, at least I hope it was good sense, and here I am with a story that makes no sense at all; but I'll tell it anyhow, because, as they say, what's going to happen's going to happen and—

CREON. Come to the point. What have you to say?

SENTRY. I did not do it. I did not see who did it. You must not punish me for what someone else has done.

CREON. A comprehensive defense! More effective, perhaps,
If I knew its purpose. Come: what is it?

SENTRY. A dreadful thing . . . I don't know how to put it—

CREON. Out with it!

SENTRY. Well, then;
The dead man—
Polyneicês—

*Pause. The Sentry is overcome, fumbles for words. Creon waits impassively.*

out there—
someone,—
New dust on the slimy flesh!

*Pause. No sign from Creon.*

Someone has given it burial that way, and
Gone . . .

*Long pause. Creon finally speaks with deadly control.*

CREON. And the man who dared do this?

SENTRY. I swear I
Do not know! You must believe me!
Listen:
The ground was dry, not a sign of digging, no,
Not a wheeltrack in the dust, no trace of anyone.
It was when they relieved us this morning: and one of them,
The corporal, pointed to it.
There it was,
The strangest—
Look:
The body, just mounded over with light dust: you see?
Not buried really, but as if they'd covered it
Just enough for the ghost's peace. And no sign
Of dogs or any wild animal that had been there.

And then what a scene there was! Every man of us
Accusing the other: we all proved the other man did it,
We all had proof that we could not have done it.
We were ready to take hot iron in our hands,
Walk through fire, swear by all the gods,
*It was not I!*
*I do not know who it was, but it was not I!*

*Creon's rage has been mounting steadily, but the sentry is too intent upon his story to notice it.*

And then, when this came to nothing, someone said
A thing that silenced us and made us stare
Down at the ground: you had to be told the news,

And one of us had to do it! We threw the dice,
And the bad luck fell to me. So here I am,
No happier to be here than you are to have me:
Nobody likes the man who brings bad news.

CHORAGOS. I have been wondering, King: can it be that the gods have done this?

CREON (*furiously*). Stop!
Must you doddering wrecks
Go out of your heads entirely? "The gods"!
Intolerable!
The gods favor this corpse? Why? How had he served them?
Tried to loot their temples, burn their images,
Yes, and the whole State, and its laws with it!
Is it your senile opinion that the gods love to honor bad men?
A pious thought!—
No, from the very beginning
There have been those who have whispered together,
Stiff-necked anarchists, putting their heads together,
Scheming against me in alleys. These are the men,
And they have bribed my own guard to do this thing.
(*Sententiously.*) Money!
There's nothing in the world so demoralizing as money.
Down go your cities,
Homes gone, men gone, honest hearts corrupted.
Crookedness of all kinds, and all for money!
(*To Sentry.*) But you—!
I swear by God and by the throne of God,
The man who has done this thing shall pay for it!
Find that man, bring him here to me, or your death
Will be the least of your problems: I'll string you up
Alive, and there will be certain ways to make you
Discover your employer before you die;
And the process may teach you a lesson you seem to have missed:
The dearest profit is sometimes all too dear:
That depends on the source. Do you understand me?
A fortune won is often misfortune.

SENTRY. King, may I speak?

CREON. Your very voice distresses me.

SENTRY. Are you sure that it is my voice, and not your conscience?

CREON. By God, he wants to analyze me now!

SENTRY. It is not what I say, but what has been done, that hurts you.

CREON. You talk too much.

SENTRY. Maybe; but I've done nothing.

CREON. Sold your soul for some silver: that's all you've done.

SENTRY. How dreadful it is when the right judge judges wrong!

CREON. Your figures of speech
May entertain you now; but unless you bring me the man,
You will get little profit from them in the end.

*Exit Creon into the palace.*

SENTRY. "Bring me the man"—!

I'd like nothing better than bringing him the man!
But bring him or not, you have seen the last of me here.
At any rate, I am safe! *(Exit Sentry.)*

## *Ode I*

CHORUS. Numberless are the world's wonders, but none *Strophe 1*
More wonderful than man; the stormgray sea
Yields to his prows, the huge crests bear him high;
Earth, holy and inexhaustible, is graven
With shining furrows where his plows have gone
Year after year, the timeless labor of stallions.

The lightboned birds and beasts that cling to cover, *Antistrophe 1*
The lithe fish lighting their reaches of dim water,
All are taken, tamed in the net of his mind;
The lion on the hill, the wild horse windy-maned,
Resign to him; and his blunt yoke has broken
The sultry shoulders of the mountain bull.

Words also, and thought as rapid as air, *Strophe 2*
He fashions to his good use; statecraft is his,
And his the skill that deflects the arrows of snow,
The spears of winter rain: from every wind
He has made himself secure—from all but one:
In the late wind of death he cannot stand.

O clear intelligence, force beyond all measure! *Antistrophe 2*
O fate of man, working both good and evil!
When the laws are kept, how proudly his city stands!
When the laws are broken, what of his city then?
Never may the anárchic man find rest at my hearth,
Never be it said that my thoughts are his thoughts.

## *Scene II*

*Reenter Sentry leading Antigonê.*

CHORAGOS. What does this mean? Surely this captive woman
Is the Princess, Antigonê. Why should she be taken?

SENTRY. Here is the one who did it! We caught her
In the very act of burying him.—Where is Creon?

CHORAGOS. Just coming from the house.

*Enter Creon, center.*

CREON. What has happened?
Why have you come back so soon?

SENTRY (*expansively*). O King,
A man should never be too sure of anything:
I would have sworn
That you'd not see me here again: your anger
Frightened me so, and the things you threatened me with;
But how could I tell then
That I'd be able to solve the case so soon?

No dice-throwing this time: I was only too glad to come!
Here is this woman. She is the guilty one:
We found her trying to bury him.
Take her, then; question her; judge her as you will.
I am through with the whole thing now, and glad of it.

CREON. But this is Antigonê! Why have you brought her here?

SENTRY. She was burying him, I tell you!

CREON (*severely*). Is this the truth?

SENTRY. I saw her with my own eyes. Can I say more?

CREON. The details: come, tell me quickly!

SENTRY. It was like this:
After those terrible threats of yours, King,
We went back and brushed the dust away from the body.
The flesh was soft by now, and stinking,
So we sat on a hill to windward and kept guard.
No napping this time! We kept each other awake.
But nothing happened until the white round sun
Whirled in the center of the round sky over us:
Then, suddenly,
A storm of dust roared up from the earth, and the sky
Went out, the plain vanished with all its trees
In the stinging dark. We closed our eyes and endured it.
The whirlwind lasted a long time, but it passed;
And then we looked, and there was Antigonê!
I have seen
A mother bird come back to a stripped nest, heard
Her crying bitterly a broken note or two
For the young ones stolen. Just so, when this girl
Found the bare corpse, and all her love's work wasted,
She wept, and cried on heaven to damn the hands
That had done this thing.
And then she brought more dust
And sprinkled wine three times for her brother's ghost.

We ran and took her at once. She was not afraid,
Not even when we charged her with what she had done.
She denied nothing.
And this was a comfort to me,
And some uneasiness: for it is a good thing
To escape from death, but it is no great pleasure
To bring death to a friend.
Yet I always say
There is nothing so comfortable as your own safe skin!

CREON (*slowly, dangerously*). And you, Antigonê,
You with your head hanging,—do you confess this thing?

ANTIGONÊ. I do. I deny nothing.

CREON (*to Sentry*). You may go.

(*Exit Sentry.*)

(*To Antigonê.*) Tell me, tell me briefly:
Had you heard my proclamation touching this matter?

ANTIGONÊ. It was public. Could I help hearing it?

CREON. And yet you dared defy the law.
ANTIGONÊ. I dared.
It was not God's proclamation. That final Justice
That rules the world below makes no such laws.

Your edict, King, was strong.
But all your strength is weakness itself against
The immortal unrecorded laws of God.
They are not merely now: they were, and shall be,
Operative for ever, beyond man utterly.
I knew I must die, even without your decree:
I am only mortal. And if I must die
Now, before it is my time to die,
Surely this is no hardship: can anyone
Living, as I live, with evil all about me,
Think Death less than a friend? This death of mine
Is of no importance; but if I had left my brother
Lying in death unburied, I should have suffered.
Now I do not.
You smile at me. Ah Creon,
Think me a fool, if you like; but it may well be
That a fool convicts me of folly.
CHORAGOS. Like father, like daughter: both headstrong, deaf to reason!
She has never learned to yield.
CREON. She has much to learn.
The inflexible heart breaks first, the toughest iron
Cracks first, and the wildest horses bend their necks
At the pull of the smallest curb.
Pride? In a slave?
This girl is guilty of a double insolence,
Breaking the given laws and boasting of it.
Who is the man here,
She or I, if this crime goes unpunished?
Sister's child, or more than sister's child,
Or closer yet in blood—she and her sister
Win bitter death for this!
(*To Servants.*) Go, some of you,
Arrest Ismenê. I accuse her equally.
Bring her: you will find her sniffling in the house there.

Her mind's a traitor: crimes kept in the dark
Cry for light, and the guardian brain shudders;
But how much worse than this
Is brazen boasting of barefaced anarchy!
ANTIGONÊ. Creon, what more do you want than my death?
CREON. Nothing.
That gives me everything.
ANTIGONÊ. Then I beg you: kill me.
This talking is a great weariness: your words
Are distasteful to me, and I am sure that mine

Seem so to you. And yet they should not seem so:
I should have praise and honor for what I have done.
All these men here would praise me
Were their lips not frozen shut with fear of you.
(*Bitterly.*) Ah the good fortune of kings,
Licensed to say and do whatever they please!

CREON. You are alone here in that opinion.

ANTIGONÊ. No, they are with me. But they keep their tongues in leash.

CREON. Maybe. But you are guilty, and they are not.

ANTIGONÊ. There is no guilt in reverence for the dead.

CREON. But Eteoclês—was he not your brother too?

ANTIGONÊ. My brother too.

CREON. And you insult his memory?

ANTIGONÊ (*softly*). The dead man would not say that I insult it.

CREON. He would: for you honor a traitor as much as him.

ANTIGONÊ. His own brother, traitor or not, and equal in blood.

CREON. He made war on his country. Eteoclês defended it.

ANTIGONÊ. Nevertheless, there are honors due all the dead.

CREON. But not the same for the wicked as for the just.

ANTIGONÊ. Ah Creon, Creon,
Which of us can say what the gods hold wicked?

CREON. An enemy is an enemy, even dead.

ANTIGONÊ. It is my nature to join in love, not hate.

CREON (*finally losing patience*). Go join them then; if you must have your love,
Find it in hell!

CHORAGOS. But see, Ismenê comes:

*Enter Ismenê, guarded.*

Those tears are sisterly, the cloud
That shadows her eyes rains down gentle sorrow.

CREON. You too, Ismenê,
Snake in my ordered house, sucking my blood
Stealthily—and all the time I never knew
That these two sisters were aiming at my throne!
Ismenê,
Do you confess your share in this crime, or deny it?
Answer me.

ISMENÊ. Yes, if she will let me say so. I am guilty.

ANTIGONÊ (*coldly*). No, Ismenê. You have no right to say so.
You would not help me, and I will not have you help me.

ISMENÊ. But now I know what you meant; and I am here
To join you, to take my share of punishment.

ANTIGONÊ. The dead man and the gods who rule the dead
Know whose act this was. Words are not friends.

ISMENÊ. Do you refuse me, Antigonê? I want to die with you:
I too have a duty that I must discharge to the dead.

ANTIGONÊ. You shall not lessen my death by sharing it.

ISMENÊ. What do I care for life when you are dead?

ANTIGONÊ. Ask Creon. You're always hanging on his opinions.

ISMENÊ. You are laughing at me. Why, Antigonê?
ANTIGONÊ. It's a joyless laughter, Ismenê.
ISMENÊ. But can I do nothing?
ANTIGONÊ. Yes. Save yourself. I shall not envy you.
There are those who will praise you; I shall have honor, too.
ISMENÊ. But we are equally guilty!
ANTIGONÊ. No more, Ismenê.
You are alive, but I belong to Death.
CREON (*to the Chorus*). Gentlemen, I beg you to observe these girls:
One has just now lost her mind; the other,
It seems, has never had a mind at all.
ISMENÊ. Grief teaches the steadiest minds to waver, King.
CREON. Yours certainly did, when you assumed guilt with the guilty!
ISMENÊ. But how could I go on living without her?
CREON. You are.
She is already dead.
ISMENÊ. But your own son's bride!
CREON. There are places enough for him to push his plow.
I want no wicked women for my sons!
ISMENÊ. O dearest Haimon, how your father wrongs you!
CREON. I've had enough of your childish talk of marriage!
CHORAGOS. Do you really intend to steal this girl from your son?
CREON. No; Death will do that for me.
CHORAGOS. Then she must die?
CREON (*ironically*). You dazzle me.
—But enough of this talk!
(*To Guards.*) You, there, take them away and guard them well:
For they are but women, and even brave men run
When they see Death coming.
*Exeunt Ismenê, Antigonê, and Guards.*

## *Ode II*

CHORUS. Fortunate is the man who has never tasted *Strophe 1*
God's vengeance!
Where once the anger of heaven has struck, that house is shaken
For ever: damnation rises behind each child
Like a wave cresting out of the black northeast,
When the long darkness under sea roars up
And bursts drumming death upon the windwhipped sand.

I have seen this gathering sorrow from time *Antistrophe 1*
long past
Loom upon Oedipus' children: generation from generation
Takes the compulsive rage of the enemy god.
So lately this last flower of Oedipus' line
Drank the sunlight! but now a passionate word
And a handful of dust have closed up all its beauty.

What mortal arrogance *Strophe 2*
Transcends the wrath of Zeus?
Sleep cannot lull him nor the effortless long months

Of the timeless gods: but he is young for ever,
And his house is the shining day of high Olympos.
All that is and shall be,
And all the past, is his.
No pride on earth is free of the curse of heaven.

The straying dreams of men *Antistrophe 2*
May bring them ghosts of joy:
But as they drowse, the waking embers burn them;
Or they walk with fixed eyes, as blind men walk.
But the ancient wisdom speaks for our own time:
*Fate works most for woe*
*With Folly's fairest show.*
Man's little pleasure is the spring of sorrow.

## *Scene III*

CHORAGOS. But here is Haimon, King, the last of all your sons.
Is it grief for Antigonê that brings him here,
And bitterness at being robbed of his bride?

*Enter Haimon.*

CREON. We shall soon see, and no need of diviners.
—Son,
You have heard my final judgment on that girl:
Have you come here hating me, or have you come
With deference and with love, whatever I do?

HAIMON. I am your son, father. You are my guide.
You make things clear for me, and I obey you.
No marriage means more to me than your continuing wisdom.

CREON. Good. That is the way to behave: subordinate
Everything else, my son, to your father's will.
This is what a man prays for, that he may get
Sons attentive and dutiful in his house,
Each one hating his father's enemies,
Honoring his father's friends. But if his sons
Fail him, if they turn out unprofitably,
What has he fathered but trouble for himself
And amusement for the malicious?
So you are right
Not to lose your head over this woman.
Your pleasure with her would soon grow cold, Haimon,
And then you'd have a hellcat in bed and elsewhere.
Let her find her husband in Hell!
Of all the people in this city, only she
Has had contempt for my law and broken it.

Do you want me to show myself weak before the people?
Or to break my sworn word? No, and I will not.
The woman dies.
I suppose she'll plead "family ties." Well, let her.
If I permit my own family to rebel,
How shall I earn the world's obedience?

Show me the man who keeps his house in hand,
He's fit for public authority.
I'll have no dealings
With lawbreakers, critics of the government:
Whoever is chosen to govern should be obeyed—
Must be obeyed, in all things, great and small,
Just and unjust! O Haimon,
The man who knows how to obey, and that man only,
Knows how to give commands when the time comes.
You can depend on him, no matter how fast
The spears come: he's a good soldier, he'll stick it out.

Anarchy, anarchy! Show me a greater evil!
This is why cities tumble and the great houses rain down,
This is what scatters armies!
No, no: good lives are made so by discipline.
We keep the laws then, and the lawmakers,
And no woman shall seduce us. If we must lose,
Let's lose to a man, at least! Is a woman stronger than we?

CHORAGOS. Unless time has rusted my wits,
What you say, King, is said with point and dignity.

HAIMON (*boyishly earnest*). Father:
Reason is God's crowning gift to man, and you are right
To warn me against losing mine. I cannot say—
I hope that I shall never want to say!—that you
Have reasoned badly. Yet there are other men
Who can reason, too; and their opinions might be helpful.
You are not in a position to know everything
That people say or do, or what they feel:
Your temper terrifies—everyone
Will tell you only what you like to hear.
But I, at any rate, can listen; and I have heard them
Muttering and whispering in the dark about this girl.
They say no woman has ever, so unreasonably,
Died so shameful a death for a generous act:
"She covered her brother's body. Is this indecent?
She kept him from dogs and vultures. Is this a crime?
Death?—She should have all the honor that we can give her!"

This is the way they talk out there in the city.

You must believe me:
Nothing is closer to me than your happiness.
What could be closer? Must not any son
Value his father's fortune as his father does his?
I beg you, do not be unchangeable:
Do not believe that you alone can be right.
The man who thinks that,
The man who maintains that only he has the power
To reason correctly, the gift to speak, the soul—
A man like that, when you know him, turns out empty.

It is not reason never to yield to reason!

In flood time you can see how some trees bend,
And because they bend, even their twigs are safe,
While stubborn trees are torn up, roots and all.
And the same thing happens in sailing:
Make your sheet fast, never slacken,—and over you go,
Head over heels and under: and there's your voyage.
Forget you are angry! Let yourself be moved!
I know I am young; but please let me say this:
The ideal condition
Would be, I admit, that men should be right by instinct;
But since we are all too likely to go astray,
The reasonable thing is to learn from those who can teach.

CHORAGOS. You will do well to listen to him, King,
If what he says is sensible. And you, Haimon,
Must listen to your father.—Both speak well.

CREON. You consider it right for a man of my years and experience
To go to school to a boy?

HAIMON. It is not right
If I am wrong. But if I am young, and right,
What does my age matter?

CREON. You think it right to stand up for an anarchist?

HAIMON. Not at all. I pay no respect to criminals.

CREON. Then she is not a criminal?

HAIMON. The City would deny it, to a man.

CREON. And the City proposes to teach me how to rule?

HAIMON. Ah. Who is it that's talking like a boy now?

CREON. My voice is the one voice giving orders in this City!

HAIMON. It is no City if it takes orders from one voice.

CREON. The State is the King!

HAIMON. Yes, if the State is a desert.

*Pause.*

CREON. This boy, it seems, has sold out to a woman.

HAIMON. If you are a woman: my concern is only for you.

CREON. So? Your "concern"! In a public brawl with your father!

HAIMON. How about you, in a public brawl with justice?

CREON. With justice, when all that I do is within my rights?

HAIMON. You have no right to trample on God's right.

CREON (*completely out of control*). Fool, adolescent fool! Taken in by a woman!

HAIMON. You'll never see me taken in by anything vile.

CREON. Every word you say is for her!

HAIMON (*quietly, darkly*). And for you.
And for me. And for the gods under the earth.

CREON. You'll never marry her while she lives.

HAIMON. Then she must die.—But her death will cause another.

CREON. Another?
Have you lost your senses? Is this an open threat?

HAIMON. There is no threat in speaking to emptiness.

CREON. I swear you'll regret this superior tone of yours!
You are the empty one!

HAIMON. If you were not my father,
I'd say you were perverse.
CREON. You girlstruck fool, don't play at words with me!
HAIMON. I am sorry. You prefer silence.
CREON. Now, by God—!
I swear, by all the gods in heaven above us,
You'll watch it, I swear you shall!
(*To the Servants.*) Bring her out!
Bring the woman out! Let her die before his eyes!
Here, this instant, with her bridegroom beside her!
HAIMON. Not here, no; she will not die here, King.
And you will never see my face again.
Go on raving as long as you've a friend to endure you.
(*Exit Haimon.*)
CHORAGOS. Gone, gone.
Creon, a young man in a rage is dangerous!
CREON. Let him do, or dream to do, more than a man can.
He shall not save these girls from death.
CHORAGOS. These girls?
You have sentenced them both?
CREON. No, you are right.
I will not kill the one whose hands are clean.
CHORAGOS. But Antigonê?
CREON (*somberly*). I will carry her far away
Out there in the wilderness, and lock her
Living in a vault of stone. She shall have food,
As the custom is, to absolve the State of her death.
And there let her pray to the gods of hell:
They are her only gods:
Perhaps they will show her an escape from death,
Or she may learn,
though late,
That piety shown the dead is piety in vain.
(*Exit Creon.*)

## *Ode III*

CHORUS. Love, unconquerable *Strophe*
Waster of rich men, keeper
Of warm lights and all-night vigil
In the soft face of a girl:
Sea-wanderer, forest-visitor!
Even the pure Immortals cannot escape you,
And mortal man, in his one day's dusk,
Trembles before your glory.

Surely you swerve upon ruin *Antistrophe*
The just man's consenting heart,
As here you have made bright anger
Strike between father and son—
And none has conquered but Love!
A girl's glánce wórking the will of heaven:

Pleasure to her alone who mocks us,
Merciless Aphroditê.°

## *Scene IV*

CHORAGOS (*as Antigonê enters guarded*). But I can no longer stand in awe of this,
Nor, seeing what I see, keep back my tears.
Here is Antigonê, passing to that chamber
Where all find sleep at last.

ANTIGONÊ. Look upon me, friends, and pity me *Strophe 1*
Turning back at the night's edge to say
Good-by to the sun that shines for me no longer;
Now sleepy Death
Summons me down to Acheron,° that cold shore:
There is no bridesong there, nor any music.

CHORUS. Yet not unpraised, not without a kind of honor,
You walk at last into the underworld;
Untouched by sickness, broken by no sword.
What woman has ever found your way to death?

ANTIGONÊ. How often I have heard the story of Niobê,° *Antistrophe 1*
Tantalos' wretched daughter, how the stone
Clung fast about her, ivy-close: and they say
The rain falls endlessly
And sifting soft snow; her tears are never done.
I feel the loneliness of her death in mine.

CHORUS. But she was born of heaven, and you
Are woman, woman-born. If her death is yours,
A mortal woman's, is this not for you
Glory in our world and in the world beyond?

ANTIGONÊ. You laugh at me. Ah, friends, friends, *Strophe 2*
Can you not wait until I am dead? O Thebes,
O men many-charioted, in love with Fortune,
Dear springs of Dircê, sacred Theban grove,
Be witnesses for me, denied all pity,
Unjustly judged! and think a word of love
For her whose path turns
Under dark earth, where there are no more tears.

CHORUS. You have passed beyond human daring and come at last
Into a place of stone where Justice sits.
I cannot tell
What shape of your father's guilt appears in this.

ANTIGONÊ. You have touched it at last: that bridal bed *Antistrophe 2*
Unspeakable, horror of son and mother mingling:

**16 Aphroditê** goddess of love **Scene IV 9 Acheron** a river of the underworld, which was ruled by Hades **15 Niobê** Niobê boasted of her numerous children, provoking Leto, the mother of Apollo, to destroy them. Niobê wept profusely, and finally was turned to stone on Mount Sipylus, whose streams are her tears.

Their crime, infection of all our family!
O Oedipus, father and brother!
Your marriage strikes from the grave to murder mine.
I have been a stranger here in my own land:
All my life
The blasphemy of my birth has followed me.

CHORUS. Reverence is a virtue, but strength
Lives in established law: that must prevail.
You have made your choice,
Your death is the doing of your conscious hand.

ANTIGONÊ. Then let me go, since all your words are bitter, *Epode*
And the very light of the sun is cold to me.
Lead me to my vigil, where I must have
Neither love nor lamentation; no song, but silence.

*Creon interrupts impatiently.*

CREON. If dirges and planned lamentations could put off death,
Men would be singing for ever.
(*To the Servants.*) Take her, go!
You know your orders: take her to the vault
And leave her alone there. And if she lives or dies,
That's her affair, not ours: our hands are clean.

ANTIGONÊ. O tomb, vaulted bride-bed in eternal rock,
Soon I shall be with my own again
Where Persephonê° welcomes the thin ghosts underground:
And I shall see my father again, and you, mother,
And dearest Polyneicês—
dearest indeed
To me, since it was my hand
That washed him clean and poured the ritual wine:
And my reward is death before my time!

And yet, as men's hearts know, I have done no wrong,
I have not sinned before God. Or if I have,
I shall know the truth in death. But if the guilt
Lies upon Creon who judged me, then, I pray,
May his punishment equal my own.

CHORAGOS. O passionate heart,
Unyielding, tormented still by the same winds!

CREON. Her guards shall have good cause to regret their delaying.

ANTIGONÊ. Ah! That voice is like the voice of death!

CREON. I can give you no reason to think you are mistaken.

ANTIGONÊ. Thebes, and you my fathers' gods,
And rulers of Thebes, you see me now, the last
Unhappy daughter of a line of kings,
Your kings, led away to death. You will remember
What things I suffer, and at what men's hands,
Because I would not transgress the laws of heaven.

**60 Persephonê** queen of the underworld

(*To the Guards, simply.*) Come: let us wait no longer.
(*Exit Antigonê, left, guarded.*)

## *Ode IV*

CHORUS. All Danaê's beauty was locked away *Strophe 1*
In a brazen cell where the sunlight could not come:
A small room still as any grave, enclosed her.
Yet she was a princess too,
And Zeus in a rain of gold poured love upon her.
O child, child,
No power in wealth or war
Or tough sea-blackened ships
Can prevail against untiring Destiny!

And Dryas' son° also, that furious king, *Antistrophe 1*
Bore the god's prisoning anger for his pride:
Sealed up by Dionysos in deaf stone,
His madness died among echoes.
So at the last he learned what dreadful power
His tongue had mocked:
For he had profaned the revels,
And fired the wrath of the nine
Implacable Sisters° that love the sound of the flute.

And old men tell a half-remembered tale *Strophe 2*
Of horror where a dark ledge splits the sea
And a double surf beats on the gráy shóres:
How a king's new woman,° sick
With hatred for the queen he had imprisoned,
Ripped out his two sons' eyes with her bloody hands
While grinning Arês° watched the shuttle plunge
Four times: four blind wounds crying for revenge,

Crying, tears and blood mingled.—Piteously born, *Antistrophe 2*
Those sons whose mother was of heavenly birth!
Her father was the god of the North Wind
And she was cradled by gales,
She raced with young colts on the glittering hills
And walked untrammeled in the open light:
But in her marriage deathless Fate found means
To build a tomb like yours for all her joy.

## *Scene V*

***Enter blind Teiresias, led by a boy. The opening speeches of Teiresias should be in singsong contrast to the realistic lines of Creon.***

**10 Dryas' son** Lycurgus, King of Thrace **18 Sisters** the Muses **22 king's new woman** Eidothea, second wife of King Phineus, blinded her stepsons. Their mother, Cleopatra, had been imprisoned in a cave. Phineus was the son of a king, and Cleopatra, his first wife, was the daughter of Boreas, the North Wind, but this illustrious ancestry could not protect his sons from violence and darkness. **25 Arês** god of war

TEIRESIAS. This is the way the blind man comes, Princes, Princes,
Lock-step, two heads lit by the eyes of one.
CREON. What new thing have you to tell us, old Teiresias?
TEIRESIAS. I have much to tell you: listen to the prophet, Creon.
CREON. I am not aware that I have ever failed to listen.
TEIRESIAS. Then you have done wisely, King, and ruled well.
CREON. I admit my debt to you. But what have you to say?
TEIRESIAS. This, Creon: you stand once more on the edge of fate.
CREON. What do you mean? Your words are a kind of dread.
TEIRESIAS. Listen, Creon:
I was sitting in my chair of augury, at the place
Where the birds gather about me. They were all a-chatter,
As is their habit, when suddenly I heard
A strange note in their jangling, a scream, a
Whirring fury; I knew that they were fighting,
Tearing each other, dying
In a whirlwind of wings clashing. And I was afraid.
I began the rites of burnt-offering at the altar,
But Hephaistos° failed me: instead of bright flame,
There was only the sputtering slime of the fat thigh-flesh
Melting: the entrails dissolved in gray smoke,
The bare bone burst from the welter. And no blaze!

This was a sign from heaven. My boy described it,
Seeing for me as I see for others.

I tell you, Creon, you yourself have brought
This new calamity upon us. Our hearths and altars
Are stained with the corruption of dogs and carrion birds
That glut themselves on the corpse of Oedipus' son.
The gods are deaf when we pray to them, their fire
Recoils from our offering, their birds of omen
Have no cry of comfort, for they are gorged
With the thick blood of the dead.
O my son,
These are no trifles! Think: all men make mistakes,
But a good man yields when he knows his course is wrong,
And repairs the evil. The only crime is pride.

Give in to the dead man, then: do not fight with a corpse—
What glory is it to kill a man who is dead?
Think, I beg you:
It is for your own good that I speak as I do.
You should be able to yield for your own good.
CREON. It seems that prophets have made me their especial province.
All my life long
I have been a kind of butt for the dull arrows
Of doddering fortune-tellers!
No, Teiresias:
If your birds—if the great eagles of God himself

**19 Hephaistos** god of fire

Should carry him stinking bit by bit to heaven,
I would not yield. I am not afraid of pollution:
No man can defile the gods.
Do what you will,
Go into business, make money, speculate
In India gold or that synthetic gold from Sardis,
Get rich otherwise than by my consent to bury him.
Teiresias, it is a sorry thing when a wise man
Sells his wisdom, lets out his words for hire!

TEIRESIAS. Ah Creon! Is there no man left in the world—
CREON. To do what?—Come, let's have the aphorism!
TEIRESIAS. No man who knows that wisdom outweighs any wealth?
CREON. As surely as bribes are baser than any baseness.
TEIRESIAS. You are sick, Creon! You are deathly sick!
CREON. As you say: it is not my place to challenge a prophet.
TEIRESIAS. Yet you have said my prophecy is for sale.
CREON. The generation of prophets has always loved gold.
TEIRESIAS. The generation of kings has always loved brass.
CREON. You forget yourself! You are speaking to your King.
TEIRESIAS. I know it. You are a king because of me.
CREON. You have a certain skill; but you have sold out.
TEIRESIAS. King, you will drive me to words that—
CREON. Say them, say them!
Only remember: I will not pay you for them.
TEIRESIAS. No, you will find them too costly.
CREON. No doubt. Speak:
Whatever you say, you will not change my will.
TEIRESIAS. Then take this, and take it to heart!
The time is not far off when you shall pay back
Corpse for corpse, flesh of your own flesh.
You have thrust the child of this world into living night,
You have kept from the gods below the child that is theirs:
The one in a grave before her death, the other,
Dead, denied the grave. This is your crime:
And the Furies and the dark gods of Hell
Are swift with terrible punishment for you.

Do you want to buy me now, Creon?

Not many days,
And your house will be full of men and women weeping,
And curses will be hurled at you from far
Cities grieving for sons unburied, left to rot
Before the walls of Thebes.

These are my arrows, Creon: they are all for you.

(*To Boy.*) But come, child: lead me home.
Let him waste his fine anger upon younger men.
Maybe he will learn at last
To control a wiser tongue in a better head. (*Exit Teiresias.*)

CHORAGOS. The old man has gone, King, but his words
Remain to plague us. I am old, too,

But I cannot remember that he was ever false.
CREON. That is true. . . . It troubles me.
Oh it is hard to give in! but it is worse
To risk everything for stubborn pride.
CHORAGOS. Creon: take my advice.
CREON. What shall I do?
CHORAGOS. Go quickly: free Antigonê from her vault
And build a tomb for the body of Polyneicês.
CREON. You would have me do this!
CHORAGOS. Creon, yes!
And it must be done at once: God moves
Swiftly to cancel the folly of stubborn men.
CREON. It is hard to deny the heart! But I
Will do it: I will not fight with destiny.
CHORAGOS. You must go yourself, you cannot leave it to others.
CREON. I will go.
—Bring axes, servants:
Come with me to the tomb. I buried her, I
Will set her free.
Oh quickly!
My mind misgives—
The laws of the gods are mighty, and a man must serve them
To the last day of his life!

(*Exit Creon.*)

## *Paean*°

CHORAGOS. God of many names *Strophe 1*
CHORUS. O Iacchos
son
of Kadmeian Sémelê
O born of the Thunder!
Guardian of the West
Regent
of Eleusis' plain
O Prince of maenad Thebes
and the Dragon Field by rippling Ismenós:°
CHORAGOS. God of many names *Antistrophe 1*
CHORUS. the flame of torches
flares on our hills
the nymphs of Iacchos
dance at the spring of Castalia:°
from the vine-close mountain
come ah come in ivy:
*Evohé evohé!* sings through the streets of Thebes

**Paean** a hymn (here dedicated to Iacchos, also called Dionysos. His father was Zeus, his mother was Sémelê, daughter of Kadmos. Iacchos's worshipers were the Maenads, whose cry was "*Evohé evohé*"). **5 Ismenós** a river east of Thebes. From a dragon's teeth, sown near the river, there sprang men who became the ancestors of the Theban nobility. **8 Castalia** a spring on Mount Parnassos

CHORAGOS. God of many names *Strophe 2*

CHORUS. Iacchos of Thebes
heavenly Child
of Sémelê bride of the Thunderer!
The shadow of plague is upon us:
come
with clement feet
oh come from Parnassos
down the long slopes
across the lamenting water

CHORAGOS. Iô Fire! Chorister of the throbbing stars! *Antistrophe 2*
O purest among the voices of the night!
Thou son of God, blaze for us!

CHORUS. Come with choric rapture of circling Maenads
Who cry *Iô Iacche!*
*God of many names!*

## *Exodos*

*Enter Messenger from left.*

MESSENGER. Men of the line of Kadmos,° you who live
Near Amphion's citadel,°
I cannot say
Of any condition of human life "This is fixed.
This is clearly good, or bad." Fate raises up,
And Fate casts down the happy and unhappy alike:
No man can foretell his Fate.
Take the case of Creon:
Creon was happy once, as I count happiness:
Victorious in battle, sole governor of the land,
Fortunate father of children nobly born.
And now it has all gone from him! Who can say
That a man is still alive when his life's joy fails?
He is a walking dead man. Grant him rich,
Let him live like a king in his great house:
If his pleasure is gone, I would not give
So much as the shadow of smoke for all he owns.

CHORAGOS. Your words hint at sorrow: what is your news for us?

MESSENGER. They are dead. The living are guilty of their death.

CHORAGOS. Who is guilty? Who is dead? Speak!

MESSENGER. Haimon.
Haimon is dead; and the hand that killed him
Is his own hand.

CHORAGOS. His father's? or his own?

MESSENGER. His own, driven mad by the murder his father had done.

CHORAGOS. Teiresias, Teiresias, how clearly you saw it all!

**1 Kadmos,** who sowed the dragon's teeth, was founder of Thebes. **2 Amphion's citadel** Amphion played so sweetly on his lyre that he charmed stones to form a wall around Thebes.

MESSENGER. This is my news: you must draw what conclusions you can from it.

CHORAGOS. But look: Eurydicê, our Queen:
Has she overheard us?

*Enter Eurydicê from the palace, center.*

EURYDICÊ. I have heard something, friends:
As I was unlocking the gate of Pallas'° shrine,
For I needed her help today, I heard a voice
Telling of some new sorrow. And I fainted
There at the temple with all my maidens about me.
But speak again: whatever it is, I can bear it:
Grief and I are no strangers.

MESSENGER. Dearest Lady,
I will tell you plainly all that I have seen.
I shall not try to comfort you: what is the use,
Since comfort could lie only in what is not true?
The truth is always best.
I went with Creon
To the outer plain where Polyneicês was lying,
No friend to pity him, his body shredded by dogs.
We made our prayers in the place to Hecatê
And Pluto,° that they would be merciful. And we bathed
The corpse with holy water, and we brought
Fresh-broken branches to burn what was left of it,
And upon the urn we heaped up a towering barrow
Of the earth of his own land.
When we were done, we ran
To the vault where Antigonê lay on her couch of stone.
One of the servants had gone ahead,
And while he was yet far off he heard a voice
Grieving within the chamber, and he came back
And told Creon. And as the King went closer,
The air was full of wailing, the words lost,
And he begged us to make all haste. "Am I a prophet?"
He said, weeping, "And must I walk this road,
The saddest of all that I have gone before?
My son's voice calls me on. Oh quickly, quickly!
Look through the crevice there, and tell me
If it is Haimon, or some deception of the gods!"

We obeyed; and in the cavern's farthest corner
We saw her lying:
She had made a noose of her fine linen veil
And hanged herself. Haimon lay beside her,
His arms about her waist, lamenting her,
His love lost under ground, crying out
That his father had stolen her away from him.

**27 Pallas** Pallas Athene, goddess of wisdom **39–40 Hecatê / And Pluto** Hecatê and Pluto (also known as Hades) were deities of the underworld.

When Creon saw him the tears rushed to his eyes
And he called to him: "What have you done, child? Speak to me.
What are you thinking that makes your eyes so strange?
O my son, my son, I come to you on my knees!"
But Haimon spat in his face. He said not a word,
Staring—
And suddenly drew his sword
And lunged. Creon shrank back, the blade missed; and the boy,
Desperate against himself, drove it half its length
Into his own side, and fell. And as he died
He gathered Antigonê close in his arms again,
Choking, his blood bright red on her white cheek.
And now he lies dead with the dead, and she is his
At last, his bride in the house of the dead.

*Exit Eurydicê into the palace.*

CHORAGOS. She has left us without a word. What can this mean?

MESSENGER. It troubles me, too; yet she knows what is best,
Her grief is too great for public lamentation,
And doubtless she has gone to her chamber to weep
For her dead son, leading her maidens in his dirge.

*Pause.*

CHORAGOS. It may be so: but I fear this deep silence.

MESSENGER. I will see what she is doing. I will go in.

*Exit Messenger into the palace.*

*Enter Creon with attendants, bearing Haimon's body.*

CHORAGOS. But here is the king himself: oh look at him,
Bearing his own damnation in his arms.

CREON. Nothing you say can touch me any more.
My own blind heart has brought me
From darkness to final darkness. Here you see
The father murdering, the murdered son—
And all my civic wisdom!

Haimon my son, so young, so young to die,
I was the fool, not you; and you died for me.

CHORAGOS. That is the truth; but you were late in learning it.

CREON. This truth is hard to bear. Surely a god
Has crushed me beneath the hugest weight of heaven,
And driven me headlong a barbaric way
To trample out the thing I held most dear.

The pains that men will take to come to pain!

*Enter Messenger from the palace.*

MESSENGER. The burden you carry in your hands is heavy,
But it is not all: you will find more in your house.

CREON. What burden worse than this shall I find there?

MESSENGER. The Queen is dead.

CREON. O port of death, deaf world,
Is there no pity for me? And you, Angel of evil,
I was dead, and your words are death again.

Is it true, boy? Can it be true?
Is my wife dead? Has death bred death?

MESSENGER. You can see for yourself.

*The doors are opened and the body of Eurydicê is disclosed within.*

CREON. Oh pity!
All true, all true, and more than I can bear!
O my wife, my son!

MESSENGER. She stood before the altar, and her heart
Welcomed the knife her own hand guided,
And a great cry burst from her lips for Megareus° dead,
And for Haimon dead, her sons; and her last breath
Was a curse for their father, the murderer of her sons.
And she fell, and the dark flowed in through her closing eyes.

CREON. O God, I am sick with fear.
Are there no swords here? Has no one a blow for me?

MESSENGER. Her curse is upon you for the deaths of both.

CREON. It is right that it should be. I alone am guilty.
I know it, and I say it. Lead me in,
Quickly, friends.
I have neither life nor substance. Lead me in.

CHORAGOS. You are right, if there can be right in so much wrong.
The briefest way is best in a world of sorrow.

CREON. Let it come,
Let death come quickly, and be kind to me.
I would not ever see the sun again.

CHORAGOS. All that will come when it will; but we, meanwhile,
Have much to do. Leave the future to itself.

CREON. All my heart was in that prayer!

CHORAGOS. Then do not pray any more: the sky is deaf.

CREON. Lead me away. I have been rash and foolish.
I have killed my son and my wife.
I look for comfort; my comfort lies here dead.
Whatever my hands have touched has come to nothing.
Fate has brought all my pride to a thought of dust.

*As Creon is being led into the house, the Choragos advances and speaks directly to the audience.*

CHORAGOS. There is no happiness where there is no wisdom;
No wisdom but in submission to the gods.
Big words are always punished,
And proud men in old age learn to be wise.

[*c.* *441* B.C.]

**114 Megareus** Megareus, brother of Haimon, had died in the assault on Thebes.

## TOPICS FOR CRITICAL THINKING AND WRITING

1. Although Sophocles called his play *Antigonê,* many critics say that Creon is the real tragic hero, pointing out that Antigonê is absent from the last third of the play. Evaluate this view.

2. In some Greek tragedies, fate plays a great role in bringing about the downfall of the tragic hero. Though there are references to the curse on the House of Oedipus in *Antigonê,* do we feel that Antigonê goes to her death as a result of the workings of fate? Do we feel that fate is responsible for Creon's fall? Is the Messenger right to introduce the notion of fate (*Exodos,* line 4)? Or are both Antigonê and Creon the creators of their own tragedy?
3. Do the words *hamartia* and *hubris* (p. 1224) apply to Antigonê? To Creon?
4. Why does Creon, contrary to the Chorus's advice (Scene V, lines 96–97), bury the body of Polyneicês before he releases Antigonê? Does his action show a zeal for piety as shortsighted as his earlier zeal for law? Is his action plausible, in view of the facts that Teiresias has dwelt on the wrong done to Polyneicês, and that Antigonê has ritual food to sustain her? Or are we not to worry about Creon's motive?
5. A *foil* is a character who, by contrast, sets off or helps to define another character. To what extent is Ismenê a foil to Antigonê? Is she entirely without courage?
6. What function does Eurydicê serve? How deeply do we feel about her fate?

# A NOTE ON THE ELIZABETHAN THEATER

Shakespeare's theater was wooden, round or polygonal (the Chorus in *Henry V* calls it a "wooden O"). About eight hundred spectators could stand in the yard in front of—and perhaps along the two sides of—the stage that jutted from the

*a* Johannes de Witt, a Continental visitor to London, made a drawing of the Swan Theater in about the year 1596. The original drawing is lost; this is Arend von Buchel's copy of it. (© The British Museum) *b* C. Walter Hodges's 1965 drawing of an Elizabethan playhouse. (Courtesy of C. Walter Hodges)

rear wall, and another fifteen hundred or so spectators could sit in the three roofed galleries that ringed the stage.

That portion of the galleries that was above the rear of the stage was sometimes used by actors. For instance, it must have served as a balcony in the famous scene in *Romeo and Juliet,* where Romeo, in the garden, speaks to Juliet, who is said to be above, at a window.

Entry to the stage was normally gained by doors at the rear, but apparently on rare occasions use was made of a curtained alcove—or perhaps a booth—between the doors, which allowed characters to be "discovered" (revealed) as in the modern proscenium theater, which normally employs a curtain. But such "discovery" scenes are rare.

Although the theater as a whole was unroofed, the stage was protected by a roof, supported by two pillars. These could serve (by an act of imagination) as trees behind which actors might pretend to conceal themselves.

A performance was probably uninterrupted by intermissions or by long pauses for the changing of scenery; a group of characters leaves the stage, another enters, and if the locale has changed, the new characters somehow tell us. (Modern editors customarily add indications of locales to help a reader, but it should be remembered that the action on the Elizabethan stage was continuous.)

## WILLIAM SHAKESPEARE

*Shakespeare (1564-1616) was born into a middle-class family in Stratford-upon-Avon. Although we have a fair number of records about his life—documents concerning marriage, the birth of children, the purchase of property, and so forth—it is not known exactly why and when he turned to the theater. What we do know, however, is important: He was an actor and a shareholder in a playhouse, and he did write the plays that are attributed to him. The dates of some of the plays can be set precisely, but the dates of some others can be only roughly set.* Hamlet *was probably written in 1600 or possibly 1600-01.*

# *Hamlet, Prince of Denmark*

[DRAMATIS PERSONAE

GHOST *of Hamlet, the former King of Denmark*
CLAUDIUS, *King of Denmark, the former King's brother*
GERTRUDE, *Queen of Denmark, widow of the former King and now wife of Claudius*
HAMLET, *Prince of Denmark, son of the late King and of Gertrude*

POLONIUS, *councillor to the King*
LAERTES, *his son*
OPHELIA, *his daughter*
REYNALDO, *his servant*

HORATIO, *Hamlet's friend and fellow student*

Kenneth Branagh as Hamlet, The Royal Shakespeare Theatre, 1993. (Mark Douet)

| | |
|---|---|
| VOLTIMAND,<br>CORNELIUS,<br>ROSENCRANTZ,<br>GUILDENSTERN,<br>OSRIC,<br>A GENTLEMAN,<br>A LORD, | *members of the Danish court* |
| BERNARDO,<br>FRANCISCO,<br>MARCELLUS, | *officers and soldiers on watch* |

FORTINBRAS, *Prince of Norway*
CAPTAIN *in his army*

*Three or four* PLAYERS, *taking the roles of* PROLOGUE, PLAYER KING, PLAYER QUEEN, *and* LUCIANUS
*Two* MESSENGERS
FIRST SAILOR
*Two* CLOWNS, *a gravedigger and his companion*
PRIEST
FIRST AMBASSADOR *from England*

*Lords, Soldiers, Attendants, Guards, other Players, Followers of Laertes, other Sailors, another Ambassador or Ambassadors from England*

Left to right: Voltimand (Jeremy Geidt), Gertrude (Christine Estabrook), Claudius (Mark Metcalf), Hamlet (Mark Rylance), and Laertes (Derek Smith) in the 1991 American Repertory Theatre production of *Hamlet,* directed by Ron Daniels. (© Richard Feldman)

**SCENE:** *Denmark*]

**1.1** *Enter Bernardo and Francisco, two sentinels,* [*meeting*].

BERNARDO. Who's there?
FRANCISCO. Nay, answer me.° Stand and unfold yourself.°
BERNARDO. Long live the King!
FRANCISCO. Bernardo?
BERNARDO. He.
FRANCISCO. You come most carefully upon your hour.
BERNARDO. 'Tis now struck twelve. Get thee to bed, Francisco.
FRANCISCO. For this relief much thanks. 'Tis bitter cold,
And I am sick at heart.
BERNARDO. Have you had quiet guard?
FRANCISCO. Not a mouse stirring.
BERNARDO. Well, good night.
If you do meet Horatio and Marcellus,
The rivals° of my watch, bid them make haste.

*Enter Horatio and Marcellus.*

FRANCISCO. I think I hear them.—Stand, ho! Who is there?
HORATIO. Friends to this ground.°
MARCELLUS. And liegemen to the Dane.°

**1.1 Location: Elsinore castle. A guard platform.** **2 me** (Francisco emphasizes that *he* is the sentry currently on watch.) **unfold yourself** reveal your identity **14 rivals** partners **16 ground** country, land **17 liegemen to the Dane** men sworn to serve the Danish king

FRANCISCO. Give° you good night.
MARCELLUS. O, farewell, honest soldier. Who hath relieved you?
FRANCISCO. Bernardo hath my place. Give you good night.
*Exit Francisco.*
MARCELLUS. Holla! Bernardo!
BERNARDO. Say, what, is Horatio there?
HORATIO. A piece of him.
BERNARDO. Welcome, Horatio. Welcome, good Marcellus.
HORATIO. What, has this thing appeared again tonight?
BERNARDO. I have seen nothing.
MARCELLUS. Horatio says 'tis but our fantasy,°
And will not let belief take hold of him
Touching this dreaded sight twice seen of us.
Therefore I have entreated him along°
With us to watch° the minutes of this night,
That if again this apparition come
He may approve° our eyes and speak to it.
HORATIO. Tush, tush, 'twill not appear.
BERNARDO. Sit down awhile,
And let us once again assail your ears,
That are so fortified against our story,
What° we have two nights seen.
HORATIO. Well, sit we down,
And let us hear Bernardo speak of this.
BERNARDO. Last night of all,°
When yond same star that's westward from the pole°
Had made his° course t' illume° that part of heaven
Where now it burns, Marcellus and myself,
The bell then beating one—
*Enter Ghost.*
MARCELLUS. Peace, break thee off! Look where it comes again!
BERNARDO. In the same figure like the King that's dead.
MARCELLUS. Thou art a scholar.° Speak to it, Horatio.
BERNARDO. Looks 'a° not like the King? Mark it, Horatio.
HORATIO. Most like. It harrows me with fear and wonder.
BERNARDO. It would be spoke to.°
MARCELLUS. Speak to it, Horatio.
HORATIO. What art thou that usurp'st° this time of night,
Together with that fair and warlike form
In which the majesty of buried Denmark°
Did sometime° march? By heaven, I charge thee, speak!
MARCELLUS. It is offended.

**18 Give** i.e., may God give **27 fantasy** imagination **30 along** to come along **31 watch** keep watch during **33 approve** corroborate **37 What** with what **39 Last . . . all** i.e., this *very* last night. (Emphatic.) **40 pole** polestar, north star **41 his** its **illume** illuminate **46 scholar** one learned enough to know how to question a ghost properly **47 'a** he **49 It . . . to** (It was commonly believed that a ghost could not speak until spoken to.) **50 usurp'st** wrongfully takes over **52 buried Denmark** the buried King of Denmark **53 sometime** formerly

BERNARDO. See, it stalks away.
HORATIO. Stay! Speak, speak! I charge thee, speak!
*Exit Ghost.*
MARCELLUS. 'Tis gone and will not answer.
BERNARDO. How now, Horatio? You tremble and look pale.
Is not this something more than fantasy?
What think you on 't?°
HORATIO. Before my God, I might not this believe
Without the sensible° and true avouch°
Of mine own eyes.
MARCELLUS. Is it not like the King?
HORATIO. As thou art to thyself.
Such was the very armor he had on
When he the ambitious Norway° combated.
So frowned he once when, in an angry parle,°
He smote the sledded° Polacks° on the ice.
'Tis strange.
MARCELLUS. Thus twice before, and jump° at this dead hour,
With martial stalk° hath he gone by our watch.
HORATIO. In what particular thought to work° I know not,
But in the gross and scope° of mine opinion
This bodes some strange eruption to our state.
MARCELLUS. Good now,° sit down, and tell me, he that knows,
Why this same strict and most observant watch
So nightly toils° the subject° of the land,
And why such daily cast° of brazen cannon
And foreign mart° for implements of war,
Why such impress° of shipwrights, whose sore task
Does not divide the Sunday from the week.
What might be toward,° that this sweaty haste
Doth make the night joint-laborer with the day?
Who is 't that can inform me?
HORATIO. That can I;
At least, the whisper goes so. Our last king,
Whose image even but now appeared to us,
Was, as you know, by Fortinbras of Norway,
Thereto pricked on° by a most emulate° pride,°
Dared to the combat; in which our valiant Hamlet—
For so this side of our known world° esteemed him—
Did slay this Fortinbras; who by a sealed° compact

**59 on 't** of it **61 sensible** confirmed by the senses **avouch** warrant, evidence **65 Norway** King of Norway **66 parle** parley **67 sledded** traveling on sleds **Polacks** Poles **69 jump** exactly **70 stalk** stride **71 to work** i.e., to collect my thoughts and try to understand this **72 gross and scope** general drift **74 Good now** (An expression denoting entreaty or expostulation.) **76 toils** causes to toil **subject** subjects **77 cast** casting **78 mart** buying and selling **79 impress** impressment, conscription **81 toward** in preparation **87 pricked on** incited. **emulate** emulous, ambitious **Thereto . . . pride** (Refers to old Fortinbras, not the Danish King.) **89 this . . . world** i.e., all Europe, the Western world **90 sealed** certified, confirmed

Well ratified by law and heraldry
Did forfeit, with his life, all those his lands
Which he stood seized° of, to the conqueror;
Against the° which a moiety competent°
Was gagèd° by our king, which had returned°
To the inheritance° of Fortinbras
Had he been vanquisher, as, by the same cov'nant°
And carriage of the article designed,°
His fell to Hamlet. Now, sir, young Fortinbras,
Of unimprovèd mettle° hot and full,
Hath in the skirts° of Norway here and there
Sharked up° a list° of lawless resolutes°
For food and diet° to some enterprise
That hath a stomach° in 't, which is no other—
As it doth well appear unto our state—
But to recover of us, by strong hand
And terms compulsatory, those foresaid lands
So by his father lost. And this, I take it,
Is the main motive of our preparations,
The source of this our watch, and the chief head°
Of this posthaste and rummage° in the land.

BERNARDO. I think it be no other but e'en so.
Well may it sort° that this portentous figure
Comes armèd through our watch so like the King
That was and is the question° of these wars.

HORATIO. A mote° it is to trouble the mind's eye.
In the most high and palmy° state of Rome,
A little ere the mightiest Julius fell,
The graves stood tenantless, and the sheeted° dead
Did squeak and gibber in the Roman streets;
As° stars with trains° of fire and dews of blood,
Disasters° in the sun; and the moist star°
Upon whose influence Neptune's° empire stands°
Was sick almost to doomsday° with eclipse.

**93 seized** possessed **94 Against the** in return for **moiety competent** corresponding portion **95 gagèd** engaged, pledged **had returned** would have passed **96 inheritance** possession **97 cov'nant** i.e., the *sealed compact* of line 90 **98 carriage . . . designed** carrying out of the article or clause drawn up to cover the point **100 unimprovèd mettle** untried, undisciplined spirits **101 skirts** outlying regions, outskirts **102 Sharked up** gathered up, as a shark takes fish **list** i.e., troop **resolutes** desperadoes **103 For food and diet** i.e., they are to serve as *food,* or "means," *to some enterprise;* also they serve in return for the rations they get **104 stomach** (1) a spirit of daring (2) an appetite that is fed by the *lawless resolutes* **110 head** source **111 rummage** bustle, commotion **113 sort** suit **115 question** focus of contention **116 mote** speck of dust **117 palmy** flourishing **119 sheeted** shrouded **121 As** (This abrupt transition suggests that matter is possibly omitted between lines 120 and 121.) **trains** trails **122 Disasters** unfavorable signs or aspects **moist star** i.e., moon, governing tides **123 Neptune** god of the sea **stands** depends **124 sick . . . doomsday** (See Matthew 24.29 and Revelation 6.12.)

And even the like precurse° of feared events,
As harbingers° preceding still° the fates
And prologue to the omen° coming on,
Have heaven and earth together demonstrated
Unto our climatures° and countrymen.

*Enter Ghost.*

But soft,° behold! Lo, where it comes again!
I'll cross° it, though it blast° me. [*It spreads his° arms.*]
Stay, *illusion!*
If thou hast any sound or use of voice,
Speak to me!
If there be any good thing to be done
That may to thee do ease and grace to me,
Speak to me!
If thou art privy to° thy country's fate,
Which, happily,° foreknowing may avoid,
O, speak!
Or if thou hast uphoarded in thy life
Extorted treasure in the womb of earth,
For which, they say, you spirits oft walk in death,
Speak of it! [*The cock crows.*] Stay and speak!—Stop it, Marcellus.

MARCELLUS. Shall I strike at it with my partisan?°

HORATIO. Do, if it will not stand. [*They strike at it.*]

BERNARDO. 'Tis here!

HORATIO. 'Tis here!

[*Exit Ghost.*]

MARCELLUS. 'Tis gone.
We do it wrong, being so majestical,
To offer it the show of violence,
For it is as the air invulnerable,
And our vain blows malicious mockery.

BERNARDO. It was about to speak when the cock crew.

HORATIO. And then it started like a guilty thing
Upon a fearful summons. I have heard
The cock, that is the trumpet° to the morn,
Doth with his lofty and shrill-sounding throat
Awake the god of day, and at his warning,
Whether in sea or fire, in earth or air,
Th' extravagant and erring° spirit hies°
To his confine; and of the truth herein
This present object made probation.°

MARCELLUS. It faded on the crowing of the cock.
Some say that ever 'gainst° that season comes

**125 precurse** heralding, foreshadowing **126 harbingers** forerunners **still** continually **127 omen** calamitous event **129 climatures** regions **130 soft** i.e., enough, break off **131 cross** stand in its path, confront **blast** wither, strike with a curse **s.d. his** its **137 privy to** in on the secret of **138 happily** haply, perchance **144 partisan** long-handled spear **156 trumpet** trumpeter **160 extravagant and erring** wandering beyond bounds. (The words have similar meaning.) **hies** hastens **162 probation** proof **164 'gainst** just before

Wherein our Savior's birth is celebrated,
This bird of dawning singeth all night long,
And then, they say, no spirit dare stir abroad;
The nights are wholesome, then no planets strike,°
No fairy takes,° nor witch hath power to charm,
So hallowed and so gracious° is that time.

HORATIO. So have I heard and do in part believe it.
But, look, the morn in russet mantle clad
Walks o'er the dew of yon high eastward hill.
Break we our watch up, and by my advice
Let us impart what we have seen tonight
Unto young Hamlet; for upon my life,
This spirit, dumb to us, will speak to him.
Do you consent we shall acquaint him with it,
As needful in our loves, fitting our duty?

MARCELLUS. Let's do 't, I pray, and I this morning know
Where we shall find him most conveniently.
*Exeunt.*

**1.2** *Flourish. Enter Claudius, King of Denmark, Gertrude the Queen, [the] Council, as° Polonius and his son Laertes, Hamlet,* cum aliis° [*including Voltimand and Cornelius*].

KING. Though yet of Hamlet our° dear brother's death
The memory be green, and that it us befitted
To bear our hearts in grief and our whole kingdom
To be contracted in one brow of woe,
Yet so far hath discretion fought with nature
That we with wisest sorrow think on him
Together with remembrance of ourselves.
Therefore our sometime° sister, now our queen,
Th' imperial jointress° to this warlike state,
Have we, as 'twere with a defeated joy—
With an auspicious and a dropping eye,°
With mirth in funeral and with dirge in marriage,
In equal scale weighing delight and dole°—
Taken to wife. Nor have we herein barred
Your better wisdoms, which have freely gone
With this affair along. For all, our thanks.
Now follows that you know° young Fortinbras,
Holding a weak supposal° of our worth,
Or thinking by our late dear brother's death

**168 strike** destroy by evil influence **169 takes** bewitches **170 gracious** full of grace
**1.2 Location: The castle. s.d. as** i.e., such as, including **cum aliis** with others **1 our** my. (The royal "we"; also in the following lines.) **8 sometime** former **9 jointress** woman possessing property with her husband **11 With . . . eye** with one eye smiling and the other weeping **13 dole** grief **17 that you know** what you know already, that; or, that you be informed as follows **18 weak supposal** low estimate

Our state to be disjoint and out of frame,
Co-leaguèd with° this dream of his advantage,°
He hath not failed to pester us with message
Importing° the surrender of those lands
Lost by his father, with all bonds° of law,
To our most valiant brother. So much for him.
Now for ourself and for this time of meeting.
Thus much the business is: we have here writ
To Norway, uncle of young Fortinbras—
Who, impotent° and bed-rid, scarcely hears
Of this his nephew's purpose—to suppress
His° further gait° herein, in that the levies,
The lists, and full proportions are all made
Out of his subject;° and we here dispatch
You, good Cornelius, and you, Voltimand,
For bearers of this greeting to old Norway,
Giving to you no further personal power
To business with the King more than the scope
Of these dilated° articles allow. [*He gives a paper.*]
Farewell, and let your haste commend your duty.°

CORNELIUS, VOLTIMAND. In that, and all things, will we show our duty.

KING. We doubt it nothing.° Heartily farewell.
[*Exeunt Voltimand and Cornelius.*]
And now, Laertes, what's the news with you?
You told us of some suit; what is 't, Laertes?
You cannot speak of reason to the Dane°
And lose your voice.° What wouldst thou beg, Laertes,
That shall not be my offer, not thy asking?
The head is not more native° to the heart,
The hand more instrumental° to the mouth,
Than is the throne of Denmark to thy father.
What wouldst thou have, Laertes?

LAERTES. My dread lord,
Your leave and favor° to return to France,
From whence though willingly I came to Denmark
To show my duty in your coronation,
Yet now I must confess, that duty done,
My thoughts and wishes bend again toward France
And bow them to your gracious leave and pardon.°

KING. Have you your father's leave? What says Polonius?

**21 Co-leaguèd with** joined to, allied with **dream . . . advantage** illusory hope of having the advantage. (His only ally is this hope.) **23 Importing** pertaining to **24 bonds** contracts **29 impotent** helpless **31 His** i.e., Fortinbras's. **gait** proceeding **31–33 in that . . . subject** since the levying of troops and supplies is drawn entirely from the King of Norway's own subjects **38 dilated** set out at length **39 let . . . duty** let your swift obeying of orders, rather than mere words, express your dutifulness **41 nothing** not at all **44 the Dane** the Danish king **45 lose your voice** waste your speech **47 native** closely connected, related **48 instrumental** serviceable **51 leave and favor** kind permission **56 bow . . . pardon** entreatingly make a deep bow, asking your permission to depart

POLONIUS. H'ath,° my lord, wrung from me my slow leave
By laborsome petition, and at last
Upon his will I sealed° my hard° consent.
I do beseech you, give him leave to go.
KING. Take thy fair hour,° Laertes. Time be thine,
And thy best graces spend it at thy will!°
But now, my cousin° Hamlet, and my son—
HAMLET. A little more than kin, and less than kind.°
KING. How is it that the clouds still hang on you?
HAMLET. Not so, my lord. I am too much in the sun.°
QUEEN. Good Hamlet, cast thy nighted color° off,
And let thine eye look like a friend on Denmark.°
Do not forever with thy vailèd lids°
Seek for thy noble father in the dust.
Thou know'st 'tis common,° all that lives must die,
Passing through nature to eternity.
HAMLET. Ay, madam, it is common.
QUEEN. If it be,
Why seems it so particular° with thee?
HAMLET. Seems, madam? Nay, it is. I know not "seems."
'Tis not alone my inky cloak, good Mother,
Nor customary° suits of solemn black,
Nor windy suspiration° of forced breath,
No, nor the fruitful° river in the eye,
Nor the dejected havior° of the visage,
Together with all forms, moods,° shapes of grief,
That can denote me truly. These indeed seem,
For they are actions that a man might play.
But I have that within which passes show;
These but the trappings and the suits of woe.
KING. 'Tis sweet and commendable in your nature, Hamlet,
To give these mourning duties to your father.
But you must know your father lost a father,
That father lost, lost his, and the survivor bound
In filial obligation for some term
To do obsequious° sorrow. But to persever°

**58 H'ath** he has **60 sealed** (as if sealing a legal document) **hard** reluctant **62 Take thy fair hour** enjoy your time of youth **63 And . . . will** and may your finest qualities guide the way you choose to spend your time **64 cousin** any kin not of the immediate family **65 A little . . . kind** i.e., closer than an ordinary nephew (since I am stepson), and yet more separated in natural feeling (with pun on *kind* meaning "affectionate" and "natural," "lawful." This line is often read as an aside, but it need not be. The King chooses perhaps not to respond to Hamlet's cryptic and bitter remark.) **67 the sun** i.e., the sunshine of the King's royal favor (with pun on *son*) **68 nighted color** (1) mourning garments of black (2) dark melancholy **69 Denmark** the King of Denmark **70 vailèd lids** lowered eyes **72 common** of universal occurrence. (But Hamlet plays on the sense of "vulgar" in line 74.) **75 particular** personal **78 customary** (1) socially conventional (2) habitual with me **79 suspiration** sighing **80 fruitful** abundant **81 havior** expression **82 moods** outward expression of feeling **92 obsequious** suited to obsequies or funerals **persever** persevere

In obstinate condolement° is a course
Of impious stubbornness. 'Tis unmanly grief.
It shows a will most incorrect to heaven,
A heart unfortified,° a mind impatient,
An understanding simple° and unschooled.
For what we know must be and is as common
As any the most vulgar thing to sense,°
Why should we in our peevish opposition
Take it to heart? Fie, 'tis a fault to heaven,
A fault against the dead, a fault to nature,
To reason most absurd, whose common theme
Is death of fathers, and who still° hath cried,
From the first corpse° till he that died today,
"This must be so." We pray you, throw to earth
This unprevailing° woe and think of us
As of a father; for let the world take note,
You are the most immediate° to our throne,
And with no less nobility of love
Than that which dearest father bears his son
Do I impart toward° you. For° your intent
In going back to school° in Wittenberg,°
It is most retrograde° to our desire,
And we beseech you bend you° to remain
Here in the cheer and comfort of our eye,
Our chiefest courtier, cousin, and our son.

QUEEN. Let not thy mother lose her prayers, Hamlet.
I pray thee, stay with us, go not to Wittenberg.

HAMLET. I shall in all my best° obey you, madam.

KING. Why, 'tis a loving and a fair reply.
Be as ourself in Denmark. Madam, come.
This gentle and unforced accord of Hamlet
Sits smiling to° my heart, in grace° whereof
No jocund° health that Denmark drinks today
But the great cannon to the clouds shall tell,
And the King's rouse° the heaven shall bruit again,°
Respeaking earthly thunder.° Come away.

*Flourish. Exeunt all but Hamlet.*

HAMLET. O, that this too too sullied° flesh would melt,
Thaw, and resolve itself into a dew!
Or that the Everlasting had not fixed

**93 condolement** sorrowing **96 unfortified** i.e., against adversity **97 simple** ignorant **99 As . . . sense** as the most ordinary experience **104 still** always **105 the first corpse** (Abel's) **107 unprevailing** unavailing, useless **109 most immediate** next in succession **112 impart toward** i.e., bestow my affection on. **For** as for **113 to school** i.e., to your studies **Wittenberg** famous German university founded in 1502 **114 retrograde** contrary **115 bend you** incline yourself **120 in all my best** to the best of my ability **124 to** i.e., at **grace** thanksgiving **125 jocund** merry **127 rouse** drinking of a draft of liquor **bruit again** loudly echo **128 thunder** i.e., of trumpet and kettledrum, sounded when the King drinks; see 1.4.8–12 **129 sullied** defiled. (The early quartos read *sallied;* the Folio, *solid.*)

His canon° 'gainst self-slaughter! O God, God,
How weary, stale, flat, and unprofitable
Seem to me all the uses° of this world!
Fie on 't, ah fie! 'Tis an unweeded garden
That grows to seed. Things rank and gross in nature
Possess it merely.° That it should come to this!
But two months dead—nay, not so much, not two.
So excellent a king, that was to° this
Hyperion° to a satyr,° so loving to my mother
That he might not beteem° the winds of heaven
Visit her face too roughly. Heaven and earth,
Must I remember? Why, she would hang on him
As if increase of appetite had grown
By what it fed on, and yet within a month—
Let me not think on 't; frailty, thy name is woman!—
A little month, or ere° those shoes were old
With which she followed my poor father's body,
Like Niobe,° all tears, why she, even she—
O God, a beast, that wants discourse of reason,°
Would have mourned longer—married with my uncle,
My father's brother, but no more like my father
Than I to Hercules. Within a month,
Ere yet the salt of most unrighteous tears
Had left the flushing in her gallèd° eyes,
She married. O, most wicked speed, to post°
With such dexterity to incestuous° sheets!
It is not, nor it cannot come to good.
But break, my heart, for I must hold my tongue.

*Enter Horatio, Marcellus, and Bernardo.*

HORATIO. Hail to your lordship!

HAMLET. I am glad to see you well.
Horatio!—or I do forget myself.

HORATIO. The same, my lord, and your poor servant ever.

HAMLET. Sir, my good friend; I'll change that name° with you.
And what make you from° Wittenberg, Horatio?
Marcellus.

MARCELLUS. My good lord.

**132 canon** law **134 all the uses** the whole routine **137 merely** completely **139 to** in comparison to **140 Hyperion** Titan sun-god, father of Helios **satyr** a lecherous creature of classical mythology, half-human but with a goat's legs, tail, ears, and horns **141 beteem** allow **147 or ere** even before **149 Niobe** Tantalus' daughter, Queen of Thebes, who boasted that she had more sons and daughters than Leto; for this, Apollo and Artemis, children of Leto, slew her fourteen children. She was turned by Zeus into a stone that continually dropped tears. **150 wants . . . reason** lacks the faculty of reason **155 gallèd** irritated, inflamed **156 post** hasten **157 incestuous** (In Shakespeare's day, the marriage of a man like Claudius to his deceased brother's wife was considered incestuous.) **163 change that name** i.e., give and receive reciprocally the name of "friend" (rather than talk of "servant") **164 make you from** are you doing away from

HAMLET. I am very glad to see you. [*To Bernardo.*] Good even, sir.—
But what in faith make you from Wittenberg?
HORATIO. A truant disposition, good my lord.
HAMLET. I would not hear your enemy say so,
Nor shall you do my ear that violence
To make it truster of your own report
Against yourself. I know you are no truant.
But what is your affair in Elsinore?
We'll teach you to drink deep ere you depart.
HORATIO. My lord, I came to see your father's funeral.
HAMLET. I prithee, do not mock me, fellow student;
I think it was to see my mother's wedding.
HORATIO. Indeed, my lord, it followed hard° upon.
HAMLET. Thrift, thrift, Horatio! The funeral baked meats°
Did coldly° furnish forth the marriage tables.
Would I had met my dearest° foe in heaven
Or ever° I had seen that day, Horatio!
My father!—Methinks I see my father.
HORATIO. Where, my lord?
HAMLET. In my mind's eye, Horatio.
HORATIO. I saw him once. 'A° was a goodly king.
HAMLET. 'A was a man. Take him for all in all,
I shall not look upon his like again.
HORATIO. My lord, I think I saw him yesternight.
HAMLET. Saw? Who?
HORATIO. My lord, the King your father.
HAMLET. The King my father?
HORATIO. Season your admiration° for a while
With an attent° ear till I may deliver,
Upon the witness of these gentlemen,
This marvel to you.
HAMLET. For God's love, let me hear!
HORATIO. Two nights together had these gentlemen,
Marcellus and Bernardo, on their watch,
In the dead waste° and middle of the night,
Been thus encountered. A figure like your father,
Armèd at point° exactly, cap-à-pie,°
Appears before them, and with solemn march
Goes slow and stately by them. Thrice he walked
By their oppressed and fear-surprisèd eyes
Within his truncheon's° length, whilst they, distilled°
Almost to jelly with the act° of fear,
Stand dumb and speak not to him. This to me
In dreadful° secrecy impart they did,

**179 hard** close **180 baked meats** meat pies **181 coldly** i.e., as cold leftovers **182 dearest** closest (and therefore deadliest) **183 Or ever** before **186 'A** he **193 Season your admiration** restrain your astonishment **194 attent** attentive **199 dead waste** desolate stillness **201 at point** correctly in every detail **cap-à-pie** from head to foot **205 truncheon** officer's staff **distilled** dissolved **206 act** action, operation **208 dreadful** full of dread

And I with them the third night kept the watch,
Where, as they had delivered, both in time,
Form of the thing, each word made true and good,
The apparition comes. I knew your father;
These hands are not more like.

HAMLET. But where was this?

MARCELLUS. My lord, upon the platform where we watch.

HAMLET. Did you not speak to it?

HORATIO. My lord, I did,
But answer made it none. Yet once methought
It lifted up its head and did address
Itself to motion, like as it would speak;°
But even then° the morning cock crew loud,
And at the sound it shrunk in haste away
And vanished from our sight.

HAMLET. 'Tis very strange.

HORATIO. As I do live, my honored lord, 'tis true,
And we did think it writ down in our duty
To let you know of it.

HAMLET. Indeed, indeed, sirs. But this troubles me.
Hold you the watch tonight?

ALL. We do, my lord.

HAMLET. Armed, say you?

ALL. Armed, my lord.

HAMLET. From top to toe?

ALL. My lord, from head to foot.

HAMLET. Then saw you not his face?

HORATIO. O, yes, my lord, he wore his beaver° up.

HAMLET. What° looked he, frowningly?

HORATIO. A countenance more in sorrow than in anger.

HAMLET. Pale or red?

HORATIO. Nay, very pale.

HAMLET. And fixed his eyes upon you?

HORATIO. Most constantly.

HAMLET. I would I had been there.

HORATIO. It would have much amazed you.

HAMLET. Very like, very like. Stayed it long?

HORATIO. While one with moderate haste might tell° a hundred.

MARCELLUS, BERNARDO. Longer, longer.

HORATIO. Not when I saw 't.

HAMLET. His beard was grizzled°—no?

HORATIO. It was, as I have seen it in his life,
A sable silvered.°

HAMLET. I will watch tonight.
Perchance 'twill walk again.

HORATIO. I warrant° it will.

**217–218 did . . . speak** began to move as though it were about to speak **219 even then** at that very instant **232 beaver** visor on the helmet **233 What** how **242 tell** count **245 grizzled** gray **247 sable silvered** black mixed with white **248 warrant** assure you

HAMLET. If it assume my noble father's person,
I'll speak to it though hell itself should gape
And bid me hold my peace. I pray you all,
If you have hitherto concealed this sight,
Let it be tenable° in your silence still,
And whatsoever else shall hap tonight,
Give it an understanding but no tongue.
I will requite your loves. So, fare you well.
Upon the platform twixt eleven and twelve
I'll visit you.
ALL. Our duty to your honor.
HAMLET. Your loves, as mine to you. Farewell.
*Exeunt* [*all but Hamlet*].
My father's spirit in arms! All is not well.
I doubt° some foul play. Would the night were come!
Till then sit still, my soul. Foul deeds will rise,
Though all the earth o'erwhelm them, to men's eyes.
*Exit.*

**1.3** *Enter Laertes and Ophelia, his sister.*

LAERTES. My necessaries are embarked. Farewell.
And, sister, as the winds give benefit
And convoy is assistant,° do not sleep
But let me hear from you.
OPHELIA. Do you doubt that?
LAERTES. For Hamlet, and the trifling of his favor,
Hold it a fashion and a toy in blood,°
A violet in the youth of primy° nature,
Forward,° not permanent, sweet, not lasting,
The perfume and suppliance° of a minute—
No more.
OPHELIA. No more but so?
LAERTES. Think it no more.
For nature crescent° does not grow alone
In thews° and bulk, but as this temple° waxes
The inward service of the mind and soul
Grows wide withal.° Perhaps he loves you now,
And now no soil° nor cautel° doth besmirch
The virtue of his will;° but you must fear,
His greatness weighed,° his will is not his own.
For he himself is subject to his birth.
He may not, as unvalued persons do,

**253 tenable** held **261 doubt** suspect
**1.3 Location: Polonius's chambers. 3 convoy is assistant** means of conveyance are available **6 toy in blood** passing amorous fancy **7 primy** in its prime, springtime **8 Forward** precocious **9 suppliance** supply, filler **11 crescent** growing, waxing **12 thews** bodily strength **temple** i.e., body **14 Grows wide withal** grows along with it **15 soil** blemish **cautel** deceit **16 will** desire **17 His greatness weighed** if you take into account his high position

Carve° for himself, for on his choice depends
The safety and health of this whole state,
And therefore must his choice be circumscribed
Unto the voice and yielding° of that body
Whereof he is the head. Then if he says he loves you,
It fits your wisdom so far to believe it
As he in his particular act and place°
May give his saying deed, which is no further
Than the main voice° of Denmark goes withal.°
Then weigh what loss your honor may sustain
If with too credent° ear you list° his songs,
Or lose your heart, or your chaste treasure open
To his unmastered importunity.
Fear it, Ophelia, fear it, my dear sister,
And keep you in the rear of your affection,°
Out of the shot and danger of desire.
The chariest° maid is prodigal enough
If she unmask° her beauty to the moon.°
Virtue itself scapes not calumnious strokes.
The canker galls° the infants of the spring
Too oft before their buttons° be disclosed,°
And in the morn and liquid dew° of youth
Contagious blastments° are most imminent.
Be wary then; best safety lies in fear.
Youth to itself rebels,° though none else near.

OPHELIA. I shall the effect of this good lesson keep
As watchman to my heart. But, good my brother,
Do not, as some ungracious° pastors do,
Show me the steep and thorny way to heaven,
Whiles like a puffed° and reckless libertine
Himself the primrose path of dalliance treads,
And recks° not his own rede.°

*Enter Polonius.*

LAERTES. O, fear me not.°
I stay too long. But here my father comes.
A double° blessing is a double grace;
Occasion smiles upon a second leave.°

POLONIUS. Yet here, Laertes? Aboard, aboard, for shame!

**20 Carve** i.e., choose **23 voice and yielding** assent, approval **26 in . . . place** in his particular restricted circumstances **28 main voice** general assent **withal** along with **30 credent** credulous **list** listen to **34 keep . . . affection** don't advance as far as your affection might lead you. (A military metaphor.) **36 chariest** most scrupulously modest **37 If she unmask** if she does no more than show her beauty **moon** (Symbol of chastity.) **39 canker galls** cankerworm destroys **40 buttons** buds **disclosed** opened **41 liquid dew** i.e., time when dew is fresh and bright **42 blastments** blights **44 Youth . . . rebels** youth is inherently rebellious **47 ungracious** ungodly **49 puffed** bloated, or swollen with pride **51 recks** heeds **rede** counsel **fear me not** don't worry on my account **53 double** (Laertes has already bid his father good-bye.) **54 Occasion . . . leave** happy is the circumstance that provides a second leave-taking. (The goddess Occasion, or Opportunity, smiles.)

The wind sits in the shoulder of your sail,
And you are stayed for. There—my blessing with thee!
And these few precepts in thy memory
Look° thou character.° Give thy thoughts no tongue,
Nor any unproportioned° thought his° act.
Be thou familiar,° but by no means vulgar.°
Those friends thou hast, and their adoption tried,°
Grapple them unto thy soul with hoops of steel,
But do not dull thy palm° with entertainment
Of each new-hatched, unfledged courage.° Beware
Of entrance to a quarrel, but being in,
Bear 't that° th' opposèd may beware of thee.
Give every man thy ear, but few thy voice;
Take each man's censure,° but reserve thy judgment.
Costly thy habit° as thy purse can buy,
But not expressed in fancy;° rich, not gaudy,
For the apparel oft proclaims the man,
And they in France of the best rank and station
Are of a most select and generous chief in that.°
Neither a borrower nor a lender be,
For loan oft loses both itself and friend,
And borrowing dulleth edge of husbandry.°
This above all: to thine own self be true,
And it must follow, as the night the day,
Thou canst not then be false to any man.
Farewell. My blessing season° this in thee!

LAERTES. Most humbly do I take my leave, my lord.

POLONIUS. The time invests° you. Go, your servants tend.°

LAERTES. Farewell, Ophelia, and remember well
What I have said to you.

OPHELIA. 'Tis in my memory locked,
And you yourself shall keep the key of it.

LAERTES. Farewell.

*Exit Laertes.*

POLONIUS. What is 't, Ophelia, he hath said to you?

OPHELIA. So please you, something touching the Lord Hamlet.

POLONIUS. Marry,° well bethought.
'Tis told me he hath very oft of late
Given private time to you, and you yourself
Have of your audience been most free and bounteous.

**59 Look** be sure that **character** inscribe **60 unproportioned** badly calculated, intemperate **his** its **61 familiar** sociable **vulgar** common **62 and their adoption tried** and also their suitability for adoption as friends having been tested **64 dull thy palm** i.e., shake hands so often as to make the gesture meaningless **65 courage** young man of spirit **67 Bear 't that** manage it so that **69 censure** opinion, judgment **70 habit** clothing **71 fancy** excessive ornament, decadent fashion **74 Are . . . that** are of a most refined and well-bred preeminence in choosing what to wear **77 husbandry** thrift **81 season** mature **83 invests** besieges, presses upon **tend** attend, wait **91 Marry** i.e., by the Virgin Mary. (A mild oath.)

If it be so—as so 'tis put on° me,
And that in way of caution—I must tell you
You do not understand yourself so clearly
As it behooves° my daughter and your honor.
What is between you? Give me up the truth.

OPHELIA. He hath, my lord, of late made many tenders°
Of his affection to me.

POLONIUS. Affection? Pooh! You speak like a green girl,
Unsifted° in such perilous circumstance.
Do you believe his tenders, as you call them?

OPHELIA. I do not know, my lord, what I should think.

POLONIUS. Marry, I will teach you. Think yourself a baby
That you have ta'en these tenders for true pay
Which are not sterling.° Tender° yourself more dearly,
Or—not to crack the wind° of the poor phrase,
Running it thus—you'll tender me a fool.°

OPHELIA. My lord, he hath importuned me with love
In honorable fashion.

POLONIUS. Ay, fashion° you may call it. Go to,° go to.

OPHELIA. And hath given countenance° to his speech, my lord,
With almost all the holy vows of heaven.

POLONIUS. Ay, springes° to catch woodcocks.° I do know,
When the blood burns, how prodigal° the soul
Lends the tongue vows. These blazes, daughter,
Giving more light than heat, extinct in both
Even in their promise as it° is a-making,
You must not take for fire. From this time
Be something° scanter of your maiden presence.
Set your entreatments° at a higher rate
Than a command to parle.° For Lord Hamlet,
Believe so much in him° that he is young,
And with a larger tether may he walk
Than may be given you. In few,° Ophelia,
Do not believe his vows, for they are brokers,°
Not of that dye° which their investments° show,
But mere implorators° of unholy suits,

**95 put on** impressed on, told to **98 behooves** befits **100 tenders** offers **103 Unsifted** i.e., untried **108 sterling** legal currency **Tender** hold, look after, offer **109 crack the wind** i.e., run it until it is broken-winded **110 tender me a fool** (1) show yourself to me as a fool (2) show me up as a fool (3) present me with a grandchild. (*Fool* was a term of endearment for a child.) **113 fashion** mere form, pretense **Go to** (An expression of impatience.) **114 countenance** credit, confirmation **116 springes** snares **woodcocks** birds easily caught; here used to connote gullibility **117 prodigal** prodigally **120 it** i.e., the promise **122 something** somewhat **123 entreatments** negotiations for surrender. (A military term.) **124 parle** discuss terms with the enemy. (Polonius urges his daughter, in the metaphor of military language, not to meet with Hamlet and consider giving in to him merely because he requests an interview.) **125 so . . . him** this much concerning him **127 In few** briefly **128 brokers** go-betweens, procurers **129 dye** color or sort **investments** clothes. (The vows are not what they seem.) **130 mere implorators** out and out solicitors

Breathing° like sanctified and pious bawds,
The better to beguile. This is for all:°
I would not, in plain terms, from this time forth
Have you so slander° any moment° leisure
As to give words or talk with the Lord Hamlet.
Look to 't, I charge you. Come your ways.°
OPHELIA. I shall obey, my lord.
*Exeunt.*

**1.4** *Enter Hamlet, Horatio, and Marcellus.*

HAMLET. The air bites shrewdly;° it is very cold.
HORATIO. It is a nipping and an eager° air.
HAMLET. What hour now?
HORATIO. I think it lacks of° twelve.
MARCELLUS. No, it is struck.
HORATIO. Indeed? I heard it not.
It then draws near the season°
Wherein the spirit held his wont° to walk.
*A flourish of trumpets, and two pieces° go off* [*within*].
What does this mean, my lord?
HAMLET. The King doth wake° tonight and takes his rouse,°
Keeps wassail,° and the swaggering upspring° reels;°
And as he drains his drafts of Rhenish° down,
The kettledrum and trumpet thus bray out
The triumph of his pledge.°
HORATIO. It is a custom?
HAMLET. Ay, marry, is 't,
But to my mind, though I am native here
And to the manner° born, it is a custom
More honored in the breach than the observance.°
This heavy-headed revel east and west°
Makes us traduced and taxed of° other nations.
They clepe° us drunkards, and with swinish phrase°
Soil our addition;° and indeed it takes
From our achievements, though performed at height,°
The pith and marrow of our attribute.°
So, oft it chances in particular men,

**131 Breathing** speaking **132 for all** once for all, in sum **134 slander** abuse, misuse **moment** moment's **136 Come your ways** come along
**1.4 Location: The guard platform.** **1 shrewdly** keenly, sharply **2 eager** biting **3 lacks of** is just short of **5 season** time **6 held his wont** was accustomed. **s.d. pieces** i.e., of ordnance, cannon **8 wake** stay awake and hold revel. **takes his rouse** carouses **9 wassail** carousal **upspring** wild German dance **reels** dances **10 Rhenish** Rhine wine **12 The triumph . . . pledge** i.e., his feat in draining the wine in a single draft **15 manner** custom (of drinking) **16 More . . . observance** better neglected than followed **17 east and west** i.e., everywhere **18 taxed of** censured by **19 clepe** call **with swinish phrase** i.e., by calling us swine **20 addition** reputation **21 at height** outstandingly **22 The pith . . . attribute** the essence of the reputation that others attribute to us

That for° some vicious mole of nature° in them,
As in their birth—wherein they are not guilty,
Since nature cannot choose his° origin—
By their o'ergrowth of some complexion,°
Oft breaking down the pales° and forts of reason,
Or by some habit that too much o'erleavens°
The form of plausive° manners, that these men,
Carrying, I say, the stamp of one defect,
Being nature's livery° or fortune's star,°
His virtues else,° be they as pure as grace,
As infinite as man may undergo,°
Shall in the general censure° take corruption
From that particular fault. The dram of evil
Doth all the noble substance often dout
To his own scandal.°

*Enter Ghost.*

HORATIO. Look, my lord, it comes!

HAMLET. Angels and ministers° of grace defend us!
Be thou° a spirit of health° or goblin damned,
Bring° with thee airs from heaven or blasts from hell,
Be thy intents° wicked or charitable,
Thou com'st in such a questionable° shape
That I will speak to thee. I'll call thee Hamlet,
King, father, royal Dane. O, answer me!
Let me not burst in ignorance, but tell
Why thy canonized° bones, hearsèd° in death,
Have burst their cerements;° why the sepulcher
Wherein we saw thee quietly inurned°
Hath oped his ponderous and marble jaws
To cast thee up again. What may this mean,
That thou, dead corpse, again in complete steel,°
Revisits thus the glimpses of the moon,°
Making night hideous, and we fools of nature°

**24 for** on account of. **mole of nature** natural blemish in one's constitution **26 his** its **27 their o'ergrowth . . . complexion** the excessive growth in individuals of some natural trait **28 pales** palings, fences (as of a fortification) **29 o'erleavens** induces a change throughout (as yeast works in dough) **30 plausive** pleasing **32 nature's livery** sign of one's servitude to nature. **fortune's star** the destiny that chance brings **33 His virtues else** i.e., the other qualities of *these men* (line 30) **34 may undergo** can sustain **35 general censure** general opinion that people have of him **36–38 The dram . . . scandal** i.e., the small drop of evil blots out or works against the noble substance of the whole and brings it into disrepute. To *dout* is to blot out. (A famous crux.) **39 ministers of grace** messengers of God **40 Be thou** whether you are **spirit of health** good angel **41 Bring** whether you bring **42 Be thy intents** whether your intentions are **43 questionable** inviting question **47 canonized** buried according to the canons of the church **hearsèd** coffined **48 cerements** grave clothes **49 inurned** entombed **52 complete steel** full armor **53 glimpses of the moon** pale and uncertain moonlight **54 fools of nature** mere men, limited to natural knowledge and subject to nature

So horridly to shake our disposition°
With thoughts beyond the reaches of our souls?
Say, why is this? Wherefore? What should we do?

[*The Ghost*] *beckons* [*Hamlet*].

HORATIO. It beckons you to go away with it,
As if it some impartment° did desire
To you alone.

MARCELLUS. Look with what courteous action
It wafts you to a more removèd ground.
But do not go with it.

HORATIO. No, by no means.

HAMLET. It will not speak. Then I will follow it.

HORATIO. Do not, my lord!

HAMLET. Why, what should be the fear?
I do not set my life at a pin's fee,°
And for my soul, what can it do to that,
Being a thing immortal as itself?
It waves me forth again. I'll follow it.

HORATIO. What if it tempt you toward the flood,° my lord,
Or to the dreadful summit of the cliff
That beetles o'er° his° base into the sea,
And there assume some other horrible form
Which might deprive your sovereignty of reason°
And draw you into madness? Think of it.
The very place puts toys of desperation,°
Without more motive, into every brain
That looks so many fathoms to the sea
And hears it roar beneath.

HAMLET. It wafts me still.—Go on, I'll follow thee.

MARCELLUS. You shall not go, my lord. [*They try to stop him.*]

HAMLET. Hold off your hands!

HORATIO. Be ruled. You shall not go.

HAMLET. My fate cries out,°
And makes each petty° artery° in this body
As hardy as the Nemean lion's° nerve.°
Still am I called. Unhand me, gentlemen.
By heaven, I'll make a ghost of him that lets° me!
I say, away!—Go on, I'll follow thee.

*Exeunt Ghost and Hamlet.*

HORATIO. He waxes desperate with imagination.

MARCELLUS. Let's follow. 'Tis not fit thus to obey him.

**55 So . . . disposition** to distress our mental composure so violently **59 impartment** communication **65 fee** value **69 flood** sea **71 beetles o'er** overhangs threateningly (like bushy eyebrows) **his** its **73 deprive . . . reason** take away the rule of reason over your mind **75 toys of desperation** fancies of desperate acts, i.e., suicide **81 My fate cries out** my destiny summons me **82 petty** weak. **artery** (through which the vital spirits were thought to have been conveyed) **83 Nemean lion** one of the monsters slain by Hercules in his twelve labors **nerve** sinew **85 lets** hinders

HORATIO. Have after.° To what issue° will this come?
MARCELLUS. Something is rotten in the state of Denmark.
HORATIO. Heaven will direct it.°
MARCELLUS. Nay, let's follow him.

*Exeunt.*

## 1.5 *Enter Ghost and Hamlet.*

HAMLET. Whither wilt thou lead me? Speak. I'll go no further.
GHOST. Mark me.
HAMLET. I will.
GHOST. My hour is almost come,
When I to sulfurous and tormenting flames
Must render up myself.
HAMLET. Alas, poor ghost!
GHOST. Pity me not, but lend thy serious hearing
To what I shall unfold.
HAMLET. Speak. I am bound° to hear.
GHOST. So art thou to revenge, when thou shalt hear.
HAMLET. What?
GHOST. I am thy father's spirit,
Doomed for a certain term to walk the night,
And for the day confined to fast° in fires,
Till the foul crimes° done in my days of nature°
Are burnt and purged away. But that° I am forbid
To tell the secrets of my prison house,
I could a tale unfold whose lightest word
Would harrow up° thy soul, freeze thy young blood,
Make thy two eyes like stars start from their spheres,°
Thy knotted and combinèd locks° to part,
And each particular hair to stand on end
Like quills upon the fretful porcupine.
But this eternal blazon° must not be
To ears of flesh and blood. List, list, O, list!
If thou didst ever thy dear father love—
HAMLET. O God!
GHOST. Revenge his foul and most unnatural murder.
HAMLET. Murder?
GHOST. Murder most foul, as in the best° it is,
But this most foul, strange, and unnatural.
HAMLET. Haste me to know 't, that I, with wings as swift

**89 Have after** let's go after him **issue** outcome **91 it** i.e., the outcome
**1.5 Location: The battlements of the castle.** **7 bound** (1) ready (2) obligated by duty and fate. (The Ghost, in line 8, answers in the second sense.) **12 fast** do penance by fasting **13 crimes** sins **of nature** as a mortal **14 But that** were it not that **17 harrow up** lacerate, tear **18 spheres** i.e., eye-sockets, here compared to the orbits or transparent revolving spheres in which, according to Ptolemaic astronomy, the heavenly bodies were fixed **19 knotted . . . locks** hair neatly arranged and confined **22 eternal blazon** revelation of the secrets of eternity **28 in the best** even at best

As meditation or the thoughts of love,
May sweep to my revenge.

GHOST. I find thee apt;
And duller shouldst thou be° than the fat° weed
That roots itself in ease on Lethe° wharf,
Wouldst thou not stir in this. Now, Hamlet, hear.
'Tis given out that, sleeping in my orchard,°
A serpent stung me. So the whole ear of Denmark
Is by a forgèd process° of my death
Rankly abused.° But know, thou noble youth,
The serpent that did sting thy father's life
Now wears his crown.

HAMLET. O, my prophetic soul! My uncle!

GHOST. Ay, that incestuous, that adulterate° beast,
With witchcraft of his wit, with traitorous gifts°—
O wicked wit and gifts, that have the power
So to seduce!—won to his shameful lust
The will of my most seeming-virtuous queen.
O Hamlet, what a falling off was there!
From me, whose love was of that dignity
That it went hand in hand even with the vow°
I made to her in marriage, and to decline
Upon a wretch whose natural gifts were poor
To° those of mine!
But virtue,° as it° never will be moved,
Though lewdness court it in a shape of heaven,°
So lust, though to a radiant angel linked,
Will sate itself in a celestial bed°
And prey on garbage.
But soft, methinks I scent the morning air.
Brief let me be. Sleeping within my orchard,
My custom always of the afternoon,
Upon my secure° hour thy uncle stole,
With juice of cursèd hebona° in a vial,
And in the porches of my ears° did pour
The leprous distillment,° whose effect
Holds such an enmity with blood of man
That swift as quicksilver it courses through
The natural gates and alleys of the body,
And with a sudden vigor it doth posset°

**33 shouldst thou be** you would have to be **fat** torpid, lethargic **34 Lethe** the river of forgetfulness in Hades **36 orchard** garden **38 forgèd process** falsified account **39 abused** deceived **43 adulterate** adulterous **44 gifts** (1) talents (2) presents **50 even with the vow** with the very vow **53 To** compared to **54 virtue, as it** as virtue **55 shape of heaven** heavenly form **57 sate . . . bed** cease to find sexual pleasure in a virtuously lawful marriage **62 secure** confident, unsuspicious **63 hebona** a poison. (The word seems to be a form of *ebony,* though it is thought perhaps to be related to *henbane,* a poison, or to *ebenus,* "yew.") **64 porches of my ears** ears as a porch or entrance of the body **65 leprous distillment** distillation causing leprosylike disfigurement **69 posset** coagulate, curdle

And curd, like eager° droppings into milk,
The thin and wholesome blood. So did it mine,
And a most instant tetter° barked° about,
Most lazar-like,° with vile and loathsome crust,
All my smooth body.
Thus was I, sleeping, by a brother's hand
Of life, of crown, of queen at once dispatched,°
Cut off even in the blossoms of my sin,
Unhouseled,° disappointed,° unaneled,°
No reckoning° made, but sent to my account
With all my imperfections on my head.
O, horrible! O, horrible, most horrible!
If thou hast nature° in thee, bear it not.
Let not the royal bed of Denmark be
A couch for luxury° and damnèd incest.
But, howsoever thou pursues this act,
Taint not thy mind nor let thy soul contrive
Against thy mother aught. Leave her to heaven
And to those thorns that in her bosom lodge,
To prick and sting her. Fare thee well at once.
The glowworm shows the matin° to be near,
And 'gins to pale his° uneffectual fire.
Adieu, adieu, adieu! Remember me.
[*Exit.*]

HAMLET. O all you host of heaven! O earth! What else?
And shall I couple° hell? O, fie! Hold,° hold, my heart,
And you, my sinews, grow not instant° old,
But bear me stiffly up. Remember thee?
Ay, thou poor ghost, whiles memory holds a seat
In this distracted globe.° Remember thee?
Yea, from the table° of my memory
I'll wipe away all trivial fond° records,
All saws° of books, all forms,° all pressures° past
That youth and observation copied there,
And thy commandment all alone shall live
Within the book and volume of my brain,
Unmixed with baser matter. Yes, by heaven!
O most pernicious woman!
O villain, villain, smiling, damnèd villain!
My tables°—meet it is° I set it down

**70 eager** sour, acid **72 tetter** eruption of scabs **barked** recovered with a rough covering, like bark on a tree **73 lazar-like** leperlike **76 dispatched** suddenly deprived **78 Unhouseled** without having received the Sacrament **disappointment** unready (spiritually) for the last journey **unaneled** without having received extreme unction **79 reckoning** settling of accounts **82 nature** i.e., the promptings of a son **84 luxury** lechery **90 matin** morning **91 his** its **94 couple** add **Hold** hold together **95 instant** instantly **98 globe** (1) head (2) world **99 table** tablet, slate **100 fond** foolish **101 saws** wise sayings **forms** shapes or images copied onto the slate; general ideas **pressures** impressions stamped **108 tables** writing tablets **meet it is** it is fitting

That one may smile, and smile, and be a villain.
At least I am sure it may be so in Denmark.
[*Writing.*]
So uncle, there you are.° Now to my word:
It is "Adieu, adieu! Remember me."
I have sworn't.

*Enter Horatio and Marcellus.*

HORATIO. My lord, my lord!
MARCELLUS. Lord Hamlet!
HORATIO. Heavens secure him!°
HAMLET. So be it.
MARCELLUS. Hilo, ho, ho, my lord!
HAMLET. Hillo, ho, ho, boy! Come, bird, come.°
MARCELLUS. How is 't, my noble lord?
HORATIO. What news, my lord?
HAMLET. O, wonderful!
HORATIO. Good my lord, tell it.
HAMLET. No, you will reveal it.
HORATIO. Not I, my lord, by heaven.
MARCELLUS. Nor I, my lord.
HAMLET. How say you, then, would heart of man once° think it?
But you'll be secret?
HORATIO, MARCELLUS. Ay, by heaven, my lord.
HAMLET. There's never a villain dwelling in all Denmark
But he's an arrant° knave.
HORATIO. There needs no ghost, my lord, come from the grave
To tell us this.
HAMLET. Why, right, you are in the right.
And so, without more circumstance° at all,
I hold it fit that we shake hands and part,
You as your business and desire shall point you—
For every man hath business and desire,
Such as it is—and for my own poor part,
Look you, I'll go pray.
HORATIO. These are but wild and whirling words, my lord.
HAMLET. I am sorry they offend you, heartily;
Yes, faith, heartily.
HORATIO. There's no offense, my lord.
HAMLET. Yes, but Saint Patrick,° but there is, Horatio,
And much offense° too. Touching this vision here,
It is an honest ghost,° that let me tell you.

**111 there you are** i.e., there, I've written that down against you **116 secure him** keep him safe **119 Hilo . . . come** (A falconer's call to a hawk in air. Hamlet mocks the hallooing as though it were a part of hawking.) **127 once** ever **130 arrant** thoroughgoing **133 circumstance** ceremony, elaboration **142 Saint Patrick** The keeper of Purgatory and patron saint of all blunders and confusion.) **143 offense** (Hamlet deliberately changes Horatio's "no offense taken" to "an offense against all decency.") **144 an honest ghost** i.e., a real ghost and not an evil spirit

For your desire to know what is between us,
O'ermaster 't as you may. And now, good friends,
As you are friends, scholars, and soldiers,
Give me one poor request.

HORATIO. What is 't, my lord? We will.

HAMLET. Never make known what you have seen tonight.

HORATIO, MARCELLUS. My lord, we will not.

HAMLET. Nay, but swear 't.

HORATIO. In faith, my lord, not I.°

MARCELLUS. Nor I, my lord, in faith.

HAMLET. Upon my sword.° [*He holds out his sword.*]

MARCELLUS. We have sworn, my lord, already.°

HAMLET. Indeed, upon my sword, indeed.

GHOST [*cries under the stage*]. Swear.

HAMLET. Ha, ha, boy, sayst thou so? Art thou there, truepenny?°
Come on, you hear this fellow in the cellarage.
Consent to swear.

HORATIO. Propose the oath, my lord.

HAMLET. Never to speak of this that you have seen,
Swear by my sword.

GHOST [*beneath*]. Swear. [*They swear.*°]

HAMLET. *Hic et ubique?*° Then we'll shift our ground.
[*He moves to another spot.*]
Come hither, gentlemen,
And lay your hands again upon my sword.
Swear by my sword
Never to speak of this that you have heard.

GHOST [*beneath*]. Swear by his sword. [*They swear.*]

HAMLET. Well said, old mole. Canst work i' th' earth so fast?
A worthy pioneer!°—Once more removed, good friends.
[*He moves again.*]

HORATIO. O day and night, but this is wondrous strange!

HAMLET. And therefore as a stranger° give it welcome.
There are more things in heaven and earth, Horatio,
Than are dreamt of in your philosophy.°
But come;
Here, as before, never, so help you mercy,°
How strange or odd soe'er I bear myself—
As I perchance hereafter shall think meet

**153 In faith . . . I** i.e., I swear not to tell what I have seen. (Horatio is not refusing to swear.) **155 sword** i.e., the hilt in the form of a cross **156 We . . . already** i.e., we swore in *faith* **159 truepenny** honest old fellow **164 s.d. They swear** (Seemingly they swear here, and at lines 170 and 190, as they lay their hands on Hamlet's sword. Triple oaths would have particular force; these three oaths deal with what they have seen, what they have heard, and what they promise about Hamlet's *antic disposition.*) **165** ***Hic et ubique*** here and everywhere. (Latin.) **172 pioneer** foot soldier assigned to dig tunnels and excavations **174 as a stranger** i.e., needing your hospitality **176 your philosophy** this subject called "natural philosophy" or "science" that people talk about **178 so help you mercy** as you hope for God's mercy when you are judged

To put an antic° disposition on—
That you, at such times seeing me, never shall,
With arms encumbered° thus, or this headshake,
Or by pronouncing of some doubtful phrase
As "Well, we know," or "We could, an if° we would,"
Or "If we list° to speak," or "There be, an if they might,"°
Or such ambiguous giving out,° to note°
That you know aught° of me—this do swear,
So grace and mercy at your most need help you.

GHOST [*beneath*]. Swear. [*They swear.*]

HAMLET. Rest, rest, perturbèd spirit! So, gentlemen,
With all my love I do commend me to you;°
And what so poor a man as Hamlet is
May do t' express his love and friending° to you,
God willing, shall not lack.° Let us go in together,
And still° your fingers on your lips, I pray.
The time° is out of joint. O cursèd spite°
That ever I was born to set it right!
[*They wait for him to leave first.*]
Nay, come, let's go together.°

*Exeunt.*

## 2.1 *Enter old Polonius with his man* [*Reynaldo*].

POLONIUS. Give him this money and these notes, Reynaldo.
[*He gives money and papers.*]

REYNALDO. I will, my lord.

POLONIUS. You shall do marvelous° wisely, good Reynaldo,
Before you visit him, to make inquire°
Of his behavior.

REYNALDO. My lord, I did intend it.

POLONIUS. Marry, well said, very well said. Look you, sir,
Inquire me first what Danskers° are in Paris,
And how, and who, what means,° and where they keep,°
What company, at what expense; and finding
By this encompassment° and drift° of question
That they do know my son, come you more nearer
Than your particular demands will touch it.°

**181 antic** fantastic **183 encumbered** folded **185 an if** if **186 list** wished. **There . . . might** i.e., there are people here (we, in fact) who could tell news if we were at liberty to do so **187 giving out** intimation. **note** draw attention to the fact **188 aught** i.e., something secret **192 do . . . you** entrust myself to you **194 friending** friendliness **195 lack** be lacking **196 still** always **197 The time** the state of affairs **spite** i.e., the spite of Fortune **199 let's go together** (Probably they wait for him to leave first, but he refuses this ceremoniousness.)

**2.1 Location: Polonius's chambers. 3 marvelous** marvelously **4 inquire** inquiry **7 Danskers** Danes **8 what means** what wealth (they have) **keep** dwell **10 encompassment** roundabout talking **drift** gradual approach or course **11–12 come . . . it** you will find out more this way than by asking pointed questions (*particular demands*)

Take you,° as 'twere, some distant knowledge of him,
As thus, "I know his father and his friends,
And in part him." Do you mark this, Reynaldo?

REYNALDO. Ay, very well, my lord.

POLONIUS. "And in part him, but," you may say, "not well.
But if 't be he I mean, he's very wild,
Addicted so and so," and there put on° him
What forgeries° you please—marry, none so rank°
As may dishonor him, take heed of that,
But, sir, such wanton,° wild, and usual slips
As are companions noted and most known
To youth and liberty.

REYNALDO. As gaming, my lord.

POLONIUS. Ay, or drinking, fencing, swearing,
Quarreling, drabbing°—you may go so far.

REYNALDO. My lord, that would dishonor him.

POLONIUS. Faith, no, as you may season° it in the charge.
You must not put another scandal on him
That he is open to incontinency;°
That's not my meaning. But breathe his faults so quaintly°
That they may seem the taints of liberty,°
The flash and outbreak of a fiery mind,
A savageness in unreclaimèd blood,
Of general assault.°

REYNALDO. But, my good lord—

POLONIUS. Wherefore should you do this?

REYNALDO. Ay, my lord, I would know that.

POLONIUS. Marry, sir, here's my drift,
And I believe it is a fetch of warrant.°
You laying these slight sullies on my son,
As 'twere a thing a little soiled wi' the working,°
Mark you,
Your party in converse,° him you would sound,°
Having ever° seen in the prenominate crimes°
The youth you breathe° of guilty, be assured
He closes with you in this consequence:°
"Good sir," or so, or "friend," or "gentleman,"
According to the phrase or the addition°
Of man and country.

**13 Take you** assume, pretend **19 put on** impute to **20 forgeries** invented tales **rank** gross **22 wanton** sportive, unrestrained **27 drabbing** whoring **29 season** temper, soften **31 incontinency** habitual sexual excess **32 quaintly** artfully, subtly **33 taints of liberty** faults resulting from free living **35–36 A savageness . . . assault** a wildness in untamed youth that assails all indiscriminately **41 fetch of warrant** legitimate trick **43 soiled wi' the working** soiled by handling while it is being made, i.e., by involvement in the ways of the world **45 converse** conversation **sound** i.e., sound out **46 Having ever** if he has ever. **prenominate crimes** before-mentioned offenses **47 breathe** speak **48 closes . . . consequence** takes you into his confidence in some fashion, as follows **50 addition** title

REYNALDO. Very good, my lord.
POLONIUS. And then, sir, does 'a this—'a does—what was I about to say? By the Mass, I was about to say something. Where did I leave?
REYNALDO. At "closes in the consequence."
POLONIUS. At "closes in the consequence," ay, marry.
He closes thus: "I know the gentleman,
I saw him yesterday," or "th' other day,"
Or then, or then, with such or such, "and as you say,
There was 'a gaming," "there o'ertook in 's rouse,"°
"There falling out° at tennis," or perchance
"I saw him enter such a house of sale,"
Videlicet° a brothel, or so forth. See you now,
Your bait of falsehood takes this carp° of truth;
And thus do we of wisdom and of reach,°
With windlasses° and with assays of bias,°
By indirections find directions° out.
So by my former lecture and advice
Shall you my son. You have° me, have you not?
REYNALDO. My lord, I have.
POLONIUS. God b'wi'° ye; fare ye well.
REYNALDO. Good my lord.
POLONIUS. Observe his inclination in yourself.°
REYNALDO. I shall, my lord.
POLONIUS. And let him ply his music.
REYNALDO. Well, my lord.
POLONIUS. Farewell.

*Exit Reynaldo.*

*Enter Ophelia.*

How now, Ophelia, what's the matter?
OPHELIA. O my lord, my lord, I have been so affrighted!
POLONIUS. With what, i' the name of God?
OPHELIA. My lord, as I was sewing in my closet,°
Lord Hamlet, with his doublet° all unbraced,°
No hat upon his head, his stockings fouled,
Ungartered, and down-gyvèd° to his ankle,
Pale as his shirt, his knees knocking each other,
And with a look so piteous in purport°
As if he had been loosèd out of hell
To speak of horrors—he comes before me.

**60 o'ertook in 's rouse** overcome by drink **61 falling out** quarreling **63 Videlicet** namely **64 carp** a fish **65 reach** capacity, ability **66 windlasses** i.e., circuitous paths. (Literally, circuits made to head off the game in hunting.) **assays of bias** attempts through indirection (like the curving path of the bowling ball, which is biased or weighted to one side) **67 directions** i.e., the way things really are **69 have** understand **70 b'wi'** be with **72 in yourself** in your own person (as well as by asking questions) **79 closet** private chamber **80 doublet** close-fitting jacket. **unbraced** unfastened **82 down-gyvèd** fallen to the ankles (like gyves or fetters) **84 in purport** in what it expressed

POLONIUS. Mad for thy love?
OPHELIA. My lord, I do not know,
But truly I do fear it.
POLONIUS. What said he?
OPHELIA. He took me by the wrist and held me hard.
Then goes he to the length of all his arm,
And, with his other hand thus o'er his brow
He falls to such perusal of my face
As° 'a would draw it. Long stayed he so.
At last, a little shaking of mine arm
And thrice his head thus waving up and down,
He raised a sigh so piteous and profound
As it did seem to shatter all his bulk°
And end his being. That done, he lets me go,
And with his head over his shoulder turned
He seemed to find his way without his eyes,
For out o' doors he went without their helps,
And to the last bended their light on me.
POLONIUS. Come, go with me. I will go seek the King.
This is the very ecstasy° of love,
Whose violent property° fordoes° itself
And leads the will to desperate undertakings
As oft as any passion under heaven
That does afflict our natures. I am sorry.
What, have you given him any hard words of late?
OPHELIA. No, my good lord, but as you did command
I did repel his letters and denied
His access to me.
POLONIUS. That hath made him mad.
I am sorry that with better heed and judgment
I had not quoted° him. I feared he did but trifle
And meant to wrack° thee. But beshrew my jealousy!°
By heaven, it is as proper to our age°
To cast beyond° ourselves in our opinions
As it is common for the younger sort
To lack discretion. Come, go we to the King.
This must be known,° which, being kept close,° might move
More grief to hide than hate to utter love.°
Come.
*Exeunt.*

**93 As** as if (also in line 97) **97 bulk** body **104 ecstasy** madness **105 property** nature **fordoes** destroys **114 quoted** observed **115 wrack** ruin, seduce **beshrew my jealousy** a plague upon my suspicious nature **116 proper . . . age** characteristic of us (old) men **117 cast beyond** overshoot, miscalculate. (A metaphor from hunting.) **120 known** made known (to the King). **close** secret **120–121 might . . . love** i.e., might cause more grief (because of what Hamlet might do) by hiding the knowledge of Hamlet's strange behavior to Ophelia than unpleasantness by telling it

**2.2** *Flourish. Enter King and Queen, Rosencrantz, and Guildenstern* [*with others*].

KING. Welcome, dear Rosencrantz and Guildenstern.
Moreover that° we much did long to see you,
The need we have to use you did provoke
Our hasty sending. Something have you heard
Of Hamlet's transformation—so call it,
Sith nor° th' exterior nor the inward man
Resembles that° it was. What it should be,
More than his father's death, that thus hath put him
So much from th' understanding of himself,
I cannot dream of. I entreat you both
That, being of so young days° brought up with him,
And sith so neighbored to° his youth and havior,°
That you vouchsafe your rest° here in our court
Some little time, so by your companies
To draw him on to pleasures, and to gather
So much as from occasion° you may glean,
Whether aught to us unknown afflicts him thus
That, opened,° lies within our remedy.
QUEEN. Good gentlemen, he hath much talked of you,
And sure I am two men there is not living
To whom he more adheres. If it will please you
To show us so much gentry° and good will
As to expend your time with us awhile
For the supply and profit of our hope,°
Your visitation shall receive such thanks
As fits a king's remembrance.°
ROSENCRANTZ. Both Your Majesties
Might, by the sovereign power you have of° us,
Put your dread° pleasures more into command
Than to entreaty.
GUILDENSTERN. But we both obey,
And here give up ourselves in the full bent°
To lay our service freely at your feet,
To be commanded.
KING. Thanks, Rosencrantz and gentle Guildenstern.
QUEEN. Thanks, Guildenstern and gentle Rosencrantz.
And I beseech you instantly to visit
My too much changèd son. Go, some of you,

**2.2 Location: The castle.** **2 Moreover that** besides the fact that **6 Sith nor** since neither **7 that** what **11 of . . . days** from such early youth **12 And sith so neighbored to** and since you are (or, and since that time you are) intimately acquainted with **havior** demeanor **13 vouchsafe your rest** please to stay **16 occasion** opportunity **18 opened** being revealed **22 gentry** courtesy **24 supply . . . hope** aid and furtherance of what we hope for **26 As fits . . . remembrance** as would be a fitting gift of a king who rewards true service **27 of** over **28 dread** inspiring awe **30 in . . . bent** to the utmost degree of our capacity. (An archery metaphor.)

And bring these gentlemen where Hamlet is.
GUILDENSTERN. Heavens make our presence and our practices°
Pleasant and helpful to him!
QUEEN. Ay, amen!
*Exeunt Rosencrantz and Guildenstern* [*with some attendants*].

*Enter Polonius.*

POLONIUS. Th' ambassadors from Norway, my good lord,
Are joyfully returned.
KING. Thou still° hast been the father of good news.
POLONIUS. Have I, my lord? I assure my good liege
I hold° my duty, as° I hold my soul,
Both to my God and to my gracious king;
And I do think, or else this brain of mine
Hunts not the trail of policy° so sure
As it hath used to do, that I have found
The very cause of Hamlet's lunacy.
KING. O, speak of that! That do I long to hear.
POLONIUS. Give first admittance to th' ambassadors.
My news shall be the fruit° to that great feast.
KING. Thyself do grace° to them and bring them in.
[*Exit Polonius.*]
He tells me, my dear Gertrude, he hath found
The head and source of all your son's distemper.
QUEEN. I doubt° it is no other but the main,°
His father's death and our o'erhasty marriage.

*Enter Ambassadors* [*Voltimand and Cornelius, with Polonius*].

KING. Well, we shall sift him.°—Welcome, my good friends!
Say, Voltimand, what from our brother° Norway?
VOLTIMAND. Most fair return of greetings and desires.°
Upon our first,° he sent out to suppress
His nephew's levies, which to him appeared
To be a preparation 'gainst the Polack,
But, better looked into, he truly found
It was against Your Highness. Whereat grieved
That so his sickness, age, and impotence°
Was falsely borne in hand,° sends out arrests°
On Fortinbras, which he, in brief, obeys,
Receives rebuke from Norway, and in fine°
Makes vow before his uncle never more
To give th' assay° of arms against Your Majesty.
Whereon old Norway, overcome with joy,

**38 practices** doings **42 still** always **44 hold** maintain **as** as firmly as **47 policy** sagacity **52 fruit** dessert **53 grace** honor (punning on *grace* said before a *feast,* line 52) **56 doubt** fear, suspect **main** chief point, principal concern **58 sift him** question Polonius closely **59 brother** fellow king **60 desires** good wishes **61 Upon our first** at our first words on the business **66 impotence** helplessness **67 borne in hand** deluded, taken advantage of **arrests** orders to desist **69 in fine** in conclusion **71 give th' assay** make trial of strength, challenge

Gives him three thousand crowns in annual fee
And his commission to employ those soldiers,
So levied as before, against the Polack,
With an entreaty, herein further shown, [*giving a paper*]
That it might please you to give quiet pass
Through your dominions for this enterprise
On such regards of safety and allowance°
As therein are set down.

KING. It likes° us well,
And at our more considered° time we'll read,
Answer, and think upon this business.
Meantime we thank you for your well-took labor.
Go to your rest; at night we'll feast together.
Most welcome home!

*Exeunt Ambassadors.*

POLONIUS. This business is well ended.
My liege, and madam, to expostulate°
What majesty should be, what duty is,
Why day is day, night night, and time is time,
Were nothing but to waste night, day, and time.
Therefore, since brevity is the soul of wit,°
And tediousness the limbs and outward flourishes,
I will be brief. Your noble son is mad.
Mad call I it, for, to define true madness,
What is 't but to be nothing else but mad?
But let that go.

QUEEN. More matter, with less art.

POLONIUS. Madam, I swear I use no art at all.
That he's mad, 'tis true; 'tis true 'tis pity,
And pity 'tis 'tis true—a foolish figure,°
But farewell it, for I will use no art.
Mad let us grant him, then, and now remains
That we find out the cause of this effect,
Or rather say, the cause of this defect,
For this effect defective comes by cause.°
Thus it remains, and the remainder thus.
Perpend.°
I have a daughter—have while she is mine—
Who, in her duty and obedience, mark,
Hath given me this. Now gather and surmise.°
[*He reads the letter.*] "To the celestial and my soul's idol, the most beautified Ophelia"—
That's an ill phrase, a vile phrase; "beautified" is a vile phrase. But you shall hear. Thus: [*He reads.*]

**79 On . . . allowance** i.e., with such considerations for the safety of Denmark and permission for Fortinbras **80 likes** pleases **81 considered** suitable for deliberation **86 expostulate** expound, inquire into **90 wit** sense or judgment **98 figure** figure of speech **103 For . . . cause** i.e., for this defective behavior, this madness, has a cause **105 Perpend** consider **108 gather and surmise** draw your own conclusions

"In her excellent white bosom,° these,° etc."

QUEEN. Came this from Hamlet to her?

POLONIUS. Good madam, stay° awhile, I will be faithful.° [*He reads.*]

"Doubt thou the stars are fire,
Doubt that the sun doth move,
Doubt° truth to be a liar,
But never doubt I love.

O dear Ophelia, I am ill at these numbers.° I have not art to reckon° my groans. But that I love thee best, O most best, believe it. Adieu.

Thine evermore, most dear lady, whilst this machine° is to him,
Hamlet."

This in obedience hath my daughter shown me,
And, more above,° hath his solicitings,
As they fell out° by° time, by means, and place,
All given to mine ear.°

KING. But how hath she
Received his love?

POLONIUS. What do you think of me?

KING. As of a man faithful and honorable.

POLONIUS. I would fain° prove so. But what might you think,
When I had seen this hot love on the wing—
As I perceived it, I must tell you that,
Before my daughter told me—what might you,
Or my dear Majesty your queen here, think,
If I had played the desk or table book,°
Or given my heart a winking,° mute and dumb,
Or looked upon this love with idle sight?°
What might you think? No, I went round° to work,
And my young mistress thus I did bespeak:°
"Lord Hamlet is a prince out of thy star;°
This must not be." And then I prescripts° gave her,
That she should lock herself from his resort,°
Admit no messengers, receive no tokens.
Which done, she took the fruits of my advice;
And he, repellèd—a short tale to make—
Fell into a sadness, then into a fast,
Thence to a watch,° thence into a weakness,
Thence to a lightness,° and by this declension°

**113 In . . . bosom** (The letter is poetically addressed to her heart.) **these** i.e., the letter **115 stay** wait **faithful** i.e., in reading the letter accurately **118 Doubt** suspect **120 ill . . . numbers** unskilled at writing verses **121 reckon** (1) count (2) number metrically, scan **123 machine** i.e., body **126 more above** moreover **127 fell out** occurred. **by** according to **128 given . . . ear** i.e., told me about **131 fain** gladly **136 played . . . table book** i.e., remained shut up, concealing the information **137 given . . . winking** closed the eyes of my heart to this **138 with idle sight** complacently or incomprehendingly **139 round** roundly, plainly **140 bespeak** address **141 out of thy star** above your sphere, position **142 prescripts** orders **143 his resort** his visits **148 watch** state of sleeplessness **149 lightness** lightheadedness **declension** decline, deterioration (with a pun on the grammatical sense)

Into the madness wherein now he raves,
And all we° mourn for.

KING [*to the Queen*]. Do you think 'tis this?

QUEEN. It may be, very like.

POLONIUS. Hath there been such a time—I would fain know that—
That I have positively said "'Tis so,"
When it proved otherwise?

KING. Not that I know.

POLONIUS. Take this from this,° if this be otherwise.
If circumstances lead me, I will find
Where truth is hid, though it were hid indeed
Within the center.°

KING. How may we try° it further?

POLONIUS. You know sometimes he walks four hours together
Here in the lobby.

QUEEN. So he does indeed.

POLONIUS. At such a time I'll loose° my daughter to him.
Be you and I behind an arras° then.
Mark the encounter. If he love her not
And be not from his reason fall'n thereon,°
Let me be no assistant for a state,
But keep a farm and carters.°

KING. We will try it.

*Enter Hamlet* [*reading on a book*].

QUEEN. But look where sadly° the poor wretch comes reading.

POLONIUS. Away, I do beseech you both, away.
I'll board° him presently.° O, give me leave.°

*Exeunt King and Queen* [*with attendants*].

How does my good Lord Hamlet?

HAMLET. Well, God-a-mercy.°

POLONIUS. Do you know me, my lord?

HAMLET. Excellent well. You are a fishmonger.°

POLONIUS. Not I, my lord.

HAMLET. Then I would you were so honest a man.

POLONIUS. Honest, my lord?

HAMLET. Ay, sir. To be honest, as this world goes, is to be one man picked out of ten thousand.

POLONIUS. That's very true, my lord.

HAMLET. For if the sun breed maggots in a dead dog, being a good kissing carrion°—Have you a daughter?

**151 all we** all of us, or, into everything that we **156 Take this from this** (The actor probably gestures, indicating that he means his head from his shoulders, or his staff of office or chain from his hands or neck, or something similar.) **159 center** middle point of the earth (which is also the center of the Ptolemaic universe) **try** test, judge **162 loose** (as one might release an animal that is being mated) **163 arras** hanging, tapestry **165 thereon** on that account **167 carters** wagon drivers **168 sadly** seriously **170 board** accost **presently** at once **give me leave** i.e., excuse me, leave me alone. (Said to those he hurries offstage, including the King and Queen.) **172 God-a-mercy** God have mercy, i.e., thank you **174 fishmonger** fish merchant **181–182 a good kissing carrion** i.e., a good piece of flesh for kissing, or for the sun to kiss

POLONIUS. I have, my lord.

HAMLET. Let her not walk i' the sun.° Conception° is a blessing, but as your daughter may conceive, friend, look to 't.

POLONIUS [*aside*]. How say you by that? Still harping on my daughter. Yet he knew me not at first; 'a° said I was a fishmonger. 'A is far gone. And truly in my youth I suffered much extremity for love, very near this. I'll speak to him again.—What do you read, my lord?

HAMLET. Words, words, words.

POLONIUS. What is the matter,° my lord?

HAMLET. Between who?

POLONIUS. I mean, the matter that you read, my lord.

HAMLET. Slanders, sir; for the satirical rogue says here that old men have gray beards, that their faces are wrinkled, their eyes purging° thick amber° and plum-tree gum, and that they have a plentiful lack of wit,° together with most weak hams. All which, sir, though I most powerfully and potently believe, yet I hold it not honesty° to have it thus set down, for yourself, sir, shall grow old° as I am, if like a crab you could go backward.

POLONIUS [*aside*]. Though this be madness, yet there is method in 't.—Will you walk out of the air,° my lord?

HAMLET. Into my grave.

POLONIUS. Indeed, that's out of the air. [*Aside*.] How pregnant° sometimes his replies are! A happiness° that often madness hits on, which reason and sanity could not so prosperously° be delivered of. I will leave him and suddenly° contrive the means of meeting between him and my daughter.—My honorable lord, I will most humbly take my leave of you.

HAMLET. You cannot, sir, take from me anything that I will more willingly part withal°—except my life, except my life, except my life.

*Enter Guildenstern and Rosencrantz.*

POLONIUS. Fare you well, my lord.

HAMLET. These tedious old fools!°

POLONIUS. You go to seek the Lord Hamlet. There he is.

ROSENCRANTZ [*to Polonius*]. God save you, sir!

[*Exit Polonius.*]

GUILDENSTERN. My honored lord!

ROSENCRANTZ. My most dear lord!

HAMLET. My excellent good friends! How dost thou, Guildenstern? Ah, Rosencrantz! Good lads, how do you both?

ROSENCRANTZ. As the indifferent° children of the earth.

**184 i' the sun** in public (with additional implication of the sunshine of princely favors) **Conception** (1) understanding (2) pregnancy **187 'a** he **191 matter** substance. (But Hamlet plays on the sense of "basis for a dispute.") **195 purging** discharging **196 amber** i.e., resin, like the resinous *plum-tree gum* **197 wit** understanding **198 honesty** decency, decorum **199 old** as old **202 out of the air** (The open air was considered dangerous for sick people.) **204 pregnant** quick-witted, full of meaning **205 happiness** felicity of expression **206 prosperously** successfully **207 suddenly** immediately **211 withal** with **213 old fools** i.e., old men like Polonius **220 indifferent** ordinary, at neither extreme of fortune or misfortune

GUILDENSTERN. Happy in that we are not overhappy.
On Fortune's cap we are not the very button.

HAMLET. Nor the soles of her shoe?

ROSENCRANTZ. Neither, my lord.

HAMLET. Then you live about her waist, or in the middle of her favors?°

GUILDENSTERN. Faith, her privates we.°

HAMLET. In the secret parts of Fortune? O, most true, she is a strumpet.° What news?

ROSENCRANTZ. None, my lord, but the world's grown honest.

HAMLET. Then is doomsday near. But your news is not true. Let me question more in particular. What have you, my good friends, deserved at the hands of Fortune that she sends you to prison hither?

GUILDENSTERN. Prison, my lord?

HAMLET. Denmark's a prison.

ROSENCRANTZ. Then is the world one.

HAMLET. A goodly one, in which there are many confines,° wards,° and dungeons, Denmark being one o' the worst.

ROSENCRANTZ. We think not so, my lord.

HAMLET. Why then 'tis none to you, for there is nothing either good or bad but thinking makes it so. To me it is a prison.

ROSENCRANTZ. Why then, your ambition makes it one. 'Tis too narrow for your mind.

HAMLET. O God, I could be bounded in a nutshell and count myself a king of infinite space, were it not that I have bad dreams.

GUILDENSTERN. Which dreams indeed are ambition, for the very substance of the ambitious° is merely the shadow of a dream.

HAMLET. A dream itself is but a shadow.

ROSENCRANTZ. Truly, and I hold ambition of so airy and light a quality that it is but a shadow's shadow.

HAMLET. Then are our beggars bodies,° and our monarchs and outstretched° heroes the beggars' shadows. Shall we to the court? For, by my fay,° I cannot reason.

ROSENCRANTZ, GUILDENSTERN. We'll wait upon° you.

HAMLET. No such matter. I will not sort° you with the rest of my servants, for, to speak to you like an honest man, I am most dreadfully attended.° But, in the beaten way° of friendship, what make° you at Elsinore?

ROSENCRANTZ. To visit you, my lord, no other occasion.

**225 favors** i.e., sexual favors **226 her privates we** i.e., (1) we are sexually intimate with Fortune, the fickle goddess who bestows her favors indiscriminately (2) we are her private citizens **227 strumpet** prostitute. (A common epithet for indiscriminate Fortune; see line 452.) **236 confines** places of confinement **wards** cells **245–246 the very . . . ambitious** that seemingly very substantial thing that the ambitious pursue **250 bodies** i.e., solid substances rather than shadows (since beggars are not ambitious) **250–251 outstretched** (1) far-reaching in their ambition (2) elongated as shadows **252 fay** faith **253 wait upon** accompany, attend. (But Hamlet uses the phrase in the sense of providing menial service.) **254 sort** class, categorize **255–256 dreadfully attended** waited upon in slovenly fashion **256 beaten way** familiar path, tried-and-true course **make** do

HAMLET. Beggar that I am, I am even poor in thanks; but I thank you, and sure, dear friends, my thanks are too dear a halfpenny.° Were you not sent for? Is it your own inclining? Is it a free° visitation? Come, come, deal justly with me. Come, come. Nay, speak.

GUILDENSTERN. What should we say, my lord?

HAMLET. Anything but to the purpose.° You were sent for, and there is a kind of confession in your looks which your modesties° have not craft enough to color.° I know the good King and Queen have sent for you.

ROSENCRANTZ. To what end, my lord?

HAMLET. That you must teach me. But let me conjure° you, by the rights of our fellowship, by the consonancy of our youth,° by the obligation of our ever-preserved love, and by what more dear a better° proposer could charge° you withal, be even° and direct with me whether you were sent for or no.

ROSENCRANTZ [*aside to Guildenstern*]. What say you?

HAMLET [*aside*]. Nay, then, I have an eye of° you.—If you love me, hold not off.°

GUILDENSTERN. My lord, we were sent for.

HAMLET. I will tell you why; so shall my anticipation prevent your discovery,° and your secrecy to the King and Queen molt no feather.° I have of late—but wherefore I know not—lost all my mirth, forgone all custom of exercises; and indeed it goes so heavily with my disposition that this goodly frame, the earth, seems to me a sterile promontory; this most excellent canopy, the air, look you, this brave° o'erhanging firmament, this majestical roof fretted° with golden fire, why, it appeareth nothing to me but a foul and pestilent congregation° of vapors. What a piece of work° is a man! How noble in reason, how infinite in faculties, in form and moving how express° and admirable, in action how like an angel, in apprehension° how like a god! The beauty of the world, the paragon of animals! And yet, to me, what is this quintessence° of dust? Man delights not me—no, nor woman neither, though by your smiling you seem to say so.

ROSENCRANTZ. My lord, there was no such stuff in my thoughts.

HAMLET. Why did you laugh, then, when I said man delights not me?

**260 too dear a halfpenny** (1) too expensive at even a halfpenny, i.e., of little worth (2) too expensive *by* a halfpenny in return for worthless kindness **261 free** voluntary **264 Anything but to the purpose** anything except a straightforward answer. (Said ironically.) **265 modesties** sense of shame **266 color** disguise **269 conjure** adjure, entreat **270 the consonancy of our youth** our closeness in our younger days **271 better** more skillful **272 charge** urge. **even** straight, honest **275 of** on **275–276 hold not off** don't hold back **278–279 so . . . discovery** in that way my saying it first will spare you from revealing the truth **279 molt no feather** i.e., not diminish in the least **284 brave** splendid **fretted** adorned (with fretwork, as in a vaulted ceiling) **286 congregation** mass. **piece of work** masterpiece **288 express** well-framed, exact, expressive **288–289 apprehension** power of comprehending **290 quintessence** the fifth essence of ancient philosophy, beyond earth, water, air, and fire, supposed to be the substance of the heavenly bodies and to be latent in all things

ROSENCRANTZ. To think, my lord, if you delight not in man, what Lenten entertainment° the players shall receive from you. We coted° them on the way, and hither are they coming to offer you service.

HAMLET. He that plays the king shall be welcome; His Majesty shall have tribute° of° me. The adventurous knight shall use his foil and target,° the lover shall not sigh gratis,° the humorous man° shall end his part in peace,° the clown shall make those laugh whose lungs are tickle o' the sear,° and the lady shall say her mind freely, or the blank verse shall halt° for 't. What players are they?

ROSENCRANTZ. Even those you were wont to take such delight in, the tragedians° of the city.

HAMLET. How chances it they travel? Their residence,° both in reputation and profit, was better both ways.

ROSENCRANTZ. I think their inhibition° comes by the means of the late° innovation.°

HAMLET. Do they hold the same estimation they did when I was in the city? Are they so followed?

ROSENCRANTZ. No, indeed are they not.

HAMLET. How comes it? Do they grow rusty?

ROSENCRANTZ. Nay, their endeavor keeps° in the wonted° pace. But there is, sir, an aerie° of children, little eyases,° that cry out on the top of question° and are most tyrannically° clapped for 't. These are now the fashion, and so berattle° the common stages°—so they call them—that many wearing rapiers° are afraid of goose quills° and dare scarce come thither.

HAMLET. What, are they children? Who maintains 'em? How are they escoted?° Will they pursue the quality° no longer than they can sing?° Will they not say afterwards, if they should grow themselves to common° players—as it is most like,° if their means are no better°—their writers do them wrong to make them exclaim against their own succession?°

**295–296 Lenten entertainment** meager reception (appropriate to Lent) **296 coted** overtook and passed by **299 tribute** (1) applause (2) homage paid in money. **of** from **299–300 foil and target** sword and shield **300 gratis** for nothing. **humorous man** eccentric character, dominated by one trait or "humor" **301 in peace** i.e., with full license **302 tickle o' the sear** easy on the trigger, ready to laugh easily. (A *sear* is part of a gunlock.) **303 halt** limp **305 tragedians** actors **306 residence** remaining in their usual place, i.e., in the city **308 inhibition** formal prohibition (from acting plays in the city) **late** recent **309 innovation** i.e., the new fashion in satirical plays performed by boy actors in the "private" theaters; or possibly a political uprising; or the strict limitations set on the theaters in London in 1600 **314 keeps** continues. **wonted** usual **315 aerie** nest. **eyases** young hawks **315–316 cry . . . question** speak shrilly, dominating the controversy (in decrying the public theaters) **316 tyrannically** outrageously **317 berattle** berate, clamor against **common stages** public theaters **318 many wearing rapiers** i.e., many men of fashion, afraid to patronize the common players for fear of being satirized by the poets writing for the boy actors **goose quills** i.e., pens of satirists **320–321 escoted** maintained **321 quality** (acting) profession **321–322 no longer . . . sing** i.e., only until their voices change **323 common** regular, adult **like** likely **323–324 if . . . better** if they find no better way to support themselves **325 succession** i.e., future careers

ROSENCRANTZ. Faith, there has been much to-do° on both sides, and the nation holds it no sin to tar° them to controversy. There was for a while no money bid for argument unless the poet and the player went to cuffs in the question.°

HAMLET. Is 't possible?

GUILDENSTERN. O, there has been much throwing about of brains.

HAMLET. Do the boys carry it away?°

ROSENCRANTZ. Ay, that they do, my lord—Hercules and his load° too.°

HAMLET. It is not very strange; for my uncle is King of Denmark, and those that would make mouths° at him while my father lived give twenty, forty, fifty, a hundred ducats° apiece for his picture in little.° 'Sblood,° there is something in this more than natural, if philosophy° could find it out.

*A flourish [of trumpets within].*

GUILDENSTERN. There are the players.

HAMLET. Gentlemen, you are welcome to Elsinore. Your hands, come then. Th' appurtenance° of welcome is fashion and ceremony. Let me comply° with you in this garb,° lest my extent° to the players, which, I tell you, must show fairly outwards,° should more appear like entertainment° than yours. You are welcome. But my uncle-father and aunt-mother are deceived.

GUILDENSTERN. In what, my dear lord?

HAMLET. I am but mad north-north-west.° When the wind is southerly I know a hawk from a handsaw.°

*Enter Polonius.*

POLONIUS. Well be with you, gentlemen!

HAMLET. Hark you, Guildenstern, and you too; at each ear a hearer. That great baby you see there is not yet out of his swaddling clouts.°

ROSENCRANTZ. Haply° he is the second time come to them, for they say an old man is twice a child.

HAMLET. I will prophesy he comes to tell me of the players. Mark it.—You say right, sir, o' Monday morning, 'twas then indeed.

**326 to-do** ado **327 tar** set on (as dogs) **327–329 There . . . question** i.e., for a while, no money was offered by the acting companies to playwrights for the plot to a play unless the satirical poets who wrote for the boys and the adult actors came to blows in the play itself **332 carry it away** i.e., win the day **333 Hercules . . . load** (Thought to be an allusion to the sign of the Globe Theatre, which was Hercules bearing the world on his shoulders.) **313–333 How . . . load too** (The passage, omitted from the early quartos, alludes to the so-called War of the Theaters, 1599–1602, the rivalry between the children's companies and the adult actors.) **335 mouths** faces **336 ducats** gold coins **336–337 in little** in miniature **337 'Sblood** by God's (Christ's) blood **338 philosophy** i.e., scientific inquiry **341 appurtenance** proper accompaniment **342 comply** observe the formalities of courtesy **garb** i.e., manner. **my extent** that which I extend, i.e., my polite behavior **343 show fairly outwards** show every evidence of cordiality **344 entertainment** a (warm) reception **347 north-north-west** just off true north, only partly **348 hawk, handsaw** i.e., two very different things, though also perhaps meaning a mattock (or *hack*) and a carpenter's cutting tool, respectively; also birds, with a play on *hernshaw,* or heron **351 swaddling clouts** cloths in which to wrap a newborn baby **352 Haply** perhaps

POLONIUS. My lord, I have news to tell you.
HAMLET. My lord, I have news to tell you. When Roscius° was an actor in Rome—
POLONIUS. The actors are come hither, my lord.
HAMLET. Buzz,° buzz!
POLONIUS. Upon my honor—
HAMLET. Then came each actor on his ass.
POLONIUS. The best actors in the world, either for tragedy, comedy, history, pastoral, pastoral-comical, historical-pastoral, tragical-historical, tragical-comical-historical-pastoral, scene individable,° or poem unlimited.° Seneca° cannot be too heavy, nor Plautus° too light. For the law of writ and the liberty,° these° are the only men.
HAMLET. O Jephthah, judge of Israel,° what a treasure hadst thou!
POLONIUS. What a treasure had he, my lord?
HAMLET. Why,
"One fair daughter, and no more,
The which he lovèd passing° well."
POLONIUS [*aside*]. Still on my daughter.
HAMLET. Am I not i' the right, old Jephthah?
POLONIUS. If you call me Jephthah, my lord, I have a daughter that I love passing well.
HAMLET. Nay, that follows not.
POLONIUS. What follows then, my lord?
HAMLET. Why,
"As by lot,° God wot,"°
and then, you know,
"It came to pass, as most like° it was"—
the first row° of the pious chanson° will show you more, for look where my abridgement° comes.
*Enter the Players.*

You are welcome, masters; welcome, all. I am glad to see thee well. Welcome, good friends. O, old friend! Why, thy face is valanced° since I saw thee last. Com'st thou to beard° me in Denmark? What, my young lady° and mistress! By 'r Lady,° your ladyship is nearer to heaven than when I saw you last, by the altitude of a chopine.° Pray God your voice, like a piece of uncurrent° gold, be not

**357 Roscius** a famous Roman actor who died in 62 B.C. **360 Buzz** (An interjection used to denote stale news.) **365 scene individable** a play observing the unity of place; or perhaps one that is unclassifiable, or performed without intermission **366 poem unlimited** a play disregarding the unities of time and place; one that is all-inclusive **Seneca** writer of Latin tragedies **Plautus** writer of Latin comedy **367 law . . . liberty** dramatic composition both according to the rules and disregarding the rules **these** i.e., the actors **368 Jephthah . . . Israel** (Jephthah had to sacrifice his daughter; see Judges 11. Hamlet goes on to quote from a ballad on the theme.) **372 passing** surpassingly **380 lot** chance **wot** knows **382 like** likely, probable **383 row** stanza. **chanson** ballad, song **384 my abridgement** something that cuts short my conversation; also, a diversion **386 valanced** fringed (with a beard) **387 beard** confront, challenge (with obvious pun) **388 young lady** i.e., boy playing women's parts **By 'r Lady** by Our Lady **389 chopine** thick-soled shoe of Italian fashion **390 uncurrent** not passable as lawful coinage

cracked within the ring.° Masters, you are all welcome. We'll e'en to 't° like French falconers, fly at anything we see. We'll have a speech straight.° Come, give us a taste of your quality.° Come, a passionate speech.

FIRST PLAYER. What speech, my good lord?

HAMLET. I heard thee speak me a speech once, but it was never acted, or if it was, not above once, for the play, I remember, pleased not the million; 'twas caviar to the general.° But it was—as I received it, and others, whose judgments in such matters cried in the top of° mine—an excellent play, well digested° in the scenes, set down with as much modesty° as cunning.° I remember one said there were no sallets° in the lines to make the matter savory, nor no matter in the phrase that might indict° the author of affectation, but called it an honest method, as wholesome as sweet, and by very much more handsome° than fine.° One speech in 't I chiefly loved: 'twas Aeneas' tale to Dido, and thereabout of it especially when he speaks of Priam's slaughter.° If it live in your memory, begin at this line: let me see, let me see—

"The rugged Pyrrhus,° like th' Hyrcanian° beast"—
'Tis not so. It begins with Pyrrhus:
"The rugged° Pyrrhus, he whose sable° arms,
Black as his purpose, did the night resemble
When he lay couchèd° in the ominous horse,°
Hath now this dread and black complexion smeared
With heraldry more dismal.° Head to foot
Now is he total gules,° horridly tricked°
With blood of fathers, mothers, daughters, sons,
Baked and impasted° with the parching streets,°
That lend a tyrannous° and a damnèd light
To their lord's° murder. Roasted in wrath and fire,

**391 cracked . . . ring** i.e., changed from adolescent to male voice, no longer suitable for women's roles. (Coins featured rings enclosing the sovereign's head; if the coin was cracked within this ring, it was unfit for currency.) **391–392 e'en to 't** go at it **393 straight** at once **quality** professional skill **398 caviar to the general** caviar to the multitude, i.e., a choice dish too elegant for coarse tastes **399 cried in the top of** i.e., spoke with greater authority than **400 digested** arranged, ordered **401 modesty** moderation, restraint **cunning** skill **402 sallets** i.e., something savory, spicy improprieties **403 indict** convict **405 handsome** well-proportioned. **fine** elaborately ornamented, showy **407 Priam's slaughter** the slaying of the ruler of Troy, when the Greeks finally took the city **409 Pyrrhus** a Greek hero in the Trojan War, also known as Neoptolemus, son of Achilles—another avenging son **Hyrcanian beast** i.e., tiger. (On the death of Priam, see Virgil, *Aeneid,* 2.506 ff.; compare the whole speech with Marlowe's *Dido Queen of Carthage,* 2.1.214 ff. On the *Hyrcanian* tiger, see *Aeneid,* 4.366–367. Hyrcania is on the Caspian Sea.) **411 rugged** shaggy, savage **sable** black (for reasons of camouflage during the episode of the Trojan horse) **413 couchèd** concealed **ominous horse** fateful Trojan horse, by which the Greeks gained access to Troy **415 dismal** ill-omened **416 total gules** entirely red. (A heraldic term.) **tricked** spotted and smeared. (Heraldic.) **418 impasted** crusted, like a thick paste **with . . . streets** by the parching heat of the streets (because of the fires everywhere) **419 tyrannous** cruel **420 their lord's** i.e., Priam's

And thus o'ersizèd° with coagulate gore,
With eyes like carbuncles,° the hellish Pyrrhus
Old grandsire Priam seeks."
So proceed you.

POLONIUS. 'Fore God, my lord, well spoken, with good accent and good discretion.

FIRST PLAYER. "Anon he finds him
Striking too short at Greeks. His antique° sword,
Rebellious to his arm, lies where it falls,
Repugnant° to command. Unequal matched,
Pyrrhus at Priam drives, in rage strikes wide,
But with the whiff and wind of his fell° sword
Th' unnervèd° father falls. Then senseless Ilium,°
Seeming to feel this blow, with flaming top
Stoops to his° base, and with a hideous crash
Takes prisoner Pyrrhus' ear. For, lo! His sword,
Which was declining° on the milky° head
Of reverend Priam, seemed i' th' air to stick.
So as a painted° tyrant Pyrrhus stood,
And, like a neutral to his will and matter,°
Did nothing.
But as we often see against° some storm
A silence in the heavens, the rack° stand still,
The bold winds speechless, and the orb° below
As hush as death, anon the dreadful thunder
Doth rend the region,° so, after Pyrrhus' pause,
A rousèd vengeance sets him new a-work
And never did the Cyclops'° hammers fall
On Mars's armor forged for proof eterne°
With less remorse° than Pyrrhus' bleeding sword
Now falls on Priam.
Out, out, thou strumpet Fortune! All you gods
In general synod° take away her power!
Break all the spokes and fellies° from her wheel,
And bowl the round nave° down the hill of heaven°
As low as to the fiends!"

POLONIUS. This is too long.

HAMLET. It shall to the barber's with your beard.—Prithee, say on. He's for a jig° or a tale of bawdry, or he sleeps. Say on; come to Hecuba.°

**421 o'ersizèd** covered as with size or glue **422 carbuncles** large fiery-red precious stones thought to emit their own light **428 antique** ancient, long-used **430 Repugnant** disobedient, resistant **432 fell** cruel **433 unnervèd** strengthless **senseless Ilium** inanimate citadel of Troy **435 his** its **437 declining** descending **milky** white-haired **439 painted** i.e., painted in a picture **440 like . . . matter** i.e., as though suspended between his intention and its fulfillment **442 against** just before **443 rack** mass of clouds **444 orb** globe, earth **446 region** sky **448 Cyclops** giant armor makers in the smithy of Vulcan **449 proof eterne** eternal resistance to assault **450 remorse** pity **453 synod** assembly **454 fellies** pieces of wood forming the rim of a wheel **455 nave** hub **hill of heaven** Mount Olympus **459 jig** comic song and dance often given at the end of a play **460 Hecuba** wife of Priam

FIRST PLAYER. "But who, ah woe! had° seen the moblèd° queen"—
HAMLET. "The moblèd queen?"
POLONIUS. That's good. "Moblèd queen" is good.
FIRST PLAYER. "Run barefoot up and down, threat'ning the flames°
With bisson rheum,° a clout° upon that head
Where late° the diadem stood, and, for a robe,
About her lank and all o'erteemèd° loins
A blanket, in the alarm of fear caught up—
Who this had seen, with tongue in venom steeped,
'Gainst Fortune's state° would treason have pronounced.°
But if the gods themselves did see her then
When she saw Pyrrhus make malicious sport
In mincing with his sword her husband's limbs,
The instant burst of clamor that she made,
Unless things mortal move them not at all,
Would have made milch° the burning eyes of heaven,°
And passion° in the gods."

POLONIUS. Look whe'er° he has not turned his color and has tears in 's eyes. Prithee, no more.

HAMLET. 'Tis well; I'll have thee speak out the rest of this soon.—Good my lord, will you see the players well bestowed?° Do you hear, let them be well used, for they are the abstract° and brief chronicles of the time. After your death you were better have a bad epitaph than their ill report while you live.

POLONIUS. My lord, I will use them according to their desert.

HAMLET. God's bodikin,° man, much better. Use every man after his desert, and who shall scape whipping? Use them after° your own honor and dignity. The less they deserve, the more merit is in your bounty. Take them in.

POLONIUS. Come, sirs.

[*Exit.*]

HAMLET. Follow him, friends. We'll hear a play tomorrow. [*As they start to leave, Hamlet detains the First Player.*] Dost thou hear me, old friend? Can you play *The Murder of Gonzago?*

FIRST PLAYER. Ay, my lord.

HAMLET. We'll ha 't° tomorrow night. You could, for a need, study° a speech of some dozen or sixteen lines which I would set down and insert in 't, could you not?

FIRST PLAYER. Ay, my lord.

HAMLET. Very well. Follow that lord, and look you mock him not. (*Exeunt Players.*) My good friends, I'll leave you till night. You are welcome to Elsinore.

**461 who . . . had** anyone who had (also in line 469) **moblèd** muffled **464 threat'ning the flames** i.e., weeping hard enough to dampen the flames **465 bisson rheum** blinding tears **clout** cloth **466 late** lately **467 all o'erteemèd** utterly worn out with bearing children **470 state** rule, managing **pronounced** proclaimed **476 milch** milky, moist with tears **burning eyes of heaven** i.e., heavenly bodies **477 passion** overpowering emotion **478 whe'er** whether **481 bestowed** lodged **482 abstract** summary account **486 God's bodikin** by God's (Christ's) little body, *bodykin.* (Not to be confused with *bodkin,* "dagger.") **487 after** according to **495 ha 't** have it **study** memorize

ROSENCRANTZ. Good my lord!

*Exeunt* [*Rosencrantz and Guildenstern*].

HAMLET. Ay, so, goodbye to you.—Now I am alone.
O, what a rogue and peasant slave am I!
Is it not monstrous that this player here,
But° in a fiction, in a dream of passion,
Could force his soul so to his own conceit°
That from her working° all his visage wanned,°
Tears in his eyes, distraction in his aspect,°
A broken voice, and his whole function suiting
With forms to his conceit?° And all for nothing!
For Hecuba!
What's Hecuba to him, or he to Hecuba,
That he should weep for her? What would he do
Had he the motive and the cue for passion
That I have? He would drown the stage with tears
And cleave the general ear° with horrid° speech,
Make mad the guilty and appall° the free,°
Confound the ignorant,° and amaze° indeed
The very faculties of eyes and ears. Yet I,
A dull and muddy-mettled° rascal, peak°
Like John-a-dreams,° unpregnant of° my cause,
And can say nothing—no, not for a king
Upon whose property° and most dear life
A damned defeat° was made. Am I a coward?
Who calls me villain? Breaks my pate° across?
Plucks off my beard and blows it in my face?
Tweaks me by the nose? Gives me the lie i' the throat°
As deep as to the lungs? Who does me this?
Ha, 'swounds,° I should take it; for it cannot be
But I am pigeon-livered° and lack gall
To make oppression bitter,° or ere this
I should ha' fatted all the region kites°
With this slave's offal.° Bloody, bawdy villain!
Remorseless,° treacherous, lecherous, kindless° villain!
O, vengeance!

**506 But** merely **507 force . . . conceit** bring his innermost being so entirely into accord with his conception (of the role) **508 from her working** as a result of, or in response to, his soul's activity **wanned** grew pale **509 aspect** look, glance **510–511 his whole . . . conceit** all his bodily powers responding with actions to suit his thought **517 the general ear** everyone's ear **horrid** horrible **518 appall** (Literally, make pale.) **free** innocent **519 Confound the ignorant** i.e., dumbfound those who know nothing of the crime that has been committed **amaze** stun **521 muddy-mettled** dull-spirited **peak** mope, pine **522 John-a-dreams** a sleepy, dreaming idler **unpregnant of** not quickened by **524 property** i.e., the crown; also character, quality **525 damned defeat** damnable act of destruction **526 pate** head **528 Gives . . . throat** calls me an out-and-out liar **530 'swounds** by his (Christ's) wounds **531 pigeon-livered** (The pigeon or dove was popularly supposed to be mild because it secreted no gall.) **532 bitter** i.e., bitter to me **533 region kites** kites (birds of prey) of the air **534 offal** entrails **535 Remorseless** pitiless **kindless** unnatural

Why, what an ass am I! This is most brave,°
That I, the son of a dear father murdered,
Prompted to my revenge by heaven and hell,
Must like a whore unpack my heart with words
And fall a-cursing, like a very drab,°
A scullion!° Fie upon 't, foh! About,° my brains!
Hum, I have heard
That guilty creatures sitting at a play
Have by the very cunning° of the scene°
Been struck so to the soul that presently°
They have proclaimed their malefactions;
For murder, though it have no tongue, will speak
With most miraculous organ. I'll have these players
Play something like the murder of my father
Before mine uncle. I'll observe his looks;
I'll tent° him to the quick.° If 'a do blench,°
I know my course. The spirit that I have seen
May be the devil, and the devil hath power
T' assume a pleasing shape; yea, and perhaps,
Out of my weakness and my melancholy,
As he is very potent with such spirits,°
Abuses° me to damn me. I'll have grounds
More relative° than this. The play's the thing
Wherein I'll catch the conscience of the King.
*Exit.*

**3.1** *Enter King, Queen, Polonius, Ophelia, Rosencrantz, Guildenstern, lords.*

KING. And can you by no drift of conference°
Get from him why he puts on this confusion,
Grating so harshly all his days of quiet
With turbulent and dangerous lunacy?
ROSENCRANTZ. He does confess he feels himself distracted,
But from what cause 'a will by no means speak.
GUILDENSTERN. Nor do we find him forward° to be sounded,°
But with a crafty madness keeps aloof
When we would bring him on to some confession
Of his true state.
QUEEN. Did he receive you well?
ROSENCRANTZ. Most like a gentleman.

**537 brave** fine, admirable. (Said ironically.) **541 drab** whore **542 scullion** menial kitchen servant (apt to be foulmouthed) **About** about it, to work **545 cunning** art, skill **scene** dramatic presentation **546 presently** at once **552 tent** probe **the quick** the tender part of a wound, the core **blench** quail, flinch **557 spirits** humors (of melancholy) **558 Abuses** deludes **559 relative** cogent, pertinent

**3.1 Location: The castle. 1 drift of conference** directing of conversation **7 forward** willing **sounded** questioned

GUILDENSTERN. But with much forcing of his disposition.°
ROSENCRANTZ. Niggard° of question,° but of our demands
Most free in his reply.
QUEEN. Did you assay° him
To any pastime?
ROSENCRANTZ. Madam, it so fell out that certain players
We o'erraught° on the way. Of these we told him,
And there did seem in him a kind of joy
To hear of it. They are here about the court,
And, as I think, they have already order
This night to play before him.
POLONIUS. 'Tis most true,
And he beseeched me to entreat Your Majesties
To hear and see the matter.
KING. With all my heart, and it doth much content me
To hear him so inclined.
Good gentlemen, give him a further edge°
And drive his purpose into these delights.
ROSENCRANTZ. We shall, my lord.

*Exeunt Rosencrantz and Guildenstern.*

KING. Sweet Gertrude, leave us too,
For we have closely° sent for Hamlet hither,
That he, as 'twere by accident, may here
Affront° Ophelia.
Her father and myself, lawful espials,°
Will so bestow ourselves that seeing, unseen,
We may of their encounter frankly judge,
And gather by him, as he is behaved,
If 't be th' affliction of his love or no
That thus he suffers for.
QUEEN. I shall obey you.
And for your part, Ophelia, I do wish
That your good beauties be the happy cause
Of Hamlet's wildness. So shall I hope your virtues
Will bring him to his wonted° way again,
To both your honors.
OPHELIA. Madam, I wish it may.

[*Exit Queen.*]

POLONIUS. Ophelia, walk you here.—Gracious,° so please you,
We will bestow° ourselves. [*To Ophelia.*] Read on this book,
[*giving her a book*]
That show of such an exercise° may color°
Your loneliness.° We are oft to blame in this—

**12 disposition** inclination **13 Niggard** stingy **question** conversation **14 assay** try to win **17 o'erraught** overtook **26 edge** incitement **29 closely** privately **31 Affront** confront, meet **32 espials** spies **41 wonted** accustomed **43 Gracious** Your Grace (i.e., the King) **44 bestow** conceal **45 exercise** religious exercise. (The book she reads is one of devotion.) **color** give a plausible appearance to **46 loneliness** being alone

'Tis too much proved°—that with devotion's visage
And pious action we do sugar o'er
The devil himself.

KING [*aside*]. O, 'tis too true!
How smart a lash that speech doth give my conscience!
The harlot's cheek, beautied with plastering art,
Is not more ugly to° the thing° that helps it
Than is my deed to my most painted word.
O heavy burden!

POLONIUS. I hear him coming. Let's withdraw, my lord.
[*The King and Polonius withdraw.*°]

*Enter Hamlet.* [*Ophelia pretends to read a book.*]

HAMLET. To be, or not to be, that is the question:
Whether 'tis nobler in the mind to suffer
The slings° and arrows of outrageous fortune,
Or to take arms against a sea of troubles
And by opposing end them. To die, to sleep—
No more—and by a sleep to say we end
The heartache and the thousand natural shocks
That flesh is heir to. 'Tis a consummation
Devoutly to be wished. To die, to sleep;
To sleep, perchance to dream. Ay, there's the rub,°
For in that sleep of death what dreams may come,
When we have shuffled° off this mortal coil,°
Must give us pause. There's the respect°
That makes calamity of so long life.°
For who would bear the whips and scorns of time,
Th' oppressor's wrong, the proud man's contumely,°
The pangs of disprized° love, the law's delay,
The insolence of office,° and the spurns°
That patient merit of th' unworthy takes,°
When he himself might his quietus° make
With a bare bodkin?° Who would fardels° bear,
To grunt and sweat under a weary life,
But that the dread of something after death,
The undiscovered country from whose bourn°
No traveler returns, puzzles the will,
And makes us rather bear those ills we have

**47 too much proved** too often shown to be true, too often practiced **53 to** compared to **the thing** i.e., the cosmetic **56 s.d. withdraw** (The King and Polonius may retire behind an arras. The stage directions specify that they "enter" again near the end of the scene.) **59 slings** missiles **66 rub** (Literally, an obstacle in the game of bowls.) **68 shuffled** sloughed, cast **coil** turmoil **69 respect** consideration **70 of . . . life** so long-lived, something we willingly endure for so long (also suggesting that long life is itself a calamity) **72 contumely** insolent abuse **73 disprized** unvalued **74 office** officialdom **spurns** insults **75 of . . . takes** receives from unworthy persons **76 quietus** acquittance; here, death **77 a bare bodkin** a mere dagger, unsheathed **fardels** burdens **80 bourn** frontier, boundary

Than fly to others that we know not of?
Thus conscience does make cowards of us all;
And thus the native hue° of resolution
Is sicklied o'er with the pale cast° of thought,
And enterprises of great pitch° and moment°
With this regard° their currents° turn awry
And lose the name of action.—Soft you° now,
The fair Ophelia. Nymph, in thy orisons°
Be all my sins remembered.

OPHELIA. Good my lord,
How does your honor for this many a day?

HAMLET. I humbly thank you; well, well, well.

OPHELIA. My lord, I have remembrances of yours,
That I have longèd long to redeliver.
I pray you, now receive them. [*She offers tokens.*]

HAMLET. No, not I, I never gave you aught.

OPHELIA. My honored lord, you know right well you did,
And with them words of so sweet breath composed
As made the things more rich. Their perfume lost,
Take these again, for to the noble mind
Rich gifts wax poor when givers prove unkind.
There, my lord. [*She gives tokens.*]

HAMLET. Ha, ha! Are you honest?°

OPHELIA. My lord?

HAMLET. Are you fair?°

OPHELIA. What means your lordship?

HAMLET. That if you be honest and fair, your honesty° should admit no discourse° to your beauty.

OPHELIA. Could beauty, my lord, have better commerce° than with honesty?

HAMLET. Ay, truly, for the power of beauty will sooner transform honesty from what it is to a bawd than the force of honesty can translate beauty into his° likeness. This was sometime° a paradox,° but now the time° gives it proof. I did love you once.

OPHELIA. Indeed, my lord, you made me believe so.

HAMLET. You should not have believed me, for virtue cannot so inoculate° our old stock but we shall relish of it.° I loved you not.

OPHELIA. I was the more deceived.

HAMLET. Get thee to a nunnery.° Why wouldst thou be a breeder of sinners? I am myself indifferent honest,° but yet I could accuse me of

**85 native hue** natural color, complexion **86 cast** tinge, shade of color **87 pitch** height (as of a falcon's flight) **moment** importance **88 regard** respect, consideration **currents** courses **89 Soft you** i.e., wait a minute, gently **90 orisons** prayers **104 honest** (1) truthful (2) chaste **106 fair** (1) beautiful (2) just, honorable **108 your honesty** your chastity **109 discourse to** familiar dealings with **110 commerce** dealings, intercourse **114 his** its **sometime** formerly **a paradox** a view opposite to commonly held opinion **115 the time** the present age **117–118 inoculate** graft, be engrafted to **118 but . . . it** that we do not still have about us a taste of the old stock, i.e., retain our sinfulness **120 nunnery** convent (with possibly an awareness that the word was also used derisively to denote a brothel) **121 indifferent honest** reasonably virtuous

such things that it were better my mother had not borne me: I am very proud, revengeful, ambitious, with more offenses at my beck° than I have thoughts to put them in, imagination to give them shape, or time to act them in. What should such fellows as I do crawling between earth and heaven? We are arrant knaves all; believe none of us. Go thy ways to a nunnery. Where's your father?

OPHELIA. At home, my lord.

HAMLET. Let the doors be shut upon him, that he may play the fool nowhere but in 's own house. Farewell.

OPHELIA. O, help him, you sweet heavens!

HAMLET. If thou dost marry, I'll give thee this plague for thy dowry: be thou as chaste as ice, as pure as snow, thou shalt not escape calumny. Get thee to a nunnery, farewell. Or, if thou wilt needs marry, marry a fool, for wise men know well enough what monsters° you° make of them. To a nunnery, go, and quickly too. Farewell.

OPHELIA. Heavenly powers, restore him!

HAMLET. I have heard of your paintings too, well enough. God hath given you one face, and you make yourselves another. You jig,° you amble,° and you lisp, you nickname God's creatures,° and make your wantonness your ignorance.° Go to, I'll no more on 't;° it hath made me mad. I say we will have no more marriage. Those that are married already—all but one—shall live. The rest shall keep as they are. To a nunnery, go.

*Exit.*

OPHELIA. O, what a noble mind is here o'erthrown!
The courtier's, soldier's, scholar's, eye, tongue, sword,
Th' expectancy° and rose° of the fair state,
The glass of fashion and the mold of form,°
Th' observed of all observers,° quite, quite down!
And I, of ladies most deject and wretched,
That sucked the honey of his music° vows,
Now see that noble and most sovereign reason
Like sweet bells jangled out of tune and harsh,
That unmatched form and feature of blown° youth
Blasted° with ecstasy.° O, woe is me,
T' have seen what I have seen, see what I see!

*Enter King and Polonius.*

KING. Love? His affections° do not that way tend;
Nor what he spake, though it lacked form a little,
Was not like madness. There's something in his soul

**123 beck** command **135–136 monsters** (An illusion to the horns of a cuckold.) **you** i.e., you women **140 jig** dance **141 amble** move coyly **you nickname . . . creatures** i.e., you give trendy names to things in place of their God-given names **142 make . . . ignorance** i.e., excuse your affectation on the grounds of pretended ignorance **on 't** of it **148 expectancy** hope **rose** ornament **149 The glass . . . form** the mirror of true fashioning and the pattern of courtly behavior **150 Th' observed . . . observers** i.e., the center of attention and honor in the court **152 music** musical, sweetly uttered **155 blown** blooming **156 Blasted** withered **ecstasy** madness **158 affections** emotions, feelings

O'er which his melancholy sits on brood,°
And I do doubt° the hatch and the disclose°
Will be some danger; which for to prevent,
I have in quick determination
Thus set it down:° he shall with speed to England
For the demand of° our neglected tribute.
Haply the seas and countries different
With variable objects° shall expel
This something-settled matter in his heart,°
Whereon his brains still° beating puts him thus
From fashion of himself.° What think you on 't?

POLONIUS. It shall do well. But yet do I believe
The origin and commencement of his grief
Sprung from neglected love.—How now, Ophelia?
You need not tell us what Lord Hamlet said;
We heard it all.—My lord, do as you please,
But, if you hold it fit, after the play
Let his queen-mother° all alone entreat him
To show his grief. Let her be round° with him;
And I'll be placed, so please you, in the ear
Of all their conference. If she find him not,°
To England send him, or confine him where
Your wisdom best shall think.

KING. It shall be so.
Madness in great ones must not unwatched go.

*Exeunt.*

## 3.2 *Enter Hamlet and three of the Players.*

HAMLET. Speak the speech, I pray you, as I pronounced it to you, trippingly on the tongue. But if you mouth it, as many of our players° do, I had as lief° the town crier spoke my lines. Nor do not saw the air too much with your hand, thus, but use all gently; for in the very torrent, tempest, and, as I may say, whirlwind of your passion, you must acquire and beget a temperance that may give it smoothness. O, it offends me to the soul to hear a robustious° periwig-pated° fellow tear a passion to tatters, to very rags, to split the ears of the groundlings,° who for the most part are capable of° nothing but in-

**161 sits on brood** sits like a bird on a nest, about to *hatch* mischief (line 162) **162 doubt** fear **disclose** disclosure, hatching **165 set it down** resolved **166 For . . . of** to demand **168 variable objects** various sights and surroundings to divert him **169 This something . . . heart** the strange matter settled in his heart **170 still** continually **171 From . . . himself** out of his natural manner **178 queen-mother** queen and mother **179 round** blunt **181 find him not** fails to discover what is troubling him

**3.2 Location: The castle. 2 our players** players nowadays **3 I had as lief** I would just as soon **7 robustious** violent, boisterous **periwig-pated** wearing a wig **9 groundlings** spectators who paid least and stood in the yard of the theater **capable of** able to understand

explicable dumb shows° and noise. I would have such a fellow whipped for o'erdoing Termagant.° It out-Herods Herod.° Pray you, avoid it.

FIRST PLAYER. I warrant your honor.

HAMLET. Be not too tame neither, but let your own discretion be your tutor. Suit the action to the word, the word to the action, with this special observance, that you o'erstep not the modesty° of nature. For anything so o'erdone is from° the purpose of playing, whose end, both at the first and now, was and is to hold as 't were the mirror up to nature, to show virtue her feature, scorn° her own image, and the very age and body of the time° his° form and pressure.° Now this overdone or come tardy off,° though it makes the unskillful° laugh, cannot but make the judicious grieve, the censure of the which one° must in your allowance° o'erweigh a whole theater of others. O, there be players that I have seen play, and heard others praise, and that highly, not to speak it profanely,° that, neither having th' accent of Christians° nor the gait of Christian, pagan, nor man,° have so strutted and bellowed that I have thought some of nature's journeymen° had made men and not made them well, they imitated humanity so abominably.°

FIRST PLAYER. I hope we have reformed that indifferently° with us, sir.

HAMLET. O, reform it altogether. And let those that play your clowns speak no more than is set down for them; for there be of them° that will themselves laugh, to set on some quantity of barren° spectators to laugh too, though in the meantime some necessary question of the play be then to be considered. That's villainous, and shows a most pitiful ambition in the fool that uses it. Go make you ready.

[*Exeunt Players.*]

*Enter Polonius, Guildenstern, and Rosencrantz.*

How now, my lord, will the King hear this piece of work?

POLONIUS. And the Queen too, and that presently.°

HAMLET. Bid the players make haste.

[*Exit Polonius.*]

**10 dumb shows** mimed performances, often used before Shakespeare's time to precede a play or each act **11 Termagant** a supposed deity of the Mohammedans, not found in any English medieval play but elsewhere portrayed as violent and blustering **Herod** Herod of Jewry. (A character in *The Slaughter of the Innocents* and other cycle plays. The part was played with great noise and fury.) **16 modesty** restraint, moderation **17 from** contrary to **19 scorn** i.e., something foolish and deserving of scorn **20 the very . . . time** i.e., the present state of affairs **his** its **20–21 pressure** stamp, impressed character **21 come tardy off** inadequately done **21–22 the unskillful** those lacking in judgment **22–23 the censure . . . one** the judgment of even one of whom **23 your allowance** your scale of values **25 not . . . profanely** (Hamlet anticipates his idea in lines 27–29 that some men were not made by God at all.) **26 Christians** i.e., ordinary decent folk **27 nor man** i.e., nor any human being at all **28 journeymen** laborers who are not yet masters in their trade **29 abominably** (Shakespeare's usual spelling, *abhominably,* suggests a literal though etymologically incorrect meaning, "removed from human nature.") **30 indifferently** tolerably **32 of them** some among them **33 barren** i.e., of wit **39 presently** at once

Will you two help to hasten them?

ROSENCRANTZ. Ay, my lord.

*Exeunt they two.*

HAMLET. What ho, Horatio!

*Enter Horatio.*

HORATIO. Here, sweet lord, at your service.

HAMLET. Horatio, thou art e'en as just a man
As e'er my conversation coped withal.°

HORATIO. O, my dear lord—

HAMLET. Nay, do not think I flatter,
For what advancement may I hope from thee
That no revenue hast but thy good spirits
To feed and clothe thee? Why should the poor be flattered?
No, let the candied° tongue lick absurd pomp,
And crook the pregnant° hinges of the knee
Where thrift° may follow fawning. Dost thou hear?
Since my dear soul was mistress of her choice
And could of men distinguish her election,°
Sh' hath sealed thee° for herself, for thou hast been
As one, in suffering all, that suffers nothing,
A man that Fortune's buffets and rewards
Hast ta'en with equal thanks; and blest are those
Whose blood° and judgment are so well commeddled°
That they are not a pipe for Fortune's finger
To sound what stop° she please. Give me that man
That is not passion's slave, and I will wear him
In my heart's core, ay, in my heart of heart,
As I do thee.—Something too much of this.—
There is a play tonight before the King.
One scene of it comes near the circumstance
Which I have told thee of my father's death.
I prithee, when thou seest that act afoot,
Even with the very comment of thy soul°
Observe my uncle. If his occulted° guilt
Do not itself unkennel° in one speech,
It is a damnèd° ghost that we have seen,
And my imaginations are as foul
As Vulcan's stithy.° Give him heedful note,
For I mine eyes will rivet to his face,
And after we will both our judgments join
In censure of his seeming.°

**45 my . . . withal** my dealings encountered **50 candied** sugared, flattering **51 pregnant** compliant **52 thrift** profit **54 could . . . election** could make distinguishing choices among persons **55 sealed thee** (Literally, as one would seal a legal document to mark possession.) **59 blood** passion **commeddled** commingled **61 stop** hole in a wind instrument for controlling the sound **69 very . . . soul** your most penetrating observation and consideration **70 occulted** hidden **71 unkennel** (As one would say of a fox driven from its lair.) **72 damnèd** in league with Satan **74 stithy** smithy, place of stiths (anvils) **77 censure of his seeming** judgment of his appearance or behavior

HORATIO. Well, my lord.
If 'a steal aught° the whilst this play is playing
And scape detecting, I will pay the theft.

*[Flourish.] Enter trumpets and kettledrums, King, Queen, Polonius, Ophelia, [Rosencrantz, Guildenstern, and other lords, with guards carrying torches].*

HAMLET. They are coming to the play. I must be idle.°
Get you a place. *[The King, Queen, and courtiers sit.]*
KING. How fares our cousin° Hamlet?
HAMLET. Excellent, i' faith, of the chameleon's dish:° I eat the air, promise-crammed. You cannot feed capons° so.
KING. I have nothing with° this answer, Hamlet. These words are not mine.°
HAMLET. No, nor mine now.° *[To Polonius.]* My lord, you played once i' th' university, you say?
POLONIUS. That did I, my lord, and was accounted a good actor.
HAMLET. What did you enact?
POLONIUS. I did enact Julius Caesar. I was killed i' the Capitol; Brutus killed me.
HAMLET. It was a brute° part° of him to kill so capital a calf° there.—Be the players ready?
ROSENCRANTZ. Ay, my lord. They stay upon° your patience.
QUEEN. Come hither, my dear Hamlet, sit by me.
HAMLET. No, good Mother, here's metal° more attractive.
POLONIUS *[to the King]*. O, ho, do you mark that?
HAMLET. Lady, shall I lie in your lap?
*[Lying down at Ophelia's feet.]*
OPHELIA. No, my lord.
HAMLET. I mean, my head upon your lap?
OPHELIA. Ay, my lord.
HAMLET. Do you think I meant country matters?°
OPHELIA. I think nothing, my lord.
HAMLET. That's a fair thought to lie between maids' legs.
OPHELIA. What is, my lord?
HAMLET. Nothing.°

**78 If 'a steal aught** if he gets away with anything **80 idle** (1) unoccupied (2) mad **82 cousin** i.e., close relative **83 chameleon's dish** (Chameleons were supposed to feed on air. Hamlet deliberately misinterprets the King's *fares* as "feeds." By his phrase *eat the air* he also plays on the idea of feeding himself with the promise of succession, of being the *heir.*) **84 capons** roosters castrated and *crammed* with feed to make them succulent **85 have . . . with** make nothing of, or gain nothing from **86 are not mine** do not respond to what I asked **87 nor mine now** (Once spoken, words are proverbially no longer the speaker's own—and hence should be uttered warily.) **93 brute** (The Latin meaning of *brutus,* "stupid," was often used punningly with the name Brutus.) **part** (1) deed (2) role **calf** fool **95 stay upon** await **97 metal** substance that is *attractive,* i.e., magnetic, but with suggestion also of *mettle,* "disposition" **103 country matters** sexual intercourse (making a bawdy pun on the first syllable of *country*) **107 Nothing** the figure zero or naught, suggesting the female sexual anatomy. (*Thing* not infrequently has a bawdy connotation of male or female anatomy, and the reference here could be male.)

OPHELIA. You are merry, my lord.

HAMLET. Who, I?

OPHELIA. Ay, my lord.

HAMLET. O God, your only jig maker.° What should a man do but be merry? For look you how cheerfully my mother looks, and my father died within 's° two hours.

OPHELIA. Nay, 'tis twice two months, my lord.

HAMLET. So long? Nay then, let the devil wear black, for I'll have a suit of sables.° O heavens! Die two months ago, and not forgotten yet? Then there's hope a great man's memory may outlive his life half a year. But, by 'r Lady, 'a must build churches, then, or else shall 'a suffer not thinking on,° with the hobbyhorse, whose epitaph is "For O, for O, the hobbyhorse is forgot."°

*The trumpets sound. Dumb show follows.*

*Enter a King and a Queen* [*very lovingly*]; *the Queen embracing him, and he her.* [*She kneels, and makes show of protestation unto him.*] *He takes her up, and declines his head upon her neck. He lies him down upon a bank of flowers. She, seeing him asleep, leaves him. Anon comes in another man, takes off his crown, kisses it, pours poison in the sleeper's ears, and leaves him. The Queen returns, finds the King dead, makes passionate action. The Poisoner with some three or four come in again, seem to condole with her. The dead body is carried away. The Poisoner woos the Queen with gifts; she seems harsh awhile, but in the end accepts love.*

[*Exeunt players.*]

OPHELIA. What means this, my lord?

HAMLET. Marry, this' miching mallico;° it means mischief.

OPHELIA. Belike° this show imports the argument° of the play.

*Enter Prologue.*

HAMLET. We shall know by this fellow. The players cannot keep counsel;° they'll tell all.

OPHELIA. Will 'a tell us what this show meant?

HAMLET. Ay, or any show that you will show him. Be not you° ashamed to show, he'll not shame to tell you what it means.

**111 only jig maker** very best composer of jigs, i.e., pointless merriment. (Hamlet replies sardonically to Ophelia's observation that he is merry by saying, "If you're looking for someone who is really merry, you've come to the right person.") **113 within 's** within this (i.e., these) **115–116 suit of sables** garments trimmed with the fur of the sable and hence suited for a wealthy person, not a mourner (but with a pun on *sable*, "black," ironically suggesting mourning once again) **119 suffer . . . on** undergo oblivion **120 For . . . forgot** (Verse of a song occurring also in *Love's Labor's Lost*, 3.1.27–28. The hobbyhorse was a character made up to resemble a horse and rider, appearing in the morris dance and such May-game sports. This song laments the disappearance of such customs under pressure from the Puritans.) **122 this' miching mallico** this is sneaking mischief **123 Belike** probably **argument** plot **124–125 counsel** secret **127 Be not you** provided you are not

OPHELIA. You are naught,° you are naught. I'll mark the play.
PROLOGUE. For us, and for our tragedy,
Here stooping° to your clemency,
We beg your hearing patiently.

[*Exit.*]

HAMLET. Is this a prologue, or the posy of a ring?°
OPHELIA. 'Tis brief, my lord.
HAMLET. As woman's love.

*Enter [two Players as] King and Queen.*

PLAYER KING. Full thirty times hath Phoebus' cart° gone round
Neptune's salt wash° and Tellus'° orbèd ground,
And thirty dozen moons with borrowed° sheen
About the world have times twelve thirties been,
Since love our hearts and Hymen° did our hands
Unite commutual° in most sacred bands.°
PLAYER QUEEN. So many journeys may the sun and moon
Make us again count o'er ere love be done!
But, woe is me, you are so sick of late,
So far from cheer and from your former state,
That I distrust° you. Yet, though I distrust,
Discomfort° you, my lord, it nothing° must.
For women's fear and love hold quantity;°
In neither aught, or in extremity.°
Now, what my love is, proof° hath made you know,
And as my love is sized,° my fear is so.
Where love is great, the littlest doubts are fear;
Where little fears grow great, great love grows there.
PLAYER KING. Faith, I must leave thee, love, and shortly too;
My operant powers° their functions leave to do.°
And thou shalt live in this fair world behind,°
Honored, beloved; and haply one as kind
For husband shalt thou—
PLAYER QUEEN. O, confound the rest!
Such love must needs be treason in my breast.
In second husband let me be accurst!
None° wed the second but who° killed the first.
HAMLET. Wormwood,° wormwood.

**129 naught** indecent. (Ophelia is reacting to Hamlet's pointed remarks about not being ashamed to show all.) **131 stooping** bowing **133 posy . . . ring** brief motto in verse inscribed in a ring **136 Phoebus' cart** the sun-god's chariot, making its yearly cycle **137 salt wash** the sea **Tellus** goddess of the earth, of the *orbèd ground* **138 borrowed** i.e., reflected **140 Hymen** god of matrimony **141 commutual** mutually **bands** bonds **146 distrust** am anxious about **147 Discomfort** distress **nothing** not at all **148 hold quantity** keep proportion with one another **149 In . . . extremity** i.e., women fear and love either too little or too much, but the two, fear and love, are equal in either case **150 proof** experience **151 sized** in size **155 operant powers** vital functions **leave to do** cease to perform **156 behind** after I have gone **161 None** i.e., let no woman **but who** except the one who **162 Wormwood** i.e., how bitter. (Literally, a bitter-tasting plant.)

PLAYER QUEEN. The instances° that second marriage move°
Are base respects of thrift,° but none of love.
A second time I kill my husband dead
When second husband kisses me in bed.
PLAYER KING. I do believe you think what now you speak,
But what we do determine oft we break.
Purpose is but the slave to memory,°
Of violent birth, but poor validity,°
Which° now, like fruit unripe, sticks on the tree,
But fall unshaken when they mellow be.
Most necessary 'tis that we forget
To pay ourselves what to ourselves is debt.°
What to ourselves in passion we propose,
The passion ending, doth the purpose lose.
The violence of either grief or joy
Their own enactures° with themselves destroy.
Where joy most revels, grief doth most lament;
Grief joys, joy grieves, on slender accident.°
This world is not for aye,° nor 'tis not strange
That even our loves should with our fortunes change;
For 'tis a question left us yet to prove,
Whether love lead fortune, or else fortune love.
The great man down,° you mark his favorite flies;
The poor advanced makes friends of enemies.°
And hitherto° doth love on fortune tend;°
For who not needs° shall never lack a friend,
And who in want° a hollow friend doth try°
Directly seasons him° his enemy.
But, orderly to end where I begun,
Our wills and fates do so contrary run°
That our devices still° are overthrown;
Our thoughts are ours, their ends° none of our own.
So think thou wilt no second husband wed,
But die thy thoughts when thy first lord is dead.
PLAYER QUEEN. Nor° earth to me give food, nor heaven light,
Sport and repose lock from me day and night,°

**163 instances** motives **move** motivate **164 base . . . thrift** ignoble considerations of material prosperity **169 Purpose . . . memory** our good intentions are subject to forgetfulness **170 validity** strength, durability **171 Which** i.e., purpose **173–174 Most . . . debt** it's inevitable that in time we forget the obligations we have imposed on ourselves **178 enactures** fulfillments **179–180 Where . . . accident** the capacity for extreme joy and grief go together, and often one extreme is instantly changed into its opposite on the slightest provocation **181 aye** ever **185 down** fallen in fortune **186 The poor . . . enemies** when one of humble station is promoted, you see his enemies suddenly becoming his friends **187 hitherto** up to this point in the argument, or, to this extent **tend** attend **188 who not needs** he who is not in need (of wealth) **189 who in want** he who, being in need **try** test (his generosity) **190 seasons him** ripens him into **192 Our . . . run** what we want and what we get go so contrarily **193 devices still** intentions continually **194 ends** results **197 Nor** let neither **198 Sport . . . night** may day deny me its pastimes and night its repose

To desperation turn my trust and hope,
An anchor's cheer° in prison be my scope!°
Each opposite that blanks° the face of joy
Meet what I would have well and it destroy!°
Both here and hence° pursue me lasting strife
If, once a widow, ever I be wife!

HAMLET. If she should break it now!

PLAYER KING. 'Tis deeply sworn. Sweet, leave me here awhile;
My spirits° grow dull, and fain I would beguile
The tedious day with sleep.

PLAYER QUEEN. Sleep rock thy brain,
And never come mischance between us twain!

[*He sleeps.*] *Exit* [*Player Queen*].

HAMLET. Madam, how like you this play?

QUEEN. The lady doth protest too much,° methinks.

HAMLET. O, but she'll keep her word.

KING. Have you heard the argument?° Is there no offense in 't?

HAMLET. No, no, they do but jest,° poison in jest. No offense° i' the world.

KING. What do you call the play?

HAMLET. *The Mousetrap.* Marry, how? Tropically.° This play is the image of a murder done in Vienna. Gonzago is the Duke's° name, his wife, Baptista. You shall see anon. 'Tis a knavish piece of work, but what of that? Your Majesty, and we that have free° souls, it touches us not. Let the galled jade° wince, our withers° are unwrung.°

*Enter Lucianus.*

This is one Lucianus, nephew to the King.

OPHELIA. You are as good as a chorus,° my lord.

HAMLET. I could interpret° between you and your love, if I could see the puppets dallying.°

OPHELIA. You are keen,° my lord, you are keen.

HAMLET. It would cost you a groaning to take off mine edge.

**200 anchor's cheer** anchorite's or hermit's fare **my scope** the extent of my happiness **201 blanks** causes to blanch or grow pale **201–202 Each . . . destroy** may every adverse thing that causes the face of joy to turn pale meet and destroy everything that I desire to see prosper **203 hence** in the life hereafter **207 spirits** vital spirits **211 doth . . . much** makes too many promises and protestations **213 argument** plot **214 jest** make believe **213–214 offense . . . offense** cause for objection . . . actual injury, crime **217 Tropically** figuratively. (The First Quarto reading, *trapically,* suggests a pun on *trap* in *Mousetrap.*) **218 Duke's** i.e., King's. (A slip that may be due to Shakespeare's possible source, the alleged murder of the Duke of Urbino by Luigi Gonzaga in 1538.) **220 free** guiltless **221 galled jade** horse whose hide is rubbed by saddle or harness **withers** the part between the horse's shoulder blades **unwrung** not rubbed sore **223 chorus** (In many Elizabethan plays, the forthcoming action was explained by an actor known as the "chorus"; at a puppet show, the actor who spoke the dialogue was known as an "interpreter," as indicated by the lines following.) **224 interpret** (1) ventriloquize the dialogue, as in puppet show (2) act as pander **225 puppets dallying** (With suggestion of sexual play, continued in *keen,* "sexually aroused," *groaning,* "moaning in pregnancy," and *edge,* "sexual desire" or "impetuosity.") **226 keen** sharp, bitter

OPHELIA. Still better, and worse.°

HAMLET. So° you mis-take° your husbands. Begin, murder; leave thy damnable faces and begin. Come, the croaking raven doth bellow for revenge.

LUCIANUS. Thoughts black, hands apt, drugs fit, and time agreeing,
Confederate season,° else° no creature seeing,°
Thou mixture rank, of midnight weeds collected,
With Hecate's ban° thrice blasted, thrice infected,
Thy natural magic and dire property°
On wholesome life usurp immediately.

[*He pours the poison into the sleeper's ear.*]

HAMLET. 'A poisons him i' the garden for his estate.° His° name's Gonzago. The story is extant, and written in very choice Italian. You shall see anon how the murderer gets the love of Gonzago's wife.

[*Claudius rises.*]

OPHELIA. The King rises.

HAMLET. What, frighted with false fire?°

QUEEN. How fares my lord?

POLONIUS. Give o'er the play.

KING. Give me some light. Away!

POLONIUS. Lights, lights, lights!

*Exeunt all but Hamlet and Horatio.*

HAMLET. "Why, let the strucken deer go weep,
The hart ungallèd° play.
For some must watch,° while some must sleep;
Thus runs the world away."°

Would not this,° sir, and a forest of feathers°—if the rest of my fortunes turn Turk with° me—with two Provincial roses° on my razed° shoes, get me a fellowship in a cry° of players?°

HORATIO. Half a share.

HAMLET. A whole one, I.

**228 Still . . . worse** more keen, always *bettering* what other people say with witty wordplay, but at the same time more offensive **229 So** even thus (in marriage) **mis-take** take falseheartedly and cheat on. (The marriage vows say "for better, for worse.") **233 Confederate season** the time and occasion conspiring (to assist the murderer) **else** otherwise **seeing** seeing me **235 Hecate's ban** the curse of Hecate, the goddess of witchcraft **236 dire property** baleful quality **238 estate** i.e., the kingship **His** i.e., the King's **243 false fire** the blank discharge of a gun loaded with powder but no shot **248–251 Why . . . away** (Probably from an old ballad, with allusion to the popular belief that a wounded deer retires to weep and die; compare with *As You Like It,* 2.1.33-66.) **249 ungallèd** unafflicted **250 watch** remain awake **251 Thus . . . away** thus the world goes **252 this** i.e., the play **feathers** (Allusion to the plumes that Elizabethan actors were fond of wearing.) **253 turn Turk with** turn renegade against, go back on **Provincial roses** rosettes of ribbon, named for roses grown in a part of France **254 razed** with ornamental slashing **cry** pack (of hounds) **fellowship . . . players** partnership in a theatrical company

"For thou dost know, O Damon° dear,
This realm dismantled° was
Of Jove himself, and now reigns here
A very, very—pajock."°

HORATIO. You might have rhymed.

HAMLET. O good Horatio, I'll take the ghost's word for a thousand pound. Didst perceive?

HORATIO. Very well, my lord.

HAMLET. Upon the talk of the poisoning?

HORATIO. I did very well note him.

*Enter Rosencrantz and Guildenstern.*

HAMLET. Aha! Come, some music! Come, the recorders.°
"For if the King like not the comedy,
Why then, belike, he likes it not, perdy."°
Come, some music.

GUILDENSTERN. Good my lord, vouchsafe me a word with you.

HAMLET. Sir, a whole history.

GUILDENSTERN. The King, sir—

HAMLET. Ay, sir, what of him?

GUILDENSTERN. Is in his retirement° marvelous distempered.°

HAMLET. With drink, sir?

GUILDENSTERN. No, my lord, with choler.°

HAMLET. Your wisdom should show itself more richer to signify this to the doctor, for for me to put him to his purgation° would perhaps plunge him into more choler.

GUILDENSTERN. Good my lord, put your discourse into some frame° and start° not so wildly from my affair.

HAMLET. I am tame, sir. Pronounce.

GUILDENSTERN. The Queen, your mother, in most great affliction of spirit, hath sent me to you.

HAMLET. You are welcome.

GUILDENSTERN. Nay, good my lord, this courtesy is not of the right breed.° If it shall please you to make me a wholesome answer, I

**257 Damon** the friend of Pythias, as Horatio is friend of Hamlet; or, a traditional pastoral name **258 dismantled** stripped, divested **258–260 This realm . . . pajock** i.e., Jove, representing divine authority and justice, has abandoned this realm to its own devices, leaving in his stead only a peacock or vain pretender to virtue (though the rhyme-word expected in place of *pajock or* "peacock" suggests that the realm is now ruled over by an "ass") **267 recorders** wind instruments of the flute kind **269 perdy** (A corruption of the French *par dieu,* "by God.") **275 retirement** withdrawal to his chambers **distempered** out of humor. (But Hamlet deliberately plays on the wider application to any illness of mind or body, as in line 307, especially to drunkenness.) **277 choler** anger. (But Hamlet takes the word in its more basic humoral sense of "bilious disorder.") **279 purgation** (Hamlet hints at something going beyond medical treatment to bloodletting and the extraction of confession.) **281 frame** order **282 start** shy or jump away (like a horse; the opposite of *tame* in line 283) **288 breed** (1) kind (2) breeding, manners

will do your mother's commandment; if not, your pardon° and my return shall be the end of my business.

HAMLET. Sir, I cannot.

ROSENCRANTZ. What, my lord?

HAMLET. Make you a wholesome answer; my wit's diseased. But, sir, such answer as I can make, you shall command, or rather, as you say, my mother. Therefore no more, but to the matter. My mother, you say—

ROSENCRANTZ. Then thus she says: your behavior hath struck her into amazement and admiration.°

HAMLET. O wonderful son, that can so stonish a mother! But is there no sequel at the heels of this mother's admiration? Impart.

ROSENCRANTZ. She desires to speak with you in her closet° ere you go to bed.

HAMLET. We shall obey, were she ten times our mother. Have you any further trade with us?

ROSENCRANTZ. My lord, you once did love me.

HAMLET. And do still, by these pickers and stealers.°

ROSENCRANTZ. Good my lord, what is your cause of distemper? You do surely bar the door upon your own liberty° if you deny° your griefs to your friend.

HAMLET. Sir, I lack advancement.

ROSENCRANTZ. How can that be, when you have the voice of the King himself for your succession in Denmark?

HAMLET. Ay, sir, but "While the grass grows"°—the proverb is something° musty.

*Enter the Players° with recorders.*

O, the recorders. Let me see one. [*He takes a recorder.*] To withdraw° with you: why do you go about to recover the wind° of me, as if you would drive me into a toil?°

GUILDENSTERN. O, my lord, if my duty be too bold, my love is too unmannerly.°

HAMLET. I do not well understand that.° Will you play upon this pipe?

GUILDENSTERN. My lord, I cannot.

HAMLET. I pray you.

GUILDENSTERN. Believe me, I cannot.

HAMLET. I do beseech you.

**289 pardon** permission to depart **298 admiration** bewilderment **301 closet** private chamber **306 pickers and stealers** i.e., hands. (So called from the catechism, "to keep my hands from picking and stealing.") **308 liberty** i.e., being freed from *distemper,* line 307; but perhaps with a veiled threat as well **deny** refuse to share **313 While . . . grows** (The rest of the proverb is "the silly horse starves"; Hamlet may not live long enough to succeed to the kingdom.) **313–314 something** somewhat **s.d. Players** actors **316 withdraw** speak privately **recover the wind** get to the windward side (thus driving the game into the *toil,* or "net") **317 toil** snare **318–319 if . . . unmannerly** if I am using an unmannerly boldness, it is my love that occasion it **320 I . . . that** i.e., I don't understand how genuine love can be unmannerly

GUILDENSTERN. I know no touch of it, my lord.

HAMLET. It is as easy as lying. Govern these ventages° with your fingers and thumb, give it breath with your mouth, and it will discourse most eloquent music. Look you, these are the stops.

GUILDENSTERN. But these cannot I command to any utterance of harmony. I have not the skill.

HAMLET. Why, look you now, how unworthy a thing you make of me! You would play upon me, you would seem to know my stops, you would pluck out the heart of my mystery, you would sound° me from my lowest note to the top of my compass,° and there is much music, excellent voice, in this little organ,° yet cannot you make it speak. 'Sblood, do you think I am easier to be played on than a pipe? Call me what instrument you will, though you can fret° me, you cannot play upon me.

*Enter Polonius.*

God bless you, sir!

POLONIUS. My lord, the Queen would speak with you, and presently.°

HAMLET. Do you see yonder cloud that's almost in shape of a camel?

POLONIUS. By the Mass and 'tis, like a camel indeed.

HAMLET. Methinks it is like a weasel.

POLONIUS. It is backed like a weasel.

HAMLET. Or like a whale.

POLONIUS. Very like a whale.

HAMLET. Then I will come to my mother by and by.° [*Aside.*] They fool me° to the top of my bent.°—I will come by and by.

POLONIUS. I will say so.

[*Exit.*]

HAMLET. "By and by" is easily said. Leave me, friends.

[*Exeunt all but Hamlet.*]

'Tis now the very witching time° of night,
When churchyards yawn and hell itself breathes out
Contagion to this world. Now could I drink hot blood
And do such bitter business as the day
Would quake to look on. Soft, now to my mother.
O heart, lose not thy nature!° Let not ever
The soul of Nero° enter this firm bosom.
Let me be cruel, not unnatural;
I will speak daggers to her, but use none.
My tongue and soul in this be hypocrites:

**326 ventages** finger-holes or *stops* (line 328) of the recorder **333 sound** (1) fathom (2) produce sound in **334 compass** range (of voice) **335 organ** musical instrument **337 fret** irritate (with a quibble on *fret,* meaning the piece of wood, gut, or metal that regulates the fingering on an instrument) **340 presently** at once **347 by and by** quite soon **347–348 fool me** trifle with me, humor my fooling **348 top of my bent** limit of my ability or endurance. (Literally, the extent to which a bow may be bent.) **351 witching time** time when spells are cast and evil is abroad **356 nature** natural feeling **357 Nero** murderer of his mother, Agrippina

How in my words soever° she be shent,°
To give them seals° never my soul consent!
*Exit.*

### 3.3 *Enter King, Rosencrantz, and Guildenstern.*

KING. I like him° not, nor stands it safe with us
To let his madness range. Therefore prepare you.
I your commission will forthwith dispatch,°
And he to England shall along with you.
The terms of our estate° may not endure
Hazard so near 's as doth hourly grow
Out of his brows.°
GUILDENSTERN. We will ourselves provide.
Most holy and religious fear° it is
To keep those many many bodies safe
That live and feed upon Your Majesty.
ROSENCRANTZ. The single and peculiar° life is bound
With all the strength and armor of the mind
To keep itself from noyance,° but much more
That spirit upon whose weal depends and rests
The lives of many. The cess° of majesty
Dies not alone, but like a gulf° doth draw
What's near it with it; or it is a massy° wheel
Fixed on the summit of the highest mount,
To whose huge spokes ten thousand lesser things
Are mortised° and adjoined, which, when it falls,°
Each small annexment, petty consequence,°
Attends° the boisterous ruin. Never alone
Did the King sigh, but with a general groan.
KING. Arm° you, I pray you, to this speedy voyage,
For we will fetters put about this fear,
Which now goes too free-footed.
ROSENCRANTZ. We will haste us.
*Exeunt gentlemen* [*Rosencrantz and Guildenstern*].

*Enter Polonius.*

**361 How . . . soever** however much by my words **shent** rebuked **362 give them seals** i.e., confirm them with deeds
**3.3 Location: The castle. 1 him** i.e., his behavior **3 dispatch** prepare, cause to be drawn up **5 terms of our estate** circumstances of my royal position **7 Out of his brows** i.e., from his brain, in the form of plots and threats **8 religious fear** sacred concern **11 single and peculiar** individual and private **13 noyance** harm **15 cess** decease, cessation **16 gulf** whirlpool **17 massy** massive **20 mortised** fastened (as with a fitted joint) **when it falls** i.e., when it descends, like the wheel of Fortune, bringing a king down with it **21 Each . . . consequence** i.e., every hanger-on and unimportant person or thing connected with the King **22 Attends** participates in **24 Arm** prepare

POLONIUS. My lord, he's going to his mother's closet.
Behind the arras° I'll convey myself
To hear the process.° I'll warrant she'll tax him home,°
And, as you said—and wisely was it said—
'Tis meet° that some more audience than a mother,
Since nature makes them partial, should o'erhear
The speech, of vantage.° Fare you well, my liege.
I'll call upon you ere you go to bed
And tell you what I know.

KING. Thanks, dear my lord.

*Exit* [*Polonius*].

O, my offense is rank! It smells to heaven.
It hath the primal eldest curse° upon 't,
A brother's murder. Pray can I not,
Though inclination be as sharp as will;°
My stronger guilt defeats my strong intent,
And like a man to double business bound°
I stand in pause where I shall first begin,
And both neglect. What if this cursèd hand
Were thicker than itself with brother's blood,
Is there not rain enough in the sweet heavens
To wash it white as snow? Whereto serves mercy
But to confront the visage of offense?°
And what's in prayer but this twofold force,
To be forestallèd° ere we come to fall,
Or pardoned being down? Then I'll look up.
My fault is past. But O, what form of prayer
Can serve my turn? "Forgive me my foul murder"?
That cannot be, since I am still possessed
Of those effects for which I did the murder:
My crown, mine own ambition, and my Queen.
May one be pardoned and retain th' offense?°
In the corrupted currents° of this world
Offense's gilded hand° may shove by° justice,
And oft 'tis seen the wicked prize° itself
Buys out the law. But 'tis not so above.
There° is no shuffling,° there the action lies°

**28 arras** screen of tapestry placed around the walls of household apartments. (On the Elizabethan stage, the arras was presumably over a door or discovery space in the tiring-house facade.) **29 process** proceedings **tax him home** reprove him severely **31 meet** fitting **33 of vantage** from an advantageous place, or, in addition **37 the primal eldest curse** the curse of Cain, the first murderer; he killed his brother Abel **39 Though . . . will** though my desire is as strong as my determination **41 bound** (1) destined (2) obliged. (The King wants to repent and still enjoy what he has gained.) **46–47 Whereto . . . offense** what function does mercy serve other than to meet sin face to face? **49 forestallèd** prevented (from sinning) **56 th' offense** the thing for which one offended **57 currents** courses **58 gilded hand** hand offering gold as a bribe **shove by** thrust aside **59 wicked prize** prize won by wickedness **61 There** i.e., in heaven **shuffling** escape by trickery **the action lies** the accusation is made manifest. (A legal metaphor.)

In his° true nature, and we ourselves compelled,
Even to the teeth and forehead° of our faults,
To give in° evidence. What then? What rests?°
Try what repentance can. What can it not?
Yet what can it, when one cannot repent?
O wretched state, O bosom black as death,
O limèd° soul that, struggling to be free,
Art more engaged!° Help, angels! Make assay.°
Bow, stubborn knees, and heart with strings of steel,
Be soft as sinews of the newborn babe!
All may be well. [*He kneels.*]

*Enter Hamlet.*

HAMLET. Now might I do it pat,° now 'a is a-praying;
And now I'll do 't. [*He draws his sword.*] And so 'a goes to heaven,
And so am I revenged. That would be scanned:°
A villain kills my father, and for that,
I, his sole son, do this same villain send
To heaven.
Why, this is hire and salary, not revenge.
'A took my father grossly, full of bread,°
With all his crimes broad blown,° as flush° as May;
And how his audit° stands who knows save° heaven?
But in our circumstance and course of thought°
'Tis heavy with him. And am I then revenged,
To take him in the purging of his soul,
When he is fit and seasoned° for his passage?
No!
Up, sword, and know thou a more horrid hent.°
[*He puts up his sword.*]
When he is drunk asleep, or in his rage,°
Or in th' incestuous pleasure of his bed,
At game,° a-swearing, or about some act
That has no relish° of salvation in 't—
Then trip him, that his heels may kick at heaven,
And that his soul may be as damned and black
As hell, whereto it goes. My mother stays.°
This physic° but prolongs thy sickly days.
*Exit.*

**62 his** its **63 to the teeth and forehead** face to face, concealing nothing **64 give in** provide. **rests** remains **68 limèd** caught as with birdlime, a sticky substance used to ensnare birds **69 engaged** entangled **assay** trial. (Said to himself.) **73 pat** opportunely **75 would be scanned** needs to be looked into, or, would be interpreted as follows **80 grossly, full of bread** i.e., enjoying his worldly pleasures rather than fasting. (See Ezekiel 16.49.) **81 crimes broad blown** sins in full bloom **flush** vigorous **82 audit** account **save** except for **83 in . . . thought** as we see it from our mortal perspective **86 seasoned** matured, readied **88 know . . . hent** await to be grasped by me on a more horrid occasion **hent** act of seizing **89 drunk . . . rage** dead drunk, or in a fit of sexual passion **91 game** gambling **92 relish** trace, savor **95 stays** awaits (me) **96 physic** purging (by prayer), or, Hamlet's postponement of the killing

KING. My words fly up, my thoughts remain below.
Words without thoughts never to heaven go.
*Exit.*

## 3.4 *Enter [Queen] Gertrude and Polonius.*

POLONIUS. 'A will come straight. Look you lay home° to him.
Tell him his pranks have been too broad° to bear with,
And that Your Grace hath screened and stood between
Much heat° and him. I'll shroud° me even here.
Pray you, be round° with him.
HAMLET [*within*]. Mother, Mother, Mother!
QUEEN. I'll warrant you, fear me not.
Withdraw, I hear him coming.
[*Polonius hides behind the arras.*]

*Enter Hamlet.*

HAMLET. Now, Mother, what's the matter?
QUEEN. Hamlet, thou hast thy father° much offended.
HAMLET. Mother, you have my father much offended.
QUEEN. Come, come, you answer with an idle° tongue.
HAMLET. Go, go, you question with a wicked tongue.
QUEEN. Why, how now, Hamlet?
HAMLET. What's the matter now?
QUEEN. Have you forgot me?°
HAMLET. No, by the rood,° not so:
You are the Queen your husband's brother's wife,
And—would it were not so!—you are my mother.
QUEEN. Nay, then, I'll set those to you that can speak.°
HAMLET. Come, come, and sit you down; you shall not budge.
You go not till I set you up a glass
Where you may see the inmost part of you.
QUEEN. What wilt thou do? Thou wilt not murder me?
Help, ho!
POLONIUS [*behind the arras*]. What ho! Help!
HAMLET [*drawing*]. How now? A rat? Dead for a ducat,° dead!
[*He thrusts his rapier through the arras.*]
POLONIUS [*behind the arras*]. O, I am slain! [*He falls and dies.*]
QUEEN. O me, what hast thou done?
HAMLET. Nay, I know not. Is it the King?
QUEEN. O, what a rash and bloody deed is this!
HAMLET. A bloody deed—almost as bad, good Mother,
As kill a King, and marry with his brother.

**3.4 Location: The Queen's private chamber.** **1 lay home** thrust to the heart, reprove him soundly **2 broad** unrestrained **4 Much heat** i.e., the King's anger **shroud** conceal (with ironic fitness to Polonius' imminent death. The word is only in the First Quarto: the Second Quarto and the Folio read "silence.") **5 round** blunt **10 thy father** i.e., your stepfather, Claudius **12 idle** foolish **15 forgot me** i.e., forgotten that I am your mother **rood** cross of Christ **18 speak** i.e., to someone so rude **25 Dead for a ducat** i.e., I bet a ducat he's dead; or, a ducat is his life's fee

QUEEN. As kill a King!
HAMLET. Ay, lady, it was my word.
[*He parts the arras and discovers Polonius.*]
Thou wretched, rash, intruding fool, farewell!
I took thee for thy better. Take thy fortune.
Thou find'st to be too busy° is some danger.—
Leave wringing of your hands. Peace, sit you down,
And let me wring your heart, for so I shall,
If it be made of penetrable stuff,
If damnèd custom° have not brazed° it so
That it be proof° and bulwark against sense.°
QUEEN. What have I done, that thou dar'st wag thy tongue
In noise so rude against me?
HAMLET. Such an act
That blurs the grace and blush of modesty,
Calls virtue hypocrite, takes off the rose
From the fair forehead of an innocent love
And sets a blister° there, makes marriage vows
As false as dicers' oaths. O, such a deed
As from the body of contraction° plucks
The very soul, and sweet religion makes°
A rhapsody° of words. Heaven's face does glow
O'er this solidity and compound mass
With tristful visage, as against the doom,
Is thought-sick at the act.°
QUEEN. Ay me, what act,
That roars so loud and thunders in the index?°
HAMLET [*showing her two likenesses*]. Look here upon this picture, and on this,
The counterfeit presentment° of two brothers.
See what a grace was seated on this brow:
Hyperion's° curls, the front° of Jove himself,
An eye like Mars° to threaten and command,
A station° like the herald Mercury°
New-lighted° on a heaven-kissing hill—
A combination and a form indeed
Where every god did seem to set his seal°
To give the world assurance of a man.
This was your husband. Look you now what follows:
Here is your husband, like a mildewed ear,°

**34 busy** nosey **38 damnèd custom** habitual wickedness **brazed** brazened, hardened **39 proof** armor **sense** feeling **45 sets a blister** i.e., brands as a harlot **47 contraction** the marriage contract **48 sweet religion makes** i.e., makes marriage vows **49 rhapsody** senseless string **49–52 Heaven's . . . act** heaven's face blushes at this solid world compounded of the various elements, with sorrowful face as though the day of doom were near, and is sick with horror at the deed (i.e., Gertrude's marriage) **53 index** table of contents, prelude or preface **55 counterfeit presentment** portrayed representation **57 Hyperion's** the sun-god's **front** brow **58 Mars** god of war **59 station** manner of standing **Mercury** winged messenger of the gods **60 New-lighted** newly alighted **62 set his seal** i.e., affix his approval **65 ear** i.e., of grain

Blasting° his wholesome brother. Have you eyes?
Could you on this fair mountain leave° to feed
And batten° on this moor?° Ha, have you eyes?
You cannot call it love, for at your age
The heyday° in the blood° is tame, it's humble,
And waits upon the judgment, and what judgment
Would step from this to this? Sense,° sure, you have,
Else could you not have motion, but sure that sense
Is apoplexed,° for madness would not err,°
Nor sense to ecstasy was ne'er so thralled,
But° it reserved some quantity of choice
To serve in such a difference.° What devil was 't
That thus hath cozened° you at hoodman-blind?°
Eyes without feeling, feeling without sight,
Ears without hands or eyes, smelling sans° all,
Or but a sickly part of one true sense
Could not so mope.° O shame, where is thy blush?
Rebellious hell,
If thou canst mutine° in a matron's bones,
To flaming youth let virtue be as wax
And melt in her own fire.° Proclaim no shame
When the compulsive ardor gives the charge,
Since frost itself as actively doth burn,
And reason panders will.°

QUEEN. O Hamlet, speak no more!
Thou turn'st mine eyes into my very soul,
And there I see such black and grainèd° spots
As will not leave their tinct.°

HAMLET. Nay, but to live
In the rank sweat of an enseamèd° bed,
Stewed° in corruption, honeying and making love
Over the nasty sty!

QUEEN. O, speak to me no more!

**66 Blasting** blighting **67 leave** cease **68 batten** gorge **moor** barren or marshy ground (suggesting also "dark-skinned") **70 heyday** state of excitement **blood** passion **72 Sense** perception through the five senses (the functions of the middle or sensible soul) **74 apoplexed** paralyzed. (Hamlet goes on to explain that, without such a paralysis of will, mere madness would not so err, nor would the five senses so enthrall themselves to *ecstasy* or lunacy; even such deranged states of mind would be able to make the obvious choice between Hamlet Senior and Claudius.) **err** so err **76 But** but that **77 To . . . difference** to help in making a choice between two such men **78 cozened** cheated **hoodman-blind** blindman's buff. (In this game, says Hamlet, the devil must have pushed Claudius toward Gertrude while she was blindfolded.) **80 sans** without **82 mope** be dazed, act aimlessly **84 mutine** incite mutiny **85–86 be as wax . . . fire** melt like a candle or stick of sealing wax held over the candle flame **86–89 Proclaim . . . will** call it no shameful business when the compelling ardor of youth delivers the attack, i.e., commits lechery, since the *frost* of advanced age burns with as active a fire of lust and reason perverts itself by fomenting lust rather than restraining it **92 grainèd** dyed in grain, indelible **93 leave their tinct** surrender their color **94 enseamèd** saturated in the grease and filth of passionate lovemaking **95 Stewed** soaked, bathed (with a suggestion of "stew," brothel)

These words like daggers enter in my ears.
No more, sweet Hamlet!

HAMLET. A murderer and a villain,
A slave that is not twentieth part the tithe°
Of your precedent lord,° a vice° of kings,
A cutpurse of the empire and the rule,
That from a shelf the precious diadem stole
And put it in his pocket!

QUEEN. No more!

*Enter Ghost* [*in his nightgown*].

HAMLET. A king of shreds and patches°—
Save me, and hover o'er me with your wings,
You heavenly guards! What would your gracious figure?

QUEEN. Alas, he's mad!

HAMLET. Do you not come your tardy son to chide,
That, lapsed° in time and passion, lets go by
Th' important° acting of your dread command?
O, say!

GHOST. Do not forget. This visitation
Is but to whet thy almost blunted purpose.
But look, amazement° on thy mother sits.
O, step between her and her fighting soul!
Conceit° in weakest bodies strongest works.
Speak to her, Hamlet.

HAMLET. How is it with you, lady?

QUEEN. Alas, how is 't with you,
That you do bend your eye on vacancy,
And with th' incorporal° air do hold discourse?
Forth at your eyes your spirits wildly peep,
And, as the sleeping soldiers in th' alarm,°
Your bedded° hair, like life in excrements,°
Start up and stand on end. O gentle son,
Upon the heat and flame of thy distemper°
Sprinkle cool patience. Whereon do you look?

HAMLET. On him, on him! Look you how pale he glares!
His form and cause conjoined,° preaching to stones,
Would make them capable.°—Do not look upon me,
Lest with this piteous action you convert
My stern effects.° Then what I have to do

**100 tithe** tenth part **101 precedent lord** former husband **vice** buffoon. (A reference to the Vice of the morality plays.) **106 shreds and patches** i.e., motley, the traditional costume of the clown or fool **111 lapsed** delaying **112 important** importunate, urgent **116 amazement** distraction **118 Conceit** imagination **122 incorporal** immaterial **124 as . . . alarm** like soldiers called out of sleep by an alarum **125 bedded** laid flat **like life in excrements** i.e., as though hair, an outgrowth of the body, had a life of its own. (Hair was thought to be lifeless because it lacks sensation, and so its standing on end would be unnatural and ominous.) **127 distemper** disorder **130 His . . . conjoined** his appearance joined to his cause for speaking **131 capable** receptive **132–133 convert . . . effects** divert me from my stern duty

Will want true color—tears perchance for blood.°
QUEEN. To whom do you speak this?
HAMLET. Do you see nothing there?
QUEEN. Nothing at all, yet all that is I see.
HAMLET. Nor did you nothing hear?
QUEEN. No, nothing but ourselves.
HAMLET. Why, look you there, look how it steals away!
My father, in his habit° as° he lived!
Look where he goes even now out at the portal!
*Exit Ghost.*
QUEEN. This is the very° coinage of your brain.
This bodiless creation ecstasy
Is very cunning in.°
HAMLET. Ecstasy?
My pulse as yours doth temperately keep time,
And makes as healthful music. It is not madness
That I have uttered. Bring me to the test,
And I the matter will reword,° which madness
Would gambol° from. Mother, for love of grace,
Lay not that flattering unction° to your soul
That not your trespass but my madness speaks.
It will but skin° and film the ulcerous place,
Whiles rank corruption, mining° all within,
Infects unseen. Confess yourself to heaven,
Repent what's past, avoid what is to come,
And do not spread the compost° on the weeds
To make them ranker. Forgive me this my virtue;°
For in the fatness° of these pursy° times
Virtue itself of vice must pardon beg,
Yea, curb° and woo for leave° to do him good.
QUEEN. O Hamlet, thou hast cleft my heart in twain.
HAMLET. O, throw away the worser part of it,
And live the purer with the other half.
Good night. But go not to my uncle's bed;
Assume a virtue, if you have it not.
That monster, custom, who all sense doth eat,°
Of habits devil,° is angel yet in this,
That to the use of actions fair and good
He likewise gives a frock or livery°
That aptly° is put on. Refrain tonight,

**134 want . . . blood** lack plausibility so that (with a play on the normal sense of *color*) I shall shed colorless tears instead of blood **141 habit** clothes **as** as when **143 very** mere **144–145 This . . . in** madness is skillful in creating this kind of hallucination **150 reword** repeat word for word **151 gambol** skip away **152 unction** ointment **154 skin** grow a skin for **155 mining** working under the surface **158 compost** manure **159 this my virtue** my virtuous talk in reproving you **160 fatness** grossness **pursy** flabby, out of shape **162 curb** bow, bend the knee **leave** permission **168 who . . . eat** which consumes all proper or natural feeling, all sensibility **169 Of habits devil** devil-like in prompting evil habits **171 livery** an outer appearance, a customary garb (and hence a predisposition easily assumed in time of stress) **172 aptly** readily

And that shall lend a kind of easiness
To the next abstinence; the next more easy;
For use° almost can change the stamp of nature,°
And either° . . . the devil, or throw him out
With wondrous potency. Once more, good night;
And when you are desirous to be blest,
I'll blessing beg of you.° For this same lord,
[*pointing to Polonius.*]
I do repent; but heaven hath pleased it so
To punish me with this, and this with me,
That I must be their scourge and minister.°
I will bestow° him, and will answer° well
The death I gave him. So, again, good night.
I must be cruel only to be kind.
This° bad begins, and worse remains behind.°
One word more, good lady.

QUEEN. What shall I do?

HAMLET. Not this by no means that I bid you do:
Let the bloat° King tempt you again to bed,
Pinch wanton° on your cheek, call you his mouse,
And let him, for a pair of reechy° kisses,
Or paddling° in your neck with his damned fingers,
Make you to ravel all this matter out°
That I essentially am not in madness,
But mad in craft.° 'Twere good° you let him know,
For who that's but a Queen, fair, sober, wise,
Would from a paddock,° from a bat, a gib,°
Such dear concernings° hide? Who would do so?
No, in despite of sense and secrecy,°
Unpeg the basket° on the house's top,
Let the birds fly, and like the famous ape,°
To try conclusions,° in the basket creep
And break your own neck down.°

QUEEN. Be thou assured, if words be made of breath,

**175 use** habit. **the stamp of nature** our inborn traits **176 And either** (A defective line, usually emended by inserting the word *master* after *either,* following the Fourth Quarto and early editors.) **178–179 when . . . you** i.e., when you are ready to be penitent and seek God's blessing, I will ask your blessing as a dutiful son should **182 their scourge and minister** i.e., agent of heavenly retribution. (By *scourge,* Hamlet also suggests that he himself will eventually suffer punishment in the process of fulfilling heaven's will.) **183 bestow** stow, dispose of **answer** account or pay for **186 This** i.e., the killing of Polonius **behind** to come **189 bloat** bloated **190 Pinch wanton** i.e., leave his love pinches on your cheeks, branding you as wanton **191 reechy** dirty, filthy **192 paddling** fingering amorously **193 ravel . . . out** unravel, disclose **195 in craft** by cunning **good** (Said sarcastically; also the following eight lines.) **197 paddock** toad **gib** tomcat **198 dear concernings** important affairs **199 sense and secrecy** secrecy that common sense requires **200 Unpeg the basket** open the cage, i.e., let out the secret **201 famous ape** (In a story now lost.) **202 try conclusions** test the outcome (in which the ape apparently enters a cage from which birds have been released and then tries to fly out of the cage as they have done, falling to its death) **203 down** in the fall; utterly

And breath of life, I have no life to breathe
What thou hast said to me.

HAMLET. I must to England. You know that?

QUEEN. Alack,
I had forgot. 'Tis so concluded on.

HAMLET. There's letters sealed, and my two schoolfellows,
Whom I will trust as I will adders fanged,
They bear the mandate; they must sweep my way
And marshal me to knavery.° Let it work.°
For 'tis the sport to have the enginer°
Hoist with° his own petard,° and 't shall go hard
But I will° delve one yard below their mines°
And blow them at the moon. O, 'tis most sweet
When in one line° two crafts° directly meet.
This man shall set me packing.°
I'll lug the guts into the neighbor room.
Mother, good night indeed. This counselor
Is now most still, most secret, and most grave,
Who was in life a foolish prating knave.—
Come, sir, to draw toward an end° with you.—
Good night, Mother.

*Exeunt* [*separately, Hamlet dragging in Polonius*].

**4.1** *Enter King and Queen,° with Rosencrantz and Guildenstern.*

KING. There's matter° in these sighs, these profound heaves.°
You must translate; 'tis fit we understand them.
Where is your son?

QUEEN. Bestow this place on us a little while.

[*Exeunt Rosencrantz and Guildenstern.*]

Ah, mine own lord, what have I seen tonight!

KING. What, Gertrude? How does Hamlet?

QUEEN. Mad as the sea and wind when both contend
Which is the mightier. In his lawless fit,
Behind the arras hearing something stir,

**211–212 sweep . . . knavery** sweep a path before me and conduct me to some *knavery* or treachery prepared for me **212 work** proceed **213 enginer** maker of military contrivances **214 Hoist with** blown up by. **petard** an explosive used to blow in a door or make a breach **214–215 't shall . . . will** unless luck is against me, I will **215 mines** tunnels used in warfare to undermine the enemy's emplacements; Hamlet will countermine by going under their mines **217 in one line** i.e., mines and countermines on a collision course, or the countermines directly below the mines **crafts** acts of guile, plots **218 set me packing** set me to making schemes, and set me to lugging (him), and, also, send me off in a hurry **223 draw . . . end** finish up (with a pun on *draw,* "pull")

**4.1 Location: The castle. s.d. Enter . . . Queen** (Some editors argue that Gertrude never exits in 3.4 and that the scene is continuous here, as suggested in the Folio, but the Second Quarto marks an entrance for her and at line 35 Claudius speaks of Gertrude's *closet* as though it were elsewhere. A short time has elapsed, during which the King has become aware of her highly wrought emotional state.) **1 matter** significance **heaves** heavy sighs

Whips out his rapier, cries, "A rat, a rat!"
And in this brainish apprehension° kills
The unseen good old man.

KING. O heavy° deed!
It had been so with us,° had we been there.
His liberty is full of threats to all—
To you yourself, to us, to everyone.
Alas, how shall this bloody deed be answered?°
It will be laid to us, whose providence°
Should have kept short,° restrained, and out of haunt°
This mad young man. But so much was our love,
We would not understand what was most fit,
But, like the owner of a foul disease,
To keep it from divulging,° let it feed
Even on the pith of life. Where is he gone?

QUEEN. To draw apart the body he hath killed,
O'er whom his very madness, like some ore°
Among a mineral° of metals base,
Shows itself pure: 'a weeps for what is done.

KING. O Gertrude, come away!
The sun no sooner shall the mountains touch
But we will ship him hence, and this vile deed
We must with all our majesty and skill
Both countenance° and excuse.—Ho, Guildenstern!

*Enter Rosencrantz and Guildenstern.*

Friends both, go join you with some further aid.
Hamlet in madness hath Polonius slain,
And from his mother's closet hath he dragged him.
Go seek him out, speak fair, and bring the body
Into the chapel. I pray you, haste in this.
[*Exeunt Rosencrantz and Guildenstern.*]
Come, Gertrude, we'll call up our wisest friends
And let them know both what we mean to do
And what's untimely done° . . . . . . . .
Whose whisper o'er the world's diameter,°
As level° as the cannon to his blank,°
Transports his poisoned shot, may miss our name
And hit the woundless° air. O, come away!
My soul is full of discord and dismay.

*Exeunt.*

**11 brainish apprehension** headstrong conception **12 heavy** grievous **13 us** i.e., me. (The royal "we"; also in line 15.) **16 answered** explained **17 providence** foresight **18 short** i.e., on a short tether. **out of haunt** secluded **22 divulging** becoming evident **25 ore** vein of gold **26 mineral** mine **32 countenance** put the best face on **40 And . . . done** (A defective line; conjectures as to the missing words include *So, haply, slander* [Capell and others]; *For, haply, slander* [Theobald and others]; and *So envious slander* [Jenkins].) **41 diameter** extent from side to side **42 As level** with as direct aim **his blank** its target at point-blank range **44 woundless** invulnerable

**4.2** *Enter Hamlet.*

HAMLET. Safely stowed.

ROSENCRANTZ, GUILDENSTERN [*within*]. Hamlet! Lord Hamlet!

HAMLET. But soft, what noise? Who calls on Hamlet? O, here they come.

*Enter Rosencrantz and Guildenstern.*

ROSENCRANTZ. What have you done, my lord, with the dead body?

HAMLET. Compounded it with dust, whereto 'tis kin.

ROSENCRANTZ. Tell us where 'tis, that we may take it thence
And bear it to the chapel.

HAMLET. Do not believe it.

ROSENCRANTZ. Believe what?

HAMLET. That I can keep your counsel and not mine own.° Besides, to be demanded of° a sponge, what replication° should be made by the son of a king?

ROSENCRANTZ. Take you me for a sponge, my lord?

HAMLET. Ay, sir, that soaks up the King's countenance,° his rewards, his authorities.° But such officers do the King best service in the end. He keeps them, like an ape, an apple, in the corner of his jaw, first mouthed to be last swallowed. When he needs what you have gleaned, it is but squeezing you, and, sponge, you shall be dry again.

ROSENCRANTZ. I understand you not, my lord.

HAMLET. I am glad of it. A knavish speech sleeps in° a foolish ear.

ROSENCRANTZ. My lord, you must tell us where the body is and go with us to the King.

HAMLET. The body is with the King, but the King is not with the body.°
The King is a thing—

GUILDENSTERN. A thing, my lord?

HAMLET. Of nothing.° Bring me to him. Hide fox, and all after!°

*Exeunt* [*running*].

**4.3** *Enter King, and two or three.*

KING. I have sent to seek him, and to find the body.
How dangerous is it that this man goes loose!

**4.2 Location: The castle.** **10 That . . . own** i.e., that I can follow your advice (by telling where the body is) and still keep my own secret **11 demanded of** questioned by **replication** reply **14 countenance** favor **15 authorities** delegated power, influence **21 sleeps in** has no meaning to **24 The . . . body** (Perhaps alludes to the legal commonplace of "the king's two bodies," which drew a distinction between the sacred office of kingship and the particular mortal who possessed it at any given time. Hence, although Claudius's body is necessarily a part of him, true kingship is not contained in it. Similarly, Claudius will have Polonius's body when it is found, but there is no kingship in this business either.) **27 Of nothing** (1) of no account (2) lacking the essence of kingship, as in lines 24–25 and note **Hide . . . after** (An old signal cry in the game of hide-and-seek, suggesting that Hamlet now runs away from them.)

**4.3 Location: The castle.**

Yet must not we put the strong law on him.
He's loved of° the distracted° multitude,
Who like not in their judgment, but their eyes,°
And where 'tis so, th' offender's scourge° is weighed,°
But never the offense. To bear all smooth and even,°
This sudden sending him away must seem
Deliberate pause.° Diseases desperate grown
By desperate appliance° are relieved,
Or not at all.

*Enter Rosencrantz,* [*Guildenstern,*] *and all the rest.*

How now, what hath befall'n?

ROSENCRANTZ. Where the dead body is bestowed, my lord,
We cannot get from him.

KING. But where is he?

ROSENCRANTZ. Without, my lord; guarded, to know your pleasure.

KING. Bring him before us.

ROSENCRANTZ. Ho! Bring in the lord.

*They enter* [*with Hamlet*].

KING. Now, Hamlet, where's Polonius?

HAMLET. At supper.

KING. At supper? Where?

HAMLET. Not where he eats, but where 'a is eaten. A certain convocation of politic worms° are e'en° at him. Your worm° is your only emperor for diet.° We fat all creatures else to fat us, and we fat ourselves for maggots. Your fat king and your lean beggar is but variable service°—two dishes, but to one table. That's the end.

KING. Alas, alas!

HAMLET. A man may fish with the worm that hath eat° of a king, and eat of the fish that hath fed of that worm.

KING. What dost thou mean by this?

HAMLET. Nothing but to show you how a king may go a progress° through the guts of a beggar.

KING. Where is Polonius?

HAMLET. In heaven. Send thither to see. If your messenger find him not there, seek him i' th' other place yourself. But if indeed you find him not within this month, you shall nose him as you go up the stairs into the lobby.

KING [*to some attendants*]. Go seek him there.

HAMLET. 'A will stay till you come.

[*Exeunt attendants.*]

**4 of** by. **distracted** fickle, unstable **5 Who . . . eyes** who choose not by judgment but by appearance **6 scourge** punishment. (Literally, blow with a whip.) **weighed** sympathetically considered **7 To . . . even** to manage the business in an unprovocative way **9 Deliberate pause** carefully considered action **10 appliance** remedies **20 politic worms** crafty worms (suited to a master spy like Polonius). **e'en** even now **Your worm** your average worm. Compare *your fat king and your lean beggar* in line 22.) **21 diet** food, eating (with a punning reference to the Diet of Worms, a famous *convocation* held in 1521) **22–23 variable service** different courses of a single meal **25 eat** eaten (Pronounced *et.*) **28 progress** royal journey of state

KING. Hamlet, this deed, for thine especial safety—
Which we do tender,° as we dearly° grieve
For that which thou hast done—must send thee hence
With fiery quickness. Therefore prepare thyself.
The bark° is ready, and the wind at help,
Th' associates tend,° and everything is bent°
For England.

HAMLET. For England!

KING. Ay, Hamlet.

HAMLET. Good.

KING. So is it, if thou knew'st our purposes.

HAMLET. I see a cherub° that sees them. But come, for England! Farewell, dear mother.

KING. Thy loving father, Hamlet.

HAMLET. My mother. Father and mother is man and wife, man and wife is one flesh, and so, my mother. Come, for England!

*Exit.*

KING. Follow him at foot;° tempt him with speed aboard.
Delay it not. I'll have him hence tonight.
Away! For everything is sealed and done
That else leans on° th' affair. Pray you, make haste.

[*Exeunt all but the King.*]

And, England,° if my love thou hold'st at aught°—
As my great power thereof may give thee sense,°
Since yet thy cicatrice° looks raw and red
After the Danish sword, and thy free awe°
Pays homage to us—thou mayst not coldly set°
Our sovereign process,° which imports at full,°
By letters congruing° to that effect,
The present° death of Hamlet. Do it, England,
For like the hectic° in my blood he rages,
And thou must cure me. Till I know 'tis done,
Howe'er my haps,° my joys were ne'er begun.

*Exit.*

## 4.4 *Enter Fortinbras with his army over the stage.*

FORTINBRAS. Go, Captain, from me greet the Danish king.
Tell him that by his license° Fortinbras
Craves the conveyance of° a promised march

**38 tender** regard, hold dear **dearly** intensely **41 bark** sailing vessel **42 tend** wait **bent** in readiness **48 cherub** (Cherubim are angels of knowledge. Hamlet hints that both he and heaven are onto Claudius's tricks.) **53 at foot** close behind, at heel **56 leans on** bears upon, is related to **57 England** i.e., King of England **at aught** at any value **58 As . . . sense** for so my great power may give you a just appreciation of the importance of valuing my love **59 cicatrice** scar **60 free awe** voluntary show of respect **61 coldly set** regard with indifference **62 process** command. **imports at full** conveys specific directions for **63 congruing** agreeing **64 present** immediate **65 hectic** persistent fever **67 haps** fortunes
**4.4 Location: The coast of Denmark. 2 license** permission **3 the conveyance of** escort during

Over his kingdom. You know the rendezvous.
If that His Majesty would aught with us,
We shall express our duty° in his eye;°
And let him know so.

CAPTAIN. I will do 't, my lord.

FORTINBRAS. Go softly° on.

[*Exeunt all but the Captain.*]

*Enter Hamlet, Rosencrantz,* [*Guildenstern,*] *etc.*

HAMLET. Good sir, whose powers° are these?

CAPTAIN. They are of Norway, sir.

HAMLET. How purposed, sir, I pray you?

CAPTAIN. Against some part of Poland.

HAMLET. Who commands them, sir?

CAPTAIN. The nephew to old Norway, Fortinbras.

HAMLET. Goes it against the main° of Poland, sir,
Or for some frontier?

CAPTAIN. Truly to speak, and with no addition,°
We go to gain a little patch of ground
That hath in it no profit but the name.
To pay° five ducats, five, I would not farm it;°
Nor will it yield to Norway or the Pole
A ranker° rate, should it be sold in fee.°

HAMLET. Why, then the Polack never will defend it.

CAPTAIN. Yes, it is already garrisoned.

HAMLET. Two thousand souls and twenty thousand ducats
Will not debate the question of this straw.°
This is th' impostume° of much wealth and peace,
That inward breaks, and shows no cause without
Why the man dies. I humbly thank you, sir.

CAPTAIN. God b'wi' you, sir.

[*Exit.*]

ROSENCRANTZ. Will 't please you go, my lord?

HAMLET. I'll be with you straight. Go a little before.

[*Exeunt all except Hamlet.*]

How all occasions do inform against° me
And spur my dull revenge! What is a man,
If his chief good and market of° his time
Be but to sleep and feed? A beast, no more.
Sure he that made us with such large discourse,°
Looking before and after,° gave us not
That capability and godlike reason
To fust° in us unused. Now, whether it be

**6 duty** respect **eye** presence **9 softly** slowly, circumspectly **10 powers** forces **16 main** main part **18 addition** exaggeration **21 To pay** i.e., for a yearly rental of. **farm it** take a lease of it **23 ranker** higher **in fee** fee simple, outright **27 debate . . . straw** settle this trifling matter **28 impostume** abscess **33 inform against** denounce, betray; take shape against **35 market of** profit of, compensation for **37 discourse** power of reasoning **38 Looking before and after** able to review past events and anticipate the future **40 fust** grow moldy

Bestial oblivion,° or some craven° scruple
Of thinking too precisely° on th' event°—
A thought which, quartered, hath but one part wisdom
And ever three parts coward—I do not know
Why yet I live to say "This thing's to do,"
Sith° I have cause, and will, and strength, and means
To do 't. Examples gross° as earth exhort me:
Witness this army of such mass and charge,°
Led by a delicate and tender° prince,
Whose spirit with divine ambition puffed
Makes mouths° at the invisible event,°
Exposing what is mortal and unsure
To all that fortune, death, and danger dare,°
Even for an eggshell. Rightly to be great
Is not to stir without great argument,
But greatly to find quarrel in a straw
When honor's at the stake.° How stand I, then,
That have a father killed, a mother stained,
Excitements of° my reason and my blood,
And let all sleep, while to my shame I see
The imminent death of twenty thousand men
That for a fantasy° and trick° of fame
Go to their graves like beds, fight for a plot°
Whereon the numbers cannot try the cause,°
Which is not tomb enough and continent°
To hide the slain? O, from this time forth
My thoughts be bloody or be nothing worth!

*Exit.*

**4.5** *Enter Horatio, [Queen] Gertrude, and a Gentleman.*

QUEEN. I will not speak with her.
GENTLEMAN. She is importunate,
Indeed distract.° Her mood will needs be pitied.
QUEEN. What would she have?
GENTLEMAN. She speaks much of her father, says she hears
There's tricks° i' the world, and hems,° and beats her heart,°

**41 oblivion** forgetfulness **craven** cowardly **42 precisely** scrupulously **event** outcome **46 Sith** since **47 gross** obvious **48 charge** expense **49 delicate and tender** of fine and youthful qualities **51 Makes mouths** makes scornful faces. **invisible event** unforeseeable outcome **53 dare** could do (to him) **54–57 Rightly . . . stake** true greatness does not normally consist of rushing into action over some trivial provocation; however, when one's honor is involved, even a trifling insult requires that one respond greatly(?) **at the stake** (A metaphor from gambling or bear-baiting.) **59 Excitements of** promptings by **62 fantasy** fanciful caprice, illusion **trick** trifle, deceit **63 plot** plot of ground **64 Whereon . . . cause** on which there is insufficient room for the soldiers needed to engage in a military contest **65 continent** receptacle; container

**4.5 Location: The castle. 2 distract** distracted **5 tricks** deceptions **hems** makes "hmm" sounds **heart** i.e., breast

Spurns enviously at straws,° speaks things in doubt°
That carry but half sense. Her speech is nothing,
Yet the unshapèd use° of it doth move
The hearers to collection;° they yawn° at it,
And botch° the words up fit to their own thoughts,
Which,° as her winks and nods and gestures yield° them,
Indeed would make one think there might be thought,°
Though nothing sure, yet much unhappily.°

HORATIO. 'Twere good she were spoken with, for she may strew
Dangerous conjectures in ill-breeding° minds.

QUEEN. Let her come in. *[Exit Gentleman.]*
[*Aside.*] To my sick soul, as sin's true nature is,
Each toy° seems prologue to some great amiss.°
So full of artless jealousy is guilt,
It spills itself in fearing to be spilt.°

*Enter Ophelia*° [*distracted*].

OPHELIA. Where is the beauteous majesty of Denmark?

QUEEN. How now, Ophelia?

OPHELIA [*she sings*].
"How should I your true love know
From another one?
By his cockle hat° and staff,
And his sandal shoon."°

QUEEN. Alas, sweet lady, what imports this song?

OPHELIA. Say you? Nay, pray you, mark.
"He is dead and gone, lady,
He is dead and gone; [*Song.*]
At his head a grass-green turf,
At his heels a stone."
O, ho!

QUEEN. Nay, but Ophelia—

OPHELIA. Pray you, mark. [*Sings.*]
"White his shroud as the mountain snow"—

*Enter King.*

QUEEN. Alas, look here, my lord.

OPHELIA.
"Larded° with sweet flowers; [*Song.*]
Which bewept to the ground did not go
With true-love showers."°

**6 Spurns . . . straws** kicks spitefully, takes offense at trifles **in doubt** obscurely **8 unshapèd use** incoherent manner **9 collection** inference, a guess at some sort of meaning **yawn** gape, wonder; grasp. (The Folio reading, *aim,* is possible.) **10 botch** patch **11 Which** which words **yield** deliver, represent **12 thought** intended **13 unhappily** unpleasantly near the truth, shrewdly **15 ill-breeding** prone to suspect the worst and to make mischief **18 toy** trifle **amiss** calamity **19–20 So . . . split** guilt is so full of suspicion that it unskillfully betrays itself in fearing betrayal **20 s.d. Enter Ophelia** (In the First Quarto, Ophelia enters, "playing on a lute, and her hair down, singing.") **25 cockle hat** hat with cockle-shell stuck in it as a sign that the wearer had been a pilgrim to the shrine of Saint James of Compostela in Spain **26 shoon** shoes **38 Larded** decorated **40 showers** i.e., tears

KING. How do you, pretty lady?

OPHELIA. Well, God 'ild° you! They say the owl° was a baker's daughter. Lord, we know what we are, but know not what we may be. God be at your table!

KING. Conceit° upon her father.

OPHELIA. Pray let's have no words of this; but when they ask you what it means, say you this:

"Tomorrow is Saint Valentine's day, [*Song.*]
All in the morning betime,°
And I a maid at your window,
To be your Valentine.
Then up he rose, and donned his clothes,
And dupped° the chamber door,
Let in the maid, that out a maid
Never departed more."

KING. Pretty Ophelia—

OPHELIA. Indeed, la, without an oath, I'll make an end on 't: [*Sings.*]

"By Gis° and by Saint Charity,
Alack, and fie for shame!
Young men will do 't, if they come to 't;
By Cock,° they are to blame.
Quoth she, 'Before you tumbled me,
You promised me to wed.' "

He answers:

" 'So would I ha' done, by yonder sun,
An° thou hadst not come to my bed.' "

KING. How long hath she been thus?

OPHELIA. I hope all will be well. We must be patient, but I cannot choose but weep to think they would lay him i' the cold ground. My brother shall know of it. And so I thank you for your good counsel. Come, my coach! Good night, ladies, good night, sweet ladies, good night, good night.

[*Exit.*]

KING [*to Horatio*]. Follow her close. Give her good watch, I pray you.

[*Exit Horatio.*]

O, this is the poison of deep grief; it springs
All from her father's death—and now behold!
O Gertrude, Gertrude,
When sorrows come, they come not single spies,°
But in battalions. First, her father slain;
Next, your son gone, and he most violent author
Of his own just remove;° the people muddied,°
Thick and unwholesome in their thoughts and whispers

**42 God 'ild** God yield or reward **owl** (Refers to a legend about a baker's daughter who was turned into an owl for being ungenerous when Jesus begged a loaf of bread.) **45 Conceit** brooding **49 betime** early **53 dupped** did up, opened **58 Gis** Jesus **61 Cock** (A perversion of "God" in oaths; here also with a quibble on the slang word for penis.) **66 An** if **77 spies** scouts sent in advance of the main force **80 remove** removal **muddied** stirred up, confused

For good Polonius' death—and we have done but greenly,°
In hugger-mugger° to inter him; poor Ophelia
Divided from herself and her fair judgment,
Without the which we are pictures or mere beasts;
Last, and as much containing° as all these,
Her brother is in secret come from France,
Feeds on this wonder, keeps himself in clouds,°
And wants° not buzzers° to infect his ear
With pestilent speeches of his father's death,
Wherein necessity,° of matter beggared,°
Will nothing stick our person to arraign
In ear and ear.° O my dear Gertrude, this,
Like to a murdering piece,° in many places
Gives me superfluous death.° *A noise within.*

QUEEN. Alack, what noise is this?

KING. Attend!°
Where is my Switzers?° Let them guard the door.

*Enter a Messenger.*

What is the matter?

MESSENGER. Save yourself, my lord!
The ocean, overpeering of his list,°
Eats not the flats° with more impetuous° haste
Than young Laertes, in a riotous head,°
O'erbears your officers. The rabble call him lord,
And, as° the world were now but to begin,
Antiquity forgot, custom not known,
The ratifiers and props of every word,°
They cry, "Choose we! Laertes shall be king!"
Caps,° hands, and tongues applaud it to the clouds,
"Laertes shall be king, Laertes king!"

QUEEN. How cheerfully on the false trail they cry!
*A noise within.*
O, this is counter,° you false Danish dogs!

*Enter Laertes with others.*

**82 greenly** in an inexperienced way, foolishly **83 hugger-mugger** secret haste **86 as much containing** as full of serious matter **88 Feeds . . . clouds** feeds his resentment or shocked grievance, holds himself inscrutable and aloof amid all this rumor **89 wants** lacks **buzzers** gossipers, informers **91 necessity** i.e., the need to invent some plausible explanation **of matter beggared** unprovided with facts **92–93 Will . . . ear** will not hesitate to accuse my (royal) person in everybody's ears **94 murdering piece** cannon loaded so as to scatter its shot **95 Gives . . . death** kills me over and over **97 Attend** i.e., guard me **98 Switzers** Swiss guards, mercenaries **100 overpeering of his list** overflowing its shore, boundary **101 flats** i.e., flatlands near shore **impetuous** violent (perhaps also with the meaning of *impiteous* [*impitious,* Q2], "pitiless") **102 head** insurrection **104 as** as if **106 The ratifiers . . . word** i.e., *antiquity* (or tradition) and *custom* ought to confirm (*ratify*) and underprop our every word or promise. **108 Caps** (The caps are thrown in the air.) **111 counter** (A hunting term, meaning to follow the trail in a direction opposite to that which the game has taken.)

KING. The doors are broke.
LAERTES. Where is this King?—Sirs, stand you all without.
ALL. No, let's come in.
LAERTES. I pray you, give me leave.
ALL. We will, we will.
LAERTES. I thank you. Keep the door. [*Exeunt followers.*] O thou vile king,
Give me my father!
QUEEN [*restraining him*]. Calmly, good Laertes.
LAERTES. That drop of blood that's calm proclaims me bastard,
Cries cuckold to my father, brands the harlot
Even here, between° the chaste unsmirchèd brow
Of my true mother.
KING. What is the cause, Laertes,
That thy rebellion looks so giantlike?
Let him go, Gertrude. Do not fear our° person.
There's such divinity doth hedge° a king
That treason can but peep to what it would,°
Acts little of his will.° Tell me, Laertes,
Why thou art thus incensed. Let him go, Gertrude.
Speak, man.
LAERTES. Where is my father?
KING. Dead.
QUEEN. But not by him.
KING. Let him demand his fill.
LAERTES. How came he dead? I'll not be juggled with.°
To hell, allegiance! Vows, to the blackest devil!
Conscience and grace, to the profoundest pit!
I dare damnation. To this point I stand,°
That both the worlds I give to negligence,°
Let come what comes, only I'll be revenged
Most throughly° for my father.
KING. Who shall stay you?
LAERTES. My will, not all the world's.°
And for° my means, I'll husband them so well
They shall go far with little.
KING. Good Laertes,
If you desire to know the certainty
Of your dear father, is 't writ in your revenge
That, swoopstake,° you will draw both friend and foe,
Winner and loser?

**121 between** in the middle of **124 fear our** fear for my **125 hedge** protect, as with a surrounding barrier **126 can . . . would** can only peep furtively, as through a barrier, at what it would intend **127 Acts . . . will** (but) performs little of what it intends **131 juggled with** cheated, deceived **134 To . . . stand** I am resolved in this **135 both . . . negligence** i.e., both this world and the next are of no consequence to me **137 throughly** thoroughly **139 My will . . . world's** I'll stop (*stay*) when my will is accomplished, not for anyone else's **140 for** as for **144 swoopstake** i.e., indiscriminately. (Literally, taking all stakes on the gambling table at once. *Draw* is also a gambling term, meaning "take from.")

LAERTES. None but his enemies.
KING. Will you know them, then?
LAERTES. To his good friends thus wide I'll ope my arms,
And like the kind life-rendering pelican°
Repast° them with my blood.
KING. Why, now you speak
Like a good child and a true gentleman.
That I am guiltless of your father's death,
And am most sensibly° in grief for it,
It shall as level° to your judgment 'pear
As day does to your eye. *A noise within.*
LAERTES. How now, what noise is that?

*Enter Ophelia.*

KING. Let her come in.
LAERTES. O heat, dry up my brains! Tears seven times salt
Burn out the sense and virtue° of mine eye!
By heaven, thy madness shall be paid with weight°
Till our scale turn the beam.° O rose of May!
Dear maid, kind sister, sweet Ophelia!
O heavens, is 't possible a young maid's wits
Should be as mortal as an old man's life?
Nature is fine in° love, and where 'tis fine
It sends some precious instance° of itself
After the thing it loves.°
OPHELIA.
"They bore him barefaced on the bier, *(Song.)*
Hey non nonny, nonny, hey nonny,
And in his grave rained many a tear—"
Fare you well, my dove!
LAERTES. Hadst thou thy wits and didst persuade° revenge,
It could not move thus.
OPHELIA. You must sing "A-down a-down," and you "call him a-down-a."° O, how the wheel° becomes it! It is the false steward° that stole his master's daughter.
LAERTES. This nothing's more than matter.°
OPHELIA. There's rosemary,° that's for remembrance; pray you, love, remember. And there is pansies;° that's for thoughts.

**149 pelican** (Refers to the belief that the female pelican fed its young with its own blood.) **150 Repast** feed **153 sensibly** feelingly **154 level** plain **158 virtue** faculty, power **159 paid with weight** repaid, avenged equally or more **160 beam** crossbar of a balance **164 fine in** refined by **165 instance** token **166 After . . . loves** i.e., into the grave, along with Polonius **171 persuade** argue cogently for **173–174 You . . . a-down-a** (Ophelia assigns the singing of refrains, like her own "Hey non nonny," to others present.) **174 wheel** spinning wheel as accompaniment to the song, or refrain **false steward** (The story is unknown.) **176 This . . . matter** this seeming nonsense is more eloquent than sane utterance **177 rosemary** (Used as a symbol of remembrance both at weddings and at funerals.) **178 pansies** (Emblems of love and courtship; perhaps from French *pensées*, "thoughts.")

LAERTES. A document° in madness, thoughts and remembrance fitted.

OPHELIA. There's fennel° for you, and columbines.° There's rue° for you, and here's some for me; we may call it herb of grace o' Sundays. You must wear your rue with a difference.° There's a daisy.° I would give you some violets,° but they withered all when my father died. They say 'a made a good end—
[*Sings.*] "For bonny sweet Robin is all my joy."

LAERTES. Thought° and affliction, passion,° hell itself,
She turns to favor° and to prettiness.

OPHELIA.
"And will 'a not come again? [*Song.*]
And will 'a not come again?
No, no, he is dead.
Go to thy deathbed,
He never will come again.

"His beard was as white as snow,
All flaxen was his poll.°
He is gone, he is gone,
And we cast away moan.
God ha' mercy on his soul!"
And of all Christian souls, I pray God. God b' wi' you.
[*Exit, followed by Gertrude.*]

LAERTES. Do you see this, O God?

KING. Laertes, I must commune with your grief,
Or you deny me right. Go but apart,
Make choice of whom° your wisest friends you will,
And they shall hear and judge twixt you and me.
If by direct or by collateral hand°
They find us touched,° we will our kingdom give,
Our crown, our life, and all that we call ours
To you in satisfaction; but if not,
Be you content to lend your patience to us,
And we shall jointly labor with your soul
To give it due content.

LAERTES. Let this be so.
His means of death, his obscure funeral—
No trophy,° sword, nor hatchment° o'er his bones,
No noble rite, nor formal ostentation°—

**179 document** instruction, lesson **180 fennel** (Emblem of flattery.) **columbines** (Emblems of unchastity or ingratitude.) **rue** (Emblem of repentance—a signification that is evident in its popular name, *herb of grace.*) **182 with a difference** (A device used in heraldry to distinguish one family from another on the coat of arms, here suggesting that Ophelia and the others have different causes of sorrow and repentance; perhaps with a play on *rue* in the sense of "ruth," "pity.") **daisy** (Emblem of dissembling, faithlessness.) **183 violets** (Emblems of faithfulness.) **186 Thought** melancholy **passion** suffering **187 favor** grace, beauty **194 poll** head **202 whom** whichever of **204 collateral hand** indirect agency **205 us touched** me implicated **212 trophy** memorial **hatchment** tablet displaying the armorial bearings of a deceased person **213 ostentation** ceremony

Cry to be heard, as 'twere from heaven to earth,
That° I must call 't in question.°

KING. So you shall,
And where th' offense is, let the great ax fall.
I pray you, go with me.

*Exeunt.*

**4.6** *Enter Horatio and others.*

HORATIO. What are they that would speak with me?

GENTLEMAN. Seafaring men, sir. They say they have letters for you.

HORATIO. Let them come in.

[*Exit Gentleman.*]

I do not know from what part of the world
I should be greeted, if not from Lord Hamlet.

*Enter Sailors.*

FIRST SAILOR. God bless you, sir.

HORATIO. Let him bless thee too.

FIRST SAILOR. 'A shall, sir, an 't° please him. There's a letter for you, sir—it came from th' ambassador° that was bound for England—if your name be Horatio, as I am let to know it is. [*He gives a letter.*]

HORATIO [*reads*]. "Horatio, when thou shalt have overlooked° this, give these fellows some means° to the King; they have letters for him. Ere we were two days old at sea, a pirate of very warlike appointment° gave us chase. Finding ourselves too slow of sail, we put on a compelled valor, and in the grapple I boarded them. On the instant they got clear of our ship, so I alone became their prisoner. They have dealt with me like thieves of mercy,° but they knew what they did: I am to do a good turn for them. Let the King have the letters I have sent, and repair° thou to me with as much speed as thou wouldest fly death. I have words to speak in thine ear will make thee dumb, yet are they much too light for the bore° of the matter. These good fellows will bring thee where I am. Rosencrantz and Guildenstern hold their course for England. Of them I have much to tell thee. Farewell.

He that thou knowest thine, Hamlet."

Come, I will give you way° for these your letters,
And do 't the speedier that you may direct me
To him from whom you brought them.

*Exeunt.*

**215 That** so that **call 't in question** demand an explanation
**4.6 Location: The castle. 8 an 't** if it **9 th' ambassador** (Evidently Hamlet. The sailor is being circumspect.) **11 overlooked** looked over **12 means** means of access **13–14 appointment** equipage **17 thieves of mercy** merciful thieves **19 repair** come **21 bore** caliber, i.e., importance **26 way** means of access

**4.7** *Enter King and Laertes.*

KING. Now must your conscience my acquittance seal,°
And you must put me in your heart for friend,
Sith° you have heard, and with a knowing ear,
That he which hath your noble father slain
Pursued my life.
LAERTES. It well appears. But tell me
Why you proceeded not against these feats°
So crimeful and so capital° in nature,
As by your safety, greatness, wisdom, all things else,
You mainly° were stirred up.
KING. O, for two special reasons,
Which may to you perhaps seem much unsinewed,°
But yet to me they're strong. The Queen his mother
Lives almost by his looks, and for myself—
My virtue or my plague, be it either which—
She is so conjunctive° to my life and soul
That, as the star moves not but in his° sphere,°
I could not but by her. The other motive
Why to a public count° I might not go
Is the great love the general gender° bear him,
Who, dipping all his faults in their affection,
Work° like the spring° that turneth wood to stone,
Convert his gyves° to graces, so that my arrows,
Too slightly timbered° for so loud° a wind,
Would have reverted° to my bow again
But not where I had aimed them.
LAERTES. And so have I a noble father lost,
A sister driven into desperate terms,°
Whose worth, if praises may go back° again,
Stood challenger on mount° of all the age
For her perfections. But my revenge will come.
KING. Break not your sleeps for that. You must not think
That we are made of stuff so flat and dull
That we can let our beard be shook with danger
And think it pastime. You shortly shall hear more.

**4.7 Location: The castle.** **1 my acquittance seal** confirm or acknowledge my innocence **3 Sith** since **6 feats** acts **7 capital** punishable by death **9 mainly** greatly **11 unsinewed** weak **15 conjunctive** closely united. (An astronomical metaphor.) **16 his** its **sphere** one of the hollow spheres in which, according to Ptolemaic astronomy, the planets were supposed to move **18 count** account, reckoning, indictment **19 general gender** common people **21 Work** operate, act **spring** i.e., a spring with such a concentration of lime that it coats a piece of wood with limestone, in effect gilding and petrifying it **22 gyves** fetters (which, gilded by the people's praise, would look like badges of honor) **23 slightly timbered** light. **loud** (suggesting public outcry on Hamlet's behalf) **24 reverted** returned **27 terms** state, condition **28 go back** i.e., recall what she was **29 on mount** set up on high

I loved your father, and we love ourself;
And that, I hope, will teach you to imagine—

*Enter a Messenger with letters.*

How now? What news?
MESSENGER. Letters, my lord, from Hamlet:
This to Your Majesty, this to the Queen.
[*He gives letters.*]
KING. From Hamlet? Who brought them?
MESSENGER. Sailors, my lord, they say. I saw them not.
They were given me by Claudio. He received them
Of him that brought them.
KING. Laertes, you shall hear them.—
Leave us.
[*Exit Messenger.*]

[*He reads.*] "High and mighty, you shall know I am set naked° on your kingdom. Tomorrow shall I beg leave to see your kingly eyes, when I shall, first asking your pardon,° thereunto recount the occasion of my sudden and more strange return. Hamlet."

What should this mean? Are all the rest come back?
Or is it some abuse,° and no such thing?°
LAERTES. Know you the hand?
KING. 'Tis Hamlet's character.° "Naked!"
And in a postscript here he says "alone."
Can you devise° me?
LAERTES. I am lost in it, my lord. But let him come.
It warms the very sickness in my heart
That I shall live and tell him to his teeth,
"Thus didst thou."°
KING. If it be so, Laertes—
As how should it be so? How otherwise?°—
Will you be ruled by me?
LAERTES. Ay, my lord,
So° you will not o'errule me to a peace.
KING. To thine own peace. If he be now returned,
As checking at° his voyage, and that° he means
No more to undertake it, I will work him
To an exploit, now ripe in my device,°
Under the which he shall not choose but fall;
And for his death no wind of blame shall breathe,
But even his mother shall uncharge the practice°
And call it accident.

**45 naked** destitute, unarmed, without following **47 pardon** permission **50 abuse** deceit **no such thing** not what it appears **51 character** handwriting **53 devise** explain to **57 Thus didst thou** i.e., here's for what you did to my father **58 As . . . otherwise** how can this (Hamlet's return) be true? Yet how otherwise than true (since we have the evidence of his letter)? **60 So** provided that **62 checking at** i.e., turning aside from (like a falcon leaving the quarry to fly at a chance bird) **that** if **64 device** devising, invention **67 uncharge the practice** acquit the stratagem of being a plot

LAERTES. My lord, I will be ruled,
The rather if you could devise it so
That I might be the organ.°
KING. It falls right.
You have been talked of since your travel much,
And that in Hamlet's hearing, for a quality
Wherein they say you shine. Your sum of parts°
Did not together pluck such envy from him
As did that one, and that, in my regard,
Of the unworthiest siege.°
LAERTES. What part is that, my lord?
KING. A very ribbon in the cap of youth,
Yet needful too, for youth no less becomes°
The light and careless livery that it wears
Than settled age his sables° and his weeds°
Importing health and graveness.° Two months since
Here was a gentleman of Normandy.
I have seen myself, and served against, the French,
And they can well° on horseback, but this gallant
Had witchcraft in 't; he grew unto his seat,
And to such wondrous doing brought his horse
As had he been incorpsed and demi-natured°
With the brave beast. So far he topped° my thought
That I in forgery° of shapes and tricks
Come short of what he did.
LAERTES. A Norman was 't?
KING. A Norman.
LAERTES. Upon my life, Lamord.
KING. The very same.
LAERTES. I know him well. He is the brooch° indeed
And gem of all the nation.
KING. He made confession° of you,
And gave you such a masterly report
For art and exercise in your defense,°
And for your rapier most especial,
That he cried out 'twould be a sight indeed
If one could match you. Th' escrimers° of their nation,
He swore, had neither motion, guard, nor eye
If you opposed them. Sir, this report of his
Did Hamlet so envenom with his envy
That he could nothing do but wish and beg

**70 organ** agent, instrument **73 Your . . . parts** i.e., all your other virtues **76 unworthiest siege** least important rank **79 no less becomes** is no less suited by **81 his sables** its rich robes furred with sable. **weeds** garments **82 Importing . . . graveness** signifying a concern for health and dignified prosperity; also, giving an impression of comfortable prosperity **85 can well** are skilled **88 As . . . demi-natured** as if he had been of one body and nearly of one nature (like the centaur) **89 topped** surpassed **90 forgery** imagining **94 brooch** ornament **96 confession** testimonial, admission of superiority **98 For . . . defense** with respect to your skill and practice with your weapon **101 escrimers** fencers

Your sudden° coming o'er, to play° with you.
Now, out of this—

LAERTES. What out of this, my lord?

KING. Laertes, was your father dear to you?
Or are you like the painting of a sorrow,
A face without a heart?

LAERTES. Why ask you this?

KING. Not that I think you did not love your father,
But that I know love is begun by time,°
And that I see, in passages of proof,°
Time qualifies° the spark and fire of it.
There lives within the very flame of love
A kind of wick or snuff° that will abate it,
And nothing is at a like goodness still,°
For goodness, growing to a pleurisy,°
Dies in his own too much.° That° we would do,
We should do when we would; for this "would" changes
And hath abatements° and delays as many
As there are tongues, are hands, are accidents,°
And then this "should" is like a spendthrift sigh,°
That hurts by easing.° But, to the quick o' th' ulcer:°
Hamlet comes back. What would you undertake
To show yourself in deed your father's son
More than in words?

LAERTES. To cut his throat i' the church.

KING. No place, indeed, should murder sanctuarize;°
Revenge should have no bounds. But good Laertes,
Will you do this,° keep close within your chamber.
Hamlet returned shall know you are come home.
We'll put on those shall° praise your excellence
And set a double varnish on the fame
The Frenchman gave you, bring you in fine° together,
And wager on your heads. He, being remiss,°
Most generous,° and free from all contriving,
Will not peruse the foils, so that with ease,

**106 sudden** immediate **play** fence **112 begun by time** i.e., created by the right circumstance and hence subject to change **113 passages of proof** actual instances that prove it **114 qualifies** weakens, moderates **116 snuff** the charred part of a candlewick **117 nothing . . . still** nothing remains at a constant level of perfection **118 pleurisy** excess, plethora. (Literally, a chest inflammation.) **119 in . . . much** of its own excess **That** that which **121 abatements** diminutions **122 As . . . accidents** as there are tongues to dissuade, hands to prevent, and chance events to intervene **123 spendthrift sigh** (An allusion to the belief that sighs draw blood from the heart.) **124 hurts by easing** i.e., costs the heart blood and wastes precious opportunity even while it affords emotional relief **quick o' th' ulcer** i.e., heart of the matter **128 sanctuarize** protect from punishment. (Alludes to the right of sanctuary with which certain religious places were invested.) **130 Will you do this** if you wish to do this **132 put on those shall** arrange for some to **134 in fine** finally **135 remiss** negligently unsuspicious **136 generous** noble-minded

Or with a little shuffling, you may choose
A sword unbated,° and in a pass of practice°
Requite him for your father.

LAERTES. I will do 't,
And for that purpose I'll anoint my sword.
I bought an unction° of a mountebank°
So mortal that, but dip a knife in it,
Where it draws blood no cataplasm° so rare,
Collected from all simples° that have virtue°
Under the moon,° can save the thing from death
That is but scratched withal. I'll touch my point
With this contagion, that if I gall° him slightly,
It may be death.

KING. Let's further think of this,
Weigh what convenience both of time and means
May fit us to our shape.° If this should fail,
And that our drift look through our bad performance,°
'Twere better not assayed. Therefore this project
Should have a back or second, that might hold
If this did blast in proof.° Soft, let me see.
We'll make a solemn wager on your cunnings°—
I ha 't!
When in your motion you are hot and dry—
As° make your bouts more violent to that end—
And that he calls for drink, I'll have prepared him
A chalice for the nonce,° whereon but sipping,
If he by chance escape your venomed stuck,°
Our purpose may hold there. [*A cry within.*] But stay, what noise?

*Enter Queen.*

QUEEN. One woe doth tread upon another's heel,
So fast they follow. Your sister's drowned, Laertes.

LAERTES. Drowned! O, where?

QUEEN. There is a willow grows askant° the brook,
That shows his hoar leaves° in the glassy stream;
Therewith fantastic garlands did she make
Of crowflowers, nettles, daisies, and long purples,°
That liberal° shepherds give a grosser name,°

**139 unbated** not blunted, having no button **pass of practice** treacherous thrust **142 unction** ointment **mountebank** quack doctor **144 cataplasm** plaster or poultice **145 simples** herb. **virtue** potency **146 Under the moon** i.e., anywhere (with reference perhaps to the belief that herbs gathered at night had a special power) **148 gall** graze, wound **151 shape** part we propose to act **152 drift . . . performance** intention should be made visible by our bungling **155 blast in proof** burst in the test (like a cannon) **156 cunnings** respective skills **159 As** i.e., and you should **161 nonce** occasion **162 stuck** thrust. (From *stoccado,* a fencing term.) **167 askant** aslant **168 hoar leaves** white or gray undersides of the leaves **170 long purples** early purple orchids **171 liberal** free-spoken **a grosser name** (The testicle-resembling tubers of the orchid, which also in some cases resemble *dead men's fingers,* have earned various slang names like "dogstones" and "cullions.")

But our cold° maids do dead men's fingers call them.
There on the pendent° boughs her crownet° weeds
Clamb'ring to hang, an envious sliver° broke,
When down her weedy° trophies and herself
Fell in the weeping brook. Her clothes spread wide,
And mermaidlike awhile they bore her up,
Which time she chanted snatches of old lauds,°
As one incapable of° her own distress,
Or like a creature native and endued°
Unto that element. But long it could not be
Till that her garments, heavy with their drink,
Pulled the poor wretch from her melodious lay
To muddy death.

LAERTES. Alas, then she is drowned?

QUEEN. Drowned, drowned.

LAERTES. Too much of water hast thou, poor Ophelia,
And therefore I forbid my tears. But yet
It is our trick;° nature her custom holds,
Let shame say what it will. [*He weeps.*] When these are gone,
The woman will be out.° Adieu, my lord.
I have a speech of fire that fain would blaze,
But that this folly douts° it. *Exit.*

KING. Let's follow, Gertrude.
How much I had to do to calm his rage!
Now fear I this will give it start again;
Therefore let's follow.

*Exeunt.*

**5.1** *Enter two Clowns°* [*with spades and mattocks*].

FIRST CLOWN. Is she to be buried in Christian burial, when she willfully seeks her own salvation?°

SECOND CLOWN. I tell thee she is; therefore make her grave straight.° The crowner° hath sat on her,° and finds it° Christian burial.

FIRST CLOWN. How can that be, unless she drowned herself in her own defense?

SECOND CLOWN. Why, 'tis found so.°

**172 cold** chaste **173 pendent** overhanging **crownet** made into a chaplet or coronet **174 envious sliver** malicious branch **175 weedy** i.e., of plants **178 lauds** hymns **179 incapable of** lacking capacity to apprehend **180 endued** adapted by nature **188 It is our trick** i.e., weeping is our natural way (when sad) **189–190 When . . . out** when my tears are all shed, the woman in me will be expended, satisfied **192 douts** extinguishes. (The Second Quarto reads "drowns.") **5.1 Location: A churchyard.** **s.d. Clowns** rustics **2 salvation** (A blunder for "damnation," or perhaps a suggestion that Ophelia was taking her own shortcut to heaven.) **3 straight** straightway, immediately. (But with a pun on *strait,* "narrow.") **4 crowner** coroner. **sat on her** conducted an inquest on her case **finds it** gives his official verdict that her means of death was consistent with **7 found so** determined so in the coroner's verdict

FIRST CLOWN. It must be *se offendendo,*° it cannot be else. For here lies the point: if I drown myself wittingly, it argues an act, and an act hath three branches—it is to act, to do, and to perform. Argal,° she drowned herself wittingly.

SECOND CLOWN. Nay, but hear you, goodman° delver—

FIRST CLOWN. Give me leave. Here lies the water; good. Here stands the man; good. If the man go to this water and drown himself, it is, will he, nill he,° he goes, mark you that. But if the water come to him and drown him, he drowns not himself. Argal, he that is not guilty of his own death shortens not his own life.

SECOND CLOWN. But is this law?

FIRST CLOWN. Ay, marry, is 't—crowner's quest° law.

SECOND CLOWN. Will you ha' the truth on 't? If this had not been a gentlewoman, she should have been buried out o' Christian burial.

FIRST CLOWN. Why, there thou sayst.° And the more pity that great folk should have countenance° in this world to drown or hang themselves, more than their even-Christian.° Come, my spade. There is no ancient° gentlemen but gardeners, ditchers, and grave makers. They hold up° Adam's profession.

SECOND CLOWN. Was he a gentleman?

FIRST CLOWN. 'A was the first that ever bore arms.°

SECOND CLOWN. Why, he had none.

FIRST CLOWN. What, art a heathen? How dost thou understand the Scripture? The Scripture says Adam digged. Could he dig without arms?° I'll put another question to thee. If thou answerest me not to the purpose, confess thyself°—

SECOND CLOWN. Go to.

FIRST CLOWN. What is he that builds stronger than either the mason, the shipwright, or the carpenter?

SECOND CLOWN. The gallows maker, for that frame° outlives a thousand tenants.

FIRST CLOWN. I like thy wit well, in good faith. The gallows does well.° But how does it well? It does well to those that do ill. Now thou dost ill to say the gallows is built stronger than the church. Argal, the gallows may do well to thee. To 't again, come.

SECOND CLOWN. "Who builds stronger than a mason, a shipwright, or a carpenter?"

FIRST CLOWN. Ay, tell me that, and unyoke.°

**8 *se offendendo*** (A comic mistake for *se defendendo,* a term used in verdicts of justifiable homicide.) **10 Argal** (Corruption of *ergo,* "therefore.") **12 goodman** (An honorific title often used with the name of a profession or craft.) **14–15 will he, nill he** whether he will or no, willy-nilly **19 quest** inquest **22 there thou sayst** i.e., that's right **23 countenance** privilege **24 even-Christian** fellow Christians **25 ancient** going back to ancient times **26 hold up** maintain **28 bore arms** (To be entitled to bear a coat of arms would make Adam a gentleman, but as one who bore a spade, our common ancestor was an ordinary delver in the earth.) **31 arms** i.e., the arms of the body **33 confess thyself** (The saying continues, "and be hanged.") **37 frame** (1) gallows (2) structure **39 does well** (1) is an apt answer (2) does a good turn **45 unyoke** i.e., after this great effort, you may unharness the team of your wits

SECOND CLOWN. Marry, now I can tell.

FIRST CLOWN. To 't.

SECOND CLOWN. Mass,° I cannot tell.

*Enter Hamlet and Horatio* [*at a distance*].

FIRST CLOWN. Cudgel thy brains no more about it, for your dull ass will not mend his pace with beating; and when you are asked this question next, say "a grave maker." The houses he makes lasts till doomsday. Go get thee in and fetch me a stoup° of liquor.

[*Exit Second Clown. First Clown digs.*]

*Song.*

"In youth, when I did love, did love,°
Methought it was very sweet,
To contract—O—the time for—a—my behove,°
O, methought there—a—was nothing—a—meet."°

HAMLET. Has this fellow no feeling of his business, 'a° sings in grave-making?

HORATIO. Custom hath made it in him a property of easiness.°

HAMLET. 'Tis e'en so. The hand of little employment hath the daintier sense.°

FIRST CLOWN. *Song.*

"But age with his stealing steps
Hath clawed me in his clutch,
And hath shipped me into the land,°
As if I had never been such."

[*He throws up a skull.*]

HAMLET. That skull had a tongue in it and could sing once. How the knave jowls° it to the ground, as if 'twere Cain's jawbone, that did the first murder! This might be the pate of a politician,° which this ass now o'erreaches,° one that would circumvent God, might it not?

HORATIO. It might, my lord.

HAMLET. Or of a courtier, which could say, "Good morrow, sweet lord! How dost thou, sweet lord?" This might be my Lord Such-a-one, that praised my Lord Such-a-one's horse when 'a meant to beg it, might it not?

HORATIO. Ay, my lord.

HAMLET. Why, e'en so, and now my Lady Worm's, chapless,° and

**48 Mass** by the Mass **52 stoup** two-quart measure **53 In . . . love** (This and the two following stanzas, with nonsensical variations, are from a poem attributed to Lord Vaux and printed in *Tottel's Miscellany,* 1557. The *O* and *a* [for "ah"] seemingly are the grunts of the digger.) **55 To contract . . . behove** i.e., to shorten the time for my own advantage. (Perhaps he means to *prolong* it.) **56 meet** suitable, i.e., more suitable **57 'a** that he **59 property of easiness** something he can do easily and indifferently **60–61 daintier sense** more delicate sense of feeling **64 into the land** i.e., toward my grave(?) (But note the lack of rhyme in *steps, land.*) **67 jowls** dashes (with a pun on *jowl,* "jawbone") **68 politician** schemer, plotter **69 o'erreaches** circumvents, gets the better of (with a quibble on the literal sense) **77 chapless** having no lower jaw

knocked about the mazard° with a sexton's spade. Here's fine revolution,° an° we had the trick to see° 't. Did these bones cost no more the breeding but° to play at loggets° with them? Mine ache to think on 't.

FIRST CLOWN. *Song.*

"A pickax and a spade, a spade,
For and° a shrouding sheet;
O, a pit of clay for to be made
For such a guest is meet."

[*He throws up another skull.*]

HAMLET. There's another. Why may not that be the skull of a lawyer? Where be his quiddities° now, his quillities,° his cases, his tenures,° and his tricks? Why does he suffer this mad knave now to knock him about the sconce° with a dirty shovel, and will not tell him of his action of battery?° Hum, this fellow might be in 's time a great buyer of land, with his statutes, his recognizances,° his fines, his double° vouchers,° his recoveries.° Is this the fine of his fines and the recovery of his recoveries, to have his fine pate full of fine dirt?° Will his vouchers vouch him no more of his purchases, and double ones too, than the length and breadth of a pair of indentures?° The very conveyances° of his lands will scarcely lie in this box,° and must th' inheritor° himself have no more, ha?

HORATIO. Not a jot more, my lord.

HAMLET. Is not parchment made of sheepskins?

HORATIO. Ay, my lord, and of calves' skins too.

HAMLET. They are sheep and calves which seek out assurance in that.° I will speak to this fellow.—Whose grave's this, sirrah?°

FIRST CLOWN. Mine, sir. [*Sings.*]

"O, pit of clay for to be made
For such a guest is meet."

**78 mazard** i.e., head. (Literally, a drinking vessel.) **78–79 revolution** turn of Fortune's wheel, change **79 an** if **trick to see** knack of seeing **79–80 cost . . . but** involve so little expense and care in upbringing that we may **80 loggets** a game in which pieces of hard wood shaped like Indian clubs or bowling pins are thrown to lie as near as possible to a stake **83 For and** and moreover **87 quiddities** subtleties, quibbles. (From Latin *quid,* "a thing.") **quillities** verbal niceties, subtle distinctions. (Variation of *quiddities.*) **88 tenures** the holding of a piece of property or office, or the conditions or period of such holding **89 sconce** head **90 action of battery** lawsuit about physical assault **91 statutes, recognizances** legal documents guaranteeing a debt by attaching land and property **91–92 fines, recoveries** ways of converting entailed estates into "fee simple" or freehold **92 double** signed by two signatories **vouchers** guarantees of the legality of a title to real estate **92–94 fine of his fines . . . fine pate . . . fine dirt** end of his legal maneuvers . . . elegant head . . . minutely sifted dirt **95–96 pair of indentures** legal document drawn up in duplicate on a single sheet and then cut apart on a zigzag line so that each pair was uniquely matched. (Hamlet may refer to two rows of teeth or dentures.) **96 conveyances** deeds **97 box** (1) deed box (2) coffin. ("Skull" has been suggested.) **inheritor** possessor, owner **101 assurance in that** safety in legal parchments **102 sirrah** (A term of address to inferiors.)

HAMLET. I think it be thine, indeed, for thou liest in 't.

FIRST CLOWN. You lie out on 't, sir, and therefore 'tis not yours. For my part, I do not lie in 't, yet it is mine.

HAMLET. Thou dost lie in 't, to be in 't and say it is thine. 'Tis for the dead, not for the quick;° therefore thou liest.

FIRST CLOWN. 'Tis a quick lie, sir; 'twill away again from me to you.

HAMLET. What man dost thou dig it for?

FIRST CLOWN. For no man, sir.

HAMLET. What woman, then?

FIRST CLOWN. For none, neither.

HAMLET. Who is to be buried in 't?

FIRST CLOWN. One that was a woman, sir, but, rest her soul, she's dead.

HAMLET. How absolute° the knave is! We must speak by the card,° or equivocation° will undo us. By the Lord, Horatio, this three years I have took° note of it: the age is grown so picked° that the toe of the peasant comes so near the heel of the courtier, he galls his kibe.°—How long hast thou been grave maker?

FIRST CLOWN. Of all the days i' the year, I came to 't that day that our last king Hamlet overcame Fortinbras.

HAMLET. How long is that since?

FIRST CLOWN. Cannot you tell that? Every fool can tell that. It was that very day that young Hamlet was born—he that is mad and sent into England.

HAMLET. Ay, marry, why was he sent into England?

FIRST CLOWN. Why, because 'a was mad. 'A shall recover his wits there, or if 'a do not, 'tis no great matter there.

HAMLET. Why?

FIRST CLOWN. 'Twill not be seen in him there. There the men are as mad as he.

HAMLET. How came he mad?

FIRST CLOWN. Very strangely, they say.

HAMLET. How strangely?

FIRST CLOWN. Faith, e'en with losing his wits.

HAMLET. Upon what ground?°

FIRST CLOWN. Why, here in Denmark. I have been sexton here, man and boy, thirty years.

HAMLET. How long will a man lie i' th' earth ere he rot?

FIRST CLOWN. Faith, if 'a be not rotten before 'a die—as we have many pocky° corpses nowadays, that will scarce hold the laying in°—'a will last you° some eight year or nine year. A tanner will last you nine year.

**110 quick** living **118 absolute** strict, precise **by the card** i.e., with precision. (Literally, by the mariner's compass-card, on which the points of the compass were marked.) **119 equivocation** ambiguity in the use of terms **120 took** taken **picked** refined, fastidious **121–122 galls his kibe** chafes the courtier's chilblain **139 ground** cause. (But, in the next line, the grave-digger takes the word in the sense of "land," "country.") **144 pocky** rotten, diseased. (Literally, with the pox, or syphilis.) **hold the laying in** hold together long enough to be interred **145 last you** last. (*You* is used colloquially here and in the following lines.)

HAMLET. Why he more than another?

FIRST CLOWN. Why, sir, his hide is so tanned with his trade that 'a will keep out water a great while, and your water is a sore° decayer of your whoreson° dead body. [*He picks up a skull.*] Here's a skull now hath lien you° i' th' earth three-and-twenty years.

HAMLET. Whose was it?

FIRST CLOWN. A whoreson mad fellow's it was. Whose do you think it was?

HAMLET. Nay, I know not.

FIRST CLOWN. A pestilence on him for a mad rogue! 'A poured a flagon of Rhenish° on my head once. This same skull, sir, was, sir, Yorick's skull, the King's jester.

HAMLET. This?

FIRST CLOWN. E'en that.

HAMLET. Let me see. [*He takes the skull.*] Alas, poor Yorick! I knew him, Horatio, a fellow of infinite jest, of most excellent fancy. He hath bore° me on his back a thousand times, and now how abhorred in my imagination it is! My gorge rises° at it. Here hung those lips that I have kissed I know not how oft. Where be your gibes now? Your gambols, your songs, your flashes of merriment that were wont° to set the table on a roar? Not one now, to mock your own grinning?° Quite chopfallen?° Now get you to my lady's chamber and tell her, let her paint an inch thick, to this favor° she must come. Make her laugh at that. Prithee, Horatio, tell me one thing.

HORATIO. What's that, my lord?

HAMLET. Dost thou think Alexander looked o' this fashion i' th' earth?

HORATIO. E'en so.

HAMLET. And smelt so? Pah! [*He throws down the skull.*]

HORATIO. E'en so, my lord.

HAMLET. To what base uses we may return, Horatio! Why may not imagination trace the noble dust of Alexander till 'a find it stopping a bunghole?°

HORATIO. 'Twere to consider too curiously° to consider so.

HAMLET. No, faith, not a jot, but to follow him thither with modesty° enough, and likelihood to lead it. As thus: Alexander died, Alexander was buried, Alexander returneth to dust, the dust is earth, of earth we make loam,° and why of that loam whereto he was converted might they not stop a beer barrel?
Imperious° Caesar, dead and turned to clay,
Might stop a hole to keep the wind away.

**149 sore** i.e., terrible, great **150 whoreson** i.e., vile, scurvy **151 lien you** lain. (See the note at line 144.) **157 Rhenish** Rhine wine **163 bore** borne **164 My gorge rises** i.e., I feel nauseated **166 were wont** used **167 mock your own grinning** mock at the way your skull seems to be grinning (just as you used to mock at yourself and those who grinned at you) **168 chopfallen** (1) lacking the lower jaw (2) dejected **169 favor** aspect, appearance **178 bunghole** hole for filling or emptying a cask **179 curiously** minutely **180 modesty** plausible moderation **183 loam** mortar consisting chiefly of moistened clay and straw **185 Imperious** imperial

O, that that earth which kept the world in awe
Should patch a wall t' expel the winter's flaw!°

*Enter King, Queen, Laertes, and the corpse* [*of Ophelia, in procession, with Priest, lords, etc.*].

But soft,° but soft awhile! Here comes the King,
The Queen, the courtiers. Who is this they follow?
And with such maimèd° rites? This doth betoken
The corpse they follow did with desperate hand
Fordo° its own life. 'Twas of some estate.°
Couch we° awhile and mark.

[*He and Horatio conceal themselves. Ophelia's body is taken to the grave.*]

LAERTES. What ceremony else?
HAMLET [*to Horatio*]. That is Laertes, a very noble youth. Mark.
LAERTES. What ceremony else?
PRIEST. Her obsequies have been as far enlarged
As we have warranty.° Her death was doubtful,
And but that great command o'ersways the order°
She should in ground unsanctified been lodged°
Till the last trumpet. For° charitable prayers,
Shards,° flints, and pebbles should be thrown on her.
Yet here she is allowed her virgin crants,°
Her maiden strewments,° and the bringing home
Of bell and burial.°
LAERTES. Must there no more be done?
PRIEST. No more be done.
We should profane the service of the dead
To sing a requiem and such rest° to her
As to peace-parted souls.°
LAERTES. Lay her i' th' earth,
And from her fair and unpolluted flesh
May violets° spring! I tell thee, churlish priest,
A ministering angel shall my sister be
When thou liest howling.°
HAMLET [*to Horatio*]. What, the fair Ophelia!
QUEEN [*scattering flowers*]. Sweets to the sweet! Farewell.
I hoped thou shouldst have been my Hamlet's wife.
I thought thy bride-bed to have decked, sweet maid,
And not t' have strewed thy grave.

**188 flaw** gust of wind **189 soft** i.e., wait, be careful **191 maimèd** mutilated, incomplete **193 Fordo** destroy. **estate** rank **194 Couch we** let's hide, lie low **199 warranty** i.e., ecclesiastical authority **200 great . . . order** orders from on high overrule the prescribed procedures **201 She should . . . lodged** she should have been buried in unsanctified ground **202 For** in place of **203 Shards** broken bits of pottery **204 crants** garlands betokening maidenhood **205 strewments** flowers strewn on a coffin **205–206 bringing . . . burial** laying the body to rest, to the sound of the bell **209 such rest** i.e., to pray for such rest **210 peace-parted souls** those who have died at peace with God **212 violets** (See 4.5.183 and note) **214 howling** i.e., in hell

LAERTES. O, treble woe
Fall ten times treble on that cursèd head
Whose wicked deed thy most ingenious sense°
Deprived thee of! Hold off the earth awhile,
Till I have caught her once more in mine arms.

[*He leaps into the grave and embraces Ophelia.*]

Now pile your dust upon the quick and dead,
Till of this flat a mountain you have made
T' o'ertop old Pelion or the skyish head
Of blue Olympus.°

HAMLET [*coming forward*]. What is he whose grief
Bears such an emphasis,° whose phrase of sorrow
Conjures the wandering stars° and makes them stand
Like wonder-wounded° hearers? This is I,
Hamlet the Dane.°

LAERTES [*grappling with him*°]. The devil take thy soul!

HAMLET. Thou pray'st not well.
I prithee, take thy fingers from my throat,
For though I am not splenitive° and rash,
Yet have I in me something dangerous,
Which let thy wisdom fear. Hold off thy hand.

KING. Pluck them asunder.

QUEEN. Hamlet, Hamlet!

ALL. Gentlemen!

HORATIO. Good my lord, be quiet.

[*Hamlet and Laertes are parted.*]

HAMLET. Why, I will fight with him upon this theme
Until my eyelids will no longer wag.°

QUEEN. O my son, what theme?

HAMLET. I loved Ophelia. Forty thousand brothers
Could not with all their quantity of love
Make up my sum. What wilt thou do for her?

KING. O, he is mad, Laertes.

QUEEN. For love of God, forbear him.°

HAMLET. 'Swounds,° show me what thou'lt do.
Woo't° weep? Woo't fight? Woo't fast? Woo't tear thyself?

**220 ingenious sense** a mind that is quick, alert, of fine qualities **225–226 Pelion, Olympus** sacred mountains in the north of Thessaly; see also *Ossa,* at line 257 **227 emphasis** i.e., rhetorical and florid emphasis. (*Phrase* has a similar rhetorical connotation.) **228 wandering stars** planets **229 wonder-wounded** struck with amazement **230 the Dane** (This title normally signifies the King; see 1.1.17 and note.) **s.d. grappling with him** The testimony of the First Quarto that "*Hamlet leaps in after Laertes*" and the "Elegy on Burbage" ("Oft have I seen him leap into the grave") seem to indicate one way in which this fight was staged; however, the difficulty of fitting two contenders and Ophelia's body into a confined space (probably the trapdoor) suggests to many editors the alternative, that Laertes jumps out of the grave to attack Hamlet.) **233 splenitive** quick-tempered **241 wag** move. (A fluttering eyelid is a conventional sign that life has not yet gone.) **247 forbear him** leave him alone **248 'Swounds** by His (Christ's) wounds **249 Woo't** wilt thou

Woo't drink up° eisel?° Eat a crocodile?°
I'll do 't. Dost come here to whine?
To outface me with leaping in her grave?
Be buried quick° with her, and so will I.
And if thou prate of mountains, let them throw
Millions of acres on us, till our ground,
Singeing his pate° against the burning zone,°
Make Ossa° like a wart! Nay, an° thou'lt mouth,°
I'll rant as well as thou.

QUEEN. This is mere° madness,
And thus awhile the fit will work on him;
Anon, as patient as the female dove
When that her golden couplets° are disclosed,°
His silence will sit drooping.

HAMLET. Hear you, sir,
What is the reason that you use me thus?
I loved you ever. But it is no matter.
Let Hercules himself do what he may,
The cat will mew, and dog will have his day.°

*Exit Hamlet.*

KING. I pray thee, good Horatio, wait upon him.

[*Exit*] *Horatio.*

[*To Laertes.*] Strengthen your patience in° our last night's speech;
We'll put the matter to the present push.°—
Good Gertrude, set some watch over your son.—
This grave shall have a living° monument.
An hour of quiet° shortly shall we see;
Till then, in patience our proceeding be.

*Exeunt.*

## 5.2 *Enter Hamlet and Horatio.*

HAMLET. So much for this, sir; now shall you see the other.°
You do remember all the circumstance?

HORATIO. Remember it, my lord!

**250 drink up** drink deeply **eisel** vinegar **crocodile** (Crocodiles were tough and dangerous, and were supposed to shed hypocritical tears.) **253 quick** alive **256 his pate** its head, i.e., top **burning zone** zone in the celestial sphere containing the sun's orbit, between the tropics of Cancer and Capricorn **257 Ossa** another mountain in Thessaly. (In their war against the Olympian gods, the giants attempted to heap Ossa on Pelion to scale Olympus.) **an** if **mouth** i.e., rant **258 mere** utter **261 golden couplets** two baby pigeons, covered with yellow down **disclosed** hatched **265–266 Let . . . day** i.e., (1) even Hercules couldn't stop Laertes's theatrical rant (2) I, too, will have my turn; i.e., despite any blustering attempts at interference, every person will sooner or later do what he or she must do **268 in** i.e., by recalling **269 present push** immediate test **271 living** lasting. (For Laertes's private understanding, Claudius also hints that Hamlet's death will serve as such a monument.) **272 hour of quiet** time free of conflict
**5.2 Location: The castle.** **1 see the other** hear the other news

HAMLET. Sir, in my heart there was a kind of fighting
That would not let me sleep. Methought I lay
Worse than the mutines° in the bilboes.° Rashly,°
And praised be rashness for it—let us know°
Our indiscretion° sometimes serves us well
When our deep plots do pall,° and that should learn° us
There's a divinity that shapes our ends,
Rough-hew° them how we will—

HORATIO. That is most certain.

HAMLET. Up from my cabin,
My sea-gown° scarfed° about me, in the dark
Groped I to find out them,° had my desire,
Fingered° their packet, and in fine° withdrew
To mine own room again, making so bold,
My fears forgetting manners, to unseal
Their grand commission; where I found, Horatio—
Ah, royal knavery!—an exact command,
Larded° with many several° sorts of reasons
Importing° Denmark's health and England's too,
With, ho! such bugs° and goblins in my life,°
That on the supervise,° no leisure bated,°
No, not to stay° the grinding of the ax,
My head should be struck off.

HORATIO. Is 't possible?

HAMLET [*giving a document*].
Here's the commission. Read it at more leisure.
But wilt thou hear now how I did proceed?

HORATIO. I beseech you.

HAMLET. Being thus benetted round with villainies—
Ere I could make a prologue to my brains,
They had begun the play°—I sat me down,
Devised a new commission, wrote it fair.°
I once did hold it, as our statists° do,
A baseness° to write fair, and labored much
How to forget that learning, but, sir, now
It did me yeoman's° service. Wilt thou know
Th' effect° of what I wrote?

HORATIO. Ay, good my lord.

**6 mutines** mutineers **bilboes** shackles **Rashly** on impulse (This adverb goes with lines 12ff.) **7 know** acknowledge **8 indiscretion** lack of foresight and judgment (not an indiscreet act) **9 pall** fail, falter, go stale. **learn** teach **11 Rough-hew** shape roughly **13 sea-gown** seaman's coat **scarfed** loosely wrapped **14 them** i.e., Rosencrantz and Guildenstern **15 Fingered** pilfered, pinched **in fine** finally, in conclusion **20 Larded** garnished **several** different **21 Importing** relating to **22 bugs** bugbears, hobgoblins **in my life** i.e., to be feared if I were allowed to live **23 supervise** reading **leisure bated** delay allowed **24 stay** await **30–31 Ere . . . play** before I could consciously turn my brain to the matter, it had started working on a plan **32 fair** in a clear hand **33 statists** statesmen **34 baseness** i.e., lower-class trait **36 yeoman's** i.e., substantial, faithful, loyal **37 effect** purport

HAMLET. An earnest conjuration° from the King,
As England was his faithful tributary,
As love between them like the palm° might flourish,
As peace should still° her wheaten garland° wear
And stand a comma° 'tween their amities,
And many suchlike "as"es° of great charge,°
That on the view and knowing of these contents,
Without debatement further more or less,
He should those bearers put to sudden death,
Not shriving time° allowed.

HORATIO. How was this sealed?

HAMLET. Why, even in that was heaven ordinant.°
I had my father's signet° in my purse,
Which was the model° of that Danish seal;
Folded the writ° up in the form of th' other,
Subscribed° it, gave 't th' impression,° placed it safely,
The changeling° never known. Now, the next day
Was our sea fight, and what to this was sequent°
Thou knowest already.

HORATIO. So Guildenstern and Rosencrantz go to 't.

HAMLET. Why, man, they did make love to this employment.
They are not near my conscience. Their defeat°
Does by their own insinuation° grow.
'Tis dangerous when the baser° nature comes
Between the pass° and fell° incensèd points
Of mighty opposites.°

HORATIO. Why, what a king is this!

HAMLET. Does it not, think thee, stand me now upon°—
He that hath killed my king and whored my mother,
Popped in between th' election° and my hopes,
Thrown out his angle° for my proper° life,
And with such cozenage°—is 't not perfect conscience
To quit° him with this arm? And is 't not to be damned
To let this canker° of our nature come
In° further evil?

HORATIO. It must be shortly known to him from England
What is the issue of the business there.

**38 conjuration** entreaty **40 palm** (An image of health; see Psalm 92:12) **41 still** always. **wheaten garland** (Symbolic of fruitful agriculture, of peace and plenty.) **42 comma** (Indicating continuity, link.) **43 "as"es** (1) the "whereases" of a formal document (2) asses. **charge** (1) import (2) burden (appropriate to asses) **47 shriving time** time for confession and absolution **48 ordinant** directing **49 signet** small seal **50 model** replica **51 writ** writing **52 Subscribed** signed (with forged signature). **impression** i.e., with a wax seal **53 changeling** i.e., substituted letter (Literally, a fairy child substituted for a human one) **54 was sequent** followed **58 defeat** destruction **59 insinuation** intrusive intervention, sticking their noses in my business **60 baser** of lower social station **61 pass** thrust. **fell** fierce **62 opposites** antagonists **63 stand me now upon** become incumbent on me now **65 election** (The Danish monarch was "elected" by a small number of high-ranking electors.) **66 angle** fishhook. **proper** very **67 cozenage** trickery **68 quit** requite, pay back **69 canker** ulcer **69–70 come In** grow into

HAMLET. It will be short. The interim is mine,
And a man's life's no more than to say "one."°
But I am very sorry, good Horatio,
That to Laertes I forgot myself,
For by the image of my cause I see
The portraiture of his. I'll court his favors.
But, sure, the bravery° of his grief did put me
Into a tow'ring passion.

HORATIO. Peace, who comes here?

*Enter a Courtier* [*Osric*].

OSRIC. Your lordship is right welcome back to Denmark.

HAMLET. I humbly thank you, sir. [*To Horatio.*] Dost know this water fly?

HORATIO. No, my good lord.

HAMLET. Thy state is the more gracious, for 'tis a vice to know him. He hath much land, and fertile. Let a beast be lord of beasts, and his crib° shall stand at the King's mess.° 'Tis a chuff,° but, as I say, spacious in the possession of dirt.

OSRIC. Sweet lord, if your lordship were at leisure, I should impart a thing to you from His Majesty.

HAMLET. I will receive it, sir, with all diligence of spirit.
Put your bonnet° to his° right use; 'tis for the head.

OSRIC. I thank your lordship, it is very hot.

HAMLET. No, believe me, 'tis very cold. The wind is northerly.

OSRIC. It is indifferent° cold, my lord, indeed.

HAMLET. But yet methinks it is very sultry and hot for my complexion.°

OSRIC. Exceedingly, my lord. It is very sultry, as 'twere—I cannot tell how. My lord, His Majesty bade me signify to you that 'a has laid a great wager on your head. Sir, this is the matter—

HAMLET. I beseech you, remember.

[*Hamlet moves him to put on his hat.*]

OSRIC. Nay, good my lord; for my ease,° in good faith. Sir, here is newly come to court Laertes—believe me, an absolute° gentleman, full of most excellent differences,° of very soft society° and great showing.° Indeed, to speak feelingly° of him, he is the card° or calendar° of gentry,° for you shall find in him the continent of what part a gentleman would see.°

**74 a man's . . . "one"** one's whole life occupies such a short time, only as long as it takes to count to 1 **79 bravery** bravado **87 crib** manger **86–87 Let . . . mess** i.e., if a man, no matter how beastlike, is as rich in livestock and possessions as Osric, he may eat at the King's table **87 chuff** boor, churl. (The Second Quarto spelling, *chough,* is a variant spelling that also suggests the meaning here of "chattering jackdaw.") **92 bonnet** any kind of cap or hat **his** its **95 indifferent** somewhat **96 complexion** temperament **101 for my ease** (A conventional reply declining the invitation to put his hat back on.) **102 absolute** perfect **103 differences** special qualities **soft society** agreeable manners **103–104 great showing** distinguished appearance **104 feelingly** with just perception **card** chart, map **104–105 calendar** guide **gentry** good breeding **105–106 the continent . . . see** one who contains in him all the qualities a gentleman would like to see. (A *continent* is that which contains.)

HAMLET. Sir, his definement° suffers no perdition° in you,° though I know to divide him inventorially° would dozy° th' arithmetic of memory, and yet but yaw° neither° in respect of° his quick sail. But, in the verity of extolment,° I take him to be a soul of great article,° and his infusion° of such dearth and rareness° as, to make true diction° of him, his semblable° is his mirror and who else would trace° him his umbrage,° nothing more.

OSRIC. Your lordship speaks most infallibly of him.

HAMLET. The concernancy,° sir? Why do we wrap the gentleman in our more rawer breath?°

OSRIC. Sir?

HORATIO. Is 't not possible to understand in another tongue?° You will do 't,° sir, really.

HAMLET. What imports the nomination° of this gentleman?

OSRIC. Of Laertes?

HORATIO [*to Hamlet*]. His purse is empty already; all 's golden words are spent.

HAMLET. Of him, sir.

OSRIC. I know you are not ignorant—

HAMLET. I would you did, sir. Yet in faith if you did, it would not much approve° me. Well, sir?

OSRIC. You are not ignorant of what excellence Laertes is—

HAMLET. I dare not confess that, lest I should compare with him in excellence. But to know a man well were to know himself.°

OSRIC. I mean, sir, for° his weapon; but in the imputation laid on him by them,° in his meed° he's unfellowed.°

HAMLET. What's his weapon?

OSRIC. Rapier and dagger.

HAMLET. That's two of his weapons—but well.°

**107 definement** definition (Hamlet proceeds to mock Osric by throwing his lofty diction back at him.) **perdition** loss, diminution **you** your description **108 divide him inventorially** enumerate his graces **dozy** dizzy. **109 yaw** swing unsteadily off course. (Said of a ship.) **neither** for all that **in respect of** in comparison with **110 in . . . extolment** in true praise (of him) **110–111 of great article** one with many articles in his inventory **111 infusion** essence, character infused into him by nature. **dearth and rareness** rarity **111–112 make true diction** speak truly **112 semblable** only true likeness **112–113 who . . . trace** any other person who would wish to follow **113 umbrage** shadow **115 concernancy** import, relevance **116 rawer breath** unrefined speech that can only come short in praising him **118 to understand . . . tongue** i.e., for you, Osric, to understand when someone else speaks your language. (Horatio twits Osric for not being able to understand the kind of flowery speech he himself uses, when Hamlet speaks in such a vein. Alternatively, all this could be said to Hamlet.) **118–119 You will do 't** i.e., you can if you try, or, you may well have to try (to speak plainly) **120 nomination** naming **127 approve** commend **129–130 I dare . . . himself** I dare not boast of knowing Laertes's excellence lest I seem to imply a comparable excellence in myself. Certainly, to know another person well, one must know oneself. **131 for** i.e., with **131–132 imputation . . . them** reputation given him by others **132 meed** merit. **unfellowed** unmatched **135 but well** but never mind

OSRIC. The King, sir, hath wagered with him six Barbary horses, against the which he° has impawned,° as I take it, six French rapiers and poniards,° with their assigns,° as girdle, hangers,° and so.° Three of the carriages,° in faith, are very dear to fancy,° very responsive° to the hilts, most delicate° carriages, and of very liberal conceit.°

HAMLET. What call you the carriages?

HORATIO [*to Hamlet*]. I knew you must be edified by the margent° ere you had done.

OSRIC. The carriages, sir, are the hangers.

HAMLET. The phrase would be more germane to the matter if we could carry a cannon by our sides; I would it might be hangers till then. But, on: six Barbary horses against six French swords, their assigns, and three liberal-conceited carriages; that's the French bet against the Danish. Why is this impawned, as you call it?

OSRIC. The King, sir, hath laid,° sir, that in a dozen passes° between yourself and him, he shall not exceed you three hits. He hath laid on twelve for nine, and it would come to immediate trial, if your lordship would vouchsafe the answer.°

HAMLET. How if I answer no?

OSRIC. I mean, my lord, the opposition of your person in trial.

HAMLET. Sir, I will walk here in the hall. If it please His Majesty, it is the breathing time° of day with me. Let° the foils be brought, the gentleman willing, and the King hold his purpose, I will win for him an I can; if not, I will gain nothing but my shame and the odd hits.

OSRIC. Shall I deliver you° so?

HAMLET. To this effect, sir—after what flourish your nature will.

OSRIC. I commend° my duty to your lordship.

HAMLET. Yours, yours. [*Exit Osric.*] 'A does well to commend it himself; there are no tongues else for 's turn.°

HORATIO. This lapwing° runs away with the shell on his head.

HAMLET. 'A did comply with his dug° before 'a sucked it. Thus has he—and many more of the same breed that I know the drossy° age

**137 he** i.e., Laertes. **impawned** staked, wagered **138 poniards** daggers. **assigns** appurtenances **hangers** straps on the sword belt (*girdle*), from which the sword hung. **and so** and so on **139 carriages** (An affected way of saying *hangers;* literally, gun carriages.) **dear to fancy** delightful to the fancy. **responsive** corresponding closely, matching or well adjusted **140 delicate** (i.e., in workmanship) **liberal conceit** elaborate design **142 margent** margin of a book, place for explanatory notes **150 laid** wagered **passes** bouts. (The odds of the betting are hard to explain. Possibly the King bets that Hamlet will win at least five out of twelve, at which point Laertes raises the odds against himself by betting he will win nine.) **153 vouchsafe the answer** be so good as to accept the challenge. (Hamlet deliberately takes the phrase in its literal sense of replying.) **157 breathing time** exercise period. **Let** i.e., if **160 deliver you** report what you say **162 commend** commit to your favor. (A conventional salutation, but Hamlet wryly uses a more literal meaning, "recommend," "praise," in line 163.) **164 for 's turn** for his purposes, i.e., to do it for him **165 lapwing** (A proverbial type of youthful forwardness. Also, a bird that draws intruders away from its nest and was thought to run about with its head in the shell when newly hatched; a seeming reference to Osric's hat.) **166 comply . . . dug** observe ceremonious formality toward his nurse's or mother's teat **167 drossy** laden with scum and impurities, frivolous

dotes on—only got the tune° of the time and, out of an habit of encounter,° a kind of yeasty° collection,° which carries them through and through the most fanned and winnowed opinions;° and do° but blow them to their trial, the bubbles are out.°

*Enter a Lord.*

LORD. My lord, His Majesty commended him to you by young Osric, who brings back to him that you attend him in the hall. He sends to know if your pleasure hold to play with Laertes, or that° you will take longer time.

HAMLET. I am constant to my purposes; they follow the King's pleasure. If his fitness speaks, mine is ready;° now or whensoever, provided I be so able as now.

LORD. The King and Queen and all are coming down.

HAMLET. In happy time.°

LORD. The Queen desires you to use some gentle entertainment° to Laertes before you fall to play.

HAMLET. She well instructs me. [*Exit Lord.*]

HORATIO. You will lose, my lord.

HAMLET. I do not think so. Since he went into France, I have been in continual practice; I shall win at the odds. But thou wouldst not think how ill all's here about my heart; but it is no matter.

HORATIO. Nay, good my lord—

HAMLET. It is but foolery, but it is such a kind of gaingiving° as would perhaps trouble a woman.

HORATIO. If your mind dislike anything, obey it. I will forestall their repair° hither and say you are not fit.

HAMLET. Not a whit, we defy augury. There is special providence in the fall of a sparrow. If it be now, 'tis not to come; if it be not to come, it will be now; if it be not now, yet it will come. The readiness is all. Since no man of aught he leaves knows, what is 't to leave betimes? Let be.°

*A table prepared.* [*Enter*] *trumpets, drums, and officers with cushions; King, Queen,* [*Osric,*] *and all the state; foils, daggers,* [*and wine borne in;*] *and Laertes.*

KING. Come, Hamlet, come and take this hand from me.
[*The King puts Laertes' hand into Hamlet's.*]

**168 tune** temper, mood, manner of speech **168–169 an habit of encounter** a demeanor in conversing (with courtiers of his own kind) **169 yeasty** frothy **collection** i.e., of current phrases **169–170 carries . . . opinions** sustains them right through the scrutiny of persons whose opinions are select and refined. (Literally, like grain separated from its chaff. Osric is both the chaff and the bubbly froth on the surface of the liquor that is soon blown away.) **170 and do** yet do **171 blow . . . out** test them by merely blowing on them, and their bubbles burst **174 that** if **177 If . . . ready** if he declares his readiness, my convenience waits on his **180 In happy time** (A phrase of courtesy indicating that the time is convenient.) **181 entertainment** greeting **189 gaingiving** misgiving **191–192 repair** coming **196–197 Since . . . Let be** since no one has knowledge of what he is leaving behind, what does an early death matter after all? Enough; don't struggle against it.

HAMLET [*to Laertes*]. Give me your pardon, sir. I have done you wrong,
But pardon 't as you are a gentleman.
This presence° knows,
And you must needs have heard, how I am punished°
With a sore distraction. What I have done
That might your nature, honor, and exception°
Roughly awake, I here proclaim was madness.
Was 't Hamlet wronged Laertes? Never Hamlet.
If Hamlet from himself be ta'en away,
And when he's not himself does wrong Laertes,
Then Hamlet does it not, Hamlet denies it.
Who does it, then? His madness. If 't be so,
Hamlet is of the faction° that is wronged;
His madness is poor Hamlet's enemy.
Sir, in this audience
Let my disclaiming from a purposed evil
Free me so far in your most generous thoughts
That I have° shot my arrow o'er the house
And hurt my brother.

LAERTES. I am satisfied in nature,°
Whose motive° in this case should stir me most
To my revenge. But in my terms of honor
I stand aloof, and will no reconcilement
Till by some elder masters of known honor
I have a voice° and precedent of peace°
To keep my name ungored.° But till that time
I do receive your offered love like love,
And will not wrong it.

HAMLET. I embrace it freely,
And will this brothers' wager frankly° play.—
Give us the foils. Come on.

LAERTES. Come, one for me.

HAMLET. I'll be your foil,° Laertes. In mine ignorance
Your skill shall, like a star i' the darkest night,
Stick fiery off° indeed.

LAERTES. You mock me, sir.

HAMLET. No, by this hand.

KING. Give them the foils, young Osric. Cousin Hamlet,
You know the wager?

HAMLET. Very well, my lord.
Your Grace has laid the odds o'° the weaker side.

KING. I do not fear it; I have seen you both.

**201 presence** royal assembly **202 punished** afflicted **204 exception** disapproval **211 faction** party **216 That I have** as if I had **217 in nature** i.e., as to my personal feelings **218 motive** prompting **222 voice** authoritative pronouncement **of peace** for reconciliation **223 name ungored** reputation unwounded **226 frankly** without ill feeling or the burden of rancor **228 foil** thin metal background which sets a jewel off (with pun on the blunted rapier for fencing) **230 Stick fiery off** stand out brilliantly **234 laid the odds o'** bet on, backed

But since he is bettered,° we have therefore odds.
LAERTES. This is too heavy. Let me see another.
[*He exchanges his foil for another.*]
HAMLET. This likes me° well. These foils have all a length?
[*They prepare to play.*]
OSRIC. Ay, my good lord.
KING. Set me the stoups of wine upon that table.
If Hamlet give the first or second hit,
Or quit in answer of the third exchange,°
Let all the battlements their ordnance fire.
The King shall drink to Hamlet's better breath,°
And in the cup an union° shall he throw
Richer than that which four successive kings
In Denmark's crown have worn. Give me the cups,
And let the kettle° to the trumpet speak,
The trumpet to the cannoneer without,
The cannons to the heavens, the heaven to earth,
"Now the King drinks to Hamlet." Come, begin.
*Trumpets the while.*
And you, the judges, bear a wary eye.
HAMLET. Come on, sir.
LAERTES. Come, my lord. [*They play. Hamlet scores a hit.*]
HAMLET. One.
LAERTES. No.
HAMLET. Judgment.
OSRIC. A hit, a very palpable hit.
*Drum, trumpets, and shot. Flourish. A piece goes off.*
LAERTES. Well, again.
KING. Stay, give me drink. Hamlet, this pearl is thine.
[*He drinks, and throws a pearl in Hamlet's cup.*]
Here's to thy health. Give him the cup.
HAMLET. I'll play this bout first. Set it by awhile.
Come. [*They play.*] Another hit; what say you?
LAERTES. A touch, a touch, I do confess 't.
KING. Our son shall win.
QUEEN. He's fat° and scant of breath.
Here, Hamlet, take my napkin,° rub thy brows.
The Queen carouses° to thy fortune, Hamlet.
HAMLET. Good, madam!
KING. Gertrude, do not drink.
QUEEN. I will, my lord, I pray you pardon me. [*She drinks.*]
KING [*aside*]. It is the poisoned cup. It is too late.
HAMLET. I dare not drink yet, madam; by and by.

**236 is bettered** has improved; is the odds-on favorite. (Laertes's handicap is the "three hits" specified in line 151.) **238 likes me** pleases me **242 Or . . . exchange** i.e., or requites Laertes in the third bout for having won the first two **244 better breath** improved vigor **245 union** pearl. (So called, according to Pliny's *Natural History,* 9, because pearls are *unique,* never identical.) **248 kettle** kettledrum **264 fat** not physically fit, out of training **265 napkin** handkerchief **266 carouses** drinks a toast

QUEEN. Come, let me wipe thy face.
LAERTES [*to King*]. My lord, I'll hit him now.
KING. I do not think 't.
LAERTES [*aside*]. And yet it is almost against my conscience.
HAMLET. Come, for the third, Laertes. You do but dally.
I pray you, pass° with your best violence;
I am afeard you make a wanton of me.°
LAERTES. Say you so? Come on. [*They play.*]
OSRIC. Nothing neither way.
LAERTES. Have at you now!

[*Laertes wounds Hamlet; then, in scuffling, they change rapiers,° and Hamlet wounds Laertes.*]

KING. Part them! They are incensed.
HAMLET. Nay, come, again. [*The Queen falls.*]
OSRIC. Look to the Queen there, ho!
HORATIO. They bleed on both sides. How is it, my lord?
OSRIC. How is 't, Laertes?
LAERTES. Why, as a woodcock° to mine own springe,° Osric;
I am justly killed with mine own treachery.
HAMLET. How does the Queen?
KING. She swoons to see them bleed.
QUEEN. No, no, the drink, the drink—O my dear Hamlet—
The drink, the drink! I am poisoned. [*She dies.*]
HAMLET. O villainy! Ho, let the door be locked!
Treachery! Seek it out.
[*Laertes falls. Exit Osric.*]
LAERTES. It is here, Hamlet. Hamlet, thou art slain.
No med'cine in the world can do thee good;
In thee there is not half an hour's life.
The treacherous instrument is in thy hand,
Unbated° and envenomed. The foul practice°
Hath turned itself on me. Lo, here I lie,
Never to rise again. Thy mother's poisoned.
I can no more. The King, the King's to blame.
HAMLET. The point envenomed too? Then, venom, to thy work.
[*He stabs the King.*]
ALL. Treason! Treason!
KING. O, yet defend me, friends! I am but hurt.
HAMLET [*forcing the King to drink*].
Here, thou incestuous, murderous, damnèd Dane,
Drink off this potion. Is thy union° here?
Follow my mother. [*The King dies.*]

**276 pass** thrust **277 make . . . me** i.e., treat me like a spoiled child, trifle with me **280 s.d. in scuffling, they change rapiers** (This stage direction occurs in the Folio. According to a widespread stage tradition, Hamlet receives a scratch, realizes that Laertes's sword is unbated, and accordingly forces an exchange.) **284 woodcock** a bird, a type of stupidity or as a decoy **springe** trap, snare **295 Unbated** not blunted with a button **practice** plot **303 union** pearl (See line 245; with grim puns on the word's other meanings: marriage, shared death.)

LAERTES. He is justly served.
It is a poison tempered° by himself.
Exchange forgiveness with me, noble Hamlet.
Mine and my father's death come not upon thee,
Nor thine on me! [*He dies.*]

HAMLET. Heaven make thee free of it! I follow thee.
I am dead, Horatio. Wretched Queen, adieu!
You that look pale and tremble at this chance,°
That are but mutes° or audience to this act,
Had I but time—as this fell° sergeant,° Death,
Is strict° in his arrest°—O, I could tell you—
But let it be. Horatio, I am dead;
Thou livest. Report me and my cause aright
To the unsatisfied.

HORATIO. Never believe it.
I am more an antique Roman° than a Dane.
Here's yet some liquor left.
[*He attempts to drink from the poisoned cup. Hamlet prevents him.*]

HAMLET. As thou'rt a man,
Give me the cup! Let go! By heaven, I'll ha 't.
O God, Horatio, what a wounded name,
Things standing thus unknown, shall I leave behind me!
If thou didst ever hold me in thy heart,
Absent thee from felicity awhile,
And in this harsh world draw thy breath in pain
To tell my story. *A march afar off* [*and a volley within*].
What warlike noise is this?

*Enter Osric.*

OSRIC. Young Fortinbras, with conquest come from Poland,
To th' ambassadors of England gives
This warlike volley.

HAMLET. O, I die, Horatio!
The potent poison quite o'ercrows° my spirit.
I cannot live to hear the news from England,
But I do prophesy th' election lights
On Fortinbras. He has my dying voice.°
So tell him, with th' occurents° more and less
Which have solicited°—the rest is silence. [*He dies.*]

HORATIO. Now cracks a noble heart. Good night, sweet prince,
And flights of angels sing thee to thy rest!
[*March within.*]
Why does the drum come hither?

**305 tempered** mixed **311 chance** mischance **312 mutes** silent observers. (Literally, actors with nonspeaking parts.) **313 fell** cruel. **sergeant** sheriff's officer **314 strict** (1) severely just (2) unavoidable. **arrest** (1) taking into custody (2) stopping my speech **318 Roman** (Suicide was an honorable choice for many Romans as an alternative to a dishonorable life.) **330 o'ercrows** triumphs over (like the winner in a cockfight) **333 voice** vote **334 occurents** events, incidents **335 solicited** moved, urged. (Hamlet doesn't finish saying what the events have prompted—presumably, his acts of vengeance, or his reporting of those events to Fortinbras.)

*Enter Fortinbras, with the* [*English*] *Ambassadors*
[*with drum, colors, and attendants*].

FORTINBRAS. Where is this sight?
HORATIO. What is it you would see?
If aught of woe or wonder, cease your search.
FORTINBRAS. This quarry° cries on havoc.° O proud Death,
What feast° is toward° in thine eternal cell,
That thou so many princes at a shot
So bloodily hast struck?
FIRST AMBASSADOR. The sight is dismal,
And our affairs from England come too late.
The ears are senseless that should give us hearing,
To tell him his commandment is fulfilled,
That Rosencrantz and Guildenstern are dead.
Where should we have our thanks?
HORATIO. Not from his° mouth,
Had it th' ability of life to thank you.
He never gave commandment for their death.
But since, so jump° upon this bloody question,°
You from the Polack wars, and you from England,
And here arrived, give order that these bodies
High on a stage° be placèd to the view,
And let me speak to th' yet unknowing world
How these things came about. So shall you hear
Of carnal, bloody, and unnatural acts,
Of accidental judgments,° casual° slaughters,
Of deaths put on° by cunning and forced cause,°
And, in this upshot, purposes mistook
Fall'n on th' inventors' heads. All this can I
Truly deliver.
FORTINBRAS. Let us haste to hear it,
And call the noblest to the audience.
For me, with sorrow I embrace my fortune.
I have some rights of memory° in this kingdom,
Which now to claim my vantage° doth invite me.
HORATIO. Of that I shall have also cause to speak,
And from his mouth whose voice will draw on more.°
But let this same be presently° performed,
Even while men's minds are wild, lest more mischance
On° plots and errors happen.
FORTINBRAS. Let four captains
Bear Hamlet, like a soldier, to the stage,
For he was likely, had he been put on,°

**341 quarry** heap of dead. **cries on havoc** proclaims a general slaughter **342 feast** i.e., Death feasting on those who have fallen. **toward** in preparation **349 his** i.e., Claudius's **352 jump** precisely, immediately. **question** dispute, affair **355 stage** platform **359 judgments** retributions. **casual** occurring by chance **360 put on** instigated. **forced cause** contrivance **366 of memory** traditional, remembered, unforgotten **367 vantage** favorable opportunity **369 voice . . . more** vote will influence still others **370 presently** immediately **372 On** on the basis of; on top of **374 put on** i.e., invested in royal office and so put to the test

To have proved most royal; and for his passage,°
The soldiers' music and the rite of war
Speak° loudly for him.
Take up the bodies. Such a sight as this
Becomes the field,° but here shows much amiss.
Go bid the soldiers shoot.
*Exeunt [marching, bearing off the dead bodies; a peal of ordnance is shot off].*

**375 passage** i.e., from life to death **377 Speak** (let them) speak **379 Becomes the field** suits the field of battle

## TOPICS FOR CRITICAL THINKING AND WRITING

### Act 1

1. The first scene (like many other scenes in this play) is full of expressions of uncertainty. What are some are these uncertainties? The Ghost first appears at 1.1.43. Does his appearance surprise us, or have we been prepared for it? Or is there both preparation and surprise? Do the last four speeches of 1.1 help to introduce a note of hope? If so, how?
2. Does the King's opening speech in 1.2 reveal him to be an accomplished public speaker—or are lines 10–14 offensive? In his second speech (lines 41–50), what is the effect of naming Laertes four times? Claudius sometimes uses the royal pronouns ("we," "our"), sometimes the more intimate "I" and "my." Study his use of these in lines 1–4 and in 106–117. What do you think he is getting at?
3. Hamlet's first soliloquy (1.2.129–159) reveals that more than just his father's death distresses him. Be as specific as possible about the causes of Hamlet's anguish here. What traits does Hamlet reveal in his conversation with Horatio (1.2.160–258)?
4. What do you make of Polonius's advice to Laertes (1.3.55–81)? Is it sound? Sound advice, but here uttered by a fool? Ignoble advice? How would one follow the advice of line 78: "to thine own self be true"? In his words to Ophelia in 1.3.102–136, what does he reveal about himself?
5. Can 1.4.17–38 reasonably be taken as a speech on the "tragic flaw"? (On this idea, see page 1224.) Or is the passage a much more limited discussion, a comment simply on Danish drinking habits?
6. Hamlet is convinced in 1.5.93–104 that the Ghost has told the truth, indeed, the only important truth. But do we detect in 105–112 a hint of a tone suggesting that Hamlet delights in hating villainy? If so, can it be said that later this delight grows, and that in some scenes (e.g., 3.3) we feel that Hamlet has almost become a diabolic revenger? Explain.

### Act 2

1. Characterize Polonius on the basis of 2.1.1–76.
2. In light of what we have seen of Hamlet, is Ophelia's report of his strange behavior when he visits her understandable?
3. Why does 2.2.33–34 seem almost comic? How do these lines help us to form a view about Rosencrantz and Guildenstern?

4. Is "the hellish Pyrrhus" (2.2.422) Hamlet's version of Claudius? Or is he Hamlet, who soon will be responsible for the deaths of Polonius, Rosencrantz and Guildenstern, Claudius, Gertrude, Ophelia, and Laertes? Explain.
5. Is the player's speech (2.2.427ff) a huffing speech? If so, why? To distinguish it from the poetry of the play itself? To characterize the bloody deeds that Hamlet cannot descend to?
6. In 2.2.504–42 Hamlet rebukes himself for not acting. Why has he not acted? Because he is a coward (line 531)? Because he has a conscience? Because no action can restore his father and his mother's purity? Because he doubts the Ghost? What reason(s) can you offer?

## Act 3

1. What do you make out of Hamlet's assertion to Ophelia: "I loved you not" (3.1.118)? Of his characterization of himself as full of "offenses" (3.1.121–27)? Why is Hamlet so harsh to Ophelia?
2. In 3.3.36–72 Claudius's conscience afflicts him. But is he repentant? What makes you say so?
3. Is Hamlet other than abhorrent in 3.3.73–96? Do we want him to kill Claudius at this moment, when Claudius (presumably with his back to Hamlet) is praying? Why?
4. The Ghost speaks of Hamlet's "almost blunted purpose" (3.4.115). Is the accusation fair? Explain.
5. How would you characterize Hamlet in 3.4.209–24?

## Act 4

1. Is Gertrude protecting Hamlet when she says he is mad (4.1.7), or does she believe that he is mad? If she believes he is mad, does it follow that she no longer feels ashamed and guilty? Explain.
2. Why should Hamlet hide Polonius's body (in 4.2)? Is he feigning madness? Is he on the edge of madness? Explain.
3. How can we explain Hamlet's willingness to go to England (4.3.52)?
4. Judging from 4.5, what has driven Ophelia mad? Is Laertes heroic, or somewhat foolish? Consider also the way Claudius treats him in 4.7.

## Act 5

1. Would anything be lost if the grave-diggers in 5.1 were omitted?
2. To what extent do we judge Hamlet severely for sending Rosencrantz and Guildenstern to their deaths, as he reports in 5.2? On the whole, do we think of Hamlet as an intriguer? What other intrigues has he engendered? How successful were they?
3. Does 5.2.193–97 show a paralysis of the will, or a wise recognition that more is needed than mere human scheming? Explain.
4. Does 5.2.280 suggest that Laertes takes advantage of a momentary pause and unfairly stabs Hamlet? Is the exchange of weapons accidental, or does Hamlet (as in Olivier's film version), realizing that he has been betrayed, deliberately get possession of Laertes's deadly weapon?
5. Fortinbras is often cut from the play. How much is lost by the cut? Explain.
6. Fortinbras gives Hamlet a soldier's funeral. Is this ridiculous? Can it fairly be said that, in a sense, Hamlet has been at war? Explain.

## General Questions

1. Hamlet in 5.2.10–11 speaks of a "divinity that shapes our ends." To what extent does "divinity" (or Fate or mysterious Chance) play a role in the happenings?
2. How do Laertes, Fortinbras, and Horatio help to define Hamlet for us?
3. T. S. Eliot says (in "Shakespeare and the Stoicism of Seneca") that Hamlet, having made a mess, "dies fairly well pleased with himself." Evaluate.

---

## ✔ Checklist: Writing about Tragedy

The checklist on page 1220, with questions concerning plot and character, is especially relevant, but here are some related questions.

The literary critic F. R. Leavis often referred to Shakespeare's plays as "dramatic poems." Of course the works are *plays* rather than *poems*—they are intended for the stage—but there is value in describing a play as, at least in part, a dramatic poem, since it reminds us of the place that *language* occupies in the best dramatic works. Read, watch, experience the play for what it is—a play; but devote careful study to it as a literary work in which language is central.

- What causes the tragedy? A flaw in the central character? A mistake (*not* the same thing as a flaw) made by this character? An outside force, such as another character, or Fate?
- Is the tragic character defined partly by other characters—for instance, by characters who help us to sense what the character *might* have done, or who in some other way reveal the strengths or weaknesses of the protagonist?
- Does a viewer know more than the tragic figure knows? More than most or all of the characters know?
- Does the tragic character achieve any sort of wisdom at the end of the play?
- To what degree do you sympathize with the tragic character?
- Is the play depressing? If not, why not?

---

# CHAPTER 31

# *Comedy*

Though etymology is not always helpful (after all, is it really illuminating to say that *tragedy* may come from a Greek word meaning "goat song"?), the etymology of *comedy* helps to reveal comedy's fundamental nature. **Comedy** (Greek: *komoidia*) is a revel-song; ancient Greek comedies are descended from fertility rituals that dramatized the joy of renewal, the joy of triumphing over obstacles, the joy of being (in a sense) reborn. Whereas the movement of tragedy, speaking roughly, is from prosperity to disaster, the movement of comedy is from some sort of minor disaster to prosperity.

Consider Shakespeare's *The Tempest.* In the first scene we are confronted with a shipwreck, and in the second we learn of a duke who has been driven out of his dukedom by an evil brother. By the end of the play the rightful duke is restored, and his daughter is betrothed to an excellent young man—in fact, to a young man who was thought by his father to have been drowned in the shipwreck. The storm that began the play is replaced, at the end, by "calm seas, auspicious gales." In the final act Gonzalo sums up the gains:

In one voyage  
Did Claribel her husband find at Tunis,  
And Ferdinand, her brother, found a wife  
Where he himself was lost; Prospero his dukedom  
In a poor isle; and all of us ourselves  
When no man was his own.

To say, however, that comedy dramatizes the triumph over obstacles is to describe it as though it were melodrama, a play in which, after hairbreadth adventures, good prevails over evil, often in the form of the hero's unlikely last-minute rescue of the fair Belinda from the clutches of the villain. What distinguishes comedy from melodrama is the pervasive high spirits of comedy. The joyous ending in comedy—usually a marriage—is in the spirit of what has gone before; the entire play, not only the end, is a celebration of fecundity.

The threats in the world of comedy are not taken very seriously; the parental tyranny that makes *Romeo and Juliet* and *Antigonê* tragedies is, in comedy, laughable throughout. Parents may fret, fume, and lock doors, but in doing so they make themselves ridiculous, for love will find a way. Villains may threaten, but the audience never takes the threats seriously.

The marriage and renewal of society, so usual at the end of comedy, may be most improbable, but they do not therefore weaken the comedy. The stuff of comedy is, in part, improbability. In *A Midsummer Night's Dream,* Puck speaks for the spectator when he says:

And those things do best please me
That befall preposterously.

In tragedy, probability is important; in comedy, *im*probability is often desirable, for at least three reasons. First, comedy seeks to include as much as possible, to reveal the rich abundance of life. The motto of comedy (and the implication in the weddings with which it usually concludes) is, The more the merrier. Second, the improbable is the surprising; surprise often evokes laughter, and laughter surely has a central place in comedy. Third, by getting the characters into improbable situations, the dramatist can show off the absurdity of their behavior. This point needs amplification.

Comedy often shows the absurdity of ideals. The miser, the puritan, the health faddist, and so on, are people of ideals, but their ideals are suffocating. The miser, for example, treats everything in terms of money; the miser's ideal causes him or her to renounce much of the abundance and joy of life. He or she is in love, but is unwilling to support a spouse; or he or she has a headache, but will not be so extravagant as to take an aspirin tablet. If a thief accosts the miser with "Your money or your life," the miser will prefer to give up life—and that is what in fact the miser has been doing all the while. Now, by putting this miser in a series of improbable situations, the dramatist can continue to demonstrate entertainingly the miser's absurdity.*

The comic protagonist's tenacious hold on his or her ideals is not very far from that of the tragic protagonist. In general, however, tragedy suggests the nobility of ideals; the tragic hero's ideals undo him or her, and they may be ideals about which we have serious reservations, but still we admire the nobility of these ideals. Romeo and Juliet will not put off their love for each other; Antigonê will not yield to Creon, and Creon holds almost impossibly long to his stern position. But the comic protagonist who is always trying to keep his or her hands

*A character who is dominated by a single trait—avarice, jealousy, timidity, and so forth—is sometimes called a **humor character.** Medieval and Renaissance psychology held that an individual's personality depended on the mixture of four liquids (humors): blood (Latin: *sanguis*), choler, phlegm, and bile. An overabundance of one fluid produced a dominant trait, and even today "sanguine," "choleric," "phlegmatic," and "bilious" describe personalities.

Not all comedy, of course, depends on humor characters placed in situations that exhibit their absurdity. **High comedy** is largely verbal, depending on witty language; **farce,** at the other extreme, is dependent on inherently ludicrous situations—for example, a hobo is mistaken for a millionaire. Situation comedy, then, may use humor characters, but it need not do so.

clean is funny; we laugh at this refusal to touch dirt with the rest of us, this refusal to enjoy the abundance life has to offer. The comic protagonist who is always talking about his or her beloved is funny; we laugh at the failure to see that the world is filled with people more attractive than the one with whom he or she is obsessed.

In short, the ideals for which the tragic protagonist loses the world seem important to us and gain, in large measure, our sympathy, but the ideals for which the comic protagonist loses the world seem trivial compared with the rich variety that life has to offer, and we laugh at their absurdity. The tragic figure makes a claim on our sympathy. The absurd comic figure continually sets up obstacles to our sympathetic interest; we feel detached from, superior to, and amused by comic figures. Something along these lines is behind William Butler Yeats's insistence that *character* is always present in comedy but not in tragedy. Though Yeats is eccentric in his notion that individual character is obliterated in tragedy, he interestingly gets at one of the important elements in comedy:

> When the tragic reverie is at its height . . . [we do not say,] "How well that man is realized. I should know him were I to meet him in the street," for it is always ourselves that we see upon the [tragic] stage. . . . Tragedy must always be a drowning and breaking of the dikes that separate man from man, and . . . it is upon these dikes comedy keeps house.

Most comic plays can roughly be sorted into one of two types: romantic comedy and satiric comedy. **Romantic comedy** presents an ideal world, a golden world, a world more delightful than our own; if there are difficulties in it, they are not briers but (to quote from Shakespeare's *As You Like It*) "burrs . . . thrown . . . in holiday foolery." It is the world of most of Shakespeare's comedies, a world of Illyria, of the Forest of Arden, of Belmont, of the moonlit Athens in *A Midsummer Night's Dream.* The chief figures are lovers; the course of their love is not smooth, but the outcome is never in doubt and the course is the more fun for being bumpy. Occasionally in this golden world there is a villain, but if so, the villain is a great bungler who never really does any harm; the world seems to be guided by a benevolent providence who prevents villains from seriously harming even themselves. In these plays, the world belongs to golden lads and lasses. When we laugh, we laugh not so much *at* them as *with* them.

If romantic comedy shows us a world with people more attractive than we find in our own, **satiric comedy** shows us a world with people less attractive. The satiric world seems dominated by morally inferior people—the decrepit wooer, the jealous spouse, the demanding parent. These unengaging figures go through their paces, revealing again and again their absurdity. The audience laughs *at* (rather than *with*) such figures, and writers justify this kind of comedy by claiming to reform society: antisocial members of the audience will see their grotesque images on the stage and will reform themselves when they leave the theater. But it is hard to believe that this theory is rooted in fact. Jonathan Swift was probably right when he said, "Satire is a sort of glass wherein beholders do generally discover everybody's face but their own."

Near the conclusion of a satiric comedy, the obstructing characters are dismissed, often perfunctorily, allowing for a happy ending—commonly the marriage of figures less colorful than the obstructionist(s). And so all-encompassing are the festivities at the end that even obstructionists are invited to join in the wedding feast. If they refuse to join, we may find them—yet again—laughable rather than sympathetic, though admittedly one may also feel lingering regret that this somewhat shabby world of ours cannot live up to the exalted (even if rigid and rather crazy) standards of the outsider who refuses to go along with the way of the world.

## WENDY WASSERSTEIN

*Wendy Wasserstein was born in Brooklyn, New York, in 1950, the daughter of immigrants from central Europe. After graduating from Mt. Holyoke College, she took creative writing courses at the City College of New York and then completed a degree program at the Yale School of Drama. Wasserstein has had a highly successful career as a playwright* (The Heidi Chronicles *won a Pulitzer Prize in 1989), and she has also achieved recognition for her television screenplays and a book of essays.*

The Man in a Case *is based on a short story by Anton Chekhov, one of her favorite writers.*

# *The Man in a Case*

LIST OF CHARACTERS

BYELINKOV

VARINKA

**SCENE:** *A small garden in the village of Mironitski. 1898.*

(*Byelinkov is pacing. Enter Varinka out of breath.*)

BYELINKOV. You are ten minutes late.

VARINKA. The most amazing thing happened on my way over here. You know the woman who runs the grocery store down the road. She wears a black wig during the week, and a blond wig on Saturday nights. And she has the daughter who married an engineer in Moscow who is doing very well thank you and is living, God bless them, in a three-room apartment. But he really is the most boring man in the world. All he talks about is his future and his station in life. Well, she heard we were to be married and she gave me this basket of apricots to give to you.

BYELINKOV. That is a most amazing thing!

VARINKA. She said to me, Varinka, you are marrying the most honorable man in the entire village. In this village he is the only man fit to speak with my son-in-law.

BYELINKOV. I don't care for apricots. They give me hives.

VARINKA. I can return them. I'm sure if I told her they give you hives she would give me a basket of raisins or a cake.

BYELINKOV. I don't know this woman or her pompous son-in-law. Why would she give me her cakes?

VARINKA. She adores you!

BYELINKOV. She is emotionally loose.

*The Man in a Case,* The Acting Company, Champaign-Urbana, Illinois, 1985. (Photograph by Diane Gorodnitzki. )

VARINKA. She adores you by reputation. Everyone adores you by reputation. I tell everyone I am to marry Byelinkov, the finest teacher in the country.

BYELINKOV. You tell them this?

VARINKA. If they don't tell me first.

BYELINKOV. Pride can be an imperfect value.

VARINKA. It isn't pride. It is the truth. You are a great man!

BYELINKOV. I am the master of Greek and Latin at a local school at the end of the village of Mironitski.

(*Varinka kisses him.*)

VARINKA. And I am to be the master of Greek and Latin's wife!

BYELINKOV. Being married requires a great deal of responsibility. I hope I am able to provide you with all that a married man must properly provide a wife.

VARINKA. We will be very happy.

BYELINKOV. Happiness is for children. We are entering into a social contract, an amicable agreement to provide us with a secure and satisfying future.

VARINKA. You are so sweet! You are the sweetest man in the world!

BYELINKOV. I'm a man set in his ways who saw a chance to provide himself with a small challenge.

VARINKA. Look at you! Look at you! Your sweet round spectacles, your dear collar always starched, always raised, your perfectly pressed pants always creasing at right angles perpendicular to the floor, and my most favorite part, the sweet little galoshes, rain or shine, just in case. My Byelinkov, never taken by surprise. Except by me.

BYELINKOV. You speak about me as if I were your pet.

VARINKA. You are my pet! My little school mouse.

BYELINKOV. A mouse?

VARINKA. My sweetest dancing bear with galoshes, my little stale babka.[1]

BYELINKOV. A stale babka?

VARINKA. I am not Pushkin.[2]

BYELINKOV (*laughs*). That depends what you think of Pushkin.

VARINKA. You're smiling. I knew I could make you smile today.

BYELINKOV. I am a responsible man. Every day I have for breakfast black bread, fruit, hot tea, and every day I smile three times. I am halfway into my translation of the *Aeneid*[3] from classical Greek hexameter into Russian alexandrines. In twenty years I have never been late to school. I am a responsible man, but no dancing bear.

VARINKA. Dance with me.

BYELINKOV. Now? It is nearly four weeks before the wedding!

VARINKA. It's a beautiful afternoon. We are in your garden. The roses are in full bloom.

BYELINKOV. The roses have beetles.

VARINKA. Dance with me!

BYELINKOV. You are a demanding woman.

VARINKA. You chose me. And right. And left. And turn. And right. And left.

BYELINKOV. And turn. Give me your hand. You dance like a school mouse. It's a beautiful afternoon! We are in my garden. The roses are in full bloom! And turn. And turn. (*Twirls Varinka around.*)

VARINKA. I am the luckiest woman!

(*Byelinkov stops dancing.*)

Why are you stopping?

BYELINKOV. To place a lilac in your hair. Every year on this day I will place a lilac in your hair.

VARINKA. Will you remember?

BYELINKOV. I will write it down. (*Takes a notebook from his pocket.*) Dear Byelinkov, don't forget the day a young lady, your bride, entered your garden, your peace, and danced on the roses. On that day every year you are to place a lilac in her hair.

VARINKA. I love you.

BYELINKOV. It is convenient we met.

VARINKA. I love you.

BYELINKOV. You are a girl.

VARINKA. I am thirty.

BYELINKOV. But you think like a girl. That is an attractive attribute.

VARINKA. Do you love me?

BYELINKOV. We've never spoken about housekeeping.

VARINKA. I am an excellent housekeeper. I kept house for my family on the farm in Gadyatchsky. I can make a beetroot soup with tomatoes and aubergines which is so nice. Awfully awfully nice.

[1]**babka** cake with almonds and raisins [2]**Pushkin** Alexander Pushkin (1799–1837), Russian poet [3]***Aeneid*** Latin epic poem by the Roman poet Virgil (70–19 B.C.)

BYELINKOV. You are fond of expletives.

VARINKA. My beet soup, sir, is excellent!

BYELINKOV. Please don't be cross. I too am an excellent housekeeper. I have a place for everything in the house. A shelf for each pot, a cubby for every spoon, a folder for favorite recipes. I have cooked for myself for twenty years. Though my beet soup is not outstanding, it is sufficient.

VARINKA. I'm sure it's very good.

BYELINKOV. No. It is awfully, awfully not. What I am outstanding in, however, what gives me greatest pleasure, is preserving those things which are left over. I wrap each tomato slice I haven't used in a wet cloth and place it in the coolest corner of the house. I have had my shoes for seven years because I wrap them in the galoshes you are so fond of. And every night before I go to sleep I wrap my bed in quilts and curtains so I never catch a draft.

VARINKA. You sleep with curtains on your bed?

BYELINKOV. I like to keep warm.

VARINKA. I will make you a new quilt.

BYELINKOV. No. No new quilt. That would be hazardous.

VARINKA. It is hazardous to sleep under curtains.

BYELINKOV. Varinka, I don't like change very much. If one works out the arithmetic the final fraction of improvement is at best less than an eighth of value over the total damage caused by disruption. I never thought of marrying till I saw your eyes dancing among the familiar faces at the headmaster's tea. I assumed I would grow old preserved like those which are left over, wrapped suitably in my case of curtains and quilts.

VARINKA. Byelinkov, I want us to have dinners with friends and summer country visits. I want people to say, "Have you spent time with Varinka and Byelinkov? He is so happy now that they are married. She is just what he needed."

BYELINKOV. You have already brought me some happiness. But I never was a sad man. Don't ever think I thought I was a sad man.

VARINKA. My sweetest darling, you can be whatever you want! If you are sad, they'll say she talks all the time, and he is softspoken and kind.

BYELINKOV. And if I am difficult?

VARINKA. Oh, they'll say he is difficult because he is highly intelligent. All great men are difficult. Look at Lermontov, Tchaikovsky, Peter the Great.

BYELINKOV. Ivan the Terrible.[4]

VARINKA. Yes, him too.

BYELINKOV. Why are you marrying me? I am none of these things.

VARINKA. To me you are.

BYELINKOV. You have imagined this. You have constructed an elaborate romance for yourself. Perhaps you are the great one. You are the one with the great imagination.

VARINKA. Byelinkov, I am a pretty girl of thirty. You're right, I am not a woman. I have not made myself into a woman because I do not deserve

[4]**Lermontov . . . Ivan the Terrible** Mikhail Lermontov (1814–41), poet and novelist; Peter Ilich Tchaikovsky (1840–93), composer; Peter the Great (1672–1725) and Ivan the Terrible (1530–84), czars credited with making Russia a great European power

that honor. Until I came to this town to visit my brother I lived on my family's farm. As the years passed I became younger and younger in fear that I would never marry. And it wasn't that I wasn't pretty enough or sweet enough, it was just that no man ever looked at me and saw a wife. I was not the woman who would be there when he came home. Until I met you I thought I would lie all my life and say I never married because I never met a man I loved. I will love you, Byelinkov. And I will help you to love me. We deserve the life everyone else has. We deserve not to be different.

BYELINKOV. Yes. We are the same as everyone else.

VARINKA. Tell me you love me.

BYELINKOV. I love you.

VARINKA (*takes his hands*). We will be very happy. I am very strong. (*Pauses.*) It is time for tea.

BYELINKOV. It is too early for tea. Tea is at half past the hour.

VARINKA. Do you have heavy cream? It will be awfully nice with apricots.

BYELINKOV. Heavy cream is too rich for teatime.

VARINKA. But today is special. Today you placed a lilac in my hair. Write in your note pad. Every year we will celebrate with apricots and heavy cream. I will go to my brother's house and get some.

BYELINKOV. But your brother's house is a mile from here.

VARINKA. Today it is much shorter. Today my brother gave me his bicycle to ride. I will be back very soon.

BYELINKOV. You rode to my house by bicycle! Did anyone see you!

VARINKA. Of course. I had such fun. I told you I saw the grocery store lady with the son-in-law who is doing very well thank you in Moscow, and the headmaster's wife.

BYELINKOV. You saw the headmaster's wife!

VARINKA. She smiled at me.

BYELINKOV. Did she laugh or smile?

VARINKA. She laughed a little. She said, "My dear, you are very progressive to ride a bicycle." She said you and your fiancé Byelinkov must ride together sometime. I wonder if he'll take off his galoshes when he rides a bicycle.

BYELINKOV. She said that?

VARINKA. She adores you. We had a good giggle.

BYELINKOV. A woman can be arrested for riding a bicycle. That is not progressive, it is a premeditated revolutionary act. Your brother must be awfully, awfully careful on behalf of your behavior. He has been careless—oh so careless—in giving you the bicycle.

VARINKA. Dearest Byelinkov, you are wrapping yourself under curtains and quilts! I made friends on the bicycle.

BYELINKOV. You saw more than the headmaster's wife and the idiot grocery woman.

VARINKA. She is not an idiot.

BYELINKOV. She is a potato-vending, sausage-armed fool!

VARINKA. Shhhh! My school mouse. Shhh!

BYELINKOV. What other friends did you make on this bicycle?

VARINKA. I saw students from my brother's classes. They waved and shouted, "Anthropos in love! Anthropos in love!!"

BYELINKOV. Where is that bicycle?

VARINKA. I left it outside the gate. Where are you going?

BYELINKOV (*muttering as he exits*). Anthropos in love, anthropos in love.

VARINKA. They were cheering me on. Careful, you'll trample the roses.

BYELINKOV (*returning with the bicycle*). Anthropos is the Greek singular for man. Anthropos in love translates as the Greek and Latin master in love. Of course they cheered you. Their instructor, who teaches them the discipline and contained beauty of the classics, is in love with a sprite on a bicycle. It is a good giggle, isn't it? A very good giggle! I am returning this bicycle to your brother.

VARINKA. But it is teatime.

BYELINKOV. Today we will not have tea.

VARINKA. But you will have to walk back a mile.

BYELINKOV. I have my galoshes on. (*Gets on the bicycle.*) Varinka, we deserve not to be different. (*Begins to pedal. The bicycle doesn't move.*)

VARINKA. Put the kickstand up.

BYELINKOV. I beg your pardon.

VARINKA (*giggling*). Byelinkov, to make the bicycle move, you must put the kickstand up.

(*Byelinkov puts it up and awkwardly falls off the bicycle as it moves.*)

(*Laughing.*) Ha ha ha. My little school mouse. You look so funny! You are the sweetest dearest man in the world. Ha ha ha!

(*Pause.*)

BYELINKOV. Please help me up. I'm afraid my galosh is caught.

VARINKA (*trying not to laugh*). Your galosh is caught! (*Explodes in laughter again.*) Oh, you are so funny! I do love you so. (*Helps Byelinkov up.*) You were right, my pet, as always. We don't need heavy cream for tea. The fraction of improvement isn't worth the damage caused by the disruption.

BYELINKOV. Varinka, it is still too early for tea. I must complete two stanzas of my translation before late afternoon. That is my regular schedule.

VARINKA. Then I will watch while you work.

BYELINKOV. No. You had a good giggle. That is enough.

VARINKA. Then while you work I will work too. I will make lists of guests for our wedding.

BYELINKOV. I can concentrate only when I am alone in my house. Please take your bicycle home to your brother.

VARINKA. But I don't want to leave you. You look so sad.

BYELINKOV. I never was a sad man. Don't ever think I was a sad man.

VARINKA. Byelinkov, it's a beautiful day, we are in your garden. The roses are in bloom.

BYELINKOV. Allow me to help you on to your bicycle. (*Takes Varinka's hand as she gets on the bike.*)

VARINKA. You are such a gentleman. We will be very happy.

BYELINKOV. You are very strong. Good day, Varinka.

(*Varinka pedals off. Byelinkov, alone in the garden, takes out his pad and rips up the note about the lilac, strews it over the garden, then carefully picks up each piece of paper and places them all in a small envelope as lights fade to black.*)

[*1986*]

## TOPICS FOR CRITICAL THINKING AND WRITING

1. You will probably agree that the scene where Byelinkov gets on the bicycle and pedals but goes nowhere is funny. But *why* is it funny? Can you formulate a theory of comedy based on this episode?
2. At the end of the play Byelinkov tears up the note but then collects the pieces. What do you interpret these actions to mean?

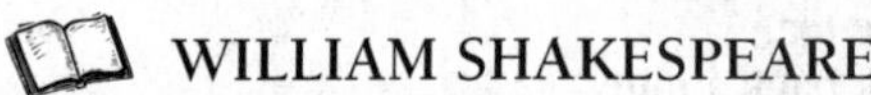

## WILLIAM SHAKESPEARE

*William Shakespeare (1564–1616) was born in Stratford, England, of middle-class parents. Nothing of interest is known about his early years, but by 1590 he was acting and writing plays in London. By the end of the following decade he had worked in all three Elizabethan dramatic genres—tragedy, comedy, and history.* Romeo and Juliet, *for example, was written about 1595, the year of* Richard II, *and in the following year he wrote* A Midsummer Night's Dream. Julius Caesar *(1599) probably preceded* As You Like It *by one year, and* Hamlet *probably followed* As You Like It *by less than a year. Among the plays that followed* King Lear *(1605–06) were* Macbeth *(1605–06) and several "romances"—plays (including* The Tempest) *that have happy endings but that seem more meditative and closer to tragedy than such comedies as* A Midsummer Night's Dream, As You Like It, *and* Twelfth Night.

# *A Midsummer Night's Dream**

*Edited by David Bevington*

[DRAMATIS PERSONAE

THESEUS, *Duke of Athens*
HIPPOLYTA, *Queen of the Amazons, betrothed to Theseus*
PHILOSTRATE, *Master of the Revels*
EGEUS, *father of Hermia*

HERMIA, *daughter of Egeus, in love with Lysander*
LYSANDER, *in love with Hermia*

**A Midsummer Night's Dream* was first published in 1600 in a small book of a type called a quarto. A second quarto edition, printed in 1616 but based on the 1600 text, introduces a few corrections, but it also introduces many errors. The 1619 text in turn was the basis for the text in the first collected edition of Shakespeare's plays, the First Folio (1623). Bevington's edition is of course based on the text of 1600, but it includes a few corrections, and it modifies the punctuation in accordance with modern usage. Material added by the editor, such as amplifications in the *dramatis personae,* is enclosed within square brackets [ ].

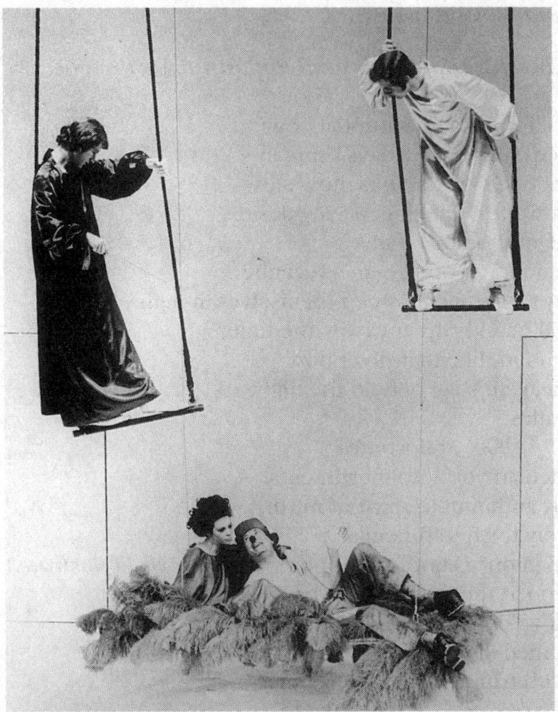

Above: Oberon (Alan Howard) and Puck (John Kane); below: Titania (Sara Kestelman) and Nick Bottom (David Waller) in a 1970 Stratford-upon-Avon production of *A Midsummer Night's Dream,* directed by Peter Brook. (Photograph by David Farrell, Shakespeare Centre Library, Stratford-upon-Avon)

DEMETRIUS, *in love with Hermia and favored by Egeus*
HELENA, *in love with Demetrius*

OBERON, *King of the Fairies*
TITANIA, *Queen of the Fairies*
PUCK, *or* ROBIN GOODFELLOW
PEASEBLOSSOM,
COBWEB,
MOTE,
MUSTARDSEED,
} *fairies attending Titania*
*Other* FAIRIES *attending*

PETER QUINCE, *a carpenter,* | PROLOGUE
NICK BOTTOM, *a weaver,* | PYRAMUS
FRANCIS FLUTE, *a bellows mender,* | THISBE
TOM SNOUT, *a tinker,* | WALL
SNUG, *a joiner,* | LION
ROBIN STARVELING, *a tailor,* | MOONSHINE
} *representing*

*Lords and Attendants on Theseus and Hippolyta*

**SCENE:** *Athens, and a wood near it*]

**[1.1]** *Enter Theseus, Hippolyta,* [*and Philostrate,*] *with others.*

THESEUS. Now, fair Hippolyta, our nuptial hour
Draws on apace. Four happy days bring in
Another moon; but, O, methinks, how slow
This old moon wanes! She lingers° my desires,
Like to a stepdame° or a dowager°
Long withering out° a young man's revenue.
HIPPOLYTA. Four days will quickly steep themselves in night,
Four nights will quickly dream away the time;
And then the moon, like to a silver bow
New bent in heaven, shall behold the night
Of our solemnities.
THESEUS. Go, Philostrate,
Stir up the Athenian youth to merriments,
Awake the pert and nimble spirit of mirth,
Turn melancholy forth to funerals;
The pale companion° is not for our pomp.° [*Exit Philostrate.*]
Hippolyta, I wooed thee with my sword°
And won thy love doing thee injuries;
But I will wed thee in another key,
With pomp, with triumph,° and with reveling.

*Enter Egeus and his daughter Hermia, and Lysander, and Demetrius.*

EGEUS. Happy be Theseus, our renowned duke!
THESEUS. Thanks, good Egeus. What's the news with thee?
EGEUS. Full of vexation come I, with complaint
Against my child, my daughter Hermia.
Stand forth, Demetrius. My noble lord,
This man hath my consent to marry her.
Stand forth, Lysander. And, my gracious Duke,
This man hath bewitched the bosom of my child.
Thou, thou, Lysander, thou hast given her rhymes
And interchanged love tokens with my child.
Thou hast by moonlight at her window sung
With feigning voice verses of feigning° love,
And stol'n the impression of her fantasy°
With bracelets of thy hair, rings, gauds,° conceits,°

**1.1 Location: Athens, Theseus' court.** **4 lingers** postpones, delays the fulfillment of **5 stepdame** stepmother. **dowager** i.e., a widow (whose right of inheritance from her dead husband is eating into her son's estate) **6 withering out** causing to dwindle **15 companion** fellow. **pomp** ceremonial magnificence **16 with my sword** i.e., in a military engagement against the Amazons, when Hippolyta was taken captive **19 triumph** public festivity **31 feigning** (1) counterfeiting (2) faining, desirous **32 And . . . fantasy** and made her fall in love with you (imprinting your image on her imagination) by stealthy and dishonest means **33 gauds** playthings. **conceits** fanciful trifles

Knacks,° trifles, nosegays, sweetmeats—messengers
Of strong prevailment in° unhardened youth.
With cunning hast thou filched my daughter's heart,
Turned her obedience, which is due to me,
To stubborn harshness. And, my gracious Duke,
Be it so° she will not here before Your Grace
Consent to marry with Demetrius,
I beg the ancient privilege of Athens:
As she is mine, I may dispose of her,
Which shall be either to this gentleman
Or to her death, according to our law
Immediately° provided in that case.

THESEUS. What say you, Hermia? Be advised, fair maid.
To you your father should be as a god—
One that composed your beauties, yea, and one
To whom you are but as a form in wax
By him imprinted, and within his power
To leave° the figure or disfigure° it.
Demetrius is a worthy gentleman.

HERMIA. So is Lysander.

THESEUS. In himself he is;
But in this kind,° wanting° your father's voice,°
The other must be held the worthier.

HERMIA. I would my father looked but with my eyes.

THESEUS. Rather your eyes must with his judgment look.

HERMIA. I do entreat Your Grace to pardon me.
I know not by what power I am made bold,
Nor how it may concern° my modesty
In such a presence here to plead my thoughts;
But I beseech Your Grace that I may know
The worst that may befall me in this case
If I refuse to wed Demetrius.

THESEUS. Either to die the death or to abjure
Forever the society of men.
Therefore, fair Hermia, question your desires,
Know of your youth, examine well your blood,°
Whether, if you yield not to your father's choice,
You can endure the livery° of a nun,
For aye° to be in shady cloister mewed,°
To live a barren sister all your life,
Chanting faint hymns to the cold fruitless moon.
Thrice blessèd they that master so their blood
To undergo such maiden pilgrimage;
But earthlier happy° is the rose distilled

**34 Knacks** knickknacks **35 prevailment in** influence on **39 Be it so** if **45 Immediately** directly, with nothing intervening **51 leave** i.e., leave unaltered. **disfigure** obliterate **54 kind** respect. **wanting** lacking. **voice** approval **60 concern** befit **68 blood** passions **70 livery** habit **71 aye** ever. **mewed** shut in. (Said of a hawk, poultry, etc.) **76 earthlier happy** happier as respects this world

Than that which, withering on the virgin thorn,
Grows, lives, and dies in single blessedness.

HERMIA. So will I grow, so live, so die, my lord,
Ere I will yield my virgin patent° up
Unto his lordship, whose unwishèd yoke
My soul consents not to give sovereignty.

THESEUS. Take time to pause, and by the next new moon—
The sealing day betwixt my love and me
For everlasting bond of fellowship—
Upon that day either prepare to die
For disobedience to your father's will,
Or° else to wed Demetrius, as he would,
Or on Diana's altar to protest°
For aye austerity and single life.

DEMETRIUS. Relent, sweet Hermia, and, Lysander, yield
Thy crazèd° title to my certain right.

LYSANDER. You have her father's love, Demetrius;
Let me have Hermia's. Do you marry him.

EGEUS. Scornful Lysander! True, he hath my love,
And what is mine my love shall render him.
And she is mine, and all my right of her
I do estate unto° Demetrius.

LYSANDER. I am, my lord, as well derived° as he,
As well possessed;° my love is more than his;
My fortunes every way as fairly° ranked,
If not with vantage,° as Demetrius';
And, which is more than all these boasts can be,
I am beloved of beauteous Hermia.
Why should not I then prosecute my right?
Demetrius, I'll avouch it to his head,°
Made love to Nedar's daughter, Helena
And won her soul; and she, sweet lady, dotes,
Devoutly dotes, dotes in idolatry,
Upon this spotted° and inconstant man.

THESEUS. I must confess that I have heard so much,
And with Demetrius thought to have spoke thereof;
But, being overfull of self-affairs,°
My mind did lose it. But, Demetrius, come,
And come, Egeus, you shall go with me;
I have some private schooling° for you both.
For you, fair Hermia, look you arm° yourself
To fit your fancies° to your father's will;
Or else the law of Athens yields you up—

**80 patent** privilege **88 Or** either **89 protest** vow **92 crazèd** cracked, unsound **98 estate unto** settle or bestow upon **99 derived** descended, i.e., as well born **100 possessed** endowed with wealth **101 fairly** handsomely **102 vantage** superiority **106 head** i.e., face **110 spotted** i.e., morally stained **113 self-affairs** my own concerns **116 schooling** admonition **117 look you arm** take care you prepare **118 fancies** likings, thoughts of love

Which by no means we may extenuate°—
To death or to a vow of single life.
Come, my Hippolyta. What cheer, my love?
Demetrius and Egeus, go° along.
I must employ you in some business
Against° our nuptial and confer with you
Of something nearly that° concerns yourselves.

EGEUS. With duty and desire we follow you.

*Exeunt* [*all but Lysander and Hermia*].

LYSANDER. How now, my love, why is your cheek so pale?
How chance the roses there do fade so fast?

HERMIA. Belike° for want of rain, which I could well
Beteem° them from the tempest of my eyes.

LYSANDER. Ay me! For aught that I could ever read,
Could ever hear by tale or history,
The course of true love never did run smooth
But either it was different in blood°—

HERMIA. O cross!° Too high to be enthralled to low.

LYSANDER. Or else misgrafted° in respect of years—

HERMIA. O spite! Too old to be engaged to young.

LYSANDER. Or else it stood upon the choice of friends°—

HERMIA. O hell, to choose love by another's eyes!

LYSANDER. Or if there were a sympathy° in choice,
War, death, or sickness did lay siege to it,
Making it momentany° as a sound,
Swift as a shadow, short as any dream,
Brief as the lightning in the collied° night,
That in a spleen° unfolds° both heaven and earth,
And ere a man hath power to say "Behold!"
The jaws of darkness do devour it up.
So quick° bright things come to confusion.°

HERMIA. If then true lovers have been ever crossed,°
It stands as an edict in destiny.
Then let us teach our trial patience,°
Because it is a customary cross,
As due to love as thoughts and dreams and sighs,
Wishes and tears, poor fancy's° followers.

LYSANDER. A good persuasion.° Therefore, hear me, Hermia:
I have a widow aunt, a dowager
Of great revenue, and she hath no child.
From Athens is her house remote seven leagues;

**120 extenuate** mitigate **123 go** i.e., come **125 Against** in preparation for **126 nearly that** that closely **130 Belike** very likely **131 Beteem** grant, afford **135 blood** hereditary station **136 cross** vexation **137 misgrafted** ill grafted, badly matched **139 friends** relatives **141 sympathy** agreement **143 momentany** lasting but a moment **145 collied** blackened (as with coal dust), darkened **146 in a spleen** in a swift impulse, in a violent flash. **unfolds** discloses **149 quick** quickly; or, perhaps, living, alive. **confusion** ruin **150 ever crossed** always thwarted **152 teach . . . patience** i.e., teach ourselves patience in this trial **155 fancy's** amorous passion's **156 persuasion** conviction

And she respects° me as her only son.
There, gentle Hermia, may I marry thee,
And to that place the sharp Athenian law
Cannot pursue us. If thou lovest me, then,
Steal forth thy father's house tomorrow night;
And in the wood, a league without the town,
Where I did meet thee once with Helena
To do observance to a morn of May,°
There will I stay for thee.

HERMIA. My good Lysander!
I swear to thee by Cupid's strongest bow,
By his best arrow° with the golden head,
By the simplicity° of Venus' doves,°
By that which knitteth souls and prospers loves,
And by that fire which burned the Carthage queen°
When the false Trojan° under sail was seen,
By all the vows that ever men have broke,
In number more than ever women spoke,
In that same place thou hast appointed me
Tomorrow truly will I meet with thee.

LYSANDER. Keep promise, love. Look, here comes Helena.

*Enter Helena.*

HERMIA. God speed, fair° Helena! Whither away?

HELENA. Call you me fair? That "fair" again unsay.
Demetrius loves your fair.° O happy fair!°
Your eyes are lodestars,° and your tongue's sweet air°
More tunable° than lark to shepherd's ear
When wheat is green, when hawthorn buds appear.
Sickness is catching. O, were favor° so!
Yours would I catch, fair Hermia, ere I go;
My ear should catch your voice, my eye your eye,
My tongue should catch your tongue's sweet melody.
Were the world mine, Demetrius being bated,°
The rest I'd give to be to you translated.°
O, teach me how you look and with what art
You sway the motion° of Demetrius' heart.

HERMIA. I frown upon him, yet he loves me still.

HELENA. O, that your frowns would teach my smiles such skill!

HERMIA. I give him curses, yet he gives me love.

**160 respects** regards **167 do . . . May** perform the ceremonies of May Day **170 best arrow** (Cupid's best gold-pointed arrows were supposed to induce love; his blunt leaden arrows, aversion.) **171 simplicity** innocence. **doves** i.e., those that drew Venus' chariot **173, 174 Carthage queen, false Trojan** (Dido, Queen of Carthage, immolated herself on a funeral pyre after having been deserted by the Trojan hero Aeneas.) **180 fair** fair-complexioned (generally regarded by the Elizabethans as more beautiful than dark-complexioned) **182 your fair** your beauty (even though Hermia is dark-complexioned). **happy fair** lucky fair one **183 lodestars** guiding stars. **air** music **184 tunable** tuneful, melodious **186 favor** appearance, looks **190 bated** excepted **191 translated** transformed **193 motion** impulse

HELENA. O, that my prayers could such affection° move!°
HERMIA. The more I hate, the more he follows me.
HELENA. The more I love, the more he hateth me.
HERMIA. His folly, Helena, is no fault of mine.
HELENA. None but your beauty. Would that fault were mine!
HERMIA. Take comfort. He no more shall see my face.
Lysander and myself will fly this place.
Before the time I did Lysander see
Seemed Athens as a paradise to me.
O, then, what graces in my love do dwell
That he hath turned a heaven unto a hell!
LYSANDER. Helen, to you our minds we will unfold.
Tomorrow night, when Phoebe° doth behold
Her silver visage in the watery glass,°
Decking with liquid pearl the bladed grass,
A time that lovers' flights doth still° conceal,
Through Athens' gates have we devised to steal.
HERMIA. And in the wood, where often you and I
Upon faint° primrose beds were wont to lie,
Emptying our bosoms of their counsel° sweet,
There my Lysander and myself shall meet;
And thence from Athens turn away our eyes,
To seek new friends and stranger companies.
Farewell, sweet playfellow. Pray thou for us,
And good luck grant thee thy Demetrius!
Keep word, Lysander. We must starve our sight
From lovers' food till morrow deep midnight.
LYSANDER. I will, my Hermia. *Exit Hermia.*
Helena, adieu.
As you on him, Demetrius dote on you! *Exit Lysander.*
HELENA. How happy some o'er other some can be!°
Through Athens I am thought as fair as she.
But what of that? Demetrius thinks not so;
He will not know what all but he do know.
And as he errs, doting on Hermia's eyes,
So I, admiring of° his qualities.
Things base and vile, holding no quantity,°
Love can transpose to form and dignity.
Love looks not with the eyes, but with the mind,
And therefore is winged Cupid painted blind.
Nor hath Love's mind of any judgment taste;°
Wings, and no eyes, figure° unheedy haste.
And therefore is Love said to be a child,

**197 affection** passion. **move** arouse **209 Phoebe** Diana, the moon **210 glass** mirror **212 still** always **215 faint** pale **216 counsel** secret thought **226 o'er . . . can be** can be in comparison to some others **231 admiring of** wondering at **232 holding no quantity** i.e., unsubstantial, unshapely **236 Nor . . . taste** i.e., nor has Love, which dwells in the fancy or imagination, any *taste* or least bit of judgment or reason **237 figure** are a symbol of

Because in choice he is so oft beguiled.
As waggish° boys in game° themselves forswear,
So the boy Love is perjured everywhere.
For ere Demetrius looked on Hermia's eyne,°
He hailed down oaths that he was only mine;
And when this hail some heat from Hermia felt,
So he dissolved, and showers of oaths did melt.
I will go tell him of fair Hermia's flight.
Then to the wood will he tomorrow night
Pursue her; and for this intelligence°
If I have thanks, it is a dear expense.°
But herein mean I to enrich my pain,
To have his sight thither and back again.

*Exit.*

**[1.2]** *Enter Quince the carpenter, and Snug the joiner, and Bottom the weaver, and Flute the bellows mender, and Snout the tinker, and Starveling the tailor.*

QUINCE. Is all our company here?

BOTTOM. You were best to call them generally,° man by man, according to the scrip.°

QUINCE. Here is the scroll of every man's name which is thought fit, through all Athens, to play in our interlude before the Duke and the Duchess on his wedding day at night.

BOTTOM. First, good Peter Quince, say what the play treats on, then read the names of the actors, and so grow to° a point.

QUINCE. Marry,° our play is "The most lamentable comedy and most cruel death of Pyramus and Thisbe."

BOTTOM. A very good piece of work, I assure you, and a merry. Now, good Peter Quince, call forth your actors by the scroll. Masters, spread yourselves.

QUINCE. Answer as I call you. Nick Bottom,° the weaver.

BOTTOM. Ready. Name what part I am for, and proceed.

QUINCE. You, Nick Bottom, are set down for Pyramus.

BOTTOM. What is Pyramus? A lover or a tyrant?

QUINCE. A lover, that kills himself most gallant for love.

BOTTOM. That will ask some tears in the true performing of it. If I do it, let the audience look to their eyes. I will move storms; I will condole° in some measure. To the rest—yet my chief humor° is for a

**240 waggish** playful, mischievous. **game** sport, jest **242 eyne** eyes. (Old form of plural.) **248 intelligence** information **249 a dear expense** i.e., a trouble worth taking. **dear** costly

**1.2 Location: Athens.** **2 generally** (Bottom's blunder for *individually.*) **3 scrip** scrap. (Bottom's error for *script.*) **8 grow to** come to **9 Marry** (A mild oath; originally the name of the Virgin Mary.) **14 Bottom** (As a weaver's term, a *bottom* was an object around which thread was wound.) **20–21 condole** lament, arouse pity **21 humor** inclination, whim

tyrant. I could play Ercles° rarely, or a part to tear a cat° in, to make all split.°

"The raging rocks
And shivering shocks
Shall break the locks
Of prison gates:
And Phibbus' car°
Shall shine from far
And make and mar
The foolish Fates."

This was lofty! Now name the rest of the players. This is Ercles' vein, a tyrant's vein. A lover is more condoling.

QUINCE. Francis Flute, the bellows mender.

FLUTE. Here, Peter Quince.

QUINCE. Flute, you must take Thisbe on you.

FLUTE. What is Thisbe? A wandering knight?

QUINCE. It is the lady that Pyramus must love.

FLUTE. Nay, faith, let not me play a woman. I have a beard coming.

QUINCE. That's all one.° You shall play it in a mask, and you may speak as small° as you will.

BOTTOM. An° I may hide my face, let me play Thisbe too. I'll speak in a monstrous little voice, "Thisne, Thisne!" "Ah Pyramus, my lover dear! Thy Thisbe dear, and lady dear!"

QUINCE. No, no, you must play Pyramus, and, Flute, you Thisbe.

BOTTOM. Well, proceed.

QUINCE. Robin Starveling, the tailor.

STARVELING. Here, Peter Quince.

QUINCE. Robin Starveling, you must play Thisbe's mother. Tom Snout, the tinker.

SNOUT. Here, Peter Quince.

QUINCE. You, Pyramus' father; myself, Thisbe's father; Snug, the joiner, you, the lion's part, and I hope here is a play fitted.

SNUG. Have you the lion's part written? Pray you, if it be, give it me, for I am slow of study.

QUINCE. You may do it extempore, for it is nothing but roaring.

BOTTOM. Let me play the lion too. I will roar that I will do any man's heart good to hear me. I will roar that I will make the Duke say, "Let him roar again, let him roar again."

QUINCE. An you should do it too terribly, you would fright the Duchess and the ladies, that they would shriek; and that were enough to hang us all.

ALL. That would hang us, every mother's son.

BOTTOM. I grant you, friends, if you should fright the ladies out of their wits, they would have no more discretion but to hang us; but I will

**22 Ercles** Hercules. (The tradition of ranting came from Seneca's *Hercules Furens.*) **tear a cat** i.e., rant **22–23 make all split** i.e., cause a stir, bring the house down **28 Phibbus' car** Phoebus's the sun-god's, chariot **40 That's all one** it makes no difference **41 small** high-pitched **42 An** if (also at line 67)

aggravate° my voice so that I will roar you° as gently as any sucking dove;° I will roar you an 'twere any nightingale.

QUINCE. You can play no part but Pyramus; for Pyramus is a sweet-faced man, a proper° man as one shall see in a summer's day, a most lovely gentlemanlike man. Therefore you must needs play Pyramus.

BOTTOM. Well, I will undertake it. What beard were I best to play it in?

QUINCE. Why, what you will.

BOTTOM. I will discharge° it in either your° straw-color beard, your orange-tawny beard, your purple-in-grain° beard, or your French-crown-color° beard, your perfect yellow.

QUINCE. Some of your French crowns° have no hair at all, and then you will play barefaced. But, masters, here are your parts. [*He distributes parts.*] And I am to entreat you, request you, and desire you to con° them by tomorrow night; and meet me in the palace wood, a mile without the town, by moonlight. There will we rehearse; for if we meet in the city, we shall be dogged with company, and our devices° known. In the meantime I will draw a bill° of properties, such as our play wants. I pray you, fail me not.

BOTTOM. We will meet, and there we may rehearse most obscenely° and courageously. Take pains, be perfect;° adieu.

QUINCE. At the Duke's oak we meet.

BOTTOM. Enough. Hold, or cut bowstrings.° *Exeunt.*

**[2.1]** *Enter a Fairy at one door, and Robin Goodfellow* [*Puck*] *at another.*

PUCK. How now, spirit, whither wander you?

FAIRY.

Over hill, over dale,
  Thorough° bush, thorough brier,
Over park, over pale,°
  Thorough flood, thorough fire,
I do wander everywhere,
Swifter than the moon's sphere;°
And I serve the Fairy Queen,

**66 aggravate** (Bottom's blunder for *moderate.*) **roar you** i.e., roar for you **66–67 sucking dove** (Bottom conflates *sitting dove* and *sucking lamb,* two proverbial images of innocence.) **69 proper** handsome **74 discharge** perform. **your** i.e., you know the kind I mean **75 purple-in-grain** dyed a very deep red. (From *grain,* the name applied to the dried insect used to make the dye.) **75–76 French-crown-color** i.e., color of a French crown, a gold coin **77 crowns** heads bald from syphilis, the "French disease" **80 con** learn by heart **83 devices** plans. **bill** list **85 obscenely** (An unintentionally funny blunder, whatever Bottom meant to say.) **86 perfect** i.e., letter-perfect in memorizing your parts **88 Hold . . . bowstrings** (An archer's expression not definitely explained, but probably meaning here "keep your promises, or give up the play.")

**2.1 Location: A wood near Athens. 3 Thorough** through **4 pale** enclosure **7 sphere** orbit

To dew her orbs° upon the green.
The cowslips tall her pensioners° be.
In their gold coats spots you see:
Those be rubies, fairy favors;°
In those freckles live their savors.°
I must go seek some dewdrops here
And hang a pearl in every cowslip's ear.
Farewell, thou lob° of spirits: I'll be gone.
Our Queen and all her elves come here anon.°

PUCK. The King doth keep his revels here tonight.
Take heed the Queen come not within his sight.
For Oberon is passing fell° and wrath,°
Because that she as her attendant hath
A lovely boy, stolen from an Indian king;
She never had so sweet a changeling.°
And jealous Oberon would have the child
Knight of his train, to trace° the forests wild.
But she perforce° withholds the lovèd boy,
Crowns him with flowers, and makes him all her joy.
And now they never meet in grove or green,
By fountain° clear, or spangled starlight sheen,°
But they do square,° that all their elves for fear
Creep into acorn cups and hide them there.

FAIRY. Either I mistake your shape and making quite,
Or else you are that shrewd° and knavish sprite°
Called Robin Goodfellow. Are not you he
That frights the maidens of the villagery,°
Skim milk, and sometimes labor in the quern,°
And bootless° make the breathless huswife° churn,
And sometimes make the drink to bear no barm,°
Mislead night wanderers, laughing at their harm?
Those that "Hobgoblin" call you, and "Sweet Puck,"
You do their work, and they shall have good luck.
Are you not he?

PUCK. Thou speakest aright;
I am that merry wanderer of the night.
I jest to Oberon and make him smile
When I a fat and bean-fed horse beguile,
Neighing in likeness of a filly foal;
And sometimes lurk I in a gossip's° bowl,
In very likeness of a roasted crab,°

**9 orbs** circles, i.e., fairy rings (circular bands of grass, darker than the surrounding area, caused by fungi enriching the soil) **10 pensioners** retainers, members of the royal bodyguard **12 favors** love tokens **13 savors** sweet smells **16 lob** country bumpkin **17 anon** at once **20 passing fell** exceedingly angry. **wrath** wrathful **23 changeling** child exchanged for another by the fairies **25 trace** range through **26 perforce** forcibly **29 fountain** spring. **starlight sheen** shining starlight **30 square** quarrel **33 shrewd** mischievous. **sprite** spirit **35 villagery** village population **36 quern** handmill **37 bootless** in vain. **huswife** housewife **38 barm** yeast, head on the ale **47 gossip's** old woman's **48 crab** crab apple

And when she drinks, against her lips I bob
And on her withered dewlap° pour the ale.
The wisest aunt,° telling the saddest° tale,
Sometimes for three-foot stool mistaketh me;
Then slip I from her bum, down topples she,
And "Tailor"° cries, and falls into a cough;
And then the whole choir° hold their hips and laugh,
And waxen° in their mirth, and neeze,° and swear
A merrier hour was never wasted there.
But, room,° fairy! Here comes Oberon.

FAIRY. And here my mistress. Would that he were gone!

*Enter* [*Oberon*] *the King of Fairies at one door, with his train; and* [*Titania*] *the Queen at another, with hers.*

OBERON. Ill met by moonlight, proud Titania.

TITANIA. What, jealous Oberon? Fairies, skip hence.
I have forsworn his bed and company.

OBERON. Tarry, rash wanton.° Am not I thy lord?

TITANIA. Then I must be thy lady; but I know
When thou hast stolen away from Fairyland
And in the shape of Corin° sat all day,
Playing on pipes of corn° and versing love
To amorous Phillida.° Why art thou here
Come from the farthest step° of India
But that, forsooth, the bouncing Amazon,
Your buskined° mistress and your warrior love,
To Theseus must be wedded, and you come
To give their bed joy and prosperity.

OBERON. How canst thou thus for shame, Titania,
Glance at my credit with Hippolyta,°
Knowing I know thy love to Theseus?
Didst not thou lead him through the glimmering night
From Perigenia,° whom he ravishèd?
And make him with fair Aegles° break his faith,
With Ariadne° and Antiopa?°

TITANIA. These are the forgeries of jealousy;

**50 dewlap** loose skin on neck **51 aunt** old woman. **saddest** most serious **54 Tailor** (possibly because she ends up sitting cross-legged on the floor, looking like a tailor.) **55 choir** company **56 waxen** increase. **neeze** sneeze **58 room** stand aside, make room **63 wanton** headstrong creature **66, 68 Corin, Phillida** (Conventional names of pastoral lovers.) **67 corn** (Here, oat stalks.) **69 step** farthest limit of travel, or, perhaps, *steep,* mountain range **71 buskined** wearing half-boots called buskins **75 Glance . . . Hippolyta** make insinuations about my favored relationship with Hippolyta **78 Perigenia** i.e., Perigouna, one of Theseus's conquests. (This and the following women are named in Thomas North's translation of Plutarch's "Life of Theseus.") **79 Aegles** i.e., Aegle, for whom Theseus deserted Ariadne according to some accounts **80 Ariadne** the daughter of Minos, King of Crete, who helped Theseus to escape the labyrinth after killing the Minotaur; later she was abandoned by Theseus. **Antiopa** Queen of the Amazons and wife of Theseus; elsewhere identified with Hippolyta, but here thought of as a separate woman

And never, since the middle summer's spring,°
Met we on hill, in dale, forest, or mead,
By pavèd° fountain or by rushy° brook,
Or in° the beachèd margent° of the sea,
To dance our ringlets° to the whistling wind,
But with thy brawls thou hast disturbed our sport.
Therefore the winds, piping to us in vain,
As in revenge, have sucked up from the sea
Contagious° fogs; which, falling in the land,
Hath every pelting° river made so proud
That they have overborne their continents.°
The ox hath therefore stretched his yoke in vain,
The plowman lost his sweat, and the green corn°
Hath rotted ere his youth attained a beard;
The fold° stands empty in the drownèd field,
And crows are fatted with the murrain° flock;
The nine-men's-morris° is filled up with mud,
And the quaint mazes° in the wanton° green
For lack of tread are undistinguishable.
The human mortals want° their winter° here;
No night is now with hymn or carol blessed.
Therefore° the moon, the governess of floods,
Pale in her anger, washes all the air,
That rheumatic diseases° do abound.
And thorough this distemperature° we see
The seasons alter: hoary-headed frosts
Fall in the fresh lap of the crimson rose,
And on old Hiems'° thin and icy crown
An odorous chaplet of sweet summer buds
Is, as in mockery, set. The spring, the summer,
The childing° autumn, angry winter, change
Their wonted liveries,° and the mazèd° world
By their increase° now knows not which is which.
And this same progeny of evils comes
From our debate,° from our dissension;
We are their parents and original.°

**82 middle summer's spring** beginning of midsummer **84 pavèd** with pebbled bottom. **rushy** bordered with rushes **85 in** on. **margent** edge, border **86 ringlets** dances in a ring. (See *orbs* in line 9.) **90 Contagious** noxious **91 pelting** paltry **92 continents** banks that contain them **94 corn** grain of any kind **96 fold** pen for sheep or cattle **97 murrain** having died of the plague **98 nine-men's-morris** i.e., portion of the village green marked out in a square for a game played with nine pebbles or pegs **99 quaint mazes** i.e., intricate paths marked out on the village green to be followed rapidly on foot as a kind of contest. **wanton** luxuriant **101 want** lack. **winter** i.e., regular winter season; or, proper observances of winter, such as the *hymn or carol* in the next line (?) **103 Therefore** i.e., as a result of our quarrel **105 rheumatic diseases** colds, flu, and other respiratory infections **106 distemperature** disturbance in nature **109 Hiems'** the winter god's **112 childing** fruitful, pregnant **113 wonted liveries** usual apparel. **mazèd** bewildered **114 their increase** their yield, what they produce **116 debate** quarrel **117 original** origin

OBERON. Do you amend it, then; it lies in you.
Why should Titania cross her Oberon?
I do but beg a little changeling boy
To be my henchman.°
TITANIA. Set your heart at rest.
The fairy land buys not the child of me.
His mother was a vot'ress of my order,
And in the spicèd Indian air by night
Full often hath she gossiped by my side
And sat with me on Neptune's yellow sands,
Marking th' embarkèd traders° on the flood,°
When we have laughed to see the sails conceive
And grow big-bellied with the wanton° wind;
Which she, with pretty and with swimming° gait,
Following—her womb then rich with my young squire—
Would imitate, and sail upon the land
To fetch me trifles, and return again
As from a voyage, rich with merchandise.
But she, being mortal, of that boy did die;
And for her sake do I rear up her boy,
And for her sake I will not part with him.
OBERON. How long within this wood intend you stay?
TITANIA. Perchance till after Theseus' wedding day.
If you will patiently dance in our round°
And see our moonlight revels, go with us;
If not, shun me, and I will spare° your haunts.
OBERON. Give me that boy and I will go with thee.
TITANIA. Not for thy fairy kingdom. Fairies, away!
We shall chide downright if I longer stay.
*Exeunt* [*Titania with her train*].
OBERON. Well, go thy way. Thou shalt not from° this grove
Till I torment thee for this injury.
My gentle Puck, come hither. Thou rememb'rest
Since° once I sat upon a promontory,
And heard a mermaid on a dolphin's back
Uttering such dulcet and harmonious breath°
That the rude° sea grew civil at her song,
And certain stars shot madly from their spheres
To hear the sea-maid's music?
PUCK. I remember.
OBERON. That very time I saw, but thou couldst not,
Flying between the cold moon and the earth,
Cupid all° armed. A certain aim he took
At a fair vestal° thronèd by the west,

**121 henchman** attendant, page **127 traders** trading vessels. **flood** flood tide **129 wanton** sportive **130 swimming** smooth, gliding **140 round** circular dance **142 spare** shun **146 from** go from **149 Since** when **151 breath** voice, song **152 rude** rough **157 all** fully **158 vestal** vestal virgin. (Contains a complimentary allusion to Queen Elizabeth as a votaress of Diana and probably refers to an actual entertainment in her honor at Elvetham in 1591.)

And loosed° his love shaft smartly from his bow
As° it should pierce a hundred thousand hearts;
But I might° see young Cupid's fiery shaft
Quenched in the chaste beams of the watery moon,
And the imperial vot'ress passèd on
In maiden meditation, fancy-free.°
Yet marked I where the bolt° of Cupid fell:
It fell upon a little western flower,
Before milk-white, now purple with love's wound,
And maidens call it "love-in-idleness."°
Fetch me that flower; the herb I showed thee once.
The juice of it on sleeping eyelids laid
Will make or man or° woman madly dote
Upon the next live creature that it sees.
Fetch me this herb, and be thou here again
Ere the leviathan° can swim a league.

PUCK. I'll put a girdle round about the earth
In forty° minutes. [*Exit.*]

OBERON. Having once this juice,
I'll watch Titania when she is asleep
And drop the liquor of it in her eyes.
The next thing then she waking looks upon,
Be it on lion, bear, or wolf, or bull,
On meddling monkey, or on busy ape,
She shall pursue it with the soul of love.
And ere I take this charm from off her sight,
As I can take it with another herb,
I'll make her render up her page to me.
But who comes here? I am invisible,
And I will overhear their conference.

*Enter Demetrius, Helena following him.*

DEMETRIUS. I love thee not; therefore pursue me not.
Where is Lysander and fair Hermia?
The one I'll slay; the other slayeth me.
Thou toldst me they were stol'n unto this wood;
And here am I, and wode° within this wood,
Because I cannot meet my Hermia.
Hence, get thee gone, and follow me no more.

HELENA. You draw me, you hardhearted adamant!°
But yet you draw not iron, for my heart
Is true as steel. Leave° you your power to draw,
And I shall have no power to follow you.

DEMETRIUS. Do I entice you? Do I speak you fair?°

**159 loosed** released **160 As** as if **161 might** could **164 fancy-free** free of love's spell **165 bolt** arrow **168 love-in-idleness** pansy, heartsease **171 or . . . or** either . . . or **174 leviathan** sea monster, whale **176 forty** (Used indefinitely.) **192 wode** mad. (Pronounced "wood" and often spelled so.) **195 adamant** lodestone, magnet (with pun on *hardhearted,* since adamant was also thought to be the hardest of all stones and was confused with the diamond) **197 Leave** give up **199 fair** courteously

Or rather do I not in plainest truth
Tell you I do not nor I cannot love you?

HELENA. And even for that do I love you the more.
I am your spaniel; and, Demetrius,
The more you beat me, I will fawn on you.
Use me but as your spaniel, spurn me, strike me,
Neglect me, lose me; only give me leave,
Unworthy as I am, to follow you.
What worser place can I beg in your love—
And yet a place of high respect with me—
Than to be usèd as you use your dog?

DEMETRIUS. Tempt not too much the hatred of my spirit,
For I am sick when I do look on thee.

HELENA. And I am sick when I look not on you.

DEMETRIUS. You do impeach° your modesty too much
To leave the city and commit yourself
Into the hands of one that loves you not,
To trust the opportunity of night
And the ill counsel of a desert° place
With the rich worth of your virginity.

HELENA. Your virtue° is my privilege.° For that°
It is not night when I do see your face,
Therefore I think I am not in the night;
Nor doth this wood lack worlds of company,
For you, in my respect,° are all the world.
Then how can it be said I am alone
When all the world is here to look on me?

DEMETRIUS. I'll run from thee and hide me in the brakes,°
And leave thee to the mercy of wild beasts.

HELENA. The wildest hath not such a heart as you.
Run when you will, the story shall be changed:
Apollo flies and Daphne holds the chase,°
The dove pursues the griffin,° the mild hind°
Makes speed to catch the tiger—bootless° speed,
When cowardice pursues and valor flies!

DEMETRIUS. I will not stay° thy questions.° Let me go!
Or if thou follow me, do not believe
But I shall do thee mischief in the wood.

HELENA. Ay, in the temple, in the town, the field,
You do me mischief. Fie, Demetrius!
Your wrongs do set a scandal on my sex.°

**214 impeach** call into question **218 desert** deserted **220 virtue** goodness or power to attract. **privilege** safeguard; warrant. **For that** because **224 in my respect** as far as I am concerned **227 brakes** thickets **231 Apollo . . . chase** (In the ancient myth, Daphne fled from Apollo and was saved from rape by being transformed into a laurel tree; here it is the female who *holds the chase,* or pursues, instead of the male.) **232 griffin** a fabulous monster with the head of an eagle and the body of a lion. **hind** female deer **233 bootless** fruitless **235 stay** wait for. **questions** talk or argument **240 Your . . . sex** i.e., the wrongs that you do me cause me to act in a manner that disgraces my sex

We cannot fight for love, as men may do;
We should be wooed and were not made to woo.
[*Exit Demetrius.*]
I'll follow thee and make a heaven of hell,
To die upon° the hand I love so well. [*Exit.*]

OBERON. Fare thee well, nymph. Ere he do leave this grove,
Thou shalt fly him and he shall seek thy love.

*Enter Puck.*

Hast thou the flower there? Welcome, wanderer.

PUCK. Ay, there it is. [*He offers the flower.*]

OBERON. I pray thee, give it me.
I know a bank where the wild thyme blows,°
Where oxlips° and the nodding violet grows,
Quite overcanopied with luscious woodbine,°
With sweet muskroses° and with eglantine.°
There sleeps Titania sometimes of the night,
Lulled in these flowers with dances and delight;
And there the snake throws° her enameled skin,
Weed° wide enough to wrap a fairy in.
And with the juice of this I'll streak° her eyes
And make her full of hateful fantasies.
Take thou some of it, and seek through this grove.
[*He gives some love juice.*]
A sweet Athenian lady is in love
With a disdainful youth. Anoint his eyes,
But do it when the next thing he espies
May be the lady. Thou shalt know the man
By the Athenian garments he hath on.
Effect it with some care, that he may prove
More fond on° her than she upon her love;
And look thou meet me ere the first cock crow.

PUCK. Fear not, my lord, your servant shall do so.
*Exeunt.*

**[2.2]** *Enter Titania, Queen of Fairies, with her train.*

TITANIA. Come, now a roundel° and a fairy song;
Then, for the third part of a minute, hence—
Some to kill cankers° in the muskrose buds,
Some war with reremice° for their leathern wings
To make my small elves coats, and some keep back
The clamorous owl, that nightly hoots and wonders

**244 upon** by **249 blows** blooms **250 oxlips** flowers resembling cowslip and primrose **251 woodbine** honeysuckle **252 muskroses** a kind of large, sweet-scented rose. **eglantine** sweetbrier, another kind of rose **255 throws** sloughs off, sheds **256 Weed** garment **257 streak** anoint, touch gently **266 fond on** doting on

**2.2 Location: The wood. 1 roundel** dance in a ring **3 cankers** cankerworms (i.e., caterpillars or grubs) **4 reremice** bats

At our quaint° spirits. Sing me now asleep.
Then to your offices, and let me rest.

*Fairies sing.*

FIRST FAIRY.
You spotted snakes with double° tongue,
Thorny hedgehogs, be not seen;
Newts° and blindworms, do no wrong,
Come not near our Fairy Queen.

CHORUS.
Philomel,° with melody
Sing in our sweet lullaby;
Lulla, lulla, lullaby, lulla, lulla, lullaby.
Never harm
Nor spell nor charm
Come our lovely lady nigh.
So good night, with lullaby.

FIRST FAIRY.
Weaving spiders, come not here;
Hence, you long-legged spinners, hence!
Beetles black, approach not near;
Worm nor snail, do no offense.

CHORUS.
Philomel, with melody
Sing in our sweet lullaby;
Lulla, lulla, lullaby, lulla, lulla, lullaby.
Never harm
Nor spell nor charm
Come our lovely lady nigh.
So good night, with lullaby.
[*Titania sleeps.*]

SECOND FAIRY.
Hence, away! Now all is well.
One aloof stand sentinel. [*Exeunt Fairies.*]

*Enter Oberon* [*and squeezes the flower on Titania's eyelids*].

OBERON.
What thou seest when thou dost wake,
Do it for thy true love take;
Love and languish for his sake.
Be it ounce,° or cat, or bear,
Pard,° or boar with bristled hair,
In thy eye that shall appear
When thou wak'st, it is thy dear.
Wake when some vile thing is near. [*Exit.*]

*Enter Lysander and Hermia.*

**7 quaint** dainty **9 double** forked **11 Newts** water lizards (considered poisonous, as were *blindworms*—small snakes with tiny eyes—and spiders) **13 Philomel** the nightingale. (Philomela, daughter of King Pandion, was transformed into a nightingale, according to Ovid's *Metamorphoses* 6, after she had been raped by her sister Procne's husband, Tereus.) **36 ounce** lynx **37 Pard** leopard

LYSANDER. Fair love, you faint with wandering in the wood;
And to speak truth, I have forgot our way.
We'll rest us, Hermia, if you think it good,
And tarry for the comfort of the day.
HERMIA. Be it so, Lysander. Find you out a bed,
For I upon this bank will rest my head.
LYSANDER. One turf shall serve as pillow for us both;
One heart, one bed, two bosoms, and one troth.°
HERMIA. Nay, good Lysander, for my sake, my dear,
Lie further off yet; do not lie so near.
LYSANDER. O, take the sense, sweet, of my innocence!°
Love takes the meaning in love's conference.°
I mean that my heart unto yours is knit
So that but one heart we can make of it;
Two bosoms interchainéd with an oath—
So then two bosoms and a single troth.
Then by your side no bed-room me deny,
For lying so, Hermia, I do not lie.°
HERMIA. Lysander riddles very prettily.
Now much beshrew° my manners and my pride
If Hermia meant to say Lysander lied.
But, gentle friend, for love and courtesy
Lie further off, in human° modesty;
Such separation as may well be said
Becomes a virtuous bachelor and a maid,
So far be distant; and good night, sweet friend.
Thy love ne'er alter till thy sweet life end!
LYSANDER. Amen, amen, to that fair prayer, say I,
And then end life when I end loyalty!
Here is my bed. Sleep give thee all his rest!
HERMIA. With half that wish the wisher's eyes be pressed!°
[*They sleep, separated by a short distance.*]

*Enter Puck.*

PUCK.
Through the forest have I gone,
But Athenian found I none
On whose eyes I might approve°
This flower's force in stirring love.
Night and silence.—Who is here?
Weeds of Athens he doth wear.
This is he, my master said,
Despisèd the Athenian maid;
And here the maiden, sleeping sound,
On the dank and dirty ground.

**48 troth** faith, trothplight **51 take . . . innocence** i.e., interpret my intention as innocent **52 Love . . . conference** i.e., when lovers confer, love teaches each lover to interpret the other's meaning lovingly **58 lie** tell a falsehood (with a riddling pun on *lie,* recline) **60 beshrew** curse. (But mildly meant.) **63 human** courteous **71 With . . . pressed** i.e., may we share your wish, so that your eyes too are *pressed,* closed, in sleep **74 approve** test

Pretty soul, she durst not lie
Near this lack-love, this kill-courtesy.
Churl, upon thy eyes I throw
All the power this charm doth owe.°
[*He applies the love juice.*]
When thou wak'st, let love forbid
Sleep his seat on thy eyelid.
So awake when I am gone,
For I must now to Oberon. *Exit.*

*Enter Demetrius and Helena, running.*

HELENA. Stay, though thou kill me, sweet Demetrius!
DEMETRIUS. I charge thee, hence, and do not haunt me thus.
HELENA. O, wilt thou darkling° leave me? Do not so.
DEMETRIUS. Stay, on thy peril!° I alone will go. [*Exit.*]
HELENA. O, I am out of breath in this fond° chase!
The more my prayer, the lesser is my grace.°
Happy is Hermia, wheresoe'er she lies,
For she hath blessèd and attractive eyes.
How came her eyes so bright? Not with salt tears;
If so, my eyes are oftener washed than hers.
No, no, I am as ugly as a bear;
For beasts that meet me run away for fear.
Therefore no marvel though Demetrius
Do, as a monster, fly my presence thus.°
What wicked and dissembling glass of mine
Made me compare° with Hermia's sphery eyne?°
But who is here? Lysander, on the ground?
Dead, or asleep? I see no blood, no wound.
Lysander, if you live, good sir, awake.
LYSANDER [*awaking*]. And run through fire I will for thy sweet sake.
Transparent° Helena! Nature shows art,
That through thy bosom makes me see thy heart.
Where is Demetrius? O, how fit a word
Is that vile name to perish on my sword!
HELENA. Do not say so, Lysander, say not so.
What though he love your Hermia? Lord, what though?
Yet Hermia still loves you. Then be content.
LYSANDER. Content with Hermia? No! I do repent
The tedious minutes I with her have spent.
Not Hermia but Helena I love.
Who will not change a raven for a dove?
The will of man is by his reason swayed,
And reason says you are the worthier maid.

**85 owe** own **92 darkling** in the dark **93 on thy peril** i.e., on pain of danger to you if you don't obey me and stay **94 fond** doting **95 my grace** the favor I obtain **102–103 no marvel . . . thus** i.e., no wonder that Demetrius flies from me as from a monster **105 compare** vie. **sphery eyne** eyes as bright as stars in their spheres **110 Transparent** (1) radiant (2) able to be seen through

Things growing are not ripe until their season;
So I, being young, till now ripe not° to reason.
And touching° now the point° of human skill,°
Reason becomes the marshal to my will
And leads me to your eyes, where I o'erlook°
Love's stories written in love's richest book.

HELENA. Wherefore° was I to this keen mockery born?
When at your hands did I deserve this scorn?
Is 't not enough, is 't not enough, young man,
That I did never, no, nor never can,
Deserve a sweet look from Demetrius' eye,
But you must flout my insufficiency?
Good troth,° you do me wrong, good sooth,° you do,
In such disdainful manner me to woo.
But fare you well. Perforce I must confess
I thought you lord of° more true gentleness.°
O, that a lady, of° one man refused,
Should of another therefore be abused!° *Exit.*

LYSANDER. She sees not Hermia. Hermia, sleep thou there,
And never mayst thou come Lysander near!
For as a surfeit of the sweetest things
The deepest loathing to the stomach brings,
Or as the heresies that men do leave
Are hated most of those they did deceive,°
So thou, my surfeit and my heresy,
Of all be hated, but the most of me!
And, all my powers, address° your love and might
To honor Helen and to be her knight! *Exit.*

HERMIA [*awaking*]. Help me, Lysander, help me! Do thy best
To pluck this crawling serpent from my breast!
Ay me, for pity! What a dream was here!
Lysander, look how I do quake with fear.
Methought a serpent ate my heart away,
And you sat smiling at his cruel prey.°
Lysander! What, removed? Lysander! Lord!
What, out of hearing? Gone? No sound, no word?
Alack, where are you? Speak, an if° you hear;
Speak, of all loves!° I swoon almost with fear.
No? Then I well perceive you are not nigh.
Either death, or you, I'll find immediately.
*Exit.* [*The sleeping Titania remains.*]

**124 ripe not** (am) not ripened **125 touching** reaching. **point** summit. **skill** judgment **127 o'erlook** read **129 Wherefore** why **135 Good troth, good sooth** i.e., indeed, truly **138 lord of** i.e., possessor of. **gentleness** courtesy **139 of** by **140 abused** ill treated **145–146 as . . . deceive** as renounced heresies are hated most by those persons who formerly were deceived by them **149 address** direct, apply **156 prey** act of preying **159 an if** if **160 of all loves** for all love's sake

**[3.1]** *Enter the clowns [Quince, Snug, Bottom, Flute, Snout, and Starveling].*

BOTTOM. Are we all met?

QUINCE. Pat, pat;° and here's a marvelous convenient place for our rehearsal. This green plot shall be our stage, this hawthorn brake° our tiring house,° and we will do it in action as we will do it before the Duke.

BOTTOM. Peter Quince?

QUINCE. What sayest thou, bully° Bottom?

BOTTOM. There are things in this comedy of Pyramus and Thisbe that will never please. First, Pyramus must draw a sword to kill himself, which the ladies cannot abide. How answer you that?

SNOUT. By 'r lakin,° a parlous° fear.

STARVELING. I believe we must leave the killing out, when all is done.°

BOTTOM. Not a whit. I have a device to make all well. Write me° a prologue, and let the prologue seem to say we will do no harm with our swords, and that Pyramus is not killed indeed; and for the more better assurance, tell them that I, Pyramus, am not Pyramus but Bottom the weaver. This will put them out of fear.

QUINCE. Well, we will have such a prologue, and it shall be written in eight and six.°

BOTTOM. No, make it two more; let it be written in eight and eight.

SNOUT. Will not the ladies be afeard of the lion?

STARVELING. I fear it, I promise you.

BOTTOM. Masters, you ought to consider with yourselves, to bring in—God shield us!—a lion among ladies° is a most dreadful thing. For there is not a more fearful° wildfowl than your lion living; and we ought to look to 't.

SNOUT. Therefore another prologue must tell he is not a lion.

BOTTOM. Nay, you must name his name, and half his face must be seen through the lion's neck, and he himself must speak through, saying thus, or to the same defect:° "Ladies"—or "Fair ladies—I would wish you"—or "I would request you"—or "I would entreat you—not to fear, not to tremble; my life for yours.° If you think I come hither as a lion, it were pity of my life.° No, I am no such thing: I am a man as other men are." And there indeed let him name his name and tell them plainly he is Snug the joiner.

**3.1 Location: The action is continuous.** **2 Pat** on the dot, punctually **3 brake** thicket **4 tiring-house** attiring area, hence backstage **7 bully** i.e., worthy, jolly, fine fellow **11 By 'r lakin** by our ladykin, i.e., the Virgin Mary. **parlous** alarming **12 when all is done** i.e., when all is said and done **13 Write me** i.e., write at my suggestion. (*Me* is used colloquially.) **19 eight and six** alternate lines of eight and six syllables, a common ballad measure **24 lion among ladies** (A contemporary pamphlet tells how at the christening in 1594 of Prince Henry, eldest son of King James VI of Scotland, later James I of England, a "blackamoor" instead of a lion drew the triumphal chariot, since the lion's presence might have "brought some fear to the nearest.") **25 fearful** fear-inspiring **30 defect** (Bottom's blunder for *effect.*) **32 my life for yours** i.e., I pledge my life to make your lives safe **33 it were . . . life** my life would be endangered

QUINCE. Well, it shall be so. But there is two hard things: that is, to bring the moonlight into a chamber; for, you know, Pyramus and Thisbe meet by moonlight.

SNOUT. Doth the moon shine that night we play our play?

BOTTOM. A calendar, a calendar! Look in the almanac. Find out moonshine, find out moonshine. [*They consult an almanac.*]

QUINCE. Yes, it doth shine that night.

BOTTOM. Why, then, may you leave a casement of the great chamber window, where we play, open, and the moon may shine in at the casement.

QUINCE. Ay; or else one must come in with a bush of thorns° and a lantern and say he comes to disfigure,° or to present,° the person of Moonshine. Then there is another thing: we must have a wall in the great chamber; for Pyramus and Thisbe, says the story, did talk through the chink of a wall.

SNOUT. You can never bring in a wall. What say you, Bottom?

BOTTOM. Some man or other must present Wall. And let him have some plaster, or some loam, or some roughcast° about him, to signify wall; or let him hold his fingers thus, and through that cranny shall Pyramus and Thisbe whisper.

QUINCE. If that may be, then all is well. Come, sit down, every mother's son, and rehearse your parts. Pyramus, you begin. When you have spoken your speech, enter into that brake, and so everyone according to his cue.

*Enter Robin* [*Puck*].

PUCK. What hempen homespuns° have we swaggering here
So near the cradle° of the Fairy Queen?
What, a play toward?° I'll be an auditor;
An actor too perhaps, if I see cause.

QUINCE. Speak, Pyramus. Thisbe, stand forth.

BOTTOM [*as Pyramus*].
"Thisbe, the flowers of odious savors sweet—"

QUINCE. Odors, odors.

BOTTOM. "—Odors savors sweet;
So hath thy breath, my dearest Thisbe dear.
But hark, a voice! Stay thou but here awhile,
And by and by I will to thee appear." *Exit.*

PUCK. A stranger Pyramus than e'er played here.° [*Exit.*]

FLUTE. Must I speak now?

QUINCE. Ay, marry, must you; for you must understand he goes but to see a noise that he heard, and is to come again.

**46 bush of thorns** bundle of thornbush faggots (part of the accoutrements of the man in the moon, according to the popular notions of the time, along with his lantern and his dog) **47 disfigure** (Quince's blunder for *figure.*) **present** represent **53 roughcast** a mixture of lime and gravel used to plaster the outside of buildings **60 hempen homespuns** i.e., rustics dressed in clothes woven of coarse, homespun fabric made from hemp **61 cradle** i.e., Titania's bower **62 toward** about to take place **71 A stranger . . . here** (Puck indicates that he has conceived of his plan to present a "stranger" Pyramus than ever seen before, and so Puck exits to put his plan into effect.)

FLUTE [*as Thisbe*].
"Most radiant Pyramus, most lily-white of hue,
Of color like the red rose on triumphant° brier,
Most brisky juvenal° and eke° most lovely Jew,°
As true as truest horse, that yet would never tire.
I'll meet thee, Pyramus, at Ninny's tomb."

QUINCE. "Ninus'° tomb," man. Why, you must not speak that yet. That you answer to Pyramus. You speak all your part° at once, cues and all. Pyramus, enter. Your cue is past; it is "never tire."

FLUTE. O—"As true as truest horse, that yet would never tire."

[*Enter Puck, and Bottom as Pyramus with the ass head.*°]

BOTTOM. "If I were fair,° Thisbe, I were° only thine."

QUINCE. O, monstrous! O, strange! We are haunted. Pray, masters! Fly, masters! Help!

[*Exeunt Quince, Snug, Flute, Snout, and Starveling.*]

PUCK. I'll follow you, I'll lead you about a round,°
Through bog, through bush, through brake, through brier.
Sometimes a horse I'll be, sometimes a hound,
A hog, a headless bear, sometimes a fire;°
And neigh, and bark, and grunt, and roar, and burn,
Like horse, hound, hog, bear, fire, at every turn. *Exit.*

BOTTOM. Why do they run away? This is a knavery of them to make me afeard.

*Enter Snout.*

SNOUT. O Bottom, thou art changed! What do I see on thee?

BOTTOM. What do you see? You see an ass head of your own, do you? [*Exit Snout.*]

*Enter Quince.*

QUINCE. Bless thee, Bottom, bless thee! Thou art translated.° *Exit.*

BOTTOM. I see their knavery. This is to make an ass of me, to fright me, if they could. But I will not stir from this place, do what they can. I will walk up and down here, and will sing, that they shall hear I am not afraid. [*Sings.*]
The ouzel cock° so black of hue,
With orange-tawny bill,
The throstle° with his note so true,
The wren with little quill°—

TITANIA [*awaking*]. What angel wakes me from my flowery bed?

**76 triumphant** magnificent **77 brisky juvenal** lively youth. **eke** also. **Jew** (Probably an absurd repetition of the first syllable of *juvenal,* or Flute's error for *jewel.*) **80 Ninus** mythical founder of Nineveh (whose wife, Semiramis, was supposed to have built the walls of Babylon where the story of Pyramus and Thisbe takes place) **81 part** (An actor's *part* was a script consisting only of his speeches and their cues.) **83 s.d. with the ass head** (This stage direction, taken from the Folio, presumably refers to a standard stage property.) **84 fair** handsome. **were** would be **87 about a round** roundabout **90 fire** will-o'-the-wisp **97 translated** transformed **102 ouzel cock** male blackbird **104 throstle** song thrush **105 quill** (Literally, a reed pipe; hence, the bird's piping song.)

BOTTOM [*sings*].
The finch, the sparrow, and the lark,
The plainsong° cuckoo gray,
Whose note full many a man doth mark,
And dares not answer nay°—
For, indeed, who would set his wit to so foolish a bird? Who would give a bird the lie,° though he cry "cuckoo" never so?°

TITANIA. I pray thee, gentle mortal, sing again.
Mine ear is much enamored of thy note;
So is mine eye enthrallèd to thy shape;
And thy fair virtue's force° perforce doth move me
On the first view to say, to swear, I love thee.

BOTTOM. Methinks, mistress, you should have little reason for that. And yet, to say the truth, reason and love keep little company together nowadays. The more the pity that some honest neighbors will not make them friends. Nay, I can gleek° upon occasion.

TITANIA. Thou art as wise as thou art beautiful.

BOTTOM. Not so, neither. But if I had wit enough to get out of this wood, I have enough to serve mine own turn.°

TITANIA. Out of this wood do not desire to go.
Thou shalt remain here, whether thou wilt or no.
I am a spirit of no common rate.°
The summer still° doth tend upon my state,°
And I do love thee. Therefore go with me.
I'll give thee fairies to attend on thee
And they shall fetch thee jewels from the deep,
And sing while thou on pressèd flowers dost sleep.
And I will purge thy mortal grossness° so
That thou shalt like an airy spirit go.
Peaseblossom, Cobweb, Mote,° and Mustardseed!

*Enter four Fairies* [*Peaseblossom, Cobweb, Mote, and Mustardseed*].

PEASEBLOSSOM. Ready.
COBWEB. And I.
MOTE. And I.
MUSTARDSEED. And I.
ALL. Where shall we go?

TITANIA. Be kind and courteous to this gentleman.
Hop in his walks and gambol in his eyes;°
Feed him with apricots and dewberries,°
With purple grapes, green figs, and mulberries;
The honey bags steal from the humble-bees,

**108 plainsong** singing a melody without variations **110 dares . . . nay** i.e., cannot deny that he is a cuckold **112 give . . . lie** call the bird a liar. **never so** ever so much **116 thy . . . force** the power of your beauty **121 gleek** scoff, jest **124 serve . . . turn** answer my purpose **127 rate** rank, value **128 still** ever, always. **doth . . . state** waits upon me as a part of my royal retinue **133 mortal grossness** materiality (i.e., the corporal nature of a mortal being) **135 Mote** i.e., speck. (The two words *moth* and *mote* were pronounced alike, and both meanings may be present.) **139 in his eyes** in his sight (i.e., before him) **140 dewberries** blackberries

And for night tapers crop their waxen thighs
And light them at the fiery glowworms' eyes,
To have my love to bed and to arise;
And pluck the wings from painted butterflies
To fan the moonbeams from his sleeping eyes.
Nod to him, elves, and do him courtesies.

PEASEBLOSSOM. Hail, mortal!

COBWEB. Hail!

MOTE. Hail!

MUSTARDSEED. Hail!

BOTTOM. I cry your worships mercy, heartily. I beseech your worship's name.

COBWEB. Cobweb.

BOTTOM. I shall desire you of more acquaintance, good Master Cobweb. If I cut my finger, I shall make bold with you.°—Your name, honest gentleman?

PEASEBLOSSOM. Peaseblossom.

BOTTOM. I pray you, commend me to Mistress Squash,° your mother, and to Master Peascod,° your father. Good Master Peaseblossom, I shall desire you of more acquaintance too.—Your name, I beseech you, sir?

MUSTARDSEED. Mustardseed.

BOTTOM. Good Master Mustardseed I know your patience° well. That same cowardly giantlike ox-beef hath devoured many a gentleman of your house. I promise you, your kindred hath made my eyes water° ere now. I desire you of more acquaintance, good Master Mustardseed.

TITANIA. Come, wait upon him; lead him to my bower.
The moon methinks looks with a watery eye;
And when she weeps,° weeps every little flower,
Lamenting some enforcèd° chastity.
Tie up my lover's tongue,° bring him silently.

[*Exeunt.*]

## [3.2] *Enter* [*Oberon,*] *King of Fairies.*

OBERON. I wonder if Titania be awaked;
Then what it was that next came in her eye,
Which she must dote on in extremity.

[*Enter*] *Robin Goodfellow* [*Puck*].

Here comes my messenger. How now, mad spirit?
What night-rule° now about this haunted° grove?

**157 If . . . you** (Cobwebs were used to stanch bleeding.) **160 Squash** unripe pea pod **161 Peascod** ripe pea pod **165 your patience** what you have endured **168 water** (1) weep for sympathy (2) smart, sting **172 she weeps** i.e., she causes dew **173 enforcèd** forced, violated; or, possibly, constrained (since Titania at this moment is hardly concerned about chastity) **174 Tie . . . tongue** (Presumably Bottom is braying like an ass.)

**3.2 Location: The wood. 5 night-rule** diversion for the night. **haunted** much frequented

PUCK. My mistress with a monster is in love.
Near to her close° and consecrated bower,
While she was in her dull° and sleeping hour,
A crew of patches,° rude mechanicals,°
That work for bread upon Athenian stalls,°
Were met together to rehearse a play
Intended for great Theseus' nuptial day.
The shallowest thick-skin of that barren sort,°
Who Pyramus presented° in their sport,
Forsook his scene° and entered in a brake.
When I did him at this advantage take,
An ass's noll° I fixèd on his head.
Anon his Thisbe must be answered,
And forth my mimic° comes. When they him spy,
As wild geese that the creeping fowler° eye,
Or russet-pated choughs,° many in sort,°
Rising and cawing at the gun's report,
Sever° themselves and madly sweep the sky,
So, at his sight, away his fellows fly;
And, at our stamp, here o'er and o'er one falls;
He "Murder!" cries and help from Athens calls.
Their sense thus weak, lost with their fears thus strong,
Made senseless things begin to do them wrong,
For briers and thorns at their apparel snatch;
Some, sleeves—some, hats; from yielders all things catch.°
I led them on in this distracted fear
And left sweet Pyramus translated there,
When in that moment, so it came to pass,
Titania waked and straightway loved an ass.

OBERON. This falls out better than I could devise.
But hast thou yet latched° the Athenian's eyes
With the love juice, as I did bid thee do?

PUCK. I took him sleeping—that is finished too—
And the Athenian woman by his side,
That, when he waked, of force° she must be eyed.

*Enter Demetrius and Hermia.*

OBERON. Stand close. This is the same Athenian.

PUCK. This is the woman, but not this the man.

[*They stand aside.*]

DEMETRIUS. O, why rebuke you him that loves you so?
Lay breath so bitter on your bitter foe.

**7 close** secret, private **8 dull** drowsy **9 patches** clowns, fools. **rude mechanicals** ignorant artisans **10 stalls** market booths **13 barren sort** stupid company or crew **14 presented** acted **15 scene** playing area **17 noll** noddle, head **19 mimic** burlesque actor **20 fowler** hunter of game birds **21 russet-pated choughs** reddish brown or gray-headed jackdaws. **in sort** in a flock **23 Sever** i.e., scatter **30 from . . . catch** i.e., everything preys on those who yield to fear **36 latched** fastened, snared **40 of force** perforce

HERMIA. Now I but chide; but I should use thee worse,
For thou, I fear, hast given me cause to curse.
If thou hast slain Lysander in his sleep,
Being o'er shoes° in blood, plunge in the deep,
And kill me too.
The sun was not so true unto the day
As he to me. Would he have stolen away
From sleeping Hermia? I'll believe as soon
This whole° earth may be bored, and that the moon
May through the center creep, and so displease
Her brother's° noontide with th' Antipodes.°
It cannot be but thou hast murdered him;
So should a murderer look, so dead,° so grim.

DEMETRIUS. So should the murdered look, and so should I
Pierced through the heart with your stern cruelty.
Yet you, the murderer, look as bright, as clear,
As yonder Venus in her glimmering sphere.

HERMIA. What's this to° my Lysander? Where is he?
Ah, good Demetrius, wilt thou give him me?

DEMETRIUS. I had rather give his carcass to my hounds.

HERMIA. Out, dog! Out, cur! Thou driv'st me past the bounds
Of maiden's patience. Hast thou slain him, then?
Henceforth be never numbered among men.
O, once tell true, tell true, even for my sake:
Durst thou have looked upon him being awake?
And hast thou killed him sleeping? O brave touch!°
Could not a worm,° an adder, do so much?
An adder did it; for with doubler tongue
Than thine, thou serpent, never adder stung.

DEMETRIUS. You spend your passion° on a misprised mood.°
I am not guilty of Lysander's blood,
Nor is he dead, for aught that I can tell.

HERMIA. I pray thee, tell me then that he is well.

DEMETRIUS. An if I could, what should I get therefor?

HERMIA. A privilege never to see me more.
And from thy hated presence part I so.
See me no more, whether he be dead or no. *Exit.*

DEMETRIUS. There is no following her in this fierce vein.
Here therefore for a while I will remain.
So sorrow's heaviness doth heavier° grow
For debt that bankrupt° sleep doth sorrow owe;

**48 o'er shoes** i.e., so far gone **53 whole** solid **55 Her brother's** i.e., the sun's. **th' Antipodes** the people on the opposite side of the earth (where the moon is imagined bringing night to noontime) **57 dead** deadly, or deathly pale **62 to** to do with **70 brave touch** noble exploit. (Said ironically.) **71 worm** serpent **74 passion** violent feelings. **misprised mood** anger based on misconception **84 heavier** (1) harder to bear (2) more drowsy **85 bankrupt** (Demetrius is saying that his sleepiness adds to the weariness caused by sorrow.)

Which now in some slight measure it will pay,
If for his tender here I make some stay.° *Lie[s] down [and sleeps]*.

OBERON. What hast thou done? Thou hast mistaken quite
And laid the love juice on some true love's sight.
Of thy misprision° must perforce ensue
Some true love turned, and not a false turned true.

PUCK. Then fate o'errules, that, one man holding troth,°
A million fail, confounding oath on oath.°

OBERON. About the wood go swifter than the wind,
And Helena of Athens look° thou find.
All fancy-sick° she is and pale of cheer°
With sighs of love, that cost the fresh blood° dear.
By some illusion see thou bring her here.
I'll charm his eyes against she do appear.°

PUCK. I go. I go, look how I go,
Swifter than arrow from the Tartar's bow.° [*Exit*].

OBERON [*applying love juice to Demetrius' eyes*].
Flower of this purple dye,
Hit with Cupid's archery,
Sink in apple of his eye.
When his love he doth espy,
Let her shine as gloriously
As the Venus of the sky.
When thou wak'st, if she be by,
Beg of her for remedy.

*Enter Puck.*

PUCK.
Captain of our fairy band,
Helena is here at hand,
And the youth, mistook by me,
Pleading for a lover's fee.°
Shall we their fond pageant° see?
Lord, what fools these mortals be!

OBERON.
Stand aside. The noise they make
Will cause Demetrius to awake.

PUCK.
Then will two at once woo one;
That must needs be sport alone.°

**86–87 Which . . . stay** i.e., to a small extent I will be able to "pay back" and hence find some relief from sorrow, if I pause here awhile (*make some stay*) while sleep "tenders" or offers itself by way of paying the debt owed to sorrow **90 misprision** mistake **92 troth** faith **93 confounding . . . oath** i.e., invalidating one oath with another **95 look** i.e., be sure **96 fancy-sick** lovesick. **cheer** face **97 sighs . . . blood** (An allusion to the physiological theory that each sigh costs the heart a drop of blood.) **99 against . . . appear** in anticipation of her coming **101 Tartar's bow** (Tartars were famed for their skill with the bow.) **113 fee** privilege, reward **114 fond pageant** foolish exhibition **119 alone** unequaled

And those things do best please me
That befall preposterously.°

[*They stand aside.*]

*Enter Lysander and Helena.*

LYSANDER. Why should you think that I should woo in scorn?
Scorn and derision never come in tears.
Look when° I vow, I weep; and vows so born,
In their nativity all truth appears.°
How can these things in me seem scorn to you,
Bearing the badge° of faith to prove them true?
HELENA. You do advance° your cunning more and more.
When truth kills truth,° O, devilish-holy fray!
These vows are Hermia's. Will you give her o'er?
Weigh oath with oath, and you will nothing weigh.
Your vows to her and me, put in two scales,
Will even weigh, and both as light as tales.°
LYSANDER. I had no judgment when to her I swore.
HELENA. Nor none, in my mind, now you give her o'er.
LYSANDER. Demetrius loves her, and he loves not you.
DEMETRIUS [*awaking*]. O Helen, goddess, nymph, perfect, divine!
To what, my love, shall I compare thine eyne?
Crystal is muddy. O, how ripe in show°
Thy lips, those kissing cherries, tempting grow!
That pure congealèd white, high Taurus'° snow,
Fanned with the eastern wind, turns to a crow°
When thou hold'st up thy hand. O, let me kiss
This princess of pure white, this seal° of bliss!
HELENA. O spite! O hell! I see you all are bent
To set against° me for your merriment.
If you were civil and knew courtesy,
You would not do me thus much injury.
Can you not hate me, as I know you do,
But you must join in souls to mock me too?
If you were men, as men you are in show,
You would not use a gentle lady so—
To vow, and swear, and superpraise° my parts,°
When I am sure you hate me with your hearts.
You both are rivals, and love Hermia;
And now both rivals, to mock Helena.
A trim° exploit, a manly enterprise,
To conjure tears up in a poor maid's eyes

**121 preposterously** out of the natural order **124 Look when** whenever **124–125 vows . . . appears** i.e., vows made by one who is weeping give evidence thereby of their sincerity **127 badge** identifying device such as that worn on servants' livery (here, his tears) **128 advance** carry forward, display **129 truth kills truth** i.e., one of Lysander's vows must invalidate the other **133 tales** lies **139 show** appearance **141 Taurus** a lofty mountain range in Asia Minor **142 turns to a crow** i.e., seems black by contrast **144 seal** pledge **146 set against** attack **153 superpraise** overpraise. **parts** qualities **157 trim** pretty, fine. (Said ironically.)

With your derision! None of noble sort°
Would so offend a virgin and extort°
A poor soul's patience, all to make you sport.

LYSANDER. You are unkind, Demetrius. Be not so;
For you love Hermia; this you know I know.
And here, with all good will, with all my heart,
In Hermia's love I yield you up my part;
And yours of Helena to me bequeath,
Whom I do love and will do till my death.

HELENA. Never did mockers waste more idle breath.

DEMETRIUS. Lysander, keep thy Hermia; I will none.°
If e'er I loved her, all that love is gone.
My heart to her but as guest-wise sojourned,°
And now to Helen is it home returned,
There to remain.

LYSANDER. Helen, it is not so.

DEMETRIUS. Disparage not the faith thou dost not know,
Lest, to thy peril, thou aby° it dear.
Look where thy love comes; yonder is thy dear.

*Enter Hermia.*

HERMIA. Dark night, that from the eye his° function takes,
The ear more quick of apprehension makes;
Wherein it doth impair the seeing sense
It pays the hearing double recompense.
Thou art not by mine eye, Lysander, found;
Mine ear, I thank it, brought me to thy sound.
But why unkindly didst thou leave me so?

LYSANDER. Why should he stay whom love doth press to go?

HERMIA. What love could press Lysander from my side?

LYSANDER. Lysander's love, that would not let him bide—
Fair Helena, who more engilds° the night
Than all yon fiery oes° and eyes of light.
Why seek'st thou me? Could not this make thee know,
The hate I bear thee made me leave thee so?

HERMIA. You speak not as you think. It cannot be.

HELENA. Lo, she is one of this confederacy!
Now I perceive they have conjoined all three
To fashion this false sport in spite of me.°
Injurious Hermia, most ungrateful maid!
Have you conspired, have you with these contrived°
To bait° me with this foul derision?
Is all the counsel° that we two have shared,
The sisters' vows, the hours that we have spent,
When we have chid the hasty-footed time

**159 sort** character, quality **160 extort** twist, torture **169 will none** i.e., want no part of her **171 to . . . sojourned** only visited with her **175 aby** pay for **177 his** its **187 engilds** brightens with a golden light **188 oes** spangles (here, stars) **194 in spite of me** to vex me **196 contrived** plotted **197 bait** torment, as one sets on dogs to bait a bear **198 counsel** confidential talk

For parting us—O, is all forgot?
All schooldays' friendship, childhood innocence?
We, Hermia, like two artificial° gods,
Have with our needles created both one flower,
Both on one sampler, sitting on one cushion,
Both warbling of one song, both in one key,
As if our hands, our sides, voices, and minds
Had been incorporate.° So we grew together
Like to a double cherry, seeming parted
But yet an union in partition,
Two lovely° berries molded on one stem;
So with two seeming bodies but one heart,
Two of the first, like coats in heraldry,
Due but to one and crowned with one crest.°
And will you rend our ancient love asunder
To join with men in scorning your poor friend?
It is not friendly, 'tis not maidenly.
Our sex, as well as I, may chide you for it,
Though I alone do feel the injury.

HERMIA. I am amazèd at your passionate words.
I scorn you not. It seems that you scorn me.

HELENA. Have you not set Lysander, as in scorn,
To follow me and praise my eyes and face?
And made your other love, Demetrius,
Who even but now did spurn me with his foot,
To call me goddess, nymph, divine and rare,
Precious, celestial? Wherefore speaks he this
To her he hates? And wherefore doth Lysander
Deny your love, so rich within his soul,
And tender° me, forsooth, affection,
But by your setting on, by your consent?
What though I be not so in grace° as you,
So hung upon with love, so fortunate,
But miserable most, to love unloved?
This you should pity rather than despise.

HERMIA. I understand not what you mean by this.

HELENA. Ay, do! Persever, counterfeit sad° looks,
Make mouths° upon° me when I turn my back.
Wink each at other, hold the sweet jest up.°
This sport, well carried,° shall be chronicled.
If you have any pity, grace, or manners,
You would not make me such an argument.°
But fare ye well. 'Tis partly my own fault,
Which death, or absence, soon shall remedy.

**203 artificial** skilled in art or creation **208 incorporate** of one body **211 lovely** loving **213–214 Two . . . crest** i.e., we have two separate bodies, just as a coat of arms in heraldry can be represented twice on a shield but surmounted by a single crest **230 tender** offer **232 grace** favor **237 sad** grave, serious **238 mouths** i.e., mows, faces, grimaces. **upon** at **239 hold . . . up** keep up the joke **240 carried** managed **242 argument** subject for a jest

LYSANDER. Stay, gentle Helena; hear my excuse,
My love, my life, my soul, fair Helena!
HELENA. O excellent!
HERMIA [*to Lysander*]. Sweet, do not scorn her so.
DEMETRIUS. If she cannot entreat,° I can compel.
LYSANDER. Thou canst compel no more than she entreat.
Thy threats have no more strength than her weak prayers.
Helen, I love thee, by my life I do!
I swear by that which I will lose for thee,
To prove him false that says I love thee not.
DEMETRIUS. I say I love thee more than he can do.
LYSANDER. If thou say so, withdraw, and prove it too.
DEMETRIUS. Quick, come!
HERMIA. Lysander, whereto tends all this?
LYSANDER. Away, you Ethiop!°
[*He tries to break away from Hermia.*]
DEMETRIUS. No, no; he'll
Seem to break loose; take on as° you would follow,
But yet come not. You are a tame man, go!
LYSANDER. Hang off,° thou cat, thou burr! Vile thing, let loose,
Or I will shake thee from me like a serpent!
HERMIA. Why are you grown so rude? What change is this,
Sweet love?
LYSANDER. Thy love? Out, tawny Tartar, out!
Out, loathèd med'cine!° O hated potion, hence!
HERMIA. Do you not jest?
HELENA. Yes, sooth,° and so do you.
LYSANDER. Demetrius, I will keep my word with thee.
DEMETRIUS. I would I had your bond, for I perceive
A weak bond° holds you. I'll not trust your word.
LYSANDER. What, should I hurt her, strike her, kill her dead?
Although I hate her, I'll not harm her so.
HERMIA. What, can you do me greater harm than hate?
Hate me? Wherefore? O me, what news,° my love?
Am not I Hermia? Are not you Lysander?
I am as fair now as I was erewhile.°
Since night you loved me; yet since night you left me.
Why, then you left me—O, the gods forbid!—
In earnest, shall I say?
LYSANDER. Ay, by my life!
And never did desire to see thee more.
Therefore be out of hope, of question, of doubt;
Be certain, nothing truer. 'Tis no jest
That I do hate thee and love Helena.

**248 entreat** i.e., succeed by entreaty **257 Ethiop** (Referring to Hermia's relatively dark hair and complexion; see also *tawny Tartar* six lines later.) **258 take on as** act as if **260 Hang off** let go **264 med'cine** i.e., poison **265 sooth** truly **268 weak bond** i.e., Hermia's arm (with a pun on *bond,* oath, in the previous line) **272 what news** what is the matter **274 erewhile** just now

HERMIA [*to Helena*]. O me! You juggler! You cankerblossom!°
You thief of love! What, have you come by night
And stol'n my love's heart from him?

HELENA. Fine, i' faith!
Have you no modesty, no maiden shame,
No touch of bashfulness? What, will you tear
Impatient answers from my gentle tongue?
Fie, fie! You counterfeit, you puppet,° you!

HERMIA. "Puppet"? Why, so!° Ay, that way goes the game.
Now I perceive that she hath made compare
Between our statures: she hath urged her height,
And with her personage, her tall personage,
Her height, forsooth, she hath prevailed with him.
And are you grown so high in his esteem
Because I am so dwarfish and so low?
How low am I, thou painted maypole? Speak!
How low am I? I am not yet so low
But that my nails can reach unto thine eyes.
[*She flails at Helena but is restrained.*]

HELENA. I pray you, though you mock me, gentlemen,
Let her not hurt me. I was never curst;°
I have no gift at all in shrewishness;
I am a right° maid for my cowardice.
Let her not strike me. You perhaps may think,
Because she is something° lower than myself,
That I can match her.

HERMIA. Lower? Hark, again!

HELENA. Good Hermia, do not be so bitter with me.
I evermore did love you, Hermia,
Did ever keep your counsels, never wronged you;
Save that, in love unto Demetrius,
I told him of your stealth° unto this wood.
He followed you; for love I followed him.
But he hath chid me hence° and threatened me
To strike me, spurn me, nay, to kill me too.
And now, so° you will let me quiet go,
To Athens will I bear my folly back
And follow you no further. Let me go.
You see how simple and how fond° I am.

HERMIA. Why, get you gone. Who is 't that hinders you?

HELENA. A foolish heart, that I leave here behind.

HERMIA. What, with Lysander?

HELENA. With Demetrius.

LYSANDER. Be not afraid; she shall not harm thee, Helena.

DEMETRIUS. No, sir, she shall not, though you take her part.

**282 cankerblossom** worm that destroys the flower bud (?) **288 puppet** (1) counterfeit (2) dwarfish woman (in reference to Hermia's smaller stature) **289 Why, so** i.e., Oh, so that's how it is **300 curst** shrewish **302 right** true **304 something** somewhat **310 stealth** stealing away **312 chid me hence** driven me away with his scolding **314 so** if only **317 fond** foolish

HELENA. O, when she is angry, she is keen° and shrewd.°
She was a vixen when she went to school,
And though she be but little, she is fierce.
HERMIA. "Little" again? Nothing but "low" and "little"?
Why will you suffer her to flout me thus?
Let me come to her.
LYSANDER. Get you gone, you dwarf!
You minimus,° of hindering knotgrass° made!
You bead, you acorn!
DEMETRIUS. You are too officious
In her behalf that scorns your services.
Let her alone. Speak not of Helena;
Take not her part. For, if thou dost intend°
Never so little show of love to her,
Thou shalt aby° it.
LYSANDER. Now she holds me not;
Now follow, if thou dar'st, to try whose right,
Of thine or mine, is most in Helena. [*Exit.*]
DEMETRIUS. Follow? Nay, I'll go with thee, cheek by jowl.°
[*Exit, following Lysander.*]
HERMIA. You, mistress, all this coil° is 'long of° you.
Nay, go not back.°
HELENA. I will not trust you, I,
Nor longer stay in your curst company.
Your hands than mine are quicker for a fray;
My legs are longer, though, to run away. [*Exit.*]
HERMIA. I am amazed and know not what to say. *Exit.*

[*Oberon and Puck come forward.*]

OBERON. This is thy negligence. Still thou mistak'st,
Or else committ'st thy knaveries willfully.
PUCK. Believe me, king of shadows, I mistook.
Did not you tell me I should know the man
By the Athenian garments he had on?
And so far blameless proves my enterprise
That I have 'nointed an Athenian's eyes;
And so far am I glad it so did sort,°
As° this their jangling I esteem a sport.
OBERON. Thou seest these lovers seek a place to fight.
Hie° therefore, Robin, overcast the night;
The starry welkin° cover thou anon
With drooping fog as black as Acheron,°
And lead these testy rivals so astray
As one come not within another's way.

**323 keen** fierce, cruel. **shrewd** shrewish **329 minimus** diminutive creature. **knotgrass** a weed, an infusion of which was thought to stunt the growth **333 intend** give sign of **335 aby** pay for **338 cheek by jowl** i.e., side by side **339 coil** turmoil, dissension. **'long of** on account of **340 go not back** i.e., don't retreat. (Hermia is again proposing a fight.) **352 sort** turn out **353 As** that (also at line 359) **355 Hie** hasten **356 welkin** sky **357 Acheron** river of Hades (here representing Hades itself)

Like to Lysander sometimes frame thy tongue,
Then stir Demetrius up with bitter wrong;°
And sometimes rail thou like Demetrius.
And from each other look thou lead them thus,
Till o'er their brows death-counterfeiting sleep
With leaden legs and batty° wings doth creep.
Then crush this herb° into Lysander's eye, [*Giving herb*]
Whose liquor hath this virtuous° property,
To take from thence all error with his° might
And make his eyeballs roll with wonted° sight.
When they next wake, all this derision°
Shall seem a dream and fruitless vision,
And back to Athens shall the lovers wend
With league whose date° till death shall never end.
Whiles I in this affair do thee employ,
I'll to my queen and beg her Indian boy;
And then I will her charmèd eye release
From monster's view, and all things shall be peace.

PUCK. My fairy lord, this must be done with haste,
For night's swift dragons° cut the clouds full fast,
And yonder shines Aurora's harbinger,°
At whose approach, ghosts, wand'ring here and there,
Troop home to churchyards. Damnèd spirits all,
That in crossways and floods have burial,°
Already to their wormy beds are gone.
For fear lest day should look their shames upon,
They willfully themselves exile from light
And must for aye° consort with black-browed night.

OBERON. But we are spirits of another sort.
I with the Morning's love° have oft made sport,
And, like a forester,° the groves may tread
Even till the eastern gate, all fiery red,
Opening on Neptune with fair blessèd beams,
Turns into yellow gold his salt green streams.
But notwithstanding, haste, make no delay.
We may effect this business yet ere day. [*Exit.*]

PUCK.

Up and down, up and down,
I will lead them up and down.

**361 wrong** insults **365 batty** batlike **366 this herb** i.e., the antidote (mentioned in 2.1.184) to love-in-idleness **367 virtuous** efficacious **368 his** its **369 wonted** accustomed **370 derision** laughable business **373 date** term of existence **379 dragons** (Supposed by Shakespeare to be yoked to the car of the goddess of night.) **380 Aurora's harbinger** the morning star, precursor of dawn **383 crossways . . . burial** (Those who had committed suicide were buried at crossways, with a stake driven through them; those drowned, i.e., buried in floods or great waters, would be condemned to wander disconsolate for want of burial rites.) **387 for aye** forever **389 Morning's love** Cephalus, a beautiful youth beloved by Aurora; or perhaps the goddess of the dawn herself **390 forester** keeper of a royal forest

I am feared in field and town.
Goblin, lead them up and down.
Here comes one.

*Enter Lysander.*

LYSANDER. Where art thou, proud Demetrius? Speak thou now.
PUCK [*mimicking Demetrius*].
Here, villain, drawn° and ready. Where art thou?
LYSANDER. I will be with thee straight.°
PUCK. Follow me, then,
To plainer° ground.
[*Lysander wanders about,° following the voice.*]

*Enter Demetrius.*

DEMETRIUS. Lysander! Speak again!
Thou runaway, thou coward, art thou fled?
Speak! In some bush? Where dost thou hide thy head?
PUCK [*mimicking Lysander*].
Thou coward, art thou bragging to the stars,
Telling the bushes that thou look'st for wars,
And wilt not come? Come, recreant;° come, thou child,
I'll whip thee with a rod. He is defiled
That draws a sword on thee.
DEMETRIUS. Yea, art thou there?
PUCK. Follow my voice. We'll try° no manhood here.
*Exeunt.*

[*Lysander returns.*]

LYSANDER. He goes before me and still dares me on.
When I come where he calls, then he is gone.
The villain is much lighter-heeled than I.
I followed fast, but faster he did fly,
That fallen am I in dark uneven way,
And here will rest me. [*He lies down.*] Come, thou gentle day!
For if but once thou show me thy gray light,
I'll find Demetrius and revenge this spite. [*He sleeps.*]

[*Enter*] *Robin* [*Puck*] *and Demetrius.*

PUCK. Ho, ho, ho! Coward, why com'st thou not?
DEMETRIUS. Abide° me, if thou dar'st; for well I wot°
Thou runn'st before me, shifting every place,
And dar'st not stand nor look me in the face.
Where art thou now?
PUCK. Come hither. I am here.
DEMETRIUS. Nay, then, thou mock'st me. Thou shalt buy° this dear,°
If ever I thy face by daylight see.
Now, go thy way. Faintness constraineth me

**402 drawn** with drawn sword **403 straight** immediately **404 plainer** more open **s.d. Lysander wanders about** (It is not clearly necessary that Lysander exit at this point; neither exit nor reentrance is indicated in the early texts.) **409 recreant** cowardly wretch **412 try** test **422 Abide** confront, face. **wot** know **426 buy** aby, pay for. **dear** dearly

To measure out my length on this cold bed.
By day's approach look to be visited.
[*He lies down and sleeps.*]

*Enter Helena.*

HELENA.
O weary night, O long and tedious night,
  Abate° thy hours! Shine comforts from the east,
That I may back to Athens by daylight,
  From these that my poor company detest;
And sleep, that sometimes shuts up sorrow's eye,
Steal me awhile from mine own company.
[*She lies down and*] *sleep*[*s*].

PUCK.
Yet but three? Come one more;
Two of both kinds makes up four.
Here she comes, curst° and sad.
Cupid is a knavish lad,
Thus to make poor females mad.

[*Enter Hermia.*]

HERMIA.
Never so weary, never so in woe,
  Bedabbled with the dew and torn with briers
I can no further crawl, no further go;
  My legs can keep no pace with my desires.
Here will I rest me till the break of day.
Heavens shield Lysander, if they mean a fray!
[*She lies down and sleeps.*]

PUCK.
On the ground
Sleep sound.
I'll apply
To your eye,
Gentle lover, remedy.
[*Squeezing the juice on Lysander's eyes.*]
When thou wak'st,
Thou tak'st
True delight
In the sight
Of thy former lady's eye;
And the country proverb known,
That every man should take his own,
In your waking shall be shown:
Jack shall have Jill;°
Naught shall go ill;
The man shall have his mare again, and all shall be well.
[*Exit. The four sleeping lovers remain.*]

**432 Abate** lessen, shorten **439 curst** ill-tempered **461 Jack shall have Jill** (Proverbial for "boy gets girl.")

**[4.1]** *Enter* [*Titania*] *Queen of Fairies, and* [*Bottom the*] *clown, and Fairies; and* [*Oberon,*] *the King, behind them.*

TITANIA.
Come, sit thee down upon this flowery bed,
While I thy amiable° cheeks do coy,°
And stick muskroses in thy sleek smooth head,
And kiss thy fair large ears, my gentle joy.
[*They recline.*]

BOTTOM. Where's Peaseblossom?

PEASEBLOSSOM. Ready.

BOTTOM. Scratch my head, Peaseblossom. Where's Monsieur Cobweb?

COBWEB. Ready.

BOTTOM. Monsieur Cobweb, good monsieur, get you your weapons in your hand, and kill me a red-hipped humble-bee on the top of a thistle; and, good monsieur, bring me the honey bag. Do not fret yourself too much in the action, monsieur, and, good monsieur, have a care the honey bag break not; I would be loath to have you overflown with a honey bag, signor. [*Exit Cobweb.*] Where's Monsieur Mustardseed?

MUSTARDSEED. Ready.

BOTTOM. Give me your neaf,° Monsieur Mustardseed. Pray you, leave your courtesy,° good monsieur.

MUSTARDSEED. What's your will?

BOTTOM. Nothing, good monsieur, but to help Cavalery° Cobweb° to scratch. I must to the barber's, monsieur, for methinks I am marvelous hairy about the face; and I am such a tender ass, if my hair do but tickle me, I must scratch.

TITANIA. What, wilt thou hear some music, my sweet love?

BOTTOM. I have a reasonable good ear in music. Let's have the tongs and the bones.°

[*Music: tongs, rural music.*°]

TITANIA. Or say, sweet love, what thou desirest to eat.

BOTTOM. Truly, a peck of provender.° I could munch your good dry oats. Methinks I have a great desire to a bottle° of hay. Good hay, sweet hay, hath no fellow.°

TITANIA. I have a venturous fairy that shall seek
The squirrel's hoard, and fetch thee new nuts.

BOTTOM. I had rather have a handful or two of dried peas. But, I pray you, let none of your people stir° me. I have an exposition° of sleep come upon me.

**4.1 Location: The action is continuous. The four lovers are still asleep onstage. 2 amiable** lovely. **coy** caress **17 neaf** fist **17–18 leave your courtesy** i.e., stop bowing, or put on your hat **20 Cavalery** cavalier. (Form of address for a gentleman.) **Cobweb** (Seemingly an error, since Cobweb has been sent to bring honey while Peaseblossom has been asked to scratch.) **25–26 tongs . . . bones** instruments for rustic music. (The tongs were played like a triangle, whereas the bones were held between the fingers and used as clappers.) **s.d. Music . . . music** (This stage direction is added from the Folio.) **28 peck of provender** one-quarter bushel of grain **29 bottle** bundle **30 fellow** equal **34 stir** disturb. **exposition** (Bottom's word for *disposition*.)

TITANIA. Sleep thou, and I will wind thee in my arms.
Fairies, begone, and be all ways° away.
[*Exeunt Fairies.*]
So doth the woodbine the sweet honeysuckle
Gently entwist; the female ivy so
Enrings the barky fingers of the elm.
O, how I love thee! How I dote on thee!
[*They sleep.*]

*Enter Robin Goodfellow* [*Puck*].

OBERON [*coming forward*].
Welcome, good Robin. Seest thou this sweet sight?
Her dotage now I do begin to pity.
For, meeting her of late behind the wood,
Seeking sweet favors° for this hateful fool,
I did upbraid her and fall out with her.
For she his hairy temples then had rounded
With coronet of fresh and fragrant flowers;
And that same dew, which sometime° on the buds
Was wont to swell like round and orient pearls,°
Stood now within the pretty flowerets' eyes
Like tears that did their own disgrace bewail.
When I had at my pleasure taunted her,
And she in mild terms begged my patience,
I then did ask of her her changeling child,
Which straight she gave me, and her fairy sent
To bear him to my bower in Fairyland.
And, now I have the boy, I will undo
This hateful imperfection of her eyes.
And, gentle Puck, take this transformèd scalp
From off the head of this Athenian swain,
That he, awaking when the other° do,
May all to Athens back again repair,°
And think no more of this night's accidents
But as the fierce vexation of a dream.
But first I will release the Fairy Queen.
[*He squeezes a herb on her eyes.*]
Be as thou wast wont to be;
See as thou wast wont to see.
Dian's bud° o'er Cupid's flower
Hath such force and blessèd power.
Now, my Titania, wake you, my sweet queen.

TITANIA [*waking*]. My Oberon! What visions have I seen!
Methought I was enamored of an ass.

**37 all ways** in all directions **45 favors** i.e., gifts of flowers **49 sometime** formerly **50 orient pearls** i.e., the most beautiful of all pearls, those coming from the Orient **62 other** others **63 repair** return **69 Dian's bud** (Perhaps the flower of the *agnus castus* or chaste-tree, supposed to preserve chastity; or perhaps referring simply to Oberon's herb by which he can undo the effects of "Cupid's flower," the love-in-idleness of 2.1.166–168.)

OBERON. There lies your love.
TITANIA. How came these things to pass?
O, how mine eyes do loathe his visage now!
OBERON. Silence awhile. Robin, take off this head.
Titania, music call, and strike more dead
Than common sleep of all these five° the sense.
TITANIA. Music, ho! Music, such as charmeth° sleep!
[*Music.*]
PUCK [*removing the ass head*].
Now, when thou wak'st, with thine own fool's eyes peep.
OBERON. Sound, music! Come, my queen, take hands with me,
And rock the ground whereon these sleepers be. [*They dance.*]
Now thou and I are new in amity,
And will tomorrow midnight solemnly°
Dance in Duke Theseus' house triumphantly,
And bless it to all fair prosperity.
There shall the pairs of faithful lovers be
Wedded, with Theseus, all in jollity.
PUCK.
Fairy King, attend, and mark:
I do hear the morning lark.
OBERON.
Then, my queen, in silence sad,°
Trip we after night's shade.
We the globe can compass soon,
Swifter than the wandering moon.
TITANIA.
Come, my lord, and in our flight
Tell me how it came this night
That I sleeping here was found
With these mortals on the ground. *Exeunt.*
*Wind horn* [*within*].

*Enter Theseus and all his train;* [*Hippolyta, Egeus*].

THESEUS. Go, one of you, find out the forester,
For now our observation° is performed;
And since we have the vaward° of the day,
My love shall hear the music of my hounds.
Uncouple° in the western valley, let them go.
Dispatch, I say, and find the forester. [*Exit an Attendant.*]
We will, fair queen, up to the mountain's top
And mark the musical confusion
Of hounds and echo in conjunction.
HIPPOLYTA. I was with Hercules and Cadmus° once,
When in a wood of Crete they bayed° the bear

**78 these five** i.e., the four lovers and Bottom **79 charmeth** brings about, as though by a charm **84 solemnly** ceremoniously **91 sad** sober **100 observation** i.e., observance to a morn of May (1.1.167) **101 vaward** vanguard, i.e., earliest part **103 Uncouple** set free for the hunt **108 Cadmus** mythical founder of Thebes. (This story about him is unknown.) **109 bayed** brought to bay

With hounds of Sparta.° Never did I hear
Such gallant chiding;° for, besides the groves,
The skies, the fountains, every region near
Seemed all one mutual cry. I never heard
So musical a discord, such sweet thunder.

THESEUS. My hounds are bred out of the Spartan kind,°
So flewed,° so sanded;° and their heads are hung
With ears that sweep away the morning dew;
Crook-kneed, and dewlapped° like Thessalian bulls;
Slow in pursuit, but matched in mouth like bells,
Each under each.° A cry° more tunable°
Was never holloed to, nor cheered° with horn,
In Crete, in Sparta, nor in Thessaly.
Judge when you hear. [*He sees the sleepers.*] But, soft!
What nymphs are these?

EGEUS. My lord, this is my daughter here asleep,
And this Lysander; this Demetrius is,
This Helena, old Nedar's Helena.
I wonder of° their being here together.

THESEUS. No doubt they rose up early to observe
The rite of May, and hearing our intent,
Came here in grace of our solemnity.°
But speak, Egeus. Is not this the day
That Hermia should give answer of her choice?

EGEUS. It is, my lord.

THESEUS. Go, bid the huntsmen wake them with their horns.

[*Exit an Attendant.*]

*Shout within. Wind horns. They all start up.*

Good morrow, friends. Saint Valentine° is past.
Begin these woodbirds but to couple now?

LYSANDER. Pardon, my lord. [*They kneel.*]

THESEUS. I pray you all, stand up.
I know you two are rival enemies;
How comes this gentle concord in the world,
That hatred is so far from jealousy°
To sleep by hate and fear no enmity?

LYSANDER. My lord, I shall reply amazedly,
Half sleep, half waking; but as yet, I swear,
I cannot truly say how I came here.
But, as I think—for truly would I speak,

**110 hounds of Sparta** (A breed famous in antiquity for their hunting skill.) **111 chiding** i.e., yelping **115 kind** strain, breed **116 So flewed** similarly having large hanging chaps or fleshy covering of the jaw. **sanded** of sandy color **118 dewlapped** having pendulous folds of skin under the neck **119–120 matched . . . each** i.e., harmoniously matched in their various cries like a set of bells, from treble down to bass **120 cry** pack of hounds. **tunable** well tuned, melodious **121 cheered** encouraged **127 wonder of** wonder at **130 in . . . solemnity** in honor of our wedding **135 Saint Valentine** (Birds were supposed to choose their mates on Saint Valentine's Day.) **140 jealousy** suspicion

And now I do bethink me, so it is—
I came with Hermia hither. Our intent
Was to be gone from Athens, where° we might,
Without° the peril of the Athenian law—

EGEUS. Enough, enough, my lord; you have enough.
I beg the law, the law, upon his head.
They would have stol'n away; they would, Demetrius,
Thereby to have defeated° you and me,
You of your wife and me of my consent,
Of my consent that she should be your wife.

DEMETRIUS. My lord, fair Helen told me of their stealth,
Of this their purpose hither° to this wood,
And I in fury hither followed them,
Fair Helena in fancy following me.
But, my good lord, I wot not by what power—
But by some power it is—my love to Hermia,
Melted as the snow, seems to me now
As the remembrance of an idle gaud°
Which in my childhood I did dote upon;
And all the faith, the virtue of my heart,
The object and the pleasure of mine eye,
Is only Helena. To her, my lord,
Was I betrothed ere I saw Hermia,
But like a sickness did I loathe this food;
But, as in health, come to my natural taste,
Now I do wish it, love it, long for it,
And will for evermore be true to it.

THESEUS. Fair lovers, you are fortunately met.
Of this discourse we more will hear anon.
Egeus, I will overbear your will;
For in the temple, by and by, with us
These couples shall eternally be knit.
And, for° the morning now is something° worn,
Our purposed hunting shall be set aside.
Away with us to Athens. Three and three,
We'll hold a feast in great solemnity.
Come, Hippolyta.

[*Exeunt Theseus, Hippolyta, Egeus, and train.*]

DEMETRIUS. These things seem small and undistinguishable,
Like far-off mountains turnèd into clouds.

HERMIA. Methinks I see these things with parted° eye,
When everything seems double.

HELENA. So methinks;
And I have found Demetrius like a jewel,
Mine own, and not mine own.°

**148 where** wherever; or, to where **149 Without** outside of, beyond **153 defeated** defrauded **157 hither** in coming hither **163 idle gaud** worthless trinket **178 for** since. **something** somewhat **185 parted** improperly focused **187–188 like . . . mine own** i.e., like a jewel that one finds by chance and therefore possesses but cannot certainly consider one's own property

DEMETRIUS. Are you sure
That we are awake? It seems to me
That yet we sleep, we dream. Do not you think
The Duke was here, and bid us follow him?
HERMIA. Yea, and my father.
HELENA. And Hippolyta.
LYSANDER. And he did bid us follow to the temple.
DEMETRIUS. Why, then, we are awake. Let's follow him,
And by the way let us recount our dreams. [*Exeunt.*]

BOTTOM [*awaking*]. When my cue comes, call me, and I will answer. My next is, "Most fair Pyramus." Heigh—ho! Peter Quince! Flute, the bellows mender! Snout, the tinker! Starveling! God's° my life, stolen hence and left me asleep! I have had a most rare vision. I have had a dream, past the wit of man to say what dream it was. Man is but an ass if he go about° to expound this dream. Methought I was—there is no man can tell what. Methought I was—and methought I had—but man is but a patched° fool if he will offer° to say what methought I had. The eye of man hath not heard, the ear of man hath not seen, man's hand is not able to taste, his tongue to conceive, nor his heart to report,° what my dream was. I will get Peter Quince to write a ballad of this dream. It shall be called "Bottom's Dream," because it hath no bottom; and I will sing it in the latter end of a play, before the Duke. Peradventure, to make it the more gracious, I shall sing it at her° death. [*Exit.*]

## [4.2] *Enter Quince, Flute,* [*Snout, and Starveling*].

QUINCE. Have you sent to Bottom's house? Is he come home yet?

STARVELING. He cannot be heard of. Out of doubt he is transported.°

FLUTE. If he come not, then the play is marred. It goes not forward, doth it?

QUINCE. It is not possible. You have not a man in all Athens able to discharge° Pyramus but he.

FLUTE. No, he hath simply the best wit° of any handicraft man in Athens.

QUINCE. Yea, and the best person° too, and he is a very paramour for a sweet voice.

FLUTE. You must say "paragon." A paramour is, God bless us, a thing of naught.°

*Enter Snug the joiner.*

SNUG. Masters, the Duke is coming from the temple and there is two or three lords and ladies more married. If our sport had gone forward, we had all been made men.°

**198 God's** may God save **201 go about** attempt **203 patched** wearing motley, i.e., a dress of various colors **204 offer** venture **204–206 The eye . . . report** (Bottom garbles the terms of 1 Corinthians 2.9) **210 her** Thisbe's (?)
**4.2 Location: Athens. 2 transported** carried off by fairies; or, possibly, transformed **5–6 discharge** perform **7 wit** intellect **8 person** appearance **10–11 a . . . naught** a shameful thing **14 we . . . men** i.e., we would have had our fortunes made

FLUTE. O sweet bully Bottom! Thus hath he lost sixpence a day during his life; he could not have scaped sixpence a day. An the Duke had not given him sixpence a day° for playing Pyramus, I'll be hanged. He would have deserved it. Sixpence a day in Pyramus, or nothing.

*Enter Bottom.*

BOTTOM. Where are these lads? Where are these hearts?°

QUINCE. Bottom! O most courageous day! O most happy hour!

BOTTOM. Masters, I am to discourse wonders.° But ask me not what; for if I tell you, I am no true Athenian. I will tell you everything, right as it fell out.

QUINCE. Let us hear, sweet Bottom.

BOTTOM. Not a word of° me. All that I will tell you is—that the Duke hath dined. Get your apparel together, good strings° to your beards, new ribbons to your pumps;° meet presently° at the palace; every man look o'er his part; for the short and the long is, our play is preferred.° In any case, let Thisbe have clean linen; and let not him that plays the lion pare his nails, for they shall hang out for the lion's claws. And, most dear actors, eat no onions nor garlic, for we are to utter sweet breath; and I do not doubt but to hear them say it is a sweet comedy. No more words. Away! Go, away! [*Exeunt.*]

**[5.1]** *Enter Theseus, Hippolyta, and Philostrate,* [*lords, and attendants*].

HIPPOLYTA. 'Tis strange, my Theseus, that° these lovers speak of.

THESEUS. More strange than true. I never may° believe
These antique° fables nor these fairy toys.°
Lovers and madmen have such seething brains,
Such shaping fantasies,° that apprehend°
More than cool reason ever comprehends.°
The lunatic, the lover, and the poet
Are of imagination all compact.°
One sees more devils than vast hell can hold;
That is the madman. The lover, all as frantic,
Sees Helen's° beauty in a brow of Egypt.°
The poet's eye, in a fine frenzy rolling,
Doth glance from heaven to earth, from earth to heaven;
And as imagination bodies forth
The forms of things unknown, the poet's pen

**17 sixpence a day** i.e., as a royal pension **19 hearts** good fellows **21 am . . . wonders** have wonders to relate **25 of** out of **26 strings** (to attach the beards) **27 pumps** light shoes or slippers. **presently** immediately **29 preferred** selected for consideration

**5.1 Location: Athens. The palace of Theseus. 1 that** that which **2 may** can **3 antique** old-fashioned (punning too on *antic,* strange, grotesque). **fairy toys** trifling stories about fairies **5 fantasies** imaginations. **apprehend** conceive, imagine **6 comprehends** understands **8 compact** formed, composed **11 Helen's** i.e., of Helen of Troy, pattern of beauty. **brow of Egypt** i.e., face of a gypsy

Turns them to shapes and gives to airy nothing
A local habitation and a name.
Such tricks hath strong imagination
That, if it would but apprehend some joy,
It comprehends some bringer° of that joy;
Or in the night, imagining some fear,°
How easy is a bush supposed a bear!

HIPPOLYTA. But all the story of the night told over,
And all their minds transfigured so together,
More witnesseth than fancy's images°
And grows to something of great constancy;°
But, howsoever,° strange and admirable.°

*Enter lovers: Lysander, Demetrius, Hermia, and Helena.*

THESEUS. Here come the lovers, full of joy and mirth.
Joy, gentle friends! Joy and fresh days of love
Accompany your hearts!

LYSANDER. More than to us
Wait in your royal walks, your board, your bed!

THESEUS. Come now, what masques,° what dances shall we have
To wear away this long age of three hours
Between our after-supper and bedtime?
Where is our usual manager of mirth?
What revels are in hand? Is there no play
To ease the anguish of a torturing hour?
Call Philostrate.

PHILOSTRATE. Here, mighty Theseus.

THESEUS. Say what abridgment° have you for this evening?
What masque? What music? How shall we beguile
The lazy time, if not with some delight?

PHILOSTRATE [*giving him a paper*].
There is a brief° how many sports are ripe.
Make choice of which Your Highness will see first.

THESEUS [*reads*]. "The battle with the Centaurs,° to be sung
By an Athenian eunuch to the harp"?
We'll none of that. That have I told my love,
In glory of my kinsman° Hercules.
[*reads.*] "The riot of the tipsy Bacchanals,
Tearing the Thracian singer in their rage"?°

**20 bringer** i.e., source **21 fear** object of fear **25 More . . . images** testifies to something more substantial than mere imaginings **26 constancy** certainty **27 howsoever** in any case. **admirable** a source of wonder **32 masques** courtly entertainments **39 abridgment** pastime (to abridge or shorten the evening) **42 brief** short written statement, summary **44 battle . . . Centaurs** (Probably refers to the battle of the Centaurs and the Lapithae, when the Centaurs attempted to carry off Hippodamia, bride of Theseus' friend Pirothous.) **47 kinsman** (Plutarch's "Life of Theseus" states that Hercules and Theseus were near kinsmen. Theseus is referring to a version of the battle of the Centaurs in which Hercules was said to be present.) **48–49 The riot . . . rage** (This was the story of the death of Orpheus, as told in *Metamorphoses* 9.)

That is an old device;° and it was played
When I from Thebes came last a conqueror.
[*Reads.*] "The thrice three Muses mourning for the death
Of Learning, late deceased in beggary"?°
That is some satire, keen and critical,
Not sorting with° a nuptial ceremony.
[*Reads.*] "A tedious brief scene of young Pyramus
And his love Thisbe; very tragical mirth"?
Merry and tragical? Tedious and brief?
That is hot ice and wondrous strange° snow.
How shall we find the concord of this discord?

PHILOSTRATE. A play there is, my lord, some ten words long,
Which is as brief as I have known a play;
But by ten words, my lord, it is too long,
Which makes it tedious. For in all the play
There is not one word apt, one player fitted.
And tragical, my noble lord, it is,
For Pyramus therein doth kill himself.
Which, when I saw rehearsed, I must confess,
Made mine eyes water; but more merry tears
The passion of loud laughter never shed.

THESEUS. What are they that do play it?

PHILOSTRATE. Hard-handed men that work in Athens here,
Which never labored in their minds till now,
And now have toiled° their unbreathed° memories
With this same play, against° your nuptial.

THESEUS. And we will hear it.

PHILOSTRATE. No, my noble lord,
It is not for you. I have heard it over,
And it is nothing, nothing in the world;
Unless you can find sport in their intents,
Extremely stretched° and conned° with cruel pain
To do you service.

THESEUS. I will hear that play;
For never anything can be amiss
When simpleness° and duty tender it.
Go bring them in; and take your places, ladies.
[*Philostrate goes to summon the players.*]

HIPPOLYTA. I love not to see wretchedness o'ercharged,°
And duty in his service° perishing.

**50 device** show, performance **52–53 The thrice . . . beggary** (Possibly an allusion to Spenser's *Tears of the Muses,* 1591, though "satires" deploring the neglect of learning and the creative arts were commonplace.) **55 sorting with** befitting **59 strange** (Sometimes emended to an adjective that would contrast with *snow,* just as *hot* contrasts with *ice.*) **74 toiled** taxed. **unbreathed** unexercised **75 against** in preparation for **80 stretched** strained. **conned** memorized **83 simpleness** simplicity **85 wretchedness o'ercharged** incompetence overburdened **86 his service** its attempt to serve

THESEUS. Why, gentle sweet, you shall see no such thing.
HIPPOLYTA. He says they can do nothing in this kind.°
THESEUS. The kinder we, to give them thanks for nothing.
Our sport shall be to take what they mistake;
And what poor duty cannot do, noble respect°
Takes it in might, not merit.°
Where I have come, great clerks° have purposèd
To greet me with premeditated welcomes;
Where I have seen them shiver and look pale,
Make periods in the midst of sentences,
Throttle their practiced accent° in their fears,
And in conclusion dumbly have broke off,
Not paying me a welcome. Trust me, sweet,
Out of this silence yet I picked a welcome;
And in the modesty of fearful duty
I read as much as from the rattling tongue
Of saucy and audacious eloquence.
Love, therefore, and tongue-tied simplicity
In least° speak most, to my capacity.°
[*Philostrate returns.*]

PHILOSTRATE. So please Your Grace, the Prologue° is addressed.°
THESEUS. Let him approach. [*A flourish of trumpets.*]

*Enter the Prologue* [*Quince*].

PROLOGUE.
If we offend, it is with our good will.
That you should think, we come not to offend,
But with good will. To show our simple skill,
That is the true beginning of our end.
Consider then, we come but in despite.
We do not come, as minding° to content you,
Our true intent is. All for your delight.
We are not here. That you should here repent you,
The actors are at hand, and, by their show,
You shall know all that you are like to know.

THESEUS. This fellow doth not stand upon points.°
LYSANDER. He hath rid° his prologue like a rough° colt; he knows not the stop.° A good moral, my lord: it is not enough to speak, but to speak true.

**88 kind** kind of thing **91 respect** evaluation, consideration **92 Takes . . . merit** values it for the effort made rather than for the excellence achieved **93 clerks** learned men **97 practiced accent** i.e., rehearsed speech; or, usual way of speaking **105 least** i.e., saying least. **to my capacity** in my judgment and understanding **106 Prologue** speaker of the prologue. **addressed** ready **113 minding** intending **118 stand upon points** (1) heed niceties or small points (2) pay attention to punctuation in his reading. (The humor of Quince's speech is in the blunders of its punctuation.) **119 rid** ridden. **rough** unbroken **120 stop** (1) the stopping of a colt by reining it in (2) punctuation mark

HIPPOLYTA. Indeed he hath played on his prologue like a child on a re-° corder; a sound, but not in government.°

THESEUS. His speech was like a tangled chain: nothing° impaired, but all disordered. Who is next?

*Enter Pyramus* [*Bottom*] *and Thisbe* [*Flute*], *and Wall* [*Snout*], *and Moonshine* [*Starveling*], *and Lion* [*Snug*].

PROLOGUE.

Gentles, perchance you wonder at this show,
  But wonder on, till truth makes all things plain.
This man is Pyramus, if you would know;
  This beauteous lady Thisbe is certain.
This man with lime and roughcast doth present
  Wall, that vile Wall which did these lovers sunder;
And through Wall's chink, poor souls, they are content
  To whisper. At the which let no man wonder.
This man, with lantern, dog, and bush of thorn,
  Presenteth Moonshine; for, if you will know,
By moonshine did these lovers think no scorn°
  To meet at Ninus' tomb, there, there to woo.
This grisly beast, which Lion hight° by name,
The trusty Thisbe coming first by night
Did scare away, or rather did affright;
And as she fled, her mantle she did fall,°
  Which Lion vile with bloody mouth did stain.
Anon comes Pyramus, sweet youth and tall,°
  And finds his trusty Thisbe's mantle slain;
Whereat, with blade, with bloody blameful blade,
  He bravely broached° his boiling bloody breast.
And Thisbe, tarrying in mulberry shade,
  His dagger drew, and died. For all the rest,
Let Lion, Moonshine, Wall, and lovers twain
At large° discourse while here they do remain.

*Exeunt Lion, Thisbe, and Moonshine.*

THESEUS. I wonder if the lion be to speak.

DEMETRIUS. No wonder, my lord. One lion may, when many asses do.

WALL.

In this same interlude° it doth befall
That I, one Snout by name, present a wall;
And such a wall as I would have you think
That had in it a crannied hole or chink,
Through which the lovers, Pyramus and Thisbe,
Did whisper often, very secretly.
This loam, this roughcast, and this stone doth show

**122–123 recorder** a wind instrument like a flute or flageolet **123 government** control **124 nothing** not at all **136 think no scorn** think it no disgraceful matter **138 hight** is called **141 fall** let fall **143 tall** courageous **146 broached** stabbed **150 At large** in full, at length **153 interlude** play

That I am that same wall; the truth is so.
And this the cranny is, right and sinister,°
Through which the fearful lovers are to whisper.

THESEUS. Would you desire lime and hair to speak better?

DEMETRIUS. It is the wittiest partition° that ever I heard discourse, my lord.

[*Pyramus comes forward.*]

THESEUS. Pyramus draws near the wall. Silence!

PYRAMUS.
O grim-looked° night! O night with hue so black!
O night, which ever art when day is not!
O night, O night! Alack, alack, alack,
I fear my Thisbe's promise is forgot.
And thou, O wall, O sweet, O lovely wall,
That stand'st between her father's ground and mine,
Thou wall, O wall, O sweet and lovely wall,
Show me thy chink to blink through with mine eyne!

[*Wall makes a chink with his fingers.*]

Thanks, courteous wall. Jove shield thee well for this.
But what see I? No Thisbe do I see.
O wicked wall, through whom I see no bliss!
Cursed by they stones for thus deceiving me!

THESEUS. The wall, methinks, being sensible,° should curse again.

PYRAMUS. No, in truth, sir, he should not. "Deceiving me" is Thisbe's cue: she is to enter now, and I am to spy her through the wall. You shall see, it will fall pat° as I told you. Yonder she comes.

*Enter Thisbe.*

THISBE.
O wall, full often hast thou heard my moans,
For parting my fair Pyramus and me.
My cherry lips have often kissed thy stones,
Thy stones with lime and hair knit up in thee.

PYRAMUS.
I see a voice. Now will I to the chink,
To spy an° I can hear my Thisbe's face.
Thisbe!

THISBE. My love! Thou art my love, I think.

PYRAMUS.
Think what thou wilt, I am thy lover's grace,°
And like Limander° am I trusty still.

THISBE.
And I like Helen,° till the Fates me kill.

PYRAMUS.
Not Shafalus to Procrus° was so true.

**161 right and sinister** i.e., the right side of it and the left; or, running from right to left, horizontally **164 partition** (1) wall (2) section of a learned treatise or oration **166 grim-looked** grim-looking **178 sensible** capable of feeling **181 pat** exactly **187 an** if **190 lover's grace** i.e., gracious lover **191, 192 Limander, Helen** (Blunders for *Leander* and *Hero.*) **193 Shafalus, Procrus** (Blunders for *Cephalus* and *Procris,* also famous lovers.)

THISBE.
As Shafalus to Procrus, I to you.
PYRAMUS.
O, kiss me through the hole of this vile wall!
THISBE.
I kiss the wall's hole, not your lips at all.
PYRAMUS.
Wilt thou at Ninny's tomb meet me straightway?
THISBE.
'Tide° life, 'tide death, I come without delay.
[*Exeunt Pyramus and Thisbe.*]
WALL.
Thus have I, Wall, my part dischargèd so;
And, being done, thus Wall away doth go. [*Exit.*]

THESEUS. Now is the mural down between the two neighbors.

DEMETRIUS. No remedy, my lord, when walls are so willful° to hear without warning.°

HIPPOLYTA. This is the silliest stuff that ever I heard.

THESEUS. The best in this kind° are but shadows;° and the worst are no worse, if imagination amend them.

HIPPOLYTA. It must be your imagination then, and not theirs.

THESEUS. If we imagine no worse of them than they of themselves, they may pass for excellent men. Here come two noble beasts in, a man and a lion.

*Enter Lion and Moonshine.*

LION.
You, ladies, you whose gentle hearts do fear
The smallest monstrous mouse that creeps on floor,
May now perchance both quake and tremble here,
When lion rough in wildest rage doth roar.
Then know that I, as Snug the joiner, am
A lion fell,° nor else no lion's dam;
For, if I should as lion come in strife
Into this place, 'twere pity on my life.

THESEUS. A very gentle beast, and of a good conscience.

DEMETRIUS. The very best at a beast, my lord, that e'er I saw.

LYSANDER. This lion is a very fox for his valor.°

THESEUS. True; and a goose for his discretion.°

DEMETRIUS. Not so, my lord; for his valor cannot carry his discretion; and the fox carries the goose.

**198 'Tide** betide, come **202 willful** willing **202–203 without warning** i.e., without warning the parents. (Demetrius makes a joke on the proverb "Walls have ears.") **205 in this kind** of this sort. **shadows** likenesses, representations **216 lion fell** fierce lion (with a play on the idea of "lion skin") **221 is . . . valor** i.e., his valor consists of craftiness and discretion **222 goose . . . discretion** i.e., as discreet as a goose, that is, more foolish than discreet

THESEUS. His discretion, I am sure, cannot carry his valor; for the goose carries not the fox. It is well. Leave it to his discretion, and let us listen to the moon.

MOON.
This lanthorn° doth the hornèd moon present—

DEMETRIUS. He should have worn the horns on his head.°

THESEUS. He is no crescent, and his horns are invisible within the circumference.

MOON.
This lanthorn doth the hornèd moon present;
Myself the man i' the moon do seem to be.

THESEUS. This is the greatest error of all the rest. The man should be put into the lanthorn. How is it else the man i' the moon?

DEMETRIUS. He dares not come there for the° candle, for you see, it is already in snuff.°

HIPPOLYTA. I am aweary of this moon. Would he would change!

THESEUS. It appears, by his small light of discretion, that he is in the wane; but yet, in courtesy, in all reason, we must stay the time.

LYSANDER. Proceed, Moon.

MOON. All that I have to say is to tell you that the lanthorn is the moon, I the man i' the moon, this thornbush my thornbush, and this dog my dog.

DEMETRIUS. Why, all these should be in the lanthorn, for all these are in the moon. But silence! Here comes Thisbe.

*Enter Thisbe.*

THISBE.
This is old Ninny's tomb. Where is my love?

LION [*roaring*]. O!

DEMETRIUS. Well roared, Lion.

[*Thisbe runs off, dropping her mantle.*]

THESEUS. Well run, Thisbe.

HIPPOLYTA. Well shone, Moon. Truly, the moon shines with a good grace.

[*The Lion worries Thisbe's mantle.*]

THESEUS. Well moused,° Lion.

*Enter Pyramus.* [*Exit Lion.*]

DEMETRIUS. And then came Pyramus.

LYSANDER. And so the lion vanished.

PYRAMUS.
Sweet Moon, I thank thee for thy sunny beams;
I thank thee, Moon, for shining now so bright;
For, by thy gracious, golden, glittering gleams,
I trust to take of truest Thisbe sight.
But stay, O spite!

**228 lanthorn** (This original spelling, *lanthorn,* may suggest a play on the *horn* of which lanterns were made, and also on a cuckold's horns; but the spelling *lanthorn* is not used consistently for comic effect in this play or elsewhere. At 5.1.134, for example, the word is *lantern* in the original.) **229 on his head** (as a sign of cuckoldry) **236 for the** because of the **237 in snuff** (1) offended (2) in need of snuffing or trimming **252 moused** shaken, torn, bitten

But mark, poor knight,
What dreadful dole° is here?
Eyes, do you see?
How can it be?
O dainty duck! O dear!
Thy mantle good,
What, stained with blood!
Approach, ye Furies° fell!°
O Fates,° come, come,
Cut thread and thrum;°
Quail,° crush, conclude, and quell!°

THESEUS. This passion, and the death of a dear friend, would go near to make a man look sad.°

HIPPOLYTA. Beshrew my heart, but I pity the man.

PYRAMUS.
O, wherefore, Nature, didst thou lions frame?
Since lion vile hath here deflowered my dear,
Which is—no, no, which was—the fairest dame
That lived, that loved, that liked, that looked with cheer.°
Come, tears, confound,
Out, sword, and wound
The pap° of Pyramus;
Ay, that left pap,
Where heart doth hop. [*He stabs himself.*]
Thus die I, thus, thus, thus.
Now am I dead,
Now am I fled;
My soul is in the sky.
Tongue, lose thy light;
Moon, take thy flight. [*Exit Moonshine.*]
Now die, die, die, die, die. [*Pyramus dies.*]

DEMETRIUS. No die, but an ace,° for him; for he is but one.°

LYSANDER. Less than an ace, man; for he is dead, he is nothing.

THESEUS. With the help of a surgeon he might yet recover, and yet prove an ass.°

HIPPOLYTA. How chance Moonshine is gone before Thisbe comes back and finds her lover?

THESEUS. She will find him by starlight.

[*Enter Thisbe.*]

Here she comes, and her passion ends the play.

**261 dole** grievous event **267 Furies** avenging goddesses of Greek myth. **fell** fierce **268 Fates** the three goddesses (Clotho, Lachesis, Atropos) of Greek myth who drew and cut the thread of human life **269 thread and thrum** the warp in weaving and the loose end of the warp **270 Quail** overpower. **quell** kill, destroy **271–272 This . . . sad** i.e., if one had other reason to grieve, one might be sad, but not from this absurd portrayal of passion **277 cheer** countenance **280 pap** breast **290 ace** the side of the die featuring the single pip, or spot. (The pun is on *die* as a singular of *dice;* Bottom's performance is not worth a whole *die* but rather one single face of it, one small portion.) **one** (1) an individual person (2) unique **293 ass** (with a pun on *ace*)

HIPPOLYTA. Methinks she should not use a long one for such a Pyramus. I hope she will be brief.

DEMETRIUS. A mote° will turn the balance, which Pyramus, which° Thisbe, is the better: he for a man, God warrant us; she for a woman, God bless us.

LYSANDER. She hath spied him already with those sweet eyes.

DEMETRIUS. And thus she means,° videlicet:°

THISBE.

Asleep, my love?
What, dead, my dove?
O Pyramus, arise!
Speak, speak. Quite dumb?
Dead, dead? A tomb
Must cover thy sweet eyes.
These lily lips,
This cherry nose,
These yellow cowslip cheeks,
Are gone, are gone!
Lovers, make moan.
His eyes were green as leeks.
O Sisters Three,°
Come, come to me,
With hands as pale as milk;
Lay them in gore,
Since you have shore°
With shears his thread of silk.
Tongue, not a word.
Come, trusty sword,
Come, blade, my breast imbrue!° [*Stabs herself.*]
And farewell, friends.
Thus Thisbe ends.
Adieu, adieu, adieu. [*She dies.*]

THESEUS. Moonshine and Lion are left to bury the dead.

DEMETRIUS. Ay, and Wall too.

BOTTOM [*starting up, as Flute does also*]. No, I assure you, the wall is down that parted their fathers. Will it please you to see the epilogue, or to hear a Bergomask dance° between two of our company? [*The other players enter.*]

THESEUS. No epilogue, I pray you; for your play needs no excuse. Never excuse; for when the players are all dead, there need none to be blamed. Marry, if he that writ it had played Pyramus and hanged himself in Thisbe's garter, it would have been a fine tragedy; and so it is, truly, and very notably discharged. But, come, your Bergomask. Let your epilogue alone. [*A dance.*]
The iron tongue° of midnight hath told° twelve.

**300 mote** small particle. **which . . . which** whether . . . or **304 means** moans, laments. **videlicet** to wit **317 Sisters Three** the Fates **321 shore** shorn **325 imbrue** stain with blood **333 Bergomask dance** a rustic dance named from Bergamo, a province in the state of Venice **340 iron tongue** i.e., of a bell. **told** counted, struck ("tolled")

Lovers, to bed, 'tis almost fairy time.
I fear we shall outsleep the coming morn
As much as we this night have overwatched.°
This palpable-gross° play hath well beguiled
The heavy° gait of night. Sweet friends, to bed.
A fortnight hold we this solemnity,
In nightly revels and new jollity. *Exeunt.*

*Enter Puck* [*carrying a broom*].

PUCK.

Now the hungry lion roars,
And the wolf behowls the moon;
Whilst the heavy° plowman snores,
All with weary task fordone.°
Now the wasted brands° do glow,
Whilst the screech owl, screeching loud
Puts the wretch that lies in woe
In remembrance of a shroud.
Now it is the time of night
That the graves, all gaping wide,
Every one lets forth his sprite,°
In the church-way paths to glide.
And we fairies, that do run
By the triple Hecate's° team
From the presence of the sun,
Following darkness like a dream,
Now are frolic.° Not a mouse
Shall disturb this hallowed house.
I am sent with broom before,
To sweep the dust behind° the door.

*Enter* [*Oberon and Titania,*] *King and Queen of Fairies, with all their train.*

OBERON.

Through the house give glimmering light,
By the dead and drowsy fire;
Every elf and fairy sprite
Hop as light as bird from brier;
And this ditty, after me,
Sing, and dance it trippingly.

TITANIA.

First, rehearse your song by rote,
To each word a warbling note.

**343 overwatched** stayed up too late **344 palpable-gross** gross, obviously crude **345 heavy** drowsy, dull **350 heavy** tired **351 fordone** exhausted **352 wasted brands** burned-out logs **358 Every . . . sprite** every grave lets forth its ghost **361 triple Hecate's** (Hecate ruled in three capacities: as Luna or Cynthia in heaven, as Diana on earth, and as Proserpina in hell.) **364 frolic** merry **367 behind** from behind. (Robin Goodfellow was a household spirit who helped good housemaids and punished lazy ones.)

Hand in hand, with fairy grace,
Will we sing, and bless this place.

[*Song and dance.*]

OBERON.

Now, until the break of day,
Through this house each fairy stray.
To the best bride-bed will we,
Which by us shall blessèd be;
And the issue there create°
Ever shall be fortunate.
So shall all the couples three
Ever true in loving be;
And the blots of Nature's hand
Shall not in their issue stand;
Never mole, harelip, nor scar,
Nor mark prodigious,° such as are
Despisèd in nativity,
Shall upon their children be.
With this field dew consecrate°
Every fairy take his gait,°
And each several° chamber bless,
Through this palace, with sweet peace;
And the owner of it blest
Ever shall in safety rest.
Trip away; make no stay;
Meet me all by break of day.

*Exeunt* [*Oberon, Titania, and train*].

PUCK [*to the audience*].

If we shadows have offended,
Think but this, and all is mended,
That you have but slumbered here°
While these visions did appear.
And this weak and idle theme,
No more yielding but° a dream,
Gentles, do not reprehend.
If you pardon, we will mend.°
And, as I am an honest Puck,
If we have unearnèd luck
Now to scape the serpent's tongue,°
We will make amends ere long;
Else the Puck a liar call.
So, good night unto you all.
Give me your hands,° if we be friends,
And Robin shall restore amends.° [*Exit.*]

**382 create** created **389 prodigious** monstrous, unnatural **392 consecrate** consecrated **393 take his gait** go his way **394 several** separate **402 That . . . here** i.e., that it is a "midsummer night's dream" **405 No . . . but** yielding no more than **407 mend** improve **410 serpent's tongue** i.e., hissing **414 Give . . . hands** applaud **415 restore amends** give satisfaction in return

## TOPICS FOR CRITICAL THINKING AND WRITING

### *Act 1*

1. On the basis of the first scene, how would you characterize Theseus? Egeus? Hermia? Do you agree with some critics that Egeus is presented comically? (Support your view.)
2. What connections can you make between 1.2 and the first scene?

### *Act 2*

1. Why do you suppose that in 2.1 Shakespeare included material about Theseus's past (lines 76–80)?
2. When the play is staged, audiences invariably laugh loudly at 2.2.109, when Lysander awakens and sees Helena. What's so funny about this?

### *Act 3*

1. What assumptions does Bottom seem to make about the nature of drama? How do they compare with your own?
2. Puck himself has said that he is mischievous, but how mischievous is he? Why did he anoint the eyes of the wrong lover?

### *Act 4*

1. Bottom is the only mortal who sees the fairies. What can we make of this? Or should we not try to make anything of it?

### *Act 5*

1. What do you make of the debate between Theseus and Hippolyta (lines 1–27)? Which of the two seems to you to come closer to the truth? Explain.
2. Do you think it is cruel to laugh at the unintentional antics of the rustic performers? Why, or why not?
3. Puck is sometimes played by a woman. What advantages or disadvantages do you see to giving the part to a woman?

### *General Questions*

1. Some critics speak of the play as a delightful fantasy that is engaging because it has so little connection with real life, but others find in it intimations of dark and dangerous elements in human beings. Where do you stand, and why?
2. Today Shakespeare's plays are sometimes done in modern dress or in costumes that reflect a particular time and place, such as the Wild West of the mid-nineteenth century or the South before the Civil War. How would you costume the play? What advantages might there be in your choice?

## ✔ Checklist: Writing about Comedy

The checklist on page 1220, with questions concerning plot and character, is especially relevant, but here are some related questions. See also the first comment, on a play as a "dramatic poem," in the checklist on tragedy, page 1404.

- Do the comic complications arise chiefly out of the personalities of the characters (for instance, pretentiousness or amorousness) or out of the situations (for instance, mistaken identity)?
- What are the chief goals of the figures? Do we sympathize with these goals, or do we laugh at persons who pursue them? If we laugh, *why* do we laugh?
- What are the personalities of those who oppose the central characters? Do we laugh at them, or do we sympathize with them?
- What is funny about the play? Is the comedy high (including verbal comedy) or chiefly situational and physical?
- Is the play predominantly genial, or is there a strong satiric tone?
- Does the comedy have any potentially tragic elements in it? Might the plot be slightly rewritten so that it would become a tragedy?
- What, if anything, do the characters learn by the end of the play?

# CHAPTER 32

# *Review: Writing about Drama*

The following questions may help you to formulate ideas for an essay on a play.

## PLOT AND CONFLICT

1. Does the exposition introduce elements that will be ironically fulfilled? During the exposition do you perceive things differently from the way the characters perceive them?
2. Are certain happenings or situations recurrent? If so, what significance do you attach to them?
3. If there is more than one plot, do the plots seem to you to be related? Is one plot clearly the main plot and another plot a subplot, a minor variation on the theme?
4. Do any scenes strike you as irrelevant?
5. Are certain scenes so strongly foreshadowed that you anticipated them? If so, did the happenings in these scenes merely fulfill your expectations, or did they also in some way surprise you?
6. What kinds of conflict are there? One character against another, one group against another, one part of a personality against another part in the same person?
7. How is the conflict resolved? By an unambiguous triumph of one side or by a triumph that is also in some degree a loss for the triumphant side? Do you find the resolution satisfying, or unsettling, or what? Why?

# CHARACTER

1. A dramatic character is not likely to be thoroughly realistic, a copy of someone we might know. Still, we can ask if the character is consistent and coherent. We can also ask if the character is complex or is, on the other hand, a simple representative of some human type.
2. How is the character defined? Consider what the character says and does and what others say about him or her and do to him or her. Also consider other characters who more or less resemble the character in question, because the similarities—and the differences—may be significant.
3. How trustworthy are the characters when they characterize themselves? When they characterize others?
4. Do characters change as the play goes on, or do we simply know them better at the end?
5. What do you make of the minor characters? Are they merely necessary to the plot, or are they foils to other characters? Or do they serve some other functions?
6. If a character is tragic, does the tragedy seem to you to proceed from a moral flaw, from an intellectual error, from the malice of others, from sheer chance, or from some combination of these?
7. What are the character's goals? To what degree do you sympathize with them? If a character is comic, do you laugh *with* or *at* the character?
8. Do you think the characters are adequately motivated?
9. Is a given character so meditative that you feel he or she is engaged less in a dialogue with others than in a dialogue with the self? If so, do you feel that this character is in large degree a spokesperson for the author, commenting not only on the world of the play but also on the outside world?

# TRAGEDY

1. What causes the tragedy? A flaw in the central character? A mistake (*not* the same thing as a flaw) made by this character? An outside force, such as another character, or fate?
2. Is the tragic character defined partly by other characters, for instance, by characters who help us to sense what the character *might* have done, or who in some other way reveal the strengths or weaknesses of the protagonist?
3. Does a viewer know more than the tragic figure knows? More than most or all of the characters know?
4. Does the tragic character achieve any sort of wisdom at the end of the play?
5. To what degree do you sympathize with the tragic character?
6. Is the play depressing? If not, why not?

## COMEDY

1. Do the comic complications arise chiefly out of the personalities of the characters (for instance, pretentiousness or amorousness), or out of the situations (for instance, mistaken identity)?
2. What are the chief goals of the figures? Do we sympathize with these goals, or do we laugh at persons who pursue them? If we laugh, *why* do we laugh?
3. What are the personalities of those who oppose the central characters? Do we laugh at them, or do we sympathize with them?
4. What is funny about the play? Is the comedy high (including verbal comedy) or chiefly situational and physical?
5. Is the play predominantly genial, or is there a strong satiric tone?
6. Does the comedy have any potentially tragic elements in it? Might the plot be slightly rewritten so that it would become a tragedy?
7. What, if anything, do the characters learn by the end of the play?

## NONVERBAL LANGUAGE

1. If the playwright does not provide full stage directions, try to imagine for at least one scene what gestures and tones might accompany each speech. (The first scene is usually a good one to try your hand at.)
2. What do you make of the setting? Does it help to reveal character? Do changes of scene strike you as symbolic? If so, symbolic of what?
3. Do certain costumes (dark suits, flowery shawls, stiff collars, etc.) or certain properties (books, pictures, toys, candlesticks, etc.) strike you as symbolic? If so, symbolic of what?

## THE PLAY IN PERFORMANCE

Often we can gain a special pleasure from, or insight into, a dramatic work when we actually see it produced onstage or made into a film. This gives us an opportunity to think about the choices that the director has made, and, even more, it may prompt us to imagine and ponder how we would direct the play for the theater or make a film version of it ourselves.

1. If you have seen the play in the theater or in a film version, what has been added? What has been omitted? Why?
2. In the case of a film, has the film medium been used to advantage—for example, in focusing attention through close-ups or reaction shots (shots showing not the speaker but a person reacting to the speaker)?
3. Do certain plays seem to be especially suited—maybe *only* suited—to the stage? Would they not work effectively as films? Is the reverse true: Are some plays best presented, and best understood, when they are done as films?

4. Critics have sometimes said about this or that play that it cannot really be staged successfully or presented well on film—that the best way to appreciate and understand it is as something to be *read,* like a poem or novel. Are there plays you have studied for which this observation appears to hold true? Which features of the work—its characters, settings, dialogue, central themes—might make it difficult to transfer the play from the page to the stage or to the movie screen?
5. Imagine that you are directing the play. What would be the important decisions you would have to make about character, setting, pacing of the action? Would you be inclined to omit certain scenes? To add new scenes that are not in the work itself? What kinds of advice would you give to the performers about their roles?

## USING SOURCES: A SAMPLE STUDENT ESSAY

In Appendix A we discuss manuscript form (pp. 1943–48) and in Appendix B the use of sources (pp. 1950–55) and documentation (pp. 1955–66). Here we give a student's documented paper on Arthur Miller's *Death of a Salesman.* (The play appears in this book on p. 1591.) The student of course had taken notes on index cards, both from the play and from secondary sources, and had arranged and rearranged the notes as her topic and thesis became clearer to her. We preface the final version of her essay with the rough outline that she prepared before she wrote her first draft.

Linda
  realistic
  encourages Willy
  foolish? loving? Both? Not so foolish; Knows how to calm him down
    prevented him from succeeding?
    doesn't understand W's needs? or nothing else to do?
    quote some critics knocking Linda

other women
5 the Woman
4 the two women in restaurant (Forsythe first, then Letta)
3 Jenny
2 W's mother (compare with father?)
    check to see exactly what the play says about her
1 Howard's wife (and daughter?) (discuss this first)
6 discuss Linda last

titles?
  Linda Loman
  Women in Miller's Salesman
  Gender in . . . Male and Female in Death . . .
  Men and Women: Arthur M's View
  Willy Loman's Women

Here is the final version of the essay.

Ruth Katz

The Women in Death of a Salesman

Death of a Salesman[1] is of course about a salesman, but it is also about the American dream of success. Somewhere in between the narrowest topic, the death of a salesman, and the largest topic, the examination of American values, is Miller's picture of the American family. This paper will chiefly study one member of the family, Willy's wife, Linda Loman, but before examining Miller's depiction of her, it will look at Miller's depiction of other women in the play in order to make clear Linda's distinctive traits. We will see that although her role in society is extremely limited, she is an admirable figure, fulfilling the roles of wife and mother with remarkable intelligence.

Linda is the only woman who is on stage much of the time, but there are several other women in the play: "the Woman" (the unnamed woman in Willy's hotel room), Miss Forsythe and her friend Letta (the two women who join the brothers in the restaurant), Jenny (Charley's secretary), the various women that the brothers talk about, and the voices of Howard's daughter and wife. We also hear a little about Willy's mother.

[1]Death of a Salesman appears in Sylvan Barnet, et al., Literature: Thinking, Reading, and Writing Critically, 2nd ed. (New York: Longman, 1997), 1591-1659. References to the play are to this edition.

We will look first at the least important (but not utterly unimportant) of these, the voices of Howard's daughter and wife on the wire recorder. Of Howard's seven-year-old daughter we know only that she can whistle "Roll Out the Barrel" and that according to Howard she "is crazy about me." The other woman in Howard's life is equally under his thumb. Here is the dialogue that tells us about her--and her relation to her husband.

> HOWARD'S VOICE. "Go on, say something." (_Pause._) "Well, you gonna talk?"
>
> HIS WIFE. "I can't think of anything."
>
> HOWARD'S VOICE. "Well, talk--it's turning."
>
> HIS WIFE (_shyly, beaten_). "Hello." (_Silence._) "Oh, Howard, I can't talk into this . . ."
>
> HOWARD (_snapping the machine off_). That was my wife. (1627)

There is, in fact, a third woman in Howard's life, the maid. Howard says that if he can't be at home when the Jack Benny program comes on, he uses the wire recorder. He tells "the maid to turn the radio on when Jack Benny comes on, and this automatically goes on with the radio. . . ." (1627). In short, the women in Howard's world exist to serve (and to worship) him.

Another woman who seems to have existed only to serve men is Willy Loman's mother. On one occasion, in speaking with Ben, Willy remembers being on her lap, and Ben, on learning that his mother is dead, utters a platitudinous description of her, "Fine specimen of a lady, Mother" (1611), but that's as much as we learn of her. Willy is chiefly interested in learning about his father, who left the family and went to Alaska. Ben characterizes the father as "a very great and a very wild-hearted man" (1613), but the fact that the father left his family and apparently had no further communication with his wife and children seems to mean nothing to Ben. Presumably the mother struggled alone to bring up the boys, but her efforts are unmentioned. Curiously, some writers defend the father's desertion of his family. Lois Gordon says, "The first generation (Willy's father) has been forced, in order to make a living, to break up the family" (278), but nothing in the play supports this assertion that the father was "forced" to break up the family.

Willy, like Ben, assumes that men are heroic and women are nothing except servants and sex machines. For instance, Willy says to Ben, "Please tell about Dad. I want my boys to hear. I want them to know the kind of stock they spring from" (1612). As Kay Stanton, a feminist critic says, Willy's words imply "an Edenic birth myth," a world "with all the Loman men springing directly from their father's side, with no commingling with a female" (69).

Another woman who, like Howard's maid and Willy's mother, apparently exists only to serve is Jenny, Charley's secretary. She is courteous, and she is treated courteously by Charley and by Charley's son, Bernard, but she has no identity other than that of a secretary. And, as a secretary--that is, as a nonentity in the eyes of at least some men--she can be addressed insensitively. Willy Loman makes off-color remarks to her:

> WILLY. . . . Jenny, Jenny, good to see you. How're ya? Workin'? Or still honest?
>
> JENNY. Fine. How've you been feeling?
>
> WILLY. Not much any more, Jenny. Ha, ha! (1633)

The first of these comments seems to suggest that a working woman is <u>not</u> honest--that is, is a prostitute or is engaged in some other sort of hanky-panky, as is the Woman who in exchange for silk stockings and sex sends Willy directly into the buyer's office. The second of Willy's jokes, with its remark about not feeling much, also refers to sex. In short, though readers or viewers of the play see Jenny as a thoroughly respectable woman, they see her not so much as an individual but as a person engaged in routine work and as a person to whom Willy can speak crudely.

It is a little harder to be certain about the characters of Miss Forsythe and Letta, the two women in the scene in Stanley's restaurant. For Happy, Miss Forsythe is "strudel," an object for a man to consume, and for Stanley she and her friend Letta are "chippies," that is, prostitutes. But is it clear that they are prostitutes? When Happy tells Miss Forsythe that he is in the business of selling, he makes a dirty joke, saying, "You don't happen to sell, do you?" (1639). She replies, "No, I don't sell," and if we take this seriously and if we believe her, we can say that she is respectable and is rightly putting Happy in his place. Further, her friend Letta says, "I gotta get up very early tomorrow. I got jury duty" (1645), which implies that she is a responsible citizen. Still, the girls do not seem especially thoughtful. When Biff introduces Willy to the girls, Letta says, "Isn't he cute? Sit down with us, Pop" (1645), and when Willy breaks down in the restaurant, Miss Forsythe says, "Say, I don't like that temper of his" (1646). Perhaps we can say this: It is going too far--on the basis of what we see--to agree with Stanley that the women are "chippies," or with Happy, who assumes that every woman is available for sex, but Miss Forsythe and Letta do not seem to be especially responsible or even interesting people. That is, as Miller presents them, they are of little substance, simply figures introduced into the play in order to show how badly Happy and Biff behave.

The most important woman in the play, other than Linda, is "the Woman," who for money or stockings and perhaps for pleasure has sex with Willy, and who will use her influence as a receptionist or secretary in the office to send Willy directly on to the buyer, without his having to wait at the desk. But even though the Woman gets something out of the relationship, she knows that she is being used. When Biff appears in the hotel room, she asks him, "Are you football or baseball?" Biff replies, "Football," and the Woman, "angry, humiliated," says, "That's me too" (1648). We can admire her vigorous response, but, again, like the other women whom we have discussed, she is not really an impressive figure. We can say that, at best, in a society that assumes women are to be exploited by men, she holds her own.

So far, then--though we have not yet talked about Linda--the world of Death of a Salesman is not notable for its pictures of impressive women. True, most of the males in the play--Willy, Biff, Happy, Ben, and such lesser characters as Stanley and Howard--are themselves pretty sorry specimens, but Bernard and Charley are exceptionally decent and successful people, people who can well serve as role models. Can any female character in the play serve as a role model?

Linda has evoked strongly contrasting reactions from the critics. Some of them judge her very severely. For instance, Lois Gordon says that Linda "encourages Willy's dream, yet she will not let him leave her for the New Continent, the only realm where the dream can be fulfilled" (280). True, Linda urges Willy not to follow Ben's advice of going to Alaska, but surely the spectator of the play cannot believe that Willy is the sort of man who can follow in Ben's footsteps and violently make a fortune. And, in fact, Ben is so vile a person (as when he trips Biff, threatens Biff's eye with the point of his umbrella, and says, "Never fight fair with a stranger, boy" [1613]), that we would not want Willy to take Ben's advice.

A second example of a harsh view of Linda is Brian Parker's comment on "the essential stupidity of Linda's behaviour. Surely it is both stupid and immoral to encourage the man you love in self-deceit and lies" (54). Parker also says that Linda's speech at the end, when she says she cannot understand why Willy killed himself, "is not only pathetic, it is also an explanation of the loneliness of Willy Loman which threw him into other women's arms" (54). Nothing in the play suggests that Linda was anything other than a highly supportive wife. If Willy turned to other women, surely it was not because Linda did not understand him. Finally, one last example of the Linda-bashing school of commentary: Guerin Bliquez speaks of "Linda's facility for prodding Willy to his doom" (383).

Very briefly, the arguments against Linda are that (1) she selfishly prevented Willy from going to Alaska, (2) she stupidly encourages him in his self-deceptions, and (3) she is materialistic, so that even at the end, in the Requiem, when she says she has made the last payment on the house, she is talking about money. But if we study the play we will see that all three of these charges are false. First, although Linda does indeed discourage Willy from taking Ben's advice and going to Alaska, she points out that there is no need for "everybody [to] conquer the world" and that Willy has "a beautiful job here" (1631), a job with excellent prospects. She may be mistaken in thinking that Willy has a good job--he may have misled her--but, given what seems to be the situation, her comment is entirely reasonable. So far as the second charge goes, that she encourages him in self-deception, there are two answers. First, on some matters she does not know that Willy has lied to her, and so her encouragement is reasonable and right. Second, on other matters she does know that Willy is not telling the truth, but she rightly thinks it is best not to let him know that she knows, since such a revelation would crush what little self-respect remains in him. Consider, for example, this portion of dialogue, early in the play, when Willy, deeply agitated about his failure to drive and about Biff, has returned from what started out as a trip to Boston. Linda, trying to take his mind off his problems, urges him to go downstairs to the kitchen to try a new kind of cheese:

> LINDA. Go down, try it. And be quiet.
>
> WILLY (turning to Linda, guiltily). You're not worried about me, are you, sweetheart?
>
> . . .
>
> LINDA. You've got too much on the ball to worry about.
>
> WILLY. You're my foundation and my support, Linda.
>
> LINDA. Just try to relax, dear. You make mountains out of molehills.
>
> WILLY. I won't fight with him any more. If he wants to go back to Texas, let him go.
>
> LINDA. He'll find his way. (1597)

Of course she does not really think he has a great deal on the ball, and she probably is not confident that Biff will "find his way," but surely she is doing the best thing possible--calming Willy, partly by using soothing words and partly by doing what she can to get Biff out of the house, since she knows that Biff and Willy can't live under the same roof.

The third charge, that she is materialistic, is ridiculous. She has to count the pennies because

<u>someone</u> has to see that the bills are paid, and Willy is obviously unable to do so. Here is an example of her supposed preoccupation with money:

> LINDA. Well, there's nine-sixty for the washing machine. And for the vacuum cleaner there's three and a half due on the fifteenth. Then the roof, you got twenty-one dollars remaining.
>
> WILLY. It don't leak, does it?
>
> LINDA. No, they did a wonderful job. Then you owe Frank for the carburetor.
>
> WILLY. I'm not going to pay that man! That goddam Chevrolet, they ought to prohibit the manufacture of that car!
>
> LINDA. Well, you owe him three and a half. And odds and ends, comes to around a hundred and twenty dollars by the fifteenth. (1606)

It might be nice if Linda spent her time taking courses at an adult education center and thinking high thoughts, but it's obvious that <u>someone</u> in the Loman family (as in all families) has to keep track of the bills.

The worst that can be said of Linda is that she subscribes to three American ideas of the time--that the man is the breadwinner, that the relationship between a father and his sons is far more important than the relationship between a mother and her sons, and that a woman's sole job is to care for the house and to produce sons for her husband. She is the maidservant to her husband and to her sons, but in this she is like the vast majority of women of her time, and she should not be criticized for not being an innovator. Compared to her husband and her sons, Linda (though of course not perfect) is a tower of common sense, virtue, and strength. In fact, far from causing Willy's failure, she does what she can to give him strength to face the facts, for instance when she encourages him to talk to Howard about a job in New York: "Why don't you go down to the place tomorrow and tell Howard you've simply got to work in New York? You're too accommodating, dear" (1595). Notice, too, her speech in which she agrees with Biff's decision that it is best for Biff to leave for good: she goes to Willy and says, "I think that's the best way, dear. 'Cause there's no use drawing it out, you'll just never get along" (1653). Linda is not the most forceful person alive, or the brightest, but she is decent and she sees more clearly than do any of the other Lomans.

There is nothing in the play to suggest that Arthur Miller was a feminist or was ahead of his time in his view of the role of women. On the contrary, the play seems to give a pre-feminist view, with women playing subordinate roles to men. The images of success of the best sort--not of Ben's ruthless sort--are Charley and Bernard, two males. Probably Miller, writing in the 1940s, could hardly conceive of a successful woman other than as a wife or mother. Notice, by the way, that Bernard--probably the most admirable male in the play--is not only an important lawyer but the father of two sons, apparently a sign of his complete success as a man. Still, Miller's picture of Linda is by no means condescending. Linda may not be a genius, but she is the brightest and the most realistic of the Lomans. Things turn out badly, but not because of Linda. The viewer leaves the theater with profound respect for her patience, her strength, her sense of decency, and, yes, her intelligence and her competence in dealing with incompetent men.

Works Cited

Bliquez, Guerin. "Linda's Role in *Death of a Salesman*." *Modern Drama* 10 (1968): 383-86.

Gordon, Lois. "*Death of a Salesman*: An Appreciation." *The Forties: Fiction, Poetry, Drama*. Ed. Warren French. Deland, Florida: Everett/Edwards, 1969. 273-83.

Koon, Helene Wickham, ed. *Twentieth Century Interpretations of* Death of a Salesman. Englewood Cliffs, New Jersey: Prentice, 1983.

Miller, Arthur. *Death of a Salesman*. *Literature: Thinking, Reading, and Writing Critically*, Eds. Sylvan Barnet et al. 2nd ed. New York: Longman, 1997. 1591-1659.

Parker, Brian. "Point of View in Arthur Miller's *Death of a Salesman*." *University of Toronto Quarterly* 35 (1966): 144-47. Rpt. in Koon. 41-55.

Stanton, Kay. "Women and the American Dream of *Death of a Salesman*." *Feminist Readings of American Drama*. Ed. Judith Schlueter. Rutherford, New Jersey: Fairleigh Dickinson UP, 1989. 67-102.

# CHAPTER 33

# Plays and Perspectives

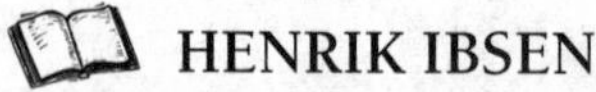

## HENRIK IBSEN

*Henrik Ibsen (1828–1906) was born in Skien, Norway, of wealthy parents who soon after his birth lost their money. Ibsen worked as a pharmacist's apprentice, but at the age of 22 he had written his first play, a promising melodrama entitled* Cataline. *He engaged in theater work first in Norway and then in Denmark and Germany. By 1865 his plays had won him a state pension that enabled him to settle in Rome. After writing romantic, historic, and poetic plays, he turned to realistic drama with* The League of Youth *(1869). Among the major realistic "problem plays" are* A Doll's House *(1879),* Ghosts *(1881), and* An Enemy of the People *(1882). In* The Wild Duck *(1884) he moved toward a more symbolic tragic comedy, and his last plays, written in the nineties, are highly symbolic.* Hedda Gabler *(1890) looks backward to the plays of the eighties rather than forward to the plays of the nineties.*

## A Doll's House

*Translated by Michael Meyer*

LIST OF CHARACTERS
TORVALD HELMER, *a lawyer*
NORA, *his wife*

*A Doll's House* (Harvard Theatre Collection)

DR. RANK
MRS. LINDE
NILS KROGSTAD, *also a lawyer*
*The Helmers' three small children*
ANNE-MARIE, *their nurse*
HELEN, *the maid*
*A Porter*

**SCENE:** *The action takes place in the Helmers' apartment.*

## Act 1

*A comfortably and tastefully, but not expensively furnished room. Backstage right a door leads out to the hall; backstage left, another door to Helmer's study. Between these two doors stands a piano. In the middle of the left-hand wall is a door, with a window downstage of it. Near the window, a round table with armchairs and a small sofa. In the right-hand wall, slightly upstage, is a door; downstage of this, against the same wall, a stove lined with porcelain tiles, with a couple of armchairs and a rocking-chair in front of it. Between the stove and the side door is a small table. Engravings on the wall. A what-not with china and other bric-a-brac; a small bookcase with leather-bound books. A carpet on the floor; a fire in the stove. A winter day.*

*A bell rings in the hall outside. After a moment, we hear the front door being opened. Nora enters the room, humming contentedly to herself. She is wearing outdoor clothes and carrying a lot of parcels, which she puts down on the table right. She leaves the door to the hall open; through it, we can see a Porter carrying a Christmas tree and a basket. He gives these to the Maid, who has opened the door for them.*

NORA. Hide that Christmas tree away, Helen. The children mustn't see it before I've decorated it this evening. (*To the porter, taking out her purse.*) How much—?

PORTER. A shilling.

NORA. Here's half a crown. No, keep it.

*The Porter touches his cap and goes. Nora closes the door. She continues to laugh happily to herself as she removes her coat, etc. She takes from her pocket a bag containing macaroons and eats a couple. Then, she tiptoes across and listens at her husband's door.*

NORA. Yes, he's here. (*Starts humming again as she goes over to the table, right.*)

HELMER (*from his room*). Is that my skylark twittering out there?

NORA (*opening some of the parcels*). It is!

HELMER. Is that my squirrel rustling?

NORA. Yes!

HELMER. When did my squirrel come home?

NORA. Just now. (*Pops the bag of macaroons in her pocket and wipes her mouth.*) Come out here, Torvald, and see what I've bought.

HELMER. You mustn't disturb me! (*Short pause; then he opens the door and looks in, his pen in his hand.*) Bought, did you say? All that? Has my little squanderbird been overspending again?

NORA. Oh, Torvald, surely we can let ourselves go a little this year! It's the first Christmas we don't have to scrape.

HELMER. Well, you know, we can't afford to be extravagant.

NORA. Oh yes, Torvald, we can be a little extravagant now. Can't we? Just a tiny bit? You've got a big salary now, and you're going to make lots and lots of money.

HELMER. Next year, yes. But my new salary doesn't start till April.

NORA. Pooh; we can borrow till then.

HELMER. Nora! (*Goes over to her and takes her playfully by the ear.*) What a little spendthrift you are! Suppose I were to borrow fifty pounds today, and you spent it all over Christmas, and then on New Year's Eve a tile fell off a roof onto my head—

NORA (*puts her hand over his mouth*). Oh, Torvald! Don't say such dreadful things!

HELMER. Yes, but suppose something like that did happen? What then?

NORA. If any thing as frightful as that happened, it wouldn't make much difference whether I was in debt or not.

HELMER. But what about the people I'd borrowed from?

NORA. Them? Who cares about them? They're strangers.

HELMER. Oh, Nora, Nora, how like a woman! No, but seriously, Nora, you know how I feel about this. No debts! Never borrow! A home that is founded on debts can never be a place of freedom and beauty. We two have stuck it out bravely up to now; and we shall continue to do so for the short time we still have to.

NORA (*goes over towards the stove*). Very well, Torvald. As you say.

HELMER (*follows her*). Now, now! My little songbird mustn't droop her wings. What's this? Is little squirrel sulking? (*Takes out his purse.*) Nora; guess what I've got here!

NORA (*turns quickly*). Money!

HELMER. Look. (*Hands her some banknotes.*) I know how these small expenses crop up at Christmas.

NORA (*counts them*). One—two—three—four. Oh, thank you, Torvald, thank you! I should be able to manage with this.

HELMER. You'll have to.

NORA. Yes, yes, of course I will. But come over here, I want to show you everything I've bought. And so cheaply! Look, here are new clothes for Ivar—and a sword. And a horse and a trumpet for Bob. And a doll and a cradle for Emmy—they're nothing much, but she'll pull them apart in a few days. And some bits of material and handkerchiefs for the maids. Old Anne-Marie ought to have had something better, really.

HELMER. And what's in that parcel?

NORA (*cries*). No, Torvald, you mustn't see that before this evening!

HELMER. Very well. But now, tell me, you little spendthrift, what do you want for Christmas?

NORA. Me? Oh, pooh, I don't want anything.

HELMER. Oh, yes, you do. Now tell me, what, within reason, would you most like?

NORA. No, I really don't know. Oh, yes—Torvald—!

HELMER. Well?

NORA (*plays with his coat-buttons; not looking at him*). If you really want to give me something, you could—you could—

HELMER. Come on, out with it.

NORA (*quickly*). You could give me money, Torvald. Only as much as you feel you can afford; then later I'll buy something with it.

HELMER. But, Nora—

NORA. Oh yes, Torvald dear, please! Please! Then I'll wrap up the notes in pretty gold paper and hang them on the Christmas tree. Wouldn't that be fun?

HELMER. What's the name of that little bird that can never keep any money?

NORA. Yes, yes, squanderbird; I know. But let's do as I say, Torvald; then I'll have time to think about what I need most. Isn't that the best way? Mm?

HELMER (*smiles*). To be sure it would be, if you could keep what I give you and really buy yourself something with it. But you'll spend it on all sorts of useless things for the house, and then I'll have to put my hand in my pocket again.

NORA. Oh, but Torvald—

HELMER. You can't deny it, Nora dear. (*Puts his arm round her waist.*) The squanderbird's a pretty little creature, but she gets through an awful lot of money. It's incredible what an expensive pet she is for a man to keep.

NORA. For shame! How can you say such a thing? I save every penny I can.

HELMER (*laughs*). That's quite true. Every penny you can. But you can't.

NORA (*hums and smiles, quietly gleeful*). Hm. If you only knew how many expenses we larks and squirrels have, Torvald.

HELMER. You're a funny little creature. Just like your father used to be. Always on the look-out for some way to get money, but as soon as you have any it just runs through your fingers, and you never know where it's gone. Well, I suppose I must take you as you are. It's in your blood. Yes, yes, yes, these things are hereditary, Nora.

NORA. Oh, I wish I'd inherited more of Papa's qualities.

HELMER. And I wouldn't wish my darling little songbird to be any different from what she is. By the way, that reminds me. You look awfully—how shall I put it?—awfully guilty today.

NORA. Do I?

HELMER. Yes, you do. Look me in the eyes.

NORA (*looks at him*). Well?

HELMER (*wags his finger*). Has my little sweet-tooth been indulging herself in town today, by any chance?

NORA. No, how can you think such a thing?

HELMER. Not a tiny little digression into a pastry shop?

NORA. No, Torvald, I promise—

HELMER. Not just a wee jam tart?

NORA. Certainly not.

HELMER. Not a little nibble at a macaroon?

NORA. No, Torvald—I promise you, honestly—

HELMER. There, there. I was only joking.

NORA (*goes over to the table, right*). You know I could never act against your wishes.

HELMER. Of course not. And you've given me your word—(*Goes over to her.*) Well, my beloved Nora, you keep your little Christmas secrets to yourself. They'll be revealed this evening, I've no doubt, once the Christmas tree has been lit.

NORA. Have you remembered to invite Dr. Rank?

HELMER. No. But there's no need; he knows he'll be dining with us. Anyway, I'll ask him when he comes this morning. I've ordered some good wine. Oh Nora, you can't imagine how I'm looking forward to this evening.

NORA. So am I. And, Torvald, how the children will love it!

HELMER. Yes, it's a wonderful thing to know that one's position is assured and that one has an ample income. Don't you agree? It's good to know that, isn't it?

NORA. Yes, it's almost like a miracle.

HELMER. Do you remember last Christmas? For three whole weeks you shut yourself away every evening to make flowers for the Christmas tree, and all those other things you were going to surprise us with. Ugh, it was the most boring time I've ever had in my life.

NORA. I didn't find it boring.

HELMER (*smiles*). But it all came to nothing in the end, didn't it?

NORA. Oh, are you going to bring that up again? How could I help the cat getting in and tearing everything to bits?

HELMER. No, my poor little Nora, of course you couldn't. You simply wanted to make us happy, and that's all that matters. But it's good that those hard times are past.

NORA. Yes, it's wonderful.

HELMER. I don't have to sit by myself and be bored. And you don't have to tire your pretty eyes and your delicate little hands—

NORA (*claps her hands*). No, Torvald, that's true, isn't it—I don't have to any longer? Oh, it's really all just like a miracle. (*Takes his arm.*) Now, I'm going to tell you what I thought we might do, Torvald. As soon as Christmas is over—(*A bell rings in the hall.*) Oh, there's the doorbell. (*Tidies up one or two things in the room.*) Someone's coming. What a bore.

HELMER. I'm not at home to any visitors. Remember!

MAID (*in the doorway*). A lady's called, madam. A stranger.

NORA. Well, ask her to come in.

MAID. And the doctor's here too, sir.

HELMER. Has he gone to my room?

MAID. Yes, sir.

*Helmer goes into his room. The Maid shows in Mrs. Linde, who is dressed in traveling clothes, and closes the door.*

MRS. LINDE (*shyly and a little hesitantly*). Good evening, Nora.

NORA (*uncertainly*). Good evening—

MRS. LINDE. I don't suppose you recognize me.

NORA. No, I'm afraid I—Yes, wait a minute—surely—(*Exclaims.*) Why, Christine! Is it really you?

MRS. LINDE. Yes, it's me.

NORA. Christine! And I didn't recognize you! But how could I—? (*More quietly.*) How you've changed, Christine!

MRS. LINDE. Yes, I know. It's been nine years—nearly ten—

NORA. Is it so long? Yes, it must be. Oh, these last eight years have been such a happy time for me! So you've come to town? All that way in winter! How brave of you!

MRS. LINDE. I arrived by the steamer this morning.

NORA. Yes, of course—to enjoy yourself over Christmas. Oh, how splendid! We'll have to celebrate! But take off your coat. You're not cold, are you? (*Helps her off with it.*) There! Now let's sit down here by the stove and be comfortable. No, you take the armchair. I'll sit here in the rocking-chair. (*Clasps Mrs. Linde's hands.*) Yes, now you look like your old self. It was just at first that—you've got a little paler, though, Christine. And perhaps a bit thinner.

MRS. LINDE. And older, Nora. Much, much older.

NORA. Yes, perhaps a little older. Just a tiny bit. Not much. (*Checks herself suddenly and says earnestly.*) Oh, but how thoughtless of me to sit here and chatter away like this! Dear, sweet Christine, can you forgive me?

MRS. LINDE. What do you mean, Nora?

NORA (*quietly*). Poor Christine, you've become a widow.

MRS. LINDE. Yes. Three years ago.

NORA. I know, I know—I read it in the papers. Oh, Christine, I meant to write to you so often, honestly. But I always put it off, and something else always cropped up.

MRS. LINDE. I understand, Nora dear.

NORA. No, Christine, it was beastly of me. Oh, my poor darling, what you've gone through! And he didn't leave you anything?

MRS. LINDE. No.

NORA. No children, either?

MRS. LINDE. No.

NORA. Nothing at all, then?

MRS. LINDE. Not even a feeling of loss or sorrow.

NORA (*looks incredulously at her*). But, Christine, how is that possible?

MRS. LINDE (*smiles sadly and strokes Nora's hair*). Oh, these things happen, Nora.

NORA. All alone. How dreadful that must be for you. I've three lovely children. I'm afraid you can't see them now, because they're out with nanny. But you must tell me everything—

MRS. LINDE. No, no, no. I want to hear about you.

NORA. No, you start. I'm not going to be selfish today, I'm just going to think about you. Oh, but there's one thing I *must* tell you. Have you heard of the wonderful luck we've just had?

MRS. LINDE. No. What?

NORA. Would you believe it—my husband's just been made manager of the bank!

MRS. LINDE. Your husband? Oh, how lucky—!

NORA. Yes, isn't it? Being a lawyer is so uncertain, you know, especially if one isn't prepared to touch any case that isn't—well—quite nice. And of course Torvald's been very firm about that—and I'm absolutely with him. Oh, you can imagine how happy we are! He's joining the bank in the New Year, and he'll be getting a big salary, and lots of percentages too. From now on we'll be able to live quite differently—we'll be able to do whatever we want. Oh, Christine, it's such a relief! I feel so happy! Well, I mean, it's lovely to have heaps of money and not to have to worry about anything. Don't you think?

MRS. LINDE. It must be lovely to have enough to cover one's needs, anyway.

NORA. Not just our needs! We're going to have heaps and heaps of money!

MRS. LINDE (*smiles*). Nora, Nora, haven't you grown up yet? When we were at school you were a terrible little spendthrift.

NORA (*laughs quietly*). Yes, Torvald still says that. (*Wags her finger.*) But "Nora, Nora" isn't as silly as you think. Oh, we've been in no position for me to waste money. We've both had to work.

MRS. LINDE. You too?

NORA. Yes, little things—fancy work, crocheting, embroidery and so forth. (*Casually.*) And other things too. I suppose you know Torvald left the Ministry when we got married? There were no prospects of promotion in his department, and of course he needed more money. But the first year he overworked himself quite dreadfully. He had to take on all sorts of extra jobs, and worked day and night. But it was too much for him, and he became frightfully ill. The doctors said he'd have to go to a warmer climate.

MRS. LINDE. Yes, you spent a whole year in Italy, didn't you?

NORA. Yes. It wasn't easy for me to get away, you know. I'd just had Ivar. But of course we had to do it. Oh, it was a marvelous trip! And it saved Torvald's life. But it cost an awful lot of money, Christine.

MRS. LINDE. I can imagine.

NORA. Two hundred and fifty pounds. That's a lot of money, you know.

MRS. LINDE. How lucky you had it.

NORA. Well, actually, we got it from my father.

MRS. LINDE. Oh, I see. Didn't he die just about that time?

NORA. Yes, Christine, just about then. Wasn't it dreadful, I couldn't go and look after him. I was expecting little Ivar any day. And then I had my poor Torvald to care for—we really didn't think he'd live. Dear, kind Papa! I never saw him again, Christine. Oh, it's the saddest thing that's happened to me since I got married.

MRS. LINDE. I know you were very fond of him. But you went to Italy—?

NORA. Yes. Well, we had the money, you see, and the doctors said we mustn't delay. So we went the month after Papa died.

MRS. LINDE. And your husband came back completely cured?

NORA. Fit as a fiddle!

MRS. LINDE. But—the doctor?

NORA. How do you mean?

MRS. LINDE. I thought the maid said that the gentleman who arrived with me was the doctor.

NORA. Oh yes, that's Doctor Rank, but he doesn't come because anyone's ill. He's our best friend, and he looks us up at least once every day. No, Torvald hasn't had a moment's illness since we went away. And the children are fit and healthy and so am I. (*Jumps up and claps her hands.*) Oh God, oh God, Christine, isn't it a wonderful thing to be alive and happy! Oh, but how beastly of me! I'm only talking about myself. (*Sits on a footstool and rests her arms on Mrs. Linde's knee.*) Oh, please don't be angry with me! Tell me, is it really true you didn't love your husband? Why did you marry him, then?

MRS. LINDE. Well, my mother was still alive; and she was helpless and bedridden. And I had my two little brothers to take care of. I didn't feel I could say no.

NORA. Yes, well, perhaps you're right. He was rich then, was he?

MRS. LINDE. Quite comfortably off, I believe. But his business was unsound, you see, Nora. When he died it went bankrupt, and there was nothing left.

NORA. What did you do?

MRS. LINDE. Well, I had to try to make ends meet somehow, so I started a little shop, and a little school, and anything else I could turn my hand to. These last three years have been just one endless slog for me, without a moment's rest. But now it's over, Nora. My poor dear mother doesn't need me any more; she's passed away. And the boys don't need me either; they've got jobs now and can look after themselves.

NORA. How relieved you must feel—

MRS. LINDE. No, Nora. Just unspeakably empty. No one to live for any more. (*Gets up restlessly.*) That's why I couldn't bear to stay out there any longer, cut off from the world. I thought it'd be easier to find some work here that will exercise and occupy my mind. If only I could get a regular job—office work of some kind—

NORA. Oh, but Christine, that's dreadfully exhausting; and you look practically finished already. It'd be much better for you if you could go away somewhere.

MRS. LINDE (*goes over to the window*). I have no Papa to pay for my holidays, Nora.

NORA (*gets up*). Oh, please don't be angry with me.

MRS. LINDE. My dear Nora, it's I who should ask you not to be angry. That's the worst thing about this kind of situation—it makes one so bitter. One has no one to work for; and yet one has to be continually sponging for jobs. One has to live; and so one becomes completely egocentric. When you told me about this luck you've just had with Torvald's new job—can you imagine?—I was happy not so much on your account, as on my own.

NORA. How do you mean? Oh, I understand. You mean Torvald might be able to do something for you?

MRS. LINDE. Yes, I was thinking that.

NORA. He will too, Christine. Just you leave it to me. I'll lead up to it so delicately, so delicately; I'll get him in the right mood. Oh, Christine, I do so want to help you.

MRS. LINDE. It's sweet of you to bother so much about me, Nora. Especially since you know so little of the worries and hardships of life.

NORA. I? You say *I* know little of—?

MRS. LINDE (*smiles*). Well, good heavens—those bits of fancy work of yours—well, really—! You're a child, Nora.

NORA (*tosses her head and walks across the room*). You shouldn't say that so patronizingly.

MRS. LINDE. Oh?

NORA. You're like the rest. You all think I'm incapable of getting down to anything serious—

MRS. LINDE. My dear—

NORA. You think I've never had any worries like the rest of you.

MRS. LINDE. Nora dear, you've just told me about all your difficulties—

NORA. Pooh—that! (*Quietly.*) I haven't told you about the big thing.

MRS. LINDE. What big thing? What do you mean?

NORA. You patronize me, Christine; but you shouldn't. You're proud that you've worked so long and so hard for your mother.

MRS. LINDE. I don't patronize anyone, Nora. But you're right—I am both proud and happy that I was able to make my mother's last months on earth comparatively easy.

NORA. And you're also proud of what you've done for your brothers.

MRS. LINDE. I think I have a right to be.

NORA. I think so too. But let me tell you something, Christine. I too have done something to be proud and happy about.

MRS. LINDE. I don't doubt it. But—how do you mean?

NORA. Speak quietly! Suppose Torvald should hear! He mustn't, at any price—no one must know, Christine—no one but you.

MRS. LINDE. But what is this?

NORA. Come over here. (*Pulls her down on to the sofa beside her.*) Yes, Christine—I too have done something to be happy and proud about. It was I who saved Torvald's life.

MRS. LINDE. Saved his—? How did you save it?

NORA. I told you about our trip to Italy. Torvald couldn't have lived if he hadn't managed to get down there—

MRS. LINDE. Yes, well—your father provided the money—

NORA (*smiles*). So Torvald and everyone else thinks. But—

MRS. LINDE. Yes?

NORA. Papa didn't give us a penny. It was I who found the money.

MRS. LINDE. You? All of it?

NORA. Two hundred and fifty pounds. What do you say to that?

MRS. LINDE. But Nora, how could you? Did you win a lottery or something?

NORA (*scornfully*). Lottery? (*Sniffs.*) What would there be to be proud of in that?

MRS. LINDE. But where did you get it from, then?

NORA (*hums and smiles secretively*). Hm; tra-la-la-la.

MRS. LINDE. You couldn't have borrowed it.

NORA. Oh? Why not?

MRS. LINDE. Well, a wife can't borrow money without her husband's consent.

NORA (*tosses her head*). Ah, but when a wife has a little business sense, and knows how to be clever—

MRS. LINDE. But Nora, I simply don't understand—

NORA. You don't have to. No one has said I borrowed the money. I could have got it in some other way. (*Throws herself back on the sofa.*) I could have got it from an admirer. When a girl's as pretty as I am—

MRS. LINDE. Nora, you're crazy!

NORA. You're dying of curiosity now, aren't you, Christine?

MRS. LINDE. Nora dear, you haven't done anything foolish?

NORA (*sits up again*). Is it foolish to save one's husband's life?

MRS. LINDE. I think it's foolish if without his knowledge, you—

NORA. But the whole point was that he mustn't know! Great heavens, don't you see? He hadn't to know how dangerously ill he was. I was the one they told that his life was in danger and that only going to a warm climate could save him. Do you suppose I didn't try to think of other ways of getting him down there? I told him how wonderful it would be for me to go abroad like other young wives; I cried and prayed; I asked him to remember my condition, and said he ought to be nice and tender to me; and then I suggested he might quite easily borrow the money. But then he got almost angry with me, Christine. He said I was frivolous, and that it was his duty as a husband not to pander to my moods and caprices—I think that's what he called them. Well, well, I thought, you've got to be saved somehow. And then I thought of a way—

MRS. LINDE. But didn't your husband find out from your father that the money hadn't come from him?

NORA. No, never. Papa died just then. I'd thought of letting him into the plot and asking him not to tell. But since he was so ill—! And as things turned out, it didn't become necessary.

MRS. LINDE. And you've never told your husband about this?

NORA. For heaven's sake, no! What an idea! He's frightfully strict about such matters. And besides—he's so proud of being a *man*—it'd be so painful and humiliating for him to know that he owed anything to me. It'd completely wreck our relationship. This life we have built together would no longer exist.

MRS. LINDE. Will you never tell him?

NORA (*thoughtfully, half-smiling*). Yes—some time, perhaps. Years from now, when I'm no longer pretty. You mustn't laugh! I mean of course, when Torvald no longer loves me as he does now; when it no longer amuses him to see me dance and dress up and play the fool for him.

Then it might be useful to have something up my sleeve. (*Breaks off.*) Stupid, stupid, stupid! That time will never come. Well, what do you think of my big secret, Christine? I'm not completely useless, am I? Mind you, all this has caused me a frightful lot of worry. It hasn't been easy for me to meet my obligations punctually. In case you don't know, in the world of business there are things called quarterly installments and interest, and they're a terrible problem to cope with. So I've had to scrape a little here and save a little there as best I can. I haven't been able to save much on the housekeeping money, because Torvald likes to live well; and I couldn't let the children go short of clothes—I couldn't take anything out of what he gives me for them. The poor little angels!

MRS. LINDE. So you've had to stint yourself, my poor Nora?

NORA. Of course. Well, after all, it was my problem. Whenever Torvald gave me money to buy myself new clothes, I never used more than half of it; and I always bought what was cheapest and plainest. Thank heaven anything suits me, so that Torvald's never noticed. But it made me a bit sad sometimes, because it's lovely to wear pretty clothes. Don't you think?

MRS. LINDE. Indeed it is.

NORA. And then I've found one or two other sources of income. Last winter I managed to get a lot of copying to do. So I shut myself away and wrote every evening, late into the night. Oh, I often got so tired, so tired. But it was great fun, though, sitting there working and earning money. It was almost like being a man.

MRS. LINDE. But how much have you managed to pay off like this?

NORA. Well, I can't say exactly. It's awfully difficult to keep an exact check on these kind of transactions. I only know I've paid everything I've managed to scrape together. Sometimes I really didn't know where to turn. (*Smiles.*) Then I'd sit here and imagine some rich old gentleman had fallen in love with me—

MRS. LINDE. What! What gentleman?

NORA. Silly! And that now he'd died and when they opened his will it said in big letters: "Everything I possess is to be paid forthwith to my beloved Mrs. Nora Helmer in cash."

MRS. LINDE. But, Nora dear, who was this gentleman?

NORA. Great heavens, don't you understand? There wasn't any old gentleman, he was just something I used to dream up as I sat here evening after evening wondering how on earth I could raise some money. But what does it matter? The old bore can stay imaginary as far as I'm concerned, because now I don't have to worry any longer! (*Jumps up.*) Oh, Christine, isn't it wonderful? I don't have to worry any more! No more troubles! I can play all day with the children, I can fill the house with pretty things, just the way Torvald likes. And, Christine, it will soon be spring, and the air will be fresh and the skies blue—and then perhaps we'll be able to take a little trip somewhere. I shall be able to see the sea again. Oh, yes, yes, it's a wonderful thing to be alive and happy!

*The bell rings in the hall.*

MRS. LINDE (*gets up*). You've a visitor. Perhaps I'd better go.

NORA. No stay. It won't be for me. It's someone for Torvald—

MAID (*in the doorway*). Excuse me, madam, a gentleman's called who says he wants to speak to the master. But I didn't know—seeing as the doctor's with him—

NORA. Who is this gentleman?

KROGSTAD (*in the doorway*). It's me, Mrs. Helmer.

*Mrs. Linde starts, composes herself; and turns away to the window.*

NORA (*takes a step toward him and whispers tensely*). You? What is it? What do you want to talk to my husband about?

KROGSTAD. Business—you might call it. I hold a minor post in the bank, and I hear your husband is to become our new chief—

NORA. Oh—then it isn't—?

KROGSTAD. Pure business, Mrs. Helmer. Nothing more.

NORA. Well, you'll find him in his study.

*Nods indifferently as she closes the hall door behind him. Then she walks across the room and sees to the stove.*

MRS. LINDE. Nora, who was that man?

NORA. A lawyer called Krogstad.

MRS. LINDE. It was him, then.

NORA. Do you know that man?

MRS. LINDE. I used to know him—some years ago. He was a solicitor's clerk in our town, for a while.

NORA. Yes, of course, so he was.

MRS. LINDE. How he's changed!

NORA. He was very unhappily married, I believe.

MRS. LINDE. Is he a widower now?

NORA. Yes, with a lot of children. Ah, now it's alight.

*She closes the door of the stove and moves the rocking-chair a little to one side.*

MRS. LINDE. He does—various things now, I hear?

NORA. Does he? It's quite possible—I really don't know. But don't let's talk about business. It's so boring.

*Dr. Rank enters from Helmer's study.*

RANK (*still in the doorway*). No, no, my dear chap, don't see me out. I'll go and have a word with your wife. (*Closes the door and notices Mrs. Linde.*) Oh, I beg your pardon. I seem to be *de trop* here too.

NORA. Not in the least. (*Introduces them.*) Dr. Rank. Mrs. Linde.

RANK. Ah! A name I have often heard in this house. I believe I passed you on the stairs as I came up.

MRS. LINDE. Yes. Stairs tire me; I have to take them slowly.

RANK. Oh, have you hurt yourself?

MRS. LINDE. No, I'm just a little run down.

RANK. Ah, is that all? Then I take it you've come to town to cure yourself by a round of parties?

MRS. LINDE. I have come here to find work.

RANK. Is that an approved remedy for being run down?

MRS. LINDE. One has to live, Doctor.

RANK. Yes, people do seem to regard it as a necessity.

NORA. Oh, really, Dr. Rank. I bet you want to stay alive.

RANK. You bet I do. However miserable I sometimes feel, I still want to go on being tortured for as long as possible. It's the same with all my patients; and with people who are morally sick, too. There's a moral cripple in with Helmer at this very moment—

MRS. LINDE (*softly*). Oh!

NORA. Whom do you mean?

RANK. Oh, a lawyer fellow called Krogstad—you wouldn't know him. He's crippled all right; morally twisted. But even he started off by announcing, as though it were a matter of enormous importance, that he had to live.

NORA. Oh? What did he want to talk to Torvald about?

RANK. I haven't the faintest idea. All I heard was something about the bank.

NORA. I didn't know that Krog—that this man Krogstad had any connection with the bank.

RANK. Yes, he's got some kind of job down there. (*To Mrs. Linde.*) I wonder if in your part of the world you too have a species of human being that spends its time fussing around trying to smell out moral corruption? And when they find a case they give him some nice, comfortable position so that they can keep a good watch on him. The healthy ones just have to lump it.

MRS. LINDE. But surely it's the sick who need care most?

RANK (*shrugs his shoulders*). Well, there we have it. It's that attitude that's turning human society into a hospital.

*Nora, lost in her own thoughts, laughs half to herself and claps her hands.*

RANK. Why are you laughing? Do you really know what society is?

NORA. What do I care about society? I think it's a bore. I was laughing at something else—something frightfully funny. Tell me, Dr. Rank—will everyone who works at the bank come under Torvald now?

RANK. Do you find that particularly funny?

NORA (*smiles and hums*). Never you mind! Never you mind! (*Walks around the room.*) Yes, I find it very amusing to think that we—I mean, Torvald—has obtained so much influence over so many people. (*Takes the paper bag from her pocket.*) Dr. Rank, would you like a small macaroon?

RANK. Macaroons! I say! I thought they were forbidden here.

NORA. Yes, well, these are some Christine gave me.

MRS. LINDE. What? I—?

NORA. All right, all right, don't get frightened. You weren't to know Torvald had forbidden them. He's afraid they'll ruin my teeth. But, dash it—for once—! Don't you agree, Dr. Rank? Here! (*Pops a macaroon into his mouth.*) You too, Christine. And I'll have one too. Just a little one. Two at the most. (*Begins to walk round again.*) Yes, now I feel really, really happy. Now there's just one thing in the world I'd really love to do.

RANK. Oh? And what is that?

NORA. Just something I'd love to say to Torvald.

RANK. Well, why don't you say it?

NORA. No, I daren't. It's too dreadful.

MRS. LINDE. Dreadful?

RANK. Well, then, you'd better not. But you can say it to us. What is it you'd so love to say to Torvald?

NORA. I've the most extraordinary longing to say: "Bloody hell!"

RANK. Are you mad?

MRS. LINDE. My dear Nora—!

RANK. Say it. Here he is.

NORA (*hiding the bag of macaroons*). Ssh! Ssh!

*Helmer, with his overcoat on his arm and his hat in his hand, enters from his study.*

NORA (*goes to meet him*). Well, Torvald dear, did you get rid of him?

HELMER. Yes, he's just gone.

NORA. May I introduce you—? This is Christine. She's just arrived in town.

HELMER. Christine—? Forgive me, but I don't think—

NORA. Mrs. Linde, Torvald dear. Christine Linde.

HELMER. Ah. A childhood friend of my wife's, I presume?

MRS. LINDE. Yes, we knew each other in earlier days.

NORA. And imagine, now she's traveled all this way to talk to you.

HELMER. Oh?

MRS. LINDE. Well, I didn't really—

NORA. You see, Christine's frightfully good at office work, and she's mad to come under some really clever man who can teach her even more than she knows already—

HELMER. Very sensible, madam.

NORA. So when she heard you'd become head of the bank—it was in her local paper—she came here as quickly as she could and—Torvald, you will, won't you? Do a little something to help Christine? For my sake?

HELMER. Well, that shouldn't be impossible. You are a widow, I take it, Mrs. Linde?

MRS. LINDE. Yes.

HELMER. And you have experience of office work?

MRS. LINDE. Yes, quite a bit.

HELMER. Well then, it's quite likely I may be able to find some job for you—

NORA (*claps her hands*). You see, you see!

HELMER. You've come at a lucky moment, Mrs. Linde.

MRS. LINDE. Oh, how can I ever thank you—?

HELMER. There's absolutely no need. (*Puts on his overcoat.*) But now I'm afraid I must ask you to excuse me—

RANK. Wait. I'll come with you.

*He gets his fur coat from the hall and warms it at the stove.*

NORA. Don't be long, Torvald dear.

HELMER. I'll only be an hour.

NORA. Are you going too, Christine?

MRS. LINDE (*puts on her outdoor clothes*). Yes, I must start to look round for a room.

HELMER. Then perhaps we can walk part of the way together.

NORA (*helps her*). It's such a nuisance we're so cramped here—I'm afraid we can't offer to—

MRS. LINDE. Oh, I wouldn't dream of it. Goodbye, Nora dear, and thanks for everything.

NORA. *Au revoir.* You'll be coming back this evening, of course. And, you too, Dr. Rank. What? If you're well enough? Of course you'll be well enough. Wrap up warmly, though.

*They go out, talking, into the hall. Children's voices are heard from the stairs.*

NORA. Here they are! Here they are!

*She runs out and opens the door. Anne-Marie, the nurse, enters with the children.*

NORA. Come in, come in! (*Stoops down and kisses them.*) Oh, my sweet darlings—! Look at them, Christine! Aren't they beautiful?

RANK. Don't stand here chattering in this draught!

HELMER. Come, Mrs. Linde. This is for mothers only.

*Dr. Rank, Helmer, and Mrs. Linde go down the stairs. The Nurse brings the children into the room. Nora follows, and closes the door to the hall.*

NORA. How well you look! What red cheeks you've got! Like apples and roses! (*The children answer her inaudibly as she talks to them.*) Have you had fun? That's splendid. You gave Emmy and Bob a ride on the sledge? What, both together? I say! What a clever boy you are, Ivar! Oh, let me hold her for a moment, Anne-Marie! My sweet little baby doll! (*Takes the smallest child from the nurse and dances with her.*) Yes, yes, Mummy will dance with Bob too. What? Have you been throwing snowballs? Oh, I wish I'd been there! No, don't—I'll undress them myself, Anne-Marie. No, please let me; it's such fun. Go inside and warm yourself; you look frozen. There's some hot coffee on the stove. (*The nurse goes into the room on the left. Nora takes off the children's outdoor clothes and throws them anywhere while they all chatter simultaneously.*) What? A big dog ran after you? But he didn't bite you? No, dogs don't bite lovely little baby dolls. Leave those parcels alone, Ivar. What's in them? Ah, wouldn't you like to know! No, no; it's nothing nice. Come on, let's play a game. What shall we play? Hide and seek. Yes, let's play hide and seek. Bob shall hide first. You want me to? All right, let me hide first.

*Nora and the children play around the room, and in the adjacent room to the left, laughing and shouting. At length Nora hides under the table. The children rush in, look, but cannot find her. Then they hear her half-stifled laughter, run to the table, lift up the cloth, and see her. Great excitement. She crawls out as though to frighten them. Further excitement. Meanwhile, there has been a knock on the door leading from the hall, but no one has noticed it. Now the door is half-opened and Krogstad enters. He waits for a moment; the game continues.*

KROGSTAD. Excuse me, Mrs. Helmer—

NORA (*turns with a stifled cry and half jumps up*). Oh! What do you want?

KROGSTAD. I beg your pardon; the front door was ajar. Someone must have forgotten to close it.

NORA (*gets up*). My husband is not at home, Mr. Krogstad.

KROGSTAD. I know.

NORA. Well, what do want here, then?

KROGSTAD. A word with you.

NORA. With—? (*To the children, quietly.*) Go inside to Anne-Marie. What? No, the strange gentleman won't do anything to hurt Mummy. When he's gone we'll start playing again.

*She takes the children into the room on the left and closes the door behind them.*

NORA (*uneasy, tense*). You want to speak to me?

KROGSTAD. Yes.

NORA. Today? But it's not the first of the month yet.

KROGSTAD. No, it is Christmas Eve. Whether or not you have a merry Christmas depends on you.

NORA. What do you want? I can't give you anything today—

KROGSTAD. We won't talk about that for the present. There's something else. You have a moment to spare?

NORA. Oh, yes. Yes, I suppose so; though—

KROGSTAD. Good. I was sitting in the café down below and I saw your husband cross the street—

NORA. Yes.

KROGSTAD. With a lady.

NORA. Well?

KROGSTAD. Might I be so bold as to ask: was not that lady a Mrs. Linde?

NORA. Yes.

KROGSTAD. Recently arrived in town?

NORA. Yes, today.

KROGSTAD. She is a good friend of yours, is she not?

NORA. Yes, she is. But I don't see—

KROGSTAD. I used to know her too once.

NORA. I know.

KROGSTAD. Oh? You've discovered that. Yes, I thought you would. Well then, may I ask you a straight question: is Mrs. Linde to be employed at the bank?

NORA. How dare you presume to cross-examine me, Mr. Krogstad? You, one of my husband's employees? But since you ask, you shall have an answer. Yes, Mrs. Linde is to be employed by the bank. And I arranged it, Mr. Krogstad. Now you know.

KROGSTAD. I guessed right, then.

NORA (*walks up and down the room*). Oh, one has a little influence, you know. Just because one's a woman it doesn't necessarily mean that— When one is in a humble position, Mr. Krogstad, one should think twice before offending someone who—hm—

KROGSTAD. —who has influence?

NORA. Precisely.

KROGSTAD (*changes his tone*). Mrs. Helmer, will you have the kindness to use your influence on my behalf?

NORA. What? What do you mean?

KROGSTAD. Will you be so good as to see that I keep my humble position at the bank?

NORA. What do you mean? Who is thinking of removing you from your position?

KROGSTAD. Oh, you don't need to play innocent with me. I realize it can't be very pleasant for your friend to risk bumping into me; and now I also realize whom I have to thank for being hounded out like this.

NORA. But I assure you—

KROGSTAD. Look, let's not beat about the bush. There's still time, and I'd advise you to use your influence to stop it.

NORA. But, Mr. Krogstad, I have no influence—

KROGSTAD. Oh? I thought you just said—

NORA. But I didn't mean it like that! I? How on earth could you imagine that I would have any influence over my husband?

KROGSTAD. Oh, I've known your husband since we were students together. I imagine he has his weaknesses like other married men.

NORA. If you speak impertinently of my husband, I shall show you the door.

KROGSTAD. You're a bold woman, Mrs. Helmer.

NORA. I'm not afraid of you any longer. Once the New Year is in, I'll soon be rid of you.

KROGSTAD (*more controlled*). Now listen to me, Mrs. Helmer. If I'm forced to, I shall fight for my little job at the bank as I would fight for my life.

NORA. So it sounds.

KROGSTAD. It isn't just the money; that's the last thing I care about. There's something else—well, you might as well know. It's like this, you see. You know of course, as every one else does, that some years ago I committed an indiscretion.

NORA. I think I did hear something—

KROGSTAD. It never came into court; but from that day, every opening was barred to me. So I turned my hand to the kind of business you know about. I had to do something; and I don't think I was one of the worst. But now I want to give up all that. My sons are growing up; for their sake, I must try to regain what respectability I can. This job in the bank was the first step on the ladder. And now your husband wants to kick me off that ladder back into the dirt.

NORA. But my dear Mr. Krogstad, it simply isn't in my power to help you.

KROGSTAD. You say that because you don't want to help me. But I have the means to make you.

NORA. You don't mean you'd tell my husband that I owe you money?

KROGSTAD. And if I did?

NORA. That'd be a filthy trick! (*Almost in tears.*) This secret that is my pride and my joy—that he should hear about it in such a filthy, beastly way—hear about it from you! It'd involve me in the most dreadful unpleasantness—

KROGSTAD. Only—unpleasantness?

NORA (*vehemently*). All right, do it! You'll be the one who'll suffer. It'll show my husband the kind of man you are, and then you'll never keep your job.

KROGSTAD. I asked you whether it was merely domestic unpleasantness you were afraid of.

NORA. If my husband hears about it, he will of course immediately pay you whatever is owing. And then we shall have nothing more to do with you.

KROGSTAD (*takes a step closer*). Listen, Mrs. Helmer. Either you've a bad memory or else you know very little about financial transactions. I had better enlighten you.

NORA. What do you mean?

KROGSTAD. When your husband was ill, you came to me to borrow two hundred and fifty pounds.

NORA. I didn't know anyone else.

KROGSTAD. I promised to find that sum for you—

NORA. And you did find it.

KROGSTAD. I promised to find that sum for you on certain conditions. You were so worried about your husband's illness and so keen to get the money to take him abroad that I don't think you bothered much about the details. So it won't be out of place if I refresh your memory. Well—I promised to get you the money in exchange for an I.O.U., which I drew up.

NORA. Yes, and which I signed.

KROGSTAD. Exactly. But then I added a few lines naming your father as security for the debt. This paragraph was to be signed by your father.

NORA. Was to be? He did sign it.

KROGSTAD. I left the date blank for your father to fill in when he signed this paper. You remember, Mrs. Helmer?

NORA. Yes, I think so—

KROGSTAD. Then I gave you back this I.O.U. for you to post to your father. Is that not correct?

NORA. Yes.

KROGSTAD. And of course you posted it at once; for within five or six days you brought it along to me with your father's signature on it. Whereupon I handed you the money.

NORA. Yes, well. Haven't I repaid the installments as agreed?

KROGSTAD. Mm—yes, more or less. But to return to what we were speaking about—that was a difficult time for you just then, wasn't it, Mrs. Helmer?

NORA. Yes, it was.

KROGSTAD. And your father was very ill, if I am not mistaken.

NORA. He was dying.

KROGSTAD. He did in fact die shortly afterwards?

NORA. Yes.

KROGSTAD. Tell me, Mrs. Helmer, do you by any chance remember the date of your father's death? The day of the month, I mean.

NORA. Papa died on the twenty-ninth of September.

KROGSTAD. Quite correct; I took the trouble to confirm it. And that leaves me with a curious little problem—(*Takes out a paper.*)—which I simply cannot solve.

NORA. Problem? I don't see—

KROGSTAD. The problem, Mrs. Helmer, is that your father signed this paper three days after his death.

NORA. What? I don't understand—

KROGSTAD. Your father died on the twenty-ninth of September. But look at this. Here your father has dated his signature the second of October. Isn't that a curious little problem, Mrs. Helmer? (*Nora is silent.*) Can you suggest any explanation? (*She remains silent.*) And there's another curious thing. The words "second of October" and the year are written in a hand which is not your father's, but which I seem to know. Well, there's a simple explanation to that. Your father could have forgotten to write in the date when he signed, and someone else could have added it before the news came of his death. There's nothing criminal about that. It's the signature itself I'm wondering about. It is genuine, I suppose, Mrs. Helmer? It was your father who wrote his name here?

NORA (*after a short silence, throws back her head and looks defiantly at him*). No, it was not. It was I who wrote Papa's name there.

KROGSTAD. Look, Mrs. Helmer, do you realize this is a dangerous admission?

NORA. Why? You'll get your money.

KROGSTAD. May I ask you a question? Why didn't you send this paper to your father?

NORA. I couldn't. Papa was very ill. If I'd asked him to sign this, I'd have had to tell him what the money was for. But I couldn't have told him in his condition that my husband's life was in danger. I couldn't have done that!

KROGSTAD. Then you would have been wiser to have given up your idea of a holiday.

NORA. But I couldn't! It was to save my husband's life. I couldn't put it off.

KROGSTAD. But didn't it occur to you that you were being dishonest towards me?

NORA. I couldn't bother about that. I didn't care about you. I hated you because of all the beastly difficulties you'd put in my way when you knew how dangerously ill my husband was.

KROGSTAD. Mrs. Helmer, you evidently don't appreciate exactly what you have done. But I can assure you that it is no bigger nor worse a crime than the one I once committed, and thereby ruined my whole social position.

NORA. You? Do you expect me to believe that you would have taken a risk like that to save your wife's life?

KROGSTAD. The law does not concern itself with motives.

NORA. Then the law must be very stupid.

KROGSTAD. Stupid or not, if I show this paper to the police, you will be judged according to it.

NORA. I don't believe that. Hasn't a daughter the right to shield her father from worry and anxiety when he's old and dying? Hasn't a wife the right to save her husband's life? I don't know much about the law but there must be something somewhere that says that such things are allowed. You ought to know about that, you're meant to be a lawyer, aren't you? You can't be a very good lawyer, Mr. Krogstad.

KROGSTAD. Possibly not. But business, the kind of business we two have been transacting—I think you'll admit I understand something about that? Good. Do as you please. But I tell you this. If I get thrown into the gutter for a second time, I shall take you with me.

*He bows and goes out through the hall.*

NORA (*stands for a moment in thought, then tosses her head*). What nonsense! He's trying to frighten me! I'm not that stupid. (*Busies herself gathering together the children's clothes; then she suddenly stops.*) But—? No, it's impossible. I did it for love, didn't I?

CHILDREN (*in the doorway, left*). Mummy, the strange gentleman's gone out into the street.

NORA. Yes, yes, I know. But don't talk to anyone about the strange gentleman. You hear? Not even to Daddy.

CHILDREN. No, Mummy. Will you play with us again now?

NORA. No, no. Not now.

CHILDREN. Oh but, Mummy, you promised!

NORA. I know, but I can't just now. Go back to the nursery. I've a lot to do. Go away, my darlings, go away. (*She pushes them gently into the other room and closes the door behind them. She sits on the sofa, takes up her embroidery, stitches for a few moments, but soon stops.*) No! (*Throws the embroidery aside, gets up, goes to the door leading to the hall, and calls.*) Helen! Bring in the Christmas tree! (*She goes to the table on the left and opens the drawer in it; then pauses again.*) No, but it's utterly impossible!

MAID (*enters with the tree*). Where shall I put it, madam?

NORA. There, in the middle of the room.

MAID. Will you be wanting anything else?

NORA. No, thank you, I have everything I need.

*The Maid puts down the tree and goes out.*

NORA (*busy decorating the tree*). Now—candles here—and flowers here. That loathsome man! Nonsense, nonsense, there's nothing to be frightened about. The Christmas tree must be beautiful. I'll do everything that you like, Torvald. I'll sing for you, dance for you—

*Helmer, with a bundle of papers under his arm, enters.*

NORA. Oh—are you back already?

HELMER. Yes. Has anyone been here?

NORA. Here? No.

HELMER. That's strange. I saw Krogstad come out of the front door.

NORA. Did you? Oh yes, that's quite right—Krogstad was here for a few minutes.

HELMER. Nora, I can tell from your face, he's been here and asked you to put in a good word for him.

NORA. Yes.

HELMER. And you were to pretend you were doing it of your own accord? You weren't going to tell me he'd been here? He asked you to do that too, didn't he?

NORA. Yes, Torvald. But—

HELMER. Nora, Nora! And you were ready to enter into such a conspiracy? Talking to a man like that, and making him promises—and then, on top of it all, to tell me an untruth!

NORA. An untruth?

HELMER. Didn't you say no one had been here? (*Wags his finger.*) My little songbird must never do that again. A songbird must have a clean beak to sing with; otherwise she'll start twittering out of tune. (*Puts his arm round her waist.*) Isn't that the way we want things? Yes, of course it is. (*Lets go of her.*) So let's hear no more about that. (*Sits down in front of the stove.*) Ah, how cozy and peaceful it is here. (*Glances for a few moments at his papers.*)

NORA (*busy with the tree; after a short silence*). Torvald.

HELMER. Yes.

NORA. I'm terribly looking forward to that fancy dress ball at the Stenborgs on Boxing Day.

HELMER. And I'm terribly curious to see what you're going to surprise me with.

NORA. Oh, it's so maddening.

HELMER. What is?

NORA. I can't think of anything to wear. It all seems so stupid and meaningless.

HELMER. So my little Nora's come to that conclusion, has she?

NORA (*behind his chair, resting her arms on its back*). Are you very busy, Torvald?

HELMER. Oh—

NORA. What are those papers?

HELMER. Just something to do with the bank.

NORA. Already?

HELMER. I persuaded the trustees to give me authority to make certain immediate changes in the staff and organization. I want to have everything straight by the New Year.

NORA. Then that's why this poor man Krogstad—

HELMER. Hm.

NORA (*still leaning over his chair, slowly strokes the back of his head*). If you hadn't been so busy, I was going to ask you an enormous favor, Torvald.

HELMER. Well, tell me. What was it to be?

NORA. You know I trust your taste more than anyone's. I'm so anxious to look really beautiful at the fancy dress ball. Torvald, couldn't you help me to decide what I shall go as, and what kind of costume I ought to wear?

HELMER. Aha! So little Miss Independent's in trouble and needs a man to rescue her, does she?

NORA. Yes, Torvald. I can't get anywhere without your help.

HELMER. Well, well, I'll give the matter thought. We'll find something.

NORA. Oh, how kind of you! (*Goes back to the tree. Pause.*) How pretty these red flowers look! But, tell me, is it so dreadful, this thing that Krogstad's done?

HELMER. He forged someone else's name. Have you any idea what that means?

NORA. Mightn't he have been forced to do it by some emergency?

HELMER. He probably just didn't think—that's what usually happens. I'm not so heartless as to condemn a man for an isolated action.

NORA. No, Torvald, of course not!

HELMER. Men often succeed in re-establishing themselves if they admit their crime and take their punishment.

NORA. Punishment?

HELMER. But Krogstad didn't do that. He chose to try and trick his way out of it; and that's what has morally destroyed him.

NORA. You think that would—?

HELMER. Just think how a man with that load on his conscience must always be lying and cheating and dissembling; how he must wear a mask even in the presence of those who are dearest to him, even his own wife and children! Yes, the children. That's the worst danger, Nora.

NORA. Why?

HELMER. Because an atmosphere of lies contaminates and poisons every corner of the home. Every breath that the children draw in such a house contains the germs of evil.

NORA (*comes closer behind him*). Do you really believe that?

HELMER. Oh, my dear, I've come across it so often in my work at the bar. Nearly all young criminals are the children of mothers who are constitutional liars.

NORA. Why do you say mothers?

HELMER. It's usually the mother; though of course the father can have the same influence. Every lawyer knows that only too well. And yet this fellow Krogstad has been sitting at home all these years poisoning his children with his lies and pretenses. That's why I say that, morally speaking, he is dead. (*Stretches out his hands towards her.*) So my pretty little Nora must promise me not to plead his case. Your hand on it. Come, come, what's this? Give me your hand. There. That's settled, now. I assure you it'd be quite impossible for me to work in the same building as him. I literally feel physically ill in the presence of a man like that.

NORA (*draws her hand from his and goes over to the other side of the Christmas tree*). How hot it is in here! And I've so much to do.

HELMER (*gets up and gathers his papers*). Yes, and I must try to get some of this read before dinner. I'll think about your costume too. And I may even have something up my sleeve to hang in gold paper on the Christmas tree. (*Lays his hand on her head.*) My precious little songbird!

*He goes into his study and closes the door.*

NORA (*softly, after a pause*). It's nonsense. It must be. It's impossible. It *must* be impossible!

NURSE (*in the doorway, left*). The children are asking if they can come in to Mummy.

NORA. No, no, no; don't let them in! You stay with them, Anne-Marie.

NURSE. Very good, madam. (*Closes the door.*)

NORA (*pale with fear*). Corrupt my little children—! Poison my home! (*Short pause. She throws back her head.*) It isn't true! It *couldn't* be true!

## *Act 2*

*The same room. In the corner by the piano the Christmas tree stands, stripped and disheveled, its candles burned to their sockets. Nora's outdoor clothes lie on the sofa. She is alone in the room, walking restlessly to and fro. At length she stops by the sofa and picks up her coat.*

NORA (*drops the coat again*). There's someone coming! (*Goes to the door and listens.*) No, it's no one. Of course—no one'll come today, it's Christmas Day. Nor tomorrow. But perhaps—! (*Opens the door and looks out.*) No. Nothing in the letter-box. Quite empty. (*Walks across the room.*) Silly, silly. Of course he won't do anything. It couldn't happen. It isn't possible. Why, I've three small children.

*The Nurse, carrying a large cardboard box, enters from the room on the left.*

NURSE. I found those fancy dress clothes at last, madam.

NORA. Thank you. Put them on the table.

NURSE (*does so*). They're all rumpled up.

NORA. Oh, I wish I could tear them into a million pieces!

NURSE. Why, madam! They'll be all right. Just a little patience.

NORA. Yes, of course. I'll go and get Mrs. Linde to help me.

NURSE. What, out again? In this dreadful weather? You'll catch a chill, madam.

NORA. Well, that wouldn't be the worst. How are the children?

NURSE. Playing with their Christmas presents, poor little dears. But—

NORA. Are they still asking to see me?

NURSE. They're so used to having their Mummy with them.

NORA. Yes, but, Anne-Marie, from now on I shan't be able to spend so much time with them.

NURSE. Well, children get used to anything in time.

NORA. Do you think so? Do you think they'd forget their mother if she went away from them—for ever?

NURSE. Mercy's sake, madam! For ever!

NORA. Tell me, Anne-Marie—I've so often wondered. How could you bear to give your child away—to strangers?

NURSE. But I had to when I came to nurse my little Miss Nora.

NORA. Do you mean you wanted to?

NURSE. When I had the chance of such a good job? A poor girl what's got into trouble can't afford to pick and choose. That good-for-nothing didn't lift a finger.

NORA. But your daughter must have completely forgotten you.

NURSE. Oh no, indeed she hasn't. She's written to me twice, once when she got confirmed and then again when she got married.

NORA (*hugs her*). Dear old Anne-Marie, you were a good mother to me.

NURSE. Poor little Miss Nora, you never had any mother but me.

NORA. And if my little ones had no one else, I know you would—no, silly, silly, silly! (*Opens the cardboard box.*) Go back to them, Anne-Marie. Now I must—Tomorrow you'll see how pretty I shall look.

NURSE. Why, there'll be no one at the ball as beautiful as my Miss Nora.

*She goes into the room, left.*

NORA (*begins to unpack the clothes from the box, but soon throws them down again*). Oh, if only I dared to go out! If I could be sure no one would come, and nothing would happen while I was away! Stupid, stupid! No one will come. I just mustn't think about it. Brush this muff. Pretty gloves, pretty gloves! Don't think about it, don't think about it! One, two, three, four, five, six—(*Cries.*) Ah—they're coming—!

*She begins to run toward the door, but stops uncertainly. Mrs. Linde enters from the hall, where she has been taking off her outdoor clothes.*

NORA. Oh, it's you, Christine. There's no one else out there, is there? Oh, I'm so glad you've come.

MRS. LINDE. I hear you were at my room asking for me.

NORA. Yes, I just happened to be passing. I want to ask you to help me with something. Let's sit down here on the sofa. Look at this. There's going to be a fancy dress ball tomorrow night upstairs at Consul Stenborg's, and Torvald wants me to go as a Neapolitan fisher-girl and dance the tarantella. I learned it on Capri.

MRS. LINDE. I say, are you going to give a performance?

NORA. Yes, Torvald says I should. Look, here's the dress. Torvald had it made for me in Italy; but now it's all so torn, I don't know—

MRS. LINDE. Oh, we'll soon put that right; the stitching's just come away. Needle and thread? Ah, here we are.

NORA. You're being awfully sweet.

MRS. LINDE (*sews*). So you're going to dress up tomorrow, Nora? I must pop over for a moment to see how you look. Oh, but I've completely forgotten to thank you for that nice evening yesterday.

NORA (*gets up and walks across the room*). Oh, I didn't think it was as nice as usual. You ought to have come to town a little earlier, Christine. . . . Yes, Torvald understands how to make a home look attractive.

MRS. LINDE. I'm sure you do, too. You're not your father's daughter for nothing. But, tell me. Is Dr. Rank always in such low spirits as he was yesterday?

NORA. No, last night it was very noticeable. But he's got a terrible disease; he's got spinal tuberculosis, poor man. His father was a frightful creature who kept mistresses and so on. As a result Dr. Rank has been sickly ever since he was a child—you understand—

MRS. LINDE (*puts down her sewing*). But, my dear Nora, how on earth did you get to know about such things?

NORA (*walks about the room*). Oh, don't be silly, Christine—when one has three children, one comes into contact with women who—well, who know about medical matters, and they tell one a thing or two.

MRS. LINDE (*sews again; a short silence*). Does Dr. Rank visit you every day?

NORA. Yes, every day. He's Torvald's oldest friend, and a good friend to me too. Dr. Rank's almost one of the family.

MRS. LINDE. But, tell me—is he quite sincere? I mean, doesn't he rather say the sort of thing he thinks people want to hear?

NORA. No, quite the contrary. What gave you that idea?

MRS. LINDE. When you introduced me to him yesterday, he said he'd often heard my name mentioned here. But later I noticed your husband had no idea who I was. So how could Dr. Rank—?

NORA. Yes, that's quite right, Christine. You see, Torvald's so hopelessly in love with me that he wants to have me all to himself—those were his very words. When we were first married, he got quite jealous if I as much as mentioned any of my old friends back home. So naturally, I stopped talking about them. But I often chat with Dr. Rank about that kind of thing. He enjoys it, you see.

MRS. LINDE. Now listen, Nora. In many ways you're still a child; I'm a bit older than you and have a little more experience of the world. There's something I want to say to you. You ought to give up this business with Dr. Rank.

NORA. What business?

MRS. LINDE. Well, everything. Last night you were speaking about this rich admirer of yours who was going to give you money—

NORA. Yes, and who doesn't exist—unfortunately. But what's that got to do with—?

MRS. LINDE. Is Dr. Rank rich?

NORA. Yes.

MRS. LINDE. And he has no dependents?

NORA. No, no one. But—

MRS. LINDE. And he comes here to see you every day?

NORA. Yes, I've told you.

MRS. LINDE. But how dare a man of his education be so forward?

NORA. What on earth are you talking about?

MRS. LINDE. Oh, stop pretending, Nora. Do you think I haven't guessed who it was who lent you that two hundred pounds?

NORA. Are you out of your mind? How could you imagine such a thing? A friend, someone who comes here every day! Why, that'd be an impossible situation!

MRS. LINDE. Then it really wasn't him?

NORA. No, of course not. I've never for a moment dreamed of—anyway, he hadn't any money to lend then. He didn't come into that till later.

MRS. LINDE. Well, I think that was a lucky thing for you, Nora dear.

NORA. No, I could never have dreamed of asking Dr. Rank—Though I'm sure that if I ever did ask him—

MRS. LINDE. But of course you won't.

NORA. Of course not. I can't imagine that it should ever become necessary. But I'm perfectly sure that if I did speak to Dr. Rank—

MRS. LINDE. Behind your husband's back?

NORA. I've got to get out of this other business; and *that's* been going on behind his back. I've *got* to get out of it.

MRS. LINDE. Yes, well, that's what I told you yesterday. But—

NORA (*walking up and down*). It's much easier for a man to arrange these things than a woman—

MRS. LINDE. One's own husband, yes.

NORA. Oh, bosh. (*Stops walking.*) When you've completely repaid a debt, you get your I.O.U. back, don't you?

MRS. LINDE. Yes, of course.

NORA. And you can tear it into a thousand pieces and burn the filthy, beastly thing!

MRS. LINDE (*looks hard at her, puts down her sewing, and gets up slowly*). Nora, you're hiding something from me.

NORA. Can you see that?

MRS. LINDE. Something has happened since yesterday morning. Nora, what is it?

NORA (*goes toward her*). Christine! (*Listens.*) Ssh! There's Torvald. Would you mind going into the nursery for a few minutes? Torvald can't bear to see sewing around. Anne-Marie'll help you.

MRS. LINDE (*gathers some of her things together*). Very well. But I shan't leave this house until we've talked this matter out.

*She goes into the nursery, left. As she does so, Helmer enters from the hall.*

NORA (*runs to meet him*). Oh, Torvald dear, I've been so longing for you to come back!

HELMER. Was that the dressmaker?

NORA. No, it was Christine. She's helping me mend my costume. I'm going to look rather splendid in that.

HELMER. Yes, that was quite a bright idea of mine, wasn't it?

NORA. Wonderful! But wasn't it nice of me to give in to you?

HELMER (*takes her chin in his hand*). Nice—to give in to your husband? All right, little silly, I know you didn't mean it like that. But I won't disturb you. I expect you'll be wanting to try it on.

NORA. Are you going to work now?

HELMER. Yes. (*Shows her a bundle of papers.*) Look at these. I've been down to the bank—(*Turns to go into his study.*)

NORA. Torvald.

HELMER (*stops*). Yes.

NORA. If little squirrel asked you really prettily to grant her a wish—

HELMER. Well?

NORA. Would you grant it to her?

HELMER. First I should naturally have to know what it was.

NORA. Squirrel would do lots of pretty tricks for you if you granted her wish.

HELMER. Out with it, then.

NORA. Your little skylark would sing in every room—

HELMER. My little skylark does that already.

NORA. I'd turn myself into a little fairy and dance for you in the moonlight, Torvald.

HELMER. Nora, it isn't that business you were talking about this morning?

NORA (*comes closer*). Yes, Torvald—oh, please! I beg of you!

HELMER. Have you really the nerve to bring that up again?

NORA. Yes, Torvald, yes, you must do as I ask! You must let Krogstad keep his place at the bank!

HELMER. My dear Nora, his is the job I'm giving to Mrs. Linde.

NORA. Yes, that's terribly sweet of you. But you can get rid of one of the other clerks instead of Krogstad.

HELMER. Really, you're being incredibly obstinate. Just because you thoughtlessly promised to put in a word for him, you expect me to—

NORA. No, it isn't that, Helmer. It's for your own sake. That man writes for the most beastly newspapers—you said so yourself. He could do you tremendous harm. I'm so dreadfully frightened of him—

HELMER. Oh, I understand. Memories of the past. That's what's frightening you.

NORA. What do you mean?

HELMER. You're thinking of your father, aren't you?

NORA. Yes, yes. Of course. Just think what those dreadful men wrote in the papers about Papa! The most frightful slanders. I really believe it would have lost him his job if the Ministry hadn't sent you down to investigate, and you hadn't been so kind and helpful to him.

HELMER. But my dear little Nora, there's a considerable difference between your father and me. Your father was not a man of unassailable reputation. But I am; and I hope to remain so all my life.

NORA. But no one knows what spiteful people may not dig up. We could be so peaceful and happy now, Torvald—we could be free from every worry—you and I and the children. Oh, please, Torvald, please—!

HELMER. The very fact of your pleading his cause makes it impossible for me to keep him. Everyone at the bank already knows that I intend to dismiss Krogstad. If the rumor got about that the new manager had allowed his wife to persuade him to change his mind—

NORA. Well, what then?

HELMER. Oh, nothing, nothing. As long as my little Miss Obstinate gets her way—Do you expect me to make a laughing-stock of myself before my entire staff—give people the idea that I am open to outside influence? Believe me, I'd soon feel the consequences! Besides—there's something else that makes it impossible for Krogstad to remain in the bank while I am its manager.

NORA. What is that?

HELMER. I might conceivably have allowed myself to ignore his moral obloquies—

NORA. Yes, Torvald, surely?

HELMER. And I hear he's quite efficient at his job. But we—well, we were school friends. It was one of those friendships that one enters into over hastily and so often comes to regret later in life. I might as well confess the truth. We—well, we're on Christian name terms. And the tactless idiot makes no attempt to conceal it when other people are present. On the contrary, he thinks it gives him the right to be familiar with me. He shows off the whole time, with "Torvald this," and "Torvald that." I can tell you, I find it damned annoying. If he stayed, he'd make my position intolerable.

NORA. Torvald, you can't mean this seriously.

HELMER. Oh? And why not?

NORA. But it's so petty.

HELMER. What did you say? Petty? You think *I* am petty?

NORA. No, Torvald dear, of course you're not. That's just why—

HELMER. Don't quibble! You call my motives petty. Then I must be petty too. Petty! I see. Well, I've had enough of this. (*Goes to the door and calls into the hall.*) Helen!

NORA. What are you going to do?

HELMER (*searching among his papers*). I'm going to settle this matter once and for all. (*The Maid enters.*) Take this letter downstairs at once. Find a messenger and see that he delivers it. Immediately! The address is on the envelope. Here's the money.

MAID. Very good, sir. (*Goes out with the letter.*)

HELMER (*putting his papers in order*). There now, little Miss Obstinate.

NORA (*tensely*). Torvald—what was in that letter?

HELMER. Krogstad's dismissal.

NORA. Call her back, Torvald! There's still time. Oh, Torvald, call her back! Do it for my sake—for your own sake—for the children! Do you hear me, Torvald? Please do it! You don't realize what this may do to us all!

HELMER. Too late.

NORA. Yes. Too late.

HELMER. My dear Nora, I forgive you this anxiety. Though it is a bit of an insult to me. Oh, but it is! Isn't it an insult to imply that I should be frightened by the vindictiveness of a depraved hack journalist? But I forgive you, because it so charmingly testifies to the love you bear me. (*Takes her in his arms.*) Which is as it should be, my own dearest Nora. Let what will happen, happen. When the real crisis comes, you will not find me lacking in strength or courage. I am man enough to bear the burden for us both.

NORA (*fearfully*). What do you mean?

HELMER. The whole burden, I say—

NORA (*calmly*). I shall never let you do that.

HELMER. Very well. We shall share it, Nora—as man and wife. And that is as it should be. (*Caresses her.*) Are you happy now? There, there, there; don't look at me with those frightened little eyes. You're simply imagining things. You go ahead now and do your tarantella, and get some practice on that tambourine. I'll sit in my study and close the door. Then I won't hear anything, and you can make all the noise you want. (*Turns in the doorway.*) When Dr. Rank comes, tell him where to find me. (*He nods to her, goes into his room with his papers, and closes the door.*)

NORA (*desperate with anxiety, stands as though transfixed, and whispers*). He said he'd do it. He will do it. He will do it, and nothing'll stop him. No, never that. I'd rather anything. There must be some escape—Some way out—! (*The bell rings in the hall.*) Dr. Rank—! Anything but that! Anything, I don't care—!

*She passes her hand across her face, composes herself, walks across, and opens the door to the hall. Dr. Rank is standing there, hanging up his fur coat. During the following scene, it begins to grow dark.*

NORA. Good evening, Dr. Rank. I recognized your ring. But you mustn't go to Torvald yet. I think he's busy.

RANK. And—you?

NORA (*as he enters the room and she closes the door behind him*). Oh, you know very well I've always time to talk to you.

RANK. Thank you. I shall avail myself of that privilege as long as I can.

NORA. What do you mean by that? As long as you *can?*

RANK. Yes. Does that frighten you?

NORA. Well, it's rather a curious expression. Is something going to happen?

RANK. Something I've been expecting to happen for a long time. But I didn't think it would happen quite so soon.

NORA (*seizes his arm*). What is it? Dr. Rank, you must tell me!

RANK (*sits down by the stove*). I'm on the way out. And there's nothing to be done about it.

NORA (*sighs with relief*). Oh, it's you—?

RANK. Who else? No, it's no good lying to oneself. I am the most wretched of all my patients, Mrs. Helmer. These last few days I've been going through the books of this poor body of mine, and I find I am bankrupt. Within a month I may be rotting up there in the churchyard.

NORA. Ugh, what a nasty way to talk!

RANK. The facts aren't exactly nice. But the worst is that there's so much else that's nasty to come first. I've only one more test to make. When that's done I'll have a pretty accurate idea of when the final disintegration is likely to begin. I want to ask you a favour. Helmer's a sensitive chap, and I know how he hates anything ugly. I don't want him to visit me when I'm in hospital—

NORA. Oh but, Dr. Rank—

RANK. I don't want him there. On any pretext. I shan't have him allowed in. As soon as I know the worst, I'll send you my visiting card with a black cross on it, and then you'll know that the final filthy process has begun.

NORA. Really, you're being quite impossible this evening. And I did hope you'd be in a good mood.

RANK. With death on my hands? And all this to atone for someone else's sin? Is there justice in that? And in every single family, in one way or another, the same merciless law of retribution is at work—

NORA (*holds her hands to her ears*). Nonsense! Cheer up! Laugh!

RANK. Yes, you're right. Laughter's all the damned thing's fit for. My poor innocent spine must pay for the fun my father had as a gay young lieutenant.

NORA (*at the table, left*). You mean he was too fond of asparagus and *foie gras?*

RANK. Yes, and truffles too.

NORA. Yes, of course, truffles, yes. And oysters too, I suppose?

RANK. Yes, oysters, oysters. Of course.

NORA. And all that port and champagne to wash them down. It's too sad that all those lovely things should affect one's spine.

RANK. Especially a poor spine that never got any pleasure out of them.

NORA. Oh yes, that's the saddest thing of all.

RANK (*looks searchingly at her*). Hm—

NORA (*after a moment*). Why did you smile?

RANK. No, it was you who laughed.

NORA. No, it was you who smiled, Dr. Rank!

RANK (*gets up*). You're a worse little rogue than I thought.

NORA. Oh, I'm full of stupid tricks today.

RANK. So it seems.

NORA (*puts both her hands on his shoulders*). Dear, dear Dr. Rank, you mustn't die and leave Torvald and me.

RANK. Oh, you'll soon get over it. Once one is gone, one is soon forgotten.

NORA (*looks at him anxiously*). Do you believe that?

RANK. One finds replacements, and then—

NORA. Who will find a replacement?

RANK. You and Helmer both will, when I am gone. You seem to have made a start already, haven't you? What was this Mrs. Linde doing here yesterday evening?

NORA. Aha! But surely you can't be jealous of poor Christine?

RANK. Indeed I am. She will be my successor in this house. When I have moved on, this lady will—

NORA. Ssh—don't speak so loud! She's in there!

RANK. Today again? You see!

NORA. She's only come to mend my dress. Good heavens, how unreasonable you are! (*Sits on the sofa.*) Be nice now, Dr. Rank. Tomorrow you'll see how beautifully I shall dance; and you must imagine that I'm doing it just for you. And for Torvald of course; obviously. (*Takes some things out of the box.*) Dr. Rank, sit down here and I'll show you something.

RANK (*sits*). What's this?

NORA. Look here! Look!

RANK. Silk stockings!

NORA. Flesh-colored. Aren't they beautiful? It's very dark in here now, of course, but tomorrow—No, no, no; only the soles. Oh well, I suppose you can look a bit higher if you want to.

RANK. Hm—

NORA. Why are you looking so critical? Don't you think they'll fit me?

RANK. I can't really give you a qualified opinion on that.

NORA (*looks at him for a moment*). Shame on you! (*Flicks him on the ear with the stockings.*) Take that. (*Puts them back in the box.*)

RANK. What other wonders are to be revealed to me?

NORA. I shan't show you anything else. You're being naughty.

*She hums a little and looks among the things in the box.*

RANK (*after a short silence*). When I sit here like this being so intimate with you, I can't think—I cannot imagine what would have become of me if I had never entered this house.

NORA (*smiles*). Yes, I think you enjoy being with us, don't you?

RANK (*more quietly, looking into the middle distance*). And now to have to leave it all—

NORA. Nonsense. You're not leaving us.

RANK (*as before*). And not to be able to leave even the most wretched token of gratitude behind; hardly even a passing sense of loss; only an empty place, to be filled by the next comer.

NORA. Suppose I were to ask you to—? No—

RANK. To do what?

NORA. To give me proof of your friendship—

RANK. Yes, yes?

NORA. No, I mean—to do me a very great service—

RANK. Would you really for once grant me that happiness?

NORA. But you've no idea what it is.

RANK. Very well, tell me, then.

NORA. No, but, Dr. Rank, I can't. It's far too much—I want your help and advice, and I want you to do something for me.

RANK. The more the better. I've no idea what it can be. But tell me. You do trust me, don't you?

NORA. Oh, yes, more than anyone. You're my best and truest friend. Otherwise I couldn't tell you. Well then, Dr. Rank—there's something you must help me to prevent. You know how much Torvald loves me—he'd never hesitate for an instant to lay down his life for me—

RANK (*leans over towards her*). Nora—do you think he is the only one—?

NORA (*with a slight start*). What do you mean?

RANK. Who would gladly lay down his life for you?

NORA (*sadly*). Oh, I see.

RANK. I swore to myself I would let you know that before I go. I shall never have a better opportunity. . . . Well, Nora, now you know that. And now you also know that you can trust me as you can trust nobody else.

NORA (*rises; calmly and quietly*). Let me pass, please.

RANK (*makes room for her but remains seated*). Nora—

NORA (*in the doorway to the hall*). Helen, bring the lamp. (*Goes over to the stove.*) Oh, dear Dr. Rank, this was really horrid of you.

RANK (*gets up*). That I have loved you as deeply as anyone else has? Was that horrid of me?

NORA. No—but that you should go and tell me. That was quite unnecessary—

RANK. What do you mean? Did you know, then—?

*The Maid enters with the lamp, puts it on the table, and goes out.*

RANK. Nora—Mrs. Helmer—I am asking you, did you know this?

NORA. Oh, what do I know, what did I know, what didn't I know—I really can't say. How could you be so stupid, Dr. Rank? Everything was so nice.

RANK. Well, at any rate now you know that I am ready to serve you, body and soul. So—please continue.

NORA (*looks at him*). After this?

RANK. Please tell me what it is.

NORA. I can't possibly tell you now.

RANK. Yes, yes! You mustn't punish me like this. Let me be allowed to do what I can for you.

NORA. You can't do anything for me now. Anyway; I don't need any help. It was only my imagination—you'll see. Yes, really. Honestly. (*Sits in the rocking-chair, looks at him, and smiles.*) Well, upon my word you *are* a fine gentleman, Dr. Rank. Aren't you ashamed of yourself, now that the lamp's been lit?

RANK. Frankly, no. But perhaps I ought to say—*adieu?*

NORA. Of course not. You will naturally continue to visit us as before. You know quite well how Torvald depends on your company.

RANK. Yes, but you?

NORA. Oh, I always think it's enormous fun having you here.

RANK. That was what misled me. You're a riddle to me, you know. I'd often felt you'd just as soon be with me as with Helmer.

NORA. Well, you see, there are some people whom one loves, and others whom it's almost more fun to be with.

RANK. Oh yes, there's some truth in that.

NORA. When I was at home, of course I loved Papa best. But I always used to think it was terribly amusing to go down and talk to the servants; because they never told me what I ought to do; and they were such fun to listen to.

RANK. I see. So I've taken their place?

NORA (*jumps up and runs over to him*). Oh, dear, sweet Dr. Rank, I didn't mean that at all. But I'm sure you understand—I feel the same about Torvald as I did about Papa.

MAID (*enters from the hall*). Excuse me, madam. (*Whispers to her and hands her a visiting card.*)

NORA (*glances at the card*). Oh! (*Puts it quickly in her pocket.*)

RANK. Anything wrong?

NORA. No, no, nothing at all. It's just something that—it's my new dress.

RANK. What? But your costume is lying over there.

NORA. Oh—that, yes—but there's another—I ordered it specially—Torvald mustn't know—

RANK. Ah, so that's your big secret?

NORA. Yes, yes. Go in and talk to him—he's in his study—keep him talking for a bit—

RANK. Don't worry. He won't get away from me. (*Goes into Helmer's study.*)

NORA (*to the Maid*). Is he waiting in the kitchen?

MAID. Yes, madam, he came up the back way—

NORA. But didn't you tell him I had a visitor?

MAID. Yes, but he wouldn't go.

NORA. Wouldn't go?

MAID. No, madam, not until he'd spoken with you.

NORA. Very well, show him in; but quietly. Helen, you mustn't tell anyone about this. It's a surprise for my husband.

MAID. Very good, madam. I understand. (*Goes.*)

NORA. It's happening. It's happening after all. No, no, no, it can't happen, it mustn't happen.

*She walks across and bolts the door of Helmer's study. The Maid opens the door from the hall to admit Krogstad, and closes it behind him. He is wearing an overcoat, heavy boots, and a fur cap.*

NORA (*goes towards him*). Speak quietly. My husband's at home.

KROGSTAD. Let him hear.

NORA. What do you want from me?

KROGSTAD. Information.

NORA. Hurry up, then. What is it?

KROGSTAD. I suppose you know I've been given the sack.

NORA. I couldn't stop it, Mr. Krogstad. I did my best for you, but it didn't help.

KROGSTAD. Does your husband love you so little? He knows what I can do to you, and yet he dares to—

NORA. Surely you don't imagine I told him?

KROGSTAD. No. I didn't really think you had. It wouldn't have been like my old friend Torvald Helmer to show that much courage—

NORA. Mr. Krogstad, I'll trouble you to speak respectfully of my husband.

KROGSTAD. Don't worry, I'll show him all the respect he deserves. But since you're so anxious to keep this matter hushed up, I presume you're better informed than you were yesterday of the gravity of what you've done?

NORA. I've learned more than you could ever teach me.

KROGSTAD. Yes, a bad lawyer like me—

NORA. What do you want from me?

KROGSTAD. I just wanted to see how things were with you, Mrs. Helmer. I've been thinking about you all day. Even duns and hack journalists have hearts, you know.

NORA. Show some heart, then. Think of my little children.

KROGSTAD. Have you and your husband thought of mine? Well, let's forget that. I just wanted to tell you, you don't need to take this business too seriously. I'm not going to take any action, for the present.

NORA. Oh, no—you won't, will you? I knew it.

KROGSTAD. It can all be settled quite amicably. There's no need for it to become public. We'll keep it among the three of us.

NORA. My husband must never know about this.

KROGSTAD. How can you stop him? Can you pay the balance of what you owe me?

NORA. Not immediately.

KROGSTAD. Have you any means of raising the money during the next few days?

NORA. None that I would care to use.

KROGSTAD. Well, it wouldn't have helped anyway. However much money you offered me now I wouldn't give you back that paper.

NORA. What are you going to do with it?

KROGSTAD. Just keep it. No one else need ever hear about it. So in case you were thinking of doing anything desperate—

NORA. I am.

KROGSTAD. Such as running away—

NORA. I am.

KROGSTAD. Or anything more desperate—

NORA. How did you know?

KROGSTAD. —just give up the idea.

NORA. How did you know?

KROGSTAD. Most of us think of that at first. I did. But I hadn't the courage—

NORA (*dully*). Neither have I.

KROGSTAD (*relieved*). It's true, isn't it? You haven't the courage either?

NORA. No. I haven't. I haven't.

KROGSTAD. It'd be a stupid thing to do anyway. Once the first little domestic explosion is over. . . . I've got a letter in my pocket here addressed to your husband—

NORA. Telling him everything?

KROGSTAD. As delicately as possible.

NORA (*quickly*). He must never see that letter. Tear it up. I'll find the money somehow—

KROGSTAD. I'm sorry, Mrs. Helmer, I thought I'd explained—

NORA. Oh, I don't mean the money I owe you. Let me know how much you want from my husband, and I'll find it for you.

KROGSTAD. I'm not asking your husband for money.

NORA. What do you want, then?

KROGSTAD. I'll tell you. I want to get on my feet again, Mrs. Helmer. I want to get to the top. And your husband's going to help me. For eighteen months now my record's been clean. I've been in hard straits all that time; I was content to fight my way back inch by inch. Now I've been chucked back into the mud, and I'm not going to be satisfied with just getting back my job. I'm going to get to the top, I tell you. I'm going to get back into the bank, and it's going to be higher up. Your husband's going to create a new job for me—

NORA. He'll never do that!

KROGSTAD. Oh, yes he will. I know him. He won't dare to risk a scandal. And once I'm in there with him, you'll see! Within a year I'll be his right-hand man. It'll be Nils Krogstad who'll be running that bank, not Torvald Helmer!

NORA. That will never happen.

KROGSTAD. Are you thinking of—?

NORA. Now I *have* the courage.

KROGSTAD. Oh, you can't frighten me. A pampered little pretty like you—

NORA. You'll see! You'll see!

KROGSTAD. Under the ice? Down in the cold, black water? And then, in the spring, to float up again, ugly, unrecognizable, hairless—?

NORA. You can't frighten me.

KROGSTAD. And you can't frighten me. People don't do such things, Mrs. Helmer. And anyway, what'd be the use? I've got him in my pocket.

NORA. But afterwards? When I'm no longer—?

KROGSTAD. Have you forgotten that then your reputation will be in my hands? (*She looks at him speechlessly.*) Well, I've warned you. Don't do anything silly. When Helmer's read my letter, he'll get in touch with me. And remember, it's your husband who's forced me to act like this. And for that I'll never forgive him. Goodbye, Mrs. Helmer. (*He goes out through the hall.*)

NORA (*runs to the hall door, opens it a few inches, and listens*). He's going. He's not going to give him the letter. Oh, no, no, it couldn't possibly happen. (*Opens the door a little wider.*) What's he doing? Standing outside the front door. He's not going downstairs. Is he changing his mind? Yes, he—!

*A letter falls into the letter-box. Krogstad's footsteps die away down the stairs.*

NORA (*with a stifled cry runs across the room towards the table by the sofa. A pause*). In the letter-box. (*Steals timidly over towards the hall door.*) There it is! Oh, Torvald, Torvald! Now we're lost!

MRS. LINDE (*enters from the nursery with Nora's costume*). Well, I've done the best I can. Shall we see how it looks—?

NORA (*whispers hoarsely*). Christine, come here.

MRS. LINDE (*throws the dress on the sofa*). What's wrong with you? You look as though you'd seen a ghost!

NORA. Come here. Do you see that letter? There—look—through the glass of the letter-box.

MRS. LINDE. Yes, yes, I see it.

NORA. That letter's from Krogstad—

MRS. LINDE. Nora! It was Krogstad who lent you the money!

NORA. Yes. And now Torvald's going to discover everything.

MRS. LINDE. Oh, believe me, Nora, it'll be best for you both.

NORA. You don't know what's happened. I've committed a forgery—

MRS. LINDE. But, for heaven's sake—!

NORA. Christine, all I want is for you to be my witness.

MRS. LINDE. What do you mean? Witness what?

NORA. If I should go out of my mind—and it might easily happen—

MRS. LINDE. Nora!

NORA. Or if anything else should happen to me—so that I wasn't here any longer—

MRS. LINDE. Nora, Nora, you don't know what you're saying!

NORA. If anyone should try to take the blame, and say it was all his fault—you understand—?

MRS. LINDE. Yes, yes—but how can you think?

NORA. Then you must testify that it isn't true, Christine. I'm not mad—I know exactly what I'm saying—and I'm telling you, no one else knows anything about this. I did it entirely on my own. Remember that.

MRS. LINDE. All right. But I simply don't understand—

NORA. Oh, how could you understand? A—miracle—is about to happen.

MRS. LINDE. Miracle?

NORA. Yes. A miracle. But it's so frightening. Christine. It *mustn't* happen, not for anything in the world.

MRS. LINDE. I'll go over and talk to Krogstad.

NORA. Don't go near him. He'll only do something to hurt you.

MRS. LINDE. Once upon a time he'd have done anything for my sake.

NORA. He?

MRS. LINDE. Where does he live?

NORA. Oh, how should I know—? Oh, yes, wait a moment—! (*Feels in her pocket.*) Here's his card. But the letter, the letter—!

HELMER (*from his study, knocks on the door*). Nora!

NORA (*cries in alarm*). What is it?

HELMER. Now, now, don't get alarmed. We're not coming in; you've closed the door. Are you trying on your costume?

NORA. Yes, yes—I'm trying on my costume. I'm going to look so pretty for you, Torvald.

MRS. LINDE (*who has been reading the card*). Why, he lives just around the corner.

NORA. Yes; but it's no use. There's nothing to be done now. The letter's lying there in the box.

MRS. LINDE. And your husband has the key?

NORA. Yes, he always keeps it.

MRS. LINDE. Krogstad must ask him to send the letter back unread. He must find some excuse—

NORA. But Torvald always opens the box at just about this time—

MRS. LINDE. You must stop him. Go in and keep him talking. I'll be back as quickly as I can.

*She hurries out through the hall.*

NORA (*goes over to Helmer's door, opens it and peeps in*). Torvald!

HELMER (*offstage*). Well, may a man enter his own drawing-room again? Come on, Rank, now we'll see what—(*In the doorway.*) But what's this?

NORA. What, Torvald dear?

HELMER. Rank's been preparing me for some great transformation scene.

RANK (*in the doorway*). So I understood. But I seem to have been mistaken.

NORA. Yes, no one's to be allowed to see me before tomorrow night.

HELMER. But, my dear Nora, you look quite worn out. Have you been practicing too hard?

NORA. No, I haven't practiced at all yet.

HELMER. Well, you must.

NORA. Yes, Torvald, I must, I know. But I can't get anywhere without your help. I've completely forgotten everything.

HELMER. Oh, we'll soon put that to rights.

NORA. Yes, help me, Torvald. Promise me you will? Oh, I'm so nervous. All those people—! You must forget everything except me this evening. You mustn't think of business—I won't even let you touch a pen. Promise me, Torvald?

HELMER. I promise. This evening I shall think of nothing but you—my poor, helpless little darling. Oh, there's just one thing I must see to—(*Goes towards the hall door.*)

NORA. What do you want out there?

HELMER. I'm only going to see if any letters have come.

NORA. No, Torvald, no!

HELMER. Why, what's the matter?

NORA. Torvald, I beg you. There's nothing there.

HELMER. Well, I'll just make sure.

*He moves towards the door. Nora runs to the piano and plays the first bars of the tarantella.*

HELMER (*at the door, turns*). Aha!

NORA. I can't dance tomorrow if I don't practice with you now.

HELMER (*goes over to her*). Are you really so frightened, Nora dear?

NORA. Yes, terribly frightened. Let me start practicing now, at once—we've still time before dinner. Oh, do sit down and play for me, Torvald dear. Correct me, lead me, the way you always do.

HELMER. Very well, my dear, if you wish it.

*He sits down at the piano. Nora seizes the tambourine and a long multi-colored shawl from the cardboard box, wraps the latter hastily around her, then takes a quick leap into the center of the room.*

NORA. Play for me! I want to dance!

*Helmer plays and Nora dances. Dr. Rank stands behind Helmer at the piano and watches her.*

HELMER (*as he plays*). Slower, slower!

NORA. I can't!

HELMER. Not so violently, Nora.

NORA. I must!

HELMER (*stops playing*). No, no, this won't do at all.

NORA (*laughs and swings her tambourine*). Isn't that what I told you?

RANK. Let me play for her.

HELMER (*gets up*). Yes, would you? Then it'll be easier for me to show her.

*Rank sits down at the piano and plays. Nora dances more and more wildly. Helmer has stationed himself by the stove and tries repeatedly to correct her, but she seems not to hear him. Her hair works loose and falls over her shoulders; she ignores it and continues to dance. Mrs. Linde enters.*

MRS. LINDE (*stands in the doorway as though tongue-tied*). Ah—!

NORA (*as she dances*). Oh, Christine, we're having such fun!

HELMER. But, Nora darling, you're dancing as if your life depended on it.

NORA. It does.

HELMER. Rank, stop it! This is sheer lunacy. Stop it, I say!

*Rank ceases playing. Nora suddenly stops dancing.*

HELMER (*goes over to her*). I'd never have believed it. You've forgotten everything I taught you.

NORA (*throws away the tambourine*). You see!

HELMER. I'll have to show you every step.

NORA. You see how much I need you! You must show me every step of the way. Right to the end of the dance. Promise me you will, Torvald?

HELMER. Never fear. I will.

NORA. You mustn't think about anything but me—today or tomorrow. Don't open any letters—don't even open the letter-box—

HELMER. Aha, you're still worried about that fellow—

NORA. Oh, yes, yes, him too.

HELMER. Nora, I can tell from the way you're behaving, there's a letter from him already lying there.

NORA. I don't know. I think so. But you mustn't read it now. I don't want anything ugly to come between us till it's all over.

RANK (*quietly, to Helmer*). Better give her her way.

HELMER (*puts his arm round her*). My child shall have her way. But tomorrow night, when your dance is over—

NORA. Then you will be free.

MAID (*appears in the doorway, right*). Dinner is served, madam.

NORA. Put out some champagne, Helen.

MAID. Very good, madam. (*Goes.*)

HELMER. I say! What's this, a banquet?

NORA. We'll drink champagne until dawn! (*Calls.*) And, Helen! Put out some macaroons! Lots of macaroons—for once!

HELMER (*takes her hands in his*). Now, now, now. Don't get so excited. Where's my little songbird, the one I know?

NORA. All right. Go and sit down—and you too, Dr. Rank. I'll be with you in a minute. Christine, you must help me put my hair up.

RANK (*quietly, as they go*). There's nothing wrong, is there? I mean, she isn't—er—expecting—?

HELMER. Good heavens no, my dear chap. She just gets scared like a child sometimes—I told you before—

*They go out right.*

NORA. Well?

MRS. LINDE. He's left town.

NORA. I saw it from your face.

MRS. LINDE. He'll be back tomorrow evening. I left a note for him.

NORA. You needn't have bothered. You can't stop anything now. Anyway, it's wonderful really, in a way—sitting here and waiting for the miracle to happen.

MRS. LINDE. Waiting for what?

NORA. Oh, you wouldn't understand. Go in and join them. I'll be with you in a moment.

*Mrs. Linde goes into the dining-room.*

NORA (*stands for a moment as though collecting herself. Then she looks at her watch*). Five o'clock. Seven hours till midnight. Then another twenty-four hours till midnight tomorrow. And then the tarantella will be finished. Twenty-four and seven? Thirty-one hours to live.

HELMER (*appears in the doorway, right*). What's happened to my little songbird?

NORA (*runs to him with her arms wide*). Your songbird is here!

## Act 3

*The same room. The table which was formerly by the sofa has been moved into the center of the room; the chairs surround it as before.*

*The door to the hall stands open. Dance music can be heard from the floor above. Mrs. Linde is seated at the table, absent-mindedly glancing through a book. She is trying to read, but seems unable to keep her mind on it. More than once she turns and listens anxiously towards the front door.*

MRS. LINDE (*looks at her watch*). Not here yet. There's not much time left. Please God he hasn't—! (*Listens again.*) Ah, here he is. (*Goes out into the hall and cautiously opens the front door. Footsteps can be heard softly ascending the stairs. She whispers.*) Come in. There's no one here.

KROGSTAD (*in the doorway*). I found a note from you at my lodgings. What does this mean?

MRS. LINDE. I must speak with you.

KROGSTAD. Oh? And must our conversation take place in this house?

MRS. LINDE. We couldn't meet at my place; my room has no separate entrance. Come in. We're quite alone. The maid's asleep, and the Helmers are at the dance upstairs.

KROGSTAD (*comes into the room*). Well, well! So the Helmers are dancing this evening? Are they indeed?

MRS. LINDE. Yes, why not?

KROGSTAD. True enough. Why not?

MRS. LINDE. Well, Krogstad. You and I must have a talk together.

KROGSTAD. Have we two anything further to discuss?

MRS. LINDE. We have a great deal to discuss.

KROGSTAD. I wasn't aware of it.

MRS. LINDE. That's because you've never really understood me.

KROGSTAD. Was there anything to understand? It's the old story, isn't it—a woman chucking a man because something better turns up?

MRS. LINDE. Do you really think I'm so utterly heartless? You think it was easy for me to give you up?

KROGSTAD. Wasn't it?

MRS. LINDE. Oh, Nils, did you really believe that?

KROGSTAD. Then why did you write to me the way you did?

MRS. LINDE. I had to. Since I had to break with you, I thought it my duty to destroy all the feelings you had for me.

KROGSTAD (*clenches his fists*). So that was it. And you did this for money!

MRS. LINDE. You mustn't forget I had a helpless mother to take care of, and two little brothers. We couldn't wait for you, Nils. It would have been so long before you'd had enough to support us.

KROGSTAD. Maybe. But you had no right to cast me off for someone else.

MRS. LINDE. Perhaps not. I've often asked myself that.

KROGSTAD (*more quietly*). When I lost you, it was just as though all solid ground had been swept from under my feet. Look at me. Now I am a shipwrecked man, clinging to a spar.

MRS. LINDE. Help may be near at hand.

KROGSTAD. It was near. But then you came, and stood between it and me.

MRS. LINDE. I didn't know, Nils. No one told me till today that this job I'd found was yours.

KROGSTAD. I believe you, since you say so. But now you know, won't you give it up?

MRS. LINDE. No—because it wouldn't help you even if I did.

KROGSTAD. Wouldn't it? I'd do it all the same.

MRS. LINDE. I've learned to look at things practically. Life and poverty have taught me that.

KROGSTAD. And life has taught me to distrust fine words.

MRS. LINDE. Then it's taught you a useful lesson. But surely you still believe in actions?

KROGSTAD. What do you mean?

MRS. LINDE. You said you were like a shipwrecked man clinging to a spar.

KROGSTAD. I have good reason to say it.

MRS. LINDE. I'm in the same position as you. No one to care about, no one to care for.

KROGSTAD. You made your own choice.

MRS. LINDE. I had no choice—then.

KROGSTAD. Well?

MRS. LINDE. Nils, suppose we two shipwrecked souls could join hands?

KROGSTAD. What are you saying?

MRS. LINDE. Castaways have a better chance of survival together than on their own.

KROGSTAD. Christine!

MRS. LINDE. Why do you suppose I came to this town?

KROGSTAD. You mean—you came because of me?

MRS. LINDE. I must work if I'm to find life worth living. I've always worked, for as long as I can remember; it's been the greatest joy of my life—my only joy. But now I'm alone in the world, and I feel so dreadfully lost and empty. There's no joy in working just for oneself. Oh, Nils, give me something—someone—to work for.

KROGSTAD. I don't believe all that. You're just being hysterical and romantic. You want to find an excuse for self-sacrifice.

MRS. LINDE. Have you ever known me to be hysterical?

KROGSTAD. You mean you really—? Is it possible? Tell me—you know all about my past?

MRS. LINDE. Yes.

KROGSTAD. And you know what people think of me here?

MRS. LINDE. You said just now that with me you might have become a different person.

KROGSTAD. I know I could have.

MRS. LINDE. Couldn't it still happen?

KROGSTAD. Christine—do you really mean this? Yes—you do—I see it in your face. Have you really the courage—?

MRS. LINDE. I need someone to be a mother to; and your children need a mother. And you and I need each other. I believe in you, Nils. I am afraid of nothing—with you.

KROGSTAD (*clasps her hands*). Thank you, Christine—thank you! Now I shall make the world believe in me as you do! Oh—but I'd forgotten—

MRS. LINDE (*listens*). Ssh! The tarantella! Go quickly, go!

KROGSTAD. Why? What is it?

MRS. LINDE. You hear that dance? As soon as it's finished, they'll be coming down.

KROGSTAD. All right, I'll go. It's no good, Christine. I'd forgotten—you don't know what I've just done to the Helmers.

MRS. LINDE. Yes, Nils. I know.

KROGSTAD. And yet you'd still have the courage to—?

MRS. LINDE. I know what despair can drive a man like you to.

KROGSTAD. Oh, if only I could undo this!

MRS. LINDE. You can. Your letter is still lying in the box.

KROGSTAD. Are you sure?

MRS. LINDE. Quite sure. But—

KROGSTAD (*looks searchingly at her*). Is that why you're doing this? You want to save your friend at any price? Tell me the truth. Is that the reason?

MRS. LINDE. Nils, a woman who has sold herself once for the sake of others doesn't make the same mistake again.

KROGSTAD. I shall demand my letter back.

MRS. LINDE. No, no.

KROGSTAD. Of course I shall. I shall stay here till Helmer comes down. I'll tell him he must give me back my letter—I'll say it was only to do with my dismissal, and that I don't want him to read it—

MRS. LINDE. No, Nils, you mustn't ask for that letter back.

KROGSTAD. But—tell me—wasn't that the real reason you asked me to come here?

MRS. LINDE. Yes—at first, when I was frightened. But a day has passed since then, and in that time I've seen incredible things happen in this house. Helmer must know the truth. This unhappy secret of Nora's must be revealed. They must come to a full understanding; there must be an end of all these shiftings and evasions.

KROGSTAD. Very well. If you're prepared to risk it. But one thing I can do—and at once—

MRS. LINDE (*listens*). Hurry! Go, go! The dance is over. We aren't safe here another moment.

KROGSTAD. I'll wait for you downstairs.

MRS. LINDE. Yes, do. You can see me home.

KROGSTAD. I've never been so happy in my life before!

*He goes out through the front door. The door leading from the room into the hall remains open.*

MRS. LINDE (*tidies the room a little and gets her hat and coat*). What a change! Oh, what a change! Someone to work for—to live for! A home to bring joy into! I won't let this chance of happiness slip through my fingers. Oh, why don't they come? (*Listens.*) Ah, here they are. I must get my coat on.

*She takes her hat and coat. Helmer's and Nora's voices become audible outside. A key is turned in the lock and Helmer leads Nora almost forcibly into the hall. She is dressed in an Italian costume with a large black shawl. He is in evening dress, with a black cloak.*

NORA (*still in the doorway, resisting him*). No, no, no—not in here! I want to go back upstairs. I don't want to leave so early.

HELMER. But my dearest Nora—

NORA. Oh, please, Torvald, please! Just another hour!

HELMER. Not another minute, Nora, my sweet. You know what we agreed. Come along, now. Into the drawing-room. You'll catch cold if you stay out here.

*He leads her, despite her efforts to resist him, gently into the room.*

MRS. LINDE. Good evening.

NORA. Christine!

HELMER. Oh, hullo, Mrs. Linde. You still here?

MRS. LINDE. Please forgive me. I did so want to see Nora in her costume.

NORA. Have you been sitting here waiting for me?

MRS. LINDE. Yes. I got here too late, I'm afraid. You'd already gone up. And I felt I really couldn't go back home without seeing you.

HELMER (*takes off Nora's shawl*). Well, take a good look at her. She's worth looking at, don't you think? Isn't she beautiful, Mrs. Linde?

MRS. LINDE. Oh, yes, indeed—

HELMER. Isn't she unbelievably beautiful? Everyone at the party said so. But dreadfully stubborn she is, bless her pretty little heart. What's to be done about that? Would you believe it, I practically had to use force to get her away!

NORA. Oh, Torvald, you're going to regret not letting me stay—just half an hour longer.

HELMER. Hear that, Mrs. Linde? She dances her tarantella—makes a roaring success—and very well deserved—though possibly a trifle too realistic—more so than was aesthetically necessary, strictly speaking. But never mind that. Main thing is—she had a success—roaring success. Was I going to let her stay on after that and spoil the impression? No, thank you. I took my beautiful little Capri signorina—my capricious little Capricienne, what?—under my arm—a swift round of the ballroom, a curtsey to the company, and, as they say in novels, the beautiful apparition disappeared! An exit should always be dramatic, Mrs. Linde. But unfortunately that's just what I can't get Nora to realize. I say, it's hot in here. (*Throws his cloak on a chair and opens the door to his study.*) What's this? It's dark in here. Ah, yes, of course—excuse me. (*Goes in and lights a couple of candles.*)

NORA (*whispers swiftly, breathlessly*). Well?

MRS. LINDE (*quietly*). I've spoken to him.

NORA. Yes?

MRS. LINDE. Nora—you must tell your husband everything.

NORA (*dully*). I knew it.

MRS. LINDE. You've nothing to fear from Krogstad. But you must tell him.

NORA. I shan't tell him anything.

MRS. LINDE. Then the letter will.

NORA. Thank you, Christine. Now I know what I must do. Ssh!

HELMER (*returns*). Well, Mrs. Linde, finished admiring her?

MRS. LINDE. Yes. Now I must say good night.

HELMER. Oh, already? Does this knitting belong to you?

MRS. LINDE (*takes it*). Thank you, yes. I nearly forgot it.

HELMER. You knit, then?

MRS. LINDE. Why, yes.

HELMER. Know what? You ought to take up embroidery.

MRS. LINDE. Oh? Why?

HELMER. It's much prettier. Watch me, now. You hold the embroidery in your left hand, like this, and then you take the needle in your right hand and go in and out in a slow, easy movement—like this. I am right, aren't I?

MRS. LINDE. Yes, I'm sure—

HELMER. But knitting, now—that's an ugly business—can't help it. Look—arms all huddled up—great clumsy needles going up and down—makes you look like a damned Chinaman. I say, that really was a magnificent champagne they served us.

MRS. LINDE. Well, good night, Nora. And stop being stubborn. Remember!

HELMER. Quite right, Mrs. Linde!

MRS. LINDE. Good night, Mr. Helmer.

HELMER (*accompanies her to the door*). Good night, good night! I hope you'll manage to get home all right? I'd gladly—but you haven't far to go, have you? Good night, good night. (*She goes. He closes the door behind her and returns.*) Well, we've got rid of her at last. Dreadful bore that woman is!

NORA. Aren't you very tired, Torvald?

HELMER. No, not in the least.

NORA. Aren't you sleepy?

HELMER. Not a bit. On the contrary, I feel extraordinarily exhilarated. But what about you? Yes, you look very sleepy and tired.

NORA. Yes, I am very tired. Soon I shall sleep.

HELMER. You see, you see! How right I was not to let you stay longer!

NORA. Oh, you're always right, whatever you do.

HELMER (*kisses her on the forehead*). Now my little songbird's talking just like a real big human being. I say, did you notice how cheerful Rank was this evening?

NORA. Oh? Was he? I didn't have a chance to speak with him.

HELMER. I hardly did. But I haven't seen him in such a jolly mood for ages. (*Looks at her for a moment, then comes closer.*) I say, it's nice to get back to one's home again, and be all alone with you. Upon my word, you're a distractingly beautiful young woman.

NORA. Don't look at me like that, Torvald!

HELMER. What, not look at my most treasured possession? At all this wonderful beauty that's mine, mine alone, all mine.

NORA (*goes round to the other side of the table*). You mustn't talk to me like that tonight.

HELMER (*follows her*). You've still the tarantella in your blood, I see. And that makes you even more desirable. Listen! Now the other guests are beginning to go. (*More quietly.*) Nora—soon the whole house will be absolutely quiet.

NORA. Yes, I hope so.

HELMER. Yes, my beloved Nora, of course you do! Do you know—when I'm out with you among other people like we were tonight, do you know why I say so little to you, why I keep so aloof from you, and just throw you an occasional glance? Do you know why I do that? It's because I pretend to myself that you're my secret mistress, my clandestine little sweetheart, and that nobody knows there's anything at all between us.

NORA. Oh, yes, yes, yes—I know you never think of anything but me.

HELMER. And then when we're about to go, and I wrap the shawl round your lovely young shoulders, over this wonderful curve of your neck—then I pretend to myself that you are my young bride, that we've just come from the wedding, that I'm taking you to my house for the first time—that, for the first time, I am alone with you—quite alone with you, as you stand there young and trembling and beautiful. All evening I've had no eyes for anyone but you. When I saw you dance the tarantella, like a huntress, a temptress, my blood grew hot, I couldn't stand it any longer! That was why I seized you and dragged you down here with me—

NORA. Leave me, Torvald! Get away from me! I don't want all this.

HELMER. What? Now, Nora, you're joking with me. Don't want, don't want—? Aren't I your husband—?

*There is a knock on the front door.*

NORA (*starts*). What was that?

HELMER (*goes towards the hall*). Who is it?

RANK (*outside*). It's me. May I come in for a moment?

HELMER (*quietly, annoyed*). Oh, what does he want now? (*Calls.*) Wait a moment. (*Walks over and opens the door.*) Well! Nice of you not to go by without looking in.

RANK. I thought I heard your voice, so I felt I had to say goodbye. (*His eyes travel swiftly around the room.*) Ah, yes—these dear rooms, how well I know them. What a happy, peaceful home you two have.

HELMER. You seemed to be having a pretty happy time yourself upstairs.

RANK. Indeed I did. Why not? Why shouldn't one make the most of this world? As much as one can, and for as long as one can. The wine was excellent—

HELMER. Especially the champagne.

RANK. You noticed that too? It's almost incredible how much I managed to get down.

NORA. Torvald drank a lot of champagne too, this evening.

RANK. Oh?

NORA. Yes. It always makes him merry afterwards.

RANK. Well, why shouldn't a man have a merry evening after a well-spent day?

HELMER. Well-spent? Oh, I don't know that I can claim that.

RANK (*slaps him across the back*). I can though, my dear fellow!

NORA. Yes, of course, Dr. Rank—you've been carrying out a scientific experiment today, haven't you?

RANK. Exactly.

HELMER. Scientific experiment! Those are big words for my little Nora to use!

NORA. And may I congratulate you on the finding?

RANK. You may indeed.

NORA. It was good, then?

RANK. The best possible finding—both for the doctor and the patient. Certainty.

NORA (*quickly*). Certainty?

RANK. Absolute certainty. So aren't I entitled to have a merry evening after that?

NORA. Yes, Dr. Rank. You were quite right to.

HELMER. I agree. Provided you don't have to regret it tomorrow.

RANK. Well, you never get anything in this life without paying for it.

NORA. Dr. Rank—you like masquerades, don't you?

RANK. Yes, if the disguises are sufficiently amusing.

NORA. Tell me. What shall we two wear at the next masquerade?

HELMER. You little gadabout! Are you thinking about the next one already?

RANK. We two? Yes, I'll tell you. You must go as the Spirit of Happiness—

HELMER. You try to think of a costume that'll convey that.

RANK. Your wife need only appear as her normal, everyday self—

HELMER. Quite right! Well said! But what are you going to be? Have you decided that?

RANK. Yes, my dear friend. I have decided that.

HELMER. Well?

RANK. At the next masquerade, I shall be invisible.

HELMER. Well, that's a funny idea.

RANK. There's a big, black hat—haven't you heard of the invisible hat? Once it's over your head, no one can see you any more.

HELMER (*represses a smile*). Ah yes, of course.

RANK. But I'm forgetting what I came for. Helmer, give me a cigar. One of your black Havanas.

HELMER. With the greatest pleasure. (*Offers him the box.*)

RANK (*takes one and cuts off the tip*). Thank you.

NORA (*strikes a match*). Let me give you a light.

RANK. Thank you. (*She holds out the match for him. He lights his cigar.*) And now—goodbye.

HELMER. Goodbye, my dear chap, goodbye.

NORA. Sleep well, Dr. Rank.

RANK. Thank you for that kind wish.

NORA. Wish me the same.

RANK. You? Very well—since you ask. Sleep well. And thank you for the light. (*He nods to them both and goes.*)

HELMER (*quietly*). He's been drinking too much.

NORA (*abstractedly*). Perhaps.

*Helmer takes his bunch of keys from his pocket and goes out into the hall.*

NORA. Torvald, what do you want out there?

HELMER. I must empty the letter-box. It's absolutely full. There'll be no room for the newspapers in the morning.

NORA. Are you going to work tonight?

HELMER. You know very well I'm not. Hullo, what's this? Someone's been at the lock.

NORA. At the lock—?

HELMER. Yes, I'm sure of it. Who on earth—? Surely not one of the maids? Here's a broken hairpin. Nora, it's yours—

NORA (*quickly*). Then it must have been the children.

HELMER. Well, you'll have to break them of that habit. Hm, hm. Ah, that's done it. (*Takes out the contents of the box and calls into the kitchen.*) Helen! Put out the light on the staircase. (*Comes back into the drawing-room with the letters in his hand and closes the door to the hall.*) Look at this! You see how they've piled up? (*Glances through them.*) What on earth's this?

NORA (*at the window*). The letter! Oh, no, Torvald, no!

HELMER. Two visiting cards—from Rank.

NORA. From Dr. Rank?

HELMER (*looks at them*). Peter Rank, M.D. They were on top. He must have dropped them in as he left.

NORA. Has he written anything on them?

HELMER. There's a black cross above his name. Look. Rather gruesome, isn't it? It looks just as though he was announcing his death.

NORA. He is.

HELMER. What? Do you know something? Has he told you anything?

NORA. Yes. When these cards come, it means he's said goodbye to us. He wants to shut himself up in his house and die.

HELMER. Ah, poor fellow. I knew I wouldn't be seeing him for much longer. But so soon—! And now he's going to slink away and hide like a wounded beast.

NORA. When the time comes, it's best to go silently. Don't you think so, Torvald?

HELMER (*walks up and down*). He was so much a part of our life. I can't realize that he's gone. His suffering and loneliness seemed to provide a kind of dark background to the happy sunlight of our marriage. Well, perhaps it's best this way. For him, anyway. (*Stops walking.*) And perhaps for us too, Nora. Now we have only each other. (*Embraces her.*) Oh, my beloved wife—I feel as though I could never hold you close enough. Do you know, Nora, often I wish some terrible danger might threaten you, so that I could offer my life and my blood, everything, for your sake.

NORA (*tears herself loose and says in a clear, firm voice*). Read your letters now, Torvald.

HELMER. No, no. Not tonight. Tonight I want to be with you, my darling wife—

NORA. When your friend is about to die—?

HELMER. You're right. This news has upset us both. An ugliness has come between us; thoughts of death and dissolution. We must try to forget them. Until then—you go to your room; I shall go to mine.

NORA (*throws her arms around his neck*). Good night, Torvald! Good night!

HELMER (*kisses her on the forehead*). Good night, my darling little songbird. Sleep well, Nora. I'll go and read my letters.

*He goes into the study with the letters in his hand, and closes the door.*

NORA (*wild-eyed, fumbles around, seizes Helmer's cloak, throws it round herself and whispers quickly, hoarsely*). Never see him again. Never. Never. Never. (*Throws the shawl over her head.*) Never see the children again. Them too. Never. Never. Oh—the icy black water! Oh—that bottomless—that—! Oh, if only it were all over! Now he's got it—he's reading it. Oh, no, no! Not yet! Goodbye, Torvald! Goodbye, my darlings!

*She turns to run into the hall. As she does so, Helmer throws open his door and stands there with an open letter in his hand.*

HELMER. Nora!

NORA (*shrieks*). Ah—!

HELMER. What is this? Do you know what is in this letter?

NORA. Yes, I know. Let me go! Let me go!

HELMER (*holds her back*). Go? Where?

NORA (*tries to tear herself loose*). You mustn't try to save me, Torvald!

HELMER (*staggers back*). Is it true? Is it true, what he writes? Oh, my God! No, no—it's impossible, it can't be true!

NORA. It *is* true. I've loved you more than anything else in the world.

HELMER. Oh, don't try to make silly excuses.

NORA (*takes a step towards him*). Torvald—

HELMER. Wretched woman! What have you done?

NORA. Let me go! You're not going to suffer for my sake. I won't let you!

HELMER. Stop being theatrical. (*Locks the front door.*) You're going to stay here and explain yourself. Do you understand what you've done? Answer me! Do you understand?

NORA (*looks unflinchingly at him and, her expression growing colder, says*). Yes. Now I am beginning to understand.

HELMER (*walking around the room*). Oh, what a dreadful awakening! For eight whole years—she who was my joy and my pride—a hypocrite, a liar—worse, worse—a criminal! Oh, the hideousness of it! Shame on you, shame!

*Nora is silent and stares unblinkingly at him.*

HELMER (*stops in front of her*). I ought to have guessed that something of this sort would happen. I should have foreseen it. All your father's recklessness and instability—be quiet!—I repeat, all your father's recklessness and instability he has handed on to you. No religion, no morals, no sense of duty! Oh, how I have been punished for closing my eyes to his faults! I did it for your sake. And now you reward me like this.

NORA. Yes. Like this.

HELMER. Now you have destroyed all my happiness. You have ruined my whole future. Oh, it's too dreadful to contemplate! I am in the power of a man who is completely without scruples. He can do what he likes with me, demand what he pleases, order me to do anything—I dare not disobey him. I am condemned to humiliation and ruin simply for the weakness of a woman.

NORA. When I am gone from this world, you will be free.

HELMER. Oh, don't be melodramatic. Your father was always ready with that kind of remark. How would it help me if you were "gone from this world," as you put it? It wouldn't assist me in the slightest. He can still make all the facts public; and if he does, I may quite easily be suspected of having been an accomplice in your crime. People may think that I was behind it—that it was I who encouraged you! And for all this I have to thank you, you whom I have carried on my hands through all the years of our marriage! Now do you realize what you've done to me?

NORA (*coldly calm*). Yes.

HELMER. It's so unbelievable I can hardly credit it. But we must try to find some way out. Take off that shawl. Take it off, I say! I must try to buy him off somehow. This thing must be hushed up at any price. As regards our relationship—we must appear to be living together just as before. Only *appear,* of course. You will therefore continue to reside here. That is understood. But the children shall be taken out of your hands. I dare no longer entrust them to you. Oh, to have to say this to the woman I once loved so dearly—and whom I still—! Well, all that must be finished. Henceforth there can be no question of happiness; we must merely strive to save what shreds and tatters—(*The front door bell rings. Helmer starts.*) What can that be? At this hour? Surely not—? He wouldn't—? Hide yourself, Nora. Say you're ill.

*Nora does not move. Helmer goes to the door of the room and opens it. The Maid is standing half-dressed in the hall.*

MAID. A letter for madam.

HELMER. Give it to me. (*Seizes the letter and shuts the door.*) Yes, it's from him. You're not having it. I'll read this myself.

NORA. Read it.

HELMER (*by the lamp*). I hardly dare to. This may mean the end for us both. No, I must know. (*Tears open the letter hastily; reads a few lines; looks at a piece of paper which is enclosed with it; utters a cry of joy.*) Nora! (*She looks at him questioningly.*) Nora! No—I must read it once more. Yes, yes, it's true! I am saved! Nora, I am saved!

NORA. What about me?

HELMER. You too, of course. We're both saved, you and I. Look! He's returning your I.O.U. He writes that he is sorry for what has happened—a happy accident has changed his life—oh, what does it matter what he writes? We are saved, Nora! No one can harm you now. Oh, Nora, Nora—no, first let me destroy this filthy thing. Let me see—! (*Glances at the I.O.U.*) No, I don't want to look at it. I shall merely regard the whole business as a dream. (*He tears the I.O.U. and both letters into pieces, throws them into the stove, and watches them burn.*) There. Now they're destroyed. He wrote that ever since Christmas Eve you've been—oh, these must have been three dreadful days for you, Nora.

NORA. Yes. It's been a hard fight.

HELMER. It must have been terrible—seeing no way out except—no, we'll forget the whole sordid business. We'll just be happy and go on telling ourselves over and over again: "It's over! It's over!" Listen to me, Nora. You don't seem to realize. It's over! Why are you looking so pale? Ah, my poor little Nora, I understand. You can't believe that I have forgiven you. But I have, Nora. I swear it to you. I have forgiven you everything. I know that what you did you did for your love of me.

NORA. That is true.

HELMER. You have loved me as a wife should love her husband. It was simply that in your inexperience you chose the wrong means. But do you think I love you any the less because you don't know how to act on your own initiative? No, no. Just lean on me. I shall counsel you. I shall guide you. I would not be a true man if your feminine helplessness did not make you doubly attractive in my eyes. You mustn't mind the hard words I said to you in those first dreadful moments when my whole world seemed to be tumbling about my ears. I have forgiven you, Nora. I swear it to you; I have forgiven you.

NORA. Thank you for your forgiveness.

*She goes out through the door, right.*

HELMER. No, don't go—(*Looks in.*) What are you doing there?

NORA (*offstage*). Taking off my fancy dress.

HELMER (*by the open door*). Yes, do that. Try to calm yourself and get your balance again, my frightened little songbird. Don't be afraid. I have broad wings to shield you. (*Begins to walk around near the door.*) How lovely and peaceful this little home of ours is, Nora. You are safe here; I shall watch over you like a hunted dove which I have snatched unharmed from the claws of the falcon. Your wildly beating little heart shall find peace with me. It will happen, Nora; it will take time, but it will happen, believe me. Tomorrow all this will seem quite different. Soon everything will be as it was before. I shall no longer need to remind you that I have forgiven you; your own heart will tell you that it is true. Do you really think I could ever bring myself to disown you, or even to reproach you? Ah, Nora, you don't understand what goes on in a husband's heart. There is something indescribably wonderful and satisfying for a husband in knowing that he has forgiven his wife—forgiven her unreservedly, from the bottom of his heart. It means that she has become his property in a double sense; he has, as it were, brought her into the world anew; she is now not only his wife but also his child. From now on that is what you shall be to me, my poor, helpless, bewildered little creature. Never be frightened of anything again, Nora. Just open your heart to me. I shall be both your will and your conscience. What's this? Not in bed? Have you changed?

NORA (*in her everyday dress*). Yes, Torvald. I've changed.

HELMER. But why now—so late—?

NORA. I shall not sleep tonight.

HELMER. But, my dear Nora—

NORA (*looks at her watch*). It isn't that late. Sit down here, Torvald. You and I have a lot to talk about.

*She sits down on one side of the table.*

HELMER. Nora, what does this mean? You look quite drawn—

NORA. Sit down. It's going to take a long time. I've a lot to say to you.

HELMER (*sits down on the other side of the table*). You alarm me, Nora. I don't understand you.

NORA. No, that's just it. You don't understand me. And I've never understood you—until this evening. No, don't interrupt me. Just listen to what I have to say. You and I have got to face facts, Torvald.

HELMER. What do you mean by that?

NORA (*after a short silence*). Doesn't anything strike you about the way we're sitting here?

HELMER. What?

NORA. We've been married for eight years. Does it occur to you that this is the first time that we two, you and I, man and wife, have ever had a serious talk together?

HELMER. Serious? What do you mean, serious?

NORA. In eight whole years—no, longer—ever since we first met—we have never exchanged a serious word on a serious subject.

HELMER. Did you expect me to drag you into all my worries—worries you couldn't possibly have helped me with?

NORA. I'm not talking about worries. I'm simply saying that we have never sat down seriously to try to get to the bottom of anything.

HELMER. But, my dear Nora, what on earth has that got to do with you?

NORA. That's just the point. You have never understood me. A great wrong has been done to me, Torvald. First by Papa, and then by you.

HELMER. What? But we two have loved you more than anyone in the world!

NORA (*shakes her head*). You have never loved me. You just thought it was fun to be in love with me.

HELMER. Nora, what kind of a way is this to talk?

NORA. It's the truth, Torvald. When I lived with Papa, he used to tell me what he thought about everything, so that I never had any opinions but his. And if I did have any of my own, I kept them quiet, because he wouldn't have liked them. He called me his little doll, and he played with me just the way I played with my dolls. Then I came here to live in your house—

HELMER. What kind of a way is that to describe our marriage?

NORA (*undisturbed*). I mean, then I passed from Papa's hands into yours. You arranged everything the way you wanted it, so that I simply took over your taste in everything—or pretended I did—I don't really know—I think it was a little of both—first one and then the other. Now I look back on it, it's as if I've been living here like a pauper, from hand to mouth. I performed tricks for you, and you gave me food and drink. But that was how you wanted it. You and Papa have done me a great wrong. It's your fault that I have done nothing with my life.

HELMER. Nora, how can you be so unreasonable and ungrateful? Haven't you been happy here?

NORA. No; never. I used to think I was; but I haven't ever been happy.

HELMER. Not—not happy?

NORA. No. I've just had fun. You've always been very kind to me. But our home has never been anything but a playroom. I've been your doll-wife, just as I used to be Papa's doll-child. And the children have been my dolls. I used to think it was fun when you came in and played with me, just as they think it's fun when I go in and play games with them. That's all our marriage has been, Torvald.

HELMER. There may be a little truth in what you say, though you exaggerate and romanticize. But from now on it'll be different. Playtime is over. Now the time has come for education.

NORA. Whose education? Mine or the children's?

HELMER. Both yours and the children's, my dearest Nora.

NORA. Oh, Torvald, you're not the man to educate me into being the right wife for you.

HELMER. How can you say that?

NORA. And what about me? Am I fit to educate the children?

HELMER. Nora!

NORA. Didn't you say yourself a few minutes ago that you dare not leave them in my charge?

HELMER. In a moment of excitement. Surely you don't think I meant it seriously?

NORA. Yes. You were perfectly right. I'm not fitted to educate them. There's something else I must do first. I must educate myself. And you can't help me with that. It's something I must do by myself. That's why I'm leaving you.

HELMER (*jumps up*). What did you say?

NORA. I must stand on my own feet if I am to find out the truth about myself and about life. So I can't go on living here with you any longer.

HELMER. Nora, Nora!

NORA. I'm leaving you now, at once. Christine will put me up for tonight—

HELMER. You're out of your mind! You can't do this! I forbid you!

NORA. It's no use your trying to forbid me any more. I shall take with me nothing but what is mine. I don't want anything from you, now or ever.

HELMER. What kind of madness is this?

NORA. Tomorrow I shall go home—I mean, to where I was born. It'll be easiest for me to find some kind of a job there.

HELMER. But you're blind! You've no experience of the world—

NORA. I must try to get some, Torvald.

HELMER. But to leave your home, your husband, your children! Have you thought what people will say?

NORA. I can't help that. I only know that I must do this.

HELMER. But this is monstrous! Can you neglect your most sacred duties?

NORA. What do you call my most sacred duties?

HELMER. Do I have to tell you? Your duties towards your husband, and your children.

NORA. I have another duty which is equally sacred.

HELMER. You have not. What on earth could that be?

NORA. My duty towards myself.

HELMER. First and foremost you are a wife and a mother.

NORA. I don't believe that any longer. I believe that I am first and foremost a human being, like you—or anyway, that I must try to become one. I know most people think as you do, Torvald, and I know there's something of the sort to be found in books. But I'm no longer prepared to accept what people say and what's written in books. I must think things out for myself, and try to find my own answer.

HELMER. Do you need to ask where your duty lies in your own home? Haven't you an infallible guide in such matters—your religion?

NORA. Oh, Torvald, I don't really know what religion means.

HELMER. What are you saying?

NORA. I only know what Pastor Hansen told me when I went to confirmation. He explained that religion meant this and that. When I get away from all this and can think things out on my own, that's one of the questions I want to look into. I want to find out whether what Pastor Hansen said was right—or anyway, whether it is right for me.

HELMER. But it's unheard of for so young a woman to behave like this! If religion cannot guide you, let me at least appeal to your conscience. I presume you have some moral feelings left? Or—perhaps you haven't? Well, answer me.

NORA. Oh, Torvald, that isn't an easy question to answer. I simply don't know. I don't know where I am in these matters. I only know that these things mean something quite different to me from what they do to you. I've learned now that certain laws are different from what I'd imagined them to be; but I can't accept that such laws can be right. Has a woman really not the right to spare her dying father pain, or save her husband's life? I can't believe that.

HELMER. You're talking like a child. You don't understand how society works.

NORA. No, I don't. But now I intend to learn. I must try to satisfy myself which is right, society or I.

HELMER. Nora, you're ill; you're feverish. I almost believe you're out of your mind.

NORA. I've never felt so sane and sure in my life.

HELMER. You feel sure that it is right to leave your husband and your children?

NORA. Yes. I do.

HELMER. Then there is only one possible explanation.

NORA. What?

HELMER. That you don't love me any longer.

NORA. No, that's exactly it.

HELMER. Nora! How can you say this to me?

NORA. Oh, Torvald, it hurts me terribly to have to say it, because you've always been so kind to me. But I can't help it. I don't love you any longer.

HELMER (*controlling his emotions with difficulty*). And you feel quite sure about this too?

NORA. Yes, absolutely sure. That's why I can't go on living here any longer.

HELMER. Can you also explain why I have lost your love?

NORA. Yes, I can. It happened this evening, when the miracle failed to happen. It was then that I realized you weren't the man I'd thought you to be.

HELMER. Explain more clearly. I don't understand you.

NORA. I've waited so patiently, for eight whole years—well, good heavens, I'm not such a fool as to suppose that miracles occur every day. Then this dreadful thing happened to me, and then I *knew:* "Now the miracle will take place!" When Krogstad's letter was lying out there, it never occurred to me for a moment that you would let that man trample over you. I *knew* that you would say to him: "Publish the facts to the world." And when he had done this—

HELMER. Yes, what then? When I'd exposed my wife's name to shame and scandal—

NORA. Then I was certain that you would step forward and take all the blame on yourself, and say: "I am the one who is guilty!"

HELMER. Nora!

NORA. You're thinking I wouldn't have accepted such a sacrifice from you? No, of course I wouldn't! But what would my word have counted for against yours? That was the miracle I was hoping for, and dreading. And it was to prevent it happening that I wanted to end my life.

HELMER. Nora, I would gladly work for you night and day, and endure sorrow and hardship for your sake. But no man can be expected to sacrifice his honor, even for the person he loves.

NORA. Millions of women have done it.

HELMER. Oh, you think and talk like a stupid child.

NORA. That may be. But you neither think nor talk like the man I could share my life with. Once you'd got over your fright—and you weren't frightened of what might threaten me, but only of what threatened you—once the danger was past, then as far as you were concerned it was exactly as though nothing had happened. I was your little songbird just as before—your doll whom henceforth you would take particular care to protect from the world because she was so weak and fragile. (*Gets up.*) Torvald, in that moment I realized that for eight years I had been living here with a complete stranger, and had borne him three children—! Oh, I can't bear to think of it! I could tear myself to pieces!

HELMER (*sadly*). I see it, I see it. A gulf has indeed opened between us. Oh, but Nora—couldn't it be bridged?

NORA. As I am now, I am no wife for you.

HELMER. I have the strength to change.

NORA. Perhaps—if your doll is taken from you.

HELMER. But to be parted—to be parted from you! No, no, Nora, I can't conceive of it happening!

NORA (*goes into the room, right*). All the more necessary that it should happen.

*She comes back with her outdoor things and a small traveling-bag, which she puts down on a chair by the table.*

HELMER. Nora, Nora, not now! Wait till tomorrow!

NORA (*puts on her coat*). I can't spend the night in a strange man's house.

HELMER. But can't we live here as brother and sister, then—?

NORA (*fastens her hat*). You know quite well it wouldn't last. (*Puts on her shawl.*) Goodbye, Torvald. I don't want to see the children. I know they're in better hands than mine. As I am now, I can be nothing to them.

HELMER. But some time, Nora—some time—?

NORA. How can I tell? I've no idea what will happen to me.

HELMER. But you are my wife, both as you are and as you will be.

NORA. Listen, Torvald. When a wife leaves her husband's house, as I'm doing now, I'm told that according to the law he is freed of any obligations towards her. In any case, I release you from any such obligations. You mustn't feel bound to me in any way, however small, just as I shall not feel bound to you. We must both be quite free. Here is your ring back. Give me mine.

HELMER. That too?

NORA. That too.

HELMER. Here it is.

NORA. Good. Well, now it's over. I'll leave the keys here. The servants know about everything to do with the house—much better than I do. Tomorrow, when I have left town, Christine will come to pack the things I brought here from home. I'll have them sent on after me.

HELMER. This is the end then! Nora, will you never think of me any more?

NORA. Yes, of course. I shall often think of you and the children and this house.

HELMER. May I write to you, Nora?

NORA. No, never. You mustn't do that.

HELMER. But at least you must let me send you—

NORA. Nothing. Nothing.

HELMER. But if you should need help?—

NORA. I tell you, no. I don't accept things from strangers.

HELMER. Nora—can I never be anything but a stranger to you?

NORA (*picks up her bag*). Oh, Torvald! Then the miracle of miracles would have to happen.

HELMER. The miracle of miracles?

NORA. You and I would both have to change so much that—oh, Torvald, I don't believe in miracles any longer.

HELMER. But I want to believe in them. Tell me. We should have to change so much that—?

NORA. That life together between us two could become a marriage. Goodbye.

*She goes out through the hall.*

HELMER (*sinks down on a chair by the door and buries his face in his hands*). Nora! Nora! (*Looks round and gets up.*) Empty! She's gone! (*A hope strikes him.*) The miracle of miracles—?

*The street door is slammed shut downstairs.*

[*1879*]

## TOPICS FOR CRITICAL THINKING AND WRITING

1. Near the beginning of the play, how does Mrs. Linde's presence help to define Nora's character? How does Nora's response to Krogstad's entrance tell us something about Nora?
2. What does Dr. Rank contribute to the play? If he were eliminated, what would be lost?
3. In view of the fact that the last act several times seems to be moving toward a "happy ending" (e.g., Krogstad promises to recall his letter), what is wrong with the alternate ending (see page 1542) that Ibsen reluctantly provided for a German production?
4. Can it be argued that although at the end Nora goes out to achieve self-realization, her abandonment of her children—especially to Torvald's loathsome conventional morality—is a crime? (By the way, exactly why does Nora leave the children? She seems to imply, in some passages, that because she forged a signature she is unfit to bring them up. But do you agree with her?)
5. Michael Meyer, in his splendid biography *Henrik Ibsen,* says that the play is not so much about women's rights as about "the need of every individual to find out the kind of person he or she really is, and to strive to become that person." What evidence can you offer to support or refute this interpretation?
6. In *The Quintessence of Ibsenism* Bernard Shaw says that Ibsen, reacting against a common theatrical preference for strange situations, "saw

that . . . the more familiar the situation, the more interesting the play. Shakespear[e] had put ourselves on the stage but not our situations. Our uncles seldom murder our fathers and . . . marry our mothers. . . . Ibsen . . . gives us not only ourselves, but ourselves in our own situations. The things that happen to his stage figures are things that happen to us. One consequence is that his plays are much more important to us than Shakespear[e]'s. Another is that they are capable both of hurting us cruelly and of filling us with excited hopes of escape from idealistic tyrannies, and with visions of intenser life in the future." How much of this do you believe? Focus on details in the play to explain your response.

# PERSPECTIVES FOR *A DOLL'S HOUSE*

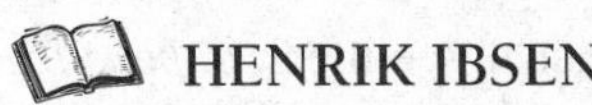

## HENRIK IBSEN

## *Notes for the Tragedy of Modern Times*

[The University Library, Oslo, has the following preliminary notes for *A Doll's House.*]

Rome 19.10.78

There are two kinds of moral law, two kinds of conscience, one in man and a completely different one in woman. They do not understand each other; but in matters of practical living the woman is judged by man's law, as if she were not a woman but a man.

The wife in the play ends up quite bewildered and not knowing right from wrong; her natural instincts on the one side and her faith in authority on the other leave her completely confused.

A woman cannot be herself in contemporary society, it is an exclusively male society with laws drafted by men, and with counsel and judges who judge feminine conduct from the male point of view.

She has committed a crime, and she is proud of it; because she did it for love of her husband and to save his life. But the husband, with his conventional views of honour, stands on the side of the law and looks at the affair with male eyes.

Mental conflict. Depressed and confused by her faith in authority, she loses faith in her moral right and ability to bring up her children. Bitterness. A mother in contemporary society, just as certain insects go away and die when she has done her duty in the propagation of the race. Love of life, of home and husband and children and family. Now and then, woman-like, she shrugs off her thoughts. Sudden return of dread and terror. Everything must be borne alone. The catastrophe approaches, ineluctably, inevitably. Despair, resistance, defeat.

[*The following note was later added in the margin:*]

Krogstad has done some dishonest business, and thus made a bit of money; but his prosperity does not help him, he cannot recover his honour.

## *Adaptation of* A Doll's House *for a German Production*

[Because Norwegian works were not copyrighted in Germany, German theaters could stage and freely adapt Ibsen's works without his consent. When he heard that a German director was going to change the ending to a happy one, Ibsen decided that he had better do the adaptation himself, though he characterized it as "a barbaric outrage" against the play.]

NORA. . . . Where we could make a real marriage out of our lives together. Goodbye. (*Begins to go.*)

HELMER. Go then! (*Seizes her arm.*) But first you shall see your children for the last time!

NORA. Let me go! I will not see them! I cannot!

HELMER (*draws her over to the door, left*). You shall see them. (*Opens the door and says softly.*) Look, there they are asleep, peaceful and carefree. Tomorrow, when they wake up and call for their mother, they will be—motherless.

NORA (*trembling*). Motherless . . . !

HELMER. As you once were.

NORA. Motherless! (*Struggles with herself, lets her traveling-bag fall, and says.*) Oh, this is a sin against myself, but I cannot leave them. (*Half sinks down by the door.*)

HELMER (*joyfully, but softly*). Nora!

THE CURTAIN FALLS.

## *Speech at the Banquet of the Norwegian League for Women's Rights*

[A month after the official birthday celebrations were over, Ibsen and his wife were invited to a banquet in his honor given by the leading Norwegian feminist society.]

Christiania, May 26, 1898

I am not a member of the Women's Rights League. Whatever I have written has been without any conscious thought of making propaganda. I have been more the poet and less the social philosopher than people generally seem inclined to believe. I thank you for the toast, but must disclaim the honor of having consciously worked for the women's rights movement. I am not even quite clear as to just what this women's rights movement really is. To me it has seemed a problem of mankind in general. And if you read my books carefully you will understand this. True enough, it is desirable to solve the woman problem, along with all the others; but that has not been the whole purpose. My task has been the *description of humanity.* To be sure, whenever such a description is felt to be reasonably true, the reader will read his own feelings and sentiments into the work of the poet. These are then attributed to the poet; but incorrectly so. Every reader remolds the work beautifully and neatly, each according to his own personality. Not only those who write but also those who read are poets. They are collaborators. They are often more poetical than the poet himself.

## TENNESSEE WILLIAMS

*Tennessee Williams (1914–83) was born Thomas Lanier Williams in Columbus, Mississippi. During his childhood his family moved to St. Louis, where his father had accepted a job as manager of a shoe company. Williams has written that neither he nor his sister Rose could adjust to the change from the South to the Midwest, but the children had already been deeply troubled. Nevertheless, at the age of 16 he achieved some distinction as a writer when his prize-winning essay in a nationwide contest was published. After high school he attended the University of Missouri but flunked ROTC and was therefore withdrawn from school by his father. He worked in a shoe factory for a while, then attended Washington University, where he wrote several plays. He finally graduated from the University of Iowa with a major in playwrighting. After graduation he continued to write, supporting himself with odd jobs such as waiting on tables and running elevators. His first commercial success was* The Glass Menagerie *(produced in Chicago in 1944, and in New York in 1945); among his other plays are* A Streetcar Named Desire *(1947),* Cat on a Hot Tin Roof *(1955), and* Suddenly Last Summer *(1958).*

# *The Glass Menagerie*

nobody, not even the rain, has such small hands.
—e. e. cummings

LIST OF CHARACTERS

AMANDA WINGFIELD, *the mother. A little woman of great but confused vitality clinging frantically to another time and place. Her characterization must be carefully created, not copied from type. She is not paranoiac, but her life is paranoia. There is much to admire in Amanda, and as much to love and pity as there is to laugh at. Certainly she has endurance and a kind of heroism, and though her foolishness makes her unwittingly cruel at times, there is tenderness in her slight person.*

LAURA WINGFIELD, *her daughter. Amanda, having failed to establish contact with reality, continues to live vitally in her illusions, but Laura's situation is even graver. A childhood illness has left her crippled, one leg slightly shorter than the other, and held in a brace. This defect need not be more than suggested on the stage. Stemming from this, Laura's separation increases till she is like a piece of her own glass collection, too exquisitely fragile to move from the shelf.*

*Left to right:* Anthony Ross (Jim), Laurette Taylor (Amanda), Eddie Dowling (Tom), and Julie Hayden (Laura) in the 1945 original production of *The Glass Menagerie,* The Playhouse, New York. (New York Public Library, The Billy Rose Theater Collection)

TOM WINGFIELD, *her son. And the narrator of the play. A poet with a job in a warehouse. His nature is not remorseless, but to escape from a trap he has to act without pity.*

JIM O'CONNOR, *the gentleman caller. A nice, ordinary, young man.*

**SCENE.** *An alley in St. Louis.*

**PART I.** *Preparation for a Gentleman Caller.*

**PART II.** *The Gentleman Calls.*

**TIME.** *Now and the Past.*

## *Scene I*

*The Wingfield apartment is in the rear of the building, one of those vast hive-like conglomerations of cellular living-units that flower as warty growths in overcrowded urban centers of lower middle-class population and are symptomatic of the impulse of this largest and fundamentally enslaved section of American society to avoid fluidity and differentiation and to exist and function as one interfused mass of automatism.*

*The apartment faces an alley and is entered by a fire-escape, a structure whose name is a touch of accidental poetic truth, for all of these huge buildings are always burning with the slow and implacable fires of human desperation. The fire-escape is included in the set—that is, the landing of it and steps descending from it.*

*The scene is memory and is therefore nonrealistic. Memory takes a lot of poetic license. It omits some details; others are exaggerated, according to the emotional value of the articles it touches, for memory is seated predominantly in the heart. The interior is therefore rather dim and poetic.*

*At the rise of the curtain, the audience is faced with the dark, grim rear wall of the Wingfield tenement. This building, which runs parallel to the footlights, is flanked on both sides by dark, narrow alleys which run into murky canyons of tangled clotheslines, garbage cans and the sinister latticework of neighboring fire-escapes. It is up and down these side alleys that exterior entrances and exits are made, during the play. At the end of Tom's opening commentary, the dark tenement wall slowly reveals (by means of a transparency) the interior of the ground floor Wingfield apartment.*

*Downstage is the living room, which also serves as a sleeping room for Laura, the sofa unfolding to make her bed. Upstage, center, and divided by a wide arch or second proscenium with transparent faded portieres (or second curtain), is the dining room. In an old-fashioned what-not in the living room are seen scores of transparent glass animals. A blown-up photograph of the father hangs on the wall of the living room, facing the audience, to the left of the archway. It is the face of a very handsome young man in a doughboy's First World War cap. He is gallantly smiling, ineluctably smiling, as if to say, "I will be smiling forever."*

*The audience hears and sees the opening scene in the dining room through both the transparent fourth wall of the building and the transparent gauze portieres of the dining-room arch. It is during this revealing scene that the fourth wall slowly ascends, out of sight.*

*This transparent exterior wall is not brought down again until the very end of the play, during Tom's final speech.*

*The narrator is an undisguised convention of the play. He takes whatever license with dramatic convention as is convenient to his purposes.*

*Tom enters dressed as a merchant sailor from alley, stage left, and strolls across the front of the stage to the fire-escape. There he stops and lights a cigarette. He addresses the audience.*

TOM. Yes, I have tricks in my pocket, I have things up my sleeve. But I am the opposite of a stage magician. He gives you illusion that has the appearance of truth. I give you truth in the pleasant disguise of illusion. To begin with, I turn back time. I reverse it to that quaint period, the thirties, when the huge middle class of America was matriculating in a school for the blind. Their eyes had failed them, or they had failed their eyes, and so they were having their fingers pressed forcibly down on the fiery Braille alphabet of a dissolving economy. In Spain there was revolution. Here there was only shouting and confusion. In Spain there was Guernica. Here there were disturbances of labor, sometimes pretty violent, in otherwise peaceful cities such as Chicago, Cleveland, Saint Louis. . . . This is the social background of the play.

(*Music.*)

The play is memory. Being a memory play, it is dimly lighted, it is sentimental, it is not realistic. In memory everything seems to happen to music. That explains the fiddle in the wings. I am the narrator of the play, and also a character in it. The other characters are my mother, Amanda, my sister, Laura, and a gentleman caller who appears in the final scenes. He is the most realistic character in the play, being an emissary from a world of reality that we were somehow set apart from. But since I have a poet's weakness for symbols, I am using this character also as a symbol; he is the long delayed but always expected something that we live for. There is a fifth character in the play who doesn't appear except in this larger-than-life photograph over the mantel. This is our father who left us a long time ago. He was a telephone man who fell in love with long distances; he gave up his job with the telephone company and skipped the light fantastic out of town. . . . The last we heard of him was a picture post-card from Mazatlan, on the Pacific coast of Mexico, containing a message of two words—"Hello—Goodbye!" and no address. I think the rest of the play will explain itself. . . .

*Amanda's voice becomes audible through the portieres.*

(*Legend on Screen: "Où Sont les Neiges?"*)

*He divides the portieres and enters the upstage area.*

*Amanda and Laura are seated at a drop-leaf table. Eating is indicated by gestures without food or utensils. Amanda faces the audience. Tom and Laura are seated in profile.*

*The interior has lit up softly and through the scrim we see Amanda and Laura seated at the table in the upstage area.*

AMANDA (*calling*). Tom?

TOM. Yes, Mother.

AMANDA. We can't say grace until you come to the table!

TOM. Coming, Mother. (*He bows slightly and withdraws, reappearing a few moments later in his place at the table.*)

AMANDA (*to her son*). Honey, don't *push* with your *fingers.* If you have to push with something, the thing to push with is a crust of bread. And chew—chew! Animals have sections in their stomachs which enable them to digest food without mastication, but human beings are supposed to chew their food before they swallow it down. Eat food leisurely, son, and really enjoy it. A well-cooked meal has lots of delicate flavors that have to be held in the mouth for appreciation. So chew your food and give your salivary glands a chance to function!

*Tom deliberately lays his imaginary fork down and pushes his chair back from the table.*

TOM. I haven't enjoyed one bite of this dinner because of your constant directions on how to eat it. It's you that makes me rush through meals with your hawk-like attention to every bite I take. Sickening—spoils my appetite—all this discussion of animals' secretion—salivary glands—mastication!

AMANDA (*lightly*). Temperament like a Metropolitan star! (*He rises and crosses downstage.*) You're not excused from the table.

TOM. I am getting a cigarette.

AMANDA. You smoke too much.

*Laura rises.*

LAURA. I'll bring in the blanc mange.

*He remains standing with his cigarette by the portieres during the following.*

AMANDA (*rising*). No, sister, no, sister—you be the lady this time and I'll be the darky.

LAURA. I'm already up.

AMANDA. Resume your seat, little sister—I want you to stay fresh and pretty—for gentlemen callers!

LAURA. I'm not expecting any gentlemen callers.

AMANDA (*crossing out to kitchenette. Airily*). Sometimes they come when they are least expected! Why, I remember one Sunday afternoon in Blue Mountain—(*Enters kitchenette.*)

TOM. I know what's coming!

LAURA. Yes. But let her tell it.

TOM. Again?

LAURA. She loves to tell it.

*Amanda returns with bowl of dessert.*

AMANDA. One Sunday afternoon in Blue Mountain—your mother received—*seventeen!*—gentlemen callers! Why, sometimes there weren't chairs enough to accommodate them all. We had to send the nigger over to bring in folding chairs from the parish house.

TOM (*remaining at portieres*). How did you entertain those gentlemen callers?

AMANDA. I understood the art of conversation!

TOM. I bet you could talk.

AMANDA. Girls in those days *knew* how to talk, I can tell you.

TOM. Yes?

(*Image: Amanda as a Girl on a Porch Greeting Callers.*)

AMANDA. They knew how to entertain their gentlemen callers. It wasn't enough for a girl to be possessed of a pretty face and a graceful figure—although I wasn't slighted in either respect. She also needed to have a nimble wit and a tongue to meet all occasions.

TOM. What did you talk about?

AMANDA. Things of importance going on in the world! Never anything coarse or common or vulgar. (*She addresses Tom as though he were seated in the vacant chair at the table though he remains by portieres. He plays this scene as though he held the book.*) My callers were gentlemen—all! Among my callers were some of the most prominent young planters of the Mississippi Delta—planters and sons of planters!

*Tom motions for music and a spot of light on Amanda.*

*Her eyes lift, her face glows, her voice becomes rich and elegiac.* (*Screen Legend: "Où Sont les Neiges?"*)

There was young Champ Laughlin who later became vice-president of the Delta Planters Bank. Hadley Stevenson who was drowned in Moon Lake and left his widow one hundred and fifty thousand in Government bonds. There were the Cutrere brothers, Wesley and Bates. Bates was one of my bright particular beaux! He got in a quarrel with that wild Wainright boy. They shot it out on the floor of Moon Lake Casino. Bates was shot through the stomach. Died in the ambulance on his way to Memphis. His widow was also well-provided for, came into eight or ten thousand acres, that's all. She married him on the rebound—never loved her—carried my picture on him the night he died! And there was that boy that every girl in Delta had set her cap for! That beautiful, brilliant young Fitzhugh boy from Green County!

TOM. What did he leave his widow?

AMANDA. He never married! Gracious, you talk as though all of my old admirers had turned up their toes to the daisies!

TOM. Isn't this the first you mentioned that still survives?

AMANDA. That Fitzhugh boy went North and made a fortune—came to be known as the Wolf of Wall Street! He had the Midas touch, whatever he touched turned to gold! And I could have been Mrs. Duncan J. Fitzhugh, mind you! But—I picked your *father!*

LAURA (*rising*). Mother, let me clear the table.

AMANDA. No dear, you go in front and study your typewriter chart. Or practice your shorthand a little. Stay fresh and pretty!—It's almost time for our gentlemen callers to start arriving. (*She flounces girlishly toward the kitchenette.*) How many do you suppose we're going to entertain this afternoon?

*Tom throws down the paper and jumps up with a groan.*

LAURA (*alone in the dining room*). I don't believe we're going to receive any, Mother.

AMANDA (*reappearing, airily*). What? No one—not one? You must be joking! (*Laura nervously echoes her laugh. She slips in a fugitive manner through the half-open portieres and draws them gently behind her. A shaft of very clear light is thrown on her face against the faded tapestry of the curtains.*) (*Music: "The Glass Menagerie" Under Faintly.*) (*Lightly.*) Not one gentleman caller? It can't be true! There must be a flood, there must have been a tornado!

LAURA. It isn't a flood, it's not a tornado, Mother. I'm just not popular like you were in Blue Mountain. . . . (*Tom utters another groan. Laura glances at him with a faint, apologetic smile. Her voice catching a little.*) Mother's afraid I'm going to be an old maid.

(*The Scene Dims Out with "Glass Menagerie" Music.*)

## *Scene II*

*"Laura, Haven't You Ever Liked Some Boy?"*

*On the dark stage the screen is lighted with the image of blue roses.*

*Gradually Laura's figure becomes apparent and the screen goes out. The music subsides.*

*Laura is seated in the delicate ivory chair at the small clawfoot table.*

*She wears a dress of soft violet material for a kimono—her hair tied back from her forehead with a ribbon.*

*She is washing and polishing her collection of glass.*

*Amanda appears on the fire-escape steps. At the sound of her ascent, Laura catches her breath, thrusts the bowl of ornaments away and seats herself stiffly before the diagram of the typewriter keyboard as though it held her spellbound. Something has happened to Amanda. It is written in her face as she climbs to the landing: a look that is grim and hopeless and a little absurd.*

*She has on one of those cheap or imitation velvety-looking cloth coats with imitation fur collar. Her hat is five or six years old, one of those dreadful cloche hats that were worn in the late twenties, and she is clasping an enormous black patent-leather pocketbook with nickel clasp and initials. This is her full-dress outfit, the one she usually wears to the D.A.R.*

*Before entering she looks through the door.*

*She purses her lips, opens her eyes wide, rolls them upward and shakes her head.*

*Then she slowly lets herself in the door. Seeing her mother's expression Laura touches her lips with a nervous gesture.*

LAURA. Hello, Mother, I was—(*She makes a nervous gesture toward the chart on the wall. Amanda leans against the shut door and stares at Laura with a martyred look.*)

AMANDA. Deception? Deception? (*She slowly removes her hat and gloves, continuing the swift suffering stare. She lets the hat and gloves fall on the floor—a bit of acting.*)

LAURA (*shakily*). How was the D.A.R. meeting? (*Amanda slowly opens her purse and removes a dainty white handkerchief which she shakes out delicately and delicately touches to her lips and nostrils.*) Didn't you go to the D.A.R. meeting, Mother?

AMANDA (*faintly, almost inaudibly*). —No.—No. (*Then more forcibly.*) I did not have the strength—to go to the D.A.R. In fact, I did not have the courage! I wanted to find a hole in the ground and hide myself in it forever! (*She crosses slowly to the wall and removes the diagram of the typewriter keyboard. She holds it in front of her for a second, staring at it sweetly and sorrowfully—then bites her lips and tears it in two pieces.*)

LAURA (*faintly*). Why did you do that, Mother? (*Amanda repeats the same procedure with the chart of the Gregg Alphabet.*) Why are you—

AMANDA. Why? Why? How old are you, Laura?

LAURA. Mother, you know my age.

AMANDA. I thought that you were an adult; it seems that I was mistaken. (*She crosses slowly to the sofa and sinks down and stares at Laura.*)

LAURA. Please don't stare at me, Mother.

*Amanda closes her eyes and lowers her head. Count ten.*

AMANDA. What are we going to do, what is going to become of us, what is the future?

*Count ten.*

LAURA. Has something happened, Mother? (*Amanda draws a long breath and takes out the handkerchief again. Dabbing process.*) Mother, has—something happened?

AMANDA. I'll be all right in a minute. I'm just bewildered—(*count five*)—by life. . . .

LAURA. Mother, I wish that you would tell me what's happened.

AMANDA. As you know, I was supposed to be inducted into my office at the D.A.R. this afternoon. (*Image: A Swarm of Typewriters.*) But I stopped off at Rubicam's Business College to speak to your teachers about your having a cold and ask them what progress they thought you were making down there.

LAURA. Oh. . . .

AMANDA. I went to the typing instructor and introduced myself as your mother. She didn't know who you were. Wingfield, she said. We don't have any such student enrolled at the school! I assured her she did, that you had been going to classes since early in January. "I wonder," she said, "if you could be talking about that terribly shy little girl who dropped out of school after only a few days' attendance?" "No," I said, "Laura, my daughter, has been going to school every day for the past six weeks!" "Excuse me," she said. She took the attendance book out and there was your name, unmistakably printed, and all the dates you were absent until they decided that you had dropped out of school. I still said, "No, there must have been some mistake! There must have been some mix-up in the records!" And she said, "No—I remember her perfectly now. Her hand shook so that she couldn't hit the right keys! The first time we gave a speed-test, she broke down completely—was sick at the stomach and almost had to be carried into the wash-room! After that morning she never showed up any more. We phoned the house but never got any answer"—while I was working at Famous and Barr, I suppose, demonstrating those—Oh! I felt so weak I could barely keep on my feet. I had to sit down while they got me a glass of water! Fifty dollars' tuition, all of our plans—my hopes and ambitions for you—just gone up the spout, just gone up the spout like that. (*Laura draws a long breath and gets awkwardly to her feet. She crosses to the victrola and winds it up.*) What are you doing?

LAURA. Oh! (*She releases the handle and returns to her seat.*)

AMANDA. Laura, where have you been going when you've gone out pretending that you were going to business college?

LAURA. I've just been going out walking.

AMANDA. That's not true.

LAURA. It is. I just went walking.

AMANDA. Walking? Walking? In winter? Deliberately courting pneumonia in that light coat? Where did you walk to, Laura?

LAURA. It was the lesser of two evils, Mother. (*Image: Winter Scene in Park.*) I couldn't go back up. I—threw up—on the floor!

AMANDA. From half past seven till after five every day you mean to tell me you walked around in the park, because you wanted to make me think that you were still going to Rubicam's Business College?

LAURA. It wasn't as bad as it sounds. I went inside places to get warmed up.

AMANDA. Inside where?

LAURA. I went in the art museum and the bird-houses at the Zoo. I visited the penguins every day! Sometimes I did without lunch and went to the movies. Lately I've been spending most of my afternoons in the Jewel-box, that big glass house where they raise the tropical flowers.

AMANDA. You did all this to deceive me, just for the deception? (*Laura looks down.*) Why?

LAURA. Mother, when you're disappointed, you get that awful suffering look on your face, like the picture of Jesus' mother in the museum!

AMANDA. Hush!

LAURA. I couldn't face it.

*Pause. A whisper of strings.*
(*Legend: "The Crust of Humility."*)

AMANDA (*hopelessly fingering the huge pocketbook*). So what are we going to do the rest of our lives? Stay home and watch the parades go by? Amuse ourselves with the glass menagerie, darling? Eternally play those worn-out phonograph records your father left as a painful reminder of him? We won't have a business career—we've given that up because it gave us nervous indigestion! (*Laughs wearily.*) What is there left but dependency all our lives? I know so well what becomes of unmarried women who aren't prepared to occupy a position. I've seen such pitiful cases in the South—barely tolerated spinsters living upon the grudging patronage of sister's husband or brother's wife!—stuck away in some little mousetrap of a room—encouraged by one in-law to visit another—little birdlike women without any nest—eating the crust of humility all their life! Is that the future that we've mapped out for ourselves? I swear it's the only alternative I can think of! It isn't a very pleasant alternative, is it? Of course—some girls *do marry.* (*Laura twists her hands nervously.*) Haven't you ever liked some boy?

LAURA. Yes. I liked one once. (*Rises.*) I came across his picture a while ago.

AMANDA (*with some interest*). He gave you his picture?

LAURA. No, it's in the year-book.

AMANDA (*disappointed*). Oh—a high-school boy.

(*Screen Image: Jim as a High-School Hero Bearing a Silver Cup.*)

LAURA. Yes. His name was Jim. (*Laura lifts the heavy annual from the clawfoot table.*) Here he is in *The Pirates of Penzance.*

AMANDA (*absently*). The what?

LAURA. The operetta the senior class put on. He had a wonderful voice and we sat across the aisle from each other Mondays, Wednesdays and Fridays in the Aud. Here he is with the silver cup for debating! See his grin?

AMANDA (*absently*). He must have had a jolly disposition.

LAURA. He used to call me—Blue Roses.

(*Image: Blue Roses.*)

AMANDA. Why did he call you such a name as that?

LAURA. When I had that attack of pleurosis—he asked me what was the matter when I came back. I said pleurosis—he thought that I said Blue Roses! So that's what he always called me after that. Whenever he saw me, he'd holler, "Hello, Blue Roses!" I didn't care for the girl that he went out with. Emily Meisenbach. Emily was the best-dressed girl at Soldan. She never struck me, though, as being sincere. . . . It says in the Personal Section—they're engaged. That's—six years ago! They must be married by now.

AMANDA. Girls that aren't cut out for business careers usually wind up married to some nice man. (*Gets up with a spark of revival.*) Sister, that's what you'll do!

*Laura utters a startled, doubtful laugh. She reaches quickly for a piece of glass.*

LAURA. But, Mother—

AMANDA. Yes? (*Crossing to photograph.*)

LAURA (*in a tone of frightened apology*). I'm—crippled!

(*Image: Screen.*)

AMANDA. Nonsense! Laura, I've told you never, never to use that word. Why, you're not crippled, you just have a little defect—hardly noticeable, even! When people have some slight disadvantage like that, they cultivate other things to make up for it—develop charm—and vivacity—and—*charm!* That's all you have to do! (*She turns again to the photograph.*) One thing your father had *plenty of*—was *charm!*

*Tom motions to the fiddle in the wings.*

(*The Scene Fades Out with Music.*)

## *Scene III*

(*Legend on the Screen: "After the Fiasco—"*)

*Tom speaks from the fire-escape landing.*

TOM. After the fiasco at Rubicam's Business College, the idea of getting a gentleman caller for Laura began to play a more important part in Mother's calculations. It became an obsession. Like some archetype of the universal unconscious, the image of the gentleman caller haunted our small apartment. . . . (*Image: Young Man at Door with Flowers.*) An evening at home rarely passed without some allusion to this image, this specter, this hope. . . . Even when he wasn't mentioned, his presence hung in Mother's preoccupied look and in my sister's frightened, apologetic manner—hung like a sentence passed upon the Wingfields! Mother was a woman of action as well as words. She began to take logical steps in the planned direction. Late that winter and in the early spring—realizing that extra money would be needed to properly feather the nest and plume the bird—she conducted a vigorous campaign on the telephone, roping in subscribers to one of those magazines for matrons called *The Home-maker's Companion,* the type of journal features the serialized sublimations of ladies of letters who think in terms of delicate cuplike breasts, slim, tapering waists, rich, creamy thighs, eyes like wood-smoke in autumn, fingers that soothe and caress like strains of music, bodies as powerful as Etruscan sculpture.

(*Screen Image: Glamor Magazine Cover.*)

*Amanda enters with phone on long extension cord. She is spotted in the dim stage.*

AMANDA. Ida Scott? This is Amanda Wingfield! We *missed* you at the D.A.R. last Monday! I said to myself: She's probably suffering with that sinus condition! How is that sinus condition? Horrors! Heaven have mercy!—You're a Christian martyr, yes, that's what you are, a Christian martyr! Well, I just now happened to notice that your subscription to the *Companion's* about to expire! Yes, it expires with the next issue, honey!—just when that wonderful new serial by Bessie Mae Hopper is getting off to such an exciting start. Oh, honey, it's something that you can't miss! You remember how *Gone With the Wind* took everybody by storm? You simply couldn't go out if you hadn't read it. All everybody *talked* was Scarlett O'Hara. Well, this is a book that critics already compare to *Gone With the Wind.* It's the *Gone With the Wind* of the post-World War generation!—What?—Burning?—Oh, honey, don't let them burn, go take a look in the oven and I'll hold the wire! Heavens—I think she's hung up!

(*Dim Out.*)

(*Legend on Screen: "You Think I'm in Love with Continental Shoemakers?"*)

*Before the stage is lighted, the violent voices of Tom and Amanda are heard. They are quarreling behind the portieres. In front of them stands Laura with clenched hands and panicky expression.*

*A clear pool of light on her figure throughout this scene.*

TOM. What in Christ's name am I—

AMANDA (*shrilly*). Don't you use that—

TOM. Supposed to do!

AMANDA. Expression! Not in my—

TOM. Ohhh!

AMANDA. Presence! Have you gone out of your senses?

TOM. I have, that's true, *driven* out!

AMANDA. What is the matter with you, you—big—big—IDIOT!

TOM. Look—I've got *no thing,* no single thing—

AMANDA. Lower your voice!

TOM. In my life here that I can call my OWN! Everything is—

AMANDA. Stop that shouting!

TOM. Yesterday you confiscated my books! You had the nerve to—

AMANDA. I took that horrible novel back to the library—yes! That hideous book by that insane Mr. Lawrence. (*Tom laughs wildly.*) I cannot control the output of diseased minds or people who cater to them—(*Tom laughs still more wildly.*) BUT I WON'T ALLOW SUCH FILTH BROUGHT INTO MY HOUSE! No, no, no, no, no!

TOM. House, house! Who pays rent on it, who makes a slave of himself to—

AMANDA (*fairly screeching*). Don't you DARE to—

TOM. No, no, *I* musn't say things! *I've* got to just—

AMANDA. Let me tell you—

TOM. I don't want to hear any more! (*He tears the portieres open. The upstage area is lit with a turgid smoky red glow.*)

*Amanda's hair is in metal curlers and she wears a very old bathrobe, much too large for her slight figure, a relic of the faithless Mr. Wingfield.*

*An upright typewriter and a wild disarray of manuscripts are on the dropleaf table. The quarrel was probably precipitated by*

*Amanda's interruption of his creative labor. A chair lying overthrown on the floor.*

*Their gesticulating shadows are cast on the ceiling by the fiery glow.*

AMANDA. You *will* hear more, you—

TOM. No, I won't hear more, I'm going out!

AMANDA. You come right back in—

TOM. Out, out, out! Because I'm—

AMANDA. Come back here, Tom Wingfield! I'm not through talking to you!

TOM. Oh, go—

LAURA (*desperately*). Tom!

AMANDA. You're going to listen, and no more insolence from you! I'm at the end of my patience! (*He comes back toward her.*)

TOM. What do you think I'm at? Aren't I supposed to have any patience to reach the end of, Mother? I know, I know. It seems unimportant to you, what I'm *doing*—what I *want* to do—having a little *difference* between them! You don't think that—

AMANDA. I think you've been doing things that you're ashamed of. That's why you act like this. I don't believe that you go every night to the movies. Nobody goes to the movies night after night. Nobody in their right minds goes to the movies as often as you pretend to. People don't go to the movies at nearly midnight, and movies don't let out at two A.M. Come in stumbling. Muttering to yourself like a maniac! You get three hours' sleep and then go to work. Oh, I can picture the way you're doing down there. Moping, doping, because you're in no condition.

TOM (*wildly*). No, I'm in no condition!

AMANDA. What right have you got to jeopardize your job? Jeopardize the security of us all? How do you think we'd manage if you were—

TOM. Listen! You think I'm crazy *about* the *warehouse?* (*He bends fiercely toward her slight figure.*) You think I'm in love with the Continental Shoemakers? You think I want to spend fifty-five *years* down there in that—*celotex interior!* with—*fluorescent—tubes!* Look! I'd rather somebody picked up a crowbar and battered out my brains—than go back mornings! I go! Every time you come in yelling that God damn *"Rise and Shine!" "Rise and Shine!"* I say to myself "How *lucky dead* people are!" But I get up. I *go!* For sixty-five dollars a month I give up all that I dream of doing and being *ever!* And you say self—*self's* all I ever think of. Why, listen, if self is what I thought of, Mother, I'd be where he is—GONE! (*Pointing to father's picture.*) As far as the system of transportation reaches! (*He starts past her. She grabs his arm.*) Don't grab at me, Mother!

AMANDA. Where are you going?

TOM. I'm going to the *movies!*

AMANDA. I don't believe that lie!

TOM (*crouching toward her, overtowering her tiny figure. She backs away, gasping*). I'm going to opium dens! Yes, opium dens, dens of vice and criminals' hang-outs, Mother. I've joined the Hogan gang, I'm a hired assassin, I carry a tommy-gun in a violin case! I run a string of cathouses in the Valley! They call me Killer, Killer Wingfield, I'm leading a double-life, a simple, honest warehouse worker by day, by night a dynamic *czar* of the *underworld, Mother.* I go to gambling casinos, I spin away fortunes on the roulette table! I wear a patch over one eye and a false mustache, sometimes I put on green whiskers. On those occasions they call me—*El Diablo!* Oh, I could tell you things to make you sleepless! My enemies plan to dynamite this place. They're going to blow us all sky-high some night! I'll be glad, very happy, and so will you! You'll go up, up on a broomstick, over Blue Mountain with seventeen gentlemen callers! You ugly—babbling old—*witch*. . . . (*He goes through a series of violent, clumsy movements, seizing his overcoat, lunging to the door, pulling it fiercely open. The women watch him, aghast. His arm catches in the sleeve of the coat as he struggles to pull it on. For a moment he is pinioned by the bulky garment. With an outraged groan he tears the coat off again, splitting the shoulders of it, and hurls it across the room. It strikes against the shelf of Laura's glass collection, there is a tinkle of shattering glass. Laura cries out as if wounded.*)

(*Music Legend: "The Glass Menagerie."*)

LAURA (*shrilly*). *My glass!*—menagerie. . . . (*She covers her face and turns away.*)

*But Amanda is still stunned and stupefied by the "ugly witch" so that she barely notices this occurrence. Now she recovers her speech.*

AMANDA (*in an awful voice*). I won't speak to you—until you apologize! (*She crosses through portieres and draws them together behind her. Tom is left with Laura. Laura clings weakly to the mantel with her face averted. Tom stares at her stupidly for a moment. Then he crosses to shelf. Drops awkwardly to his knees to collect the fallen glass, glancing at Laura as if he would speak but couldn't.*)

*"The Glass Menagerie" steals in as*
(*The Scene Dims Out.*)

## *Scene IV*

*The interior is dark. Faint light in the alley.*

*A deep-voiced bell in a church is tolling the hour of five as the scene commences.*

*Tom appears at the top of the alley. After each solemn boom of the bell in the tower, he shakes a little noise-maker or rattle as if to express the tiny spasm of man in contrast to the sustained power and dignity of the Almighty. This and the unsteadiness of his advance make it evident that he has been drinking.*

*As he climbs the few steps to the fire-escape landing light steals up inside. Laura appears in night-dress, observing Tom's empty bed in the front room.*

*Tom fishes in his pockets for the door-key, removing a motley assortment of articles in the search, including a perfect shower of movie-ticket stubs and an empty bottle. At last he finds the key, but just as he is about to insert it, it slips from his fingers. He strikes a match and crouches below the door.*

TOM (*bitterly*). One crack—and it falls through!

*Laura opens the door.*

LAURA. Tom! Tom, what are you doing?

TOM. Looking for a door-key.

LAURA. Where have you been all this time?

TOM. I have been to the movies.

LAURA. All this time at the movies?

TOM. There was a very long program. There was a Garbo picture and a Mickey Mouse and a travelogue and a newsreel and a preview of coming attractions. And there was an organ solo and a collection for the milk-fund—simultaneously—which ended up in a terrible fight between a fat lady and an usher!

LAURA (*innocently*). Did you have to stay through everything?

TOM. Of course! And, oh, I forgot! There was a big stage show! The headliner on this stage show was Malvolio the Magician. He performed wonderful tricks, many of them, such as pouring water back and forth between pitchers. First it turned to wine and then it turned to beer and then it turned to whiskey. I know it was whiskey it finally turned into because he needed somebody to come up out of the audience to help him, and I came up—both shows! It was Kentucky Straight Bourbon. A very generous fellow, he gave souvenirs. (*He pulls from his back pocket a shimmering rainbow-colored scarf.*) He gave me this. This is his magic scarf. You can have it, Laura. You wave it over a canary cage and you get a bowl of gold-fish. You wave it over the gold-fish bowl and they fly away canaries. . . . But the wonderfullest trick of all was the coffin trick. We nailed him into a coffin and he got out of the coffin without removing one nail. (*He has come inside.*) There is a trick that would come in handy for me—get me out of this 2 by 4 situation! (*Flops onto bed and starts removing shoes.*)

LAURA. Tom—Shhh!

TOM. What you shushing me for?

LAURA. You'll wake up Mother.

TOM. Goody, goody! Pay 'er back for all those "Rise an' Shines." (*Lies down, groaning.*) You know it don't take much intelligence to get yourself into a nailed-up coffin, Laura. But who in hell ever got himself out of one without removing one nail?

*As if in answer, the father's grinning photograph lights up.*

(*Scene Dims Out.*)

*Immediately following: The church bell is heard striking six. At the sixth stroke the alarm clock goes off in Amanda's room, and after a few moments we hear her calling: "Rise and Shine! Rise and Shine! Laura, go tell your brother to rise and shine!"*

TOM (*sitting up slowly*). I'll rise—but I won't shine.

*The light increases.*

AMANDA. Laura, tell your brother his coffee is ready.

*Laura slips into front room.*

LAURA. Tom! It's nearly seven. Don't make Mother nervous. (*He stares at her stupidly. Beseechingly.*) Tom, speak to Mother this morning. Make up with her, apologize, speak to her!

TOM. She won't to me. It's her that started not speaking.

LAURA. If you just say you're sorry she'll start speaking.

TOM. Her not speaking—is that such a tragedy?

LAURA. Please—please!

AMANDA (*calling from kitchenette*). Laura, are you going to do what I asked you to do, or do I have to get dressed and go out myself?

LAURA. Going, going—soon as I get on my coat! (*She pulls on a shapeless felt hat with nervous, jerky movement, pleadingly glancing at Tom. Rushes awkwardly for coat. The coat is one of Amanda's, inaccurately made-over, the sleeves too short for Laura.*) Butter and what else?

AMANDA (*entering upstage*). Just butter. Tell them to charge it.

LAURA. Mother, they make such faces when I do that.

AMANDA. Sticks and stones may break my bones, but the expression on Mr. Garfinkel's face won't harm us! Tell your brother his coffee is getting cold.

LAURA (*at door*). Do what I asked you, will you, will you, Tom?

*He looks sullenly away.*

AMANDA. Laura, go now or just don't go at all!

LAURA (*rushing out*). Going—going! (*A second later she cries out. Tom springs up and crosses to the door. Amanda rushes anxiously in. Tom opens the door.*)

TOM. Laura?

LAURA. I'm all right. I slipped, but I'm all right.

AMANDA (*peering anxiously after her*). If anyone breaks a leg on those fire-escape steps, the landlord ought to be sued for every cent he possesses! (*She shuts door. Remembers she isn't speaking and returns to other room.*)

*As Tom enters listlessly for his coffee, she turns her back to him and stands rigidly facing the window on the gloomy gray vault of the areaway. Its light on her face with its aged but childish features is cruelly sharp, satirical as a Daumier print.*

*(Music Under: "Ave Maria.")*

*Tom glances sheepishly but sullenly at her averted figure and slumps at the table. The coffee is scalding hot; he sips it and gasps and spits it back in the cup. At his gasp, Amanda catches her breath and half turns. Then catches herself and turns back to window.*

*Tom blows on his coffee, glancing sidewise at his mother. She clears her throat. Tom clears his. He starts to rise. Sinks back down again, scratches his head, clears his throat again. Amanda coughs. Tom raises his cup in both hands to blow on it, his eyes staring over the rim of it at his mother for several moments. Then he slowly sets the cup down and awkwardly and hesitantly rises from the chair.*

TOM (*hoarsely*). Mother. I—I apologize. Mother. (*Amanda draws a quick, shuddering breath. Her face works grotesquely. She breaks into child-like tears.*) I'm sorry for what I said, for everything that I said, I didn't mean it.

AMANDA (*sobbingly*). My devotion has made me a witch and so I make myself hateful to my children!

TOM. No you *don't.*

AMANDA. I worry so much, don't sleep, it makes me nervous!

TOM (*gently*). I understand that.

AMANDA. I've had to put up a solitary battle all these years. But you're my right-hand bower! Don't fall down, don't fail!

TOM (*gently*). I try, Mother.

AMANDA (*with great enthusiasm*). Try and you will SUCCEED! (*The notion makes her breathless.*) Why, you—you're just *full* of natural endowments! Both of my children—they're *unusual* children! Don't you think I know it? I'm so—*proud!* Happy and—feel I've—so much to be thankful for but—Promise me one thing, son!

TOM. What, Mother?

AMANDA. Promise, son, you'll—never be a drunkard!

TOM (*turns to her grinning*). I will never be a drunkard, Mother.

AMANDA. That's what frightened me so, that you'd be drinking! Eat a bowl of Purina!

TOM. Just coffee, Mother.

AMANDA. Shredded wheat biscuit?

TOM. No. No, Mother, just coffee.

AMANDA. You can't put in a day's work on an empty stomach. You've got ten minutes—don't gulp! Drinking too-hot liquids makes cancer of the stomach. . . . Put cream in.

TOM. No, thank you.

AMANDA. To cool it.

TOM. No! No, thank you, I want it black.

AMANDA. I know, but it's not good for you. We have to do all that we can to build ourselves up. In these trying times we live in, all that we have to cling to is—each other. . . . That's why it's so important to—Tom, I—I sent out your sister so I could discuss something with you. If you hadn't spoken I would have spoken to you. (*Sits down.*)

TOM (*gently*). What is it, Mother, that you want to discuss?

AMANDA. Laura!

*Tom puts his cup down slowly.*

(*Legend on Screen: "Laura."*)

(*Music: "The Glass Menagerie."*)

TOM. —Oh.—Laura . . .

AMANDA (*touching his sleeve*). You know how Laura is. So quiet but—still water runs deep! She notices things and I think she—broods about them. (*Tom looks up.*) A few days ago I came in and she was crying.

TOM. What about?

AMANDA. You.

TOM. Me?

AMANDA. She has an idea that you're not happy here.

TOM. What gave her that idea?

AMANDA. What gives her any idea? However, you do act strangely. I—I'm not criticizing, understand *that!* I know your ambitions do not lie in the warehouse, that like everybody in the whole wide world—you've had to—make sacrifices, but—Tom—Tom—life's not easy, it calls for—Spartan endurance! There's so many things in my heart that I cannot describe to you! I've never told you but I—*loved* your father. . . .

TOM (*gently*). I know that, Mother.

AMANDA. And you—when I see you taking after his ways! Staying out late—and—well, you *had* been drinking the night you were in that—terrifying condition! Laura says that you hate the apartment and that you go out nights to get away from it! Is that true, Tom?

TOM. No. You say there's so much in your heart that you can't describe to me. That's true of me, too. There's so much in my heart that I can't describe to *you!* So let's respect each other's—

AMANDA. But, why—*why,* Tom—are you always so *restless?* Where do you go to, nights?

TOM. I—go to the movies.

AMANDA. Why do you go to the movies so much, Tom?

TOM. I go to the movies because—I like adventure. Adventure is something I don't have much of at work, so I go to the movies.

AMANDA. But, Tom, you go to the movies *entirely too much!*

TOM. I like a lot of adventure.

*Amanda looks baffled, then hurt. As the familiar inquisition resumes he becomes hard and impatient again. Amanda slips back into her querulous attitude toward him.*

(*Image on Screen: Sailing Vessel with Jolly Roger.*)

AMANDA. Most young men find adventure in their careers.

TOM. Then most young men are not employed in a warehouse.

AMANDA. The world is full of young men employed in warehouses and offices and factories.

TOM. Do all of them find adventure in their careers?

AMANDA. They do or they do without it! Not everybody has a craze for adventure.

TOM. Man is by instinct a lover, a hunter, a fighter, and none of those instincts are given much play at the warehouse!

AMANDA. Man is by instinct! Don't quote instinct to me! Instinct is something that people have got away from! It belongs to animals! Christian adults don't want it!

TOM. What do Christian adults want, then, Mother?

AMANDA. Superior things! Things of the mind and the spirit! Only animals have to satisfy instincts! Surely your aims are somewhat higher than theirs! Than monkeys—pigs—

TOM. I reckon they're not.

AMANDA. You're joking. However, that isn't what I wanted to discuss.

TOM (*rising*). I haven't much time.

AMANDA (*pushing his shoulders*). Sit down.

TOM. You want me to punch in red at the warehouse, Mother?

AMANDA. You have five minutes. I want to talk about Laura.

(*Legend: "Plans and Provisions."*)

TOM. All right! What about Laura?

AMANDA. We have to be making plans and provisions for her. She's older than you, two years, and nothing has happened. She just drifts along doing nothing. It frightens me terribly how she just drifts along.

TOM. I guess she's the type that people call home girls.

AMANDA. There's no such type, and if there is, it's a pity! That is unless the home is hers, with a husband!

TOM. What?

AMANDA. Oh, I can see the handwriting on the wall as plain as I see the nose in the front of my face! It's terrifying! More and more you remind me of your father! He was out all hours without explanation—Then *left! Goodbye!* And me with the bag to hold. I saw that letter you got from the Merchant Marine. I know what you're dreaming of. I'm not standing here blindfolded. Very well, then. Then *do* it! But not till there's somebody to take your place.

TOM. What do you mean?

AMANDA. I mean that as soon as Laura has got somebody to take care of her, married, a home of her own, independent—why, then you'll be free to go wherever you please, on land, on sea, whichever way the wind blows! But until that time you've got to look out for your sister. I don't say me because I'm old and don't matter! I say for your sister because she's young and dependent. I put her in business college—a dismal failure! Frightened her so it made her sick to her stomach. I took her over to the Young People's League at the church. Another fiasco. She spoke to nobody, nobody spoke to her. Now all she does is fool with those pieces of glass and play those worn-out records. What kind of a life is that for a girl to lead!

TOM. What can I do about it?

AMANDA. Overcome selfishness! Self, self, self is all that you ever think of! (*Tom springs up and crosses to get his coat. It is ugly and bulky. He pulls on a cap with earmuffs.*) Where is your muffler? Put your wool muffler on! (*He snatches it angrily from the closet and tosses it around his neck and pulls both ends tight.*) Tom! I haven't said what I had in mind to ask you.

TOM. I'm too late to—

AMANDA (*catching his arms—very importunately. Then shyly*). Down at the warehouse, aren't there some—nice young men?

TOM. No!

AMANDA. There *must* be—*some.*

TOM. Mother—

*Gesture.*

AMANDA. Find out one that's clean-living—doesn't drink and—ask him out for sister!

TOM. What?

AMANDA. For *sister!* To *meet!* Get *acquainted!*

TOM (*stamping to door*). Oh, my *go-osh!*

AMANDA. Will you? (*He opens door. Imploringly.*) Will you? (*He starts down.*) Will you? *Will* you dear?

TOM (*calling back*). YES!

*Amanda closes the door hesitantly and with a troubled but faintly hopeful expression.*

(*Screen Image: Glamor Magazine Cover.*)

*Spot Amanda at phone.*

AMANDA. Ella Cartwright? This is Amanda Wingfield! How are you honey? How is that kidney condition? (*Count five.*) *Horrors!* (*Count five.*) You're a Christian martyr, yes, honey, that's what you are, a Christian martyr! Well, I just happened to notice in my little red book that your subscription to the *Companion* has just run out! I knew that you wouldn't want to miss out on the wonderful serial starting in this new issue. It's by Bessie Mae Hopper, the first thing she's written since *Honeymoon for Three.* Wasn't that a strange and interesting story? Well, this one is even lovelier, I believe. It has a sophisticated society background. It's all about the horsey set on Long Island!

(*Fade Out.*)

### *Scene V*

(*Legend on Screen: "Annunciation."*) *Fade with music.*

*It is early dusk of a spring evening. Supper has just been finished at the Wingfield apartment. Amanda and Laura in light-colored dresses are removing dishes from the table, in the upstage area, which is shadowy, their movements formalized almost as a dance or ritual, their moving forms as pale and silent as moths.*

*Tom, in white shirt and trousers, rises from the table and crosses toward the fire-escape.*

AMANDA (*as he passes her*). Son, will you do me a favor?

TOM. What?

AMANDA. Comb your hair! You look so pretty when your hair is combed! (*Tom slouches on sofa with evening paper. Enormous caption "Franco Triumphs."*) There is only one respect in which I would like you to emulate your father.

TOM. What respect is that?

AMANDA. The care he always took of his appearance. He never allowed himself to look untidy. (*He throws down the paper and crosses to fire-escape.*) Where are you going?

TOM. I'm going out to smoke.

AMANDA. You smoke too much. A pack a day at fifteen cents a pack. How much would that amount to in a month? Thirty times fifteen is how much, Tom? Figure it out and you will be astounded at what you could save. Enough to give you a night-school course in accounting at Washington U! Just think what a wonderful thing that would be for you, son!

*Tom is unmoved by the thought.*

TOM. I'd rather smoke. (*He steps out on landing, letting the screen door slam.*)

AMANDA (*sharply*). I know! That's the tragedy of it. . . . (*Alone, she turns to look at her husband's picture.*)

(*Dance Music: "All the World Is Waiting for the Sunrise!"*)

TOM (*to the audience*). Across the alley from us was the Paradise Dance Hall. On evenings in spring the windows and doors were open and the music came outdoors. Sometimes the lights were turned out except for a large glass sphere that hung from the ceiling. It would turn slowly about and filter the dusk with delicate rainbow colors. Then the orchestra played a waltz or a tango, something that had a slow and sensuous rhythm. Couples would come outside, to the relative privacy of the alley. You could see them kissing behind ashpits and telephone poles. This was the compensation for lives that passed like mine, without any change or adventure. Adventure and change were imminent in this year. They were waiting around the corner for all these kids. Suspended in the mist over Berchtesgaden, caught in the folds of Chamberlain's umbrella—In Spain there was Guernica! But here there was only hot swing music and liquor, dance halls, bars, and movies, and sex that hung in the gloom like a chandelier and flooded the world with brief, deceptive rainbows. . . . All the world was waiting for bombardments!

*Amanda turns from the picture and comes outside.*

AMANDA (*sighing*). A fire-escape landing's a poor excuse for a porch. (*She spreads a newspaper on a step and sits down, gracefully and demurely as if she were settling into a swing on a Mississippi veranda.*) What are you looking at?

TOM. The moon.

AMANDA. Is there a moon this evening?

TOM. It's rising over Garfinkel's Delicatessen.

AMANDA. So it is! A little silver slipper of a moon. Have you made a wish on it yet?

TOM. Um-hum.

AMANDA. What did you wish for?

TOM. That's a secret.

AMANDA. A secret, huh? Well, I won't tell mine either. I will be just as mysterious as you.

TOM. I bet I can guess what yours is.

AMANDA. Is my head so transparent?

TOM. You're not a sphinx.

AMANDA. No, I don't have secrets. I'll tell you what I wished for on the moon. Success and happiness for my precious children! I wish for that whenever there's a moon, and when there isn't a moon, I wish for it, too.

TOM. I thought perhaps you wished for a gentleman caller.

AMANDA. Why do you say that?

TOM. Don't you remember asking me to fetch one?

AMANDA. I remember suggesting that it would be nice for your sister if you brought some nice young man from the warehouse. I think I've made that suggestion more than once.

TOM. Yes, you have made it repeatedly.

AMANDA. Well?

TOM. We are going to have one.

AMANDA. *What?*

TOM. A gentleman caller!

(*The Annunciation Is Celebrated with Music.*)

*Amanda rises.*

(*Image on Screen: Caller with Bouquet.*)

AMANDA. You mean you have asked some nice young man to come over?

TOM. Yep. I've asked him to dinner.

AMANDA. You really did?

TOM. I did!

AMANDA. You did, and did he—*accept?*

TOM. He did!

AMANDA. Well, well—well, well! That's—lovely!

TOM. I thought that you would be pleased.

AMANDA. It's definite, then?

TOM. Very definite.

AMANDA. Soon?

TOM. Very soon.

AMANDA. For heaven's sake, stop putting on and tell me some things, will you?

TOM. What things do you want me to tell you?

AMANDA. Naturally I would like to know when he's *coming!*

TOM. He's coming tomorrow.

AMANDA. *Tomorrow?*

TOM. Yep. Tomorrow.

AMANDA. But, Tom!

TOM. Yes, Mother?

AMANDA. Tomorrow gives me no time!

TOM. Time for what?

AMANDA. Preparations! Why didn't you phone me at once, as soon as you asked him, the minute that he accepted? Then, don't you see, I could have been getting ready!

TOM. You don't have to make any fuss.

AMANDA. Oh, Tom, Tom, Tom, of course I have to make a fuss! I want things nice, not sloppy! Not thrown together. I'll certainly have to do some fast thinking, won't I?

TOM. I don't see why you have to think at all.

AMANDA. You just don't know. We can't have a gentleman caller in a pigsty! All my wedding silver has to be polished, the monogrammed table linen ought to be laundered! The windows have to be washed and fresh curtains put up. And how about clothes? We have to *wear* something, don't we?

TOM. Mother, this boy is no one to make a fuss over!

AMANDA. Do you realize he's the first young man we've introduced to your sister? It's terrible, dreadful, disgraceful that poor little sister has never received a single gentleman caller! Tom, come inside! (*She opens the screen door.*)

TOM. What for?

AMANDA. I want to ask you some things.

TOM. If you're going to make such a fuss, I'll call it off, I'll tell him not to come.

AMANDA. You certainly won't do anything of the kind. Nothing offends people worse than broken engagements. It simply means I'll have to work like a Turk! We won't be brilliant, but we'll pass inspection. Come on inside. (*Tom follows, groaning.*) Sit down.

TOM. Any particular place you would like me to sit?

AMANDA. Thank heavens I've got that new sofa! I'm also making payments on a floor lamp I'll have sent out! And put the chintz covers on, they'll brighten things up! Of course I'd hoped to have these walls repapered. . . . What is the young man's name?

TOM. His name is O'Connor.

AMANDA. That, of course, means fish—tomorrow is Friday! I'll have that salmon loaf—with Durkee's dressing! What does he do? He works at the warehouse?

TOM. Of course! How else would I—

AMANDA. Tom, he—doesn't drink?

TOM. Why do you ask me that?

AMANDA. Your father *did!*

TOM. Don't get started on that!

AMANDA. He *does* drink, then?

TOM. Not that I know of!

AMANDA. Make sure, be certain! The last thing I want for my daughter's a boy who drinks!

TOM. Aren't you being a little premature? Mr. O'Connor has not yet appeared on the scene!

AMANDA. But will tomorrow. To meet your sister, and what do I know about his character? Nothing! Old maids are better off than wives of drunkards!

TOM. Oh, my God!

AMANDA. Be still!

TOM (*leaning forward to whisper*). Lots of fellows meet girls whom they don't marry!

AMANDA. Oh, talk sensibly, Tom—and don't be sarcastic! (*She has gotten a hairbrush.*)

TOM. What are you doing?

AMANDA. I'm brushing that cow-lick down! What is this young man's position at the warehouse?

TOM (*submitting grimly to the brush and the interrogation*). This young man's position is that of a shipping clerk, Mother.

AMANDA. Sounds to me like a fairly responsible job, the sort of a job *you* would be in if you just had more *get-up.* What is his salary? Have you got any idea?

TOM. I would judge it to be approximately eighty-five dollars a month.

AMANDA. Well—not princely, but—

TOM. Twenty more than I make.

AMANDA. Yes, how well I know! But for a family man, eighty-five dollars a month is not much more than you can just get by on. . . .

TOM. Yes, but Mr. O'Connor is not a family man.

AMANDA. He might be, mightn't he? Some time in the future?

TOM. I see. Plans and provisions.

AMANDA. You are the only man that I know of who ignores the fact that the future becomes the present, the present the past, and the past turns into everlasting regret if you don't plan for it!

TOM. I will think that over and see what I can make of it.

AMANDA. Don't be supercilious with your mother! Tell me some more about this—what do you call him?

TOM. James D. O'Connor. The D. is for Delaney.

AMANDA. Irish on *both* sides! *Gracious!* And doesn't drink?

TOM. Shall I call him up and ask him right this minute?

AMANDA. The only way to find out about those things is to make discreet inquiries at the proper moment. When I was a girl in Blue Mountain and it was suspected that a young man drank, the girl whose attentions he had been receiving, if any girl *was,* would sometimes speak to the minister of his church, or rather her father would if her father was living, and sort of feel him out on the young man's character. That is the way such things are discreetly handled to keep a young woman from making a tragic mistake!

TOM. Then how did you happen to make a tragic mistake?

AMANDA. That innocent look of your father's had everyone fooled! He *smiled*—the world was *enchanted!* No girl can do worse than put herself at the mercy of a handsome appearance! I hope that Mr. O'Connor is not too good-looking.

TOM. No, he's not too good-looking. He's covered with freckles and hasn't too much of a nose.

AMANDA. He's not right-down homely, though?

TOM. Not right-down homely. Just medium homely, I'd say.

AMANDA. Character's what to look for in a man.

TOM. That's what I've always said, Mother.

AMANDA. You've never said anything of the kind and I suspect you would never give it a thought.

TOM. Don't be suspicious of me.

AMANDA. At least I hope he's the type that's up and coming.

TOM. I think he really goes in for self-improvement.

AMANDA. What reason have you to think so?

TOM. He goes to night school.

AMANDA (*beaming*). Splendid! What does he do, I mean study?

TOM. Radio engineering and public speaking!

AMANDA. Then he has visions of being advanced in the world! Any young man who studies public speaking is aiming to have an executive job some day! And radio engineering? A thing for the future! Both of these facts are very illuminating. Those are the sort of things that a mother should know concerning any young man who comes to call on her daughter. Seriously or—not.

TOM. One little warning. He doesn't know about Laura. I didn't let on that we had dark ulterior motives. I just said, why don't you come have dinner with us? He said okay and that was the whole conversation.

AMANDA. I bet it was! You're eloquent as an oyster. However, he'll know about Laura when he gets here. When he sees how lovely and sweet and pretty she is, he'll thank his lucky stars he was asked to dinner.

TOM. Mother, you mustn't expect too much of Laura.

AMANDA. What do you mean?

TOM. Laura seems all those things to you and me because she's ours and we love her. We don't even notice she's crippled any more.

AMANDA. Don't say crippled! You know that I never allow that word to be used!

TOM. But face facts, Mother. She is and—that's not all—

AMANDA. What do you mean "not all"?

TOM. Laura is very different from other girls.

AMANDA. I think the difference is all to her advantage.

TOM. Not quite all—in the eyes of others—strangers—she's terribly shy and lives in a world of her own and those things make her seem a little peculiar to people outside the house.

AMANDA. Don't say peculiar.

TOM. Face the facts. She is.

(*The Dance-Hall Music Changes to a Tango that Has a Minor and Somewhat Ominous Tone.*)

AMANDA. In what way is she peculiar—may I ask?

TOM (*gently*). She lives in a world of her own—a world of—little glass ornaments, Mother. . . . (*Gets up. Amanda remains holding brush, looking at him, troubled.*) She plays old phonograph records and—that's about all—(*He glances at himself in the mirror and crosses to door.*)

AMANDA (*sharply*). Where are you going?

TOM. I'm going to the movies. (*Out screen door.*)

AMANDA. Not to the movies, every night to the movies! (*Follows quickly* to screen door.) I don't believe you always go to the movies! (*He is gone. Amanda looks worriedly after him for a moment. Then vitality and optimism return and she turns from the door. Crossing to portieres.*) Laura! Laura! (*Laura answers from kitchenette.*)

LAURA. Yes, Mother.

AMANDA. Let those dishes go and come in front! (*Laura appears with dish towel. Gaily.*) Laura, come here and make a wish on the moon!

LAURA (*entering*). Moon—moon?

AMANDA. A little silver slipper of a moon. Look over your left shoulder, Laura, and make a wish! (*Laura looks faintly puzzled as if called out of sleep. Amanda seizes her shoulders and turns her at angle by the door.*) Now! Now, darling, *wish!*

LAURA. What shall I wish for, Mother?

AMANDA (*her voice trembling and her eyes suddenly filling with tears*). Happiness! Good Fortune!

*The violin rises and the stage dims out.*

## *Scene VI*

(*Image: High School Hero.*)

TOM. And so the following evening I brought Jim home to dinner. I had known Jim slightly in high school. In high school Jim was a hero. He had tremendous Irish good nature and vitality with the scrubbed and polished look of white chinaware. He seemed to move in a continual spotlight. He was a star in basketball, captain of the debating club, president of the senior class and the glee club and he sang the male lead in the annual light operas. He was always running or bounding, never just walking. He seemed always at the point of defeating the law of gravity. He was shooting with such velocity through his adolescence that you would logically expect him to arrive at nothing short of the White House by the time he was thirty. But Jim apparently ran into more interference after his graduation from Soldan. His speed had definitely slowed. Six years after he left high school he was holding a job that wasn't much better than mine.

(*Image: Clerk.*)

He was the only one at the warehouse with whom I was on friendly terms. I was valuable to him as someone who could remember his former glory, who had seen him win basketball games and the silver cup in debating. He knew of my secret practice of retiring to a cabinet of the washroom to work on poems when business was slack in the warehouse. He called me Shakespeare. And while the other boys in the warehouse regarded me with suspicious hostility, Jim took a humorous attitude toward me. Gradually his attitude affected the others, their hostility wore off and they also began to smile at me as people smile at an oddly fashioned dog who trots across their path at some distance.

I knew that Jim and Laura had known each other at Soldan, and I had heard Laura speak admiringly of his voice. I didn't know if Jim remembered her or not. In high school Laura had been as unobtrusive as Jim had been astonishing. If he did remember Laura, it was not as my sister, for when I asked him to dinner, he grinned and said, "You know, Shakespeare, I never thought of you as having folks!"

He was about to discover that I did. . . .

(*Light up Stage.*)

(*Legend on Screen: "The Accent of a Coming Foot."*)

*Friday evening. It is about five o'clock of a late spring evening which comes "scattering poems in the sky."*

*A delicate lemony light is in the Wingfield apartment.*

*Amanda has worked like a Turk in preparation for the gentleman caller. The results are astonishing. The new floor lamp with its rose-silk shade is in place, a colored paper lantern conceals the broken light fixture in the ceiling, new billowing white curtains are at the windows, chintz covers are on chairs and sofa, a pair of new sofa pillows make their initial appearance.*

*Open boxes and tissue paper are scattered on the floor.*

*Laura stands in the middle with lifted arms while Amanda crouches before her, adjusting the hem of the new dress, devout and ritualistic. The dress is colored and designed by memory. The arrangement of Laura's hair is changed; it is softer and more becoming. A fragile, unearthly prettiness has come out in Laura: she is like a piece of translucent glass touched by light, given a momentary radiance, not actual, not lasting.*

AMANDA (*impatiently*). Why are you trembling?

LAURA. Mother, you've made me so nervous!

AMANDA. How have I made you nervous?

LAURA. By all this fuss! You make it seem so important!

AMANDA. I don't understand you, Laura. You couldn't be satisfied with just sitting home, and yet whenever I try to arrange something for you, you seem to resist it. (*She gets up.*) Now take a look at yourself. No, wait! Wait just a moment—I have an idea!

LAURA. What is it now?

*Amanda produces two powder puffs which she wraps in handkerchiefs and stuffs in Laura's bosom.*

LAURA. Mother, what are you doing?

AMANDA. They call them "Gay Deceivers"!

LAURA. I won't wear them!

AMANDA. You will!

LAURA. Why should I?

AMANDA. Because, to be painfully honest, your chest is flat.

LAURA. You make it seem like we were setting a trap.

AMANDA. All pretty girls are a trap, a pretty trap, and men expect them to be. (*Legend: "A Pretty Trap."*) Now look at yourself, young lady. This is the prettiest you will ever be! I've got to fix myself now! You're going to be surprised by your mother's appearance! (*She crosses through portieres, humming gaily.*)

*Laura moves slowly to the long mirror and stares solemnly at herself.*

*A wind blows the white curtains inward in a slow, graceful motion and with a faint, sorrowful sighing.*

AMANDA (*off stage*). It isn't dark enough yet. (*She turns slowly before the mirror with a troubled look.*)

(*Legend on Screen: "This Is My Sister: Celebrate Her with Strings!" Music.*)

AMANDA (*laughing, off*). I'm going to show you something. I'm going to make a spectacular appearance!

LAURA. What is it, Mother?

AMANDA. Possess your soul in patience—you will see! Something I've resurrected from that old trunk! Styles haven't changed so terribly much after all. . . . (*She parts the portieres.*) Now just look at your mother! (*She wears a girlish frock of yellowed voile with a blue silk sash. She carries a bunch of jonquils—the legend of her youth is nearly revived. Feverishly.*) This is the dress in which I led the cotillion. Won the cakewalk twice at Sunset Hill, wore one spring to the Governor's ball in Jackson! See how I sashayed around the ballroom, Laura? (*She raises her skirt and does a mincing step around the room.*) I wore it on Sundays for my gentlemen callers! I had it on the day I met your father—I had malaria fever all that spring. The change of climate from East Tennessee to the Delta—weakened resistance—I had a little temperature all the time—not enough to be serious—just enough to make me restless and giddy! Invitations poured in—parties all over the Delta!—"Stay in bed," said Mother, "you have fever!"—but I just wouldn't.—I took quinine but kept on going, going!—Evenings, dances!—Afternoons, long, long rides! Picnics—lovely!—So lovely, that country in May.—All lacy with dogwood, literally flooded with jonquils!—That was the spring I had the craze for jonquils. Jonquils became an absolute obsession. Mother said, "Honey, there's no more room for jonquils." And still I kept bringing in more jonquils. Whenever, wherever I saw them, I'd say, "Stop! Stop! I see jonquils!" I made the young men help me gather the jonquils! It was a joke, Amanda and her jonquils! Finally there were no more vases to hold them, every available space was filled with jonquils. No vases to hold them? All right, I'll hold them myself! And then I—(*She stops in front of the picture.*) (*Music.*) met your father! Malaria fever and jonquils and then—this—boy. . . . (*She switches on the rose-colored lamp.*) I hope they get here before it starts to rain. (*She crosses upstage and places the jonquils in bowl on table.*) I gave your brother a little extra change so he and Mr. O'Connor could take the service car home.

LAURA (*with altered look*). What did you say his name was?

AMANDA. O'Connor.

LAURA. What is his first name?

AMANDA. I don't remember. Oh, yes, I do. It was—Jim!

*Laura sways slightly and catches hold of a chair.*

(*Legend on Screen: "Not Jim!"*)

LAURA (*faintly*). Not—Jim!

AMANDA. Yes, that was it, it was Jim! I've never known a Jim that wasn't nice!

(*Music: Ominous.*)

LAURA. Are you sure his name is Jim O'Connor?

AMANDA. Yes. Why?

LAURA. Is he the one that Tom used to know in high school?

AMANDA. He didn't say so. I think he just got to know him at the warehouse.

LAURA. There was a Jim O'Connor we both knew in high school—(*Then, with effort.*) If that is the one that Tom is bringing to dinner—you'll have to excuse me, I won't come to the table.

AMANDA. What sort of nonsense is this?

LAURA. You asked me once if I'd ever liked a boy. Don't you remember I showed you this boy's picture?

AMANDA. You mean the boy you showed me in the year-book?

LAURA. Yes, that boy.

AMANDA. Laura, Laura, were you in love with that boy?

LAURA. I don't know, Mother. All I know is I couldn't sit at the table if it was him!

AMANDA. It won't be him! It isn't the least bit likely. But whether it is or not, you will come to the table. You will not be excused.

LAURA. I'll have to be, Mother.

AMANDA. I don't intend to humor your silliness, Laura. I've had too much from you and your brother, both! So just sit down and compose yourself till they come. Tom has forgotten his key so you'll have to let them in, when they arrive.

LAURA (*panicky*). Oh, Mother—*you* answer the door!

AMANDA (*lightly*). I'll be in the kitchen—busy!

LAURA. Oh, Mother, please answer the door, don't make me do it!

AMANDA (*crossing into kitchenette*). I've got to fix the dressing for the salmon. Fuss, fuss—silliness!—over a gentleman caller!

*Door swings shut. Laura is left alone.*

(*Legend: "Terror!"*)

*She utters a low moan and turns off the lamp—sits stiffly on the edge of the sofa, knotting her fingers together.*

(*Legend on Screen: "The Opening of a Door!"*)

*Tom and Jim appear on the fire-escape steps and climb to landing. Hearing their approach, Laura rises with a panicky gesture. She retreats to the portieres.*

*The doorbell. Laura catches her breath and touches her throat. Low drums.*

AMANDA (*calling*). Laura, sweetheart! The door!

*Laura stares at it without moving.*

JIM. I think we just beat the rain.

TOM. Uh-huh. (*He rings again, nervously. Jim whistles and fishes for a cigarette.*)

AMANDA (*very, very gaily*). Laura, that is your brother and Mr. O'Connor! Will you let them in, darling?

*Laura crosses toward kitchenette door.*

LAURA (*breathlessly*). Mother—you go to the door!

*Amanda steps out of kitchenette and stares furiously at Laura. She points imperiously at the door.*

LAURA. Please, please!

AMANDA (*in a fierce whisper*). What is the matter with you, you silly thing?

LAURA (*desperately*). Please, you answer it, *please!*

AMANDA. I told you I wasn't going to humor you, Laura. Why have you chosen this moment to lose your mind?

LAURA. Please, please, please, you go!

AMANDA. You'll have to go to the door because I can't!

LAURA (*despairingly*). I can't either!

AMANDA. Why?

LAURA. I'm *sick!*

AMANDA. I'm sick, too—of your nonsense! Why can't you and your brother be normal people? Fantastic whims and behavior! (*Tom gives a long ring.*) Preposterous goings on! Can you give me one reason—(*Calls out lyrically.*) COMING! JUST ONE SECOND!—why should you be afraid to open a door? Now you answer it, Laura!

LAURA. Oh, oh, oh . . . (*She returns through the portieres. Darts to the victrola and winds it frantically and turns it on.*)

AMANDA. Laura Wingfield, you march right to that door!

LAURA. Yes—yes, Mother!

*A faraway, scratchy rendition of "Dardanella" softens the air and gives her strength to move through it. She slips to the door and draws it cautiously open.*

*Tom enters with caller, Jim O'Connor.*

TOM. Laura, this is Jim. Jim, this is my sister, Laura.

JIM (*stepping inside*). I didn't know that Shakespeare had a sister!

LAURA (*retreating stiff and trembling from the door*). How—how do you do?

JIM (*heartily extending his hand*). Okay!

*Laura touches it hesitantly with hers.*

JIM. Your hand's *cold,* Laura!

LAURA. Yes, well—I've been playing the victrola. . . .

JIM. Must have been playing classical music on it! You ought to play a little hot swing music to warm you up!

LAURA. Excuse me—I haven't finished playing the victrola. . . .

*She turns awkwardly and hurries into the front room. She pauses a second by the victrola. Then catches her breath and darts through the portieres like a frightened deer.*

JIM (*grinning*). What was the matter?

TOM. Oh—with Laura? Laura is—terribly shy.

JIM. Shy, huh? It's unusual to meet a shy girl nowadays. I don't believe you ever mentioned you had a sister.

TOM. Well, now you know. I have one. Here is the *Post Dispatch.* You want a piece of it?

JIM. Uh-huh.

TOM. What piece? The comics?

JIM. Sports! (*Glances at it.*) Ole Dizzy Dean is on his bad behavior.

TOM (*disinterest*). Yeah? (*Lights cigarette and crosses back to fire-escape door.*)

JIM. Where are *you* going?

TOM. I'm going out on the terrace.

JIM (*goes after him*). You know, Shakespeare—I'm going to sell you a bill of goods!

TOM. What goods?

JIM. A course I'm taking.

TOM. Huh?

JIM. In public speaking! You and me, we're not the warehouse type.

TOM. Thanks—that's good news. But what has public speaking got to do with it?

JIM. It fits you for—executive positions!

TOM. Awww.

JIM. I tell you it's done a helluva lot for me.

(*Image: Executive at Desk.*)

TOM. In what respect?

JIM. In every! Ask yourself what is the difference between you an' me and men in the office down front? Brains?—No!—Ability?—No! Then what? Just one little thing—

TOM. What is that one little thing?

JIM. Primarily it amounts to—social poise! Being able to square up to people and hold your own on any social level!

AMANDA (*off stage*). Tom?

TOM. Yes, Mother?

AMANDA. Is that you and Mr. O'Connor?

TOM. Yes, Mother.

AMANDA. Well, you just make yourselves comfortable in there.

TOM. Yes, Mother.

AMANDA. Ask Mr. O'Connor if he would like to wash his hands.

JIM. Aw—no—no—thank you—I took care of that at the warehouse. Tom—

TOM. Yes?

JIM. Mr. Mendoza was speaking to me about you.

TOM. Favorably?

JIM. What do you think?

TOM. Well—

JIM. You're going to be out of a job if you don't wake up.

TOM. I am waking up—

JIM. You show no signs.

TOM. The signs are interior.

(*Image on Screen: The Sailing Vessel with Jolly Roger Again.*)

TOM. I'm planning to change. (*He leans over the rail speaking with quiet exhilaration. The incandescent marquees and signs of the first-run movie houses light his face from across the alley. He looks like a voyager.*) I'm right at the point of committing myself to a future that doesn't include the warehouse and Mr. Mendoza or even a night-school course in public speaking.

JIM. What are you gassing about?

TOM. I'm tired of the movies.

JIM. Movies!

TOM. Yes, movies! Look at them—(*a wave toward the marvels of Grand Avenue.*) All of those glamorous people—having adventures—hogging it all, gobbling the whole thing up! You know what happens? People go to the *movies* instead of *moving!* Hollywood characters are supposed to have all the adventures for everybody in America, while everybody in America sits in a dark room and watches them have them! Yes, until there's a war. That's when adventure becomes available to the masses! *Everyone's* dish, not only Gable's! Then the people in the dark room come out of the dark room to have some adventures themselves—Goody, goody—It's our turn now, to go to the South Sea Island—to make a safari—to be exotic, far-off—But I'm not patient. I don't want to wait till then. I'm tired of the *movies* and I am *about* to *move!*

JIM (*incredulously*). Move?

TOM. Yes.

JIM. When?

TOM. Soon!

JIM. Where? Where?

(*Theme Three: Music Seems to Answer the Question, while Tom Thinks it Over. He Searches among his Pockets.*)

TOM. I'm starting to boil inside. I know I seem dreamy, but inside—well, I'm boiling! Whenever I pick up a shoe, I shudder a little thinking how short life is and what I am doing!—Whatever that means. I know it doesn't mean shoes—except as something to wear on a traveler's feet! (*Finds paper.*) Look—

JIM. What?

TOM. I'm a member.

JIM (*reading*). The Union of Merchant Seamen.

TOM. I paid my dues this month, instead of the light bill.

JIM. You will regret it when they turn the lights off.

TOM. I won't be here.

JIM. How about your mother?

TOM. I'm like my father. The bastard son of a bastard! See how he grins? And he's been absent going on sixteen years!

JIM. You're just talking, you drip. How does your mother feel about it?

TOM. Shhh—Here comes Mother! Mother is not acquainted with my plans!

AMANDA (*enters portieres*). Where are you all?

TOM. On the terrace, Mother.

*They start inside. She advances to them. Tom is distinctly shocked at her appearance. Even Jim blinks a little. He is making his first con-*

*tact with girlish Southern vivacity and in spite of the night-school course in public speaking is somewhat thrown off the beam by the unexpected outlay of social charm.*

*Certain responses are attempted by Jim but are swept aside by Amanda's gay laughter and chatter. Tom is embarrassed but after the first shock Jim reacts very warmly. Grins and chuckles, is altogether won over.*

(*Image: Amanda as a Girl.*)

AMANDA (*coyly smiling, shaking her girlish ringlets*). Well, well, well, so this is Mr. O'Connor. Introductions entirely unnecessary. I've heard so much about you from my boy. I finally said to him, Tom—good gracious!—why don't you bring this paragon to supper? I'd like to meet this nice young man at the warehouse!—Instead of just hearing him sing your praises so much! I don't know why my son is so standoffish—that's not Southern behavior! Let's sit down and—I think we could stand a little more air in here! Tom, leave the door open. I felt a nice fresh breeze a moment ago. Where has it gone? Mmm, so warm already! And not quite summer, even. We're going to burn up when summer really gets started. However, we're having—we're having a very light supper. I think light things are better fo' this time of year. The same as light clothes are. Light clothes an' light food are what warm weather calls fo'. You know our blood gets so thick during th' winter—it takes a while fo' us to *adjust* ou'selves!—when the season changes. . . . It's come so quick this year. I wasn't prepared. All of a sudden—heavens! Already summer!—I ran to the trunk an' pulled out this light dress—Terribly old! Historical almost! But feels so good—so good an' co-ol, y'know. . . .

TOM. Mother—

AMANDA. Yes, honey?

TOM. How about—supper?

AMANDA. Honey, you go ask Sister if supper is ready! You know that Sister is in full charge of supper! Tell her you hungry boys are waiting for it. (*To Jim.*) Have you met Laura?

JIM. She—

AMANDA. Let you in? Oh, good, you've met already! It's rare for a girl as sweet an' pretty as Laura to be domestic! But Laura is, thank heavens, not only pretty but also very domestic. I'm not at all. I never was a bit. I never could make a thing but angel-food cake. Well, in the South we had so many servants. Gone, gone, gone. All vestiges of gracious living! Gone completely! I wasn't prepared for what the future brought me. All of my gentlemen callers were sons of planters and so of course I assumed that I would be married to one and raise my family on a large piece of land with plenty of servants. But man proposes—and woman accepts the proposal!—To vary that old, old saying a little bit—I married no planter! I married a man who worked for the telephone company!—that gallantly smiling gentleman over there! (*Points to the picture.*) A telephone man who—fell in love with long distance!—Now he travels and I don't even know where!—But what am I going on for about my—tribulations! Tell me yours—I hope you don't have any! Tom?

TOM (*returning*). Yes, Mother?

AMANDA. Is supper nearly ready?

TOM. It looks to me like supper is on the table.

AMANDA. Let me look—(*She rises prettily and looks through portieres.*) Oh, lovely—But where is Sister?

TOM. Laura is not feeling well and she says that she thinks she'd better not come to the table.

AMANDA. What?—Nonsense!—Laura? Oh, Laura!

LAURA (*off stage, faintly*). Yes, Mother.

AMANDA. You really must come to the table. We won't be seated until you come to the table! Come in, Mr. O'Connor. You sit over there and I'll—Laura? Laura Wingfield! You're keeping us waiting, honey! We can't say grace until you come to the table!

*The back door is pushed weakly open and Laura comes in. She is obviously quite faint, her lips trembling, her eyes wide and staring. She moves unsteadily toward the table.*

(*Legend: "Terror!"*)

*Outside a summer storm is coming abruptly. The white curtains billow inward at the windows and there is a sorrowful murmur and deep blue dusk.*

*Laura suddenly stumbles—She catches a chair with a faint moan.*

TOM. Laura!

AMANDA. Laura! (*There is a clap of thunder.*) (*Legend: "Ah!"*) (*Despairingly.*) Why, Laura, you *are* sick, darling! Tom, help your sister into the living room, dear! Sit in the living room, Laura—rest on the sofa. Well! (*To the gentleman caller.*) Standing over the hot stove made her ill!—I told her that it was just too warm this evening, but—(*Tom comes back in. Laura is on the sofa.*) Is Laura all right now?

TOM. Yes.

AMANDA. What *is* that? Rain? A nice cool rain has come up! (*She gives the gentleman caller a frightened look.*) I think we may—have grace—now . . . (*Tom looks at her stupidly.*) Tom, honey—you say grace!

TOM. Oh . . . "For these and all thy mercies—" (*They bow their heads, Amanda stealing a nervous glance at Jim. In the living room Laura, stretched on the sofa, clenches her hand to her lips, to hold back a shuddering sob.*) God's Holy Name be praised—

(*The Scene Dims Out.*)

## *Scene VII*

### *A Souvenir*

*Half an hour later. Dinner is just being finished in the upstage area which is concealed by the drawn portieres.*

*As the curtain rises Laura is still huddled upon the sofa, her feet drawn under her, her head resting on a pale blue pillow, her eyes wide and mysteriously watchful. The new floor lamp with its shade of rose-colored silk gives a soft, becoming light to her face, bringing out the fragile, unearthly prettiness which usually escapes attention. There is a steady murmur of rain, but it is slackening and stops soon after the scene begins; the air outside becomes pale and luminous as the moon breaks out.*

*A moment after the curtain rises, the lights in both rooms flicker and go out.*

JIM. Hey, there, Mr. Light Bulb!

*Amanda laughs nervously.*

(*Legend: "Suspension of a Public Service."*)

AMANDA. Where was Moses when the lights went out? Ha-ha. Do you know the answer to that one, Mr. O'Connor?

JIM. No, Ma'am, what's the answer?

AMANDA. In the dark! (*Jim laughs appreciatively.*) Everybody sit still. I'll light the candles. Isn't it lucky we have them on the table? Where's a match? Which of you gentlemen can provide a match?

JIM. Here.

AMANDA. Thank you, sir.

JIM. Not at all, Ma'am!

AMANDA. I guess the fuse has burnt out. Mr. O'Connor, can you tell a burnt-out fuse? I know I can't and Tom is a total loss when it comes to mechanics. (*Sound: Getting Up: Voices Recede a Little to Kitchenette.*) Oh, be careful you don't bump into something. We don't want our gentleman caller to break his neck. Now wouldn't that be a fine howdy-do?

JIM. Ha-ha! Where is the fuse-box?

AMANDA. Right here next to the stove. Can you see anything?

JIM. Just a minute.

AMANDA. Isn't electricity a mysterious thing? Wasn't it Benjamin Franklin who tied a key to a kite? We live in such a mysterious universe, don't we? Some people say that science clears up all the mysteries for us. In my opinion it only creates more! Have you found it yet?

JIM. No, Ma'am. All these fuses look okay to me.

AMANDA. Tom!

TOM. Yes, Mother?

AMANDA. That light bill I gave you several days ago. The one I told you we got the notices about?

TOM. Oh.—Yeah.

(*Legend: "Ha!"*)

AMANDA. You didn't neglect to pay it by any chance?

TOM. Why, I—

AMANDA. Didn't! I might have known it!

JIM. Shakespeare probably wrote a poem on that light bill, Mrs. Wingfield.

AMANDA. I might have known better than to trust him with it! There's such a high price for negligence in this world!

JIM. Maybe the poem will win a ten-dollar prize.

AMANDA. We'll just have to spend the remainder of the evening in the nineteenth century, before Mr. Edison made the Mazda lamp!

JIM. Candlelight is my favorite kind of light.

AMANDA. That shows you're romantic! But that's no excuse for Tom. Well, we got through dinner. Very considerate of them to let us get through dinner before they plunged us into everlasting darkness, wasn't it, Mr. O'Connor?

JIM. Ha-ha!

AMANDA. Tom, as a penalty for your carelessness you can help me with the dishes.

JIM. Let me give you a hand.

AMANDA. Indeed you will not!

JIM. I ought to be good for something.

AMANDA. Good for something? (*Her tone is rhapsodic.*) *You?* Why, Mr. O'Connor, nobody, *nobody's* given me this much entertainment in years—as you have!

JIM. Aw, now, Mrs. Wingfield!

AMANDA. I'm not exaggerating, not one bit! But Sister is all by her lonesome. You go keep her company in the parlor! I'll give you this lovely old candelabrum that used to be on the altar at the church of the Heavenly Rest. It was melted a little out of shape when the church burnt down. Lightning struck it one spring. Gypsy Jones was holding a revival at the time and he intimated that the church was destroyed because the Episcopalians gave card parties.

JIM. Ha-ha.

AMANDA. And how about coaxing Sister to drink a little wine? I think it would be good for her! Can you carry both at once?

JIM. Sure. I'm Superman!

AMANDA. Now, Thomas, get into this apron!

*The door of kitchenette swings closed on Amanda's gay laughter; the flickering light approaches the portieres.*

*Laura sits up nervously as he enters. Her speech at first is low and breathless from the almost intolerable strain of being alone with a stranger.*

*(Legend: "I Don't Suppose You Remember Me at All!")*

*In her first speeches in this scene, before Jim's warmth overcomes her paralyzing shyness, Laura's voice is thin and breathless as though she has run up a steep flight of stairs.*

*Jim's attitude is gently humorous. In playing this scene it should be stressed that while the incident is apparently unimportant, it is to Laura the climax of her secret life.*

JIM. Hello, there, Laura.

LAURA (*faintly*). Hello. (*She clears her throat.*)

JIM. How are you feeling now? Better?

LAURA. Yes. Yes, thank you.

JIM. This is for you. A little dandelion wine. (*He extends it toward her with extravagant gallantry.*)

LAURA. Thank you.

JIM. Drink it—but don't get drunk! (*He laughs heartily. Laura takes the glass uncertainly; laughs shyly.*) Where shall I set the candles?

LAURA. Oh—oh, anywhere . . .

JIM. How about here on the floor? Any objections?

LAURA. No.

JIM. I'll spread a newspaper under to catch the drippings. I like to sit on the floor. Mind if I do?

LAURA. Oh, no.

JIM. Give me a pillow?

LAURA. What?

JIM. A pillow!

LAURA. Oh . . . (*Hands him one quickly.*)

JIM. How about you? Don't you like to sit on the floor?

LAURA. Oh—yes.

JIM. Why don't you, then?

LAURA. I—will.

JIM. Take a pillow! (*Laura does. Sits on the other side of the candelabrum. Jim crosses his legs and smiles engagingly at her.*) I can't hardly see you sitting way over there.

LAURA. I can—see you.

JIM. I know, but that's not fair, I'm in the limelight. (*Laura moves her pillow closer.*) Good! Now I can see you! Comfortable?

LAURA. Yes.

JIM. So am I. Comfortable as a cow. Will you have some gum?

LAURA. No, thank you.

JIM. I think that I will indulge, with your permission. (*Musingly unwraps it and holds it up.*) Think of the fortune made by the guy that invented the first piece of chewing gum. Amazing, huh? The Wrigley Building is one of the sights of Chicago.—I saw it summer before last when I went up to the Century of Progress. Did you take in the Century of Progress?

LAURA. No, I didn't.

JIM. Well, it was quite a wonderful exposition. What impressed me most was the Hall of Science. Gives you an idea of what the future will be in America, even more wonderful than the present time is! (*Pause. Smiling at her.*) Your brother tells me you're shy. Is that right, Laura?

LAURA. I—don't know.

JIM. I judge you to be an old-fashioned type of girl. Well, I think that's a pretty good type to be. Hope you don't think I'm being too personal—do you?

LAURA (*hastily, out of embarrassment*). I believe I *will* take a piece of gum, if you—don't mind. (*Clearing her throat.*) Mr. O'Connor, have you—kept up with your singing?

JIM. Singing? Me?

LAURA. Yes. I remember what a beautiful voice you had.

JIM. When did you hear me sing?

(*Voice Offstage in the Pause.*)

VOICE (*offstage*).

O blow, ye winds, heigh-ho.
A-roving I will go!
I'm off to my love
With a boxing glove—
Ten thousand miles away!

JIM. You say you've heard me sing?

LAURA. Oh, yes! Yes, very often . . . I—don't suppose you remember me—at all?

JIM (*smiling doubtfully*). You know I have an idea I've seen you before. I had that idea soon as you opened the door. It seemed almost like I was about to remember your name. But the name that I started to call you—wasn't a name! And so I stopped myself before I said it.

LAURA. Wasn't it—Blue Roses?

JIM (*springs up, grinning*). Blue Roses! My gosh, yes—Blue Roses! That's what I had on my tongue when you opened the door! Isn't it funny what tricks your memory plays? I didn't connect you with the high school somehow or other. But that's where it was; it was high school. I didn't even know you were Shakespeare's sister! Gosh, I'm sorry.

LAURA. I didn't expect you to. You—barely knew me!

JIM. But we did have a speaking acquaintance, huh?

LAURA. Yes, we—spoke to each other.

JIM. When did you recognize me?

LAURA. Oh, right away!

JIM. Soon as I came in the door?

LAURA. When I heard your name I thought it was probably you. I knew that Tom used to know you a little in high school. So when you came in the door—Well, then I was—sure.

JIM. Why didn't you *say* something, then?

LAURA (*breathlessly*). I didn't know what to say, I was—too surprised!

JIM. For goodness' sakes! You know, this sure is funny!

LAURA. Yes! Yes, isn't it, though. . . .

JIM. Didn't we have a class in something together?

LAURA. Yes, we did.

JIM. What class was that?

LAURA. It was—singing—Chorus!

JIM. Aw!

LAURA. I sat across the aisle from you in the Aud.

JIM. Aw.

LAURA. Mondays, Wednesdays and Fridays.

JIM. Now I remember—you always came in late.

LAURA. Yes, it was so hard for me, getting upstairs. I had a brace on my leg—it clumped so loud!

JIM. I never heard any clumping.

LAURA (*wincing at the recollection*). To me it sounded like—thunder!

JIM. Well, well, well. I never even noticed.

LAURA. And everybody was seated before I came in. I had to walk in front of all those people. My seat was in the back row. I had to go clumping all the way up the aisle with everyone watching!

JIM. You shouldn't have been self-conscious.

LAURA. I know, but I was. It was always such a relief when the singing started.

JIM. Aw, yes, I've placed you now! I used to call you Blue Roses. How was it that I got started calling you that?

LAURA. I was out of school a little while with pleurosis. When I came back you asked me what was the matter. I said I had pleurosis—you thought I said Blue Roses. That's what you always called me after that!

JIM. I hope you didn't mind.

LAURA. Oh, no—I liked it. You see, I wasn't acquainted with many—people. . . .

JIM. As I remember you sort of stuck by yourself.

LAURA. I—I—never had much luck at—making friends.

JIM. I don't see why you wouldn't.

LAURA. Well, I—started out badly.

JIM. You mean being—

LAURA. Yes, it sort of—stood between me—

JIM. You shouldn't have let it!

LAURA. I know, but it did, and—

JIM. You were shy with people!

LAURA. I tried not to be but never could—

JIM. Overcome it?

LAURA. No, I—I never could!

JIM. I guess being shy is something you have to work out of kind of gradually.

LAURA (*sorrowfully*). Yes—I guess it—

JIM. Takes time!

LAURA. Yes—

JIM. People are not so dreadful when you know them. That's what you have to remember! And everybody has problems, not just you, but practically everybody has got some problems. You think of yourself as having the only problems, as being the only one who is disappointed. But just look around you and you will see lots of people as disappointed as you are. For instance, I hoped when I was going to high school that I would be further along at this time, six years after, than I am now—You remember that wonderful write-up I had in *The Torch?*

LAURA. Yes! (*She rises and crosses to table.*)

JIM. It said I was bound to succeed in anything I went into! (*Laura returns with the annual.*) Holy Jeez! *The Torch!* (*He accepts it reverently. They smile across it with mutual wonder. Laura crouches beside him and they begin to turn through it. Laura's shyness is dissolving in his warmth.*)

LAURA. Here you are in *Pirates of Penzance!*

JIM (*wistfully*). I sang the baritone lead in that operetta.

LAURA (*rapidly*). So—*beautifully!*

JIM (*protesting*). Aw—

LAURA. Yes, yes—beautifully—beautifully!

JIM. You heard me?

LAURA. All three times!

JIM. No!

LAURA. Yes!

JIM. All three performances?

LAURA (*looking down*). Yes.

JIM. Why?

LAURA. I—wanted to ask you to—autograph my program.

JIM. Why didn't you ask me to?

LAURA. You were always surrounded by your own friends so much that I never had a chance to.

JIM. You should have just—

LAURA. Well, I—thought you might think I was—

JIM. Thought I might think you was—what?

LAURA. Oh—

JIM (*with reflective relish*). I was beleaguered by females in those days.

LAURA. You were terribly popular!

JIM. Yeah—

LAURA. You had such a—friendly way—

JIM. I was spoiled in high school.

LAURA. Everybody—liked you!

JIM. Including you?

LAURA. I—yes, I—I did, too—(*She gently closes the book in her lap.*)

JIM. Well, well, well!—Give me that program, Laura. (*She hands it to him. He signs it with a flourish.*) There you are—better late than never!

LAURA. Oh, I—what a—surprise!

JIM. My signature isn't worth very much right now. But some day—maybe—it will increase in value! Being disappointed is one thing and being discouraged is something else. I am disappointed but I'm not discouraged. I'm twenty-three years old. How old are you?

LAURA. I'll be twenty-four in June.

JIM. That's not old age!

LAURA. No, but—

JIM. You finished high school?

LAURA (*with difficulty*). I didn't go back.

JIM. You mean you dropped out?

LAURA. I made bad grades in my final examinations. (*She rises and replaces the book and the program. Her voice strained.*) How is—Emily Meisenbach getting along?

JIM. Oh, that kraut-head!

LAURA. Why do you call her that?

JIM. That's what she was.

LAURA. You're not still—going with her?

JIM. I never see her.

LAURA. It said in the Personal Section that you were—engaged!

JIM. I know, but I wasn't impressed by that—propaganda!

LAURA. It wasn't—the truth?

JIM. Only in Emily's optimistic opinion!

LAURA. Oh—

(*Legend: "What Have You Done since High School?"*)

*Jim lights a cigarette and leans indolently back on his elbows smiling at Laura with a warmth and charm which light her inwardly with altar candles. She remains by the table and turns in her hands a piece of glass to cover her tumult.*

JIM (*after several reflective puffs on a cigarette*). What have you done since high school? (*She seems not to hear him.*) Huh? (*Laura looks up.*) I said what have you done since high school, Laura?

LAURA. Nothing much.

JIM. You must have been doing something these six long years.

LAURA. Yes.

JIM. Well, then, such as what?

LAURA. I took a business course at business college—

JIM. How did that work out?

LAURA. Well, not very—well—I had to drop out, it gave me—indigestion—

*Jim laughs gently.*

JIM. What are you doing now?

LAURA. I don't do anything—much. Oh, please don't think I sit around doing nothing! My glass collection takes up a good deal of my time. Glass is something you have to take good care of.

JIM. What did you say—about glass?

LAURA. Collection I said—I have one—(*She clears her throat and turns away again, acutely shy.*)

JIM (*abruptly*). You know what I judge to be the trouble with you? Inferiority complex! Know what that is? That's what they call it when someone low-rates himself! I understand it because I had it, too. Although my case was not so aggravated as yours seems to be. I had it until I took up public speaking, developed my voice, and learned that I had an aptitude for science. Before that time I never thought of myself as being outstanding in any way whatsoever! Now I've never made a regular study of it, but I have a friend who says I can analyze people better than doctors that make a profession of it. I don't claim that to be necessarily true, but I can sure guess a person's psychology, Laura! (*Takes out his gum.*) Excuse me, Laura. I always take it out when the flavor is gone. I'll use this scrap of paper to wrap it in. I know how it is to get it stuck on a shoe. Yep—that's what I judge to be your principal trouble. A lack of confidence in yourself as a person. You don't have the proper amount of faith in yourself. I'm basing that fact on a number of your remarks and also on certain observations I've made. For instance that clumping you thought was so awful in high school. You say that you even dreaded to walk into class. You see what you did? You dropped out of school, you gave up an education because of a clump, which as far as I know was practically nonexistent! A little physical defect is what you have. Hardly noticeable even! Magnified thousands of times by imagination! You know what my strong advice to you is? Think of yourself as *superior* in some way!

LAURA. In what way would I think?

JIM. Why, man alive, Laura! Just look about you a little. What do you see? A world full of common people! All of 'em born and all of 'em going to die! Which of them has one-tenth of your good points! Or mine! Or anyone else's, as far as that goes—Gosh! Everybody excels in some one thing. Some in many! (*Unconsciously glances at himself in the mirror.*) All you've got to do is discover in *what!* Take me, for instance. (*He adjusts his tie at the mirror.*) My interest happens to lie in electrodynamics. I'm taking a course in radio engineering at night school, Laura, on top of a fairly responsible job at the warehouse. I'm taking that course and studying public speaking.

LAURA. Ohhhh.

JIM. Because I believe in the future of television! (*Turning back to her.*) I wish to be ready to go up right along with it. Therefore I'm planning to get in on the ground floor. In fact, I've already made the right connections and all that remains is for the industry itself to get under way! Full steam—(*His eyes are starry.*) *Knowledge*—Zzzzzp! *Money*—Zzzzzzp!—*Power!* That's the cycle democracy is built on! (*His attitude is convincingly dynamic. Laura stares at him, even her shyness eclipsed in her absolute wonder. He suddenly grins.*) I guess you think I think a lot of myself!

LAURA. No—o-o-o, I—

JIM. Now how about you? Isn't there something you take more interest in than anything else?

LAURA. Well, I do—as I said—have my—glass collection—

*A peal of girlish laughter from the kitchen.*

JIM. I'm not right sure I know what you're talking about. What kind of glass is it?

LAURA. Little articles of it, they're ornaments mostly! Most of them are little animals made out of glass, the tiniest little animals in the world. Mother calls them a glass menagerie! Here's an example of one, if you'd like to see it! This one is one of the oldest. It's nearly thirteen. (*He stretches out his hand.*) (*Music: "The Glass Menagerie."*) Oh, be careful—if you breathe, it breaks!

JIM. I'd better not take it. I'm pretty clumsy with things.

LAURA. Go on, I trust you with him! (*Places it in his palm.*) There now—you're holding him gently! Hold him over the light, he loves the light! You see how the light shines through him?

JIM. It sure does shine!

LAURA. I shouldn't be partial, but he is my favorite one.

JIM. What kind of a thing is this one supposed to be?

LAURA. Haven't you noticed the single horn on his forehead?

JIM. A unicorn, huh?

LAURA. Mmm-hmmm!

JIM. Unicorns, aren't they extinct in the modern world?

LAURA. I know!

JIM. Poor little fellow, he must feel sort of lonesome.

LAURA (*smiling*). Well, if he does he doesn't complain about it. He stays on a shelf with some horses that don't have horns and all of them seem to get along nicely together.

JIM. How do you know?

LAURA (*lightly*). I haven't heard any arguments among them!

JIM (*grinning*). No arguments, huh? Well, that's a pretty good sign! Where shall I set him?

LAURA. Put him on the table. They all like a change of scenery once in a while!

JIM (*stretching*). Well, well, well, well—Look how big my shadow is when I stretch!

LAURA. Oh, oh, yes—it stretches across the ceiling!

JIM (*crossing to door*). I think it's stopped raining. (*Opens fire-escape door.*) Where does the music come from?

LAURA. From the Paradise Dance Hall across the alley.

JIM. How about cutting the rug a little, Miss Wingfield?

LAURA. Oh, I—

JIM. Or is your program filled up? Let me have a look at it. (*Grasps imaginary card.*) Why, every dance is taken! I'll just have to scratch some out. (*Waltz Music: "La Golondrina."*) Ahhh, a waltz! (*He executes some sweeping turns by himself then holds his arms toward Laura.*)

LAURA (*breathlessly*). I—can't dance!

JIM. There you go, that inferiority stuff!

LAURA. I've never danced in my life!

JIM. Come on, try!

LAURA. Oh, but I'd step on you!

JIM. I'm not made out of glass.

LAURA. How—how—how do we start?

JIM. Just leave it to me. You hold your arms out a little.

LAURA. Like this?

JIM. A little bit higher. Right. Now don't tighten up, that's the main thing about it—relax.

LAURA (*laughing breathlessly*). It's hard not to.

JIM. Okay.

LAURA. I'm afraid you can't budge me.

JIM. What do you bet I can't? (*He swings her into motion.*)

LAURA. Goodness, yes, you can!

JIM. Let yourself go, now, Laura, just let yourself go.

LAURA. I'm—

JIM. Come on!

LAURA. Trying!

JIM. Not so stiff—Easy does it!

LAURA. I know but I'm—

JIM. Loosen th' backbone! There now, that's a lot better.

LAURA. Am I?

JIM. Lots, lots better! (*He moves her about the room in a clumsy waltz.*)

LAURA. Oh, my!

JIM. Ha-ha!

LAURA. Oh, my goodness!

JIM. Ha-ha-ha! (*They suddenly bump into the table. Jim stops.*) What did we hit on?

LAURA. Table.

JIM. Did something fall off it? I think—

LAURA. Yes.

JIM. I hope that it wasn't the little glass horse with the horn!

LAURA. Yes.

JIM. Aw, aw, aw. Is it broken?

LAURA. Now it is just like all the other horses.

JIM. It's lost its—

LAURA. Horn! It doesn't matter. Maybe it's a blessing in disguise.

JIM. You'll never forgive me. I bet that that was your favorite piece of glass.

LAURA. I don't have favorites much. It's no tragedy, Freckles. Glass breaks so easily. No matter how careful you are. The traffic jars the shelves and things fall off them.

JIM. Still I'm awfully sorry that I was the cause.

LAURA (*smiling*). I'll just imagine he had an operation. The horn was removed to make him feel less—freakish! (*They both laugh.*) Now he will feel more at home with the other horses, the ones that don't have horns . . .

JIM. Ha-ha, that's very funny! (*Suddenly serious.*) I'm glad to see that you have a sense of humor. You know—you're—well—very different! Surprisingly different from anyone else I know! (*His voice becomes soft and hesitant with a genuine feeling.*) Do you mind me telling you that? (*Laura is abashed beyond speech.*) You make me feel sort of—I don't know how to put it! I'm usually pretty good at expressing things, but—This is something that I don't know how to say! (*Laura touches her throat and clears it—turns the broken unicorn in her hands.*) (*Even softer.*) Has anyone ever told you that you were pretty? (*Pause: Music.*) (*Laura looks up slowly, with wonder, and shakes her head.*) Well, you are! In a very different way from anyone else. And all the nicer because of the difference, too. (*His voice becomes low and *husky. Laura turns away, nearly faint with the novelty of her emotions.*) I wish that you were my sister. I'd teach you to have some confidence in yourself. The different people are not like other people, but being different is nothing to be ashamed of. Because other people are not such wonderful people. They're one hundred times one thousand. You're one times one! They walk all over the earth. You just stay here. They're common as—weeds, but—you—well, you're *Blue Roses!*

(*Image on Screen: Blue Roses.*)
(*Music Changes.*)

LAURA. But blue is wrong for—roses . . .

JIM. It's right for you—You're—pretty!

LAURA. In what respect am I pretty?

JIM. In all respects—believe me! Your eyes—your hair—are pretty! Your hands are pretty! (*He catches hold of her hand.*) You think I'm making this up because I'm invited to dinner and have to be nice. Oh, I could do that! I could put on an act for you, Laura, and say lots of things without being very sincere. But this time I am. I'm talking to you sincerely. I happened to notice you had this inferiority complex that keeps you from feeling comfortable with people. Somebody needs to build your confidence up and make you proud instead of shy and turning away and—blushing—Somebody ought to—ought to—*kiss* you. Laura! (*His hand slips slowly up her arm to her shoulder.*) (*Music Swells Tumultuously.*) (*He suddenly turns her about and kisses her on the lips. When he releases her Laura sinks on the sofa with a bright, dazed look. Jim backs away and fishes in his pocket for a cigarette.*) (*Legend on Screen: "Souvenir."*) Stumble-john! (*He lights the cigarette, avoiding her look. There is a peal of girlish laughter from Amanda in the kitchen. Laura slowly raises and opens her hand. It still contains the little broken glass animal. She looks at it with a tender, bewildered expression.*) Stumble-john! I shouldn't have done that—That was way off the beam. You don't smoke, do you? (*She looks up, smiling, not hearing the question. He sits beside her a little gingerly. She looks at him speechlessly—waiting. He coughs decorously and moves a little farther aside as he considers the situation and senses her feelings, dimly, with perturbation. Gently.*) Would you—care for a—mint? (*She doesn't seem to hear him but her look grows brighter even.*) Peppermint—Life Saver? My pocket's a regular drug store—wherever I go . . . (*He pops a mint in his mouth. Then gulps and decides to make a clean breast of it. He speaks slowly and gingerly.*) Laura, you know, if I had a sister like you, I'd do the same thing as Tom. I'd bring out fellows—introduce her to them. The right type of boys—of a type to—appreciate her. Only—well—he made a mistake about me. Maybe I've got no call to be saying this. That may not have been the idea in having me over. But what if it was? There's nothing wrong about that. The only trouble is that in my case—I'm not in a situation to—do the right thing. I can't take down your number and say I'll phone. I can't call up next week and—ask for a date. I thought I had better explain the situation in case you misunderstood it and—hurt your feelings. . . . (*Pause. Slowly, very slowly, Laura's look changes, her eyes returning slowly from his to the ornament in her palm.*)

*Amanda utters another gay laugh in the kitchen.*

LAURA (*faintly*). You—won't—call again?

JIM. No, Laura, I can't. (*He rises from the sofa.*) As I was just explaining, I've—got strings on me, Laura, I've—been going steady! I go out all the time with a girl named Betty. She's a home-girl like you, and Catholic, and Irish, and in a great many ways we—get along fine. I met her last summer on a moonlight boat trip up the river to Alton, on the *Majestic.* Well—right away from the start it was—love! (*Legend: Love!*) (*Laura sways slightly forward and grips the arm of the sofa. He fails to notice, now enrapt in his own comfortable being.*) Being in love has made a new man of me! (*Leaning stiffly forward, clutching the arm of the sofa, Laura struggles visibly with her storm. But Jim is oblivious, she is a long way off.*) The power of love is really pretty tremendous! Love is something that—changes the whole world, Laura! (*The storm abates a little and Laura leans back. He notices her again.*) It happened that Betty's aunt took sick, she got a wire and had to go to Centralia. So Tom—when he asked me to dinner—I naturally just accepted the invitation, not knowing that you—that he—that I—(*He stops awkwardly.*) Huh—I'm a stumble-john! (*He flops back on the sofa. The holy candles in the altar of Laura's face have been snuffed out! There is a look of almost infinite desolation. Jim glances at her uneasily.*) I wish that you would—say something. (*She bites her lip which was trembling and then bravely smiles. She opens her hand again on the broken glass ornament. Then she gently takes his hand and raises it level with her own. She carefully places the unicorn in the palm of his hand, then pushes his fingers closed upon it.*) What are you—doing that for? You want me to have him?—Laura? (*She nods.*) What for?

LAURA. A—souvenir . . .

*She rises unsteadily and crouches beside the victrola to wind it up.*

(*Legend on Screen: "Things Have a Way of Turning Out So Badly."*)

(*Or Image: "Gentleman Caller Waving Good-Bye!—Gaily."*)

*At this moment Amanda rushes brightly back in the front room. She bears a pitcher of fruit punch in an old-fashioned cut-glass pitcher and a plate of macaroons. The plate has a gold border and poppies painted on it.*

AMANDA. Well, well, well! Isn't the air delightful after the shower? I've made you children a little liquid refreshment. (*Turns gaily to the gentleman caller.*) Jim, do you know that song about lemonade?

"Lemonade, lemonade
Made in the shade and stirred with a spade—
Good enough for any old maid!"

JIM (*uneasily*). Ha-ha! No—I never heard it.

AMANDA. Why, Laura! You look so serious!

JIM. We were having a serious conversation.

AMANDA. Good! Now you're better acquainted!

JIM (*uncertainly*). Ha-ha! Yes.

AMANDA. You modern young people are much more serious-minded than my generation. I was so gay as a girl!

JIM. You haven't changed, Mrs. Wingfield.

AMANDA. Tonight I'm rejuvenated! The gaiety of the occasion, Mr. O'Connor! (*She tosses her head with a peal of laughter. Spills lemonade.*) Oooo! I'm baptizing myself!

JIM. Here—let me—

AMANDA (*setting the pitcher down*). There now. I discovered we had some maraschino cherries. I dumped them in, juice and all!

JIM. You shouldn't have gone to that trouble, Mrs. Wingfield.

AMANDA. Trouble, trouble? Why it was loads of fun! Didn't you hear me cutting up in the kitchen? I bet your ears were burning! I told Tom how outdone with him I was for keeping you to himself so long a time! He should have brought you over much, much sooner! Well, now that you've found your way, I want you to be a very frequent caller! Not just occasional but all the time. Oh, we're going to have a lot of gay times together! I see them coming! Mmm, just breathe that air! So fresh, and the moon's so pretty! I'll skip back out—I know where my place is when young folks are having a—serious conversation!

JIM. Oh, don't go out, Mrs. Wingfield. The fact of the matter is I've got to be going.

AMANDA. Going, now? You're joking! Why, it's only the shank of the evening, Mr. O'Connor!

JIM. Well, you know how it is.

AMANDA. You mean you're a young workingman and have to keep workingmen's hours. We'll let you off early tonight. But only on the condition that next time you stay later. What's the best night for you? Isn't Saturday night the best night for you workingmen?

JIM. I have a couple of time-clocks to punch, Mrs. Wingfield. One at morning, another one at night!

AMANDA. My, but you *are* ambitious! You work at night, too?

JIM. No, Ma'am, not work but—Betty! (*He crosses deliberately to pick up his hat. The band at the Paradise Dance Hall goes into a tender waltz.*)

AMANDA. Betty? Betty? Who's—Betty! (*There is an ominous cracking sound in the sky.*)

JIM. Oh, just a girl. The girl I go steady with! (*He smiles charmingly. The sky falls.*)

(*Legend: "The Sky Falls."*)

AMANDA (*a long-drawn exhalation*). Ohhhh . . . Is it a serious romance, Mr. O'Connor?

JIM. We're going to be married the second Sunday in June.

AMANDA. Ohhhh—how nice! Tom didn't mention that you were engaged to be married.

JIM. The cat's not out of the bag at the warehouse yet. You know how they are. They call you Romeo and stuff like that. (*He stops at the oval mirror to put on his hat. He carefully shapes the brim and the crown to give a discreetly dashing effect.*) It's been a wonderful evening, Mrs. Wingfield. I guess this is what they mean by Southern hospitality.

AMANDA. It really wasn't anything at all.

JIM. I hope it don't seem like I'm rushing off. But I promised Betty I'd pick her up at the Wabash depot, an' by the time I get my jalopy down there her train'll be in. Some women are pretty upset if you keep 'em waiting.

AMANDA. Yes, I know—The tyranny of women! (*Extends her hand.*) Goodbye, Mr. O'Connor. I wish you luck—and happiness—and success! All three of them, and so does Laura!—Don't you, Laura?

LAURA. Yes!

JIM (*taking her hand*). Goodbye, Laura. I'm certainly going to treasure that souvenir. And don't you forget the good advice I gave you. (*Raises his voice to a cheery shout.*) So long, Shakespeare! Thanks again, ladies—good night!

*He grins and ducks jauntily out.*

*Still bravely grimacing, Amanda closes the door on the gentleman caller. Then she turns back to the room with a puzzled expression. She and Laura don't dare to face each other. Laura crouches beside the victrola to wind it.*

AMANDA (*faintly*). Things have a way of turning out so badly. I don't believe that I would play the victrola. Well, well—well—Our gentleman caller was engaged to be married! Tom!

TOM (*from back*). Yes, Mother?

AMANDA. Come in here a minute. I want to tell you something awfully funny.

TOM (*enters with macaroon and a glass of the lemonade*). Has the gentleman caller gotten away already?

AMANDA. The gentleman caller has made an early departure. What a wonderful joke you played on us!

TOM. How do you mean?

AMANDA. You didn't mention that he was engaged to be married.

TOM. Jim? Engaged?

AMANDA. That's what he just informed us.

TOM. I'll be jiggered! I didn't know about that.

AMANDA. That seems very peculiar.

TOM. What's peculiar about it?

AMANDA. Didn't you call him your best friend down at the warehouse?

TOM. He is, but how did I know?

AMANDA. It seems extremely peculiar that you wouldn't know your best friend was going to be married!

TOM. The warehouse is where I work, not where I know things about people!

AMANDA. You don't know things anywhere! You live in a dream; you manufacture illusions! (*He crosses to door.*) Where are you going?

TOM. I'm going to the movies.

AMANDA. That's right, now that you've had us make such fools of ourselves. The effort, the preparations, all the expense! The new floor lamp, the rug, the clothes for Laura! All for what? To entertain some other girl's fiancé! Go to the movies, go! Don't think about us, a mother deserted, an unmarried sister who's crippled and has no job! Don't let anything interfere with your selfish pleasure! Just go, go, go—to the movies!

TOM. All right, I will! The more you shout about my selfishness to me the quicker I'll go, and I won't go to the movies!

AMANDA. Go, then! Then go to the moon—you selfish dreamer!

*Tom smashes his glass on the floor. He plunges out on the fire-escape, slamming the door. Laura screams—cut by door.*

*Dance-hall music up. Tom goes to the rail and grips it desperately, lifting his face in the chill white moonlight penetrating the narrow abyss of the alley.*

*(Legend on Screen: "And So Good-Bye . . .")*

*Tom's closing speech is timed with the interior pantomime. The interior scene is played as though viewed through sound-proof glass. Amanda appears to be making a comforting speech to Laura who is huddled upon the sofa. Now that we cannot hear the mother's speech, her silliness is gone and she has dignity and tragic beauty. Laura's dark hair hides her face until at the end of the speech she lifts it to smile at her mother. Amanda's gestures are slow and graceful, almost dancelike, as she comforts the daughter. At the end of her speech she glances a moment at the father's picture—then withdraws through the portieres. At close of Tom's speech, Laura blows out the candles, ending the play.*

TOM. I didn't go to the moon, I went much further—for time is the longest distance between two places—Not long after that I was fired for writing a poem on the lid of a shoe-box. I left Saint Louis. I descended the steps of this fire-escape for a last time and followed, from then on, in my father's footsteps, attempting to find in motion what was lost in space—I traveled around a great deal. The cities swept about me like dead leaves, leaves that were brightly colored but torn away from the branches. I would have stopped, but I was pursued by something. It always came upon me unawares, taking me altogether by surprise. Perhaps it was a familiar bit of music. Perhaps it was only a piece of transparent glass—Perhaps I am walking along a street at night, in some strange city, before I have found companions. I pass the lighted window of a shop where perfume is sold. The window is filled with pieces of colored glass, tiny transparent bottles in delicate colors, like bits of a shattered rainbow. Then all at once my sister touches my shoulder. I turn around and look into her eyes . . . Oh, Laura, Laura, I tried to leave you behind me, but I am more faithful than I intended to be! I reach for a cigarette, I cross the street, I run into the movies or a bar, I buy a drink, I speak to the nearest stranger—anything that can blow your candles out! (*Laura bends over the candles.*)—for nowadays the world is lit by lightning! Blow out your candles, Laura—and so goodbye . . .

*She blows the candles out.*

*(The Scene Dissolves.)*

[*1944*]

## TOPICS FOR CRITICAL THINKING AND WRITING

1. On page 1590 Williams explains why he used magic-lantern slides, but when the play was produced in New York, the slides were omitted. Is the device an extraneous gimmick? Might it interfere with the play, by over-simplifying and thus in a way belittling the actions?

2. What does the victrola offer to Laura? Why is the typewriter a better symbol (for the purposes of the play) than, say, a piano? After all, Laura could have been taking piano lessons. Explain the symbolism of the unicorn, and the loss of its horn. What is Laura saying to Jim in the gesture of giving him the unicorn?
3. Laura escapes to her glass menagerie. To what do Amanda and Tom escape? How complete is Tom's escape at the end of the play?
4. What is meant at the end when Laura blows out the candles? Is she blowing out illusions? Or life? Or both?
5. Did Williams make a slip in having Amanda say Laura is "crippled" on page 1587?
6. There is an implication that had Jim not been going steady he might have rescued Laura, but Jim also seems to represent (for example, in his lines about money and power) the corrupt outside world that no longer values humanity. Is this a slip on Williams's part, or is it an interesting complexity?
7. On page 1588 Williams says, in a stage direction, "Now that we cannot hear the mother's speech, her silliness is gone and she has dignity and tragic beauty." Is Williams simply dragging in the word "tragic" because of its prestige, or is it legitimate? "Tragedy" is often distinguished from "pathos": in the tragic, the suffering is experienced by persons who act and are in some measure responsible for their suffering; in the pathetic, the suffering is experienced by the passive and the innocent. For example, in discussing Aeschylus's *The Suppliants* (in *Greek Tragedy*), H. D. F. Kitto says: "The Suppliants are not only pathetic, as the victims of outrage, but also tragic, as the victims of their own misconceptions." Given this distinction, to what extent are Amanda and Laura tragic? Pathetic?

## A PERSPECTIVE FOR *THE GLASS MENAGERIE*

 TENNESSEE WILLIAMS

### *Production Notes*

Being a "memory play," *The Glass Menagerie* can be presented with unusual freedom of convention. Because of its considerably delicate or tenuous material, atmospheric touches and subtleties of direction play a particularly important part. Expressionism and all other unconventional techniques in drama have only one valid aim, and that is a closer approach to truth. When a play employs unconventional techniques, it is not, or certainly shouldn't be, trying to escape its responsibility of dealing with reality, or interpreting experience, but is actually or should be attempting to find a closer approach, a more penetrating and vivid expression of things as they are. The straight realistic play with its genuine frigidaire and authentic ice cubes, its characters that speak exactly as its audience speaks, corresponds to the academic landscape and has the same virtue of a photographic likeness. Everyone should know nowadays the unimportance of the photographic in art: that truth, life, or reality is an organic thing which the poetic imagination can represent or suggest, in essence, only through transformation, through changing into other forms than those which were merely present in appearance.

These remarks are not meant as comments only on this particular play. They have to do with a conception of a new, plastic theater which must take the place of the exhausted theater of realistic conventions if the theater is to resume vitality as a part of our culture.

## *The Screen Device*

There is *only one important difference between the original and acting version of the play* and that is the *omission* in the latter of the device which I tentatively included in my *original* script. This device was the use of a screen on which were projected magic-lantern slides bearing images or titles. I do not regret the omission of this device from the . . . Broadway production. The extraordinary power of Miss Taylor's performance made it suitable to have the utmost simplicity in the physical production. But I think it may be interesting to some readers to see how this device was conceived. So I am putting it into the published manuscript. These images and legends, projected from behind, were cast on a section of wall between the front-room and dining-room areas, which should be indistinguishable from the rest when not in use.

The purpose of this will probably be apparent. It is to give accent to certain values in each scene. Each scene contains a particular point (or several) which is structurally the most important. In an episodic play, such as this, the basic structure or narrative line may be obscured from the audience; the effect may seem fragmentary rather than architectural. This may not be the fault of the play so much as a lack of attention in the audience. The legend or image upon the screen will strengthen the effect of what is merely allusion in the writing and allow the primary point to be made more simply and lightly than if the entire responsibility were on the spoken lines. Aside from this structural value, I think the screen will have a definite emotional appeal, less definable but just as important. An imaginative producer or director may invent many other uses for this device than those indicated in the present script. In fact the possibilities of the device seem much larger to me than the instance of this play can possibly utilize.

## *The Music*

Another extra-literary accent in this play is provided by the use of music. A single recurring tune, "The Glass Menagerie," is used to give emotional emphasis to suitable passages. This tune is like circus music, not when you are on the grounds or in the immediate vicinity of the parade, but when you are at some distance and very likely thinking of something else. It seems under those circumstances to continue almost interminably and it weaves in and out of your preoccupied consciousness; then it is the lightest, most delicate music in the world and perhaps the saddest. It expresses the surface vivacity of life with the underlying strain of immutable and inexpressible sorrow. When you look at a piece of delicately spun glass you think of two things: how beautiful it is and how easily it can be broken. Both of those ideas should be woven into the recurring tune, which dips in and out of the play as if it were carried on a wind that changes. It serves as a thread of connection and allusion between the narrator with his separate point in time and space and the subject of his story. Between each episode it returns as reference to the emotion, nostalgia, which is the first condition of the play. It is primarily Laura's music and therefore comes out most clearly when the play focuses upon her and the lovely fragility of glass which is her image.

### *The Lighting*

The lighting in the play is not realistic. In keeping with the atmosphere of memory, the stage is dim. Shafts of light are focused on selected areas or actors, sometimes in contradistinction to what is the apparent center. For instance, in the quarrel scene between Tom and Amanda, in which Laura has no active part, the clearest pool of light is on her figure. This is also true of the supper scene. The light upon Laura should be distinct from the others, having a peculiar pristine clarity such as light used in early religious portraits of female saints or madonnas. A certain correspondence to light in religious paintings, such as El Greco's, where the figures are radiant in atmosphere that is relatively dusky, could be effectively used throughout the play. (It will also permit a more effective use of the screen.) A free, imaginative use of light can be of enormous value in giving a mobile, plastic quality to plays of a more or less static nature.

*[1944]*

## ARTHUR MILLER

*Arthur Miller was born in New York in 1915. In 1938 he graduated from the University of Michigan, where he won several prizes for drama. Six years later he had his first Broadway production,* The Man Who Had All the Luck, *but the play was unlucky and closed after four days. By the time of his first commercial success,* All My Sons *(1947), he had already written several plays. In 1949 he won a Pulitzer Prize with* Death of a Salesman *and achieved an international reputation. Among his other works are an adaptation (1950) of Ibsen's* Enemy of the People *and a play about the Salem witch trials,* The Crucible *(1953), both containing political implications, and* The Misfits *(1961, a screenplay),* After the Fall *(1964), and* Incident at Vichy *(1965).*

# *Death of a Salesman*

Certain Private Conversations in Two Acts and a Requiem

LIST OF CHARACTERS

WILLY LOMAN
LINDA
BIFF

Lee J. Cobb as Willy Loman in the 1949 original Broadway production of *Death of a Salesman.* (Courtesy of the Theatre Arts Library, Harry Ransom Humanities Research Center, The University of Texas at Austin)

Dustin Hoffman as Willy Loman, and John Malkovich as Biff, in the 1984 production. (© 1984 by Inge Morath. Magnum Photos, Inc.)

HAPPY
BERNARD
THE WOMAN
CHARLEY
UNCLE BEN
HOWARD WAGNER
JENNY
STANLEY
MISS FORSYTHE
LETTA

**SCENE:** *The action takes place in Willy Loman's house and yard and in various places he visits in the New York and Boston of today.*

## Act 1

**SCENE:** *A melody is heard, played upon a flute. It is small and fine, telling of grass and trees and the horizon. The curtain rises.*

*Before us is the Salesman's house. We are aware of towering, angular shapes behind it, surrounding it on all sides. Only the blue light of the sky falls upon the house and forestage; the surrounding area shows an angry glow of orange. As more light appears, we see a solid vault of apartment houses around the small, fragile-seeming home. An air of the dream clings to the place, a dream rising out of reality. The kitchen at center seems actual enough, for there is a kitchen table with three chairs, and a refrigerator. But no other fixtures are seen. At the back of the kitchen there is a draped entrance, which leads to the living room. To the right of the kitchen, on a level raised two feet, is a bedroom furnished only with a brass bedstead and a straight chair. On a shelf over the bed a silver athletic trophy stands. A window opens onto the apartment house at the side.*

*Behind the kitchen, on a level raised six and a half feet, is the boys' bedroom, at present barely visible. Two beds are dimly seen, and at the back of the room a dormer window. (This bedroom is above the unseen living room.) At the left a stairway curves up to it from the kitchen.*

*The entire setting is wholly or, in some places, partially transparent. The roof-line of the house is one-dimensional; under and over it we see the apartment buildings. Before the house lies an apron, curving beyond the forestage into the orchestra. This forward area serves as the back yard as well as the locale of all Willy's imaginings and of his city scenes. Whenever the action is in the present the actors observe the imaginary wall-lines, entering the house only through its door at the left. But in the scenes of the past these boundaries are broken, and characters enter or leave a room by stepping "through" a wall onto the forestage.*

*From the right, Willy Loman, the Salesman, enters, carrying two large sample cases. The flute plays on. He hears but is not aware of it. He is past sixty years of age, dressed quietly. Even as he crosses the stage to the doorway of the house, his exhaustion is apparent. He unlocks the door, comes into the kitchen, and thankfully lets his burden down, feeling the soreness of his palms. A word-sigh escapes his lips—it might be "Oh, boy, oh, boy." He closes the door, then carries his cases out into the living room, through the draped kitchen doorway.*

*Linda, his wife, has stirred in her bed at the right. She gets out and puts on a robe, listening. Most often jovial, she has developed an iron repression of her exceptions to Willy's behavior—she more than loves him, she admires him, as though his mercurial nature, his temper, his massive dreams and little cruelties, served her only as sharp reminders of the turbulent longings within him, longings which she shares but lacks the temperament to utter and follow to their end.*

LINDA (*hearing Willy outside the bedroom, calls with some trepidation*). Willy!

WILLY. It's all right. I came back.

LINDA. Why? What happened? (*Slight pause.*) Did something happen, Willy?

WILLY. No, nothing happened.

LINDA. You didn't smash the car, did you?

WILLY (*with casual irritation*). I said nothing happened. Didn't you hear me?

LINDA. Don't you feel well?

WILLY. I'm tired to the death. (*The flute has faded away. He sits on the bed beside her, a little numb.*) I couldn't make it. I just couldn't make it, Linda.

LINDA (*very carefully, delicately*). Where were you all day? You look terrible.

WILLY. I got as far as a little above Yonkers. I stopped for a cup of coffee. Maybe it was the coffee.

LINDA. What?

WILLY (*after a pause*). I suddenly couldn't drive any more. The car kept going off onto the shoulder, y'know?

LINDA (*helpfully*). Oh. Maybe it was the steering again. I don't think Angelo knows the Studebaker.

WILLY. No, it's me, it's me. Suddenly I realize I'm goin' sixty miles an hour and I don't remember the last five minutes. I'm—I can't seem to—keep my mind to it.

LINDA. Maybe it's your glasses. You never went for your new glasses.

WILLY. No, I see everything. I came back ten miles an hour. It took me nearly four hours from Yonkers.

LINDA (*resigned*). Well, you'll just have to take a rest, Willy, you can't continue this way.

WILLY. I just got back from Florida.

LINDA. But you didn't rest your mind. Your mind is overactive, and the mind is what counts, dear.

WILLY. I'll start out in the morning. Maybe I'll feel better in the morning. (*She is taking off his shoes.*) These goddam arch supports are killing me.

LINDA. Take an aspirin. Should I get you an aspirin? It'll soothe you.

WILLY (*with wonder*). I was driving along, you understand? And I was fine. I was even observing the scenery. You can imagine, me looking at scenery, on the road every week of my life. But it's so beautiful up there, Linda, the trees are so thick, and the sun is warm. I opened the windshield and just let the warm air bathe over me. And then all of a sudden I'm goin' off the road! I'm tellin' ya, I absolutely forgot I was driving. If I'd've gone the other way over the white line I might've killed somebody. So I went on again—and five minutes later I'm dreamin' again, and I nearly . . . (*He presses two fingers against his eyes.*) I have such thoughts, I have such strange thoughts.

LINDA. Willy, dear. Talk to them again. There's no reason why you can't work in New York.

WILLY. They don't need me in New York. I'm the New England man. I'm vital in New England.

LINDA. But you're sixty years old. They can't expect you to keep traveling every week.

WILLY. I'll have to send a wire to Portland. I'm supposed to see Brown and Morrison tomorrow morning at ten o'clock to show the line. Goddammit, I could sell them! (*He starts putting on his jacket.*)

LINDA (*taking the jacket from him*). Why don't you go down to the place tomorrow and tell Howard you've simply got to work in New York? You're too accommodating, dear.

WILLY. If old man Wagner was alive I'd a been in charge of New York now! That man was a prince, he was a masterful man. But that boy of his, that Howard, he don't appreciate. When I went north the first time, the Wagner Company didn't know where New England was!

LINDA. Why don't you tell those things to Howard, dear?

WILLY (*encouraged*). I will, I definitely will. Is there any cheese?

LINDA. I'll make you a sandwich.

WILLY. No, go to sleep. I'll take some milk. I'll be up right away. The boys in?

LINDA. They're sleeping. Happy took Biff on a date tonight.

WILLY (*interested*). That so?

LINDA. It was so nice to see them shaving together, one behind the other, in the bathroom. And going out together. You notice? The whole house smells of shaving lotion.

WILLY. Figure it out. Work a lifetime to pay off a house. You finally own it, and there's nobody to live in it.

LINDA. Well, dear, life is a casting off. It's always that way.

WILLY. No, no, some people—some people accomplish something. Did Biff say anything after I went this morning?

LINDA. You shouldn't have criticized him, Willy, especially after he just got off the train. You mustn't lose your temper with him.

WILLY. When the hell did I lose my temper? I simply asked him if he was making any money. Is that a criticism?

LINDA. But, dear, how could he make any money?

WILLY (*worried and angered*). There's such an undercurrent in him. He became a moody man. Did he apologize when I left this morning?

LINDA. He was crestfallen, Willy. You know how he admires you. I think if he finds himself, then you'll both be happier and not fight any more.

WILLY. How can he find himself on a farm? Is that a life? A farm hand? In the beginning, when he was young, I thought, well, a young man, it's good for him to tramp around, take a lot of different jobs. But it's more than ten years now and he has yet to make thirty-five dollars a week!

LINDA. He's finding himself, Willy.

WILLY. Not finding yourself at the age of thirty-four is a disgrace!

LINDA. Shh!

WILLY. The trouble is he's lazy, goddammit!

LINDA. Willy, please!

WILLY. Biff is a lazy bum!

LINDA. They're sleeping. Get something to eat. Go on down.

WILLY. Why did he come home? I would like to know what brought him home.

LINDA. I don't know. I think he's still lost, Willy. I think he's very lost.

WILLY. Biff Loman is lost. In the greatest country in the world a young man with such—personal attractiveness, gets lost. And such a hard worker. There's one thing about Biff—he's not lazy.

LINDA. Never.

WILLY (*with pity and resolve*). I'll see him in the morning; I'll have a nice talk with him. I'll get him a job selling. He could be big in no time. My God! Remember how they used to follow him around in high school? When he smiled at one of them their faces lit up. When he walked down the street . . . (*He loses himself in reminiscences.*)

LINDA (*trying to bring him out of it*). Willy, dear, I got a new kind of American-type cheese today. It's whipped.

WILLY. Why do you get American when I like Swiss?

LINDA. I just thought you'd like a change . . .

WILLY. I don't want a change! I want Swiss cheese. Why am I always being contradicted?

LINDA (*with a covering laugh*). I thought it would be a surprise.

WILLY. Why don't you open a window in here, for God's sake?

LINDA (*with infinite patience*). They're all open, dear.

WILLY. The way they boxed us in here. Bricks and windows, windows and bricks.

LINDA. We should've bought the land next door.

WILLY. The street is lined with cars. There's not a breath of fresh air in the neighborhood. The grass don't grow any more, you can't raise a carrot in the back yard. They should've had a law against apartment houses. Remember those two beautiful elm trees out there? When I and Biff hung the swing between them?

LINDA. Yeah, like being a million miles from the city.

WILLY. They should've arrested the builder for cutting those down. They massacred the neighborhood. (*Lost.*) More and more I think of those days, Linda. This time of year it was lilac and wisteria. And then the peonies would come out, and the daffodils. What fragrance in this room!

LINDA. Well, after all, people had to move somewhere.

WILLY. No, there's more people now.

LINDA. I don't think there's more people. I think . . .

WILLY. There's more people! That's what's ruining this country! Population is getting out of control. The competition is maddening! Smell the stink from that apartment house! And another one on the other side . . . How can they whip cheese?

*On Willy's last line, Biff and Happy raise themselves up in their beds, listening.*

LINDA. Go down, try it. And be quiet.

WILLY (*turning to Linda, guiltily*). You're not worried about me, are you, sweetheart?

BIFF. What's the matter?

HAPPY. Listen!

LINDA. You've got too much on the ball to worry about.

WILLY. You're my foundation and my support, Linda.

LINDA. Just try to relax, dear. You make mountains out of molehills.

WILLY. I won't fight with him any more. If he wants to go back to Texas, let him go.

LINDA. He'll find his way.

WILLY. Sure. Certain men just don't get started till later in life. Like Thomas Edison, I think. Or B. F. Goodrich. One of them was deaf. (*He starts for the bedroom doorway.*) I'll put my money on Biff.

LINDA. And Willy—if it's warm Sunday we'll drive in the country. And we'll open the windshield, and take lunch.

WILLY. No, the windshields don't open on the new cars.

LINDA. But you opened it today.

WILLY. Me? I didn't. (*He stops.*) Now isn't that peculiar! Isn't that a remarkable . . . (*He breaks off in amazement and fright as the flute is heard distantly.*)

LINDA. What, darling?

WILLY. That is the most remarkable thing.

LINDA. What, dear?

WILLY. I was thinking of the Chevvy. (*Slight pause.*) Nineteen twenty-eight . . . when I had that red Chevvy . . . (*Breaks off.*) That funny? I coulda sworn I was driving that Chevvy today.

LINDA. Well, that's nothing. Something must've reminded you.

WILLY. Remarkable. Ts. Remember those days? The way Biff used to simonize that car? The dealer refused to believe there was eighty thousand miles on it. (*He shakes his head.*) Heh! (*To Linda.*) Close your eyes, I'll be right up. (*He walks out of the bedroom.*)

HAPPY (*to Biff*). Jesus, maybe he smashed up the car again!

LINDA (*calling after Willy*). Be careful on the stairs, dear! The cheese is on the middle shelf. (*She turns, goes over to the bed, takes his jacket, and goes out of the bedroom.*)

*Light has risen on the boys' room. Unseen, Willy is heard talking to himself; "Eighty thousand miles," and a little laugh. Biff gets out of bed, comes downstage a bit, and stands attentively. Biff is two years older than his brother Happy, well built, but in these days bears a worn air and seems less self-assured. He has succeeded less, and his dreams are stronger and less acceptable than Happy's. Happy is tall, powerfully made. Sexuality is like a visible color on him, or a scent that many women have discovered. He, like his brother, is lost, but in a different way, for he has never allowed himself to turn his face toward defeat and is thus more confused and hard-skinned, although seemingly more content.*

HAPPY (*getting out of bed*). He's going to get his license taken away if he keeps that up. I'm getting nervous about him, y'know, Biff?

BIFF. His eyes are going.

HAPPY. No, I've driven with him. He sees all right. He just doesn't keep his mind on it. I drove into the city with him last week. He stops at a green light and then it turns red and he goes. (*He laughs.*)

BIFF. Maybe he's color-blind.

HAPPY. Pop? Why he's got the finest eye for color in the business. You know that.

BIFF (*sitting down on his bed*). I'm going to sleep.

HAPPY. You're not still sour on Dad, are you, Biff?

BIFF. He's all right, I guess.

WILLY (*underneath them, in the living room*). Yes, sir, eighty thousand miles—eighty-two thousand!

BIFF. You smoking?

HAPPY (*holding out a pack of cigarettes*). Want one?

BIFF (*taking a cigarette*). I can never sleep when I smell it.

WILLY. What a simonizing job, heh!

HAPPY (*with deep sentiment*). Funny, Biff, y'know? Us sleeping in here again? The old beds. (*He pats his bed affectionately.*) All the talk that went across those beds, huh? Our whole lives.

BIFF. Yeah. Lotta dreams and plans.

HAPPY (*with a deep and masculine laugh*). About five hundred women would like to know what was said in this room. (*They share a soft laugh.*)

BIFF. Remember that big Betsy something—what the hell was her name—over on Bushwick Avenue?

HAPPY (*combing his hair*). With the collie dog!

BIFF. That's the one. I got you in there, remember?

HAPPY. Yeah, that was my first time—I think. Boy, there was a pig. (*They laugh, almost crudely.*) You taught me everything I know about women. Don't forget that.

BIFF. I bet you forgot how bashful you used to be. Especially with girls.

HAPPY. Oh, I still am, Biff.

BIFF. Oh, go on.

HAPPY. I just control it, that's all. I think I got less bashful and you got more so. What happened, Biff? Where's the old humor, the old confidence? (*He shakes Biff's knee. Biff gets up and moves restlessly about the room.*) What's the matter?

BIFF. Why does Dad mock me all the time?

HAPPY. He's not mocking you, he . . .

BIFF. Everything I say there's a twist of mockery on his face. I can't get near him.

HAPPY. He just wants you to make good, that's all. I wanted to talk to you about Dad for a long time, Biff. Something's—happening to him. He—talks to himself.

BIFF. I noticed that this morning. But he always mumbled.

HAPPY. But not so noticeable. It got so embarrassing I sent him to Florida. And you know something? Most of the time he's talking to you.

BIFF. What's he say about me?

HAPPY. I can't make it out.

BIFF. What's he say about me?

HAPPY. I think the fact that you're not settled, that you're still kind of up in the air . . .

BIFF. There's one or two other things depressing him, Happy.

HAPPY. What do you mean?

BIFF. Never mind. Just don't lay it all to me.

HAPPY. But I think if you just got started—I mean—is there any future for you out there?

BIFF. I tell ya, Hap, I don't know what the future is. I don't know—what I'm supposed to want.

HAPPY. What do you mean?

BIFF. Well, I spent six or seven years after high school trying to work myself up. Shipping clerk, salesman, business of one kind or another. And it's a measly manner of existence. To get on that subway on the hot mornings in summer. To devote your whole life to keeping stock, or making phone calls, or selling or buying. To suffer fifty weeks of the year for the sake of a two-week vacation, when all you really desire is to be outdoors, with your shirt off. And always to have to get ahead of the next fella. And still—that's how you build a future.

HAPPY. Well, you really enjoy it on a farm? Are you content out there?

BIFF (*with rising agitation*). Hap, I've had twenty or thirty different kinds of jobs since I left home before the war, and it always turns out the same. I just realized it lately. In Nebraska when I herded cattle, and the Dakotas, and Arizona, and now in Texas. It's why I came home now, I guess, because I realized it. This farm I work on, it's spring there now, see? And they've got about fifteen new colts. There's nothing more inspiring or—beautiful than the sight of a mare and a new colt. And it's cool there now, see? Texas is cool now, and it's spring. And whenever spring comes to where I am, I suddenly get the feeling, my God, I'm not gettin' anywhere! What the hell am I doing, playing around with horses, twenty-eight dollars a week! I'm thirty-four years old, I oughta be makin' my future. That's when I come running home. And now, I get here, and I don't know what to do with myself. (*After a pause.*) I've always made a point of not wasting my life, and everytime I come back here I know that all I've done is to waste my life.

HAPPY. You're a poet, you know that, Biff? You're a—you're an idealist!

BIFF. No, I'm mixed up very bad. Maybe I oughta get married. Maybe I oughta get stuck into something. Maybe that's my trouble. I'm like a boy. I'm not married, I'm not in business, I just—I'm like a boy. Are you content, Hap? You're a success, aren't you? Are you content?

HAPPY. Hell, no!

BIFF. Why? You're making money, aren't you?

HAPPY (*moving about with energy, expressiveness*). All I can do now is wait for the merchandise manager to die. And suppose I get to be merchandise manager? He's a good friend of mine, and he just built a terrific estate on Long Island. And he lived there about two months and sold it, and now he's building another one. He can't enjoy it once it's finished. And I know that's just what I would do. I don't know what the hell I'm workin' for. Sometimes I sit in my apartment—all alone. And I think of the rent I'm paying. And it's crazy. But then, it's what I always wanted. My own apartment, a car, and plenty of women. And still, goddammit, I'm lonely.

BIFF (*with enthusiasm*). Listen, why don't you come out West with me?

HAPPY. You and I, heh?

BIFF. Sure, maybe we could buy a ranch. Raise cattle, use our muscles. Men built like we are should be working out in the open.

HAPPY (*avidly*). The Loman Brothers, heh?

BIFF (*with vast affection*). Sure, we'd be known all over the counties!

HAPPY (*enthralled*). That's what I dream about, Biff. Sometimes I want to just rip my clothes off in the middle of the store and outbox that goddam merchandise manager. I mean I can outbox, outrun, and outlift anybody in that store, and I have to take orders from those common, petty sons-of-bitches till I can't stand it any more.

BIFF. I'm tellin' you, kid, if you were with me I'd be happy out there.

HAPPY (*enthused*). See, Biff, everybody around me is so false that I'm constantly lowering my ideals . . .

BIFF. Baby, together we'd stand up for one another, we'd have someone to trust.

HAPPY. If I were around you . . .

BIFF. Hap, the trouble is we weren't brought up to grub for money. I don't know how to do it.

HAPPY. Neither can I!

BIFF. Then let's go!

HAPPY. The only thing is—what can you make out there?

BIFF. But look at your friend. Builds an estate and then hasn't the peace of mind to live in it.

HAPPY. Yeah, but when he walks into the store the waves part in front of him. That's fifty-two thousand dollars a year coming through the revolving door, and I got more in my pinky finger than he's got in his head.

BIFF. Yeah, but you just said . . .

HAPPY. I gotta show some of those pompous, self-important executives over there that Hap Loman can make the grade. I want to walk into the store the way he walks in. Then I'll go with you, Biff. We'll be together yet, I swear. But take those two we had tonight. Now weren't they gorgeous creatures?

BIFF. Yeah, yeah, most gorgeous I've had in years.

HAPPY. I get that any time I want, Biff. Whenever I feel disgusted. The only trouble is, it gets like bowling or something. I just keep knockin' them over and it doesn't mean anything. You still run around a lot?

BIFF. Naa. I'd like to find a girl—steady, somebody with substance.

HAPPY. That's what I long for.

BIFF. Go on! You'd never come home.

HAPPY. I would! Somebody with character, with resistance! Like Mom, y'know? You're gonna call me a bastard when I tell you this. That girl Charlotte I was with tonight is engaged to be married in five weeks. (*He tries on his new hat.*)

BIFF. No kiddin'!

HAPPY. Sure, the guy's in line for the vice-presidency of the store. I don't know what gets into me, maybe I just have an over-developed sense of competition or something, but I went and ruined her, and furthermore I can't get rid of her. And he's the third executive I've done that to. Isn't that a crummy characteristic? And to top it all, I go to their weddings! (*Indignantly, but laughing.*) Like I'm not supposed to take bribes. Manufacturers offer me a hundred-dollar bill now and then to throw an order their way. You know how honest I am, but it's like this girl, see. I hate myself for it. Because I don't want the girl, and, still, I take it and—I love it!

BIFF. Let's go to sleep.

HAPPY. I guess we didn't settle anything, heh?

BIFF. I just got one idea that I think I'm going to try.

HAPPY. What's that?

BIFF. Remember Bill Oliver?

HAPPY. Sure, Oliver is very big now. You want to work for him again?

BIFF. No, but when I quit he said something to me. He put his arm on my shoulder, and he said, "Biff, if you ever need anything, come to me."

HAPPY. I remember that. That sounds good.

BIFF. I think I'll go to see him. If I could get ten thousand or even seven or eight thousand dollars I could buy a beautiful ranch.

HAPPY. I bet he'd back you. 'Cause he thought highly of you, Biff. I mean, they all do. You're well liked, Biff. That's why I say to come back here, and we both have the apartment. And I'm tellin' you, Biff, any babe you want . . .

BIFF. No, with a ranch I could do the work I like and still be something. I just wonder though. I wonder if Oliver still thinks I stole that carton of basketballs.

HAPPY. Oh, he probably forgot that long ago. It's almost ten years. You're too sensitive. Anyway, he didn't really fire you.

BIFF. Well, I think he was going to. I think that's why I quit. I was never sure whether he knew or not. I know he thought the world of me, though. I was the only one he'd let lock up the place.

WILLY (*below*). You gonna wash the engine, Biff?

HAPPY. Shh!

*Biff looks at Happy, who is gazing down, listening. Willy is mumbling in the parlor.*

HAPPY. You hear that?

*They listen. Willy laughs warmly.*

BIFF (*growing angry*). Doesn't he know Mom can hear that?

WILLY. Don't get your sweater dirty, Biff!

*A look of pain crosses Biff's face.*

HAPPY. Isn't that terrible? Don't leave again, will you? You'll find a job here. You gotta stick around. I don't know what to do about him, it's getting embarrassing.

WILLY. What a simonizing job!

BIFF. Mom's hearing that!

WILLY. No kiddin', Biff, you got a date? Wonderful!

HAPPY. Go on to sleep. But talk to him in the morning, will you?

BIFF (*reluctantly getting into bed*). With her in the house. Brother!

HAPPY (*getting into bed*). I wish you'd have a good talk with him.

*The light on their room begins to fade.*

BIFF (*to himself in bed*). That selfish, stupid . . .

HAPPY. Sh . . . Sleep, Biff.

*Their light is out. Well before they have finished speaking, Willy's form is dimly seen below in the darkened kitchen. He opens the refrigerator, searches in there, and takes out a bottle of milk. The apartment houses are fading out, and the entire house and surroundings become covered with leaves. Music insinuates itself as the leaves appear.*

WILLY. Just wanna be careful with those girls, Biff, that's all. Don't make any promises. No promises of any kind. Because a girl, y'know, they always believe what you tell 'em, and you're very young, Biff, you're too young to be talking seriously to girls.

*Light rises on the kitchen. Willy, talking, shuts the refrigerator door and comes downstage to the kitchen table. He pours milk into a glass. He is totally immersed in himself, smiling faintly.*

WILLY. Too young entirely, Biff. You want to watch your schooling first. Then when you're all set, there'll be plenty of girls for a boy like you. (*He smiles broadly at a kitchen chair.*) That so? The girls pay for you? (*He laughs.*) Boy, you must really be makin' a hit.

*Willy is gradually addressing—physically—a point offstage, speaking through the wall of the kitchen, and his voice has been rising in volume to that of a normal conversation.*

WILLY. I been wondering why you polish the car so careful. Ha! Don't leave the hubcaps, boys. Get the chamois to the hubcaps. Happy, use newspaper on the windows, it's the easiest thing. Show him how to do it, Biff! You see, Happy? Pad it up, use it like a pad. That's it, that's it, good work. You're doin' all right, Hap. (*He pauses, then nods in approbation for a few seconds, then looks upward.*) Biff, first thing we gotta do when we get time is clip that big branch over the house. Afraid it's gonna fall in a storm and hit the roof. Tell you what. We get a rope and sling her around, and then we climb up there with a couple of saws and take her down. Soon as you finish the car, boys, I wanna see ya. I got a surprise for you, boys.

BIFF (*offstage*). Whatta ya got, Dad?

WILLY. No, you finish first. Never leave a job till you're finished—remember that. (*Looking toward the "big trees."*) Biff, up in Albany I saw a beautiful hammock. I think I'll buy it next trip, and we'll hang it right between those two elms. Wouldn't that be something? Just swingin' there under those branches. Boy, that would be . . .

*Young Biff and Young Happy appear from the direction Willy was addressing. Happy carries rags and a pail of water. Biff, wearing a sweater with a block "S," carries a football.*

BIFF (*pointing in the direction of the car offstage*). How's that, Pop, professional?

WILLY. Terrific. Terrific job, boys. Good work, Biff.
HAPPY. Where's the surprise, Pop?
WILLY. In the back seat of the car.
HAPPY. Boy! (*He runs off.*)
BIFF. What is it, Dad? Tell me, what'd you buy?
WILLY (*laughing, cuffs him*). Never mind, something I want you to have.
BIFF (*turns and starts off*). What is it, Hap?
HAPPY (*offstage*). It's a punching bag!
BIFF. Oh, Pop!
WILLY. It's got Gene Tunney's signature on it!

*Happy runs onstage with a punching bag.*

BIFF. Gee, how'd you know we wanted a punching bag?
WILLY. Well, it's the finest thing for the timing.
HAPPY (*lies down on his back and pedals with his feet*). I'm losing weight, you notice, Pop?
WILLY (*to Happy*). Jumping rope is good too.
BIFF. Did you see the new football I got?
WILLY (*examining the ball*). Where'd you get a new ball?
BIFF. The coach told me to practice my passing.
WILLY. That so? And he gave you the ball, heh?
BIFF. Well, I borrowed it from the locker room. (*He laughs confidentially.*)
WILLY (*laughing with him at the theft*). I want you to return that.
HAPPY. I told you he wouldn't like it!
BIFF (*angrily*). Well, I'm bringing it back!
WILLY (*stopping the incipient argument, to Happy*). Sure, he's gotta practice with a regulation ball, doesn't he? (*To Biff.*) Coach'll probably congratulate you on your initiative!
BIFF. Oh, he keeps congratulating my initiative all the time, Pop.
WILLY. That's because he likes you. If somebody else took that ball there'd be an uproar. So what's the report, boys, what's the report?
BIFF. Where'd you go this time, Dad? Gee we were lonesome for you.
WILLY (*pleased, puts an arm around each boy and they come down to the apron*). Lonesome, heh?
BIFF. Missed you every minute.
WILLY. Don't say? Tell you a secret, boys. Don't breathe it to a soul. Someday I'll have my own business, and I'll never have to leave home any more.
HAPPY. Like Uncle Charley, heh?
WILLY. Bigger than Uncle Charley! Because Charley is not—liked. He's liked, but he's not—well liked.
BIFF. Where'd you go this time, Dad?
WILLY. Well, I got on the road, and I went north to Providence. Met the Mayor.
BIFF. The Mayor of Providence!
WILLY. He was sitting in the hotel lobby.
BIFF. What'd he say?
WILLY. He said, "Morning!" And I said, "Morning!" And I said, "You got a fine city here, Mayor." And then he had coffee with me. And then I went to Waterbury. Waterbury is a fine city. Big clock city, the famous Waterbury clock. Sold a nice bill there. And then Boston—Boston is the cradle of the Revolution. A fine city. And a couple of other towns in Mass., and on to Portland and Bangor and straight home!

BIFF. Gee, I'd love to go with you sometime, Dad.

WILLY. Soon as summer comes.

HAPPY. Promise?

WILLY. You and Hap and I, and I'll show you all the towns. America is full of beautiful towns and fine, upstanding people. And they know me, boys, they know me up and down New England. The finest people. And when I bring you fellas up, there'll be open sesame for all of us, 'cause one thing, boys: I have friends. I can park my car in any street in New England, and the cops protect it like their own. This summer, heh?

BIFF AND HAPPY (*together*). Yeah! You bet!

WILLY. We'll take our bathing suits.

HAPPY. We'll carry your bags, Pop!

WILLY. Oh, won't that be something! Me comin' into the Boston stores with you boys carryin' my bags. What a sensation!

*Biff is prancing around, practicing passing the ball.*

WILLY. You nervous, Biff, about the game?

BIFF. Not if you're gonna be there.

WILLY. What do they say about you in school, now that they made you captain?

HAPPY. There's a crowd of girls behind him everytime the classes change.

BIFF (*taking Willy's hand*). This Saturday, Pop, this Saturday—just for you, I'm going to break through for a touchdown.

HAPPY. You're supposed to pass.

BIFF. I'm takin' one play for Pop. You watch me, Pop, and when I take off my helmet, that means I'm breakin' out. Then you watch me crash through that line!

WILLY (*kisses Biff*). Oh, wait'll I tell this in Boston!

*Bernard enters in knickers. He is younger than Biff, earnest and loyal, a worried boy.*

BERNARD. Biff, where are you? You're supposed to study with me today.

WILLY. Hey, looka Bernard. What're you lookin' so anemic about, Bernard?

BERNARD. He's gotta study, Uncle Willy. He's got Regents next week.

HAPPY (*tauntingly, spinning Bernard around*). Let's box, Bernard!

BERNARD. Biff! (*He gets away from Happy.*) Listen, Biff, I heard Mr. Birnbaum say that if you don't start studyin' math he's gonna flunk you, and you won't graduate. I heard him!

WILLY. You better study with him, Biff. Go ahead now.

BERNARD. I heard him!

BIFF. Oh, Pop, you didn't see my sneakers! (*He holds up a foot for Willy to look at.*)

WILLY. Hey, that's a beautiful job of printing!

BERNARD (*wiping his glasses*). Just because he printed University of Virginia on his sneakers doesn't mean they've got to graduate him, Uncle Willy!

WILLY (*angrily*). What're you talking about? With scholarships to three universities they're gonna flunk him?

BERNARD. But I heard Mr. Birnbaum say . . .

WILLY. Don't be a pest, Bernard! (*To his boys.*) What an anemic!

BERNARD. Okay, I'm waiting for you in my house, Biff.

*Bernard goes off. The Lomans laugh.*

WILLY. Bernard is not well liked, is he?

BIFF. He's liked, but he's not well liked.

HAPPY. That's right, Pop.

WILLY. That's just what I mean. Bernard can get the best marks in school, y'understand, but when he gets out in the business world, y'understand, you are going to be five times ahead of him. That's why I thank Almighty God you're both built like Adonises. Because the man who makes an appearance in the business world, the man who creates personal interest, is the man who gets ahead. Be liked and you will never want. You take me, for instance. I never have to wait in line to see a buyer. "Willy Loman is here!" That's all they have to know, and I go right through.

BIFF. Did you knock them dead, Pop?

WILLY. Knocked 'em cold in Providence, slaughtered 'em in Boston.

HAPPY (*on his back, pedaling again*). I'm losing weight, you notice, Pop?

*Linda enters as of old, a ribbon in her hair, carrying a basket of washing.*

LINDA (*with youthful energy*). Hello, dear!

WILLY. Sweetheart!

LINDA. How'd the Chevvy run?

WILLY. Chevrolet, Linda, is the greatest car ever built. (*To the boys.*) Since when do you let your mother carry wash up the stairs?

BIFF. Grab hold there, boy!

HAPPY. Where to, Mom?

LINDA. Hang them up on the line. And you better go down to your friends, Biff. The cellar is full of boys. They don't know what to do with themselves.

BIFF. Ah, when Pop comes home they can wait!

WILLY (*laughs appreciatively*). You better go down and tell them what to do, Biff.

BIFF. I think I'll have them sweep out the furnace room.

WILLY. Good work, Biff.

BIFF (*goes through wall-line of kitchen to doorway at back and calls down*). Fellas! Everybody sweep out the furnace room! I'll be right down!

VOICES. All right! Okay, Biff.

BIFF. George and Sam and Frank, come out back! We're hangin' up the wash! Come on, Hap, on the double! (*He and Happy carry out the basket.*)

LINDA. The way they obey him!

WILLY. Well, that's training, the training. I'm tellin' you, I was sellin' thousands and thousands, but I had to come home.

LINDA. Oh, the whole block'll be at that game. Did you sell anything?

WILLY. I did five hundred gross in Providence and seven hundred gross in Boston.

LINDA. No! Wait a minute. I've got a pencil. (*She pulls pencil and paper out of her apron pocket.*) That makes your commission . . . Two hundred—my God! Two hundred and twelve dollars!

WILLY. Well, I didn't figure it yet, but . . .

LINDA. How much did you do?

WILLY. Well, I—I did—about a hundred and eighty gross in Providence. Well, no—it came to—roughly two hundred gross on the whole trip.

LINDA (*without hesitation*). Two hundred gross. That's . . . (*She figures.*)

WILLY. The trouble was that three of the stores were half-closed for inventory in Boston. Otherwise I woulda broke records.

LINDA. Well, it makes seventy dollars and some pennies. That's very good.

WILLY. What do we owe?

LINDA. Well, on the first there's sixteen dollars on the refrigerator . . .

WILLY. Why sixteen?

LINDA. Well, the fan belt broke, so it was a dollar eighty.

WILLY. But it's brand new.

LINDA. Well, the man said that's the way it is. Till they work themselves in, y'know.

*They move through the wall-line into the kitchen.*

WILLY. I hope we didn't get stuck on that machine.

LINDA. They got the biggest ads of any of them!

WILLY. I know, it's a fine machine. What else?

LINDA. Well, there's nine-sixty for the washing machine. And for the vacuum cleaner there's three and a half due on the fifteenth. Then the roof, you got twenty-one dollars remaining.

WILLY. It don't leak, does it?

LINDA. No, they did a wonderful job. Then you owe Frank for the carburetor.

WILLY. I'm not going to pay that man! That goddam Chevrolet, they ought to prohibit the manufacture of that car!

LINDA. Well, you owe him three and a half. And odds and ends, comes to around a hundred and twenty dollars by the fifteenth.

WILLY. A hundred and twenty dollars! My God, if business don't pick up I don't know what I'm gonna do!

LINDA. Well, next week you'll do better.

WILLY. Oh, I'll knock 'em dead next week. I'll go to Hartford. I'm very well liked in Hartford. You know, the trouble is, Linda, people don't seem to take to me.

*They move onto the forestage.*

LINDA. Oh, don't be foolish.

WILLY. I know it when I walk in. They seem to laugh at me.

LINDA. Why? Why would they laugh at you? Don't talk that way, Willy.

*Willy moves to the edge of the stage. Linda goes into the kitchen and starts to darn stockings.*

WILLY. I don't know the reason for it, but they just pass me by. I'm not noticed.

LINDA. But you're doing wonderful, dear. You're making seventy to a hundred dollars a week.

WILLY. But I gotta be at it ten, twelve hours a day. Other men—I don't know—they do it easier. I don't know why—I can't stop myself—I talk too much. A man oughta come in with a few words. One thing about Charley. He's a man of few words, and they respect him.

LINDA. You don't talk too much, you're just lively.

WILLY (*smiling*). Well, I figure, what the hell, life is short, a couple of jokes. (*To himself:*) I joke too much! (*The smile goes.*)

LINDA. Why? You're . . .

WILLY. I'm fat. I'm very—foolish to look at, Linda. I didn't tell you, but Christmas time I happened to be calling on F. H. Stewarts, and a salesman I know, as I was going in to see the buyer I heard him say something about—walrus. And I—I cracked him right across the face. I won't take that. I simply will not take that. But they do laugh at me. I know that.

LINDA. Darling . . .

WILLY. I gotta overcome it. I know I gotta overcome it. I'm not dressing to advantage, maybe.

LINDA. Willy, darling, you're the handsomest man in the world . . .

WILLY. Oh, no, Linda.

LINDA. To me you are. (*Slight pause.*) The handsomest.

*From the darkness is heard the laughter of a woman. Willy doesn't turn to it, but it continues through Linda's lines.*

LINDA. And the boys, Willy. Few men are idolized by their children the way you are.

*Music is heard as behind a scrim, to the left of the house; The Woman, dimly seen, is dressing.*

WILLY (*with great feeling*). You're the best there is. Linda, you're a pal, you know that? On the road—on the road I want to grab you sometimes and just kiss the life outa you.

*The laughter is loud now, and he moves into a brightening area at the left, where The Woman has come from behind the scrim and is standing, putting on her hat, looking into a "mirror" and laughing.*

WILLY. 'Cause I get so lonely—especially when business is bad and there's nobody to talk to. I get the feeling that I'll never sell anything again, that I won't make a living for you, or a business, a business for the boys. (*He talks through The Woman's subsiding laughter; The Woman primps at the "mirror."*) There's so much I want to make for . . .

THE WOMAN Me? You didn't make me, Willy. I picked you.

WILLY (*pleased*). You picked me?

THE WOMAN (*who is quite proper-looking, Willy's age*). I did. I've been sitting at that desk watching all the salesmen go by, day in, day out. But you've got such a sense of humor, and we do have such a good time together, don't we?

WILLY. Sure, sure. (*He takes her in his arms.*) Why do you have to go now?

THE WOMAN. It's two o'clock . . .

WILLY. No, come on in! (*He pulls her.*)

THE WOMAN. . . . my sisters'll be scandalized. When'll you be back?

WILLY. Oh, two weeks about. Will you come up again?

THE WOMAN. Sure thing. You do make me laugh. It's good for me. (*She squeezes his arm, kisses him.*) And I think you're a wonderful man.

WILLY. You picked me, heh?

THE WOMAN. Sure. Because you're so sweet. And such a kidder.

WILLY. Well, I'll see you next time I'm in Boston.

THE WOMAN. I'll put you right through to the buyers.

WILLY (*slapping her bottom*). Right. Well, bottoms up!

THE WOMAN (*slaps him gently and laughs*). You just kill me, Willy. (*He suddenly grabs her and kisses her roughly.*) You kill me. And thanks for the stockings. I love a lot of stockings. Well, good night.

WILLY. Good night. And keep your pores open!

THE WOMAN. Oh, Willy!

*The Woman bursts out laughing, and Linda's laughter blends in. The Woman disappears into the dark. Now the area at the kitchen table brightens. Linda is sitting where she was at the kitchen table, but now is mending a pair of her silk stockings.*

LINDA. You are, Willy. The handsomest man. You've got no reason to feel that . . .

WILLY (*coming out of The Woman's dimming area and going over to Linda*). I'll make it all up to you, Linda, I'll . . .

LINDA. There's nothing to make up, dear. You're doing fine, better than . . .

WILLY (*noticing her mending*). What's that?

LINDA. Just mending my stockings. They're so expensive . . .

WILLY (*angrily, taking them from her*). I won't have you mending stockings in this house! Now throw them out!

*Linda puts the stockings in her pocket.*

BERNARD (*entering on the run*). Where is he? If he doesn't study!

WILLY (*moving to the forestage, with great agitation*). You'll give him the answers!

BERNARD. I do, but I can't on a Regents! That's a state exam! They're liable to arrest me!

WILLY. Where is he? I'll whip him, I'll whip him!

LINDA. And he'd better give back that football, Willy, it's not nice.

WILLY. Biff! Where is he? Why is he taking everything?

LINDA. He's too rough with the girls, Willy. All the mothers are afraid of him!

WILLY. I'll whip him!

BERNARD. He's driving the car without a license!

*The Woman's laugh is heard.*

WILLY. Shut up!

LINDA. All the mothers . . .

WILLY. Shut up!

BERNARD (*backing quietly away and out*). Mr. Birnbaum says he's stuck up.

WILLY. Get outa here!

BERNARD. If he doesn't buckle down he'll flunk math! (*He goes off.*)

LINDA. He's right, Willy, you've gotta . . .

WILLY (*exploding at her*). There's nothing the matter with him! You want him to be a worm like Bernard? He's got spirit, personality . . .

*As he speaks, Linda, almost in tears, exits into the living room. Willy is alone in the kitchen, wilting and staring. The leaves are gone. It is night again, and the apartment houses look down from behind.*

WILLY. Loaded with it. Loaded! What is he stealing? He's giving it back, isn't he? Why is he stealing? What did I tell him? I never in my life told him anything but decent things.

*Happy in pajamas has come down the stairs; Willy suddenly becomes aware of Happy's presence.*

HAPPY. Let's go now, come on.

WILLY (*sitting down at the kitchen table*). Huh! Why did she have to wax the floors herself? Everytime she waxes the floors she keels over. She knows that!

HAPPY. Shh! Take it easy. What brought you back tonight?

WILLY. I got an awful scare. Nearly hit a kid in Yonkers. God! Why didn't I go to Alaska with my brother Ben that time! Ben! That man was a genius, that man was success incarnate! What a mistake! He begged me to go.

HAPPY. Well, there's no use in . . .

WILLY. You guys! There was a man started with the clothes on his back and ended up with diamond mines!

HAPPY. Boy, someday I'd like to know how he did it.

WILLY. What's the mystery? The man knew what he wanted and went out and got it! Walked into a jungle, and comes out, the age of twenty-one, and he's rich! The world is an oyster, but you don't crack it open on a mattress!

HAPPY. Pop, I told you I'm gonna retire you for life.

WILLY. You'll retire me for life on seventy goddam dollars a week? And your women and your car and your apartment, and you'll retire me for life! Christ's sake, I couldn't get past Yonkers today! Where are you guys, where are you? The woods are burning! I can't drive a car!

*Charley has appeared in the doorway. He is a large man, slow of speech, laconic, immovable. In all he says, despite what he says, there is pity, and, now, trepidation. He has a robe over pajamas, slippers on his feet. He enters the kitchen.*

CHARLEY. Everything all right?

HAPPY. Yeah, Charley, everything's . . .

WILLY. What's the matter?

CHARLEY. I heard some noise. I thought something happened. Can't we do something about the walls? You sneeze in here, and in my house hats blow off.

HAPPY. Let's go to bed, Dad. Come on.

*Charley signals to Happy to go.*

WILLY. You go ahead, I'm not tired at the moment.

HAPPY (*to Willy*). Take it easy, huh? (*He exits.*)

WILLY. What're you doin' up?

CHARLEY (*sitting down at the kitchen table opposite Willy*). Couldn't sleep good. I had a heartburn.

WILLY. Well, you don't know how to eat.

CHARLEY. I eat with my mouth.

WILLY. No, you're ignorant. You gotta know about vitamins and things like that.

CHARLEY. Come on, let's shoot. Tire you out a little.

WILLY (*hesitantly*). All right. You got cards?

CHARLEY (*taking a deck from his pocket*). Yeah, I got them. Someplace. What is it with those vitamins?

WILLY (*dealing*). They build up your bones. Chemistry.

CHARLEY. Yeah, but there's no bones in a heartburn.

WILLY. What are you talkin' about? Do you know the first thing about it?

CHARLEY. Don't get insulted.

WILLY. Don't talk about something you don't know anything about.

*They are playing. Pause.*

CHARLEY. What're you doin' home?

WILLY. A little trouble with the car.

CHARLEY. Oh. (*Pause.*) I'd like to take a trip to California.

WILLY. Don't say.

CHARLEY. You want a job?

WILLY. I got a job, I told you that. (*After a slight pause.*) What the hell are you offering me a job for?

CHARLEY. Don't get insulted.

WILLY. Don't insult me.

CHARLEY. I don't see no sense in it. You don't have to go on this way.

WILLY. I got a good job. (*Slight pause.*) What do you keep comin' in here for?

CHARLEY. You want me to go?

WILLY (*after a pause, withering*). I can't understand it. He's going back to Texas again. What the hell is that?

CHARLEY. Let him go.

WILLY. I got nothin' to give him, Charley, I'm clean, I'm clean.

CHARLEY. He won't starve. None a them starve. Forget about him.

WILLY. Then what have I got to remember?

CHARLEY. You take it too hard. To hell with it. When a deposit bottle is broken you don't get your nickel back.

WILLY. That's easy enough for you to say.

CHARLEY. That ain't easy for me to say.

WILLY. Did you see the ceiling I put up in the living room?

CHARLEY. Yeah, that's a piece of work. To put up a ceiling is a mystery to me. How do you do it?

WILLY. What's the difference?

CHARLEY. Well, talk about it.

WILLY. You gonna put up a ceiling?

CHARLEY. How could I put up a ceiling?

WILLY. Then what the hell are you bothering me for?

CHARLEY. You're insulted again.

WILLY. A man who can't handle tools is not a man. You're disgusting.

CHARLEY. Don't call me disgusting, Willy.

*Uncle Ben, carrying a valise and an umbrella, enters the forestage from around the right corner of the house. He is a stolid man, in his sixties, with a mustache and an authoritative air. He is utterly certain of his destiny, and there is an aura of far places about him. He enters exactly as Willy speaks.*

WILLY. I'm getting awfully tired, Ben.

*Ben's music is heard. Ben looks around at everything.*

CHARLEY. Good, keep playing; you'll sleep better. Did you call me Ben?

*Ben looks at his watch.*

WILLY. That's funny. For a second there you reminded me of my brother Ben.

BEN. I only have a few minutes. (*He strolls, inspecting the place. Willy and Charley continue playing.*)

CHARLEY. You never heard from him again, heh? Since that time?

WILLY. Didn't Linda tell you? Couple of weeks ago we got a letter from his wife in Africa. He died.

CHARLEY. That so.

BEN (*chuckling*). So this is Brooklyn, eh?

CHARLEY. Maybe you're in for some of his money.

WILLY. Naa, he had seven sons. There's just one opportunity I had with that man . . .

BEN. I must make a train, William. There are several properties I'm looking at in Alaska.

WILLY. Sure, sure! If I'd gone with him to Alaska that time, everything would've been totally different.

CHARLEY. Go on, you'd froze to death up there.

WILLY. What're you talking about?

BEN. Opportunity is tremendous in Alaska, William. Surprised you're not up there.

WILLY. Sure, tremendous.

CHARLEY. Heh?

WILLY. There was the only man I ever met who knew the answers.

CHARLEY. Who?

BEN. How are you all?

WILLY (*taking a pot, smiling*). Fine, fine.

CHARLEY. Pretty sharp tonight.

BEN. Is Mother living with you?

WILLY. No, she died a long time ago.

CHARLEY. Who?

BEN. That's too bad. Fine specimen of a lady, Mother.

WILLY (*to Charley*). Heh?

BEN. I'd hoped to see the old girl.

CHARLEY. Who died?

BEN. Heard anything from Father, have you?

WILLY (*unnerved*). What do you mean, who died?

CHARLEY (*taking a pot*). What're you talkin' about?

BEN (*looking at his watch*). William, it's half-past eight!

WILLY (*as though to dispel his confusion he angrily stops Charley's hand*). That's my build!

CHARLEY. I put the ace . . .

WILLY. If you don't know how to play the game I'm not gonna throw my money away on you!

CHARLEY (*rising*). It was my ace, for God's sake!

WILLY. I'm through, I'm through!

BEN. When did Mother die?

WILLY. Long ago. Since the beginning you never knew how to play cards.

CHARLEY (*picks up the cards and goes to the door*). All right! Next time I'll bring a deck with five aces.

WILLY. I don't play that kind of game!

CHARLEY (*turning to him*). You ought to be ashamed of yourself!

WILLY. Yeah?

CHARLEY. Yeah! (*He goes out.*)

WILLY (*slamming the door after him*). Ignoramus!

BEN (*as Willy comes toward him through the wall-line of the kitchen*). So you're William.

WILLY (*shaking Ben's hand*). Ben! I've been waiting for you so long! What's the answer? How did you do it?

BEN. Oh, there's a story in that.

*Linda enters the forestage, as of old, carrying the wash basket.*

LINDA. Is this Ben?

BEN (*gallantly*). How do you do, my dear.

LINDA. Where've you been all these years? Willy's always wondered why you . . .

WILLY (*pulling Ben away from her impatiently*). Where is Dad? Didn't you follow him? How did you get started?

BEN. Well, I don't know how much you remember.

WILLY. Well, I was just a baby, of course, only three or four years old . . .

BEN. Three years and eleven months.

WILLY. What a memory, Ben!

BEN. I have many enterprises, William, and I have never kept books.

WILLY. I remember I was sitting under the wagon in—was it Nebraska?

BEN. It was South Dakota, and I gave you a bunch of wild flowers.

WILLY. I remember you walking away down some open road.

BEN (*laughing*). I was going to find Father in Alaska.

WILLY. Where is he?

BEN. At that age I had a very faulty view of geography, William. I discovered after a few days that I was heading due south, so instead of Alaska, I ended up in Africa.

LINDA. Africa!

WILLY. The Gold Coast!

BEN. Principally diamond mines.

LINDA. Diamond mines!

BEN. Yes, my dear. But I've only a few minutes . . .

WILLY. No! Boys! Boys! (*Young Biff and Happy appear.*) Listen to this. This is your Uncle Ben, a great man! Tell my boys, Ben!

BEN. Why, boys, when I was seventeen I walked into the jungle, and when I was twenty-one I walked out. (*He laughs.*) And by God I was rich.

WILLY (*to the boys*). You see what I been talking about? The greatest things can happen!

BEN (*glancing at his watch*). I have an appointment in Ketchikan Tuesday week.

WILLY. No, Ben! Please tell about Dad. I want my boys to hear. I want them to know the kind of stock they spring from. All I remember is a man with a big beard, and I was in Mamma's lap, sitting around a fire, and some kind of high music.

BEN. His flute. He played the flute.

WILLY. Sure, the flute, that's right!

*New music is heard, a high, rollicking tune.*

BEN. Father was a very great and a very wild-hearted man. We would start in Boston, and he'd toss the whole family into the wagon, and then he'd drive the team right across the country; through Ohio, and Indiana, Michigan, Illinois, and all the Western states. And we'd stop in the towns and sell the flutes that he'd made on the way. Great inventor, Father. With one gadget he made more in a week than a man like you could make in a lifetime.

WILLY. That's just the way I'm bringing them up, Ben—rugged, well liked, all-around.

BEN. Yeah? (*To Biff.*) Hit that, boy—hard as you can. (*He pounds his stomach.*)

BIFF. Oh, no, sir!

BEN (*taking boxing stance*). Come on, get to me! (*He laughs.*)

WILLY. Go to it. Biff! Go ahead, show him!

BIFF. Okay! (*He cocks his fists and starts in.*)

LINDA (*to Willy*). Why must he fight, dear?

BEN (*sparring with Biff*). Good boy! Good boy!

WILLY. How's that, Ben, heh?

HAPPY. Give him the left, Biff!

LINDA. Why are you fighting?

BEN. Good boy! (*Suddenly comes in, trips Biff, and stands over him, the point of his umbrella poised over Biff's eye.*)

LINDA. Look out, Biff!

BIFF. Gee!

BEN (*patting Biff's knee*). Never fight fair with a stranger, boy. You'll never get out of the jungle that way. (*Taking Linda's hand and bowing.*) It was an honor and a pleasure to meet you, Linda.

LINDA (*withdrawing her hand coldly, frightened*). Have a nice—trip.

BEN (*to Willy*). And good luck with your—what do you do?

WILLY. Selling.

BEN. Yes. Well . . . (*He raises his hand in farewell to all.*)

WILLY. No, Ben, I don't want you to think . . . (*He takes Ben's arm to show him.*) It's Brooklyn, I know, but we hunt too.

BEN. Really, now.

WILLY. Oh, sure, there's snakes and rabbits and—that's why I moved out here. Why, Biff can fell any one of these trees in no time! Boys! Go right over to where they're building the apartment house and get some sand. We're gonna rebuild the entire front stoop right now! Watch this, Ben!

BIFF. Yes, sir! On the double, Hap!

HAPPY (*as he and Biff run off*). I lost weight, Pop, you notice?

*Charley enters in knickers, even before the boys are gone.*

CHARLEY. Listen, if they steal any more from that building the watchman'll put the cops on them!

LINDA (*to Willy*). Don't let Biff . . .

*Ben laughs lustily.*

WILLY. You shoulda seen the lumber they brought home last week. At least a dozen six-by-tens worth all kinds a money.

CHARLEY. Listen, if that watchman . . .

WILLY. I gave them hell, understand. But I got a couple of fearless characters there.

CHARLEY. Willy, the jails are full of fearless characters.

BEN (*clapping Willy on the back, with a laugh at Charley*). And the stock exchange, friend!

WILLY (*joining in Ben's laughter*). Where are the rest of your pants?

CHARLEY. My wife bought them.

WILLY. Now all you need is a golf club and you can go upstairs and go to sleep. (*To Ben.*) Great athlete! Between him and his son Bernard they can't hammer a nail!

BERNARD (*rushing in*). The watchman's chasing Biff!

WILLY (*angrily*). Shut up! He's not stealing anything!

LINDA (*alarmed, hurrying off left*). Where is he? Biff, dear! (*She exits.*)

WILLY (*moving toward the left, away from Ben*). There's nothing wrong. What's the matter with you?

BEN. Nervy boy. Good!

WILLY (*laughing*). Oh, nerves of iron, that Biff!

CHARLEY. Don't know what it is. My New England man comes back and he's bleedin', they murdered him up there.

WILLY. It's contacts, Charley, I got important contacts!

CHARLEY (*sarcastically*). Glad to hear it, Willy. Come in later, we'll shoot a little casino. I'll take some of your Portland money. (*He laughs at Willy and exits.*)

WILLY (*turning to Ben*). Business is bad, it's murderous. But not for me, of course.

BEN. I'll stop by on my way back to Africa.

WILLY (*longingly*). Can't you stay a few days? You're just what I need, Ben, because I—I have a fine position here, but I—well, Dad left when I was such a baby and I never had a chance to talk to him and I still feel—kind of temporary about myself.

BEN. I'll be late for my train.

*They are at opposite ends of the stage.*

WILLY. Ben, my boys—can't we talk? They'd go into the jaws of hell for me, see, but I . . .

BEN. William, you're being first-rate with your boys. Outstanding, manly chaps!

WILLY (*hanging on to his words*). Oh, Ben, that's good to hear! Because sometimes I'm afraid that I'm not teaching them the right kind of—Ben, how should I teach them?

BEN (*giving great weight to each word, and with a certain vicious audacity*). William, when I walked into the jungle, I was seventeen. When I walked out I was twenty-one. And, by God, I was rich! (*He goes off into darkness around the right corner of the house.*)

WILLY. . . . was rich! That's just the spirit I want to imbue them with! To walk into a jungle! I was right! I was right! I was right!

*Ben is gone, but Willy is still speaking to him as Linda, in nightgown and robe, enters the kitchen, glances around for Willy, then goes to the door of the house, looks out and sees him. Comes down to his left. He looks at her.*

LINDA. Willy, dear? Willy?

WILLY. I was right!

LINDA. Did you have some cheese? (*He can't answer.*) It's very late, darling. Come to bed, heh?

WILLY (*looking straight up*). Gotta break your neck to see a star in this yard.

LINDA. You coming in?

WILLY. Whatever happened to that diamond watch fob? Remember? When Ben came from Africa that time? Didn't he give me a watch fob with a diamond in it?

LINDA. You pawned it, dear. Twelve, thirteen years ago. For Biff's radio correspondence course.

WILLY. Gee, that was a beautiful thing. I'll take a walk.

LINDA. But you're in your slippers.

WILLY (*starting to go around the house at the left*). I was right! I was! (*Half to Linda, as he goes, shaking his head.*) What a man! There was a man worth talking to. I was right!

LINDA (*calling after Willy*). But in your slippers, Willy!

*Willy is almost gone when Biff, in his pajamas, comes down the stairs and enters the kitchen.*

BIFF. What is he doing out there?

LINDA. Sh!

BIFF. God Almighty, Mom, how long has he been doing this?

LINDA. Don't, he'll hear you.

BIFF. What the hell is the matter with him?

LINDA. It'll pass by morning.

BIFF. Shouldn't we do anything?

LINDA. Oh, my dear, you should do a lot of things, but there's nothing to do, so go to sleep.

*Happy comes down the stair and sits on the steps.*

HAPPY. I never heard him so loud, Mom.

LINDA. Well, come around more often; you'll hear him. (*She sits down at the table and mends the lining of Willy's jacket.*)

BIFF. Why didn't you ever write me about this, Mom?

LINDA. How would I write to you? For over three months you had no address.

BIFF. I was on the move. But you know I thought of you all the time. You know that, don't you, pal?

LINDA. I know, dear, I know. But he likes to have a letter. Just to know that there's still a possibility for better things.

BIFF. He's not like this all the time, is he?

LINDA. It's when you come home he's always the worst.

BIFF. When I come home?

LINDA. When you write you're coming, he's all smiles, and talks about the future, and—he's just wonderful. And then the closer you seem to come, the more shaky he gets, and then, by the time you get here, he's arguing, and he seems angry at you. I think it's just that maybe he can't bring himself to—to open up to you. Why are you so hateful to each other? Why is that?

BIFF (*evasively*). I'm not hateful, Mom.

LINDA. But you no sooner come in the door than you're fighting!

BIFF. I don't know why. I mean to change. I'm tryin', Mom, you understand?

LINDA. Are you home to stay now?

BIFF. I don't know. I want to look around, see what's doin'.

LINDA. Biff, you can't look around all your life, can you?

BIFF. I just can't take hold, Mom. I can't take hold of some kind of a life.

LINDA. Biff, a man is not a bird, to come and go with the spring time.

BIFF. Your hair . . . (*He touches her hair.*) Your hair got so gray.

LINDA. Oh, it's been gray since you were in high school. I just stopped dyeing it, that's all.

BIFF. Dye it again, will ya? I don't want my pal looking old. (*He smiles.*)

LINDA. You're such a boy! You think you can go away for a year and . . . You've got to get it into your head now that one day you'll knock on this door and there'll be strange people here . . .

BIFF. What are you talking about? You're not even sixty, Mom.

LINDA. But what about your father?

BIFF (*lamely*). Well, I meant him too.

HAPPY. He admires Pop.

LINDA. Biff, dear, if you don't have any feeling for him, then you can't have any feeling for me.

BIFF. Sure I can, Mom.

LINDA. No. You can't just come to see me, because I love him. (*With a threat, but only a threat, of tears.*) He's the dearest man in the world to me, and I won't have anyone making him feel unwanted and low and blue. You've got to make up your mind now, darling, there's no leeway any more. Either he's your father and you pay him that respect, or else you're not to come here. I know he's not easy to get along with—nobody knows that better than me—but . . .

WILLY (*from the left, with a laugh*). Hey, hey, Biffo!

BIFF (*starting to go out after Willy*). What the hell is the matter with him? (*Happy stops him.*)

LINDA. Don't—don't go near him!

BIFF. Stop making excuses for him! He always, always wiped the floor with you. Never had an ounce of respect for you.

HAPPY. He's always had respect for . . .

BIFF. What the hell do you know about it?

HAPPY (*surlily*). Just don't call him crazy!

BIFF. He's got no character—Charley wouldn't do this. Not in his own house—spewing out that vomit from his mind.

HAPPY. Charley never had to cope with what he's got to.

BIFF. People are worse off than Willy Loman. Believe me, I've seen them!

LINDA. Then make Charley your father, Biff. You can't do that, can you? I don't say he's a great man. Willy Loman never made a lot of money. His name was never in the paper. He's not the finest character that ever lived. But he's a human being, and a terrible thing is happening to him. So attention must be paid. He's not to be allowed to fall into his grave like an old dog. Attention, attention must be finally paid to such a person. You called him crazy . . .

BIFF. I didn't mean . . .

LINDA. No, a lot of people think he's lost his—balance. But you don't have to be very smart to know what his trouble is. The man is exhausted.

HAPPY. Sure!

LINDA. A small man can be just as exhausted as a great man. He works for a company thirty-six years this March, opens up unheard-of territories to their trademark, and now in his old age they take his salary away.

HAPPY (*indignantly*). I didn't know that, Mom.

LINDA. You never asked, my dear! Now that you get your spending money someplace else you don't trouble your mind with him.

HAPPY. But I gave you money last . . .

LINDA. Christmas time, fifty dollars! To fix the hot water it cost ninety-seven fifty! For five weeks he's been on straight commission, like a beginner, an unknown!

BIFF. Those ungrateful bastards!

LINDA. Are they any worse than his sons? When he brought them business, when he was young, they were glad to see him. But now his old friends, the old buyers that loved him so and always found some order to hand him in a pinch—they're all dead, retired. He used to be able to make six, seven calls a day in Boston. Now he takes his valises out of the car and puts them back and takes them out again and he's exhausted. Instead of walking he talks now. He drives seven hundred miles, and when he gets there no one knows him any more, no one welcomes him. And what goes through a man's mind, driving seven hundred miles home without having earned a cent? Why shouldn't he talk to himself? Why? When he has to go to Charley and borrow fifty dollars a week and pretend to me that it's his pay? How long can that go on? How long? You see what I'm sitting here and waiting for? And you tell me he has no character? The man who never worked a day but for your benefit? When does he get the medal for that? Is this his reward—to turn around at the age of sixty-three and find his sons, who he loved better than his life, one a philandering bum . . .

HAPPY. Mom!

LINDA. That's all you are, my baby! (*To Biff.*) And you! What happened to the love you had for him? You were such pals! How you used to talk to him on the phone every night! How lonely he was till he could come home to you!

BIFF. All right, Mom. I'll live here in my room, and I'll get a job. I'll keep away from him, that's all.

LINDA. No, Biff. You can't stay here and fight all the time.

BIFF. He threw me out of this house, remember that.

LINDA. Why did he do that? I never knew why.

BIFF. Because I know he's a fake and he doesn't like anybody around who knows!

LINDA. Why a fake? In what way? What do you mean?

BIFF. Just don't lay it all at my feet. It's between me and him—that's all I have to say. I'll chip in from now on. He'll settle for half my paycheck. He'll be all right. I'm going to bed. (*He starts for the stairs.*)

LINDA. He won't be all right.

BIFF (*turning on the stairs, furiously*). I hate this city and I'll stay here. Now what do you want?

LINDA. He's dying, Biff.

*Happy turns quickly to her, shocked.*

BIFF (*after a pause*). Why is he dying?

LINDA. He's been trying to kill himself.

BIFF (*with great horror*). How?

LINDA. I live from day to day.

BIFF. What're you talking about?

LINDA. Remember I wrote you that he smashed up the car again? In February?

BIFF. Well?

LINDA. The insurance inspector came. He said that they have evidence. That all these accidents in the last year—weren't—weren't—accidents.

HAPPY. How can they tell that? That's a lie.

LINDA. It seems there's a woman . . . (*She takes a breath as:*)

BIFF (*sharply but contained*). What woman?

LINDA (*simultaneously*). . . . and this woman . . .

LINDA. What?

BIFF. Nothing. Go ahead.

LINDA. What did you say?

BIFF. Nothing. I just said what woman?

HAPPY. What about her?

LINDA. Well, it seems she was walking down the road and saw his car. She says that he wasn't driving fast at all, and that he didn't skid. She says he came to that little bridge, and then deliberately smashed into the railing, and it was only the shallowness of the water that saved him.

BIFF. Oh, no, he probably just fell asleep again.

LINDA. I don't think he fell asleep.

BIFF. Why not?

LINDA. Last month . . . (*With great difficulty.*) Oh, boys, it's so hard to say a thing like this! He's just a big stupid man to you, but I tell you there's more good in him than in many other people. (*She chokes, wipes her eyes.*) I was looking for a fuse. The lights blew out, and I went down the cellar. And behind the fuse box—it happened to fall out—was a length of rubber pipe—just short.

HAPPY. No kidding!

LINDA. There's a little attachment on the end of it. I knew right away. And sure enough, on the bottom of the water heater there's a new little nipple on the gas pipe.

HAPPY (*angrily*). That—jerk.

BIFF. Did you have it taken off?

LINDA. I'm—I'm ashamed to. How can I mention it to him? Every day I go down and take away that little rubber pipe. But, when he comes home, I put it back where it was. How can I insult him that way? I don't know what to do. I live from day to day, boys. I tell you, I know every thought in his mind. It sounds so old-fashioned and silly, but I tell you he put his whole life into you and you've turned your backs on him. (*She is bent over in the chair, weeping, her face in her hands.*) Biff, I swear to God! Biff, his life is in your hands!

HAPPY (*to Biff*). How do you like that damned fool!

BIFF (*kissing her*). All right, pal, all right. It's all settled now. I've been remiss. I know that, Mom. But now I'll stay, and I swear to you, I'll apply myself. (*Kneeling in front of her, in a fever of self-reproach.*) It's just—you see, Mom, I don't fit in business. Not that I won't try. I'll try, and I'll make good.

HAPPY. Sure you will. The trouble with you in business was you never tried to please people.

BIFF. I know, I . . .

HAPPY. Like when you worked for Harrison's. Bob Harrison said you were tops, and then you go and do some damn fool thing like whistling whole songs in the elevator like a comedian.

BIFF (*against Happy*). So what? I like to whistle sometimes.

HAPPY. You don't raise a guy to a responsible job who whistles in the elevator!

LINDA. Well, don't argue about it now.

HAPPY. Like when you'd go off and swim in the middle of the day instead of taking the line around.

BIFF (*his resentment rising*). Well, don't you run off? You take off sometimes, don't you? On a nice summer day?

HAPPY. Yeah, but I cover myself!

LINDA. Boys!

HAPPY. If I'm going to take a fade the boss can call any number where I'm supposed to be and they'll swear to him that I just left. I'll tell you something that I hate to say, Biff, but in the business world some of them think you're crazy.

BIFF (*angered*). Screw the business world!

HAPPY. All right, screw it! Great, but cover yourself!

LINDA. Hap, Hap!

BIFF. I don't care what they think! They've laughed at Dad for years, and you know why? Because we don't belong in this nuthouse of a city! We should be mixing cement on some open plain or—or carpenters. A carpenter is allowed to whistle!

*Willy walks in from the entrance of the house, at left.*

WILLY. Even your grandfather was better than a carpenter. (*Pause. They watch him.*) You never grew up. Bernard does not whistle in the elevator, I assure you.

BIFF (*as though to laugh Willy out of it*). Yeah, but you do, Pop.

WILLY. I never in my life whistled in an elevator! And who in the business world thinks I'm crazy?

BIFF. I didn't mean it like that, Pop. Now don't make a whole thing out of it, will ya?

WILLY. Go back to the West! Be a carpenter, a cowboy, enjoy yourself!

LINDA. Willy, he was just saying . . .

WILLY. I heard what he said!

HAPPY (*trying to quiet Willy*). Hey, Pop, come on now . . .

WILLY (*continuing over Happy's line*). They laugh at me, heh? Go to Filene's, go to the Hub, go to Slattery's, Boston. Call out the name Willy Loman and see what happens! Big shot!

BIFF. All right, Pop.

WILLY. Big!

BIFF. All right!

WILLY. Why do you always insult me?

BIFF. I didn't say a word. (*To Linda.*) Did I say a word?

LINDA. He didn't say anything, Willy.

WILLY (*going to the doorway of the living room*). All right, good night, good night.

LINDA. Willy, dear, he just decided . . .

WILLY (*to Biff*). If you get tired hanging around tomorrow, paint the ceiling I put up in the living room.

BIFF. I'm leaving early tomorrow.

HAPPY. He's going to see Bill Oliver, Pop.

WILLY (*interestedly*). Oliver? For what?

BIFF (*with reserve, but trying; trying*). He always said he'd stake me. I'd like to go into business, so maybe I can take him up on it.

LINDA. Isn't that wonderful?

WILLY. Don't interrupt. What's wonderful about it? There's fifty men in the City of New York who'd stake him. (*To Biff.*) Sporting goods?

BIFF. I guess so. I know something about it and . . .

WILLY. He knows something about it! You know sporting goods better than Spalding, for God's sake! How much is he giving you?

BIFF. I don't know, I didn't even see him yet, but . . .

WILLY. Then what're you talkin' about?

BIFF (*getting angry*). Well, all I said was I'm gonna see him, that's all!

WILLY (*turning away*). Ah, you're counting your chickens again.

BIFF (*starting left for the stairs*). Oh, Jesus, I'm going to sleep!

WILLY (*calling after him*). Don't curse in this house!

BIFF (*turning*). Since when did you get so clean?

HAPPY (*trying to stop them*). Wait a . . .

WILLY. Don't use that language to me! I won't have it!

HAPPY (*grabbing Biff, shouts*). Wait a minute! I got an idea. I got a feasible idea. Come here, Biff, let's talk this over now, let's talk some sense here. When I was down in Florida last time, I thought of a great idea to sell sporting goods. It just came back to me. You and I, Biff—we have a line, the Loman Line. We train a couple of weeks, and put on a couple of exhibitions, see?

WILLY. That's an idea!

HAPPY. Wait! We form two basketball teams, see? Two water-polo teams. We play each other. It's a million dollars' worth of publicity. Two brothers, see? The Loman Brothers. Displays in the Royal Palms—all the hotels. And banners over the ring and the basketball court: "Loman Brothers." Baby, we could sell sporting goods!

WILLY. That is a one-million-dollar idea!

LINDA. Marvelous!

BIFF. I'm in great shape as far as that's concerned.

HAPPY. And the beauty of it is, Biff, it wouldn't be like a business. We'd be out playin' ball again.

BIFF (*enthused*). Yeah, that's . . .

WILLY. Million-dollar . . .

HAPPY. And you wouldn't get fed up with it, Biff. It'd be the family again. There'd be the old honor, and comradeship, and if you wanted to go off for a swim or somethin'—well, you'd do it! Without some smart cooky gettin' up ahead of you!

WILLY. Lick the world! You guys together could absolutely lick the civilized world.

BIFF. I'll see Oliver tomorrow. Hap, if we could work that out . . .

LINDA. Maybe things are beginning to . . .

WILLY (*wildly enthused, to Linda*). Stop interrupting! (*To Biff.*) But don't wear sport jacket and slacks when you see Oliver.

BIFF. No, I'll . . .

WILLY. A business suit, and talk as little as possible, and don't crack any jokes.

BIFF. He did like me. Always liked me.

LINDA. He loved you!

WILLY (*to Linda*). Will you stop! (*To Biff.*) Walk in very serious. You are not applying for a boy's job. Money is to pass. Be quiet, fine, and serious. Everybody likes a kidder, but nobody lends him money.

HAPPY. I'll try to get some myself, Biff. I'm sure I can.

WILLY. I see great things for you kids, I think your troubles are over. But remember, start big and you'll end big. Ask for fifteen. How much you gonna ask for?

BIFF. Gee, I don't know . . .

WILLY. And don't say "Gee." "Gee" is a boy's word. A man walking in for fifteen thousand dollars does not say "Gee!"

BIFF. Ten, I think, would be top though.

WILLY. Don't be so modest. You always started too low. Walk in with a big laugh. Don't look worried. Start off with a couple of your good stories to lighten things up. It's not what you say, it's how you say it—because personality always wins the day.

LINDA. Oliver always thought the highest of him . . .

WILLY. Will you let me talk?

BIFF. Don't yell at her, Pop, will ya?

WILLY (*angrily*). I was talking, wasn't I?

BIFF. I don't like you yelling at her all the time, and I'm tellin' you, that's all.

WILLY. What're you, takin' over this house?

LINDA. Willy . . .

WILLY (*turning to her*). Don't take his side all the time, goddammit!

BIFF (*furiously*). Stop yelling at her!

WILLY (*suddenly pulling on his cheek, beaten down, guilt ridden*). Give my best to Bill Oliver—he may remember me. (*He exits through the living room doorway.*)

LINDA (*her voice subdued*). What'd you have to start that for? (*Biff turns away.*) You see how sweet he was as soon as you talked hopefully? (*She goes over to Biff.*) Come up and say good night to him. Don't let him go to bed that way.

HAPPY. Come on, Biff, let's buck him up.

LINDA. Please, dear. Just say good night. It takes so little to make him happy. Come. (*She goes through the living room doorway, calling upstairs from within the living room.*) Your pajamas are hanging in the bathroom, Willy!

HAPPY (*looking toward where Linda went out*). What a woman! They broke the mold when they made her. You know that, Biff.

BIFF. He's off salary. My God, working on commission!

HAPPY. Well, let's face it: he's no hot-shot selling man. Except that sometimes, you have to admit, he's a sweet personality.

BIFF (*deciding*). Lend me ten bucks, will ya? I want to buy some new ties.

HAPPY. I'll take you to a place I know. Beautiful stuff. Wear one of my striped shirts tomorrow.

BIFF. She got gray. Mom got awful old. Gee, I'm gonna go in to Oliver tomorrow and knock him for a . . .

HAPPY. Come on up. Tell that to Dad. Let's give him a whirl. Come on.

BIFF (*steamed up*). You know, with ten thousand bucks, boy!

HAPPY (*as they go into the living room*). That's the talk, Biff, that's the first time I've heard the old confidence out of you! (*From within the living room, fading off*) You're gonna live with me, kid, and any babe you want just say the word . . . (*The last lines are hardly heard. They are mounting the stairs to their parents' bedroom.*)

LINDA (*entering her bedroom and addressing Willy, who is in the bathroom. She is straightening the bed for him*). Can you do anything about the shower? It drips.

WILLY (*from the bathroom*). All of a sudden everything falls to pieces. Goddam plumbing, oughta be sued, those people. I hardly finished putting it in and the thing . . . (*His words rumble off.*)

LINDA. I'm just wondering if Oliver will remember him. You think he might?

WILLY (*coming out of the bathroom in his pajamas*). Remember him? What's the matter with you, you crazy? If he'd've stayed with Oliver he'd be on top by now! Wait'll Oliver gets a look at him. You don't know the average caliber any more. The average young man today—(*he is getting into bed*)—is got a caliber of zero. Greatest thing in the world for him was to bum around.

*Biff and Happy enter the bedroom. Slight pause.*

WILLY (*stops short, looking at Biff*). Glad to hear it, boy.

HAPPY. He wanted to say good night to you, sport.

WILLY (*to Biff*). Yeah. Knock him dead, boy. What'd you want to tell me?

BIFF. Just take it easy, Pop. Good night. (*He turns to go.*)

WILLY (*unable to resist*). And if anything falls off the desk while you're talking to him—like a package or something—don't you pick it up. They have office boys for that.

LINDA. I'll make a big breakfast . . .

WILLY. Will you let me finish? (*To Biff.*) Tell him you were in the business in the West. Not farm work.

BIFF. All right, Dad.

LINDA. I think everything . . .

WILLY (*going right through her speech*). And don't undersell yourself. No less than fifteen thousand dollars.

BIFF (*unable to bear him*). Okay. Good night, Mom. (*He starts moving.*)

WILLY. Because you got a greatness in you, Biff, remember that. You got all kinds of greatness . . . (*He lies back, exhausted. Biff walks out.*)

LINDA (*calling after Biff*). Sleep well, darling!

HAPPY. I'm gonna get married, Mom. I wanted to tell you.

LINDA. Go to sleep, dear.

HAPPY (*going*). I just wanted to tell you.

WILLY. Keep up the good work. (*Happy exits.*) God . . . remember that Ebbets Field game? The championship of the city?

LINDA. Just rest. Should I sing to you?

WILLY. Yeah. Sing to me. (*Linda hums a soft lullaby.*) When that team came out—he was the tallest, remember?

LINDA. Oh, yes. And in gold.

*Biff enters the darkened kitchen, takes a cigarette, and leaves the house. He comes downstage into a golden pool of light. He smokes, staring at the night.*

WILLY. Like a young god. Hercules—something like that. And the sun, the sun all around him. Remember how he waved to me? Right up from the field, with the representatives of three colleges standing by? And the buyers I brought, and the cheers when he came out—Loman, Loman, Loman! God Almighty, he'll be great yet. A star like that, magnificent, can never really fade away!

*The light on Willy is fading. The gas heater begins to glow through the kitchen wall, near the stairs, a blue flame beneath red coils.*

LINDA (*timidly*). Willy dear, what has he got against you?

WILLY. I'm so tired. Don't talk any more.

*Biff slowly returns to the kitchen. He stops, stares toward the heater.*

LINDA. Will you ask Howard to let you work in New York?

WILLY. First thing in the morning. Everything'll be all right.

*Biff reaches behind the heater and draws out a length of rubber tubing. He is horrified and turns his head toward Willy's room, still dimly lit, from which the strains of Linda's desperate but monotonous humming rise.*

WILLY (*staring through the window into the moonlight*). Gee, look at the moon moving between the buildings!

*Biff wraps the tubing around his hand and quickly goes up the stairs.*

## *Act 2*

**SCENE:** *Music is heard, gay and bright. The curtain rises as the music fades away. Willy, in shirt sleeves, is sitting at the kitchen table, sipping coffee, his hat in his lap. Linda is filling his cup when she can.*

WILLY. Wonderful coffee. Meal in itself.

LINDA. Can I make you some eggs?

WILLY. No. Take a breath.

LINDA. You look so rested, dear.

WILLY. I slept like a dead one. First time in months. Imagine, sleeping till ten on a Tuesday morning. Boys left nice and early, heh?

LINDA. They were out of here by eight o'clock.

WILLY. Good work!

LINDA. It was so thrilling to see them leaving together. I can't get over the shaving lotion in this house!

WILLY (*smiling*). Mmm . . .

LINDA. Biff was very changed this morning. His whole attitude seemed to be hopeful. He couldn't wait to get downtown to see Oliver.

WILLY. He's heading for a change. There's no question, there simply are certain men that take longer to get—solidified. How did he dress?

LINDA. His blue suit. He's so handsome in that suit. He could be a—anything in that suit!

*Willy gets up from the table. Linda holds his jacket for him.*

WILLY. There's no question, no question at all. Gee, on the way home tonight I'd like to buy some seeds.

LINDA (*laughing*). That'd be wonderful. But not enough sun gets back there. Nothing'll grow any more.

WILLY. You wait, kid, before it's all over we're gonna get a little place out in the country, and I'll raise some vegetables, a couple of chickens . . .

LINDA. You'll do it yet, dear.

*Willy walks out of his jacket. Linda follows him.*

WILLY. And they'll get married, and come for a weekend. I'd build a little guest house. 'Cause I got so many fine tools, all I'd need would be a little lumber and some peace of mind.

LINDA (*joyfully*). I sewed the lining . . .

WILLY. I could build two guest houses, so they'd both come. Did he decide how much he's going to ask Oliver for?

LINDA (*getting him into the jacket*). He didn't mention it, but I imagine ten or fifteen thousand. You going to talk to Howard today?

WILLY. Yeah. I'll put it to him straight and simple. He'll just have to take me off the road.

LINDA. And Willy, don't forget to ask for a little advance, because we've got the insurance premium. It's the grace period now.

WILLY. That's a hundred . . . ?

LINDA. A hundred and eight, sixty-eight. Because we're a little short again.

WILLY. Why are we short?

LINDA. Well, you had the motor job on the car . . .

WILLY. That goddam Studebaker!

LINDA. And you got one more payment on the refrigerator . . .

WILLY. But it just broke again!

LINDA. Well, it's old, dear.

WILLY. I told you we should've bought a well-advertised machine. Charley bought a General Electric and it's twenty years old and it's still good, that son-of-a-bitch.

LINDA. But, Willy . . .

WILLY. Whoever heard of a Hastings refrigerator? Once in my life I would like to own something outright before it's broken! I'm always in a race with the junkyard! I just finished paying for the car and it's on its last legs. The refrigerator consumes belts like a goddam maniac. They time those things. They time them so when you finally paid for them, they're used up.

LINDA (*buttoning up his jacket as he unbuttons it*). All told, about two hundred dollars would carry us, dear. But that includes the last payment on the mortgage. After this payment, Willy, the house belongs to us.

WILLY. It's twenty-five years!

LINDA. Biff was nine years old when we bought it.

WILLY. Well, that's a great thing. To weather a twenty-five year mortgage is . . .

LINDA. It's an accomplishment.

WILLY. All the cement, the lumber, the reconstruction I put in this house! There ain't a crack to be found in it any more.

LINDA. Well, it served its purpose.

WILLY. What purpose? Some stranger'll come along, move in, and that's that. If only Biff would take this house, and raise a family . . . (*He starts to go.*) Good-by, I'm late.

LINDA (*suddenly remembering*). Oh, I forgot! You're supposed to meet them for dinner.

WILLY. Me?

LINDA. At Frank's Chop House on Forty-eighth near Sixth Avenue.

WILLY. Is that so! How about you?

LINDA. No, just the three of you. They're gonna blow you to a big meal!

WILLY. Don't say! Who thought of that?

LINDA. Biff came to me this morning, Willy, and he said, "Tell Dad, we want to blow him to a big meal." Be there six o'clock. You and your two boys are going to have dinner.

WILLY. Gee whiz! That's really somethin'. I'm gonna knock Howard for a loop, kid. I'll get an advance, and I'll come home with a New York job. Goddammit, now I'm gonna do it!

LINDA. Oh, that's the spirit, Willy!

WILLY. I will never get behind a wheel the rest of my life!

LINDA. It's changing, Willy, I can feel it changing!

WILLY. Beyond a question. G'by, I'm late. (*He starts to go again.*)

LINDA (*calling after him as she runs to the kitchen table for a handkerchief*). You got your glasses?

WILLY (*feels for them, then comes back in*). Yeah, yeah, got my glasses.

LINDA (*giving him the handkerchief*). And a handkerchief.

WILLY. Yeah, handkerchief.

LINDA. And your saccharine?

WILLY. Yeah, my saccharine.

LINDA. Be careful on the subway stairs.

*She kisses him, and a silk stocking is seen hanging from her hand. Willy notices it.*

WILLY. Will you stop mending stockings? At least while I'm in the house. It gets me nervous. I can't tell you. Please.

*Linda hides the stocking in her hand as she follows Willy across the forestage in front of the house.*

LINDA. Remember, Frank's Chop House.

WILLY (*passing the apron*). Maybe beets would grow out there.

LINDA (*laughing*). But you tried so many times.

WILLY. Yeah. Well, don't work hard today. (*He disappears around the right corner of the house.*)

LINDA. Be careful!

*As Willy vanishes, Linda waves to him. Suddenly the phone rings. She runs across the stage and into the kitchen and lifts it.*

LINDA. Hello? Oh, Biff! I'm so glad you called, I just . . . Yes, sure, I just told him. Yes, he'll be there for dinner at six o'clock, I didn't forget. Listen, I was just dying to tell you. You know that little rubber pipe I told you about? That he connected to the gas heater? I finally decided to go down the cellar this morning and take it away and destroy it. But it's gone! Imagine? He took it away himself, it isn't there! (*She listens.*) When? Oh, then you took it. Oh—nothing, it's just that I'd hoped he'd taken it away himself. Oh, I'm not worried, darling, because this morning he left in such high spirits, it was like the old days! I'm not afraid any more. Did Mr. Oliver see you? . . . Well, you wait there then. And make a nice impression on him, darling. Just don't perspire too much before you see him. And have a nice time with Dad. He may have big news too! . . . That's right, a New York job. And be sweet to him tonight, dear. Be loving to him. Because he's only a little boat looking for a harbor. (*She is trembling with sorrow and joy.*) Oh, that's wonderful, Biff, you'll save his life. Thanks, darling. Just put your arm around him when he comes into the restaurant. Give him a smile. That's the boy . . . Good-by, dear. . . . You got your comb? . . . That's fine. Good-by, Biff dear.

*In the middle of her speech, Howard Wagner, thirty-six, wheels in a small typewriter table on which is a wire-recording machine and proceeds to plug it in. This is on the left forestage. Light slowly fades on Linda as it rises on Howard. Howard is intent on threading the machine and only glances over his shoulder as Willy appears.*

WILLY. Pst! Pst!

HOWARD. Hello, Willy, come in.

WILLY. Like to have a little talk with you, Howard.

HOWARD. Sorry to keep you waiting. I'll be with you in a minute.

WILLY. What's that, Howard?

HOWARD. Didn't you ever see one of these? Wire recorder.

WILLY. Oh. Can we talk a minute?

HOWARD. Records things. Just got delivery yesterday. Been driving me crazy, the most terrific machine I ever saw in my life. I was up all night with it.

WILLY. What do you do with it?

HOWARD. I bought it for dictation, but you can do anything with it. Listen to this. I had it home last night. Listen to what I picked up. The first one is my daughter. Get this. (*He flicks the switch and "Roll out the Barrel" is heard being whistled.*) Listen to that kid whistle.

WILLY. That is lifelike, isn't it?

HOWARD. Seven years old. Get that tone.

WILLY. Ts, ts. Like to ask a little favor if you . . .

*The whistling breaks off, and the voice of Howard's daughter is heard.*

HIS DAUGHTER. "Now you, Daddy."

HOWARD. She's crazy for me! (*Again the same song is whistled.*) That's me! Ha! (*He winks.*)

WILLY. You're very good!

*The whistling breaks off again. The machine runs silent for a moment.*

HOWARD. Sh! Get this now, this is my son.

HIS SON. "The capital of Alabama is Montgomery; the capital of Arizona is Phoenix; the capital of Arkansas is Little Rock; the capital of California is Sacramento . . ." (*and on, and on.*)

HOWARD (*holding up five fingers*). Five years old, Willy!

WILLY. He'll make an announcer some day!

HIS SON (*continuing*). "The capital . . ."

HOWARD. Get that—alphabetical order! (*The machine breaks off suddenly.*) Wait a minute. The maid kicked the plug out.

WILLY. It certainly is a . . .

HOWARD. Sh, for God's sake!

HIS SON. "It's nine o'clock, Bulova watch time. So I have to go to sleep."

WILLY. That really is . . .

HOWARD. Wait a minute! The next is my wife.

*They wait.*

HOWARD'S VOICE. "Go on, say something." (*Pause.*) "Well, you gonna talk?"

HIS WIFE. "I can't think of anything."

HOWARD'S VOICE. "Well, talk—it's turning."

HIS WIFE (*shyly, beaten*). "Hello." (*Silence.*) "Oh, Howard, I can't talk into this . . ."

HOWARD (*snapping the machine off*). That was my wife.

WILLY. That is a wonderful machine. Can we . . .

HOWARD. I tell you, Willy, I'm gonna take my camera, and my bandsaw, and all my hobbies, and out they go. This is the most fascinating relaxation I ever found.

WILLY. I think I'll get one myself.

HOWARD. Sure, they're only a hundred and a half. You can't do without it. Supposing you wanna hear Jack Benny, see? But you can't be at home at that hour. So you tell the maid to turn the radio on when Jack Benny comes on, and this automatically goes on with the radio . . .

WILLY. And when you come home you . . .

HOWARD. You can come home twelve o'clock, one o'clock, any time you like, and you get yourself a Coke and sit yourself down, throw the switch, and there's Jack Benny's program in the middle of the night!

WILLY. I'm definitely going to get one. Because lots of times I'm on the road, and I think to myself, what I must be missing on the radio!

HOWARD. Don't you have a radio in the car?

WILLY. Well, yeah, but who ever thinks of turning it on?

HOWARD. Say, aren't you supposed to be in Boston?

WILLY. That's what I want to talk to you about, Howard. You got a minute? (*He draws a chair in from the wing.*)

HOWARD. What happened? What're you doing here?

WILLY. Well . . .

HOWARD. You didn't crack up again, did you?

WILLY. Oh, no. No . . .

HOWARD. Geez, you had me worried there for a minute. What's the trouble?

WILLY. Well, tell you the truth, Howard. I've come to the decision that I'd rather not travel any more.

HOWARD. Not travel! Well, what'll you do?

WILLY. Remember, Christmas time, when you had the party here? You said you'd try to think of some spot for me here in town.

HOWARD. With us?

WILLY. Well, sure.

HOWARD. Oh, yeah, yeah. I remember. Well, I couldn't think of anything for you, Willy.

WILLY. I tell ya, Howard. The kids are all grown up, y'know. I don't need much any more. If I could take home—well, sixty-five dollars a week, I could swing it.

HOWARD. Yeah, but Willy, see I . . .

WILLY. I tell ya why, Howard. Speaking frankly and between the two of us, y'know—I'm just a little tired.

HOWARD. Oh, I could understand that, Willy. But you're a road man, Willy, and we do a road business. We've only got a half-dozen salesmen on the floor here.

WILLY. God knows, Howard. I never asked a favor of any man. But I was with the firm when your father used to carry you in here in his arms.

HOWARD. I know that, Willy, but . . .

WILLY. Your father came to me the day you were born and asked me what I thought of the name Howard, may he rest in peace.

HOWARD. I appreciate that, Willy, but there just is no spot here for you. If I had a spot I'd slam you right in, but I just don't have a single solitary spot.

*He looks for his lighter. Willy has picked it up and gives it to him. Pause.*

WILLY (*with increasing anger*). Howard, all I need to set my table is fifty dollars a week.

HOWARD. But where am I going to put you, kid?

WILLY. Look, it isn't a question of whether I can sell merchandise, is it?

HOWARD. No, but it's business, kid, and everybody's gotta pull his own weight.

WILLY (*desperately*). Just let me tell you a story, Howard . . .

HOWARD. 'Cause you gotta admit, business is business.

WILLY (*angrily*). Business is definitely business, but just listen for a minute. You don't understand this. When I was a boy—eighteen, nineteen—I was already on the road. And there was a question in my mind as to whether selling had a future for me. Because in those days I had a yearning to go to Alaska. See, there were three gold strikes in one month in Alaska, and I felt like going out. Just for the ride, you might say.

HOWARD (*barely interested*). Don't say.

WILLY. Oh, yeah, my father lived many years in Alaska. He was an adventurous man. We've got quite a little streak of self-reliance in our family. I thought I'd go out with my older brother and try to locate him, and maybe settle in the North with the old man. And I was almost decided to go, when I met a salesman in the Parker House. His name was Dave Singleman. And he was eighty-four years old, and he'd drummed merchandise in thirty-one states. And old Dave, he'd go up to his room, y'understand, put on his green velvet slippers—I'll never forget—and pick up his phone and call the buyers, and without ever leaving his room, at the age of eighty-four, he made his living. And when I saw that, I realized that selling was the greatest career a man could want. 'Cause what could be more satisfying than to be able to go, at the age of eight-four, into twenty or thirty different cities, and pick up a phone, and be remembered and loved and helped by so many different people? Do you know? when he died—and by the way he died the death of a salesman, in his green velvet slippers in the smoker of the New York, New Haven and Hartford, going into Boston—when he died, hundreds of salesmen and buyers were at his funeral. Things were sad on a lotta trains for months after that. (*He stands up, Howard has not looked at him.*) In those days there was personality in it, Howard. There was respect, and comradeship, and gratitude in it. Today, it's all cut and dried, and there's no chance for bringing friendship to bear—or personality. You see what I mean? They don't know me any more.

HOWARD (*moving away, to the right*). That's just the thing, Willy.

WILLY. If I had forty dollars a week—that's all I'd need. Forty dollars, Howard.

HOWARD. Kid, I can't take blood from a stone, I . . .

WILLY (*desperation is on him now*). Howard, the year Al Smith was nominated, your father came to me and . . .

HOWARD (*starting to go off*). I've got to see some people, kid.

WILLY (*stopping him*). I'm talking about your father! There were promises made across this desk! You mustn't tell me you've got people to see—I put thirty-four years into this firm, Howard, and now I can't pay my insurance! You can't eat the orange and throw the peel away—a man is not a piece of fruit! (*After a pause.*) Now pay attention. Your father—in 1928 I had a big year. I averaged a hundred and seventy dollars a week in commissions.

HOWARD (*impatiently*). Now, Willy, you never averaged . . .

WILLY (*banging his hand on the desk*). I averaged a hundred and seventy dollars a week in the year of 1928! And your father came to me—or rather, I was in the office here—it was right over this desk—and he put his hand on my shoulder . . .

HOWARD (*getting up*). You'll have to excuse me, Willy, I gotta see some people. Pull yourself together. (*Going out.*) I'll be back in a little while.

*On Howard's exit, the light on his chair grows very bright and strange.*

WILLY. Pull myself together! What the hell did I say to him? My God, I was yelling at him! How could I? (*Willy breaks off, staring at the light, which occupies the chair, animating it. He approaches this chair, standing across the desk from it.*) Frank, Frank, don't you remember what you told me that time? How you put your hand on my shoulder, and Frank . . . (*He leans on the desk and as he speaks the dead man's name he accidentally switches on the recorder, and instantly*)

HOWARD'S SON. ". . . of New York is Albany. The capital of Ohio is Cincinnati, the capital of Rhode Island is . . ." (*The recitation continues.*)

WILLY (*leaping away with fright, shouting*). Ha! Howard! Howard! Howard!

HOWARD (*rushing in*). What happened?

WILLY (*pointing at the machine, which continues nasally, childishly, with the capital cities*). Shut it off! Shut it off!

HOWARD (*pulling the plug out*). Look, Willy . . .

WILLY (*pressing his hands to his eyes.*) I gotta get myself some coffee. I'll get some coffee . . .

*Willy starts to walk out. Howard stops him.*

HOWARD (*rolling up the cord*). Willy, look . . .

WILLY. I'll go to Boston.

HOWARD. Willy, you can't go to Boston for us.

WILLY. Why can't I go?

HOWARD. I don't want you to represent us. I've been meaning to tell you for a long time now.

WILLY. Howard, are you firing me?

HOWARD. I think you need a good long rest, Willy.

WILLY. Howard . . .

HOWARD. And when you feel better, come back, and we'll see if we can work something out.

WILLY. But I gotta earn money, Howard. I'm in no position to . . .

HOWARD. Where are your sons? Why don't your sons give you a hand?

WILLY. They're working on a very big deal.

HOWARD. This is no time for false pride, Willy. You go to your sons and you tell them that you're tired. You've got two great boys, haven't you?

WILLY. Oh, no question, no question, but in the meantime . . .

HOWARD. Then that's that, heh?

WILLY. All right, I'll go to Boston tomorrow.

HOWARD. No, no.

WILLY. I can't throw myself on my sons. I'm not a cripple!

HOWARD. Look, kid, I'm busy this morning.

WILLY (*grasping Howard's arm*). Howard, you've got to let me go to Boston!

HOWARD (*hard, keeping himself under control*). I've got a line of people to see this morning. Sit down, take five minutes, and pull yourself together, and then go home, will ya? I need the office, Willy. (*He starts to go, turns, remembering the recorder, starts to push off the table holding the recorder.*) Oh, yeah. Whenever you can this week, stop by and drop off the samples. You'll feel better, Willy, and then come back and we'll talk. Pull yourself together, kid, there's people outside.

*Howard exits, pushing the table off left. Willy stares into space, exhausted. Now the music is heard—Ben's music—first distantly, then closer, closer. As Willy speaks, Ben enters from the right. He carries valise and umbrella.*

WILLY. Oh, Ben, how did you do it? What is the answer? Did you wind up the Alaska deal already?

BEN. Doesn't take much time if you know what you're doing. Just a short business trip. Boarding ship in an hour. Wanted to say good-by.

WILLY. Ben, I've got to talk to you.

BEN (*glancing at his watch*). Haven't the time, William.

WILLY (*crossing the apron to Ben*). Ben, nothing's working out. I don't know what to do.

BEN. Now, look here, William. I've bought timberland in Alaska and I need a man to look after things for me.

WILLY. God, timberland! Me and my boys in those grand outdoors!

BEN. You've a new continent at your doorstep, William. Get out of these cities, they're full of talk and time payments and courts of law. Screw on your fists and you can fight for a fortune up there.

WILLY. Yes, yes! Linda, Linda!

*Linda enters as of old, with the wash.*

LINDA. Oh, you're back?

BEN. I haven't much time.

WILLY. No, wait! Linda, he's got a proposition for me in Alaska.

LINDA. But you've got . . . (*To Ben.*) He's got a beautiful job here.

WILLY. But in Alaska, kid, I could . . .

LINDA. You're doing well enough, Willy!

BEN (*to Linda*). Enough for what, my dear?

LINDA (*frightened of Ben and angry at him*). Don't say those things to him! Enough to be happy right here, right now. (*To Willy, while Ben laughs.*) Why must everybody conquer the world? You're well liked, and the boys love you, and someday—(*To Ben*)—why, old man Wagner told him just the other day that if he keeps it up he'll be a member of the firm, didn't he, Willy?

WILLY. Sure, sure. I am building something with this firm, Ben, and if a man is building something he must be on the right track, mustn't he?

BEN. What are you building? Lay your hand on it. Where is it?

WILLY (*hesitantly*). That's true, Linda, there's nothing.

LINDA. Why? (*To Ben.*) There's a man eighty-four years old . . .

WILLY. That's right, Ben, that's right. When I look at that man I say, what is there to worry about?

BEN. Bah!

WILLY. It's true, Ben. All he has to do is go into any city, pick up the phone, and he's making his living and you know why?

BEN (*picking up his valise*). I've got to go.

WILLY (*holding Ben back*). Look at this boy!

*Biff, in his high school sweater, enters carrying suitcase. Happy carries Biff's shoulder guards, gold helmet, and football pants.*

WILLY. Without a penny to his name, three great universities are begging for him, and from there the sky's the limit, because it's not what you do, Ben. It's who you know and the smile on your face! It's contacts, Ben, contacts! The whole wealth of Alaska passes over the lunch table at the Commodore Hotel, and that's the wonder, the wonder of this country, that a man can end with diamonds here on the basis of being liked! (*He turns to Biff.*) And that's why when you get out on that field today it's important. Because thousands of people will be rooting for you and loving you. (*To Ben, who has again begun to leave.*) And Ben! when he walks into a business office his name will sound out like a bell and all the doors will open to him! I've seen it, Ben, I've seen it a thousand times! You can't feel it with your hand like timber, but it's there!

BEN. Good-by, William.

WILLY. Ben, am I right? Don't you think I'm right? I value your advice.

BEN. There's a new continent at your doorstep, William. You could walk out rich. Rich! (*He is gone.*)

WILLY. We'll do it here, Ben! You hear me? We're gonna do it here!

*Young Bernard rushes in. The gay music of the Boys is heard.*

BERNARD. Oh, gee, I was afraid you left already!

WILLY. Why? What time is it?

BERNARD. It's half-past one!

WILLY. Well, come on, everybody! Ebbets Field next stop! Where's the pennants? (*He rushes through the wall-line of the kitchen and out into the living room.*)

LINDA (*to Biff*). Did you pack fresh underwear?

BIFF (*who has been limbering up*). I want to go!

BERNARD. Biff, I'm carrying your helmet, ain't I?

HAPPY. No, I'm carrying the helmet.

BERNARD. Oh, Biff, you promised me.

HAPPY. I'm carrying the helmet.

BERNARD. How am I going to get in the locker room?

LINDA. Let him carry the shoulder guards. (*She puts her coat and hat on in the kitchen.*)

BERNARD. Can I, Biff? 'Cause I told everybody I'm going to be in the locker room.

HAPPY. In Ebbets Field it's the clubhouse.

BERNARD. I meant the clubhouse. Biff!

HAPPY. Biff!

BIFF (*grandly, after a slight pause*). Let him carry the shoulder guards.

HAPPY (*as he gives Bernard the shoulder guards*). Stay close to us now.

*Willy rushes in with the pennants.*

WILLY (*handing them out*). Everybody wave when Biff comes out on the field. (*Happy and Bernard run off.*) You set now, boy?

*The music has died away.*

BIFF. Ready to go, Pop. Every muscle is ready.

WILLY (*at the edge of the apron*). You realize what this means?

BIFF. That's right, Pop.

WILLY (*feeling Biff's muscles*). You're comin' home this afternoon captain of the All-Scholastic Championship Team of the City of New York.

BIFF. I got it, Pop. And remember, pal, when I take off my helmet, that touchdown is for you.

WILLY. Let's go! (*He is starting out, with his arm around Biff, when Charley enters, as of old, in knickers.*) I got no room for you, Charley.

CHARLEY. Room? For what?

WILLY. In the car.

CHARLEY. You goin' for a ride? I wanted to shoot some casino.

WILLY (*furiously*). Casino! (*Incredulously.*) Don't you realize what today is?

LINDA. Oh, he knows, Willy. He's just kidding you.

WILLY. That's nothing to kid about!

CHARLEY. No, Linda, what's goin' on?

LINDA. He's playing in Ebbets Field.

CHARLEY. Baseball in this weather?

WILLY. Don't talk to him. Come on, come on! (*He is pushing them out.*)

CHARLEY. Wait a minute, didn't you hear the news?

WILLY. What?

CHARLEY. Don't you listen to the radio? Ebbets Field just blew up.

WILLY. You go to hell! (*Charley laughs. Pushing them out.*) Come on, come on! We're late.

CHARLEY (*as they go*). Knock a homer, Biff, knock a homer!

WILLY (*the last to leave, turning to Charley*). I don't think that was funny, Charley. This is the greatest day of his life.

CHARLEY. Willy, when are you going to grow up?

WILLY. Yeah, heh? When this game is over, Charley, you'll be laughing out of the other side of your face. They'll be calling him another Red Grange. Twenty-five thousand a year.

CHARLEY (*kidding*). Is that so?

WILLY. Yeah, that's so.

CHARLEY. Well, then, I'm sorry, Willy. But tell me something.

WILLY. What?

CHARLEY. Who is Red Grange?

WILLY. Put up your hands. Goddam you, put up your hands!

*Charley, chuckling, shakes his head and walks away, around the left corner of the stage. Willy follows him. The music rises to a mocking frenzy.*

WILLY. Who the hell do you think you are, better than everybody else? You don't know everything, you big, ignorant, stupid . . . Put up your hands!

*Light rises, on the right side of the forestage, on a small table in the reception room of Charley's office. Traffic sounds heard. Bernard, now mature, sits whistling to himself. A pair of tennis rackets and an old overnight bag are on the door beside him.*

WILLY (*offstage*). What are you walking away for? Don't walk away! If you're going to say something say it to my face! I know you laugh at me behind my back. You'll laugh out of the other side of your goddam face after this game. Touchdown! Touchdown! Eighty thousand people! Touchdown! Right between the goal posts.

*Bernard is a quiet, earnest, but self-assured young man. Willy's voice is coming from right upstage now. Bernard lowers his feet off the table and listens. Jenny, his father's secretary, enters.*

JENNY (*distressed*). Say, Bernard, will you go out in the hall?

BERNARD. What is that noise? Who is it?

JENNY. Mr. Loman. He just got off the elevator.

BERNARD (*getting up*). Who's he arguing with?

JENNY. Nobody. There's nobody with him. I can't deal with him any more, and your father gets all upset every time he comes. I've got a lot of typing to do, and your father's waiting to sign it. Will you see him?

WILLY (*entering*). Touchdown! Touch—(*He sees Jenny.*) Jenny, Jenny, good to see you. How're ya? Workin'? Or still honest?

JENNY. Fine. How've you been feeling?

WILLY. Not much any more, Jenny. Ha, ha! (*He is surprised to see the rackets.*)

BERNARD. Hello, Uncle Willy.

WILLY (*almost shocked*). Bernard! Well, look who's here! (*He comes quickly, guiltily, to Bernard and warmly shakes his hand.*)

BERNARD. How are you? Good to see you.

WILLY. What are you doing here?

BERNARD. Oh, just stopped by to see Pop. Get off my feet till my train leaves. I'm going to Washington in a few minutes.

WILLY. Is he in?

BERNARD. Yes, he's in his office with the accountant. Sit down.

WILLY (*sitting down*). What're you going to do in Washington?

BERNARD. Oh, just a case I've got there, Willy.

WILLY. That so? (*Indicating the rackets.*) You going to play tennis there?

BERNARD. I'm staying with a friend who's got a court.

WILLY. Don't say. His own tennis court. Must be fine people, I bet.

BERNARD. They are, very nice. Dad tells me Biff's in town.

WILLY (*with a big smile*). Yeah, Biff's in. Working on a very big deal, Bernard.

BERNARD. What's Biff doing?

WILLY. Well, he's been doing very big things in the West. But he decided to establish himself here. Very big. We're having dinner. Did I hear your wife had a boy?

BERNARD. That's right. Our second.

WILLY. Two boys! What do you know!

BERNARD. What kind of a deal has Biff got?

WILLY. Well, Bill Oliver—very big sporting-goods man—he wants Biff very badly. Called him in from the West. Long distance, carte blanche, special deliveries. Your friends have their own private tennis court?

BERNARD. You still with the old firm, Willy?

WILLY (*after a pause*). I'm—I'm overjoyed to see how you made the grade, Bernard, overjoyed. It's an encouraging thing to see a young man really—really . . . Looks very good for Biff—very . . . (*He breaks off, then.*) Bernard . . . (*He is so full of emotion, he breaks off again.*)

BERNARD. What is it, Willy?

WILLY (*small and alone*). What—what's the secret?

BERNARD. What secret?

WILLY. How—how did you? Why didn't he ever catch on?

BERNARD. I wouldn't know that, Willy.

WILLY (*confidentially, desperately*). You were his friend, his boyhood friend. There's something I don't understand about it. His life ended after that Ebbets Field game. From the age of seventeen nothing good ever happened to him.

BERNARD. He never trained himself for anything.

WILLY. But he did, he did. After high school he took so many correspondence courses. Radio mechanics; television; God knows what, and never made the slightest mark.

BERNARD (*taking off his glasses*). Willy, do you want to talk candidly?

WILLY (*rising, faces Bernard*). I regard you as a very brilliant man, Bernard. I value your advice.

BERNARD. Oh, the hell with the advice, Willy. I couldn't advise you. There's just one thing I've always wanted to ask you. When he was supposed to graduate, and the math teacher flunked him . . .

WILLY. Oh, that son-of-a-bitch ruined his life.

BERNARD. Yeah, but, Willy, all he had to do was go to summer school and make up that subject.

WILLY. That's right, that's right.

BERNARD. Did you tell him not to go to summer school?

WILLY. Me? I begged him to go. I ordered him to go!

BERNARD. Then why wouldn't he go?

WILLY. Why? Why! Bernard, that question has been trailing me like a ghost for the last fifteen years. He flunked the subject, and laid down and died like a hammer hit him!

BERNARD. Take it easy, kid.

WILLY. Let me talk to you—I got nobody to talk to. Bernard, Bernard, was it my fault? Y'see? It keeps going around in my mind, maybe I did something to him. I got nothing to give him.

BERNARD. Don't take it so hard.

WILLY. Why did he lay down? What is the story there? You were his friend!

BERNARD. Willy, I remember, it was June, and our grades came out. And he'd flunked math.

WILLY. That son-of-a-bitch!

BERNARD. No, it wasn't right then. Biff just got very angry, I remember, and he was ready to enroll in summer school.

WILLY (*surprised*). He was?

BERNARD. He wasn't beaten by it at all. But then, Willy, he disappeared from the block for almost a month. And I got the idea that he'd gone up to New England to see you. Did he have a talk with you then?

*Willy stares in silence.*

BERNARD. Willy?

WILLY (*with a strong edge of resentment in his voice*). Yeah, he came to Boston. What about it?

BERNARD. Well, just that when he came back—I'll never forget this, it always mystifies me. Because I'd thought so well of Biff, even though he'd always taken advantage of me. I loved him, Willy, y'know? And he came back after that month and took his sneakers—remember those sneakers with "University of Virginia" printed on them? He was so proud of those, wore them every day. And he took them down in the cellar, and burned them up in the furnace. We had a fist fight. It lasted at least half an hour. Just the two of us, punching each other down the cellar, and crying right through it. I've often thought of how strange it was that I knew he'd given up his life. What happened in Boston, Willy?

*Willy looks at him as at an intruder.*

BERNARD. I just bring it up because you asked me.

WILLY (*angrily*). Nothing. What do you mean, "What happened?" What's that got to do with anything?

BERNARD. Well, don't get sore.

WILLY. What are you trying to do, blame it on me? If a boy lays down is that my fault?

BERNARD. Now, Willy, don't get . . .

WILLY. Well, don't—don't talk to me that way! What does that mean, "What happened?"

*Charley enters. He is in his vest, and he carries a bottle of bourbon.*

CHARLEY. Hey, you're going to miss that train. (*He waves the bottle.*)

BERNARD. Yeah, I'm going. (*He takes the bottle.*) Thanks, Pop. (*He picks up his rackets and bag.*) Good-by, Willy, and don't worry about it. You know, "If at first you don't succeed . . ."

WILLY. Yes, I believe in that.

BERNARD. But sometimes, Willy, it's better for a man just to walk away.

WILLY. Walk away?

BERNARD. That's right.

WILLY. But if you can't walk away?

BERNARD (*after a slight pause*). I guess that's when it's tough. (*Extending his hand.*) Good-by, Willy.

WILLY (*shaking Bernard's hand*). Good-by, boy.

CHARLEY (*an arm on Bernard's shoulder*). How do you like this kid? Gonna argue a case in front of the Supreme Court.

BERNARD (*protesting*). Pop!

WILLY (*genuinely shocked, pained, and happy*). No! The Supreme Court!

BERNARD. I gotta run. 'By, Dad!

CHARLEY. Knock 'em dead, Bernard!

*Bernard goes off.*

WILLY (*as Charley takes out his wallet*). The Supreme Court! And he didn't even mention it!

CHARLEY (*counting out money on the desk*). He don't have to—he's gonna do it.

WILLY. And you never told him what to do, did you? You never took any interest in him.

CHARLEY. My salvation is that I never took any interest in anything. There's some money—fifty dollars. I got an accountant inside.

WILLY. Charley, look . . . (*with difficulty.*) I got my insurance to pay. If you can manage it—I need a hundred and ten dollars.

*Charley doesn't reply for a moment; merely stops moving.*

WILLY. I'd draw it from my bank but Linda would know, and I . . .

CHARLEY. Sit down, Willy.

WILLY (*moving toward the chair*). I'm keeping an account of everything, remember. I'll pay every penny back. (*He sits.*)

CHARLEY. Now listen to me, Willy.

WILLY. I want you to know I appreciate . . .

CHARLEY (*sitting down on the table*). Willy, what're you doin'? What the hell is going on in your head?

WILLY. Why? I'm simply . . .

CHARLEY. I offered you a job. You make fifty dollars a week. And I won't send you on the road.

WILLY. I've got a job.

CHARLEY. Without pay? What kind of a job is a job without pay? (*He rises.*) Now, look, kid, enough is enough. I'm no genius but I know when I'm being insulted.

WILLY. Insulted!

CHARLEY. Why don't you want to work for me?

WILLY. What's the matter with you? I've got a job.

CHARLEY. Then what're you walkin' in here every week for?

WILLY (*getting up*). Well, if you don't want me to walk in here . . .

CHARLEY. I'm offering you a job.

WILLY. I don't want your goddam job!

CHARLEY. When the hell are you going to grow up?

WILLY (*furiously*). You big ignoramus, if you say that to me again I'll rap you one! I don't care how big you are! (*He's ready to fight.*)

*Pause.*

CHARLEY (*kindly, going to him*). How much do you need, Willy?

WILLY. Charley, I'm strapped. I'm strapped. I don't know what to do. I was just fired.

CHARLEY. Howard fired you?

WILLY. That snotnose. Imagine that? I named him. I named him Howard.

CHARLEY. Willy, when're you gonna realize that them things don't mean anything? You named him Howard, but you can't sell that. The only thing you got in this world is what you can sell. And the funny thing is that you're a salesman, and you don't know that.

WILLY. I've always tried to think otherwise, I guess. I always felt that if a man was impressive, and well liked, that nothing . . .

CHARLEY. Why must everybody like you? Who liked J. P. Morgan? Was he impressive? In a Turkish bath he'd look like a butcher. But with his pockets on he was very well liked. Now listen, Willy, I know you don't like me, and nobody can say I'm in love with you, but I'll give you a job because—just for the hell of it, put it that way. Now what do you say?

WILLY. I—I just can't work for you, Charley.

CHARLEY. What're you, jealous of me?

WILLY. I can't work for you, that's all, don't ask me why.

CHARLEY (*angered, takes out more bills*). You been jealous of me all your life, you damned fool! Here, pay your insurance. (*He puts the money in Willy's hand.*)

WILLY. I'm keeping strict accounts.

CHARLEY. I've got some work to do. Take care of yourself. And pay your insurance.

WILLY (*moving to the right*). Funny, y'know? After all the highways, and the trains, and the appointments, and the years, you end up worth more dead than alive.

CHARLEY. Willy, nobody's worth nothin' dead. (*After a slight pause.*) Did you hear what I said?

*Willy stands still, dreaming.*

CHARLEY. Willy!

WILLY. Apologize to Bernard for me when you see him. I didn't mean to argue with him. He's a fine boy. They're all fine boys, and they'll end up big—all of them. Someday they'll all play tennis together. Wish me luck, Charley. He saw Bill Oliver today.

CHARLEY. Good luck.

WILLY (*on the verge of tears*). Charley, you're the only friend I got. Isn't that a remarkable thing? (*He goes out.*)

CHARLEY. Jesus!

*Charley stares after him a moment and follows. All light blacks out. Suddenly raucous music is heard, and a red glow rises behind the screen at right. Stanley, a young waiter, appears, carrying a table, followed by Happy, who is carrying two chairs.*

STANLEY (*putting the table down*). That's all right, Mr. Loman, I can handle it myself. (*He turns and takes the chairs from Happy and places them at the table.*)

HAPPY (*glancing around*). Oh, this is better.

STANLEY. Sure, in the front there you're in the middle of all kinds of noise. Whenever you got a party, Mr. Loman, you just tell me and I'll put you back here. Y'know, there's a lotta people they don't like it private, because when they go out they like to see a lotta action around them because they're sick and tired to stay in the house by theirself. But I know you, you ain't from Hackensack. You know what I mean?

HAPPY (*sitting down*). So how's it coming, Stanley?

STANLEY. Ah, it's a dog life. I only wish during the war they'd a took me in the Army. I coulda been dead by now.

HAPPY. My brother's back, Stanley.

STANLEY. Oh, he come back, heh? From the Far West.

HAPPY. Yeah, big cattle man, my brother, so treat him right. And my father's coming too.

STANLEY. Oh, your father too!

HAPPY. You got a couple of nice lobsters?

STANLEY. Hundred per cent, big.

HAPPY. I want them with the claws.

STANLEY. Don't worry, I don't give you no mice. (*Happy laughs.*) How about some wine? It'll put a head on the meal.

HAPPY. No. You remember, Stanley, that recipe I brought you from overseas? With the champagne in it?

STANLEY. Oh, yeah, sure. I still got it tacked up yet in the kitchen. But that'll have to cost a buck apiece anyways.

HAPPY. That's all right.

STANLEY. What'd you, hit a number or somethin'?

HAPPY. No, it's a little celebration. My brother is—I think he pulled off a big deal today. I think we're going into business together.

STANLEY. Great! That's the best for you. Because a family business, you know what I mean?—that's the best.

HAPPY. That's what I think.

STANLEY. 'Cause what's the difference? Somebody steals? It's in the family. Know what I mean? (*Sotto voce.*) Like this bartender here. The boss is goin' crazy what kinda leak he's got in the cash register. You put it in but it don't come out.

HAPPY (*raising his head*). Sh!

STANLEY. What?

HAPPY. You notice I wasn't lookin' right or left, was I?

STANLEY. No.

HAPPY. And my eyes are closed.

STANLEY. So what's the . . . ?

HAPPY. Strudel's comin'.

STANLEY (*catching on, looks around*). Ah, no, there's no . . .

*He breaks off as a furred, lavishly dressed Girl enters and sits at the next table. Both follow her with their eyes.*

STANLEY. Geez, how'd ya know?

HAPPY. I got radar or something. (*Staring directly at her profile.*) Oooooooo . . . Stanley.

STANLEY. I think that's for you, Mr. Loman.

HAPPY. Look at that mouth. Oh, God. And the binoculars.

STANLEY. Geez, you got a life, Mr. Loman.

HAPPY. Wait on her.

STANLEY (*going to the Girl's table*). Would you like a menu, ma'am?

GIRL. I'm expecting someone, but I'd like a . . .

HAPPY. Why don't you bring her—excuse me, miss, do you mind? I sell champagne, and I'd like you to try my brand. Bring her a champagne, Stanley.

GIRL. That's awfully nice of you.

HAPPY. Don't mention it. It's all company money. (*He laughs.*)

GIRL. That's a charming product to be selling, isn't it?

HAPPY. Oh, gets to be like everything else. Selling is selling, y'know.

GIRL. I suppose.

HAPPY. You don't happen to sell, do you?

GIRL. No, I don't sell.

HAPPY. Would you object to a compliment from a stranger? You ought to be on a magazine cover.

GIRL (*looking at him a little archly*). I have been.

*Stanley comes in with a glass of champagne.*

HAPPY. What'd I say before, Stanley? You see? She's a cover girl.

STANLEY. Oh, I could see, I could see.

HAPPY (*to the Girl*). What magazine?

GIRL. Oh, a lot of them. (*She takes the drink.*) Thank you.

HAPPY. You know what they say in France, don't you? "Champagne is the drink of the complexion"—Hya, Biff!

*Biff has entered and sits with Happy.*

BIFF. Hello, kid. Sorry I'm late.

HAPPY. I just got here. Uh, Miss . . . ?

GIRL. Forsythe.

HAPPY. Miss Forsythe, this is my brother.

BIFF. Is Dad here?

HAPPY. His name is Biff. You might've heard of him. Great football player.

GIRL. Really? What team?

HAPPY. Are you familiar with football?

GIRL. No, I'm afraid I'm not.

HAPPY. Biff is quarterback with the New York Giants.

GIRL. Well, that is nice, isn't it? (*She drinks.*)

HAPPY. Good health.

GIRL. I'm happy to meet you.

HAPPY. That's my name. Hap. It's really Harold, but at West Point they called me Happy.

GIRL (*now really impressed*). Oh, I see. How do you do? (*She turns her profile.*)

BIFF. Isn't Dad coming?

HAPPY. You want her?

BIFF. Oh, I could never make that.

HAPPY. I remember the time that idea would never come into your head. Where's the old confidence, Biff?

BIFF. I just saw Oliver . . .

HAPPY. Wait a minute. I've got to see that old confidence again. Do you want her? She's on call.

BIFF. Oh, no. (*He turns to look at the Girl.*)

HAPPY. I'm telling you. Watch this. (*Turning to the Girl.*) Honey? (*She turns to him.*) Are you busy?

GIRL. Well, I am . . . but I could make a phone call.

HAPPY. Do that, will you, honey? And see if you can get a friend. We'll be here for a while. Biff is one of the greatest football players in the country.

GIRL (*standing up*). Well, I'm certainly happy to meet you.

HAPPY. Come back soon.

GIRL. I'll try.

HAPPY. Don't try, honey, try hard.

*The Girl exits. Stanley follows, shaking his head in bewildered admiration.*

HAPPY. Isn't that a shame now? A beautiful girl like that? That's why I can't get married. There's not a good woman in a thousand. New York is loaded with them, kid!

BIFF. Hap, look . . .

HAPPY. I told you she was on call!

BIFF (*strangely unnerved*). Cut it out, will ya? I want to say something to you.

HAPPY. Did you see Oliver?

BIFF. I saw him all right. Now look, I want to tell Dad a couple of things and I want you to help me.

HAPPY. What? Is he going to back you?

BIFF. Are you crazy? You're out of your goddam head, you know that?

HAPPY. Why? What happened?

BIFF (*breathlessly*). I did a terrible thing today, Hap. It's been the strangest day I ever went through. I'm all numb, I swear.

HAPPY. You mean he wouldn't see you?

BIFF. Well, I waited six hours for him, see? All day. Kept sending my name in. Even tried to date his secretary so she'd get me to him, but no soap.

HAPPY. Because you're not showin' the old confidence, Biff. He remembered you, didn't he?

BIFF (*stopping Happy with a gesture*). Finally, about five o'clock, he comes out. Didn't remember who I was or anything. I felt like such an idiot, Hap.

HAPPY. Did you tell him my Florida idea?

BIFF. He walked away. I saw him for one minute. I got so mad I could've torn the walls down! How the hell did I ever get the idea I was a salesman there? I even believed myself that I'd been a salesman for him! And then he gave me one look and—I realized what a ridiculous lie my whole life has been! We've been talking in a dream for fifteen years. I was a shipping clerk.

HAPPY. What'd you do?

BIFF (*with great tension and wonder*). Well, he left, see. And the secretary went out. I was all alone in the waiting room. I don't know what came over me, Hap. The next thing I know I'm in his office—paneled walls, everything. I can't explain it. I—Hap. I took his fountain pen.

HAPPY. Geez, did he catch you?

BIFF. I ran out. I ran down all eleven flights. I ran and ran and ran.

HAPPY. That was an awful dumb—what'd you do that for?

BIFF (*agonized*). I don't know, I just—wanted to take something, I don't know. You gotta help me, Hap. I'm gonna tell Pop.

HAPPY. You crazy? What for?

BIFF. Hap, he's got to understand that I'm not the man somebody lends that kind of money to. He thinks I've been spiting him all these years and it's eating him up.

HAPPY. That's just it. You tell him something nice.

BIFF. I can't.

HAPPY. Say you got a lunch date with Oliver tomorrow.

BIFF. So what do I do tomorrow?

HAPPY. You leave the house tomorrow and come back at night and say Oliver is thinking it over. And he thinks it over for a couple of weeks, and gradually it fades away and nobody's the worse.

BIFF. But it'll go on forever!

HAPPY. Dad is never so happy as when he's looking forward to something!

*Willy enters.*

HAPPY. Hello, scout!

WILLY. Gee, I haven't been here in years!

*Stanley has followed Willy in and sets a chair for him. Stanley starts off but Happy stops him.*

HAPPY. Stanley!

*Stanley stands by, waiting for an order.*

BIFF (*going to Willy with guilt, as to an invalid*). Sit down, Pop. You want a drink?

WILLY. Sure, I don't mind.

BIFF. Let's get a load on.

WILLY. You look worried.

BIFF. N-no. (*To Stanley.*) Scotch all around. Make it doubles.

STANLEY. Doubles, right. (*He goes.*)

WILLY. You had a couple already, didn't you?

BIFF. Just a couple, yeah.

WILLY. Well, what happened, boy? (*Nodding affirmatively, with a smile.*) Everything go all right?

BIFF (*takes a breath, then reaches out and grasps Willy's hand*). Pal . . . (*He is smiling bravely, and Willy is smiling too.*) I had an experience today.

HAPPY. Terrific, Pop.

WILLY. That so? What happened?

BIFF (*high, slightly alcoholic, above the earth*). I'm going to tell you everything from first to last. It's been a strange day. (*Silence. He looks *around, composes himself as best he can, but his breath keeps breaking the rhythm of his voice.*) I had to wait quite a while for him, and . . .

WILLY. Oliver?

BIFF. Yeah, Oliver. All day, as a matter of cold fact. And a lot of—instances—facts, Pop, facts about my life came back to me. Who was it, Pop? Who ever said I was a salesman with Oliver?

WILLY. Well, you were.

BIFF. No, Dad, I was a shipping clerk.

WILLY. But you were practically . . .

BIFF (*with determination*). Dad, I don't know who said it first, but I was never a salesman for Bill Oliver.

WILLY. What're you talking about?

BIFF. Let's hold on to the facts tonight, Pop. We're not going to get anywhere bullin' around. I was a shipping clerk.

WILLY (*angrily*). All right, now listen to me . . .

BIFF. Why don't you let me finish?

WILLY. I'm not interested in stories about the past or any crap of that kind because the woods are burning, boys, you understand? There's a big blaze going on all around. I was fired today.

BIFF (*shocked*). How could you be?

WILLY. I was fired, and I'm looking for a little good news to tell your mother, because the woman has waited and the woman has suffered. The gist of it is that I haven't got a story left in my head, Biff. So don't give me a lecture about facts and aspects. I am not interested. Now what've you got to say to me?

*Stanley enters with three drinks. They wait until he leaves.*

WILLY. Did you see Oliver?

BIFF. Jesus, Dad!

WILLY. You mean you didn't go up there?

HAPPY. Sure he went up there.

BIFF. I did. I—saw him. How could they fire you?

WILLY (*on the edge of his chair*). What kind of a welcome did he give you?

BIFF. He won't even let you work on commission?

WILLY. I'm out! (*Driving.*) So tell me, he gave you a warm welcome?

HAPPY. Sure, Pop, sure!

BIFF (*driven*). Well, it was kind of . . .

WILLY. I was wondering if he'd remember you. (*To Happy.*) Imagine, man doesn't see him for ten, twelve years and gives him that kind of a welcome!

HAPPY. Damn right!

BIFF (*trying to return to the offensive*). Pop, look . . .

WILLY. You know why he remembered you, don't you? Because you impressed him in those days.

BIFF. Let's talk quietly and get this down to the facts, huh?

WILLY (*as though Biff had been interrupting*). Well, what happened? It's great news, Biff. Did he take you into his office or'd you talk in the waiting room?

BIFF. Well, he came in, see, and . . .

WILLY (*with a big smile*). What'd he say? Betcha he threw his arm around you.

BIFF. Well, he kinda . . .

WILLY. He's a fine man. (*To Happy.*) Very hard man to see, y'know.

HAPPY (*agreeing*). Oh, I know.

WILLY (*to Biff*). Is that where you had the drinks?

BIFF. Yeah, he gave me a couple of—no, no!

HAPPY (*cutting in*). He told him my Florida idea.

WILLY. Don't interrupt. (*To Biff.*) How'd he react to the Florida idea?

BIFF. Dad, will you give me a minute to explain?

WILLY. I've been waiting for you to explain since I sat down here! What happened? He took you into his office and what?

BIFF. Well—I talked. And—and he listened, see.

WILLY. Famous for the way he listens, y'know. What was his answer?

BIFF. His answer was—(*He breaks off, suddenly angry.*) Dad, you're not letting me tell you what I want to tell you!

WILLY (*accusing, angered*). You didn't see him, did you?

BIFF. I did see him!

WILLY. What'd you insult him or something? You insulted him, didn't you?

BIFF. Listen, will you let me out of it, will you just let me out of it!

HAPPY. What the hell!

WILLY. Tell me what happened!

BIFF (*to Happy*). I can't talk to him!

*A single trumpet note jars the ear. The light of green leaves stains the house, which holds the air of night and a dream. Young Bernard enters and knocks on the door of the house.*

YOUNG BERNARD (*frantically*). Mrs. Loman, Mrs. Loman!

HAPPY. Tell him what happened!

BIFF (*to Happy.*) Shut up and leave me alone!

WILLY. No, no! You had to go and flunk math!

BIFF. What math? What're you talking about?

YOUNG BERNARD. Mrs. Loman, Mrs. Loman!

*Linda appears in the house, as of old.*

WILLY (*wildly*). Math, math, math!

BIFF. Take it easy, Pop!

YOUNG BERNARD. Mrs. Loman!

WILLY (*furiously*). If you hadn't flunked you'd've been set by now!

BIFF. Now, look, I'm gonna tell you what happened, and you're going to listen to me.

YOUNG BERNARD. Mrs. Loman!

BIFF. I waited six hours . . .

HAPPY. What the hell are you saying?

BIFF. I kept sending in my name but he wouldn't see me. So finally he . . . (*He continues unheard as light fades low on the restaurant.*)

YOUNG BERNARD. Biff flunked math!

LINDA. No!

YOUNG BERNARD. Birnbaum flunked him! They won't graduate him!

LINDA. But they have to. He's gotta go to the university. Where is he? Biff! Biff!

YOUNG BERNARD. No, he left. He went to Grand Central.

LINDA. Grand—You mean he went to Boston!

YOUNG BERNARD. Is Uncle Willy in Boston?

LINDA. Oh, maybe Willy can talk to the teacher. Oh, the poor, poor boy!

*Light on house area snaps out.*

BIFF (*at the table, now audible, holding up a gold fountain pen*). . . . so I'm washed up with Oliver, you understand? Are you listening to me?

WILLY (*at a loss*). Yeah, sure. If you hadn't flunked . . .

BIFF. Flunked what? What're you talking about?

WILLY. Don't blame everything on me! I didn't flunk math—you did! What pen?

HAPPY. That was awful dumb, Biff, a pen like that is worth—

WILLY (*seeing the pen for the first time*). You took Oliver's pen?

BIFF (*weakening*). Dad, I just explained it to you.

WILLY. You stole Bill Oliver's fountain pen!

BIFF. I didn't exactly steal it! That's just what I've been explaining to you!

HAPPY. He had it in his hand and just then Oliver walked in, so he got nervous and stuck it in his pocket!

WILLY. My God, Biff!

BIFF. I never intended to do it, Dad!

OPERATOR'S VOICE. Standish Arms, good evening!

WILLY (*shouting*). I'm not in my room!

BIFF (*frightened*). Dad, what's the matter? (*He and Happy stand up.*)

OPERATOR. Ringing Mr. Loman for you!

WILLY. I'm not there, stop it!

BIFF (*horrified, gets down on one knee before Willy*). Dad, I'll make good, I'll make good. (*Willy tries to get to his feet. Biff holds him down.*) Sit down now.

WILLY. No, you're no good, you're no good for anything.

BIFF. I am, Dad, I'll find something else, you understand? Now don't worry about anything. (*He holds up Willy's face.*) Talk to me, Dad.

OPERATOR. Mr. Loman does not answer. Shall I page him?

WILLY (*attempting to stand, as though to rush and silence the Operator*). No, no, no!

HAPPY. He'll strike something, Pop.

WILLY. No, no . . .

BIFF (*desperately, standing over Willy*). Pop, listen! Listen to me! I'm telling you something good. Oliver talked to his partner about the Florida idea. You listening? He—he talked to his partner, and he came to me . . . I'm going to be all right, you hear? Dad, listen to me, he said it was just a question of the amount!

WILLY. Then you . . . got it?

HAPPY. He's gonna be terrific, Pop!

WILLY (*trying to stand*). Then you got it, haven't you? You got it! You got it!

BIFF (*agonized, holds Willy down*). No, no. Look, Pop. I'm supposed to have lunch with them tomorrow. I'm just telling you this so you'll know that I can still make an impression, Pop. And I'll make good somewhere, but I can't go tomorrow, see.

WILLY. Why not? You simply . . .

BIFF. But the pen, Pop!

WILLY. You give it to him and tell him it was an oversight!

HAPPY. Sure, have lunch tomorrow!

BIFF. I can't say that . . .

WILLY. You were doing a crossword puzzle and accidentally used his pen!

BIFF. Listen, kid, I took those balls years ago, now I walk in with his fountain pen? That clinches it, don't you see? I can't face him like that! I'll try elsewhere.

PAGE'S VOICE. Paging Mr. Loman!

WILLY. Don't you want to be anything?

BIFF. Pop, how can I go back?

WILLY. You don't want to be anything, is that what's behind it?

BIFF (*now angry at Willy for not crediting his sympathy*). Don't take it that way! You think it was easy walking into that office after what I'd done to him? A team of horses couldn't have dragged me back to Bill Oliver!

WILLY. Then why'd you go?

BIFF. Why did I go? Why did I go! Look at you! Look at what's become of you!

*Off left, The Woman laughs.*

WILLY. Biff, you're going to go to that lunch tomorrow, or . . .

BIFF. I can't go. I've got no appointment!

HAPPY. Biff, for . . . !

WILLY. Are you spiting me?

BIFF. Don't take it that way! Goddammit!

WILLY (*strikes Biff and falters away from the table*). You rotten little louse! Are you spiting me?

THE WOMAN. Someone's at the door, Willy!

BIFF. I'm no good, can't you see what I am?

HAPPY (*separating them*). Hey, you're in a restaurant! Now cut it out, both of you! (*The girls enter.*) Hello, girls, sit down.

*The Woman laughs, off left.*

MISS FORSYTHE. I guess we might as well. This is Letta.

THE WOMAN. Willy, are you going to wake up?

BIFF (*ignoring Willy*). How're ya, miss, sit down. What do you drink?

MISS FORSYTHE. Letta might not be able to stay long.

LETTA. I gotta get up very early tomorrow. I got jury duty. I'm so excited! Were you fellows ever on a jury?

BIFF. No, but I been in front of them! (*The girls laugh.*) This is my father.

LETTA. Isn't he cute? Sit down with us, Pop.

HAPPY. Sit him down, Biff!

BIFF (*going to him*). Come on, slugger, drink us under the table. To hell with it! Come on, sit down, pal.

*On Biff's last insistence, Willy is about to sit.*

THE WOMAN (*now urgently*). Willy, are you going to answer the door!

*The Woman's call pulls Willy back. He starts right, befuddled.*

BIFF. Hey, where are you going?

WILLY. Open the door.

BIFF. The door?

WILLY. The washroom . . . the door . . . where's the door?

BIFF (*leading Willy to the left*). Just go straight down.

*Willy moves left.*

THE WOMAN. Willy, Willy, are you going to get up, get up, get up, get up?

*Willy exits left.*

LETTA. I think it's sweet you bring your daddy along.

MISS FORSYTHE. Oh, he isn't really your father!

BIFF (*at left, turning to her resentfully*). Miss Forsythe, you've just seen a prince walk by. A fine, troubled prince. A hardworking, unappreciated prince. A pal, you understand? A good companion. Always for his boys.

LETTA. That's so sweet.

HAPPY. Well, girls, what's the program? We're wasting time. Come on, Biff. Gather round. Where would you like to go?

BIFF. Why don't you do something for him?

HAPPY. Me!

BIFF. Don't you give a damn for him, Hap?

HAPPY. What're you talking about? I'm the one who . . .

BIFF. I sense it, you don't give a good goddam about him. (*He takes the rolled-up hose from his pocket and puts it on the table in front of Happy.*) Look what I found in the cellar, for Christ's sake. How can you bear to let it go on?

HAPPY. Me? Who goes away? Who runs off and . . .

BIFF. Yeah, but he doesn't mean anything to you. You could help him—I can't! Don't you understand what I'm talking about? He's going to kill himself, don't you know that?

HAPPY. Don't I know it! Me!

BIFF. Hap, help him! Jesus . . . help him . . . Help me, help me, I can't bear to look at his face! (*Ready to weep, he hurries out, up right.*)

HAPPY (*starting after him*). Where are you going?

MISS FORSYTHE. What's he so mad about?

HAPPY. Come on, girls, we'll catch up with him.

MISS FORSYTHE (*as Happy pushes her out*). Say, I don't like that temper of his!

HAPPY. He's just a little overstrung, he'll be all right!

WILLY (*off left, as The Woman laughs*). Don't answer! Don't answer!

LETTA. Don't you want to tell your father . . .

HAPPY. No, that's not my father. He's just a guy. Come on, we'll catch Biff, and, honey, we're going to paint this town! Stanley, where's the check! Hey, Stanley!

*They exit. Stanley looks toward left.*

STANLEY (*calling to Happy indignantly*). Mr. Loman! Mr. Loman!

*Stanley picks up a chair and follows them off. Knocking is heard off left. The Woman enters, laughing. Willy follows her. She is in a black slip; he is buttoning his shirt. Raw, sensuous music accompanies their speech:*

WILLY. Will you stop laughing? Will you stop?

THE WOMAN. Aren't you going to answer the door? He'll wake the whole hotel.

WILLY. I'm not expecting anybody.

THE WOMAN. Whyn't you have another drink, honey, and stop being so damn self-centered?

WILLY. I'm so lonely.

THE WOMAN. You know you ruined me, Willy? From now on, whenever you come to the office, I'll see that you go right through to the buyers. No waiting at my desk anymore, Willy. You ruined me.

WILLY. That's nice of you to say that.

THE WOMAN. Gee, you are self-centered! Why so sad? You are the saddest, self-centeredest soul I ever did see-saw. (*She laughs. He kisses her.*) Come on inside, drummer boy. It's silly to be dressing in the middle of the night. (*As knocking is heard.*) Aren't you going to answer the door?

WILLY. They're knocking on the wrong door.

THE WOMAN. But I felt the knocking. And he heard us talking in here. Maybe the hotel's on fire!

WILLY (*his terror rising*). It's a mistake.

THE WOMAN. Then tell him to go away!

WILLY. There's nobody there.

THE WOMAN. It's getting on my nerves, Willy. There's somebody standing out there and it's getting on my nerves!

WILLY (*pushing her away from him*). All right, stay in the bathroom here, and don't come out. I think there's a law in Massachusetts about it, so don't come out. It may be that new room clerk. He looked very mean. So don't come out. It's a mistake, there's no fire.

*The knocking is heard again. He takes a few steps away from her, and she vanishes into the wing. The light follows him, and now he is facing Young Biff, who carries a suitcase. Biff steps toward him. The music is gone.*

BIFF. Why didn't you answer?

WILLY. Biff! What are you doing in Boston?

BIFF. Why didn't you answer? I've been knocking for five minutes, I called you on the phone . . .

WILLY. I just heard you. I was in the bathroom and had the door shut. Did anything happen home?

BIFF. Dad—I let you down.

WILLY. What do you mean?

BIFF. Dad . . .

WILLY. Biffo, what's this about? (*Putting his arm around Biff.*) Come on, let's go downstairs and get you a malted.

BIFF. Dad, I flunked math.

WILLY. Not for the term?

BIFF. The term. I haven't got enough credits to graduate.

WILLY. You mean to say Bernard wouldn't give you the answers?

BIFF. He did, he tried, but I only got a sixty-one.

WILLY. And they wouldn't give you four points?

BIFF. Birnbaum refused absolutely. I begged him, Pop, but he won't give me those points. You gotta talk to him before they close the school. Because if he saw the kind of man you are, and you just talked to him in your way, I'm sure he'd come through for me. The class came right before practice, see, and I didn't go enough. Would you talk to him? He'd like you, Pop. You know the way you could talk.

WILLY. You're on. We'll drive right back.

BIFF. Oh, Dad, good work! I'm sure he'll change it for you!

WILLY. Go downstairs and tell the clerk I'm checkin' out. Go right down.

BIFF. Yes, sir! See, the reason he hates me, Pop—one day he was late for class so I got up at the blackboard and imitated him. I crossed my eyes and talked with a lithp.

WILLY (*laughing*). You did? The kids like it?

BIFF. They nearly died laughing!

WILLY. Yeah? What'd you do?

BIFF. The thquare root of thixthy twee is . . . (*Willy bursts out laughing; Biff joins.*) And in the middle of it he walked in!

*Willy laughs and The Woman joins in offstage.*

WILLY (*without hesitation*). Hurry downstairs and . . .

BIFF. Somebody in there?

WILLY. No, that was next door.

*The Woman laughs offstage.*

BIFF. Somebody got in your bathroom!

WILLY. No, it's the next room, there's a party . . .

THE WOMAN (*enters, laughing; she lisps this*). Can I come in? There's something in the bathtub, Willy, and it's moving!

*Willy looks at Biff; who is staring open-mouthed and horrified at The Woman.*

WILLY. Ah—you better go back to your room. They must be finished painting by now. They're painting her room so I let her take a shower here. Go back, go back . . . (*He pushes her.*)

THE WOMAN (*resisting*). But I've got to get dressed, Willy, I can't . . .

WILLY. Get out of here! Go back, go back . . . (*Suddenly striving for the ordinary.*) This is Miss Francis, Biff, she's a buyer. They're painting her room. Go back, Miss Francis, go back . . .

THE WOMAN. But my clothes, I can't go out naked in the hall!

WILLY (*pushing her offstage*). Get outa here! Go back, go back!

*Biff slowly sits down on his suitcase as the argument continues offstage.*

THE WOMAN. Where's my stockings? You promised me stockings, Willy!

WILLY. I have no stockings here!

THE WOMAN. You had two boxes of size nine sheers for me, and I want them!

WILLY. Here, for God's sake, will you get outa here!

THE WOMAN (*enters holding a box of stockings*). I just hope there's nobody in the hall. That's all I hope. (*To Biff.*) Are you football or baseball?

BIFF. Football.

THE WOMAN (*angry, humiliated*). That's me too. G'night. (*She snatches her clothes from Willy, and walks out.*)

WILLY (*after a pause*). Well, better get going. I want to get to the school first thing in the morning. Get my suits out of the closet. I'll get my valise. (*Biff doesn't move.*) What's the matter! (*Biff remains motionless, tears falling.*) She's a buyer. Buys for J. H. Simmons. She lives down the hall—they're painting. You don't imagine—(*He breaks off. After a pause.*) Now listen, pal, she's just a buyer. She sees merchandise in her room and they have to keep it looking just so . . . (*Pause. Assuming command.*) All right, get my suits. (*Biff doesn't move.*) Now stop crying and do as I say. I gave you an order. Biff, I gave you an order! Is that what you do when I give you an order? How dare you cry! (*Putting his arm around Biff.*) Now look, Biff, when you grow up you'll understand about these things. You mustn't—you mustn't overemphasize a thing like this. I'll see Birnbaum first thing in the morning.

BIFF. Never mind.

WILLY (*getting down beside Biff.*) Never mind! He's going to give you those points. I'll see to it.

BIFF. He wouldn't listen to you.

WILLY. He certainly will listen to me. You need those points for the U. of Virginia.

BIFF. I'm not going there.

WILLY. Heh? If I can't get him to change that mark you'll make it up in summer school. You've got all summer to . . .

BIFF (*his weeping breaking from him*). Dad . . .

WILLY (*infected by it*). Oh, my boy . . .

BIFF. Dad . . .

WILLY. She's nothing to me, Biff. I was lonely, I was terribly lonely.

BIFF. You—you gave her Mama's stockings! (*His tears break through and he rises to go.*)

WILLY (*grabbing for Biff*). I gave you an order!

BIFF. Don't touch me, you—liar!

WILLY. Apologize for that!

BIFF. You fake! You phony little fake! You fake! (*Overcome, he turns quickly and weeping fully goes out with his suitcase. Willy is left on the floor on his knees.*)

WILLY. I gave you an order! Biff, come back here or I'll beat you! Come back here! I'll whip you!

*Stanley comes quickly in from the right and stands in front of Willy.*

WILLY (*shouts at Stanley*). I gave you an order . . .

STANLEY. Hey, let's pick it up, pick it up, Mr. Loman. (*He helps Willy to his feet.*) Your boys left with the chippies. They said they'll see you home.

*A second waiter watches some distance away.*

WILLY. But we were supposed to have dinner together.

*Music is heard, Willy's theme.*

STANLEY. Can you make it?

WILLY. I'll—sure, I can make it. (*Suddenly concerned about his clothes.*) Do I—I look all right?

STANLEY. Sure, you look all right. (*He flicks a speck off Willy's lapel.*)

WILLY. Here—here's a dollar.

STANLEY. Oh, your son paid me. It's all right.

WILLY (*putting it in Stanley's hand*). No, take it. You're a good boy.

STANLEY. Oh, no, you don't have to . . .

WILLY. Here—here's some more, I don't need it any more. (*After a slight pause.*) Tell me—is there a seed store in the neighborhood?

STANLEY. Seeds? You mean like to plant?

*As Willy turns, Stanley slips the money back into his jacket pocket.*

WILLY. Yes. Carrots, peas . . .

STANLEY. Well, there's hardware stores on Sixth Avenue, but it may be too late now.

WILLY (*anxiously*). Oh, I'd better hurry. I've got to get some seeds. (*He starts off to the right.*) I've got to get some seeds, right away. Nothing's planted. I don't have a thing in the ground.

*Willy hurries out as the light goes down. Stanley moves over to the right after him, watches him off. The other waiter has been staring at Willy.*

STANLEY (*to the waiter*). Well, whatta you looking at?

*The waiter picks up the chairs and moves off right. Stanley takes the table and follows him. The light fades on this area. There is a long pause, the sound of the flute coming over. The light gradually rises on the kitchen, which is empty. Happy appears at the door of the house, followed by Biff. Happy is carrying a large bunch of long-stemmed roses. He enters the kitchen, looks around for Linda. Not seeing her, he turns to Biff, who is just outside the house door, and makes a gesture with his hands, indicating "Not here, I guess." He looks into the living room and freezes. Inside, Linda, unseen, is seated, Willy's coat on her lap. She rises ominously and quietly and moves toward Happy, who backs up into the kitchen, afraid.*

HAPPY. Hey, what're you doing up? (*Linda says nothing but moves toward him implacably.*) Where's Pop? (*He keeps backing to the right, and now Linda is in full view in the doorway to the living room.*) Is he sleeping?

LINDA. Where were you?

HAPPY (*trying to laugh it off*). We met two girls, Mom, very fine types. Here, we brought you some flowers. (*Offering them to her.*) Put them in your room, Ma.

*She knocks them to the floor at Biff's feet. He has now come inside and closed the door behind him. She stares at Biff, silent.*

HAPPY. Now what'd you do that for? Mom, I want you to have some flowers . . .

LINDA (*cutting Happy off, violently to Biff*). Don't you care whether he lives or dies?

HAPPY (*going to the stairs*). Come upstairs, Biff.

BIFF (*with a flare of disgust, to Happy*). Go away from me! (*To Linda.*) What do you mean, lives or dies? Nobody's dying around here, pal.

LINDA. Get out of my sight! Get out of here!

BIFF. I wanna see the boss.

LINDA. You're not going near him!

BIFF. Where is he? (*He moves into the living room and Linda follows.*)

LINDA (*shouting after Biff*). You invite him for dinner. He looks forward to it all day—(*Biff appears in his parents' bedroom, looks around, and exits*)—and then you desert him there. There's no stranger you'd do that to!

HAPPY. Why? He had a swell time with us. Listen, when I—(*Linda comes back into the kitchen*)—desert him I hope I don't outlive the day!

LINDA. Get out of here!

HAPPY. Now look, Mom . . .

LINDA. Did you have to go to women tonight? You and your lousy rotten whores!

*Biff re-enters the kitchen.*

HAPPY. Mom, all we did was follow Biff around trying to cheer him up! (*To Biff.*) Boy, what a night you gave me!

LINDA. Get out of here, both of you, and don't come back! I don't want you tormenting him any more. Go on now, get your things together! (*To Biff.*) You can sleep in his apartment. (*She starts to pick up the flowers and stops herself.*) Pick up this stuff, I'm not your maid any more. Pick it up, you bum, you!

*Happy turns his back to her in refusal. Biff slowly moves over and gets down on his knees, picking up the flowers.*

LINDA. You're a pair of animals! Not one, not another living soul would have had the cruelty to walk out on that man in a restaurant!

BIFF (*not looking at her*). Is that what he said?

LINDA. He didn't have to say anything. He was so humiliated he nearly limped when he came in.

HAPPY. But, Mom, he had a great time with us . . .

BIFF (*cutting him off violently*). Shut up!

*Without another word, Happy goes upstairs.*

LINDA. You! You didn't even go in to see if he was all right!

BIFF (*still on the floor in front of Linda, the flowers in his hand; with self-loathing*). No. Didn't. Didn't do a damned thing. How do you like that, heh? Left him babbling in a toilet.

LINDA. You louse. You . . .

BIFF. Now you hit it on the nose! (*He gets up, throws the flowers in the wastebasket.*) The scum of the earth, and you're looking at him!

LINDA. Get out of here!

BIFF. I gotta talk to the boss, Mom. Where is he?

LINDA. You're not going near him. Get out of this house!

BIFF (*with absolute assurance, determination*). No. We're gonna have an abrupt conversation, him and me.

LINDA. You're not talking to him.

*Hammering is heard from outside the house, off right. Biff turns toward the noise.*

LINDA (*suddenly pleading*). Will you please leave him alone?

BIFF. What's he doing out there?

LINDA. He's planting the garden!

BIFF (*quietly*). Now? Oh, my God!

*Biff moves outside, Linda following. The light dies down on them and comes up on the center of the apron as Willy walks into it. He is carrying a flashlight, a hoe, and a handful of seed packets. He raps the top of the hoe sharply to fix it firmly, and then moves to the left, measuring off the distance with his foot. He holds the flashlight to look at the seed packets, reading off the instructions. He is in the blue of night.*

WILLY. Carrots . . . quarter-inch apart. Rows . . . one-foot rows. (*He measures it off.*) One foot. (*He puts down a package and measures off.*) Beets. (*He puts down another package and measures again.*) Lettuce. (*He reads the package, puts it down.*) One foot—(*He breaks off as Ben appears at the right and moves slowly down to him.*) What a proposition, ts, ts. Terrific, terrific. 'Cause she's suffered, Ben, the woman has suffered. You understand me? A man can't go out the way he came in, Ben, a man has got to add up to something. You can't, you can't—(*Ben moves toward him as though to interrupt.*) You gotta consider now. Don't answer so quick. Remember, it's a guaranteed twenty-thousand-dollar proposition. Now look, Ben, I want you to go through the ins and outs of this thing with me. I've got nobody to talk to, Ben, and the woman has suffered, you hear me?

BEN (*standing still, considering*). What's the proposition?

WILLY. It's twenty thousand dollars on the barrelhead. Guaranteed, gilt-edged, you understand?

BEN. You don't want to make a fool of yourself. They might not honor the policy.

WILLY. How can they dare refuse? Didn't I work like a coolie to meet every premium on the nose? And now they don't pay off? Impossible!

BEN. It's called a cowardly thing, William.

WILLY. Why? Does it take more guts to stand here the rest of my life ringing up a zero?

BEN (*yielding*). That's a point, William. (*He moves, thinking, turns.*) And twenty thousand—that is something one can feel with the hand, it is there.

WILLY (*now assured, with rising power*). Oh, Ben, that's the whole beauty of it! I see it like a diamond, shining in the dark, hard and rough, that I can pick up and touch in my hand. Not like—like an appointment! This would not be another damned-fool appointment, Ben, and it changes all the aspects. Because he thinks I'm nothing, see, and so he spites me. But the funeral . . . (*Straightening up.*) Ben, that funeral will be massive! They'll come from Maine, Massachusetts, Vermont, New Hampshire! All the old-timers with the strange license plates—that boy will be thunderstruck, Ben, because he never realized—I am known! Rhode Island, New York, New Jersey—I am known, Ben, and he'll see it with his eyes once and for all. He'll see what I am, Ben! He's in for a shock, that boy!

BEN (*coming down to the edge of the garden*). He'll call you a coward.

WILLY (*suddenly fearful*). No, that would be terrible.

BEN. Yes. And a damned fool.

WILLY. No, no, he mustn't, I won't have that! (*He is broken and desperate.*)

BEN. He'll hate you, William.

*The gay music of the Boys is heard.*

WILLY. Oh, Ben, how do we get back to all the great times? Used to be so full of light, and comradeship, the sleigh-riding in winter, and the ruddiness on his cheeks. And always some kind of good news coming up, always something nice coming up ahead. And never even let me carry the valises in the house, and simonizing, simonizing that little red car! Why, why can't I give him something and not have him hate me?

BEN. Let me think about it. (*He glances at his watch.*) I still have a little time. Remarkable proposition, but you've got to be sure you're not making a fool of yourself.

*Ben drifts off upstage and goes out of sight. Biff comes down from the left.*

WILLY (*suddenly conscious of Biff, turns and looks up at him, then begins picking up the packages of seeds in confusion*). Where the hell is that seed? (*Indignantly.*) You can't see nothing out here! They boxed in the whole goddam neighborhood!

BIFF. There are people all around here. Don't you realize that?

WILLY. I'm busy. Don't bother me.

BIFF (*taking the hoe from Willy*). I'm saying good-by to you, Pop. (*Willy looks at him, silent, unable to move.*) I'm not coming back any more.

WILLY. You're not going to see Oliver tomorrow?

BIFF. I've got no appointment, Dad.

WILLY. He put his arm around you, and you've got no appointment?

BIFF. Pop, get this now, will you? Everytime I've left it's been a—fight that sent me out of here. Today I realized something about myself and I tried to explain it to you and I—I think I'm just not smart enough to make any sense out of it for you. To hell with whose fault it is or anything like that. (*He takes Willy's arm.*) Let's just wrap it up, heh? Come on in, we'll tell Mom. (*He gently tries to pull Willy to left.*)

WILLY (*frozen, immobile, with guilt in his voice*). No, I don't want to see her.

BIFF. Come on! (*He pulls again, and Willy tries to pull away.*)

WILLY (*highly nervous*). No, no, I don't want to see her.

BIFF (*tries to look into Willy's face, as if to find the answer there*). Why don't you want to see her?

WILLY (*more harshly now*). Don't bother me, will you?

BIFF. What do you mean, you don't want to see her? You don't want them calling you yellow, do you? This isn't your fault; it's me, I'm a bum. Now come inside! (*Willy strains to get away.*) Did you hear what I said to you?

*Willy pulls away and quickly goes by himself into the house. Biff follows.*

LINDA (*to Willy*). Did you plant, dear?

BIFF (*at the door, to Linda*). All right, we had it out. I'm going and I'm not writing any more.

LINDA (*going to Willy in the kitchen*). I think that's the best way, dear. 'Cause there's no use drawing it out, you'll just never get along.

*Willy doesn't respond.*

BIFF. People ask where I am and what I'm doing, you don't know, and you don't care. That way it'll be off your mind and you can start brightening up again. All right? That clears it, doesn't it? (*Willy is silent, and Biff goes to him.*) You gonna wish me luck, scout? (*He extends his hand.*) What do you say?

LINDA. Shake his hand, Willy.

WILLY (*turning to her, seething with hurt*). There's no necessity—to mention the pen at all, y'know.

BIFF (*gently*). I've got no appointment, Dad.

WILLY (*erupting fiercely*). He put his arm around . . . ?

BIFF. Dad, you're never going to see what I am, so what's the use of arguing? If I strike oil I'll send you a check. Meantime forget I'm alive.

WILLY (*to Linda*). Spite, see?

BIFF. Shake hands, Dad.

WILLY. Not my hand.

BIFF. I was hoping not to go this way.

WILLY. Well, this is the way you're going. Good-by.

*Biff looks at him a moment, then turns sharply and goes to the stairs.*

WILLY (*stops him with*). May you rot in hell if you leave this house!

BIFF (*turning*). Exactly what is it that you want from me?

WILLY. I want you to know, on the train, in the mountains, in the valleys, wherever you go, that you cut down your life for spite!

BIFF. No, no.

WILLY. Spite, spite, is the word of your undoing! And when you're down and out, remember what did it. When you're rotting somewhere beside the railroad tracks, remember, and don't you dare blame it on me!

BIFF. I'm not blaming it on you!

WILLY. I won't take the rap for this, you hear?

*Happy comes down the stairs and stands on the bottom step, watching.*

BIFF. That's just what I'm telling you!

WILLY (*sinking into a chair at a table, with full accusation*). You're trying to put a knife in me—don't think I don't know what you're doing!

BIFF. All right, phony! Then let's lay it on the line. (*He whips the rubber tube out of his pocket and puts it on the table.*)

HAPPY. You crazy . . .

LINDA. Biff! (*She moves to grab the hose, but Biff holds it down with his hand.*)

BIFF. Leave it there! Don't move it!

WILLY (*not looking at it*). What is that?

BIFF. You know goddam well what that is.

WILLY (*caged, wanting to escape*). I never saw that.

BIFF. You saw it. The mice didn't bring it into the cellar! What is this supposed to do, make a hero out of you? This supposed to make me sorry for you?

WILLY. Never heard of it.

BIFF. There'll be no pity for you, you hear it? No pity!

WILLY (*to Linda*). You hear the spite!

BIFF. No, you're going to hear the truth—what you are and what I am!

LINDA. Stop it!

WILLY. Spite!

HAPPY (*coming down toward Biff*). You cut it now!

BIFF (*to Happy*). The man don't know who we are! The man is gonna know! (*To Willy.*) We never told the truth for ten minutes in this house!

HAPPY. We always told the truth!

BIFF (*turning on him*). You big blow, are you the assistant buyer? You're one of the two assistants to the assistant, aren't you?

HAPPY. Well, I'm practically . . .

BIFF. You're practically full of it! We all are! and I'm through with it. (*To Willy.*) Now hear this, Willy, this is me.

WILLY. I know you!

BIFF. You know why I had no address for three months? I stole a suit in Kansas City and I was in jail. (*To Linda, who is sobbing.*) Stop crying. I'm through with it.

*Linda turns away from them, her hands covering her face.*

WILLY. I suppose that's my fault!

BIFF. I stole myself out of every good job since high school!

WILLY. And whose fault is that?

BIFF. And I never got anywhere because you blew me so full of hot air I could never stand taking orders from anybody! That's whose fault it is!

WILLY. I hear that!

LINDA. Don't, Biff!

BIFF. It's goddam time you heard that! I had to be boss big shot in two weeks, and I'm through with it!

WILLY. Then hang yourself! For spite, hang yourself!

BIFF. No! Nobody's hanging himself, Willy! I ran down eleven flights with a pen in my hand today. And suddenly I stopped, you hear me? And in the middle of that office building, do you hear this? I stopped in the middle of that building and I saw—the sky. I saw the things that I love in this world. The work and the food and time to sit and smoke. And I looked at the pen and said to myself, what the hell am I grabbing this for? Why am I trying to become what I don't want to be? What am I doing in an office, making a contemptuous, begging fool of myself, when all I want is out there, waiting for me the minute I say I know who I am! Why can't I say that, Willy? (*He tries to make Willy face him, but Willy pulls away and moves to the left.*)

WILLY (*with hatred, threateningly*). The door of your life is wide open!

BIFF. Pop! I'm a dime a dozen, and so are you!

WILLY (*turning on him now in an uncontrolled outburst*). I am not a dime a dozen! I am Willy Loman, and you are Biff Loman!

*Biff starts for Willy, but is blocked by Happy. In his fury, Biff seems on the verge of attacking his father.*

BIFF. I am not a leader of men, Willy, and neither are you. You were never anything but a hard-working drummer who landed in the ash can like all the rest of them! I'm one dollar an hour, Willy! I tried seven states and couldn't raise it. A buck an hour! Do you gather my meaning? I'm not bringing home any prizes any more, and you're going to stop waiting for me to bring them home!

WILLY (*directly to Biff*). You vengeful, spiteful mutt!

*Biff breaks from Happy. Willy, in fright, starts up the stairs. Biff grabs him.*

BIFF (*at the peak of his fury*). Pop! I'm nothing! I'm nothing, Pop. Can't you understand that? There's no spite in it any more. I'm just what I am, that's all.

*Biff's fury has spent itself and he breaks down, sobbing, holding on to Willy, who dumbly fumbles for Biff's face.*

WILLY (*astonished*). What're you doing? What're you doing? (*To Linda.*) Why is he crying?

BIFF (*crying, broken*). Will you let me go, for Christ's sake? Will you take that phony dream and burn it before something happens? (*Struggling to contain himself he pulls away and moves to the stairs.*) I'll go in the morning. Put him—put him to bed. (*Exhausted, Biff moves up the stairs to his room.*)

WILLY (*after a long pause, astonished, elevated*). Isn't that—isn't that remarkable? Biff—he likes me!

LINDA. He loves you, Willy!

HAPPY (*deeply moved*). Always did, Pop.

WILLY. Oh, Biff! (*Staring wildly.*) He cried! Cried to me. (*He is choking with his love, and now cries out his promise.*) That boy—that boy is going to be magnificent!

*Ben appears in the light just outside the kitchen.*

BEN. Yes, outstanding, with twenty thousand behind him.

LINDA (*sensing the racing of his mind, fearfully, carefully*). Now come to bed, Willy. It's all settled now.

WILLY (*finding it difficult not to rush out of the house*). Yes, we'll sleep. Come on. Go to sleep, Hap.

BEN. And it does take a great kind of a man to crack the jungle.

*In accents of dread, Ben's idyllic music starts up.*

HAPPY (*his arm around Linda*). I'm getting married, Pop, don't forget it. I'm changing everything. I'm gonna run that department before the year is up. You'll see, Mom. (*He kisses her.*)

BEN. The jungle is dark but full of diamonds, Willy.

*Willy turns, moves, listening to Ben.*

LINDA. Be good. You're both good boys, just act that way, that's all.

HAPPY. 'Night, Pop. (*He goes upstairs.*)

LINDA (*to Willy*). Come, dear.

BEN (*with greater force*). One must go in to fetch a diamond out.

WILLY (*to Linda, as he moves slowly along the edge of the kitchen, toward the door*). I just want to get settled down, Linda. Let me sit alone for a little.

LINDA (*almost uttering her fear*). I want you upstairs.

WILLY (*taking her in his arms*). In a few minutes, Linda. I couldn't sleep right now. Go on, you look awful tired. (*He kisses her.*)

BEN. Not like an appointment at all. A diamond is rough and hard to the touch.

WILLY. Go on now. I'll be right up.

LINDA. I think this is the only way, Willy.

WILLY. Sure, it's the best thing.

BEN. Best thing!

WILLY. The only way. Everything is gonna be—go on, kid, get to bed. You look so tired.

LINDA. Come right up.

WILLY. Two minutes.

*Linda goes into the living room, then reappears in her bedroom. Willy moves just outside the kitchen door.*

WILLY. Loves me. (*Wonderingly.*) Always loved me. Isn't that a remarkable thing? Ben, he'll worship me for it!

BEN (*with promise*). It's dark there, but full of diamonds.

WILLY. Can you imagine that magnificence with twenty thousand dollars in his pocket?

LINDA (*calling from her room*). Willy! Come up!

WILLY (*calling into the kitchen*). Yes! Yes. Coming! It's very smart, you realize that, don't you, sweetheart? Even Ben sees it. I gotta go, baby. 'By! 'By! (*Going over to Ben, almost dancing.*) Imagine? When the mail comes he'll be ahead of Bernard again!

BEN. A perfect proposition all around.

WILLY. Did you see how he cried to me? Oh, if I could kiss him, Ben!

BEN. Time, William, time!

WILLY. Oh, Ben, I always knew one way or another we were gonna make it, Biff and I.

BEN (*looking at his watch*). The boat. We'll be late. (*He moves slowly off into the darkness.*)

WILLY (*elegiacally, turning to the house*). Now when you kick off, boy, I want a seventy-yard boot, and get right down the field under the ball, and when you hit, hit low and hit hard, because it's important, boy. (*He swings around and faces the audience.*) There's all kinds of important people in the stands, and the first thing you know . . . (*Suddenly realizing he is alone.*) Ben! Ben, where do I . . . ? (*He makes a sudden movement of search.*) Ben, how do I . . . ?

LINDA (*calling*). Willy, you coming up?

WILLY (*uttering a gasp of fear, whirling about as if to quiet her*). Sh! (*He turns around as if to find his way; sounds, faces, voices, seem to be swarming in upon him and he flicks at them, crying.*) Sh! Sh! (*Suddenly music, faint and high, stops him. It rises in intensity, almost to an unbearable scream. He goes up and down on his toes, and rushes off around the house.*) Shhh!

LINDA. Willy?

*There is no answer. Linda waits. Biff gets up off his bed. He is still in his clothes. Happy sits up. Biff stands listening.*

LINDA (*with real fear*). Willy, answer me! Willy!

*There is the sound of a car starting and moving away at full speed.*

LINDA. No!

BIFF (*rushing down the stairs*). Pop!

*As the car speeds off the music crashes down in a frenzy of sound, which becomes the soft pulsation of a single cello string. Biff slowly returns to his bedroom. He and Happy gravely don their jackets. Linda slowly walks out of her room. The music has developed into a dead march. The leaves of day are appearing over everything. Charley and Bernard, somberly dressed, appear and knock on the kitchen door. Biff and Happy slowly descend the stairs to the kitchen as Charley and Bernard enter. All stop a moment when Linda, in clothes of mourning, bearing a little bunch of roses, comes through the draped doorway into the kitchen. She goes to Charley and takes his arm. Now all move toward the audience, through the wall-line of the kitchen. At the limit of the apron, Linda lays down the flowers, kneels, and sits back on her heels. All stare down at the grave.*

## *Requiem*

CHARLEY. It's getting dark, Linda.

*Linda doesn't react. She stares at the grave.*

BIFF. How about it, Mom? Better get some rest, heh? They'll be closing the gate soon.

*Linda makes no move. Pause.*

HAPPY (*deeply angered*). He had no right to do that. There was no necessity for it. We would've helped him.

CHARLEY (*grunting*). Hmmm.

BIFF. Come along, Mom.

LINDA. Why didn't anybody come?

CHARLEY. It was a very nice funeral.

LINDA. But where are all the people he knew? Maybe they blame him.

CHARLEY. Naa. It's a rough world, Linda. They wouldn't blame him.

LINDA. I can't understand it. At this time especially. First time in thirty-five years we were just about free and clear. He only needed a little salary. He was even finished with the dentist.

CHARLEY. No man only needs a little salary.

LINDA. I can't understand it.

BIFF. There were a lot of nice days. When he'd come home from a trip; or on Sundays, making the stoop; finishing the cellar; putting on the new porch; when he built the extra bathroom; and put up the garage. You know something, Charley, there's more of him in that front stoop than in all the sales he ever made.

CHARLEY. Yeah. He was a happy man with a batch of cement.

LINDA. He was so wonderful with his hands.

BIFF. He had the wrong dreams. All, all, wrong.

HAPPY (*almost ready to fight Biff*). Don't say that!

BIFF. He never knew who he was.

CHARLEY (*stopping Happy's movement and reply; to Biff*). Nobody dast blame this man. You don't understand: Willy was a salesman. And for a salesman, there is no rock bottom to the life. He don't put a bolt to a nut, he don't tell you the law or give you medicine. He's a man way out there in the blue, riding on a smile and a shoeshine. And when they start not smiling back—that's an earthquake. And then you get yourself a couple of spots on your hat, and you're finished. Nobody dast blame this man. A salesman is got to dream, boy. It comes with the territory.

BIFF. Charley, the man didn't know who he was.

HAPPY (*infuriated*). Don't say that!

BIFF. Why don't you come with me, Happy?

HAPPY. I'm not licked that easily. I'm staying right in this city, and I'm gonna beat this racket! (*He looks at Biff, his chin set.*) The Loman Brothers!

BIFF. I know who I am, kid.

HAPPY. All right, boy. I'm gonna show you and everybody else that Willy Loman did not die in vain. He had a good dream. It's the only dream you can have—to come out number-one man. He fought it out here, and this is where I'm gonna win it for him.

BIFF (*with a hopeless glance at Happy, bends toward his mother*). Let's go, Mom.

LINDA. I'll be with you in a minute. Go on, Charley. (*He hesitates.*) I want to, just for a minute. I never had a chance to say good-by.

*Charley moves away, followed by Happy. Biff remains a slight distance up and left of Linda. She sits there, summoning herself. The flute begins, not far away, playing behind her speech.*

LINDA. Forgive me, dear. I can't cry. I don't know what it is, but I can't cry. I don't understand it. Why did you ever do that? Help me, Willy, I can't cry. It seems to me that you're just on another trip. I keep expecting you. Willy, dear, I can't cry. Why did you do it? I search and search and I search, and I can't understand it, Willy. I made the last payment on the house today. Today, dear. And there'll be nobody home. (*A sob rises in her throat.*) We're free and clear. (*Sobbing mournfully, released.*) We're free. (*Biff comes slowly toward her.*) We're free . . . We're free . . .

*Biff lifts her to her feet and moves out up right with her in his arms. Linda sobs quietly. Bernard and Charley come together and follow them, followed by Happy. Only the music of the flute is left on the darkening stage as over the house the hard towers of the apartment buildings rise into sharp focus and the curtain falls.*

## TOPICS FOR CRITICAL THINKING AND WRITING

1. Miller said (p. 1661) that tragedy shows man's struggle to secure "his sense of personal dignity," and that "his destruction in the attempt posits a wrong or an evil in his environment." Does this make sense when applied to some earlier tragedy (for example, *Oedipus Rex* or *Hamlet*), and does it apply convincingly to *Death of a Salesman*? Is this the tragedy of an individual's own making? Or is society at fault for corrupting and exploiting Willy? Or both?
2. Is Willy pathetic rather than tragic? If pathetic, does this imply that the play is less worthy than if he is tragic?

3. Do you feel that Miller is straining too hard to turn a play about a little man into a big, impressive play? For example, do the musical themes, the unrealistic setting, the appearances of Ben, and the speech at the grave seem out of keeping in a play about the death of a salesman?
4. We don't know what Willy sells, and we don't know whether or not the insurance will be paid after his death. Do you consider these uncertainties to be faults in the play?
5. Is Howard a villain?
6. Characterize Linda.
7. It is sometimes said that Biff and Happy can be seen as two aspects of Willy. In this view, Biff more or less represents Willy's spiritual needs, and Happy represents his materialism and his sexuality. If you were directing the play, would you take this line? Whatever your interpretation, how would you costume the brothers?
8. Although Miller envisioned Willy as a small man (literally small), the role was first performed by Lee J. Cobb, a large man. If you were casting the play, what actor would you select? Why? And whom would you choose for Linda, Biff, Happy, Bernard, and Charley?
9. Take a passage of dialogue of some 30 lines and discuss the movements—gestures and blocking—that as a director you would suggest to the performers.

## A PERSPECTIVE FOR *DEATH OF A SALESMAN*

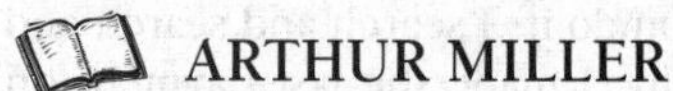

### ARTHUR MILLER

# *Tragedy and the Common Man*

[This essay appeared in the *New York Times* in 1949, while *Death of a Salesman* was running on Broadway.]

In this age few tragedies are written. It has often been held that the lack is due to a paucity of heroes among us, or else that modern man has had the blood drawn out of his organs of belief by the skepticism of science, and the heroic attack on life cannot feed on an attitude of reserve and circumspection. For one reason or another, we are often held to be below tragedy—or tragedy above us. The inevitable conclusion is, of course, that the tragic mode is archaic, fit only for the very highly placed, the kings or the kingly, and where this admission is not made in so many words it is most often implied.

I believe that the common man is as apt a subject for tragedy in its highest sense as kings were. On the face of it this ought to be obvious in the light of modern psychiatry, which bases its analysis upon classic formulations, such as the Oedipus and Orestes complexes, for instances, which were enacted by royal beings, but which apply to everyone in similar emotional situations.

More simply, when the question of tragedy in art is not at issue, we never hesitate to attribute to the well-placed and the exalted the very same mental processes as the lowly. And finally, if the exaltation of tragic action were truly a property of the high-bred character alone, it is inconceivable that the mass of mankind should cherish tragedy above all other forms, let alone be capable of understanding it.

As a general rule, to which there may be exceptions unknown to me, I think the tragic feeling is evoked in us when we are in the presence of a character who is ready to lay down his life, if need be, to secure one thing—his sense of personal dignity. From Orestes to Hamlet, Medea to Macbeth, the underlying struggle is that of the individual attempting to gain his "rightful" position in his society.

Sometimes he is one who has been displaced from it, sometimes one who seeks to attain it for the first time, but the fateful wound from which the inevitable events spiral is the wound of indignity, and its dominant force is indignation. Tragedy, then, is the consequence of a man's total compulsion to evaluate himself justly.

In the sense of having been initiated by the hero himself, the tale always reveals what has been called his "tragic flaw," a failing that is not peculiar to grand or elevated characters. Nor is it necessarily a weakness. The flaw, or crack in the character, is really nothing—and need be nothing, but his inherent unwillingness to remain passive in the face of what he conceives to be a challenge to his dignity, his image of his rightful status. Only the passive, only those who accept their lot without active retaliation, are "flawless." Most of us are in that category.

But there are among us today, as there always have been, those who act against the scheme of things that degrades them, and in the process of action everything we have accepted out of fear or insensitivity or ignorance is shaken before us and examined, and from this total onslaught by an individual against the seemingly stable cosmos surrounding us—from this total examination of the "unchangeable" environment—comes the terror and the fear that is classically associated with tragedy.

More important, from this total questioning of what has previously been unquestioned, we learn. And such a process is not beyond the common man. In revolutions around the world, these past thirty years, he has demonstrated again and again this inner dynamic of all tragedy.

Insistence upon the rank of the tragic hero, or the so-called nobility of his character, is really but a clinging to the outward forms of tragedy. If rank or nobility of character was indispensable, then it would follow that the problems of those with rank were the particular problems of tragedy. But surely the right of one monarch to capture the domain from another no longer raises our passions, nor are our concepts of justice what they were to the mind of an Elizabethan king.

The quality in such plays that does shake us, however, derives from the underlying fear of being displaced, the disaster inherent in being torn away from our chosen image of what and who we are in this world. Among us today this fear is as strong, and perhaps stronger, than it ever was. In fact, it is the common man who knows this fear best.

Now, if it is true that tragedy is the consequence of a man's total compulsion to evaluate himself justly, his destruction in the attempts posits a wrong or an evil in his environment. And this is precisely the morality of tragedy and its lesson. The discovery of the moral law, which is what the enlightenment of tragedy consists of, is not the discovery of some abstract or metaphysical quantity.

The tragic right is a condition of life, a condition in which the human personality is able to flower and realize itself. The wrong is the condition which suppresses man, perverts the flowing out of his love and creative instinct. Tragedy enlightens—and it must, in that it points the heroic finger at the enemy of man's freedom. The thrust for freedom is the quality in tragedy which exalts. The revolutionary questioning of the stable environment is what terrifies. In no way is the common man debarred from such thoughts or such actions.

Seen in this light, our lack of tragedy may be partially accounted for by the turn which modern literature has taken toward the purely psychiatric view of life, or the purely sociological. If all our miseries, our indignities, are born and bred within our minds, then all action, let alone the heroic action, is obviously impossible.

And if society alone is responsible for the cramping of our lives, then the protagonist must needs be so pure and faultless as to force us to deny his validity as a character. From neither of these views can tragedy derive, simply because neither represents a balanced concept of life. Above all else, tragedy requires the finest appreciation by the writer of cause and effect.

No tragedy can therefore come about when its author fears to question absolutely everything, when he regards any institution, habit or custom as being either everlasting, immutable or inevitable. In the tragic view the need of man to wholly realize himself is the only fixed star, and whatever it is that hedges his nature and lowers it is ripe for attack and examination. Which is not to say that tragedy must preach revolution.

The Greeks could probe the very heavenly origin of their ways and return to confirm the rightness of laws. And Job could face God in anger, demanding his right and end in submission. But for a moment everything is in suspension, nothing is accepted, and in this stretching and tearing apart of the cosmos, in the very action of so doing, the character gains "size," the tragic stature which is spuriously attached to the royal or the highborn in our minds. The commonest of men may take on that stature to the extent of his willingness to throw all he has into the contest, the battle to secure his rightful place in his world.

There is a misconception of tragedy with which I have been struck in review after review, and in many conversations with writers and readers alike. It is the idea that tragedy is of necessity allied to pessimism. Even the dictionary says nothing more about the word than that it means a story with a sad or unhappy ending. This impression is so firmly fixed that I almost hesitate to claim that in truth tragedy implies more optimism in its author than does comedy, and that its final result ought to be the reinforcement of the onlooker's brightest opinions of the human animal.

For, if it is true to say that in essence the tragic hero is intent upon claiming his whole due as a personality, and if this struggle must be total and without reservation, then it automatically demonstrates the indestructible will of man to achieve his humanity.

The possibility of victory must be there in tragedy. Where pathos rules, where pathos is finally derived, a character has fought a battle he could not possibly have won. The pathetic is achieved when the protagonist is, by virtue of his witlessness, his insensitivity or the very air he gives off, incapable of grappling with a much superior force.

Pathos truly is the mode for the pessimist. But tragedy requires a nicer balance between what is possible and what is impossible. And it is curious, although edifying, that the plays we revere, century after century, are the tragedies. In them, and in them alone, lies the belief—optimistic, if you will—in the perfectibility of man.

It is time, I think, that we who are without kings, took up this bright thread of our history and followed it to the only place it can possibly lead in our time—the heart and spirit of the average man.

## LUIS VALDEZ

*Luis Valdez was born into a family of migrant farm workers in Delano, California, in 1940. After completing high school he entered San Jose State College on a scholarship. He wrote his first plays while still an undergraduate, and after receiving his degree (in English and drama) from San Jose in 1964 he joined the San Francisco Mime Troupe, a left-wing group that performed in parks and streets. Revolutionary in technique as well as in political content, the Mime Troupe rejected the traditional forms of drama and instead drew on the traditions of the circus and the carnival.*

*In 1965 Valdez returned to Delano, California, where Cesar Chavez had organized a strike of farm workers and a boycott against grape growers. It was here, under the wing of the United Farm Workers, that he established El Teatro Campesino (the Farm Workers' Theater), which at first specialized in doing short, improvised, satirical skits called* actos. *When the* teatro *moved to Del Rey, California, it expanded its repertoire beyond farm issues, and it became part of a cultural center that gave workshops (in English and Spanish) in such subjects as history, drama, and politics.*

*The* actos, *performed by amateurs on college campuses and on flatbed trucks and at the edges of vineyards, were highly political. Making use of stereotypes (the boss, the scab), the* actos *sought not to present the individual thoughts of a gifted playwright but to present the social vision of ordinary people—the* pueblo*—though it was acknowledged that in an oppressive society the playwright might have to help guide the people to see their own best interests.*

*Valdez moved from* actos *to* mitos *(myths)—plays that drew on Aztec mythology, Mexican folklore, and Christianity—and then to* Zoot Suit, *a play that ran for many months in California and that became the first Mexican-American play to be produced on Broadway. More recently he wrote and directed a hit movie,* La

Bamba, *and in 1991 received an award from the A.T.&T. Foundation for his musical,* Bandido, *to be presented by El Teatro Campesino.*

Los Vendidos *was written in 1967, when Ronald Reagan was governor of California.*

# *Los Vendidos**

LIST OF CHARACTERS

HONEST SANCHO
SECRETARY
FARM WORKER
JOHNNY
REVOLUCIONARIO
MEXICAN-AMERICAN

**SCENE:** *Honest Sancho's Used Mexican Lot and Mexican Curio Shop. Three models are on display in Honest Sancho's shop: to the right, there is a Revolucionario, complete with sombrero, carrilleras*[1] *and carabina 30-30. At center, on the floor, there is the Farm Worker, under a broad straw sombrero. At stage left is the Pachuco,*[2] *filero*[3] *in hand.*

(*Honest Sancho is moving among his models, dusting them off and preparing for another day of business.*)

SANCHO. Bueno, bueno, mis monos, vamos a ver a quien vendemos ahora, ¿no?[4] (*To audience.*) ¡Quihubo! I'm Honest Sancho and this is my shop. Antes fui contratista pero ahora logré tener mi negocito.[5] All I need now is a customer. (*A bell rings offstage.*) Ay, a customer!

SECRETARY (*Entering*). Good morning, I'm Miss Jiménez from—

SANCHO. ¡Ah, una chicana! Welcome, welcome Señorita Jiménez.

SECRETARY (*Anglo pronunciation*). JIM-enez.

SANCHO. ¿Qué?

SECRETARY. My name is Miss JIM-enez. Don't you speak English? What's wrong with you?

SANCHO. Oh, nothing, Señorita JIM-enez. I'm here to help you.

SECRETARY. That's better. As I was starting to say, I'm a secretary from Governor Reagan's office, and we're looking for a Mexican type for the administration.

SANCHO. Well, you come to the right place, lady. This is Honest Sancho's Used Mexican lot, and we got all types here. Any particular type you want?

SECRETARY. Yes, we were looking for somebody suave—

SANCHO. Suave.

SECRETARY. Debonair.

***Los Vendidos** the sellouts [1]**carrilleras** cartridge belts [2]**Pachuco** an urban tough guy [3]**filero** blade [4]**Bueno . . . no?** Well, well, darlings, let's see who we can sell now, O.K.? [5]**Antes . . . negocito** I used to be a contractor, but now I've succeeded in having my little business.

Scene from TV adaptation, "El Teatro Campesino Special: *Los Vendidos.*" KNBC, Los Angeles, 1972.

SANCHO. De buen aire.

SECRETARY. Dark.

SANCHO. Prieto.

SECRETARY. But of course not too dark.

SANCHO. No muy prieto.

SECRETARY. Perhaps, beige.

SANCHO. Beige, just the tone. Así como cafecito con leche,[6] ¿no?

SECRETARY. One more thing. He must be hard-working.

SANCHO. That could only be one model. Step right over here to the center of the shop, lady. (*They cross to the Farm Worker.*) This is our standard farm worker model. As you can see, in the words of our beloved Senator George Murphy, he is "built close to the ground." Also take special notice of his four-ply Goodyear huaraches, made from the rain tire. This wide-brimmed sombrero is an extra added feature—keeps off the sun, rain, and dust.

SECRETARY. Yes, it does look durable.

SANCHO. And our farmworker model is friendly. Muy amable.[7] Watch. (*Snaps his fingers.*)

FARM WORKER (*Lifts up head*). Buenos días, señorita. (*His head drops.*)

SECRETARY. My, he's friendly.

SANCHO. Didn't I tell you? Loves his patrones! But his most attractive feature is that he's hard working. Let me show you. (*Snaps fingers. Farm Worker stands.*)

[6]**Así . . . leche** like coffee with milk [7]**Muy amable** very friendly

FARM WORKER. ¡El jale![8] (*He begins to work.*)

SANCHO. As you can see, he is cutting grapes.

SECRETARY. Oh, I wouldn't know.

SANCHO. He also picks cotton. (*Snap. Farm Worker begins to pick cotton.*)

SECRETARY. Versatile isn't he?

SANCHO. He also picks melons. (*Snap. Farm Worker picks melons.*) That's his slow speed for late in the season. Here's his fast speed. (*Snap. Farm Worker picks faster.*)

SECRETARY. ¡Chihuahua! . . . I mean, goodness, he sure is a hard worker.

SANCHO (*Pulls the Farm Worker to his feet*). And that isn't the half of it. Do you see these little holes on his arms that appear to be pores? During those hot sluggish days in the field, when the vines or the branches get so entangled, it's almost impossible to move; these holes emit a certain grease that allow our model to slip and slide right through the crop with no trouble at all.

SECRETARY. Wonderful. But is he economical?

SANCHO. Economical? Señorita, you are looking at the Volkswagen of Mexicans. Pennies a day is all it takes. One plate of beans and tortillas will keep him going all day. That, and chile. Plenty of chile. Chile jalapeños, chile verde, chile colorado. But, of course, if you do give him chile (*Snap. Farm Worker turns left face. Snap. Farm Worker bends over.*) then you have to change his oil filter once a week.

SECRETARY. What about storage?

SANCHO. No problem. You know these new farm labor camps our Honorable Governor Reagan has built out by Parlier or Raisin City? They were designed with our model in mind. Five, six, seven, even ten in one of those shacks will give you no trouble at all. You can also put him in old barns, old cars, river banks. You can even leave him out in the field overnight with no worry!

SECRETARY. Remarkable.

SANCHO. And here's an added feature: Every year at the end of the season, this model goes back to Mexico and doesn't return, automatically, until next Spring.

SECRETARY. How about that. But tell me: does he speak English?

SANCHO. Another outstanding feature is that last year this model was programmed to go out on STRIKE! (*Snap.*)

FARM WORKER. ¡HUELGA! ¡HUELGA! Hermanos, sálganse de esos files.[9] (*Snap. He stops.*)

SECRETARY. No! Oh no, we can't strike in the State Capitol.

SANCHO. Well, he also scabs. (*Snap.*)

FARM WORKER. Me vendo barato, ¿y qué?[10] (*Snap.*)

SECRETARY. That's much better, but you didn't answer my question. Does he speak English?

SANCHO. Bueno . . . no, pero[11] he has other—

SECRETARY. No.

SANCHO. Other features.

SECRETARY. NO! He just won't do!

[8]**El jale** the job [9]**Huelga . . . files** Strike! Strike! Brothers, leave those rows. [10]**Me . . . qué?** I come cheap. So what? [11]**Bueno . . . no, pero** Well, no, but

SANCHO. Okay, okay pues. We have other models.

SECRETARY. I hope so. What we need is something a little more sophisticated.

SANCHO. Sophisti—¿qué?

SECRETARY. An urban model.

SANCHO. Ah, from the city! Step right back. Over here in this corner of the shop is exactly what you're looking for. Introducing our new 1969 JOHNNY PACHUCO model! This is our fast-back model. Streamlined. Built for speed, low-riding, city life. Take a look at some of these features. Mag shoes, dual exhausts, green chartreuse paint-job, dark-tint windshield, a little poof on top. Let me just turn him on. (*Snap. Johnny walks to stage center with a pachuco bounce.*)

SECRETARY. What was that?

SANCHO. That, señorita, was the Chicano shuffle.

SECRETARY. Okay, what does he do?

SANCHO. Anything and everything necessary for city life. For instance, survival: He knife fights. (*Snap. Johnny pulls out switchblade and swings at Secretary.*)

(*Secretary screams.*)

SANCHO. He dances. (*Snap.*)

JOHNNY (*Singing*). "Angel Baby, my Angel Baby . . ." (*Snap.*)

SANCHO. And here's a feature no city model can be without. He gets arrested, but not without resisting, of course. (*Snap.*)

JOHNNY. ¡En la madre, la placa![12] I didn't do it! I didn't do it! (*Johnny turns and stands up against an imaginary wall, legs spread out, arms behind his back.*)

SECRETARY. Oh no, we can't have arrests! We must maintain law and order.

SANCHO. But he's bilingual!

SECRETARY. Bilingual?

SANCHO. Simón que yes.[13] He speaks English! Johnny, give us some English. (*Snap.*)

JOHNNY (*Comes downstage*). Fuck-you!

SECRETARY (*Gasps*). Oh! I've never been so insulted in my whole life!

SANCHO. Well, he learned it in your school.

SECRETARY. I don't care where he learned it.

SANCHO. But he's economical!

SECRETARY. Economical?

SANCHO. Nickels and dimes. You can keep Johnny running on hamburgers, Taco Bell tacos, Lucky Lager beer, Thunderbird wine, yesca—

SECRETARY. Yesca?

SANCHO. Mota.

SECRETARY. Mota?

SANCHO. Leños[14] . . . Marijuana. (*Snap; Johnny inhales on an imaginary joint.*)

SECRETARY. That's against the law!

JOHNNY (*Big smile, holding his breath*). Yeah.

[12]**¡En . . . la placa!** Wow, the cops! [13]**Simón que yes** Yea, sure. [14]**Leños** joints (marijuana)

SANCHO. He also sniffs glue. (*Snap. Johnny inhales glue, big smile.*)

JOHNNY. That's too much man, ése.[15]

SECRETARY. No, Mr. Sancho, I don't think this—

SANCHO. Wait a minute, he has other qualities I know you'll love. For example, an inferiority complex. (*Snap.*)

JOHNNY (*To Sancho*). You think you're better than me, huh ése? (*Swings switchblade.*)

SANCHO. He can also be beaten and he bruises, cut him and he bleeds; kick him and he—(*He beats, bruises and kicks Pachuco.*) would you like to try it?

SECRETARY. Oh, I couldn't.

SANCHO. Be my guest. He's a great scapegoat.

SECRETARY. No, really.

SANCHO. Please.

SECRETARY. Well, all right. Just once. (*She kicks Pachuco.*) Oh, he's so soft.

SANCHO. Wasn't that good? Try again.

SECRETARY (*Kicks Pachuco*). Oh, he's so wonderful! (*She kicks him again.*)

SANCHO. Okay, that's enough, lady. You ruin the merchandise. Yes, our Johnny Pachuco model can give you many hours of pleasure. Why, the L.A.P.D. just bought twenty of these to train their rookie cops on. And talk about maintenance. Señorita, you are looking at an entirely self-supporting machine. You're never going to find our Johnny Pachuco model on the relief rolls. No, sir, this model knows how to liberate.

SECRETARY. Liberate?

SANCHO. He steals. (*Snap. Johnny rushes the Secretary and steals her purse.*)

JOHNNY. ¡Dame esa bolsa, vieja![16] (*He grabs the purse and runs. Snap by Sancho. He stops.*)

(*Secretary runs after Johnny and grabs purse away from him, kicking him as she goes.*)

SECRETARY. No, no, no! We can't have any *more* thieves in the State Administration. Put him back.

SANCHO. Okay, we still got other models. Come on, Johnny, we'll sell you to some old lady. (*Sancho takes Johnny back to his place.*)

SECRETARY. Mr. Sancho, I don't think you quite understand what we need. What we need is something that will attract the women voters. Something more traditional, more romantic.

SANCHO. Ah, a lover. (*He smiles meaningfully.*) Step right over here, señorita. Introducing our standard Revolucionario and/or Early California Bandit type. As you can see he is well-built, sturdy, durable. This is the International Harvester of Mexicans.

SECRETARY. What does he do?

SANCHO. You name it, he does it. He rides horses, stays in the mountains, crosses deserts, plains, rivers, leads revolutions, follows revolutions, kills, can be killed, serves as a martyr, hero, movie star—did I say movie star? Did you ever see *Viva Zapata? Viva Villa? Villa Rides? Pancho Villa Returns? Pancho Villa Goes Back? Pancho Villa Meets Abbott and Costello—*

[15]**ése** fellow [16]**¡Dame . . . vieja!** Give me that bag, old lady!

SECRETARY. I've never seen any of those.

SANCHO. Well, he was in all of them. Listen to this. (*Snap.*)

REVOLUCIONARIO (*Scream*). ¡VIVA VILLAAAAA!

SECRETARY. That's awfully loud.

SANCHO. He has a volume control. (*He adjusts volume. Snap.*)

REVOLUCIONARIO (*Mousey voice*). ¡Viva Villa!

SECRETARY. That's better.

SANCHO. And even if you didn't see him in the movies, perhaps you saw him on TV. He makes commercials. (*Snap.*)

REVOLUCIONARIO. Is there a Frito Bandito in your house?

SECRETARY. Oh yes, I've seen that one!

SANCHO. Another feature about this one is that he is economical. He runs on raw horsemeat and tequila!

SECRETARY. Isn't that rather savage?

SANCHO. Al contrario,[17] it makes him a lover. (*Snap.*)

REVOLUCIONARIO (*To Secretary*). ¡Ay, mamasota, cochota, ven pa'ca![18] (*He grabs Secretary and folds her back—Latin-Lover style.*)

SANCHO (*Snap. Revolucionario goes back upright.*). Now wasn't that nice?

SECRETARY. Well, it was rather nice.

SANCHO. And finally, there is one outstanding feature about this model I KNOW the ladies are going to love: He's a GENUINE antique! He was made in Mexico in 1910!

SECRETARY. Made in Mexico?

SANCHO. That's right. Once in Tijuana, twice in Guadalajara, three times in Cuernavaca.

SECRETARY. Mr. Sancho, I thought he was an American product.

SANCHO. No, but—

SECRETARY. No, I'm sorry. We can't buy anything but American-made products. He just won't do.

SANCHO. But he's an antique!

SECRETARY. I don't care. You still don't understand what we need. It's true we need Mexican models such as these, but it's more important that he be *American.*

SANCHO. American?

SECRETARY. That's right, and judging from what you've shown me, I don't think you have what we want. Well, my lunch hour's almost over: I better—

SANCHO. Wait a minute! Mexican but American?

SECRETARY. That's correct.

SANCHO. Mexican but . . . (*A sudden flash.*) AMERICAN! Yeah, I think we've got exactly what you want. He just came in today! Give me a minute. (*He exits. Talks from backstage.*) Here he is in the shop. Let me just get some papers off. There. Introducing our new 1970 Mexican-American! Ta-ra-ra-ra-ra-RA-RAAA!

(*Sancho brings out the Mexican-American model, a clean-shaven middle-class type in a business suit, with glasses.*)

SECRETARY (*Impressed*). Where have you been hiding this one?

[17]**Al contrario** on the contrary [18]**¡Ay . . . pa'ca!** —, get over here!

SANCHO. He just came in this morning. Ain't he a beauty? Feast your eyes on him! Sturdy US STEEL frame, streamlined, modern. As a matter of fact, he is built exactly like our Anglo models except that he comes in a variety of darker shades: naugahyde, leather, or leatherette.

SECRETARY. Naugahyde.

SANCHO. Well, we'll just write that down. Yes, señorita, this model represents the apex of American engineering! He is bilingual, college educated, ambitious! Say the word "acculturate" and he accelerates. He is intelligent, well-mannered, clean—did I say clean? (*Snap. Mexican-American raises his arm.*) Smell.

SECRETARY (*Smells*). Old Sobaco, my favorite.

SANCHO (*Snap. Mexican-American turns toward Sancho*). Eric! (*To Secretary.*) We call him Eric García. (*To Eric.*) I want you to meet Miss JIM-enez, Eric.

MEXICAN-AMERICAN. Miss JIM-enez, I am delighted to make your acquaintance. (*He kisses her hand.*)

SECRETARY. Oh, my, how charming!

SANCHO. Did you feel the suction? He has seven especially engineered suction cups right behind his lips. He's a charmer all right!

SECRETARY. How about boards? Does he function on boards?

SANCHO. You name them, he is on them. Parole boards, draft boards, school boards, taco quality control boards, surf boards, two-by-fours.

SECRETARY. Does he function in politics?

SANCHO. Señorita, you are looking at a political MACHINE. Have you ever heard of the OEO, EOC, COD, WAR ON POVERTY? That's our model! Not only that, he makes political speeches.

SECRETARY. May I hear one?

SANCHO. With pleasure. (*Snap.*) Eric, give us a speech.

MEXICAN-AMERICAN. Mr. Congressman, Mr. Chairman, members of the board, honored guests, ladies and gentlemen. (*Sancho and Secretary applaud.*) Please, please. I come before you as a Mexican-American to tell you about the problems of the Mexican. The problems of the Mexican stem from one thing and one thing alone: He's stupid. He's uneducated. He needs to stay in school. He needs to be ambitious, forward-looking, harder-working. He needs to think American, American, American, AMERICAN, AMERICAN, AMERICAN. GOD BLESS AMERICA! GOD BLESS AMERICA! GOD BLESS AMERICA!! (*He goes out of control.*)

(*Sancho snaps frantically and the Mexican-American finally slumps forward, bending at the waist.*)

SECRETARY. Oh my, he's patriotic too!

SANCHO. Sí, señorita, he loves his country. Let me just make a little adjustment here. (*Stands Mexican-American up.*)

SECRETARY. What about upkeep? Is he economical?

SANCHO. Well, no, I won't lie to you. The Mexican-American costs a little bit more, but you get what you pay for. He's worth every extra cent. You can keep him running on dry Martinis, Langendorf bread.

SECRETARY. Apple pie?

SANCHO. Only Mom's. Of course, he's also programmed to eat Mexican food on ceremonial functions, but I must warn you: an overdose of beans will plug up his exhaust.

SECRETARY. Fine! There's just one more question: HOW MUCH DO YOU WANT FOR HIM?

SANCHO. Well, I tell you what I'm gonna do. Today and today only, because you've been so sweet, I'm gonna let you steal this model from me! I'm gonna let you drive him off the lot for the simple price of—let's see taxes and license included—$15,000.

SECRETARY. Fifteen thousand DOLLARS? For a MEXICAN!

SANCHO. Mexican? What are you talking, lady? This is a Mexican-AMERICAN! We had to melt down two pachucos, a farm worker and three gabachos[19] to make this model! You want quality, but you gotta pay for it! This is no cheap run-about. He's got class!

SECRETARY. Okay, I'll take him.

SANCHO. You will?

SECRETARY. Here's your money.

SANCHO. You mind if I count it?

SECRETARY. Go right ahead.

SANCHO. Well, you'll get your pink slip in the mail. Oh, do you want me to wrap him up for you? We have a box in the back.

SECRETARY. No, thank you. The Governor is having a luncheon this afternoon, and we need a brown face in the crowd. How do I drive him?

SANCHO. Just snap your fingers. He'll do anything you want.

(*Secretary snaps. Mexican-American steps forward.*)

MEXICAN-AMERICAN. RAZA QUERIDA, ¡VAMOS LEVANTANDO ARMAS PARA LIBERARNOS DE ESTOS DESGRACIADOS GABACHOS QUE NOS EXPLOTAN! VAMOS.[20]

SECRETARY. What did he say?

SANCHO. Something about lifting arms, killing white people, etc.

SECRETARY. But he's not supposed to say that!

SANCHO. Look, lady, don't blame me for bugs from the factory. He's your Mexican-American; you bought him, now drive him off the lot!

SECRETARY. But he's broken!

SANCHO. Try snapping another finger.

(*Secretary snaps. Mexican-American comes to life again.*)

MEXICAN-AMERICAN. ¡ESTA GRAN HUMANIDAD HA DICHO BASTA! Y SE HA PUESTO EN MARCHA! ¡BASTA! ¡BASTA! ¡VIVA LA RAZA! ¡VIVA LA CAUSA! ¡VIVA LA HUELGA! ¡VIVAN LOS BROWN BERETS! ¡VIVAN LOS ESTUDIANTES![21] ¡CHICANO POWER!

(*The Mexican-American turns toward the Secretary, who gasps and backs up. He keeps turning toward the Pachuco, Farm Worker, and Revolucionario, snapping his fingers and turning each of them on, one by one.*)

PACHUCO (*Snap. To Secretary*). I'm going to get you, baby! ¡Viva La Raza!

[19]**gabachos** whites [20]**Raza . . . Vamos** Beloved Raza [persons of Mexican descent], let's take up arms to liberate ourselves from those damned whites who exploit us. Let's get going. [21]**¡Esta . . . Estudiantes!** This great mass of humanity has said enough! And it has begun to march. Enough! Enough! Long live La Raza! Long live the Cause! Long live the strike! Long live the Brown Berets! Long live the students!

FARM WORKER (*Snap. To Secretary*). ¡Viva la huelga! ¡Viva la Huelga! ¡VIVA LA HUELGA!

REVOLUCIONARIO (*Snap. To Secretary*). ¡Viva la revolución! ¡VIVA LA REVOLUCIÓN!

(*The three models join together and advance toward the Secretary who backs up and runs out of the shop screaming. Sancho is at the other end of the shop holding his money in his hand. All freeze. After a few seconds of silence, the Pachuco moves and stretches, shaking his arms and loosening up. The Farm Worker and Revolucionario do the same. Sancho stays where he is, frozen to his spot.*)

JOHNNY. Man, that was a long one, ése.[22] (*Others agree with him.*)

FARM WORKER. How did we do?

JOHNNY. Perty good, look at all that lana,[23] man! (*He goes over to Sancho and removes the money from his hand. Sancho stays where he is.*)

REVOLUCIONARIO. En la madre, look at all the money.

JOHNNY. We keep this up, we're going to be rich.

FARM WORKER. They think we're machines.

REVOLUCIONARIO. Burros.

JOHNNY. Puppets.

MEXICAN-AMERICAN. The only thing I don't like is—how come I always got to play the godamn Mexican-American?

JOHNNY. That's what you get for finishing high school.

FARM WORKER. How about our wages, ése?

JOHNNY. Here it comes right now. $3,000 for you, $3,000 for you, $3,000 for you, and $3,000 for me. The rest we put back into the business.

MEXICAN-AMERICAN. Too much, man. Heh, where you vatos[24] going tonight?

FARM WORKER. I'm going over to Concha's. There's a party.

JOHNNY. Wait a minute, vatos. What about our salesman? I think he needs an oil job.

REVOLUCIONARIO. Leave him to me.

(*The Pachuco, Farm Worker, and Mexican-American exit, talking loudly about their plans for the night. The Revolucionario goes over to Sancho, removes his derby hat and cigar, lifts him up and throws him over his shoulder. Sancho hangs loose, lifeless.*)

REVOLUCIONARIO (*To audience*). He's the best model we got! ¡Ajua![25]

(*Exit.*)

THE END

[22]**ése** man [23]**lana** money [24]**vatos** guys [25]**¡Ajua!** Wow!

## TOPICS FOR CRITICAL THINKING AND WRITING

1. If you are an Anglo (shorthand for a Caucasian with traditional Northern European values), do you find the play deeply offensive? Why, or why not? If you are a Mexican-American, do you find the play entertain-

ing—or do you find parts of it offensive? What might Anglos enjoy in the play, and what might Mexican-Americans find offensive?

2. What stereotypes of Mexican-Americans are presented here? At the end of the play what image of the Mexican-American is presented? How does it compare with the stereotypes?
3. If you are a member of some other minority group, in a few sentences indicate how *Los Vendidos* might be adapted into a play about that group.
4. Putting aside the politics of the play (and your own politics), what do you think are the strengths of *Los Vendidos?* What do you think are the weaknesses?
5. The play was written in 1967. Putting aside a few specific references, for instance to Governor Reagan, do you find it dated? If not, why not?
6. In 1971 when *Los Vendidos* was produced by El Teatro de la Esperanza, the group altered the ending by having the men decide to use the money to build a community center. Evaluate this ending.
7. When the play was videotaped by KNBC in Los Angeles for broadcast in 1973, Valdez changed the ending. In the revised version we discover that a scientist (played by Valdez) masterminds the operation, placing Mexican-American models wherever there are persons of Mexican descent. These models soon will become Chicanos (as opposed to persons with Anglo values) and will aid rather than work against their fellows. Evaluate this ending.
8. In his short essay "The Actos," Valdez says, "Actos: Inspire the audience to social action. Illuminate specific points about social problems. Satirize the opposition. Show or hint at a solution. Express what people are feeling." How many of these do you think *Los Vendidos* does?
9. Many people assume that politics get in the way of serious art. That is, they assume that artists ought to be concerned with issues that transcend politics. Does this point make any sense to you? Why, or why not?

## A PERSPECTIVE FOR *LOS VENDIDOS*

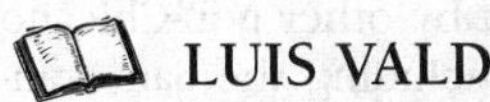

### LUIS VALDEZ

## *The* Actos

Nothing represents the work of El Teatro Campesino (and other teatros Chicanos) better than the acto. In a sense, the acto is Chicano theatre, though we are now moving into a new, more mystical dramatic form we have begun to call the mito. The two forms are, in fact, cuates[1] that complement and balance each other as day goes into night, el sol la sombra, la vida la muerte, el pájaro la serpiente.[2] Our rejection of white western European (gabacho) proscenium theatre makes the birth of new Chicano forms necessary, thus, los actos y los mitos; one through the eyes of man, the other through the eyes of God.

[1]**cuates** twins [2]**el sol . . . serpiente** sun and shade, life and death, the bird and the serpent

The actos were born quite matter of factly in Delano. Nacieron hambrientos de la realidad. Anything and everything that pertained to the daily life, la vida cotidiana, of the huelguistas[3] became food for thought, material for actos. The reality of campesinos on strike had become dramatic (and theatrical as reflected by newspapers, TV newscasts, films, etc.), and so the actos merely reflected the reality. Huelguistas portrayed huelguistas, drawing their improvised dialogue from real words they exchanged with the esquiroles (scabs) in the fields every day.[4]

"Hermanos, compañeros, sálganse de esos files."
"Tenemos comida y trabajo para ustedes afuera de la huelga."
"Esquirol, ten vergüenza."
"Unidos venceremos."
"¡Sal de ahí barrigón!"

The first huelguista to portray an esquirol in the teatro did it to settle a score with a particularly stubborn scab he had talked with in the fields that day. Satire became a weapon that was soon aimed at known and despised contractors, growers and mayordomos. The effect of those early actos on the huelguistas de Delano packed into Filipino Hall was immediate, intense and cathartic. The actos rang true to the reality of the huelga.

Looking back at those early, crude, vital, beautiful, powerful actos of 1965, certain things have now become clear about the dramatic form we were just beginning to develop. There was, of course, no conscious deliberate plan to develop the acto as such. Even the name we gave our small presentations reflects the hard pressing expediency under which we worked from day to day. We could have called them "skits," but we lived and talked in San Joaquin Valley Spanish (with a strong Tejano influence), so we needed a name that made sense to the raza. Cuadros, pasquines, autos, entremeses[5] all seemed too highly intellectualized. We began to call them actos for lack of a better word, lack of time and lack of interest in trying to sound like classical Spanish scholars. De todos modos éramos raza, ¿quién se iba a fijar?[6]

The acto, however, developed its own structure through five years of experimentation. It evolved into a short dramatic form now used primarily by los teatros de Aztlán, but utilized to some extent by other non-Chicano guerrilla theatre companies throughout the U.S., including the San Francisco Mime Troupe and the Bread and Puppet Theatre. (Considerable creative crossfeeding has occurred on other levels, I might add, between the Mime Troupe, the Bread and Puppet, and the Campesino.) Each of these groups may have their own definition of the acto, but the following are some of the guidelines we have established for ourselves over the years:

Actos: Inspire the audience to social action. Illuminate specific points about social problems. Satirize the opposition. Show or hint at a solution. Express what people are feeling.

[3]**huelguistas** strikers [4]The following five lines of dialogue can be translated thus: Brothers, friends, leave those rows. / We have food and work for you outside of the strike. / Scab, you ought to be ashamed. / United we will conquer. / Get out of here, fatso! [5]**Cuadros . . . entremeses** various Spanish words for short plays [6]**De todos . . . fijar?** In all ways we are the Race (i.e., indigenous Americans mixed with European and African blood); who was going to pay attention?

So what's new, right? Plays have been doing that for thousands of years. True, except that the major emphasis in the acto is the social vision, as opposed to the individual artist or playwright's vision. Actos are not written; they are created collectively, through improvisation by a group. The reality reflected in an acto is thus a social reality, whether it pertains to campesinos or to batos locos, not psychologically deranged self-projections, but rather, group archetypes. Don Sotaco, Don Coyote, Johnny Pachuco, Juan Raza, Jorge el Chingón, la Chicana, are all group archetypes that have appeared in actos.

The usefulness of the acto extended well beyond the huelga into the Chicano movement, because Chicanos in general want to identify themselves as a group. The teatro archetypes symbolize the desire for unity and group identity through Chicano heroes and heroines. One character can thus represent the entire Raza, and the Chicano audience will gladly respond to his triumphs or defeats. What to a non-Chicano audience may seem like oversimplification in an acto, is to the Chicano a true expression of his social state and therefore reality.

[*1970*]

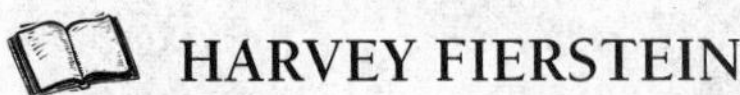

## HARVEY FIERSTEIN

*Harvey Fierstein was born in Brooklyn, New York, the son of parents who had emigrated from Eastern Europe. While studying painting at Pratt Institute he acted in plays and revues, and one of his plays was produced in 1973, but he did not achieve fame until his* Torch Song Trilogy *(1976–79) moved from Off Broadway to Broadway in 1982.* Torch Song Trilogy *won the Theatre World Award, the Tony Award, and the Drama Desk Award. In addition, Fierstein won the Best Actor Tony Award and the Best Actor Drama Desk Award. He later received a third Tony Award for the book for the musical version of* La Cage aux Folles *(1983).*

# *On Tidy Endings*

*The curtain rises on a deserted, modern Upper West Side apartment. In the bright daylight that pours in through the windows we can see the living room of the apartment. Far Stage Right is the galley kitchen, next to it the multilocked front door with intercom. Stage Left reveals a hallway that leads to the two bedrooms and baths.*

*Though the room is still fully furnished (couch, coffee table, etc.), there are boxes stacked against the wall and several photographs and paintings are on the floor leaving shadows on the wall where they once hung. Obviously someone is moving out. From the way the boxes are neatly labeled and stacked, we know that this is an organized person.*

*From the hallway just outside the door we hear the rattling of keys and two arguing voices:*

Harvey Fierstein, Ricky Addison Reed, and Anne de Salvo in the 1987 production of *On Tidy Endings*, Lyceum Theater, New York. (Photograph by Peter Cunningham)

JIM (*offstage*). I've got to be home by four. I've got practice.

MARION (*offstage*). I'll get you to practice, don't worry.

JIM (*offstage*). I don't want to go in there.

MARION (*offstage*). Jimmy, don't make Mommy crazy, alright? We'll go inside, I'll call Aunt Helen and see if you can go down and play with Robbie.

(*The door opens. Marion is a handsome woman of forty. Dressed in a business suit, her hair conservatively combed, she appears to be going to a business meeting. Jim is a boy of eleven. His playclothes are typical, but someone has obviously just combed his hair. Marion recovers the key from the lock.*)

JIM. Why can't I just go down and ring the bell?

MARION. Because I said so.

(*As Marion steps into the room she is struck by some unexpected emotion. She freezes in her path and stares at the empty apartment. Jim lingers by the door.*)

JIM. I'm going downstairs.

MARION. Jimmy, please.

JIM. This place gives me the creeps.

MARION. This was your father's apartment. There's nothing creepy about it.

JIM. Says you.

MARION. You want to close the door, please?

(*Jim reluctantly obeys.*)

MARION. Now, why don't you go check your room and make sure you didn't leave anything.

JIM. It's empty.

MARION. Go look.

JIM. I looked last time.

MARION (*trying to be patient*). Honey, we sold the apartment. You're never going to be here again. Go make sure you have everything you want.

JIM. But Uncle Arthur packed everything.

MARION (*less patiently*). Go make sure.

JIM. There's nothing in there.

MARION (*exploding*). I said make sure!

(*Jim jumps, then realizing that she's not kidding, obeys.*)

MARION. Everything's an argument with that one. (*She looks around the room and breathes deeply. There is sadness here. Under her breath:*) I can still smell you. (*Suddenly not wanting to be alone.*) Jimmy? Are you okay?

JIM (*returning*). Nothing. Told you so.

MARION. Uncle Arthur must have worked very hard. Make sure you thank him.

JIM. What for? Robbie says, (*fey mannerisms*) "They love to clean up things!"

MARION. Sometimes you can be a real joy.

JIM. Did you call Aunt Helen?

MARION. Do I get a break here? (*Approaching the boy understandingly.*) Wouldn't you like to say good-bye?

JIM. To who?

MARION. To the apartment. You and your daddy spent a lot of time here together. Don't you want to take one last look around?

JIM. Ma, get a real life.

MARION. "Get a real life." (*Going for the phone.*) Nice. Very nice.

JIM. Could you call already?

MARION (*dialing*). Jimmy, what does this look like I'm doing?

(*Jim kicks at the floor impatiently. Someone answers the phone at the other end.*)

MARION (*into the phone*). Helen? Hi, we're upstairs. . . . No, we just walked in the door. Jimmy wants to know if he can come down. . . . Oh, thanks.

(*Hearing that, Jim breaks for the door.*)

MARION (*yelling after him*). Don't run in the halls! And don't play with the elevator buttons!

(*The door slams shut behind him.*)

MARION (*back to the phone*). Hi. . . . No, I'm okay. It's a little weird being here. . . . No. Not since the funeral, and then there were so many people. Jimmy told me to get "a real life." I don't think I could handle anything realer. . . . No, please. Stay where you are. I'm fine. The doorman said Arthur would be right back and my lawyer should have been here already. . . . Well, we've got the papers to sign and a few other odds and ends to clean up. Shouldn't take long.

(*The intercom buzzer rings.*)

MARION. Hang on, that must be her. (*Marion goes to the intercom and speaks.*) Yes? . . . Thank you. (*Back to the phone.*) Helen? Yeah, it's the lawyer. I'd better go. . . . Well, I could use a stiff drink, but I drove down. Listen, I'll stop by on my way out. Okay? Okay. 'Bye.

(*She hangs up the phone, looks around the room. That uncomfortable feeling returns to her quickly. She gets up and goes to the front door, opens it and looks out. No one there yet. She closes the door, shakes her head knowing that she's being silly and starts back into the room. She looks around, can't make it and retreats to the door. She opens it, looks out, closes it, but stays right there, her hand on the doorknob. The bell rings. She throws open the door.*)

MARION. That was quick.

(*June Lowell still has her finger on the bell. Her arms are loaded with contracts. Marion's contemporary, June is less formal in appearance and more hyper in her manner.*)

JUNE. *That* was quicker. What, were you waiting by the door?

MARION (*embarrassed*). No. I was just passing it. Come on in.

JUNE. Have you got your notary seal?

MARION. I think so.

JUNE. Great. Then you can witness. I left mine at the office and thanks to gentrification I'm double-parked downstairs. (*Looking for a place to dump her load.*) Where?

MARION (*definitely pointing to the coffee table*). Anywhere. You mean you're not staying?

JUNE. If you really think you need me I can go down and find a parking lot. I think there's one over on Columbus. So, I can go down, park the car in the lot and take a cab back if you really think you need me.

MARION. Well . . . ?

JUNE. But you shouldn't have any problems. The papers are about as straightforward as papers get. Arthur is giving you power of attorney to sell the apartment and you're giving him a check for half the purchase price. Everything else is just signing papers that state that you know that you signed the other papers. Anyway, he knows the deal, his lawyers have been over it all with him, it's just a matter of signatures.

MARION (*not fine*). Oh, fine.

JUNE. Unless you just don't want to be alone with him . . . ?

MARION. With Arthur? Don't be silly.

JUNE (*laying out the papers*). Then you'll handle it solo? Great. My car thanks you, the parking lot thanks you, and the cab driver that wouldn't have gotten a tip thanks you. Come have a quick look-see.

MARION (*joining her on the couch*). There are a lot of papers here.

JUNE. Copies. Not to worry. Start here.

(*Marion starts to read.*)

JUNE. I ran into Jimmy playing Elevator Operator.

(*Marion jumps.*)

JUNE. I got him off at the sixth floor. Read on.

MARION. This is definitely not my day for dealing with him.

(*June gets up and has a look around.*)

JUNE. I don't believe what's happening to this neighborhood. You made quite an investment when you bought this place.

MARION. Collin was always very good at figuring out those things.

JUNE. Well, he sure figured this place right. What, have you tripled your money in ten years?

MARION. More.

JUNE. It's a shame to let it go.

MARION. We're not ready to be a two-dwelling family.

JUNE. So, sublet it again.

MARION. Arthur needs the money from the sale.

JUNE. Arthur got plenty already. I'm not crying for Arthur.

MARION. I don't hear you starting in again, do I?

JUNE. Your interests and your wishes are my only concern.

MARION. Fine.

JUNE. I still say we should contest Collin's will.

MARION. June . . . !

JUNE. You've got a child to support.

MARION. And a great job, and a husband with a great job. Tell me what Arthur's got.

JUNE. To my thinking, half of everything that should have gone to you. And more. All of Collin's personal effects, his record collection . . .

MARION. And I suppose their three years together meant nothing.

JUNE. When you compare them to your sixteen-year marriage? Not nothing, but not half of everything.

MARION (*trying to change the subject*). June, who gets which copies?

JUNE. Two of each to Arthur. One you keep. The originals and anything else come back to me. (*Looking around.*) I still say you should've sublet the apartment for a year and then sold it. You would've gotten an even better price. Who wants to buy an apartment when they know someone died in it. No one. And certainly no one wants to buy an apartment when they know the person died of AIDS.

MARION (*snapping*). June. Enough!

JUNE (*catching herself*). Sorry. That was out of line. Sometimes my mouth does that to me. Hey, that's why I'm a lawyer. If my brain worked as fast as my mouth I would have gotten a real job.

MARION (*holding out a stray paper*). What's this?

JUNE. I forgot. Arthur's lawyer sent that over yesterday. He found it in Collin's safety-deposit box. It's an insurance policy that came along with some consulting job he did in Japan. He either forgot about it when he made out his will or else he wanted you to get the full payment. Either way, it's yours.

MARION. Are you sure we don't split this?

JUNE. Positive.

MARION. But everything else . . . ?

JUNE. Hey, Arthur found it, his lawyer sent it to me. Relax, it's all yours. Minus my commission, of course. Go out and buy yourself something. Anything else before I have to use my cut to pay the towing bill?

MARION. I guess not.

JUNE (*starting to leave*). Great. Call me when you get home. (*Stopping at the door and looking back.*) Look, I know that I'm attacking this a little coldly. I am aware that someone you loved has just died. But there's a time and place for everything. This is about tidying up loose ends, not holding hands. I hope you'll remember that when Arthur gets here. Call me.

(*And she's gone.*)

(*Marion looks ill at ease to be alone again. She nervously straightens the papers into neat little piles, looks at them and then remembers:*)

MARION. Pens. We're going to need pens.

(*At last a chore to be done. She looks in her purse and finds only one. She goes to the kitchen and opens a drawer where she finds two more. She starts back to the table with them but suddenly remembers something else. She returns to the kitchen and begins going through the cabinets until she finds what she's looking for: a blue Art Deco teapot. Excited to find it, she takes it back to the couch. Guilt strikes. She stops, considers putting it back, wavers, then:*)

MARION (*to herself*). Oh, he won't care. One less thing to pack.

(*She takes the teapot and places it on the couch next to her purse. She is happier. Now she searches the room with her eyes for any other treasures she may have overlooked. Nothing here. She wanders off into the bedroom. We hear keys outside the front door. Arthur lets himself into the apartment carrying a load of empty cartons and a large shopping bag. Arthur is in his mid-thirties, pleasant looking though sloppily dressed in work clothes and slightly overweight. Arthur enters the apartment just as Marion comes out of the bedroom carrying a framed watercolor painting. They jump at the sight of each other.*)

MARION. Oh, hi, Arthur. I didn't hear the door.

ARTHUR (*staring at the painting*). Well hello, Marion.

MARION (*guiltily*). I was going to ask you if you were thinking of taking this painting because if you're not going to then I'll take it. Unless, of course, you want it.

ARTHUR. No. You can have it.

MARION. I never really liked it, actually. I hate cats. I didn't even like the show. I needed something for my college dorm room. I was never the rock star poster type. I kept it in the back of a closet for years until Collin moved in here and took it. He said he liked it.

ARTHUR. I do too.

MARION. Well, then you keep it.

ARTHUR. No. Take it.

MARION. We've really got no room for it. You keep it.

ARTHUR. I don't want it.

MARION. Well, if you're sure.

ARTHUR (*seeing the teapot*). You want the teapot?

MARION. If you don't mind.

ARTHUR. One less thing to pack.

MARION. Funny, but that's exactly what I thought. One less thing to pack. You know, my mother gave it to Collin and me when we moved in to our first apartment. Silly sentimental piece of junk, but you know.

ARTHUR. That's not the one.

MARION. Sure it is. Hall used to make them for Westinghouse back in the thirties. I see them all the time at antiques shows and I always wanted to buy another, but they ask such a fortune for them.

ARTHUR. We broke the one your mother gave you a couple of years ago. That's a reproduction. You can get them almost anywhere in the Village for eighteen bucks.

MARION. Really? I'll have to pick one up.

ARTHUR. Take this one. I'll get another.

MARION. No, it's yours. You bought it.

ARTHUR. One less thing to pack.

MARION. Don't be silly. I didn't come here to raid the place.

ARTHUR. Well, was there anything else of Collin's that you thought you might like to have?

MARION. Now I feel so stupid, but actually I made a list. Not for me. But I started thinking about different people; friends, relatives, you know, that might want to have something of Collin's to remember him by. I wasn't sure just what you were taking and what you were throwing out. Anyway, I brought the list. (*Gets it from her purse.*) Of course these are only suggestions. You probably thought of a few of these people yourself. But I figured it couldn't hurt to write it all down. Like I said, I don't know what you are planning on keeping.

ARTHUR (*taking the list*). I was planning on keeping it all.

MARION. Oh, I know. But most of these things are silly. Like his high school yearbooks. What would you want with them?

ARTHUR. Sure. I'm only interested in his Gay period.

MARION. I didn't mean it that way. Anyway, you look it over. They're only suggestions. Whatever you decide to do is fine with me.

ARTHUR (*folding the list*). It would have to be, wouldn't it. I mean, it's all mine now. He did leave this all to me.

(***Marion is becoming increasingly nervous, but tries to keep a light approach as she takes a small bundle of papers from her bag.***)

MARION. While we're on the subject of what's yours. I brought a batch of condolence cards that were sent to you care of me. Relatives mostly.

ARTHUR (*taking them*). More cards? I'm going to have to have another printing of thank-you notes done.

MARION. I answered these last week, so you don't have to bother. Unless you want to.

ARTHUR. Forge my signature?

MARION. Of course not. They were addressed to both of us and they're mostly distant relatives or friends we haven't seen in years. No one important.

ARTHUR. If they've got my name on them, then I'll answer them myself.

MARION. I wasn't telling you not to, I was only saying that you don't have to.

ARTHUR. I understand.

(***Marion picks up the teapot and brings it to the kitchen.***)

MARION. Let me put this back.

ARTHUR. I ran into Jimmy in the lobby.

MARION. Tell me you're joking.

ARTHUR. I got him to Helen's.

MARION. He's really racking up the points today.

ARTHUR. You know, he still can't look me in the face.

MARION. He's reacting to all of this in strange ways. Give him time. He'll come around. He's really very fond of you.

ARTHUR. I know. But he's at that awkward age: under thirty. I'm sure in twenty years we'll be the best of friends.

MARION. It's not what you think.

ARTHUR. What do you mean?

MARION. Well, you know.

ARTHUR. No I don't know. Tell me.

MARION. I thought that you were intimating something about his blaming you for Collin's illness and I was just letting you know that it's not true. (*Foot in mouth, she braves on.*) We discussed it a lot and . . . uh . . . he understands that his father was sick before you two ever met.

ARTHUR. I don't believe this.

MARION. I'm just trying to say that he doesn't blame you.

ARTHUR. First of all, who asked you? Second of all, that's between him and me. And third and most importantly, of course he blames me. Marion, he's eleven years old. You can discuss all you want, but the fact is that his father died of a "fag" disease and I'm the only fag around to finger.

MARION. My son doesn't use that kind of language.

ARTHUR. Forget the language. I'm talking about what he's been through. Can you imagine the kind of crap he's taken from his friends? That poor kid's been chased and chastised from one end of town to the other. He's got to have someone to blame just to survive. He can't blame you, you're all he's got. He can't blame his father; he's dead. So, Uncle Arthur gets the shaft. Fine, I can handle it.

MARION. You are so wrong, Arthur. I know my son and that is not the way his mind works.

ARTHUR. I don't know what you know. I only know what I know. And all I know is what I hear and see. The snide remarks, the little smirks . . . And it's not just the illness. He's been looking for a scapegoat since the day you and Collin first split up. Finally he has one.

MARION (*getting very angry now*). Wait. Are you saying that if he's going to blame someone it should be me?

ARTHUR. I think you should try to see things from his point of view.

MARION. Where do you get off thinking you're privy to my son's point of view?

ARTHUR. It's not that hard to imagine. Life's rolling right along, he's having a happy little childhood, when suddenly one day his father's moving out. No explanations, no reasons, none of the fights that usually accompany such things. Divorce is hard enough for a kid to understand when he's listened to years of battles, but yours?

MARION. So what should we have done? Faked a few months' worth of fights before Collin moved out?

ARTHUR. You could have told him the truth, plain and simple.

MARION. He was seven years old at the time. How the hell do you tell a seven-year-old that his father is leaving his mother to go sleep with other men?

ARTHUR. Well, not like that.

MARION. You know, Arthur, I'm going to say this as nicely as I can: Butt out. You're not his mother and you're not his father.

ARTHUR. Thank you. I wasn't acutely aware of that fact. I will certainly keep that in mind from now on.

MARION. There's only so much information a child that age can handle.

ARTHUR. So it's best that he reach his capacity on the street.

MARION. He knew about the two of you. We talked about it.

ARTHUR. Believe me, he knew before you talked about it. He's young, not stupid.

MARION. It's very easy for you to stand here and criticize, but there are aspects that you will just never be able to understand. You weren't there. You have no idea what it was like for me. You're talking to someone who thought that a girl went to college to meet a husband. I went to protest rallies because I liked the music. I bought a guitar because I thought it looked good on the bed! This lifestyle, this knowledge that you take for granted, was all a little out of left field for me.

ARTHUR. I can imagine.

MARION. No, I don't think you can. I met Collin in college, married him right after graduation and settled down for a nice quiet life of Kids and Careers. You think I had any idea about this? Talk about life's little surprises. You live with someone for sixteen years, you share your life, your bed, you have a child together, and then you wake up one day and he tells you that to him it's all been a lie. A lie. Try that on for size. Here you are the happiest couple you know, fulfilling your every life fantasy and he tells you he's living a lie.

ARTHUR. I'm sure he never said that.

MARION. Don't be so sure. There was a lot of new ground being broken back then and plenty of it was muddy.

ARTHUR. You know that he loved you.

MARION. What's that supposed to do, make things easier? It doesn't. I was brought up to believe, among other things, that if you had love that was enough. So what if I wasn't everything he wanted. Maybe he wasn't exactly everything I wanted either. So, you know what? You count your blessings and you settle.

ARTHUR. No one has to settle. Not him. Not you.

MARION. Of course not. You can say, "Up yours!" to everything and everyone who depends and needs you, and go off to make yourself happy.

ARTHUR. It's not that simple.

MARION. No. This is simpler. Death is simpler. (*Yelling out:*) Happy now?

(*They stare at each other. Marion calms the rage and catches her breath. Arthur holds his emotions in check.*)

ARTHUR. How about a nice hot cup of coffee? Tea with lemon? Hot cocoa with a marshmallow floating in it?

MARION. (*laughs*). I was wrong. You *are* a mother.

(*Arthur goes into the kitchen and starts preparing things. Marion loafs by the doorway.*)

MARION. I lied before. He *was* everything I ever wanted.

(*Arthur stops, looks at her, and then changes the subject as he goes on with his work.*)

ARTHUR. When I came into the building and saw Jimmy in the lobby I absolutely freaked for a second. It's amazing how much they look alike. It was like seeing a little miniature Collin standing there.

MARION. I know. He's like Collin's clone. There's nothing of me in him.

ARTHUR. I always kinda hoped that when he grew up he'd take after me. Not much chance, I guess.

MARION. Don't do anything fancy in there.

ARTHUR. Please. Anything we can consume is one less thing to pack.

MARION. So you've said.

ARTHUR. So *we've* said.

MARION. I want to keep seeing you and I want you to see Jim. You're still part of this family. No one's looking to cut you out.

ARTHUR. Ah, who'd want a kid to grow up looking like me anyway. I had enough trouble looking like this. Why pass on the misery?

MARION. You're adorable.

ARTHUR. Is that like saying I have a good personality?

MARION. I think you are one of the most naturally handsome men I know.

ARTHUR. Natural is right, and the bloom is fading.

MARION. All you need is a few good nights' sleep to kill those rings under your eyes.

ARTHUR. Forget the rings under my eyes, (*grabbing his middle*) . . . how about the rings around my moon?

MARION. I like you like this.

ARTHUR. From the time that Collin started using the wheelchair until he died, about six months, I lost twenty-three pounds. No gym, no diet. In the last seven weeks I've gained close to fifty.

MARION. You're exaggerating.

ARTHUR. I'd prove it on the bathroom scale, but I sold it in working order.

MARION. You'd never know.

ARTHUR. Marion, *you'd* never know, but ask my belt. Ask my pants. Ask my underwear. Even my stretch socks have stretch marks. I called the ambulance at five A.M., he was gone at nine and by nine-thirty, I was on a first-name basis with Sara Lee. I can quote the business hours of every ice-cream parlor, pizzeria and bakery on the island of Manhattan. I know the location of every twenty-four-hour grocery in the greater New York area, and I have memorized the phone numbers of every Mandarin, Szechuan and Hunan restaurant with free delivery.

MARION. At least you haven't wasted your time on useless hobbies.

ARTHUR. Are you kidding? I'm opening my own Overeater's Hotline. We'll have to start small, but expansion is guaranteed.

MARION. You're the best, you know that? If I couldn't be everything that Collin wanted then I'm grateful that he found someone like you.

ARTHUR (*turning on her without missing a beat*). Keep your goddamned gratitude to yourself. I didn't go through any of this for you. So your thanks are out of line. And he didn't find "someone like" me. It was me.

MARION (*frightened*). I didn't mean . . .

ARTHUR. And I wish you'd remember one thing more: He died in my arms, not yours.

(*Marion is totally caught off guard. She stares disbelieving, open-mouthed. Arthur walks past her as he leaves the kitchen with place mats. He puts them on the coffee table. As he arranges the papers and place mats he speaks, never looking at her.*)

ARTHUR. Look, I know you were trying to say something supportive. Don't waste your breath. There's nothing you can say that will make any of this easier for me. There's no way for you to help me get through this. And that's your fault. After three years you still have no idea or understanding of who I am. Or maybe you do know but refuse to accept it. I don't know and I don't care. But at least understand, from my point of view, who you are: You are my husband's *ex*-wife. If you like, the mother of *my* stepson. Don't flatter yourself into thinking you're any more than that. And whatever you are, you're certainly not my friend.

(*He stops, looks up at her, then passes her again as he goes back to the kitchen. Marion is shaken, working hard to control herself. She moves toward the couch.*)

MARION. Why don't we just sign these papers and I'll be out of your way.

ARTHUR. Shouldn't you say *I'll* be out of *your* way? After all, I'm not just signing papers. I'm signing away my home.

MARION (*resolved not to fight, she gets her purse*). I'll leave the papers here. Please have them notarized and returned to my lawyer.

ARTHUR. Don't forget my painting.

MARION (*exploding*). What do you want from me, Arthur?

ARTHUR (*yelling back*). I want you the hell out of my apartment! I want you out of my life! And I want you to leave Collin alone!

MARION. The man's dead. I don't know how much more alone I can leave him.

(*Arthur laughs at the irony, but behind the laughter is something much more desperate.*)

ARTHUR. Lots more, Marion. You've got to let him go.

MARION. For the life of me, I don't know what I did or what you think I did, for you to treat me like this. But you're not going to get away with it. You will not take your anger out on me. I will not stand here and be badgered and insulted by you. I know you've been hurt and I know you're hurting but you're not the only one who lost someone here.

ARTHUR (*topping her*). Yes I am! You didn't just lose him. I did! You lost him five years ago when he divorced you. This is not your moment of grief and loss, it's mine! (*Picking up the bundle of cards and throwing it toward her.*) These condolences do not belong to you, they're mine. (*Tossing her list back to her.*) His things are not yours to give away, they're mine! This death does not belong to you, it's mine! Bought and paid for outright. I suffered for it, I bled for it.

I was the one who cooked his meals. I was the one who spoon-fed them. I pushed his wheelchair. I carried and bathed him. I wiped his backside and changed his diapers. I breathed life into and wrestled fear out of his heart. I kept him alive for two years longer than any doctor thought possible and when it was time I was the one who prepared him for death.

I paid in full for my place in his life and I will *not* share it with you. We are not the two widows of Collin Redding. Your life was not here. Your husband didn't just die. You've got a son and a life somewhere else. Your husband's sitting, waiting for you at home, wondering, as I am, what the hell you're doing here and why you can't let go.

(*Marion leans back against the couch. She's blown away. Arthur stands staring at her.*)

ARTHUR (*quietly*). Let him go, Marion. He's mine. Dead or alive; mine.

(*The teakettle whistles. Arthur leaves the room, goes to the kitchen and pours the water as Marion pulls herself together. Arthur carries the loaded tray back into the living room and sets it down on the coffee table. He sits and pours a cup.*)

ARTHUR. One marshmallow or two?

(*Marion stares, unsure as to whether the attack is really over or not.*)

ARTHUR (*placing them in her cup*). Take three, they're small.

(*Marion smiles and takes the offered cup.*)

ARTHUR (*campily*). Now let me tell you how I *really* feel.

(*Marion jumps slightly, then they share a small laugh. Silence as they each gather themselves and sip their refreshments*)

MARION (*calmly*). Do you think that I sold the apartment just to throw you out?

ARTHUR. I don't care about the apartment . . .

MARION. . . . Because I really didn't. Believe me.

ARTHUR. I know.

MARION. I knew the expenses here were too much for you, and I knew you couldn't afford to buy out my half . . . I figured if we sold it, that you'd at least have a nice chunk of money to start over with.

ARTHUR. You could've given me a little more time.

MARION. Maybe. But I thought the sooner you were out of here, the sooner you could go on with your life.

ARTHUR. Or the sooner you could go on with yours.

MARION. Maybe. (*Pauses to gather her thoughts.*) Anyway, I'm not going to tell you that I have no idea what you're talking about. I'd have to be worse than deaf and blind not to have seen the way you've been treated. Or mistreated. When I read Collin's obituary in the newspaper and saw my name and Jimmy's name and no mention of you . . . (*Shakes her head, not knowing what to say.*) You know that his secretary was the one who wrote that up and sent it in. Not me. But I should have done something about it and I didn't. I know.

ARTHUR. Wouldn't have made a difference. I wrote my own obituary for him and sent it to the smaller papers. They edited me out.

MARION. I'm sorry. I remember, at the funeral, I was surrounded by all of Collin's family and business associates while you were left with your friends. I knew it was wrong. I knew I should have said something but it felt good to have them around me and you looked like you were holding up. . . . Wrong. But saying that it's all my fault for not letting go . . . ? There were other people involved.

ARTHUR. Who took their cue from you.

MARION. Arthur, you don't understand. Most people that we knew as a couple had no idea that Collin was Gay right up to his death. And even those that did know only found out when he got sick and the word leaked out that it was AIDS. I don't think I have to tell you how stupid and ill-informed most people are about homosexuality. And AIDS . . . ? The kinds of insane behavior that word inspires . . . ?

Those people at the funeral, how many times did they call to see how he was doing over these years? How many of them ever went to see him in the hospital? Did any of them even come here? So, why would you expect them to act any differently after his death?

So, maybe that helps to explain their behavior, but what about mine, right? Well, maybe there is no explanation. Only excuses. And excuse number one is that you're right, I have never really let go of him. And I am jealous of you. Hell, I was jealous of anyone that Collin ever talked to, let alone slept with . . . let alone loved.

The first year, after he moved out, we talked all the time about the different men he was seeing. And I always listened and advised. It was kind of fun. It kept us close. It kept me a part of his intimate life. And the bottom line was always that he wasn't happy with the men he was meeting. So, I was always allowed to hang on to the hope that one day he'd give it all up and come home. Then he got sick.

He called me, told me he was in the hospital and asked if I'd come see him. I ran. When I got to his door there was a sign, INSTRUCTIONS FOR VISITORS OF AN AIDS PATIENT. I nearly died.

ARTHUR. He hadn't told you?

MARION. No. And believe me, a sign is not the way to find these things out. I was so angry. . . . And he was so sick . . . I was sure that he'd die right then. If not from the illness then from the hospital staff's neglect. No one wanted to go near him and I didn't bother fighting with them because I understood that they were scared. I was scared. That whole month in the hospital I didn't let Jimmy visit him once.

You learn.

Well, as you know, he didn't die. And he asked if he could come stay with me until he was well. And I said yes. Of course, yes. Now, here's something I never thought I'd ever admit to anyone: had he asked to stay with me for a few weeks I would have said no. But he asked to stay with me until he was well and knowing there was no cure I said yes. In my craziness I said yes because to me that meant forever. That he was coming back to me forever. Not that I wanted him to die, but I assumed from everything I'd read. . . . And we'd be back together for whatever time he had left. Can you understand that?

(*Arthur nods.*)

MARION (*gathers her thoughts again*). Two weeks later he left. He moved in here. Into this apartment that we had bought as an investment. Never to live in. Certainly never to live apart in. Next thing I knew, the name Arthur starts appearing in every phone call, every dinner conversation.

"Did you see the doctor?"

"Yes. Arthur made sure I kept the appointment."

"Are you going to your folks for Thanksgiving?"

"No. Arthur and I are having some friends over."

I don't know which one of us was more of a coward, he for not telling or me for not asking about you. But eventually you became a given. Then, of course, we met and became what I had always thought of as friends.

(*Arthur winces in guilt.*)

MARION. I don't care what you say, how could we not be friends with someone so great in common: love for one of the most special human beings there ever was. And don't try and tell me there weren't times when you enjoyed me being around as an ally. I can think of a dozen occasions when we ganged up on him, teasing him with our intimate knowledge of his personal habits.

(*Arthur has to laugh.*)

MARION. Blanket stealing? Snoring? Excess gas, no less? (*Takes a moment to enjoy this truce.*) I don't think that my loving him threatened your relationship. Maybe I'm not being truthful with myself. But I don't. I never tried to step between you. Not that I ever had the opportunity. Talk about being joined at the hip! And that's not to say I wasn't jealous. I was. Terribly. Hatefully. But always lovingly. I was happy for Collin because there was no way to deny that he was happy. With everything he was facing, he was happy. Love did that. You did that.

He lit up with you. He came to life. I envied that and all the time you spent together, but more, I watched you care for him (sometimes *overcare* for him), and I was in awe. I could never have done what you did. I never would have survived. I really don't know how you did.

ARTHUR. Who said I survived?

MARION. Don't tease. You did an absolutely incredible thing. It's not as if you met him before he got sick. You entered a relationship that you knew in all probability would end this way and you never wavered.

ARTHUR. Of course I did. Don't have me sainted, Marion. But sometimes you have no choice. Believe me, if I could've gotten away from him I would've. But I was a prisoner of love.

(*He makes a campy gesture and pose.*)

MARION. Stop.

ARTHUR. And there were lots of pluses. I got to quit a job I hated, stay home all day and watch game shows. I met a lot of doctors and learned a lot of big words. (*Arthur jumps up and goes to the pile of boxes where he extracts one and brings it back to the couch.*)

And then there was all the exciting traveling I got to do. This box has a souvenir from each one of our trips. Wanna see? (*Marion nods. He opens the box and pulls things out one by one. Holding up an old bottle.*)

This is from the house we rented in Reno when we went to clear out his lungs. (*Holding handmade potholders.*)

This is from the hospital in Reno. Collin made them. They had a great arts and crafts program. (*Copper bracelets.*)

These are from a faith healer in Philly. They don't do much for a fever, but they look great with a green sweater. (*Glass ashtrays.*)

These are from our first visit to the clinic in France. Such lovely people. (*A Bible.*)

This is from our second visit to the clinic in France. (*A bead necklace.*)

A Voodoo doctor in New Orleans. Next time we'll have to get there earlier in the year. I think he sold all the pretty ones at Mardi Gras. (*A tiny piñata.*)

Then there was Mexico. Black market drugs and empty wallets. (*Now pulling things out at random.*)

L.A., San Francisco, Houston, Boston . . . We traveled everywhere they offered hope for sale and came home with souvenirs. (*Arthur quietly pulls a few more things out and then begins to put them all back into the box slowly. Softly as he works:*) Marion, I would have done anything, traveled anywhere to avoid . . . or delay. . . . Not just because I loved him so desperately, but when you've lived the way we did for three years . . . the battle becomes your life. (*He looks at her and then away.*) His last few hours were beyond any scenario I had imagined. He hadn't walked in nearly six months. He was totally incontinent. If he spoke two words in a week I was thankful. Days went by without his eyes ever focusing on me. He just stared out at I don't know what. Not the meals as I fed him. Not the TV I played constantly for company. Just out. Or maybe in.

It was the middle of the night when I heard his breathing become labored. His lungs were filling with fluid again. I knew the sound. I'd heard it a hundred times before. So, I called the ambulance and got him to the hospital.

They hooked him up to the machines, the oxygen, shot him with morphine and told me that they would do what they could to keep him alive.

But, Marion, it wasn't the machines that kept him breathing. He did it himself. It was that incredible will and strength inside him. Whether it came from his love of life or fear of death, who knows. But he'd been counted out a hundred times and a hundred times he fought his way back.

I got a magazine to read him, pulled a chair up to the side of his bed and holding his hand, I wondered whether I should call Helen to let the cleaning lady in or if he'd fall asleep and I could sneak home for an hour. I looked up from the page and he was looking at me. Really looking right into my eyes. I patted his cheek and said, "Don't worry, honey, you're going to be fine."

But there was something else in his eyes. He wasn't satisfied with that. And I don't know why, I have no idea where it came from, I just heard the words coming out of my mouth, "Collin, do you want to die?"

His eyes filled and closed, he nodded his head.

I can't tell you what I was thinking, I'm not sure I was. I slipped off my shoes, lifted his blanket and climbed into bed next to him. I helped him to put his arms around me, and mine around him, and whispered as gently as I could into his ear, "It's alright to let go now. It's time to go on." And he did.

Marion, you've got your life and your son. All I have is an intangible place in a man's history. Leave me that. Respect that.

MARION. I understand.

(*Arthur suddenly comes to life, running to get the shopping bag that he'd left at the front door.*)

ARTHUR. Jeez! With all the screamin' and sad storytelling I forgot something. (*He extracts a bouquet of flowers from the bag.*) I brung you flowers and everything.

MARION. You brought *me* flowers?

ARTHUR. Well, I knew you'd never think to bring me flowers and I felt that on an occasion such as this somebody oughta get flowers from somebody.

MARION. You know, Arthur, you're really making me feel like a worthless piece of garbage.

ARTHUR. So what else is new? (*He presents the flowers.*) Just promise me one thing: Don't press one in a book. Just stick them in a vase and when they fade just toss them out. No more memorabilia.

MARION. Arthur, I want to do something for you and I don't know what. Tell me what you want.

ARTHUR. I want little things. Not much. I want to be remembered. If you get a Christmas card from Collin's mother make sure she sent me one too. If his friends call to see how you are, ask if they've called me. Have me to dinner so I can see Jimmy. Let me take him out now and then. Invite me to his wedding. (*They both laugh.*)

MARION. You've got it.

ARTHUR (*clearing the table*). Let me get all this cold cocoa out of the way. We still have the deed to do.

MARION (*checking her watch*). And I've got to get Jimmy home in time for practice.

ARTHUR. Band practice?

MARION. Baseball. (*Picking her list off the floor.*) About this list, you do what you want.

ARTHUR. Believe me, I will. But I promise to consider your suggestions. Just don't rush me. I'm not ready to give it all away. (*Arthur is off to the kitchen with his tray and the phone rings. He answers in the kitchen.*) "Hello? . . . Just a minute. (*Calling out.*) It's your eager Little Leaguer.

(*Marion picks up the living room extension and Arthur hangs his up.*)

MARION (*into phone*). Hello, honey. . . . I'll be down in five minutes. No. You know what? You come up here and get me. . . . No, I said you should come up here. . . . I said I want you to come up here. . . . Because I said so. . . . Thank you. (*She hangs the receiver.*)

ARTHUR (*rushing to the papers*). Alright, where do we start on these?

MARION (*getting out her seal*). I guess you should just start signing everything and I'll stamp along with you. Keep one of everything on the side for yourself.

ARTHUR. Now I feel so rushed. What am I signing?

MARION. You want to do this another time?

ARTHUR. No. Let's get it over with. I wouldn't survive another session like this.

(*He starts to sign and she starts her job.*)

MARION. I keep meaning to ask you; how are you?

ARTHUR (*at first puzzled and then:*) Oh, you mean my health? Fine. No. I'm fine. I've been tested, and nothing. We were very careful. We took many precautions. Collin used to make jokes about how we should invest in rubber futures.

MARION. I'll bet.

ARTHUR (*stops what he's doing*). It never occurred to me until now. How about you?

MARION (*not stopping*). Well, we never had sex after he got sick.

ARTHUR. But before?

MARION (*stopping but not looking up*). I have the antibodies in my blood. No signs that it will ever develop into anything else. And it's been five years so my chances are pretty good that I'm just a carrier.

ARTHUR. I'm so sorry. Collin never told me.

MARION. He didn't know. In fact, other than my husband and the doctors, you're the only one I've told.

ARTHUR. You and your husband . . . ?

MARION. Have invested in rubber futures. There'd only be a problem if we wanted to have a child. Which we do. But we'll wait. Miracles happen every day.

ARTHUR. I don't know what to say.

MARION. Tell me you'll be be there if I ever need you.

(*Arthur gets up, goes to her and puts his arm around her. They hold each other. He gently pushes her away to make a joke.*)

ARTHUR. Sure! Take something else that should have been mine.

MARION. Don't even joke about things like that.

(*The doorbell rings. They pull themselves together.*)

ARTHUR. You know we'll never get these done today.

MARION. So, tomorrow.

(*Arthur goes to open the door as Marion gathers her things. He opens the door and Jimmy is standing in the hall.*)

JIM. C'mon, Ma. I'm gonna be late.

ARTHUR. Would you like to come inside?

JIM. We've gotta go.

MARION. Jimmy, come on.

JIM. Ma!

(*She glares. He comes in. Arthur closes the door.*)

MARION (*holding out the flowers*). Take these for Mommy.

JIM (*taking them*). Can we go?

MARION (*picking up the painting*). Say good-bye to your Uncle Arthur.

JIM. 'Bye, Arthur. Come on.

MARION. Give him a kiss.

ARTHUR. Marion, don't.

MARION. Give your uncle a kiss good-bye.

JIM. He's not my uncle.

MARION. No. He's a hell of a lot more than your uncle.

ARTHUR (*offering his hand*). A handshake will do.

MARION. Tell Uncle Arthur what your daddy told you.

JIM. About what?

MARION. Stop playing dumb. You know.

ARTHUR. Don't embarrass him.

MARION. Jimmy, please.

JIM (*He regards his mother's softer tone and then speaks*). He said that after me and Mommy he loved you the most.

MARION (*standing behind him*). Go on.

JIM. And that I should love you too. And make sure that you're not lonely or very sad.

ARTHUR. Thank you.

(*Arthur reaches down to the boy and they hug. Jim gives him a little peck on the cheek and then breaks away.*)

MARION (*going to open the door*). Alright, kid, you done good. Now let's blow this joint before you muck it up.

(*Jim rushes out the door. Marion turns to Arthur.*)

MARION. A child's kiss is magic. Why else would they be so stingy with them. I'll call you.

(*Arthur nods understanding. Marion pulls the door closed behind her. Arthur stands quietly as the lights fade to black.*)

THE END

**NOTE:** *If being performed on film, the final image should be of Arthur leaning his back against the closed door on the inside of the apartment and Marion leaning on the outside of the door. A moment of thought and then they both move on.*

[*1987*]

## TOPICS FOR CRITICAL THINKING AND WRITING

1. We first hear about AIDS on page 1679. Were you completely surprised, or did you think the play might introduce the subject? That is, did the author in any way prepare you for the subject? If so, how?
2. So far as the basic story goes, June (the lawyer) is not necessary. Marion could have brought the papers with her. Why do you suppose Fierstein introduces June? What function(s) does she serve? How would you characterize her?
3. On page 1680 Marion says of the teapot, "One less thing to pack." Arthur says the same words a moment later, and then he repeats them

yet again. A little later, while drinking cocoa, he repeats the words, and Marion says, "So you've said," to which Arthur replies, "So *we've* said." Exactly what tone do you think should be used when Marion first says these words? When Arthur says them? And what significance, if any, do you attach to the fact that both characters speak these words?

4. A reviewer of the play said that Arthur is "bitchy" in many of his responses to Marion. What do you suppose the reviewer meant by this? Does the term imply that Fierstein presents a stereotype of the homosexual? If so, what is this stereotype? If you think that the term applies (even though you might not use such a word yourself), do you think that Fierstein's portrayal of Arthur is stereotypical? If it is stereotypical, is this a weakness in the play?
5. Arthur says that Jimmy blames him for Collin's death, but Marion denies it. Who do you think is right? Can a reader be sure? Why, or why not?
6. When Arthur tells Marion that she should have told Jimmy why Collin left her, Marion says, "How the hell do you tell a seven-year-old that his father is leaving his mother to go sleep with other men?" Arthur replies, "Well, not like that." What does Arthur mean? How *might* Marion have told Jimmy? Do you think she should have told Jimmy?
7. Do you agree with a reader who found Marion an unconvincing character because she is "so passive and unquestioningly loving in her regard for her ex-husband"? If you disagree, how would you argue your case?
8. During the course of the play, what (if anything) does Marion learn? What (if anything) does Arthur learn? What (if anything) does Jimmy learn? What (if anything) does the reader or viewer learn from the play?
9. One reader characterized the play as "propaganda." Do you agree? Why, or why not? And if you think *On Tidy Endings* is propaganda, are you implying that it is therefore deficient as a work of art?

## MARSHA NORMAN

*Marsha Norman was born in Louisville, Kentucky, in 1947. After receiving a bachelor's degree from Agnes Scott College and a master of arts in teaching from the University of Louisville, she taught gifted children and disturbed children. Her reputation as a playwright was established with a two-act play,* Getting Out, *which was produced in Louisville (1977) and subsequently in New York (1978).* 'night, Mother, *which had its world premiere in Cambridge, Massachusetts, in 1983, won the Pulitzer Prize for drama in that year.*

# *'night, Mother*

LIST OF CHARACTERS

JESSIE CATES, *in her late thirties or early forties, is pale and vaguely unsteady physically. It is only in the last year that Jessie has gained control of her mind and body, and tonight she is determined to hold on to that control. She wears pants and a long black sweater with deep*

Kathy Bates as Jessie, and Anne Pitoniak as Mama, in the Pulitzer Prize–winning original production of *'night Mother,* American Repertory Theatre, Cambridge, 1982–83. (© 1994–95 by Richard Feldman)

***pockets, which contain scraps of paper, and there may be a pencil behind her ear or a pen clipped to one of the pockets of the sweater.***

***As a rule, Jessie doesn't feel much like talking. Other people have rarely found her quirky sense of humor amusing. She has a peaceful energy on this night, a sense of purpose, but is clearly aware of the time passing moment by moment. Oddly enough, Jessie has never been as communicative or as enjoyable as she is on this evening, but we must know she has not always been this way. There is a familiarity between these two women that comes from having lived together for a long time. There is a shorthand to the talk and a sense of routine comfort in the way they relate to each other physically. Naturally, there are also routine aggravations.***

THELMA CATES, ***"Mama," is Jessie's mother, in her late fifties or early sixties. She has begun to feel her age and so takes it easy when she can, or when it serves her purpose to let someone help her. But she speaks quickly and enjoys talking. She believes that things* are *what she says they are. Her sturdiness is more a mental quality than a physical one, finally. She is chatty and nosy, and this is* her *house.***

***The play takes place in a relatively new house built way out on a country road, with a living room and connecting kitchen, and a cen-***

*ter hall that leads off to the bedrooms. A pull cord in the hall ceiling releases a ladder which leads to the attic. One of these bedrooms opens directly onto the hall, and its entry should be visible to everyone in the audience. It should be, in fact, the focal point of the entire set, and the lighting should make it disappear completely at times and draw the entire set into it at others. It is a point of both threat and promise. It is an ordinary door that opens onto absolute nothingness. That door is the point of all the action, and the utmost care should be given to its design and construction.*

*The living room is cluttered with magazines and needlework catalogues, ashtrays and candy dishes. Examples of Mama's needlework are everywhere—pillows, afghans, and quilts, doilies and rugs, and they are quite nice examples. The house is more comfortable than messy, but there is quite a lot to keep in place here. It is more personal than charming. It is not quaint. Under no circumstances should the set and its dressing make a judgment about the intelligence or taste of Jessie and Mama. It should simply indicate that they are very specific real people who happen to live in a particular part of the country. Heavy accents, which would further distance the audience from Jessie and Mama, are also wrong.*

*The time is the present, with the action beginning about 8:15. Clocks onstage in the kitchen and on a table in the living room should run throughout the performance and be visible to the audience.*

*There will be no intermission.*

*Mama stretches to reach the cupcakes in a cabinet in the kitchen. She can't see them, but she can feel around for them, and she's eager to have one, so she's working pretty hard at it. This may be the most serious exercise Mama ever gets. She finds a cupcake, the coconut-covered, raspberry-and-marshmallow-filled kind known as a snowball, but sees that there's one missing from the package. She calls to Jessie, who is apparently somewhere else in the house.*

MAMA (*unwrapping the cupcake*). Jessie, it's the last snowball, sugar. Put it on the list, O.K.? And we're out of Hershey bars, and where's that peanut brittle? I think maybe Dawson's been in it again. I ought to put a big mirror on the refrigerator door. That'll keep him out of my treats, won't it? You hear me, honey? (*Then more to herself.*) I hate it when the coconut falls off. Why does the coconut fall off?

*Jessie enters from her bedroom, carrying a stack of newspapers.*

JESSIE. We got any old towels?

MAMA. There you are!

JESSIE (*holding a towel that was on the stack of newspapers*). Towels you don't want anymore. (*Picking up Mama's snowball wrapper.*) How about this swimming towel Loretta gave us? Beach towel, that's the name of it. You want it? (*Mama shakes her head no.*)

MAMA. What have you been doing in there?

JESSIE. And a big piece of plastic like a rubber sheet or something. Garbage bags would do if there's enough.

MAMA. Don't go making a big mess, Jessie. It's eight o'clock already.

JESSIE. Maybe an old blanket or towels we got in a soap box sometime?

MAMA. I said don't make a mess. Your hair is black enough, hon.

JESSIE (*continuing to search the kitchen cabinets, finding two or three more towels to add to her stack*). It's not for my hair, Mama. What about some old pillows anywhere, or a foam cushion out of a yard chair would be real good.

MAMA. You haven't forgot what night it is, have you? (*Holding up her fingernails.*) They're all chipped, see? I've been waiting all week, Jess. It's Saturday night, sugar.

JESSIE. I know. I got it on the schedule.

MAMA (*crossing to the living room*). You want me to wash 'em now or are you making your mess first? (*Looking at the snowball.*) We're out of these. Did I say that already?

JESSIE. There's more coming tomorrow. I ordered you a whole case.

MAMA (*checking the* TV Guide). A whole case will go stale, Jessie.

JESSIE. They can go in the freezer till you're ready for them. Where's Daddy's gun?

MAMA. In the attic.

JESSIE. Where in the attic? I looked your whole nap and couldn't find it anywhere.

MAMA. One of his shoeboxes, I think.

JESSIE. Full of shoes. I looked already.

MAMA. Well, you didn't look good enough, then. There's that box from the ones he wore to the hospital. When he died, they told me I could have them back, but I never did like those shoes.

JESSIE (*pulling them out of her pocket*). I found the bullets. They were in an old milk can.

MAMA (*as Jessie starts for the hall*). Dawson took the shotgun, didn't he? Hand me that basket, hon.

JESSIE (*getting the basket for her*). Dawson better not've taken that pistol.

MAMA (*stopping her again*). Now my glasses, please. (*Jessie returns to get the glasses.*) I told him to take those rubber boots, too, but he said they were for fishing. I told him to take up fishing.

*Jessie reaches for the cleaning spray, and cleans Mama's glasses for her.*

JESSIE. He's just too lazy to climb up there, Mama. Or maybe he's just being smart. That floor's not very steady.

MAMA (*getting out a piece of knitting*). It's not a floor at all, hon, it's a board now and then. Measure this for me. I need six inches.

JESSIE (*as she measures*). Dawson could probably use some of those clothes up there. Somebody should have them. You ought to call the Salvation Army before the whole thing falls in on you. Six inches exactly.

MAMA. It's plenty safe! As long as you don't go up there.

JESSIE (*turning to go again*). I'm careful.

MAMA. What do you want the gun for, Jess?

JESSIE (*not returning this time. Opening the ladder in the hall*). Protection. (*She steadies the ladder as Mama talks.*)

MAMA. You take the TV way too serious, hon. I've never seen a criminal in my life. This is way too far to come for what's out here to steal. Never seen a one.

JESSIE (*taking her first step up*). Except for Ricky.

MAMA. Ricky is mixed up. That's not a crime.

JESSIE. Get your hands washed. I'll be right back. And get 'em real dry. You dry your hands till I get back or it's no go, all right?

MAMA. I thought Dawson told you not to go up those stairs.

JESSIE (*going up*). He did.

MAMA. I don't like the idea of a gun, Jess.

JESSIE (*calling down from the attic*). Which shoebox, do you remember?

MAMA. Black.

JESSIE. The box was black?

MAMA. The shoes were black.

JESSIE. That doesn't help much, Mother.

MAMA. I'm not trying to help, sugar. (*No answer.*) We don't have anything anybody'd want, Jessie. I mean, I don't even want what we got, Jessie.

JESSIE. Neither do I. Wash your hands. (*Mama gets up and crosses to stand under the ladder.*)

MAMA. You come down from there before you have a fit. I can't come up and get you, you know.

JESSIE. I know.

MAMA. We'll just hand it over to them when they come, how's that? Whatever they want, the criminals.

JESSIE. That's a good idea, Mama.

MAMA. Ricky will grow out of this and be a real fine boy, Jess. But I have to tell you, I wouldn't want Ricky to know we had a gun in the house.

JESSIE. Here it is. I found it.

MAMA. It's just something Ricky's going through. Maybe he's in with some bad people. He just needs some time, sugar. He'll get back in school or get a job or one day you'll get a call and he'll say he's sorry for all the trouble he's caused and invite you out for supper someplace dress-up.

JESSIE (*coming back down the steps*). Don't worry. It's not for him, it's for me.

MAMA. I didn't think you would shoot your own boy, Jessie. I know you've felt like it, well, we've all felt like shooting somebody, but we don't do it. I just don't think we need . . .

JESSIE (*interrupting*). Your hands aren't washed. Do you want a manicure or not?

MAMA. Yes, I do, but . . .

JESSIE (*crossing to the chair*). Then wash your hands and don't talk to me any more about Ricky. Those two rings he took were the last valuable things *I* had, so now he's started in on other people, door to door. I hope they put him away sometime. I'd turn him in myself if I knew where he was.

MAMA. You don't mean that.

JESSIE. Every word. Wash your hands and that's the last time I'm telling you.

*Jessie sits down with the gun and starts cleaning it, pushing the cylinder out, checking to see that the chambers and barrel are empty, then putting some oil on a small patch of cloth and pushing it through the barrel with the push rod that was in the box. Mama goes to the kitchen and washes her hands, as instructed, trying not to show her concern about the gun.*

MAMA. I shoulda got you to bring down that milk can. Agnes Fletcher sold hers to somebody with a flea market for forty dollars apiece.

JESSIE. I'll go back and get it in a minute. There's a wagon wheel up there, too. There's even a churn. I'll get it all if you want.

MAMA (*coming over, now, taking over now*). What are you doing?

JESSIE. The barrel has to be clean, Mama. Old powder, dust gets in it . . .

MAMA. What for?

JESSIE. I told you.

MAMA (*reaching for the gun*). And I told you, we don't get criminals out here.

JESSIE (*quickly pulling it to her*). And I told you . . . (*Then trying to be calm.*) The gun is for me.

MAMA. Well, you can have it if you want. When I die, you'll get it all, anyway.

JESSIE. I'm going to kill myself, Mama.

MAMA (*returning to the sofa*). Very funny. Very funny.

JESSIE. I am.

MAMA. You are not! Don't even say such a thing, Jessie.

JESSIE. How would you know if I didn't say it? You want it to be a surprise? You're lying there in your bed or maybe you're just brushing your teeth and you hear this . . . noise down the hall?

MAMA. Kill yourself.

JESSIE. Shoot myself. In a couple of hours.

MAMA. It must be time for your medicine.

JESSIE. Took it already.

MAMA. What's the matter with you?

JESSIE. Not a thing. Feel fine.

MAMA. You feel fine. You're just going to kill yourself.

JESSIE. Waited until I felt good enough, in fact.

MAMA. Don't make jokes, Jessie. I'm too old for jokes.

JESSIE. It's not a joke, Mama.

*Mama watches for a moment in silence.*

MAMA. That gun's no good, you know. He broke it right before he died. He dropped it in the mud one day.

JESSIE. Seems O.K. (*She spins the chamber, cocks the pistol, and pulls the trigger. The gun is not yet loaded, so all we hear is the click, but it will definitely work. It's also obvious that Jessie knows her way around a gun. Mama cannot speak.*) I had Cecil's all ready in there, just in case I couldn't find this one, but I'd rather use Daddy's.

MAMA. Those bullets are at least fifteen years old.

JESSIE (*pulling out another box*). These are from last week.

MAMA. Where did you get those?

JESSIE. Feed store Dawson told me about.

MAMA. Dawson!

JESSIE. I told him I was worried about prowlers. He said he thought it was a good idea. He told me what kind to ask for.

MAMA. If he had any idea . . .

JESSIE. He took it as a compliment. He thought I might be taking an interest in things. He got through telling me all about the bullets and then he said we ought to talk like this more often.

MAMA. And where was I while this was going on?

JESSIE. On the phone with Agnes. About the milk can, I guess. Anyway, I asked Dawson if he thought they'd send me some bullets and he said he'd just call for me, because he knew they'd send them if he told them to. And he was absolutely right. Here they are.

MAMA. How could he do that?

JESSIE. Just trying to help, Mama.

MAMA. And then I told you where the gun was.

JESSIE (*smiling, enjoying this joke*). See? Everybody's doing what they can.

MAMA. You told me it was for protection!

JESSIE. It *is!* I'm still doing your nails, though. Want to try that new Chinaberry color?

MAMA. Well, I'm calling Dawson right now. We'll just see what he has to say about this little stunt.

JESSIE. Dawson doesn't have any more to do with this.

MAMA. He's your brother.

JESSIE. And that's all.

MAMA (*stands up, moves toward the phone*). Dawson will put a stop to this. Yes he will. He'll take the gun away.

JESSIE. If you call him, I'll just have to do it before he gets here. Soon as you hang up the phone, I'll just walk in the bedroom and lock the door. Dawson will get here just in time to help you clean up. Go ahead, call him. Then call the police. Then call the funeral home. Then call Loretta and see if *she'll* do your nails.

MAMA. You will not! This is crazy talk, Jessie!

*Mama goes directly to the telephone and starts to dial, but Jessie is fast, coming up behind her and taking the receiver out of her hand, putting it back down.*

JESSIE (*firm and quiet*). I said no. This is private. Dawson is not invited.

MAMA. Just me.

JESSIE. I don't want anybody else over here. Just you and me. If Dawson comes over, it'll make me feel stupid for not doing it ten years ago.

MAMA. I think we better call the doctor. Or how about the ambulance. You like that one driver, I know. What's his name, Timmy? Get you somebody to talk to.

JESSIE (*going back to her chair*). I'm through talking, Mama. You're it. No more.

MAMA. We're just going to sit around like every other night in the world and then you're going to kill yourself? (*Jessie doesn't answer.*) You'll miss. (*Again there is no response.*) You'll just wind up a vegetable. How would you like that? Shoot your ear off? You know what the doctor said about getting excited. You'll cock the pistol and have a fit.

JESSIE. I think I can kill myself, Mama.

MAMA. You're not going to kill yourself, Jessie. You're not even upset! (*Jessie smiles, or laughs quietly, and Mama tries a different approach.*) People don't really kill themselves, Jessie. No, mam, doesn't make sense, unless you're retarded or deranged, and you're as normal as they come, Jessie, for the most part. We're all *afraid* to die.

JESSIE. I'm not, Mama. I'm cold all the time, anyway.

MAMA. That's ridiculous.

JESSIE. It's exactly what I want. It's dark and quiet.

MAMA. So is the back yard, Jessie! Close your eyes. Stuff cotton in your ears. Take a nap! It's quiet in your room. I'll leave the TV off all night.

JESSIE. So quiet I don't know it's quiet. So nobody can get me.

MAMA. You don't know what dead is like. It might not be quiet at all. What if it's like an alarm clock and you can't wake up so you can't shut it off. Ever.

JESSIE. Dead is everybody and everything I ever knew, gone. Dead is dead quiet.

MAMA. It's a sin. You'll go to hell.

JESSIE. Uh-huh.

MAMA. You will!

JESSIE. Jesus was a suicide, if you ask me.

MAMA. You'll go to hell just for saying that. Jessie!

JESSIE (*with genuine surprise*). I didn't know I thought that.

MAMA. Jessie!

*Jessie doesn't answer. She puts the now-loaded gun back in the box and crosses to the kitchen. But Mama is afraid she's headed for the bedroom.*

MAMA (*in a panic*). You can't use my towels! They're my towels. I've had them for a long time. I like my towels.

JESSIE. I asked you if you wanted that swimming towel and you said you didn't.

MAMA. And you can't use your father's gun, either. It's mine now, too. And you can't do it in my house.

JESSIE. Oh, come on.

MAMA. No. You can't do it. I won't let you. The house is in my name.

JESSIE. I have to go in the bedroom and lock the door behind me so they won't arrest you for killing me. They'll probably test your hands for gunpowder, anyway, but you'll pass.

MAMA. Not in my house!

JESSIE. If I'd known you were going to act like this, I wouldn't have told you.

MAMA. How am I supposed to act? Tell you to go ahead? O.K. by me, sugar? Might try it myself. What took you so long?

JESSIE. There's just no point in fighting me over it, that's all. Want some coffee?

MAMA. Your birthday's coming up, Jessie. Don't you want to know what we got you?

JESSIE. You got me dusting powder, Loretta got me a new housecoat, pink probably, and Dawson got me new slippers, too small, but they go with the robe, he'll say. (*Mama cannot speak.*) Right? (*Apparently Jessie is right.*) Be back in a minute.

*Jessie takes the gun box, puts it on top of the stack of towels and garbage bags, and takes them into her bedroom. Mama, alone for a moment, goes to the phone, picks up the receiver, looks toward the bedroom, starts to dial, and then replaces the receiver in its cradle as Jessie walks back into the room. Jessie wonders, silently. They have lived together for so long there is very rarely any reason for one to ask what the other was about to do.*

MAMA. I started to, but I didn't. I didn't call him.

JESSIE. Good. Thank you.

MAMA (*starting over, a new approach*). What's this all about, Jessie?

JESSIE. About?

*Jessie now begins the next task she had "on the schedule," which is refilling all the candy jars, taking the empty papers out of the boxes of chocolates, etc. Mama generally snitches when Jessie does this. Not tonight, though. Nevertheless, Jessie offers.*

MAMA. What did I do?

JESSIE. Nothing. Want a caramel?

MAMA (*ignoring the candy*). You're mad at me.

JESSIE. Not a bit. I am worried about you, but I'm going to do what I can before I go. We're not just going to sit around tonight. I made a list of things.

MAMA. What things?

JESSIE. How the washer works. Things like that.

MAMA. I know how the washer works. You put the clothes in. You put the soap in. You turn it on. You wait.

JESSIE. You do something else. You don't just wait.

MAMA. Whatever else you find to do, you're still mainly waiting. The waiting's the worst part of it. The waiting's what you pay somebody else to do, if you can.

JESSIE (*nodding*). O.K. Where do we keep the soap?

MAMA. I could find it.

JESSIE. See?

MAMA. If you're mad about doing the wash, we can get Loretta to do it.

JESSIE. Oh now, that might be worth staying to see.

MAMA. She'd never in her life, would she?

JESSIE. Nope.

MAMA. What's the matter with her?

JESSIE. She thinks she's better than we are. She's not.

MAMA. Maybe if she didn't wear that yellow all the time.

JESSIE. The washer repair number is on a little card taped to the side of the machine.

MAMA. Loretta doesn't ever have to come over here again. Dawson can just leave her at home when he comes. And we don't ever have to see Dawson either if he bothers you. Does he bother you?

JESSIE. Sure he does. Be sure you clean out the lint tray every time you use the dryer. But don't ever put your house shoes in, it'll melt the soles.

MAMA. What does Dawson do, that bothers you?

JESSIE. He just calls me Jess like he knows who he's talking to. He's always wondering what I do all day. I mean, I wonder that myself, but it's my day, so it's mine to wonder about, not his.

MAMA. Family is just accident, Jessie. It's nothing personal, hon. They don't mean to get on your nerves. They don't even mean to be your family, they just are.

JESSIE. They know too much.

MAMA. About what?

JESSIE. They know things about you, and they learned it before you had a chance to say whether you wanted them to know it or not. They were there when it happened and it don't belong to them, it belongs to you, only they got it. Like my mail-order bra got delivered to their house.

MAMA. By accident!

JESSIE. All the same . . . they opened it. They saw the little rosebuds on it. (*Offering her another candy.*) Chewy mint?

MAMA (*shaking her head no*). What do they know about you? I'll tell them never to talk about it again. Is it Ricky or Cecil or your fits or your hair is falling out or you drink too much coffee or you never go out of the house or what?

JESSIE. I just don't like their talk. The account at the grocery is in Dawson's name when you call. The number's on a whole list of numbers on the back cover of the phone book.

MAMA. Well! Now we're getting somewhere. They're none of them ever setting foot in this house again.

JESSIE. It's not them, Mother. I wouldn't kill myself just to get away from them.

MAMA. You leave the room when they come over, anyway.

JESSIE. I stay as long as I can. Besides, it's you they come to see.

MAMA. That's because I stay in the room when they come.

JESSIE. It's not them.

MAMA. Then what is it?

JESSIE (*checking the list on her note pad*). The grocery won't deliver on Saturday anymore. And if you want your order the same day, you have to call before ten. And they won't deliver less than fifteen dollars' worth. What I do is tell them what we need and tell them to add on cigarettes until it gets to fifteen dollars.

MAMA. It's Ricky. You're trying to get through to him.

JESSIE. If I thought I could do that, I would stay.

MAMA. Make him sorry he hurt you, then. That's it, isn't it?

JESSIE. He's hurt me, I've hurt him. We're about even.

MAMA. You'll be telling him killing is O.K. with you, you know. Want him to start killing next? Nothing wrong with it. Mom did it.

JESSIE. Only a matter of time, anyway, Mama. When the call comes, you let Dawson handle it.

MAMA. Honey, nothing says those calls are always going to be some new trouble he's into. You could get one that he's got a job, that he's getting married, or how about he's joined the army, wouldn't that be nice?

JESSIE. If you call the Sweet Tooth before you call the grocery, that Susie will take your fudge next door to the grocery and it'll all come out together. Be sure you talk to Susie, though. She won't let them put it in the bottom of a sack like that one time, remember?

MAMA. Ricky could come over, you know. What if he calls us?

JESSIE. It's not Ricky, Mama.

MAMA. Or anybody could call us, Jessie.

JESSIE. Not on Saturday night, Mama.

MAMA. Then what is it? Are you sick? If your gums are swelling again, we can get you to the dentist in the morning.

JESSIE. No. Can you order your medicine or do you want Dawson to? I've got a note to him. I'll add that to it if you want.

MAMA. Your eyes don't look right. I thought so yesterday.

JESSIE. That was just the ragweed. I'm not sick.

MAMA. Epilepsy is sick, Jessie.

JESSIE. It won't kill me. (*A pause.*) If it would, I wouldn't have to.

MAMA. You don't *have* to.

JESSIE. No, I don't. That's what I like about it.

MAMA. Well, I won't let you!

JESSIE. It's not up to you.

MAMA. Jessie!

JESSIE. I want to hang a big sign around my neck, like Daddy's on the barn. GONE FISHING.

MAMA. You don't like it here.

JESSIE (*smiling*). Exactly.

MAMA. I meant here in my house.

JESSIE. I know you did.

MAMA. You never should have moved back in here with me. If you'd kept your little house or found another place when Cecil left you, you'd have made some new friends at least. Had a life to lead. Had your own things around you. Give Ricky a place to come see you. You never should've come here.

JESSIE. Maybe.

MAMA. But I didn't force you, did I?

JESSIE. If it was a mistake, we made it together. You took me in. I appreciate that.

MAMA. You didn't have any business being by yourself right then, but I can see how you might want a place of your own. A grown woman should . . .

JESSIE. Mama . . . I'm just not having a very good time and I don't have any reason to think it'll get anything but worse. I'm tired. I'm hurt. I'm sad. I feel used.

MAMA. Tired of what?

JESSIE. It all.

MAMA. What does that mean?

JESSIE. I can't say it any better.

MAMA. Well, you'll have to say it better because I'm not letting you alone till you do. What were those other things? Hurt . . . (*Before Jessie can answer.*) You had this all ready to say to me, didn't you? Did you write this down? How long have you been thinking about this?

JESSIE. Off and on, ten years. On all the time, since Christmas.

MAMA. What happened at Christmas?

JESSIE. Nothing.

MAMA. So why Christmas?

JESSIE. That's it. On the nose.

*A pause. Mama knows exactly what Jessie means. She was there, too, after all.*

JESSIE (*putting the candy sacks away*). See where all this is? Red hots up front, sour balls and horehound mixed together in this one sack. New packages of toffee and licorice right in back there.

MAMA. Go back to your list. You're hurt by what?

JESSIE (*Mama knows perfectly well*). Mama . . .

MAMA. O.K. Sad about what? There's nothing real sad going on right now. If it was after your divorce or something, that would make sense.

JESSIE (*looking at her list, then opening the drawer*). Now, this drawer has everything in it that there's no better place for. Extension cords, batteries for the radio, extra lighters, sandpaper, masking tape, Elmer's glue, thumbtacks, that kind of stuff. The mousetraps are under the sink, but you call Dawson if you've got one and let him do it.

MAMA. Sad about what?

JESSIE. The way things are.

MAMA. Not good enough. What things?

JESSIE. Oh, everything from you and me to Red China.

MAMA. I think we can leave the Chinese out of this.

JESSIE (*crosses back into the living room*). There's extra light bulbs in a box in the hall closet. And we've got a couple of packages of fuses in the fuse box. There's candles and matches in the top of the broom closet, but if the lights go out, just call Dawson and sit tight. But don't open the refrigerator door. Things will stay cool in there as long as you keep the door shut.

MAMA. I asked you a question.

JESSIE. I read the paper. I don't like how things are. And they're not any better out there than they are in here.

MAMA. If you're doing this because of the newspapers, I can sure fix that!

JESSIE. There's just more of it on TV.

MAMA (*kicking the television set*). Take it out, then!

JESSIE. You wouldn't do that.

MAMA. Watch me.

JESSIE. What would you do all day?

MAMA (*desperately*). Sing. (*Jessie laughs.*) I would, too. You want to watch? I'll sing till morning to keep you alive, Jessie, please!

JESSIE. No. (*Then affectionately.*) It's a funny idea, though. What do you sing?

MAMA (*has no idea how to answer this*). We've got a good life here!

JESSIE (*going back into the kitchen*). I called this morning and canceled the papers, except for Sunday, for your puzzles; you'll still get that one.

MAMA. Let's get another dog, Jessie! You liked a big dog, now, didn't you? That King dog, didn't you?

JESSIE (*washing her hands*). I did like that King dog, yes.

MAMA. I'm so dumb. He's the one run under the tractor.

JESSIE. That makes him dumb, not you.

MAMA. For bringing it up.

JESSIE. It's O.K. Handi-Wipes and sponges under the sink.

MAMA. We could get a new dog and keep him in the house. Dogs are cheap!

JESSIE (*getting big pill jars out of the cabinet*). No.

MAMA. Something for you to take care of.

JESSIE. I've had you, Mama.

MAMA (*frantically starting to fill pill bottles*). You do too much for me. I can fill pill bottles all day, Jessie, and change the shelf paper and wash the floor when I get through. You just watch me. You don't have to do another thing in this house if you don't want to. You don't have to take care of me, Jessie.

JESSIE. I know that. You've just been letting me do it so I'll have something to do, haven't you?

MAMA (*realizing this was a mistake*). I don't do it as well as you. I just meant if it tires you out or makes you feel used . . .

JESSIE. Mama, I know you used to ride the bus. Riding the bus and it's hot and bumpy and crowded and too noisy and more than anything in the world you want to get off and the only reason in the world you don't get off is it's still fifty blocks from where you're going? Well, I can get off right now if I want to, because even if I ride fifty more years and get off then, it's the same place when I step down to it. Whenever I feel like it, I can get off. As soon as I've had enough, it's my stop. I've had enough.

MAMA. You're feeling sorry for yourself!

JESSIE. The plumber's helper is under the sink, too.

MAMA. You're not having a good time! Whoever promised you a good time? Do you think I've had a good time?

JESSIE. I think you're pretty happy, yeah. You have things you like to do.

MAMA. Like what?

JESSIE. Like crochet.

MAMA. I'll teach you to crochet.

JESSIE. I can't do any of that nice work, Mama.

MAMA. Good time don't come looking for you, Jessie. You could work some puzzles or put in a garden or go to the store. Let's call a taxi and go to the A&P!

JESSIE. I shopped you up for about two weeks already. You're not going to need toilet paper till Thanksgiving.

MAMA (*interrupting*). You're acting like some little brat, Jessie. You're mad and everybody's boring and you don't have anything to do and you don't like me and you don't like going out and you don't like staying in and you never talk on the phone and you don't watch TV and you're miserable and it's your own sweet fault.

JESSIE. And it's time I did something about it.

MAMA. Not something like killing yourself. Something like . . . buying us all new dishes! I'd like that. Or maybe the doctor would let you get a driver's license now, or I know what let's do right this minute, let's rearrange the furniture.

JESSIE. I'll do that. If you want. I always thought if the TV was somewhere else, you wouldn't get such a glare on it during the day. I'll do whatever you want before I go.

MAMA (*badly frightened by those words*). You could get a job!

JESSIE. I took that telephone sales job and I didn't even make enough money to pay the phone bill, and I tried to work at the gift shop at the hospital and they said I made people real uncomfortable smiling at them the way I did.

MAMA. You could keep books. You kept your dad's books.

JESSIE. But nobody ever checked them.

MAMA. When he died, they checked them.

JESSIE. And that's when they took the books away from me.

MAMA. That's because without him there wasn't any business, Jessie!

JESSIE (*putting the pill bottles away*). You know I couldn't work. I can't do anything. I've never been around people my whole life except when I went to the hospital. I could have a seizure any time. What good would a job do? The kind of job I could get would make me feel worse.

MAMA. Jessie!

JESSIE. It's true!

MAMA. It's what you think is true!

JESSIE (*struck by the clarity of that*). That's right. It's what I think is true.

MAMA (*hysterically*). But I can't do anything about that!

JESSIE (*quietly*). No. You can't. (*Mama slumps, if not physically, at least emotionally.*) And I can't do anything either, about my life, to change it, make it better, make me feel better about it. Like it better, make it work. But I can stop it. Shut it down, turn it off like the radio when there's nothing on I want to listen to. It's all I really have that belongs to me and I'm going to say what happens to it. And it's going to stop. And I'm going to stop it. So. Let's just have a good time.

MAMA. Have a good time.

JESSIE. We can't go on fussing all night. I mean, I could ask you things I always wanted to know and you could make me some hot chocolate. The old way.

MAMA (*in despair*). It takes cocoa, Jessie.

JESSIE (*gets it out of the cabinet*). I bought cocoa, Mama. And I'd like to have a caramel apple and do your nails.

MAMA. You didn't eat a bite of supper.

JESSIE. Does that mean I can't have a caramel apple?

MAMA. Of course not. I mean . . . (*Smiling a little.*) Of course you can have a caramel apple.

JESSIE. I thought I could.

MAMA. I make the best caramel apples in the world.

JESSIE. I know you do.

MAMA. Or used to. And you don't get cocoa like mine anywhere anymore.

JESSIE. It takes time, I know, but . . .

MAMA. The salt is the trick.

JESSIE. Trouble and everything.

MAMA (*backing away toward the stove*). It's no trouble. What trouble? You put it in the pan and stir it up. All right. Fine. Caramel apples. Cocoa. O.K.

*Jessie walks to the counter to retrieve her cigarettes as Mama looks for the right pan. There are brief near-smiles, and maybe Mama clears her throat. We have a truce, for the moment. A genuine but nevertheless uneasy one. Jessie, who has been in constant motion since the beginning, now seems content to sit.*

*Mama starts looking for a pan to make the cocoa, getting out all the pans in the cabinets in the process. It looks like she's making a mess on purpose so Jessie will have to put them all away again. Mama is buying time, or trying to, and entertaining.*

JESSIE. You talk to Agnes today?

MAMA. She's calling me from a pay phone this week. God only knows why. She has a perfectly good Trimline at home.

JESSIE (*laughing*). Well, how is she?

MAMA. How is she every day, Jessie? Nuts.

JESSIE. Is she really crazy or just silly?

MAMA. No, she's really crazy. She was probably using the pay phone because she had another little fire problem at home.

JESSIE. Mother . . .

MAMA. I'm serious! Agnes Fletcher's burned down every house she ever lived in. Eight fires, and she's due for a new one any day now.

JESSIE (*laughing*). No!

MAMA. Wouldn't surprise me a bit.

JESSIE (*laughing*). Why didn't you tell me this before? Why isn't she locked up somewhere?

MAMA. 'Cause nobody ever got hurt, I guess. Agnes woke everybody up to watch the fires as soon as she set 'em. One time she set out porch chairs and served lemonade.

JESSIE (*shaking her head*). Real lemonade?

MAMA. The houses they lived in, you knew they were going to fall down anyway, so why wait for it, is all I could ever make out about it. Agnes likes a feeling of accomplishment.

JESSIE. Good for her.

MAMA (*finding the pan she wants*). Why are you asking about Agnes? One cup or two?

JESSIE. One. She's your friend. No marshmallows.

MAMA (*getting the milk, etc.*). You have to have marshmallows. That's the old way, Jess. Two or three? Three is better.

JESSIE. Three, then. Her whole house burns up? Her clothes and pillows and everything? I'm not sure I believe this.

MAMA. When she was a girl, Jess, not now. Long time ago. But she's still got it in her, I'm sure of it.

JESSIE. She wouldn't burn her house down now. Where would she go? She can't get Buster to build her a new one, he's dead. How could she burn it up?

MAMA. Be exciting, though, if she did. You never know.

JESSIE. You do too know, Mama. She wouldn't do it.

MAMA (*forced to admit, but reluctant*). I guess not.

JESSIE. What else? Why does she wear all those whistles around her neck?

MAMA. Why does she have a house full of birds?

JESSIE. I didn't know she had a house full of birds!

MAMA. Well, she does. And she says they just follow her home. Well, I know for a fact she's still paying on the last parrot she bought. You gotta keep your life filled up, she says. She says a lot of stupid things. (*Jessie laughs, Mama continues, convinced she's getting somewhere.*) It's all that okra she eats. You can't just willy-nilly eat okra two meals a day and expect to get away with it. Made her crazy.

JESSIE. She really eats okra twice a day? Where does she get it in the winter?

MAMA. Well, she eats it a lot. Maybe not two meals, but . . .

JESSIE. More than the average person.

MAMA (*beginning to get irritated*). I don't know how much okra the average person eats.

JESSIE. Do you know how much okra Agnes eats?

MAMA. No.

JESSIE. How many birds does she have?

MAMA. Two.

JESSIE. Then what are the whistles for?

MAMA. They're not real whistles. Just little plastic ones on a necklace she won playing Bingo, and I only told you about it because I thought I might get a laugh out of you for once even if it wasn't the truth, Jessie. Things don't have to be true to talk about 'em, you know.

JESSIE. Why won't she come over here?

*Mama is suddenly quiet, but the cocoa and milk are in the pan now, so she lights the stove and starts stirring.*

MAMA. Well now, what a good idea. We should've had more cocoa. Cocoa is perfect.

JESSIE. Except you don't like milk.

MAMA (*another attempt, but not as energetic*). I hate milk. Coats your throat as bad as okra. Something just downright disgusting about it.

JESSIE. It's because of me, isn't it?

MAMA. No, Jess.

JESSIE. Yes, Mama.

MAMA. O.K. Yes, then, but she's crazy. She's as crazy as they come. She's a lunatic.

JESSIE. What is it exactly? Did I say something, sometime? Or did she see me have a fit and's afraid I might have another one if she came over, or what?

MAMA. I guess.

JESSIE. You guess what? What's she ever said? She must've given you some reason.

MAMA. Your hands are cold.

JESSIE. What difference does that make?

MAMA. "Like a corpse," she says, "and I'm gonna be one soon enough as it is."

JESSIE. That's crazy.

MAMA. That's Agnes. "Jessie's shook the hand of death and I can't take the chance it's catching, Thelma, so I ain't comin' over, and you can understand or not, but I ain't comin'. I'll come up the driveway, but that's as far as I go."

JESSIE (*laughing, relieved*). I thought she didn't like me! She's scared of me! How about that! Scared of me.

MAMA. I could make her come over here, Jessie. I could call her up right now and she could bring the birds and come visit. I didn't know you ever thought about her at all. I'll tell her she just has to come and she'll come, all right. She owes me one.

JESSIE. No, that's all right. I just wondered about it. When I'm in the hospital, does she come over here?

MAMA. Her kitchen is just a tiny thing. When she comes over here, she feels like . . . (*Toning it down a little.*) Well, we all like a change of scene, don't we?

JESSIE (*playing along*). Sure we do. Plus there's no birds diving around.

MAMA. I hate those birds. She says I don't understand them. What's there to understand about birds?

JESSIE. Why Agnes likes them, for one thing. Why they stay with her when they could be outside with the other birds. What their singing means. How they fly. What they think Agnes is.

MAMA. Why do you have to know so much about things, Jessie? There's just not that much *to* things that I could ever see.

JESSIE. That you could ever *tell*, you mean. You didn't have to lie to me about Agnes.

MAMA. I didn't lie. You never asked before!

JESSIE. You lied about setting fire to all those houses and about how many birds she has and how much okra she eats and why she won't come over here. If I have to keep dragging the truth out of you, this is going to take all night.

MAMA. That's fine with me. I'm not a bit sleepy.

JESSIE. Mama . . .

MAMA. All right. Ask me whatever you want. Here.

*They come to an awkward stop, as the cocoa is ready and Mama pours it into the cups Jessie has set on the table.*

JESSIE (*as Mama takes her first sip*). Did you love Daddy?

MAMA. No.

JESSIE (*pleased that Mama understands the rules better now*). I didn't think so. Were you really fifteen when you married him?

MAMA. The way he told it? I'm sitting in the mud, he comes along, drags me in the kitchen, "She's been there ever since"?

JESSIE. Yes.

MAMA. No. It was a big fat lie, the whole thing. He just thought it was funnier that way. God, this milk in here.

JESSIE. The cocoa helps.

MAMA (*pleased that they agree on this, at least*). Not enough, though, does it? You can still taste it, can't you?

JESSIE. Yeah, it's pretty bad. I thought it was my memory that was bad, but it's not. It's the milk, all right.

MAMA. It's a real waste of chocolate. You don't have to finish it.

JESSIE (*putting her cup down*). Thanks, though.

MAMA. I should've known not to make it. I knew you wouldn't like it. You never did like it.

JESSIE. You didn't ever love him, or he did something and you stopped loving him, or what?

MAMA. He felt sorry for me. He wanted a plain country woman and that's what he married, and then he held it against me the rest of my life like I was supposed to change and surprise him somehow. Like I remember this one day he was standing on the porch and I told him to get a shirt on and he went in and got one and then he said, real peaceful, but to the point, "You're right, Thelma. If God had meant for people to go around without any clothes on, they'd have been born that way."

JESSIE (*sees Mama's hurt*). He didn't mean anything by that, Mama.

MAMA. He never said a word he didn't have to, Jessie. That was probably all he'd said to me all day, Jessie. So if he said it, there was something to it, but I never did figure that one out. What did that mean?

JESSIE. I don't know. I liked him better than you did, but I didn't know him any better.

MAMA. How could I love him, Jessie. I didn't have a thing he wanted. (*Jessie doesn't answer.*) He got his share, though. You loved him enough for both of us. You followed him around like some . . . Jessie, all the man ever did was farm and sit . . . and try to think of somebody to sell the farm to.

JESSIE. Or make me a boyfriend out of pipe cleaners and sit back and smile like the stick man was about to dance and wasn't I going to get a kick out of that. Or sit up with a sick cow all night and leave me a chain of sleepy stick elephants on my bed in the morning.

MAMA. Or just sit.

JESSIE. I liked him sitting. Big old faded blue man in the chair. Quiet.

MAMA. Agnes gets more talk out of her birds than I got from the two of you. He could've had that GONE FISHING sign around his neck in that chair. I saw him stare off at the water. I saw him look at the weather rolling in. I got where I could practically see that boat myself. But you, you knew what he was thinking about and you're going to tell me.

JESSIE. I don't know, Mama! His life, I guess. His corn. His boots. Us. Things. You know.

MAMA. No, I don't know, Jessie! You had those quiet little conversations after supper every night. What were you whispering about?

JESSIE. We weren't whispering, you were just across the room.

MAMA. What did you talk about?

JESSIE. We talked about why black socks are warmer than blue socks. Is that something to go tell Mother? You were just jealous because I'd rather talk to him than wash the dishes with you.

MAMA. I was jealous because you'd rather talk to him than anything! (*Jessie reaches across the table for the small clock and starts to wind it.*) If I had died instead of him, he wouldn't have taken you in like I did.

JESSIE. I wouldn't have expected him to.

MAMA. Then what would you have done?

JESSIE. Come visit.

MAMA. Oh, I see. He died and left you stuck with me and you're mad about it.

JESSIE (*getting up from the table*). Not anymore. He didn't mean to. I didn't have to come here. We've been through this.

MAMA. He felt sorry for you, too, Jessie, don't kid yourself about that. He said you were a runt and he said it from the day you were born and he said you didn't have a chance.

JESSIE (*getting the canister of sugar and starting to refill the sugar bowl*). I know he loved me.

MAMA. What if he did? It didn't change anything.

JESSIE. It didn't have to. I miss him.

MAMA. He never really went fishing, you know. Never once. His tackle box was full of chewing tobacco and all he ever did was drive out to the lake and sit in his car. Dawson told me. And Bennie at the bait shop, he told Dawson. They all laughed about it. And he'd come back from fishing and all he'd have to show for it was a . . . a whole pipe cleaner *family*—chickens, pigs, a dog with a bad leg—it was creepy strange. It made me sick to look at them and I hid his pipe cleaners a couple of times but he always had more somewhere.

JESSIE. I thought it might be better for you after he died. You'd get interested in things. Breathe better. Change somehow.

MAMA. Into what? The Queen? A clerk in a shoe store? Why should I? Because he said to? Because you said to? (*Jessie shakes her head.*) Well I wasn't here for his entertainment and I'm not here for yours either, Jessie. I don't know what I'm here for, but then I don't think about it. (*Realizing what all this means.*) But I bet you wouldn't be killing yourself if he were still alive. That's a fine thing to figure out, isn't it?

JESSIE (*filling the honey jar now*). That's not true.

MAMA. Oh no? Then what were you asking about him for? Why did you want to know if I loved him?

JESSIE. I didn't think you did, that's all.

MAMA. Fine then. You were right. Do you feel better now?

JESSIE (*cleaning the honey jar carefully*). It feels good to be right about it.

MAMA. It didn't matter whether I loved him. It didn't matter to me and it didn't matter to him. And it didn't mean we didn't get along. It wasn't important. We didn't talk about it. (*Sweeping the pots off the cabinet.*) Take all these pots out to the porch!

JESSIE. What for?

MAMA. Just leave me this one pan. (*She jerks the silverware drawer open.*) Get me one knife, one fork, one big spoon, and the can opener, and put them out where I can get them. (*Starts throwing knives and forks in one of the pans.*)

JESSIE. Don't do that! I just straightened that drawer!

MAMA (*throwing the pan in the sink*). And throw out all the plates and cups. I'll use paper. Loretta can have what she wants and Dawson can sell the rest.

JESSIE (*calmly*). What are you doing?

MAMA. I'm not going to cook. I never liked it, anyway. I like candy. Wrapped in plastic or coming in sacks. And tuna. I'll eat tuna, thank you.

JESSIE (*taking the pan out of the sink*). What if you want to make apple butter? You can't make apple butter in that little pan. What if you leave carrots on cooking and burn up that pan?

MAMA. I don't like carrots.

JESSIE. What if the strawberries are good this year and you want to go picking with Agnes.

MAMA. I'll tell her to bring a pan. You said you would do whatever I wanted! I don't want a bunch of pans cluttering up my cabinets I can't get down to, anyway. Throw them out. Every last one.

JESSIE (*gathering up the pots*). I'm putting them all back in. I'm not taking them to the porch. If you want them, they'll be here. You'll bend down and get them, like you got the one for the cocoa. And if somebody else comes over here to cook, they'll have something to cook in, and that's the end of it!

MAMA. Who's going to come cook here?

JESSIE. Agnes.

MAMA. In my pots. Not on your life.

JESSIE. There's no reason why the two of you couldn't just live here together. Be cheaper for both of you and somebody to talk to. And if the birds bothered you, well, one day when Agnes is out getting her hair done, you could take them all for a walk!

MAMA (*as Jessie straightens the silverware*). So that's why you're pestering me about Agnes. You think you can rest easy if you get me a new babysitter? Well, I don't want to live with Agnes. I barely want to talk with Agnes. She's just around. We go back, that's all. I'm not letting Agnes near this place. You don't get off as easy as that, child.

JESSIE. O.K., then. It's just something to think about.

MAMA. I don't like things to think about. I like things to go on.

JESSIE (*closing the silverware drawer*). I want to know what Daddy said to you the night he died. You came storming out of his room and said I could wait it out with him if I wanted to, but you were going to watch *Gunsmoke.* What did he say to you?

MAMA. He didn't have *anything* to say to me, Jessie. That's why I left. He didn't say a thing. It was his last chance not to talk to me and he took full advantage of it.

JESSIE (*after a moment*). I'm sorry you didn't love him. Sorry for you, I mean. He seemed like a nice man.

MAMA (*as Jessie walks to the refrigerator*). Ready for your apple now?

JESSIE. Soon as I'm through here, Mama.

MAMA. You won't like the apple, either. It'll be just like the cocoa. You never liked eating at all, did you? Any of it! What have you been living on all these years, toothpaste?

JESSIE (*as she starts to clean out the refrigerator*). Now, you know the milkman comes on Wednesdays and Saturdays, and he leaves the order blank in an egg box, and you give the bills to Dawson once a month.

MAMA. Do they still make that orangeade?

JESSIE. It's not orangeade, it's just orange.

MAMA. I'm going to get some. I thought they stopped making it. You just stopped ordering it.

JESSIE. You should drink milk.

MAMA. Not anymore, I'm not. That hot chocolate was the last. Hooray.

JESSIE (*getting the garbage can from under the sink*). I told them to keep delivering a quart a week no matter what you said. I told them you'd run out of Cokes and you'd have to drink it. I told them I knew you wouldn't pour it on the ground . . .

MAMA (*finishing her sentence*). And you told them you weren't going to be ordering anymore?

JESSIE. I told them I was taking a little holiday and to look after you.

MAMA. And they didn't think something was funny about that? You who doesn't go to the front steps? You, who only sees the driveway looking down from a stretcher passed out cold?

JESSIE (*enjoying this, but not laughing*). They said it was about time, but why didn't I take you with me? And I said I didn't think you'd want to go, and they said, "Yeah, everybody's got their own idea of vacation."

MAMA. I guess you think that's funny.

JESSIE (*pulling jars out of the refrigerator*). You know there never was any reason to call the ambulance for me. All they ever did for me in the emergency room was let me wake up. I could've done that here. Now, I'll just call them out and you say yes or no. I know you like pickles. Ketchup?

MAMA. Keep it.

JESSIE. We've had this since last Fourth of July.

MAMA. Keep the ketchup. Keep it all.

JESSIE. Are you going to drink ketchup from the bottle or what? How can you want your food and not want your pots to cook it in? This stuff will all spoil in here, Mother.

MAMA. Nothing I ever did was good enough for you and I want to know why.

JESSIE. That's not true.

MAMA. And I want to know why you've lived here this long feeling the way you do.

JESSIE. You have no earthly idea how I feel.

MAMA. Well, how could I? You're real far back there, Jessie.

JESSIE. Back where?

MAMA. What's it like over there, where you are? Do people always say the right thing or get whatever they want, or what?

JESSIE. What are you talking about?

MAMA. Why do you read the newspaper? Why don't you wear that sweater I made for you? Do you remember how I used to look, or am I just any old woman now? When you have a fit, do you see stars or what? How did you fall off the horse, really? Why did Cecil leave you? Where did you put my old glasses?

JESSIE (*stunned by Mama's intensity*). They're in the bottom drawer of your dresser in an old Milk of Magnesia box. Cecil left me because he made me choose between him and smoking.

MAMA. Jessie, I know he wasn't that dumb.

JESSIE. I never understood why he hated it so much when it's so good. Smoking is the only thing I know that's always just what you think it's going to be. Just like it was the last time, right there when you want it and real quiet.

MAMA. Your fits made him sick and you know it.

JESSIE. Say seizures, not fits. Seizures.

MAMA. It's the same thing. A seizure in the hospital is a fit at home.

JESSIE. They didn't bother him at all. Except he did feel responsible for it. It *was* his idea to go horseback riding that day. It was his idea I could do *anything* if I just made up my mind to. I fell off the horse because I didn't know how to hold on. Cecil left for pretty much the same reason.

MAMA. He had a girl, Jessie. I walked right in on them in the toolshed.

JESSIE (*after a moment*). O.K. That's fair. (*Lighting another cigarette.*) Was she very pretty?

MAMA. She was Agnes's girl, Carlene. Judge for yourself.

JESSIE (*as she walks to the living room*). I guess you and Agnes had a good talk about that, huh?

MAMA. I never thought he was good enough for you. They moved here from Tennessee, you know.

JESSIE. What are you talking about? You liked him better than I did. You flirted him out here to build your porch or I'd never even met him at all. You thought maybe he'd help you out around the place, come in and get some coffee and talk to you. God knows what you thought. All that curly hair.

MAMA. He's the best carpenter I ever saw. That little house of yours will still be standing at the end of the world, Jessie.

JESSIE. You didn't need a porch, Mama.

MAMA. All right! I wanted you to have a husband.

JESSIE. And I couldn't get one on my own, of course.

MAMA. How were you going to get a husband never opening your mouth to a living soul?

JESSIE. So I was quiet about it, so what?

MAMA. So I should have let you just sit here? Sit like your daddy? Sit here?

JESSIE. Maybe.

MAMA. Well, I didn't think so.

JESSIE. Well, what did you know?

MAMA. I never said I knew much. How was I supposed to learn anything living out here? I didn't know enough to do half the things I did in my life. Things happen. You do what you can about them and you see what happens next. I married you off to the wrong man, I admit that. So I took you in when he left, I'm sorry.

JESSIE. He wasn't the wrong man.

MAMA. He didn't love you, Jessie, or he wouldn't have left.

JESSIE. He wasn't the wrong man, Mama. I loved Cecil so much. And I tried to get more exercise and I tried to stay awake. I tried to learn to ride a horse. And I tried to stay outside with him, but he always knew I was trying, so it didn't work.

MAMA. He was a selfish man. He told me once he hated to see people move into his houses after he built them. He knew they'd mess them up.

JESSIE. I loved that bridge he built over the creek in back of the house. It didn't have to be anything special, a couple of boards would have been just fine, but he used that yellow pine and rubbed it so smooth . . .

MAMA. He had responsibilities here. He had a wife and son here and he failed you.

JESSIE. Or that baby bed he built for Ricky. I told him he didn't have to spend so much time on it, but he said it had to last, and the thing ended up weighing two hundred pounds and I couldn't move it. I said, "How long does a baby bed have to last, anyway?" But maybe he thought if it was strong enough, it might keep Ricky a baby.

MAMA. Ricky is too much like Cecil.

JESSIE. He is not. Ricky is as much like me as it's possible for any human to be. We even wear the same size pants. These are his, I think.

MAMA. That's just the same size. That's not you're the same person.

JESSIE. I see it on his face. I hear it when he talks. We look out at the world and we see the same thing: Not Fair. And the only difference between us is Ricky's out there trying to get even. And he knows not to trust anybody and he got it straight from me. And he knows not to try to get work, and guess where he got that. He walks around like there's loose boards in the floor, and you know who laid that floor, I did.

MAMA. Ricky isn't through yet. You don't know how he'll turn out!

JESSIE (*going back to the kitchen*). Yes I do and so did Cecil. Ricky is the two of us together for all time in too small a space. And we're tearing each other apart, like always, inside that boy, and if you don't see it, then you're just blind.

MAMA. Give him time, Jess.

JESSIE. Oh, he'll have plenty of that. Five years for forgery, ten years for armed assault . . .

MAMA (*furious*). Stop that! (*Then pleading.*) Jessie, Cecil might be ready to try it again, honey, that happens sometimes. Go downtown. Find him. Talk to him. He didn't know what he had in you. Maybe he sees things different now, but you're not going to know that till you see him. Or call him up! Right now! He might be home.

JESSIE. And say what? Nothing's changed, Cecil, I'd just like to look at you, if you don't mind? No. He loved me, Mama. He just didn't know how things fall down around me like they do. I think he did the right thing. He gave himself another chance, that's all. But I did beg him to take me with him. I did tell him I would leave Ricky and you and everything I loved out here if only he would take me with him, but he couldn't and I understood that. (*Pause.*) I wrote that note I showed you. I wrote it. Not Cecil. I said "I'm sorry, Jessie, I can't fix it all for you." I said I'd always love me, not Cecil. But that's how he felt.

MAMA. Then he should've taken you with him!

JESSIE (*picking up the garbage bag she has filled*). Mama, you don't pack your garbage when you move.

MAMA. You will not call yourself garbage, Jessie.

JESSIE (*taking the bag to the big garbage can near the back door*). Just a way of saying it, Mama. Thinking about my list, that's all. (*Opening the can, putting the garbage in, then securing the lid.*) Well, a little more than that. I was trying to say it's all right that Cecil left. It was . . . a relief in a way. I never was what he wanted to see, so it was better when he wasn't looking at me all the time.

MAMA. I'll make your apple now.

JESSIE. No thanks. You get the manicure stuff and I'll be right there.

*Jessie ties up the big garbage bag in the can and replaces the small garbage bag under the sink, all the time trying desperately to regain her calm. Mama watches, from a distance, her hand reaching unconsciously for the phone. Then she has a better idea. Or rather she thinks of the only other thing left and is willing to try it. Maybe she is even convinced it will work.*

MAMA. Jessie, I think your daddy had little . . .

JESSIE (*interrupting her*). Garbage night is Tuesday. Put it out as late as you can. The Davis's dogs get in it if you don't. (*Replacing the garbage bag in the can under the sink.*) And keep ordering the heavy black bags. It doesn't pay to buy the cheap ones. And I've got all the ties here with the hammers and all. Take them out of the box as soon as you open a new one and put them in this drawer. They'll get lost if you don't, and rubber bands or something else won't work.

MAMA. I think your daddy had fits, too. I think he sat in his chair and had little fits. I read this a long time ago in a magazine, how little fits go, just little blackouts where maybe their eyes don't even close and people just call them "thinking spells."

JESSIE (*getting the slipcover out of the laundry basket*). I don't think you want this manicure we've been looking forward to. I washed this cover for the sofa, but it'll take both of us to get it back on.

MAMA. I watched his eyes. I know that's what it was. The magazine said some people don't even know they've had one.

JESSIE. Daddy would've known if he'd had fits, Mama.

MAMA. The lady in this story had kept track of hers and she'd had eighty thousand of them in the last eleven years.

JESSIE. Next time you wash this cover, it'll dry better if you put it on wet.

MAMA. Jessie, listen to what I'm telling you. This lady had anywhere between five and five hundred fits a day and they lasted maybe fifteen seconds apiece, so that out of her life, she'd only lost about two weeks altogether, and she had a full-time secretary job and an IQ of 120.

JESSIE (*amused by Mama's approach*). You want to talk about the fits, is that it?

MAMA. Yes. I do. I want to say . . .

JESSIE (*interrupting*). Most of the time I wouldn't even know I'd had one, except I wake up with different clothes on, feeling like I've been run over. Sometimes I feel my head start to turn around or hear myself scream. And sometimes there *is* this dizzy stupid feeling a little before it, but if the TV's on, well, it's easy to miss.

*As Jessie and Mama replace the slipcover on the sofa and the afghan on the chair, the physical struggle somehow mirrors the emotional one in the conversation.*

MAMA. I can tell when you're about to have one. Your eyes get this big! But, Jessie, you haven't . . .

JESSIE (*taking charge of this*). What do they look like? The seizures.

MAMA (*reluctant*). Different each time, Jess.

JESSIE. O.K. Pick one, then. A good one. I think I want to know now.

MAMA. There's not much to tell. You just . . . crumple, in a heap, like a puppet and somebody cut the strings all at once, or like the firing squad in some Mexican movie, you just slide down the wall, you know. You don't know what happens? How can you not know what happens?

JESSIE. I'm busy.

MAMA. That's not funny.

JESSIE. I'm not laughing. My head turns around and I fall down and then what?

MAMA. Well, your chest squeezes in and out, and you sound like you're gagging, sucking air in and out like you can't breathe.

JESSIE. Do it for me. Make the sound for me.

MAMA. I will not. It's awful-sounding.

JESSIE. Yeah. It felt like it might be. What's next?

MAMA. Your mouth bites down and I have to get your tongue out of the way fast, so you don't bite yourself.

JESSIE. Or you. I bite you, too, don't I?

MAMA. You got me once real good. I had to get a tetanus! But I know what to watch for now. And then you turn blue and the jerks start up. Like I'm standing there poking you with a cattle prod or you're sticking your finger in a light socket as fast as you can . . .

JESSIE. Foaming like a mad dog the whole time.

MAMA. It's bubbling, Jess, not foam like the washer overflowed, for God's sake; it's bubbling like a baby spitting up. I go get a wet washcloth, that's all. And then the jerks slow down and you wet yourself and it's over. Two minutes tops.

JESSIE. How do I get to bed?

MAMA. How do you think?

JESSIE. I'm too heavy for you now. How do you do it?

MAMA. I call Dawson. But I get you cleaned up before he gets here and I make him leave before you wake up.

JESSIE. You could just leave me on the floor.

MAMA. I want you to wake up someplace nice, O.K.? (*Then making a real effort.*) But, Jessie, and this is the reason I even brought this up! You haven't had a seizure for a solid year. A whole year, do you realize that?

JESSIE. Yeah, the phenobarb's about right now, I guess.

MAMA. You bet it is. You might never have another one, ever! You might be through with it for all time!

JESSIE. Could be.

MAMA. You are. I know you are!

JESSIE. I sure am feeling good. I really am. The double vision's gone and my gums aren't swelling. No rashes or anything. I'm feeling as good as I ever felt in my life. I'm even feeling like worrying or getting mad and I'm not afraid it will start a fit if I do, I just go ahead.

MAMA. Of course you do! You can even scream at me, if you want to. I can take it. You don't have to act like you're just visiting here, Jessie. This is your house, too.

JESSIE. The best part is, my memory's back.

MAMA. Your memory's always been good. When couldn't you remember things? You're always reminding me what . .

JESSIE. Because I've made lists for everything. But now I remember what things mean on my lists. I see "dish towels," and I used to wonder whether I was supposed to wash them, buy them, or look for them because I wouldn't remember where I put them after I washed them, but now I know it means wrap them up, they're a present for Loretta's birthday.

MAMA (*finished with the sofa now*). You used to go looking for your lists, too, I've noticed that. You always know where they are now! (*Then suddenly worried.*) Loretta's birthday isn't coming up, is it?

JESSIE. I made a list of all the birthdays for you. I even put yours on it. (*A small smile.*) So you can call Loretta and remind her.

MAMA. Let's take Loretta to Howard Johnson's and have those fried clams. I *know* you love that clam roll.

JESSIE (*slight pause*). I won't be here, Mama.

MAMA. What have we just been talking about? You'll be here. You're well, Jessie. You're starting all over. You said it yourself. You're remembering things and . . .

JESSIE. I won't be here. If I'd ever had a year like this, to think straight and all, before now, I'd be gone already.

MAMA (*not pleading, commanding*). No, Jessie.

JESSIE (*folding the rest of the laundry*). Yes, Mama. Once I started remembering, I could see what it all added up to.

MAMA. The fits are over!

JESSIE. It's not the fits, Mama.

MAMA. Then it's me for giving them to you, but I didn't do it!

JESSIE. It's not the fits! You said it yourself, the medicine takes care of the fits.

MAMA (*interrupting*). Your daddy gave you those fits, Jessie. He passed it down to you like your green eyes, and your straight hair. It's not my fault!

JESSIE. So what if he had little fits? It's not inherited. I fell off the horse. It was an accident.

MAMA. The horse wasn't the first time, Jessie. You had a fit when you were five years old.

JESSIE. I did not.

MAMA. You did! You were eating a popsicle and down you went. He gave it to you. It's *his* fault, not mine.

JESSIE. Well, you took your time telling me.

MAMA. How do you tell that to a five-year-old?

JESSIE. What did the doctor say?

MAMA. He said kids have them all the time. He said there wasn't anything to do but wait for another one.

JESSIE. But I didn't have another one.

*Now there is a real silence.*

JESSIE. You mean to tell me I had fits all the time as a kid and you just told me I fell down or something and it wasn't till I had the fit when Cecil was looking that anybody bothered to find out what was the matter with me?

MAMA. It wasn't *all the time,* Jessie. And they changed when you started to school. More like your daddy's. Oh, that was some swell time, sitting here with the two of you turning off and on like light bulbs some nights.

JESSIE. How many fits did I have?

MAMA. You never hurt yourself. I never let you out of my sight. I caught you every time.

JESSIE. But you didn't tell anybody.

MAMA. It was none of their business.

JESSIE. You were ashamed.

MAMA. I didn't want anybody to know. Least of all you.

JESSIE. Least of all me. Oh, right. That was mine to know, Mama, not yours. Did Daddy know?

MAMA. He thought you were . . . you fell down a lot. That's what he thought. You were careless. Or maybe he thought I beat you. I don't know what he thought. He didn't think about it.

JESSIE. Because you didn't tell him!

MAMA. If I told him about you, I'd have to tell him about him!

JESSIE. I don't like this. I don't like this one bit.

MAMA. I didn't think you'd like it. That's why I didn't tell you.

JESSIE. If I'd known I was an epileptic, Mama, I wouldn't have ridden any horses.

MAMA. Make you feel like a freak, is that what I should have done?

JESSIE. Just get the manicure tray and sit down!

MAMA (*throwing it to the floor*). I don't want a manicure!

JESSIE. Doesn't look like you do, no.

MAMA. Maybe I did drop you, you don't know.

JESSIE. If you say you didn't, you didn't.

MAMA (*beginning to break down*). Maybe I fed you the wrong thing. Maybe you had a fever sometime and I didn't know it soon enough. Maybe it's a punishment.

JESSIE. For what?

MAMA. I don't know. Because of how I felt about your father. Because I didn't want any more children. Because I smoked too much or didn't eat right when I was carrying you. It has to be something I did.

JESSIE. It does not. It's just a sickness, not a curse. Epilepsy doesn't mean anything. It just is.

MAMA. I'm not talking about the fits here, Jessie! I'm talking about this killing yourself. It has to be me that's the matter here. You wouldn't be doing this if it wasn't. I didn't tell you things or I married you off to the wrong man or I took you in and let your life get away from you or all of it put together. I don't know what I did, but I did it, I know. This is all my fault, Jessie, but I don't know what to do about it now!

JESSIE (*exasperated at having to say this again*). It doesn't have anything to do with you!

MAMA. Everything you do has to do with me, Jessie. You can't do *anything,* wash your face or cut your finger, without doing it to me. That's right! You might as well kill me as you, Jessie, it's the same thing. This has to do with me, Jessie.

JESSIE. Then what if it does! What if it has everything to do with you! What if you are all I have and you're not enough? What if I could take all the rest of it if only I didn't have you here? What if the only way I can get away from you for good is to kill myself? What if it is? I can *still* do it!

MAMA (*in desperate tears*). Don't leave me, Jessie! (*Jessie stands for a moment, then turns for the bedroom.*) No! (*She grabs Jessie's arm.*)

JESSIE (*carefully taking her arm away*). I have a box of things I want people to have. I'm just going to go get it for you. You . . . just rest a minute.

*Jessie is gone. Mama heads for the telephone, but she can't even pick up the receiver this time and, instead, stoops to clean up the bottles that have spilled out of the manicure tray.*

*Jessie returns, carrying a box that groceries were delivered in. It probably says Hershey Kisses or Starkist Tuna. Mama is still down on the floor cleaning up, hoping that maybe if she just makes it look nice enough, Jessie will stay.*

MAMA. Jessie, how can I live here without you? I need you! You're supposed to tell me to stand up straight and say how nice I look in my pink dress, and drink my milk. You're supposed to go around and lock up so I know we're safe for the night, and when I wake up, you're supposed to be out there making the coffee and watching me get older every day, and you're supposed to help me die when the time comes. I can't do that by myself, Jessie. I'm not like you, Jessie. I hate the quiet and I don't want to die and I don't want you to go, Jessie. How can I . . . (*Has to stop a moment.*) How can I get up every day knowing you had to kill yourself to make it stop hurting and I was here all the time and I never even saw it. And then you gave me this chance to make it better, convince you to stay alive, and I couldn't do it. How can I live with myself after this, Jessie?

JESSIE. I only told you so I could explain it, so you wouldn't blame yourself, so you wouldn't feel bad. There wasn't anything you could say to change my mind. I didn't want you to save me. I just wanted you to know.

MAMA. Stay with me just a little longer. Just a few more years. I don't have that many more to go, Jessie. And as soon as I'm dead, you can do whatever you want. Maybe with me gone, you'll have all the quiet you want, right here in the house. And maybe one day you'll put in some begonias up the walk and get just the right rain for them all summer. And Ricky will be married by then and he'll bring your grandbabies over and you can sneak them a piece of candy when their daddy's not looking and then be real glad when they've gone home and left you to your quiet again.

JESSIE. Don't you see, Mama, everything I do winds up like this. How could I think you would understand? How could I think you would want a manicure? We could hold hands for an hour and then I could go shoot myself? I'm sorry about tonight, Mama, but it's exactly why I'm doing it.

MAMA. If you've got the guts to kill yourself, Jessie, you've got the guts to stay alive.

JESSIE. I know that. So it's really just a matter of where I'd rather be.

MAMA. Look, maybe I can't think of what you should do, but that doesn't mean there isn't something that would help. *You* find it. *You* think of it. You can keep trying. You can get brave and try some more. You don't have to give up!

JESSIE. I'm *not* giving up! This *is* the other thing I'm trying. And I'm sure there are some other things that might work, but *might* work isn't good enough anymore. I need something that *will* work. *This* will work. That's why I picked it.

MAMA. But something might happen. Something that could change everything. Who knows what it might be, but it might be worth waiting for! (*Jessie doesn't respond.*) Try it for two more weeks. We could have more talks like tonight.

JESSIE. No, Mama.

MAMA. I'll pay more attention to you. Tell the truth when you ask me. Let you have your say.

JESSIE. No, Mama! We wouldn't have more talks like tonight, because it's this next part that's made this last part so good, Mama. No, Mama. *This* is how I have my say. This is how I say what I thought about it *all* and I say no. To Dawson and Loretta and the Red Chinese and epilepsy and Ricky and Cecil and you. And me. And hope. I say no! (*Then going to Mama on the sofa.*) Just let me go easy, Mama.

MAMA. How can I let you go?

JESSIE. You can because you have to. It's what you've always done.

MAMA. You are my child!

JESSIE. I am what became of your child. (*Mama cannot answer.*) I found an old baby picture of me. And it was somebody else, not me. It was somebody pink and fat who never heard of sick or lonely, somebody who cried and got fed, and reached up and got held and kicked but didn't hurt anybody, and slept whenever she wanted to, just by closing her eyes. Somebody who mainly just laid there and laughed at the colors waving around over her head and chewed on a polka-dot whale and woke up knowing some new trick nearly every day, and rolled over and drooled on the sheet and felt your hand pulling my quilt back up over me. That's who I started out and this is who is left. (*There is no self-pity here.*) That's what this is about. It's somebody I lost, all right, it's my own self. Who I never was. Or who I tried to be and never got there. Somebody I waited for who never came. And never will. So, see, it doesn't much matter what else happens in the world or in this house, even. I'm what was worth waiting for and I didn't make it. Me . . . who might have made a difference to me . . . I'm not going to show up, so there's no reason to stay, except to keep you company . . . not reason enough because I'm not . . . very good company. (*Pause.*) Am I?

MAMA (*knowing she must tell the truth*). No. And neither am I.

JESSIE. I had this strange little thought, well, maybe it's not so strange. Anyway, after Christmas, after I decided to do this, I would wonder, sometimes, what might keep me here, what might be worth staying for, and you know what it was? It was maybe if there was something I really liked, like maybe if I really liked rice pudding or cornflakes for breakfast or something, that might be enough.

MAMA. Rice pudding is good.

JESSIE. Not to me.

MAMA. And you're not afraid?

JESSIE. Afraid of what?

MAMA. I'm afraid of it, for me, I mean. When my time comes. I know it's coming, but . . .

JESSIE. You don't know when. Like in a scary movie.

MAMA. Yeah, sneaking up on me like some killer on the loose, hiding out in the back yard just waiting for me to have my hands full someday and how am I supposed to protect myself anyhow when I don't know what he looks like and I don't know how he sounds coming up behind me like that or if it will hurt or take very long or what I don't get done before it happens.

JESSIE. You've got plenty of time left.

MAMA. I forget what for, right now.

JESSIE. For whatever happens, I don't know. For the rest of your life. For Agnes burning down one more house or Dawson losing his hair or . . .

MAMA (*quickly*). Jessie. I can't just sit here and say O.K., kill yourself if you want to.

JESSIE. Sure you can. You just did. Say it again.

MAMA (*really startled*). Jessie! (*Quiet horror.*) How dare you! (*Furious.*) How dare you! You think you can just leave whenever you want, like you're watching television here? No, you can't, Jessie. You make me feel like a fool for being alive, child, and you are so wrong! I like it here, and I will stay here until they make me go, until they drag me screaming and I mean screeching into my grave, and you're real smart to get away before then because, I mean, honey, you've never heard noise like that in your life. (*Jessie turns away.*) Who am I talking to? You're gone already, aren't you? I'm looking right through you! I can't stop you because you're already gone! I guess you think they'll all have to talk about you now! I guess you think this will really confuse them. Oh yes, ever since Christmas you've been laughing to yourself and thinking, "Boy, are they all in for a surprise." Well, nobody's going to be a bit surprised, sweetheart. This is just like you. Do it the hard way, that's my girl, all right. (*Jessie gets up and goes into the kitchen, but Mama follows her.*) You know who they're going to feel sorry for? Me! How about that! Not you, me! They're going to be *ashamed* of you. Yes. *Ashamed!* If somebody asks Dawson about it, he'll change the subject as fast as he can. He'll talk about how much he has to pay to park his car these days.

JESSIE. Leave me alone.

MAMA. It's the truth!

JESSIE. I should've just left you a note!

MAMA (*screaming*). Yes! (*Then suddenly understanding what she has said, nearly paralyzed by the thought of it, she turns slowly to face Jessie, nearly whispering.*) No. No. I . . . might not have thought of all the things you've said.

JESSIE. It's O.K., Mama.

*Mama is nearly unconscious from the emotional devastation of these last few moments. She sits down at the kitchen table, hurt and angry and desperately afraid. But she looks almost numb. She is so far beyond what is known as pain that she is virtually unreachable and Jessie knows this, and talks quietly, watching for signs of recovery.*

JESSIE (*washes her hands in the sink*). I remember you liked that preacher who did Daddy's, so if you want to ask him to do the service, that's O.K. with me.

MAMA (*not an answer, just a word*). What.

JESSIE (*putting on hand lotion as she talks*). And pick some songs you like or let Agnes pick, she'll know exactly which ones. Oh, and I had your dress cleaned that you wore to Daddy's. You looked real good in that.

MAMA. I don't remember, hon.

JESSIE. And it won't be so bad once your friends start coming to the funeral home. You'll probably see people you haven't seen for years, but I thought about what you should say to get you over that nervous part when they first come in.

MAMA (*simply repeating*). Come in.

JESSIE. Take them up to see their flowers, they'd like that. And when they say, "I'm so sorry, Thelma," you just say, "I appreciate your coming, Connie." And then ask how their garden was this summer or what they're doing for Thanksgiving or how their children . . .

MAMA. I don't think I should ask about their children. I'll talk about what they have on, that's always good. And I'll have some crochet work with me.

JESSIE. And Agnes will be there, so you might not have to talk at all.

MAMA. Maybe if Connie Richards does come, I can get her to tell me where she gets that Irish yarn, she calls it. I know it doesn't come from Ireland. I think it just comes with a green wrapper.

JESSIE. And be sure to invite enough people home afterward so you get enough food to feed them all and have some left for you. But don't let anybody take anything home, especially Loretta.

MAMA. Loretta will get all the food set up, honey. It's only fair to let her have some macaroni or something.

JESSIE. No, Mama. You have to be more selfish from now on. (*Sitting at the table with Mama.*) Now, somebody's bound to ask you why I did it and you just say you don't know. That you loved me and you know I loved you and we just sat around tonight like every other night of our lives, and then I came over and kissed you and said, " 'Night, Mother," and you heard me close my bedroom door and the next thing you heard was the shot. And whatever reasons I had, well, you guess I just took them with me.

MAMA (*quietly*). It was something personal.

JESSIE. Good. That's good, Mama.

MAMA. That's what I'll say, then.

JESSIE. Personal. Yeah.

MAMA. Is that what I tell Dawson and Loretta, too? We sat around, you kissed me, " 'Night, Mother"? They'll want to know more, Jessie. They won't believe it.

JESSIE. Well, then, tell them what we did. I filled up the candy jars. I cleaned out the refrigerator. We made some hot chocolate and put the cover back on the sofa. You had no idea. All right? I really think it's better that way. If they know we talked about it, they really won't understand how you let me go.

MAMA. I guess not.

JESSIE. It's private. Tonight is private, yours and mine, and I don't want anybody else to have any of it.

MAMA. O.K., then.

JESSIE (*standing behind Mama now, holding her shoulders*). Now, when you hear the shot, I don't want you to come in. First of all, you won't be able to get in by yourself, but I don't want you trying. Call Dawson, then call the police, and then call Agnes. And then you'll need something to do till somebody gets here, so wash the hot-chocolate pan. You wash that pan till you hear the doorbell ring and I don't care if it's an hour, you keep washing that pan.

MAMA. I'll make my calls and then I'll just sit. I won't need something to do. What will the police say?

JESSIE. They'll do that gunpowder test, I guess, and ask you what happened, and by that time, the ambulance will be here and they'll come in and get me and you know how that goes. You stay out here with Dawson and Loretta. You keep Dawson out here. I want the police in the room first, not Dawson, O.K.?

MAMA. What if Dawson and Loretta want me to go home with them?

JESSIE (*returning to the living room*). That's up to you.

MAMA. I think I'll stay here. All they've got is Sanka.

JESSIE. Maybe Agnes could come stay with you for a few days.

MAMA (*standing up, looking into the living room*). I'd rather be by myself, I think. (*Walking toward the box Jessie brought in earlier.*) You want me to give people those things?

JESSIE (*they sit down on the sofa, Jessie holding the box on her lap*). I want Loretta to have my little calculator. Dawson bought it for himself, you know, but then he saw one he liked better and he couldn't bring both of them home with Loretta counting every penny the way she does, so he gave the first one to me. Be funny for her to have it now, don't you think? And all my house slippers are in a sack for her in my closet. Tell her I know they'll fit and I've never worn any of them, and make sure Dawson hears you tell her that. I'm glad he loves Loretta so much, but I wish he knew not everybody has her size feet.

MAMA (*taking the calculator*). O.K.

JESSIE (*reaching into the box again*). This letter is for Dawson, but it's mostly about you, so read it if you want. There's a list of presents for you for at least twenty more Christmases and birthdays, so if you want anything special you better add it to this list before you give it to him. Or if you want to be surprised, just don't read that page. This Christmas, you're getting mostly stuff for the house, like a new rug in your bathroom and needlework, but next Christmas, you're really going to cost him next Christmas. I think you'll like it a lot and you'd never think of it.

MAMA. And you think he'll go for it?

JESSIE. I think he'll feel like a real jerk if he doesn't. Me telling him to, like this and all. Now, this number's where you call Cecil. I called it last week and he answered, so I know he still lives there.

MAMA. What do you want me to tell him?

JESSIE. Tell him we talked about him and I only had good things to say about him, but mainly tell him to find Ricky and tell him what I did, and tell Ricky you have something for him, out here, from me, and to come get it. (*Pulls a sack out of the box.*)

MAMA (*the sack feels empty*). What is it?

JESSIE (*taking it off*). My watch. (*Putting it in the sack and taking a ribbon out of the sack to tie around the top of it.*)

MAMA. He'll sell it!

JESSIE. That's the idea. I appreciate him not stealing it already. I'd like to buy him a good meal.

MAMA. He'll buy dope with it!

JESSIE. Well, then, I hope he gets some good dope with it, Mama. And the rest of this is for you. (*Handing Mama the box now. Mama picks up the things and looks at them.*)

MAMA (*surprised and pleased*). When did you do all this? During my naps, I guess.

JESSIE. I guess. I tried to be quiet about it. (*As Mama is puzzled by the presents.*) Those are just little presents. For whenever you need one. They're not bought presents, just things I thought you might like to look at, pictures or things you think you've lost. Things you didn't know you had, even. You'll see.

MAMA. I'm not sure I want them. They'll make me think of you.

JESSIE. No they won't. They're just things, like a free tube of toothpaste I found hanging on the door one day.

MAMA. Oh. All right, then.

JESSIE. Well, maybe there's one nice present in there somewhere. It's Granny's ring she gave me and I thought you might like to have it, but I didn't think you'd wear it if I gave it to you right now.

MAMA (*taking the box to a table nearby*). No. Probably not. (*Turning back to face her.*) I'm ready for my manicure, I guess. Want me to wash my hands again?

JESSIE (*standing up*). It's time for me to go, Mama.

MAMA (*starting for her*). No, Jessie, you've got all night!

JESSIE (*as Mama grabs her*). No, Mama.

MAMA. It's not even ten o'clock.

JESSIE (*very calm*). Let me go, Mama.

MAMA. I can't. You can't go. You can't do this. You didn't say it would be so soon, Jessie. I'm scared. I love you.

JESSIE (*takes her hands away*). Let go of me, Mama. I've said everything I had to say.

MAMA (*standing still a minute*). You said you wanted to do my nails.

JESSIE (*taking a small step backward*). I can't. It's too late.

MAMA. It's not too late!

JESSIE. I don't want you to wake Dawson and Loretta when you call. I want them to still be up and dressed so they can get right over.

MAMA (*As Jessie backs up, Mama moves in on her, but carefully*). They wake up fast, Jessie, if they have to. They don't matter here, Jessie. You do. I do. We're not through yet. We've got a lot of things to take care of here. I don't know where my prescriptions are and you didn't tell me what to tell Dr. Davis when he calls or how much you want me to tell Ricky or who I call to rake the leaves or . . .

JESSIE. Don't try and stop me, Mama, you can't do it.

MAMA (*grabbing her again, this time hard*). I can too! I'll stand in front of this hall and you can't get past me. (*They struggle.*) You'll have to knock me down to get away from me, Jessie. I'm not about to let you . . .

*Mama struggles with Jessie at the door and in the struggle Jessie gets away from her and—*

JESSIE (*almost a whisper*). 'Night, Mother. (*She vanishes into her bedroom and we hear the door lock just as Mama gets to it.*)

MAMA (*screams*). Jessie! (*Pounding on the door.*) Jessie, you let me in there. Don't you do this, Jessie. I'm not going to stop screaming until you open this door, Jessie. Jessie! Jessie! What if I don't do any of the things you told me to do! I'll tell Cecil what a miserable man he was to make you feel the way he did and I'll give Ricky's watch to Dawson if I feel like it and the only way you can make sure I do what you want is you come out here and make me, Jessie! (*Pounding again.*) Jessie! Stop this! I didn't know! I was here with you all the time. How could I know you were so alone?

*And Mama stops for a moment, breathless and frantic, putting her ear to the door, and when she doesn't hear anything, she stands up straight again and screams once more.*

Jessie! Please!

*And we hear the shot, and it sounds like an answer, it sounds like No.*

*Mama collapses against the door, tears streaming down her face, but not screaming anymore. In shock now.*

Jessie, Jessie, child . . . Forgive me. (*Pause.*) I thought you were mine.

*And she leaves the door and makes her way through the living room, around the furniture, as though she didn't know where it was, not knowing what to do. Finally, she goes to the stove in the kitchen and picks up the hot-chocolate pan and carries it with her to the telephone, and holds on to it while she dials the number. She looks down at the pan, holding it tight like her life depended on it. She hears Loretta answer.*

MAMA. Loretta, let me talk to Dawson, honey.

## TOPICS FOR CRITICAL THINKING AND WRITING

1. Early in the play, on page 1696, Jessie says she wants the gun for "protection." In the context of the entire play, what do you take this to mean?
2. Why do you think Jessie says, on page 1698, that she would rather use her father's gun than her husband's?
3. The playwright specifies that "the time is the present, with the action beginning about 8:15. Clocks onstage in the kitchen and on a table in the living room should run throughout the performance and be visible to the audience." Why?
4. Jessie insists (p. 1714) that Ricky is like her, and not like his father, Cecil. What do you think she is getting at?
5. On page 1699 Mama says, "People don't really kill themselves, Jessie. No, mam, doesn't make sense, unless you're retarded or deranged." Specify the various reasons that Mama assumes are the motives for Jessie's suicide. Most theories of suicide can be classified into one of two groups, psychoanalytical and sociological. Psychoanalytical theories (usually rooted in Freud) assume that human beings have dual impulses, *eros* (life instinct) and *thanatos* (death instinct). When the death instinct, expressed as hostility and aggression, is turned against others it takes the form of homicide, but when it is turned against the self it takes the form of suicide. Most sociological theories assume that suicide occurs among three types of people: egoistic suicides, people who are excessively individualistic (i.e., who are not integrated into society); altruistic suicides, people who have an excessive sense of duty to society and who die willingly to serve society; and, third, anomic suicides, people who find their usual lifestyles disrupted by sudden social changes such as the loss of a job during an economic depression. Do any of these theories seem helpful in explaining Jessie's suicide? In your opinion why *does* Jessie kill herself? (You may want to do some research on suicide, for instance, by consulting Freud's *Civilization and Its Discontents,* or Andrew F. Henry and James F. Short, *Homicide and Suicide,* or Edwin S. Scheidman, ed., *Essays in Self-Destruction,* or A. Alvarez, *The Savage God.*)
6. The greatest tragedies somehow suggest that the tragic figures are not only particular individuals—Oedipus, Hamlet, and so forth—but also are universal figures who somehow embody our own hopes and fears. Another way of putting it is to say that the greatest plays are not case histories but are visions of a central aspect of life. To what extent, in your opinion, does *'night, Mother* meet this criterion?

# A PERSPECTIVE FOR *'NIGHT, MOTHER*

## MARSHA NORMAN

## *Talking about* 'night, Mother

NORMAN. . . . I'm also always exploring the rules. I want to know which ones are breakable and which ones are not. I'm convinced that there are absolutely unbreakable rules in the theater, and that it doesn't matter how good you are, you can't break them.

INTERVIEWER. Do you care to list them?

NORMAN. Sure. It's real easy, you could put this on the back of a cereal box! You must state the issue at the beginning of the play. The audience must know what is at stake; they must know when they will be able to go home: "This is a story of a little boy who lost his marbles." They must know, when the little boy either gets his marbles back or finds something that is better than his marbles, or kills himself because he can't live without his marbles, that the play will end and they can applaud and go home. He can't *not* care about the marbles. He has to want them with such a passion that you are interested, that you connect to that passion. The theater is all about wanting things that you can or can't have or you do or do not get. Now, the boy himself has to be likable. It has to matter to you whether he gets his marbles or not. The other things—language, structure, et cetera,—are variables. One other thing: You can't stop the action for detours. On the way to finding his marbles, the boy can't stop and go swimming. He might do that in a novel, but not in a play.

I like to talk about plays as pieces of machinery. A ski lift. When you get in it, you must feel absolutely secure; you must know that this thing can hold you up. And the first movement of it must be so smooth that whatever residual fears you had about the machine or the mountain are allayed. The journey up the mountain on the ski lift must be continuous. You can't stop and just dangle. If you do, people will realize how far down it is, and they will suddenly get afraid and start grasping the corners of their chairs, which you don't want them to do.

INTERVIEWER. You've said the main character must want something. Is *'night, Mother,* then, Thelma's play? It seems that Jessie, the suicidal daughter, has lost all desire.

NORMAN. Well, Jessie certainly doesn't want to have anything more to do with *her* life, but she does want Mama to be able to go on, and that's a very strong desire on Jessie's part. She *wants* Mama to be able to do the wash and know where everything is. She wants Mama to live, and to live free of the guilt that Mama might have felt had Jessie just left her a note. Jessie's desires are so strong in the piece. The play exists because Jessie wants something for Mama. Then, of course, Mama wants Jessie to stay. So you have two conflicting goals. And at that point it is a real struggle. It might as well be armed warfare. Only very late in the piece do they realize that both goals are achievable given some moderation.

What Mama does understand, finally, is that there wasn't anything she could do. And so Jessie does win. Mama certainly loses in the battle to keep her alive, but Mama does gain other things in the course of the evening.

INTERVIEWER. Why doesn't Thelma go a bit further? Why doesn't she attack her daughter physically to prevent the suicide?

NORMAN. Well, there is that final moment at the door, and it posed an interesting dilemma. At that moment in the script, Thelma is reaching for something to hit Jessie with. In the early versions of the script, there was a line that said, "I'll knock you out cold before I'll let you . . ." In my mind I saw Thelma reaching for the frying pan. Like, "I am going to hurt you now. And we will straighten this out when you wake up." [Laughter] Then Tom Moore, the director, pointed out that while it may be tragedy to pick up a frying pan, it is farce when you put it down.

INTERVIEWER. You weren't willing then to risk humor at that point?

NORMAN. Right. And you can't leave Thelma standing there at the door holding the frying pan.

INTERVIEWER. But did you try it that way during rehearsal?

NORMAN. We tried to make the fight as violent as we could. Thelma only has one thing left to try and that is physical harm. But I don't know if the audience ever understands that effort.

INTERVIEWER. Did the fact that you could not demonstrate Thelma's passion in a physical way put more weight on her final verbal plea to Jessie?

NORMAN. The struggle at the door is one of the most difficult moments for both of them. The actress, Anne Pitoniak, as a human being inside that character, realizes she must fight and she must lose.

INTERVIEWER. Does she let go of Jessie in that moment?

NORMAN. Thelma's crucial letting go has occurred earlier in the piece. This fight is pure instinct. This has nothing to do with thinking or feeling, this is just physical. This is that last moment when you realize you're cornered, and you're not going to try to talk to the grizzly bear anymore. . . . She *does* know that she has lost. Jessie is simply too powerful. But that doesn't mean that Thelma is just going to stand there.

INTERVIEWER. The play is due to go to Japan soon, where I believe that suicide is considered a civil right. I should think the audiences there will experience your story very differently than a Western audience.

NORMAN. It's going to be fascinating, isn't it? I thought the same thing. I have no idea. Americans have a life-at-all-costs attitude. It's a very privileged point of view, actually. My sense of *'night, Mother* is that it is, by my own definitions of these words, a play of nearly total triumph. Jessie is able to get what she feels she needs. That is not a despairing act. It may look despairing from the outside, but it has cost her everything she has. If Jessie says it's worth it, then it is.

INTERVIEWER. But suicide is not survival. That's what I'm questioning.

NORMAN. But see, by Jessie's definition of survival, it is. As Jessie says, "My life is all I really have that belongs to me, and I'm going to say what happens to it." . . . Jessie has taken an action on her own behalf that for her is the final test of all that she has been. That's how I see it. Now you don't have to see it that way; nor does anybody else have to see it that way.

INTERVIEWER. Better death with honor than a life of humiliation?

NORMAN. Right. I think that the question the play asks is, "What does it take to survive? What does it take to save your life?" Now Jessie's answer is "It takes killing myself." Mama's answer is "It takes cocoa and marshmallows and doilies and the *TV Guide* and Agnes and the birds and trips to the grocery." Jessie feels, "No, I'm sorry. That's not enough."

## AUGUST WILSON

*August Wilson was born in Pittsburgh in 1945, the son of a black woman and a white man. After dropping out of school at the age of 15, Wilson took various odd jobs, such as stock clerk and short-order cook, in his spare time educating himself in the public library, chiefly by reading works by such black writers as Richard Wright, Ralph Ellison, Langston Hughes, and Amiri Baraka (LeRoi Jones). In 1978 the director of a black theater in St. Paul, Minnesota, who had known Wilson in Pittsburgh, invited him to write a play for the theater. Six months later Wilson moved permanently to St. Paul.*

*The winner of the Pulitzer Prize for drama in 1987, Wilson's* Fences *was first presented as a staged reading in 1983 and was later performed in Chicago, Seattle, Rochester (New York), and New Haven (Connecticut) before reaching New York City in 1987. An earlier play,* Ma Rainey's Black Bottom, *was voted Best Play of the Year 1984–85 by the New York Drama Critics' Circle. In 1981 when* Ma Rainey *was first read at the O'Neill Center in Waterford, Connecticut, Wilson met Lloyd Richards, a black director with whom he has continued to work closely.* The Piano Lesson, *directed by Richards, won Wilson a second Pulitzer Prize in 1990.*

# *Fences*

*for Lloyd Richards,*
*who adds to whatever he touches*

When the sins of our fathers visit us
We do not have to play host.
We can banish them with forgiveness
As God, in His Largeness and Laws.
—August Wilson

LIST OF CHARACTERS

TROY MAXSON
JIM BONO, *Troy's friend*
ROSE, *Troy's wife*
LYONS, *Troy's oldest son by previous marriage*
GABRIEL, *Troy's brother*
CORY, *Troy and Rose's son*
RAYNELL, *Troy's daughter*

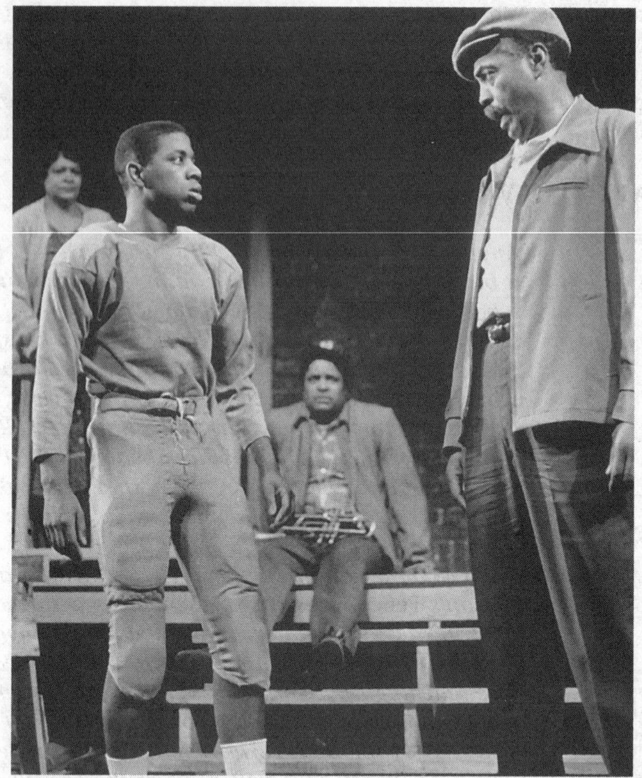

Left to right: Frances Foster as Rose, Keith Amos as Cory, William Jay as Gabriel, and Gilbert Lewis as Troy, in the Seattle Repertory Theatre production of *Fences*. (Photograph © Chris Bennion)

**SETTING:** ***The setting is the yard which fronts the only entrance to the Maxson household, an ancient two-story brick house set back off a small alley in a big-city neighborhood. The entrance to the house is gained by two or three steps leading to a wooden porch badly in need of paint.***

***A relatively recent addition to the house and running its full width, the porch lacks congruence. It is a sturdy porch with a flat roof. One or two chairs of dubious value sit at one end where the kitchen window opens onto the porch. An old-fashioned icebox stands silent guard at the opposite end.***

***The yard is a small dirt yard, partially fenced, except for the last scene, with a wooden saw horse, a pile of lumber, and other fence-building equipment set off to the side. Opposite is a tree from which hangs a ball made of rags. A baseball bat leans against the tree. Two oil drums serve as garbage receptacles and sit near the house at right to complete the setting.***

**THE PLAY:** ***Near the turn of the century, the destitute of Europe sprang on the city with tenacious claws and an honest and solid dream. The city devoured them. They swelled its belly until it burst***

*into a thousand furnaces and sewing machines, a thousand butcher shops and bakers' ovens, a thousand churches and hospitals and funeral parlors and money-lenders. The city grew. It nourished itself and offered each man a partnership limited only by his talent, his guile, and his willingness and capacity for hard work. For the immigrants of Europe, a dream dared and won true.*

*The descendants of African slaves were offered no such welcome or participation. They came from places called the Carolinas and the Virginias, Georgia, Alabama, Mississippi, and Tennessee. They came strong, eager, searching. The city rejected them and they fled and settled along the riverbanks and under bridges in shallow, ramshackle houses made of sticks and tarpaper. They collected rags and wood. They sold the use of their muscles and their bodies. They cleaned houses and washed clothes, they shined shoes, and in quiet desperation and vengeful pride, they stole, and lived in pursuit of their own dream. That they could breathe free, finally, and stand to meet life with the force of dignity and whatever eloquence the heart could call upon.*

*By 1957, the hard-won victories of the European immigrants had solidified the industrial might of America. War had been confronted and won with new energies that used loyalty and patriotism as its fuel. Life was rich, full, and flourishing. The Milwaukee Braves won the World Series, and the hot winds of change that would make the sixties a turbulent, racing, dangerous, and provocative decade had not yet begun to blow full.*

## *Act 1*

### *Scene 1*

*It is 1957. Troy and Bono enter the yard, engaged in conversation. Troy is fifty-three years old, a large man with thick, heavy hands; it is this largeness that he strives to fill out and make an accommodation with. Together with his blackness, his largeness informs his sensibilities and the choices he has made in his life.*

*Of the two men, Bono is obviously the follower. His commitment to their friendship of thirty-odd years is rooted in his admiration of Troy's honesty, capacity for hard work, and his strength, which Bono seeks to emulate.*

*It is Friday night, payday, and the one night of the week the two men engage in a ritual of talk and drink. Troy is usually the most talkative and at times he can be crude and almost vulgar, though he is capable of rising to profound heights of expression. The men carry lunch buckets and wear or carry burlap aprons and are dressed in clothes suitable to their jobs as garbage collectors.*

BONO. Troy, you ought to stop that lying!

TROY. I ain't lying! The nigger had a watermelon this big. (*He indicates with his hands.*) Talking about . . . "What watermelon, Mr. Rand?" I liked to fell out! "What watermelon, Mr. Rand?" . . . And it sitting there big as life.

BONO. What did Mr. Rand say?

TROY. Ain't said nothing. Figure if the nigger too dumb to know he carrying a watermelon, he wasn't gonna get much sense out of him. Trying to hide that great big old watermelon under his coat. Afraid to let the white man see him carry it home.

BONO. I'm like you . . . I ain't got no time for them kind of people.

TROY. Now what he look like getting mad cause he see the man from the union talking to Mr. Rand?

BONO. He come to me talking about . . . "Maxson gonna get us fired." I told him to get away from me with that. He walked away from me calling you a troublemaker. What Mr. Rand say?

TROY. Ain't said nothing. He told me to go down the Commissioner's office next Friday. They called me down there to see them.

BONO. Well, as long as you got your complaint filed, they can't fire you. That's what one of them white fellows tell me.

TROY. I ain't worried about them firing me. They gonna fire me cause I asked a question? That's all I did. I went to Mr. Rand and asked him, "Why? Why you got the white mens driving and the colored lifting?" Told him, "what's the matter, don't I count? You think only white fellows got sense enough to drive a truck. That ain't no paper job! Hell, anybody can drive a truck. How come you got all whites driving and the colored lifting?" He told me "take it to the union." Well, hell, that's what I done! Now they wanna come up with this pack of lies.

BONO. I told Brownie if the man come and ask him any questions . . . just tell the truth! It ain't nothing but something they done trumped up on you cause you filed a complaint on them.

TROY. Brownie don't understand nothing. All I want them to do is change the job description. Give everybody a chance to drive the truck. Brownie can't see that. He ain't got that much sense.

BONO. How you figure he be making out with that gal be up at Taylor's all the time . . . that Alberta gal?

TROY. Same as you and me. Getting just as much as we is. Which is to say nothing.

BONO. It is, huh? I figure you doing a little better than me . . . and I ain't saying what I'm doing.

TROY. Aw, nigger, look here . . . I know you. If you had got anywhere near that gal, twenty minutes later you be looking to tell somebody. And the first one you gonna tell . . . that you gonna want to brag to . . . is me.

BONO. I ain't saying that. I see where you be eyeing her.

TROY. I eye all the women. I don't miss nothing. Don't never let nobody tell you Troy Maxson don't eye the women.

BONO. You been doing more than eyeing her. You done bought her a drink or two.

TROY. Hell yeah, I bought her a drink! What that mean? I bought you one, too. What that mean cause I buy her a drink? I'm just being polite.

BONO. It's all right to buy her one drink. That's what you call being polite. But when you wanna be buying two or three . . . that's what you call eyeing her.

TROY. Look here, as long as you known me . . . you ever known me to chase after women?

BONO. Hell yeah! Long as I done known you. You forgetting I knew you when.

TROY. Naw, I'm talking about since I been married to Rose?

BONO. Oh, not since you been married to Rose. Now, that's the truth, there. I can say that.

TROY. All right then! Case closed.

BONO. I see you be walking up around Alberta's house. You supposed to be at Taylors' and you be walking up around there.

TROY. What you watching where I'm walking for? I ain't watching after you.

BONO. I seen you walking around there more than once.

TROY. Hell, you liable to see me walking anywhere! That don't mean nothing cause you see me walking around there.

BONO. Where she come from anyway? She just kinda showed up one day.

TROY. Tallahassee. You can look at her and tell she one of them Florida gals. They got some big healthy women down there. Grow them right up out the ground. Got a little bit of Indian in her. Most of them niggers down in Florida got some Indian in them.

BONO. I don't know about that Indian part. But she damn sure big and healthy. Woman wear some big stockings. Got them great big old legs and hips as wide as the Mississippi River.

TROY. Legs don't mean nothing. You don't do nothing but push them out of the way. But them hips cushion the ride!

BONO. Troy, you ain't got no sense.

TROY. It's the truth! Like you riding on Goodyears!

*Rose enters from the house. She is ten years younger than Troy, her devotion to him stems from her recognition of the possibilities of her life without him: a succession of abusive men and their babies, a life of partying and running the streets, the Church, or aloneness with its attendant pain and frustration. She recognizes Troy's spirit as a fine and illuminating one and she either ignores or forgives his faults, only some of which she recognizes. Though she doesn't drink, her presence is an integral part of the Friday night rituals. She alternates between the porch and the kitchen, where supper preparations are under way.*

ROSE. What you all out here getting into?

TROY. What you worried about what we getting into for? This is men talk, woman.

ROSE. What I care what you all talking about? Bono, you gonna stay for supper?

BONO. No, I thank you, Rose. But Lucille say she cooking up a pot of pigfeet.

TROY. Pigfeet! Hell, I'm going home with you! Might even stay the night if you got some pigfeet. You got something in there to top them pigfeet, Rose?

ROSE. I'm cooking up some chicken. I got some chicken and collard greens.

TROY. Well, go on back in the house and let me and Bono finish what we was talking about. This is men talk. I got some talk for you later. You know what kind of talk I mean. You go on and powder it up.

ROSE. Troy Maxson, don't you start that now!

TROY (*puts his arm around her*). Aw, woman . . . come here. Look here, Bono . . . when I met this woman . . . I got out that place, say, "Hitch up my pony, saddle up my mare . . . there's a woman out there for me somewhere. I looked here. Looked there. Saw Rose and latched on to her." I latched on to her and told her—I'm gonna tell you the truth—I told her, "Baby, I don't wanna marry, I just wanna be your man." Rose told me . . . tell him what you told me, Rose.

ROSE. I told him if he wasn't the marrying kind, then move out the way so the marrying kind could find me.

TROY. That's what she told me. "Nigger, you in my way. You blocking the view! Move out the way so I can find me a husband." I thought it over two or three days. Come back—

ROSE. Ain't no two or three days nothing. You was back the same night.

TROY. Come back, told her . . . "Okay, baby . . . but I'm gonna buy me a banty rooster and put him out there in the backyard . . . and when he see a stranger come, he'll flap his wings and crow . . ." Look here, Bono, I could watch the front door by myself . . . it was that back door I was worried about.

ROSE. Troy, you ought not talk like that. Troy ain't doing nothing but telling a lie.

TROY. Only thing is . . . when we first got married . . . forget the rooster . . . we ain't had no yard!

BONO. I hear you tell it. Me and Lucille was staying down there on Logan Street. Had two rooms with the outhouse in the back. I ain't mind the outhouse none. But when that goddamn wind blow through there in the winter . . . that's what I'm talking about! To this day I wonder why in the hell I ever stayed down there for six long years. But see, I didn't know I could do no better. I thought only white folks had inside toilets and things.

ROSE. There's a lot of people don't know they can do no better than they doing now. That's just something you got to learn. A lot of folks still shop at Bella's.

TROY. Ain't nothing wrong with shopping at Bella's. She got fresh food.

ROSE. I ain't said nothing about if she got fresh food. I'm talking about what she charge. She charge ten cents more than the A&P.

TROY. The A&P ain't never done nothing for me. I spends my money where I'm treated right. I go down to Bella, say, "I need a loaf of bread, I'll pay you Friday." She give it to me. What sense that make when I got money to go and spend it somewhere else and ignore the person who done right by me? That ain't in the Bible.

ROSE. We ain't talking about what's in the Bible. What sense it make to shop there when she overcharge?

TROY. You shop where you want to. I'll do my shopping where the people been good to me.

ROSE. Well, I don't think it's right for her to overcharge. That's all I was saying.

BONO. Look here . . . I got to get on. Lucille going be raising all kind of hell.

TROY. Where you going, nigger? We ain't finished this pint. Come here, finish this pint.

BONO. Well, hell, I am . . . if you ever turn the bottle loose.

TROY (*hands him the bottle*). The only thing I say about the A&P is I'm glad Cory got that job down there. Help him take care of his school clothes and things. Gabe done moved out and things getting tight around here. He got that job . . . He can start to look out for himself.

ROSE. Cory done went and got recruited by a college football team.

TROY. I told that boy about that football stuff. The white man ain't gonna let him get nowhere with that football. I told him when he first come to me with it. Now you come telling me he done went and got more tied up in it. He ought to go and get recruited in how to fix cars or something where he can make a living.

ROSE. He ain't talking about making no living playing football. It's just something the boys in school do. They gonna send a recruiter by to talk to you. He'll tell you he ain't talking about making no living playing football. It's a honor to be recruited.

TROY. It ain't gonna get him nowhere. Bono'll tell you that.

BONO. If he be like you in the sports . . . he's gonna be all right. Ain't but two men ever played baseball as good as you. That's Babe Ruth and Josh Gibson.[1] Them's the only two men ever hit more home runs than you.

TROY. What it ever get me? Ain't got a pot to piss in or a window to throw it out of.

ROSE. Times have changed since you was playing baseball, Troy. That was before the war. Times have changed a lot since then.

TROY. How in hell they done changed?

ROSE. They got lots of colored boys playing ball now. Baseball and football.

BONO. You right about that, Rose. Times have changed, Troy. You just come along too early.

TROY. There ought not never have been no time called too early! Now you take that fellow . . . what's that fellow they had playing right field for the Yankees back then? You know who I'm talking about, Bono. Used to play right field for the Yankees.

ROSE. Selkirk?

TROY. Selkirk! That's it! Man batting .269, understand? .269. What kind of sense that make? I was hitting .432 with thirty-seven home runs! Man batting .269 and playing right field for the Yankees! I saw Josh Gibson's daughter yesterday. She walking around with raggedy shoes on her feet. Now I bet you Selkirk's daughter ain't walking around with raggedy shoes on her feet! I bet you that!

ROSE. They got a lot of colored baseball players now. Jackie Robinson[2] was the first. Folks had to wait for Jackie Robinson.

TROY. I done seen a hundred niggers play baseball better than Jackie Robinson. Hell, I know some teams Jackie Robinson couldn't even make! What you talking about Jackie Robinson. Jackie Robinson wasn't nobody. I'm talking about if you could play ball then they ought to have let you play. Don't care what color you were. Come telling me I come along too early. If you could play . . . then they ought to have let you play.

*Troy takes a long drink from the bottle.*

ROSE. You gonna drink yourself to death. You don't need to be drinking like that.

TROY. Death ain't nothing. I done seen him. Done wrassled with him. You can't tell me nothing about death. Death ain't nothing but a fastball on

[1]**Josh Gibson** African-American ballplayer (1911–47), known as the Babe Ruth of the Negro Leagues [2]**Jackie Robinson** In 1947 Robinson (1919–72) became the first African-American to play baseball in the major leagues.

the outside corner. And you know what I'll do to that! Lookee here, Bono . . . am I lying? You get one of them fastballs, about waist high, over the outside corner of the plate where you can get the meat of the bat on it . . . and good god! You can kiss it goodbye. Now, am I lying?

BONO. Naw, you telling the truth there. I seen you do it.

TROY. If I'm lying . . . that 450 feet worth of lying! (*Pause.*) That's all death is to me. A fastball on the outside corner.

ROSE. I don't know why you want to get on talking about death.

TROY. Ain't nothing wrong with talking about death. That's part of life. Everybody gonna die. You gonna die, I'm gonna die. Bono's gonna die. Hell, we all gonna die.

ROSE. But you ain't got to talk about it. I don't like to talk about it.

TROY. You the one brought it up. Me and Bono was talking about baseball . . . you tell me I'm gonna drink myself to death. Ain't that right, Bono? You know I don't drink this but one night out of the week. That's Friday night. I'm gonna drink just enough to where I can handle it. Then I cuts it loose. I leave it alone. So don't you worry about me drinking myself to death. 'Cause I ain't worried about Death. I done seen him. I done wrestled with him.

Look here, Bono . . . I looked up one day and Death was marching straight at me. Like Soldiers on Parade! The Army of Death was marching straight at me. The middle of July, 1941. It got real cold just like it be winter. It seem like Death himself reached out and touched me on the shoulder. He touch me just like I touch you. I got cold as ice and Death standing there grinning at me.

ROSE. Troy, why don't you hush that talk.

TROY. I say . . . what you want, Mr. Death? You be wanting me? You done brought your army to be getting me? I looked him dead in the eye. I wasn't fearing nothing. I was ready to tangle. Just like I'm ready to tangle now. The Bible say be ever vigilant. That's why I don't get but so drunk. I got to keep watch.

ROSE. Troy was right down there in Mercy Hospital. You remember he had pneumonia? Laying there with a fever talking plumb out of his head.

TROY. Death standing there staring at me . . . carrying that sickle in his hand. Finally he say, "You want bound over for another year?" See, just like that . . . "You want bound over for another year?" I told him, "Bound over hell! Let's settle this now!"

It seem like he kinda fell back when I said that, and all the cold went out of me. I reached down and grabbed that sickle and threw it just as far as I could throw it . . . and me and him commenced to wrestling.

We wrestled for three days and three nights. I can't say where I found the strength from. Everytime it seemed like he was gonna get the best of me, I'd reach way down deep inside myself and find the strength to do him one better.

ROSE. Everytime Troy tell that story he find different ways to tell it. Different things to make up about it.

TROY. I ain't making up nothing. I'm telling you the facts of what happened. I wrestled with Death for three days and three nights and I'm standing here to tell you about it. (*Pause.*) All right. At the end of the third night we done weakened each other to where we can't hardly move. Death stood up, throwed on his robe . . . had him a white robe with a hood on it. He throwed on that robe and went off to look for his sickle. Say, "I'll be back." Just like that. "I'll be back." I told him, say, "Yeah, but . . . you gonna have to find me!" I wasn't no fool. I wasn't going looking for him. Death ain't nothing to play with. And I know he's gonna get me. I know I got to join his army . . . his camp followers. But as long as I keep my strength and see him coming . . . as long as I keep up my vigilance . . . he's gonna have to fight to get me. I ain't going easy.

BONO. Well, look here, since you got to keep up your vigilance . . . let me have the bottle.

TROY. Aw hell, I shouldn't have told you that part. I should have left out that part.

ROSE. Troy be talking that stuff and half the time don't even know what he be talking about.

TROY. Bono know me better than that.

BONO. That's right. I know you. I know you got some Uncle Remus[3] in your blood. You got more stories than the devil got sinners.

TROY. Aw hell, I done seen him too! Done talked with the devil.

ROSE. Troy, don't nobody wanna be hearing all that stuff.

*Lyons enters the yard from the street. Thirty-four years old, Troy's son by a previous marriage, he sports a neatly trimmed goatee, sport coat, white shirt, tieless and buttoned at the collar. Though he fancies himself a musician, he is more caught up in the rituals and "idea" of being a musician than in the actual practice of the music. He has come to borrow money from Troy, and while he knows he will be successful, he is uncertain as to what extent his lifestyle will be held up to scrutiny and ridicule.*

LYONS. Hey, Pop.

TROY. What you come "Hey, Popping" me for?

LYONS. How you doing, Rose? (*He kisses her.*) Mr. Bono. How you doing?

BONO. Hey, Lyons . . . how you been?

TROY. He must have been doing all right. I ain't seen him around here last week.

ROSE. Troy, leave your boy alone. He come by to see you and you wanna start all that nonsense.

TROY. I ain't bothering Lyons. (*Offers him the bottle.*) Here . . . get you a drink. We got an understanding. I know why he come by to see me and he know I know.

LYONS. Come on, Pop . . . I just stopped by to say hi . . . see how you was doing.

TROY. You ain't stopped by yesterday.

ROSE. You gonna stay for supper, Lyons? I got some chicken cooking in the oven.

LYONS. No, Rose . . . thanks. I was just in the neighborhood and thought I'd stop by for a minute.

TROY. You was in the neighborhood all right, nigger. You telling the truth there. You was in the neighborhood cause it's my payday.

LYONS. Well, hell, since you mentioned it . . . let me have ten dollars.

[3]**Uncle Remus** narrator of traditional black tales in a book by Joel Chandler Harris

TROY. I'll be damned! I'll die and go to hell and play blackjack with the devil before I give you ten dollars.

BONO. That's what I wanna know about . . . that devil you done seen.

LYONS. What . . . Pop done seen the devil? You too much, Pops.

TROY. Yeah, I done seen him. Talked to him too!

ROSE. You ain't seen no devil. I done told you that man ain't had nothing to do with the devil. Anything you can't understand, you want to call it the devil.

TROY. Look here, Bono . . . I went down to see Hertzberger about some furniture. Got three rooms for two-ninety-eight. That what it say on the radio. "Three rooms . . . two-ninety-eight." Even made up a little song about it. Go down there . . . man tell me I can't get no credit. I'm working every day and can't get no credit. What to do? I got an empty house with some raggedy furniture in it. Cory ain't got no bed. He's sleeping on a pile of rags on the floor. Working every day and can't get no credit. Come back here—Rose'll tell you—madder than hell. Sit down . . . try to figure what I'm gonna do. Come a knock on the door. Ain't been living here but three days. Who know I'm here? Open the door . . . devil standing there bigger than life. White fellow . . . white fellow . . . got on good clothes and everything. Standing there with a clipboard in his hand. I ain't had to say nothing. First words come out of his mouth was . . . "I understand you need some furniture and can't get no credit." I liked to fell over. He say, "I'll give you all the credit you want, but you got to pay the interest on it." I told him, "Give me three rooms worth and charge whatever you want." Next day a truck pulled up here and two men unloaded them three rooms. Man what drove the truck give me a book. Say send ten dollars, first of every month to the address in the book and every thing will be all right. Say if I miss a payment the devil was coming back and it'll be hell to pay. That was fifteen years ago. To this day . . . the first of the month I send my ten dollars, Rose'll tell you.

ROSE. Troy lying.

TROY. I ain't never seen that man since. Now you tell me who else that could have been but the devil? I ain't sold my soul or nothing like that, you understand. Naw, I wouldn't have truck with the devil about nothing like that. I got my furniture and pays my ten dollars the first of the month just like clockwork.

BONO. How long you say you been paying this ten dollars a month?

TROY. Fifteen years!

BONO. Hell, ain't you finished paying for it yet? How much the man done charged you?

TROY. Ah hell, I done paid for it. I done paid for it ten times over! The fact is I'm scared to stop paying it.

ROSE. Troy lying. We got that furniture from Mr. Glickman. He ain't paying no ten dollars a month to nobody.

TROY. Aw hell, woman. Bono know I ain't that big a fool.

LYONS. I was just getting ready to say . . . I know where there's a bridge for sale.

TROY. Look here, I'll tell you this . . . it don't matter to me if he was the devil. It don't matter if the devil give credit. Somebody has got to give it.

ROSE. It ought to matter. You going around talking about having truck with the devil . . . God's the one you gonna have to answer to. He's the one gonna be at the Judgment.

LYONS. Yeah, well, look here, Pop . . . Let me have that ten dollars. I'll give it back to you. Bonnie got a job working at the hospital.

TROY. What I tell you, Bono? The only time I see this nigger is when he wants something. That's the only time I see him.

LYONS. Come on, Pop, Mr. Bono don't want to hear all that. Let me have the ten dollars. I told you Bonnie working.

TROY. What that mean to me? "Bonnie working." I don't care if she working. Go ask her for the ten dollars if she working. Talking about "Bonnie working." Why ain't you working?

LYONS. Aw, Pop, you know I can't find no decent job. Where am I gonna get a job at? You know I can't get no job.

TROY. I told you I know some people down there. I can get you on the rubbish if you want to work. I told you that the last time you came by here asking me for something.

LYONS. Naw, Pop . . . thanks. That ain't for me. I don't wanna be carrying nobody's rubbish. I don't wanna be punching nobody's time clock.

TROY. What's the matter, you too good to carry people's rubbish? Where you think that ten dollars you talking about come from? I'm just supposed to haul people's rubbish and give my money to you cause you too lazy to work. You too lazy to work and wanna know why you ain't got what I got.

ROSE. What hospital Bonnie working at? Mercy?

LYONS. She's down at Passavant working in the laundry.

TROY. I ain't got nothing as it is. I give you that ten dollars and I got to eat beans the rest of the week. Naw . . . you ain't getting no ten dollars here.

LYONS. You ain't got to be eating no beans. I don't know why you wanna say that.

TROY. I ain't got no extra money. Gabe done moved over to Miss Pearl's paying her the rent and things done got tight around here. I can't afford to be giving you every payday.

LYONS. I ain't asked you to give me nothing. I asked you to loan me ten dollars. I know you got ten dollars.

TROY. Yeah, I got it. You know why I got it? Cause I don't throw my money away out there in the streets. You living the fast life . . . wanna be a musician . . . running around in them clubs and things . . . then, you learn to take care of yourself. You ain't gonna find me going and asking nobody for nothing. I done spent too many years without.

LYONS. You and me is two different people, Pop.

TROY. I done learned my mistake and learned to do what's right by it. You still trying to get something for nothing. Life don't owe you nothing. You owe it to yourself. Ask Bono. He'll tell you I'm right.

LYONS. You got your way of dealing with the world . . . I got mine. The only thing that matters to me is the music.

TROY. Yeah, I can see that! It don't matter how you gonna eat . . . where your next dollar is coming from. You telling the truth there.

LYONS. I know I got to eat. But I got to live too. I need something that gonna help me to get out of the bed in the morning. Make me feel like I belong in the world. I don't bother nobody. I just stay with the music cause that's the only way I can find to live in the world. Otherwise there ain't no telling what I might do. Now I don't come criticizing you and how you live. I just come by to ask you for ten dollars. I don't wanna hear all that about how I live.

TROY. Boy, your mamma did a hell of a job raising you.

LYONS. You can't change me, Pop. I'm thirty-four years old. If you wanted to change me, you should have been there when I was growing up. I come by to see you . . . ask for ten dollars and you want to talk about how I was raised. You don't know nothing about how I was raised.

ROSE. Let the boy have ten dollars, Troy.

TROY (*to Lyons*). What the hell you looking at me for? I ain't got no ten dollars. You know what I do with my money. (*To Rose.*) Give him ten dollars if you want him to have it.

ROSE. I will. Just as soon as you turn it loose.

TROY (*handing Rose the money*). There it is. Seventy-six dollars and forty-two cents. You see this, Bono? Now, I ain't gonna get but six of that back.

ROSE. You ought to stop telling that lie. Here, Lyons. (*She hands him the money.*)

LYONS. Thanks, Rose. Look . . . I got to run . . . I'll see you later.

TROY. Wait a minute. You gonna say, "thanks, Rose" and ain't gonna look to see where she got that ten dollars from? See how they do me, Bono?

LYONS. I know she got it from you, Pop. Thanks. I'll give it back to you.

TROY. There he go telling another lie. Time I see that ten dollars . . . he'll be owing me thirty more.

LYONS. See you, Mr. Bono.

BONO. Take care, Lyons!

LYONS. Thanks, Pop. I'll see you again.

*Lyons exits the yard.*

TROY. I don't know why he don't go and get him a decent job and take care of that woman he got.

BONO. He'll be all right, Troy. The boy is still young.

TROY. The *boy* is thirty-four years old.

ROSE. Let's not get off into all that.

BONO. Look here . . . I got to be going. I got to be getting on. Lucille gonna be waiting.

TROY (*puts his arm around Rose*). See this woman, Bono? I love this woman. I love this woman so much it hurts. I love her so much . . . I done run out of ways of loving her. So I got to go back to basics. Don't you come by my house Monday morning talking about time to go to work . . . 'cause I'm still gonna be stroking!

ROSE. Troy! Stop it now!

BONO. I ain't paying him no mind, Rose. That ain't nothing but gin-talk. Go on, Troy. I'll see you Monday.

TROY. Don't you come by my house, nigger! I done told you what I'm gonna be doing.

*The lights go down to black.*

## *Scene 2*

*The lights come up on Rose hanging up clothes. She hums and sings softly to herself. It is the following morning.*

ROSE (*sings*).

> Jesus, be a fence all around me every day
> Jesus, I want you to protect me as I travel on my way.
> Jesus, be a fence all around me every day.

*Troy enters from the house.*

> Jesus, I want you to protect me
> As I travel on my way.

(*To Troy.*) 'Morning. You ready for breakfast? I can fix it soon as I finish hanging up these clothes?

TROY. I got the coffee on. That'll be all right. I'll just drink some of that this morning.

ROSE. That 651 hit yesterday. That's the second time this month. Miss Pearl hit for a dollar . . . seem like those that need the least always get lucky. Poor folks can't get nothing.

TROY. Them numbers don't know nobody. I don't know why you fool with them. You and Lyons both.

ROSE. It's something to do.

TROY. You ain't doing nothing but throwing your money away.

ROSE. Troy, you know I don't play foolishly. I just play a nickel here and a nickel there.

TROY. That's two nickels you done thrown away.

ROSE. Now I hit sometimes . . . that makes up for it. It always comes in handy when I do hit. I don't hear you complaining then.

TROY. I ain't complaining now. I just say it's foolish. Trying to guess out of six hundred ways which way the number gonna come. If I had all the money niggers, these Negroes, throw away on numbers for one week—just one week—I'd be a rich man.

ROSE. Well, you wishing and calling it foolish ain't gonna stop folks from playing numbers. That's one thing for sure. Besides . . . some good things come from playing numbers. Look where Pope done bought him that restaurant off of numbers.

TROY. I can't stand niggers like that. Man ain't had two dimes to rub together. He walking around with his shoes all run over bumming money for cigarettes. All right. Got lucky there and hit the numbers . . .

ROSE. Troy, I know all about it.

TROY. Had good sense, I'll say that for him. He ain't throwed his money away. I seen niggers hit the numbers and go through two thousand dollars in four days. Man bought him that restaurant down there . . . fixed it up real nice . . . and then didn't want nobody to come in it! A Negro go in there and can't get no kind of service. I seen a white fellow come in there and order a bowl of stew. Pope picked all the meat out of the pot for him. Man ain't had nothing but a bowl of meat! Negro come behind him and ain't got nothing but the potatoes and carrots. Talking about what numbers do for people, you picked a wrong example. Ain't done nothing but make a worser fool out of him than he was before.

ROSE. Troy, you ought to stop worrying about what happened at work yesterday.

TROY. I ain't worried. Just told me to be down there at the Commissioner's office on Friday. Everybody think they gonna fire me. I ain't worried about them firing me. You ain't got to worry about that. (*Pause.*) Where's Cory? Cory in the house? (*Calls.*) Cory?

ROSE. He gone out.

TROY. Out, huh? He gone out 'cause he know I want him to help me with this fence. I know how he is. That boy scared of work.

*Gabriel enters. He comes halfway down the alley and, hearing Troy's voice, stops.*

TROY (*continues*). He ain't done a lick of work in his life.

ROSE. He had to go to football practice. Coach wanted them to get in a little extra practice before the season start.

TROY. I got his practice . . . running out of here before he get his chores done.

ROSE. Troy, what is wrong with you this morning? Don't nothing set right with you. Go on back in there and go to bed . . . get up on the other side.

TROY. Why something got to be wrong with me? I ain't said nothing wrong with me.

ROSE. You got something to say about everything. First it's the numbers . . . then it's the way the man runs his restaurant . . . then you done got on Cory. What's it gonna be next? Take a look up there and see if the weather suits you . . . or is it gonna be how you gonna put up the fence with the clothes hanging in the yard.

TROY. You hit the nail on the head then.

ROSE. I know you like I know the back of my hand. Go on in there and get you some coffee . . . see if that straighten you up. 'Cause you ain't right this morning.

*Troy starts into the house and sees Gabriel. Gabriel starts singing. Troy's brother, he is seven years younger than Troy. Injured in World War II, he has a metal plate in his head. He carries an old trumpet tied around his waist and believes with every fiber of his being that he is the Archangel Gabriel. He carries a chipped basket with an assortment of discarded fruits and vegetables he has picked up in the strip district and which he attempts to sell.*

GABRIEL (*singing*).

Yes, ma'am I got plums
You ask me how I sell them
Oh ten cents apiece
Three for a quarter
Come and buy now
'Cause I'm here today
And tomorrow I'll be gone

*Gabriel enters.*

Hey, Rose!

ROSE. How you doing Gabe?

GABRIEL. There's Troy . . . Hey, Troy!

TROY. Hey, Gabe.

*Exit into kitchen.*

ROSE (*to Gabriel*). What you got there?

GABRIEL. You know what I got, Rose. I got fruits and vegetables.

ROSE (*looking in basket*). Where's all these plums you talking about?

GABRIEL. I ain't got no plums today, Rose. I was just singing that. Have some tomorrow. Put me in a big order for plums. Have enough plums tomorrow for St. Peter and everybody.

*Troy reenters from kitchen, crosses to steps.*

(*To Rose.*) Troy's mad at me.

TROY. I ain't mad at you. What I got to be mad at you about? You ain't done nothing to me.

GABRIEL. I just moved over to Miss Pearl's to keep out from in your way. I ain't mean no harm by it.

TROY. Who said anything about that? I ain't said anything about that.

GABRIEL. You ain't mad at me, is you?

TROY. Naw . . . I ain't mad at you, Gabe. If I was mad at you I'd tell you about it.

GABRIEL. Got me two rooms. In the basement. Got my own door too. Wanna see my key? (*He holds up a key.*) That's my own key! My two rooms!

TROY. Well, that's good, Gabe. You got your own key . . . that's good.

ROSE. You hungry, Gabe? I was just fixing to cook Troy his breakfast.

GABRIEL. I'll take some biscuits. You got some biscuits? Did you know when I was in heaven . . . every morning me and St. Peter would sit down by the gate and eat some big fat biscuits? Oh, yeah! We had us a good time. We'd sit there and eat us them biscuits and then St. Peter would go off to sleep and tell me to wake him up when it's time to open the gates for the judgment.

ROSE. Well, come on . . . I'll make up a batch of biscuits.

*Rose exits into the house.*

GABRIEL. Troy . . . St. Peter got your name in the book. I seen it. It say . . . Troy Maxson. I say . . . I know him! He got the same name like what I got. That's my brother!

TROY. How many times you gonna tell me that, Gabe?

GABRIEL. Ain't got my name in the book. Don't have to have my name. I done died and went to heaven. He got your name though. One morning St. Peter was looking at his book . . . marking it up for the judgment . . . and he let me see your name. Got it in there under M. Got Rose's name . . . I ain't seen it like I seen yours . . . but I know it's in there. He got a great big book. Got everybody's name what was ever been born. That's what he told me. But I seen your name. Seen it with my own eyes.

TROY. Go on in the house there. Rose going to fix you something to eat.

GABRIEL. Oh, I ain't hungry. I done had breakfast with Aunt Jemimah. She come by and cooked me up a whole mess of flapjacks. Remember how we used to eat them flapjacks?

TROY. Go on in the house and get you something to eat now.

GABRIEL. I got to sell my plums. I done sold some tomatoes. Got me two quarters. Wanna see? (*He shows Troy his quarters.*) I'm gonna save them and buy me a new horn so St. Peter can hear me when it's time to open the gates. (*Gabriel stops suddenly. Listens.*) Hear that? That's the hellhounds. I got to chase them out of here. Go on get out of here! Get out!

*Gabriel exits singing.*

Better get ready for the judgment
Better get ready for the judgment
My Lord is coming down

*Rose enters from the house.*

TROY. He's gone off somewhere.

GABRIEL (*offstage*).

Better get ready for the judgment
Better get ready for the judgment morning
Better get ready for the judgment
My God is coming down

ROSE. He ain't eating right. Miss Pearl say she can't get him to eat nothing.

TROY. What you want me to do about it, Rose? I done did everything I can for the man. I can't make him get well. Man got half his head blown away . . . what you expect?

ROSE. Seem like something ought to be done to help him.

TROY. Man don't bother nobody. He just mixed up from that metal plate he got in his head. Ain't no sense for him to go back into the hospital.

ROSE. Least he be eating right. They can help him take care of himself.

TROY. Don't nobody wanna be locked up, Rose. What you wanna lock him up for? Man go over there and fight the war . . . messin' around with them Japs, get half his head blown off . . . and they give him a lousy three thousand dollars. And I had to swoop down on that.

ROSE. Is you fixing to go into that again?

TROY. That's the only way I got a roof over my head . . . cause of that metal plate.

ROSE. Ain't no sense you blaming yourself for nothing. Gabe wasn't in no condition to manage that money. You done what was right by him. Can't nobody say you ain't done what was right by him. Look how long you took care of him . . . till he wanted to have his own place and moved over there with Miss Pearl.

TROY. That ain't what I'm saying, woman! I'm just stating the facts. If my brother didn't have that metal plate in his head . . . I wouldn't have a pot to piss in or a window to throw it out of. And I'm fifty-three years old. Now see if you can understand that!

*Troy gets up from the porch and starts to exit the yard.*

ROSE. Where you going off to? You been running out of here every Saturday for weeks. I thought you was gonna work on this fence?

TROY. I'm gonna walk down to Taylors'. Listen to the ball game. I'll be back in a bit. I'll work on it when I get back.

*He exits the yard. The lights go to black.*

### *Scene 3*

*The lights come up on the yard. It is four hours later. Rose is taking down the clothes from the line. Cory enters carrying his football equipment.*

ROSE. Your daddy like to had a fit with you running out of here this morning without doing your chores.

CORY. I told you I had to go to practice.

ROSE. He say you were supposed to help him with this fence.

CORY. He been saying that the last four or five Saturdays, and then he don't never do nothing, but go down to Taylors'. Did you tell him about the recruiter?

ROSE. Yeah, I told him.

CORY. What he say?

ROSE. He ain't said nothing too much. You get in there and get started on your chores before he gets back. Go on and scrub down them steps before he gets back here hollering and carrying on.

CORY. I'm hungry. What you got to eat, Mama?

ROSE. Go on and get started on your chores. I got some meat loaf in there. Go on and make you a sandwich . . . and don't leave no mess in there.

*Cory exits into the house. Rose continues to take down the clothes. Troy enters the yard and sneaks up and grabs her from behind.*

Troy! Go on, now. You liked to scared me to death. What was the score of the game? Lucille had me on the phone and I couldn't keep up with it.

TROY. What I care about the game? Come here, woman. (*He tries to kiss her.*)

ROSE. I thought you went down Taylors' to listen to the game. Go on, Troy! You supposed to be putting up this fence.

TROY (*attempting to kiss her again*). I'll put it up when I finish with what is at hand.

ROSE. Go on, Troy. I ain't studying you.

TROY (*chasing after her*). I'm studying you . . . fixing to do my homework!

ROSE. Troy, you better leave me alone.

TROY. Where's Cory? That boy brought his butt home yet?

ROSE. He's in the house doing his chores.

TROY (*calling*). Cory! Get your butt out here, boy!

*Rose exits into the house with the laundry. Troy goes over to the pile of wood, picks up a board, and starts sawing. Cory enters from the house.*

TROY. You just now coming in here from leaving this morning?

CORY. Yeah, I had to go to football practice.

TROY. Yeah, what?

CORY. Yessir.

TROY. I ain't but two seconds off you noway. The garbage sitting in there overflowing . . . you ain't done none of your chores . . . and you come in here talking about "Yeah."

CORY. I was just getting ready to do my chores now, Pop . . .

TROY. Your first chore is to help me with this fence on Saturday. Everything else come after that. Now get that saw and cut them boards.

*Cory takes the saw and begins cutting the boards. Troy continues working. There is a long pause.*

CORY. Hey, Pop . . . why don't you buy a TV?

TROY. What I want with a TV? What I want one of them for?

CORY. Everybody got one. Earl, Ba Bra . . . Jesse!

TROY. I ain't asked you who had one. I say what I want with one?

CORY. So you can watch it. They got lots of things on TV. Baseball games and everything. We could watch the World Series.

TROY. Yeah . . . and how much this TV cost?

CORY. I don't know. They got them on sale for around two hundred dollars.

TROY. Two hundred dollars, huh?

CORY. That ain't that much, Pop.

TROY. Naw, it's just two hundred dollars. See that roof you got over your head at night? Let me tell you something about that roof. It's been over ten years since that roof was last tarred. See now . . . the snow come this winter and sit up there on that roof like it is . . . and it's gonna seep inside. It's just gonna be a little bit . . . ain't gonna hardly notice it. Then the next thing you know, it's gonna be leaking all over the house. Then the wood rot from all that water and you gonna need a whole new roof. Now, how much you think it cost to get that roof tarred?

CORY. I don't know.

TROY. Two hundred and sixty-four dollars . . . cash money. While you thinking about a TV, I got to be thinking about the roof . . . and whatever else go wrong here. Now if you had two hundred dollars, what would you do . . . fix the roof or buy a TV?

CORY. I'd buy a TV. Then when the roof started to leak . . . when it needed fixing . . . I'd fix it.

TROY. Where you gonna get the money from? You done spent it for a TV. You gonna sit up and watch the water run all over your brand new TV.

CORY. Aw, Pop. You got money. I know you do.

TROY. Where I got it at, huh?

CORY. You got it in the bank.

TROY. You wanna see my bankbook? You wanna see that seventy-three dollars and twenty-two cents I got sitting up in there?

CORY. You ain't got to pay for it all at one time. You can put a down payment on it and carry it on home with you.

TROY. Not me. I ain't gonna owe nobody nothing if I can help it. Miss a payment and they come and snatch it right out of your house. Then what you got? Now, soon as I get two hundred dollars clear, then I'll buy a TV. Right now, as soon as I get two hundred and sixty-four dollars, I'm gonna have this roof tarred.

CORY. Aw . . . Pop!

TROY. You go on and get you two hundred dollars and buy one if ya want it. I got better things to do with my money.

CORY. I can't get no two hundred dollars. I ain't never seen two hundred dollars.

TROY. I'll tell you what . . . you get you a hundred dollars and I'll put the other hundred with it.

CORY. All right, I'm gonna show you.

TROY. You gonna show me how you can cut them boards right now.

*Cory begins to cut the boards. There is a long pause.*

CORY. The Pirates won today. That makes five in a row.

TROY. I ain't thinking about the Pirates. Got an all-white team. Got that boy . . . that Puerto Rican boy . . . Clemente. Don't even half-play him. That boy could be something if they give him a chance. Play him one day and sit him on the bench the next.

CORY. He gets a lot of chances to play.

TROY. I'm talking about playing regular. Playing every day so you can get your timing. That's what I'm talking about.

CORY. They got some white guys on the team that don't play every day. You can't play everybody at the same time.

TROY. If they got a white fellow sitting on the bench . . . you can bet your last dollar he can't play! The colored guy got to be twice as good before he get on the team. That's why I don't want you to get all tied up in them sports. Man on the team and what it get him? They got colored on the team and don't use them. Same as not having them. All them teams the same.

CORY. The Braves got Hank Aaron and Wes Covington. Hank Aaron hit two home runs today. That makes forty-three.

TROY. Hank Aaron ain't nobody. That what you supposed to do. That's how you supposed to play the game. Ain't nothing to it. It's just a matter of timing . . . getting the right follow-through. Hell, I can hit forty-three home runs right now!

CORY. Not off no major-league pitching, you couldn't.

TROY. We had better pitching in the Negro leagues. I hit seven home runs off of Satchel Paige.[4] You can't get no better than that!

CORY. Sandy Koufax. He's leading the league in strikeouts.

TROY. I ain't thinking of no Sandy Koufax.

CORY. You got Warren Spahn and Lew Burdette. I bet you couldn't hit no home runs off of Warren Spahn.

TROY. I'm through with it now. You go on and cut them boards. (*Pause.*) Your mama tell me you done got recruited by a college football team? Is that right?

CORY. Yeah. Coach Zellman say the recruiter gonna be coming by to talk to you. Get you to sign the permission papers.

TROY. I thought you supposed to be working down there at the A&P. Ain't you suppose to be working down there after school?

CORY. Mr. Stawicki say he gonna hold my job for me until after the football season. Say starting next week I can work weekends.

TROY. I thought we had an understanding about this football stuff? You suppose to keep up with your chores and hold that job down at the A&P. Ain't been around here all day on a Saturday. Ain't none of your chores done . . . and now you telling me you done quit your job.

CORY. I'm going to be working weekends.

TROY. You damn right you are! And ain't no need for nobody coming around here to talk to me about signing nothing.

[4]**Satchel Paige** (1906–82) pitcher in the Negro leagues

CORY. Hey, Pop . . . you can't do that. He's coming all the way from North Carolina.

TROY. I don't care where he coming from. The white man ain't gonna let you get nowhere with that football noway. You go on and get your book-learning so you can work yourself up in that A&P or learn how to fix cars or build houses or something, get you a trade. That way you have something can't nobody take away from you. You go on and learn how to put your hands to some good use. Besides hauling people's garbage.

CORY. I get good grades, Pop. That's why the recruiter wants to talk with you. You got to keep up your grades to get recruited. This way I'll be going to college. I'll get a chance . . .

TROY. First you gonna get your butt down there to the A&P and get your job back.

CORY. Mr. Stawicki done already hired somebody else 'cause I told him I was playing football.

TROY. You a bigger fool than I thought . . . to let somebody take away your job so you can play some football. Where you gonna get your money to take out your girlfriend and whatnot? What kind of foolishness is that to let somebody take away your job?

CORY. I'm still gonna be working weekends.

TROY. Naw . . . naw. You getting your butt out of here and finding you another job.

CORY. Come on, Pop! I got to practice. I can't work after school and play football too. The team needs me. That's what Coach Zellman say . . .

TROY. I don't care what nobody else say. I'm the boss . . . you understand? I'm the boss around here. I do the only saying what counts.

CORY. Come on, Pop!

TROY. I asked you . . . did you understand?

CORY. Yeah . . .

TROY. What?!

CORY. Yessir.

TROY. You go on down there to that A&P and see if you can get your job back. If you can't do both . . . then you quit the football team. You've got to take the crookeds with the straights.

CORY. Yessir. (*Pause.*) Can I ask you a question?

TROY. What the hell you wanna ask me? Mr. Stawicki the one you got the questions for.

CORY. How come you ain't never liked me?

TROY. Liked you? Who the hell say I got to like you? What law is there say I got to like you? Wanna stand up in my face and ask a damn foolass question like that. Talking about liking somebody. Come here, boy, when I talk to you.

*Cory comes over to where Troy is working. He stands slouched over and Troy shoves him on his shoulder.*

Straighten up, goddammit! I asked you a question . . . what law is there say I got to like you?

CORY. None.

TROY. Well, all right then! Don't you eat every day? (*Pause.*) Answer me when I talk to you! Don't you eat every day?

CORY. Yeah.

TROY. Nigger, as long as you in my house, you put that sir on the end of it when you talk to me.

CORY. Yes . . . sir.

TROY. You eat every day.

CORY. Yessir!

TROY. Got a roof over your head.

CORY. Yessir!

TROY. Got clothes on your back.

CORY. Yessir.

TROY. Why you think that is?

CORY. Cause of you.

TROY. Ah, hell I know it's cause of me . . . but why do you think that is?

CORY (*hesitant*). Cause you like me.

TROY. Like you? I go out of here every morning . . . bust my butt . . . putting up with them crackers every day . . . cause I like you? You are the biggest fool I ever saw. (*Pause.*) It's my job. It's my responsibility! You understand that? A man got to take care of his family. You live in my house . . . sleep you behind on my bedclothes . . . fill you belly up with my food . . . cause you my son. You my flesh and blood. Not cause I like you! Cause it's my duty to take care of you. I owe a responsibility to you! Let's get this straight right here . . . before it go along any further . . . I ain't got to like you. Mr. Rand don't give me my money come payday cause he likes me. He give me cause he owe me. I done give you everything I had to give you. I gave you your life! Me and your mama worked that out between us. And liking your black ass wasn't part of the bargain. Don't you try and go through life worrying about if somebody like you or not. You best be making sure they doing right by you. You understand what I'm saying boy?

CORY. Yessir.

TROY. Then get the hell out of my face, and get on down to that A&P.

*Rose has been standing behind the screen door for much of the scene. She enters as Cory exits.*

ROSE. Why don't you let the boy go ahead and play football, Troy? Ain't no harm in that. He's just trying to be like you with the sports.

TROY. I don't want him to be like me! I want him to move as far away from my life as he can get. You the only decent thing that ever happened to me. I wish him that. But I don't wish him a thing else from my life. I decided seventeen years ago that boy wasn't getting involved in no sports. Not after what they did to me in the sports.

ROSE. Troy, why don't you admit you was too old to play in the major leagues? For once . . . why don't you admit that?

TROY. What do you mean too old? Don't come telling me I was too old. I just wasn't the right color. Hell, I'm fifty-three years old and can do better than Selkirk's .269 right now!

ROSE. How's was you gonna play ball when you were over forty? Sometimes I can't get no sense out of you.

TROY. I got good sense, woman. I got sense enough not to let my boy get hurt over playing no sports. You been mothering that boy too much. Worried about if people like him.

ROSE. Everything that boy do . . . he do for you. He wants you to say "Good job, son." That's all.

TROY. Rose, I ain't got time for that. He's alive. He's healthy. He's got to make his own way. I made mine. Ain't nobody gonna hold his hand when he get out there in that world.

ROSE. Times have changed from when you was young, Troy. People change. The world's changing around you and you can't even see it.

TROY (*slow, methodical*). Woman . . . I do the best I can do. I come in here every Friday. I carry a sack of potatoes and a bucket of lard. You all line up at the door with your hands out. I give you the lint from my pockets. I give you my sweat and my blood. I ain't got no tears. I done spent them. We go upstairs in that room at night . . . and I fall down on you and try to blast a hole into forever. I get up Monday morning . . . find my lunch on the table. I go out. Make my way. Find my strength to carry me through to the next Friday. (*Pause.*) That's all I got, Rose. That's all I got to give. I can't give nothing else.

*Troy exits into the house. The lights go down to black.*

### *Scene 4*

*It is Friday. Two weeks later. Cory starts out of the house with his football equipment. The phone rings.*

CORY (*calling*). I got it! (*He answers the phone and stands in the screen door talking.*) Hello? Hey, Jesse. Naw . . . I was just getting ready to leave now.

ROSE (*calling*). Cory!

CORY. I told you, man, them spikes is all tore up. You can use them if you want, but they ain't no good. Earl got some spikes.

ROSE (*calling*). Cory!

CORY (*calling to Rose*). Mam? I'm talking to Jesse. (*Into phone.*) When she say that? (*Pause.*) Aw, you lying, man. I'm gonna tell her you said that.

ROSE (*calling*). Cory, don't you go nowhere!

CORY. I got to go to the game, Ma! (*Into the phone.*) Yeah, hey, look, I'll talk to you later. Yeah, I'll meet you over Earl's house. Later. Bye, Ma.

*Cory exits the house and starts out the yard.*

ROSE. Cory, where you going off to? You got that stuff all pulled out and thrown all over your room.

CORY (*in the yard*). I was looking for my spikes. Jesse wanted to borrow my spikes.

ROSE. Get up there and get that cleaned up before your daddy get back in here.

CORY. I got to go to the game! I'll clean it up *when I get back.*

*Cory exits.*

ROSE. That's all he need to do is see that room all messed up.

*Rose exits into the house. Troy and Bono enter the yard. Troy is dressed in clothes other than his work clothes.*

BONO. He told him the same thing he told you. Take it to the union.

TROY. Brownie ain't got that much sense. Man wasn't thinking about nothing. He wait until I confront them on it . . . then he wanna come crying seniority. (*Calls.*) Hey, Rose!

BONO. I wish I could have seen Mr. Rand's face when he told you.

TROY. He couldn't get it out of his mouth! Liked to bit his tongue! When they called me down there to the Commissioner's office . . . he thought they was gonna fire me. Like everybody else.

BONO. I didn't think they was gonna fire you. I thought they was gonna put you on the warning paper.

TROY. Hey, Rose! (*To Bono.*) Yeah, Mr. Rand like to bit his tongue.

*Troy breaks the seal on the bottle, takes a drink, and hands it to Bono.*

BONO. I see you run right down to Taylors' and told that Alberta gal.

TROY (*calling*). Hey Rose! (*To Bono.*) I told everybody. Hey, Rose! I went down there to cash my check.

ROSE (*entering from the house*). Hush all that hollering, man! I know you out here. What they say down there at the Commissioner's office?

TROY. You supposed to come when I call you, woman. Bono'll tell you that. (*To Bono.*) Don't Lucille come when you call her?

ROSE. Man, hush your mouth. I ain't no dog . . . talk about "come when you call me."

TROY (*puts his arm around Rose*). You hear this, Bono? I had me an old dog used to get uppity like that. You say, "C'mere, Blue!" . . . and he just lay there and look at you. End up getting a stick and chasing him away trying to make him come.

ROSE. I ain't studying you and your dog. I remember you used to sing that old song.

TROY (*he sings*).

Hear it ring! Hear it ring! I had a dog his name was Blue.

ROSE. Don't nobody wanna hear you sing that old song.

TROY (*sings*).

You know Blue was mighty true.

ROSE. Used to have Cory running around here singing that song.

BONO. Hell, I remember that song myself.

TROY (*sings*).

You know Blue was a good old dog.
Blue treed a possum in a hollow log.

That was my daddy's song. My daddy made up that song.

ROSE. I don't care who made it up. Don't nobody wanna hear you sing it.

TROY (*makes a song like calling a dog*). Come here, woman.

ROSE. You come in here carrying on, I reckon they ain't fired you. What they say down there at the Commissioner's office?

TROY. Look here, Rose . . . Mr. Rand called me into his office today when I got back from talking to them people down there . . . it come from up top . . . he called me in and told me they was making me a driver.

ROSE. Troy, you kidding!

TROY. No I ain't. Ask Bono.

ROSE. Well, that's great, Troy. Now you don't have to hassle them people no more.

*Lyons enters from the street.*

TROY. Aw hell, I wasn't looking to see you today. I thought you was in jail. Got it all over the front page of the *Courier* about them raiding Sefus's place . . . where you be hanging out with all them thugs.

LYONS. Hey, Pop . . . that ain't got nothing to do with me. I don't go down there gambling. I go down there to sit in with the band. I ain't got nothing to do with the gambling part. They got some good music down there.

TROY. They got some rogues . . . is what they got.

LYONS. How you been, Mr. Bono? Hi, Rose.

BONO. I see where you playing down at the Crawford Grill tonight.

ROSE. How come you ain't brought Bonnie like I told you? You should have brought Bonnie with you, she ain't been over in a month of Sundays.

LYONS. I was just in the neighborhood . . . thought I'd stop by.

TROY. Here he come . . .

BONO. Your daddy got a promotion on the rubbish. He's gonna be the first colored driver. Ain't got to do nothing but sit up there and read the paper like them white fellows.

LYONS. Hey, Pop . . . if you knew how to read you'd be all right.

BONO. Naw . . . naw . . . you mean if the nigger knew how to drive he'd be all right. Been fighting with them people about driving and ain't even got a license. Mr. Rand know you ain't got no driver's license?

TROY. Driving ain't nothing. All you do is point the truck where you want it to go. Driving ain't nothing.

BONO. Do Mr. Rand know you ain't got no driver's license? That's what I'm talking about. I ain't asked if driving was easy. I asked if Mr. Rand know you ain't got no driver's license.

TROY. He ain't got to know. The man ain't got to know my business. Time he find out, I have two or three driver's licenses.

LYONS (*going into his pocket*). Say, look here, Pop . . .

TROY. I knew it was coming. Didn't I tell you, Bono? I know what kind of "Look here, Pop" that was. The nigger fixing to ask me for some money. It's Friday night. It's my payday. All them rogues down there on the avenue . . . the ones that ain't in jail . . . and Lyons is hopping in his shoes to get down there with them.

LYONS. See, Pop . . . if you give somebody else a chance to talk sometimes, you'd see that I was fixing to pay you back your ten dollars like I told you. Here . . . I told you I'd pay you when Bonnie got paid.

TROY. Naw . . . you go ahead and keep that ten dollars. Put it in the bank. The next time you feel like you wanna come by here and ask me for something . . . you go on down there and get that.

LYONS. Here's your ten dollars, Pop. I told you I don't want you to give me nothing. I just wanted to borrow ten dollars.

TROY. Naw . . . you go on and keep that for the next time you want to ask me.

LYONS. Come on, Pop . . . here go your ten dollars.

ROSE. Why don't you go on and let the boy pay you back, Troy?

LYONS. Here you go, Rose. If you don't take it I'm gonna have to hear about it for the next six months. (*He hands her the money.*)

ROSE. You can hand yours over here too, Troy.

TROY. You see this, Bono. You see how they do me.

BONO. Yeah, Lucille do me the same way.

*Gabriel is heard singing off stage. He enters.*

GABRIEL. Better get ready for the Judgment! Better get ready for . . . Hey! . . . Hey! . . . There's Troy's boy!

LYONS. How are you doing, Uncle Gabe?

GABRIEL. Lyons . . . The King of the Jungle! Rose . . . hey, Rose. Got a flower for you. (*He takes a rose from his pocket.*) Picked it myself. That's the same rose like you is!

ROSE. That's right nice of you, Gabe.

LYONS. What you been doing, Uncle Gabe?

GABRIEL. Oh, I been chasing hellhounds and waiting on the time to tell St. Peter to open the gates.

LYONS. You been chasing hellhounds, huh? Well . . . you doing the right thing, Uncle Gabe. Somebody got to chase them.

GABRIEL. Oh, yeah . . . I know it. The devil's strong. The devil ain't no pushover. Hellhounds snipping at everybody's heels. But I got my trumpet waiting on the judgment time.

LYONS. Waiting on the Battle of Armageddon, huh?

GABRIEL. Ain't gonna be too much of a battle when God get to waving that Judgment sword. But the people's gonna have a hell of a time trying to get into heaven if them gates ain't open.

LYONS (*putting his arm around Gabriel*). You hear this, Pop. Uncle Gabe, you all right!

GABRIEL (*laughing with Lyons*). Lyons! King of the Jungle.

ROSE. You gonna stay for supper, Gabe? Want me to fix you a plate?

GABRIEL. I'll take a sandwich, Rose. Don't want no plate. Just wanna eat with my hands. I'll take a sandwich.

ROSE. How about you, Lyons? You staying? Got some short ribs cooking.

LYONS. Naw, I won't eat nothing till after we finished playing. (*Pause.*) You ought to come down and listen to me play, Pop.

TROY. I don't like that Chinese music. All that noise.

ROSE. Go on in the house and wash up, Gabe . . . I'll fix you a sandwich.

GABRIEL (*to Lyons, as he exits*). Troy's mad at me.

LYONS. What you mad at Uncle Gabe for, Pop?

ROSE. He thinks Troy's mad at him cause he moved over to Miss Pearl's.

TROY. I ain't mad at the man. He can live where he want to live at.

LYONS. What he move over there for? Miss Pearl don't like nobody.

ROSE. She don't mind him none. She treats him real nice. She just don't allow all that singing.

TROY. She don't mind that rent he be paying . . . that's what she don't mind.

ROSE. Troy, I ain't going through that with you no more. He's over there cause he want to have his own place. He can come and go as he please.

TROY. Hell, he could come and go as he please here. I wasn't stopping him. I ain't put no rules on him.

ROSE. It ain't the same thing, Troy. And you know it.

*Gabriel comes to the door.*

Now, that's the last I wanna hear about that. I don't wanna hear nothing else about Gabe and Miss Pearl. And next week . . .

GABRIEL. I'm ready for my sandwich, Rose.

ROSE. And next week . . . when that recruiter come from that school . . . I want you to sign that paper and go on and let Cory play football. Then that'll be the last I have to hear about that.

TROY (*to Rose as she exits into the house*). I ain't thinking about Cory nothing.

LYONS. What . . . Cory got recruited? What school he going to?

TROY. That boy walking around here smelling his piss . . . thinking he's grown. Thinking he's gonna do what he want, irrespective of what I say. Look here, Bono . . . I left the Commissioner's office and went down to the A&P . . . that boy ain't working down there. He lying to me. Telling me he got his job back . . . telling me he working weekends . . . telling me he working after school . . . Mr. Stawicki tell me he ain't working down there at all!

LYONS. Cory just growing up. He's just busting at the seams trying to fill out your shoes.

TROY. I don't care what he's doing. When he get to the point where he wanna disobey me . . . then it's time for him to move on. Bono'll tell you that. I bet he ain't never disobeyed his daddy without paying the consequences.

BONO. I ain't never had a chance. My daddy came on through . . . but I ain't never knew him to see him . . . or what he had on his mind or where he went. Just moving on through. Searching out the New Land. That's what the old folks used to call it. See a fellow moving around from place to place . . . woman to woman . . . called it searching out the New Land. I can't say if he ever found it. I come along, didn't want no kids. Didn't know if I was gonna be in one place long enough to fix on them right as their daddy. I figured I was going searching too. As it turned out I been hooked up with Lucille near about as long as your daddy been with Rose. Going on sixteen years.

TROY. Sometimes I wish I hadn't known my daddy. He ain't cared nothing about no kids. A kid to him wasn't nothing. All he wanted was for you to learn how to walk so he could start you to working. When it come time for eating . . . he ate first. If there was anything left over, that's what you got. Man would sit down and eat two chickens and give you the wing.

LYONS. You ought to stop that, Pop. Everybody feed their kids. No matter how hard times is . . . everybody care about their kids. Make sure they have something to eat.

TROY. The only thing my daddy cared about was getting them bales of cotton in to Mr. Lubin. That's the only thing that mattered to him. Sometimes I used to wonder why he was living. Wonder why the devil hadn't come and got him. "Get them bales of cotton in to Mr. Lubin" and find out he owe him money . . .

LYONS. He should have just went on and left when he saw he couldn't get nowhere. That's what I would have done.

TROY. How he gonna leave with eleven kids? And where he gonna go? He ain't knew how to do nothing but farm. No, he was trapped and I think he knew it. But I'll say this for him . . . he felt a responsibility toward us. Maybe he ain't treated us the way I felt he should have . . . but without that responsibility he could have walked off and left us . . . made his own way.

BONO. A lot of them did. Back in those days what you talking about . . . they walk out their front door and just take on down one road or another and keep on walking.

LYONS. There you go! That's what I'm talking about.

BONO. Just keep on walking till you come to something else. Ain't you never heard of nobody having the walking blues? Well, that's what you call it when you just take off like that.

TROY. My daddy ain't had them walking blues! What you talking about? He stayed right there with his family. But he was just as evil as he could be. My mama couldn't stand him. Couldn't stand that evilness. She run off when I was about eight. She sneaked off one night after he had gone to sleep. Told me she was coming back for me. I ain't never seen her no more. All his women run off and left him. He wasn't good for nobody.

When my turn come to head out, I was fourteen and got to sniffing around Joe Canewell's daughter. Had us an old mule we called Greyboy. My daddy sent me out to do some plowing and I tied up Greyboy and went to fooling around with Joe Canewell's daughter. We done found us a nice little spot, got real cozy with each other. She about thirteen and we done figured we was grown anyway . . . so we down there enjoying ourselves . . . ain't thinking about nothing. We didn't know Greyboy had got loose and wandered back to the house and my daddy was looking for me. We down there by the creek enjoying ourselves when my daddy come up on us. Surprised us. He had them leather straps off the mule and commenced to whupping me like there was no tomorrow. I jumped up, mad and embarrassed. I was scared of my daddy. When he commenced to whupping on me . . . quite naturally I run to get out of the way. (*Pause.*) Now I thought he was mad cause I ain't done my work. But I see where he was chasing me off so he could have the gal for himself. When I see what the matter of it was, I lost all fear of my daddy. Right there is where I become a man . . . at fourteen years of age. (*Pause.*) Now it was my turn to run him off. I picked up them same reins that he had used on me. I picked up them reins and commenced to whupping on him. The gal jumped up and run off . . . and when my daddy turned to face me, I could see why the devil had never come to get him . . . cause he was the devil himself. I don't know what happened. When I woke up, I was laying right there by the creek, and Blue . . . this old dog we had . . . was licking my face. I thought I was blind. I couldn't see nothing. Both my eyes were swollen shut. I laid there and cried. I didn't know what I was gonna do. The only thing I knew was the time had come for me to leave my daddy's house. And right there the world suddenly got big. And it was a long time before I could cut it down to where I could handle it.

Part of that cutting down was when I got to the place where I could feel him kicking in my blood and knew that the only thing that separated us was the matter of a few years.

*Gabriel enters from the house with a sandwich.*

LYONS. What you got there, Uncle Gabe?

GABRIEL. Got me a ham sandwich. Rose gave me a ham sandwich.

TROY. I don't know what happened to him. I done lost touch with everybody except Gabriel. But I hope he's dead. I hope he found some peace.

LYONS. That's a heavy story, Pop. I didn't know you left home when you was fourteen.

TROY. And didn't know nothing. The only part of the world I knew was the forty-two acres of Mr. Lubin's land. That's all I knew about life.

LYONS. Fourteen's kinda young to be out on your own. (*Phone rings.*) I don't even think I was ready to be out on my own at fourteen. I don't know what I would have done.

TROY. I got up from the creek and walked on down to Mobile. I was through with farming. Figured I could do better in the city. So I walked the two hundred miles to Mobile.

LYONS. Wait a minute . . . you ain't walked no two hundred miles, Pop. Ain't nobody gonna walk no two hundred miles. You talking about some walking there.

BONO. That's the only way you got anywhere back in them days.

LYONS. Shhh. Damn if I wouldn't have hitched a ride with somebody!

TROY. Who you gonna hitch it with? They ain't had no cars and things like they got now. We talking about 1918.

ROSE (*entering*). What you all out here getting into?

TROY (*to Rose*). I'm telling Lyons how good he got it. He don't know nothing about this I'm talking.

ROSE. Lyons, that was Bonnie on the phone. She say you supposed to pick her up.

LYONS. Yeah, okay, Rose.

TROY. I walked on down to Mobile and hitched up with some of them fellows that was heading this way. Got up here and found out . . . not only couldn't you get a job . . . you couldn't find no place to live. I thought I was in freedom. Shhh. Colored folks living down there on the riverbanks in whatever kind of shelter they could find for themselves. Right down there under the Brady Street Bridge. Living in shacks made of sticks and tarpaper. Messed around there and went from bad to worse. Started stealing. First it was food. Then I figured, hell, if I steal money I can buy me some food. Buy me some shoes too! One thing led to another. Met your mama. I was young and anxious to be a man. Met your mama and had you. What I do that for? Now I got to worry about feeding you and her. Got to steal three times as much. Went out one day looking for somebody to rob . . . that's what I was, a robber. I'll tell you the truth. I'm ashamed of it today. But it's the truth. Went to rob this fellow . . . pulled out my knife . . . and he pulled out a gun. Shot me in the chest. I felt just like somebody had taken a hot branding iron and laid it on me. When he shot me I jumped at him with my knife. They told me I killed him and they put me in the penitentiary and locked me up for fifteen years. That's where I met Bono. That's where I learned how to play baseball. Got out that place and your mama had taken you and went on to make life without me. Fifteen years was a long time for her to wait. But that fifteen years cured me of that robbing stuff. Rose'll tell you. She asked me when I met her if I had gotten all that foolishness out of my system. And I told her, "Baby, it's you and baseball all what count with me." You hear me, Bono? I meant it too. She say, "Which one comes first?" I told her, "Baby, ain't no doubt it's baseball . . . but you stick and get old with me and we'll both outlive this baseball." Am I right, Rose? And it's true.

ROSE. Man, hush your mouth. You ain't said no such thing. Talking about, "Baby you know you'll always be number one with me." That's what you was talking.

TROY. You hear that, Bono. That's why I love her.

BONO. Rose'll keep you straight. You get off the track, she'll straighten you up.

ROSE. Lyons, you better get on up and get Bonnie. She waiting on you.

LYONS (*gets up to go*). Hey, Pop, why don't you come on down to the Grill and hear me play?

TROY. I ain't going down there. I'm too old to be sitting around in them clubs.

BONO. You got to be good to play down at the Grill.

LYONS. Come on, Pop . . .

TROY. I got to get up in the morning.

LYONS. You ain't got to stay long.

TROY. Naw, I'm gonna get my supper and go on to bed.

LYONS. Well, I got to go. I'll see you again.

TROY. Don't you come around my house on my payday.

ROSE. Pick up the phone and let somebody know you coming. And bring Bonnie with you. You know I'm always glad to see her.

LYONS. Yeah, I'll do that, Rose. You take care now. See you, Pop. See you, Mr. Bono. See you, Uncle Gabe.

GABRIEL. Lyons! King of the Jungle!

*Lyons exits.*

TROY. Is supper ready, woman? Me and you got some business to take care of. I'm gonna tear it up too.

ROSE. Troy, I done told you now!

TROY (*puts his arm around Bono*). Aw hell, woman . . . this is Bono. Bono like family. I done known this nigger since . . . how long I done know you?

BONO. It's been a long time.

TROY. I done know this nigger since Skippy was a pup. Me and him done been through some times.

BONO. You sure right about that.

TROY. Hell, I done know him longer than I known you. And we still standing shoulder to shoulder. Hey, look here, Bono . . . a man can't ask for no more than that. (*Drinks to him.*) I love you, nigger.

BONO. Hell, I love you too . . . I got to get home see my woman. You got yours in hand. I got to get mine.

*Bono starts to exit as Cory enters the yard, dressed in his football uniform. He gives Troy a hard, uncompromising look.*

CORY. What you do that for, Pop?

*He throws his helmet down in the direction of Troy.*

ROSE. What's the matter? Cory . . . what's the matter?

CORY. Papa done went up to the school and told Coach Zellman I can't play football no more. Wouldn't even let me play the game. Told him to tell the recruiter not to come.

ROSE. Troy . . .

TROY. What you Troying me for. Yeah, I did it. And the boy know why I did it.

CORY. Why you wanna do that to me? That was the one chance I had.

ROSE. Ain't nothing wrong with Cory playing football, Troy.

TROY. The boy lied to me. I told the nigger if he wanna play football . . . to keep up his chores and hold down that job at the A&P. That was the conditions. Stopped down there to see Mr. Stawicki . . .

CORY. I can't work after school during the football season, Pop! I tried to tell you that Mr. Stawicki's holding my job for me. You don't never want to listen to nobody. And then you wanna go and do this to me!

TROY. I ain't done nothing to you. You done it to yourself.

CORY. Just cause you didn't have a chance! You just scared I'm gonna be better than you, that's all.

TROY. Come here.

ROSE. Troy . . .

*Cory reluctantly crosses over to Troy.*

TROY. All right! See. You done made a mistake.

CORY. I didn't even do nothing!

TROY. I'm gonna tell you what your mistake was. See . . . you swung at the ball and didn't hit it. That's strike one. See, you in the batter's box now. You swung and you missed. That's strike one. Don't you strike out!

*Lights fade to black.*

## *Act 2*

### *Scene 1*

*The following morning. Cory is at the tree hitting the ball with the bat. He tries to mimic Troy, but his swing is awkward, less sure. Rose enters from the house.*

ROSE. Cory, I want you to help me with this cupboard.

CORY. I ain't quitting the team. I don't care what Poppa say.

ROSE. I'll talk to him when he gets back. He had to go see about your Uncle Gabe. The police done arrested him. Say he was disturbing the peace. He'll be back directly. Come on in here and help me clean out the top of this cupboard.

*Cory exits into the house. Rose sees Troy and Bono coming down the alley.*

Troy . . . what they say down there?

TROY. Ain't said nothing. I give them fifty dollars and they let him go. I'll talk to you about it. Where's Cory?

ROSE. He's in there helping me clean out these cupboards.

TROY. Tell him to get his butt out here.

*Troy and Bono go over to the pile of wood. Bono picks up the saw and begins sawing.*

TROY (*to Bono*). All they want is the money. That makes six or seven times I done went down there and got him. See me coming they stick out their hands.

BONO. Yeah. I know what you mean. That's all they care about . . . that money. They don't care about what's right. (*Pause.*) Nigger, why you got to go and get some hard wood? You ain't doing nothing but building a little old fence. Get you some soft pine wood. That's all you need.

TROY. I know what I'm doing. This is outside wood. You put pine wood inside the house. Pine wood is inside wood. This here is outside wood. Now you tell me where the fence is gonna be?

BONO. You don't need this wood. You can put it up with pine wood and it'll stand as long as you gonna be here looking at it.

TROY. How you know how long I'm gonna be here, nigger? Hell, I might just live forever. Live longer than old man Horsely.

BONO. That's what Magee used to say.

TROY. Magee's a damn fool. Now you tell me who you ever heard of gonna pull their own teeth with a pair of rusty pliers.

BONO. The old folks . . . my granddaddy used to pull his teeth with pliers. They ain't had no dentists for the colored folks back then.

TROY. Get clean pliers! You understand? Clean pliers! Sterilize them! Besides we ain't living back then. All Magee had to do was walk over to Doc Goldblum's.

BONO. I see where you and that Tallahassee gal . . . that Alberta . . . I see where you all done got tight.

TROY. What you mean "got tight"?

BONO. I see where you be laughing and joking with her all the time.

TROY. I laughs and jokes with all of them, Bono. You know me.

BONO. That ain't the kind of laughing and joking I'm talking about.

*Cory enters from the house.*

CORY. How you doing. Mr. Bono?

TROY. Cory? Get that saw from Bono and cut some wood. He talking about the wood's too hard to cut. Stand back there, Jim, and let that young boy show you how it's done.

BONO. He's sure welcome to it.

*Cory takes the saw and begins to cut the wood.*

Whew-e-e! Look at that. Big old strong boy. Look like Joe Louis. Hell, must be getting old the way I'm watching that boy whip through that wood.

CORY. I don't see why Mama want a fence around the yard noways.

TROY. Damn if I know either. What the hell she keeping out with it? She ain't got nothing nobody want.

BONO. Some people build fences to keep people out . . . and other people build fences to keep people in. Rose wants to hold on to you all. She loves you.

TROY. Hell, nigger, I don't need nobody to tell me my wife loves me. Cory . . . go on in the house and see if you can find that other saw.

CORY. Where's it at?

TROY. I said find it! Look for it till you find it!

*Cory exits into the house.*

What's that supposed to mean? Wanna keep us in?

BONO. Troy . . . I done known you seem like damn near my whole life. You and Rose both. I done know both of you all for a long time. I remember when you met Rose. When you was hitting them baseball out the park. A lot of them old gals was after you then. You had the pick of the litter. When you picked Rose, I was happy for you. That was the first time I knew you had any sense. I said . . . My man Troy knows what he's doing . . . I'm gonna follow this nigger . . . he might take me somewhere. I been following you too. I done learned a whole heap of things about life watching you. I done learned how to tell where the shit lies. How to tell it from the alfalfa. You done learned me a lot of things. You showed me how to not make the same mistakes . . . to take life as it comes along and keep putting one foot in front of the other. (*Pause.*) Rose a good woman, Troy.

TROY. Hell, nigger, I know she a good woman. I been married to her for eighteen years. What you got on your mind, Bono?

BONO. I just say she a good woman. Just like I say anything. I ain't got to have nothing on my mind.

TROY. You just gonna say she a good woman and leave it hanging out there like that? Why you telling me she a good woman?

BONO. She loves you, Troy. Rose loves you.

TROY. You saying I don't measure up. That's what you trying to say. I don't measure up cause I'm seeing this other gal. I know what you trying to say.

BONO. I know what Rose means to you, Troy. I'm just trying to say I don't want to see you mess up.

TROY. Yeah, I appreciate that, Bono. If you was messing around on Lucille I'd be telling you the same thing.

BONO. Well, that's all I got to say. I just say that because I love you both.

TROY. Hell, you know me . . . I wasn't out there looking for nothing. You can't find a better woman than Rose. I know that. But seems like this woman just stuck onto me where I can't shake her loose. I done wrestled with it, tried to throw her off me . . . but she just stuck on tighter. Now she's stuck on for good.

BONO. You's in control . . . that's what you tell me all the time. You responsible for what you do.

TROY. I ain't ducking the responsibility of it. As long as it sets right in my heart . . . then I'm okay. Cause that's all I listen to. It'll tell me right from wrong every time. And I ain't talking about doing Rose no bad turn. I love Rose. She done carried me a long ways and I love and respect her for that.

BONO. I know you do. That's why I don't want to see you hurt her. But what you gonna do when she find out? What you got then? If you try and juggle both of them . . . sooner or later you gonna drop one of them. That's common sense.

TROY. Yeah, I hear what you saying, Bono. I been trying to figure a way to work it out.

BONO. Work it out right, Troy. I don't want to be getting all up between you and Rose's business . . . but work it so it come out right.

TROY. Ah hell, I get all up between you and Lucille's business. When you gonna get that woman that refrigerator she been wanting? Don't tell me you ain't got no money now. I know who your banker is. Mellon don't need that money bad as Lucille want that refrigerator. I'll tell you that.

BONO. Tell you what I'll do . . . when you finish building this fence for Rose . . . I'll buy Lucille that refrigerator.

TROY. You done stuck your foot in your mouth now!

*Troy grabs up a board and begins to saw. Bono starts to walk out the yard.*

Hey, nigger . . . where you going?

BONO. I'm going home. I know you don't expect me to help you now. I'm protecting my money. I wanna see you put that fence up by yourself. That's what I want to see. You'll be here another six months without me.

TROY. Nigger, you ain't right.

BONO. When it comes to my money . . . I'm right as fireworks on the Fourth of July.

TROY. All right, we gonna see now. You better get out your bankbook.

*Bono exits, and Troy continues to work. Rose enters from the house.*

ROSE. What they say down there? What's happening with Gabe?

TROY. I went down there and got him out. Cost me fifty dollars. Say he was disturbing the peace. Judge set up a hearing for him in three weeks. Say to show cause why he shouldn't be recommitted.

ROSE. What was he doing that cause them to arrest him?

TROY. Some kids was teasing him and he run them off home. Say he was howling and carrying on. Some folks seen him and called the police. That's all it was.

ROSE. Well, what's you say? What'd you tell the judge?

TROY. Told him I'd look after him. It didn't make no sense to recommit the man. He stuck out his big greasy palm and told me to give him fifty dollars and take him on home.

ROSE. Where's he at now? Where'd he go off to?

TROY. He's gone about his business. He don't need nobody to hold his hand.

ROSE. Well, I don't know. Seem like that would be the best place for him if they did put him into the hospital. I know what you're gonna say. But that's what I think would be best.

TROY. The man done had his life ruined fighting for what? And they wanna take and lock him up. Let him be free. He don't bother nobody.

ROSE. Well, everybody got their own way of looking at it I guess. Come on and get your lunch. I got a bowl of lima beans and some cornbread in the oven. Come and get something to eat. Ain't no sense you fretting over Gabe.

*Rose turns to go into the house.*

TROY. Rose . . . got something to tell you.

ROSE. Well, come on . . . wait till I get this food on the table.

TROY. Rose!

*She stops and turns around.*

I don't know how to say this. (*Pause.*) I can't explain it none. It just sort of grows on you till it gets out of hand. It starts out like a little bush . . . and the next thing you know it's a whole forest.

ROSE. Troy . . . what is you talking about?

TROY. I'm talking, woman, let me talk. I'm trying to find a way to tell you . . . I'm gonna be a daddy. I'm gonna be somebody's daddy.

ROSE. Troy . . . you're not telling me this? You're gonna be . . . what?

TROY. Rose . . . now . . . see . . .

ROSE. You telling me you gonna be somebody's daddy? You telling your *wife* this?

*Gabriel enters from the street. He carries a rose in his hand.*

GABRIEL. Hey, Troy! Hey, Rose!

ROSE. I have to wait eighteen years to hear something like this.

GABRIEL. Hey, Rose . . . I got a flower for you. (*He hands it to her.*) That's a rose. Same rose like you is.

ROSE. Thanks, Gabe.

GABRIEL. Troy, you ain't mad at me is you? Them bad mens come and put me away. You ain't mad at me is you?

TROY. Naw, Gabe, I ain't mad at you.

ROSE. Eighteen years and you wanna come with this.

GABRIEL (*takes a quarter out of his pocket*). See what I got? Got a brand new quarter.

TROY. Rose . . . it's just . . .

ROSE. Ain't nothing you can say, Troy. Ain't no way of explaining that.

GABRIEL. Fellow that give me this quarter had a whole mess of them. I'm gonna keep this quarter till it stop shining.

ROSE. Gabe, go on in the house there. I got some watermelon in the Frigidaire. Go on and get you a piece.

GABRIEL. Say, Rose . . . you know I was chasing hellhounds and them bad mens come and get me and take me away. Troy helped me. He come down there and told them they better let me go before he beat them up. Yeah, he did!

ROSE. You go on and get you a piece of watermelon, Gabe. Them bad mens is gone now.

GABRIEL. Okay, Rose . . . gonna get me some watermelon. The kind with the stripes on it.

*Gabriel exits into the house.*

ROSE. Why, Troy? Why? After all these years to come dragging this in to me now. It don't make no sense at your age. I could have expected this ten or fifteen years ago, but not now.

TROY. Age ain't got nothing to do with it, Rose.

ROSE. I done tried to be everything a wife should be. Everything a wife could be. Been married eighteen years and I got to live to see the day you tell me you been seeing another woman and done fathered a child by her. And you know I ain't never wanted no half nothing in my family. My whole family is half. Everybody got different fathers and mothers . . . my two sisters and my brother. Can't hardly tell who's who. Can't never sit down and talk about Papa and Mama. It's your papa and your mama and my papa and my mama . . .

TROY. Rose . . . stop it now.

ROSE. I ain't never wanted that for none of my children. And now you wanna drag your behind in here and tell me something like this.

TROY. You ought to know. It's time for you to know.

ROSE. Well, I don't want to know, goddamn it!

TROY. I can't just make it go away. It's done now. I can't wish the circumstance of the thing away.

ROSE. And you don't want to either. Maybe you want to wish me and my boy away. Maybe that's what you want? Well, you can't wish us away. I've got eighteen years of my life invested in you. You ought to have stayed upstairs in my bed where you belong.

TROY. Rose . . . now listen to me . . . we can get a handle on this thing. We can talk this out . . . come to an understanding.

ROSE. All of a sudden it's "we." Where was "we" at when you was down there rolling around with some godforsaken woman? "We" should have come to an understanding before you started making a damn fool of yourself. You're a day late and a dollar short when it comes to an understanding with me.

TROY. It's just . . . She gives me a different idea . . . a different understanding about myself. I can step out of this house and get away from the pressures and problems . . . be a different man. I ain't got to wonder how I'm gonna pay the bills or get the roof fixed. I can just be a part of myself that I ain't never been.

ROSE. What I want to know . . . is do you plan to continue seeing her. That's all you can say to me.

TROY. I can sit up in her house and laugh. Do you understand what I'm saying. I can laugh out loud . . . and it feels good. It reaches all the way down to the bottom of my shoes. (*Pause.*) Rose, I can't give that up.

ROSE. Maybe you ought to go on and stay down there with her . . . if she's a better woman than me.

TROY. It ain't about nobody being a better woman or nothing. Rose, you ain't the blame. A man couldn't ask for no woman to be a better wife than you've been. I'm responsible for it. I done locked myself into a pattern trying to take care of you all that I forgot about myself.

ROSE. What the hell was I there for? That was my job, not somebody else's.

TROY. Rose, I done tried all my life to live decent . . . to live a clean . . . hard . . . useful life. I tried to be a good husband to you. In every way I knew how. Maybe I come into the world backwards, I don't know. But . . . you born with two strikes on you before you come to the plate. You got to guard it closely . . . always looking for the curve ball on the inside corner. You can't afford to let none get past you. You can't afford a call strike. If you going down . . . you going down swinging. Everything lined up against you. What you gonna do. I fooled them, Rose. I bunted. When I found you and Cory and a halfway decent job . . . I was safe. Couldn't nothing touch me. I wasn't gonna strike out no more. I wasn't going back to the penitentiary. I wasn't gonna lay in the streets with a bottle of wine. I was safe. I had me a family. A job. I wasn't gonna get that last strike. I was on first looking for one of them boys to knock me in. To get me home.

ROSE. You should have stayed in my bed, Troy.

TROY. Then when I saw that gal . . . she firmed up my backbone. And I got to thinking that if I tried . . . I just might be able to steal second. Do you understand after eighteen years I wanted to steal second.

ROSE. You should have held me tight. You should have grabbed me and held on.

TROY. I stood on first base for eighteen years and I thought . . . well, goddamn it . . . go on for it!

ROSE. We're not talking about baseball! We're talking about you going off to lay in bed with another woman . . . and then bring it home to me. That's what we're talking about. We ain't talking about no baseball.

TROY. Rose, you're not listening to me. I'm trying the best I can to explain it to you. It's not easy for me to admit that I been standing in the same place for eighteen years.

ROSE. I been standing with you! I been right here with you, Troy. I got a life too. I gave eighteen years of my life to stand in the same spot with you. Don't you think I ever wanted other things? Don't you think I had dreams and hopes? What about my life? What about me. Don't you think it ever crossed my mind to want to know other men? That I wanted to lay up somewhere and forget about my responsibilities? That I wanted someone to make me laugh so I could feel good? You not the only one who's got wants and needs. But I held on to you, Troy. I took all my feelings, my wants and needs, my dreams . . . and I buried them inside you. I planted a seed and watched and prayed over it. I planted myself inside you and waited to bloom. And it didn't take me no eighteen years to find out the soil was hard and rocky and it wasn't never gonna bloom.

But I held on to you, Troy. I held you tighter. You was my husband. I owed you everything I had. Every part of me I could find to give you. And upstairs in that room . . . with the darkness falling in on me . . . I gave everything I had to try and erase the doubt that you wasn't the finest man in the world. And wherever you was going . . . I wanted to be there with you. Cause you was my husband. Cause that's the only way I was gonna survive as your wife. You always talking about what you give . . . and what you don't have to give. But you take too. You take . . . and don't even know nobody's giving!

*Rose turns to exit into the house; Troy grabs her arm.*

TROY. You say I take and don't give!

ROSE. Troy! You're hurting me!

TROY. You say I take and don't give!

ROSE. Troy . . . you're hurting my arm! Let go!

TROY. I done give you everything I got. Don't you tell that lie on me.

ROSE. Troy!

TROY. Don't you tell that lie on me!

*Cory enters from the house.*

CORY. Mama!

ROSE. Troy. You're hurting me.

TROY. Don't you tell me about no taking and giving.

*Cory comes up behind Troy and grabs him. Troy, surprised, is thrown off balance just as Cory throws a glancing blow that catches him on the chest and knocks him down. Troy is stunned, as is Cory.*

ROSE. Troy. Troy. No!

*Troy gets to his feet and starts at Cory.*

Troy . . . no. Please! Troy!

*Rose pulls on Troy to hold him back. Troy stops himself.*

TROY (*to Cory*). All right. That's strike two. You stay away from around me, boy. Don't you strike out. You living with a full count. Don't you strike out.

*Troy exits out the yard as the lights go down.*

## *Scene 2*

*It is six months later, early afternoon. Troy enters from the house and starts to exit the yard. Rose enters from the house.*

ROSE. Troy, I want to talk to you.

TROY. All of a sudden, after all this time, you want to talk to me, huh? You ain't wanted to talk to me for months. You ain't wanted to talk to me last night. You ain't wanted no part of me then. What you wanna talk to me about now?

ROSE. Tomorrow's Friday.

TROY. I know what day tomorrow is. You think I don't know tomorrow's Friday? My whole life I ain't done nothing but look to see Friday coming and you got to tell me it's Friday.

ROSE. I want to know if you're coming home.

TROY. I always come home, Rose. You know that. There ain't never been a night I ain't come home.

ROSE. That ain't what I mean . . . and you know it. I want to know if you're coming straight home after work.

TROY. I figure I'd cash my check . . . hang out at Taylors' with the boys . . . maybe play a game of checkers . . .

ROSE. Troy, I can't live like this. I won't live like this. You livin' on borrowed time with me. It's been going on six months now you ain't been coming home.

TROY. I be here every night. Every night of the year. That's 365 days.

ROSE. I want you to come home tomorrow after work.

TROY. Rose . . . I don't mess up my pay. You know that now. I take my pay and I give it to you. I don't have no money but what you give me back. I just want to have a little time to myself . . . a little time to enjoy life.

ROSE. What about me? When's my time to enjoy life?

TROY. I don't know what to tell you, Rose. I'm doing the best I can.

ROSE. You ain't been home from work but time enough to change your clothes and run out . . . and you wanna call that the best you can do?

TROY. I'm going over to the hospital to see Alberta. She went into the hospital this afternoon. Look like she might have the baby early. I won't be gone long.

ROSE. Well, you ought to know. They went over to Miss Pearl's and got Gabe today. She said you told them to go ahead and lock him up.

TROY. I ain't said no such thing. Whoever told you that is telling a lie. Pearl ain't doing nothing but telling a big fat lie.

ROSE. She ain't had to tell me. I read it on the papers.

TROY. I ain't told them nothing of the kind.

ROSE. I saw it right there on the papers.

TROY. What it say, huh?

ROSE. It said you told them to take him.

TROY. Then they screwed that up, just the way they screw up everything. I ain't worried about what they got on the paper.

ROSE. Say the government send part of his check to the hospital and the other part to you.

TROY. I ain't got nothing to do with that if that's the way it works. I ain't made up the rules about how it work.

ROSE. You did Gabe just like you did Cory. You wouldn't sign the paper for Cory . . . but you signed for Gabe. You signed that paper.

*The telephone is heard ringing inside the house.*

TROY. I told you I ain't signed nothing, woman! The only thing I signed was the release form. Hell, I can't read, I don't know what they had on that paper! I ain't signed nothing about sending Gabe away.

ROSE. I said send him to the hospital . . . you said let him be free . . . now you done went down there and signed him to the hospital for half his money. You went back on yourself, Troy. You gonna have to answer for that.

TROY. See now . . . you been over there talking to Miss Pearl. She done got mad cause she ain't getting Gabe's rent money. That's all it is. She's liable to say anything.

ROSE. Troy, I seen where you signed the paper.

TROY. You ain't seen nothing I signed. What she doing got papers on my brother anyway? Miss Pearl telling a big fat lie. And I'm gonna tell her about it too! You ain't seen nothing I signed. Say . . . you ain't seen nothing I signed.

*Rose exists into the house to answer the telephone. Presently she returns.*

ROSE. Troy . . . that was the hospital. Alberta had the baby.

TROY. What she have? What is it?

ROSE. It's a girl.

TROY. I better get on down to the hospital to see her.

ROSE. Troy . . .

TROY. Rose . . . I got to go see her now. That's only right . . . what's the matter . . . the baby's all right, ain't it?

ROSE. Alberta died having the baby.

TROY. Died . . . you say she's dead? Alberta's dead?

ROSE. They said they done all they could. They couldn't do nothing for her.

TROY. The baby? How's the baby?

ROSE. They say it's healthy. I wonder who's gonna bury her.

TROY. She had family, Rose. She wasn't living in the world by herself.

ROSE. I know she wasn't living in the world by herself.

TROY. Next thing you gonna want to know if she had any insurance.

ROSE. Troy, you ain't got to talk like that.

TROY. That's the first thing that jumped out your mouth. "Who's gonna bury her?" Like I'm fixing to take on that task for myself.

ROSE. I am your wife. Don't push me away.

TROY. I ain't pushing nobody away. Just give me some space. That's all. Just give me some room to breathe.

*Rose exits into the house. Troy walks about the yard.*

TROY (*with a quiet rage that threatens to consume him*). All right . . . Mr. Death. See now . . . I'm gonna tell you what I'm gonna do. I'm gonna take and build me a fence around this yard. See? I'm gonna build me a fence around what belongs to me. And then I want you to stay on the other side. See? You stay over there until you're ready for me. Then you come on. Bring your army. Bring your sickle. Bring your wrestling clothes. I ain't gonna fall down on my vigilance this time. You ain't gonna sneak up on me no more. When you ready for me . . . when the top of your list say Troy Maxson . . . that's when you come around here. You come up and knock on the front door. Ain't nobody else got nothing to do with this. This is between you and me. Man to man. You stay on the other side of that fence until you ready for me. Then you come up and knock on the front door. Anytime you want. I'll be ready for you.

*The lights go down to black.*

*Scene 3*

*The lights come up on the porch. It is late evening three days later. Rose sits listening to the ball game waiting for Troy. The final out of the game is made and Rose switches off the radio. Troy enters the yard carrying an infant wrapped in blankets. He stands back from the house and calls.*

*Rose enters and stands on the porch. There is a long, awkward silence, the weight of which grows heavier with each passing second.*

TROY. Rose . . . I'm standing here with my daughter in my arms. She ain't but a wee bittie little old thing. She don't know nothing about grownups' business. She innocent . . . and she ain't got no mama.

ROSE. What you telling me for, Troy?

*She turns and exits into the house.*

TROY. Well . . . I guess we'll just sit out here on the porch.

*He sits down on the porch. There is an awkward indelicateness about the way he handles the baby. His largeness engulfs and seems to swallow it. He speaks loud enough for Rose to hear.*

A man's got to do what's right for him. I ain't sorry for nothing I done. It felt right in my heart. (*To the baby.*) What you smiling at? Your daddy's a big man. Got these great big old hands. But sometimes he's scared. And right now your daddy's scared cause we sitting out here and ain't got no home. Oh, I been homeless before. I ain't had no little baby with me. But I been homeless. You just be out on the road by your lonesome and you see one of them trains coming and you just kinda go like this . . .

*He sings as a lullaby.*

Please, Mr. Engineer let a man ride the line
Please, Mr. Engineer let a man ride the line
I ain't got no ticket please let me ride the blinds

*Rose enters from the house. Troy, hearing her steps behind him, stands and faces her.*

She's my daughter, Rose. My own flesh and blood. I can't deny her no more than I can deny them boys. (*Pause.*) You and them boys is my family. You and them and this child is all I got in the world. So I guess what I'm saying is . . . I'd appreciate it if you'd help me take care of her.

ROSE. Okay, Troy . . . you're right. I'll take care of your baby for you . . . cause . . . like you say . . . she's innocent . . . and you can't visit the sins of the father upon the child. A motherless child has got a hard time. (*She takes the baby from him.*) From right now . . . this child got a mother. But you a womanless man.

*Rose turns and exits into the house with the baby. Lights go down to black.*

*Scene 4*

*It is two months later. Lyons enters the street. He knocks on the door and calls.*

LYONS. Hey, Rose! (*Pause.*) Rose!

ROSE (*from inside the house*). Stop that yelling. You gonna wake up Raynell. I just got her to sleep.

LYONS. I just stopped by to pay Papa this twenty dollars I owe him. Where's Papa at?

ROSE. He should be here in a minute. I'm getting ready to go down to the church. Sit down and wait on him.

LYONS. I got to go pick up Bonnie over her mother's house.

ROSE. Well, sit it down there on the table. He'll get it.

LYONS (*enters the house and sets the money on the table*). Tell Papa I said thanks. I'll see you again.

ROSE. All right, Lyons. We'll see you.

*Lyons starts to exit as Cory enters.*

CORY. Hey, Lyons.

LYONS. What's happening, Cory? Say man, I'm sorry I missed your graduation. You know I had a gig and couldn't get away. Otherwise, I would have been there, man. So what you doing?

CORY. I'm trying to find a job.

LYONS. Yeah I know how that go, man. It's rough out here. Jobs are scarce.

CORY. Yeah, I know.

LYONS. Look here, I got to run. Talk to Papa . . . he know some people. He'll be able to help get you a job. Talk to him . . . see what he say.

CORY. Yeah . . . all right, Lyons.

LYONS. You take care. I'll talk to you soon. We'll find some time to talk.

*Lyons exits the yard. Cory wanders over to the tree, picks up the bat, and assumes a batting stance. He studies an imaginary pitcher and swings. Dissatisfied with the result, he tries again. Troy enters. They eye each other for a beat. Cory puts the bat down and exits the yard. Troy starts into the house as Rose exits with Raynell. She is carrying a cake.*

TROY. I'm coming in and everybody's going out.

ROSE. I'm taking this cake down to the church for the bake sale. Lyons was by to see you. He stopped by to pay you your twenty dollars. It's laying in there on the table.

TROY (*going into his pocket*). Well . . . here go this money.

ROSE. Put it in there on the table, Troy. I'll get it.

TROY. What time you coming back?

ROSE. Ain't no use in you studying me. It don't matter what time I come back.

TROY. I just asked you a question, woman. What's the matter . . . can't I ask you a question?

ROSE. Troy, I don't want to go into it. Your dinner's in there on the stove. All you got to do is heat it up. And don't you be eating the rest of them cakes in there. I'm coming back for them. We having a bake sale at the church tomorrow.

*Rose exits the yard. Troy sits down on the steps, takes a pint bottle from his pocket, opens it, and drinks. He begins to sing.*

TROY.

Hear it ring! Hear it ring!
Had an old dog his name was Blue
You know Blue was mighty true
You know Blue as a good old dog
Blue trees a possum in a hollow log
You know from that he was a good old dog

*Bono enters the yard.*

BONO. Hey, Troy.

TROY. Hey, what's happening, Bono?

BONO. I just thought I'd stop by to see you.

TROY. What you stop by and see me for? You ain't stopped by in a month of Sundays. Hell, I must owe you money or something.

BONO. Since you got your promotion I can't keep up with you. Used to see you every day. Now I don't even know what route you working.

TROY. They keep switching me around. Got me out in Greentree now . . . hauling white folks' garbage.

BONO. Greentree, huh? You lucky, at least you ain't got to be lifting them barrels. Damn if they ain't getting heavier. I'm gonna put in my two years and call it quits.

TROY. I'm thinking about retiring myself.

BONO. You got it easy. You can drive for another five years.

TROY. It ain't the same, Bono. It ain't like working the back of the truck. Ain't got nobody to talk to . . . feel like you working by yourself. Naw, I'm thinking about retiring. How's Lucille?

BONO. She all right. Her arthritis get to acting up on her sometime. Saw Rose on my way in. She going down to the church, huh?

TROY. Yeah, she took up going down there. All them preachers looking for somebody to fatten their pockets. (*Pause.*) Got some gin here.

BONO. Naw, thanks. I just stopped by to say hello.

TROY. Hell, nigger . . . you can take a drink. I ain't never known you to say no to a drink. You ain't got to work tomorrow.

BONO. I just stopped by. I'm fixing to go over to Skinner's. We got us a domino game going over his house every Friday.

TROY. Nigger, you can't play no dominoes. I used to whup you four games out of five.

BONO. Well, that learned me. I'm getting better.

TROY. Yeah? Well, that's all right.

BONO. Look here . . . I got to be getting on. Stop by sometime, huh?

TROY. Yeah, I'll do that, Bono. Lucille told Rose you bought her a new refrigerator.

BONO. Yeah, Rose told Lucille you had finally built your fence . . . so I figured we'd call it even.

TROY. I knew you would.

BONO. Yeah . . . okay. I'll be talking to you.

TROY. Yeah, take care, Bono. Good to see you. I'm gonna stop over.

BONO. Yeah. Okay, Troy.

*Bono exits. Troy drinks from the bottle.*

TROY.

Old Blue died and I dig his grave
Let him down with a golden chain
Every night when I hear old Blue bark
I know Blue treed a possum in Noah's Ark.
Hear it ring! Hear it ring!

*Cory enters the yard. They eye each other for a beat. Troy is sitting in the middle of the steps. Cory walks over.*

CORY. I got to get by.

TROY. Say what? What's you say?

CORY. You in my way. I got to get by.

TROY. You got to get by where? This is my house. Bought and paid for. In full. Took me fifteen years. And if you wanna go in my house and I'm sitting on the steps . . . you say excuse me. Like your mama taught you.

CORY. Come on, Pop . . . I got to get by.

*Cory starts to maneuver his way past Troy. Troy grabs his leg and shoves him back.*

TROY. You just gonna walk over top of me?

CORY. I live here too!

TROY (*advancing toward him*). You just gonna walk over top of me in my own house?

CORY. I ain't scared of you.

TROY. I ain't asked if you was scared of me. I asked you if you was fixing to walk over top of me in my own house? That's the question. You ain't gonna say excuse me? You just gonna walk over top of me?

CORY. If you wanna put it like that.

TROY. How else am I gonna put it?

CORY. I was walking by you to go into the house cause you sitting on the steps drunk, singing to yourself. You can put it like that.

TROY. Without saying excuse me???

*Cory doesn't respond.*

I asked you a question. Without saying excuse me???

CORY. I ain't got to say excuse me to you. You don't count around here no more.

TROY. Oh, I see . . . I don't count around here no more. You ain't got to say excuse me to your daddy. All of a sudden you done got so grown that your daddy don't count around here no more . . . Around here in his own house and yard that he done paid for with the sweat of his brow. You done got so grown to where you gonna take over. You gonna take over my house. Is that right? You gonna wear my pants. You gonna go in there and stretch out on my bed. You ain't got to say excuse me cause I don't count around here no more. Is that right?

CORY. That's right. You always talking this dumb stuff. Now, why don't you just get out my way?

TROY. I guess you got someplace to sleep and something to put in your belly. You got that, huh? You got that? That's what you need. You got that, huh?

CORY. You don't know what I got. You ain't got to worry about what I got.

TROY. You right! You one hundred percent right! I done spent the last seventeen years worrying about what you got. Now it's your turn, see? I'll tell you what to do. You grown . . . we done established that. You a man. Now, let's see you act like one. Turn your behind around and walk out this yard. And when you get out there in the alley . . . you can forget about this house. See? Cause this is my house. You go on and be a man and get your own house. You can forget about this. Cause this is mine. You go on and get yours cause I'm through with doing for you.

CORY. You talking about what you did for me . . . what'd you ever give me?

TROY. Them feet and bones! That pumping heart, nigger! I give you more than anybody else is ever gonna give you.

CORY. You ain't never gave me nothing! You ain't never done nothing but hold me back. Afraid I was gonna be better than you. All you ever did was try and make me scared of you. I used to tremble every time you called my name. Every time I heard your footsteps in the house. Wondering all the time . . . what's Papa gonna say if I do this? . . . What's he gonna say if I do that? . . . What's Papa gonna say if I turn on the radio? And Mama, too . . . she tries . . . but she's scared of you.

TROY. You leave your mama out of this. She ain't got nothing to do with this.

CORY. I don't know how she stand you . . . after what you did to her.

TROY. I told you to leave your mama out of this!

*He advances toward Cory.*

CORY. What you gonna do . . . give me a whupping? You can't whup me no more. You're too old. You just an old man.

TROY (*shoves him on his shoulder*). Nigger! That's what you are. You just another nigger on the street to me!

CORY. You crazy! You know that?

TROY. Go on now! You got the devil in you. Get on away from me!

CORY. You just a crazy old man . . . talking about I got the devil in me.

TROY. Yeah, I'm crazy! If you don't get on the other side of that yard . . . I'm gonna show you how crazy I am! Go on . . . get the hell out of my yard.

CORY. It ain't your yard. You took Uncle Gabe's money he got from the army to buy this house and then you put him out.

TROY (*advances on Cory*). Get your black ass out of my yard!

*Troy's advance backs Cory up against the tree. Cory grabs up the bat.*

CORY. I ain't going nowhere! Come on . . . put me out! I ain't scared of you.

TROY. That's my bat!

CORY. Come on!

TROY. Put my bat down!

CORY. Come on, put me out.

*Cory swings at Troy, who backs across the yard.*

What's the matter? You so bad . . . put me out!

*Troy advances toward Cory.*

CORY (*backing up*). Come on! Come on!

TROY. You're gonna have to use it! You wanna draw that bat back on me . . . you're gonna have to use it.

CORY. Come on! . . . Come on!

*Cory swings the bat at Troy a second time. He misses. Troy continues to advance toward him.*

TROY. You're gonna have to kill me! You wanna draw that bat back on me. You're gonna have to kill me.

*Cory, backed up against the tree, can go no farther. Troy taunts him. He sticks out his head and offers him a target.*

Come on! Come on!

*Cory is unable to swing the bat. Troy grabs it.*

TROY. Then I'll show you.

*Cory and Troy struggle over the bat. The struggle is fierce and fully engaged. Troy ultimately is the stronger and takes the bat from Cory and stands over him ready to swing. He stops himself.*

Go on and get away from around my house.

*Cory, stung by his defeat, picks himself up, walks slowly out of the yard and up the alley.*

CORY. Tell Mama I'll be back for my things.

TROY. They'll be on the other side of that fence.

*Cory exits.*

TROY. I can't taste nothing. Helluljah! I can't taste nothing no more. (*Troy assumes a batting posture and begins to taunt Death, the fastball on the outside corner.*) Come on! It's between you and me now! Come on! Anytime you want! Come on! I be ready for you . . . but I ain't gonna be easy.

*The lights go down on the scene.*

### *Scene 5*

*The time is 1965. The lights come up in the yard. It is the morning of Troy's funeral. A funeral plaque with a light hangs beside the door. There is a small garden plot off to the side. There is noise and activity in the house as Rose, Lyons, and Bono have gathered. The door opens and Raynell, seven years old, enters dressed in a flannel nightgown. She crosses to the garden and pokes around with a stick. Rose calls from the house.*

ROSE. Raynell!
RAYNELL. Mam?
ROSE. What you doing out there?
RAYNELL. Nothing.

*Rose comes to the door.*

ROSE. Girl, get in here and get dressed. What you doing?
RAYNELL. Seeing if my garden growed.
ROSE. I told you it ain't gonna grow overnight. You got to wait.
RAYNELL. It don't look like it never gonna grow. Dag!
ROSE. I told you a watched pot never boils. Get in here and get dressed.
RAYNELL. This ain't even no pot, Mama.
ROSE. You just have to give it a chance. It'll grow. Now you come on and do what I told you. We got to be getting ready. This ain't no morning to be playing around. You hear me?
RAYNELL. Yes, mam.

*Rose exits into the house. Raynell continues to poke at her garden with a stick. Cory enters. He is dressed in a Marine corporal's uniform, and carries a duffelbag. His posture is that of a military man, and his speech has a clipped sternness.*

CORY (*to Raynell*). Hi. (*Pause.*) I bet your name is Raynell.
RAYNELL. Uh huh.
CORY. Is your mama home?

*Raynell runs up on the porch and calls through the screen door.*

RAYNELL. Mama . . . there's some man out here. Mama?

*Rose comes to the door.*

ROSE. Cory? Lord have mercy! Look here, you all!

*Rose and Cory embrace in a tearful reunion as Bono and Lyons enter from the house dressed in funeral clothes.*

BONO. Aw, looka here . . .
ROSE. Done got all grown up!
CORY. Don't cry, Mama. What you crying about?
ROSE. I'm just so glad you made it.
CORY. Hey Lyons. How you doing, Mr. Bono.

*Lyons goes to embrace Cory.*

LYONS. Look at you, man. Look at you. Don't he look good, Rose. Got them Corporal stripes.

ROSE. What took you so long?

CORY. You know how the Marines are, Mama. They got to get all their paperwork straight before they let you do anything.

ROSE. Well, I'm sure glad you made it. They let Lyons come. Your Uncle Gabe's still in the hospital. They don't know if they gonna let him out or not. I just talked to them a little while ago.

LYONS. A Corporal in the United States Marines.

BONO. Your daddy knew you had it in you. He used to tell me all the time.

LYONS. Don't he look good, Mr. Bono?

BONO. Yeah, he remind me of Troy when I first met him. (*Pause.*) Say, Rose, Lucille's down at the church with the choir. I'm gonna go down and get the pallbearers lined up. I'll be back to get you all.

ROSE. Thanks, Jim.

CORY. See you, Mr. Bono.

LYONS (*with his arm around Raynell*). Cory . . . look at Raynell. Ain't she precious? She gonna break a whole lot of hearts.

ROSE. Raynell, come and say hello to your brother. This is your brother, Cory. You remember Cory.

RAYNELL. No, Mam.

CORY. She don't remember me, Mama.

ROSE. Well, we talk about you. She heard us talk about you. (*To Raynell.*) This is your brother, Cory. Come on and say hello.

RAYNELL. Hi.

CORY. Hi. So you're Raynell. Mama told me a lot about you.

ROSE. You all come on into the house and let me fix you some breakfast. Keep up your strength.

CORY. I ain't hungry, Mama.

LYONS. You can fix me something, Rose. I'll be in there in a minute.

ROSE. Cory, you sure you don't want nothing? I know they ain't feeding you right.

CORY. No, Mama . . . thanks. I don't feel like eating. I'll get something later.

ROSE. Raynell . . . get on upstairs and get that dress on like I told you.

*Rose and Raynell exit into the house.*

LYONS. So . . . I hear you thinking about getting married.

CORY. Yeah, I done found the right one, Lyons. It's about time.

LYONS. Me and Bonnie been split up about four years now. About the time Papa retired. I guess she just got tired of all them changes I was putting her through. (*Pause.*) I always knew you was gonna make something out yourself. Your head was always in the right direction. So . . . you gonna stay in . . . make it a career . . . put in your twenty years?

CORY. I don't know. I got six already, I think that's enough.

LYONS. Stick with Uncle Sam and retire early. Ain't nothing out here. I guess Rose told you what happened with me. They got me down the workhouse. I thought I was being slick cashing other people's checks.

CORY. How much time you doing?

LYONS. They give me three years. I got that beat now. I ain't got but nine more months. It ain't so bad. You learn to deal with it like anything else. You got to take the crookeds with the straights. That's what Papa used to say. He used to say that when he struck out. I seen him strike out three times in a row . . . and the next time up he hit the ball over the grandstand. Right out there in Homestead Field. He wasn't satisfied hitting in the seats . . . he want to hit it over everything! After the game he had two hundred people standing around waiting to shake his hand. You got to take the crookeds with the straights. Yeah, Papa was something else.

CORY. You still playing?

LYONS. Cory . . . you know I'm gonna do that. There's some fellows down there we got us a band . . . we gonna try and stay together when we get out . . . but yeah, I'm still playing. It still helps me to get out of bed in the morning. As long as it do that I'm gonna be right there playing and trying to make some sense out of it.

ROSE (*calling*). Lyons, I got these eggs in the pan.

LYONS. Let me go on and get these eggs, man. Get ready to go bury Papa. (*Pause.*) How you doing? You doing all right?

*Cory nods. Lyons touches him on the shoulder and they share a moment of silent grief. Lyons exits into the house. Cory wanders about the yard. Raynell enters.*

RAYNELL. Hi.

CORY. Hi.

RAYNELL. Did you used to sleep in my room?

CORY. Yeah . . . that used to be my room.

RAYNELL. That's what Papa call it. "Cory's room." It got your football in the closet.

*Rose comes to the door.*

ROSE. Raynell, get in there and get them good shoes on.

RAYNELL. Mama, can't I wear these? Them other one hurt my feet.

ROSE. Well, they just gonna have to hurt your feet for a while. You ain't said they hurt your feet when you went down to the store and got them.

RAYNELL. They didn't hurt then. My feet done got bigger.

ROSE. Don't you give me no backtalk now. You get in there and get them shoes on.

*Raynell exits into the house.*

Ain't too much changed. He still got that piece of rag tied to that tree. He was out here swinging that bat. I was just ready to go back in the house. He swung that bat and then he just fell over. Seem like he swung it and stood there with this grin on his face . . . and then he just fell over. They carried him on down to the hospital, but I knew there wasn't no need . . . why don't you come on in the house?

CORY. Mama . . . I got something to tell you. I don't know how to tell you this . . . but I've got to tell you . . . I'm not going to Papa's funeral.

ROSE. Boy, hush your mouth. That's your daddy you talking about. I don't want hear that kind of talk this morning. I done raised you to come to this? You standing there all healthy and grown talking about you ain't going to your daddy's funeral?

CORY. Mama . . . listen . . .

ROSE. I don't want to hear it, Cory. You just get that thought out of your head.

CORY. I can't drag Papa with me everywhere I go. I've got to say no to him. One time in my life I've got to say no.

ROSE. Don't nobody have to listen to nothing like that. I know you and your daddy ain't seen eye to eye, but I ain't got to listen to that kind of talk this morning. Whatever was between you and your daddy . . . the time has come to put it aside. Just take it and set it over there on the shelf and forget about it. Disrespecting your daddy ain't gonna make you a man, Cory. You got to find a way to come to that on your own. Not going to your daddy's funeral ain't gonna make you a man.

CORY. The whole time I was growing up . . . living in his house . . . Papa was like a shadow that followed you everywhere. It weighed on you and sunk into your flesh. It would wrap around you and lay there until you couldn't tell which one was you anymore. That shadow digging in your flesh. Trying to crawl in. Trying to live through you. Everywhere I looked, Troy Maxson was staring back at me . . . hiding under the bed . . . in the closet. I'm just saying I've got to find a way to get rid of that shadow, Mama.

ROSE. You just like him. You got him in you good.

CORY. Don't tell me that, Mama.

ROSE. You Troy Maxson all over again.

CORY. I don't want to be Troy Maxson. I want to be me.

ROSE. You can't be nobody but who you are, Cory. That shadow wasn't nothing but you growing into yourself. You either got to grow into it or cut it down to fit you. But that's all you got to make life with. That's all you got to measure yourself against that world out there. Your daddy wanted you to be everything he wasn't . . . and at the same time he tried to make you into everything he was. I don't know if he was right or wrong . . . but I do know he meant to do more good than he meant to do harm. He wasn't always right. Sometimes when he touched he bruised. And sometimes when he took me in his arms he cut.

When I first met your daddy I thought . . . Here is a man I can lay down with and make a baby. That's the first thing I thought when I seen him. I was thirty years old and had done seen my share of men. But when he walked up to me and said, "I can dance a waltz that'll make you dizzy," I thought, Rose Lee, here is a man that you can open yourself up to and be filled to bursting. Here is a man that can fill all them empty spaces you been tipping around the edges of. One of them empty spaces was being somebody's mother.

I married your daddy and settled down to cooking his supper and keeping clean sheets on the bed. When your daddy walked through the house he was so big he filled it up. That was my first mistake. Not to make him leave some room for me. For my part in the matter. But at that time I wanted that. I wanted a house that I could sing in. And that's what your daddy gave me. I didn't know to keep up his strength I had to give up little pieces of mine. I did that. I took on his life as mine and mixed up the pieces so that you couldn't hardly tell which was which anymore. It was my choice. It was my life and I didn't have to live it like that. But that's what life offered me in the way of being a woman and I took it. I grabbed hold of it with both hands.

By the time Raynell came into the house, me and your daddy had done lost touch with one another. I didn't want to make my blessing off of nobody's misfortune . . . but I took on to Raynell like she was all them babies I had wanted and never had.

*The phone rings.*

Like I'd been blessed to relive a part of my life. And if the Lord see fit to keep up my strength . . . I'm gonna do her just like your daddy did you . . . I'm gonna give her the best of what's in me.

RAYNELL (*entering, still with her old shoes*). Mama . . . Reverend Tollivier on the phone.

*Rose exits into the house.*

RAYNELL. Hi.

CORY. Hi.

RAYNELL. You in the Army or the Marines?

CORY. Marines.

RAYNELL. Papa said it was the Army. Did you know Blue?

CORY. Blue? Who's Blue?

RAYNELL. Papa's dog what he sing about all the time.

CORY (*singing*).

Hear it ring! Hear it ring!
I had a dog his name was Blue
You know Blue was mighty true
You know Blue was a good old dog
Blue treed a possum in a hollow log
You know from that he was a good old dog.
Hear it ring! Hear it ring!

*Raynell joins in singing.*

CORY AND RAYNELL.

Blue treed a possum out on a limb
Blue looked at me and I looked at him
Grabbed that possum and put him in a sack
Blue stayed there till I came back
Old Blue's feets was big and round
Never allowed a possum to touch the ground.

Old Blue died and I dug his grave
I dug his grave with a silver spade
Let him down with a golden chain
And every night I call his name
Go on Blue, you good dog you
Go on Blue, you good dog you.

RAYNELL.

Blue laid down and died like a man
Blue laid down and died . . .

BOTH.

Blue laid down and died like a man
Now he's treeing possums in the Promised Land
I'm gonna tell you this to let you know
Blue's gone where the good dogs go
When I hear old Blue bark
When I hear old Blue bark
Blue treed a possum in Noah's Ark
Blue treed a possum in Noah's Ark.

*Rose comes to the screen door.*

ROSE. Cory, we gonna be ready to go in a minute.

CORY (*to Raynell*). You go on in the house and change them shoes like Mama told you so we can go to Papa's funeral.

RAYNELL. Okay, I'll be back.

*Raynell exits into the house. Cory gets up and crosses over to the tree. Rose stands in the screen door watching him. Gabriel enters from the alley.*

GABRIEL (*calling*). Hey, Rose!

ROSE. Gabe?

GABRIEL. I'm here, Rose. Hey Rose, I'm here!

*Rose enters from the house.*

ROSE. Lord . . . Look here, Lyons!

LYONS. See, I told you, Rose . . . I told you they'd let him come.

CORY. How you doing, Uncle Gabe?

LYONS. How you doing, Uncle Gabe?

GABRIEL. Hey, Rose. It's time. It's time to tell St. Peter to open the gates. Troy, you ready? You ready, Troy. I'm gonna tell St. Peter to open the gates. You get ready now.

*Gabriel, with great fanfare, braces himself to blow. The trumpet is without a mouthpiece. He puts the end of it into his mouth and blows with great force, like a man who has been waiting some twenty-odd years for this single moment. No sound comes out of the trumpet. He braces himself and blows again with the same result. A third time he blows. There is a weight of impossible description that falls away and leaves him bare and exposed to a frightful realization. It is a trauma that a sane and normal mind would be unable to withstand. He begins to dance. A slow, strange dance, eerie and life-giving. A dance of atavistic signature and ritual. Lyons attempts to embrace him. Gabriel pushes Lyons away. He begins to howl in what is an attempt at song, or perhaps a song turning back into itself in an attempt at speech. He finishes his dance and the gates of heaven stand open as wide as God's closet.*

That's the way that go!

BLACKOUT

[*1987*]

## TOPICS FOR CRITICAL THINKING AND WRITING

1. What do you think Bono means when he says, early in Act 2 (p. 1759), "Some people build fences to keep people out . . . and other people build fences to keep people in"? Why is the play called *Fences?* What is Troy fencing in? (You'll want to take account of Troy's last speech in 2.2, but don't limit your response to this speech.)
2. Would you agree that Troy's refusal to encourage his son's aspirations is one of the "fences" of the play? What do you think Troy's reasons are—conscious and unconscious—for not wanting Cory to play football at college?
3. Compare and contrast Cory and Lyons. Consider, too, in what ways they resemble Troy, and in what ways they differ from him.
4. In what ways is Troy like his father, and in what ways unlike?
5. What do you make of the prominence given to the song about Blue?
6. There is a good deal of anger in the play, but there is also humor. Which passages do you find humorous, and why?
7. Characterize Rose Maxson.
8. Some scenes begin by specifying that "the lights come up." Others do not, presumably beginning with an illuminated stage. All scenes except the last one—which ends with a sudden blackout—end with the lights slowly going down to blackness. How would you explain Wilson's use of lighting?

## A PERSPECTIVE FOR *FENCES*

### AUGUST WILSON

# *Talking about* Fences

[Part of an interview conducted with David Savran on 13 March 1987]

***In reading* Fences, *I came to view Troy more and more critically as the play progressed, sharing Rose's point of view. We see that Troy has been crippled by his father. That's being replayed in Troy's relationship with Cory. Do you think there's a way out of that cycle?***

Surely. First of all, we're all like our parents. The things we are taught early in life, how to respond to the world, our sense of morality—everything, we get from them. Now you can take that legacy and do with it anything you want to do. It's in your hands. Cory is Troy's son. How can he be Troy's son without sharing Troy's values? I was trying to get at why Troy made the choices he made, how they have influenced his values and how he attempts to pass those along to his son. Each generation gives the succeeding generation what they think they need. One question in the play is, "Are the tools we are given sufficient to compete in a world that is different from the one our parents knew?" I think they are—it's just that we have to do different things with the tools. That's all Troy has to give. Troy's flaw is that he does not recognize that the world was changing. That's because he spent fifteen years in a penitentiary.

As African-Americans, we should demand to participate in society as Africans. That's the way out of the vicious cycle of poverty and neglect that exists in 1987 in America, where you have a huge percentage of blacks living in the equivalent of South African townships, in housing projects. No one is inviting these people to participate in society. Look at the poverty levels—$8,500 for a family of four, if you have $8,501 you're not counted. Those statistics would go up enormously if we had an honest assessment of the cost of living in America. I don't know how anybody can support a family of four on $8,500. What I'm saying is that 85 or 90 percent of blacks in America are living in abject poverty and, for the most part, are crowded into what amount to concentration camps. The situation for blacks in America is worse than it was forty years ago. Some sociologists will tell you about the tremendous progress we've made. They didn't put me out when I walked in the door. And you can always point to someone who works on Wall Street, or is a doctor. But they don't count in the larger scheme of things.

***Do you have any idea how these political changes could take place?***

I'm not sure. I know that blacks must be allowed their cultural differences. I think the process of assimilation to white American society was a big mistake. We don't want to be like you. Blacks living in housing projects are isolated from the society, for the most part—living as they choose, as Africans. Only they don't realize the value in what they're doing because they have accepted their victimization. They've marked themselves as victims. Once they recognize that, they can begin to move through society in a different manner, from a stronger position, and claim what is theirs.

***A project of yours is to point up what happens when oppression is internalized.***

Yes, transfer of aggression to the wrong target. I think it's interesting that the two roads open to blacks for "full participation" are entertainment and sports. *Ma Rainey* and *Fences,* and I didn't plan it that way. I don't think that they're the correct roads. I think Troy's right. Now with the benefit of historical perspective, I can say that the athletic scholarship was actually a way of exploiting. Now you've got two million kids who think they're going to play in the NBA. In the sixties the universities made a lot of money off of athletics. You had kids playing for free who, by and large, were not getting educated, were taking courses in basketweaving. Some of them could barely read.

***Troy may be right about that issue, but it seems that he has passed on certain destructive traits in spite of himself. Take the hostility between father and son.***

I think every generation says to the previous generation: you're in my way. I've got to get by. The father-son conflict is actually a normal generational conflict that happens all the time.

***So it's a healthy and a good thing?***

Oh, sure. Troy is seeing this boy walk around, smelling his piss. Two men cannot live in the same household. Troy would have been tremendously disappointed if Cory had not challenged him. Troy knows that this boy has to go out and do battle with that world: "So I had best prepare him because I know that's a harsh, cruel place out there. But that's going to be easy compared to what he's getting here. Ain't nobody gonna whip your ass like I'm gonna whip it." He has a tremendous love for the kid. But he's not going to say, "I love you," he's going to demonstrate it. He's carrying garbage for seventeen years just for the kid. The only world Troy knows is the one that he made. Cory's going to go on to find another one, he's going to arrive at the same place as Troy. I think one of the most important lines in the play is when Troy is talking about his father: "I got to the place where I could feel him kicking in my blood and knew that the only thing that separated us was the matter of a few years."

Hopefully, Cory will do things a bit differently with his son. For Troy, sports was not the way to go, the white man wouldn't let him get away with that. "Get you a job, with your hands, something that nobody can take away from you." The idea of school—he doesn't know what that is. That's for white folks. Very few blacks had paperwork jobs. But if you knew how to fix cars, you could always make some money. That's what Troy wants for Cory. There aren't many people who ever jumped up in Troy's face. So he's proud of the kid at the same time that he expresses a hurt that all men feel. You got to cut your kid loose at some point. There's that sense of loss and separation. You find out how Troy left his father's house and you see how Cory leaves his house. I suspect with Cory it will repeat with some differences and maybe, after five or six generations, they'll find a different way to do it.

***Where Cory ends up is very ambiguous, as a marine in 1965.***

Yes. For the average black kid on the street, that was an alternative. You went into the army because you could learn how to do something. I can remember my parents talking about the son of some friends: "He's in the navy. He *did* something"—as opposed to standing on the street corner, shooting drugs, drinking wine, and robbing stores. Lyons says to Cory, "I always knew you were going to make something out of yourself." It really wounds me. He's a corporal in the marines. For blacks, that is a sense of accomplishment. Therein lies one of the tragedies of blacks in America. Cory says, "I don't know. I put in six years. That's enough." Anyone who goes into the army and makes a career out of it is a loser. They sit there and are nurtured by the army and they don't have to confront life. Then they get out of the army and find there's nothing to do. They didn't learn any skills. And if they did, they can't find a job. Four months later, they're shooting dope. In the sixties a whole bunch of blacks went over, fought and died in the Vietnam War. The survivors came back to the same street corners and found out nothing had changed. They still couldn't get a job.

At the end of *Fences* every person, with the exception of Raynell, is institutionalized. Rose is in a church. Lyons is in a penitentiary. Gabriel's in a mental hospital and Cory's in the marines. The only free person is the girl, Troy's daughter, the hope for the future. That was conscious on my part because in '57 that's what I saw. Blacks have relied on institutions which are really foreign—except for the black church, which has been our saving grace. I have some problems with it but I recognize it as a central social organization and sometimes an economic organization for the black community. I would like to see blacks develop their own institutions that respond to their needs.

## DAVID HENRY HWANG

*David Henry Hwang (pronounced Wong), the son of first-generation Chinese immigrants, was born in 1957 in San Gabriel, a suburb of Los Angeles. When he was an undergraduate at Stanford University he wrote and directed his first play,* FOB *(1979; the letters stand for "Fresh Off the Boat"), in a production financed in part by the student-run Stanford Asian American Theater Project. In the following year* FOB *was staged in New York, at the New York Shakespeare Festival Public Theater, and won an Obie Award (best play staged Off-Broadway). Among Hwang's later plays are* The Sound of a Voice *(1983) and* M. Butterfly *(1988). Together with another of Hwang's short plays,* The House of Sleeping Beauties, The Sound of a Voice *was staged under the collective title of* Sound and Beauty.

# *The Sound of a Voice*

CHARACTERS

MAN, *fifties, Japanese*

WOMAN, *fifties, Japanese*

**SETTING:** *Woman's house, in a remote corner of the forest.*

**SCENE I.** *Woman pours tea for Man. Man rubs himself, trying to get warm.*

MAN. You're very kind to take me in.

WOMAN. This is a remote corner of the world. Guests are rare.

MAN. The tea—you pour it well.

WOMAN. No.

MAN. The sound it makes—in the cup—very soothing.

WOMAN. That is the tea's skill, not mine. (*She hands the cup to him.*) May I get you something else? Rice, perhaps?

MAN. No.

WOMAN. And some vegetables?

MAN. No, thank you.

WOMAN. Fish? (*Pause.*) It is at least two days' walk to the nearest village. I saw no horse. You must be very hungry. You would do a great honor to dine with me. Guests are rare.

MAN. Thank you.

WOMAN (*Woman gets up, leaves. Man holds the cup in his hands, using it to warm himself. He gets up, walks around the room. It is sparsely furnished, drab, except for one shelf on which stands a vase of brightly colored flowers. The flowers stand out in sharp contrast to the starkness of the room. Slowly, he reaches out towards them. He touches them. Quickly, he takes one of the flowers from the vase, hides it in his clothes. He returns to where he had sat previously. He waits. Woman re-enters. She carries a tray with food.*) Please. Eat. It will give me great pleasure.

An archetypal dramatic situation—a man and a woman.

MAN. This—this is magnificent.

WOMAN. Eat.

MAN. Thank you. (*He motions for Woman to join him.*)

WOMAN. No, thank you.

MAN. This is wonderful. The best I've tasted.

WOMAN. You are reckless in your flattery. But anything you say, I will enjoy hearing. It's not even the words. It's the sound of a voice, the way it moves through the air.

MAN. How long has it been since you last had a visitor? (*Pause.*)

WOMAN. I don't know.

MAN. Oh?

WOMAN. I lose track. Perhaps five months ago, perhaps ten years, perhaps yesterday. I don't consider time when there is no voice in the air. It's pointless. Time begins with the entrance of a visitor, and ends with his exit.

MAN. And in between? You don't keep track of the days? You can't help but notice—

WOMAN. Of course I notice.

MAN. Oh.

WOMAN. I notice, but I don't keep track. (*Pause.*) May I bring out more?

MAN. More? No. No. This was wonderful.

WOMAN. I have more.

MAN. Really—the best I've had.

WOMAN. You must be tired. Did you sleep in the forest last night?

MAN. Yes.

WOMAN. Or did you not sleep at all?

MAN. I slept.

WOMAN. Where?

MAN. By a waterfall. The sound of the water put me to sleep. It rumbled like the sounds of a city. You see, I can't sleep in too much silence. It scares me. It makes me feel that I have no control over what is about to happen.

WOMAN. I feel the same way.

MAN. But you live here—alone?

WOMAN. Yes.

MAN. It's so quiet here. How can you sleep?

WOMAN. Tonight, I'll sleep. I'll lie down in the next room, and hear your breathing through the wall, and fall asleep shamelessly. There will be no silence.

MAN. You're very kind to let me stay here.

WOMAN. This is yours. (*She unrolls a mat; there is a beautiful design of a flower on the mat. The flower looks exactly like the flowers in the vase.*)

MAN. Did you make it yourself?

WOMAN. Yes. There is a place to wash outside.

MAN. Thank you.

WOMAN. Goodnight.

MAN. Goodnight. (*Man starts to leave.*)

WOMAN. May I know your name?

MAN. No. I mean, I would rather not say. If I gave you a name, it would only be made-up. Why should I deceive you? You are too kind for that.

WOMAN. Then what should I call you? Perhaps—"Man Who Fears Silence"?

MAN. How about, "Man Who Fears Women"?

WOMAN. That name is much too common.

MAN. And you?

WOMAN. Yokiko.

MAN. That's your name?

WOMAN. It's what you may call me.

MAN. Goodnight, Yokiko. You are very kind.

WOMAN. You are very smart. Goodnight. (*Man exits. Hanako*[1] *goes to the mat. She tidies it, brushes it off. She goes to the vase. She picks up the flowers, studies them. She carries them out of the room with her. Man re-enters. He takes off his outer clothing. He glimpses the spot where the vase used to sit. He reaches into his clothing, pulls out the stolen flower. He studies it. He puts it underneath his head as he lies down to sleep, like a pillow. He starts to fall asleep. Suddenly, a start. He picks up his head. He listens.*)

**SCENE II.** *Dawn. Man is getting dressed. Woman enters with food.*

WOMAN. Good morning.

MAN. Good morning, Yokiko.

WOMAN. You weren't planning to leave?

MAN. I have quite a distance to travel today.

WOMAN. Please. (*She offers him food.*)

MAN. Thank you.

WOMAN. May I ask where you're travelling to?

[1]**Hanako** the woman

MAN. It's far.

WOMAN. I know this region well.

MAN. Oh? Do you leave the house often?

WOMAN. I used to. I used to travel a great deal. I know the region from those days.

MAN. You probably wouldn't know the place I'm headed.

WOMAN. Why not?

MAN. It's new. A new village. It didn't exist in "those days." (*Pause.*)

WOMAN. I thought you said you wouldn't deceive me.

MAN. I didn't. You don't believe me, do you?

WOMAN. No.

MAN. Then I didn't deceive you. I'm travelling. That much is true.

WOMAN. Are you in such a hurry?

MAN. Travelling is a matter of timing. Catching the light. (*Woman exits; Man finishes eating, puts down his bowl. Woman re-enters with the vase of flowers.*) Where did you find those? They don't grow native around these parts, do they?

WOMAN. No; they've all been brought in. They were brought in by visitors. Such as yourself. They were left here. In my custody.

MAN. But—they look so fresh, so alive.

WOMAN. I take care of them. They remind me of the people and places outside this house.

MAN. May I touch them?

WOMAN. Certainly.

MAN. These have just blossomed.

WOMAN. No; they were in bloom yesterday. If you'd noticed them before, you would know that.

MAN. You must have received these very recently. I would guess—within five days.

WOMAN. I don't know. But I wouldn't trust your estimate. It's all in the amount of care you show to them. I create a world which is outside the realm of what you know.

MAN. What do you do?

WOMAN. I can't explain. Words are too inefficient. It takes hundreds of words to describe a single act of caring. With hundreds of acts, words become irrelevant. (*Pause.*) But perhaps you can stay.

MAN. How long?

WOMAN. As long as you'd like.

MAN. Why?

WOMAN. To see how I care for them.

MAN. I *am* tired.

WOMAN. Rest.

MAN. The light?

WOMAN. It will return.

**SCENE III.** *Man is carrying chopped wood. He is stripped to the waist. Woman enters.*

WOMAN. You're very kind to do that for me.

MAN. I enjoy it, you know. Chopping wood. It's clean. No questions. You take your axe, you stand up the log, you aim—pow!—you either hit it or you don't. Success or failure.

WOMAN. You seem to have been very successful today.

MAN. Why shouldn't I be? It's a beautiful day. I can see to those hills. The trees are cool. The sun is gentle. Ideal. If a man can't be successful on a day like this, he might as well kick the dust up into his own face. (*Man notices Woman staring at him. Man pats his belly, looks at her.*) Protection from falls.

WOMAN. What? (*Man pinches his belly, showing some fat.*) Oh. Don't be silly. (*Man begins slapping the fat on his belly to a rhythm.*)

MAN. Listen—I can make music—see?—that wasn't always possible. But now—that I've developed this—whenever I need entertainment.

WOMAN. You shouldn't make fun of your body.

MAN. Why not? I saw you. You were staring.

WOMAN. I wasn't making fun. (*Man inflates his cheeks.*) I was just—stop that!

MAN. Then why were you staring?

WOMAN. I was—

MAN. Laughing?

WOMAN. No.

MAN. Well?

WOMAN. I was—Your body. It's . . . strong. (*Pause.*)

MAN. People say that. But they don't know. I've heard that age brings wisdom. That's a laugh. The years don't accumulate here. They accumulate here. (*Pause; he pinches his belly.*) But today is a day to be happy, right? The woods. The sun. Blue. It's a happy day. I'm going to chop wood.

WOMAN. There's nothing left to chop. Look.

MAN. Oh. I guess . . . that's it.

WOMAN. Sit. Here.

MAN. But—

WOMAN. There's nothing left. (*Man sits; Woman stares at his belly.*) Learn to love it.

MAN. Don't be ridiculous.

WOMAN. Touch it.

MAN. It's flabby.

WOMAN. It's strong.

MAN. It's weak.

WOMAN. And smooth.

MAN. Do you mind if I put on my shirt?

WOMAN. Of course not. Shall I get it for you?

MAN. No. No. Just sit there. (*Man starts to put on his shirt. He pauses, studies his body.*) You think it's cute, huh?

WOMAN. I think you should learn to love it. (*Man pats his belly, talks to it.*)

MAN (*to belly*). You're okay, sir. You hang onto my body like a great horseman.

WOMAN. Not like that.

MAN (*Ibid.*). You're also faithful. You'll never leave me for another man.

WOMAN. No.

MAN. What do you want me to say? (*Woman walks over to Man. She touches his belly with her hand. They look at each other.*)

**SCENE IV.** *Night. Man is alone. Flowers are gone from stand. Mat is unrolled. Man lies on it, sleeping. Suddenly, he starts. He lifts up his* *head. He listens. Silence. He goes back to sleep. Another start. He lifts up his head, strains to hear. Slowly, we begin to make out the strains of a single* shakuhachi[2] *playing a haunting line. It is very soft. He strains to hear it. The instrument slowly fades out. He waits for it to return, but it does not. He takes out the stolen flower. He stares into it.*

**SCENE V.** *Day. Woman is cleaning, while Man relaxes. She is on her hands and knees, scrubbing. She is dressed in a simple outfit, for working. Her hair is tied back. Man is sweating. He has not, however, removed his shirt.*

MAN. I heard your playing last night.

WOMAN. My playing?

MAN. *Shakuhachi.*

WOMAN. Oh.

MAN. You played very softly. I had to strain to hear it. Next time, don't be afraid. Play out. Fully. Clear. It must've been very beautiful, if only I could've heard it clearly. Why don't you play for me sometime?

WOMAN. I'm very shy about it.

MAN. Why?

WOMAN. I play for my own satisfaction. That's all. It's something I developed on my own. I don't know if it's at all acceptable by outside standards.

MAN. Play for me. I'll tell you.

WOMAN. No; I'm sure you're too knowledgeable in the arts.

MAN. Who? Me?

WOMAN. You being from the city and all.

MAN. I'm ignorant, believe me.

WOMAN. I'd play, and you'd probably bite your cheek.

MAN. Ask me a question about music. Any question. I'll answer incorrectly. I guarantee it.

WOMAN. Look at this.

MAN. What?

WOMAN. A stain.

MAN. Where?

WOMAN. Here? See? I can't get it out.

MAN. Oh. I hadn't noticed it before.

WOMAN. I notice it every time I clean.

MAN. Here. Let me try.

WOMAN. Thank you.

MAN. Ugh. It's tough.

WOMAN. I know.

MAN. How did it get here?

WOMAN. It's been there as long as I've lived here.

MAN. I hardly stand a chance. (*Pause.*) But I'll try. Uh—one—two—three—four! One—two—three—four! See, you set up . . . gotta set up . . . a rhythm—two—three—four. Like fighting! Like battle! One—two—three—four! Used to practice with a rhythm . . . beat . . . battle! Yes! (*The stain starts to fade away.*) Look—it's—yes!—whoo!—there it

[2]**shakuhachi** a Japanese bamboo flute

goes—got the sides—the edges—yes!—fading quick—fading away—ooo—here we come—towards the center—to the heart—two—three—four—slow—slow death—tough—dead! (*Man rolls over in triumphant laughter.*)

WOMAN. Dead.

MAN. I got it! I got it! Whoo! A little rhythm! All it took! Four! Four!

WOMAN. Thank you.

MAN. I didn't think I could do it—but there—it's gone—I did it!

WOMAN. Yes. You did.

MAN. And you—you were great.

WOMAN. No—I was carried away.

MAN. We were a team! You and me!

WOMAN. I only provided encouragement.

MAN. You were great! You were! (*Man grabs Woman. Pause.*)

WOMAN. It's gone. Thank you. Would you like to hear me play *shakuhachi?*

MAN. Yes I would.

WOMAN. I don't usually play for visitors. It's so . . . I'm not sure. I developed it—all by myself—in times when I was alone. I heard nothing—no human voice. So I learned to play *shakuhachi.* I tried to make these sounds resemble the human voice. The *shakuhachi* became my weapon. To ward off the air. It kept me from choking on many a silent evening.

MAN. I'm here. You can hear my voice.

WOMAN. Speak again.

MAN. I will.

**SCENE VI.** *Night. Man is sleeping. Suddenly, a start. He lifts his head up. He listens. Silence. He strains to hear. The* shakuhachi *melody rises up once more. This time, however, it becomes louder and more clear than before. He gets up. He cannot tell from what direction the music is coming. He walks around the room, putting his ear to different places in the wall, but he cannot locate the sound. It seems to come from all directions at once, as omnipresent as the air. Slowly, he moves towards the wall with the sliding panel through which the Woman enters and exits. He puts his ear against it, thinking the music may be coming from there. Slowly, he slides the door open just a crack, ever so carefully. He peeks through the crack. As he peeks through, the Upstage wall of the set becomes transparent, and through the scrim, we are able to see what he sees. Woman is Upstage of the scrim. She is tending a room filled with potted and vased flowers of all variety. The lushness and beauty of the room Upstage of the scrim stands out in stark contrast to the barrenness of the main set. She is also transformed. She is a young woman. She is beautiful. She wears a brightly colored kimono. Man observes this scene for a long time. He then slides the door shut. The scrim returns to opaque. The music continues. He returns to his mat. He picks up the stolen flower. It is brown and wilted, dead. He looks at it. The music slowly fades out.*

**SCENE VII.** *Morning. Man is half-dressed. He is practicing sword maneuvers. He practices with the feel of a man whose spirit is willing, but the flesh is inept. He tries to execute deft movements, but is* *dissatisfied with his efforts. He curses himself, and returns to basic exercises. Suddenly, he feels something buzzing around his neck—a mosquito. He slaps his neck, but misses it. He sees it flying near him. He swipes at it with his sword. He keeps missing. Finally, he thinks he's hit it. He runs over, kneels down to recover the fallen insect. He picks up two halves of a mosquito on two different fingers. Woman enters the room. She looks as she normally does. She is carrying a vase of flowers, which she places on its shelf.*

MAN. Look.

WOMAN. I'm sorry?

MAN. Look.

WOMAN. What? (*He brings over the two halves of mosquito to show her.*)

MAN. See?

WOMAN. Oh.

MAN. I hit it—chop!

WOMAN. These are new forms of target practice?

MAN. Huh? Well—yes—in a way.

WOMAN. You seem to do well at it.

MAN. Thank you. For last night. I heard your *shakuhachi.* It was very loud, strong—good tone.

WOMAN. Did you enjoy it? I wanted you to enjoy it. If you wish, I'll play it for you every night.

MAN. Every night!

WOMAN. If you wish.

MAN. No—I don't—I don't want you to treat me like a baby.

WOMAN. What? I'm not.

MAN. Oh, yes. Like a baby. Who you must feed in the middle of the night or he cries. Waaah! Waaah!

WOMAN. Stop that!

MAN. You need your sleep.

WOMAN. I don't mind getting up for you. (*Pause.*) I would enjoy playing for you. Every night. While you sleep. It will make me feel—like I'm shaping your dreams. I go through long stretches when there is no one in my dreams. It's terrible. During those times, I avoid my bed as much as possible. I paint. I weave. I play *shakuhachi.* I sit on mats and rub powder into my face. Anything to keep from facing a bed with no dreams. It is like sleeping on ice.

MAN. What do you dream of now?

WOMAN. Last night—I dreamt of you. I don't remember what happened. But you were very funny. Not in a mocking way. I wasn't laughing at you. But you made me laugh. And you were very warm. I remember that. (*Pause.*) What do you remember about last night?

MAN. Just your playing. That's all. I got up, listened to it, and went back to sleep. (*Man gets up, resumes practicing with his sword.*)

WOMAN. Another mosquito bothering you?

MAN. Just practicing. Ah! Weak! Too weak! I tell you, it wasn't always like this. I'm telling you, there were days when I could chop the fruit from a tree without ever taking my eyes off the ground. (*He continues practicing.*) You ever use one of these?

WOMAN. I've had to pick one up, yes.

MAN. Oh?

WOMAN. You forget—I live alone—out here—there is . . . not much to sustain me but what I manage to learn myself. It wasn't really a matter of choice.

MAN. I used to be very good, you know. Perhaps I can give you some pointers.

WOMAN. I'd really rather not.

MAN. C'mon—a woman like you—you're absolutely right. You need to know how to defend yourself.

WOMAN. As you wish.

MAN. Do you have something to practice with?

WOMAN. Yes. Excuse me. (*She exits. He practices more. She re-enters with two wooden sticks. He takes one of them.*) Will these do?

MAN. Nice. Now, show me what you can do.

WOMAN. I'm sorry?

MAN. Run up and hit me.

WOMAN. Please.

MAN. Go on—I'll block it.

WOMAN. I feel so . . . undignified.

MAN. Go on. (*She hits him playfully with stick.*) Not like that!

WOMAN. I'll try to be gentle.

MAN. What?

WOMAN. I don't want to hurt you.

MAN. You won't—Hit me! (*Woman charges at Man, quickly, deftly. She scores a hit.*) Oh!

WOMAN. Did I hurt you?

MAN. No—you were—let's try that again. (*They square off again. Woman rushes forward. She appears to attempt a strike. He blocks that apparent strike, which turns out to be a feint. She scores.*) Huh?

WOMAN. Did I hurt you? I'm sorry.

MAN. No.

WOMAN. I hurt you.

MAN. No.

WOMAN. Do you wish to hit me?

MAN. No.

WOMAN. Do you want me to try again?

MAN. No.

WOMAN. Thank you.

MAN. Just practice there—by yourself—let me see you run through some maneuvers.

WOMAN. Must I?

MAN. Yes! Go! (*She goes to an open area.*) My greatest strength was always as a teacher. (*Woman executes a series of deft movements. Her whole manner is transformed. Man watches with increasing amazement. Her movements end. She regains her submissive manner.*)

WOMAN. I'm so embarrassed. My skills—they're so—inappropriate. I look like a man.

MAN. Where did you learn that?

WOMAN. There is much time to practice here.

MAN. But you—the techniques.

WOMAN. I don't know what's fashionable in the outside world. (*Pause.*) Are you unhappy?

MAN. No.

WOMAN. Really?

MAN. I'm just . . . surprised.

WOMAN. You think it's unbecoming for a woman.

MAN. No, no. Not at all.

WOMAN. You want to leave.

MAN. No!

WOMAN. All visitors do. I know. I've met many. They say they'll stay. And they do. For a while. Until they see too much. Or they learn something new. There are boundaries outside of which visitors do not want to see me step. Only who knows what those boundaries are? Not I. They change with every visitor. You have to be careful not to cross them, but you never know where they are. And one day, inevitably, you step outside the lines. The visitor knows. You don't. You didn't know that you'd done anything different. You thought it was just another part of you. The visitor sneaks away. The next day, you learn that you had stepped outside his heart. I'm afraid you've seen too much.

MAN. There are stories.

WOMAN. What?

MAN. People talk.

WOMAN. Where? We're two days from the nearest village.

MAN. Word travels.

WOMAN. What are you talking about?

MAN. There are stories about you. I heard them. They say that your visitors never leave this house.

WOMAN. That's what you heard?

MAN. They say you imprison them.

WOMAN. Then you were a fool to come here.

MAN. Listen.

WOMAN. Me? Listen? You. Look! Where are these prisoners? Have you seen any?

MAN. They told me you were very beautiful.

WOMAN. Then they are blind as well as ignorant.

MAN. You are.

WOMAN. What?

MAN. Beautiful.

WOMAN. Stop that! My skin feels like seaweed.

MAN. I didn't realize it at first. I must confess—I didn't. But over these few days—your face has changed for me. The shape of it. The feel of it. The color. All changed. I look at you now, and I'm no longer sure you are the same woman who had poured tea for me just a week ago. And because of that I remembered—how little I know about a face that changes in the night. (*Pause.*) Have you heard those stories?

WOMAN. I don't listen to old wives' tales.

MAN. But have you heard them?

WOMAN. Yes. I've heard them. From other visitors—young—hotblooded—or old—who came here because they were told great glory was to be had by killing the witch in the woods.

MAN. I was told that no man could spend time in this house without falling in love.

WOMAN. Oh? So why did you come? Did you wager gold that you could come out untouched? The outside world is so flattering to me. And you—are you like the rest? Passion passing through your heart so powerfully that you can't hold onto it?

MAN. No! I'm afraid!

WOMAN. Of what?

MAN. Sometimes—when I look into the flowers, I think I hear a voice—from inside—a voice beneath the petals. A human voice.

WOMAN. What does it say? "Let me out"?

MAN. No. Listen. It hums. It hums with the peacefulness of one who is completely imprisoned.

WOMAN. I understand that if you listen closely enough, you can hear the ocean.

MAN. No. Wait. Look at it. See the layers? Each petal—hiding the next. Try and see where they end. You can't. Follow them down, further down, around—and as you come down—faster and faster—the breeze picks up. The breeze becomes a wail. And in that rush of air—in the silent midst of it—you can hear a voice.

WOMAN (*Woman grabs flower from Man*). So, you believe I water and prune my lovers? How can you be so foolish? (*She snaps the flower in half, at the stem. She throws it to the ground.*) Do you come only to leave again? To take a chunk of my heart, then leave with your booty on your belt, like a prize? You say that I imprison hearts in these flowers? Well, bits of my heart are trapped with travellers across this land. I can't even keep track. So kill me. If you came here to destroy a witch, kill me now. I can't stand to have it happen again.

MAN. I won't leave you.

WOMAN. I believe you. (*She looks at the flower that she has broken, bends to pick it up. He touches her. They embrace.*)

**SCENE VIII.** ***Day. Woman wears a simple undergarment, over which she is donning a brightly colored kimono, the same one we saw her wearing Upstage of the scrim. Man stands apart.***

WOMAN. I can't cry. I don't have the capacity. Right from birth, I didn't cry. My mother and father were shocked. They thought they'd given birth to a ghost, a demon. Sometimes I've thought myself that. When great sadness has welled up inside me, I've prayed for a means to release the pain from my body. But my prayers went unanswered. The grief remained inside me. It would sit like water, still. (*Pause; she models her kimono.*) Do you like it?

MAN. Yes, it's beautiful.

WOMAN. I wanted to wear something special today.

MAN. It's beautiful. Excuse me. I must practice.

WOMAN. Shall I get you something?

MAN. No.

WOMAN. Some tea, maybe?

MAN. No. (*Man resumes swordplay.*)

WOMAN. Perhaps later today—perhaps we can go out—just around here. We can look for flowers.

MAN. All right.

WOMAN. We don't have to.

MAN. No. Let's.

WOMAN. I just thought if—

MAN. Fine. Where do you want to go?

WOMAN. There are very few recreational activities around here, I know.

MAN. All right. We'll go this afternoon. (*Pause.*)

WOMAN. Can I get you something?

MAN (*turning around*). What?

WOMAN. You might be—

MAN. I'm not hungry or thirsty or cold or hot.

WOMAN. Then what are you?

MAN. Practicing. (*Man resumes practicing; Woman exits. As soon as she exits, he rests. He sits down. He examines his sword. He runs his finger along the edge of it. He takes the tip, runs it against the soft skin under his chin. He places the sword on the ground with the tip pointed directly upwards. He keeps it from falling by placing the tip under his chin. He experiments with different degrees of pressure. Woman re-enters. She sees him in this precarious position. She jerks his head upward; the sword falls.*)

WOMAN. Don't do that!

MAN. What?

WOMAN. You can hurt yourself!

MAN. I was practicing!

WOMAN. You were playing!

MAN. I was practicing!

WOMAN. It's dangerous.

MAN. What do you take me for—a child?

WOMAN. Sometimes wise men do childish things.

MAN. I knew what I was doing!

WOMAN. It scares me.

MAN. Don't be ridiculous. (*He reaches for the sword again.*)

WOMAN. Don't! Don't do that!

MAN. Get back! (*He places the sword back in its previous position, suspended between the floor and his chin, upright.*)

WOMAN. But—

MAN. Sssssh!

WOMAN. I wish—

MAN. Listen to me! The slightest shock, you know—the slightest shock—surprise—it might make me jerk or—something—and then . . . so you must be perfectly still and quiet.

WOMAN. But I—

MAN. Sssssh! (*Silence.*) I learned this exercise from a friend—I can't even remember his name—good swordsman—many years ago. He called it his meditation position. He said, like this, he could feel the line between this world and the others because he rested on it. If he saw something in another world that he liked better, all he would have to do is let his head drop, and he'd be there. Simple. No fuss. One day, they found him with the tip of his sword run clean out the back of his neck. He was smiling. I guess he saw something he liked. Or else he'd fallen asleep.

WOMAN. Stop that.

MAN. Stop what?

WOMAN. Tormenting me.

MAN. I'm not.

WOMAN. Take it away!

MAN. You don't have to watch, you know.

WOMAN. Do you want to die that way—an accident?

MAN. I was doing this before you came in.

WOMAN. If you do, all you need to do is tell me.

MAN. What?

WOMAN. I can walk right over. Lean on the back of your head.

MAN. Don't try to threaten—

WOMAN. Or jerk your sword up.

MAN. Or scare me. You can't threaten—

WOMAN. I'm not. But if that's what you want.

MAN. You can't threaten me. You wouldn't do it.

WOMAN. Oh?

MAN. Then I'd be gone. You wouldn't let me leave that easily.

WOMAN. Yes, I would.

MAN. You'd be alone.

WOMAN. No. I'd follow you. Forever. (*Pause.*) Now, let's stop this nonsense.

MAN. No! I can do what I want! Don't come any closer!

WOMAN. Then release your sword.

MAN. Come any closer and I'll drop my head.

WOMAN (*Woman slowly approaches Man. She grabs the hilt of the sword. She looks into his eyes. She pulls it out from under his chin.*) There will be no more of this. (*She exits with the sword. He starts to follow her, then stops. He touches under his chin. On his finger, he finds a drop of blood.*)

**SCENE IX.** *Night. Man is leaving the house. He is just about out, when he hears a* shakuhachi *playing. He looks around, trying to locate the sound. Woman appears in the doorway to the outside.* Shakuhachi *slowly fades out.*

WOMAN. It's time for you to go?

MAN. Yes. I'm sorry.

WOMAN. You're just going to sneak out? A thief in the night? A frightened child?

MAN. I care about you.

WOMAN. You express it strangely.

MAN. I leave in shame because it is proper. (*Pause.*) I came seeking glory.

WOMAN. To kill me? You can say it. You'll be surprised at how little I blanche. As if you'd said, "I came for a bowl of rice," or "I came seeking love" or "I came to kill you."

MAN. Weakness. All weakness. Too weak to kill you. Too weak to kill myself. Too weak to do anything but sneak away in shame. (*Woman brings out Man's sword.*)

WOMAN. Were you even planning to leave without this? (*He takes sword.*) Why not stay here?

MAN. I can't live with someone who's defeated me.

WOMAN. I never thought of defeating you. I only wanted to take care of you. To make you happy. Because that made me happy and I was no longer alone.

MAN. You defeated me.

WOMAN. Why do you think that way?

MAN. I came here with a purpose. The world was clear. You changed the shape of your face, the shape of my heart—rearranged everything—created a world where I could do nothing.

WOMAN. I only tried to care for you.

MAN. I guess that was all it took. (*Pause.*)

WOMAN. You still think I'm a witch. Just because old women gossip. You are so cruel. Once you arrived, there were only two possibilities: I would die or you would leave. (*Pause.*) If you believe I'm a witch, then kill me. Rid the province of one more evil.

MAN. I can't—

WOMAN. Why not? If you believe that about me, then it's the right thing to do.

MAN. You know I can't.

WOMAN. Then stay.

MAN. Don't try and force me.

WOMAN. I won't force you to do anything. (*Pause.*) All I wanted was an escape—for both of us. The sound of a human voice—the simplest thing to find, and the hardest to hold onto. This house—my loneliness is etched into the walls. Kill me, but don't leave. Even in death, my spirit would rest here and be comforted by your presence.

MAN. Force me to stay.

WOMAN. I won't. (*Man starts to leave.*) Beware.

MAN. What?

WOMAN. The ground on which you walk is weak. It could give way at any moment. The crevice beneath is dark.

MAN. Are you talking about death? I'm ready to die.

WOMAN. Fear for what is worse than death.

MAN. What?

WOMAN. Falling. Falling through the darkness. Waiting to hit the ground. Picking up speed. Waiting for the ground. Falling faster. Falling alone. Waiting. Falling. Waiting. Falling.

(*Woman wails and runs out through the door to her room. Man stands, confused, not knowing what to do. He starts to follow her, then hesitates, and rushes out the door to the outside. Silence. Slowly, he re-enters from the outside. He looks for her in the main room. He goes slowly towards the panel to her room. He throws down his sword. He opens the panel. He goes inside. He comes out. He unrolls his mat. He sits on it, cross-legged. He looks out into space. He notices near him a* shakuhachi. *He picks it up. He begins to blow into it. He tries to make sounds. He continues trying through the end of the play. The Upstage scrim lights up. Upstage, we see the Woman. She is young. She is hanging from a rope suspended from the roof. She has hung herself. Around her are scores of vases with flowers in them whose blossoms have been blown off. Only the stems remain in the vases. Around her swirl the thousands of petals from the flowers. They fill the Upstage scrim area like a blizzard of color. Man continues to attempt to play. Lights fade to black.*)

[*1983*]

## TOPICS FOR CRITICAL THINKING AND WRITING

1. As the play unfolds, we learn the characters' names, but Hwang identifies them at first as simply "Man" and "Woman." What do these terms suggest about how we should understand them? Note also the age of the characters. Why is this detail important, and how is it highlighted at various points in the action and dialogue?
2. Soon after the play begins, the Woman refers to "the sound of a voice," the phrase which Hwang has taken as his title. How is this phrase connected to the main themes of the play? In considering this question, pay close attention to the uses of, and references to, silence and sound in the work as a whole.
3. Is it possible to generalize about the atmosphere of *The Sound of a Voice*—its mood, the tone of its language? Students have sometimes used words like *captivating* and *haunting* about this play. Would you say these words are accurate, or would different words be more faithful to your sense of the work? Make sure to give evidence from the text for your responses.
4. Scene VII opens with the Man swiping at a mosquito with a sword. A student in one of our classes said that this scene struck her as a "mistake"—that it seemed almost farcical. Do you think that this scene does or does not contribute effectively to the impact of the play?
5. Imagine that you are directing this play. What specific pieces of advice would you want to give to the actors about their roles and how most effectively to play them? Zero in on a moment in the text that, in your view, will be especially challenging for the two actors.
6. Focus on the ending. Could the play have ended with the Woman's words, or does it require the actions that the concluding stage directions describe? What would be lost if the last we saw and heard, before the lights fade to black, was the woman speaking her final lines?

# A PERSPECTIVE FOR *THE SOUND OF A VOICE*

## DAVID HENRY HWANG

## *Thoughts about "Ethnic Theater"*

[On 28 June 1989 Jean W. Ross interviewed David Henry Hwang on behalf of *Contemporary Authors.*]

CA. You told Jeremy Gerard for the *New York Times Magazine* that when you were growing up, you thought being Chinese was "a minor detail, like having red hair." How did you begin to feel otherwise and to start exploring your heritage?

HWANG. A lot of that happened in college. I was in college in the mid- to late 1970s, and whereas most people seem to associate collegiate life in the seventies with [actor] John Travolta, there was at that time a third-world consciousness, a third-world power movement, in the universities, particularly among Hispanics and Asians. The blacks really started it in the late sixties and early seventies, and it took a while to trickle down into the other third-world communities. Asians probably picked it up last; we got interested in the late seventies, when many of the other ethnic communities had become less politicized. I think my political consciousness, such as it is, evolved out of that third-world, Marxist setting at the university. While I was never a very ardent Marxist, I studied the ideas and I was interested in the degree to which we all may have been affected by certain prejudices in the society without having realized it, and to what degree we had incorporated that into our persons by the time we'd reached our early twenties.

The other thing that I think fascinated me about exploring my Chineseness at that time was consistent with my interest in playwriting. I had become very interested in Sam Shepard, particularly in the way in which Shepard likes to create a sort of American mythology. In his case it's the cowboy mythology, but nonetheless it's something that is larger than simply our present-day, fast-food existence. In my context, creating a mythology, creating a past for myself, involved going into Chinese history and Chinese-American history. I think the combination of wanting to delve into those things for artistic reasons and being exposed to an active third-world-consciousness movement was what started to get me interested in my roots when I was in college.

CA. You've told earlier interviewers how the amazing true story of a French diplomat and his Chinese lover, a Beijing Opera star who turned out to be a man, called to your mind the Puccini opera *Madama Butterfly* and became your award-winning play *M. Butterfly.* Earlier you had felt some concern about "riding the hyphen," as Jeremy Gerard titled his article—becoming stereotyped as a Chinese-American writer. Has *M. Butterfly* helped you overcome that worry to some extent?

HWANG. I first became aware of the simplistic nature of this stereotyping when I did the two Japanese plays *The Sound of a Voice* and *The House of Sleeping Beauties.* I thought this work was a departure because these were the first plays I'd written that didn't deal with being Chinese-American, with race and assimilation; I felt that they were really tragic love stories. Yet they were not perceived as being a departure, because they had Asian actors. So I realized that the stereotyping is based on the color of the actors. . . .

CA. I wonder if there will come a time when the expression "ethnic theater" won't have any meaning.

HWANG. I'm hopeful that there will be a time at some point, but I think it's going to be fifty years or so down the road. The whole idea of being ethnic only applies when it's clear what the dominant culture is. Once it becomes less clear and the culture is acknowledged to be more multicultural, then the idea of what's ethnic becomes irrelevant. I think even today we're starting to see that. The mono-ethnic theaters—that is, the Asian theaters, the black theaters, the Hispanic theaters—are really useful; they serve a purpose. But I think, if we do our jobs correctly, we will phase out our own need for existence and the future of theaters will be in multicultural theaters, theaters that do a black play and a Jewish play and a classic and whatever. That sort of thing is already starting to happen. In San Francisco, for example, there's now a coalition being built between the Oakland Ensemble Theater, which is a black theater; Teatro Campesino, which is Hispanic; and the Asian-American Theater Company. They will pool their resources and do a season. I think that sort of thing is great.

There are so many people now who can't be labeled. I know a couple in which the man is Japanese and Jewish and the woman is Haitian and Filipino. They have a child, and sociologists have told them that a child of that stock probably hasn't existed before. When someone like that becomes a writer, what do we call him? Do we say he's an Asian writer, or what? As those distinctions become increasingly muddled, the whole notion of what is ethnic as opposed to what is mainstream is going to become more and more difficult to define.

## DAVID MAMET

*David Mamet was born in Chicago in 1947, and was educated at Goddard College. A screenwriter and director as well as a playwright, he has occasionally taught courses in film. In 1976 his play* American Buffalo *won the New York Drama Critics Circle Award for the best American play, and in 1984* Glengarry Glen Ross *won the Pulitzer Prize.* Oleanna *was first produced in 1992. "All my plays," he has said, "attempt to bring out the poetry in the plain, everyday language people use."*

# *Oleanna*

The want of fresh air does not seem much to affect the happiness of children in a London alley: the greater part of them sing and play as though they were on a moor in Scotland. So the absence of a genial mental atmosphere is not commonly recognized by children who have never known it. Young people have a marvelous faculty of either dying or adapting themselves to circumstances. Even if they are unhappy—very unhappy—it is astonishing how easily they can be prevented from finding it out, or at any rate from attributing it to any other cause than their own sinfulness.

—Samuel Butler, *The Way of All Flesh*

"Oh, to be in *Oleanna,*
That's where I would rather be.
Than be bound in Norway
And drag the chains of slavery."

—Folk Song

CHARACTERS
CAROL *A woman of twenty*
JOHN *A man in his forties*

*The play takes place in John's office.*

Rebecca Pidgeon and W. H. Macy in *Oleanna*, 1992. (© Brigitte Lacombe)

## *One*

***John is talking on the phone. Carol is seated across the desk from him.***

JOHN (*on phone*). And what about the land. (*Pause*) The land. And what about the land? (*Pause*) What about it? (*Pause*) No. I don't understand. Well, yes, I'm I'm . . . no, I'm *sure* it's signif . . . I'm sure it's significant. (*Pause*) Because it's significant to mmmmmm . . . did you call Jerry? (*Pause*) Because . . . no, no, no, no, no. What did they say . . . ? Did you speak to the *real* estate . . . where *is* she . . . ? Well, well, all right. Where are her notes? Where are the notes we took with her. (*Pause*) I thought you were? No. No, I'm sorry, I didn't mean that, I just thought that I saw you, when we were there . . . what . . . ? I thought I saw you with a *pencil.* WHY NOW? is what I'm say . . . well, that's why I say "call Jerry." Well, I can't right now, be . . . no, I *didn't* schedule any . . . Grace: I *didn't* . . . I'm well aware . . . Look: Look. Did you call Jerry? Will you call Jerry . . . ? Because I can't now. I'll be there, I'm sure I'll be there in fifteen, in twenty. I intend to. No, we aren't *going* to lose the, we aren't *going* to lose the house. Look: Look, I'm not minimizing it. The "easement." Did she say "easement"? (*Pause*) What did she *say; is* it a "term of art," are we *bound* by it . . . I'm sorry . . . (*Pause*) are: we: yes. *Bound* by . . . Look: (*He checks his watch.*) before the other side *goes home,* all right? "a term of art." Because: that's right (*Pause*) The yard for the boy. Well, that's the whole . . . Look: I'm going to meet you there . . . (*He checks his watch.*) Is the realtor there? All right, tell her to show you the basement again. Look at the *this* because . . . Bec . . .

I'm leaving in, I'm leaving in ten or fifteen . . . Yes. No, no, I'll meet you at the new . . . That's a good. If he thinks it's necc . . . you tell Jerry to meet . . . All right? We *aren't* going to lose the deposit. All right? I'm sure it's going to be . . . (*Pause*) I hope so. (*Pause*) I love you, too. (*Pause*) I love you, too. As soon as . . . I will.

(*He hangs up.*) (*He bends over the desk and makes a note.*) (*He looks up.*) (*To Carol:*) I'm sorry . . .

CAROL. (*Pause*) What is a "term of art"?

JOHN. (*Pause*) I'm sorry . . . ?

CAROL. (*Pause*) What is a "term of art"?

JOHN. Is that what you want to talk about?

CAROL. . . . to talk about . . . ?

JOHN. Let's take the mysticism out of it, shall we? Carol? (*Pause*) Don't you think? I'll tell you: when you have some "thing." Which must be broached. (*Pause*) Don't you think . . . ? (*Pause*)

CAROL. . . . don't I think . . . ?

JOHN. Mmm?

CAROL. . . . did I . . . ?

JOHN. . . . what?

CAROL. Did . . . did I . . . did I say something wr . . .

JOHN. (*Pause*) No. I'm sorry. No. You're right. I'm very sorry. I'm somewhat rushed. As you see. I'm sorry. You're right. (*Pause*) What is a "term of art"? It seems to mean a *term,* which has come, through its use, to mean something *more specific* than the words would, to someone *not acquainted* with them . . . indicate. That, I believe, is what a "term of art," would mean. (*Pause*)

CAROL. You don't know what it means . . . ?

JOHN. I'm not sure that I know what it means. It's one of those things, perhaps you've had them, that, you look them up, or have someone explain them to you, and you say "aha," and, you immediately *forget* what . . .

CAROL. You don't do that.

JOHN. . . . I . . . ?

CAROL. You don't do . . .

JOHN. . . . I don't, what . . . ?

CAROL. . . . for . . .

JOHN. . . . I don't for . . .

CAROL. . . . no . . .

JOHN. . . . forget things? Everybody does that.

CAROL. No, they don't.

JOHN. They don't . . .

CAROL. No.

JOHN. (*Pause*) No. Everybody does that.

CAROL. Why would they do that . . . ?

JOHN. Because. I don't know. Because it doesn't interest them.

CAROL. No.

JOHN. I think so, though. (*Pause*) I'm sorry that I was distracted.

CAROL. You don't have to say that to me.

JOHN. You paid me the compliment, or the "obeisance"—all right—of coming in here . . . All right. *Carol.* I find that I am at a *standstill.* I find that I . . .

CAROL. . . . what . . .

JOHN. . . . one moment. In regard to your . . . to your . . .

CAROL. Oh, oh. You're buying a new house!

JOHN. No, let's get on with it.

CAROL. "Get on"? (*Pause*)

JOHN. I know how . . . *believe* me. I know how . . . potentially *humiliating* these . . . I have no desire to . . . I have no desire other than to help you. But: (*He picks up some papers on his desk.*) I won't even say "but." I'll say that as I go back over the . . .

CAROL. I'm just, I'm just trying to . . .

JOHN. . . . no, it will not do.

CAROL. . . . what? What will . . . ?

JOHN. No. I see, I see what you, it . . . (*He gestures to the papers.*) but your work . . .

CAROL. I'm just: I sit in class I . . . (*She holds up her notebook.*) I take notes . . .

JOHN (*simultaneously with* "notes"). Yes. I understand. What I am trying to *tell* you is that some, some basic . . .

CAROL. . . . I . . .

JOHN. . . . one moment: some basic missed communi . . .

CAROL. I'm doing what I'm told. I bought your book, I read your . . .

JOHN. No, I'm sure you . . .

CAROL. No, no, no. I'm doing what I'm told. It's *difficult* for me. It's *difficult* . . .

JOHN. . . . but . . .

CAROL. I don't . . . lots of the *language* . . .

JOHN. . . . please . . .

CAROL. The *language,* the "things" that you say . . .

JOHN. I'm sorry. No. I don't think that that's true.

CAROL. It *is* true. I . . .

JOHN. I think . . .

CAROL. It *is* true.

JOHN. . . . I . . .

CAROL. Why would I . . . ?

JOHN. I'll tell you why: you're an incredibly bright girl.

CAROL. . . . I . . .

JOHN. You're an incredibly . . . you have no problem with the . . . Who's kidding who?

CAROL. . . . I . . .

JOHN. No. No. I'll tell you why. I'll tell. . . . I think you're *angry,* I . . .

CAROL. . . . why would I . . .

JOHN. . . . wait one moment. I . . .

CAROL. It *is* true. I have *problems* . . .

JOHN. . . . every . . .

CAROL. . . . I come from a different *social* . . .

JOHN. . . . ev . . .

CAROL. a different economic . . .

JOHN. . . . Look:

CAROL. No. I: when I *came* to this school:

JOHN. Yes. Quite . . . (*Pause*)

CAROL. . . . does that mean nothing . . . ?

JOHN. . . . but look: look . . .

CAROL. . . . I . . .

JOHN. (*Picks up paper.*) Here: Please: Sit down. (*Pause*) Sit down. (*Reads from her paper.*) "I think that the ideas contained in this work express the author's feelings in a way that he intended, based on his results." What can that mean? Do you see? What . . .

CAROL. I, the best that I . . .

JOHN. I'm saying, that perhaps this course . . .

CAROL. No, no, no, you can't, you can't . . . I have to . . .

JOHN. . . . how . . .

CAROL. . . . I have to pass it . . .

JOHN. Carol, I:

CAROL. I *have* to pass this course, I . . .

JOHN. Well.

CAROL. . . . don't you . . .

JOHN. Either the . . .

CAROL. . . . I . . .

JOHN. . . . either the, I . . . either the *criteria* for judging progress in the class are . . .

CAROL. No, no, no, no, I have to pass it.

JOHN. Now, look: I'm a human being, I . . .

CAROL. I did what you told me. I did, I did everything that, I read your *book,* you told me to buy your book and read it. Everything you *say* I . . . (*She gestures to her notebook.*) (*The phone rings.*) I do. . . . Ev . . .

JOHN. . . . look:

CAROL. . . . everything I'm told . . .

JOHN. Look. Look. I'm not your *father.* (*Pause*)

CAROL. What?

JOHN. I'm.

CAROL. Did I say you were my father?

JOHN. . . . no . . .

CAROL. Why did you say that . . . ?

JOHN. I . . .

CAROL. . . . why . . . ?

JOHN. . . . in class I . . . (*He picks up the phone.*) (*Into phone:*) Hello. I can't talk now. Jerry? Yes? I underst . . . I can't talk now. I know . . . I know . . . Jerry. I can't *talk* now. Yes, I. Call me back in . . . Thank you. (*He hangs up.*) (*To Carol:*) What do you want me to do? We are two people, all right? Both of whom have subscribed to . . .

CAROL. No, no . . .

JOHN. . . . certain arbitrary . . .

CAROL. No. You have to help me.

JOHN. Certain institutional . . . you tell me what you want me to do. . . . You tell me what you want me to . . .

CAROL. How can I go back and tell them the *grades* that I . . .

JOHN. . . . what can I do . . . ?

CAROL. *Teach* me. *Teach* me.

JOHN. . . . I'm trying to teach you.

CAROL. I read your book. I read it. I don't under . . .

JOHN. . . . you don't understand it.

CAROL. No.

JOHN. Well, perhaps it's not well *written* . . .

CAROL (*simultaneously with* "written"). No. No. No. I want to *understand* it.

JOHN. What don't you understand? (*Pause*)

CAROL. *Any* of it. What you're trying to say. When you talk about . . .

JOHN. . . . yes . . . ? (*She consults her notes.*)

CAROL. "Virtual warehousing of the young" . . .

JOHN. "Virtual warehousing of the young." If we artificially prolong adolescence . . .

CAROL. . . . and about "The Curse of Modern Education."

JOHN. . . . well . . .

CAROL. I don't . . .

JOHN. Look. It's just a *course,* it's just a *book,* it's just a . . .

CAROL. No. No. There are *people* out there. People who came *here.* To know something they didn't *know.* Who *came* here. To be *helped.* To be *helped.* So someone would *help* them. To *do* something. To *know* something. To get, what do they say? "To get on in the world." How can I do that if I don't, if I fail? But I don't *understand.* I don't *understand.* I don't understand what anything means . . . and I walk around. From morning 'til night: with this one thought in my head. I'm *stupid.*

JOHN. No one thinks you're stupid.

CAROL. No? What am I . . . ?

JOHN. I . . .

CAROL. . . . what am I, then?

JOHN. I think you're angry. Many people are. I have a *telephone* call that I have to make. And an *appointment,* which is rather *pressing;* though I sympathize with your concerns, and though I wish I had the time, this was not a previously scheduled meeting and I . . .

CAROL. . . . you think I'm nothing . . .

JOHN. . . . have an appointment with a *realtor,* and with my wife and . . .

CAROL. You think that I'm stupid.

JOHN. No. I certainly don't.

CAROL. You said it.

JOHN. No. I did not.

CAROL. You did.

JOHN. When?

CAROL. . . . you . . .

JOHN. No. I never did, or never would say that to a student, and . . .

CAROL. You said, "What can that mean?" (*Pause*) "What can that mean?" . . . (*Pause*)

JOHN. . . . and what did that mean to you . . . ?

CAROL. That meant I'm stupid. And I'll never learn. That's what that meant. And you're right.

JOHN. . . . I . . .

CAROL. But then. But then, what am I doing here . . . ?

JOHN. . . . if you thought that I . . .

CAROL. . . . when nobody wants me, and . . .

JOHN. . . . if you interpreted . . .

CAROL. Nobody *tells* me anything. And I *sit* there . . . in the *corner.* In the *back.* And everybody's talking about "this" all the time. And "concepts," and "precepts" and, and, and, and, and, WHAT IN THE WORLD

ARE YOU *TALKING* ABOUT? And I read your book. And they said, "Fine, go in that class." Because you talked about responsibility to the young. I DON'T KNOW WHAT IT MEANS AND I'M *FAILING* . . .

JOHN. May . . .

CAROL. No, you're right. "Oh, hell." I failed. Flunk me out of it. It's garbage. Everything I do. "The ideas contained in this work express the author's feelings." That's right. That's right. I know I'm stupid. I know what I am. (*Pause*) I know what I am, Professor. You don't have to tell me. (*Pause*) It's pathetic. Isn't it?

JOHN. . . . Aha . . . (*Pause*) Sit down. Sit down. Please. (*Pause*) Please sit down.

CAROL. Why?

JOHN. I want to talk to you.

CAROL. Why?

JOHN. Just sit down. (*Pause*) Please. Sit down. Will you, please . . . ? (*Pause. She does so.*) Thank you.

CAROL. What?

JOHN. I want to tell you something.

CAROL. (*Pause*) What?

JOHN. Well, I know what you're talking about.

CAROL. No. You don't.

JOHN. I think I do. (*Pause*)

CAROL. How can you?

JOHN. I'll tell you a story about myself. (*Pause*) Do you mind? (*Pause*) I was raised to think myself stupid. That's what I want to tell you. (*Pause*)

CAROL. What do you mean?

JOHN. Just what I said. I was brought up, and my earliest, and most persistent memories are of being told that I was stupid. "You have such *intelligence*. Why must you behave so *stupidly?*" Or, "Can't you *understand?* Can't you *understand?*" And I could *not* understand. I could *not* understand.

CAROL. What?

JOHN. The simplest problem. Was beyond me. It was a mystery.

CAROL. What was a mystery?

JOHN. How people learn. How *I* could learn. Which is what I've been speaking of in class. And of *course* you can't hear it. Carol. Of *course* you can't. (*Pause*) I used to speak of "real people," and wonder what the *real* people did. The *real* people. Who were they? *They* were the people other than myself. The *good* people. The *capable* people. The people who could do the things, *I* could not do: learn, study, retain . . . all that *garbage*—which is what I have been talking of in class, and that's *exactly* what I have been talking of—If you are told . . . Listen to this. If the young child is told he cannot understand. Then he takes it as a *description* of himself. What am I? I am *that which can not understand.* And I saw you out there, when we were speaking of the concepts of . . .

CAROL. I can't understand any of them.

JOHN. Well, then, that's *my* fault. That's not your fault. And that is not verbiage. That's what I firmly hold to be the truth. And I am sorry, and I owe you an apology.

CAROL. Why?

JOHN. And I suppose that I have had some *things* on my mind. . . . We're buying a *house,* and . . .

CAROL. People said that you were stupid . . . ?

JOHN. Yes.

CAROL. When?

JOHN. I'll tell you when. Through my life. In my childhood; and, perhaps, they stopped. But I heard them continue.

CAROL. And what did they say?

JOHN. They said I was incompetent. Do you see? And when I'm tested the, the, the *feelings* of my youth about the *very subject of learning* come up. And I . . . I become, I feel "unworthy," and "unprepared." . . .

CAROL. . . . yes.

JOHN. . . . eh?

CAROL. . . . yes.

JOHN. And I feel that I must fail. (*Pause*)

CAROL. . . . but then you *do* fail. (*Pause*) You have to. (*Pause*) Don't you?

JOHN. A *pilot.* Flying a plane. The pilot is flying the plane. He thinks: Oh, my *God,* my mind's been drifting! Oh, my God! What kind of a cursed imbecile am I, that I, with this so precious cargo of *Life* in my charge, would allow my attention to wander. Why was I born? How deluded are those who put their trust in me, . . . et cetera, so on, and he crashes the plane.

CAROL. (*Pause*) He could just . . .

JOHN. That's right.

CAROL. He could say:

JOHN. My attention *wandered* for a moment . . .

CAROL. . . . uh huh . . .

JOHN. I had a *thought* I did not like . . . but now:

CAROL. . . . but now it's . . .

JOHN. That's what I'm telling you. It's time to put my attention . . . see: it is not: this is what I learned. It is Not Magic. Yes. Yes. *You.* You are going to be frightened. When faced with what may or may not be but which you are going to perceive as a test. You will become frightened. And you will say: "I am incapable of . . ." and everything *in* you will think these two things. "I must. But I can't." And you will think: Why was I born to be the laughingstock of a world in which everyone is better than I? In which I am entitled to nothing. Where I can not learn.

(*Pause*)

CAROL. Is that . . . (*Pause*) Is that what I have . . . ?

JOHN. Well. I don't know if I'd put it that way. Listen: I'm talking to you as I'd talk to my son. Because that's what I'd like him to have that I never had. I'm talking to you the way I wish that someone had talked to me. I don't know how to do it, other than to be *personal,* . . . but . . .

CAROL. Why would you want to be personal with me?

JOHN. Well, you see? That's what I'm saying. We can only interpret the behavior of others through the screen we . . . (*The phone rings.*) Through . . . (*To phone:*) Hello . . . ? (*To Carol:*) Through the screen we create. (*To phone:*) Hello. (*To Carol:*) Excuse me a moment. (*To phone:*) Hello? No, I can't talk nnn . . . I know I did. In a few . . . I'm . . . is he coming to the . . . yes. I talked to him. We'll meet you at the No, because I'm with a *student.* It's going to be fff . . . This is important, too. I'm with a *student,* Jerry's going to . . . Listen: the sooner I get off, the sooner I'll be down, all right. I love you. Listen, listen, I said "I love you," it's going to work *out* with the, because I feel that it is, I'll be right down. All right? Well, then it's going to take as long as it takes. (*He hangs up.*) (*To Carol:*) I'm sorry.

CAROL. What was that?

JOHN. There are some problems, as there usually are, about the final agreements for the new house.

CAROL. You're buying a new house.

JOHN. That's right.

CAROL. Because of your promotion.

JOHN. Well, I suppose that that's right.

CAROL. Why did you stay here with me?

JOHN. Stay here.

CAROL. Yes. When you should have gone.

JOHN. Because I like you.

CAROL. You like me.

JOHN. Yes.

CAROL. Why?

JOHN. Why? Well? Perhaps we're similar. (*Pause*) Yes. (*Pause*)

CAROL. You said "everyone has problems."

JOHN. Everyone has problems.

CAROL. Do they?

JOHN. Certainly.

CAROL. You do?

JOHN. Yes.

CAROL. What are they?

JOHN. Well. (*Pause*) Well, you're perfectly right. (*Pause*) If we're going to take off the Artificial *Stricture,* of "Teacher," and "Student," why should *my* problems be any more a mystery than your own? Of *course* I have problems. As you saw.

CAROL. . . . with what?

JOHN. With my *wife* . . . with *work* . . .

CAROL. With work?

JOHN. Yes. And, and, perhaps my problems are, do you see? *Similar* to yours.

CAROL. Would you tell me?

JOHN. All right. (*Pause*) I came *late* to teaching. And I found it Artificial. The notion of "I know and you do not"; and I saw an *exploitation* in the education process. I told you. I hated school, I hated teachers. I hated everyone who was in the position of a "boss" because I *knew*—I didn't *think,* mind you, I *knew* I was going to fail. Because I was a fuckup. I was just no goddamned good. When I . . . late in life . . . (*Pause*) When I *got out from under* . . . when I worked my way out of the need to fail. When I . . .

CAROL. How do you do that? (*Pause*)

JOHN. You have to look at what you are, and what you feel, and how you act. And, finally, you have to look at how you act. And say: If that's what I *did,* that must be how I think of myself.

CAROL. I don't understand.

JOHN. If I fail all the time, it must be that I think of myself as a failure. If I do not want to think of myself as a failure, perhaps I should begin by *succeeding* now and again. Look. The tests, you see, which you encounter, in school, in college, in life, were designed, in the most part, for idiots. *By* idiots. There is no need to fail at them. They are not a test of your worth. They are a test of your ability to retain and spout back misinformation. Of *course* you fail them. They're *nonsense.* And I . . .

CAROL. . . . no . . .

JOHN. Yes. They're *garbage.* They're a *joke.* Look at me. Look at me. The Tenure Committee. The Tenure Committee. Come to judge me. The Bad Tenure Committee.

The "Test." Do you see? They put me to the test. Why, they had people voting on me I wouldn't employ to wax my car. And yet, I go before the Great Tenure Committee, and I have an urge, to *vomit,* to, to, to puke my *badness* on the table, to show them: "I'm no good. Why would you pick *me?*"

CAROL. They granted you tenure.

JOHN. Oh no, they announced it, but they haven't *signed.* Do you see? "At any moment . . ."

CAROL. . . . mmm . . .

JOHN. "They might not *sign*" . . . I might not . . . the *house* might not go through . . . Eh? Eh? They'll find out my "dark secret." (*Pause*)

CAROL. . . . what is it . . . ?

JOHN. There *isn't* one. But *they* will find an index of my badness . . .

CAROL. Index?

JOHN. A ". . . pointer." A "Pointer." You see? Do you see? I *understand* you. I. Know. That. Feeling. Am I entitled to my job, and my nice *home,* and my *wife,* and my *family,* and so on. This is what I'm saying: That theory of education which, that *theory:*

CAROL. I . . . I . . . (*Pause*)

JOHN. What?

CAROL. I . . .

JOHN. What?

CAROL. I want to know about my grade. (*Long pause*)

JOHN. Of course you do.

CAROL. Is that bad?

JOHN. No.

CAROL. Is it bad that I asked you that?

JOHN. No.

CAROL. Did I upset you?

JOHN. No. And I apologize. Of *course* you want to know about your grade. And, of course, you can't concentrate on anyth . . . (*The telephone starts to ring.*) Wait a moment.

CAROL. I should go.

JOHN. I'll make you a deal.

CAROL. No, you have to . . .

JOHN. Let it ring. I'll make you a deal. You stay here. We'll start the whole course over. I'm going to say it was not you, it was I who was not paying attention. We'll start the whole course over. Your grade is an "A." Your final grade is an "A." (*The phone stops ringing.*)

CAROL. But the class is only half over . . .

JOHN (*simultaneously with* "over"). Your grade for the whole term is an "A." If you will come back and meet with me. A few more times. Your grade's an "A." Forget about the paper. You didn't like it, you didn't like writing it. It's not important. What's important is that I awake your interest, if I can, and that I answer your questions. Let's start over. (*Pause*)

CAROL. Over. With what?

JOHN. Say this is the beginning.

CAROL. The beginning.

JOHN. Yes.

CAROL. Of what?

JOHN. Of the class.

CAROL. But we can't start over.

JOHN. I say we can. (*Pause*) I say we can.

CAROL. But I don't believe it.

JOHN. Yes, I know that. But it's true. What is The Class but you and me? (*Pause*)

CAROL. There are rules.

JOHN. Well. We'll break them.

CAROL. How can we?

JOHN. We won't tell anybody.

CAROL. Is that all right?

JOHN. I say that it's fine.

CAROL. Why would you do this for me?

JOHN. I like you. Is that so difficult for you to ...

CAROL. Um ...

JOHN. There's no one here but you and me. (*Pause*)

CAROL. All right. I did not understand. When you referred ...

JOHN. All right, yes?

CAROL. When you referred to hazing.

JOHN. Hazing.

CAROL. You wrote, in your book. About the comparative ... the comparative ... (*She checks her notes.*)

JOHN. Are you checking your notes ... ?

CAROL. Yes.

JOHN. Tell me in your own ...

CAROL. I want to make sure that I have it right.

JOHN. No. Of course. You want to be exact.

CAROL. I want to know everything that went on.

JOHN. ... that's good.

CAROL. ... so I ...

JOHN. That's very good. But I was suggesting, many times, that that which we wish to retain is retained oftentimes, I think, *better* with less expenditure of effort.

CAROL. (*Of notes*) Here it is: you wrote of *hazing.*

JOHN. ... that's correct. Now: I said "hazing." It means ritualized annoyance. We shove this book at you, we say read it. Now, you say you've read it? I think that you're *lying.* I'll *grill* you, and when I find you've lied, you'll be disgraced, and your life will be ruined. It's a sick game. Why do we do it? Does it educate? In no sense. Well, then, what is higher education? It is something-other-than-useful.

CAROL. What is "something-other-than-useful?"

JOHN. It has become a ritual, it has become an article of faith. That all must be subjected to, or to put it differently, that all are entitled to Higher Education. And my point . . .

CAROL. You disagree with that?

JOHN. Well, let's address that. What do you think?

CAROL. I don't know.

JOHN. What do you think, though? (*Pause*)

CAROL. I don't know.

JOHN. I spoke of it in class. Do you remember my example?

CAROL. Justice.

JOHN. Yes. Can you repeat it to me? (*She looks down at her notebook.*) Without your notes? I ask you as a favor to me, so that I can see if my idea was interesting.

CAROL. You said "justice" . . .

JOHN. Yes?

CAROL. . . . that all are entitled . . . (*Pause*) I . . . I . . . I . . .

JOHN. Yes. To a speedy trial. To a fair trial. But they needn't be given a trial *at all* unless they stand accused. Eh? Justice is their right, should they choose to avail themselves of it, they should have a fair trial. It does not follow, of necessity, a person's life is incomplete without a trial in it. Do you see? My point is a confusion between equity and *utility* arose. So we confound the *usefulness* of higher education with our, granted, right to equal access to the same. We, in effect, create a *prejudice* toward it, completely independent of . . .

CAROL. . . . that it is prejudice that we should go to school?

JOHN. Exactly. (*Pause*)

CAROL. How can you say that? How . . .

JOHN. Good. Good. *Good.* That's right! Speak up! What is a prejudice? An unreasoned belief. We are all subject to it. None of us is not. When it is threatened, or opposed, we feel anger, and feel, do we not? As you do now. Do you not? Good.

CAROL. . . . but how can you . . .

JOHN. . . . let us examine. Good.

CAROL. How . . .

JOHN. Good. Good. When . . .

CAROL. I'M SPEAKING . . . (*Pause*)

JOHN. I'm sorry.

CAROL. How can you . . .

JOHN. . . . I beg your pardon.

CAROL. That's all right.

JOHN. I beg your pardon.

CAROL. That's all right.

JOHN. I'm sorry I interrupted you.

CAROL. That's all right.

JOHN. You were saying?

CAROL. I was saying . . . I was saying . . . (*She checks her notes.*) How can you say in a class. Say in a college class, that college education is prejudice?

JOHN. I said that our predilection for it . . .

CAROL. Predilection . . .

JOHN. . . . you know what that means.

CAROL. Does it mean "liking"?

JOHN. Yes.

CAROL. But how can you say that? That College . . .

JOHN. . . . that's my *job,* don't you know.

CAROL. What is?

JOHN. To provoke you.

CAROL. No.

JOHN. Oh. Yes, though.

CAROL. To provoke me?

JOHN. That's right.

CAROL. To make me mad?

JOHN. That's right. To force you . . .

CAROL. . . . to make me mad is your job?

JOHN. To force you to . . . listen: (*Pause*) Ah. (*Pause*) When I was young somebody told me, are you ready, the rich copulate less often than the poor. But when they do, they take more of their clothes off. Years. Years, mind you, I would compare experiences of my own to this dictum, saying, aha, this fits the norm, or ah, this is a variation from it. What did it mean? Nothing. It was some jerk thing, some school kid told me that took up room inside my head. (*Pause*)

Somebody told *you,* and you hold it as an article of faith, that higher education is an unassailable good. This notion is so dear to you that when I question it you become angry. Good. Good, I say. Are not those the very things which we should question? I say college education, since the war, has become so a matter of course, and such a fashionable necessity, for those either of or aspiring *to* the new vast middle class, that we *espouse* it, as a matter of right, and have ceased to ask, "What is it good for?" (*Pause*)

What might be some reasons for pursuit of higher education?

*One:* A love of learning.

*Two:* The wish for mastery of a skill.

*Three:* For economic betterment.

(*Stops. Makes a note.*)

CAROL. I'm keeping you.

JOHN. One moment. I have to make a note . . .

CAROL. It's something that I said?

JOHN. No, we're buying a house.

CAROL. You're buying the new house.

JOHN. To go with the tenure. That's right. Nice *house,* close to the *private school* . . . (*He continues making his note.*) . . . We were talking of economic *betterment* (*Carol writes in her notebook.*) . . . I was thinking of the School Tax. (*He continues writing.*) (*To himself:*) . . . *where is it written* that I have to send my child to public school. . . . Is it a law that I have to improve the City Schools at the expense of my own interest? And, is this not simply *The White Man's Burden?* Good. And (*Looks up to Carol*) . . . does this interest you?

CAROL. No. I'm taking notes . . .

JOHN. You don't have to take notes, you know, you can just listen.

CAROL. I want to make sure I remember it. (*Pause*)

JOHN. I'm not lecturing you, I'm just trying to tell you some things I think.

CAROL. What do you think?

JOHN. Should all kids go to college? *Why* . . .

CAROL. (*Pause*) To learn.

JOHN. But if he does not learn.

CAROL. If the child does not learn?

JOHN. Then why is he in college? Because he was told it was his "right"?

CAROL. Some might find college instructive.

JOHN. I would hope so.

CAROL. But how do they feel? Being told they are wasting their time?

JOHN. I don't think I'm telling them that.

CAROL. You said that education was "prolonged and systematic hazing."

JOHN. Yes. It can be so.

CAROL. . . . if education is so *bad*, why do you do it?

JOHN. I do it because I love it. (*Pause*) Let's . . . I suggest you look at the demographics, wage-earning capacity, college- and non-college-educated men and women, 1855 to 1980, and let's see if we can wring some worth from the statistics. Eh? And . . .

CAROL. No.

JOHN. What?

CAROL. I can't understand them.

JOHN. . . . you . . . ?

CAROL. . . . the "charts." The *Concepts*, the . . .

JOHN. "Charts" are simply . . .

CAROL. When I leave here . . .

JOHN. Charts, do you see . . .

CAROL. No, I can't . . .

JOHN. You can, though.

CAROL. NO, NO—I DON'T UNDERSTAND. DO YOU SEE??? I DON'T *UNDERSTAND* . . .

JOHN. What?

CAROL. *Any* of it. *Any* of it. I'm *smiling* in class, I'm *smiling*, the whole time. What are you *talking* about? What is everyone *talking* about? I don't *understand*. I don't know what it *means*. I don't know what it means to *be* here . . . you tell me I'm intelligent, and then you tell me I should not be *here*, what do you *want* with me? What does it *mean?* Who should I *listen* to . . . I . . .

(*He goes over to her and puts his arm around her shoulder.*)

NO! (*She walks away from him.*)

JOHN. Sshhhh.

CAROL. No, I don't under . . .

JOHN. Sshhhhh.

CAROL. I don't know what you're *saying* . . .

JOHN. Sshhhhh. It's all right.

CAROL. . . . I have no . . .

JOHN. Sshhhhh. Sshhhhh. Let it go a moment. (*Pause*) Sshhhhh . . . let it go. (*Pause*) Just let it go. (*Pause*) Just let it go. It's all right. (*Pause*) Sshhhhh. (*Pause*) I understand . . . (*Pause*) What do you feel?

CAROL. I feel bad.

JOHN. I know. It's all right.

CAROL. I . . . (*Pause*)

JOHN. What?

CAROL. I . . .

JOHN. What? Tell me.

CAROL. I don't understand you.

JOHN. I know. It's all right.

CAROL. I . . .

JOHN. What? (*Pause*) What? *Tell* me.

CAROL. I can't tell you.

JOHN. No, you must.

CAROL. I can't.

JOHN. No. Tell me. (*Pause*)

CAROL. I'm bad. (*Pause*) Oh, God. (*Pause*)

JOHN. It's all right.

CAROL. I'm . . .

JOHN. It's all right.

CAROL. I can't talk about this.

JOHN. It's all right. Tell me.

CAROL. Why do you want to know this?

JOHN. I don't want to know. I want to know whatever you . . .

CAROL. I always . . .

JOHN. . . . good . . .

CAROL. I always . . . all my life . . . I have never told anyone this . . .

JOHN. Yes. Go on. (*Pause*) Go on.

CAROL. All of my life . . . (*The phone rings.*) (*Pause. John goes to the phone and picks it up.*)

JOHN (*into phone*). I can't talk now. (*Pause*) What? (*Pause*) Hmm. (*Pause*) All right, I . . . I. Can't. Talk. Now. No, no, no, I *Know* I did, but. . . . What? Hello. What? She *what?* She *can't,* she said the agreement is void? How, how is the agreement *void? That's Our House.*

I have the *paper;* when we come down, next week, with the payment, and the paper, that house is . . . wait, wait, wait, wait, wait, wait, wait: Did Jerry . . . is Jerry there? (*Pause*) Is *she* there . . . ? Does she have a *lawyer . . . ?* How the *hell,* how the *Hell.* That is . . . it's a question, you said, of the *easement.* I don't underst . . . it's not the *whole agreement.* It's just the *easement,* why would she? Put, put, put, *Jerry* on. (*Pause*) Jer, *Jerry:* What the *Hell* . . . that's my *house.* That's . . . Well, I'm no, no, no, I'm *not* coming ddd . . . List, *Listen, screw* her. You *tell* her. You, listen: I want you to take *Grace,* you take Grace, and get out of that house. You *leave* her there. Her and her lawyer, and you *tell* them, we'll see them in court next . . . no. No. Leave her there, leave her to *stew* in it: You tell her, we're *getting* that house, and we are going to . . . No. I'm *not* coming down. I'll be damned if I'll sit in the same rrr . . . the next, you tell her the next time I *see* her is in court . . . I . . . (*Pause*) What? (*Pause*) What? I don't understand. (*Pause*) Well, what about the house? (*Pause*) There isn't any problem with the hhh . . . (*Pause*) No, no, no, that's all right. All ri . . . All right . . . (*Pause*) Of course. Tha . . . Thank you. No, I will. Right away. (*He hangs up.*) (*Pause*)

CAROL. What is it? (*Pause*)

JOHN. It's a surprise party.

CAROL. It is.

JOHN. Yes.

CAROL. A party for you.

JOHN. Yes.

CAROL. Is it your birthday?

JOHN. No.

CAROL. What is it?

JOHN. The tenure announcement.

CAROL. The tenure announcement.

JOHN. They're throwing a party for us in our new house.

CAROL. Your new house.

JOHN. The house that we're buying.

CAROL. You have to go.

JOHN. It seems that I do.

CAROL. (*Pause*) They're proud of you.

JOHN. Well, there are those who would say it's a form of aggression.

CAROL. What is?

JOHN. A surprise.

## *Two*

*John and Carol seated across the desk from each other.*

JOHN. You see, (*pause*) I love to teach. And flatter myself I am *skilled* at it. And I love the, the aspect of *performance.* I think I must confess that.

When I found I loved to teach I swore that I would not become that cold, rigid automaton of an instructor which I had encountered as a child.

Now, I was not unconscious that it was given me to err upon the other side. And, so, I asked and *ask* myself if I engaged in heterodoxy, I will not say "gratuitously" for I do not care to posit orthodoxy as a given good—but, "to the detriment of, of my students." (*Pause*)

As I said. When the possibility of tenure opened, and, of course, I'd long pursued it, I was, of course *happy,* and *covetous* of it.

I asked myself if I was wrong to covet it. And thought about it long, and, I hope, truthfully, and saw in myself several things in, I think, no particular order. (*Pause*)

That I *would* pursue it. That I *desired* it, that I was not pure of longing for security, and that that, perhaps, was not reprehensible in me. That I had duties *beyond* the school, and that my duty to my home, for instance, was, or should be, if it were not, of an equal weight. That tenure, and security, and yes, and *comfort,* were not, of themselves, to be scorned; and were even worthy of honorable pursuit. And that it was given me. Here, in this place, which I enjoy, and in which I find comfort, to assure myself of—as far as it rests in The Material—a continuation of that joy and comfort. In exchange for what? Teaching. Which I love.

What was the price of this security? To obtain *tenure.* Which tenure the committee is in the process of granting me. And on the basis of which I contracted to purchase a house. Now, as you don't have your own family, at this point, you may not know what that means. But to me it is important. A home. A Good Home. To raise my family. Now: The Tenure Committee will meet. This is the process, and a *good* process. Under which the school has functioned for quite a long time. They will meet, and hear your complaint—which you have the right to make; and they will dismiss it. They will *dismiss* your complaint; and, in the intervening period, I will lose my house. I will not be able to close on my house. I will lose my *deposit,* and the home I'd picked out for my wife and son will go by the boards. Now: I see I have angered you. I understand your anger at teachers. I was angry with mine. I felt hurt and humiliated by them. Which is one of the reasons that I went into education.

CAROL. What do you want of me?

JOHN. (*Pause*) I was hurt. When I received the report. Of the tenure committee. I was shocked. And I was hurt. No, I don't mean to subject you to my weak sensibilities. All right. Finally, I didn't understand. Then I thought: is it not always at those points at which we reckon ourselves unassailable that we are most vulnerable and . . . (*Pause*) Yes. All right. You find me pedantic. Yes. I am. By nature, by *birth,* by profession, I don't know . . . I'm always looking for a *paradigm* for . . .

CAROL. I don't know what a paradigm is.

JOHN. It's a model.

CAROL. Then why can't you use that word? (*Pause*)

JOHN. If it is important to you. Yes, all right. I was looking for a model. To continue: I feel that one point . . .

CAROL. I . . .

JOHN. One second . . . upon which I am unassailable is my unflinching concern for my students' dignity. I asked you here to . . . in the spirit of *investigation,* to ask you . . . to ask . . . (*Pause*) What have I done to you? (*Pause*) And, and, I suppose, how I can make amends. Can we not settle this now? It's pointless, really, and I want to know.

CAROL. What you can do to force me to retract?

JOHN. That is not what I meant at all.

CAROL. To bribe me, to convince me . . .

JOHN. . . . No.

CAROL. To retract . . .

JOHN. That is not what I meant at all. I think that you know it is not.

CAROL. That is not what I know. I *wish* I . . .

JOHN. I do not want to . . . you wish what?

CAROL. No, you said what amends can you make. To force me to retract.

JOHN. That is not what I said.

CAROL. I have my notes.

JOHN. Look. Look. The Stoics say . . .

CAROL. The Stoics?

JOHN. The Stoical Philosophers say if you remove the phrase "I have been injured," you have removed the injury. Now: Think: I know that you're upset. Just tell me. Literally. Literally: what wrong have I done you?

CAROL. Whatever you have done to me—to the extent that you've done it to *me,* do you know, rather than to me as a *student,* and, so, to the student body, is contained in my report. To the tenure committee.

JOHN. Well, all right. (*Pause*) Let's see. (*He reads.*) I find that I am sexist. That I am *elitist.* I'm not sure I know what that means, other than it's a derogatory word, meaning "bad." That I . . . That I insist on wasting time, in nonprescribed, in self-aggrandizing and theatrical *diversions* from the prescribed *text* . . . that these have taken both sexist and pornographic forms . . . here we find listed . . . (*Pause*) Here we find listed . . . instances ". . . closeted with a student" . . . "Told a rambling, sexually explicit story, in which the frequency and attitudes of fornication of the poor and rich are, it would seem, the central point . . . moved to *embrace* said student and . . . all part of a pattern . . ." (*Pause*)

(*He reads.*) That I used the phrase "The White Man's Burden" . . . that I told you how I'd asked you to my room because I quote like you. (*Pause*)

(*He reads.*) "He said he 'liked' me. That he 'liked being with me.' He'd let me write my examination paper over, if I could come back oftener to see him in his office." (*Pause*) (*To Carol:*) It's *ludicrous.* Don't you know that? It's not *necessary.* It's going to *humiliate* you, and it's going to cost me my *house,* and . . .

CAROL. It's "*ludicrous* . . ."?

(*John picks up the report and reads again.*)

JOHN. "He told me he had problems with his wife; and that he wanted to take off the artificial stricture of Teacher and Student. He put his arm around me . . ."

CAROL. Do you deny it? Can you deny it . . . ? Do you see? (*Pause*) Don't you see? You don't see, do you?

JOHN. I don't see . . .

CAROL. You think, you think you can deny that these things happened; or, if they *did,* if they *did,* that they meant what you *said* they meant. Don't you see? You drag me in here, you drag us, to listen to you "go on"; and "go on" about this, or that, or we don't "express" ourselves very well. We don't say what we mean. Don't we? Don't we? We *do* say what we mean. And you say that "I don't understand you . . .": Then *you* . . . (*Points.*)

JOHN. "Consult the Report"?

CAROL. . . . that's right.

JOHN. You see. You see. Can't you . . . You see what I'm saying? Can't you tell me in your own words?

CAROL. Those are my own words. (*Pause*)

JOHN. (*He reads.*) "He told me that if I would stay alone with him in his office, he would change my grade to an A." (*To Carol:*) What have I done to you? Oh. My God, are you so hurt?

CAROL. What I "feel" is irrelevant. (*Pause*)

JOHN. Do you know that I tried to help you?

CAROL. What I know I have reported.

JOHN. I would like to help you now. I would. Before this escalates.

CAROL (*simultaneously with* "escalates"). You see. I don't think that I need your help. I don't think I need anything you have.

JOHN. I feel . . .

CAROL. I don't *care* what you feel. Do you see? DO YOU SEE? You can't *do* that anymore. You. Do. Not. Have. The. Power. Did you misuse it? *Someone* did. Are you part of that group? *Yes. Yes.* You Are. You've *done* these things. And to say, and to say, "Oh. Let me help you with your problem . . ."

JOHN. Yes. I understand. I understand. You're *hurt.* You're *angry.* Yes. I think your *anger* is *betraying* you. Down a path which helps no one.

CAROL. I don't *care* what you think.

JOHN. You don't? (*Pause*) But you talk of *rights.* Don't you see? *I* have rights too. Do you see? I have a *house* . . . part of the *real* world; and The Tenure Committee, Good Men and True . . .

CAROL. . . . Professor . . .

JOHN. . . . Please: *Also* part of that world: you understand? This is my *life.* I'm not a *bogeyman.* I don't "stand" for something, I . . .

CAROL. . . . Professor . . .

JOHN. . . . I . . .

CAROL. Professor. I came here as a *favor.* At your personal request. Perhaps I should not have done so. But I did. On my behalf, and on behalf of my group. And you speak of the tenure committee, one of whose members is a woman, as you know. And though you might call it Good Fun, or An Historical Phrase, or An Oversight, or, All of the Above, to refer to the committee as Good Men and True, it is a demeaning remark. It is a sexist remark, and to overlook it is to countenance continuation of that method of thought. It's a remark . . .

JOHN. OH COME ON. Come on. . . . Sufficient to deprive a family of . . .

CAROL. Sufficient? Sufficient? Sufficient? Yes. It is a *fact* . . . and that story, which I quote, is *vile* and *classist,* and *manipulative* and *pornographic.* It . . .

JOHN. . . . it's pornographic . . . ?

CAROL. What gives you the *right.* Yes. To speak to a *woman* in your private . . . Yes. Yes. I'm sorry. I'm sorry. You feel yourself empowered . . . you say so yourself. To *strut.* To *posture.* To "perform." To "Call me in here . . ." Eh? You say that higher education is a joke. And treat it as such, you *treat* it as such. And *confess* to a taste to play the *Patriarch* in your class. To grant *this.* To deny *that.* To embrace your students.

JOHN. How can you assert. How can you stand there and . . .

CAROL. How can you *deny* it. You did it to me. *Here.* You *did.* . . . You *confess.* You love the Power. To *deviate.* To *invent,* to transgress . . . to *transgress* whatever norms have been established for us. And you think it's charming to "question" in yourself this taste to mock and destroy. But you should question it. Professor. And you pick those things which you feel *advance* you: publication, *tenure,* and the steps to get them you call "harmless rituals." And you perform those steps. Although you say it is hypocrisy. But to the aspirations of your students. Of *hard-working students,* who come here, who *slave* to come here—you have no idea what it cost me to come to this school—you *mock* us. You call education "hazing," and from your so-protected, so-elitist seat you hold our confusion as a *joke,* and our hopes and efforts with it. Then you sit there and say "what have I done?" And ask me to understand that *you* have aspirations too. But I tell you. I tell you. That you are vile. And that you are exploitative. And if you possess one ounce of that inner honesty you describe in your book, you can look in yourself and see those things that I see. And you can find revulsion equal to my own. Good day. (*She prepares to leave the room.*)

JOHN. Wait a second, will you, just one moment. (*Pause*) Nice day today.

CAROL. What?

JOHN. You said "Good day." I think that it is a nice day today.

CAROL. *Is* it?

JOHN. Yes, I think it is.

CAROL. And why is that important?

JOHN. Because it is the essence of all human communication. I say something conventional, you respond, and the information we exchange is not about the "weather," but that we both agree to converse. In effect, we agree that we are both human. (*Pause*)

I'm not a . . . "exploiter," and you're not a . . . "deranged," what? *Revolutionary* . . . that we may, that we may have . . . positions, and that we may have . . . desires, which are in *conflict*, but that we're just human. (*Pause*) That means that sometimes we're *imperfect.* (*Pause*) Often we're in conflict . . . (*Pause*) *Much* of what we do, you're right, in the name of "principles" is *self-serving* . . . much of what we do is *conventional.* (*Pause*) You're right. (*Pause*) You said you came in the class because you wanted to learn about *education.* I don't know that I can teach you about education. But I know that I can tell you what I *think* about education, and then *you* decide. And you don't have to fight with me. *I'm* not the subject. (*Pause*) And where I'm *wrong* . . . perhaps it's not your job to "fix" me. I don't want to fix *you.* I would like to tell you what I *think,* because that *is* my job, conventional as it is, and flawed as I may be. And then, if you can show me some better *form,* then we can proceed from there. But, just like "nice day, isn't it . . . ?" I don't think we can proceed until we accept that each of us is human. (*Pause*) And we still can have difficulties. We *will* have them . . . that's all right too. (*Pause*) Now:

CAROL. . . . wait . . .

JOHN. Yes. I want to hear it.

CAROL. . . . the . . .

JOHN. Yes. Tell me frankly.

CAROL. . . . my position . . .

JOHN. I want to hear it. In your own words. What you want. And what you feel.

CAROL. . . . I . . .

JOHN. . . . yes . . .

CAROL. My Group.

JOHN. Your "Group" . . . ? (*Pause*)

CAROL. The people I've been talking to . . .

JOHN. There's no shame in that. Everybody needs advisers. Everyone needs to expose themselves. To various points of view. It's not wrong. It's essential. Good. Good. Now: You and I . . . (*The phone rings.*)

You and I . . .

(*He hesitates for a moment, and then picks it up.*) (*Into phone*) Hello. (*Pause*) Um . . . no, I know they do. (*Pause*) I know she does. Tell her that I . . . can I call you back? . . . Then tell her that I think it's going to be fine. (*Pause*) Tell her just, just hold on, I'll . . . can I get back to you? . . . Well . . . no, no, no, we're *taking* the house . . . we're . . . no, no, nn . . . no, she will nnn, it's not a *question* of refunding the dep . . . no . . . it's not a *question* of the deposit . . . will you call Jerry?

Babe, baby, will you just call Jerry? Tell him, nnn . . . tell him they, well, they're to keep the deposit, because the deal, be . . . because the deal is going to go *through* . . . because I know . . . be . . . will you please? Just *trust* me. Be . . . well, I'm dealing with the complaint. Yes. Right *Now.* Which is why I . . . yes, no, no, it's really, I can't *talk* about it now. Call Jerry, and I can't talk now. Ff . . . fine. Gg . . . good-bye. (*Hangs up.*) (*Pause*) I'm sorry we were interrupted.

CAROL. No . . .

JOHN. I . . . I was saying:

CAROL. You said that we should agree to talk about my complaint.

JOHN. That's correct.

CAROL. But we *are* talking about it.

JOHN. Well, that's correct too. You see? This is the *gist* of education.

CAROL. No, no. I mean, we're talking about it at the Tenure Committee Hearing. (*Pause*)

JOHN. Yes, but I'm saying: we can talk about it *now,* as easily as . . .

CAROL. No. I think that we should stick to the process . . .

JOHN. . . . wait a . . .

CAROL. . . . the "conventional" process. As you said. (*She gets up.*) And you're right, I'm sorry if I was, um, if I was "discourteous" to you. You're right.

JOHN. Wait, wait a . . .

CAROL. I really should go.

JOHN. Now, look, granted. I have an interest. In the status quo. All right? Everyone does. But what I'm saying is that the *committee* . . .

CAROL. Professor, you're right. Just don't impinge on me. We'll take our differences, and . . .

JOHN. You're going to make a . . . look, look, look, you're going to . . .

CAROL. I shouldn't have come here. They told me . . .

JOHN. One moment. No. No. There are *norms,* here, and there's no reason. Look: I'm trying to *save* you . . .

CAROL. No one *asked* you to . . . you're trying to save *me?* Do me the courtesy to . . .

JOHN. I *am* doing you the courtesy. I'm talking *straight* to you. We can settle this *now.* And I want you to sit *down* and . . .

CAROL. You must excuse me . . . (*She starts to leave the room.*)

JOHN. Sit down, it seems we each have a . . . Wait one moment. Wait one moment . . . just do me the courtesy to . . .

(*He restrains her from leaving.*)

CAROL. LET ME GO.

JOHN. I have no desire to *hold* you, I just want to *talk* to you . . .

CAROL. LET ME GO. LET ME GO. WOULD SOMEBODY *HELP* ME? WOULD SOMEBODY *HELP* ME PLEASE . . . ?

## *Three*

(*At rise, Carol and John are seated.*)

JOHN. I have asked you here. (*Pause*) I have asked you here against, against my . . .

CAROL. I was most surprised you asked me.

JOHN. . . . against my better *judgment,* against . . .

CAROL. I was most surprised . . .

JOHN. . . . against the . . . yes. I'm sure.

CAROL. . . . If you would like me to leave, I'll leave. I'll go right now . . . (*She rises.*)

JOHN. Let us begin *correctly,* may we? I feel . . .

CAROL. That is what I wished to do. That's why I came here, but now . . .

JOHN. . . . I feel . . .

CAROL. But now perhaps you'd like me to leave . . .

JOHN. I don't want you to leave. I asked you to come . . .

CAROL. I didn't have to come here.

JOHN. No. (*Pause*) Thank you.

CAROL. All right. (*Pause*) (*She sits down.*)

JOHN. Although I feel that it *profits,* it would *profit* you something, to . . .

CAROL. . . . what I . . .

JOHN. If you would hear me out, if you would hear me out.

CAROL. I came here to, the court officers told me not to come.

JOHN. . . . the "court" officers . . . ?

CAROL. I was shocked that you asked.

JOHN. . . . wait . . .

CAROL. Yes. But I did *not* come here to hear what it "profits" me.

JOHN. The "court" officers . . .

CAROL. . . . no, no, perhaps I should leave . . . (*She gets up.*)

JOHN. Wait.

CAROL. No. I shouldn't have . . .

JOHN. . . . wait. Wait. Wait a moment.

CAROL. Yes? What is it you want? (*Pause*) What is it you want?

JOHN. I'd like you to stay.

CAROL. You want me to stay.

JOHN. Yes.

CAROL. You do.

JOHN. Yes. (*Pause*) Yes. I would like to have you hear me out. If you would. (*Pause*) Would you please? If you would do that I would be in your debt. (*Pause*) (*She sits.*) Thank You. (*Pause*)

CAROL. What is it you wish to tell me?

JOHN. All right. I cannot . . . (*Pause*) I cannot help but feel you are owed an apology. (*Pause*) (*Of papers in his hands*) I have read. (*Pause*) And reread these accusations.

CAROL. What "accusations"?

JOHN. The, the tenure comm . . . what other accusations . . . ?

CAROL. The tenure committee . . . ?

JOHN. Yes.

CAROL. Excuse me, but those are not accusations. They have been *proved.* They are facts.

JOHN. . . . I . . .

CAROL. No. Those are not "accusations."

JOHN. . . . those?

CAROL. . . . the committee (*The phone starts to ring.*) the committee has . . .

JOHN. . . . All right . . .

CAROL. . . . those are not accusations. The Tenure Committee.

JOHN. ALL RIGHT. ALL RIGHT. ALL RIGHT. (*He picks up the phone.*) Hello. Yes. No. I'm here. Tell Mister . . . No, I can't talk to him now . . . I'm sure he has, but I'm fff . . . I know . . . No, I have no time t . . . tell Mister . . . tell Mist . . . tell Jerry that I'm *fine* and that I'll call him right aw . . . (*Pause*) My wife . . . Yes. I'm sure she has. Yes, thank you. Yes, I'll call her too. I cannot talk to you now. (*He hangs up.*) (*Pause*) All right. It was good of you to come. Thank you. I have studied. I have spent some time studying the indictment.

CAROL. You will have to explain that word to me.

JOHN. An "indictment" . . .

CAROL. Yes.

JOHN. Is a "bill of particulars." A . . .

CAROL. All right. Yes.

JOHN. In which is alleged . . .

CAROL. No. I cannot allow that. I cannot allow that. Nothing is alleged. Everything is proved . . .

JOHN. Please, wait a sec . . .

CAROL. I cannot *come* to allow . . .

JOHN. If I may . . . If I may, from whatever you feel is "established," by . . .

CAROL. The issue here is not what I "feel." It is not my "feelings," but the feelings of women. And men. Your superiors, who've been "polled," do you see? To whom *evidence* has been presented, who have *ruled,* do you see? Who have weighed the testimony and the evidence, and have *ruled,* do you see? That you are *negligent.* That you are *guilty,* that you are found *wanting,* and in *error;* and are *not,* for the reasons so-told, to be given tenure. That you are to be disciplined. For facts. For *facts.* Not "alleged," what is the word? But *proved.* Do you see? *By your own actions.*

That is what the tenure committee has said. That is what my lawyer said. For what you did in class. For what you did *in this office.*

JOHN. They're going to discharge me.

CAROL. As full well they should. You don't understand? You're angry? What has *led* you to this place? Not your sex. Not your race. Not your class. YOUR OWN ACTIONS. And you're *angry.* You *ask* me here. What *do* you want? You want to "charm" me. You want to "convince" me. You want me to recant. I will *not* recant. Why should I . . . ? What I say is right. You tell me, you are going to tell me that you have a wife and child. You are going to say that you have a career and that you've worked for twenty years for this. Do you know what you've *worked* for? *Power.* For *power.* Do you understand? And you sit there, and you tell me *stories.* About your *house,* about all the private *schools,* and about *privilege,* and how you are entitled. To *buy,* to *spend,* to *mock,* to *summon.* All your stories. All your silly weak *guilt,* it's all about *privilege;* and you won't know it. Don't you see? You worked twenty years for the right to *insult* me. And you feel entitled to be *paid* for it. Your Home. Your Wife . . . Your sweet "deposit" on your house . . .

JOHN. Don't you have feelings?

CAROL. That's my point. You see? Don't you have feelings? Your final argument. What is it that has no feelings. *Animals.* I don't take your side, you question if I'm Human.

JOHN. Don't you have feelings?

CAROL. I have a responsibility. I . . .

JOHN. . . . to . . . ?

CAROL. To? This institution. To the *students.* To my *group.*

JOHN. . . . your "group." . . .

CAROL. Because I speak, yes, not for myself. But for the group; for those who suffer what I suffer. On behalf of whom, even if I, were, inclined, to what, forgive? Forget? What? Overlook your . . .

JOHN. . . . my behavior?

CAROL. . . . it would be wrong.

JOHN. Even if you were inclined to "forgive" me.

CAROL. It would be wrong.

JOHN. And what would transpire.

CAROL. Transpire?

JOHN. Yes.

CAROL. "Happen?"

JOHN. Yes.

CAROL. Then *say* it. For Christ's sake. Who the *hell* do you think that you are? You want a post. You want unlimited power. To do and to say what you want. As it pleases you—Testing, Questioning, Flirting . . .

JOHN. I never . . .

CAROL. Excuse me, one moment, will you?

(*She reads from her notes.*)

The twelfth: "Have a good day, dear."

The fifteenth: "Now, don't *you* look fetching . . ."

April seventeenth: "If you girls would come over here . . ." I saw you. I saw you, Professor. For two semesters sit there, stand there and exploit our, as you thought, "paternal prerogative," and what is that but rape; I swear to God. You asked me in here to explain something to me, as a child, that I did not understand. But I came to explain something to you. You Are Not God. You ask me why I came? I came here to instruct you.

(*She produces his book.*)

And your book? You think you're going to show me some "light"? You "*maverick.*" Outside of tradition. No, no, (*She reads from the book's liner notes.*) "*of* that fine tradition of *inquiry.* Of Polite *skepticism*" . . . and you say you believe in free intellectual discourse. YOU BELIEVE IN NOTHING. YOU BELIEVE IN NOTHING AT ALL.

JOHN. I believe in freedom of thought.

CAROL. Isn't that fine. *Do* you?

JOHN. Yes. I do.

CAROL. Then why do you question, for one moment, the committee's decision refusing your tenure? Why do you question your suspension? You believe in what *you call* freedom of thought. Then, fine. *You* believe in freedom-of-thought *and* a home, and, *and* prerogatives for your kid, *and* tenure. And I'm going to tell you. You believe *not* in "freedom of thought," but in an elitist, in, in a protected hierarchy which rewards you. And for whom you are the clown. And you mock and exploit the system which pays your rent. You're wrong. I'm not wrong. You're wrong. You think that I'm full of hatred. I know what you think I am.

JOHN. Do you?

CAROL. You think I'm a, of course I do. You think I am a frightened, repressed, confused, I don't know, abandoned young thing of some doubtful sexuality, who wants, power and revenge. (*Pause*) *Don't* you? (*Pause*)

JOHN. Yes. I do. (*Pause*)

CAROL. Isn't that better? And I feel that that is the first moment which you've treated me with respect. For you told me the truth. (*Pause*) I did not come here, as you are assured, to gloat. Why would I want to gloat? I've profited nothing from your, your, as you say, your "misfortune." I came here, as you did me the honor to *ask* me here, I came here to *tell* you something.

(*Pause*) That I think . . . that I think you've been wrong. That I think you've been terribly wrong. Do you hate me now? (*Pause*)

JOHN. Yes.

CAROL. Why do you hate me? Because you think me wrong? No. Because I have, you think, *power* over you. Listen to me. Listen to me, Professor. (*Pause*) It is the power that you hate. So deeply that, that any atmosphere of free discussion is impossible. It's not "unlikely." It's *impossible.* Isn't it?

JOHN. Yes.

CAROL. *Isn't* it . . . ?

JOHN. Yes. I suppose.

CAROL. Now. The thing which you find so cruel is the selfsame process of selection I, and my group, go through *every day of our lives.* In admittance to school. In our tests, in our class rankings. . . . Is it unfair? I can't tell you. But, if it is fair. Or even if it is "unfortunate but necessary" for us, then, by God, so must it be for you. (*Pause*) You write of your "responsibility to the young." Treat us with respect, and that will *show* you your responsibility. You write that education is just hazing. (*Pause*) But we worked to get to this school. (*Pause*) And some of us. (*Pause*) Overcame prejudices. Economic, sexual, you cannot begin to imagine. And endured humiliations I *pray* that you and those you love never will encounter. (*Pause*) To gain admittance here. To pursue that same dream of security *you* pursue. We, who, who are, at any moment, in danger of being deprived of it. By . . .

JOHN. . . . by . . . ?

CAROL. By the administration. By the teachers. By *you.* By, say, one low grade, that keeps us out of graduate school; by one, say, one capricious or inventive answer on our parts, which, perhaps, you don't find amusing. Now you *know,* do you see? What it is to be subject to that power. (*Pause*)

JOHN. I don't understand. (*Pause*)

CAROL. My charges are not trivial. You see that in the haste, I think, with which they were accepted. A *joke* you have told, with a sexist tinge. The language you use, a verbal or physical caress, yes, yes, I know, you say that it is meaningless. I understand. I differ from you. To lay a hand on someone's shoulder.

JOHN. It was devoid of sexual content.

CAROL. I say it was not. I SAY IT WAS NOT. Don't you begin to *see* . . . ? Don't you begin to understand? IT'S NOT FOR YOU TO SAY.

JOHN. I take your point, and I see there is much good in what you refer to.

CAROL. . . . do you think so . . . ?

JOHN. . . . but, and this is not to say that I cannot change, in those things in which I am deficient . . . But, the . . .

CAROL. Do you hold yourself harmless from the charge of sexual exploitativeness . . . ? (*Pause*)

JOHN. Well, I . . . I . . . I . . . You know I, as I said. I . . . think I am not too old to *learn,* and I *can* learn, I . . .

CAROL. Do you hold yourself innocent of the charge of . . .

JOHN. . . . wait, wait, wait . . . All right, let's go back to . . .

CAROL. YOU FOOL. Who do you think I am? To come here and be taken in by a *smile.* You little yapping fool. You think I want "revenge." I don't want revenge. I WANT UNDERSTANDING.

JOHN. . . . *do* you?

CAROL. I do. (*Pause*)

JOHN. What's the use. It's over.

CAROL. Is it? What is?

JOHN. My job.

CAROL. Oh. Your job. That's what you want to talk about. (*Pause*) (*She starts to leave the room. She steps and turns back to him.*) All right. (*Pause*) What if it were possible that my Group withdraws its complaint. (*Pause*)

JOHN. What?

CAROL. That's right. (*Pause*)

JOHN. Why.

CAROL. Well, let's say as an act of friendship.

JOHN. An act of friendship.

CAROL. Yes. (*Pause*)

JOHN. In exchange for what.

CAROL. Yes. But I don't think, "exchange." Not "in exchange." For what do we derive from it? (*Pause*)

JOHN. "Derive."

CAROL. Yes.

JOHN. (*Pause*) Nothing. (*Pause*)

CAROL. That's right. We derive nothing. (*Pause*) Do you see that?

JOHN. Yes.

CAROL. That is a little word, Professor. "Yes." "I see that." But you will.

JOHN. And you might speak to the committee . . . ?

CAROL. To the committee?

JOHN. Yes.

CAROL. Well. Of course. That's on your mind. We might.

JOHN. "If" what?

CAROL. "Given" what. Perhaps. I think that that is more friendly.

JOHN. GIVEN WHAT?

CAROL. And, believe me, I understand your rage. It is not that I don't feel it. But I do not see that it is deserved, so I do not resent it. . . . All right. I have a list.

JOHN. . . . a list.

CAROL. Here is a list of books, which we . . .

JOHN. . . . a list of books . . . ?

CAROL. That's right. Which we find questionable.

JOHN. What?

CAROL. Is this so bizarre . . . ?

JOHN. I can't believe . . .

CAROL. It's not necessary you believe it.

JOHN. Academic freedom . . .

CAROL. Someone chooses the books. If you can choose them, others can. What are you, "God"?

JOHN. . . . no, no, the "dangerous." . . .

CAROL. You have an agenda, we have an agenda. I am not interested in your feelings or your motivation, but your actions. If you would like me to speak to the Tenure Committee, here is my list. You are a Free Person, you decide. (*Pause*)

JOHN. Give me the list. (*She does so. He reads.*)

CAROL. I think you'll find . . .

JOHN. I'm capable of reading it. Thank you.

CAROL. We have a number of *texts* we need re . . .

JOHN. I see that.

CAROL. We're amenable to . . .

JOHN. Aha. Well, let me look over the . . . (*He reads.*)

CAROL. I think that . . .

JOHN. LOOK. I'm reading your demands. All right?! (*He reads.*) (*Pause*) You want to ban my book?

CAROL. We do not . . .

JOHN (*of list*). It says here . . .

CAROL. . . . We want it removed from inclusion as a representative example of the university.

JOHN. Get out of here.

CAROL. If you put aside the issues of personalities.

JOHN. Get the fuck out of my office.

CAROL. No, I think I would reconsider.

JOHN. . . . you think you can.

CAROL. We can and we *will.* Do you want our support? That is the only quest . . .

JOHN. . . . to ban my *book* . . . ?

CAROL. . . . that is correct

JOHN. . . . this . . . this is a *university* . . . we . . .

CAROL. . . . and we have a statement . . . which we need you to . . . (*She hands him a sheet of paper.*)

JOHN. No, no. It's out of the question. I'm sorry. I don't know what I was thinking of. I want to tell you something. I'm a teacher. I am a teacher. Eh? It's my *name* on the door, and *I* teach the class, and that's what I do. I've got a book with my name on it. And my son will *see* that *book* someday. And I have a respon . . . No, I'm sorry I have a *responsibility* . . . to *myself,* to my *son,* to my *profession*. . . . I haven't been *home* for two days, do you know that? Thinking this out.

CAROL. . . . you haven't?

JOHN. I've been, no. If it's of interest to you. I've been in a *hotel. Thinking.* (*The phone starts ringing.*) *Thinking* . . .

CAROL. . . . you haven't been home?

JOHN. . . . *thinking,* do you see.

CAROL. Oh.

JOHN. And, and, I owe you a debt, I see that now. (*Pause*) You're *dangerous,* you're *wrong* and it's my *job* . . . to say no to you. That's my job. You are absolutely right. You want to ban my book? Go to *hell,* and they can do whatever they want to me.

CAROL. . . . you haven't been home in two days . . .

JOHN. I think I told you that.

CAROL. . . . you'd better get that phone. (*Pause*) I think that you should pick up the phone. (*Pause*)

(*John picks up the phone.*)

JOHN (*on phone*). Yes. (*Pause*) Yes. Wh . . . I. I. I had to be away. All ri . . . did they wor . . . did they worry ab . . . No. I'm all right, now, Jerry. I'm f . . . I got a little turned *around,* but I'm *sitting* here and . . . I've got it figured out. I'm fine. I'm fine don't worry about me. I got a little bit mixed up. But I am not sure that it's not a blessing. It cost me my job? Fine. Then the job was not worth having. Tell Grace that I'm coming home and everything is fff . . . (*Pause*) What? (*Pause*) *What?* (*Pause*) What do you *mean?* WHAT? Jerry . . . Jerry. They . . . Who, who, what can they do . . . ? (*Pause*) NO. (*Pause*) NO. They can't do th . . . What do you mean? (*Pause*) But how . . . (*Pause*) She's, she's, she's *here* with me. To . . . Jerry. I don't underst . . . (*Pause*) (*He hangs up.*) (*To Carol:*) What does this mean?

CAROL. I thought you knew.

JOHN. What. (*Pause*) What does it mean. (*Pause*)

CAROL. You tried to rape me. (*Pause*) According to the law. (*Pause*)

JOHN. . . . what . . . ?

CAROL. You tried to rape me. I was leaving this office, you "pressed" yourself into me. You "pressed" your body into me.

JOHN. . . . I . . .

CAROL. My Group has told your lawyer that we may pursue criminal charges.

JOHN. . . . no . . .

CAROL. . . . under the statute. I am told. It was battery.

JOHN. . . . no . . .

CAROL. Yes. And attempted rape. That's right. (*Pause*)

JOHN. I think that you should go.

CAROL. Of course. I thought you knew.

JOHN. I have to talk to my lawyer.

CAROL. Yes. Perhaps you should.

(*The phone rings again.*) (*Pause*)

JOHN. (*Picks up phone. Into phone:*) Hello? I . . . Hello . . . ? I . . . Yes, he just called. No . . . I. I can't talk to you now, Baby. (*To Carol:*) Get out.

CAROL. . . . your wife . . . ?

JOHN. . . . who it is is no concern of yours. Get out. (*To phone:*) No, no, it's going to be all right. I. I can't talk now, Baby. (*To Carol:*) Get out of here.

CAROL. I'm going.

JOHN. Good.

CAROL (*exiting*). . . . and don't call your wife "baby."

JOHN. What?

CAROL. Don't call your wife baby. You heard what I said.

(*Carol starts to leave the room. John grabs her and begins to beat her.*)

JOHN. You vicious little bitch. You think you can come in here with your political correctness and destroy my life?

(*He knocks her to the floor.*)

After how I treated you . . . ? You should be ... *Rape you* . . . ? Are you kidding me . . . ?

(*He picks up a chair, raises it above his head, and advances on her.*)

I wouldn't touch you with a ten-foot pole. You little *cunt* ...

(*She cowers on the floor below him. Pause. He looks down at her. He lowers the chair. He moves to his desk, and arranges the papers on it. Pause. He looks over at her.*)

. . . well . . .

(*Pause. She looks at him.*)

CAROL: Yes. That's right.

(*She looks away from him, and lowers her head. To herself:*)

. . . yes. That's right.

END

## TOPICS FOR CRITICAL THINKING AND WRITING

1. Did you find that on the whole you were on the side of one character rather than the other, or did your sympathies change, and if they changed did they change once and for all? (Incidentally, Mamet in an interview said that both characters are "altogether right" and both are "altogether wrong." Does this statement help you?)
2. Each of the three scenes begins with a stage direction informing the reader that the two characters are seated. In the first two scenes, they are "seated across the desk." The third scene does not specify the desk. How would you begin the third scene? Explain your decision.
3. Nothing is said of the costumes. How would you dress the two performers? Would you have them wear the same clothing in all three scenes, or different costumes in each scene? Why?
4. Toward the end of the first scene, John tells Carol that it is his job (as a professor) to "provoke" her, that is, to stimulate students to question traditional values. Reread the play, paying close attention to all of the comments on education, especially to Carol's comments in Scene Two—for instance, to her charge that by saying that education may be a form of "hazing" he mocks "*hardworking students,* who come here." Summarize—if it is possible—John's view of education, and Carol's. In your opinion, how much validity is there to what either character says about education? Explain.
5. Near the end of Scene One, we hear one side of a telephone conversation, which at first seems to suggest that John is in danger of losing the

house he is about to buy. It turns out that this is a friendly ruse to get him to come to the house, where he will find a party in his honor. Why do you suppose Mamet included this bit?

6. Although in much of Scene Three Carol is dominant, the play ends with her cowering on the floor, and saying—indeed repeating—"That's right." Mamet said, in an interview, "I think that people are generally more happy with a mystery than with an explanation." Is the ending mysterious? If so, do you agree with Mamet's generalization about mystery? Explain.
7. What do you take to be the relevance of the quotation from Samuel Butler (page 1798)? (By the way, we strongly recommend Butler's *The Way of All Flesh,* a witty, highly autobiographical and often moving novel published in 1903, a year after Butler's death.)
8. "Oleanna" is never mentioned in the play, but (as you know) the printed version includes as a sort of preface a quotation from a song, mentioning Oleanna, where it is contrasted with an oppressive Norwegian state. A student tells us of another stanza:

   So if you'd like a happy life,
   To Oleanna you must go,
   The poorest man from the old country
   Becomes a king in a year or so.

   Judging from this stanza, Oleanna is a never-never land, a dream world. We have also heard that Oleanna was the name of a nineteenth-century Norwegian-American utopian community, and that as a youth Mamet once went camping on the site. In any case, what do you think of the title?

# A PERSPECTIVE FOR *OLEANNA*

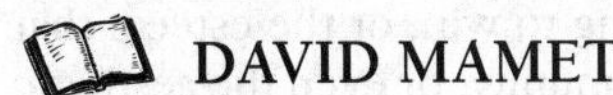

## DAVID MAMET

## *Talking about Drama*

[Part of an interview conducted with David Savran on 11 February 1987]

***In your plays the through-line is so strong that the characters can be saying things that are very, very different from what is really being communicated in the subtext.***

That's why theatre's like life, don't you think? No one really says what they mean, but they always mean what they mean.

***Also, in acting, subtext is usually defined as a power dynamic.***

I've been teaching acting for about twenty years now, and I love it. It's all about two people who want something different. If the two people don't want something different, what the hell is the scene about? Stay home. The same is true for writing. If two people don't want something from each other, then why are you having the scene? Throw the goddam scene out—which might seem like an overly strict lesson to be learned in a schoolroom but is awfully helpful in the theatre. If the two people don't want something different, the audience is going to go to sleep. Power, that's another way of putting it.

All of us are trying all the time to create the best setting and the best expression we can, not to communicate our wishes to each other, but to *achieve* our wishes *from* each other. I think awareness of this is the difference between good and bad playwriting. Whether it's a politician trying to get votes or a guy trying to go to bed with a girl or somebody trying to get a good table at a restaurant, the point is not to speak the desire but to speak that which is most likely to bring about the desire.

***Your plays are confrontational only indirectly, insofar as they're about asking questions rather than providing answers or delineating a mystery.***

In *Writing in Restaurants* I say that the purpose of the theatre is to deal with things that can't be dealt with rationally. If they can be dealt with rationally, they probably don't belong in my theatre. There are other people who feel differently and who work that way brilliantly. One of them is Arthur Miller. *Incident at Vichy, The Crucible,* also his new play, *Clara.* Or Wally Shawn, in *Aunt Dan and Lemon.* Or Fugard, for example.

***You say that, as a writer, you don't have a political agenda. Then what effect do you want to have on your audience?***

When I write a play, what I'm trying to do is write that play. As for the effect . . . it's not that it doesn't interest me, but it's really not my job to manipulate the audience, whether for a political motive or to get them to "like" my play. My job with the play succeeds according to its own logical syllogism. If this, then that. That's the difference between a playwright and a writer of advertising. The writer of advertising should be concerned, as Mr. Ogilvy tells us, solely with the effect it's going to have on the reader or the viewer, to persuade to buy the product or service advertised. If the writer of advertising is worried about the awards that he or she is going to win, or the esteem that he or she is going to win in the advertising community, or even the aesthetic beauty of the ad—absent its ability to influence the viewer—that person is not doing his or her job. Playwriting is exactly the opposite. Somebody said that if everybody likes everything you do, then you're doing something wrong.

# CHAPTER 34

# *Critical Perspectives on William Shakespeare's* The Tempest

## *A Casebook*

In this chapter we give *The Tempest* and the following related material:

1. An extract from a probable source, Montaigne's essay titled "Of the Cannibals"
2. An essay by Jane Lee, arguing that although the play is rooted in its own age it nevertheless speaks to us
3. An essay by Stephen Greenblatt, perhaps the most eminent critic of the New Historicist school, emphasizing the need to face the "cruelty, injustice, and pain" that is part of our civilization
4. Part of a discussion between a scholar, Ralph Berry, and a director of the play, Jonathan Miller
5. Part of an essay by Errol G. Hill, a theater historian, on possible racist implications in the roles of Caliban and Ariel
6. An essay by a scholar, Linda Bamber, on "the traffic in women"

## WILLIAM SHAKESPEARE

*Shakespeare (1564–1616) was born into a middle-class family in Stratford-upon-Avon. Although we have a fair number of records about his life—documents concerning marriage, the birth of children, the purchase of property, and so forth—it is not known exactly why and when he turned to the theater. What we do know, however, is important: He was an actor and a shareholder in a playhouse, and he did write the plays that are attributed to him. The dates of some of the plays can be set precisely, but the dates of some others can be set only roughly. It is known that* The Tempest *was performed before the King on 1 November 1611, and all scholars assume that the play was written in the months immediately preceding this production.*

## The Tempest*

*Edited by David Bevington*

NAMES OF THE ACTORS
ALONSO, *King of Naples*
SEBASTIAN, *his brother*
PROSPERO, *the right Duke of Milan*
ANTONIO, *his brother, the usurping Duke of Milan*
FERDINAND, *son to the King of Naples*
ADRIAN *and* FRANCISCO, } *lords*
CALIBAN, *a savage and deformed slave*
TRINCULO, *a jester*
STEPHANO, *a drunken butler*
MASTER *of a ship*
BOATSWAIN
MARINERS

MIRANDA, *daughter to Prospero*

ARIEL, *an airy spirit*
IRIS, CERES, JUNO, NYMPHS, REAPERS, } *[presented by] spirits*

*[Other Spirits attending on Prospero]*
**THE SCENE:** *An uninhabited island*

### 1.1 *A Tempestuous Noise of Thunder and Lightning Heard. Enter a Shipmaster and a Boatswain.*

MASTER. Boatswain!
BOATSWAIN. Here, Master. What cheer?
MASTER. Good,° speak to the mariners. Fall to 't yarely,° or we run ourselves aground. Bestir, bestir!

*Exit.*

*Enter Mariners.*

BOATSWAIN. Heigh, my hearts! Cheerly, cheerly, my hearts! Yare, yare! Take in the topsail. Tend° to the Master's whistle.—Blow° till thou burst thy wind, if room enough!°

**1.1 Location: On board ship, off the island's coast. 3 Good** i.e., it's good you've come, or, my good fellow. **yarely** nimbly **6 Tend** attend **Blow** (Addressed to the wind.) **7 if room enough** as long as we have sea room enough
*Words or phrases followed by a degree symbol are explained at the foot of the page.

Morris Carnovsky as Prospero in *The Tempest.* (Photograph by Martha Swope)

*Enter Alonso, Sebastian, Antonio, Ferdinand, Gonzalo, and others.*

ALONSO. Good Boatswain, have care. Where's the Master? Play the men.°

BOATSWAIN. I pray now, keep below.

ANTONIO. Where is the Master, Boatswain?

BOATSWAIN. Do you not hear him? You mar our labor. Keep° your cabins! You do assist the storm.

GONZALO. Nay, good,° be patient.

BOATSWAIN. When the sea is. Hence! What cares these roarers° for the name of king? To cabin! Silence! Trouble us not.

GONZALO. Good, yet remember whom thou hast aboard.

BOATSWAIN. None that I more love than myself. You are a councillor; if you can command these elements to silence and work the peace of the present,° we will not hand° a rope more. Use your authority. If you cannot, give thanks you have lived so long and make yourself ready in your cabin for the mischance of the hour, if it so hap.°—Cheerly, good hearts!—Out of our way, I say.

*Exit.*

**8–9 Play the men** act like men (?) ply, urge the men to exert themselves (?) **12 Keep** remain in **14 good** good fellow **15 roarers** waves or winds, or both; spoken to as though they were "bullies" or "blusterers" **19–20 work . . . present** bring calm to our present circumstances **20 hand** handle **22 hap** happen

GONZALO. I have great comfort from this fellow. Methinks he hath no drowning mark upon him; his complexion is perfect gallows.° Stand fast, good Fate, to his hanging! Make the rope of his destiny our cable, for our own doth little advantage.° If he be not born to be hanged, our case is miserable.°

*Exeunt* [*courtiers*].

*Enter Boatswain.*

BOATSWAIN. Down with the topmast! Yare! Lower, lower! Bring her to try wi' the main course.° (*A cry within.*) A plague upon this howling! They are louder than the weather or our office.°

*Enter Sebastian, Antonio, and Gonzalo.*

Yet again? What do you here? Shall we give o'er° and drown? Have you a mind to sink?

SEBASTIAN. A pox o' your throat, you bawling, blasphemous, incharitable dog!

BOATSWAIN. Work you, then.

ANTONIO. Hang, cur! Hang, you whoreson, insolent noisemaker! We are less afraid to be drowned than thou art.

GONZALO. I'll warrant him for drowning,° though the ship were no stronger than a nutshell and as leaky as an unstanched° wench.

BOATSWAIN. Lay her ahold, ahold!° Set her two courses.° Off to sea again! Lay her off!

*Enter Mariners, wet.*

MARINERS. All lost! To prayers, to prayers! All lost!
[*The Mariners run about in confusion, exiting at random.*]

BOATSWAIN. What, must our mouths be cold?°

GONZALO. The King and Prince at prayers! Let's assist them,
For our case is as theirs.

SEBASTIAN. I am out of patience.

ANTONIO. We are merely° cheated of our lives by drunkards.
This wide-chapped° rascal! Would thou mightst lie drowning
The washing of ten tides!°

GONZALO. He'll be hanged yet,
Though every drop of water swear against it
And gape at wid'st° to glut° him.
(*A confused noise within:*) "Mercy on us!"—

**25 complexion . . . gallows** appearance shows he was born to be hanged (and therefore, according to the proverb, in no danger of drowning) **27 our . . . advantage** our own cable is of little benefit **28 case is miserable** circumstances are desperate **29–30 Bring . . . course** sail her close to the wind by means of the mainsail **31 our office** i.e., the noise we make at our work **32 give o'er** give up **39 warrant him for drowning** guarantee that he will never be drowned **40 unstanched** insatiable, loose, unrestrained (suggesting also "incontinent" and "menstrual") **41 ahold** ahull, close to the wind. **courses** sails, i.e., foresail as well as mainsail, set in an attempt to get the ship back out into open water **44 must . . . cold** i.e., must we drown in the cold sea, or, let us heat up our mouths with liquor **47 merely** utterly **48 wide-chapped** with mouth wide open **48–49 lie . . . tides** (Pirates were hanged on the shore and left until three tides had come in.) **51 at wid'st** wide open. **glut** swallow

"We split,° we split!"—"Farewell my wife and children!"—
"Farewell, brother!"—"We split, we split, we split!"
[*Exit Boatswain.*]

ANTONIO. Let's all sink wi' the King.
SEBASTIAN. Let's take leave of him.
*Exit* [*with Antonio*].

GONZALO. Now would I give a thousand furlongs of sea for an acre of barren ground: long heath,° brown furze,° anything. The wills above be done! But I would fain° die a dry death.
*Exit.*

**1.2** *Enter Prospero* [*in his magic cloak*] *and Miranda.*

MIRANDA. If by your art,° my dearest father, you have
Put the wild waters in this roar, allay° them.
The sky, it seems, would pour down stinking pitch,
But that the sea, mounting to th' welkin's cheek,°
Dashes the fire out. O, I have suffered
With those that I saw suffer! A brave° vessel,
Who had, no doubt, some noble creature in her,
Dashed all to pieces. O, the cry did knock
Against my very heart! Poor souls, they perished.
Had I been any god of power, I would
Have sunk the sea within the earth or ere°
It should the good ship so have swallowed and
The freighting° souls within her.
PROSPERO. Be collected.°
No more amazement.° Tell your piteous° heart
There's no harm done.
MIRANDA. O, woe the day!
PROSPERO. No harm.
I have done nothing but° in care of thee,
Of thee, my dear one, thee, my daughter, who
Art ignorant of what thou art, naught knowing
Of whence I am, nor that I am more better°
Than Prospero, master of a full° poor cell,
And thy no greater father.
MIRANDA. More to know
Did never meddle° with my thoughts.
PROSPERO. 'Tis time
I should inform thee farther. Lend thy hand
And pluck my magic garment from me. So,

**52 split** break apart **57 heath** heather. **furze** gorse, a weed growing on wasteland **58 fain** rather

**1.2 Location: The island, near Prospero's cell.** On the Elizabethan stage, this cell is implicitly at hand throughout the play, although in some scenes the convention of flexible distance allows us to imagine characters in other parts of the island. **1 art** magic **2 allay** pacify **4 welkin's cheek** sky's face **6 brave** gallant, splendid **11 or ere** before **13 freighting** forming the cargo. **collected** calm, composed **14 amazement** consternation. **piteous** pitying **16 but** except **19 more better** of higher rank **20 full** very **22 meddle** mingle

[*laying down his magic cloak and staff*]
Lie there, my art.—Wipe thou thine eyes. Have comfort.
The direful spectacle of the wreck,° which touched
The very virtue° of compassion in thee,
I have with such provision° in mine art
So safely ordered that there is no soul—
No, not so much perdition° as an hair
Betid° to any creature in the vessel
Which° thou heard'st cry, which thou saw'st sink. Sit down,
For thou must now know farther.

MIRANDA [*sitting*]. You have often
Begun to tell me what I am, but stopped
And left me to a bootless inquisition,°
Concluding, "Stay, not yet."

PROSPERO. The hour's now come;
The very minute bids thee ope thine ear.
Obey, and be attentive. Canst thou remember
A time before we came unto this cell?
I do not think thou canst, for then thou wast not
Out° three years old.

MIRANDA. Certainly, sir, I can.

PROSPERO. By what? By any other house or person?
Of anything the image, tell me, that
Hath kept with thy remembrance.

MIRANDA. 'Tis far off,
And rather like a dream than an assurance
That my remembrance warrants.° Had I not
Four or five women once that tended me?

PROSPERO. Thou hadst, and more, Miranda. But how is it
That this lives in thy mind? What seest thou else
In the dark backward and abysm of time?°
If thou rememberest aught° ere thou cam'st here,
How thou cam'st here thou mayst.

MIRANDA. But that I do not.

PROSPERO. Twelve year since, Miranda, twelve year since,
Thy father was the Duke of Milan and
A prince of power.

MIRANDA. Sir, are not you my father?

PROSPERO. Thy mother was a piece° of virtue, and
She said thou wast my daughter; and thy father
Was Duke of Milan, and his only heir
And princess no worse issued.°

MIRANDA. O the heavens!
What foul play had we, that we came from thence?
Or blessèd was 't we did?

**26 wreck** shipwreck **27 virtue** essence **28 provision** foresight **30 perdition** loss **31 Betid** happened **32 Which** whom **35 bootless inquisition** profitless inquiry **41 Out** fully **45–46 assurance . . . warrants** certainty that my memory guarantees **50 backward . . . time** abyss of the past **51 aught** anything **56 piece** masterpiece, exemplar **59 no worse issued** no less nobly born, descended

PROSPERO. Both, both, my girl.
By foul play, as thou sayst, were we heaved thence,
But blessedly holp° hither.
MIRANDA. O, my heart bleeds
To think o' the teen that I have turned you to,°
Which is from° my remembrance! Please you, farther.
PROSPERO. My brother and thy uncle, called Antonio—
I pray thee mark me—that a brother should
Be so perfidious!—he whom next° thyself
Of all the world I loved, and to him put
The manage° of my state, as at that time
Through all the seigniories° it was the first,
And Prospero the prime° duke, being so reputed
In dignity, and for the liberal arts
Without a parallel; those being all my study,
The government I cast upon my brother
And to my state grew stranger,° being transported°
And rapt in secret studies. Thy false uncle—
Dost thou attend me?
MIRANDA. Sir, most heedfully.
PROSPERO. Being once perfected° how to grant suits,
How to deny them, who t' advance and who
To trash° for overtopping,° new created
The creatures° that were mine, I say, or changed 'em,
Or else new formed 'em;° having both the key°
Of officer and office, set all hearts i' the state
To what tune pleased his ear, that° now he was
The ivy which had hid my princely trunk
And sucked my verdure° out on 't.° Thou attend'st not.
MIRANDA. O, good sir, I do.
PROSPERO. I pray thee, mark me.
I, thus neglecting worldly ends, all dedicated
To closeness° and the bettering of my mind
With that which, but by being so retired,
O'erprized all popular rate,° in my false brother
Awaked an evil nature; and my trust,

**63 holp** helped **64 teen . . . to** trouble I've caused you to remember or put you to **65 from** out of **68 next** next to **70 manage** management, administration **71 seigniories** i.e., city-states of northern Italy **72 prime** first in rank and importance **76 to . . . stranger** i.e., withdrew from my responsibilities as duke. **transported** carried away **79 perfected** grown skillful **81 trash** check a hound by tying a cord or weight to its neck. **overtopping** running too far ahead of the pack; surmounting, exceeding one's authority **82 creatures** dependents **82–83 or changed . . . formed 'em** i.e., either changed their loyalties and duties or else created new ones **83 key** (1) key for unlocking (2) tool for tuning stringed instruments **85 that** so that **87 verdure** vitality. **on 't** of it **90 closeness** retirement, seclusion **91–92 but . . . rate** i.e., were it not that its private nature caused me to neglect my public responsibilities, had a value far beyond what public opinion could appreciate, or, simply because it was done in such seclusion, had a value not appreciated by popular opinion

Like a good parent,° did beget of° him
A falsehood in its contrary as great
As my trust was, which had indeed no limit,
A confidence sans° bound. He being thus lorded°
Not only with what my revenue yielded
But what my power might else° exact, like one
Who, having into° truth by telling of it,
Made such a sinner of his memory
To° credit his own lie,° he did believe
He was indeed the Duke, out o'° the substitution
And executing th' outward face of royalty°
With all prerogative. Hence his ambition growing—
Dost thou hear?

MIRANDA. Your tale, sir, would cure deafness.

PROSPERO. To have no screen between this part he played
And him he played it for,° he needs will be°
Absolute Milan.° Me, poor man, my library
Was dukedom large enough. Of temporal royalties°
He thinks me now incapable; confederates°—
So dry° he was for sway°—wi' the King of Naples
To give him annual tribute, do him° homage,
Subject his coronet to his° crown, and bend°
The dukedom yet° unbowed—alas, poor Milan!—
To most ignoble stooping.

MIRANDA. O the heavens!

PROSPERO. Mark his condition° and th' event,° then tell me
If this might be a brother.

MIRANDA. I should sin
To think but° nobly of my grandmother.
Good wombs have borne bad sons.

PROSPERO. Now the condition.
This King of Naples, being an enemy
To me inveterate, hearkens° my brother's suit,
Which was that he,° in lieu o' the premises°

**94 good parent** (Alludes to the proverb that good parents often bear bad children; see also line 120.) **of** in **97 sans** without. **lorded** raised to lordship, with power and wealth **99 else** otherwise, additionally **100 into** unto, against. **102 To** so as to **100–102 Who . . . lie** i.e., who, by repeatedly telling the lie (that he was indeed Duke of Milan), made his memory such a confirmed sinner against truth that he began to believe his own lie **103 out o'** as a result of **104 And . . . royalty** and (as a result of) his carrying out all the visible functions of royalty **107–108 To have . . . it for** to have no separation or barrier between his role and himself. (Antonio wanted to act in his own person, not as substitute.) **108 needs will be** insisted on becoming **109 Absolute Milan** unconditional Duke of Milan **110 temporal royalties** practical prerogatives and responsibilities of a sovereign **111 confederates** conspires, allies himself **112 dry** thirsty. **sway** power **113 him** i.e., the King of Naples **114 his . . . his** Antonio's . . . the King of Naples's **bend** make bow down **115 yet** hitherto **117 condition** pact. **event** outcome **119 but** other than **122 hearkens** listens to **123 he** the King of Naples. **in . . . premises** in return for the stipulation

Of homage and I know not how much tribute,
Should presently extirpate° me and mine
Out of the dukedom and confer fair Milan,
With all the honors, on my brother. Whereon,
A treacherous army levied, one midnight
Fated to th' purpose did Antonio open
The gates of Milan, and, i' the dead of darkness,
The ministers for the purpose° hurried thence°
Me and thy crying self.

MIRANDA. Alack, for pity!
I, not remembering how I cried out then,
Will cry it o'er again. It is a hint°
That wrings° mine eyes to 't.

PROSPERO. Hear a little further,
And then I'll bring thee to the present business
Which now's upon 's, without the which this story
Were most impertinent.°

MIRANDA. Wherefore° did they not
That hour destroy us?

PROSPERO. Well demanded,° wench.°
My tale provokes that question. Dear, they durst not,
So dear the love my people bore me, nor set
A mark so bloody° on the business, but
With colors fairer° painted their foul ends.
In few,° they hurried us aboard a bark,°
Bore us some leagues to sea, where they prepared
A rotten carcass of a butt,° not rigged,
Nor tackle,° sail, nor mast; the very rats
Instinctively have quit° it. There they hoist us,
To cry to th' sea that roared to us, to sigh
To th' winds whose pity, sighing back again,
Did us but loving wrong.°

MIRANDA. Alack, what trouble
Was I then to you!

PROSPERO. O, a cherubin
Thou wast that did preserve me. Thou didst smile,
Infusèd with a fortitude from heaven,
When I have decked° the sea with drops full salt,

**125 presently extirpate** at once remove **131 ministers . . . purpose** agents employed to do this. **thence** from there **134 hint** occasion **135 wrings** (1) constrains (2) wrings tears from **138 impertinent** irrelevant. **Wherefore** why **139 demanded** asked. **wench** (Here a term of endearment.) **141–142 set . . . bloody** i.e., make obvious their murderous intent. (From the practice of marking with the blood of the prey those who have participated in a successful hunt.) **143 fairer** apparently more attractive **144 few** few words. **bark** ship **146 butt** cask, tub **147 Nor tackle** neither rigging **148 quit** abandoned **151 Did . . . wrong** (i.e., the winds pitied Prospero and Miranda, though of necessity they blew them from shore) **155 decked** covered (with salt tears); adorned **156 which** i.e., the smile

Under my burden groaned, which° raised in me
An undergoing stomach,° to bear up
Against what should ensue.

MIRANDA. How came we ashore?

PROSPERO. By Providence divine.
Some food we had, and some fresh water, that
A noble Neapolitan, Gonzalo,
Out of his charity, who being then appointed
Master of this design, did give us, with
Rich garments, linens, stuffs,° and necessaries,
Which since have steaded much.° So, of° his gentleness,
Knowing I loved my books, he furnished me
From mine own library with volumes that
I prize above my dukedom.

MIRANDA. Would° I might
But ever° see that man!

PROSPERO. Now I arise.
[*He puts on his magic cloak.*]
Sit still, and hear the last of our sea sorrow.°
Here in this island we arrived; and here
Have I, thy schoolmaster, made thee more profit°
Than other princess'° can, that have more time
For vainer° hours and tutors not so careful.

MIRANDA. Heavens thank you for 't! And now, I pray you, sir—
For still 'tis beating in my mind—your reason
For raising this sea storm?

PROSPERO. Know thus far forth:
By accident most strange, bountiful Fortune,
Now my dear lady,° hath mine enemies
Brought to this shore; and by my prescience
I find my zenith° doth depend upon
A most auspicious star, whose influence°
If now I court not, but omit,° my fortunes
Will ever after droop. Here cease more questions.
Thou art inclined to sleep. 'Tis a good dullness,°
And give it way.° I know thou canst not choose.
[*Miranda sleeps.*]
Come away,° servant, come! I am ready now.
Approach, my Ariel, come.

*Enter Ariel.*

**157 undergoing stomach** courage to go on **165 stuffs** supplies **166 steaded much** been of much use. **So, of** similarly, out of **169 Would** I wish **170 But ever** i.e., someday **171 sea sorrow** sorrowful adventure at sea **173 more profit** profit more **174 princess'** princesses. (Or the word may be *princes*, referring to royal children both male and female.) **175 vainer** more foolishly spent **180 my dear lady** (Refers to Fortune, not Miranda.) **182 zenith** height of fortune. (Astrological term.) **183 influence** astrological power **184 omit** ignore **186 dullness** drowsiness **187 give it way** let it happen (i.e., don't fight it) **188 Come away** come

ARIEL. All hail, great master, grave sir, hail! I come
To answer thy best pleasure; be 't to fly,
To swim, to dive into the fire, to ride
On the curled clouds, to thy strong bidding task°
Ariel and all his quality.°
PROSPERO. Hast thou, spirit,
Performed to point° the tempest that I bade thee?
ARIEL. To every article.
I boarded the King's ship. Now on the beak,°
Now in the waist,° the deck,° in every cabin,
I flamed amazement.° Sometimes I'd divide
And burn in many places; on the topmast,
The yards, and bowsprit would I flame distinctly,°
Then meet and join. Jove's lightning, the precursors
O' the dreadful thunderclaps, more momentary
And sight-outrunning° were not.° The fire and cracks
Of sulfurous roaring the most mighty Neptune°
Seem to besiege and make his bold waves tremble,
Yea, his dread trident shake.
PROSPERO. My brave spirit!
Who was so firm, so constant, that this coil°
Would not infect his reason?
ARIEL. Not a soul
But felt a fever of the mad° and played
Some tricks of desperation. All but mariners
Plunged in the foaming brine and quit the vessel,
Then all afire with me. The King's son, Ferdinand,
With hair up-staring°—then like reeds, not hair—
Was the first man that leapt; cried, "Hell is empty,
And all the devils are here!"
PROSPERO. Why, that's my spirit!
But was not this nigh shore?
ARIEL. Close by, my master.
PROSPERO. But are they, Ariel, safe?
ARIEL. Not a hair perished.
On their sustaining garments° not a blemish,
But fresher than before; and, as thou bad'st° me,
In troops° I have dispersed them 'bout the isle.
The King's son have I landed by himself,
Whom I left cooling of° the air with sighs
In an odd angle° of the isle, and sitting,
His arms in this sad knot.° *[He folds his arms.]*

**193 task** make demands upon **194 quality** (1) fellow spirits (2) abilities **195 to point** to the smallest detail **197 beak** prow **198 waist** midships. **deck** poop deck at the stern **199 flamed amazement** struck terror in the guise of fire, i.e., Saint Elmo's fire **201 distinctly** in different places **204 sight-outrunning** swifter than sight. **were not** could not have been **205 Neptune** Roman god of the sea **208 coil** tumult **210 of the mad** i.e., such as madmen feel **214 up-staring** standing on end **219 sustaining garments** garments that buoyed them up in the sea **220 bad'st** ordered **221 troops** groups **223 cooling of** cooling **224 angle** corner **225 sad knot** (Folded arms are indicative of melancholy.)

PROSPERO. Of the King's ship,
The mariners, say how thou hast disposed,
And all the rest o' the fleet.
ARIEL. Safely in harbor
Is the King's ship; in the deep nook,° where once
Thou called'st me up at midnight to fetch dew°
From the still-vexed Bermudas,° there she's hid;
The mariners all under hatches stowed,
Who, with a charm joined to their suffered labor,°
I have left asleep. And for the rest o' the fleet,
Which I dispersed, they all have met again
And are upon the Mediterranean float°
Bound sadly home for Naples,
Supposing that they saw the King's ship wrecked
And his great person perish.
PROSPERO. Ariel, thy charge
Exactly is performed. But there's more work.
What is the time o' the day?
ARIEL. Past the mid season.°
PROSPERO. At least two glasses.° The time twixt six and now
Must by us both be spent most preciously.
ARIEL. Is there more toil? Since thou dost give me pains,°
Let me remember° thee what thou hast promised,
Which is not yet performed me.
PROSPERO. How now? Moody?
What is 't thou canst demand?
ARIEL. My liberty.
PROSPERO. Before the time be out? No more!
ARIEL. I prithee,
Remember I have done thee worthy service,
Told thee no lies, made thee no mistakings, served
Without or grudge or grumblings. Thou did promise
To bate° me a full year.
PROSPERO. Dost thou forget
From what a torment I did free thee?
ARIEL. No.
PROSPERO. Thou dost, and think'st it much to tread the ooze
Of the salt deep,
To run upon the sharp wind of the north,
To do me° business in the veins° o' the earth
When it is baked° with frost.
ARIEL. I do not, sir.

**228 nook** bay **229 dew** (Collected at midnight for magical purposes; compare with line 324.) **230 still-vexed Bermudas** ever stormy Bermudas. (Perhaps refers to the then recent Bermuda shipwreck. The Folio text reads "Bermoothes.") **232 with . . . labor** by means of a spell added to all the labor they have undergone **235 float** sea **240 mid season** noon **241 glasses** hourglasses **243 pains** labors **244 remember** remind **251 bate** remit, deduct **256 do me** do for me. **veins** veins of minerals, or, underground streams, thought to be analogous to the veins of the human body **257 baked** hardened

PROSPERO. Thou liest, malignant thing! Hast thou forgot
The foul witch Sycorax, who with age and envy°
Was grown into a hoop?° Hast thou forgot her?

ARIEL. No, sir.

PROSPERO. Thou hast. Where was she born? Speak. Tell me.

ARIEL. Sir, in Argier.°

PROSPERO. O, was she so? I must
Once in a month recount what thou hast been,
Which thou forgett'st. This damned witch Sycorax,
For mischiefs manifold and sorceries terrible
To enter human hearing, from Argier,
Thou know'st, was banished. For one thing she did°
They would not take her life. Is not this true?

ARIEL. Ay, sir.

PROSPERO. This blue-eyed° hag was hither brought with child°
And here was left by the sailors. Thou, my slave,
As thou report'st thyself, was then her servant;
And, for° thou wast a spirit too delicate
To act her earthy and abhorred commands,
Refusing her grand hests,° she did confine thee,
By help of her more potent ministers
And in her most unmitigable rage,
Into a cloven pine, within which rift
Imprisoned thou didst painfully remain
A dozen years; within which space she died
And left thee there, where thou didst vent thy groans
As fast as mill wheels strike.° Then was this island—
Save° for the son that she did litter° here,
A freckled whelp,° hag-born°—not honored with
A human shape.

ARIEL. Yes, Caliban her son.°

PROSPERO. Dull thing, I say so:° he, that Caliban
Whom now I keep in service. Thou best know'st
What torment I did find thee in. Thy groans
Did make wolves howl, and penetrate the breasts
Of ever-angry bears. It was a torment
To lay upon the damned, which Sycorax
Could not again undo. It was mine art,
When I arrived and heard thee, that made gape°
The pine and let thee out.

ARIEL. I thank thee, master.

**259 envy** malice **260 grown into a hoop** i.e., so bent over with age as to resemble a hoop **263 Argier** Algiers **268 one . . . did** (Perhaps a reference to her pregnancy, for which her life would be spared.) **271 blue-eyed** with dark circles under the eyes or with blue eyelids, implying pregnancy. **with child** pregnant **274 for** because **276 hests** commands **283 as mill wheels strike** as the blades of a mill wheel strike the water **284 Save** except. **litter** give birth to **285 whelp** offspring. (Used of animals.) **hag-born** born of a female demon **286 Yes . . . son** (Ariel is probably concurring with Prospero's comments about a "freckled whelp," not contradicting the point about "A human shape.") **287 Dull . . . so** i.e., exactly, that's what I said, you dullard **294 gape** open wide

PROSPERO. If thou more murmur'st, I will rend an oak
And peg thee in his° knotty entrails till
Thou hast howled away twelve winters.

ARIEL. Pardon, master.
I will be correspondent° to command
And do my spriting° gently.°

PROSPERO. Do so, and after two days
I will discharge thee.

ARIEL. That's my noble master!
What shall I do? Say what? What shall I do?

PROSPERO. Go make thyself like a nymph o' the sea. Be subject
To no sight but thine and mine, invisible
To every eyeball else. Go take this shape
And hither come in 't. Go, hence with diligence!

*Exit* [*Ariel*].

Awake, dear heart, awake! Thou hast slept well.
Awake!

MIRANDA. The strangeness of your story put
Heaviness° in me.

PROSPERO. Shake it off. Come on,
We'll visit Caliban, my slave, who never
Yields us kind answer.

MIRANDA. 'Tis a villain, sir,
I do not love to look on.

PROSPERO. But, as 'tis,
We cannot miss° him. He does make our fire,
Fetch in our wood, and serves in offices°
That profit us.—What ho! Slave! Caliban!
Thou earth, thou! Speak.

CALIBAN (*within*). There's wood enough within.

PROSPERO. Come forth, I say! There's other business for thee.
Come, thou tortoise! When?°

*Enter Ariel like a water nymph.*

Fine apparition! My quaint° Ariel,
Hark in thine ear. [*He whispers.*]

ARIEL. My lord, it shall be done.

*Exit.*

PROSPERO. Thou poisonous slave, got° by the devil himself
Upon thy wicked dam,° come forth!

*Enter Caliban.*

CALIBAN. As wicked° dew as e'er my mother brushed
With raven's feather from unwholesome fen°
Drop on you both! A southwest° blow on ye
And blister you all o'er!

**297 his** its **299 correspondent** responsive, submissive **300 spriting** duties as a spirit. **gently** willingly, ungrudgingly **310 Heaviness** drowsiness **314 miss** do without **315 offices** functions, duties **319 When** (An exclamation of impatience.) **320 quaint** ingenious **322 got** begotten, sired **323 dam** mother. (Used of animals.) **324 wicked** mischievous, harmful **325 fen** marsh, bog **326 southwest** i.e., wind thought to bring disease

PROSPERO. For this, be sure, tonight thou shalt have cramps,
Side-stitches that shall pen thy breath up. Urchins°
Shall forth at vast° of night that they may work
All exercise on thee. Thou shalt be pinched
As thick as honeycomb,° each pinch more stinging
Than bees that made 'em.°

CALIBAN. I must eat my dinner.
This island's mine, by Sycorax my mother,
Which thou tak'st from me. When thou cam'st first,
Thou strok'st me and made much of me, wouldst give me
Water with berries in 't, and teach me how
To name the bigger light, and how the less,°
That burn by day and night. And then I loved thee
And showed thee all the qualities o' th' isle,
The fresh springs, brine pits, barren place and fertile.
Cursed be I that did so! All the charms°
Of Sycorax, toads, beetles, bats, light on you!
For I am all the subjects that you have,
Which first was mine own king; and here you sty° me
In this hard rock, whiles you do keep from me
The rest o' th' island.

PROSPERO. Thou most lying slave,
Whom stripes° may move, not kindness! I have used thee,
Filth as thou art, with humane° care, and lodged thee
In mine own cell, till thou didst seek to violate
The honor of my child.

CALIBAN. Oho, Oho! Would 't had been done!
Thou didst prevent me; I had peopled else°
This isle with Calibans.

MIRANDA. Abhorrèd slave,
Which any print° of goodness wilt not take,
Being capable of all ill! I pitied thee,
Took pains to make thee speak, taught thee each hour
One thing or other. When thou didst not, savage,
Know thine own meaning, but wouldst gabble like
A thing most brutish, I endowed thy purposes°
With words that made them known. But thy vile race,°
Though thou didst learn, had that in 't which good natures
Could not abide to be with; therefore wast thou
Deservedly confined into this rock,
Who hadst deserved more than a prison.°

**329 Urchins** hedgehogs; here, suggesting goblins in the guise of hedgehogs **330 vast** lengthy, desolate time. (Malignant spirits were thought to be restricted to the hours of darkness.) **332 As thick as honeycomb** i.e., all over, with as many pinches as a honeycomb has cells **333 'em** i.e., the honeycomb **338 the bigger . . . less** i.e., the sun and the moon. (See Genesis 1.16: "God then made two great lights: the greater light to rule the day, and the less light to rule the night.") **342 charms** spells **345 sty** confine as in a sty **348 stripes** lashes **349 humane** (Not distinguished as a word from *human.*) **353 peopled else** otherwise populated **355 print** imprint, impression **360 purposes** meanings, desires **361 race** natural disposition; species, nature **354–365 Abhorrèd . . . prison** (Sometimes assigned by editors to Prospero.)

CALIBAN. You taught me language, and my profit on 't
Is I know how to curse. The red plague° rid° you
For learning° me your language!
PROSPERO. Hagseed,° hence!
Fetch us in fuel, and be quick, thou'rt best,°
To answer other business.° Shrugg'st thou, malice?
If thou neglect'st or dost unwillingly
What I command, I'll rack thee with old° cramps,
Fill all thy bones with aches,° make thee roar
That beasts shall tremble at thy din.
CALIBAN. No, pray thee.
[*Aside.*] I must obey. His art is of such power
It would control my dam's god, Setebos,°
And make a vassal of him.
PROSPERO. So, slave, hence!

*Exit Caliban.*

*Enter Ferdinand; and Ariel, invisible,° playing and singing.*
[*Ferdinand does not see Prospero and Miranda.*]

*Ariel's Song.*

ARIEL.
Come unto these yellow sands,
And then take hands;
Curtsied when you have,° and kissed
The wild waves whist;°
Foot it featly° here and there,
And, sweet sprites,° bear
The burden.° Hark, hark!

*Burden, dispersedly°* [*within*]. Bow-wow.

The watchdogs bark.

[*Burden, dispersedly within.*] Bow-wow.

Hark, hark! I hear
The strain of strutting chanticleer
Cry Cock-a-diddle-dow.
FERDINAND. Where should this music be? I' th' air or th' earth?
It sounds no more; and sure it waits upon°
Some god o' th' island. Sitting on a bank,°
Weeping again the King my father's wreck,
This music crept by me upon the waters,

**367 red plague** plague characterized by red sores and evacuation of blood. **rid** destroy **368 learning** teaching. **Hagseed** offspring of a female demon **369 thou'rt best** you'd be well advised **370 answer other business** perform other tasks **372 old** such as old people suffer, or, plenty of **373 aches** (Pronounced "aitches.") **376 Setebos** (A god of the Patagonians, named in Robert Eden's *History of Travel,* 1577.) **377 s.d. Ariel, invisible** (Ariel wears a garment that by convention indicates he is invisible to the other characters.) **380 Curtsied . . . have** when you have curtsied **380–381 kissed . . . whist** kissed the waves into silence, or, kissed while the waves are being hushed **382 Foot it featly** dance nimbly **383 sprites** spirits **384 burden** refrain, undersong **385 s.d. dispersedly** i.e., from all directions, not in unison **392 waits upon** serves, attends **393 bank** sandbank

Allaying both their fury and my passion°
With its sweet air. Thence° I have followed it,
Or it hath drawn me rather. But 'tis gone.
No, it begins again.

*Ariel's Song.*

ARIEL.
Full fathom five thy father lies.
Of his bones are coral made.
Those are pearls that were his eyes.
Nothing of him that doth fade
But doth suffer a sea change
Into something rich and strange.
Sea nymphs hourly ring his knell.°
*Burden* [*within*]. Ding dong.
Hark, now I hear them, ding dong bell.

FERDINAND. The ditty does remember° my drowned father.
This is no mortal business, nor no sound
That the earth owes.° I hear it now above me.

PROSPERO [*to Miranda*]. The fringèd curtains of thine eye advance°
And say what thou seest yond.

MIRANDA. What is 't? A spirit?
Lord, how it looks about! Believe me, sir,
It carries a brave° form. But 'tis a spirit.

PROSPERO. No, wench, it eats and sleeps and hath such senses
As we have, such. This gallant which thou seest
Was in the wreck; and, but° he's something stained°
With grief, that's beauty's canker,° thou mightst call him
A goodly person. He hath lost his fellows
And strays about to find 'em.

MIRANDA. I might call him
A thing divine, for nothing natural
I ever saw so noble.

PROSPERO [*aside*]. It goes on,° I see,
As my soul prompts it.—Spirit, fine spirit, I'll free thee
Within two days for this.

FERDINAND [*seeing Miranda*]. Most sure, the goddess
On whom these airs° attend!—Vouchsafe° my prayer
May know° if you remain° upon this island,
And that you will some good instruction give
How I may bear me° here. My prime° request,
Which I do last pronounce, is—O you wonder!°—
If you be maid or no?°

**396 passion** grief **397 Thence** i.e., from the bank on which I sat **406 knell** announcement of a death by the tolling of a bell **409 remember** commemorate **411 owes** owns **412 advance** raise **415 brave** excellent **418 but** except that. **something stained** somewhat disfigured **419 canker** cankerworm (feeding on buds and leaves) **423 It goes on** i.e., my plan works **426 airs** songs. **Vouchsafe** grant **427 May know** i.e., that I may know. **remain** dwell **429 bear me** conduct myself. **prime** chief **430 wonder** (Miranda's name means "to be wondered at.")

MIRANDA. No wonder, sir,
But certainly a maid.
FERDINAND. My language? Heavens!
I am the best° of them that speak this speech,
Were I but where 'tis spoken.
PROSPERO [*coming forward*]. How? The best?
What wert thou if the King of Naples heard thee?
FERDINAND. A single° thing, as I am now, that wonders
To hear thee speak of Naples.° He does hear me,°
And that he does I weep.° Myself am Naples,
Who with mine eyes, never since at ebb,° beheld
The King my father wrecked.
MIRANDA. Alack, for mercy!
FERDINAND. Yes, faith, and all his lords, the Duke of Milan
And his brave son° being twain.
PROSPERO [*aside*]. The Duke of Milan
And his more braver° daughter could control° thee,
If now 'twere fit to do 't. At the first sight
They have changed eyes.°—Delicate Ariel,
I'll set thee free for this. [*To Ferdinand.*] A word, good sir.
I fear you have done yourself some wrong.° A word!
MIRANDA [*aside*]. Why speaks my father so ungently? This
Is the third man that e'er I saw, the first
That e'er I sighed for. Pity move my father
To be inclined my way!
FERDINAND. O, if a virgin,
And your affection not gone forth, I'll make you
The Queen of Naples.
PROSPERO. Soft, sir! One word more.
[*Aside.*] They are both in either's° pow'rs; but this swift business
I must uneasy° make, lest too light winning
Make the prize light.° [*To Ferdinand.*] One word more: I charge thee
That thou attend° me. Thou dost here usurp
The name thou ow'st° not, and hast put thyself
Upon this island as a spy, to win it
From me, the lord on 't.°
FERDINAND. No, as I am a man.
MIRANDA. There's nothing ill can dwell in such a temple.

**431 maid or no** i.e., a human maiden as opposed to a goddess or married woman **433 best** i.e., in birth **436 single** (1) solitary, being at once King of Naples and myself (2) feeble **437, 438 Naples** the King of Naples **437 He does hear me** i.e., the King of Naples does hear my words, for I am King of Naples **438 And . . . weep** i.e., and I weep at this reminder that my father is seemingly dead, leaving me heir **439 at ebb** i.e., dry, not weeping **442 son** (The only reference in the play to a son of Antonio.) **443 more braver** more splendid. **control** refute **445 changed eyes** exchanged amorous glances **447 done . . . wrong** i.e., spoken falsely **454 both in either's** each in the other's **455 uneasy** difficult **455–456 light . . . light** easy . . . cheap **457 attend** follow, obey **458 ow'st** ownest **460 on 't** of it

If the ill spirit have so fair a house,
Good things will strive to dwell with 't.°

PROSPERO. Follow me.—
Speak not you for him; he's a traitor.—Come,
I'll manacle thy neck and feet together.
Seawater shalt thou drink; thy food shall be
The fresh-brook mussels, withered roots, and husks
Wherein the acorn cradled. Follow.

FERDINAND. No!
I will resist such entertainment° till
Mine enemy has more power.

*He draws, and is charmed° from moving.*

MIRANDA. O dear father,
Make not too rash° a trial of him, for
He's gentle,° and not fearful.°

PROSPERO. What, I say,
My foot° my tutor?—Put thy sword up, traitor,
Who mak'st a show but dar'st not strike, thy conscience
Is so possessed with guilt. Come, from thy ward,°
For I can here disarm thee with this stick
And make thy weapon drop. [*He brandishes his staff.*]

MIRANDA [*trying to hinder him*]. Beseech you, father!

PROSPERO. Hence! Hang not on my garments.

MIRANDA. Sir, have pity!
I'll be his surety.°

PROSPERO. Silence! One word more
Shall make me chide thee, if not hate thee. What,
An advocate for an impostor? Hush!
Thou think'st there is no more such shapes as he,
Having seen but him and Caliban. Foolish wench,
To° the most of men this is a Caliban,
And they to him are angels.

MIRANDA. My affections
Are then most humble; I have no ambition
To see a goodlier man.

PROSPERO [*to Ferdinand*]. Come on, obey.
Thy nerves° are in their infancy again
And have no vigor in them.

FERDINAND. So they are.
My spirits,° as in a dream, are all bound up.
My father's loss, the weakness which I feel,
The wreck of all my friends, nor this man's threats
To whom I am subdued, are but light° to me,
Might I but through my prison once a day

**463 strive . . . with 't** i.e., expel the evil and occupy the *temple,* the body **469 entertainment** treatment **470 s.d. charmed** magically prevented **471 rash** harsh **472 gentle** wellborn. **fearful** frightening, dangerous, or perhaps, cowardly **473 foot** subordinate. (Miranda, the foot, presumes to instruct Prospero, the head.) **475 ward** defensive posture (in fencing) **479 surety** guarantee **484 To** compared to **488 nerves** sinews **490 spirits** vital powers **493 light** unimportant

Behold this maid. All corners else° o' th' earth
Let liberty make use of; space enough
Have I in such a prison.

PROSPERO [*aside*]. It works. [*To Ferdinand.*] Come on.—
Thou hast done well, fine Ariel! [*To Ferdinand.*] Follow me.
[*To Ariel.*] Hark what thou else shalt do me.°

MIRANDA [*to Ferdinand*]. Be of comfort.
My father's of a better nature, sir,
Than he appears by speech. This is unwonted°
Which now came from him.

PROSPERO [*to Ariel*]. Thou shalt be as free
As mountain winds; but then° exactly do
All points of my command.

ARIEL. To th' syllable.

PROSPERO [*to Ferdinand*]. Come, follow. [*To Miranda.*] Speak not for him.

*Exeunt.*

**2.1** *Enter Alonso, Sebastian, Antonio, Gonzalo, Adrian, Francisco, and others.*

GONZALO [*to Alonso*]. Beseech you, sir, be merry. You have cause,
So have we all, of joy, for our escape
Is much beyond our loss. Our hint° of woe
Is common; every day some sailor's wife,
The masters of some merchant, and the merchant,°
Have just our theme of woe. But for the miracle,
I mean our preservation, few in millions
Can speak like us. Then wisely, good sir, weigh
Our sorrow with° our comfort.

ALONSO. Prithee, peace.

SEBASTIAN [*aside to Antonio*]. He receives comfort like cold porridge.°

ANTONIO [*aside to Sebastian*]. The visitor° will not give him o'er° so.

SEBASTIAN. Look, he's winding up the watch of his wit; by and by it will strike.

GONZALO [*to Alonso*]. Sir—

SEBASTIAN [*aside to Antonio*]. One. Tell.°

GONZALO. When every grief is entertained that's offered, comes to th' entertainer°—

**495 corners else** other corners, regions **499 me** for me **501 unwonted** unusual
**503 then** until then, or, if that is to be so
**2.1 Location: Another part of the island.** **3 hint** occasion **5 masters . . . the merchant** officers of some merchant vessel and the merchant himself, the owner **9 with** against **10 porridge** (punningly suggested by *peace,* i.e., "peas" or "pease," a common ingredient of porridge) **11 visitor** one taking nourishment and comfort to the sick, as Gonzalo is doing. **give him o'er** abandon him **15 Tell** keep count **16–17 When . . . entertainer** when every sorrow that presents itself is accepted without resistance, there comes to the recipient

SEBASTIAN. A dollar.°

GONZALO. Dolor comes to him, indeed. You have spoken truer than you purposed.

SEBASTIAN. You have taken it wiselier than I meant you should.

GONZALO [*to Alonso*]. Therefore, my lord—

ANTONIO. Fie, what a spendthrift is he of his tongue!

ALONSO [*to Gonzalo*]. I prithee, spare.°

GONZALO. Well, I have done. But yet—

SEBASTIAN [*aside to Antonio*]. He will be talking.

ANTONIO [*aside to Sebastian*]. Which, of he or Adrian, for a good wager, first begins to crow?°

SEBASTIAN. The old cock.°

ANTONIO. The cockerel.°

SEBASTIAN. Done. The wager?

ANTONIO. A laughter.°

SEBASTIAN. A match!°

ADRIAN. Though this island seem to be desert°—

ANTONIO. Ha, ha, ha!

SEBASTIAN. So, you're paid.°

ADRIAN. Uninhabitable and almost inaccessible—

SEBASTIAN. Yet—

ADRIAN. Yet—

ANTONIO. He could not miss 't.°

ADRIAN. It must needs be° of subtle, tender, and delicate temperance.°

ANTONIO. Temperance° was a delicate° wench.

SEBASTIAN. Ay, and a subtle,° as he most learnedly delivered.°

ADRIAN. The air breathes upon us here most sweetly.

SEBASTIAN. As if it had lungs, and rotten ones.

ANTONIO. Or as 'twere perfumed by a fen.

GONZALO. Here is everything advantageous to life.

**18 dollar** widely circulated coin, the German thaler and the Spanish piece of eight. (Sebastian puns on *entertainer* in the sense of innkeeper; to Gonzalo, *dollar* suggests "dolor," grief.) **24 spare** forbear, cease **27–28 Which . . . crow** which of the two, Gonzalo or Adrian, do you bet will speak (crow) first? **29 old cock** i.e., Gonzalo **30 cockerel** i.e., Adrian **32 laughter** (1) burst of laughter (2) sitting of eggs. (When Adrian, the *cockerel,* begins to speak two lines later, Sebastian loses the bet. The Folio speech prefixes in lines 35–36 are here reversed so that Antonio enjoys his laugh as the prize for winning, as in the proverb "He who laughs last laughs best" or "He laughs that wins." The Folio assignment can work in the theater, however, if Sebastian pays for losing with a sardonic laugh of concession.) **33 A match** a bargain; agreed **34 desert** uninhabited **36 you're paid** i.e., you've had your laugh **40 miss 't** (1) avoid saying "Yet" (2) miss the island **41 must needs be** has to be. **temperance** mildness of climate **42 Temperance** a girl's name. **delicate** (Here it means "given to pleasure, voluptuous"; in line 41, "pleasant." Antonio is evidently suggesting that *tender, and delicate temperance* sounds like a Puritan phrase, which Antonio then mocks by applying the words to a woman rather than an island. He began this bawdy comparison with a double entendre on *inaccessible,* line 37.) **43 subtle** (Here it means "tricky, sexually crafty"; in line 41, "delicate.") **delivered** uttered. (Sebastian joins Antonio in baiting the Puritans with his use of the pious cant phrase *learnedly delivered.*)

ANTONIO. True, save° means to live.

SEBASTIAN. Of that there's none, or little.

GONZALO. How lush and lusty° the grass looks! How green!

ANTONIO. The ground indeed is tawny.°

SEBASTIAN. With an eye° of green in 't.

ANTONIO. He misses not much.

SEBASTIAN. No. He doth but° mistake the truth totally.

GONZALO. But the rarity of it is—which is indeed almost beyond credit—

SEBASTIAN. As many vouched rarities° are.

GONZALO. That our garments, being, as they were, drenched in the sea, hold notwithstanding their freshness and glosses, being rather new-dyed than stained with salt water.

ANTONIO. If but one of his pockets° could speak, would it not say he lies?

SEBASTIAN. Ay, or very falsely pocket up° his report.°

GONZALO. Methinks our garments are now as fresh as when we put them on first in Afric, at the marriage of the King's fair daughter Claribel to the King of Tunis.

SEBASTIAN. 'Twas a sweet marriage, and we prosper well in our return.

ADRIAN. Tunis was never graced before with such a paragon to° their queen.

GONZALO. Not since widow Dido's° time.

ANTONIO [*aside to Sebastian*]. Widow? A pox o' that! How came that "widow" in? Widow Dido!

SEBASTIAN. What if he had said "widower Aeneas" too? Good Lord, how you take° it!

ADRIAN [*to Gonzalo*]. "Widow Dido" said you? You make me study of° that. She was of Carthage, not of Tunis.

GONZALO. This Tunis, sir, was Carthage.

ADRIAN. Carthage?

GONZALO. I assure you, Carthage.

ANTONIO. His word is more than the miraculous harp.°

SEBASTIAN. He hath raised the wall, and houses too.

ANTONIO. What impossible matter will he make easy next?

**48 save** except **50 lusty** healthy **51 tawny** dull brown, yellowish **52 eye** tinge, or spot (perhaps with reference to Gonzalo's eye or judgment) **54 but** merely **57 vouched rarities** allegedly real though strange sights **61 pockets** i.e., because they are muddy **63 pocket up** i.e., conceal, suppress; often used in the sense of "receive unprotestingly, fail to respond to a challenge." **his report** (Sebastian's jest is that the evidence of Gonzalo's soggy and sea-stained pockets would confute Gonzalo's speech and his reputation for truth telling.) **68 to** for **70 widow Dido** Queen of Carthage, deserted by Aeneas. (She was, in fact, a widow when Aeneas, a widower, met her, but Antonio may be amused at Gonzalo's prudish use of the term "widow" to describe a woman deserted by her lover.) **74 take** understand, respond to, interpret **75 study of** think about **80 miraculous harp** (Alludes to Amphion's harp, with which he raised the walls of Thebes; Gonzalo has exceeded that deed by re-creating ancient Carthage—*wall and houses*—mistakenly on the site of modern-day Tunis. Some Renaissance commentators believed, like Gonzalo, that the two sites were near each other.)

SEBASTIAN. I think he will carry this island home in his pocket and give it his son for an apple.

ANTONIO. And, sowing the kernels° of it in the sea, bring forth more islands.

GONZALO. Ay.°

ANTONIO. Why, in good time.°

GONZALO [*to Alonso*]. Sir, we were talking° that our garments seem now as fresh as when we were at Tunis at the marriage of your daughter, who is now queen.

ANTONIO. And the rarest° that e'er came there.

SEBASTIAN. Bate,° I beseech you, widow Dido.

ANTONIO. O, widow Dido? Ay, widow Dido.

GONZALO. Is not, sir, my doublet° as fresh as the first day I wore it? I mean, in a sort.°

ANTONIO. That "sort"° was well fished for.

GONZALO. When I wore it at your daughter's marriage.

ALONSO. You cram these words into mine ears against
The stomach of my sense.° Would I had never
Married° my daughter there! For, coming thence,
My son is lost and, in my rate,° she too,
Who is so far from Italy removed
I ne'er again shall see her. O thou mine heir
Of Naples and of Milan, what strange fish
Hath made his meal on thee?

FRANCISCO. Sir, he may live.
I saw him beat the surges° under him
And ride upon their backs. He trod the water,
Whose enmity he flung aside, and breasted
The surge most swoll'n that met him. His bold head
'Bove the contentious waves he kept, and oared
Himself with his good arms in lusty° stroke
To th' shore, that o'er his° wave-worn basis bowed,°
As° stooping to relieve him. I not doubt
He came alive to land.

ALONSO. No, no, he's gone.

SEBASTIAN [*to Alonso*]. Sir, you may thank yourself for this great loss,
That° would not bless our Europe with your daughter,
But rather° loose° her to an African,

**85 kernels** seeds **87 Ay** (Gonzalo may be reasserting his point about Carthage, or he may be responding ironically to Antonio, who, in turn, answers sarcastically.) **88 in good time** (An expression of ironical acquiescence or amazement, i.e., "sure, right away.") **89 talking** saying **92 rarest** most remarkable, beautiful **93 Bate** abate, except, leave out. (Sebastian says sardonically, surely you should allow widow Dido to be an exception.) **95 doublet** close-fitting jacket **96 in a sort** in a way **97 sort** (Antonio plays on the idea of drawing lots and on "fishing" for something to say.) **100 The stomach . . . sense** my appetite for hearing them **101 Married** given in marriage **102 rate** estimation, opinion **107 surges** waves **112 lusty** vigorous **113 his** its. **that . . . bowed** i.e., that projected out over the base of the cliff that had been eroded by the surf, thus seeming to bend down toward the sea **114 As** as if **117 That** you who **118 rather** would rather. **loose** (1) release, let loose (2) lose

Where she at least is banished from your eye,°
Who hath cause to wet the grief on 't.°

ALONSO. Prithee, peace.

SEBASTIAN. You were kneeled to and importuned° otherwise
By all of us, and the fair soul herself
Weighed between loathness and obedience at
Which end o' the beam should bow.° We have lost your son,
I fear, forever. Milan and Naples have
More widows in them of this business' making°
Than we bring men to comfort them.
The fault's your own.

ALONSO. So is the dear'st° o' the loss.

GONZALO. My lord Sebastian,
The truth you speak doth lack some gentleness
And time° to speak it in. You rub the sore
When you should bring the plaster.°

SEBASTIAN. Very well.

ANTONIO. And most chirurgeonly.°

GONZALO [*to Alonso*]. It is foul weather in us all, good sir,
When you are cloudy.

SEBASTIAN [*to Antonio*]. Fowl° weather?

ANTONIO [*to Sebastian*]. Very foul.

GONZALO. Had I plantation° of this isle, my lord—

ANTONIO [*to Sebastian*]. He'd sow 't with nettle seed.

SEBASTIAN. Or docks, or mallows.°

GONZALO. And were the king on 't, what would I do?

SEBASTIAN. Scape° being drunk for want° of wine.

GONZALO. I' the commonwealth I would by contraries°
Execute all things; for no kind of traffic°
Would I admit; no name of magistrate;
Letters° should not be known; riches, poverty,
And use of service,° none; contract, succession,°
Bourn, bound of land, tilth,° vineyard, none;

**119 is banished from your eye** is not constantly before your eye to serve as a reproachful reminder of what you have done **120 Who . . . on 't** i.e., your eye, which has good reason to weep because of this, or, Claribel, who has good reason to weep for it **121 importuned** urged, implored **122–124 the fair . . . bow** Claribel herself was poised uncertainly between unwillingness to marry and obedience to her father as to which end of the scales should sink, which should prevail **126 of . . . making** on account of this marriage and subsequent shipwreck **129 dear'st** heaviest, most costly **132 time** appropriate time **133 plaster** (A medical application.) **134 chirurgeonly** like a skilled surgeon. (Antonio mocks Gonzalo's medical analogy of a *plaster* applied curatively to a wound.) **136 Fowl** (with a pun on *foul,* returning to the imagery of lines 135–136) **137 plantation** colonization (with subsequent wordplay on the literal meaning, "planting") **138 docks, mallows** (Weeds used as antidotes for nettle stings.) **140 Scape** escape. **want** lack. (Sebastian jokes sarcastically that this hypothetical ruler would be saved from dissipation only by the barrenness of the island.) **141 by contraries** by what is directly opposite to usual custom **142 traffic** trade **144 Letters** learning **145 use of service** custom of employing servants. **succession** holding of property by right of inheritance **146 Bourn . . . tilth** boundaries, property limits, tillage of soil

No use of metal, corn,° or wine, or oil;
No occupation; all men idle, all,
And women too, but innocent and pure;
No sovereignty—

SEBASTIAN. Yet he would be king on 't.

ANTONIO. The latter end of his commonwealth forgets the beginning.

GONZALO. All things in common nature should produce
Without sweat or endeavor. Treason, felony,
Sword, pike,° knife, gun, or need of any engine°
Would I not have; but nature should bring forth,
Of its own kind, all foison,° all abundance,
To feed my innocent people.

SEBASTIAN. No marrying 'mong his subjects?

ANTONIO. None, man, all idle—whores and knaves.

GONZALO. I would with such perfection govern, sir,
T' excel the Golden Age.°

SEBASTIAN. 'Save° His Majesty!

ANTONIO. Long live Gonzalo!

GONZALO. And—do you mark me, sir?

ALONSO. Prithee, no more. Thou dost talk nothing to me.

GONZALO. I do well believe Your Highness, and did it to minister occasion° to these gentlemen, who are of such sensible° and nimble lungs that they always use° to laugh at nothing.

ANTONIO. 'Twas you we laughed at.

GONZALO. Who in this kind of merry fooling am nothing to you; so you may continue, and laugh at nothing still.

ANTONIO. What a blow was there given!

SEBASTIAN. An° it had not fallen flat-long.°

GONZALO. You are gentlemen of brave mettle;° you would lift the moon out of her sphere° if she would continue in it five weeks without changing.

*Enter Ariel* [*invisible*] *playing solemn music.*

SEBASTIAN. We would so, and then go a-batfowling.°

ANTONIO. Nay, good my lord, be not angry.

GONZALO. No, I warrant you, I will not adventure my discretion so weakly.° Will you laugh me asleep? For I am very heavy.°

ANTONIO. Go sleep, and hear us.°

**147 corn** grain **154 pike** lance. **engine** instrument of warfare **156 foison** plenty **161 the Golden Age** the age, according to Hesiod, when Cronus, or Saturn, ruled the world; an age of innocence and abundance. **'Save** God save **164–165 minister occasion** furnish opportunity. **sensible** sensitive. **166 use** are accustomed **171 An** if. **flat-long** with the flat of the sword, i.e., ineffectually. (Compare with "fallen flat.") **172 mettle** temperament, courage. (The sense of *metal,* indistinguishable as a form from *mettle,* continues the metaphor of the sword.) **173 sphere** orbit. (Literally, one of the concentric zones occupied by planets in Ptolemaic astronomy.) **175 a-batfowling** hunting birds at night with lantern and *bat,* or "stick"; also, gulling a simpleton. (Gonzalo is the simpleton, or fowl, and Sebastian will use the moon as his lantern.) **177–178 adventure . . . weakly** risk my reputation for discretion for so trivial a cause (by getting angry at these sarcastic fellows) **178 heavy** sleepy **179 Go . . . us** i.e., get ready for sleep, and we'll do our part by laughing

[*All sleep except Alonso, Sebastian, and Antonio.*]

ALONSO. What, all so soon asleep? I wish mine eyes
Would, with themselves, shut up my thoughts.° I find
They are inclined to do so.

SEBASTIAN. Please you, sir,
Do not omit° the heavy° offer of it.
It seldom visits sorrow; when it doth,
It is a comforter.

ANTONIO. We two, my lord,
Will guard your person while you take your rest,
And watch your safety.

ALONSO. Thank you. Wondrous heavy.

[*Alonso sleeps. Exit Ariel.*]

SEBASTIAN. What a strange drowsiness possesses them!

ANTONIO. It is the quality o' the climate.

SEBASTIAN. Why
Doth it not then our eyelids sink? I find not
Myself disposed to sleep.

ANTONIO. Nor I. My spirits are nimble.
They° fell together all, as by consent;°
They dropped, as by a thunderstroke. What might,
Worthy Sebastian, O, what might—? No more.
And yet methinks I see it in thy face,
What thou shouldst be. Th' occasion speaks thee,° and
My strong imagination sees a crown
Dropping upon thy head.

SEBASTIAN. What, art thou waking?

ANTONIO. Do you not hear me speak?

SEBASTIAN. I do, and surely
It is a sleepy° language, and thou speak'st
Out of thy sleep. What is it thou didst say?
This is a strange repose, to be asleep
With eyes wide open—standing, speaking, moving—
And yet so fast asleep.

ANTONIO. Noble Sebastian,
Thou lett'st thy fortune sleep—die, rather; wink'st°
Whiles thou art waking.

SEBASTIAN. Thou dost snore distinctly;°
There's meaning in thy snores.

ANTONIO. I am more serious than my custom. You
Must be so too if heed° me, which to do
Trebles thee o'er.°

SEBASTIAN. Well, I am standing water.°

**181 Would . . . thoughts** would shut off my melancholy brooding when they close themselves in sleep **183 omit** neglect. **heavy** drowsy **192 They** the sleepers. **consent** common agreement **197 occasion speaks thee** opportunity of the moment calls upon you, i.e., proclaims you usurper of Alonso's crown **200 sleepy** dreamlike, fantastic **205 wink'st** (you) shut your eyes **206 distinctly** articulately **209 if heed** if you heed **210 Trebles thee o'er** makes you three times as great and rich. **standing water** water that neither ebbs nor flows, at a standstill

ANTONIO. I'll teach you how to flow.
SEBASTIAN. Do so. To ebb°
Hereditary sloth° instructs me.
ANTONIO. O,
If you but knew how you the purpose cherish
Whiles thus you mock it!° How, in stripping it,
You more invest° it!° Ebbing men, indeed,
Most often do so near the bottom° run
By their own fear or sloth.
SEBASTIAN. Prithee, say on.
The setting° of thine eye and cheek proclaim
A matter° from thee, and a birth indeed
Which throes° thee much to yield.°
ANTONIO. Thus, sir:
Although this lord° of weak remembrance,° this
Who shall be of as little memory
When he is earthed,° hath here almost persuaded—
For he's a spirit of persuasion, only
Professes to persuade°—the King his son's alive,
'Tis as impossible that he's undrowned
As he that sleeps here swims.
SEBASTIAN. I have no hope
That he's undrowned.
ANTONIO. O, out of that "no hope"
What great hope have you! No hope that way° is
Another way so high a hope that even
Ambition cannot pierce a wink° beyond,
But doubt discovery there.° Will you grant with me
That Ferdinand is drowned?
SEBASTIAN. He's gone.
ANTONIO. Then tell me,
Who's the next heir of Naples?
SEBASTIAN. Claribel.

**211 ebb** recede, decline **212 Hereditary sloth** natural laziness and the position of younger brother, one who cannot inherit **213–214 If . . . mock it** if you only knew how much you really enhance the value of ambition even while your words mock your purpose **215 invest** clothe. (Antonio's paradox is that, by skeptically stripping away illusions, Sebastian can see the essence of a situation and the opportunity it presents or that, by disclaiming and deriding his purpose, Sebastian shows how valuable it really is.) **214–215 How . . . invest it** i.e., how the more you speak flippantly of ambition, the more you, in effect, affirm it. **216 the bottom** i.e., on which unadventurous men may go aground and miss the tide of fortune **218 setting** set expression (of earnestness) **219 matter** matter of importance **220 throes** causes pain, as in giving birth. **yield** give forth, speak about **221 this lord** i.e., Gonzalo. **remembrance** (1) power of remembering (2) being remembered after his death **223 earthed** buried **224–225 only . . . persuade** whose whole function (as a privy councillor) is to persuade **229 that way** i.e., in regard to Ferdinand's being saved **231 wink** glimpse **231–232 Ambition . . . there** ambition itself cannot see any further than that hope (of the crown), is unsure of finding anything to achieve beyond it or even there

ANTONIO. She that is Queen of Tunis; she that dwells
Ten leagues beyond man's life;° she that from Naples
Can have no note,° unless the sun were post°—
The Man i' the Moon's too slow—till newborn chins
Be rough and razorable;° she that from° whom
We all were sea-swallowed, though some cast° again,
And by that destiny to perform an act
Whereof what's past is prologue, what to come
In yours and my discharge.°

SEBASTIAN. What stuff is this? How say you?
'Tis true my brother's daughter's Queen of Tunis,
So is she heir of Naples, twixt which regions
There is some space.

ANTONIO. A space whose every cubit°
Seems to cry out, "How shall that Claribel
Measure us° back to Naples? Keep° in Tunis,
And let Sebastian wake."° Say this were death
That now hath seized them, why, they were no worse
Than now they are. There be° that can rule Naples
As well as he that sleeps, lords that can prate°
As amply and unnecessarily
As this Gonzalo. I myself could make
A chough of as deep chat.° O, that you bore
The mind that I do! What a sleep were this
For your advancement! Do you understand me?

SEBASTIAN. Methinks I do.

ANTONIO. And how does your content°
Tender° your own good fortune?

SEBASTIAN. I remember
You did supplant your brother Prospero.

ANTONIO. True.
And look how well my garments sit upon me,
Much feater° than before. My brother's servants
Were then my fellows. Now they are my men.

SEBASTIAN. But, for your conscience?

ANTONIO. Ay, sir, where lies that? If 'twere a kibe,°
'Twould put me to° my slipper; but I feel not
This deity in my bosom. Twenty consciences
That stand twixt me and Milan,° candied° be they°

**236 Ten . . . life** i.e., further than the journey of a lifetime **237 note** news, intimation. **post** messenger **239 razorable** ready for shaving. **from** on our voyage from **240 cast** were disgorged (with a pun on *casting* of parts for a play) **243 discharge** performance **247 cubit** ancient measure of length of about twenty inches **249 Measure us** i.e., traverse the cubits, find her way. **Keep** stay. (Addressed to Claribel.) **250 wake** i.e., to his good fortune **252 There be** there are those **253 prate** speak foolishly **255–256 I . . . chat** I could teach a jackdaw to talk as wisely, or, be such a garrulous talker myself **259 content** desire, inclination **260 Tender** regard, look after **263 feater** more becomingly, fittingly **266 kibe** chilblain, here a sore on the heel **267 put me to** oblige me to wear **269 Milan** the dukedom of Milan. **candied** frozen, congealed in crystalline form. **be they** may they be

And melt ere they molest!° Here lies your brother,
No better than the earth he lies upon,
If he were that which now he's like—that's dead,
Whom I, with this obedient steel, three inches of it,
Can lay to bed forever; whiles you, doing thus,°
To the perpetual wink° for aye° might put
This ancient morsel, this Sir Prudence, who
Should not° upbraid our course. For all the rest,
They'll take suggestion° as a cat laps milk;
They'll tell the clock° to any business that
We say befits the hour.

SEBASTIAN. Thy case, dear friend,
Shall be my precedent. As thou gott'st Milan,
I'll come by Naples. Draw thy sword. One stroke
Shall free thee from the tribute° which thou payest,
And I the king shall love thee.

ANTONIO. Draw together;
And when I rear my hand, do you the like
To fall it° on Gonzalo. [*They draw.*]

SEBASTIAN. O, but one word.
[*They talk apart.*]

*Enter Ariel [invisible], with music and song.*

ARIEL [*to Gonzalo*]. My master through his art foresees the danger
That you, his friend, are in, and sends me forth—
For else his project dies—to keep them living.
*Sings in Gonzalo's ear.*

While you here do snoring lie,
Open-eyed conspiracy
His time° doth take.
If of life you keep a care,
Shake off slumber, and beware.
Awake, awake!

ANTONIO. Then let us both be sudden.°

GONZALO [*waking*]. Now, good angels preserve the King!
[*The others wake.*]

ALONSO. Why, how now, ho, awake? Why are you drawn?
Wherefore this ghastly looking?

GONZALO. What's the matter?

SEBASTIAN. Whiles we stood here securing° your repose,
Even now, we heard a hollow burst of bellowing
Like bulls, or rather lions. Did 't not wake you?
It struck mine ear most terribly.

ALONSO. I heard nothing.

ANTONIO. O, 'twas a din to fright a monster's ear,

**270 molest** interfere **274 thus** similarly. (The actor makes a stabbing gesture.) **275 wink** sleep, closing of eyes. **aye** ever **277 Should not** would not then be able to **278 take suggestion** respond to prompting **279 tell the clock** i.e., agree, answer appropriately, chime **283 tribute** (See 1.2.113–124.) **286 fall it** let it fall **292 time** opportunity **296 sudden** quick **300 securing** standing guard over

To make an earthquake! Sure it was the roar
Of a whole herd of lions.

ALONSO. Heard you this, Gonzalo?

GONZALO. Upon mine honor, sir, I heard a humming,
And that a strange one too, which did awake me.
I shaked you, sir, and cried.° As mine eyes opened,
I saw their weapons drawn. There was a noise,
That's verily.° 'Tis best we stand upon our guard,
Or that we quit this place. Let's draw our weapons.

ALONSO. Lead off this ground, and let's make further search
For my poor son.

GONZALO. Heavens keep him from these beasts!
For he is, sure, i' th' island.

ALONSO. Lead away.

ARIEL [*aside*]. Prospero my lord shall know what I have done.
So, King, go safely on to seek thy son.

*Exeunt* [*separately*].

## **2.2** *Enter Caliban With a Burden of Wood. A Noise of Thunder Heard.*

CALIBAN. All the infections that the sun sucks up
From bogs, fens, flats,° on Prosper fall, and make him
By inchmeal° a disease! His spirits hear me,
And yet I needs must° curse. But they'll nor° pinch,
Fright me with urchin shows,° pitch me i' the mire,
Nor lead me, like a firebrand,° in the dark
Out of my way, unless he bid 'em. But
For every trifle are they set upon me,
Sometimes like apes, that mow° and chatter at me
And after bite me; then like hedgehogs, which
Lie tumbling in my barefoot way and mount
Their pricks at my footfall. Sometimes am I
All wound with° adders, who with cloven tongues
Do hiss me into madness.

*Enter Trinculo.*

Lo, now, lo!
Here comes a spirit of his, and to torment me
For bringing wood in slowly. I'll fall flat.
Perchance he will not mind° me. [*He lies down.*]

TRINCULO. Here's neither bush nor shrub to bear off° any weather at all. And another storm brewing; I hear it sing i' the wind. Yond same black cloud, yond huge one, looks like a foul bombard° that would

**310 cried** called out **312 verily** true

**2.2 Location: Another part of the island. 2 flats** swamps **3 By inchmeal** inch by inch **4 needs must** have to. **nor** neither **5 urchin shows** elvish apparitions shaped like hedgehogs **6 like a firebrand** they in the guise of a will-o'-the-wisp **9 mow** make faces **13 wound with** entwined by **17 mind** notice **18 bear off** keep off **20 foul bombard** dirty leather jug

shed his° liquor. If it should thunder as it did before, I know not where to hide my head. Yond same cloud cannot choose but fall by pailfuls. [*Seeing Caliban.*] What have we here, a man or a fish? Dead or alive? A fish, he smells like a fish; a very ancient and fishlike smell; a kind of not-of-the-newest Poor John.° A strange fish! Were I in England now, as once I was, and had but this fish painted,° not a holiday fool there but would give a piece of silver. There would this monster make a man.° Any strange beast there makes a man. When they will not give a doit° to relieve a lame beggar, they will lay out ten to see a dead Indian. Legged like a man, and his fins like arms! Warm, o' my troth!° I do now let loose my opinion, hold it° no longer: this is no fish, but an islander, that hath lately suffered° by a thunderbolt. [*Thunder.*] Alas, the storm is come again! My best way is to creep under his gaberdine.° There is no other shelter hereabout. Misery acquaints a man with strange bedfellows. I will here shroud° till the dregs° of the storm be past.

[*He creeps under Caliban's garment.*]

*Enter Stephano, singing,* [*a bottle in his hand*].

STEPHANO.

"I shall no more to sea, to sea,
Here shall I die ashore—"

This is a very scurvy tune to sing at a man's funeral. Well, here's my comfort. *Drinks.*

*(Sings.)*

"The master, the swabber,° the boatswain, and I,
The gunner and his mate,
Loved Mall, Meg, and Marian, and Margery,
But none of us cared for Kate.
For she had a tongue with a tang,°
Would cry to a sailor, 'Go hang!'
She loved not the savor of tar nor of pitch,
Yet a tailor might scratch her where'er she did itch.°
Then to sea, boys, and let her go hang!"

This is a scurvy tune too. But here's my comfort. *Drinks.*

CALIBAN. Do not torment me!° O!

STEPHANO. What's the matter?° Have we devils here? Do you put tricks upon 's° with savages and men of Ind,° ha? I have not scaped drowning to be afeard now of your four legs. For it hath been said,

**21 his** its **25 Poor John** salted fish, type of poor fare **27 painted** i.e., painted on a sign set up outside a booth or tent at a fair **28 make a man** (1) make one's fortune (2) be indistinguishable from an Englishman **29 doit** small coin **31 o' my troth** by my faith **32 hold it** hold it in **33 suffered** i.e., died **34 gaberdine** cloak, loose upper garment **36 shroud** take shelter. **dregs** i.e., last remains (as in a *bombard* or jug, line 20) **41 swabber** crew member whose job is to wash the decks **45 tang** sting **48 tailor . . . itch** (A dig at tailors for their supposed effeminacy and a bawdy suggestion of satisfying a sexual craving.) **51 Do . . . me** (Caliban assumes that one of Prospero's spirits has come to punish him.) **52 What's the matter** what's going on here? **52–53 put tricks upon 's** trick us with conjuring shows. **Ind** India

"As proper° a man as ever went on four legs° cannot make him give ground"; and it shall be said so again while Stephano breathes at'° nostrils.

CALIBAN. This spirit torments me! O!

STEPHANO. This is some monster of the isle with four legs, who hath got, as I take it, an ague.° Where the devil should he learn° our language? I will give him some relief, if it be but for that.° If I can recover° him and keep him tame and get to Naples with him, he's a present for any emperor that ever trod on neat's leather.°

CALIBAN. Do not torment me, prithee. I'll bring my wood home faster.

STEPHANO. He's in his fit now and does not talk after the wisest.° He shall taste of my bottle. If he have never drunk wine afore,° it will go near to° remove his fit. If I can recover° him and keep him tame, I will not take too much° for him. He shall pay for him that hath° him,° and that soundly.

CALIBAN. Thou dost me yet but little hurt; thou wilt anon,° I know it by thy trembling. Now Prosper works upon thee.

STEPHANO. Come on your ways. Open your mouth. Here is that which will give language to you, cat. Open your mouth.° This will shake your shaking, I can tell you, and that soundly. [*Giving Caliban a drink.*] You cannot tell who's your friend. Open your chaps° again.

TRINCULO. I should know that voice. It should be—but he is drowned, and these are devils. O, defend me!

STEPHANO. Four legs and two voices—a most delicate° monster! His forward voice now is to speak well of his friend; his backward voice° is to utter foul speeches and to detract. If all the wine in my bottle will recover him,° I will help° his ague. Come. [*Giving a drink.*] Amen! I will pour some in thy other mouth.

TRINCULO. Stephano!

STEPHANO. Doth thy other mouth call me?° Mercy, mercy! This is a devil, and no monster. I will leave him. I have no long spoon.°

TRINCULO. Stephano! If thou beest Stephano, touch me and speak to me, for I am Trinculo—be not afeard—thy good friend Trinculo.

STEPHANO. If thou beest Trinculo, come forth. I'll pull thee by the lesser legs. If any be Trinculo's legs, these are they. [*Pulling him out.*]

**55 proper** handsome. **four legs** (The conventional phrase would supply *two legs,* but the creature Stephano thinks he sees has four.) **57 at'** at the **60 ague** fever. (Probably both Caliban and Trinculo are quaking; see lines 51 and 71.) **should he learn** could he have learned **61 for that** i.e., for knowing our language **61–62 recover** restore **63 neat's leather** cowhide **65 after the wisest** in the wisest fashion **66 afore** before **67 go near to** be in a fair way to. **recover** restore **68 I will . . . much** i.e., no sum can be too much **69 hath** possesses, receives **68–69 He shall . . . hath him** i.e., anyone who wants him will have to pay dearly for him **70 anon** presently **73 cat . . . mouth** (Allusion to the proverb "Good liquor will make a cat speak.") **75 chaps** jaws **78 delicate** ingenious **79 backward voice** (Trinculo and Caliban are facing in opposite directions. Stephano supposes the monster to have a rear end that can emit *foul speeches* or foul-smelling wind at the monster's *other mouth,* line 82.) **80–81 If . . . him** even if it takes all the wine in my bottle to cure him **81 help** cure **84 call me** i.e., call me by name, know supernaturally who I am **85 long spoon** (Allusion to the proverb "He that sups with the devil has need of a long spoon.")

Thou art very Trinculo indeed! How cam'st thou to be the siege° of this mooncalf?° Can he vent° Trinculos?

TRINCULO. I took him to be killed with a thunderstroke. But art thou not drowned, Stephano? I hope now thou art not drowned. Is the storm overblown?° I hid me under the dead mooncalf's gaberdine for fear of the storm. And art thou living, Stephano? O Stephano, two Neapolitans scaped! [*He capers with Stephano.*]

STEPHANO. Prithee, do not turn me about. My stomach is not constant.°

CALIBAN. These be fine things, an if° they be not spirits.
That's a brave° god, and bears° celestial liquor.
I will kneel to him.

STEPHANO. How didst thou scape? How cam'st thou hither? Swear by this bottle how thou cam'st hither. I escaped upon a butt of sack° which the sailors heaved o'erboard—by this bottle,° which I made of the bark of a tree with mine own hands since° I was cast ashore.

CALIBAN [*kneeling*]. I'll swear upon that bottle to be thy true subject, for the liquor is not earthly.

STEPHANO. Here. Swear then how thou escapedst.

TRINCULO. Swum ashore, man, like a duck. I can swim like a duck, I'll be sworn.

STEPHANO. Here, kiss the book.° Though thou canst swim like a duck, thou art made like a goose.

[*Giving him a drink.*]

TRINCULO. O Stephano, hast any more of this?

STEPHANO. The whole butt, man. My cellar is in a rock by the seaside, where my wine is hid.—How now, mooncalf? How does thine ague?

CALIBAN. Hast thou not dropped from heaven?

STEPHANO. Out o' the moon, I do assure thee. I was the Man i' the Moon when time was.°

CALIBAN. I have seen thee in her, and I do adore thee.
My mistress showed me thee, and thy dog, and thy bush.°

STEPHANO. Come, swear to that. Kiss the book. I will furnish it anon with new contents. Swear.

[*Giving him a drink.*]

TRINCULO. By this good light,° this is a very shallow monster! I afeard of him? A very weak monster! The Man i' the Moon? A most poor credulous monster! Well drawn,° monster, in good sooth!°

CALIBAN [*to Stephano*]. I'll show thee every fertile inch o' th' island,
And I will kiss thy foot. I prithee, be my god.

**90 siege** excrement **91 mooncalf** monstrous or misshapen creature (whose deformity is caused by the malignant influence of the moon). **vent** excrete, defecate **94 overblown** blown over **97 not constant** unsteady **98 an if** if **99 brave** fine, magnificent. **bears** he carries **102 butt of sack** barrel of Canary wine **103 by this bottle** i.e., I swear by this bottle **104 since** after **110 book** i.e., bottle (but with ironic reference to the practice of kissing the Bible in swearing an oath; see *I'll be sworn* in lines 108–109) **118 when time was** once upon a time **120 dog . . . bush** (The Man in the Moon was popularly imagined to have with him a dog and a bush of thorn.) **123 By . . . light** by God's light, by this good light from heaven **125 Well drawn** well pulled (on the bottle). **in good sooth** truly, indeed

TRINCULO. By this light, a most perfidious and drunken monster! When 's god's asleep, he'll rob his bottle.°

CALIBAN. I'll kiss thy foot. I'll swear myself thy subject.

STEPHANO. Come on then. Down, and swear.

[*Caliban kneels.*]

TRINCULO. I shall laugh myself to death at this puppy-headed monster. A most scurvy monster! I could find in my heart to beat him—

STEPHANO. Come, kiss.

TRINCULO. But that the poor monster's in drink.° An abominable monster!

CALIBAN. I'll show thee the best springs. I'll pluck thee berries.
I'll fish for thee and get thee wood enough.
A plague upon the tyrant that I serve!
I'll bear him no more sticks, but follow thee,
Thou wondrous man.

TRINCULO. A most ridiculous monster, to make a wonder of a poor drunkard!

CALIBAN. I prithee, let me bring thee where crabs° grow,
And I with my long nails will dig thee pignuts,°
Show thee a jay's nest, and instruct thee how
To snare the nimble marmoset.° I'll bring thee
To clustering filberts, and sometimes I'll get thee
Young scamels° from the rock. Wilt thou go with me?

STEPHANO. I prithee now, lead the way without any more talking.—Trinculo, the King and all our company else° being drowned, we will inherit° here.—Here, bear my bottle.—Fellow Trinculo, we'll fill him by and by again.

CALIBAN (*sings drunkenly*).
Farewell, master, farewell, farewell!

TRINCULO. A howling monster; a drunken monster!

CALIBAN.
No more dams I'll make for fish,
Nor fetch in firing°
At requiring,
Nor scrape trenchering,° nor wash dish.
'Ban, 'Ban, Ca-Caliban
Has a new master. Get a new man!°
Freedom, high-day!° High-day, freedom! Freedom, high-day, freedom!

STEPHANO. O brave monster! Lead the way.

*Exeunt.*

**128–129 When . . . bottle** i.e., Caliban wouldn't even stop at robbing his god of his bottle if he could catch him asleep **135 in drink** drunk **144 crabs** crab apples, or perhaps crabs **145 pignuts** earthnuts, edible tuberous roots **147 marmoset** small monkey **149 scamels** (Possibly *seamews,* mentioned in a contemporary account, or shellfish, or perhaps from *squamelle,* "furnished with little scales." Contemporary French and Italian travel accounts report that the natives of Patagonia in South America ate small fish described as *fort scameux* and *squame.*) **151 else** in addition, besides ourselves **152 inherit** take possession **157 firing** firewood **159 trenchering** trenchers, wooden plates **161 Get a new man** (Addressed to Prospero.) **162 high-day** holiday

**3.1** *Enter Ferdinand, bearing a log.*

FERDINAND. There be some sports are painful, and their labor
Delight in them sets off.° Some kinds of baseness°
Are nobly undergone,° and most poor° matters
Point to rich ends. This my mean° task
Would be as heavy to me as odious, but°
The mistress which I serve quickens° what's dead
And makes my labors pleasures. O, she is
Ten times more gentle than her father's crabbed,
And he's composed of harshness. I must remove
Some thousands of these logs and pile them up,
Upon a sore injunction.° My sweet mistress
Weeps when she sees me work and says such baseness
Had never like executor.° I forget;°
But these sweet thoughts do even refresh my labors,
Most busy lest when I do it.°

*Enter Miranda; and Prospero [at a distance, unseen].*

MIRANDA. Alas now, pray you,
Work not so hard. I would the lightning had
Burnt up those logs that you are enjoined° to pile!
Pray, set it down and rest you. When this° burns,
'Twill weep° for having wearied you. My father
Is hard at study. Pray now, rest yourself.
He's safe for these° three hours.

FERDINAND. O most dear mistress,
The sun will set before I shall discharge°
What I must strive to do.

MIRANDA. If you'll sit down,
I'll bear your logs the while. Pray, give me that.
I'll carry it to the pile.

FERDINAND. No, precious creature,
I had rather crack my sinews, break my back,
Than you should such dishonor undergo
While I sit lazy by.

MIRANDA. It would become me
As well as it does you; and I should do it
With much more ease, for my good will is to it,
And yours it is against.

**3.1 Location: Before Prospero's cell.** **1–2 There . . . sets off** some pastimes are laborious, but the pleasure we get from them compensates for the effort. (Pleasure is *set off* by labor as a jewel is set off by its foil.) **2 baseness** menial activity **3 undergone** undertaken. **most poor** poorest **4 mean** lowly **5 but** were it not that **6 quickens** gives life to **11 sore injunction** severe command **13 Had . . . executor** i.e., was never before undertaken by so noble a being. **I forget** i.e., I forget that I'm supposed to be working, or, I forget my happiness, oppressed by my labor **15 Most . . . it** i.e., busy at my labor but with my mind on other things (?) (The line may be in need of emendation.) **17 enjoined** commanded **18 this** i.e., the log **19 weep** i.e., exude resin **21 these** the next **22 discharge** complete

PROSPERO [*aside*]. Poor worm, thou art infected!
This visitation° shows it.

MIRANDA. You look wearily.

FERDINAND. No, noble mistress, 'tis fresh morning with me
When you are by° at night. I do beseech you—
Chiefly that I might set it in my prayers—
What is your name?

MIRANDA. Miranda.—O my father,
I have broke your hest° to say so.

FERDINAND. Admired Miranda!°
Indeed the top of admiration, worth
What's dearest° to the world! Full many a lady
I have eyed with best regard,° and many a time
The harmony of their tongues hath into bondage
Brought my too diligent° ear. For several° virtues
Have I liked several women, never any
With so full soul but some defect in her
Did quarrel with the noblest grace she owed°
And put it to the foil.° But you, O you,
So perfect and so peerless, are created
Of° every creature's best!

MIRANDA. I do not know
One of my sex; no woman's face remember,
Save, from my glass, mine own. Nor have I seen
More that I may call men than you, good friend,
And my dear father. How features are abroad°
I am skilless° of; but, by my modesty,°
The jewel in my dower, I would not wish
Any companion in the world but you;
Nor can imagination form a shape,
Besides yourself, to like of.° But I prattle
Something° too wildly, and my father's precepts
I therein do forget.

FERDINAND. I am in my condition°
A prince, Miranda; I do think, a king—
I would,° not so!—and would no more endure
This wooden slavery° than to suffer
The flesh-fly° blow° my mouth. Hear my soul speak:
The very instant that I saw you did

**32 visitation** (1) Miranda's visit to Ferdinand (2) visitation of the plague, i.e., infection of love **34 by** nearby **37 hest** command. **Admired Miranda** (Her name means "to be admired or wondered at.") **39 dearest** most treasured **40 best regard** thoughtful and approving attention **42 diligent** attentive. **several** various (also in line 43) **45 owed** owned **46 put . . . foil** (1) overthrew it (as in wrestling) (2) served as a *foil,* or "contrast," to set it off **48 Of** out of **52 How . . . abroad** what people look like in other places **53 skilless** ignorant. **modesty** virginity **57 like of** be pleased with, be fond of **58 Something** somewhat **59 condition** rank **61 would** wish (it were) **62 wooden slavery** being compelled to carry wood **63 flesh-fly** insect that deposits its eggs in dead flesh. **blow** befoul with fly eggs

My heart fly to your service, there resides
To make me slave to it, and for your sake
Am I this patient log-man.

MIRANDA. Do you love me?

FERDINAND. O heaven, O earth, bear witness to this sound,
And crown what I profess with kind event°
If I speak true! If hollowly,° invert°
What best is boded° me to mischief!° I
Beyond all limit of what° else i' the world
Do love, prize, honor you.

MIRANDA [*weeping*]. I am a fool
To weep at what I am glad of.

PROSPERO [*aside*]. Fair encounter
Of two most rare affections! Heavens rain grace
On that which breeds between 'em!

FERDINAND. Wherefore weep you?

MIRANDA. At mine unworthiness, that dare not offer
What I desire to give, and much less take
What I shall die° to want.° But this is trifling,
And all the more it seeks to hide itself
The bigger bulk it shows. Hence, bashful cunning,°
And prompt me, plain and holy innocence!
I am your wife, if you will marry me;
If not, I'll die your maid.° To be your fellow°
You may deny me, but I'll be your servant
Whether you will° or no.

FERDINAND. My mistress,° dearest,
And I thus humble ever.

MIRANDA. My husband, then?

FERDINAND. Ay, with a heart as willing°
As bondage e'er of freedom. Here's my hand.

MIRANDA [*clasping his hand*]. And mine, with my heart in 't. And now farewell
Till half an hour hence.

FERDINAND. A thousand thousand!°

*Exeunt* [*Ferdinand and Miranda, separately*].

PROSPERO. So glad of this as they I cannot be,
Who are surprised with all;° but my rejoicing
At nothing can be more. I'll to my book,
For yet ere suppertime must I perform
Much business appertaining.°

*Exit.*

**69 kind event** favorable outcome **70 hollowly** insincerely, falsely. **invert** turn **71 boded** in store for. **mischief** harm **72 what** whatever **79 die** (Probably with an unconscious sexual meaning that underlies all of lines 77–81.) **to want** through lacking **81 bashful cunning** coyness **84 maid** handmaiden, servant. **fellow** mate, equal **86 will** desire it. **My mistress** i.e., the woman I adore and serve (not an illicit sexual partner) **89 willing** desirous **92 A thousand thousand** i.e., a thousand thousand farewells **94 with all** by everything that has happened, or, *withal,* "with it" **97 appertaining** related to this

## 3.2 *Enter Caliban, Stephano, and Trinculo.*

STEPHANO. Tell not me. When the butt is out,° we will drink water, not a drop before. Therefore bear up and board 'em.° Servant monster, drink to me.

TRINCULO. Servant monster? The folly of° this island! They say there's but five upon this isle. We are three of them; if th' other two be brained° like us, the state totters.

STEPHANO. Drink, servant monster, when I bid thee. Thy eyes are almost set° in thy head. [*Giving a drink.*]

TRINCULO. Where should they be set° else? He were a brave° monster indeed if they were set in his tail.

STEPHANO. My man-monster hath drowned his tongue in sack. For my part, the sea cannot drown me. I swam, ere I could recover° the shore, five and thirty leagues° off and on.° By this light,° thou shalt be my lieutenant, monster, or my standard.°

TRINCULO. Your lieutenant, if you list;° he's no standard.°

STEPHANO. We'll not run,° Monsieur Monster.

TRINCULO. Nor go° neither, but you'll lie° like dogs and yet say nothing neither.

STEPHANO. Mooncalf, speak once in thy life, if thou beest a good mooncalf.

CALIBAN. How does thy honor? Let me lick thy shoe.
I'll not serve him. He is not valiant.

TRINCULO. Thou liest, most ignorant monster, I am in case to jostle a constable.° Why, thou debauched° fish, thou, was there ever man a coward that hath drunk so much sack° as I today? Wilt thou tell a monstrous lie, being but half a fish and half a monster?

CALIBAN. Lo, how he mocks me! Wilt thou let him, my lord?

TRINCULO. "Lord," quoth he? That a monster should be such a natural!°

CALIBAN. Lo, lo, again! Bite him to death, I prithee.

STEPHANO. Trinculo, keep a good tongue in your head. If you prove a mutineer—the next tree!° The poor monster's my subject, and he shall not suffer indignity.

**3.2 Location: Another part of the island. 1 out** empty **2 bear . . . 'em** (Stephano uses the terminology of maneuvering at sea and boarding a vessel under attack as a way of urging an assault on the liquor supply.) **4 folly of** i.e., stupidity found on **5–6 be brained** are endowed with intelligence **8 set** fixed in a drunken stare, or, sunk, like the sun **9 set** placed. **brave** fine, splendid **12 recover** gain, reach **13 leagues** units of distance, each equaling about three miles. **off and on** intermittently. **By this light** (An oath: by the light of the sun.) **14 standard** standard-bearer, ensign (as distinguished from *lieutenant,* lines 14–15) **15 list** prefer. **no standard** i.e., not able to stand up **16 run** (1) retreat (2) urinate (taking Trinculo's *standard,* line 15, in the old sense of "conduit") **17 go** walk. **lie** (1) tell lies (2) lie prostrate (3) excrete **23–24 in case . . . constable** i.e., in fit condition, made valiant by drink, to taunt or challenge the police **24 debauched** (1) seduced away from proper service and allegiance (2) depraved **25 sack** Spanish white wine **28 natural** (1) idiot (2) natural as opposed to unnatural, monsterlike **31 the next tree** i.e., you'll hang

CALIBAN. I thank my noble lord. Wilt thou be pleased
To hearken once again to the suit I made to thee?

STEPHANO. Marry,° will I. Kneel and repeat it. I will stand, and so shall Trinculo. [*Caliban kneels.*]

*Enter Ariel, invisible.°*

CALIBAN. As I told thee before, I am subject to a tyrant,
A sorcerer, that by his cunning hath
Cheated me of the island.

ARIEL [*mimicking Trinculo*]. Thou liest.

CALIBAN.
Thou liest, thou jesting monkey, thou!
I would my valiant master would destroy thee.
I do not lie.

STEPHANO. Trinculo, if you trouble him any more in 's tale, by this hand, I will supplant° some of your teeth.

TRINCULO. Why, I said nothing.

STEPHANO. Mum, then, and no more.—Proceed.

CALIBAN. I say by sorcery he got this isle;
From me he got it. If thy greatness will
Revenge it on him—for I know thou dar'st,
But this thing° dare not—

STEPHANO. That's most certain.

CALIBAN. Thou shalt be lord of it, and I'll serve thee.

STEPHANO. How now shall this be compassed?° Canst thou bring me to the party?

CALIBAN. Yea, yea, my lord. I'll yield him thee asleep,
Where thou mayst knock a nail into his head.

ARIEL. Thou liest; thou canst not.

CALIBAN. What a pied ninny's° this! Thou scurvy patch!°—
I do beseech thy greatness, give him blows
And take his bottle from him. When that's gone
He shall drink naught but brine, for I'll not show him
Where the quick freshes° are.

STEPHANO. Trinculo, run into no further danger. Interrupt the monster one word further° and, by this hand, I'll turn my mercy out o' doors° and make a stockfish° of thee.

TRINCULO. Why, what did I? I did nothing. I'll go farther off.°

STEPHANO. Didst thou not say he lied?

ARIEL. Thou liest.

STEPHANO. Do I so? Take thou that. [*He beats Trinculo.*]
As you like this, give me the lie° another time.

TRINCULO. I did not give the lie. Out o' your wits and hearing too? A pox

**35 Marry** i.e., indeed. (Originally an oath, "by the Virgin Mary.") **36 s.d. invisible** i.e., wearing a garment to connote invisibility, as at 1.2.377 **45 supplant** uproot, displace **51 this thing** i.e., Trinculo **54 compassed** achieved **59 pied ninny** fool in motley. **patch** fool **63 quick freshes** running springs **65 one word further** i.e., one more time **65–66 turn . . . doors** i.e., forget about being merciful. **66 stockfish** dried cod beaten before cooking **67 off** away **71 give me the lie** call me a liar to my face

o' your bottle! This can sack and drinking do. A murrain° on your monster, and the devil take your fingers!

CALIBAN. Ha, ha, ha!

STEPHANO. Now, forward with your tale. [*To Trinculo.*] Prithee, stand further off.

CALIBAN. Beat him enough. After a little time
I'll beat him too.

STEPHANO. Stand farther.—Come, proceed.

CALIBAN. Why, as I told thee, 'tis a custom with him
I' th' afternoon to sleep. There thou mayst brain him,
Having first seized his books; or with a log
Batter his skull, or paunch° him with a stake,
Or cut his weasand° with thy knife. Remember
First to possess his books, for without them
He's but a sot,° as I am, nor hath not
One spirit to command. They all do hate him
As rootedly as I. Burn but his books.
He has brave utensils°—for so he calls them—
Which, when he has a house, he'll deck withal.°
And that most deeply to consider is
The beauty of his daughter. He himself
Calls her a nonpareil. I never saw a woman
But only Sycorax my dam and she;
But she as far surpasseth Sycorax
As great'st does least.

STEPHANO. Is it so brave° a lass?

CALIBAN. Ay, lord. She will become° thy bed, I warrant,
And bring thee forth brave brood.

STEPHANO. Monster, I will kill this man. His daughter and I will be king and queen—save Our Graces!—and Trinculo and thyself shall be viceroys. Dost thou like the plot, Trinculo?

TRINCULO. Excellent.

STEPHANO. Give me thy hand. I am sorry I beat thee; but, while thou liv'st, keep a good tongue in thy head.

CALIBAN. Within this half hour will he be asleep.
Wilt thou destroy him then?

STEPHANO. Ay, on mine honor.

ARIEL [*aside*]. This will I tell my master.

CALIBAN. Thou mak'st me merry; I am full of pleasure.
Let us be jocund.° Will you troll the catch°
You taught me but whilere?°

STEPHANO. At thy request, monster, I will do reason, any reason.°—Come on, Trinculo, let us sing. *Sings.*

**73 murrain** plague (Literally, a cattle disease.) **84 paunch** stab in the belly **85 weasand** windpipe **87 sot** fool **90 brave utensils** fine furnishings **91 deck withal** furnish it with **98 brave** splendid, attractive **99 become** suit (sexually) **112 jocund** jovial, merry. **troll the catch** sing the round **113 but whilere** only a short time ago **114 reason, any reason** anything reasonable

"Flout° 'em and scout° 'em
And scout 'em and flout 'em!
Thought is free."

CALIBAN. That's not the tune.

*Ariel plays the tune on a tabor° and pipe.*

STEPHANO. What is this same?

TRINCULO. This is the tune of our catch, played by the picture of Nobody.°

STEPHANO. If thou beest a man, show thyself in thy likeness. If thou beest a devil, take 't as thou list.°

TRINCULO. O, forgive me my sins!

STEPHANO. He that dies pays all debts.° I defy thee. Mercy upon us!

CALIBAN. Art thou afeard?

STEPHANO. No, monster, not I.

CALIBAN. Be not afeard. The isle is full of noises,
Sounds, and sweet airs, that give delight and hurt not.
Sometimes a thousand twangling instruments
Will hum about mine ears, and sometimes voices
That, if I then had waked after long sleep,
Will make me sleep again; and then, in dreaming,
The clouds methought would open and show riches
Ready to drop upon me, that when I waked
I cried to dream° again.

STEPHANO. This will prove a brave kingdom to me, where I shall have my music for nothing.

CALIBAN. When Prospero is destroyed.

STEPHANO. That shall be by and by.° I remember the story.

TRINCULO. The sound is going away. Let's follow it, and after do our work.

STEPHANO. Lead, monster; we'll follow. I would I could see this taborer! He lays it on.°

TRINCULO. Wilt come? I'll follow, Stephano.

*Exeunt [following Ariel's music].*

**3.3** *Enter Alonso, Sebastian, Antonio, Gonzalo, Adrian, Francisco, etc.*

GONZALO. By 'r lakin,° I can go no further, sir.
My old bones aches. Here's a maze trod indeed
Through forthrights and meanders!° By your patience,
I needs must° rest me.

**116 Flout** scoff at. **scout** deride **119 s.d. tabor** small drum **121–122 picture of Nobody** (Refers to a familiar figure with head, arms, and legs but no trunk.) **124 take 't . . . list** i.e., take my defiance as you please, as best you can **126 He . . . debts** i.e., if I have to die, at least that will be the end of all my woes and obligations **137 to dream** desirous of dreaming **141 by and by** very soon **145 lays it on** i.e., plays the drum vigorously

**3.3 Location: Another part of the island. 1 By 'r lakin** by our Ladykin, by our Lady **3 forthrights and meanders** paths straight and crooked **4 needs must** have to

ALONSO. Old lord, I cannot blame thee,
Who am myself attached° with weariness,
To th' dulling of my spirits.° Sit down and rest.
Even here I will put off my hope, and keep it
No longer for° my flatterer. He is drowned
Whom thus we stray to find, and the sea mocks
Our frustrate° search on land. Well, let him go.
[*Alonso and Gonzalo sit.*]

ANTONIO [*aside to Sebastian*]. I am right° glad that he's so out of hope.
Do not, for° one repulse, forgo the purpose
That you resolved t' effect.

SEBASTIAN [*to Antonio*]. The next advantage
Will we take throughly.°

ANTONIO [*to Sebastian*]. Let it be tonight,
For, now° they are oppressed with travel,° they
Will not, nor cannot, use° such vigilance
As when they are fresh.

SEBASTIAN [*to Antonio*]. I say tonight. No more.

*Solemn and strange music; and Prospero on the top,° invisible.*

ALONSO. What harmony is this? My good friends, hark!

GONZALO. Marvelous sweet music!

*Enter several strange shapes, bringing in a banquet, and dance about it with gentle actions of salutations; and, inviting the King, etc., to eat, they depart.*

ALONSO. Give us kind keepers,° heavens! What were these?

SEBASTIAN. A living° drollery.° Now I will believe
That there are unicorns; that in Arabia
There is one tree, the phoenix'° throne, one phoenix
At this hour reigning there.

ANTONIO. I'll believe both;
And what does else want credit,° come to me
And I'll be sworn 'tis true. Travelers ne'er did lie,
Though fools at home condemn 'em.

GONZALO. If in Naples
I should report this now, would they believe me
If I should say I saw such islanders?
For, certes,° these are people of the island,
Who, though they are of monstrous° shape, yet note,
Their manners are more gentle, kind, than of
Our human generation you shall find

**5 attached** seized **6 To . . . spirits** to the point of being dull-spirited **8 for** as **10 frustrate** frustrated **11 right** very **12 for** because of **14 throughly** thoroughly **15 now** now that. **travel** (Spelled *trauaile* in the Folio and carrying the sense of labor as well as traveling.) **16 use** apply **17 s.d. on the top** at some high point of the tiring-house or the theater, on a third level above the gallery **20 kind keepers** guardian angels **21 living** with live actors. **drollery** comic entertainment, caricature, puppet show **23 phoenix** mythical bird consumed to ashes every five hundred to six hundred years, only to be renewed into another cycle **25 want credit** lack credence **30 certes** certainly **31 monstrous** unnatural

Many, nay, almost any.
PROSPERO [*aside*]. Honest lord,
Thou hast said well, for some of you there present
Are worse than devils.
ALONSO. I cannot too much muse°
Such shapes, such gesture, and such sound, expressing—
Although they want° the use of tongue—a kind
Of excellent dumb discourse.
PROSPERO [*aside*]. Praise in departing.°
FRANCISCO. They vanished strangely.
SEBASTIAN. No matter, since
They have left their viands° behind, for we have stomachs.°
Will 't please you taste of what is here?
ALONSO. Not I.
GONZALO. Faith, sir, you need not fear. When we were boys,
Who would believe that there were mountaineers°
Dewlapped° like bulls, whose throats had hanging at 'em
Wallets° of flesh? Or that there were such men
Whose heads stood in their breasts?° Which now we find
Each putter-out of five for one° will bring us
Good warrant° of.
ALONSO. I will stand to° and feed,
Although my last°—no matter, since I feel
The best° is past. Brother, my lord the Duke,
Stand to, and do as we. [*They approach the table.*]

*Thunder and lightning. Enter Ariel, like a harpy,° claps his wings upon the table, and with a quaint device° the banquet vanishes.°*

ARIEL. You are three men of sin, whom Destiny—
That hath to instrument this lower world
And what is in 't—the never-surfeited sea
Hath caused to belch up you,° and on this island
Where man doth not inhabit, you 'mongst men
Being most unfit to live. I have made you mad;

**36 muse** wonder at **38 want** lack **39 Praise in departing** i.e., save your praise until the end of the performance. (Proverbial.) **41 viands** provisions. **stomachs** appetites **44 mountaineers** mountain dwellers **45 Dewlapped** having a dewlap, or fold of skin hanging from the neck, like cattle **46 Wallets** pendent folds of skin, wattles **47 in their breasts** (i.e., like the Anthropophagi described in *Othello,* 1.3.146) **48 putter-out . . . one** one who invests money or gambles on the risks of travel on the condition that the traveler who returns safely is to receive five times the amount deposited; hence, any traveler **49 Good warrant** assurance. **stand to** fall to; take the risk **50 Although my last** even if this were to be my last meal **51 best** best part of life **52 s.d. harpy** a fabulous monster with a woman's face and breasts and a vulture's body, supposed to be a minister of divine vengeance. **quaint device** ingenious stage contrivance. **the banquet vanishes** i.e., the food vanishes; the table remains until line 82 **53–56 whom . . . up you** you whom Destiny, controller of the sublunary world as its instrument, has caused the ever hungry sea to belch up

And even with suchlike valor° men hang and drown
Their proper° selves.

*[Alonso, Sebastian, and Antonio draw their swords.]*

You fools! I and my fellows
Are ministers of Fate. The elements
Of whom° your swords are tempered° may as well
Wound the loud winds, or with bemocked-at° stabs
Kill the still-closing° waters, as diminish
One dowl° that's in my plume. My fellow ministers
Are like° invulnerable. If° you could hurt,
Your swords are now too massy° for your strengths
And will not be uplifted. But remember—
For that's my business to you—that you three
From Milan did supplant good Prospero;
Exposed unto the sea, which hath requit° it,
Him and his innocent child; for which foul deed
The powers, delaying, not forgetting, have
Incensed the seas and shores, yea, all the creatures,
Against your peace. Thee of thy son, Alonso,
They have bereft; and do pronounce by me
Ling'ring perdition,° worse than any death
Can be at once, shall step by step attend
You and your ways; whose° wraths to guard you from—
Which here, in this most desolate isle, else° falls
Upon your heads—is nothing° but heart's sorrow
And a clear° life ensuing.

*He vanishes in thunder; then, to soft music, enter the shapes again, and dance, with mocks and mows,° and carrying out the table.*

PROSPERO. Bravely° the figure of this harpy hast thou
Performed, my Ariel; a grace it had devouring.°
Of my instruction hast thou nothing bated°
In what thou hadst to say. So,° with good life°
And observation strange,° my meaner° ministers
Their several kinds° have done. My high charms work,
And these mine enemies are all knit up

**59 suchlike valor** i.e., the reckless valor derived from madness **60 proper** own **62 whom** which. **tempered** composed and hardened **63 bemocked-at** scorned **64 still-closing** always closing again when parted **65 dowl** soft, fine feather **66 like** likewise, similarly. **If** even if **67 massy** heavy **71 requit** requited, avenged **77 perdition** ruin, destruction **79 whose** (Refers to the heavenly powers.) **80 else** otherwise **81 is nothing** there is no way **82 clear** unspotted, innocent. **s.d. mocks and mows** mocking gestures and grimaces **83 Bravely** finely, dashingly **84 a grace . . . devouring** i.e., you gracefully caused the banquet to disappear as if you had consumed it (with puns on *grace,* meaning "gracefulness" and "a blessing on the meal," and on *devouring,* meaning "a literal eating" and "an all-consuming or ravishing grace") **85 bated** abated, omitted **86 So** in the same fashion. **good life** faithful reproduction **87 observation strange** exceptional attention to detail. **meaner** i.e., subordinate to Ariel **88 several kinds** individual parts

In their distractions.° They now are in my power;
And in these fits I leave them, while I visit
Young Ferdinand, whom they suppose is drowned,
And his and mine loved darling.

[*Exit above.*]

GONZALO. I' the name of something holy, sir, why° stand you
In this strange stare?

ALONSO. O, it° is monstrous, monstrous!
Methought the billows° spoke and told me of it;
The winds did sing it to me, and the thunder,
That deep and dreadful organ pipe, pronounced
The name of Prosper; it did bass my trespass.°
Therefor° my son i' th' ooze is bedded; and
I'll seek him deeper than e'er plummet° sounded,°
And with him there lie mudded.

*Exit.*

SEBASTIAN. But one fiend at a time,
I'll fight their legions o'er.°

ANTONIO. I'll be thy second.

*Exeunt* [*Sebastian and Antonio*].

GONZALO. All three of them are desperate.° Their great guilt,
Like poison given to work a great time after,
Now 'gins to bite the spirits.° I do beseech you,
That are of suppler joints, follow them swiftly
And hinder them from what this ecstasy°
May now provoke them to.

ADRIAN. Follow, I pray you.

*Exeunt omnes.*

## 4.1 *Enter Prospero, Ferdinand, and Miranda.*

PROSPERO. If I have too austerely punished you,
Your compensation makes amends, for I
Have given you here a third° of mine own life,
Or that for which I live; who once again
I tender° to thy hand. All thy vexations
Were but my trials of thy love, and thou
Hast strangely° stood the test. Here, afore heaven,

**90 distractions** trancelike state **94 why** (Gonzalo was not addressed in Ariel's speech to the *three men of sin,* line 53, and is not, as they are, in a maddened state; see lines 105–107.) **95 it** i.e., my sin (also in line 96) **96 billows** waves **99 bass my trespass** proclaim my trespass like a bass note in music **100 Therefor** in consequence of that **101 plummet** a lead weight attached to a line for testing depth. **sounded** probed, tested the depth of **104 o'er** one after another **105 desperate** despairing and reckless **107 bite the spirits** sap their vital powers through anguish **109 ecstasy** mad frenzy

**4.1 Location: Before Prospero's cell. 3 a third** i.e., Miranda, into whose education Prospero has put a third of his life (?) or who represents a large part of what he cares about, along with his dukedom and his learned study (?) **5 tender** offer

I ratify this my rich gift. O Ferdinand,
Do not smile at me that I boast her off,°
For thou shalt find she will outstrip all praise
And make it halt° behind her.

FERDINAND. I do believe it
Against an oracle.°

PROSPERO. Then, as my gift and thine own acquisition
Worthily purchased, take my daughter. But
If thou dost break her virgin-knot before
All sanctimonious° ceremonies may
With full and holy rite be ministered,
No sweet aspersion° shall the heavens let fall
To make this contract grow; but barren hate,
Sour-eyed disdain, and discord shall bestrew
The union of your bed with weeds° so loathly
That you shall hate it both. Therefore take heed,
As Hymen's lamps shall light you.°

FERDINAND. As I hope
For quiet days, fair issue,° and long life,
With such love as 'tis now, the murkiest den,
The most opportune place, the strong'st suggestion°
Our worser genius° can,° shall never melt
Mine honor into lust, to° take away
The edge° of that day's celebration
When I shall think or° Phoebus' steeds are foundered°
Or Night kept chained below.

PROSPERO. Fairly spoke.
Sit then and talk with her. She is thine own.
[*Ferdinand and Miranda sit and talk together.*]
What,° Ariel! My industrious servant, Ariel!

*Enter Ariel.*

ARIEL. What would my potent master? Here I am.

PROSPERO. Thou and thy meaner fellows° your last service
Did worthily perform, and I must use you
In such another trick.° Go bring the rabble,°
O'er whom I give thee power, here to this place.

**7 strangely** extraordinarily **9 boast her off** i.e., praise her so, or, perhaps an error for "boast of her"; the Folio reads "boast her of" **11 halt** limp **12 Against an oracle** even if an oracle should declare otherwise **16 sanctimonious** sacred **18 aspersion** dew, shower **21 weeds** (in place of the flowers customarily strewn on the marriage bed) **23 As . . . you** i.e., as you long for happiness and concord in your marriage. (Hymen was the Greek and Roman god of marriage; his symbolic torches, the wedding torches, were supposed to burn brightly for a happy marriage and smokily for a troubled one.) **24 issue** offspring **26 suggestion** temptation **27 worser genius** evil genius, or, evil attendant spirit. **can** is capable of **28 to** so as to **29 edge** keen enjoyment, sexual ardor **30 or** either. **foundered** broken down, made lame. (Ferdinand will wait impatiently for the bridal night.) **33 What** now then **35 meaner fellows** subordinates **37 trick** device. **rabble** band, i.e., the *meaner fellows* of line 35

Incite them to quick motion, for I must
Bestow upon the eyes of this young couple
Some vanity° of mine art. It is my promise,
And they expect it from me.

ARIEL. Presently?°

PROSPERO. Ay, with a twink.°

ARIEL.
Before you can say "Come" and "Go,"
And breathe twice, and cry "So, so,"
Each one, tripping on his toe,
Will be here with mop and mow.°
Do you love me, master? No?

PROSPERO. Dearly, my delicate Ariel. Do not approach
Till thou dost hear me call.

ARIEL. Well; I conceive.°

*Exit.*

PROSPERO. Look thou be true;° do not give dalliance
Too much the rein. The strongest oaths are straw
To the fire i' the blood. Be more abstemious,
Or else good night° your vow!

FERDINAND. I warrant° you, sir,
The white cold virgin snow upon my heart°
Abates the ardor of my liver.°

PROSPERO. Well.
Now come, my Ariel! Bring a corollary,°
Rather than want° a spirit. Appear, and pertly!°—
No tongue!° All eyes! Be silent. *Soft music.*

*Enter Iris.°*

IRIS. Ceres,° most bounteous lady, thy rich leas°
Of wheat, rye, barley, vetches,° oats, and peas;
Thy turfy mountains, where live nibbling sheep,
And flat meads° thatched with stover,° them to keep;
Thy banks with pionèd and twillèd° brims,
Which spongy° April at thy hest° betrims
To make cold nymphs chaste crowns; and thy broom groves,°
Whose shadow the dismissèd bachelor° loves,

**41 vanity** (1) illusion (2) trifle (3) desire for admiration, conceit **42 Presently** immediately **43 with a twink** in the twinkling of an eye **47 mop and mow** gestures and grimaces **50 conceive** understand **51 true** true to your promise **54 good night** i.e., say good-bye to. **warrant** guarantee **55 The white . . . heart** i.e., the ideal of chastity and consciousness of Miranda's chaste innocence enshrined in my heart **56 liver** (as the presumed seat of the passions) **57 corollary** surplus, extra supply **58 want** lack. **pertly** briskly **59 No tongue** all the beholders are to be silent (lest the spirits vanish). **s.d. Iris** goddess of the rainbow and Juno's messenger **60 Ceres** goddess of the generative power of nature. **leas** meadows **61 vetches** plants for forage, fodder **63 meads** meadows. **stover** winter fodder for cattle **64 pionèd and twillèd** undercut by the swift current and protected by roots and branches that tangle to form a barricade **65 spongy** wet. **hest** command **66 broom groves** clumps of broom, gorse, yellow-flowered shrub

Being lass-lorn; thy poll-clipped° vineyard;
And thy sea marge,° sterile and rocky hard,
Where thou thyself dost air:° the queen o' the sky,°
Whose watery arch° and messenger am I,
Bids thee leave these, and with her sovereign grace,
*Juno descends*° [*slowly in her car*].
Here on this grass plot, in this very place,
To come and sport. Her peacocks° fly amain.°
Approach, rich Ceres, her to entertain.°

*Enter Ceres.*

CERES. Hail, many-colored messenger, that ne'er
Dost disobey the wife of Jupiter,
Who with thy saffron° wings upon my flowers
Diffusest honeydrops, refreshing showers,
And with each end of thy blue bow° dost crown
My bosky° acres and my unshrubbed down,°
Rich scarf° to my proud earth. Why hath thy queen
Summoned me hither to this short-grassed green?

IRIS. A contract of true love to celebrate,
And some donation freely to estate°
On the blest lovers.

CERES. Tell me, heavenly bow,
If Venus or her son,° as° thou dost know,
Do now attend the Queen? Since they did plot
The means that° dusky° Dis my daughter got,°
Her and her° blind boy's scandaled° company
I have forsworn.

IRIS. Of her society°
Be not afraid. I met her deity°
Cutting the clouds towards Paphos,° and her son
Dove-drawn° with her. Here thought they to have done°
Some wanton charm° upon this man and maid,
Whose vows are that no bed-right shall be paid
Till Hymen's torch be lighted; but in vain.
Mars's hot minion° is returned° again;

**67 dismissèd bachelor** rejected male lover **68 poll-clipped** pruned, lopped at the top, or *pole-clipped,* "hedged in with poles" **69 sea marge** shore **70 thou . . . air** you take the air, go for walks. **queen o' the sky** i.e., Juno **71 watery arch** rainbow **72 s.d. Juno descends** i.e., starts her descent from the "heavens" above the stage (?) **74 peacocks** birds sacred to Juno and used to pull her chariot. **amain** with full speed **75 entertain** receive **78 saffron** yellow **80 bow** i.e., rainbow **81 bosky** wooded. **unshrubbed down** open upland **82 scarf** (The rainbow is like a colored silk band adorning the earth.) **85 estate** bestow **87 son** i.e., Cupid. **as** as far as **89 that** whereby. **dusky** dark. **Dis . . . got** (Pluto, or *Dis,* god of the infernal regions, carried off Proserpina, daughter of Ceres, to be his bride in Hades.) **90 her** i.e., Venus's. **scandaled** scandalous **91 society** company **92 her deity** i.e., Her Highness **93 Paphos** place on the island of Cyprus, sacred to Venus **94 Dove-drawn** (Venus's chariot was drawn by doves.) **done** placed **95 wanton charm** lustful spell

Her waspish-headed° son has broke his arrows,
Swears he will shoot no more, but play with sparrows°
And be a boy right out.°

[*Juno alights.*]

CERES. Highest Queen of state,°
Great Juno, comes; I know her by her gait.°

JUNO. How does my bounteous sister?° Go with me
To bless this twain, that they may prosperous be,
And honored in their issue.° *They sing:*

JUNO.
Honor, riches, marriage blessing,
Long continuance, and increasing,
Hourly joys be still° upon you!
Juno sings her blessings on you.

CERES.
Earth's increase, foison plenty,°
Barns and garners° never empty,
Vines with clustering bunches growing,
Plants with goodly burden bowing;

Spring come to you at the farthest
In the very end of harvest!°
Scarcity and want shall shun you;
Ceres' blessing so is on you.

FERDINAND. This is a most majestic vision, and
Harmonious charmingly.° May I be bold
To think these spirits?

PROSPERO. Spirits, which by mine art
I have from their confines called to enact
My present fancies.

FERDINAND. Let me live here ever!
So rare a wondered° father and a wife
Makes this place Paradise.

*Juno and Ceres whisper, and send Iris on employment.*

PROSPERO. Sweet now, silence!
Juno and Ceres whisper seriously;
There's something else to do. Hush and be mute,
Or else our spell is marred.

IRIS [*calling offstage*]. You nymphs, called naiads,° of the windring°
brooks,
With your sedged° crowns and ever-harmless° looks,

**129 sedged** made of reeds. **ever-harmless** ever innocent **98 Mars's hot minion** i.e., Venus, the beloved of Mars. **returned** i.e., returned to Paphos **99 waspish-headed** hotheaded, peevish **100 sparrows** (Supposed lustful, and sacred to Venus.) **101 right out** outright. **Highest . . . state** most majestic Queen **102 gait** i.e., majestic bearing **103 sister** i.e., fellow goddess (?) **105 issue** offspring **108 still** always **110 foison plenty** plentiful harvest **111 garners** granaries **115 In . . . harvest** i.e., with no winter in between **119 charmingly** enchantingly **123 wondered** wonder-performing, wondrous **128 naiads** nymphs of springs, rivers, or lakes. **windring** wandering, winding (?)

Leave your crisp° channels, and on this green land
Answer your summons; Juno does command.
Come, temperate° nymphs, and help to celebrate
A contract of true love. Be not too late.

*Enter certain nymphs.*

You sunburned sicklemen,° of August weary,°
Come hither from the furrow° and be merry.
Make holiday; your rye-straw hats put on,
And these fresh nymphs encounter° every one
In country footing.°

*Enter certain reapers, properly° habited. They join with the nymphs in a graceful dance, towards the end whereof Prospero starts suddenly, and speaks; after which, to a strange, hollow, and confused noise, they heavily° vanish.*

PROSPERO [*aside*]. I had forgot that foul conspiracy
Of the beast Caliban and his confederates
Against my life. The minute of their plot
Is almost come. [*To the Spirits.*] Well done! Avoid;° no more!

FERDINAND [*to Miranda*]. This is strange. Your father's in some passion
That works° him strongly.

MIRANDA. Never till this day
Saw I him touched with anger so distempered.

PROSPERO. You do look, my son, in a moved sort,°
As if you were dismayed. Be cheerful, sir.
Our revels° now are ended. These our actors,
As I foretold you, were all spirits and
Are melted into air, into thin air;
And, like the baseless fabric° of this vision,
The cloud-capped towers, the gorgeous palaces,
The solemn temples, the great globe° itself,
Yea, all which it inherit,° shall dissolve,
And, like this insubstantial pageant faded,
Leave not a rack° behind. We are such stuff
As dreams are made on,° and our little life
Is rounded° with a sleep. Sir, I am vexed.
Bear with my weakness. My old brain is troubled.
Be not disturbed with° my infirmity.
If you be pleased, retire° into my cell

**130 crisp** curled, rippled **132 temperate** chaste **134 sicklemen** harvesters, field workers who cut down grain and grass. **of August weary** i.e., weary of the hard work of the harvest **135 furrow** i.e., plowed fields **137 encounter** join **138 country footing** country dancing. **s.d. properly** suitably. **heavily** slowly, dejectedly **142 Avoid** withdraw **144 works** affects, agitates **146 moved sort** troubled state, condition **148 revels** entertainment, pageant **151 baseless fabric** unsubstantial theatrical edifice or contrivance **153 great globe** (With a glance at the Globe Theatre.) **154 which it inherit** who subsequently occupy it **156 rack** wisp of cloud **157 on** of **158 rounded** surrounded (before birth and after death), or crowned, rounded off **160 with** by **161 retire** withdraw, go

And there repose. A turn or two I'll walk
To still my beating° mind.
FERDINAND, MIRANDA. We wish your peace.
*Exeunt [Ferdinand and Miranda].*
PROSPERO. Come with a thought!° I thank thee, Ariel. Come.
*Enter Ariel.*
ARIEL. Thy thoughts I cleave° to. What's thy pleasure?
PROSPERO. Spirit,
We must prepare to meet with Caliban.
ARIEL. Ay, my commander. When I presented° Ceres,
I thought to have told thee of it, but I feared
Lest I might anger thee.
PROSPERO. Say again, where didst thou leave these varlets?
ARIEL. I told you, sir, they were red-hot with drinking;
So full of valor that they smote the air
For breathing in their faces, beat the ground
For kissing of their feet; yet always bending°
Towards their project. Then I beat my tabor,
At which, like unbacked° colts, they pricked their ears,
Advanced° their eyelids, lifted up their noses
As° they smelt music. So I charmed their ears
That calflike they my lowing° followed through
Toothed briers, sharp furzes, pricking gorse,° and thorns,
Which entered their frail shins. At last I left them
I' the filthy-mantled° pool beyond your cell,
There dancing up to the chins, that the foul lake
O'erstunk° their feet.
PROSPERO. This was well done, my bird.
Thy shape invisible retain thou still.
The trumpery° in my house, go bring it hither,
For stale° to catch these thieves.
ARIEL. I go, I go. *Exit.*
PROSPERO. A devil, a born devil, on whose nature
Nurture can never stick; on whom my pains,
Humanely taken, all, all lost, quite lost!
And as with age his body uglier grows,
So his mind cankers.° I will plague them all,
Even to roaring.

**163 beating** agitated **164 with a thought** i.e., on the instant, or, summoned by my thought, no sooner thought of than here **165 cleave** cling, adhere **167 presented** acted the part of, or, introduced **174 bending** aiming **176 unbacked** unbroken, unridden **177 Advanced** lifted up **178 As** as if **179 lowing** mooing **180 furzes, gorse** prickly shrubs **182 filthy-mantled** covered with a slimy coating **184 O'erstunk** smelled worse than, or, caused to stink terribly **186 trumpery** cheap goods, the *glistering apparel* mentioned in the following stage direction **187 stale** (1) decoy (2) out-of-fashion garments (with possible further suggestions of "horse piss," as in line 198, and "steal," pronounced like *stale*). *For stale* could also mean "fit for a prostitute." **192 cankers** festers, grows malignant

*Enter Ariel, loaden with glistering apparel, etc.*

Come, hang them on this line.°

[*Ariel hangs up the showy finery; Prospero and Ariel remain,° invisible.*] *Enter Caliban, Stephano, and Trinculo, all wet.*

CALIBAN. Pray you, tread softly, that the blind mole may
Not hear a foot fall. We now are near his cell.

STEPHANO. Monster, your fairy, which you say is a harmless fairy, has done little better than played the jack° with us.

TRINCULO. Monster, I do smell all horse piss, at which my nose is in great indignation.

STEPHANO. So is mine. Do you hear, monster? If I should take a displeasure against you, look you—

TRINCULO. Thou wert but a lost monster.

CALIBAN. Good my lord, give me thy favor still.
Be patient, for the prize I'll bring thee to
Shall hoodwink this mischance.° Therefore speak softly.
All's hushed as midnight yet.

TRINCULO. Ay, but to lose our bottles in the pool—

STEPHANO. There is not only disgrace and dishonor in that, monster, but an infinite loss.

TRINCULO. That's more to me than my wetting. Yet this is your harmless fairy, monster!

STEPHANO. I will fetch off my bottle, though I be o'er ears° for my labor.

CALIBAN. Prithee, my king, be quiet. Seest thou here,
This is the mouth o' the cell. No noise, and enter.
Do that good mischief which may make this island
Thine own forever, and I thy Caliban
For aye thy footlicker.

STEPHANO. Give me thy hand. I do begin to have bloody thoughts.

TRINCULO [*seeing the finery*]. O King Stephano! O peer!° O worthy Stephano! Look what a wardrobe here is for thee!

CALIBAN. Let it alone, thou fool, it is but trash.

TRINCULO. Oho, monster! We know what belongs to a frippery.° O King Stephano! [*He puts on a gown.*]

STEPHANO. Put off° that gown, Trinculo. By this hand, I'll have that gown.

TRINCULO. Thy Grace shall have it.

CALIBAN. The dropsy° drown this fool! What do you mean
To dote thus on such luggage?° Let 't alone
And do the murder first. If he awake,

**193 line** lime tree or linden. **s.d. Prospero and Ariel remain** (The staging is uncertain. They may instead exit here and return with the spirits at line 249.) **197 jack** (1) knave (2) will-o'-the-wisp **205 hoodwink this mischance** (Misfortune is to be prevented from doing further harm by being hooded like a hawk and also put out of remembrance.) **212 o'er ears** i.e., totally submerged and perhaps drowned **219 King . . . peer** (Alludes to the old ballad beginning, "King Stephen was a worthy peer.") **222 frippery** place where cast-off clothes are sold **224 Put off** put down, or, take off **227 dropsy** disease characterized by the accumulation of fluid in the connective tissue of the body **228 luggage** cumbersome trash

From toe to crown° he'll fill our skins with pinches,
Make us strange stuff.

STEPHANO. Be you quiet, monster.—Mistress line,° is not this my jerkin?° [*He takes it down.*] Now is the jerkin under the line.° Now, jerkin, you are like° to lose your hair and prove a bald° jerkin.

TRINCULO. Do, do!° We steal by line and level,° an 't like° Your Grace.

STEPHANO. I thank thee for that jest. Here's a garment for 't. [*He gives a garment.*] Wit shall not go unrewarded while I am king of this country. "Steal by line and level" is an excellent pass of pate.° There's another garment for 't.

TRINCULO. Monster, come, put some lime° upon your fingers, and away with the rest.

CALIBAN. I will have none on 't. We shall lose our time,
And all be turned to barnacles,° or to apes
With foreheads villainous° low.

STEPHANO. Monster, lay to° your fingers. Help to bear this° away where my hogshead° of wine is, or I'll turn you out of my kingdom. Go to,° carry this.

TRINCULO. And this.

STEPHANO. Ay, and this.

[*They load Caliban with more and more garments.*]

*A noise of hunters heard. Enter divers spirits, in shape of dogs and hounds, hunting them about, Prospero and Ariel setting them on.*

PROSPERO. Hey, Mountain, hey!

ARIEL. Silver! There it goes, Silver!

PROSPERO. Fury, Fury! There, Tyrant, there! Hark! Hark!

[*Caliban, Stephano, and Trinculo are driven out.*]

Go, charge my goblins that they grind their joints
With dry° convulsions,° shorten up their sinews

**230 crown** head **232 Mistress line** (Addressed to the linden or lime tree upon which, at line 193, Ariel hung the *glistering apparel.*) **jerkin** jacket made of leather **233 under the line** under the lime tree (with punning sense of being south of the equinoctial line or equator; sailors on long voyages to the southern regions were popularly supposed to lose their hair from scurvy or other diseases. Stephano also quibbles bawdily on losing hair through syphilis, and in *Mistress* and *jerkin.*) **234 like** likely. **bald** (1) hairless, napless (2) meager **235 Do, do** i.e., bravo. (Said in response to the jesting or to the taking of the jerkin, or both.) **by line and level** i.e., by means of plumb line and carpenter's level, methodically (with pun on *line,* "lime tree," line 233, and *steal,* pronounced like *stale,* i.e., prostitute, continuing Stephano's bawdy quibble). **an 't like** if it please **238 pass of pate** sally of wit. (The metaphor is from fencing.) **240 lime** birdlime, sticky substance (to give Caliban sticky fingers) **243 barnacles** barnacle geese, formerly supposed to be hatched from barnacles attached to trees or to rotting timber; here, evidently used, like *apes,* as types of simpletons **244 villainous** miserably **245 lay to** start using. **this** i.e., the *glistering apparel.* **246 hogshead** large cask **246–247 Go to** (An expression of exhortation or remonstrance.) **254 dry** associated with age, arthritic (?) **convulsions** cramps

With agèd° cramps, and more pinch-spotted make them
Than pard° or cat o' mountain.°

ARIEL. Hark, they roar!

PROSPERO. Let them be hunted soundly.° At this hour
Lies at my mercy all mine enemies.
Shortly shall all my labors end, and thou
Shalt have the air at freedom. For a little°
Follow, and do me service.

*Exeunt.*

**5.1** *Enter Prospero in His Magic Robes,* [*With His Staff,*] *and Ariel.*

PROSPERO. Now does my project gather to a head.
My charms crack° not, my spirits obey, and Time
Goes upright with his carriage.° How's the day?

ARIEL. On° the sixth hour, at which time, my lord,
You said our work should cease.

PROSPERO. I did say so,
When first I raised the tempest. Say, my spirit,
How fares the King and 's followers?

ARIEL. Confined together
In the same fashion as you gave in charge,
Just as you left them; all prisoners, sir,
In the line grove° which weather-fends° your cell.
They cannot budge till your release.° The King,
His brother, and yours abide all three distracted,°
And the remainder mourning over them,
Brim full of sorrow and dismay; but chiefly
Him that you termed, sir, the good old lord, Gonzalo.
His tears runs down his beard like winter's drops
From eaves of reeds.° Your charm so strongly works 'em
That if you now beheld them your affections°
Would become tender.

PROSPERO. Dost thou think so, spirit?

ARIEL. Mine would, sir, were I human.°

PROSPERO. And mine shall.
Hast thou, which art but air, a touch,° a feeling
Of their afflictions, and shall not myself,

**255 agèd** characteristic of old age **256 pard** panther or leopard. **cat o' mountain** wildcat **257 soundly** thoroughly (and suggesting the sounds of the hunt) **260 little** little while longer

**5.1 Location: Before Prospero's cell.** **2 crack** collapse, fail. (The metaphor is probably alchemical, as in *project* and *gather to a head,* line 1.) **3 his carriage** its burden. (Time is no longer heavily burdened and so can go *upright,* "standing straight and unimpeded.") **4 On** approaching **10 line grove** grove of lime trees. **weather-fends** protects from the weather **11 your release** you release them **12 distracted** out of their wits **17 eaves of reeds** thatched roofs **18 affections** disposition, feelings **20 human** (Spelled *humane* in the Folio and encompassing both senses.) **21 touch** sense, apprehension

One of their kind, that relish all as sharply
Passion as they,° be kindlier° moved than thou art?
Though with their high wrongs I am struck to the quick,
Yet with my nobler reason 'gainst my fury
Do I take part. The rarer° action is
In virtue than in vengeance. They being penitent,
The sole drift of my purpose doth extend
Not a frown further. Go release them, Ariel.
My charms I'll break, their senses I'll restore,
And they shall be themselves.

ARIEL. I'll fetch them, sir.

*Exit.*

[*Prospero traces a charmed circle with his staff.*]

PROSPERO. Ye elves of hills, brooks, standing lakes, and groves,
And ye that on the sands with printless foot
Do chase the ebbing Neptune, and do fly him
When he comes back; you demi-puppets° that
By moonshine do the green sour ringlets° make,
Whereof the ewe not bites; and you whose pastime
Is to make midnight mushrooms,° that rejoice
To hear the solemn curfew;° by whose aid,
Weak masters° though ye be, I have bedimmed
The noontide sun, called forth the mutinous winds,
And twixt the green sea and the azured vault°
Set roaring war; to the dread rattling thunder
Have I given fire,° and rifted° Jove's stout oak°
With his own bolt;° the strong-based promontory
Have I made shake, and by the spurs° plucked up
The pine and cedar; graves at my command
Have waked their sleepers, oped, and let 'em forth
By my so potent art.° But this rough° magic
I here abjure, and when I have required°
Some heavenly music—which even now I do—
To work mine end upon their senses that°
This airy charm° is for, I'll break my staff,
Bury it certain fathoms in the earth,

**23–24 that . . . they** I who experience human passions as acutely as they **24 kindlier** (1) more sympathetically (2) more naturally, humanly **27 rarer** nobler **36 demi-puppets** puppets of half size, i.e., elves and fairies **37 green sour ringlets** fairy rings, circles in grass (actually produced by mushrooms) **39 midnight mushrooms** mushrooms appearing overnight **40 curfew** evening bell, usually rung at nine o'clock, ushering in the time when spirits are abroad **41 Weak masters** i.e., subordinate spirits, as in 4.1.35 (?) **43 the azured vault** i.e., the sky **44–45 to . . . fire** I have discharged the dread rattling thunderbolt **45 rifted** riven, split. **oak** a tree that was sacred to Jove **46 bolt** lightning bolt **47 spurs** roots **33–50 Ye . . . art** (This famous passage is an embellished paraphrase of Golding's translation of Ovid's *Metamorphoses,* 7.197–219.) **50 rough** violent **51 required** requested **53 their senses that** the senses of those whom **54 airy charm** i.e., music

And deeper than did ever plummet sound
I'll drown my book. *Solemn music.*

*Here enters Ariel before; then Alonso, with a frantic gesture, attended by Gonzalo; Sebastian and Antonio in like manner, attended by Adrian and Francisco. They all enter the circle which Prospero had made, and there stand charmed; which Prospero observing, speaks:*

[*To Alonso.*] A solemn air,° and° the best comforter
To an unsettled fancy,° cure thy brains,
Now useless, boiled° within thy skull! [*To Sebastian and Antonio.*]
There stand,
For you are spell-stopped.—
Holy Gonzalo, honorable man,
Mine eyes, e'en sociable° to the show° of thine,
Fall° fellowly drops. [*Aside.*] The charm dissolves apace,
And as the morning steals upon the night,
Melting the darkness, so their rising senses
Begin to chase the ignorant fumes° that mantle°
Their clearer° reason.—O good Gonzalo,
My true preserver, and a loyal sir
To him thou follow'st! I will pay thy graces°
Home° both in word and deed.—Most cruelly
Didst thou, Alonso, use me and my daughter.
Thy brother was a furtherer° in the act.—
Thou art pinched° for 't now, Sebastian. [*To Antonio.*] Flesh and blood,
You, brother mine, that entertained ambition,
Expelled remorse° and nature,° whom,° with Sebastian,
Whose inward pinches therefore are most strong,
Would here have killed your king, I do forgive thee,
Unnatural though thou art.—Their understanding
Begins to swell, and the approaching tide
Will shortly fill the reasonable shore°
That now lies foul and muddy. Not one of them
That yet looks on me, or would know me.—Ariel,
Fetch me the hat and rapier in my cell.
[*Ariel goes to the cell and returns immediately.*]
I will discase° me and myself present
As I was sometime Milan.° Quickly, spirit!
Thou shalt ere long be free.

**58 air** song. **and** i.e., which is **59 fancy** imagination **60 boiled** i.e., extremely agitated **63 sociable** sympathetic. **show** appearance **64 Fall** let fall **67 ignorant fumes** fumes that render them incapable of comprehension. **mantle** envelop **68 clearer** growing clearer **70 pay thy graces** requite your favors and virtues **71 Home** fully **73 furtherer** accomplice **74 pinched** punished, afflicted **76 remorse** pity. **nature** natural feeling. **whom** i.e., who **81 reasonable shore** shores of reason, i.e., minds. (Their reason returns, like the incoming tide.) **85 discase** disrobe **86 As . . . Milan** in my former appearance as Duke of Milan

*Ariel sings and helps to attire him.*

ARIEL.
Where the bee sucks, there suck I.
In a cowslip's bell I lie;
There I couch° when owls do cry.
On the bat's back I do fly
After° summer merrily.
Merrily, merrily shall I live now
Under the blossom that hangs on the bough.

PROSPERO. Why, that's my dainty Ariel! I shall miss thee,
But yet thou shalt have freedom. So, so, so.°
To the King's ship, invisible as thou art!
There shalt thou find the mariners asleep
Under the hatches. The Master and the Boatswain
Being awake, enforce them to this place,
And presently,° I prithee.

ARIEL. I drink the air before me and return
Or ere° your pulse twice beat.

*Exit.*

GONZALO. All torment, trouble, wonder, and amazement
Inhabits here. Some heavenly power guide us
Out of this fearful° country!

PROSPERO. Behold, sir King,
The wrongèd Duke of Milan, Prospero.
For more assurance that a living prince
Does now speak to thee, I embrace thy body;
And to thee and thy company I bid
A hearty welcome. [*Embracing him.*]

ALONSO. Whe'er thou be'st he or no,
Or some enchanted trifle° to abuse° me,
As late° I have been, I not know. Thy pulse
Beats as of flesh and blood; and, since I saw thee,
Th' affliction of my mind amends, with which
I fear a madness held me. This must crave°—
An if this be at all°—a most strange story.°
Thy dukedom I resign,° and do entreat
Thou pardon me my wrongs.° But how should Prospero
Be living, and be here?

PROSPERO [*to Gonzalo*]. First, noble friend,
Let me embrace thine age,° whose honor cannot
Be measured or confined. [*Embracing him.*]

**90 couch** lie **92 After** i.e., pursuing **96 So, so, so** (Expresses approval of Ariel's help as valet.) **101 presently** immediately **103 Or ere** before **106 fearful** frightening **112 trifle** trick of magic. **abuse** deceive **113 late** lately **116 crave** require **117 An . . . all** if this is actually happening. **story** i.e., explanation **118 Thy . . . resign** (Alonso made arrangement with Antonio at the time of Prospero's banishment for Milan to pay tribute to Naples; see 1.2.113–127.) **119 wrongs** wrongdoings **121 thine age** your venerable self

GONZALO. Whether this be
Or be not, I'll not swear.

PROSPERO. You do yet taste
Some subtleties° o' th' isle, that will not let you
Believe things certain. Welcome, my friends all!
[*Aside to Sebastian and Antonio.*] But you, my brace° of lords, were I so minded,
I here could pluck His Highness' frown upon you
And justify you° traitors. At this time
I will tell no tales.

SEBASTIAN. The devil speaks in him.

PROSPERO. No.
[*To Antonio.*] For you, most wicked sir, whom to call brother
Would even infect my mouth, I do forgive
Thy rankest fault—all of them; and require
My dukedom of thee, which perforce° I know
Thou must restore.

ALONSO. If thou be'st Prospero,
Give us particulars of thy preservation,
How thou hast met us here, whom° three hours since
Were wrecked upon this shore; where I have lost—
How sharp the point of this remembrance is!—
My dear son Ferdinand.

PROSPERO. I am woe° for 't, sir.

ALONSO. Irreparable is the loss, and Patience
Says it is past her cure.

PROSPERO. I rather think
You have not sought her help, of whose soft grace°
For the like loss I have her sovereign° aid
And rest myself content.

ALONSO. You the like loss?

PROSPERO. As great to me as late,° and supportable
To make the dear loss, have I° means much weaker
Than you may call to comfort you; for I
Have lost my daughter.

ALONSO. A daughter?
O heavens, that they were living both in Naples,
The king and queen there! That° they were, I wish
Myself were mudded° in that oozy bed
Where my son lies. When did you lose your daughter?

PROSPERO. In this last tempest. I perceive these lords
At this encounter do so much admire°

**124 subtleties** illusions, magical powers (playing on the idea of "pastries, concoctions") **126 brace** pair **128 justify you** prove you to be **133 perforce** necessarily **136 whom** i.e., who **139 woe** sorry **142 of . . . grace** by whose mercy **143 sovereign** efficacious **145 late** recent **145–146 supportable . . . have I** to make the deeply felt loss bearable, I have **151 That** so that **152 mudded** buried in the mud **155 admire** wonder

That they devour their reason° and scarce think
Their eyes do offices of truth, their words
Are natural breath.° But, howsoever you have
Been jostled from your senses, know for certain
That I am Prospero and that very duke
Which was thrust forth of° Milan, who most strangely
Upon this shore, where you were wrecked, was landed
To be the lord on 't. No more yet of this,
For 'tis a chronicle of day by day,°
Not a relation for a breakfast nor
Befitting this first meeting. Welcome, sir.
This cell's my court. Here have I few attendants,
And subjects none abroad.° Pray you, look in.
My dukedom since you have given me again,
I will requite° you with as good a thing,
At least bring forth a wonder to content ye
As much as me my dukedom.

*Here Prospero discovers° Ferdinand and Miranda, playing at chess.*

MIRANDA. Sweet lord, you play me false.°
FERDINAND. No, my dearest love,
I would not for the world.
MIRANDA. Yes, for a score of kingdoms you should wrangle,
And I would call it fair play.°
ALONSO. If this prove
A vision° of the island, one dear son
Shall I twice lose.
SEBASTIAN. A most high miracle!
FERDINAND [*approaching his father*]. Though the seas threaten, they are merciful;
I have cursed them without cause. [*He kneels.*]
ALONSO. Now all the blessings
Of a glad father compass° thee about!
Arise, and say how thou cam'st here. [*Ferdinand rises.*]
MIRANDA. O, wonder!
How many goodly creatures are there here!

**156 devour their reason** i.e., are openmouthed, dumbfounded **156–158 scarce . . . breath** scarcely believe that their eyes inform them accurately as to what they see or that their words are naturally spoken **161 of** from **164 of day by day** requiring days to tell **168 abroad** away from here, anywhere else **170 requite** repay **172 s.d. discovers** i.e., by opening a curtain, presumably rearstage **173 play me false** i.e., press your advantage **176–177 Yes . . . play** i.e., yes, even if we were playing for twenty kingdoms, something less than the whole world, you would still press your advantage against me, and I would lovingly let you do it as though it were fair play, or, if you were to play not just for stakes but literally for kingdoms, my complaint would be out of order in that your "wrangling" would be proper **178 vision** illusion **182 compass** encompass, embrace

How beauteous mankind is! O brave° new world
That has such people in 't!
PROSPERO. 'Tis new to thee.
ALONSO. What is this maid with whom thou wast at play?
Your eld'st° acquaintance cannot be three hours.
Is she the goddess that hath severed us,
And brought us thus together?
FERDINAND. Sir, she is mortal;
But by immortal Providence she's mine.
I chose her when I could not ask my father
For his advice, nor thought I had one. She
Is daughter to this famous Duke of Milan,
Of whom so often I have heard renown,
But never saw before; of whom I have
Received a second life; and second father
This lady makes him to me.
ALONSO. I am hers.
But O, how oddly will it sound that I
Must ask my child forgiveness!
PROSPERO. There, sir, stop.
Let us not burden our remembrances with
A heaviness° that's gone.
GONZALO. I have inly° wept,
Or should have spoke ere this. Look down, you gods,
And on this couple drop a blessèd crown!
For it is you that have chalked forth the way°
Which brought us hither.
ALONSO. I say amen, Gonzalo!
GONZALO. Was Milan° thrust from Milan, that his issue
Should become kings of Naples? O, rejoice
Beyond a common joy, and set it down
With gold on lasting pillars: In one voyage
Did Claribel her husband find at Tunis,
And Ferdinand, her brother, found a wife
Where he himself was lost; Prospero his dukedom
In a poor isle; and all of us ourselves
When no man was his own.°
ALONSO [*to Ferdinand and Miranda*]. Give me your hands.
Let grief and sorrow still° embrace his° heart
That° doth not wish you joy!
GONZALO. Be it so! Amen!

*Enter Ariel, with the Master and Boatswain amazedly following.*

**185 brave** splendid, gorgeously appareled, handsome **188 eld'st** longest **202 heaviness** sadness. **inly** inwardly **205 chalked . . . way** marked as with a piece of chalk the pathway **207 Was Milan** was the Duke of Milan **214–215 all . . . own** all of us have found ourselves and our sanity when we all had lost our senses **216 still** always. **his** that person's **217 That** who

O, look, sir, look, sir! Here is more of us.
I prophesied, if a gallows were on land,
This fellow could not drown.—Now, blasphemy,°
That swear'st grace o'erboard,° not an oath° on shore?
Hast thou no mouth by land? What is the news?

BOATSWAIN. The best news is that we have safely found
Our King and company; the next, our ship—
Which, but three glasses° since, we gave out° split—
Is tight and yare° and bravely° rigged as when
We first put out to sea.

ARIEL [*aside to Prospero*]. Sir, all this service
Have I done since I went.

PROSPERO [*aside to Ariel*]. My tricksy° spirit!

ALONSO. These are not natural events; they strengthen°
From strange to stranger. Say, how came you hither?

BOATSWAIN. If I did think, sir, I were well awake,
I'd strive to tell you. We were dead of sleep,°
And—how we know not—all clapped under hatches,
Where but even now, with strange and several° noises
Of roaring, shrieking, howling, jingling chains,
And more diversity of sounds, all horrible,
We were awaked; straightway at liberty;
Where we, in all her trim, freshly beheld
Our royal, good, and gallant ship, our Master
Cap'ring to eye° her. On a trice,° so please you,
Even in a dream, were we divided from them°
And were brought moping° hither.

ARIEL [*aside to Prospero*]. Was 't well done?

PROSPERO [*aside to Ariel*]. Bravely, my diligence. Thou shalt be free.

ALONSO. This is as strange a maze as e'er men trod,
And there is in this business more than nature
Was ever conduct° of. Some oracle
Must rectify our knowledge.

PROSPERO. Sir, my liege,
Do not infest° your mind with beating on°
The strangeness of this business. At picked° leisure,
Which shall be shortly, single° I'll resolve° you,

**220 blasphemy** i.e., blasphemer **221 That swear'st grace o'erboard** i.e., you who banish heavenly grace from the ship by your blasphemies. **not an oath** aren't you going to swear an oath **225 glasses** i.e., hours. **gave out** reported, professed to be **226 yare** ready. **bravely** splendidly **228 tricksy** ingenious, sportive **229 strengthen** increase **232 dead of sleep** deep in sleep **234 several** diverse **240 Cap'ring to eye** dancing for joy to see. **On a trice** in an instant **241 them** i.e., the other crew members **242 moping** in a daze **246 conduct** guide **248 infest** harass, disturb. **beating on** worrying about **249 picked** chosen, convenient **250 single** privately, by my own human powers. **resolve** satisfy, explain to

Which to you shall seem probable,° of every
These° happened accidents;° till when, be cheerful
And think of each thing well.° [*Aside to Ariel.*] Come hither, spirit.
Set Caliban and his companions free.
Untie the spell. [*Exit Ariel.*] How fares my gracious sir?
There are yet missing of your company
Some few odd° lads that you remember not.

*Enter Ariel, driving in Caliban, Stephano, and Trinculo, in their stolen apparel.*

STEPHANO. Every man shift° for all the rest,° and let no man take care for himself; for all is but fortune. Coragio,° bully monster,° coragio!

TRINCULO. If these be true spies° which I wear in my head, here's a goodly sight.

CALIBAN. O Setebos, these be brave° spirits indeed!
How fine° my master is! I am afraid
He will chastise me.
SEBASTIAN. Ha, ha!
What things are these, my lord Antonio?
Will money buy 'em?
ANTONIO. Very like. One of them
Is a plain fish, and no doubt marketable.
PROSPERO. Mark but the badges° of these men, my lords,
Then say if they be true.° This misshapen knave,
His mother was a witch, and one so strong
That could control the moon, make flows and ebbs,
And deal in her command without her power.°
These three have robbed me, and this demidevil—
For he's a bastard° one—had plotted with them
To take my life. Two of these fellows you
Must know and own.° This thing of darkness I
Acknowledge mine.
CALIBAN. I shall be pinched to death.
ALONSO. Is not this Stephano, my drunken butler?
SEBASTIAN. He is drunk now. Where had he wine?
ALONSO. And Trinculo is reeling ripe.° Where should they

**251 probable** plausible **251–252 of every These** about every one of these **252 accidents** occurrences **253 well** favorably **257 odd** unaccounted for **258 shift** provide. **for all the rest** (Stephano drunkenly gets wrong the saying "Every man for himself.") **259 Coragio** courage. **bully monster** gallant monster. (Ironical.) **260 true spies** accurate observers (i.e., sharp eyes) **262 brave** handsome **263 fine** splendidly attired **269 badges** emblems of cloth or silver worn by retainers to indicate whom they serve. (Prospero refers here to the stolen clothes as emblems of their villainy.) **270 true** honest **273 deal . . . power** wield the moon's power, either without her authority or beyond her influence, or, even though to do so was beyond Sycorax's own power **275 bastard** counterfeit **277 own** recognize, admit as belonging to you **281 reeling ripe** stumblingly drunk

Find this grand liquor that hath gilded° 'em?
[*To Trinculo.*] How cam'st thou in this pickle?°

TRINCULO. I have been in such a pickle since I saw you last that, I fear me, will never out of my bones. I shall not fear flyblowing.°

SEBASTIAN. Why, how now, Stephano?

STEPHANO. O, touch me not! I am not Stephano, but a cramp.

PROSPERO. You'd be king o' the isle, sirrah?°

STEPHANO. I should have been a sore° one, then.

ALONSO [*pointing to Caliban*]. This is a strange thing as e'er I looked on.

PROSPERO. He is as disproportioned in his manners
As in his shape.—Go, sirrah, to my cell.
Take with you your companions. As you look
To have my pardon, trim° it handsomely.

CALIBAN. Ay, that I will; and I'll be wise hereafter
And seek for grace.° What a thrice-double ass
Was I to take this drunkard for a god
And worship this dull fool!

PROSPERO. Go to. Away!

ALONSO. Hence, and bestow your luggage where you found it.

SEBASTIAN. Or stole it, rather.

[*Exeunt Caliban, Stephano, and Trinculo.*]

PROSPERO. Sir, I invite Your Highness and your train
To my poor cell, where you shall take your rest
For this one night; which, part of it, I'll waste°
With such discourse as, I not doubt, shall make it
Go quick away: the story of my life,
And the particular accidents° gone by
Since I came to this isle. And in the morn
I'll bring you to your ship, and so to Naples,
Where I have hope to see the nuptial
Of these our dear-belovèd solemnized;
And thence retire me° to my Milan, where
Every third thought shall be my grave.

ALONSO. I long
To hear the story of your life, which must
Take° the ear strangely.

PROSPERO. I'll deliver° all;
And promise you calm seas, auspicious gales,

**282 gilded** (1) flushed, made drunk (2) covered with gilt (suggesting the horse urine) **283 pickle** (1) fix, predicament (2) pickling brine (in this case, horse urine) **285 flyblowing** i.e., being fouled by fly eggs (from which he is saved by being pickled) **288 sirrah** (Standard form of address to an inferior, here expressing reprimand.) **289 sore** (1) tyrannical (2) sorry, inept (3) wracked by pain **294 trim** prepare, decorate **296 grace** pardon, favor **303 waste** spend **306 accidents** occurrences **311 retire me** return **314 Take** take effect upon, enchant. **deliver** declare, relate

And sail so expeditious that shall catch
Your royal fleet far off.° [*Aside to Ariel.*] My Ariel, chick,
That is thy charge. Then to the elements
Be free, and fare thou well!—Please you, draw near.°
*Exeunt omnes* [*except Prospero*].

## Epilogue *Spoken by Prospero.*

Now my charms are all o'erthrown,
And what strength I have 's mine own,
Which is most faint. Now, 'tis true,
I must be here confined by you
Or sent to Naples. Let me not,
Since I have my dukedom got
And pardoned the deceiver, dwell
In this bare island by your spell,
But release me from my bands°
With the help of your good hands.°
Gentle breath° of yours my sails
Must fill, or else my project fails,
Which was to please. Now I want°
Spirits to enforce,° art to enchant,
And my ending is despair,
Unless I be relieved by prayer,°
Which pierces so that it assaults°
Mercy itself, and frees° all faults.
As you from crimes° would pardoned be,
Let your indulgence° set me free.
*Exit.*

**316–317 catch . . . far off** enable you to catch up with the main part of your royal fleet, now afar off en route to Naples (see 1.2.235–236) **319 draw near** i.e., enter my cell

**Epilogue.** **9 bands** bonds **10 hands** i.e., applause (the noise of which would break the spell of silence) **11 Gentle breath** favorable breeze (produced by hands clapping or favorable comment) **13 want** lack **14 enforce** control **16 prayer** i.e., Prospero's petition to the audience **17 assaults** rightfully gains the attention of **18 frees** obtains forgiveness for **19 crimes** sins **20 indulgence** (1) humoring, lenient approval (2) remission of punishment for sin

# TOPICS FOR CRITICAL THINKING AND WRITING

## Act 1

1. Some directors of stage productions of *The Tempest* show, at the very beginning of the play, Ariel or Prospero presiding over the storm. What do you think of this idea, and why?
2. How would you characterize the Boatswain? And how would you characterize (on the basis of 1.1 only) Antonio? Sebastian? Gonzalo?

3. In 1.2, Prospero's speeches from line 23 to line 185 are Shakespeare's attempt to provide necessary exposition. Some readers and spectators find the speeches tedious, and they find unsuccessful Shakespeare's efforts to make them dramatic by means of Miranda's brief comments. Your opinion? If you agree with these critics, try (for the sake of argument) to make a case on the other side. You might, for instance, take any one speech and show that it contains interestingly varied tones of voice—variations that, in effect, *are* dramatic action.
4. Some producers distribute parts of 1.1 throughout 1.2 in an effort to enliven 1.2. What do you think of this idea? If you think it has some merit, exactly how would you divide 1.1, and exactly where in 1.2 would you put the pieces?
5. In 1.2.89–90, Prospero speaks of himself as "neglecting worldly ends." To what degree do you think Prospero is responsible for what his enemies did to him?
6. How would you characterize Prospero's response to Ariel in 1.2.241–95? Are his speeches appropriate, or are they those of a tyrant? Or what?
7. In your opinion, how valid is Caliban's claim to the island in 1.2.334?

## Act 2

1. In 2.1, Gonzalo gives his version of an ideal society (derived in part from an essay by Montaigne, printed on p. 1896). How does Gonzalo's society compare with the society governed by Prospero?
2. In 2.1, Antonio presumably has nothing to gain by urging Sebastian to kill Alonso. Why do you suppose Shakespeare decided to have Sebastian make this suggestion?
3. In 2.2.26–30, Stephano says that he hopes he can get Caliban back to Naples, where he will make money from him. Do you think Shakespeare is implying that Prospero exploits Caliban in a more or less similar way? Or is Shakespeare implying a contrast? Or both?
4. In his song at the end of 2.2, Caliban thinks he has achieved freedom. How free is he?

## Act 3

1. In the first scene of this act, why does Prospero assign hard labor to Ferdinand?
2. In Scene 3, read aloud, two or three times, Alonso's last speech (lines 95–102). How does Alonso's mental condition compare with Sebastian's and Antonio's? Exactly how do you think each line in Alonso's speech should be spoken?

## Act 4

1. Some directors of the play find Prospero's theatrical production (of Iris, and others) tedious, and they present it as comic. What do you think of this approach?
2. Look closely at Prospero's speech beginning "Our revels now are ended" (4.1.148). Many directors move this speech to the end of the

play, thereby making it a sort of epilogue. If you were directing the play, would you make this change? Explain.

3. In 4.1.166, Prospero says, "We must prepare to meet with Caliban." Assuming that we tend to see some or all of the characters in the play at least somewhat symbolically (for instance, symbolic of power, or of goodness, or of stupidity), what might Caliban seem to stand for at this point in the play? Or is this a thoroughly wrong way of thinking about the characters?

## Act 5

1. In 5.1.18–19, Ariel says that if Prospero saw the enchanted men he would pity them ("your affections / Would become tender"). What episodes do you find in the play where a character pities another character?
2. Do you think Prospero's punishment of Caliban is cruel, just, or merciful—or what? And why?
3. Prospero gives up his magic ("this rough magic / I here abjure" [5.1.50–51]). Shakespeare never tells us exactly *why* Prospero gives up his magic. What do you make of this action?
4. Many readers and spectators find Prospero still—despite his talk of forgiveness—very bitter in the last scene. What do you take his mental state to be? Do you think it is appropriate? Dramatically effective?
5. What *can* Prospero accomplish? What *has* he accomplished?

## Additional Topics

1. *The Tempest* is Shakespeare's last play. Prospero's talk of retirement, and his putting away of magic, is sometimes seen as suggesting that Shakespeare is bidding farewell to the theater, the world of enchanting but insubstantial characters and stories. Do you think a biographical interpretation along these lines is useful? Explain.
2. *A foil* in drama is a character who contrasts with (and thereby helps to define) another character. Thus, Ariel and Caliban are often said to be foils, the one airy and light, the other earthy and clumsy. Take another pair of characters and show how they make an interesting contrast.
3. What, if anything, do Trinculo and Stephano contribute to the play?
4. Prospero has been seen as a racist-colonist. Do you agree? Support your argument with evidence.
5. *The Times Literary Supplement,* 2 September 1994, carried a favorable review of a production of *The Tempest.* The reviewer praised the company for performing the play

> as though it actually meant what it says, namely, that Prospero is wise and good; that his authority is educational; that self-restraint is both a virtue and the precondition of any meaningful freedom; that maturity, understanding and fulfillment are accessible only to innocence, which thus demands our protection; in short, that if only we go the right way about living them, our lives will prove to be self-justified, full of meaning and their own joyous reward. Such intuitions are, of course, not fashionable. One can see why a recent production had to have Ariel spit in Prospero's face on receiving

> his freedom. But why not just spit on Shakespeare, the play and on life while you're about it, and have done with the lot?

There's a great deal here to think about. Take some or all of it and offer your response.

## PERSPECTIVES FOR *THE TEMPEST*

### MICHEL EYQUEM DE MONTAIGNE

*No source is known for the plot of* The Tempest, *but various bits in the play can be traced. For instance, Robert Eden's* History of Travail *(1577) mentions that the Patagonians worship a "great devil Setebos," and several writings concerning an English expedition that found its way from the Caribbean to Virginia in 1609 provided details about a shipwreck and about encounters with Indians.*

*Gonzalo's description of an ideal commonwealth (2.1.141ff) probably is indebted to an essay by the French writer Montaigne (1533–92), first published in French in 1588 and translated into English by John Florio in 1603. Montaigne's essay concerns a topic that was much debated at the time: What is the nature of the "natural man"? Did the Indians before the encounter with Europeans live lives of "natural" virtue, or were they savages who were elevated by the religion and the civilization that the whites brought to them? To take a simple instance: Was their nudity a sign of their innocent and natural purity, or was it a sign of their ignorance, sexual corruption, and need for civilization? Which is superior,* nature or nurture? *(The view that nature is in need of nurture of course provided a moral justification for colonization, and it was widely invoked later, especially during the Victorian period.)*

*We print part of Montaigne's essay, in which he suggests that civilized people are prone to call barbaric any customs other than their own. Further, what civilized people call "wild" may be more properly regarded as "natural," whereas their own products of civilization may be regarded as* unnatural, *or as bastard. Elsewhere in the essay he suggests that although the natives of the New World had the habit of eating human flesh, they were very decent folk, superior to Europeans who tortured their own people and did not hesitate to torture the natives of the New World. (Shakespeare's Caliban is not said to eat human flesh, but his name probably is an anagram of* cannibal, *a word derived from* Caribales, *the name of a people Columbus encountered in the Caribbean.)*

# *Of the Cannibals*

. . . I find (as far as I have been informed) there is nothing in that (Native American) nation that is either barbarous or savage, unless men call that barbarism which is not common to them. As indeed, we have no other aim of truth and reason than the example and idea of the opinions and customs of the country we live in. There is ever perfect religion, perfect policy, perfect and complete use of all things. They are even savage, as we call those fruits wild which nature of herself and of her ordinary progress hath produced; whereas indeed, they are those which ourselves have altered by our artificial devices, and diverted from their common order, we should rather term savage. In those are the true and most profitable virtues and natural properties most lively and vigorous, which in these we have bastardized, applying them to the pleasure of our corrupted taste. And if notwithstanding, in divers fruits of those countries that were never tilled, we shall find that, in respect of ours, they are most excellent and as delicate unto our taste, there is no reason art should gain the point of honor of our great and puissant mother Nature. We have so much by our inventions surcharged the beauties and riches of her works that we have altogether overchoked her; yet wherever her purity shineth, she makes our vain and frivolous enterprises wonderfully ashamed. . . .

It is a nation . . . that hath no kind of traffic, no knowledge of letters, no intelligence of numbers, no name of magistrate, nor of politic superiority; no use of service, of riches, or of poverty; no contracts, no successions, no partitions, no occupation but idle; no respect of kindred but common, no apparel but natural, no manuring of lands, no use of wine, corn, or metal. The very words that import lying, falsehood, treason, dissimulations, covetousness, envy, detraction, and pardon, were never heard of amongst them. How dissonant would he find his imaginary commonwealth from this perfection? . . .

Furthermore, they live in a country of so exceeding pleasant and temperate situation that, as my testimonies have told me, it is very rare to see a sick body amongst them; and they have further assured me they never saw any man there either shaking with the palsy, toothless, with eyes dropping, or crooked and stooping through age.

## TOPICS FOR CRITICAL THINKING AND WRITING

1. Reread Montaigne's first sentence. Do you think that people have a tendency to slip into calling customs barbaric that are "not common to them"? What might be some examples? Is it clear to you that, for instance, corporal punishment (practiced in many parts of the world) is barbaric whereas imprisonment is humane?
2. What does Montaigne mean when he says that cultivated fruits are "bastardized"? Would you agree that at least some fruits and other products of civilization (or nurture) are inferior to those produced by nature?

What do you think of extending the argument, saying that some tribes or races (or cultures?) are good by *nature* and are spoiled by *nurture* (codes of civilization)?

3. Some critics have suggested that in Gonzalo's description of an ideal community (2.1.141ff) Shakespeare is satirizing Montaigne. Your view? Your reasons?

## JANE LEE

*Jane Lee, formerly of Tufts University, contributed this short essay to the playbill for a local production of* The Tempest.

# *The Tempest in Its Age and in Our Time*

"He was not of an age, but for all time." Thus Ben Jonson on Shakespeare, in a memorial poem published in 1623, seven years after Shakespeare's death. Jonson may or may not have been sincere, but as a professional poet he knew what was expected of him, and he obliged with the expected sentiment—which happens to be true.

Let's begin with Shakespeare and his own age. No writer, not even the greatest, can wholly escape from his age, and Shakespeare can be profitably examined in his Elizabethan and Jacobean context. When we think of the Renaissance we think of the great voyages of discovery and of the widespread interest in what for Europe was the New World. Although Shakespeare displays only the slightest interest in the New World (he mentions America only once), and although for him a sea journey is of interest chiefly because it can lead to a shipwreck and thus get a comedy started, *The Tempest* indeed is influenced by Elizabethan literature of voyages. Shakespeare had been reading, or had heard of, accounts of *The Sea-Venture,* a ship that sailed from Plymouth for Virginia in 1609, carrying the new governor of the Virginia colony. *The Sea-Venture* was caught in a storm off the Bermudas and was thought to have been destroyed, but it was (miraculously, so it seemed) preserved. Numerous connections can be made between Shakespeare's play and the pamphlets describing the voyage to Bermuda and thence to Virginia, but one connection, very much of its time, is especially interesting. After recording that the governor tried to deal peaceably with the Indians but came to learn, when the Indians killed one of his men, "how little a fair and noble entreaty works upon a barbarous disposition," the writer wonders, "Can a leopard change his spots? Can a savage remaining savage be civil?" Such a reflection as this, of course, is relevant to Caliban, the "savage" of *The Tempest,* and to Prospero, who first sought to educate Caliban with "kindness" but who came to find kindness less effective than "stripes," i.e., lashes.

*The Tempest,* then, although set on an island in the Mediterranean, owes much to English and European thinking about the nature of the inhabitants of the New World, that is, to thinking about the nature of the "natural" man. Was the Indian a sort of unfallen man, a noble savage in an unfallen Eden, or was he even lower than the sinful European, who had been brought to some degree of civility by Christ's teachings and also by the stern discipline of governors?

And so the play can be seen as an early document in the history of English colonialism. Prospero, having enslaved the brutish Caliban and having seized his island, is now dependent on the slave: "We cannot miss [i.e. do without] him. He does make our fire, / Fetch in our wood, and serves in offices / That profit us." Caliban has the qualities that the imperialistic white man customarily attributes to what Kipling almost three hundred years later called "the lesser breeds without the Law": he is lazy, smelly, and drunken, he worships devils, and he is lecherous and treacherous. The loyal courtier Gonzalo, unaware of Caliban, finds the air of the island sweet, the grass lush, a place fit for a utopian society in which there would be no crime and no need for hard labor, but Prospero finds that he must govern severely so long as Caliban and most of the shipwrecked people are on the island. All of this is to say, again, that *The Tempest* is of its own age, for it toys with the idea of Utopia—a word (meaning "no place" in Greek) invented by Sir Thomas More early in the English Renaissance. More gives the name to an imaginary society supposedly discovered during one of Amerigo Vespucci's voyages to the New World. His book, entitled *Utopia,* was widely read and discussed in Europe and in England.

5 Much can be said about *The Tempest* as a work of its age, but space is short and we must turn to the play as a work for all time. If *The Tempest* can be seen as a document in the history of colonialism, or in the history of Renaissance utopian thought, it can—and should—also be seen as a play that has very little to do with colonialism and very little to do with utopian thought, if by utopian thought we mean naive proposals for systems of government that will bring happiness to all citizens. In this, paradoxically, *The Tempest* resembles More's *Utopia,* for despite More's description of the admirable government of his imaginary people, More is not, at bottom, setting forth a proposal for a new kind of government that will convert European savages into moral people. Rather, More seems chiefly to be telling us not what government must do but what *individuals* must do if life is to be decent. What is needed is not an ideal government, but wise or enlightened *self*-government of the individual.

Let's look at one of Prospero's speeches. Prospero has at his mercy his treacherous brother, who had usurped the throne and set Prospero and Prospero's infant daughter adrift in a flimsy boat without a sail. Also under Prospero's magic spell are several other "men of sin." Prospero says:

Though with their high wrongs I am struck to th' quick,
Yet with my nobler reason 'gainst my fury
Do I take part. The rarer action is
In virtue than in vengeance. They being penitent,
The sole drift of my purpose doth extend
Not a frown further. Go, release them, Ariel.
My Charms I'll break, their senses I'll restore,
And they shall be themselves.

"The rarer action is / In virtue than in vengeance." "Virtue," here contrasted with "vengeance," obviously includes mercy; earlier in the play Prospero spoke of "The virtue of compassion." To put it a little differently, Prospero has conquered not only his wicked foes but his own quite understandable desire for vengeance, substituting forgiveness for it. This self-conquest, his greatest achievement, can be contrasted to the explosive passion of Caliban, who sought to rape Prospero's daughter, and to the murderous assertiveness of Prospero's brother and his allies. When, near the end of the play, Prospero says, "This thing of darkness I / Acknowledge mine," he is explicitly speaking of Caliban, but we can sense that he is also glancing at an enemy more dangerous than the savage islander; he is glancing at the dark impulse in himself, over which, however, he has triumphed.

And so, if Shakespeare was "of an age," he is also "for all time," just as, for example, More's *Utopia* is also both a Renaissance comment on the New World and (more important) a vision of how the individual—even in the corrupt Old World—should and can govern himself or herself. *The Tempest,* despite Gonzalo's utopian speech, like *Utopia* and like Plato's *Republic,* is not a treatise on government but on self-government. The connection with *The Republic* can be pursued for a moment. *The Republic* is a myth whose subject is the mind, for Plato's philosopher-kings are symbols of reason ruling over the passions of the enlightened man. When in *The Republic,* Glaucon (who doesn't quite get the point) doubts that Socrates' ideal state exists anywhere on earth, the reply is, "In heaven there is laid up a pattern of it, which he who desires may behold, and beholding, may set his own house in order."

*The Tempest,* like all good drama, gives us heightened images of our life, not merely life as it was lived at some remote historical period but life as we know it and feel it. To take a simple example, we feel the truth of even the loutish Trinculo's bitter observation that in England men will not give a coin "to relieve a lame beggar, [but] will lay out ten to see a dead Indian." But *The Tempest* goes further than giving us a vivid image of life as we know it; like all other great drama, it gives us a memorable image of life *to live up to,* and thus perhaps it can, at least so far as any work of art can, help us to set our house in order. If Shakespeare was a colonialist, he was one in the sense that any great artist is: he explored the remote territory of the self, brought back his discoveries, and put them at our service.

[*1993*]

##  TOPICS FOR CRITICAL THINKING AND WRITING

1. In her second paragraph Lee says that Prospero "first sought to educate Caliban with 'kindness' but . . . came to find kindness less effective than 'stripes,' i.e., lashes." Examine Prospero's treatment of Caliban, from beginning to end. Does Prospero always rely on physical punishment? Is he sometimes—or always or often or never—cruel?
2. Does it make sense to say that *The Tempest* is (or may be) "for all time"? Explain.

##  STEPHEN GREENBLATT

*Stephen Greenblatt, a professor of English at the University of California, Berkeley, is a specialist in the literature of the Renaissance. He is especially associated with a school of thought that he called the New Historicism, an approach discussed on page 1929.*

*This essay originally appeared in 1991, in* Chronicle of Higher Education, *a publication aimed chiefly at college and university teachers and administrators.*

# *The Best Way to Kill Our Literary Inheritance Is to Turn It Into a Decorous Celebration of the New World Order*

The columnist George F. Will recently declared that Lynne V. Cheney, the chairman of the National Endowment for the Humanities, is "secretary of domestic defense."

"The foreign adversaries her husband, Dick, must keep at bay," Mr. Will wrote, "are less dangerous, in the long run, than the domestic forces with which she must deal." Who are these homegrown enemies, more dangerous even than Saddam Hussein with his arsenal of chemical weapons? The answer: professors of literature. You know, the kind of people who belong to that noted terrorist organization, the Modern Language Association.

Mr. Will, who made these allegations in *Newsweek* (April 22), doesn't name names—I suppose the brandishing of a list of the insidious fifth column's members is yet to come—but he does mention, as typical of the disease afflicting Western civilization, the professor who suggests that Shakespeare's *Tempest* is somehow about imperialism.

This is a curious example—since it is very difficult to argue that *The Tempest is not* about imperialism. (It is, of course, about many other things, as well, including the magical power of the theater.) The play—set on a mysterious island over whose inhabitants a European prince has assumed absolute control—is full of conspicuous allusions to contemporary debates over the project of colonization: The Virginia Company's official report on the state of its New World colony and the account by William Strachey, secretary of the settlement at Jamestown, of a violent storm and shipwreck off the coast of Bermuda, are examples.

5 Colonialism was not simply a given of the period. The great Spanish Dominican Bartolomé de Las Casas argued that his countrymen should leave the New World, since they were bringing only exploitation and violence. Spanish jurists like Francisco de Vitoria presented cases against the enslavement of the Indians and against the claim to imperial possession of the Americas. The most searing attack on colonialism in the 16th century was written by the French essayist Montaigne, who in "Of Cannibals" wrote admiringly of the Indians and in "Of Coaches" lamented the whole European enterprise: "So many cities razed, so many nations exterminated, so many millions of people put to the sword, and the richest and most beautiful part of the world turned upside down, for the traffic in pearls and pepper!" We know that Shakespeare read Montaigne; one of the characters in *The Tempest* quotes from "Of Cannibals."

Shakespeare's imagination was clearly gripped by the conflict between the prince and the "savage" Caliban (is it too obvious to note the anagrammatic play on "cannibal"?). Caliban, enslaved by Prospero, bitterly challenges the European's right to sovereignty. The island was his birthright, he claims, and was unjustly taken from him. Caliban's claim is not upheld in *The Tempest,* but neither is it simply dismissed, and at the enigmatic close of the play all of the Europeans—every one of them—leave the island.

These are among the issues that literary scholars investigate and encourage their students to consider, and I would think that the columnists who currently profess an ardent interest in our cultural heritage would approve.

But for some of them such an investigation is an instance of what is intolerable—a wicked plot by renegade professors bent on sabotaging Western civilization by delegitimizing its founding texts and ideas. Such critics want a tame and orderly canon. The painful, messy struggles over rights and values, the political and sexual and ethical dilemmas that great art has taken upon itself to articulate and to grapple with, have no place in their curriculum. For them, what is at stake is the staunch reaffirmation of a shared and stable culture that is, as Mr. Will puts it, "the nation's social cement." Also at stake is the transmission of that culture to passive students.

But art, the art that matters, is not cement. It is mobile, complex, elusive, disturbing. A love of literature may help to forge community, but it is a community founded on imaginative freedom, the play of language, and scholarly honesty, not on flag waving, boosterism, and conformity.

10 The best way to kill our literary inheritance is to turn it into a decorous liturgical celebration of the new world order. Poets cannot soar when their feet are stuck in social cement.

The student of Shakespeare who asks about racism, misogyny, or anti-Semitism is not on the slippery slope toward what George Will calls "collective amnesia and deculturation." He or she is on the way to understanding something about *Othello, The Taming of the Shrew,* and *The Merchant of Venice.* It is, I believe, all but impossible to understand these plays without grappling with the dark energies upon which Shakespeare's art so powerfully draws.

And it is similarly difficult to come to terms with what *The Tempest* has to teach us about forgiveness, wisdom, and social atonement if we do not also come to terms with its relations to colonialism.

If we allow ourselves to think about the extent to which our magnificent cultural tradition—like that of every civilization we know of—is intertwined with cruelty, injustice, and pain, do we not, in fact, run the risk of "deculturation"? Not if our culture includes a regard for truth. Does this truth mean that we should despise or abandon great art?

Of course not.

15 Like most teachers, I am deeply committed to passing on the precious heritage of our language, and I take seriously the risk of collective amnesia. Yet there seems to me a far greater risk if professors of literature, frightened by intemperate attacks upon them in the press, refuse to ask the most difficult questions about the past—the risk that we might turn our artistic inheritance into a simple, reassuring, soporific lie.

[*1991*]

## TOPICS FOR CRITICAL THINKING AND WRITING

1. In paragraph 3 Greenblatt says that in *Newsweek* (22 April 1991) George Will mentions, "as typical of the disease afflicting Western civilization, the professor who suggests that Shakespeare's *Tempest* is somehow about imperialism." Will's exact words are that some professors say "Shakespeare's *Tempest* reflects the imperialist rape of the Third World." Has Greenblatt reported Will's view fairly? Explain.
2. There is no doubt that Shakespeare derived some details of *The Tempest* from reports of the New World. Does this in itself mean that the play must in some degree be about the New World? Do *you* think it is about the New World? Entirely? In part? A little? Not at all? Explain.
3. In paragraph 12 Greenblatt says that *The Tempest* can "teach us about forgiveness, wisdom, and social atonement." Do you agree? If so, *what* can it teach us about these things?

## RALPH BERRY AND JONATHAN MILLER

***Ralph Berry is the author of several books on Shakespeare. Jonathan Miller, a physician by training, is a noted director of plays. We print part of an interview in which Berry questions Miller about his 1970 production of*** The Tempest.

# *A Production of* The Tempest

JM. It's in disease that one understands health and I think that we can actually now by hindsight understand a great deal more of the relationship of white Europe to the black world. Knowing what we now know about the emergence of the black world and its revolt against the world of white Europe, I just don't think that we would have had the conceptual apparatus, the cognitive skills to visualise that until it began to break down. Now this is not because I wish to seize *The Tempest* or to hijack *The Tempest* and to fly it to a modern airport and make it do the work of anti-colonial radicalism, that would be I think a very crude and brutal thing to do. It is just that by bringing out that particular theme in *The Tempest* something rather rich happens which wouldn't occur if one simply played the rather romantic version of *The Tempest* where both Caliban and Ariel are impalpable spirits or gross clods. I mean I think that there is something very interesting also in seeing the trio of Prospero, Caliban and Ariel in the light of some metaphysical idea of the division of the human soul and the tripartite nature of the mind.

RB. How did your approach to *The Tempest* come into being?

JM. Well, it came into being in two ways. Very often I find that, although I spoke previously about not being exposed to theatrical clichés I've been exposed to a certain number of them and certainly some of my moves in the theatre have been prompted by a revulsion against certain well-established clichés, which are so glaring that hardly anyone who is aware of simply being at school could fail to notice them. Now the one which stuck in my gorge was the sequin-spangled, pointed-eared, flitting figure of Ariel on wires, his hands held stiffly behind him as he flew *à la* Peter Pan on and off the stage. This seemed to me to be sentimental and diminishing and similarly the scaly, web-footed monster of Caliban just didn't tell me anything about anyone, it wasn't a monster which meant anything in my imagination and it actually clotted my imagination and stopped it from thinking. But I had been reading some years before a book by an anthropologist called Mannoni, who had written a book on the revolt in Madagascar in 1947, and he had used as a metaphor in order to explain the relationships of the very protagonists of the revolt the image of *The Tempest* and he saw Caliban and Ariel as different forms of black response to white paternalism. In Caliban he saw the demoralised, detribalised, dispossessed shuffling field hand and in Ariel a rather deft accomplished black who actually absorbs all the techniques and skills of the white master; the house servant, who is then in a position to assume political power when the white master goes back home. And of course we had this situation only a few years ago in Nigeria, with the skilled civil servant Ibos and the unskilled tribal Hausas. Now once again I wasn't using *The Tempest* as a political cartoon to illustrate the Nigerian dilemma nor as it were to castigate modern colonialism or to expose the wickedness of Rhodesia, but to use the images of Rhodesia, Nigeria, and indeed the whole colonial theme as knowledge which the audience brought to bear on Shakespeare's play. They could scarcely avoid thinking of that situation when the two characters were represented as blacks. Now by doing it in this way I hoped to bring them into a closer relationship with the whole notion of subordination and mastery which I think is one of the things which Shakespeare is talking about with great eloquence in that play. And I think he is also talking about, in a sense, infantilism and about the way in which maturity is only arrived at by surrendering one's claim to control the whole of nature. A child after all arrives at maturity by appreciating the reality principle, and after all what is the reality principle? The reality principle is simply the understanding that there are certain things over which one has control, and there are most things over which one has no control.

RB. I think that the reality principle is certainly one of the immutable touchstones of Shakespeare's whole work.

JM. I think that this in a sense comes out very clearly in this play, particularly if you slant it in this manner. After all one of the most important aspects of the reality principle is that there is a limited control over other people's destinies, not just over the physical world, but over the moral world, and that certain infantile personalities flourish in the colonial situation because they meet people whose power to resist their will is diminished by their lack of skills and so you often get rather immature personalities flourishing in the colonial situation because the colonial situation has in it people who cannot resist the superior technology of advanced society, and Prospero achieves his maturity in surrendering his power over his slaves, in leaving the island and returning to the world in which he must actually face his peers and equals, in a society where everyone has access to the same skills.

RB. And indeed he looks forward to surrendering his power to his children.

JM. He surrenders three things: he surrenders the power over his own children, he surrenders the power over subordinates, or at least over helpless subordinates, and he surrenders this impractical desire for power over the forces of nature. By breaking his staff he is doing what the child really does after the age of five, of realising that his rage will not call down the tempest but only contempt.

[*1977*]

## TOPICS FOR CRITICAL THINKING AND WRITING

1. In his first paragraph Miller suggests that today we can see *The Tempest* in interesting ways that were unavailable to earlier ages. If you find this approach attractive, apply it to some literary work other than *The Tempest.* For instance, can we now see meanings in *Huckleberry Finn* that were unavailable to Mark Twain and his contemporary readers?
2. In paragraph 3 Miller summarizes an interpretation of Caliban and Ariel. Do you think this interpretation makes sense? Explain.
3. If you were producing *The Tempest* might you (like Miller) present Caliban and Ariel as black? Why? (You may want to take into account the next essay, by Errol G. Hill, in this book.)
4. Miller says (paragraph 3) that *The Tempest* is partly about "the whole notion of subordination and mastery." But *what* does it say about these notions?
5. Summarize Miller's view of "infantilism" (paragraphs 3–7) and its relation to Prospero. Next, indicate the degree to which you think this view of infantilism helps you to understand the play.

## ERROL G. HILL

***Errol G. Hill, a theater historian, is the author of many studies, including*** Shakespeare in Sable: A History of Black Shakespearean Actors. ***We reprint part of an essay that originally appeared in*** Theatre History Studies.

# *Caliban and Ariel: A Study in Black and White*

When the establishment theatre slowly began to overcome its opposition to interracial casting in Shakespeare, Caliban was one of the first nonblack roles offered to black actors. The occasion was the 1944 production by Margaret Webster which opened at the Alvin Theatre in New York on January 25, 1945, after short tryout runs in Philadelphia and Boston. In the cast were Arnold Moss as Prospero, Canada Lee as Caliban, and the ballerina Vera Zorina as Ariel. Webster had, a few years earlier, created a breakthrough of sorts by casting Paul Robeson as Othello in the record-breaking

Theatre Guild production of that play and now she was building on that success. The February 1945 issue of *Theatre Arts* defended her choice of Canada Lee for the role of Caliban:

> In picking the Negro actor for the role, Miss Webster made it clear that she meant to exploit his particular intensity, his power to come to grips with character, and not the pigmentation of his skin. "I do not intend," she insists, "to make Caliban a parable of the current state of the American Negro." Yet her willing eyes discover a ready parallel.

Webster may not have intended it, but she was setting a dangerous precedent. In his first night review of the production, one of the major New York critics observed that "Caliban is a perfect role for a Negro." The production ran for one hundred performances at the Alvin Theatre and was revived later that year at City Center, New York, for a further three weeks.

Now it is true that to the medieval and Elizabethan mind, blackness was associated with evil and hence with the devil who is "the prince of darkness" and personifies evil. Caliban, we are told in the play, was fathered by the devil and is referred to by Prospero as "a devil, a born devil" and "a thing of darkness." It can therefore be argued that he ought originally to have been played black. However, to my knowledge, there is no tradition of playing the role in blackface or of using a black actor prior to Webster's production, and certainly from a modern viewpoint there is no logical justification for casting a black actor as Caliban when the counterpart role of Ariel is given to a sylphlike white actor or, quite often, actress. If anything, the reverse is more appropriate.

Caliban's mother, we recall, was a foul blue-eyed witch called Sycorax who, pregnant with him, had been banished from Algiers to the island. She was either European or Mediterannean in origin and her misshapen son who, Shakespeare tells us, is freckled, must have shared his mother's ethnic pedigree. The delicate Ariel, on the other hand, was found on the island by Sycorax and imprisoned in a pine tree until freed by Prospero who promptly enslaved him as his personal genie. Though unhuman and free of the elements, Ariel inhabited the island prior to the arrival of foreigners and is presumably indigenous to the Caribbean—in any case hardly European. These considerations have been generally ignored in filling the roles. Instead Ariel, the creature of air and native to the Caribbean, is white. Caliban, the savage monster and would-be rapist from the Mediterranean, is black. It is beauty and the beast all over again, with white equating beauty and black bestiality.

[*1984*]

##  TOPICS FOR CRITICAL THINKING AND WRITING

1. Do you think that a director should or should not cast an African-American in the role of Caliban? Or is the matter of color irrelevant?
2. Browse through the issues constituting the last two or three years of *Shakespeare Quarterly*, or the last two or three issues of *Shakespeare Survey* (an annual publication), taking special note of the comments on Caliban and Ariel in various productions. Summarize these, and then in-

dicate which interpretations seem to you to be especially interesting and fruitful.

## LINDA BAMBER

*Linda Bamber, author of* Comic Women, Tragic Men: A Study of Gender and Genre in Shakespeare, *teaches English literature at Tufts University.*

# The Tempest *and* The Traffic in Women

*The Tempest,* as many readers have noticed, recapitulates several themes from Shakespeare's earlier plays. Sometimes it seems to be doing so "consciously," if a play can be said to be conscious of its own procedures. First of all, in a series of swift and virtuosic variations, it recapitulates the theme of the masculine struggle for power against other men. Antonio and Sebastian conspire to kill Alonso for his crown; Caliban, Trinculo, and Stephano plot to kill Prospero for his power on the island; Ferdinand is accused of being a usurper of Prospero's power and is temporarily enslaved as punishment; and, of course, Antonio has conspired with Alonso to usurp Prospero's power in Milan and "extirpate"* Prospero himself. Behind this array of murderous conspiracies lie the history plays and the tragedies, in which men fight and kill each other for political power and revenge.

The mating of Miranda is another theme with a long history behind it. We may think of all the fathers in Shakespeare who have battled their daughters for the power to choose the daughter's sexual partner; more broadly, we may think of all the men—fathers, husbands, and lovers—who have suffered and made others suffer when they lose control of "their" women's sexuality. Capulet, Brabantio, Egeus, and Lear fall into the first category; Othello, Leontes, Antony, and perhaps Hamlet fall into the second. In *The Tempest,* of course, the father and daughter do not struggle against each other. They are in perfect agreement as to the choice of Miranda's mate. And yet the play strips to its essentials—and thus makes legible—the father-daughter issue as well as the male power issue. Moreover, it is the play in which the fundamental connection between the two themes is most clearly spelled out.

In a brilliant essay called "The Traffic in Women: Notes on the 'Political Economy' of Sex,"[1] Gayle Rubin has appropriated for feminist purposes the insights of Claude Levi-Strauss's *The Elementary Structures of Kinship* in ways that may be pertinent to a reading of *The Tempest.* Levi-Strauss, as Rubin puts it, "sees the essence of kinship systems to lie in an exchange of women between men" (171). To give a woman to another family or tribe creates reciprocal obligations on the one hand and "affines" or allies on the other. It can make allies, in fact, out of enemies, and expand the scope and power of the man who gives the woman as a gift. This description of primitive social structure applies neatly to the action of *The Tempest,* in which

*All references are to the Signet Classic editions of Shakespeare's plays, Sylvan Barnet, gen. ed. (New York: NAL, 1987). 1.2.125.

Prospero's gift of Miranda to Alonso's family creates a kinship alliance with a former enemy and supersedes the bond between Alonso and Antonio. Miranda is Prospero's ticket home; or rather Prospero's ownership in her newly acquired sexuality is his ticket home. It may be objected that this is too harsh a description of Prospero's relationship to his daughter. He does, after all, negotiate quite delicately with her over her feelings for Ferdinand when Ferdinand first appears, and he seems to behave as if the marriage could not take place without her desire for it. But Levi-Strauss makes clear that the woman remains an "object in the exchange, not . . . one of the partners . . . even when the girl's feelings are taken into consideration, as, moreover, is usually the case." The partners are not "a man and a woman, . . . but two groups of men," and "in acquiescing to the proposed union, [the woman only] precipitates or allows the exchange to take place, she cannot alter its nature."[2]

Fragments of the picture drawn by Rubin and Levi-Strauss appear in earlier plays, where they often seem somewhat inexplicable. For instance, in *A Midsummer Night's Dream* Egeus's will to control his daughter's choice of a husband seems utterly irrational, since Lysander and Demetrius are clearly meant to be indistinguishable from one another. But if we understand Egeus to be asserting his ownership in Hermia's sexuality, then his control is valuable for its own sake, not for its influence over Hermia's choice. "[Demetrius] hath my love," declares Egeus,

> And what is mine my love shall render him.
> And she is mine, and all my right of her
> I do estate unto Demetrius. (1.1.95–98)

The actual husband is irrelevant. What matters are Egeus's rights of possession in his daughter, without which he has nothing to trade with other men.

5 Another puzzling moment that clears up in the light of the idea of the exchange of women is the one in which Othello responds to the news that Desdemona has been unfaithful to him. "Farewell content!" he cries, which is understandable enough; but then he goes on,

> Farewell the plumed troops, and the big wars
> That makes ambition virtue! O, farewell!
> Farewell . . . all quality,
> Pride, pomp, and circumstance of glorious war!
> . . .
> Farewell! Othello's occupation's gone! (3.3.345–48, 350–51, 354)

There is no logical reason why Othello should not continue to perform his duties as a Venetian general even if his wife has been unfaithful. And yet Othello assumes that his relations with other men—the men who confer and acknowledge his power—have been catastrophically damaged by this event. Having lost his ownership in this daughter of Venice, Othello loses his connection to Venice itself and thus his "occupation." Prospero, by contrast, loses his occupation first but regains it when the woman *he* "owns" becomes marriageable.

Is the exchange of women part of the ideology of *The Tempest* or not? Does *The Tempest* simply reveal the mechanisms of the traffic in women (thus making it available for criticism) or is it committed to the system it depends on for its plot? The answer, as usual in Shakespeare, is "Both." Think, for instance, of *The Merchant of Venice,* which is both an anti-Semitic play and a play about anti-Semitism. And certainly when dealing with patriarchal structures of all kinds Shakespeare goes back and forth between endorsing and criticizing what he describes. I will begin, then, with some evidence of Shakespeare's commitment to the traffic in women and proceed to his uneasiness with it.

The journey that brings Alonso and his group to Prospero's island was originally a wedding journey, undertaken to deliver Alonso's daughter Claribel to the King of Tunis. In giving his daughter to a foreigner Alonso seems to be serving the "social aim of exogamy and alliance"[3] so important to the formation of kinship systems. But apparently Alonso has gone too far. Tunis is *too* far outside the immediate family, *too* "exo." After the shipwreck, Sebastian refuses to console Alonso for the presumed death of Ferdinand, berating him instead for his behavior toward Claribel:

> Sir, you may thank yourself for this great loss,
> That would not bless our Europe with your daughter,
> But rather loose her to an African.
> . . .
> You were kneeled to and importuned otherwise
> By all of us; and the fair soul herself
> Weighed, between loathness and obedience, at
> Which end o' th' beam should bow. (2.1.128–30; 133–36)

Not only has Prospero given to an African what he should have given to a European, but he has also failed to find an accommodation with his daughter's own desire. Clearly Alonso has played his hand badly. Sebastian tells him he will never see Claribel again, and neither, presumably, will he profit from his alliance with the King of Tunis.

The contrast with Prospero is obvious. While Alonso imposes his will on his daughter crudely, Prospero is full of subtlety and technique. While Alonso makes a useless alliance, Prospero makes a useful one. Like a conduct book or an instruction manual, the play teaches by negative as well as positive examples: *don't* do it that way, *do* do it this way. But like a conduct book or an instruction manual, the play never doubts that "it" should be done. The presence of the negative example is evidence of the play's commitment to the traffic in women. Because Alonso does it wrong, Prospero seems to do it right. It is Alonso's failures that invite us to approve of Prospero's liberal, benevolent use of his patriarchal powers, to notice the effort he puts into their exercise, and to applaud his ultimate success. The reader's judgment is deflected onto Alonso, and the system itself is protected from criticism.

10 But the play does register a price for the traffic in women, and that price is the incest taboo. Levi-Strauss argues that the incest taboo "should best be understood as a mechanism to insure that . . . exchanges [of women] take place between families and between groups" (Rubin 173). He quotes an informant as follows:

> What, would you like to marry your sister? What is the matter with you? Don't you want a brother-in-law? Don't you realize that if you marry another man's sister and another man marries your sister, you will have at least two brothers-in-law, while if you marry your own sister you will

> have none? With whom will you hunt, with whom will you garden, whom will you go visit? (Levi-Strauss 485)

This quotation makes it clear that there is something to be given up as well as something to be gained in the exchange of women. In *Civilization and Its Discontents* Freud argues that what we value about organized society is purchased at the price of the repression or sublimation of our instinctual life, and *The Tempest* can be read as a kind of gloss on that argument. By obeying the rules of exogamy Prospero creates a kinship alliance with Alonso; and "kinship," as Rubin says, "is organization, and organization gives power" (174). The power that Prospero gains, however, requires the renunciation of his own sexual gratification. The drama of that renunciation is played out in his relations with Caliban.

Caliban is most often read as the native "other" degraded by the European imagination and enslaved by European power. But he may also be read as *self*-difference, the otherness we reject within ourselves and specifically as the otherness of the body. "This thing of darkness," Prospero says at the end of the play, "I / Acknowledge mine" (5.1.275–6). Caliban has far more of a body than anyone else in the play; only Ferdinand offers any competition at all. Caliban is a suffering body, first of all, pinched and stung and cramped by Prospero's punishments. Then he is an alcoholic body, drunk and rowdy; a humiliated body, dunked in a cesspool; and, most relevant to my discussion, a sexual body with desire for Miranda. It must be admitted that even Caliban's desire for Miranda is mixed with a "civilized" desire for kinship, power, and alliances with men. Reminded of the attempted rape, an unrepentant Caliban says,

> O ho, O ho! Would 't had been done!
> Thou didst prevent me; I had peopled else
> This isle with Calibans. (1.2.349–51)

And Caliban "offers" Miranda to Stephano to lure him into the conspiracy against Prospero:

> And that most deeply to consider is
> The beauty of his daughter.
>
> . . .
>
> She will become thy bed, I warrant,
> And bring thee forth brave brood. (3.2.102–3; 108–9)

But although Caliban is at one level a player in the male power game, at another level he is that which Prospero must control in order to succeed at the game, that is, his own instinctual life. Only Caliban has the power to elicit an intense emotional reaction from Prospero; the reaction is rage, and it interrupts the wedding masque that Prospero produces to celebrate Miranda's engagement to Ferdinand. As I argue elsewhere,[4] this rage may be related to the wedding masque itself, which marks the moment when Prospero gives up his sexual rights to his daughter. The rape that Caliban attempted and Prospero prevented can be seen as the site or symbol of Prospero's struggle with himself. It is worth noting in this context that Prospero has lived in involuntary celibacy during his entire stay on the island and that the return to Milan is in no way imagined as a return to a sexual partner.

Prospero's control of Caliban hurts. For one thing, Caliban's claim to have been himself usurped by Prospero is never answered, so it calls into question Prospero's own legitimacy and perhaps legitimacy per se. More significantly for my purposes, Caliban is a demonstration that we cannot actually separate repression of the body from something even closer to home, something like the repression of desire itself. Caliban's great speech about the music on the island concludes,

> . . . and then, in dreaming,
> The clouds methought would open and show riches
> Ready to drop upon me, that when I waked
> I cried to dream again. (3.3.145–48)

The enslavement of the grotesque, incestuous body is also, in *The Tempest*, the enslavement of the delicate soul. So much is given up, the play suggests, for the sake of social organization—for the sake of *having* a woman to exchange—that the whole system must be understood as problematic. Thus *The Tempest* questions its own ideology.

Does the play have any "consciousness" of the cost to *women* of the system it both supports and questions, or is it only the man who pays the price? Claribel, the violated woman, is remembered only by Gonzalo in his cheerful summing-up speech at the end of the play:

> . . . In one voyage
> Did Claribel her husband find at Tunis,
> And Ferdinand, her brother, found a wife
> Where he himself was lost. (5.1.208–11)

At first glance this appears to be a complete erasure of Claribel's experience. Her situation is exactly what it has always been, and yet now it is described as a joyful affair, and the description is allowed to stand. But of course it is Gonzalo who is speaking, and the play invites skepticism toward Gonzalo. The ending of the play is much more somber than Gonzalo realizes—perhaps even a little bitter. Is Gonzalo's fleeting mention of Claribel the opposite of what it seems, a reminder of a difficulty rather than a dismissal of it? Perhaps. But even if we grant that it is, this moment seems a most minimal acknowledgment of the price that is paid by women for kinship, for exogamy, for the traffic in women. The play accepts as inevitable the "distinction," as Rubin puts it, "between gift and giver" (174) and does not concern itself unduly with the tragedy for a woman of *being* the gift.

[*1995*]

## Notes

[1]Gayle Rubin, "The Traffic in Women: Notes on the 'Political Economy' of Sex," in Rayna R. Reiter, ed., *Toward an Anthropology of Women* (New York: Monthly Review, 1975).

[2]Claude Levi-Strauss, *The Elementary Structures of Kinship* (Boston: Beacon, 1969), p. 115.

[3]Rubin, p. 173.

[4]Linda Bamber, *Comic Women, Tragic Men: A Study of Gender and Genre in Shakespeare* (Palo Alto: Stanford UP, 1982), p. 177.

## TOPICS FOR CRITICAL THINKING AND WRITING

1. In paragraphs 3 and 4 Bamber points to scenes in *A Midsummer Night's Dream* and *Othello* that are clarified by the idea of "the traffic in women." If you are familiar with any other scenes in Shakespeare that are thus clarified, specify them and briefly explain how they fit into the pattern.
2. Bamber suggests that "the rape that Caliban attempted and Prospero prevented can be seen as the site or symbol of Prospero's struggle with himself." How might you support this assertion?
3. Bamber ends by saying that the play "does not concern itself unduly with the tragedy for a woman of *being* the gift." Assuming the truth of her observation, do you think the play is therefore at fault? Explain.

# SAMPLE ESSAY BY A STUDENT

Rudy Swinton

English 150G

May 1, 1996

King Caliban?

Almost the first thing that Caliban does, when we meet him in The Tempest, is to announce his claim to the island. He says to Prospero:

> This island's mine, by Sycorax my mother,
> Which thou tak'st from me. When thou
>     cam'st first,
> Thou strok'st me and made much of me,
>     wouldst give me
> Water with berries in 't, and teach me how
> To name the bigger light, and how the less,
> That burn by day and night. And then
>     I loved thee
> And showed thee all the qualities o'
>     th' isle,
> The fresh springs, brine pits, barren
>     place and fertile.

Cursed be I that did so! All the charms
Of Sycorax, toads, beetles, bats,
light on you!
For I am all the subjects that you have,
Which first was mine own king. . . .
(1.2.334-45)

There are three very interesting things here. First, as I have said, Caliban announces his claim to the throne: it is his because his mother ruled the island. Second, he shows a special closeness with nature. He obviously is especially fond of "water with berries in 't," and he was thoroughly familiar with the island--with its "fresh springs, brine pits, barren place and fertile." Third, he hates Prospero.

How strong is Caliban's claim that the island is his? Stephen Greenblatt says: "Caliban, enslaved by Prospero, bitterly challenges the European's right to sovereignty. The island was his birthright, he claims, and was unjustly taken from him. Caliban's claim is not upheld in The Tempest, but neither is it simply dismissed . . ." (1901). Somewhat similarly, Linda Bamber says that "Caliban's claim to have been himself usurped by Prospero is never answered, so it calls into question Prospero's own legitimacy . . ." (1910). I disagree with both of these comments. I think Shakespeare clearly dismisses Caliban's claim and indicates that when Prospero made a slave of Caliban he did the only thing possible.

Caliban says the island is his because it was his mother's. But his mother was exiled from Algiers and dumped on the island, so she was not one of the native people. In fact, there seem to have been no native people at all, only the spirit Ariel. Prospero says that Caliban's mother was a "damned witch" (1.2.265). Actually, no one else in the play verifies Prospero's statement, but I think we assume it is true, since no one in the play denies it. Now, if it _is_ true, as I think it is, then Caliban really does not have much claim on the island. All he can say is that he was there first, before Prospero. But he is there only because his mother was exiled there. Further, his mother imprisoned the only inhabitant, Ariel, so if the island "naturally" and fairly belongs to anyone, it is Ariel, who was put into a tree by Sycorax. Prospero released Ariel, on the condition that Ariel would serve Prospero. Ariel did not have much choice, but he made the deal, and a deal is a deal, so the island is Prospero's, since it was given to him by the one truly original inhabitant.

If Caliban were truly an original inhabitant, and if he were the sort of person that Montaigne describes in his famous essay on Native Americans, we certainly would feel that Prospero has no right to enslave him. This is what Montaigne says about the people in the New World:

> It is a nation . . . that hath . . . no name of magistrate, nor of political superiority; . . . no partitions, no occupation but idle; no respect of kindred but common, no apparel but natural, no manuring of lands, no use of wine, corn, or metal. The very words that import lying, falsehood, treason, dissimulations,

covetousness, envy, detraction, and pardon, were never heard of amongst them. (1896)

But this ideal society is not the society that Caliban represents. True, Caliban is especially close to nature, but that is because there was no one else on the island, except his mother and Ariel, and of course he did not have any books, and he was illiterate. Prospero taught him how to speak, and in fact Caliban does speak very well, but he seems to be unable to learn anything else. We learn that Caliban tried to rape Prospero's daughter, Miranda. Since Miranda is the only woman on the island, and she is very beautiful, it is not at all surprising that Caliban wants to possess her sexually, but still it is obviously horrible, and it indicates that Caliban has no self-control. Judging from what we see in the play, Miranda is correct when she says that no "print of goodness" will stick to Caliban, and he is "capable of all ill" (1.2.355-56).

Since Caliban does not have any right to the island, other than the fact that he was there before Prospero was, and since he is thoroughly wicked even if he does speak effectively about the beauty of the island, and since his wickedness led him to try to rape Miranda, Prospero really has no course other than to try to control Caliban. If Caliban were fully human, enslavement would be totally wrong, but Caliban seems to be half human and half a beast, the offspring of a witch and a devil, and so Prospero has to take strong means to control him. It is a very bad situation, but it is not of Prospero's making. And notice that far from wishing to enslave Caliban and to colonize the island, Prospero wants to go home, and at the end he does go home, leaving Caliban behind. Prospero does not want Caliban as a slave; he enslaves him only because he had to protect himself and his daughter. Prospero is quite willing to let Caliban be king--provided that Prospero and Miranda are far away. And so at last Caliban is back where he was before Prospero drifted to the island, when Caliban could say of himself that he "was mine own king." We wish him well in his island monarchy--but we don't want to be around him.

Works Cited

Bamber, Linda. "The Tempest and The Traffic in Women." Barnet et al. 1906-10.

Barnet, Sylvan et al., eds. Literature: Thinking, Reading, and Writing Critically, 2nd ed. New York: Longman, 1997.

Greenblatt, Stephen. "The Best Way to Kill Our Literary Inheritance Is to Turn It Into a Decorous Celebration of the New World Order." Barnet et al. 1900-1901.

Montaigne, Michel Eyquem de. "Of the Cannibals." Barnet et al. 1896.

Shakespeare, William. The Tempest. Barnet et al. 1830-92.

## TOPICS FOR CRITICAL THINKING AND WRITING

1. What is the author's thesis?
2. Do you think the thesis is adequately supported? Explain.
3. Do you think the student has made good use of the other texts presented in this chapter? Explain.

# PART FIVE

## *Critical Perspectives*

# CHAPTER 35

# Critical Approaches
## The Nature of Criticism

Formalist (or New) Criticism
Deconstruction
Reader-Response Criticism
Archetypal (or Myth) Criticism
Historical Scholarship, Marxist Criticism,
The New Historicism, and Biographical Criticism
Psychological (or Psychoanalytic) Criticism
Gender (Feminist, and Lesbian and Gay) Criticism

In everyday talk the commonest meaning of **criticism** is something like "finding fault." And to be critical is to be censorious. But a critic can see excellences as well as faults. Because we turn to criticism with the hope that the critic has seen something we have missed, the most valuable criticism is not that which shakes its finger at faults but that which calls our attention to interesting things going on in the work of art. Here is a statement by W. H. Auden (1907–73), suggesting that criticism is most useful when it calls our attention to things worth attending to:

> What is the function of a critic? So far as I am concerned, he can do me one or more of the following services:
>
> 1. Introduce me to authors or works of which I was hitherto unaware.
> 2. Convince me that I have undervalued an author or a work because I had not read them carefully enough.
> 3. Show me relations between works of different ages and cultures which I could never have seen for myself because I do not know enough and never shall.
> 4. Give a "reading" of a work which increases my understanding of it.
> 5. Throw light upon the process of artistic "Making."
> 6. Throw light upon the relation of art to life, science, economics, ethics, religion, etc.
>
> —*The Dyer's Hand* (New York, 1963), pp. 8–9

Auden does not neglect the delight we get from literature, but he extends (especially in his sixth point) the range of criticism to include topics beyond the literary work itself. Notice too the emphasis on observing, showing, and illuminating, which suggests that the function of critical writing is not very different from the commonest view of the function of imaginative writing.

Whenever we talk about a work of literature or of art, or, for that matter, even about a so-so movie or television show, what we say depends in large measure on certain conscious or unconscious assumptions that we make: "I liked it; the characters were very believable" (here the assumption is that characters ought to be believable); "I didn't like it; there was too much violence" (here the assumption is that violence ought not to be shown, or if it is shown it should be made abhorrent); "I didn't like it; it was awfully slow" (here the assumption probably is that there ought to be a fair amount of physical action, perhaps even changes of scene, rather than characters just talking); "I didn't like it; I don't think topics of this sort ought to be discussed publicly" (here the assumption is a moral one, that it is indecent to present certain topics); "I liked it partly because it was refreshing to hear such frankness" (here again the assumption is moral, and more or less the reverse of the previous one).

In short, whether we realize it or not, we judge the work from a particular viewpoint—its realism, its morality, or whatever.

Professional critics, too, work from assumptions, but their assumptions are usually highly conscious, and the critics may define their assumptions at length. They regard themselves as, for instance, Freudians or Marxists or gay critics. They read all texts through the lens of a particular theory, and their focus enables them to see things that otherwise might go unnoticed. It should be added, however, that if a lens or critical perspective or interpretive strategy helps us to see certain things, it also limits our vision. Many critics therefore regard their method not as an exclusive way of thinking but only as a useful tool.

What follows is a brief survey of the chief current approaches to literature. You may find, as you read these pages, that one or another approach sounds especially congenial, and therefore you may want to make use of it in your reading and writing. On the other hand, it's important to remember, first, that works of literature are highly varied, and, second, that we read them for various purposes—to kill time, to enjoy fanciful visions, to be amused, to explore alien ways of feeling, and to learn about ourselves. It may be best to try to respond to each text in the way that the text seems to require rather than to read all texts according to a single formula. You'll find that some works will lead you to want to think about them from several angles. A play by Shakespeare may stimulate you to read a book about the Elizabethan playhouse, and another that offers a Marxist interpretation of the English Renaissance, and still another that offers a feminist analysis of Shakespeare's plays. All of these approaches, and others, will help you to deepen your understanding of the literary works that you read.

## FORMALIST (OR NEW) CRITICISM

**Formalist criticism** emphasizes the work as an independent creation, a self-contained unit, something to be studied in itself, not as part of some larger context, such as the author's life or a historical period. This kind of study is called formalist criticism because the emphasis is on the *form* of the work, the relationships between the parts—the construction of the plot, the contrasts between characters, the functions of rhymes, the point of view, and so on.

Cleanth Brooks, perhaps America's most distinguished formalist critic, in an essay in the *Kenyon Review* (Winter 1951), reprinted in *The Modern Critical Spectrum*, eds. Gerald Jay Goldberg and Nancy Marmer Goldberg (1962), set forth what he called his "articles of faith":

> That literary criticism is a description and an evaluation of its object.
>
> That the primary concern of criticism is with the problem of unity—the kind of whole which the literary work forms or fails to form, and the relation of the various parts to each other in building up this whole.
>
> That the formal relations in a work of literature may include, but certainly exceed, those of logic.
>
> That in a successful work, form and content cannot be separated.
>
> That form is meaning.

If you have read the earlier pages of this book you are already familiar with most of these ideas, but in the next few pages we will look into some of them in detail.

Formalist criticism is, in essence, *intrinsic* criticism, rather than extrinsic, for (at least in theory) it concentrates on the work itself, independent of its writer and the writer's background—that is, independent of biography, psychology, sociology, and history. The discussions of Langston Hughes's "Harlem" (p. 830) and of Yeats's "The Balloon of the Mind" (p. 35) are examples. The gist is that a work of literature is complex, unified, and freestanding. In fact, of course, we usually bring outside knowledge to the work. For instance, a reader who is familiar with, say, *Hamlet* can hardly study another tragedy by Shakespeare, let's say *Romeo and Juliet,* without bringing to the second play some conception of what Shakespearean tragedy is or can be. A reader of Alice Walker's *The Color Purple* inevitably brings unforgettable outside material (perhaps the experience of being an African-American, or at least some knowledge of the history of African-Americans) to the literary work. It is very hard to talk only about *Hamlet* or *The Color Purple* and not at the same time talk about, or at least have in mind, aspects of human experience.

Formalist criticism begins with a personal response to the literary work, but it goes on to try to account for the response by closely examining the work. It assumes that the author shaped the poem, play, or story so fully that the work guides the reader's responses. The assumption that "meaning" is fully and completely presented within the text is not much in favor today, when many literary critics argue that the active or subjective reader (or even what Judith Fetterley, a feminist critic, has called "the resisting reader") and not the author of the text makes the "meaning." Still, even if one grants that the reader is active, not passive or coolly objective, one can hold with the formalists that the author is active too, constructing a text that in some measure controls the reader's responses. During the process of writing about our responses we may find that our responses change. A formalist critic would say that we see with increasing clarity what the work is really like, and what it really means. (Similarly, when authors write and revise a text they may change their understanding of what they are doing. A story that began as a lighthearted joke may turn into something far more serious than the writer imagined at the start, but, at least for the formalist critic, the final work contains a stable meaning that all competent readers can perceive.)

In practice, formalist criticism usually takes one of two forms, **explication** (the unfolding of meaning, line by line or even word by word) or **analysis** (the examination of the relations of parts). The essay on Yeats's "The Balloon of the Mind" (p. 35) is an explication, a setting forth of the implicit meanings of the words. The essay on Kate Chopin's "The Story of an Hour" (p.32–33) is an analysis. The three essays on Frost's "Stopping by Woods on a Snowy Evening" (pp. 1144–54) are chiefly analyses but with some passages of explication.

To repeat: Formalist criticism assumes that a work of art is stable. An artist constructs a coherent, comprehensible work, thus conveying to a reader an emotion or an idea. T. S. Eliot said that the writer can't just pour out emotions onto the page. Rather, Eliot said in an essay entitled "Hamlet and His Problems" (1919), "The only way of expressing emotion in the form of art is by finding an 'objective correlative'; in other words, a set of objects, a situation, a chain of events which shall be the formula of the *particular* emotion." With this in mind, consider Robert Frost's "The Span of Life":

> The old dog barks backward without getting up.
> I can remember when he was a pup.

The image of an old dog barking backward, and the speaker's memory—apparently triggered by the old dog's bark—of the dog as a pup, presumably is the "objective correlative" of Frost's emotion or idea; Frost is "expressing emotion" through this "formula." And all of us, as competent readers, can grasp pretty accurately what Frost expressed. Frost's emotion, idea, meaning, or whatever is "objectively" embodied in the text. Formalist critics try to explain how and why literary works—*these* words, in *this* order—constitute unique, complex structures that embody or set forth meanings.

Formalist criticism, also called the **New Criticism** (to distinguish it from the historical and biographical writing that in earlier decades had dominated literary study), began to achieve prominence in the late 1920s and was the dominant form from the late 1930s until about 1970, and even today it is widely considered the best way for a student to begin to study a work of literature. For one thing, formalist criticism empowers the student; that is, the student confronts the work immediately, and is not told first to spend days or weeks or months, for instance, reading Freud and his followers in order to write a psychoanalytic essay or reading Marx and Marxists in order to write a Marxist essay, or doing research on "necessary historical background" in order to write a historical essay.

## DECONSTRUCTION

**Deconstruction,** or deconstructive or poststructuralist criticism, can almost be characterized as the opposite of everything formalist criticism stands for. Deconstruction begins with the assumptions that the world is unknowable and that language is unstable, elusive, unfaithful. (Language is all of these things because meaning is largely generated by opposition: "Hot" means something in opposition to "cold," but a hot day may be 90 degrees whereas a hot oven is at least 400 degrees; and a "hot item" may be of any temperature.) Deconstructionists seek to show that a literary work (usually called "a text" or "a discourse") inevitably is self-contradictory. Unlike formalist critics—who hold that a competent author constructs a coherent work with a stable meaning, and that competent readers can perceive this meaning—deconstructionists (e.g., Barbara

Johnson, in *The Critical Difference* [1980]) hold that a work has no coherent meaning at the center. Jonathan Culler, in *On Deconstruction* (1982), says that "to deconstruct a discourse is to show how it undermines the philosophy it asserts" (86). (Johnson and Culler provide accessible introductions, but the major document is Jacques Derrida's seminal, difficult work, *Of Grammatology* [1967, trans. 1976].) The text is only marks on paper, and therefore so far as a reader goes the author of a text is not the writer but the reader; texts are "indeterminate," "open," and "unstable."

Despite the emphasis on indeterminacy, one sometimes detects in deconstructionist interpretations a view associated with Marxism. This is the idea that authors are "socially constructed" from the "discourses of power" or "signifying practices" that surround them. Thus, although authors may think they are individuals with independent minds, their works usually reveal—unknown to the authors—the society's economic base. Deconstructionists "interrogate" a text, and they reveal what the authors were unaware of or had thought they had kept safely out of sight. That is, deconstructionists often find a rather specific meaning—though this meaning is one that might surprise the author.

Deconstruction is valuable insofar as—like the New Criticism—it encourages close, rigorous attention to the text. Furthermore, in its rejection of the claim that a work has a single stable meaning, deconstruction has had a positive influence on the study of literature. The problem with deconstruction, however, is that too often it is reductive, telling the same story about every text—that here, yet again, and again, we see how a text is incoherent and heterogeneous. There is, too, an irritating arrogance in some deconstructive criticism: "The author could not see how his/her text is fundamentally unstable and self-contradictory, but *I* can and now will interrogate the text and will issue my report." Readers, of course, should not prostrate themselves before texts, but there is something askew about an approach—however intense and detailed—that often leads readers to conclude that they know a good deal more than the benighted author.

Aware that their emphasis on the instability of language implies that their own texts are unstable or even incoherent, some deconstructionists seem to aim at entertaining rather than at edifying. They probably would claim that they do not deconstruct meaning in the sense of destroying it; rather, they might say, they exuberantly multiply meanings, and to this end they may use such devices as puns, irony, and allusions, somewhat as a poet might, and just as though (one often feels) they think they are as creative as the writers they are commenting on. Indeed, for many deconstructionists, the traditional conception of "literature" is merely an elitist "construct." All "texts" or "discourses" (novels, scientific papers, a Kewpie doll on the mantel, watching TV, suing in court, walking the dog, and all other signs that human beings make) are of a piece; all are unstable systems of signifying, all are fictions, all are "literature." If literature (in the usual sense) occupies a special place in deconstruction it is because literature delights in its playfulness, its fictiveness, whereas other discourses nominally reject playfulness and fictiveness.

## READER-RESPONSE CRITICISM

Probably all reading includes some sort of response—"This is terrific," "This is a bore," "I don't know what's going on here"—and probably almost all writing about literature begins with some such response, but specialists in literature disagree greatly about the role that response plays, or should play, in experiencing literature and in writing about it.

At one extreme are those who say that our response to a work of literature should be a purely aesthetic response—a response to a work of art—and not the response we would have to something comparable in real life. To take an obvious point: If in real life we heard someone plotting a murder, we would intervene, perhaps by calling the police or by attempting to warn the victim. But when we hear Macbeth and Lady Macbeth plot to kill King Duncan, we watch with deep *interest;* we hear their words with *pleasure,* and maybe we even look forward to seeing the murder and to seeing what the characters then will say and what will happen to the murderers.

When you think about it, the vast majority of the works of literature do not have a close, obvious resemblance to the reader's life. Most readers of *Macbeth* are not Scots, and no readers are Scottish kings or queens. (It's not just a matter of older literature; no readers of Toni Morrison's *Beloved* are nineteenth-century African-Americans.) The connections readers make between themselves and the lives in most of the books they read are not, on the whole, connections based on ethnic or professional identities, but, rather, connections with states of consciousness, for instance a young person's sense of isolation from the family, or a young person's sense of guilt for initial sexual experiences. Before we reject a work either because it seems too close to us ("I'm a man and I don't like the depiction of this man"), or on the other hand too far from our experience ("I'm not a woman, so how can I enjoy reading about these women?"), we probably should try to follow the advice of Virginia Woolf, who said, "Do not dictate to your author; try to become him." Nevertheless, some literary works of the past may today seem intolerable, at least in part. There are passages in Mark Twain's *Huckleberry Finn* that deeply upset us today. We should, however, try to reconstruct the cultural assumptions of the age in which the work was written. If we do so, we may find that if in some ways it reflected its age, in other ways it challenged that culture.

Still, some of our experiences, some of *what we are,* may make it virtually impossible for us to read a work sympathetically or "objectively," experiencing it only as a work of art and not as a part of life. Take so humble a form of literature as the joke. A few decades ago jokes about nagging wives and mothers-in-law were widely thought to be funny. Our fairly recent heightened awareness of sexism today makes those jokes unfunny. Twenty years ago the "meaning" of a joke about a nagging wife or about a mother-in-law was, in effect, "Here's a funny episode that shows what women typically are." Today the "meaning"—at least as the hearer conceives it—is "The unfunny story you have just told shows that you have stupid, stereotypical views of women." In short, the joke may "mean" one thing to the teller, and a very different thing to the hearer.

Reader-response criticism, then, says that the "meaning" of a work is not merely something put into the work by the writer; rather, the "meaning" is an interpretation created or constructed or produced by the reader as well as the writer. Stanley Fish, an exponent of reader-response theory, in *Is There a Text in This Class?* (1980), puts it this way: "Interpretation is not the art of construing but of constructing. Interpreters do not decode poems; they make them" (327).

Let's now try to relate these ideas more specifically to comments about literature. If "meaning" is the production or creation not simply of the writer but also of the perceiver, does it follow that there is no such thing as a "correct" interpretation of the meaning of a work of literature? Answers to this question differ. At one extreme, the reader is said to construct or reconstruct the text under the firm guidance of the author. That is, the author so powerfully shapes or constructs the text—encodes an idea—that the reader is virtually compelled to perceive or reconstruct or decode it the way the author wants it to be perceived. (We can call this view *the objective view,* since it essentially holds that readers look objectively at the work and see what the author put into it.) At the other extreme, the reader constructs the meaning according to his or her own personality—that is, according to the reader's psychological identity. (We can call this view *the subjective view,* since it essentially holds that readers inevitably project their feelings into what they perceive.) An extreme version of the subjective view holds that there is no such thing as literature; there are only texts, some of which some readers regard in a particularly elitist way.

Against the objective view one can argue thus: No author can fully control a reader's response to every detail of the text. No matter how carefully constructed the text is, it leaves something—indeed, a great deal—to the reader's imagination. For instance, when Macbeth says that life "is a tale / Told by an idiot, full of sound and fury / Signifying nothing," are we getting a profound thought from Shakespeare or, on the contrary, are we getting a shallow thought from Macbeth, a man who does not see that his criminal deeds have been played out against a heaven that justly punishes his crimes? In short, the objective view neglects to take account of the fact that the author is not continually at our shoulder making sure that we interpret the work in a particular way.

It is probably true, as Flannery O'Connor says in *Mystery and Manners* (1957), that good writers select "every word, every detail, for a reason, every incident for a reason" (75), but there are always *gaps* or *indeterminacies,* to use the words of Wolfgang Iser, a reader-response critic. Readers always go beyond the text, drawing inferences, and evaluating the text in terms of their own experience. In the Old Testament, for instance, in Genesis, the author tells us (Chapter 22) that God commanded Abraham to sacrifice his son Isaac, and then says that "Abraham rose up early in the morning" and prepared to fulfill the command. We are not explicitly told *why* Abraham "rose up early in the morning," or how he spent the intervening night, but some readers take "early in the morning" to signify (reasonably?) that Abraham has had a sleepless night. Others take it to signify (reasonably?) that Abraham is prompt in obeying God's command. Some readers fill the gap with both explanations, or with neither. Doubtless much depends on the reader, but there is no doubt that readers "naturalize"—make natural, according to their own ideas—what they read.

In an extreme form the subjective view denies that authors can make us perceive the meanings that they try to put into their works. This position suggests that every reader has a different idea of what a work means, an idea that reflects the reader's own ideas. Every reader, then, is Narcissus, who looked into a pool of water and thought he saw a beautiful youth but really saw only a reflection of himself. But does every reader see his or her individual image in each literary work? Of course not. Even *Hamlet,* a play that has generated an enormous range of interpretation, is universally seen as a tragedy, a play that deals with painful realities. If someone were to tell us that *Hamlet* is a comedy, and that the end, with a pile of corpses, is especially funny, we would not say, "Oh, well, we all see things in our own way." Rather, we would make our exit as quickly as possible.

Many people who subscribe to one version or another of a reader-response theory would agree that they are concerned not with all readers but with what they call *informed readers* or *competent readers.* Thus, informed or competent readers are familiar with the conventions of literature. They understand, for instance, that in a play such as *Hamlet* the characters usually speak in verse. Such readers, then, do not express amazement that Hamlet often speaks metrically, and that he sometimes uses rhyme. These readers understand that verse is the normal language for most of the characters in the play, and therefore such readers do not characterize Hamlet as a poet. Informed, competent readers, in short, know the rules of the game. There will still, of course, be plenty of room for differences of interpretation. Some people will find Hamlet not at all blameworthy; others will find him somewhat blameworthy; and still others may find him highly blameworthy. In short, we can say that a writer works against a background that is *shared* by readers. As readers, we are familiar with various kinds of literature, and we read or see *Hamlet* as a particular kind of literary work, a tragedy, a play that evokes (in Shakespeare's words) "woe or wonder," sadness and astonishment. Knowing (to a large degree) how we ought to respond, our responses thus are not merely private.

Consider taking, as a guide to reading, a remark made by Mencius (372–289 B.C.), the Chinese Confucian philosopher. Speaking of reading *The Book of Odes,* the oldest Chinese anthology, Mencius said that "a reader must let his thought go to meet the intention as he would a guest." We often cannot be sure about the author's intention (we do not know what Shakespeare intended to say in *Hamlet;* we have only the play itself), and even those relatively few authors who have explicitly stated their intentions may be untrustworthy for one reason or another. Yet there is something highly attractive in Mencius's suggestion that when we read we should—at least for a start—treat our author not with suspicion or hostility but with goodwill and with the expectation of pleasure.

*What are the implications of reader-response theory for writing an essay on a work of literature?* Even if we agree that we are talking only about competent readers, does this mean that *almost* anything goes in setting forth one's responses in an essay? Almost all advocates of any form of reading-response criticism agree on one thing: There are agreed-upon rules of *writing* if not of reading. This one point of agreement can be amplified to contain at least two aspects: (1) we all agree (more or less) as to what constitutes evidence, and (2) we all agree that a written response should be coherent. If you say that you find Hamlet to be less noble than his adversary, Claudius, you will be expected to provide evidence by pointing to specific passages, to specific things that Hamlet and Claudius say and do. And you will be expected to order the material into an effective, coherent sequence, so that the reader can move easily through your essay and will understand what you are getting at.

## ARCHETYPAL (OR MYTH) CRITICISM

Carl G. Jung, the Swiss psychiatrist, in *Contributions to Analytical Psychology* (1928), postulates the existence of a "collective unconscious," an inheritance in our brains consisting of "countless typical experiences [such as birth, escape from danger, selection of a mate] of our ancestors." Few people today believe in an inherited "collective unconscious," but many people agree that certain repeated experiences, such as going to sleep and hours later awakening, or the perception of the setting and of the rising sun, or of the annual death and rebirth of vegetation, manifest themselves in dreams, myths, and literature—in these instances, as stories of apparent death and rebirth. This archetypal plot of death and rebirth is said to be evident in Coleridge's *The Rime of the Ancient Mariner,* for example. The ship suffers a deathlike calm and then is miraculously restored to motion, and, in a sort of parallel rebirth, the mariner moves from spiritual death to renewed perception of the holiness of life. Another archetypal plot is the quest, which usually involves the testing and initiation of a hero, and thus essentially represents the movement from innocence to experience. In addition to archetypal plots there are archetypal characters, since an archetype is any recurring unit. Among archetypal characters are the Scapegoat (as in Shirley Jackson's "The Lottery," page 484–90), the Hero (savior, deliverer), the Terrible Mother (witch, stepmother—even the wolf "grandmother" in the tale of Little Red Riding Hood), and the Wise Old Man (father figure, magician).

Because, the theory holds, both writer and reader share unconscious memories, the tale an author tells (derived from the collective unconscious) may strangely move the reader, speaking to his or her collective unconscious. As Maud Bodkin puts it, in *Archetypal Patterns in Poetry* (1934), something within us "leaps in response to the effective presentation in poetry of an ancient theme" (4). But this emphasis on ancient (or repeated) themes has made archetypal criticism vulnerable to the charge that it is reductive. The critic looks for certain characters or patterns of action and values the work if the motifs are there, meanwhile overlooking what is unique, subtle, distinctive, and truly interesting about the work. That is, to put the matter crudely, a work is regarded as good if it is pretty much like other works, with the usual motifs and characters. A second weakness in some archetypal criticism is that in the search for the deepest meaning of a work the critic may crudely impose a pattern, seeing (for instance) The Quest in every walk down the street. But perhaps to say this is to beg the question; it is the critic's job to write so persuasively that the reader at least tentatively accepts the critic's view. For a wide-ranging study of one particular motif, see Barbara Fass Leavy's *In Search of the Swan Maiden* (1994), a discussion of the legend of a swan maiden who is forced to marry a mortal because he possesses something of hers, usually a garment or an animal skin. Leavy analyzes several versions of the story, which she takes to be a representation not only of female rage against male repression but also a representation of male fear of female betrayal. Leavy ends her book by examining this motif in Ibsen's *A Doll's House.* Her claim is that when Nora finds a lost object, the dance costume, she can flee from the tyrannical domestic world and thus she regains her freedom.

If archetypal criticism sometimes seems farfetched, it is nevertheless true that one of its strengths is that it invites us to use comparisons, and comparing is often an excellent way to see not only what a work shares with other works but what is distinctive in the work. The most successful practitioner of archetypal criticism was the late Northrop Frye (1912–91), whose numerous books help readers to see fascinating connections between works. For Frye's explicit comments about archetypal criticism, as well as for examples of such criticism in action, see especially his *Anatomy of Criticism* (1957) and *The Educated Imagination* (1964). On archetypes see also Chapter 16, "Archetypal Patterns," in Norman Friedman, *Form and Meaning in Fiction* (1975).

## HISTORICAL SCHOLARSHIP

**Historical criticism** studies a work within its historical context. Thus, a student of *Julius Caesar, Hamlet,* or *Macbeth*—plays in which ghosts appear—may try to find out about Elizabethan attitudes toward ghosts. We may find that the Elizabethans took ghosts more seriously than we do, or, on the other hand, we may find that ghosts were explained in various ways, for instance, sometimes as figments of the imagination and sometimes as shapes taken by the devil in order to mislead the virtuous. Similarly, a historical essay concerned with *Othello* may be devoted to Elizabethan attitudes toward Moors, or to Elizabethan ideas of love, or, for that matter, to Elizabethan ideas of a daughter's obligations toward her father's wishes concerning her suitor. The historical critic assumes (and one can hardly dispute the assumption) that writers, however individualistic, are shaped by the particular social contexts in which they live. One can put it this way: The goal of historical criticism is to understand how people in the past thought and felt. It assumes that such understanding can enrich our understanding of a particular work. The assumption is, however, disputable, since one may argue that the artist—let's say Shakespeare—may *not* have shared the age's view on this or that. All of the half-dozen or so Moors in Elizabethan plays other than *Othello* are villainous or foolish, but this evidence, one can argue, does not prove that *therefore* Othello is villainous or foolish.

## MARXIST CRITICISM

One form of historical criticism is **Marxist criticism,** named for Karl Marx (1818–83). Actually, to say "one form" is misleading, since Marxist criticism today is varied, but essentially it sees history primarily as a struggle between socioeconomic classes, and it sees literature (and everything else) as the product of economic forces of the period.

For Marxists, economics is the "base" or "infrastructure"; on this base rests a "superstructure" of ideology (law, politics, philosophy, religion, and the arts, including literature), reflecting the interests of the dominant class. Thus, literature is a material product, produced—like bread or battleships—in order to be consumed in a given society. Like every other product, literature is the product of work, and it *does* work. A bourgeois society, for example, will produce literature that in one way or another celebrates bourgeois values, such as individualism. These works serve to assure the society that produces them that its values are solid, even universal. The enlightened Marxist writer or critic, on the other hand, exposes the fallacy of traditional values and replaces them with the truths found in Marxism. In the heyday of Marxism in the United States, during the depression of the 1930s, it was common for such Marxist critics as Granville Hicks to assert that the novel must show the class struggle.

Few critics of any sort would disagree that works of art in some measure reflect the age that produced them, but most contemporary Marxist critics go further. First, they assert—in a repudiation of what has been called "'vulgar' Marxist theory"—that the deepest historical meaning of a literary work is to be found in what it does *not* say, what its ideology does not permit it to express. Second, Marxists take seriously Marx's famous comment that "the philosophers have only *interpreted* the world in various ways; the point is to *change* it." The critic's job is to change the world, by revealing the economic basis of the arts. Not surprisingly, most Marxists are skeptical of such concepts as "genius" and "masterpiece." These concepts, they say, are part of the bourgeois myth that idealizes the individual and detaches it from its economic context. For an introduction to Marxist criticism, see Terry Eagleton, *Marxism and Literary Criticism* (1976).

# THE NEW HISTORICISM

A recent school of scholarship, called the **New Historicism,** insists that there is no "history" in the sense of a narrative of indisputable past events. Rather, the New Historicism holds that there is only our version—our narrative, our representation—of the past. In this view, each age projects its own preconceptions on the past; historians may think they are revealing the past but they are revealing only their own historical situation and their personal preferences. Thus, in the nineteenth century and in the twentieth almost up to 1992, Columbus was represented as the heroic benefactor of humankind who discovered the New World. But even while plans were being made to celebrate the five-hundredth anniversary of his first voyage across the Atlantic, voices were raised in protest: Columbus did not "discover" a New World; after all, the indigenous people knew where they were, and it was Columbus who was lost, since he thought he was in India. People who wrote history in, say, 1900, projected onto the past their current views (colonialism was a good thing), and people who in 1992 wrote history projected onto that same period a very different set of views (colonialism was a Bad Thing). Similarly, ancient Greece, once celebrated by historians as the source of democracy and rational thinking, is now more often regarded as a society that was built on slavery and on the oppression of women. And the Renaissance, once glorified as an age of enlightened thought, is now often seen as an age that tyrannized women, enslaved colonial people, and enslaved itself with its belief in witchcraft and astrology. Thinking about these changing views, one feels the truth of the witticism that the only thing more uncertain than the future is the past.

The New Historicism is especially associated with Stephen Greenblatt, who popularized the term in 1982 in the preface to a collection of essays published in the journal *Genre.* Greenblatt himself has said of the New Historicism that "it's no doctrine at all" (*Learning to Curse* [1990]) but the term is nevertheless much used, and, as the preceding remarks have suggested, it is especially associated with power, most especially with revealing the tyrannical practices of a society that others have glorified. The New Historicism was in large measure shaped by the 1960s; the students who in the 1960s protested against the war in Vietnam by holding demonstrations, in the 1980s—they were now full professors—protested against Ronald Reagan by writing articles exposing Renaissance colonialism. Works of literature were used as a basis for a criticism of society. Academic writing of this sort was not dry, impartial, unimpassioned scholarship; rather, it connected the past with the present, and it offered value judgments. In Greenblatt's words,

> Writing that was not engaged, that withheld judgments, that failed to connect the present with the past seemed worthless. Such connection could be made either by analogy or causality; that is, a particular set of historical circumstances could be represented in such a way as to bring out homologies with aspects of the present or, alternatively, those circumstances could be analyzed as the generative forces that led to the modern condition. (*Learning to Curse* 167)

For a collection of 15 essays exemplifying the New Historicism, see H. Aram Veeser, ed., *The New Historicism* (1989).

# BIOGRAPHICAL CRITICISM

One kind of historical research is the study of *biography,* which for our purposes includes not only biographies but also autobiographies, diaries, journals, letters, and so on. What experiences did (for example) Mark Twain undergo? Are some of the apparently sensational aspects of *Huckleberry Finn* in fact close to events that Twain experienced? If so, is he a "realist"? If not, is he writing in the tradition of the "tall tale"?

The really good biographies not only tell us about the life of the author but they enable us to return to the literary texts with a deeper understanding of how they came to be what they are. If you read Richard B. Sewall's biography of Emily Dickinson, you will find a wealth of material concerning her family and the world she moved in—for instance, the religious ideas that were part of her upbringing.

Biographical study may illuminate even the work of a living author. If you are writing about the poetry of Adrienne Rich, for example, you may want to consider what she has told us in many essays about her life, especially about her relations with her father and her husband.

# PSYCHOLOGICAL (OR PSYCHOANALYTIC) CRITICISM

One form that biographical study may take is **psychological** or **psychoanalytic criticism,** which usually examines the author and the author's writings in the framework of Freudian psychology. A central doctrine of Sigmund Freud (1856–1939) is the Oedipus complex, the view that all males (Freud seems not to have made his mind up about females) unconsciously wish to displace their fathers and to sleep with their mothers. According to Freud, hatred for the father and love of the mother, normally repressed, may appear disguised in dreams. Works of art, like dreams, are disguised versions of repressed wishes.

Consider the case of Edgar Allan Poe. An orphan before he was three years old, he was brought up in the family of John Allan, but he was never formally adopted. His relations with Allan were stormy, though he seems to have had better relations with Allan's wife and still better relations with an aunt, whose daughter he married. In the Freudian view, Poe's marriage to his cousin (the daughter of a mother figure) was a way of sleeping with his mother. According to psychoanalytic critics, if we move from Poe's life to his work, we see, it is alleged, this hatred for his father and love for his mother. Thus, the murderer in "The Cask of Amontillado" is said to voice Poe's hostility toward his father, and the wine vault in which much of the story is set (an encompassing structure associated with fluids) is interpreted as symbolizing Poe's desire to return to his mother's womb. In Poe's other works, the longing for death is similarly taken to embody his desire to return to the womb.

Other psychoanalytic interpretations of Poe have been offered. Kenneth Silverman, author of a biography titled *Edgar Allan Poe* (1991) and the editor of a collection titled *New Essays on Poe's Major Tales* (1993), emphasizes the fact that Poe was orphaned before he was three, and was separated from his brother and his infant sister. In *New Essays* Silverman relates this circumstance to the "many instances of engulfment" that he finds in Poe's work. Images of engulfment, he points out, "are part of a still larger network of images having to do with biting, devouring, and similar oral mutilation." Why are they common in Poe? Here is Silverman's answer:

> Current psychoanalytic thinking about childhood bereavement explains the fantasy of being swallowed up as representing a desire, mixed with dread, to merge with the dead; the wish to devour represents a primitive attempt at preserving loved ones, incorporating them so as not to lose them. (20)

Notice that psychoanalytic interpretations usually take us away from what the author consciously intended; they purport to tell us what the work reveals, whether or not the author was aware of this meaning. The "meaning" of the work is found not in the surface content of the work but in the author's psyche.

One additional example—and it is the most famous—of a psychoanalytic study of a work of literature may be useful. In *Hamlet and Oedipus* (1949) Ernest Jones, amplifying some comments by Freud, argued that Hamlet delays killing Claudius because Claudius (who has killed Hamlet's father and married Hamlet's mother) has done exactly what Hamlet himself wanted to do. For Hamlet to kill Claudius, then, would be to kill himself.

If this approach interests you, take a look at Norman N. Holland's *Psychoanalysis and Shakespeare* (1966), or Frederick Crews's study of Hawthorne, *The Sins of the Fathers* (1966). Crews finds in Hawthorne's work evidence of unresolved Oedipal conflicts, and he accounts for the appeal of the fictions thus: The stories "rest on fantasy, but on the shared fantasy of mankind, and this makes for a more penetrating fiction than would any illusionistic slice of life" (263). For applications to other authors, look at Simon O. Lesser's *Fiction and the Unconscious* (1957), or at an anthology of criticism, *Literature and Psychoanalysis,* edited by Edith Kurzweil and William Phillips (1983).

Psychological criticism can also turn from the author and the work to the reader, seeking to explain why we, as readers, respond in certain ways. Why, for example, is *Hamlet* so widely popular? A Freudian answer is that it is universal because it deals with a universal (Oedipal) impulse. One can, however, ask whether it appeals as strongly to women as to men (again, Freud was unsure about the Oedipus complex in women) and, if so, why it appeals to them. Or, more generally, one can ask if males and females read in the same way.

## GENDER (FEMINIST, AND LESBIAN AND GAY) CRITICISM

This last question brings us to **gender criticism.** As we have seen, writing about literature usually seeks to answer questions. Historical scholarship, for instance, tries to answer such questions as, What did Shakespeare and his contemporaries believe about ghosts? or How did Victorian novelists and poets respond to Darwin's theory of evolution? Gender criticism, too, asks questions. It is especially concerned with two issues, one about reading and one about writing: Do men and women read in different ways, and Do they write in different ways?

**Feminist criticism** can be traced back to the work of Virginia Woolf (1882–1941), but chiefly it grew out of the women's movement of the 1960s. The women's movement at first tended to hold that women are pretty much the same as men and therefore should be treated equally, but much recent feminist criticism has emphasized and explored the differences between women and men. Because the experiences of the sexes are different, the argument goes, the values and sensibilities are different, and their responses to literature are different. Further, literature written by women is different from literature written by men. Works written by women are seen by some feminist critics as embodying the experiences of a minority culture—a group marginalized by the dominant male culture. (If you have read Charlotte Perkins Gilman's "The Yellow Wallpaper" or Susan Glaspell's "Trifles," you'll recall that these literary works themselves are largely concerned about the differing ways in which men and women perceive the world.) Not all women are feminist critics, and not all feminist critics are women. Further, there are varieties of feminist criticism. For a good introduction see *The New Feminist Criticism: Essays on Women, Literature, and Theory* (1985), edited by Elaine Showalter. For the role of men in feminist criticism, see *Engendering Men* (1990), edited by Joseph A. Boone and Michael Cadden (1990). At this point it should also be said that some theorists, who hold that identity is socially constructed, strongly dispute the value of establishing "essentialist" categories such as *heterosexual, gay,* and *lesbian*—a point that we will consider in a moment.

Feminist critics rightly point out that men have established the conventions of literature and that men have established the canon—that is, the body of literature that is said to be worth reading. Speaking a bit broadly, in this patriarchal or male-dominated body of literature, men are valued for being strong and active, whereas women are expected to be weak and passive. Thus, in the world of fairy tales, the admirable male is the energetic hero (Jack, the Giant-Killer) but the admirable female is the passive Sleeping Beauty. Active women such as the wicked stepmother or—a disguised form of the same thing—the witch are generally villainous. (There are of course exceptions, such as Gretel, in "Hansel and Gretel.") A woman hearing or reading the story of Sleeping Beauty or of Little Red Riding Hood (rescued by the powerful woodcutter) or any other work in which women seem to be trivialized will respond differently from a man. For instance, a woman may be socially conditioned into admiring Sleeping Beauty, but only at great cost to her mental well-being. A more resistant female reader may recognize in herself no kinship with the beautiful, passive Sleeping Beauty and may respond to the story indignantly. Another way to put it is this: The male reader perceives a romantic story, but the resistant female reader perceives a story of oppression.

For discussions of the ways in which, it is argued, women *ought* to read, you may want to look at *Gender and Reading* (1986), edited by Elizabeth A. Flynn and Patrocino Schweickart, and especially at Judith Fetterley's book *The Resisting Reader* (1978). Fetterley's point, briefly, is that women should resist the meanings (that is, the visions of how women ought to behave) that male authors—or female authors who have inherited patriarchal values—bury in their books. "To read the canon of what is currently considered classic American literature is perforce to identify as male," Fetterley says. "It insists on its universality in specifically male terms." Fetterley argues that a woman must read as a woman, "exorcising the male mind that has been implanted in women." In resisting the obvious meanings—for instance, the false claim that male values are universal values—women may discover more significant meanings. Fetterley argues that Faulkner's "A Rose for Emily"

> is a story not of a conflict between the South and the North or between the old order and the new; it is a story of the patriarchy North and South, new and old, and of the sexual conflict within it. As Faulkner himself has implied, it is a story of a woman victimized and betrayed by the system of sexual politics, who nevertheless has discovered, within the structures that victimize her, sources of power for herself. . . . "A Rose for Emily" is the story of how to murder your gentleman caller and get away with it. (34-35)

Fetterley goes on to state that the society made Emily a "lady"—society dehumanized her by elevating her. Emily's father, seeking to shape her life, stood in the doorway of their house and drove away her suitors. So far as he was concerned, Emily was a nonperson, a creature whose own wishes were not to be regarded; he alone would shape her future. Because society (beginning with her father) made her a "lady"—a creature so elevated that she is not taken seriously as a passionate human being—she is able to kill Homer Barron and not be suspected. Here is Fetterley speaking of the passage in which the townspeople crowd into her house when her death becomes known:

> When the would-be "suitors" finally get into her father's house, they discover the consequences of his oppression of her, for the violence contained in the rotted corpse of Homer Barron is the mirror image of the violence represented in the tableau, the back-flung front door flung back with a vengeance. (42)

Feminist criticism has been concerned not only with the depiction of women and men in a male-determined literary canon and with female responses to these images but also with yet another topic: women's writing. Women have had fewer opportunities than men to become writers of fiction, poetry, and drama—for one thing, they have been less well educated in the things that the male patriarchy valued—but even when they *have* managed to write, men sometimes have neglected their work simply because it had been by a woman. Feminists have further argued that certain forms of writing have been especially the province of women—for instance, journals, diaries, and letters; and predictably, these forms have not been given adequate space in the traditional, male-oriented canon.

In 1972, in an essay titled "When We Dead Awaken: Writing as ReVision," the poet and essayist Adrienne Rich effectively summed up the matter:

> A radical critique of literature, feminist in its impulse, would take the work first of all as a clue to how we live, how we have been living, how we have been led to imagine ourselves, how our language has trapped as well as liberated us; and how we can begin to see—and therefore live—afresh. . . . We need to know the writing of the past and know it differently than we have ever known it; not to pass on a tradition but to break its hold over us.

Much feminist criticism concerned with women writers has emphasized connections between the writer's biography and her art. Suzanne Juhasz, in her introduction to *Feminist Critics Read Emily Dickinson* (1983), puts it this way:

> The central assumption of feminist criticism is that gender informs the nature of art, the nature of biography, and the relation between them. Dickinson is a woman poet, and this fact is integral to her identity. Feminist criticism's sensitivity to the components of female experience in general and to Dickinson's identity as a woman generates essential insights about her. . . . Attention to the relationship between biography and art is a requisite of feminist criticism. To disregard it further strengthens those divisions continually created by traditional criticism, so that nothing about the woman writer can be seen whole. (1-5)

**Lesbian and gay criticism** have their roots in feminist criticism; feminist criticism introduced many of the questions that these other, newer developments are now exploring.

In 1979, in a book called *On Lies, Secrets, and Silence,* Adrienne Rich reprinted a 1975 essay on Emily Dickinson, "Vesuvius at Home." In her new preface to the reprinted essay she said that a lesbian-feminist reading of Dickinson would not have to prove that Dickinson slept with another woman. Rather, lesbian-feminist criticism "will ask questions hitherto passed over; it will not search obsessively for heterosexual romance as the key to a woman artist's life and work" (157-58). Obviously such a statement is also relevant to a male artist's life and work. It should be mentioned, too, that Rich's comments on lesbian reading and lesbianism as an image of creativity have been much discussed. For a brief survey, see Marilyn R. Farwell, "Toward a Definition of the Lesbian Literary Imagination," *Signs* 14 (1988): 100-18.

Before turning to some of the questions that lesbian and gay critics address, it is necessary first to say that lesbian criticism and gay criticism are not—to use a word now current in much criticism—symmetrical, chiefly because lesbian and gay relationships themselves are not symmetrical. Straight society has traditionally been more tolerant of—or blinder to—lesbianism than to male homosexuality. Further, lesbian literary theory has tended to see its affinities more with feminist theory than with gay theory; the emphasis has been on gender (male/female) rather than on sexuality (homosexuality/bisexuality/heterosexuality). On the other hand, some gays and lesbians have been writing what is now being called *queer theory.*

Now for some of the questions that this criticism addresses: (1) Do lesbians and gays read in ways that differ from the ways straight people read? (2) Do they write in ways that differ from those of straight people? (Gregory Woods argues in *Lesbian and Gay Writing: An Anthology of Critical Essays* [1990], edited by Mark Lilly, that "modern gay poets . . . use . . . paradox, as weapon and shield, against a world in which heterosexuality is taken for granted as being exclusively natural and healthy" [176]. Another critic, Jeffrey Meyers, writing in *Journal of English and Germanic Philology* 88 [1989]:126-29, in an unsympathetic review of a book on gay writers contrasts gay writers of the past with those of the present. According to Meyers, closeted homosexuals in the past, writing out of guilt and pain, produced a distinctive literature that is more interesting than the productions of today's uncloseted writers.) (3) How have straight writers portrayed lesbians and gays, and how have lesbian and gay writers portrayed straight women and men? (4) What strategies did lesbian and gay writers use to make their work acceptable to a general public in an age when lesbian and gay behavior was unmentionable?

Questions such as these have stimulated critical writing especially about bisexual and lesbian and gay authors (for instance, Virginia Woolf, Gertrude Stein,

Elizabeth Bishop, Walt Whitman, Oscar Wilde, E. M. Forster, Hart Crane, Tennessee Williams), but they have also led to interesting writing on such a topic as Nathaniel Hawthorne's attitudes toward women. "An account of Hawthorne's misogyny that takes no account of his own and his culture's gender anxieties," Robert K. Martin says in Boone and Cadden's *Engendering Men,* "is necessarily inadequate" (122).

Shakespeare's work—and not only the sonnets, which praise a beautiful male friend—has stimulated a fair amount of gay criticism. Much of this criticism consists of "decoding" aspects of the plays. Seymour Kleinberg argues, in *Essays on Gay Literature* (1985), ed. Stuart Kellogg, that Antonio in *The Merchant of Venice,* whose melancholy is not made clear by Shakespeare, is melancholy because (again, this is according to Kleinberg) Antonio's lover, Bassanio, is deserting him, and because Antonio is ashamed of his own sexuality:

> Antonio is a virulently anti-Semitic homosexual and is melancholic to the point of despair because his lover, Bassanio, wishes to marry an immensely rich aristocratic beauty, to leave the diversions of the Rialto to return to his own class and to sexual conventionality. Antonio is also in despair because he despises himself for his homosexuality, which is romantic, obsessive, and exclusive, and fills him with sexual shame. (113)

Several earlier critics had suggested that Antonio is a homosexual, hopelessly pining for Bassanio, but Kleinberg goes further, and argues that Antonio and Bassanio are lovers, not just good friends, and that Antonio's hopeless and shameful (because socially unacceptable) passion for Bassanio becomes transformed into hatred for the Jew, Shylock. The play, according to Kleinberg, is partly about "a world where . . . sexual guilt is translated into ethnic hatred" (124).

Examination of matters of gender can help to illuminate literary works, but it should be added, too, that some—perhaps most—critics write also as activists, reporting their findings not only to help us to understand and to enjoy the works of (say) Whitman, but also to change society's view of sexuality. Thus, in *Disseminating Whitman* (1991), Michael Moon is impatient with earlier critical rhapsodies about Whitman's universalism. It used to be said that Whitman's celebration of the male body was a sexless celebration of brotherly love in a democracy, but the gist of Moon's view is that we must neither whitewash Whitman's poems with such high-minded talk, nor reject them as indecent; rather, we must see exactly what Whitman is saying about a kind of experience that society had shut its eyes to, and we must take Whitman's view seriously. Somewhat similarly, Gregory Woods in *Articulate Flesh* (1987) points out that until a few years ago discussions of Hart Crane regularly condemned his homosexuality, as is evident in L. S. Dembo's characterization of Crane (quoted by Woods) as "uneducated, alcoholic, homosexual, paranoic, suicidal" (140). Gay and lesbian writers do not adopt this sort of manner. But it should also be pointed out that today there are straight critics who study lesbian or gay authors and write about them insightfully and without hostility.

One assumption in much lesbian and gay critical writing is that although gender greatly influences the ways in which we read, reading is a skill that can be learned, and therefore straight people—aided by lesbian and gay critics—can learn to read, with pleasure and profit, lesbian and gay writers. This assumption of course also underlies much feminist criticism, which often assumes that men must stop ignoring books by women and must learn (with the help of feminist critics) how to read them, and, in fact, how to read—with newly opened eyes—the sexist writings of men of the past and present.

In addition to the titles mentioned earlier concerning gay and lesbian criticism, consult Eve Kosofsky Sedgwick, *Between Men: English Literature and Male Homosocial Desire* (1985) and an essay by Sedgwick, "Gender Criticism," in *Redrawing the Boundaries,* ed. Stephen Greenblatt and Giles Gunn (1992).

While many in the field of lesbian and gay criticism have turned their energies toward examining the effects that an author's—or a character's—sexual identity may have upon the text, others have begun to question, instead, the concept of sexual identity itself.* Drawing upon the work of the French social historian Michel Foucault, critics such as David Halperin (*One Hundred Years of Homosexuality and Other Essays on Greek Love* [1990]) and Judith Butler (*Gender Trouble* [1989]) explore how various categories of identity, such as "heterosexual" and "homosexual," represent ways of defining human beings that are distinct to particular cultures and historical periods. These critics, affiliated with what is known as the "social constructionist" school of thought, argue that the way a given society (modern American or ancient Greek) interprets sexuality will determine the particular categories within which individuals come to understand and to name their own desires. For such critics the goal of a lesbian or gay criticism is not to define the specificity of a lesbian or gay literature or mode of interpretations, but to show how the ideology (the normative understanding of a given culture) makes it seem natural to think about sexuality in terms of such identities as lesbian, gay, bisexual, or straight. By challenging the authority of those terms, or "denaturalizing" them, and by calling attention to moments in which literary (and nonliterary) representations make assumptions that reinforce the supposed inevitability of those distinctions, such critics attempt to redefine our understandings of the relations between sexuality and literature. They hope to make clear that sexuality is always, in a certain sense, "literary"; it is a representation of a fiction that society has constructed in order to make sense out of experience.

Because such critics have challenged the authority of the opposition between heterosexuality and homosexuality, and have read it as a historical construct rather than as a biological or psychological absolute, they have sometimes resisted the very terms *lesbian* and *gay.* Many now embrace what is called queer theory as an attempt to mark their resistance to the categories of identity they see our culture as imposing upon us.

Works written within this mode of criticism are often influenced by deconstructionist or psychoanalytic thought. They examine works by straight authors as frequently as they do works by writers who might be defined as lesbian or gay. Eve Kosofsky Sedgwick's reading of *Billy Budd* in her book *Epistemology of the Closet* (1990) provides a good example of this sort of criticism. Reading Claggart as "the homosexual" in the text of Melville's novella, Sedgwick is not interested in defining his difference from other characters. Instead, she shows how the novella sets up a large number of oppositions—such as public and private, sincerity and sentimentality, health and illness—all of which have a relationship to the way in which a distinct "gay" identity was being produced by American society at the end of the nineteenth century. Other critics whose work in this field may be useful for students of literature are D. A. Miller, *The*

*This paragraph and the next two are by Lee Edelman of Tufts University.

*Novel and the Police* (1988); Diana Fuss, *Essentially Speaking* (1989) and *Identification Papers* (1995); Judith Butler, *Bodies That Matter* (1993); and Lee Edelman, *Homographesis: Essays in Gay Literary and Cultural Theory* (1993).

• • •

This chapter began by making the obvious point that all readers, whether or not they consciously adopt a particular approach to literature, necessarily read through particular lenses. More precisely, a reader begins with a frame of interpretation—historical, psychological, sociological, or whatever—and from within the frame a reader selects one of the several competing methodologies. Critics often make great—even grandiose—claims for their approaches. For example, Frederic Jameson, a Marxist, begins *The Political Unconscious: Narrative as a Socially Symbolic Act* (1981) thus:

> This book will argue the priority of the political interpretation of literary texts. It conceives of the political perspective not as some supplemental method, not as an optional auxiliary to other interpretive methods current today—the psychoanalytic or the myth-critical, the stylistic, the ethical, the structural—but rather as the absolute horizon of all reading and all interpretation. (7)

Readers who are chiefly interested in politics may be willing to assume "the priority of the political interpretation . . . as the absolute horizon of all reading and all interpretation," but other readers may respectfully decline to accept this assumption.

In talking about a critical approach, it is sometimes said that readers decode a text by applying a grid to it; the grid enables them to see certain things clearly. Good; but what is sometimes forgotten is that (since there is no such thing as a free lunch) a lens or a grid—an angle of vision or interpretive frame and a methodology—also prevents a reader from seeing certain other things. This is to be expected. What is important, then, is to remember this fact, and thus not to deceive ourselves by thinking that our keen tools enable us to see the whole. A psychoanalytic reading of, say, *Hamlet,* may be helpful, but it does not reveal all that is in *Hamlet,* and it does not refute the perceptions of another approach, let's say a historical study. Each approach may illuminate aspects neglected by others.

It is too much to expect a reader to apply all useful methods (or even several) at once—that would be rather like looking through a telescope with one eye and through a microscope with the other—but it is not too much to expect readers to be aware of the limitations of their methods. If one reads much criticism, one finds two kinds of critics. There are, on the one hand, critics who methodically and mechanically peer through a lens or grid, and they find what one can easily predict they will find. On the other hand, there are critics who (despite what may be inevitable class and gender biases) are at least relatively open-minded in their approach—critics who, one might say, do not at the outset of their reading believe that their method assures them that (so to speak) they have got the text's number and that by means of this method they will expose the text for what it is. The philosopher Richard Rorty engagingly makes a distinction somewhat along these lines, in an essay he contributed to Umberto Eco's *Interpretation and Overinterpretation* (1992). There is a great difference, Rorty suggests,

> between knowing what you want to get out of a person or thing or text in advance and [on the other hand] hoping that the person or thing or text will help you want something different—that he or she or it will help you to change your purposes, and thus to change your life. This distinction, I think, helps us highlight the difference between methodical and inspired readings of texts. (106)

Rorty goes on to say he has seen an anthology of readings on Conrad's *Heart of Darkness,* containing a psychoanalytic reading, a reader-response reading, and so on. "None of the readers had, as far as I could see," Rorty says,

> been enraptured or destabilized by *Heart of Darkness.* I got no sense that the book had made a big difference to them, that they cared much about Kurtz or Marlow or the woman "with helmeted head and tawny cheeks" whom Marlow sees on the bank of the river. These people, and that book, had no more changed these readers' purposes than the specimen under the microscope changes the purpose of the histologist. (107)

The kind of criticism that Rorty prefers he calls "unmethodical" criticism and "inspired" criticism. It is, for Rorty, the result of an "encounter" with some aspect of a work of art "which has made a difference to the critic's conception of who she is, what she is good for, what she wants to do with herself . . ." (107). This is not a matter of "respect" for the text, Rorty insists. Rather, he says, "love" and "hate" are better words, "For a great love or a great loathing is the sort of thing that changes us by changing our purposes, changing the uses to which we shall put people and things and texts we encounter later" (107).

## SUGGESTIONS FOR FURTHER READING

Because a massive list of titles may prove discouraging rather than helpful, it seems advisable here to give a short list of basic titles. (Titles already mentioned in this chapter—which are good places to begin—are *not* repeated in the following list.)

A good sampling of contemporary criticism (60 or so essays or chapters from books), representing all of the types discussed in this commentary except lesbian and gay criticism, can be found in *The Critical Tradition: Classic Texts and Contemporary Trends,* ed. David H. Richter (1989).

For a readable introduction to various approaches, written for students who are beginning the study of literary theory, see Steven Lynn, *Texts and Contexts* (1994). For a more advanced survey, that is, a work that assumes some familiarity with the material, see a short book by K. M. Newton, *Interpreting the Text: A Critical Introduction to the Theory and Practice of Literary Interpretation* (1990). A third survey, though considerably longer than the books by Lynn and Newton, is narrower because it confines itself to a study of critical writings about Shakespeare: Brian Vickers, *Appropriating Shakespeare: Contemporary Critical Quarrels* (1993), offers an astringent appraisal of deconstruction, New Historicism, psychoanalytic criticism, feminist criticism, and Marxist criticism. For a collection of essays on Shakespeare written from some of the points of view that Vickers deplores, see John Drakakis, ed., *Shakespearean Tragedy* (1992).

Sympathetic discussions (usually two or three pages long) of each approach, with fairly extensive bibliographic suggestions, are given in the appropriate articles in three encyclopedic works: Wendell V. Harris, *Dictionary of Concepts in Literary Criticism and Theory* (1992); Irene Makaryk, ed., *Encyclopedia of Contemporary Literary Theory* (1963); Michael Goden and Martin Kreiswirth, eds., *The Johns Hopkins Guide to Literary Theory and Criticism* (1994). For essays discussing feminist, gender, Marxist, psychoanalytic, deconstructive, New Historicism, and cultural criticism—as well as other topics not covered in this chapter—see Stephen Greenblatt and Giles Gunn, eds., *Redrawing the Boundaries: The Transformation of English and American Literary Studies* (1992).

## Formalist (or New) Criticism

Cleanth Brooks, *The Well Wrought Urn: Studies in the Structure of Poetry* (1947), especially Chapters 1 and 11 ("The Language of Paradox" and "The Heresy of Paraphrase"); W. K. Wimsatt, *The Verbal Icon* (1954), especially "The Intentional Fallacy" and "The Affective Fallacy"; Murray Krieger, *The New Apologists for Poetry* (1956); and, for an accurate overview of a kind of criticism often misrepresented today, Chapters 9–12 in volume 6 of René Wellek, *A History of Modern Criticism: 1750–1950* (1986).

## Deconstruction

Christopher Norris, *Deconstruction: Theory and Practice* (1982; rev. ed. 1991); Vincent B. Leitch, *Deconstructive Criticism: An Advanced Introduction and Survey* (1983); Christopher Norris, *The Deconstructive Turn* (1984); Christopher Norris, *Deconstruction and the Interests of Theory* (1989).

## Reader-Response Criticism

Wolfgang Iser, *The Act of Reading: A Theory of Aesthetic Response* (1978); Wolfgang Iser, *Prospecting: From Reader Response to Literary Anthropology* (1993); Susan Suleiman and Inge Crosman, eds., *The Reader in the Text* (1980); Jane P. Tompkins, ed., *Reader-Response Criticism* (1980); Norman N. Holland, *The Dynamics of Literary Response* (1973, 1989); Steven Mailloux, *Interpretive Conventions: The Reader in the Study of American Fiction* (1982).

## Archetypal (or Myth) Criticism

G. Wilson Knight, *The Starlit Dome* (1941); Richard Chase, *Quest for Myth* (1949); Murray Krieger, ed., *Northrop Frye in Modern Criticism* (1966); Frank Lentricchia, *After the New Criticism* (1980).

## Historical Criticism

For a brief survey of some historical criticism of the first half of this century, see René Wellek, *A History of Modern Criticism: 1750–1950,* volume 6 (1986), Chapter 4 ("Academic Criticism"). E. M. W. Tillyard, *The Elizabethan World Picture* (1943) and Tillyard's *Shakespeare's History Plays* (1944), both of which related Elizabethan literature to the beliefs of the age, are good examples of the historical approach.

## Marxist Criticism

Raymond Williams, *Marxism and Literature* (1977); Tony Bennett, *Formalism and Marxism* (1979); Lydia Sargent, ed., *Women and Revolution: A Discussion of the Unhappy Marriage of Marxism and Feminism* (1981); and for a brief survey of American Marxist writers of the 1930s and 1940s, see Chapter 5 of volume 6 of René Wellek, *A History of Modern Criticism* (1986).

## New Historicism

Stephen Greenblatt, *Renaissance Self-Fashioning from More to Shakespeare* (1980), especially the first chapter; Brook Thomas, *The New Historicism and Other Old-Fashioned Topics* (1991).

## Biographical Criticism

Leon Edel, *Literary Biography* (1957); Estelle C. Jellinek, ed., *Women's Autobiography: Essays in Criticism* (1980); James Olney, *Metaphors of Self: The Meaning of Autobiography* (1981). Among the most distinguished twentieth-century literary biographies is Richard Ellmann, *James Joyce* (1959, rev. ed. 1982).

## Psychological (or Psychoanalytic) Criticism

Edith Kurzweil and William Phillips, eds., *Literature and Psychoanalysis* (1983); Maurice Charney and Joseph Reppen, eds., *Psychoanalytic Approaches to Literature and Film* (1987); Madelon Sprengnether, *The Spectral Mother: Freud, Feminism, and Psychoanalysis* (1990); Frederick Crews, *Out of My System* (1975).

## Gender (Feminist, and Lesbian and Gay) Criticism

Gayle Greene and Coppèlia Kahn, eds., *Making a Difference: Feminist Literary Criticism* (1985), including an essay by Bonnie Zimmerman on lesbian criticism; Catherine Belsey and Jane Moore, eds., *The Feminist Reader: Essays in Gender and the Politics of Literary Criticism* (1989); Toril Moi, ed., *French Feminist Thought* (1987); Elizabeth A. Flynn and Patrocinio P. Schweickart, eds., *Gender and Reading: Essays on Readers, Texts, and Contexts* (1986); Barbara Christian, *Black Feminist Criticism: Perspectives on Black Women Writers* (1985); Shoshana Felman, *What Does a Woman Want? Reading and Sexual Difference* (1993); Robert K. Martin, *The Homosexual Tradition in American Poetry* (1979). Henry Abelove et al., eds., *The Lesbian and Gay Studies Reader* (1993), has only a few essays concerning literature, but it has an extensive bibliography on the topic.

*A last word:* If you want to read only a few pages about the nature and value of criticism, look at Helen Vendler's introduction and "The Function of Criticism" in a collection of her essays, *The Music of What Happens* (1988). Vendler is aware that most criticism today is ideological—Marxist, Freudian, or whatever, and it is therefore concerned with the interpretation of meaning—but she is less concerned with ideology and meaning than with the causes of "the aesthetic power of the art work":

> It is natural that people under new cultural imperatives should be impelled to fasten new interpretations (from the reasonable to the fantastic) onto aesthetic objects from the past. But criticism cannot stop there. The critic may well begin, "Look at it this way for a change," but the sentence must continue, "and now don't you see it as more intelligibly beautiful and moving?" That is, if the interpretation does not reveal some hitherto occluded aspect of the aesthetic power of the art work, it is useless as art criticism (though it may be useful as cultural history or sociology or psychology or religion). (2)

# APPENDIX A

# *Remarks about Manuscript Form*

## BASIC MANUSCRIPT FORM

Much of what follows is nothing more than common sense.

- Use good quality **$8\frac{1}{2}$" × 11"** paper. Make a photocopy, or, if you have written on a word processor print out a second copy, in case the instructor's copy goes astray.
- If you write on a typewriter or a word processor, **double-space,** and type on one side of the page only; use a reasonably fresh ribbon. If you submit handwritten copy, use lined paper and write on one side of the page only in black or dark blue ink, on every other line.
- Use **one-inch margins** on all sides.
- Within the top margin, put your last name and then (after hitting the space bar twice) the **page number** (in arabic numerals), so that the number is flush with the right-hand margin.
- On the first page, below the top margin and flush with the left-hand margin, put **your full name,** your **instructor's name,** the **course number** (including the section), and the **date,** one item per line, double-spaced.
- **Center the title** of your essay. Remember that the title is important—it gives the readers their first glimpse of your essay. **Create your own title**—one that reflects your topic or thesis. For example, a paper on Charlotte Perkins Gilman's "The Yellow Wallpaper" should not be called "The Yellow Wallpaper" but might be called

  Disguised Tyranny
  in Gilman's "The Yellow Wallpaper"

  or

  How to Drive a Woman Mad

These titles do at least a little in the way of rousing a reader's interest.

- **Capitalize the title thus:** Begin the first word of the title with a capital letter, and capitalize each subsequent word except articles (*a, an, the*), conjunctions (*and, but, if, when,* etc.), and prepositions (*in, on, with,* etc.):

    A Word on Behalf of Love

    Notice that you do *not* enclose your title within quotation marks, and you do not underline it—though if it includes the title of a story, *that* is enclosed within quotation marks, or if it includes the title of a novel or play, *that* is underlined (to indicate italics), thus:

    Gilman's "The Yellow Wallpaper"<br>and Medical Practice

    and

    Gender Stereotypes in <u>Macbeth</u>

- **After writing your title, double-space,** indent five spaces, and begin your first sentence.
- Unless your instructor tells you otherwise, **use a paper clip** to hold the pages together. (Do not use a stiff binder; it will only add to the bulk of the instructor's stack of papers.)
- Extensive revisions should have been made in your drafts, but minor **last-minute revisions** may be made—neatly—on the finished copy. Proofreading may catch some typographical errors, and you may notice some small weaknesses. You can make corrections using the following proofreader's symbols.

## CORRECTIONS IN THE FINAL COPY

**Changes** in wording may be made by crossing through words and rewriting them:

The influence of Poe and Hawthorne ~~have~~ has greatly diminished.

**Additions** should be made above the line, with a caret below the line at the appropriate place:

The influence of Poe and Hawthorne has ^greatly diminished.

**Transpositions** of letters may be made thus:

The inlfuence of Poe and Hawthorne has greatly diminished.

**Deletions** are indicated by a horizontal line through the word or words to be deleted. Delete a single letter by drawing a vertical or diagonal line through it; then indicate whether the letters on either side are to be closed up by drawing a connecting arc:

```
The influence of Poe and Hawthorne has greatlly
diminished.
```

**Separation** of words accidentally run together is indicated by a vertical line, **closure** by a curved line connecting the letters to be closed up:

```
The influence|of Poe and Hawthorne has g reatly
diminished.
```

**Paragraphing** may be indicated by the symbol ¶ before the word that is to begin the new paragraph:

```
The influence of Poe and Hawthorne has greatly
diminished. ¶The influence of Borges has very
largely replaced that of earlier writers of fantasy.
```

## QUOTATIONS AND QUOTATION MARKS

First, a word about the *point* of using quotations. Don't use quotations to pad the length of a paper. Rather, give quotations from the work you are discussing so that your readers will see the material you are discussing and (especially in a research paper) so that your readers will know what some of the chief interpretations are and what your responses to them are.

*Note:* The next few paragraphs do *not* discuss how to include citations of pages, a topic taken up in the next chapter under the heading "How to Document: Footnotes and Internal Parenthetical Citations."

**The Golden Rule:** If you quote, *comment on* the quotation. Let the reader know what you make of it and why you quote it.

Additional principles:

1. **Identify the speaker or writer of the quotation** so that the reader is not left with a sense of uncertainty. Usually, in accordance with the principle of letting readers know where they are going, this identification precedes the quoted material, but occasionally it may follow the quotation, especially if it will provide something of a pleasant surprise. For instance, in a discussion of Flannery O'Connor's stories, you might quote a disparaging comment on one of the stories and then reveal that O'Connor herself was the speaker.

2. If the quotation is part of your own sentence, **be sure to fit the quotation grammatically and logically into your sentence.**

*Incorrect:* Holden Caulfield tells us very little about "what my lousy childhood was like."

*Correct:* Holden Caulfield tells us very little about what his "lousy childhood was like."

3. **Indicate any omissions or additions.** The quotation must be exact. Any material that you add—even one or two words—must be enclosed within square brackets, thus:

```
Hawthorne tells us that "owing doubtless to the depth
of the gloom at that particular spot [in the forest],
neither the travellers nor their steeds were
visible."
```

If you wish to omit material from within a quotation, indicate the ellipsis by three spaced periods. If your sentence ends in an omission, add a closed-up period and then three spaced periods to indicate the omission. The following example is based on a quotation from the sentences immediately above this one:

```
The instructions say, "If you . . . omit material
from within a quotation, [you must] indicate the
ellipsis. . . . If your sentence ends in an omission,
add a closed-up period and then three spaced
periods. . . .
```

Notice that although material preceded "If you," periods are not needed to indicate the omission because "If you" began a sentence in the original. Customarily, initial and terminal omissions are indicated only when they are part of the sentence you are quoting. Even such omissions need not be indicated when the quoted material is obviously incomplete—when, for instance, it is a word or phrase.

4. **Distinguish between short and long quotations,** and treat each appropriately. **Short quotations** (usually defined as fewer than five lines of typed prose or three lines of poetry) are enclosed within quotation marks and run into the text (rather than being set off, without quotation marks), as in the following example:

```
Hawthorne begins the story by telling us that "Young
Goodman Brown came forth at sunset into the street at
Salem village," thus at the outset connecting the
village with daylight. A few paragraphs later, when
Hawthorne tells us that the road Brown takes was
"darkened by all of the gloomiest trees of the
forest," he begins to associate the forest with
darkness--and a very little later with evil.
```

If your short quotation is from a poem, be sure to follow the capitalization of the original, and use a slash mark (with a space before and after it) to indicate separate lines. Give the line numbers, if your source gives them, in parentheses, immediately after the closing quotation marks and before the closing punctuation, thus:

```
In Adrienne Rich's "Aunt Jennifer's Tigers," Rich
says that "Uncle's wedding band / Sits heavily upon
Aunt Jennifer's hand" (7-8). The band evidently is a
sign of her oppression.
```

To set off a **long quotation** (more than four typed lines of prose or more than two lines of poetry), indent the entire quotation ten spaces from the left margin. Usually, a long quotation is introduced by a clause ending with a colon—for instance, "The following passage will make this point clear:" or "The closest we come to hearing an editorial voice is a long passage in the middle of the story:" or some such lead-in. After typing your lead-in, double-space, and then type the quotation, indented and double-spaced.

5. **Commas and periods go inside the quotation marks.**

```
Chopin tells us in the first sentence that "Mrs.
Mallard was afflicted with heart trouble," and in the
last sentence the doctors say that Mrs. Mallard "died
of heart disease."
```

**Exception:** If the quotation is immediately followed by material in parentheses or in square brackets, close the quotation, then give the parenthetic or bracketed material, and then—after closing the parenthesis or bracket—put the comma or period.

```
Chopin tells us in the first sentence that "Mrs.
Mallard was afflicted with heart trouble" (17), and
in the last sentence the doctors say that Mrs.
Mallard "died of heart disease" (18).
```

**Semicolons, colons, and dashes** go outside the closing quotation marks.

**Question marks and exclamation points** go inside if they are part of the quotation, outside if they are your own.

In the following passage from a student's essay, notice the difference in the position of the question marks. The first is part of the quotation, so it is enclosed within the quotation marks. The second question mark, however, is the student's, so it comes after the closing quotation mark.

```
The older man says to Goodman Brown, "Sayest thou
so?" Doesn't a reader become uneasy when the man
```

```
immediately adds, "We are but a little way in the
  forest yet"?
```

## Quotation Marks or Underlining?

Use quotation marks around titles of short stories and other short works—that is, titles of chapters in books, essays, and poems that might not be published by themselves. Underline (to indicate italics) titles of books, periodicals, collections of essays, plays, and long poems such as *The Rime of the Ancient Mariner.* Word processing software probably will let you use italic type (instead of underlining) if you wish.

# APPENDIX B

# *Writing a Research Paper*

First things first: On page 1477 we print a sample research paper by a student, Ruth Katz's "The Women in *Death of a Salesman.*"

Because a research paper requires its writer to collect and interpret evidence—usually including the opinions of earlier investigators—one sometimes hears that a research paper, unlike a critical essay, is not the expression of personal opinion. But such a view is unjust both to criticism and to research. A critical essay is not a mere expression of personal opinions; if it is any good, it offers evidence that supports the opinions and thus persuades the reader of their objective rightness. And a research paper is in the final analysis largely personal, because the author continuously uses his or her own judgment to evaluate the evidence, deciding what is relevant and convincing. A research paper is not the mere presentation of what a dozen scholars have already said about a topic; it is a thoughtful evaluation of the available evidence, and so it is, finally, an expression of what the author thinks the evidence adds up to.

Research can be a tedious and frustrating business; there are hours spent reading books and articles that prove to be irrelevant, there are contradictory pieces of evidence, and there is never enough time.

Still, even though research has its difficult moments, those who engage in it feel (at least sometimes) an exhilaration, a sense of triumph at having studied a problem thoroughly and arrived at conclusions that—for the moment, anyway—seem objective and irrefutable. Later, new evidence may turn up and require a new conclusion, but until that time one has built something that will endure wind and weather.

# PRIMARY AND SECONDARY MATERIALS

The materials of literary research can be conveniently divided into two sorts, primary and secondary. The *primary materials,* or sources, are the real subject of study; the *secondary materials* are critical and historical accounts already written about these primary materials. For example, Langston Hughes wrote poems, stories, plays, and essays. For a student of Hughes, these works are the primary materials. If you want to study his ways of representing African-American speech or his representations of whites, or his collaboration with Zora Neale Hurston, you will read the primary material—his own writings (and Hurston's, in the case of the collaborative work). But in an effort to reach a thoughtful understanding of some aspect of his work, you will also want to look at later biographical and critical studies of his works and perhaps also at scholarly writing on such topics as Black English. You may even find yourself looking at essays on Black English that do not specifically mention Hughes but that nevertheless may prove helpful.

Similarly, if you are writing about Charlotte Perkins Gilman (we include one of her stories), the primary material includes not only other stories but also her social and political writing. If you are writing about her views of medical treatment of women, you will want to look not only at the story we reprint ("The Yellow Wallpaper") but also at her autobiography. Further, you will also want to look at some secondary material, such as recent scholarly books and articles on medical treatment of women in the late nineteenth and early twentieth centuries.

## Locating Material: First Steps

The easiest way to locate articles and books on literature written in a modern language—that is, on a topic other than literature of the ancient world—is to consult the

*MLA International Bibliography* (1922- ),

which until 1969 was published as part of *PMLA* (*Publications of the Modern Language Association*) and since 1969 has been published separately. It is also available on CD-ROM through WILSONDISC, and in fact the disc is preferable since it is updated quarterly, whereas the print version is more than a year behind the times.

*MLA International Bibliography* lists scholarly studies—books as well as articles in academic journals—published in a given year. Because of the great number of items listed, the print version of the bibliography runs to more than one volume, but material on writing in English (including, for instance, South African authors who write in English) is in one volume. To see what has been published on Langston Hughes in a given year, then, in this volume you turn to the section on American literature (as opposed to English, Canadian, Irish, and so forth), and then to the subsection labeled 1900-99, to see if anything that sounds relevant is listed.

Because your time is limited, you probably cannot read everything published on your topic. At least for the moment, therefore, you will use only the last five or ten years of this bibliography. Presumably, any important earlier material will have been incorporated into some of the recent studies listed, and if, when you come to read these recent studies, you find references to an article of, say, 1975 that sounds essential, of course you will read that article too.

Although *MLA International Bibliography* includes works on American literature, if you are doing research on an aspect of American literature you may want to begin with

*American Literary Scholarship* (1965- ),

an annual publication noted for its broad coverage of articles and books on major and minor American writers, and perhaps especially valuable for its frank comments on the material that it lists.

On some recent topics—for instance, the arguments for and against dropping *Huckleberry Finn* from high school curricula—there may be few or no books, and there may not even be material in the scholarly journals indexed in *MLA International Bibliography*. Popular magazines, however, such as *Atlantic, Ebony,* and *Newsweek*—unlisted in *MLA*—may include some useful material. These magazines, and about 200 others, are indexed in

*Readers' Guide to Periodical Literature* (1900- ).

If you want to write a research paper on the controversy over *Huckleberry Finn,* or on the popular reception given to Kenneth Branagh's films of Shakespeare's *Henry V* and *Much Ado about Nothing,* you can locate material (for instance, reviews of Branagh's films) through *Readers' Guide.* For that matter, you can also locate reviews of older films, let's say Olivier's films of Shakespeare's plays, by consulting the volumes for the years in which the films were released.

On many campuses *Readers' Guide* has been supplanted by

*InfoTrac* (1985- ),

on CD-ROM. The disc is preinstalled in a microcomputer that can be accessed from a computer terminal. This index to authors and subjects in popular and scholarly magazines and in newspapers provides access to several database indexes, including:

- The *General Periodicals Index,* available in the Academic Library Edition (about 1,100 general and scholarly periodicals) and in the Public Library Edition (about 1,100 popular magazines).
- The *Academic Index* (400 general-interest publications, all of which are also available in the Academic Library Edition of the *General Periodicals Index*).
- The *Magazine Index Plus* (the four most recent years of the *New York Times,* the two most recent months of the *Wall Street Journal,* and 400 popular magazines, all of which are included in the Public Library Edition of the *General Periodicals Index*).
- The *National Newspaper Index* (the four most recent years of the *New York Times,* the *Christian Science Monitor,* the *Washington Post,* and the *Los Angeles Times*).

## Other Bibliographic Aids

There are hundreds of guides to publications and to reference works. For instance, *American Women Writers: Bibliographical Essays* (1983), edited by Maurice Duke, Jackson R. Bryer, and M. Thomas Inge, includes scholarship through 1981 on 24 authors, including Bradstreet, Jewett, Chopin, Stein, O'Connor, Hurston, and Plath. *Black American Writers: Bibliographical Essays* (1978), edited by M. Thomas Inge, Maurice Duke, and Jackson R. Bryer, covers slave narratives, as well as such later African-American writers as Hughes, Ellison, and Baldwin.

How do you find such books? Two invaluable guides to reference works (that is, to bibliographies and to such helpful compilations as handbooks of mythology, place names, and critical terms) are

James L. Harner, *Literary Research Guide: A Guide to Reference Sources for the Study of Literatures in English and Related Topics,* 2nd ed. (1993)

and

Michael J. Marcuse, *A Reference Guide for English Studies* (1990).

And there are guides to these guides: reference librarians. If you don't know where to turn to find something, turn to the librarian.

## TAKING NOTES

Let's assume now that you have checked some bibliographies and that you have a fair number of references you must read to have a substantial knowledge of the evidence and the common interpretations of the evidence. Most researchers find it convenient, when examining bibliographies and the library catalog, to write down each reference on a 3" × 5" index card—one title per card. On the card put the author's full name (last name first), the exact title of the book or of the article, and the name of the journal (with dates and pages). Titles of books and periodicals (publications issued periodically—for example, monthly or four times a year) are underlined; titles of articles and of essays in books are put within quotation marks. It's also a good idea to put the library catalog number on the card to save time if you need to get the item for a second look.

Next, start reading or scanning the materials whose titles you have collected. Some of these items will prove irrelevant or silly; others will prove valuable in themselves and also in the leads they give you to further references, which you should duly record on 3" × 5" cards. Notes—aside from these bibliographic notes—are best taken on 4" × 6" cards. Smaller cards do not provide enough space for summaries of useful materials, but 4" × 6" cards—rather than larger cards—will serve to remind you that you should not take notes on everything. Be selective in taking notes.

### Two Mechanical Aids: The Photocopier and the Word Processor

The **photocopier** enables you to take home from the library, with very little effort, lots of material (including material that does not circulate) that you might otherwise have to copy laboriously by hand. If you are writing a paper on feminist responses to Faulkner's "A Rose for Emily," you can simply scan the material to locate the relevant pages, and then can photocopy the essays in journals, or the appropriate passages in books. Later, at your convenience, without making another trip to the library you can read or reread the photocopied material, highlighting or underlining the chief points. But (and this point is so important that it will be made again, in a moment) because it is easy to highlight or underline, you may mark almost everything. That is, you may not *think* about the material, as you would if you were taking notes by hand, where you would have a powerful incentive to think about whether the material really is noteworthy.

If you take notes on the **word processor,** print them out and then scissor them apart. Although the slips will not be identical in size, you can still arrange them into appropriate packets, and (as with index cards) you can then arrange the packets into an appropriate sequence. At this point you can begin to draft your paper, working from your organized notes, or—and this is probably a better method—you can rearrange the sequence of notes in your word processor. That is, guided by the sequence of slips, you can move blocks of notes on the word processor into the sequence that you have tentatively settled on. After you have done this, you can start drafting your paper, writing a lead-in to the first quotation, printing the quotation (or part of it, or a summary of it), and commenting on it. *Caution:* Do not feel that you must use all of your notes. Your reader does not want to read a series of notes that are linked by thin connectives.

## A Guide to Note Taking

1. **In the upper-left corner of the card (if you are not using a word processor), specify the source in an abbreviated form.** The author's last name, or the name and the first word of the title are usually enough (unless the first word is *A, An,* or *The*).

2. **Write summaries, not paraphrases** (that is, write abridgments rather than restatements which in fact may be as long as or longer than the original). There is rarely any point to paraphrasing. Generally speaking, either quote exactly (and put the passage in quotation marks, with a notation of the source, including the page number or numbers) or summarize, reducing a page or even an entire article or chapter of a book to a single 4" × 6" card. Even when you summarize, indicate your source (including the page numbers) on the card, so that you can give appropriate credit in your paper.

3. **Quote sparingly.** Of course, in your summary you will sometimes quote a phrase or a sentence—putting it in quotation marks—but quote sparingly. You are not doing stenography; rather you are assimilating knowledge and you are thinking, and so for the most part your source should be digested rather than engorged whole. Thinking now, while taking notes, will also help you later to avoid plagiarism. If, on the other hand, when you take notes you mindlessly copy material at length, later when you are writing the paper you may be tempted to copy it yet again, perhaps without giving credit. Similarly, if you photocopy pages from articles or books, and then merely underline some passages, you probably will not be thinking; you will just be underlining. But if you make a terse summary on a note card you will be forced to think and to find your own words for the idea. Quote directly only those passages that are particularly effective, or crucial, or memorable. In your finished paper these quotations will provide authority and emphasis.

4. **Quote accurately.** After copying a quotation, check your card against the original, correct any misquotation, and then put a check mark after your

quotation to indicate that it is accurate. Verify the page number also, and then put a check on your card, after the page number. If a quotation runs from the bottom of page 306 to the top of 307, on your card put a distinguishing mark (for instance two parallel vertical lines after the last word of the first page), so that if you later use only part of the quotation, you will know the page on which it appeared.

**Use ellipses** (three spaced periods) to indicate the omission of any words within a sentence. If the omitted words are at the end of the quoted sentence, put a period immediately at the point where you end the sentence, and then add three spaced periods to indicate the omission. Example:

```
If the . . . words are at the end of the quoted
sentence, put a period immediately at the point where
you end. . . .
```

**Use square brackets to indicate your additions** to the quotation. Here is an example.

```
Here is an [uninteresting] example.
```

5. **Never copy a passage by changing an occasional word,** under the impression that you are thereby putting it into your own words. Notes of this sort may find their way into your paper, your reader will sense a style other than yours, and suspicions of plagiarism may follow. (For a detailed discussion of plagiarism, see pp. 1955–56.)

6. **Write on one side of the card only.** Because when you set out to draft your paper you will probably want to spread out your notes so that you can see all of the material simultaneously, notes on the back of a card are of little use and they will probably get overlooked. If a note won't fit on one side of a card, continue the note on a second card (and a third, if necessary), and put the appropriate number on each card.

7. **Comment on your notes.** Feel free to jot down your responses to the note. Indeed, consider it your obligation to *think* about the material, evaluating it and using it as a stimulus to further thought. For example, you may want to say, "Gold seems to be generalizing from insufficient evidence," or "Corsa made the same point five years earlier"; but make certain that later you will be able to distinguish between these comments and the notes summarizing or quoting your source. A suggestion: Surround all comments recording your responses with double parentheses, thus: ((. . .)).

8. **In the upper corner of each note card write a brief key**—for example, "Swordplay in *Hamlet*"—so that later you can tell at a glance what is on the card.

As you work, you'll find yourself returning again and again to your primary materials—and you'll probably find to your surprise that a good deal of the secondary material is unconvincing or even wrong, despite the fact that it is printed in a handsome book or a scholarly journal. At times, under the weight of evidence, you will have to abandon some of your earlier views, but at times you will have your own opinions reinforced and you will feel that your ideas have more validity than those you are reading. One of the things we learn from research is that not everything in print is true; this discovery is one of the pleasures we get from research.

# DRAFTING THE PAPER

The difficult job of writing up your findings remains, but if you have taken good notes and have put useful headings on each card, you are well on your way. Read through the cards and sort them into packets of related material. Discard all notes, however interesting, that you now see are irrelevant to your paper. Go through the cards again and again, sorting and re-sorting, putting together what belongs together. Probably you will find that you have to do a little additional research—somehow you aren't quite clear about this or that—but after you have done this additional research, you should be able to arrange the packets into a reasonable and consistent sequence. You now have a kind of first draft, or at least a tentative organization for your paper. Two further pieces of advice:

1. Beware of the compulsion to include every note card in your essay; that is, beware of telling the reader, "*A* says . . . ; *B* says . . . ; *C* says. . . ."
2. You must have a point, a thesis.

The final version of the paper should be a finished piece of work, without the inconsistencies, detours, and occasional dead ends of an early draft. Your readers should feel that they are moving toward a conclusion (by means of your thoughtful evaluation of the evidence) rather than merely reading an anthology of commentary on the topic. And so we should get some such structure as: "There are three common views on . . . The first two are represented by *A* and *B;* the third, and by far the most reasonable, is *C*'s view that . . . *A* argues . . . but . . . The second view, *B*'s, is based on . . . but . . . Although the third view, *C*'s, is not conclusive, still . . . Moreover, *C*'s point can be strengthened when we consider a piece of evidence that she does not make use of. . . ."

Be sure, when you quote, to *write a lead-in,* such as "*X* concisely states the common view" or "*Z,* without offering any proof, asserts that . . ." Let the reader know where you are going, or, to put it a little differently, let the reader know how the quotation fits into your argument.

Quotations and summaries, in short, are accompanied by judicious analyses of your own so that by the end of the paper your readers not only have read a neatly typed paper (see page 1943–48) and have gained an idea of what previous writers have said, but also are persuaded that under your guidance they have seen the evidence, heard the arguments justly summarized, and reached a sound conclusion.

A bibliography or list of works consulted (see pages 1961–67) is usually appended to a research paper so that readers may easily look further into the primary and secondary material if they wish; but if you have done your job well, readers will be content to leave the subject where you left it, grateful that you have set matters straight.

# DOCUMENTATION

## What to Document: Avoiding Plagiarism

Honesty requires that you acknowledge your indebtedness for material, not only when you quote directly from a work, but also when you appropriate an idea that is not common knowledge. Not to acknowledge such borrowing is plagiarism. If in doubt whether to give credit, give credit.

You ought, however, to develop a sense of what is considered **common knowledge.** Definitions in a dictionary can be considered common knowledge, so there is no need to say, "According to Webster, a novel is. . . ." (This is weak in three ways: It's unnecessary, it's uninteresting, and it's unclear, since "Webster" appears in the titles of several dictionaries, some good and some bad.) Similarly, the date of first publication of *The Scarlet Letter* can be considered common knowledge. Few can give it when asked, but it can be found out from innumerable sources, and no one need get the credit for providing you with the date. The idea that Hamlet delays is also a matter of common knowledge. But if you are impressed by So-and-so's argument that Claudius has been much maligned, you should give credit to So-and-so.

Suppose that in the course of your research for a paper on Langston Hughes you happen to come across Arnold Rampersad's statement, in an essay in *Voices and Visions* (ed. Helen Vendler), that

> Books alone could not save Hughes from loneliness, let alone give him the strength to be a writer. At least one other factor was essential in priming him for creative obsession. In the place in his heart, or psychology, vacated by his parents entered the black masses. (355)

This is an interesting idea, and in the last sentence the shift from heart to psychology is perhaps especially interesting. You certainly can*not* say—with the implication that the idea and the words are your own—something like

> Hughes let enter into his heart, or his psychology--a place vacated by his parents--the black masses.

The writer is simply lifting Rampersad's ideas and making only tiny changes in the wording. But even a larger change in the wording is unacceptable unless Rampersad is given credit. Here is a restatement that is an example of plagiarism even though the words differ from Rampersad's:

> Hughes took into himself ordinary black people, thus filling the gap created by his mother and father.

In this version, the writer presents Rampersad's idea as it were the writer's own—and presents it less effectively than Rampersad.

What to do? Give Rampersad credit, perhaps along these lines:

> As Arnold Rampersad has said, "in the place in his heart, or his psychology" where his parents had once been, Hughes now substituted ordinary black people (355).

You can use another writer's ideas, and even some of the very words, but you must give credit, and you must use quotation marks when you quote.

You can (1) give credit and quote directly, or (2) give credit and summarize the writer's point, or (3) give credit and summarize the point but include—within quotation marks—some phrase you think is especially interesting.

## How to Document: Footnotes and Internal Parenthetical Citations (MLA Format)

A student's documented essay on Arthur Miller's *Death of a Salesman* appears on pages 1477-87 of this book.

Documentation tells your reader exactly what your sources are. Until recently, the standard form was the footnote, which, for example, told the reader that the source of such-and-such a quotation was a book by So-and-so. But in 1984 the Modern Language Association, which had established the footnote form used in hundreds of journals, university presses, and classrooms, substituted a new form. It is this new form—parenthetical citation *within* the text (rather than at the foot of the page or the end of the essay)—that we will discuss at length. Keep in mind, though, that footnotes still have their uses.

***Footnotes.*** If you are using only one source, your instructor may advise you to give the source in a footnote. (Check with your instructors to find out their preferred forms of documentation.)

Let's say that your only source is this textbook. Let's say, too, that all of your quotations will be from a single story—Kate Chopin's "The Story of an Hour"—printed in this book on pages 19-21. If you use a word processor, the software program can probably format the note for you. If, however, you are using a typewriter, type the digit 1 (elevated, and *without* a period after it) after your first reference to (or quotation from) the story, and then put a footnote at the bottom of the page, explaining where the story can be found. After your last line of text on the page, triple-space, indent five spaces from the left-hand margin, raise the typewriter carriage half a line, and type the arabic number 1. Do *not* put a period after it. Then lower the carriage half a line and type a statement (double-spaced) to the effect that all references are to this book. Notice that although the footnote begins by being indented five spaces, if the note runs to more than one line the subsequent lines are given flush left.

[1]Chopin's story appears in Sylvan Barnet et al., eds. Literature: Thinking, Reading, and Writing Critically, 2nd ed. (New York: Longman, 1997), 19-21.

(If a book has more than three authors or editors, give the name of only the first author or editor, and follow it with a comma and *et al.,* the Latin abbreviation for "and others.")

Even if you are writing a comparison of, say, two stories in this book, you can use a note of this sort. It might run thus:

[1]All page references given parenthetically within the essay refer to stories in Sylvan Barnet et al., eds. Literature: Thinking, Reading, and Writing Critically, 2nd ed. (New York: Longman, 1997).

If you use such a note, you do not need to use a footnote after each quotation that follows. You can give the citations right in the body of the paper, by putting the page references in parentheses after the quotations.

***Internal Parenthetical Citations.*** On pages 1946-47 we distinguish between embedded quotations (which are short, are run right into your own sentence, and are enclosed within quotation marks) and quotations that are set off on the page and are not enclosed within quotation marks (for example, three or more lines of poetry, five or more lines of typed prose).

For an embedded quotation, put the page reference in parentheses immediately after the closing quotation mark, *without* any intervening punctuation. Then, after the parenthesis that follows the number, put the necessary punctuation (for instance, a comma or a period):

```
     Woolf says that in the struggling moth there was
"something marvelous as well as pathetic" (74). She
goes on to explain . . .
```

Notice that the period comes *after* the parenthetical citation. Notice, similarly, that in the next example *no* punctuation comes after the first citation—because none is needed—and a comma comes *after* (not before or within) the second citation, because a comma is needed in the sentence:

```
This is ironic because almost at the start of the
story, in the second paragraph, Richards with the
best of motives "hastened" (19) to bring his sad
message; if he had at the start been "too late" (21),
Mallard would have arrived at home first.
```

For a quotation that is not embedded within the text but is set off (by being indented ten spaces), put the parenthetical citation on the last line of the quotation, one space *after* the period that ends the quoted sentence.

Four additional points:

1. The abbreviations *p., pg.,* and *pp.* are *not* used in citing pages.
2. If a story is very short—perhaps running for only a page or two—your instructor may tell you there is no need to keep citing the page reference for each quotation. Simply mention in the footnote that the story appears on, say, pages 35-36.
3. If you are referring to a poem, your instructor may tell you to use parenthetical citations of line numbers rather than of page numbers. But, again, your footnote will tell the reader that the poem can be found in this book, and on what page.
4. If you are referring to a play with numbered lines, your instructor may prefer that in your parenthetical citations you give act, scene, and line, rather than page numbers. Use arabic (not roman) numerals, separating the act from the scene, and the scene from the line, by periods. Here, then, is how a reference to Act 3, Scene 2, line 118 would be given:

   ```
   (3.2.118)
   ```

***Parenthetical Citations and List of Works Cited.*** Footnotes have fallen into disfavor. Parenthetical citations are now usually clarified not by means of a footnote but by means of a list, headed Works Cited, given at the end of the essay. In this list you give alphabetically (last name first) the authors and titles that you have quoted or referred to in the essay.

Briefly, the idea is that the reader of your paper encounters an author's name and a parenthetical citation of pages. By checking the author's name in Works Cited, the reader can find the passage in the book. Suppose you are writing about Kate Chopin's "The Story of an Hour." Let's assume that you have already mentioned the author and the title of the story—that is, you have let the reader know the subject of the essay—and now you introduce a quotation from the story in a sentence such as this. (Notice the parenthetical citation of page numbers immediately after the quotation.)

> True, Mrs. Mallard at first expresses grief when she hears the news, but soon (unknown to her friends) she finds joy in it. So, Richards's "sad message" (19), though sad in Richard's eyes, is in fact a happy message.

Turning to Works Cited, the reader, knowing the quoted words are by Chopin, looks for Chopin and finds the following:

> Chopin, Kate. "The Story of an Hour." <u>Literature: Thinking, Reading, and Writing Critically</u>, 2nd ed. Eds. Sylvan Barnet et al. New York: Longman, 1997.

Thus the essayist is informing the reader that the quoted words ("sad message") are to be found on page 19 of this anthology.

If you have not mentioned Chopin's name in some sort of lead-in, you will have to give her name within the parentheses so that the reader will know the author of the quoted words:

> What are we to make out of a story that ends by telling us that the leading character has died "of joy that kills" (Chopin 21)?

(Notice, by the way, that the closing quotation marks come immediately after the last word of the quotation; the citation and the final punctuation—in this case, the essayist's question mark—come *after* the closing quotation marks.)

If you are comparing Chopin's story with Gilman's "The Yellow Wallpaper," in Works Cited you will give a similar entry for Gilman—her name, the title of the story, the book in which it is reprinted, and the page numbers that the story occupies.

If you are referring to several works reprinted within one volume, instead of listing each item fully, it is acceptable in Works Cited to list each item simply by giving the author's name, the title of the work, then a period, a space, and the name of the anthologist, followed by the page numbers that the selection spans. Thus a reference to Chopin's "The Story of an Hour" would be followed only by: Barnet 19-21. This form requires that the anthology itself be cited under the name of the first-listed editor, thus:

Barnet, Sylvan, et al., eds. Literature: Thinking, Reading, and Writing Critically, 2nd ed. New York: Longman, 1997.

If you are writing a research paper, you will use many sources. Within the essay itself you will mention an author's name, quote or summarize from this author, and follow the quotation or summary with a parenthetical citation of the pages. In Works Cited you will give the full title, place of publication, and other bibliographic material.

Here are a few examples, all referring to an article by Joan Templeton, "The *Doll House* Backlash: Criticism, Feminism, and Ibsen." The article appeared in *PMLA* 104 (1989): 28–40, but this information is given only in Works Cited, not within the text of the student's essay.

If in the text of your essay you mention the author's name, the citation following a quotation (or a summary of a passage) is merely a page number in parentheses, followed by a period, thus:

> In 1989 Joan Templeton argued that many critics, unhappy with recognizing Ibsen as a feminist, sought "to render Nora inconsequential" (29).

Or:

> In 1989 Joan Templeton noted that many critics, unhappy with recognizing Ibsen as a feminist, have sought to make Nora trivial (29).

If you don't mention the name of the author in a lead-in, you will have to give the name within the parenthetical citation:

> Many critics, attempting to argue that Ibsen was not a feminist, have tried to make Nora trivial (Templeton 29).

Notice in all of these examples that the final period comes after the parenthetical citation. *Exception:* If the quotation is longer than four lines and, therefore, is set off by being indented ten spaces from the left margin, end the quotation with the appropriate punctuation (period, question mark, or exclamation mark), hit the space bar twice, and type (in parentheses) the page number. In this case, do not put a period after the citation.

*Another point:* If your list of Works Cited includes more than one work by an author, in your essay when you quote or refer to one or the other you'll have to identify *which* work you are drawing on. You can provide the title in a lead-in, thus:

> In "The Doll House Backlash: Criticism, Feminism, and Ibsen," Templeton says, "Nora's detractors have often been, from the first, her husband's defenders" (30).

Or you can provide the information in the parenthetic citation, giving a shortened version of the title—usually the first word, unless it is *A, An,* or *The,* in which case the second word usually will do, though certain titles may require still another word or two, as in this example:

```
According to Templeton, "Nora's detractors have often
been, from the first, her husband's defenders" ("Doll
House Backlash" 30).
```

***Forms of Citation in Works Cited.*** In looking over the following samples of entries in Works Cited, remember:

1. The list of Works Cited appears at the end of the paper. It begins on a new page, and the page continues the numbering of the text.
2. The list of Works Cited is arranged alphabetically by author (last name first).
3. If a work is anonymous, list it under the first word of the title unless the first word is *A, An,* or *The,* in which case list it under the second word.
4. If a work is by two authors, although the book is listed alphabetically under the first author's last name, the second author's name is given in the normal order, first name first.
5. If you list two or more works by the same author, the author's name is not repeated but is represented by three hyphens followed by a period and a space.
6. Each item begins flush left, but if an entry is longer than one line, subsequent lines in the entry are indented five spaces.

For details about almost every imaginable kind of citation, consult Joseph Gibaldi, *MLA Handbook for Writers of Research Papers,* 4th ed. (New York: Modern Language Association, 1995). We give here, however, information concerning the most common kinds of citations.

Here are samples of the kinds of citations you are most likely to include in your list of Works Cited.

**A book by one author:**

```
Douglas, Ann. The Feminization of American Culture.
     New York: Knopf, 1977.
```

Notice that the author's last name is given first, but otherwise the name is given as on the title page. Do not substitute initials for names written out on the title page, but you may shorten the publisher's name—for example, from Little, Brown and Company to Little.

Take the title from the title page, not from the cover or the spine, but disregard unusual typography—for instance, the use of only capital letters or the use of *&* for *and.* Underline the title and subtitle with one continuous underline, but do not underline the period. The place of publication is indicated by the name of the city. If the city is not well known or if several cities have the same name (for instance, Cambridge, Massachusetts, and Cambridge, England) the name of the state is added. If the title page lists several cities, give only the first.

**A book by more than one author:**

Gilbert, Sandra, and Susan Gubar. The Madwoman in the Attic: The Woman Writer and the Nineteenth-Century Literary Imagination. New Haven: Yale UP, 1979.

Notice that the book is listed under the last name of the first author (Gilbert) and that the second author's name is then given with first name (Susan) first. *If the book has more than three authors,* give the name of the first author only (last name first) and follow it with *et al.* (Latin for "and others.")

**A book in several volumes:**

McQuade, Donald, et al., eds. The Harper American Literature. 2nd ed. 2 vols. New York: HarperCollins, 1994.

Pope, Alexander. The Correspondence of Alexander Pope. 5 vols. Ed. George Sherburn. Oxford: Clarendon, 1955.

Notice that the total number of volumes is given after the title, regardless of the number that you have used.

If you have used more than one volume, within your essay you will parenthetically indicate a reference to, for instance, page 30 of volume 3 thus: (3: 30). If you have used only one volume of a multivolume work—let's say you used only volume 2 of McQuade's anthology—in your entry in Works Cited write, after the period following the date, Vol. 2. In your parenthetical citation within the essay you will therefore cite only the page reference (without the volume number), since the reader will (on consulting Works Cited) understand that in this example the reference is in volume 2.

If, instead of using the volumes as a whole, you used only an independent work within one volume—say, an essay in volume 2—in Works Cited omit the abbreviation *Vol.* Instead, give an arabic 2 (indicating volume 2) followed by a colon, a space, and the page numbers that encompass the selection you used:

McPherson, James Alan. "Why I Like Country Music." The Harper American Literature. 2nd ed. 2 vols. New York: HarperCollins, 1994. 2: 2304-15.

Notice that this entry for McPherson specifies not only that the book consists of two volumes, but also that only one selection ("Why I Like Country Music," occupying pages 2304-15 in volume 2) was used. If you use this sort of citation in Works Cited, in the body of your essay a documentary reference to this work will be only to the page; the volume number will *not* be added.

**A book with a separate title in a set of volumes:**

Churchill, Winston. <u>The Age of Revolution</u>. Vol. 3 of <u>A History of the English-Speaking Peoples</u>. New York: Dodd, 1957.

Jonson, Ben. <u>The Complete Masques</u>. Ed. Stephen Orgel. Vol. 4 of <u>The Yale Ben Jonson</u>. New Haven: Yale UP, 1969.

**A revised edition of a book:**

Chaucer, Geoffrey. <u>The Works of Geoffrey Chaucer</u>. Ed. F. N. Robinson. 2nd ed. Boston: Houghton, 1957.

Ellmann, Richard. <u>James Joyce</u>. Rev. ed. New York: Oxford UP, 1982.

**A reprint, such as a paperback version of an older hardcover book:**

Rourke, Constance. <u>American Humor</u>. 1931. Garden City, New York: Doubleday, 1953.

Notice that the entry cites the original date (1931) but indicates that the writer is using the Doubleday reprint of 1953.

**An edited book other than an anthology:**

Keats, John. <u>The Letters of John Keats</u>. Ed. Hyder Edward Rollins. 2 vols. Cambridge, Mass.: Harvard UP, 1958.

**An anthology.** You can list an anthology either under the editor's name or under the title.

**A work in a volume of works by one author:**

Sontag, Susan. "The Aesthetics of Silence." In <u>Styles of Radical Will</u>. New York: Farrar, 1969. 3-34.

This entry indicates that Sontag's essay, called "The Aesthetics of Silence," appears in a book of hers entitled *Styles of Radical Will.* Notice that the page numbers of the short work are cited (not page numbers that you may happen to refer to, but the page numbers of the entire piece).

**A work in an anthology, that is, in a collection of works by several authors.** Begin with the author and the title of the work you are citing, not with the name of the anthologist or the title of the anthology. The entry ends with the pages occupied by the selection you are citing:

> Ng, Fae Myenne. "A Red Sweater." Charlie Chan Is Dead: An Anthology of Contemporary Asian American Fiction. Ed. Jessica Hagedorn. New York: Penguin, 1993. 358-68.

Normally, you will give the title of the work you are citing (probably an essay, short story, or poem) in quotation marks. If you are referring to a book-length work (for instance, a novel or a full-length play), underline it to indicate italics. If the work is translated, after the period that follows the title, write *Trans.* and give the name of the translator, followed by a period and the name of the anthology.

If the collection is a multivolume work and you are using only one volume, in Works Cited you will specify the volume, as in the example (p. 1962) of McPherson's essay. Because the list of Works Cited specifies the volume, your parenthetical documentary reference within your essay will specify (as mentioned earlier) only the page numbers, not the volume. Thus, although McPherson's essay appears on pages 2304-15 in the second volume of a two-volume work, a parenthetical citation will refer only to the page numbers because the citation in Works Cited specifies the volume.

Remember that the pages specified in the entry in your list of Works Cited are to the *entire selection,* not simply to pages you may happen to refer to within your paper.

If you are referring to a *reprint of a scholarly article,* give details of the original publication, as in the following example:

> Mack, Maynard. "The World of Hamlet." Yale Review 41 (1952): 502-23. Rpt. in Hamlet. By William Shakespeare. Ed. Edward Hubler. New York: New American Library, 1963. 234-56.

**Two or more works in an anthology.** If you are referring to more than one work in an anthology in order to avoid repeating all the information about the anthology in each entry in Works Cited, under each author's name (in the appropriate alphabetical place) give the author and title of the work, then a period, a space, and the name of the anthologist, followed by the page numbers that the selection spans. Thus, a reference to Shakespeare's *Hamlet* would be followed only by

> Barnet 1292-1402

rather than by a full citation of Barnet's anthology. This form requires that the anthology itself also be listed, under Barnet.

**Two or more works by the same author.** Notice that the works are given in alphabetical order (*Fables* precedes *Fools*) and that the author's name is not repeated but is represented by three hyphens followed by a period and a space. If the author is the translator or editor of a volume, the three hyphens are followed not by a period but by a comma, then a space, then the appropriate abbreviation (*Trans.* or *Ed.*), then the title:

Frye, Northrop. Fables of Identity: Studies in Poetic Mythology. New York: Harcourt, 1963.

---. Fools of Time: Studies in Shakespearean Tragedy. Toronto: U of Toronto P, 1967.

**A translated book:**

Gogol, Nikolai. Dead Souls. Trans. Andrew McAndrew. New York: New American Library, 1961.

If you are discussing the translation itself, as opposed to the book, list the work under the translator's name. Then put a comma, a space, and "trans." After the period following "trans." skip a space, then give the title of the book, a period, a space, and then "By" and the author's name, first name first. Continue with information about the place of publication, publisher, and date, as in any entry to a book.

**An introduction, foreword, or afterword, or other editorial apparatus:**

Fromm, Erich. Afterword. 1984. By George Orwell. New American Library, 1961.

Usually a book with an introduction or some such comparable material is listed under the name of the author of the book rather than the name of the author of the editorial material (see the citation to Pope on p. 1962). But if you are referring to the editor's apparatus rather than to the work itself, use the form just given.

Words such as *preface, introduction, afterword,* and *conclusion* are capitalized in the entry but are neither enclosed within quotation marks nor underlined.

**A book review.** First, an example of a review that does not have a title:

Vendler, Helen. Rev. of Essays on Style. Ed. Roger Fowler. Essays in Criticism 16 (1966): 457-63.

If the review has a title, give the title after the period following the reviewer's name, before "Rev." If the review is unsigned, list it under the first word of the title, or the second word if the first word is *A, An,* or *The.* If an unsigned review has no title, begin the entry with "Rev. of" and alphabetize it under the title of the work being reviewed.

**An encyclopedia.** The first example is for a signed article, the second for an unsigned article:

Lang, Andrew. "Ballads." Encyclopaedia Britannica. 1910 ed.

"Metaphor." The New Encyclopaedia Britannica: Micropaedia. 1974 ed.

**An article in a scholarly journal.** Some journals are paginated consecutively; that is, the pagination of the second issue picks up where the first issue left off. Other journals begin each issue with a new page 1. The forms of the citations in Works Cited differ slightly.

First, the citation of *a journal that uses continuous pagination:*

Burbick, Joan. "Emily Dickinson and the Economics of Desire." American Literature 58 (1986): 361-78.

This article appeared in volume 58, which was published in 1986. (Notice that the volume number is followed by a space, then by the year in parentheses, and then by a colon, a space, and the page numbers of the entire article.) Although each volume consists of four issues, you do *not* specify the issue number when the journal is paginated continuously.

For *a journal that paginates each issue separately* (a quarterly journal will have four page 1's each year), give the issue number directly after the volume number and a period, with no spaces before or after the period:

Spillers, Hortense J. "Martin Luther King and the Style of the Black Sermon." The Black Scholar 3.1 (1971): 14-27.

**An article in a weekly, biweekly, or monthly publication:**

McCabe, Bernard. "Taking Dickens Seriously." Commonweal 14 May 1965: 24.

Notice that the volume number and the issue number are omitted for popular weeklies or monthlies such as *Time* and *Atlantic.*

**An article in a newspaper.** Because newspapers usually consist of several sections, a section number may precede the page number. The example indicates that an article begins on page 3 of section 2 and is continued on a later page:

Wu, Jim. "Authors Praise New Forms." New York Times 8 March 1996, sec. 2: 3+.

You may also have occasion to cite something other than a printed source, for instance, a lecture. Here are the forms for the chief nonprint sources.

**An interview:**

Saretta, Howard. Personal interview. 3 Nov. 1996.

**A lecture:**

Heaney, Seamus. Lecture. Tufts University. 15 Oct. 1996.

**A television or radio program:**

60 Minutes. CBS. 30 Jan. 1994.

**A film or videotape:**

Modern Times. Dir. Charles Chaplin. United Artists, 1936.

**A recording:**

Frost, Robert. "The Road Not Taken." Robert Frost Reads His Poetry. Caedmon, TC 1060, 1956.

**A performance:**

The Cherry Orchard. By Anton Chekhov. Dir. Ron Daniels. American Repertory Theatre, Cambridge, Mass. 3 Feb. 1994.

# APPENDIX C

# *Glossary of Literary Terms*

The terms briefly defined here are for the most part more fully defined earlier in the text. Hence many of the entries below are followed by page references to the earlier discussions.

**Absurd, Theater of the** plays, especially written in the 1950s and 1960s, that call attention to the incoherence of character and of action, the inability of people to communicate, and the apparent purposelessness of existence

**accent** stress given to a syllable (946)

**act** a major division of a play (1208)

**action** (1) the happenings in a narrative or drama, usually physical events (*B* marries *C*, *D* kills *E*), but also mental changes (*F* moves from innocence to experience); in short, the answer to the question, "What happens?" (2) less commonly, the theme or underlying idea of a work (1207–08)

**allegory** a work in which concrete elements (for instance, a pilgrim, a road, a splendid city) stand for abstractions (humanity, life, salvation), usually in an unambiguous, one-to-one relationship. The literal items (the pilgrim, and so on) thus convey a meaning, which is usually moral, religious, or political. To take a nonliterary example: The Statue of Liberty holds a torch (enlightenment, showing the rest of the world the way to freedom), and at her feet are broken chains (tyranny overcome). A caution: Not all of the details in an allegorical work are meant to be interpreted. For example, the hollowness of the Statue of Liberty does not stand for the insubstantiality or emptiness of liberty. (123)

**alliteration** repetition of consonant sounds, especially at the beginnings of words (*f*ree, *f*orm, *ph*antom) (949)

**allusion** an indirect reference; thus when Lincoln spoke of "a nation dedicated to the proposition that all men are created equal," he was making an allusion to the Declaration of Independence.

**ambiguity** multiplicity of meaning, often deliberate, that leaves the reader uncertain about the intended significance

**anagnorisis** a recognition or discovery, especially in tragedy—for example, when the hero understands the reason for his or her fall (1225)

**analysis** an examination, which usually proceeds by separating the object of study into parts (34, 45–48, 51)

**anapest** a metrical foot consisting of two unaccented syllables followed by an accented one. Example, showing three anapests: "As I came / to the edge / of the wood" (947)

**anecdote** a short narrative, usually reporting an amusing event in the life of an important person (342)

**antagonist** a character or force that opposes (literally, "wrestles") the protagonist (the main character). Thus, in *Hamlet* the antagonist is King Claudius, the protagonist is Hamlet; in Antigonê, the antagonist is Creon, the protagonist Antigonê.

**antecedent action** happenings (especially in a play) that occurred before the present action (1208)

**apostrophe** address to an absent figure or to a thing as if it were present and could listen. Example: "O rose, thou art sick!" (895)

**approximate rhyme** see *half-rhyme*

**archetype** a theme, image, motive, or pattern that occurs so often in literary works it seems to be universal. Examples: a dark forest (for mental confusion), the sun (for illumination) (1926–27, 1939)

**aside** in the theater, words spoken by a character in the presence of other characters, but directed to the spectators—i.e., understood by the audience to be inaudible to the other characters (1208)

**assonance** repetition of similar vowel sounds in stressed syllables. Example: *light/bride* (949)

**atmosphere** the emotional tone (for instance, joy, or horror) in a work, most often established by the setting

**ballad** a short narrative poem, especially one that is sung or recited, often in a stanza of four lines, with 8, 6, 8, 6 syllables, with the second and fourth lines rhyming. A **folk** or **popular ballad** is a narrative song that has been transmitted orally by what used to be called "the folk"; a **literary ballad** is a conscious imitation (without music) of such a work, often with complex symbolism. (1043–44)

**blank verse** unrhymed iambic pentameter—that is, unrhymed lines of ten syllables, with every second syllable stressed (953)

**cacophony** an unpleasant combination of sounds

**caesura** a strong pause within a line of verse (948)

**canon** a term originally used to refer to those books accepted as Holy Scripture by the Christian church. The term has come to be applied to literary works thought to have a special merit by a given culture—for instance, the body of literature traditionally taught in colleges and universities. Such works are sometimes called "classics" and their authors are "major authors." As conceived in the United States until recently, the canon consisted chiefly of works by dead white European and American males—partly, of course, because middle-class and upper-class white males were in fact the people who did most of the writing in the Western Hemisphere, but also because white males (for instance, college professors) were the people who chiefly established the canon. Not surprisingly the canon-makers valued (or valorized or "privileged") writings that revealed, asserted, or reinforced the canon-makers' own values. From about the 1960s feminists and Marxists and others argued that these works had been regarded as central not because they were inherently better than other works but because they reflected the interests of the dominant culture, and that other work, such as slave narratives and the diaries of women, had been "marginalized."

In fact, the literary canon has never been static (in contrast to the biblical canon, which has not changed for more than a thousand years), but it is true that certain authors, such as Homer, Chaucer, and Shakespeare have been permanent fixtures. Why? Partly because they do indeed support the values of those who in large measure control the high cultural purse strings, and perhaps partly because these books are rich enough to invite constant reinterpretation from age to age—that is, to allow each generation to find its needs and its values in them.

**catastrophe** the concluding action, especially in a tragedy

**catharsis** Aristotle's term for the purgation or purification of the pity and terror supposedly experienced while witnessing a tragedy

**character** (1) a person in a literary work (Romeo); (2) the personality of such a figure (sentimental lover, or whatever). Characters (in the first sense) are sometimes classified as either "flat" (one-dimensional) or "round" (fully realized, complex). (86, 91–93, 103–04, 1221, 1474)

**characterization** the presentation of a character, whether by direct description, by showing the character in action, or by the presentation of other characters who help to define each other

**cliché** an expression that through overuse has ceased to be effective. Examples: *acid test, sigh of relief, the proud possessor*

**climax** the culmination of a conflict; a turning point, often the point of greatest tension in a plot (1207)

**comedy** a literary work, especially a play, characterized by humor and by a happy ending (1405–08, 1472, 1475)

**comparison and contrast** to compare is strictly to note similarities; to contrast is to note differences. But *compare* is now often used for both activities. (38–39)

**complication** an entanglement in a narrative or dramatic work that causes a conflict

**conflict** a struggle between a character and some obstacle (for example, another character or fate) or between internal forces, such as divided loyalties (85–86, 1208, 1473)

**connotation** the associations (suggestions, overtones) of a word or expression. Thus *seventy* and *three score and ten* both mean "one more than sixty-nine," but because *three score and ten* is a biblical expression, it has an association of holiness; see *denotation.* (896)

**consistency building** the process engaged in during the act of reading, of reevaluating the details that one has just read in order to make them consistent with the new information that the text is providing

**consonance** repetition of consonant sounds, especially in stressed syllables. Also called *half-rhyme* or slant rhyme. Example: *arouse/doze* (949)

**convention** a pattern (for instance, the 14-line poem, or sonnet) or motif (for instance, the bumbling police officer in detective fiction) or other device occurring so often that it is taken for granted. Thus it is a convention that actors in a performance of *Julius Caesar* are understood to be speaking Latin, though in fact they are speaking English. Similarly, the soliloquy (a character alone on the stage speaks his or her thoughts aloud) is a convention, for in real life sane people rarely talk aloud to themselves.

**couplet** a pair of lines of verse, usually rhyming (951)

**crisis** a high point in the conflict that leads to the turning point (1207)

**criticism** the analysis or evaluation of a literary work (1919–41)

**cultural criticism** criticism that sets literature in a social context, often of economics or politics or gender. Borrowing some of the methods of anthropology, cultural criticism usually extends the canon to include popular material—for instance, comic books and soap operas

**dactyl** a metrical foot consisting of a stressed syllable followed by two unstressed syllables. Example: *underwear* (947)

**deconstruction** a critical approach that assumes language is unstable and ambiguous and is therefore inherently contradictory. Because authors cannot control their language, texts reveal more than their authors are aware of. For instance, texts (like such institutions as the law, the churches, and the schools) are likely, when closely scrutinized, to reveal connections to a society's economic system, even though the authors may have believed they were outside of the system. (1922–23, 1939)

**denotation** the dictionary meaning of a word. Thus *soap opera* and *daytime serial* have the same denotation, but the connotations (associations, emotional overtones) of *soap opera* are less favorable. (896)

**dénouement** the resolution or the outcome (literally, the "unknotting") of a plot (86, 91, 1207)

**deus ex machina** literally, "a god out of a machine"; any unexpected and artificial way of resolving the plot—for example, by introducing a rich uncle, thought to be dead, who arrives on the scene and pays the debts that otherwise would overwhelm the young hero

**dialogue** exchange of words between characters; speech

**diction** the choice of vocabulary and of sentence structure. There is a difference in diction between "One never knows" and "You never can tell." (870–71)

**didactic** pertaining to teaching; having a moral purpose

**dimeter** a line of poetry containing two feet (947)

**discovery** see *anagnorisis* (1225, 1969)

**drama** (1) a play; (2) conflict or tension, as in "The story lacks drama" (1203–09)

**dramatic irony** see *irony*

**dramatic monologue** a poem spoken entirely by one character but addressed to one or more other characters whose presence is strongly felt (868)

**effaced narrator** a narrator who reports but who does not editorialize or enter into the minds of any of the characters in the story

**elegy** a lyric poem, usually a meditation on a death (837)

**elision** omission (usually of a vowel or unstressed syllable), as in *o'er* (for *over*) and in "Th' inevitable hour"

**end rhyme** identical sounds at the ends of lines of poetry (949)

**end-stopped line** a line of poetry that ends with a pause (usually marked by a comma, semicolon, or period) because the grammatical structure and the sense reach (at least to some degree) completion. It is contrasted with a *run-on line.* (948)

**English (or Shakespearean) sonnet** a poem of 14 lines (three quatrains and a couplet), rhyming *ababcdcdefefgg* (951)

**enjambment** a line of poetry in which the grammatical and logical sense run on, without pause, into the next line or lines (948)

**epic** a long narrative, especially in verse, that usually records heroic material in an elevated style

**epigram** a brief, witty poem or saying

**epigraph** a quotation at the beginning of the work, just after the title, often giving a clue to the theme

**epiphany** a "showing forth," as when an action reveals a character with particular clarity

**episode** an incident or scene that has unity in itself but is also a part of a larger action

**epistle** a letter, in prose or verse

**essay** a work, usually in prose and usually fairly short, that purports to be true and that treats its subject tentatively. In most literary essays the reader's interest is as much in the speaker's personality as in any argument that is offered.

**euphony** literally, "good sound," a pleasant combination of sounds

**explication** a line-by-line unfolding of the meaning of a text (34–38, 959–60)

**exposition** a setting forth of information. In fiction and drama, introductory material introducing characters and the situation; in an essay, the presentation of information, as opposed to the telling of a story or the setting forth of an argument (91, 1208)

**eye-rhyme** words that look as though they rhyme, but do not rhyme when pronounced. Example: *come/home* (949)

**fable** a short story (often involving speaking animals) with an easily grasped moral (85)

**farce** comedy based not on clever language or on subtleties of characters but on broadly humorous situations (for instance, a man mistakenly enters the women's locker room) (1406)

**feminine rhyme** a rhyme of two or more syllables, with the stress falling on a syllable other than the last. Examples: *fatter/batter; tenderly/slenderly* (949)

**feminist criticism** an approach especially concerned with analyzing the depiction of women in literature—what images do male authors present of female characters?—and also with the reappraisal of work by female authors (1931–37, 1940)

**fiction** an imaginative work, usually a prose narrative (novel, short story), that reports incidents that did not in fact occur. The term may include all works that invent a world, such as a lyric poem or a play.

**figurative language** words intended to be understood in a way that is other than literal. Thus *lemon* used literally refers to a citrus fruit, but *lemon* used figuratively refers to a defective machine, especially a defective automobile. Other examples: "He's a beast," "She's a witch," "A sea of troubles." Literally, such expressions are nonsense, but writers use them to express meanings inexpressible in literal speech. Among the commonest kinds of figures of speech are *apostrophe, metaphor,* and *simile* (see the discussions of these words in this glossary) (888–904)

**flashback** an interruption in a narrative that presents an earlier episode

**flat character** a one-dimensional character (for instance, the figure who is only and always the jealous husband or the flirtatious wife) as opposed to a round or many-sided character (92)

**fly-on-the-wall narrator** a narrator who never editorializes and never enters a character's mind but reports only what is said and done (108)

**foil** a character who makes a contrast with another, especially a minor character who helps to set off a major character

**foot** a metrical unit, consisting of two or three syllables, with a specified arrangement of the stressed syllable or syllables. Thus the iambic foot consists of an unstressed syllable followed by a stressed syllable. (946–47)

**foreshadowing** suggestions of what is to come (93)

**formalist criticism** analysis that assumes a work of art is a constructed object with a stable meaning that can be ascertained by studying the relationships between the elements of the work. Thus a poem is like a chair; a chair *can* of course be stood on, or used for firewood, but it was created with a specific purpose that was evident and remains evident to all viewers. (1920–22, 1939)

**free verse** poetry in lines of irregular length, usually unrhymed (953–54)

**gap** a term from reader-response criticism, referring to a reader's perception that something is unstated in the text, requiring the reader to fill in the material—for instance, to draw a conclusion as to why a character behaves as she does. Filling in the gaps is a matter of "consistency building." Different readers of course may fill the gaps differently, and readers may even differ as to whether a gap exists at a particular point in the text. (10)

**gay criticism** see **gender criticism**

**gender criticism** criticism concerned especially with alleged differences in the ways that males and females read and write, and also with the representations of gender (straight, bisexual, gay, lesbian) in literature (164–66, 1931–37, 1940)

**genre** kind or type, roughly analogous to the biological term *species*. The four chief literary genres are nonfiction, fiction, poetry, and drama, but these can be subdivided into further genres. Thus fiction obviously can be divided into the short story and the novel, and drama obviously can be divided into tragedy and comedy. But these can be still further divided—for instance, tragedy into heroic tragedy and bourgeois tragedy, comedy into romantic comedy and satirical comedy.

**gesture** physical movement, especially in a play (1204)

**haiku** a Japanese form having three unrhymed lines of five, seven, and five syllables (921–23)

**half-rhyme** repetition in accented syllables of the final consonant sound but without identity in the preceding vowel sound; words of similar but not identical sound. Also called near rhyme, slant rhyme, approximate rhyme, and off-rhyme. See *consonance*. Examples: *light/bet; affirm/perform* (949)

**hamartia** a flaw in the tragic hero, or an error made by the tragic hero (1224)

**heptameter** a metrical line of seven feet (947)

**hero, heroine** the main character (not necessarily heroic or even admirable) in a work; cf. *protagonist*

**heroic couplet** an end-stopped pair of rhyming lines of iambic pentameter (951)

**hexameter** a metrical line of six feet (947)

**historical criticism** the attempt to illuminate a literary work by placing it in its historical context (1927–28, 1939–40)

**hubris, hybris** a Greek word, usually translated as "overweening pride," "arrogance," "excessive ambition," and often said to be characteristic of tragic figures (1224)

**hyperbole** figurative language using overstatement, as in "He died a thousand deaths" (925)

**iamb, iambic** a poetic foot consisting of an unaccented syllable followed by an accented one. Example: *alone* (947)

**image, imagery** imagery is established by language that appeals to the senses, especially sight ("deep blue sea") but also other senses ("tinkling bells," "perfumes of Arabia") (905)

**indeterminacy** a passage that careful readers agree is open to more than one interpretation. According to some poststructural critics, because language is unstable and because contexts can never be objectively viewed, all texts are indeterminate (10–11)

**innocent eye** a naive narrator in whose narration the reader sees more than the narrator sees (107)

**internal rhyme** rhyme within a line (949)

**interpretation** the assignment of meaning to a text (54–56, 700–01)

**intertextuality** all works show the influence of other works. If an author writes (say) a short story, no matter how original she thinks she is, she inevitably brings to her own story a knowledge of other stories—for example, a conception of what a short story is, and, speaking more generally, an idea of what a story (long or short, written or oral) is. In opposition to formalist critics, who see a literary work as an independent whole containing a fixed meaning, some contemporary critics emphasize the work's *intertextuality* —that is, its connections with a vast context of writings and indeed of all aspects of culture, and in part depending also on what the reader brings to the work. Because different readers bring different things, meaning is thus ever-changing. In this view, then, no text is self-sufficient, and no writer fully controls the meaning of the text. Because we are talking about connections of which the writer is unaware, and because "meaning" is in part the creation of the reader, the author is by no means an authority. Thus the critic should see a novel (for instance) in connection not only with other novels, past and present, but also in connection with other kinds of narratives, such as TV dramas and films, even though the author of the book lived before the age of film and TV. See Jay Clayton and Eric Rothstein, eds., *Influences and Intertextuality in Literary History* (1991).

**irony** a contrast of some sort. For instance, in **verbal irony** or **Socratic irony** (924), the contrast is between what is said and what is meant ("You're a great guy," meant bitterly). In **dramatic irony** or **Sophoclean irony** (also called **tragic irony**) (1225), the contrast is between what is intended and what is accomplished (Macbeth usurps the throne, thinking he will then be happy, but the action leads him to misery), or between what the audience knows (a murderer waits in the bedroom) and what a character says (the victim enters the bedroom, innocently saying, "I think I'll have a long sleep")

**Italian (or Petrarchan) sonnet** a poem of 14 lines, consisting of an octave (rhyming *abbaabba*) and a sestet (usually *cdecde* or *cdccdc*) (951)

**lesbian criticism** see **gender criticism**

**litotes** a form of understatement in which an affirmation is made by means of a negation; thus "He was not underweight," meaning "He was grossly overweight"

**lyric poem** a short poem, often songlike, with the emphasis not on narrative but on the speaker's emotion or reverie (836–60)

**Marxist criticism** the study of literature in the light of Karl Marx's view that economic forces, controlled by the dominant class, shape the literature (as well as the law, philosophy, religion, etc.) of a society (1928, 1940)

**masculine rhyme** rhyme of one-syllable words (*lies/cries*) or, if more than one syllable, words ending with accented syllables (*behold/foretold*) (949)

**mask** a term used to designate the speaker of a poem, equivalent to *persona* or *voice* (861-67)

**meaning** critics seek to interpret "meaning," variously defined as what the writer intended the work to say about the world and human experience, or as what the work says to the reader irrespective of the writer's intention. Both versions imply that a literary work is a nut to be cracked, with a kernel that is to be extracted. Because few critics today hold that meaning is clear and unchanging, the tendency now is to say that a critic offers "an interpretation" or "a reading" rather than a "statement of the meaning of a work." Many critics today would say that an alleged interpretation is really a creation of meaning.

**melodrama** a narrative, usually in dramatic form, involving threatening situations but ending happily. The characters are usually stock figures (virtuous heroine, villainous landlord).

**metaphor** a kind of figurative language equating one thing with another: "This novel is garbage" (a book is equated with discarded and probably inedible food), "a piercing cry" (a cry is equated with a spear or other sharp instrument) (892)

**meter** a pattern of stressed and unstressed syllables (940-48)

**metonymy** a kind of figurative language in which a word or phrase stands not for itself but for something closely related to it: *saber rattling* means "militaristic talk or action" (894)

**monologue** a relatively long, uninterrupted speech by a character

**monometer** a metrical line consisting of only one foot (947)

**montage** in film, quick cutting; in fiction, quick shifts

**mood** the atmosphere, usually created by descriptions of the settings and characters

**motif** a recurrent theme within a work, or a theme common to many works

**motivation** grounds for a character's action (92-93)

**myth** (1) a traditional story reflecting primitive beliefs, especially explaining the mysteries of the natural world (why it rains, or the origin of mountains); (2) a body of belief, not necessarily false, especially as set forth by a writer. Thus one may speak of Yeats and Alice Walker as myth-makers, referring to the visions of reality that they set forth in their works.

**myth criticism** see **archetype**

**narrative, narrator** a narrative is a story (an anecdote, a novel); a narrator is one who tells a story (not the author, but the invented speaker of the story). On kinds of narrators, see *point of view.* (105-09, 122)

**New Criticism** a mid-twentieth-century movement (also called formalist criticism) that regarded a literary work as an independent, carefully constructed object; hence it made little or no use of the author's biography or of historical context and it relied chiefly on explication (1920-22, 1939)

**New Historicism** a school of criticism holding that the past cannot be known objectively. According to this view, because historians project their own "narrative"—their own invention or "construction"—on the happenings of the past, historical writings are not objective but are, at bottom, political statements. (1929, 1940)

**novel** a long work of prose fiction, especially one that is relatively realistic (602–05)

**novella** a work of prose fiction longer than a short story but shorter than a novel—say, about 40 to 80 pages

**objective point of view** a narrator reports but does not editorialize or enter into the minds of any of the characters in the story (108)

**octave, octet** an eight-line stanza, or the first eight lines of a sonnet, especially of an Italian sonnet (951)

**octosyllabic couplet** a pair of rhyming lines, each line with four iambic feet (951)

**ode** a lyric exalting someone (for instance, a hero) or something (for instance, a season) (837)

**off-rhyme** see *half-rhyme*

**omniscient narrator** a speaker who knows the thoughts of all of the characters in the narrative (107–08)

**onomatopoeia** words (or the use of words) that sound like what they mean. Examples: *buzz, whirr* (949)

**open form** poetry whose form seems spontaneous rather than highly patterned

**oxymoron** a compact paradox, as in *a mute cry, a pleasing pain, proud humility*

**parable** a short narrative that is at least in part allegorical and that illustrates a moral or spiritual lesson (8–9, 54–56, 85)

**paradox** an apparent contradiction, as in Jesus's words "Whosoever will save his life shall lose it; but whosoever will lose his life for my sake, the same shall save it" (925)

**paraphrase** a restatement that sets forth an idea in diction other than that of the original (4)

**parody** a humorous imitation of a literary work, especially of its style

**pathos** pity, sadness

**pentameter** a line of verse containing five feet (947)

**peripeteia** a reversal in the action (1225)

**persona** literally, a mask; the "I" or speaker of a work, sometimes identified with the author but usually better regarded as the voice or mouthpiece created by the author (861–87)

**personification** a kind of figurative language in which an inanimate object, animal, or other nonhuman is given human traits. Examples: *the creeping tide* (the tide is imagined as having feet), *the cruel sea* (the sea is imagined as having moral qualities) (895)

**Petrarchan sonnet** see *Italian sonnet*

**plot** the episodes in a narrative or dramatic work—that is, what happens. (But even a lyric poem can be said to have a plot; for instance, the speaker's mood changes from anger to resignation.) Sometimes *plot* is defined as the author's particular arrangement (sequence) of these episodes, and *story* is the episodes in their chronological sequence. Until recently it was widely believed that a good plot had a logical structure: *A* caused *B* (*B* did not simply happen to follow *A*), but in the last few decades some critics have argued that such a concept merely represents the white male's view of experience. (103, 1207–08, 1220–21, 1473)

**poem** an imaginative work in meter or in free verse, usually employing figurative language (829–35)

**point of view** the perspective from which a story is told—for example, by a major character or a minor character or a fly on the wall; see also *narrative, narrator, omniscient narrator* (105–09, 122)

**postmodernism** the term came into prominence in the 1960s, to distinguish the contemporary experimental writing of such authors as Samuel Beckett and Jorge Luis Borges from such early twentieth-century classics of modernism as James Joyce's *Ulysses* (1922) and T. S. Eliot's *The Waste Land* (1922). Although the classic modernists had been thought to be revolutionary in their day, after World War II they seemed to be conservative, and their works seemed remote from today's society with its new interests in such things as feminism, gay and lesbian rights, and pop culture. Postmodernist literature, though widely varied and not always clearly distinct from modernist literature, usually is more politically concerned, more playful—it is given to parody and pastiche—and more closely related to the art forms of popular culture than is modernist literature.

**prosody** the principles of versification (946)

**protagonist** the chief actor in any literary work. The term is usually preferable to *hero* and *heroine* because it can include characters—for example, villainous or weak ones—who are not aptly called heroes or heroines. (1207)

**psychological criticism** a form of analysis especially concerned both with the ways in which authors unconsciously leave traces of their inner lives in their works and with the ways in which readers respond, consciously and unconsciously, to works (1930–31, 1940)

**pyrrhic foot** in poetry, a foot consisting of two unstressed syllables (947)

**quatrain** a stanza of four lines (951)

**reader-response criticism** criticism emphasizing the idea that various readers respond in various ways and therefore that readers as well as authors "create" meaning (1923–26, 1939)

**realism** presentation of plausible characters (usually middle class) in plausible (usually everyday) circumstances, as opposed, for example, to heroic characters engaged in improbable adventures. Realism in literature seeks to give the illusion of reality.

**recognition** see *anagnorisis* (1225)

**refrain** a repeated phrase, line, or group of lines in a poem, especially in a ballad

**resolution** the dénouement or untying of the complication of the plot (85–86)

**reversal** a change in fortune, often an ironic twist (1225)

**rhetorical question** a question to which no answer is expected or to which only one answer is plausible. Example: "Do you think I am unaware of your goings-on?"

**rhyme** similarity or identity of accented sounds in corresponding positions, as, for example, at the ends of lines: *love/dove; tender/slender* (948–49)

**rhythm** in poetry, a pattern of stressed and unstressed sounds; in prose, some sort of recurrence (for example, of a motif) at approximately identical intervals (938–41, 948)

**rising action** in a story or play, the events that lead up to the *climax* (1207)

**rising meter** a foot (for example, iambic or anapestic) ending with a stressed syllable

**romance** narrative fiction, usually characterized by improbable adventures and love (602–03)

**round character** a many-sided character, one who does not always act predictably, as opposed to a "flat" or one-dimensional, unchanging character (92)

**run-on line** a line of verse whose syntax and meaning require the reader to go on, without a pause, to the next line; an *enjambed* line (948)

**sarcasm** crudely mocking or contemptuous language; heavy verbal irony (925)

**satire** literature that entertainingly attacks folly or vice; amusingly abusive writing (879–81)

**scansion** description of rhythm in poetry; metrical analysis (946–48)

**scene** (1) a unit of a play, in which the setting is unchanged and the time continuous; (2) the setting (locale, and time of the action); (3) in fiction, a dramatic passage, as opposed to a passage of description or of summary (1208)

**selective omniscience** a point of view in which the author enters the mind of one character and for the most part sees the other characters only from the outside

**sentimentality** excessive emotion, especially excessive pity, treated as appropriate rather than as disproportionate

**sestet** a six-line stanza, or the last six lines of an Italian sonnet (951)

**sestina** a poem with six stanzas of six lines each and a concluding stanza of three lines. The last word of each line in the first stanza appears as the last word of a line in each of the next five stanzas but in a different order. In the final (three-line) stanza, each line ends with one of these six words, and each line includes in the middle of the line one of the other three words.

**setting** the time and place of a story, play, or poem (for instance, a Texas town in winter, about 1900) (86, 91, 126)

**Shakespearean sonnet** see *English sonnet*

**short story** a fictional narrative, usually in prose, rarely longer than 30 pages and often much briefer (342–45)

**simile** a kind of figurative language explicitly making a comparison—for example, by using *as, like,* or a verb such as *seems* (891)

**soliloquy** a speech in a play, in which a character alone on the stage speaks his or her thoughts aloud (1208)

**sonnet** a lyric poem of 14 lines; see *English sonnet, Italian sonnet* (951)

**speaker** see *persona* (871–87, 887)

**spondee** a metrical foot consisting of two stressed syllables (947)

**stage direction** a playwright's indication to the actors or readers—for example, offering information about how an actor is to speak a line (1203–05, 1404)

**stanza** a group of lines forming a unit that is repeated in a poem (951)

**stereotype** a simplified conception, especially an oversimplification—for example, a stock character such as the heartless landlord, the kindly old teacher, the prostitute with a heart of gold. Such a character usually has only one personality trait, and this is boldly exaggerated.

**stream of consciousness** the presentation of a character's unrestricted flow of thought, often with free associations, and often without punctuation (108)

**stress** relative emphasis on one syllable as compared with another (946)

**structuralism** a critical theory holding that a literary work consists of conventional elements that, taken together by a reader familiar with the conventions, give the work its meaning. Thus just as a spectator must know the rules of a game (e.g., three strikes and you're out) in order to enjoy the game, so a reader must know the rules of, say, a novel (coherent, realistic, adequately motivated characters, a plausible plot, for instance *The Color Purple*) or of a satire (caricatures of contemptible figures in amusing situations that need not be at all plausible, for instance *Gulliver's Travels*). Structuralists normally have no interest in the origins of a work (i.e., in the historical background, or in the author's biography), and no interest in the degree to which a work of art seems to correspond to reality. The interest normally is in the work as a self-sufficient construction. Consult Robert Scholes, *Structuralism in Literature: An Introduction,* and two books by Jonathan Culler, *Structuralist Poetics* (1976) and (for the critical shift from structuralism to poststructuralism) *On Deconstruction* (1982).

**structure** the organization of a work, the relationship between the chief parts, the large-scale pattern—for instance, a rising action or complication followed by a crisis and then a resolution

**style** the manner of expression, evident not only in the choice of certain words (for instance, colloquial language) but in the choice of certain kinds of sentence structure, characters, settings, and themes

**subplot** a sequence of events often paralleling or in some way resembling the main story

**summary** a synopsis or condensation (1951)

**symbol** a person, object, action, or situation that, charged with meaning, suggests another thing (for example, a dark forest may suggest confusion, or perhaps evil), though usually with less specificity and more ambiguity than an allegory. A symbol usually differs from a metaphor in that a symbol is expanded or repeated and works by accumulating associations. (123–26, 148, 905–23)

**synecdoche** a kind of figurative language in which the whole stands for a part (*the law,* for a police officer), or a part (*all hands on deck,* for all persons) stands for the whole (895)

**tale** a short narrative, usually less realistic and more romantic than a short story; a yarn

**tercet** see *triplet*

**tetrameter** a verse line of four feet (947)

**theme** what the work is about; an underlying idea of a work; a conception of human experience suggested by the concrete details. Thus the theme of *Macbeth* is often said to be that "vaulting ambition o'erleaps itself." (91, 93–94, 104, 958)

**thesis** the point or argument that a writer announces and develops. A thesis differs from a *topic* by making an assertion. "The fall of Oedipus" is a topic, but "Oedipus falls because he is impetuous" is a thesis, as is "Oedipus is impetuous, but his impetuosity has nothing to do with his fall." (26–27, 34, 41, 45)

**thesis sentence** a sentence summarizing, as specifically as possible, the writer's chief point (argument and perhaps purpose) (26)

**third-person narrator** the teller of a story who does not participate in the happenings (107–08)

**tone** the prevailing attitude (for instance, ironic, genial, objective) as perceived by the reader. Notice that a reader may feel that the tone of the persona of the work is genial while the tone of the author of the same work is ironic. (870–71, 887)

**topic** a subject, such as "Hamlet's relation to Horatio." A topic becomes a *thesis* when a predicate is added to this subject, thus: "Hamlet's relation to Horatio helps to define Hamlet."

**tragedy** a serious play showing the protagonist moving from good fortune to bad and ending in death or a deathlike state (1223–28, 1474)

**tragic flaw** a supposed weakness (for example, arrogance) in the tragic protagonist. If the tragedy results from an intellectual error rather than from a moral weakness, it is better to speak of "a tragic error." (1224)

**tragicomedy** a mixture of tragedy and comedy, usually a play with serious happenings that expose the characters to the threat of death but that ends happily

**transition** a connection between one passage and the next (30, 31)

**trimeter** a verse line with three feet (947)

**triplet** a group of three lines of verse, usually rhyming (951)

**trochee** a metrical foot consisting of a stressed syllable followed by an unstressed syllable. Example: *garden* (947)

**understatement** a figure of speech in which the speaker says less than what he or she means; an ironic minimizing, as in "You've done fairly well for yourself" said to the winner of a multimillion-dollar lottery (924–25)

**unity** harmony and coherence of parts, absence of irrelevance (30)

**unreliable narrator** a narrator whose report a reader cannot accept at face value, perhaps because the narrator is naive or is too deeply implicated in the action to report it objectively (107)

**verbal irony** see **irony**

**verse** (1) a line of poetry; (2) a stanza of a poem (951)

**vers libre** free verse, unrhymed poetry (953–54)

**villanelle** a poem with five stanzas of three lines rhyming *aba,* and a concluding stanza of four lines, rhyming *abaa.* The entire first line is repeated as the third line of the second and fourth stanzas; the entire third line is repeated as the third line of the third and fifth stanzas. These two lines form the final two lines of the last (four-line) stanza. (945)

**voice** see *persona, style,* and *tone* (861–87)

# Acknowledgments

## PHOTO ACKNOWLEDGMENTS

Frontispiece: by permission of the Houghton Library, Harvard University; **7**: Courtesy of Arte Público Press—University of Houston; **12**: Courtesy, Farrar, Straus and Giroux; **73**: The Bettmann Archive; **272**: AP/Wide World; **273**: © by Regina O'Connor, used with the permission of the literary executor, Robert Giroux; **318**: © Jerry Bauer; **553**: © 1995 Sigrid Estrada; **702**: UPI/Bettmann; **741**: UPI/Bettmann; **908–909**: University of Virginia; **943**: Kunsthistorisches Museum, Vienna; **960**: Stanford News Service; **973**: Boston Athenaeum; **974**: National Anthropological Archives/Smithsonian Institution; **977**: Pocahontas and John Smith: Artist: Victor Nehig/© Courtesy Museum of Art, Brigham Young University. All rights reserved; **982**: Library of Congress; **984**: Virginia Military Institute; **987**: © 1995 Estate of Tseng Kwong Chi-MTDP/Artists Rights Society (ARS), New York; **989**: William Williams Collection of Photographs. Miriam and Ira. D. Wallach Division of Art, Prints and Photographs. New York Public Library; **990**: Brown Brothers; **991**: War Relocation Authority/The National Archives; **996**: AP/Wide World; **999**: UPI/Bettmann; **1004**: Edward S. Curtis: Blackfoot Travois, Vol. 18 No. 637, The North American Indian. Courtesy of Laboratory of Anthropology/Museum of Indian Arts and Culture; **1101:** Kuboso Memorial Museum of Arts, Osaka; **1012:** Rijksmuseum Vincent van Gogh, Amsterdam; **1014:** The Metropolitan Museum of Art, New York, The Alfred Steiglitz Collection, 1949 (49.59.1); **1016:** Smith College Museum of Art; **1018:** Courtesy Bibliothèque Nationale, Paris; **1020:** Jeu de Paume, Paris/Art Resource; **1022:** van Gogh, Vincent. The Starry Night (1889) oil on canvas, 29 × 36¼″ (73.7 × 92.1 cm). The Museum of Modern Art, New York. Acquired through the Lillie P. Bliss Bequest. Photograph © 1997 The Musuem of Modern Art, New York; **1024:** Scala,Art Resource, New York; **1026:** Duchamp, Marcel. Nude Descending a Staircase, No. 2. Philadelphia Museum of Art. The Louise and Walter Arensberg Collection; **1035**: The Metropolitan Museum of Art, Gift of Thomas F. Ryan, 1910. [11.173.9]; **1120**: Courtesy, Trustees of Amherst College; **1122**: by permission of the Houghton Library, Harvard University; **1140**: Courtesy of the Jones Library Inc., Amherst, MA; **1142**: Courtesy of the Jones Library Inc., Amherst, MA; **1171**: AP/Wide World; **1210**: Courtesy of the New York Public Library Billy Rose Theatre Collection; **1227**: Frederick Ayer/Photo Researchers; **1229**: John Vickers; **1265**: © Donald Cooper/Photostage; **1291 left**: Stock Montage; **1291 right**: Courtesy, C. Walter Hodges; **1293**: Mark Douet; **1294**: © Richard Feldman; **1408**: AP/Wide World; **1409**: Diane Gorodnitzki; **1415**: David Farrrell, Shakespeare Centre Library, Stratford-upon-Avon; **1489**: Harvard Theater Collection; **1544**: Courtesy of the New York Public Library, Billy Rose Theatre Collection; **1591**: © 1995 Inge Morath/Magnum Photos; **1592 top**: Eileen Darby; **1592 bottom**: © 1995 Inge Morath/Magnum Photos; **1665**: El Teatro Campesino; **1676**: Peter Cunningham; **1694**: © Richard Feldman; **1730**: Chris Bennion; **1782**: Courtesy, Writers and Artists Agency; **1783**: Martha Swope © TIME Inc.; **1798**: AP/Wide World; **1799**: © Brigitte Lacombe; **1831**: Martha Swope © TIME Inc.

## TEXT ACKNOWLEDGMENTS

Chinua Achebe. "Civil Peace" from *Girls at War and Other Stories* by Chinua Achebe. Copyright © 1972, 1973 by Chinua Achebe. Used by permission of Doubleday, a division of Bantam Doubleday Dell Publishing Group, Inc., and Harold Ober Associates Incorporated; excerpt from "An Image of Africa: Racism in Conrad's *Heart of Darkness.*" *Massachusetts Review* 18:4, Winter 1977. Reprinted by permission of Massachusetts Review.

Sherman Alexie. "On the Amtrak from Boston to New York City" reprinted from *First Indian on the Moon.* Copyright © 1993 by Sherman Alexie, by permission of Hanging Loose Press.

Paula Gunn Allen. "Pocahontas to Her English Husband, John Rolfe" from *Skins and Bones* by Paula Gunn Allen. West End Press. Reprinted by permission of the author.

Anjana Appachana. "To Rise Above" from *The Forbidden Stitch, an Asian American Women's Anthology,* edited by Shirley Geok-lin Lim et al. Copyright © 1989 CALYX Books. By permission of the publisher.

Gloria Anzaldua. "To live in the Borderlands means you" from *Borderlands/La Frontera: The New Mestiza.* Copyright © 1987 by Gloria Anzaldua. Reprinted by permission from Aunt Lute Books.

Margaret Atwood. "Rape Fantasies" from *Dancing Girls* by Margaret Atwood. Copyright © 1977, published in Canada by McClelland & Stewart. Reprinted in the United States with permission of the author and McClelland & Stewart, Toronto.

W. H. Auden. "The Unknown Citizen," "Musée des Beaux Arts," and "Stop All the Clocks." Copyright © 1940 and renewed 1968 by W. H. Auden. Reprinted from *Collected Poems* by W. H. Auden. By permission of Random House, Inc., and Faber and Faber Ltd.

Jimmy Santiago Baca. "So Mexicans Are Taking Jobs from Americans" in *Immigrants in Our Own Land.* Copyright © 1982 by Jimmy Santiago Baca. Reprinted by permission of New Directions Publishing Corporation.

Toni Cade Bambara. "The Lesson" from *Gorilla, My Love* by Toni Cade Bambara. Copyright © 1972 by Toni Cade Bambara. Reprinted by permission of Random House, Inc.

Linda Bamber. "*The Tempest* and the Traffic in Women" by Linda Bamber. Reprinted by permission of the author.

Amiri Baraka. "A Poem for Black Hearts" from *Wise.* Copyright © 1964 by Amiri Baraka. Reprinted by permission of Sterling Lord Literistic, Inc.

Basho. "On the withered bough" from *The Japanese Haiku* by Kenneth Yasuda. Reprinted by permission of Charles E. Tuttle Co., Inc.

Ralph Berry and J. Miller. "A Production of *The Tempest*" from *On Directing Shakespeare* by Ralph Berry. Barnes and Noble, 1977.

Elizabeth Bishop. "Filling Station," "The Fish," "Poem," and "To a Tree" from *The Complete Poems 1927–1979* by Elizabeth Bishop. Copyright © 1979, 1983 by Alice Helen Methfessel. Reprinted by permission of Farrar, Straus & Giroux, Inc.

Elizabeth Bowen. "The Demon Lover" from *Collected Stories* by Elizabeth Bowen. Copyright © 1946, renewed 1974 by Elizabeth Bowen. Reprinted by permission of Alfred A. Knopf, Inc.

Elizabeth Bowman. "An Interpretation of 'The Soul selects her own Society'." *Explicator* 29:2 (October 1970), Item 13. Reprinted with permission of the Helen Dwight Reid Educational Foundation. Copyright © 1970. Published by Heldref Publications, 1319 Eighteenth Street., N.W., Washington, DC 20036-1802.

Gwendolyn Brooks. "We Real Cool" and "The Mother" from *Blacks.* Copyright © 1987, published by The David Company, Chicago; "Martin Luther King, Jr." from *Riot* by Gwendolyn Brooks. Reprinted by permission of the author.

Joseph Bruchac. "Ellis Island" from *The Remembered Earth,* edited by Geary Hobson. Albuquerque: Red Earth Press, 1979. Reprinted by permission of the author.

Raymond Carver. "Cathedral" from *Cathedral* by Raymond Carver. Copyright © 1981 by Raymond Carver; "Popular Mechanics" and "What We Talk About When We Talk About Love" from *What We Talk About When We Talk About Love* by Raymond Carver. Copyright © 1980, 1981 by Raymond Carver. All of the above reprinted by permission of Alfred A. Knopf, Inc.

Lorna Dee Cervantes. "Refugee Ship" by Lorna Dee Cervantes is reprinted with permission from the publisher of *A Decade of Hispanic Literature: An Anniversary Anthology.* Houston: Arte Público Press–University of Houston, 1982.

Diana Chang. "The Oriental Contingent" by Diana Chang from *The Forbidden Stitch: An Asian American Women's Anthology,* edited by Shirley Geok-lin Lim et al. Copyright © 1989 CALYX Books, by permission of the publisher.

Anton Chekhov. "Misery" reprinted with the permission of Simon & Schuster from *The Schoolmistress and Other Stories* by Anton Chekhov, translated from the Russian by Constance Garnett. Copyright © 1921 by Macmillan Publishing Company, renewed 1949 by David Garnett.

Kate Chopin. "The Storm" reprinted by permission of Louisiana State University Press from *The Complete Works of Kate Chopin,* edited by Per Seyersted. Copyright © 1969 by Louisiana State University Press.

Sandra Cisneros. "One Holy Night" from *Woman Hollering Creek.* Copyright © 1991 by Sandra Cisneros. Published by Vintage Books, a division of Random House, Inc., New York, and originally in hardcover by Random House, Inc. Reprinted by permission of Susan Bergholz Literary Services. All rights reserved.

Lucille Clifton. "in the inner city." Copyright © 1969 by Lucille Clifton. Reprinted from *Good Woman: Poems and a Memoir 1969–1980* by Lucille Clifton, with the permission of BOA Editions, Ltd., 92 Park Avenue, Brockport, NY 14420.

Judith Ortiz Cofer. "My Father in the Navy" and "Latin Women Pray" from *Reaching for the Mainland* by Judith Ortiz Cofer, appearing in *Triple Crown* (1987). Reprinted by permission of Bilingual Press, Arizona State University, Tempe.

A. R. Coulthard. "Joyce Carol Oates's 'Where Are You Going, Where Have You Been?' as Pure Realism." *Studies in Short Fiction* 26 (1989): 505–510. Copyright © 1989 by Newberry College.

Countee Cullen. "For a Lady I Know" and "Incident" reprinted by permission of GRM Associates, Inc., Agents for the Estate of Ida M. Cullen. From the book *Color* by Countee Cullen. Copyright © 1925 by Harper & Brothers; copyright renewed 1953 by Ida M. Cullen.

e. e. cummings. "anyone lived in a pretty how town." Copyright 1940, © 1968, 1991 by the Trustees for the E. E. Cummings Trust; "next to of course god america i." Copyright 1926, 1954, © 1991 by the Trustees for the E. E. Cummings Trust. Copyright © 1985 by George James Firmage; "in Just—." Copyright 1923, 1951 © 1991 by the Trustees for the E. E. Cummings Trust. Copyright © 1976 by George James Firmage, from *Complete Poems, 1904–1962* by E. E. Cummings, edited by George J. Firmage. Reprinted by permission of Liveright Publishing Corporation.

Alice Elliott Dark. "In the Gloaming." Copyright © 1993 by Alice Elliott Dark. Originally appeared in *The New Yorker,* May 3, 1993. Reprinted by permission of Melanie Jackson Agency.

Walter de la Mare. "An Epitaph" from *The Complete Poems* by Walter de la Mare. Reprinted by permission of The Literary Trustees of Walter de la Mare and The Society of Authors as their representative.

Emily Dickinson. "These are the days when Birds come back," "Wild Nights—Wild Nights!" "There's a certain Slant of light," "The Soul selects her own Society," "I heard a Fly buzz—when I died," "This World is not Conclusion," "I like to see it lap the Miles,"

"Because I could not stop for Death," "A narrow Fellow in the Grass," "Further in Summer than the Birds," "Tell all the Truth but tell it slant," "A Route of Evanescence," "Those—dying then," "Apparently with no surprise," "Papa above," "This was a Poet," "I'm Nobody," "I got so I could hear his name" reprinted by permission of the publishers and the Trustees of Amherst College from *The Poems of Emily Dickinson,* edited by Thomas H. Johnson. Cambridge, MA: The Belknap Press of Harvard University Press. Copyright © 1951, 1955, 1983 by the President and Fellows of Harvard College; "I got so I could hear his name" and "This was a Poet" from *The Complete Poems of Emily Dickinson,* edited by Thomas H. Johnson. Copyright © 1929 by Martha Dickinson Bianchi, copyright renewed 1957 by Mary L. Hampson. Reprinted by permission of Little, Brown and Company.

Rita Dove. "Daystar" from *Thomas and Beulah.* Copyright © 1986 by Rita Dove. Reprinted by permission of the author; "Second-Hand Man" by Rita Dove from *Fifth Sunday* (1985). Reprinted by permission of the author.

Bob Dylan. "The Times They Are A-Changin'." Copyright © 1963, 1964 by Warner Bros. Music. Copyright renewed 1991 by Special Rider Music. All rights reserved. International copyright secured. Reprinted by permission.

T. S. Eliot. "The Love Song of J. Alfred Prufrock" from *Collected Poems 1909–1962* by T. S. Eliot. Copyright © 1936 by Harcourt Brace Inc., copyright © 1964, 1963 by T. S. Eliot. Reprinted by permission of Faber and Faber Ltd.

Ralph Ellison. "Battle Royal" from *Invisible Man* by Ralph Ellison. Copyright © 1947, 1948, 1952 by Ralph Ellison. Reprinted by permission of Random House, Inc.

Louise Erdrich. "Indian Boarding School: The Runaways" and "Dear John Wayne" from *Jacklight: Poems* by Louise Erdrich. Copyright © 1984 by Louise Erdrich. Reprinted by permission of Henry Holt and Company, Inc.; "Fleur" by Louise Erdrich. Copyright © 1986 by Louise Erdrich. Reprinted by permission of the author.

Martín Espada. "Tony Went to the Bodega but He Didn't Buy Anything" from *Trumpets from the Islands of Their Eviction* by Martín Espada (1987). Reprinted by permission of Bilingual Review Press, Arizona State University, Tempe; "Bully" from *Rebellion Is the Circle of a Lover's Hands* by Martín Espada. Curbstone Press, 1990. Reprinted by permission of Curbstone Press. Distributed by Consortium.

Judith Farr. Excerpt from *The Passion of Emily Dickinson* by Judith Farr. Copyright © 1992 by the President and Fellows of Harvard College. Reprinted by permission of the publishers. Cambridge, MA: Harvard University Press.

William Faulkner. "A Rose for Emily" from *Collected Stories of William Faulkner* by William Faulkner. Copyright © 1930 and renewed 1958 by William Faulkner. Reprinted by permission of Random House, Inc.

Jessie Fauset. "On Reading 'The Negro Speaks of Rivers'." *Crisis* 30–31 (March 1926): 239.

Lawrence Ferlinghetti. "Constantly Risking Absurdity" from *A Coney Island of the Mind* by Lawrence Ferlinghetti. Copyright © 1958 by Lawrence Ferlinghetti. Reprinted by permission of New Directions Publishing Corporation.

Harvey Fierstein. "On Tidy Endings" reprinted with the permission of Atheneum Publishers, an imprint of Macmillan Publishing Company, from *Safe Sex* by Harvey Fierstein. Copyright © 1987 by Harvey Fierstein. This play may not be reprinted in whole or in part without written permission of the publishers. No performance of any kind may be given without permission in writing from the author's agent, William Morris Agency, 1350 Avenue of the Americas, New York, NY 10019.

Jane Flanders. "Van Gogh's Bed" from *Timepiece* by Jane Flanders. Copyright © 1988. Reprinted by permission of the University of Pittsburgh Press.

Jack D. Forbes. "Only Approved Indians Can Play" from *Earth Power Coming: Short Fiction in Native American Literature,* edited by Simon Ortiz. Reprinted by permission of Jack D. Forbes.

Carolyn Forché. "The Colonel" from *The Country Between Us* by Carolyn Forché. Copyright © 1981 by Carolyn Forché. Originally appeared in *Pequod.* Reprinted by permission of HarperCollins Publishers Inc.

Robert Francis. "The Pitcher" reprinted from *The Orb Weaver.* Copyright © 1960 by Robert Francis, Wesleyan University Press. By permission of University Press of New England.

Robert Frost. "Stopping by Woods on a Snowy Evening," "The Need of Being Versed in Country Things," "The Aim Was Song," "The Look at Two," and "The Draft Horse" from *The Poetry of Robert Frost,* edited by Edward Connery Lathem. Copyright 1951, © 1962 by Robert Frost. Copyright 1923, © 1969 by Henry Holt and Company, Inc.; excerpts from *The Selected Prose of Robert Frost,* edited by Hyde Cox and Edward Connery Lathem. Copyright 1939, © 1967 by Holt, Rinehart and Winston; Letter 53 and Letter 73 from *Selected Letters of Robert Frost,* edited by Lawrance Thompson. Copyright © 1964 by Lawrance Thompson and Holt, Rinehart and Winston. All of the above reprinted by permission of Henry Holt and Company, Inc.

Tess Gallagher. "The Hug." Copyright © 1987 by Tess Gallagher. Reprinted from *Amplitude* with the permission of Graywolf Press, Saint Paul, MN.

Federico García Lorca. "Despedida" by Federico García Lorca from *Obras Completas.* Aguilar, 1993 edition. Copyright © Herederos de Federico García Lorca. Translation by Merryn Williams © Merryn Williams and Herederos de Federico García Lorca. All rights reserved. For information regarding rights and permissions for works by Federico García Lorca, please contact William Peter Kosmas, Esq., 77 Rodney Court, 6/8 Maida Vale, London W9 1TJ, England.

Gabriel García Márquez. "A Very Old Man with Enormous Wings" from *Leaf Storm and Other Stories* by Gabriel García Márquez. Copyright © 1971 by Gabriel García Márquez. Reprinted by permission of HarperCollins Publishers Inc.

Allen Ginsberg. "A Supermarket in California" from *Collected Poems 1947–1980* by Allen Ginsberg. Copyright © 1955 by Allen Ginsberg. Reprinted by permission of HarperCollins Publishers Inc.

Nikki Giovanni. "MasterCharge Blues" from *Re: Creation* by Nikki Giovanni. Copyright © 1970 by Nikki Giovanni; "Nikki-Rosa" from *Black Judgment.* Both poems are reprinted by permission of the author.

Susan Glaspell. "Trifles" is reprinted by permission of Daphne C. Cook.

Louise Gluck. "The School Children" from *The House on Marshland* by Louise Gluck. Copyright © 1975 by Louise Gluck. First published by The Ecco Press in 1985. Reprinted by permission.

Patricia Grace. "Butterflies" from *Electric City and Other Stories.* Reprinted by permission of Penguin Books New Zealand.

Gerald Graff. "Teaching the Politics of *Heart of Darkness*" from *Beyond the Culture Wars: How Teaching the Conflicts Can Revitalize American Education* by Gerald Graff. Copyright © 1992 by Gerald Graff. Reprinted by permission of W. W. Norton & Company, Inc.

Stephen Greenblatt. "The Best Way to Kill Our Literary Inheritance Is to Turn It into a Decorous Celebration of the New World Order." *The Chronicle of Higher Education,* June 12, 1991. Reprinted by permission of the author.

H. D. (Hilda Doolittle). "Helen" by H. D. from *Collected Poems 1912–1944.* Copyright © 1982 by the Estate of Hilda Doolittle. Reprinted by permission of New Directions Publishing Corporation.

John Haines. "The Whale in the Blue Washing Machine" from *Cicada.* Copyright © 1977 by John Haines, Wesleyan University Press. Reprinted by permission of University Press of New England.

Daniel Halpern. "How to Eat Alone" from *Selected Poems* by Daniel Halpern. Copyright © 1994 by Daniel Halpern. Reprinted by permission of Alfred A. Knopf, Inc.

Joy Harjo. "Visions" from *She Had Some Horses* by Joy Harjo. Copyright © 1982 by Thunder's Mouth Press. Used by permission of the publisher, Thunder's Mouth Press.

Robert Hayden. "Frederick Douglass" and "Those Winter Sundays" are reprinted from *Angle of Ascent: New and Selected Poems* by Robert Hayden. Copyright © 1966 by Robert Hayden. By permission of Liveright Publishing Corporation.

Seamus Heaney. "Digging" from *Selected Poems 1966–1987* by Seamus Heaney. Copyright © 1990 by Seamus Heaney. Reprinted by permission of Farrar, Straus & Giroux, Inc., and Faber and Faber Ltd.

Anthony Hecht. "The Dover Bitch" from *Collected Earlier Poems* by Anthony Hecht. Copyright © 1990 by Anthony E. Hecht. Reprinted by permission of Alfred A. Knopf, Inc.

Liliana Heker. "The Stolen Party." Copyright © 1982 by Liliana Hecker. Translation copyright © 1985 by Alberto Manguel. Reprinted from *Other Fires: Short Fiction by Latin American Women,* edited by Alberto Manguel. By permission of Clarkson N. Potter Publishers, published by Crown Publishers, a division of Random House, Inc., and by permission of Random House Canada Limited.

Ernest Hemingway. "Cat in the Rain" reprinted with permission of Scribner, a division of Simon & Schuster, Inc., from *In Our Time* by Ernest Hemingway. Copyright © 1925 by Charles Scribner's Sons; copyright renewed 1953 by Ernest Hemingway.

Errol G. Hill. Excerpt from "Caliban and Ariel." *Theatre History Studies,* Volume 4, 1984. Reprinted by permission of Theatre History Studies.

John Hollander. "Disagreements" from *Selected Poetry* by John Hollander. Copyright © 1993 by John Hollander. Reprinted by permission of Alfred A. Knopf, Inc.

A. E. Housman. "Eight O'Clock" from *The Collected Poems of A. E. Housman* by A. E. Housman. Copyright © 1939, 1940 by Holt, Rinehart and Winston, Inc. Copyright © 1967 by Robert E. Symons. Reprinted by permission of Henry Holt and Company, Inc.

Langston Hughes. "Evenin' Air Blues," "Dream Boogie," "Passing," "Theme for English B," "Harlem (Dream Deferred)," "Ballad of the Landlord," "Harlem (1)," "Let America be America Again," "Mother to Son," "The Negro Speaks of Rivers," "Poet to Bigot," "Poet to Patron," "Ruby Brown," "The South," "Too Blue," "The Weary Blues" from *Collected Poems* by Langston Hughes. Copyright © 1994 by the Estate of Langston Hughes. Reprinted by permission of Alfred A. Knopf, Inc.; "Writers: Black and White" by Langston Hughes from *The American Negro Writer and His Roots.* Copyright © 1960 by the American Society of African Culture. Reprinted by permission of Harold Ober Associates Incorporated; "Making Poetry Pay: On Public Reading" from *I Wonder as I Wander: An Autobiographical Journey* by Langston Hughes. Copyright © 1956 by Langston Hughes. Copyright renewed © 1993 by Arnold Rampersad; "The Negro and the Racial Mountain." *The Nation,* June 23, 1926, pp. 692–694. Copyright © 1926 by Langston Hughes. Copyright renewed 1980 by George Houston Bass. Reprinted by permission of Harold Ober Associates; "On the Cultural Achievements of African Americans" from the James Weldon Johnson Collection; Langston Hughes Papers in *The Life of Langston Hughes* by Arnold Rampersad, reprinted by permission of the Yale Collection of American Literature, Beinecke Rare Book and Manuscript Library, Yale University; "The Negro Speaks of Rivers" and additional excerpt from *The Big Sea: An Autobiography* by Langston Hughes. Copyright © 1940 by Langston Hughes. Copyright renewed © 1968 by Arna Bontemps and George Houston Bass. Reprinted by permission of Farrar, Straus & Giroux, Inc.

David Henry Hwang. *The Sound of a Voice* from *FOB and Other Plays.* Copyright © 1990 by David Henry Hwang. Reprinted by permission of Dutton Signet, a division of Penguin Books USA; "Thoughts About Ethnic Theatre," extracts from an interview with Jean W. Ross (June 28, 1989) in *Contemporary Authors,* Volume 132. Reprinted by permission of Gale Research Inc.

Henrik Ibsen. Excerpt from "Speech at the Banquet of the Norwegian League for Women's Rights" from *Ibsen: Letters and Speeches,* edited by Evert Sprinchorn. Copyright © 1964 by Evert Sprinchorn. Reprinted by permission of Hill and Wang, a division of Farrar, Straus & Giroux, Inc.; excerpts from *The Oxford Ibsen,* Volume 5, translated and edited by J. W. McFarlane. Copyright © 1961 Oxford University Press. Reprinted from *The Oxford Ibsen,* Volume 5, translated and edited by J. W. McFarlane (1961) by permission of Oxford University Press; *A Doll's House* from *The Plays of Ibsen* by Henrik Ibsen, translated by Michael Meyer. Copyright © 1966 by Michael Meyer. Reprinted by permission of Harold Ober Associates Incorporated. *Caution:* These plays are fully protected, in whole, in part or in any form under the copyright laws of the United States of America, the British Empire including the Dominion of Canada, and all other countries of the Copyright Union, and are subject to royalty. All rights including motion picture, radio, television, recitation, public reading are strictly reserved. For professional rights and amateur rights all inquiries should be addressed to the author's agent: Robert A. Freedman Dramatic Agency Inc., 1501 Broadway, New York, NY 10036.

Kazuo Ishiguro. "A Family Supper." Copyright © 1990 by Kazuo Ishiguro. Reprinted by permission of International Creative Management, Inc. First appeared in *Esquire.*

Shirley Jackson. "The Lottery" from *The Lottery* by Shirley Jackson. Copyright © 1948, 1949 by Shirley Jackson. Renewal copyright © 1976, 1977 by Laurence Hyman, Barry Hyman, Mrs. Sarah Webster, and Mrs. Joanne Schnurer. Reprinted by permission of Farrar, Straus & Giroux, Inc.

Randall Jarrell. "The Death of the Ball Turret Gunner" from *The Complete Poems* by Randall Jarrell. Copyright © 1945 and renewal copyright © 1972 by Mrs. Randall Jarrell. Reprinted by permission of Farrar, Straus & Giroux, Inc.

Onwuchekwa Jemie. "On the Power of 'The Negro Speaks of Rivers'" from *Langston Hughes: An Introduction to the Poetry* by Onwuchekwa Jemie. Copyright © 1977 by Columbia University Press. Reprinted by permission of the publisher.

Franz Kafka. "The Metamorphosis" from *The Metamorphosis, the Penal Colony and Other Stories* by Franz Kafka, translated by Willa and Edwin Muir. Copyright © 1948 by Schocken Books, Inc. Copyright renewed 1975 by Schocken Books, Inc. Reprinted by permission of Schocken Books, published by Pantheon Books, a division of Random House, Inc.

X. J. Kennedy. "Nothing in Heaven Functions as It Ought" from *Cross Ties: Selected Poems* by X. J. Kennedy. Copyright © 1969 by X. J. Kennedy; "Nude Descending a Staircase" from *Nude Descending a Staircase* by X. J. Kennedy. Copyright © 1961 by X. J. Kennedy, renewed. Both poems reprinted by permission of Curtis Brown Ltd.

Jamaica Kincaid. "Girl" from *At the Bottom of the River* by Jamaica Kincaid. Copyright © 1978, 1983 by Jamaica Kincaid. Reprinted by permission of Farrar, Straus & Giroux, Inc.

Galway Kinnell. "Blackberry Eating" from *Three Books* by Galway Kinnell. Copyright © 1993 by Galway Kinnell. Previously published in *Mortal Acts, Mortal Words* (1980). Reprinted by permission of Houghton Mifflin Company. All rights reserved.

Yusef Komunyakaa. "Facing It" from *Dien Cai Dau.* Copyright © 1988 by Yusef Komunyakaa, Wesleyan University Press. By permission of University Press of New England.

D. H. Lawrence. "Snake" from *The Complete Poems of D. H. Lawrence* by D. H. Lawrence, edited by V. de Sola Pinto and F. W. Roberts. Copyright © 1964, 1971 by Angelo Ravagli and C. M. Weekley, Executors of the Estate of Frieda Lawrence Ravagli; "The Horse-Dealer's Daughter." Copyright © 1922 by Thomas B. Seltzer, Inc., renewed 1950 by Frieda Lawrence from *Complete Short Stories of D. H. Lawrence* by D. H. Lawrence. Used by permission of Viking Penguin, a division of Penguin Books USA Inc.

David Leavitt. "Territory" from *Family Dancing* by David Leavitt. Copyright © 1983, 1984 by David Leavitt. Reprinted by permission of Alfred A. Knopf, Inc.

Li-Young Lee. "I Ask My Mother to Sing." Copyright © 1986 by Li-Young Lee. Reprinted from *Rose* by Li-Young Lee, with the permission of BOA Editions, Ltd., 92 Park Avenue, Brockport, NY 14420.

Doris Lessing. "A Woman on a Roof" from *Stories* by Doris Lessing. Copyright ©

1978 by Doris Lessing. Reprinted by permission of Alfred A. Knopf, Inc. Also from *A Man and Two Women* by Doris Lessing. Copyright © 1963 by Doris Lessing. Reprinted by kind permission of Jonathan Clowes Ltd., London, on behalf of Doris Lessing.

Lyn Lifshin. "My Mother and the Bed" from *Tangled Vines,* edited by Lyn Lifshin. Reprinted by permission of the author.

Larry McCaffrey and Sinda Gregory. Interview with Raymond Carver from *Alive and Writing* by Larry McCaffrey and Sinda Gregory. Copyright © 1987 by The Board of Trustees of the University of Illinois Press. Reprinted by permission of the authors and the University of Illinois Press.

Claude McKay. "America" from *Selected Poems of Claude McKay.* Copyright © 1981. Reprinted by permission of The Archives of Claude McKay, Carl Cowl Administrator.

Archibald MacLeish. "Ars Poetica" from *Collected Poems 1917–1982* by Archibald MacLeish. Copyright © 1985 by the Estate of Archibald MacLeish. Reprinted by permission of Houghton Mifflin Company. All rights reserved.

Naguib Mahfouz. "The Answer Is No" from *The Time and the Place and Other Stories* by Naguib Mahfouz. Copyright © 1991 by the American University in Cairo Press. Used by permission of Doubleday, a division of Bantam Doubleday Dell Publishing Group, Inc.

David Mamet. "Oleanna" from *Oleanna* by David Mamet. Copyright © 1992 by David Mamet. Reprinted by permission of Vintage Books, a division of Random House, Inc.; selections from an interview with David Mamet by David Savaran from *In Their Own Words.* Reprinted by permission of Theatre Communications Group.

Laureen Mar. "My Mother, Who Came from China, Where She Never Saw Snow." Copyright © 1977 by Laureen Mar. Reprinted by permission of the author.

Bobbie Ann Mason. "Shiloh" from *Shiloh and Other Stories* by Bobbie Ann Mason. Copyright © 1982 by Bobbie Ann Mason. Reprinted by permission of HarperCollins Publishers Inc. "Shiloh" originally appeared in *The New Yorker* magazine.

Edna St. Vincent Millay. Sonnet XXX of *Fatal Interview* and "The Spring and the Fall" by Edna St. Vincent Millay. From *Collected Poems,* HarperCollins. Copyright © 1923, 1931, 1951, 1958 by Edna St. Vincent Millay and Norma Millay Ellis. Reprinted by permission of Elizabeth Barnett, literary executor.

Arthur Miller. *Death of a Salesman* by Arthur Miller from *Death of a Salesman* by Arthur Miller. Copyright 1949, renewed © 1977 by Arthur Miller. Used by permission of Viking Penguin, a division of Penguin Books USA Inc.; "Tragedy and the Common Man" from *The New York Times,* February 27, 1949, Section 2. Copyright © 1949 by Arthur Miller. Reprinted by permission of International Creative Management, Inc.

R. Baxter Miller. "Africa as the Source of Civilization and History" from the *Art and Imagination of Langston Hughes.* Copyright © 1989 by the University Press of Kentucky. Reprinted by permission of the publishers.

Susan Minot. "Lust" from *Lust and Other Stories* by Susan Minot. Copyright © 1989 by Susan Minot. Reprinted by permission of Houghton Mifflin Co./Seymour Lawrence. All rights reserved.

Gabriela Mistral. "El Pensador de Rodin." Copyright 1961, 1964, 1970, 1971 by Doris Dana. Reprinted by arrangement with Doris Dana, c/o the Joan Daves Agency as agent for the proprietor.

James Masao Mitsui. "Shrike on a Dead Tree" from *Journal of the Sun* (1974). Reprinted by permission of the author.

Marianne Moore. "Poetry" reprinted with permission of Simon & Schuster from *The Collected Poems of Marianne Moore.* Copyright © 1935 by Marianne Moore, renewed 1963 by Marianne Moore and T. S. Eliot.

Pat Mora. "Immigrants" and "Sonrisas" by Pat Mora are reprinted with permission from the publisher of *Borders.* Houston: Arte Público Press–University of Houston, 1986.

Aurora Levins Morales. "Child of the Americas" from *Getting Home Alive* by Aurora

Levins Morales. Copyright © 1986 by Aurora Levins Morales and Rosario Morales. Ithaca, NY: Firebrand Books.

Moritake. "Fallen petals rise" from *An Introduction to Haiku* by Harold G. Henderson. Copyright © 1958 by Harold G. Henderson. Used by permission of Doubleday, a division of Bantam Doubleday Dell Publishing Group, Inc.

Alice Munro. "Boys and Girls" from *Dance of the Happy Shades* by Alice Munro. Copyright © 1968 by Alice Munro. Published by McGraw-Hill Ryerson Limited. Reprinted by arrangement with the Virginia Barber Literary Agency. All rights reserved.

David Mura. "An Argument: On 1942" from *After We Lost Our Way* by David Mura. Reprinted by permission of the author.

V. S. Naipaul. "The Night Watchman's Occurrence Book." Copyright © 1967 by V. S. Naipaul. Reprinted with the permission of Wylie, Aitken & Stone, Inc.

Gloria Naylor. "The Two" excerpted from *The Women of Brewster Place* by Gloria Naylor. Copyright © 1980, 1982 by Gloria Naylor. Used by permission of Viking Penguin, a division of Penguin Books USA Inc.

Marsha Norman. *'night, Mother* by Marsha Norman. Copyright © 1983 by Marsha Norman. *Caution:* Professionals and amateurs are hereby warned that *'night, Mother,* being fully protected under the Copyright Laws of the United States of America and other countries of the Berne and Universal Copyright Conventions, is subject to a royalty. All rights, including but not limited to, professional, amateur, recording, motion picture, recitation, lecturing, public reading, radio and television broadcasting, video or sound taping, photocopying, all other forms of mechanical or electronic reproduction, and the rights of translation into foreign languages are expressly reserved. All inquiries concerning rights (other than stock and amateur rights) should be addressed to the author's agent, Charmaine Ferenezi, The Tantleff Office, 375 Greenwich Street, Suite 700, New York, NY 10013. The stock and amateur production rights for *'night, Mother* are controlled exclusively by the Dramatists Play Service, Inc., 440 Park Avenue South, New York, NY 10016. No amateur performance of the play may be given without obtaining in advance the written permission of the Dramatists Play Service, Inc., and paying the requisite fee; "Marsha Norman Talking about *'night, Mother*" from *Interviews with Contemporary Woman Playwrights* by Kathleen Betsko and Rachel Koenig. Copyright © 1987 by Kathleen Betsko and Rachel Koenig. Reprinted by permission of William Morrow & Company, Inc.

Nila northSun. "Moving Camp Too Far" from *Diet Pepsi.* Reprinted by permission of the author.

Joyce Carol Oates. "Where Are You Going, Where Have You Been?" from *The Wheel of Love and Other Stories* by Joyce Carol Oates. Copyright © 1970 by Joyce Carol Oates. Reprinted by permission of John Hawkins & Associates, Inc.; excerpt from *Woman Writer: Occasions and Opportunities* by Joyce Carol Oates. Copyright © 1988 by the Ontario Review. Used by permission of the publisher, Dutton, an imprint of New American Library, a division of Penguin Books USA Inc.; "Interview with Joyce Carol Oates" from *Mirrors: An Introduction to Literature,* 3rd edition, edited by John R. Knott and Christopher R. Reaske. Copyright © 1988 by John R. Knott, Jr., and Christopher R. Reaske. Reprinted by permission of HarperCollins Publishers Inc.

Tim O'Brien. "The Things They Carried" from *The Things They Carried.* Copyright © 1990 by Tim O'Brien. Reprinted by permission of Houghton Mifflin Co./Seymour Lawrence. All rights reserved.

Flannery O'Connor. "Parker's Back" and "Revelation" from *The Complete Stories* by Flannery O'Connor. Copyright © 1964, 1965, 1971 by the Estate of Mary Flannery O'Connor; excerpts from *Mystery and Manners* by Flannery O'Connor. Copyright © 1969 by the Estate of Mary Flannery O'Connor; excerpts from *The Habit of Being* by Flannery O'Connor. Copyright © 1979 by Regina O'Connor. All of the above reprinted by permission of Farrar, Straus & Giroux, Inc.; "A Good Man Is Hard to Find" from *A Good Man Is*

*Hard to Find.* Copyright © 1953 by Flannery O'Connor and renewed 1981 by Mrs. Regina O'Connor. Reprinted by permission of Harcourt Brace Inc.

Frank O'Connor. "Guests of the Nation" from *Collected Stories* by Frank O'Connor. Copyright © 1931, 1936, 1937, 1944, 1945, 1946, 1947, 1948, 1949, 1950, 1952, 1953, 1954, 1955, 1956, 1957, 1958, 1959, 1960, 1961, 1965 by Frank O'Connor. Copyright © 1981 by Harriet O'Donovan Sheehy, Executrix of the Estate of Frank O'Connor. Reprinted by permission of Alfred A. Knopf, Inc., and Joan Daves Agency.

Sharon Olds. "Rite of Passage" from *The Dead and the Living* by Sharon Olds. Copyright © 1983 by Sharon Olds. Reprinted by permission of Alfred A. Knopf, Inc.

Mary Oliver. "The Black Walnut Tree" from *Twelve Moons* by Mary Oliver. Copyright © 1978 by Mary Oliver. First appeared in *The Ohio Review.* Reprinted by permission of Little, Brown and Company.

Simon J. Ortiz. "The San Francisco Indians" from *The Man to Send Rain Clouds.* Reprinted by permission of the author.

Wilfred Owen. "Dulce et Decorum Est" from *Collected Poems of Wilfred Owen.* Copyright © 1963 by Chatto & Windus, Ltd. Reprinted by permission of New Directions Publishing Corporation.

Grace Paley. "Samuel" and "A Conversation with My Father" from *Enormous Changes at the Last Minute* by Grace Paley. Copyright © 1968, 1974 by Grace Paley. Reprinted by permission of Farrar, Straus & Giroux, Inc.

Dorothy Parker. "A General Review of the Sex Situation" from *The Portable Dorothy Parker.* Copyright 1926, renewed © 1954 by Dorothy Parker. Reprinted by permission of Viking Penguin, a division of Penguin Books USA Inc.

Linda Pastan. "Ethics" is reprinted from *Waiting for My Life,* Poems by Linda Pastan, by permission of W. W. Norton & Company, Inc. Copyright © 1981 by Linda Pastan; "Marks" is reprinted from *The Five Stages of Grief,* Poems by Linda Pastan, by permission of W. W. Norton & Company, Inc. Copyright © 1978 by Linda Pastan; "Jump Cabling" is reprinted from *Light Year '85,* published by W. W. Norton, by permission of the author. Copyright © 1985 by Linda Pastan.

Carl Phillips. "Luncheon on the Grass" is reprinted by permission of the author.

Marge Piercy. "Barbie Doll," "What's That Smell in the Kitchen?" and "A Work of Artifice" from *Circles on the Water* by Marge Piercy. Copyright © 1969, 1971, 1973, 1982 by Marge Piercy. Reprinted by permission of Alfred A. Knopf, Inc.

Sylvia Plath. "Metaphors" from *The Collected Poems* by Sylvia Plath, edited by Ted Hughes. Copyright © 1960 by Ted Hughes; "Daddy" from *Ariel* by Sylvia Plath. Copyright © 1963 by Ted Hughes. Reprinted by permission of HarperCollins Publishers and Faber and Faber Ltd.

Katherine Anne Porter. "The Jilting of Granny Weatherall" from *The Flowering Judas and Other Stories.* Copyright 1930 and renewed © 1958 by Katherine Anne Porter. Reprinted by permission of Harcourt Brace & Company.

Ezra Pound. "An Immortality" from *Collected Early Poems of Ezra Pound.* Copyright © 1976 by the Trustees of The Ezra Pound Literary Property Trust; "In a Station of the Metro" and "The River Merchant's Wife" from *Personae* by Ezra Pound. Copyright © 1926 by Ezra Pound. Reprinted by permission of New Directions Publishing Corporation.

Craig Raine. "A Martian Sends a Postcard Home." Copyright © 1979 by Craig Raine. Reprinted from *A Martian Sends a Postcard Home* by Craig Raine (1979). By permission of Oxford University Press.

Arnold Rampersad. "On the Cultural Achievements of African Americans" from *The Life of Langston Hughes,* Volume II, by Arnold Rampersad. Reprinted by permission of the author.

Dudley Randall. "The Melting Pot" from *The City's Burning.* Broadside Press, 1968. Reprinted by permission.

John Crowe Ransom. "Piazza Piece" from *Selected Poems,* 3rd edition, revised and enlarged by John Crowe Ransom. Copyright © 1924, 1927 by Alfred A. Knopf, Inc. Copyright © renewed 1952, 1955 by John Crowe Ransom. Reprinted by permission of Alfred A. Knopf, Inc.

Henry Reed. "Naming of Parts" from *Collected Poems* by Henry Reed, edited by Jon Stallworthy (1991). Reprinted by permission of Oxford University Press.

Adrienne Rich. "Living in Sin," "Diving into the Wreck," "Rape," "Aunt Jennifer's Tigers," and "Mourning Picture" reprinted from *The Fact of a Doorframe, Poems Selected and New, 1950-1984* by Adrienne Rich. By permission of W. W. Norton & Company, Inc. Copyright © 1984 by Adrienne Rich. Copyright © 1975, 1978 by W. W. Norton & Company, Inc. Copyright © 1981 by Adrienne Rich; "For the Felling of an Elm in the Harvard Yard." Copyright © 1993, 1951 by Adrienne Rich, from *Collected Early Poems: 1950-1970* by Adrienne Rich. Reprinted by permission of the author and W. W. Norton & Company, Inc.

Theodore Roethke. "My Papa's Waltz." Copyright © 1942 by Hearst Magazines, Inc., from *The Collected Poems of Theodore Roethke* by Theodore Roethke. Used by permission of Doubleday, a division of Bantam Doubleday Dell Publishing Group, Inc.

Wendy Rose. "Three Thousand Dollar Death Song" from *Lost Copper* (1980). Reprinted by permission of Malki Museum Press.

Larry Rubin. "Oates's 'Where Are You Going, Where Have You Been?'" *Explicator* 42:4 (Summer 1984), pp. 57-60; "Response to Elizabeth Bowman's Interpretation of 'The Soul selects her own Society'." *Explicator* 30:8 (April 1972), Item 67. Reprinted with permission of the Helen Dwight Reid Educational Foundation. Published by Heldref Publications, 1319 Eighteenth Street, N.W., Washington, DC 20036-1802. Copyright © 1984.

Edward W. Said. Excerpt from *Culture and Imperialism* by Edward W. Said. Copyright © 1992 by Edward W. Said. Reprinted by permission of Alfred A. Knopf, Inc.

David Savran. Excerpt from *In Their Own Words* by David Savran. Copyright © 1988 by David Savran. Reprinted by permission of Theatre Communications Group.

Anne Sexton. "The Starry Night" from *All My Pretty Ones* by Anne Sexton. Copyright © 1962 by Anne Sexton, renewed 1990 by Linda G. Sexton. Reprinted by permission of Houghton Mifflin Company. All rights reserved.

William Shakespeare. *Hamlet, A Midsummer Night's Dream,* and *The Tempest* from *The Complete Works of Shakespeare,* edited by David Bevington. Reprinted by permission of HarperCollins Publishers Inc.

Elaine Showalter. "The Double Worlds of Men and Women" from *Sexual Anarchy* by Elaine Showalter. Copyright © 1990 by Elaine Showalter. Reprinted by permission of Viking Penguin, a division of Penguin Books USA Inc.

Leslie Marmon Silko. "The Man to Send Rain Clouds." Copyright © 1981 by Leslie Marmon Silko from *Storyteller* by Leslie Marmon Silko. Reprinted with the permission of Seaver Books, New York.

Isaac Bashevis Singer. "The Son from America" from *A Crown of Feathers* by Isaac Bashevis Singer. Copyright © 1973 by Isaac Bashevis Singer. Reprinted by permission of Farrar, Straus & Giroux, Inc.

Stevie Smith. "Not Waving but Drowning" from *The Collected Poems of Stevie Smith* by Stevie Smith. Copyright © 1972 by Stevie Smith. Reprinted by permission of New Directions Publishing Corporation.

Gary Snyder. "Hitch Haiku" from *The Back Country* by Gary Snyder. Reprinted by permission of New Directions Publishing Corporation.

Sokan. "If only we could" from *The Japanese Haiku* by Kenneth Yasuda (1957). Reprinted by permission of Charles E. Tuttle Co., Inc.

Cathy Song. "Beauty and Sadness" from *Picture Bride.* Copyright © 1983 by Cathy Song. Reprinted by permission of Yale University Press.

Sophocles. *Antigone* from *Sophocles: The Oedipus Cycle, an English Version* by Dudley Fitts and Robert Fitzgerald. Copyright © 1939 by Harcourt Brace & Company and renewed 1967 by Dudley Fitts and Robert Fitzgerald. Reprinted by permission of the publisher; *Oedipus Rex* from *Sophocles: The Oedipus cycle, an English Version* by Dudley Fitts and Robert Fitzgerald. Copyright © 1949 by Harcourt Brace & Company and renewed 1977 by Cornelia Fitts and Robert Fitzgerald. Reprinted by permission of the publisher. *Caution:* For both plays, all rights, including professional, amateur, motion picture, recitation, lecturing, performance, public reading, radio broadcasting, and television are strictly reserved. Inquiries on all rights should be addressed to Harcourt Brace & Company, Permissions Department, Orlando, FL 32887-6777.

William Stafford. "Traveling Through the Dark" from *Stories That Could Be True* by William Stafford. Harper & Row, 1977. Reprinted by permission of the Estate of William Stafford.

John Steinbeck. "The Chrysanthemums" from *The Long Valley* by John Steinbeck. Copyright 1937, copyright © renewed 1965 by John Steinbeck. Reprinted by permission of Viking Penguin, a division of Penguin Books USA Inc.

Wallace Stevens. "Emperor of Ice Cream" from *The Collected Poems of Wallace Stevens* by Wallace Stevens. Copyright © 1923 and renewed 1951 by Wallace Stevens. Reprinted by permission of Alfred A. Knopf, Inc.

Taigi. "Look, O look, there go" from *The Japanese Haiku* by Kenneth Yasuda. Reprinted by permission of Charles E. Tuttle Co., Inc.

Elizabeth Tallent. "No One's a Mystery" from *Time with Children* by Elizabeth Tallent. Copyright © 1986, 1987 by Elizabeth Tallent. Reprinted by permission of Alfred A. Knopf, Inc.

Amy Tan. "Two Kinds" reprinted by permission of G. P. Putnam's Sons from "Two Kinds" from *The Joy Luck Club* by Amy Tan. Copyright © 1989 by Amy Tan.

Dylan Thomas. "Fern Hill" and "Do not go gentle into that good night" from Dylan Thomas, *The Poems of Dylan Thomas.* Copyright © 1945 by the Trustees for the Copyrights of Dylan Thomas; 1952 by Dylan Thomas. Reprinted by permission of New Directions Publishing Corporation and David Higham Associates Ltd.

Mike Tierce and John Michael Crafton. "Connie's Tambourine Man: A New Reading of Arnold Friend." *Studies in Short Fiction* 22 (1985): 219–224.

Anne Tyler. "The Artificial Family" from *Selected Stories from the Southern Review 1965–1985,* edited by Lewis P. Simpson et al. Copyright © 1988. Louisiana State University Press. Reprinted by permission of Russell & Volkening as agents for the author.

John Updike. "The Rumor" from *The Afterlife* by John Updike. Copyright © 1994 by John Updike. Reprinted by permission of Alfred A. Knopf, Inc.; "A & P" from *Pigeon Feathers and Other Stories* by John Updike. Copyright © 1960 and renewed 1988 by John Updike. Originally appeared in *The New Yorker;* "Youth's Progress." Copyright © 1955 by John Updike. Reprinted from *The Carpentered Hen and Other Tame Creatures* by John Updike. By permission of Alfred A. Knopf, Inc.

Luis Valdéz. "Los Vendidos" and "The Actos" by Luis Valdéz are reprinted with permission from the publisher of *Luis Valdéz—Early Works: Actos, Bernabe, Pensamiento Serpentino.* Houston: Arte Público Press–University of Houston, 1990.

Helena María Viramontes. "The Moths" by Helena María Viramontes is reprinted with permission from the publisher of *The Moths and Other Stories.* Houston: Arte Público Press–University of Houston, 1985.

Derek Walcott. "A Far Cry from Africa" from *Collected Poems 1948–1984* by Derek Walcott. Copyright © 1986 by Derek Walcott. Reprinted by permission of Farrar, Straus & Giroux, Inc.

Alice Walker. "Everyday Use" from *In Love & Trouble: Stories of Black Women.* Copyright © 1973 by Alice Walker. Reprinted by permission of Harcourt Brace & Company.

Wendy Wasserstein. "The Man in a Case" from *Orchards: 7 Stories by Anton Chekhov & 7 Plays Where They Have Inspired* by Anton Chekhov et al. Copyright © 1986 by Wendy Wasserstein. Reprinted by permission of Alfred A. Knopf, Inc.

Ian Watt. "The Symbolism of the Two Knitters" from *Conrad in the Nineteenth Century* by Ian Watt. Reprinted by permission of the University of California Press.

Eudora Welty. "A Worn Path" from *A Curtain of Green and Other Stories.* Copyright © 1941 and renewed 1969 by Eudora Welty. Reprinted by permission of Harcourt Brace & Company.

John Hall Wheelock. "Earth" reprinted with permission of Scribner an imprint of Simon & Schuster from *The Gardner and Other Poems* by John Hall Wheelock. Copyright © 1961 by John Hall Wheelock. Copyright renewed 1989.

Richard Wilbur. "A Simile for Her Smile" from *Ceremony and Other Poems.* Copyright © 1950 and renewed 1978 by Richard Wilbur. Reprinted by permission of Harcourt Brace & Company; "The Albatross" by Charles Baudelaire, translated by Richard Wilbur from *The Flowers of Evil.* Copyright © 1965 by New Directions Publishing Corporation. Reprinted by permission of New Directions Publishing Corporation.

Tennessee Williams. Excerpt from *Where I Live* by Tennessee Williams. Copyright © 1951 by Tennessee Williams. Reprinted by permission of New Directions Publishing Corporation; *The Glass Menagerie* from *The Glass Menagerie* by Tennessee Williams. Copyright © 1945 by Tennessee Williams and Edwina D. Williams. Copyright renewed 1973 by Tennessee Williams. Reprinted by permission of Random House, Inc.

William Carlos Williams. "The Red Wheelbarrow," "The Great Figure," and "Spring and All" from William Carlos Williams, *The Collected Poems 1909–1939,* Volume I. Copyright © 1938 by New Directions Publishing Corporation; "The Dance" from William Carlos Williams, *The Collected Poems 1939–1962,* Volume II. Copyright © 1944 by William Carlos Williams. Reprinted by permission of New Directions Publishing Corporation.

August Wilson. *Fences* from *Fences* by August Wilson. Copyright © 1986 by August Wilson. Used by permission of New American Library, a division of Penguin Books USA Inc.

Tobias Wolff. "Powder." Copyright © 1992 by Tobias Wolff. Reprinted by permission of International Creative Management, Inc.; "Say Yes." Copyright © 1985 by Tobias Wolff. Reprinted by permission of International Creative Management, Inc.

James Wright. "Lying in a Hammock at William Duffy's Farm in Pine Island, Minnesota" from *The Branch Will Not Break.* Copyright © 1963 by James Wright, Wesleyan University Press. By permission of University Press of New England.

Richard Wright. "Four Haiku" by Richard Wright. Copyright © 1978 by Richard Wright. Reprinted by permission of John Hawkins & Associates, Inc.

Mitsuye Yamada. "To the Lady" and "The Question of Loyalty" from *Camp Notes and Other Poems.* Copyright © 1992 by Mitsuye Yamada. Reprinted by permission of the author and Kitchen Table: Women of Color Press, P.O. Box 40-4920, Brooklyn, NY 11240-4920.

W. B. Yeats. "For Anne Gregory" reprinted with permission of Simon & Schuster from *The Poems of W. B. Yeats: A New Edition,* edited by Richard J. Finneran. Copyright © 1933 by Macmillan Publishing Company, renewed 1961 by Bertha Georgie Yeats; "Leda and the Swan" and "Sailing to Byzantium" reprinted with permission of Simon & Schuster from *The Poems of W. B. Yeats: A New Edition* edited by Richard J. Finneran. Copyright © 1928 by Macmillan Publishing Company, renewed 1956 by Bertha Georgie Yeats; "The Balloon of the Mind" reprinted with permission of Macmillan Publishing Company from *The Poems of W. B. Yeats: A New Edition,* edited by Richard J. Finneran. New York: Macmillan, 1983.

# Index of Terms

# Index of Authors, Titles, and First Lines of Poems

*Quotation marks indicate the first line of a poem.*